WÖRTERBUCH
DER RECHTS- UND WIRTSCHAFTSSPRACHE

TEIL II

DEUTSCH – ENGLISCH

VON

ALFRED ROMAIN

Dr. jur., B. A., Rechtsanwalt

in Zusammenarbeit mit

Karina MacMahon M. A. (Cantab.)

Solicitor of the Supreme Court
of England and Wales

and

Derek Rutter

ehemaliger Chefübersetzer
der Britischen Botschaft in Bonn

Dritte, neubearbeitete Auflage

C. H. BECK'SCHE VERLAGSBUCHHANDLUNG
MÜNCHEN 1994

Die Deutsche Bibliothek – CIP-Einheitsaufnahme

Romain, Alfred:
Wörterbuch der Rechts- und Wirtschaftssprache / von Alfred Romain. – München : Beck.
(Beck'sche Rechts- und Wirtschaftswörterbücher)
Parallelsacht.: Dictionary of legal and commercial terms
NE: HST

Teil 2. Deutsch-Englisch / in Zusammenarbeit mit Karina MacMahon und Derek Rutter. – 3., neubearb. Aufl. – 1994
ISBN 3 406 35836 5

ISBN 3 406 35836 5

© C. H. Beck'sche Verlagsbuchhandlung (Oscar Beck), München 1993
Druck der C. H. Beck'schen Buchdruckerei, Nördlingen
Printed in Germany

Vorwort zur dritten Auflage

Der dritten Auflage liegt eine Neubearbeitung und Aktualisierung des Wortschatzes zugrunde, der sich im letzten Jahrzehnt erweitert hat – besonders durch die Europäische Gemeinschaft und die Wiedervereinigung Deutschlands sowie zahlreiche Gesetzesinitiativen. Trotz einiger Straffungen ist der Umfang gegenüber der Vorauflage (1985) wiederum gestiegen (um 56 Seiten). Die freundliche und stetige Aufnahme, welche die Vorauflage gefunden hat, läßt hoffen, daß dieses Wörterbuch den Anforderungen der Praxis der Fachübersetzer und der juristischen und wirtschaftlichen Berufe mit Auslandsberührung auch weiterhin gerecht wird.

Karina MacMahon, M. A. (Cantab.), Solicitor of the Supreme Court of England and Wales, schwerpunktmäßig in einer deutsch-angloamerikanischen Anwaltssozietät in München tätig, hat das gesamte Manuskript überarbeitet und aktualisiert und ist damit Mitverfasserin geworden.

Für wertvolle Beiträge bei der Vorbereitung dieser Auflage bedanke ich mich besonders bei der Fachübersetzerin für den gewerblichen Rechtsschutz Andrea Braams, München, meinen Kollegen am Sprachen- und Dolmetscher-Institut München, Hans Berger und Rudolf Sachs, bei dem Fachübersetzer für Wirtschaft und Recht, Herbert Breese, München, meiner Assistentin Frau Hannelore Blumenthal und den Studierenden des Sprachen- und Dolmetscher-Instituts für ihre Anregungen bei juristischen Übersetzungen und Terminologiearbeit im Unterricht.

München, im Dezember 1993   *Alfred Romain*

Preface to the Third Edition

The terms included in this, the Third Edition of the German-English volume have undergone not only a complete revision and update but have also been supplemented with further terminology, particularly vocabulary arising out of and used in connection with the European Community, the Reunification of Germany, and new legislation. Although the dictionary has been streamlined, it nevertheless contains 56 more pages than the previous edition (1985). The friendly and continued positive reception accorded the previous edition promotes hope that this edition will continue to meet the practical needs of specialist translators and members of the legal and financial professions.

Karina MacMahon M. A. (Cantab.), Solicitor of the Supreme Court of England and Wales who currently works for a major German law firm specialising in German-Anglo-American matters has revised and updated the entire manuscript and thus joins me as co-editor.

I would especially like to thank friends and colleagues who have given me their invaluable assistance in preparing this dictionary. Those who deserve particular thanks are: Andrea Braams, specialist translator for intellectual property law, Hans Berger and Rudolf Sachs, both of the Sprachen- und Dolmetscher-Institut, Munich, Herbert Breese, specialist translator for commercial terms, my assistant Mrs Hannelore Blumenthal and last but not least my students at the Munich Institute for Interpreters who have given me plenty of interesting suggestions.

Munich, December 1993 *Alfred Romain*

Abkürzungen – Abbreviations

adj	adjective	Adjektiv, Eigenschaftswort
adv	adverb	Adverb
bal	balance-sheet term	bilanztechnischer Ausdruck
Brit	British	britischer Sprachgebrauch
crim	criminal law	Strafrecht
D	Federal Republic of Germany	Bundesrepublik Deutschland
eccl	ecclesiastical	kirchlich bzw. kirchenrechtlich
econ	economical	wirtschaftlich, ökonomisch
esp	especially	besonders, speziell
etc	etcetera	und so weiter
etw	something	etwas
exch	stock-exchange	börsenfachlich
f	feminine (gender)	weiblich (Genus)
fig	figurative(ly)	im übertragenen Sinn
GB	Great Britain	Großbritannien
infra	see below	siehe unten
ins	insurance	versicherungstechnisch
int	international	international, völkerrechtlich
lit	literal(ly)	wörtlich
m	masculine (gender)	männlich (Genus)
n	neuter	sächlich (Genus)
obs	obsolete	obsolet, veraltet
opp	opposite, as opposed to	im Gegensatz zu
o.s.	oneself	sich, selbst
parl	parliamentary	Parlament(ssprache)
pat	patent (law)	patent(rechtlich)
pl	plural	Plural, Mehrzahl
pol	political	politisch
qv	quod vide	siehe dort
s	noun	Substantiv
scot	Scottish (law)	Schottisch(es Recht)
sl	slang	Slang, Jargon
s.o.	some one	jemand
sth	something	etwas
supra	see above	siehe oben
tax	taxation	steuerrechtlich
US	United States (of America)	USA, US-amerikanisch
v/i	intranstive verb	intransitives Verb
v/t	transitive verb	transitives Verb

Sonderabkürzungen sind bei einigen längeren Stichworten am Anfang der Eintragung angegeben.
Special abbreviations will be found at the beginning of some of the lengthy entries.
(=) bedeutet, daß im Englischen das gleiche Wort stehen kann.
(=) means that the same word may be used in English.

Abkürzungen — Abbreviations

Kursivsatz bedeutet eine Erläuterung oder Umschreibung.
Italics indicate an explanation or paraphrase.

Häufig vorkommende orthographische Verschiedenheiten zwischen britischen und amerikanischen Sprachgebrauch:
Frequent differences in spelling between British und American usage:

GB	US
behaviour	behavior
cancelled	canceled
centre	center
cheque	check
colourable	colorable
defence	defense
endeavour	endeavor
enrolment	enrollment
fulfil	fulfill
fulfilment	fulfillment
habour	harbor
honour	honor
honourable	honorable
labour	labor
licence *(n)*	license
offence	offense
per cent	percent
plough	plow
pretence	pretense
programme	program
trade mark	trademark
traveller	traveler
tyre	tire
wilful	willful

A

abänderbar *adj* modifiable, alterable, commutable (*sentence*).

abändern *v/t* to alter, to amend.

Abänderung *f* alteration, variation, modification, amending, amendment; *in ~ von*: in derogation of.

Abänderungs|antrag motion for amendment (*of a bill*); *e-n ~ ~ stellen* to move an amendment; application for variation (*maintenance*); **~befugnis** power to amend; **~gesetz** amending act, amending law; **~klage** petition to modify a judgment (*periodical payments*); **~patent** revised patent, reissued patent; **~urkunde** amending document, amendment scheme; **~urteil** amending judgment; **~vorbehalt** reserved right to amend, (amending) reservation.

Abandon *m* relinquishment, abandonment; **~erklärung** declaration of abandonment; **~klausel** abandonment clause (*insurance*).

abandonnieren *v/t* to relinquish, to abandon, to withdraw from.

Abartigkeit *f* abnormality; **seelische ~** mental abnormality, freakishness.

Abbau reduction; exploitation (*min*), removal, cancellation, run-down; **~ der Auftragspolster** working off the backlog of orders; **~ der Belegschaft** reduction in personnel, jobcuts, job pruning; **~ der Handelsschranken** reduction in trade barriers; **~ der Lagerbestände** reduction in stock; **~ der Zölle** reduction in tariffs; **~ der Zwangswirtschaft** decontrol, liberalization; **~entschädigung** compensation for depletion (*of mineral deposits*); **~gebiet** mining territory; **~genehmigung** licence (permit) to exploit mineral resources; **~gerechtigkeit** mining concession; **~rechte** quarrying (mining) rights (*in exploitation contracts*); **~vertrag** mining contract; **~verlust** depletion loss; **~ von Steuervergünstigungen** reduction in tax benefits.

abbaufähig *adj* depletable, exploitable; wasting.

abbedingen *v/t* to exclude (*legal limitations*) by agreement, to contract out.

Abbedingung *f* contracting out.

abbefördern *v/t* to transport (away), to remove.

abberufen *v/t* to recall (*ambassador*), to dismiss (*manager*).

Abberufung *f* (*dipl*) recall; dismissal; **~sabstimmung** vote to remove s. o. (*from an office*); **~srecht** *n* (*dipl*) right to demand a recall; right to remove s. o. from office; **~sschreiben** letter of recall.

abbestellen *v/t* to cancel an order, to discontinue *subscriptions*.

Abbestellung *f* cancellation of an order, discontinuation *of subscriptions*; **~ vorbehalten** right to cancel reserved.

abbezahlen *v/t* to pay off *in full or by instalments*.

Abbiegeverbot *n* no turning.

abbieten *v/t* to outbid.

Abbildung *f* depiction, illustration; **beleidigende ~** defamatory *or* insulting depiction.

Abblendepflicht *f* requirement that headlights be dimmed (*or* dipped).

abbrechen *v/t* to discontinue, to disrupt; to stop (*work*), to break off, to drop out (*of university*), to interrupt (*session*), to demolish (*building*), to drop (*connection*).

Abbrecherquote *f* dropout rate.

Abbruch *m* (*1*) rupture; discontinuation; **~ der diplomatischen Beziehungen** breaking off of (*rupture of*) diplomatic relations; **~ der Verhandlungen** breakdown of

1

Abbruch

negotiations, breaking off of negotiations, discontinuance.

Abbruch *m (2)* demolition, dismantling; ~**anordnung** condemnation order *(buildings)*; ~**arbeiten** *f/pl* demolition works; ~**sbewilligung** demolition permit, demolition licence; ~**unternehmer** demolition contractor; ~**verfügung** demolition order, demolition permit; ~**wert** demolition value.

Abbruch *(3)* = *Schwangerschaftsabbruch q. v.*

abbuchen *v/t* to debit an account, to deduct *(by authorization)* from an account; *sometimes used in the sense of ausbuchen q. v.*

Abbuchung *f* debit-entry; authorized deduction from an account, *also → Ausbuchung*; ~ **im Bankeinzugverfahren** direct debit; ~**skreditkarte** direct debit card.

Abbüßen *n* serving one's sentence; **nach ~ der Strafe** after the expiry of the sentence, after serving one's sentence.

abbüßen *v/t* to serve a sentence; to serve time; to do time; to atone.

ABC Waffen *f/pl* ABC A*(tomic)*, B*(iological)*, and C*(hemics)* weapons.

abdanken *v/i* to abdicate.

Abdankung *f* abdication; ~**sdekret** decree of abdication; ~**surkunde** instrument of abdication.

abdecken *v/t* to cover *(an overdraft, deficit)*, to furnish collateral.

Abdeckung *f* providing cover; ~ **des Marktes** market coverage.

abdingbar *adj* not mandatory *(rules)*, subject to be contracted away *(legal provisions)*, transactionable.

abdisponieren *v/t* to transfer funds *from bank to bank*, to withdraw *(funds)*.

Abdisposition *f* transfer of funds *from bank to bank*, withdrawal.

Abdruck *m* print, copy, impression, proof, reproduction, reprinting; ~**srecht** copyright, authority to reprint, right of reproduction; ~ **in Fortsetzungen**: serial rights; **unbefugter ~** unauthorized reproduction.

abfertigen

Abendverkauf *m* late night opening *(of shops)*.

Aberdepot *n (antiquated form of)* irregular deposit of fungible securities *(where title passes to bank)*.

aberkennen *v/t* to deprive *s.o. of a right,* to dismiss *(a claim)*, to disallow.

Aberkennung *f* deprivation; disqualification; ~ **der bürgerlichen Ehrenrechte** suspension *(or* deprivation) of civic rights; ~ **der Staatsangehörigkeit** forfeiture of nationality, expatriation; ~ **des Ruhegehalts** deprivation of pension rights; ~**sfrist** disqualification period.

aberratio ictus *Fehlgehen der Tat* miscarriage of criminal act, transferred malice.

Abfahrts|datum sailing date; ~**erlaubnis** clearance for departure.

Abfall *m (1)* defection, desertion, secession.

Abfall *m (2)* litter, rubbish; waste, scraps; **a~arm** *adj* low-waste; ~**beseitigung** disposal of refuse; ~**entsorgungsanlage** waste disposal installation; **a~los** non-waste; ~**mengenplanung** planning of mass waste, scrap, and spoilage; ~**produkt** waste product, residual product, by-product; ~**stoffe zu Rohstoffen verarbeiten** to recycle; ~**sünder** litter bug; ~**vermeidung** avoidance of waste production; ~**verwertung** waste utilization, recycling; ~**wirtschaft** (solid) waste management.

abfangen *v/t* to intercept *(letters, telephone calls)*; to pull out of a skid *(vehicle)*; to underpin *(foundations)*.

Abfangen *n* interception *(of letters, telephone calls)*; regaining control *(of vehicle)*; ~ **von Kursschwankungen** price cushioning *(shares)*.

abfassen *v/t* to formulate *(a document)*, to compose *(a manuscript)*, to draw up *(a contract)*.

Abfassung *f* formulation, composition, drawing up.

abfertigen *v/t* to dispatch *(luggage,*

2

Abfertiger

freight); to clear (*customs*); *nicht abgefertigt*: uncleared.

Abfertiger *m* dispatching clerk (*luggage, freight*).

Abfertigung *f* dispatching, handling, clearance; *normale* ~: normal handling; ~ **der Waren** clearance of goods; ~ **im Reiseverkehr** control of tourist traffic.

Abfertigungs|abteilung despatch (= *dispatch*) department; ~**antrag** application for clearance (*customs*); ~**sbeamter** clearance officer; ~**bescheinigung** certificate of acceptance (*customs*); ~**dienst** dispatch service; ~**frist** clearance deadline; ~**gebühr** forwarding charge; ~**hafen** port of clearance, port of shipment; ~**schalter** passport control point; ~**schein** dispatch certificate; ~**spediteur** truck haulage; dispatch agent; ~**stelle** dispatch office; ~**zollstelle** office of clearance.

abfinden *v/t* to settle (*a claim*), to pay off (*a creditor*), to buy out (*a partner*), to compound (*one's creditors with a lump sum*); to indemnify (*for an accident*).

Abfindung *f* settlement, lump sum settlement, accord and satisfaction; ~ *an ausscheidende Führungskräfte*: "golden handshake"; ~ **e-s Teilhabers** paying off a partner, indemnifying an outgoing partner; ~ **für** (*wegen*) **Verlust des Arbeitsplatzes** redundancy pay, severance pay, compensation for dismissal; ~ **von Gläubigern** compounding with creditors, arrangement with one's creditors; **als endgültige** ~ in full and final settlement; **ausgehandelte** ~ negotiated settlement; **freiwillige** ~ voluntary settlement, ex gratia payment; **soziale** ~ *bei Kündigung* redundancy pay; **vergleichsweise** ~ payment by way of compromise.

Abfindungs|angebot offer of lump-sum compensation; early retirement offer; ~**anspruch** right to a settlement; ~**betrag** amount of the settlement; ~**erklärung** general release (*accidents*), acceptance declaration, *allgemeine* ~~: general release; ~**geld** settlement moneys, indemnification funds; ~**guthaben** credit balance upon withdrawal (*partner*); ~**klausel** general release clause (*insurance*), acceptance declaration clause; ~**summe** amount of settlement; sum in full settlement of all claims; settlement sum, settlement moneys; ~**vereinbarung** settlement agreement; ~**vergleich** compromise; nuisance settlement (*to avoid nominal liability litigation*); ~**vertrag** settlement agreement; ~**zahlung** payment in full settlement; redundancy payment, severance payment; ~**zahlungen an weichende Erben** estate payments to heirs in settlement of inheritance share.

Abfluß *m* efflux, outflow; ~ **liquider Mittel** cash drain.

abfordern *v/t* to claim, to demand, to request.

abführen (1) *v/t* to deduct and pay over, to transfer (*wage tax, social insurance premiums*); ~ (2) *v/t* to lead away, to take a person away (*into custody*).

Abführung (1) paying over, transfer; ~ **an den Bund** the paying of funds (*by a Land*) to the Federal Government; ~ **der Steuer** remittance of the tax, payment of tax to collector.

Abführung (2) leading away the prisoner (*into custody*); ~**sbefehl** order to remove (*a prisoner*).

Abgabe *f* (1) submission, handing over (*a statement*), handing in (*a telegram*), filing (*an offer*), delivery (*of a letter*), casting (*of a vote*); ~ **der Sache an ein anderes Gericht** transferring a case to another court; ~**druck** selling pressure, sales pressure (*exch*); ~ **e-r Erklärung** making a declaration, issuing a statement; ~ **e-r Willenserklärung** act, external manifestation of will (*with legal effect*); ~**frist** deadline for filing (*declaration, tax*); ~**kurs** issuing price (*exch*); ~**land**

3

Abgabe sending country; **~preis** selling price; issuing price; **~satz** selling rate for money market securities; **~sätze der Bundesbank** Bundesbank's selling rates for money market securities; **~termin** due date (*for tax return, etc*); ~ **zum Verbrauch** putting on the market; **verspätete ~** late filing.

Abgabe *f* (2) tax, duty, levy, fiscal charge; ~ **auf das Grundvermögen** levy on real estate; **~n auf alkoholische Getränke** tax on alcoholic beverages; **~n, die kostendeckenden Gebühren entsprechen** charges similar in nature to fees; **freiwillige soziale ~n** non-obligatory employee benefit contributions; **gesetzliche soziale ~n** statutory social service expenditure; **inländische ~** internal tax, *pl also:* internal taxation; **öffentliche ~n** public charges; **sonstige ~n** other duties and taxes; **soziale ~n** social insurance and welfare dues; **steuerähnliche ~n** parafiscal taxes.

Abgaben|befreiung exemption from taxes, duties and other revenue charges; **~bescheid** order concerning tax (*etc*) liability; **~eintreibung** enforcement of the tax collection; ~ **erheben** to raise revenue(s); **a~frei** exempt from taxes and duties, duty-free; **~freiheit** immunity from taxes (and duties); **~hinterziehung** defrauding of tax revenue, tax evasion; **~hoheit** fiscal jurisdiction; **~ordnung** fiscal code; **a~pflichtig** *adj* subject to levy, taxable, rateable, chargeable; **~pflichtiger** taxpayer; **~recht** revenue law; **~schulden** tax liabilities; **~schuldner** person liable to pay taxes and/or duties; **~streitigkeiten** tax disputes; **~system** revenue system; **~überhöhung** excessive taxation; **~umgehung** tax avoidance (*legally permissible*); tax evasion (*illegal*); **~veranlagung** tax assessment; **~verfahren** tax levy procedure; **~vergünstigung** tax concession, tax relief; **~verordnung** tax levy regulation; **~verpflichtung** tax liability; *öffentlich-rechtliche:* **~~** *tax liability under public law;* **~voranschlag** revenue estimate(s); **~wesen** the revenue system.

Abgang *m* (*1*) departure, dispatch.

Abgang *m* (*2*) (*pl Abgänge*) outflow withdrawal, wastage loss, retirement; a decrease in assets (*in balance sheet*); persons leaving; **~e bei Beteiligungen** divestitures of investment in subsidiaries and associated companies; **~sgeld** severance pay; **~zeugnis** leaving certificate, diploma.

Abgangs|bahnhof departure station; **~flughafen** departure airport; **~hafen** port of departure; port of sailing; port of clearance; **~land** country of departure, **~ort** place of departure, point of shipment; **~quote** rate of outflow; **~tag** day of dispatch; **~zollstelle** customs station at point of departure.

Abgas *n* (pl **~e:**) emissions, exhaust, flue gas, off-gas, gaseous emissions; pollutant emissions; **~entgiftungsvorrichtungen** *f/pl* anti-pollution equipment; **~normen** emission standard levels of exhaust; **umweltschädliche ~e** emissions of gaseous pollutants.

abgeändert *adj* amended, changed.

abgeben *v/t* to give up (*part of a claim*), to dispose of (*part of land*), to hand in (*import declaration*).

abgehen *v/t* to digress, to depart from (*standard*); to leave (*station*); to be missing (*item*); **A~n vom Goldstandard:** *abandonment of the gold standard.*

abgeholt *adj* picked up, collected; **nicht ~** unclaimed, not collected.

abgekürzt *adj* abbreviated, abridged.

abgelaufen *adj* expired, lapsed (*policy*).

Abgeld *n* discount; **mit ~:** *at a discount.*

abgelten *v/t* to discharge, to settle, to pay in settlement of claim, to reimburse; *als abgegolten gelten: to be deemed discharged.*

Abgeltung *f* discharge (*of claim*); settlement, reimbursement; indemnification; ~ **nach dem Äquivalenzprinzip** payment on the equivalence (*or:* quid pro quo) principle; ~ **von Besatzungsschäden** indemnification for damage by occupying forces; ~ **von Leistungen** reimbursement for the discharge of obligations; **pauschale** ~ lump-sum settlement; compounded settlement; **zur** ~ **der Schadensansprüche** in settlement of claims for damage; **zur** ~ **von Barleistungen** in lieu of cash payment.

Abgeltungs|bereich scope of compensation; **~betrag** amount of indemnity; **a~fähig** *adj* capable of redemption; **~gesetz** indemnity law; **~klausel** general release clause **~maßnahmen** payment measures; **~svergleich** full settlement, overall settlement.

abgeneigt *adj* disinclined.

Abgeordneten|eid parliamentary oath; **~haus** lower house (*of parliament, Bundestag*), House of Representatives (Congress) *US,* House of Commons *GB;* **~immunität** privilege of parliamentary immunity; **~indemnität** parliamentary privilege; **~kammer** (legislative) chamber; **~mandat** parliamentary mandate, term of office; **~sitz** parliamentary seat, seat in the House.

Abgeordneter *m* (*der Abgeordnete*) delegate, representative, Member of Parliament, congressman, lawmaker, deputy.

abgerechnet *adj* accounted for, settled.

abgeschlossen *adj* consummated, completed, executed, closed, self-contained; **formgerecht** ~ in due form, proper; in the prescribed form.

Abgeschlossenheit *f* completeness, self-containment; **~sbescheinigung** certificate of completeness (*as a self-contained condominium unit*).

abgesehen von *adv* apart from, regardless of, except for, save.

abgesondert *adj* separate.

abgestuft *adj* graduated, marked at intervals.

abgezeichnet *adj* initialled.

abgleichen *v/t* to square.

abgrenzen *v/t* to mark, to demarcate; to delimit; to define; to stake out, to apportion; **gegeneinander** ~ to define the respective functions, to demarcate.

Abgrenzung *f* delimitation, demarcation, apportionment; accrual accounting, accruals and deferrals; ~ **der Hoheitsgewässer** fixing the limits of territorial waters; ~ **des Geldvolumens** delimitation of the money in circulation; **internationale** ~ international demarcation; **periodische** ~ periodical delimitation *of deferred items* (*in accounting*); **transitorische** ~ periodical delimitation *of deferred items* (*in accounting*); **unterschiedliche ~en** differences in delimitation; **unterschiedliche methodische** ~ different methods of delimitation; **unterschiedliche begriffliche** **~en** differences of definition.

Abgrenzungs|ergebnis result of expense allocation statement; **~konten** (accounts showing) accruals and deferrals, transitory accounts; **~merkmale** classification criteria; **~posten** accruals, transitory items; **~rechnung** statement of apportionment; **~streitigkeit** demarcation dispute.

Abgruppierung *f* down-grading (*of a job*).

abhaken *v/t* to check off (*items, names*); to tick off.

abhalten *v/t* to hold (*a meeting*), to keep (*s.o. from working*), to deter (*from crime*), hinder.

abhandeln *v/t* to bargain, to beat down someone's price.

Abhandenkommen *n* loss, getting lost, the mislaying of sth.

abhanden kommen *v/i* to get lost, to be mislaid (*document, keys*).

Abhandlung *f* treatise; essay; **juristische** ~ legal treatise; ~~ *über Gesetzestechnik*: monograph.

abhängig *adj* contingent upon, de-

5

Abhängige

pendent upon, subject to; **gegenseitig** ~ interdependent.
Abhängige *m/pl f/pl* dependants.
Abhängigkeit *f* dependence; **~sbericht** subordinate status report *(subsidiary corporation's report on controlling influence of parent company)*; **~sverhältnis** dependent condition; **gegenseitige** ~ interdependence.
Abhebung *f* withdrawal; **~sbefugnis** drawing right; **tägliche ~en** day-to-day withdrawals.
abhelfen *v/i* to remedy, to relieve, to grant relief; to satisfy *(a need)*; **e-m Unrecht** ~ to redress a wrong.
Abhilfe *f* redress, relief, remedy, interlocutory revision; **~antrag** application for relief; **~behörde** authority in charge of remedial action; **~bescheid** redress decision, remedial decision; **~bestimmungen** remedial provisions, terms of relief; **~gesetz** remedial statute; **~gesuch** petition for relief; **~gewähren** to grant relief, to remedy sth, to rectify sth; ~ **im Verwaltungswege** administrative relief; **~maßnahme** remedial measure; **~mitteilung** notice of relief; **~recht** right to redress; ~ **schaffen** to remedy, to provide relief; **~verfahren** remedial action, redress proceedings; **etwas erfordert** ~ sth needs to be remedied; **um** ~ **bitten** to ask for relief.
abhilfefähig *adj* capable of relief, remediable.
Abhör|affäre bugging affair, wiretapping scandal; **~aktion** bugging campaign, electronic surveillance operation; **~anlage** bugging devices, bugs; **~gesetz** *(D 1968)* Exemptions from Telecommunication Secrecy Act; **~skandal** wiretapping scandal, bugging scandal.
Abhören *m* interception, monitoring; ~ **von Telefongesprächen** telephone tapping, wire-tapping, phone-tapping.
abhören *v/t* to intercept, to tap, to monitor electronically, to bug.

Abkommen

Abhol|dienst pick-up service; **~fach** post office box.
Abholung *f* collection, pick up; **~sanspruch** right to recover possession *of chattels from third-party's property;* collection right.
Abholzung *f* deforestation; **~srecht** right to harvest forest.
Abitur *n* (=) final secondary-school examination, upper secondary leaving certificate, „A" levels *(GB)*.
abklingen *v/i* to fall off; to slacken.
Abkommen *n* agreement, convention, accord, treaty; ~ **über den Gefangenenaustausch** convention concerning exchange of prisoners; ~ **über die internationale Zivilluftfahrt** international civil aviation convention; ~ **über e-n Bereitschaftskredit** standby agreement; ~ **über kulturelle Zusammenarbeit** cultural exchange agreement; ~ **über wirtschaftliche Zusammenarbeit** agreement on economic cooperation; ~ **zur Vermeidung der Doppelbesteuerung** double taxation agreement, double tax treaty; **aus dem** ~ **ausscheiden** to cease to be a party to the convention; to withdraw from an understanding; **dies** ~ **liegt bis zum ... zur Unterzeichnung auf** this agreement shall be left open for signature until ...; **diplomatisches** ~ diplomatic agreement; **ein** ~ **legalisieren lassen** to have a treaty legalized (authenticated); **internationales** ~ **über Betäubungsmittel** international agreement on narcotics; **internationales** ~ **zur Vollstreckung ausländischer Schiedssprüche** international agreement on the execution of foreign arbitral awards; **langfristiges** ~ long-term agreement; **laufendes** ~ continuing agreement, valid agreement; **mehrseitiges** ~ multilateral agreement; **multilaterales** ~ multilateral treaty, convention; **revidiertes** ~ modified convention; **vertragliches** ~ contractual understanding; **völkerrechtliches** ~ interna-

Abkommensbereich / **Ablehnung**

tional convention, treaty; **zweiseitiges ~** bilateral agreement.

Abkommens|bereich scope of the agreement; **~land** convention country, treaty country; **~währung** convention-currency.

Abkömmling *m* descendant; *pl: offspring, descendants, progeny, issue*;- **~e gerader Linie** direct descendants; **direkter ~ ersten Grades** direct descendant in first degree lineage; **erbberechtigter ~** descendant entitled to an inheritance; **nichtehelicher ~** illegitimate offspring.

Abkopplung *f* de-coupling, disconnection.

Abkunft *f* parentage, descent, lineage, ancestry.

Ablade|erlaubnis *f* (*für das Schiff*) permission to unload (*after customs clearance of ship*); **~gebühren** *f/pl* unloading charges (*ship, railway*); **~gewicht** unloading weight; **~hafen** port of discharge; **~kontrolldienstleistung** unloading control service; **~ort** place of unloading.

Abladen *n* shipping (*sea transport*), unloading (*land transport*).

abladen *v/t* to ship, to unload.

Ablader *m* shipper, forwarder (*to carrier*); unloader.

Abladung *f* unloading; **~shafen** port of discharge; **~skosten** unloading charges; **~stermin** deadline for discharging cargo.

Ablage *f* filing; filing tray, filing system, filing basket; **~nverzeichnis** old files index.

Ablauf *m* expiration (*end of period*); procedure, operations, sequence of operations; **~ der Bezugsrechte** expiration of subscription rights (*to shares, bonds*); **~ der Frist** expiry of a period, expiration of the deadline; **~ e-r angemessenen Frist**: *expiry of a reasonable period*; **~ der Gültigkeitsdauer** expiry of the period of validity; **~ der Kündigungsfrist** expiration of notice period (*lease, employment termination, bank withdrawal*); **~ des Mietverhältnisses** expiration of tenancy; **~ e-s Patents** expiration of validity of a patent; **~ e-s Vertrages** termination of a contract; **~shemmung** tolling, suspension of the running of time, *sth.* to stop time running; **~szeitpunkt eines Patents** expiry date of a patent; **bei ~** at the time of expiry; **den ~ der Frist hemmen** to suspend the running of time; **der konkrete ~ der Geschehnisse** the real course of events; **mit dem ~ von ...** upon the expiration of ...; **nach ~ der Amtszeit** after the expiration of the term of office; **nach ~ von zwei Monaten** after two months.

ablaufen *v/i* to expire (*policy, lease, term*), to run out.

Ableben *n* death, decease; **~sversicherung** burial insurance; **bei ~** in the event of death; **nach seinem ~** after his decease.

ablegen *v/t* to file.

Ablegung *f* **e-s Eides** the taking of an oath, swearing of an oath; **~ e-s Geständnisses** making a confession; **~ einer Verklarung** making a sworn statement concerning a maritime accident.

ablehnen *v/t* to decline, to refuse, to rule out; *strikt ~*: *to absolutely refuse, to emphatically decline*.

ablehnend *adj* negative, censorious, critical.

Ablehnung *f* refusal, rejection, repudiation; **~ der Verantwortung** denial of responsibility; **~ e-s Angebots** decline of an offer, rejection of an offer; **~ e-s Antrags** refusal to grant an application, dismissal of a motion (*court*); **~ e-s Gesuchs** rejection of a petition; **~ e-s Patentantrags** refusal of a patent application; **~ e-s Richters** challenge to a member of the court, objection to a member of the court; **~ e-s Richters wegen Besorgnis der Befangenheit** motion to disqualify a judge, challenging a judge on a suspicion of prejudice (*or* propter affectum *or* on grounds of

7

Ablehnungs|antrag / **abmarken**

bias); **bei ~** in case of refusal; **willkürliche ~** arbitrary denial, wilful refusal.

Ablehnungs|antrag challenging motion (*court*); **~bereich** rejection region (*statistics*); **~bescheid** decision concerning the rejection; **~erklärung** declaration of challenge, statement of challenge; **~gesuch** challenging petition; **~recht** right of refusal.

ableiten to deduce; to derive from.

Ableitung *f* (*von Schadstoffen*) discharge of waste.

ablenken *v/t* to divert.

Ablenkung *f* diversion, distraction; **~smanöver** diversion, diversionary tactics; red-herring; device.

ablesen *v/t* to read (off, from).

Ableugnen *m* denial (*of a fact*), disavowal (*of action*).

ableugnen *v/t* to deny, to disown.

Ablichtung *f* photostatic copy, photocopy, photostat; **beglaubigte ~** certified photocopy.

abliefern *v/t* to deliver, to surrender; *wieder ~:* to redeliver.

Ablieferung *f* delivery; surrender; **~ beim Empfänger** storage door delivery; **gebrauchsfertige ~** turnkey delivery.

Ablieferungs|bescheinigung certificate of delivery; **~frist** delivery deadline; **~gewicht** weight delivered; **~kontingent** delivery quota; **~ort** place of delivery; **~pflicht** statutory obligation to surrender (*weapons, foreign currency*); **a~pflichtig** required to be surrendered; **~preis** delivery price, price of delivery; **~schein** delivery sheet; **~Soll** deliveries required (*from farmers etc*); **~zwang** compulsory delivery.

ablösbar redeemable (*bonds, mortgage*).

ablösen *v/t* to supersede, to replace (*old model*), to redeem (*a loan*); to refund.

Ablösung *f* replacement, redemption; refunding; **~ der Kapitalertragsteuer** discharging the liability for capital income tax; **~ e-r Dienstbarkeit** payment for the discharge of an easement; **~ von Abgaben** anticipatory paying of levies; **~ von Krediten** repayment (*or:* redemption) of a loan; **~ von Lehen** enfranchisement, redemption of feudal tenure; **vorzeitige ~** early redemption (*of loan*).

Ablösungs|anleihe commutation loan; **~anspruch** right of redemption; **~berechtigter** party entitled to redeem; **~betrag** redemption amount; **~fonds** sinking fund, redemption fund; **~recht** right of redemption; **~rente** redeemable annuity; **~ ~ für Lehensdienste:** quit rent, scutage; **~schuld** refunding debt, commutation debt; **~schuldverschreibung** refunding bond, commutation bond (*issued in lieu of payment*); **~summe** redemption price, commutation; **~vertrag** contract to redeem; **~wert** cash surrender value (*life insurance*); **~zinssatz** redemption; rate of interest (*discount*); **~zusage** assurance of redemption.

abmachen *v/t* to arrange for, to agree, to bargain; **etwas gütlich ~** to settle amicably.

Abmachung *f* arrangement, settlement, stipulation; **außergerichtliche ~** private agreement, out-of-court settlement; **bindende ~** binding settlement; **faire ~** square deal (*colloquial*), fair deal; **handelspolitische ~** trade agreement; **internationale ~en** international conventions; **vertragliche ~** conventional arrangement, contractual stipulation; **vorläufige ~** provisional agreement.

Abmahn|kosten legal expenses of a warning notice (*or* of a letter before action) **~verein** association to watch against unfair practices.

abmahnen *v/t* to warn (*against doing sth.*).

Abmahnung *f* warning, warning notice; **~sschreiben** (written) warning notice, letter before action, (seven) day letter.

abmarken *v/t* to mark the boundaries (*of real estate*).

8

Abmarkung *f* marking the boundary (line), demarcation; ~**sgesetz** cadastral survey law; ~**slinie** dividing line, boundary (line); ~**szeichen** bench marks.

Abmelde|formular *n* official form for giving notice of one's departure, form for notification of moving; **polizeiliche** ~**bescheinigung** police certification of notice of departure.

abmelden *v/t* to cancel (*a registration*), to give notice of withdrawal; to deregister, to sign off, to log off; **sich** ~ to give notice of departure, to cancel one's visit officially; **sich polizeilich** ~ to notify police of one's departure from present address.

Abmeldung *f* notice of one's departure from present address; notice of cancellation (*registration*); **polizeiliche** ~ notice to police of one's removal from present address.

abmessen *v/t* to measure, to gauge.

Abmessungs-, Konstruktions- und Qualitätsnormen *pl* standards of dimensions, designs and quality.

abmustern *v/i* to sign off on discharge (*sailors*).

Abmusterung *f* discharge of crew (*at trip's end*).

Abnahme *f* taking delivery (*of goods*), acceptance (*of performance*), final inspection; acceptance inspection; ~**attest** acceptance certificate (*upon acceptance of tested product*); *provisorisches* ~: *interim acceptance certificate*; ~ **e-r Verklarung** recording of a maritime accident; ~ **e-s Werks** acceptance of performance; ~**frist** deadline for acceptance; ~**garantie** guarantee to purchase, guarantee of acceptance, underwriting (guarantee); ~**kontrolle** delivery check; ~**pflicht** obligation to accept delivery of goods; ~**protokoll** acceptance certificate, test report; ~**prüfung** acceptance inspection, inspection test upon receipt; ~**schein** receipt, acceptance certificate; ~ **unter Vorbehalt** conditional acceptance; ~**verfahren** acceptance procedure; ~**verpflichtung** purchase commitment, obligation to take delivery, ~ ~ *aus Devisentermingeschäften: commitment to accept delivery of foreign exchange in forward transactions*; ~**vereinbarung** agreement to accept securities (*by investor*); ~**verweigerung** refusal to accept delivery, refusal of goods, rejection; ~**verzug** delay in taking delivery of purchased goods; ~ **von Waren** physical acceptance of merchandise, taking delivery of goods; **förmliche** ~ formal acceptance (*of construction work, with joint inspection and protocol*); **konkludente** ~ implied acceptance (*by occupation and use*).

abnehmen *v/t* to take delivery (*of goods*), to take possession (*of goods*); to accept (*performance, work done*); *v/i*: to diminish (*sales volume*); to slow down (*business activity*).

Abnehmer *m* purchaser, consumer; ~ **des Käufers** subpurchaser; ~ **finden** to find a market; ~**gruppe** buying combine, consumer group, category of consumers; ~**land** consumer country, target country; **alleiniger** ~ sole purchaser; **ausländische** ~ *pl* foreign purchasers; **späterer** ~ subsequent purchaser.

Abneigung *f* aversion; **unüberwindliche** ~ insurmountable aversion.

Abnutzung *f* wear and tear, wearing off (*in use*); ~ **der Straßen** wear and tear of roads; ~ **infolge normalen Verbrauchs** wear and tear through normal use; **angemessene** ~ fair wear and tear; reasonable wear and tear; **natürliche** ~ normal wear and tear, physical depreciation; **übliche** ~ normal wear and tear.

Abnutzungs|absetzung depreciation for wear and tear; ~**entschädigung** compensation for wear and tear; ~**satz** rate of wear and tear; ~**schaden** damage due to wear and tear.

Abolition *f* general pardon, (general)

9

Abonnement

quashing of criminal proceedings *for a certain type of offence*; amnesty.

Abonnement *n* subscription; ~**fernsehen** pay-TV; ~**sdauer** subscription period; ~**(s)karte** season ticket, subscriber('s) ticket *(season)*; ~**smahnung** renewal reminder; ~**(s)preis** subscription rate, subscription fee; ~**svertrag** subscription contract.

Abonnent *m* subscriber; ~**en werben** to solicit subscribers *(or* subscriptions); ~**en-Unfallversicherung** subscribers' accident insurance; ~**enversicherung** subscribers' insurance.

abonnieren *v/t* to subscribe, to have a subscription for.

abordnen *v/t* to delegate.

Abordnung *f* delegation; ~ **e-s Mitarbeiters** delegation, posting (transfer) of employee to another location.

Abpackbeutel *m* repackaging bag *(retail sales)*.

Abpacken *n* packaging.

abraten *v/i* to advise against.

Abrategebühr *f* lawyer's fee for examining and advising against an appeal.

abräumen *v/t* to clear (away), to strip, to remove.

abrechnen *v/i* to render an account, to invoice, to account, to bill; **netto** ~ to render a net statement.

Abrechner *m* settlement clerk *(banking)*.

Abrechnung *f* settlement of accounts, invoicing, statement, invoice statement; ~**sbank** clearing bank *(drawn on)*; ~**sbescheid** fiscal authority's statement of account; contract note *(Stock Exchange)*; ~**sbetrug** false accounting; ~**sbogen** summary, accounting sheet; ~**skurs** making up net price *(by broker)*, settling price-rate; ~**smanipulation** accounting manipulation; ~**speriode** accounting period; **a~reif** billable, accountable; ~**ssaldo** clearing balance; ~**sschlüssel** settlement formula; ~**sstelle** clearing office;

Absage

~**stag** accounting reference date, day for settling accounts; ~**sverfahren** clearing procedure; accounting method; ~**swährung** currency of payment; ~**szeit** accounting period; ~**szeitraum** accounting (reference) period, period of settlement; **anerkannte** ~ acknowledged settlement statement; **e-e** ~ **nachprüfen** to audit an account, to check a settlement statement; **gegenseitige** ~ mutual invoicing; *(der Kommissionäre und Makler:)* exch ringing up; **jährliche** ~ annual accounting; **laut** ~ as per account rendered; **nach** ~ **der Spesen** after deduction of expenses; **tägliche** ~ daily settlement of accounts; **zentrale** ~**sstelle** central clearing house

Abrede *f* informal agreement, understanding; **das ist gegen unsere** ~ that is contrary to our understanding; **e-e** ~**treffen** to agree *(informally)*; **in** ~ **stellen** to deny, to disavow; **mündliche** ~ oral understanding, verbal agreement; **stillschweigende** ~ tacit agreement.

abreisefertig *adj* ready to sail *(ship)*.

abreißen *v/t* to demolish *(building)*, to pull down, to tear down.

Abreißkalender *m* sheet calendar, tear-off calendar.

Abriß *m* (1) synopsis *(digest of law)*.

Abriß *m* (2) demolition *(of building etc)*.

Abruf *m* call, request for delivery of goods ordered *(deliverable on call)*, request for funds on loan *(loan on call)*; ~**arbeit** employment at call *(at employer's request)*; ~**auftrag** order for goods to be delivered on demand; ~ **bestellter Ware** request for delivery; ~ **von Geldern** calling of funds; **auf** ~ *(goods)* on call, ready for delivery; **künftige** ~**e** future calls.

abrufen *v/t* to call, to request delivery of goods ordered.

abrunden *v/t* to round down.

Abrundung *f* rounding down.

Absage *f* refusal, cancellation.

absagen *v/i* to decline, to cancel, to refuse.

Absatz *(1) m* paragraph, subparagraph, clause, sub-clause; **der rot angekreuzte** ~ the paragraph marked with a red "X"; **der rotangestrichene** ~ the paragraph sidelined in red.

Absatz *(2) m* marketing, selling, sale(s); ~**abkommen** sales agreement; ~ **an Private** sales to private takers, sales to the private sector; ~**bedingungen** conditions on the market; ~**behinderung** blocking sales, sales impediment; impeding the marketing; ~**belebung** stimulating sales, increased sales; ~**beschränkungen** sales limitations; ~**chancen** sales potential; *bequeme ~~: convenient sales potential; weltwirtschaftliche ~~: world-wide economic potential;* ~**erwartungen** sales expectations; ~**fachmann** marketing man; ~**fähigkeit** selling capacity; ~**finanzierung** financing of sales, customer financing, instalment sales financing; ~**finanzierungsszessionar** factor; ~ **finden** to find a market, to sell *v/i*; ~**flaute** sales slump; ~**fondgesetz** Act on Agricultural Marketing Fund *(D, 1976)*; ~**förderung** sales promotion; trade promotion; ~**forschung** market research; ~**garantie** sales guarantee; ~**gebiet** sales territory; *neue ~~e erschließen: to open up new markets;* ~**genossenschaft** marketing co-operative; *landwirtschaftliche ~~: agricultural (marketing) cooperative;* ~**kartell** sales cartel, distribution cartel; ~**kontingente** marketing quotas; ~**kontingentierung** quota system for sales, sales quotas; ~**kosten** distribution expenses, marketing expenses, marketing costs; ~**kredit** sales credit; ~**krise** sales crisis; ~**lage** sales situation, current state of sales; ~**lager** dealers' inventories of merchandise; ~**land** importing country; ~**lenkung** controlled distribution, steering of sales; ~**mangel** lack of sales; ~**markt** sales market; ~**menge** quantity of sales; ~**möglichkeit** sales outlet; *mit sicherer ~~: certain to sell;* ~**netz** sales network; ~**organisation** sales organization; *landwirtschaftliche ~~: agricultural marketing association;* ~**plan** sales plan, marketing scheme; ~**politik** marketing policy, sales policy, distribution policy; ~**prognose** sales forecast; ~**provision** sales commission; ~**quote** sales quota; ~**regelung** market control; ~**richtung** direction of trade; ~**risiko** marketing risk; ~**rückgang** decline in sales, reduction in sales; ~**schwankung** sales fluctuation; ~**schwierigkeiten** sales difficulties; ~**spielraum** scope for sales; ~**statistik** distribution statistics, sales statistics; ~**steigerung** increase in sales; ~**stockung** sales stagnation, slump in sales; ~**tempo** sales pace; ~**verhältnisse** market conditions; ~**volumen** sales volume; ~**wege** distribution channels; ~**werbung** sales promotion; ~**werte** sales figures; ~**wesen** marketing; ~**wirtschaft** marketing; **erzielbarer** ~ sales potential; **gerade noch rentabler** ~ sale of marginal value; **langsamer** ~ slow sale(s); **regionaler** ~ regional market; **reißend** ~ **finden** to sell rapidly; **reißender** ~ rapid sales; **schneller** ~ ready sales; *schnellen ~ finden: to find a ready market.*

abschaffen *v/t* to abolish, to repeal, get rid of.

Abschaffung *f* abolition, abolishment, repeal, *sth.* which can be estimated; ~ **der Todesstrafe** abolition of the death penalty.

abschätzbar *adj* appraisable.

abschätzen *v/t* to appraise, to estimate

abschicken *v/t* to dispatch.

abschieben *v/t* to pass *forged notes or bills*; to deport *(undesirable alien)*; to remove.

Abschiebung *f (unerwünschter Ausländer)* (summary) deportation *(of undesirable alien)*, removal; summary return to native country; **~sandrohung** warning, that deportation could be imposed; **~sbefugnis** power of removal; **~shaft** detention for deportation; custody prior to deportation; **~sschutz** temporary protection from summary deportation.

Abschied *m* resignation, departure, farewell; **~saudienz** farewell audience, valedictory audience; **~sgesuch** resignation; *das ~~ einreichen: to tender one's resignation; to hand in one's resignation;* **~srede** farewell speech, valedictory address; **den ~ erhalten** to be retired; **den ~ nehmen** to quit (*the service*), to resign (*from a post*).

Abschirmdienst *f* (military) counter-intelligence, agency; **Militärischer ~ (MAD)** Military Screening Service.

abschirmen *v/t* to screen, to shield.

Abschirmung *f* screening (*device*); **atomare ~** nuclear umbrella.

Abschlag *m* discount, rebate, markdown price reduction; **~sdividende** interim dividend; **~srechnung** invoice on account; **~szahlung** (part) payment on account, interim payment, progress payment, anticipation payment; **pauschaler ~** flat-rate reduction.

abschlagen *v/t* to refuse (*a request*).

abschlägig *adj* negative (*reply*).

Abschleppen *n* towing-away.

Abschleppfahrzeug *n* towing vehicle, vehicle lifting truck.

abschließen *v/t* to conclude, to complete, (*a contract*), to close (*an account*), to balance (*an account*), to finalize (*negotiations*).

Abschluß *m* completition, conclusion of contract; closing the accounts, bargain, termination, ultimate balance, final accounts, financial statements; **~agent** agent with power to conclude a contract; underwriting agent (*insurance*); **~bedingungen** terms of business; **~bericht** final report; **~besprechung** final discussion; **~bilanz** closing balance; **~buchung** closing entry; **~ der Bücher** closing of the account books, balancing of accounts; **~ der Sitzungsperiode** conclusion of a session *parliament*; **~ergebnis** final results; **~freiheit** freedom to contract; **~gebühren** closing fees (*in mortgages*), completion fees, front-end fees; **~gliederungsprinzip** principle of account classification; **~konten** closing accounts, final accounts; **~kosten** closing expenses; **~kurs** closing price (*securities*); trading price; **~nota** closing note; **~ort** place of contracting, place where deal is closed; **~prämie** sales premium; **~preis** strike price; **~provision** commission for closing business; **~prüfer** accountant, auditor; **~prüfung** final examination, audit (*of annual accounts*); **~rechnung** final accounting, final settlement; **~saldo** closing balance; **~schreiben** final warning notice (*unfair competition*); **~stichtag** accounting reference date, fixed date for closing; **~termin** target date for closing, closing records; **~unterlagen** closing records; **~vergütung** end-of-year-bonus (*to staff*); **~vertreter** = **~agent** *qv*; **~vollmacht** power (of attorney) to close deal (*or:* to complete) a deal; **~ von Deckungsgeschäften** hedging *in securities;* **~zahlung** final payment (*instalments*); **~~ für das Rechnungsjahr**: *closing payment for the accounting year;* **~ziffern** profit and loss figures (*in company reports*); **~ zu festem Verkaufspreis** outright sale; **bei ~ des Berichts** at the time the report went to press (*or:* to print), (*or:* was concluded); **~ tätigen** to close a deal; **fester ~** confirmed deal; **maßgebender ~zeitpunkt** effective balance sheet date; **neuer ~** new business transaction.

Abschnitt *m* section, subdivision, part, chapter, phase, counterfoil, stub; **~sbesteuerung** taxation by fixed assessment periods.

abschöpfen *v/t* to skim off, to siphon

Abschöpfung

off, to tax away, absorb (*excessive buying power*).
Abschöpfung *f* siphoning off, taxing away, price-adjustment levy, agricultural levy.
Abschöpfungs|anleihe loan designed to absorb surplus money; **~bescheid** price-adjustment levy (*EEC price adjustment*); **~betrag** price-adjustment levy; *innergemeinschaftlicher ~~:* price adjustment levy within the EEC.; **~regelung** adjustment levy regulation; **~satz** price-adjustment rate.
abschotten *v/t* to seal off (*bulkhead*).
abschrecken *v/t* to deter, to frighten off, to scare away.
Abschreckung *f* deterrence; **~sprinzip** principle of deterrence; **~swirkung** deterrent effect; **atomare ~** nuclear deterrence.
abschreiben *(1) v/t* to copy, to transcribe, to plagiarize.
abschreiben *(2) v/i – v/t* to write off, to take depreciation (on), to mark down, to charge off, to make a deduction for depreciation; **als uneinbringlich ~** to write off as an irrecoverable loss.
Abschreibung *f* write-off, depreciation, allowable tax depreciation, removal (*of an item*) from a register; write-down; *removal of plot of real estate from land register folio;* **~en auf Anlagevermögen** depreciation of fixed assets, write-down of investments; **~ auf Basis der Wiederbeschaffungskosten** replacement-cost method of depreciation; **~ auf Basis des geschätzten Nutzens** estimated service-yield basis of depreciation; **~en auf Beteiligungen** write-down of investment in shares of subsidiaries and associated companies; **~en auf den Zugang** depreciation on newly acquired assets; **~en auf Finanzanlagen** write-down of investments; **~en auf Geschäftswert** write-down of goodwill; **~ auf Sachanlagen** depreciation of fixed assets; **~en auf Warenbestände** inventory depreciation; **~en auf**

Abschreibung

Zugänge des Geschäftsjahres depreciation and write-downs on additions made during the fiscal year; **~en vornehmen** to undertake depreciation; **~ für Abnützung** depreciation for wear and tear; **~ für Wertminderung** loss-in-value depreciation, depreciation allowance **~ nach proportionaler Gesamtleistung** (*zB e-r Maschine*) production depreciation; **~ nach Wiederbeschaffungskosten** replacement method of depreciation; **arithmetische degressive ~** sum-of-digits depreciation; **aufgelaufene ~** accumulated depreciation; **außerordentliche ~** extraordinary write-off, extraordinary depreciation; **außerplanmäßige ~** non-scheduled depreciation, extraordinary depreciation; **beschleunigte ~** accelerated write-off; **buchmäßige ~** recorded depreciation; **degressive ~** reducing-balance (*method of*) depreciation; **digitale ~** sum-of-digits depreciation, sum-of-the-years-digits method; **entstandene ~en** depreciation accruals; **erste ~ bei Neubauten** initial allowance for depreciation of new buildings; **fiskalisch zugelassene ~** allowable tax depreciation; **jährliche ~** annual depreciation; **kalkulatorische ~** calculated depreciation; depreciation for cost-accounting purposes; **lineare ~** straight-line depreciation, depreciation at a constant rate; **planmäßige ~** scheduled depreciation; **progressive ~** progressive rate of depreciation (*increasing instalments*); **reinvestierte ~** amount written off in respect of depreciation and subsequently reinvested; **scharf degressive ~** depreciation on a steeply degressive scale; **schwankende ~** varying rates of depreciation; **steuerliche ~** tax depreciation; **steuerliche ~sbegünstigung** tax privilege in respect of depreciation; **verdiente ~en** earned depreciation; **vorzeitige ~** anticipatory write-off.

Abschreibungs|aufwand depreciation expenses; ~**betrug** fraudulent writing-off practices; ~**dauer** period of depreciation; ~**erleichterung** write-off facilities, relief by way of depreciation; ~**fonds** investment fund for depreciation, depreciation reserve; ~**freiheit** depreciation allowance; ~**gegenstand** depreciation unit; ~**gesellschaft** tax shelter company; ~**konto** depreciation account; ~**korrekturen** adjustment for depreciation; ~**kosten** depreciation charges; ~**kriterium** depreciation criterion; ~**methode** accounting method of depreciation; ~**möglichkeiten für Investitionen** writing-off possibilities in respect of capital expenditure; ~**objekt** item to be depreciated, property suitable for special depreciation; ~**plan** depreciation plan, plan for the utilization of depreciation, depreciation scheme; ~**präferenz** special depreciation allowance; ~**quote** rate of depreciation, rate of wear and tear; ~**regelungen** rules governing depreciation *(for tax purposes)*; ~**reserve** reserve fund for accrued depreciation; ~**rhythmus** rate at which assets are written off; ~**rückstellung** special reserve fund for depreciation; ~**satz** *(annual)* depreciation rate, rate of depreciation; ~**tabelle** table of depreciation; ~**vergünstigung** tax privilege in respect of depreciation; ~**zeitraum** asset depreciation range.

Abschrift *f* copy, carbon copy, transcript; ~ **e-s Wechsels** transcript of bill of exchange; **amtliche** ~ official copy, certified copy; **beglaubigte** ~ attested copy, certified copy, authenticated copy; ~ ~ *aus e-m Staatsarchiv*: record office copy; **eigenhändige** ~ copy in one's own hand(writing); **genaue** ~ identical copy, exact copy; **gerichtlich beglaubigte** ~ court attested copy, court-sealed copy; **gleichlautende** ~ conformed copy, true (and exact) copy; **mit der Urschrift übereinstimmende** ~ a true copy; **notariell beglaubigte** ~ notarized copy; **vollständige** ~ full copy, complete copy.

abschwächen *v reflex* to decline, to slacken *(economic activity)*, to weaken.

Abschwächung *f* decline, sagging, softening, downturn, easing *(market)*; ~ **der Expansion** slowdown in expansion; ~**serscheinung** sign of approaching downturn; *lagerzyklisch bedingte* ~~*en*: signs of weakening caused by the stock cycle; ~**smöglichkeit** downside risk *(equities)*, downside potential; ~**stendenz** recessionary trend; **konjunkturelle** ~ cyclical slowdown.

abschweifen *v/i* to digress *(from a subject)*.

Abschweifung *f* digression.

abschwören *v/t* to abjure, to swear off.

Abschwung *m* downward swing *(in market)*, down-turn; ~**sphase** downward cycle *(in economics)*.

absehbar *adj* foreseeable, **in** ~**er Zeit** within a reasonable time, within the foreseeable future.

absehen (von) *v/t* to refrain from.

Absehen *n* **von Strafe** exemption from punishment.

Absendebescheinigung *f* certificate of posting.

absenden *v/t* to send, to post *(a letter)* *(GB)*, to mail *(US)*, to dispatch *(freight)*, to ship *(cargo)*.

Absender *m* the sender *(of a letter)*, consignor *(of freight)*, shipper *(of merchandise)*; ~**-Freistempel** postage will be paid by sender.

Absendetag *m* date of mailing, day of posting.

Absendung *f* dispatch(ing).

Absenkung *f* lowering ground-water level.

absetzbar *adj* deductible *(from taxes)*, marketable *(securities)*, dismissible *(official)*; **steuerlich** ~ tax deduct-

Absetzbarkeit   **Abstammung**

ible; **voll** ~ allowable in full against taxable profits.
Absetzbarkeit *f* marketability, salability, deductibility.
absetzen *v/t* to sell, to market, to distribute; *mehr* ~: to increase sales, to outsell; to oust *(from office)*, to remove; to deduct *(expenses)*; **sich** ~ to abscond.
Absetzung *f* removal from office, dismissal, ouster, discharge, deduction *(costs)*; ~ **e-s Termins** cancellation of trial date; **~en für Abnutzung** depreciation for wear and tear; ~ **für Substanzverringerung** depletion allowance; **erhöhte** ~ increased rate of depreciation; **gewaltsame** ~ forcible ouster *(from office)*; **zulässige ~en** admissible deductions.
absichern to secure, to guard against.
Absicherung *f* safeguarding, providing collateral for a loan; ~ **gegen Marktrisiken** providing cover against market risks; ~ **im Warentermingeschäft** facilities for covering risks in commodity futures trading.
Absicht *f* intention, intent; ~ **der Parteien** intention of the parties; ~ **der Wohnsitzbildung** the intention to establish a permanent residence; **~sanfechtung** *petition to have a transaction rescinded because of intent to give creditor preferential treatment*; **~serklärung** declaration of intention, letter of intent; **betrügerische** ~ fraudulent intent(ion); **böse** ~ evil intention, spirit of mischief; *in* ~*r* ~: *maliciously*; **böswillige** ~ malicious intent; *in* ~*r* ~*:* *maliciously, with malice*; **e-e** ~ **dartun** to evince *or* express an intention; **gegenteilige** ~ contrary intention; **gesetzgeberische** ~ legislative intent; **gewinnsüchtige** ~ avaricious intent, motive of lucre; **in bester** ~ with the best intentions; **in betrügerischer** ~ with fraudulent intent; **in böser** ~ with malice; **in der** ~ with a view to; **in verbrecherischer** ~ with felonious intent; **mutmaßliche** ~ presumed intention; **rechtsgeschäftliche** ~ intention to create legal effect; **verfassungsfeindliche** ~ treasonable intent, subversive intent.
absichtlich *adv* intentionally, wilfully, purposely, on purpose.
absolut *adj* absolute, out and out.
Absolvent *m* degree holder, graduate, academic.
absondern *v/t* to sever, to segregate, to separate, to obtain preferential treatment *(as lienholder in bankruptcy)*.
Absonderung *f* preferential treatment for secured creditor, separate satisfaction of lienholders in bankruptcy.
Absonderungs|anspruch preferential claim of secured creditor; **~gläubiger** preferred creditor; **~recht** preferential right, *right of preferential satisfaction of secured creditor*.
Absorptionsprinzip *n* lesser included offence principle.
abspalten *v/t* to segregate *(cost components, etc)*.
Abspalter *m* dissident.
Abspaltung *f* segregation, split, spin-off.
abspecken *v/i* to slim down *(firm)*.
abspenstig machen to entice *(a customer)* away.
Absperrungs|gitter barrier, railings, restraining bar; **~maßnahmen** *f/pl* cordoning off *(by police)*.
Absprache *f* understanding, accord, agreement, gentleman's agreement *(unsigned)*, arrangement, civil conspiracy; **geheime** ~ collusive agreement; **verbotene** ~ *(civil or criminal)* conspiracy.
absprachegemäß *adv* as per understanding, as agreed.
absprechen *v/t* to disallow a claim *(judicially)*; to come to an informal agreement with s. o.
abstammen *v/i* to descend (from).
Abstammung *f* origin, national origin; parentage, descent; lineage descent; **außereheliche** ~ illegitimate descent; **blutschänderische**

15

~ incestuous descent; **ehebrecherische** ~ adulterous descent; **eheliche** ~ legitimate descent; **uneheliche** ~ illegitimate descent.

Abstammungs|feststellung certification of parentage (*by court*); **~feststellungsklage** paternity suit; **~gutachten** expert opinion on someone's lineage; **~nachweis** proof of parentage; **~prinzip** jus sanguinis (*as to nationality*); **~surkunde** certificate of descent and personal status; **~urteil** judgment concerning descent.

Abstand *m* distance; ~ **halten** to keep one's distance; ~ **nehmen** to refrain from; **mit** ~ by a margin; **zeitlicher** ~ time lag.

Abstands|fläche space (*between buildings*); **~geld** premium, forfeit money, key money (*tenancy*); **~summe** compensation, indemnity; **~zahlung** release payment.

abstellen *v/t* to park, to garage; to abolish (*corruption*), to abate (*nuisance*); to remedy, to cut off, to refer to as authoritative, to be guided by; to assign (*an employee*).

Abstellgleis *n* storage siding.

Abstellung *f* assignment (*of employee to a special task*).

Abstellung *f* **e-s Übelstandes** redress of a grievance.

abstempeln *v/t* to postmark (*a letter*), to cancel (*tax stamps*); *fig* to label.

Abstimmbarkeit *f* reconcilability (*of accounts*).

abstimmen (1) *v/i* to vote (*on a motion*), to ballot (*for division*); ~ **lassen** to put to the vote; **namentlich** ~ to take a roll-call vote.

abstimmen (2) *v/t* to reconcile (*accounts*), to reach an understanding (*on measures to be taken*).

Abstimmende *pl* voters.

Abstimmung *f* (1) coordination, matching; mutual understanding; ~ **von Konten:** reconciliation; ~ **der Wirtschaftspolitik** coordination of general economic policy; ~ **innerstaatlicher Maßnahmen** harmonization of national measures (*with treaty obligations*); ~ **über interessierende Fragen** reconciliation of views on problems of common interest; **gegenseitige** ~ harmonization, *nach* ~ *r* ~: *as mutually understood*; **ressortmäßige** ~ coordination of departmental views.

Abstimmung *f* (2) vote, voting, poll, referendum (*by population*), plebiscite (*on national issue*), division (*parliament*); ~ **durch Erheben von den Sitzen** voting by rising from the seats; ~ **durch getrennte Zählung** vote by division; ~ **durch Hammelsprung** division, dividing, voting on division; ~ **durch Handaufheben** vote by show of hands; ~ **durch Namensaufruf** voting by call of names, voting by roll call; ~ **durch Vertreter** voting by proxies; ~ **durch Zuruf** vote by acclamation, voice vote, oral vote, vote viva voce; ~ **ohne Fraktionszwang** free vote; ~ **zur Sache** vote on the merits (*not procedural*), vote on substantive motion; **ablehnende** ~ negative vote; **e-e schriftliche** ~ **verlangen** to demand a poll; **geheime** ~ secret vote, vote by (secret) ballot; **knappes** ~ **sergebnis** close vote; **namentliche** ~ roll-call vote, polling by calling out voters' names, voting on a poll (*company meeting*); **offene** ~ open balloting, open vote; **öffentliche** ~ public voting; **schriftliche** ~ voting by written ballot, voting by correspondence, postal vote; **überraschende** ~ surprising vote, upset vote; **unentschiedene** ~ (voting) tie; **zur** ~ **bringen** to put to the vote; **zur** ~ **schreiten** to proceed to the vote; **zur** ~ **stellen** to put to the vote.

Abstimmungs|antrag voting proposal, motion that the vote be taken; **a~berechtigt** entitled to vote; **~berechtigter** qualified voter; **~bezirk** voting precinct, constituency; **~ergebnis** vote, voting result, election returns, *knappes* ~~: close vote; *positives* ~~: *affirmative vote*; **~gebiet** plebiscitary area;

abstoßen | **Abtretung**

~**geheimnis** voting secrecy, confidentiality of voting; ~**handlung** (act of) voting; ~**lokal** voting place, ballot station; ~**machine** voting machine; ~**mechanismus** coordinating mechanism; ~**modus** voting procedure; ~**niederlage** voting defeat, election defeat; ~**niederschrift** voting record; ~**räume** voting premises; ~**recht** right to vote, franchise right; ~**reglement** voting system; ~**schutzvorrichtungen** voting security devices; ~**verfahren** voting procedure, voting method; ~**zettel** ballot paper.

abstoßen v/t to unload (*securities*), to clear out (*inventory*); **A~** n sell-off.

abstrakt adj abstract, isolated from other transactions, absolute.

Abstraktionsprinzip n *the principle of the abstract nature of rights in rem.*

Abstreiten n denial.

abstreiten v/t to deny (*a charge*), to contest (*a right*).

Abstrich m curtailment, reduction, cutback (*of expenses*).

abstrus adj abstruse, recondite.

Abstufung f graduation (*into shades*); lowering the class (*of a road*).

abstützen v/t to shore up (*prices, rates*).

absuchen v/t to search, to comb (*area for fugitives*).

abtakeln v/t to unrig (*ship*).

abtasten v/t to feel, to frisk (*clothing*), to pat down (*for weapons*); to try out, to sound.

Abtastverfahren n scanning method.

abteilen v/t to parcel, to divide (*into parts*), to partition, to sever, to compartmentalise, to departmentalise.

Abteilung f department, section, directorate, directorate-general (*government*); division (*of a business*), ward (*in hospital*); **technische ~** engineering department.

Abteilungs|direktor departmental manager, head of directorate (-general); ~**gemeinkosten** departmental overhead; ~**kalkulation** departmental costing; ~**leiter** superintendent, head of a department; ~**prämiensystem** department incentive system; **organisatorisch getrennte ~en** separately organized departments.

Abtötung f **der Leibesfrucht** feticide (= *foeticide*).

abtragen v/t to pay off (*in instalments*); to discharge (*obligations*); to place in a dead file, to close the file.

abträglich adj detrimental, derogatory, prejudicial.

Abtragung f paying off (*debt*), amortization.

Abtransport m transport, removal.

abtransportieren v/t to transport away, to remove, to evacuate (*population*).

abtreiben v/t to cause or perform an abortion, to abort.

Abtreibung f abortion; **~ der eigenen Leibesfrucht** self-induced abortion; ~**seingriff** abortion operation; ~**smittel** abortifacient.

abtrennbar adj severable, detachable.

abtrennen v/t to sever (*court proceedings*), to separate, to detach (*coupon from bond*), to partition off (*a department*).

Abtrennung f severance *of a suit* (*court*); clipping (*interest coupons*), partitioning (off); (*part of a room*); **die ~ des Verfahrens anordnen** to order that a suit be severed; ~**srecht** right of severance.

abtretbar adj assignable, transferable.

Abtretbarkeit f assignability.

abtreten v/t to assign (*a claim*), to transfer (*an account*); to relinquish (*rights*); to cede (*territory*).

Abtretender m, (*der Abtretende, die Abtretende*) assignor, transferor, relinquisher, ceding (*state*).

Abtretung f assignment (*of claims, outstanding accounts, rights*); transfer, conventional subrogation, cession (*of territory by one state to another*); surrender (*of land to a public authority*); **~ an Zahlungsstatt** assignment as payment (= *in lieu of payment*); **~ der Ersatzansprüche** assignment of compensation claims *against tortfeasor*; ~**sanzeige** notice

17

Abtrünniger / **Abwehr**

of assignment; ~**saussschluß** prohibition of assignment (clause); ~**sbegünstigter** allottee, assignee, transferee; ~**sempfänger** assignee, transferee; ~**serklärung** declaration of assignment, act of assignment; ~**sgebiet** ceded territory; ~**surkunde** assignment document, instrument of assignment; ~**sverbot** covenant not to assign; ~**svertrag** contract of assignment, treaty of cession; ~ **von Lohn- und Gehaltsansprüchen** assignment of wages; ~ **zahlungshalber** assignment for the purpose of payment (*principal debt remains undischarged until full collection of assigned claim has been effected*); **gütliche** ~ voluntary assignment; **zwangsweise** ~ assignment by operation of law, forced sale (*of land to public authority*); compulsory cession (*of territory*).

Abtrünniger m (*der Abtrünnige*) defector, secessionist, deserter.

aburteilen v/t to adjudge (*in criminal law*); **summarisch** ~: to sentence summarily.

Aburteilung f conviction, sentencing, adjudgment for a criminal offence; **erneute** ~ resentencing; **nach strafgerichtlicher** ~ upon conviction by a criminal court; **zur** ~ **bringen** to commit for trial, to bring to trial; **zur** ~ **überweisen** to remand for trial, to commit for trial.

abverdienen v/t to earn by labo(u)r, to work off (*a debt.*).

abverlangen v/t to demand (*sth. of s.o.; e.g. letter from post office*).

abvermieten v/t to sublet (*a room*).

abwägen v/t to weigh (*one thing against the other*), to balance; **das Für und Wider** ~ to weigh the pros and cons.

Abwägung f consideration, weighing; ~**sfehler** error of judgment, error in obtaining a judicial balance; **bei** ~ **aller Umstände** on balance; considering the facts and circumstances (*of the case*), all things considered.

Abwahl f recall election, vote to remove from office.

abwählen v/t to vote out (*of office*).

abwälzen v/t to pass on, to shift (*burden, tax*).

Abwälzung f passing on (*price increase, tax etc.*) to another.

abwandeln v/t to modify.

Abwandelung f modification (*of draft contract etc.*).

abwandern v/i to migrate (*to another area*).

Abwanderung f migration (*from*), outflow, exodus; ~ **auf andere Verkehrsträger** transfer to other types of carriers; ~ **von Kapital** exodus of capital funds; ~ **von Kunden** drifting away of customers, gradual loss of customers.

Abwärtsbewegung f downward movement, downtrend, bearish tendency.

Abwasser n waste water, sewage; ~**abgaben** sewage charges, water pollution control levy; ~**behandlung** waste water treatment; ~**beseitigung** sewage disposal; ~**gebühren** sewer charges; **gereinigtes** ~ treated sewage.

abwechseln v/i to alternate (between).

abwechselnd adv alternately.

abwegig adj fallacious (*reasoning*), irrelevant (*argument*), (entirely) mistaken (*point of view*), (absolutely) wrong, ill-founded.

Abwegigkeit f fallacy, irrelevance, erroneousness.

Abwehr f defence (*US: defense*), warding off (*danger*), parrying (*blow*), counter-intelligence; ~**anspruch** right to defensive demand; ~**aussperrung** defensive lockout; ~ **e-s gegenwärtigen Angriffs** repulse of an actual attack; ~**klage** injunction porceedings, petition for injunction (*to restrain s.o. from commiting a nuisance or wrongful act*); ~**konditionen** defensive conditions; ~**maßnahme** defensive measures ~**werbung** counter publicity; ~**zeichen** defensive trade mark; ~**zölle** protective tariffs.

18

Abweichen *n* deviation.
abweichen *v/i* to differ, to deviate *(from course, from standard)*, to depart *(from subject matter)*, to digress *(from a rule)*, to go off *at a tangent*.
abweichend *adj* divergent, differing, dissenting, out of line; ~ **von §..** notwithstanding section.., deviating from section... contrary to section..
Abweichler *m* deviationist.
Abweichlertum *n* deviationism.
Abweichung *f* variance, deviation, divergence, derogation; **~en nach oben oder unten** plus or minus variations; **~sanalyse** analysis of cost divergence; **~sklausel** deviation clause; ~ **vom Standard** deviation from the standard (*or*: from the norm); ~ **vom Thema** digression from the subject; ~ **von der Rechtsprechung** deviation from legal precedent; ~ **von der Route** deviation from the (travel) route; **geringfügige** ~ immaterial deviation, minimal deviation, nominal deviation, slight deviation; **in ~ von** by way of derogation from, deviating from, notwithstanding; ~~~ *den Vorschriften des ..; notwithstanding the provisions of ..;* **mengenmäßige** ~ quantitative deviation, difference in quantity; **unerhebliche** ~ insignificant departure; **zulässige** ~ allowable deviation, tolerable deviation, permissable deviation.
abweisen *v/t* to reject, to dismiss, to turn down, to repudiate; **kostenpflichtig** ~ to dismiss with costs.
Abweisung *f* dismissal *(of action)*; ~ **mangels Masse** rejection of bankruptcy petition due to lack of funds *(to cover the costs of the proceedings)*.
abwendbar *adj* avoidable.
Abwendbarkeit *f* avoidability.
Abwendung *f* warding off, prevention, avoidance *of a danger*; **zur ~ der Zwangsvollstreckung (be-)-zahlen** to pay in order to ward off execution *(without acknowledging the claim)*.
Abwerben *n* (*von Arbeitskräften*) enticing personnel away; poaching labour.
abwerben *v/t* to entice away *(customers from competitors)*, to attract *(workers away from employer)*, to cause s. o. to defect from *(his party etc)*.
Abwerbung *f* enticement *(to join new employer, or of a customer from competitor)*; labo(u)r piracy.
abwerfen *v/t* to yield *(a profit)*.
abwerten *v/t* to devalue *(a currency)*.
Abwertung *f* devaluation *(of currency)*, downward adjustment *(of inventory)*; **~sgewinn** devaluation profit; **~sklausel** devaluation clause; a**~sverdächtig** devaluation-prone; ~ **wegen Mengenrisikos** adjustment for quantitative risks; ~ **wegen Preisrisikos** adjustment for price risks; ~ **wegen Skonti und Niederstwert** adjustment for cash discounts and lowest value; ~ **wegen Sonderlager- und Leihwarenrisikos** adjustment for risks arising from special storage and equipment lent to customers; ~ **wegen technischen Risikos** adjustment for technical risks.
Abwesender *m* (*der Abwesende*) absentee.
Abwesenheit *f* absence; ~ **in der Hauptverhandlung** absence from trial; non-appearance at trial; **eigenmächtige** ~ absence without leave.
Abwesenheits|erkenntnis judgment in absentia; in default of appearance; **~geld** fee for out-of-town services *(of lawyer)*; **~pfleger** curator of the estate of an absentee; curator absentis; **~pflegschaft** curatorship of absentees; **~urteil** sentence in absentia; **~verfahren** proceedings against absentee; **~vertreter** absentee's representative.
abwickeln *v/t* to wind up *(a business)*, to liquidate *(a company)*; to transact, to complete *(contract, assignment)*.
Abwickler *m* liquidator, receiver, adjuster *(insurance claim)*, claims adjuster.

Abwicklung *f* liquidation; handling; ~ **e–s Versicherungsbestandes** winding up insurance contracts on hand; **~bilanz** → *Liquidationsbilanz qv*; **~shandlung** liquidation act (or measure); **~ von Krediten** repaying credits, loans; **bankmäßige ~** handling by banks, processing by a bank; **gerichtliche ~** court ordered liquidation; **verfahrensmäßige ~** procedural management, handling procedure.

Abwicklungs|bank liquidating bank, settling bank; **~eröffnungsbilanz** = *Liquidationseröffnungsbilanz qv*; **~gesellschaft** liquidating company; **~konto** settlement account, liquidation account; **~masse** liquidation assets, total assets and liabilities under liquidation; **~stelle** clearing office, liquidating agency; **~termin** settlement date (*exch*); **~verfahren** winding-up (proceedings); **~verhältnis** winding-up relationship.

abwiegen *v/t* to weigh (*goods*).

Abwiegler *m a person attempting to calm down a riotous crowd.*

abwracken *v/t* to scrap, to dismantle (*a ship*); to wreck (*automobiles*).

Abwrackfirma *f* wreckers.

abzahlbar *adj* repayable, redeemable.

abzahlen *v/t* to pay off, to pay by instalments, to settle.

Abzahlung *f* paying off (*in instalments*), gradual payment, *US:* time payment; **auf ~** on deferred terms, on an instalment plan (=*system*).

Abzahlungs|darlehen loan repayable in instalments; **~geschäft** instalment plan business; **~kauf** (retail) installment sale *US*, hire-purchase transaction *GB*; **~kredit** instalment credit.

Abzeichen *n* badge, *pl* insignia; ~ (*n/pl*) **verbotener Vereinigungen**: *insignia of prohibited organizations.*

abzeichnen *v/t* to initial (*a document*); *am Rande ~: to initial in the margin.*

abziehen *v/t* to deduct, to subtract, to withhold (*tax*), to take (*amount, percentage*) off the total.

Abziehplakat *n* paint transfer poster.

abzielen *v/t* to aim (*at sth*).

abzinsen *v/t* to discount unaccrued interest (*on a bill of lading etc*).

Abzinsung *f* deduction of unaccrued interest; discounting the interest; **~ auf Darlehen** deduction of unaccrued interest on loans; **~sbetrag** amount of discount in respect of unaccrued interest; **~sfaktor** factor used in calculation of present value; **~ssatz** discount rate for unaccrued interest.

Abzug *m* (*pl Abzüge* = ~*e*) deduction, subtraction, discount, rebate, allowance, withholding, recoupment; **~ an der Quelle** deduction at source, withholding at source; **~e für eigene Ansprüche** deductions for own demands (*or ... for own use*); **~e für Sonderausgaben** tax allowance for special expenditure (= *Sonderausgaben qv*); **~e vom steuerpflichtigen Einkommen** deductions from taxable income; **~ neu für alt** deduction for the excess value of a new replacement or repair (*repairing damage*); **anteilige ~e** proportional deductions, pro rata deductions; **bar ohne ~** cash without discount; **e–n ~ gewähren** to allow a rebate; **e–n ~ von 3% machen** to strike off (*or* knock off) 3%; **frei von ~en** free from deductions, *net*; **im ~swege** by way of deduction; **in ~ bringen** to deduct, to allow a deduction; **jährlicher ~** annual allowance (*tax*); **massierte ~e** large-scale withdrawals; **nach ~ der Kosten** after deduction of costs; **nach ~ der Steuern** after (deducting) taxes; **nach ~ von** after deduction of, after allowance for; **ohne ~** without deduction; **ohne ~e jeder Art** free from any deductions, without deductions of any kind; **rein netto, ohne ~e jeder Art** net, without any deduction; **zulässiger ~** admissible allowance (*or* deductions) (*tax*).

Abzug(shahn) *m* trigger.

abzüglich *prep* less, deducting, minus.

Abzugs|beträge statutory deductions; **a~fähig** deductible, tax-deductible; **~fähigkeit** deductibility; **~ von Schuldzinsen:** *interest relief on loans;* **~posten** deductible item; **~steuer** withholding tax; **~tabelle** schedule of deductions; **~verbot** restriction on tax deductions.

abzweigen *v/t* to branch off; to divert from; to earmark *special funds.*

Abzweigung *f* junction *(road),* turn-off, branching off; diversion *(capital).*

Achsenkilometer-Vergütung *f* reimbursement based upon the number of axles and the distance in kilometers.

Achsgewicht *n* axle weight.

Achslast *f* axle weight.

achten *v/t* to regard, to observe, to take care, to respect.

ächten *v/t* to proscribe, to outlaw, to ban; **den Atomkrieg ~** to ban atomic warfare.

Achtgeben *n* watching out; *gehöriges ~:* proper lookout *(traffic).*

Achtlosigkeit *f* inattention, heedlessness, carelessness, neglect.

Achtung *f* attention, esteem, respect; **~!** look out! danger!; **~, Halt!** attention, stop; **~ vor dem Gesetz** respect for the law.

Ächtung *f* proscription, outlawing, ban.

Acker *m* farmland, arable land; soil; **~land** tillable land.

Ackerbau *m* agriculture, farming, cultivation of land; **~kunde** agriculture, agronomy; **~lehre** agronomy; **~ und Viehzucht** farming and (stock) breeding.

actio libera in causa (=) *criminal responsibility of person who knowingly brought about a condition of alcoholic incapacity in order to commit an offence (or negligently foresaw or failed to foresee the commission of the act) in such a condition.*

actio pro socio (=) *an action by a partner against one or several of his associates in respect of recovery for the partnership as a whole.*

ad acta legen to shelve, to put into the files.

Adäquanzprüfung *f* reasonable contemplation test.

Adäquanztheorie *f* theory of adequate *(i. e. not absolute)* causation *(in law of damages).*

adäquat *adj* adequate; appropriate.

Adaptionsrecht *n* right of adaption.

Adel *m* nobility, aristocracy.

adeln *v/t* to ennoble, to raise to nobility, to raise to the peerage, to make s. o. a peer.

Adels|anmaßung assumption of spurious title *(of nobility);* **~brief** patent of nobility; **~herrschaft** feudal government; **~prädikat** title of nobility; **~stand** nobility, peerage; **~titel** title of nobility.

Adgo *f (Allgemeine Deutsche Gebührenordnung) General German Fees Regulation governing doctors' fees.*

Adhärenz *f* adherence; *obs* accessories, appurtenances.

Adhäsions|verfahren *n* adhesive procedure *(damage claim linked with criminal proceedings);* **~vertrag** adhesion contract, supplementary agreement; **~verschluß** adhesion flap *(for "printed matter").*

Adjudikation *f obs* adjudication, award.

adjudizieren *v/t* to adjudge, to adjudicate, to award to s. o.

Administration *f* administration, management.

Administrativenteignung *f* expropriation *(or* condemnation) by administrative authorities.

adoptieren *v/t* to adopt.

Adoptierende(r) *m (= der Adoptierende)* adopting parent.

Adoptierter *m (= der Adoptierte)* adopted person, adoptee.

Adoptierung *f = Adoption qv.*

Adoption *f* adoption.

Adoptions|beschluß adoption order; **~dekret** adoption order; **~fürsorge** adoption service; **~hilfe** adoption service; **~pflege** personal care prior to adoption; **~probezeit** adoption probationary period; **~register** register of adopted children; **~verein** adoption society; **~verhältnis** adoptive

Adoptiveltern   **Agio**

relationship; ~**vermittlung** placement for adoption; ~~ *sstelle placement agency, adoption agency*.

Adoptiv|eltern *pl* adopting parents, adoptive parents; ~**kind** *n* adoptee, adopted child; ~**mutter** *f* adoptive mother; ~**vater** *m* adoptive father; ~**verwandtschaft** relationship by adoption.

Adressat *m* addressee (*recipient of letter*), consignee (*receiver of goods*), payee (*remittance*), offeree (*contractual offer*).

Adreßbuch *n* directory, postal book, trade book, address book.

Adresse *f* address, destination; house, firm; *name of a party on a bill of exchange*; ~**nänderung** change of address; ~**nbüro** agency which sells sets of addresses; **erste** ~ top-rated borrower, triple A rating; **gute** ~ party in good standing (*credit rating*), prime name (*eg bank*); **per** ~ care of = *c/o*; **zweite** ~**n** *pl* second-class names (*firms*).

adressieren *v/t* to address, to direct (*letter etc*).

Adressiermaschine *f* addressograph, addressing machine.

Adreßrecht *m* (ambassador's) right to address (*monarch, head of state*).

ADSp (*Allgemeine Deutsche Spediteurbedingungen*) General Terms and Conditions of German Forwarding Agents.

Advaloremzoll *m* ad valorem duty, stamp duty.

Advokat *m* advocate, attorney at law, lawyer; ~**enkniff** lawyer's sharp practices.

Advokatur *f* law practice, law office, law firm, profession of a lawyer.

Affekt *m* emotional impulse, irresistible impulse; **im** ~in the (sudden) heat of the moment (*or* of passion).

Affektionswert *m* sentimental value, imaginary value.

Affidavierung *f* certification by affidavit.

Affiliation *f* affiliation (*to a subsidiary company*); *obs for* adoption.

Affinität *f* affinity, relationship by marriage.

Affirmation *f* affirmation, assurance.

affirmativ *adj* affirmative.

Affront *m* offence, indignity.

à fonds perdu non-reimbursable; given outright, à fonds perdu.

Afterbelehnung *f* subinfeudation (*of under-vassal*).

Afterbürge *m* second bail, surety for a surety.

Afterbürgschaft *f obs* = Nachbürgschaft *qv*.

Afterlehen *n* arriere fee, inferior fief.

Afterpfand *m* secondary security.

Aftervermietung *f obs* = Untervermietung *qv*.

AGB-Gesetz (*Gesetz zur Regelung des Rechts der Allgemeinen Geschäftsbedingungen, D 1976*) (the German) Unfair Contract Terms Act, Standard Contracts Act.

Agent *m* agent, secret agent, operative; commercial representative; ~**enführer** control agent; ~**enprovision** agent's commission; ~**entätigkeit** secret service activity; ~ **provocateur** entrapping person, agent provocateur, "sting" agent, *US*.

Agentur *f* agency, agency business; sub-branch; ~**vertrag** agency agreement.

Aggravation *f* exaggeration (*of medical complaint*), aggravation.

Aggregat *n* aggregate, unit of machinery, assemblage; ~**zustand** condition, *(solid, liquid, gaseous)* state.

Aggression *f* aggression; ~**skrieg** war of aggression.

Aggressor *m pol* aggressor.

Agio *n* premium; ~**geschäft** *business speculating in capital issues sold at a premium* ~**gewinn** gain in respect of premium, *profit upon capital issue at a premium*; ~**jäger** premium hunter; ~**konto** premium account; ~**notierung** premium quotation, quotation in terms of premium (*securities*); ~**papiere** securities redeemable at a premium; ~**überschuß** premium surplus (*arising from an increase in capital*), share premium reserve.

Agiotage *f* jobbing, speculating in share premium reserves.

Agioteur *m* broker speculating in share premium reserves.

Agitation *f* political agitation, rabble rousing; **aufrührerische** ~ sedition.

Agitator *m* political agitator.

Agnat descendants of the same father's through males; ~**en** *m/pl* agnates, male line of relatives.

Agrar|abschöpfung *agr* (agricultural) levy, ~**bank** farmers' bank, rural credit bank; ~**erzeugnis** *agr* produce, farm product; ~**fonds** *agr* fund; ~**genossenschaft** farmer's cooperative; ~**gesetzgebung** *agr* laws; ~**hypothek** mortgage (loan); ~**kredit** *agr* credit, credit facilities for farmers, farm loan; ~**kreditinstitut** farm loan bank; ~**kultur** agriculture, economy based on agriculture; ~**land** country with predominantly agrarian economy; ~**markt** *agr* market; ~**marktordnung** farm marketing code, agrarian market regulations; ~**marktregelung** *agr* market regulation, *agr* marketing; ~**pfandbrief** farm mortgage bond; ~**politik** *agr* policy, farm policy; ~**preis** price of farm products, *agr* price; ~**preisbildung** price regulation for farm products; ~**preisgefüge** price structure of farm products; ~**preisniveau** level of *agr* prices; ~**preispolitik** *agr* pricing policy; ~**preissubventionen** farm-price subsidies; ~**produktion** *agr* production; ~**programm** *agr* program; ~**recht** *agr* law; ~**rohstoff** agrarian raw material; ~**schutz** protective measures for agriculture; ~**sektor** *agr* sector; ~**staat** *agr* state, farm state; ~**subvention** grant for farmers, *agr* subsidy; ~**überschüsse** farm-product surpluses; ~**verordnung** *agr* regulation; ~**wirtschaft** *agr* economy; ~**wirtschaftler** agronomist; ~**wissenschaft** agronomy, agronomics; ~**zoll** *agr* tariff.

Agrément *n* agrément (*intimation that diplomat is acceptable*); **das** ~ **erteilen** to grant agrément.

Agroindustrie *f* agricultural business.

Agronom *m* agronomist.

Agronomie *f* agronomy, husbandry.

ahnden *v/t* to punish (*for an offence*).

Ahndung *f* punishment (*for an offence*).

Ahne *m* (*pl Ahnen*) ancestor, progenitor.

Ahnen|reihe line of ancestors; ~**tafel** *f* genealogical tree, family tree, pedigree.

Ähnlichkeit *f* similarity; ~**sbereich** area of similarity (*where confusion is possible*); ~**sbeschluß** order to obtain expert opinion on similarity (*of child to putative father*); ~**sbeweis** evidence of similarity, proof on the basis of similarity (*paternity*); ~**sgutachten** expert opinion on similarity (*of child to putative father*); ~**verhältnis** ratio of similitude.

Aide-mémoire *n* aide-mémoire, memorandum.

Akademiker *m* university (*College US*) graduate, professional man, academic; ~**in** female graduate.

Akklamation *f* acclamation, vote by voice, viva voce.

Akkord *m* agreement, piece-work, job-work; ~**arbeit** job-work, piece-work, jobbing; ~**arbeiter** piece-worker; ~**lohn** piece-work pay, piece wage(s), job wage, job rate pay, task wage; ~**lohnsatz** = *Akkordsatz qv*; ~**revision** revising piece work rate; ~**richtsatz** standard piece rate; ~**satz** piece rate, piece-work rate, rate for the job; ~**schere** piece-work squeeze; ~**system** piece-rate plan, work contract system; ~**vertrag** agreement on piece-rate work; ~**zulage** bonus for piece-rate work; **im** ~ **arbeiten** to work by the job.

akkordieren *v/i* to agree, to reach an agreement; to enter into a collective bargaining agreement.

akkreditieren *v/t* to accredit (*to a country*).

Akkreditierung *f* accreditation (*of diplomat*); ~**sbrief** letter of accreditation.

Akkreditiv *n* letter of credit; commercial credit; ~**abwicklung** processing of letter of credit; ~**anzeige** notification of credit; ~**auftrag** order to open a credit; ~**auftraggeber** applicant for the credit; ~**bank** originating bank for a letter of credit, issuing bank; ~**bedingungen** terms and conditions of the (letter of) credit; ~**begünstigter** beneficiary of a letter of credit; ~**deckungsguthaben** customers' balances held as cover for letter of credit; ~**einrede** *defence that seller must first seek satisfaction through the letter of credit;* ~**erlös** proceeds from honouring letter of credit; ~**ermächtigung** letter of authority; ~**eröffnung** establishment of a credit; ~**geschäfte** documentary credit operations; ~**gestellung** opening of credit for; ~**skonto** discount for letter of credit; ~**steller** party providing letter of credit facility; ~**stellung** opening of a letter of credit; ~**verbindlichkeit** liability in respect of credits opened; ~**ziehung** opening of letter of credit; ~**zwang** requirement that letter of credit facilities be used; **bestätigtes ~** confirmed letter of credit; **ein ~ eröffnen** to open a letter of credit; **ein ~ stellen** to open a letter of credit; **einfaches ~** clean letter of credit; **für ~ gebunden** earmarked to cover liability for letters of credit; **negoziierbares ~** negotiable credit; **reines ~** clean letter of credit; **revolvierendes ~** revolving letter of credit; **unbestätigtes ~** unconfirmed letter of credit; **unwiderrufliches ~** irrevocable letter of credit; **unwiderrufliches, bestätigtes ~** confirmed irrevocable letter of credit; **widerrufliches ~** conditional letter of credit.

Akkreszenz *(obs for Anwachsung qv)* accretion, continuous growth.

Akkumulation *f* accumulation.

akkumulieren *v/t* to accumulate, to pile up, to amass.

Akkusationsmaxime *f* (principle of) accusatorial procedure; ~ **prozess** criminal proceedings by accusation and indictment.

Akontozahlung *f* down-payment, payment on account.

Akquisiteur *m* canvasser, agent soliciting orders.

Akquisition *f* (1) canvassing, soliciting of orders, sales promotion; ~**skosten** sales promotion costs (2) acquisition, merger.

Akribie *f* absolute precision; utmost accuracy.

Akronym *n* acronym.

Akt *m* act, deed; sexual act, coitus; *dialect:* = *Akte qv*; **feindlicher ~** hostile act; **notarieller ~** notarization (of deed); **unfreundlicher ~** unfriendly act.

Akte *f (pl Akten)* file *(of documents)*, record *(of a case)*, (police) dossier *or* file *pl* papers, files, written proceedings; ~**n ablegen** to file documents *(or* papers); ~**n anfordern** to ask for records; ~**n vorlegen** to present the files, to place the record before *(a senior official, judge, lawyer)*; **bei den ~n** on file, on record; **e-e ~ ausfertigen** to execute a document; **notarielle ~** notarial document, deed or document recorded and authenticated by a notary; notary's file; **zu den ~n nehmen** to file, to add to the file; to include in the record; **zu den ~n reichen** to put on the file, to file in the records, to submit to the court's records.

Akten|abschrift copy of the file, copy *(of parts)* of the record; ~**auszug** abstract of record, excerpt from the record; ~**beiziehung** supplementing the record, ordering a case-record to be submitted to the court *(for evidentiary purposes)*; ~**beweis** evidence by court record; ~**blatt** leaf *or* sheet from the file; ~**bündel** bundle of files, records; ~**deckel** file cover; ~**durchsicht** checking the files; ~**einforderung** order for the return of a court-record; ~**einsicht** access to records *(searching and inspecting)*, inspection of files; ~**exemplar** record copy; ~**führung** keeping of the files, record-keeping; ~**kopie** file copy; a~**kundig** on (in) the record, known to the court (*from the records*), ~~ *werden: to become a matter of record*; ~**lage** the (present) status of the case, the record as it stands; *nach* ~~ *entscheiden: to adjudicate the case on the record (without further hearing)*; ~**lageentscheidung** *f* ex officio decision *on the basis of the record as it stands (in the event of default of one or both parties)*; a~**mäßig** according to the record; ~**mappe** briefcase, portfolio for documents; ~**notiz** file note, memo; ~**ordnung** filing system; ~**schwanz** index tail, flag; ~**stück** file copy of document, document on file, paper forming part of the record; ~**übersendung** transfer of file; ~**vermerk** file note, memo; ~**vernichtung** destruction of records, shredding; ~**verzeichnis** file index; ~**vorgang** subject of records; what has happened on a file; ~**vorlage** production of the file; ~**vormerkung** advance note (*or* reminder) on file; ~**widrigkeit** non-conformity with matters in the record; ~**wolf** paper-shredder; ~**zeichen** file reference, reference number, file number, case number, number of action, ~ ~ *unbekannt": crime stopper's program (TV).*

Aktie *f* share, share of corporate stock, *pl* (*also*) equities, (equity) securities.

Aktien|agio premium on newly issued shares; ~**anteile** units of shares, premium on stock; share participation; ~**aufgeld** premium on newly issued shares; ~ **auflegen** to issue shares, to offer (for subscription); ~**aufteilung** stock split; ~**ausgabe** issue of shares; ~**ausgeben** to issue shares; ~**bank** joint-stock bank; bank in corporate form; ~**baugesellschaft** building company in corporate form; ~**besitz** shareholdings, stockholding; ~ **besitzen** to hold shares; ~**besitzer** shareholder, stockholder; ~**besitzzeit** duration of possession of shares; ~**bestand** portfolio of shares; ~**beteiligung** share participation; ~**betrug** securities fraud; ~**bewertung** stock valuation; ~ **beziehen** to take up shares, to buy shares; ~**bezugsrecht** subscription right to new shares, stock subscription right; ~**bezugsrechtsschein** warrant (*for new issue*); ~**bonus** share bonus; stock dividend; ~**börse** stock exchange; ~**buch** register of shareholders, register of members; *US:* stock record book, stock transfer journal, register of members, shareholders' roll; ~**dividende** share dividend(s); ~**einlösung** redemption of stock, repurchase of shares; ~**einzahlung** payment for shares; ~ **einziehen** to buy back shares (*by company*); to declare shares forfeited; ~**einziehung** calling in of shares, forfeiture of shares; ~**erwerbsoption** stock option; ~**gattung** class of shares; ~**gesellschaft** → *Aktiengesellschaft*; ~**gesetz** Companies Act, (Stock) Corporation Act; ~**handel** dealing in shares, stockjobbing, stockbroking; ~**händler** dealer in shares, stock-jobber; stockbroker; ~**index** share price index; ~ ~-*Termingeschäfte* stock-index futures; ~**inhaber** shareholder, stockholder; ~**kapital** → *Aktienkapital*; ~**kauf** stock purchase, purchase of shares; ~**konsortium** securities syndicate (*placing new issues*); ~ **im Publikumsbesitz** shares in public possession, outstanding stock; ~**kupon** (dividend) coupon, dividend warrant; ~**kurs** (market) price (*of shares*), market quotation, share quotation; ~**kurszettel** list of quotations; ~ **lauten auf den Namen** shares are issued in the name of s. o.; ~**liste** list of shareholders; ~**majorität** = *Aktienmehrheit qv*; ~**makler** stock broker; share broker; jobber; ~**mantel** share structure of company, company shell;

Aktienmarkt   **genehmigte Aktien**

~**markt** equity market, stock market, share market; ~**material** supply of shares on offer; ~**mehrheit** majority of shares, stock majority; ~ **mit garantierter Mindestdividende** shares with a guaranted minimum dividend rate; ~ **mit Nachbezugsrecht** shares with subsequent subscription (or dividend) rights; ~ **mit Nennwert** par-value shares; ~ **mit rückwirkender Dividende** cumulative dividend shares; ~ **mit Stimmrecht** voting shares; voting stock; ~**mittelwert** par line (*of stock exchange trading*); ~**notierung** share quotation; ~**option** stock option, share option (*in futures trading*); ~**paket** block of shares, parcel of shares, stock package; *beherrschendes* ~ ~: *controlling stock*; ~**papier** share certificate; ~**pool-Vereinbarung** stock pooling agreement; ~**promesse** share warrant, provisional scrip; ~**prospekt** stock prospectus; ~**recht** company law, *US*: corporation law; ~**rechtsnormen** corporation law norms *US*, company law norms *GB*; ~**rechtsreform** company law reform; ~**rendite** yield on stocks or shares; ~**rückkauf** stock buy-back, redemption of stocks or shares, repurchase of stocks; ~**schwindel** share pushing, fraudulent marketing of shares; ~**schwindler** share pusher, fraudulent share salesman; ~**spaltung** share splitting, stock splitting; ~**spekulant** stock exchange speculator; ~**spekulation** playing the (stock) market, speculating in stocks; ~**spitze** share fraction (*left over on rights issue etc.*); ~**split** share splitting, stock split-up; ~**streubesitz** diversified share holdings; ~**stückelung** subdivision of shares, denomination of shares; ~**tausch** stock swap; ~**teilung** stock split; ~**übertragung** stock transfer; ~**umtausch** exchange of shares, switch of shares; ~**unternehmung** stock enterprise; ~**urkunde** *GB* share certificate, *US* stock certificate, certificate of stock; ~ **von der Notierung absetzen** to remove shares from the stock exchange list, to de-list; ~**wert** (*actual*) value of a share; ~**wesen** company law and practice, the capital-share system, matters pertaining to shares and stock corporations; ~ **zeichnen** to subscribe for shares; ~**zeichner** share *or* stock subscriber, new shares buyer; ~**zeichnung** capital stock subscription, subscription for shares; ~**zeichnungsbuch** subscription ledger; ~**zeichnungsliste** allotment sheet; ~**zertifikat** share certificate, stock certificate; *vorläufiges* ~ ~: *stub*; ~ **zurückkaufen** to buy back shares; ~ **zur Zeichnung öffentlich auflegen** to invite applications for the public subscription of shares, to open for subscription; to offer shares to the public; ~ **zusammenlegen** to consolidate stock, to reduce shares; ~**zusammenlegung** reverse split, splitdown, splitback, reduction in shares, consolidation of shares (stock); ~ **zuteilen** to allot shares; ~**zuteilung** allotment of shares; **alte** ~ old shares (*from previous issue*); **amtlich eingeführte** ~ listed shares, officially quoted shares; **auf den Inhaber lautende** ~ bearer shares, shares made out to bearer; **auf den Namen lautende** ~ registered shares; **ausgegebene** ~ issued shares, outstanding (capital) stock; **begebene** ~ issued stock; **börsenfähige** ~ listed stock; **börsengängige** ~ listed shares, marketable stock; **dividendenberechtigte** ~ dividend-paying shares; participating stock; **eigene** ~ company's own shares; **eingezogene** ~ redeemed shares; **emittierte** ~ shares issued (and outstanding); **endgültige** ~ definite shares; **erstklassige** ~ blue-chip stock; blue chips; **fluktuierendes** ~**material** floating supply of shares on offer; **genehmigte** (*noch nicht ausgegebene*) ~ authorized capital, au-

26

thorized (but unissued) stock, unissued treasury stock, reserved shares; **gewinnberechtigte** ~ participating preferred (preference) shares; **gezeichnete** ~ subscribed shares; **hochwertige** ~ blue-chip stock; **junge** ~ new shares, new issue of shares; **kaduzierte** ~ forfeited shares; **nachschußpflichtige** ~ assessable stock (*US*); **nennwertlose** ~ non-par-value shares (= no par value stock), unvalued stock; **nicht amtlich notierte** ~ over-the-counter (*OTC*) shares, unlisted shares, unquoted shares; **nicht gezeichnete** ~ unsubscribed *or*: non-subscribed shares/stock; **nicht im Börsenhandel zugelassene** ~ over-the-counter shares, unquoted shares; **nicht nachschußpflichtige** ~ non-contribution shares; **nicht voll einbezahlte** ~ not fully paid-up shares partly paid shares; **noch nicht ausgegebene** ~ unissued shares; **notierte** ~ listed stock (or shares); **stimmberechtigte** ~ voting shares, voting stock; **stimmrechtslose** ~ non-voting shares, non-voting stock; **unbegebene** ~ unissued shares, unsold shares; **vinkulierte** ~ restricted shares; **voll einbezahlte** ~ (*= einbezahlte*) fully paid-up shares; **zurückerworbene** ~ redeemed shares, reacquired stock.

Aktiengesellschaft joint-stock company, *US* (stock) corporation, *Brit* public (limited) company; **e-e ~gesellschaft gründen** to form (to found) a public company (*or US*: corporation); **gemischtwirtschaftliche** ~ semi-public enterprise; partly public company.

Aktienkapital *n* share-capital, capital stock, joint stock; ~ **erhöhen** to increase the capital (of a company); ~ **herabsetzen** to reduce capital stock; **ausgegebenes** ~ issued capital; **begebenes** ~ capital issued; **dividendenberechtigtes** ~ dividend bearing capital stock; **eingezahltes** ~ paid-up capital; **genehmigtes** ~ (*unissued*) authorized capital; **noch nicht eingezahltes** ~ unpaid capital (stock); **stimmberechtigtes** ~ voting (capital) stock; **verwässertes** ~ watered stock, diluted shares; **voll eingezahltes** ~ fully paid-up (capital) stock.

Aktion *f* action; campaign; operation; **~sfähigkeit** ability to act; **~sfreiheit** freedom to action; **~sgemeinschaft** joint venture group; society for promoting (*the environment*); **~sprogramm** programme of action, campaign plan, scheme; **~sradius** radius of action.

Aktionär *m* shareholder; stockholder *US*, member (*of a company GB*), member (*of a corporation US*); **~sbrief** letter of information to shareholders; **~sbuch** = *Aktienbuch* *qv*; **~sstimmrecht** shareholder's voting right; **~sversammlung** general meeting (of shareholders), general meeting of a company; **außenstehender** ~ outside shareholder; **bezugsberechtigter** ~ shareholder entitled to subscription; allottee; **eingetragener** ~ registered shareholder (stockholder); **freie ~e** outside shareholders.

Aktiv|bestand net assets; **~bilanz** favo(u)rable balance; **~forderungen** outstanding debts, accounts receivable; **~geschäfte der Banken** (banks') lending and investment business; **~handel** active trade; **~hypotheken** mortgage lendings; **~kapital** working capital (*opp. = land and buildings*); **~konto** asset account, account having a credit balance; **~legitimation** → *Aktivlegitimation*; **~legitimiert** entitled to the claim (*as the proper party*); **~masse** the bankrupt's estate; **~mitglied** active member; **~posten** asset item; **~salden der Leistungsbilanz** surpluses achieved on goods and services; **~saldo** credit balance; **~seite** assets side (*of the balance sheet*), credit side; **~überschuß** net surplus; **~- und Passivgeschäft** transactions on

Aktiva / **Akzept**

both sides of the balance sheet; ~**vermögen** assets; ~**vollmacht** active power-of-attorney; ~**wert** asset value; ~**zinsen** interest receivable, interest earned.

Aktiva *n/pl* (= *die Aktiven*) assets; ~ **und Passiva** assets and liabilities; **antizipative** ~ accrued assets, accrued receivables, deferred receivables; **die ~ und Passiva übernehmen** to take over the assets and liabilities; **festliegende** ~ permanent assets, fixed assets; **flüssige** ~ liquid assets, circulating assets; **freie** ~ freely disposable assets; **immaterielle** ~ intangible assets, intangibles; **notleidende** ~ non-performing assets; **produktive** ~ active assets; **realisierbare** ~ realizable assets; **sofort realisierbare** ~ immediately realizable assets; **sonstige** ~ other assets; **transferbeschwerte** ~ assets subject to transfer difficulties; **transitorische** ~ transitory assets; assets on suspense account; unexpired expense; prepaid expenses; deferred charges; **unechte** ~ fictitious assets; **verfügbare** ~ available assets; **verwertbare** ~ disposable assets; **werbende** ~ earning assets; productive assets.

Aktivieren *n* = *Aktivierung qv*.

aktivieren *v/t* to set up as assets, to capitalize, to activate; to enter on the assets side (*of the balance sheet*); to revaluate (*depreciated assets according to current value*); to reassign to active duty (*official*).

Aktivierung *f* activation; including an item on the assets side of the balance sheet; capitalization; revaluation (*of depreciated assets according to current value*); reassignment to active duty; ~ **der Zahlungsbilanz** improvement in the balance of payments; ~ **des Außenhandels** improving the export trade, achieving an export surplus; ~ **des Warenverkehrs** promoting trade; ~ **von Abschreibungen bei der Veräußerung** raising written-down assets to current value upon disposal (*of plant*) (*dissolving hidden reserves*).

aktivierungs|fähig capable of being used to improve the asset position; **A~pflicht** *f* duty to capitalize: *duty to disclose or revive items on the assets side of the balance sheet*; ~**pflichtig** *adj* liable to be disclosed or revived on assets side of the balance sheet; **A~recht** right to capitalize; **A~wahlrecht** option either to capitalize items or not.

Aktivist *m* activist; militant.

Aktivität *f* (1) activity, vigo(u)r, energy; (2) surplus on balance-sheet, excess of assets over liabilities; **kreditäre** ~ lending activity.

Aktivlegitimation *f* right of action as the proper party; **mangelnde** ~ incapacity to sue as the proper party, wrong plaintiff.

aktualisieren *v/t* to update, to bring up to date.

Aktualisierung *f* updating, update; ~**sprogramm** updating programme.

Akzept *n* acceptance (*of bill*); accepted bill, time draft; ~**bank** accepting bank, drawee bank; ~**bestand** portfolio of accepted bills, bill holdings; ~ **ehrenhalber** acceptance for (*or* out of) honour, acceptance supra protest; ~ **einholen** to obtain acceptance; ~**einholung** presentation for acceptance; ~ **einlösen** to pay a bill of exchange; ~**einlösung** cashing an acceptance, payment of a bill of exchange; ~ **erster Bankadressen** acceptances of first-class banks; **a~fähig** suitable for acceptance, bankable; ~**frist** deadline for acceptance; ~**geschäft** acceptance business, bill brokerage; ~**konto** bills payable account, acceptance account (bills payable); ~**kredit** acceptance credit, term credit; *unbestätigter* ~~: *unconfirmed acceptance credit*; ~**leistung** (giving of an) acceptance, accepting; ~**linie** ceiling for acceptances (*of a bank's customer*), acceptance limit; ~**obligo** bills payable;

Akzeptant   **Alkohol**

~**obligobuch** ledger of bills-payable; ~**provision** commission on acceptance, acceptance commission; ~**schuldner** acceptor, acceptance debtor; ~**umlauf** amount of acceptances in circulation; ~**verbindlichkeiten** liability in respect of (trade) acceptances; ~**vermerk** acceptance (*words of acceptance on draft*); ~**verpflichtung** acceptance liability; ~**verweigerung** non-acceptance, refusal to accept; ~**vorlage** presentation for acceptance; presentation of acceptance, bill for payment; **bedingtes** ~ conditional acceptance; **bedingungsloses** ~ unconditional acceptance; **eingeschränktes** ~ qualified acceptance; **mangels** ~ for (*or* because of) non-acceptance; ~~ *zurückgegangener Wechsel*: draft returned because of nonacceptance; **mit** ~ **versehen** appearing with an acceptance; *v. t.* to provide with acceptance; **reines** ~ clean (no interest) bill; **unbeschränktes** ~ general acceptance, clean acceptance; **ungedecktes** ~ acceptance without sufficient collateral; **vor Fälligkeit bezahltes** ~ anticipated acceptance, early acceptance.

Akzeptant *m* acceptor, drawee (*who accepted bill*).

Akzeptanz *f* acceptability, suitability, eligibility.

akzeptieren *v/t* to accept (*a bill; an offer; conditions imposed*).

Akzeptierung *f* acceptance (*of a bill*).

Akzession *f* accession.

Akzessions|klausel accession clause; ~**urkunde** *f* instrument of accession; ~**vertrag** treaty of accession.

Akzessorietät *f* accessoriness, dependence (of collateral) on principal debt; **strenge** ~ strict accessoriness (*collateral obligation automatically follows principal obligation*).

akzessorisch *adj* accessory, incidental (*of collateral or surety obligation*).

Alarm *m* alarm, alert; ~**anlage** antiburglary device, burglar alarm; ~**bereitschaft** status; alert, stand-by, *erhöhte* ~ ~: heightened alert;

~**dienst** alarm service, emergency service; ~ **zustand** alert *cf. Alarmbereitschaft*; **blinder** ~ false alarm.

aleatorisch *adj* aleatory, hazardous, uncertain, doubtful.

alias alias, also known as, otherwise known as (*cover-name*); *A* ~ *B*: *A otherwise B, A alias B.*

Alibi *n* alibi; **ein** ~ **beibringen** to establish one's alibi, to provide an alibi.

Alimentationsprinzip *n* principle of adequate remuneration of public officials.

Alimente *n/pl* maintenance payments (support) (*for illegitimate child*); ~**nbeiträge** maintenance (support) payments (*for illegitimate child*), payments under an affiliation order *GB*; ~**nbeschluß** affiliation order; ~**nprozeß** *m* maintenance proceedings *cf Alimente,* affiliation proceedings *GB*.

alimentieren *v/t* to provide funds for; to support.

Alimentierung *f* providing funds for; support.

Aliud-Lieferung *f* delivery of other goods (*from those ordered*).

Alkohol *m* alcohol; ~~**Atemmeßgerät** breathalyser, intoximeter; ~**ausschank** sale of alcoholic beverages (liquor), licensed premises; ~**beratungsstelle** alcohol counselling agency; ~**einwirkung** influence of alcohol; (under the) influence of drink; ~**gehalt** alcohol content, proof alcoholic strength; ~**genuß** alcohol consumption; *mäßig im* ~~: *temperate in habits;* ~**messung** alcoholometry, measuring of alcohol content; ~ **mißbrauch** abuse of alcohol; ~ **monopol** monopoly on alcoholic beverages; ~**nachweis** proof of alcohol-content (in the blood); ~**probe** sobriety test; ~**steuer** tax on alcohol; **a~süchtig** addicted to alcohol; ~**süchtiger** alcohol addict, dipsomaniac; ~**süchtigkeit** alcoholism, dipsomania; ~**test** alcohol test, blood test, breathalyser test; ~ **unter Steuerverschluß**

29

Alkoholiker   **Allgemein|begriff**

bonded alcohol, alcohol in bond; ~**verbot** alcohol ban, prohibition (of sale and consumption of alcoholic beverages); ~**vergiftung** alcoholic intoxication, alcohol poisoning; **gereinigter** ~ rectified alcohol; **unter** ~**einfluß** under the influence of alcohol (*or* of drink); **vergällter** ~ denatured alcohol.

Alkoholiker *m* alcoholic (patient), drunk, problem drinker; ~**fürsorge** welfare service for alcoholics.

Allbeteiligungsklausel *f* general participation clause.

Allein|auftrag exclusive (broker) agreement *or* contract; ~**benutzung** sole *or* exclusive use; a~**berechtigt** exclusively entitled, having exclusive rights; ~**berechtigung** exclusive rights, exclusive authorization; ~**besitz** sole possession, exclusive occupation; ~**bezugsvertrag** solus agreement; ~**eigentum** sole ownership, exclusive ownership; *in* ~~ *stehend:* (*solely and*) *independently owned*; ~**eigentümer** sole owner, sole proprietor, sole and unconditional owner; ~**erbe** sole heir, universal heir; ~**erbschein** sole-heir certificate of inheritance (*total estate to one heir*); ~**erfinder** sole inventor; ~**gang** single-handed effort; ~**gebrauch** sole use; ~**geschäftsführer** sole (managing) director (*of an enterprise esp a German private limited company*), sole manager (*commercial*); ~**gesellschafter** sole shareholder, shareholder of a one-man-company (*having acquired all shares*), ~**gewahrsam** sole custody; ~**händler** independent trader; ~**herrschaft** autocracy; ~**hersteller** sole manufacturer; ~**herstellungsrecht** monopoly of production, exclusive manufacturing licence (license *US*); ~**inhaber** sole holder; ~**pacht** sole tenancy, entire tenancy; ~**recht** sole right(s); ~**schuldner** sole debtor; a~**stehend** single, sole, unmarried, living alone; detached (*building*), isolated, island position (*newspaper advertisement*); ~**stehende** *f* feme sole, single woman; ~**stehender** *m* bachelor, single person; ~**stellung** singularly outstanding position; ~**ursache** sole cause; ~**verkauf** exclusive sale(s), sole distributors; ~**verkaufsabrede** informal exclusive sales agreement; ~**verkaufsrecht** sole selling right, exclusive selling rights; ~**veröffentlichungsrecht** sole right of publication; ~**verschulden** sole fault; ~**vertreter** sole agent, exclusive representative; exclusive sales agent, sole selling agent, sole distributor; ~**vertretervertrag** exclusive agency agreement; ~**vertretung** exclusive agency, sole agency, exclusive representation; ~**vertretungsanspruch** *pol* claim to be the only legitimate (*international*) representative (*of a divided country*); ~**vertretungsberechtigung** having sole power of representation; ~**vertretungsvertrag** exclusive agency agreement; ~**vertrieb** exclusive sale; sole distributors; ~**vertriebsrecht** sole selling right, exclusive right to sell, exclusive right of distribution; ~**vertriebsvertrag** exclusive distribution contract; ~**zeichnungsberechtigter** person entitled to sign alone, single signatory; ~**zeichnungsberechtigung** right of single signature.

Allgemein|begriff general conception; ~**besitz** common possession, communal property; ~**bildung** general knowledge, general education; a~**gültig** generally valid, of general validity; ~**gültigkeit** universal validity, universality, generality; *ohne die* ~~ *einzuschränken: without restricting the generality;* ~**heit** *f* the general public, ~**interesse** public interest; a~**kundig** notorious, of common knowledge; ~**kundigkeit** common knowledge, public knowledge; a~**verbindlich** *adj* generally binding; ~**verbindlichkeit** universal validity (and binding character of collec-

Allmende   **Alternativangebot**

tive bargaining agreements) (*irrespective of individual employment contract*); ~**verbindlicherklärung** declaration of generally binding validity (*of collective bargaining agreements*), declaration of universal validity; ~**verfügungen** general dispositions; ~**verständlichkeit** general comprehensibility, understandability for the general public; ~**vollmacht** general power-of-attorney; **a**~**wirtschaftlich** *adj* from the standpoint of the economy as a whole; ~**wissen** general knowledge; ~**wohl** → *Gemeinwohl.*

Allmende *f* common land, commons *hist* folkland; ~**nutzung** use of the commons; ~**recht** right of common.

Allod *n hist* al(l)od, absolute property in land (*no reversion to the lord*).

Allonge *f* allonge, extension slip (*bill of exchange*), sider.

Allphasen|besteuerung multi-stage cumulative system; ~**steuer** all-phase tax; all-stage tax (*a tax imposed on each stage of handling or disposition*); **kumulative** ~**-Umsatzsteuer** cumulative (all-phase) turnover tax, cascade tax.

Allzuständigkeit *f* comprehensive jurisdiction (*of local authorities*).

Almosen *n* alms, charity; ~**empfänger** receiver of charity.

Als-ob-Tarif *m* tariff fixed to meet potential competition.

Alt|anleihe *f* pre-currency-reform loan (*under the Altsparergesetz qv*); ~**bankengesetz** *Berlin enactment of 1953 concerning pre-war Berlin banks*; ~**bau** → *Altbau*; ~**besitz** old holding, ownership under former economic conditions, pre-currency reform ownership; ~**besitzer** previous (prior) owner; ~**bundeskanzler** ex-Chancellor, former Federal Chancellor; ~**bürgermeister** ex-mayor, former mayor (*courtesy title*); ~**-Emission** former issue, pre-currency reform issue; ~**geld-Guthaben** *n* pre-currency-reform credit balance → *Altsparergesetz*; ~**gläubiger** previous creditor, assignor; ~**hausbesitz** ownership of pre-war dwellings; ~**hypothek** pre-currency-reform mortgage loan; ~**lasten** pre-unification burdens; *soil and water pollution by former waste disposal, "inherited" environmental liabilities*; ~**metalle** old metals, scrap metals.

Altbau *m house or flat completed before June 20, 1948 (date of Currency Reform)*; ~**mieten** rents of pre-currency-reform dwellings; ~**mietenverordnung** (*AMVO, 1958*) *control ordinance for pre-currency reform dwellings*; ~**sanierung** redevelopment (*or* refurbishing, *or* renovation) of old buildings, renovation of existing buildings; ~~**sbeihilfe:** *house improvement grant;* ~**wohnung** pre-currency-reform dwelling; **historischer** ~ ancient house, historical old building.

Altenhilfe *f* old age relief, help for old people.

Altenpfleger *m* (old people's) care assistant.

Altenteil *m* retired farmer's portion (*of an estate and of the mansion house*); ~**slasten** charges to provide for an old farmer's livelihood; ~**svertrag** contract for granting old age pension and support (*to farmer*).

Altenwohnheim *n* old people's home, residential home, rest home, home for the aged.

Alter *n* age, seniority; **arbeitsfähiges** ~ employable age; **erwerbsfähiges** ~ employable age; **heiratsfähiges** ~ marriageable age; **pensionsfähiges** ~ pensionable age, retirement age; **schulpflichtiges** ~ school age, compulsory school attendance age; **wehrpflichtiges** ~ draft age, age liable to military service; **zugelassenes** ~ admitted age, age for admission; **zurechnungsfähiges** ~ age of responsibility.

Alternat *n int* alternat.

Alternativ|angebot alternative offer (*or* bid); ~**anklage** alternative charge; ~**bedingungen** disjunc-

31

Alternative — **amortisieren**

tive terms, alternative terms; ~-**Energiequellen** alternative energy sources; ~**obligation** alternative obligation; ~**steuer** alternative tax; ~**straftatbestände** alternative counts (*in a charge*); ~**urteil** alternative finding (*in a judgement*); ~**vermächtnis** alternative legacy; ~**verpflichtung** alternative obligation; ~**vorbringen** disjunctive allegations, alternative allegations; ~**währung** alternative currency.

Alternative *f* alternative, choice.

Alters|aufbau age structure, age grouping, age pattern; ~**beihilfe** old age assistance; old-age allowance; ~**dispens** waiving the age-limit; ~**erfordernis** age-requirement; ~**freibetrag** old-age allowance, old-age exemption, age allowance, age (tax) relief; ~~ *für Rentner: tax reduction for retired persons*; ~**fürsorge** care of the aged; ~**fürsorgeausschuß** old people's welfare council; ~**geld** old-age allowance; ~**gliederung** (*von Außenständen*) aging; ~**grenze** age limit, retirement age; *flexible* ~~: *flexible retirement age; variable age limit*; ~**gruppe** age group; age cohort; ~**kapital** endowment sum for old age; ~**heim** rest home, old folks home; home for the aged; ~**hilfe für Landwirte** farmers' old age benefits; ~**jahrgang** age cohort; ~**klasse** age bracket, age group; ~**klasseneinstufung** age grouping; ~**pension** old-age pension; ~**pensionierung** superannuation; ~**präsident** chairman by seniority, the oldest member, Father of the House; ~**privileg** seniority privilege; ~**pyramide** (statistical) age-structure; ~**rente** old-age pension, retirement pension, retirement annuity (*ins*); ~ ~ *für Freiberufler: self-employed retirement annuity*; *vorgezogene* ~~: *early retirement pension*; ~**rentner** (old-age) pensioner; ~**risiko** age-risk (*in insurance premiums*); ~**ruhegeld** old-age pension; ~**schwäche** old-age infirmity; ~**schwachsinn** senile dementia, dotage, senility; **a**~**spezifisch** age-specific; ~**struktur** age structure; ~- **und Hinterbliebenenversorgung** old-age and surviving dependants pensions; ~**unterhalt** maintenance claim of old divorced spouse; ~**unterstützung** retirement allowance; ~**versicherung** old-age insurance (*or assurance*); ~**versorgung** → *Altersversorgung*; ~**vorsorge** provision for old age; ~ ~**konto**: *individual retirement account*; ~**zulage** superannuation allowance, age bonus, seniority bonus.

Altersversorgung *f* provision for old age, retirement pension, ~ **der Mitarbeiter** retirement pensions for the staff, employee (*or staff*) pension scheme; ~**skasse** old-age pension fund; ~**sversicherung** old-age endowment insurance, pension insurance; ~**swerk** pension scheme; **betriebliche** ~ company pension scheme, employee pension scheme; **freiwillige** ~ non-obligatory retirement pension; **steuerabzugsfähiger** ~**s- und Gewinnbeteiligungsplan** (*e-r Firma*) qualified pension plan.

Alterung *f* aging, growing old.

Ältestenrat *m* D parl Council of Elders, Speaker's advisory committee (*consisting of the Speaker, the Deputy Speaker and designated members of the parliamentary parties to advise on parliamentary business*).

Ältestenrecht *n* right of primogeniture (*of a farmer's eldest son*).

Altstadtsanierung *f* urban renewal, improvement *or* reconstruction of historic town centres.

Amiable Compositeur *m* amiable compositeur; amicable compounder, friendly compositeur.

Amnestie *f* amnesty, general pardon; ~**gesetz** *n* amnesty Act, Act of oblivion; ~**vorlage** amnesty bill.

amnestieren *v/t* to grant an amnesty, to grant a general pardon.

amortisierbar *adj* amortizable, redeemable.

amortisieren *v/t* to amortize, to re-

Amortisation　　　　　　　　　　　　　　　　　　　　　　　　　　　　　　**amtierend**

pay gradually, to redeem in instalments.
Amortisation *f* amortization, redemption, sinking fund payments, repayment in equal instalments.
Amortisations|betrag (*Hypothek*) sum required for redemption; **~darlehen** amortizable loan; loan redeemable by scheduled repayments; **~dauer** repayment (*or* payback) period; **~fonds** redemption fund, sinking fund; **~hypothek** amortizable mortgage loan; **~kasse** sinking fund, redemption fund; **~konto** redemption account; **~obligation** sinking fund bond; **~plan** terms of amortization, terms of redemption; **~quote** amortization rate; **~schein** amortization certificate, redemption bond; **~schuld** amortization debt, redeemable bond; **~tabelle** amortization table of payments, amortization schedule of payments; **~verfahren** amortization method; **~zahlung** amortization payment.
Ampel *f* → *Verkehrsampel*.
Amt *n* office, executive office, post, appointment, tenure of office, function, station, service; statutory office; **~ auf Lebenszeit** office for life, life tenure; **~ für landwirtschaftliche Marktordnung** Office for Farm Market Regulations; **~ für Öffentliche Ordnung** Local Government Office; **~ für Rüstungskontrolle** Agency for the Control of Armaments; **~ in der Justiz** judicial office; **~ in der Verwaltungsbehörde** administrative office; **aus dem ~ ausscheiden** to cease to hold office, to vacate one's office, to retire; **aus dem ~ entfernen** to remove from office; **Auswärtiges ~** → *Auswärtiges*; **besoldetes ~** salaried position, paid office, stipendiary (*magistrate*); **bisheriges ~** previous official position; **ein ~ antreten** to take up office; **ein ~ aufgeben** to relinquish an office, to retire; **ein ~ ausüben** to exercise an official function; **ein ~ bekleiden** to hold office, to occupy a position; **ein ~ besetzen** to fill an office; **ein ~ innehaben** to occupy an office; **ein ~ niederlegen** to resign (from office), to retire from office; **ein ~ versehen** to officiate, to discharge official duties; **ein ~ verwalten** to hold an office; **federführendes ~** drafting office, main office, head office; **geistliches ~** ecclesiastical office; **in ~ und Würden** in a position of esteem; **jmdn seines ~es entheben** to dismiss a person from office, to oust s. o. from office; **jmdn vorläufig des ~es entheben** to suspend s. o. from office; **jmdn zu einem ~ berufen** to call s. o. to an office, to appoint s. o. to a position; **kraft seines ~es** by virtue of his office; **~~~es handeln**: *to act in one's official capacity;* **öffentliches ~** public office, public appointment; **richterliches ~** judicial office; **seines ~es enthoben sein** to be functus officio, to be stripped of one's official duties; **sich für ein ~ eignen** to be suitable (qualified) for an official position; **statistisches ~** statistical office; **vom ~ auszufüllen** for official (office) use only; **von ~s wegen** ex officio; proprio motu; **von e-m ~ ausgeschlossen sein** to be disqualified from holding office; **von e-m ~ entbinden** to release from office; **weisungsgebundenes ~** subordinate office, duties subject to superior orders or instructions.
Ämter|handel office-jobbing; **~häufung** accumulation of offices *by same incumbent*; **~kauf** selling public offices, *eccl* simony; **~patronage** patronage (*of offices*), spoils system; **~schacher** bargaining for public offices; higgling and haggling.
amtieren *v/i* to hold office, to be in office, to exercise one's functions, to officiate; to serve in office, to administer an office.
amtierend *adj* officiating (*clergyman at marriage ceremony etc*); holding an

33

amtlich

office for an interim period, sitting (*of a judge*); *vorübergehend* ~: *pro tem (pore).*

amtlich *adj* official, *adv* officially, in an official capacity; **nicht** ~ unofficial, non-official, not official; private(ly), in one's private capacity.

Amts|ablösung release from office, change of office; ~**abzeichen** official insignia; ~**akten** official files; ~**anklage** ex officio charge, impeachment (*of public officer*); ~**anmaßung** usurpation of office, false assumption of authority, fraudulent exercise of a public office; ~**antritt** taking up of office; ~**anwalt** official solicitor, public prosecutor *at local court;* ~**anwaltschaft** *office of the public prosecutor at a local court;* ~**arzt** official physician, official surgeon, medical officer of health *GB;* ~**aufsicht** internal supervision (*or* review) of administrative decisions;~**ausübung** exercise of an office; ~**befugnis** official competence; **a~bekannt** (*to be*) known to the authority, (*to have*) official knowledge *of s.th.;* ~~ *ohne pfändbare Habe: officially notified as being without attachable belongings; nihil;* ~**bekanntheit** notoriety; ~**bekräftigung** official confirmation; ~**beleidigung** insulting a public official; ~**bereich** the jurisdiction of an office; ~~*e-s Gerichts: precincts of a court, range of jurisdiction of a court;* ~**bescheid** official notification; Patent Office ruling (*US*), (Patent) Office Action; ~**bescheinigung** official certificate; ~**bestätigung** official confirmation; ~**besucher** visitor to a public office; ~**betrieb** ex officio proceedings; ~**bezeichnung** official description, official designation, title of an office, official title; ~**bezirk** official district, administrative district, jurisdictional area of an office; ~**blatt** official gazette, official journal; ~**bonus** advantage of incumbency; ~**bote** office messenger; ~**buch** official register; ~**bürgschaft** official fidelity

Amtskosten

guarantee; ~**dauer** period of appointment, tenure (of office), term of office; ~**delikte** criminal offences by a public official, felonies and misdemeanours in office, malpractices in office; ~**eid** oath of office, official oath; ~**einführung** initiation into office; ~**einkünfte** emoluments, salary; ~**einsetzung** inauguration (*into office*), appointment; ~**enthebung** removal from office, dismissal of an official; ~**entlassung** discharge from office; ~**ermittlung** official investigation (*by public prosecutor*); ~**ermittlungspflicht** duty to make official investigation; ~**etat** official fund, official budget; ~**fähigkeit** eligibility for office; ~**folge** sequence of tenure of office; ~**führung** tenure of office, administration of office, conduct of official functions; ~**gebühren** official fees; ~**geheimnis** official secret(s); ~**gehilfe** office assistant, tipstaff *GB,* usher; ~**gelder** official funds; ~**gericht** → *Amtsgericht* ~**geschäfte** official business, official functions; ~**gewalt** official authority, official powers; ~**haftung** public liability, liability of the state for a public officer; ~**haftungsklage** legal action for public liability claim; ~**handlung** official action; ~**hilfe** secondment, administrative aid (*as between government agencies*); ~~ *ersuchen: letters rogatory;* ~~ *und Rechtshilfe: administrative and legal cooperation;* ~**immunität** immunity in office, privilege in office; ~**inhaber** office bearer, holder of an office, incumbent, officer, appointee; ~~ *von Rechts wegen;* officer de jure, titular officer; *faktischer* ~~: *officer de facto, actual office holder;* ~**jahr** year of office; ~**kasse** cash office; ~**kaution** official fidelity guarantee; ~**kenntnis** official notice, official knowledge (*of a fact*); ~**kette** chain of office (*worn by town mayor at ceremony*); ~**kleidung** official attire, robe of office; ~**kosten** official

Amtslöschung

charges, fees; ~**löschung** ex officio deletion from a public register (*extinction of corporation etc.*); ~**mißbrauch** abuse of official functions, undue use of authority, malpractice by public officer; ~**mündel** ward of the (*youth*) office; child under guardianship of the (*youth*) office; ~**nachfolger** successor (in office); ~**niederlegung** resignation from office; ~**organ** official organ, government agency; ~**ort** official residence; *am ~~ wohnhaft sein: to be in residence;* ~**periode** term of office; ~**person** official; person in authority; ~**personal** official staff; ~**pfleger** ex officio guardian (*of illegitimate child*); ~**pflegschaft** ex officio curatorship; ~**pflicht** official duty; ~**pflichtverletzung** breach of official duty; ~**prinzip** principle of ex officio proceedings; ~**rat** executive officer, third secretary (*embassy*); ~**räume des Gerichts** court premises, court administration rooms; ~**register** official registry; ~**richter** judge of a local court (*in Germany*) ≈ district (court) judge ≈ magistrate (*in criminal matters*), ≈ justice of the peace; ~**richterin** woman judge at local court, woman magistrate; ~**robe** robe, official gown; ~**sache** official business; ~**schild** office sign; ~**schimmel** red tape, red-tapism; ~**siegel** official seal, public seal; ~**sitz** seat, official residence, location of office; ~**sprache** official language; ~**stellung** official status, official position; ~**stunden** authorized hours, official working hours, opening hours; ~**tätigkeit** official functions, official activities; ~**tracht** official attire; official robe (*or* gown); ~**träger** functionary, officer, incumbent, office-holder; ~**übergabe** surrender of office, transfer of office; ~**übernahme** assumption of office; **a~üblich** customary (official) procedure; ~**unterschlagung** misappropriation by a public official, embezzlement by an official, malversation, depecula-

Amtsgerichtsbezirk

tion; ~**verfassung** constitution of office; ~**vergehen** malfeasance in office, offence(s) committed by a public official; ~**vermerk** official memo(randum); ~**verschwiegenheit** official secrecy, confidentiality; ~**verteidiger** = *Pflichtverteidiger qv*; ~**vertretung** official representation; ~**verweigerung** refusal to admit appointee to office; official refusal, denial; ~**verweser** temporary administrator, deputy administrator; ~**vorgänger** predecessor in office; ~**vormund** official guardian (*youth welfare office for illegitimate children*); ~**vormundschaft** ex officio guardianship; ~**vorstand** head of an executive department, chief of a bureau, superintendent; ~**vorsteher** office supervisor; ~**waltung** performance of official duties; ~**wechsel** change of office; *turnusmäßiger ~~: rotation in office*; ~**weg** official channels; ~**widerspruch** ex officio objection, official opposition; **a~widrig** contrary to official regulations; ~**widrigkeit** default in official duty, breach of official regulations, dereliction of duty; ~**würde** decorum; ~**zeichen** *pl* insignia; ~**zeit** term of office, incumbency; *verbleibende ~~: remainder of the term of office;* ~**zeugnis** official testimonial; ~**zustellung** service ordered by the court ex officio; service upon official request; **von ~ wegen** ex officio, of its (the court's) own motion; *~~~ bekannt sein: to have official notice of sth.*

Amtsgericht *n* (=) local court *in Germany* ≈ magistrates' court, ≈ county court, ≈ district court; ~-**Familiengericht** family division of the ~; ~ **in Strafsachen** criminal division of the ~ ≈ petty sessions; ~ - **Streitgericht** civil litigation division of the ~; ~ - **Vollstreckungsgericht** *division for execution of civil claims at local German court.*

Amtsgerichts|**bezirk** magisterial precinct, district of local court;

analog   **Änderung**

~**direktor** (*formerly*) senior judge at local court; ~**gebäude** local court house; ~**präsident** president of the local court; ~**praxis** customary procedure in the local court.

analog *adj* analogic, analogical, analogous, by analogy, mutatis mutandis; ~ **anwendbar** applicable mutatis mutandis.

Analogie *f* analogy; ~**schluß** parity of reasoning, conclusion by analogy; ~**verbot** prohibition of analogy: *rule of German criminal law forbidding the creation of charges for criminal offences by way of analogy with existing statutory definitions of crimes*; ~**verfahren** (method of) reasoning by analogy.

Anatomievertrag *m agreement to release body or organs upon death for anatomical or surgical use.*

anbahnen *v/t* to prepare the ground, to pave the way, to introduce; *sich* ~ to be in the offing.

Anbau *m* (1) cultivation, tillage, crop growing; ~**beschränkung** restriction on cultivation; acreage restriction; crop restriction; ~**fläche** area under cultivation, acreage; ~**prämie** premium for cultivation; ~**teile** add-on components; ~**verträge** planting contracts.

Anbau *m* (2) (*pl Anbauten*) annex, extension, out-building; construction of an annex etc, enlargement of a building, *pl*: structural additions, attachments to buildings.

anbauen (*1*) *v/t* to plant, to cultivate (*land, vegatables etc*).

anbauen (*2*) *v/t* to add (*to a building*), to annex, to make a structural addition to, to add an extension.

anbelangen *v/t* to concern.

anberaumen *v/t* to set down, to fix a date (*for a hearing, a meeting*).

Anberaumung *f* setting down (for trial).

anbetreffen *v/t* to concern.

Anbieten *n* solicitation, offering, holding for sale; ~ **zur Abtreibung** offering to procure an abortion; **kartellmäßiges** ~ collusive pricing.

anbieten *v/t* to offer, to tender, to propound, to bid.

Anbietender *m* offeror.

Anbieter *m* tenderer, bidder, supplier; ~**inflation** supply inflation.

Anbietungspflicht *f* obligation to offer for sale, obligation to treat.

anbringen, *v/t* to affix, to attach, to instal; *ständig gut sichtbar anzubringen: to be kept constantly exhibited/easily visible.*

Anbringung *f* attachment, installation.

Ancienniät *f* seniority.

andauern *v/i* to continue, to persist.

Anderdepot *n* trust deposit (account), third-party securities deposit.

anderenorts *adv (a. a. O.)* in alio loco (*citation*).

Anderkonto *n* trust account (*of lawyer or notary*), client account, third party security account.

ändern *v/t* to change, to alter, to modify, to amend; *sich* ~ to vary, to change.

Änderung *f* change, alteration, modification, variation; ~ **der Rechtsprechung** change in (the trend) of court findings; ~ **der Verhältnisse** variation of the circumstances; ~ **der Gesellschaftsform** change in the (legal) structure of a business, business form (*corporate, partnership etc*); ~ **des Grundkapitals** change in the stock capital, change in the capitalization; ~ **des rechtlichen Gesichtspunkts** change of the legal aspect (*concerning a criminal charge*); ~ **e-s Gesetzes** amendment to an Act; ~ **im Strafmaß** change of sentence; ~ **oder Wegfall der Geschäftsgrundlage** ≈ frustration of contract, *fundamental change or cessation of the conditions underlying the transaction*; ~**en und Ergänzungen** modifications and amendments; changes and additions; ~ **von Amts wegen** amendment by the court of its own motion; ~ **vorbehalten** subject to change without notice, subject to alterations; **bauliche** ~ structural

36

Änderungsantrag

alteration; **etwaige** ~**en** changes as they occur; any changes; **grundlegende** ~ fundamental change; **nachträgliche** ~ retrospective modification; **redaktionelle** ~ drafting amendment; **stufenweise** ~ **des Interventionspunktes** crawling peg, step-by-step changes in the intervention point; **unbefugte** ~ **von Urkunden** unauthorized alteration of documents; **wesentliche** ~ substantial change, material alteration.

Änderungs|antrag motion for an amendment; ~**auftrag** change order, instructions to change; *technischer* ~ ~: *engineering change order;* ~**befugnis** power to vary; authority to make changes or amendments; ~**bescheid** amending decision; ~**beschluß** amending order, amending resolution; ~**buchung** corrective entry, offsetting entry; ~**eintragung** recording of changes, amending entry (*in a register*); ~**gesetz** amending Act; ~**klausel** escape clause; ~**kündigung** notice of termination pending a change of contract; ~**protokoll** minutes recording a change or correction; ~**recht** right to require a change; ~**svorbehalt** proviso to make unilateral changes (*price, other terms*); ~**vorschläge machen** to make proposals for amendment.

andeuten *v/t* to indicate, to hint at, to allude to, to intimate.

Andeutung *f* a hint, allusion, indication; **versteckte** ~ innuendo (*defamatory*), hidden allusion, intimation.

andienen *v/t* to tender, to offer to sell to a public authority, to offer one's services.

Andienung *f* tendering, offering for sale to public authorities, delivery; ~**srecht** right of tender.

Andreaskreuz *n* railway crossing sign.

Andrehen *n* (*jmdm etw. andrehen*) twisting, churning.

androhen *v/t* to threaten, to warn of.

anerkennen

Androhung *f* threat, warning; ~ **der Entlassung** threat of dismissal; ~ **der Kaduzierung von Kapitalanleihen** threat of a possible forfeiture of shares; ~ **einer Ausschlußfrist** warning of a final time limit (*after which no further submissions will be accepted by the court*); ~ **e-s Versäumnisurteils** warning that judgment in default will be obtained (*if lawyer fails to appear again*); ~ **gemeingefährlicher Verbrechen** threat of felonies entailing common danger; **bei** ~ **von Freiheitsstrafe** by threatening a penalty of imprisonment; **ohne weitere** ~ without further warning; **unter** ~ **e-r Gefängnisstrafe** under pain of imprisonment.

aneignen *v/t v reflex* (*sich etw.* ~) to appropriate (improperly), to usurp, to appropriate for one's own use and benefit, to possess oneself of s. th.; **sich etwas widerrechtlich** ~ to appropriate unlawfully.

Aneignung *f* appropriation, occupancy, original occupation (*of property which belongs to nobody*); ~**srecht** right of appropriation; **rechtswidrige** ~ conversion, misappropriation; **widerrechtliche** ~ conversion, misappropriation.

Anerbe *m* exclusive heir to a farm, heir to farm property in fee tail.

Anerben|gericht hereditary farm court; ~**gut** entailed farm estate; ~**recht** entail on farm property (*in the former British Occupation Zone of Germany*).

anerbieten *v/reflex* to offer (*one's services*), to tender.

Anerbieten *n* offer (*of services, to do s.th.*); ~ **von Dienstleistungen** offer of services.

anerkannt *adj* approved, accepted, acknowledged, recognized; **als gültig** ~ recognized as valid, accepted.

anerkanntermaßen *adv* avowedly, admittedly.

anerkennen *v/t* to recognize, to acknowledge, to accept; **nicht** ~ to disown, to repudiate, to deny.

37

Anerkenntnis

Anerkenntnis *n* recognition, acknowledg(e)ment, cognovit (*in court*); ~ **der Vaterschaft** (*recorded*) acknowledgment of paternity, recognition of paternity; **~schreiben** letter of acknowledg(e)ment; **~urteil** judgment by confession; **schriftliches** ~ acknowledg(e)ment in writing.

Anerkennung *f* acknowledg(e)ment, recognition, acceptance; ~ **der Vaterschaft** acknowledg(e)ment of paternity; ~ **e-s Testaments** acceptance of legality of a will; **~sgebühr** nominal fee, symbolical fee; ~ **von Ansprüchen** acceptance of the claims; **de facto** ~ de facto recognition, recognition as a de facto government; **de jure** ~ de jure recognition, formal recognition (*of a state, a government*); **diplomatische** ~ diplomatic recognition; **einseitige** ~ unilateral recognition; **endgültige völkerrechtliche** ~ final public recognition, formal (= *de jure*) recognition, definitive recognition under international law; **gegenseitige** ~ mutual recognition, reciprocal recognition; **gerichtliche** ~ recognition in court, →*Anerkenntnis*, recognition by the court; **ohne** ~ **einer Rechtspflicht** ex gratia, without prejudice, without admitting legal responsibility; **staatliche** ~ governmental recognition; **steuerliche** ~ admission for tax purposes.

Anfahrtswege *m/pl* access routes; approach roads.

Anfall *m* incidence, accrual, devolution, yield; ~ **des Fonds** items accruing to a fund; ~ **e-r Erbschaft** devolution of an inheritance; ~ **e-r Steuer** incidence of a tax; ~ **e-s Rechts** giving rise to a right, accrual of a right, accession of right; **~sberechtigter** beneficiary, reversioner; **~srecht** right to reversion; **~stag** date of accrual.

anfallen *v/t* to accrue, to become available, to occur, to devolve upon.

anfällig *adj* susceptible; sensitive, prone.

38

Anfechtung

Anfälligkeit *f* sensitivity; susceptibility; proneness (to).

Anfang *m* beginning, commencement, inception, opening, start; **von** ~ **an** from the beginning, ab initio, ex tunc.

Anfangs|**bestand** opening inventory, opening balance, initial balance; **~bestellung** initial order; **~bilanz** opening balance; *steuerliche* ~~: *opening balance for tax purposes;* **~dividende** initial dividend; **~gehalt** starting salary, initial salary; **~guthaben** initial credit balance, opening credit; **~kapital** original assets, initial capital, start-up capital; **~kurs** opening price (*for listed securities*), first quotation; **~plädoyer** opening statement (*in court*), counsel's opening speech; **~schuld** initial liabilities; **~stadium** initial stage; **~tag** date of commencement; **~termin** commencing date; **~vermögen** original assets, initial property (of a spouse); **~vermögensübersicht** initial survey of assets, initial status; **~verpflichtung(en)** initial liabilities; **~verzug** initial delay; **~wert** initial value, original value.

Anfänger *m* novice, beginner, learner, tyro.

anfechtbar *adj* voidable; annullable, defeasible, challengeable, contestable, controversial; debatable, subject to appeal, not final; **nicht** ~ noncontestable; final.

Anfechtbarkeit *f* voidability, annullability, defeasibility, relative nullity; contestability, appealability.

anfechten *v/t* to rescind, to avoid, to annul (*an instrument, an obligation, a contract*); to challenge, to contest (*a will, the validity, of s.th.*); to revoke; to appeal (*from judgment*).

Anfechtung *f* rescission, avoidance nullification (*act, instrument, contract etc*); contesting, challenging, appeal (*judgment, decision*); ~ **der Ausschlagung** revocation of a disclaimer (*to an inheritance*); ~ **e-s Patents** contesting a patent; **außerkonkursmäßige** ~ non-bankruptcy avoidance (*of debtor's preferential transactions*).

Anfechtungs|befugnis authority to rescind; **~berechtigter** party legally entitled to rescind; **~erklärung** notice of avoidance; **~frist** statutory time limit for an avoidance (*or the lodging of a legal remedy or an appeal*); **~gegner** addressee of a notice of avoidance; **~gesetz** →*Gläubigeranfechtungsgesetz*; **~gründe** grounds for avoidance, grounds for appeal; **~klage** action to rescind, action for avoidance, action to set aside, rescissory action, impeachment action; **~klausel** avoidance clause; **~recht** right of rescission, right to nullify, right of avoidance; **~streit** annulment suit.

anfertigen *v/t* to make, to manufacture to order, to prepare (*a brief, a translation*); to taylor-make.

Anfertigung *f* production, manufacture, fabrication by a craftsman, producing s.th. to order.

anfinanzieren *v/t* to provide initial credit, to provide initial finance.

Anfinanzierung *f* initial financing.

anfliegen *v/t* to provide an air service to, to fly regularly to (*airline*).

Anflughafen *m* a port of call.

anfordern *v/t* to demand (*delivery, shipment*), to ask for, to request, to require (*s.th. to be supplied*), to requisition.

Anforderung *f* demand, request, requisition; requirement; **~en an die Beweisführung** standard of proof; **~sbehörden** procurement authorities (*military*); **~sbescheid** requisition (decision); **~sprofil am Arbeitsplatz** job requirements; **~sschein** requisition form; **auf ~** upon request, on demand; **den gesetzlichen ~en genügen** to meet the legal requirements; **strenge ~ an die Sorgfaltspflicht** high degree of care and diligence required; **terminbedingte ~** liabilities due on specified dates.

Anfrage *f* inquiry, question, interpellation; **e–e ~ positiv beantworten** to give a positive answer to a question, to answer a query affirmatively (or positively); **große ~** major interpellation (*signed by all members of parliamentary party – German federal parliament*); **kleine ~** written question, minor interpellation, question (*in parliament*); **mündliche ~** oral question (*by a member of parliament during question time*); **parlamentarische ~** interpellation.

anfragen *v/i* to inquire, to make inquiries; **schriftlich ~** to inquire in writing.

anführen *v/t* to quote (*author, authority*), to cite (*a precedent, a case*), to adduce (*evidence, arguments*), to allege (*reasons, facts*), to state (*s.th. in support of an argument*).

Anführer *m* leader, leader of a group, gang leader, ringleader.

Angabe *f* indication, statement, specification, declaration, representation, instruction; *pl*: information, data, representations, particulars, details, further facts; **~ des Inhalts e-r Sendung** declaration of the contents of a consignment; **~ des Versicherungsnehmers** statement by the insured person; **~pflichten** disclosure requirements; **~n zur Person** personal data (*of person interrogated or examined in court*), name and description; **~ zur Sache** statement(s) concerning the case as such, testimony concerning the issue of the case; **anfallende ~n** supplied data; **ausreichende ~n** sufficient data; **bereinigte ~n** real terms; **bewußt falsche ~n** knowingly false statements; **entstellte ~n** distorted information; **falsche ~(n)** false representation(s); **~~ machen: to make false statements**; **falsche ~ an Eides statt** false statement in lieu of an oath; **gegenwartsnahe ~n** up-to-date figures and data; **irreführende ~n** fraudulent representation(s), misleading statements; **konkrete ~n** definite data; **laut ~** as per statement, according to (your) instruction(s);

angeben

mit ~ der Gehaltsansprüche stating salary; **nach** ~ pursuant to (the description); **nach ~ des Kunden gefertigt** made to order; **nach ~n des Zeugen** according to the testimony of the witness; **nach unseren** ~n according to our instructions; **nachprüfbare** ~n verifiable allegations; **nähere** ~n further (and better) particulars; **ohne** ~ not stated; **ohne ~ von Gründen** without giving (any) reasons, without stating reasons; **rechtserhebliche** ~n relevant statements, relevant information; **sachdienliche** ~n pertinent data, relevant information; **seine** ~n **beschwören** to swear to the truth of one's statement, to give one's testimony on oath; **statistische** ~n statistical data; **tatsächliche** ~n (factual) data, facts and figures; **unrichtige** ~n incorrect data, misrepresentation(s); **unter ~ von Gründen** setting forth the reasons, with the giving of reasons; **vierteljährliche** ~n quarterly data; **vollständige** ~n full particulars; **wahrheitsgetreue** ~n truthful statement, true statement; **wesentliche** ~n material representations; **widersprechende** ~n contradictory statements; **zweckdienliche** ~n relevant information.

angeben *v/t* to state, to utter, to name (a person, a witness); *(wie) oben angegeben: (as) stated above*; **näher** ~ to specify, to itemize; **zu hoch** ~ to overstate.

angeblich *adj* alleged, ostensible, purported, reputed, would-be.

Angebot *n* offer *(contract)*, proffer, proposal, bid *(auction)*, tender *(performance, payment)*, supply *(market)*; ~ **an Arbeitskräften** availability of labour; ~ **der Wiedergutmachung** offer of amends *(defamation)*; ~ **zur Unzucht** indecent proposal; ~ **und Nachfrage** supply and demand; **abgeändertes** ~ qualified offer, amended offer; „**annehme** ~" „take" *(telegram)*; **befristetes** ~ offer open until a specified time only; **bemustertes** ~ sampled offer; **bindendes** ~ firm offer, binding offer; **ein** ~ **abgeben** to submit a tender; **ein** ~ **machen** to offer, to make an offer, to tender; **ein** ~ **zurücknehmen** to withdraw an offer; **ernstgemeintes** ~ serious offer, serious-minded offer; **freibleibendes** ~ offer without engagement, non-binding offer, revocable offer, offer subject to confirmation; **gekoppeltes** ~ combination offer, joint offer; **laufendes** ~ current offer; **mündliches** ~ verbal offer, oral offer; **öffentliches** ~public offer, general offer; **reichhaltiges** ~ abundant choice of goods; **schriftliches** ~ offer in writing, written proposal; **ständig aufrechterhaltenes** ~ standing offer; **stillschweigendes** ~ implied offer; **unverändertes** ~ standing offer; **unverlangtes** ~ unsolicited offer; **ursprüngliches** ~ original offer; **verbindliches** ~ firm bid, binding offer; **vorbehaltloses** ~ unconditional offer.

Angebots|ausschreibung invitation to tender; ~**bindefrist** bid acceptance period; acceptance deadline; ~**druck** supply-push, pressure of supply *(on the market)*; ~**einholung** request to submit offer; ~**empfänger** offeree; **a~induziert** supply-induced *(recession)*; ~**kalkulation** pricing of an offer; pricing of a quotation; ~**lage** supply situation; ~**liste** list of what is on offer, offering sheet *(bank)*; ~**monopol** monopoly of supply; ~**muster** sample offer; ~**potential** supply potential; ~**preis des Verkäufers** price quoted by seller; vendor's price; ~**zwang** compulsory requirement to offer s. th. *(to a public authority or to a bidder)*.

angebracht *adj* appropriate, suitable, proper; *soweit ~: where appropriate*.

angefochten *adj* avoided, annulled, rescinded; **nicht** ~ unrescinded, unchallenged.

Angehöriger *m* (*der Angehörige*) (*pl*

Angeklagter *Angehörige ~e)*; (1) relatives *jur: persons related by blood or marriage, adoption or betrothal (including ex-spouses)*; (2) member *(of a public service or community)*; ~ **des öffentlichen Diensts** public servant, official; ~ **e-s Staates** national of a country (*or:* citizen).

Angeklagter *m (der Angeklagte)* the accused *(after committal for trial)*, the defendant *(in a criminal case)*, prisoner at the bar *(if under arrest)*; **der ~ in der Hauptverhandlung** the defendant *(during the trial)*, the accused.

Angeld *n* earnest (money), deposit.

Angelegenheit *f* the matter; the case; **~en der freiwilligen Gerichtsbarkeit** ex parte jurisdiction matters; ~ **von Bedeutung** a matter of importance; **amtliche ~** official matter; **auswärtige ~en** foreign affairs, external affairs; **die bewußte ~** the matter referred to, the (afore)said case; **e-e ~ e-m Anwalt übergeben**, to pass a matter on to a lawyer (a solicitor); to put a matter in the hands of an attorney; **innere ~en** home affairs, internal matters; **innerstaatliche ~** matter of domestic concern, internal affairs; **nationale ~en** matters of national concern; **öffentliche ~** s. th. of public concern, public affair; **personelle ~en** private affairs; **persönliche ~** private matter; **soziale ~en** matters of social concern; **streitige ~** controversial matter.

angelernt *adj* semi-skilled; trained-on-the job.

Angelschein *m* licence to fish, rod licence.

angemeldet *adj* registered, notified; declared *(customs)*.

angemessen *adj* adequate, reasonable, fair and reasonable, appropriate, reasonable und proportionate.

Angemessenheit *f* reasonableness, adequacy, sufficiency.

angenommen *pp* accepted *(offer)*; *conj* assuming that.

angerechnet werden (→*anrechnen*) to be credited, to be given credit for, to be considered *(in sentencing)*, to make an allowance for *(pre-trial confinement)*.

angereichert *adj* enriched, augmented.

angeschlossen *adj* attached to, affiliated to, joined to.

Angeschuldigter *m (der Angeschuldigte)* the person charged; indictee, indicted person, the accused, *(a person charged but not yet committed for trial)*.

angesehen *adj* reputable.

angesichts in view of, whereas, aware (of).

angespannt *adj* strained, tight *(financial condition, money market)*.

Angestellter *m (der Angestellte)* (salaried) employee, salary earner, white collar worker; ~ **im öffentlichen Dienst** employee in the civil service; **~nberuf** white-collar occupation; **~ngehälter** staff salaries; **~ngewerkschaft** employees' union; **~nkasse** employee pension fund; **~nrente** employees' pension *(from Social Insurance)*; **~nunterstützungskasse** employee provident fund; **~nversicherung** social insurance for (salaried) employees; obligatory employees' insurance; **~nversicherungspflichtig** subject to social insurance for employees; **auf Probe ~r** trial employee, employee working for a trial period; probationer; **leitende ~** *(high-up)* managerial employees, senior executive, executive employees, *(entitled to employ and discharge others)*; managerial staff.

Angewiesener *m (der Angewiesene)* drawee.

angleichen *v/t* to harmonize, to adjust, to assimilate.

Angleichung *f* alignment, adjustment, harmonization, approximation; ~ **der Steuersätze** alignment of rates; ~ **der Besteuerungsverfahren** approximation of methods of taxation; ~ **von Zollsätzen** alignment of customs duties.

angliedern

angliedern v/t to join, to attach, to affiliate with (to), to annex.
Angliederung f inclusion, affiliation; *pol* annexation.
angreifen v/t to attack, to assail, to assault (*with physical violence*).
Angreifer m assailant, attacker *pol/mil* aggressor.
angrenzen v/i to border (upon), to be adjacent (to).
angrenzend adj adjacent, abutting, contiguous, adjoining.
Angrenzer m immediate neighbour, abutting owner, abutter; **~land** contiguous territory, adjoining territory, neighbouring country.
Angriff m attack; **~ auf das Leben** attempt to kill s.o.; **~ auf den Leumund des Zeugen** imputation on the character of the witness, discrediting a witness; **~ auf den Luftverkehr** aggressive acts against air transport; **~ auf die Menschenwürde** attack upon human dignity; **bewaffneter ~** armed attack; **e-n ~ abwehren** to ward off an assault; **gegenwärtiger rechtswidriger ~** imminent unlawful attack; **räuberischer ~** predatory assault; **rechtswidriger ~** unlawful attack, assault; **tätlicher ~** assault.
Angriffs|bündnis offensive alliance; **~handlung** act of aggression; **~krieg** *mil* offensive war; war of aggression, aggressive war; **~mittel** means of prosecuting a case, *mil* offensive means, resources; for offensive action; **selbständige ~~:** *independent points to support the appeal*; **~punkt** point of attack; target for an attack; **~streik** positive strike; **~waffe** offensive weapon *pl* armaments for offensive war; **~ziel** objective, target.
Angst|käufe m/pl panic buying, scare buying; **~klausel** „without recourse" clause (*on bill of exchange endorsement*); **~verkauf** panic sale.
anhaken v/t to tick off, to check off.
Anhalt m supporting fact, clue, criterion.
Anhalterecht n right to stop a person

anheimstellen

in the street; right of stoppage in transitu.
Anhalte- und Umladerechte n/pl (*e–s Versenders*) privilege of transit.
Anhalter m hitchhiker; **~verkehr** hitchhiking.
Anhalteweg m distance required to bring a vehicle to a stop.
Anhaltspunkt m clue, indication, criterion; **konkreter ~** definite point, clue, clear indication.
Anhang m supplement, addition, annex, appendage, appendix, rider (*to a bill*), schedule (*to an Act*), allonge (*to a bill of exchange*), codicil (*to a will*), dependants (*family*); following (*pol*); **~sbudget** supplemental budget; **~steuer** supplementary tax; **im ~ zu diesem Vertrag** annexed to this contract.
Anhängeadresse f tag, tie-on label, luggage label.
anhängen v/t to affix, to annex, to append.
Anhänger m (1) *pol* follower, supporter, adherent partisan.
Anhänger m (2) trailer; **~last** towed load; **~vorrichtung** trailer hitch; **leichter ~** light trailer.
Anhängeverfahren n supplementary proceedings.
anhängig adj pending, pendente lite.
Anhängigkeit f pendency; **~ e–s Strafverfahrens** pendency of prosecution.
anhäufen v/t to accumulate, to amass, to stock-pile, to pile up, to snowball; *v reflex* to accrue, to accumulate.
Anhäufung f accumulation (*of capital*), agglomeration, long series (of); **~ von Reserven** pyramiding of reserves.
anheben v/t to increase (*prices*), to raise, to mark up.
Anhebung f price increase, upward price adjustment.
anheimfallen v/i to devolve upon, to revert to, to escheat *cf Heimfall*.
anheimgeben v/i to suggest to s. o. (*judge to a party or counsel*).
anheimstellen v/i to suggest for consideration, to leave it to s.o. (*to

42

anheuern — **ankreuzen**

s. o.'s. discretion), to request (*indirectly*), to submit to.

anheuern v/t to recruit, to hire, to sign on (up), to sign articles (*seamen*).

Anheuerung f hiring, signing up.

Anhören m = *Anhörung qv*; **nach ~** after giving an opportunity for an explanation, after having heard.

anhören v/t to hear s. o., to give s. o. an opportunity to be heard, to grant a hearing to s. o., to give s. o. an audience.

Anhörung f informal hearing, granting a hearing; opportunity to be heard; **~srecht** right to be heard; **~sverfahren** (public) hearing (procedure); **nach ~ der Zeugen** after hearing the witnesses informally; **mündliche ~** informal hearing; **öffentliche ~** public hearing.

Ankauf m purchase, buying; **~konsortium** buying syndicate; **~rechte** option, to purchase; **freihändiger ~** purchase by private treaty, private purchase.

ankaufen v/t to purchase, to buy.

Ankäufer m purchaser, buyer.

Ankaufs|ermächtigung authority to purchase; **~genehmigung** purchase approval, permission to buy; **~kurs** buying rate; **~option** option to purchase; **~preis** purchase price, buying-in price; *An- oder Verkaufspreise: purchase or selling prices*; **~rechnung** invoice (*covering a purchase*); **~recht** right of purchase;**~(s)wert** purchase value.

ankaufsfähig adj purchasable (*goods, valuables*); discountable (*bills of exchange*).

Ankergebühr f anchorage, groundage, keelage.

Ankerrecht n right of anchoring, anchorage, keelage.

anklagbar adj prosecutable, indictable.

Anklage f accusation, charge, indictment; (the) prosecution; **~bank** dock; **~behörde** the prosecution, the public prosecutor, the Director of Public Prosecutions *GB*, the District Attorney *US*; **~ erheben** to charge, to indict, to prefer charges; **~erhebung** formal accusation, preferring charges, preferment, indictment; **~erzwingung** compelling the public prosecutor to prefer charges *cf Klageerzwingungsverfahren*; **~grundsatz** = **~ prinzip** *qv*; **~monopol** sole right of the state to institute criminal proceedings; **~prinzip** principle of ex officio prosecution; **~punkt** count of a charge; **~rede** opening statement by the prosecutor; **~schrift** bill of indictment, charge, charge sheet, charge and bill of particulars, indictment, written accusation; **~nverbindung** joinder of indictments; **~vertreter** counsel for the prosecution, prosecutor, prosecuting attorney, prosecuting counsel; **~zwang** compulsory public prosecution of crimes; **die ~ vertreten** to prosecute, to act for the Prosecution; **e–e ~ erhärten** to support a charge; **e–e ~ fallenlassen** to drop a charge; **e–e ~ verfolgen** to prosecute, to press charges; to proceed with a charge; **jmdn in den ~zustand versetzen** to commit s. o. for trial; **öffentliche ~** = *Anklage qv*; **unter ~ stehen** to be accused; **unter ~ stellen** (*wegen*) to charge *with*, to arraign *for*, to indict; **von e–r ~ absehen** to drop a charge.

anklagefähig adj suitable for a criminal charge, indictable.

anklagen v/t to accuse, to charge (*with a crime, for trial*), to indict, to impeach (*in impeachment proceedings only*); **erneut ~** to reaccuse, to charge again.

Ankläger m accuser, arraigner, public prosecutor, counsel for the prosecution.

Anknüpfungs|punkt connecting factor, point of reference, point of linkage, jurisdictional basis, point of contact; **~tatsachen** tying-in facts, facts of reference.

ankreuzen v/t to tick, to mark with a

ankündigen

cross; **das Kästchen ~** to mark the box with a cross, to tick the box.
ankündigen *v/t* to announce, to give prior notice.
Ankündigung *f* announcement, notification, notice, warning; **~sschreiben** written notice; **öffentliche ~** public announcement; **ohne ~** without a moment's warning, without notice; **ohne vorherige ~** without prior notice.
Ankunft *f* arrival; **planmäßige ~** scheduled arrival; **voraussichtliche ~** expected time of arrival (*E. T. A.*).
Ankunfts|flughafen airport of arrival, **~hafen** port of arrival; **~meldung** notice of arrival (*consignment*); **~ort** place of arrival; **~schiff** incoming ship; **~wert** value upon arrival; **~zeit** time of arrival *wahrscheinliche ~~*: *expected time of arrival*.
ankurbeln *v/t* to stimulate (*business*).
Ankurbelung *f* stimulation (*business*), pump-priming, boosting (*of the economy*).
Anlage *f* (*1*) investment, placement; invested capital, capital assets, fixed assets; **~aktien** investment stocks; **~bedarf** investment requirements; **~berater** investment adviser, investment consultant; **~bereitschaft** willingness to invest, propensity to invest; **~bewertung** investment rating; **~dispositionen** investment decisions; **~erträge** investment income; **~fonds** investment funds; **~form** form of investment, type of investment; **~gesellschaft** investment company; **~güter** capital goods; capital equipment; *bewegliche ~~*: *movable assets*; *geringwertige ~~*: *low-value capital goods*; **~investitionen** investment in fixed assets; **~investitionen der Unternehmen** fixed investment by companies; **~kapital** invested capital, investment capital, permanent capital, fixed capital, business capital; **~käufe** investment buying, portfolio buying; **~klima** investment climate;

Anlagenvermittlungsbüro

~konto investment account; **~kosten** plant expenses; initial capital expenditure; **~kredit** investment credit; **~kundschaft** investing customers; **~mittel** investment resources; **~möglichkeit** opportunity for employment of funds, investment opportunity; **~nabgänge** disposals of fixed assets, retirements (*US*); **~nabschreibung** equipment depreciation, investment depreciation; **~nbewertung** investment evaluation; **~nbuch** property ledger; **~nbuchhaltung** fixed asset accounting; investment accounting; **~nfinanzierung** financing of investments; **~ninvestitionen** fixed investment; **~nkonto** fixed asset account; investment account; **~nmiete** investment rental; *kalkulatorische ~~*: *calculated systems rental*; **~npalette** range of investments; **~nrendite** investment yield, compound yield; **~nsicherheit** safety of (nuclear) installations; **~nspiegel** investors' guide; **~nstreuung** investment diversification; **~nüberträge** transfer of fixed assets; **~numbuchungen** reclassification of fixed assets; **~nwagnis** fixed asset contingency, fixed asset risk, investment risk; **~nwerte** investment securities, investments, fixed assets; *festverzinsliche ~~*: *fixed income investment*; **~nzugänge** additional fixed assets; **~objekt** object of investment, investment item; **~papiere** investment stocks and shares, investment securities; **~plan** investment plan; **~politik** investment policy; investment strategy; strategy of investment; **a~scheu** reluctant to invest, reluctant to put capital at risk; **~titel** investment security; **~umdisposition** policy of switching investments, changing form of investment; investment switch; *langfristige ~~*: *long-term policy of switching investments*; **~vermittler** investment broker; **~nvermittlungs-**

Anlage | **Anleihe**

büro investment exchange, investment brokerage; **~vermögen** capital assets, fixed assets, net tangible assets, invested capital, fixed capital, fixed property investment; **~~ zum Anschaffungswert**: *fixed assets valued at cost, bewegliches ~~*: *movable property investment*; **~ von Bankgeldern** investment of bank funds; **~wagnis** investment risk; **~wechsel** change of investment; **~wert** investment value; **~werte** investments, assets; *immaterielle ~~*: *intangible assets*; **~wertpapier** investment (security); **~williger** would-be investor, person willing to invest; **~zuwachs** growth in capital assets; **einträgliche ~** remunerative investment; **ertragbringende ~** remunerative investment, with-profits investment; **festverzinsliche ~** (fixed-) interest-bearing investment; **gewinnbringende ~** profitable investment; **immaterielle ~werte** intangible assets; **kurzfristige ~n** short-term investment; **langfristige ~** long-term investment; **liquide ~n** liquid assets, quick assets; **mündelsichere ~** legal investment, trustee investment; **werbende ~** productive investment.

Anlage *f* (2) installation, plant, works (*of an enterprise*); facilities; **~n im Bau** works in progress; **bauliche ~n** building structures; **feuergefährliche ~n** fire hazardous installations; **genehmigungspflichtige ~n** installations requiring official permit; **gewerbliche ~n** industrial plant and equipment; **maschinelle ~n** plant facilities; **militärische ~n** military property; **öffentliche ~n** public grounds, ornamental grounds, public gardens; **sanitäre ~n** hygiene facilities; **störende ~n** disturbing installations.

Anlage *f* (3) enclosure, annex; exhibit (*Schriftsatz*); **aus der ~ ersichtlich** set forth in the enclosure; **in der ~** enclosed (*herewith*).

anlanden *v/t* to land.

Anlandsetzen *n* putting ashore.
Anlandung *f* landing, accretion (*washing up of sand or soil*), alluvion.
Anlaß *m* occasion, cause, motive; **~aufsicht** supervision when required (*by an occurence*); **begründeter ~** just cause, good cause; **berechtigter ~** good grounds (for), reasonable cause; **erheblicher ~** perfectly good cause; **früherer ~** previous occasion; **konkreter ~** definite cause, certain occasion.
anläßlich *prep* on the occasion of, in the course of, incidental to.
anlastbar *adj* chargeable, imputable (to).
anlasten *v/t* to blame (for), to accuse of being at fault, to impute, to put the blame on.
Anlaufhafen *m* port of call.
Anlauf|kosten launching costs, start-up costs; **~kredit** pump-priming credit; **~produktion** initial production; **~sfrist** start-up period, initial period; **~verlust** initial loss; **~zeit** warming-up time (*production, workers*), start-up period, time for adaptation, warm-up.
Anlege|gebühr(en) *f* (*pl*) moorage, quayage, moorage fees; quay dues, dockage; **~stelle** *f* dock, mooring platform; **öffentlicher ~platz** public wharf.
anlegen *v/t* to invest; **befristet ~** to invest for a fixed term; **verzinslich ~** to invest for interest.
Anleger *m* investor; **~publikum** investors, investing public; **~schicht** class of investors; **~schutz** protection of investors; **institutioneller ~** institutional investor(s) (*banks, insurance companies*); **liquide öffentliche ~** public authorities with liquid funds available.
Anlegung *f* investment; planning.
Anlehnung *f* dependence, imitation, borrowing; **in ~ an** analogous to, by analogy to, in conformity with, following.
Anleihe *f* loan, (*borrowing by issuing bearer bonds*), bond issue; **~ablösung** loan redemption, redemption of a bond issue (or series);

45

Anleiheablösungsschuld

~**ablösungsschuld** bond redemption indebtedness; ~**aufnahme** raising (floating) of a loan; borrowing; ~**ausstattung** loan terms; ~**bedarf** demand for public loans; borrowing requirements; ~**bedingungen** loan terms; ~**begebung** = ~ emission *qv;* ~**dienst** service of the loan; ~**emission** issue of a loan; ~**erlös** proceeds of bonded loan; ~**ermächtigung** authority to borrow; ~**finanzierung** raising funds by way of bonds; financing by placing fixed interest-bearing securities; ~**forderung** (claim to repayment of) bonded debt; ~**garantie** bond guarantee; ~**gläubiger** bond creditor(s); ~**kapital** loan capital, bonded debt; ~**konsortium** loan placement syndicate, consortium; ~**konversion** conversion of bonds (*into shares*); ~**laufzeit** term of a loan; ~**markt** bond market; ~ **mit variablem Zinssatz** floating rate bond; ~**mittel** resources derived from the issue of bonds; ~ **der öffentlichen Hand** public; ~**nehmer** borrower; ~**n im Umlauf** bonds in circulation; ~**papier** bond certificate; ~**politik** borrowing policy; ~**rendite** loan yield; ~**schuld** bonded debt, bond obligation, indebtedness under a bond issue; ~**schuldner** debtor (*public loan*); ~**schuldverschreibung** public bond, debenture; ~**stock** loan fund; ~**tilgung** repayment of loan, redemption of bonds; ~**typ** type (or category) of bonds, class of bonds; ~**umschuldung** loan roll-over, rescheduling; ~**umwandlung** bond conversion into shares; ~**verpflichtung** obligation under a loan issue; obligation to grant a loan; ~**zeichner** bond subscriber, subscriber to a public bond issue; ~**zeichnung** bond subscription; ~**zins** bond *or* loan interest rate; **ähnlich ausgestattete** ~**n** loans issued on similar terms; **auf dem** ~**weg** (raising funds) by means of bonds; **aufgerufene** ~**n** loans called for repayment; **e–e** ~ **auflegen** to float a loan, to issue a loan; **e–e** ~ **aufnehmen** to take up a loan, to contract a loan; **e–e** ~ **bedienen** to service a loan; **e–e** ~ **begeben** to issue a loan; **e–e** ~ **placieren** to place a loan; **e–e** ~ **tilgen** to repay a loan, to redeem a bond issue; **e–e** ~ **unterbringen** to place a loan; **e–e** ~ **zeichnen** to subscribe for a loan; **dinglich gesicherte** ~ secured bonds; **fundierte** ~ funded bonds; **garantierte** ~ guaranteed loan; **konsolidierte** ~ consolidated loan; **hypothekarisch gesicherte** ~ mortgage bonds, loan secured by a mortgage; **kündbare** ~ callable loan, redeemable loan; **kurzfristige** ~ short-term loan; **langfristige** ~ long-term loan, long-term bonds (issue); **nicht bediente** ~ non-performing loan; **nicht zweckgebundene** ~ general purpose loan; **notleidende** ~ troubled loan; **private** ~ private loan; **öffentliche** ~**n** loans of public authorities, bonds issued by public authorities; **öffentliche** ~**titel** bonds of public authorities; **steuerbefreite** ~ tax-free bonds, tax-free loan; **steuerbegünstigte** ~ tax-privileged bonds, preferentially taxed bonds; **ungesicherte** ~ unsecured loan; **unkündbare** ~ perpetual bonds, non-callable bonds; **untilgbare** ~ non-callable bonds, non-redeemable loan; **üppig ausgestattete** ~ loans on generous terms; **verbriefte** ~ bonded loan; **wertbeständige** ~ constant value bonds, stable-value bond; **zinsvariable** ~ floating-rate loan, escalator loan; **zweckgebundene** ~ tied loan.

Anleitung *f* direction, instruction; ~**shandbuch** book of instructions, service manual.

Anlernen *n* **von Arbeitskräften** on the job training.

Anlernkosten *pl* training costs.

Anlernling *m* trainee, learner, beginner.

Anlernung *f* on the job training.

Anlieferung *f* delivery; ~ **frei Haus**

anliegend | **Anmeldung**

door to door delivery; ~**skosten** delivery charge; ~**sstelle** place of delivery.

anliegend *presp, adj* enclosed, attached hereto; ~**senden wir Ihnen** enclosed please find, we enclose.

Anlieger *m* adjacent owner, contiguous occupier, abutter, abutting owner, neighbour, riparian proprietor; ~**beiträge** municipal development charges (*for properties next to public streets*); ~**gebrauch** (*privileged*) use by adjacent owners (*by occupiers of premises bordering a public street*); ~**grundstück** adjoining real estate, adjoining premises; ~**kosten** adjacent property charges, road charges; ~**nutzung** → ~ *gebrauch*; ~**recht** adjoining property rights; ~**siedlung** adjoining housing estate; ~**staat** littoral state, bordering state, neighbouring state, riparian state; ~**verkehr** passage (*or* through way) for "residents only", resident traffic (*lawful traffic to and from place in closed street*); ~**verpflichtung** adjacent owners' obligation.

anlocken *v/t* to allure, to entice, to bait (*customers*).

anmahnen *v/t* to remind (*s. o. of overdue account*), to request payment, to issue a warning (*to pay outstanding accounts*).

Anmahnung *f* reminder; ~ **säumiger Schuldner** sending of reminders to dilatory debtors.

anmaßen *v reflex* to arrogate oneself to, to usurp (*title, office*).

Anmaßung *f* unwarranted assumption of authority; usurpation of office, presumption.

Anmelde|amt receiving office; ~**amtsexemplar** home copy; ~**bestimmungen** instructions to applicants, instructions for registration; ~**datum** registration date, filing date; ~**erfordernisse** registration requirements; ~**formular** registration form; a~**frei** nothing to declare (*customs*); ~**frist** time allowed for filing, time for applications; ~**gebühr** registration fee, filing fee, application fee (*patent etc*), entrance fee (*association*); ~**pflicht** compulsory registration, duty to report; a~**pflichtig** liable to file (*bankruptcy petition*), notifiable; ~**prinzip** first-to-file system; ~**priorität** priority of filing date; ~**recht** right to file, right to apply (*for patents*); ~**schein** registration form; ~**schluß** deadline for registration, closing date for filing; ~**stelle** registration office; ~**tag** date of filing; ~**unterlagen** application documents; ~**verfahren** application procedure (*patents*); ~**vordruck** registration form; ~**zeichen** filed trademark; ~**zeitraum** stipulated tax period, declaration period.

anmelden *v/t* to apply for registration, to register, to announce, to file, to apply for (*patent*), to declare (*customs*); *v reflex* to register, to enroll, to sign on; **sich polizeilich** ~ to register with the police.

Anmelder *m* registrant, applicant (*patent*), declarant (*customs*); ~ **e-s Patents** applicant for a patent; **früherer** ~ *pat* prior applicant; **mehrere** ~ multiple applicants; **späterer** ~ *pat* subsequent applicant.

Anmeldung *f* registration, notification, application for registration, advancement (*of a claim*); filing application (*patent*), declaration (*customs*); ~ **des Konkurses** bankruptcy notice; ~ **e-r Forderung** notice of a claim; = ~ *e-r Konkursforderung qv*; ~ **e-r Konkursforderung** proof (of debt) in bankruptcy, proof of debt; ~ **e-s Warenzeichens** (application for) registration of a trademark; ~ **für eigene Rechnung** declaration on one's own behalf; ~ **für fremde Rechnung** declaration on behalf of another person; ~ **von Vermögen** declaration of property (*or* assets); ~ **wegen Wohnungswechsel** notice of change of domicile (*or* of address); ~ **zum Handelsregister** application for registration in the Commercial Register; ~ **zum Verkehr** movement certificate; ~

Anmeldungsfrist / **Annahme**

zur Eintragung in ein Register application for registration; **e-e ~ tätigen** to effect an application; **e-e ~ weiterverfolgen** to pursue an application; **~svordruck** declaration form (*customs*); **e-e ~ zurückweisen** to refuse a patent application; **e-r ~ entgegenstehen** to oppose (*or* interfere with) an application (*industrial property rights registration*); **entgegenstehende ~** interfering (*or* opposing) application; **frühere ~** prior application; **laufende ~** pending application; **noch nicht verbeschiedene ~** pending application; **polizeiliche ~** registration with the police authorities; **prioritätsbegründende ~** application establishing priority; **schwebende ~** pending application; **spätere ~** subsequent application.

Anmeldungsǀfrist time limit for filing (*an application for registration*); **~gebühr** registration fee; **~schein** application blank, registration form; **~termin** registration deadline; **~unterlagen** documents in support of registration, registration papers.

anmerken *v/t* to make annotations, to annotate; to comment.

Anmerkung *f* annotation, note, comment, *pl also*: explanatory notes.

anmustern *v/t* to sign up (*seamen*) *cf* Anmusterung.

Anmusterung *f* hiring, signing up engagement of merchant marine staff (*i. e. officers, sailors or other employees by the Mercantile Marine Office*) (*Seemannsamt*).

Annäherung *f* approximation, *pol* rapprochement; **~spolitik** policy of rapprochement; **~sprozeß** convergence; **~swert** approximation, approximate value; **schrittweise ~** progressive approximation.

Annahme *f* (1) acceptance (= *acc*), adoption, taking delivery (*of goods*); **~ an Erfüllungs statt** *acc* in lieu of specific performance (*acc of sth. different in full discharge of the obligation*); **~ an Kindes Statt** (= *~ als Kind*) adoption; **~ des Geschäftsberichts** approval of the annual report; **~ ehrenhalber** *acc* on an honorary basis, *acc* for honour, *acc* supra protest; **~ e-s Angebots** *acc* of an offer; **~ e-s Antrags** adoption (*or* passing) of a resolution, passing of a motion (*meetings*); **~ e-s Gesetzes** passing (passage) of a law, enactment; **~ e-s Vertrages als verbindlich** adoption of contract as binding; **~ erfüllungshalber** conditional *acc*, *acc* subject to performance (*of the contractual obligation, esp the payment of a cheque or bill of exchange*); **~erklärung** *acc*, declaration of *acc*; **~frist** time for *acc*, term for *acc*, *acc* period; **~kurs** *acc*-rate (*for shares*); **~ mit Einschränkungen** qualified *acc*; **~ nach Protest** *acc* supra protest; **~pflicht** obligation to accept; **~protest** protested refusal to accept; **~schreiben** letter of *acc*; **~urkunde** instrument of *acc*; **~verhinderung** obstruction of *acc*, inability to take delivery; „**~verweigert**" "refused", delivery refused (*postal service*); **~verweigerung** denial of *acc*, refusal of *acc*, non-*acc*, refusal to accept delivery; **~verweigerungsvermerk** note of refusal, description of refusal; **~verzug** mora accipiendi, default in *acc*, default in taking delivery; **~wille** intention to accept; **ausdrückliche ~erklärung** express *acc*; **bedingte ~** conditional *acc*, qualified *acc*; **die ~ der Leistung ablehnen** to refuse to accept the performance; **die ~ verweigern** to refuse *acc*, to refuse to take delivery; **eingeschränkte ~** qualified *acc*; **glatte ~** clear *acc*; **mangels ~ protestieren** to protest for non-payment; **mangels ~ zurück** returned for want of *acc*, returned for non-acceptance; **stillschweigende ~** tacit *acc*, implied *acc*; **uneingeschränkte und unbedingte ~** general acceptance, unqualified and unconditional *acc*,

Annahme   **Anpassung**

general *acc*; **verspätete** ~ late *acc*; **vorbehaltlose** ~ outright *acc*, *acc* without reservation.

Annahme *f* (2) assumption, supposition; **ehrliche** ~ firm belief.

annehmbar *adj* acceptable, reasonable, plausible.

annehmen (1) *v/t* to accept, to agree to, to adopt; **annehmen** (2) *v/i* to assume; **einstimmig** ~ to adopt unanimously.

Annehmender *m* acceptor (*of a bill of exchange*); the accepting party, the offeree (*who accepts the offer*).

Annehmlichkeit *f* convenience, ease, facility, amenity.

annektieren *v/t* to annex (*territory*).

Annektierung *f* annexation.

Annex *m* appendage, annex schedule.

Annexion *f* annexation (*by occupation or by conquest*); ~**spolitik** policy of annexation.

Annonce *f* advertisement, *esp* small advertisement, small ad; ~**n-Expedition** advertising agency.

annoncieren *v/i* to advertise, to publish an advertisement.

Annuität *f* annuity, annual payment; ~**sdarlehen** annuity loan; ~**enhypothek** redemption mortgage (*equal instalment of interest and repayment*).

annullierbar *adj* cancellable.

annullieren *v/t* to nullify, to annul, to cancel, to avoid, to declare null and void.

Annullierung *f* annulment, annulation, rescission, cancellation; ~ **von Aufträgen** cancellation of orders.

anordnen *v/t* to direct, to order, to enjoin, to require, to rule; **letztwillig** ~ to direct by last will and testament.

Anordnung *f* (1) order, directive, precept, regulation, rule; ~ **auf Vorlage** (*von Urkunden*) **bei Gericht** order to produce (documents in court); ~ **der Haftentlassung** release order; ~**der Haftfortdauer** recommitment, remand, order to continue confinement; ~ **der Nachlaßverwaltung** administration order (*in respect of a deceased person's estate*); ~ **der Untersuchungshaft** order for pretrial confinement, order to remand s. o. in custody (*pending further investigation*), interim committitur; ~ **des Erscheinens** judicial order to appear in person; ~ **des Strafvollzugs nach Widerruf der Strafaussetzung zur Bewährung** reactivation of a suspended sentence; **allgemeine** ~ general instruction; **auf** ~ **des Gerichts** by (*court*) order; **bis auf weitere** ~ until further notice; **einstweilige** ~ provisional order, temporary order, interlocutory order, interim order, interim measure (*by the court*), interlocutory relief, mesne process; **einstweilige** ~ **auf Unterhaltszahlung** maintenance order, *court order for alimony and/or support for child(en) pendente lite i. e. during divorce proceedings;* **einstweilige** ~ **zur Sicherung des Streitgegenstandes** temporary decree to secure the controversial object, quia timet action; **gerichtliche** ~ court order; ~~ **des Getrenntlebens?** separation order; **letztwillige** ~ testamentary disposition; **richterliche** ~ judicial order; *auf Grund* ~*r* ~*:* by order of the court; **sich nach der amtlichen** ~ **richten** to comply with the official instruction.

Anordnung *f* (2) structure, configuration, set-up, arrangement.

Anordnungs|**behörde** *public authority issuing the directive;* ~**gebühr** charge for an adminstrative order; ~**recht** regulatory power.

anpassen *v/t* to adjust, to adapt; *v reflex* to become adapted, to adjust onself, to accord with.

Anpassung *f* adaptation, adjustment, matching; ~ **an den veränderten Status** adaptation to the (changed) legal status; ~ **an die Entwicklung der Lebenshaltungskosten** cost of living adjustment; ~ **der Löhne** wage adjustment; **außenwirtschaftliche** ~ external adjust-

49

Anpassungsfähigkeit — Anrufung

ment; **stufenweise** ~ adaptation by stages.

Anpassungs|fähigkeit adaptability; ~**fonds** adjustment fund; ~**gesetz** matching law, adjustment law; ~**investition** matching investment; adjustment investment; ~**klausel** adjustment clause; *automatische* ~~ *des Versicherungswertes (bei beliehenen Versicherungen):* self-reducing clause; ~**skoeffizient** conversion factor (*agrarian market*); ~**prozeß** adaptation, process of adjustment.

anprangern *v/t* to expose, to denounce, to pillory (*a wrongdoer*).

anpreisen *v/t* to praise (extravagantly); to puff (*by salesman*), to push (*certain articles*).

Anpreisung *f* (extravagant) praise, sales talk; **marktschreierische** ~ puffing, aggressive salesmanship; **unverbindliche** ~**en** non-binding sales talk.

Anrainer *m* adjoining owner, owner *or* occupant of adjacent land, abutter, neighbouring farmer; ~**staat** bordering state.

anraten *v/t* to advise, to recommend.

anrechenbar *adj* allowable.

anrechnen *v/t* to take into account, to make allowance for, to allow as a credit against, to credit (against), to set off (against), to put (*a sum*) to s.o.'s credit, to apply (*a payment to a particular debt*); ~ **auf etw.** to count against s. th. (*and see above*).

Anrechnung *f* taking into account, allowance, credit; charge; ~ **auf den Erbteil** taking into account for the portion of the estate; ~ **der Untersuchungshaft** making allowance for the time of pre-trial custody; ~ **von Dienstzeiten** reckoning of length of service; ~ **von Vorausempfängen** crediting advance receipts; **in** ~ **bringen** to make allowance for.

Anrechnungs|betrag credit; **a~fähig** *adj* allowable, deductible; ~**fähigkeit** allowability; **a~pflichtig** *adj* subject to be taken into account, chargeable, deductible, eligible; ~**verfahren** (tax) credit method(s); ~**vorschrift von Teilleistungen** (*auf Zinsen, Hauptsache*) rule of partial payments; ~**zeitraum** (*tax*) credit period.

Anrecht *n* entitlement, interest, expectancy, (inchoate) right, claim; ~ **auf den Heimfall** (right to the) reversion; ~ **auf eine Altersversorgung** accrued retirement benefits, pension expectancy; ~ **auf Pfandeinlösung** equity of redemption; **bedingtes** ~ conditional interest, conditional title, conditional future right; **wohlerworbenes** ~ vested interest.

anregen *v/t* to suggest.

Anregung *f* suggestion.

Anreicherung *f* augmentation, accumulation; ~ **der Substanz** accumulation of permanent assets; ~**sfond** cumulative trust, growth fund.

Anreise *f* journey to a destination.

Anreiz *m* incentive, stimulus, inducement; sweetener; ~**blockierung** disincentive; ~**maßnahme** incentive scheme; ~**prämie** incentive bonus; **steuerlicher** ~ fiscal stimulus, tax incentive; **steuerpolitische** ~**e** tax incentives.

anreizen *v/t* to incite, to stir up, to inflame, to stimulate, to spur.

Anreizung *f* incitement; ~ **zum Rassenhaß** incitement of race hatred, racism; ~ **zum Zweikampf** provoking another person to duel.

Anrempeln und Berauben mugging; theft by jostling the victim.

anrüchig *adj* of ill repute, disreputable, fishy.

Anrüchigkeit *f* disreputableness, shadiness, fishiness, notoriety.

Anrufbeantworter telephone answering machine.

anrufen *v/t* to invoke, to have recourse (*to the law*), to bring the matter before (court), to resort to, to appeal (*to a higher instance*).

Anrufung *f* invocation, resort (*to courts of law*), submission (*to court of*

ansammeln / **Anschluß**

arbitration); ~**schance** (*equal*) opportunity to resort to courts of law.
ansammeln *v/t* to accumulate (*capital*), to collect (*art objects*); *v reflex* to accrue (*interest*).
Ansammlung *f* gathering, assembly (*persons*); accumulation (*money, profits*); **unerlaubte ~ auf öffentlichen Straßen** unlawful assembly in public thoroughfares.
ansässig *adj* resident, residing at; **~ werden** to become a resident, to take up one's abode; **nicht hier ~** non-resident, not living here.
Ansässiger *m* (*der Ansässige*) resident, local inhabitant.
Ansässigkeit *f* residence, status of a resident.
Ansatz *m* (*pl Ansätze* = ~**e**) initial stage for an action, entry in an account *or* estimate, valuation, carrying value; ~**punkt** (*of an argument*), point of reference; **~ zur Tatbestandsverwirklichung** overt act; **außer ~ bleiben** to remain out of account; **ein niedriger ~** an item at a lower value; **~e des Haushaltsplans** budget appropriations; **kalkulatorischer ~** calculated base data.
anschaffen *v/t* to acquire; to procure.
Anschaffung *f* acquisition; purchase; providing cover (*banking*); **~ zum Zwecke der Weiterveräußerung** purchase for resale; **für ~ sorgen** to provide for cover, to provide for sufficient payment into the bank account.
Anschaffungs|darlehen personal instalment credit, consumer loan; **~geschäfte** purchase of securities transactions, stock-exchange acquisitions; **~kosten** cost of acquisition, acquisition cost, initial outlay, prime cost, original cost; **~kostenprinzip** historical cost accounting; **~kurs** purchasing rate; **~nebenkosten** incidental acquisition costs; **~preis** first price, cost price, original price, buying price; **~~ des Anteilsinhabers**: shareholder's cost; **~tag** date of acquisition; **~wert** acquisition value, cost, original cost, prime cost, purchasing value; **zum ~~**: at cost (*price*); **~wertprinzip** cost value principle.
Anschein *m* appearance, semblance; **~ der Gerechtigkeit** semblance of justice; **allem ~ nach** in all probability; **auf den ersten ~** prima facie, at first glance; **den ~ erwecken** to pretend, to make believe, to give the (deceptive) impression; **den ~ haben** to have the appearance of; **den ~ wahren** to keep up appearances; **falscher ~** false appearance, make-believe; **ohne den ~ e-s Rechts** without a semblance of right.
anscheinend *adj* apparent, ostensible.
Anscheins|beweis *m* prima facie evidence, half proof; **~vertreter** apparent agent; ostensible agent; **~vollmacht** apparent authority, ostensible authority.
Anschlag *m* (1) plot, attack; **e-n ~ verüben** to make an assassination attempt; **hochverräterischer ~** treasonable assault; **terroristischer ~** act of terrorism.
Anschlag *m* (2) notice on the bulletin board, announcement on the notice-board; poster, placard; **~säule** advertising pillar, poster pillar; **~stelle** billboard boarding, poster site; **~tafel** billboard, bulletin, board, poster panel; **~werbung** poster advertising; **öffentlicher ~** poster, public notice by wall-poster.
anschlagen *v/t* to post on the bulletin board, to put up a notice/poster.
Anschließungsantrag *m* rider, annexed motion, seconding motion.
Anschluß *m* connection, joinder, affiliation, follow-up; **~anmeldung** (*Patent*) in-part application; **~auftrag** a follow-up order; **~bahnhof** junction; **~bereich** service area (*public utilities*); **~berufung** cross appeal, counter-appeal, respondent's notice of appeal; **~beschwerde** cross-complaint, respondent's notice of (joining a) complaint; **~finanzierung** follow-up financing; **~frachten** forward-

51

ing carriage charges; ~**gleis** siding, side track; ~**konkurs** „follow-up" bankruptcy (*when composition proceedings fail*); ~**markt** aftermarket; ~**pacht** renewal lease; ~**pfändung** second distress, secondary attachment; ~**pflicht** compulsory connection (*to sewers, other services*); ~**plan** recovery plan; ~-**Rediskontzusage** undertaking to rediscount for an additional period; ~**reeder** on-carrying shipowner, connecting carrier; ~**revision** counter-appeal (*to higher court on points of law only*), cross-appeal in error; ~**transporte** forwarding carriage; ~**verfahren** connecting procedure, subsequent proceedings; ~**vertrag** follow-up agreement; treaty of accession, contract of association; ~**zone** contiguous zone (*maritime law*); ~**zug** connection, connecting train; ~**zwang** compulsory participation (*in public utility services*); **allgemeine** ~- **und Versorgungspflicht** general obligation to provide and maintain public utility services (*vested in public corporations*).

Anschnallpflicht *f* (statutory) duty to fasten a safety-belt; ~**gesetz** mandatory seatbelt law.

anschreiben lassen *v/t* to take on credit, to buy on credit (*at the grocer's or baker's*), to buy on tick (*slang*), to charge to s.o.'s account, to have s. th. chalked up (*drinks*).

Anschreibenlassen *n* taking (buying) on credit; charging to customer's account.

Anschrift *f* address; ~**enermittlung** tracing addresses (*of bad debtors etc*); ~**sänderung** change of address; **ladungsfähige** ~ address for service (of a court summons).

anschuldigen *v/t* to accuse, to charge, to incriminate.

Anschuldigung *f* accusation, charge, incrimination; ~ **zurückweisen** to reject accusations; **aus den Fingern gesogene** ~ trumped-up charge, fabricated charge; malicious accusation; **falsche** ~ false accusation (of crime); **falsche** ~ **erheben** to make false accusations; **vorsätzlich falsche** ~ malicious accusation, trumped-up charge; **wissentlich falsche** ~ deliberate false charge.

anschwärzen *v/t* to disparage s.o., to slander (commercially), to slander goods.

Anschwärzung *f* malicious falsehood, disparagement of goods, trade libel, running down (of s. o.), disparagement (of competitor), blackening the reputation (of s. o.).

Anschwemmung *f* alluvion (*washing up of sand or soil*).

Ansehen *n* credit, esteem, reputation; **das** ~ **herabsetzen** to diminish the reputation of, to disparage, to belittle; **geschäftliches** ~ business reputation; **ohne** ~ **der Person** irrespective of the person concerned, disregarding (the social status) of the person concerned.

ansehen *v/t* to regard, to consider; **als erwiesen** ~ to take for granted, to consider sth. to have been proved; to take sth. as given; **etwas als geringfügig** ~ to hold sth. (to be) a trivial matter.

Ansehung *f* regard, respect; **in** ~ taking into consideration, with due regard for (the fact that).

ansetzen *v/t* to fix, to make an appointment, to set a date for, to schedule (*date, hearing etc*); to rate, to assess (*costs*), to appropriate.

Ansetzung *f* fixing (*a day in court*); assessment (*costs*), the beginning of an attempt.

Ansicht *f* opinion, view, inspection. ~ **des Gerichts** opinion of the court; **e-r** ~ **beipflichten** to concur (with s. o.'s opinion); **für e-e** ~ **eintreten** to support a view; **private** ~ personal point of view, personal opinion; **radikale** ~**en** extreme opinions, extremist views, radical views; **zur** ~ for inspection, on approval (*consignment of unordered books etc*); ~~ **schicken: to send on approval*).

Ansichts|sache a matter of opinion;

Ansiedlung | **Anspruch**

~**exemplar** specimen copy. ~**muster** sample specimen; ~**sendung** consignment for inspection, sample consignment (*for approval or return*); ~**zeichnung** sketch.

Ansiedlung *f* settlement, housing estate, locality, village.

Anspannung *f* stress, strain, tightening; ~ **der Devisenbilanz** foreign exchange difficulties, hardening of the foreign exchange market; ~ **der Kassenlage** tightening of liquidity; ~ **der Reserven** drain on the reserves; ~ **des Geldmarktes** strain on the money market, monetary strain; ~**ssymptome** signs of strain.

ansparen *v/i* to save for a specific purpose; to accumulate by saving.

Ansparleistung *f* minimum savings for home financing.

Anspielung *f* allusion, hint; **beleidigende** ~ innuendo.

Ansporn *f* incentive, stimulus.

Ansprechpartner *m* addressee target.

Ansprechstelle *f* point of contact, liaison (office).

Anspruch *m* claim (= *cl*), demand, right, title, interest; ~ **auf Auskunftserteilung** entitlement to information; ~ **auf bevorrechtigte Befriedigung** prior *cl* to satisfaction; ~ **auf Erfindernennung** inventor's right to be mentioned; ~ **auf Erfüllung** *cl* to (specific) performance; ~ **auf Herausgabe** right to claim restitution; ~ **auf Rechnungslegung** *cl or* entitlement to the rendering of accounts; ~ **auf Schadenersatz** *cl* for damages, entitlement to damages; ~~ *erheben: to claim damages*; ~ **auf ungestörte Intimsphäre** right of privacy; ~ **aus e-m Recht** a legal right, title (under a right); ~ **aus e-m Vermächtnis** *cl* to a legacy, *cl* under a legacy; ~ **aus e-m Vertrag** *cl* under a contract, contractual *cl*; ~ **erheben** to claim, to lodge a *cl*; to lay *cl* to; to sth; **allumfassender** ~ comprehensive *cl*, omnibus *cl*; **älterer** ~ prior *cl*; **auf e-n** ~ **verzichten** to waive a *cl*, to give up a *cl*, to relinquish a *cl*; **bedingter** ~ conditional *cl*; **befristeter** ~ *cl* subject to a time-limit, *cl* due after a period of time; **begründeter** ~ substantiated *cl*, justified *cl*, good *cl*; sound *cl*; **berechtigter** ~ *cl*, rightful *cl*; **betagter** ~ deferred *cl*; **deliktischer** ~ tortious *cl*, *cl* under the law of torts; **dinglicher** ~ real right, (*cl* under a) right in rem, ad rem *cl*; **ein** ~**ist verjährt** a *cl* has become statute-barred; **e-n** ~**aberkennen** to dismiss a *cl*; **e-n** ~ **abtreten** assign a right (of action), to assign a *cl*; **e-n** ~ **anerkennen** to acknowledge a *cl*; to recognize a *cl*, to allow a *cl*; **e-n** ~ **anmelden** to register a *cl*, to prove a *cl*, to announce a *cl*; **e-n** ~ **aufrechterhalten** to sustain a *cl*; **e-n** ~ **begründen** to substantiate a *cl*, to state reasons for a *cl*, to justify a *cl*, to support a *cl*; **e-n** ~ **bestreiten** to deny a *cl*, to resist a *cl*; **e-n** ~ **dem Grunde nach anerkennen** to recognize the basis of a *cl*; **e-n** ~ **durchsetzen** to enforce a *cl*, to prosecute a *cl*; **e-n** ~ **erheben** to raise a *cl*, to lodge a *cl*, to put in a *cl*, to claim title to; **e-n** ~ **geltend machen** to assert a *cl*; **e-n** ~ **gerichtlich geltend machen** to prosecute a *cl*, to assert a *cl* by legal action; **e-n** ~ **glaubhaft machen** to establish a *cl* by prima facie evidence; **e-n** ~ **substantiieren** to substantiate a *cl*, to state particulars in support of a *cl*; **e-n** ~ **zu Fall bringen** to defeat a *cl*, to thwart a *cl*; **e-n** ~ **zurückweisen** to repudiate a *cl*; **geheimer** ~ **im Innenverhältnis** secret equity, secret *cl* inter se, *cl* arising from secret internal arrangement; **geldwerter** ~ monetary *cl*; **gesetzlicher** ~ legal *cl*; **gewohnheitsrechtlicher** ~ customary right; **höchstpersönlicher** ~ (highly) personal *cl*, nontransferable *cl*, a *cl* in personam; **in** ~ **nehmen** to make a *cl* on, to claim sth. from s. o, to hold liable, to demand, to utilize, to employ

53

the services (of); ~~ **genommene Beträge**: amounts drawn (under a credit), **noch nicht ~~ genommener Teil e–s Kredits**: undrawn portion of a loan; **naturrechtlicher** ~ natural right; **nichtvermögensrechtlicher** ~ non-pecuniary claim; **obligatorischer** ~ personal right, right in personam, cl founded in obligation, obligatory right; **possessorischer** ~ possessory claim, right based on possession; **prioritätsälterer** ~ prior cl; cl of earlier priority date; **rechtmäßiger** ~ legal cl; **rechtsgültiger** ~ valid cl, good title; **schuldrechtlicher** ~ = obligatorischer ~ qv; **seerechtlicher** ~ maritime cl; **sich e–s ~ begeben** to remit a cl, to give up a cl; to concede a cl; **territorialer** ~ territorial cl; **titulierter** ~ directly enforceable cl (judgment, decree, order, deed with judgment note etc); **über e–n ~ erkennen** to adjudicate over a cl; **übertragener** ~ assigned cl, transferred right; **unbegründeter** ~ unfounded cl; **unberechtigter** ~ pretence, unjustified cl, bogus cl; **unbestreitbarer** ~ unchallengeable right; **uneinklagbarer** ~ unenforceable claim; **vermögensrechtlicher** ~ pecuniary cl; **vermögenswerter** ~ claim in the nature of an asset; **vertraglicher** ~ contractual cl; **vertretbarer** ~ sustainable claim; **verwirkter** ~ lapsed right, stale demand; **vorgehender** ~ prior cl; **vorrangiger** ~ prior cl, prior charge; **widerstreitende ~e** (pl) interfering claims; **wohlerworbener** ~ vested right; valid right; **zivilrechtlicher** ~ civil cl; **zusammenfassender** ~ omnibus cl; **zweifelhafter** ~ doubtful cl, pretence.

Anspruchs|befriedigung (cl = claim) satisfaction of cl; realization of cl; **~begründung** founding of a cl, establishment of a cl; **a~berechtigt** entitled to a cl (or right); **~berechtigter** rightful claimant, the party entitled to claim, beneficiary; award holder, awardee; **~fassung** draft cl; vorläufige **~~**: draft cl, temporary cl, patent pending right; **~gebühr** pat claims fee; **~grund** legal basis for a cl, foundation of a cl; glaubhaft gemachter **~~**: probable ground; **~grundlage** foundation of cl, basis of cl; glaubhaft gemachte **~~**: probable cause, credible cl; **~häufung** joinder of causes of action, accumulation of cl–s; **~konkurrenz** concurring claims; **~steller** claimant; unberechtigter ~: unauthorized claimant; **~stellerin** claimant (female); **~übergang** devolution of claims, passing of cl; **~verbrauch** pre-exhaustion of rights; **~verjährung** limitation (of claims), barring of claims (under the Statute of Limitations); **~verlust** disentitlement; **~verwirkung** forfeiture of claim, estoppel of claim; **~verzicht** waiver of a cl; **~voraussetzungen** conditions of entitlement, qualifying conditions, eligibility criteria; **~vorbehalt** reservation of cl.

Anstalt f institution, establishment, foundation; ~ **des öffentlichen Rechts** (incorporated) public-law institution; **geschlossene** ~ secure place; **öffentlich-rechtliche** ~ = ~ des öffentlichen Rechts qv; **sozialtherapeutische** ~ institution for social therapy (reform of offenders).

Anstalts|abteilung ward (of mental hospital); **~arzt** resident doctor (mental hospital etc); **~erziehung** reform-education (for juveniles), education in an approved school (or reformatory); **~gewalt** authority vested in a public institution; liability of a public institution; **~pflege** institutional care; **~ordnung** regulations of a public institution; institution; **~unterbringung** committal to an institution.

Anstand m decency, propriety, decorum.

Anstands|gefühl sense of decency, sense of propriety; **~pflicht** moral obligation; **~regeln** (rules of) decorum, propriety, etiquette; **~schenkung** customary present, gift arising from a moral obligation.

Ansteckung *f* contagion, infection, communication of disease; ~**sgefahr** risk of contamination, risk of infection; ~**sverdacht** suspicion of infection.

anstellen *v/t* to engage, to employ.

Anstellung *f* engagement, employment, appointment; ~ **auf Probe** trial engagement, probationary appointment; ~ **auf Zeit** temporary appointment, temporary employment; **befristete** ~ limited-term (*or* fixed-term) appointment; **feste** ~ regular employment, contractual employment; **planmäßige** ~ establishment.

Anstellungs|bedingungen conditions (terms) of employment; ~**behörde** appointing authority; ~**betrug** employment fraud, (*employment obtained by fraud*); ~**körperschaft** the employing corporate body; ~**urkunde** document of appointment; contract, ~**verhältnis** employment contract, terms of employment; ~**vertrag** contract of employment, service contract.

Anstiegstendenz *f* rising tendency.

anstiften *v/t* to instigate, to incite, to abet (*another to commit a crime*).

Anstifter *m* instigator, abettor, suborner.

Anstiftung *f* incitement, instigation, solicitation (*to commit crime*); ~**sversuch** attempted instigation (*to commit a crime*); ~ **zum Meineid** subornation of perjury; ~ **zum Selbstmord** inciting s.o. to commit suicide; ~ **zum unsittlichen Lebenswandel** incitement to lead an immoral life.

Anstoß *m* offence, annoyance; ~ **erregen** to give offence; ~ **nehmen** to take offence.

anstößig *adj* objectionable, offensive, scandalous, obnoxious.

Anstößigkeit *f* objectionableness, impropriety, scandalous nature.

Anstrengung *f* effort; **echte** ~**en** genuine efforts; **gemeinsame** ~ common endeavour (*preamble*).

Ansturm *m* run, wild rush (*customers, bargain sale*); ~ **auf eine Bank** run on a bank; ~ **der Gläubiger** run of creditors.

Anteil *m* share, part, participation, portion, quota, proportion, quota interest, stake; ~ **am Gesellschaftskapital** share of company's capital; ~ **am Gewinn** share of (the) profits; ~ **an der Erbschaft** share of the inheritance, portion of the estate; ~ **an der Förderung** working interest; ~ **an e-r Kapitalgesellschaft** share in a corporation, share in a company (limited); ~ **aus e-r Auseinandersetzung** portion from a settlement; ~**e in Fremdbesitz** shares held by outsiders; **abrufbare** ~**e** callable shares; **eigener** ~ own interest; **fremder** ~ interest of outside shareholder, share held by a third party; **seinen** ~ **zahlen** to pay one's share; **steuerpflichtiger** ~ taxable portion; **unbestimmter** ~ indefinite share, slice; **verhältnismäßiger** ~ proportionate share, quota, rateable portion; **zu erwartender** ~ presumptive share, expected share.

anteilig *adj* ratable (= *rateable*), pro rata; proportionate; ~ **verrechnet** taken into account in due proportion, calculated on a pro rata basis; ~ **verteilen** to pro-rate.

Anteils|besitz shareholding, share of property interests; ~**eigner** owner of a share, shareholder, stockholder, equity holder; unit holder; ~**empfänger** recipient of a share, shareholder; ~**inhaber** certificate holder, shareholder; **a**~**mäßig** on a pro rata basis; ~**nießbrauch** usufruct of part of a property, use and benefit of a capital share; ~**recht** right to a share, proportionate right; ~**rechte an Wertpapierfonds** participation rights in portfolio property, investment fund shares; ~**satz** proportion quota, rateable portion, rate; ~**schein** share certificate; ~**zoll** compensatory levy.

Anthropotechnik *f* human engineering.
Antialkoholbewegung *f* temperance movement, teetotalism.
Antichrese *n* antichresis, Welsh mortgage (*income from pledged property instead of interest*), *cf Nutzpfand*.
Antidiskriminierung *f* affirmative action.
Antidumpingzoll *m* anti-dumping duty.
Antikartellgesetzgebung *f* antitrust legislation.
Antinomie *f* antinomy, conflicting provisions of the same statute.
Antirezessionspolitik *f* anti-recession policy.
Antiselektion *f* (*Ausscheiden der besseren Risiken*) adverse selection.
Antiterrorismusgesetz *n* Prevention of Terrorism Act.
Antitrustgesetze *n/pl* Anti-trust Acts.
antizipieren *v/t* to anticipate, to preempt.
Antrag *m* application; application form; motion, petition, demand, request, claim; proposal, proposition, submission; ~ **auf Abschluß e-s Vertrages** offer (to conclude a contract), application to conclude a contract; ~ **auf Abweisung der Klage** motion to dismiss the complaint; ~ **auf Anberaumung eines Termins** application for trial date; ~ **auf Anordnung e-r Sicherheitsleistung** application for security of costs; ~ **auf Aufhebung der Immunität** motion to lift immunity; ~ **auf Aufhebung des Konkursverfahrens** petition for discharge (*of bankruptcy proceedings*); ~ **auf Auszahlung von Hinterlegungsgeldern** application for release of deposited moneys; ~ **auf Beitritt** application (*or* request) for membership; ~ **auf e-n Beschluß im Bürowege** motion for a decision in chambers; ~ **auf Einstellung des Verfahrens** application to stay proceedings; ~ **auf einstweilige Einstellung der Zwangsvollstreckung** motion for stay of execution proceedings; ~ **auf Eintragung** application for registration, motion to record; ~ **auf Entmündigung** petition in lunacy, petition for incompetence (*in lunacy*); ~ **auf Entscheidung ohne Anhören des Gegners** ex parte application; ~ **auf Entscheidung ohne mündliche Verhandlung** application for summons in chambers; ~ **auf Erlaß einer einstweiligen Verfügung** application for an interim injunction; ~ **auf Eröffnung des Konkursverfahrens** petition in bankruptcy; ~ **auf Erteilung des Armenrechts** *GB* ≈ application for legal aid; petition to sue (or defend) in forma pauperis (as a poor party); ~ **auf Fristverlängerung** request for an extension of time; ~ **auf Genehmigung** request for ratification; ~ **auf gerichtliche Entscheidung** motion for judgment; ~ **auf gütliche Beilegung** motion for a friendly settlement; ~ **auf Liquidation** winding-up petition, petition for winding-up (*company*); ~ **auf Nachprüfung** application for judicial review; ~ **auf Nichtigkeitserklärung e-s Patents stellen** to avoid a patent, to petition for annulment of a patent; ~ **auf Rechnungslegung** application for the rendering of accounts; ~ **auf Urteilsberichtigung** motion to correct judgment; ~ **auf Verfolgung** petition for prosecution; ~ **auf Versetzung in den Ruhestand** application to be retired; ~ **auf Vollstreckungsaufschub** petition for reprieve; ~ **auf Vorlage von Urkunden** application for an order for discovery; ~ **auf vordringliche Behandlung** motion for urgent handling, an urgent application; ~ **auf Vornahme e-r gerichtlichen Handlung** praecipe; ~ **auf Vertagung** motion for adjournment; ~ **auf Wiederaufnahme des Verfahrens** motion (bill) for a new trial (*or* a fresh trial); ~ **auf**

Wiederaufnahme e–s (ruhenden) Verfahrens application for revivor; ~ **auf Zulassung der Berufung** petition for leave to appeal; ~ **e–s Mitglieds** motion submitted by a member; a member's application; ~ **im Verfahren der freiwilligen Gerichtsbarkeit** ex parte application; ~ **in e–m Nebenverfahren** motion for ancillary relief; ~**steller** → *Antragsteller;* ~**stellung** → *Antragstellung;* ~ **unter Anwesenden** personal offer; ~ **zur Geschäftsordnung** procedural motion, motion on a point of order *(parl and other meetings)*; **auf** ~ on application, on motion, upon requisition; at the request (of), at the instance (of), on the application (of); **auf** ~ **des Klägers** at the plaintiff's suit; **auf formlosen** ~ on simple application; **auf eigenen** ~ proprio motu; **ausgefüllter** ~ completed application; **den** ~ **aus der Klage stellen** to ask for relief; **der** ~ **ist abgelehnt** the motion is dismissed, the nays have it; **der** ~ **ist angenommen** the motion is passed; the ayes have it; the application is granted; **die den** ~ **stützenden Tatsachen** the facts supporting the motion; ~~~~~ *müssen glaubhaft gemacht werden: the application must be supported by evidence raising a prima facie case; the evidence must be credible;* **e–m** ~ **stattgeben** to allow a petition, to pass a motion, to find for the petitioner, to sustain a motion, to grant an application; **e–m** ~ **nicht stattgeben** to deny (*or:* to dismiss) a motion; **e–n** ~ **ablehnen** to decline an application, to reject a motion; to vote against a motion, to overrule a motion, to deny a motion, to dismiss a petition; **e–n** ~**annehmen** to accept a proposal, to pass a resolution, (*der* ~ *wird angenommen: the motion is carried*); **e–n** ~ **auf Abstimmung stellen** to put the question to the vote; **e–n** ~ **genehmigen** to allow an application; **e–n** ~ **absetzen** to remove a motion from the agenda, to table a motion *(US)* *(GB: to table a motion = Antrag einbringen);* **e–n** ~ **begründen** to substantiate a motion (*or* an application), to state reasons for a motion; **e–n** ~ **durchbringen** to get a motion adopted *(meetings)*; **e–n** ~ **einbringen** to bring in a motion, *parl* to introduce a bill, to table a motion *(GB)*; **e–n** ~ **einreichen** to file (*or* to submit) an application, **e–n** ~ **ohne weiteres zurückweisen** to dismiss a claim summarily; **e–n** ~ **stellen** to move, to put an application, to apply; **e–n** ~ **stützen auf** to support a motion on; **e–n** ~ **unterstützen** to second a motion *(meetings, parl)*; **e–n** ~ **zum Beschluß erheben** to carry a motion; **e–n** ~ **zum Scheitern bringen** *parl* to defeat a bill; **einseitiger** ~ex parte application; **erneuter** ~ a fresh application, resubmission; **formloser** ~ informal application; **unerledigter** ~ outstanding application; **vorsorglich gestellter** ~ precautionary motion.

Antrags|**befugnis** legal possibility to institute proceedings; ~**berechtigung** right to apply, cause for the petition, entitlement to the petition (or application); ~**berechtigter** the rightful petitioner, the authorized petitioner; ~**bestand** outstanding applications, person with *locus standi* to petition; ~**delikt** offence requiring an application for prosecution *(to the prosecutor or court by victim, relatives of the victim, superior);* ~**ersuchen** petition; ~**formular** application form, claims form; ~**frist** application period, time for filing (a motion); ~**gegner** opponent of the petition, respondent; ~**muster** application form, precedent for an application; ~**recht** (formal) right of motion, right of application; ~**rücknahme** withdrawal of motion *(meeting)*, withdrawal of petition *(in court)*; ~**schrift** written application, written statement of request, brief containing the motion; ~~ **und**

Antragsteller

Schreibarbeiten forms and paperwork; ~**verfahren** proceeding initiated upon petition.

Antragsteller *m* applicant, petitioner, submitter, claimant, raiser (*of a motion*), mover (*meetings*), moving party, proponent (*of a motion*), proposer, postulant, propounder (*probate*); *pro forma* ~~: *nominal raiser (of the motion)*

Antragstellung *f* proposal (*or* introduction) of a motion (*meeting*), submission of the prayers for relief, reading of a motion for judgment (*court*), filing of an application; *bei* ~~: *on application, on a claim being made.*

Antriebskräfte *f/rf* expansionary forces, stimulating forces.

Antritt *m* commencement, assumption (*of an office*); ~ **von Beweisen** offer of evidence, provision of evidence; ~**sbesuch** first visit; visit to present one's credentials; ~**srede** (*bei Amtsübernahme*) inauguration address, inaugural speech.

Antwort *f* answer, replication, response, reply; rejoinder (*defendant's answer to plaintiff's replication*); ~ **bezahlt** reply paid, answer prepaid (*telegram*); ~**karte** reply card, reply-paid postcard; ~**note** note in reply; ~**schreiben** letter in reply, written answer; ~**telegramm** telegram with answer paid, prepaid answering telegram; **ablehnende** ~ negative reply, answer in the negative, negative response (*market research*); **abschlägige** ~ = *ablehnende* ~ *qv*; **bejahende** ~ affirmative reply, positive reply; **postwendende** ~ reply by return of mail; **telegrafische** ~ telegraphic reply; **umgehende** ~ immediate reply.

antworten *v/t* to answer, to reply; **ausweichend** ~ to give an evasive answer; **frech** ~ to give an impudent (*or* a cheecky) answer; **mit ja oder nein** ~ to answer yes or no; **was haben Sie darauf zu** ~? what do you have to say in reply (*or* to that)?

Anwalt

anvertrauen *v/t* to entrust (*s. o. with sth*).

anwachsen *v/i* to augment, to increase, to accrue; ~ *lassen:* to allow to run up.

Anwachsung *f* accretion, increase, accrual, allusion; ~ (*durch Zurückweichen von Gewässern*): reliction; ~ **durch Anschwemmung** alluvion; **allmähliche** ~ imperceptible accretion.

Anwachsungsrecht *n* right to accruals, right of accrual, accruing right, jus accrescendi; right of survivorship (*joint owners or joint holders of rights*).

Anwalt *m* = *Rechtsanwalt qv*, lawyer, solicitor, attorney-at-law, counsel (*appearing in court*), advocate (*also fig*); ~ **als Rechtspflegeorgan** lawyer as officer of the court; ~**, der Parteiverrat begeht** prevaricator, a lawyer who betrays his client; a lawyer who commits prevarication; ~ **des Beklagten** counsel for the defendant (*in a civil case in court*); ~ **des Klägers** counsel for the plaintiff (*appearing in court*); ~ **für Steuersachen** tax attorney, tax accountant, lawyer specializing in taxation matters; ~ **mit 10jähriger Berufszeit** lawyer of ten years' standing; ~**schaft** → *Anwaltschaft*; **aktenkundiger** ~ lawyer acquainted with the file of a case; **als** ~ **auftreten** to appear as counsel (attorney) (*in court*); **angestellter** ~ in-house lawyer, staff lawyer, fee earner; **beratender** ~ counsellor, consulting (*or* advising) counsel; legal adviser; **der gegnerische** ~ the opposing lawyer, the lawyer for the other side; **durch e-n** ~ **vertreten sein** to be legally represented, to have a lawyer ceeting for one; **e-n** ~ **bevollmächtigen** to give power of attorney to a lawyer; **e- n** ~ **in Anspruch nehmen** to engage (the services of) a lawyer; to instruct a lawyer; **e-n** ~ **mandieren** to retain a lawyer; **e-n** ~ **nehmen** to engage (the services of) a lawyer; **freiberuflicher** ~ self-

Anwältin

employed private practitioner; **klägerischer** ~ counsel for the plaintiff, plaintiff's attorney; **prozeßerfahrener** ~ case-hardened lawyer; **prozeßführender** ~ counsel, lawyer conducting a law-suit.

Anwältin f woman solicitor, female solicitor.

Anwalts|assessor trainee-lawyer (*before full admission to bar*), junior barrister; ~**beruf** the legal profession; *den ~~ ausüben: to practise law, to be a member of the legal profession*; ~**bestellung** retainer; ~**büro** law office(s); ~**firma** firm of lawyers; ~**gebühren** legal fees, solicitor's fees, counsel's (*or* barrister's) fees; ~**gebührenvorschuß** case retainer; ~**geheimnis** attorney-client privilege, solicitor-client privilege; ~**gehilfe** legal secretary, trainee; ~**gutachten** legal opinion by a lawyer, counsel's opinion *GB*; ~**honorar** attorney's fee, barrister's, (*solicitor's*) fee; ~**kammer** bar association, Law Society (*GB, for solicitors*); Bar Council (*GB, for barristers*); ~**kanzlei** law office, lawyer's office; *große ~~: law firm*; ~**kosten** lawyer's charges, lawyer's fees; ~**lehrling** apprentice (in a law office); ~ **mandierung** retainer; ~~ *im Einzelfall: special retainer*; ~**notar** lawyer commissioned as notary, notary-advocate; ~**pflichten** legal professional duties; ~**pflichtverletzung** legal malpractice, professional misconduct; ~**plädoyer** summary argument, barrister's speech; ~**praxis** law practice; ~**prozeß** litigation with necessary representation by lawyers; ~**rechnung** legal bill; ~**referendar** pupil; ~**robe** lawyer's gown; ~**sachen** litigation about lawyer's rights; *cases concerning professional admission and standing of lawyers*; ~**senat** lawyers' appeal court, *appellate division of German Supreme Court for lawyers' professional and disciplinary litigation*; solicitor's disciplinary tribunal; **sozietät** law firm; ~**stand** the legal profession; *in*

Anwartschaftsberechtigter

den ~~ aufnehmen: to admit to the bar; ~**streitigkeit** lawyers' professional and disciplinary litigation; ~**tag** lawyers' congress, lawyers' conference; ~**tätigkeit** advocacy, work as a practising lawyer; *forensische ~~: trial advocacy*; ~~ **und Gerichtskosten** legal expenses (and court fees); ~**verein** association of lawyers (*not the official professional body*); ~**versorgung** (obligatory) retirement pension scheme for lawyers; ~**vertrag** contract retaining a lawyer; ~**verzeichnis** Law List, *GB* lawyers' directory; ~**vorschuß** retaining fee, retainer (payment on account of lawyer's fees); ~**wechsel** change of attorney; ~**zustellung** direct service between lawyers; ~**zwang** mandatory representation by lawyers (*in court proceedings*).

Anwaltschaft f the legal profession, the bar, attorneyship, advocacy, the legal fraternity; **aus der** ~ **ausschließen** to disbar, to be struck off the roll (*of solicitors*); **zur** ~ **zulassen** to admit to the bar, to call to the bar, to be admitted to the roll (*of solicitors*).

Anwärter *m* candidate for office; ~**bezüge** trainees' remuneration; ~**dienst** service as trainee for clerical court service.

Anwartschaft f expectancy, future interest, inchoate interest, inchoate title; future estate, prospect; ~ **auf Verlängerung des Urheberrechts** inchoate right to renew copyright; **bedingte** ~ contingent remainder, conditional future interest.

Anwartschafts|berechtigter person entitled in expectancy, prospective beneficiary, reversionary, remainderman; ~**dividende** reversionary dividend; ~**patent** reversionary patent; ~**recht** expectancy, expectant right, contingent right; *dingliches ~~: estate in expectancy*; ~**rente** deferred annuity; ~**vermögen** property in expectancy; ~**zeit** qualifying period, waiting time (*social insurance*).

59

anweisen *v/t* to order (*s.o. to pay or deliver to a third party*), to draw (*upon s. o.*), to direct, to give directions (instructions), to require, to remit (*money to an account*).

Anweisender *m* (*der Anweisende*) drawer, remittor.

Anweisung *f* order, (*esp order to pay to a third party*); unnegotiable order (*to a third party to pay or deliver fungible goods*), warrant (*to remit*), instruction, directive, direction; **~en abwarten!** await instructions; **~en einholen** to seek instructions; **~en entgegennehmen** to take instructions; **~en über die Reiseroute** route instructions; **~ zum Schulbesuch** school attendance order; **~ zur Auslieferung von Lagergut** delivery order; **bedingte ~** conditional order; **genaue ~** strict instructions; **schriftliche ~** written instructions; **telegrafische ~** telegraphic transfer; **verbindliche ~** binding (mandatory) instructions; **unbedingte ~** unconditional order to pay (*bill of exchange*).

Anweisungsblatt *n* transit sheet, instruction sheet.

Anweisungsempfänger *m* payee, third-party beneficiary (*under an order to pay or deliver*).

anwendbar applicable, pertinent, relevant, usable; **~ sein** to be applicable, to apply.

Anwendbarkeit *f* usability, applicability; **~ e-s Gesetzes** operation of a law; **beeinträchtigen nicht die ~** shall not prejudice the applicability (of . .); **gewerbliche ~** industrial applicability.

anwenden *v/t* to apply; **entsprechend ~** to apply mutatis mutandis; **nebeneinander ~** to apply concurrently; **praktisch ~** to put into practice; to use in practice.

Anwenderecht *n* right to use; user's right.

Anwendung *f* application, use, utilization; **~ der besseren Sachnorm** better-law-approach (*international private law*); **~ e-s Gesetzes** application of a law; **auch auf ... ~ finden** to extend the provisions to . . .; **entsprechende ~ finden** to apply mutatis mutandis; **räumliche ~** territorial application (*of statute*); **rückwirkende ~** retroactive application; **sinngemäß ~ finden** to apply mutatis mutandis; **strenge ~** strict application (*of the law*); **zur ~ bringen** to apply, to put to use; **~ von Gewalt** use of force; application of force.

Anwendungs|bereich scope of application, field of application, applicability; **~ e-s Gesetzes:** *scope of an Act; purview of a law; räumlicher ~~: territorial (or geographical) field of application; zeitlicher ~~: (scope of) time of application;* **~erfindung** invention of a new application (*of a known substance or method*); **~fall** applicable case; **~modalitäten** particulars of application, requirements of application; **~gebiet** field of application; **~zeitraum** period of application.

anwenden *v/t* to apply, to employ, to use; **falsch ~** to misapply.

anwerben *v/t* to recruit, to enlist.

Anwerben *n* **zum ausländischen Militärdienst** recruiting for foreign military service.

Anwerbestop *m* recruitment ban.

Anwerbung *f* recruitment, enlistment; **~skommission** recruitment commission (*of employers, soldiers*); **~ von Arbeitskräften** recruitment of labo(u)r; **~ von Freiberuflern** professional recruitment.

Anwesen *n* (built-upon) property; **eigengenutztes gewerbliches ~** business homestead, trade property for own use; **hausbesetztes ~** squatted property; **landwirtschaftliches ~** farm property; (*pfändungsfreies*), **eigenbewirtschaftetes landwirtschaftliches ~** (*Neusiedlerhof*) homestead, *self-operated farm not subject to an attachment order.*

anwesend *adj* in attendance, present; **~ sein** to attend, to be present; **unmittelbar ~** actually present.

Anwesende (*die Anwesenden*) *m/f/pl* persons present, those present.

Anwesenheit *f* presence; **in ~ von** in the presence of; **physische ~** actual presence, physical presence.

Anwesenheits|appell roll call, calling of the register; **~gelder** attendance allowance; **~liste** attendance list, attendance sheet, attendance roster; *die ~~ verlesen*: *to call the roll, to call the register*; **~pflicht** requirement of attendance; **~prämie** attendance bonus; **~zeit** hours of attendance, attendance time.

Anwohner *m* occupant of adjacent building, *pl* residents (*of the same street*), persons living nearby.

Anzahl *f* number, quantity.

anzahlen *v/t* to pay on account, to deposit, to make a down payment, to pay a first instalment.

Anzahlung *f* down payment, payment on account; **~sgarantie** down-payment guarantee, advance payment bond; **e–e ~ leisten** = *e–e ~ machen qv*; **e–e ~ machen** to pay a deposit, to make a down payment, to pay s.th. on account.

anzapfen *v/t* to tap.

Anzapfen *n* **von Telefonleitungen** telephone tapping, wire-tapping, interception of calls.

Anzeichen *n* indication, symptom; **~beweis** prima facie evidence.

Anzeige *f* announcement, notice, notification, advice note; letter of advice, report, information (*police*); advertisement (*press*); **a~bedürftig** notifiable; **~bereitschaft** readiness of the public to inform the police; **~ der Verteidigungsabsicht** notice of intention to defend; **~ e-s Versicherungsfalles** trouble notice (*indemnity insurance*), prior notice of pending insurance claim; **~ erstatten** to lay an information (*against s.o. with the police*), to inform against s.o., to report s.o. (*to the police*), to deliver a denunciation (*against s.o.*); **~erstatter** *m* informer, person laying an information, prosecuting witness, private prosecutor, relator; **~erstatterin** *f* prosecutrix, relatrix, female person laying an information; **~frist** advertising deadline, deadline for disclosure (*or reporting*); **~ gegen Unbekannt** *information about a criminal offence committed by persons unknown*; **~kosten** cost of notification, advertising cost; **~nblätter** free advertisement papers; **~nausschnitt** press cutting, clipping; **~nbeleg** voucher copy; **~nbelegung** buying of advertising space; **~nschluß** closing date for advertisements; **~nwerbung** press advertising; **~obliegenheit** policy-holder's notification requirement; **~pflicht** obligation to notify, duty to report, duty to give notice (*in insurance policy*), obligation to inform the authorities, duty to disclose, duty to inform the police (*of crime*); **a~pflichtig** notifiable, reportable, subject to obligation to inform (*the authorities, the police*); **~ über die Absendung** notice of consignment (*or shipment*); **angeschnittene ~** bleed advertisement; **bebilderte ~** pictorial advertisement, illustrated advertisement; **doppelseitige ~** double-page spread advertisement, double spread advertisement; **e~ aufgeben** to have an advertisement inserted; **großformatige ~** big splurge ad, spectacular ad, large advertisement; **schriftliche ~** written information, written complaint; **seitenbeherrschende ~** advertisement dominating the page; **sensationell aufgemachte ~** spectacular advertisement, sensational layout of an advertisment; **umrandete ~** boxed advertisement; **unterlassene ~** failure to report a crime to the police.

anzeigen *v/t* to report (s.o. to the police), to give notice, to indicate, to lay an information (*against s.o*).

anziehen *v/i exch* to pick up, to harden.

Anziehen *n* rise, stiffening (*of prices*), improvement (*exch market, prices*).

anzweifeln *v/t* to doubt, to have

one's doubts about s. th., to question, to call into question.
Apostille *f* official authentication (*without consular certificate*).
Apothekerkammer *f professional corporate organisation of pharmacists*.
Apparat *m* apparatus, device, appliance; machinery (*government, administration*); **lebenserhaltene** ~**e** life-support machine.
Appellationsgericht *n* court of appeal.
appellieren *v/i* to appeal.
Appretur *f* dressing, finishing.
Approbation *f* admission to medical practice.
Äquidistanzverfahren equidistance method (*law of the sea*).
Äquivalenz ~**parität** parity of exchange; ~**prinzip** principle of equivalent consideration, compensatory principle (*in taxation of charging fees*).
Arbeit *f* work; job, employment, workmanship; ~ **in wechselnden Schichten** (alternating) shift work; ~ **leisten** to work, to do a job; ~ **suchen** to seek employment, to look for a job; **beschwerliche** ~**en** work of a particularly arduous nature; **die** ~ **in Angriff nehmen** to get the work started, to get on with the job; **die** ~ **niederlegen** to quit, to walk out, to down tools, to sign off (*individually*); **gefahrengeneigte** ~ dangerous work (per se), accident-prone work, hazardous work; **handwerkliche** ~ custom-workmanship, work involving the skills of a craftsman; **im Stücklohn geleistete** ~ contract work; **körperliche** ~ manual labour, physical work; **nach Akkord bezahlte** ~ work paid at piece-rates; **nach Zeit bezahlte** ~ work charged on a time basis; **nichtgewerbliche** ~**en** non-industrial work; **nichtselbständige** ~ dependent personal services; **öffentliche** ~**en** public works; **projektmäßige und konstruktive** ~ planning and design work; **schlampige** ~ sloppy workmanship, slovenly work; **schlechte** ~ **durchgehen lassen** to let bad work(manship) pass; **schriftliche** ~ paper work; **selbständige** ~ independent personal services, free lance work; **sich bei der** ~ **ablösen** to relieve one another at work, to work in relays, to take over work from one another, to rotate; **soziale** ~ social work; **übermäßig viel** ~ too much work, an awful lot of work, a huge work load; **übernommene** ~ work undertaken; **unselbständige** ~ dependent personal services; **vorbereitende** ~**en** preparatory work; **wissenschaftliche** ~ scientific work, scientific paper; **zugeteilte** ~ allotted task, delegated task, allotted duties; **die** ~ **niederlegen** to stop working, to down tools, to go on strike.
arbeiten *v/i* to work; **schwarz** ~ to moonlight, to work "off the books".
Arbeiter *f* worker, manual worker, blue-collar worker, workman, wage-earner, labo(u)rer; operative, workman employed; *collectively* labo(u)r; ~**aussperrung** lockout (*of workers*); ~**berufsverkehr** (work) rush hour traffic; ~**bewegung** labour movement; ~**genossenschaft** workers' cooperative; ~**gewerkschaft** labo(u)r union, trade union; ~**haushaltung** workman's household (*budget*); ~**klasse** working class; ~**kolonie** workers' housing estate; ~**leihverhältnis** labo(u)r lending arrangement, loan out arrangement, body shop arrangement; ~**partei** Labour Party; ~**räte** *hist* workers' committees (*German revolutionary organizations at end of First World War*); ~**rentenanspruch** workers' retirement pension rights; ~**rentenneuregelung** workers' pension adjustment; ~**rentenversicherung** workers' pension insurance; ~**schaft** (the) workers; ~**selbstverwaltung** workers' self-management; ~**siedlung** workers' housing estate;

Arbeiterschaft   **Arbeitsabkommen**

~**stand** working classes; ~**stunde** manpower hour, man-hour; ~**versicherung** industrial insurance; ~**vertretung** labo(u)r representation; ~**unfallversicherung** workers' accident insurance; ~ **wiedereinstellen** to reinstate workers; ~**wohlfahrt** workers' social aid; ~**wohnstätten** workmen's dwellings, workers' homes; **angelernter** ~ semi-skilled worker, pl semi-skilled labo(u)rers; **bewährter** ~ successful worker (*of good standing*); **eingesetzter** ~ employed worker; **geistiger** ~ professional, academic, white-collar employee; **gelernter** ~ skilled worker, skilled workman, pl skilled labo(u)rers; **ungelernter** ~ unskilled worker, pl unskilled labo(u)rers; **gewerbliche** ~ workers, workmen.

Arbeiterschaft f labo(u)r; **gewerkschaftlich organisierte** ~ organized labo(u)r.

Arbeitgeber m employer, principal, pl employers, management; ~**anteil** employer's share, employer's contribution (*to social insurance premiums*); ~-**Arbeitnehmerbeziehungen** management-labo(u)r relations, relations between management and workforce, personnel relations, industrial relations; ~**beisitzer** associate judge representing employers (*in German labo(u)r court*); ~**beitrag** employer's contribution; ~**beiträge zur Rentenversicherung** employer's contributions to worker's pension insurance, (*US*) payroll tax for social security; ~**bescheinigung** employer's certificate; ~**haftpflichtversicherung** employers' liability insurance; ~**kartei** employer's file; ~**pflichten** employers' (legal) obligations; ~**schaft** management, the employers; ~ **und Arbeitnehmer** management and workforce; ~**verband** employers' association; ~**vereinigung** employers' association; ~**vertreter** employers' representative; ~**zuschuß** additional allowance by employer, employer's bonus; *freiwilliger* ~~ *employer's voluntary contribution.*

Arbeitnehmer m jobholder, employed person, person in dependent employment, employee, (*salaried employee or wage earner*); **nicht gewerkschaftlich organisierte** ~ free labour, unorganized labour workforce without a trade union; **tarifvertraglich beschäftigter** ~ person employed under a collective wage agreement.

Arbeitnehmer|aktien employee shares (*in employee-ownership corporations*); ~**anteil** employee's share, employee's contribution (*to social insurance premimium*); ~-**Arbeitgeberausschuß** employee-employer committee, labo(u)r-management committee; ~**beförderung** promotion of employee; ~**beratung** job counsel(l)ing; ~**erfinder** employed inventor, employee-inventor; ~**erfindung** employee-invention (= *employee's invention*); ~**erfindungsgesetz** Employee-Invention Act *D 25. 7. 1957;* ~**freibetrag** earned income relief, allowance for employed persons, employee exempted amount (*in income tax*); ~**kündigung** notice of termination by employee; ~**organisation** labour organization; ~**politik** industrial relations policy, labour-management policy; ~**schaft** the employees, the staff, the work force; ~**schutz** protection of employees; ~**überlassung** supply of temps (*or* temporary workers *or* employees *or* staff); ~**überlassungsgesetz** (*1972*) Personnel Leasing Act; ~**verband** trade union; ~**vereinigung** labour union; ~**vertreter** employee representative; ~**vertretung** worker(s') representation.

Arbeits|abkommen working agreement; ~**ablauf** flow of work, work process, routine; ~**ablaufdiagramm** process chart; ~ **analyse** job analysis; ~ **blatt** spread sheet; ~**laufkarte** route card; ~**abmachungen** working agreements;

63

Arbeitsamt — **Arbeitsgericht**

~**amt** (German) employment office, public employment agency, labour exchange (GB); ~**anfall** volume of work (arising), amount of work to be done; ~**anforderung(en)** job requirement(s); ~**angebot** job offer; unfilled jobs, vacant positions; ~**anweisungen** job instructions, work regulations; ~**auflagen** conditions attached to work performance; ~**aufnahme** commencement of work; ~**aufsicht** labour inspection; ~**aufteilung** distribution of work; ~**auftrag** work order, job order, commission; ~**aufwand** amount of work done; ~**aufwandsentschädigung** compensation for labour used, compensation for work done; ~**ausfall** loss of working time, time not worked; ~**ausfallkasse** redundancy scheme; ~**ausschuß** working committee; ~**bedarf** work requirements, ~**bedingungen** terms of employment, working conditions (*at place of work*); ~**befreiung** (temporary) release from work; ~**behörde** labour exchange, official employment agency; ~**belastung** workload; ~**berater** employment adviser; ~**beratung** employment advisory service, vocational guidance, careers' service; ~**bereich** field of work; ~**bereitschaft** willingness to work; ~**beschaffung** creation of jobs; ~**beschaffungsprogramm** job-creating program(me), public employment scheme; ~**bescheinigung** certificate from last employer, statement of employment (*stating beginning, end and type of employment*); ~**bestand** work at hand, outstanding orders; ~**bewertung** job rating; ~**blatt** worksheet; ~**diagramm** work-diagram; ~**direktor** labour-relations director; ~**disposition** directive on work to be done, allocation of work; ~**effekt** effectiveness of labour; ~**einkommen** earned occupational income; wages and salaries, income from employment, earned income (*tax GB*); *mittelbares* ~~ *indirect earnings from employment; pfändbares* ~~: *attachable working income; unpfändbares* ~~: *income from employment not subject to garnishment; verschleiertes* ~~: *masked (or concealed) working income;* ~**einrichtung** equipment for the job; work environment; plant; ~**einsatz** employment of labour, allocation of labour; ~**einstellung** cessation of work, suspension of work, stoppage of work; ~**einteilung** work-allotment; distribution of work; ~**entgelt** employment remuneration, wages or salaries; ~**erfahrung** work experience; ~**erfolgsprämie** bonus for good results; ~**erlaubnis** work(ing) permit, employment permit; ~**ertrag** output (*per employee*), work yield; ~**essen** working luncheon; a~**extensiv** having a low labour content; a~**fähig** able to work, fit for work, employable, able-bodied; ~**fähigkeit** working capacity, ability to work, fitness for work; ~**förderung** employment promotion, promotion of job creation; ~**förderungsgesetz** Employment Promotion Act; ~**fortschrittsbescheinigung** progress certificate; a~**frei** off duty, idle; ~**freistellung** granting time-off, exemption from work; ~**freudigkeit** keenness (at work), zeal; ~**frieden** peace in labour relations, industrial peace; ~**fürsorge** workers' welfare, (*care for workers' health and employment conditions*); ~**gang** work process, production phase, stage of operations; ~**gebiet** field of activity, sphere of operations, competence; ~**gefahren** occupational risks, industrial hazards; ~**gemeinschaft** (*ARGE*) joint venture; ~**gemeinschaftsvertrag** joint venture agreement; ~**genehmigung** labour permit, work permit; ~**geräte** (*n/pl*) work implements, tools of one's trade, work tools, work appliances, working equipment; ~**gericht**

Arbeitsgerichtsbarkeit

(German) labour court, labour tribunal, industrial (relations) court; **~gerichtsbarkeit** jurisdiction of (German) labour courts, industrial jurisdiction; **~gerichtsgesetz** Labour Courts Act (*German industrial relations court system*); **~gesetzgebung** labour legislation, employment legislation; **~gestaltung** job design, work structuring; **~gruppe** work group, team of workers, working party, workgang; **~hygiene** employee healthcare, industrial hygiene; **~instrument** (work) tool; **~intensität** rate of labour required (*per unit output*); **a~intensiv** labour intensive, having a high labour-content; **~jahrgang** employable age in a given year; **~kampf** industrial dispute, labour struggle; **~kampfmaßnahmen** industrial action; **~kapital** working capital; **~kollegen** fellow employees, colleagues at work; **~konferenz** working conference; **~konflikt** industrial conflict; **~kosten** cost of labour, labour costs; ~~ *pro Produktionseinheit: labour-cost per unit of output;* **~kraft** (*pl ~kräfte → Arbeitskräfte*) manpower, working strength, workman; **~kräftepotential** human resources; **~kraftreserven** manpower reserves, reserves of labour; **~kreis** working party; **~lager** forced labour camp; **~laufkarte** job card; **~laufzettel** work process (*or* progress) voucher; **~leistung** performance at work service, output of labour, productivity of labour; **~lenkung** directing labour supply; **~lohn** wage, pay; *entgangener* ~~ *lost pay, lost remuneration;* **a~los** → *arbeitslos*; **~loser** → *Arbeitsloser*; **~losigkeit** → *Arbeitslosigkeit*; **~mangel** lack of work; defective work performance; **~markt** labour market, job market, employment market; **~marktabgabe** labour-market levy; **~marktausgleich** levelling out of labour market conditions; **~marktlage** condition of the

Arbeitsrechtler

labour market, current labour market situation, employment situation; **~marktpolitik** employment policy, labour policy; **~marktungleichgewicht** labour market disequilibrium; **a~mäßig** workwise, as far as work is concerned; **~medizin** occupational therapy, medical care for employed persons; **~minister** Minister of Labo(u)r, Secretary of State for Employment *GB*, Secretary of Labor *US*; **~ministerium** Department of Employment *GB*, Department of Labor *US*; **~mittel** working implements; work materials; ~~ *patent: working device patent;* **~mobilität** mobility of labour; **~möglichkeit** job opportunity; **~moral** morale at work; **~mündigkeit** minimum age for employment; **~nachweis** vacancies; employment agency; **~niederlegung** (work) stoppage, walkout (at work); **~not** shortage of work, lack of employment, unemployment crisis; **~- oder Gebrauchsgegenstände** utensils; **~-oder Gebrauchszweck** purpose of utilization; **~ordnung** work rules, employment regulations, workshop regulations; **~papier** working paper; draft memorandum, exposure draft; **~papiere** employee papers, working papers; **~pause** break (from work); **~pensum** work quota, amount of work to be done (in a given time); **~pflicht** obligation to work, compulsory work; **~plan** work schedule; **~platz** → *Arbeitsplatz*; **~podest** working platform; **~potential** working capacity; potential of labour supply; **~produktivität** productivity of labour, labour efficiency, per capita productivity; **~programm** work program(me), working program(me); **~prozeß** operation, production process; **~raum** workroom; **~recht** employment, law, labour law, industrial relations law; **~rechtler** *lawyer specialising in the law of employment and labour rela-*

65

tions; ~**richter** judge in a labour court; (labour tribunal); ~**ruhe** rest period; ~**sachen** employment law cases; a ~**scheu** idle, work-shy, averse to work; ~**scheue** work dodgers, shirkers; ~**schicht** (work-)shift; ~**schluß** end of the working day, close of business; ~**schutz** employment safety (regulations) ~**schutzgesetze** industrial safety legislation, *GB* Factory Acts; ~**sicherheit** safety at work; a~-**sparend** labour-saving; ~**spitze** work peak, excessive work load; ~**sprache** working language (*at meetings*); ~**stätte** workplace, place of work, working environment; ~**stelle** place of employment; place of work; job; ~**stoffe** material supplies; ~**strecke** production line; ~**streitigkeit** labour conflict, industrial dispute; ~**stück** work piece, processed item; ~**studie** work study, time and motion study; ~**stunde** man hour, hour worked, *pl* (~*n*) working hours; ~**stundenbuch** employees' time-book; ~**suche** job seeking, job hunting, looking for a job; ~**suchender** job seeker, person in search of a job; ~**tag** work day, working day (*not a Sunday or holiday*); ~**tagebuch** work-diary; a~**täglich** per working day, every work day; ~**tagung** business meeting, working conference; ~**tarifvertrag** (industrial) collective agreement (*on wages and work conditions*), collective wage agreement; a~**teilig** based on division of labour, by proportionate labour cost; ~**teilung** division of labour, work sharing, job share; ~**trupp** squad, group of workmen; ~**überlastung** excessive work load; a~**u-nfähig** unable to work, incapable of working, disabled; ~**unfähiger** (*der Arbeitsunfähige*) disabled person; ~**unfähigkeit** incapacity to work, inability to work, unfitness to work; *dauernde* ~~: *permanent disablement; vorübergehende* ~~: *temporary incapacity;* ~**unfähigkeits-bescheinigung** certificate of disability to work; ~**unfall** accident at work, occupational accident; ~**unfallversicherung** occupational accident insurance; ~**unruhen** labour disturbances; strikes and lockouts; ~**unterbrechung** interruption of work, work stoppage; ~**unterlagen** working papers; ~**unterweisung** job instruction; ~**verbot** prohibition of (gainful) employment; ~**verdienst** wage(s), remuneration for work; ~**vereinfachung** work simplification; ~**verfahren** operating process, work process; ~**verhältnis** employment, employment relationship, employer-employee relationship, employed earner's employment; *abhängiges* ~~: *paid employment;* ~**verhinderung** temporary incapacity to work; ~**verletzung** industrial injury; ~**vermittler** placement officer, employment adviser; employment agent; ~**vermittlung** labour exchange, arranging employment, placing of employees, employment placement (service); ~**vermittlungsfähigkeit** employability; ~**verpflichtung** industrial conscription, obligation to perform services; ~**verrichtung** performance of work; ~**verteilungsprogramm** work schedule; ~**vertrag** employment contract, contract of employment, contract of service, labour contract; ~**vertragsrecht** employment contract law; ~**verwaltung** labour administration, manpower administration; *staatliche* ~~: *public employment service; employment authorities, employment services;* ~**verweigerung** refusal to work; a~-**verwendbar** employable; ~**verwendbarkeit** (*der Arbeitslosen*) employability (*of the jobless*); ~**vorbereitung** job preparation, planning engineering; ~**vorgang** work process, operation; ~**vorrat** order-book totals; current number of outstanding orders; ~**vorrichtung** working device; ~**wahl** choice of

Arbeitskräfte   **Arbeitsplatz**

employment; ~**wechsel** change of employment, change of job; ~**weise** operation, method of work *(man, machine)*; ~**werttheorie** labour theory of value; **a~willig** willing to work; **a~wirtschaftlich** *adj* efficient in man-hours *(in respect of economies in the use of labour)*; ~**woche** working week, work-week (= *workweek US*); ~**zeit** → *Arbeitszeit*; ~**zerlegung** specialization of labour; division of labour, allocation of work; ~**zettel** time sheet *of worker*; ~**zeugnis** certificate of employment, (job) reference; ~**zimmer** private office; ~**zwang** compulsory employment, compulsory work, forced labour.

Arbeitskräfte *f/pl* labour, workmen, labour force, work force, manpower; ~ **abbauen** to shed labour, to cut down on manpower; to reduce the labour force; ~**bedarf** manpower requirements; ~**angebot** labour supply, manpower supply; ~**bewegung** turnover of labour *(or* workmen*)*; ~**einsatz** deployment of labour; ~**engpaß** manpower bottleneck; ~**mangel** manpower shortage; ~**potential** human resources, manpower potential; ~**überschuß** excess (supply of) manpower; ~**volumen** resources of manpower; ~**vorausschätzung** manpower forecast; **angelernte ~** semi-skilled labour; **gewerkschaftlich nicht organisierte ~** unorganized labour; **gewerkschaftlich organisierte ~** union labour; organized labour; **inländische ~** domestic labour; **verfügbare ~** manpower resources; **weibliche ~** female labour.

arbeitslos *adj* unemployed, jobless, out of work, on the dole.

Arbeitslosen|fürsorge *f* welfare measures for the unemployed; ~**geld** unemployment benefit; ~**hilfe** unemployment relief *(on a reduced scale after initial period of full benefits)*, ~**quote** unemployment rate; ~**unterbringungsprojekt** statutory redundancy scheme; ~**unterstützung** unemployment, benefit, dole; unemployment compensation *US*; *(full benefits according to regulations)*; ~**versicherung** unemployment insurance; ~**versicherungsbeitrag** unemployment insurance contribution.

Arbeitsloser *m (der Arbeitslose)* s.o. who is unemployed, unemployed person, jobless person *pl* the jobless; *pl* (~*e*) the unemployed; **gemeldete ~e** registered unemployed; **langfristig ~** long-term unemployed; **unterstützte ~e** unemployed persons receiving benefits; **vermittelte ~e** unemployed persons placed in vacancies.

Arbeitslosigkeit *f* unemployment (= *un*); ~**squote** *un* rate; ~**ssockel** hard-core *un*; **entwicklungsmäßig bedingte ~** technological *un*; **fluktuierende ~** fluctuating scale of *un*; **friktionelle ~** frictional *un*; **jahreszeitlich bedingte ~** seasonal *un*; **konjunkturbedingte ~** cyclical *un*; **konjunkturelle ~** cyclical *un,* recession *un*; **nachfragebedingte ~** *un* because of lack of demand, demand-deficient *un*; **saisonbedingte ~** seasonal *un*; **strukturbedingte ~** structural *un*; **unechte ~** distorted *un* figures; **verdeckte ~** concealed *un*; **zeitweise ~** intermittent *un*.

Arbeitsplatz *m* position, job, post, place of work, work station, place of employment; **unfallsicherer ~~**: *safe place to work*; ~**beschaffung** creation of new jobs; ~**beschreibung** job profile, job description; ~**bewertung** job rating, job evaluation, performance appraisal; ~**darlehen** loan to finance jobs; ~**einrichtung** work-facilities; ~**erhalt** job preservation; ~**gestaltung** human engineering, design (layout) of workplace; ~**garantie** reinstatement guarantee; ~**rechte** job rights; ~**schutz** job preservation *(for service-men)*; ~**sicherheit** job security, employment security; ~**teilung** job shar-

67

Arbeitszeit — **Arrest**

ing, job-share; ~**untersuchung** job analysis; ~**vermittlung** job placement; ~**vernichtung** destruction of jobs; erosion of workplaces; ~**wahl** job choice, (freedom of) choice of employment; ~**wechsel** labour turnover, change of employment, *häufiger* ~~: *job switching;* **unbesetzter** ~ (job) vacancy.

Arbeitszeit *f* work hours, working time; **gesetzliche** ~ hours of work prescibed by law; **normale** ~ straight time; **tarifliche** ~ collectively agreed working hours; ~**nachweise** time records; ~**ordnung** working time regulations; ~**verkürzung** reducing working hours; **gleitende** ~ flexitime; **verkürzte** ~ reduced working hours, short time work.

Arbitrage *f* arbitrage; **a**~**fähig** eligible for arbitrage dealings; ~**geschäfte** arbitrage dealings; ~**klausel** *clause among merchants to settle warranty claims by an assessed reduction in the purchase price, excluding the right of redhibition;* ~**rechnung** arbitrage calculation.

Arbitrageur *m* arbitrageur, arbitrager (*US*).

Architekt *m* architect; ~**engebühr** architect's fee; ~**engebührenordnung** regulation on architects' fees; ~**kammer** professional body of architects; ~**liste** official register of architects; ~**envertrag** *m* architect's contract (of service); **bauleitender** ~ architect directing construction work.

Archiv *n* archives, records, morgue (*for newspaper work*), record office, filing-room, storage; ~**exemplar** copy for the records, copy on file; ~**gut** archive material.

Archivar *m* archivist, recorder, keeper of the records.

Ärgernis *n* annoyance; nuisance; ~ **erregen** to give offence; *dazu bestimmt,* ~ *zu* ~: *calculated to give offence;* **öffentliches** ~ public nuisance, scandal, outrage upon decency.

Arglist *f* malice, cunning; ~**einrede** plea of fraud, exceptio doli, *defence that other party acted in bad faith.*

arglistig *adj* malicious, cunning, treacherous; (*acting*) with intent to deceive.

arglos *adj* unsuspecting, innocent.

Arglosigkeit *f* unsuspecting state of mind, innocence.

Argument *n* argument, reasoning, reason; ~**e für etwas vorbringen** to build up a case; **juristisches** ~ legal point; **stichhaltiges** ~ valid argument, sound argument.

argumentativ *adj* argumentative.

argumentieren *v/i* to argue, to plead *in court.*

Argumentation *f* reasoning, line of reasoning.

Argwohn *m* suspicion, mistrust; ~ **erregen** arouse suspicion; ~ **schöpfen** to become (= *get*) suspicious.

Arm m arm; **senkrecht erhobener** ~ arm raised upright (*traffic policeman*); **waagerecht ausgestreckte** ~**e** arms stretched out horizontally.

arm *adj* poor; needy, indigent (*of persons*), deficient (*resources*).

Armen|anwalt counsel representing legally-aided party; ~**fürsorge** public welfare (or assistance) for the needy; ~**grab** pauper's grave; ~**pflege** public assistance for people in need; ~**pfleger** welfare worker, public relief officer; ~**recht** → *Armenrecht.*

Armenrecht *n* → *Prozeßkostenhilfe* legal aid.

Armut *f* poverty, indigence, destitution, penury, distressed circumstances; ~**szeugnis** certificate of poverty, certificate of entitlement to legal aid.

arrangieren *v/t* to make arrangements, to arrange (for); *v/ reflex* to come to terms, to compromise.

Arrest *m* apprehension (*of suspect*), taking into custody; civil arrest (*by court order*); attachment; ~**anspruch** claim for an arrest: *claim or outstanding debt to be secured by an arrest*; ~**befehl** (*civil judicial*) arrest

arrondieren / **Arzt**

order (*personal and/or in rem*); ~**beklagter** defendant in arrest proceedings *on the validity of the arrest order*; ~**beschlagnahme** provisional seizure; (*by arrest order*) ~**beschluß** writ of attachment, order of (civil) arrest; ~**bruch** illegal interference with attached property: *breach of lien imposed by arrest proceedings*; ~**gericht** competent court for arrest proceedings; ~**gläubiger** attaching creditor, applicant in arrest proceedings; ~**grund** (urgent) reason for granting an order of civil arrest (*or*: writ of attachment); ~**hypothek** provisional judicial mortgage *by way of a civil arrest order*; ~**kläger** plaintiff in arrest proceedings; ~**lokal** detention room; ~**pfandrecht** attachment lien; ~**pfändung** attachment of a claim, charging order; ~**schuldner** respondent in arrest proceedings; ~**urteil** judgment on *the validity of a civil arrest* (*after an oral hearing*); ~**verfahren** (civil) arrest proceedings; ~**vollziehung** enforcement of a civil arrest (*by levying attachment etc*); ~**zelle** detention cell; **dinglicher** ~ in rem arrest order, attachment; **offener** ~ receiving order (*bankruptcy, freezing all assets of debtor*); **persönlicher** ~ arrest of debtor *at the instance of creditor in arrest proceedings*, domestic attachment.

arrondieren to round off.

Arrondierung *f* rounding-off (*property by purchase*), consolidation of small farm-holdings *setting up economically-sized farming units*; ~**skauf** rounding-off purchase.

Art *f* kind, type, nature; ~**en von Beihilfen** categories of aid; ~**(handlungs)vollmacht** *authority limited to a particular type of transaction*; ~**verzeichnis** classified directory; **dieser** ~ such; **eigener** ~ sui generis; **mittlerer** ~ **und Güte** of average kind and quality, of merchantable quality; **üblicher** ~ of the usual kind, of customary quality; **von durchschnittlicher** ~ **und Güte** of average kind and quality; **von gleicher** ~ **und Güte** of the same type and quality.

Artenschutz *m* protection of endangered species.

Artikel *m* (1) article, section (*of a law or Act*); clause (*of a contract*); ~**gesetz** Amending Act (*Act amending specified articles*); ~ **im Parteiprogramm** plank of the party platform; **dieser** ~ **schließt nicht aus, daß** ... nothing in this article (*section, clause*) shall be construed to preclude ...

Artikel *m* (2) article, item, *pl*. goods, merchandise; **hochwertige** ~ articles of high quality; **schlechtgehender** ~ article which sells badly (*or* poorly); sleeper; **schnellverkäuflicher** ~ fastselling item, article which is quickly sold; **zugkräftiger** ~ fast selling article, puller.

Arznei *f* medicine, medicament, medication; ~**abgabe** dispensing, selling medicines; **(amtliches)** ~**buch** dispensatory, pharmacopeia; **verschreibungspflichtige** ~ medicine requiring (a doctor's) prescription.

Arzneimittel *n* medication, medicine *pl*: pharmaceutical products; ~**gesetz** Medical Preparations Act: *Act governing the production and distribution of medicines*; ~**industrie** pharmaceutical industry; ~**kunde** pharmacology; **gesetzlich geschützte** ~ proprietary medicines.

Arzt *m* physician, doctor, surgeon, health professional; G. P. (General Practitioner); ~**beruf** medical profession; **Ä**~**egesetz** Medical Profession Act; ~**geheimnis** doctors secrecy obligation; ~**haftung** a medical practitioner's liability; ~**helferin** doctor's assistant; **Ä**~**ekammer** medical association (*disciplinary powers*), medical council; ~**kosten** medical expenses; ~**kostenversicherung** → *Versicherung*; **Ä**~**eordnung** professional regulations relating to doctors; ~**praxis** doctor's practice; ~**rechnung** doctor's bill, state-

Asbestgeschädigte / **attestieren**

ment of medical fees; **Ä~eversorgung** (1) retirement pension system for doctors, (2) medical attention; **~vertrag** doctor-patient contract, **Ä~everzeichnis** directory of doctors; **~wahl** choice of doctor; **approbierter ~** a licensed physician, a qualified doctor; **behandelnder ~** the attending physician, the doctor in charge; **der abbrechende ~** the doctor who performs a legal abortion; **niedergelassener ~** licensed medical practitioner; **praktischer ~** (general) practitioner, (qualified) medical practitioner.

Asbestgeschädigte *m, f, pl* asbestosis sufferers.

Asoziale *pl* vagrants, delinquents, the disadvantaged members of society.

Asperationsprinzip *n* principle of asperity: *principle of punishment for multiple offences forming one aggregate sentence based on the severest penalty for the individual offence.*

Assekurant *m obs* insurer, underwriter.

Assekuranz *f* insurance business, underwriting.

Assekuranzmakler *m obs* insurance broker.

Asservantenkonto *n* suspense account, special-purpose account.

Asservat *n* exhibit (*in the custody of the court*); **~enabteilung** exhibit section; **~enkammer** court storeroom for exhibits; **~enliste** list of exhibits (*in the custody of the court*); **~enraum** property room.

Assessor *m obs* = *Beisitzer qv*; junior judge, associate judge; junior executive officer; = *Notarassessor qv*.

Assimilation *f* assimilation, adaption (= *adaptation*); **gesellschaftliche ~** social adaption.

Assoziation *f* association, entering into a partnership, adherence (*to a convention*), formation of a society.

assoziieren (*v/reflex*) to associate, to go into partnership, to join, to form a partnership.

Assoziierung *f* association, entering into a partnership, process of confederating; **~sabkommen** treaty of accession, treaty of confederacy; **~ssystem** arrangements of association; **~svertrag** = *Assoziierungsabkommen qv*.

Asyl *n* asylum, sanctuary, refuge; **~bewerber** asylum seeker; **~gewährung** (the) granting of asylum; **~recht** law of asylum, right of sanctuary *or* asylum; **diplomatisches ~** diplomatic asylum, *refuge in an embassy*; **politisches ~** political asylum.

Asylant *m* asylum seeker.

Aszendent *m* ascendant (= *ascendent*), ancestor.

Atlantik|-Charta *f* Atlantic Charter (*1941*); **~pakt** Atlantic-Pact, North Atlantic Treaty Organization = NATO.

Atemprobe *f* breath test, specimen of breath, breathalyser test.

Atom|anlage nuclear installation, nuclear plant; **~gemeinschaft** atomic pool; **~gesetz** atomic energy Act; **~kraftwerk** atomic power plant; **~kriegsführung** atomic warfare, nuclear warfare; **~müll** nuclear waste; **~~-Entsorgung**: *disposal of nuclear waste; geringverstrahlter: low-level waste;* **~risiko** atomic risk; **~test-Stoppvertrag** Test Ban Treaty; **~sperrvertrag** Non-proliferation Treaty; **~sprengkörper** nuclear explosive device; **~streitkräfte** nuclear forces; **~versicherungsrecht** atomic risks insurance law.

Attaché *m* attaché.

Attentat *n* assassination attempt (*for political motives*).

Attentäter *m* assassinator, assassin, would-be assassin, *perpetrator of an assassination attempt or other crime of violence for political motives.*

Attentismus *m* wait-and-see attitude, prevarication, attentisme.

Attest *n* certificate, attestation, testimonial; **ärztliches ~** health certificate, medical certificate, doctor's certificate.

attestieren to certify.

atypisch *adj* atypical, not conforming to a standard type (*of contract*).

Audienz *f* audience, formal reception.

aufarbeiten *v/t* to get through (*work*), to catch up (*on a backlog*), to use up (*material, supplies*), to work off (*unfilled orders*), to get up to date (*with one's work*).

Aufarbeitung *f* reconditioning (*upholstery*); *cf aufarbeiten*.

Aufbau *m* construction; building-up; organization, structure, system set-up; composition, makeup (*Br*: make-up); development, establishing; assembly, mounting; superstructure (*vehicle*), ~**darlehen** reconstruction loan (*as part of the Lastenausgleich qv*); ~ **der Bank** structure of the bank; ~ **der Verwaltung** organization of the administration; ~ **der wirtschaftlichen Existenz** establishing a livelihood; ~**finanzierung** financing of *post-war* reconstruction; ~**hilfe-Fonds** Aid for Reconstruction Fund; ~**kredit** credit facilities for *post-war* reconstruction; ~**leistungen** construction and assembly; ~**möbel** ready-to-assemble furniture; ~**unterstützung** benefits for reconstruction purposes (*for refugees etc*); ~**zug** late transfers stream (*secondary school*); ~**vertrag** reconstruction contract; **organisatorischer** ~ organization and structure.

aufbereiten *v/t* to refine, to process, to treat (*crude oil*), to dress (*ore, hides*).

Aufbereitung *f* refining; processing; treating, dressing; *cf aufbereiten*; ~**sanlagen** reprocessing plants.

aufbessern *v/t* to raise (*salary*); to improve (*market*).

Aufbesserung *f* increase, raise, improvement.

aufbewahren *v/t* to keep in safe custody (*in storage, on file*), to store, to keep safe.

Aufbewahrer *m* keeper, custodian, depositary.

Aufbewahrung *f* storage, safekeeping, safe deposit, preservation; ~ **entzündlicher Waren** storage of inflammables; ~ **von Akten** storage of files.

Aufbewahrungs|frist period of storage, record retention period; period of custody; ~**gebühr** storage fee, storage charge, safe deposit charge, charge for safe-deposit services (*bank*); ~**ort** place of storage, depository, place of safe-keeping; ~**pflicht** obligation to keep, obligation to preserve (*business records*); ~**schein** deposit receipt, claim check; chit to acknowledge deposit.

aufbieten *v/t* to muster (*strength*); to publish the banns, to give public notice (*of impending forfeiture etc*), *cf Aufgebot*.

Aufblähung *f* inflation, overexpansion (*credit, turnover*).

aufblenden *v/i* to turn on the full lights, to turn the headlights up (*automobile*); to fade in (*motion picture photography*).

aufbrauchen *v/t* to use up (*stores*).

Aufbrauchsfrist *f* deadline for using up (*infringing article*).

aufbrechen *v/t* to pry open (*receptacle*), to break open, to pick (*a lock*), to unseal.

Aufbrechen *n* breaking open a receptacle, forcing open (*of receptacle by burglar*); ~ **des Zollverschlusses** breaking of customs seal.

aufbringen *v/t* to raise (*funds*), to contribute; to capture (*ship as prize*), to recapture.

Aufbringung *f* raising (*of funds*), levy, contribution, capture (*ship*).

Aufbringungs|erklärung contributor's statement; **a~pflichtig** liable to contribute funds; ~**schlüssel** seal of contributions; ~**schuld** liability to contribute; obligation to contribute; ~**schuldner** party liable to contribute (*funds to cover deficit*); ~**- u. Beschlagnahmeklausel** F.C. & S. Clause (free of capture and seizure).

aufbürden *v/t* to charge, to burden, to impose.

Aufbürdung *f* charge, burdening, imposition.

aufdecken *v/t* to expose (*scandal*), to disclose (*defects*), to detect (*crime*).

Aufdeckung *f* exposure, disclosure, discovery, detection; ~ **der Unwahrheit** detection of falsehood; ~ **einer Verschwörung** exposure of a plot.

Aufdruck *m* imprint, impression.

aufdrucken *v/t* to imprint, to print upon, to overprint.

aufdrücken *v/t* to impress (*seal*), to stamp.

Aufeinanderfolge *f* succession, sequence; ~ **der Ereignisse** sequence of events; **turnusmäßige** ~ succession by rotation; **zeitliche** ~ chronological order.

aufeinanderfolgend *adj* consecutive, successive, in sequence, following on from each other, following one after the other.

Aufenthalt *m* stay, sojourn; residence, abode; **dauernder** ~ permanent residence, fixed abode; **gewöhnlicher** ~ habitual residence; **ohne festen** ~ of no fixed abode; **ständiger** ~ = *dauernder Aufenthalt qv*; **unbekannter** ~ unknown whereabouts; **vorübergehender** ~ temporary stay.

Aufenthalts|anweisung instruction to stay in vicinity of (*location*); ~**berechtigung** right of abode, right (*or* entitlement) of residence; ~**bescheinigung** residence certificate; ~**beschränkung** residence restriction(s), limitation of stay (*for foreigner*); ~**bestimmung** determining the place of abode; ~**bestimmungsrecht** right to determine the place of abode; ~**bewilligung** permit for stay; ~**dauer** length of stay; ~**erlaubnis** residence permit; ~**genehmigung** residence permit; ~**gestattung** temporary permission to stay (in the country); ~**kosten** subsistence expenses; ~**ort** abode, (place of) residence, habitation, whereabouts; *den jeweiligen* ~~ *ermitteln:* to establish whereabouts; *dauernder* ~~: *fixed abode, permanent residence, permanent abode*; *gewöhnlicher* ~~: *habitual place of residence, usual place of abode*; *ständiger* ~~: *permanent residence*; ~**raum** room suitable for habitation; ~**recht** right of abode; law concerning residence of aliens; ~**regelung** residence regulation(s), rules as to residence (*of aliens*); ~**regelungsgesetz** residence law; ~**sichtvermerk** residence control stamp; ~**staat** state of residence; ~**verbot** residence ban, exclusion order; ~**verlängerung** extension of residence permit.

auferlegen *v/t* to impose (*restrictions, duties, taxes*); to require, to inflict (*punishment*).

Auferlegung *f* imposition, infliction.

auffahren *v/i* to run into (a car from behind), to collide from behind.

Auffahrunfall *m* rear-end collision, nose-to-tail collision, *Serie von* ~*unfällen;* pile-up.

auffangen *v/t* to absorb (*wage increase*).

Auffang|gebiet reception area (*refugees*); ~**gesellschaft** successor company (*in case of winding-up reorganization*), absorbing company, rescue company; ~**organisation** recipient company (*temporary successor organization*); ~**tatbestand** omnibus clause, subsidiary clause of an enactment.

auffassen *v/t* to comprehend, to understand, to construe.

Auffassung *f* understanding, comprehension, opinion; ~**sgabe** perceptive faculty; *rasche* ~~: *quick grasp of issues;* **e-e** ~ **vertreten** to hold, to maintain, to sustain an opinion.

auffinden *v/t* to find, to discover.

Auffindung *f* (= *Auffinden n*) discovery, detection.

auffordern *v/t* to request, to demand.

Aufforderung *f* request, demand, requisition; ~**sschreiben** letter of request; ~ **zu Gewaltmaßnahmen** provocation to commit acts of violence; ~**zu Straftaten** incitement to crime; ~ **zum Kauf** invitation to buy; ~ **zum Kon-**

aufforsten   **Aufgebot**

toausgleich balance-order; ~ **zum Ungehorsam gegen Gesetze** incitement to break the law; ~ **zur Abgabe eines Angebots** invitation to submit an offer (tender), invitation to treat; ~ **zur Abgabe von Submissionen** invitation to bid; ~ **zur Einzahlung auf Aktien** call (to pay in capital); ~ **zur Offerte** invitation to offer, invitation for tender, invitation to treat; ~ **zur Preisabgabe** (= *Preisaufgabe*) request for a (price) quotation; ~ **zur Unzucht** solicitation for immoral purposes; ~ **zur Urkundenvorlage** notice to produce (documents); **gerichtliche** ~ judicial request; **gütliche** ~ amicable request; **öffentliche** ~ public request; **schriftliche** ~ demand in writing, request in writing; **zahlbar bei** ~ payable on demand.

aufforsten *v/t* to afforest, to reafforest.

Aufforstung *f* afforestation; ~ **der Reserven** building up the reserves.

Auffrischungskurs *m* refresher course.

aufführen *v/t* to present (*play*), to perform.

Aufführender *m* (*der Aufführende*) presenter, performer.

Aufführung *f* performance, presentation (*play*), listing (*items*); ~**sort** place of dramatic entertainment; ~**srecht** right of representation and performance, right(s) of performance; *pl*: performing rights, dramatic rights, stage rights; ~**svertrag** performing rights contract; **öffentliche** ~ public performance.

auffüllen *v/t* to refill (*hole in the ground*), to replenish (*stocks*).

Auffüllung *f* replenishment.

Aufgabe *f* (1) task, function, job, duty; ~ **e-s Patents** subject matter of a patent, object of a patent; ~**nbereich** province, jurisdiction, competence; ~**ngebiet** field, sphere of functions *cf Aufgabenbereich*; ~**ngliederungsplan** organisation (of functions) plan; ~**nträger** commissioned agency; ~**n übernehmen** to take over the job of ..; ~**nverteilung** allocation of tasks, job assignment; ~**n wahrnehmen** to exercise (the) functions; **hoheitsrechtliche** ~**n** governmental functions; **kapitalmarktpolitische** ~ objective of capital market policy; **öffentliche** ~**n** public duties (*or* functions); **öffentlich-rechtliche** ~**n** functions in the sphere of public law; **repräsentative** ~**n** representative functions; **zugewiesene** ~**n** delegated functions, tasks (to), allocated duties.

Aufgabe *f* (2) abandonment, discontinuance; termination; ~ **der Prämie** abandonment of the option money; ~ **des Gewerbebetriebes** cessation of the business; ~ **e-r Tätigkeit** termination of an activity; ~ **e-s Amtes** resignation (from office); ~ **e-s Betriebs** closing down of a business; ~ **e-s Rechts** abandonment (*or* giving up of) of a right, renunciation; ~ **von Produktionszweigen** line dropping (*by dealer*).

Aufgabe *f* (3) posting, mailing, dispatch; ~**bahnhof** dispatch station; ~ **des Gepäcks** check(ing) in the luggage; ~**ort** place of posting, place of mailing; ~**schein** (postal) receipt; ~**stempel** stamp of dispatch; ~**zeit** time of dispatch, (= *time of sending, time of mailing, time of posting*); ~ **zur Post** posting, mailing (*cf Zustellung*).

Aufgabe *f* (4) **einer Bestellung** (the) placing of an order, ordering

Aufgabe (5) accounting advice.

aufgeben *v/t* to surrender (*a right*), to give up (*position, right, claim, prosecution, search*), to resign, to abandon (*ship, claim, case*), to quit, to part with (*possession*), to post (*letter*), to place (*an order*), to enjoin, to request (*by court*).

Aufgebot *n* (1) public invitation to assert claims (*subject to exclusion or forfeiture*); (2) banns of matrimony, publication of banns, notice of an intended marriage; ~ **der Nach-laßgläubiger** public notice to creditors of an estate (to prove their claims); ~ **der Verlobten** banns (of matrimony), notice of an intended marriage; ~**seinrede** *dilatory plea of an heir pending marshalling of creditors of an estate*; ~**stermin** deadline fixed by public summons (*threatening forfeiture or exclusion*); ~**sverfahren** public citation, proceedings by public summons; forfeiture proceedings (*after warning by public notice*), cancellation proceedings (*for shares, licences, other documents*); **ein** ~ **bestellen** to publish the banns.

Aufgeld *n* premium, agio, surcharge, extra charge, additional charge; ~**konto** agio account, premium account.

aufgelegt *adj* open for subscription.

aufgeschoben *adj* deferred, postponed, stayed; ~ **werden** → *aufschieben*.

aufgliederbar *adj* classifiable, itemizable.

aufgliedern *v/t* to itemize, to break down; to classify.

Aufgliederung breakdown; itemization; ~ **des Aufkommens an Steuern und Sozialbeiträgen**: *breakdown of total tax receipts and social welfare contributions*.

aufgreifen *v/t* to pick up (*vagabond by police*); to take up (*subject*).

aufhalten *v/reflex* to stay, to reside.

aufhäufen *v/t* to accumulate (*money, profits*).

Aufhäufung *f* accumulation.

aufheben *v/t* to lift, to cancel, to set aside, to reverse, to repeal, to quash, to overrule, to rescind; **sich gegenseitig** ~ to cancel each other out.

Aufhebung *f* reversal, repeal *etc cf aufheben*, setting aside; ~ **der Annahme an Kindes statt** revocation *or*: cancellation of an adoption; ~ **der Beschränkung** abolition of the restriction (*or* limit); ~ **der Ehe** annulment of marriage; ~ **der ehelichen Lebensgemeinschaft** dissolution of conjugal community, separation (from bed and board), judicial separation; ~ **der Entmündigung** revocation of order of lunacy, termination of guardianship; dewarding; ~ **der häuslichen Gemeinschaft** cessation of domestic life; ~ **der Immunität** suspension of *parliamentary* immunity; ~ **der Kosten** mutual discharge of cost claims; ~ **der Pfändung** release of the attachment lien, release from distraint; ~ **der Vormundschaft** termination of guardianship, dewarding; ~ **des Haftbefehls gegen Sicherheitsleistung** release on bail; ~ **des Konkursverfahrens** termination of bankruptcy; ~ **e-r Dienstbarkeit** extinguishment of an easement; ~ **e-r Ehe** = *Eheaufhebung* ~; ~ **e-s Gesetzes** repeal of an Act, repeal of statute; ~ **e-s Urteils** reversal of a judgment, quashing of a judgment; ~ **e-s Vertrages** cancellation of a contract *by mutual consent*; ~ **und Rückverweisung** reversal and remand; **einverständliche** ~ termination by mutual consent, surrender (*lease*).

Aufhebungs|anspruch right to demand dissolution (*of marriage*); ~**begehren** prayer for dissolution (*of marriage*); ~**gesetz** repealing statute; ~**prämie** cancellation premium; ~**klage** petition for dissolution (*of marriage*) (*cf Eheaufhebung*); ~**recht** right of cancellation; ~**vertrag** termination agreement; ~**urteil** reversing judgment, judgment allowing an appeal.

aufhetzen *v/t* to incite, to agitate, to stir up hatred (*against s. o.*).

Aufhetzung *f* incitement, agitation, rabble-rousing.

Aufhol|arbeit *f* make-up work; ~**bewegung** process of catching up; ~**konjunktur** backlog boom.

Aufkauf *m* buying-up, buy-out; buying out; bulk buying, forestalling *exch*, cornering the market

aufkaufen / **Auflassung**

exch; ~ **von Beherrschungsrechten** (*mit Leihkapital finanziert*) leverage buyout.

aufkaufen *v/t* to buy up, to forestall *exch*; **billig** ~ to buy up cheaply; **den Markt** ~ to corner the market.

Aufkäufer *m* buying-agent, speculative buyer, forestaller *exch*; ~**gruppe** corner group of speculative buyers.

aufklären *v/t* to clear up, to clarify.

Aufklärung *f* clarification, clearing-up; enlightenment; detection (*crime*); successful investigation; ~**sbeschluß** clarifying order (*of the court*), order to produce clarifying evidence; ~**spflicht** duty to provide clarification, duty to explain, duty to give advice on proper procedure; *ärztliche* ~~: *surgeon's obligation to inform patient of nature and gravity of intended operation*; *richterliche* ~~: (1) *judge's obligation to give proper directions for pleading*, (2) *duty of judicial inquiry* (*criminal law*); ~**squote** detection rate, clear-up rate; ~**srüge** plea (or exception) that the court failed to give clarifying directions or to clarify the issue; ~**swerbung** explanatory advertising, "reason-why" advertising.

Aufkleber *m* sticker, slip, gummed label.

Aufklebezettel *m* sticker, adhesive label.

aufkommen (*für etwas*) *v/i* to account for, to be responsible (*for s. th.*), to be answerable (*for sth.*), to support (*child*).

Aufkommen *n* proceeds, accrual; yield (*revenue*).

aufkündigen *v/t* to call in, to call for redemption (*loan*), to give notice of termination (*contract*).

Aufkündigung *f* recall (*loan, capital*), notice of termination (*contract*).

aufladen *v/t* to load, to put a load on sth.

Aufladen und Abladen *n* loading and unloading.

Auflage *f* (1) edition (*book*), circulation (*newspaper, periodical*), press run; ~ **mit Anmerkungen** annotated edition; ~**nbeglaubigung** certified statement of circulation; ~**nhöhe** number of printed copies, circulation figures; **abgesetzte** ~ paid circulation; **beschränkte** ~ limited circulation, controlled circulation; **die beste** ~ the best edition (*deposit for copyright protection*); **erweiterte** ~ enlarged (or expanded) edition; **neubearbeitete** ~ revised edition; **revidierte** ~ revised edition.

Auflage *f* (2) imposition (*of burden, obligation*), requisition, requirements, burden (*attached to a grant*), direction (*by the court to a party*), proviso, condition; ~**beschluß** (order with) directions of the court; ~~ **mit Ausschlußfrist** "*unless*" *order*; ~**n der Bewährungszeit** conditions of probation; ~**nfrist** time for carrying out directions; ~**n machen** to impose conditions (or terms), to impose requirements; ~**nschenkung** = *Schenkung unter e-r Auflage qv*; ~**nüberwachungsstelle** supervisory office (*probation*); **gerichtliche** ~ request (or direction) by the court, obligation imposed by judge; **mit** ~**n belastet** charged with obligations to be performed; **mit der** ~ subject to the condition that; **ohne** ~**n** (with) no strings attached, unconditional.

auflassen *v/t* to convey (*title to land before a notary*), to agree on passing of ownership to land in notarial deed; to terminate public use (*road*), to close down (*plant, mine*).

Auflassung *f* (1) conveyance of land, *mutual declaration of conveyance of ownership to land before notary*, transfer of fee simple; closing of title; ~**sanspruch** entitlement to a conveyance of land; ~**anwartschaft** the expectancy in rem (*created by the notarial declaration*) of conveyance; ~**seintragung** registration of conveyance; ~**sklausel** conveyance clause; ~**surkunde** record of conveyance of land (*notarial*), transfer (of land) certificate, conveyance of

Auflassung / **Aufnahme**

title deed; ~**svollmacht** power of conveyance (*notarial record*), authority to transfer ownership to land (*on behalf of another*); ~**svormerkung** priority notice of conveyance, caution of *notarially executed* conveyance *entered, or to be entered, in the Land Title Register*.

Auflassung *f* (2) withdrawal from public use (*road etc*), abandonment, closing down (*plant, mine*); ~ **von Geschäftszweigen** closing down lines of business; ~ **von Landstraßen** extinguishment of highways, closing of highways.

Auflauf *m* unlawful assembly, riotous gathering (*gathering of people who will not disperse after police order to move on*).

auflaufen *v/i* to accrue (*interest*), to accumulate.

Auflaufen *n* **von Zinsen** accrual of interest.

aufleben *v/i* to revive, *etwas wiederaufleben lassen v/t*: to revive.

auflegen *v/t* to lay out (*for inspection*); to invite subscriptions, to launch (*a new series of production*); to float.

Auflegung *f* disclosure, display, flotation (*bonds*).

auflehnen *v/reflex* to revolt, to rebel.

Auflehnung *f* insurrection.

aufliegen *v/i* to be exposed, to be offered, (for subscription); to be open (for signature).

Auflockerung *f* easing (*of restrictions*); **schrittweise** ~**en** successive relaxations, gradual relaxation.

Auflösbarkeit *f* dissolvability, terminability.

auflösen *v/t* to dissolve (*relationship*), to break up (*meeting*), to break off (*engagement*), to annul (*contract*), to resolve (*a tie, problem*); *auflösende Bedingung*: *condition subsequent*.

Auflösung *f* dissolution, annulment; ~ **des Arbeitsverhältnisses** judicial termination of employment; ~ **e-r Rückstellung** release of a reserve, writing back of provisions;

~**sbeschluß** dissolution order; ~**sklage** petition for judicial dissolution, legal action to obtain a judicial dissolution.

Aufmachung *f* presentation, get-up (= *getup US*), type of display; **äußere** ~ outward appearance.

Aufmaß *n* measurements (of work done) on the site; ~**liste** measurement list.

Aufmerksamkeit *f* attention, attentiveness, care, caution.

aufmerksam machen to draw one's attention to, to warn, to give a fair warning.

Aufnahme *f* adoption, admittance, taking up, initiation; recording (*sound*); ~**antrag** application for admission; ~**bedingungen** terms of admission (*membership*); ~**beitrag** initial contribution, joining fee; ~**beschränkung** admission restriction (*university*), limited admission; ~ **der diplomatischen Beziehungen** establishing diplomatic relations; ~ **der Verhandlungen mit** entering into negotiations with; ~ **des Verfahrens** resumption of proceedings (*after a stay*); ~ **des Vertriebs** commencement of distribution; ~ **e-r Anleihe** flotation of a loan (*of bonds*); ~ **e-r Gesellschaft** absorption of a company (*amalgamation*), take-over (bid); ~ **e-s Darlehens** taking-up of a loan, acceptance of a loan, borrowing; ~ **e-s Kredits** borrowing; ~ **e-s Mitglieds** admission of a member; ~**fähigkeit** capacity to absorb, market receptivity; ~**gebühr** joining fee; ~ **in die Tagesordnung** inclusion on the agenda; ~**land** receiving country, country of reception; ~**prüfung** entrance examination; ~**staat** receiving state, host state; ~**verfahren** regulations of admission; ~ **von Bedingungen** inclusion of conditions (*in a draft agreement*); ~**zwang** mandatory admission (*to an association*); **vor** ~ **der Geschäftstätigkeit** before undertaking any business.

aufnehmen v/t to start (*work, operations*), to establish (*contacts, relations*), to admit, to receive (*members*), to absorb (*a company, goods*), to draw up (*minutes*), to take down (*dictation*), to borrow (*money*), to honour (*bill*).

Aufopferung f **für große Havarie** general average sacrifices.

Aufopferungsanspruch m denial damage: *compensation for loss or impairment of use imposed by a public authority short of expropriation, disturbance claim.*

Aufprall m impact, collision (*car accident*).

Aufpreis m extra charge (*contract price*), surcharge, premium (*issue of securities*).

aufrechenbar adj offsettable, admissible for set-off, capable of being set-off (*debts*), capable of mutual compensation (*guilt*).

aufrechnen v/i to set off (*a claim against that of another*), US to offset, to discharge by way of counterclaim.

Aufrechnung f set-off (= setoff, US); **~sanspruch** set-off claim, claim used for set-off; **~seinrede** defence of set-off, **~serklärung** notice (*or* statement) of set-off, **~sforderung** = **~sanspruch** qv; **~srecht** right of set-off; **~sverbot** unlawfulness of set-off, contractual exclusion of set-off; **die ~ erklären** to exercise the right of set-off; **die ~ ist unzulässig** there can be no set-off (*e.g. against the Crown*); **gerichtliche ~** set-off in court proceedings; **unbestrittene ~** undisputed set-off, uncontested discharge by way of set-off.

aufrechterhalten v/t to maintain (*order, good relations*); to keep up (*insurance*), to uphold (*a charge, a decision*); to abide by (*an offer*).

Aufrechterhaltung f maintenance, preservation; **~ der öffentlichen Ruhe und Ordnung** preservation of the public peace, preservation of law and order; **~ des Patents** maintenance of the patent; **~ wohlerworbener Rechte** preservation of acquired rights; **unter ~ der persönlichen Einreden** subject to equities (*negotiable instruments*), subject to a plea of demurrer.

aufreizen to incite, to stir up, to inflame the minds of others.

Aufreizung f incitement; **~ zum Rassenhaß** incitement to racial hatred.

Aufriß m vertical section.

aufrollen v/t to reopen.

aufrücken v/i to move up, to be promoted (*to a higher position*).

Aufruf m proclamation (*to the people*), public notice; roll call (*soldiers; parliamentary session*); call[ing] (*next witness, next case*), calling in (*bank notes, bonds etc*); **~ der Namen** roll call, calling of the register.

aufrufen v/t to call, to summon, to give notice of redemption; **namentlich ~** to call the roll, to call the register.

Aufruhr m insurrection, rebellion, revolt, riot; riotous assembly; **~versicherung** riot (and civil commotion) insurance.

Aufrührer m insurgent, insurrectionist, rebel, rioter.

aufrührerisch adj rebellious, riotous, inflammatory, insurgent, insurrectionist, seditious.

aufrunden v/t to round up.

Aufrundung f rounding up.

aufrüsten v/i, v/t to rearm.

Aufrüstung f rearmament.

Aufschieben n postponement, deferment, putting off.

aufschieben v/t to postpone, to defer, to put off; *aufgeschoben werden: to stand over, to be delayed, to be adjourned.*

aufschiebend adj dilatory, suspensive; **~ bedingt** subject to a suspensive (suspensory) condition, subject to a condition precedent.

Aufschiebung f = Aufschieben qv, Aufschub qv; **~ der Vollstreckung** = Strafaufschub qv; = Vollstreckungsaufschub qv.

Aufschlag m mark-up, surcharge,

aufschlagen / **Aufspaltung**

additional charge; ~ **auf den Einfuhrpreis** import mark-up.
aufschlagen *v/t* to surcharge, to charge more, to add to the price, to mark up.
Aufschließung *f* development, *cf. Erschließung*; ~**sarbeiten** development work (*drainage, gas, water etc*); ~**sbohrungen** development drilling, development wells; ~**smaßnahmen** development; ~ **von Wohnsiedlungsgebieten** development of housing areas.
Aufschlußarbeiten *f/pl* development work, exploration.
Aufschlüsselung *f* itemization, breakdown (*figures*), allocation (*between different categories*), apportionment.
aufschreiben *v/t* to note sth, to jot down sth, (*jmdn*) to take down a person's name (*police*).
Aufschrift *f* inscription, inscription label, word markings.
Aufschub *m* deferment, deferral, suspense, reprieve; delay, postponement, continuance, extension; ~ **bewilligen** to grant additional time, to grant a respite; ~ **des Strafvollzugs** = *Strafaufschub qv;* ~**frist** period of deferment, time limit (for payment).
aufschwindeln *v/t* to palm off (on s. o.), to con s. o. (*into buying sth*).
Aufschwung *m* rise, upsurge, upturn, upswing, uptrend, revival; ~**skraft** expansive force (*business*); ~**stendenz** uptrend, upsurge; **konjunktureller** ~ business recovery.
Aufseher *m* supervisor, warder, guard (*prison, institution*), controller (*factory*).
Aufseherin *f* wardress, matron (*prison, institution*), woman overseer (*factory*).
aufsetzen *v/t* to draw up (*contract, document*).
Aufsicht *f* supervision; **mangelnde** ~ lack of supervision; **unter** ~ **stellen** to put s. o. under surveillance; **unter polizeilicher** ~ under police surveillance.

Aufsichts|amt control-board; ~**beamter** supervisor, superintendent, surveyor; ~**befugnis** supervisory authority, controlling authority; right of supervision; ~**behörde** regulatory authority, regulatory agency; authority; superior authority, supervising authority, supervisory board; ~**nbeschwerde** complaint to superior authority; ~**führender** superintendent; ~**gewalt** supervisory power; ~**maßnahmen** supervisory measures; ~**maßregeln** disciplinary action; ~**organ** supervisory body; ~**person** supervisor, superintendent; ~**pflicht** duty to supervise; ~**pflichtiger** person liable to supervise; person whose duty is to supervise; ~**pflichtverletzung** breach of supervisory duties; ~**rat** → *Aufsichtsrat;* ~**recht** right of supervision, visitorial power, right of inspection; ~**verschulden** negligence in supervising s. o.
Aufsichtsrat *m* supervisory board (*German stock company*), board of supervision ≈ board of directors ≈ board of trustees.
Aufsichtsrats|mitglied member of the supervisory board, non-executive director; **geschäftsführendes** ~~: managing director; ~**präsidium** supervisory board's presiding committee; presiding group of the supervisory board; ~**sitz** directorship, seat on the supervisory board; ~**sitzung** meeting of the supervisory board, board meeting; ~**steuer** *tax on remuneration of member of supervisory board of German stock company*; ~**tantieme** remuneration of directors (of supervisory board), directors' royalty; –~ **und Verwaltungsratsvergütungen** directors' fees; ~**vorsitzender** chairman of the board (of directors), chairman of the supervisory board, president (*of a corporation US*).
Aufspaltung *f* splitting, split up, disaggregation (*statistics*); ~ **des Vermögens** property-splitting, divi-

Aufsplitterung

sion of property; ~ **in Teilklagen** splitting a cause of action.

Aufsplitterung *f* fragmentation.

Aufstachelung *f* incitement; ~ **zum Angriffskrieg** incitement to wage a war of aggression; ~ **zum Aufruhr** inciting to riot; ~ **zum Rassenhaß** incitement to race hatred.

Aufstand *m* uprising, insurgency, insurrection, revolt; ~ **niederschlagen** to squash a riot.

aufständisch *adj* insurgent.

Aufständischer *m* insurgent.

Aufstecker *m* sticker, crowner (*in shop*), badge.

Aufsteller *m* show card.

Aufstellplakat *n* show card, counter card.

Aufstellung *f* statement (*accounts*), scheme, preparation (*balance sheet*), nomination (*candidate*), installation (*machine*); **genaue** ~ specification; **spezifizierte** ~ detailed statement, elaborate account; **statistische** ~ statistical table; *pl also*: statistical returns.

Aufstempelung stamping.

Aufstieg *m* career advancement, occupational advancement, rise, promotion, ~**schance** opportunity for advancement, opportunity for promotion.

Aufstiegsbeamter *m civil servant entitled to promotion*.

Aufstiegsmöglichkeit *f* opportunity for promotion, promotion prospects.

aufstocken *v/t* to increase, to step up, to accumulate, to strengthen (*cash position, reserves*).

Aufstockung *f* increase; accumulation; stockpiling; ~ **des Plafonds** rallonge; ~**saktien** capitalization shares; ~**schance** *f* prospect of bonus issue.

Aufstufung *f* rate-increase promotion.

aufsuchen *v/t* to prospect (*for minerals, oil*).

Aufsuchen *n* visiting (customers), canvassing; ~ **von Bestellungen** canvassing for orders.

Auftrag

Aufsuchung *f* prospecting (*minerals, oil*); ~**s- und Gewinnungskonzession** prospecting concession.

aufteilbar *adj* divisible, severable, classifiable, apportionable.

aufteilen *v/t* to divide (up), to apportion, to allot (*land*), to distribute (*estate*).

Aufteilung *f* apportionment, partition, division, allotment, distribution, break-up; ~ **der Gewinne** distribution of profits; ~ **der Kosten** distribution of costs; ~ **im Innenverhältnis** equitable apportionment, *partition by owners inter se*; ~ **von Gewinnen** apportionment of profit (*to several assessment periods*); **anteilsmäßige** ~ pro rata apportionment; **ausgewogene** ~ equitable distribution; **prozentuale** ~ distribution on a percentage basis.

Aufteilungs|bescheid partition order; ~**grundlagen** underlying data for a partition; ~**maßstab** proportions for a partition, ratio of allocation; ~**plan** partition plan; ~**verfahren** method of partition; ~**verhältnis** ratio of allocation.

Auftrag *m* (*pl Aufträge*) mandate (*contract to do some act without reward*), commission, request; *econ*: order; contract; ~ **auf Abruf** option order, order subject to call; ~**e gemeinsam erteilen** to pool orders; ~ **hereinholen** to canvass orders; ~**sfreigabe** order release; ~ **zu Festpreisen** fixed-price contract; **auf Widerruf gültiger** ~ open order; **ausgeführter** ~ completed order; **den** ~ **übernehmen** to accept the commission, to take on an assignment; **e–n** ~ **erlangen** to secure an order, to obtain an order; **e–n** ~ **erteilen** to order, to award a contract; **e–n** ~ **stornieren** to withdraw an order, to cancel an order; **e–n** ~ **streichen** to cancel an order; **e–n** ~ **untervergeben** to farm out, to subcontract; **e–n** ~ **vergeben** to place a contract; **e–n** ~ **zurücknehmen** to withdraw an order; **eingehende**

79

Auftraggeber

Aufträge incoming orders; **fester ~** firm order; **freibleibender ~** order without engagement; **Ihrem ~ gemäß** in accordance with your instructions; **im ~** (for and) on behalf of, by order of (*public administration*), i. A. (*before signature*) by order; **im ~ und für Rechnung** by order and for account (of); **im gerichtlichen ~** by order of the court; **in ~ gegeben** ordered, contracted for; **innerbetrieblicher ~** internal order, shop order; **kein ~** no order(s) (*N/O*); **limitierter ~** limited (price) order (*exch*); **namens und im ~** in the name and on behalf of; **öffentlicher ~** government contract, government order, cost-plus contract; **periodischer ~** repeat order; **sich um ~e bemühen** to solicit orders; **unerledigte ~e** unfilled orders, outstanding orders; **unlimitierter ~** unlimited order; **verlust-stoppender ~** stop loss order; **vorliegende ~e** orders in hand.

Auftraggeber *m* mandator (*contract of mandate*); principal, ordering party, customer, client, contracting agency, contract placing authority, (*government contracts*), buyer (*in sales contracts*), owner (*building contracts*), tenderee (*in invitations for tenders*); **verdeckter ~** undisclosed principal.

Auftragnehmer *m* contractor, supplier, seller, order(ing) party, party with whom the order is placed.

Auftrags|abrechnung job (order cost) accounting; **~änderung** change in the order; **~angelegenheiten** delegated functions, matters handled upon request (*of another authority*); **~annahme** acceptance of an order; **~ausgaben** agency work, functions carried out on behalf of other government bodies; **~ausgaben** expenses incurred by agent (*or* contract for); **~beendigung** termination (*or* completion) of job; **~bereinigung** elimination of dead orders; **~besorgung** commission, solicitation of orders;

Auftragsrecht

~bestand orders in hand; outstanding orders, *reichliche ~bestände: well-filled order books; überhängender ~~: backlog of orders*; **~bestandsbuch** order book; **~bestätigung** acknowledg(e)ment of an order (*by supplier etc*), confirmation of an order; (*exch:*) contract note, sale note; confirmation of a commission; **~bewegung** changes in order backlog; **~blatt** work sheet; **~dienst** telephone answering service; **~eingang** new orders booked, incoming orders, inflow of orders; **~eingänge aus dem Inland:** *home-market orders*; **~entziehung** cancellation of (building) contract (by customer); **~erfindung** invention made under contract; **~erledigung** completion of job, execution of an order (*administration, military*), disposal of a commission; **~erteilung** placing of order(s), awarding of contract, acceptance of tender; *exch: hektische ~~: feverish placing of orders;* **~flaute** sluggishness of market, slowness of incoming orders; **~formular** order form, order sheet; **~gegenstand** the goods and services to be supplied, the contracted-for goods, the contractual article(s); **a~gemäß** according to instructions, as per order; as agreed; **~geschäft** commission business; **~index** index of new orders; **~kennzeichen** job order code, job number, job reference; **~kosten** job order costs; *unverrechnete ~~: unbilled job order costs; vorverrechnete ~~: job order costs billed in advance;* **~kostensammelblatt** job cost sheet; **~kostenverfahren** job order costing; **~kurve** rate of booking of new orders; **~lage** level of incoming orders; *knappe ~~: thin market* (*exch*); **~lenkung** allocation of contracts; **~not** shortage of orders; **~nummer** order number, job number, job reference; **~papiere** securities taken on a commission basis (*exch*); **~polster** backlog of orders on (= in) hand; **~produzent** agent producer; **~recht** law of

auftreten

mandate; rights arising from a commission; ~**rückgang** drop in orders, fall in the number of orders; ~**rückstand** backlog of orders; ~**schreiben** letter containing an order, written order; ~**überhang** backlog of orders on hand; *den* ~~*abbauen: to work off the backlog (of unfilled orders)*; ~**vergabe** awarding contracts; award of the contract (*after tenders*); ~**verhältnis** agency, mandate relationship, agency contract; ~**verwaltung** administration by commission; **a~weise** on instructions; on a commission basis, on a contract basis; ~**welle** wave of new orders; (sudden) influx of orders; ~**werbung** solicitation of business, advertising for business; ~**wert** contract value, amount of the contract sum; **a~widrig** contrary to instructions; ~**zeit** time of the order; order man-hours; ~**zettel** order slip, order sheet.

auftreten *v/i* to appear (*in court*), to act (*in a capacity*), to occur; **immer wieder** ~ to recur; **persönlich** ~ to act in person; to appear in person (*or* in personam).

Auftrieb *m* upsurge, upswing, upward turn, boom tendency (*business trend*); supply at market place (*livestock*); ~**selement** stimulating factor; ~**skraft** buoyancy (*exch*); propellant forces, buoyant forces; ~**smoment** stimulating factor; ~**stendenz** upward trend, boom trend; **konjunktureller** ~ cyclical upsurge.

Auftrittsverbot *n* stage ban, ban on a stage performance.

Aufwand *m* expenditure, expense, cost; ~**sart** type of expense; ~**sentschädigung** expense allowance, representation allowance, entertainment allowance; ~**sposten** expense item; ~**sprinzip** sumptuary principle (*tax*); ~**steuer** luxury tax; **aktivierungspflichtiger** ~ expense to be capitalized, expense treatable as an addition to assets; **als** ~ **buchen** to charge to expense; **anschaffungsnaher** ~ asset-related expense, *subsequent expense incurred in connection with the purchase of an asset*; aquisition expenses; **betrieblicher** ~ operating expense; **betriebsfremder** ~ non-operating expense; **erfolgswirksamer** ~ expense affecting the operating result; **fehlender** ~ unaccrued cost; **periodenfremder** ~ expense not relating to the period under review.

Aufwärtstrend *m* uptrend.

aufwenden *v/t* to expend, to lay out.

Aufwendungen *f/pl* expenses incurred, expenditure, outlay, outgoings; ~ **der Schuldentilgung** amounts used for debt redemption; ~ **für Altersversorgung und Unterstützung** expenditure related to pension plans and other employee benefits; ~ **für Fahrten zwischen Wohnung und Arbeitsstätte** commuting expenses; ~ **und Erträge** revenue and expense; **angemessene tatsächliche** ~ actual out-of-pocket expenses reasonably incurred; appropriate and factual expenses; **außerbetriebliche** ~ non-operational expenditures; **begünstigte** ~ (tax-)favoured expenditures; **betriebliche** ~ operating expenditure; **entstandene, aber noch nicht fällige** ~ accrued payable accounts; **finanzierungsfähige** ~ expenditure eligible for financing; **massierte** ~ concentration of outgoings; **notwendige** ~ necessaries, necessary outgoings, necessary expenses; **rein buchmäßige** ~ items of purely accounting expenditure; **werterhöhende** ~ (expenditure for) improvements, valuable improvements, meliorations; **wertsteigernde** ~ (= *werterhöhende Aufwendungen qv.*); **zinsähnliche** ~ interest-related expense.

Aufwendungs|ersatz reimbursement of expenses; ~**ersatzansprüche** claims for reimbursement of expenses; ~**ersparnis** savings in expenses; ~**quote** expense ratio.

aufwerten *v/t* to revaluate, to valorize, to raise the exchange rate, to

Aufwertung

revalue upwards, to revalue at a higher price (value), to appreciate.

Aufwertung f (upward) revaluation, exchange rate appreciation; upvaluation.

Aufwertungs|erlös proceeds from revaluation; ~**gesetz** Revaluation Act (*German Act of 1924 to revalorize claims destroyed by inflation*); ~**gewinn** revaluation surplus, revalorization profit; ~**gutschrift** credit entry for revaluation; ~**satz** official rate of increase of exchange rate, revaluation rate.

aufwiegeln v/t to incite, to stir up (*population by agitators*).

Aufwiegelung f incitement, sedition (*to disobedience*); ~ **zum Landfriedensbruch** inciting to riot.

Aufwiegler m agitator, demagogue.

aufzählen v/t to enumerate, to itemize, to count up, to list.

Aufzählung f enumeration, itemization, recital, listing.

aufzeichnen v/t to record; **amtlich** ~ to record (officially).

Aufzeichnung f record; memorandum, recording; ~**en der Kundenbuchhaltung** accounts receivable records; ~**spflicht** f duty to keep records and accounts (*tax laws*); **a~spflichtig** liable to be recorded (*in books and accounts*) ~**ssystem** system of records; **interne** ~ internal memo, intercompany memo, in-house memo.

aufziehen v/t to arrange; to make a display of; to bring up (*children*).

aufzinsen v/t to revalue for accrued interest, to mark up for accrued interest, to add unaccrued interest.

Aufzinsung f compounding, accumulating of interest; *adding unaccrued interest to determine final capital sum.*

Aufzugsverordnung f ordinance concerning *the construction, operation and supervision of elevators.*

aufzwingen v/t to force upon, to impose.

Augenblick|des Todes moment of death, in articulo mortis; **lichter** ~ lucid interval.

ausbessern

augenfällig adj obvious, clear.

Augenfälligkeit f obviousness.

Augenmerk n attention.

Augenschein m inspection (*judicial*), judicial view; ~**nahme** inspection (by the court); ~**sbeweis** evidence by inspection, real evidence, ocular evidence, auto-optic evidence, demonstrative evidence, visual evidence; **in** ~ **nehmen** to view, to inspect, to visit the scene; **richterlicher** ~ judicial inspection; **sich durch** ~ **überzeugen** to convince oneself by inspection.

augenscheinlich adj evident, obvious, clear.

Augenscheinlichkeit f obviousness, clearness.

Augenzeuge m eye witness; ~ **sein** to (eye-)witness; ~**nbericht** eye-witness account.

Auktion f auction, public sale, sale by public auction; **zur** ~ **bringen** to put s. th. up for auction, to auction.

Auktions|ankündigung notice of public auction; ~**gebühren** auction fees; ~**liste** auction catalogue; ~**lokal** auction room; ~**partie** sale lot; ~**posten** auction lot; ~**preis** auction price; ~**system** system of establishing prices by auction.

Auktionator m auctioneer.

auktionieren v/t (= *verauktionieren*) to auction, to sell by (public) auction, to put up for auction.

Ausbau m development, completion, expansion; improvement (*roads*); ~**arbeiten** interior work, extension work; ~**firma** finishing contractor.

ausbauen v/t to develop, to improve, to extend.

ausbaufähig adj capable of development, expandable, capable of extension.

ausbedingen v/t to stipulate, to reserve, to require.

Ausbedingung f stipulation.

ausbedungen adj stipulated, agreed upon.

ausbessern v/t to repair (*street, work*), to correct (*errors*).

Ausbesserung *f* repair (work), correction; ~**swerft** repair yard.
Ausbeute *f* yield, return, produce.
ausbeuten *v/t* to exploit, to take advantage of.
Ausbeutung *f* exploitation, utilization, working, depletion (*by excessive exploitation*), sweating (*labour*); ~ **der Notlage eines anderen** taking advantage of the predicament of another; ~ **des Meeresbodens** exploitation of the sea bed; ~ **durch Heimarbeit** sweating system, sweated labour; ~ **e–r Dirne** exploiting a female prostitute; **e–s Minderjährigen** exploitation of (the inexperience of) a minor; ~**sgeschäft** unconscionable transaction; ~**slizenz** licence to exploit; ~**srecht** right of exploitation; **mißbräuchliche** ~ abusive exploitation.
ausbezahlen *v/t* to pay (*wages*), to pay off (*joint interest in property*), to buy out (*partner*).
ausbieten *v/t* to call for bids (*auction*).
Ausbieter *m* auctioneer.
Ausbietung *f* calling for bids (*auction*); ~**sgarantie** bidding guarantee (*to make a definitive bid at an auction*); ~**sverfahren** calling for bids (*stage of the proceedings at a public sale of landed property*).
ausbilden *v/t* to train (*apprentices etc*).
Ausbildender *m* vocational instructor; master craftsman.
Ausbilder *m* instructor.
Ausbildung *f* training, schooling, education; further education, professional training, vocational training; ~ **am Arbeitsplatz** in-plant training, in-house training, on-the-job-training; ~ **vor Arbeitsaufnahme** pre-employment training; **berufliche Aus- und Weiterbildung** vocational instruction and advanced training; **betriebliche** ~ in-plant training, in-house training; **gewerbliche** ~ vocational training; **handwerkliche** ~ training for a trade (*or for a craft*); **juristische** ~ legal training; **kaufmännische** ~ business (*or* commercial) training; **militärische** ~ military training; **praktische** ~ practical training; **schulische** ~ schooling.
Ausbildungs|beihilfe vocational education allowance, training grant; ~**beruf** recognised job-training, recognized trade; ~**betrieb** firm providing vocational (*or* occupational) training; ~**förderung** promotion of vocational training; ~**freibetrag** educational allowance; ~**gang** course of vocational (professional) training; ~**geld** training allowance; ~**kosten** training costs, expenses involved in vocational training; ~**ordnung(en)** rules for vocational training; ~**pflicht** statutory duty to provide vocational training; ~**platz** apprenticeship, training place; ~**reform** reform of the system of vocational training; ~**stand** level of professional training; ~**stätte** place of vocational training, training facilities, training centre; **überbetriebliche** ~~: joint training establishment; ~**umlage** industrial training levy; ~**unterhalt** vocational promotion support (*to divorced spouse*); ~**unterstützung** vocational education support; ~**verhältnis** vocational (*or*: professional) training relationship; ~**werkstatt** training shop; ~**zeit** time allotted for vocational training; ~**zulage** extra pay during vocational training; ~**zuschuß** (vocational) training subsidy.
Ausbleiben *n* non-appearance, non-attendance, failure to appear, default of appearance; **unentschuldigtes** ~ absence without valid excuse, absence without apology.
ausbleiben *v/t* to fail to appear, to be absent.
ausbrechen *v/i* to break jail, to escape from prison.
Ausbruch *m* prison breaking, jailbreak, escape from prison; ~ **aus dem Gefängnis** jail breaking, prison breaking; ~**sversuch** attempt to escape from prison.
ausbuchen *v/t* to write off; to delete

from the accounts *and/or* to delete from the inventory; *ausgebucht: written off, booked up (theatre)*.

Ausbuchung *f* writing off (*as uncollectible, fully depreciated*), deletion from the inventory *and/or* the accounts, abandonment.

ausbürgern *v/t* to denationalize, to expatriate, to deprive of one's citizenship.

Ausbürgerung *f* expatriation, denaturalization, depriving s. o. of his (her) citizenship.

ausdeuten *v/t* to explain (*the meaning*), to construe (*text*).

Ausdeutung *f* explanation, construction.

ausdisponiert *adj* fully allocated; fully disposed of.

Ausdruck *m* (*pl: Ausdrücke*) expression, term, phrase; ~ **der Rechtssprache** legal term, term of art; ~ **des Willens** manifestation of intension; expression of intention, expression of will; **~sweise** mode of expression, phraseology; *juristische* ~~: *legal parlance* (*or* terminology); **beschreibende ~e** *pl* descriptive terms; **juristischer** ~ legal term, legal phrase; **zum ~ bringen** to express, to indicate, to state, to enunciate.

ausdrücken *v/t* to express, to phrase, to put in words, to utter, to purport, to couch (*in legal terms*).

ausdrücklich *adj* (*bzw adv* ~*ly*) express, explicit; definite, positive; **soweit nicht ~ etwas anderes bestimmt ist** in the absence of any provision to the contrary, in the absence of anything to the contrary, unless otherwise stated.

auseinandergehen *v/t* to part, to diverge, to differ (*opinion*), to dissolve (*meeting*), to be broken off (*engagement*).

auseinandersetzen (1) *v/t* to explain, to elucidate, to expound, to set out; *v/reflex* to argue, to disagree, to struggle, to have a dispute.

auseinandersetzen (2) *v/i, v/t* to settle up (*estate, liquidation*), to partition, to divide, to distribute (*net assets*).

Auseinandersetzung *f* (1) argument, disagreement, dispute, struggle; **kriegerische** ~ armed conflict; **interne** ~ internal dispute, infighting; **juristische** ~ legal dispute; **lohnpolitische** ~ wage dispute, dispute about wage policy;

Auseinandersetzung *f* (2) partition, final division, final distribution (*estate*), settlement, division of net assets, apportionment, repartition; **vereinbarte** ~ voluntary partition; **vermögensrechtliche** ~ distribution of property, distribution of assets and liabilities; **zwangsweise** ~ compulsory partition.

Auseinandersetzungs|anspruch claim to a distribution-quota; **~beschluß** order of distribution; **~bilanz** winding-up balance-sheet, apportioning balance sheet, final balance sheet; **~guthaben** credit balance in case of partition; **~klage** legal action over an apportionment of assets and liabilities, action for partition; **~plan** winding-up and distribution scheme; **~verbindlichkeiten** liabilities to be discharged upon winding-up a firm; **~verbot** prohibition of (*or*: inhibition of) partition (*of estate*); **~versteigerung** *public sale by auction for the purpose of dividing and distributing joint property*; **~vertrag** settlement agreement, partition agreement.

ausfahren *v/t* to deliver goods (*to customers*); to occupy capacity by operating (*a machine, a plant*).

Ausfahrt *f* exit, driveway; ~ **freihalten!** keep exit clear! no parking!

Ausfall *m* (*pl Ausfälle*: ~*e*) shortfall, loss, failure (*machine*), out-turn (*US* = *outturn*) (*pattern*), deficiency (*uncollectible amount*), irretrievable amount; **~bürge** deficiency guarantor; **~bürgschaft** deficiency guarantee, secondary guarantee, ordinary guarantee, simple guarantee; **~dauer** dead time, down time; ~ **der Sinneswahrnehmung** sensory aphasia; ~ **e-r Bedingung** absence of a precondition, non-occurrence (of an event), of a condition (to materialize), *the non-occurrence of an uncertain event on which condition depends;* **~forderung** claim (of partly secured creditor) for the deficiency; **~haftung** contingent liability, liability for irretrievable debts; **~muster** pattern reference, output sample, outturn sample, pilot sample; **~quote** loan loss; **~risiko** risk of non-payment, default risk; **~stunden** hours not worked, lost hours; **~vergütung** deficiency compensation; **~versicherung** insurance for irretrievable receivables; **~zeit(en)** lost period(s) of time, (social) insurance shortfall; periods during which no insurance contributions were paid (*due to unemployment, illness, higher education, training etc, for which credit will be given for pension expectancy*).

ausfechten *v/t* to fight out (*not to settle a case*), to contest, to dispute.

ausfeilen *v/t* to polish the style (*of a brief etc*), to polish up.

ausfertigen *v/t* to exemplify, to execute (*a document*), to issue, to engross, to make out, to make a final and fair copy; to make a counterpart copy; to make an authentic copy (*equivalent to the original document*); **doppelt ~** to duplicate, to issue in counterpart copies, to make two engrossments.

Ausfertigung counterpart, office copy, official copy; antigraphy, engrossment, exemplification, exemplified copy; **~sgebühr** fee for executing a deed, issuing fee; **~szollstelle** issuing (customs) office; **amtliche ~** office copy, official copy; **dritte ~** copy 3, triplicate; **erste ~** first of exchange (*bill of exchange*); **gerichtliche ~** court-sealed copy; **in doppelter ~** engrossed in duplicate; **in dreifacher ~** in triplicate; **in einfacher ~** in a single copy; **in fünffacher ~ einreichen** to file in quintuplicate, to file five copies; **in vierfacher ~** in quadruplicate; **mehrfache ~** in multiple copies; **in ~r ~:** *(done in) several counterparts, issued (executed) in several copies;* **nochmalige ~** re-execution; **vollstreckbare ~** enforceable official copy; **zweite ~** duplicate, counterpart.

Ausfindigmachen *m* discovery, tracing.

Ausfischung *f* devastation of fishery resources.

Ausflucht *f* (*pl: Ausflüchte*) evasion, prevarication; **~e** *pl* **machen** to prevaricate, trying to evade a question, to equivocate, to quibble, to beat around the bush.

Ausflug *m* departure by air.

ausfolgen *v/t* to deliver, to hand over, to surrender.

Ausfolgung *f* delivery, handing-over, surrender; **~sprotest** protest for non-delivery (*bill of exchange*).

ausforschen *v/t* to sound out, to pump, to explore, to go on a fishing expedition (*cross-examination*).

Ausforschung *f* exploratory soundings, sounding out, *seeking disclosure by adversary of facts supporting a case;* **~santrag** (improper) application to carry out inquiries; **~sbeweis** (purely) exploratory questioning of a witness (*seeking to prove a point by improper exploratory offers of evidence or endeavouring to induce opponent to disclose a point in one's favour*); **~sdurchsuchung** exploratory search; **~sfragen** exploratory questioning, questions to sound out, fishing exploration, fishing expedition; **~sklage** exploratory action.

ausfragen *v/t* to question, to interrogate, to pump for information.

Ausfuhr *f* export, exportation, exporting, exports (*= exported goods*); **~abfertigung** export clearance; **~abschöpfung** export levy; **~ auf Zeit** temporary exports; **~belebung** recovery of exports; **~be-**

85

Ausfuhrbescheinigung

scheinigung certificate of export; ~**bestimmungen** export regulations; ~**bewilligung** export permit, export licence; ~**bürgschaft** export guarantee; ~**deklaration** export declaration, shipper's manifest; ~**dokumente** export documents (*or* papers); ~**einheit** export unit (*in volume of exports*); ~**erklärung** export declaration; ~**erlaubnis** export permit, export clearance; ~**erstattungen** export refunds; ~**förderung** export promotion, encouragement to export; ~**förderungsgesetz** Export Promotion Act; ~**förderungskredit** export promotion credit; ~**förmlichkeiten** export formalities; ~**genehmigung** export permit; ~**geschäfte** export business, export transactions; ~**hafen** port of export; ~**handel** export trade; ~**händler** exporter, export trader; ~**händlervergütung** refund (of value-added tax) to exporters; ~**höchstmengen** quantitative export limits; ~**kartell** export cartel; ~**kontingent** export quota; ~**kontrolle** export controls; ~**land** country of export, exporting country; ~**lieferungen** exports, export deliveries; ~**lizenz** export licence, export permit; ~ **nach aktiver Veredelung** exportation after inward processing; ~**nachweis** export certificate, proof of export; ~**ort** exit point; ~**papier** export document; ~**prämie** exports bonus, export premium, drawback; ~**quote,** ratio of exports to imports; ~**politik** export policy; ~**schein** export licence certificate; ~**sortiment** range of exports; ~**sperre** stoppage of exports, embargo; ~**steuer** export tax; ~**tag** day of exportation; ~**überschuß** export surplus, overbalance of exports; ~**verantwortlicher** person responsible for exports; ~**verbot** export ban, embargo, prohibition of export ~**vergütung** export rebate, export refund; ~**verträge** export

Ausführungsanweisung

agreements, export contracts; ~**ware** export goods, goods to be exported; ~**wirtschaft** export trade; exporting industries; ~**zoll** customs duty on exportation; ~ **zur passiven Veredelung** exportation for outward processing; **einseitiges** ~**geschäft** unrequited exports, unilateral exports; **endgültige** ~ outright exportation; **entgeltliche** ~ exports against payment, exports on a payment basis; **gewerbliche** ~ industrial exports; **sichtbare** ~ visible exports; **unbezahlte** ~ unpaid exports; **unsichtbare** ~ invisible exports.

ausführbar *adj* feasible, practicable; **nicht** ~ unworkable, unfeasible.

Ausführbarkeit *f* feasibility.

ausführen *v/t* to accomplish (*task, job*), to perform (*work*), to implement (*law*), to perpetrate (*criminal act*), to execute (*order*), to export (*goods*), to submit (*pleadings, argument*), to elaborate (*in detail*).

ausführend *adj* executive, performing.

Ausführer *m* exporter; **ermächtigter** ~ approved exporter.

Ausführung *f* accomplishment, performance; implementation, execution; perpetration; workmanship, design; ~ **der Straftat** commission of the act; **bei der** ~ (*der Tat*) in faciendo, in the act of (committing an offence); **fachgerechte** ~ good workmanship; **in** ~ **begriffene Arbeit** work-in-progress; **in** ~ **von** pursuant to, implementing (*a law*); **zur** ~ **bringen** to carry out, to carry into effect, to execute.

Ausführungs|anweisung regulation, regulatory instruction, instructions who is to carry out (do, execute, implement etc); ~**anzeige** advice of execution (*orders*), notice of completion, report of completion of performance; ~**behörden** executive authorities, implementing authorities; ~**beispiel** embodiment (*of invention*); ~**beschluß** executory decision; ~**bestimmungen** implementing regu-

Ausführungen

lations, regulatory statute, administrative regulations; ~**frist** time for performance, time for completion; ~**geschäft** implementing transaction, follow-up business; ~**gesetz** implementing law, regulatory statute; ~**verordnung** implementing ordinance, rules, statutory instrument; ~**vorschrift** regulatory instructions; **zur ~handlung schreiten** to enter upon the fulfilment of (duties).

Ausführungen *f/pl* argument, pleading(s), submissions (*to the court*), remarks, observations; ~ **machen** to make observations, to present arguments; ~ **zum Sachverhalt** argument on fact; **einleitende ~machen** to make opening remarks, to open a case; **mündliche ~** oral pleadings.

ausfüllen *v/t* to fill in (*a form, a questionnaire*), to complete (*a blank*), to fill out (*a form*).

Ausfüllung *f* completion (*of a form etc*); ~**sbefugnis** authority to complete (*a blank*).

Ausgabe *f* (1) issue, (*securities*); ~**aufgeld** premium; ~**bank** bank of issue, issuing bank; ~**bedingungen** terms of issue; ~**betrag** issue price; ~**kurs** issue price, issue quotation; *günstiger* ~~: "*to get in on the ground floor*", "*to get a basement bargain*"; ~**land** country of issue (*carnet passport*); ~**ort** place of issue; ~**preis** issue price; offering price; ~**stelle** issuing agency, issuing office; ~**tag** date of issue, day of issue; ~ **über dem Nennwert** issue above par; ~ **von Aktien** issue of shares (*stock*).

Ausgabe *f* (2) expense item, expenditure; outlay, disbursement; **abzugsfähige ~** tax-deductible expense.

Ausgaben|**abstrich** cut in expenditure; ~**ansatz** estimated expenditure; ~**beleg** voucher (receipt, counterfoil), for payment; ~**beschlüsse** expenditure (votes), expenditure decisions; ~**bewilligung** expenditure allowance,

Ausgaben

grant, appropriation; ~**buch** expenditure ledger; ~**budget** expenditure budget; ~ **des Privatverbrauchers** personal consumption expenditure; ~**dispositionen** expenditure arrangements; ~**erhöhungen** increase in expenditure; ~**erstattung** reimbursement of expenses; **a~freudig** *adj* ready to spend, munificent; ~**gestaltung** pattern of expenditure; ~**gruppe** category of expenditure; ~**konto** expense account; ~**kontrollbogen** expenditure check-list; ~**kurve** outlay graph, expenditure graph; ~**kürzung** spending cut, retrenchment, reduction in expenditure; ~ **machen** to spend, to incur expenses; ~**-Plafond** expenditure ceiling; ~**posten** expense items; ~**programm** expenditure programme, expenditure plan; ~**quote** proportion of expenditure, spending rate; ~**rechnung** calculation of expenses, expenditure bill (*or* invoice); ~**spitze** maximum expenditure; ~**struktur** pattern of expenditure; ~**überschreitung** excess expenditure; ~**überschuß** excess expenditure; ~**verpflichtung** liability to incur expenditure of ...; **abzugsfähige ~** (tax-)deductible expenses; **außergewöhnliche ~** unusual (extraordinary) expenditure; **außerplanmäßige ~** expenditure not budgeted for, extraordinary expenditure; **buchmäßige ~** non-cash expenditure; **die ~ umlegen auf ...** to apportion the expenses among ...; **einmalige ~** unique expenditure, non-recurring (non-recurrent) expenditure; **feste ~** fixed cost, permanent expenditure; **konsumptive ~** expenditure on consumption; **laufende ~** current expense, running expenses, recurrent expenditure, ordinary expenditure; **nichtabzugsfähige ~**non-deductible expense; **öffentliche ~** public expenditure, government(al) spending; **ordentliche ~** ordinary expenditure, proper expenditure;

Ausgang — Ausgleich

reguläre ~ ordinary expenditure; **sachliche** ~ expenditure on material; **sachlich richtige** ~ proper outgoings, proper expenditure, appropriate disbursements; **sonstige** ~ other payments; **überplanmäßige** ~ unbudgeted expenditure; **unmittelbare** ~ direct expenditure; **unvorhergesehene** ~ unforeseen expenses, **vermögensvermehrende** ~ asset-increasing expenditure; **voraussichtliche** ~ **decken** to cover the foreseeable expenses; **vordatierte** ~ pre-dated payments.

Ausgang *m* exit (*building*), outcome, result, outgo, outlet, initial point, point of departure; ~ **des Rechtsstreits** outcome of the law-suit.

Ausgangs|abfertigung clearance outwards; ~**abschnitt** exit sheet; ~**annahme** initial assumption; ~**basis** initial position; ~**behörde** originating office; ~**bescheinigung** exit visa; ~**deklaration** exit declaration; ~**fracht** outgoing freight; ~**frage** the initial question, threshold question; ~**hafen** port of departure; ~**kapital** original capital; ~**land** country of departure; ~**material** basic material, starting material, source material; ~**miete** original rent, basic rent; ~**parität** initial par value; ~**produkt** primary product; ~**punkt** starting point, terminus a quo, initial terminus; ~**rechnung** sales invoice; ~**sperre** curfew (*civilians*), confinement to barracks (*soldiers*); *nächtliche* ~~: *night-time curfew, dusk-to-dawn curfew;* ~**stand** initial position, starting total; ~**stoff** primary material, source material; ~**tarif** basic rate; ~**urteil** original judgment, judgment of the first instance; ~**wert** initial value, initial figure; ~**zahlen** initial figures, *figures taken as basis of calculation*; ~**zeitraum** initial period, *period taken as the basis of comparison*; ~**zollsatz** basic (customs) duty; ~**zollstelle** customs office at point of exit, office of exit.

ausgeben *v/t* to spend, to expend (*money*), to issue, to emit (*securities*); ~ **als** to pass off as (*own manufacture*); **sich** ~ **als** to pose as (*a representative; a nobleman, s.o. else*); **sich fälschlich** ~ to pretend to be, to pose as, to personate; **sich für jmdn anderes** ~ to personate.

ausgebildet *adj* (fully) trained; **juristisch** ~ legally trained.

Ausgebot *n* (judicial auction) offer of real estate.

Ausgebürgerte(r) *m* expatriate, a person deprived of citizenship.

ausgefertigt *adj* done, executed, engrossed, exemplified → *ausfertigen*; **noch nicht** ~ drafted, in draft form only not yet engrossed.

Ausgehverbot *n* curfew (*civilian population*); confinement to barracks (*soldiers*).

Ausgelieferte(r) *m* extradited person.

ausgeliehen *adj* loaned, on loan; **verzinslich** ~ loaned out at interest.

ausgemacht *adj* agreed, settled (*arrangement, bargain*), arranged.

ausgenommen *adj* except, with the exception of, save for.

ausgeschlossen *adj* excluded, foreclosed (*after deadline*), disqualified (*from office, etc*).

Ausgestoßene(r) *f/m* outcast.

Ausgewiesene(r) *f/m* expellee.

ausgewogen *adj* balanced, equable.

Ausgewogenheit *f* balance, well-balanced proportion, equilibrium; ~ **der Zahlungsbilanz** state of equilibrium in balance of payments; ~**sgrundsatz** fairness doctrine; doctrine of fairness; equal (*broadcasting*) time.

ausgezeichnet *adj* (*Preis*) priced, with the price marked.

Ausgleich *m* adjustment, equation, offset, balance (*accounts*), hotchpot (*advancements, share of inheritance*), compensation (*damage*), equalization (*burdens*), levelling out (*market rates, curves*); ~ **der Handelsbilanz** redressing (*or:* squaring) the balance of trade; ~ **der Risiken** spreading of risks; ~ **der**

ausgleichen | **Ausgleichszahlung**

Zahlungsbilanz squaring (*or:* evening out) the balance of payments, balance of payments equilibrium; ~ **e–r Spanne** bridging a gap; ~ **unter Gesamtschuldnern** settlement by contribution(s) (*to a joint debtor who had paid off a common debt*); **angemessener ~ in Geld** reasonable monetary compensation; **automatischer ~** automatic adjustment, escalator clause; **finanzieller ~** pecuniary compensation; **formaler ~** a balance on paper only; **organischer ~** natural equilibrium (*in balance of payments*); **sozialer ~** social equilibrium, adjustment on grounds of social policy; **überörtlicher ~** regional compensation; **zum ~ bringen** to bring into hotchpot (*advancements*), to balance (*accounts*) to even-out; **zum ~ Ihres Kontos** in settlement of your account; **zum ~ unserer Rechnung** in full discharge (*or* payment) of our accounts; **zum vollständigen ~** in full satisfaction (*of a claim*).

ausgleichen *v/t* to equalize, to balance (*accounts*), to make up (*for deficit*), to settle (*debts*), to square, to spread evenly, to even out, to set off (= offset) (*debts by counterclaims*); **gegeneinander ~** to offset; **nach oben ~** to level up.

ausgleichend *adj* compensatory, compensative, balancing, retributive.

Ausgleichs|abgabe equalization levy (*under German post-war equalization of burdens legislation*); countervailing levy, countervailing charge, compensatory tax; ~**amt** Equalization of Burdens Office; ~**anspruch** compensation claim of commercial agent (*on termination of agency by principal*); equalization claim (*German Equalization of Burdens legislation*); right of contribution (*among joint debtors*); compensation for claims (*damage*); ~**arbitrage** arbitrage in exchange (*foreign currencies*); ~**ausschuß** Equalization Committee (*German Equalization of Burdens administration*); ~**behörden** Equalization of Burdens authorities; ~**belastung** countervailing charge; ~**berechtigt** entitled to contribution (*joint debtors*); ~**betrag** compensatory amount; payment to settle an amount, amount of adjustment; ~**bevorzugung** reverse discrimination; ~**bewegung** compensatory movement; ~**buchung** adjusting entry; equal but opposite entry; ~**dividende** equalizing dividend; ~**entschädigung** compensation (money); **a~fähig** compensable, equalizable, capable of being compensated; ~**fonds** Equalization of Burdens Fund; compensation fund; ~**forderung** equalization claim: *claim for compensation of losses under "Equalization of Burdens Act"*, compensation claim; ~**guthaben** compensatory credit balance; ~**haftung** contributory liability (*of joint debtors*); ~**kasse** equalization fund; compensation fund (*Equalization of Burdens*); ~**konto** countervailing account, adjustments account, overs and shorts account; ~**kredit** stop-gap loan, compensatory credit; ~**lager(bestände)** buffer stocks; ~**leistung** compensatory payment, equalization benefits; ~**lohn** make-up wages, wage adjustment; ~**masse** sum applied to adjusting payments; ~**maßnahme** carry-over arrangement; ~**pflicht** duty to compensate; ~**pool** buffer pool; ~**posten** compensatory item, balancing item; ~**prämie** adjustment premium; ~**quittung** general discharge, mutual release (*certificate*); ~**rücklage** compensatory reserve; ~**schuld** equalization charge; ~**stelle** clearing office; ~**steuer** equalizing tax; ~**tendenz** levelling-off tendency, tendency towards equilibrium, ~**termin** settlement date; ~**umlage** equalization assessment; ~**verfahren** equalization method, compensation; ~**zahlung** deficiency payment, compensation payment; ~**zoll** countervailing customs duty; ~**zulage** compensatory allowance, additional compensation; ~**zuweisungen** allocation of funds *under Equalization of Burdens scheme*.

Ausgleichung *f* adjustment, settlement, graduation (*insurance*), arranging a hotchpot (*advancements upon succession*); ~**spflicht** duty to compensate; ~ **von Vorempfängen** hotchpot.

ausgliedern *v/t* to set apart, to show separately, to hive off.

Ausgliederung *f* separation, setting up as a separate unit, spin off.

ausgründen *v/t* to form separate enterprises (*out of a combine*), to hive off.

aushandeln *v/t* to settle by negotiation, to bargain (*prices*).

aushändigen *v/t* to hand over, to deliver (up), to surrender, to hand out.

Aushändigung *f* handing over, delivery, surrender; ~ **e-r Urkunde** delivery of a document; ~**spflicht** obligation to surrender (*a document*); **gegen** ~ **des Wechsels** against (*or* on) surrender of the bill of exchange.

Aushang *m* publication on the notice board, posting on the bulletin board.

aushängen *v/t* to post, to give public notice by posting, to put up a notice.

ausheben *v/t* to enlist, to recruit, to draft (*soldiers*), to clean out (*gangsters' den*).

Aushebung *f* (*Mil.*) *obs.* enlistment, recruiting, drafting; (*Police*) raid (*on gangsters' den*).

aushelfen *v/i* to help out, to assist temporarily.

Aushilfe *f* temporary assistance, temporary helper, a temp; ~**tätigkeit** substitute work, stopgap work, temporary work.

Aushilfs|arbeitsverhältnis employment as temporary help; ~**kräfte** casual workers, temporary helpers; ~**personal** temporary staff; ~**stellung** temporary job; ~**tätigkeit** stint; **a**~**weise** as a deputy, as a temporary helper, as a stopgap.

aushöhlen *v/t* to erode, to undermine (*constitution*), to water down, to dilute (*capital, strength*).

Aushöhlung *f* erosion, undermining, watering down, dilution; ~ **der Landeszuständigkeit** indirect reduction of the competence of a German state (*Land*) *in favour of the federal government's jurisdiction and power*; ~ **der Steuerbasis** tax erosion; ~ **der Verfassung** undermining the constitution, depriving the constitution of its substance.

Auskämmaktion *f* combing-out raid.

auskämmen *v/t* to comb out, to mop up.

auskämpfen *v/t* to fight to the finish.

auskehren *v/t* to pay out, to distribute (*a profit*).

ausklagen *v/t* to decide by litigation, to recover by court action.

ausklammern *v/t* to exclude for the time being; to leave s. th. in abeyance temporarily.

Ausklammerung *f* (temporary) exclusion.

ausklarieren *v/i* to clear *outward-bound ship*.

Ausklarieren *n* (*Ausklarierung*) clearance outwards, outclearance (*from port*).

Auskommen *n* livelihood, sustenance, subsistence, self-dependence.

auskratzen *v/i* to slip (out), to abscond.

auskundschaften *v/t* to explore, to spy out, to reconnoitre, to ferret out, to find out; to trace, to locate, to pinpoint.

Auskunft *f* (*pl Auskünfte*= ~*e*) information, disclosure; ~**e einholen** to seek information; ~ **erlangen** to obtain information; ~**e erteilen** to supply information; ~ **über Bonität** information about financial soundness; **beschränkte** ~ **über Strafen** restricted disclosure regarding previous convictions (*only to judicial authorities*); **die ~ verweigern** to refuse disclosure, to refuse to disclose sth.; **hinlängliche ~ einziehen** to obtain sufficient intelligence (data, information); **mündliche ~** oral information; **sachdienliche ~e** relevant information.

Auskunfts|anspruch claim to be entitled to discovery, right to be informed; **~berechtigter** person entitled to be informed, authorized person to accept disclosure; **~blatt** information sheet; **~büro** inquiry-office, detective agency; **~ersuchen** request for information; **~erteilung** discovery, disclosure of information; **~erzwingung** enforcement of discovery, judicial order for disclosure; **~kartei** information record card; **~person** informant, informer; **~pflicht** obligation (*or* duty) to disclose, duty to provide information; **a~pflichtig** obliged to disclose sth., obliged to provide information; **~recht** right to demand information; **~stelle** enquiry office, information desk; **~verweigerung** refusal to disclose sth.; **~verweigerungsrecht** right to refuse to give information, privilege of non-disclosure, right to rely on privileged communications; **~wesen** detective business, provision of information.

Auskunftei *f* detective agency, reference agency, commercial agency, mercantile agency, credit (reporting) agency.

ausladen *v/t* to unload, to discharge, to unship.

Auslade|hafen port of unloading; **~platz** unloading berth; **~stelle** unloading place; wharf.

Auslader *m* unloader, discharger, docker, stevedore, longshoreman.

Ausladung *f* unloading, act of discharging.

Auslage *f* (*1*) display, show (*shop window*).

Auslage *f* (*2*) expense, expense item; *pl* (*~n*) expenses, out-of-pocket expenses, disbursements, outlay.

Auslagen|aufstellung statement of disbursement; **~deckung** collateral for expenses, sufficient funds for expenses; **~ des Zeugen** witness expenses; **~ersatz** reimbursement of expenses; **~ erstattet bekommen** to recover (one's) expenses, to recoup disbursements; **~erstattung** reimbursement of expenses; **~erstattungsansprüche** claims for reimbursement of expenses; **~freiheit** exemption from payment of expenses (*to court*); **~haben** to incur expenses; **~pauschale** flat-rate for expenses (*for a lawyer's postage, telephone charges etc*); **~rechnung** note of expenses; **~schuldner** party liable to pay the expenses; **~ und Gebühren** fees and expenses; **~vorschuß** advance payment in respect of expenses; **außerordentliche ~** extra-budgetary expenses; **bare ~** out-of-pocket expenses; **erstattungsfähige ~** reimbursable expenses (*to be paid by court or losing party*); **notwendige ~** necessary expenses; **persönliche ~** personal expenses, out-of-pocket expenses.

auslagern *v/t* to remove to a safe place of storage, to evacuate (*e.g. valuable paintings during war*); to deposit elsewhere (*not in main office or general storage place*), to sell from stock.

Auslagerung *f* evacuation to a safe place of storage; removal to a separate place of storage, exit from the warehouse.

Ausland *n* foreign countries, abroad; overseas (*as seen from GB*); **europäisches ~** a European foreign country; **im ~** abroad, in foreign countries, on the Continent, overseas; **im ~ wohnhaft** resident abroad, expatriate; **im ~ zahlbar** payable abroad.

Ausländer *m* foreigner, foreign national, non-national, alien; **~amt**

ausländisch

office for foreigners, aliens' registration office; ~**behandlung** treatment of aliens (or foreigners); ~ **britischer Geburt** GB: statutory alien; ~-**DM-Konto** non-resident's DM account; ~**eigenschaft** status of alien(s); ~**feindlichkeit** xenophobia, hostility towards foreigners; ~**gesetz** law concerning foreigners (*entrance, residence, surveillance, deportation etc*), Aliens Act; ~**kartei** card-index of aliens; ~**konto** non-resident's account, external account; ~**konvertibilität** convertibility of non-residents' funds; ~**kriminalität** crime rate of aliens; (and foreigners); ~**meldeamt** aliens' registration office; ~ **mit Wohnsitz im Inland** non-national resident, foreign resident, resident alien; ~ **ohne Wohnsitz im Inland** non-resident alien; ~**polizei** police department for foreign nationals; ~**recht** (the) law concerning foreign nationals; ~**sicherheit** *security to be furnished by non-resident plaintiffs of foreign nationality*; ~**sonderkonto** foreign resident's special account; ~**überwachung** supervision of aliens; ~**zentralregister** central register of foreign residents; **beschränkt steuerpflichtiger** ~ non-resident alien subject to limited taxation (*taxable for domestic income and property only*); **feindlicher** ~ alien enemy, enemy alien; **heimatloser** ~ stateless alien; **im Inland ansässiger** ~ resident alien; **unerwünschter** ~ undesirable alien.

ausländisch *adj* foreign, alien.

Auslands|absatz sales abroad, sales in foreign markets; ~**abteilung** overseas department; ~**akkreditiv** credit opened in a foreign country; ~**akzept** bill accepted abroad; ~**angebote** offers from abroad, foreign offers; ~**anlage** investment abroad; foreign investment; ~**anleihe** external loan, foreign loan, foreign bond issue; ~**anmeldung** *patent* application in a foreign country, foreign application, application

Auslandskapital

abroad; ~**arbitrage** foreign arbitrage; ~**aufenthalt** foreign residence, stay abroad, time spent abroad; ~**auftrag** order from abroad, foreign order; ~**belegschaft** employees outside Germany, employees abroad; ~**besitz** foreign holdings, property situated abroad; ~**beteiligung** foreign investment, foreign capital participation; ~**beurkundung** execution and authentication (*of an act or statement*) in a foreign country; ~**bevollmächtigter** foreign agent, representative in a foreign country; agent abroad; ~**bewohner** non-resident; ~**bond** external bond; *geregelte ~~s: external bonds covered by service arrangements;* ~**deutscher** German national living abroad, ethnic German; ~**dienst** service abroad, international agency; ~**dienststelle** foreign agency; *diplomatische ~~: diplomatic agency;* ~**direktion** overseas headquarters; ~**einlagen** foreigners' deposits; ~**einsatz** overseas posting, job abroad; ~**emission** foreign issue (or flotation); ~-**Entschädigungsgesetz** *law on the compensation of war losses incurred abroad (due to confiscations etc)*; ~**entscheidungen** foreign decisions, judgments by foreign courts; ~**filiale** foreign branch; ~**flug** international flight; ~**forderungen** foreign receivables, outstanding foreign debts, external claims; *claims against debtor residing abroad, debt owed by foreign debtor;* ~**forderungen und -verbindlichkeiten** external assets and liabilities; ~**gelder** foreign money, foreigners' deposits; ~**geschäft** foreign business; ~**gespräch** international call (*phone*); ~**grundstück(e)** real estate located abroad; ~**güter** foreign assets; ~**guthaben** foreign deposits; funds deposited abroad; ~**hilfe** external aid, foreign aid, aid to overseas countries; ~**investitionen** investments abroad; ~**kapital** foreign capital, foreign capital groups, foreign in-

Auslandskontakte

vestors; ~**kontakte** contacts abroad; ~**konten** accounts in foreign banks; ~**korrespondent** foreign correspondent; employee in charge of foreign correspondence; ~**kredit** credit facilities abroad; ~**markt** foreign (*or* external) market; ~**nachfrage** demand from abroad; ~**niederlassung** branch office in a foreign country, business establishment abroad; ~**patent** foreign patent, patent granted abroad; ~**postanweisung** international money order; ~**preise** prices abroad; ~**provisionsvertreter** foreign commission agent, foreign representative; ~**reise** journey overseas, trip abroad, travel to foreign countries; ~**rente** pension payable to a foreigner residing abroad, foreign social security pension; ~**saldo** net balance on foreign business accounts; ~**scheck** foreign cheque (*US: check*), foreign currency cheque, cheque drawn on a foreign bank; ~**schulden** foreign liabilities, debts abroad, foreign debts, external debts; ~**schuldverschreibungen** external bond(s); ~**status** position in a foreign market, external status; ~**stelle** office for foreign affairs, foreign agency; ~**strafregister** criminal register of offences committed abroad; ~**straftaten** offences committed abroad; ~**stück** foreign-owned certificate (*of a bond, share, etc*); ~**umsatz** international sales, turnover in foreign markets, export sales, foreign sales; *unsichtbare ~umsätze: invisible trade abroad*; ~**verbindlichkeiten** external liabilities, liabilities to non-residents; ~**vermögen** external assets, property situate(d) abroad, foreign possession; ~**verschuldung** external borrowing, indebtedness to foreign creditors, foreign indebtedness; ~**vertreter** representative abroad, overseas representative; ~**vertretungen** diplomatic and consular missions abroad, diplomatic and consular agencies; ~**währung** foreign currency; ~**wechsel** foreign bill of exchange, external bill; ~**werte** foreign securities, foreign quotations; ~**wertpapierbereinigungsverfahren** external securities validation procedure; **a~wirksam** *adj* effective in other countries, valid abroad; ~**wohnsitz** foreign domicile, residence abroad (*cf Wohnsitz*); ~**zulage** expatriation allowance, foreign service allowance; ~**zustellung** service beyond national jurisdiction, service abroad.

auslassen *v/t* to leave out, to omit, to pass over, to skip.

Auslassung *f* omission, omittance; **versehentliche** ~ accidental omission.

auslasten *v/t* to use to capacity, to utilize to the full.

Auslastung *f* utilization, degree of utilization, engagement to capacity, load factor.

Auslaufen *n* expiry (*of a period of time*), phasing out, gradual termination; running out (*production*).

auslaufen *v/i* to be phased out (*legal provisions*), to expire (*period of time*), to run out (*production*), to be in its final stage, to be discontinued.

Auslaufkosten *pl* run-down costs, phasing-out costs.

Auslaufzeit *f* time of departure.

auslegen *v/t* (*1*) to display (*goods*), to exhibit, to make available for inspection (*patent specification*).

auslegen *v/t* (*2*) to interpret, to construe; **einschränkend** ~ to interpret (construe) restrictively; **eng** ~ to interpret (construe) restrictively (or strictly), to give a narrow interpretation; **falsch** ~ to misconstrue, to misinterpret; **großzügig** ~ to interpret liberally; **weit** ~ to interpret (construe) widely, to give abroad interpretation.

Auslegehalle *f* public inspection hall (*in patent office*), display room.

Auslegeschrift *f* patent specification *laid open to public inspection*, second publication.

Auslegung *f* interpretation (= *i*), construction, reading; ~ **von Gesetzen** statutory *i*; **abweichende** ~ divergent *i*; **althergebrachte** ~ orthodox *i*, traditional *i*; **authentische** ~ official (authentic) *i*; **begriffliche** ~, conceptual *i*; doctrinal *i* (*not related to context*); **buchstäbliche** ~ literal *i*; **einschränkende** ~ restrictive *i*; **enge** ~ narrow *i*, strict *i*, close *i*; **grammatikalische** ~ grammatical *i*; **großzügige** ~ liberal *i*; **gültige** ~ valid *i*; ~~ *e-s Gesetzes*: *official interpretation of an Act;* **konventionelle** ~ orthodox *i*; **richterliche** ~ judicial construction; **sinngemäße** ~ equitable construction; logical *i*; **sinnwidrige** ~ misinterpretation, *i* incompatible with the context, misleading *i*; **strenge** ~ strict *i*; **unzulässig weite** ~ extravagant *i*, too wide an *i*; **vereinbarte** ~ agreed *i*; **vergleichende** ~ comparative *i*; **weite** ~ wide *i*, broad *i*, liberal construction; **wörtliche** ~ literal *i*.

Auslegungs|bedürftigkeit necessity of interpretation (*due to ambiguity*); ~**bestimmung** interpretation clause; ~**freiheit** permissible (extent of) interpretation; ~**grundsätze** canons of construction, basic (or fundamental) principles of construction; ~**protokoll** minutes on (agreed) interpretation; ~**regel** rule of interpretation (*or* construction), *pl* ~*n* canons of construction, rules of construction; *einheitliche* ~~*n*: *common interpretation;* ~**vorschrift** *statutory* rule(s) of interpretation.

Auslegungsfrist *f* presentation period.

Ausleihe *f* lending (out); issuing desk (*library*); ~**- und Diskontgeschäft** *n* bank loans and discounts; ~**verpflichtung** lending obligation; ~~*n der Gläubiger*: *creditors' obligations to grant loans*.

Ausleihen *m* lending (*money by banks*); borrowing (*book from library*).

ausleihen *v/t* to lend (*money*), to borrow (*temporarily; book from library, tool from fellow-worker*).

Ausleiher *m* lender, borrower (= *Entleiher qv*); (= *Verleiher qv*).

Ausleihung *f* lending (*by bank*); *pl* ~*en*: *total lendings;* ~**sgrenzen** lending limits, lending ceiling; ~**skapital** loan capital, revolving fund; ~**squote** lending ratio; ~**sstand** amount of lendings (loans) outstanding; **langfristige** ~ long-term lending, long-term loans.

Auslese *f* selection, process of selection, shakeout, sifting; ~**prüfung** competitive examination, selection examination (*or* test); **negative** ~ adverse selection (*insurance risks*).

auslieferbar *adj* (1) = *lieferbar qv*; (2) extraditable, deportable.

ausliefern *v/t* to deliver (*from storage or production*); to extradite.

Auslieferschein *n written authority to pick up goods from factory or storage*.

Auslieferung *f* (1) delivery on sale, surrender, rendition *cf Lieferung*.

Auslieferung *f* (2) extradition.

Auslieferungs|agent distributing agent; ~**anweisung** (1) delivery order (D/O); ~**auftrag** delivery order; ~**buch** delivery book; ~**lager** supply depot (*of distributor*), consignment stock; ~**schein** delivery order; = *Auslieferschein qv*; ~**stelle** publisher's trade counter.

Auslieferungs|abkommen (2) extradition treaty; ~**antrag** request for extradition; ~**beschluß** (*gerichtlich*) writ of extradition; ~**delikt** extraditable offence; ~**ersuchen** extradition request; ~**gesetz** Extradition Act; ~**haft** custody (*or* arrest), pending extradition; ~**haftbefehl** warrant of arrest pending extradition; ~**hindernisse** bars to extradition; ~**pflicht** extradition committal; obligation to extradite; ~**sachen** extradition matters; ~**übereinkommen** extradition convention; ~**verbot** prohibition of extraditing s.o.; ~**verfahren** extradition proceedings; ~**vertrag** extradition treaty; ~**verweige-**

rung refusal to extradite; ~ **von flüchtigen Straftätern** extradition of fugitives, surrender of fugitives.

ausliegen *v/i* to be on display (*goods*), to be available (*for inspection or entry*) (*lists*).

ausloben *v/i* to promise a reward for s.th. (*for finding s.th.; for information leading to arrest*).

Auslobung *f* (public) promise of reward, public offer of a reward, public advertisement of a reward.

auslosbar *adj* redeemable by drawings, callable by lot.

auslöschen *v/t* to delete, to obliterate, to destroy.

Auslöschung *f* deletion, obliteration.

Auslösepreis trigger action price; ~**vorrichtung** trigger mechanism.

auslosen *v/t* to choose by lot, to redeem (*bonds*) by lot.

auslösen *v/t* to trigger (off); to redeem (*pawn, mortgaged property*).

Auslosung *f* drawing (of lots), premature redemption of bonds (*selected by lot*); ~**sanleihe** bond which is redeemable by lot; ~**srecht** right to participate in drawings (*for premature redemption of bonds*).

Auslösung *f* redemption (*pawn, mortgaged property*), daily allowance, separation allowance (*for workers assigned to places other than their usual place of work*); ~**spreis** (*Agrarmarktordnung*) activating price; ~**srecht** right of redemption, right to redeem (*mortgaged property*).

Ausmarkung *f* exclusion of land from local jurisdiction.

Ausmaß *n* extent, size; ~ **des Verschuldens** degree of fault (*or* negligence).

ausmustern *v/t* to clear out, to remove from the inventory.

Ausmusterung *f* exemption from military service.

Ausnahme *f* exception, exemption; ~**bescheinigung** certificate of exemption; ~**bestimmung** exemption clause, extraordinary provision, saving clause; ~**bewilligung** exceptional grant; ~**fall** exceptional case; ~**frachtsätze** differential rates; ~**genehmigung** special permit (*or* licence), exceptional permission; ~**gericht** special tribunal; ~**gesetz** Emergency Act; ~**liste** list of exceptions; ~**preis** exceptional price; ~**recht fremder Staatsangehöriger** special legal status of foreigners; ~**regel** exceptional rule; ~**tarif** special rate(s); ~**verordnung** special ordinance, *statutory instrument concerning exceptions and/or exemptions*; ~ **von der Besteuerung** exemption from taxation; ~**vorschriften** exemption provisions; **mit** ~ **von** except, other than; with the exception of...

Ausnahmezustand *m* state of emergency; **den** ~ **verhängen** declare a state of emergency.

ausnahmsweise *adj* exceptionally, by way of exception, as an exception.

ausnehmen *v/t* to exempt, to make an exception (*from a rule, a charge etc*), to set aside.

Ausnüchterungszelle *f* sobering-up cell.

Ausnutzung *f* utilization, exploitation, taking undue advantage (of s. o.); ~**sspielraum der Kapazitäten** margin of employable capacity; ~ **des innerstaatlichen Rechtsweges** exhaustion of local (domestic) remedies; **mißbräuchliche** ~ abuse; ~~ **e-r beherrschenden Stellung**: *improper exploitation of a dominant position*.

ausnutzen *v/t* to utilize, to exploit (*resources*), to use to capacity (*plant*), to take advantage (*of s. o.'s weakness*).

auspfänden *v/t* to levy upon completely, to sell out, to distrain upon all belongings of a debtor, to strip a debtor of all belongings by execution.

ausplaudern *v/t* to disclose, to divulge, to let out (*a secret*).

ausplündern *v/t* to pillage, to sack, to loot, to ransack.

ausprobieren *v/t* to test, to sample, to try out.

ausradieren *v/t* to erase, to rub out, *pol mil* to wipe out.

ausrangieren *v/t* to discard (*inventory items*), get rid of (*employee*).

ausräumen *v/t* to vacate, to clear out, to empty (*a room*), to strip, to remove (from); to dispel (*doubts*); to negative (*an inference*); to settle finally (*problems, disputes*).

Ausrede *f* excuse, feeble excuse, pretext.

ausreichen *v/t* to pay out (*loan money*), to make sth available.

Ausreise *f* departure, outward journey; ~**erlaubnis** permission to leave the country; ~**kontrolle** exit check, check on leaving customs territory; ~**land** country of exit; ~**sperre** prohibition to leave the country; ~**sichtvermerk** exit visa; ~**visum** exit visa.

ausreisen *v/i* to leave (a country), to depart.

Ausreißer *m* (*1*) runaway, fugitive (*2*) faulty product (*or* part) (*quality testing*).

ausrichten *v/t* to align, to bring into conformity (with).

Ausrichtung *f* orientation; alignment, policy, guidance; **sozial- und allgemeinpolitische** ~ social or political policies.

ausrotten *v/t* to exterminate; to eradicate (*evil*), to eliminate.

Ausrottung *f* extermination, eradication.

Ausruf *m* proclamation (*notice*), sudden cry, exclamation; **spontaner** ~ spontaneous exclamation.

ausrufen *v/t* to proclaim, to announce (*over the loudspeaker system*).

Ausrufung *f* proclamation.

ausrüsten *v/t* to equip, to fit out, to furnish, to prepare s. th.; **neu** ~ to retool, to re-equip.

Ausrüster *m* fitter, ship's chandler.

Ausrüstung *f* equipment (*plant*), finish(ing) (*textiles*); ~**güter** (items of) equipment, furnishing and fittings; production equipment; ~**sinvestitionen** equipment investment, production investment, investment for plant and machinery; ~**skosten** tooling costs, equipment costs; ~**svermietung** equipment leasing; ~**sversicherung** equipment insurance.

Aussage *f* testimony, statement of a witness (oral) evidence; ~ **e-s Sachverständigen** expert('s) testimony; ~**erpressung** extortion of statements (*in police interrogation*), sweating (*US*); ~**freiheit** liberty to testify; ~**genehmigung** permission to give evidence (*by superior authority*); ~**kraft** legal weight given to evidence, probative strength; ~**(n) des Angeklagten** statements by the accused; ~**notstand** testimony under duress; ~**pflicht** duty to give evidence, compulsory testimony; ~**protokoll** deposition, record of evidence, minutes of the examination of a witness; ~ **unter Eid** evidence on oath, sworn testimony; ~**verweigerung** refusal to testify, refusal to give evidence (*court*); refusal to answer questions (*police*); ~~ *des Angeklagten*: silence *of* accused; ~**verweigerungsrecht** → *Aussageverweigerungsrecht;* ~**wert** indicative value; evidentiary value of testimony; **abträgliche** ~ detrimental testimony; **belastende** ~ incriminating testimony (*or* evidence); **beschworene** ~ = *eidliche* ~ *qv*; **die** ~ **verweigern** to refuse to give evidence; **eidliche** ~ sworn testimony, sworn evidence; **e-e** ~ **beschwören** to swear that evidence is true; **e-e** ~ **widerrufen** to retract a statement; **falsche uneidliche** ~ false unsworn testimony; **freiwillige** ~ voluntary statement; **nichteidliche** ~ unsworn statement; **unbeeidigte** ~ unsworn testimony, unsworn evidence, unsworn statement; **uneidliche** ~ unsworn testimony, unsworn evidence, unsworn statement; **widersprechende** ~**n** (= *widersprüchliche* ~*n*) divergent testimonies, conflicting evidence; **zur falschen** ~ **verleiten** to suborn.

aussagen *v/i, v/t* to testify, to give evidence; **falsch** ~ to give false evidence.

Aussageverweigerungsrecht *n* privilege to refuse to give evidence; ~ **des Rechtsanwalts** legal professional privilege, privilege of lawyers; ~ **des Zeugen** privilege of witness; ~ **wegen Gefahr der Selbstbezichtigung** right against self-incrimination; **anwaltschaftliches** ~ attorney-client privilege, privilege of communications between client and solicitor; **berufliches** ~ professional privilege; **durch ein** ~ **geschützte Mitteilung** privileged communication, privileged information; **sich auf das** ~ **berufen** to claim privilege.

ausschalten *v/t* to eliminate (*adversary*), to rule out.

Ausschaltung *f* elimination; ~ **der Konkurrenz** elimination of competition; ~ **des Überraschungsmoments** elimination of the element of surprise (*criminal procedure*).

Ausschank *m* sale of alcoholic beverages on the premises; ~**genehmigung** = *Schankerlaubnis qv;* ~ **im Lokal** sale of alcoholic beverages on the premises; ~**verbote** prohibitions concerning the on-premise sale of alcoholic beverages; ~**zeiten** licensing hours.

Ausscheiden *n* retirement, withdrawal (*partner*), discontinuance; ~ **e-s Gesellschafters** retirement of a partner; ~ **durch Tod** ceasing to hold office due to death; **turnusmäßiges** ~ retirement by rotation.

ausscheiden *v/i* to withdraw, to retire from office, to drop out, to cease to be a member, to set aside (*funds*), to earmark (*money for special purpose*); **turnusmäßig** ~ to retire in (by) rotation, to rotate.

ausscheidend *adj* outgoing, retiring, leaving.

Ausscheidetafel *f* decrement table (*life insurance*).

Ausscheidungsanmeldung *pat f* divisional application, continuation-in-part (application).

Ausscheren *n* lane-switching.
Ausschiffen *n* disembarkation.
Ausschiffungskarte *f* disembarkation card.

ausschlachten *v/t* to cannibalize, to strip the assets of a firm.

Ausschlachtung *f* cannibalization (*dismantling machines etc.*), company stripping.

Ausschlag *m* the deciding factor; **den** ~ **geben** to be decisive, to tip the scales.

ausschlagen *v/t* to decline (*an offer*), to disclaim (*inheritance*), to renounce, to waive (*a right of choice*), to relinquish.

Ausschlagung *f* turning down, (*offer*), disclaimer (*inheritance*), non-acceptance, renouncement, relinquishment; ~ **e-r Erbschaft** renunciation of a succession, disclaimer of inheritance; ~ **e-s Vermächtnisses** disclaimer of legacy; ~**sfrist** period for filing a disclaimer, period during which one may renounce (*term for deliberating on the non-acceptance*); ~**srecht** right to disclaim (*an inheritance or legacy*), jus deliberandi.

ausschließen *v/t* to exclude, to rule out, to preclude (*error, misunderstanding*), to foreclose (*redemption*), to expel (*a member*), to debar (*from entrance*), to disbar (*a barrister*); *to* strike off the roll (*of solicitors*), to bar (*a remedy*), to negative (*a contingency*).

ausschließlich *adj* exclusive, sole; **nicht** ~ non-exclusive.

Ausschließlichkeit *f* exclusivity, exclusiveness; ~ **der Firma** exclusiveness of firm name.

Ausschließlichkeits|bindung exclusive commitment, exclusive dealing; ~**erklärung** assurance of exclusive commitment (*to a bank or firm*); ~**klausel** exclusivity clause, clause providing for exclusive dealing; ~**recht** exclusive right, right to exclude (all others), monopoly right, peremptory right; *geistiges und künstlerisches* ~~: *copyright in literary, dramatic, musical and artistic*

Ausschließung

works; gewerbliches ~~: exclusive industrial property right; **~vereinbarung** exclusivity clause; **~vertrag** exclusive agreement.

Ausschließung *f* exclusion, preclusion, expulsion, disqualification, proscription; **~ aus der Rechtsanwaltschaft** → *Ausschluß;* **~ der Öffentlichkeit** excluding the public (from the court room); **~ e-s Gesellschafters** expulsion of a partner *or* member; **~sbescheid** notice of preclusion; **~sfrist** = *Ausschlußfrist qv*; **~srecht** right of exclusion; **~urteil** court order to exclude a partner; **~sverfügung** exclusion order.

Ausschluß *f* exclusion, preclusion, foreclosure, expulsion, disbarment (*cf ausschließen*); **~ aus der Rechtsanwaltschaft** disbarment, striking off the roll; **~ bei unvorhergesehenen Ereignissen** unforeseen contingencies excepted; **~ der Aufrechnung** exclusion of set-off: *payment shall be made without set-off for any claim arising*; **~ der Brieferteilung** clause excluding right to issue mortgage certificate; **~ der Doppelbesteuerung** avoidance of double taxation; **~ des allgemeinen Gerichtsstandes** exclusion of general jurisdiction; **~frist** time bar, preclusive period, preclusive time limit; *jmdm e–e ~~ setzen:* to foreclose s.o.; **~ jeder Haftung** exclusion of all liability; **~frist** term of preclusion, preclusive period; **~klausel** exclusivity stipulation; **~recht** power (or right) to expel; **~urteil** judgment barring claims, exclusory judgment; **~ wegen eigenen Interesses** disqualification because of personal interest (*partiality*); **unter ~ aller persönlichen Einwendungen** (*negotiable instruments*), excluding all personal objections; **unter ~ der Gefahr** without risk; **unter ~ der Öffentlichkeit** excluding the public, in closed court, in camera; *~~~~ verhandeln: to sit in camera, to sit in closed court*; **unter ~ des**

Ausschreitung

Rechtsweges without recourse to courts of law, no legal recourse; **unter ~ der Zollbelastung** excluding customs duties; **unter ~ jeder Diskriminierung** on a non-discriminatory basis; **unter ~ jeder Haftung** without liability whatsoever; **unter ~ jeder Sachmängelhaftung** excluding all liabilities for defects; **unter ~ von** excluding; **zeitweiliger ~** suspension.

ausschöpfen *v/t* to exhaust (*remedies, reserves*), to deplete.

Ausschöpfung *f* exhaustion; full utilization; **~ des Rechtsweges** exhaustion of legal remedies; full utilization of one's rights of appeal.

ausschreiben *v/t* to write out (*invoice, receipt*), to offer (by public announcement) (*position, reward*), to invite tenders, to put up for tender; **öffentlich ~** to invite tenders.

Ausschreibung *f* public tender, tendering (for), (notice of) invitation to tender, invitation to bid (*or* to apply), allocation by tenders, *(US:)* request for bids; **an e–r ~ teilnehmen** to participate in a tender; **beschränkte ~** limited invitation to tender; **durch ~** by tender; **erstmalige ~** initial invitation for tenders; **freie ~** competitive bidding; **nachträgliche ~** subsequent request for proposal; **offene ~** unrestricted invitation to tender; **staatliche ~** government tender.

Ausschreibungs|bedingungen terms of the tender; **~frist** deadline for filing tender, bidding period; **~garantie** tender guarantee; **~konsortium** bidding syndicate; **~schluß** closing date (for tenders); **~verfahren** competitive bidding, bidding procedure; *offenes ~~: free competitive bidding*; **~verpflichtung** obligation to invite applications (*for position of employee*), obligation to put out to public tender; **~wettbewerb** competitive bidding.

Ausschreitung *f* (*pl ~en*) outrage(s), disturbance(s), tumult, violence, riot.

Ausschuß *m* (1) committee (= *c*); ~**beratung** consultation in *c*, (= *at committee-level, in the committee-stage*); ~**bericht** *c* report; ~**beschluß** *c* resolution; ~ **für Forschung und Technologie** *c* on research and technology; ~ **für Innerdeutsche Beziehungen** *c* on intra-German relations; ~ **für Raumordnung, Bauwesen und Städtebau** *c* on regional planning, construction and urban development; ~ **für Wahlprüfung, Immunität und Geschäftsordnung** *c* on scrutiny of elections, immunities and rules of procedure; ~**mitglied** *c* member; ~**sitzung** *c* meeting; **an einen ~ zurückverweisen** to recommit to a *c*; **auswärtiger ~** foreign affairs *c*; **beratender ~** advisory *c*; consultative *c*; **beschließender ~** *c* with power to pass resolutions, executive *c*; **Dreier~** *c* of three; **e-n ~ einsetzen** to set up a *c*; **engerer ~** small *c*; **federführender ~** main *c*, responsible *c*; **gemischter ~** mixed *c*, joint *c*; **geschäftsführender ~** executive *c*; management *c*; **leitender ~** steering committee; **mitberatender ~** co-advisory *c*; **paritätischer Ausschuß** equally divided bipartisan *c*, *c* set up on a parity basis; **ständiger ~** permanent *c*, standing *c*; **vorberatender ~** predeliberating *c*, preparatory *c*.

Ausschuß *m* (2) spoilage, rejects, spoiled work, outcast; ~**prozentsatz** scrap factor; ~**quote** reject quota; ~**ware** rejects, throw-outs, spoils, imperfects.

ausschütten *v/t* to distribute (*dividends, profits*), to pay (out).

Ausschüttung *f* payout, distribution (*dividends, profits*); amount distributed; ~**sanspruch** claim for distribution, right to receive dividends; **a~sfähig** distributable; ~**ssatz** payout rate; **steuerfreie ~en** tax-free distributions; **zur ~ kommender Gewinn** distributable profits.

Außen|**abteilung** outlying agency, outpost; ~**anlagen** external installations, land improvements (*building*); ~**arbeit** outdoor job; field work; ~**beamter** field worker, field officer, field official; ~**bereich** external sphere, external undeveloped land, open country; **im ~~:** *extramural*; ~**beruf** outdoor occupation; ~**bezirke** outer districts, outlying districts; ~**bezirk e-r Gefangenenanstalt** jail liberties, prison area; ~**bilanz** balance of payments; ~**dienst** field service; ~~*leiter:* field sales executive; ~~*mitarbeiter:* field worker, solo representative, staff salesman, travelling salesman, *pl* outdoor staff, staff salesman; ~**finanzierung** external financing; ~**gebäude** outbuilding; ~**grenzen der Gemeinschaft** the Community's external frontiers; ~**haftung** external liability; ~**handel →** *Außenhandel*; ~**markt** external market; ~**investitionsrecht** law on external investments; ~**minister** foreign minister, *GB*: Foreign Secretary, Secretary of State for Foreign and Commonwealth Affairs, *US*: Secretary of State; (*Commonwealth*:) Minister of External Affairs; ~**ministerium** Foreign Ministry, Foreign Office (= *The Foreign and Commonwealth Office*) *GB*, State Department (= *Department of State*) *US*; ~**montage** field assembly, field installation; ~**montagelöhne** field installation wages; ~**politik** foreign policy; ~**prüfer** external auditor *or* examiner; ~**prüfung** field auditing, independent audit; ~**revision** independent post audit; ~**revisor** travel(l)ing auditor; ~**seiter** outsider, maverick; unorganized labour and management; ~**stand** account, outstanding debt, amount owing, item to be collected; *pl* Außenstände → *Außenstände*; ~**stehender** third party, stranger, outsider; uninitiated layman; ~**stelle** field office, outside agency, branch office; ~**steuer** external (involvement) tax (*tax assessments resulting*

Außenhandel / **Äußerung**

from international or other external connections); ~**steuerrecht** law of external taxation ~**tarif** external customs tariff; ~**umsatz** sales to outside parties; ~**umsatzerlöse** (proceeds from) external sales, customer sales; ~**verhältnis** external relationship, relation to the outside world, relation to third parties; ~**wanderung** external migration; ~**welt** the outside world; *streng von der* ~~ *abgeschlossen*: incommunicado; ~**werbung** outdoor advertizing; ~**wert** external value; *der gewogene* ~~: *the trade-weighted rate*; ~**wirkung** effect on the outside world, effect as against others; ~**wirtschaft** foreign trade, external economy, international economic relations; a~**wirtschaftlich** *adj* pertaining to foreign trade; ~**wirtschaftsgesetz** External Economic Relations Act (*D 1961, as amended, 1971 AWG*); ~**wirtschaftsverkehr** foreign trade and payments; ~**zoll** external tariff, *pl:* (~*zölle*) external duties; ~**zollsatz** external rate of duty.

Außenhandel *m* external trade, foreign trade; ~ **mit Gütern** visible trade.

Außenhandels|bank foreign trade bank (*authorized to handle foreign exchange transactions*); ~**beirat** foreign trade advisory council; ~**bilanz** foreign trade balance; ~**defizit** trade gap; ~**kaufmann** import and export merchant, international trader; ~**klima** export climate; ~**monopol** foreign trade monopoly; a~**orientiert** *adj* adapted (geared) to foreign trade; ~**partner** foreign trade partner (*a state or a business enterprise*); ~**platz** foreign trade centre; ~**statistik** foreign trade statistics, import/export statistics; ~**stelle** foreign trade agency; ~**überschuß** trade surplus; ~**verflechtung** interlocking relationship with international trade; ~**vertretung** foreign trade mission; ~**volumen** total foreign trade turnover.

Außenstände *m/pl* receivables, debts due and owing, active debts, book debts, outstanding debts, money owing, sums of money due and owing; **abgetretene** ~ assigned accounts; **diverse** ~ sundry debtors; **langfristige** ~ accounts receivable; **nicht beitreibbare** ~ bad debts.

außer|betrieblich external (to the enterprise), non-operational; ~**börslich** over the counter, in the outside market; ~**dienstlich** off duty, in a private capacity, outside one's functions; ~**ehelich** extramarital, illegitimate; ~**etatmäßig** extra budgetary; ~**gerichtlich** extrajudicial, out of court, private; ~**gesetzlich** extra-legal; ~**gewöhnlich** extraordinary; ~**ordentlich** anomalous, extraordinary, exceptional; ~**parlamentarisch** extra-parliamentary; ~**planmäßig** extraordinary, supernumerary (*position*), non-budgetary (*expenditure*); ~**staatlich** out of the state; ~**tariflich** outside the collective agreement (*wages, fringe benefits*).

Außerachtlassen *n* disregard; ~**der im Verkehr erforderlichen Sorgfalt** (driving) without due care and attention.

Außerkraftsetzung *f* abrogation; repeal.

Außerkrafttreten *n* abrogation, repeal, ceasing to be in force, expiration.

Außerkurssetzen *n* demonetization, withdrawal from circulation; suspension of a quotation (*stock exchange*).

Außerkurssetzung *f* = *Außerkurssetzen qv*.

Äußerlichkeiten *f/pl* externals, appearances, formalities.

äußern to utter, to enunciate, to express, to state (one's opinion).

Äußerung *f* utterance, remark, statement; ~**en in Wort und Schrift** words spoken or written; ~**stheorie** doctrine of utterance (*of legal intention*); **dienstliche** ~ official statement, official comment (*by* *a judge or civil servant*); **ehrenrührige** ~ disparaging statement; **geringschätzige** ~ disparaging statement; **gutachtliche** ~ expertise, expert's view; **herabsetzende** ~ disparaging statement, degrading remarks, aspersion; **hochverräterische** ~(en) seditious utterance(s); **zustimmende** ~ assenting opinion, "pro", assent.

Außerverfolgungsetzung *f* discharge by the court before completion of trial, quashing (of case).

Aussetzen *n* suspension (*of proceedings, execution*); promise (*reward, prize*), grant (*bequest*).

aussetzen *v/t* to suspend temporarily, to stay; to discontinue; to promise publicly (*reward*), to expose, to abandon (*children, helpless persons*); to subject to sth.

Aussetzung *f* (*1*) suspension, stay; ~ **der Strafe zur Bewährung** suspension of sentence on probation; ~ **der (Straf)Vollstreckung** stay of execution; ~ **der Zwangsvollstreckung** suspension of (civil) execution (upon a judgment); ~ **des Verfahrens** suspension of proceedings.

Aussetzung *f* (*2*) exposure, abandonment (*children, helpless persons*).

Aussetzung *f* (*3*) public offer; ~ *e–r Belohnung*: *offering of a reward*.

Aussicht *f* prospect, opportunity; ~**enprüfung** examination of prospects of success (*litigation, appeal etc*) **hinreichende** ~ reasonable prospect (*of . . .*).

Aussiedler *m* repatriate; *repatriated German national or ethnic German*; newly settled farmer; ~**hof** new farm in the open country, new farm settlement.

Aussiedlung *f* isolated farm settlement.

aussöhnen *v/reflex* to reconcile.

Aussöhnung *f* reconciliation.

Aussöhnungsgebühr *f* reconciliation fee (*of lawyer in a divorce case*).

aussondern *v/t* to segregate, to release from bankrupt's estate.

Aussonderung *f* assertion of rights of ownership against the bankrupt's estate, segregation from s.o.'s estate.

Aussonderungs|anspruch claim for release from bankrupt's estate; **a~berechtigt** entitled to release from bankrupt's estate (*as not belonging to the bankrupt*); **a~fähig sein** to be severable from bankrupt's estate, not to be in the bankrupt's order and disposition; ~**gläubiger** creditor entitled to recovery (*and repossession of goods not belonging to bankrupt debtor*); ~**recht** (*bankruptcy:*) right of separation and recovery (*from bankrupt's estate*), right of reclamation, right of seclusion, right to segregation; ~**verfahren** reclamation proceedings, segregation proceedings.

Ausspähen *n* spying out clandestinely.

aussperren *v/t* to lock out.

Aussperrung *f* lockout.

Ausspielung *f* drawing of a lottery; **öffentliche** ~ public lottery.

Aussprache *f* discussion, dialogue; **freie** ~ wide-ranging debate, free discussion.

aussprechen *v/t*, to pronounce, to pass sentence; *v/reflex* **sich für etwas** ~ to advocate; **sich gegen etwas** ~ to declare oneself against s.th.

Ausspruch *m* award, pronouncement; ~ **im Schiedsverfahren** arbitral award; **richterlicher** ~ judicial pronouncement, court award.

Ausstand *m* strike, walkout.

Ausstandsverzeichnis *n* list of outstanding debts (*for social security contributions*).

ausstatten *v/t* to furnish, to equip (*rooms, business enterprise*), to equip, to clothe, to vest (*s.o. with powers*), to endow (*with capital*), to confer (*powers*).

Ausstattung *f* equipment, furnishings, (*rooms, enterprise*); terms of issue (*bonds etc*), endowment (*capital, foundation*); advancements (*for children*); get-up (*outward appearance and presentation of goods*), style of pack-

ausstehen   **Austritt**

age; ~ **e- r Anleihe** terms of a loan; ~**sbeihilfe** *initial assistance to children helping them to become independent*; ~**sschutz** protection of style of packing, protection of typical get-up and appearance of goods; ~**sversicherung** child endowment insurance; **einmalige** ~ once-and-for-all allocation; **finanzielle** ~ funding; **irreführende** ~ misleading presentation of goods; **serienmäßige** ~ standard equipment of the series; **technische** ~ technical equipment, machinery; **ungenügende** ~ underfunding.

ausstehen *v/i* to be owed, to be overdue (*payments*), to be pending (*court decision*).

ausstehend *adj* outstanding, unpaid.

ausstellen *v/t* to issue (*passport, document*), to make (out) (*receipt*), to draw up, to exhibit (*goods*), to display.

Aussteller *m* drawer (*bill of exchange*), issuer (*securities, debentures*), maker, giver (*promissory note*), (*debentures*), exhibitor (*participant in exhibition*); ~ **e-r eidesstattlichen Versicherung** affirmant; ~**haftung** liability of drawer; „**zurück an den** ~" (*bei ungedecktem Scheck*) refer to drawer (*R/D*), returned to drawer.

Ausstellung *f* (1) drawing (*bill of exchange*); issue (*documents, passport, securities*); ~ **e-r Urkunde** issue of a certificate, execution of a document; ~**sdatum** date of issue; ~ **von ungedeckten Schecks** drawing of uncovered cheques; ~**sort** place of drawing, place of issue; ~**stag** day of issue.

Ausstellung *f* (2) exhibition, exposition, show; ~**sbescheinigung** certificate of exhibition; ~**sgelände** exhibition site, exhibition grounds; ~**sgut** exhibited articles; ~**slokal** show-room; ~**sschutz** patent protection of recent display at an exhibition; ~**sstück** artifact.

Ausstellung *f* (3) layoff, dismissal of workers.

Aussteuer trousseau, dowry; ~**versicherung** child endowment insurance, children's assurance.

aussteuern *v/t* to provide a dowry; *ausgesteuert werden: to exhaust sickness insurance cover* (*due to extremely protracted illness*).

Aussteuerung *f* premature payment of benefits in full discharge of accrued social insurance.

Ausstoß *m* output (*production*).

ausstoßen *v/t* to expel, to discharge dishono(u)rably.

Ausstoßung *f* expulsion (*of a member*), dishono(u)rable discharge (*soldier*).

Ausstrahlung *f* exhibition.

ausstreichen *v/t* to delete, to cross out, to strike (from the record), to rule out.

Ausstreichung *f* deletion, erasure.

ausstreuen *v/t* to disseminate, to spread (*rumours*).

Ausstreuung *f* dissemination, spreading.

Aussuchen *n* sorting, selection.

aussuchen *v/t* to choose, to pick, to sort out, to select.

Austausch *m* exchange, interchange; substitution (*of worn-out or defective parts*); ~ **der Ratifikationsurkunden** exchange of the instruments of ratification; ~**dienst** exchange service (*students*); ~**geschäft** barter transaction; ~**pfändung** levy upon a valuable indispensable item of property and replacing it by a simple and inexpensive one; ~**relation** terms of trade; ~**vertrag** reciprocal agreement; ~**volumen** volume of exports and imports; ~ **von Gefangenen** exchange of prisoners (of war); ~ **von Lizenzen** cross licences.

austauschbar *adj* interchangeable.

Austauschbarkeit *f* interchangeability.

Austrag *m* retirement of a farmer (*continuing to live on the farm*).

austragen *v/t* to take the matter to court, to litigate (*not to compromise*).

austreten *v/i* to resign from membership, to withdraw.

Austritt *m* resignation of member-

102

ship, withdrawal, retirement, dissociation; ~ **e-s Mitglieds** withdrawal of a member; **~serklärung** notice of withdrawal.

ausüben v/t to exercise, to practise.

Ausübung f exercise (*rights*), execution (*official duties*); ~ **der Gerichtsbarkeit** exercise of jurisdiction; ~ **der öffentlichen Gewalt** exercise of public (*or* official) authority; ~ **des Anwaltsberufes** practice of law; ~ **des Dienstes** discharge of duty, exercise of official function(s); ~ **des Ermessens** exercise of discretion; ~ **e-r Banktätigkeit** exercise of the banking profession, banking; ~ **e-r Befugnis** excercise of a faculty (*or* power); ~ **e-r Erfindung** application of an invention; ~ **e-s Amtes** execution of an office, exercise of a function, performance of one's duty; ~ **e-s Rechts** exercise of a right; **~sfrist** period of time for the exercise of (*an option*); **~srecht** right of use(r) (*industrial property rights*); **~szwang für Patente** compulsory application of patents; **in ~ öffentlicher Funktionen** in the discharge of public functions; **unbefugte ~ e-s Berufs** unauthorized practice of a profession or vocation, practising without a licence; **unbefugte ~ e-s öffentlichen Amtes** usurpation of public office; **unerlaubte ~ e-s Berufs** illicit (*or* unlawful) practice of a profession.

Ausverkauf m clearance sale, sale, selling off; ~ **wegen Aufgabe des Geschäfts** liquidation sale (*of a company*); closing-down sale (*of a shop*); **~sware** sale goods.

ausverkaufen v/t to sell out, to sell off.

ausverkauft adj sold out.

Auswahl f choice, selection, variety; **~aufs Geratewohl** random selection; ~ **der Investitionsobjekte** investment selection; **~erfindung** invention by a special selection of a technical process; **~erklärung** election; **~ermessen** discretionary choice; **~fehler** sampling error; **~frage** multiple-choice question; **~käufe** selective buying; **~kriterium** eligibility criterion; **~plan** sample design; **~prüfung** selective examination; **~richtlinien** selection directives; **~sendung** samples sent for selection; **~verfahren** selection procedure, competition; *gezieltes ~~*: *purposive sample*; **~verschulden** fault in selecting an agent (*culpa in eligendo*); **bewußte ~** purposive sample (*opinion polls*); **geschichtete ~** stratified sample (*opinion polls*); **repräsentative ~** representative sample.

Auswanderer m emigrant; **~beratung** prospective emigrants' advisory service.

auswandern v/i to emigrate.

Auswanderung f emigration; **überseeische ~** emigration overseas.

Auswanderungs|agent passage broker; **~behörde** emigration authority; **~beratungsstelle** advisory board for emigrants; **~freiheit** right of unhindered emigration, freedom to emigrate; **~land** emigration country, target country of emigration, **~betrug** fraudulent enticement to emigrate; **~recht** right of emigration; **~überschuß** excess of emigration (*as compared to immigration*); **~wesen** emigration matters.

auswärtig adj exterior, foreign.

Auswärtiger Dienst m (*der Auswärtige Dienst*) Foreign Service.

Auswärtiges Amt n (*das Auswärtige Amt*) Federal Foreign Office (*D*), the Foreign and Commonwealth Office *GB*, State Department *US*.

auswechselbar adj interchangeable.

auswechseln v/t to exchange, to replace.

Auswechselung f exchange, replacement.

ausweichen v/i to evade; to avoid oncoming traffic, to get out of the way.

Ausweichklausel f escape clause.

Ausweichmöglichkeit f chance of avoiding (*accident*), evading (*question*), loophole (*in the law*), alternative (*logic*); **letzte ~** last opportunity of escape (*or* evasion).

Ausweis m (1) proof of identity, means of identification; identity card (*ID*); identification document, pass, laissez-passer; **~einziehung** cancellation of identification document; **~fälschung** forgery of identification document; **~kontrolle** identity control; identification check; **~mißbrauch** misuse of identification papers; **~papiere** identification documents, identity papers; **~pflicht** obligation to carry identification papers, requirement in respect of publication; **~wesen** identity card matters, issue of identification papers.

Ausweis m (2) bank return; **~posten** item in the return; **~schema** form of return; breakdown; **~Stichtag** bank-return date; **zusammengefaßter ~** combined return.

ausweisen v/t (1) to show (*in the accounts*), to disclose; to present, to itemize, to report; v/reflex (*sich ~*) to identify oneself; to prove one's identity, to establish one's identity, to produce identification.

ausweisen v/t (2) to expel, to order to leave a country, to deport.

Ausweisung f (1) entry in the accounts, showing, proof of identity.

Ausweisung f (2) expulsion, deportation; **~ aus dem Besitz** dispossession

Ausweisungs|antrag official request for expulsion; **~befehl** order to leave the country, deportation order; **~beschluß** deportation order; **~schutz** legal protection against deportation; **~verfahren** alien deportation proceedings.

ausweislich prep according to, as shown in, as evidenced by, as appears from.

ausweispflichtig adj subject to disclosure in the accounts; required to be entered in the accounts.

auswerten v/t to evaluate (*data*), to utilize, to exploit (*invention*).

Auswertung f evaluation, utilization, exploitation; **~ der Bilanzen** analysis of balance sheets; **~ von Entdeckungen** utilization of discoveries.

Auswiegen n weighing-in, exact weighing.

auswiegen v/t to weigh (exactly).

"aus wohlunterrichteten Kreisen" on good authority.

auszahlen v/t to pay (*a sum of money*; *wages etc*), to pay off (*a partner, co-heirs*), to distribute (*profits*).

Auszahlung f payout, disbursement; **~ der Gerichtskasse** payment out of court; **~ der Kreditvaluta** paying out loan funds; **~ gesperrt** payment stopped; **~ von Einlagen** payment of bank deposits (*to customer*); **~von Hinterlegungsgeldern** payment out (of court); **telegrafische ~** cable (*or*) telegraphic transfer; **vorfristige ~** early payment.

Auszahlungs|anweisung instruction to pay, payment voucher; **~beleg** voucher, cash voucher; **~berechtigung** authorization of payment; **~ermächtigung** authority to pay; **~kurs** net percentage of loan paid to borrower, out-payment rate; **~schein** payment slip; **~ssperre** stop payment order; **~stelle** payment agency; **~überschuß** excess of out-payments; **~verfügung** payment order; **~wert** net proceeds (*of disposition of property*).

auszählen v/t to make a full count.

Auszählung f count, counting; **~ der Stimmen** official counting of the votes.

auszeichnen v/t to tag, to mark the price, to price.

Auszeichnung f marking of price (*on goods*) (*openly or in code*).

ausziehen v/i (1) to vacate (*premises*), to move out, to quit.

ausziehen *v/t* (2) to extract *(figures from accounts)*.

Auszubildender *m* *("Azubi")* trainee, apprentice; pupil *(trainee barrister)*, articled clerk *(trainee solicitor)*, ~**envertretung** representative body of apprentices.

Auszug *m* (1) removal, moving out *(from house etc)*, walkout *(opposition from parliament)*; ~**svertrag** agreement to vacate premises *(voluntarily, waiving eviction)*.

Auszug *m* (2) excerpt, extract, statement (of account); (bank) summary; ~ **aus dem Handelsregister** extract from the commercial register; ~ **aus den Grundakten** extract from the land registry file; ~ **aus dem Strafregister** extract from the register of previous convictions; ~ **aus der Konkurstabelle** *(enforceable)* extract from the bankrupty schedule; **e-n ~ machen** to make an extract.

autark *adj* self-supporting *(economically)*, autarchic.

Autarkie *f* autarchy, absolute sovereignty, (policy of) national self-sufficiency.

Autobahn *f* autobahn *(in Germany)*, superhighway, freeway *US*, motorway, dual two-lane motorway *GB*; ~~**-amt** motorway office; Autobahn administration; ~**ausfahrt** motorway exit; ~**gebühr** *(superhighway etc)* toll; ~**kontrollpunkt** (autobahn) checkpoint; ~**zubringer** motorway slipway, feeder road *(to an autobahn)*.

Autodidakt *m* self-educated person, self-made man.

Auto|**diebstahl** car theft; ~**fähre** roll-on, roll-off ferry; ~**fahrer** driver, motorist; ~**fahrergruß** offensive gesture by another motorist; ~**falle** criminal highway trap; police trap *(on highway)*, speed trap; ~**führer** = *Kraftfahrzeugführer qv*; ~**haftpflichtversicherung** third party motor insurance; (statutory) motor vehicle liability insurance; car insurance against third party risk; ~**halter** = *Kraftfahrzeughalter qv*; ~**händler** car dealer; ~**händlerhaftpflicht** automobile dealer's risk; ~**insassenunfallversicherung** = *Insassenunfallversicherung qv*; ~~**-Kaskoversicherung** = *Kraftfahrzeug-Kaskoversicherung qv*; ~**schalter** drive-in teller; ~**unfall** car accident, road traffic accident; ~**vermietung** car rental (service).

Autokrat *m* autocrat.

Autokratie *f* autocracy.

Automat *m* automatic machine, slot machine, → *Verkaufsautomat*; ~**enaufstellung** contract authorizing placement of an automatic *(vending or dispensing)* machine; ~**endiebstahl** theft from a vending machine; ~**enmietvertrag** rental agreement for vending machines; ~**enmißbrauch** purloining (vending) machines, misuse of vending machines; ~**enplatz** automatic work station, place of installation for vending machine, vending machine location.

Automatik *f* automatism; **marktwirtschaftliche** ~ automatic working of the free market, free-market automatism.

Automatismus *m* automatism; *state or quality of being automatic*.

Automobil|**aktien** motor shares; ~**haftpflichtversicherung** *statutory* automobile third party risk insurance; ~**halter** *m* = *Kraftfahrzeughalter qv*.

autonom *adj* autonomous, self-regulating, independent.

Autonomie *f* autonomy, regionalism; ~**recht** right to autonomous administration.

Autopsie *f* autopsy, post-mortem (examination), necrocopsy.

Autor *m* author, writer.

Autoren|**anteil** author's fee, royalty; ~**exemplar** presentation copy; ~**honorar** author's fee, royalty; ~**rabatt** author's percentage of retail price; ~**manuskript** manuscript; ~**recht** author's rights, copyright.

Autorisation *f* authorization.

autorisieren *v/t* to authorize, to empower, to approve.
Autorisierung *f* authorization.
autoritär *adj* authoritarian.
Autorität *f* authority; ~**smißbrauch** abuse of authority; ~**sverletzung** breach of authority; ~**szeichen** symbol of authority.
autoritativ *adj* authoritative.
Autosuggestion *f* auto-suggestion.
Aval *m* (*rarely: s*) recourse guarantee, bank guarantee (*for customer's benefit*); ~**akzept** collateral acceptance (*by bank*); ~**kredit** guarantee credit; ~**linie** line of guarantee (*by bank*), guarantee line; ~**provision** commission on bank guarantee *or* bank suretyship; ~**wechsel** bill of exchange guaranteed by a bank.
avalieren *v/t* to accept (a bill of exchange) by way of guarantee, to provide a bank guarantee.
Avalierung *f* providing a guarantee *or* suretyship (*spec for bill of exchange or promissory note*).
Avis (*m, s*) notice, advice note; **mangels** ~ for non-advice.
avisieren *v/t* to advise, to notify; **rechtzeitig** ~ to advise in good time.
Azubi *m* (= *Auszubildender*) apprentice, trainee.
azyklisch *adj* acyclic; not cyclic; noncyclic, (*disregarding cyclical trend*).

B

Bagatell|betrag petty sum; **~delikt** petty offence; **~diebstahl** petty theft, pilferage; **~fall** negligible case; **~sache** petty case, trivial matter; **~schaden** trivial damage; **~steuer** trifling tax, secondary tax; **~strafsachen** petty offences, summary offences.

bagatellisieren to minimize; to belittle, to play down; to scorn.

Bahn (*GB.: railway = US: railroad*) **~abzweigung** rail junction, branch line; **b~amtlich** *official(ly) by the railway company*; **~anlagen** railway installations; **~anschluß** rail connection; **~anschlußgleis** railway siding; **~betriebshaftung** statutory liability for railway operation; **~fracht** rail charges, railway freight; **~grundbuch** railway land title register; **~(hofs)- speditionsgesellschaft** railway transfer company, contract carrier; **~körper** road bed, railway trackbed, permanent way; **b~lagernd** left at station to be called for, to be collected at the station; **~polizei** railway police; **b~postlagernd** *adj* to be called for at station office; **~spediteur** railway agent, cartage contractor; **~spedition** haulage from and to railway station; **~transport** rail transport; **~überführung** railway bridge, overpass; **~übergang** level crossing; *beschrankter ~~: crossing with gates (or barriers)*; *niveaugleicher ~~: level crossing, US: grade crossing*; *unbeschrankter ~~: crossing without gates (or barriers)*; **~unterführung** railway underpass; **~zustellung** railway delivery.

bahnbrechend *adj* pioneering, revolutionary.

Baisse *f* slump, drop in the market, sharp fall; **~bewegung** bearish movement; **~engagement** engagement to sell short, engagement to operate for a fall, short position; **~geschäft** short selling, bear transaction; **~lage** bearish market; **~moment** depressive factor; **~position** bear position, short position; **~spekulant** operator for a fall, speculator for a fall, bear, bear seller; **~spekulation** speculation for a fall, bearish operation, bear operation, going short; **~stimmung** bearish mood; **~tendenz** bearish tendency; *auf ~ spekulieren* to operate for a fall, to speculate for a fall, to sell (at) a bear, to sell short; *e-n ~angriff machen* to launch a bear attack; *e-n ~verkauf tätigen* to sell short; *konjunkturelle ~* recessionary slump.

Baissier *m* speculator (= operator) for a fall, bear, short (seller).

Ballast *m* ballast; **~ laden** to go in ballast, to load ballast; **~ladung** ballast; **lebender ~** shifting ballast; **unnötigen ~ abwerfen** to jettison superfluous ballast.

Ballen *m* bundle, bale (*cotton*), pack (*wool, yarn*).

Ballotage *f* secret ballot (*with black and white balls*).

Ballungs|gebiet agglomeration (area); **~raum** *m* congested urban area, conurbation, urban sprawl.

Bancomat *m* cash dispenser, cash point.

Bandaufnahme *f* tape recording.

Bandbreite *f* range of variation, margin of fluctuation, spread (*e. g. exchange rates*), parity band.

Bande *f* (*pl ~ n*) gang.

Banden|diebstahl theft committed by a gang, gang theft; **~mitglied** member of a gang, gangster, member of a terrorist group.

Bandenwerbung *f* background, advertizing on perimeter boards.

Banderole *f pasted label with revenue stamp,* revenue stamp *(on cigarette packs, cigars, liquor);* ~**nsteuer** excise stamp tax *(on pasted labels).*
Bandit *m* bandit, gangster, outlaw.
Bandware(n) *f (pl)* narrow goods, small wares, ribbons.
Bank *f* bank (= *b*), banking house, banking establishment, banker; ~**adresse** *b* address, bank as reference; ~**agent** *b* representative; ~**agio** premium charged by banks *(selling new issue of shares or bonds);* ~**aktien** *b* shares, *b* stock; ~**aktiengesellschaft** banking company, banking corporation; ~**akzept** *b* acceptance credit; banker's acceptance; *fremdes* ~~: *acceptance of another bank; privatdiskontfähige* ~~*e: b acceptances qualifying as prime acceptances;* ~**an-**~ **Kredit** inter-bank lending; ~**angestellter** *b* employee, *b* clerk; ~**anweisung** *b* remittance, order for payment (drawn on a *b*); ~**auftrag** *b* order, instruction to a *b*; ~**auskunft** *b* reference, banker's reference; ~**ausweis** *b* statement; ~**auszug** *b* statement; ~**beamter** *b* official; ~**bedingungen** general terms and conditions of a *b*; ~~**bei-**~**-Einlage** inter-bank deposit; ~**bescheinigung** *b* certificate, *b* confirmation; ~**bestätigung** *b* certificate, *b* confirmation; ~**betrieb** banking activities, banking operations; **b**~**betrieblich** *adj* banking, pertaining to the business of a *b*, **b**~**betriebswirtschaftlich** pertaining to bank management; ~**bezirk** banking area; ~**bilanz** *b* balance sheet; ~**buchhaltung** accounting system of a *b*, the books and accounts of a *b*, accounting department of a *b*; ~**büchlein** savings account pass-book; ~**bürgschaft** *b* guarantee, security note of a bank; ~**darlehen** *b* loan; ~~-**Dauerauftrag** (bank) standing-order, banker's order; ~**deckung** bankable collateral, cover provided by bank; ~**depositen** *b* deposits; ~**depot** safe custody (account) at a *b*; *b* safe; ~**direktor** banking director; *b* manager; ~**diskont** *b* discount, official rate of discount; ~**diskontsatz** *b* discount rate; ~**eigenschaft** *b* status; ~**einbruchsversicherung** *b* burglary insurance; ~**einlage** *b* deposit, savings deposit; ~**einlagenversicherung** guaranty of deposits insurance; ~**fach** bank safe; ~**fachmann** banker, banking specialist; **b**~**fähig** bankable; *nicht* ~: *unbankable;* ~**fähigkeit** eligibility (for borrowing at a bank); bankable nature *(of a bill of exchange);* ~**fazilitäten** bank facilities, credit facilities at a bank; ~**filiale** branch of a *b*; ~**forderungen** outstanding accounts of a *b*; **b**~**fremd** incompatible with sound banking practice, outside the sphere of banking; ~ **für internationalen Zahlungsausgleich** (*BIZ*) Bank for International Settlements; ~**fusion** *b* consolidation, *b* merger; ~**fusionsvertrag** *b* merger agreement; ~**garantie** *b* guarantee, banker's guarantee, standby letter of credit, guarantee credit; ~**garantiefonds** *b* guarantee funds; ~**gebühren** *b* charges; ~**geheimnis** banking secrecy, banker's privilege *(right to refuse testimony);* ~**geld** *b* money, money from banks; ~**geschäft** banking, bank transaction; **b**~**geschäftlich** relating to banking business; ~**gesetz** Act relating to a central *b*, *hist* an Act concerning the Reichsbank *(1875, 1924, 1930);* ~**gesetzgebung** banking legislation; ~**gewerbe** banking, the banking business, the banking trade; **b**~**giriert** *adj* bank-endorsed; ~**giro** *b* giro, transfer under *b* clearing; ~**gläubiger** *b* creditor *(b as a creditor);* ~**guthaben** credit balance with a *b* cash in, stock in; *termingebundene* ~~: *time balances at banks;* ~**guthaben staatlicher Organe** government deposits (with banks); ~**haus** *b*, banking house; ~**institut** banking establishment; ~**justitiar** legal ad-

viser of a *b*, in-house lawyer of a bank; ~**kanäle** banking channels, banking outlets; ~**kapital** capital-stock of a *b*; ~-**Kassenjournal** teller's cash book; ~**kaufmann** banker; ~**konditionen** credit conditions of a *b*; ~**konto** *b* account; *debitorisches* ~~: *b account showing debit balance*; *kreditorisches* ~~: *b account showing credit balance*; *ohne* ~~:*, without a bank account*; ~**konzern** banking group, group of *b–s*; ~**konzerngeschäfte** group banking; ~**krach** *b* (or banking) collapse; banking failure; ~**kredit** *b* credit, credit facilities by *b–s*; ~**kredite an die Wirtschaft** lending by banks to business; ~**kreise** banking circles; ~**krise** banking crisis; ~**kunde** (regular) customer of a *b*; ~**leitzahl** *b* code, (*b's*) number, sorting code; ~**lombardgeschäft** collateral loan business (of banks); **b~mäßig** in accordance with banking procedure, banking *adj or adv*; ~**note** *b* note, *US also b* bill; ~**noten aus dem Verkehr ziehen** to withdraw *b* notes from circulation; ~**notenausgabe** note issue; ~**noten einziehen** to withdraw *b* notes from circulation; ~**notenfälschung** forgery of bank notes; ~**noten in Umlauf setzen** to issue *b* notes, to introduce *b* notes; ~**notenmonopol** monopoly of issuing *b* notes; ~**notenumlauf** notes in circulation, paper circulation; ~**papier** *b* notes, securities issued by a *b*; ~**platz** banking center (*US*), centre (*GB*); ~**politische Fragen** problems of banking policy; ~**preise** *b* charges; ~**prokurist** *Prokurist of a b, holder of b's Prokura, b officer holding full powers of representation (except real estate transactions)* cf *Prokurist*, authorized signatory of a *b*; ~**provision** bank(ing) commission; ~**quittung** *b* receipt; ~**rate** central bank's discount rate cf *Diskontsatz*; ~**raub** *b* holdup, *b* raid; ~**recht** banking law; ~**referenz** banker's reference; ~**rembourskredit** external trade credit facilities (*by banks*); ~**reserve** bank's reserves; ~**revision** *b* audit(s); ~**revisor** *b* auditor, *b* examiner; ~**rücklage** *b's* reserves; ~**safegebühren** safe charges (of a bank); ~**saldo** *b* balance, balance of a *b* account; ~**satz** central bank's discount rate; ~**schalter** *b* counter *automatischer* ~~ *automatic teller machine, care point, automatic cash dispenser;* ~~*bus; mobile bank;* ~**scheck** banker's cheque (*US* check); *b* draft (*cheque or bill drawn by one bank upon another*); ~**schließfach** (customer's) safe; safe deposit box; ~**schulden** *b* debts, due to banks, *b* receivables ~**schuldner** *b's* debtor, borrower from a *b*; ~**schuldverschreibungen** *b* bonds, *b* debentures; ~**sicherheit** security (*usually a guarantee*) posted (provided) by a *b*; ~**sparen** saving through a *b*; ~**sperre** freezing of *b* account (*ordered by court*); ~**spesen** *b* charges; **b~technisch** banking *adj or adv*, according to banking procedure; ~**transaktion** banking operation, banking transaction; ~**tratte** banker's draft; ~**tresor** *b* safe, vault, safe vault; ~**überweisung** *b* transfer, *b* remittance, *b* giro; ~**überweisungsauftrag** *b* payment order; ~**überweisungsformular** *b* giro credit slip; ~**überziehungskredit** *b* overdraft facilities; **b~üblich** in line with banking practice; customary in banking; ~**umsätze** *b* turnover(s); ~**- und Börsenverkehr** banking and stock exchange transactions; ~**unternehmen** banking establishment, *b* enterprise, *b*; ~**unternehmer** banker, owner of a *b*; ~**unterschrift** (formal) *b* signature; ~**usance** banking usage, banking practice; ~**valoren** *b* securities, *b* valuables; ~**verbindlichkeit** *b* liabilities; ~**verbindung** *b* reference; ~**verein** bankers' association; ~**verkehr** inter-bank relations, inter-bank dealings;

Bankvertrag

~**vertrag** *b* contract; ~**vollmacht** power of attorney to a *b*; ~**vorschuß** *b* advance, short term credit by *b*; ~**wechsel** *b* draft, banker's draft, *b* bill, *b* acceptance; ~**welt** the banking world; ~**werte** *b* shares, *b* stock; ~**wesen** banking; ~**wirtschaftlich** banking, relating to the business of banking; ~**woche** bank-return week; ~**wochenstichtag** weekly bank-return date; ~**ziehungen** drawings of bills of exchange *by banks on their customers to provide credit*; ~**zinsen** bank interest; ~-**zu**-~-**Ausleihungen** interbank lendings; ~-**zu**-~-**Kredite** interbank lendings; ~**zulage** bank allowance; ~**zusammenbruch** bank failure, collapse of a *b*; ~**zusammenschlüsse** banking concentration; **angeschlossene** ~ associated *b*, affiliated *b*; **avisierende** ~ advising *b*, notifying *b*; **bei der** ~ **einzahlen** to pay into the *b*; **bezogene** ~ *b* drawn upon, payor *b*; **die** ~ **stellt ihre Zahlungen ein** the *b* closes its doors; **die überweisende** ~the remitting *b*; **die übliche** ~**provision** usual *b* charges; **ein** ~**konto überziehen** to overdraw a *b* account; **eingeschaltete** ~ intermediary *b*; **emittierende** ~ *b* of issue, issuing *b*; **erstschuldende** ~ *b* which is the primary debtor; **falsche** ~**note** dud note, forged *b* note; **federführende** ~ lead *b*, leading *b*; **fremdes** ~**akzept** acceptance of another *b*; **gegenseitige** ~**forderungen** interbank balances; **insolvente** ~ insolvent *b*; **kontoführende** ~ bank in charge of the account(s); **konzessionierte** ~ chartered *b*; **korrespondierende** ~ correspondent *b*; **negoziierende** ~ negotiating *b*; **notleidende** ~ *b* in difficulties; **private** ~**en** private *b–s*; **privatdiskontfähige** ~ *b* which ranks in the prime acceptance category; **seriöse** ~**geschäfte** sound banking; **staatseigene** ~ state-owned *b*; **überregionale** ~ national *b*; **un-**

Bann

seriöses ~**unternehmen** wildcat bank; **verwahrende** ~ custodian *b*; **von der** ~ **nicht zu vertretende Umstände** circumstances not attributable to the *b*; **wie von** ~**seite mitgeteilt wurde** according to information from a banking source; **zahlende** ~ paying banker, paying *b*, payer *b*; **zweckgebundenes** ~**guthaben** earmarked bank account.

Banken|aufsicht banking supervision (*by government*); ~**aufsichtsbehörde** bank supervisory authority; ~**gelder** interbank funds; deposits of banks; ~**geldschöpfung** *bank* money creation; ~**gruppe** banking group; ~**konsortium** *bank* consortium, banking syndicate; ~**kreditoren** balances of other banks and bankers; ~**liquidität** *bank* liquidity; ~**markt** interbank market; ~**moratorium** moratorium by the banks concerned; ~**organisation** banking organization; ~**system** banking system; ~**verfahren** bank procedure; ~**verordnung** bank regulation.

Bankett *n* hard shoulder; **unbefestigtes** ~ soft shoulder.

Bankier *m* banker (*strictly, an individual operating a bank, also used for members of banking partnership and directors of banking corporations*).

Bankrott *s/m* insolvency, insolvency offence; **betrügerischer** ~ fraudulent insolvency offence (*fraudulent preference and/or concealment or removal of insolvent's property*); **einfacher** ~ (simple) insolvency offence.

bankrott *adj* insolvent, broke.

Bankrotteur *m* defaulter, the bankrupt.

Bann *m* interdiction, outlawing; *hist* jurisdiction; privileged protection; power of punishment, interdiction of fire and water; ~**bruch** customs violation, *unlawful import, export or transit of goods without customs clearance*; ~**kreis** = ~**meile** *qv*; ~**kreisverletzung** violation (*or:* infringe-

bar   **Bargeld**

ment) of protected parliamentary zone; ~**meile** precincts *(territory of a town)*; protected zone around a parliament *(where demonstrations are prohibited)*; ~**meilengesetz** protection of parliamentary zone Act; ~**wald** (especially) protected forest; ~**ware** *illegally loaded goods which endanger ship or cargo.*

bar *adj, adv* cash; *in* ~: *in cash, in specie*; *in* ~ *oder in Sachleistungen*: *in cash or in kind.*

Bar|abgeltung discharge by cash payment, cash settlement; ~**abhebung** cash withdrawal; ~**ablösung** cash redemption; ~**ablösungswert** cash redemption value; ~**abschluß** cash bargain; ~**abzug** cash deduction; ~**anschaffung** providing cash; ~**aufwendungsschätzung** net cost estimate; ~**ausgabe** cash disbursement, cash expenditure; ~**ausgleich** settlement in cash; ~**auslagen** out-of-pocket expenses (or expenditure), actual expenses, cash expenses, cash outlay, (cash) disbursement(s); ~**auszahlung** cash payment; *pl also* cash disbursements; ~**ausschüttung** cash distribution, (dividend) payment in cash; ~**bestand** cash in hand, amount of ready money; ~**betrag** amount in cash; ~**deckung** cover in form of money; ~**depot** cash deposit; ~**depotgestellung** putting up of cash deposits; ~**depotpflicht** cash deposit requirement; ~**diskont** cash discount; ~**dividende** cash dividend; ~**einforderung** cash call; ~**eingänge** cash receipts; ~**einkauf** cash purchase; ~**einlage** cash deposit, cash subscription; ~**einlösung** redemption in cash, cash payment *(for a cheque etc)*; ~**einnahmen** cash income, cash receipts; ~**einschuß** cash margin, cash contribution; ~**einschußpflicht** cash-margin requirement; ~**einzahlung** cash deposit; ~**entnahmen** drawings in cash; ~**erlös** proceeds in cash; ~**erstattung** cash refund; ~**forderung** money claim; ~**freimachung** postage prepaid, bulk franking; ~**gebot** bid in cash, portion payable in cash by the highest bidder *(difference between minimum bid and highest bid, plus costs of auction)*; ~**geld** → *Bargeld*; ~**geschäft** cash transaction, *pl also* dealings in cash; ~**gründung** formation by founders' cash subscriptions; ~**guthaben** cash balance; ~**hinterlegung** money paid into court *(as security)*; ~**kauf** cash purchase; ~**kaution** cash deposit; ~**kredit** cash credit, bank overdraft; *persönlicher* ~~: *personal loan*; ~**leistungen** cash benefits; ~**liquidität** cash position, liquid cash resources; ~**löhne** wages in cash; ~**mittel** cash, monetary funds; ~**preis** cash price; ~**reserve** liquid reserves, cash reserves; ~**schaft** ready money, cash in s. o.'s possession, money in s. o.'s pocket; ~**scheck** open cheque *(US: check)*, uncrossed cheque, cheque made out to cash, cashable cheque; ~**sicherheit** cash deposit; ~**überschuß** cash balance, balance in hand; ~**überweisung** cash remittance; ~**unterhalt** (periodical) maintenance payments made in cash; ~**verkauf** cash sale; ~**verkehr** trade on cash terms; ~**vermögen** liquid assets, quick assets; ~**wert** cash value, value in cash, present value, realization value, cash equivalent; ~~-*anwartschaft*: present value of an expectancy; ~~-*rechnung*: discounted cash flow method; ~**werte** cash assets, liquid funds; ~**zahlung** → *Barzahlung.*

Bargeld *n* cash, ready cash, ready money, notes and coin; ~**automat** automatic teller, cash point (machine); ~**bestand** cash in hand; ~**durchfluß** cash flow; ~**knappheit** money shortage; **b**~**los** *adj* cashless *(remittance by cheque, bank transfer or postal transfer)*, non-cash; ~**rückfluß** reflux of notes and coin(s) *(to the banks)*; ~**umlauf** circulation of notes and coin(s);

111

Barren   **Bau**

~**volumen** total number of notes and coin(s) in circulation; **aufgerufenes** ~ bank notes or coins called in for cancellation.

Barren *m* bar, ingot, pig; ~**gold** gold bullion, gold bars; ~**silber** silver bullion.

Barzahlung *f* cash, cash payment, payment in cash, ready cash; ~ **bei sofortiger Abrechnung** spot payment; ~ **gegen Dokumente oder Auslieferungsanweisung** payment in cash against documents or delivery order; ~ **und Selbstabholung** cash and carry; ~ **von Spitzen** *cash payments for small balances in the current account*; **elektronischer** ~ electronic cash; **gegen** ~ for cash; ~~ *verkaufen: to sell for cash*; **nur gegen** ~ terms strictly cash; **sofortige** ~ prompt cash (payment), payment on the spot.

Barzahlungs|basis cash basis, terms, cash; ~**forderung** demand for cash payment, debt to be paid in cash only; ~**nachlaß** cash discount; ~**preis** cash price; ~**rabatt** cash discount; ~**skonto** cash discount, prompt-payment discount; ~**vertrag** contract on cash basis.

basieren *v/i* to be based (on), to rest on.

Basis *f* basis, foundation; *pol* grass roots; ~**einstandspreis** base cost, basic (standard) cost; ~**gesellschaft** base company; ~**kalkulation** base unit cost accounting; ~**laufzeit** effective base period; ~**jahr** base year; ~**kurs** initial rate (or price); ~**linie** baseline(s); ~**marke** base trade mark (*international registration*); ~**steuer** US: normal tax; ~**stichtag** base reference date; ~**wert** base value; ~**zeitraum** base period; **auf gleicher** ~ on equal terms; **auf handelsgewichteter** ~ on the trade-weighted basis; **tragfähige** ~ sound basis.

Bau *m* (*pl Bauten,* in first sense only) building, edifice, structure, erection; construction (work), building (*activity*); building site, construction site; type of construction, design (*machine*); ~**abnahme** final inspection of construction work; acceptance of construction work (*by customer*); ~**abnahmegebühr** inspection fee; ~**abstand** set back; ~**amt** building authority, building office (*in charge of particular building operations*); ~**anfrage** request for preliminery planning permission; ~**anlage** complex; ~**antrag** application for building permission (*or* planning permission); ~**antragsteller** planning permission applicant; ~**anzeige** notice of building works, *report that building work is undertaken*; ~**arbeit** construction (*or* building) work; ~**arbeiter** builder, mason, construction worker; ~**artgenehmigung** *permission for the type of machine to be constructed*; type approval mark; ~**artzulassung** engineering type licence; ~**auflage** building condition (*by building authority*); ~**aufseher** building surveyor, *GB* clerk of the works; ~**aufsicht** building inspection; ~**aufsichtsbehörde** inspector of works, supervisory authority for building; *oberste* ~~: *supreme inspection of works authority*; ~**auftrag** building order ~*aufträge der öffentlichen Hand*: *public (sector) building orders*; ~**aufwand** building expenditure; ~**ausführung** building, construction, type of construction, design, finish of a building; ~**ausnahmegenehmigung** exceptional building permission; ~**ausschreibung** invitation to tender for construction work; ~**beginn** start of building works, commencement of construction; ~**behörde** building authority *Oberste* ~~: ≈ *supreme building authority*; ~**beobachtung** supervisory observation of works (clearance) ~**beratung** building consultation; ~**beratungsstelle** advisory office for housing construction; ~**berufe** building vocations; ~**beschrän-**

Baubeschreibung | **Bauleitplan**

kungen building restrictions, zoning restrictions; **~beschreibung** building specifications; **~bestandszeichnung** plan of current state of a building; **~beteiligte** parties to a construction undertaking (*i.e. the owner, the builder, the contractor*); **~betreuer** agent, building development agent; **~betrieb** construction business; **~bewilligung** building permission, building licence; **~darlehen** building loan, construction loan; *nachstelliges ~~: building loan secured by junior mortgage*; **~darlehensvertrag** building loan agreement; **~denkmal** (*geschütztes*) ancient monument, historic building; **~dispens** exceptional waiver of building restrictions; **~einstellung** stoppage of work at building site; **~~sbescheid:** *stop order,* **~erlaubnis** building permission, planning permission, building licence; **~erwartungsland** near ripe land, development land, prospective building land; **b~fällig** dilapidated; **b~fällig werden** to fall into disrepair; **~fälligkeit** disrepair, dilapidated condition; **~fehler** structural fault; **~fertigstellungsanzeige** completion notice; **~feuchtigkeit** damp; **~firma** builder, building firm, construction company; **~flächen** building areas, building sites; **~fluchtlinie** building line, straight line, row; **~forderungen** outstanding accounts for construction work; **~führer** site supervisor, building foreman, engineer; **~gebiet** building zone; **~gebot** requirement to build (*on empty lot*); **~gefährdung** violation of building rules endangering the safety of others; **~gelände** building site; *erschlossenes ~~: building site cleared and prepared*; **~geld** building capital; **~gelddarlehen** building loan; **~geldhypothek** building mortgage; **~geldkredit** credit for building purposes; **~genehmigung** building permission, building licence planning permission (*GB*); **~genossenschaft** cooperative building society; **~gesetzbuch** building code; **~gestaltung** form and design of building(s); **~gesuch** application for a building permit (*or:* licence); *or* planning permission (*GB*); **~gewährleistung** construction warranty; **~gewerbe** building industry, building trade; **~grundstück** building plot, building land; **~haftpflichtversicherung** builder's risk insurance; **~handwerker** builder, *pl* building craftsmen; **~handwerkersicherungshypothek** builder's lien, *security charge on building and site for builder's money claim*; **~hauptgewerbe** building trades; **~herr** principal of a building contract, builder-owner, placer of building order; **~herrenhaftung** liability of building-principal; **~herrenmodell** builder-owner model, house-builders scheme; *building-by-proprietor system of condominium construction*; **~hilfsgewerbe** ancillary building trade(s); **~hof** builder's yard, yard of a construction firm, timber yard; **~hypothek** building mortgage; **~industrie** the building industry; **~ingenieur** building engineer, civil engineer (*if referring to Tiefbau qv*); **~investition** capital expenditure on building; **~jahr** year of construction, model year, date of a building, year of manufacture (*motorcar, machine*), year (*of a car*); **~kastenverfahren** building block process; **~konjunktur** economic trends in the building business; **~kontingent** building quota; **~kosten** → *Baukosten*; **~kredit** construction loan; **~kunst** architecture; **~land** → *Bauland*; **~last** obligation to construct and maintain (*church, school, highway etc*); **~leistung** building work, construction work performed; **~leiter** project manager, site supervisor, *GB* clerk of the works; **~leitplan** zoning map,

113

Bauleitplanung

general municipal real estate utilization plan; ~**leitplanung** zoning: *local authority planning for real estate utilization and building;* ~**linie** building line, general line; ~**lücke** building pattern; ~**lust** propensity to build; ~**lustiger** *(der ~lustige)* person interested in building *(a house for himself);* ~**mangel** defect of construction work, structural defect; ~**maßnahmen** construction works; ~**material** building materials; ~**meister** master builder, builder; ~**meisterprüfung** master builder's examination; ~**nebengewerbe** ancillary building trade(s); ~**nutzungsverordnung** *ordinance on use of buildings (for dwelling purposes, commercial purposes),* use order; ~**objekt** the building under construction, the subject matter of a building contract, building project; *beleihungsreifes ~~: building project qualifying for mortgage-loans;* ~**ordnung** building regulations; ~**ordnungsrecht** building regulations law; ~**pflicht** obligation to build *(on empty plot);* ~**plan** building plan, construction plan, layout of a building; ~**planbearbeitungsgebühr** plan fee; ~**planung** planning of building work; ~**planungsrecht** *the law on planning for building projects;* ~**platz** building lot *(before construction),* building land; building site *(during construction);* ~**polizei** official inspectors of buildings, municipal survey office; ~**prämie** building grant; ~**preise** building prices; ~**produktion** building output; ~**projekt** building (construction) project; ~**recht** right to build, construction law; **b~reif** developed *(land),* suitable for building purposes; ready for building; *noch nicht ~: undeveloped;* ~**risikoversicherung** builder's risk insurance; ~**sachen** cases concerning building disputes; ~**sachverständiger** building expert; quantity surveyor; ~**schäden** structural damage; ~**schädenver-**

Bauvorbescheid

sicherung building liability insurance; ~**schein** building certificate; ~**schutt** building-site débris; ~**schutzbereich** safety zone around building site; *beschränkter ~~: restricted safety building zone;* ~**sektor** (the) building sector *(of the economy);* ~**spar** ... → *Bauspar* ...; ~**sparen** → *Bauspar* ...; ~**sparer** → *Bauspar* ...; ~**sperre** building freeze, prohibition to continue building, all building prohibited; ~**stelle** building site, site; ~**stoffe** building materials; ~**stoffhandlung** building supplies firm; ~**stoffindustrie** building material industry; ~**stoffwechsel** building-material bill *(bill of exchange to finance building material);* ~**summe** total building cost; ~**tätigkeit** building; *öffentliche ~~: building for public account;* ~**technik** structural engineering; ~**teil** component part of a building; ~**träger** builder, developer; *commercial builder who sells completed dwelling; gemeinnütziger ~~: nonprofit making builder;* ~**-Überhang** carry-over of unfinished building projects; ~**überwachung** building inspection; ~**- und Bodenbank** *bank for building and real estate transactions;* ~**- und Nutzholz** timber (for building and other purposes); ~**- und Wohnungsgenossenschaft** (cooperative) building society; ~**unternehmen** building firm, building contractors, construction company; ~**unternehmer** building contractor; ~**unternehmerhaftungspflichtversicherung** builder's risk policy; ~**unternehmerkaution** construction bond; ~**vergabe** awarding a building contact; ~**verbot** building prohibition; ~**vertrag** building contract; *~~ bis zur schlüsselfertigen Übergabe: turnkey-contract;* ~**verwaltung** building authorities; ~**volumen** amount of building output; ~**voranfrage** application for outline, planning permission; ~**vorbescheid** provisional planning permission; ~**vorhaben** building project; *anzeigepflichtiges* ~~: *building-project requiring notice to the authorities; notifiable building project; anzeigefreies* ~~: *building-project exempt from notice to the authorities, finanziell gesicherte* ~~: *building-projects for which finance is secured*; ~**vorlagen** building specifications; ~**vorschriften** building regulations, building code, structural requirements; ~**werk** building, edifice, structure, erection, building or erection, structure or work; ~~ *im Erbbaurecht: building owned under hereditary building right*; ~**wert** value in terms of building costs, construction cost; ~**wesen** building; ~**wesenversicherung** comprehensive building liability insurance; ~**wich** minimum spacing of buildings: *(legally required) lateral distance from neighbo(u)ring border*; ~**wirtschaft** building trade; ~**zeichnungen** construction drawings; ~**zinsen** interest for building finance; ~**zwecke** (*zu* ~*zwecken*) (for) building purposes; ~**zwischenfinanzierungen** bridging loan, interim financing for building mortgage; **angrenzender** ~**teil** party structure; **durchgehendes** ~**grundstück** through lot; **gewerbliche** ~**ten** non-residential constructions, commercial and industrial buildings; **gewerblicher und industrieller** ~ industrial building; **im** ~ **befindlich** under construction; **öffentliches** ~**wesen** public building; **privates** ~**wesen** non-government building, private-sector building; **saniertes** ~**gebiet** upgraded area, rehabilitated area.

Bauer *m* farmer, peasant, peasant farmer.

Bauern|betrieb peasant farm; ~**fänger** trickster, confidence man, con man; ~**fängerei** trickery, confidence trick(s); ~**hof** *m* farm, farmstead; ~**verband** farmers' union.

Baukosten *pl* building costs, expenditure for the construction of a building; ~**anschlag** building estimate, builder's estimate; ~**index** statistical index of building costs; ~**voranschlag** = *Baukostenanschlag qv*; ~**zuschuß** (tenant's) contribution to building costs; *verlorener* ~~: *non-repayable contribution to building costs*.

Bauland *n* building land, developed land, ~**bereitstellung** *making land available for family housing at reasonable prices (an obligation of local authorities)*; ~**beschaffung** procurement of land for development; ~**besteuerung** site value rating; ~**erschließung** real estate development; ~**gericht** lands tribunal; ~**kammer** lands tribunal panel; ~**sachen** lands tribunal, land cases; ~**senat** lands tribunal appeal court; ~**steuer** tax on (unused) building land.

Baulichkeit *f* erection; **uralte** ~ ancient messuage, ancient building.

Baumschutzverordnung *f* preservation of trees ordinance.

Baumwoll|börse *f* cotton exchange; ~**terminbörse** cotton futures market.

Bauspar|beitrag *contribution to building and loan association or building society*; ~**darlehen** loan from a building and loan association, saver's building loan (*granted to a member after quota of savings reached*); ~**einzahlung** deposit paid to building and loan association; ~**en** *n* saving through building and loan associations; ~**er** *m* person saving through building society; ~**guthaben** *balance on savings account (with building and loan association or building society)*; ~**kasse** building and loan association, *GB* building society, saving and loan association; ~**kassenbeitrag** = *Bausparbeitrag qv*; ~**prämie** state grant for homestead saving, (*allowance to supplement savings under building and loan association arrangement*), premium allowed on building society

Bayerisches Oberstes Landesgericht   **beanstanden**

savings; ~**summe** savings target for building loan (*under savings and loan agreement*); ~**vertrag** building society savings contract.

Bayerisches Oberstes Landesgericht Bavarian Supreme Court (*in matters of state law*).

beachten *v/t* to observe, to adhere to, to comply with, to take into consideration, to take note (of sth); to consider; **nicht** ~ to disregard, to ignore, to fail to observe (*etc*).

Beachtenspflicht *f* requirement of compliance.

beachtlich *adj* considerable, noteworthy, significant, notable.

Beachtung *f* observance, compliance (with); ~ **der Verbote** compliance with the prohibitions; **unter** ~ **von** subject to, in compliance with; taking into consideration; **unter gebührender** ~ with due observance of.

Beamten|anwärter candidate for a position in the civil service; ~**beleidigung** insulting a civil servant; ~**besoldung** remuneration of civil servants, public officials' emoluments; ~**bestechung** corruption of public officials, bribery of civil servant; ~**bund** association of public officials; ~**eid** oath of office (*of public official*); ~**gesetz** Civil Service Act; ~**gewerkschaft** civil servants union; ~**haftung** public liability, *liability of public authorities for their officials and agents*; ~**laufbahn** civil service career; ~**nötigung** coercion against public officials; ~**pension** civil servant's (retirement) pension; ~**recht** *law regulating the rights and duties of civil servants*; ~**rechtsrahmengesetz** (*German federal unification law of 1971*) *General Act governing the public service*; ~**schaft** officialdom, the public of officials; ~**status** status of a public official; ~**stellen** positions for civil servants; ~**tum** officialdom; ~**verhältnis** status of a public official; ~**versorgung** *retirement pensions for civil servants*; ~**vertretung** *organization representing public officials*; ~**wirtschaft** officialdom, red-tapism, officialdom.

Beamter *m* (*der Beamte*) officer (*including any person authorized to perform public functions*), public servant; official, public official, administrative officer, ministerial officer, civil officer, public officer, public agent, civil servant (*usually for life and pensionable*); ~ **am Einzahlungsschalter** receiving teller, receiving clerk; ~ **auf Dienstreise** official on temporary official mission; ~ **auf Lebenszeit** civil servant; ~ **des einfachen Dienstes** official of the subclerical class (*or of the messengerial service*); permanent official; ~ **auf Probe** probationer, government officer on probation; ~ **auf Widerruf** official on recall; ~ **auf Zeit** public official for a fixed term; ~ **des höheren Dienstes** official of the administrative class, A class civil servant; ~ **des mittleren Dienstes** clerical officer, civil servant of the clerical class; ~ **des Rechnungshofes** state auditor; ~ **zur Wiederverwendung** *civil officer suspended from active duty*; **außerplanmäßiger** ~ extraordinary administrative officer; **diensttuender** ~ officer on duty, duty official; **e-m** ~ **den Diensteid abnehmen** to swear in an official; **hoher** ~ high-ranking official (or civil servant); **höherer** ~ senior civil servant; **im dienstlichen Auftrag reisender** ~ official on mission; **leitender** ~ executive official, *civil officer in a leading position*; **pensionsberechtigter** ~ civil servant with pension rights; **planmäßiger** ~ regular civil servant; **richterlicher** ~ judicial officer.

Beamtin *f* female civil servant.

beanspruchen *v/t* to demand, to claim, to lay claim to, to assert.

Beanspruchung *f* demand, laying claim to s. th; stress (*quality testing*).

beanstanden *v/t* to complain (of), to object (to), to criticize; **zu** ~ objectionable.

Beanstandung *f* complaint, objection, criticism.

beantragen *v/t* to apply for (*an administrative act*), to make an application, to move (*meetings, legislative bodies, procedural matters*), to propose, to bring forward a motion, to petition, to pray (*court, for judgment etc*), to request, to ask (for), to put in a claim (for); **schriftlich** ~ to apply in writing, to file written application.

Beantragung *f* application, request.

beantworten to answer, to reply (to).

Beantwortung *f* answer, reply; ~ **e-s Rechtshilfeersuchens** answer to letters rogatory; **~sfrist** time for (filing a) reply; **ungenügende ~** insufficient answer.

bearbeiten *v/t* to work (on), to process, to deal (with) (*administration*), to treat, to process, to finish (*production*), to adapt, to arrange (*literary works, music*).

Bearbeiter *m* the official responsible, the person in charge; **~urheberrecht** adapter's copyright, copyright of the arranger.

Bearbeitung *f* handling, treatment, working, dealing with; processing (*industry*), adaptation (*literary work*), derivation (*law of copyright*), paraphrase (*idea, text*); ~ **e-s Kunden** cultivating a customer, dealing with a customer; **~sboykott** blocking of goods; boykott; **~sgebühr** handling fee, processing fee, service charge; **~skosten** claim expenses (*insurance*); **~srechte** rights of adaptation; **~sschädenklausel** clause covering processing risks; **~svorgang** manufacturing (*or* proceeding) operation; **~zeiten** processing times; **etwas in ~ nehmen** to start to work officially on s. th., to start to handle s. th.; **in ~ befindliche Aufträge** work in progress; **steuerunschädliche ~** operating without tax disadvantages.

Beauschlagung overhead cost allocation, indirect cost allocation.

beaufsichtigen *v/t* to supervise, to superintend, to oversee, to invigilate (*examinations*).

Beaufsichtigung *f* supervision, surveillance, invigilation (*examinations*).

beauftragen *v/t* to charge (or to commission) s. o. with a task, to instruct (*a lawyer*), to mandate, to empower, to retain.

Beauftragter *m* mandatee, mandatary; private attorney, commissioner, director; agent, representative agent, delegate; proxy (*for voting*).

Beauftragung *f* commissioning, conferring of a mandate, placing of an order, instructions, briefing (*lawyer*).

bebaubar *adj* suitable for development.

Bebaubarkeit *f* suitability for constructions and development.

bebaut *adj* built-upon, built up (*plot of land*), cultivated (*area*), **zu dicht ~**: overbuilt.

Bebauung *f* development (*agriculture*), type (and extent) of building; **~sdichte** residential density; **b~sfähig** *adj* suitable for development; **~sgenehmigung** provisional planning permission; **~sgruppe** residential cluster; **~splan** building plan, development plan; **~stiefe** maximum rear building distance; **~svorschriften** building regulations; zoning classification, zoning laws; **~szusammenhang** building coherence, coherent appearance of built-up section.

Bedachter *m* (*der Bedachte*) beneficiary (under a will), prospective legatee, grantee; **alternativ ~** alternative beneficiary; **in einem Testament ~** beneficiary under a will; **testamentarisch ~** beneficiary under a will.

Bedarf *m* need(s), requirement(s), demand; **~ an Arbeitskräften** labour requirements; **aufgestauter ~** pent-up demand; **bei ~** if required; **dem tatsächlichen ~ anpassen** to bring in line with actual needs; **der aktuelle** ~ the current requirements; **der übliche** ~ usual requirements; **elastischer** ~ selective demand; **lebenswichtiger** ~ essential supplies, necessities of life; **nach** ~ as (and when) required; **potentieller** ~ potential requirements; **pro-Kopf-**~ per capita demand; **unseren gesamten** ~ all our requirements; **voraussichtlicher** ~ foreseeable needs, anticipated requirements.

Bedarfs|anmeldung purchase notice; ~**artikel** necessaries, provisions; ~**bestätigung** certificate of need; ~**deckung** satisfaction of wants; ~**fall** (in) case of need; ~**gegenstände** implements, articles required for human needs; ~**güter** consumer goods, essential commodities; ~**lenkung** consumer guidance, influencing consumption; ~**lücke** unsatisfied demand; **b~orientiert** demand-oriented; ~**plan** public requirement plan; ~**prämie** required premium *(for a particular risk)*; ~**quote** vacancy *or* employment ratio; ~**spanne** required margin, net expense ratio, cover-requiring margin; ~**spanne des Kreditgeschäfts** margin required on lending business; ~**termin** date by which b. is required *(e.g. funds)*; **b~theoretisch** theoretically demand-related; ~**träger** party requiring *(the goods, services and/or credit)*, consumer, would-be borrower; ~**verwaltung** procurement (administration); ~**zunahme** increase in demand; ~**zuweisungen** allotments in accordance with requirements; **im** ~**falle** if required, in case of need.

Bedeckung *f* provision of cover *(for obligations or reserves)*.

Bedenken *n (mostly pl die* ~) doubt(s), misgivings, hesitation, scruples; ~ **haben** to hesitate, to have doubts; **keine** ~ no objection(s), "no problems"; without any scruples; **ohne** ~ without any scruples; without hesitation.

bedenken *v/t* to consider, to take into account, to think of; **jmdn testamentarisch** ~ to remember s. o. in one's will.

bedenkenlos *adj* without hesitation, unscrupulous, ruthless.

bedenklich *adj* questionable, risky, open to objections, doubtful.

Bedenkzeit *f* time for consideration, time to think it over.

bedeuten *v/i* to mean, to imply, to import, to represent, to indicate, to purport; **anscheinend** ~ to purport; **darüber hinaus** ~ to include and extend beyond; **nichts zu** ~ **haben** to be irrelevant, to mean nothing.

bedeutend *adj* important, relevant.

bedeutsam *adj* significant.

Bedeutung *f* meaning, sense, significance, relevance, importance; **allgemeine** ~ common intent; **an** ~ **gewinnen** to gain importance; **buchstäbliche** ~ literal meaning; **die eigentliche** ~ the actual meaning; **die gleiche** ~ the same meaning; **die natürliche** ~ natural meaning; **entscheidende** ~ decisive significance; **grundsätzliche** ~ fundamental importance; **laienhafte** ~ popular sense; **materiellrechtliche** ~ significance in substantive law; **natürliche** ~ *(e-s Wortes)* common intent; **quantitative** ~ significance in terms of figures, quantitative significance; **rechtliche** ~ legal meaning, legal significance; **rechtserhebliche** ~ relevance in law; **übertragene** ~ figurative meaning, metaphorical sense; **universelle** ~ universal meaning; **von allgemeiner** ~ of general import; **von großer** ~ **sein** to be of major importance; **von höchster** ~ of paramount importance; **wörtliche** ~ literal sense, literal meaning; **zwingende** ~ necessary implication.

bedeutungslos *adj* insignificant, unimportant, irrelevant.

Bedeutungslosigkeit *f* unimportance, insignificance, irrelevance, meaninglessness.

bedeutungsvoll *adj* important, significant, weighty.

Bediensteter *m* (*der Bedienstete, pl Bedienstete ~e*) staff member, public servant, official; **~e der EG** servants of the European Communities, EEC officials; **öffentliche ~e** public servants.

Bedienung, *f* service, operation (*of a machine*); **~sanleitung** = **~sanweisung** *qv*; **~sanweisung(en)** technical instructions, operating instructions; **~sperson** operator.

bedingt *adj* conditional, contingent, qualified; **~ vorsätzlich** reckless(ly), with indirect intent; **auflösend ~** subject to a resolutory (*or* dissolving) condition; **aufschiebend ~** subject to a suspensive condition.

Bedingtgeschäft *n* conditional transaction.

Bedingtheit *f* conditionality.

Bedingtlieferung *f* sale on approval.

Bedingung *f* condition (= *c, pl: c–s*), term, stipulation, proviso; **~ auferlegen** to impose *c–s*; **~en bei sofortiger Barzahlung** spot *c–s*; **~en der Strafbarkeit** necessary collateral elements of crime; **~en einhalten** to adhere to the *c–s*, to keep to the *c–s*; **~en festsetzen** to stipulate *c–s*, to agree upon *c–s*; **~en nicht erfüllen** to fail to meet *c–s*; **~en vereinbaren** to settle the terms, to agree on the *c–s*; **allgemeine ~en** standard (*or* general) terms and *c–s*; **angemessene ~en** reasonable terms and *c–s*; **auf ~en eingehen** to yield to *c–s*; **auflösende ~** resolutory *c*, dissolving *c*.; **aufschiebende ~** *c* precedent, suspensive *c*; **ausdrückliche ~** express term, explicit *c* (of an agreement); **den ~en entsprechen** to satisfy the *c–s*; **~ gesetzlichen ~~:** *to satisfy or comply with legal requirements*; **der Eintritt der ~** the occurrence of the contingency, the fulfilment of the *c*, occurrence of the event (insured against); **die ~en erfüllen** to comply with the *c–s*, to perform the *c–s*, to fulfil the qualifications; **e–e ~ tritt ein** a *c* occurs, a contingency comes to pass (*or* happens); **einschränkende ~** restrictive covenant; **entsprechende ~en zur Annahme** the appropriate provisions for adoption; **gegenseitige ~en** mutual *c–s*; **gemäß nachstehender ~en** subject as hereafter provided; **günstige ~en** favourable terms ; **lästige ~** onerous *c*; **notwendige ~** necessary *c*; **rechtliche ~** legal *c*; **rechtlich unzulässige ~** illegal *c*; **sittenwidrige ~** immoral term, *c* contra bonos mores; **stillschweigende ~** implied *c*, implied term; **übliche ~en** usual terms, usual *c–s*; **unerlaubte ~** illegal *c*, unlawful term; **unerläßliche ~** sine qua non *c*, absolute precondition, necessary *c*, indispensable *c*; **unmögliche ~** impossible *c*; **unter annehmbaren ~en** on accommodating terms; **unter der ~, daß** on *c* that, upon the *c* that, under the proviso that, provided that, sub modo; **unter der ~ der eigenen proportionalen Schadenstragung bei Unterversicherung** subject to average; **unzulässige ~** improper *c*; **wesentliche ~** essential *c*, *c* that goes to the roots of an agreement; **wettbewerbsneutrale steuerliche ~en** fiscal *c* with a neutral effect on competition; **zu geschäftlichen ~en** on commercial terms, at arm's length; **zu gleichen ~en** on the same terms, on equal terms; **zur ~ machen, daß** to make it a *c* that; **zu vernünftigen ~en** on reasonable terms; **zwingend notwendige ~** indispensable *c*, mandatory *c*.

Bedingungs|eintritt occurrence of the conditional event, happening of the contingency; **b~sfeindlich** absolute, not permitting a condition, unconditional; **b~slos** unconditional, without qualification.

bedrohen *v/t* to threaten, to menace; **gewalttätig ~** to assault, to threaten with violence.

Bedrohung threat(s), threatening,

bedürfen

threatening utterances and/or gestures; ~ **der öffentlichen Ordnung** danger to public order, threat to public peace; ~ **mit e-m Verbrechen** threatening a felony; ~ **von Beamten** threatening public officers; **gewalttätige** ~ assault, violent threat.

bedürfen *v/i* to need, to require.

Bedürfnis *n* need, requirement; ~**se des täglichen Lebens**: necessaries; *daily needs*; ~**anstalt** structural convenience, public toilet; ~**befriedigung** satisfaction of needs; ~**frage** question of public need *(for a licensed trade etc)*; ~**prüfung** public need test, *examination concerning the existence of a public need for a trade or establishment before granting licence;* **dringendes** ~ urgent requirement.

bedürftig poor and needy, indigent.

Bedürftige *pl* persons in need (of), indigent persons; **sozial** ~ those in need of help on social grounds.

Bedürftigkeit *f* indigence, need, lack of means; ~**snachweis** proof of need; ~**sprüfung** means test; ~**schwelle** standard of need; ~**szeugnis** certificate of poverty.

beehren *v/reflex* to have the honour (to).

beeiden *v/t* to confirm upon oath, to swear to the truth of s. th.

beeidet *adj* sworn *(testimony, statement)*.

beeidigen *v/t* to administer the oath, to swear a witness (in); ~ **lassen** to have s. o. *(a witness)* sworn (in), to have an oath administered to s. o.

beeidigt *adj* sworn (in) *(of a witness, expert etc)*.

Beeidigung *f* administration of oath, swearing in; **nachträgliche** ~ subsequent administration of the oath.

beeinflussen *v/t* to influence; **leicht zu** ~ (to be) easily influenced.

Beeinflussung *f* influencing, exercise of influence; ~ **von Zeugen** tampering with witnesses, exercising undue influence on witnesses; **sittenwidrige** ~ improper influence; **unzulässige** ~ undue influence.

beeinträchtigen *v/t* to impair, to af-

Befähigung

fect unfavo(u)rably (*or* adversely); to derogate (from).

Beeinträchtigung *f* impairment (of), encroachment (on), detraction (from), interference (with); ~ **der Erwerbsfähigkeit** impairment of earning capacity; ~ **der Heiratschancen** impairment of (marriage) prospects; ~ **der persönlichen Freiheit** invasion of personal liberty; ~ **der Rechte** impairment of rights, interference with s.o.'s rights; ~ **der Sicherheit des Verkehrs** impairment of road safety; **e-e** ~ **beseitigen** to remove a nuisance, to eliminate a disadvantage; **ohne** ~ **durch Dritte** peaceably and quietly, without any interference by third parties.

beenden *v/t* to finish, to conclude, to put to an end.

beendigen *v/t* to terminate, to determine, to complete.

Beendigung *f* termination, expiration, cessation, completion; ~ **der Kriegshandlungen** cessation of hostilities; ~ **des Kriegszustandes** termination of the state of war; ~ **e-s Vertrages** termination of a contract; ~**skündigung** notice of termination.

beerben *v/t* to be s. o.'s heir, to succeed to, to inherit from; **gesetzlich** ~ to inherit under the statutory rules, to succeed s. o. by intestate succession.

Beerbung *f* inheriting, succession upon death.

Beerdigung *f* burial, funeral; ~**sfeierlichkeit** burial ceremony, obsequies; ~**skosten** funeral expenses; ~**sort** place of burial.

befähigen *v/i* to enable, to qualify.

Befähigung *f* qualification, aptitude; ~ **für e-n akademischen Beruf** professional qualification; ~ **für ein öffentliches Amt** qualification for public office; ~ **zum Richteramt** qualification for holding judicial office; ~ **zur Patenterteilung** patent power; **allgemeine** ~ general competence; **berufliche** ~ occupational aptitude, professional qualification; **fachliche** ~ professional qualification, qualification in a particular field.

Befähigungs|nachweis certificate of qualification, certificate of proficiency, proof of ability, evidence of formal qualifications; **~schein** qualification certificate.

befangen *adj* prejudiced, bias(s)ed; **für ~ erklären** to declare s. o. to be prejudiced; to challenge on the grounds of partiality; **sich für ~ erklären** to disqualify oneself; to state that one is not unprejudiced (*of a judge, declining to act*), to declare oneself bias(s)ed.

Befangenheit *f* lack of impartiality, prejudice, bias; **wegen ~ ablehnen** to challenge because of prejudice, to challenge propter affectum.

befassen *v reflex* to deal with, to occupy oneself with, to process.

Befehl *m* order, command; **~ ausgeführt!** mission accomplished; **~ssprache** computer language; **auf ~ handeln** to act under (superior) orders; **den ~ übernehmen** to assume command; **e-m ~ zuwiderhandeln** to contravene an order; **e-n ~ verweigern** to refuse to obey an order; **laut ~** by order; **höherer ~** superior order(s); **richterlicher ~** bench warrant, court order.

befehlen *v/t* to order, to command.

Befehls|befugnis power of command; **~ebene** echelon, level of command; **~gehorsam** obedience to orders; **~gewalt** power of command, military control; **~mißbrauch** abuse of authority, abuse of power of command; **~notstand** acting under superior orders (*plea to excuse an offence, e.g. war crime*); **~recht** right of command; **~- und Kommandogewalt** supreme power of command; **~verweigerung** refusal to obey an order.

Befinden *n* opinion, (judicial) determination, finding.

befinden *v/t* to find, to adjudge, to hold, to rule, to pass (*judgment*); **etwas für gut ~** to approve of sth.

Beflaggung *f* flagging, putting out flags.

Befleckung *f* defilement, tarnishing.

befolgen *v/t* to comply with, to obey, to observe.

Befolgung *f* observance, compliance (with); **genaue ~** strict observance.

Beförderer *m* carrier.

befördern *v/t(1)* to transport, to convey, to forward.

befördern *v/t(2)* to upgrade, to promote.

Beförderung *f* (= *Befördern n*) (1) transportation, transport, haulage, dispatch, forwarding, shipment, conveyance; transmission (*telegrams, messages*); **~ auf dem Landweg** land transport; **~ auf dem Luftwege** air transport; **~ durch öffentliche Verkehrsmittel** by public transport; **~ im Straßenverkehr** road transport, cartage, haulage; **~ per Achse** road transport; **~ per Bahn** rail transport; **~ per Schiff** waterborne transport; **~ von Haus zu Haus** door-to-door transport; **frachtfreie ~** freight-prepaid transportation, transportation without charge to the customer; **gewerbsmäßige ~ von Waren** (common) carrier's business; **öffentliche ~** public transport.

Beförderung *f* (2) upgrading, advancement, promotion; **~** (*in e-e höhere Gehaltsstufe*) in-class promotion, incremental rise.

Beförderungs(1)art mode of transport; **~entgelte** transport charges, transport rates; **~geschäft** transport business; **~gut** cargo; **~kosten** transport expenses, cost of transport; carriage; **~kunden** transport users; **~leistung** traffic performance, amount of passenger and goods traffic carried; *steuerfreie ~ ~:* *tax-free transport;* **~mittel** means of transport, transportation facilities; **~papier** transport document; **~pflicht** statutory obliga-

Beförderungsanspruch

tion to undertake transportation (*by public carriers*); ~**preis** transport charges; ~**risiko** risk of transport; ~**schein** way-bill; ~**steuer** transportation tax (*persons*); ~**steuerbefreiungen** exemptions from transportation tax; ~**strecken** transportation routes; ~**tarife** scale of transport charges, passenger tariff; ~**unternehmen** transport company, carrier; ~**unternehmer** carrier, haulage contractor; ~**verkehr** haulage transport; ~**vertrag** (*persons*) transport contract, contract of carriage, passage contract; ~**vorbehalt** reservation of postal transport monopoly; ~**vorschriften** forwarding instructions; ~**weg** (transport) route, transit route.

Beförderungs(2)anspruch right to be promoted, seniority right; ~**aussichten** career prospects; promotion prospects; ~**hindernis** impediment to promotion; ~**richtlinien** civil servants rules on promotion; ~**tabelle** promotional chart; ~**tag** date of promotion, day of nomination; ~**vorbehalt** reservation in respect of promotion; ~**zulage** seniority pay.

befrachten *v/t* to freight, to load on board a ship; to contract for sea transport (*with a carrier*), to put cargo at sea-carrier's disposal for transport.

Befrachter *f* freighter (*party contracting with sea-carrier to transport a cargo*); inland waterway forwarding agent(s), consignor.

Befrachtung *f* freighting, surrendering cargo to sea-carrier; ~**skontor** shipping agency; ~**svertrag** contract of affreightment; contract of transport of goods by sea (*rarely: by inland waterways*), charter-party.

befragen *v/t* to question, to interrogate, to consult.

Befragter *m* respondent, interviewee.

Befragung *f* questioning, interrogation, interview; **peinliche** ~ interrogation under torture *hist*.

Befriedigung

befreien *v/t* to liberate, to exempt, to dispense (from), to release, to free.

befreit *adj* exempt, immune, freed (from); **gesetzlich** ~ legally exempt.

Befreiung *f* liberation, exemption, immunity, dispensation, enfranchisement (*from bonds of tenure*); ~ **des Zeugen vom persönlichen Erscheinen** relieving a witness from duty to appear in court; ~**sanspruch** right to be relieved of an obligation, right of indemnity, right of exemption; ~**bescheinigung** certificate of exemption; ~**sgründe** grounds for exemption; *gesetzliche* ~~: *legal exemptions*; ~**svorschriften** exemption rules; ~ **vom Alterserfordernis** dispensation from the age requirement; ~ **vom Aufgebot** waiving the banns; ~ **vom Ehehindernis** marriage dispensation; ~ **vom Militärdienst** exemption from military service; ~**vom Unterricht** leave of absence from classes; ~ **von der Gerichtsbarkeit** jurisdictional immunity, exemption from jurisdiction; ~ **von der MWSt** exemption from VAT; ~ **von e-r Verbindlichkeit** release from an obligation, exemption; ~ **von Gefangenen** obtaining the release of prisoners (by force), freeing prisoners; ~ **von Sicherheitsleistung** dispensation (or exemption) from requirement of posting security; **persönliche** ~ personal exemption; **sachliche** ~ exemption in respect of the subject matter.

befrieden *v/t* to pacify, to quiet.

befriedigen *v/t* to satisfy, to discharge (*an obligation*), to gratify.

Befriedigung *f* satisfaction; ~**saussicht(en)** prospect(s) of satisfaction; ~**srecht** right to be paid (*from estate*); ~**svorrecht** right to preferential payment; ~ **von Gläubigern** paying off creditors; **abgesonderte** ~ separate realization for a secured creditor (*of lien,*

122

apart from bankrupt's estate); **anteilige** ~ pro rata payment (or settlement), proportionate share; **anteilmäßige** ~ = *anteilige ~qv*; **bevorzugte** ~ preferential payment(s); **quotenmäßige** ~ pro rata payment; **teilweise** ~ part satisfaction, discharge in part; **vorzugsweise** ~ preferential satisfaction.

Befriedung *f* pacification.

befristen *v/t* to set a time limit, to limit, to fix a deadline.

befristet *adj* limited in time, fixed-term.

Befristung *f* fixing a deadline, time limit imposed; ~ **der Spareinlagen** fixed time for savings deposits.

Befruchtung *f* fertilization; **künstliche** ~ in vitro fertilization.

Befugnis *f* authority, power, competence; **~se übertragen** to delegate powers; ~ **zur Darlehensgewährung** lending authority; **dazugehörige ~se** incidental powers; **delegierte** ~ delegated power; **gesetzliche** ~ statutory power, statutory authority; **hoheitsrechtliche ~se** governmental powers, sovereign powers; **ohne gesetzliche** ~ without legal authority, ultra vires; **originäre ~se** inherent powers; **rechtsgeschäftliche ~se** competence for legal transactions; **satzungsmäßige ~se** *e-r juristischen Person* corporate powers; **seine ~se überschreiten** to exceed one's authority, to act ultra vires; **ständige ~se** permanent authority, established powers; **zugewiesene ~se** powers conferred (upon), assigned powers.

befugt *adj* authorized, empowered, competent, qualified; **nicht** ~ unauthorized, incompetent.

Befund *m* test, result, findings, *esp:* results of a medical examination, medical findings, medical report; **~bericht** report (of the findings).

befürworten *v/t* to sponsor, to recommend, to endorse, to second (*a motion*), to authorize.

Befürworter *m* (*pl* =) sponsor, supporter; seconder (*of a motion*); ~ **des Gemeinsamen Marktes** marketeer, supporter of the EEC.

Befürwortung *f* recommendation, support, backing.

Begabten|abitur *special university entrance qualification for persons of above-average intellectual ability;* **~förderung** benefits for gifted pupils/students; **~prüfung** extra-school examinations for gifted persons (*for university entrance level*).

Begabung *f* intelligence, talent, aptitude; **erfinderische** ~ inventive faculty; **manuelle** ~ manual aptitude.

begebbar *adj* negotiable; **nicht** ~ not negotiable, non-negotiable.

Begebbarkeit *f* negotiability, negotiable character; **~sklausel** negotiable words, negotiability clause.

begeben *v/t* to negotiate (*instruments*), to issue, to emit, to float (*shares, bonds*).

Begebung *f* negotiation, issue, flotation (*marketable securities*); ~ **e– s Wechsels** negotiation of a bill of exchange; ~ **von Aktien** issue of shares; ~ **von Auslandsanleihen** issue of foreign bonds.

Begebungs|avis advice of negotiation; **~fähigkeit** negotiability; **~konsortium** issuing syndicate; **~kosten** *e-r Anleihe* floating costs *of a loan;* **~kurs** issue price; **~recht** power to negotiate; **~vertrag** *transfer agreement for negotiable instruments.*

Begegnungsschule *f* bi-cultural school, multi-cultural school.

begehbar *adj* passable (*path*).

Begehen *n* commission, perpetration (*of crime*).

begehen *v/t* to commit, to perpetrate.

Begehren *n* petition, demand, desire, request (*in judicial proceedings*).

begehren *v/t* to require, to demand (*redress*), to pray (for), to petition (for) (*relief*).

Begehung *f* (1) perpetration, commission (*of an offence*); ~ **e-r uner-**

laubten Handlung ~malfeasance, commission of a tort, (*generally*: commission of an offence); **~sdelikt** offence by commission (*of an act*); **~gefahr** risk of further commission of an offence; **~sort** the place the offence was committed, locus criminis, locus delicti; **fahrlässige** ~ negligent commission; **gemeinschaftliche** ~ joint commission (*of a crime*); **versuchte** ~ attempted commission (of a crime).

Begehung *f (2)* perambulation, procession (on the fields), walking over (land) for inspection purposes, inspection of the building site; **öffentliches ~srecht** public right of way.

Beginn *m* beginning, commencement, start, opening; ~ **der Hauptverhandlung** the opening of the trial (*or* hearing); ~ **der Laufzeit** beginning of the term of validity, commencement (*of a policy*).

beginnen *v/t* to begin, to initiate, to open, to commence, to start.

beglaubigen *v/t* to attest to the authenticity of (*signatures*), to authenticate, to verify, to prove; **notariell** ~ to notarize, to authenticate, to certify, to attest (by a notary); **notariell** ~ **lassen** to have *a signature* notarized, to have a signature attested by a notary.

Beglaubigender *m* (*der Beglaubigende*) attestor.

beglaubigt *adj* authenticated, certified (*copy, translation*); **amtlich** ~ officially certified; **notariell** ~ notarially authenticated, notarially certified (as correct); **öffentlich** ~ certified by public notarial act, officially acknowledged, officially authenticated.

Beglaubigung *f* attestation, verification, certification; ~ **e-r Unterschrift** attestation of a signature; ~ **von Urkunden** attestation of deeds, certification of (conformity of) documents; legalization; **gerichtliche** ~ attestation by the court, court's authentication (of signature etc); **notarielle** ~ notarial attestation, notarial authentication; **öffentliche** ~ official attestation, official authentication (*by public officer, esp a notary*); **zur** ~ **dessen** in witness whereof (*in formal documents*).

Beglaubigungs|befugnis authority to attest, authority to authenticate (*documents*); **~formel** attestation clause; **~gebühr** certification fee, attestation charge; **~klausel** attestation clause, witnessing clause; **~schreiben** credentials; *das* ~~ *überreichen:* to present credentials; **~stempel** seal for authentication, certification stamp; **~vermerk** attestation clause, testimonium ("*In witness whereof . . .*"), certificate of acknowledgement (*authenticity of signature*).

begleichen *v/t* to pay, to discharge, to defray (*expenses*), to settle (a bill), to hono(u)r (a bill of exchange), to square.

Begleichung *f* payment, discharge, settlement, satisfaction; **vollständige** ~ full discharge.

Begleit|blatt summary sheet, back-up sheet; **~brief** covering letter, transmittal letter; **~dokument** accompanying documents; **~erscheinung** attendant symptom, accompanying manifestation, concomitant; **~name** assumed additional name; **~papiere** accompanying documents; **~personen** companions, accompanying staff, mail guards (*on train*); **~schreiben** accompanying letter; **~umstände** surrounding (*or* attendant *or* collateral) circumstances, concomitants.

begnadigen *v/t* to pardon, to grant a pardon (to), to reprieve; (*begnadigt werden: to be pardoned, to receive a pardon*).

Begnadigung *f* pardon, the granting of a pardon; **allgemeine** ~ general pardon, amnesty; **unbeschränkte** ~ absolute pardon, full pardon; **volle** ~ full pardon.

Begnadigungs|akt the act of clemency; **~befugnis** the power to pardon, the prerogative of mercy; **~gesuch** petition for clemency; **~kommission** clemency board; **~möglichkeit** remissibility; **~recht** prerogative of mercy; **~sachen** clemency matters.

Begräbnis *n* burial, interment, funeral; **~kosten** *pl* funeral expenses; **~schein** burial licence; **~stätten** burial grounds, cemetery.

begreiflich *adj* comprehensible, conceivable, intelligible.

begrenzen *v/t* to limit, to terminate.

begrenzt *adj* limited, determinable.

Begrenzung *f* limitation, restriction; **~sleuchten** position (side) lights; **gesetzliche** ~ limitation in law; **ohne** ~ without limitation, without restriction; **zeitliche** ~ limitation as to time.

Begriff *m* concept, notion, term; **allgemeine ~e des Rechts** general legal concepts; **juristischer** ~ legal term, legal concept.

begrifflich *adj* notional, conceptual; ~ **völlig verschieden** of an absolutely different conceptual character.

Begriffsbestimmung *f* definition; **dehnbare** ~ elastic definition; **gemäß der** ~ **des Gesetzes** as defined in the Act.

Begriffsinhalt *m* (*e-s Warenzeichens*) connotation, implied meaning.

Begriffsjurisprudenz *f* analytical jurisprudence.

begründen *v/t* to give (*or* state) reasons, to substantiate, to justify.

Begründer *m* founder, originator.

begründet *adj* well founded, justified; **für** ~ **halten** to deem valid; **rechtlich** ~ legally founded, legally established, legally justified.

Begründetheit *f* reasonable justification, merits (*of a claim*), justification, arguments (for).

Begründung *f* statement of reasons, grounds, foundation, argument (*for s.th.*), findings of law (*of a judgment*); reasoning; ~ **e-r Schuld** establishment of an obligation, the arising of an obligation, incurring an obligation; ~ **e-s Antrags** grounds for a motion; ~ **e-s Gesellschaftsverhältnisses** establishment of a partnership; ~ **e-s Gerichtsstandes** establishment of a (legal) forum; ~ **e-s Rechts** creation of a right (or title); ~ **e-s Urteils** grounds for a judgment, findings of the court *in a judgment*; **~sfrist** time for stating reasons (*in support of claim*); **~szwang** requirement to file supporting argument; **ausführliche** ~ amplified (*or* more detailed) reasons; **bestechende** ~ specious argumentation; **die** ~ **e-r Entscheidung** the reasons for a decision; **e-e** ~ **vortragen** to state a case; **mangelnde** ~ lack of supporting argument, lack of justification; **nähere** ~ substantiation; **rechtliche** ~ legal reasoning; **schlüssige** ~ cogent argument, sound reasoning; **schriftliche** ~ written reasons; **vertretbare** ~ tenable (valid, cogent) argument; **zur** ~ **von** in support of.

Begrüßungsgeld *n* welcome money.

begünstigen *v/t* to benefit, to favo(u)r, to be partial to sth., to show favo(u)r; *crim:* to abet, to act as accessory after the fact, to connive (at); to give aid and comfort (*to the enemy*); **persönlich ~:** *to receive, harbour and maintain.*

Begünstiger *m* accessory after the fact, abettor, criminal protector.

Begünstigter *m* beneficiary.

Begünstigung *f* designation of a beneficiary; preference, preferential treatment; showing favo(u)rs; abetting, connivance, acting as accessory after the fact; ~ **im Amt** favo(u)ritism in office; **gleichmäßige** ~ equal benefit; **steuerliche** ~ tax privilege.

Begünstigungs|absicht intention of benefiting s.o.; **~klausel** benefit clause (*insurance*); **~vertrag** beneficial contract.

begutachten *v/t* to give an opinion, to deliver an expert opinion, to appraise.

Begutachter *m* surveyor, → *Gutachter*.

Begutachtung *f* appraisal, expert valuation; **negative** ~ negative expert's opinion; **positive** ~ favo(u)rable expert's opinion; **schriftliche** ~ written opinion.

Behältnis *n* receptacle, container.

behandeln *v/t* to treat, to deal with; **erkennungsdienstlich** ~ to check a person's identity (*for the police records*); **gleich** ~ to place on the same footing (as), to treat equally (to); **ungerecht** ~ to discriminate, to treat s. o. unfairly; **verschieden** ~ to discriminate; **vertraulich** ~ to keep in confidence, to treat confidentially.

Behandlung *f* treatment; **~sabbruch** stopping medical treatment (*of terminally ill patient*); **~sfehler** medical negligence; medical malpractice; **~sgebühr** medical fee; processing fee, handling charge; **~kosten** handling charges; **~sverfahren** method of medical treatment; processing method; **~szwang** legal obligation to give medical treatment; **ambulante** ~ outpatient treatment; **ärztliche** ~ medical treatment, medical attendance; **bevorzugte** ~ preferential treatment; **die ~ zurückstellen** to defer a matter, *US*: to table a matter; **diskriminierende** ~ discriminatory treatment; **disparitätische** ~ unequal treatment; **einkommensteuerliche** ~ treatment for income tax purposes; **fachgerechte** ~ competent (medical) treatment; **freie ärztliche** ~ free medical treatment; **grausame** ~ cruel treatment; **stationäre** ~ inpatient treatment; **steuerliche** ~ tax treatment, tax status; **ungleiche** ~ discrimination, discriminatory treatment; **unterschiedliche** ~ difference in treatment, discrimination; **zollrechtliche** ~ customs treatment.

beharren *v/i* to persist, to persevere.

beharrlich *adj* persistent, persevering, unwavering.

Beharrung *f* insistence, perseverance; ~ **auf e-m Standpunkt** insisting on a point of view, sticking to a point of view, inflexibility; **~stendenz** tendency to inertia.

behaupten *v/t* to claim, to allege (*facts*), to contend, to assert (*rights*), to aver (*legal argument*), to maintain (*against counter-arguments*), to say; *v reflex* to stand up well, to remain steady, to stand one's ground.

Behauptung *f* claim, allegation, contention, (positive) assertion, averment; ~ **gegen** ~ one man's word against another's; ~ **ohne Beweisantritt** assertion unsupported by evidence, nude matter; **~slast** burden of (sufficient) allegations; **abträgliche** ~ harmful assertion; **abwegige** ~ frivolous claim; **anfechtbare** ~ refutable assertion; **beleidigende** ~ defamatory statement; **die ~en der Gegenpartei bestreiten** to deny the opponent's allegations; **die ~ entbehrt jeder Grundlage** the allegation (assertion) is without substance (*or* is absolutely unfounded); **e-e ~ aufstellen** to claim, to assert; **e-e ~ zu den Akten nehmen** to take down an allegation (*for the record*); **einseitige ~en** one-sided (*or* unilateral) allegations; **erhebliche tatsächliche ~en** material allegations; **irrelevante** ~ irrelevant assertion; **negative** ~ negative averment (*or* allegation); **neue tatsächliche ~en** new factual allegations; **nichtssagende ~en aufstellen** to express meaningless assertions; **rechtserhebliche ~en** allegations material to the merits of the case, allegations relevant to the issue; **seine ~en beweisen** to prove one's assertions; **ständig wiederholte ~en** continual statements, reiterated statements; **unbewiesene** ~ unproved assertion; **tatsächliche** ~ statement of fact, factual statement, allegation.

behebbar *adj* remediable (*damage*), amendable, rectifiable; available (*account*); ~ **gegen Faktura und**

Konnossement available against invoice and bill of lading.

beheben v/t to remedy (*a defect, a breach*), to repair (*damage*), to remove (*difficulties*), to rectify.

Behebung f repair, remedying, removal (*of a defect*); **gütliche ~ aller Schwierigkeiten** friendly settlement of any difficulty.

beheimatet adj being a native of, residing in, registered at (*ship*).

Behelf m makeshift; cf *Rechtsbehelf*; **~sbauten** (temporary) makeshift structures; **~sheim** emergency dwelling, makeshift home; **b~smäßig** adj makeshift, improvised, temporary.

Beherbergung f (providing) accommodation, lodgings, shelter.

Beherbungs|betrieb small hotel, bed and breakfast business, meal and bed enterprise; **~betrug** hotel fraud; **~gewerbe** hotel and lodging industry, the hotel trade; **~stätten** hotels and lodgings; **~vertrag** contract for lodging, hotel contract, innkeeper's contract; **~wesen** lodging and hotel business.

beherrschen v/t to dominate, to control, to rule, to master.

Beherrschung f domination, control; **~svertrag** controlling agreement; **im ~sbereich** subject to control, in the sphere of control.

behindern v/t to obstruct, to impede.

behindert adj handicapped, disabled; **geistig ~** mentally handicapped; **körperlich ~** physically disabled.

Behinderter m disabled person.

Behinderung f hindrance, obstruction, restraint; disablement, impairment; **~ der Rechtspflege** (the) obstruction of justice, obstructing the course of justice; **~ der Schiffahrt** obstruction to navigation (*or* shipping); **~ des Konkursverfahrens** obstruction to bankruptcy proceedings; **~ des öffentlichen Verkehrs** obstructing traffic; **~ des Wettbewerbs** restraint of competition; **~sverbot** prohibition of obstructing sth; **~swettbewerb** obstructive competitive practices; **~ von Parlamentsmitgliedern** restraining members of Parliament, obstruction of members; **körperliche oder geistige ~** physical or mental impairment; **vorsätzliche ~** (wilful) obstruction; **widerrechtliche ~ durch Streikposten** unlawful picketing.

Behörde f government body; government subdivision; public authority, official authority, administrative body (*or* agency), regulatory body; **~ für Umweltschutzfragen** environmental authority; **angegliederte ~n** affiliated authorities; **die Hohe B~** (*der Montanunion*) the High Authority (*of the European Coal and Steel Community*); **die maßgebende ~** the appropriate authority; **ersuchende ~** public authority requesting (another) *to perform an official function*; **ersuchte ~** the requested authority (*public authority officially requested to perform a function*); **nachgeordnete ~** subsidiary authority, lower (echelon) authority; **oberste ~** supreme authority; **örtliche ~** local office, local authority; **sachlich unzuständige ~** (functionally) incompetent authority; **staatliche ~** governmental agency; **unterstellte ~** subordinate authority, **vollziehende ~** executive office, executive public body; **vorgesetzte ~** superior authority; **zuständige ~** (the) proper authority, competent authority, appropriate authority.

Behörden|angestellte salaried civil servant; **~apparat** official machinery; **~aufbau** structure of the public administration; **~eigenschaft** character of a public office, official status; **~gliederung** subdivisions of the administration; **~hierarchie** administrative hierarchy; **~leiter** chief of a government agency, head of a public authority; **~sitz** seat of a public administrative body;

behördlich | **Beiordnung**

~**sprache** officialese, gobbledygook; ~**weg** administrative channels, recourse to public authorities, echelons of public service; ~**wirtschaft** red tape, bureaucracy; ~**zug** echelons of public service, channels of public service.

behördlich *adj* official, magisterial; ~**erseits** *adj* officially, on the part of the authorities.

bei *prep* care of (c/o) (*in an address*).

Beiakte *f* related file; *pl* (~n): supplementary files.

beibehalten *v/t* to maintain, to keep unchanged, to retain.

Beibehaltung *f* maintenance, continuation (*of a state, condition or rule*).

beibringen *v/t* to adduce, to furnish, to supply, to provide.

Beibringung *f* production (*documents in court*), adduction; obtaining; causing; ~**sfrist** deadline for submission, *time for the production of documents, names and addresses of witnesses etc;* ~**sgrundsatz** principle of party presentation (*not ex officio*), accusatorial procedure; ~ **von Gift** administering poison.

Beichtgeheimnis *n* seal of confession, confessional secret.

beiderseitig *adj* mutual, reciprocal.

beidrücken *v/t* to affix (*seal*), to impress.

Beifahrer *m* (front-seat) passenger, co-driver (*passenger car*), driver's mate (*lorry*).

beifügen *v/t* to add, to enclose, to annex, to append, to subjoin.

Beifügung *f* addition, added matter, annex, enclosure.

Beigeladener *m* summoned third party.

beigetrieben *adj* collected, recovered; **nicht** ~ unrecovered, not retrieved.

beigeordnet *adj* associate(d), affiliated, subsidiary.

Beigeordneter *m* councillor.

Beihilfe *f* (1) grant, aid, grant-in-aid, allowance, *pl also:* aids granted, *esp. contribution granted by the state to established civil servants for costs of illness, births and deaths;* ~**empfänger** recipient of aid (*esp official receiving compensation for expenses of illness, births and deaths*); ~**regelung** system of aid for public servants; **degressive** ~**n** aids on diminishing scales; **nicht rückzahlungspflichtige** ~ non-returnable aid; **staatliche** ~ government(al) grant, government aid to public servants.

Beihilfe *f* (2) aiding and abetting (*before and during commission of crime*); ~ **leisten** to assist in the commission of crime, to counsel and procure, to aid and abet; ~ **zum Selbstmord** assisting suicide.

Beiladung *f* (1) additional cargo, cargo added, extra cargo.

Beiladung *f* (2) third-party summons to attend proceedings (*as a person whose rights may be affected*).

Beilage *f* enclosure (*to a letter or brief*); ~ **zur Anlage** appendix to annex, schedule to annex.

beiläufig *adv* incidentally, accidentally, casually.

beilegen *v/t* to enclose; to reconcile, to settle.

Beilegung *f* settlement, adjustment, accommodation; ~ **im Wege des Vergleichs** settlement by compromise; ~ **von Meinungsverschiedenheiten** settlement of differences; ~ **von Streitigkeiten** settlement of disputes; **friedliche** ~ peaceful settlement; **gerichtliche** ~ court settlement; **gütliche** ~ amicable settlement, out-of-court settlement; **schiedsgerichtliche** ~ settlement by way of arbitration.

beimessen *v/t* to attribute (to), to ascribe (to), to credit s. o. with.

Beimessung *f* attribution, the ascribing.

Beimischung *f* admixture; additive; **ohne** ~ without additives, unadulterated.

beinhalten *v/t* to contain, to comprise, to include, to imply, to amount to.

beiordnen *v/t* to assign as counsel or advisor (*to a poor or helpless party*).

Beiordnung *f* assignment as counsel

Beipackzettel

(or advisor) to s. o; ~ **im Armenrecht** *hist* assignment to a pauper.

Beipackzettel *m* information leaflet in medical packing.

beipflichten *v/i* to concur (with).

Beirat *m* advisory board, advisory council, advisory committee, supervisory board; **wissenschaftlicher** ~ scientific advisory council.

Beischlaf *m* sexual intercourse; carnal knowledge; **~erschleichung** fraudulently obtaining sexual intercourse; **~erzwingung** obtaining sexual intercourse by force; rape; **außerehelicher** ~ extra-marital intercourse.

Beischreibung *f* addition and/or correction of register entry.

Beiseiteschaffen *n* removing by stealth, secreting; ~ **der Familienhabe** secret removal of family property (*esp: household things*); ~ **einer Leiche** secret removal of a corpse; ~ **gepfändeter Sachen** secret removal of attached objects; ~ **von Vermögensgegenständen** secret removal of property (*by bankrupt*).

beiseiteschaffen *v/t* to secrete, to remove secretly, to make away (*with the loot*), to stash away.

Beisitzer *m* associate judge, assessor, puisne judge; ~ **der Arbeitsgerichte** lay-assessors in industrial tribunals; **beamteter** ~ civil servant as board member; **landwirtschaftlicher** ~ agricultural assessor; **schiffssachverständiger** ~ nautical assessor.

Beispiel *n* example, instance; **praktisches** ~ practical example, object lesson, case in point; **zum** ~ (*z. B.*) for example, for instance, *e.g.* (= *exempli gratia*).

beispiellos *adj* unprecedented.

Beistand *m* (1) support, aid, assistance; ~ **leisten** to render assistance; **~sabkommen** standby arrangement; **~sfazilität** support facility; **~sleistung in Seenot** salvage service; **~spakt** mutual assistance pact, pact of mutual assistance;

Beitragsentgelt

~spflicht duty to help and assist s. o.; **~sverpflichtung** duty to render military aid, duty to help an ally militarily; **gegenseitiger** ~ mutual assistance.

Beistand *m* (2) assistant; legal advisor, counsel.

beistehen *v/i* to support, to second, to back.

beisteuern *v/t* to contribute (to) (*esp money to a cause*).

Beitrag *m* (financial) contribution, subscription, premium; pro rata share, *pl* Beiträge (~*e*) membership dues; ~ **des Bundes** pro rata grant of the federal government; **abgeführter** ~ delivered contribution; **anteilsmäßiger** ~ pro rata share; **berücksichtigungsfähige** ~**e** qualifying contributions; **freiwilliger** ~ voluntary contribution, voluntary subscription; **laufender** ~ periodical contribution; **unwirksame** ~ ineffective (social insurance) contributions; **zugesagter** ~ pledged contribution.

Beitrags|abführung remittance of dues, *esp. of social security contributions*; **~abrechnung** accounting for dues (*or contributions*) collected; **~abzug** deduction of (*social security*) contributions (*by employer*); **~aufkommen** yield from contributions; ~~ **der Sozialversicherungen**: parafiscal (*social insurance*) *revenue*; **~befreiung** exemption from (*social insurance*) contributions; **~bemessungsgrenze** upper income limit (for social security); **~bemessungsgrundlage** facts underlying the assessment of contributions; **~berechnung** computation of contributions; **~bescheid** *official notice of social insurance charges*; **~einnahmen** collected contributions, premium income; **~einziehung** forcible collection, enforcement of contributions; **~einzug** = *~einziehung qv*; **~einzugsverfahren** enforcement procedure for collection of contributions (*social insurance*); **~entgelt**

129

membership contribution; ~**entrichtung** payment of contributions, of premiums, of dues; ~**ermäßigung** premium rebate, reduction of dues; ~**erstattung** refunding of contributions, reimbursement of dues; ~**forderungen** outstanding dues (*or* contributions); **b**~**frei** non-contributory; ~**freiheit** exemption from (*social security*) contributions; ~**freistellung** waiving requirement to pay dues; ~**hinterziehung** evasion of social security contributions; ~**klasse** class of social security contributors, contributions scale; ~**kürzung** (*unlawful*) reduction of social security contributions; ~**leistung** payment of contributions; ~**pflicht** liability to contribute; ~**pflichtig** liable to contribution; subject to social security contributions, ~**pflichtiger** party liable to pay contributions (*or* dues, *or* premiums); *person subject to compulsory social security;* ~**rückerstattung** → ~*erstattung;* ~**rückstände** arrears of contributions (*or* of dues, of premiums); ~**satz** rate of contribution; ~**schlüssel** coefficients (for contributions); ~**staffelung** *ins* grading of premiums, scale of premiums; ~**streit** litigation concerning (*social insurance*) contributions; ~**überwachung** control of collections of contributions (*social insurance*); ~**verfahren** procedure for dues collection (*or* collection of social insurance contributions); ~**vollstreckung** enforcement of contribution debts by execution; ~**zahler** contributor, party paying contibutions (*or* dues *or* premiums); ~**zahlung** remittance (*or* payment) of contributions (*or of* dues, *of* premiums), payment of subscription (*club*); ~**zeiten** paid-up periods (*social security contributions*).

beitragen *v/t* to contribute (to), to subscribe (to), to be conducive to.

beitreibbar *adj* recoverable, collectible; **nicht** ~ irrecoverable, uncollectible.

beitreiben *v/t* to collect, to recover, to enforce the payment of.

Beitreibung *f* recovery, enforced collection, (*esp. by execution*), enforcement of the payment of money; ~ **der Steuerschuld** enforced collection of tax payable; ~**skosten** collection expenses; ~**smaßnahmen** execution for collection of money debts; ~**sverfahren** collection procedure, recovery proceedings; ~**ssachen** collection cases; ~ **von Außenständen** recovery of outstanding debts, collection of outstanding accounts; **außergerichtliche** ~ collection without judicial process.

beitreten *v/i* to join, to become a member, to enter, *int* to accede (to), to enter.

Beitritt *m* entry, joining, becoming a member, *int* accession; ~ **zu e-m Staatsvertrag** accession to a treaty.

Beitritts|antrag application for membership; ~**ausgleichsbetrag** accession; compensatory amount; ~**berechtigung** entitlement to membership; ~**erklärung** enrolment, declaration of membership, *int* declaration of accession; ~**klausel** association clause, accession clause (*treaty*); ~**land** acceding country; ~**protokoll** protocol of accession; ~**urkunde** instrument of accession; ~**vertrag** treaty of accession, accession treaty; ~**zwang** compulsory membership.

beiwohnen *v/i* to attend; to cohabit, to have sexual intercourse, to copulate, to have carnal knowledge.

Beiwohnung *f* cohabitation, sexual intercourse, the sex act copulation; ~**sunfähigkeit** incapacity to consummate; **außereheliche** ~ extramarital intercourse; **Gelegenheit zur** ~ access.

beiziehen *v/t* to call in, to obtain the file (*of another case*).

Beiziehung *f* order to obtain the file (*of another case*).

bejahen *v/t* to answer in the affirmative, to affirm.

bejahend *adj* affirmative, positive.

bejahendenfalls *adv* if so; in case you agree; if the answer is ‚yes'.

Bejahung *f* an affirmative answer, consent, affirmation.

bekämpfen *v/t* to combat, to oppose, to fight against s. th.; **sich bis aufs Messer** ~ to fight each other tooth and nail.

Bekämpfung *f* struggle, fight (against s. th.).

bekannt *adj* known, well known, notorious; **hierdurch wird ~ gemacht** notice is hereby given; **polizeilich ~ sein** to have a police record.

Bekanntgabe *f* announcement, publication, notification.

bekanntgeben *v/t* to make public, to make known, to announce.

Bekanntheitsgrad *m* (national) name recognition, awareness level; **~ e-r Marke** brand awareness.

bekanntmachen *v/t* to publish, to make known, to announce; **öffentlich ~** to make public, to announce (publicly).

Bekanntmachung *f* announcement, publication, proclamation; **~ der Börsenorgane** notification by the stock exchange authorities; **~ der Firmenänderung** notification of change of a firm's (or corporation's) name; **amtliche ~** official announcement; public announcement; **gerichtliche ~en** court notices; **öffentliche ~** public notice, public notification, public announcement; **vereinfachte ~** simplified notification.

Bekanntmachungs|befugnis authorization to publish (*a conviction for slander; a public apology etc.*); **~gebühr** publication fee; **~pflicht** (statutory) duty to disclose publicly; **~tag** date of publication.

bekennen *v/t, v/i* to own up (to), to confess (to), to acknowledge; *v reflex* to acknowledge, to profess (*a faith*), to avow; to claim responsibility ; **sich schuldig ~** to plead guilty, to confess (to).

Bekennerbrief *m* (*von Terroristen*) a letter claiming responsibility for an outrage (*bombing attack*), terrorists' letter of confession.

Bekenntnis *n* confession (*of guilt, of commission of a crime*); religious affiliation, creed, denomination (*religion*); **~freiheit** freedom to profess a faith; *negative* **~~**: *freedom not to profess a faith;* **~schule** denominational school; **politisches ~** political belief; **religiöses ~** denomination, religious confession, religious belief.

beklagen *v/t* to deplore, to mourn, to bewail; *jur* = *verklagen qv*; *v reflex* to complain.

Beklagter *m* (*der Beklagte*) defendant (*in a civil case*), respondent (*in divorce and equity proceedings*); **~nhäufung** plurality of defendants.

bekräftigen *v/t* to affirm, to reaffirm, to corroborate (*by evidence*), to vouch (for); **eidlich ~** to affirm by oath.

Bekräftigung *f* affirmation, corroboration, confirmation; **~ der Wahrheit** affirmation (of the truth).

Bekräftigungs|eid *m* assertory oath, confirmatory oath; **~formel** words of affirmation (*in lieu of religious oath*).

bekunden *v/t* to testify, to give evidence, to depose (and say).

Bekundung *f* testimony, statement (*of a witness or party*), deposition; **schriftliche ~** deposition.

Beladen *n* loading, lading; **~ und Entladen** loading and unloading.

beladen *v/t* to load.

Beladung *f* loading, lading; **~sgrenze** load limit, maximum load.

belagern *v/t* to besiege, to beleaguer.

Belagerung *f* siege.

Belagerungszustand *m* state of siege; **den ~ verhängen** to proclaim the state of siege.

Belang *m* concern, relevance; **öffentliche ~e** *pl* matters of public concern, (the) interests of the public; **von ~** of some importance, material, relevant; **von keinem ~**

belangbar

of no importance, immaterial, irrelevant.

belangbar *adj* liable to court action, subject to legal proceedings, suable.

belangen *v/t* to hold s. o. responsible, to take legal action (steps) (*against s. o.*), to prosecute s. o.; **gerichtlich** ~ to take legal action against s. o.

belanglos *adj* irrelevant, inconsequential, immaterial, petty.

Belanglosigkeit *f* insignificance, irrelevance, impertinence.

Belangung *f* (the) prosecution (of), legal action, the taking of proceedings (*against s. o.*).

belassen *v/t* to leave the matter where it stands, to leave it at that, to let sth rest, to leave in abeyance, to leave things as they are; to allow s. o. to obtain (keep) sth.

Belassung *f* permitted retention; ~**squote** permitted quota to be retained.

Belastbarkeit *f* capacity to bear a burden; capacity to meet the costs, loading capacity; inherent strength.

belasten *v/t* to charge, to burden, to load, to encumber (*property by mortgage etc*), to debit (*an account*), to incriminate (*suspected person*); **sich selbst** ~ to incriminate oneself.

belastend *adj* onerous, inculpatory, incriminating, incriminating.

belastet *pp* → *belasten*, *adj* burdened, incriminated, encumbered (*property*); **nicht** ~ unmortgaged, unencumbered, cleared of a charge, free of suspicion.

Belasteter *m* (*der Belastete*) a politically incriminated person (*ex-Nazi*).

belästigen *v/t* to molest, to annoy.

belästigend *adj* annoying, offensive, troublesome.

Belästigung *f* nuisance, molestation, annoyance, importuning (*for purposes of prostitution*); ~**sverbot** non-molestation order; **nachbarrechtliche** ~ private nuisance, nuisance by adjacent owner; **rechtserhebliche** ~ actionable nuisance.

Beleg

Belastung *f* charge, burden, load, encumbrance, debit, incrimination, incidence (tax); *cf belasten*; ~**en der Devisenbilanz** pressure on the net foreign exchange movement; ~ **des Arbeitsmarktes** depressive effect on the labo(u)r market; **außergewöhnliche** ~**en** extraordinary expenses (*deductible from income tax*); **dauernde** ~ standing charge; **dingliche** ~ encumbrance (in rem), fixed charge; **finanzielle** ~ financial burden; **finanzielle** ~ **durch Löhne und Gehälter** pay load; **hypothekarische** ~ mortgage charge; **objektsteuerartige** ~ in rem fiscal charge; **politische** ~ political incrimination; **steuerliche** ~ tax load, tax burden, fiscal charges; **von** ~**en freistellen** to disencumber.

Belastungs|anzeige debit advice, debit note, ~~*n auf Kundenkonten verbuchen: to post charges to customer's account*; ~**aufgabe** debit advice, debit memo, debit note; ~~ *an e-m Scheck: cheque voucher;* ~**grenze** maximum for encumbrances; capacity to stand (*price rises*); ~**material** incriminating material (*or evidence*), ~**probe** test, ordeal; ~**quote** load ratio; ~**verbot** prohibition to submit property to charges or encumbrances; ~**verschiebungen** shifts in the total encumbrance; ~**zeuge** detrimental witness, prosecution witness.

belaufen *v reflex* to aggregate, to total.

Belebungskomponenten *f/pl* stimulating factors.

Beleg *m* supporting document, voucher, receipt, slip; ~**abschnitt** stub, counterfoil; ~~ *an e-m Scheck: cheque voucher;* ~ **anliegend** voucher attached; ~**e beibringen** to furnish documentary material, to tender proofs and vouchers; ~**buch** slip book; ~**buchhaltung** voucher bookkeeping, voucher system; ~**doppel** copy voucher; ~**leser** video scan document reader; ~**nummer** voucher number; ~**prüfung** voucher audit; ~**regi-**

ster voucher register; **~sichtung** vouching, inspection of vouchers; **~e vorlegen** to submit documentary material; **anerkannter ~** approved voucher; **geprüfter ~** audited voucher.

Belegarzt *m* outside doctor who has hospital beds at his disposal; **~vertrag** hospital facilities contract with outside doctor.

belegbar *adj* provable by documents.

belegen *v/t* to document, to substantiate, to produce evidence (for), to prove; to occupy; **~** *adj* situate, locally situate, situated, located; **~ sein** to be located (at).

Belegenheit *f* situs, locus rei sitae; **~sfinanzamt** revenue office where taxable property is situate; **~sgemeinden** local districts where the (real) property is situate; **~sland** country of situs, country where property is situate; **~sstaat** state of situs, state where property is situate.

Belegexemplar *n* copy voucher, author's copy, specimen, file copy, courtesy copy.

Belegschaft *f* staff, operating staff, personnel, workforce, the employees; **~saktien** employees' shares; **~~ plan:** *employee share scheme*; *stock purchase plan;* **~sversammlung** staff meeting.

Belegstelle *f* supporting authority, locus citatus, reference.

Belegung *f* occupation, occupancy; documentation, verification; **~szeit** utilization time.

belehnbar *adj* eligible as security for credit = *beleihbar qv, hist* suitable as a fief.

belehnen *v/t* to enfeoff.

Belehnter *m* (*der Belehnte*), donee, feoffee, liegeman, vassal.

Belehnung *f* investiture, infeoffment (= *enfeoffment*), infeudation, seisin (= *seizin*).

belehren *v/t* to instruct, to advise (*s.o. of his rights*); to caution, to warn (*that anything you say may be used as evidence*), to direct (*the jury*); **falsch ~** to misdirect.

Belehrung *f* instruction, advice, caution, warning, direction (*jury*); **~ des Angeklagten** *über sein Recht, einen Verteidiger zu haben* notifying the accused *of his right to counsel*; **~spflicht** obligation to caution (*a suspect*); **~ zum Schutz des Beschuldigten** cautionary instruction; **falsche ~** misdirection (*of jury*).

beleidigen *v/t* to insult, to offend; **grob ~** to outrage, to insult grossly.

beleidigend *adj* offensive, defamatory, libel(l)ous, slanderous.

Beleidigung *f* insult, defamation, indignity, libel (*written or other permanent form*), slander (*verbal*), verbal injury, outrage (*extreme*); **~ ausländischer Staatsmänner** insulting foreign statesmen; **~ der Gesetzgebungsorgane** insult against (*or* to) the legislative organs; **~ des Gerichts** insulting the court, (*Mißachtung:* contempt of court); **~ e-r Behörde** insult to an authority; **~sklage** action for defamation, libel action; **grundlose ~** gratuitous insult; **tätliche ~** assault with intent to insult; **schwere ~** gross insult; **wechselseitige ~** mutual insult.

beleihbar *adj* suitable as collateral security, suitable to serve as collateral.

beleihen *v/t* to lend against collateral security, to use as collateral.

Beleihung *f* lending against collateral security, using as collateral; **~ e-r Police** policy loan; **~ von Ansprüchen** assigning rights as collateral.

beleihungsfähig *adj* = *beleihbar qv*.

Beleihungs|grenze limit of credit with reference to the collateral security, lending limit; **~objekt** property used as collateral security; **~ prozentsatz** loan ratio; **~quote** loan-to-value ratio; **~raum** loan category, lending limit (*with reference to collateral security*); **~satz** rate for advances on securities; **~stop** bar to further lendings; **~wert** hy-

beleumdet   **Benennung**

pothecary value, collateral value, value as collateral security, loan value (*of a policy*).

beleumdet *adj* = *beleumundet qv*.

beleumundet *adj* reputed; **gut ~ sein** to have a good reputation; **übel ~** ill reputed, disreputable.

Belieben *n* discretion; **freies ~** free discretion, uncontrolled discretion; **nach ~** at one's discretion, at (one's) pleasure, at will; **nach ~ des Gerichts** as the court may think fit.

beliebig *adj* optional, as desired, discretionary.

Belieferung *f* supply, supplies; **~ des Hofes** purveyance; **~sanspruch** entitlement to regular supplies; **~spflicht** obligation to supply as required; **~sstockung** temporary stop of deliveries.

belohnen *v/t* to reward, to remunerate.

Belohnung *f* reward, premium; **~ für die Ergreifung** reward for information leading to the arrest of s. o.; **amtliche ~** official reward, prize; **e-e ~ aussetzen** to promise (*or* offer) a reward; **gebührende ~** due reward.

bemächtigen *v/reflex* to seize.

bemängeln *v/t* to find fault (with), to criticize, to cavil at.

Bemängelung *f* fault-finding.

bemänteln *v/t* to disguise, to cover up, to palliate, to gloss over.

bemessen *v/t* to award (*punishment, damages*), to assess, to scale.

Bemessung *f* assessment, awarding, determination; **~ der Geldstrafe** assessment of fine, computation of a fine.

Bemessungsgrundlage *f* evaluation basis, basis of assessment, (*or* yardstick for); **~maßstab** standard of assessment; **~zeitraum** (*tax*) basis period, chargeable accounting period, period of assessment.

Bemühung *f* effort, endeavo(u)r; **größte ~en** best endeavo(u)rs.

bemustern *v/t* to supply samples (of), to attach samples to an offer.

Bemusterung *f* sampling.

benachbart *adj* neighbo(u)ring, contiguous, abutting.

benachrichtigen *v/t* to notify, to inform, to advise; **jmdn schriftlich ~** notify s. o. in writing.

Benachrichtigung *f* notification, notice, information, advice (*commercial*); **~sschreiben** letter of advice, advice note; **~sverfahren** notification procedure; **~ über Anhängigkeit bei einem Schiedsgericht** notice of reference; **~ von Aktionären** notice to members.

benachteiligen *v/t* to discriminate against, to affect adversely, to place at a disadvantage.

benachteiligt *adj* adversely affected, disadvantaged; **sozial oder wirtschaftlich ~** underprivileged, disadvantaged.

Benachteiligung *f* discrimination (against); **~ durch Schikane** discrimination by way of victimization; **~sverbot** prohibition of discrimination; *geschlechtsbezogenes* **~~:** *prohibition of sex discrimination;* **steuerliche ~** tax discrimination, fiscal discrimination.

benannt *adj* named, nominated, said, such, aforesaid, above-mentioned.

Benannter *m/sing* (*der Benannte*) the person named, the aforesaid.

beneficium excussionis → *Einrede der Vorausklage*.

Benefizium *n eccl* benefice.

Benehmen *n* (*1*) behaviour, conduct, demeanour; **ungebührliches ~** misconduct, improper behaviour.

Benehmen *n* (*2*) consultation, consent (*after consultation, esp of equal ranking authorities*); **im ~ mit** in consultation with; **im gemeinsamen ~** by common accord; **sich ins ~ setzen** to communicate (with), to consult.

benennen *v/t* to nominate, to name.

Benennung *f* nomination, designation, description, naming; **~sgebühr** *part* designation fee; **~**

134

Benennungssystem

von Zeugen offering the testimony of a particular witness, naming a witness *(to the court)*; **gemeinsame** ~ joint designation.
Benennungssystem *n* nomenclature.
benötigen *v/t* to require, to want, to need.
benutzen *v/t* to use, to utilize, to occupy *(room)*.
Benutzer *m* (= *Benützer*) user; **~ e-s Warenzeichens** (rightful) user of a trade-mark; **gutgläubiger** ~ user in good faith.
Benutzung *f* use, utilization; **~ der Erfindung** use of invention; **~ und Gewahrsam** actual use or occupation *(of rooms)*; **~ verwendeter Postwertzeichen** use of cancelled stamps; **allgemein zulässige** ~ *(geschützter Werke)* fair use *(copyright)*; **bei ordnungsgemäßer** ~ when properly used; **erlaubnisfreie** ~ free use (for everyone), free availability; **gewöhnliche** ~ ordinary use, natural use; **mißbräuchliche** ~ misuse, improper use; **öffentliche** ~ public use; **widerrechtliche** ~ **e-r gepfändeten Sache** abuse of distress; **zulässige** ~ permitted use.
Benutzungsǀbedingungen terms and conditions of use; **~gebühr** charge for the use of sth, *(toll roads, bridges)*; **~genehmigung** permission (licence) to use sth; **~kosten** user cost; **~lizenz** licence to use; **~ordnung** regulation(s) for the use of sth; **~recht** right of user, user, right to use sth; **~zwang** compulsory usage, compulsory use *(of public utility services)*.
Benzin *n, GB:* petrol, *US:* gas(oline); **bleifreies** ~ unleaded petrol; **Normal** ~ two-star petrol; **Super** ~ four-star petrol.
beobachten *v/t* to observe, to keep under observation, to survey.
Beobachter *m* observer; **~delegation** team of observers; **als** ~ **fungieren** to act as observer, to hold a watching brief *(lawyer at trial)*, to act as rapporteur *(conference)*;

Berechnung

politischer ~ political observer, rapporteur *(conference)*.
Beobachtung *f* observation, monitoring, supervision; **~zeitraum** period under observation; **unter** ~ **stellen** to place under observation.
beraten *v/t* to advise, to give advice, *v/i* to deliberate, to confer, to consider, to consult; *v/reflex* to deliberate, to consider; **nochmals** ~ to reconsider; **sich anwaltschaftlich** ~ **lassen** to seek legal advice.
beratend *adj* advisory, consultant.
Berater *m* consultant, adviser; **juristischer** ~ legal adviser; **technischer** ~ technical consultant.
Beratung *f* advice, conselling; deliberation *(judges, members of parliament etc)*, consultation *(with lawyer, doctor)*; **e-e geheime** ~ **abhalten** to deliberate in camera; **neutrale (juristische)** ~ independent legal advice; **nochmalige** ~ reconsideration; **sich zur** ~ **zurückziehen** to retire for deliberation; **unparteiische** ~ independent advice; **wirtschaftliche** ~ economic consultancy.
Beratungsǀausschuß advisory board, advisory committee; **~befugnis** advisory power; **~gegenstand** item for discussion, point on the agenda; **~geheimnis** the secrecy of (judicial) deliberations; **~gremium** compulative body; **~hilfe** legal advice and assistance; **~kosten** consultation fee(s); **~organ** consultative organ (committee); **~pflicht** legal duty to give advice; **~stelle** advisory bureau; **~tätigkeit** consultancy, advisory work; **~vertrag** consultancy agreement.
berauben to rob s. o., to divest s. o. of sth (by violence).
Beraubung *f* robbing, robbery, spoliation, deprivation.
berechnen *v/t* to calculate, to compute; to bill, to invoice, to charge, to evaluate; **zu niedrig** ~ to underbill, to undercharge, to charge too little; **zuviel** ~ to overcharge.
Berechnung *f* calculation, computa-

tion; ~ **der Fristen** computation of time limits.

Berechnungs|art method *or* mode of calculation; **~formel** formula used for the calculation; **~grundlage** basis of computation; **~methode** method of calculation; *gemeinsame ~~: common method of calculation*; **~tabelle** calculation table; **~verordnung** computation ordinance (*concerning rent*); **~weise** mode of calculation; **~zeitraum** period of computation.

berechtigen *v/i* to entitle, to authorize, to qualify.

berechtigend *adj* entitling, facultative.

berechtigt *adj* entitled, justified, duly authorized, competent, qualified, rightful; **nicht ~ (zu)** without authority (to), unauthorized.

Berechtigter *m* (*der Berechtigte, pl Berechtigte ~e*) the party (absolutely) entitled, promisee, obligee, rightful claimant, beneficiary; **der wirklich ~e** the party actually entitled; **dinglich ~**person entitled in rem; **mehrere ~** several holders, several entitled parties; **wertpapiermäßig ~** holder in due course.

Berechtigung *f* right, privilege, entitlement; justification; authority; **~serfordernisse** eligibility requirements, qualification requirements; **~snachweis** proof of authority, licence, certificate of eligibility; **~schein** certificate of authority (*or entitlement*), warrant, licence; **~ zur Darlehensaufnahme** entitlement to borrow; **dingliche ~** legal interest, right in rem; **ohne ~** without authority, without justification.

Berechtsamsbuch *n* mining rights register.

bereden *v/t* to discuss, to confer; to persuade, to talk over.

Bereich *m* range, scope, purview, sphere, division, group, domain, field of jurisdiction, region; **~ der öffentlichen Finanzen** sphere of public finances; **~ der Wirtschaft** the economic sphere; **abgebender**

~ transferring division; **alle ~e des Marktes** all sections of the market; **empfangender ~** receiving division; **geschäftsführender ~** management sector; **militärischer ~** military zone; **in den ~ fallen** to come within the scope; **in den ~ jmds. gehören** to be in s. o.'s province; **öffentlicher ~** the public sector.

bereichern *v/reflex* to enrich oneself, to feather one's nest.

Bereicherung *f* (unjust) enrichment, gain; **sittenwidrige ~** lucre, immoral enrichment; **ungerechtfertigte ~** unjust (*or* undue) enrichment; *Herausgabe e-r ~~: restitution of sth obtained without legal cause.*

Bereicherungs|absicht intent to profit; **~anspruch** claim on account of unjust enrichment; *claim for the recovery of sth obtained without legal cause*, condictio sine causa; **~einrede** plea of unjust enrichment; **~klage** *Klage aus ungerechtfertigter Bereicherung qv;* **~verbot** impermissibility of enrichment by insurance benefits.

bereinigen *v/t* to adjust, to clear up, to correct, to straighten out; to regularize, to validate, to reassess (*securities after devaluation*), to settle (*debts, accounts*), to audit and verify (*balance sheet*).

bereinigt *adj* adjusted, regularized, revised.

Bereinigung *f* corrective adjustment, clearing-up, settlement, regularization, validation, reassessment, *cf bereinigen;* **~ des Sortiments** simplifying the range of products; **~sgesetz** validating statute; **~ und Neufassung von Gesetzen** revision of statutes.

bereit *adj* ready, prepared, willing.

bereithalten *v/t* to keep available, to hold ready.

Bereitschaft *f* readiness, preparedness; **~ zum Gespräch** willingness to discuss (*or* to talk, *or* to negotiate).

Bereitschafts|akkreditiv standby letter of credit; **~dienst** standby

bereitstellen

duty, office standby, emergency service; ~**fall** state of military standby duty; ~**kredit** stand-by facility; ~~-*Vereinbarung: stand-by arrangement*; ~**polizei** mobile police, riot police, flying squad; ~**reserve** ready reserve, standby reserves; ~**zusagen erteilen** to indicate readiness to grant credit; **in** ~ **stehen** to stand by.

bereitstellen *v/t* to place at s.o.'s disposal, to hold available, to allocate, to provide.

Bereitstellung *f* providing, allocation, earmarking, appropriation (*of funds*), loan accomodation, making (and/or holding) available, lining up; ~**sbescheid** advice about availability of credit, notification of the provision of a stand-by credit; ~**sfonds** earmarked funds; ~**sgebühren** commitment charge; ~**skonto** allocation fund, credit account available for drawings (*subject to providing cover by collateral security*); ~**splafond** commitment ceiling; ~**preis** basic energy supply price; basic rate; ~**sprovision** commitment fee; facility fee, standby fee; ~**szinsen** commitment interest; ~ **von Finanzierungsmitteln** allocation of funds for financing purposes.

bereuen *v/t* to repent, to regret, to rue.

Berg|amt *n* local mining authority, board of mines; ~**arbeiter** → *Bergarbeiter*; ~**bau** → *Bergbau*; ~**bauer** mountain farmer; ~**behörden** mining authorities; ~**gesetz** mining law; ~**polizei** *f* safety authorities for mines; ~**recht** mining law; ~**regalabgabe** mining royalty; ~**schäden** damage caused by mining operations; ~**schadensersatzanspruch** claim in respect of mining damage; ~**verordnungen** mining safety regulations; ~**verwaltung** administration of mines; ~**werk** →*Bergwerk*.

Bergarbeiter *m* miner, mine-worker, pitman; ~**kolonie** miners'

Bergwerksschäden

housing estate; ~-**Wohnungsbau** miners' homes.

Bergbau *m* mining, mining industry, extractive industry; ~**berechtigung** mining licence; ~**betrieb** mining enterpreise; ~**berufsgenossenschaft** compulsory accident insurance for miners; ~**ingenieur** mining engineer; ~**produktion** mining output; ~**regal** mining rights; ~**unternehmen** mining enterprise.

Berge|geld *n* salvage (money); ~**lohn** salvage, salvage money; ~**lohnforderung** salvage claim; ~**wert** *m* salvage value, damaged value, residual value.

bergen *v/t* to salvage, to rescue.

Bergmann *m* miner; ~**sprämie** bonus (extra pay) for miners (*tax free, statutory compensation for work in the pit*); ~**srente** miners pension.

Bergung *f* salvage; ~ **und Hilfeleistung** maritime assistance, maritime salvage.

Bergungs|dienst salvage service; ~**fälle** salvage cases; ~**gesellschaft** salvage company; ~**gut** salvage; ~**kosten** salvage charges; ~**recht** right of salvage; ~**schaden** salvage loss; ~**unternehmen** professional salvage; ~**verlust** salvage loss; ~**vertrag** salvage agreement.

Bergwerk *n* mine pit, mining concession.

Bergwerks|abgaben mining tax, mining royalties; ~**aktie** mining share; ~**berechtigung** mining rights, mining lease; ~**eigentum** proprietary mining rights (*right to prospect and extract minerals*); ~**eigentümer** holder of mining property, holder of mineral rights, mine owner; ~**feld** mining concession territory; ~**gesellschaft** mining company, colliery (*coal mining*); ~**konzession** mining licence; ~**pacht** mining lease; ~**recht** mining law, right to work minerals, mining right(s); ~**schäden** mining damage, dam-

137

Bericht

age to a mine; ~**unternehmungen** mines, mining enterprises.

Bericht *m* report, narration; ~**e aus erster Hand** first hand reports; ~ **e-r Auskunftei** mercantile report, status report (on a company); ~ **erstatten** to report ~**erstatter** reporter, reporting judge, judge rapporteur; rapporteur *(conference)*; ~**erstattung** reporting; ~ **über die Vermögenslage** statement of affairs; **amtlicher** ~ official report, bulletin; **e-n** ~ **ausarbeiten** to draw up a report; **e-n** ~ **vorlegen** to submit a report; **eingehender** ~ detailed account, full report **vertraulicher** ~ confidential report; **zusammenfassender** ~ summary account, comprehensive statement.

berichten *v/t* to report, to narrate.

Berichter *m* rapporteur.

berichtigen *v/t* to correct, to rectify, to adjust, to amend.

Berichtigung *f* correction, rectification of mistake, adjustment; ~ **des Grundbuchs** rectification of the land register *(esp if changes extraneous to the register have occurred)*; ~ **des Klagevorbringens** amendment of the statement of claim; ~ **e-r Buchung** rectification of an entry; ~ **e-s Urteils** rectification of a judgment; ~ **falscher Aussagen** correction of false statements; ~ **von Amts wegen** ex officio correction, amendment by the court of its own motion; **rückwirkende** ~ retroactive correction.

Berichtigungs|anspruch right to have sth corrected, claim for rectification; ~**anzeige** notice of error, notification of error; ~**betrag** corrective amount; ~**bewilligung** granting permission to rectify *(a register)*; ~**buchung** rectifying entry, period-end adjusting entry, transfer and counter warrant; **b~fähig** *adj* rectifiable; ~**feststellung** rectifying statement; ~**haushalt** amended budget; ~**konto** adjustment account, suspense account, reconciliation account; ~**protokoll** protocol of amendment, rectifying

Beruf

minutes, record of rectification; ~**satz** rate of adjustment; ~**veranlagung** corrective assessment, reassessment of taxes.

Berichts|daten reporting items; ~**jahr** year under review; ~**kreis** 1. scope of reporting; 2. group of reporting firms; **b~pflichtig** *adj* required to render returns, obliged to report; ~**termin** reporting date; ~**woche** week under review; reference week; ~**zeitpunkt** key date, date referred to in the report, reporting date, return date; ~**zeitraum** period under review, reference period.

Berliner Testament *n* Berlin Testament: *(reciprocal will whereby the spouses appoint each other universal heir and their child (children) final heir(s) of spouse surviving)*.

Berner|Übereinkunft *f* Berne Convention 1886 *(on international literary and artistic copyright protection)*; ~ **Verband** Berne Union *(established by the Berne Convention qv)*.

berüchtigt *adj* notorious, infamous.

berücksichtigen *v/t* to take into account, to make allowance for, to take into consideration, to respect.

Berücksichtigung *f* consideration, regard; ~ **finden** to be taken into consideration; **nach gebührender** ~ after due consideration; **unter** ~ **aller Umstände** having considered all the facts and circumstances.

berücksichtigungsfähig *adj* allowable *(tax)*, deductible.

Beruf *m* profession or business, occupation *(the principal business of one's life)*, vocation, calling, trade, *(craftsmen)*, profession *(self-employed, university graduates)*, pursuit; **akademischer** ~ academic profession, graduate profession; **ausgeübter** ~ actual occupation; **erlernter** ~ skilled trade, occupation; for which a person was trained; original occupation; **freier** ~ independent profession, liberal profession, self-employment, professional services, free-lance work; *die freien* ~*e*: the professions, the profes-

138

sional classes, professional occupations; **gefährdeter** ~ hazardous occupation; **graphische** ~**e** printing and allied trades; **handwerklicher** ~ trade, craft; **hauswirtschaftliche** ~**e** domestic callings, domestic service; **kaufmännische** ~**e** mercantile callings; **nicht selbständiger** ~ employment; **ständiger** ~ regular occupation; **von** ~ by occupation, by trade.

berufen *v/t* to appoint *(to an office)*, to co-opt *(to a committee)*, to call *(to a chair)*; *v/reflex* to rely on sth, to plead sth *(ignorance, force majeure etc)*, to vouch.

berufen *adj* qualified, competent.

beruflich *adj* professional, occupational, vocational.

Berufs|akademie college of advanced vocational studies; ~**anfänger** person beginning a vocation; learner, tyro; novice; ~**angabe** calling, statement of one's occupation; *pl/n* vocational data, occupational status, profession or vocation; ~**aufbauschule** vocational extension school; ~**auffassung** professional standard, ethical standard of a profession or trade; ~**aufgaben** occupational functions; ~**ausbildung** pre-employment training, occupational *(or* vocational) training *(or* education); ~~ *am Arbeitsplatz: vocational training on the job; betriebliche* ~~ *in-house training; schulische* ~~~: *vocational training in (vocational) school*; ~**ausbildungskosten** cost of vocational education, expenditure on vocational education; ~**ausbildungsstelle** vocational training centre; ~**ausbildungsunterstützung** training allowance; ~**ausbildungswerk** training opportunities scheme; ~**ausrüstung** professional equipment; ~**aussichten** job prospects; career prospects, occupational outlook; ~**ausstattung** professional equipment; ~**ausübung** vocational practice, exercise of one's profession; *unbefugte* ~*ausübung: unlawful practice (of a profession)*; ~**beamtentum** permanent civil service, officialdom; ~**beamter** career civil servant; established *(or* permanent) civil servant; ~**bedingt** occupational; ~**befähigung** occupational predisposition *(or* capacity), eligibility for office; ~**benennung** job title, occupational title; ~**berater** vocational advisor, career counsellor; vocational consultant; occupational guidance counsellor; ~**beratung** vocational guidance, careers advice, job counselling; ~**bezeichnung** occupational title, job title; ~**bild** occupational pattern; ~**bildung** vocational *or* professional education; ~**diplomat** career diplomat; ~**ehre** professional honour; ~**eid** professional oath; ~**einschränkungen** job restrictions; ~**erfahrung** vocational experience, post qualification experience; ~**erlaubnis** licence for practising a trade or profession; ~**ethos** professional ethics; ~**fachschule** specialised vocational *(or* trade) school; ~**feuerwehr** full-time fire brigade; ~**förderung** promotion of vocational advancement; ~**förderungszentrum** vocational advancement centre *(center, US)*; ~**fortbildung** advanced vocational training *(of jobholders)*; ~**freiheit** occupational liberty; **b**~**fremd** non-occupational, unacquainted with the trade or profession concerned; ~**gefahr** occupational hazard(s); ~**geheimnis** professional secret *(or* secrecy), professional discretion; ~**genossenschaft** social insurance for occupational accidents; mutual indemnity association; ~**gericht** professional disciplinary tribunal; ~**gerichtsbarkeit** disciplinary jurisdiction for the professions; ~**gruppe** occupational group; ~**gewerkschaft** craft union; ~**gruppeneinteilung** vocational classification; ~**haftpflichtversicherung** professional liability insurance, professional indemnity cover; ~**haftung für uner-**

Berufshandel

laubte Handlungen tortious professional liability *(legal profession etc)*; ~**handel** professional traders; ~**hilfe** vocational rehabilitation *(after occupational disease or accident)*; ~**jahr** years of service; ~**klassifizierung** job classification, job grade; ~**konsul** career consul; ~**krankheit** occupational *(or* vocational, *or* industrial*)* disease; ~**laufbahn** career (pattern); occupational history; ~**leben** professional life, working life, active life; **b**~**mäßig** professionally, in a professional way, in keeping with one's profession; ~**merkmal** job characteristic; ~**offizier** regular officer; ~**ordnung** occupational regulations; ~**ordnungsrecht** law of professional rules and regulations; ~**organisation** professional *(or* trade*)* association; ~**pflicht** professional duty, occupational duty; ~**pflichtverletzung** professional misconduct; ~**politiker** politician (by career), a career politician; ~**qualifikation** professional qualification; ~**prognose** occupational forecast, ~**richter** professional judge, salaried judge; ~**risiko** occupational hazard, industrial hazard; ~**schicht** occupational category; ~**schule** (part-time) vocational *(or* industrial*)* school; ~**schulinternat** boarding school for vocational training; ~**schulwesen** vocational education; ~**soldat** regular soldier; ~**spieler** professional *(or:* notorious*)* gambler; professional player *(sport)*; ~**sprache** vernacular, professional jargon; ~**stand** profession, professional group; ~**statistik** occupational statistics; ~**stellung** occupational position; ~**struktur** occupational pattern, career structure; ~**systematik** structure of occupational groups; occupational classification; **b**~**tätig** gainfully employed, working; ~**tätigkeit** employment, work, occupation, professional activity; *entgeltliche oder unentgeltliche* ~~: *occupation, whether gainful or*

Berufung

not; ~**umschulung** vocational retraining *(for a new career)*; ~**unfähigkeit** occupational disability *(less than 50% of normal capacity)*; ~**unfähigkeitsrente** occupational disability pension; ~**unfall** occupational accident; ~**unfallversicherung** occupational accident insurance; ~**verband** professional organization *(or* society *or* association*)*, vocational association; ~**verbot** disqualification from public service, prohibition to practise a profession, non-admission to a profession; ~**verbrecher** career criminal; habitual criminal, professional criminal; ~**verbrechertum** organized crime, professional crime; ~**vergehen** professional misconduct, unethical professional conduct; ~**verhalten** work habits; ~**verhältnis** occupational status; ~**verkehr** rush hour traffic, commuter traffic; ~**verlauf** career; ~**verschwiegenheit** professional duty of confidentiality ~**vertretung** representation of professional group; ~**vorbereitung** vocational preparation; ~**wahl** career choice; *freie* ~~: *freedom to choose one's profession, free choice of one's career;* ~**wechsel** change of occupation *(or* profession*)*, job change: *häufiger* ~~: *job-hopping;* ~**wunsch** career aspiration; ~**zeuge** convenient witness, amenable witness; ~**zugehörigkeit** occupational category, membership of a profession *or* occupational group; ~**zulassung** admission to a profession; ~**zuschlag** *ins* extra premium for occupational risks; ~**zweig** branch of a profession; occupation.

Berufung *f (1)* plea, appointment, call; ~ **auf den Diensteid** invoking one's oath of office; ~ **auf den Nachtrunk** hip-flask defence; ~ **auf die Wahrnehmung berechtigter Interessen** plea in justification based on points of private *or* public interest; ~ **auf höheren Befehl** plea of superior orders, *or* of acting under military orders; ~ **auf Prozeßunfähigkeit** *(wegen Gei-*

140

Berufung

steskrankheit) plea of insanity; ~**sgründe** grounds for being named as beneficiary under a will; ~**zum Erben** status as prospective heir.

Berufung *f* (2) appeal (*on questions of fact and law*); ~ **einlegen** to appeal (from), to lodge an appeal; ~ **gegen das Strafmaß** appeal against sentence; ~ **in Strafsachen** criminal appeal; ~ **in Zivilsachen** appeal in civil cases; ~ **nach Fristablauf** appeal out of time; **beschränkte** ~ limited appeal; **der** ~ **stattgeben** to allow the appeal; **e-e** ~ **als unbegründet zurückweisen** to dismiss an appeal on the merits, *or* as unfounded; **e-e** ~ **frist- und formgerecht einlegen** to lodge an appeal in due form and time; **e-e** ~ **für zulässig erklären** to grant leave to appeal; **e-e** ~ **ist zulässig** an appeal is (procedurally) admissible; **e-e** ~**verwerfen** to dismiss an appeal (on procedural grounds); **e-e** ~**zurückweisen** to dismiss an appeal (on the merits); **e-r** ~ **stattgeben** to allow an appeal; **erfolglose** ~ unsuccessful appeal; **in die** ~ **gehen** (to go) to appeal; **über** ~**en beschließen** to hear and decide (any) appeals.

Berufungs|akten papers on the appeal, records of the appeal; ~**anschlußschrift** notice of cross-appeal; ~**antrag** petition of appeal, ~**anträge** points of appeal; ~**antwort** respondent's answer on appeal; ~**ausschuß** review board (*administrative decisions*); ~**begründung** (statement of) grounds of appeal, brief in support of appeal; ~**begründungsfrist** time-limit for filing appellant's (statement of) grounds of appeal; ~**beklagter** respondent; ~**beschränkung** limiting the scope of an appeal; ~**einlegung** (lodging of) an appeal; ~**entscheidung** appellate decision; ~**erwiderung** response to the appeal; **b~fähig** appealable; ~**frist** time-limit for appealing; ~**führer** appellant, party appealing; ~**gebühren** appeal fees; ~**gegner** appellee, respondent; ~**gericht** court of appeal, appellate court; ~**gerichtsbarkeit** appellate jurisdiction; ~**gründe** grounds of (for) appeal, arguments in support of the appeal; ~**instanz** appellate instance; *in der* ~ *instanz freigesprochen werden*: to be acquitted on appeal; ~**kläger** appellant (*in a civil case*); ~**möglichkeit** remedy of appeal; ~**recht** right of appeal; ~**richter** appellate judge, appeal judge; ~**rücknahme** withdrawal of appeal; ~**sache** case on appeal; ~**schrift** petition for appeal, notice of appeal; ~**stelle** board of appeals (*from administrative decisions*); ~**summe** sum *or* amount subject to appeal, sum involved in the appeal; ~**urteil** appeal judgment; ~**verfahren** appellate procedure (*in the rules*); appeal proceedings (*in the particular case*); ~**verhandlung** hearing of an appeal, sitting of the appellate court; ~**verzicht** abandonment (*or* waiver) of the appeal.

beruhen (auf) *v/i* to be based (on), to rest (on); **auf sich** ~ **lassen** to leave sth undecided, to let sth rest.

Beruhigungs|frist *f* cooling-off period; ~**zelle** *f* cooling-off cell, „bull pen".

berühmen *v/reflex* to assert, to claim to oneself, to arrogate.

Berühmung *f* assertion (of a claim), pretension(s), jactitation, arrogation.

berühren *v/t* to touch, to affect.

Berührung *f* touch; ~**spunkt** point of contact.

besagen *v/t* to purport, to mean, to imply; **anscheinend** ~ to purport, to appear to mean, to imply.

Besamung *f* (artificial) insemination; ~**shauptstelle** centre for artificial insemination (of domestic animals); ~**sstation** insemination centre.

Besatz *m* trim, trimmings (*dress*), facings (*shoes*), stemming, tamping bags (*drilling for oil*), admixture (*to seeds, farming*); ~**waren** trimmings.

Besatzung *f* occupation, occupation forces; crew.

Besatzungsamt ⁣ **Beschäftigung**

Besatzungs|amt occupation office, administative office of the military government; **~aufträge** contracts of supply for the occupying power; **~behörden** occupation authorities; **~folgekosten** occupation-induced costs; **~gebiet** zone of occupation, territory of occupation; **~liste** crew list.

beschädigen *v/t* to injure, to damage.

Beschädigtenrente *f* disablement pension: *pension for (partly) disabled persons.*

Beschädigtenversorgung *f* care for the disabled.

Beschädigter *m* (*der Beschädigte*) disabled (person).

Beschädigung *f* damaging, damage, injury; ~ **ausländischer Hoheitszeichen** violation of foreign flags and national emblems; ~ **fremder Sachen** damage to property of another; ~ **öffentlicher Anlagen** malicious damage to public places and grounds; ~ **öffentlicher Bekanntmachungen** destruction of official proclamations (notices); ~ **von Denkmälern** malicious damage to public monuments; ~ **von Siegeln** damaging official seals; ~ **wichtiger Anlagen** damage to important public installations; **absichtliche** ~ wilful (*or* wanton) damage; **böswillige** ~ malicious damage; **geringfügige** ~ slight damage, trivial deterioration or spoilage; **vorsätzliche** ~ wilful damage.

beschaffen *v/t* to procure, to obtain, to furnish, to supply, to secure.

Beschaffenheit *f* nature, condition, state, quality; **~sangabe** quality description; **~smerkmal** characteristic feature; **~szeugnis** certificate of inspection; **etwa gleiche** ~ **und Qualität** like grade and quality.

Beschaffung *f* procurement, provision, acquisition; ~ **e–s Darlehens** procuring a loan; ~ **von Kreditmitteln** procurement of resources by borrowing, obtaining a loan.

Beschaffungs|amt procurement division, procurement office, supply office; **~beamter** procurement officer, purveyor; **~ermächtigung** procurement authorization; **~kosten** original cost(s), prime cost; **~liste** procurement list, list of supplies; **~offizier** procurement officer; **~preis** cost of obtaining goods; **~recht** law of official procurement, law of supply to governmental agencies; **~schwindel** procurement fraud; **~stelle** procurement agency; **~~ und Fertigungsphase** acquisition and operational phase; **~vertrag** procurement contract, contract to supply (a public agency); **~wesen** government procurement, defence procurement.

beschäftigen *v/t* to occupy, to keep occupied; to give employment to; *v/reflex* (*sich mit etwas*) to be concerned with, to consider, to busy oneself with; **jmdn entgeltlich** ~ to employ for remuneration, to give remunerative employment to s. o.

beschäftigt *adj* employed, occupied; **gewerblich** ~ gainfully employed.

Beschäftigte *pl* employed (persons), jobholders, employees, persons in remunerative employment; wage and salary earners; **~nstand** level of employment, number of persons employed; **~nstatistik** employment statistics; **~r im öffentlichen Dienst** public servant; **abhängig** ~ employees, wage and salary earners; **ständig** ~ regularly employed, permanently employed; **unselbständig** ~ employees wage and salary earners, paid workers; **unständige** ~ temporarily employed persons.

Beschäftigung *f* occupation, vocation, employment, job, activity, engagement, pursuit; ~ **im Angestelltenverhältnis** salaried employment; ~ **im öffentlichen Dienst** public sector employment, public service employment;

Beschäftigungsabfall / **beschenken**

abhängige ~ dependent employment (*wage-earning or salaried employment*); entgeltliche ~ remunerated (*or* paid) employment; gefahrgeneigte ~ hazardous occupation; geringfügige ~ minor occupation; small-scale employment; hauptamtliche ~ full-time employment; lohnsteuerpflichtige ~ employment subject to wage tax (*wage-earning or salaried employment*); nebenberufliche ~ part-time job, work on the side, side-line job; probeweise ~ probationary employment; regelmäßige ~ regular employment; versicherungsfreie ~ (social) insurance-free employment.

Beschäftigungsabfall decline in employment; ~**abweichung** deviation in; ~**anspruch** right to one's job; ~**art** employment category; ~**aussichten** employment prospects; ~**bedingungen** conditions of employment; ~**bescheinigung** certificate of employment, employment record card; ~**dauer** duration (*or* period) of employment; ~**einbruch** falling off in activity, sudden decline in employment figures; ~**engpass** employment bottleneck; ~**grad** capacity utilization rate; ~**lage** employment situation, current employment figures; ~**lose** unemployed (persons); *vermittlungsfähige* ~~~: *employable unemployed;* ~**möglichkeiten** employment opportunities; ~**nachweis** certificate of employment, employment record card; ~**ort** place of employment; ~**pflicht** obligation to continue the actual employment; ~**politik** employment policy; ~**potential** potential labour force; ~**reserve** reserve of employable labour; ~**stand** level of employment; ~**statistik** employment statistics; ~**therapie** occupational therapy; ~**verbot** prohibition to employ (*individuals or groups, aliens*); ~**verhältnis** employment (relationship); ~**zeit** period of employment, duration of employment.

beschatten *v/t* (*jmdn*) to shadow s. o.
Beschau *f* (physical) inspection, examination; ~ **der Warenladung** examination of the loads.
Bescheid *m* ruling, official reply, order, official information, (administrative) decision; ~**serledigung** ruling carrying out the terms of an administrative decision, compliance with an administrative decision; ~**serteilung** notification, rendering of an administrative decision, issuing an official information, official reply; **abschlägiger** ~ denial, refusal; negative reply; **endgültiger** ~ final (*or* definite) decision; **schriftlicher** ~ written notification, written ruling; **vorläufiger** ~ provisional ruling.

bescheiden *v/t* to render an administrative decision, to notify of a decision; **jmdn abschlägig** ~ to inform s.o. of a negative decision, to reject.

Bescheidungsurteil *n administrative court judgment instructing a public authority to make a certain ruling.*

bescheinigen *v/t* to certify, to confirm in writing, to attest.

Bescheinigung *f* certification, certificate, certificate "to whom it may concern", attestation, written confirmation; ~ **der Echtheit** authentication; ~ **über die Aufteilung von Partien** certificate for splitting of consignments; ~ **über die Zulassung nach dem Konstruktionsprinzip** certificate of approval by design type; ~ **über vom Arbeitgeber bezahlte Lohnsteuer** withholding statement, proof of wage taxes paid by employer; **amtliche** ~ official certificate; **ärztliche** ~ doctor's certificate, medical certificate; **e-e** ~ **beibringen** to provide a certificate, to furnish a certificate; **konsularische** ~ consular certificate; **notarielle** ~ notarial certification (*or* attestation), notary's certificate; **vorläufige** ~ interim certificate; **zollamtliche** ~ customs certificate.

beschenken *v/t* to make a gift to s.o., to donate.

143

Beschenkter *m* (*der Beschenkte*) donee, presentee, recipient of a gift.
Beschilderung *f* signposting.
beschimpfen *v/t* to abuse, to revile, to vituperate.
Beschimpfung *f incl pl* (*~en*): abuse, revilement, invective, vituperation, abusive language, offensive language; ~ **der Bundesrepublik** abusive language against the Federal Republic; ~ **der Kirche** revilement of the church(es); ~ **des Staates und seiner Symbole** vilification of the State and its emblems; ~ **Verstorbener** disparaging the memory of the dead.
Beschlagnahme *f* (legal) seizure attachment, court-ordered receivership; distraint (*by landlord*), arrest (*of a ship*), order of attachment of debts (*garnishment*), levy (*in execution*), requisition (*military purposes*), confiscation; ~**anordnung** order of attachment, writ of sequestration, seizing order; ~**beschluß** order of attachment; ~**des Führerscheins** seizure (*or* taking away) of driving licence; ~ **durch Eingriff von hoher Hand** arrest of princes, intervention by government agencies (*insurance policy*); ~ **durch Pfändungs- und Überweisungsbeschluß** attachment by garnishee order; ~ **durch Wegnahme** actual seizure, physical seizure; ~ **e-r Druckschrift** confiscation of printed matter; ~**freiheit** exemption from attachment and seizure; ~**protokoll** record(s) of a seizure (*or* attachment); ~**recht** right of seizure; *int*: right of angary; ~**risiko** *ins* risk of seizure; *ausgeschlossen free of capture and seizure;* ~**verfügung** charging order, warrant of attachment; ~ **von Forderungen** attachment of debts; ~ **von Schutzrechten** sequestration of industrial property rights; ~**wert** condemnation value; **e-e** ~ **aufheben** to set aside an attachment order, to release sth. from attachment, to grant replevin; **gerichtliche** ~ judicial seizure; **physische** ~ actual seizure, physical seizure; **rechtswidrige** ~ illegal seizure, improper seizure.
beschlagnahmefähig *adj* liable to be seized, attachable.
beschlagnahmen *v/t* to seize, to attach, to distrain, to levy, to requisition (*cf Beschlagnahme*), to impound, to place (*or* impose) an embargo (on), to arrest, to confiscate.
Beschleunigung *f* expedition, acceleration, speeding up; ~ **des Verfahrens** expediting proceedings; ~**spflicht** obligation to expedite (*proceedings, the handling of sth.*); ~**streifen** acceleration lane (*highway*).
beschließen *v/t* to adopt (*resolution*), to pass a resolution, to resolve, to decide, to pass (*motion, bill*), to vote, to declare (*dividend*); **durch Konsens** ~ to resolve by informal consent, to agree informally.
beschlossen *pp, adj* resolved; ~ **und verkündet** ordered (and pronounced as follows); ordered, adjudged and decreed.
Beschluß *m* order, court order, intermediate order (*court*), ruling (*in proceedings*), resolution (*meeting, parl*), vote; ~**abteilung** decision-making department, *division for labour-court matters decided by order (not judgment)*; ~ **auf einseitigen Antrag** order ex parte; ~ **auf Verwerfung e-s Rechtsmittels** order to dismiss; ~ **auf Wiederaufnahme e-s ruhenden Verfahrens** order of revivor; ~ **auf Zulassung der öffentlichen Zustellung** order for service by publication; ~**ausschuß** executive committee; **b**~**fähig** *adj* qualified to decide by vote; being a quorum; having (*or* constituting) a quorum; ~**fähigkeit** *f* (presence of a) quorum; ~**fassung** (passing of a) resolution, voting; ~ **im Bürowege** order in chambers; ~**feststellung** (*chairman's*) statement whether a resolution has been adopted; ~**kammer** *labour court division for matters decided by order (not judgment) cf. Beschlußverfahren;* ~

mit einfacher Mehrheit ordinary resolution, resolution by simple majority; ~ **nur auf Antrag** ex parte order, special rule; ~**recht** authority to issue (*directly applicable*) orders and regulations; **b~reif** *adj* ready to be voted on; ~ **über die Aufhebung des Haftbefehls** release order to set aside a warrant of arrest; ~ **über (die) Eröffnung des Konkursverfahrens** order of adjudication in bankruptcy; ~**unfähigkeit** lack of a quorum; ~**verfahren** decision-making by vote; court-order proceedings (*decisions by orders not judgments*); **außerordentlicher ~** extraordinary resolution; **der angefochtene ~** the order (decision) appealed from, the resolution in dispute; **der ~ wurde schriftlich gefaßt** the resolution was passed in writing, adopted by a written vote; **durch ~ bestimmen** to decide by resolution (or by order); **e–n ~ aufheben** to discharge an order; **e–n ~ erlassen** to issue an order, to pass a resolution; **e–n ~ fassen** to pass a resolution; **einstimmiger ~** unanimous vote, unanimous resolution; **es ergeht folgender ~** be it resolved, that it is ordered and decreed as follows; **gerichtlicher ~** court order; **mit qualifizierter Mehrheit gefaßter ~** extraordinary resolution, resolution passed by a qualified (*or* the neccessary, *or* due) majority; **nicht b~fähig sein** to lack (*or* not to have) a quorum; **qualifizierter ~** special resolution (*after notice*), qualified resolution; **rechtsgültiger ~** (legally) valid resolution; **rechtskräftiger ~** non-appealable order, final ruling (*of a court*); **richterlicher ~ im Bürowege** judge's order, order in chambers; **unqualifizierter ~** ordinary resolution; **zur ~fassung geeignet** votable; **zwingender ~** peremptory order.

bescholten *adj* unchaste, having lived an unchaste life.

Bescholtenheit *f* stained reputation, unchastity.

beschränken *v/t* to limit, to restrict, to restrain.

beschränkend *adj* restrictive, limiting.

beschränkt *adj* limited, restricted, qualified; ~**steuerpflichtig** subject to limited tax liability (*of non-residents*); **zeitlich ~** qualified as to time, limited in time.

Beschränkung *f* restriction, limitation, limit, qualification; ~ **der Erbenhaftung** limiting the liability for debts of the estate; ~ **der Zuständigkeit** limitation of jurisdiction; ~**en auferlegen** to impose restrictions; ~**en aufheben** to withdraw (*or* remove) restrictions; ~**en im Wirtschaftsverkehr** restrictions on trade; trade barriers; **gesetzliche ~** statutory restriction, legal restriction; **haushaltsrechtliche ~en** budgetary restrictions; **immanente ~** self-qualifying element; **keinen ~en unterworfen** without restrictions; **mengenmäßige ~** quantitative restriction; **ohne jede ~** without any restrictions, without let or hindrance; **verschleierte ~** disguised restriction; **zeitliche ~** limitation (in time).

beschreiben *v/t* to describe, to outline, to set out, to give an account; **ausführlich ~** to give a detailed description of sth.

Beschreibung *f* description, account, report, narration, specification (*patents*); **deutliche ~ e–s Patentanspruchs** distinct statement of the invention claimed, clear description of a (patent) claim; **e–e genaue ~ des Verbrechers** an exact description of the criminal; **gleicher ~** of (a) like description; **vorläufige ~** provisional specification.

beschriften *v/t* to letter, to provide with an inscription; to mark in writing, to write on (*envelope, document*), to caption (*illustration*), to label, to mark (*goods*).

Beschriftung *f* inscription, superscription, marking *cf.* **beschriften**; ~**sschild** placard, name plate, marking label.

beschuldigen *v/t* to blame, to lay (*or* put) the blame on s. o., to charge s. o. (*with having committed an offence; with a crime*), to accuse (*formally in court*), to inculpate, to incriminate; **jmdn** ~ to lay a charge at s. o.'s door (*etc cf beschuldigen*); **sich selbst** ~ to incriminate oneself, to blame oneself.

beschuldigend *adj* accusatory, inculpatory, incriminatory.

Beschuldigter *m* (*der Beschuldigte*) the person charged, suspect (*during investigation*), defendant (*before trial, non-technically during trial*), accused (*in court,* → *Angeschuldigter* → *Angeklagter*).

Beschuldigung *f* inculpation, charge, accusation, imputation; **e-e** ~ **gegen jmdn vorbringen** = *beschuldigen qv*; **falsche** ~ false accusation (*or* allegation); **grundlose** ~ baseless charge.

Beschußwesen *n* examination and licencing of fire arms.

Beschützer *m* protector.

Beschwer *f* grievance, gravamen, cause of complaint.

Beschwerde *f* plaint, complaint (*injustice, grievance to superior etc.*), grievance, request for relief; remonstrance, appeal against an administrative act; interlocutory appeal, appeal from a court order (*from interlocutory or final decisions in the form of a Beschluss qv*); ~**antrag** application for relief in an appeal (*from a court order*); ~**ausschuß** appeals board, grievance committee, complaints commission; ~**begründung** argument in support of the appeal (*from court order*); ~**behörde** public authority competent for the complaint; ~**belehrung** instructions for an appeal, *advice as to the legality, time and formalities of an appeal* (*or* complaint); ~**berechtigter** person aggrieved, person entitled to appeal, complainant, appellant; ~**bescheid** information about the determination of a complaint (*or* appeal); ~**brief** letter of complaint; ~**buch** book of complaints, requests book; ~**einlegung** taking appeal (*or* filing), lodging of a complaint (*or* appeal); ~ **erheben** to lodge an appeal (*from an order*), to remonstrate; ~**entscheidung** determination of a complaint (*or* appeal); **b~fähig** *adj* appealable, subject to appeal; ~**frist** time for lodging an appeal; ~ **führen** to complain, to lodge a complaint; ~**führer** complainant; appellant, remonstrant, petitioner; ~**gebühr** appeal fee, *pl* ~*en* appeal charges; ~ **gegen e-e Entscheidung einlegen** to file an appeal (= to appeal) against (from) a decision; ~**gegenstand** cause of appeal; matter of complaint; ~**gegner** appellee, respondent; ~**gericht** appeal court, court of appeal; appellate division; ~**grund** gravamen, reason for complaint; ~**instanz** appellate instance; ~**kammer** appellate division (*from orders of the local court or regional court*), board of appeal (*administration, patents*); ~**kommissar** ombudsman; ~**punkt** subject matter of complaint, *pl*: points of complaint; ~**recht** right of complaint, right of appeal; ~**rücknahme** withdrawal of appeal; ~**schrift** petition for review; ~**senat** appellate division; ~**stelle** complaints department; ~**summe** sum involved in (interlocutory) appeal; ~ **und Petitionsrecht** right to complain and petition (*in case of a grievance*); ~**verfahren** appellate procedure (*concerning a court order*); ~**weg** appeals procedure, channels of complaint, grievance procedure, complaints procedure; course of remedial action, **den** ~*weg* **beschreiten** to lodge a complaint; ~**wert** *amount assessed as* appellate value; **e-e** ~ **verwerfen** to refuse an appeal; **e-r** ~ **abhelfen** to take remedial action upon complaint, to grant a remedy upon the lodging of a complaint (*or* appeal) *by the agency or court against whom the complaint or appeal is directed*; to remedy as directed; *generally*: to remedy a grievance, to si-

beschweren

lence a complaint, to remove cause of complaint; **einfache ~** ordinary appeal (from a court order) (*no time-limit*); **sofortige ~** immediate appeal (from a court order) (*to be filed within the statutory period*); **weitere ~** further appeal on points of law (*against a court order*).

beschweren *v/i* to aggrieve; *v reflex* to complain, to make complaint, to state one's grievance.

beschwerlich *adj* onerous, arduous, tiresome, inconvenient.

Beschwerlichkeit *f* inconvenience, arduousness.

beschwert *adj* aggrieved, adversely affected; **sich ~ fühlen** to feel aggrieved.

Beschwerter *m* (*der Beschwerte*) person aggrieved.

beschwichtigen *v/t* to appease, to soothe.

Beschwichtigungspolitik *f* policy of appeasement.

beschwindeln *v/t* to cheat, to swindle.

beschwören *v/t* to swear (*to the truth of s. th.*), to take (swear) an oath, to affirm (on oath).

besehen *v/t* to inspect, to examine (*goods*) *cf wie besehen*.

beseitigen *v/t* to eliminate, to remove; **schrittweise ~** to progressively eliminate.

Beseitigung *f* elimination, removal; **~e-r Störung** abatement of a nuisance; *in equipment*: removal of a defect, remedial maintenance; **~ des Strafmakels** extinction of the blemish of punishment (young offenders); **~ radioaktiven Abfalls** disposal of radioactive waste material; **~sanspruch** right to the abatement of a nuisance, right to have s. th. removed (*or* eliminated); **~sbefugnis** authority to require the removal (*or* elimination) of s.th.; **~sklage** action for abatement (or suppression) of a nuisance; **~sverfügung** condemnation order; **~ von Elendsvierteln** slum clearance; **~ von**

Besitz

Rechtsmängeln removing a defect of title (*deficiency in title, defect in substance*).

besetzen *v/t* to occupy, take possession of (*territory, premises*), to fill (*vacancy*), to appoint s.o. (*to a post*).

Besetztzeichen *n* "engaged" signal.

Besetzung *f* occupation; appointment, placement; **~ des Gerichts** composition of the bench; attendance of judges in court; ; **~ feindlichen Gebietes** occupation of enemy territory; **~srüge** objection to the composition of the panel of judges; **~srecht** right of patronage; **~ von Arbeitsplätzen** filling of jobs; **kriegerische ~** belligerent occupation.

besichern *v/t* to secure, to provide collateral.

Besicherung *f* providing security (*or* collateral) for a loan; **~svereinbarung** security agreement; **dingliche ~** providing (in rem) collateral (security), providing security by mortgage.

Besicht *m* inspection (*upon sale*), (superficial) examination; **auf ~ kaufen** to buy subject to inspection; **nach ~ kaufen** to buy after examination; **ohne ~** without inspection.

besichtigen *v/t* to inspect, to view, to examine, to tour.

Besichtigung *f* inspection, view, examination; **~ des Tatorts** inspection (*or* viewing) of the scene of a crime; **~sbericht** survey (*or* inspection) report; **~sprotokoll** survey report, mutual record of inspection; **gerichtliche ~** judicial inspection, view taken by the court; **nach ~ kaufen** to buy after inspection; **ohne ~** without previous inspection; **unverbindliche ~** non-binding inspection, free inspection; **zur ~** on show, for examination.

Besitz *m* possession = *p* (*in the legal sense*), occupancy (*of rooms, houses*), holding (*of shares, securities, also of land*), property (*in an*

147

Besitzanspruch   **Besitzwille**

economic, not juristic sense); ~**anspruch** possessory claim, claim for *p*; ~**antritt** entry into *p*, taking *p*; ~**aufgabe** surrender of *p*; ~ **aufgeben** to part with *p*, to surrender *p*; ~ **auf Grund e-s Besitzmittlungsverhältnisses** derivative *p*; ~**dauer** holding period; ~**diener** possessor's agent, possessory servant, custodian, person exercising actual control (*e.g.* caretaker); ~**einräumung** granting of *p*, delivery of *p*; ~**einweisung** putting into *p*; ~**entziehung** dispossession, divestment, exclusion and ouster, ejection ouster; *widerrechtliche* ~~: *unlawful ouster, unlawful dispossession*; ~ **entziehen** to dispossess, to oust, to turn s. o. out of *p*; ~**entziehungsklage** action for (recovery of) *p*; ~ **ergreifen** to take *p* (of); ~**ergreifer** occupant, person taking *p* unilaterally; ~**ergreifung** taking *p*, taking up occupation; ~**ergreifungsrecht** right of occupation; ~ **erlangen** to obtain *p*; ~**erlangung** gaining *p*, obtaining *p* (of); ~**erwerb** obtaining *p* (of), taking *p* (of); ~ **erwerben** to acquire (*or* to obtain *or* to gain) *p*; ~**fehler** legal deficiency of *p*; ~**gehilfe** = ~ *diener qv*; ~**genuß** (actual) enjoyment of *p*; ~**gesellschaft** property-holding company; ~**größe** size of holdings; ~ **im Rechtssinn** legal *p*; ~**institut** (*constitution possessorium*), possessory agreement, agreement for indirect *p*, *granting possessor* (*debtor*) *the right to hold possession on behalf of another* (*the creditor*); ~**klage** action for (recovery of) *p*, possessory action, writ of entry; ~**konto** property account; ~ **mit der Absicht der Veräußerung** (*Rauschgift*) *p* with the intent to supply; ~**mittler** bailor, *person allowing indirect p to another*; ~**mittlungsverhältnis** bailment *relationship allowing indirect possession* (*tenancy, deposit etc*); ~**nachfolger** subsequent holder, subsequent possessor; ~ **nach Vertragsablauf** holding over; ~**nachweis** proof of *p*; ~**nahme** taking *p* (of) (*or* occupation); ~ **ohne Gewahrsam** *p* in law; ~ **ohne Rechtstitel** naked *p*, *p* without due legal title; ~**pfand** possessor's lien, possessory lien; ~**recht** right of *p*, right to *p*, possessive right, possessory interest, possessory title *pl also*: occupancy rights; **b**~**rechtlich** *adj* possessory; ~**rückgabe** surrender of *p*; ~**schutz** legal protection of *p*; ~**stand** acquired status, vested rights; ~**standsklausel** grandfather clause; ~**steuern** taxes on income and property, taxes on earned and unearned income; ~**störer** trespasser, *person who disturbs quiet p*; ~**störung** disturbance (of *p*), (unlawful) interference with *p*, trespass, private (*or* civil) nuisance; ~**störungsklage** action for disturbance of *p*, action of trespass; ~**titel** possessory title, right to *p*; *nicht verkehrsfähiger* ~~: *unmarketable title*; *rechtsfehlerhafter* ~~: *want of title*; ~**tum** property, possessions; ~**übergang** change of *p*; ~**übernahme** entry into *p*; ~**übertragung** transfer of *p*; *cf Tag der Besitzübertragung.*; ~**umschreibung** transfer of title registration; ~- **und Gebrauchsvorteile** *p* and enjoyment; ~ **und Nutzung entziehen** to oust, to dispossess, to eject; ~- **und Verkehrssteuern** taxes on property and transactions; ~**urkunde** title-deed, document of title; ~**veränderung** change of *p*; ~**verbot** prohibition of owning sth; ~**verhältnisse** the property situation; ~**verlust** loss of possession, loss of property; ~**vermutung** presumption of ownership of possessing sponse (*as against execution creditors*); ~**vorenthaltung** deprivation of the enjoyment of property, ouster; ~**wechsel** (*1*) change of *p*, change in ownership; ~**wechsel** (*2*) bills receivable (*balance sheet item*); ~**wehr** defence of *p* and custody (*by self help*); ~**wille** intention of

148

Besitzzeit — **Besoldungsordnung**

possessing, animus possidenti; (*or* wish) to possess; ~**zeit** duration of *p* (~ of continuous holding); ~**zersplitterung** fragmentation of holdings; **abgeleiteter** ~ derivative *p*; **aus dem** ~ **vertreiben** to oust, to eject; **ausschließlicher** ~ exclusive *p*; **bestrittener** ~ adverse *p*; **den** ~ **wiedererlangen** to recover *p*; **der jeweilige** ~**berechtigte** the person for the time being entitled to *p*; **fehlerhafter** ~ faulty *p*, adverse *p*; **fiktiver** ~ constructive *p*; **fingierter** ~ constructive *p*, indirect *p*; **fortwährender** ~ continuous *p*; **geduldeter** ~ *p* by tacit consent, tenancy at will; **gemeinschaftlicher** ~ joint possession, joint holding; **gutgläubiger** ~ bona fide *p*; **im** ~having *p* (of); **im** ~ **angetroffen** found in *p*; **im** ~ **sein von** to be in *p* of; **im ausschließlichen** ~ **von etw sein** to have sole *p* of sth; **im unmittelbaren** ~ **habend in** *p*; **in** ~ **nehmen** to take *p* of, to occupy; **in** ~ **setzen** to give *p*, to bestow *p* upon; **in unmittelbarem** ~ **und Gewahrsam** in actual *p*; **in vollem** ~ **seiner geistigen Kräfte** in (full) *p* of his faculties, being of sound mind (and memory); **jederzeit entziehbarer** ~ precarious *p*; **jmdn in den** ~ **einweisen** to give *p*; **landwirtschaftlich genutzter** ~ agricultural holding; **mittelbarer** ~ indirect *p*, constructive *p*; **rechtlicher** ~ legal *p*; **rechtmäßiger** ~ lawful *p*; **rechtswidriger** ~ unlawful *p*; **redlicher** ~ honest *p*; in good faith; **reiner** ~ naked *p*, natural *p*; **tatsächlicher** ~ actual *p*; **treuhänderischer** ~fiduciary *p*; **unbefugter** ~ unauthorized *p*; **unbeschränkter** ~ full *p*; **unerlaubter** ~ illegal *p*; **ungestörter** ~ quiet *p*; **in** ~ **haben**: *to enjoy quiet p*; **unmittelbarer** ~ immediate *p*, direct *p*, actual *p*, physical *p*, corporeal *p*; **unrechtmäßiger** ~ unlawful *p*, *p* without title; **uralter** ~ immemorial *p*; **widerrechtlicher** ~ unlawful *p*; **wieder in** ~ **nehmen** to repossess, to resume *p* of; **wieder in den** ~ **setzen** to restore to *p*; **wohlerworbener** ~ vested *p*, vested right of *p*.

besitzen *v/t* to possess, to have possession (of), to hold, to occupy; *generally econ*: to own; **treuhänderisch** ~ to hold on (*or* in) trust, to hold as a trustee.

Besitzer *m* possessor, holder, occupier, occupant, man in possession; *econ* proprietor; ~ **auf Lebenszeit** holder for life, life tenant; **bösgläubiger** ~ possessor mala fide; **früherer** ~prepossessor, former occupant; **gutgläubiger** ~ possessor bona fide, innocent holder for value (*bill of exchange*), holder in good faith; **mittelbarer** ~ bailor, indirect possessor; **nicht berechtigter** ~ adverse possessor; **prekarischer** ~ occupant at will, occupant upon sufferance; **rechtmäßiger** ~ lawful holder, lawful possessor; **tatsächlicher** ~ actual possessor; **treuhänderischer** ~ fiduciary bailee, holder in trust; **unmittelbarer** ~ direct holder, actual possessor.

Besitztum *n* property, estate, possession(s); **befriedetes** ~enclosed premises.

Besitzung *f* esp. *pl*. landed estate, properties, possessions.

besolden *v/t* to remunerate for one's services, to pay a salary to (*a public official*), to pay a stipend (*to a magistrate etc*).

besoldet *adj* salaried, stipendiary.

Besoldung *f* salary, remuneration of employment (*of an official or officer*); stipend (*judges, clergymen*); pay (*soldiers*).

Besoldungs|anpassung salary adjustment; ~**dienstalter** seniority for salary purposes, age for purposes of remuneration; ~**gesetz** Act for the remuneration of public officials, salary law; ~**gruppe** salary bracket, grade, salary class; pay grade, salary scale; ~**niveau** level of remuneration; ~**ordnung** salary scheme, pay plan, system of re-

149

besonnen | **Bestandskontrolle**

muneration, *pl* ~*en* salary regulations; ~**plan** remuneration plan for public officials; ~**reform** reform of the system of remuneration (*for public officers*); ~**stelle** pay office; ~**stufe** salary grade; ~**tarif** rate of pay.

besonnen *adj* circumspect, sensible.

Besonnenheit *f* circumspection.

besorgen *v/t* to procure, to look after, to attend to (s.o.'s affairs).

besorgen *v/i* to apprehend, to suspect.

Besorgnis *f* apprehension; ~ **der Befangenheit** reasonable grounds to suspect partiality, fear of prejudice; *wegen* ~~~ (*also:*) *propter affectum, on account of some prejudice.*

Besorgung *f* commission, procurement, provision; handling, errand; ~ **fremder Geschäfte** handling matters of third parties.

besprechen *v/t* to discuss, to confer (with s.o.), to review (*a book*).

Besprechung *f* discussion, talk, conference, review, critique; ~**sexemplar** review copy, press copy; ~**sgebühr** *lawyers' fee for out-of-court negotiations*; **einleitende** ~ opening talks; **interne** ~ private discussion.

Besserverdienende *pl* the better off, higher income earners, employees of the higher income brackets.

Besserung *f* reformation, improvement (of deliquents); ~**sanstalt** *f* (*obs*) house of correction, detention home, reform school, reformatory; **b**~**sfähig** *adj* reclaimable, corrigible; ~**sklausel** *debtor's conditional promise of additional payments in case of improved earnings position, betterment clause;* ~**smaßregeln** measures for improvement and correction (of convicted persons); ~**sschein** income and adjustment bond, bond to pay when able, debtor warrant, *promise in writing to pay upon improvement of the debtor's financial circumstances.*

Bestabrechnung *f* charging most favourable rate to consumer (*electricity*).

bestallen *v/t* to appoint (*s.o. to public office*), to license (*professions*).

Bestallung *f* appointment, order of appointment, the granting of a licence (*to practice*); ~**surkunde** instrument of appointment, certificate of appointment, letter of appointment, letters patent, patent vesting deed.

Bestand *m* (*pl Bestände* = ~*e*) holdings, portfolio, stock (in hand), inventory; balance (*of an account*), cash balance, cash in hand; orders in hand; (~*e:*) resources; legal validity, legal continuity; ~ **an ausstehenden Einfuhrlizenzen** "float" of outstanding import licences; ~ **an Lebensversicherungen** holdings of life insurance contracts (*by an insurance agent*); ~ **an Termineinlagen** total time deposits; ~ **aufnehmen** to take stock, to take inventory; ~**e in zweiter Hand** stocks in the hands of subsequent holders (*after the producers*); **abgetretener** ~ assigned outstanding accounts; **den** ~ **körperlich aufnehmen** to take inventory by actual checking; **ein gegebener** ~(*von Geld und Kapital*) a given sum (*or* amount) (*of money and capital*), currently available stock; **eiserner** ~ base stock, reserve stock, last reserve, reserve fund; **flottierender** ~ float; **offener** ~ open-end account; **unverkäufliche** ~**e** dead stock; **valutarische** ~**e** gold and foreign exchange reserves.

Bestands|aufnahme stock taking, stock check, inventory; *belegmäßige* ~~: *voucher-monitored material inventory*; *karteimäßige* ~~: *card-file monitored material inventory*; ~**bewertung** inventory valuation; ~**buch** stock book; ~**dichte** crop density (*forestry*); ~**erhaltung** preservation of amenity; ~**führung** asset accountability; ~**karte** inventory card; *laufende* ~~: *perpetual inventory card*; ~**konto** asset account, real account, *pl* books of original entry; ~**kontrolle** stock check, in-

Bestandteil

ventory control; ~**kraft** administrative finality; ~~**klausel**: *finality clause*; **b** ~ **kräftig** final and absolute; ~**liste** inventory, stock-list; ~**lockerung** thinning (out) (*forest*); ~**meldung** stock report, report on present assets (*or* holdings); ~**minderung** decrease in stock; ~**prüfer** stock chaser, inventory checker; ~**prüfung** inventory audit; ~**rente** present pension; ~**schutz** protection of vested rights; ~**übernahme** inventory take-over; ~**übertragung** transfer of total stock (*or* holdings); ~**veränderung** stock change, change in book value (of an asset), change in portfolio holdings; ~**verlust** inventory shrinkage, inventory loss; ~**verzeichnis** property report, inventory list, schedule of properties, register (*and description*) *of items* of landed property (*in land title register*); ~**wagnis** inventory contingency, inventory risk; ~**zahl** present total; stock figure.

Bestandteil *m* component, constituent part, integral part; ~ **des Grundstückseigentums bilden** to run with the land; **e–n** ~ **darstellen** to form an integral part (of); **organischer** ~ natural component (*or* element); **unwesentlicher** ~ separable part, removable component (part); **wesentlicher** ~ vital component part, integral part, part and parcel, irremovable part, (immovable) fixture (*realty*); *etw zum* ~*n* ~ *e–r Urkunde machen*: *to incorporate by reference*.

bestätigen *v/t* to confirm, to ratify, to endorse, to validate; to acknowledge; to sustain, to uphold (*decision*); to certify (*copy, cheque*); to corroborate (*testimony*); **amtlich oder gerichtlich** ~ to homologate, to confirm officially or judicially, to certify.

bestätigt *pp, adj*; **es wird hierdurch** ~**, daß** this is to certify that, it is hereby certified that; **unterschriftlich** ~ witness our hands; signed and approved.

Bestätigung *f* confirmation, ratifica-

Bestechung

tion, endorsement, validation, acknowledgment; ~ **der Ordnungsgemäßheit** certificate of compliance; ~ **der Zeugenaussage** corroboration of witness; ~ **e–s Urteils** confirmation of a judgment; **eidliche** ~ confirmation upon oath; **gerichtliche** ~ judicial confirmation; **gültig nur bei** ~ subject to confirmation; **rückseitige** ~ endorsement (overleaf); **um** ~ **des Empfangs wird gebeten** please acknowledge receipt.

Bestätigungs|brief letter of acknowledgment (*or* confirmation), *cf*. ~**schreiben**; **b**~**fähig** affirmable; ~**patent** confirmation patent; ~**recht** right of approval (of nominations etc.); ~**schreiben** letter of acknowledgment; letter of confirmation, confirmation note, confirmation of an order; *kaufmännisches* ~~: *commercial letter of confirmation*; ~**urkunde** confirmation certificate, document of ratification; ~**vermerk** attestation; ~~ *des Wirtschaftsprüfers*: *auditor's report*; audit opinion; ~**zeichen** confirmatory sign (*traffic*).

Bestattung *f* funeral, burial, interment, cremation; ~**sanstalt** undertaker's establishment, funeral parlor (*US*); ~**sfeierlichkeiten** funeral ceremonies, obsequies; ~**sgeld** funeral expenses compensation; ~**gewerbe** undertaking; ~**skosten** funeral expenses; ~**sort** burial place, resting place; ~**swesen** funeral matters.

Bestbietender *m* (*der Bestbietende*) (the) highest bidder.

bestechen *v/t* to bribe, to buy (over), to corrupt, to grease s. o.'s palm; **sich** ~ **lassen** take (*or* accept) a bribe (*or* bribes).

bestechlich *adj* corruptible, open (*or* amenable) to bribery, venal

Bestechlichkeit *f* corruptibility, corruption, venality, openness to accepting bribes; bribery; *acceptance of benefit by public official for an act in violation of his duty*.

Bestechung *f* bribing, bribery; cor-

151

bestehen / **bestimmbar**

ruption, corrupt practices, graft (*US*); **aktive** ~ offering a bribe, bribing (an official); **passive** ~ acceptance of a bribe, taking a bribe, taking kickbacks; ~**sfond** slush fund; ~**sgeld** bribe money, slush, boodle; ~**smanöver** corrupt practices; ~**sversuch** attempt to bribe.

bestehen *v/i* to exist; **noch** ~ to subsist, to survive; *bestehen aus: to be composed of*.

bestehend *adj* existing, in esse, extant, prevailing.

Bestell|buch order-book; ~**eingang** (number of) incoming orders; *laufender* ~~: *amount of orders currently being placed*; ~**formular** purchase order form; ~**geld** delivery charge; ~**index** index of incoming orders; ~**karte** return coupon; ~**liste** list of orders; ~**schein** order form, subscription form; ~**vertrag** *publisher's contract with an author for a specific work to be created*; b~**wirksam** *adj* as per order date; ~**zeitraum** order period; ~**zettel** order form, order slip; ~**zuschlag** order margin.

bestellen *v/t* to order (*goods, food*), to place an order (for), to appoint (*s.o. to a public office*), to create (*or* execute) a mortgage; to till, to cultivate.

Besteller *m* person (*or* firm) ordering (*goods etc*), orderer, customer; person (*or* firm) commissioning.

bestellt *adj* ordered, booked, on order; **ordnungsgemäß** ~ duly appointed, named, appointed and constituted.

Bestellung *f* order, purchase order; appointment; tillage (land), sowing; ~ **e–r Hypothek** granting of a mortage, execution and registration of a mortgage; ~ **e–r Sicherheit** putting up of collateral, providing security (*for a loan*); ~ **e–s Verteidigers** appointment of defence counsel; ~ **zum Postversand** mail order; **auf** ~ by order, as ordered; **auf** ~ **(an)fertigen** to make to order; **e–e** ~ **annehmen** to accept a commission, to take an order; **e–e** ~ **aufgeben** to place an order; **öffentliche** ~ (public) appointment; **schriftliche** ~ written order; **verbindliche** ~ binding order.

bestens *adv* at best, at best market price, at lowest possible price.

Bestens|auftrag order at best *or* at the best rate obtainable; ~**-Order** = ~*auftrag qv*; ~**verkauf** sale at most favourable rate (*without limitation*).

besteuerbar *adj* taxable, subject to excise tax.

Besteuerbarkeit taxability.

besteuern *v/t* to tax, to levy taxes (*on s.o. or s.th.*), to rate.

Besteuerung *f* taxation (= *t*), imposition of tax, taxing, levy of taxes; ~ **im Abzugsverfahren** withholding tax; ~**sunterschiede** taxation disparities; ~**szeitraum** tax period; **direkte** ~ direct taxation; **gegenseitige** ~ mutual *t*; **gleichmäßige** ~ equal and uniform *t*; **indirekte** ~ indirect *t*, imposition of excise taxes; **maßvolle** ~ commensurate *t*; **mehrfache** ~ multiple *t*; **progressive** ~ progressive *t* **proportionale** ~proportional *t*; **rückbezügliche** ~ retroactive *t*; **übermäßige** ~ excessive *t*; **übersetzte** ~ excessive *t*; **unterschiedliche** ~ discriminatory *t*.

Besteuerungs|art type of tax; b~**fähig** *adj* liable to be taxed, taxable; ~**fähigkeit** taxability; ~**freigrenze** tax-free allowance, limit of tax exemption; ~**grenze** tax limit; ~**grundlage** tax base, basis of taxation; ~**hoheit** taxing power (*of a state*); ~**maßstab** standard for assessment, basis for taxation; ~**recht** taxing power, right to tax; ~**unterlagen** documents and materials for tax assessment, tax records; ~**verfahren** taxation procedure; ~**zeitraum** assessment period.

bestimmbar *adj* ascertainable, determinable; **quantitativ** ~ quantifiable.

bestimmen *v/t* to determine, to decide, to provide, *v/reflex* to be governed by (*a law*).

bestimmt *adj* definite, clear, peremptory; *pp* provided (for), determined; ~ **für** intended for, destined for; **gesetzlich** ~ provided (for) by law; **soweit nichts anderes** ~ **ist** except as otherwise provided.

Bestimmtheit *f* certainty, definiteness; determination, peremptoriness; **~grundsatz** principle of clarity and definiteness *of the wording of enactments*.

Bestimmung *f* term, provision (*law, contract*), regulation, rule; destination (*transport*), disposition (*choice*) direction, instruction; ~ **der Zuständigkeit** ruling as to jurisdiction; ~ **des Durchlaufs der Produktionsstufen** routing; ~ **des Gesellschaftszwecks** definition of the objects of a company (*objects clause*); ~ **durch das Los** determination by lot; **ausdrückliche** ~ express stipulation; **bankgesetzliche** ~**en** provisions of the banking laws; **bestehende** ~**en** prevailing regulations; **den** ~**en zuwiderlaufen** to contravene the regulations, to be in breach of legal provisions; **derzeit geltende** ~**en** the provisions in force; **die** ~**en von § 2 sind erfüllt** the requirements of section 2 have been satisfied; **durchzuführende** ~ provisions to be implemented; **eindeutige** ~ explicit provision; **e-e** ~ **entfällt** a provision does not apply; **einleitende** ~ preamble, introductory clause; **einschlägige** ~**en** relevant provisions, **ergänzende** ~**en** supplementary provisions; **gegenteilige** ~ stipulation to the contrary; **gemäß den** ~**en dieses Vertrages** according to the terms of the present agreement (*or* hereof); in accordance with the terms of this contract; **gemäß nachstehenden** ~**en** as hereinafter provided; **gesetzliche** ~ legal provision, legal rule, statutory provision; **den** ~**n** ~**en entsprechen**: to satisfy the legal requirements; **haushaltsrechtliche** ~ budgetary regulations; **mangels gegenteiliger** ~ in the absence of any contrary provision; **nachgiebige** ~ deviation clause; **nichttarifäre** ~**en** non-tariff provisions; **sich auf gesetzliche** ~**en berufen** to invoke the statutory provisions; **statutarische** ~**en** regulatory provisions; **subsidiäre** ~**en** subordinate regulations; **umsatzsteuerrechtliche** ~**en** turnover tax provisions, VAT provisions; **vorbehaltlich anderslautender** ~**en** except as otherwise (herein) provided; **vorbehaltlich der** ~**en** subject to the terms (of); **zwingende** ~ imperative (*or* mandatory) provision.

Bestimmungs|amt (*e.s. Beamten*) designated office; **~bahnhof** destination station; **~faktor** determining factor, determinant; **~flughafen** airport of destination; **~gebühr** *pat* designation fee; **b~gemäß** *adj* according to regulations, according to the terms (*of the contract*), for (*or* in accordance with) the intended use, in accordance with the instructions; **~hafen** port of destination; **~land** country of destination; ~~**prinzip**: country of destination principle (*turnover tax in transfrontier trade*); **~ort** (place of) destination, ultimate (*or* final) destination; **~postamt** (post) office of destination; **~recht** right of control, power of appointment; **~staat** designated State.

Bestkauf *m* purchase at the lowest price; purchase at the most favourable price.

Bestpreis *m* highest price, best price; **zum** ~ **verkaufen** sell at highest price, sell at best.

bestrafen *v/t* to punish, to sentence *bestraft werden: to suffer punishment*.

Bestrafung *f* punishment (= *p*); ~ **durch Parlamentsgesetz** act of attainder; **der** ~ **entgehen** to escape *p*, to go scot free; **disziplinarische** ~ disciplinary *p*;

Bestreben | **Beteiligung**

ehrengerichtliche ~ professional *p*; **sich der** ~ **aussetzen** to be liable to *p*; **strenge** ~ severe *p*; **von e-r** ~ **absehen** to refrain from *p*, to waive *p*.

Bestreben *n* endeavour, desire; **in dem** ~ anxious (to), desiring.

Bestrebung *f* endeavour, effort, attempt; ~**en sind im Gange** efforts are being made; **staatsfeindliche** ~**en** subversive activities; **von dem** ~ **getragen** ... inspired by a desire (to).

bestreiken *v/t* to be on strike (*against a plant or company*), to picket.

bestreikt *adj* strikebound.

Bestreikung *f* maintaining a strike, picketing.

bestreitbar *adj* (*1*) deniable, open to question, contestable, disputable, impugnable, challengeable; (*2*) defrayable, payable.

Bestreitbarkeit *f* deniability.

Bestreiten *n* (*1*) denial, contestation, traverse; ~ **der Echtheit e-r Urkunde** impeachment of a document, plea of non est factum (*or* nient le fait*) *(not his deed)*; ~~~ *der Unterschrift:* disowning of one's signature; ~ **der Identität** pleading diversity (*accused person and perpetrator*); ~ **der Schlüssigkeit** plea in demurrer, plea that there is no proper cause of action; ~ **der Schuldverpflichtung** denial of indebtedness, plea of onerari non; ~ ~ **einzelner Klagebehauptungen** special denial; ~ **mit Nichtwissen** plea of ignorance; **allgemeines** ~ general denial, general (*or* common) traverse, general issue; ~~ *der Einwendungen des Beklagten: general replication;* **formelles** ~ formal denial, negative averment; **im** ~**sfall** in case of denial, if denied; **substantiiertes** ~ substantiated denial, special traverse, special denial.

Bestreiten *n* (*2*) defrayment, defrayal (*expenses*).

bestreiten (*1*) to contest, to deny, to traverse, to repudiate, to impugn.

bestreiten (*2*) to defray (*expenses, charges*), to bear (*costs*).

Bestreitung *f* payment, defrayal.

Bestrittensein *n* contested nature of ..., denial

Bestsellerparagraph *m* renegotiation provision for authors of unexpected bestsellers (*s. 36 German Copyright Act*).

Besucher|kreis group of visitors, patronage; ~**tribühne** strangers' gallery, public gallery (*parl*); ~**visum** visitor's visa, tourist visa.

Besuchs|erlaubnis visitor's pass (*prison*); ~**recht** right of access, visiting rights; ~**verbot** no visitors!, visiting forbidden; ~**verkehr** prison visits (rules).

Betätigen *n* operating; ~ **der Bremse** operating the brake.

betätigen *v/reflex* to work, to have a job, to be active; to act (as, to act) in the capacity of; **sich gewerblich** ~ to carry on a trade or business.

Betätigung *f* occupation, activity, work; ~**sfeld** scope of work; **parteipolitische** ~ party-political activity; **politische** ~ political activity; **schriftstellerische** ~ literary activity; **wissenschaftliche** ~ pursuit of science, scientific activities, academic pursuits.

betäuben *v/t* to stupefy, to narcotize, to numb.

Betäubung *f* stunning (*blow, slaughtering*), anaesthetization.

Betäubungsmittel *n* narcotic(s), narcotic drug; anaesthetic (*med*); **erlaubnispflichtiges** ~ controlled drug.

beteiligen *v/t* to give a share (*in the profits*), to grant an interest (*in the capital*); *v/reflex* to participate, to acquire an interest, to take part, to contribute.

beteiligt *adj* participating, holding an interest (in), involved.

Beteiligter *m* (*der Beteiligte, pl Beteiligte:* ~*e*) participant, participator, concerned, party or privy (in) (*crime*); partner (in interest), an accessory (to); **den** ~**n e-e Frist zur Äußerung setzen**: to give notice to the parties concerned to submit their statements.

Beteiligung *f* participation, hold-

Beteiligungsbetrag   **Betrag**

ing(s) of equity capital, *major investment in the capital stock of another company (over 25%)*, interest in the capital of a company, equity interest, stake; ~ **am Gewinn** profit-sharing, share in the profits; ~ **am Stammkapital** equity participation; ~ **an e-m Unternehmen** participation in an enterprise; ~ **an der Patentverwertung** interest in patent exploitation (*exploitation of a patent*); ~**en an haftendem Kapital** risk capital operations; ~ **zur Hälfte** half interest; **Abstoßen e-r** ~ (*Tochtergesellschaft*) divestment; **angemessene** ~ a fair share; **beherrschende** ~ controlling interest; **formale** ~ nominal participation; **interne** ~**en** intercompany participations; **kommanditistische** ~ limited-partnership participation; **maßgebliche** ~substantial interest, controlling interest, controlling participation; **persönliche** ~ personal participation, personal investment; **stille** ~ sleeping partner's interest, sleeping partner's holding.

Beteiligungs|betrag amount of capital investment; ~**darlehen** = *partiarisches Darlehen qv*; ~**erträge** direct investment income, income from affiliated companies; ~**finanzierung** equity financing; financing by additional contribution (of partners); ~**fonds** equity fund; ~**geschäft** participation (transaction), *investing in the capital of other companies for purposes of control or major influence*; ~**gesellschaft** associated company, company in which a capital investment is held; mixed public and private sector company; ~**gewinn** profit from participation, investment earnings; ~**-Investitionen** portfolio investments, trade investment; ~**kapital** direct investment capital, outside equity capital; ~**konto** trade investments account, participation account; ~**papier** security representing a participation, investment certificate, equity certificate; ~**quote** participation quota; ~**sparen** capital investment savings, savings to acquire equities; ~**unternehmen** enterprise in which shares (*or* an interest) is held, associate, affiliate; ~**verhältnis** participation quota; participating relationship; ~**vertrag** participation agreement; ~**wert** book value of investment in subsidiaries and associated companies; ~**zusage** promise to participate; ~~ *der Seeversicherung zur Beweissicherung u. bei Klage*: suing and labouring clause.

beteuern *v/t* to assert, to declare solemnly, to affirm, to protest (*one's innocence*), to aver.

Beteuerung *f* affirmation, solemn assertion, protestation; ~ **unter Eid** assertion oath; **eidesgleiche** ~ solemn affirmation; words of affirmation having the force of an oath.

Betracht *m* consideration, regard (*used only in phrases such as the following*): **in** ~ **kommen** to be considered *as a possibility*, to be eligible *as a candidate*; **in** ~ **ziehen** to take into account, to consider, to take into consideration; **nicht in** ~ **kommen** to be out of the question, to be unsuitable, to be ineligible.

betrachten *v/t* to consider, to regard; **als erledigt** ~ to consider the matter closed, to regard as settled.

beträchtlich *adj* considerable, substantial.

Betrachtung *f* consideration, contemplation; **nüchterne** ~ conservative view, dispassionate view.

Betrachtungsweise *f* (mental) approach, attitude (*to things*), stance; **objektive** ~ objectivist(ic) approach; **subjektive** ~ subjectiv approach; **wirtschaftliche** ~ commercial considerations, economic school of thought.

Betrag *m* amount, sum, sum of money, quantum; ~ **dankend erhalten** (amount) received with thanks, this is to acknowledge the receipt of; ~ **erhalten** amount received; ~ **pro Einheit** unit amount; ~ **pro Kopf**

Betragsgebühr   **Betreten**

amount per head; **~sgebühr** fixed-sum charge; **~sspalte** amount column; **~sverfahren** *separate proceedings concerning the amount of the claim*; **abgebuchter** ~ debit (*on bank account*), amount debited; **abgehobener** ~ amount withdrawn (*from bank account*); **abgezweigter** ~ earmarked amount, amount earmarked for a special purpose; **abzugsfähiger** ~ deductible amount (*or* item); **anteiliger** ~ pro-rata amount; **ausgezahlter** ~ amount paid out (*to borrower under a loan arrangement*), disbursement; **ausstehender** ~ outstanding amount; **der angegebene** ~ (the) amount indicated, stated amount; **der benötigte** ~ the sum required; **der doppelte** ~ double the amount, twice the amount; **der eingeplante** ~ the amount included in the plan, the budgeted amount; **der fällige** ~ the amount due; **e-n ~ a conto zahlen** to make (*or* effect) a payment on account ...; **e-n ~ anrechnen** to credit an amount, to make allowance for an amount (*a refund, a discount etc*); **e-n ~ auf ein Konto einzahlen** to pay in a sum to s.o.'s credit; **e-n ~ flüssig machen** to realize (*or* to mobilize) an amount; **e-n ~ für Ausleihungen abzweigen** to earmark a sum for loans, to hive off a sum for loans; **e-n ~ in Abrechnung bringen** to debit a sum; **e-n ~ in Abzug bringen** to deduct an amount; **e-n ~ kürzen** to cut (*or* to delete) an item (*in an invoice*); **eingeforderter** ~ call (on shares), amount called; **eingeklagter** ~ amount sued for, amount endorsed (*on originating summons*), sum in dispute; **einmaliger** ~ non-recurring sum, once-and-for-all sum; **erheblicher** ~ substantial amount; **erzielter** ~ amount realized; **fälliger** ~ amount due, sum due; **ganzer** ~ full amount; **geringer** ~ small sum, petty amount; **geschuldeter** ~ sum due, sum owing, debt due; **gesicherter** ~ secured amount; **gezeichneter** ~ subscribed amount, subscription; **gleicher** ~ equivalent *or* equal amount; **hinterlegter** ~ deposited sum; **im ~e von** amounting to; **namhafter** ~ substantial amount (*or* sum); **nicht geschuldeter** ~ undue debt, amount not owed; **nomineller** ~ nominal sum; **pro forma** ~ nominal amount; **runder** ~ round sum; **steuerfreier** ~ tax-free amount; **strittiger** ~ amount in dispute; **überfälliger** ~ amount overdue; **überzogener** ~ overdrawn amount; **vereinbarter** ~ agreed sum; **zu erwartender** ~ expected sum, anticipated amount (*earnings*); **zuviel berechneter** ~ overcharged amount; **zuwenig berechneter** ~ undercharged amount.

Betragen *n* behavio(u)r, conduct; **ungebührliches** ~ unbecoming conduct.

betragen *v/i* to amount to, to total, to add up to, to come to; **durchschnittlich** ~ to average; **im ganzen** ~ to total.

betragsmäßig as regards the amount, in figures, mathematically.

betrauen *v/t* to entrust (*s.o. with a task*), to appoint (*s.o. to an office*).

Betreff *m* reference, subject, (*Betr.* = *Ref. or re:*).

betreffen *v/t* to concern, to relate to, to pertain to, to be in respect of.

betreffend *prep* concerning, regarding, with reference to, referring to, with respect to.

betreffs *prep* with reference to, concerning, regarding, (= *re:*, = *ref:*); **~sangabe** *f* reference, title.

Betreiben *n* operation, running; prompting, inducing, contriving; **auf ~ von** at the instigation of.

betreiben *v/t* to operate, to pursue, to carry on, to conduct, to run.

Betreiber *m* (plant) operator, person or company in charge of the operation of a (*nuclear*) plant; **~pflichten** duties of plant operators.

Betreten *n* entry, entering; ~ **bei**

betreten

Strafe verboten trespassers will be prosecuted; ~ **verboten** keep off, no entrance, no trespassing; **unbefugtes** ~ trespass; **widerrechtliches** ~ trespass.

betreten *v/t* to enter, to set foot on (*or* in), (*unbefugterweise*) to trespass.

Betretungs|recht right freely to enter (public forests and lands), right to enter premises temporarily; **~verbot** absolute prohibition to enter premises; no trespassing, positively no admittance.

betreuen *v/t* to take (good) care of s. th. (*or* s. o.), to look after s. th.

Betreuung *f* care; maintenance; **~sgebühr** (notary's) fee for advisory care; **~sstelle** welfare centre, assistance agency; **~sunterhalt** maintenance (payments) for looking after a dependant; support as compensation for taking care of infirm person; **soziale** ~ social care, social welfare.

Betrieb *m* business, enterprise, undertaking, plant; the firm, the company; operation, working, running (*of the firm*); **aktiver** ~ going concern; **arbeitender** ~ operating business, going concern; **den** ~ **aufnehmen** to begin working, to start business; **den** ~ **einstellen** to cease working; to close (down), to stop business; **ernährungswirtschaftlicher** ~ *firm engaged in the production or processing of foodstuffs*; **forstwirtschaftlicher** ~ forestry undertaking; **gemeinwirtschaftlicher** ~ collective economic enterprise; **gemischtwirtschaftlicher** ~ public utility company, semi-public enterprise; **gewerblicher** ~ trade or business, commercial (industrial) enterprise; ~~ **von Körperschaften des öffentlichen Rechts**: business enterprises belonging to public authorities; **gewerkschaftlich** (*vollständig*) **organisierter** ~ closed shop; **gewerkschaftsfreier** ~ non-union shop; **graphischer** ~ printing works, printing firm; **großbäuerlicher** ~ large farm; **handwerklicher** ~ handicraft undertaking, craftsman's shop; **in** ~ **befindliches Unternehmen** going concern; **in** ~ **nehmen** to put into operation; **in** ~ **sein** to be in operation, to operate; **in** ~ **setzen** to put into operation; **industrieller** ~ industrial enterprise; industrial concern (industrial) plant; **konzessionierter** ~ licensed enterprise; **landwirtschaftlicher** ~ agricultural holding, farm; **milchverarbeitender** ~ milk-processing factory, dairy; **mittelbäuerlicher** ~ medium-sized farm; **nahestehende** ~**e** affiliated enterprises, closely related enterprises; **öffentlicher** ~ public enterprise; **rationell wirtschaftender** ~ efficiently run enterprise; **staatseigener** ~ state-owned enterprise; **volkseigener** ~ (*VEB*) people's enterprise.

betrieblich *adj* relating to an enterprise, operational, internal, in-house.

Betriebs|abgaben rates (and local taxes) to be paid by an enterprise; **~ablauf** operational procedure, course of operations, sequence of operations; **~abrechnung** (internal) operational accounting, (performance) cost accounting, shop accounting, income account, cost and revenue statement; **~absprache** *informal understanding between management and staff representation;* **~aktiven** assets used for operations; **~altersversorgung** company pension scheme; **~analyse** operational analysis; **~änderung** change in the object of an enterprise; **~angehörige** staff, employees of a firm, shop employees, personnel; **~anlage** plant, production facilities, operating equipment, production layout; *nicht ausgenutzte* ~*n*: *idle equipment*; **~anlagenbuch** plant ledger; **~anlagenvermieter** plant hire operator; **~anleitung** operating instructions, service manual; **~anweisung** = ~*anleitung qv*; **~anwesenheitslohn**

Betriebsanwesenheitslohn

portal-to-portal pay (*mining*); ~**arzt** works doctor, company doctor; ~**assistent** assistant to the works manager; ~**aufgabe** closing down of an enterprise; ~**aufnahme** (1) going into operation, start-up of business, establishment of a firm; (2) industrial census; ~**aufseher** works manager, factory supervisor; ~**aufspaltung** split-up of an enterprise (*to form two legally separate companies (eg operating and property owning)*); ~**aufwand** working expense, operating expenditure; ~**aufzeichnungen** company records; ~**ausflug** staff outing, works' outing, office outing; ~**ausgabe** operating costs, operating expenditure, business expense, trade expense; *abzugsfähige* ~~: *deduction for expenses; allgemeine* ~~*n*: *general operating expenses, overheads; vorausbezahlte* ~~*n*: *deferred charges to operations*; ~**ausrüstung** machinery and equipment, plant; ~**ausschuß** staff representation committee; ~**ausstattung** = ~*ausrüstung qv*; ~**beamte** company officials, management officials; ~**bedingungen** conditions of operation, business conditions; ~**berater** management consultant, industrial advisor; ~**beratung** management consultancy; ~**bereitschaft** readiness for use; *technische* ~~: *ready for use*; ~**bilanz** operating statement; ~**blindheit** plant blindness, *lack of common sense due to overinvolvement with company problems*, an excessively parochial approach; ~**bremse** operating brake; ~**buchführung** industrial accounting, internal accounting, operating accounts, internal operations bookkeeping, cost accounting; ~**buchhaltung** (1) = ~*buchführung qv*, (2) internal accounts department; ~**buße** company penalty; ~**ebene** establishment level, plant, level; ~**einheit** operating unit, operating holding; ~**einkommen** business income, operating returns; ~**einnahme** operating receipt; *pl* ~*n* operating revenue, business gains; ~**einrichtungen** production equipment, operating equipment, plant operating facilities, factory installations; ~**einrichtung und Maschinen** plant and machinery; ~**einschränkung** cutting down of operations, reduction in (*or* curtailment of) operations; ~**einstellung** closing-down (*of business enterprise*), stoppage of business; ~**erfahrung** industrial know-how, business experience; ~**erfindung** works invention, employee's invention; ~**erfolg** operating results; ~**erfordernisse** operating requirements; ~**ergebnis** operating profit or loss, production result, operating result(s); *pl* ~*se*: trading results; ~**ergebnisrechnung** operating statement, trading profit or loss; ~**erlaubnis** operating licence, type approval, production permit; motor vehicle licence; ~**eröffnung** opening of the business; ~**ertrag** operating earnings; ~**erweiterungsverbot** prohibition to enlarge plant facilities, prohibition of plant enlargement; ~**erwerb** acquisition of a business; ~**erwerber** party acquiring an enterprise, transferee of a business *or* an undertaking; buyer of a firm; **b**~**fähig** usable, in working order; *nicht* ~*fähig*: *unworkable*; ~**fähigkeit** operating ability; ~**ferien** works holiday, staff vacations; ~~ *machen*: *to close down for the holidays; geschlossene* ~~: *holidays for the entire staff;* **b**~**fertig** *adj* ready for operation, ready to use; ~**finanzamt** (*locally*) competent revenue office for an enterprise (*or for the domestic permanent establishment of a foreign enterprise*); ~**fläche** area of an industrial enterprise; *landwirtschaftliche* ~~: *farm land, acreage of a farm;* ~**fonds** working fund, trading fund; ~**forschung** operational research; **b**~**fremd** not belonging to the business or enterprise, extraneous, non-operating; ~**fremder**

Betriebsfrieden   **Betriebspachtvertrag**

person not belonging to the firm or company, outsider, third party; ~**frieden** peaceful management – staff relations, internal peace in the firm; ~**führer** manager, operator; ~**führung** management; ~**führungslehre** management science, management techniques, modern management; ~**führungsvertrag** business management agreement; ~**gebäude** factory building; *landwirtschaftliches* ~~: *farming building;* ~**gefahr** operational risk (*or* hazard) *(motor vehicle, machinery)*; ~**geheimnis** business secret, trade secret, manufacturing secret, industrial secret; ~**gemeinde** municipality of employing enterprise *(for employees residing elsewhere)*; ~**gemeinkosten** (operating) overheads, plant overheads, indirect operating costs; ~**gemeinschaft** (community of) staff and management, joint business, joint venture, joint working arrangement; ~**genehmigung** operating permit, licence; ~**gesellschaft** operating company *(subsidiary of a holding company)*; *internationale* ~~: *international operating agency;* ~**gewerkschaft** company union; ~**gewinn** operating profit (*or* surplus), trading profit, earned surplus; ~**gleis** industrial track, plant (railway) line; ~**grundstück** factory premises, company premises, plant site; ~**gutachten** expert opinion (*or* expertise) about (the status of) an enterprise; ~**guthaben** working balance; ~**haftpflichtversicherung** employer's liability insurance; ~**haftung** operational liability; ~**handbuch** operating manual; ~**hauptbuch** factory ledger; ~**hilfe** farmer's emergency help; ~**hygiene** industrial hygiene; ~**ingenieur** production engineer; ~**inhaber** owner, work proprietor, owner of an establishment, proprietor of a firm (*or* business); *mitarbeitender* ~~: *working employer;* ~**jahr** operating year, year of operation; ~**justiz** internal "administration of justice" in a company, internal disciplinary rules (*in a company*); ~**kalkulator** cost accountant; ~**kapazität** plant capacity, works capacity, operating capacity (*in production*); ~**kapital** (net) working capital, (*capital* = *c*) circulating *c; also:* floating *c,* active *c,* trading *c,* rolling *c,* trading fund, business *c,* available *c*; ~~*verhältnis: working capital ratio;* ~**kassenmittel** cash funds (of an enterprise); ~**klima** work climate, working atmosphere; ~**konto** working account, trading account; ~**konzession** trade licence; ~**kosten** operating cost (*plant, installation*), overhead, working expenses, *agr* farm expenses; *laufende* ~~: *running expenditure;* ~**kostenermittlung** cost accounting; ~**kostenkalkulation** cost effectiveness analysis; ~**kostenkoeffizient** ratio of working expenses; ~**kostensatz** operating cost ratio; ~**krankenkasse** plant health insurance, company's social health insurance (*as a public corporation*); *landwirtschaftliche* ~~: *farmers' social health insurance*; ~**kredit** working capital credit; industrial credit(s), advance for current operations, short-term loan, working funds loan; ~**leiter** production manager, works manager, operations manager; ~**leitung** management, factory management; *oberste* ~~: *top management;* ~**material** working material, working stock, stock-in-trade, factory supplies; ~**mittel** → *Betriebsmittel*; ~**nachfolge** succession of the enterprise; b~**notwendig** *adj* necessary for running a business, required for operations; ~**obmann** shop steward, staff representative; ~**optimum** ideal capacity (*of an enterprise*), optimal production; ~**ordnung** factory regulations, shop regulations, internal regulations of a firm or company; ~**organisation** industrial organization; ~**nachfolge** succession of the enterprise; ~**pachtvertrag**

159

lease of company premises; ~**personal** staff, personnel (*of a firm or company*), operating staff (*engineering*); ~**pflicht** legal obligation to operate (*railway, public utility*); ~**plan** business plan; ~**planpflicht** mine operator's obligation to submit exploitation plan; ~**politik** business policy, operational policy, company policy; ~**prüfer** tax investigator, revenue investigator, public auditor; ~**prüfung** external audit(s), fiscal tax audit (*or* examination), revenue investigation, tax office inspection (*of a firm's accounts*), field audit; ~**prüfungsbilanz** fiscal tax audit balance sheet, tax investigation balance sheet; ~**rat** (*1*) staff committee, works council; (*2*) member of a staff committee, shop-steward; ~**ratsfähigkeit** capacity to set up a staff representation; ~**ratsvorsitzender** shop chairman, chairman of staff committee *etc, cf Betriebsrat*; ~**ratswahl** election of staff committee members; ~**rechnung** trading account, operating account; ~**rente** company-provided pension; ~**risiko** business risk, risk of running a business, industrial hazard; ~**schließung** plant closing, plant shutdown, closing down of the business; ~**schluß** closing hours; ~**schulden** (current) debts of a firm or company; ~**schutz** industrial safety; ~**sicherheit** industrial safety, safety at work, a firm's safety record; ~**sitz** company headquarters, principal place of business of a firm, principal offices of the firm, registered office; ~**spaltung** separation of factory units; ~**stadium** operational stage; ~**stätte** permanent establishment, regular and established place of business; *inländische ~~: domestic establishment; mehrgemeindliche ~~n: joint communal plants*; ~**stätteninhaber** person in charge of permanent establishment (*or* branch enterprise), branch manager; ~**steuer** operating tax; ~**stillegung** closing-down (*or* closure); ~**stoff** fuel; ~**stoffe** operating supplies; ~**störung** operating trouble, breakdown, stoppage, shutdown; ~**struktur** business structure, corporate structure; ~**tätigkeit** operation, operating activities; ~**technik** industrial engineering, management engineering; ~**teil** unit (of an enterprise), plant; ~**übereinkommen** operating agreement; ~**übergabe** the handing over of factory premises, transfer of a business *or* of an enterprise; ~**überlassungsvertrag** lease of a running concern: *agreement between corporations to transfer the enterprise for a limited time;* ~**übernahme** takeover of a firm *or* plant; ~**überschuß** operating surplus, trading surplus; ~**- und Geschäftsausstattung** equipment and fittings, plant and equipment, plant and machinery; ~**unfall** →*Betriebsunfall;* ~**unkosten** running costs, overhead expenses, overheads; ~**unterbrechung** interruption of business, temporary cessation of work, stoppage; ~**unterbrechungsversicherung** loss-of-profit insurance, use and occupancy insurance; ~**unternehmer** entrepreneur, business propietor, contractor; ~**suntersagung** ban on operations of a plant; ~**urlaub** company vacation; ~**veranstaltungen** (annual) staff parties (*or* events), *educational or recreational activities organized by the firm or company;* ~**veräußerung** transfer of the business as a whole; ~**vereinbarung** shop agreement, union contract, single plant bargaining agreement, individual works agreement, internal wage and salary agreement; ~**verfassung** organization of industrial relations, labo(u)r-management relations, industrial democracy; ~**verfassungsgesetz** Employees' Representation Act; ~**verfassungsrecht** *the law concerning employees' representation and co-determination in business* *and industry;* ~**vergleich** interfactory comparative studies, intra-industrial studies; ~**verhältnisse** operating conditions; ~**verlagerung** relocation of the business; ~**verlust** operating loss, trading loss; ~**verlustversicherung** business insurance, consequential loss insurance; insurance of trading loss; ~**vermögen** business assets, commercial assets, business property, operating assets, trading capital; *bewegliches* ~~: *movable assets; gewillkürtes* ~~: *voluntary business property; landwirtschaftliches* ~~: *farming stock and effects; notwendiges* ~~: *necessary business property;* ~**versammlung** staff meeting, factory meeting, assembly of employees, shop floor meeting, works meeting; ~**versicherung** factory insurance, group insurance (*for employees*); *eigene* ~~: *self-insurance;* ~**vertretung** employees' representation; ~**verwaltungen (des Bundes)** operating agencies (of the Federal Government), federal public undertakings; ~**verwaltungsgemeinkosten** plant administration overheads; ~**vorräte** working stocks; ~**vorrichtungen** installations; ~**vorschrift** shop regulation(s), firm rules; service instructions; ~**wert** value as a going concern; ~**wirt** graduate in business administration, MBA (*master of business administration*); graduate in managerial economics, (business) economist; ~**wirtschaft** business economics, managerial economics, applied economics, business (*or* industrial) management; ~**wirtschaftslehre** business economics, management theory, science of managerial economics, science of business (*or* industrial) management; *allgemeine* ~~: *managerial economics; forstliche* ~~: *forestry economics;* **b**~**wirtschaftlich** managerial, operational; related to business management; ~~~*es Studium*: *business management studies;* ~**wirtschaftlichkeitsquotient** operating ratio; ~**zugehörigkeit** length of service, job tenure; staff membership in a firm or company, seniority; ~**zugehörigkeitsdauer** length of employment (*or* service), duration of employment; ~**zuschuß** operating subsidy, operational grant; ~**zweig** branch of business (*or* of industry).

Betriebsmittel *n/pl* production equipment and facilities, working funds, operating funds, operating resources, working cash, corporate cash; ~**bereitstellung** provision of production equipment and manufacturing facilities; ~**fonds** working capital fund; ~~**Grundzeit** machine equipment base time; ~**kredit** business loan, credit to provide working funds, working capital credit; ~**rücklage** operating cash reserve; ~~**Rüstzeit** machine set-up time; ~**überweisung** remittance of operating cash, payment of working funds; ~**zuweisung** allotment of operating cash (*or* of working funds); **handelsübliche** ~ commercial supplies; **landwirtschaftliche** ~ agricultural equipment and resources; **umlaufende** ~ current assets.

Betriebsunfall *m* industrial accident, on-the-job accident, accident at work; ~**schutz** workmen's compensation, protection from industrial accidents; ~**verhütung** prevention of industrial accidents; ~**verletzung** industrial injury; ~**versicherung** industrial injuries insurance.

betroffen *adj* affected, concerned; **nachteilig** ~adversely affected.

Betroffener *m* (*der Betroffene*) the person affected, the person interested, the party concerned.

Betrug *m* fraud, obtaining by false pretences, cheating, swindling, deceit; ~ **aus Not** petty fraud due to indigence; ~ **begehen** to commit fraud, to obtain by false pretences, to cheat; ~ **im zweiten Rückfall** fraud recidivism; **ausgemachter** ~ a clear case of fraud; **sich des** ~**es**

Betrugsabsicht   **Bevölkerung**

schuldig machen to be guilty of fraud.
Betrugs|absicht fraudulent purpose; *in* ~~ *handeln*: to intend to defraud; ~**handlung** fraudulent act; **zu** ~**zwecken** (for a) fraudulent purpose.
betrügen *v/t* to commit fraud, to cheat, to defraud.
Betrüger *m* swindler, defrauder, sharper, cheat, fraud.
Betrügerei *f* cheating, swindling, swindle, trickery.
betrügerisch *adj* fraudulent, surreptitious, deceptive; ~ **erlangen** to obtain fraudulently, to obtain by false pretences, to obtain by fraud; ~ **erwerben** to acquire by fraud; ~ **in Verkehr bringen** to palm off on a person (*false money*), to market fraudulently, to swindle into the market.
betrunken *adj* drunk, intoxicated.
Betrunkener *m* (*der Betrunkene*) drunken person, drunk, intoxicated person.
Betrunkenheit *f* (state of) drunkenness, intoxication, inebriation.
Bettel|betrug fraudulent begging; ~**brief** begging letter (*also: fraudulent begging letter*).
Bettelei *f* begging; mendicancy; pestering.
Betteln *n* begging, beggary; ~ **und Hausieren verboten!** begging and hawking prohibited!
Bettler *m* beggar, scrounger, mendicant; ~**sprache** beggar's cant.
Beugehaft *f* coercive detention (*in case of obstruction or refusal to attend etc*).
Beugemittel *n/pl* disciplinary means of coercion, measures to enforce compliance with court orders.
Beugestrafe *f* coercive penalty, contempt of court penalty.
beurkunden *v/t* to record, to place on record, to record in a notarial deed, to register.
beurkundet *adj* recorded (in notarial form); **amtlich** ~ officially recorded, on record; **notariell** ~ recorded by a notary.

Beurkundung *f* (notarial or judicial) recording (*of an act or transaction*); executing a (notarial) deed, record of acknowledgment (*of deeds and conveyances*); ~**sbefugnis** power of certification; ~**sgebühren** notary's fees for recording (*an act or transaction*); ~**smonopol** (notary's recording monopoly); ~**s- und Beglaubigungsgebühren** notary's recording and certification fees; **gerichtliche** ~ judicial certification, entry in court records (*of court settlement*); **notarielle** ~ executing a notarial instrument, notarial protocolization, recording of an act or transaction before (and by) a notary, recording by a notary, notarization (*required of conveyances etc*); **notarieller** ~**svermerk über erfolglose Wechselvorlage** noting (*of a bill of exchange*); **öffentliche** ~ public registration (*or recording*).
beurlauben *v/t* to grant leave of absence; to suspend (*from office*).
Beurlaubung *f* leave, suspension (from office).
beurteilen *v/t* to judge, to give an opinion, to assess; **falsch** ~ to misjudge; **erneut** ~ to rejudge; **positiv** ~ to give a positive assessment, to regard with favour, to give a good performance rating, to rate well.
Beurteilung *f* appraisal, opinion, judgment, assessment; performance report; ~**sfehler** error of judgment; ~**sspielraum** latitude of evaluation *or* interpretation; ~**sgrundsatz** rule for grading performance and behaviour; **dienstliche** ~ efficiency report, personnel assessment, reference by a superior; **kontroverse** ~controversial opinions; **strafgerichtliche** ~ assessment under criminal law.
Beute *f* booty, loot; ~**gut** loot, captured goods; ~**politik** *pol* spoils system; ~**recht** right of capture, right to take booty.
Bevölkerung *f* population; **arbeitsfähige** ~ able-bodied people, employable population; **berufstätige**

Bevölkerungsaufbau **Bewährungsauflagen**

~ employed and self-employed persons, (number of) people in work; **erwerbstätige** ~ the gainfully employed population; **wahlberechtigte** ~ voting population; **werktätige** ~ working population.

Bevölkerungs|aufbau (statistical) structure of the population; ~**dichte** density of population; ~**druck** population pressure; ~**explosion** population explosion; ~**kreis** section of the population; ~**politik** population policy, policy of influencing the birth rate; ~**pyramide** population pyramid; age pyramid; ~**schicht** social stratum, class of society; *die ärmeren* ~~**en**: *the poorer classes*; ~**schutz** civil defence, protection of the civil population; ~**statistik** vital statistics, demography; ~**struktur** population structure; ~**überschuß** surplus population; ~**wachstum** population growth.

bevollmächtigen *v/t* to authorize, to empower, to give power of attorney, to appoint s. o. one's lawful agent (*or* attorney in fact).

bevollmächtigt *adj* duly authorized, empowered, having power of attorney; **nicht** ~ unauthorized, lacking power of attorney; **ordnungsgemäß** ~ duly authorized.

Bevollmächtigte *f* female attorney (in fact).

Bevollmächtigter *m* (*der Bevollmächtigte*) authorized person, attorney (in fact), donee of a power; *dipl* plenipotentiary, authorized (*or* private) agent, proxy; *durch e-n ~n abstimmen*: *to vote by proxy*; **allgemein** ~ general attorney, generally empowered person; **als** ~ per pro (*signature, usually*: *in Vertretung i. V. qv*); **die hierzu gehörig befugten** ~ the duly authorized plenipotentiaries; **privatrechtlicher** ~ attorney in fact, private agent.

Bevollmächtigung *f* authorization, power of attorney.

bevorraten *v/i* to stock up, to provide with stocks, to stockpile.

Bevorratung *f* building up of stocks, stockpiling, keeping stocks in supply, provisioning, ~**spflicht** stock-piling obligation.

bevorrechtigen *v/t* to privilege, to grant privileges; to grant preferences (*by insolvent debtor*).

bevorrechtigt *adj* privileged, preferred, preferential; **nicht** ~ non-privileged, unprivileged, deferred.

Bevorrechtigung *f* preference, preferment, priority, privilege.

bevorschussen *v/t* to advance money (*on current account*), to allow an overdraft, to grant an advance (*salary*).

Bevorschussung *f* advance, granting an advance.

bevorstehend *adj* forthcoming, nearing; **unmittelbar** ~ imminent (*danger*), impending (*death*).

bevorzugen *v/t* to prefer, to give preference to, to grant special privilege (to), to privilege.

bevorzugt *v/t* preferred, preferential, privileged.

Bevorzugung *f* (granting) preferential treatment (of), preferment.

bewachen *v/t* to guard, to keep watch (over).

Bewachung *f* guarding, guard, escort; ~**sdienst** guard duties; ~**sfahrzeug** escort vessel (ship), escort car; ~**sgewerbe** guard and watch service industry; ~**svertrag** guarding contract, agreement for the services of watchmen (*to guard, patrol and oversee a building or other property*).

bewaffnet *adj* armed.

Bewaffnung *f* arms, equipment, weapons carried *by s. o.*, armament (*military forces*).

bewahren *v* to keep (*unchanged*), to preserve, to protect, to save.

Bewährung *f* probation (*suspension of sentence on probation*); ~ **gewähren** to grant probation, to suspend a sentence on probation; **auf** ~ **entlassen** to release on probation; **unter** ~ **stellen** to place (*put*) on probation.

Bewährungs|auflagen conditions of

probation; ~**aufsicht** supervision of the probationer; ~**aufstieg** automatic promotion or upgrading of civil servants with a satisfactory record, promotion by seniority (*after satisfactory service*); ~**frist** probation period; ~**helfer** probation officer; ~**hilfe** probation service; ~**plan** rehabilitation scheme for probationers; ~**probe** (acid) test, trial (run); ~**system** probation system; ~**zeit** probation period.

Bewässerungsprojekt *n* irrigation scheme.

Beweggrund *m* (*pl Beweggründe*) motive, motivation, inducement; **niedrige** ~*pl* base motives, turpitude.

beweglich *adj* movable, tangible, personal (*property*).

Beweglichkeit *f* movability, flexibility, agility.

Bewegtbildzeit *f* animated film time.

Bewegung *f* movement; ~**s- und Reisefreiheit** freedom of movement and travel; **staatsgefährdende** ~ subversive movement.

Beweis *m* proof, evidence; ~ **anbieten** to offer evidence; ~**angebot** offer of proof, offer of evidence; ~**anordnung** directions for (the taking of) evidence; ~**anregung** suggestion as to the taking of evidence; ~**antrag** motion to take evidence, offer of evidence; ~ **antreten** to adduce evidence, to tender evidence; ~**antritt** offer of evidence, submission of evidence, production of evidence (*documents*), presentation of evidence (*documents, exhibits*); *fehlender* ~*antritt: failure of evidence*; ~**antritt durch Urkundenvorlage** submitting documents, producing documents as evidence; ~**anzeichen** indicative evidence; ~**aufnahme** → *Beweisaufnahme;* ~**bedürftigkeit** necessity to be proved; ~**beschluß** order for evidence, directions for evidence; ~ ~*zur Vernehmung von Zeugen: orders for examination;* ~ **der Bösgläubigkeit** proof of bad faith; ~ **der Kenntnis** proof of scienter; ~ **des ersten Anscheins** prima facie evidence; *den* ~ *des ersten Anscheins erbringen: to establish a prima facie case*; ~ **des Nichtgeschehenseins** negative evidence; ~ **des Nichtvorhandenseins** negative evidence; ~ **durch Mittäter** evidence by accomplices; ~**einrede** objection to the admission of evidence; ~ **erbringen** to prove, to furnish proof; *e–n* ~ *nicht erbringen: to fail to prove s.th.;* ~**ergebnis** evidence (in the case), the outcome of the evidence; *zum* ~~ *plädieren: to sum up evidence;* ~**erhärtung** corroboration of evidence; ~ **erheben** to take evidence; **b**~**erheblich** relevant to the issues of the case, of probative value; ~**erheblichkeit** relevancy of evidence; ~**erhebung** taking evidence, hearing of evidence; ~**vermittlung** exploratory, examination of a witness; **b**~**fähig** susceptible of proof, demonstrable, provable, having probative value; ~**fähigkeit** provability, probative value; **b**~**fällig** unable to produce proof, lacking proof, unsuccessful in proving sth, not proven; ~**fälligkeit** failure to furnish proof, inability to furnish proof, failure of evidence; ~**frage** evidential issue; ~**frist** time granted for producing evidence; ~**führer** party submitting evidence, party bearing the burden of proof; ~**führung** production of evidence, marshalling of evidence; ~**führungslast** burden of producing evidence; ~**funktion** probative function; ~**gebühr** fee for taking evidence, fee for evidentiary proceedings (*charged by lawyers and for the court*); ~**gegenstand** point of evidence, subject matter of the (taking of) evidence; ~**indiz** point of circumstantial evidence; ~**kette** chain of evidence; ~**kraft** probatory force, probative value, conclusiveness; ~ ~ *e–r Aussage: the strength of testimony;* ~ ~ *e–r Urkunde: internal evidence;* **b**~**kräftig** *adj* probative, conclusive (cogent), substantiating; *nicht ~~: non-probative*; ~**last** onus (probandi), burden of proof; *die ~~ umkehren: to shift the burden of proof*; *trotz der ~~ e-n Beweis erbringen: to sustain the burden of proof; formelle (= subjektive) ~~: burden of producing evidence; materielle = objektive ~~: onus: (= burden) of proof*; ~**lastklausel** stipulation *(in terms and conditions)* fixing the burden of proof; ~**lastverschiebung** shift in the burden of proof, change in the onus of proof; ~**liefern** to prove, to furnish evidence; ~**mangel** lack of evidence; b~**mäßig** evidential; ~**material** evidence, means of evidence, documents; *belastendes ~~: incriminating evidence*; *neues ~~: fresh evidence*; *widersprüchliches ~~: contradictory evidence*; *~~ beibringen: to furnish (supply) evidence*; ~**mittel** → *Beweismittel*; ~**nachholung** introduction of new evidence; ~**not** inability to produce proof; difficulty of discharging the burden of proof, lack of evidence; ~**offerte** offer to furnish evidence; ~**pflicht** (legal) obligation to furnish proof, onus of proof; ~**pflichtiger** *(der ~pflichtige)* the party who has to prove sth; ~**protokoll** transcript of evidence, record of proof; ~**recht** law of evidence; b~**rechtlich** evidentiary, probative; ~**regel** rule of evidence; ~**schwierigkeit** difficulty of proving sth; ~**sicherung** preservation of evidence, perpetuating evidence, perpetuating testimony; ~**stück** exhibit; ~**termin** (date fixed for the) hearing of evidence; ~**thema** the subject of the hearing of evidence, the points in issue; ~**umkehrung** shift in (reversal of) the burden of proof; ~**unerheblichkeit** irrelevance of evidence; ~**unterlage** evidencing instrument, document introduced as evidence; ~**unterschlagung** concealing evidence; ~**urkunde** exhibit (in the form of a document), documentary evidence; ~**urkunden- und Asservatenliste** list of exhibits; ~**verbindung** producing joint evidence; ~**verbot** inadmissibility of evidence; ~**vereinbarung** evidential stipulation; ~**vereitelung** obstructing the obtaining of evidence; ~**verfahren** the taking of evidence, proceedings for the introduction of evidence; ~**verhandlungen** argument in court concerning the admission of evidence; ~**vermutung** evidential presumption; ~**vernichtung** destruction of evidence; ~**verwertung** using sth as evidence; *~~sverbot: non-admissibility of (improperly obtained) evidence*; ~ **vom Hörensagen** hearsay evidence; ~**wert** probative value; ~**würdigung** consideration of the evidence; weighing of the evidence, evaluation of the evidence, *die ~~ vornehmen: to consider (= weigh) the evidence*; *freie ~~: free evaluation of the evidence*; ~**zeichen** token; **angetretener** ~ evidence adduced; **aus Mangel an** ~**en** for want of proof, due to lack of evidence; **ausreichender** ~ sufficient evidence; **bis zum** ~ **des Gegenteils** unless the contrary is proved, in the absence of proof to the contrary; **die** ~**last trifft den Kläger** the burden of proof lies with the plaintiff; **direkter** ~ direct evidence; **e-n** ~ **entkräften** to refute evidence; **eindeutiger** ~ clear evidence, proof; **e-n** ~ **anbieten für** to offer evidence for; **einwandfreier** ~ absolute proof; **hinreichender** ~ sufficient evidence; **indirekter** ~ circumstantial evidence; **lückenhafter** ~ incomplete evidence; **mangels** ~**es** because of lack of proof, in the absence of proof, for want of sufficient evidence; **mangels** ~**es des Gegenteils** in the absence of proof to the contrary; **mittelbarer** ~ indirect evidence, circumstantial evidence; **mündlicher** ~ (oral) testimony; **neuer** ~**fresh** evidence; **sachdienlicher** ~ relevant evidence; **schlüssiger** ~ substantial proof, clear proof, conclusive evidence; **schriftliche ~e** written proof, written evidence, evidence in writing; **überzeugender ~** convincing evidence; **unmittelbarer ~** direct evidence; **unter ~ stellen** to offer (*or* adduce) evidence, to furnish proof, to prove; **unwiderlegbarer ~** unchallengeable evidence, irrefutable evidence; **urkundlicher ~** proof by documentary evidence; **voller ~** full proof, conclusive proof, absolute proof; **vorläufiger ~** preliminary proof; **zulässiger ~** admissible evidence; **zulässiges ~angebot** admissible (offer of) evidence; **zum ~ dafür** as evidence thereof; **zwingender ~** (absolute) proof.

Beweisaufnahme *f* the taking of evidence, hearing of the evidence, receiving evidence; **~gebühr** (lawyer's) fee for the taking of evidence; **~protokoll** record of the evidence, transcript of the testimony; **~termin** evidential hearing; **~ zum Strafmaß** evidence to determine sentence; **die ~findet unter Ausschluß der Öffentlichkeit statt** evidence is being heard in camera; **die ~ schließen** to close the case; **in die ~ eintreten:** to proceed to take evidence.

beweisbar *adj* provable, verifiable.

beweisen *v/t* to prove; to establish, to make evident, to demonstrate; **gerichtlich ~** to prove ~ to the court (*or* in court).

Beweismittel *n* judicial evidence, (formal) means of evidence; (*witnesses, experts, documents, exhibits*), evidence presented to the court; **neu aufgefundene ~** fresh evidence, newly discovered evidence; **nicht zugelassenes ~** non-admitted (*or* inadmissible) evidence; **notwendiges ~** indispensable evidence, crucial evidence; **primäres ~** primary evidence; **ungeeignetes ~** unsuitbale evidence; **zulässiges ~** admissible evidence.

bewerben *v/reflex* (*sich um etwas ~*) to apply (*for a post or job*), to compete for s.th., to submit a tender.

Bewerber *m* applicant, candidate, aspirant, postulant, suitor (*company take-overs*); bidder, pretender (*crown*); **ohne ~** unapplied for.

Bewerbung *f* application (*for a position*); **~sbedingungen** conditions for tendering; **~bogen** application form; application requirements; **~sprüfung** application examination; **~sschreiben** letter of application, written application; **~sunterlagen** papers in support of application.

bewertbar *adj* assessable, appraisable, eligible for consideration.

bewerten *v/t* to assess, to appraise, to value, to evaluate; **höher ~** to write up.

bewertet *pp adj* assessed, valued, appraised; **nicht ~** unassessed, not valued.

Bewertung *f* appraisal, assessment (of value), valuation, rating; **~ der Aktiva** valuation of assets; **~ des Schadens** assessment of the damage; **kursmässige ~** quoted value; **steuerliche ~** tax valuation; **vorsichtige ~** conservative valuation; **zollamtliche ~** official valuation (by customs authority).

Bewertungs|abschlag reduction in valuation; deduction of asset value; **~freiheit** discretionary valuation (at taxpayer's choice) *c.f. equipment of small value*; **~gesetz** tax valuation Act; **~grundlage** basis of valuation; **~grundsätze** principles of (balance sheet) valuation; **~irrtum** error in valuation; **~maßstab** standard of valuation; **~smethode** method of valuation, procedure for determining value, valuation technique; **~stetigkeit** consistency of valuation; **~stichtag** valuation date; **~system** valuation (system); **~unterlagen** valuation papers; **~verfahren** valuation method; **~vorschriften** (tax) valuation rules; *steuerliche ~ ~: valuation rules according to tax laws;*

bewiesen   **bezahlt**

~**wahlrecht** valuation alternatives; ~**zeitpunkt** time of valuation.

bewiesen *pp adj* proved, proven; **unwiderlegbar** ~ absolutely proved, proved beyond all doubt.

bewilligen *v/t* to grant, to allow, to appropriate (*budget*), to allocate.

Bewilligung *f* grant, appropriation, vote (*finance bill*); ~ **auf Widerruf** revocable grant; ~ **des Parlaments** parliamentary grant, appropriation; ~**santrag** application for a grant; ~**sausschuß** appropriations committee; ~**sbescheid** decision on an application (for a grant); ~**sgesuch** petition for a grant; ~**sgrundsatz** *principle that changes of entries in the land title register require the consent of the owner or entitled party if their rights are affected*; ~**sinhaber** holder of the authorization, grantee; ~**srecht** *parl* right to make appropriations; ~**sstelle** authority in charge of allowing an expenditure; ~**sverfahren** authorization procedure, (*procedure for allowing a grant*) (*or other public expenditure*); **unverausgabte** ~**en** unused appropriations.

bewirken *v/t* to operate, to effect, to cause, to give rise to.

bewirtschaften *v/t* to manage, to run (*an enterprise*), to cultivate (*land*), to ration (*scarce goods*), to control (*housing, rent*).

Bewirtschaftung *f* (*cf bewirtschaften*) management, cultivation, rationing, control; ~**smaßnahmen** control measures, controls, rationing; ~**spflicht** duty of cultivation; ~**ssystem** system of controls, controls, rationing system; **aus der** ~ **herausnehmen** to decontrol; **kollektive** ~ collective enterprise, collective farming; **staatliche** ~ government control, rationing.

Bewirtung *f* hospitality, business entertainment; ~**skosten** entertainment expenses; ~**sspesen** business entertainment expenses, entertainment allowance (*business friends, clients etc.*).

bewohnbar *adj* habitable, fit to live in, fit for human habitation; **nicht** ~ unfit for human habitation, uninhabitable.

Bewohnbarkeit *f* habitability, fitness for human habitation.

Bewohnen *n* occupation, occupancy (*house, apartment*), dwelling (*in living quarters*); **eigenes** ~ personal occupation, self occupation.

bewohnen *v/t* to inhabit, to live in, to occupy, to reside in.

Bewohner *m* inhabitant, resident, residental occupier, occupant, occupier; ~ **e-s fremden Gebietes** non-resident; **mietergeschützter** ~ protected occupier.

bewußt *adj* conscious, aware (of sth), deliberate; **sich** ~ **sein** to realize, to be aware of.

Bewußtsein *n* awareness, consciousness; ~ **der Rechtswidrigkeit** awareness of illegality; **im vollen** ~ **der Folgen** fully aware of the consequences; **in dem** ~ **der Schuld** conscious of being guilty, having guilty knowledge; **in dem** ~ **der Unschuld** aware (*or* conscious) of one's innocence.

Bewußtseins|grad degree of awareness; ~**lücke** momentary blackout; ~**schwelle** threshold of consciousness; ~**spaltung** schizophrenia, dissociation; ~**störung** mental disturbance, derangement of the senses; ~**stufe** level of awareness; ~**trübung** *f* clouded consciousness, transitory mental disturbance, confusion of the mind.

bezahlen *v/t* to pay, to pay for, to pay off (*debts*), to defray (*expenses*) to settle (*a bill*); **bezahlt werden**: to get paid; **sich bezahlt machen**: to pay (*for itself*), to become profitable; **bar** ~ to pay in cash; **schlecht** ~ to pay badly, to underpay (*employees*); **sofort** ~ to pay cash down, to pay on the nail.

bezahlt *adj* paid, paid-up, settled; ~ **Brief** (*bB*) sellers over; ~ **Geld** (*bG*) buyers over; ~ **und Brief** more sellers than buyers; ~ **und Geld** more buyers than sellers; ~ **und quittiert** discharged and ac-

167

quitted; **nicht** ~ unpaid, outstanding; **voll** ~ paid in full, fully paid up (*shares*).

Bezahlung *f* payment, pay (*employees*), disbursement (*expenses*), settlement (*of debts*); ~ **e-r Schuld** satisfaction of a debt, settlement of a debt; ~ **für den Anmarschweg** dead-heading pay, payment for travel expenses; ~ **gegen offene Rechnung** clean payment; ~ **nach Erfolg** payment by result; ~ **nach Leistung** performance-related pay; ~ **unter Vorbehalt** payment under protest, payment with reservations; ~ **von Rechnungen** settling of accounts; ~ **von Schulden** payment of debts; **bei** ~ on payment; **fristgerechte** ~ due payment, payment within the time limit; **gegen** ~ against payment; **nachträgliche** ~ payment in arrears, subsequent payment; **sofortige** ~ immediate payment, on-the-spot payment; **teilweise** ~ part payment; **vollständige** ~ payment (settlement) in full.

bezeichnen *v/t* to designate, to mark, to indicate, to denote.

bezeichnend *adj* representative, significant, typical.

Bezeichnung *f* designation, description, mark; ~ **der Erfindung** title of the invention, designation of the invention; **geschützte** ~ proprietary designation; **handelsübliche** ~ trade description, customary designation; **kurze** ~ short title (*of an enactment*); **mehrdeutige** ~ ambiguous (*or* equivocal) description; **nähere** ~ **des Klägers** plaintiff's description.

Bezeichnungsweise *f* nomenclature, terminology.

bezeugen *v/t* to testify (to), to give evidence (of sth), to bear testimony, to bear witness (to), to attest (*signature*).

Bezeugung *f* witnessing, attestation → *Bekundung*: → *Beglaubigung*.

bezichtigen *v/t* to accuse (*of having committed a crime*), to impute, to incriminate, to ascribe.

Bezichtigung *f* accusation, imputation, incrimination; ~ **e-s Unrechts** imputation of wrong, accusation of wrong-doing.

beziehbar *adj* obtainable (*goods*), ready for occupancy (= occupation) (*house, flat etc*); **sofort** ~ vacant possession, ready for immediate occupancy (= occupation).

beziehen *v/t* to subscribe, to obtain, to draw, to collect; *v reflex* (*auf*) to refer to.

Bezieher *m* recipient, subscriber.

Beziehung *f* regard, relation, relationship, *pl* connections, relations.

Beziehungen (*pl*): ~ **zwischen den Sozialpartnern** industrial relations, labour-management, relations; **außereheliche** ~ extra-marital relationships (*or* affairs); **auswärtige** ~ foreign relations; **besondere** ~ special relationship; **diplomatische** ~ diplomatic relations; ~~*aufnehmen*: *to establish diplomatic relations*; ~~*abbrechen*: *to sever diplomatic relations, to break off diplomatic relations*; ~~*unterhalten*: *to maintain diplomatic relations*; **ehebrecherische** ~ adulterous relationships; *in ehebrecherischen leben*: *to live in adultery*; **eheliche** ~marital relations, conjugal relations; **ehewidrige** ~ intimacy, illicit relations, extra-marital relations; **freundschaftliche** ~ friendly relations, bonds of friendship; **geschäftliche** ~ business connections; **geschlechtliche** ~ sexual intercourse; **gespannte** ~ strained relations; **gutnachbarliche** ~ good neighbourly relations; **internationale** ~ international relations; **landesverräterische** ~ treasonable relations; **schuldrechtliche** ~ contractual relations, relations based on an obligation; **vermögensrechtliche** ~ relationships arising out of property rights, economic relationship; **verräterische** ~ treasonable relations; **vertragliche** ~ contractual relations; **wirtschaftliche** ~ commercial relations; **zwischenstaatliche**

Beziehungskauf | **Bezüge**

~ international relations, inter-State relations.
Beziehungskauf *m* direct purchase (*from producer or wholesaler*).
beziehungsweise *conj* as the case may be, respectively, and/or.
bezifferbar *adj* quantifiable; **nicht** ~ unliquidated, not quantifiable, unquantifiable.
beziffern *v/t* to state (*or* put) in figures, to amount (to), to number, to mark with numbers, to quantify.
Bezirk *m* district, (*administrative county in former German Democratic Republic*); region → *Regierungsbezirk* (*D*); **befriedete** ~**e** pacified areas; **ländlicher** ~ rural district; **postalischer** ~ postal district.
Bezirks|ausschuß regional committee; ~**direktor** (*ins*) area manager, regional director; ~**filiale** regional head office; ~**finanzdirektion** regional finance department; ~**gebiet** district territory; ~**sgericht** district court, local court (*Austria*); ~**güterfernverkehr** limited long distance haulage; (*150 km radius*); ~**hauptmann** *Austr.* chief officer of a county, district commissioner; ~**haushalt** budget for regional administration (*Bezirk*), regional budget; ~**hoheit** regional autonomy; ~**karte** regional season ticket; ~**lasten** regional expenditure: *public expenditures to be met by the regional administration*; ~**leiter** district manager; ~**notar** district notary (*in Württemberg: public notary with judicial functions for the land title register and for probate matters*); ~**ordnung** regional by-laws, by-laws of a *Bezirk*; ~**planungsstellen** district planning authorities; ~**recht** law applicable to regional administration, regional by-laws; ~**regierung** upper regional authority, district government; ~**revisor** official auditor for a court district; ~**satzung** regional by-laws (*Bezirk*); ~**schornsteinfeger** official (district) chimney-sweep; ~**tag** regional chamber of deputies, regional parliament; ~**tagsmitglieder** deputies of the *Bezirkstag qv*; ~**tagspräsident** president of the *Bezirkstag qv*; ~**umlage** *assessment* (*imposed*) *upon the local authorities by the Bezirkstag qv,* regional charges (levy); ~**verband** district cooperative association; ~**vermögen** property of an administrative district, regional authorities' assets; ~**verordnungen** ordinances issue by a *Bezirk qv*; ~**vertreter** regional representative, distributor; ~**verwaltung** district (*Bezirk*) authorities; ~**wahlen** regional elections (*for a Bezirkstag qv*); ~**wehrersatzamt** district draft board.
Bezogener *m* (*der Bezogene*) drawee.
Bezug *m* (*1*) reference (to a letter), regard, respect; relationship; ~ **haben auf** to have a bearing upon; ~**nahme** reference; ~~ **auf rückseitige Bedingungen:** *for conditions see back*; ~ **nehmen** to refer; *es wird ~ genommen auf: reference is made to*; **in** ~ **auf** with regard to, in relation to, with reference to, referring to; **ohne** ~ without reference (*to any previous letter*); **unter** ~ **auf** with reference to.
Bezug *m* (*2*) buying (*of goods*), supply, subscription (*periodicals, newspaper*), moving in (*dwelling*), occupation; ~ **aus dem Ausland** importing (goods from abroad); ~ **von Leistungen** drawing benefits; ~ **von neuen Aktien** allocation of new shares; **zum** ~ **angeboten** offered for subscription.
Bezüge *m/pl* salary, earnings, emoluments, remuneration, pay; ~ **mit Pensionsberechtigung** pensionable salary; **bedingt pfändbare** ~ benefits subject to qualified garnishment (*pensions and similar recurrent benefits where garnishment may be applied for in exceptional cases*); **einmalige** ~ non-recurring remuneration, once-only payments; **fortlaufende** ~ continuous (regular) remuneration, salary; **pfändbare** ~ wages and salaries subject to execution, garnishable earnings, attach-

bezüglich — **bieten**

able earnings; **pro forma** ~ nominal remuneration; **steuerfreie** ~ tax-free earnings; **unpfändbare** ~ earnings exempt from garnishment.

bezüglich *prep* with regard to, in respect of, concerning.

Bezugs|(1)**basis** basis of comparison; ~**datum** reference date; ~**größe** yard stick, reference figure, reference quantity, standard for (*or* of) comparison; ~**grundlage** base level; ~**jahr** reference year, basis year; ~**menge** datum quantity, amount purchased; ~**patent** related patent; ~**urkunde** reference document; ~**zeichen** reference code/number/signs; ~**zeitraum** reference period.

Bezugs|(2)**aktien** rights-shares, new issue shares, preemptive shares; ~**angebot** subscription offer; ~**anweisung** order to deliver goods; ~**aufforderung** request to take delivery; request to exercise option rights; ~**bedingungen** terms and conditions of sale, sales conditions; ~**berechtigter** allottee (*new shares*); beneficiary (*insurance*); ~**berechtigung** entitlement to (life) insurance benefit; ~**bescheinigung** subscription rights certificate, allotment certificate; ~**beschränkung** rationing, imposing quota restrictions (on buying); ~**erklärung** notice of exercise of option; ~**fähigkeitsbescheinigung** certificate of occupancy; ~**frist** term of subscription, time-limit for subscription; ~**gebiet** supplying area; ~**gebühr** subscription fee; ~**genossenschaft** (agricultural) co-operative purchasing association; ~**größe** reference figure, reference amount; ~**kosten** delivery costs; ~**kurs** subscription price; ~**land** supplying country (*imports*), customer country (*exports*); ~**option** option on new shares; ~**pflicht** obligation to buy (from the licensor); ~**preis** price of delivery, subscription price; ~**quelle** source of supply; ~**quellennachweis** proof of origin; (*Verzeichnis*) directory of suppliers; ~**recht** → *Bezugsrecht*; ~**schein** talon; ration card, subscription rights certificate, certificate of entitlement; ~**tag** day of issue, allotment day; ~**termin** fixed date for delivery, delivery date; ~**verhältnis 5:1** ratio of 1 new for 5 old shares; ~**vertrag** contract of (regular) supply, multiple delivery contract.

Bezugsrecht *n* (1) subscription right, stock right (*US*), pre-emptive right, (*US*); *ohne* ~~: *ex rights; mit* ~~: *cum rights*; ~ **ausgeübt** ex rights; ~**sangebot** rights offer; ~**sausgabe** rights issue; ~**semission** rights issue; ~**shandel** trading in subscription rights, rights trading; ~**sobligation** option bond; ~**surkunde** letter of rights; ~**svereinbarung** option agreement; ~**swert** security carrying subscription rights; **ein** ~ **ausüben** to take up an option, to exercise an option.

Bezugsrecht *n* (2) right to life insurance benefits.

bezuschußbar *adj* subsidizable, eligible for a grant (*or* subsidy).

bezweifeln *v/t* to doubt, to dispute.

BGB *n* → *Bürgerliches Gesetzbuch*; ~**-Gesellschaft** non-trading partnership, civil partnership; ~**-Gesellschafter** members of a non-trading partnership.

Bibliotheksordnung *f* library regulations, library user's rules.

Bier *n* beer, ~**steuer** beer tax; ~**lieferungsvertrag** regular beer supply contract; ~**verlag** brewery depot; ~**verleger** brewery agent, porter merchant; **obergäriges** ~ top fermented beer; **untergäriges** ~ bottom-fermented beer.

Bietabkommen *n* bidding arrangement; **negatives** ~ agreement to abstain from bidding.

Bieten *n* (the) bidding, ~ *zwecks Höhertreiben*: *by-bidding*.

bieten *v/i*, *v/t* to offer (*to buy at a stated price*), to make a bid (*or* bids); *niedrig* ~: *to bid low*.

170

Bieter *m* bidder; **~kaution** bid bond.
Bietungs|garantie *v* bid bond, tender guarantee; **~kaution** tender bond; **~konsortium** bidding syndicate.
Bietvereinbarung *f* knock-out agreement.
Bigamie *f* bigamy.
bigamisch *adj* bigamous.
Bigamist *m* bigamist.
Bilanz *f* balance, balance sheet (= *b.s.*) balance sheets (= *b.s.–s*); **~abschluß** closing entries (for the *b.s.*), drawing the *b.s*; **~abteilung** central accounting department; **~analyse** *b.s.* analysis; **~änderung** change (*or* amendment) to the *b.s.*; **~ansatz** *b.s.* item, value shown; *disclosure of an item in the b.s.;* **~aufbereitung** preparing data for the *b.s.*; **~ausgleich** *b.s.* equilibrium, settlement of the *b.s.* difference; *externer* **~~**: *balance of payments equilibrium*; **~ausgleichsposten** *b.s.* adjustment item; **~auszug** summarized *b.s.*; abstract from the *b.s.*, summary of assets and liabilities; **~bereinigung** adjustment of the *b.s.*; **~bericht** accounting report, explanatory remarks on the *b.s.*; **~berichtigung** rectification of the *b.s.*; **~buchhalter** qualified accountant (*capable of preparing b.s.–s*); **~deckungskapital** *b.s.* capital assets; **~delikte** *b.s.* offences, cooking of *b.s.–s*, juggling of financial statements; **~ der laufenden Leistungen** balance of current transactions; **~ des langfristigen Kapitalverkehrs** balance of long-term capital transactions; **~details** *b.s.* items (*or* details); **~entwurf** draft balance; **~ergebnis** *b.s.* profit or loss, net result; **~fälschung** falisification of the *b.s.*, cooking of the *b.s.*; **~frisur** window-dressing; **~gewinn** *b.s.* profit, unappropriated retained earnings; net earnings shown in the *b.s.*; **~gliederung** *b.s* structure (*or* system); **~identität** *b.s.* identity; **~jahr** financial year; **~kennzahl** *b.s.* ratio; **~kontinuität** *b.s.* continuity, consistency in statement presentation; **~kosmetik** window dressing; **b~mäßig** pertaining to the *b.s.*, shown by the *b.s.*; **~periode** accounting period (*from one b.s. date to the next*); **~position** *b.s.* item; **~posten** *b.s.* item; **~prüfer** auditor of the financial statement; **~prüfung** *b.s.* audit; **~relation** ratio between *b.s.* items; **~revision** *b.s.* audit; **~richtliniengesetz** Account Directives Law (*adapting EC directives*); **~saldo** capital balance, *b.s.* ratio; **~sanierung** restructuring; **~statistik** *b.s.* statistics; **~stichtag** *b.s.* date; **~summe** *b.s.* total; **~überschuß** surplus of assets over liabilities on the *b.s.*; **~urkunde** original *b.s.*; **~verkürzung** *b.s.* contraction; **~verlust** loss (as shown by the *b.s.*), net loss for the year; **~verschleierung** window dressing; *betrügerische* **~~**: *fraudulent statement*; **~volumen** *b.s.* total; **~vorlage** presentation of the *b.s.*; **~wahrheit** correct (*or* accurate) and true presentation of *b.s.* items; **~wert** *b.s.* value; book value, carrying value; **~ ziehen** to strike a balance; **~zusammenhang** *b.s.* continuity; **aktive ~** *b.s.* showing a profit; **außenwirtschaftliche ~** the balance of payments; **die ~ aufstellen** to draw up the *b.s.*, to prepare the *b.s.*; **die ~ der gesamten Wirtschaftstätigkeit** net result of the overall economic activity; **die ~ frisieren** to cook (*or* doctor) the *b.s.*, to window-dress; **die ~ verschleiern** to cook the *b.s.*; **die ~ vorlegen** to submit the *b.s.*; **fiktive ~** fictitious balance (*or b.s.*); **geprüfte ~** audited balance; **konjunkturpolitische ~** assessment of cyclical trends, appraisal of economic policy; **konsolidierte ~** consolidated *b.s.*; **passive ~** *b.s.* showing a loss; **rohe ~** rough balance, trial balance; **steuerliche ~** *b.s.* for tax purposes; **verschleierte**

bilanzieren / **Billigung**

~ veiled *b.s.*; **versicherungstechnische** ~ actuarial statement, actuarial valuation *b.s.*; **vorläufige** ~ trial balance.

bilanzieren to prepare the balance sheet, to balance the accounts, to strike a balance, to make out a balance sheet, to show in the balance sheet.

Bilanzierung *f* striking the balance, preparing the balance sheet; **~sgrundsätze** accounting principles; **~speriode** period covered by the balance sheet; **~srichtlinien** directives (*or* regulations) for the preparation of balance sheets; **~sschema** method of making up a financial statement, balance sheet system; **~stag** balance sheet date, date of closing entries; **~stricks** accounting gimmickry; **~svorschriften** accounting rules, regulating for the preparation of balance sheets; **inflationsbereinigte** ~ inflation accounting.

Bild|archiv picture library, photographic archives; **~dokumentation** pictorial (*or* photographic) documentation; **~funk** telephoto; **~gegendarstellung** correction by publishing the correct picture; **~geschichte** comic strip; **~plakat** pictorial poster; **~schirmterminal** video display unit; **~schirmtext** videotext, picture-screen text; viewdata (*GB*); **~schirmzeitung** vid news; **~träger** picture carrier, film visual recording; **~werbung** pictorial advertising; **~zeichen** pictorial trade-mark, device trademark, logo.

Bildnisschutz *m* (copyright) protection of one's own image.

Bildungs|abschluß educational qualification, educational attainment; **~bereitschaft** readiness to be educated; **~chancen** educational opportunities; **~einrichtung** educational establishment; **~notstand** educational emergency, educationally backward state of affairs; **~~gebiet**: *educational wasteland, educational wilderness, educational priority area*; **~planning** educational planning; **~politik** educational policy; **~urlaub** educational leave; *bezahlter ~~*: *paid educational leave;* **~vorschriften** educational requirements, educational rules; **~weg** educational career; school background; **~wesen** education system, educational matters, education.

billigen *v/t* to approve, to sanction; **stillschweigend** ~ to acquiesce in, to approve tacitly.

billigerweise *adj* equitably, in all fairness, justly.

Billigflagge *f* flag of convenience (*FOC*); **~nländer** flag of convenience states.

Billigkeit *f* (1) cheapness, inexpensiveness.

Billigkeit *f* (2) equitableness, equity, fairness; **aus Gründen der** ~ for reasons of equity; **nach** ~according to equity, as seems fair and reasonable.

Billigkeits|abwägung balancing the equities; **~anspruch** equitable claim; **~entscheidung** equitable decision, decision ex aequo et bono; **~erlaß** equitable decree, equitable tax relief; **~erwägung** equitable consideration(s); **~haftung** liability on the grounds of equitable principles; **~maßnahmen** measures taken on equitable principles; **~recht** equity, equitable law (*nach ~~*: *in equity*); **b~rechtlich** equitable; in equity; **~verfahren** equity procedure; **~verpflichtung** equitable obligation.

Billigläden *m/pl* off-price stores.

billigst *adv* cheapest, at lowest possible price.

Billigst-Order *f* order to buy at the lowest possible price.

Billigtarif cut-price fare, cheap rate.

Billigung *f* approval, sanction; ~ **e-s Geschäfts** adoption of a transaction (*e.g. a purchase*), approval of a business (transaction); **~sfrist** time limit for granting approval; ~ **von Straftaten** approving criminal acts; **gerichtliche** ~ sanction of court; **stillschweigende** ~ acquiescence, tacit approval.

Billigwarengeschäft *n* cut-price store, penny store.

Bimetallismus *m* bi-metallism, double standard currency.

binden *v/t* to bind, to commit, to tie; *v/reflex* to stand committed, to engage oneself, to commit o. s.

bindend *adj* binding, firm (*offer*).

Bindung *f* tie, binding arrangement, commitment, linking, tying-up; ~**sentgelt** earnest (*in contracting*); ~**sermächtigung** commitment authorization; ~**sfrist** commitment period, fixed investment period, fixed-rate period (*interest*); ~**wille** willingness to enter into a commitment; ~**swirkung** commitment (1) binding effect; ~ **von Geldmitteln** earmarking of funds; **vertragliche** ~ contractual commitment; **zwangswirtschaftliche** ~ public control.

Binnen|beziehung internal relationship (= *Innenverhältnis qv.*); ~**fischerei** freshwater fishery; ~**flotte** inland waterways fleet; ~**gewässer** inland waters; ~**hafen** inland port, inland-waterway harbo(u)r; ~**handel** domestic trade (*or* commerce), internal trade, home trade; ~**kartell** domestic cartel; ~**konjunktur** internal economic trends; ~**land** inland, interior of a country; ~**luftverkehr** domestic flights; ~**markt** domestic market; home market; ~~ *der Gemeinschaft*: internal Community market: *europäischer* ~~: *Internal Market, single (unit) market*; **b**~**markt orientiert** based on home market requirements; ~**meer** land-locked sea; ~**nachfrage** internal demand, domestic demand; ~**schifffahrt** → *Binnenschiffahrt*; ~**schiffe** ships on inland waterways; ~**schiffer** inland waterways navigators, (*or* irland waterways operators); ~**schifffahrtverkehr** inland waterways transport; ~**staat** land-locked state (*or* country); ~**tarif** inland rate, home tariff; ~**transportversicherung** inland marine insurance; ~**verkehr** inland transport; ~**verkehrsschadensversicherung** inland transportation policy; ~**versand** interior transit; ~**währung** home currency, internal currency; ~**wanderung** internal migration; ~**wasserstraßen** inland waterways; ~**wert** internal value; ~**wirtschaft** internal economy; **b**~**wirtschaftlich** *adj* relating to the domestic economy; concerning internal trade, pertaining to internal economic matters; ~**zoll** internal tariff, internal duty; ~**zollsatz** internal rate of duty; ~**zollstelle** inland customs office.

Binnenschiffahrt *f* inland navigation, inland waterway transportation; ~**sgesetz** Inland Waterways (civil liabilities) Act; ~**srecht** the law governing inland navigation; ~**ssachen** inland navigation matters (*or* cases); ~**straßen-Ordnung** inland waterway transportation rules; ~**versicherung** inland waterways insurance.

Biotopschutz *m* protection of biological sites.

bis | auf weiteres pending further notice, until further notice; ~ **vor kurzem** until recently, up to the present time; ~ **zum ...** (*ausschließlich*) before the (*date*); ~ **zum ...** up to and including (the date); (*einschließlich*) on or before the (*date*).

Bitte *f* request, petition; **letztwillige** ~ precatory words, dying request.

bitten *v/t* to beg, to entreat, to solicit, to ask, to invite.

Bittschrift *f* petition.

Bittsteller *m* petitioner, solicitant, supplicant.

Blankett *n* blank (*form*), specimen (*share certificate*); ~**fälschung** forgery by misusing a blank form; ~**gesetz** blanket law; ~**mißbrauch** fraudulent use of documents signed in blank; ~**norm** blanket provision of the law; ~**police** blank policy; ~**strafge**-

blanko

setz outline penal law *subject to implementing ordinance,* ~**vorschrift** blanket provision, blanket enactment.
blanko *adv* in blank; ~ **übertragen** to assign in blank; ~ **verkaufen** to sell short; **in** ~ **ausstellen** to make out in blank.
Blanko|abtretung assignment in blank; ~**adoption** unqualified adoption release; ~**akzept** acceptance in blank, blank acceptance; ~**formular** blank form, skeleton letter; ~**geschäft** uncovered transaction, selling short; ~**giro** blank endorsement; ~**indossament** blank endorsement, general endorsement, endorsement in blank; *mit ~~ versehen: endorsed in blank*; ~**kredit** open credit, unsecured loan (*or* credit); ~**offerte** offer in blank; ~**police** blank policy; ~**quittung** blank receipt; ~**scheck** blank cheque; ~**übertragungsallonge** fly-power; ~**unterschrift** signature on a blank, blank signature; ~**verkauf** *exch* short sale, bearish sale; ~**verkäufer** uncovered bear; ~**vollmacht** proxy in blank, carte blanche, unlimited power, dormant warrant; ~**wechsel** blank draft; ~**zession** assignment in blank; **ungedeckter** ~**vorschuß** uncovered advance.
Blatt *n* sheet (of paper), folio (*manuscript; register*).
Blaues Kreuz *n* temperance union.
Blaulicht *n* flashing light (*police car*).
bleifrei *adj* unleaded.
Blendung *f* blinding (*by headlight of oncoming car*), dazzling.
blenden *v/t* to blind, to dazzle.
Blick *m* look, glance; ~**fangwerbung** advertizing through attention-getters; ~**feld** range of vision, field of vision, purview; ~**richtung** line of vision (*or* sight); **auf den ersten** ~ at first sight, prima facie.
Blinden|anstalt institution for the blind; ~**arbeit** blindcraft; ~**führhund** guide dog, ~**fürsorge** public care of the blind; ~**geld** public assistance allowance for the blind; ~**heim** home for the blind; ~**hilfe** public financial help for the blind; ~**hund** = ~*führhund, qv;* ~**pflegegeld** public maintenance contributions for the blind; ~**schrift** braille; ~**waren** products made by the blind; ~**warenvertriebsausweis** identity card authorizing sale of goods produced by blind persons; ~**zulagen** additional benefits for the blind.
Blindsekunde *f* sudden blinding, time to react to dazzle from oncoming traffic.
Blink|bake *mar* flashing beacon; ~**feuer** flashing light; ~**leuchte** indicator light; ~**licht** flashing red warning light; ~~ *bei Bahnübergängen: level crossing signal.*
Blinker *m* winker, (direction) indicator (light).
Blitzschlag *m* lightning; ~**versicherung** lightning insurance.
Blitzschutzanlage *f* lightning-arrester equipment.
Blockade *f* blockade; ~**brecher** blockade-runner; ~**politik** embargo policy, blockade policy.
Blockbuchstaben *m/pl* block letters.
blockfrei *adj pol* uncommitted, non-committed, non-aligned.
Blockfreiheit *f* non-alignment.
blockieren *v/t* to block, to stymie.
Blockierpatent *n* blocking-off patent.
Blockierung *f* blockage, obstruction (*traffic*), *pol* deadlock, stalemate, freezing (*accounts etc*), momentary blackout (*mentally*).
Blockpolice *f ins* block policy.
Blockpolitik *f* bloc-alignment policy.
Blockschrift *f* block letters, capital letters; *in ~~schreiben: to print, to write in block letters, to write in capital letters (caps).*
Blockwahl *f* uniform ticket election (of candidates), election en-bloc.
Blut|alkoholgehalt percentage of alcohol in the blood, blood-alcohol level; ~**alkoholgutachten** medical opinion on blood-alcohol level;

Bluter

~**alkoholmeßgerät** intoximeter, breathalyzer; ~**bad** massacre, slaughter; ~**entnahme** taking of a blood sample, extraction (*or* taking) of blood; ~**fehde** (= *Blutsfehde*) blood feud, vendetta; ~**gruppe** blood group; ~**gruppenbestimmung** blood typing; ~**gruppengutachten** paternity test based on blood groups; ~**gruppenuntersuchung** blood group test; ~**lust** blood lust; ~**probe** blood test, blood sample; ~**rache** blood-vengeance, blood revenge; ~**risikenuntersuchung** blood screening; ~**schande** incest; ~**schänder** incestuous person; b~**schänderisch** incestuous; ~**spender** blood-donor; ~**tat** bloody deed, act of murder; ~**schuld** blood guilt, hereditary taint of murder; b~**sverwandt** related by blood, of the same blood, consanguineous, akin; ~**sverwandte** blood relatives; *die nächsten* ~~*n: the next of kin in blood;* ~**verwandtschaft** blood relationship, consanguinity, kin; ~~ *in gerader Linie: lineal consanguinity; durch* ~~ *verbundene Personen: persons related by blood, privies of blood.*

Bluter *m* haemophiliac (*US:* hemo..).

Boden *m* soil, land; ~**altertümer** archeological finds; ~**bearbeitung** cultivation of the soil; ~**beschaffungsplan** land-acquisition program(me); ~**bewirtschaftung** cultivation of land, utilization of the soil, (arable) farming; ~**denkmal** ancient monument found in the ground; ~**entwässerung** land drainage; ~**erosion** soil erosion; ~**erschließung** soil development; ~**ertrag** profits from the soil, crop yield, gainage; ~**erzeugnis** produce of the soil; ~**fläche** floor space (*inside a building*), ground area (*outside*); ~**fruchtbarkeit** fertility of the soil; ~**früchte** produce of the soil, fruits of the land, natural fruits, *hist* esplees; ~**kredit** mortgage credit, credit secured by land;

Bodmerei

~**kreditanstalt** land credit company, land bank, land (mortgage) bank, real estate credit institution; *landwirtschaftliche* ~~: *agricultural mortgage corporation*; ~**kreditbank** land mortgage bank; ~**krieg** ground war; ~**melioration** = *Bodenverbesserung qv*; ~**nutzung** use of the soil, enjoyment of land; ~**ordnung** regulations concerning agricultural land; ~**parzelle** parcel of land, plot (of land), lot; ~**potential** soil resources; ~**preis** land price; ~**prinzip** jus soli; ~**probe** soil specimen; ~**produkte** products of the soil; ~**recht** land law, law of landed property; ~**reform** land reform, agrarian reform; ~**reformgesetze** land reform laws; ~**rente** ground rent, rack rent; ~**schätze** natural resources, mineral resources; ~~*e-s Landes: national resources; energiehaltige* ~~: *primary fuels*; ~**schätzung** appraisal of (farm) land; ~**spekulation** speculation in landed property, real estate speculation (*or* venture); ~**verband** land development association; ~**verbesserung** land improvement, amelioration; ~**verkehr** land transactions (*especially: agricultural*); ~~ *mit Grundbuch: registered conveyancing matters;* ~~ *ohne Grundbuch: private conveyancing matters;* ~**verkehrsgenehmigung** permission to transfer (agricultural) land; ~**verkehrsrecht** law of development and land transfer; ~**verseuchung** soil contamination; ~**verteilung** (equitable) distribution of the land; ~**wert** land value, site value; **marginaler** ~ marginal land; **ungenutzter** ~ unused land, uncultivated land, *US* unseated land.

Bodmerei *f* bottomry; ~ **auf die Schiffsladung** repondentia (loan); ~**briefe** bottomry bond, maritime loan, bill of gross adventure, sea bill; ~**darlehen** bottomry loan, gross adventure; ~**gelder** bottomry money; ~**gewinn** profit from bottomry; ~**prämie** bottomry in-

175

Bogenerneuerung — **Börsenauftrag**

terest; ~**schein** bottomry bond, hypothecation bond; ~**versicherung** bottomry insurance; ~**vertrag** letter of bottomry; ~**zinsen** bottomry interest, marine interest.

Bogenerneuerung *f* renewal of coupon sheets.

Bohr|anlage drilling rig; ~**anteil** share (quota) of production (of a well); ~**loch** drill hole, well (*oil and gas*); ~**trupp** drilling team; ~**turm** (drilling) derrick; ~**versuch** trial drilling.

Bohrung *f* drilling; ~ **fündig** productive drilling.

Bombenteppichwurf *m* carpet bombing.

Bon *m* chit, slip, ticket, cash register receipt.

bona fide *adv* bona fide, in good faith.

Bonifikation *f* the granting of a bonus (*or* premium), allowance, rebate, the crediting of a commission; ~**srückvergütung** repayment of a bonus (*or* premium), subtaker's commission repayment.

bonifizieren *v/t* to grant a bonus (*or* premium), to make an allowance (*or* rebate), to give a commission.

Bonität *f* soundness, credit solvency, financial standing, financial reliability, credit standing, credit-worthiness; quality of the soil; ~**sanforderungen** credit standards; ~**seinstufung** credit rating; ~**sprüfung** rating (of credit-worthiness).

Boniteur *m* valuer, assessor, appraiser (*of land*).

bonitieren *v/t* to classify (*land*), to assess (*soil quality*), to appraise (*value*), to evaluate.

Bonitierung *f* classification of land, appraisal of soil quality.

Bonus *m* bonus, premium; extra dividend, special dividend; ~**ausgabe** scrip; ~**lohn** bonus scheme.

Bonzentum *n pol* corrupt rule, boss rule.

Bord|arrest arrest on board ship; ~**konossement** on board bill of lading (= *on board B/L*), shipped bill of lading, ship's bill; ~**papiere** ship's papers; plane's papers; ~**überladung** ship-to-ship transshipment; ~**vertretung** staff committee on board a ship; ~**vorräte** ship's stores, aircraft stores; **über** ~ **werfen** to jettison, to throw overboard.

Bordell *n* brothel, bawdy house, lewd house, whorehouse; ~**bezirk** red-light district.

Börse *f* stock exchange, stockmarket, the Exchange; **an der** ~ **gehandelt** obtainable on the market, quoted on (at) the stock exchange; **an der** ~ **spekulieren** to play the (stock) market; **an der** ~ **zur amtlichen Notierung zulassen** to list on the stock exchange; **der** ~ **Auftrieb geben** to give a fillip to the market; **empfindlich reagierende** ~ sensitive market; **fast umsatzlose** ~ flat (inactive) market; **federführende** ~ the leading stock exchange (*for a security issue*); **freundliche** ~ cheerful market; **lebhafte** ~ brisk market; **lustlose** ~ dull market, listless trading; **überregionale** ~ national securities exchange.

Börsen|abkürzungen ticker abbreviations; ~**abrechnung** stock exchange settlement, securities trading settlement; ~**abschluß** (stock exchange) transaction; ~**abschlußeinheit** regular lot, full lot; ~**agent** stock exchange agent (*or* representative) *of a bank*; **b**~**amtlich** *adj* under the rules (*securities trading*), pursuant to stock exchange regulations; ~**angebot** tender-offer; ~**aufsichtsamt** supervisory authority for stock markets, *US*: Securities and Exchange Commission; ~**aufsichtsbehörde** supervisory authority for stock markets and exchanges, *US*: Securities and Exchange Commission *sl* stockmarket watchdog agency; ~**auftrag** stock exchange *or* market order; *für einen Monat gültiger* ~~: *month order*; *unlimitierter* ~~: *market order*; *nur für e-n Tag gültiger* ~~:

Börsenauftragnehmer **Börsenschluß**

day order; ~**auftragnehmer** account executive; ~**ausschuß** stock exchange committee; ~**beobachter** market watcher(s); ~**bericht** exchange report, market report, stock exchange account; ~**besucher** person authorized to enter the stock exchange; ~**blatt** financial paper, stock exchange gazette, financial newspaper; *D (=) German book-trade gazette;* ~**brauch** stock exchange usage, market terms; ~**effekten** securities traded on the stock exchange; ~**einführung** admission to stock exchange dealing, admission to official quotation, introduction to the stock exchange; ~**einführungsgebühr** stock exchange admission fee; ~**einführungsprovision** stock exchange introduction commission; ~**engagement** stock exchange commitment; ~**eröffnung** the opening of the stock exchange; ~**fachmann** trading specialist; b~**fähig** admissible for trading, marketable (*or* negotiable) on the stock exchange; ~**fähigkeit** qualification for trading (on a stock exchange); ~**fernschreiber** stock ticker; ~**flaute** dullness of the market; b~**gängig** listed on the stock exchange, marketable (*securities*); ~**gepflogenheiten** stock exchange practices; ~**geschäft** stock exchange transaction, transaction on the exchange, dealing; *abgeschlossenes* ~~: *round transaction, gekoppelte* ~~*e*: *matched sales;* ~**geschehen** activities on the stock exchange, stock exchange business; ~**gesetz** German Stock Exchange Act (*of 1896 as amended 1975*); b~**ngültig** valid for one day; ~**halle** Stock Exchange floor, trading floor; ~**handel** stock exchange trading; ~**händler** stock-jobber, deal maker, dealer; *US:* floor trader; ~**index** stock exchange index; ~**klima** atmosphere (*or* tone) of the stock exchange; trading climate; ~**kommissionsfirma** commission brokers; ~**kommissionsgeschäft** stock-broking transaction; ~**konjunktur** stock exchange trends; ~**konsortium** stock exchange syndicate, (stock market) pool; ~**krach** collapse of the market, crash; ~**kredit** (bank)-lendings for financing stock exchange business; ~**krise** market crisis; ~**kurs** stock exchange price, market rate (*or* price), (stock exchange) quotation; ~**kursregistriergerät** stockmaster; ~**kurswiedergabegerät** desk-top terminal; ~**makler** stock-broker, (stock) exchange broker, floor broker, dealer, stock jobber, broker-member of the stock exchange; ~**maklerfirma** firm of stock brokers; ~**maklergeschäft** stock-broking; ~**maklerstand** pitch; ~**manöver** market jobbery, market-rigging; ~**markt** stock market; b~**mäßig** in accordance with stock exchange rules; b~**mäßig handelbar** negotiable on the stock exchange; ~**mitglied** member of a stock exchange; ~**nachrichten** financial (market) news; b~**notiert** quoted (on the stock exchange); ~**notierung** quotation; ~**notiz** quotation; *amtliche* ~~: *official quotation, letzte* ~~: *last price;* ~~ **oder Marktpreis** current market price; ~**ordnung** stock exchange regulations (*or* rules); ~**organe** stock exchange authorities; ~**papiere** listed securities; ~**parkett** floor; ~**pflichtblatt** official bourse gazette; ~**platz** exchange centre, stock exchange (city); ~**preis** exchange price, market price, exchange quotation; ~**premiere** stockmarket launch; stockmarket première; ~**prospekt** prospectus; ~**recht** law of the stock exchange, law governing stock exchange transactions; ~**saal** trading floor, dealing room; ~**scheinverkauf** fictitious sale of a security, wash sale; ~**schiedsgericht** stock exchange arbitration tribunal; ~**schluß** (*1*) closing of the exchange, final hour of trading, close

Börsenschwindel

of business of the stock exchange; *nach ~~:* after official hours; (2) trading unit; *gebrochener ~~:* odd lot (*less than 100 shares or 1000 bonds*); *voller ~~:* even lot, full lot; ~**schwindel** stock exchange swindle; ~**schwindler** stock exchange swindler; ~**sitz** (exchange) seat; ~**sitzung** trading session; ~**spekulant** stock exchange speculator (*or* gambler), stag, punter; ~**spekulation** stock exchange speculation, a stock-exchange flutter; ~**spiel** exchange gambling, a hazardous transaction; ~**spieler** manipulator, stock exchange gambler, speculator; ~**sprache** stock exchange parlance; ~**stand** pitch, trading post; ~**stempel** stamp for stock exchange dealings (*stamp duty*); ~**steuer** = ~*umsatzsteuer qv*; ~**stimmung** tone of the market, atmosphere; ~**stunden** stock exchange hours, official hours; ~**tag** market-day, trading session, official day of business on the stock exchange; b~**täglich** *adj* per (every) stock-exchange business day; b~**technisch bedingt** due to technical lities of the stock exchange; ~**tendenz** (stock) market trend; ~**terminauftrag auf Wochenfrist** week order; ~**termingeschäft** trading in futures, forward transaction, futures deal; ~**ticker** tape, ticker; ~**tickerabkürzungen** tape abbreviations; ~**tickernotierung** tape quotation, ticker quotation; ~**tipgeber** tipster; ~**transaktionen** stock exchange transactions, bargains; ~**turbulenzen** market turmoil; ~**umsatzsteuer** stock exchange turnover tax; ~**usancen** exchange usages, market terms; ~**verfahren** stock exchange procedure; ~**verkehr** stock exchange dealings; ~**versionen** stock exchange rumours; ~**vertreter** representative (of a bank) at the stock exchange; ~**vorschriften** stock exchange rules; ~**vorstand** stock exchange committee, board of gover-

Botschafter

nors of the stock exchange; (*London:*) The Council of the Stock Exchange; (*New York:*) Governing Committee of the New York Stock Exchange; ~**werte** securities quoted on the stock exchange, quoted securities; *führende ~~: market leaders;* ~**wesen** stock exchange matters, stock exchange market, bourse system; ~**zeit** official hours (*or* trading hours) (of a stock exchange); ~**zeitung** stock exchange journal, financial newspaper; ~**zettel** official price list, stock list, list of quotations, market report, (*London:*) Stock Exchange Daily Official List; ~**zulassung** admission of securities to the stock exchange, stock exchange introduction; ~**zulassungsprospekt** prospectus; ~**zulassungsverfahren** listing procedure; ~**zwang** stock exchange monopoly, *legal requirement of trading all listed securities exclusively on official stock exchange;* **bei ~beginn** when trading starts, when the market opens; **bei ~schluß höher notieren** to close at a higher price (or up ... points); **gestützte ~kurse** pegged market; **nicht genehmigter ~einführungsprospekt** red herring prospectus; **nur sofort ausführbarer ~auftrag** immediate (*or* cancel) order; **selbständiges ~mitglied** floor trader; **zum ~handel zulassen** to list on the exchange.

Börsianer *m* stock-exchange operator, market operator.

bösartig *adj* malicious, vicious.

bösgläubig *adv* in bad faith, mala fide.

Bösgläubigkeit *f* bad faith, mala fides.

böslich *adv* in bad faith, maliciously.

böswillig *adj* malicious, wanton.

Böswilligkeit *f* malevolence, malice.

Bote *m* messenger; *durch Boten:* by hand.

Botenlohn *m* messenger's fee, delivery fee.

Botschaft *f* embassy.

Botschafter *m* ambassador; ~ **zur**

besonderen Verwendung Special Representative, Ambassador at Large; ~**ebene** ambassadorial level; ~**konferenz** ambassadorial conference; ~**lenkungsausschuß** ambassadorial group; ~**posten** ambassadorship; **außerordentlicher und bevollmächtigter** ~ ambassador plenipotentiary.

Botschafts|gebäude embassy; ~**personal** embassy staff; ~**rat** embassy councillor.

Boykott *m* boycott; ~**streik** boycott-strike; *mittelbarer* ~~: *secondary boycott-strike*.

boykottieren *v/t* to boycott, to black.

Brachialgewalt *f* brute force.

Brachland *n* fallow land, a site in its natural state; ~**programm** land set-aside scheme.

brachlegen *v/t* to lay fallow.

brachliegen *v* to lie fallow (*fields*), to lie idle (*equipment*); to go to waste.

Brachliegenlassen *n* non-cultivation.

Brachzeit *f* machine down time; fallowing season.

Branche *f* branch of business, line of business, trade; **lagerintensive** ~ type of business requiring large stocks; **zukunftsträchtige** ~ promising line of business, growth industry.

Branchen|adreßbuch trade directory; **b~bedingt** due to the conditions in a particular line of business; ~**gewerkschaft** craft union; **b~mäßig** applicable to a certain line (*or* certain lines) of business; ~**konjunktur** economic trends in a certain branch; ~**risiko** industrial risk; **b~üblich** customary in this branch of business; ~**untersuchung** study of particular business lines, study of a given industry; ~**verzeichnis** classified directory; ~**zyklen** business cycles peculiar to certain lines of business.

Brand *f* fire, conflagration; fuel (*coal for domestic use*); ~**bombe** *f* fire bomb; ~**brief** letter asking urgently for money, dunning letter; ~**diebstahl** theft committed during a fire; ~**feststellung** inquest on the cause of a fire; ~**gefahr** fire risk (= *risk of fire*), fire hazard(s); ~**gefährdung** exposing to the risk of fire; ~**geruch** smell of burning; ~**kasse** fire insurance; ~**mauer** fire wall, partition-wall; ~**meldung** reporting of fire; ~**schaden** fire damage; ~**schadensprüfer** fire-loss assessor; ~**schutz** fire prevention and protection; ~**stifter** incendiary, arsonist, fire raiser; *pyromanischer* ~~: *fire bug*; ~**stiftung** *f* arson, incendiarism, intentional fire, setting fire, house-burning, fire-raising; *einfache* ~~: *simple arson*, *schwere* ~~: *aggravated arson*, *fahrlässige* ~~: *causing fire by negligence*; ~**ursache** cause of (a) fire; ~**verhütung** fire prevention, fire loss prevention; ~**versicherung** fire insurance, fire policy; ~**versicherungsgesellschaft** fire (insurance) company; ~**wache** fire guard, fire-watch; ~**wand** fire-resisting wall; **zu e–m** ~ **anstiften** to incite to commit arson.

Branntwein *m* distilled spirits, liquor; ~**ausschank** liquor sale on licensed premises; ~**brenner** distiller; ~**brennerei** distillery; ~**monopol** monopoly of distilled spirits; ~**steuer** tax on distilled spirits.

Brauanzeige *f* brewing declaration.

Brauch *m* usage, custom; **allgemeiner** ~ general (*or* common) usage; **althergebrachter** ~ standing custom, established usage; **ständiger** ~ established usage, established custom; **stehender** ~ established custom, established use; **uralter** ~ ancient custom.

brauchbar *adj* useful, usable, serviceable, reliable.

Brauchbarkeit *f* usefulness, usability, serviceability; ~**sdauer** useful life; **praktische** ~ practicability, feasibility.

Brauchwasser *n* industrial water, water for non-human consumption.

Brauerei *f* brewery; ~**aktien** brewery stock (*or* shaves); ~**genossenschaft** brewers' cooperative; ~**gewerbe** brewing industry.

Brau|gerechtigkeit *f* brewing privilege; ~**meister** *m* brewmaster, (master) brewer.

Braunkohlenbergbau *m* soft coal mining, lignite mining.

Braut *f* betrothed, bride-to-be, fiancée; bride (*on day of marriage*); ~**ausstattung** trousseau; ~**aussteuerversicherung** wedding-outfit insurance; ~**geschenke** engagement presents: *presents given to (or exchanged by) the betrothed*; ~**kind** child born by a girl engaged to be married, premarital child.

Bräutigam *m* fiancé (*formally engaged*), bridegroom (*on wedding day*).

Breitbandkabel *n* wide band cable.

Brems|anlagen braking devices, brakes; ~**licht** brake light, stop light; ~**sicherheit** brake efficiency; ~**spur** brake marks, skid marks; ~**strecke** = ~**weg** *qv*; ~**system** braking system; *zwei voneinander unabhängige* ~~*e*: *two independent brakes*; ~**weg** braking distance, (overall) stopping distance.

Brenn|holzrecht right to cut fire wood; ~**material** (solid) fuel; ~**recht** distilling licence; ~**spiritussteuer** denatured alcohol tax.

Brennerei *f* distillery, still.

Brett *n* board, plank (*more than 2 inches thick*); **schwarzes** ~ bulletin board.

brevi manu traditio = *traditio brevi manu qv*.

Brief *m* letter, certificate; asked price, offer quotation; *the rate at which securities are offered, without transactions;* ~**adel** titled nobility conferred by letters patent; ~**entwurf** draft letter; ~**fach** post-office box; ~ **gegen Empfangsbescheinigung** letter sent against certificate of delivery; ~**geheimnis** secrecy of mails, privacy of correspondence, inviolability of letters; *das* ~~ *verletzen*: *to violate the secrecy of correspondence, to tamper with mail*; ~**grundschuld** certificated (German) land charge (*land charge = Grundschuld entered in the land title register for which an official transferable document has been issued*); ~**hypothek** certificated mortgage (*cf note at* ~**grundschuld**); ~**kastenfirma** letter-box company, letter drop; ~**kastenwerbung** distribution of advertising material through the letter-box; junk mail (advertising); ~**kontrolle** official checking of mail, (prison) censorship of correspondence; ~**kurs** selling rate (*at which bank sells foreign currency to customer*); asked price, offering price; ~**kursnotiz** offer quotation; ~**laufzeit** regular time for mail service, time needed (*or* taken) for postal delivery; ~**marke** (postage) stamp, postal stamp; ~**markenfälschung** forgery of postal stamps; stamp forgery; ~**markenhandel** trading in stamps; ~**notiz** offer quotation (*cf* ~*kurs*); ~**post** letter post, *US* first-class mail (*includes postal cards*); ~**post mit Zustellungsnachweis** certified mail; ~**sendung** consignment by letter post; ~**sperre** stoppage of mail; ~**tasche** wallet, billfold; **b**~**telegrafisch** by letter-telegram; ~**telegramm** lettergram, letter telegram, day letter, telegram delivered by mail; ~**träger** postman, *US* mailman, mail carrier; ~**übergabe** delivery of a letter (*or* of a certificate); ~ **und Geld** *exch* asked and bid, sellers and buyers; ~**unterschlagung** diversion of letters from addressee, theft of a letter; ~**verkehr** correspondence, exchange of letters; ~**vorlage** specimen letter; presentation of the mortgage certificate (*for foreclosure*); ~**wahl** postal voting, absentee voting, vote by correspondence, mail ballot; ~**wahlscheine** mailed-in ballot; ~**wähler** absentee-voter, outvoter; ~**wechsel** correspondence, exchange of letters; ~**zensur** censorship of the mail, postal

Bringschuld   **Bruttoinvestitionsquote**

censorship; ~**zustellung** delivery of letters, mail delivery; **auslaufender** ~ outgoing letter; **der vorliegende** ~ the letter in hand; **eingeschriebener** ~ registered letter; *durch* ~*n* ~: *by registered post*; **frankierter** ~ prepaid letter; **gehandelt und** ~ sellers ahead; **in den** ~**kasten werfen** to post; **mehr** ~ *exch* sellers over; **nicht abgeholter** ~ unclaimed letter; **offener** ~ open letter, published letter; **postlagernder** ~ letter to be called for, poste restante; **unfrankierter** ~ unpaid letter; **unzustellbarer** ~undeliverable letter, returned letter; **vervielfältigter** ~ process letter, multigraphed letter, duplicated letter.

Bringschuld *f* obligation which debtor has to perform at creditor's address.

Brite *m* Briton; **gebürtiger** ~ British born person, British by birth, s. o. with British nationality by birth.

Broschüre *f* booklet, pamphlet, brochure, folder.

Bruch infringement, violation (*agreement, legal provision*), breach, rupture, breakage; ~ **der Amtsverschwiegenheit** breach of official secrecy; ~**probe** breaking test; ~**risiko** risk of breakage; ~**schaden** damage by breakage; ~**schadenversicherung** insurance against breakage; ~**teil** → *Bruchteil*; ~**zins** interest for a broken period, broken interest; **frei von** ~ free from breakage (*as a clause*), free of breakage (*as a fact*).

Bruchteil *m* fraction, fractional part; ~ **einer Erbschaft** fractional part of an inheritance.

Bruchteils|aktie fractional share; ~**anteil** fractional share; ~**eigentum** ownership by undivided (fractional) shares, fractional co-ownership, tenancy in common, fractional share of property; ~**eigentümer** part owner, *sing*: owner of a fractional part of property; *pl*: co-owners by undivided shares, tenants in common; ~**gemeinschaft** community of part-owners; tenancy in common; ~**gratisaktien-Zertifikat** scrip certificate.

Brücke *f* bridge; ~**nzoll** bridge toll, pontage; **mautpflichtige** ~ toll bridge.

Bruder *m* brother; ~**mord** fratricide; ~**schaft** brotherhood, fraternity, guild; ~**volk** sister nation; **leiblicher** ~ full brother, one's own brother, brother-german.

Brunnenvergiftung *f* (wilful) poisoning of wells; *fig* vicious (political) calumny.

brutto *adj, adv* gross.

Brutto|arbeitseinkommen earned income before deductions (*taxes and social insurance contributions*); ~**bestand** gross total, total holdings, total stock before any deductions; ~**betrag** gross amount, amount including VAT; ~**bilanz** rough balance, trial balance; ~**-Bodenproduktion** gross production of the soil; ~**buchwert** book value before any adjustments; ~**dividende** gross dividend; ~**einkommen** gross income; ~**einkünfte** total gross income (*from all taxable sources*); ~**einkünfte vor Abschreibung** total gross income before depreciation; ~**einnahmen** gross receipts, gross takings, gross earnings, gross returns; ~**entlohnung** total remuneration before any deductions; ~**erlös** gross profit on sales; ~**ersparnis** gross savings; ~**ertrag** gross proceeds (*from sale*), gross yield (*from investment*), gross revenue; *bereinigter* ~~: *adjusted gross income*; ~**fracht** gross freight; **b**~ **für netto** gross for net (*price charged by weight including packing*); ~**gehalt** gross salary (*total salary before any deductions*); ~**geschäftsgewinn** gross trading profit; ~**gewicht** gross weight (*including packing materials*), tare weight; *höchstes* ~~: *maximum operating gross weight* (*containers*); ~**gewinn** gross profits; ~**inlandsprodukt** gross domestic product; ~**investition** gross investment; ~**investitionsquote** gross investment ratio;

~**jahresarbeitsentgelt** annual gross wages, total annual remuneration before deductions; ~**jahreserträge** gross annual income; ~**kapitalbildung** gross capital formation; ~**ladefähigkeit** deadweight cargo; ~**lohnsumme** total wages; ~**lohnurteil** judgment expressed in the amount of the total wage (*or* salary) (*before deductions for withholding tax etc*); ~**mietwert** gross annual value (*of rented premises*); ~**pachtwert** gross annual value (*of farm property etc*); ~**prämie** gross premium; ~**preis** gross price (*before rebate and/or discounts*); long price; ~**prinzip** overall principle; ~**registertonne** registered ton (*100 cubic feet*); ~**rendite** gross yield; ~**rente** gross annual return (*on invested capital*); ~**reserven** gross reserve assets; ~**sozialprodukt** gross national product (GNP); ~**spanne ohne Skontoabzug** gross merchandising margin; ~**steuerbelastung** gross burden of taxes, gross tax load (ratio); ~**tonnage** gross tonnage; ~**umsatz** gross turnover; ~**verdienst** gross earnings; ~**verleiheinnahmen** gross rental (*motion pictures*); ~**verlust** gross loss; ~**verzinsung** gross interest return; ~**warengewinn** gross trading profit; ~**warenumsatz** gross sales; ~**zins** gross interest.

Buch *n* book, account book, ledger, volume, official register *pl Bücher*: *books, accounts*; ~*er führen*: *to keep books*; ~*er und Geschäftspapiere*: *books and records*; ~**abschluß** closing of accounts, balancing of the books; *e-n* ~~ *vornehmen*: *to make up books*; *die Bücher abschließen*: *to balance the books, to close the accounts*; ~**außenstände** book debts (*due to a firm*); outstanding accounts, accounts receivable; ~**auszug** abstract of accounts; ~**berechtigter** person entitled according to register entry; ~**eigentum** registered ownership, ownership of property registered in the land title register;

~**einsicht** access to the books and accounts, inspection of books; ~**ersitzung** *acquisition of a prescriptive title to land through an official register* (*where the entry has remained unchallenged for 30 years or longer, coupled with possession*); ~**forderung** book debt, outstanding account; *pl* accounts receivable; **b**~**führen** *v/i* to keep a record (of), to keep accounts; *pl Bücher führen*: *to keep books*; *ordnungsgemäß* ~ *führen*: *to keep regular accounts*; ~**führung** →*Buchführung*; ~**geld** deposit currency; **b**~**gemäß** as shown by the books; ~**gewinn** book profit; notional profit by upward revaluation; ~**gemeinschaft** book-club; ~**gläubiger** book creditor, creditor of outstanding accounts; ~**grundschuld** registered land charge; ~**guthaben** credit balance in the account; ~**halter** accountant, book-keeper; ~**haltung** → *Buchhaltung*; ~**handel** book-trade, bookselling; ~**händler** bookseller, bookdealer; ~**handlung** bookshop; ~**hypothek** registered mortgage (*without deed*); ~**inventur** book inventory, record inventory; ~**korrektur** accountancy adjustment; ~**kredit** current account credit, bank advance facilities; ~**macher** bookmaker, bookie; **b**~**mäßig** *adj* according to the books, for bookkeeping purposes, as shown by the books; -~ **oder Kontensparen** bank saving, saving through accounts; ~**prüfer** auditor (*obsolete term,* → *vereidigter* ~~), certified public accountant; *vereidigter* ~~: *sworn public accountant, sworn auditor, chartered accountant*; ~**prüfung** audit, *betriebseigene* ~~: *internal audit*; *betriebsfremde* ~~: *external audit*; ~**prüfungsgesellschaft** auditing firm, firm of auditors; ~**rechte** non-certificated mortgage rights; (*merely exist in land title register*); ~**sachverständiger** accountancy expert, auditing expert; ~**schulden** stated liabilities; ~**stabe** → *Buchstabe*;

buchen | **Buchungsabschluß**

~**stelle** booking office, accounting agency; ~~ **und Betriebsprüfung** tax examination of a business enterprise; ~**verlust** book loss, loss according to the books, accounting loss; ~**wert** book value, *nominal value carried in the books of account*; ~~ *vor Abschreibung*: *gross book value*; ~**zwang** legal obligation to keep books; **öffentliches** ~ public book, public register.

buchen *v/t* to book, to enter in the books, to make an entry in the accounts; *gleichlautend* ~ *to make a corresponding entry* (*of a debit and/or credit item in two different firms*).

Bücherrevisor *m obs* → *Buchprüfer*.

Buchführung *f* bookkeeping, keeping accounts, accounting, accountancy; ~ **in Loseblattform** looseleaf ledger; **amerikanische** ~ columnar bookkeeping, tabular bookkeeping; **doppelte** ~ bookkeeping by double entry, double-entry bookkeeping, double account system; **einfache** ~ bookkeeping by single entry, single-entry bookkeeping; **kameralistische** ~ single-entry bookkeeping, governmental accounting; **kaufmännische** ~ commercial bookkeeping; **ordnungsmäßige** ~ sound accounting practice, proper bookkeeping.

Buchführungsangaben accounting information; ~**daten** accounting information, bookkeeping data; ~**grundsätze** principles of sound accounting practice; ~**shelfer** bookkeeping assistant; ~**maschine** accounting machine; ~**pflicht** requirement to keep accounts; ~**richtlinien** accounting rules; ~**sachverständiger** accountancy expert; ~**system** accounting system; ~**vorschriften** bookkeeping rules; ~**wesen** accountancy.

Buchhaltung *f* bookkeeping, accounting *cf Buchführung*; bookkeeping department, accounts (*or* accounting) department.

Buchstabe *m* letter; subparagraph, subclause (*in citations*), sub-item; *an dem* ~*n kleben*: *to stick to the letter*; *auf den* ~*n genau*: *punctilious*; ~ **des Gesetzes** letter of the law, litera legis; **toter** ~ dead letter, dead verbality.

Buchstabierungswörter *n/pl* (*Ida, Nordpol etc.*) identification words.

buchstäblich *adj* literal, (verbatim et) literatim, word-for-word.

Buchung *f* posting, booking, reservation (*flight, hotel*); entering (in the books); (bookkeeping) entry; ~ **ohne Gegenbuchung** unbalanced entry; **debitorische** ~ debit-side entry; **e–e** ~ **berichtigen** to correct an entry (*of an item*); **e** ~ **stornieren** to delete an entry, to cancel an entry, to reverse an entry; **e–e** ~ **vornehmen** to enter in the books; **einfache** ~ single entry; **fiktive** ~ imputed entry; **gleichlautende** ~ entry in conformity; **kreditorische** ~ credit-side entry; **nachträgliche** ~ post-entry, subsequent entry; **transitorische** ~ suspense entry on suspense account, expense prepaid, income item received in advance; **zusammengefaßte** ~ compound entry.

Buchungsabschluß closing of (the) accounts; ~**aufgabe** statement of accounting entry; ~**beleg** voucher, journal voucher, accounting voucher, accounting record; ~**bescheinigung** booking certificate, written confirmation of a reservation; ~**bestätigung** confirmation of reservation; ~**fehler** bookkeeping error, misentry; ~**maschine** posting machine, (automatic) bookkeeping machine; ~**methoden** accounting methods; ~**nummer** number of an entry; ~**posten** bookkeeping item, entry, *e–n* ~~ *übertragen*: *to post up*; ~**schluß** closing of the accounts; ~**stand** state of the accounts, accounts position; ~**stelle** accounts department; ~**streifen** booking strip, bookkeeping voucher; **b**~**technisch** relating to accoun-

183

tancy technicalities; ~*e Gründe*: *reasons due to the technicalities of accounting*; ~**text** entry description; ~**unterlage** accounting voucher, bookkeeping document(s), *pl* accounting records; ~**vorgang** bookkeeping (operation), posting.

Budget *n* budget, annual estimates, appropriation; ~**abstrich** budget cut; ~**aufschlüsselung** breakdown of the budget; ~**aufstellung** budgeting, preparing the budget; ~**ausgleich** balancing (of) the budget; ~**ausschuß** budget committee; ~**debatte** budget debate, debate on the finance bill; ~**gesetz** Finance Act; ~**kürzung** budget cut; ~**periode** budget period, budgetary spending period; ~**posten** budget item; ~**recht** constitutional right (*of parliament*) to decide on the budget; ~**überschreitung** exceeding budgetary appropriations; ~**überschuß** budget surplus; ~**voranschlag** budgetary estimates; ~**vorlage** presentation of the budget; **das** ~ **vorlegen** to open (*or* to submit) the budget.

Büdnerrechte *n/pl* small holders' rights.

Bugsierlohn *n* towage.

Bühnen|arbeitsrecht theatrical employment law; ~**arbeitsverhältnis** theatrical employment; ~**aufführung** theatrical performance; ~**dienstvertrag** contract of theatrical employment; ~**künstler** stage artist, actor, performer; ~**mitglieder** members of the theatrical profession; ~**rechte** dramatic rights, stage rights, rights of performance; ~**schaffende** persons working for the theatre; ~**schiedsgerichtsbarkeit** arbitration for theatrical performers; ~**schiedsgericht** performing rights tribunal (*copyrights*), court of arbitration for the theatrical profession; ~**verlag** publisher of dramatic works; ~**vermittlung** official employment agency for the theatre profession; ~**werk** dramatic work.

Buhrufe *m/pl pol* booing, hissing.

Bummelant *m* loafer, dawdler, slowcoach.

Bummelantentum *n* absenteeism (*work*), loafing; truancy (*school*).

Bummelstreik *m* slowdown (strike), go-slow (strike), work to rule; *e-n* ~ *machen*: *to go slow*.

Bummler *m* = *Bummelant qv*.

Bund *m* bond; alliance, pact; confederacy, (con)federation; association; Federal Government, *esp* Government of the German Federal Republic; ~ **der Ehe** the bond of marriage.

Bundes|adler *the eagle symbol as shown in the German Federal coat of arms*; ~**amt** → *Bundesamt*; ~**angelegenheit** a matter within federal jurisdiction; ~**anleihe** federal loan, federal bond; ~**anleihekonsortium** federal loan syndicate; ~**anstalt** → *Bundesanstalt*; ~**anwalt** federal attorney, federal prosecutor; ~**anwaltschaft** Federal Prosecutor's Department; ~**anzeiger** Federal Gazette; ~**arbeitsgemeinschaft der freien Wohlfahrtspflege** Federal Association of Voluntary Welfare Work; ~**arbeitsgericht** Federal Labour Court (*court of last resort*); ~**arbeitsminister** Federal Minister of Labour; ~**archiv** Federal Record Office; ~**ärzteordnung** federal rules for the medical profession; ~**aufgaben** functions of the Federal Administration; ~**aufsicht** federal supervision; ~**aufsichtsamt** Federal Supervisory Office; ~**aufsichtsamt für das Kreditwesen** Federal Banking Supervisory Board; ~**aufsichtsamt für das Versicherungswesen** Federal Insurance Supervisory Authority; ~**auftragsverwaltung** (Laender)administration on behalf of the Federation); ~**ausbildungsförderungsgesetz** Federal Student Aid Act; ~**ausführungsbehörde** federal (implementing) agency; ~**ausgaben** federal expenditure; ~**autobahn** German motorway, German autobahn; ~**bahn** German Federal

Railways (*West Germany*); **~bahnpolizei** federal railway police; **~bank** German Federal Bank; **b~bankfähig** *adj* eligible (for discount) at the Bundesbank (*bills of exchange*); **~bankfähigkeit** eligibility (*of negotiable instruments*) at the Bundesbank; **~baublatt** Federal Building Gazette; **~baudirektion** Federal Building Board; **~baugesetz** Federal Building Law; **~beamte** federal officials, federal civil servants; **~beamtenrecht** *law governing the German federal civil service*; **~beauftragter** federal commissioner; **~beauftragter für den Datenschutz** Federal Data Protection Commissioner; **~beauftragter für den Steinkohlenbergbau und die Steinkohlenbergbaugebiete** Federal Commissioner for the Hard Coal Industry and the Hard Coal Mining Areas; **~bediensteter** federal employee, federal civil servant, public servant in federal service; **~behörde** federal authority, federal department; *mittelbare* ~~: *independent federal agency*; *oberste* ~~*n*: *supreme federal authorities*; **~beihilfe** federal grant; **~bürger** citizen of the German Federal Republic, German citizen; **~bürgschaft** federal guarantee; **~darlehenswohnungen** *housing financed by federal loans*; **~dienstgerichte** federal disciplinary tribunals; **~dienststelle** federal agency (*or* department); **~dienststrafgerichte** federal disciplinary courts; **~disziplinaranwalt** *federal prosecutor in disciplinary matters;* **~disziplinarhof** supreme federal disciplinary tribunal; **~disziplinarordnung** federal disciplinary rules; **~disziplinarrecht** federal disciplinary law; **~druckerei** *German Federal Government's Printers*; **~ebene** (at) federal level; **b~eigen** federally owned, owned by the national government, property of the (German) Federal Republic; **~einkommen** federal income; **~entschädigungsgesetz** Federal Indemnification Law (*for victims of Nazi persecution*); **~entschädigungsrecht** law pertaining to indemnification of persecutees; **~ergänzungsgesetz** Federal Amending Law; **~ernährungsministerium** Federal Ministry of Food; **~etat** Federal Government budget; **~fernstraße** federal highway; **~finanzbehörden** federal revenue authorities; **~finanzhof** Federal Fiscal Court; **~finanzminister** Federal Minister of Finance; **~finanzministerium** Federal Ministry of Finance; **~finanzverwaltung** federal revenue administration; **~fiskus** federal treasury; **~flagge** federal flag; **~forschungsanstalt für Landeskunde und Raumordnung** Federal Research Institute for Regional Geography and Regional Planning; **~forschungsanstalt für Viruskrankheiten der Tiere** Federal Research Institute for Animal Virus Diseases; **~gebiet** federal territory; **~gebührenordnung** federal fee scale regulation; **~genosse** ally; **~gericht** federal court; *obere* ~~*e*: highest federal courts; **~gerichtshof** (= *BGH*) Federal Supreme Court of Justice (*civil and criminal jurisdiction*); **~gesetz** federal law, German Federal Act; *US*: Congressional Act; **~gesetzblatt** Federal Law Gazette; **~gesetzgeber** federal law-maker, federal legislator; **~gesetzgebung** federal legislation; **~gesundheitsamt** Federal Health Office; **~grenzschutz** Federal Frontier Guards; **~hauptkasse** Federal Chief Cash Office; **~haus** *German Parliament (building)*; **~haushalt** federal budget; **~haushaltsgesetz** Federal Budget Act; **~heer** the Federal Army; **~hilfe** Federal aid and assistance; **~hoheit** federal sovereignty; **~institut für Berufsbildungsforschung** Federal Institute for Research into Vocational Education and Training; **~-Immissionsschutzgesetz** Federal Pollution

Bundesjustizminister   **Bundessprachenamt**

Control Act; ~**justizminister** Federal Minister of Justice; ~**justizministerium** Federal Ministry of Justice; ~**kabinett** Federal Cabinet; ~**kanzler** *D*: Chancellor of the Federal Republic of Germany; Federal Chancellor; ~**kanzleramt** Federal Chancellery; ~**kartellamt** Federal Cartel Office, Federal Cartel Authority; ~**kasse** Federal Cash Office, Federal Treasury; ~**kompetenzen** federal responsibilities; ~**kriminalamt** (German) Federal Bureau of Investigation, Federal Office of Criminal Investigation; ~**land** Land of the (German) Federal Government, Land; federal real estate; ~**laufbahnverordnung** Federal Civil Service Careers Ordinance; ~**leistungsgesetz** Federal Requisitioning Law; ~**lotsenkammer** Federal Chamber of Pilots; ~**mietengesetze** Federal Rents Acts ~**minister** → *Bundesminister*; ~**ministerium** → *Bundesministerium*; ~**mittel** federal funds; ~**mittelbehörde** intermediate Federal authority; ~**monopolverwaltung** Federal Monopoly Administration; ~**nachrichtendienst** Federal Intelligence Service; ~**notarkammer** (=) national association of notaries *(professional body)*; ~**notarordnung** national rules and regulations for (German) notaries; ~**oberbehörden** federal superior authorities; ~**oberseeamt** Federal High Court of Inquiry into Marine Casualties; ~**organe** constitutional organs of the Federal Government; ~**parlament** Federal Parliament; ~**patentamt** (Federal) German Patent Office; ~**patentgericht** (German) Federal Patent Tribunal; ~**personalausschuß** Federal Civil Service Commission; ~**pflichten** *constitutional obligations incumbent upon the Federation*; ~**polizei** federal police; ~**post** Federal Postal Administration, the German postal service; ~**präsident** President of the Federal Republic of Germany

(Federal President); ~**präsidialamt** Office of the Federal President; ~**presseamt** Federal Press Office; ~**pressechef** Head of (German) Federal Press Office *(official government spokesman)*; ~**prüfstelle für jugendgefährdende Schriften** Federal Review Board for Publications Harmful to Young Persons: ~**rat** Federal Council, Bundesrat, Senate of the Federal Parliament *(representing the German states)*, *in Switzerland:* Executive National Council; ~**rechnungshof** Federal Audit Office; ~**recht** federal law; ~~ *bricht Landesrecht: federal law supersedes state law*; b~**rechtlich** *adj* according to federal law, pursuant to federal legislation; ~**rechtsanwaltsgebührenordnung** *BRAGO* (German Federal) Attorneys' Fees Act; ~**rechtsanwaltskammer** German Federal Lawyers' Association; ~**rechtsanwaltsordnung** *Rules and Regulations for the German Bar*; ~**regierung** the Federal Government; ~**republik Deutschland** Federal Republic of Germany; ~**ressort** federal department; *das beteiligte* ~~: *the federal department concerned*; ~**richter** federal judge; ~**rückerstattungsgesetz** Federal Restitution Law *(concerning property transferred during the Nazi regime)*; ~**schatz** (property of the) Federal Treasury; ~**schatzanweisung** Federal treasury note; ~**schatzbrief** Federal treasury bill; ~**schuld** federal debt; ~**schuldbuch** Federal Debt Register; ~**schuldenverwaltung** Federal Debt Administration; ~**schuldverschreibung** federal bond; ~**seuchengesetz** *(German) federal law concerning prevention of epidemics*; ~**siegel** federal seal; ~**sozialgericht** Supreme Social Insurance Tribunal; ~**sozialhilfegesetz** *federal public assistance (for poor persons) Act*; ~**sozialrichter** justice at the Bundessozialgericht *qv*; ~**sprachenamt** Federal Office of Languages, Federal Linguistic Service; ~**staat** federal state, (*individual*) state (of a confederation); ~~**sklausel**: *federal clause*; **b**~**staatlich** federal, national; ~**statistik** federal (government) statistics; ~**stelle** federal agency; ~**stelle für Außenhandelsinformation** German Foreign Trade Information Office ~**steuerblatt** Federal Taxation Gazette; ~**strafregister** Federal Criminal Records Register; ~**straße** federal highway; ~**tag** the „Bundestag" (*lower House of the German Parliament*); Federal Diet (*obsolescent*); ~**tagsabgeordneter** Member of the Bundestag *qv*, M.P., deputy; ~**tagsbeamte** German Federal Parliament officials, Bundestag officials; ~**tagspräsident** President (Speaker) of the *Bundestag qv*; ~**tagswahl** general federal elections; ~**treue** allegiance (of the Länder) to the Federal Government (*and mutual loyalty*); ~**unterstützung** federal aid; ~**urlaubsgesetz** Federal Vacations Law; ~**verband** national association; ~**verband der deutschen Industrie** National Association of German Industry; ~**verband des privaten Bankgewerbes** National Association of Private Banks; ~**verband für den Selbstschutz** Federal Self-Protection Association; ~**verdienstorden** Federal Order of Merit; ~**vereinigung der Arbeitgeberverbände** National Union of Employers' Associations; ~**verfassung** federal constitution; ~**verfassungsgericht** Federal Constitutional Court; ~**verfassungsgerichtsbarkeit** federal jurisdiction on constitutional questions; ~**vermögen** federal (government) property, federal funds; ~**vermögensstelle** Federal Property Agency; ~**vermögensverwaltung** federal property administration; ~**versammlung** Federal Electoral Assembly (*election of the Federal President*), Federal Convention, Electoral College; ~**versicherungsamt** Federal (Social) Insurance Authority; ~**versicherungsanstalt für Angestellte** Federal Insurance Institution for Salaried Employees; ~**versorgungsgesetz** War Pensioners Act, Federal (War Victims') Pension Law; ~**verteidigung** national defence; ~**vertriebenengesetz** Federal Law on Expelled Persons; ~**verwaltung** federal administration; ~**verwaltungsamt** Federal Office of Administration; ~**verwaltungsgericht** (Supreme) Federal Administrative Tribunal; ~**wahlgesetz** Federal Electoral Act; ~**wahlleiter** Federal Electoral Supervisor, (federal) election officer, (federal) returning officer; ~**wappen** coat of arms of the Federal Republic, federal arms; ~**wehr** German Federal Armed Forces; ~**wehrverwaltung** Federal Armed Forces Administration; ~**wehrverwaltungsamt** Federal Armed Forces Administrative Office; ~**zentrale für gesundheitliche Aufklärung** Federal Centre for Health Education; ~**zentralregister** Federal Central Register of previous convictions); ~**zollblatt** Federal Customs Gazette; ~**zollverwaltung** Federal Customs Administration; ~**zuschuß** federal subsidy, federal grant; ~**zuständigkeit** federal jurisdiction; ~**zwang** federal cumpulsory action (*in relation to the Länder or a particular German federal state*).

Bundesamt *n* federal office, federal agency; ~ **für gewerbliche Wirtschaft** Federal Office for Trade and Industry; ~ **für Schiffsvermessung** Federal Office for Ship Tonnage Measurement; ~ **für Sera und Impfstoffe** Federal Agency for Sera and Vaccines; ~ **für Verfassungsschutz** Federal Office for the Protection of the Constitution; ~ **für Wehrtechnik und Beschaffung** Federal Office for Military Technology and Procurement; ~ **für Zivilschutz** Federal Civil Defence Office.

Bundesanstalt *f* federal institution, federal institute, federal administration, federal corporation, independent federal agency; ~ **für Arbeit** Federal Labour Office; ~ **für den Güterfernverkehr** Federal Office for Long-Distance Goods Transport; ~ **für Flugsicherung** Federal Administration of Air Navigation Services; ~ **für Geowissenschaften und Rohstoffe** Federal Institute for Geosciences and Natural Resources; ~ **für Gewässerkunde** Federal Institute for Hydrology; ~ **für Materialprüfung** Federal Institute for Materials Testing; ~ **für Straßenwesen** Federal Institute for Road Research; ~ **für Wasserbau** Federal Institute for Waterway Engineering.

Bundesminister *m* federal minister; ~ **der Finanzen** Federal Minister of Finance; ~ **der Justiz** Federal Minister of Justice; ~ **der Verteidigung** Federal Minister of Defence; ~ **des Auswärtigen** Federal Minister for Foreign Affairs; ~ **des Innern** Federal Minister of the Interior; ~ **für Arbeit und Sozialordnung** Federal Minister of Labour and Social Affairs; ~ **für Bildung und Wissenschaft** Federal Minister of Education and Science; ~ **für Ernährung, Landwirtschaft und Forsten** Federal Minister of Food, Agriculture and Forests; ~ **für Forschung und Technologie** Federal Minister for Research and Technology; ~ **für Jugend, Familie und Gesundheit** Federal Minister for Youth, Family Affairs and Health; ~ **für Raumordnung, Bauwesen und Städtebau** Federal Minister for Regional Planning, Building and Urban Development; ~ **für Verkehr und für das Post- und Fernmeldewesen** Federal Minister of Transport, Postal and Telecommunications; ~ **für Wirtschaft** Federal Minister of Economics; ~ **für wirtschaftliche Zusammenarbeit** Federal Minister for Economic Co-operation; **~gesetz** Federal Minister (Official Position) Act (1971).

Bundesministerium *n* federal ministry; Federal Department (*US*); ~ **der Finanzen** Federal Ministry of Finance; ~ **der Justiz** Federal Ministry of Justice; ~ **der Verteidigung** Federal Ministry of Defence; ~ **des Innern** Federal Ministry of the Interior; ~ **für Arbeit und Sozialordnung** Federal Ministry of Labour and Social Affairs; ~ **für Bildung und Wissenschaft** Federal Ministry of Education and Science; ~ **für das Post- und Fernmeldewesen** Federal Ministry of Postal and Telecommunications; ~ **für Ernährung, Landwirtschaft und Forsten** Federal Ministry of Food, Agriculture and Forests; ~ **für Forschung und Technologie** Federal Ministry for Research and Technology; ~ **für Jugend, Familie und Gesundheit** Federal Ministry for Youth, Family Affairs and Health; ~ **für Raumordnung, Bauwesen und Städtebau** Federal Ministry for Regional Planning, Building and Urban Development; ~ **für Verkehr** Federal Ministry of Transport; ~ **für Wirtschaft** Federal Ministry of Economics, ~ **für wirtschaftliche Zusammenarbeit** Federal Ministry for Economic Co-operation.

Bündigkeit *f* conciseness, coherence.

Bündnis *m* alliance, pact; **~fall** casus foederis (*contingency provided for in a treaty of alliance, military intervention pursuant to the alliance*); **~freiheit** nonalignment; **~politik** alliance policy, alignment policy; **~vertrag** treaty of alliance, mutual assistance pact.

Bürde *f* onerous task, burden, chore.

Bürge *m* surety, guarantor (for payment), voucher, sponsor; *e-n ~n bringen:* to find surety, to provide a guarantor; *den ~n stellen:* to stand surety, to stand bail; **bezahlter ~**

bürgen — **Büro**

compensated surety; **der leistende ~** paying surety; **selbstschuldnerischer ~** primarily liable guarantor, directly suable guarantor; **tauglicher ~** proper guarantor.

bürgen *v/i* to guarantee, to stand surety (for), to sponsor.

Bürger *m* citizen, *hist*: burgher; **~antrag** citizen's initiative; **~ausschuß** citizens' committee; **~befragung** opinion poll; **~begehren** local citizens' referendum; **~beteiligung** participation of local citizens in decision-making; **~brief** act of naturalization, certificate of citizenship; **~initiative** citizens' action group; **~krieg** civil war, internal war; **~kunde** civics; **~meister** *m* mayor; *Regierender ~: Governing Mayor (Berlin)*; **~meisteramt** mayor's office, town hall; city hall; **~meisterwahl(en)** mayoral elections; **b~nah** *adj* comprehensible (*or* helpful) to the man in the street; citizen-orientated; **~mitwirkung** participation of local citizens in the public affairs; **~pflicht** civic duty, obligation as a citizen; **~recht** freedom of a borough, political liberty, franchise; **~rechtler** civil rights activist; **~schaft** citizenry; **~sinn** sense of good citizenship, public spirit, service for the welfare of the community; **~stand** (the) middle classes; **~steig** pavement, *US* sidewalk; **~steigseite** kerb side, near side, *US*: curb side; **~steuer** poll tax, community charge; **~versammlung** town meeting; **~wehr** vigilance unit; **~~mitglied:** *vigilante*.

Bürgerliches Gesetzbuch *n* = *BGB* (German) Civil Code.

Bürgschaft *f* suretyship, contract of suretyship, surety bond, guarantee; **~ leisten** to stand surety, to grant (*or* accept *or* undertake) a guarantee (for s. o.); **~snehmer** guaranteed creditor; creditor secured by suretyship; **e–e ~ übernehmen** to stand surety; *für jmdn ~~~ : to stand surety for another*; **einfache ~** secondary guarantee; **selbstschuldnerische ~** personal guarantee, absolute suretyship, directly enforceable guarantee, absolute guarantee (*waiving the defence that the principal debtor be sued and levied upon first*); **solidarische ~** joint and several suretyship.

Bürgschafts|erklärung suretyship declaration (*or* instrument); guarantor's undertaking, statement of guarantee; **~geber** guarantor; **~kredit** guaranteed credit; **~leistung** standing surety, the undertaking of a guarantee, furnishing of guarantee; providing a suretyship; **~nehmer** guarantee; **~provision** guarantee commission; **~schein** suretyship instrument, certificate of guarantee; **~schuld** guarantee indebtedness, principal debt (*secured by guarantee or suretyship*); **~stellung** = *~leistung qv*; **~übernahme** = *~leistung qv*; **~urkunde** = *~schein qv*; **~verhältnis** principal and surety, (suretyship) relationship; **~verpflichtung** suretyship obligation; **~vertrag** (contract of) suretyship, contract of guarantee; **~volumen** total guarantees; **~wechsel** bill of exchange as a guarantee, guarantee bill; **~zusage** guarantee undertaking.

Büro *n* office, bureau (*administration*); **~angestellter** office employee, clerk, clerical worker; **~arbeiten** office work, clerical work; **~beamter** official, clerical officer; **~bedarf** stationery (requirements); **~beruf** clerical occupation, office job; **~gehilfe** junior clerk, office junior; **~gemeinschaft** shared offices (*of lawyers*); **~handel** unofficial dealings; **~kraft** office employee, clerk; **~material** office supplies, stationery; **~personal** clerical staff; **~schluß** closing time; **~termin** hearing in chambers; **~unkosten** office expenditure, overheads; **~vorsteher** senior clerk (*in a law office*); office manager; **~weg** administrative channels; *im ~~~e: in chambers, without a court hearing*; **~zeit** office hours.

Bürokrat *m* bureaucrat.
Bürokratie *f* bureaucracy.
Bürokratismus *m* red tape.
Buße *f* penance, atonement; penalty, civil (*or* administrative) fine.
Bußgeld *n* civil penalty, regulatory; fine; non-criminal fine; ~**bescheid** penalty notice; ~**katalog** schedule of penalties *(for traffic offences);* ~**sache** summary offence; ~**verfahren** summary proceedings concerning administrative penalties.
Büttel *m* (*obs.*) beadle.

C

cessio legis *f* assignment by operation of law.

Chance *f* chance, opportunity, prospect; **~ngleichheit** equality of opportunities; **~nungleichheit im Wettbewerb** inequality of competition; **~test** personality test, test of character; **bessere wirtschaftliche ~n** better business prospects, brighter business outlook.

Charakter|anlage disposition, nature; **~bild** character study; **~eigenschaft** trait, trait of character, distinctive feature; **~mangel** failing(s), bad character; **~schwäche** weakness of character, failings; **~test** personality test, test of character; **~untersuchung** character analysis; **~veränderung** change of personality; **~zug** distinguishing feature; **amtlicher ~** official character (*or* nature); **obligatorischer ~** obligatory character (*of an engagement*); **simultaner ~** simultaneous character (*of offences*).

charakteristisch *adj* characteristic, distinctive (*mark or feature of a trade mark etc*).

Charta *f* charter (*historically or relating to international bodies or declarations*).

Charter *f* charter; **~flug** charter flight; **~flugzeug** charter plane; **~gesellschaft** charter company, charter carrier; **~partie** charter-party; **~vertrag** charter-party; **~~ auf Zeit**: time charter; **~vertragsrecht** the law of chartering.

Charterer *m* charterer.

chartern *v/t* to charter, to hire.

Chef *m* principal, boss, chief; **~anwalt** leader, leading counsel, lead attorney; **~arzt** doctor in charge of a hospital (*or department of a hospital*), senior medical officer; **~delegierter** head of a delegation; **~ des Bundeskanzleramts** Head of the Federal Chancellery; **~ des Bundespräsidialamts** Head of the Office of the Federal President; **~ des Generalstabs** chief of staff; **~des Protokolls** chief (*or* head) of protocol department; **~dolmetscher** chief interpreter; **~konstrukteur** chief designer; **~redakteur** editor-in-chief, chief editor; **~sekretärin** head secretary; **~übersetzer** chief translator; **~ vom Dienst** desk editor, duty editor.

Chemiewerte *m/pl exch* chemical industry securities.

Chiffre *f* cipher, code; box number (*newspaper ads*), key number; **~anzeige** box-number advertisement, keyed advertisement; **~telegramm** code(d) telegram.

chiffrieren *v/t* to (en)cipher, to code, to write (*or* wire) in code.

Chiffriermaschine *f* cipher machine, coder.

Christlich-Demokratische Union Christian Democratic Union; **~Soziale Union** Christian Social Union (*Bavaria*).

Cif *s*, *adj* (= *CIF*) cost, insurance and freight; **~~Preis** cif price.

clausula rebus sic stantibus *f referred to usually as*: the rebus sic stantibus clause (*i. e treaties to become inoperative if conditions have changed fundamentally*).

Clearing *n* = *Verrechnung(sverfahren)* clearing; **~abkommen** clearing agreement; **~bank** clearing bank (*GB: a member of the London Bankers' Clearing House, generally: a commercial bank*); **~guthaben** *n/pl* clearing assets; **~konto** clearing account; **~stelle** clearing house; **~verkehr** clearing (transactions); **~vertrag** clearing agreement; **~ zum Pariwert** par clearance.

Code *m* code (*e.g. ABC Code for cablegrams*); **~buch** code book.

Computer|delikte *n/pl* computer

(-related) offences; **~kriminalität** computer-related crime.

conditio sine qua non *f* (=) (absolute) condition (precedent).

constitutum possessorium *n* = *Besitzmittlungsverhältnis*, bailment, agreement granting indirect possession, constructive possession (*Sicherungsübereignung*) *i.e. without transfer of physical possession*.

contra *prep* (= *gegen*) versus (*v.*).

Copyright *n* copyright; **~-Register** register of copyrights.

coram publico *adv* in public, publicly.

corps diplomatique *n* diplomatic corps, corps diplomatique.

corpus delicti corpus delicti, the material evidence (of a crime), the actual commission of a particular offence.

Coupon *m* (= *Kupon*) coupon, dividend-warrant, return coupon; **~steuer** coupon tax.

Courtage *f* broker's fee, brokerage; **~gebühr** (amount of) broker's commission, brokerage; **~rechnung** brokerage account.

culpa in contrahendo *f* negligence in the course of contracting (*causing damage to other party*), faulty happening prior to conclusion of contract.

D

Dach|antenne roof antenna, roof aerial; **~deckerhandwerk** roofing trade; **~fonds** pyramiding fund, fund of funds; **~geschoßwohnung** attic apartment (*or* flat), penthouse apartment; **~gesellschaft** umbrella company, holding company, controlling company; **~kammer** attic room; **~konzern** umbrella group; **~organisation** holding company, umbrella organization, parent enterprise; **~verband** national federation.

Dafürhalten *n* opinion, view.

dahingestellt *adj* undecided; *etwas ~ sein lassen*: *to leave s. th. undecided.*

Daktyloskopie *f* dactyloscopy *the taking and classification of fingerprints.*

Damnationslegat *n* civil law legacy (*obligation of the heir to satisfy the legatee*).

Damnum *n* mortgage discount *deducted from the face amount of a mortgage*; *exch:* difference between nominal and lower issue price.

Dämpfung *f* slowing down (*boom etc*) an economic downturn; **~ der Exportkonjunktur** check to expansion of exports; **~ der Investitionstätigkeit** measures to slow down rate of capital investment; **konjunkturelle ~** an economic downturn, recession, slowdown.

danach *adv* thereafter, subsequently.

Dank|adresse address of thanks; **~sagungsbeschluß** vote of thanks; **e-e ~sagung beschließen** to adopt a vote of thanks.

Darbietung *f* presentation, show, production, account.

darlegen *v/t* to set forth (*in court*); *im einzelnen ~*: *to particularize, to state in detail.*

Darlegung *f* presentation, explanation, argument, submission, statement; **~ des Falles** statement of the case; **~slast** the onus of presentation; **~spflicht** *the* (*procedural*) obligation to present the case to the court; **~spflichtiger** proponent; **kurze ~** summary statement; **vollständige ~ des Sachverhalts** a complete presentation of the facts and circumstances, complete statement.

Darlehen *n* loan, personal loan, fixed-sum credit; *jur* loan for consumption; **~ und Hypotheken** mortgage and other loans; **~ an Börsenmakler** stock exchange loan(s); **~ gegen Pfandbestellung** loan secured by chattel mortgage; loan against collateral; **~ mit täglicher Kündigung** loan at call; **~ zu Wucherzinsen** = *wucherisches ~ qv*; **befristetes ~** loan for a fixed term; **besichertes ~** loan against collateral, secured loan; **ein ~ absichern** to secure a loan, to provide collateral for a loan; **ein ~ aufnehmen** to borrow (money), to take up a loan; **ein ~ geben** to grant a loan, to extend a loan to s.o.; **ein ~ kündigen** to call in a loan, to recall a loan; **ein ~ tilgen** to repay a loan, to redeem a loan; **für ein ~ Sicherheit leisten** to secure a loan; **gesichertes ~** secured loan; **hypothekarisches ~** mortgage loan; **kapitalersetzendes ~** blocked loan; **kommunalverbürgtes ~** loan guaranteed by local authorities, publicly guaranteed loan; **kündbares ~** callable loan; *jederzeit kündbares ~*: call loan; **kurzfristiges ~** short-term loan; **langfristiges ~** loan, long-term loan; **mittelfristiges ~** medium-term credit; **nachrangiges ~** subordinated loan; **partiarisches ~** loan coupled with a share in the profits; **ungesichertes ~** unsecured loan; **unkündbares ~** blocked loan, uncallable loan; **unverzinsliches ~** in-

193

terest-free loan, free loan; **vertragliches** ~ contractual loan; **verzinsliches** ~ interest-bearing loan; loan at interest; **wucherisches** ~ usurious loan; **zinsfreies** ~ = *unverzinsliches Darlehen qv*; **zinsgünstiges** ~ low-interest loan.

Darlehens|antrag application for a loan; ~**aufnahme** (the) taking up of a loan, borrowing; ~**betrag** loan amount; ~**empfänger** borrower, recipient of a loan; ~**forderung** money due under a loan, debt; ~**geber** lender, creditor; ~**geschäft** lending transaction, loan business; ~**gewährung** (the) granting of a loan, lending; ~ *gewährung auf fremde Rechnung:* loan for account of others; ~**hypothek** mortgage (securing a loan); ~**interessent** would-be borrower; ~**kapital** principal moneys, principal, loan capital; ~**kasse** loan society, savings bank; ~**kassenverein** loan society, cooperative banking association; ~**konto** loan account; ~**kosten** loan charges; ~**nehmer** borrower, ~**politik** loan policy; ~**restschuld** balance of loan indebtedness; ~**schuld** debt under a loan, amount of a loan, loan indebtedness; ~**schuldner** borrower; ~**stock** total amount of loans outstanding, total lendings; ~**summe** amount of the loan; ~**titel** loan instrument, document of entitlement of the lender; ~**valuta** loan proceeds, the advanced sum; ~**verbindlichkeiten** loan indebtedness; ~**verhandlungen führen** to negotiate a loan; ~**vermittler** loan arranger; loan agent; ~**versprechen** promise to grant a loan, assurance of a loan; ~**vertrag** loan agreement; ~**vorvertrag** preliminary agreement for a loan; ~**zinsen** loan interest, interest on a loan; ~**zinssatz** loan interest (rate); ~**zusage** promise to grant a loan, loan commitment.

darstellen *v/t* to represent, to describe, to constitute, to portray.

Darstellung *f* presentation (*of facts*), statement, description (*of an object*), illustration; ~ **der Erfindung** disclosure of invention; ~ **des Sachverhalts** statement (of the facts and circumstances); ~ **des Tatbestandes** statement of the facts (and circumstances), recital of facts; ~ **e-s Musters** representation of a design; **anfechtbare** ~ disputable (*or* contestable) statement; **bildliche** ~ illustration; **e-e** ~ **eidlich erhärten** to affirm a statement upon oath, to corroborate upon oath; **falsche** ~ misrepresentation; **knappe** ~ concise presentation, succinct account; **kontenmäßige** ~ account-type representation; **schematische** ~ scheme, outline; **umfassende** ~ comprehensive account, full statement.

dartun *v/t* to show, to set forth, to suggest, to make evident.

darüberhinaus *adv* beyond that, over and above s.th., furthermore.

Daseinsvorsorge *f* provision for elementary requirements.

das heißt *d. h.* id est = i. e., that is to say, to wit, namely.

Datei *f* data (collection); ~**enregister** central register of data.

Daten *pl* data, facts, particulars; ~**abgleich** counter-checking of data; ~**ausgabe** data output; ~**bank** data bank, data exchange; ~**eingabe** data input; ~**erfassung** data collecting; ~**erhebung** gathering of data; ~**geheimnis** data secrecy; ~**schutz** data protection; ~**schutzbeauftragter** Commissioner for Data Protection; ~**schutzgesetz** Data Protection Act; ~**sicherheit** data security; ~**sicherung** data protection; ~**speicherung** storing of data; ~**sperrung** blocking of data; ~**übermittlung** data transmission; ~**träger** data carrier; ~**verarbeiter** data-processing machine, data processor; ~**verarbeitung** data processing; ~**verarbeitungsanlagen** data processing systems; ~**verarbeitungskosten** data processing costs; ~**verbund** data-pro-

datieren — **Dauerprüfung**

cessing interoperation; **~verknüpfung** linkage of data, data matching; **~weitergabe** data transmission, data disclosure; **~zentrale** data centre; **~zweckbindung** purpose-related nature of data; **analytische** ~ analytical data; **angefallene** ~ incoming data, available data; **anonymisierte** ~ data rendered anonymous; **einwandfreie** ~ unimpeachable data, reliable data; **elektronische ~verarbeitung** electronic data processing; **personenbezogene** ~ personal data; **statistische** ~ statistical data.

datieren *v/t* to date.

dato *adv* (today); *bis* ~: *to date, up to this date*.

Datowechsel *m* fixed-date bill.

Datum *n* date; ~ **des Inkrafttretens** effective date; ~ **des Poststempels** postmark date; **angegebenes** ~ stated date; **gleichen ~s** of the same date; **maßgebliches** ~ decisive date; **nach dem heutigen** ~ after date, after today's date; **unter dem** ~ dated the ..., bearing the date of ...; **zum festgesetzten** ~ on the appointed day for a fixed date.

Datums|angabe date; *ohne ~~*: *undated; Tag der ~~*: *day of date;* code date *(milk, butter etc)*; **~aufdruck** date mark; **~grenze** date line; **~stempel** date marker, date stamp.

Dauer *f* duration, length of time, term; **~angestellter** permanent employee; **~anlage** long-term investment; **~anleger** long-term investor; **~anleihe** permanent loan; **~arbeitslosigkeit** chronic unemployment; **~arbeitsplatz** fixed place of employment, permanent post; **~arbeitsplatzdarlehen** lasting-employment loan; **~arbeitsverhältnis** continuous employment; **~arrest** custody for an indefinite time; **~aufenthaltsberechtigung** resident status; **~auftrag** standing order *(for recurring remittances by bank transfer)*; preauthorized debits; **~ausschreibungsverfahren** standing invitation to tender; **~ausschuß** standing committee; **~ausstellung** permanent exhibition; **~beanspruchung** endurance stress, fatigue stress, continuous strain; **~delikt** continuing offence; **~belästigung** continuing nuisance; **~belastung** continuous load, permanent strain; **~beschäftigung** permanent occupation; **~besitz** permanent possession; **~betrieb** continuous operation *(machine)*; **~debatte** filibuster; **~delikt** continuing offence; ~ **der Gefängnisstrafe** period of imprisonment, term of imprisonment; ~ **der Haftung** indemnity period; **~eigenschaften** permanent properties; ~ **e–s Patents** duration of patent; **~einladung** standing invitation; **~emission** tap issue; **~emittent** constant issuer; **~ertragsfähigkeit** long-time productivity; **~existenz** existence in perpetuity, perpetual succession, artificial succession *(of a legal entity)*; permanent position *(employment)*; **~folgen e–r Verletzung** continuing effects of injury; **~garantie** continuing warranty; **~geschwindigkeit** cruising speed, sustained speed *(motor vehicle)*; **~invalidität** permanent disability; **~karte** season ticket *(transport)*, commutation ticket *(US)*, pass; **~kredit** permanent loan, long-term loan; **~kunde** standing *(or* regular) customer; **~lehen** perpetual lease, permanent estate; **~leistung** continuous output *(machine)*; **~mandat** mandate of indefinite duration, employment of a lawyer on a permanent basis; **~miete** permanent tenancy, long-term tenancy; **~mieter** permanent tenant, long-term tenancy; **~nutzungsrecht** registered perpetual lease (of business premises) *entered as a charge in the German land register,* proprietary lease; **~pacht** perpetual lease; **~parken** permanent parking; **~pflegschaft** permanent curatorship; **~prüfung** endurance test; ~**rente** permanent pension; ~**recht** perpetual interest (*or* right) (*with renewal clause*); ~**redner** marathon speaker, filibuster speaker; ~**regelung** permanent arrangement (*or* settlement); ~**rente** perpetual annuity; ~**schaden** permanent impairment; *verbleibender* ~~: *residual damage*; ~**schuld** fixed debt, long-term debt, permanent debt; ~**schuldverhältnis** continuous obligation; ~**staatsangehörigkeit** permanent nationality; ~**stellung** permanent employment, permanent appointment, permanent job; ~**straftat** continuing offence, continuing crime; ~**treuhand** perpetual trust; ~**unterhalt** long-term maintenance; ~**verlust** constant loss; ~**vertrag** continuing agreement; continuous contract; ~**vollmacht** enduring power of attorney; ~**waren** durable goods, nonperishable goods (*or* food-stuff); ~**werbung** permanent publicity; ~**wohnrecht** permanent residential right; ~**wohnrechtsvertrag** contract conferring permanent residential rights, contract of permanent residence; ~**wohnsitz** permanent residence, domicile; **für die ~ des Verfahrens** for the duration of the proceedings; **für die ~ e-s laufenden Monats** for the duration of one continuous month; **für die ~ von** for a period of.

Daumenabdruck *m* thumb-mark (*left accidentally*), thumb-print (*police*).

dazwischentreten *v/i* to interfere with, to intervene, to supervene.

debellatio (=) complete conquest (of a defeated state).

Debet *n* debit (side); ~**buchung** debit-entry; ~**note** debit note; ~**posten** debit item; ~**saldo** debit balance, balance due, balance payable; ~~ *abdecken*: *to cover a short account*; ~~ *stehen lassen*: *to leave a balance to one's debit*; ~**spalte** debit column; ~**zins** interest on debit balance; **als ~posten buchen** to debit; **bank-übliche ~zinsen** normal bank interest on debit balances.

debitieren *v/t* to debit, to charge.

Debitor *m* debtor (*bookkeeping*).

Debitoren *pl* accounts receivable, receivables; ~ **aus Wechselforderungen** = ~ *aus Wechseln qv*; ~ **aus Wechseln** bills receivable; ~**buch** customers' ledger, sales ledger; ~**buchhalter** accounts receivable clerk; ~**buchhaltung** accounts receivable department (*US*); ~**geschäft** lending (business), advances and overdrafts; ~**guthaben** accounts receivable; ~**konto** debtor-account; ~**kredit** accounts receivable loan; ~**risiko** default risk; ~**saldo** balance payable; ~**sätze** lending rates; ~**verkauf** factoring, selling accounts receivable outright; ~**verluste** bad debt losses, losses on receivables; ~**versicherung** trade credit insurance, accounts receivable insurance; ~**wagnis** accounts receivable risk; ~**ziehung** bill drawn on debtor, promissory note issued by debtor; **zedierter ~bestand** assigned accounts receivable.

deblockieren *v/t* to unfreeze.

dechiffrieren *v/t* to decode, to decipher.

Deck|adresse *f* a cover address, accommodation address; ~**mantel** cloak, disguise, veil; ~**name** assumed name, fictitious name, alias, nom de plume, pseudonym.

decken *v/t* to cover (*losses*), to provide cover for (*debit balance*), to secure; to shield (*an offender*); *v|reflex* to be coextensive with, to meet.

Deckoffizier *m* warrant officer.

Decks|güter deck-stowed goods; ~**ladung** *f* deck-cargo, deck-load; ~**verladung** shipment on deck.

Deckung *f* cover, security, collateral backing (*credit*), ~ **anschaffen** to supply funds to cover (a cheque); ~ **des Krankheitsrisikos** sickness cover; ~ **e-s Verlusts** (the) covering of a loss; ~ **von Risiken** cover of risks; **anteilige ~ bei Sammelpolice** pro rata distribution on a collective policy; **bankmäßige ~** collateral accepted by banks; **keine ~** no funds (*on an account*), not covered; no (insurance) cover; **mangelnde ~** returned for want of funds (*cheque*); **mangels ~** for want of cover, for want of funds, for want of provision; **ohne ~ sein** to be without cover, to be without funds in hand; **ohne ~ verkaufen** *exch* to sell short; **volle ~** full cover; **vorläufige ~** *ins* provisional cover; **ungenügende ~** insufficient cover.

Deckungs|anschaffung provision of cover; **~aufstockungsklausel** topping-up clause; **~auftrag** covering order; **~beitrag** contribution, variable gross margin, profit contribution, marginal (variable gross) income; **~beschaffer** purveyor of cover; **~darlehen** loan needed as a cover; **~fonds wegen Umstellungskosten** fund to cover conversion costs; **~forderung** covering claim; *claims on Government held in trust for savers compensated for losses through Currency Reform*; **~frist** *ins* duration of cover; **~geschäft** hedging transaction; **~grenze** required margin of cover, (lower) cover limit; **~guthaben** covering balance; **~hypothek** mortgage investment as insurance reserve, mortgage loan serving as cover; **~kapital** *ins* policy reserve, unearned premium reserve, actuarial reserve, balance sheet reserves (*US*); *das versicherungsmathematisch berechnete ~~*: *the actuarially calculated policy reserve*; **~kauf** *exch* covering purchase, short covering, buying in, purchase of goods in replacement; **~klausel** cover clause; **~kongruenz** correctness of cover; **~konto** cover account, balance serving as cover; **~lücke** deficit (*budget*); **~masse** cover(ing) fund, fund formed to cover specified liabilities; **~mittel** resources, cover, covering funds (*available to meet liabilities*), covering resources; *ordentliche ~~*: *ordinary budget receipts*; *ungeeignete ~~*: *non-admitted assets*; **~order** covering order; **~prämie** net level annual premium; **~quote** cover ratio; **~register** cover register; **~rücklage** insurance reserve, unearned premium reserve; **~satz** reserve ratio, cover ratio; **~schutz** insurance protection; **~sicherheit** collateral security, insurance reserve; **~stock** *ins* premium reserve stock, cover fund, reserve value fund, unearned premium reserve; guarantee stock (*building society*); **~stockfähig** *adj* eligible for premium reserve stock; **~stockfähigkeit** eligibility for investment in premium reserve stock; **~stockprinzip** principle of providing a premium reserve, cover fund principle; **~summe** *ins* insured sum, amount insured, amount covered; **~verhältnis** cover ratio (*currency to gold, foreign exchange*); (*ins*) *gesetzlich vorgeschriebenes ~~*: *legal reserve requirements*; **~verkauf** hedging sale, covering sale, resale of goods by unpaid seller; **~vorsorge** provisions for sufficient cover; **~währung** currency serving as cover; **~werte** covering assets; **~zusage** cover note, binding receipt; *vorläufige ~~*: *interim cover note, binder, binding slip*; (*ins*); **~zuschuß** additional cover.

Découvert *n* uncovered position.

Delcredere *n* collection guarantee.

Defektenverfahren *n* recover (of a deficiency) procedure.

Defensiv|bündnis *n* defensive alliance; **~streik** negative strike; **~zeichen** *n* defensive trade-mark (*registered to ward off similar signs*).

definieren *v/t* to define; **recht generell ~** to define in fairly general terms.

definiert *adj* defined, expressed in terms of.

definitorisch *adj*, *adv* definitional, by definition, in defined terms.

Defizit *n* deficit, short, shortfall, shortage, adverse variance; **~ der Dienstleistungsbilanz** deficit on services, shortfall on invisible ac-

defizitär / **Deliktsanspruch**

count; ~ **der Zahlungsbilanz** external deficit, deficit on balance of payments; ~**finanzierung** deficit financing, deficit spending; ~**haushalt** budget showing a deficit, adverse budget, budget in deficit; ~**politik** policy of deficit financing, deficit (budgeting) policy; ~**wirtschaft** deficit financing; **aus dem** ~ **kommen** to get out of the red; **budgetmäßiges** ~ budget deficit; **mit e-m** ~ **abschließen** to show a (final) deficit.

defizitär *adj* in deficit.

Deflation *f* deflation; ~**sdruck** deflationary pressure.

Deflationismus *m* deflationism, deflationary policy.

deflationistisch *adj* deflationary, deflationist.

degradieren *v/t* to degrade, to demote, to reduce to the ranks.

Degradierung *f* degradation, demotion, reduction to the ranks.

Degressivsteuer *f* degressive tax.

Deich *m* dike, dyke; ~**amt** dike authority; ~**aufseher** dike master; ~**genossenschaft** dike association; ~**geschworene** sworn dike inspectors; ~**graf** "dyke-reed", dike master; ~**hauptmann** dike master; ~**ordnung** dike ordinances, dike law; ~**polizei** dike police; ~**recht** dike-law, legislation concerning dikes; ~**verband** dike district corporation; ~**wesen** diking, matters concerning dikes and embankments.

Dekartellisierung (= *Dekartellierung*) *f* decartelization (*of German industry after World War II*).

Deklaration *f* (customs) declaration, declaring (*dutiable goods*); ~ **für zollfreie Waren** entry for duty-free goods; ~ **zur Einlagerung unter Zollverschluß** warehousing entry.

Deklarations|etikett declaration label; ~**pflicht** obligation to declare; ~**schein** declaration certificate; ~**wert** declared value, value at point of entry; ~**zwang** compulsory declaration.

deklaratorisch *adj* declaratory, declarative (*not operative, outward*).

deklarieren *v/t* to declare (*dutiable goods*); *nicht deklariert:* unentered; **zollamtlich** ~ to declare officially (to the customs authority).

Dekonzentration *f* deconcentration, dispersal; ~ **von Vermögenswerten** dispersal of assets.

Dekorateur *m* decorator, interior decorator, curtain fitter; window-dresser, display artist; set designer.

Dekoration *f* window display, window dressing; set (*TV, motion pictures*).

Dekret *n* decree, (*imperial, royal*) order, ordinance.

dekretieren *v/t* to decree, to order (by decree), to ordain.

Dekulpation *f* diminished criminal responsibility.

Delegation *f* delegation deputation; (*act of*) delegating (*authority*); ~**sbefugnis** power of substitution; ~**sführer** head of a delegation; ~**sleiter** head of the delegation; ~ **von Kompetenzen** delegation of authority; **öffentlich-rechtliche** ~ delegation under public law (*or* by a public authority).

delegieren *v/t* to delegate.

Delegierter *m* (*der Delegierte*) delegate, deputy.

Delegierung *f* → *Delegation (2)*.

deliberalisieren *v/t* to deliberalize, to reimpose restrictions.

Deliberalisierung *f* deliberalization.

Delikt *n* offence (*US: offense*), tort, tortious act, civil wrong; **fortgesetztes** ~ continued offence; **geringfügiges** ~ petty offence; **politisches** ~ political offence; **seerechtliches** ~ admiralty offence maritime; **sittlich verwerfliches** ~ offence involving moral turpitude; **verwandte** ~**e** related offences; **völkerrechtswidriges** ~ offence under international law; **zivilrechtliches** ~ actionable tort.

Delikts|anspruch tort claim, tortious claim; **d~fähig** *capable of tortious liability (age requirement etc)*; ~**fähigkeit** *capacity for tortious* lia-

deliktisch / **Denaturalisierung**

bility (*age requirement etc*); **~haftung** liability in tort; **~handlung** tortious act; **~klage** tort action; **~ort** place where the offence took place, scene of the crime; **~statut** lex loci delicti (commissi), *the law of the place where the crime took place*.

deliktisch *adj* tortious.

Delinquent *m* offender, delinquent.

Delkredere *n* del credere guarantee; **~agent** del credere agent; **~fonds** contingent fund as del credere security; **~geschäft** del credere business; **~haftung** del credere liability; **~klausel** del credere clause (*providing for del credere liability of agent*); **~konto** provision for doubtful debts, contingent account for del credere agents; **~provision** del credere commission; **~reserve** = *Delkredererückstellung qv*; **~risiko** collection risk; **~rückstellung** (general) contingency reserve, bad debts reserve (*for del credere liability*); **~ stellen** to stand del credere, to stand security; **~und Vertrauensschadenversicherung** commercial insurance, credit insurance; **~versicherung** accounts receivable insurance, credit insurance, doubtful debts insurance; **~vertrag** del credere agreement (*with agent or broker*); **~wertberichtigung** allowance for doubtful accounts; **das ~ übernehmen** to stand del credere.

Démarche *f* formal diplomatic step, démarche.

Demarkations|linie line of demarcation; **~vertrag** demarcation agreement (*between electricity companies*).

Dementi *n* official denial.

dementieren *v/t* to deny (officially); to disown; **etwas förmlich ~** to issue an official denial.

Demenz *f med jur* dementia, idiocy.

demgemäß *adv* pursuant.

Demission *f* resignation (*from office*); **seine ~ einreichen**: *to tender one's resignation*.

demobilisieren *v/t* to demobilize.

Demobilisierung *f* demobilization.

Demobilmachung *f* demobilization, demob.

Demographie *f* demography.

demographisch *adj* (= *demografisch*) demographic.

Demokrat *m* democrat.

Demokratie *f* democracy; **mittelbare ~** = *repräsentative ~ qv*; **parlamentarische ~** parliamentary democracy; **plebiszitäre ~** plebiscitary democracy; **repräsentative ~** representative democracy; **unmittelbare ~** direct democracy.

demokratisch *adj* democratic; **~es Mehrheitssystem** democratic majority rule.

demokratisieren *v/t* to democratize, to make (*a country etc*) (more) democratic.

Demokratisierung *f* democratization; **~sprozess** process of democratization.

demonetisieren *v/t* to demonetize (*metal etc*), to withdraw from circulation, to deprive of the status of money.

Demonetisierung *f* demonetization, withdrawal from circulation (*coin*).

Demonstrant *f* demonstrator.

Demonstration *f* demonstration, manifestation; **~srecht** right to demonstrate publicly; **~sschäden** damage caused by demonstrations, riot damage.

demonstrieren *v/i* to demonstrate, to hold a demonstration; *v/t* to establish (*the truth of a proposition*).

Demontage *f pol* dismantling (*of heavy industry in occupied Germany after 1945*); **~liste** dismantling list; **~maßnahmen** dismantling measures.

demontieren *v/t* to dismantle.

Demoskopie *f* public opinion research, opinion polls.

Denaturalisation *f* denaturalization (*depriving of citizenship*).

denaturalisieren *v/t* to denaturalize, to withdraw s. o.'s citizenship (*or* nationality).

Denaturalisierung *f* → *Denaturalisation*.

denaturieren v/t to denature (*alcohol*); pervert the nature of.

Denaturierung f denaturing (*alcohol*).

Denkgesetze n/pl rules of logic.

Denkmal n (ancient) monument, public monument; ~**schutz** protection of ancient monuments; *unter ~schutz stellen: to preserve as a historical site*; ~**schutzgesetz** Act for the protection of ancient monuments.

Denkschrift f memorandum.

Denunziant m informer.

Denunziation f denunciation.

denunzieren v/t to denounce, to inform (*the police*).

Deponent m depositor (*of money in bank*), bailor (*for safe-keeping*).

Deponie f (refuse) dump; dumping; **wilde ~** indiscriminate dumping.

deponieren v/t to deposit, to hand over for safe-keeping, to lodge.

Deponierung f lodgment, deposition; dumping.

Deport m *exch* backwardation, forward discount; ~**satz** backwardation rate, forward discount.

Deportation f deportation.

deportieren v/t to deport; v/i *exch* to do backwardation business.

Deportierung f deportation.

Depositar m depositary.

Depositen pl (*obs term for Einlagen qv*) deposits (in a bank), deposited funds; ~**anstalt** commercial bank, deposit bank; ~**bank** commercial bank, deposit bank; ~**geschäft** deposit banking; ~**heft** deposit book; ~**kasse** deposit bank, deposit bank branch; ~**konto** deposit account; ~**schein** deposit receipt; ~**versicherung** (bank) deposit insurance; ~**volumen** total deposits; ~**zertifikat** certificate of deposit; ~**zinsen** deposit interest; **befristete ~** time deposits, fixed term deposits; **sofort fällige ~** demand deposits.

depositum regulare (=) regular deposit (of specific goods), regular security deposit, bailment.

Depot n securities deposit, safe custody; depot; ~**abteilung** safe-custody; department, securities (deposit) department; ~**aktien** deposited shares; ~**aufstellung** statement of securities (deposited); ~**auszug** statement of deposit, list of deposited securities, statement of securities; ~**bank** *bank at which securities etc. are deposited*, custodian bank, depositary bank; ~**berechtigter** depositor, party entitled to deposit; ~**bescheinigung** deposit certificate; ~**besitz** deposit holding securities; ~**bewertung** portfolio analysis; ~**brief** letter of deposit; ~**buch** deposit ledger, securities ledger; ~**buchhaltung** safe-deposit accounting; ~**gebühr** custody account charge; ~**geschäft** safe-deposit service; ~**gesetz** Securities Deposit Act; ~**inhaber** depositor, person entitled to a safe-deposit; ~**konto** safe-custody account, security deposit account, custodianship account; ~**kosten** safe-custody charges; ~**kunde** securities account holder, customer holding securities on deposit; ~**pflicht** → *Bardepotpflicht*; ~**prüfung** audit of safe-custody holdings (*by official auditors annually*); ~**quittung** safe-custody receipt; ~**schein** certificate of deposit; deposit slip, safe custody receipt; ~**steuer** bank deposit tax; ~**stimmrecht** proxy voting power for deposited shares (*held by banks*); ~**stück** security or item deposited (*at authorized depository, i.e. bank*); ~**unterlagen** documents relating to safe custody; ~**unterschlagung** misappropriation of deposited securities; ~ **unter Streifband** → *Streifbanddepot*; ~**verpfändung** pledge of securities deposited (*by a debtor with his bank*); ~**versicherung** deposit insurance; ~**vertrag** safe-custody agreement (*with a bank*); ~**verwaltung** administration of deposited items; ~**wechsel** bill of exchange deposited (*with a bank*) as collateral; **im ~** in the safe-custody department; **offenes ~** open deposit (*bank arranges for collection of dividends*).

Deputat *n* allowance in kind (*in addition to wages*), remuneration in kind, non-cash remuneration; ~**kohle** free coal *for mine workers*; ~**wohnung** company-owned housing, tied cottage.

Deputation *f* delegation.

Deputierter *m* (*der Deputierte*) deputy, delegate.

Deregulierung *f* deregulation.

derelinquieren *v/t* to abandon (the ownership of) movable goods.

Dereliktion *f* dereliction, voluntary abandonment of goods.

dergleichen *pron*, such, such like.

Derogation *f* derogation *part-repeal of a statute and replacement by another enactment*.

derogieren *v/t* to repeal and replace parts of a statute.

Deroute *f* collapse of the market, slump, a free fall (of share prices).

deroutieren *v/t obs* to throw into confusion, to upset (the market).

derzeitig *adj* present, presently subsisting, actual; *die ~en Verhältnisse*: *the present state of affairs*.

Designation *f* designation; ~**srecht** right of designation; right of proposal.

designieren *v/t* to designate; *der designierte Botschafter*: *the ambassador designate*.

Desinflation *f* disinflation.

Desinteresse *n* hands-off attitude, unconcern, lack of interest, indifference.

Destinatär *m* beneficiary of an endowment.

Deszendent *m* descendant.

Detail|**geschäft** retail shop, retail trade; ~**handel** (*obs for Einzelhandel*) retail trade; ~**preis** retail price; ~**schilderung** detailed description.

detaillieren *v/t* to give (*or* to state) full particulars, to specify.

Detektiv *m* detective, plain clothes man, *colloq* sleuth, dick, undercoverman; ~**büro** detective agency.

deutlichkeitshalber *adv* for the sake of clarity.

Deutscher *m* (*der Deutsche*) German, German national, German subject.

Deutscher Bund *m* German Federation (1815–1866) (*created at Congress of Vienna*).

Deutscher Einheitsmietvertrag *m* German standard tenancy agreement.

Deutscher Gemeindetag *m Congress of German local communities*.

Deutscher Gewerkschaftsbund *m* (*DGB*) German Trade Union Federation.

Deutscher Industrie- und Handelstag *m* (*DIHT*) German Industrial and Trade Association (*chambers of industry and commerce*).

Deutscher Paritätischer Wohlfahrtsverband German Non-denominational Welfare Association.

Deutscher Richtertag (=) *Congress of German Judges*.

Deutscher Städtetag *m* German Cities' Assembly, Assembly of County Boroughs.

Deutscher Wetterdienst German Meteorological Service.

Deutsches Hydrographisches Institut German Hydrographic Institute.

Deutsches Institut für Medizinische Dokumentation und Information German Institute for Medical Documentation and Information.

Deutsches Müttergenesungswerk The German Mothers' Convalescence and Recuperation Scheme.

Deutsches Nationalkomitee für Internationale Jugendarbeit German National Committee for International Youth Work.

Deutsches Patentamt German Patent Office.

Deutsches Reich *n hist* German Reich (Empire), *Holy Roman Empire; also: the Weimar Republic and Germany 1933–1945*.

Deutsches Rotes Kreuz German Red Cross.

Deutschland *n* Germany (*as a whole*); ~**vertrag** Bonn Convention of 26 May 1952 (*ending occupation status*), German Treaty.

Devastationsklage *f action to prevent deterioration of mortgaged property*.
Deviation *f* deviation from route *(maritime law)*.
Devisen *pl* foreign currency, foreign exchange; ~**abfluß** loss of foreign currency; ~**abkommen** foreign exchange agreement; ~**berechnung** foreign exchange settlement; ~**arbitrage** foreign arbitrage; ~**ausgang** foreign exchange expenditure; ~**ausgleichsabkommen** offset agreement; ~**ausgleichsfond** exchange equalization fund (account); ~**ausländer** non-resident *(for purposes of exchange control)*; ~**behörde** exchange control authority; ~**belastung** burden on the foreign exchange position; ~**bescheinigung** foreign exchange certificate; ~**beschränkung** exchange restriction; ~**bestände** exchange holdings; ~**bestimmungen** exchange regulations; ~**bewirtschaftung** foreign exchange control; ~**bilanz** balance of foreign exchange payments; ~**bonus** percentage allowance for earners of foreign currency; ~**börse** foreign exchange market; ~**eigenhandel** foreign exchange dealings for (bank's) own account; ~**eingangsmeldung** notification of foreign exchange received; ~**einnahmen** foreign exchange proceeds; ~**erleichterung** easing of foreign exchange restrictions; ~**freibetrag** foreign currency allowance; ~**freigrenze** free quota of foreign exchange; ~**genehmigung** foreign exchange permit *or* licence; ~**geschäft** transaction in foreign exchange; ~**gesetze** foreign exchange laws; ~**guthaben** foreign exchange holdings; ~**handel** currency trading, foreign exchange dealings; *intervalutarischer* ~~: *cross-exchange dealings, multi-lateral exchange dealings*; ~**händler** foreign exchange dealer; ~**haushalt** foreign exchange position, foreign exchange receipts and expenditure; ~**inländer** resident, foreigner permanently resident in Germany *(for purposes of exchange control)*; ~**kassageschäft** exchange for spot delivery, spot exchange transaction; ~**kassahandel** spot business in foreign exchange, spot exchange dealing; ~**kassakurs** spot exchange rate; ~**knappheit** shortage of foreign exchange; ~**kontingent** foreign exchange quota; ~**kontingentierung** foreign exchange rationing; ~**konto** foreign currency account; ~**kontrolle** foreign exchange control; ~ ~(*an der Grenze*) *currency check at border*; ~**kontrollerklärung** exchange control declaration; ~**kredite** foreign currency loans; ~**kurs** exchange rate, *pl also*: foreign exchange rates; currency rates, *freier* ~~: *free rate (of exchange)*; *gespaltener* ~~: *two-tiered exchange rate*; ~**kurszettel** list of foreign exchange, foreign exchange list; ~**lage** foreign exchange position; ~**makler** foreign exchange broker, foreign broker; ~**mangel** shortage of foreign exchange; ~**markt** (foreign) exchange market; ~**plafond** foreign exchange limit (*or* ceiling); **d**~**politisch** according to foreign exchange policies; ~**polster** foreign exchange cushion; ~**portefeuille** foreign currency holding; ~**position** foreign exchange position; ~**positionsmeldung** exchange position return; ~**recht** foreign exchange law; **d**~**rechtlich** according to exchange regulations; under foreign exchange control law; ~~ *genehmigt*: *approved by exchange control authority*; ~**reportgeschäft** swap; ~**reserven** foreign currency reserves, ~**sachen** foreign exchange matters; ~**schieber** illegal currency dealer; ~**schiebung** illegal foreign exchange transaction, currency racket; ~**schmuggel** currency smuggling; ~**schwankungen** fluctuations of exchange (rate); ~**spekulationsgewinn** profit on foreign exchange speculation; ~**spielraum** available foreign ex-

Devolutionsrecht — **dienen**

change (fluctuation-) margin; ~**stabilisierungsfonds** exchange stabilization fund; ~**stelle** exchange control agency; ~**strafrecht** penal foreign currency law; ~**tausch** switch in foreign currencies; ~**termingeschäft** forward (foreign)-exchange transaction; ~**transfer** currency transfer; ~~~**risiko**; *transfer risk*; ~**verkehr** foreign exchange (transactions); ~**überlassungsquote** quota of foreign exchange to be surrendered; ~**überwachung** exchange control; ~**überwachungsstelle** exchange control office; ~**verfügbarkeit** availability of foreign currency; ~**vergehen** currency offence, violation of foreign exchange regulations; ~**verkehr** foreign exchange transactions; ~**verkehrsbeschränkungen** foreign exchange restrictions; ~**vorleistung** advance of funds in foreign currency; ~**vorschriften** exchange rules, currency requirements; ~**währung** currency-exchange standard; ~**wechsel** bill in foreign currency; ~**wertberichtigung** foreign exchange adjustment; ~**werte** foreign exchange assets; d~**wirtschaftlich** *adj* from a foreign exchange point of view; foreign-exchange ...; ~**zufluß** inflow of foreign currency; ~**zugang** accrual of foreign currency; ~**zuteilung** exchange allowance, foreign exchange allocation; ~~ *für Reisezwecke*: travel allowance; ~**zuteilungsbestätigung** confirmed allocation of foreign exchange; ~**zuwiderhandlungen** violations of foreign exchange regulations; ~**zwangswirtschaft** exchange control.

Devolutionsrecht *m* chief prosecutor's right to take over the proceedings.

Devotionalien *f/pl* religious articles.

Dezentralisation *f* decentralization, regionalization.

dezentralisieren *v/t* to decentralize, to regionalize.

Dezernat *n* (administrative) department, section (*of police department*).

Dezernent *m* chief of a section, departmental head.

Diagramm *n* diagram, scheme.

Diäten *pl* emolument of members of parliament (*including sessional expense allowance*), per diem allowances.

Dichotomie *f* dichotomy, classification of offences.

Dichtkunst *f* creative writing, literature; **dramatische** ~ drama.

Dieb *m* thief; **gewerbsmäßiger** ~ common thief, professional thief; **kleiner** ~ petty thief, pilferer; **vermeintlicher** ~ reputed thief, presumed thief.

Dieberei *f* (habitual) thievery.

Diebes|bande pack of thieves; ~**gut** stolen goods, loot (of thieves); **d~sicher** thief-proof, burglar-proof; ~**werkzeug** thieves' tools and instruments.

Diebin *f* (female) thief.

diebisch *adj* thievish, thieving.

Diebstahl *m* theft, larceny, stealing; ~ **aus Transportgut** pilfering; ~ **e-r Erfindung** piracy of an invention; ~ **geistigen Eigentums** → *geistiger* ~; ~ **im zweiten Rückfall** larceny recidivism (*second repeated offence of theft*); ~ **in flagranti** open theft; theft in flagranti; ~**sicherung** anti-theft device; ~ **von Genußmitteln** petty theft of consumables; **einfacher** ~ theft, plain theft, simple larceny; **geistiger** ~ theft of ideas, plagiarism, literary theft, piracy; **geringfügiger** ~ petty theft; **räuberischer** ~ theft accompanied by violence, mugging; **schwerer** ~ compound larceny, aggravated theft (*or* larceny).

Diebstahls|risiko pilferage and theft risk; ~**sicherung** anti-theft measures; ~**sucht** kleptomania; ~**versicherung** theft insurance; ~**vorsatz** intent to steal, animus furandi.

dienen *v/i* to serve, to be of service (*to s.o.*), to be in service (*as a domes-*

tic servant), to serve (*in the Army, Navy etc.*).

Diener *m* servant, attendant (*dipl.*), domestic servant, manservant.

dienlich *adj* useful, conducive (*to a purpose*), helpful.

Dienst *m* service; ~**abzeichen** service mark; ~**alter** length of service, years of service, job seniority, seniority in rank; *höheres* ~~: *seniority*; *nach dem* ~~: *according to seniority*; **d~älter** *adj* senior; ~**altersstufe** grade of seniority; ~**alterszulage** seniority allowance; ~**angelegenheit** official matter; ~**antritt** commencement of duties; *bei* ~*antritt*: *on taking up one's duties*; ~**anweisung** standing instructions, staff regulations, office circular; ~**aufsicht** supervision (*of a public authority*); ~**aufsichtsbehörde** inspectorate, superior authority; ~**aufsichtsbeschwerde** complaint about the conduct of an official, disciplinary complaint; ~**auftrag** official order; ~**aufwandsentschädigung** expense allowance (*for public servant*); ~**ausübung** discharge of duty; ~**ausweis** official identification card (*of public servant*); official pass, identity card; ~**barkeit** → *Dienstbarkeit*; ~**befehl** official order; ~**befreiung** (*mil.*) leave of absence; ~**behinderung** obstruction of an official; ~**behörde** public authority; *oberste* ~~: *top-level authority*; ~**berechtigter** person entitled to the services of another; ~**bereich** jurisdiction of an official, sphere of competence; ~**bereitschaft** (readiness for) service, stand-by-duty; ~**besprechung** (staff) conference; ~**bezeichnung** official title; ~**bezüge** remuneration of an official, official emoluments (*salary including allowances of public servant*); *ruhegehaltsfähige* ~~: *pensionable emoluments*; ~**bote** servant, domestic help; ~**e anbieten** to offer services; ~**eid** oath of office, official oath; ~**einkommen** earnings (of public servant), emoluments;

~**einsatzplan** duty roster; ~**e leisten** to render services; ~**enthebung** dismissal, suspension from service; ~**entlassung** dismissal (from service), discharge; ~**entziehung** deprivation of services; ~**erfindung** employee invention; ~**erfüllung** performance of one's duties; ~**erschwerung** impediment to the exercise of one's duties; ~**fahrt** official journey, official (or business) trip; ~**fahrzeug** service vehicle; ~**flagge** official flag; ~**gang** errand (*by employee or official*); ~**gebäude** official quarters; ~**gebrauch** official use, *nur für den* ~~: *for official use only, restricted matter*; ~**geheimnis** official secret; ~**gericht** disciplinary tribunal; ~**geschäfte** official business; ~**gespräch** official call, business call; ~**grad** grade (*civil servant*), rank (*soldier, officer*); ~**gradabzeichen** badge of rank, rank marking; ~**gradherabsetzung** demotion, degrading; ~**grundstück** official compound, office premises; **d~habend** *adj* on duty, in charge, desk (*officer*); ~**handlung** official act; ~**herr** employer, master; ~**jahre** years of service; ~**jubiläum** long-service anniversary; ~**kleidung** uniform; ~**kräfte** staff, personnel; ~**kraftfahrzeug** service vehicle; ~**leistung** → *Dienstleistung*; ~**liste** roster; ~**lohn** wages, pay; ~ **nach Vorschrift** work to rule (*auch*: ~ *streng nach Vorschrift*); ~**ordnung** service regulations, staff regulations: *allgemeine* ~~: *general service regulations*; ~**ordnungsvorschrift** a rule under official regulations; ~**ort** station, location of official functions; ~**person** servant, staff member; ~**personal** personnel; ~**pflicht** official duty, public duty, conscription; *von seinen* ~~*en entbinden*: *to suspend s.o. from office*; ~**pflichtiger** draftee, person liable to do military service (*or other public service*); ~**pflichtverletzung** violation of official duty; ~**plan** job/

Dienstposten duty roster, list of work assignments; time-table; **~posten** official position (in the service); **~rang** (seniority in) rank; **~rangliste** seniority list; **~räume** official quarters, official premises; **~recht** service regulations; **~reise** travelling on official business, official tour, business trip; **~sache** official business, official matter; *gebührenpflichtige ~~: (auf Briefen)* = *on Her Majesty's service* (O.H.M.S.); *geheime ~~ classified as secret*; **~siegel** official seal, seal of office; **~stelle** (administrative) office, government agency, official agency, *ausführende ~~: implementing agency, leitende ~~: executive office, staatliche ~~: government agency*; **~stellung** position; *pensionsberechtigte ~~: pensionable office*; **~stempel** official stamp; **~strafe** disciplinary penalty; **~strafgerichte** disciplinary tribunal; **~strafkammer** disciplinary court (for officials); **~strafordnung** disciplinary rules; **~strafrecht** disciplinary law; **~strafverfahren** disciplinary proceedings; **~stunden** hours of attendance, office hours; **d~tauglich** fit for military service; *für ~~ erklären: to pass for military service*; **~telegramm** service telegram; **d~tuend** adj serving on duty; **~umschlag** official envelope; *frankierter ~~: prepaid official envelope, penalty envelope (US)*, **d~unfähig** unfit for service; **~unfähigkeit** unfitness for service, inability to work; **~unfall** accident while on duty; **d~untauglich** unfit for military service; **~untauglichkeit** unfitness for military service; **~unterbrechung** interruption of official work; **~vereinbarung** agreement with staff representation; **~verfehlung** official misconduct; **~vergehen** offence against regulations, neglect of duty, disciplinary offence: *offence committed while acting in an official capacity*; **~verhältnis** employment, employer-employee relationship; **~vermerk** official entry, official memo; **~verpflichtung** requisition order, engagement for (compulsory) services; **~versäumnis** neglect of duty; absence from duty; **~verschaffungsvertrag** contract for the procurement of services; **~verschwiegenheit** official discretion, confidentiality, secrecy; **~vertrag** contract of services (*to client, patient etc*); contract of service (*by employees*), contract of employment; **~vorgesetzter** superior official, supervisor; **~vorschriften** internal regulations; **~vorschuß** business-expense advance; **~weg** official channels, usual channels, the proper channels; **~widrigkeit** irregularity (*of a public servant*); acting contrary to the regulations; **~wohnung** official quarters, company-owned apartment, tied cottage, service occupancy; **~zeit** official hours, office (or business) hours, attendance hours, hours of service; length (or period) of service, term of office; *anwartschaftsberechtigte ~~: qualifying service, ruhegehaltsfähige ~~: time of service recognized for pension rights*; **~bescheinigung** certificate of time of (military or equivalent) service; **~versorgung** transitional financial support for ex-servicemen; **~zeugnis** testimonial, reference (*for a public servant*); **~zulage** service bonus, salary increase; **anwaltschaftliche ~e** professional services (of a lawyer); **aus dem ~ entlassen** to dismiss from office, to discharge; **außer ~** off duty; **außer ~ stellen** to lay up, to put out of service (*ship*); **dem ~ fernbleiben** to absent oneself from work; **den ~ antreten** to take up duties; **die Guten ~e** good offices (*international relations*); **diplomatischer ~** diplomatic service; **einfacher ~** subclerical class; **e-n ~ erweisen** to render a service; **e-n ~leisten** to render a service; **entgangene ~e** loss of services; **freiberufliche ~e** free-lance services; **für den öffentlichen ~ qualifiziert sein** to

Dienstbarkeit / **Differenzierung**

qualify for a civil service position; **gehobener** ~ executive class; **geleistete** ~**e** services rendered; **höherer** ~ administrative class (*university graduates*); **im** ~ on duty; **im** ~ **bewährt** with creditable records, of proven ability, time-tested; **in** ~ **stellen** to put into service (*ship*); **konsularischer** ~ consular service; **mittlerer** ~ clerical class; **neutralitätswidrige** ~**e** services in breach of neutrality; **öffentlicher** ~ public service, civil service; **seine** ~**e anbieten** to offer one's services; **sich zum** ~ **melden** to report for duty; **technischer** ~ technical service; **unentgeltliche** ~**e** gratuitous service; **vorläufig vom** ~ **entheben** to suspend from public service.

Dienstbarkeit *f* servitude, easement; subservience; **beschränkt persönliche** ~ restricted easement, easement for the benefit of an individual (*does not run with the land*); **negative** ~ negative servitude; **persönliche** ~ personal servitude; **positive** ~ affirmative (*or* positive) servitude.

Dienstleistung service, *pl.* services rendered; ~**en erbringen** to render services; **gebührenpflichtige** ~**en** services against charge, sold support; **der zur** ~ **Verpflichtete** person under the obligation to render a service; **fremde** ~**en** purchased services; **häusliche** ~ domestic services; **passive** ~**en** services rendered by aliens (*in the foreign country*); **pensionsanwartschaftsberechtigende** ~**en** pensionable services; **persönliche** ~**en** personal services; **seemännische** ~ maritime service;

Dienstleistungs|bereich service sector; ~**abend** late night closing for (shopping and) public services; ~**beruf** service (-rendering) occupation; ~**betrieb** service (rendering) business, utility undertaking (*electricity company*); ~**bilanz** balance of service transactions, net services, net invisibles; *Saldo der*

~~: *net position on services; Überschüsse in der* ~~: *surpluses arising from net services*; ~**geschäft** service transactions; ~**geschäfte** sale of services, service transactions; ~**gewerbe** service (rendering) business, service-rendering sector; service industries; ~**handwerk** service-rendering handicraft enterprises; ~**körperschaft** (personal) service corporation; ~**kosten** cost of materials and services; ~**marke** service mark; ~**pflicht** obligation to perform services; ~**unternehmen** establishment for the provision of services; service-rendering enterprise; ~**verkehr** services transactions, *aktiver* ~~: *services rendered by residents; passiver* ~~: *residents' use of foreigners' services; freier* ~~: *freedom of provision of services;* ~**vertrag** service contract; ~**wirtschaft** services industry.

dienstlich *adj* official; *adv* in an official capacity.

diesbezüglich *adj* as regards this, with reference to this, referenced (*US*).

Dietrich *m* pick-lock, skeleton key.

diffamieren *v/t* to bring into disrepute, to defame, to calumniate.

Diffamierung *f* defamation, slander, calumny.

Differential|kostenspanne cost differential; ~**zoll** discriminating duty, differential duty.

Differenz|abgabe (*EG*) differential charge; ~**betrag** residual balance (*or* quantity); ~**gebühr** differential fee (*between two scale brackets*); ~**geschäft** margin business, marginal trading, gambling in futures, wagering transaction; ~**handel** margin business, marginal trading, gambling in futures; ~**lohn** differential pay; ~**zahlung** marginal payment, payment of the balance of an account.

differenzieren *v/i* to differentiate.

Differenzierung *f* differentiation, variation; ~**sverbot** prohibition of discrimination (*due to sex, race, descent, religion, faith*); **branchen-**

mäßige ~ variation as between different trades or industries.

differieren v/i to differ, to be of a different opinion.

Diktat n pol (1) dictate, (2) dictation; **~frieden** dictated peace; **~zeichen** reference number (or initials); **nach ~ genehmigt** (n.D.g.) approved as dictated; **nach ~ verreist** dictated by ... and signed in his absence, dictated but not signed.

Diktator m dictator.

Diktatur f dictatorship.

Diktion f diction, phraseology.

dilatorisch adj dilatory.

Dimensionsaufpreis m extra charge for size.

DIN-Vorschriften (DIN-) standard rules (of German Official Standards Committee)).

dinglich adj real, in rem; adv: **~ gesichert**: secured by property (pledge, mortgage etc.).

Dinglichkeit f reality, in rem quality.

Diplom n diploma, degree; **ein ~ verleihen**: to award a diploma; **~-Ingenieur** graduate engineer; **~-Kaufmann** Master of Business Administration (MBA); bachelor of commerce; **~-Landwirt** graduate in agriculture; **~volkswirt** graduate economist.

Diplomat m diplomat, diplomatic agent, diplomatist.

Diplomaten|bezüge diplomat's salary (or emoluments); **~paß** diplomatic passport, diplomat's passport; **~sichtvermerk** visa for diplomatic officials.

Diplomatisches Korps n diplomatic corps, corps diplomatique.

Direkt|absatz direct selling; **~bezug** direct purchasing (from suppliers); **~einkauf** direct buying; **~forderung** direct claim, immediate demand; **~geschäft** direct transaction (without intermediaries); **~händler** dealer (selling directly without agents); **~investitionen** direct investments; **~kredit** direct lending (by government agencies), direct loan (credit); **~schuldner** direct debtor; **~verkauf** direct sale (producer to consumer), house-to-house selling; **~versicherer** original insurer.

Direktion f management, main office, headquarters, directorate, abstractly: control; **~sassistent** personal assistant to the general manager; a P.A.; **~sausschuß** steering committee; **~srecht** entitlement to give instructions, right of control; authority.

Direktor m director, manager, departmental head, senior vice-president (US); school: headmaster; **geschäftsführender ~** managing director, head manager; **kaufmännischer ~** commercial director, business manager, sales manager; **stellvertretender ~** deputy director, deputy manager; **technischer ~** engineering director, technical manager, head of the engineering section.

Direktive f directive.

Direktorat n directorate, directorship, headmaster's office, principal's office.

Direktorium n board of management, board of governors (central bank) directorate.

Dirigismus m dirigism, dirigisme, controls, (economic) regimentation; **wirtschaftspolitischer ~** policy of governmental economic controls.

Dirnenwesen n prostitution.

Disagio n discount, disagio, below par; **~ auf Termindollars** discount on forward dollars; **mit ~** at a discount.

Discountpreis n discount price.

Diskont m discount; domestic bill; pl **Diskonten**: inland trade bills; **~ à forfait** bill of exchange discount without recourse; **~abrechnung** discount note; **~bedingungen** discount terms; **~erlös** discount earned; **~erhöhung** raising of the discount rate; **d~fähig** discountable, eligible for discount (bills of exchange); **~fähigkeit** eligibility

Diskontant

for discount; **~gefälle** divergence between discount rates; **~geschäft** discount business, cut-price business, price-cutting; **~haus** (*referring to UK*) discount house; cut-price shop; **~kredit** discount credit; **~laden** cut-price store; **~makler** bill-broker, discount broker; **~markt** discount market; **~note** discount note; **~ ohne Regress** discount without recourse; **~provision** discount commission; **~satz** discount rate, *esp* official rate of discount, bank rate, *US*: rediscount rate; **~~ der Geschäftsbanken**: market rate; **~rechnung** discount note (*statement of charges for discounted bills, including discount*); **~senkung** bank rate reduction; **~spesen** discount charges; **~wechsel** discount bill, discounted bill; **~wert** discount value.

Diskontant *m* party presenting a bill for discount.

diskontieren *v/t* to discount, to take (a bill) on discount.

Diskontierer *m* discounting banker.

Diskontierung *f* discounting (*of a bill*); **~szeitraum** discount period.

Diskonto *m* discount *m* (= *Diskont qv*); **ab ~** less discount; **abzüglich ~** less discount.

diskreditieren *v* to discredit, to bring into disrepute.

Diskrepanz *f* discrepancy, disparity (between), gap; **zeitliche ~** time-lag.

Diskretion *f* discretion; **~stage** days of grace; **~ wahren** to preserve (strict) confidence, to keep s. th. confidential.

diskriminieren *v/i* to discriminate against, to deal unfairly with s. o.; **~d behandeln**: *to make subject to discriminatory treatment*, to treat unfairly.

Diskriminierung *f* discrimination (against); **~ am Arbeitsplatz** job discrimination, discrimination at work; **~ durch die Behörde** administrative discrimination; **~sverbot** prohibition of discrimi-

Disposition

nation, ban on discrimination, rule of non-discrimination; **~sverbotsbescheid** non-discrimination notice; **geschlechtsbezogene ~** sexual (*or* sex-based) dicrimination; **steuerliche ~** taxation (*or* fiscal) discrimination.

Dispache *f marine ins* average statement, average adjustment, settlement of average; **~kosten** adjustment charges; **~prüfungsstelle** average adjustment, verification agency; **die ~ aufmachen** to make up the average, to settle the average, to state the average.

Dispacheur *m* average adjuster, average-stater, arbitrator of averages.

dispachieren *v/t* to adjust averages.

Dispachierung *f* adjustment of average(s).

Disparität *f* disparity.

Dispens *m* exemption, dispensation; **~erteilung** dispensation, the granting of an exemption, official waiver of a restriction.

dispensieren *v/t* (*1*) to dispense (from), to excuse; (*2*) to dispense (*medicine*).

Dispensierrecht *n* right to dispense medicines.

Dispensionsprivileg (*des Monarchen*) dispensing power.

Disponent *m* managing clerk.

disponibel *adj* disposable, available, accessible.

disponieren *v/i* to dispose of, to make arrangements; to place orders, to allot; **knapp ~** to show caution in the placing of orders, to plan cautiously.

Disposition *f* (*1*) disposition, disposal, arrangement; **~en des Handels** trade orders, forward planning; **~ des Kapitalmarktes** state of the capital market; **jmdn zur ~ stellen** to place s. o. in temporary retirement; **kurzfristige ~en der Kundschaft** customer orders at short notice; **längerfristige ~** relatively long-term planning; **privatwirtschaftliche ~en** measures by private firms, private-sector planning; **saisonale ~en**

Disposition   **Dividende**

seasonal preparations (*for placing orders*).

Disposition *f* (2) order processing department, contract management.

Dispositions|befugnis power of control; ~**grundsatz** = ~*maxime qv*; ~**guthaben** balance available; ~**kredit** overdraft facility, unresticted-use credit, running-account credit; ~**maxime** principle of party disposition (*of facts and remedies in legal proceedings as distinguished from ex officio disposition*); ~**fonds** funds at the free disposal (*of the chancellor etc.*); ~**möglichkeit** possibility of disposition, availability for disposal, scope of action; ~**papier** (transferable) instrument of title, document of title ; ~**reserve** general operating reserve, available reserve; ~**stellung** availability, putting s. th. at s. o.'s disposal.

dispositiv *adj* optional.

Dispositivnormen *f/pl* non-mandatory provisions of the law, optional rules.

Disput *m* verbal dispute, (*scientific, legal etc*) controversy, argument.

Disqualifikation *f* disqualification.

disqualifizieren *v/t* to disqualify, to incapacitate.

disqualifiziert *adj* disqualified.

Disqualifizierung *f* disqualification.

Dissens *m* dissent, lack of agreement (*between contracting parties*); **offener** ~ patent ambiguity, disagreement, clear lack of agreement; **versteckter** ~ hidden discrepancy of meaning, latent ambiguity; hidden disagreement.

Dissenter *m* (religious) dissenter, nonconformist (*referring in German to Church of England*).

Dissident *m* non-conformist, dissenter.

Dissimulation *f* dissimulation, dissembled (*or* concealed) intention (*or* meaning).

dissimulieren *v/t* to dissimulate, to dissemble (*real intention*).

Distanz|delikt offence committed over a distance (*at several places or with effect in other localities than the original act*); ~**fracht** (long) distance freight, pro rata freight; ~**geschäft** non-local transaction; ~**scheck** out-of-town cheque (*US check*): *cheque not drawn on a bank at the place of residence of the drawer*; ~**handel** long distance trading, mail-order business; ~**wechsel** out-of-town bill.

Distrikt *m* district, region, section.

Disziplinar|anzeige information alleging a disciplinary offence; ~**ausschuß** disciplinary committee, grievance committee; ~**befugnis** disciplinary power; ~**behörde** disciplinary authority; ~**bestrafung** disciplinary punishment; ~**bücher** disciplinary records; ~**gericht** disciplinary tribunal; ~**gerichtsbarkeit** disciplinary jurisdiction; ~**gewalt** disciplinary power, disciplinary authority; ~**kammer** disciplinary (court) division; ~**maßnahme** *sing u. pl*: disciplinary action; ~**ordnung** disciplinary regulations, code of ethics; ~**recht** disciplinary law; ~**richter** judge of a disciplinary tribunal; ~**sache** disciplinary case; ~**strafe** disciplinary punishment; ~**strafgewalt** disciplinary punitive power; ~**strafrecht** disciplinary penal law; ~**untersuchung** disciplinary investigation; ~**verfahren** disciplinary proceedings; ~**vergehen** disciplinary offence, misconduct by public officer; ~**vorgesetzter** (disciplinary) superior of a public servant.

Divergenz *f* divergence; ~**Koeffizient** diversity factor; ~**revision** appeal on points of law because of conflicting precedents.

Divergieren *n* divergence.

divergieren *v/i* to diverge (from), to differ from.

divergierend *adj* divergent.

Diverses *n* sundries.

Diversifikation *f* diversification.

Diversifizierung *f* diversification (*of investments*); ~ **der Versorgung** diversification of supplies.

Dividende *f* dividend (= *d*); ~ **auf Stammaktien** ordinary *d*; ~ **aus-**

Dividendenabrechnung / **Dokument**

schütten to pay a *d*, to distribute a *d*; ~ **erklären** to declare a *d*; ~ **festsetzen** to fix a *d*, to declare a *d*; ~ **in Gratisaktien** stock *d*; ~**nabrechnung** *d* note; ~**nabschlag** reduction in *d–s*, ex-dividend markdown; ~**nanspruch** right to a *d*; ~**n aus Beteiligungen** participation *d–s*; ~**nausgleichsrücklage** *d* equalization reserve; ~**nausschüttung** distribution of a *d*; ~**nauszahlungsstelle** *d* disbursing agent; **d~nberechtigt** entitled to a *d*; ~**nberechtigung** entitlement to a *d*; **d~nbevorrechtigt** ranking first in *d* rights; ~**n beziehen** to draw *d–s*; ~**neinkommen** *d* income; ~**neinkünfte** income from *d–s*; ~**n erheben** to collect *d–s*; ~**nerklärung** declaration of a *d*; ~**nertrag** income from *d–s*; ~**nfonds** bonus fund, *d* fund; ~**ngarantie** dividend guarantee; ~**ngarantierücklage** special reserve for future guaranteed *d–s*; ~**n in Streubesitz** *d–s* on portfolio investment; ~**nkürzung** reduction of *d–s*; **d~nlos** *adj* without *d*, dividendless; ~**nnachzahlung** payment of accumulated *d–s*; ~**noptik** dividend payout for window-dressing purposes; ~**npapiere** *d*-bearing securities, equities; ~**nreserve** *d* reserve fund; ~**nrückstände** arrears of *d–s*; ~**nsatz** *d* rate; ~**nschein** *d* coupon, *d* warrant; ~**nsenkung** *d* cut; ~**nstock** *d* fund; ~**nstop** curb on *d–s*, *d* ceiling, *d* limitation; ~**nverteilung** distribution of *d– s*; ~**nvorschlag** *d* proposal; ~**nwerte** *d*-bearing securities; ~**nzahlstelle** *d* disbursing agent; **abzüglich** ~ ex dividend; **aufgelaufene** ~ accumulated *d*; **ausgeschüttete** ~ distributed *d*; **außerordentliche** ~ special *d*; **e–e ~ festsetzen** to declare a *d*; **einschließlich** ~ cum *d*; **ertragsorientierte** ~**n** *d–s* conforming to earnings; **fällige** ~**n** payable *d–s*, **keine ~n ausschütten** to pass the *d*; **kumulative** ~ **mit Nachholungsrecht** cumulative *d*;

laufende ~ accrued *d–s*; **mit ~** cum *d*; **noch nicht ausgezahlte** ~ unpaid *d*; **ohne** ~ ex *d*, dividendless; **unerhobene** ~**n** unclaimed *d–s*; **vorläufige** ~ interim *d*.

DM|Abkommenskonten DM agreement accounts; ~**-Agenten-Konto** Agent's DM Account; ~**Anleihen** DM-denominated bonds, DM bonds; ~**-Aufwertung** DM revaluation, revaluation of the DM; ~**-Bilanzgesetz** (= *Gesetz über die Eröffnungsbilanz in Deutscher Mark und die Kapitalneufestsetzung vom 21. 8. 1949*) German post-currency reform balance-sheet Act; ~**-Exportabwicklungskonto** DM export settlement account; ~**-Konto** DM account; *beschränkt konvertierbare* ~~: DM accounts of limited convertibility; ~**Konten von Ausländern** non-resident's DM accounts; ~**-Quote bei der Weltbank** DM quota in the World Bank (International Bank for Reconstruction and Development); ~**-Referenzzins** FIBOR (Frankfurt Interbank Offered Rate); ~**-Sperrguthaben** blocked DM account; ~**-Vertreterkonto** representative's (or agent's) DM account.

Dock *n* dock, wharf; ~**arbeiter** *m sing* longshoreman (*pl* longshoremen); ~**empfangsschein** dock warrant; ~**gebühren** dock charges, dock dues; ~**lagerschein** dock warrant; ~**meister** dockmaster; ~**möglichkeit** dockage, docking facilities.

Doktorgrad *m* doctorate, doctor's degree; ~ **erwerben** to take one's doctor's degree; ~ **verleihen** to confer a doctor's degree.

Dokument *n* document, instrument; ~**e gegen Akzept** documents against acceptance; ~**e gegen Kasse** documents against payment (in cash); ~**e gegen Zahlung** documents against payment; ~**enakkreditiv** documentary letter of credit, commercial letter of credit,

Dokumentation

documentary credit; *unwiderrufliches ~~*: *irrevocable documentary credit*, *widerrufliches ~~*: *revocable documentary credit*; **~enandienung** tendering of documents; **~enaufnahme** taking up of documents; **d~enecht** *adj* accepted for use on official documents (*ball pen etc*); **~engegenwert** currency equivalent of documents; **~eninkasso** collecting of commercial documents (*through a bank*); **~enkredit** documentary credit; **~enpfand** documentary pledge; **~entratte** documentary draft, documentary bill, draft with documents attached; **~enwechsel** documentary bill (of exchange).

Dokumentation *f* documentation, source material, set of documents.

dokumentieren *v/t* to document, to establish by documents, to prove by documents, to demonstrate.

Dollar|abfluß dollar drain outflow of dollars; **~abhebungen** dollar drawings; **~akzept** dollar acceptance; **~anleihen** dollar bonds; **~bestände** dollar holdings; **~bilanz** dollar balance of payments; **~guthaben** dollar balance; **~klausel** *contract term that payment is to be made in US dollars*; **~parität** dollar parity; **~rembours** dollar documentary credit; **~wechsel** dollar acceptance.

Dolmetscher *n* interpreter; **~eid** interpreter's oath; **allgemein beeidigter ~** sworn interpreter; **freiberuflicher ~** free-lance interpreter; **öffentlich bestellter ~** officially appointed interpreter, state-certificated interpreter; **staatlich geprüfter ~** state-certificated interpreter; **vereidigter ~** sworn interpreter.

dolos *adj*, dolose, with criminal intent, malicious.

dolus *m* intent (*criminal or tortious*); **~ directus** direct intent; **~ eventualis** contingent intent.

Domäne *f* domain, estate, state-owned farm, demesne.

Doppelgesellschafter

Dominion *n* dominion (*i.e. a British d.*); **~status** dominion status.

Dominium *n* sovereignty, supreme control, dominion.

Domizil *n* residence, domicile (*place at which a bill is made payable*); **~gesellschaft** domiciliary company; **~land** country of domicile, home country; **~ort** place of payment of a domiciled bill; **~provision** domicile commission; **~statut** the domicile law, lex domicilii; **~stelle** place for presentment; **~vermerk** domicile note; **~wechsel** domiciled bill, domiciliated bill, addressed bill, indirect bill; *echter ~~*: *typical domiciled bill* (*place of residence of drawee is different from place of payment*); **unechter ~~** *non-typical domiciled bill* (*residence of drawee and place of payment in the same city*); **franko ~** free consignee's home address.

Domiziliant *m* payer of a domiciled bill.

domizilieren *v/t* to domicile, to domiciliate (*bill of exchange*).

Domizilierung *f* domiciling, domiciliation (*making a bill of exchange payable at a place other than that of the acceptor*); **~sbank** bank of payment for a domiciled bill; **~svermerk** domicile note.

Dontgeschäft *n risky speculation*, *exch* trading in puts and calls, premium trading, premium bargain.

Doppel|agent double agent, *secret agent for both sides*; **~beschäftigung** double employment; **~beschluß** two-track decision; **~besteuerung** → *Doppelbesteuerung*; **~bestrafung** punishing twice for the same offence, double punishment; **~boden** (*Zollkontrolle e-s Fahrzeuges*) false bottom; **~brief** overweight letter; **~buchhaltung** bookkeeping by double entry; **d~deutig** *adj* equivocal, ambiguous; **~ehe** bigamous marriage; **~funktion** dual function; **~gesellschafter** simultaneous partner (*or member*) in two part-

211

nerships (*or companies*); ~**haus** double-fronted house, *building consisting of two semi-detached houses*, duplex house; ~**mandat** double mandate, double retainer (*of lawyer by two clients*); ~**mitgliedschaft** dual membership; ~**- oder Vielfachbesteuerung** double or multiple taxation; ~**prämie** compound option, double premium; ~**provision** double commission (*buyer and seller*); ~**schutz** double protection, simultaneous protection; ~**selbstmord** double suicide, suicide pact; ~**sinn** double meaning, equivocation, ambiguity; **d~sinnig** *adj* having a double meaning, equivocal; ~**staater** person of dual nationality; ~**staatsangehörigkeit** dual nationality; ~**veranlagung** double assessment; ~**verdiener** double earner, two-job man, *pl*: husband and wife who are both gainfully employed; ~**verfolgungsverbot** prohibition of double jeopardy, bar against repeated prosecution for same offence (*ne bis in idem*); ~**vermietung** double letting of (a room or appartment) to different parties; ~**versicherung** double insurance, additional insurance; ~**versicherungsklausel** double indemnity clause (*for death by accident*); ~**versorgung** „double dipping"; ~**währung** double standard currency; ~~**ssystem;** *dual currency standard*; ~**wechsel** second of exchange; ~**wohnsitz** dual domicile; ~**zählung** duplication, counting s. th. twice; ~**züngigkeit** duplicity, double talk, double-dealing; ~**zustellung** double service; ~**zuständigkeit** dual competence, dual jurisdiction.

Doppelbesteuerung *f* double taxation; ~**sabkommen** double taxation treaty (*or*: convention); ~**svergünstigung** double taxation relief.

Dorf|anger *m* village green; ~**bewohner** villager; ~**flur** *f* village land; ~**gemeinde** village community, rural community; ~**gemeinderat** rural council, parish council; ~**sanierung** village improvement; ~**testament** last will executed before a village mayor (*extreme need*).

Dosisgrenzwerte *m/pl* maximum tolerable radiation data.

Dossier *n* dossier, file, (*esp by police*).

Dotalgelder *n/pl* endowment funds.

Dotation *f* general financial grant, endowment; allocation; ~**sauflagen** conditions (for the use) of a government grant; ~**skapital** endowment capital.

dotieren *v/t* to endow (*a foundation*); to remunerate (*position, office*); *nicht dotiert*: *unendowed*.

Dotierung *f* allocation (*of funds*), endowment, provision (of resources); *rare*: remuneration (*connected with an office*); ~ **der Rücklagen** allocation to reserves.

Doyen *m* doyen, dean (*of the diplomatic corps*).

Draht|akzept *n* telegraphic acceptance; ~**adresse** cable address; ~**anschrift** cable address, telegram address; ~**antwort** telegraphic reply; ~**überweisung** telegraphic transfer (or remittance); ~**wort** telegraphic address, cable address.

drakonisch *f* draconian, draconic, harsh, cruel, radical.

Drall *m* twist, spin (*of bullet*).

Dramatisierungsrecht *n* drama adaptation right.

Drang *m* impulse, urge; **unwiderstehlicher** ~ irresistible impulse, overpowering urge.

Draufgabe *f* earnest, earnest money, deposit, handsel (= *Handgeld*).

Draufgeld *n* (1) = *Draufgabe qv*; (2) premium, contango.

draufzahlen *v/i* to pay too much.

Dreh|beginn *m* commencement of principal photography; ~**buch** film script; ~**schluß** completion of principal photography.

Drei-Bogen-Plakat *n* three-sheet poster.

Dreiecks|arbitrage *f* triangular exchange (arbitrage); ~**geschäft** triangular transaction *or*: operation;

triangular trade; ~**verhältnis** triangle relationship, ménage à trois.
Dreierausschuß *m* committee of three, tripartite committee.
Dreierbündnis *n* tripartite alliance.
dreifach *adj*, *adv* in triplicate (*of a document*), treble, triple.
Dreigewaltenlehre *f* trichotomy of governmental powers, separation of powers doctrine.
Dreijahresfrist *f* three-year period.
Dreimächteabkommen *n* tripartite pact, three power agreement.
Dreimeilenzone *f* three mile zone.
Dreimonatsakzept *n* three months' paper (acceptance).
Dreimonatseinrede *f* three months' plea (*of the heir during which he can refuse or delay payment of debts in respect of the estate and claim exemption from execution*).
Dreimonatsgeld *n* ninety days' loan, 90-day deposits; three-months' money.
Dreimonatswechsel *m* three months' bill, bill at three months, three months' paper.
Dreimonatsziel *n* payable three months after date, payment due in 3 months.
dreiprozentig *adj* bearing three percent interest.
dreiseitig *adj* tripartite.
Dreißigster *m* (*der Dreißigste*) thirty days' maintenance: *legal obligation to maintain servants for 30 days after the death of their master*.
Dreistufigkeit *f* three-tier system.
dreiteilig *adj* tripartite, in three parts.
Dreiteilung *f* **der Straftaten** tripartition of offences, triple classification of offences (*e.g. treason, felonies misdemeanours*).
Dreiviertelmehrheit *f* three-quarters majority.
Dreizeugentestament *n* oral last will and testimony before three witnesses (*in an emergency*).
dringlich *adj* urgent.
Dringlichkeit *f* urgency, priority.
Dringlichkeits|antrag urgency motion, privileged motion; ~**bescheinigung** certificate of priority; ~**erklärung** declaration of urgency; ~**fall** urgent case; ~**frage** question of urgency; ~**klausel** urgency clause (*special priority for legislation*); ~**liste** priority list; ~**stufe** priority rating, precedence rating; degree of priority; *höchste* ~~: *top priority*; ~**verfahren** summary procedure, emergency procedure; ~**vorlage** urgent business.
Dritt|anspruch third-party claim; ~**ausfertigung** third copy (*bill of exchange*); ~**begünstigter** third party beneficiary, donee beneficiary; ~~ *e- r Klage*: *use plaintiff*; ~**berechtigter** the entitled third party; ~**beteiligung** joinder by a third party; ~**eigentümer** third-party owner; ~**erwerber** third-party purchaser; ~**gläubiger** third-party creditor; ~**haftung für fahrlässige Schädigung** collateral negligence; ~**kontrahent** third contracting party; ~**land** third country, non-member-country; non-EEC state, (*pl* ~**länder**): *outside countries*, ~~*er regelung*: *third country rules*; ~**markt** *market other than the home market*, outside market, export market; ~**schaden** third-party damage; ~**schadensliquidation** realization of third-party damage (*by directly injured party*); ~**schuldner** third-party debtor, garnishee, assigned debtor; ~**schuldnererklärung** statutory declaration by garnishee (*as to validity of garnished claim*); ~**schuldnerklage** action against garnishee; ~**schuldnerpfändung** garnishment; ~**vermögen** property of an unspecified person, third-party assets; ~**verpflichteter** third-party obligee; ~**verwahrung** custody by a third party, escrow; ~**widerspruch** third-party intervention against execution, third-party opposition; ~**widerspruchsklage** third-party action against execution; ~**widerspruchskläger** plain-

tiff in a third-party opposition case (*against execution upon a debtor*); ~**wirkung** effect on third party.

Dritter *m* (*der Dritte*) third party (*pl: third parties*), outsider, stranger, such other person; **gutgläubiger** ~ innocent third party, third party acting in good faith.

Droge *f* drug, pharmaceutical product; ~**nmißbrauch** drug abuse, drug addiction; ~**nspürhund** narcotics sniffing dog; ~**nsüchtiger** drug addict; **gesundheitsgefährdende** ~ deleterious (*or* harmful) drug.

Drogerie *f* druggist's shop (*selling toiletries and patent medicines exempt from medical prescription*); *US*: drugstore.

Drohbrief *m* threatening letter.

drohen *v/t* to threaten *s. o. with s. th.*

drohend *adj* threatening; impending; imminent (*danger*).

Drohung *f* threat(s); ~ **mit Gefahr für Leib und Leben** threat to life and limb; ~ **mit polizeilicher Anzeige** threatening to inform the police; **versteckte** ~ veiled threat; **widerrechtliche** ~ unlawful threat; illegitimate threat.

drosseln *v/t* to curb, to cut down; to throttle; to choke, to slow down.

Druck|auftrag printing order; ~**bogenhonorar** author's fee by printed sheet; ~**erlaubnis** licence to print, printing permit; **d**~**fähig** *adj* printable, fit for printing; ~**fahne** galley-proof; ~**fehler** misprint, printing error; ~**fehlerliste** list of misprints; **d**~**fertig** ready to go to press; ~**genehmigung** imprimatur, permission to print; ~**kostengebühr** *pat* printing fee; ~ **im Staatsauftrag** public printing; ~**legung** printing, going to press; ~**legungsgebühr** printing fee; ~**nebenrechte** ancillary printing rights; **d**~**reif** *adj* fit for printing, ready for printing, printable; ~**sache** printed matter, printed papers, *US*: second- (*respectively third*-) class mail, document (*parl*); *großformatige* ~~: *broadsheet*; ~**sachenwerbung** direct-mail advertizing; ~**schrift** (1) printed publication, printed document; *öffentliche* ~~: *printed publication, periodische* ~~: *periodical; unzüchtige* ~~*en: obscene writings*; (2) block letters; „*in* ~~": *print*; ~**stock** printing block, cut, engraving, plate, electrotype; ~**vermerk** imprint; ~**werk** printed work, printed publication.

Drückeberger *m* draft dodger (*military service*), truant (*school*), shirker, slacker (*work*), malingerer, dodger, workshy person.

Drückebergerei *f* dodging, shirking, playing truant.

Druckereigewerbe *n* printing industry.

dubios *adj* dubious, doubtful.

Dubiosen *pl* bad debts, doubtful debts, shady doubtful receivables; ~**konto** bad debts account; ~**reserven** contingent reserves for bad debts.

dulden *v/t* to acquiesce, to suffer, to tolerate, to bear, to be passive; **stillschweigend** ~ to acquiesce, to suffer, to connive (at).

Duldung *f* acquiescence, sufferance, toleration, tacit permission; ~ **des Rechtsscheins** holding out; ~**sbescheid** *official information that sth will be tolerated until further order;* ~**sklage** *petition requiring respondent to tolerate s. th.*; ~**spflicht** *obligation to tolerate s. th.*; ~**stitel** *judgment, deed, or court settlement requiring s. o. to tolerate s. th.*; ~**svollmacht** power of representation by estoppel (*by acquiescence*).

Dumping *n* dumping; ~**bekämpfungszoll** anti-dumping tariff; ~**Praktiken** dumping; ~**preis** dumping price; ~**verbot** ban on dumping; ~**verbotsgesetz** anti-dumping law.

Dunkel|männer back-stage conspirators; ~**ziffer** percentage of undetected crime.

Duplik *f* (defendant's) rejoinder, duplicatio.

Duplikat *n* duplicate.

duplizieren *v/t* to duplicate; to rejoin (*cf Duplik*).

Durchbeförderung *f* transit transportation.

durcherkennen *v/t* to render a final decision as to the merits (*by a court of error*).

Durchfahrt *f* passage, thoroughfare; ~**sfreiheit** freedom of transit; ~**shöhe** headroom (*under a bridge*); ~**srecht** right of passage; wayleave (*minerals from mine or quarry over or through land*); öffentliches ~~ (*inland waterways*): *public passage*; ~**sstraße** through street, thoroughfare; ~**sverbot** no entry, no through road, no passage, no thoroughfare; ~ **verboten!** "no thoroughfare"; **bloße** ~ simple passage (*maritime law*); **enge** ~narrow passage; **friedliche** ~ innocent passage.

Durchfallquote *f* drop-out rate, failure rate.

Durchfinanzierung *f* financing to completion, continuous provision of funds.

Durchfracht|konnossement through bill of lading; ~**transportpapier** through document of transport; ~**verladung** through-freight shipment.

Durchfuhr transit; ~**abgaben** transit duties; ~**abschnitt** transit sheet; ~**land** country of transit; ~**handel** transit trade; ~**staat oder –hoheitsgebiet** territory of transit; ~**verbot** prohibitions on transit; ~**verfahren** transit procedure; ~**verkehr** traffic in transit.

Durchführbarkeit practicability, workability, feasibility; ~**sstudie** feasibility study.

Durchführung *f* implementation, accomplishment, consummation.

Durchführungs|abkommen implementing agreement; ~**anordnung** implementing order; ~**bestimmungen** implementing regulations, rules and regulations; ~**gesetz** implementing law, executive Act; ~**verordnung** implementing order (*or* ordinance), executive decree.

Durchgangs|arzt provisional doctor *for work accident cases*; ~**fracht** through freight, through shipment; ~**güter** transit goods; ~**konnossement** through bill of lading; ~**konto** transit account, suspense account, provisional account; ~**ladung** through shipment; ~**lager** transit camp, provisional camp; ~**land** transit country; ~**tarif** through rate; ~**transport** transport in transit; ~**verbindung** through route; ~**verkehr** through traffic, traffic passing through; ~**waren** goods in transit, transit goods; ~**zoll** pass duty, transit duty; ~**zollstelle** customs office en route.

durchgehend *adj, adv* non-stop.

durchgreifen *v/i* to take drastic measures, to get tough.

Durchgriff *m* (1) drastic action; (2) enforcement of liability against capital owner; ~ **des Verbrauchers gegen den Produzenten** enforcement of liability by the end-user (or consumer) against the producer (or manufacturer), vertical privity; ~**serinnerung** exception to a ruling: *objection to the decision of a master (Rechtspfleger qv) which must be treated by his superior judge as an appeal from the order*; ~**shaftung** piercing the corporate veil; direct liability of controlling shareholder (*of one-man company or controlling limited partner acting in bad faith*).

durchhalten, *v/i* to hold out (to the end), to see it through.

durchkämpfen *v/t* to fight it out.

Durchkonnossement *n* through bill of lading.

Durchlauf|konto suspense account; ~**posten** transitory item, item on a suspense account; ~**termin** summary first hearing; ~**zeit** processing time.

Durchleit|gelder transmitted monies; ~**kredit** transmitted credit; ~**marge** commission for passing on funds to the final borrower, the transmitting bank's margin on the credit.

Durchleitung *f* transmission.

Durchlieferung *f* transit deportation.

durchpeitschen *v/t* to rush through, to railroad (*a bill*) (*US*).

Durchreisegenehmigung *f* transit permit.

Durchreisender *m* transit passenger.

Durchreisesichtvermerk *m* transit visa.

Durchreisevisum *n* transit visa.

Durchsatz *m* throughput (*oil pipe etc*).

Durchschlag *m* carbon, carbon copy; **abgezeichneter** ~initialled carbon copy.

Durchschlagskraft *f* force of the argument, punch, effectiveness.

Durchschlupf *m* average outgoing quality.

Durchschnitt *m* average; *im* ~: *on average*; **den** ~ **nehmen** to take the average; **gewogener** ~ weighted average; **gleitender 4-Wochen** ~ 4-week moving average; **repräsentativer** ~ representative cross-section.

durchschnittlich *adj* averaging, on average.

Durchschnitts|beförderungsentgelt average transport charges; ~**beitragssatz** average contribution, average rate of social security payments; ~**betrag** average amount; ~**einkommen** average income; ~**entgelt** average remuneration; ~**ertrag** average yield; ~**fachmann** skilled workman of average capabilities; ~**gewinn** average profits; ~**kosten** average charge; ~**kurs** market average; ~**leistung** norm, average performance, standard capacity; ~**lohn** average wage; ~**menschen** ordinary people, average men in the street; ~**miete** average rent; ~**preis** average price; ~**qualität** average quality; *mittlere* ~~: *run-of-the-mill*; ~**rechnung** calculation of average; ~**satz** average rate; ~**tagessaldo** average daily balance; ~**ware** articles of average quality; ~**wert** average value, ~~ *je Einheit: unit value*; mean value; ~**zinsen** average interest rates.

Durchschreibe|block carbon-copy pad; ~**buchhaltung** *f* manual mechanical bookkeeping, multiple copy bookkeeping, duplicate recording system; ~**papier** copying paper, carbon paper.

Durchschrift *f* carbon copy, carbon.

durchsehen *v/t* to peruse, to glance through, to check, to take a cursory look at *sth*.

durchsetzbar *adj* enforceable, recoverable; **nicht** ~ unenforceable, imperfect.

durchsetzen *v/t* to enforce, to put through; *v/reflex* to achieve one's objectives, to assert o.s., to get one's way.

Durchsetzung *f* getting s.th. through, enforcement.

Durchsicht *f* perusal, cursory examination; **flüchtige** ~ taking a glance at s.th.; **nochmalige** ~ second inspection (*of the books, of a paper etc.*) revision, reexamination; **zur** ~ for perusal; **zur gefälligen** ~ for your kind inspection.

Durchstreichen *n* deletion, cancellation, crossing out.

durchstreichen *v/t* to cross out, to delete, to cancel.

durchsuchen *v/t* to search (*under a search warrant*), to ransack (*esp. in a disorderly manner*).

Durchsuchung *f* search, visit and search (*of ships*), rummage; ~**sbefehl** search warrant; ~**befugnis** (*or* authority) power to search; ~**srecht** right of search, right of visit and search (*at sea*); ~ **und Beschlagnahme** search and seizure; ~ **von Wohnungen** search of private homes.

Durchwahl *f* direct (*or* through) dialling, trunk dialling by subscribers; ~**nummer** direct number; ~**system** direct dialling system.

durchweg *adv* altogether, throughout.

durchwinken *v/t* to wave (*or* whisk) through (*border*).

Durchzugsrecht *n* right of passage, right to march through (*by an army through neutral territory*).

Dürftigkeit *f* neediness (*persons*), meagreness (*resources*), scantiness (*knowledge*), feebleness (*arguments*); ~**seinrede** plea of insufficient assets in an estate.

Dutzendware *f* cheap merchandise, mass-produced articles.

Dynamisierung *f* periodic adjustment of pensions *according to current wage-level*.

Ebenbürtigkeit *f* equality of birth, equality of rank; *staatsrechtliche und diplomatische* ~: *equality of status*.

ebenda *adv* ibidem, ibid. (*in citations*).

Ebene *f* level (administration); **auf höherer** ~ high-level (*talks*); **auf nationaler** ~ at national level; **die staatliche** ~ government level; **handelspolitische** ~ (at) trade policy level.

echt *adj* authentic, true, genuine (*signature, document*).

Echtheit *f* authenticity, genuineness; ~ **der Unterschrift** genuineness of the signature; **die** ~ **bestätigen** to authenticate; **die** ~ **feststellen** to establish the authenticity; **die** ~ **von Münzen prüfen** to pix (= *pyx*), to test at the trial of the pyx; **die** ~ **von Urkunden bestätigen** to authenticate documents.

Echtheits|beweis proof of authenticity, authentication, proof of genuineness; ~ *e–r Handschrift*: *proof of writing*; ~**bürgschaft** guarantee of genuineness; ~**probe** forge test (*metallurgic*); ~**prüfung** test of genuineness, test of authenticity; test of colo(u)r fastness; ~**zeugnis** certificate of genuineness, certificate of authenticity.

Eck|grundstück corner lot; ~**haus** house on a corner; ~**lohn** standard wage, collectively agreed wage; ~**wert** prime value, benchmark figure; ~~-*Aktienindex*: *Real Time Index*; ~**zins** standard interest rate, basic rate of interest.

Edelmetall *n* precious metal; ~**börse** market for precious metals; ~**gewicht** troy weight; ~**prägezeichen** hallmark; ~**prüfer** assayer.

Edikt *n* edict, (*royal etc.*) decree.

Editionseid *m* disclosure on oath, discovery on oath.

Editionspflicht *f* duty to produce a document.

Effekt *m* effect, result, outcome.

Effekten *pl* (marketable) securities, (= *s–s*), stocks and bonds; ~**abrechnung** contract note, statement of transactions of *s–s*; ~**abteilung** investment department, *s–s* department; ~**anlage** investment in *s–s*; ~**anlageberater** investment adviser; ~**arbitrage** arbitrage in *s–s*, stock arbitrage; ~**austausch** portfolio switch (*investment fund*); ~**bank** bank dealing in *s–s*, investment bank; ~ **beleihen** to advance money on *s–s*; ~**beleihung** advance on *s–s*; ~**berechnung** stock-account; ~**bestand** holdings (in *s–s*); ~**börse** stock-market, stock-exchange; ~**buch** *s–s* ledger; ~**depot** portfolio, *s–s* (safe custody) account; ~**differenzgeschäft** margin business, margin trading; ~**einführung** marketing of *s–s*; ~**emission** issue of *s–s*; ~**emissionsgeschäft** underwriting business; ~**engagements** (stock-exchange) commitments; ~**gattung** type of *s–s*; ~**geschäft** dealing in *s–s*; ~**giroverkehr** clearing system for settling transactions in *s–s*; (*without physical delivery*); ~**gruppe** category of *s–s*; ~**handel** stock trading, *s–s* dealings; ~**händler** stock trader, stock dealer, investment dealer, dealer in *s–s*, stock broker, jobber (*GB*); ~**inhaber** holder of *s–s*; ~**käufe** *s–s* purchases; ~**kennummer** *s–s* code number; ~**kommissionsgeschäft** stock exchange dealing (*on customer's behalf*); ~**konto** stock account, *a bank account for s–s holdings and transactions*; ~**kredit** collateral loan on *s–s*; loan to finance stock transactions; ~**kundschaft** customers investing in *s–s*; ~**kurs** quoted price of s–s on the stock exchange; ~**liste** list of s–s; ~**lombard** (collateral) loan on (marketable) s–s, collateral advance; ~ **lombardieren** to borrow on s–s; ~**makler** stockbroker; ~**markt** stock market; ~ **mit täglichem Umsatz** active s–s, heavily traded shares; ~**notierungen** stock-exchange quotations; ~-**Optionshandel** trading in securities options; ~**order** order to buy or sell s–s; ~**paket** block of s–s, package of shares; ~**plazierung** placing of newly issued s–s; ~**portefeuille** investment portfolio, s–s in hand; ~**posten** lot (*of stocks, shares etc*); *geringer* ~~: *odd lot*; ~**rechnung** stock account, calculation of price of s–s; ~**sammeldepot** omnibus deposit of s–s, collective deposit; ~**schalter** s–s counter; ~**scheck** s–s transfer cheque for s–s; ~**sektor** dealings in s–s; ~**sparen** saving through investment in s–s; ~**spekulation** speculating in s–s; ~**steuer** stamp duty on s–s; ~**termingeschäfte** forward operations in s–s; ~**umsatzsteuer** transfer duty on s–s; ~**verkauf** security sales; *freihändiger* ~~: *over-the-counter trading*; ~~ *an Kapitalsammelstellen*: *institutional selling*; ~**verwaltung** portfolio management; **an der Börse gehandelte** ~ stock exchange s–s, s–s listed on the stock exchange; **beleihbare** ~ eligible paper, s–s eligible as collateral; **börsengängige** ~ marketable s–s; **lombardierte** ~ s–s held in pledge, shares pledged as security for a loan; **marktgängige** ~ marketable s–s; **nicht an der Börse notierte** ~ unlisted s–s; **nicht plazierte** ~ non-placed s–s.

Effektiv|bestand actual amount, actual balance, realizable assets; ~**bezüge** remuneration actually earned; ~**einnahmen** actual takings; ~**geschäft** actual business, spot market transaction(s); ~**klausel** specified currency clause *on bill of exchange or cheque*; specified coin clause; *clause that collective pay increase must be added to actual wage;* ~**lohn** actual wage, real wage; ~**preis** cash price, effective earnings; ~**vermerk** exclusive foreign currency notice on a bill or note; ~**verzinsung**, effective annual rate; real return, true yield of interest; ~**wert** actual value; ~**zins** effective annual rate.

Effektivitätsprinzip *n* principle of de facto effectiveness.

Effizienz *f* efficiency.

Egalitätsprinzip *n* principle of equality before the law.

EG-Binnenmarkt *m* EC internal market, single market.

Ehe *f* marriage (= *ma*), matrimony, wedlock; e~**ähnlich** connubial; ~**anbahnung** introducing prospective *ma* partners to one another; ~**anbahnungsinstitut** *dating agency, dating bureau;* ~**anerkennung** recognition of *ma* (*by another state*); ~**anfechtbarkeit** voidability of *ma*; ~**aufgebot** banns; ~**aufhebung** dissolution of *ma* (*due to error, fraud, threats etc at the time of marriage*) ~**aufhebungsgründe** grounds for dissolution of a *ma*; ~**aufhebungsklage** petition to dissolve a *ma cf Eheaufhebung*; ~**auflösung** dissolution of *ma*; ~**band** matrimonial ties, the bonds of wedlock; ~**beratung** *ma* guidance, *ma* counselling; ~**beratungsstelle** *ma* guidance bureau; ~**betrug** *ma* under false pretences; ~**brecher** adulterer; ~**brecherin** adulteress; e~**brecherisch** adulterous; ~**bruch** adultery; ~~ *begehen: to commit adultery;* ~~*szeuge: co-respondent; aus* ~~ *erzeugt: adulterine;* ~**dispens** exemption from *ma* impediments; e~**fähig** marriageable, legally capable of getting married, suitable for *ma*; ~**fähigkeit** capacity to marry; ~**fähigkeitsattest** = *Ehefähigkeitszeugnis qv*; ~**fähigkeitszeugnis** certificate of no impediment (*of one's home country*); certificate of nubility; ~**feststellungsklage** *action for a judicial decla-*

Ehefrau

ration on the existence or non-existence of a marriage; ~**frau** married woman, wife, feme covert; *rechtmäßige* ~~: *lawful wedded wife; getrennt lebende* ~~: *wife living separately, grass widow; mitverdienende* ~~: *wife contributing to the family income by working;* ~**gatte** → *Ehegatte;* ~**gelöbnis** *ma* vow(s); ~**gesetz** matrimonial law, *ma* Act, Matrimonial Causes Act *(court proceedings);* ~**gemeinschaft** conjugal community; ~**güterrecht** matrimonial property law; ~**herstellungsklage** petition for restitution of conjugal rights; ~**hindernis** → *Ehehindernis;* ~**konflikt** marital dispute; ~**kontrakt** *obs for Ehevertrag qv;* ~**leute** spouses, husband and wife; ~**paar** married couple; **e**~**lich** → *ehelich;* ~**lichkeit** → *Ehelichkeit;* ~**losigkeit** unwedded state, celibacy; ~**makler** matchmaker, *ma* broker, *ma* agent; ~**mann** husband, married man; **e**~**mündig** of marriageable age, nubile; ~**mündigkeit** marriageable age; ~**name** married name *(of a spouse);* ~**nichtigkeit** → *Ehenichtigkeit;* ~**paar** married couple; ~**partner** spouse; ~**prozeß** matrimonial cause; ~**recht** matrimonial law; ~**sache** matrimonial cause; ~**scheidung** → *Ehescheidung;* ~**schließender** party contracting a *ma;* ~**schließung** *f* → *Eheschließung;* ~**stand** matrimony, married state, wedlock; ~**standsbeihilfe** *ma* grant; ~**standsdarlehen** state loan to newly married couple; ~**störung** disturbance of *ma by outside party;* ~**streitigkeit** marital quarrel, matrimonial cause; ~**tauglichkeit** fitness for *ma (esp medical);* ~**trennung** separation (from bed and board); ~**unbedenklichkeitszeugnis** *ma* clearance certificate; **e**~**unmündig** *adj* not of marriageable age, too young to marry; ~**verbot** *ma* prohibition, prohibitive impediment to (or restraint of) of *ma,* absolute bar to *ma;* ~**verfehlung** matrimonial offence;

Ehegatte

~**versprechen** promise of *ma; beiderseitiges* ~~: *espousals;* ~**vertrag** matrimonial property agreement *(ante-nuptial or post-nuptial), ma* articles; **e**~**widrig** *adj* constituting a matrimonial offence; ~**widrigkeit** matrimonial offence; ~**wirkungen** effects of *ma; persönliche* ~~: *personal effects of ma;* ~**wohnung** marital home; ~**zeit** duration of the *ma; period of time during which the ma existed;* ~**zerrüttung** irretrievable breakdown of a *ma;* **anfechtbare** ~voidable *ma;* **aus erster** ~ of (*or* from) the first *ma;* **bigame** ~ bigamous *ma;* **die** ~ **betreffend** nuptial; **die** ~ **schließen** to marry, to get married, to solemnize (*ma*), to celebrate a *ma;* **e-e** ~ **aufheben** to dissolve a *ma (due to fraud, error, threats at the time of ma);* **e-e** ~ **brechen** to commit adultery; **e-e** ~ **eingehen** to be (*or* get) married, to marry, to enter into *ma,* to wed; **e-e** ~ **scheiden** to grant a divorce, to dissolve a *ma;* **freie** ~ common-law marriage, informal marital relationship; **gemischt nationale** ~ mixed *ma,* a *ma* between persons of different nationalities; **geschiedene** ~ divorced *ma;* **glaubensverschiedene** ~ *marriage between spouses of different religious denominations;* **internationales** ~**- und Kindschaftsrecht** private international law on marriage, parenthood and childhood; **morganatische** ~morganatic *ma;* **nachfolgende** ~ subsequent marriage; **nichtige** ~ void *ma;* **rechtsgültige** ~ legal *ma;* **vernichtbare** ~ voidable *ma;* **Vollziehung der** ~ consummation of *ma;* **vollzogene** ~ consummated *ma;* **wilde** ~ concubinage, living together as man and wife; **zerrüttete** ~ wrecked *ma,* irretrievably broken-down *ma.*

Ehegatte *m* spouse, marriage partner, marital partner, husband *or* wife; ~**naussagen** spousal testimony; ~**naussageverweigerungsrecht** husband – wife privilege; **~nerbrecht** entitlement to inheritance of surviving spouse; **~nfreibetrag** marital deduction; **~ngesellschaft** business partnership between spouses; **~nhaftung** legal liability of one spouse for the other; **~npflichtteil** (excluded) surviving spouse's compulsory share (*cf. Pflichtteil*); **~testament** mutual will of spouses; **~unterhalt** provision for a spouse; **~~** *während der Scheidung maintenance pending svit*; **~verträge** contracts between spouses **getrennt lebender ~** separated marital partner; **überlebender ~** surviving spouse.

Ehehindernis *n* impediment to *ma*; **~ der Verwandtschaft** marriage impediment in respect of relatives; **absolutes ~** absolute impediment; **als ~ geltende Verwandtschaftsgrade** levitical degress; **aufschiebendes ~** suspensive impediment; **gesetzliches ~** legal impediment; **relatives ~** relative impediment (*in relation to certain persons*).

ehelich *adj* matrimonial, conjugal, marital, connubial, legitimate; **~ geboren** born in (lawful) wedlock; **durch nachfolgende Eheschließung ~ werden** to be legitimated by subsequent marriage; **für ~ erklären** to legitimate, to legitimize.

Ehelichkeit *f* legitimacy, status of legitimacy; **~sanfechtung** denial of legitimacy, petition to have a child declared illegitimate; **~sbestreitung** denial of legitimacy; **~serklärung** act of legitimation, declaration of legitimacy; **~svermutung** presumption of legitimacy.

Ehenichtigkeit *f* nullity of marriage, invalidity of marriage; **~serklärung** annulment of marriage; **~sfeststellungsurteil** judicial declaration of nullity; **~sgrund** diriment impediment, reason for invalidity of marriage; **~sklage** petition for nullity of marriage, nullity suit; **~surteil** nullity decree.

Ehescheidung *f* divorce; **~sgrund** ground(s) for divorce, *pl*: grounds for petition for divorce; **~sklage** petition for divorce; **~sprozeß** divorce suit; **~srecht** law relating to divorce; **~surteil** divorce decree; **~sverfahren** divorce proceedings; **endgültige ~** divorce a vinculo matrimonii, decree absolute; **für ~ zuständiges Gericht** divorce court.

Eheschließung marriage, the act of marrying, celebration of marriage, solemnization of the marriage; *bei ~*: *on marriage*; **~sakt** act of marrying, marriage ceremony; **bürgerliche ~** civil marriage, registry office marriage; **e-e ~ vornehmen** to contract a marriage; **nach der ~** after the marriage, post-nuptial; **nachfolgende ~** subsequent marriage; **standesamtliche ~** registry office marriage, marriage by certificate, civil marriage.

Ehr|abschneidung *f* defamation of character; **e~los** infamous, dishono(u)rable; **~losigkeit** infamy; **~loserklärung** attainder; **~verletzung** injuring a person's reputation, defamation, defamatory statement, derogatory statement; **~verlust** loss of hono(u)r.

Ehren|akzept acceptance supra protest; **~akzeptant** acceptor for honour; **~amt** honorary position, office of honour; **e~amtlich** honorary, in an honorary capacity; **~annahme** acceptance for honour; **~beamter** honorary officer; **~bezeigung** salute; **~bürger** honorary citizen, honorary freeman (*town*), honorary member (*university*); **~bürgerbrief** certificate of honorary citizenship; **~bürgerrecht** honorary freedom; *das ~~ verleihen*: *to confer the freedom of a city*; **~eintritt** intervention supra protest, act of honour; **~erklärung** declaration of honour, *public withdrawal of a defamatory remark, public acknowledgment of the honorary character of a person;* **~gericht** professional tribunal; **e~halber** for reasons of *h*, honoris

221

causa, for *h*'s sake; ~**karte** complimentary ticket; ~**kodex** code of honour, moral code; ~**kränkung** affront, insult; defamation; ~**mitglied** honorary member; ~**präsident** honorary president; ~ **rechte** honorary rights; *bürgerliche* ~~: *civic rights*; ~**rechtsverlust** loss of civic rights; e~**rührig** discreditable, disgraceful, dishonourable; ~**sache** matter of honour; ~**schuld** debt of honour; ~**schutz** protection of honour; legal protection against defamation; ~**sold** honorary pension, *mostly: honorary remuneration coupled with a high decoration*; ~**söldner** honorary pensioner; ~**strafe** degrading punishment, penalty imposed by a disciplinary court; ~**vorsitzender** honorary chairman; ~**wort** word of honour, parole (*upon release*); *sein* ~~ *geben: to pledge one's word, to give one's word of honour*; ~**zeichen** badge of honour, decoration.

Eich|amt *n* bureau of standards, office of weights and measures; ~**frequenz** standard frequency; ~**gebühr** *fee for determining official weight or measure*; ~**gesetz** (German) Standard Weights and Measures Law; ~**gewicht** standard weight; ~**maß** standard measure; ~**meister** inspector of weights and measures, gauger, sealer; ~**stempel** gauger's mark, stamp of bureau of standards (*official measure*); ~**wesen** control of standard weights and measures; ~**zeugnis** gauger's certificate.

eichen *v/t* to calibrate, to standardize.

Eichung *f* calibration, adjustment.

Eid *m* oath; **assertorischer** ~ assertory oath; **außergerichtlicher** ~ extrajudicial oath; **beschränkter** ~ qualified oath; **den** ~ **ablegen** to take the oath, to be sworn (in); **den** ~ **abnehmen** to administer the oath, to swear (a person) in; **den** ~ **leisten** to swear (*or* take) take the oath, to swear; **den** ~ **nachsprechen** to repeat the oath (*after the person administering it*); **den** ~ **verweigern** to refuse to take the oath; **durch** ~ **bekräftigen** to affirm upon oath; **e-n** ~ **auferlegen** to put a person upon his oath; **e-n** ~ **brechen** to break one's oath; **e-n** ~ **leisten** to swear an oath, to take (an) oath; **e-n** ~ **schwören** to swear, to take an oath; **er erklärt unter** ~ he deposes upon oath and says (*or:* states); **falscher** ~ false oath; **gerichtlicher** ~ oath administered in court; **jmdm den** ~ **zuschieben** to tender an oath to s. b.; **jmdn unter** ~ **vernehmen** to examine s. o. on oath; **promissorischer** ~ promissory oath; **richterlicher** ~ oath by a judge; oath before a judge; **unter** ~ on (upon) oath; **unter** ~ **aussagen** to testify on oath, to make oath and say; **vom** ~ **entbinden** to release from oath.

Eides|abnahme administration of an oath; ~**belehrung** caution concerning the oath (*before the oath is administered*); ~**bruch** breaking of an oath; ~**delikt** offence of false swearing, perjury; ~**fähigkeit** capacity to swear (or take) oath; ~**formel** standard form of oath; the oath; *religiöse* ~~: *religious form of the oath*; ~**förmlichkeiten** oath-rite, form of the oath; ~**helfer** *hist* oath helper; ~**leistung** administration of the oath; the act of swearing the oath; ~**mündigkeit** minimum age for taking (swearing) an oath; ~**notstand** exceptional circumstances excusing a false oath; ~**pflicht** legal duty to swear (or take) the oath; e~**stattlich** in lieu of an oath; e~*stattliche Versicherung* → *Versicherung;* ~**unfähigkeit** disqualification from taking the oath; ~**verletzung** violation of one's oath; ~**verweigerer** *a person who refuses to take the oath (on principle)*; ~**verweigerung** refusal to take the oath; **an** ~ **Statt** in lieu of an oath; ~~~ *versichern: to affirm in lieu of an oath, to state in an affidavit,* → *eidesstattliche Versicherung*.

Eidgenosse *m* Swiss national.

eidgenössisch f Swiss, confederate.
eidlich adj sworn, on oath.
eigen adj own, of one's own, personal, proprietary, individual.
Eigen|aktien treasury stock; *zurückerworbene ~~* reacquired stock, treasury stock; **~anfall** (*a foundry's*) own accumulation (*of scrap*); **~anlage** a firm's own plant; **~anteilsklausel** excess clause; **~anzeige** self-accusation; **~arbeit** one's own handy work, do-it-yourself work (*DIY.*); **~art** individuality, originality; **~bedarf** one's own requirements, personal requirements, personal use; domestic requirements (*of a country*); *~~ geltend machen*: to require the premises for occupation as residence; **~bedarfsklage** action for self-possession (*of premises required by landlord for himself or his family*); **~behalt** retention (*insurance*): portion to be paid by insured party himself; **~belastung** dead load (*own weight of vehicle*); **~beleg** internal voucher, self-prepared voucher; **~besitz** owner occupation, proprietary possession, owner-possession, own holding (*possession with intent to hold for oneself*); own property; **~besitzanmaßung** actual ouster; **~besitzer** proprietary possessor, owner-occupier, exclusive possessor (*person holding with intent to have possession for himself*); **~betrieb** one's own business, enterprise operated by its owner, owner-operated municipal enterprise; **~bewirtschaftung** owner cultivation (*of land*); **~darstellung über die Kreditfähigkeit** one's own representation of credit worthiness (*or:* of capacity to borrow); **~deckung** collateral put up by the debtor (*from his own capital*); **~depot** own securities deposit; **~erzeugnis** company-manufactured product; **~erzeugung** domestic production, own product; **~fertigung** own products, own manufacture; **~fertigungskapazität** own available manufacturing capacity; **~fertigungsprogramm** company manufacturing program; **~finanzierung** self-financing, financing from one's own resources, equity financing; **~finanzierungsmittel** internal resources; **~gefahr** individual (*or* own) risk; **~geld** prisoner's own money (account); **~geschäft** business transaction for one's own account, own business, independent operation(s); **~gesetzlichkeit** development of its own inherent laws, development subject to its own (economic) laws; **~gewicht** own weight, empty weight, dead weight, tare weight (*railway*); **~handel** private trade, business for one's account; **e~händig** by one's own hand, in one's own handwriting, manu propria, holographic; *~~ unterschrieben*: *signed personally*; **~händler** (authorized) dealer, trader (*not an agent*); **~händlervertrag** authorized dealer's agreement, exclusive dealer arrangement; **~heim** private dwelling house, privately owned residence, owner-occupied house *~~ mit Einliegerwohnung: owner-occupied house with separate apartment*; **~investition** self-financed investment, investment from one's own resources, own capital investment; **~jagd** land owner's right to hunt (*on his own estate*); **~jagdrevier** owner's hunting district; **~kosten** primary costs, one's own costs; **~leistung** borrower's own funding; borrower's capital resources (*building*) pl *~en*: services rendered for own account, work performed and materials supplied by owner; *andere aktivierte ~~*: *other company-produced additions to plant and equipment*; **~macht** self-given authority; *verbotene ~~*: *unlawful interference with possession*; **e~mächtig** high-handed, acting without proper authority, arbitrary; **~marke** house brand; **~masse** net mass; **~mittel** (one's own) resources, private means, capital resources, building capital; *~~ des Darlehensnehmers:*

Eigenkapital / **Eigentum**

borrower's own funds; ~**name** proper name, surname (*not an alias*); ~**nutz** self-interest, one's own use, for one's personal use; personal profit; *strafbarer* ~~: *punishable greed*; ~**nutzer** private occupier; ~**nutzung** proprietor's own use, internal use; ~**nutzungswert** imputed rent of owner-occupied premises); ~**obligo** own commitment; ~**produktion** domestic production; ~**rechtserbschein** *Erbschein*; ~**rettung** self-rescue; ~**schuld** one's own indebtedness; ~**staatlichkeit** autonomous statehood, sovereignty; e~**ständig** independent, autonomous, for own goal; e~**trassiert** drawn by the drawer on himself; ~**tum** → *Eigentum*; ~**tümer** → *Eigentümer*; ~**verbrauch** consumption for one's own use; personal consumption, in-house consumption; ~**veredelung** processing (of goods) for (the manufacturer's) own account; ~**vermögen** capital and reserves, one's own assets, own resources; ~**verschulden** (injured party's) own fault (*or* negligence); *zurücktretendes* ~~ *des Verletzten*: *supervening negligence*; ~**versicherung** self-insurance, insurance for one's own account; ~**versorgung** self-support, self-supply, *pol* graft (*of politicians*); ~**verwaltung** a local authority's inherent administrative functions; ~**vorteil** self-benefit, one's own advantage; ~**wechsel** negotiable promissory note; ~**werbung** house advertising; ~**wert** actual value, intrinsic value; ~**wirtschaftlichkeit** viability of a public enterprise (*without support*).

Eigenkapital *m* net worth, equity capital, proprietary capital, capital resources of the owner of a business, shareholder's (*or* stockholder's) equity, equity resources, surplus earnings; *haftendes* ~~: *net worth*; ~**ausstattung** equity position; ~**bildung** equity capital formation; ~**leistung** borrower's capital resources (*building*); ~**quote** equity ratio; ~**rendite** return on equity; ~**verzinsung** return on net worth; ~ **von ...%** dent-equity ratio of ...%.

Eigenschaft *f* quality, attribute, characteristic, nature, capacity, property; ~**zeichen** individual trade mark; **berufliche** ~ professional character; **besondere** ~**en** peculiar characteristics, special features; **erforderliche** ~ requirement; **in amtlicher** ~ in an official capacity, colore officii; **in aufsichtsführender** ~ in a supervisory capacity; **in beratender** ~ in an advisory capacity; **in der** ~ **als Vertreter** in one's representative capacity; **in dienstlicher** ~ in one's official capacity; **in privater** ~ in one's personal capacity; **in seiner** ~ **als** in one's capacity as; **in treuhänderischer** ~ in a fiduciary capacity; **körperliche** ~**en** physical characteristics; **notwendige** ~ essential quality; **persönliche** ~ personal characteristics; **rechtliche** ~ legal status; **wesentliche** ~ essentiality, indispensable feature; **zufällige** ~ accidental quality; **zugesicherte** ~ warranted quality;

Eigentum *n* ownership, beneficial ownership, owner's title, (the right of) property, proprietorship, title, fee simple (*land*), legal estate (*land*); ~ **an beweglichen Sachen** personal property, ownership of chattels; ~**an unbeweglichen Sachen** ownership of real, property; ~ **auf Zeit** ownership for a limited time; ~ **der Erbengemeinschaft** joint property of the heirs, parcenary; ~ **der öffentlichen Hand** public property; ~**erwerben** to acquire (*or* obtain) the ownership (of sth), to acquire the title (to sth); ~ **geht auf den Erben über** the title passes to the heir; ~ **nach Bruchteilen** tenancy in common, common ownership (*by fractional undivided interests*); ~ **übertragen** to transfer the title (to sth); ~ **zur gesamten Hand** joint property, joint tenancy; **als** ~ as absolute property, in fee

Eigentümer ... **Eigentumsanspruch**

(*land*); **belastetes** ~ encumbered property; **beschränktes** ~ restricted ownership; **das ~ geht über** the title passes (to); **das ~ haben** to own, to hold the title (to); **das ~ lastenfrei machen** to clear the title; **das ~ übergehen lassen** to pass title, to convey the property; **entgeltlich erworbenes** ~ title (property) acquired by payment; **erbrechtlich beschränktes** ~ fee tail, estate in tail; **fremdes** ~ third party's property; **geistiges** ~ intellectual property (*copyrights, patents, trade marks*); his "brain-child", brainwork; **gemeinschaftliches** ~ joint ownership; **gewerbliches** ~ proprietary right, industrial property, commercial property; **im gemeinsamen** ~ jointly owned; **in ausländischem** ~ foreign-owned; **juristisches** ~ legal ownership; **künstlerisches** ~ proprietary rights of an artist; **lastenfreies** ~ perfect ownership, clear title (*land*), unencumbered title; **mit Rechtsmängeln behaftetes** ~ bad title; **öffentliches** ~ public property; **originäres** ~ original ownership; **rechtlich geschütztes gewerbliches** ~ (legally protected) industrial property right; **rechtmäßiges** ~ good title; **sich das ~ vorbehalten** to reserve one's proprietary rights, to reserve title; **treuhänderisches** ~ trust property; **unbeschränktes** ~ absolute ownership; **unentziehbares** ~ indefeasible title; **vermutetes** ~ reputed (*or* supposed) ownership; **volles** ~ good title.

Eigentümer *m* (absolute, legal) owner, beneficial owner; proprietor; ~ **auf Lebenszeit** life owner, owner holding property for life; ~ **auf Zeit** owner pro tempore; ~**Besitzer-Verhältnis** owner-possessor relationship; ~ **im Innenverhältnis** equitable owner; ~**gebrauch** proprietary use; ~**grundschuld** owner's (land) charge; ~**haftpflichtversicherung** owner's public liability insurance; ~**hypothek** owner's mortgage (*for his own benefit*); ~**nießbrauch** owner's right of usufruct; ~**recht** owner's right(s); ~ **sein** to own, to be owner (*or* proprietor); ~**weg** privately owned road; ~ **zu Bruchteilen** tenant in common *in undivided fractional interests*; ~ **zur gesamten Hand** *pl* joint tenants; **alleiniger, absoluter** ~ sole and unconditional owner; **alleinverfügungsberechtigter** ~ owner with exclusive right of disposal, sole and unconditional owner; **als ~ auftreten** to act in one's capacity as owner; **derzeitiger** ~ present owner; **eingetragener** ~ registered owner; **gutgläubiger** ~ bona fide owner; **jeweiliger** ~ respective owner for the time being; **dem jeweiligen ~ zustehen:** *to run with the land*; **mutmaßlicher** ~ putative owner; **neuer** ~ new owner, incomer, alienee; **rechtmäßiger** ~ rightful owner; **treuhänderischer** ~ trustee, fiduciary owner; **unumschränkter** ~ absolute owner; **vermutlicher** ~ reputed owner, putative owner; **wirklicher** ~ real owner, true owner; **wirtschaftlicher** ~ beneficial owner.

Eigentümerin *f* proprietress.

Eigentums|anspruch right of ownership, title to property, property claim; ~**aufgabe** abandonment of goods, dereliction; ~**bildung** formation of property, property formation; ~~ **in Arbeitnehmerhand**: *acquisition of property by employees*; ~**entziehung** conversion, expropriation; ~**erwerb** acquisition of ownership (*or*: of title), accession of title; ~~ **durch Vermischung**: *accession by confusion*; ~~ **durch Verschmelzung**: *accession by merger* (*or*: *confusion*); **derivativer** ~~: *succession of title*; **originärer** ~~: *primary acquisition of title (by operation of law)*; ~**feststellungsklage** action for a declaration concerning the ownership; ~**garantie** constitutional guarantee of the right of ownership; ~**herausgabeanspruch** claim

225

Eigner   **Einäscherung**

for possession based on ownership; ~**klage** action based on ownership; ~**nachweis** (prima facie) evidence of title (*or* ownership), abstract of title; ~**ordnung** system of property ownership; property arrangements; ~**papiere** documents of title (*to goods, to a car etc*); ~**recht** title, ownership, right of ownership, proprietorship, dominion, domain (*public*); ~**recht am Grundstück** ownership of land, property rights in land, fee simple, freehold estate; ~**recht an e-m Patent** ownership of a patent, proprietary rights in respect of a patent; ~**recht an Waren** title to goods; ~**schutz** legal protection of ownership; ~**störung** actionable nuisance, infringement of property rights; ~**streuung** dispersal of assets; ~**titel** title to property; *rechtsmängelfreier* ~~: clear title (*of record*); ~**übergang** passing of title; ~**übertragung** transfer of ownership, transfer of title (to); ~**übertragungsurkunde** deed of conveyance (*unregistered land*), transfer certificate (*registered land*); ~**urkunde** certificate of title, title document; ~**ursprung** root of title, origin of ownership; ~**verflechtung** cross ownership; ~**vergehen** offence against property rights; ~**verhältnis** status of ownership; ~~*se: proprietorship*; ~**verletzung** violation of property rights; ~**verlust** loss of ownership; ~**vermutung** presumption of ownership; ~**versicherung** title insurance; ~**verzicht** abandonment of title; ~**vorbehalt** reservation of title, reservation of ownership, retention of title, title retention; *verlängerter* ~~: *extended reservation of proprietary rights*; ~**wechsel** change in ownership; ~**wohnung** freehold flat, condo, condominium apartment; *eigengenutzte* ~~: *owner-occupied apartment (flat)*.

Eigner *m* owner, proprietor (*of a business, of real estate*).

Eignung *f* suitability, eligibility, fitness aptitude, qualifications; ~ **für Wohnzwecke** fitness for habitation; **berufliche** ~ vocational aptitude, occupational competence; **fachliche** ~ professional qualification; **geistige** ~ mental fitness; **körperliche** ~physical fitness.

Eignungs|garantie warranty of fitness; ~**prüfung** qualifying examination; aptitude test (*persons*), fitness test (*health*); ~**untersuchung** fitness examination; qualifying examination; ~**wert** service value, suitability.

Eil|abfertigung quick dispatch; ~**auftrag** urgent (*or* rush) job, urgent work, urgent (*or* rush) order; ~**bestellung** rush (*or* urgent) order; ~**bote** express messenger, special delivery messenger, expressman; *durch* ~~~!: *express, by special delivery*; ~**brief** express letter, special delivery letter; ~**dienst** expedited service, express service; ~**fracht** express freight, fast freight; ~**frachtbrief** special consignment note for express freight (*or* for fast goods); ~**gebühr** express delivery charge, special charge for urgent work; ~**geld** dispatch money; ~**gut** express matter, express goods; ~~*beförderung: express carriage; als* ~~: *by passenger train*; ~**maßregeln** urgent measures; ~**paket** express parcel; ~**post** express postal service; ~**verfahren** summary proceeding(s); ~**zuständigkeit** competence for urgent matters; ~**zustellung** express delivery, special delivery.

einarbeiten *v/t* to learn on the job, to train on the job; *v/reflex* to acquaint oneself with a new job, to settle into a new job, to familiarize o. s. with new work.

Einarbeitung *f* breaking in, adjustment to a new job, familiarization with new work; ~**szeit** period of vocational adjustment, familiarization period.

einäschern *v/t* to cremate (*corpses*).

Einäscherung *f* cremation.

Einbahn|straße one-way street, one-way only; **~verkehr** one-way traffic.

Einbau *m* installation, assembly; **~möbel** built-in furniture, unit furniture; **~schrank** built-in wardrobe, unit cupboard; **~vorschrift** assembly instructions.

einbauen *v/t* to instal, to mount, to build in; to incorporate (*in a brief*).

Einbauten *pl* fixtures and fittings, fitments (*equipment built in by the tenant*); **~ in Mietobjekte** tenant's (*or* leasehold) improvements; **gewerbliche ~** trade fixtures.

Einbehalt *m* retention money.

einbehalten *v/t* to withhold, to retain.

Einbehaltung *f* withholding (*of wage tax etc*), retention *cf Zurückbehaltung*; **~ von Gewinnen** retention of profits.

Einbenennung *f* conferring one's family name upon an illegitimate child.

einberufen *v/t* to call (*a meeting*), to convene; to summon (*parliament*); to draft (*soldiers*).

Einberufung *f* convocation, summons, convening; call to arms, call-up, draft (*army*); **~ e-r Konferenz** convening (*or* calling) a conference; **~sbefehl** call-up order, draft order; **~sbekanntmachung** notice of meeting, convening notice; **~sbescheid** call-up order, draft order; **~sdekret** letter of summons to parliament; **~sfrist** notice period (*for a meeting*).

einbezahlen *v/t* to pay in.

einbezahlt *adj* paid-in, paid-up; *voll ~: fully paid-up* (*capital*).

einbeziehen *v/t* to incorporate (by reference), to include, to adopt.

Einbeziehung *f* inclusion, incorporation; **~ durch Bezugnahme** incorporation by reference; **~in den Pfandverband** extension of mortgage; **unter ~** including, together with.

Einbiegeverkehr *m* traffic turning into a major (*or US:* priority) road.

Einblicksrecht *n* inspection right(s), right to inspect papers, documents, records of the other party.

einbrechen *v/i* to break in, to burgle, to commit burglary.

Einbrecher *m* burglar.

Einbringen *n* contribution, investment.

einbringen *v/t* to contribute, to invest, to introduce, to bring in (*assets into a partnership*, *capital into a company*); to harvest; to table (*a motion*); to file (*a petition*); to earn, to yield (*interest*).

Einbringlichkeit *f* lucrativeness, collectibility, soundness (*of an outstanding debt*).

Einbringung *f* bringing in, contribution, investment; entry; harvesting; **~ e-s Antrags** introduction of a motion; **~svertrag** agreement, contract on contribution to capital; **~swert** value of capital investment (*at the time it is made*), value of asset when brought in; **~ von Sachwerten** contribution of physical assets (*to partnership capital*).

Einbruch *m* (1) burglary, (*GB and US*: not necessarily at night time; common law: at night), housebreaking; **~(s)diebstahl** burglary, housebreaking and theft, theft by breaking and entering; **~diebstahlversicherung** burglary insurance, **e~sicher** burglar-proof; **~sversuch** attempted burglary; **~swerkzeug** housebreaking implements, burglary tools.

Einbruch *m* (2) break, recession; **saisonbedingter ~** seasonal recession.

einbürgern *v/t* to naturalize.

Einbürgerung *f* naturalization (*of foreigners*), granting of citizenship.

Einbürgerungs|antrag application for naturalization; **~bedingungen** qualification(s) for naturalisation; **~fähigkeit** eligibility for naturalization; **~urkunde** certificate of naturalization, citizenship papers; **~verfahren** naturalization proceedings, procedure for obtaining citizenship.

Einbuße *f* impairment, loss, damage.

einbüßen *v/i* to be impaired, to lose.

Eindämmung *f* containment, checking; ~ **der Kreditexpansion** curbing of credit expansion; **~spolitik** policy of containment.

eindecken *v/reflex* to meet one's requirements, to buy ahead.

Eindeckung *f* precautionary buying, stocking up, replenishment (*of stocks, funds etc*).

eindeutig *adj* explicit; clear, definite, unambiguous, unequivocal.

Eindringen *n* intrusion, penetration; ~ **in fremde Räume** unlawful entering of enclosed premises.

eindringen *v/i* to intrude, to penetrate, to enter forcibly.

Eindringling *m* intruder, squatter.

Einehe *f* monogamy.

Einfachbier *n* small beer.

Einfahrt *f* entry, entrance, way in, drive, driveway; descent (*pit*); ~ **verboten** no entry; no thoroughfare.

Einfamilienhaus *n* detached house, single house, house for one family, family residence.

Einflug oder Ausflug *m* admission to, stay in, departure from (*airport*).

Einfluß *m* (*pl Einflüsse*) influence; **~bereich** sphere of influence, orbit, purview; **~nahme** influencing, influence peddling; **~zone** zone of influence, zone of operations; **außersaisonale ~e** *pl* nonseasonal influences; **beherrschender** ~ controlling interest; **ungebührlicher** ~ undue influence.

einfordern *v/t* to exact, to call in, to collect.

Einforderung *f* call, (*capital*) collection, calling-in.

Einfriedung *f* enclosure (= inclosure), fence; **~smauer** surrounding wall; **~srecht** right of enclosure; **~szaun** surrounding fence.

Einfrieren *n* freezing, blocking, immobilization.

einfrieren *v/t* to freeze, to block (*accounts*).

einfügen *v/t* to insert, to interpolate.

Einfügung *f* insertion, interpolation;

~sgebot requirement to be in harmony with surroundings.

Einfühlungsvermögen *n* empathy, intuitive understanding, intuitive flair, tactfulness, sensitive mental perception.

Einfuhr *f* importation, imports, import trade, imported goods; **~abfertigung** clearance inwards; **~~ im Betrieb**: *local import control;* **~abgaben** import duties; **~abschöpfung** import levy; **~anrecht** right to import; **~anschlußlieferungen** follow-up imports; **~ auf dem Seeweg** importation by sea; **~-Ausgleichsabgabe** import equalization levy (*or* tax); **~ausschuss** advisory committee on imports; **~bedarf** import requirements; **~belastung** import charges; **~bescheinigung** certificate of importation; **~beschränkung** import restrictions; *mengenmäßige* **~~**: *quantitative restriction of imports*; **~besteuerung** imposition of tax on importation; **~bestimmungen** import regulations; **~bewilligung** import permit; **~bewilligungsantrag** application for import permit; **~blatt** importation sheet (counter foil; voucher); **~deklaration** import declaration, import entry; **~dispositionen** import arrangements; **~einheit** unit of imported goods, import unit; **~erklärung** import declaration; **~erlaubnis** import licence, import permit; **~freigabe** release for importation; **~-Freiliste** import freelist; **~genehmigung** import authorization, import permit; **~handel** import trade, passive trade; **~händler** importer; **~kontingent** import quota; **~kontingentierung** imposing import quotas, limitation (by quotas) on imports; **~kredit** import credit; **~kurve** trend in imports; **~kürzungen** import cuts; **~land** country from which imports are obtained; (*also*:) importing country; **~lieferungen** import shipments; **~liste** import list; **~lizenz**

Einfuhrmonopol

import licence; ~**monopol** monopoly of imports; ~**müdigkeit** reluctance to import; ~**ort** place of importation; ~**papier** import document; ~**plafond** import "ceiling"; ~**potential** importing capacity; ~**prämie** bounty on imports, import bonus; ~**preis** import price; ~**prognose** forecasting the course of imports; ~**regelung** import rule (*or* regulation); ~**restriktionen** import restrictions; ~**schein** import licence; ~**sog** demand for imports, import pull, pressure to import; ~**sonderabgabe** import surcharge; ~**sperre** embargo on imports; ~**stelle** import agency; ~**steuern** import duties; ~**stop** import ban; ~**tief** an import low, low level of imports; ~**überschuß** import surplus; ~**umsatzsteuer** turnover tax on imports; ~**-Unbedenklichkeitsbescheinigung** import clearance certificate; ~**- und Vorratsstelle** import and storage agency; ~ **unter Zollverschluß** import(ation) in bond; ~**ventil** import opening, the import tap; ~**verbot** import prohibition, import ban; ~**verlagerung** shift in the type of imports; ~**vorausdispositionen** preliminary arrangements for imports; ~**vorgenehmigung** preliminary import permit; ~**waren** import goods, imported article; *nicht kontingentierte* ~~: *non-quota imports*; ~**wert** value of imports; ~**ziel** deferred payment for imports; ~**zoll** customs duty on imports; ~~*anmeldung: import declaration*; ~**zuschuß** import subsidy; **abschöpfungsfreie** ~ free-of-levy import; **die** ~ **lenken** to steer imports; **entgeltliche** ~ imports against (upon) payment; ~**endgültige** ~ outright importation, permanent importation; **gewerbliche** ~ commercial and industrial imports; **kommerzielle** ~ commercial imports; **liberalisierte** ~ liberalized imports; **nichtkommerzielle** ~ non-commercial imports; **private** ~ imports on private account; **sichtbare** ~ visible imports; **unentgeltliche** ~ imports free of payment; **unsichtbare** ~ invisible imports; **vorübergehende** ~ temporary admission (*or* importation); **zollfreie** ~ duty-free entry, free import.

einführen *v/t* to introduce, to initiate; to inaugurate; to import; **schrittweise** ~ to establish by steps (gradually).

Einführer *m* importer.

Einführung *f* introduction, initiation.

Einführungs|anzeige launch advertisement; ~**gesetz** introductory act (law); ~**kurs** introductory price, issuing price (*exch*); introductory course (*education*); ~**nummer** introductory number; ~**prospekt** listing prospectus; pathfinder prospectus; introductory prospectus; ~**preis** placing price, introductory price; ~**schreiben** letter of introduction; ~**werbung** initial advertising, launch advertising (*or* publicity).

Eingabe *f* petition, application to an authority, presentation of a request (*or* grievance); ~**frist** time limit for applications; ~**termin** closing date for applications.

Eingang *m* way in, entrance, introduction, entry receipt, incomings, incoming mail, arrival receipt (*of mail, documents, money*); ~ **vorbehalten** subject to collection (*cheque*).

Eingangs|abfertigung inward clearance, formalities on arrival (of persons), receipt (of thing); ~**abteilung** receiving department; ~**amt** first position of a career; ~**anzeige** acknowledgment of receipt, advice of receipt; ~**beleg** (*der Handkasse*) petty-cash receipt; ~**bescheinigung** (acknowledgment of) receipt; ~**besoldung** entrance level pay, starting salary; ~**bestätigung** confirmation of receipt, notice of arrival; ~**buch** book of entries, (inward) goods

eingedenk dessen / **Eingriff**

book, register of mail (or articles) received; ~**buchung** original entry; ~**datum** date of receipt (or arrival); ~~**Durchgangszollstelle** office of entry en route; ~**formel** preamble (*of an Act*); ~**gehalt** commencing salary; ~**gewicht** weight delivered; ~**meldung** receiving report (*goods received*); ~**nummer** serial number (*of mail*); ~**ort** place of entry; ~**prüfung** receiving inspection; *pat* examination on filing; ~**rechnung** purchase invoice; ~**stempel** date stamp, receipt stamp; ~**stufe** entrance level; ~**tag** date of receipt; ~**tarif** basic rate; ~**vermerk** file mark; ~**zoll** import duty, inward duty; ~**zollamt** import customs office; ~**zollstelle** office of entry; entry processing unit.

eingedenk dessen (*Präambel*) mindful of.

eingehalten *adj* observed, complied with, kept; **nicht** ~ unkept, unobserved, not complied with.

eingehen *v/i* to incur (*risk*), to undertake, to enter into (*obligations*); to be received, to come in (*mail, remittance*).

Eingehungsbetrug *m* fraudulent representation to obtain a contract, fraud in treaty.

eingeklagt *adj* sued for.

eingemeinden *v/t* to incorporate (*into a city or town*), to suburbanize.

Eingemeindung *f* incorporation (*of village etc into a city or other local community*), suburbanization.

eingerechnet *adj* inclusive, included.

eingeschlossen *adj* included, implied.

eingeschrieben registered (*mail*), enrolled (*student*).

eingestanden *pp + adj* acknowledged, admitted → *eingestehen*.

eingestandenermaßen *adv* admittedly, avowedly, concededly.

Eingeständnis *n* admission, avowal; ~ **e–r Prozeßpartei**: admission of a party.

eingestehen *v/t* to admit, to concede.

eingetragen *adj* registered, on record, recorded; enrolled (*member*), booked; **gerichtlich** ~ registered with the court; **nicht** ~ not registered, not recorded.

Eingeweide *pl* viscera (*autopsy*).

eingezahlt *adj* paid-up; *voll* ~: *fully paid up*.

eingliedern *v/t* to incorporate, to include, to integrate, to classify.

Eingliederung *f* incorporation, integration; ~ **in den Arbeitsprozeß** intregration into employment; ~**sdarlehen** integration loan, rehabilitation loan; ~**shilfe** integration assistance; ~**leistungen** integration aid, grants and benefits for the economic integration (*of refugees*); **wirtschaftliche** ~ integration (*or* absorption) into the economic system, economic integration.

Eingreifen *n* intervention; **gerichtliches** ~ judicial intervention; **polizeiliches** ~ intervention by the police.

eingreifen *v/i* to encroach upon, to interfere with (*rights*).

eingrenzen *v/t* to delimit, to restrict the scope of.

Eingriff *m* intrusion, interference (with), encroachment (on, upon sth), official action, infringement (*of rights*); ~ **in das Privateigentum** interference with private property, violation of private property; ~ **in den Gewerbebetrieb** interference with business; ~ **in die grundrechtlich geschützten Freiheiten** interference with civil liberties; ~ **in die persönliche Freiheit** interference with personal liberty; ~ **in die Rechte anderer** encroachment upon; infringement of other people's rights; ~**sbefugnisse** powers of intervention; ~**snormen** statutory requirements for (Government) intervention; ~**sschwelle** threshold of interference; ~**sverwaltung** executive administration (*affecting the individual*); **dirigistische** ~**e** governmental interference; ~**enteignungsgleicher** ~ inverse condemnation;

Eingruppierung — **einig**

hoheitsrechtliche ~**e** intervention by sovereign power(s); **staatlicher** ~ state (*or* governmental) intervention.

Eingruppierung *f* classification, grouping.

einhalten *v/t* to observe, to comply with, to adhere to.

Einhaltung *f* observance (of), compliance (with); ~ **der gegenseitigen Verpflichtungen** adherence to mutual obligations; ~ **der Gesetze** observance of the laws; ~ **e–r Bedingung** compliance with a condition; ~ **e–r Frist** meeting a deadline, observance of a time limit; ~ **e–s Vertrages** adherence to (the terms of) a contract; ~ **in allen wesentlichen Punkten** substantial compliance, compliance with the essential requirements; ~ **von Handelsbräuchen** observance of commercial usages; **unter** ~ **einer Frist (von)** subject to a term (time-limit) of.

einhandeln *v/t* to obtain by bargaining.

einheben *v/t* to collect, to levy.

Einhebung collection (*of public charges*), levy.

einheften *v/t* to file (away), to put sth in a loose-leaf file.

Einhegungsrecht *n* right of enclosure.

einheimisch *adj* local, domestic, indigenous.

Einheirat *f* marriage into a family business or farm.

einheiraten *v/i* to marry into (*a family business or farm*).

Einheit *f* unit, entity, point (*statistical*), *fig* unity; **in sich abgeschlossene** ~ self-contained unit (*rooms*); **nationale** ~ national unity; **selbständige** ~ separate unit; **wirtschaftliche** ~ economic unit.

einheitlich *adj* unitary, uniform, standardized, concerted (*action*).

Einheitlichkeit *f* uniformity; ~ **der Erfindung** unity of invention.

Einheits|bank unitary bank (*bank without branches*); ~**bedingungen** standard conditions; ~**beiträge** flat-rate contributions; ~**bestrebung** unification movement; ~**betrag** flat rate; ~**bewertung** valuation of economic units (*of the taxpayer*); ~**formular** standard form; ~**front** united front; ~**geschäfte** standardized transactions; ~**gesellschaft** unit company, unified company; consolidated limited partnership; ~**gewerkschaft** industrial union, multi-craft union; *fachliche* ~~: *horizontal union*; ~**gründung** single-step foundation (*foundation and capital issue at the same time*); ~**kosten** unit cost; ~**kurs** standard quotation, official rate, single figure quotation (*stock exchange*); ~**liste** *pol* single list; ~**markt** standard market; ~**mietvertrag** standard tenancy agreement; ~**muster** standard pattern, standard sample; ~**partei** *pol* unity party; ~**police** standard policy; ~**prämie** uniform premium; ~**preis** standard price, uniform price, flat price, unit price, single price, all-at-one price; ~**preisgeschäft** one-price store; ~**preissystem** standard price system; ~**qualität durchschnittlicher Güte** standard quality, marketable quality; ~**recht** unified standard law; ~**satz** standard rate; ~**schule** normal school, standard school; ~**staat** unitary state; ~**steuer** uniform tax, single tax; ~**strafe** consolidated single penalty; ~**stücklohn** standard piece wage; ~**tarif** uniform tariff, single-schedule tariff; ~**vertrag** standard contract, standard agreement; ~**versicherung** all risks insurance; ~**vordruck** standard printed form; ~**wert** rateable (*or* taxable) value, assessment unit value (*of real estate*), assessable value, standard value; ~**wertbescheid** tax value assessment notice; ~**zoll** uniform duty; ~**zolltarif** single-schedule tariff.

einholen *v/t* to call for, to seek, to obtain (*advice, an expert opinion*).

einig *adj* in agreement with; ~ **sein**: *to agree v/i, to be in agreement*.

einigen *v/reflex* to come to (*or* reach) an agreement, to agree; *v/t pol* to unite; **sich außergerichtlich** ~ to settle out of court; **sich gütlich** ~ to settle amicably.

Einigkeit *f* mutual consent, harmony, agreement; *es besteht* ~ *darüber*: *it is mutually understood and agreed*.

Einigung *f* agreement, mutual consent, concurrence of will, meeting of (the) minds (*law of contract*); consensus ad idem; *pol*: unification; *zu e–r* ~ *kommen*: *to reach an agreement, to come to terms*; **außergerichtliche** ~ out-of-court settlement; **gütliche** ~ amicable settlement, private agreement.

Einigungs|amt conciliation board; ~**grundsatz** principle of formal agreement (*in land registery matters for conveyances*); ~**mangel** lack of agreement, disagreement, failure to agree (*contract*); ~**stelle** board of conciliation; ~**urkunde** certificate of conciliation; ~**verfahren** conciliation proceedings; ~**vorschlag** proposal for a settlement.

einkalkulieren *v/t* to take into account.

Einkammergesetzgebung *f* unicameral legislation, single-chamber enactment of laws, single-chamber system.

Einkammersystem *n* unicameral system.

einkassieren *v/t* to collect.

Einkassierung *f* collection.

Einkauf *m* purchase, *colloq* shopping; **bargeldloser** ~ cashless shopping.

einkaufen to purchase, to buy, to shop.

Einkäufer *m* buyer, purchasing agent; **ortsansässiger** ~ resident buyer, local buyer.

Einkaufs|abteilung purchasing (*or* buying) department; ~**akkreditiv** buying letter of credit; ~**bedingungen** conditions of purchase, purchase terms; ~**beleg** purchase voucher; ~**buch** voucher register; ~**dispositionen** buying arrangements; ~**ermächtigung** purchasing authorization; ~**gemeinschaft** purchasing pool; ~**genossenschaft** purchasing cooperative, purchasers' association; ~**kartell** purchase cartel; ~**kommission** buying commission, order to buy on commission; ~**kommissionär** purchasing commission merchant; ~**kontingent** purchase quota, buying quota; ~**konto** purchase account; ~**kredit** loan to finance purchases; ~**preis** purchase price, cost price; ~**provision** buying commission, buying brokerage; ~**rabatt** purchase discount; ~**rechnung** invoice for a purchase, purchase account; ~**sachbearbeiter** purchasing agent; ~**sitzung** purchasing session; ~**vereinigung** purchasing association; ~**vertreter** buying agent; ~**vollmacht** purchasing authority; e~**wirksam** as per purchasing date; ~**zentrum** shopping centre; ~**zusammenschluß** joint purchase.

einkerkern *v/t* to incarcerate.

einklagbar *adj* suable, actionable, **nicht** ~: unenforceable, non-actionable; **selbständig** ~ actionable per se.

Einklagbarkeit *f* suability, enforceability, recoverability.

einklagen *v/t* to file a suit for, to sue for, to sue, to issue a writ against.

Einklagung *f* suing (*for a claim*), taking legal action (*for the recovery of a debt*).

Einklang *m* accord, agreement, congruity; **im** ~ **mit** in keeping with, in step with; **in** ~ **bringen** to reconcile, to harmonize.

Einklarieren *m* = *Einklarierung qv*.

einklarieren *v/t* to clear (inward-bound ship), to clear in.

Einklarierung *f* clearance inwards, inward clearance; ~**stag** day of entry.

Einkommen *n* income, ordinary income, (total) earnings; ~ **aus freier Berufstätigkeit** professional earnings; ~ **aus Gewerbebetrieb** trading income, income from trade or industry; ~ **aus Grundbesitz** in-

einkommensabhängig

come from landed property; ~ **aus Kapital- und Vermögensbesitz** income from capital and property; ~ **aus Kapitalvermögen** income from capital, *GB*: unearned income; ~ **aus selbständiger Arbeit** professional earnings, free-lance earnings; ~ **aus unselbständiger Arbeit** income from wages and salaries; ~ **nach (Abzug der) Steuern** income after (deduction of) taxes, net income, income net of taxes; ~ **von Körperschaften** corporate income; ~ **vor Abzug der Steuern** gross income, pre-tax income; **beitragspflichtiges** ~ income liable to payment of contributions *(for social security etc)*; **die laufenden ~s- und Vermögensteuern** current taxes on income and wealth; **effektives** ~ real income; **festes** ~ regular income, fixed income; **freiberufliches** ~ independent income, income from self-employment, free-lance income; **freies** ~ free income; **gewerbliches** ~ income derived from trade or industry, business income; **persönliches** ~ personal income; **Pro-Kopf-Einkommen** individual earnings, per capita income; **ruhegeldfähiges** ~ pensionable income; **sozialversicherungspflichtiges** ~ income liable to payment of social insurance contributions; **spärliches** ~ pittance, modest income; **steuerbares** ~ taxable income; **steuerfreies** ~ tax-free income; **steuerpflichtiges** ~ taxable income; **unselbständiges** ~ wage and salary income; **verfügbares** ~ disposable income; **zu versteuerndes** ~ taxable income, assessable income.

einkommensabhängig *adj* income-dependent.

Einkommens|ausgleich income equalization; ~**besteuerung** taxation of income; ~**bezieher** recipient of income; *selbständiger* ~~: *independent recipient of income*; ~**elastizität** income elasticity; ~**entstehung** origin *or* source of in-

Einkommenssteuer

come; ~**entwicklung** movement in incomes; ~**erhöhung** increase in income; *exogene* ~~: *increase in income originating elsewhere*; ~**erklärung** statement of income, income-tax return; ~**ermittlung** determination of (taxable) income; ~**grenze** income limit; ~**gruppe** income group, income bracket; ~**klasse** income class; ~**nachholbedarf** earnings lag; ~**niveau** level of income; ~**pfändung** garnisheeing of earnings, attachment of earnings; ~**politik** incomes policy; ~**quelle** source of income; ~**quellenbesteuerung** taxation of income at source; **e~reagibel** sensitive to variations in income; ~**rücklage** income reserve(s), unspent income; ~**schicht** income group, income bracket; ~**schichtung** income stratification; ~**schmälerung** reduction of earnings; ~**schwelle** income threshold; ~**sicherung** income maintenance; ~**steuer** → *Einkommensteuer*; ~**streuung** distribution of income, income spread; ~**stufe** income bracket; ~**teile** portions of income; ~**übertragung** income transfer; ~**umlagerung** income switching; ~**umschichtung** shift in income; ~**verlagerung** shifting income; **e~vermehrend** *adj* income-increasing; ~**verschiebung** shift in income; ~**verteilung** distribution (*or* redistribution) of income; ~**zuwachs** increase of earnings; *inflationsbereinigter* ~~: *increase in income (earnings) adapted to inflationary changes*.

Einkommenssteuer *f* (individual) income tax, personal income tax; ~**ausfall** shortfall in income tax; ~**bescheid** income tax assessment, income tax bill; ~**erklärung** income tax return; *gemeinsame* ~~: *joint income tax return (of husband and wife)*; ~**erleichterungen** income-tax relief; **e~frei** *adj* free of income tax, tax-free; ~**freiheit** exemption from income tax; ~**gesetz** Income Tax Act; ~**Grundtabelle** basic table for calculating income tax; ~**novelle** income-tax amending law, tax amending bill; ~**pflicht** income tax liability; *beschränkte* ~~: *limited income tax liability (for non-residents' earnings from inland sources)*; **e**~**pflichtig** *adj* liable to income tax; ~**pflichtiger** income-tax payer; ~**recht** income tax law; ~**richtlinie** income tax directive; ~**rückvergütung** refund of income tax; ~**senkungen** income-tax reductions; ~**-Splitting-Tabelle** joint marital income tax scale; ~**tabelle** income-tax table; ~**tarif** income tax rate, tax scale; ~**veranlagung** assessment of individual income tax; ~**vergünstigung** income tax relief; ~**-Vorauszahlung** prepayment (*or* advance payment) of income tax; **ausländische** ~ foreign income tax; **die** ~ **ist durch den Steuerabzug abgegolten** income tax is settled by deduction at source; **progressive** ~ progressive income tax; **unbeschränkte** ~**pflicht** unlimited income tax liability (*for residents*); **zur** ~ **kommen noch hinzu** the following surcharges are added to the (income) tax assessment; **zur** ~ **veranlagen** to assess the amount of income tax payable.

Einkreisung *f* encirclement; integration into a district authority.

Einkreisungs|kette *f* (*bei Fahndung*) drag-net technique; ~**patent** fencing-in patent; ~**politik** policy of encirclement, isolation.

Einkünfte *pl* revenue, earnings, income, taxable proceeds, (*from certain types of sources*); ~ **aus Aktien** income from shares; ~ **aus Arbeitsleistung und gewerblicher Tätigkeit** earned income (*professional and employee income*); ~ **aus der unmittelbaren Nutzung** income derived from direct use; ~ **aus eigener Arbeit** personal earnings; ~ **aus Erwerbstätigkeit** earned income, trading receipts; ~ **aus Gewerbebetrieb** income from trade or industry, industrial and commercial profits; ~ **aus Grundbesitz** income from real estate; ~ **aus Kapitalvermögen** unearned income, income from capital assets, investment income; ~ **aus Landbesitz** income from real estate; ~ **aus nichtselbständiger Arbeit** income from employment; ~ **aus selbständiger Arbeit** self-employment income, free-lance earnings; ~ **aus unbeweglichem Vermögen** income from real (*or* immovable) property; ~ **aus Vermietung und Verpachtung** income from immovable property, income derived from letting (property); ~ **aus Wertpapiervermögen** income from securities; ~ **der öffentlichen Hand** public revenue; ~ **von natürlichen Personen** personal income; **ausländische** ~ foreign income; **betriebliche** ~ operating income; **echte** ~ actual income; **entgangene** ~ lost earnings; **feste** ~ fixed income; **feste oder bestimmbare** ~ fixed or determinable income; **freiberufliche** ~ free-lance income, earnings from self-employment; **inländische** ~ domestic income; **nichtgewerbliche** ~ nonbusiness income; **pauschalbesteuerte** ~ income taxed at a flat rate; **sonstige** ~ other income, miscellaneous revenues; **ständige** ~ permanent income; **steuerfreie** ~ tax-free income; **wiederkehrende** ~ regular income, recurring receipts; **zu versteuernde** ~ taxable income.

Einkunfts|arten types of (taxable) income, classes of revenue; ~**quelle** source of income.

Einlage *f* deposit (*bank account*); initial capital share; capital contribution; enclosure (*letter*).

Einlagen|bestand total deposits; ~**buch** pass-book (*bank account*); ~**entwicklung** movement of deposits; ~**forderung** call; ~ **geschäft** deposit business (*banks*); ~ **in Sachwerten** investment in non-monetary assets; ~**konto** deposit account; capital contribution account; ~ **mit 3% verzinsen** to pay 3% interest on deposit accounts; ~**rückstand** arrears on calls, unpaid calls; ~**sicherung** deposit security arrangements; ~**sicherungsfonds** deposit guaranty fund; ~**verbindlichkeiten** deposit liability ties; ~**-zertifikat** certificate of deposit (*CD*); ~**zins** interest on deposits; **ausstehende** ~ unpaid capital, unpaid subscriptions; **befristete** ~ deposits for a fixed term, time deposits; **erste** ~ original investment, initial share; **feste** ~ fixed deposits; **gebietsfremde** ~ non-resident deposits; **gesetzliche** ~ legal minimum deposits; **kommunale** ~ deposits by local authorities; **kündbare** ~ time deposits, deposits at notice, investment subject to call; **kurzfristige** ~ deposits on short notice, short-term deposits; **langfristige** ~ long-term deposits; **mindestreservepflichtige** ~ deposits subject to minimum reserve obligation; **öffentliche** ~ public deposits; **täglich fällige** ~ demand deposits, deposits payable on demand; **terminierte** ~ time (*or* fixed term) deposits; **unverzinsliche** ~ non-interest-bearing deposits.

Einlagerer *m* depositor, warehouse customer.

einlagern *v/t* to store, to warehouse, to place in a warehouse.

Einlagerung *f* storage, storing, warehousing; ~**smaßnahme** storage arrangement; ~ **unter Zollverschluß** bonding; **jeder Zeit zugängliche** ~ live storage, permanently accessible storage.

Einlagerungs|gebühr storage charge; ~**kapazität** storage space, warehousing space; ~**kredit** warehouse loan; ~**land** country of warehousing; ~**schein** warehouse receipt; ~**wechsel** storage bill, warehouse bill.

einlassen *v/reflex* to enter an appearance (*civil procedure*), to defend a case; to take up one's defence.

Einlassung *f* appearance, submission to the jurisdiction of a court; answer to the charge, statement of accused in court; ~ **auf die Anklage** pleading to the charge; ~**sfrist** period for filing a defence; ~**stermin** day to show cause, stipulated date for entering an appearance; ~ **zur Hauptsache** plea to the merits of plaintiff's claim; ~ **zur Anklage verweigern** to stand mute; ~ **zur Sache** defence relating to the substance of the dispute; pleading on the merits of a case.

Einlauf *m* incoming mail; arrival; ~**hafen** port of entry; ~**stelle** filing office, filing department (*of a court, administrative agency for incoming mail and pleadings*).

einlaufend *adj* incoming.

einlegen *v/t* to lodge, to file (*a remedy*), to insert.

Einleger *m* depositor, contributor (*to company's capital*); **gewerbetreibender** ~ business depositor.

Einlegung *f* lodging, filing; ~ **der Berufung** filing of appeal, lodging of the appeal; ~ **e-s Rechtsbehelfs** lodging of a legal remedy; ~ **e-s Rechtsmittels** lodging of an appeal.

einleiten *v/t* to initiate, to introduce.

einleitend *adj* introductory, initial.

Einleitung *f* introduction, institution, initiation (*proceedings*); ~**sbehörde** initiating authority (*in disciplinary proceedings*); ~**sbeschluß** decision to institute (disciplinary) proceedings, receiving order; ~**sformel** caption (*indictment, pleading*), title; ~~ **e-r Entschließung: resolving clause;** ~ **e-s Strafverfahrens** institution of a prosecution (*or* of criminal proceedings).

Einlieferer *m* (= *der Einliefernde*) depositor; committing officer.

einliefern *v/t* to commit (*a person to an institution or prison*); to deliver.

Einlieferung *f* commitment, committal, official assignment and delivery *of a person to prison, a mental hospital etc.*; taking over of an ex-

einliegend

tradicted person for trial; ~**sbefehl** warrant of commitment, committal order; ~**sbescheinigung** postal receipt *for registered letters etc*; certificate of deposit; ~**sliste** list of commitments to prison; ~**sschein** paying-in slip, certificate of posting, postal receipt; ~ **in die Haftanstalt** committal to prison.

einliegend *adv* enclosed.

Einliegerwohnung *f* internal flat (*within an apartment or dwelling house*); lodging contained in a dwelling.

einlösbar *adj* redeemable (*pledge, security*), payable (*cheque, bill of exchange*), convertible; *nicht ~*: *irredeemable, uncollectible*.

Einlösbarkeit *f* redeemability, payability, convertibility.

einlösen *v/t* to redeem, to pay, to discharge, to hono(u)r (*bill of exchange*); *nicht ~*: *to dishono(u)r; nicht eingelöst: unclaimed* (*cheque*).

Einlösung *f* redemption, payment, discharge, honouring; ~ **e-s Versprechens** keeping a promise; ~ **e-s Wechsels** payment (*or* hono(u)ring; *or* discharge) of a bill of exchange; ~ **von Banknoten** redemption of bank notes; ~ **von Wertpapieren** redemption of securities.

Einlösungs|betrag redemption amount, redemption price; ~**bedingungen** terms of redemption; ~**ermächtigung** authority to pay; ~**garantie** garantee (GB: guarantee) to honour a cheque; ~**frist** date of maturity, redemption period „~~ *abgelaufen*": *out of date* (*cheque*); ~**klausel** redemption clause; ~**kurs** redemption rate (*or* price); ~**pflicht** obligation to redeem, compulsory convertibility (*gold currency*); ~**papiere** documents that must be presented for payment; ~**provision** collection commission; ~**recht** right of redemption; ~**stelle** paying agent; ~**tag** redemption date, maturity date.

Einmal|behälter disposable contain-

Einnahmenausfall

er, one-way container; ~**beitrag** *ins* single premium; ~**betrag** lump sum, single payment; ~**kosten** non-recurring costs, non-recurrent expenditure; ~**prämie** single premium; ~**prämien-Lebensversicherung** single premium life policy; ~**rückstellung** non-recurring allocation to reserve, non-recurrent provision; ~**-Sparbeträge** single savings inpayment; ~**tarif** one-time rate (advertising).

einmalig *adj* non-recurrent, non-recurring, "one-off", once only.

Einmann|betrieb one-man business; ~**gesellschaft** one-man company; ~**-GmbH** one-man private limited company; ~**wahlkreis** single candidate constituency.

Einmischung *f* interference, intervention; ~**sklage** *f* = *Hauptintervention qv;* ~**spolitik** interventionist policy; **fremde** ~ foreign interference; **staatliche** ~ state interference; **unbefugte** ~ unauthorized intervention.

Einmündung *f* mouth, estuary (*river*); junction (*roads*).

Einnahme *f* receipt, *pl* (*~n*): takings, earnings, proceeds; **ordentliche** ~ ordinary receipt (*budget*).

Einnahmen|ausfall revenue shortfall; ~**-Ausgaben-Buchführungssystem** costbook principle of accounting; ~**-Ausgabenrechnung** cash-based accounting, bill of receipts and expenditures; ~ **aus laufender Rechnung** current receipts; ~**buch** receipts book; ~**decke** general revenue position, revenue cover-ratio; ~**kasse** cash receiving office; ~**politik** revenue policy; *gezielte* ~~ *purposive* (*or:* ad hoc) *revenue policy*; ~**posten** revenue items; ~**quelle** source of revenue; ~**rückgang** decline in revenue; ~**spitze** peak in receipts; ~**struktur** structure of revenue, revenue pattern; ~**überschuß** excess of receipts over expenditure; ~ **und Ausgaben** receipts and expenditure, receipts and payments; ~**- und Ausgabenplan** cash budget;

einordnen / **Einrede**

~- **und Ausgabenrechnung** receipt and expenditure accounting (*without balance sheet*); ~- **und Ausgabensätze** amounts entered as receipts and expenditures; ~- **und Ausgabenübersicht** cash survey; ~**vakuum** gap in receipts; **alle** ~ **und Ausgaben** all items of revenue and expenditure; **aufzeichnungspflichtige** ~ notifiable receipts, receipts required to be entered in the books; **bare** ~ cash receipts; **einmalige** ~ non-recurring receipts; **laufende** ~ regular income items; **ordentliche** ~ ordinary receipts (*budget*); **zweckgebundene** ~ earmarked receipts.

einordnen *v/t* to file; *v/reflex* to get in (*into the correct*) lane (*traffic*); ~!: *get in lane.*

Einordnung *f* classification, integration, filing (*letters*); ~**sfahrstreifen vor Kreuzungen** approach lane(s) to intersections.

Einparteienstaat *m* one-party state.

einpendeln *v/i* to find a level, to even out, to reach equilibrium.

Einpendeln *n* plateauing.

Einpersonenhaushalt *m* single person household.

Einphasensteuer *f* single-stage tax.

einplanen *v/t* to include in the plan, to plan, to budget for.

Einplanung *f* planning, inclusion in the plan, making provisions.

einquartieren *v/t* to billet, to quarter.

Einquartierung *f* quartering, billeting.

einräumen *v/t* to concede, to accord; to grant facilities (*credit*).

Einräumung *f* admission, concession, allowance, granting.

einrechnen *v/t* to count in, to include in one's calculations, to take into account.

Einrechnung *f* inclusion (*in the calculation or charge*).

Einrede *f* plea, defence plea, procedural defence, (negative) plea, objection, demurrer; ~ **der Arglist** defence that the pleading of another person is malicious, objection on the ground of malice, defence of fraud; ~ **der Aufrechnung** defence of set-off; ~ **der Dürftigkeit des Nachlasses** plene administravit, plea that assets are not sufficient to satisfy the plaintiff; ~ **der Erfüllung** plea in discharge; ~ **der mangelnden Aktivlegitimation** defence plea that plaintiff is not the proper party, plea of incompetence of plaintiff; ~ **der mangelnden Passivlegitimation** plea that defendant is the wrong party to be sued; ~ **der mangelnden Prozeßfähigkeit** defence of "unfit to plead", *plea of lack of legal capacity for court pleadings;* ~ **der örtlichen und sachlichen Unzuständigkeit** plea of want of jurisdiction; ~ **der Rechtshängigkeit** plea of another action pending, plea of lis pendens; ~ **der Rechtskraft** plea of res judicata, plea of estoppel per rem judicatam, (plea of) former adjudication; ~ **der Schikane** plea of chicanery; ~ **der ungenügenden Sicherheitsleistung** plea of insufficient security; ~ **der Unzulässigkeit** equitable estoppel, plea that action does not lie; ~ **der Unzurechnungsfähigkeit** defence of "unfit to plead", plea of lack of legal capacity of the other party, plea of insanity (*criminal procedure*); ~ **der Unzuständigkeit** plea of lack of competence, objection to the jurisdiction; ~ **der Verjährung** plea of lapse of time, plea that claim is statute-barred; *die* ~~~ *geltend machen: to plead lapse of time (criminal procedure) or: to plead the Statute of Limitations (civil cases);* ~ **der Vorausklage** (= *beneficium excussionis, beneficium ordinis*) benefit of discussion: *privilege of a surety that the creditor should first proceed against the debtor and exhaust his remedy against him,* plea of unexhausted remedies; ~ **der Vorbenutzung** plea of prior use (*patents*); ~ **des Mehrverkehrs** plea of multiple access (*paternity suit*); ~ **des nicht erfüllten Vertrags** plea

237

einreichen

of non-performance; ~ **des Schiedsgerichts** plea that arbitration had been agreed upon; ~ **schlechter Prozeßführung** plea of negligent litigation; ~**verzicht** waiver of a plea; **absolute** ~ absolute defence; peremptory plea; **aufschiebende** ~ dilatory plea, plea in suspension, plea of preliminary defence; **e-e begründete** ~ a good defence, a well-founded defence, a valid defence; **e-e** ~ **erheben** to put forward a defence, to enter a plea, to set up a defence, to plead as a defence; **e-e** ~ **vorbringen** to plead as a defence; **hemmende** ~ dilatory exception (*or plea*); **peremptorische** ~ peremptory plea, plea in bar, complete defence; **persönliche** ~ personal defence (*negotiable instrum. law*); **prozeßhindernde** ~ plea in abatement, preliminary objection, plea in bar of trial; **rechtshindernde** ~ plea in law; **rechtsvernichtende** ~ plea in bar, peremptory plea; **unbegründete** ~ bad plea, unfounded plea; **unzulässige** ~ inadmissible plea, improper plea; **verzögerliche** ~ dilatory plea.

einreichen *v/t* to submit, to present, to file, to lodge; to pay in for collection.

Einreicher *m* presenter, applicant for discount, discounter (*bills of exchange*).

Einreicher-Obligo *n* liability of party lodging a bill (for discount).

Einreichung *f* filing, presentation, *pl* ~*en*: *discounts* (*banking*); ~ **der Klage** filing of the action, presentation of the petition; ~ **e-r Patentanmeldung** filing of a patent application; ~ **e-r Strafanzeige** laying an information; bringing a criminal charge against; ~ **e-s Antrags** filing of an application; ~ **e-s Konkursantrags** presentation (*or* filing) of a bankruptcy petition; ~ **von Schriftsätzen** delivery of pleadings; ~ **von Urkunden** filing of documents.

Einreichungs|amt office for delivery

Einsatz

(*of pleadings*), filing office; ~**datum** filing date; ~**frist** deadline for filing, deadline (*or* period) for presentation, tender period, closing date; ~**termin** filing date.

Einreihung *f* classification.

Einreise|erlaubnis entry permit, entry clearance; ~**erlaubnisschein** entry clearance certificate; ~**flughafen** airport of entry, gateway airport; ~**kontrolle** check on entering a customs territory; ~**sichtvermerk** entry visa, entrance visa; ~**verbot für Ausländer** prohibition of entry for foreigners; exclusion of aliens; ~**visum** entry visa.

Einreisender *m* entrant, incoming passenger.

einrichten *v/t* to establish, to institute, to organize.

Einrichter *m* setup man.

Einrichtezeit *f* setup time.

Einrichtung *f* establishment, institution, facility, installation; ~**en des öffentlichen Rechts** bodies governed by public law; **gastgebende** ~ host establishment; **gemeinnützige** ~ socially beneficial institution; **gewerbliche** ~**en** commercial establishments; **öffentliche** ~ public institution; **schadenverhütende** ~**en** safety devices, safety facilities; **soziale** ~**en** social services; **städtische** ~**en** municipal services.

Einrichtungs|gegenstände equipment, furniture and fixtures; ~**haus** furniture store; ~**konto** equipment account; ~**kosten** initial capital expenditure; ~**kredit** credit for household furniture; ~**patent** device patent.

einrücken *v/t* to indent (*typewritten line*), to insert (*classified ad*), *v/i* to join the armed services.

Einrückung *f* indent, indention; insertion.

Einsatz *m* action, employment (*workers*), tour of duty (*official*), deposit (*pledge*), stake, stake money (*game, betting*); sortie (*war, plane*); ~**auftrag** mission; ~**beratung** applica-

238

tion consultation; **~bereitschaft** willingness to serve; readiness for use; *mil*: alert, operational readiness; **~dienst** special service, emergency service; **e~fähig** operational (*military equipment*); **~fahrzeug** emergency vehicle (*fire brigade etc*); **~form** method of employment; **~freudigkeit** drive, zeal, keenness, enterprise; **~gebiet** operational area; **~gruppe** task force, detail; **~horn** siren *of vehicle on (emergency) duty*; **~leiter** squad leader, officer in charge of the operation; **~plan** employee roster; **~preis** starting price (*auction*), reserve price; **~stab** staff-headquarters, action group; **~strafe** individual penalty merged in a compound sentence; **~wert** entered value, book value; **~zeit** uptime (*machine*); **~zug** relief train; **bestmöglicher ~** optimum utilization; **zum ~ bringen** to apply, to employ.

einsatzfähig *adj* employable, fit for employment, able-bodied.

Einschaltquote *f* audience rating.

einschätzen *v/t* to assess, to size up, to estimate, to appraise.

Einschätzung *f* assessment, appraisal, appreciation; **~ der Kreditwürdigkeit** credit rating; **~ des Risikos** appraisal of the risk.

einscheren *v/i* to duck into line.

einschicken *v* to send in, to submit, to tender.

einschieben *v/t* to insert, to interpolate (*text*).

Einschiebung *f* insertion, interpolation.

einschießen *v/t* to contribute (*money to an enterprise*), to put money (*into a business*), to make money available (*for a business venture or speculation*).

einschiffen *v/reflex* to embark, to go on board.

Einschiffung *f* embarkation (*or* embarcation); **~shafen** port of embarkation, port of lading, port of shipping; **~skarte** embarkation card.

Einschlafen *n* **am Steuer** falling asleep at the wheel (*or* while driving).

Einschlag *m* amount of timber cut, felling rate.

einschlägig *adj* pertinent, relevant; **~ vorbestraft →** *vorbestraft*.

einschleichen *v/i* to sneek in, to creep in, to steal in, to enter by stealth, to enter surreptitiously.

Einschleifung *f* curved motorway approach.

Einschleppen *n* towing in (*ship*); bringing into the country (*contagious disease*).

einschleppen *v/t* to tow in (*ship*); to carry in (*contagious disease*).

einschleusen *v/t* to lock(in) (*ship*); to introduce surreptitiously (*agents*), to put sth into circulation.

Einschleusung *f* passing (a ship) into a lock, channelling into, entry (*of goods into a market*); **~spreis** *EEC*: "sluice-gate" price.

einschließlich *prep* inclusive; **bis ~** up to and including.

Einschließung *f* inclusion, confinement (*in a fortress etc, for political offences*), incarceration.

einschmuggeln *v/t* to smuggle in.

einschneidend *adj* drastic.

Einschnitt *m fig* break, important event, turning point, upheaval.

einschränken *v/t* to restrict, to limit.

einschränkend *adj* restrictive.

Einschränkung *f* restriction, limitation, curtailment; **mit der ~:** subject to the proviso, sub modo; **~ der Pressefreiheit** restriction of the freedom of the press; **~ des Absatzes** limitation of markets; **~ des freien Wettbewerbs** restraint of competition; **~en auferlegen** to impose restrictions on; **~en des Wehretats** defence cuts; **~en und Entbehrungen** austerity, scrimping and pinching; **bedingte zeitliche ~** contingent limitation.

Einschreibe|brief registered letter, *US*: certified mail; **~gebühr** registration fee; **~päckchen** registered small package; **~sendung** registered mail, certified mail.

Einschreiben *n* registered; *US*: registration or registry of mailable matter; by registered mail; ~ **mit Rückschein** recorded delivery, registered mail including return receipt.

einschreiben v/t to register, to inscribe, to enrol.

Einschreibung f enrolment (= *enrollment*), matriculation.

Einschreiten n intervention.

einschreiten v/i to intervene.

einschüchtern v/t to intimidate.

Einschüchterung f intimidation.

Einschulung f school enrolment.

Einschuß m (pl *Einschüsse*) contribution of money, capital funds invested, *exch*: margin, requirement (*deposited with broker*), initial margin, margin deposit, collateral security margin, trading margin, marginal deposit.

einsehen v/i to inspect, to check in a register.

einseitig adj one-sided, unilateral; ~ **verpflichtend** → *verpflichtend;* ~ **zu beschriften** only one side of each sheet shall be used.

Einseitigkeit f one-sidedness, partiality, prejudiced character (*of one's judgment*).

einsenden v/t to send (in), to submit.

Einsender m sender, submitter, contributor (*articles to a newspaper*).

Einsendeschluß m closing day for entries.

einsetzen v/t to insert (*word, a clause*), to institute, to establish (*committee etc*), to appoint (*a person to an office*), to stake (*money for risk venture*), to constitute, to employ (*labo(u)r, machinery*).

Einsetzung f (*cf einsetzen*) insertion inclusion, institution, establishment, appointment, employment; ~ **der Geschworenen** panellation, impanelling of the jury; ~ **e-s Ersatzerben** substitution of an heir; ~ **e-s Nacherben** nomination of a secondary (*or* subsequent) heir (*in a will, as contingent successor of the heir*); ~ **e-s Testamentsvollstreckers** appointment of an executor.

Einsetzungsbefugnis f power of appointment.

Einsicht f inspection, examination (*books etc*); insight, understanding; ~ **in die Akten** inspection of the files; ~ **in die Bücher** inspection of books; ~ **in ein Register** inspection of a register; ~ **nehmen** to examine, to inspect; **mangelnde** ~ lack of self-critical understanding; **zur ~ ausliegen** to be open to inspection; **zur ~ vorlegen** to submit for inspection.

einsichtig adj reasonably self-critical, appreciating one's own faults.

Einsichtnahme f inspection, examination; ~ **in Urkunden** inspection of documents.

Einsichtsfähigkeit f capacity to understand (the wrongfulness of an act).

Einsichtsrecht n right of inspection; ~ **in die Bücher** (right of) access to the books.

einsichtsvoll adj reasonable, showing understanding.

einsparen v/t to economize, to cut expenses, to save.

Einsparung f economizing, curtailing expenditure, reduction (*of costs positions etc*); **~en vornehmen** to make economies; **erzwungene ~en** forced savings, compulsory savings; **geringfügige ~en** marginal savings, minimal savings.

einsortieren v/t to sort; **alphabetisch ~** to file s. th. in alphabetical order.

Einsparung f saving, economy.

einspeisen v/t to feed (*into a machine, computer, etc*).

Einspeisung f feeding in, input.

Einsperren n locking s.o. up, confinement (in an institution or jail), imprisonment; **widerrechtliches** ~ false imprisonment, unlawful imprisonment.

einsperren v v/t to lock up, to take into custody, to imprison, to incarcerate; ~ **lassen** to have s. o. put in gaol (= jail).

einspielen *v/t* to bring in, to gross (*film*); *v/reflex* to get going properly, to level out (*interest rate*).

Einspielergebnis *n* trade shown (*motion picture*), box office takings.

Einspielerlös *m* = *Einspielergebnis qv*.

einsprechen *v/i* to oppose.

Einsprechender *m* opposer, opponent.

einspringen *v/i* to step in, to help out, to deputize for.

Einspruch *m* objection, protest, exception, *pat* opposition; ~ **einlegen** to lodge (*or* file) an objection; ~ **erheben** to object, to raise objections; *pat*: to raise (to lodge, to file) an opposition, to oppose, to give notice of opposition; ~ **gegen ein Versäumnisurteil** notice of objection to a judgment by default; ~ **gegen Erteilung eines Patents** opposition to the grant of a patent; ~ **wegen mangelnder Neuheit** objection for lack (*or* want) of novelty; ~ **wurde nicht erhoben** *pat* the application was left unopposed; **begründeter** ~ well-founded objection; **dem** ~ **wird nicht stattgegeben** objection overruled; **e–m** ~ **stattgeben** to allow (*or* uphold) an objection; **e–n** ~ **verwerfen** to overrule an objection; *pat* to reject an opposition; **e–n** ~ **zurücknehmen** to withdraw an oppostion (*or* an objection); **e–n** ~ **zurückweisen** to overrule an objection (*at a trial*), to reject an opposition (*patent*); **für ~szwecke ausliegen** *pat* to lie open to opposition; **nachträglicher** ~ *pat* belated opposition; **rechtzeitiger** ~*pat* objection filed in due time, opposition entered in time; **über e–n** ~ **entscheiden** *pat* to take a decision on an opposition; **unbegründeter** ~ unfounded opposition; **unzulässiger** ~ inadmissible opposition; **verspäteter** ~ belated (*or* late) objection, *pat* late opposition.

Einspruchs|abteilung *pat* Opposition Division; **~begründung** argument (brief) in support of the objection, *pat* grounds for (*or* of) opposition; **~einlegung** filing of the objection, *pat* notice of opposition; **~entscheid** ruling on an objection, *pat* official decision concerning an opposition, award of priority; **~ergänzung** *pat* supplementary argument in support of opposition; **~erwiderung** *pat* reply (*or* rejoinder) to an opposition, counterstatement (*or* counter-brief) to an opposition; **~frist** period for objection, period for filing protest, *pat* period for entering an opposition; **~gebühr** *pat* opposition fee; **~partei** *pat* opponent, party in opposition, party to an interference; **~recht** right of objection, right to protest; **~schrift** written notice of exceptions to a ruling, preliminary statement in support of an interference (*or* opposition to a grant of patent*); **~schriftsatz** *pat* notice of opposition, opposition brief; memorandum in support of opposition; **~verfahren** *pat* interference proceedings, opposition proceedings; ~~ *einleiten (gegen Erteilung); to give notice of opposition, to enter an opposition to a grant*.

Einstand *m* entry, celebrating the beginning of a new job, house-warming party.

Einstands|bedingungen initial terms, terms of issue; **~berechnung** cost accounting; **~kosten** initial cost, prime cost; **~preis** cost price, prime cost, first cost, original cost; *Zugänge zu ~~en (bil): additions at cost;* **~wert** value at cost, (all-in) cost value; **~zinssatz** effective rate of interest to the borrower.

einstechen *v/t* (*auf jmdn*) to stab (at) s.o.

einstehen *v/i* (*für etwas*) to answer for sth, to vouch for, to take the responsibility for sth; ~ **müssen** to be responsible for, to be liable for.

einstehlen *v/reflex* to sneak in; *cf einschleichen*.

Einsteigediebstahl *m* larceny by means of climbing in, theft by a cat burglar.

einsteigen v/i to embark; to take part (*enterprise*), to get in on sth (*business venture*); *crim* to climb in.

einsteigern v/t to obtain sth at an auction (*as the highest bidder*).

Einsteigerung f buying in at an auction.

einstellen v/t (1) to hire; to employ; **sich ~ lassen** to sign on.

einstellen v/t (2) to discontinue, to stay, to suspend; **einstweilen ~ to** suspend temporarily, to suspend until further notifice.

einstellen v/t (3) to engage, to take on, to allocate.

einstellig adj single-figure, single-digit.

Einstellung f (1) employment, hiring; **~ von Arbeitskräften** hiring of labour.

Einstellungs|liste list of appointments for public office; **~prüfung** entrance examination; constitutional loyalty check of candidates for public office; **~stab** recruiting staff; **~stop** stoppage of recruiting, hiring freeze; **~termin** date of entry into the service; **~untersuchung** medical check of draftees; **~vertrag** employment contract; **~voraussetzung** (pre)condition of employment; qualifications for admission.

Einstellung f (2) stay, discontinuance, suspension (*of proceedings*); **der Feindseligkeiten** cessation of hostilities; **~ der Kampfhandlungen** ending of combat action; **~ der Strafvollstreckung** stay of execution, stopping execution of sentence; **~ der Zwangsvollstreckung** discontinuance of civil execution; **~ des Betriebes** suspension of operations; **~ des Ermittlungsverfahrens** discontinuation of criminal investigations, nolle prosequi, withdrawal of prosecution; **~ des Geschäftsbetriebes** suspension of business, suspension of operations; **~ des Konkursverfahrens** discontinuance of bankruptcy proceedings; **~ des Strafverfahrens** dismissal of a criminal case; **~sbeschluß** order to dismiss a case, order to stop proceedings; **~sverfügung** stop notice; **~ einstweilige ~** suspension of the proceedings.

Einstellung f (3) mental attitude, approach; **freundliche ~** friendly spirit; **innere ~** mental attitude; **politische ~** political convictions; **überparteiliche ~** non-party spirit, non-partisan view.

Einstellungen pl **in Rücklagen** transfers to reserves.

einstimmig adj unanimous, nemine contradicente (*nem. con*).

Einstimmigkeit f unanimity; **kommt keine ~ zustande ...** failing unanimity ...

einstufen v/t to grade, to categorize, to classify, to scale; **höher ~** to upgrade, to put into a higher group (*or* income bracket); **neu ~** to reclassify; **niedriger ~** to downgrade, to put into a lower group (*or* income bracket).

einstufig adj single-stage.

Einstufung categorization, classification, employee rating, grading assessment (*tax*); **~ nach Leistungsfähigkeit** performance rating; **höhere ~** promotional classification change, upgrading; **niedrigere ~** demotional classification, demotion, downgrading.

Einsturz m collapse, foundering; **~gefahr** danger of collapse; *Vorsicht ~~!: danger – building unsafe*.

einstweilig adj temporary, provisional, interim, interlocutory.

Eintausch m barter, exchange, trade; **~wagen** trade-in (car); **~wert** trade-in value.

eintauschen to trade in, to barter, to take in exchange for sth, to sell in part-exchange for.

eintaxieren v/t to appraise.

einteilen v/t to divide up, to class, to grade, to classify.

Einteilung f division, subdivision, classification, gradation, graduation (*scale*).

Eintrag m entry (*in a register*); **~ ohne Gegenbuchung** single en-

eintragen   **Eintrittsalter**

try; **kein** ~ no entry; no previous convictions.

eintragen *v/t* to enter, to make an entry, to register; to post; to enrol.

einträglich *adj* lucrative, profitable.

Einträglichkeit *f* lucrativeness, profitableness.

Eintragsrolle *f* registration list.

Eintragung *f* registration; entry, recordation; ~ **e-s Warenzeichens** registration of a trade mark; ~ **im Grundbuch** entry in the land register; ~ **im Handelsregister** (= *in das H.*) entry (*or* registration) in the commercial register; ~ **in ein Register** entry in a register, registration; **e-e** ~ **löschen** to delete an entry, to cancel an entry; **gegenstandslose** ~ entry no longer applicable; **im Rang nachgehende** ~ inferior entry; **nachträgliche** ~ post-entry, subsequent entry; **polizeiliche** ~ police registration; **unrichtige** ~ false entry; **zur** ~ **einreichen** to file for registration; **zur** ~ **vorlegen** to file for registration.

Eintragungs|antrag application for registration, application for entry in the register (*land register*); **~ausschluß** exclusion from the professional list; **~beschluß** registration order, ruling that sth be entered in the register; **~bewilligung** grant of consent for an entry in the register (*by the party charged*); **~erfordernisse** recording (*or* registration) requirements; **e~fähig** registrable, eligible for registration, capable of registration, recordable; **~fähigkeit** eligibility for registration; registrability; **~gebühr** registration fee; **~hindernisse** grounds for refusal (to register); **e~pflichtig** *adj* requiring registration; **~verbote** (*Warenzeichenrecht*) bars to registration; **~verfahren** registration procedure; **~vermerk in einem Register** note of entry, registration; **~voraussetzungen** recording (*or* registration) requirements; **~wirkung** legal effect of registration; **~zwang** compulsory registration.

eintreibbar *adj* collectible, recoverable.

eintreiben *v/t* to collect, to enforce the collection (*of outstanding accounts*).

Eintreibung *f* collection, enforcing the collection (*of outstanding accounts*), measures for the recovery of a debt; **gerichtliche** ~ collection through judicial proceedings; **zwangsweise** ~ enforcement of the collection, collection by levying execution.

Eintreten *n* entry, occurrence, intervention; *cf Eintritt;* ~ **des Erbfalls** the event of an inheritance.

eintreten *v/i* to step in, to enter, to occur, ~ **für:** *to stand up for, to answer for, to be liable.*

eintretendenfalls *adj* should the case arise, if so, if that happens.

Eintretender *m* (*der Eintretende*) entrant, incoming member, new member.

Eintritt *m* entry, entrance, occurrence; ~ **als Teilhaber** entering (joining) a firm as partner; ~ **in die Rechte** subrogation to the rights (of); ~ **der Bedingung** happening of the contingency, occurrence of the event; ~ **des den Klageanspruch begründenden Ereignisses** accrual of the cause of action; ~ **des Versicherungsfalles** happening of the insured event; ~ **e-s Ereignisses** occurrence of an event; ~ **e-s Schadenfalles** occurrence of a loss insured against; ~ **in die Tagesordnung** proceeding to the points of the agenda; *vor* ~ ...: *before proceeding to the business of the meeting;* ~ **in ein Geschäft** joining a business, becoming a partner of a firm; ~ **in e-e Laufbahn** embarking upon a career; ~ **in e-e Partei** joining a party; ~ **verboten** no entry, no admittance; **bei** ~ **der Volljährigkeit** upon reaching majority, when coming of age; **bei** ~ **des Todes** upon death; **kein** ~ no entry.

Eintritts|alter age at entry; required minimum age; **~erlaubnis** admis-

243

einverleiben / **einwandfrei**

sion; ~**gebühr** admission fee; ~**geld** entrance fee, admission; ~**grenzzollamt** customs office at place of entry; ~**hafen** port of entry; ~**häufigkeit** frequency with which sth happens; probability of occurrence; ~**karte** admission (*or* entry) ticket; ~**klausel** automatic accrual of partnership status clause; succession- by-entry clause; ~**prämie** take-over premium, entry premium; ~**preis** admission (fee, charge); entrance fee; ~**prüfung** entrance examination; ~**recht** right of entry, right to succeed a partner; right of preemption: *the right of accepting an offer in preference to others*; ~**sperre** restriction of entry; ~**voraussetzungen** entrance requirements.

einverleiben *v/t* to incorporate, to include, to annex.

Einverleibung *f* incorporation, inclusion, annexation.

Einvernahme *f* examination (*of witness*), interrogation.

Einvernehmen *n* understanding, agreement, accord, tacit agreement, consent; **geheimes** ~ secret understanding, collusion; **gutes** ~ **unter den Nationen** comity of nations; **in gegenseitigem** ~ (= *im gegenseitigen* ~) by mutual consent, by common agreement, by common accord; **in gutem** ~ on friendly terms.

Einvernehmenserklärung *f* declaration of understanding.

einvernehmlich *adv* by mutual consent (or agreement).

einverstanden agreed, understood, I (we) agree.

einverständlich *adv* by mutual agreement (*or* consent), by stipulation.

Einverständnis *n* agreement, consent, accord, approval; ~ **über etwas erzielen** to come to an understanding; **beiderseitiges** ~ mutual agreement, (*or* consent); **geheimes** ~ secret understanding; **hierzu ist ihr** ~ **erforderlich** subject to their agreement; **mündliches** ~ verbal consent; **restloses** ~ full consent; **schriftliches** ~ written consent; **wenn kein** ~ **erreicht wird** if no agreement is reached, failing agreement.

Einwand *m* objection, defence (*US: defense*), plea, demurrer; ~ **der Arglist** defence of malice; ~ **der mangelnden Passivlegitimation** plea that defendant is the wrong party; ~ **der mangelnden Schlüssigkeit** demurrer; ~ **der materiellen Rechtskraft** issue preclusion; ~ **der Nichtigkeit** plea of nullity; ~ **der Rechtskraftwirkung** plea of res judicata, estoppel by judgment; ~ **der Rechtsunwirksamkeit** plea of nullity; ~ **der unzulässigen Rechtsausübung** plea of estoppel; ~ **der Unzuständigkeit** → *Einrede der U.*; ~ **der Verwirkung** (defence of) laches, implied waiver; **dem** ~ **abhelfen** to meet objections; **der** ~ **ist berechtigt** the objection is justified (*or* sound); **ein berechtigter** ~ a good defence; **e-m** ~ **stattgeben** to sustain an objection; **e-n** ~ **entkräften** to refute an objection; **e-n** ~ **machen** to raise an objection; **e-n** ~ **vorbringen** to set up a defence; **formaler** ~ technical objection; **geringer** ~ slight objection; **rechtstechnischer** ~ technical defence; **schikanöser** ~ frivolous plea.

Einwanderer *m* immigrant.

einwandern *v/i* to immigrate.

Einwanderung *f* immigration.

Einwanderungs|beamter immigration officer; ~**behörden** immigration authorities; ~**beschränkungen** immigration restrictions; ~**gesetz** immigration law; ~**kontingent** immigration quota; ~**kontrolle** immigration control; ~**land** immigration country, country encouraging immigration; ~**quote** immigration quota; ~**recht** right of immigration; ~**visum** immigration visa.

einwandfrei *adj* faultless, perfect, unimpeachable, proper, impecc-

244

able, unblemished; **fachlich** ~ in a good and workmanlike manner; **juristisch** ~ legally correct, legally watertight.

Einwegflasche *f* one-trip container, non-returnable bottle, one-way bottle.

einweihen *v/i* to inaugurate, to consecrate, to dedicate; *j-n in etw.* ~*:* to initiate s. o. in *(a science, an art)*/into *(an office, a secret)*.

Einweihung *f* inauguration, consecration, initiation.

einwechseln *v/t* to cash *(cheque)*, to exchange *(foreign currency)*.

einweisen *v/t* to commit *(to an institution)*; to put into possession *(land, rooms)*; to familiarize, to train *(worker at new machine)*, to acquaint with *(conditions of employment)*.

Einweisung *f* (*cf einweisen*) commitment, compulsory admission, putting into possession, breaking-in, training, instruction, initiation, familiarization; ~ **in die Haftanstalt** committal to prison; ~**sbeschluß** order granting possession; commitment; ~**sverfügung** order granting possession.

einwenden *v/t* to object, to oppose, to remonstrate, to plead.

Einwendung *f* objection, defence *(US: defense)*, remonstration, plea, representation; ~ **der Nichtigkeit** plea of nullity; ~ **der verspäteten Zustellung** plea of late service; ~ **des Selbsteintrittsrechts** claiming the right of self-performance, claiming the right to contract for one's principal or oneself; ~**en erheben** to raise objections; ~**en vorbringen** to show cause, to plead defences, to disclose a defence; **materielle** ~ = *materiell-rechtliche* ~; **materiellrechtliche** ~ defence for reasons of substantive law, material factor defence; **rechtliche** ~ objection in (point of) law; **rechtsvernichtende** ~ plea in bar; **unzulässige** ~ inadmissible defence; **vertraglich begründete** ~ defence arising out of the contract; **verzögerliche** ~ dilatory plea.

einwilligen *v/i* to consent, to agree to *in advance*.

Einwilligung *f* consent *in advance*; **die ~ bis auf weiteres verweigern** to withhold consent; **die ~ einholen** to obtain consent; **die ~ erteilen** to give one's consent; **die ~ verweigern** to refuse one's consent; **elterliche** ~ parental consent; **höchstpersönliche** ~ strictly personal consent; **stillschweigende** ~ acquiescence.

einwirken *v/i* to act (upon), to operate (upon), to influence.

Einwirkung *f* effect, influence, impact; **liquiditätspolitische** ~**en** measures taken to affect monetary liquidity; **notenbankpolitische** ~ measure of Central Bank policy; **wechselseitige** ~ interaction.

Einwohner *m* inhabitant, resident; ~**daten** population data; ~**informationssystem** information system regarding the registration of residents; ~**meldeamt** registration office (for inhabitants), residents' registration office; police registration bureau; population register; ~**register** population register; ~**schaft** inhabitants, population *(of a town, city etc.)*.

Einwurf *m* objection, interposition, interruption, interposed remark.

einzahlen *v/t* to pay in(to) *(an account)*, to deposit *(with a bank)*, to pay up *(capital contribution)*.

Einzahler *m* depositor, payer.

Einzahlung *f* paying in, payment in, lodging, deposit *(of money)*; ~ **auf Aktien** payment (of a call) on shares; ~ **auf Kapitalanteile gemäß Abruf** payments of calls, subscription (for securities issue); ~**en und Auszahlungen** deposits and drawings; ~ **verlangen** to request payment, to call up capital, to make a call *(on shares)*; **zur ~ auffordern** to call, to request payment, to make a call *(on shares)*.

Einzahlungs|aufforderung notice of call; request for payment; ~**beleg** paying-in slip, credit slip, deposit slip, deposit receipt; ~**buch**

pass-book, paying-in book, bankbook; ~**quittung** deposit receipt, call receipt; ~**schein** deposit slip, paying-in (credit) slip; ~**ströme** cash inflows; ~**überschuß** excess of payments in (*or* deposits); ~**verpflichtung** liability in respect of calls (*on shares*).

einzeichnen *v/t* to draw in, to plot on a map etc; *v/reflex* to write down one's name (*on a list*).

Einzel|abnehmer individual purchaser; ~**abrede** special arrangement, individual agreement; ~**abstimmung** voting by roll call; checking in detail (*accounts*); ~**akkord** individual piece work (rate), piece-work rate, piece-rate work; ~**akt** single act, individual regulation, individual order; ~**anerkennung** individual recognition; ~**anfertigung** work (*or* manufacture) to customer's specification, job work, single-part production, special construction; ~**angaben** particulars, detailed information, specification(s); ~**anleger** individual investor(s); ~**arbeitsvertrag** individual employment contract; ~**aufgliederung** detailed classification (*or* break-down); ~**aufstellung** itemized list, itemized schedule, specification; ~**auftrag** individual order, special order; ~**ausgebot** inviting separate bids (*for each plot of land or each item – auctioneering*); ~**beratung** *pol* discussion at the committe stage; ~**bericht** separate report; ~**besteuerung** individual taxation; e~**betrieblich** relating to individual enterprises; ~**bewertung** individual valuation; ~**bilanz** individual balance-sheet; ~**bürgschaft** individual guarantee; ~**eigentum** individual proprietorship; ~**erfinder** sole inventor; ~**erscheinung** isolated instance; ~**ersparnisse** individual savings; ~**ertragswert** individual productive value (*or* earning power); ~**fahrkarte** single (fare); ~**fall** (*pl*: *Einzelfälle*), a particular case, an individual case, an isolated case, a given instance, a particular occasion; *im konkreten* ~~: *in the actual case*; *in vergleichbaren* ~~*en*: *in cases of a similar nature*; ~**fertigung** *(1) = Einzelanfertigung qv*; *(2)* production of individual units, job production, construction by hand; ~**finanzierungssystem** system for financing individual transactions; ~**firma** private firm, individual enterprise; ~**garantie** individual guarantee; ~**genehmigung** special permit, individual licence; ~**genehmigungsverfahren** individual licence procedure; ~**geschäft** individual store, retail store; ~**geschäftsführung** single power of management; ~-**gewerkschaft** craft union, single-industry union; ~**haft** solitary confinement; ~**handel** → *Einzelhandel*; ~**händler** retailer, retail trader, retail dealer, *selbständiger* ~~: *independent retailer*; ~**händler-Einkaufsgenossenschaft** retailer cooperative; ~**händlerrabatt** retail discount; ~**handlungsvollmacht** sole agency, individual power of representation, power (authorizing s. o.) to act alone; ~**häuser** detached houses; ~**heit** → *Einzelheit*; ~**hof** solitary farm; ~**honorar** fee for specific services; ~**kalkulation** unit calculation; ~**kaufmann** sole trader; ~**konto** sole account, individual account, personal account; ~**konzession** licence in a particular case, individual licence; ~**kredit** individual loan, personal credit; ~**ladenpreis** retail price; ~**lizenz** individual licence, single licence; ~**lizenzkosten** product-oriented licence costs; ~**lohn** individual wage; ~**miete** single-person tenancy, rent in a particular case, hiring of a special object; ~**mieter** sole tenant; ~**nachfolge** individual succession; ~**nachweis** proof of the particulars, proof of each item; ~**objekt** individual property; ~**pächter** sole tenant; ~**person** private individual, individual per-

Einzelpolice — **Einzelhandelsabteilung**

son; ~**police** single policy; ~**preis** unit price; ~**plan** individual plan; departmental budget; ~**prokura** individual „Prokura": *full power of commercial representation vested in one person (who can sign alone)*, single representation; ~**punkt** point, item; ~~*e für die Bemessungsgrundlage: components for calculating assessment basis*; ~**rechtsnachfolge** individual succession; ~**rechtsnachfolger** individual successor (*person succeeding to the rights and obligations concerning individual items of property, not the estate as a whole*); ~**refinanzierung** individual refinancing, loan to finance an individual firm's lending; ~**reisender** individual passenger, lone traveller; ~**richter** judge sitting alone, single judge, sole judge; ~**schuld** individual debt; ~**schuldner** sole debtor; ~**schuldverhältnis** individual debt relationship, obligation in one particular case (*involving one transaction only*); ~**staat** state (of a union), member state (of a federation); e~**staatlich** *US*: State (*relating to a member state of a union*); ~**statut** conflict of laws rule concerning specific matters; ~**strafe** individual sentence, part sentence (*of several sentences for the same group of acts*); ~**straftat** single act, single crime; ~**stück** odd piece; ~**tarifverhandlung** single-part bargaining, individual bargaining, *collective bargaining for a particular enterprise*; ~**teil** part, component part; ~**teillager** parts inventory, replacement parts storage; ~**transport** individual shipment; ~**treuhänder** sole trustee; ~**unfallversicherung** personal accident insurance; ~**unterlagen** particular (*or* specific) documents, data, detailed documentation; ~**unternehmen** individually owned enterprise, sole proprietorship business; ~**unternehmer** individual proprietor, sole proprietor; ~**urkunde** separate instrument; ~**verbindlichkeit** sole obligation, obligation of a sole debtor, individual debt; ~**verbraucher** individual consumer; ~**vermächtnis** specific gift, specific legacy; ~**vermächtnisnehmer** sole legatee, beneficiary of a specific bequest; ~**vernehmung** individual interrogation or examination of a witness *in the absence of other witnesses*; ~**verpackung** individual packaging; ~**verpflichtung** several debt, separate obligation; ~**versicherer** individual insurer, underwriting member; ~**versicherung** individual insurance, insurance of individual risks; ~**versteuerung** separate assessment, individual taxation; ~**vertrag** individual agreement; ~**vertretung (-smacht)** sole agency, individual power of represention; ~**verwahrung** separate custody of securities, jacket custody, individual safe-keeping, special deposit; ~**vollmacht** specific power of attorney; ~**vormundschaft** guardianship by one guardian, regular guardianship; ~**vorschläge** individual proposals; ~**vorstand** one-man board of directors, sole governing director; ~**wahl** separate election of candidates; ~**wechsel** single bill of exchange; ~**weisungen** special directions (*or* orders); ~**werbung** direct advertising, canvassing; ~**wertberichtigung** individual value adjustment, adjustment of value of an individual asset, specific loan loss provision; ~**wesen** individual (being); e~**wirtschaftlich** *adj* relating to an individual enterprise; ~**zeichnungsberechtigung** separate power to sign on behalf of the firm; ~**zelle** single cell, one-man cell.

Einzelhandel *m* retail trade.

Einzelhandels|abteilung retail department; ~**artikel** retail goods; ~**betrieb** retail business; ~**firma** retail firm, retailer, retail store; ~**geschäft** retail business, retail store; ~**gewerbe** retail trade; ~**kette** retail chain; ~**kredit** retail credit; ~**organisation** retail sales

247

Einzelheit

organization; ~**preis** retail price, *empfohlener* ~~: *suggested retail price*; ~**preisindex** retail price index (*RPI*); ~**richtpreis** recommended retail price; ~**spanne** retail margin; ~**umsatz** retail store sales, retail sales; ~**vertrieb** retail sales, retail marketing.

Einzelheit *f* detail; *pl* details, particulars; ~**en des schriftsätzlichen Vorbringens** particulars of pleadings; ~**en zur Anklage** bill of particulars; **auf** ~**en eingehen** to go into details; **genaue** ~**en** full particulars; **kleinste** ~ minuta (*pl.-ae*); **mit allen** ~**en** with full particulars, in detail.

einzeln *adj* single, individual *adv*; one by one, seriatim; ~ **aufführen** to specify, to itemize; ~ **haftbar** severally liable; **im** ~**en** in detail, one by one, specified.

einziehbar *adj* recoverable, collectible, seizable (*goods*).

einziehen *v/t* to collect, to recover by levying execution, to redeem (*bond*), to withdraw from circulation (*bank notes*), to confiscate (*instruments of crime*), to seize.

Einziehung *f* collection (*debts, taxes*), redemption (*bonds*), withdrawal (*bank notes*), confiscation; criminal forfeiture (*obscene matter etc*); ~ **des Führerscheins** forfeiture of driver's licence; ~ **des Passes** (cancellation and) withdrawal of passport; ~ **des Vermögens** confiscation of property; ~ **von Außenständen** collection of accounts (*or* of receivables); ~ **von Falschgeld** confiscation of counterfeit money; **zur** ~ for collection.

Einziehungs|**abtretung** assignment for collection; ~**auftrag** postal collection order; ~**beschluß** forfeiture order; ~**erkenntnisverfahren** judicial forfeiture proceedings; ~**gebühr** collecting charge; ~**verfahren** forfeiture proceedings; ~**vollmacht** authority to collect, power of collection.

Einzug *m* (*1*) entry, moving in, occuption, collection, advent.

Eisenbahn

Einzug *m* (*2*) collection, direct debiting.

Einzugs|**ermächtigung** direct debit authorization; ~**gebiet** catchment basin (*river*), catchment area (*of a business, branch*); ~**kosten** collecting charges, ~~ *zahlt Remittent*: *with exchange*; ~**posten** item(s) for collection; ~**spesen** collecting expenses; *zahlbar zuzüglich* ~: *payable with exchange*; ~**stelle** collecting agency; ~**tag** moving-in day; ~**verfahren** direct debiting, method of collection; ~**verkehr** bank collections; ~**vollmacht** direct debiting (authorization); ~**wechsel** bill for collection.

einzuhalten *adj* observable.

Eisen|**bau** iron and steel construction; ~**erzbergbau** iron ore mining; ~**handel** iron trade, hardware business; ~**händler** hardware dealer, ironmonger; ~**handlung** hardware store, ironmongery; ~**industrie** iron (and steel) industry; *bearbeitende* ~~: *ironworking industry*; ~**hüttenwerk** ironworks, metallurgical plant; ~ **und Metallwarenbranche** hardware trade; ~ **und Stahlindustrie** steel industry; ~**waren** hardware, ironware.

Eisenbahn *f* railway(s), *US*: railroad; ~**aktien** railway shares, rails, *US*: railroad stocks; ~**anleihe** railway loan; ~**ausbesserungswerk** railway repair shop; ~**beförderungsrecht** railway transportation law; ~**betrieb** railway service; ~**betriebshaftung** railway operation liability; ~**diebstahl** railway larceny; ~**-Expreßgutverkehr** railway express service; ~**fahrplan** railway timetable, schedule of trains; ~**fiskus** public railway administration; ~**frachtbrief** waybill, railroad bill of lading; ~**frachtrecht** railway freight (transportation) law; ~**geleise** tracks; *normalspuriges* ~*geleis*: *standard-gauge track*; ~**gesetze** railway Acts; ~**gütertarif** railway freight tariff; ~**güterverkehr** rail transport; ~**hotel** terminus hotel; ~**knoten-**

Eisenbahnerstreik — **Emission**

punkt railway junction; ~**kreuzung** A level crossing; ~**netz** railway system; ~**stillegung** closing down of railway lines; ~**tarife** rail charges; ~**transport** rail transport; ~**übergänge** level crossings, grade crossings; ~**unternehmen** railway company; ~**verkehr** railway traffic; ~**verkehrsordnung** Railway Traffic Regulations; ~**verwaltung** Railway Executive, management of a railroad company; ~**werte** railway securities; ~**zubehör** railway equipment; ~**zulieferer** railway supplier; **nichtbundeseigene ~en** non-federally-owned railway companies.

Eisenbahnerstreik *m* rail strike, railway workers' strike.

Elefantenhochzeit *f* mega merger (between two firms).

Elektrizitäts|entziehung abstraction of electricity; ~**gesellschaft** (electric) power company; ~**sicherungsverordnung** ordinance to secure power supply in an emergency (*D 1982*); ~**versorgung** electricity supply; ~**versorgungsunternehmen** (*EVU*) electricity enterprise; ~**werk** power station; ~**wirtschaft** electricity supply services, electric power industry; ~**zähler** electricity meter, electric meter.

Elektro|aktien electricity shares; ~**fahrzeug** electric power-driven vehicle; electro-vehicle; ~**gerät** electric appliance; ~**händler** electrical retailer; ~**ingenieur** electrical engineer; ~**markt** market for electrical equipment; ~**meister** master-craftsman in electrical engineering, qualified electrician; ~**technik** electrical engineering, electrical technology; ~**techniker** electrician; ~**werte** electricals, electrical equipment industry shares, electricity shares; ~**zaun** electric fence.

Elementar|begriff fundamental concept, basic idea; ~**ereignis** manifestation of the elements, Act of God; ~**erkenntnis** fundamental knowledge, basic knowledge; ~**schulbildung** elementary education, primary education.

Elendsviertel *n* slum; **nicht sanierungsfähiges ~** irredeemable slum, non-rehabitable slum.

eliminieren *v/t* to eliminate, to expunge (*from the record*).

Eliminierung *f* elimination.

elterlich *adj* parental; ~**e Sorge** → *Sorge*.

Eltern *pl* parents; ~**beirat** parents' council, parent-teacher committee; ~**haftung** liability involved in parental care; ~**liebe** parental love and affection; ~**mord** parenticide; ~**recht** parental right; ~**rente** pension for parents (*of servicemen*); ~**pflicht** parental duty; ~**recht** parentel right(s); ~**schaft** parenthood; ~**schlafzimmer** master bedroom; ~**teil** parent; *alleinerziehender ~~: single parent, parent with sole-custody*; *sorgeberechtigter ~~: natural guardian, parent vested with parental control, custodial parent*; *testamentslos verstorbener ~~: intestate parent*; ~**urlaub** parental leave; ~**verantwortung** parent's responsibility; ~**verhältnis** parent-and-child relationship; ~**versagen** parent's failure to fulfil their responsibilities; **an ~ statt** (in) loco parentis; **leibliche ~** natural parents.

Emanzipation *f* emancipation.

Emballage *f* packing, packing material, packaging.

Embargo *n* embargo; ~**bestimmungen** embargo regulations; **ein ~ aufheben** to lift an embargo; **ein ~ verhängen** to impose an embargo.

Emblem *n* emblem, symbol; *pl* ~**e:** *insignia*.

emeritieren *v/i, v/t* to retire from an academic chair, to give emeritus status.

Emeritierung *f* retirement from academic chair (*retaining the status of a professor*).

Emission *f* (1) issue (*of marketable securities*), flotation; **~ von Schuld-**

Emission | Empfangsanzeige

verschreibungen debenture issue; **neue ~en an den Mann bringen** to place new capital issues (*with takers*).

Emission *f* (2) emission (gas, fumes); **~snorm** emission standard; **~sschutz** protection from obnoxious substances *emanating from plant or property*.

Emissions (*nur Bedeutung zu 1*) **agio** underwriting premium, premium for the issue of securities; **~bank** issuing house, issuing bank; **~bedingungen** terms and conditions of an issue; **~disagio** discount to subscribers of a share (*or* bond) issue, discount; **~erlös** proceeds of an issue; **~garantie** underwriting (guarantee); **~genehmigung** issue permit; **~geschäft** issuing business, security-issue, underwriting business securities; **~gesellschaft** security flotation company, issuing house, company issuing its own shares; **~gesetz** Issue Act, Act concerning the issue of securities; **~gewinn** paid-in surplus (*realized at a capital issue*); **~haus** (security) issuing house; **~institut** issuing house, investment bank, underwriter; **~klima** climate for new issues; **~konsortialvertrag** underwriting agreement; **~konsortium** issue syndicate, distributing syndicate, underwriting syndicate, underwriting group, selling consortium; **~kontingentierung** allotting quotas for new issues, security issue rationing; **~kontrolle** official control of capital issues; **~kosten** issuing expenses; **~kredit** credit obtained through an issue of securities; **~kurs** issue price; **~land** country of issue; **~markt** issue market; **~modalitäten** terms and conditions of an issue; **~pause** pause before placing a new issue, (security) issue suspension; **~politik** security issues policy; **~preis** issuing price; **~prospekt** underwriting prospectus; **~recht** right to issue securities; **~reife** ability to absorb new issues, readiness for capital issues; **~sperre** ban on new issues; capital issue restrictions; **~spitze** unsold portion of an issue; **~statistik** statistics of fresh issues; **~syndikat** = **~konsortium** *qv;* **~termin** date of issue; **~typ** type of issue; **~überhang** excess issue, issue backlog; **~übernahmegeschäft** underwriting; **~vergütung** issue commission; **~vertrag** underwriting contract, agreement concerning a capital issue; **~währung** currency of issue; **~welle** spate of new issues; **~wunsch** request to issue securities.

Emittent *m* issuer, issuing institution; **öffentliche ~en** official issuers.

emittieren *v/t* to issue (*shares, bonds*).

Empfang *m* receipt (*letter, communication*); **den ~ bestätigen** to acknowledge receipt; **den ~ der Waren quittieren** to sign for the goods, to acknowledge receipt of the goods; **in ~ nehmen** to take delivery, to accept; **nach ~** on receipt, (up)on delivery; **zahlbar bei ~** payable on receipt, cash on delivery, C.O.D.

Empfänger *m* recipient, consignee, addressee, allottee (*of securities*); **~ e~s Geldvermächtnisses** pecuniary legatee; **~gesellschaft** *f* receiving entity; **~land** donee country (*aid*); **~partei** recipient party.

Empfangnahme *f* receipt, taking delivery, acceptance.

Empfängnis *f* conception; **~verhütung** contraception; **~zeit** period of (possible) conception, the beginning of pregnancy.

Empfangs|anzeige notice of receipt; **~bedürftigkeit** requirement of receipt; **~bekenntnis** acknowledgment of receipt; **e~berechtigt** authorized to receive; **~berechtigter** authorized recipient, legitimate consignee, legitimate beneficiary; **~bescheinigung,** receipt, acknowledgment of receipt, certificate of delivery, acknowledgment of service; **~bestätigung** receipt,

empfehlen | Energie

acknowledgment of receipt, acknowledgment of service; ~**bevollmächtigter** resident agent, authorized receiving agent, party entitled to take delivery; ~**bote** receiving agent, *auxiliary person to effect the receipt (of a message, document, declaration) on behalf of the principal addressee*); ~**chef** shop walker (*department store*); ~**schein** advice of delivery, ~~: certificate of delivery; *gegen ~~: against receipt*; ~**spediteur** forwarding agent at place of destination; ~**staat** receiving state (*for a diplomat*), host state; ~**theorie** doctrine of receipt; ~**zeit** time of arrival (*of goods*), time of delivery.

empfehlen *v/t* to recommend.

empfehlenswert *adj* recommendable, advisable.

Empfehlung *f* recommendation; ~**sschreiben** letter of recommendation, letter of introduction, testimonial; ~**svereinbarungen** recommended arrangements; **unverbindliche** ~ recommendation without prejudice.

En-bloc-Lizenz *f* bloc licence.

End|abnehmer ultimate buyer, ultimate consumer, ultimate user, end customer; ~**abrechnung** final accounts, final bill; ~**absatz** sales to ultimate buyers (*or* consumers); ~**absicht** final aim, ultimate goal; ~**alter** maturity age, age at expiration; ~**bahnhof** terminal station; ~**bank** final bank; *die empfangende ~~: the bank which finally receives*; ~**bedarf** demand from ultimate users, ultimate demand; ~**bescheid** final decision, definite decision; ~**bestand** final balance, total; ~**boje** end buoy, *westlichste ~~: westernmost end buoy*; ~**entscheidung** final determination (*possibly subject to appeal*); ~**ergebnis** final result; ~**erzeugnis** finished product; ~**fabrikat** final product; (*valid only if actually or constructively received by addressee*); ~**finanzierung** residual financing; ~**gehalt** final salary (*before termination*), retiring salary; ~**gerätemarkt** market for final products (*or* terminals); ~**gruppenbestimmung** final group determination; ~**gültigkeit** finality; ~**kreditnehmer** ultimate borrower; ~**lager** nuclear waste dump; ~**lagerung** ultimate deposit (*nuclear waste*); ~**montage** final assembly; ~**preis** price to the ultimate consumer, retail price; ~**produkt** finished product; ~**produktpreis** price of the finished product; ~**prüfung** final inspection; ~**punkt** (final) terminus, destination, final point, terminal point; ~**saldo** final balance, closing balance; ~**schiedsspruch** final arbitral award; ~**stand** final position; ~**station** terminal (station); ~**termin** final date, deadline; ~**summe** grand total, total (sum); ~**ursache** final cause; ~**urteil** judgment (*completing the case at the trial court*), (final) decree, final appealable order; ~**verbleibskontrollvorschriften** destinational control regulations; ~**verbleibsnachweis** final destination certificate; ~**verbraucher** (ultimate) consumer ~~~-*Nachfrage: demand from ultimate consumers*; ~*nachweis: certificate proving the ultimate consumer*; ~**verkaufspreis** retail price, consumer price; ~**vermögen** final assets (*of a spouse being divorced*); ~**wert** final amount, accumulated value; ~~ *e-r Annuität: accumulation of an annuity*; ~**zeitpunkt** final date; cut-off point; ~**zinssatz** interest rate to the borrower, all-in interest rate.

Energie *f* energy, power (*comprising power from electricity, coal, gas, nuclear fission etc.*); ~**anlagen** power installations; ~**anlagenhaftung** liability for power installations; ~**anleihe** electricity loan, loan to finance power supply projects; ~**aufsichtsbehörden** power supply supervisory authorities; ~**einsparung** energy saving; ~~*sgesetz: energy saving Act D 1976*; ~**kosten** cost of electric power and other energy; **e~intensiv** *adj* power-in-

251

Engagement

tensive; ~**markt** market for power supply, fuel and electricity market; ~**notstand** power supply crisis, power shortage; ~**programm** programme of power-plant building, power programme; ~**sektor** power supply sector (*of the economy*), fuel and power industries; ~**sicherungsgesetz** emergence security Act for the protection and control of energy *D 1974*; ~**träger** source of power (energy), fuel; ~**unternehmen** power supply company; ~**verbrauch** power consumption; ~**versorgung** supply of energy; ~**sunternehmen** public utilities in the field of power supply; ~**wirtschaft** energy-supply industry; ~**wirtschaftsgesetz** Act for the Promotion of the Fuel and Electricity Industries; ~**wirtschaftsrecht** power-industry legislation.

Engagement *n* commitment, investment, loan; ~**s lösen** to liquidate commitments.

Engpaß *m* bottleneck, shortage; ~**investition** investment in a bottleneck situation; ~**leistung** peak-load capacity, achievement in spite of a bottleneck.

en gros *adj, adv* wholesale, bulk-purchased.

Engros|abnehmer wholesale buyer; ~**bezug** wholesale purchase; ~**einkauf** wholesale purchase; ~**geschäft** wholesale business; ~**verkauf** wholesale, direct sale.

Enkelgesellschaft *f* sub-subsidiary, company controlled through a subsidiary.

Enklave *f* enclave.

Enquête *f* official inquiry; ~**kommission** commission of inquiry, royal commission; ~**recht** parliamentary enquiry privilege.

Ensembleschutz *m* protection of historic groups of buildings.

entäußern *v/reflex* to part with, to dispose of, to divest o. s. of.

Entäußerung *f* abandonment, relinquishment, alienation.

entfallen

entbehrlich *adj* dispensable, non-essential, superfluous.

Entbehrlichkeit *f* dispensability.

entbinden *v/t* to dispense, release, to discharge, to set free.

Entbindung *f* dispensation, release (*from duties*), exemption.

Entbindungs|anstalt *f* maternity hospital; ~**beihilfe** confinement grant; ~**heim** maternity home; ~**kosten** expenses incurred by childbirth, maternity costs.

Entbürokratisierung *f* deregulation.

enteignen *v/t* to expropriate.

enteignend *adj* expropriatory.

Enteignung *f* (compulsory) expropriation, taking under eminent domain (*US*); ~ **ausländischen Vermögens** expropriation of alien property; ~ **im öffentlichen Interesse** expropriation in the public interest; **entschädigungslose** ~ expropriation without compensation.

Enteignungs|anordnung expropriation (= e.)-order; ~**befugnis** authority to expropriate; ~**behörde** e. authority; ~**beschluß** e. order, vesting order; ~**bescheid** notice of e.; ~**entschädigung** compensation for expropriated property, indemnity for e.; ~**gesetz** Act of eminent domain, e. Act; **e~gleich** expropriatory, equivalent to e.; ~**plan** e. plan; ~**recht** right of e., eminent domain; ~**verfahren** e. proceedings, eminent domain proceedings.

enterben *v/t* to disinherit, to exclude from (intestate) succession.

Enterbung *f* disinheritance, exclusion from (intestate) succession; **die testamentarische** ~**sverfügung anfechten** *to seek to have the testamentary exclusion from (intestate) succession set aside by court decision.*

Enteuropäisierung *f* de-Europeanization.

entfallen *v/i* (1) to be allotted to, to fall to; (2) to be omitted, to be dropped; *entfällt:* not applicable (*in forms*), inapplicable.

Entfaltung *f* unfolding, development; **~ der Persönlichkeit** development of one's personality, pursuit of happiness, leading a rich full life.

entfernen *v/t* to remove, to oust *v/reflex* to leave, to withdraw, to retire, to go away, to abscond.

Entfernung *(1) f* removal, ouster; withdrawal; **~ aus dem Amt** removal from office, dismissal; **~ aus dem Dienst** removal from office, removal from post; **unerlaubte ~** absenting oneself without leave; **~~ von der Truppe**: *absence without leave (AWL)*.

Entfernung *(2) f* distance; **~ in der Luftlinie** distance in a straight line, airline distance, distance as the crow flies; **~sstaffel** scale of graded mileage charges; **die zurückgelegte ~** the distance covered.

entflechten *v/t* to deconcentrate (*combines*), to decartelize.

Entflechtung *f* deconcentration, decartelization, demerger; demergerisation; **~sabkommen** disengagement agreement.

Entfremdung *f* estrangement.

entführen *v/t* to abduct (*minor, girl*), to kidnap.

Entführer *m* kidnapper, abductor (*of a minor or girl*).

Entführung *f* abduction (*of a minor or girl*), kidnapping, hijacking (*plane*); **~ e–s Kindes zwecks Erpressung** extortionary child kidnapping; **~ Minderjähriger** abduction of young persons, abduction of minors; **~ mit Willen der Minderjährigen** ravishment of ward, elopement; **~ zur Ehe** abduction without consent, elopement.

entgegenhalten *v/t* to reply, to answer an argument, to say sth in rebuttal, *pat* to cite.

Entgegenhaltung *f* replication, argumentative answer, rejoinder, *pat* citation (*as against an application*), reference (cited against ..) prior art document.

Entgegennahme *f* acceptance (*gift, goods, contributions*), receiving (*of orders*), receipt.

entgegennehmen *v/t* to accept, to receive, to take.

entgegensehen *v/t* to await, to expect (*message, answer*), to face (*crisis etc*), to look forward to sth (*pleasant*).

entgegensetzen *v/t* to counter (*argument, reproach*), to oppose.

entgegenstehen *v/i* to impair, to stand in s. o. 's way; *dem steht nichts entgegen*: *there are no objections to it*.

entgegenstehend *adj* adverse (*claim, right*).

entgegenstellen *v/reflex* to oppose.

entgegentreten *v/i* to confront sth.

entgegenwirken to counteract.

entgegnen *v/i, v/t* to reply, to retort.

Entgegnung *f* replication, rejoinder.

Entgelt *n* remuneration, compensation, consideration; **~bescheinigung** receipt; **~ für Leistungen** charges for services; **~ für Schädigung** compensation for damage; **~nachweis** evidence of remuneration received; **~tarifvertrag** collective wage agreement; **~vereinbarung** agreement concerning remuneration for services; **abzugsfähige ~e** deductible charges for services; **gegen das ~ eines angemessenen Zinses** in return for an adequate rate of interest; **umsatzsteuerbare ~e** receipts liable to turnover tax.

entgelten *v/t* to compensate, to remunerate, to repay.

entgeltlich *adj, adv* for (valuable) consideration, on a payment basis; for reward, lucrative; **~ oder unentgeltlich abtreten** to assign against or without valuable consideration.

Entgeltlichkeit *f* remunerativeness, payment basis.

enthaften *v/t* to release from liability, to disencumber.

Enthaftung *f* release (*or* discharge) from liability; **~sklausel** general release clause.

Enthaltungspflicht *f* obligation to refrain from exercising a right or privilege.

enthaupten *v/t* to decapitate, to behead, to execute by decapitation.
Enthauptung *f* decapitation, beheading.
entheben *v/t* to relieve (*of duties*); to remove (*from an office*).
entheiligen *v/t* to profane (*Sabbath*), to desecrate.
Entheiligung *f* profanation, desecration.
enthoben *adj* deprived from, dismissed.
Enthortung *f* dishoarding.
enthüllen *v/t* to expose, to disclose, to reveal, to divulge.
Enthüllung *f* disclosure, discovery.
entkolonisieren *v/t* to decolonize.
entkommen *v/i* to escape, get away; *jmdm ~: to give s.o. the slip*.
entkräften to weaken, to invalidate, to refute (*an argument, evidence*).
Entkräftung *f* invalidation (*of evidence*), refutation.
Entkriminalisierung *f* decriminalization.
Entlade|beginn breaking bulk; **~frist** unloading period; **~gerät** unloading equipment; **~hafen** port of discharge, port of unloading; *letzter ~~: final port*; **~kosten** unloading fee, discharging fee; **~rampe** unloading platform.
entladen *v/t* to unload.
Entladung *f* unloading, discharge; **~shafen** port of discharge.
entlassen *v/t* to discharge; to dismiss, to release, to oust; to excuse (*a witness after examination*); **fristlos ~** to dismiss summarily (*or* instantly), to dismiss without notice, to fire, to give the sack; **bedingt ~** to parole; *bedingt E~er: parolee*.
Entlassung *f* dismissal, discharge, release, removal from office; **~ auf Antrag** resignation; **~ aus dem Amt** dismissal from service, release from service; **~ aus dem Militärdienst** discharge from military service, release from military service; **~ aus dem Pfandverband** release from charge; **~ aus dem Staatsangehörigkeitsverhältnis** release from nationality; **~ aus der Haft** release from custody; **~ aus der Vormundschaft** dewarding; releasing s.o. from wardship; **~ aus e-r Verbindlichkeit** discharge from an obligation; **~ aus Haftung** release from liability; **~ von Gefangenen** release of prisoners; **~ wegen unzulänglicher Leistungen** dismissal for incompetence; **bedingte ~** conditional release, parole; **ehrenhafte ~** honourable discharge; **endgültige ~** discharge from parole (*of prisoner*); **fristlose ~** dismissal without notice, summary dismissal, instant dismissal; **kollektive ~** collective dismissal; **unehrenhafte ~** dishonourable discharge, discharge with ignominy; *die ~~ aussprechen: to discharge with ignominy*; **ungerechtfertigte ~** wrongful dismissal (*common law claim*), unfair dismissal (*statutory claim*); **vorzeitige ~** premature release, release before due date; **widerrechtliche fristlose ~** wrongful dismissal.
Entlassungs|abfindung severance pay, soldier's pay at discharge from service; **~beschluß** order of dismissal; **~entschädigung** dismissal compensation; *großzügige ~~; a „golden handshake"*, **~geld** severance pay = *abfindung qv*; **~grund** grounds for discharge, reason for dismissal; **~lager** discharge camp, separation centre; **~papiere** discharge papers, walking papers; *~~ verlangen: "to ask for one's cards"*; **~schein** certificate of discharge; **~stelle** demobilization centre.
entlasten *v/t* to relieve, to ease, to disengage; to discharge, to pass a vote of approval; to give formal approval; to exonerate (*a suspect, defendant*); *nicht entlastet: undischarged (debtor)*.
Entlastung *f* relief, easing, exculpation, personal discharge, exoneration (*suspect, accused*), remission; formal approval of (*an officer's, a board's) activities, acceptance of reports and accounts*; **~ des Vorstands** formal approval of the actions of the

Entlastungsanzeige   **Entschädigung**

managing board; ~ **erteilen** to give a discharge; ~ **e–s Treuhänders** formal approval of trustee's work; ~ **von Grundbesitz** disencumbering of real estate; **liquiditätsmäßige** ~ improvement in liquidity; **zur ~ meines Kontos** to reduce the debit (amount) on my account.

Entlastungs|anzeige credit note; ~**auftrag** relief order; ~**beschluß** vote of approval; ~**beweis** exculpatory evidence, proof by principal of proper care and diligence in selecting servants; evidence in exoneration, exonerating evidence; ~**erteilung** acceptance of reports and accounts, vote of formal approval; ~**grund** reason for relief; ~**straße** by-pass (road); ~**symptom** sign of improvement; ~**zeuge** witness for the defence; ~**zug** relief train, extra train.

Entlehnungsfreiheit *f* liberty to quote or copy (*from copyrighted work*).

entleihen to borrow (*book from library*).

Entleiher *m* borrower.

entliberalisieren *v/t* to deliberalize (*trade, rents*), to reimpose state controls.

Entliberalisierung *f* deliberalization, reimposing state controls.

entloben *v/reflex* to break off one's engagement.

Entlobung *f* breaking off of the engagement.

entlohnen *v/t* to remunerate, to pay for one's work.

Entlohnung remuneration, emolument, payment; **tägliche** ~ daily pay, per diem pay; **angemessene** ~ adequate remuneration, fair pay.

entmachten *v/t* to deprive (of one's) power, to render powerless.

Entmachtung *f* deprivation of power, rendering powerless.

entmilitarisieren *v/t* to demilitarize.

Entmilitarisierung *f* demilitarization.

entmonetisieren *v/t* to demonetize.

Entmonetisierung *f* demonetization.

entmündigen *v/t* to declare a person legally incapable, to place under guardianship.

Entmündigter *m* (*der Entmündigte*) adult person placed under guardianship; a person subject to an order of the Court of Protection; ~ **wegen Verschwendungssucht** ~ prodigal, person placed under guardianship because of squandermania.

Entmündigung *f* placing s. o. under the control of a guardian, legal incapacitation, deprivation of legal capacity.

Entmündigungs|antrag petition to declare s. o. mentally incapable, petition in lunacy, application for guardianship *or* for an order of the Court of Protection; ~**ausschuß** commission in lunacy, committee of inquisition (*concerning the mental incapacity of a patient*); ~**beschluß** order placing an adult person under the control of a guardian, order certifying the mental incapacity of s. o.; ~**sachen** proceedings for guardianship, mental incapacity cases; ~**verfahren** proceedings to certify s. o. mentally incapable, inquisition of lunacy, proceedings in the Court of Protection, proceedings to place an adult person under guardianship.

Entnahme *f* withdrawal (of payment); *pl* drawings; taking out of money; sampling (*of test specimens*); ~**recht** drawing right.

entnehmen *v/t* to take, to take out, to withdraw, to quote from.

Entpflichtung *f* release from allegiance; release from service obligation.

entrechten *v/t* to deprive of one's rights.

Entrechtung *f* deprivation of (fundamental) rights, disfranchisement.

entrichten *v/t* to pay (*dues, fees etc*).

Entrichtung *f* payment (*of a money debt, esp. a fee*), discharge.

entschädigen *v/t* to compensate, to indemnify, to reimburse.

Entschädigung *f* compensation, in-

255

Entschädigungsanspruch | **Entscheidung**

demnification, reimbursement; ~**für Ersatzbeschaffung** reimbursement of replacements; ~ **für immateriellen Schaden** solace, solatium; ~ **für nationalsozialistisches Unrecht** compensation for Nazi wrongs; ~ **für unschuldig verbüßte Untersuchungshaft** compensation for pre-trial custody of an innocent person; ~ **für Verdienstausfall** compensation for loss of earnings; ~ **in Geld** pecuniary compensation; **angemessene** ~ (fair and) reasonable compensation, just compensation; **billige** ~ fair compensation; **finanzielle** ~ pecuniary compensation (*or* reward); **freiwillige** ~ ex gratia payment as (*by way of*) compensation; **quotale** ~ pro rata compensation; **soziale** ~ compensation in keeping with social considerations; **vereinnahmte** ~ allowance received; **vertraglich vereinbarte** ~ contractually agreed compensation, liquidated damages; **volle** ~ full compensation.

Entschädigungs|anspruch compensation claim; ~**antrag** petition for compensation; **e~berechtigt** entitled to compensation; ~**berechtigung** entitlement to compensation; ~**beschluß** (*im Adhäsionsverfahren*) compensation order; ~**fonds** compensation fund; ~**forderung** compensation claim, indemnity claim; ~**gericht** claims tribunal; ~**kammer des Landgerichts** indemnification panel of the regional court (Landgericht) (*in claims by Nazi prosecutees*); ~**last** compensation burden (*as a public charge*), indemnification charges; ~**leistung** compensatory payment, indemnity benefit, payment of damages; ~**pflicht** obligation to compensate; **e~pflichtig** *adj* obliged to compensate, to compensate; ~**pflichtiger** person obliged to compensate; ~**recht** right to compensation; ~**rente** compensation pension, regular compensation payments; ~**sachen** compensation cases (*for Nazi prosecutees*); ~**summe** amount of indemnification, (*or* of compensation); ~**vereinbarung** agreement for compensation; ~**verfahren** compensation proceedings, legal proceedings for damages; ~**zahlung** payment of compensation, compensating grant.

entschärfen to unprime (*shell*); to render (*mine, unexploded bomb*) harmless; to remove the detonator of (bomb); to neutralize.

Entschärfungskommando bomb (mine-)disposal squad.

Entscheid *m* decision, ruling, decree.

entscheiden *v/t, v/i* to decide, to adjudge, to adjudicate upon, to hold, to rule, to determine, to dispose; *v/reflex* to resolve, to opt (for), to decide; **gerichtlich** ~ to adjudicate, to adjudge, to rule; **rechtsfehlerhaft** ~ to err in law, to err on a point of law, to err on a legal technicality.

entscheidend *adj* decisive, vital, crucial, conclusive.

Entscheidung *f* decision, determination, adjudication, ruling; ~ **im schriftlichen Verfahren** paper adjudication, decision according to written pleadings (without further hearing); ~ **nach Aktenlage** judgment in accordance with the state of the pleadings, decision as the case lies (*without considering fresh arguments or evidence*); ~ **nach Gutdünken** discretionary decision, decision at the court's pleasure (*or* discretion); ~ **über die Kosten** decision on costs; **abschließende** ~ final decision; **abweisende** ~ dismissal; **an ~en gebunden sein** to be bound by precedents; **beschwerdefähige** ~ appealable decision; **bindende** ~ binding decision; **die angefochtene** ~ the decision appealed from (*or* against); **die** ~ **der unteren Instanz aufheben** to overrule the lower court; **die** ~ **durch ein Schiedsgericht vereinbaren** to agree to submit a dispute to arbitration; **e-e** ~ **aufhe-**

Entscheidungsbefugnis / **entschulden**

ben to set aside (*or* to reverse) a decision; **e-e ~ aufrechterhalten** to uphold a decision; **e-e ~ fällen** to render a decision, to give a ruling; **e-e ~ in zweiter Instanz bestätigen** to uphold a decision on appeal; **e-e ~ mit Gründen versehen** to state the reasons for a decision; **e-e ~ nachprüfen** to review a decision; **e-e ~ umstoßen** to quash a decision; **e-e ~ vertagen** to postpone a decision; **einschlägige ~** precedent, a case in point; **erstinstanzliche ~** the decision at first instance; **gerichtliche ~** court decision, adjudication, judicial ruling; **grundsätzliche ~** decision of principle, fundamental ruling; **künstlerische ~** creative decision; **maßgebliche ~** precedent; **mit Gründen versehene ~** (a) reasoned decision; **nicht veröffentlichte ~** unreported decision; **rechtlich einwandfreie ~** (legally) correct decision; **rechtsfehlerhafte ~** (*e-s Richters*) self-misdirection, erroneous decision; **rechtskräftige ~** (final and) non-appealable decision, irreversible ruling; **richterliche ~** judicial decision, the judge's ruling; **sachliche ~** objective decision; **sachlich-rechtliche ~** decision on the merits (of a case); **schiedsgerichtliche ~** arbitration award; **schiedsrichterliche ~** arbitration award, award by an arbitrator; **schriftliche ~** written decision, decision in written proceedings; **sich e-r ~ fügen** to accept a decision; **sorgfältig durchdachte ~** carefully considered decision; **unternehmerische ~**(*sfindung*) entrepreneurial decision-making; **vorbehaltlich e-r endgültigen ~** subject to final decision; **vorläufige ~** provisional decision.

Entscheidungs|befugnis competence to decide, authority to adjudicate, power to take decisions; **~begründung** reasons, reasoning leading to the decision; **~delegation** delegation of decision-making; **~einklang** conformity of decisions in different jurisdictions; **e~erheblich** relevant to the issue; **~erheblichkeit** relevance to the issues of the case; **~findung** decision-making; **~gewalt** power to decide; *freie ~~: uncontrolled discretion;* **~gründe** reasons for the decision, grounds of judgment; *die ~~ absetzen: to state the reasons for a decision in writing;* **~grundlage** basis of the decision; **~merkmal** criterion for a decision; **~pflicht** obligation to render a decision, duty to decide; **~prozeß** decision-making process; **~rahmen** latitude of judgment; **~recht** authority to adjudicate; **e~reif** ripe for judgment; **~sammlung** reports; **~spielraum** latitude of judgment, discretion, **~träger** decision maker; **~unfähigkeit** division of opinion, inability to reach a decision; **~verbund** joint decisions (*divorce and supplementary matters*).

Entschleierung *f* unmasking, disclosure, removing a disguise.

Entschiedenheit *f* determination, resoluteness, peremptoriness.

entschließen *v/reflex* to come to a decision, to resolve, to make up one's mind, to decide.

Entschließung *f* resolution (*meeting*), order (*administrative authority*); **~santrag** motion for resolution; **~sentwurf** draft resolution.

Entschluß *m* decision (*to reach a decision*); **aus eigenem ~** on his own initiative; **fester ~** firm decision; **unerschütterlicher ~** unshakeable resolution, firm decision.

entschlüsseln to decipher, to decrypt, to decode, to break *or* to crack a code.

Entschlüsselung *f* deciphering, decoding.

entschuldbar *adj* excusable, pardonable, venial.

Entschuldbarkeit *f* excusability, pardonable nature (of), venial character of sth.

entschulden *v/t* to disencumber, to clear of debts, to free of debts.

entschuldigen

entschuldigen *v/t* to excuse, to pardon; *v/reflex* to apologize.
Entschuldigung *f* excuse, apology; **ausreichende** ~ full (*or* adequate) apology; **ohne ausreichende** ~ without reasonable excuse, without good cause; **ohne triftigen** ~**sgrund** without lawful excuse.
Entschuldung *f* reduction of indebtedness, disencumberment; debt relief; ~**sverfahren** *administrative proceedings to reduce mortgage indebtedness of agricultural properties*.
Entschwefelung *f* desulphurization.
entsenden *v/t* to send on a mission, to delegate.
Entsendestaat *m* sending state.
Entsendung *f* sending, secondment.
Entsetzung *f mil* relief, rescue, deforcement; (*aus Besitz*) dispossession, ouster.
entseuchen *v/t* to decontaminate.
Entseuchung *f* decontamination.
entsichern to cock, to release the safety device of (*a fire arm*).
entsiegeln *v/t* to unseal, to break open (*letter*), to break the seal.
Entsiegelung *f* unsealing, taking off the seal(s).
Entsorgung *f* waste disposal; ~**sgut** waste and sewage.
Entspannung *f* easing of tension, disengagement, de-escalation, détente; ~ **am Geldmarkt** easing of money rates.
Entspannungssymptom *m* sign of slackening tension, of détente.
Entsparung *f* (= *Entsparen n*) dissaving.
entsperren *v/t* to unblock, to deblock (*an account*), to release.
Entsperrung *f* unblocking, release.
entsprechen *v/i* to correspond, to conform, to be in agreement with, to comply (with *an order*), to meet (expectations), to accord with.
entsprechend *adj, adv* in accordance with, in conformity with, corresponding, appropriate, analogous, mutatis mutandis; equivalent, akin, as the case may be; **weitmöglichst** ~ as close(ly) as possible.
Entsprechung *f* analogy, correspondence, agreement; **volle** ~ equivalent, complete identity.
Entstehung *f* accrual (*of a right*), origin (*of a title*), formation (*of a company*), emergence, accrual, incurrence, creation; ~**sdatum** date of origin; ~**geschichte** genesis; ~**sursache** original cause; ~**szeitpunkt** date of origin; ~**szustand** nascent state.
entstellen *v/i* to distort, to disfigure, to deface, to deform, to pervert.
Entstellung *f* disfigurement, distortion, deformation, defacement; ~ **der Wahrheit** perversion of the truth; ~ **des Gesichts** disfigurement, deformation of the face; ~ **von Tatsachen** misrepresentation, distortion (*or* twisting) of the facts.
Entstempeln *n* cancellation of licence-plate.
Entstörungsdienst *m* fault-clearing service, trouble-shooting service.
Entstrickung *f* release from attachment.
Enttarnung *f* unmasking *of spies*.
Enttrümmerung *f* rubble clearance.
entvölkern *v/t* to depopulate.
Entvölkerung *f* depopulation.
entwaffnen *v/t* to disarm.
Entwaffnung *f* disarming (*a criminal*).
entwarnen *v/i* to sound the "all clear" signal.
Entwarnung *f* "all clear" signal, off-signal, cancellation of a warning.
entwässern *v/t* to drain, to dry up.
Entwässerung *f* drainage (*land*).
Entwehrung *f surrender of purchased object in order to claim damages based on warranty of title*.
entweichen *v/i* to abscond, to escape; to leak (*gas*).
Entweichen *n* absconding, escape.
Entweichenlassen *n* allowing a prisoner to escape; **fahrlässiges** ~ negligent allowing of an escape.
entweihen *v/t* to profane, to desecrate, to soil, to sully.
Entweihung *f* profanation, desecration.
entwenden *v/t* to deprive one of possession, to obtain unauthorized control, to take away (unlawfully).

Entwenden *f* unlawful taking of another's property.
entwerfen *v/t* to draft, to make a draft, to sketch.
entwerten *v/t* to cancel, to invalidate, to obliterate.
Entwertung *f* cancellation, depreciation, devaluation; **~sstempel** cancellation stamp (*postmark*).
Entwicklung *f* development, trend, movement; **defizitäre ~** trend towards a deficit; **diskriminierungsfreie ~** non-discriminatory development; **gleichgewichtige ~ beider Seiten** even development of the two sides; **kassenmäßige ~** movement in cash position; **konjunkturelle ~** cyclical trend.
Entwicklungs|abschnitt phase in the development; **~bedingungen der Konjunktur** conditions affecting the economic trend; **~fonds** development fund, fund for developing countries; **~gebiet** development area, growth area; **~gebot** requirement to develop (*an area, a project etc*); **~gesellschaft** development corporation; **~helfer** development agent; **~hilfe** development aid; *förderungswürdige ~~*: *development aid deserving government grants*; **~kredit** development loan, credit made available for development projects; **~land** developing country, *pl also emerging nations*; **~linie** line of development, trend; **~pause** temporary standstill (in development); **~richtung** trend; **~schema** pattern of development; **~vorhaben** development project.
entwidmen *v/t* to release from public use, to reclassify as private (*road*).
Entwidmung *f* release from public use, reclassification for private use.
entwöhnen *v/t, v reflex* to break (*or* give up) a habit, to cure from an addiction.
Entwöhnung *f* cure from an addiction, breaking of a habit; **~skur** treatment for curing addicts (*or* alcoholics), detoxication.

entwürdigen *v/t* to debase, to degrade, to disgrace.
Entwürdigung *f* debasement, disgrace, degrading, humiliation.
Entwurf *f* draft (*document*), outline, design (*machine etc*); **~der Stellungnahme** draft opinion; **~ des Haushaltsplans** draft budget, budget estimates; **erster ~** first draft, rough draft.
Entwurfs|fassung *e-s Vertrages* draft agreement; **~schreiben** draft letter; **~stadium** planning stage, blueprint stage; **~verfasser** draftsman; **~zeichner** draftsman.
entzerren *v/t* to straighten out, to eliminate distortion, to rectify.
Entzerrung *f* rectification, straightening out (*what is distorted*), distortion compensation.
entziehen *v/t* to deprive, to divest, to take away, *v/reflex* to elude, to avoid, to escape, to slip away.
Entziehung *f* deprivation, divestment; **~ der bürgerlichen Ehrenrechte** suspension of civic rights, deprivation of civic rights; **~ der elterlichen Gewalt** withdrawal of parental control; **~ der Fahrerlaubnis** disqualification from driving (motor vehicles), suspension (of driver's licence); driving ban; *zwingend vorgeschriebene ~~~*: *mandatory disqualification from driving*; **~ der Staatsangehörigkeit** expatriation, deprivation of citizenship; **~ der Vollmacht** revocation of the power of attorney; **~ der Zulassung** striking off the roll, debarring, disqualification; **~ des Besitzes** dispossession; **~ des Führerscheins** forfeiture of the driving licence; **~ des Wahlrechts** disfranchisement; **~ e-r Lizenz** revocation of a licence; **~ von Elektrizität** abstraction of electricity, tapping electric power.
Entziehungs|anstalt detoxication centre; **~~ für Alkoholiker**: alcoholics' home; **~beschluß** declaration of withdrawal; **~kur** detoxication treatment, cure from addiction; **~recht** power of revocation.

entziffern *v/t* to decipher, to decode, to make out.
Entzifferung *f* deciphering, decoding.
Entzug *m* → *Entziehung*; **steuerliche ~swirkungen** fiscal drag.
entzünden *v/reflex* to ignite, to catch fire spontaneously.
entzweien *v/t* to disunite, to turn *persons* against each other.
Erachten *n* view, opinion; **handeln Sie nach eigenem ~!** do as you think fit; **meines ~s** in my opinion, as I see it, in my view.
erarbeiten *v/t* to gain by (hard) work, to acquire.
Erarbeitung *f* acquisition (of wealth) by work; **zur ~ der Grundlinien** to evolve the broad lines.
Erb|abfindung settlement for an inheritance; *compensation for a beneficiary (or co-heir) in satisfaction of his (her) right of inheritance*; **~anfall** (accrual of an) inheritance, devolution of an inheritance, succession to the estate of a deceased person; **~anspruch** right of inheritance, inheritance claim; *bedingter ~~: contingent remainder*; **~anteil** inherited share of estate; **~anwärter** apparent heir, expectant heir; *übergangener ~~: pretermitted heir, a passed-over heir*; **~anwartschaft** expectancy of inheritance, estate in expectancy; **~auseinandersetzung** partition of an inheritance, division of the estate, distribution of the estate; **~ausgleich** money compensation in lieu of future inheritance; (2) collation of goods, hotchpot of advancements; **~ausschlagung** disclaimer of inheritance, repudiation of an inheritance; **~baurecht** *etc* → *Erbbau...*; **e~berechtigt** entitled to inherit; **~berechtigter** (*der Erbberechtigte*) person entitled to inherit; *der nächste gesetzliche ~~: next heir*; **~berechtigung** title to an inheritance; **~bescheinigung** *f Sw* = *Erbschein qv*; **~besitz** possession by inheritance, inheritable (*or* inherited) property, hereditament; **e~eigen** hereditable, belonging (*to s.o.*) by right of inheritance, allodial; **~einsetzung** appointment as an heir; *gegenseitige ~~: mutual appointment as heir, double will*; **~ersatzanspruch** substituted inheritance right (*of illegitimate children, since 1970*); **~erschleichung** gaining an inheritance by fraud, legacy-hunting; **~fähigkeit** legal capacity to inherit; **~fall** devolution of an inheritance, (the event of) succession; **~fallschulden** debts incurred upon the inheritance; **~folge** → *Erbfolge*; **~gang** succession upon death, devolution of inheritance, devolution of the estate (of a deceased person); *im ~~ anfallen: to accrue by way of succession*; **e~gesund** *adj* not afflicted with a hereditary disease; **~gesundheit** eugenics, freedom from hereditary disease; **~gut** inherited property, hereditament, patrimony, *hist* allodium, freehold estate; **~hof** hereditary farm (*estate tail*); inherited farm; **~kranker** person afflicted with a hereditary disease; **~krankheit** hereditary disease; **~lasser** estate-leaver, decedent, the deceased (person), (*the intestate or the testator (m) or testatrix (f)*); **~lasserschuld** ancestral debt, testator's debts; **~lasserin** the female decedent; testatrix; **~legitimation** evidence of the right to an inheritance, certificate of inheritance; **~lehen** hereditary fief; **e~lich** *adj* hereditary (*right, disease*), inheritable (*property*), inherited; **~lichkeit** inheritability, hereditary character; **~linie** line of succession; **~masse** assets of the estate; **~monarchie** hereditary monarchy; **~nachweis** proof of inheritance; **~pacht** hereditary tenancy; **~pächter** holder of a hereditary tenancy, fee-farmer; **~pachtgelände** hereditary leasehold land; **~pachtheimstätte** hereditary leasehold homestead; **~pachtrecht** right of inheritable tenancy; **~pachtvertrag** inheritable lease (agreement); **~pachtzins**

ground rent; **~quote** proportional right to an inheritance, fraction of the inheritance; **~recht** → *Erbrecht*; **~schaft** → *Erbschaft*; **~schein** → *Erbschein*; certificate of inheritance; **~schleicher** legacy hunter, fortune hunter; **~statut** *the law of decedent's nationality urhuch governs the inheritance*; **~stück** heirloom; **~teil** → *Erbteil*; **~teilung** partition of a succession, division of the estate;**~unfähigkeit** legal incapacity to inherit; **e~unwürdig** unworthy to inherit; **~unwürdigkeit** unworthiness to inherit, moral ineligibility for an inheritance; **~vergleich** inheritance settlement; **~vermutung des Fiskus** presumptive inheritance by the state (*in the absence of any other heirs*); **~vertrag** contract of succession by inheritance, deed of inheritance (*appointing an heir or heirs inter vivos*); **~verzicht** renunciation of inheritance, relinquishment of an inheritance; **~zins** ground rent, perpetual rent, rent charge; **~zuwachs** accretion by inheritance.

Erbbau|berechtigter tenant under a building lease, tenant on ground rent; **~grundbuch** land register for building leases; **~recht** building lease, heritable building right, the law concerning building leases; superficies; **~rechtsvertrag** building lease agreement; **~zins** ground rent (for a building lease).

Erbe *m* heir, *as a civil law concept, the universal successor of a deceased person*, successor; **~ erster Ordnung** heir of the first degree; **~ in der Seitenlinie** heir collateral; **~naufgebot** public notice designed to trace the heirs to an estate; **~n, die mit dem Erblasser in gerader Linie verwandt sind** lineal heirs, natural heirs; **~ngemeinschaft** community of heirs, joint heirs; **~nhaftung** personal liability of the heir; **~nlosigkeit** default of heirs, absence of heirs; **~nmehrheit** plurality of heirs; **~nmutter** indigent expectant mother of an heir (*legal maintenance claim*); **alleiniger ~** sole heir; **als ~ berufen sein** to be called to the succession; **gesetzlicher ~** heir by intestacy, heir at law, statutory heir; **keine ~n hinterlassen** to die without issue; **künftiger ~** heir apparent; **leiblicher ~** heir of the body; **mutmaßlicher ~** heir presumptive; **rechtmäßiger ~** lawful heir; **testamentarischer ~** testamentary heir.

Erbe *n* inheritance, heritage, estate; **ein ~ antreten** to take possession of an inheritance, to accept an inheritance, *fig* to step into the shoes of s. b.; **ein ~ ausschlagen** to refuse (*or* to disclaim) an inheritance; **väterliches ~** patrimony.

erben *v/t, v/i* to inherit.

Erbeserbe *m* heir to an heir.

Erbeserbengemeinschaft *f* subparticipation in community of heirs (*by the heirs of a deceased member*).

Erbfolge *f* succession (upon death), heritable succession, inheritance; **~ in der Seitenlinie** collateral inheritance; **~ in gerader Linie** lineal succession; **~ nach Stämmen** succession per stirpes, stirpital succession; **~ordnung** order of succession; **~persönlichkeitsrecht** personal rights of an inventor, right to be named as inventor; **~verteilung nach Stämmen** stirpital distribution; **gesetzliche ~** intestate succession, succession ab intestato; legal succession; **gewillkürte ~** testamentary succession; **testamentarische ~** testamentary (*or* testate) succession.

Erbin *f* heiress, female heir.

Erbrecht *n* law of succession, right (*or* title) to an inheritance, right to succeed; **gesetzliches ~** law of intestate succession, legal right to an inheritance, right to an inheritance from an intestate; **gesetzliches ~ des Fiskus** the State's right to succeed to heirless property; **testamentarisches ~** law of testamentary succession, legal right to an inheritance under a will.

Erbschaft inheritance, estate; **angefallene** ~ accrued inheritance; e–e ~ **antreten** to enter upon an inheritance; e–e ~ **erschleichen** to obtain a legacy by intrigue (*or* by fraud, by false pretences); **ruhende** ~ contingent inheritance; **verschuldete** ~ estate encumbered with debts.

Erbschafts|anfall accrual of an inheritance, transfer of the deceased's estate to the heir; ~**angelegenheiten** matters of inheritance, questions pertaining to the inheritance; ~**annahme** acceptance of an inheritance; *unbedingte* ~~: *unconditional acceptance of an inheritance*; ~**anspruch** right of succession, claim to an inheritance; ~**anteil** share in an inheritance; ~**antritt** accession to an estate, entry upon an inheritance; ~**anwärter** expectant heir, heir in expectancy; ~**anzeige** notice of accrual of inheritance; ~**auseinandersetzung** partition of a succession; ~**ausschlagung** renunciation of succession, refusal to accept an inheritance (*filed with probate court in notarized form*); ~**besitzer** possessor of the estate *under (alleged) right of inheritance*; ~**erklärung** inheritance declaration: *declaration accepting or refusing an inheritance*; ~**erwerber** purchaser of an inheritance as a whole; ~**gegenstände** items of property in the estate; ~**geschäfte** transactions concerning the estate; ~**gläubiger** creditors of the estate; ~**inventar** inventorized list of the estate; ~**kauf** purchase of a total inheritance; ~**käufer** purchaser of a total inheritance; ~**klage** inheritance recovery action, action to establish claim to an inheritance; ~**masse** estate, bulk of the estate, inherited property; ~**prozesse** death litigation; ~**sachen** inheritance cases, probate matters; ~**steuer** inheritance tax, estate tax, succession tax; ~**steuergesetz** inheritance tax law *US:* Unified Estate and Gift Tax Act; ~**steuerpflicht** liability to (pay) inheritance tax; ~**streit** litigation about an inheritance; ~**teilung** partition of the estate of a deceased person; ~~ *vornehmen*: *to parcel an inheritance*; ~**übergang** devolution of an estate of a deceased person; ~**vermächtnis** legacy of a whole estate; ~**vermögen** inherited assets.

Erbschein *m* certificate of inheritance (*testate or intestate succession*); ~ **des Alleinerben** = *Alleinerbschein qv;* ~**santrag** application for a certificate of inheritance; ~**sverfahren** proceedings (*in German probate court*) for the issue of a certificate of inheritance; **Eigenrechts**~ certificate of inheritance based on German law (*deceased alien*); **Fremdrechts**~ (German) certificate of inheritance based on foreign law; **gegenständlich beschränkter** ~ certificate of inheritance limited to assets within the country; **gemeinschaftlicher** ~ joint certificate of inheritance (*several heirs*); **Sammel**~ collective certificate of inheritance (*several successions*); **Teil**~ → *Teilerbschein;* **vereinigter** ~ = *Sammelerbschein qv.*

Erbteil *n* share of the inheritance, part-inheritance; ~**skauf** purchase of the share of an inheritance; ~**sübertragung** transfer of one's share of an inheritance; **gemeinschaftlicher** ~ joint share in the inheritance; **gesetzlicher** ~ legal portion, distributive share (*intestacy*); **künftiger** ~ future interest on an inheritance; **mütterlicher** ~ matrimonial estate; **väterlicher** ~ patrimonial estate, patrimony.

Erd|abfuhr site clearance and excavation; ~**arbeiten** earthwork, groundwork; ~**arbeiter** digger, excavation labourer, groundman; ~**aufschüttungsarbeiten** terracing; ~**bebenversicherung** earthquake insurance; ~**bewegung(en)** soil movement; ~**gas** oil gas, natural gas; ~**öl** → *Erdöl;* ~**rutsch** landslide (*also in elections*);

erdenken / **Erfinder**

~schicht bed, layer, stratum of soil.

erdenken *v/t* to devise, to think up, to invent, to imagine.

erdenklich *adj* imaginable, conceivable, possible.

erdichten *v/t* to fabricate, to concoct, to cook up, to trump up.

Erdichtung *f* fabrication, concoction, invention of a story.

Erdöl *n* (crude) oil, petroleum; **~aktien** oil shares; **~belieferung** oil supply; **~bevorratung** oil stockkeeping; **~bohrinsel** drilling platform; **~förderung** oil production, petroleum extraction; **~konzession** oil concession, oil lease.

erdolchen *v/t* to stab (to death).

erdrosseln *v/t* to strangle (to death).

Erdrosselung *f* strangulation; **~steuer** strangulation tax, prohibitive tax.

ereignen *v/reflex* to occur, to happen, to take place.

Ereignis *n* occurrence, event, happening; **~ mit überholender Kausalität** supervening cause; **bestimmtes ~** specified event; **kriegerische ~se** hostilities, events of war; **sicher eintretendes ~** definite event; **unabwendbares ~** unavoidable accident, inavoidable casualty, inevitable event, fortuitous event; **ungewisses ~** contingency, contingent event; **unvorhergesehenes ~** unforeseen event; **versichertes ~** event insured against; **zufälliges ~** fortuitous event, accident, fortuitous occurrence, *durch ~~*: *by accidental means*.

Ererbtes *n* inherited property, heritage.

erfahren *v/t* to learn, to discover, to come to one's knowledge; to experience; *v/i* to undergo (*processing, changes*).

Erfahrung *f* experience, know-how, background; **gewerbliche ~en** business and industrial experience, commercial know how; **in ~ bringen** to learn, to find out; **praktische ~** practical experience, know-how.

Erfahrungs|austausch interchange of know-how; **~bericht** progress report, case history; **~beweis** proof a posteriori; **e~gemäß** in accordance with experience, according to past experience; **~grundsatz** principle derived from experience, empirical rule; **~lehre** empiricism; **~kreis** sphere of experience; **~methode** empirical method, rule of thumb; **~regel** rule of thumb; **~satz** rule of experience; **~wert** empirical value, empirical experience; **~wissen** know-how; *technisches ~~*: *technical know-how*.

erfaßbar *adj* ascertainable, recordable, registrable, calculable; **statistisch ~** statistically ascertainable.

erfassen *v/t* (*officialese*) to comprise, to include, to cover.

Erfassung *f* scope of coverage, assessment, scope of conscription, marshalling (the assets); **~ an der Quelle** taxation at source; **~ der Wehrpflichten** conscription; **~sbereich** scope (*of assessment, survey etc*); **~sbreite** scope of coverage (*etc → Erfassung*); **~smerkmal** statistical criterion; **~ von Auskünften** pooling of information.

erfinden *v/t* to invent, to devise.

Erfinder *m* inventor; **~benennung** declaration of inventorship; right to be named as inventor; **~ der Haupterfindung** original inventor; **~eid** inventor's oath; **~eigenschaft** inventorship, inventive faculty; **~erklärung** declaration of inventorship; **~gemeinschaft** joint inventors, association of inventors; **~identität** identity of the inventor; **~nennung** mention of the inventor, naming of the inventor; **~prämie** award to inventors; **~prinzip** frist-to-invent system; **~recht** inventor's right; **~schein** inventor's certificate; **~schutz** protection of inventors; **~tätigkeit** the work of the inventor; **~vergütung** inventor's compensation; **abhängiger~** dependent inventor; **alleiniger ~** sole inventor; **angeblicher ~** alleged (supposed, pre-

erfinderisch / **Erfolgsabwendung**

tended) inventor; **beamteter** ~ inventor in an official position; **freier** ~ independent inventor; **früherer** ~ preceding inventor; **gemeinsame** ~ joint inventors; **späterer** ~ subsequent inventor; **wahrer** ~ actual inventor, true and first inventor.

erfinderisch *adj* inventive, imaginative.

Erfindung *f* invention (= *i, pl i–s*); ~**en oder sonstige Erkenntnis** *i–s* or other knowledge; **ältere** ~ prior *i*; **beanspruchte** ~ claimed *i*; **biologische** ~ biological *i*; **chemische** ~ chemical *i*; **den Umfang der** ~ **abgrenzen** to define (*or* limit) the scope of an *i*; **die** ~ **abgrenzen (gegen)** to delimit the *i* (from); **die** ~ **beschreiben** to describe (specify) the *i*; **die** ~ **ist gerichtet auf** the *i* is directed to (addressed to, relates to); **die** ~ **mangelt der Neuheit** the *i* lacks novelty; **die vorliegende** ~ the present *i*; **ein Ausführungsbeispiel der** ~ **vorführen** to demonstrate an embodiment of the *i*; **ein Hilfsmittel nutzende** ~ factor-using *i*; **ein Hilfsmittel sparende** ~ factor-saving *i*; **e–e** ~ **machen** to make an *i*, to invent sth; **e–e** ~ **nutzen** to exploit an *i*, to make use of an *i*; **e–e** ~ **praktisch verwendbar machen** to reduce an *i* to practice, put an *i* to practical use; **e–e** ~ **unzulässig abhändern** to alter (modify) an *i* in an inadmissible manner; **e–e** ~ **verkaufen** to vend (*or* sell) an *i*; **e–e** ~ **vollbringen** to achieve an *i*; **e–e** ~ **zum Patent anmelden** to file a patent application for an *i*, to apply for a patent of an *i*; **gebundene** ~ *i* subject to a commitment, employee's *i* made available to the employer; **gegen die guten Sitten verstoßende** ~ scandalous *i*, vicious *i*; **kollidierende** ~**en** interfering *i–s*; **menschliche Arbeitskraft sparende** ~ labour-saving *i*; **patentfähige** ~ patentable *i*; *es liegt keine* ~~ *vor*: *no patentable invention is involved*; **patentierte** ~ patented *i*;

unvollständige ~ incomplete (*or* unaccomplished) *i*; **vollendete** ~ (fully) accomplished *i*; **umwälzende** ~ revolutionary *i*; **Verbesserungs**~ improvement *i*; **verwandte** ~**en** related *i–s*, cognate *i–s*; **Wesen e–r** ~ gist of an *i*; **Zusatz**~ developmental *i*, additional *i*.

Erfindungs|aufgabe problem of the *i*; object of the invention; ~**besitz** possession of an *i*; ownership of an invention; ~**bezeichnung** title of an invention; ~**eigenschaft** sufficiency (of an *i*); *fehlende* ~~: *lack of invention*; ~**gabe** ingenuity; inventiveness; ~**gedanke** inventive idea, inventive concept; ~**gegenstand** subject-matter of an *i*; ~**geheimnisse** secrets of an *i*; ~**höhe** inventive step, inventive merit, inventive level, inventivity, degree of inventive ingenuity; (*US:*) non-obviousness; *mangelnde* ~~: *lack of inventiveness*; ~~ *aberkennen*: *to deny inventive step*; ~~ *verneinen*: *to deny inventive step*; ~**leistung** inventive step; *zusätzliche* ~~: *inventive step*, ~**maßstab** standard of *i*; ~**patent** patent for *i*, letters patent; ~**priorität** priority of *i*; ~**vorteil** benefit (*or* advantage) of the *i*; ~**swert** inventive merit; **e**~**wesentlich** essential to the *i*, important, salient (features).

Erfolg *m* success, result, outcome.

Erfolgs|abwendung preventing the effect (*of a criminal act*); ~**anteil** share in the results, share in the profit; ~**anteilsystem** profit sharing scheme, bonus system; ~**aussichten** chances of success, prospect of success; ~**eintritt** (the) case of success, happening of the contingency; ~**beitrag** contribution to profits; ~**beteiligung** profit sharing (plan) *for employees*; ~**delikt** objective crime; ~**erlebnis** sense of achievement; ~**gebühr** →~**honorar**; ~**haftung** strict liability, liability without fault; ~**honorar** contingent fee, payment by result; ~~**vertrag**: *contingency contract*;

erforderlich / **Erfüllungsangebot**

~konto nominal account, income and expenditure account (*concerning the particular type of income such as trade, rents, interest etc*); **~lohn** incentive wage; **e~neutral** without P/L (profit/loss) effect; **~ort** place of effect (*place where the result of an act occurs*); **~posten** item on the income and expenditure account; **~prämie** efficiency bonus; **~quote** success rate; **~rechnung** income statement, profit and loss accounting; **e~wirksam** *adj* affecting net income, affecting the operating result.

erforderlich *adj* necessary, required, requisite; *nicht ~: unnecessary, not required; etw. ~ machen: to necessitate.*

erforderlichenfalls *adv* if required, in case of need, if necessary, where necessary.

Erforderliches *n* (*das Erforderliche*) that which is required, the necessities, necessaries; *das ~ veranlassen: to take the necessary steps*.

Erforderlichkeit *f* necessity, requirement, need; **~sgrundsatz** (= **~~prinzip**) *principle of the least oppressive consequence, of a choice of administrative steps.*

erfordern *v/t* to require, to necessitate, to demand, to exact.

Erfordernis *n* requirement, necessity; **~ der Schriftform** necessity of written form (*written, typed, printed etc and signed*); **allen ~sen gerecht werden** to meet all requirements; **unbedingtes ~** absolute necessity, a "must"; **unterschiedliche haushaltspolitische ~e** differing budgetary needs; **verfassungsmäßige ~** constitutional requirements.

erforschen *v/t* to explore, to inquire (into), to examine, to find out (*the truth, the actual facts*).

Erforschung *f* exploration, inquiry, investigation, examination.

erfrieren *v/i* to freeze to death, to die of cold.

erfüllen *v/t* to fulfil(l), to perform, to discharge (*obligations*); to meet (*conditions*).

erfüllt *adj* fulfilled, performed, satisfied; *nicht ~: unfulfilled, unperformed, unsatisfied.*

Erfüllung *f* fulfil(l)ment; performance, satisfaction, compliance (with); **~ der Aufgaben** performance of the tasks; **~ des Kaufpreises** payment of the purchase price; **~ des Vertrages** performance of the contract, satisfaction of the contractual terms; *die ~ e–s Vertrages wird unmöglich: performance of a contract becomes impossible;* **~ e-r Amtspflicht** performance of an official duty, execution of duty; **~ e-s Anspruchs** discharge of a right, satisfaction of a claim; **~ e-r Bedingung** satisfaction of condition, compliance with a condition; **~ e-r Forderung** discharge of a debt, satisfaction of a claim; **~ e-r Pflicht** discharge of a duty; **~ e-r Verpflichtung** discharge of an obligation, discharge of a liability; **~ fälliger Verpflichtungen** discharge of matured obligations; **~ in bar** performance in cash, cash payment; **~ in natura** specific performance; **~ Zug um Zug** mutual simultaneous performance; **an ~s statt** in lieu of performance, in full satisfaction, (acceptance) as a discharge; **auf ~ klagen** to sue for performance; **die ~ dieser Abkommen** the carrying out of these agreements; **freiwillige ~** voluntary performance; **mangelhafte ~** defective performance; **restlose ~** full discharge; **teilweise ~** part satisfaction, part performance; **vergleichsweise ~** performance under a settlement; **vertragsgetreue ~** performance pursuant to contract, performance in specie.

Erfüllungs|angebot tender (*or* offer) of performance; **~annahme** acceptance as performance; **~anspruch** claim for performance; **~frist** time for performance; **~betrug** fraud in the performance; **~garantie(verpflichtung)** performance bond; **~gegenstand** obligation to be performed, subject

ergänzen / **Erhalt**

matter of the contract; ~**gehilfe** *person employed in performing an obligation for whom the principal is vicariously liable*; ~**geschäft** transaction to perform a contract; **e~halber** by way of provisional performance; on account of performance, as conditional payment (*e.g. a bill of exchange which will not operate as a discharge until it is honoured*); ~**interesse** interest in the complete satisfaction of an obligation, positive interest; ~**klage** action for (specific) performance; ~**ort** place of performance; ~**pflicht** obligation to perform; ~**politik** policy of unconditional fulfilment (*of Versailles Treaty*); ~**tag** date for performance, settlement day, pay day; ~**übernahme** assumption of an obligation to perform, vicarious performance; ~**vereitelung** rendering the performance impossible; ~**vergütung** contingency fee; ~**vertrag** agreement specifying performance; ~**verpflichtung** obligation to perform; ~**verweigerung** refusal to fulfill an obligation; ~**zeit** time of performance (→for an obligation).

ergänzen *v/t* to supplement.
ergänzend *adj* supplementary.
Ergänzung *f* supplementary addition, completion, supplement; ~ **des Pflichtteils** completion of the compulsory portion (*adding equivalent of donations to estate-value*); ~ **e~s Urteils** amendment of a judgment; ~**en zu den Erklärungen** additional explanations.
Ergänzungs|abgabe special levy, surtax, surcharge; ~**abkommen** supplementary agreement; ~**anweisung** supplementary regulation; ~**bescheid** supplementary ruling; ~**bestimmungen** supplementary provisions; ~**blatt** continuation sheet; ~**eid** suppletory oath (*of party to supplement oath of one witness or to verify documents*); ~**gesetz** amending law, supplementary act; ~**pflegschaft** supplementary curatorship (*in case of prevention or disablement of parents or guardian*); ~**police** supplementary policy; ~**richter** substitute judge; ~**schöffen** substitute lay judges; ~**testamentsvollstreckung** supplemental executorship; ~**- und Rahmengesetz** supplementing and co-ordinating law; ~**urteil** supplementary judgment; ~**versicherung** additional insurance; ~**vordruck** supplementary form; ~**vorlage** supplementary bill; ~**vorschrift** supplementary regulation; ~**wahl** by-election; ~**zuweisung** additional grant.

Ergebnis *n* result, yield, outcome; ~**abführungsvertrag** profit-and-loss transfer agreement; ~**anteil** share of the income (*or* profits); ~**ausschlußvereinbarung** profit-and-loss exclusion agreement; ~**beteiligung** profit participation; ~ **der Beweisaufnahme** result of the taking of evidence, summary of evidence; ~ **der Ermittlungen** = *Ermittlungsergebnis qv.*; **e~neutral** *adj* not affecting the operating result; ~**rechnung** statement of operating results, income and expenditure account; ~**übernahmevertrag** profit-and-loss assumption agreement (*with a subsidiary*); ~**übersicht** statement of results, earnings statement; **buchmäßiges** ~ result according to the books; **neutrales** ~ non-operating profit or loss.

ergehen *v/i* to be rendered, to be promulgated, to be issued.
ergiebig *adj* productive, fertile.
Ergiebigkeit *f* productiveness, productive capacity.
Ergonomie *f* ergonomics (*adaptation of working conditions to suit the worker*).
ergreifen *v/t* to apprehend, to seize.
Ergreifung *f* apprehension, seizure; ~**sort** place of arrest.
ergründen *v/t* to explore, to probe into, to find out, to fathom.
Ergründung *f* exploration.
Erhalt *m* receipt; **den ~ Ihres Schreibens bestätigend** this is to

erhalten / **Erinnerungshilfe**

acknowledge (the) receipt of your letter, in acknowledgement of your letter.

erhalten *pp* of *erhalten v/t* in receipt; *richtig* ~: duly received.

erhältlich *adj* obtainable, available.

Erhaltung *f* preservation, maintenance, upkeep; ~ **des Friedens** maintenance of peace, preservation of peace; ~ **von Arbeitsplätzen** job preservation, safeguarding of jobs.

Erhaltungs|arbeiten plant preservation work (*during strike*); ~**aufwand** maintenance expense; ~**kosten** expense of maintenance; ~**pflicht** duty to preserve (*ancient monuments*); ~**zustand** state of repair; *einwandfreier* ~~: *good and tenantable repair* (*rooms*), *good condition*; *schlechter* ~~: *disrepair, non-repair, (in) bad repair.*

erhängen *v/reflex* to hang oneself.

erhärten *v/t* to confirm, to corroborate, to substantiate.

Erhärtung *f* confirmation, corroboration, substantiation.

erheben *v/t* to raise, to lodge, to levy (*taxes*), to charge, to impose.

erheblich *adj* relevant, material, substantial, significant, of legal relevance.

Erheblichkeit *f* relevancy, significance, substantialness.

Erhebung *f* inquiry, investigation, official collection of data; ~ **an der Quelle** collection at source; ~**en an Ort und Stelle** *über etw.* inquiry on the spot *into s. th.* ~**en anstellen** to make investigations; ~ **durch Veranlagung** collection by means of assessment; ~ **e-r Klage** commencement of (legal) proceedings, the taking of an action; ~ **zum Gesetz** enactment; **amtliche** ~ official inquiry; **finanzstatistische** ~ collection of financial statistics; **örtliche** ~ on-site investigation; **statistische** ~ statistics, collection of statistical data.

Erhebungs|angaben statistical data; ~**gebiet** collection area; ~**kosten** collection costs; ~**monat** month for which statistics are collected; **e**~**mäßig** relating to collection of data; ~**reihe** series of collection of data; ~**stichtag** statistical return date, statistical reference date; ~**termin** date of collection; ~**verfahren** collection procedure; ~**zeitraum** period of collection.

erhellen *v/i* to become clear, to appear from, to become evident.

erhöhen *v/t* to increase, to enhance, to raise.

Erhöhung *f* increase, increment, enhancement, rise; ~ **der Sätze** raising of duties, rise in rates; ~ **des Grundkapitals** increase of the share capital; ~ **des Lebensstandards** rise in the standard of living; **konjunkturautonome** ~ rise independent of cyclical causes; **lohnseitig bedingte** ~ **der Kosten** rise in costs caused by wage increases.

Erholung *f* recovery, recreation; **durchgreifende** ~ all-round recovery.

Erholungs|anlagen recreation facilities; ~**aufenthalt** rest-cure, holiday, vacation; ~**bedürftiger** (*der Erholungsbedürftige*) person in need of a vacation; ~**beihilfe** vacation allowance, (employee's) holiday grant; ~**flächen** pleasure grounds; ~**gebiet** recreation area; ~**kur** rest cure; ~**möglichkeiten** recreational facilities, amenities; ~**ort** resort; ~**pause** breather, a pause for rest; ~**urlaub** vacation, holiday, recreational leave, convalescent leave; ~**wald** recreational forest; ~**zeit** recovery period, rest period (*piece work job*).

erinnern *v/t* to remind (s. o. of sth); *v/reflex* to remember, to recollect; *soweit ich mich erinnern kann*: *as far as I can remember*; *to the best of my recollection*.

Erinnerung *f* memory, recollection, reminder; *esp pl* ~*en* opposition, objection(s) (*to an administrative step on the same level*); ~**en gegen den Kostenfestsetzungsbeschluß** summons to review the taxation.

Erinnerungs|hilfe memory aid,

267

aide-mémoire; ~**lücke** gap in one's memory, partial amnesia; ~**posten** pro memoria item; ~**schreiben** follow-up letter; ~**schwäche** weakness of memory; ~**täuschung** amnesic delusion, delusion of one's memory; ~**verlust** loss of memory, amnesia; ~**vermögen** memory, power of recollection; ~**werbung** institutional advertising, follow-up advertising; ~**wert** reminder value, pro memoria figure.

erkannt (*pp erkennen*) held (*by a court*), ruled.

erkennen *v/t* to discern, to know, distinguish, perceive; to hold (*by a judge*), to pass judgment; to enter on an account, to credit; to enter in a ledger; **antragsgemäß** ~ to find for the plaintiff.

erkennend *adj* discerning; adjudicative, recognizing.

Erkenntnis *f* realization, understanding, perception; finding, decision, judgment; ~**se e–s Berichts** findings of a report; ~ **e–s Gerichts** finding of a court, court ruling; **e–mäßig** *adj* as regards cognitive discernment; relating to perception; perceptive; ~**verfahren** contentious proceedings, trial; court procedure leading to a judgment; ~**vermögen** cognitive faculty, cognition, intellectual capacity; ~**wert** informative value, evidential value, value as a pointer.

Erkennungs|**dienst** records department (*police*), (criminal) identification department; **e**~**dienstlich** by way of police identification service, identifying; ~**karte** identification card; ~**kartei** identification register; ~**marke** identity disc, identification tag, *sl* dog tag; ~**merkmal** distinguishing mark; ~**nummer** identification number; ~**wort** password, watchword; ~**zeichen** identification mark, markings (*aeroplane*); ~**zeuge** identifying witness.

erklären *v/t* to explain, to expound; to declare, to state, to assert, to say; to give notice; to declare (*customs*), *v/reflex*: to give an explanation, to plead (*to the charge*); **eidlich** ~ to state under oath; to swear an affidavit (that); **feierlich** ~ to asseverate, to solemnly declare, to state in solemn form (of law); **für rechtmäßig** ~ to legitimate, legitimize; **jmdn für befangen** ~ → *befangen*; **sich bereit** ~ to undertake, to offer, to agree to.

Erklärung *f* explanation, interpretation; declaration, statement; ~ **auf dem Sterbebett** dying declaration; ~ **über Nichtbestreiten** admission of fact; **Allgemeine** ~ **der Menschenrechte** Universal Declaration of Human Rights; **amtliche** ~ official statement; **ärgerniserregende** ~ scandalous statement; **beeidete schriftliche** ~ affidavit; **begründete** ~ explanation, reasoned statement; **belastende** ~ incriminatory statement; **ehrenwörtliche** ~ declaration of honour; **eidesstattliche** ~ declaration in lieu of an oath, statutory declaration; **eidliche** ~ statement on oath; **e–e** ~ **abgeben** to make a declaration (*or* statement); **freiwillige** ~ voluntary statement; **gewillkürte** ~ voluntary act; **mündliche** ~ verbal statement, parol declaration (*or* act); **rechtsgeschäftliche** ~ private act legal declaration; **rechtsgestaltende** ~**en** dispositive acts; **schriftliche** ~ written statement, written declaration; **spontane** ~ spontaneous statement; **unberechtigte** ~ unauthorized statement; **vorvertragliche** ~ representation, pre-contractual declaration; **zu Protokoll gegebene** ~ statement made for the record, official statement, a protocol note, statement placed on record.

Erklärungs|**bewußtsein** awareness of expressing one's will; ~**bote** communicating messenger (*merely transmitting a declaration, not an agent*); ~**empfänger** addressee, recipient of a declaration; ~**frist** time to answer, deadline for reply; ~**irr-**

tum mistake in the utterance, mistake in the declaration itself; **~pflicht** obligation to make a statement, obligation to plead; **~tag** *exch* contango-day, making-up day, option day; **~termin** deadline for a declaration (*or* plea), time-limit for effecting a declaration; **~theorie** doctrine of declaratory effect of an act (*regardless of intention or lack of it*); **~wille** intention of expressing one's will.

erklärungsbedürftig *adj* needing an explanation, requiring further explanation.

erkranken *v/i* to fall ill, to become sick, to contract a disease.

Erkrankung *f* illness, sickness; **~shäufigkeit** frequency of illness; **im ~sfall** in case of illness.

erkundigen *v/reflex* to inquire (after) (= *enquire*), to make inquiries (= *enquiries*).

Erkundigung *f* query, inquiry (= *enquiry*); **~en einziehen** to gather information *about sth. or s.b.*, to make inquiries, to inquire into; **~spflicht** duty to make enquiries (= *inquiries*), requirement to obtain further information.

Erkundung *f* exploration, investigation, reconnaissance; **~sgespräche** soundings, exploratory talks.

erlangen *v/t* to obtain, to gain, to reach, to acquire.

Erlangung *f* obtainment, acquisition, recovery attainment; **~ durch Betrug** obtaining by false pretences; **~ von Schadensersatz** recovery of damages.

Erlaß *m* decree, order; rendition, pronouncement, passing; remission, release, waiver; **~bescheid des Finanzamts** order for remission of tax liability; **~ der Zinszahlung** waiver of the interest payment; **~ des Strafrests** remission of the unserved part of the sentence; **~ e-r Schuld** release from a debt, waiver of a debt; **~ e-s Urteils** rendering a judgment, pronouncement of a judgment; **~ von Gebühren** cancellation of charges; **~ von Rückständen** remission of arrears; **~vergleich** composition agreement, composition by waiver; **~vertrag** acquittal contract, (general) release agreement; **~zeitraum** time covered by the release (from an obligation); **amtlicher ~** official decree; **königlicher ~** royal proclamation; **ministerieller ~** ministerial order; **öffentlich-rechtlicher ~** order by a public authority.

erlassen *v/t* to issue (*order, decree, writ*), to pass, to render (*judgment*), to remit (*sentence, debt*), to release (from) (*debt, liability*), to dispense (from).

erläßlich *adj* (= *erlaßbar*) dispensable, remissible, venial, forgivable.

erlauben *v/t* to allow, to permit *v/reflex* to permit oneself (to); to take the liberty (*of doing sth*); *ich erlaube mir festzustellen*: *I beg to state (to point out); ich erlaube mir, Ihnen mitzuteilen*: *I am pleased to inform (or: advise) you.*

Erlaubnis *f* permission, authority, licence; **~antrag** application for a permit; **~erteilung** granting of permission; **~irrtum** error concerning permissibility; **~kartell** permitted cartel (*joint agreement of business undertakings*); **~schein** permit, licence; **~scheininhaber** permit (licence) holder; **~urkunde** permit, licence; **~verfahren** procedure for obtaining a permit (licence); toleration of business combines procedure; **~vorbehalt** reservation on the granting of permission; **behördliche ~** official permit; **beschränkte ~** limited permission; **gerichtliche ~** leave of court; **polizeiliche ~** permission by the police; **vertragliche ~** contractual licence.

erlaubt *adj* permissible, permitted; **generell ~** generally permitted.

erläutern *v/t* to explain, to elucidate, to comment.

erläuternd *adj* explanatory.

Erläuterung *f* explanation, elucidation, comment, explanatory

Erläuterungsbericht

note(s); ~ **an Hand von Beispielen** explanation by way of illustrative examples; ~ **verdienen** to deserve amplification; **~en zur Bilanz und Gewinn- und Verlustrechnung** notes to financial statements.

Erläuterungs|bericht explanatory report; **~beschluß** explanatory order; **~gesetz** declaratory statute, expository statute; **~werk** commentary.

Erlebensfall *m* survival, the case that a person is still alive; **~bonifikation** guaranteed maturity bonus; **~versicherung** endowment policy, pure endowment assurance; **im ~ zahlbare Summe** sum payable if the insured (person) survives (*at the date of the policy*).

erledigen *v/t* to dispose of, to settle, to deal with, to get sth done, to finish, to arrange, to dispatch; *endgültig erledigt: finally disposed of; für erledigt erklären: to declare sth finally disposed of* (or dealt with), *to clear off;* (*a backlog of work*); **förmlich ~** to solemnize; **rein geschäftsmäßig ~** to deal with s.o. at arm's length, to dispose of in a business-like manner.

Erledigung *f* disposal, disposition, discharge, arrangement; **~ am gleichen Tag** same-day service; **~ der Hauptsache** termination of the substantive dispute (*leaving the issue of costs to be decided by the court*); **~ eigener Angelegenheiten** conduct of one's own affairs; **~ e-s Rechtsstreits** termination of the case; **~sausschuß** executive committee; **~sbescheinigung** certificated discharge; **~sgebühr** fee for out of court settlement; **~ von Formalitäten** compliance with formalities; **bis zur ~** pending arrangement; **endgültige ~** final disposition; **gütliche ~** amicable arrangement; **prompte ~ der geschäftlichen Angelegenheiten** dispatch of business; **rasche ~** prompt (*or* expeditious) settlement; **schiedsrichterliche ~** submission

270

Erlöschen

to arbitration; **vollständige ~** complete performance, final settlement.

erleichtern *v/t* to ease, to relieve, to alleviate.

Erleichterung *f* alleviation, relaxation, relief; **~smaßnahmen** relief measures.

Erlös *m* proceeds, profit (*from a sale or venture*); **~anteil** share of the proceeds; **~bindung** tying-up proceeds; **~einbuße** shortfall in profits, fall in sales revenue; **~konten** income accounts; **~stabilisierungssystem** earnings stabilization system; **~verbesserungen** increased proceeds, higher proceeds; **sich aus dem ~ befriedigen** to pay oneself out of the proceeds.

erloschen *adj* expired, extinct.

Erlöschen *n* extinguishment, extinction, lapse, discharge (*of an obligation*); **~ der Verbindlichkeiten** discharge of indebtedness; **~ der Verbindlichkeit durch Bezahlung** discharge by payment; **~ der Vollmacht** termination of authority; **~ des Völkerrechtssubjekts** debellatio, extinguishment of the state; **~ e-r Dienstbarkeit** extinguishment of an easement; **~ e-r Forderung** discharge of a debt; **~ e-r Hypothek** cancellation of a mortgage, discharge from a mortgage; **~ e-r Versicherung** expiration of an insurance; **~ e-r Zahlungsverpflichtung** discharge of an obligation to pay; **~ e-s Patents** lapse of patent; **~ e-s Pfandrechts** voidance of a lien, discharge of a lien; redemption of mortgage; **~ e-s Rechts** extinction of a right, lapse of a right; **~ e-s Schuldverhältnisses** discharge of an obligation, cancellation of a debt; **~~~ durch Erfüllung**: *discharge by performance;* **~ e-s Urheberrechts** lapse of copyright, expiry of copyright; **~ e-s Warenzeichens** lapse of a trade-mark; **~ von Schuldverpflichtungen** extinguishment of debts, cancellation of debts; **~ von Wegerechten** ex-

erlöschen

tinguishment of ways; **zum ~ bringen** to extinguish, to cause to be discharged.

erlöschen v/i to become extinct, to expire, to lapse, to become discharged.

ermächtigen v/t to empower, to vest s. o. with authority, to authorize; *der Ermächtigende: the donor of a power, person granting an authority*; *der Ermächtigte: donee of a power, authorized person*; *ordnungsgemäß ermächtigt: duly authorized*.

Ermächtigung f power, grant of authority, delegated power, authorization; **~ zum Erlaß von Rechtsvorschriften** delegated power(s) to issue legal regulations (*statutory instruments*); **die mir erteilte ~** the power(s) conferred upon me; **gerichtliche ~ zur gewaltsamen Öffnung** warrant to open doors; **gesetzliche ~** statutory power; **richterliche ~** judicial authority; **uneingeschränkte ~** full authority, unlimited power.

Ermächtigungs|gesetz Enabling Act; **~indossament** restrictive endorsement, endorsement for collection only; **~schreiben** letter of delegation, letter of authority; **~vorschriften** regulations about delegating authority.

ermahnen v/t to admonish, to reprimand, to reprove, to warn.

Ermahnung f admonition, warning.

ermangeln v/i to lack, to be wanting.

ermangelnd adj devoid (of), lacking.

Ermangelung f lack; **in ~** in default (of, whereof), failing, for want of, for lack of, in the absence of; **in ~ besonderer Bestimmungen** in the absence of special provisions; **in ~ e-r besonderen Vereinbarung** failing special agreement; **in ~ e-s Gegenbeweises** in the absence of proof to the contrary, unless proof to the contrary exists.

ermäßigen v/t to reduce, to lower, to curtail, to mark down.

Ermäßigung f reduction, cut; **~ bei**

Ermessensakt

Mengenabnahme quantity discount.

Ermessen n discretion; **behördliches ~** administrative discretion; **billiges ~** equitable discretion; **dem ~ überlassen** to leave to the discretion (of); **es ist ins ~ des Richters gestellt** it is a question for the discretion of the judge; **freies ~** (unqualified) discretion; **gerichtliches ~** discretion of the court; **im ~ des Gerichts** at the discretion of the court, as the court may determine; **in jmds freiem ~ stehen** to be in the absolute discretion of; **in jmds ~ stellen** to leave sth. to s.o.'s discretion; **nach bestem ~** to the best of one's judgment; **nach billigem ~** ex aequo et bono; **nach eigenem ~ handeln** to use one's own discretion; **nach ~ des Gerichts** as the court may determine, as the court may think fit; **nach freiem ~** in one's discretion, at s. o. 's uncontrolled (*or* unqualified) discretion; *ich überlasse es Ihrem ~~: I leave it to your discretion*; **nach pflichtgemäßem ~** according to one's best judgment; *~~~für richtig halten: to think fit*; **rechtliches ~** legal discretion; **richterliches ~** judicial discretion, discretion of (the) judge; **uneingeschränktes ~** absolute discretion, unqualified discretion.

Ermessens|akt act of discretion, discretionary decision; **~ansprüche** discretionary claims; **~beamter** official entitled to decide at his (own) discretion; **~befugnis** discretionary power; **unbeschränkte ~** (unlimited) arbitrary power; *~~ überschreiten: to exceed one's discretionary power;* **~bereich** field of discretion, limits of discretionary power, scope of discretion; **~entscheidung** discretionary decision; **~fehler** abuse of discretion; **~frage** a matter of discretion; **~freiheit** discretion; liberty to decide at one's own discretion; **~gebrauch** exercise of discretion; **~grundsatz** principle of discre-

271

ermitteln

tion; ~**handlung** discretionary act; ~**mißbrauch** abuse of discretion; ~**nachprüfung** review of (administrative) discretion; ~**recht** discretionary power; ~**spielraum** scope of (administrative) discretion; ~**überschreitung** exceeding one's scope of discretion; ~**vorschrift** discretionary rule (of law).

ermitteln v/t to investigate, to trace, to ferret (out), to discover, to locate, to ascertain.

Ermittler m investigator, inquiry agent; **verdeckter** ~ undercover agent.

Ermittlung f (spec pl ~en) criminal investigation(s), tracing, locating, ascertainment, discovery, inquiries; ~ **an Ort und Stelle** investigations at the scene of the crime; ~ **der Einkünfte** determination of the income; ~ **des Gewinns** determination of the profits; **des Leistungsumfangs** ascertainment of quantity of performance; ~**en anstellen** to institute an investigation, to carry out investigations; ~ **von Amts wegen** ex officio inquiries; **polizeiliche** ~**en blieben erfolglos** investigations by the police produced no results; **während der weiteren** ~**en** pending further investigation.

Ermittlungs|akten investigation records; ~**beamter** investigator, investigating officer; ~**befugnisse** power of investigation; ~**behörde** investigating authority; ~**dienst** investigation service; ~**ergebnis** result of the investigations; ~**fehler** mistake in investigation; *statistischer* ~~: *error in statistical ascertainment*; ~**grundsatz** principle of ex-officio inquiries; ~**journalismus** investigative reporting; ~**maßnahmen** investigative measures; ~**pflicht** duty to investigate, duty to make enquiries; ~**richter** examing judge, committing magistrate, summary judge; ~**tätigkeit** investigations, preliminary investigation, investigation

ernannt

before trial; ~**verfahren** preliminary investigation (or proceedings); *das* ~~ *einstellen*: to drop the charge; *gegen jmdn ein Ermittlungsverfahren eröffnen*: to place sb under inverstigation by the public prosecutor; ~**zeitraum** investigation period.

ermöglichen v/t to render possible, to render feasible, to allow, to permit.

Ermöglichung f making sth possible.

ermorden v/t to murder; *der Ermordete*: the murdered person.

Ermordung f murder, murdering, assassination (*political*).

Ermüdungserscheinung f symptom of fatigue, sign of fatigue.

ermutigen v/t to encourage.

Ermutigung f encouragement.

ernähren v/t to feed, to nourish, to support; v/reflex to live (on), to subsist; *sich selbst* ~: to earn one's own living.

Ernährer m breadwinner (*of family*).

Ernährung f feeding, nutrition, food, nourishment, alimentation, maintenance, sustenance, support; **für die menschliche** ~ **ungeeignet** unfit for human consumption; **künstliche** ~ artificial feeding.

Ernährungs|aufwand amount spent on food; ~**fachmann** nutritional expert, nutritionist; ~**güter** foods, foodstuffs; ~**industrie** food-processing industry; ~**lage** food position; ~**minister** Minister of (Agriculture, Fisheries and) Food; ~**politik** food policy; ~**sicherstellungsgesetz** emergency food supply law; ~**sicherung** food security; ~**standard** standard of nutrition; ~- **und Landwirtschaftsorganisation der Vereinten Nationen** Food and Agriculture Organization of the United Nations; ~**wirtschaft** agricultural and food industries, economics of food supply; food production and distribution; **e**~**wirtschaftlich** relating to agriculture and food supply.

ernannt *adj* named, designated,

272

ernennen / **Erpressung**

nominated; *der E~e: nominee, person appointed.*

ernennen *v/t* to appoint, to nominate, to designate, to name.

Ernennung *f* appointment (*of a public official*), nomination, designation.

Ernennungs|ausschuß nomination committee; **~befugnis** power of appointment; *unbeschränkte ~~:* arbitrary power of appointment; **~behörde** appointing authority; **~grundsätze** principles for appointment to an office; **~recht** power of appointment; **~urkunde** letter of appointment, certificate of appointment; **~verfahren** appointment procedure.

erneuern *v/t* to renew, to revive, to renovate, to repair, to replace.

Erneuerung *f* renewal, revival, renovation; **stillschweigende ~** renewal by tacit agreement; automatic renewal.

Erneuerungs|fonds renewals fund; **~konto** renewal account, reserve account for replacements; **~maßnahme** renewal (*or* improvement) measure; **~police** renewal policy; **~prämie** renewal bonus; **~provision** renewal commission; **~rücklage** reserve funds for replacements, renewals reserve; **~schein** talon, renewal coupon; **~tag** renewal date.

erniedrigen *v/t* to degrade, to debase, to humble, to humiliate.

Erniedrigung *f* degradation, debasement, humiliation.

Ernstfall *m* emergency, case of emergency, casus belli.

Ernte *f* harvest, crop(s); **~arbeit** harvest work; **~arbeiter** harvester, harvestman; **~aussichten** crop prospects; **~beurteilung** crop forecast; **~einlagerung** stockpiling of agricultural products, storage of crops; **~ertrag** produce, yield; **~erzeugnisse** agricultural products; **~helfer** volunteer harvester; **~jahr** crop year; **~maschine** harvester, harvesting machine; **~stützungskredit** loan to finance crop production; **~versicherung** growing crop insurance; **~verzeichnis** crop register; **~zeit** harvest, harvesting time.

eröffnen *v/t* to open, to inaugurate; to disclose, to establish; *neu eröffnet: newly established.*

Eröffnung *f* opening, inauguration, establishment, disclosure; **~ des Hauptverfahrens** opening of the trial; order to proceed with the trial; committal for trial; **~ des Konkursverfahrens** commencement of bankruptcy proceedings, adjudication.

Eröffnungs|ansprache inaugural address, opening speech; **~antrag** petition to institute proceedings; **~beschluß** order committing s.b. for trial; committal for trial, finding of an indictment; bankruptcy order; **~bilanz** opening balance, initial statement of affairs; **~feierlichkeit** inaugural ceremony; **~gebot** opening bid; **~inventar** opening inventory; **~kurs** opening quotation, opening price; **~notierung** opening quotation; **~protokoll** record of probate proceedings; **~sitzung** opening session; **~verfahren** committal proceedings; **~verhandlung** hearing on sufficiency of criminal charge; hearing in probate proceedings.

erörtern *v/t* to discuss, to argue about; **eingehend ~** to discuss at length.

Erörterung *f* discussion, argument; **~sgebühr** (lawyer's fee for discussing the case in court); **~spflicht** obligation (*for the court*) to discuss a case *with the litigants.*

erpressen *v/t* to blackmail, to extort, to demand with menaces.

Erpressen *n* **von Aussagen** extortion of statements *from a suspect.*

Erpresser *m* extortionist, blackmailer; **~brief** blackmail letter.

erpresserisch *adj* extortionate, blackmailing.

Erpressung *f* extortion, blackmail; **~ e-s Geständnisses** extraction of a confession under duress; **~ im Amt** extortion by public officials;

273

erproben

~**sversuch** attempted blackmail; ~ **von Aussagen** extortion of statements (*of suspects or witnesses*); **nukleare** ~ nuclear blackmail; **organisierte Banden-**~ racketeering; **räuberische** ~ robbery by blackmail, larceny by extortion (*threatening to inflict bodily harm*), demanding with menaces (*involving danger to life and limb*); **schwere** ~ aggravated extortion.

erproben *v/t* to test, to try (out).

Erprobung *f* trial, tryout; ~**szeit** trial period.

errechnen *v/t* to calculate, to compute, to reckon.

Errechnung *f* calculation, computation; ~ **der Rücklage** computation of reserve; ~ **des Barwerts** computation of cash value; ~ **des Fondswerts** validation of fund.

Erregung *f* incitement, provocation; ~ **e-s geschlechtlichen Ärgernisses** (*durch exhibitionistische Handlung*) indecent exposure, public indecency; ~ **öffentlichen Ärgernisses** offence against public order and decency; disorderly conduct.

erreichbar *adj* obtainable, accessible, available, feasible.

erreichen *v/t* to obtain, to gain, to reach, to achieve; *Erreichen* (*n*) *der Volljährigkeit* → *Volljährigkeit*.

errichten *v/t* to erect (*building*), to establish, to form, to set up (*enterprise*), to make, to draw up, to execute (*deed, will*).

Errichtung *f* erection; formation, establishment, foundation; drawing-up, execution; ~ **e-r Gesellschaft** formation of a company, incorporation of a company; ~ **e-s gemeinsamen Marktes** establishing a common market; ~ **e-s Testaments** valid execution of a will; **formgültige** ~ execution (of a deed etc); **schrittweise** ~ progressive establishment.

error in persona mistake about the identity *of the contracting party*; *in German criminal law*: offender's mistake about the identity of his victim.

274

Ersatzgeschworener

Errungenschaft *f* acquisition, achievement, attainments; ~**sgemeinschaft** matrimonial regime of joint ownership of subsequently acquired property (*abrogated 1958*).

Ersatz *m* substitute, replacement; compensation, indemnification, restitution, alternative; ~**absonderung** substitute for the loss of lienholder's preferential interest; ~**anspruch** claim for compensation; *pl*: *compensation claims, damage claims*; ~**aussonderung** substitutional segration (*recovery of the consideration for repleviable goods sold by bankrupt or trustee*); ~**bedarf** replacement needs; **e–berechtigt** *adj* entitled to compensation (*or* replacement), eligible for compensation; ~**beschaffung** replacement (purchase), procuring a substitute; ~**bescheinigung** replacement certificate; ~**betrag** alternative amount, substitute amount, replacement figure; ~**blatt** replacement sheet; ~**deckung** substitute cover; ~**deckungswerte** substitute cover assets; ~**dienst** (*now: Zivildienst qv*) alternative non-military service (*for conscientious objectors*); ~**dienstbeschädigter** person injured in alternative non-military service; ~**dienstbeschädigung** injury (*or* disablement) suffered during alternative non-military service; ~**dienstleistender** person (*conscientious objector*) doing alternative non-military service; ~**einheitswert** substituted standard tax value; ~**erbe** substituted heir, substitutional heir, alternate heir, reversionary heir; ~**erbfolge** substituted succession, reversionary succession; ~**erfüllung e-s Vermächtnisses** ademption of a legacy; ~**forderung** claim for compensation (*or* reimbursement); ~**freiheitsstrafe** imprisonment in default of payment of fine; ~**geld** token money; ~**geldstrafe** fine in the alternative; option of fine in lieu of imprisonment (*up to 6 months*); ~**geschworener** alternate juror;

Ersatzimport

~**import** relief imports; ~**investition** replacement investment *for capital assets*; ~**kasse** substitutional social health insurance institution; ~**land** lieu land(s) (*in lieu of expropriated land*); ~ **leisten** to effect compensation, to compensate; ~**leistung** compensation, indemnification; ~**leistungspflicht** obligation to effect compensation; ~**lieferung** substitute delivery; replacement; ~**linie** substituted line; ~**-Lohnsteuerkarte** replacement card for a (*lost*) wage tax card; ~**mann** alternate, substitute; ~**mitglied** substitute member; ~**nacherbe** substitute reversionary heir; ~**nacherbfolge** substitute reversionary succession; ~**nachfolge** substitute succession; ~**pflicht** obligation to render compensation, liability to pay damages; e~**pflichtig** liable to pay damages; liable for compensation; ~**raum** alternative accommodation; ~**raumbeschaffungspflicht** obligation to supply alternative accommodation *for evicted tenants*; ~**revision** writ of error in lieu of appeal; ~**richter** alternate judge; ~**schöffe** alternate lay judge; ~**schule** independent school; ~**steuer** substitute tax; ~**stoff** substitute (material); ~**strafe** substitute penalty; ~**summe** amount of compensation; ~**teil** spare part; ~**teillager** stock of spare parts, inventory of parts; ~**testamentsvollstrecker** administrator de bonis non; ~**unterbringung** alternative accommodation; ~**urkunde** substitute document, replacement certificate; ~**veranlagung** substitute assessment; ~**verbindlichkeit** substitute obligation, secondary obligation; ~**verkündung** substitute pronouncement (of a judgement); ~**vermächtnis** substitutional legacy, substitutional bequest; ~**vermächtnisklausel** shifting clause, clause providing for a substitutional legacy (*in the event that legatee fails to accept or has died*); ~**vermächt-**

Erschleichen

nisnehmer substitute legatee; ~**vornahme** substitute performance; ~**wahl** by-election; ~**ware** equivalent goods, replacement; ~**weise** as a substitute for, substitutional; ~**wert** replacement value; ~**wirtschaft** economy using substitute material; ~**wohnung** alternative accommodation; ~**zeiten** substitute(d) qualifying periods (*for social insurance, such as war service, prisoner of war time, internment, unemployment, persecution, evacuation, expulsion from East Germany*); ~**zustellung** substitute(d) service, constructive service of process; ~**zustimmung** constructive consent.

Erscheinen *n* appearance, attendance; publication, issue; ~**sfolge** frequency; ~ **von Zeugen** attendance of witnesses; ~ **vor Gericht** appearance in court; **freigestelltes persönliches** ~ voluntary appearance; **persönliches** ~ personal appearance, appearance in person; **vom** ~ **in der Hauptverhandlung entbinden** to grant permission to be absent from trial.

erscheinen *v/i* to appear, to make one's appearance; *der Erschienene*: (*the*) *person appearing*; **nicht im Termin** ~ to fail to appear; **persönlich** ~ to appear in person; **Sie werden gebeten zu** ~ your presence is requested.

Erscheinungsort *m* place of publication.

erschießen *v/t* to shoot, to shoot, to kill; **standrechtlich** ~ to shoot by order of a court martial, to execute by a firing squad.

Erschießung *f* execution by shooting; ~**sbefehl** order to execute by shooting; ~**skommando** firing squad; **standrechtliche** ~ shooting by order of a court martial.

erschlagen *v/t* to beat to death, to kill by violent means, to slay.

Erschleichen *n* obtaining surreptitiously, obtaining by artifice; ~ **des Beischlafs durch Täuschung** inducing (extra-marital) sexual inter-

275

erschleichen course under false pretences; ~ **freien Eintritts** evasion of entrance fees; ~ **von Beförderungsmitteln** avoiding payment on public transport.

erschleichen v/t to obtain surreptitiously, to obtain by artifice.

Erschleichung f = Erschleichen qv.

erschließen v/t to develop (*territory, industries*), to open up (*markets*), to improve, to prepare for exploitation, to tap, to exploit.

Erschließung f (site) development, improvement; ~ **von Baugelände** site development; **wasserwirtschaftliche** ~ development of water resources.

Erschließungs|abgabe development charge; **~aufwendungen** development and improvement costs; **~beitrag** development charge (*or* assessment); **~beitragsbereich** development district, improvement district; **~bezirk** improvement district; **~gelände** development land, land ready for building; **~gewinnabgabe** development land tax; **~kosten** development costs; **~recht** land development law; **~und Bauentwicklungserlaubnis** planning permission; **~unternehmer** developer.

erschöpfen v/t to exhaust, to treat exhaustively, to deplete.

Erschöpfung f exhaustion, depletion (*resources*); ~ **der innerstaatlichen Rechtsmittel** exhaustion of national remedies; ~ **der natürlichen Hilfsquellen** depletion of resources; ~ **des Instanzenzuges** exhaustion of appellate instances; **nach** ~ **der innerstaatlichen Rechtsmittelverfahren** after all domestic remedies have been exhausted; **~des Rechtsweges** exhaustion of ordinary legal remedies.

Erschöpfungs|delirium delirium due to exhaustion; **~einrede** plea of depletion of the estate (*as against creditors*); **~grad** degree of exhaustion (*or* depletion); **~tod** death from exhaustion; **~zustand** state of exhaustion.

erschweren v/t to render more difficult, to impede.

Erschwernis n impediment, added difficulty; **~zulage** extra pay for difficult working conditions.

Erschwerung f added difficulty, aggravation (*of crime*).

ersehen v/t to gather from sth, to infer, to deduce.

ersetzbar adj substitutable, replaceable.

ersetzen v/t to substitute, to replace; to make up for, to compensate (for *damage*), to reimburse.

Ersetzung f substitution, replacement, reimbursement; **~sbefugnis** (facultative) alternative performance, authority to provide a substitute; **dingliche** ~ physical substitution.

ersichtlich adj apparent, evident, manifest, *woraus* ~ *wird, daß* ...: *from which it appears that* ...

ersinnen v/t to devise, to contrive, to invent, to excogitate.

ersitzbar adj prescribable, capable of being acquired by adverse possession (*land*) or prescription.

ersitzen v/t to acquire by adverse possession in good faith, to obtain title by long possession.

Ersitzer m person acquiring title by adverse possession (*or* prescription).

Ersitzung f acquisition by (long) adverse possession (*or* prescription); ~ **von Grund und Boden** acquisition of land by long adverse possession.

Ersitzungs|besitz long adverse possession (*leading to prescription*), aquisition by squatting rights; ~~ *am Grundstück*: *pedal possession*; **~eigentum** title by adverse possession or prescription; **e~fähig** prescribable, capable of (being acquired by) adverse possession or prescription; **~frist** time of prescription, prescriptive period; **~recht** title by prescription, squatter's title; **~zeit** = ~*frist qv*.

ersparen v/t to save (*money, labour*); to spare (*trouble, embarrassment*).

Ersparnis f saving (*in time, manpower*) (*pl Ersparnisse = ~e: savings*); **~bereicherung** unjust enrichment by saving other expenses; **~bildung** formation of savings; **echte ~se** genuine savings; **freie ~se** voluntary savings; **volkswirtschaftliche ~se** the country's savings.

Ersparung f saving.

Erst|absatz initial sales, first sale; ~~ *von Wertpapieren: initial placing of securities*; **~abschreibung** initial capital allowance; **~anlage** original investment; **~anmeldung** original application *pat* initial application; **~auftrag** opening-order, initial order; **~ausbildung** initial training; **~ausfertigung** original, engrossed document, script, principal (*or* original) instrument; **~ausleihung** initial lending; **~ausstattung** initial equipment, initial allocation; **~begünstigster** primary beneficiary; **~begünstigung** primary insurance benefit; **~belehnung** original fief; **~beleihung** original charge for a loan; **~bescheid** first ruling; **~besteller** launching customer; **~dauer** initial term; **~einlage** original investment; **~emission** original issue; **~erfinder** true and first inventor, original inventor; **~erwerb** first acquisition, acquisition by first taker; **~erwerber** first buyer, first taker, original subscriber; **~finanzierung** initial financing; **e~geboren** first-born; **~gebot** first bid; **~geburtsrecht** primogeniture; **e~genannt** (*party*) of the first part; **~gericht** trial court, court of first instance, nisi prius court; **~gutschrift** original amount credited, initial crediting; **~hypothek** first mortgage; **e~instanzlich** adj of the court of first instance, of the trial court, at the first instance; **~käufer** first-time buyer; **e~klassig** adj first-class, first-rate, first-grade, of top quality; **~montage** original assembly, green assembly; **~plazierung** initial placing (*of securities*); **~prämie** first premium; **~prüfung** original inspection; **e~rangig** of the first rank, ranking first, first-rate, top-rate; **~richter** trial judge, original judge; **~risikoversicherung** first loss insurance; **~schrift** original; **~schuldner** primary debtor; **~schürfrecht** original mining licence, ore-leave; **e~stellig** first, first-rank, ranking first; **~stimme** first vote; **~täter** first offender; **~verarbeiter** primary processor; **~verbüßung** serving a prison term for the first time, first imprisonment (*of an offender*); **~verkauf** initial sale; **~veröffentlichung** first publication; **~verpflichteter** primarily liable party; **~versicherer** original insurer, direct insurer, direct writing company, leading underwriter, prime underwriter; **~versicherung** original insurance; **~zeichner** original subscriber; **~zeichnung** initial subscription.

erstatten v/t to reimburse, to refund.

Erstattung f reimbursement, refund; **~ der Gebühren** refund of charges; **~ gerechtfertigter Auslagen** reimbursement of expenses properly incurred; **~ notwendiger Aufwendungen** exceptional circumstances allowance; reimbursement of a party's necessary expenses (*as party to party costs*); **auf ~ der Kosten wird gegenseitig verzichtet** the parties mutually waive all claims to costs; **gegen ~ der Unkosten** with out-of-pocket expenses.

Erstattungs|anspruch refund claim, claim to reimbursement (*of costs*), claim for restitution; **~antrag** application for reimbursement; **~bescheid** notice of repayment (*or* restitution); **~beschluß** order for repayment of (*misappropriated or missing*) funds to the Treasury; **~betrag** refunded amount; **e~fähig** adj taxable (*costs*), recoverable, undisbursed; **~fähigkeit** eligibility for cost assessment (*from party to party*); **~forderung** claim for reimbursement, claim for repayment; ~**frist** time limit for recovery of (*misappropriated or missing*) public funds; ~**gesetz** Recovery of Public Funds Law (*1937 as amended*); ~**gründe** grounds for restitution; ~**pflicht** duty to repay (*or* to reimburse); **e**~**pflichtig** requiring reimbursement, reimbursable; ~**rückstände** arrears of repayments; ~**streitigkeiten** disputes concerning the liability for restitution of public funds; ~**verfahren** repayment procedure; ~**zinsen** interest on amounts to be reimbursed.

erstechen *v/t* to stab (to death), to knife (to death).

erstehen *v/t* to purchase.

Ersteher *m* purchaser.

Erstehung *f* purchase.

Ersteigerer *m* auction buyer, highest bidder.

ersteigern *v/t* to buy at an auction; **selbst** ~ to buy in, to bid oneself successfully.

erstellen *v/t* to make, to provide, to make available, to build.

Erstellung *f* provision, production, construction; ~**skosten** cost of construction.

Erstickungstod *m* death from suffocation.

Erstlingsrede *f parl* maiden speech.

erstrecken *v/reflex* to extend, to comprise, to cover, to embrace.

Erstreckung *f* extent, extension, ~ **e–r Frist**: extension of a deadline, granting additional time.

erstreiten *v/t* to recover, to gain by a law-suit, to gain by litigation.

Ersuchen *n* request *from one authority to another*, intergovernmental request; requisition; ~ **um Unterstützung** request for assistance; **behördliches** ~ official request.

ersuchen *v/t* to request, to petition for; *Sie werden (höflich) ersucht*: *you are kindly requested* (*to*).

ersuchend *adj* requesting.

erteilen *v/t* to confer, to grant, to bestow (on sb).

Erteilung *f* grant, bestowal; ~ **des Agréments** the granting of the agrément (*intimation that an ambassador will be acceptable*); ~ **des letzten Wortes an den Angeklagten** allocution, court's inquiry of defendant as to whether he has anything to say before judgment is pronounced; ~ **e–r Vollmacht** conferring power of attorney, appointment of an attorney (*or* agent); ~ **e–s Patents** the granting of a patent; ~**santrag** request for grant; ~**sgebühr** *pat* fee for grant; ~ **von Genehmigungen** issue of licences, granting of permits.

Ertrag *m* (*pl Erträge* = ~*e*) yield, return, proceeds, earnings, revenue; ~**e aus Beteiligungen** revenue from participations; ~**e aus Beteiligungen an Tochtergesellschaften** income from subsidiaries; ~**e festverzinslicher Wertpapiere** earnings from fixed interest bearing securities; **abnehmender** ~ diminishing return; **aus laufenden** ~**en bezahlen** to pay as you go; **ausschüttungsgleiche** ~**e** undistributed yields, profits deemed to be distributed; **außergewöhnliche** ~**e** income of non-recurrent nature; **betriebsfremde** ~**e** non-operating income; **geringfügige** ~**e** small earnings, minor earnings; **gewerblicher** ~ income from trade and industry, commercial income; **jährliche** ~**e** annual profits; **nicht realisierter** ~ unrealized profit; **unversteuerter** ~ untaxed earnings.

ertragbringend *adj* productive, remunerative, profitable, lucrative.

ertragfähig *adj* yielding a return, productive.

Erträgnis (*pl Erträgnisse* = ~*e*) = *Ertrag, qv*; ~**e aus Kapitalanlagen** income (*or* returns) from investment; ~**e aus Vermögensanlagen** income from investments; ~**e, Tilgungsbeträge oder Kapitalrückzahlungen** income, amortisation or capital repayments; **alle** ~**e aus Darlehen** all income arising from loans; **andere** ~**e** other income (items); **betriebsfremde** ~**e** non-operating income; **einmaliges** ~ non-recurring income; **sonstige** ~**e** non-operating revenue.

ertragreich *adj* productive, profitable, lucrative, paying.

Ertrags|abnahme diminishing of returns; ~**anteil** portion (share) of proceeds, taxable proportion of a pension (*from insurance or an annuity*); ~**aufteilung** earnings apportionment; ~**ausfall** loss of earnings; ~**aussichten** prospective earnings; ~**bedingungen** conditions of profitability; ~**besteuerung** taxation of earnings; ~**beteiligung** profit sharing; ~**bilanz** balance of payments on current account; ~**chancen** prospective return; ~**denken** thinking in terms of profit; ~**entwicklung** trend in earnings, profitability; ~**fähigkeit** earning capacity, productive capacity; ~**gesetz** *econ* law of variable proportions; ~**hoheit** tax sovereignty; ~**kraft** earning power, earnings capability; ~**lage** income position, earnings situation, earnings picture, profit and loss position; **e**~**los** non-accruing (*bond*); ~**minderung** reduction in earnings; **e**~**orientiert** earnings orientated; ~**pacht** royalty rent; ~**planziel** earnings target; ~**position** profit and loss position; ~**rechnung** income account, income statement; ~**rückgang** reduction in earnings; ~**rücklage** revenue reserve; ~**schein** coupon, dividend warrant; *aufgerufene* ~~*e*: *coupons called for payment*; ~**schwelle** break-even point; ~**situation** earnings picture; ~**spitze** peak yield; ~**steigerung** earnings growth; ~**steuern** taxation of proceeds (*from income-yielding objects*), taxes on earnings; ~**steuertarif** scale of taxation on earnings; ~**umdispositionen** coupon switching; ~~ **- und Aufwandposten** income and expense rates; ~~ **- und Aufwandsollrechnung** income and expenditure account; ~**vergleich** comparison of yield; ~**wert** capitalized income value, earning-capacity value, earning power (*capitalized value of potential yield*); *jährlicher* ~~: *net annual value*; *steuerlicher* ~~: *rateable value (of a property)*; ~**wertanalyse** income value analysis; ~**wertverfahren** income value appraisal method; **e**~**wirtschaftlich** in terms of profit and loss; ~**zahlen** trading figures; ~**zinsen** interest earned or received.

Ertrinkungstod *m* death by drowning.

Erwachsenen|adoption adult adoption; ~**bildung** adult education; ~**unterhaltsverpflichtung** adult maintenance obligation; ~**wahlrecht** adult suffrage.

Erwachsenheitssumme *f* = *Beschwerdewert qv*.

erwägen *v/t* to consider, to weigh, to ponder, to deliberate.

Erwägung *f* consideration, deliberation; *in der* ~, *daß* ...: *considering; whereas;* ~**en anstellen** to consider; **nach reiflicher** ~ after due consideration; **nochmalige** ~ reconsideration; **wohlwollende** ~ favo(u)rable consideration.

erwähnen *v/t* to mention, to refer to.

erwähnt *pp, adj* mentioned, named; **bereits** ~ mentioned before, aforesaid; **oben** ~ above-mentioned, (a)forementioned, aforesaid, as stated above; **unten** ~ as below, mentioned below, see below; **zuletzt** ~ last mentioned, latter; **zuvor** ~ aforementioned.

Erwähnung *f* mention (of), reference (to); **ehrenvolle** ~ honourable mention.

Erwarten *n* expectation, *wider* ~: *against all expectations*.

erwarten *v/t* to expect, to await.

Erwartung *f* expectation, expectancy, anticipation; **den** ~**en entsprechen** to meet s.o.'s expectations; **den** ~**en nicht entsprechen** to fall short of expectations; **die** ~**en erfüllen** to come up to s. o.'s expectations.

Erwartungs|kauf sale by expectancy; **~struktur** expectation (structure); **e~voll** *adj* expectant; **~wert** anticipated value (*e.g. pension*).

erweisen *v/reflex* to prove to be (*true, correct, false etc*).

erweislich *adj* demonstrably, verifiably.

erweitern *v/t* to extend, to enlarge, to expand.

Erweiterung *f* extension, enlargement, expansion; **~des Klageantrags** extending the claim of the action.

Erweiterungs|bau extension, annex (building); **~investition** capital expenditure for purposes of expansion, extension project; **~kosten** expansion cost.

Erwerb *m* acquisition; earnings, income; ~ **aus zweiter Hand** second-hand purchase; ~ **der Staatsangehörigkeit** obtaining citizenship, naturalization; ~ **durch Verschmelzung** acquisition by absorption, acquisition by (virtue of a) merger; ~ **unter Lebenden** acquisition inter vivos; ~ **vom Nichtberechtigten** (bona fide) acquisition from non-entitled party; ~ **von Grundeigentum** acquisition of immovable property; ~ **von Todes wegen** acquisition mortis causa; **abgeleiteter** ~ derivative acquisition; **bedingter** ~ conditional acquisition; **gutgläubiger** ~ acquisition in good faith (*by the innocent buyer without notice*), innocent receipt, bona fide purchase; **mehrfacher** ~ multiple acquisition; **nachhändiger** ~ acquisition by subsequent takers; **originärer** ~ original acquisition; **steuerpflichtiger** ~ taxable earnings; **unentgeltlicher** ~ gratuitous transfer of property; **zufälliger** ~ chance acquisition.

erwerben *v/t* to acquire, to obtain, to gain, to get; **betrügerisch** ~ to obtain by fraud; **gutgläubig** ~ to acquire (a good title) in good faith; **käuflich** ~ to acquire by purchase, to purchase, to buy; **rechtmäßig** ~ to obtain a good title, to acquire lawfully.

Erwerber *m* the acquiring party, acquirer, transferee, allottee (*shares*), alienee; ~ **auf Grund e-s Vorkaufsrechts** pre-emptor; **bösgläubiger** ~ acquirer in bad faith, fraudulent transferee; **gutgläubiger** ~ bona fide transferee, bona fide purchaser, purchaser for value without notice, innocent purchaser without notice; **späterer** ~ subsequent transferee (*or* purchaser); **steuerpflichtiger** ~ taxable recipient; **unentgeltlicher** ~ acquirer by way of gratuitous transfer, acquirer for no consideration.

Erwerbs|berechtigter party entitled to acquire title to sth, authorized transferee; **~bereitschaft** willingness to acquire, willingness to exercise an option; **~beschränkungen** occupational restrictions; **~betrieb** business undertaking; **~einkommen** earned income; **~einkünfte** receipts from earnings; **e~fähig** capable of gainful employment; **~fähiger** *m* (*der ~fähige*) person capable of earning a living, person of employable age; **~fähigkeit** earning capacity, ability to earn a living; *geminderte ~~: reduced earning capacity*; **~gelegenheit** job, position of employment; **~genossenschaft** co-operative industrial society, trading co-operative; **~geschäft** trade or business, transaction for profit, trading transaction; **~gesellschaft** commercial company (*or* partnership), trading firm; **~grundlage** means of livelihood; **~interessent** potential purchaser; **~kosten** cost of acquisition; **~leben** business life, business and vocational activities, working life, gainful activity; **e~los** *adj* unemployed, out of work, not gainfully employed; **~losenfürsorge** public assistance for the unemployed, unemployment relief; **~losenquote** unemployment ratio; **~losenunterstützung** unemploy-

Erwerbslosenversicherung

ment benefit, "dole" (*to be on the dole*); ~**losenversicherung** unemployment insurance; ~**loser** unemployed (person); ~**losigkeit** unemployment, redundancy; ~**minderung** reduction in earning capacity; ~**möglichkeit** means of earning a living; ~**nebenkosten** transaction cost; ~**obliegenheit** requirement to seek remunerative occupation; ~**person** gainfully employed person; *unselbständige* ~~*en*: *wage and salary earners*; ~**preis** purchase price; ~**quelle** source of income; ~**schaden** damage to one's trade or occupation; ~**suchender** person seeking employment; **e~tätig** gainfully employed; ~**tätiger** gainfully employed person; *pl* the gainfully employed; *zivile* ~~*e*: *persons in civilian employment*; *selbständig* ~~: *self-employed person*; ~**tätigkeit** gainful occupation, gainful employment, remunerative employment; *selbständige* ~~: *self-employment*; ~**titel** (legal) title of acquisition; **e~unfähig** *adj* unable to work, (wholly and permanently) disabled, incapacitated; ~**unfähiger** person unable to work, disabled person; ~**unfähigkeit** invalidity, (permanent and total) disability, disablement, total incapacity; ~**unfähigkeitsrente** disability pension, invalidity allowance; ~**unternehmen** business enterprise; ~**verbot** prohibition from acquiring sth; ~**verhalten** employment behaviour; ~**verhältnisse** economic conditions; ~**vermögen** productive property, earning assets; ~**vorgänge** business transactions; ~**wert** purchase cost, (value) at cost; ~**wirtschaft** free enterprise, business (activities), trading; **e~wirtschaftlich** *adj* operating on a profit basis, trading, business (activity); ~**zweck** purpose of the acquisition; *ohne* ~~: *non-profit-making*; ~**zweig** branch of industry, line of business.

Erzeuger

Erwerbung *f* acquisition; the object bought, the purchase.

erwidern *v/t* to answer, to reply to; to rejoin, to respond to; to retort; to reciprocate.

Erwiderung *f* answer, reply, rejoinder, response; ~ **des Beklagten** defendant's reply, rejoinder; ~ **des Klägers** replication; ~**sfrist** deadline for answering, time to reply; ~**sschrift** reply, brief in replication, statement in reply; **erschöpfende** ~ full answer; **geschickte** ~ a clever reply; **kurzfristige** ~ a reply at short notice.

erwiesen *adj* proven, established.

erwirken *v/t* to obtain (*an official act; pardon*), to effect, to bring about (*a result*), to succeed in getting (*a thing*), to achieve.

erwirtschaften *v/t* to produce, to earn, to obtain (by economic activity).

erwischen *v/t* to catch (*a thief etc*).

erwürgen *v/t* to strangle, to strangulate, to choke to death, to garrotte.

Erwürgung *f* strangulation, choking to death, garrotting, strangling.

Erz *n* (*1*) ore; ~**abbau** ore-mining, ore production; ~**ader** (mineral) vein; ~**aufbereitung** ore preparation, dressing of ore; **e~führend** ore-bearing; ~**grube** ore-pit; ~**haltigkeit** ore content (*of rock*); ~**hütte** smelting works; **geringwertiges** ~ low-grade ore; **hochwertiges** ~ high-grade ore.

Erz ... (*2*); ~**diakon** archdeacon; ~**feind** arch-enemy; ~**herzog** archduke; ~**herzogtum** archduchy, archdukedom; ~**gauner** arch-rogue, crook, arch-swindler.

erzeugen *v/t* to produce, to manufacture, to make.

Erzeuger *m* producer, manufacturer, maker; procreator, begetter; ~**beihilfen** producer subsidies; ~**benennungsschwindel** palming off, holding out, *deception as to the identity of the manufacturer*; ~**gemeinschaft** combination of

Erzeugnis

(agricultural) producers; ~**großmarkt** central market; ~**grundpreis** basic production price; ~**handel** direct selling (*by manufacturer to ultimate consumer*); ~**kosten** cost of production; ~**land** producer country, country of origin; ~**preis** producer's price; ~**richtpreis** producer target price; ~**vereinigung** association of manufacturers.

Erzeugnis *n* (*pl Erzeugnisse*: ~*e*) product; ~**gruppe** product group; ~**patent** product patent; ~**spektrum** product range; ~**e der ersten Verarbeitungsstufe** products of first-stage processing; **ausländische** ~**e** goods of foreign origin, foreign products; **deutsches** ~ made in Germany; **eigenes** ~ our own produce (*or* product); **einheimische** ~**e** domestic products; **erlösgünstige** ~**e** high-yielding products, products yielding a high return; **forstwirtschaftliche** ~**e** forest products, products of forest management; **gekoppeltes** ~ tied product; **gewerbliche** ~**e** industrial products; **gleiche oder gleichartige** ~**e** identical or similar products; **handwerkliche** ~**e** craft products; **hochwertige** ~**e** high-quality products; **konkurrenzlose** ~**e** unrivalled goods; **landwirtschaftliche** ~**e** farm products, agricultural produce; **leichtverderbliche** ~**e** perishable (food) products; **milchwirtschaftliche** ~**e** dairy produce; **neuartiges** ~ novel product; **schwer verkäufliche** ~**e** hard-to-move products; **steuerpflichtige** ~**e** taxable products; **strategisch wichtige** ~**e** strategic products; **unfertige** ~**e** unfinished goods, (*Bilanzposten*) work in progress; **veredelte** ~**e** improved goods, products improved by processing; **vermietete** ~**e** equipment leased to customers, products on lease; **weiterverarbeitete** ~**e** processed products.

Erzeugung *f* production, manufacture; ~**sgebiet** production area, country of origin; ~**skosten** production cost, prime cost; ~**sland** country of origin, producer country; ~ **und Verbrauch von Energie** energy production and consumption; **gewerbliche** ~ industrial production; **produktionstägliche** ~ output per "production day".

erziehen *v/t* to educate, to bring up.

Erzieher *m* educator, tutor, instructor, teacher.

Erziehung *f* education, upbringing.

Erziehungs|anstalt reformatory school, approved school, remand home, *now:* community home *GB*; ~**beihilfe** education grant, education allowance; ~**beistand** educational supervisor (*of delinquent youths*); ~**beistandschaft** official educational care and supervision (*juvenile delinquency*); ~**berechtigter** person in charge of minor's upbringing, person having parental power; ~**geld** *periodical payments from public funds to non-working parent of small child*, child-raising benefit; ~**gewalt** parental control, parental power, disciplinary power over minors; ~**heim** community home (*GB*), reform school (*US*), approved school; ~**hilfe** disciplinary aid and supervision (*in respect of minors in military service*); ~**kosten** cost of upbringing and education; ~**maßregeln** disciplinary measures for juvenile delinquents; ~**minister** Education Minister; ~**pflicht** obligation in respect of care and upbringing (of children and young persons); ~**recht** right of care and custody, *right of control concerning upbringing and education of minors*; ~**register** correctional register of juvenile delinquents; ~**ministerium** ministry of education, department of education; ~**rente** child benefits, *social insurance pension for surviving or divorced spouse for the upbringing of children*; ~**wesen** education, education system, education matters; ~**zulage** education allowance.

erzwingbar *adj* enforceable; **nicht ~** unenforceable.

erzwingen *v/t* to compel, to enforce, to obtain by compulsion.

Erzwingung enforcement, compulsion; **~ des Erscheinens** compulsion to attend; **~sgeld** contempt fine, compulsion money; **~shaft** arrest to enforce a court order, confinement to prison for contempt; **~srecht** compulsory power; **~sstrafe** penalty to enforce a court order.

eskomptieren *v/t* to discount in advance.

Eskortefahrer *m* outrider (*police*).

Essen auf Rädern meals on wheels.

Essensmarke *f* luncheon voucher.

Eßwaren *f/pl* edibles, comestibles, food products, victuals.

etablieren *v/t reflex* to establish, to set oneself up in business, to found.

Etablissement *m* business establishment, fancy (*or* ill-reputed) restaurant or club; **~sbezeichnung** business name, trade name (*of a small shop or restaurant, bar etc not entitled to a registered business name;* **anrüchiges ~** house of ill fame, brothel.

Etagenwohnung *f* (self-contained) flat, apartment.

Etat *m* budget, estimates; **~abstrich** budget cut; **~anforderung** budget requirement; **~ansatz** budgetary vote, budgetary estimate, budget appropriation, proposed budget figure(s); *unausgenutzter* **~**: *unused budgetary vote*; **~aufschlüsselung** breakdown of budget, details of budget; **~ausgleich** balancing of the budget; **~einsparungen** budgetary savings; **~genehmigung** budget approval; **~jahr** financial year, fiscal year, budgetary year; **e~mäßig** budgetary; **~mittel** appropriated funds, voted funds; *allgemeine* **~~**: *general fund*; **~planung** budget estimates; **~recht** budget law; **~titel** budget item, heading in the budget; **~überschreitung** excess of appropriated funds; **~überschüsse** carry-over funds, non-expended appropriations; **~zuweisung** budgetary allotment; **~zuweisungsplan** allotment schedule.

etatisieren *v/t* to budget (*an item*), to provide for in the budget, to include in the budget.

Etikett *n* label, price tag; **~beschreibung** informative label(l)ing; **~enausdrucker** label printer; **~enschwindel** fraudulent label(l)ing; **~fälschung** false label(l)ing; **~ierung** label(l)ing; **~ierungsmaschine** label(l)ing machine; **~ zum Aufkleben** adhesive label, sticky label.

etwa *adv* about, approximately, on or about, thereabouts.

Eurogeldmarktgeschäfte *n/pl* eurocurrency business (*or* transactions).

Europäische/Atomgemeinschaft European Atomic Energy Community (*Euratom*); **~ Freihandelszone** *f* European Free Trade Association (*EFTA*); **~ Gemeinschaften** *the* European Communities; **~ Gemeinschaft für Kohle und Stahl** (*Montanunion*) European Coal and Steel Community (*Coal and Steel Pool, ECSC*); **~ Gesellschaft für die Chemische Aufbereitung Bestrahlter Kernbrennstoffe** European Company for the Chemical Processing of Irradiated Nuclear Fuels; **~ Gesellschaft für die Finanzierung von Eisenbahnmaterial** European Company for the Financing of Railway Rolling Stock; **~ Investitionsbank** European Investment Bank; **~ Kernenergie-Agentur** European Nuclear Energy Agency; **~ Kommission für Menschenrechte** European Commission of Human Rights; **~ Konferenz für Molekularbiologie** European Molecular Biology Conference; **~ Menschenrechtskonvention** European Convention on Human Rights; **~ Molekularbiologie-Organisation** European Molecular Biology Organization; **~ Organi-**

sation für Astronomische Forschung in der Südlichen Hemisphäre European Southern Observatory; ~ **Organisation für experimentelle photogrammetrische Untersuchungen** European Organization for Experimental Photogrammetric Research; ~ **Organisation für kernphysikalische Forschung** European Organization for Nuclear Research; ~ **Patentorganisation** European Patent Organization; ~ **Rechnungseinheit** (*ERE*) European Unit of Account (*E.U.A.*); ~ **Währungseinheit** *f* (*EWE*) European Currency Unit (*ECU*); ~ **Weltraumorganisation** European Space Agency; ~ **Wirtschaftsgemeinschaft** (*EWG*) European Economic Community (*EEC*); ~ **Zahlungsunion** (*EPU*) European Payments Union; ~ **Zivilluftfahrt-Kommission** European Civil Aviation Conference; ~ **Zollunion** European Customs Union; ~**r Ausrichtungs- und Garantiefonds für die Landwirtschaft** European Agricultural Guidance and Guarantee Fund; ~**r Fonds für währungspolitische Zusammenarbeit** European Monetary Co-operation Fund; ~**r Gerichtshof** European Court of Justice; ~**r Gerichtshof für Menschenrechte** European Court of Human Rights; ~**r Rat** European Council (*of heads of state*); ~**r Wirtschaftsrat** Organization for European Economic Cooperation (*OEEC*); ~**s Atomforschungszentrum** European Nuclear Research Centre; ~**s Gerichtsstands- und Vollstreckungsübereinkommen** (*EuGVÜ* European Convention on Jurisdictions and Enforcement); ~**s Jugendwerk** European Youth Foundation; ~**s Jugendzentrum** European Youth Centre; ~**s Laboratorium für Molekularbiologie** European Molecular Biology Laboratory; ~**s Parlament** European Parliament; ~**s Patentamt** European Patent Office; ~**s Terrorismus-Übereinkommen** European Convention on Terrorism; ~**s Waffenübereinkommen** European Arms Convention; ~**s Patentregister** Register of European Patents; ~**s Patentübereinkommen** European Patent Convention; ~**s Währungssystem** European Monetary System (*EMS*); ~**s Zentrum für mittelfristige Wettervorhersage** European Centre for Medium-Range Weather Forecasts; ~**s Zentrum für Weltraumtechnik** European Space Technology Centre.

Europa|-Patent Europatent; ~**rat** Council of Europe; ~**recht** European law.

Europäisierung *f* Europeanisation.

Euthanasie *f* euthanasia.

evakuieren *v/t* to evacuate.

Evakuiertenrecht *n* law concerning (*the status etc of*) evacuees.

Evakuierter *m* (*der Evakuierte*) evacuated person, evacuee.

Evakuierung *f* evacuation.

Eventual|anspruch contingent claim; ~**antrag** motion in the alternative; ~**aufrechnung** cautionary setting-off (*by a counter claim*); ~**forderung** contingent claim; ~**haftung** contingent liability; ~**maxime** alternative pleading; contingency motion; ~**obligo** contingent commitment; ~**standpunkt** alternative argument, cautionary contention; ~**verbindlichkeit** contingent liability, cautionary obligation, indirect liability, secondary liability; ~**verpflichtung** contingent liability, cautionary obligation; ~**vorsatz** indirect intent (*of a* [mentally accepted] *contingent result*).

Eventualität *f* contingency.

eventuell *adj* (*adv*) possible (*possibly*), if occasion arises, contingent.

evident *adj* evident, obvious, manifest, clear.

Evidenztheorie *f principle of nullity of administrative acts which are evidently faulty.*

Evidenzzentrale *f* information centre, credit recording centre.
Evisszeration *f* disembowelling.
Evokationsrecht *n* the right to withdraw a matter from the cognizance of another court or authority, *right to claim exclusive jurisdiction in a matter pending elsewhere* ≈ right to issue a writ of certiorari.
E-Werk *n* = *Elektrizitätswerk qv*.
EWG-Vertrag *m* Treaty of Rome, EEC Treaty.
Ewiggeld *n* (*hist*) perpetual annuity.
Ewigkeitsentscheidung *f* decision for all time; unchangeable fundamental constitutional principle.
ex lege *adv* by operation of law.
ex nunc *adv* from now (on).
ex tunc *adv* ab initio.
ex officio *adv* (=) ex officio.
exceptio doli *f* (= *Einrede der Arglist*) plea of fraud (*or* of bad faith).
exceptio plurium *f* (=) *denial of paternity because others had sexual intercourse with the mother of the child*.
Exekution *f* execution, forced realization, final settlement in a forward foreign exchange transaction; forced sale of collaterals.
Exekutions|befehl order to carry out death sentence; ~**kauf** *exch* buying in, (en)forced realization; ~**kommando** execution squad, firing squad; ~**recht** right of execution; ~**verkauf** *exch* selling out, forced sale.
Exekutiv|ausschuß *m* executive committee; ~**gewalt** executive power; ~**organ** executive organ of; ~**rat** executive council.
Exekutive *f* the executive, executive power, administrative power, magistracy; executive organ.
Exequatur *n* exequatur.
Exhibitionismus *m* exhibitionism, indecent exposure.
Exhibitionist *m* exhibitionist.
exhumieren *v/t* to exhume, to disinter.
Exhumierung *f* exhumation, disinterment.
Exil *n* exile; ~**regierung** *f* exile government, government in exile.

existent *adj* in being, in esse, in existence; **möglicherweise** ~ in posse, possibly existing.
Existenz *f* existence, livelihood, subsistence; ~**aufbauhilfe** (*financial*) *assistance to enable persons to (re)establish a business or practice*; ~**fähigkeit** viability; ~**gründer** a person setting up in business; founder of a firm; ~**gründung** setting up in business; ~**grundlage** basis of subsistence; ~**kampf** struggle for existence, life's struggle, the "rat race"; ~**minimum** a living wage, subsistence minimum, subsistence level, poverty line; *am Rande des* ~~~*s: to be living on the poverty line*; ~**neugründungsprogramm** restart programme; ~**sicherung** ensuring a (means of) livelihood.
existieren *v/i* to exist, to subsist, to manage to live; **früher** ~ to pre-exist, to exist beforehand.
Exitus *m* exitus, death, demise.
Exklave *f* exclave.
Exklusiv|recht exclusive right; ~-**Vertrag** exclusive rights agreement, exclusive licence.
Exkulpation *f* exculpation; ~**sbeweis** exculpatory proof *against vicarious liability* (*by principal that he instructed and supervised the agent properly*).
exkulpieren *v/reflex* to be excused, to free from fault (and liability).
Exmatrikulation *f* leaving, or removal from university.
Exotenfonds *m/pl* off-shore funds.
Expansion *f* expansion; **inflationsfreie** ~ non-inflationary expansion.
Expatriation *f* *compulsory* expatriation.
expatriieren to deprive of citizenship, to exile, to expatriate *cf ausbürgern*.
Expedieut *m* forwarding clerk, dispatching clerk, shipping clerk.
expedieren *v/t* to dispatch, to ship, to forward.
Expedition *f* (1) expedition, forwarding shipping; (2) = ~*sabteilung qv*; ~**sabteilung** forwarding

Experte

department, shipping department; **~sbuch** shipping book.
Experte *m* expert, specialist *cf Sachverständiger*.
Expertise *f* expertise, expert opinion (*on a painting etc*).
Exploration *f* exploration (*minerals, oil etc*).
Explosionsschaden *m* explosion damage.
Export *m* export(s), exportation, exporting; **~abgabe** export tax; **~abhängigkeit** export dependency; **~abteilung** export department; **~abwicklungskonto** export settlement account; **~akkreditiv** export letter of credit; **~-Akkreditiv-Deckungskonto** export credit-cover account; **~angebot** exports tender; **~artikel** export article, export item; **~auflage** requirements for exports, required export quota; **~auftrag** export order; **~bedingungen** export terms; **~beratungsstelle** export consultancy service; **~beschränkung** export restriction; **~bestimmungen** export regulations; **~bewilligung** export licence, permission to export; **~bonus** premium for export, export bounty; **~daten** export data; *prognostische ~~~: data permitting a forecast of exports*; **~deklaration** entry outwards; **~druck** pressure to export, inducement to export; **~einnahmen** export revenue; *laufende ~~~: current export receipts*; **~erfahrung** exporting experience; **~erlös** export earnings, proceeds from exports; **~finanzierung** financing of exports; **~finanzierungsinstrument** export financing instrument, instrument of credit for exports; **~firma** export company (*or* business), export house; **~förderung** export promotion, export drive; **~forderungen** export claims, outstanding accounts from exports; **~freudigkeit** readiness to export, a taste for exporting; **~gemeinschaft** group of exporting firms, export association; **~geschäft** export business,

Exportselbstbeschränkung

export transaction; *das ~~~ forcieren: to push exports;* **~hafen** port of export(ation); **~handel** export trade; **~industrie** export industry; **e~induziert** *adj* export-led, export-induced; **~intensität** export ratio, ratio of exports to output; **e~intensiv** *adj* having a high export ratio, export-promoting (*investment*); **~interesse** interest in exporting, incentive to export; **~investition** investment for promoting exports; **~kartell** export cartel; **~kaufmann** exporter, export merchant; **~kommissionär** export commission merchant; **~konjunktur** trend in exports, export business development; **~konossement** outward bill of lading; **~kontingent** export quota; **~kredit** credit to finance exports, export credit; **~kreditbrief** export letter of credit; **~kreditversicherung** export credit insurance; **~land** (*1*) exporting country, country dependent on exports, (*2*) country of destination for exports; **~lastigkeit** excessive export dependence, disproportionally large export quota, predominance of exports; **~leiter** export manager, head of the export department; **~liste** export list; **~lizenz** export licence, export permit; **~markt** export market; **~messe** export fair, export exhibition; **~müdigkeit** lack of willingness to promote exports, reluctance to export; **e~nah** *adj* closely connected with exporting, directly concerned with exporting; **~- oder Reimportverbote** regulations prohibiting exports or reimports; **e~orientiert** *adj* export-oriented, export-minded; **~prämie** export premium; **~preis** export price; *stark ausgehandelte ~~~e: export prices resulting from close bargaining*; **~risikogarantie** export risk guarantee; **~risikohaftung** liability for export risk, export (risk) guarantee; **~sachbearbeiter** export clerk; **~selbstbeschränkung** voluntary export restraint; **~sper-**

Exportsteuer

re embargo on exports; ~**steuer** export tax; ~**steigerung** rise in exports; ~**subvention** subsidy on exports, export subsidy; ~**tarif** special transport rates for export goods; e~**trächtig** *adj* likely to induce exports, exports-promoting; ~**Tratte** export draft; *anfallende* ~ *--n: export drafts arising*; ~**überschuß** export surplus; *bilateraler* ~~: *"unrequited" exports*; ~**unternehmung** exporting undertaking, exporting company; ~**valutaerklärung** export currency declaration; ~**-Ventil** outlet in the shape of exports, export "safety-valve"; ~**verbot** export ban, export prohibition; ~**vergütung** drawback, tax rebate (*to exporters*); ~**vertreter** (manufacturer's) export agent; ~**ware** exported article(s), articles suitable for exporting; ~**werbung** export advertising, publicity to promote exports; e~**wichtig** important for exports; ~**wirtschaft** export trade, export business, export sector; ~**zoll** export duty; ~**zuteilung** allotment for exports.

Exporteur *m* exporter, export firm.

exportieren *v/t, v/i* to export.

Expressgut *n* railway express, fast freight.

Expropriation *f* = *Enteignung qv*.

exproprieren *v/t* = *enteignen qv*.

exterritorial *adj* exterritorial, extraterritorial.

Exterritorialer *m* (= *der Exterritoriale*) person enjoying extraterritorial status, person with diplomatic status.

Exterritorialität *f* exterritoriality; extraterritoriality.

Extraaufgeld *n* overagio.

Extradividende *f* bonus, additional dividend, *sl* melon.

Extraprämie *f* overagio.

Extrarisiko *n* special risk.

Extremfall *m* extreme case.

Exzedentenrückversicherung *f* excess loss reinsurance, surplus reinsurance.

exzerpieren *v/t* to make excerpts (from).

F

Fabrik *f* factory, works, mill; ~**abgabepreis** selling price ex works; ~**anlage(n)** plant; ~**arbeit** factory work, manufactured goods; ~**arbeiter** factory worker, factory hand, operative; ~**auftrag** manufacturing order; ~**bauten** factory buildings, plant facilities; ~**besitzer** factory owner; ~**gebäude** factory building, plant; ~**grundstück** factory site; ~**klausel** ex works' stipulation; ~**leitung** factory (*or* plant) management; ~**marke** manufacturer's trade mark, brand; ~**musterlager** permanent display of sample products at factory; f~**neu** *adj* brand-new; ~**nummer** (manufacturer's) serial number; ~**ordnung** factory regulations, shop rules; ~**preis** factory price, manufacturing price, selling price ex works, factory-transfer price; ~**unternehmung** factory; ~**zeichen** manufacturer's mark, brand, trade mark; **ab** ~ ex works; **auswärtige** ~ external factory, group-linked plant.

Fabrikant *m* manufacturer, factory owner.

Fabrikat *n* product, manufacture, article; ~**egemeinkosten** product overheads; ~**egruppe** product group; **angearbeitete** ~**e** goods in process; **ausländisches** ~ foreign make (*or* product); **entwicklungsintensive** ~**e** products involving high development costs; **inländisches** ~ home manufacture.

Fabrikation *f* manufacture.

Fabrikations|anlagen production plant, manufacturing facilities; ~**auftrag** manufacturing order, production order, job order; ~**auftragsnummer** job order number; ~**betrieb** manufacturing concern; ~**einrichtungen** plant equipment; ~**fehler** flaw, manufacturing defect; ~**geheimnis** manufacturing secret; ~**gemeinkosten** manufacturing overhead; ~**grundstück** manufacturing premises; ~**konto** work-in-process account, production account; ~**kosten** factory expenses, production costs; ~**lizenz** manufacturing licence; ~**monopol** production monopoly; ~**name** style, style name; ~**nummer** serial number, manufacturer's number; ~**partie** job lot; ~**reife** finished-product stage; ~**recht** manufacturing right; ~**risiko** manufacturing risk; ~**stätte** workshop; ~**und Vertriebsrecht** shop right, manufacturing and sales rights; ~**und Gewerbezwecke** manufacturing and industrial purposes; ~**verfahren** manufacturing process; ~**zweig** line of manufacture.

fabrizieren *v/t* to manufacture.

Fach *n* subject, discipline, subject matter (*learning*), special area, special list, field (*vocation*), province; ~**abteilung** specialized department; ~**akademie** technical college (*below university and Fachhochschule qv level*); ~**anwalt** specialized solicitor; ~~ **für Steuerrecht**: *tax lawyer, tax counsellor*; ~**arbeiter** skilled worker, *pl* skilled labourer, skilled manpower; *freie* ~~~: *available skilled workers*; ~**arbeiterbrief** skilled worker's certificate, craft certificate; ~**arbeiterlohn** wage of a skilled labourer (worker); ~**arzt für Berufskrankheiten** occupational therapist; ~**aufsicht** (substantive) supervisory power, supervising authority; ~**aufsichtsbehörde** supervisory authority (*competent to supervise the work of lower authorities*); ~**ausbildung** specialized training (*in a particular field*), technical training; ~**ausdruck** technical term,

Fachausschuß — **Fähigkeit**

term of art; *juristischer* ~~: *legal term*; ~**ausschuß** specialized committee, technical committee; ~**behörde** specialized government, department; ~**berater** technical adviser; ~**bereich** specialized field, faculty *(university)*; ~**bildung** vocational training (education); technical training, professional training; ~**blatt** trade publication, trade journal; ~**einzelhandel** specialist retail trade; ~**gebiet** specialized field, subject area, domain; ~**gelehrter** specialist, expert, specialized academic; f~**gerecht** workmanlike, *adv: in a proper and workmanlike manner*; ~**geschäft** specialist shop, speciality store, limited-line retailer; ~**gewerkschaft** craft union; ~**gremium** technical body, technical committee; ~**großhandel** specialist wholesale trade; ~**gruppe** functional group, specialist group, working party; ~**handel** specialized trade; specialist retailers (dealers), limited-line trade; ~**hochschule** technical college, vocational college; ~**hochschulreife** entrance qualification for a specialized (technical) college or university *(limited field of study)*; ~**kammer** specialized court (panel); ~**kenntnis** f specialized knowledge, technical knowledge, know-how; *ausreichende* ~*se*: *reasonable skill and knowledge*; ~**kraft** specialist, skilled person; *pl Fachkräfte*: *skilled personnel, specialists, technical manpower*; ~~*emangel*: *skills shortage*; ~**kreis** special trade or professional group; f~**kundig** *adj* skilled, expert, competent; f~**lich** → *fachlich*; *adj*; ~**literatur** pertinent literature, special literature; ~**makler** *exch* official broker; ~**mann** expert, specialist, person skilled in the art; f~**männisch** professional, in a professional manner; ~**messe** trade fair (exhibition); ~**minister** (departmental) minister, government minister; ~**ministerium** government department; ~**oberschule** senior technical school; ~**organisation** special agency; f~**orientiert** *adj* specialized; ~**personal** skilled personnel, technical staff, specialist personnel; ~**presse** trade press; ~**schule** vocational school, technical school; ~**schulausbildung** vocational school training; ~**schulwesen** vocational school system; *landwirtschaftliches* ~~: *agricultural education*; ~**senat** specialized division in court of appeal; ~**sparte** administrative branch; ~**sprache** technical language, nomenclature; *juristische* ~~: *legal parlance, legalese*; ~**stellenverfahren** technical agency procedure; ~**studium** specialized professional studies; ~**tagung** trade conference; ~**übersetzer** specialized translator, technical translator; ~**unternehmer** specialized entrepreneur, owner of a specialized business undertaking, manufacturer of a special product line; ~**verband** trade association, professional association; ~**wahl** subject choice; ~**welt** professional circles, the trade; ~**wissen** technical knowledge, expert knowledge; ~**wissenschaft** special scientific knowledge; ~**zeitschrift** trade paper, technical journal.

fachlich *adj* professional, specialist, technical; ~~ *geeignet*: *technically qualified*.

Façonwert *m* goodwill.

Factoring n factoring (business): *financing through the purchase of accounts receivable*, receivable financing; ~**-Firma** factor, factoring company; ~**vertrag** factoring agreement; **echtes** ~ non-recourse factoring; **unechtes** ~ recourse factoring; **verdeckte** ~ non-notification factoring.

facultas alternativa f optional right of performance.

fähig *adj* capable, eligible, able.

Fähigkeit f capacity, ability, eligibility; ~ **zum Richteramt** eligibility to act as a judge; ~ **zum Schiedsrichteramt** eligibility to act as an

289

fahnden

arbitrator; **berufliche** ~ professional (*or* vocational) ability; **rechtliche** ~ legal capacity; **verminderte geistige** ~ impaired mental capacity.

fahnden *v/i* to pursue, to search (for).

Fahnder *m* police detective.

Fahndung *f* police investigation to detect and locate a suspect.

Fahndungs|abteilung investigative unit, tracing and search department; ~**ausschreibung** a "wanted" notice; ~**blätter** police gazette, "wanted" list; ~**dienste** investigation services; ~**kartei** wanted-person file; ~**liste** wanted-person file; ~**meldung** investigation message.

Fahnenabzug *m* galley proof.

Fahneneid *m* oath of enlistment.

Fahnenflucht *f* desertion; *Verleitung zur* ~: *subornation to desertion;* **jmdn zur** ~ **anstiften** to procure s. o. to desert, to incite s. o. to desert.

fahnenflüchtig *adj* being a deserter, deserting, deserting the colours; ~ **werden** to desert (*a military unit*).

Fahr|anfänger learner; ~**auftrag** transport order; ~**ausweis** ticket; ~**bahn** → *Fahrbahn*: ~**erlaubnis** → *Fahrerlaubnis*; ~**gast** passenger, transport user; ~**gastaufkommen** ridership; ~**beförderung** passenger transport; ~**gastschiff** passenger ship; ~**geld** fare, passage-money; ~**geldhinterziehung** fare evasion; ~**geldpreller** fares dodger; ~**geldvergütungen** travel allowance; ~**gemeinschaft** ride-sharing group, petrol-sharing group, car pool; ~**geschwindigkeit** speed; *übermäßige* ~~: *excessive speed*; ~**gestellnummer** chassis number; ~**karte** ticket, passenger ticket; *einfache* ~~: *single ticket, one-way ticket;* ~**kartenautomat** automatic ticket dispenser; ~**lehrer** driving instructor; ~**leistung** travel distance, mileage; ~**personal** transport employees; ~**plan** *m* timetable, schedule; *den* ~*einhalten*: *to keep to the timetable*;

Fahrer

~**preis** fare, transportation charge; ~**prüfung** driving test, driver's test; ~**recht** right of passage; ~**schein** ticket; ~**scheinheft** ticket book; ~**schule** driving school; ~**schüler** learner-(driver); ~**spuren** vehicle tracks; (traffic) lanes; ~**straße** drive, road, carriageway, roadway; ~**streifen** lane; *seitlicher* ~ *side lane;* ~**tüchtigkeit** fitness to drive (*driver*), roadworthiness (*car*); navigability (*ship*); ~- **und Gehrechte** easement of passage; ~**unterricht** driving school instruction; *polizeilicher* ~~: *driving rectification course*; ~**untüchtigkeit** unfitness to drive; ~**verbot** prohibition from driving (a motor vehicle), driving ban; ~**wasser** navigable water; ~**weise** way of driving, driving style.

Fahrbahn *f* carriageway, US: driveway; roadway, pavement; ~**hälfte** half of the carriageway; lane; *die eigene* ~~: *the near side, one's own lane*; ~**markierungen** markings on the carriage way; ~**rand** edge of carriageway; ~**verengung** carriageway narrows, narrow sections of road, merging of lanes; ~**wechsel** lane change; *plötzlicher* ~~: *lane switching;* **die** ~ **freigeben** authorizing vehicles to proceed; **die gesamte Breite der** ~ **ausnutzen** to take advantage of the full width of the carriageway.

Fahren *n* driving; ~ **nach Entzug der Fahrerlaubnis** driving whilst disqualified; ~ **unter Alkoholeinfluß** driving while under the influence of alcohol; **grob fahrlässiges** ~ reckless driving; **grob verkehrsgefährdendes** ~ furious driving, reckless driving; **leichtsinniges** ~ reckless driving; **rücksichtsloses** ~ wanton driving, reckless driving, inconsiderate driving; **unvorsichtiges** ~ careless driving; **verkehrsgefährdendes** ~ dangerous driving; **zu schnelles** ~ speeding.

Fahrer *m* driver, operator, person in charge (of a motor vehicle); ~**, der**

Fahrerflucht begeht hit-and-run driver; **~flucht** hit-and-run offence, unauthorized leaving of scene of accident; **~fluchtfall** hit-and-run case; **~ ohne Führerschein** driver without a licence; **flüchtiger ~** hit-and-run driver; **nicht versicherter ~** uninsured driver; **rücksichtsloser ~** reckless driver; **~~,** *der den Weg nicht freigibt*: road hog; **wegen häufiger Unfälle unerwünschte ~** undesirable risks, undesired driver because prone to accident; **zuverlässiger ~** safe driver.

Fahrerin *f* woman driver.

Fahrerlaubnis *f* driving licence, *US: driver's licence*; **~antrag** application for a driving licence, application form for a driving licence; **~entziehung** disqualification from driving; **~sperre** suspension of driving licence.

fahrlässig *adj* negligent, careless.

Fahrlässigkeit *f* negligence, carelessness, want of diligence, heedlessness; **~sdelikt** negligence offence; **~sklausel** negligence clause; **arbeitsbedingte ~** carelessness at work; **bewußte ~** recklessness, conscious negligence; **eigene ~** personal negligence; **geringer Grad von ~** slight negligence; **gewöhnliche ~** ordinary negligence; **grobe ~** gross negligence; **leichte ~** ordinary negligence; **rechtserhebliche ~** actionable negligence, **strafbare ~** criminal negligence; **unbewußte ~** inadvertent negligence; **zu vertretende ~** imputed negligence, liability for negligence (of others).

Fahrnis *n* personal property, personalty, movable property, movables, chattels; **~hypothek** chattel mortgage; **~pfändung** levy of execution, levying movable property, distraint of chattels; **~versicherung** insurance of movable property.

Fahrrad *n* bicycle; **~ mit Hilfsmotor**: auto cycle; bicycle with auxiliary engine.

Fährrecht *n* right of ferry.

Fahrt *f* journey, voyage, trip; **~anweisungen** sailing instructions; **~auslagen** travel expenses; **~bericht** travel journal, travel report; **~enbuch** *n* compulsory driver's log, vehicle log, (*obligatory record of all vehicle movements*); **~ennachweis** vehicle log, personal record of transport (*of professional drivers*); **~enschreiber** vehicle travel recorder; tachigraph; **~genehmigung** journey authorization; **~kosten** transportation cost, travel expenses, commuting costs; **~kostenentschädigung** reimbursement of travel expenses, expense; **~kostenzulage** travel allowance; **~kostenzuschuß** travel allowance; **~richtung** → *Fahrtrichtung*; **~strecke** itinerary; **~teilnehmer** passenger; **einfache ~** single ticket; **große ~** deep-sea navigation, ocean voyage.

Fahrtrichtung *f* direction (of travel); **~sänderung** change of direction; **~sänderungsanzeige** indication of change of direction; **~sanzeiger** direction indicator; **vorgeschriebene ~** prescribed direction.

Fahrverbot *n* prohibition to drive motor vehicles

Fahrzeug *n* vehicle; **~brief** → *Kraftfahrzeugbrief*; **~ der öffentlichen Verkehrsbetriebe** public service vehicle; **~führer** driver of a vehicle, operator; **~halter** → *Kraftfahrzeughalter*; **~hersteller** car (vehicle) manufacturer; **~mitte** broadside; **~steuer** vehicle (car) tax; boat dues (*inland navigation*); **~schein** → *Kraftfahrzeugschein*; **~verkehr** vehicular traffic; **~~** *in beiden Richtungen verboten*: *closed to all vehicles in both directions;* **~(kasko)versicherung** vehicle (own damage) insurance, *cf Vollkaskoversicherung*; **~vollversicherung** comprehensive car insurance, fully comprehensive insurance; **~werte** motor shares; **gewerbliches ~** commercial vehicle; **miteinander verbundene ~e** a combination of vehicles;

schienengebundenes ~ rail vehicle, rail-bound vehicle; **überlanges** ~ long vehicle.

Faksimile *n* facsimile; **~stempel** facsimile stamp, signature stamp; **~unterschrift** facsimile signature.

faktisch *adj* actual, de facto.

Faktor *m* factor; **~enentgelt** factor's remuneration, factor's compensation; **~markt** factor market; **alle sachdienlichen ~en** all pertinent factors; **außerbetriebliche ~en** external factors; **entlastender ~** exonerating factor *or* circumstance; **innerwirtschaftliche ~en** domestic economic factors.

Faktura *f* invoice, bill, statement of account; **laut ~:** *as invoiced*; **e-e ~ ausstellen** to invoice.

Fakturenbuch *n* invoice book.

Fakturenwert *m* invoiced amount.

fakturieren *v/t* to invoice.

Fakturierung *f* invoicing.

Fakturist *m* invoice clerk.

Fakultät *f* faculty, department of a university (*now: Fachbereich qv*); **juristische ~** law school, law faculty.

fakultativ *adj* facultative, optional, permissive.

Fakultativ|klausel *f* optional clause; **~protokoll** optional protocol.

Fall *m* (*pl Fälle:* ~e) case, precedent; **~gerechtigkeit** equity and justice in the individual case; **~recht** case law; **~sammlung** law report(s), law reporters, collection of leading cases; table of cases; **f ~weise** *adj* relating to a particular case, ad hoc; **außergewöhnlicher ~** extreme case, unusual case; **bahnbrechender ~** seminal case, pioneer case; unprecedented case; **den ~ durch Sachverständigen begutachten lassen** to appoint an expert to report on the case; **der betreffende ~** the case concerned, the case in question; **der hier strittige ~** the matter in dispute; **der vorliegende ~** the present case, the case at issue; **der zur Entscheidung stehende ~** the case at issue, the matter in hand; **ein besonders krasser ~** an extreme case, a blatant example; **ein einschlägiger ~** a case in point, a precedent; **ein ~ höherer Gewalt** a case of force majeure; **ein ~ tritt ein** a case arises; **e-n ~ wiederaufrollen** to reopen a case; **ein ~ wird im Schnellverfahren behandelt** a case is disposed of summarily; **e-n ~ absetzen** to strike out; **e-n ~ bearbeiten** to handle a case, to deal with a case; **e-n ~ erledigen** dispose of a case; **e-n ~ schlüssig vortragen** to state a case coherently; **e-n ~ verhandeln** to try a case; **e-n ~ vor Gericht anhängig machen** to begin legal proceedings, to take a matter to court; **erstmalig zu entscheidender ~** case of first impression; **gleichgelagerter ~** similar case, analagous case; **hypothetischer ~** hypothetical case; **im analogen ~** in an analogous case, in pari materia, mutatis mutandis; **im betrachteten ~** in the case at hand, in the case under discussion; **im ~e des Verstoßes gegen** in case of non-compliance with; **im ~e des Verzuges** in case of undue delay, in default of (*payment etc*); **im konkreten ~** in the case under consideration; **im vorliegenden ~** in the case under consideration; **in begründeten ~en** in cases where there is adequate reason; **in besonders gelagerten ~en** in cases of a special nature; **je nach Lage des ~es** as the case may be; **leichtere ~e** non-serious cases; **seerechtlicher ~** case involving maritime law; **seinen ~ vortragen** to plead one's cause (*or* case); **unerledigter ~** unsettled case; **von ~ zu ~** as the case arises, on an ad hoc basis; **von ~ zu ~ entscheiden** to decide each case on its merits.

Falle *f* trap, snare; **~nstellen** = *Fallenstellerei qv*; **~nstellerei** snaring.

Fallgrube *f* pitfall.

fallen *v/i* to fall, to drop, to decline, to decrease, to recede, to depreciate; **~ lassen** to dismiss, to drop, to withdraw; **unter etwas ~** to come

fällen within the scope of, to fall within the terms of; to come under the heading of.

fällen *v/t* to render (*judgment*), to pass, to pronounce, to rule.

fällig *adj* (now) due, overdue, due und payable, owing, payable, matured; ~ **werden** to fall due, to become due; ~ *werdend*: *accruing, becoming due*; **jederzeit** ~ due at call, on demand; **nicht** ~ not due; **noch nicht** ~ unmatured; **täglich** ~ due at call.

Fälligkeit *f* maturity, due date, time for payment; **auf monatliche** ~ **abstellen** to set upon the basis of monthly maturities; **bei** ~ at (= on) maturity, when due, as it matures, after falling due; *bei* ~ *zahlbar*: *payable when due*; **vor** ~ prior to maturity; **vorzeitige** ~ accelerated maturity; **vor** ~ **zahlen** to anticipate payment.

Fälligkeits|avis reminder of due date; ~**datum** date of maturity, maturity date, due date; ~**factoring** maturity factoring; ~**frist** maturity period; maturity deadline; ~**gliederung** spacing of the maturities; ~**jahr** year of maturity; ~**klausel** accelerating clause; ~**steuern** fixed-date taxes; ~**tabelle** aging schedule; ~**tag** date of maturity, maturity date, due date, accrual date (*interest, annuities*), date of payment, term day; *nach dem* ~~*e*: *post diem*; ~**termin** date of maturity, maturity date, due date, date of expiration.

Fallitenmasse *f* bankrupt's estate.

Fallstrick *m* snare, pitfall; **rechtliche** ~**e** legal pitfalls, legal traps.

falsch *adj* false, falsified, wrong, erroneous, mistaken, fallacious.

Falsch|anzeige false information, false accusation; ~**auskünfte** erroneous information; ~**aussage** false testimony; ~**belehrung** misdirection; ~**beurkundung** making false entry, false certification; *mittelbare* ~~: *false declaration (for entry in a public register), constructive false certification*; ~**beurkundung im Amt** false certification by public officer; ~**bezeichnung von Waren** false trade description, misbranding of goods; ~**buchung** false entry, fraudulent entry, mis-entry; ~**eid** false oath, false swearing (by negligence) *außergerichtlicher* ~~: *false swearing*; ~**geld** false money, counterfeit money, false coin; ~~ *in Umlauf bringen*: *to circulate (utter) counterfeit money*; ~**geldabschieber** distributor of counterfeit money; ~**lieferung** wrong shipment, mistaken delivery, delivery of the wrong goods (*different from those ordered*); ~**meldung** false report, canard, hoax; **f~münzen** *v/i* to counterfeit, to forge banknotes, to adulterate; ~**münzer** counterfeiter, forger; ~**münzerei** counterfeiting, making and circulating (uttering) of counterfeit money; ~**parker** parking offender; ~**spieler** card-sharper; ~**urkunde** fabricated document; ~**verteilung** maldistribution.

fälschen *v/t* to forge, to falsify, to fake.

fälschlich *adv* falsely, erroneously.

Fälschung *f* forgery, falsification, fabrication, fake, imitation; ~ **der Wahlergebnisse** election fraud; **f~ssicher** counterfeit-proof; ~ **von Metallgeld** counterfeiting coins; ~ **von Postwertzeichen** forgery of postal stamps; ~ **von Urkunden** → *Urkundenfälschung*.

Falsifikat *n* forgery.

Faltblatt *n* leaflet, *US*: folder.

Faltprospekt *m* leaflet, *US*: folder.

Faltschachtel *f* folding box, collapsible carton.

falsus procurator agent without authority.

Familie *f* family; **kinderreiche** ~ large family.

Familien|angehörige family-members, kinsfolk; *mithelfende* ~~: *assisting family-members*; ~**angehörigkeit** kin, family-membership, family relationship; ~**angelegenheiten** family affairs, domestic matters; ~**arbeitskräfte** working fam-

Familienausgleichskasse

ily-members; ~**ausgleichskasse** family allowance fund; *gewerbliche* ~~: *occupational family allowance fund*; ~**beihilfe** family allowance; ~**betrieb** family concern, family-owned enterprise, family-operated business; *bäuerlicher* ~~: *family-operated farm*; ~**buch** genealogical register, family abstract from register of births and marriages; ~**diebstahl** larceny from members of the family; ~**fideikommiß** large entailed estate held by a (noble) family; ~**frau** housewife; ~**fürsorge** family welfare; ~**geld** family allowance; ~**gericht** family court, family division of the local court, domestic court; ~**gesellschaft** family concern, family-held partnership (*or* company); ~**gut** entailed estate, family estate; ~**habe** family assets, family property; ~**haupt** head of a family; ~**heimfahrt** trip home (to the family); ~**heimgesetz** law on family accommodation; ~**hilfe** family support; f~**intern** domestic, within a family; ~**leistungen** family allowances; ~**lohn** family wage; ~**ministerium** Ministry for Family Affairs; ~**mitarbeit** employment within a family; ~**mitglied** family-member; *mithelfendes* ~~: *assisting family-member*; ~**name** family name, last name, surname; *zusammengesetzter* ~~: *compound family name*; ~**oberhaupt** head of a family; ~**oder Kleinbetriebe** family and small-scale firms; ~**packung** family-size pack; ~**papiere** family documents; ~**paß** joint passport (for a family); ~**pflege** child care within a family (*of foster, parents relatives, adoptive parents etc*); fostering; ~**planung** family planning; ~**rat** family council, family meeting; ~**recht** law of domestic relations, family law; f~**rechtlich** *adj* under family law; ~**rechtsänderungsgesetz** Family Law Alteration Act; ~**rechtsanwalt** matrimonial practitioner; ~**rechtssa-**

Fangabkommen

chen cases involving family law; ~**rechtsschutz** legal expenses insurance for family law matters; ~**sache** family law case; ~**register** family register; ~**richter** family court judge; ~**senat** family law panel at appellate court; ~**stamm** stirps (*pl. stirpes*), family stock, lineage; ~**stammbaum** lineage, genealogical table; ~**stammbuch** family book; ~**stand** personal status, marital status; ~**sterbegeld** funeral allowance for family members; ~**stiftung** family foundation; ~**stück** family heirloom; ~**unterhalt** family living expenses, upkeep of a family; ~**unternehmen** family concern, family-owned enterprise; ~**unterstützung** allowance for dependants; ~**vater** pater familias, father of a family, male head of a household; ~**verhältnisse** family background, family circumstances; *in geordneten* ~~*n leben*: *to have a normal home life*; ~**versicherung** family insurance; ~**versorgungsversicherung** family income insurance policy, family protection policy; ~**vorstand** head of the family; ~**wohnsitz** family residence; ~**wohnung** family home, family residence; ~**zulage** family allowance (*a wage supplement*); ~**zusammenführung** family reunion (*or* reunification); ~**zusatzdarlehen** additional loan for a family; ~**zuschlag** special family allowance.

Fang|abkommen fishing-limit agreement; ~**beschränkung** fishing limitation; ~**brief** letter constituting a police trap; ~**frage** a trick question, deliberate trap; ~**geräte** fishing implements; ~**gründe** fishing grounds; ~**plätze** fishing grounds; ~**quote** allowable catch, catch quota; ~**prämie** reward for catching a shoplifter; ~**rechte** fishery rights; ~**schaltung** telephone trap; ~**und Schonzeiten** open and close seasons; ~**verbot** ban on fishing.

Fantasiewort *n* fancy word *(firm name)*, imaginary name.

Farbdrucksiegel *n* rubber-stamp seal.

Farbe *f* colo(u)r, shade; ~ **bekennen** to show one's hand, to come clean, to own up; **~nmarkt** market for dyestuff and chemical shares; **~nsektor** paint and dyestuff industry; **~nwerte** shares *(or other securities)* of IG Farben successors; **licht- und waschechte** ~ fast colo(u)r.

färben *fig* to dye; to slant, to tinge, to embroider *(a report, an article)*.

Farbstoffindustrie *f* dyestuffs industry.

Faß *n* barrel.

Fassadenkletterer *m* cat-burglar.

Fasson *f* make, shape *(of dresses etc)*.

Fassonwert *m* goodwill.

Faßraum *m* barrelage space.

Fassung *f* wording, version, formulation, form of words; **alte** ~ original version, unamended version; **... erhält folgende geänderte** ~ ... shall be amended and shall read as follows; **folgende** ~ the following text; **geänderte** ~ amended version; **neueste** ~ with latest amendments, latest version (draft); **verbindliche** ~ authentic text, binding text, governing version.

Faustpfand *n* pawn, pledge, dead-pledge; **~darlehen** loan on the security of a pawn, chattel mortgage, loan against a pledge; **~gläubiger** pawnee, pledgee; **~kredit** loan against pledge; **~recht** law of pledge, right to hold on pledged collateral.

Faustrecht *n* club-law, law of the jungle, right of private warfare; ~ **üben** to take the law into one's own hands.

Faustregel *f* rule of thumb, rule based on practice, rough-and-ready guide.

Fautfracht *f* dead freight.

Favoriten *m/pl* favourites *(stock exchange)*, glamour stock.

Fax *n* fax, telefacsimile.

federführend *adj* (acting as) central coordinator, holding the main responsibility for, leading, principal.

Federführung *f* central coordination, main responsibility (for), central handling (of), central administration (of).

Fehlanpassung maladjustment; **~anzeige** blank return, nil return, negative report; **~auffassung** misconception, erroneous conception; **~bedarf** uncovered demand, shortfall, deficit; **~bestand** deficiency *(in stock, of men etc)*, inventory deficiency; **~betrag** deficiency, deficit, shortage, shortfall, missing sum; ~~ *der Gesamtrechnung:* overall accounting deficit; **den ~~ decken:** to make up for the deficit; *geringfügige ~~e:* small amounts lacking; *rechnerischer ~~:* arithmetical shortage; **~beurteilung** misjudgment (= *misjudgement*); **~bewertung** erroneous appraisal, misjudgment; **~bitte** futile request, unsuccessful plea; **~buchung** incorrect entry; **~disposition** misguided action, misplanning; **~einsatz** misdirection, erroneous, disposition; **~einschätzung** miscalculation; **~entscheidung** misjudgment, wrong decision; **~entwicklung** undesirable trend, aberration; **~ernte** crop failure; **~fabrikat** defective article; **~fracht** dead freight; **~gebrauch** wrong use; **~geburt** miscarriage; **~geld** risk-money, allowance to cashier for errors; ~~*entschädigung:* lump-sum allowance to cashier for possible cash deficits; **~gewicht** deficiency in weight, shortweight; **~investition** bad investment, investment failure; **~konstruktion** faulty design; **~leistung** poor performance; **~leitung** *f* misdirection, misguidance; **~menge** deficiency, shortage, missing quantity, quantity considered as lost; **~paarung** mismatching; **~rechnung** miscalculation; **~schätzung** wrong estimate; **~schichten** shifts which workers fail to do, absenteeism; **~schluß** wrong inference, wrong

Fehlen | **Feindbegünstigung**

conclusion; ~**spekulation** bad speculation, misconjecture; ~**spruch** judicial error, *rare for Fehlurteil qv*; ~**steuerung** misdirection; ~**urteil** wrong judgment (= *judgement*), misjudgment, error of judgment, miscarriage of justice; ~**verhalten** misconduct, malconduct, misbehaviour; *grobes* ~~: *wanton misconduct*, *schwerwiegendes* ~~: *grave misconduct*, *vorsätzliches* ~~: *wilful misconduct*; ~**zeiten** times of absence from work, absentee periods, periods of time off; ~**zeitenquote** rate of absenteeism.

Fehlen *n* lack, absence; ~ **der Unterlagen** documents missing; ~ **e-r gesetzlichen Grundlage** lack of any legal basis; ~ **e-r Stellungnahme** absence of an opinion, failure to comment; **unentschädigtes** ~ unexcused absence, absence without leave.

Fehler *m* mistake, defect, fault, error, imperfection, vice; ~**bereich** margin of error; ~**berichtigung** correction of errors; ~ **der Ausführung** faulty workmanship; ~ **des Gerichts** judicial error; ~ **des Materials** faulty material; **f~frei** faultless, without any fault or defect, free from defect(s); ~**grenze** margin of error, limit of error, tolerance; *hohe* ~~*n*: *wide limits of error*; **f** ~**haft** faulty, defective; ~**haftigkeit** faultiness, incorrectness; ~ **im Rubrum** defect in title; ~**quelle** source of error; ~**suche** trouble shooting; ~**verbesserung** rectification; **e-n** ~ **zugeben** to stand corrected, to admit one's mistake; **innerer** ~ inherent vice, (*or* defect), intrinsic error, inherent mistake; **inhaltlicher** ~ defect of (= in) substance; **natürlicher** ~ inherent vice; **offenbarer** ~ patent defect, obvious error; **verborgener** ~ latent defect.

Feierschicht *f* dropped shift, idle shift, unworked shift; ~**en einlegen** to drop shifts.

Feiertag *m* (bank) holiday, non-working day, non-business day; ~**sarbeit** work on a public holiday; ~**sgesetze** laws regulating public holidays; ~**slohn** (bank) holiday pay; ~**slohnzahlungsanspruch** right to (claim) holiday pay; ~**sruhe** public holiday observance; ~**svergütung** regular pay for public holidays; ~**szuschlag** holidaywork bonus; *additional payment for work done on a public holiday*; **gesetzlicher** ~ public holiday, legal holiday, statutory holiday, non-working day; **gesetzlich geschützter** ~ recognized holiday, statutory public holiday; **nationaler** ~ national holiday, bank holiday (*GB*); **ungeschützter** ~ working holiday, non-statutory public holiday.

Feilbieten *n* offering for sale.

feilbieten *v/t* to offer for sale, to put up for sale, to tender (for sale).

Feilhalten *n* offering for sale, exhibition (*or* exposure) for sale, having on sale.

feilhalten *v/t* to offer for sale, to have for sale, to display for sale.

Fein|gehalt standard of fineness, fineness; ~**gehaltsstempel** hallmark, standard mark; ~**gehaltswert** assay office value; ~**gehaltszeichen** assay mark; ~**gold** fine gold, refined gold; ~**goldgewicht** weight of fine gold; ~**heitsgrad des Goldes** fineness of gold; ~**kostgeschäft** delicatessen store (shop); ~**mechanik** precision engineering; ~**mechaniker** precision mechanic; ~**regulierung** fine adjustment; *die konjunkturelle* ~~: *the fine adjustment of cyclical policy*; ~**steuerung** fine tuning.

Feind|begünstigung *obs.* aiding the enemy; ~**besitz** enemy property; ~**einwirkung** enemy action; ~**esgewalt** enemy action, act of the Queen's enemy; ~**esland** enemy territory; ~**gebiet** hostile territory, enemy territory; ~**handlung** hostile act; ~**seligkeiten** hostilities; ~**staat** enemy state, hostile state; ~**staatenklausel** (*UN-Charter*) enemy state clause *reserving*

Feldarbeit

enemy-state status (of 2nd world war); ~**unterstützung** supporting the enemy; ~**vermögen** enemy property; ~**vermögensverwalter** alien property custodian.

Feld|arbeit farm work, field work; ~**arbeiter** farm worker, *pl* agricultural labo(u)r; ~**beschädigung** damage to the fields; crop damage; ~**diebstahl** theft of crops in the fields; ~**früchte** crops in the fields; ~**gefährdung** endangering the fields; ~**geschworener** rural boundary juror; ~**jäger** military police; ~**jägerkommandant** provost-marshal; ~**markung** landmark, field boundary; ~**polizei** rural guard force; ~**post** military postal service; ~**schaden** damage done to the fields; ~**- und Forstdiebstahl** theft from fields or forests; ~**weg** farm road (*US:*) dirt road; ~**webel** warrant officer; ~**zeugwesen** ordnance.

Femegericht *n* unlawful secret court, vehmic court.

Fememord *m* secret political murder, unlawful execution pursuant to the verdict of a secret court.

Fenster|klebeplakat window sticker; ~**recht** window right(s), (easement of) light, right of prospect; ~**umschlag** visible envelope, window envelope.

Ferien|arbeit vacation work; ~**einsatz** vacation work, holiday work; ~**haus** holiday house; ~**kammer** vacation court; ~**ordnung** school holiday (vacation) order for schools; ~**sache** vacation business; ~**sitzung** vacation sitting, sitting after term, post-terminal sitting; ~**vergütung** vacation pay, holiday money; ~**vertreter** deputy during vacations; ~**wetterversicherung** holiday weather insurance; ~**wohnung** holiday flat *or* flatlet.

Fern|adoption adoption in absentia (*by undisclosed adopting parents*); ~**amt** trunk exchange; ~~ *mit Handvermittlung: manual exchange*; ~**anschluß** long distance connection; ~**bedienung** remote control;

Fernverbindungen

~**beglaubigung** notarial certification by indirect acknowledgment; ~**belastung** collection from another place; ~**bleiben** absence, nonappearance; ~~ *vom Dienst: absence from duty*; *unentschuldigtes* ~~: *unexcused absence, unexcused failure to appear;* ~**fischerei** long-range fishing; ~**gasversorgung** town gas supply, long-distance gas supply; ~**gespräch** telephone call, trunk call, long-distance call; ~**giroverkehr** distance giro transfers, bank transfers over long distances; ~**heizung** district heating; ~**lastunternehmen** long haulage business; ~**lastverkehr** long haulage; ~**lehrgang** correspondence course; ~**leitung** long-distance power line; ~**licht** driving lights, full beam, full headlights; ~**meldeanlagen** telecommunication installations; ~**meldegeheimnis** secrecy of telecommunications; ~**meldeordnung** telecommunication regulations; ~**melderechnungsdienst** telecommunication accounts office; ~**melderecht** law governing telecommunications; ~**meldeverkehr** telecommunications; ~**meldewesen** telecommunications; ~**schreiben** telex; ~**schreiber** telex machine; ~**schreibgebühren** telex charges; ~**schreibmaschine** teletypewriter, teleprinter; ~**schreibverkehr** communications; f ~**schriftlich** by telex or facsimile; ~**seh**... → *Fernseh|*...; ~**setzanlagen** teletypesetting systems; ~**sprech**... → *Fernsprech|*...; ~**straße** arterial road, trunk road, highway, dual carriage way; ~**straßengesetz** Highway Maintenance Act; ~**studium** distance learning, studies by correspondence; ~**trauung** marriage by proxy; ~**übertragung** long-distance transmission; ~**unterricht** distance teaching; ~**unterrichtsschutzgesetz** *(1974)* Correspondence Courses Act; ~**verbindungen** telecommunications, trunk connections;

297

Fernsehanstalt

~**verkehr** long-distance transport; ~**verkehrsstraße** = *Fernstraße qv*; ~**verkehrszug** long-distance train, express train; ~**wärmelieferung** distance heating supply; ~**wärmenetz** long-distance heating system; ~**wärmeverbund** integrated system of district heating; ~**wirkung** remote effect, indirect effect, long-term effect; ~**ziel** remote objective, ultimate object, end goal, long-range goal.

Fernseh|anstalt television corporation; ~**freiheit** freedom of (reporting and opinion in) television broadcasting; ~**funk** television (broadcasting); ~**kette(n)** network syndication; ~**recht** television law, ~**streit** dispute about television rights; ~**teilnehmer** (tele)viewer; ~**technik** television engineering, video technique (*US*); ~**übereinkommen** International Television Convention (*of Straßburg 1965–75*); ~**werk** television work (*copyright*).

Fernsprech|amt telephone exchange (*or* office); ~**anlage** telephone (installation); ~**anschluß** telephone connection; ~**buch** telephone directory; ~**dienst** telephone system; ~**gebühren** telephone charges; ~**geheimnis** telephone secrecy, secrecy of telephone communications; ~**hauptanschluß** telephone main station; ~**linien** telephone lines; ~**netz** telephone system; ~**nummer** telephone number, subscriber's number; ~**ordnung** telephone regulations; ~**teilnehmer** telephone subscriber; ~**teilnehmerverzeichnis** telephone directory, phone book; ~**verbindung** telephone connection; *e-e* ~~ *herstellen*: *to put through a call*; ~**verkehr** telephone communications; ~**wesen** telephony; ~**zelle** telephone box, telephone booth; ~**zentrale** exchange.

fertig *adj*, ready, ready-made.

Fertig|bau prefabricated house, prefab; ~**erzeugnis** finished product, (fully) manufactured article; ~**fabrikat** finished product, (fully)

Fertigungsablauf

manufactured article; ~**haus** prefab (building); ~**keit** → *Fertigkeit*; ~**kleidung** ready-made clothing; ~**montage** final assembly, assembly of the finished product; ~**packung** prepack, packaging; ~**produkte** finished products; **f**~**stellen** to complete, to finish; ~**stellung** completion; ~**stellungsbürge** completion guarantor; ~**stellungsgarantie** completion bond (*or* guarantee); ~**ung** → *Fertigung*; ~**waren** finished goods, finished products; ~**waren-Enderzeugnisse** finally finished goods; ~**waren-Vorerzeugnisse** primary products to be further processed

fertigen *v/t* to manufacture, to produce, to complete.

Fertigkeit *f* skill, proficiency.

Fertigung *f* manufacure, making; **bedarfsorientierte** ~ demand-oriented production.

Fertigungs|ablauf production flow; ~**auslastung** utilization of production capacity; ~**bereich** manufacturing sector; ~**betrieb** manufacturing enterprise; ~**einheit** unit of product; ~**einleitung** production start-up, production launch; ~**einrichtungen** manufacturing facilities; ~**einzelkosten** production cost of individual product, prime cost; ~**fehler** defect due to workmanship; ~**frist** production time, period stipulated for completion; ~**gehälter** direct labour salaries; ~**gemeinkosten** manufactoring overhead, production overhead, indirect production cost, factory overhead; ~~*lohn*: *indirect labour*; ~~ *material*: *indirect material*; *allgemeine* ~~: *general manufacturing overhead*; ~**industrie** manufacturing industries; ~**ingenieur** production engineer; ~**kapazität** production capacity; ~**kontrolle** supervision of manufacture; ~**kosten** manufacturing cost, processing cost, (*direct and indirect*) costs of production; *bookkeeping*: conversion costs; ~**kostenrechnung** statement of production costs;

fesseln

~**kostenstelle** productive burden centre; ~**lohn** productive wages, productive labour; ~**lohnstunde** direct labour hour; ~**plan** work schedule, production schedule, production plan; ~**planung** production planning; ~**sonderkosten** special production costs; ~**sortiment** product mix; ~**spektrum** range of products, product line; ~**stätte** workshop, manufacturing plant; ~**stellengemeinkosten** workshop overheads; ~**überwachung** production monitoring; production control; ~**verfahren** production method, manufacturing process, process of manufacture; ~**vorbereitung** production scheduling, preparations for production; ~**zeit** production time; *großzügig bemessene* ~~: *generously computed production times*.

fesseln *v/t* to fetter, to shackle, to manacle, to handcuff, to tie.

Fesselung *f* fettering.

Fest|**angestellte** permanently employed persons, established employees, permanent staff; ~**auftrag** definite order, exclusive uncancellable broker's contract; ~**gebot** firm bid; ~**gebühr** fixed charge *or* fee; ~**gehalt** fixed salary; ~**geld** → *Festgeld*; ~**genommener** arrested person, person under arrest; ~**kauf** definite purchase, concluded sale; ~**konto** blocked account, fixed-date time account; ~**landsockel** continental shelf; ~**landswechsel** continental bill; **f**~**legen** → *festlegen*; ~**legung** → *Festlegung*; ~**meter** solid cubic metre (*US*: meter); ~**mietvertrag** fixed-term tenancy; ~**nahme** → *Festnahme*; **f**~**nehmen** to seize, to apprehend, to arrest, to take into custody; ~**preis** → *Festpreis*; **f**~**schreiben** to settle in writing, to lay down in permanent form; ~**schreibungsfrist** period for which securities must be held; **f**~**setzen** to fix, to determine, to assess; ~**setzung** → *Festsetzung*; **f**~**stehen** to be certain, to be beyond doubt, to be established;

Festsetzung

f~**stellbar** determinable, ascertainable, identifiable; *nicht* ~~: *incapable of being ascertained, untraceable*; **f**~**stellen** to determine, to ascertain, to locate, to find out; to state, to declare; ~**stellung** → *Feststellung*; ~**stoff-Emissionen** particle emissions; ~**übernahme** firm underwriting; ~**verkauf** fixed sale, sold; **f**~**verzinslich** bearing stated interest, fixed interest-bearing; ~**wert** base value, fixed value; ~**zinsdarlehen** fixed-rate term loan.

Festgeld *n* time deposit, term deposit, fixed deposit; ~**anlage** money deposited for a fixed term; ~**konto** time deposit; ~**zinsen** interest on fixed-term deposits.

festlegen *v/t* to fix, to stipulate, to fix, to settle; to immobilize, to invest; **anteilig** ~ to apportion, to allocate; **vertraglich** ~ to stipulate (by contract).

Festlegung *f* determination, stipulation; establishment, immobilization (*of funds*), locking-up (*of capital*); ~ **von Haftungsquoten** apportionment of liability; **gesetzliche** ~ statutory determination; **stärkere fristmäßige** ~ **der Ersparnisse** depositing of savings for longer periods.

Festnahme *f* apprehension, arrest, seizure, taking a person into custody, *sl* pinch; ~ **auf frischer Tat** apprehension in the very act; ~ **durch jedermann** citizen's arrest; **vorläufige** ~ (provisional) apprehension, summary arrest, detention for questioning, **widerrechtliche** ~ unlawful arrest, false imprisonment.

Festpreis *m* fixed price, firm price, flat price; ~**auftrag** firm-price order; ~**politik** one-price policy, policy of controlled prices; ~**zuschlag** firm-price surcharge.

festsetzbar *adj* determinable; taxable (*costs*).

Festsetzung *f* fixing, determination, assessment; ~ **der Dringlichkeiten** priority rating; ~ **der Pro-**

feststellbar / **Fettausgleichsabgabe**

ze߈kosten taxing of costs; ~ **der Quotenhöhe** fixing quota levels; ~ **der Steuer in e~m Pauschbetrag** lump sum tax assessment; ~ **des Steuergegenstandes** determination of the tax basis; ~ **e-r Entschädigung** assessment of compensation; ~ **höherer Prämien** rating up; ~ **von Dividenden** declaration of dividends; ~ **von Höchstbeträgen** fixing of limits; ~ **von Schadenersatz** assessment of damages; **gerichtliche** ~ judicial determination; taxation (*costs*).

feststellbar *adj* determinable, ascertainable, capable of ascertainment.

Feststellbremse *f* hand brake, parking brake.

Feststellung *f* determination, ascertainment, declaration (*by judgment*); ~ **der Echtheit** verification, authentication; ~ **der Personalangaben e-s Zeugen** identification of witness; ~ **der Personalien** identification; ~ **der Kautionsstellungsfähigkeit** determination on granting bail, perfecting bail; ~ **der Steuerschuld** establishing the amount of tax to be paid; ~ **der Vaterschaft** ascertainment of paternity, court finding of paternity; ~ **der Warenbeschaffenheit** identification of goods; ~ **des Alkoholgehalts** determination of alcoholic strength; ~ **des Aufenthaltsorts** finding out a person's whereabouts, tracing s.b.'s address; ~ **des Erfinders** determination of the identity of the inventor; ascertainment of the inventor's identity; ~ **des Invaliditätsgrades** determination of the degree of disablement; ~ **des Jahresabschlusses** adoption of the annual statement of accounts; ~ **des Rechtsanspruches** proof of title; ~ **des Sachverhalts** fact finding, ascertainment of the facts; ~ **des Schadens** ascertainment of loss; ~ **des Tatbestandes** ascertainment of the facts; ~ **e-r Forderung** official recognition of claim; ~ **e-r Konkursforderung** proving a claim in bankruptcy; **aktenmäßige** ~ recording (*of facts, names etc.*); **diese** ~ **wird getroffen** this finding shall be made; **die zur** ~ **seiner Person erforderlichen Angaben machen** to identify oneself; **einheitliche** ~ uniform assessment; **gerichtliche** ~ declaration by the court; **patentamtliche** ~ **der Kollision von Patentansprüchen** interference ruling; **rechtliche** ~ legal findings, declaration; **rechtskräftige** ~ final and absolute finding of the court, non-appealable declaratory judgment; **richterliche** ~**(en)** judicial finding; **tatsächliche** ~ acertainment of facts, finding of facts.

Feststellungs|anspruch claim for (*or* entitlement to) a declaratory judgment; ~**beamter** assessing official, appraiser; ~**befund** official findings; ~**behörde** loss-assessing authority; ~**bescheid** notice assessment, declaratory administrative ruling; ~**interesse** interest to seek a declaratory judgment; ~**klage** declaratory action, declaratory proceeding, action for a declaratory judgment; suit for a declaration, bill of peace; *positive* ~~: *positive declaratory action*; *negative* ~~: *action for a negative declaration, jactitation suit*; ~**slast** onus of correct ascertainment of facts; ~**protokoll** record of the facts; ~**streit** declaratory proceedings; ~**urteil** declaratory judgment, declaration judgment, declaration as to rights, declaration of title; ~**verfahren** declaratory proceedings; ~**widerklage** declaratory cross petition; ~**zeitpunkt** point in time when sth was determined (*or* ascertained); ~**zeitraum** period for determination; ~**zwischenurteil** declaratory interlocutory order.

Festungshaft *f obs* confinement in a fortress, incarceration.

Fett|ausgleichsabgabe fat price equalization levy; ~**druck** bold print; ~**gehalt** fat content; ~**rohstoff** raw material for the production of fats; ~**wert** fat equivalent.

Feuchtigkeitsschaden *m* damage due to moisture.
Feudalsystem *n* feudalism.
Feuer *n* fire, destructive burning, conflagration; **f~beständig** *adj* fire-resistant, fire-proof, incombustible; **~beständigkeit** fire-proof quality, fire resistance; **~bestattung** cremation, incineration; **~bestattungsanlage** crematorium; **~einstellung** cease fire; **f~-gefährlich** inflammable; **f~hemmend** fire-resistant; **~leiter** fire escape; **~löschapparat** fire fighting machine; **~löscher** fire extinguisher; **~löscheinrichtungen** fire-extinguishing equipment; **~meldesystem** fire-alarm system; **~risiko** fire hazard; **~schaden** fire damage, damage by reason of fire; **~schadensabteilung** fire department (*of an insurance company*); **~schiff** lightship; **~schutz** fire prevention, fire protection; **~schutzabgabe** fire prevention levy; **~schutzdienst** fire prevention service; **~schutzsteuer** fire protection tax, fire-brigade tax; **f~sicher** fire-proof; **~sicherheit** fire-proof quality, fire safety; **~snot** fire emergency, danger from fire; **~stätte** fire-place; **~versicherer** fire insurer; **~versicherung** fire insurance, insurance against loss by fire; insurance against fire-risks; **~versicherungsgesellschaft** fire insurance company, fire underwriter; **~versicherungsteuer** fire insurance tax; **~wache** fire station; **~waffe** firearm; **~wehr** → *Feuerwehr*.
Feuerwehr *f* fire-brigade, fire service; **~bezirk** fire district; **~fonds** fire-fighting fund (*of bank for a crash*); **~zufahrt** fire lane; **freiwillige ~** voluntary fire brigade.
FIATA *n* Combined Transport Bill of Lading.
Fideikommiß *m* estate in fee-tail, entailed estate; **~auflösung** disentailment; **~land** settled land; **~lehen** estate in fee-tail; **~nachfolger** successor to disentailed estates; **~sachen** cases involving estates in fee-tail.
Fiduziant *m* creator of a trust, cestui que trust.
Fiduziar *m* fiduciary, trustee.
fiduziarisch *adj* fiduciary.
Fiktion *f* fiction; **~ des Kennens** imputed knowledge; **gesetzliche ~** legal fiction; **juristische ~** legal fiction.
Filial|bank bank branch, branch of a bank; **~betrieb** branch, chain store; **~buchführung** branch accounting; **~buchhaltung** branch accounting; **~geschäft** branch, branch business, chain store; **~handlungsvollmacht** power of attorney for a branch; **~grossbank** major bank with a branch system; **~-Kreditinstitut** credit institution with branch system; **~leiter** branch manager; **~netz** branch network; **~prokura** „Prokura" (*qv*) limited to a branch; **~vergleich** comparison as between branches; **~wechsel** house bill.
Filiale *f* branch store, branch.
Film|abgabe motion picture promotion levy (*per ticket*); **~bearbeitung** screen adaptation; **~bewertungsstelle** film assessment boad (*rating cultural value*); **~bezugsvertrag** motion-picture distribution agreement; **~förderung** official promotion of (valuable) motion pictures; **~freiheit** freedom of producing and showing (uncensored) film; **~hersteller** producer, moviemaker, motion picture producer; **~produktionszentrum** film producing centre; **~prüfstelle** film review board, board of film censors; **~rechte** film rights; **~regisseur** film director; **~schaffende** film production workers, motion picture staff; **~selbstkontrolle** internal motion picture industry control; **~stoff** screen story; **~urheber** film copyright owner; **~urheberrecht** film copyright; **~verleiher** distributor; **~verwertungsrechte** film (exploitation) rights; **~vorführungs-**

Filz — **finanzschwach**

konzession cinemas and films licence; ~**werk** cinematographic work; ~**wesen** motion-picture industry, film branch; ~**wirtschaft** film business, motion picture industry; ~**zensur** motion picture censorship.

Filz *m* cronyism; nepotism.

filzen *v/t* to frisk.

Filzokratie *f* corrupt politics, the old-boy's network (*GB*), nepotism.

Finanz|abkommen monetary convention, financial treaty; ~**abteilung** financial department; ~**amt** tax office, revenue board, revenue-office, Inland Revenue Office *GB*; ~**amtsbescheid** revenue ruling, tax inspector's ruling; ~**amtssachbearbeiter** (*pl*) inland revenue minders, (*or* personnel); ~**angelegenheiten** financial business; ~**anlagen** financial assets; ~**anteil** fiscal element; ~**aufkommen** budgetary revenue; ~**ausgleich** fiscal adjustment, fiscal compensation, equalization of financial burdens, financial compensation; ~**ausschuß** committee on finance; ~**autonomie** self-administrative financial system, fiscal autonomy; ~**bankrott** financial bankruptcy; ~**beamter** fiscal officer, revenue officer; ~**behörde** revenue authority, Internal Revenue (*UK*), Internal Revenue Service (*US*); ~**berater** financial adviser; ~**bericht** fiscal report, financial statement; ~**buchhaltung** general (*or* financial) accounting department; ~**gebarung** financial management, fiscal policy; ~**gericht** first-instance fiscal court, tax court, revenue court; ~**gerichtsbarkeit** fiscal court jurisdiction; ~**gerichtsordnung** code of procedure for fiscal courts; ~**gerichtsverfahren** fiscal proceedings; ~**gesellschaft** finance company; ~**gesetz** Revenue Act, Finance Act; ~**gesetzesvorlage** finance bill; ~**gesetzgebung** financial legislation, budgetary laws; ~**hilfe** financial aid; ~**hoheit** financial sovereignty, fiscal autonomy, independent power to levy taxes etc; **f~iell** → *finanziell*; **f~ieren** → *finanzieren*; ~**ierung** → *Finanzierung*; ~**jahr** fiscal year, financial year, tax year; ~**kabinett** budget committee of the (Federal Chancellor's) cabinet; ~**kapital** financing capital; ~**kompetenz** financial responsibility; ~**konsortium** financial syndicate; ~**kraft** financial strength, financial capacity; **f~kräftig** *adj* financially strong, financially sound; ~**kredit** financing credit, financial loan; ~**kreise** financial circles; ~**krise** financial crisis; ~**lage** financial position, financial standing; ~**makler** finance broker; ~**mann** financier; ~**markt** capital market; ~**masse** total financial resources, total revenue and expenditure; ~**minister** Minister of Finance, Chancellor of the Exchequer *GB*, Secretary of the Treasury *US*; ~**ministerium** ministry of finance, Treasury, treasury department; ~**mittelaufbringung** source of working capital, raising of capital; ~**mittelbindung** absorption of funds, earmarking of funds; ~**mittelverwendung** application of funds; ~**monopol** revenue-producing monopoly, fiscal monopoly; ~**ordnung** financial regulations, financing rules; ~**periode** financial period, budgetary period; ~**plafond** financial ceiling, financial limit; ~**plan** finance plan, budget; ~**planung** budgetary planning; ~~-*srat*: *financial planning board* (*of the Federal Government*); ~**platz** financial centre; ~**politik** fiscal policy, financial policy; ~**prüfungsabteilung** auditing department; ~**recht** law of public finance; ~**rechtsweg** resort to tax courts; ~**reform** fiscal (*or* tax) reform; ~**sachverständiger** financial expert, fiscal expert; ~**schuld** monetary debt, financial indebtedness; **f~schwach** *adj* financially weak;

Finanzen

~**schwierigkeiten** financial difficulties; ~**sperre** financial embargo; ~**spritze** injection of fresh funds; ~**stabilität** financial stability; ~**statistik** financial statistics; f~**statistisch** relating to financial statistics; ~**status** statement of financial position, financial status, list of assets and liabilities; ~**struktur** financial structure; ~**system** financial system; ~**termingeschäfte** financial futures; ~**transaktion** financial operation; ~**- und Kassengeschäft** financial and cash business; ~**- und Steuerausschuß** Finance and Taxation Committee; ~**- und Steuerhoheit der Mitgliedstaaten** financial and fiscal powers of the Member States; ~**- und Zollkasse** Tax and Customs Collector's Office; ~**verfassung** financial system, constitutional rules governing public finances; ~**verhältnisse** financial conditions; ~**vermögen** financial assets, revenue-producing assets (*of the state*); ~**vertrag** financing agreement; ~**verwaltung** fiscal administration, Inland Revenue (*GB*), taxation authorities; ~**volumen** financial volume; ~**vorlage** finance bill, appropriations bill; ~**wechsel** finance bill, accommodation bill; ~**welt** financial circles; ~**wesen** finance, financial matters; ~**wirtschaft** financing business, public finances; *betriebliche* ~~: *business financing*; ~**wissenschaft** public finances; ~**wissenschaftler** (academic) expert on public finance; ~**zoll** revenue tariff, customs duty of a fiscal nature; ~**zuweisung** financial allocation, allocation of funds; ~**zwang** enforcement by Revenue authorities.

Finanzen *f/pl* finance, financial policy; **gesunde** ~ sound finances; **kommunale** ~ local-authority finances; **öffentliche** ~ public finances; **zerrüttete** ~ shattered finances, financial ruination.

finanziell *adj* financial, pecuniary.

Finanzieller Beistandsfonds der Organisation für Wirtschaftliche Zusammenarbeit und Entwicklung Financial Support Fund of the Organization for Economic Cooperation and Development.

finanzieren *v/t* to finance, to provide funds for a transaction, to supply capital for, to fund, to bankroll; *frei finanziert*: *privately financed*.

Finanzierung *f* financing, funding, financial backing, financial management; ~ **aus Abschreibungen** financing by accrued depreciation; ~ **des Haushalts** providing revenue for the budget; ~ **mit Lieferantenkredit** trade credit financing; **anteilige** ~ proportionate financing, pro rata financing; **ausgleichende** ~ compensatory financing; **bankmäßige** ~ financing by banks; **externe** ~ external financing; **interne** ~ internal financing; **kurzfristige** ~ providing short-term finance; **langfristige** ~ providing long-term finance; **nachstellige** ~ provision of money on second or junior mortgages.

Finanzierungs|abkommen financing agreement; ~**art** type of financing; ~**bank** financing bank, issuing house; ~**basis** financial base, basis for providing loans; ~**bedarf** financing requirements, borrowing requirement; ~**beitrag** financial contribution; ~**darlehen** loan for financing purposes; ~**defizit** financing deficit; ~**fragen** questions of financing; ~**firma** financing firm; ~**gebühr** financing charge; ~**geschäft** financing, transaction; ~**gesellschaft** finance company; ~~ *für Industriebedarf*: *industrial trust*; ~**hilfe** financing aid; *einmalige* ~~: *non-recurring appropriation*; ~**institut** finance company; ~**instrument** a means of raising funds, financing instrument; ~**konsortium** financing syndicate; ~**kredit** credit for financing purposes; ~**last** burden of financing charges; ~ **leasing** finance lease; ~**lücke** funding gap; gap in the financing; ~**makler** credit broker; ~**mittel** funds for financing purposes; *endgültige* ~~: *funds for ultimate investment*; *erwirtschaftete* ~~: *cash flow*; *längerfristige* ~~: *funds medium and longer term financing*; *langfristige* ~~: *long-term financing*; *nachweisbare* ~~: *ascertainable resources*; ~**modalitäten** financing terms, financing arrangements, arrangements for providing funds; ~**plan** financing scheme, financial paper, finance plan; ~**quelle** source of funds, source for financial operations; *letzte* ~~: *bank of last resort*; ~**reserven** reserves for financing; ~**rückhalt** reserve for financing; ~**saldo** financing surplus or deficit; ~**satz** financing rate; ~**träger** provider of finance, financing institution, financial backer; ~**übersicht** financing table, financing schedule; ~**unterlagen** finance documents; ~**vertrag** financing agreement; ~**verpflichtung** obligation to provide finance; ~**wechsel** finance bill (*bill of exchange or negotiable promissory note for financing purposes*); ~**zusage** promise to finance, commitment to provide finance; ~**zuschuß** public grant for financing purposes.

Finder *m* finder (of lost property); ~**lohn** finder's reward, finder's fee.

Fingerabdruck *m* finger print, dactylogram; **genetischer** ~ DNA-fingerprint.

fingiert *adj* fictitious, feigned, sham.

Finte *f* feint, trick, red herring.

Firma *f* (1) firm name, business name, name of the company, corporate name; (2) firm, business entity, enterprise or company; **e-r Kapitalgesellschaft** corporate name; **alteingesessene** ~ old-established firm; **e-e** ~ **löschen** to deregister, expunge a firm (*or* company) (*from the Commercial Register*); **e-e** ~ **sanieren** to salvage a business, to restructure a firm; **eingetragene** ~ registered firm; **erloschene** ~ defunct firm; **selbständige** ~ independent firm; **unter der** ~ **klagen oder verklagt werden** to sue or be sued in the firm's name; **unter eigener** ~ **auftreten** to trade in one's own name.

Firmen|**änderung** change of firm name; ~**anmeldung** registration of a firm; ~**aquisiteur** taker-over; ~**ausschließlichkeit** exclusive right to a firm's name; ~**bezeichnung** style (of a firm), firm-name; ~**chef** head of a firm, executive head; **f**~**eigen** *adj* company-owned; ~**eintragung** registration of business names; ~**erwerb** acquisition of a firm; ~**fortführung** continuation of a firm (*or* firm-name); ~**gebrauch** use of firm-name; *unbefugter* ~~: *improper use of a firm's name*; ~**hai** corporate raider; ~**inhaber** business proprietor; **f**~**intern** in-house; ~**jäger** corporate raider; ~**kennzeichen** fascio, logo; ~**kern** essential words of a firm name; ~**konto** a firm's bank(ing) account, corporate account; ~**kreis** range of firms covered; ~**kundengeschäft** wholesale banking; ~**leitung** senior management; ~**mantel** legal title to (and registration of) a firm, bare shell, corporate fold, corporate shell; ~**mißbrauchsverfahren** legal proceedings against misuse of a firm name; ~**nachfolger** successor in business; ~**name** = *Firma (1) qv*; ~**öffentlichkeit** compulsory registration of commercial undertakings; ~**pension** retirement pension (*from one's firm or company*); ~**recht** (1) right to a firm-name; *über die* ~~*e verfügen*: *to make use of the rights to a firm-name*, (2) law relating to firm-names; ~**register** register of firm-names; ~**rembourse** firms' documentary credits; ~**schild** sign board, trade sign, name-plate of a firm or company; ~**schutz** legal protection of firm-name; ~**siedlung** industrial site; ~**siegel** company seal, corporate seal; ~**sitz** domicile of a firm or company, registered office; ~**stempel** official stamp of a firm or company; ~**tarifvertrag** single firm collective wage agreement; ~**übergang** transfer of a firm (*or* firm-name), assignment of a firm; ~**verletzung** violation of the rights in respect of a firm-name; ~**vermögen** assets of a firm, company assets; ~**vertreter** manufacturer's agent, firm's representative; ~**wagen** company car; ~**wahrheit** genuineness of a firm's style, truthfulness of a firm's name; ~**wert** goodwill, intangible value of a business, value of plant in successful operation; *derivativer* ~~: *acquired goodwill*; *negativer* ~~: *negative goodwill*; *originärer* ~~: *created goodwill, self-generated goodwill, developed goodwill*; ~**zeichen** firm's logo; manufacturer's emblem, producer's mark; trader's name and address (*on brochures*).

firmieren *v/i* to trade under the name, to have (*or* use) the firm-name (*or* corporate name).

Firmierung *f* use of a firm-name or corporate name, choice of name.

Fisch|erlaubnis fishing licence; ~**gründe** fishing grounds; ~**recht** common of piscary, right of fishery; ~**verarbeitungsschiff** factory vessel; ~**wilderei** fish poaching; ~**wirtschaft** fishing industry; ~**zucht** breeding and raising of fish, pisciculture.

Fischerei|abkommen fishery convention; ~**ausübung** fishing; exercise of fishing rights; ~**behörden** fishery authorities; ~**beschränkungen** fishery restrictions; ~**berechtigter** holder of fishing rights; ~**berechtigung** fishing rights; ~**erzeugnisse** fish products; ~**erlaubnis** fishing licence (*US*: license); ~**fahrzeug** fishing vessel; ~**genossenschaft** fishery cooperative; ~**gerechtigkeit** fishing rights, common of piscary; ~**gesetze** fishery Acts; ~**grenzen** fishery limits; *staatliche* ~~: *national fishing limits*; ~**hoheit** jurisdiction over fisheries; ~**pachtvertrag** fishing lease; ~**pächter** holder of a fishing lease; ~**prüfung** (= Fischerprüfung) fishing licence examination; ~**rechte** fishing rights, fishery; ~**schein** fishing licence; ~**schutzzone** fishery conservation zone; ~**verwaltung** fishery administration; ~**zone** fishing zone.

Fiskal|gelder tax monies; ~**jahr** fiscal year; ~**politik** fiscal policy, government tax policy.

fiskalisch *adj* fiscal, relating to taxation.

Fiskus *m* Inland Revenue (GB), (public) treasury, revenue authorities, royal treasury, tax authorities, exchequer, *the state as financial body*, fisc, *scot*: fisk; ~**privileg** privilege of the revenue authorities.

Fix|auftrag firm order; ~**geschäft** transaction where time is of the essence, transaction at a fixed date; ~**handelskauf** fixed-date sale: *mercantile contract of sale with absolutely fixed delivery date*; ~**kauf** fixed-date purchase; ~**klausel** fixed-date clause; ~**kosten** fixed costs, overheads; ~~ *bestandteil*: *fixed-cost component*.

fixen *v/i* to sell short, to speculate for a fall in prices; to inject narcotic (by an addict).

Fixer *m* intravenous drug addict.

Fixierung *f* fixation, fixing, encapsulation; ~ **von Bedingungen** stipulation of conditions.

Fixum *n* fixed allowance, fixed remuneration, fixed salary, fixed level of remuneration.

Flächen|bedarf floor space required; ~**berechnung** area calculation; ~**bombardierung** *f* pattern bombing; ~**eigentum** surface ownership; ~**einheit** unit of area; ~**mehrerträge** greater yields per unit of area; ~**nutzungsplan** municipal development plan, land use plan, zoning map; ~**produktivität** productivity per unit of area; ~**sanierung** area rehabilitation; ~**stichprobe** area sample; ~**stillegung** taking land out of

305

production; laying an area fallow; ~~*sprogramm: soil bank (programme; US: program), set-aside program.*
Flagge *f* flag, colo(u)rs; **billige ~** flag of convenience, *(ships sailing under flags of convenience)*; **unter falscher ~** under false colo(u)rs.
Flaggen|attest certificate of registry; ~**diskriminierung** flag discrimination; ~**führung** flying a flag; ~**gruß** dipping to warships; ~**mißbrauch** misuse of flag; ~**recht** law of flag, right of flag; ~**rechtsgesetz** law concerning the right of flag; ~**wechsel** reflagging; ~**zeugnis** certificate of registry.
Flaschen|gebinde bottle container, bottle; ~**pfand** *n* returnable bottle deposit.
flau *adj exch* sluggish, inanimate, stagnant.
Flaute *f exch* slackness, dullness, sluggishness, *econ* dullness, flat season.
Fleisch|beschau meat inspection; ~**beschauer** meat inspector; ~**beschaugesetz** meat inspection law; ~**erzeugnis** meat product; ~**gesetz** law on meat production; ~**konservenhersteller** manufacturer of tinned meat; ~**waren** meat products; ~**wunde** flesh wound.
Fliegeralarm *m* air raid warning.
fliehen *v/i* to escape, to flee.
Fließband *n* assembly line, production line, conveyor-belt; ~**arbeit** assembly-line work; ~**arbeiter** assembly-line worker; ~**fertigung** assembly-line production; ~**montage** conveyor-belt assembly, assembly-line production; ~**prinzip** conveyor-belt system.
Flößereirecht *n* right of floating logs.
Flotten|abkommen naval agreement; ~**gericht** naval court-martial; ~**stützpunkt** naval base; ~**vertrag** naval treaty; ~**vorlage** navy bill.
Flöz *n* seam.
Flucht *f* escape, flight; **die ~ begünstigen** to aid the escape; ~**gefahr** risk of escape, risk of flight, danger of absconding, danger of defendant's fleeing; ~**gelder** hot money, fugitive money, flight money; ~**helfer** accessory to an escape; escape agent; ~**kapital** flight capital, hot money, fugitive money; ~**verdacht** suspicion of flight (*or* absconding); *es besteht* ~~: *there is reason to expect that he will abscond*; **f~verdächtig** suspected of intending to abscond; ~**versuch** attempt to escape, attempt to abscond.
flüchtig *adj* fugitive, unapprehended; at large; ~ **werden** to abscond, to flee from justice.
Flüchtiger *m* person on the run, fugitive.
Fluchtlinie *f* building line (of street), frontage line; ~**nplan** building regulations governing frontage lines.
Flüchtling *m* fugitive, refugee; ~**e und Vertriebene** refugees and expellees; **politischer ~** political refugee, political émigré.
Flüchtlings|amt refugee office; ~**ausweis** refugee's identity card; ~**betrieb** refugee-operated business; ~**einsatz** employment of refugees; ~**fürsorge** refugee welfare; ~**gesetz** refugee law; ~**-Jugendwohnheim** home for young refugees; ~**konvention** refugee convention; ~**rente** social-security pension for refugees; ~**siedlungsgesetz** refugee settlement law; ~**siedlungskredit** refugee settlement loan.
Flug|dienst air service; ~**gast** passenger, airline passenger; ~**hafen** → *Flughafen*; ~**lärm** noise by aircraft; ~**lehrer** pilot instructor; ~**linie** airline; ~**n** *des Durchgangsverkehrs*: *through airline operation*; ~**linienverkehr** airline traffic, air service; *internationaler* ~~: *international air service*; *planmäßiger* ~~: *scheduled air services*; ~**lotse** air traffic controller; ~**netz** airline network; ~**platz** airfield; ~**preis** air fare; ~**regeln** aviation rules; ~**risiko** flying risk; ~**schüler** trainee pilot; ~**schreiber** voice and data recorder „black box";

Flughafen / **Folge**

~**sicherheit** flight safety; ~**sicherung** air traffic control; air safety control; ~**sicherungsbehörde** air safety authority; ~**tüchtigkeit** airworthiness; ~**unfallentschädigung** air accident compensation; ~**verkehr** aviation, air travel, air transport, air service; ~**verkehrsrisiko** aviation risk; ~**wesen** aviation, aeronautics.

Flughafen *m* airport; ~**bereich** airport zone, airport control area; ~**betriebe** airport companies; ~**brauch** custom of the airport; *dem ~~ entsprechend*: *in the manner customary at the airport*; ~**polizeigruppe** airport police; ~**zollstelle** airport customs.

Flugzeug *n* aircraft, aeroplane, plane; ~**entführer** hijacker; ~**entführung** (aircraft) high jacking; ~**führer** pilot; ~**wesen** aviation, air navigation; **frei** ~ free on aircraft.

Fluktuation *f* fluctuation, turnover (of labour), job-changing, „jobhopping", flow of funds; ~**sarbeitslosigkeit** frictional unemployment; ~**sbestand** frictional float; ~**srate** level of frictional unemployment; **starke** ~ **der Belegschaft** quick turnover in staff.

fluktuieren *v/i* to fluctuate, to float, to flow.

Flur *f* village lands; cadastral district (or unit); ~**bereinigung** → *Flurbereinigung*; ~**buch** cadastral survey register; ~**hüter** field guard; ~**schaden** field damage, damage to agricultural land; ~**schutz** protection of the fields (crops); ~**stück** lot, plot *(cadastral unit)*; ~**zersplitterung** fragmented holdings; ~**zwang** compulsory cultivation.

Flurbereinigung *f* (farm)land consolidation, consolidation of fragmented holdings; re-allocation of land; ~**samt** farmland consolidation authority; ~**sdienst** farmland consolidation service; ~**sgericht** farmland consolidation tribunal; ~**sgesetz** farmland consolidation law; ~**splan** farmland consolidation plan; ~**recht** farmland consolidation law; ~**sverfahren** farmland consolidation proceedings; ~**swesen** farmland consolidation.

Fluß *m* river; flux, flow; ~**anlieger** riparian owner, owner of riparian land; ~**anliegerstaaten** riparian states; ~**bauämter** river authorities; ~**deich** river embankment; ~**diagramm** flow chart; ~**einzugsgebiet** drainage basin; ~**frachtgeschäft** carriage of goods on inland waterways; ~**frachtsendung** consignment carried by inland waterway; ~**hafen** river port; ~**konnossement** = *Ladeschein qv*; ~**ladeschein** = *Ladeschein qv*; ~**ordnung** river regulations; ~**verkehr** river traffic; ~**verschmutzung** pollution of rivers; **internationalisierter** ~ international (or internationalized) river; **öffentlicher** ~ public river; **öffentlicher schiffbarer** ~ public navigable river; **schiffbarer** ~ navigable river.

Flüssigkeitsverhältnis *n* current position (ratio), *(finance)*.

Flüssigkeitsverlust *m* ullage *(in a container of liquid)*.

Flüssigmachung *f* realization *(of assets)*; ~ **seiner Vermögenswerte** realization of one's assets; ~ **von Kapital** setting free of capital.

Flüster|dolmetschen whispered interpretation, whispering; ~**propaganda** *f* whispering campaign, whispered propaganda, smear campaign.

Flutgebiet *n* tide-land.
Föderalismus *m* federalism.
Föderalist *m* federalist.
Föderation *f* federation.
Folge *f* effect, result, consequence, succession, sequence, outcome, continuation; ~**erzeugnis** derived product; ~**kosten** consequential charges; ~**lasten** consequential burdens; ~ **leisten** to obey, to observe, to answer, to comply with; ~**nbeseitigungsanspruch** claim to remedial action, claim to nullify consequences *(of administrative acts)*;

307

folgen

~**nbeseitigungsurteil** judgment for remedial action; **f~ndermaßen** as follows; ~**pflicht** duty of compliance; ~**prämie** renewal premium, current premium; ~**prozesse** successive actions; ~**recht** right to follow the asset, right of stoppage in transitu; droit de suite (*copyright*); **f~richtig** *adj* consistent, coherent, rational, logical, logically correct; ~**richtigkeit** consistency, correct reasoning, valid conclusion; *mangelnde* ~: *inconsequence, inconsistency*; ~**sachen** ancillary proceedings (in divorce cases); ~**schaden** consequential damage (*or* loss); ~~-*Versicherung*: *consequential loss insurance*; *nicht adäquater* ~~: *remote damage*; ~**treffen** follow-up meeting; ~**verzug** consequential delay; **f~widrig** inconsequent, illogical, inconsistent; ~**widrigkeit** inconsequence; ~**wirkung** consequential effect; **adäquate** ~**n** natural (and probable) consequences; **den** ~**n begegnen** to counter (*or* to meet) the consequences; **die** ~**n auf sich nehmen** to face the consequences; **in ununterbrochener** ~ in uninterrupted succession; **lückenlose** ~ chain of causation; **unmittelbare** ~ direct result; **zur** ~ **haben** to involve, to result in, to follow.

folgen *v/i* to follow, to result in; **im f~nden** hereinafter, below; ~~ *kurz bezeichnet: hereinafter called.*

folgern *v/i* to conclude, to deduce, to infer from, to gather from.

Folgerung *f* conclusion, consequence, deduction, inference, implication.

Folien|deckel *m* (stick fast) foil lid; ~**verpackung** blister packaging.

Folioblatt *m* folio.

Folter *f* torture; ~**kammer** torture chamber.

Folterer *m* torturer.

foltern *v/t* to torture.

Folterung *f* torture; ~**sverhör** third degree practices, interrogation with torture.

Fond *m* (= *Fonds*) fund; ~**anlagen**

308

Forderung

fund investment; ~**anteil** (fund)-unit, share; ~**auflösung** liquidation of the fund; ~**beitrag** contribution to the fund; ~**s Deutsche Einheit** German Unity Fund; ~ **für unvorhergesehene Ausgaben** contingency fund; ~**überschuß** fund surplus; ~**vermögen** total funds, fund's assets; ~**verwaltung** fund management; **gemeinsamer** ~ community fund; **schwarzer** ~ surreptitious fund, slush fund (*for secret service*); **selbständig wirtschaftender öffentlichrechtlicher** ~ autonomous public fund; **thesaurierender** ~ cumulative fund, accumulative investment fund.

foppen *v/t* to fool, to tease, to rig.

Förder|(1)abgaben mining royalties; ~**ausfall** *m* decline in mining production; ~**band** conveyor belt; ~**ergebnis** mining output; ~**gebiete** development areas; ~**menge** output, tonnage (*mining*); ~**quote** output quota; ~-**Soll** planned output, output target; ~**strecke** haulage way; ~**zahl** output; ~**ziel** output target; ~**ziffern** production figures, output figures.

Förder|(2)programm economic promotion program(me), development scheme; ~**stufe** advanced primary education level (*5th and 6th classes*); ~**unterricht** remedial instruction; remedial lesson.

fordern *v/t* to demand, to claim, to require.

fördern *v/t* (*1*) to sponsor, to promote, to encourage; (*2*) *v/t* to produce *from a mine or well,* to win, to extract.

Förderer *m* sponsor, patron, promoter.

Forderung *f* demand, claim, debt due, account receivable; requirement, postulation; *pl* ~*en*: debts due and owing, receivables, outstanding accounts, accounts receivable; choses in action; ~**en an verbundene Unternehmen** receivables from affiliated companies; ~ **aus Schuldverschreibung** bonded

Forderung

claim; ~ **aus Warenlieferungen und Leistungen** accounts receivable (trade), receivables for goods and services; **~en an Konzernunternehmen** due from affiliates; **~en an Kunden** accounts receivable; **~en aus Lieferungen und Leistungen** trade debtors (*accounting*); **abgetretene** ~ assigned debt; **anerkannte** ~ admitted claim, recognized claim; **angemeldete** ~ claim submitted to the bankruptcy court; **auf e-e** ~ **verzichten** to renounce a claim, to withdraw a claim; **auf e-r** ~ **hartnäckig bestehen** to persist with (*or* on) a demand; **ausstehende** ~**en** outstanding (and open) accounts; **bedingte** ~ conditional claim; **berechtigte** ~ justified claim; **bestehende** ~ existing debt; **bestrittene** ~ disputed debt; **bevorrechtigte** ~ preferred claim, preferential claim, preferential debt, privileged claim, prior claim; **bezifferte** ~ liquidated demand, demand in (terms of) figures; **buchmäßige** ~ book debt; **dinglich gesicherte** ~ security for money, secured debt; **dubiose** ~ doubtful debt, problematic debts; **e-e** ~ **abgelten** to discharge a debt; **e-e** ~ **abtreten** to assign a claim, to transfer a debt; **e-e** ~ **anmelden** to prove a debt (*in bankruptcy*), to prove against the estate; **e-e** ~ **auf etwas erheben** to claim sth; **e-e** ~ **einklagen** to sue for the recovery of a debt; **e-e** ~ **eintreiben** to collect a debt; **e-e** ~ **erlassen** to forgo a debt; **e-e** ~ **geltend machen** to claim, to prefer a claim; **e-e** ~ **gerichtlich geltend machen** to assert a claim by legal action, to sue for a debt; **e-e** ~ **im Gesellschaftskonkurs nachweisen** to prove a debt in liquidation; **e-e** ~ **ist abgewiesen worden** a claim has been dismissed; **e-e** ~ **unterstützen** to endorse (*or* support) a claim (*or* plea); **einklagbare** ~ debt recoverable by action; **entstandene** ~ accruals receivable (*not yet matured*); **erdichtete** ~ fictitious claim; **erloschene** ~ discharged debt; **fällige** ~ debt due, liquid debt, due and payable debt, matured claim; **festgestellte** ~ ascertained claim (*bankruptcy*); **freiverfügbare** ~**en gegen das Ausland** freely convertible foreign balances; **gegenseitige** ~**en** mutual claims; **gegenwärtige und zukünftige** ~ debts owing and accruing; **gepfändete** ~ garnished debt; **geldwerte** ~ monetary claim; **geringfügige** ~ minor claim; **gesetzliche** ~ legal claim; **gesicherte** ~ secured claim; **gestundete** ~ deferred claim; **hartnäckige** ~ persistent demand (*or* claim); **hypothekarisch gesicherte** ~ mortgage debt; **langfristige** ~ long-term receivables; **laufende** ~ current outstanding accounts; **liquide** ~ liquidated demand, matured debt; **nachrangige** ~ subordinate debt; **nicht bevorrechtigte** ~ ordinary debt; **nicht gesicherte** ~ unsecured claim; **nichtübertragbare** ~ non-assignable right; **nichtverbriefte** ~ non-bonded claim; **sichere** ~ good debts, reliable debtors; **sonstige** ~**en** other accounts, miscellaneous debts; **streitgegenständliche** ~ litigious claim; **strittige** ~ disputed claim; **täglich fällige** ~**en** claims payable on demand; **titulierte** ~ enforceable claim, judgment debt, debt of record; debt in the form of an enforceable instrument; **unbestrittene** ~ undisputed debt; **uneinbringliche** ~**n** irrecoverable outstanding accounts, uncollectable reiceivables, uncollectibles; **ungedeckte** ~ unsecured claim; **unpfändbare** ~**n** ungarnishable third-party debts, outstanding accounts exempt from garnishment; **unverzinsliche** ~**en** non-interest-bearing debts; **verbriefte** ~ bonded claim; **verjährte** ~ statute-barred debt, outlawed debt, debt barred by prescription; **verzinsliche** ~ active debt, interest-bearing debt; **vollstreckbare** ~

Forderungsabschreibung

judgment debt, enforceable claim; **vorrangige** ~ preferred debt, prior claim; **zivilrechtliche** ~ civil claim; **zweifelhafte** ~ doubtful claim, *pl* doubtful debts.

Forderungs|abschreibung writing-off of bad debts; ~**abtretung** assignment (*of claims or of debts*); *formlose* ~~: *equitable assignment*; *gesetzliche* ~~: *assigment by operation of law*; ~**anerkennung** allowance of claims; ~**anmeldung** proof of debt (*in bankruptcy*); ~**arrest** order of attachment of debts; ~**ausfälle** bad debt losses; ~**ausfallskosten** bad debt expense; ~**ausfallversicherung** accounts receivable insurance; **f~berechtigt** entitled to claim; ~**berechtigter** obligee, promisee, rightful claimant; ~**eingänge** collections; ~**kauf** purchase of accounts receivable; ~**nachweis** proof of debts, proof of claims; ~**pfändung** garnishment, attachment of a debt, order of attachment; ~**pfändungsverfahren** garnishee proceedings; ~**posten** (current) asset item; ~**recht** right to recover (*a debt*); right to claim, chose in action; ~**saldo** net claims; ~**stundung** respite; ~**tilgung** discharge of a debt by payment, redemption of a debt; ~**übernahme** assumption of a claim; ~**übergang** subrogation, transmission of claims; *gesetzlicher* ~~: *assignment by operation of law, legal subrogation*; ~**übertragung** transfer of claim, assignment; ~**vermächtnis** legacy of an outstanding account, testamentary disposition of claims; ~**verletzung** breach of an obligation; *positive* ~~: *breach of contract, breach of an obligation other than by delay or impossibility*.

Förderung (1) *f* promotion, backing; ~ **der Bildung** advancement of education; ~ **der Ersparnisbildung** promotion of savings.

Förderung (2) *f* production (*from mine, oil well etc*), extraction.

Förderungsbedürftigkeit financial need for vocational promotion;

310

Form

~**fähigkeit** suitability for promotion; *or* grants-in-aid; **gebiet** development area; ~**maßnahmen** measures of encouragement, aid scheme; ~**pflicht** duty to expedite the case, requirement of promptness in court proceedings; ~**plan** development target; ~**prämie** output bonus; ~**programm** promotion scheme; ~**wille** beneficial intention; **f~würdig** *adj* deserving encouragement, worthy of promotion, eligible for promotion; ~**zuschlag** incentive bonus, subsidy; ~**zuwendungen** promotional subsidies.

forensisch *adj* forensic.

Forfaitierung *f* non-recourse financing, forfaiting.

Form *adj* form, formalities; ~**blatt** blank, form, preprinted form; ~**bogengutachten** expert opinion on a standard form; ~**enmißbrauch** misuse of legal forms; ~**erfordernis** form requirement, compulsion to use a specified form, physical requirement; ~**fehler** error in the form, formal defect, want of form, irregularity in form, flaw; **f~frei** exempt from formalities, informal; ~**freiheit** informality, absence of formal requirements; ~**gebung** industrial design, styling; **f~gerecht** *adj* correct as to form, in the proper form, in due form, *adv* duly; ~**gestalter** industrial designer; **f~gültig** formally correct; ~**gültigkeit** formal validity; ~**kaufmann** merchant by legal form: *incorporated organization having the status of a merchant*; **f~los** informal, without formality, verbal, common form; ~**losigkeit** absence of formal requirements, informality; ~**mangel** want of legal form, noncompliance with required form; ~**mißbrauch** abuse of formal requirements; ~**nichtigkeit** nullity due to lack of legally prescribed form; ~**prüfer** *pat* formalities examiner; ~**prüfung** *pat* formalities examination; ~**sachbearbeiter** *pat* formalities officer;

~sache matter of form, formality, pro forma matter, routine; *reine* ~~: *just a formality*; **~verletzung** want of legal form, noncompliance with required form; **~vorschrift** formal requirement, prescribed form; *pl*: formalities, formal requisites, formal requirements, formal rules; *gesetzliche* ~~: *formal legal requirements, Statute of Frauds (written form)*; *wesentliche* ~~: *essential formalities*; **f~widrig** contrary to form, not in compliance with formal requirements; **f~zulässig** formally admissible; **~zwang** compulsory legal form, mandatory compliance with statutory form; *gewillkürter* ~~: *form stipulated by contract*; **ästhetische ~schöpfungen** *pat* aesthetic creations; **äußere ~** physical form; **die ~ wahren** to comply with the formalities, to fulfill the formal requirements; **feierliche ~** solemn form; **gesetzliche ~** statutory form, form required by law, legal form; **in der vom Gesetz vorgesehenen ~** in the manner prescribed by law; **in e–e ~ bringen** to reduce to a form, to draft; **in gehöriger ~** in due form; **notarielle ~** notarial form, (in the) form of a notarial document; **strenge ~** stringent form; **vorgeschriebene ~** prescribed form, legal form, due form.

formal *adj* formal, regular; technical.

Formal|beleidigung verbal insult, abusive language, *utterance defamatory per se*; **~delikt** technical offence; **~einwand** technical objection, technical traverse; **~jurist** legal purist; **~prüfung** *pat* formalities examination; **~prüfer** *pat* formalities examiner; **f~rechtlich** technical, formalistic, in accordance with the letter of law; **~versicherung** social insurance by estoppel; **~vertrag** pro forma agreement; a contract in the usual form, standard agreement.

Formalien *f/pl* formalities, matters of form, formal requirements.

Formalismus *m* formalism.
Formalität *f* formality; **e–e bloße ~** a mere matter of form.
Format-Normen *f/pl* standard formats.
Formel *f* formula, phrase.
formell *adj* formal, ceremonial, procedural; **~ und materiell** in form and in fact, in procedural and substantive law.
förmlich *adj* in due form, official.
Förmlichkeit *f* formality, formal requirement(s); **leere ~** formalism, mere formalities.
Formular *n* form, printed form, blank form; **~brief** form letter; **~buch** book of precedents, collection of standard forms; **~klausel** standard form clause; **~kommentar** *commentary based on standard documents*; **f~mässig** (rendered) on standard forms, on a form, according to (printed) form; **~vertrag** standard-form contract; **~wesen** *matters concerned with printed forms*, paperwork;
formulieren *v/t* to formulate, to word, to couch, to draft;
Formulierung *f* wording, formulation, form of words, phrasing, drafting; **~sfehler** drafting error; **genaue ~** precise wording, concise wording; **zutreffende ~** apt words.
Forschung *f* research; **angewandte ~** applied research; **betriebspsychologische ~** work attitude and morale research; **betriebswissenschaftliche ~** business research; **freie ~** uncontrolled research; **wissenschaftliche ~** scientific research; **zweckfreie ~** pure research.
Forschungs|abteilung research department; **~anstalt** research institute; **~arbeit** research work; **~haushalt** research budget; **~hilfe** research aid; **~kosten** research costs; **~vorhaben** research project; **~zulage** extra allowance for research work.
Forst *m* (cultivated) forest, woodland, (managed) forest; **~akade-**

mie school for forestry (studies); ~**amt** (Woodland and) Forestry, Commissioners; ~**aufsichtsbehörde** forest supervisory office; ~**beamter** forester, forest officer, forestry official; ~**benutzung** forest utilization; ~**einrichtung** forest inventory and planning; ~**ertrag** forest produce, yield of a forest; ~**frevel** serious infringement of forest laws; ~**gesetz** Forest Act; ~**polizei** forest (police) inspectorate; ~**recht** forest law; ~**rechtegesetz** Act concerning (ancient) forest rights; ~**regal** sovereign rights in respect of forest; ~**rügesache** case involving violation of forest regulations; ~**sachverständiger** forestry expert; ~**schutz** forest protection; ~**strafrecht** law of forest offences; ~**verwaltung** forest administration; ~**widerstand** obstruction of a forestry officer; ~**wirtschaft** forestry, forest managements, sylviculture; forest economics; ~**wirtschaftsjahr** forestry year; ~**wirtschaftspolitik** forestry policy, lumbering industry policy.

Fort|bestand continued existence; ~**bestehen** continued existence, continuation; f~**bilden** v/t to provide further education, (cf. Fortbildung); ~**bildung** → Fortbildung; ~**bleiben** non-attendance; ~**dauer** continuance, continuation; f~**dauern** v/i to continue, to last, to persist; ~**entwicklung** continued development; lineare ~~: growth at the same rate; ~**fall** cessation, discontinuance, disappearance; ~**führung** continuation; ~**gang** continuance; ~~ des Verfahrens: continuation of the proceedings; ~**geltung** continued validity; f~**gesetzt** continued, continual, constant, incessant; ~**kommen** career advancement, occupational advancement; promotion; f~**lassen** to omit, to delete; ~**lassung** omission, deletion; ~**laufen** m continuance; escape, elopement; f~**laufend** adj continuous, consecutive; ~~ numeriert: numbered consecutively; ~**pflanzung** procreation; ~**schaffen** m removal, asportation; widerrechtliches ~~: asportation (theft); ~**schätzung** estimated forward projection; f~**schreiben** v/t to carry forward, to project to a subsequent date, to extrapolate, to keep listed, to continue as a register; ~**schreibung** continuation of registration, renewal of assessment of value, updating, forward projection, extrapolation; ~~sbescheid: notice of revaluation for assessment, ~~sveranlagung: revaluation for assessment; f~**schreitend** adj progressive; ~**schritt** → Fortschritt; ~**setzung** → Fortsetzung; ~**wirkung** continued effect, after-effect.

Fortbildung f further education, advanced training, adult education; **berufliche ~** further vocational training; ~s ~swesen: extension work; **betriebliche ~** in-house training, executive training.

Fortschritt f progress, advancement, improvement; ~**spartei** progress party; ~**srate** growth ratio; **auffallender ~ der Technik** marked technological advancement; **merklicher ~** marked advancement; **sozialer ~** social progress; **ständiger ~** progressive advancement; **technischer ~** technological progress, technical advancement, advance in the art (pat), technical advance.

Fortsetzung f continuation, sequel; **~ der Sitzung** adjourned meeting, continuation of the meeting; **~ des Mietverhältnisses** continuation of tenancy; **~ e-s ruhenden Verfahrens** revival of an action; **~ folgt** to be continued; ~**stat** continuing offence; ~**sverbot** prohibition to continue (unlawful activity), order to desist; injunction; ~**szusammenhang** continuation of offence; **automatische ~sklausel** renewal clause (by stated terms), continuation (of partnership) clause; **in ~en veröffentlichen** to serialize.

Fracht f freight, load, cargo, goods for transport, carriage; voraus-

bezahlte ~: *prepaid freight*; **~abnahme** acceptance of shipment; **~abschluss** freight fixing; **~angebot** freight offered; **~ankunftsbenachrichtigung** landing notice; **~annahme** freights office, acceptance of transport goods; **~annahmeschein** shipping note; **~anspruch** freight claim; **~ausgangspunktsystem** basing point system; **~ausgleich** freight equalization; **~basis** freight basis, *agreed delivery point from which freight is charged;* **~bedingungen** terms of freight; **~behälter** container; **~berechnung** calculation of freight, freight charges; ~ **bezahlt** freight paid; ~ **bezahlt der Empfänger** freight forward; **~bezahlung im voraus** advance freight; **~brief** consignment note, (railway) waybill, straight bill of lading; railroad bill of lading *US*; ~~*doppel*: *duplicate consignment note, counterfoil waybill*; **~buch** book of cargo (loading); **~buchung** freight booking; **~büro** freight office; **~dampfer** freighter; **~enausgleich** adjustment of freight rates, equalization of freight rates; **~enmakler** shipping-broker; **~enmaklergeschäft** ship brokerage; **~enprüfung** examination of transportation charges; **~ermäßigung** freight reduction; **~ertrag** freight receipts, freight revenue; *die zu erwartenden* ~*erträge*: *anticipated freight*; **~flugverkehr** air freight service; **~flugzeug** freight carrier (plane), freighter; **f~frei** carriage paid, freight prepaid, transport at no charge to customer; freight or carriage paid; **~führer** carrier, haulage contractor *by land or inland waterways*, shipper (US); **~führerpfandrecht** carrier's lien; ~ **für die ganze Reise** voyage freight; **~gebühr** freight, freight charge, carriage charge; **~geschäft** carrying trade, carriage of goods, freight transaction; **f~günstig** *adj* favourably located from the point of view

of freight costs; **~gut** cargo, goods for transport; goods sent by freight service; ordinary freight; ~~*sendung*: *consignment by goods train*; *als* ~~: *by freight train* (= *goods train*); ~~*verkehr*: *slow goods traffic*; **~halle** freight centre; **~handbuch** cargo manual; **~hilfegebiet** area of publicly supported freight rates; ~ **im voraus bezahlt** freight prepaid; **~inkasso** collection of freight charges; **f~intensiv** *adj* involving a large volume of freight; high-freight; **~kosten** freight costs, freight charges, shipping expense; **~kostennachnahme** carriage forward, collect shipment; **~kostenübernahme durch den Verkäufer** freight absorption, carriage charged to seller of goods; **~kosten zahlt der Empfänger** charges forward; **~kredit** credit allowed for freight payment; **~leistung** transportation service, freight earnings; **~lohn** freight; **~makler** freight broker; **~manifest des Luftfahrzeugs** aircraft cargo manifest; **~notierung** freight quotation; **~papier** transport document; **~parität** freight parity; ~ **per Nachnahme** freight collect, freight forward; **~police** freight policy; **~prüfer** freight examiner (*law agent in freight disputes*); **~rabatt** freight discount; **~raten** freight rates; *unwirtschaftliche* ~~: *uncommercial rates (dumping)*; **~raum** freight capacity, shipping space; **~rechnung** freight note, freight account; **~recht** law concerning carriage of goods; **~satz** freight rate, rate of freight; **~schiff** cargo vessel, cargo ship; **~stundung** freight deferment; **~tarif** freight rates; ~~*liste*: *rates tariff*; **~tonne** freight ton; **~traditionspapier** bill of lading; **~- und Liegegeld** freight and demurrage; **f~ungünstig** *adj* unfavourably located in regard to freight; **~urkunden** freight documents, shipping documents; **~verkehr** freight traffic; **~vermittler** freight agent;

Frage   **Fraktionsbeschluß**

~**versicherung** cargo insurance, freight insurance; ~**versender** consignor, shipper; ~**vertrag** contract of carriage, freight contract; ~**vorausbezahlt** freight prepaid; ~**waggon** freight waggon, boxcar; ~ **zahlbar am Bestimmungsort** freight payable at destination; ~ **zahlt der Empfänger** freight payable at destination; ~**zettel** way bill; ~**zuschlag** charge for excess freight, primage; ~**zustellgebühren** terminal charges; ~**zustellung** freight delivery; **vorausbezahlte** ~ prepaid freight.

Frage *f* question, problem, query; ~**bogen** questionnaire; ~**pflicht** *duty (of the court) to put questions to the parties (in order to clarify the issue);* ~**recht** right to interrogate *(witnesses);* ~**steller** questioner, interrogator; ~**stellung** formulation of a question, statement of a problem; ~**stunde** question time; **der** ~ **ausweichen** to evade the question; **die** ~ **erhebt sich** = *es erhebt sich die* ~ *qv;* **die** ~ **wird zugelassen** the question is admitted, objection overruled; **die zur Entscheidung stehende** ~ the question at issue; **e-e** ~ **aufwerfen** to raise a point; **e-e** ~ **entstehen lassen** to raise a point; **e-e** ~ **nur mit ja oder nein zu beantwortende** ~ categorical question *(answer yes or no!);* **e-e** ~ **vorlegen** to propound a question, to submit a question; **entscheidende** ~ crucial question, critical question, key question, fundamental issue; **entscheidungserhebliche** ~ determinative issue, issue, material issue, question in dispute; **erledigte** ~ closed issue; **es erhebt sich die** ~ the question arises *(whether ..., as to whether);* **etwas in** ~ **ziehen** to question; **hypothetische** ~ hypothetical question; **informatorische** ~ exploratory question; **in** ~ **stellen** to question, dispute; **juristische** ~ legal question; **justistiable** ~ justiciable issue; **materiell-rechtliche** ~ matter of substance, point of substantive law; **nebensächliche** ~ secondary question; **offene** ~ a question that remains open, undecided question, moot point; **präjudizielle** ~ question involving a precedent; **rechtserhebliche** ~ issue of legal relevance, genuine issue; **schwebende** ~ unsolved problem, undecided question, a matter that is in abeyance, a pending matter; **schwierige** ~ vexed question; **sich genauer mit e-r** ~**befassen** to deal with a question in more detail; **streitige** ~ = *strittige* ~ *qv;* **strittige** ~ question in dispute; **umstrittene** ~ controversial question; **verfahrensrechtliche** ~ procedural question.

fragen *v/t* to question, to put a question (to s. o), to pose a question.

fraglich *adj* questionable, under discussion, before the court; disputable, dubious, involved, at issue, in question.

Fraglichkeit *f* questionableness, disputability, dubious nature.

fraglos *adv* unquestionably, beyond dispute.

fragwürdig *adj* questionable, doubtful, problematical, suspect.

Fraktion *f* parliamentary group, parliamentary party, fraction, odd lot.

Fraktions|beschluß resolution adopted by a parliamentary party; ~**disziplin** obligation to vote for the party (line); ~**führer** parliamentary leader of a party, floor leader *(US);* ~**geschäftsführer** chief whip; ~~ *der Regierungspartei*: *chief government whip, parliamentary manager;* **f**~**los** *adj* independent; ~**mitglied** parliamentary party member; ~**sitzung** meeting of the parliamentary party; ~**vorlage** bill introduced by a parliamentary party; ~**vorsitzender** chairman (or leader) of a parliamentary party, floor leader; ~**wechsel** changing sides, switching from one political party to another; ~**wechsler** defector; ~**zwang** obligation to vote according to the parliamentary party's decision, obligation to take the party line, whip; *den ~ aufheben*: *to take off the whips, to allow a free vote*; *den ~~ nicht einhalten*: *to break the whip.*

Franchise *f* franchise (*in the meaning of a business license only*); exemption, margin; **~geber** franchisor; **~-Geschäfte** franchising-business; **~klausel** franchise clause; **~nehmer** franchisee, licencee under a franchising agreement; **~-Unternehmen** franchise enterprise; **~vertrag** franchising (agreement).

Frankatur *f* prepayment of postage, prepayment of carriage (= *freight*); **~vermerk** freight payment marking; **~zwang** compulsory prepayment (of freight).

frankieren *v/t* to stamp, to prepay postage.

Frankiermaschine *f* franking machine, postage meter.

frankiert *adj* stamped, postage-free, post paid.

franko *adv* free of charge, postpaid, prepaid, postage-free, free delivered at ..., carriage paid, freight free, freight paid, all charges paid, uncharged.

Frau *f* woman; **alleinstehende ~** single woman; **berufstätige ~** gainfully employed woman; **friedensstörende ~** perturbatrix; **geschiedene ~** divorced woman, divorcée, feme discovert; **ledige ~** unmarried female, single woman; **unbescholtene ~** innocent woman, a woman of stainless character, unblemished woman; **unverheiratete ~** single woman, unmarried female, spinster, feme sole.

Frauen|arbeit women's work, a woman's job, work done by women, employment of women; **~arbeitsschutz** employment and work protection of women; **~bekanntschaft** female acquaintance; **~bewegung** feminist movement; **~emanzipation** emancipation (of women); **~gut** married women's property; **~handel** white slave trade; **~haus** refuge for battered women, shelter for battered wives; **~kriminalität** crime rate of female offenders; **~löhne** wages paid to female workers; **~rechtlerin** feminist, suffragette; **~sperson** female person; *ledige ~~*: *feme sole, spinster*; **~wahlrecht** women's suffrage, female suffrage; **~zuschläge** premium for women's work.

Frei|aktie bonus share, stock dividend; **f~ an Bord** free on board (f.o.b.); **~antwort** prepaid answer; **~bank** public meat, cheap-meat department; **f~ Bau** free to building site; **~berufler** self-employed person, free-lance(r), (lawyer) in private practice; **f~beruflich** *adj* self-employed, in private practice, freelance, independent, on a (purely) contractual basis; **~betrag** → *Freibetrag*; **~beweis** moral evidence, informal evidence; **~bezirk** free zone (of port); **f~bleibend** *adj* subject to change (without notice), subject to prior sale, not binding, without obligation; **~bordzeugnis** loadline certificate, freeboard certificate; **~brief** carte blanche; **~exemplar** free copy, presentation copy; **~fahrkarte** free ticket, free pass, complimentary ticket; **~fahrschein** = *~fahrkarte qv*; **~fahrt** free ride, free trip; **~gabe** → *Freigabe*; **~gang** *m* free passage within goal liberties, *employment of privileged prisoners outside of prison;* **~gänger** prisoner privileged to be out of prison temporarily (*for work etc*); **f~geben** *v/t* to release, to decontrol, to derequisition; **~gelände** open ground; **f~gemacht** prepaid, postage-free; **~gepäck** free (allowance of) luggage; **f~gestellt** optional, privileged, exempt; **~gewicht** weight allowance, weight allowed free; **~grenze** exemption limit, tax allowance; free quota, permitted limit, limit of tax exemption; **~gut** *hist* alod; goods in free circulation, duty-free goods; **~gutsbesitzer** *hist* alodiary; **~hafen** free port; **~haltebedürfnis** (*e-s*

315

Warenzeichens) a need to keep free the use (*of a trademark*); **f~halten** *v/t* to keep open (*offer*); **~haltung** keeping (offer) open, indemnification; ~~*sverpflichtung*: *indemnity, obligation to save harmless;* **~handel** free trade; **~sabkommen** free-trade agreement; **~handelsregelung** free-trade rules; **~handelszone** free-trade area; **f~händig** *adv* by private contract (*or* treaty), in the open market, freely negotiated, (sold) by bargaining; **~händlerisch** marketeering; **~heit** → *Freiheit;* **~heitsstrafe** → *Freiheitsstrafe;* **~jahr** year of grace, year of exemption (*from redemption, annuities, interest etc.*), redemption-free year; **~karte** complimentary ticket, free ticket; **~kauf** ransom, redemption (*of a hostage, prisoner etc.*); **~konto** unrestricted account; **f~ konvertierbar** freely convertible; **~ladebahnhof** station with a direct loading ramp; **~ladeverkehr** full truck traffic (*US*); **~lager** bonded warehouse; dump; **~land** open land; **f~ Längsseite Seeschiff** free alongside ship (*f.a.s.*); **f~lassen** to release; **~lassung** release (*from custody*); ~~ *gegen Kaution*: *release on bail, discharge on recognisance;* *bedingte* ~~: *conditional discharge;* **~lassungsbeschluß** release order; **~leitung** overhead (transmission) line, open wire; **~liste** free list (*list of tax-free goods, or of goods allowed to be imported*); **f~ Lkw** free on truck (*lorry*); **f~machen** to vacate (*a seat, a room*); to disengage o.s.; to prepay postage, to stamp; **~machung** vacating, disengagement; prepayment (of postage); **~marke** postage stamp; **~markt** free market; **~passagier** deadhead, passenger using a free ticket; **~porto** return postage; **~portoprivileg** franking privilege; **~raum** margin of choice, sphere of uncontrolled activity; **~raumklausel** clear space clause; **~rechtslehre** (=) (*adjudication based on equitable principles only*); **~sasse** freeholder, frank(-)tenant,

yeoman, owner of allodial land; **~sassengut** frank tenement, freehold; **~schaffender** free-lance worker, self-employed person; **f~ Schiff** free on board ship; **~schärler** franc-tireur, guerilla; **~schärlerei** guerilla-warfare, actions by franc-tireurs; **~schicht** free shift, nonwork shift, **f~setzen** to lay off, to make redundant; **~setzung** release, laying off; **f~sprechen** to acquit (*s.o. of a charge*); to release (*apprentice*) from articles; **~gesprochen**: *acquitted; tried and discharged;* **~sprechung** acquittal; exoneration, release of an apprentice from articles; **~spruch** acquittal, verdict of not-guilty, order of discharge; ~~ *aus Rechtsgründen*: *acquittal on a point of law;* ~~ *mangels Beweises*: *discharge, verdict of "not proven" Scot;* ~~ *wegen erwiesener Unschuld*: *honourable acquittal;* ~~ *von allen Anklagepunkten*: *acquittal on all charges;* ~~ *wegen Unzurechnungsfähigkeit*: *verdict of guilty but insane;* **~staat** republic; **~stätte** sanctuary; **f~stellen** to indemnify s.o. against (*or from*), to hold s.o. harmless against, to exempt, to give s.o. a choice; to hold safeguarded (against a risk); to release from work; **~stellung** → *Freistellung;* **~stempler** postage meter, franking machine; **~tod** suicide; **~treppe** outdoor steps; **~umschlag** stamped addressed envelope; **~veranlagung** voluntary assessment; **~verband** voluntary district combination (*between local communities for a special purpose*); **~verkauf** voluntary sale; **~verkehr** → *Freiverkehr;* **f~ von Beschädigung** free from damage, free from leakage; **f~ Werk** free at factory gate; **f~ Waggon** free on rail (*f.o.r.*); **~werden e-s Sitzes** occurrence of vacancy; **~wild** unprotected game, easy victim, fair game; **f~willig** voluntary, non-obligatory, spontaneous; **~willigkeit** voluntariness, optionality, spontaneity; ~~*sprinzip*: *principle* *of voluntary action, voluntarism*; **f~wirtschaftlich** *adj* pertaining to free enterprise, free-enterprise *adj*; **~zeichen** free mark, unprotected mark, non-registrable trade-mark; ringing tone (*tel.*); **f~zeichnen** *v/reflex* to exempt (*from liabilities*) by standard terms of contract, to stipulate exemption, to contract (oneself) out (*of liability etc*), to sign a saving clause; **~zeichnung** → *Freizeichnung*; **~zeit** → *Freizeit*; **f~zügig** *adj* unrestricted, at large, free to move, liberal; **~zügigkeit** → *Freizügigkeit*.

Freibetrag *m* free allowance, tax-free allowance, relief, personal allowance, (flat) exemption; ~ **für außergewöhnliche Belastungen** allowance for exceptional charges; **~sgrenze** threshold; **allgemeiner** ~ general tax-free margin; **persönlicher** ~ personal tax exemption, personal relief; **steuerlicher** ~ tax allowance.

Freier *m* (1) freemen, (2) customer of a prostitute.

Freigabe *f* release, clearance, liberalization, decontrol; **~bescheid** advance permission; ; ~ **e-s gesperrten Kontos** release of a blocked account; **~erklärung** clearance certificate; **~klausel** partial release (of collateral) clause; **~mitteilung** release note; **~nummer** release number; **~vertrag** release contract; ~ **von Mitteln** release of funds; ~ **zur Veröffentlichung** release (for publication).

Freiheit *f* freedom, liberty; ~ **der Lehre** "freedom of the chair"; ~ **der Hohen See** freedom of the high seas; ~ **der Meere** freedom of the seas; ~ **der öffentlichen Meinungsäußerung** freedom of speech; ~ **der Person** personal freedom; ~ **der Schiffahrt** freedom of navigation; ~ **des Fischfangs** freedom of fishing; ~ **von Furcht** freedom from fear; ~ **von Not** freedom from want; **akademische** ~ academic freedom; **natürliche** ~ natural liberty; **persönliche** ~ personal liberty.

freiheitlich *adj* liberal, free (and constitutional), freedom-loving.

Freiheits|beraubung false imprisonment, duress of imprisonment, false arrest, unlawful detention, detaining a person against his will; deprivation of liberty; ~~ *im Amt*: *false imprisonment by an official*; **~beschränkung** restraint, restriction of liberty; **~delikte** offenses against a person's liberty; **~entziehung** restraint, detention, deprivation of liberty, incarceration; **~entzug** = *~entziehung qv*; *~~srate*: *rate of incarceration*; **~schutz** protection of a person's liberty (*by the criminal law*); **~strafe** → *Freiheitsstrafe*.

Freiheitsstrafe *f* imprisonment, prison sentence, jail sentence; ~ **mit unbestimmter Strafdauer** indeterminate sentence; **ersatzweise verhängte** ~ imprisonment for failure to pay a fine; **kurzfristige** ~ short term of imprisonment; **lebenslängliche** ~ (= *lebenslange*) imprisonment for life, life sentence; **mit** ~ **bedroht** imprisonable, threatened with imprisonment; **seine** ~ **verbüßen** to serve one's term of imprisonment; **teilverbüßte** ~ partly served sentence; **zeitige** ~ prison sentence for a term of years, determinate sentence.

Freiraum *m* freedom to develop.

Freistellung *f* exemption; release, dispensation, (grant of a) leave of absence, relief from work; ~ **von Haftung** indemnity against liability; ~ **von Steuern** exemption from taxation.

Freistellungs|anspruch right of indemnity, right of recourse (against debtor); claim to be held safeguarded; **~bescheid** notice of exemption; **~erklärung** deed of general release, saving declaration; declaration of inapplicability; **~garantie** guarantee of indemnity; ~**klausel** exemption clause; ~**verfahren** exemption proceedings; ~**verfügung** notice of exemption, release order; ~**verpflichtung** indemnity obligation.

Freiverkehr *m exch* curb market, unofficial market, unofficial stock transactions, unofficial business, over-the-counter market (*or* trade), open market, curb trading; ~**aktie** unquoted share; **geregelter** ~ regulated unofficial dealing; **im** ~ **gehandelt** over-the-counter.

Freiverkehrs|börse Unlisted Securities Market; curb exchange, unofficial market, over-the-counter market; ~**kurs** street market price, free market rate, *pl* street prices; ~**makler** curb(stone) broker, outside broker, outsider; ~**markt** street market, unofficial market, outside market, *cf* ~*börse*; ~**notierung** unquoted list; ~**umsätze** outside transactions; ~**werte** unlisted securities, curb stock, over-the-counter securities.

Freiwilligkeit *f* voluntariness, voluntary nature, non-obligatory nature.

Freizeichnung *f* agreed exemption from liability, contracting out; ~**sklausel** (liability) exemption clause, *ins* excepted perils clause, non-liability clause, memorandum clause, non warranty clause, saving clause, saving errors and omissions clause (S.E.A.O.), negligence clause.

Freizeit *f* spare time, leisure time, free time, time off; ~**aktivitäten** leisure activities; ~**arrest**; free-time custody ~**arrestanstalt** detention centre; ~**ausgleich** compensation for overtime by time off, time-off in lieu (*of overtime pay*); ~**bedürfnisse** leisure-time needs; ~**beschäftigung** leisure-time occupation, spare-time job; ~**gesellschaft** leisure society; ~**gestalter** recreation director; ~**gestaltung** organization of leisure time; ~**kleidung** leisure wear; ~**heim** leisure centre, recreational centre; ~**programm** recreational program(me); ~**veranstaltung** leisure-time event; ~**wert** value of free time, recreational value; **absolute** ~ discretionary time; **bezahlte** ~ paid holiday schemes.

Freizügigkeit *f* freedom of movement, (*vocation and/or residential mobility*); free choice of residence and occupation, free movement of labour, free movement, unrestricted mobility; ~ **der Arbeitskräfte**: industrial mobility, mobility of labour; ~ **des Devisenverkehrs**: freedom of exchange movements; **berufliche** ~ freedom to provide services.

Fremd|abtreibung abortion by a third party; ~**anzeige** third-party deposit notice (*deposited security belongs to someone else*); ~**arbeiter** foreign worker, *collectively:* "guest workers", immigrant workers, foreign labo(u)r, outside labour (*not family*); ~**aufwendungen** extraneous expenses; ~**begünstigung** aiding and abetting another; ~**beilagen** inserted printed matter; ~**beleg** external voucher; ~**belieferung** outsourcing deliveries to/from a third party; ~**besitz** possession for another, possession as a bailee; ~**besitzer** possessor as bailee, a person who possesses on behalf of someone else; ~**bestimmung** outside control; **f~bezogen** obtained from third parties; ~**depot** deposit for a third party, safekeeping for another; ~**emissionsgeschäft** issuing securities for the account of others; ~**erzeugnis** another maker's product, not our own make; ~~**se**: *products/equipment purchased;* ~**fabrikat** outside product; ~**finanzierung** debt financing, external financing, financing with borrowed money, debt financing; ~**finanzierungsquote** proportion financed with outside funds, borrowing ratio; ~**geld** third-party money, trust money, trust funds; borrowed

Fremdenfeindlichkeit

funds; ~~er: third-party funds; deposits and borrowed funds; ~herrschaft foreign rule; ~kapital loan capital, borrowed capital, debt capital, loan stock; outside capital; langfristiges ~~: long-term loans; ~~geber: debt supplier; ~konto third-party account, trust account; ~körper foreign matter, extraneous element, alien element; ~leistung service rendered by an outside party (or third party), outside service; ~material bought material, material from outside source; ~mittel borrowed funds, borrowings, debts; ~rechtserbschein → Erbschein; ~rente social insurance pension for refugees, stateless aliens and others allowing for previous employment in a third country (before flight or expulsion); ~rettung rescue of another person; ~scheck third-party cheque; ~stoffverbot prohibition of adding adulterating substances, ban on impurities; ~stoffverordnung : anti-adulteration ordinance (of D 1959); ~umsatz external sales, sales to outside parties (excluding inter-company sales); ~vergleich dealing-at-arm's-length test; ~vermutung constructive notice of third-party bailment (to a bank by depositor in bank safe-deposit); ~versicherung insurance of third-party interests, third-party insurance; ~währung → Fremdwährung.

Fremden|feindlichkeit xenophobia; ~freundlichkeit xenophilia; ~heim lodging house, boarding house, guest house; ~paß alien's passport (issued to aliens in Germany who cannot otherwise prove their identity); ~pension = ~heim qv; ~polizei aliens' police department, aliens' (registration) office; ~recht law concerning aliens, law governing the registration of aliens; ~übernachtungen tourists' overnight reservations; ~verkehr tourism, tourist trade; ~verzeichnis guest list; number of overnight stays.

Fremdenverkehrs|abgabe tourist tax; ~förderung promotion of tourism; ~gebiet tourist area; ~gemeinde tourist centre; ~gewerbe tourist trade, tourist industry; ~verband tourist association; ~verein local tourist association; ~werbung promotion of tourism.

Fremdwährung f foreign currency.

Fremdwährungs|anleihe foreign currency loan, foreign currency bond issue; ~klausel foreign currency clause (clause relating a monetary debt to a foreign currency); ~konto (foreign) currency account; ~kredit credit in foreign currency; ~obligation currency bonds; ~schuld debt expressed in a foreign currency; ~~en: foreign currency liabilities; foreign currency debts; ~urteil judgment in foreign currency; ~versicherung insurance in foreign currency terms; ~wechsel foreign currency bill, foreign bill, bill drawn in a foreign currency.

Freundschafts|besuch goodwill visit; ~dienst friendly service, act of friendship; ~-, **Handels- und Schiffahrtsvertrag** treaty of friendship, commerce and navigation; ~pakt treaty of friendship; ~verhältnis friendship, friendly relationship; ~wechsel accommodation bill.

Frevel m outrage, sacrilege, social crime, blasphemy.

freveln v/i to commit an outrage, to perpetrate an outrage.

Freveltat f outrage, atrocious crime, heinous crime.

Frieden m peace; **sozialer** ~ social peace, peace in labour relations; ~ **und Freiheit** (the cause of) peace and liberty.

Friedens|angebot peace offer, offer of peace; ~appell appeal for peace; ~aussichten prospects of peace; ~bedingungen peace terms, peace conditions; ~bewegung peace campaign; ~bruch breach of the peace, violation of the peace, violation of a peace treaty; ~diktat dictated peace (treaty); ~**erklärung** declaration of peace; ~**gefährdung** threat to peace; ~**konferenz** peace conference; ~**marsch** peace demonstration (by a procession); ~**miete** pre-war rent; ~**partei** the "doves"; ~**pflicht** obligation to keep the peace (*to refrain from strikes and lockouts during negotiations*); ~**politik** peaceful policy, policy promoting peace; ~**recht** the international law of peace; ~**regelung** peace settlement; ~**richter** justice of the peace; ~**schluß** conclusion of a peace treaty; ~**stifter** peacemaker; ~**unterhändler** peace negotiator; ~**verhandlungen** peace negotiations; ~**verrat** treasonably endangering the pacific status, ~**vertrag** peace treaty; ~**ware** pre-war goods; ~**wirtschaft** peacetime economy.

Friedhofsverwaltung *f* burial authority, cemetery board.

frisieren *v/t* to doctor (*a balance sheet, a report*), to slant (*news*), to cook (the accounts).

Frist *f* time-limit, period (of time), limited time, fixed (*or* definite) period, term; time allowed, deadline; ~**ablauf** time-limit, deadline, expiration of time, lapse of time, time elapsing; *nach* ~~: *after the deadline, post terminum*; ~**beginn** the beginning of a period, commencement of the term; ~**berechnung** computation of time; ~**bestimmung** calculation of the final date; ~**bewilligung** granting additional time; ~**einhaltung** meeting the deadline, observance of the time-limit; ~**enlösung** tolerated abortion within first three months of pregnancy; ~**ende** end of the stipulated term, time-limit; **f~gemäß** *adj, adv* within the timelimit, within the specified time, by the due date; **f~gerecht** within time, within the set period, within the prescibed time limit; = *f~gemäß qv*; ~**gesuch** petition for an extension of time, petition for

respite, request for time; ~**hemmung** suspension of prescription (*Statute of Limitations*), suspension of time-limit (*for legal action etc*); ~**igkeit** maturity, period to maturity; **f~los** *adj, adv* without notice, instant(ly), at a minute's notice; **f~mäßig** *adj* on the due date, within the agreed time-limit, before the deadline; ~**sache** case (*or* matter) where a deadline must be observed; ~**setzung** fixing of a time-limit (*or* deadline); *gerichtliche* ~~: *peremptory order for time*; ~**tag** day allowed within time-limit, day of respite, day of grace; ~**überschreitung** failure to observe the time-limit, exceeding the deadline, overshooting the deadline; ~**unterbrechung** interruption of the running of the period, interruption of a period of time (*or* term); ~**verlängerung** enlargement of time, extension of the time limit; ~~*abrede: extension agreement*; ~~*santrag: application for an extension of time*; ~~*sbeschluß: order extending time, time order*; ~~*sgesuch: petition for more time*; ~**versäumnis** failure to observe the time-limit; ~**wahrung** compliance with the (agreed) time-limit, observance of the deadline; ~ **zur Klagebeantwortung** time for defence, time for answer; ~ **zur Klageerhebung** time for commencement of action, time within which the action must be brought; stipulated period for commencement of proceedings; ~ **zur Vorbereitung der mündlichen Verhandlung** time to prepare for trial; **abgelaufene** ~ expired term, lapsed time; **angegebene** ~ stated period (*or* deadline); **angemessene** ~ reasonable (period of) time, adequate time; *in* ~ *r* ~: *within a reasonable time*; **äußerst knappe** ~**en** barely sufficient time, extremely limited periods of time; **bei Ablauf dieser** ~ after the expiry of such period (*or* deadline); **bestimmte** ~ specified period, definite period, fixed period; **die ~ beginnt** time begins to run; **die ~ läuft** time runs; **e–e ~ bewilligen** to grant time, to allow further time, to consent to a delay; **e–e ~ einhalten** to keep a date, adhere to a time-limit, observe a deadline; **e–e ~ festsetzen** to fix a final date, to determine a time-limit, to stipulate a (certain) period of time; **e–e ~ gewähren** to grant (additional) time, to give a respite; **e–e ~ hemmen** to stay the running of the period (of limitation), to suspend the running of (prescriptive) time; **e–e ~ setzen** to set a time-limit, to fix a deadline, to specify a period of time; **e–e ~ verkürzen** to shorten a time-limit; **e–e ~ verlängern** to extend the time (*or* time-limit); **e–e ~ versäumen** to fail to meet the deadline; **e–e ~ verpassen** to neglect a time-limit; **e–e ~ wahren** to observe (*or* to adhere to) a time-limit; **eingeräumte ~** time granted, time allowed; **gesetzliche ~** legal time-limit, statutory period; **gewährte ~** time allowed; **innerhalb der ~** not later than, before the deadline of; **innerhalb der vorgeschriebenen ~** within the prescribed time-limit; **innerhalb der vorgesehenen ~** within the prescribed period; **kurze ~** short period, *in ~r ~: at short notice*; **laufende ~** unexpired period of time, the current period of time; **nicht abgelaufene ~** unexpired time (*or* term); **nichtverlängerbare ~** strict time-limit, non-renewable term; **offene ~** unexpired time; **ohne ~angabe** without day, without a time-limit; **präklusive ~** absolute deadline; **richterliche ~** time allowed by the court; **strenge ~** strict time (limit); **vereinbarte ~** stipulated term.

Fristeninkongruenz *f* maturity mismatch, mismatching maturity.

Frontalzusammenstoß *m* smash-up, head-on collision.

Frost|aufbruch patch of frost damage; **~schäden** frost damage; **~schutzmittel** anti-freeze (mixture, solution); **~schutzscheibe** screen defroster; **~versicherung** insurance against frost; **~warnung** frost warning.

Frucht *f* (*pl Früchte: ~e*) fruit, *pl also*: proceeds, benefits, natural fruits, civil fruits; **~e auf dem Halm** growing crop, standing crop; **~~~** *verkaufen: to sell the crop standing*; **~e der Saison** products of the season; **~e e-r Erfindung** benefits of an invention; **~epfandrecht** lien on the fruits of the land; **~erwerb** acquisition of (civil *and/or* natural) fruits; **~genuß** enjoyment of fruits and benefits; **f~los** *adj* fruitless, unsuccessful, useless; **~losigkeit** fruitlessness; **~ziehung** harvesting, collecting the fruits and benefits; **~wechsel** succession of crops, rotation of crops; **gezogene ~** gathered fruits, harvested crops, collected proceeds; **natürliche ~e** natural fruits, fructus naturales, products of nature.

Früh|bezugsrabatt seasonal allowance; **~druschprämie** early threshing premium; **~geburt** premature birth, premature delivery; **~invalidität** disablement before retirement age; **~kapitalismus** early capitalism; **~pensionierung** early retirement, premature retirement; **~rentner** early retirer, early leaver, premature pensioner; **~schicht** morning shift; **~stückskartell** informal cartel agreement (*arranged at luncheon of executives*); **~verrentung** early retirement on a pension; **~symptom** advance pointer; **~warnung** early (bird) warning (*nuclear attack; strikes*); **~zustellung** early morning delivery.

früher *adj* antecedent, former.

frühestens *adj* no earlier than, at the earliest (by).

Fühlungnahme *f* exploratory contacts (soundings).

Fuhr|geld cartage, carriage; **~lohn** = *Fuhrgeld qv*; **~mann** carter, waggoner, teamster; **~park** car (vehicle) fleet, motor pool; **~un-**

ternehmen transport business, haulage contractors; ~**unternehmer** carrier, hauling contractor; ~**wesen** the carrying trade, the haulage contracting sector.

Fuhre *f* cartload, waggon-load.

Führen *n* operation, guidance, management; ~ **akademischer Titel** use of academic titles; **unbefugtes** ~ **e–s Titels** unauthorized use of a title; **unbefugtes** ~ **von Amtsbezeichnungen** unauthorized use of official titles; ~ **von Kraftfahrzeugen** operation (*or* driving) of motor vehicles.

Führer des Kraftfahrzeugs driver of the vehicle.

Führerschein *m* driving licence *GB*, driver's licence *US*, operator's licence; ~ **auf Probe** probationary driving licence; ~**entzug** withdrawal of driving licence, revocation of driving licence; *befristeter* ~~: *suspension of driver's licence*; **f~frei** exempt from driving licence (*motor bikes*); ~**klasse** class (*or* category) of driving licence (*type of vehicle covered*); ~**pflicht** obligation to obtain a driving licence, statutory requirement in respect of driving licences; ~**prüfung** driving test; ~**sperre** suspension of driving licence; **internationaler** ~ international driving licence (*or* permit); **nationaler** ~ domestic driving licence.

Führung *f* (1) management, leadership, direction, guidance, use; ~ **der Bücher** keeping of the books, accounting; ~ **der Geschäfte** conduct of the business, management; *mit der* ~~~ *betraut*: *to be responsible for managing the business*; ~ **der Haushaltsbücher** family accounting; ~ **des Prozesses** conduct of the suit; ~ **des Urkundenbeweises** proof by documentary evidence; ~ **e–s Namens** use of a name; ~ **von Verhandlungen** conduct of negotiations; **kollektive** ~ collective leadership.

Führung *f* (2) conduct, behaviour; ~**saufsicht** supervision of conduct (*of repeated offender*); ~**sliste** record of good conduct, police record; ~**szeugnis** certificate of good conduct, police clearance, certificate of character, *mil*: service record; *polizeiliches* ~~: *police reference*; **einwandfreie** ~ good behaviour, good conduct; *bei* ~*r* ~: *subject to good behaviour*, good conduct; **gute** ~ good behaviour, good conduct; **schlechte** ~ bad behaviour, misconduct.

Führungs|(1)anspruch claim to leadership; ~**ausschuß** management committee; ~**befähigung** management talent, managerial qualities; ~**befugnis** managerial authority; ~**ebene** executive level, management level, level of command; ~**eigenschaft** leadership, managerial quality; ~**entscheidung** executive (management) decision; ~**gremium** governing group, management committee; ~**grundsatz** management principle; ~**gruppe** management team; ~**instrument** instrument of control; ~**kräfte** executive personnel, senior executives, senior management, management staff; *untergeordnete* ~~: *junior executives*; ~**nachwuchs** future executives, rising generation of managers, junior (*or* younger) managers; ~**nachwuchsgruppe** management reserve group; ~**spitze** top management, top echelons in a firm, top-level executives; ~**stab** operational staff, command.

Füllauftrag *m* = *Füllorder q.v.*

Füllorder *f* stop-gap order, fill-in order.

Fund *m* finding lost property; found object, find; ~**büro** lost-property office; ~**diebstahl** unlawful appropriation of s.th. found, larceny by finder; ~**ort** *min* pit bottom; ~**recht** law concerning lost property; rights of the finder of lost property; ~**sache** object found, lost property; ~**stelle** place where an object was found; citation (*of a precedent or legal authority*), source reference, indication of source;

fundieren | **Fürsorge**

~**stellensammlung**: *Citator*; ~**stellenverzeichnis** list of source references; ~**unterschlagung** unlawfully keeping lost property, larceny by finder.

fundieren *v/t* to fund (*debt, loan*); to lay the foundation of.

fundiert *adj* funded, consolidated; solid, founded, informed; **nicht** ~ unfunded.

Fundierung *f* funding, foundation, basis, consolidation; ~**sanleihe** funding loan, consolidation loan; ~**sschuldverschreibung** funding bond; ~**szertifikat** funding certificate; **vertragsrechtliche** ~ basis in the law of contract.

Fünf|jahresfrist period of five years, quinquennial period; **f~jährig** quinquennial; **f~seitig** quinquepartite; **f~teilig** quinquepartite.

fungibel *adj* fungible, interchangeable; marketable.

Fungibilität *f* fungibility, interchangeability.

fungieren *v/i* to function, to act (as), to serve, to officiate.

Funk|aufklärung radio intelligence, *interception of enemy radio messages*; ~**ausrüstung** radio equipment; ~**bearbeitung** adaptation for radio broadcasting; ~**piraten** radio pirates; ~**recht** law regulating radio communications, broadcasting right; ~**regal** (*federal*) broadcasting prerogative; ~**spruch** radio message ~**streife** police patrol car, squad car; ~**telegramm** wireless message; ~**verkehr** radio communications, radio contact.

Funktion *f* function, capacity; **amtliche** ~ official function; *in* ~*r* ~: *in his official capacity*; **beratende** ~ advisory function (or capacity); **betriebsleitende** ~ managerial function; **hoheitsrechtliche** ~ sovereign function; **richterähnliche** ~ quasi-judicial function; **richterliche** ~ judicial function.

Funktionalreform *f* reform of administrative functions.

Funktionär *m* officer, official, functionary.

funktionell *adj* functional.

funktionieren *v/i* to function, to operate; **schlecht** ~ malfunction *v/i*.

Funktions|dauer period of office, term of office; ~**erfindung** invention of a new function; **f~fähig** *adj* capable of functioning, workable, efficient; ~**mangel** functional deficiency, functional shortcomings; ~**nachfolge** succession in governmental functions (*said of the German Federal Republic with reference to the German Reich*); ~**rabatt** functional discount; ~**raum** functional region, nodal region; **f~schwach** inefficient; ~**schwäche** functional weakness; ~**unfähigkeit** inability to function, unworkability, failure to function properly.

Fürsorge *f* public assistance, provident care, relief, welfare (work), social assistance, after-care (*for discharged prisoners*); ~**amt** welfare centre, public relief office, assistance authority; ~**anspruch** right to receive public social assistance, eligibility for public relief; ~**anstalt** welfare institution; reformatory (*young delinquents*); ~**ausschuß** welfare committee; ~**beamter** social worker; ~**bedürftige** persons eligible for public relief; ~**behörde** welfare agency, welfare authority; ~**bezirk** parish, welfare district; ~**einrichtung** (public) welfare institution; ~**empfänger** person on welfare, welfare recipient; ~**erziehung** correctional education, education in approved school; (corrective) treatment of young offenders; residential care and custody; ~**erziehungsanstalt** community home, *GB* child care home, youth treatment centre; ~**erziehungsbehörde** authority in charge of child care; ~**erziehungssachen** matters of care proceedings, public assistance matters; ~**erziehungsverfahren** care pro-

323

ceedings; ~**heim** child care home; ~**last** welfare charge, welfare liability; ~**lehrling** apprentice in a welfare institution; ~**leistungen** welfare benefits; ~**patient** rate-aided patient; ~**pflicht** duty in respect of care and supervision, obligation to provide welfare services, employer's duty of care and welfare maintenance; ~**recht** welfare law, legislation relating to welfare services; ~**rente** relief pension; ~**richtsätze** standard rates for social welfare benefits; ~**stelle** social assistance (or relief) office; ~**tätigkeit** welfare work, social work; ~**- und Versorgungsbezüge** public assistance and pension receipts; ~**unterstützung** public assistance benefits, outdoor relief, public relief; ~**verband** welfare association, charitable association; ~**wesen** social welfare; ~**zögling** ward of a welfare service; **geschlossene** ~ indoor relief; **öffentliche** ~ public assistance, public relief, public welfare work; **private** ~ private charity, voluntary welfare work; **soziale** ~ social service; **väterliche** ~ paternal care.

Fürsorger *m* welfare officer.

Fürsprache *f* intercession, interposition, plea; ~ **einlegen** to intercede (*with s.o. for s.o.*).

Fürstenǀrecht sovereign's right to regulate succession; ~**stand** princedom; ~**tum** principality.

furtum usus larceny for temporary use.

Fusiomanie *f* merger mania.

Fusion *f* fusion, merger, amalgamation; **echte** ~ merger, amalgamation; **unechte** ~ take over (*GB*); ~ **durch Neugründung** consolidation, amalgamation.

Fusionär *m* mergerite.

fusionieren *v/i* to merge, to amalgamate.

Fusionsǀabkommen merger agreement; ~**befürworter** mergerite; ~**bilanz** merger balance sheet, consolidated balance sheet; ~**gegner** antimergerite; ~**gesellschaft** merging company; ~**gewinn** surplus from consolidation, consolidation profits; ~**kontrolle** supervision of mergers, merger control; ~**kontrollamt** takeover panel; ~**Kontroll-Richtlinien** merger guidelines; ~**neigung** willingness to merge; ~**vertrag** merger agreement, agreement (*or* articles) of consolidation, contract of merger.

Fußǀabdrücke footprints; ~**angel** mantrap, snare; ~**block** stocks; ~**bodenheizung** underfloor heating; ~**bremse** foot-brake; ~**eisen** leg irons, (leg) shackles; ~**fesseln** leg irons, (leg) shackles; ~**gänger** → *Fußgänger*; ~**note** footnote; ~**spuren** foot-prints; ~**weg** path, footpath; **auf freiem** ~ **befindlich** to be at liberty (*or* at large); **auf freien** ~ **setzen** to set free, to release, to discharge.

Fußgänger *m* pedestrian; ~**ampel** traffic beacon, pedestrian crossing; ~**bereich** pedestrian precinct, pedestrianized area; ~**insel** traffic island; ~**überweg** pedestrian crossing; ~~ **an Schulen**: school crossing; ~**zone** pedestrian precinct, pedestrian mall; **entgegenkommender** ~: oncoming pedestrian; **unachtsamer** ~ jay walker.

Futterkrippenwirtschaft *f* spoils system (*US*); old-boys' network (*GB*).

Futtermittel *n* animal food, feed; ~**kredit** feed loan; ~**recht** law of animal foods.

G

Gage *f* remuneration (*of artists*), fee.
Galanteriewaren *f/pl* fancy goods.
Galgen *m* gallows; ~**frist** last respite, brief respite.
gängig *adj* common, prevalent; marketable, salable (= *saleable*).
Gängigkeit *f* salability (= *saleability*), marketability.
ganz|oder teilweise *adv* in whole or in part; ~ **und gar** *adv* completely and utterly.
Ganztagsbeschäftigung *f* full-time employment.
Garant *m* guarantor, warrantor, underwriter; ~**enpflicht** guarantor's obligation, guarantee; ~**enstellung** (the) position of being a guarantor.
Garantie *f* guarantee (GB), guaranty (US), full warranty, product warranty; (*capital issues:*) underwriting; indemnity; ~**abteilung** underwriting department; ~**akkreditiv** standby letter of credit; ~**deckungskonto** guarantee cover account; ~ **der Geldrückgabe bei Nichtgefallen** money-back guarantee; ~**einbehalt** retention money; ~**erklärung** guarantee-undertaking, statement of indemnity; ~**fall** circumstances (*or* event) bringing guarantee into operation; ~**fonds** guarantee fund; ~**frist** period of guarantee, guarantee period, indemnity period; *Beginn der* ~~: *commencement of the guarantee period*; ~ **für Kreditaufnahmen** undertaking for borrowing; ~**gemeinschaft** joint guarantors, guarantee association; ~**geschäft** guarantee transaction, indemnity transaction; ~**haftung** liability under a guarantee (*or* indemnity); ~**indossament** endorsement by way of collateral security; ~**kapital** capital backing, capital serving as a safeguard for depositors, protective capital resources; ~**klausel** warranty clause (*in contract*); ~**konsortium** underwriting syndicate; ~**leisten** to furnish a guarantee, to give an indemnity; ~**leistung** giving of a guarantee; ~**lohn** guaranteed wage; ~**nehmer** beneficiary under a guarantee, guaranteed creditor; ~**pflicht** obligation under a guarantee; ~**provision** underwriting commission; ~**rahmen** guarantee ceiling, indemnity ceiling; ~**reparaturen** (*Autohändler etc*) warranty work; ~**schein** (certificate of) guarantee, (certificate of) warranty; ~**schreiben** letter of guarantee, letter of indemnity; ~**sicherheitskonto** guarantee collateral account; ~**stock** special reserve for doubtful claims, indemnity collateral; ~**übernahmeverpflichtung** covenant to honor guaranty (*US*); ~ **übernehmen** to give a guarantee; ~**verletzung** breach of warranty, breach of indemnity; ~**verpflichtung** obligation under a guarantee; ~**vertrag** (*1*) contract of guarantee; (*2*) contract of indemnity, indemnity; collateral assurance; ~ **von Effektenemissionen** underwriting; ~**werte** non-forfeiture values; ~**zeit** guarantee period; indemnity period; ~**zusage** indemnity commitment; **ohne** ~ no guarantee.
garantieren *v/t* to guarantee, to warrant.
garantiert *adj adv* guaranteed, warranted; ~ **rein** warranted pure.
Garottierung *f* garrotting (*capital punishment by strangulation*).
Gartenbau *m* horticulture; ~**erzeugnisse** horticultural products; ~**gestaltung** landscape gardening, horticultural landscaping.
Gärtnereibetrieb *m* market garden, garden centre.
Gas|automat *obs.* gas slot-machine,

325

Gastarbeiter

coin-in-the-slot gas-meter; ~**beton** aerated concrete; ~**erzeugung** gas production; ~**fabrik** gasworks; ~**heizung** gas heating; ~**kammer** gas chamber; ~**kampfstoff** war gas, chemical warfare agent; ~**krieg** gas war, chemical warfare; ~**pistole** gas pistol; ~**schutz** anti-gas measures.

Gast|arbeiter foreign worker, migrant worker, "guest worker", *pl* foreign labour; ~**aufnahmevertrag** lodging agreement; ~**gewerbe** hotel and restaurant industry; ~**haus** inn; ~**land** host country, receiving country; ~**recht** laws of hospitality, (right of) hospitality; ~**spiel** guest performance, guest appearance; *einmaliges* ~~: *one-night stand*; ~**spielvertrag** agreement on guest performances; ~**stätte** → *Gaststätte*; ~**wirt** innkeeper; ~**wirtschaft** restaurant, licensed premises; ~**wirtshaftung** innkeeper's liability; ~**wirtspfandrecht** inkeeper's lien.

Gaststätte *f* restaurant, *brauereigebundene* ~~: *tied house*; ~**nbesitzer** restaurant owner.

Gaststätten|erlaubnis licence to operate a bar, restaurant or inn; ~**gesetz** Licensing Act, *German law (1970) regulating the restaurant business*; ~**gewerbe** hotel and restaurant industry; restaurant business; ~**lieferant** caterer; ~**recht** *the law regulating licensed premises, restaurants and the hotel business*; ~~**und Beherbergungsgewerbe** hotel and catering trade; ~**verbot** prohibition to enter licensed premises; ~**wesen** the catering industry, restaurant trade.

Gatte *m* husband, spouse; *pl* ~*n*: spouses, husband and wife.

Gattin *f* wife, spouse.

Gattung *f* species, kind, class.

Gattungs|anspruch generic claim; ~**begriff** generic term; ~**bezeichnung** generic name, generic term; ~**kauf** sale of unascertained goods *of the same kind*; ~**sache** unascer-

Gebäude

tained thing of one kind or type; ~**schenkung** gift of money or fungible goods; ~**schuld** indeterminate obligation, obligation to supply unascertained goods; *konkretisierte* ~: *obligation to supply ascertained (segregated) fungible goods*; ~**vermächtnis** (unspecified) legacy of things of the same type general bequest; *beschränktes* ~~: *legacy of things of the same type if available in the estate*; ~**ware(n)** unascertained goods, fungible commodity; ~**warenschuld** obligation to supply unascertained goods of a particule kind.

Gauner *m* swindler, crook; ~**sprache** thieves' cant, thieves' latin.

Gaunerei *f* sharp practices, racket, swindling.

geächtet *adj* outlawed, hors de la loi.

Geächteter *m* (*der Geächtete*) outlaw.

Gebärdenspiel *n* pantomime.

Gebaren *n* behaviour, conduct, management, life-style.

Gebäude *n* building (= *b*); erection, structure; ~**abnahme** final acceptance of a new *b*; ~**abstand** legally required distance from other *b–s*; ~**ausbesserungen** repair of *b–s*; ~**bestand** total of *b–s*; ~**bewertung** valuation of *b–s*; ~**buch** register of *b–s*; ~**ertragswert** annual value of *b–s*; ~~**-Feuerversicherungsanstalt** fire insurance company (*specializing in real estate risks*); ~**haftpflicht** premises liability, house owner's liability; ~**haftung** = ~*haftpflicht qv*; ~**instandhaltung** keeping a *b* in good repair; ~**nutzfläche** usable *b* space; ~**schaden** structural damage to a *b*; ~**steuer** house-duty, tax on *b–s*; ~**substanzschaden** structural damage (to a *b*); ~**versicherung** insurance of a *b*; ~**wertschätzung** building's valuation, structural survey; **angrenzendes** ~ adjacent *b*, adjoining *b*; **bewohntes** ~ inhabited *b*; **ein** ~ **schätzen** to assess a *b*; **leerstehendes** ~empty *b*; **öffentliches** ~ public *b*.

Geber *m* donor, giver, presenter.

Gebiet *f* territory (= *t*), region, area; domain, province, scope; **abgetretenes** ~ ceded *t*; **annektiertes** ~ annexed *t*; **befriedetes** ~ pacified *t*; **besetztes** ~ occupied *t*; **das fällt nicht in mein** ~ that is not within my province, that is outside my jurisdiction; **entlegene** ~**e** outlying districts; **entmilitarisiertes** ~ demilitarized area; **gemeindefreie** ~**e** lands not subject to local authorities' jurisdiction; **ölträchtiges** ~ "proven territory"; **überseeische** ~**e** overseas *t-s*; **unterentwickelte** ~**e** underdeveloped areas; **unterversorgtes** ~ deprived area; **zum Ödland gewordenes** ~ derelict land.

gebieten *v/t* to command, to impose, to order.

Gebieter *m* ruler, master.

Gebiets|abtretung (territory = *t*) cession of *t*; ~**änderung** territorial change; ~**ansässiger** resident; ~**anspruch** territorial claim; ~**ausschuß** regional committee; ~**austausch** exchange of *t*; ~**beauftragter** regional representative; ~**bereinigung** territorial adjustment; ~**einheit** subarea, areal unit; ~**entwicklungsplan** subregional development plan; ~**erweiterung** territorial enlargement (*or* expansion); ~**forderung** territorial claim; ~**fremder** non-resident; ~**gewalt** territorial authority; ~**herrschaft** territorial sovereignty, territorial domain; ~**hoheit** territorial sovereignty; ~**kartell** regional cartel, area-apportioning cartel; ~**körperschaft** territorial entity, political subdivision, local authority; *kommunale* ~~: *a local authority (as a body corporate)*; ~**leiter** district manager, area manager; ~**provision** overriding commission (*of a commercial agent*); ~**reform** territorial reorganization of local government; ~**schutz** territorial monopoly; ~**stand** the territorial status, *t* within the borders of a state; ~**statut** lex territorialis; ~**übertragung** transfer of *t*; ~**veränderung** territorial change; ~**verletzung** violation of *t*, invasion; ~**vertreter** distributing agent (*for a t*), regional commercial representative; ~**zentrum** regional centre.

Gebilde *n* thing, fabric, entity, formation, structure.

Gebinde *n* bundle, packet, rap (*thread*); spray (*flowers*); row of tiles, truss (*roof*); cask, tun (*wine*); barrel; tin, *US*: can (*oil*).

geboren *adj* born, ~*e*: née (*maiden name*); **vorehelich** ~ born before marriage.

Gebot *n* command, order, precept, requirement; bid, offer; (*relig*): Commandment; **das erste** ~ the opening bid (*auction*); **ein festes** ~ a fixed offer; **das geringste** ~ the legal minimum bid; **das letzte** ~ the last bid, the closing bid; **gegen ein** ~ **verstoßen** to break a rule, to break a Commandment.

Gebotszeichen mandatory sign (*traffic*).

Gebrauch *m* use, usage; **allgemein in** ~ in common usage; **außer** ~ out of use, no longer used, obsolete; ~~*kommen*: *to fall into disuse, to become obsolete*; **bestimmungsmäßiger** ~ use as required, contractual use, prescribed end use; **gewöhnlicher** ~ ordinary use; **nur zum eigenen** ~ for private use only; **öffentlicher** ~ public use; **ordnungsgemäßer** ~ proper use (*of a machine*); **rechtmäßiger** ~ legal use; **redlicher** ~ fair use (*copyright*), fair usage; **sachgemäßer** ~ proper use, proper usage; **unbefugter** ~ unauthorized use, adverse use; **ununterbrochener** ~ uninterrupted use; **vorschriftswidriger** ~ improper use; **widerrechtlicher** ~ unlawful use, unauthorized use.

Gebraucher *m* user; **g~freundlich** user-friendly.

Gebrauchs|abnahme acceptance for ready use; ~**abschreibung** physical depreciation, depreciation for wear and tear; ~**abweichung** use variance; ~**anforderung** requirement(s) for use; ~**anmaßung** conversion to one's own use, unauthorized use, illicit use; ~**anweisung** instruction(s) for use, directions for use, instruction booklet; ~**artikel** object in daily use; *pl* consumer goods; ~**beschränkung** restraint of use; ~**diebstahl** stealing for temporary use (*and subsequent abandonment*); ~~ an e-m *Kraftfahrzeug*: stealing a ride; ~**entziehung** deprivation of use; ~**entzug** loss of use; ~**fahrzeug** utility vehicle; **g~fertig** ready for use; ~**gegenstand** utility article, article for daily use; *persönliche ~ e: personal effects*; ~**gestattung** permission to use (sth); ~**gewährung** granting the use of sth; ~**graphik** commercial art; ~**güter** utility goods; *gewerbliche ~~: goods used in trade and industry; langlebige ~~: durable consumer goods; persönliche ~~: convenience goods*; ~**information** on how to use sth; ~**kategorien** use classes (*city zoning rules*); ~**leihe** loan for use (= *Leihe qv*); ~**lizenz** licence for use; ~**mittelentwendung** petty theft of consumer goods; ~**möglichkeit** opportunity of use, possibility to use sth; ~**muster** → *Gebrauchsmuster;* ~**recht** right of user, use as of right, right to use sth; ~**regelung** regulations for the use of sth; ~**störung** interference with the proper use of sth; ~**überlassung** transfer for use; ~~*svertrag: usage contract*; ~**untauglichkeit** unfitness for use, unsuitability for use; ~**vorteile** the amenity and advantage of using, use and enjoyment; ~**wert** utility value, service value, value in use; ~**zolltarif** working tariff; ~**zweck** intended use.

Gebrauchsmuster *n* utility model, utility patent, patent of a lesser degree (*protected minor invention of every-day usefulness*); ~**abteilung** utility model division; ~**anmeldung** utility model application; ~**berühmung** holding out sth as a utility-patented article; ~**eintragung** model registration utility; ~**gebühren** (*Patent Office*) charge for registration of utility models; ~**gesetz** Utility Models Act (*German law originally enacted in 1891, as amended*); ~**hilfsanmeldung** auxiliary utility model registration (*for the event that full patent should not be granted*); ~**löschung** utility model cancellation; ~**rolle** Utility Model Register; ~**schrift** utility model specification; ~**schutz** legal protection of inventions registered as utility models; ~**streitsachen** utility model litigation cases; ~**urkunde** utility model certificate; ~**verletzung** utility model infringement; **registriertes ~modell** registered model under a utility patent.

Gebraucht|maschinen used equipment; ~**wagen** second-hand car, used car; ~**warenbuch** second-hand goods journal (*for specified goods*) ~**warenladen** thrift shop; ~**warenhandel** second-hand trade; ~**warenmarkt** second-hand market.

Gebrechen *n* infirmity; **körperliches ~** physical defect.

Gebrechlichkeit *f* infirmity; ~**spfleger** protector, curator for a helpless person; ~**spflegschaft** curatorship due to infirmity.

Gebrüder *Schmidt* (*Firma*): *Schmidt Brothers* (*a firm*).

Gebühr *f* fee, charge, rate; ~**en** (*e-s Anwalts, Steuerberaters etc*): *professional charges*; **amtliche ~** official fee; **einmalige ~** non-recurrent charge, one-off fee; **ermäßigte ~** reduced rate; **fortlaufend wiederkehrende ~en** recurrent charges; **gesetzliche ~** legal fee; **übliche ~en** usual charges **zusätzliche ~en** additional charges.

Gebühren|anteil portion of the fees; ~**aufstellung** statement of fees, account of charges; ~**aufteilung** fee splitting; ~**befreiung** remission of fees; ~**bemessung** assess-

Gebührenberechnung   **Gedanke**

ment of charges; ~**berechnung** calculation of charges; ~**einheit** unit of charge (*telephone*); ~**einzug** collection of charges; ~ **erheben** to levy fees; ~**erhebung** charging of fees, collection of fees; *übermäßige* ~~: *excessive charge, overcharging (fees)*; ~**erlaß** waiver of a fee (*or* charge); ~**ermäßigung** reduction of fees; ~**erstattung** refund of fees; ~**forderung** claim for professional charges; g~**frei** free of charge, exempt from duty; ~**freiheit** exemption from fees (*or* charges); ~**hinterziehung** evasion of public charges; ~**marke** fee stamp; ~**nachlaß** reduction of public charges; ~**ordnung** fee scale, schedule of charges, rules relating to fees, official regulation for fees; g~**pflichtig** subject to a fee, liable to charges, chargeable; ~**quittung** receipt (for fees); ~**rahmen** official scale of fees; ~**rechnung** invoice in respect of fees, bill of costs; ~**rückerstattung** refund of fees; ~**satz** full rate of a fee or charge; ~**schuldner** debtor owing fees; ~ **städtischer Einrichtungen** dues collected by municipal departments; ~**streitwert** litigation fee value; ~**tabelle** table of fees, scale of fees; *gerichtliche* ~~: *table of costs;* ~**tarif** rate of charges, fee schedule; ~**teilung** fee sharing; ~**überhebung** overcharging, excessive rates; ~**überweisung** remittance of fees; ~ **und Auslagen** fees and expenses, fees and costs; ~**vereinbarung** agreement concerning (lawyer's) fees; ~**verzeichnis** list of charges, fee schedule; ~**vorschuß** retaining fee, advance for charges, retainer (*lawyer, consultant*), money on account; ~ **zahlt der Empfänger** charges collected, reverse charge; ~**zahlung** payment of fees (*or* charges); ~~*svordruck: voucher for the settlement of fees; unterlassene* ~~: *failure to pay fees, non-payment of fees*; ~**zuschlag** surcharge, excess fee.

gebühren *v/t* to be due to s. o., *v/reflex* to be fitting and proper.

gebührend *adj* proper, appropriate.

gebührlich *adj* = *gebührend qv*.

Gebundenheit *f* commitment, binding nature, obligatory nature.

Geburt *f* birth, childbirth; **eheliche** ~ legitimate birth; **nach der** ~ **eintretend** post-natal; **uneheliche** ~ illegitimate birth.

Geburten|ausfall decline in birthrate; ~**berg** birthrate bulge; babyboom years; ~**beschränkung** birth control; ~**buch** register of births; ~**eintragung** registration of births; ~**rate** birth rate; ~**regelung** birth control, planned parenthood; ~**register** register of births, table of births, birth record; ~**rückgang** decline in the birth rate; g~**stark** having a high birthrate; ~**überschuß** surplus of births over deaths, survival rate; ~**ziffer** birth rate; number of births; ~**zulage** birth grant.

Geburts|anzeige notice of birth, announcement of birth; ~**beihilfe** maternity benefit; ~**datum** date of birth, day of birth; ~**fehler** congenital defect; ~**land** native country; ~**name** name at birth; ~**ort** place of birth; ~**recht** birth right; ~**register** register of births; ~**schein** certificate of birth; ~**urkunde** certificate of birth.

Gedächtnis *n* memory, recollection; ~**auffrischung** refreshing one's memory; ~**ausfall** lapse of memory; ~**bild** image retained in the memory; ~**fehler** lapse of memory; ~**feier** commemoration ceremony; ~**kraft** strength of memory; ~**protokoll** memorandum; minutes (*or* statement) from memory; ~**schwund** loss of memory, amnesia; ~**störung** partial amnesia; ~**stütze** memory aid, mnemonic aid, memo; ~**vermögen** capacity of recollection, memory retention, quality of memory; **sein** ~ **erforschen** to search one's memory.

Gedanke *m* thought, idea; **selbstän-**

Gedankenarmut

diger ~ self-supporting idea, independent concept; **sich von e-m ~ leiten lassen** to be guided by an idea.

Gedanken|armut poverty of ideas; lack of imagination; ~**austausch** exchange of views; ~**freiheit** freedom of thought; ~**gang** way of thinking, thought, line of thought, train of ideas, train of reasoning; *lückenloser ~~*: *coherent line of thought*; ~**gut** stock of ideas, ideology; **g~los** thoughtless; ~**losigkeit** thoughtlessness; ~**lücke** gap in the line of thought, incoherence; ~**sprung** illogical break in the line of thought, inconsistency; ~**verbindung** association of ideas; ~**vorbehalt** mental reservation.

gedeckt *adj* covered, provided with funds; „**nicht ~**" refer to drawer (*R/D*).

Gedinge *n* piece work, contract work; ~**lohn** piece wage, job wage.

geeignet *adj* suitable, qualified, proper.

Geeignetheit *f* suitability.

Gefahr *f* danger, peril; risk, hazard; ~ **beim Eigentümer** owner's risk; ~ **der zufälligen Verschlechterung** risk of deterioration; ~ **e-r erneuten Verurteilung** double jeopardy; ~ **erhöhung** increase of risk; ~ **für Leib und Leben** danger to life and limb; **g~geneigt** dangerous per se, accident-prone; ~ **im Verzug** apprehended danger, imminence of danger, imminent danger, increased danger in any delay, periculum in mora; ~**klassen** classes of risk; ~**stelle** dangerous part of road; ~**tarif** rate for increased risk; ~**tragung** bearing of the risk; ~**übergang** passing of (the) risk; ~**übernahme** acceptance of the risk; *gemeinschaftliche ~~*: *pooling of risk*; ~**verschollenheit** *total and permanent disappearance of a person in dangerous circumstances*; ~**zeichen** danger sign; **abzuwendende** ~ avoidable danger (*or* risk); **akute** ~ imminent peril, immedi-

330

Gefahrenabwehr

ate danger; **auf eigene** ~ at one's own risk, at one's peril; **auf ~ des Befrachters** shipper's risk; **auf ~ des Empfängers** at receiver's risk; **auf ~ des Käufers** at purchaser's risk; **die ~ geht über** the risk passes; **die ~ trägt A.** the risk lies (*or* rests) with A., the risk shall be borne by A.; **drohende** ~ imminent danger; **echte** ~ genuine risk; **erkennbare** ~ perceivable risk, discernible risk; **für die ~ haften** to bear the risk; **gegenwärtige** ~ present danger, imminent danger, apparent danger; ~~~ *für Leib und Leben*: *imminent danger to life and limb*; **gemeine** ~ common danger; **gemeinsame** ~ common danger; **objektive** ~ actual danger; **übernommene** ~ assumed risk; **unabwendbare** ~ unavoidable danger; **versicherte ~(en)** risk(s) covered, perils insured against.

Gefahren|abwehr accident prevention, averting dangers; ~**abwehrrecht** right to ward off dangers; ~**abwendung** avoiding dangers, minimizing risk; ~**abwendungspflicht** duty to avoid dangers; ~**änderung** alteration of risk *ins*; ~**ausgleich** equalization of risks, offsetting risks; ~**beseitigung** removal of dangerous objects; ~**blindheit** blindness to risks; inadvertent negligence; ~ **der Meere** dangers of the sea; ~ **der Seefahrt** dangers of navigation; ~ **durch den Straßenzustand** dangers of the roads; ~**entlastung** risk mitigation; ~**erhöhung** increase of risk; **g~geneigt** = *gefahrgeneigt qv*; ~**grenze** critical point; ~**klasse** risk class, class of risk, category of hazard (*accident branch*); ~**klausel** perils clause, emergency clause; ~**lage** emergency, dangerous situation; ~**merkmale** particulars of the risk; ~**moment** element of danger; ~**prämie** (extraordinary) risk premium; ~**punkt** danger point; ~**quelle** source of danger, unusual danger, safety hazard, nuisance; *ständige ~~*: *permanent nui-*

gefährden

sance; ~~, *die Kinder anzieht*: attractive nuisance; ~**rückstellung** reserve for special risks; ~**stelle** dangerous place; ~**übergang** passing of the risk; ~**übernahme** assumption of risk; ~**verhütung** accident prevention; ~**warnzeichen** danger warning (sign); ~**zone** danger zone; ~**zulage** danger money, danger-zone bonus, hazard bonus; penalty rate; **die** ~ **e-s Importsogs** the danger of a spate of imports; **gedeckte** ~ risks and perils (insured against), covered risks; **gegen alle** ~ against all risks; **versicherungsfähige** ~ insurable risks, insurable hazards.

gefährden *v/t* to endanger, to expose to danger, to pose danger to; to imperil, to jeopardize.

gefährdend *adj* dangerous.

Gefährdeter *m* (*der Gefährdete*) person in a dangerous position, endangered person; predelinquent.

Gefährdetenfürsorge *f* care and protection for morally endangered persons, social service for predelinquents.

Gefährdung *f* danger, endangerment, imperilment, jeorpardizing; ~ **der Allgemeinheit** danger to the public, a public danger; ~ **der öffentlichen Ordnung** endangering public peace and order; ~ **der öffentlichen Sicherheit** endangering public safety; ~ **der Sittlichkeit** danger to public morals; ~ **des Luftverkehrs** intentional endangering of air travel; ~**von Arbeitsplätzen** threat to jobs; ~ **des Verkehrs** endangering transport facilities; **vorsätzliche** ~ **anderer Personen** wilful interference with the safety of others; **zusätzliche** ~ added peril, additional danger.

Gefährdungs|delikt strict-liability tort; ~**haftung** liability regardless of fault, strict liability.

gefährlich *adj* dangerous, likely to cause danger, hazardous.

Gefährlichkeit *f* dangerousness, dangerous nature, perilousness, gravity of danger.

Gefälle *n* descent; **gefährliches** ~ dangerous descent.

Gefälligkeit *f* gratuitous service, an act of courtesy, voluntary courtesy, act done as a favo(u)r, accommodation.

Gefälligkeits|abrede accommodation agreement, courtesy arrangement; ~**adresse** accommodation address; ~**akzept** accommodation acceptance; ~**brief** letter written as a favo(u)r; ~**demokratie** complacency democracy; ~**fahrt** hitchhiking ride, free ride in other people's car; ~**girant** accommodation endorser; ~**indossament** accommodation endorsement; ~**mitfahrer** gratuitous passenger; ~**vereinbarung** sweetheart deal; ~**verhältnis** purely social relationship, courtesy-relationship; ~**vertrag** accommodation agreement; ~**wechsel** accommodation paper (*bill or promissory note*), accommodation bill, accommodation note; ~**zeichner** accommodation maker, accommodation party; ~**zusage** gratuitous promise.

Gefangenen|anstalt prison; ~**arbeit** convict labour; goods made by prisoners; ~**aufseher** prison warder; ~**aufstand** prison riot; ~**aussage** prisoner's statement, testimony of s.o. in custody; ~**austausch** exchange of prisoners; ~**befreiung** freeing prisoners, rescue of prisoners; ~**beschäftigung** occupation of prisoners, work for prisoners; ~**brief** letter from prison; ~**flucht** escape of prisoners; ~**fürsorge** prison welfare; ~**hilfe** discharged prisoners' aid; ~**lager** prisoner of war camp; ~**meuterei** mutiny by prisoners; ~**mitverantwortung** prisoner's co-responsibility; ~**post** prisoners' mail; ~**schulwesen** prisoners' education; ~**selbstbefreiung** prisoners' self-liberation; ~**transport** transportation of prisoners, convoy of prisoners; ~**transportwagen** prison van, "Black Maria"; ~**unfallfürsorge** accident-care for prisoners; ~**ware** prison-made goods.

Gefangener *m* (*der Gefangene*) prisoner, prison inmate, person under arrest, detainee; **streng bewachter** ~ heavily guarded prisoner.

Gefangenhaltung *f* detention, confinement, imprisonment.

Gefangennahme *f* capture, apprehension, imprisonment, arrest, seizure.

Gefangenschaft *f* captivity, confinement, being a prisoner (of war).

Gefängnis *n* prison, gaol (= *jail, US*), penitentiary, imprisonment, confinement in a prison (*now: Freiheitsstrafe*); **in ein ~ einweisen**: *to commit to prison*; **~aufseher** = ~wärter qv; **~abteilung** prison ward; **~ausbruch** escape from prison, jailbreak; **~ bis zu 2 Jahren** imprisonment (for a term) not exceeding 2 years; **~direktor** prison governor, (prison) warden; **~geistlicher** prison chaplain; **~hof** prison yard; **~insasse** (prison) inmate; **~mauer** perimeter wall; **~ nicht unter 2 Jahren** imprisonment of not less than 2 years; **~ordnung** prison rules; **~personal** prison staff; **~revolte** prison riot; **~strafe** prison sentence, jail sentence, imprisonment (*without hard labour*), prison term; **bei ~~~**: *under pain of imprisonment, on pain of committal to prison*; **zu ~~ verurteilen**: *to sentence to a term of imprisonment*; **~verwaltung** prison administration; **~wärter** prison warden; warder, turnkey, gaoler (= *jailer, US*).

Gefolgschaft *f* adherents, followers, vassals; **~streue** allegiance, party loyalty.

gefördert *adj* promoted, state-aided, subsidized; **öffentlich** ~ supported by the public authorities; **staatlich** ~ government-sponsored.

gefragt *adj* in demand, sought after.

Gefrier|anlage refrigerating plant; **~verfahren** freezing process; **~ware** frozen goods.

Gefüge *n* structure, composition, set-up, nature.

gefügig *adj* docile, manageable, amenable.

gegebenenfalls *adj* if so, as occasion arises, should the opportunity arise, if applicable, where appropriate.

Gegebenheiten *f/pl* given facts, existing circumstances; **geografische** ~ natural objects; **wirtschaftliche** ~ economic background, business climate.

gegen *prep* against, versus.

Gegen|abrede mutual understanding, informal compensatory agreement; **~akkreditiv** mutual letter of credit, countervailing credit, back-to-back credit; **~angebot** counter-offer, counterbid; **~anklage** counter-accusation, counter-charge; **~anspruch** counterclaim; **~antrag** counter-motion, cross motion; **~anwalt** opposing counsel; **~anzeige** contra-indication; **~argument** counter-argument; **~aussage** testimony to the contrary; **~äußerung** answer, replication; **~begutachtung** opposing expert opinion; **~beschuldigung** recrimination, counter-charge; **~en vorbringen**: *to recriminate*; **~bestätigung** counter-confirmation; **~beweis** proof to the contrary, rebutting evidence, evidence in rebuttal, counter-evidence; **den ~~ antreten**: *to introduce rebutting evidence; to put forward counter-evidence*; **den ~~ erbringen**: *to furnish proof to the contrary*; **g~beweislich** disprobative; **~beziehung** reciprocal relationship; **~bieter** competitive bidder; **~buchung** balancing entry, offsetting entry, per contra, counter-entry, counter-item; **ohne ~~**: *unbalanced*; **~bürge** counter-surety; **~darstellung** reply (*to a charge*), counter-statement; **~~sanspruch**: *right to have a counter-statement published*; **~deckung** counter-security; hedging; **~demonstrant** participant in a counter-demonstration; **~demonstration** counter-demonstration; **~denkschrift** counter-memorial; **~dienst** return

Gegeneinrede service, reciprocal service; **~einrede** counterplea; **~einwand** counter-plea; **~entwurf** alternative draft; **~erklärung** reply, answer, rejoinder, denial, counter-statement, counter-notice; **~faktor** opposing factor; **~forderung** counterclaim, cross-claim; *e-e ~~ erheben: to interpose (submit) a counterclaim, to counterclaim;* **~frage** counter-question; **~geschäft** back-to-back transaction, quid pro quo *pl*: countertrade; **~gewicht** counterweight, compensating factor; **g~gezeichnet** counter-signed counter-executed; **~grund** counter-argument; **~gutachten** counter-opinion (of an expert); **~kandidat** rival candidate; **~klage** counter claim, cross-action; cross-petition, counter-suit; **~kläger** counter-claimant, cross-petitioner; **~konto** contra account; **~kredit** back-to-back credit; **~läufigkeit** contrary course, opposite movement; **~leistung** (valuable) consideration, counter-performance, quid pro quo; *als ~~: in return for, in consideration of; angemessene ~~: fair and reasonable consideration;* **~leistungspolitik** give-and-take policy; **~manifest** anti-manifesto; **~maßnahme** counter-measure, counteraction, preventive measure; **~offerte** counter-offer; **~partei** opposing party, opponent, the other side; **~posten** contra-item, counter-item, opposite entry; *passivischer ~~: counterpart on the liabilities side;* **~probe** counter-verification, cross-check; **~propaganda** counter-propaganda; **~protest** counter-protest; **~reaktion** reaction, opposite movement; **~rechnung** controlling account, check account, account for checking purposes, bill in return, invoice for set-off purposes; **~recht** adverse right, adverse title; **~regierung** counter-government; **~revolution** counter-revolution; **~saldo** counterbalance; **~schlag** retaliation; **~seite** opposite side; **g~seitig** *adj* mutual, reciprocal; **~seitigkeit** → *Gegenseitigkeit;* **~spionage** counter-espionage; **~stand** → *Gegenstand;* **g~steuern** counter-steering; **~stimme** adverse vote, "No"-vote, vote "against"; *ohne ~~: unanimous, unopposed;* **~stück** counterpart; **~teil** (the) contrary, (the) opposite; *das ~~ beweisen: to disprove;* **g~teilig** *adj* contrary, to the contrary; **g~über** *prep* as between, as against, vis-à-vis, towards; **g~überstellen** *v/t* to confront s. o. (with); **~überstellung** comparative analysis; confrontation, identification parade, police line-up; **~verkauf** sale in return, counter-sale; **~verkehr** oncoming traffic, contra-flow (system); two-way traffic; **~verpflichtung** cross-undertaking, reciprocal insurance; *treuhänderische ~~: back-bond;* **~versicherung** mutual insurance; **~vertrag** counter-treaty; **~vorbringen** replication, affirmative plea; *neues ~~ zur Klageerwiderung: special replication; offensichtlich unschlüssiges ~~: frivolous answer; substantiiertes ~~: special plea; verspätetes ~~ pretermitted defence; vertretbares ~~ arguable defence;* **~vormund** co-guardian, supervisory guardian; **~vormundschaft** supervisory guardianship; **~vorstellung** remonstration, arguments; *~~en erheben: to remonstrate, to take exception to;* **~wechsel** cross-bill; **~werbung** aggressive advertizing; **~wert** → *Gegenwert;* **g~zeichnen** *v/t* to countersign, to back; **~zeichnung** counter-signature; **~zug** counter-move *(negotiations).*

Gegenseitigkeit *f* mutuality, reciprocity; **~ bei der Strafverfolgung** reciprocity of punishment; **~ gewähren** to grant reciprocal treatment; **~ verbürgen** to guarantee reciprocity; *auf ~ on mutual terms.*

Gegenseitigkeits|abkommen reciprocity agreement; **~ausfuhr** barter

Gegenstand | **Gehaltsabrechnung**

exports; ~**behandlung** reciprocity of treatment; ~**erklärung** mutual declaration; ~**geschäft** barter transaction, reciprocal deal, barter; ~**gesellschaft** mutual association; ~**klausel** reciprocity stipulation; ~**prinzip** principle of reciprocity (*in recognizing foreign judgments*); ~**verpflichtung** mutual promise; ~**versicherung** mutual insurance, reciprocal insurance; ~**vertrag** reciprocity treaty.

Gegenstand *m* (*pl Gegenstände*: ~*e*) object, thing, subject-matter, article, res; ~ **der Anmeldung** subject(-matter) of the application; ~ **der Klage** substance of the action; ~ **des Berufungsverfahrens** matter arising in an appeal; ~ **des Schutzbegehrens** matter for which protection is sought; ~**e des täglichen Bedarfs** necessaries; ~**e des Verbrechens** products and tools of the offence; ~ **e-r Gesellschaft** objects of a company; ~ **e-s Patents** subject-matter of a patent; ~ **e-s Unternehmens** objects of enterprise; ~ **e-s Vertrages** subject-matter of a contract; ~**e öffentlichen Interesses** matters of public interest; **als Waffe geeigneter** ~ sth which is suitable as a weapon; **besprochener** ~ points discussed, subject-matter under discussion; **bewegliche** ~**e** movable objects; **fabrikmäßig hergestellte** ~**e** manufactured articles; **immaterielle** ~**e** incorporeal things; **inventarisierte** ~**e** inventorized items; **körperlich** ~ tangible thing, corporeal object; **lebensgefährlicher** ~ life-endangering article; **patentrechtlich geschützter** ~ patented article; **schädlicher** ~ noxious thing; **steuerpflichtiger** ~ taxable object; **streitbefangener** ~ object involved in the litigation; **unkörperliche** ~**e** intangibles; **versicherter** ~ subject-matter insured, risk.

gegenständlich *adj* objective, concrete, involved in the transaction.

gegenstandslos *adj* nugatory, irrelevant, purposeless, pointless, no longer valid, invalid.

Gegenstandswert *m* value of the subject matter, amount involved.

gegenüber *prep* vis-à-vis; as against, opposite, in relation to.

gegenwärtig *adj* present, in praesenti, in attendance, current.

Gegenwartswert *m* present value, actual value, value (*for taxing the costs*); ~ **der Anwartschaft**: present value of an expectancy.

Gegenwert *m* consideration, equivalent, currency equivalent, equivalent sum, countervalue; ~ **der begebenen Aktien** nominal value of shares issued; ~**mittel** counterpart funds; *originäre* ~~: *original counterpart funds*; **gleicher** ~ equivalent value.

Gegner *m* opponent, adversary, the opposing party, the other side, opposing counsel; ~**unabhängigkeit** independent status of adversary (*collective bargaining*); **der** ~ **blieb aus** the opposing party (*or* counsel) failed to appear; **ein ebenbürtiger** ~ an equally skilled adversary, a worthy opponent; **mutmaßlicher** ~ purported adversary; **über den** ~ **obsiegen** to defeat the opponent, to win one's case.

gegnerisch *adj* adverse, opposing, opposite.

Gehalt *n* salary, fixed salary; ~ **bei Einstellung** initial salary, starting salary; ~ **beziehen** to draw one's salary; ~ **nach Vereinbarung** salary by arrangement; **festes** ~ fixed salary; **volles** ~ full pay.

Gehalts|abrechnung salary account, salary printout; ~**abzug** payroll deduction, deduction from salary; ~**ansatz** salary rate; ~**anspruch** salary required, desired salary; ~**aufbesserung** raise (in salary), pay increase; ~**aufstellung** statement of salary; ~**basis** salary basis, *reine* ~~: *straight salary* (*no share of profits*); ~**bogen** salary schedule; ~**empfänger** salary-earner, salaried worker; ~**erhöhung** salary increase; *laufbahnmäßige* ~~:

within-grade salary increase; ~**forderung** salary claim; ~**fortzahlung** continued payment of salary (*in case of illness etc*); ~**gefälle** salary differential; ~**gruppe** salary class, salary group, salary bracket; ~**klasse** salary class, salary bracket; ~**konto** salary account; ~**kosten** salary costs; ~**kürzung** salary cut, deduction from salary; ~**liste** payroll, payroll sheet, pay sheet; ~**nachzahlung** back pay, payment of salary in arrears; ~**pfändung** garnishment of salary, attachment of earnings; ~**rückstände** accrued salary, arrears in pay; ~**scheck** pay cheque, salary cheque; ~**staffelung** salary scale; ~**steigerung** salary raise, pay increase; ~**streifen** pay slip; ~**stufe** salary bracket; *in e–e niedrigere ~~ zurückversetzen: to reduce to a lower salary, to reclassify in a lower salary group*; ~**tarif** salary schedule; ~**tüte** wage-packet, pay envelope; ~**überzahlung** excess payment of salary; ~**verrechnungskonto** payroll transitory account; ~**vorschuß** salary advance; ~**wünsche** desired salary; ~**zahlung** salary payment; ~**zulage** additional salary.

geheim *adj* secret, restricted, confidential, surreptitious, clandestine; „**streng ~**" top secret.

Geheim|abkommen secret pact; ~**agent** secret agent, intelligence agent; ~**befehl** secret order; ~**bereich** sphere of privacy; ~**bericht** secret report; ~**buchführung** undisclosed accounting; ~**bund** secret society; ~**bündelei** (association with) secret societies; ~**dienst** secret service, intelligence service; ~**diplomatie** secret diplomacy; ~**haltung** → *Geheimhaltung*; ~**konto** secret account; ~**mittel** secret funds; ~**nachrichten** intelligence reports; ~**nummer** ex-directory number, unlisted telephone number; ~**pakt** secret pact; ~**patent** secret patent; ~**polizei** secret police; ~**polizist** member of the secret police; plain-clothes (police-)man; ~**sache** secret matter, classified item; ~**schublade** secret drawer; ~**schutz** secrecy, maintenance of secrecy; *unter ~~ stehende Angaben: restricted data, classified information*; ~~~**abkommen**: Security Protection Treaty; ~**sender** clandestine transmitter; ~**sitzung** secret session; ~**sphäre** sphere of secrecy, intimacy; ~**tinte** invisible ink; ~**urteil** judgment of a secret court; ~**verbindung** secret society, secret connection; ~**verfahren** secret (manufacturing) process; ~**vertrag** secret agreement.

Geheimhaltung *f* secrecy, maintenance of secrecy.

geheimhaltungsbedürftig *adj* sensitive, classified, subject to classification.

Geheimhaltungs|kontrolle spill control; ~**pflicht** duty of secrecy, obligation to maintain secrecy; ~**stufe** degree of security, security grading; ~**system** security system; ~**verpflichtung** pledge of secrecy; ~**versprechen** promise of secrecy; ~**vorschriften** secrecy rules.

Geheimnis *n* secret; ~**schutz** security, maintenance of secrecy; ~**verletzung** violation of secrecy; ~**verrat** betrayal of secrets; **ein ~ preisgeben** to disclose a secret; **ein ~ verraten** to betray a secret; **gewissensbelastendes ~** guilty secret; **strenges ~** top secret.

Gehilfe *m* assistant, helper, skilled worker; *crim* accessory, aider and abettor; ~**nhaftung** respondent superior (*in tort*), vicarious liability (*of master for servant*).

Gehirn|blutung cerebral (*or* brain) haemorrhage (*US:* hemorrhage); ~**erschütterung** concussion; ~**quetschung** cerebral contusion; ~**tod** brain death; ~**trust** brains trust; ~**wäsche** brainwashing.

Gehöft *n* farmstead, homestead.

Gehör *n* hearing; **rechtliches ~** opportunity of being heard, fair hearing, full hearing, day in court, right of audience; *das ~~ versagen: to*

gehorchen | **Geld**

deny s. o. an opportunity of being heard; **richterliches** ~ right to be heard in court; **sich ~ verschaffen** to gain a hearing, to make oneself heard.

gehorchen *v/t* to obey; **nicht ~** to disobey, to fail to obey.

gehörend *adj* belonging (to), incident, appertaining to.

gehörig *adj* belonging (to), rightfully due to s. o., forming part of sth; *adv* appropriately, duly, in due form, properly, in due terms.

Gehorsam *m* obedience; **~ gegen das Gesetz** obedience to the law; **~ schulden** to owe obedience to s. o.; **~spflicht** duty to obey; **~sverweigerung** refusal to obey, disobedience, insubordination; **unbedingter ~** absolute obedience.

Gehrecht *n* pedestrian's right of way.

Geh- und Fahrtrecht *n* easement of access.

Gehweg *m* (compulsory) footpath, pavement, sidewalk.

Geisel *f* hostage; **~befreiung** freeing of hostages; **~erschießung** shooting of hostages; **~nahme** taking of hostages, seizure of hostages, ~~ *begehen: to seize hostages*.

Geist *m* **des Rechts** spirit of the law.

Geisterfahrer *m* ghost driver, phantom driver.

Geistes|abwesenheit absent-mindedness; **~arbeiter** brain-worker; **~gegenwart** presence of mind; **~fähigkeit** mental ability; **g~gestört** mentally deranged (or disturbed); **~gestörter** person of unsound mind, mentally deranged person, mental defective; **~gestörtheit** mental derangement, unsoundness of mind, mental disturbance; **~gut** intellectual product; **g~krank** insane, mentally ill, lunatic, of unsound mind; *unheilbar ~~: incurably insane;* **~kranker** person of unsound mind; insane person, lunatic; *mittelloser ~~: indigent insane person; unheilbarer ~~: incurably insane person;* ~~ *als Kläger: patient plaintiff;* **~krankheit** insanity, lunacy, mental disease; *angeborene ~~: congenital insanity; unheilbare ~~: incurable insanity;* **g~schwach** weak-minded, mentally deficient; **~schwäche** weakness of mind, feeble-mindedness, mental deficiency, mental infirmity, imbecility; **~schwacher** feeble-minded person, person of unsound mind, mental defective, imbecile; **~störung** mental disorder, mental derangement; **~tätigkeit** mental activity, mental work; *gestörte ~~: unbalanced mind;* **~verfassung** mental condition; **~zustand** mental state, state of mind; *gesunder ~~: soundness (of mind); normaler ~~: sanity.*

Gekränktheit *f* sense of grievance, offence.

Geladener *m* (*der Geladene*) the person summoned.

Gelände *n* terrain, area, tract of land, ground, site; **~aufbereitung** site preparation; **~aufnahme** topographical survey; **~gängigkeit** cross-country performance; **~punkt** bench mark, landmark; **bebautes ~** built-up area; **ebenes ~** level ground; **erschlossenes ~** developed (tract of) land, improved site; **landwirtschaftlich genutztes ~** agricultural land; **unbebautes ~** open space(s), idle land, clear area of land.

Gelbbuch *n* fallow book (*official goverment report, similar to a blue book*).

Geld *n* money (= *m*); **~abfindung** pecuniary compensation, cash settlement; **~abfluß** drain of *m*; **~ abgezählt bereithalten** please have correct change; no change given; **~abhebung** withdrawal of *m* (from an account); **~abschöpfung** taking *m* out of circulation, sterilization of *m*; **~abwertung** currency depreciation, devaluation; **~akkord** money piecework; **~angelegenheiten** monetary (or *m*) matters, pecuniary affairs; **~anlage** investment, employment of *m*, placing of *m*; ~~ *bei ersten Adressen: monies placed at first class banks;* **~ anlegen** to invest *m*, to

336

Geldanleger   **Geldmarkt**

place *m*, to invest capital; ~**anleger** investor(s); ~**anspruch** monetary claim; ~**aristokratie** plutocracy, timocracy; ~ **auf Abruf** call money; ~**(er) aufbringen** to raise funds; ~**auflagen** monetary conditions; ~**aufnahme** borrowing; ~ **aufnehmen** to take up *m*; ~**aufwertung** revaluation of *m*; ~**ausfuhr** exportation of *m*; ~**ausgabe** expenditure; ~**ausgleich** settlement of payments; ~**ausweitung** monetary expansion; ~**automat** cash dispenser, service till, automatic teller machine, bancomat; ~**automatenkarte** cash card; ~**bedarf** monetary need; ~**beschaffungskosten** cost of procuring *m*; ~**beschaffungsverkäufe** *m*-raising sales; ~**bestand** stock of *m*, monetary holding(s), cash-in-hand; ~**betrag** amount, sum (of *m*); *beigetriebener* ~~: *amount collected by way of execution; ein bestimmter* ~~: *fixed sum; jmdn e-n* ~~ *gutschreiben: to credit s.o. with an amount;* ~**bewilligung** allocation of funds, appropriation of funds; ~**bezüge** monetary remuneration; ~**brief** registered letter containing *m* (or valuables); ~**briefträger** postman authorized to make cash payments; ~**börse** purse; ~**buße** penalty; administrative fine; *e-e* ~~ *verhängen: to impose a fine;* ~**darlehen** loan; ~**disponent** *m* manager; ~**disponibilitäten** available liquid funds; ~**disposition** employment of funds, *m* management; ~**eingang** receipt (of *m*); ~**einlage** investment, contribution in the form of funds; ~**einnehmer** collector; ~**einschuß** injection of *m*; ~ **einsenden** to send (in) *m*; ~**einziehung** collection of *m*; ~**einziehung durch die Post** postal collection; ~**empfang** receipt of *m*; ~**empfänger** payee, recipient of a *m* remittance; ~**empfangsvollmacht** authority to accept *m*; ~**entschädigung** pecuniary compensation, pecuniary satisfaction; ~**entwertung** depreciation of currency, currency devaluation, inflation; ~**entwertungsausgleich** equalization for *m* depreciation; ~**entzug** loss of funds, drain of *m*; ~**er abziehen** to withdraw deposits; ~**er mit Verwendungsauflagen** monies subject to instructions as to their use; ~**er nutzbar anlegen** to invest, to employ monies usefully; ~**ersatz** monetary compensation; ~ **fest anlegen** to tie up *m*, to invest *m*; ~**forderung** pecuniary claim, money due, outstanding debt, active debt; liquidated demand; ~~*en des Kapitalverkehrs: financial debts, bestimmte* ~~: *claim in a liquidated amount, e–e* ~~ *einklagen: to sue for a debt;* ~**fülle** abundance of *m*; ~ **für den Prozeß aufbringen** to invest *m* in a law-suit; ~**geber** lender of capital, financier; ~**geschäft** monetary transaction, financial transaction; ~-**Güterbilanz** relationship between *m* and goods; ~**handel** *m*-market business, currency trading; ~**hortung** hoarding of *m*; ~ **in ein Unternehmen stecken** to sink (or put) *m* into an enterprise; ~ **in den Wirtschaftskreislauf einschleusen** to pump *m* into the economic system; ~**inflation** monetary inflation; ~**institut** financial institution, bank; ~**kapital** monetary capital; ~~*bildung: formation of (monetary) capital;* ~~*(s)anlage: pecuniary investment;* ~**karte** debit card; ~**kasse** till, cash register; ~**kassette** cash box; ~**knappheit** scarcity of *m*, lack of *m*, shortage of *m*, financial squeeze; *zeitweilige* ~~: *money pinch;* ~**kredit** *m* loan, advance; ~**kreislauf** circulation of *m*; ~**krise** monetary crisis; ~**kurs** rate of exchange; *exch* buying rate, buying price, bid price, bid quotations, demand rate; ~**leiher** money-lender; ~**leistung** performance in money, payment, cash benefit, pecuniary consideration; ~**leute** rich people, plutocrats; ~**mangel** scarcity of *m*, lack of funds; ~**markt** *m* market; *ange-*

Geldmarktkredite — **Geldwäsche**

spannter ~~: *tight moneymarket*; ~**marktkredite** *m*-market lendings, *m*-market loan; ~**marktpapiere** *m*-market paper; ~**marktregulativ** means of regulating the *m*-market; ~**marktverschuldung** *m*-market indebtedness; ~**menge** money supply, quantity of currency; ~~*nziel*: *money supply target*; ~~~*nzuwachs*: *money supply growth*; ~**mittel** pecuniary resources, *m*, funds; ~**notiz** *exch* demand quotation; **g~politisch** from the point of view of monetary policy; ~~ *neutral*: *neutral in monetary policy*; ~**preis** price in *m*, cash price, price of *m*, interest rate on very short-term loans; prize in the form of a payment of *m*; ~**quelle** source of *m*, source of capital; ~~~*n*: *pecuniary resources*; ~**reform** currency reform, monetary reform; ~**rente** periodical payments; ~**reserve** monetary reserve; ~**sammlung** collection of *m*; ~**satz** money rate, buying rate; ~**schein** note, banknote, bill; *gekennzeichneter* ~~: *marked m*; ~**schneiderei** sharp practice; ~**schnitt** cut in the supply of *m*; ~**schöpfung** creation of *m*; ~~~*skredit*: *credit with money-creating effect; hoheitliche* ~~: *creation of m by the state*; *kreditäre* ~~: *creation of m in the form of a bank credit*; ~**schrank** safe, strong-box, safe deposit box; ~**schrankknacker** safe-cracker, safe-blower; ~**schuld** pecuniary debt, *m* debt; ~~~*en*: *pecuniary obligations*; ~**schwemme** glut (*or* flood) of *m*; ~**sendung** remittance (of *m*); ~**sog** drain of *m*; ~**sorten** notes and coin(s); ~~~*schuld*: *debt to be paid in a specified currency*; ~**sortiermaschine** coin-counting machine; ~**spende** donation of *m*, financial contribution; ~**stillegung** tying up of *m*, locking up *m*, freezing of funds; ~**strafe** → *Geldstrafe*; ~**stück** coin; ~**summe** sum of *m*; ~~~*nschuld*: *obligation to pay an amount of m*; ~~~*n vermächtnis*: *general pecuniary legacy*; ~**surrogat** representative *m*, ~**taschenraub** purse snatching; ~**-Taxkurs** estimated price; ~**transport** transport of *m*; ~**transportwagen** armoured car; ~ **überfülle** excessive supply of *m*; ~**überhang** surplus of *m* supply; ~ **überweisung** *m* transfer; *telegrafische* ~~: *money order telegram*; ~**umlauf** circulation of *m*; ~~~*geschwindigkeit*: *velocity of monetary circulation*; ~**umstellung** currency conversion; ~**umtausch** exchange of *m*, exchange of invalidated notes and coins (*at currency reform*); ~ **und Brief** bid and asked; ~ **und Kreditpolitik** *m* and credit policy; ~- **und Sachbezüge** remuneration in *m* and in kind; ~**unterschlagung** embezzlement, peculation; ~**verbindlichkeit** pecuniary obligation; ~**verfassung** monetary structure; ~**verkehr** movements, *m* transactions; ~**verknappung** scarcity of *m*; ~**verleih** *m* lending; ~**verleiher** *m*-lender; *wucherischer* ~~: *loan shark*; ~**vermächtnis** pecuniary legacy; ~**vermehrung** increase in *m*; expansion in the *m* supply; ~**vermittler** *m*-broker; ~**vermögen** monetary wealth, pecuniary assets, monetary capital; *ruhendes* ~~: *inactive monetary wealth*; ~**vermögensbildung** monetary wealth formation; ~**vermögenswert** monetary asset, monetary value; ~**vernichtung** destruction of monetary wealth; ~**verschlechterung** deterioration of currency; ~**verschwendung** squandering of *m*, wasting *m*; ~**versorgung** supply of *m*; ~ **verzinslich anlegen** to invest *m* for interest; to put out *m* at interest; ~**volumen** quantity (*or* volume) of *m* (in circulation); *rechnerisches* ~~: *statistical volume of money*; *volkswirtschaftliches* ~~: *overall volume of money*; ~ **von e-m Konto abheben** to withdraw *m* from an account; ~**vorrat** available funds, cash reserve, cash in hand; supply of *m*; ~ **vorteilhaft anlegen** to invest *m* profitably; ~**waschanlage** *m* laundering (bank); ~**wäsche** *m*

Geldwäscherei — **Gelegenheitsarbeit**

laundering; ~**wäscherei** *m* laundering; ~**wechselautomat** change (giving) machine; ~**wechselgeschäft** exchange transaction, exchange business; ~ **wechseln** to exchange *m*; ~**wechsler** money-changer, *m* dealer; **g~wert** *adj* monetary, in terms of *m*; ~**wert** monetary value, value of *m*; *abnehmender* ~~: *monetary erosion*; **g~wertbereinigt** real monetary value, real terms; ~**wertschuld** pecuniary obligation; ~**wertschwankungen** fluctuations in the value of *m*; ~**wertstabilität** monetary stability; ~**wertverschlechterung** currency depreciation; ~**wesen** monetary matters, currency matters; ~**wirtschaft** *m* monetary economy; ~**wucher** usury; ~**zeichen** monetary token(s); ~**zins** *m* interest, rate of interest on *m*; nominal interest; ~**zuwachs** increase in the supply of *m*; ~**zuwachsrate** rate of increase in the supply of money; **anlagebereite** ~**er** funds, available for investment; **angelegtes** ~ invested *m*, investment; **aufgenommene** ~**er** *bil* creditors' account; **außer Kurs gesetztes** ~ *m* withdrawn from circulation; **bares** ~ cash; **bei Gericht hinterlegtes** ~ funds in court; **billiges** ~ cheap *m*; **das restliche** ~ the residue of *m*; **durchlaufende** ~**er** transitory funds; **eingefrorene** ~**er** frozen funds; **falsches** ~ counterfeit *m*; **feste** ~**er** fixed *m-s*, time deposits, fixed term deposits; **festgelegte** ~**er** tied-up funds, immobilized *m*; **flüssige** ~**er** liquid funds; **fremde** ~**er** funds from outside sources, borrowings; **gefälschtes** ~ counterfeit *m*; **gepfändetes** ~ distrained *m*; **gewaschenes** ~ laundered *m*; **heißes** ~ hot *m*; **knappes** ~ tight *m*; **krankes** ~ unsound *m*; **kurzfristiges** ~ *m* at call, *m* at short notice; **längerfristig verfügbares** ~ medium-term funds; **mit** ~ **abfinden** to settle with *m* (or for cash); **öffentliche** ~**er** public funds; ~~**er veruntreuen**: *to peculate, to misappropriate public funds*; **originäres** ~ original *m*; **sämtliche** ~**er** all *m-s*; **stillgelegte** ~**er** non-earning reserve; **tägliches** ~ call *m*, day-to-day *m*, *m* at one day's notice; **täglich fälliges** ~ day *m*; **übriges** ~ loose *m*, loose capital; **umlaufendes** ~ *m* in circulation; **zweckgebundene** ~**er** ear-marked monies, ad hoc monies.

geldlich *adj* pecuniary, monetary.

Geldstrafe *f* (judicial) fine, pecuniary penalty; **an Stelle e-r** ~ in lieu of a fine; **e-e** ~ **festsetzen** to assess a fine; **e-e** ~ **verhängen** to impose a fine; **es wird auf** ~ **erkannt** a fine is imposed; **mit e-r** ~ **bestrafen** to punish with a fine; **mit** ~ **bedroht** liable to a fine; **zu e-r** ~ **verurteilen** to impose a fine, to sentence to a fine.

gelegen *adj* situate, situated, located.

Gelegenheit *f* chance, occasion, opportunity, bargain; ~ **zu schriftlicher und mündlicher Äußerung** the opportunity to submit one's case orally and in writing; ~ **zur Erwiderung** opportunity to respond; ~ **zur Stellungnahme** opportunity for an explanation; ~ **zur Replik** opportunity to rebut; ~ **zur Verleumdung** occasion for scandal, opportunity to defame; **bei** ~ as occasion arises, if and when the occasion arises; **die** ~ **nützen** to avail oneself of the opportunity (chance), to seize the chance, to take the opportunity

Gelegenheits|arbeit casual work, casual job, odd jobs, jobbing; ~**arbeiter** casual worker, odd job man, jobber; ~**arbeitkräfte** casual staff; ~**beschäftigung** casual employment; ~**diebstahl** casual theft, petty theft; ~**einkünfte** casual emoluments, income from odd jobs; ~**einnahmen** receipts from casual employment; ~**frachtführer** occasional carrier, private carrier; ~**geschäft** occasional deal, chance business; ~**geschenke** occasional presents; ~**gesellschaft** ad hoc as-

gelegentlich

sociation, special (*or* temporary) association, occasional partnership, single venture partnership, joint venture, joint enterprise, temporary association; ~**kauf** chance purchase, bargain; ~**käufer** casual buyer, bargain hunter; ~**kunde** casual customer; ~**schiffahrt** occasional navigation (*or* shipping); ~**spediteur** occasional forwarder; ~**täter** infrequent offender; ~**trinker** social drinker; ~**verbrecher** infrequent offender, accidental criminal; ~**verkehr** occasional transportation.

gelegentlich *adj* occasional, discontinuous, incidental, casual; *adv* on occasion, when the occasion arises, at times, from time to time, occasionally.

Geleit *adj* escort, conduct; ~**brief** letters of safe conduct; ~**schiff** escort, convoy-ship; ~**schutz** escort, convoy-protection; ~**zug** convoy; **freies** ~ safe conduct; *Verletzung des freien* ~*s*: violation of safe conduct; **sicheres** ~ safe conduct.

gelernt *adj* skilled, trained by trade.

gelesen und genehmigt read and approved.

Geliebte *f* mistress, paramour; ~**ntestament** last will in favour of a mistress.

Geliebter *m* (*der Geliebte*) lover.

geliefert *adj* delivered.

geliefert (benannter Bestimmungsort im Einfuhrland) verzollt, delivered (named place of destination in the country of importation), duty paid.

geloben *v/t* to promise solemnly, to vow, to pledge, to swear.

Gelöbnis *n* vow, solemn declaration, pledge; taking oath on enlistment.

gelten *v/i* to be valid, to prevail, to be in effect, to be in force, to hold true, to apply, to be applicable; ~ **als**: to be deemed, to be considered as, to be regarded as, to pass for; ~ **lassen** to accept sth as founded, to acknowledge, to al-

340

low; **als richtig** ~ to be deemed to be true; **dies gilt auch wenn** notwithstanding the fact that; **entsprechend** ~ to apply mutatis mutandis; **jeweils** ~ to be applicable for the time being; **sinngemäß** ~ to apply mutatis mutandis.

geltend *adj* valid, effective, in force, in operation, applicable, existing; ~ **machen** to raise, to put forward, to assert, to claim to argue; *gerichtlich* ~~: *to assert by court action.*

Geltendmachung *f* assertion, claiming, enforcement; ~ **des Zeugnisverweigerungsrechts** plea of privilege (*witness*); ~ **e-r Teilklage** proceeding on part of a claim; ~ **e-s Rechts** assertion of a right, insistence on one's right; ~ **e-s Vermieterpfandrechts** distress (under a landlord's lien); ~ **e-s Verpächterpfandrechts** *cf supra;* **gerichtliche** ~ **e-s Anspruchs** assertion of a claim in court, legal action to enforce a claim; **nachträgliche** ~ subsequent reliance, subsequent assertion; **verspätete** ~ delay in asserting (a right), laches.

Geltung *f* validity, recognition, operation, prevalence; ~ **haben** to be operative, to be in force, to apply; **zur** ~ **bringen** to put forward, to assert.

Geltungs|bedürfnis need for recognition; ~**bereich** extent (of validity), scope (*or* area) of application, sphere of operation, purview, area of application; *örtlicher* ~~: *territory covered, territorial application; persönlicher* ~~: *personal scope;* ~**bereichsklausel** territorial application clause; ~**dauer** duration, term of validity, life (*patent*); period of validity; ~**gebiet** purview, territory of application *cf* ~*bereich.*

Gelübde *n* vow, solemn promise, pledge.

Gemarkung *f* local subdistrict (*for survey map*); boundary; area.

GEMA *f* German Society for Musical Performance and Mechanical Reproduction Rights.

gemäß *prep* in accordance with, in pursuance of, pursuant to, subject to, in compliance with, under, in keeping with.

gemäßigt *adj* moderate.

gemein *adj* common, ordinary, usual, average.

Gemeinbedarf *m* public requirements.

Gemeinde *f adm: (basic unit of local government)* local authority, local government unit, municipality, commune, parish, community; ~**abgaben** (parochial) rates, local taxes; ~**abgabengesetz** law concerning local revenue; ~**abwässerverband** sewage disposal district board; ~**amt** local government office; ~**angehöriger** local resident; ~**angelegenheiten** local government matters; ~**anleihe** municipal loan; ~**aufgaben** functions of local authorities; ~**aufsichtsbehörde** local government supervisory authority; ~**autonomie** local government; ~**bank** municipal bank; ~**beamter** local government official, parochial officer; ~**bedienstete** local government employees, municipal employees; ~**behörde** local authority, municipal authority; ~**betrieb** local authority enterprise, municipal enterprise; ~**bewohner** local resident, parishioner; ~**bezirke** local districts; ~**bürger** freeman; ~**bürgerrecht** local citizenship, freedom of a city; ~**dienste** local goverment services, municipal services; ~**eigentum** municipal property, parish property; ~**einwohner** local resident; ~**finanzen** municipal finances, local finances, communal finances; g~**frei** (*land*) outside of a local government district; ~**freiheiten** privileges of local government units, municipal freedoms; ~**fürsorge** parochial relief, local government relief; ~**gebiet** local authority area, local administrative area; ~**gesundheitsamt** local board of health; ~**gruppen** local government groups; ~**gut** municipal (*or* parochial) property; ~**haushalt** municipal budget; ~**haushaltsrecht** local government budget law, local finance legislation; ~**hoheit** exclusive local government jurisdiction; ~**kasse** municipal treasury, local authority treasury; ~**lasten** municipal charges, local charges; ~**nutzungsrechte** rights of use vested in local authority; ~**ordnung** local government code, municipal regulations; ~**organe** local authority agencies; ~**polizei** local police, municipal police; ~**polizist** parish constable, local police officer; ~**rat** (local) council, municipal council, parish council, community council, village council, urban district council; ~**ratsbeschluß** council resolution, council decision; ~**ratsmitglied** member of local council, councillor; ~**ratswahlen** local government elections; ~**recht** local government law; ~**satzung** municipal by(e)-laws, municipal code; ~**schulden** municipal debts, debts of local authorities; ~**schule** local school, parish school; ~**schwester** parish nurse, district nurse; ~**steuern** local taxes, municipal taxes, local rates, municipal rates, personal community charge, poll tax; ~**steuerzahler** rate-payer; ~**straße** local street, local road; ~**testament** last will executed before the mayor (*in an emergency*); ~**verband** local government regional authority, district board, association of local authorities; ~**verfassung** constitution of a local authority; ~**verfassungsrecht** local government law; ~**vermögen** municipal property, property of a town (*or* parish); council property; ~**verordnung** municipal ordinance, local authority regulations; ~**versammlung** parish meeting, town meeting; ~**vertretung** council (of a local au-

Gemeineigentum

thority), representation of a local authority; ~**verwaltung** local administration, local government administration, municipal administration, local government office; town meeting, village meeting; ~**vorstand** municipal executive board; ~**vorsteher** (*eccl*) chairman of the parish council; ~**wahl** municipal election, local election; ~**wahlberechtigter** parochial elector, *person entitled to vote in a local government election*; ~**wahlgesetz** local government election law; ~**wahlordnung** regulations governing local elections; ~**waisenrat** communal orphan council; ~**weg** local road; ~**wohnhaus** council house; ~**wohnungsamt** local housing office; ~**zentrum** community centre; **abgelegene** ~**n** remote communities; **hebeberechtigte** ~ *local authority entitled to charge municipal taxes and rates*; **kreisangehörige** ~ community forming part of a county; **kreisfreie** ~ county borough.

Gemeineigentum *n* public ownership, nationalized property; **in** ~ **überführen** to nationalize.

gemeinfrei *adj* in the public domain, of common knowledge, *unprotected by copyright or industrial property rights*.

Gemeingebrauch *n* common use, public use; ~**sinteressierter** person having a legitimate interest in the public use of sth.

Gemeingefahr *f* common danger, collective danger, public danger.

gemeingefährlich *adj* dangerous to the public, constituting a public danger, dangerous to public safety.

Gemeingefährlichkeit *f* public danger, danger to public safety.

Gemeingläubiger *m* general creditor in bankruptcy, non-preferential creditor.

gemeingültig *adj* generally accepted, universally valid.

Gemeingut *n* common property, public property, public domain.

Gemeinschaft

Gemeininteresse *n* interest of the general public.

Gemeinkosten *pl* overhead, overhead costs, indirect costs, fixed costs, basic expense, general expenditure; ~**abweichung** overhead cost variance; ~**ansatz** standard overhead cost data; ~**konto** overhead charges account; ~**lohn** indirect labour costs; ~**satz** overhead rate; ~**überdeckung** overabsorbed overhead; ~**umlage** overhead cost allocation; ~**unterdeckung** under-absorbed indirect costs; ~**verrechnungssatz** overhead cost absorption rate; ~**zuschlag** overhead rate, establishment charge; **abschreibungsabhängige** ~ depreciation-related overhead (costs); **anteilige** ~ prorated overhead, pro-rata overhead; **steuerlich zulässige** ~ overhead rate permissible under tax laws; **umzulegende** ~ overhead costs to be prorated, overhead costs to be assessed on a pro rata basis; **verrechnete** ~ absorbed overhead.

Gemeinlast *f* burden-sharing, common burden, overhead charges.

Gemeinnutz *m* public benefit.

gemeinnützig *adj* useful for general welfare, for public use, for the public benefit; charitable, pro bono publico.

Gemeinnützigkeit *f* usefulness for the benefit of the public; promotion of general welfare, public charity; charitable nature; ~**sverordnung** *ordinance regulating tax advantages for promotion of public benefits*.

gemeinsam *adj* joint, common, mutual, combined; ~ **mit**: jointly with, in conjunction with.

Gemeinsamer Markt → *Markt*.

gemeinschädlich *adj* damaging to the public.

Gemeinschaft *f* community, association; ~ **nach Bruchteilen** → *Bruchteilsgemeinschaft*; ~ **nach bürgerlichem Recht** ownership in common *according to the German*

Civil Code; ~ **zur gesamten Hand** → *Gesamthandsgemeinschaft*; **Atlantische** ~ Atlantic Community; **eheliche** ~ conjugal community, matrimony; **erweiterte** ~ enlarged Community; **häusliche** ~ common household; **ursprüngliche** ~ original Community.

Gemeinschafter *m* associate, group member.

gemeinschaftlich *adj* joint, common, in common; *adv* jointly, conjointly, in conjunction with; ~ **berechtigt sein** to hold concurrently.

Gemeinschafts|anlage collectively owned installation; ~**aktion** joint action, synergy; ~**anschluß** (two-) party line, shared line (*telephone*); ~**antenne** shared aerial, party aerial; ~~*nanlage*: master TV aerial (*US: antenna*); ~**arbeit** team work, cooperative work; ~**aufgabe** joint task; ~**besitz** joint possession, *generally*: joint property; ~**behandlung** Community treatment, intra-Community treatment; ~**besteller** joint buyers, joint subscribers (*newspaper, periodicals*); ~**beteiligung** joint interest, joint participation, joint capital share, jointly owned company; ~**bilanz** consolidated balance sheet; ~**depot** joint custody account, joint deposit of securities; ~**dienst** joint service; ~**eigentum** common parts (*block of residential flats*); ~**einrichtung** jointly used installation; ~**emission** joint issue; ~**erfindung** joint invention; ~**erzeugnis** Community product; ~**felder** open fields, common land; ~**finanzierung** group financing; ~**geschäfte** joint business, syndicate transactions; ~**haft** group confinement; ~**haftung** joint liability; ~**hilfe** mutual assistance; ~**kasse** common funds, common treasury, common kitty; ~**konto** joint account, partnership account; ~**kredit** syndicate credit, joint loan; ~**land** Community country; ~**marke** Community trade mark; ~**ordnung** condominium bye-laws, declaration of restrictions; ~**organ** jointly used agency, community organ; ~**patentgesetz** (1979) Community Patent Act; ~**plafond** Community ceiling; ~**präferenz** Community Preference; ~**produktion** joint production; ~**projekt** joint venture, community project; ~**recht** Community law, EEC law; ~**regelungen** Community rules, common rules; ~**schule** non-denominational school, coeducational school; ~**stelle** joint office; ~**stunde** joint instruction hour, staff meeting; ~**tochter** joint subsidiary; ~**treue** Community loyalty; ~**unterkünfte** (joint) employee accomodations; ~**unternehmen** joint venture, cooperative venture; ~**ursprung** Community origin; ~**vermögen** collective property; ~**verpflegung** communal feeding; ~**versicherung** group insurance; ~**vertrag** joint contract; ~**weide** open meadows; ~**werbung** joint advertizing; ~**zentrum** community centre, civic centre; ~**zoll** Community tariff.

Gemeinschuldner *m* debtor in bankruptcy, (adjudicated) bankrupt, undischarged bankrupt.

Gemeinwesen *n* body politic.

Gemeinwirtschaft *f* the socio-economic sector of business.

gemeinwirtschaftlich *adj* socio-economic.

Gemeinwohl *n* general welfare.

Gemischtwaren *pl* groceries, general goods; ~**laden** variety store; ~**handlung** general store, grocery store.

gemischtwirtschaftlich *adj* semi-public (*enterprise*), publicly owned in part, pertaining to a mixed (*capitalist/socialist*) economy.

Gemütskrankheit *f* emotional illness, emotional disturbance, melancholia, nervous breakdown.

Gemütsverfassung *f* state of mind, emotional condition.

genehm *adj* agreeable, acceptable.

genehmigen *v/t* to approve of, to

genehmigt | **Generalabrechnung**

sanction, to ratify, to adopt, to affirm, to give one's assent to.
genehmigt *adj* approved, authorized (*capital*).
Genehmigung *f* approval, permit, sanction, ratification, authorization; adoption, affirmation, assent; leave (*of court*); ~**auf Zeit** period authorization; ~ **der Bilanz** adoption (*or* approval) of the balance sheet; ~ **des Gerichts** leave of the court; ~ **des Jahresberichts** adoption of the annual report; **allgemeine** ~ general licence; **amtliche** ~ official approval, official authorization; **atomrechtliche** ~ permission under nuclear law; **behördliche** ~ licence, permit; **der** ~ **unterliegen** to require consent, to be subject to approval; **devisenrechtliche** ~ exchange control permit, exchange authorization; **die** ~ **für etwas erhalten** to get sth affirmed (*or* approved), to obtain a permit; **die** ~ **für etwas einholen** to seek permission, to obtain the approval for sth; **die** ~ **verweigern** to disaffirm, to refuse permission; **finanzamtliche** ~ approval of the fiscal authorities; **gerichtliche** ~ court sanction, leave of court; ~~ *der Adoption*: granting letters of adoption; **gewerbliche** ~ trade permit; **ministerielle** ~ approval by the ministry; **nachträgliche** ~ ratification, (subsequent) approval; **rechtsaufsichtliche** ~ approval by the supervisory authority; **seine** ~ **zurücknehmen** to revoke one's consent; **staatliche** ~ governmental approval; **zur** ~ **vorlegen** to submit for approval (*or* authorization).
Genehmigungsantrag application for a permit (*or* licence); ~**bedürftig** subject to approval, requiring official approval; ~**bedürftigkeit** requirement of official approval; ~**befugnis** authority to approve; ~**behörde** approving authority, authorizing body; ~**bescheid** notice of approval, permit, licence; ~**bescheinigung** certificate of approval; ~**erfordernis** requirement of official approval; **g**~**fähig** approvable, capable of being approved; **g**~**frei** exempt from licensing; ~**pflicht** requirement of official permission; **g**~**pflichtig** subject to authorization, subject to approval, requiring official approval, subject to licence, licensable; ~**schreiben** letter of approval, letter of approbation; ~**urkunde** instrument of approval, licence; ~**verfahren** licence procedure, ratification procedure; ~**vermerk** "approved" endorsement, "approved" stamp, note of approval; ~**vorschriften** regulation for public permits; ~**widerruf** revocation of ratification; ~**zeichen** approval mark.

General|abrechnung, general settlement of accounts, full settlement; ~**abtretung** deed of general assignment; ~**agent** chief agent, general agent; ~**agentur** general agency business; ~**amnestie** general pardon; ~**anwalt** solicitor general; ~**bevollmächtigter** executive manager; general agent; (*pol*) plenipotentiary; ~**bundesanwalt** federal attorney general; ~~ *beim Bundesgerichtshof*: Public Prosecutor General at the Federal Court of Justice; ~**direktor** president (*of a corporation*), chairman of the board of directors, executive director, managing director, general manager, director general; ~**embargo** universal embargo; ~**gouverneur** governor general, ~**inventur** cradle-to-grave inventory; ~**klausel** comprehensive clause, blanket clause; ~**konsul** consul general; ~**konsulat** consulate general; ~**konto** general account; ~**mobilmachung** general mobilization; ~**police** floating policy, open policy, block policy; ~**prävention** (principle of) crime prevention; ~**quartiermeister** Quartermaster General; ~**quittung** receipt in full, comprehensive receipt; ~**repräsentanz** general representatives;

Generationenvertrag   **Genuß**

~**schlüssel** skeleton key; ~**schuldverschreibung** general debenture; ~**sekretär** secretary general; ~**staatsanwalt** chief public prosecutor, Director of Public Prosecutions, Attorney General; ~**stabschef** chief of staff; ~**stabskarte** ordnance map; ~**streik** general strike, mass strike; ~**überholung** reconditioning, overhaul; ~**übernehmer** s.o taking over the enterprise (*or* company) as a whole; ~**unkosten** overhead (expenses), undistributed cost; ~**unternehmer** general contractor, prime contractor; ~**verpfändung** floating charge; ~**versammlung** general meeting, general assembly; *außerordentliche* ~~: *extraordinary meeting, special meeting; konstituierende* ~~: *statutory meeting (GB), ordentliche* ~~ *annual general meeting*; ~**vertrag** Bonn Convention = *Convention on Relations Between the Three Powers and the Federal Republic of Germany (1952, ending military occupation of West Germany)*; ~**vertreter** general agent; ~**vertretung** general agency, head agency; ~**vertretungsabkommen** general agency agreement; ~**vertrieb** general sales agency; ~**vollmacht** general authority, general power (of attorney), plenary power, unlimited power (of attorney); ~**zahlmeister** Paymaster General; ~**zolldirektor** Director-General of Customs.

Generationenvertrag *m* generational transfer program(-me); the social contract between the generations.

Genesungsurlaub *m* convalescent leave.

Genfer Konventionen *f/pl* Geneva Conventions (*conventions on prisoners of war, wounded soldiers etc.*)

Genfer Welturheberrechtsabkommen *n* World Copyright Convention (*of 1952*).

Genosse *m* member (of a co-operative society), *pol*: comrade.

Genossenschaft *f* co-operative (*US*: cooperative) (= *cp*) society, co-op, co-operative enterprise; **eingetragene** ~ (*eG*) registered *cp* society (*body corporate*); **eingetragene** ~ **mit beschränkter Haftpflicht** (*eGmbH*) registered *cp* society with limited liability; **eingetragene** ~ **mit unbeschränkter Haftung** (*eGmuH*) registered *cp* society with unlimited liability; **gewerbliche** ~ industrial *cp*; **ländliche** ~ agricultural *cp*, rural *cp*; **landwirtschaftliche (Absatz)**~ producers' *cp*.

Genossenschafts|anteil share in a co-operative society (*co-operative = cp*); ~**bank** *cp* bank, bank for *cp-s*, *cp* banking association, people's bank; *landwirtschaftliche* ~~: *agricultural credit society*; ~**gesetz** co-operative association law; ~**kapital** capital of a *cp*, a (credit) co-operative's credit; ~**kasse** *cp* bank; *cp* funds; ~**recht** law of *cp* societies; ~**register** Register of Co-operative Societies; ~**sektor** institutions in the field of *cp-s*; ~**verband** association of *cp* societies; ~**versammlung** meeting of members of a *cp* society; ~**vertrag** articles of association of a *cp*; ~**wald** collectively owned forest; ~**wesen** *cp* movement, the *cp* system; ~**wohnung** cooperative apartment, co-op (owned) apartment.

Gen|schaden *m* congenital disability; ~**technikgesetz** law on genetic technology.

Genugtuung *f* satisfaction, legal redress, amends, gratification.

Genus *m* genus, type, kind; *gram* gender (*of a noun*); ~**kauf** sale of unascertained goods; ~~-**Sachen** unascertained goods, fungibles; ~~-**Schuld** obligation to provide fungibles, unascertained debt.

Genuß *f* enjoyment, use; ~**aktie** bonus share (*non-voting*); ~**mittel** articles consumed for stimulation and enjoyment (*mainly beverages*); ~**mittelentwendung** petty larceny of consumables; ~**recht** special dividend right, participation right (*without membership obligations or liabilities*); ~**schein** (profit) participating certificate, bonus share, dividend right certificate; ~**schuld** obligations under bonus rights; ~**tauglichkeitsbescheinigung** health certificate for human consumption; **tatsächlicher** ~ actual enjoyment; **ungestörter** ~ quiet enjoyment, undisturbed enjoyment.

Gepäck *n* luggage, *esp. US*: baggage; ~**abfertigung** luggage office; checking-in of luggage, clearing of luggage (*customs*); ~**annahme** "in" counter of left-luggage office; ~**aufbewahrung** left-luggage office, baggage deposit; ~**ausgabe** ("out" section of) left-luggage office; ~**ausgabebereich** baggage delivery area; ~**durchleuchtungsgerät** screening machine; ~**kreisel** baggage carousel; ~**meister** baggage master; ~ **mit Übergewicht** over-luggage, excess baggage; ~**schalter** luggage office; ~**schein** luggage receipt, luggage ticket, left-luggage ticket; ~**selbstbedienung** self-claim luggage (= baggage) system; ~**verkehr** registered luggage transportation; ~**versicherung** luggage insurance; **aufgegebenes** ~ registered baggage; **mitgeführtes** ~ accompanied baggage; **nicht mitgeführtes** ~ unaccompanied baggage; **persönliches** ~ ordinary luggage.

gepfändet *adj* attached (*by way of execution*), distrained; **fruchtlos** ~ not satisfied, "nulla bona".

Gepflogenheit *f* usage, custom, standard practice; **diplomatische** ~ diplomatic usage; **internationale** ~ international usage; **parlamentarische** ~ parliamentary usage, parliamentary form; **den** ~**n** ~**en entsprechend:** *parliamentary*; **uralte** ~ immemorial usage.

geprüft *adj* tested, examined, checked.

Gerät *n* appliance, utensil, piece of equipment, implement; ~**ebau** construction of equipment; ~**elieferplan** equipment delivery scheme; ~**emiete** equipment lease; ~**eschuppen** tool-shed; ~**esicherheitsgesetz** Equipment-Safety Law; ~**schaften** implements, tools, utensils; **landwirtschaftliche** ~ agricultural implements, farming implements.

Geräuschpegel *m* noise level.

gerechnet vom ... to be computed from, reckoning from, calculated as from.

gerecht *adj* just, fair; ~ **und angemessen** just and proper.

gerechtfertigt *adj* justified.

Gerechtigkeit *f* justice, justness, fairness; franchise, licence; ~ **in der Sache selbst** substantial justice; ~ **walten lassen** to do justice, to let justice be done; ~ **widerfahren lassen** (*jmdm*) to do s. b. justice, to dispense justice; **ausgleichende** ~ distributive justice; **materielle** ~ substantial justice, substantive justice; **natürliche** ~ natural justice; **soziale** ~ social justice.

Gerechtigkeits|begriff concept of justice; ~**empfinden** sense of fairness, fair-mindedness; ~**gefühl** sense of fairness; ~**liebe** love of justice; ~**sinn** sense of justice.

Gerechtsame *f* franchise, privilege, right of exploitation.

geregelt *adj* regular, settled, disposed of, arranged; **gütlich** ~ settled amicably, disposed of by agreement; **vertraglich** ~ contractually settled, agreed by contract.

Gericht *n* court of law, (law) court, court of justice; tribunal; ~ **der belegenen Sache** the court where the thing in controversy is situated, forum rei sitae; ~ **des Urteilsstaates** original court, the national court; ~ **erster Instanz** court of first instance, trial court, court of original jurisdiction; ~ **für Wettbewerbsbeschränkungen** restrictive practices court; ~ **letzter Instanz** court of last resort; ~ **zweiter Instanz** court of second instance, appellate court; **an ein anderes** ~ **verweisen** to refer (*or* transfer) the case to another court;

Gericht   **gerichtlich**

ausschließlich zuständiges ~ sole court of competence; **außerordentliches** ~ extraordinary court; **bei** ~ at (in) court; **bei** ~ **anhängig** pending before a court; ~~~*er Fall: a (the) case before the court*; **bei** ~ **einreichen** to hand into court, to file at court; **bei** ~ **hinterlegen** to pay into court, to deposit with the court; **bei** ~ **mündlich vortragen** to address the court; **bei** ~ **vortragen** to submit to the court; **das angerufene** ~ the invoked court, the court seized of the case; **das** ~ **anrufen** to take legal (*or* court) action, to resort to courts of law; **das** ~ **erachtete dies für unwesentlich** the court considered this to be immaterial; **das erkennende** ~ the trial court; **das** ~ **erkennt ihm die Berechtigung ab** the Court holds him to be disqualified (from); **das** ~ **erkennt über den Anspruch** the court adjudicates on a claim; **das** ~ **hat die Ansprüche materiell geprüft** the Court examined the merits of the claims; **das** ~ **hat entschieden** the court held (that); **das** ~ **ist berufen, darüber zu befinden (ob)** the Court is called upon to consider (whether); **das** ~ **ist überzeugt, (daß)** the Court is satisfied (that); **das Jüngste** ~ the Last Judgment, Doomsday; **das** ~ **kommt zu dem Ergebnis...** the Court is led to the conclusion...; **das** ~ **überzeugen** to satisfy the court; **dem** ~ **etwas plausibel machen** to explain to the court; **dem** ~ **glaubhaft machen** to give prima facie evidence that; **dem** ~ **vorlegen** to submit to the court; **durch das** ~ by the court, per curiam; **ein** ~ **mit einer Frage befassen,** to make a court cognizant of a question; **ein** ~ **parteilich besetzen** to pack a court; **erkennendes** ~ this court, trial court, judging court; **erstinstanzliches** ~ court of first instance; **ersuchendes** ~ court issuing letters rogatory, the requesting court; **ersuchtes** ~ requested court, authority to which the letters rogatory are transmitted; **für Ehescheidungen zuständiges** ~ divorce court; **gleichgeordnetes** ~ court of equal authority; „**Hohes** ~" your Honour; **innerstaatliche** ~**e** municipal courts, domestic courts, national courts; **jmdn auffordern, vor** ~ **zu erscheinen** to summon s. o. to appear in court; **jmdn vor** ~ **laden** to summon (before the court); **jmdn vor** ~ **verklagen** to sue s. o.; **jmdn vor** ~ **vertreten** to represent s. o. in court (*or* in legal proceedings); **letztinstanzliches** ~ court of last resort; **nachgeordnetes** ~ subordinate court; **nicht ortsgebundenes** ~ ambulatory court, assize court; **ordentlich bestelltes** ~ regularly constituted court; **ordentliches** ~ court of record, ordinary court; law court; **sich vor** ~ **verantworten** to stand trial; **übergeordnetes** ~ higher court; **unteres** ~ subordinate court (*or* tribunal); **unzuständiges** ~ a court that lacks jurisdiction, incompetent court; **vor** ~ **auftreten** to appear in court; **vor** ~ **aussagen** to give evidence in court, to testify in court; **vor** ~ **beweisen** to prove to the satisfaction of the court; **vor** ~ **bringen** to put on trial, to bring before a court, to bring to trial; **vor** ~ **erscheinen** to appear in court; **vor** ~ **gehen** to take legal (*or* court) action; **vor** ~ **geltend machen** to plead (in court), to assert a claim in court; **vor** ~ **klagen** to sue, to bring a court action against; **vor** ~ **plädieren** to plead at the bar; **vor** ~ **stehen** to be on trial, to stand trial; to be a party to legal proceedings; **vor** ~ **stellen** to put on trial; **zu** ~ **sitzen** to sit in judgment; **zuständiges** ~ competent court, court of competent jurisdiction, appropriate court.

gerichtlich *adj* judicial, legal, per curiam, forensic; ~ **und außergerichtlich** judicial and extrajudicial; **nicht** ~ out of court, non-judicial.

Gerichts|akte case record, case file, record of trial, record of proceedings, *pl*: court files, court records, records of the court, judicial documents, court papers; *zu den ~~n einreichen*: *to put on file, to file with the court*; **~archiv** court archives, "paper mill"; **~arzt** medical officer of the court, court-appointed doctor; **~assessor** junior judicial officer (*acting as assistant judge or prosecuting officer*); **~barkeit** → *Gerichtsbarkeit*; **~beamter** judicial officer, law-court official; **~beauftragter** judicial agent, person commissioned by a court of justice; **~befehl** court order; **g~bekannt** known to the court, *s.th. of which the court takes judicial notice*; **~bekanntmachungen** legal notices; **~berichterstattung** reporting of court proceedings; **~bescheid** summary court decision (*administrative court*); **~beschluß** order of the court, court order, judicial order; *e-n ~~ erlassen*: *to order, to rule*; *e-e ~ erwirken*: *to obtain a court order*; **~besetzung** appointment of court judges; **~bezirk** judicial district, circuit, venue; *im ~~*: *in the judicial district, within the jurisdiction*; **~bote** court messenger; **~diener** court attendant, (court) usher, tipstaff; **~dolmetscher** court interpreter; **~eingang** court entrance; received at the court; **~eingangsstelle** filing office, seal office (*for petitions, writs*); **~entscheidung** court decision, judicial decision; **~ferien** vacation (of the courts), non-term, recess; *in den ~~*: *out of term, during the vacation*; **~gebrauch** judicial custom; **~gebühren** court fees; **g~hängig** *adj* pending at court; **~hilfe** court assistance; **~hof** court of justice, court of judicature; *~ der Europäischen Gemeinschaften*: *Court of Justice of the European Communities*; *oberster ~~*: *supreme court*; **~hoheit** jurisdiction, (supreme) judicial sovereignty; **~hügel** *hist* parle hill (parling hill); **~instanz** (court) instance; **~jahr** legal year; **~kanzlei** court registry, clerk's office (at a court), record office; **~kasse** court cashier; **~kommissar** judicial commissioner; **~kosten** costs, court fees; *die ~ auferlegen*: *to order to pay the costs (of the proceedings)*; **~kostengesetz** Court Fees Act; **~kostenmarke** court fee stamp; **~kostentabelle** table of costs; **g~kundig** known to the court, *s.th. of judicial notice*; **~kundigkeit** notoriety, judicial notice; **~medizin** forensic medicine, legal medicine, medical jurisprudence; **g~medizinisch** medico-legal, relating to forensic medicine; **g~notorisch** known to the court; *s.th. of judicial notice*; *~~sein*: *to be of judicial notice*; **~ordnung** system of judicature, rules of the court; **~organisation** organization of the courts, judicial set-up; **~ort** place of trial, place of court; **~periode** term, law-term, session; **~personen** court officials, court officers; **~polizei** bailiff, court police; **~präsident** president of the court, chief presiding judge; **~praxis** judicial custom; **~protokoll** record, court stenographer's transcript; **~psychiatrie** forensic psychiatry; **~referendar** (=) *law graduate in the course of court training*, judicial trainee **~saal** courtroom; **~sache** matter, case (*being tried in court*) **~sachverständiger** court-appointed expert; **~schranke** bar; **~schutz** court protection; **~siegel** court seal; **~sitz** seat of a court; **~sitzung** court hearing, sitting (of a court), court session; *e-e ~~ abhalten*: *to hold court*, *öffentliche ~~*: *open court*; **~sprache** official language (used in court); **~sprengel** court district; **~spruch** court judgment, court decision, court ruling; **~stand** → *Gerichtsstand*; **~stätte** place of the court; **~stelle** location of the court, seat of the court; **~tafel** court notice-board; **~tag** judicial day, day of the hearing, *a day on which the court is in*

Gerichtsbarkeit

session; ~**tagebuch** court diary; ~**tätigkeit** judicial activity; ~**termin** day of hearing, court hearing, date fixed for the trial; ~**urkunden** court record, judicial document; ~**urteil** court judgment, (court) decree, (judicial) sentence (*crim. law*); ~**usance** judicial custom, court practice; ~**verfahren** legal proceedings, court proceedings, judicial proceedings; ~**verfassung** court system, system of judicature, structure of the judiciary, constitution of the courts; ~**verfassungsgesetz** Judicature Act, *law governing court jurisdiction and organization*, Constitution of Courts Act; ~**verhandlung** court hearing; *öffentliche* ~~: *hearing in open court*; ~**verwaltung** administration of the courts; ~**vollzieher** bailiff, sheriff's officer, committing officer; ~**vollzieherkosten** bailiff's fees, sheriff's poundage; ~**vorsitzender** presiding judge; ~**wachtmeister** tipstaff, serjeant (of the peace); ~**wesen** judicial system; ~**zeiten** juridical days, legal days; ~**zuständigkeit** jurisdiction, competence of the judiciary; ~**zweige** branches of the courts.

Gerichtsbarkeit *f* jurisdiction (= *j*), judicial authority; ~**des Staats des Wohnsitzes** domiciliary *j*; ~**erster Instanz** *j* of first instance, original *j*; **ausschließliche** ~ exclusive *j*; **der** ~ **unterliegen** to be subject to the *j*; **die** ~ **ausschließen** to oust the *j* of the courts; **deutsche** ~ German *j*; **e~r** ~ **unterstehen** to come within the jurisdiction of; **freiwillige** ~ non-contentious proceedings, non-contentious litigation, *Gesetz über* ~~ (*FGG*): *German Ex Parte Jurisdiction Act*; **inländische** ~ domestic *j*, national *j*; **internationale** ~ international *j*; **keiner** ~ **unterworfen sein** to be immune from legal process, to be exempt from court-*j*; **kirchliche** ~ ecclesiastical *j*; **nicht ausschließliche** ~ concurrent *j*; **obligatorische** ~ mandatory *j*, compulsory *j*; **or-**

geringschätzen

dentliche ~ ordinary *j*, *j* of courts of record; **streitige** ~ contentious *j*, contentious litigation.

Gerichtsstand *m* jurisdictional venue, legal venue, forum, place of jurisdiction, place of litigation, purview of a court's competence; ~ **der belegenen Sache** = *dinglicher Gerichtsstand qv*; ~ **der Erbschaft** probate *j*; ~ **der Geschäftsniederlassung** *j* at (the place of) branch establishment; ~ **der unerlaubten Handlung** forum actus in tort cases; ~ **des Erfüllungsortes** *j* at the place of performance; ~ **des Sachzusammenhangs** *j* on the ground of factual connection; ~ **des Tatortes** forum actus, place of competent *j* in criminal cases; ~ **des Vermögens** *j* on grounds of the location of (an) asset(s); ~ **des Wohnsitzes** forum by reason of domicile of the defendant, forum domicilii; ~**sklausel** jurisdictional clause, clause as to the venue of the action; ~**svereinbarung** stipulation as to venue, agreement as to the *j* of the court in the event of litigation; **allgemeiner** ~ place of general jurisdiction (*at the defendant's domicile or general residence*); residuary jurisdiction, natural forum; **ausschließlicher** ~ exclusive venue, exclusive place of *j*; **besonderer** ~ **des Sachzusammenhangs** supplementary forum for personal actions connected with real actions (*at the forum rei sitae*); **den** ~ **vereinbaren** stipulate a *j*; **dinglicher** ~ in rem jurisdiction; **inländischer** ~ domestic *j*; **vereinbarter** ~ consent (*or* agreed) jurisdiction, stipulated venue, mutually agreed place of *j*.

gerieren *v/reflex* to behave (as), to act, to conduct oneself.

geringfügig *adj* slight, trivial, petty, minor; disregardable; **ganz** ~ inappreciable (*quantity*), very slight, very small.

Geringfügigkeit *f* triviality, insignificance, pettiness, bagatelle.

geringschätzen *v/t* to disregard, to despise, to hold in contempt.

349

Geringschätzigkeit *f* contempt, disdain.

Geringschätzung *f* disdain, contempt, disregard.

Geringstland *n* lowest-yield land, land valueless for cultivation.

geringwertig *adj* of low value, low grade, inferior, trivial.

gerissen *adj* shrewd, cunning, tricky.

Geruchsbelästigung *f* molestation by smell, nuisance of malodours.

Geruchssinn *m* sense of smell.

Gerüst *n* scaffold.

Gesamt|abfindung separation package (*termination of employment*); ~**abmessungen** over-all dimensions; ~**absatz** total sales; ~**abschluß** total account, overall result; blanket contract; *rechnerischer* ~~: *arithmetical net total*; ~**abwägung** general consideration of the merits (*or of the issue*), overall weighing of the pros and cons; ~**angebot** aggregate supply (*economy*); ~**annuität** total annuity, cumulative annuity; ~**arbeitsverträge** collective labour agreements; ~**aufkommen** total revenue, total yield; ~**auftragswert** total contract value; value of total-orders-received; ~**aufwand** aggregate expenditure, total disbursements; ~**aufwendungen** = *Gesamtaufwand qv*; ~**ausbeute** total recovery, total exploitation; ~**ausfuhr** total exports, national exports; ~**ausgabe** complete edition, full edition; ~**ausgaben** aggregate expenditure; ~**ausgebot** combined auction-offer (*of several parcels of land*); ~**ausgleich** full settlement, total net position; ~**ausrüstung** complete equipment; ~**ausweis** consolidated statement of financial position; ~**bank** entire bank; ~**bedarf** total need, total requirements; ~**belastung** total load; total encumbrances; *steuerliche* ~~: (*the*) *total tax burden*; ~**bereich** the whole sphere, total field; ~**bereinigung** overall validation; ~**beschäftigtenzahl** (*e–s Landes*) work force; ~**besitz** common possession, collective property; ~**betrachtung** overall view, general survey, comprehensive survey; ~**betrag** sum total, total amount, aggregate sum; *den* ~~ *bilden*: *to amount to*; ~~ *der Einkünfte*: *aggregate income*; ~~ *der Verbindlichkeiten*: *total liabilities*; ~**betrieb** the entire concern; ~**betriebsrat** central works council; ~**bewertung** total evaluation, total assessment; ~**bezüge** total emoluments; *jährliche* ~~: *annual emolument*; ~**bilanz** consolidated balance sheet, overall balance sheet, combined balance sheet; *volkswirtschaftliche* ~~: *national accounts*; ~**blattzahl** total number of sheets; ~**bürgschaft** joint guarantee, joint suretyship; **g~deutsch** all-German, pan-German (*comprising the whole territory of pre-war Germany*); ~**disposition** overall lay-out, the overall arrangement; ~**dividende** total dividend; ~**durchschnitt** total average; ~**eigentum** joint ownership, joint property, undivided ownership; ~**einkommen** total income; ~**einnahme** total income, gross receipts; ~**entschädigung** total compensation, general compensation; ~**entwicklung** general development, overall trend; ~**erbbaurecht** joint hereditary building right; ~**erbe** universal heir, sole beneficiary; ~**erbfolge** universal succession of a deceased by inheritance; ~**ergebnis** total result; ~**ergebnisrechnung** statement of income and accumulated earnings, combined profit and loss account; ~**erhebung** complete statistics, complete census, all-embracing census; ~**ertrag** total proceeds, aggregate output; ~**erzeugnis** joint product; ~**erzeugung** overall production; ~**etat** overall budget; ~**forderung** total claim; ~**genehmigung** joint permit (*or* licence), block licence; ~**geschäftsführung** joint management; ~**gewicht** total weight, total load, combined weight; *das höchstzulässige* ~~: *total authorized*

Gesamtgläubiger   **Gesamtschuldneranteil**

loaded weight; zulässiges ~~: *licence (US: license) weight*; **~gläubiger** joint creditor; **~grundschuld** comprehensive land charge (*on two or more properties to secure one debt*); **~gut** joint marital property, common property; **~gutsverbindlichkeit** liability in respect of joint marital property; **~gutsverwaltung** administration of joint marital property; **~haftung** joint and several liability, joint responsibility; **~hand** joint title, collective ownership; **~handelsbilanz** overall trade balance; **~händer** joint holder of property; **g~händerisch** joint, in common; **~handsberechtigung** joint entitlement, entirety of interests; **~handsbesitz** undivided interest, joint property; ~~ *mit Anwachsungsrecht im Todesfall*: *estate in joint tenancy*; **~handseigentum** joint ownership; **~handseigentümer** joint owner; ~ *am Nachlaß*: *parcener*; **~handsgemeinschaft** community of joint owners; **~handsgläubiger** co-creditor of a joint claim; **~handsklage** *shareholder's action for the benefit of the partnership as a whole*; **~handsrecht** undivided right (*of a collective group*) *pl*: undivided interests; **~handsverhältnis** joint-property relationship; **~handsvermögen** joint property, joint assets, joint capital; **~handsverpflichtung** joint obligation (*of several debtors*); **~haushalt** overall budget, national budget; **~hochschule** amalgamated university; **~hypothek** collective mortgage, comprehensive mortgage, blanket mortgage; **~index** overall index; **~jahreseinkommen** total annual revenue; **~kapazität** overall capacity; **~kapital** total capital, resources; **~kapitalausstattung** total capitalization; **~konjunktur** general economic trend, general level of economic activity; **~kosten** total cost, total outlay; **~kostenberechnung** calculation of total costs; **~kredit** bulk credit; **~kreditlinie** overall line of credit; **~lage** the general position, the overall situation; *wirtschaftliche* ~~: *general economic situation, the overall economic outlook;* **~leistung** total output, overall performance; **~liquidität** overall liquidity, total liquidity; **~liquidation** complete winding-up; **~masse** the total estate; **~meldung** combined statement; **~nachfolge** universal succession (*of all assets and liabilities*); **~nachfolger** universal successor; **~nachfrage** overall demand, aggregate demand; **~nachlaß** the complete estate, the real and personal estate; **~nichtigkeit** complete nullity; **~nutzung** joint use; **~nutzungsdauer** physical life (*of a machine*), total time of utility; **~organisation** overall organization, group of enterprises; **~personalrat** combined works council; **~plan** master plan, overall plan; **~planung** overall planning; **~preis** total price, lump-sum price; **~produkt** total product; **~prokura** joint power of Prokura (→ *Prokura*); **~quittung** receipt in full, total receipt; **~rechnung** overall accounts; *monetäre* ~~: *overall monetary account; volkswirtschaftliche* ~~: *national accounts*; **~rechtsnachfolge** universal succession; **~rechtsnachfolger** universal successor, general successor; **~regelung** overall settlement; **~rendite** compound yield, overall yield; **~risiko** overall risk, total hazard; **~rücklage** total reserve; **~saldo** overall balance; **~schadenhaftung** liability for total loss; **~schema** overall plan; **~schiffshypothek** comprehensive ship-mortgage (on several vessels); **~schuld** joint obligation, joint (and several) debt; **~schuldklage** action for recovery of a joint debt; **~schuldner** joint debtor, co-debtor; *pl*. joint and several debtors; *als* ~~ *haften*: *to be jointly and severally liable; ausgleichspflichtiger* ~~: *contributory*; **~schuldneranteil** contribution; **g~schuldnerisch** as joint and several debtors, jointly and severally liable; **~schuldschein** joint promissory note; **~schuldverhältnis** solidarity, joint indebtedness; **~schule** comprehensive school; **~staat** the nation (as a whole); **g~staatlich** national; **~status** consolidated statement, overall position; **~statut** universal law; general charter, joint property jurisdiction (*international private law*); **~steueraufkommen** total tax revenue; **~steuereinnahmen** total tax revenue; **~stimmenzahl** total votes cast, total number of votes; **~strafe** compound sentence, adjusted cumulative punishment (*adding up individual sentences, reducing the total*); **~strafenbildung** merger of sentences (*with total increase*); **~summe** (sum) total, grand total, total amount, gross sum, global sum; **~~** *der Abschreibungen*: *accumulated depreciation*; **~überschuß** total surplus; **~umlaufvermögen** total current assets; **~umsatz** aggregate turnover, aggregate sales, total business; **~umsatzrabatt** total turnover rebate, total-sales discount; **~umschuldung** total debt rescheduling (*or* restructuring); **~unternehmen** the enterprise as a whole; **~urkunde** all-in document; **~veranlagung** overall assessment; **~verantwortung** overall responsibility, collective responsibility, joint liability; **~verband** general association, national association; **~verbindlichkeit** total liabilities, joint indebtednes; **~vereinbarung** collective agreement; **~vergleich** full settlement, overall settlement; **~vergütung** total remuneration; **~verhalten** general conduct, collective behavio(u)r; **~verlust** overall loss, total loss; **~vermächtnis** universal legacy; **~vermächtnisnehmer** universal legatee; **~vermögen** aggregate property, all the property, total assets, real and personal estate, the estate and effects; *steuerpflichtiges* **~~**: *aggregate taxable property*; **~versicherung** comprehensive insurance, all loss insurance; **~versorgung** integrated retirement provisions; **~vertrag** integrated contract, the entire agreement, joint contract, master agreement; **~vertreter** co-agent, joint agents; **~vertretung** collective representation, joint agency; overall representation; **~vollmacht** joint (*or* collective) power of attorney, joint procuration, joint authority; **~volumen** total volume; **~vorsatz** general intent; **~vorstand** the national executive; **~werk** complete works (*author, artist*); **~wert** aggregate value, total value; **~wirkung** overall effect; **~wirtschaft** overall economy, the whole economic system, the national economy; **g~wirtschaftlich** *adj* macro-economic; **~wohl** general welfare, commonwealth, the general public interest; **~zahlungsbilanz** overall balance of payments; **~zeichnung** joint signature; **g~zeichnungsberechtigt** entitled to sign jointly; **~zeichnungsberechtigung** joint signature; **~zeit** total time, aggregate period; *anteilig zur Gesamtzeit*: *pro rata temporis*.

Gesandter *m* (*der Gesandte*) (embassy) minister; **päpstlicher** **~** nuncio.

Gesandtschaft *f* legation.

Gesandtschafts|attaché attaché (at a legation); **~gebäude** legation building; **~personal** legation staff; **~rat** legation counsellor; **~recht** right to establish a legation, droit de légation.

geschädigt *adj* damaged, injured, aggrieved; **~** *sein*: *to suffer damages, to be the aggrieved party*.

Geschädigter *m* the injured party, person unjured, the wronged party, sufferer, the aggrieved party; **mittelbar** **~** indirect victim (of damage).

Geschäft *n* business; transaction, deal, bargain; store, shop; **für**

Geschäft

den, **den es angeht** transaction for the benefit of whom it may concern; ~ **für eigene und fremde Rechnung besorgen** to transact business for one's own account and for third-party account; ~ **mit kleiner Marge** transaction providing a small return, business with small margin; ~ **tätigen** to transact business; **abgeschlossenes** ~ closed (*or* completed) transaction; **an e-e Lieferfirma gebundenes** ~ tied shop; **auf Gewinn gerichtetes** ~ lucrative business, profitable transaction; **bankähnliches** ~ quasi-banking transaction; **bankfremdes** ~ non-bank business; **darlehensähnliches** ~ quasi-loan; **das überwiesene** ~ the portfolio transferred (*investment*); **das vermittelte** ~ the transaction arranged (*by the intermediary*); **das zugrunde liegende** ~ the underlying transaction; **ein** ~ **abschließen** to conclude a bargain, to place a contract, to enter into a transaction; **ein** ~ **abwickeln** to wind up a business, to handle a deal; to carry out a transaction; **ein** ~ **aufgeben** to give up a business, to discontinue a business, to close down (a shop); **ein** ~ **ausführen** to effect a transaction; **ein** ~ **ausüben** to carry on a trade, to operate a business; **ein** ~ **betreiben** to run a business, to carry on a business, to operate a business; **ein** ~ **rückgängig machen** to cancel an order; **ein** ~ **zustande bringen** to negotiate a transaction; **gebührenfreies** ~**e** gratuitous, transactions; **juristisch vollzogenes** ~ legal transaction; **konzerninternes** ~ interaffiliate deal, internal group trading; **laufende** ~**e** current transactions, day-to-day transactions; **persönliche** ~**e** personal trading (*of a board member, official etc*); **rentables** ~ paying business, lucrative business; **richterliche** ~**e** matters handled by judges; **schwebende** ~**e** pending transactions; **sittenwidriges** ~ transaction contra bonos mores; immoral transaction; **verdecktes** ~ colourable transaction; **vorteilhaftes** ~ bargain; **zweifelhafte** ~**e** shady dealings, doubtful transactions.

Geschäftemacher *m* shrewd businessman, speculator, profiteer.

Geschäftemacherei *f* profiteering, crafty business deals; **interne** ~ insider dealing.

geschäftlich *adj* commercial, businesslike, business..., on business, from a business point of view; **rein** ~: *at arm's length*; ~**e Gewandtheit** business acumen.

Geschäfts|ablauf course of business; *normaler* ~~: *regular (or ordinary) course of business*; ~**abschluß** (business) transaction, business contract, conclusion of a business deal; *den* ~~ *vorlegen*: *to submit the annual accounts*; ~**abschlüsse**: *orders secured;* ~**abwicklung** the handling (*or* settling) of a business, winding-up of an enterprise; ~**abzeichen** logo; ~**adresse** business address; ~**andrang** run, crush, pressure of business; ~**anmaßung** usurpation of the business of an enterprise; ~**anteil** participation (*GmbH*), share, interest in a business firm; ~~ *an e-r GmbH: capital share in a private company limited (under German law)*, *GmbH-participation*; ~**anweisung** company instructions; ~**art** type of business; ~**aufgabe** abandonment of the business; ~**aufsicht** trade supervision; ~**ausfallversicherung** loss of profits insurance; ~**aussichten** business outlook; ~**ausstattung** business equipment, furniture and fittings; ~**ausweitung** expansion of trade; ~**bank** commercial bank, merchant bank, private credit bank; ~**bedarf** business requirements; ~**bedingungen** terms and conditions, terms of business, trading conditions; *allgemeine* ~~: *general terms and conditions of trade*; ~**beginn** commencement of business; ~**belebung** revival of business; ~**bereich** sphere (*or* line) of business, portfolio (*gov-*

353

Geschäftsbericht   **Geschäftskapital**

ernment); *ohne* ~~: *without portfolio*; ~**bericht** business report, report and accounts; ~~ *des Vorstands*: *directors' report*; ~**besorgung** a transaction for the benefit of another, agency business; act done by an agent; ~**besorgungsvertrag** contract for services, contract to manage s.th. for s.o.; ~**betrieb** conduct of a business, course of business, business establishment, business concern; *eingerichteter* ~~: *established business*; *im gewöhnlichen* ~~: *in the usual course of business*; *kaufmännischer* ~~: *commercial undertaking*; ~**bezeichnung** trade name; *die übliche* ~~: *the usual trade name*; ~**beziehungen** trade (*or* trading) relations, business connections; ~**bezirk** business district, bailiwick (*of bailiff*); ~**briefe** business letters, business correspondence; ~**bücher** business records, books of account, the books of a business; ~**einkommen** business income; ~**einlage** capital contribution, investment in a business; ~**einrichtung** business equipment, business fixtures and fittings; ~**erfahrung** business experience; ~**ergebnis** business result, operating result; ~**erlaubnis** trading licence; ~**eröffnung** opening of a business; ~**erweiterung** expansion of business; g~**fähig** legally competent, capable of contracting, *beschränkt* ~~: *of restricted capacity to contract, under legal disability* (*as a minor or patient*); *nicht* ~~: *incompetent*; *nicht voll* ~~ = *beschränkt geschäftsfähig qv*: *voll* ~~: *fully capable* (*to contract*); ~**fähiger** (*der* ~*fähige*) legally competent person, person with contractual capacity (*to enter into legal transactions*); *beschränkt* ~~: *person with limited capacity* (*minor, infirm person*); *nicht* ~~: *incompetent (person)*; *person without legal capacity*; ~**fähigkeit** (legal) capacity to contract; *beschränkte* ~~: *limited capacity* (*to contract*); *mangelnde* ~~: *lacking legal capacity*; *partielle* ~~: *partial capacity to contract*; ~**fahrten** business trips; ~**finanzen** business finance, financial matters of a firm; ~**fortführung** continuation of business; ~**frau** businesswoman; g~**frei** non-business (*day*); ~**freund** business acquaintance; g~**führend** *adj* managing; ~**führer** → *Geschäftsführer*; ~**führung** → *Geschäftsführung*; ~**gang** course of business, official procedure; *gewöhnlicher* ~~: *normal course of business*; *normaler* ~~: *normal conduct of business*; *ordentlicher* ~~: *ordinary course of business*; *patentamtlicher* ~~: *Patent Office procedure*; ~**gebaren** → *Geschäftsgebaren*; ~**gebarung** = *Geschäftsgebaren qv*; ~**gebiet** field (*or* line) of business; *vertragliches* ~~: *contractual field of business*; ~**gebühr** general fee for out-of-court work (*of German lawyers*); ~**gegenstand** subject matter (of the proceedings); ~**geheimnis** trade secret, business secret; *ein* ~~ *preisgeben*: *to divulge a trade secret*; ~**gewinn** business profits, profit of the business, trading profit, operating profit, earned surplus (tax); ~**grundlage** the basis of a transaction; *die* ~~ *für e-n Vertrag ist weggefallen*: *a contract becomes frustrated*; ~**grundsätze** business policies; ~**grundstücke** business premises; ~**guthaben** credit balance (*in a business*); ~~ *bei e-r Genossenschaft*: *membership shares in a cooperative society*; ~**haus** business premises, office building; ~**herr** principal; ~~ *bei Geschäftsführung ohne Auftrag* (*qv*): *involuntary principal*; *ungenannter* ~~: *undisclosed principal*; ~**inhaber** business proprietor, owner of a business, principal, owner manager; ~**interesse** interest in a business transaction; ~**inventar** office furniture and equipment; ~**irrtum** mistake as to the substance of the transaction; ~**jahr** business year, fiscal year, financial year; ~~*esabschluß*: *end-of-year accounts*; *laufendes* ~~: *current business year*; ~**kapital** (business)

354

Geschäftskosten   **Geschäftsvermögen**

capital; ~**kosten** costs, business expenditure; *allgemeine* ~~: *overhead charges*; ~**kreis** scope of operations, scope of business; ~**kreislauf** circulation of business deposits; ~**kunde** customer; ~**lage** business, situation; ~**leistung** business performance; ~**leiter** manager, person in charge of a business; ~**leitung** management, executive management; administrative office; ~*spersonal: managerial staff; oberste* ~~: *general management*; ~**lokal** business premises; ~**los** slack; ~**losigkeit** stagnation of business; ~**mann** businessman; *kleiner* ~~: *petty trader*; **g**~**mäßig** businesslike; ~**methoden** business practices; *unlautere* ~~: *unfair trade practices, unfair dealing*; ~**nachfolger** trade successor; ~**neugründung** new establishment; ~**nummer** reference number; ~**ordnung** → *Geschäftsordnung*; ~**papiere** commercial papers, business papers; ~**partner** party to a transaction; partner; ~**personal** staff (*or* employees) of a business undertaking; ~**plan** insurance business plan; ~**politik** business policy; ~**praktiken** business practices; ~**praxis** normal business usage, commercial practice; ~**prüfung** auditing (of the accounts of a business); ~**raum** store, office; ~*räume: business premises*; ~**raummiete** business premises tenancy, rent for business premises; ~**reise** business trip; ~**risiko** commercial risk, trade risk, business hazard; ~**rückgang** decline of business, downturn, business recession; ~**schädigung** discrediting the business of a trader; trade libel; ~**schluß** closing time, close of business; ~**schulden** business liabilities, trade debts; ~**sitz** place of business, (registered) office of a firm; ~**sparte** type of transaction, line of business; ~**spartenkalkulation** business sector costing, business category costing; ~**sprache** official language, commercial language; ~**statistik** business statistics, current statistics; ~**stelle** office, agency, executive secretary's office; court office, clerk's office, registry, record office; ~**stellenleiter** manager of a sub-branch, branch manager; ~**stil** business style, commercial style; ~**stille** dullness, slackness in trade; ~**stillstand** business stoppage; ~**struktur** business structure; ~**stunden** opening hours, business hours, banking hours; **g**~**tätig** doing business, active in business; ~**tätigkeit** commercial activities, business operations, doing business; *ordentliche* ~~: *ordinary course of business*; ~**träger** chargé d'affaires (ad interim); ~**übergang** assignment of a business enterprise (*to a successor*), devolution of a business; ~**übernahme** take-over (*of a business, firm, enterprise*); *nach der* ~~: *under new management*; ~**übersicht** business report, statement of operations; ~**umfang** volume of business; **g**~**unfähig** incompetent (to contract); ~**unfähiger** (*der Geschäftsunfähige*) person without legal capacity to contract; ~**unfähigkeit** juridical incapacity; ~**unkosten** expense in carrying on business; operating expenses, business expenses; *allgemeine* ~~: *overhead expenses, overheads;* ~**unterbrechung** interruption of business; ~**unterlagen** business records; ~**unternehmung** business enterprise, commercial undertaking, commercial establishment; ~**veräußerung** transfer of a business, sale of a business; ~**verbindlichkeit** business obligation; ~**verbindung(en)** business relations; ~**verfahren** business practice; *betrügerisches* ~~: *fraudulent business practice*; ~**verkehr** business dealings, transactions; *im gewöhnlichen* ~~: *in the ordinary course of business*; ~**verlauf** course of business, business trend; ~**verlegung** removal of business; ~**verlust** business loss, loss of earnings; ~**vermögen** business as-

355

Geschäftsführer

sets; ~**verteilung** allocation of duties, allocation of business, distribution of business; ~**verteilungsplan** distribution of business plan, organizational chart, functional distribution schedule, schedule of responsibility; ~**verzeichnis** cause list (*in a court*); ~**viertel** shopping centre; ~**volumen** volume of business, balance sheet total; ~**vorfall** business transaction; ~**vorgänger** predecessor in business; ~**vorhaben** business project; ~**vorteil** trading advantage; ~**welt** business world, business community; ~**wert** goodwill (of a business), trade interest; value of subject matter (*for computation of fees*); ~**wille** intention underlying a transaction; ~**zeichen** reference (number), file number, file reference, mark; ~**zeit** business hours, office hours, opening hours; ~**zentrum** business centre, trading centre, shopping centre; ~**zusammenbruch** trading failure, collapse of a business; ~**zweck** object (of a business), business purpose; ~**zweig** line of business.

Geschäftsführer *m* manager, general manager, managing director, executive director (*GmbH*); ~**losigkeit** total vacancy on managing board, unoccupied (sole) directorship, company being without a director; ~ **ohne Auftrag** manager without mandate, voluntary agent, negotiorum gestor; **alleiniger** ~ general manager, sole manager; **alleinvertretungsberechtigter** ~ manager with sole power of representation; **faktischer** ~ de facto director; **parlamentarischer** ~ parliamentary manager, whip.

Geschäftsführung *f* management; ~ **ohne Auftrag** *management without mandate*; spontaneous agency without authority, necessitous intervention; ~**sbefugnis** power to conduct the business, power to direct (a business), power of management; ~**sgenehmigung** licence to conduct business; ~**skosten** executive

Geschichtserzählung

expenses; ~**sorgan** management body; ~**s- und allgemeine Verwaltungskosten** executive and general administrative expenses; **die** ~ **ausüben** to manage the business; **fahrlässige** ~ (grossly) negligent management; **kaufmännische** ~ business management; **oberste** ~ top management; **ordentliche** ~ proper business management, conduct of affairs; **ordnungsmäßige** ~ proper management; **schlechte** ~ mismanagement; **tatsächliche** ~ actual management.

Geschäftsgebaren *n* business practices, way of doing business, business methods; ~**anständiges** ~ fair practices; **betrügerisches** ~ fraudulent manipulation; **korrektes** ~ straight dealings; **ordentliches** ~ proper business methods; **redliches** ~ fair dealing; **reelles** ~ honest dealings; **unlauteres** ~ dishonest (*or* dubious) business practices, unfair competition.

Geschäftsordnung rules of procedure, rules and regulations, (standing) rules; ~ **des Vorstands** proceedings of directors; **parlamentarische** ~ parliamentary procedure; standing orders; ~**sausschuß** standing orders committee; ~**spunkt** (= *Punkt der* ~) point of order; „**zur** ~" „on a point of order".

Geschehen *n* happenings, events; **das konjunkturelle** ~ cyclical trends; **marktwirtschaftliches** ~ operation of the free market.

geschehen *v/i* to happen, to occur, to take place; (*prep*.) ~ ... *am* ... : *done at ... this ... day of ...*; ~ *zu Bonn*: *... done at Bonn* (*in treaties*).

Geschenk *n* present, gift; ~**annahme** ~ acceptance of gifts (*intended as a bribe*); ~**artikel** gift article(s), *pl* fancy goods, articles suitable as presents; ~**packung** gift in presentation wrapping, gift box; ~**sendung** gift parcel; „~~", *keine Handelsware*": "*gift parcel without commercial value*".

Geschichtserzählung *f* (*in der*

Geschicklichkeit

Klagebegründung) statement of the facts of the case, plaintiff's narrative of his case, account of the events.

Geschicklichkeit *f* skill, dexterity, adroitness; **handwerksübliche** ~ ordinary skill (of a craftsman).

geschieden *adj* divorced; *schuldig ~: divorced as the guilty party; schuldlos ~: divorced as the innocent party; ~ werden: to be divorced, to obtain a divorce.*

Geschiedene *f* divorcée, a divorced woman.

Geschiedenenunterhalt *f* maintenance allowance, permanent alimony.

Geschiedener *m* (*der Geschiedene*) a divorced man, divorcé.

Geschlecht *n* sex; lineage, species.

Geschlechts|akt sexual act, coitus; ~**befriedigung** sexual gratification; ~**drang** sexual impulse, sexual urge; ~**ehre** woman's honour in sexual respects; ~**gemeinschaft** cohabitation; ~**kranker** venereal patient, person suffering from a venereal disease; ~**krankheit** venereal disease; ~**krankheitengesetz** Venereal Diseases Act (*German law of 1953*); **g~spezifisch** sex-specific; ~**teil** genital organ, sex organ, *pl* genitals, private parts; *die männlichen ~e: virilia, male sex organs etc* ~**umwandlung** transsexuality, sex change; ~**verkehr** sexual intercourse, carnal knowledge; ~~ *ohne Einwilligung: non-consensual intercourse; außerehelicher ~~: extramarital intercourse, fornication; fehlende Gelegenheit zum ~~: non-access; unzüchtiger ~~: illicit connection, fornication, stuprum; vorehelicher ~~: premarital intercourse.*

geschlossen *adj* closed, private, in camera, as a whole, en bloc, self-contained, unanimous (*vote*).

Geschlossenheit *f* homogeneity.

Geschmacksmuster *n* design, registered design, ornamental design, design patent; ~**eintragung** registration of design; ~**gesetz** Registered Designs Act; ~**recht** law of registered designs; ~**rolle** Register

Geschworenenablehnung

of Designs; ~**schutz** protection of registered designs; ~**urkunde** certificate of registration of a design; design letters patent; ~**verletzung** piracy of design.

Geschoßflächenplan *m* (outline) floor plan.

geschuldet *adj* legally due, owing, owing and accruing.

geschützt *adj* protected; **gesetzlich** ~ legally protected, protected by law, registered; **nicht** ~ unprotected, uncopyrighted, unpatented; **nicht urheberrechtlich** ~ uncopyrighted, non-copyrighted; **patentrechtlich** ~ protected by patent.

geschwängert *adj* pregnant, *pp* made pregnant (by).

Geschwängerte *f* pregnant woman, woman made pregnant (by).

Geschwindigkeit *f* speed; **angemessene** ~ reasonable and proper speed; **gefahrlose** ~ safe (limit of) speed; **gestoppte** ~ timed speed; **ohne triftigen Grund mit ungewöhnlich niedriger** ~ **fahren** travel at an abnormally slow speed without proper cause; **überhöhte** ~ excessive speed; **zulässige** ~ lawful speed, permitted speed.

Geschwindigkeits|begrenzung speed limit; ~**begrenzungsschild** speed-limit sign; ~**beschränkung** speed restriction; ~**kontrolle** speed control, speed check; ~**messer** speedometer, speed indicator, tachometer; ~**überschreitung** exceeding the speed limit; ~**vorschriften** speed regulations, speed restrictions.

Geschwister *pl* brothers and sisters, siblings; ~**kind** nephew (*or* niece).

Geschworene *pl* (*die Geschworenen*) the jury; ~ **belehren**: to instruct the jury; **unvoreingenommene** ~ impartial jury.

Geschworenen|ablehnung challenging the jury, objection to the jury; ~**anklage** indictment; ~**anklageschrift** bill of indictment; ~**bank** jury box; ~**beeinflussung** tampering with jurors; ~**beste-**

357

Geschworener / **Gesellschaft**

chung bribing jurors, corruption of the jury, fixing the jury; **~gericht** court with a jury, jury trial; *ranggleiches ~~*: *trial by a jury of one's peers*; **~liste** jury list, panel, jury panel; *in die ~~ eintragen*: *to impanel*; **~prozeß** trial by jury; **~spruch** verdict, finding of a jury; **~urteil** verdict; *unerträgliches ~~*: *perverse verdict*; **~verfahren** trial by jury.

Geschworener *m* (*der Geschworene*) juror, member of a jury; *~ sein*: *to act as juror, to sit in a jury*.

gesehen und genehmigt seen and approved.

Geselle *m* tradesman; craftsman *who has served his apprenticeship*, qualified craftsman; journeyman (*hist*); **~nbrief** certificate of qualification as craftsman, certificate of completed apprenticeship; **~njahre** a tradesman's years of service; **~nlohn** rate of pay for qualified craftsmen; **~nprüfung** final appenticeship examination, tradesman's qualifying examination; **~nstück** piece of work in apprentice's final examination; **~nzeit** tradesman's years of service, period as a journeyman (*hist*).

Gesellschaft *f* society, social order; association, company, *US*: corporation; partnership; *pl* **~en**: companies or firms; **~ auf Gegenseitigkeit** mutual society; **~ auf Widerruf** partnership at will, revocable partnership; **~ des bürgerlichen Rechts** civil-law partnership, non-commercial partnership, non-trading partnership; **~en des Handelsrechts** commercial law associations; **~en, die keinen Erwerbszweck verfolgen** non-profit companies; **~ für Absatzfinanzierung** sales finance company; **~ für Wirtschafts- und Sozialwissenschaften** Society for Economic and Social Services; **~ in ausschließlichem Schachtelbesitz** wholly-owned group company; **~ mit beschränkter Haftung** (German) private limited company, private company limited by shares; **~ mit beschränkter Nachschußpflicht** company limited by guarantee, company with reserve liability; **~ mit widerrechtlichen Zwecken** illegal partnership; **~ ohne Geschäftsbetrieb** inactive company; **~ ohne (Haupt-)Geschäftssitz im Inland** non-resident company; **~ ohne Prospekt** non-prospectus company; **abgebende ~** vendor company; **abhängige ~** dependent company, controlled company; **angegliederte ~** affiliated company; **aufgelöste ~** dissolved company; **aufnehmende ~** absorbing company (*in merger*); **aus e-r ~ austreten** to withdraw from a partnership (*or* society); **ausländische ~** non-resident company; **ausschüttende ~** distributing company; **befreundete ~** associated company, closely related company; **beherrschende ~** controlling company, holding; **beherrschte ~** controlled company; **bergrechtliche ~** mining company; **beteiligte ~** participating company; **börsennotierte ~** quoted company; **bürgerlich-rechtliche ~** = *Gesellschaft des bürgerlichen Rechts qv*; **dividendenlose ~** company paying no dividends; **effektiv tätige ~** operating company; **einbringende ~** vendor company; **e-e ~ auflösen** to dissolve a partnership, to wind up a company; **e-e ~ ausgliedern** to remove a subsidiary from a group, to take a company out of a combine (*or* group of firms); **e-e ~ beherrschen** to control another company; **e-e ~ errichten** to establish a company, to set up a firm, to found a firm; **e-e ~ gründen** to establish a company (*or* partnership), to found a company, to form a company, to float a company, to promote a company; **eingegliederte ~** integrated company; **emittierende ~** issuing company; **gelöschte ~** defunct company, deregistered company, struck-off

Gesellschafter company; **gemeinnützige** ~ friendly society, non-profit association; **gemischtwirtschaftliche** ~ quasi-public company, partly publicly-owned company, part publicly-owned company; **jederzeit kündbare** ~ partnership at will, partnership subject to notice on either side; **herrschende** ~ controlling company; **inländische** ~ resident company; **klassenlose** ~ classless society; **konzernnahe** ~ quasi group company; **konzessionierte** ~ licensed company, chartered corporation; **leonistische** ~ leonine partnership, leonina societas, *partnership where one party is to bear all losses and will not participate in the profits*; **nahestehende** ~ affiliated company, associated company; **nicht mehr bestehende** ~ defunct company; **nichtrechtsfähige** ~ unincorporated society; **öffentlich rechtliche** ~ public (law) corporation; **rechtsfähige** ~ company with legal personality, incorporated company; **selbständige** ~ unaffiliated company, independent company; **stille** ~ partnership in commendam, undisclosed participation *in the business of another with share in profits and losses but no voice in the management*; ≈ dormant (silent, secret) partnership; *atypische* ~~: *atypical silent partnership; silent quasi-partnership (undisclosed contractual partnership rights and an interest in the liquidation proceeds)*; **übernehmende** ~ transferee company; **verstaatlichte** ~ nationalized company; **wissenschaftliche** ~ scientific society; **zum Börsenhandel zugelassene** ~ quoted company.

Gesellschafter *m* partner; shareholder (*GmbH*); ~ **als Abwickler** liquidating partner; ~ **als Geschäftsführer** managing member; ~ **als Liquidator** liquidating partner; ~**anteil** partner's interest, share, business interest; ~**beschluß** resolution adopted by the partners; ~**darlehen** a partner's loan to the partnership, proprietor's loan; ~**einlage** partner's contribution; ~**-Geschäftsführer** managing partner; ~**kapital** partner's capital; ~ **kraft Rechtsscheins** partner by estoppel, ostensible partner; ~ **nach BGB** = *BGB-Gesellschafter qv*; ~**versammlung** company meeting (*GmbH*); partners' meeting; ~**verzeichnis** register of members; ~**wechsel** change of partners; **atypischer stiller** ~ pseudo dormant partner, (atypical) silent partner (*with managerial rights*); **ausscheidender** ~ outgoing partner, retiring partner, withdrawing partner; **beschränkt haftender** ~ limited partner; **geschäftsführender** ~ managing partner, active partner; **jeder** ~ **hat seinen Gewinnanteil zu versteuern** each partner's profits are taxed separately; **neu eintretender** ~ incoming partner; **persönlich haftender** ~ personally liable partner, general partner, unlimited partner, ordinary partner; **stiller** ~ *person holding an undisclosed participation in a firm without partnership status or liability, imprecisely*: dormant partner, silent partner, sleeping partner, secret partner, undisclosed partner; → *stille Gesellschaft*; *atypischer* ~~: *atypical silent partner (with managerial rights)*; **tätiger** ~ active partner, acting partner, working partner; **typischer stiller** ~ genuine dormant partner, typical sleeping partner; **unbeschränkt haftender** ~ = *persönlich haftender Gesellschafter qv*; **verbleibender** ~ surviving partner (*upon the death of a partner*), continuing partner.

Gesellschafts|anspruch partnership claim; claim submitted by a company; ~**anteil** partnership interest, capital share; ~**bilanz** partnership balance-sheet, company balance sheet; ~**bücher** the partnership (*or* company's) books; ~**darlehen** a partner's (*or* shareholder's) loan to his firm, internal partnership loan; ~**eigentum** corporate property, company property, partnership

Gesellschaftseinkommen   **Gesetz**

property; ~**einkommen** corporate income, company earnings; ~**einkünfte** corporate income, company earnings; ~**einlage** contribution (to the partnership capital), investment in a company; ~**erfindung** company-owned invention; g~**feindlich** anti-social; ~**firma** partnership name, name of the company, corporate name; ~**forderung** partnership claim, claim by the company; ~**form** legal form of association, corporate structure; ~**gewinn** company's profit, corporate profit; ~**gläubiger** creditor of a (the) company; ~**gründer** promoter, founder of a company; ~**gründung** company foundation, formation of a (the) company, establishment of a partnership (*or* company); ~**handlung** corporate act; ~**justitiar** company's legal adviser, legal officer of a company, company solicitor; ~**kapital** partnership capital, corporate capital, joint capital, capital stock; ~**klasse** social class; ~**konkurs** involuntary liquidation, compulsory winding-up, winding-up by the court; ~**lehre** social science, social studies; ~**mittel** partnership funds, corporate funds; ~**name** corporate name; ~**ordnung** social order; *gerechte* ~~: *just social order, square deal*; ~**organe** company organs; ~**politik** social policy (and action), socio-politics; g~**politisch** relating to social policy, sociopolitical; ~**rechnung** corporate statement of accounts; ~**recht** law of associations (*law of partnership and company law*), company law, partnership law; ~**register** register of companies and partnerships; ~**reise** guided tour, package tour, group tour, conducted tour; ~**reingewinn** corporate surplus, net profits of a company (*or partnership*); ~**satzung** memorandum and articles of association (*GB*), (corporate) charter (*US*); ~**schuld** partnership debt, debt of a company; ~**schulden** corporate debts, partnership debts, company liabilities; ~**sitz** (place of) registered office (*GB*), domicile (*or* residence) of a company (*or* corporation), principal office (*of a company*); ~**statut** = ~*satzung qv*; ~**steuer** capital contribution and transfer tax, company tax; ~**steuerpflicht** liability to pay capital contribution and transfer tax; ~**struktur** company structure, corporate structure; ~**stufe** social scale; ~**system** social system; ~**verbindlichkeiten** corporate liabilities, company debts; ~**verhältnis** corporate relationship, relationship between partners (*or* associates); ~**vermögen** partnership property, partnership funds, company assets; ~**versammlung** company meeting, general meeting, partners' meeting; ~**vertrag** memorandum of association, partnership agreement, articles of partnership, partnership deed, deed of partnership; *social science*: social contract; ~**zweck** object(s) of the company, partnership purpose; ~**zweckbestimmung** objects clause of the company.

Gesetz *n* law, Act, Act of Parliament, statute, public statute, Act of Legislature (*US state-law*); ~**blatt** legal gazette; law gazette; ~**buch** law code, code, statute book; ~ **des abnehmenden Bodenertrags** law of diminishing agricultural marginal productivity; ~**geber**, g~**geberisch** → *gesetzgeberisch*; ~**gebung** → *Gesetzgebung*; ~ **gegen den unlauteren Wettbewerb** Act Against Unfair Competition; ~ **gegen Wettbewerbsbeschränkungen** Anti-Cartel Act; ~ **in der Fassung vom**... law as revised on ..., an Act as amended on...; ~ **in geänderter Fassung** law as amended; g~**lich** → *gesetzlich*; ~**lichkeit** → *Gesetzlichkeit*; g~**los** → *gesetzlos*; ~**loser** → *Gesetzloser*; ~**losigkeit** → *Gesetzlosigkeit*; g~**mäßig** → *gesetzmäßig*; ~**mäßigkeit** → *Gesetzmäßigkeit*, ~ **mit rückwirkender Kraft** retro-

Gesetz

active law, law with retroactive effect, retrospective law; ~ **über die Besteuerung von Auslandsbeziehungen** (*Außensteuergesetz*) Act on External Tax Relations; ~ **über die Wahrnehmung von Urheberrechten und verwandten Schutzrechten** Act on Performing Rights Associations; ~ **über vorzeitiges Ausscheiden von Arbeitnehmern** Job Release Act; ~**und Verordnungsblatt** Gazette of Laws and Ordinances; ~ **vom abnehmenden Ertragszuwachs** law of diminishing returns; ~ **von Ursache und Wirkung** law of cause and effect; ~ **werden** to become law, to be enacted, to pass into law; **g~widrig** → *gesetzwidrig*; ~**widrigkeit** → *Gesetzwidrigkeit*; ~ **zur Bekämpfung der Umweltkriminalität** Act on Combatting Environmental Criminality; ~ **zur Heilung von fehlerhaften Verwaltungsakten** Validating Statute; ~ **zur Neuordnung des Arzneimittelrechts** Act to Revise the Law Concerning Pharmaceuticals; ~ **zur Neuordnung des Geldwesens** Monetary Reform Act; ~ **zur Verbesserung der betrieblichen Altersversorgung** Act on the Improvement of Works Pension Schemes (*GB*), Act on the Improvement of Corporate Pension Plans (*US*); ~ **zur Verminderung von Luftverunreinigungen durch Bleiverbindungen in Autokraftstoffen für Kraftfahrzeuge** (*Benzinbleigesetz*) Act to Reduce Air Pollution due to Lead in Fuel; **allgemeines** ~ law of a general nature, general statute, public statute; **aufhebendes** ~ repealing Act (*or* statute); **auf Grund des** ~**es** on the strength of a law, by virtue of the law; **befristetes** ~ temporary statute; **das** ~ **findet Anwendung** the law applies (*or* operates), the law shall apply; **das** ~ **in der Fassung vom** ... the statute (*or* Act) as amended on; **das** ~ **tritt am Tage seiner Verkündung in Kraft** the Act shall become effective on the date of its promulgation; **das** ~ **übertreten** to contravene the law; **ein** ~~: to breach (*or* violate) a law, to offend against a law; **das** ~ **umgehen** to evade the law; **das** ~ **von Angebot und Nachfrage** the law of supply and demand; **das** ~ **verlangt** ... it is a statutory requirement, the law requires you to ...; **die vom** ~ **angedrohte Strafe** the punishment laid down by law; **durch** ~ **geregelt** regulated by law, the subject of legislation; **ein** ~ **abändern** to revise a law, to amend an Act, to alter a law; **ein** ~ **ändern** = *ein* ~ *abändern qv*; **ein** ~ **annehmen** to pass an Act, to enact a statute; **ein** ~ **anwenden** to apply a law; **ein** ~ **aufheben** to repeal a law, to abrogate a law (= an Act); **ein** ~ **außer Kraft setzen** to rescind a law, to abrogate an Act, to invalidate a law; **ein** ~ **beachten** to comply with a law, to observe a law, to adhere to a statute; **ein** ~ **beschließen** to enact a law, to pass a law; **ein** ~ **durchführen** to implement a law; **ein** ~ **einbringen** to introduce a bill, to initiate legislation, to table a bill *GB*; **ein** ~ **einhalten** to observe a law, to adhere to a law; **ein** ~ **ergehen lassen** to pass an Act; **ein** ~ **erklären** to explain a law, to expound a legal enactment; **ein** ~ **erlassen** to enact a law, *pl* to enact legislation, to legislate; **ein** ~ **handhaben** to implement a law, to operate a law; **ein** ~ **in Kraft setzen** to enact a law, to bring a law into operation, to put a law into force; **ein** ~ **ist in Kraft** a law is in force; **ein** ~ **ist überholt** a law is obsolete, an Act is superseded by; **ein** ~ **umgehen** to evade a law, to elude a law; **ein** ~ **verabschieden** to pass a bill, to pass an Act, to pass a law; **ein** ~ **verkünden** to promulgate a law; **einheitliches** ~ uniform law, uniform Act, standard(ized) law; **einschlägiges** ~

361

relevant law, applicable law; **formelles** ~ formally enacted law; **gegen ein** ~**verstoßen** to violate the provisions of a law, to infringe a law, to offend against a law; **geltendes** ~ law in force (for the time being), current law, applicable law; **gültiges** ~ operative law, applicable law; **in e-m** ~ **enthalten sein** to be embodied in a law, to be set out in a law; **kraft** ~**es** by (operation of) law, ipso jure, by virtue of the law; **nach dem** ~ according to law, under the law; **nach** ~ **und Recht** in accordance with the law, according to law; **ökonomisches** ~ economic law; **rückwirkendes** ~ retroactive law, ex post facto law; **ungeschriebenes** ~ unwritten law, lex inscripta; **unter ein** ~ **fallen** to come under a law, to be covered by an Act, to fall within (the purview of) a law; **verfassungswidriges** ~ unconstitutional law; **zeitlich unbeschränktes** ~ perpetual statute; **zwingendes** ~ mandatory statute, obligatory law.

Gesetzes|akzessorität *compliance with legislation on the part of administrative organs;* ~**analogie** analogous application of laws; ~**änderung** alteration of statute, amendment of a law; ~**anwendung** application of a (the) law; ~**aufhebung** repeal of a law, abrogation of a statute; ~**auslegung** interpretation of law (*of a law or of the law*), construing an Act; ~**begriff** statutory concept, legal term ~**beratung** legislative deliberation(s); ~**bereinigung** statute law revision; ~**beschluß** enactment; ~**beschreibung** nomography; ~**bestimmung** provision of law, statutory provision; ~**bruch** breach of law, infringement of the law; ~**einheit** unity of the law; **e-n** ~~ **einbringen**: *to table a bill (GB)*; ~**fiktion** legal fiction, fictitious legal situation; ~**form** form of a law, statutory form; ~**formel** enacting clause, enacting words, legal formula, legal form of words; ~**initiative** legislative initiative, right to introduce a bill, (private member's) bill; ~**kodex** legal code, code of law; ~**kollision** conflict of laws, collision between two laws; ~**kommentar** legal commentary; ~**komplex** series of laws, nexus of laws; ~**konkurrenz** concurrence of laws; necessarily included lesser offence; merger of offences; inclusion of a lesser offence in the greater one; ~**kraft** force of law, legal force; ~~ *verleihen: to enact, to give legal force to*; ~**lücke** loophole in the law, gap: *e-e* ~~ *ausfüllen to remedy a gap*; ~**novelle** amending law (bill); ~**paragraph** section of an Act, paragraph; ~**pergament** statute roll; ~**recht** statutory law, statute law, written law, enacted law; ~**sammlung** statute book, consolidated statutes; *bereinigte* ~~: *Revised Statutes*; ~**sprache** legal language, statutory language, legal terminology; ~**staat** state strictly bound by legislation; ~**text** wording of the law, legal text; ~**titel** title of the Act, designation of a law, rubric of a statute; ~**treue** obedience to the law; ~**übertretung** offence, infringement of an Act, contravention of the law; ~**umgehung** evasion of the law; ~**ungehorsam** disobedience to statute (*or* the law); ~**unkenntnis** ignorance of the law; *sich auf* ~~ *berufen: to plead ignorance of the law*; ~**verabschiedung** the passing of a bill, enactment of a law; ~**verächter** a despiser of the law; ~**verbot** statutory prohibition; ~**verkündung** promulgation of a law; ~**verletzung** infringement of an Act, violation of the law, legal offence; *fahrlässige* ~~: *negligent violation of statute*; *rechtsirrtümliche* ~~: *good-faith violation of law*; ~**verordnung** ordinance, decree; ~**verstoß** violation of (a/the) law; ~**vollziehung** execution of the law; ~**vollzug** law enforcement; ~**vorbehalt** legal reservation, legal proviso, constitutional requirement of a specific enactment (*if constitutional rights are to be restricted by statute*); **~vorlage** bill, draft of an Act, draft law; *e–e ~~ abwürgen*: *to strangle a bill*; *e–e ~~ einbringen*: *to table a bill (GB), to initiate legislation*; *e–e ~~ dem Plenum wieder vorlegen*: *to report a bill*; **~vorschlag** proposal for a law, bill, proposed statute; **~vorschrift** legal provision, statutory rule; **~werk** legal code; **g~widrig** illegal, unlawful, contrary to law, in contravention of the law, in breach of the law; **~wortlaut** statutory language; **~zuständigkeit** legislative competence; **~zweck** legal purpose, object of the law.

Gesetzgeber *m* legislator, law-maker, the legislature.

gesetzgeberisch *adj* legislative; *~ tätig sein*: *to legislate*.

Gesetzgebung *f* legislation, lawmaking; laws and regulations; *~ auf dem Verordnungswege* secondary legislation, legislation in the form of ordinances; *~ des Bundes und der Länder* Federal and Land legislation; *~ des Handelsrechts* commercial legislation; *~ durch die Verwaltung* administrative legislation; **arbeitsrechtliche ~** labour legislation; **ausländische ~** foreign legislation; **ausschließliche ~** exclusive legislation; **gewerkschaftsfeindliche ~** anti-labour legislation; **inländische ~** domestic legislation; **innerstaatliche ~** municipal legislation, domestic legislation; **interessengebundene ~** special pleading legislation, laws biassed by special interests; **jetzige ~** current legislation; **konkurrierende ~** concurrent legislation; **nationale ~** national legislation; **rückwirkende ~** retroactive legislation.

Gesetzgebungs|akt act of legislation, enactment; **~autonomie** autonomic legislation; **~befugnis** legislative power, legislative authority, lawmaking power; *konkurrierende ~~*: *concurrent power*; **~delegation** delegated legislation; **~funktion** legislative function, the function of legislation; **~kompetenz** legislative authority; **~maßnahme** legislative act; **~materialien** travaux préparatoires; **~notstand** legislative state of emergency, emergency legislation; **~organe** legislative organs; **~recht** right to legislate, legislative authority; **~technik** legislative methods, technical legislative procedure; **~übersicht** survey of (recent) legislation; **~verfahren** legislative procedure, process of legislation; **~weg** channel of legislation; **~werk** body of legislation; **~zuständigkeit** legislative competence.

gesetzlich *adj* lawful, legal, statutory, in law, by operation of law; **~ geschützt** protected by law, registered, patented.

Gesetzlichkeit *f* legality, lawfulness.

gesetzlos *adj* lawless, illegal, not covered by (a) statute.

Gesetzloser *m* (*der Gesetzlose*) outlaw.

Gesetzlosigkeit *f* lawlessness, outlawry, defiance of the law.

gesetzmäßig *adj* lawful, legal, in accordance with (the) law, statutory, pursuant to law.

Gesetzmäßigkeit *f* legality, lawfulness.

gesetzwidrig *adj* unlawful, contrary to law, illegal.

Gesetzwidrigkeit *f* illegality, unlawfulness.

gesichert *adj* secured, safe, certain; **dinglich ~** secured, secured by mortgage, secured in rem; **nicht ~** unsecured, without collateral.

Gesichtspunkt *m* point of view, aspect; *e–n* **vortragen** to submit a proposition; **ein vertretbarer ~** a debatable point; **nach wirtschaftlichen ~en** from an economic point of view, pursuant to commercial principles; **rechtlicher ~** legal point; **unter bankgeschäftlichen ~en** for banking reasons.

Gesinnung f mental attitude, mentality, way of thinking, state of mind; ~**smerkmale** criteria of mental attitude; ~**sschutz** protection of (editor's) ideological opinions; ~**sstrafrecht** n *penal law based on mental attitudes or political convictions*; ~**stäter** m ideological criminal, perpetrator for ideological motives, fanatical criminal.

gesondert *adj* separate, on its own merits; under separate cover.

Gespannfahrzeug n animal-drawn vehicle.

Gespräch n conversation, discussion, discourse; ~**e am runden Tisch** round table talks; ~ **auf Botschafterebene** discussion at ambassador(ial) level; ~**e auf hoher Ebene** high-level talks; ~**sgegenstand** topic (*or* subject-matter) of the discussion; ~**snotiz** memo (of a discussion); ~**spartner** interlocutor, opposite number; ~ **unter vier Augen** private talks, confidential discussion, face-to-face discussion; **ein ~ anmelden** to announce a call; **dienstliches** ~ business call, official call; **R-~** call with reversed charges, collect call; **vorbereitendes** ~ preparatory discussion, initial talk.

gesprochen *adj* spoken, oral.

gestaffelt *adj* staggered, graduated.

Gestaltung f formation, structure, shape, configuration, design, presentation; ~ **von Rechtsverhältnissen** arrangement of legal relations; **redaktionelle** ~ draftsmanship (*legal texts*).

Gestaltungs|akt formative act; ~**arbeit** creative (art) work; ~**freiheit** freedom of design *or* arrangement; ~**höhe** level of design; *künstlerische* ~~: *artistic level;* ~**klage** action for a modification of rights, action for a change of legal relationship (*e.g. a divorce decree*); ~**mangel** defect of outward design; ~**merkmale** criteria of design; *individuelle* ~~: *creative design;* ~**mißbrauch** (taxpayer's) abuse of formally admissible arrangements; ~**mittel** creative means; ~**recht** right to alter a legal relationship; right to establish, change or terminate a legal relationship; dispositive right; ~**urteil** judgment establishing or altering a legal relationship.

geständig self-confessed, confessed, inclined to confess.

Geständnis n *crim* confession; *civil procedure*: admission; ~**zwang** obtaining of a confession by coercion; **ausdrückliches** ~ direct confession; **außergerichtliches** ~ confession out of court; **ein freiwilliges** ~ **ablegen** to volunteer a confession; **ein** ~ **ablegen** to make a confession; **ein** ~ **gegen Mitbeschuldigte ablegen** to give evidence against one's co-accused; to "squeal"; **ein** ~ **widerrufen** to retract (*or* withdraw) a confession; **erzwungenes** ~ forced confession; **gerichtliches** ~ confession in open court, judicial confession; **qualifiziertes** ~ qualified confession, limited confession, admission against interest; **umfassendes** ~ a full confession; **unfreiwilliges** ~ involuntary confession; **von jmdm ein** ~ **erpressen** to extort a confession from s. o.

gestatten *v/t* to permit, to allow, to suffer, to consent to sth; **geflissentlich** ~ to allow knowingly, to give implied permission; **nicht** ~ to disallow, not to permit.

Gestattung f permission, consent, licence; ~**svertrag** licence agreement; **stets widerrufliche** ~ (permanently) revocable right, licence subject to revocation at any time, precarious right, sufferance.

gestehen *v/t, v/i* to admit, to confess, to own up.

Gestehungskosten *pl* cost of acquisition, prime cost, production costs, cost-price.

Gestehungspreis m cost-price, prime cost.

Gestehungswert m cost-price, price without a profit-margin.

Gestellung f provision, making available, presentation for inspection; ~ **der Waren** (*Zoll*) presentation of goods to the customs office; ~ **e-s Akkreditivs** opening of a credit, providing a letter of credit; **~sbefehl** call-up order, *US*: draft order; **~skosten** original cost; **~sverzeichnis** (customs) declaration list, reporting list.

Gestionsgebühren *f/pl* management fees.

gestorben deceased, ob (= obiit).

gestrichen *adj* cancelled, expunged, stricken (*from the record*); no quotation *exch.*

Gesuch *n* petition, request, application; **ein ~ ablehnen** to refuse a request; **ein ~ abschlägig bescheiden** to decline a petition; **ein ~ abweisen** to reject a petition; **ein ~ aufsetzen** to draw up a petition; **ein ~ bearbeiten** to be in charge of a petition; **ein ~ befürworten** to support a petition; **ein ~ bewilligen** to grant an application; **ein ~ einbringen** to present (*or* lodge) a petition; **ein ~ einreichen** to present a petition, to file a petition; **ein ~ genehmigen** to grant a petition (*or* an application); **schriftliches ~** petition in writing.

Gesuchsteller *m* petitioner, applicant.

gesucht *pp; adj* wanted, sought after, in demand; **für sofort ~** wanted immediately; **steckbrieflich ~** wanted by the police.

Gesuchter *m* (*der Gesuchte, ein Gesuchter*) wanted person.

gesund *adj* healthy, of sound health, wholesome; **geistig ~** of sound mind.

Gesundheit *f* health, *econ* soundness; **garantierte ~** warranted sound (*of horses*), a clean bill of health.

Gesundheits|amt board of health, public health department; *pl* **~ämter**: sanitary authorities; **~attest** health certificate; **~behörde** health office, *pl* **~~n**: health authorities; **~beschädigung** personal injury; **~dienst** health service; *staatlicher* **~~**: *public health service;* **~fürsorge** medical welfare, medical care; **g~gefährdend** health-endangering, unhealthy, harmful; **~gefährdung** hazard to human health; **~kontrolle** sanitary control; **~maßnahmen** public health measures; **~paß** bill of health; **~~** *mit Vermerk*: *„ansteckungsverdächtig"*: *suspected bill of health*; **~polizei** sanitary police; **~reformgesetz** (German) Health Reform Act (*1989*); **~schaden** injury to health; health impairment; **g~schädlich** injurious to health, unwholesome, noxious; **~schutz** protection of public health, health protection; **~~** *bei der Arbeit*: *occupational hygiene*; **~störung** ill health; **~verletzung** injury to health; **~vorschriften** sanitary regulations; public health regulations; **~wesen** public health, sanitation; **~zerstörung** destruction of health; **~zeugnis** health certificate; **~zustand** physical condition, state of health; *einwandfreier* **~~**: *sound health.*

Gesundschrumpfung *f* slimming down, down-sizing.

Getötetenrate *f* death rate.

Getränke|automat automatic drink dispenser; **~herstellung** manufacture of beverages; **~industrie** beverage industry; **~steuer** beverage tax; **geistige ~** alcoholic beverages; **kohlensäurehaltige und schäumende ~** aerated or sparkling beverages; **steuerpflichtige ~e** excisable liquor, drinks subject to the beverage tax.

Getreide *n* grain, cereals; **~anbau** cultivation of grain; **~ausfuhr** exportation of grain, grain exports; **~ausfuhrland** grain-exporting country; **~bilanz** estimate of the supplies and consumption of grain; **~börse** corn-exchange; **~einfuhr** grain importation, grain imports; **~einfuhr- und Vorratsstelle** grain import and storage agency; **~gesetz** grain marketing law (*D*: *internal trade*); **~handel** grain trade, trading in grain; grain merchant's firm; **~händler** grain merchant, grain dealer; **~konsortialkredit**

syndicate credit on grain; ~**marktregelung** grain market regulation; ~**preis** grain price; ~**silo** grain silo, grain elevator; ~**speicher** granary, store house for grain; ~**terminsgeschäfte** grain futures; ~**überhang** carry-over of grain; ~**wirtschaft** grain-producing, grain production and marketing; ~**zoll** duty on imported grain.

getrennt *adj* separate, separated, several; ~ *leben* →*leben*.

Getrenntbesteuerung *f* separate taxation (*of spouses or divorced persons*).

Getrenntleben *n* separation (of spouses), living separate, living apart; **eheliches** ~ separation of spouses; **einvernehmliches** ~ consensual separation; **gerichtlich gestattetes** ~ judicial separation.

Gewächshausversicherung *f* greenhouse insurance.

gewählt *pp* → *wählen*; ~ **werden** to be elected, to get in; **einstimmig** ~ **werden** to be elected unanimously.

Gewähr *f* guarantee (*GB*), warranty, guaranty (*US*); ~ **für Rechtsmängel** = *Gewährleistung für Rechtsmängel qv*; ~ **für Sachmängel** = *Gewährleistung für Sachmängel qv*; **die** ~ **für etwas übernehmen** to (represent and) warrant, to accept a guarantee for; **mit** ~ warranted ..., with recourse; **ohne** ~ unwarranted, no guarantee, without recourse, without engagement, subject to correction; **stillschweigende** ~ implied warranty; **volle** ~ **für** fully guaranteed against; **wir übernehmen keine** ~ we accept no responsibility (for).

gewähren *v/t* to grant, to accord, to allow; **ohne weiteres zu** ~ to be granted as a matter of course.

Gewährfrist *f* period of guarantee, warranty period.

gewährleisten *v/t* to warrant, to guarantee, to ensure.

Gewährleistender *m* (*der Gewährleistende*) warrantor, guarantor.

Gewährleistung *f* (statutory) warranty, guarantee: *liability of the seller (lender, contractor) for faults or deficiencies of the goods, services, premises, etc*; ~ **für Rechtsmängel** warranty of title, title guarantee; ~ **für Sachmängel** (implied) warranty of soundness, warranty of fitness, warranty of merchantable quality, *seller's legal responsibility that the goods are of proper quality and fit for the contractual use*; ~ **übernehmen** to give a warranty, to warrant, to assume responsibility for; **ausdrückliche oder stillschweigende** ~ express or implied warranty; **gesetzliche** ~ implied warranty, statutory warranty; **stillschweigende** ~ implied warranty.

Gewährleistungs|anspruch warranty claim; ~**erklärung** express warranty; ~**frist** period of guarantee, warranty period; ~**garantie** performance guarantee, warranty; ~**klage** action under a warranty; ~~ *wegen Sachmängeln*: *legal action based on a warranty of soundness* (*etc*); ~**klausel** warranty clause; ~**mangel** a defect covered by a warranty; ~**pflicht** obligation under a warranty; *liability for proper quality and good title*; ~**vertrag** → *Gewährvertrag*.

Gewährs|mangel fault for which seller is responsible, defect under a warranty; ~**mann** reliable authority, reliable source, informant; warrantor; ~**pflicht** *f* warranty; ~**träger** guarantor, warrantor's guaranteeing authority (*or* person); ~**verband** *m* guaranteeing authority (*savings bank system*).

Gewahrsam *m* (actual) custody of sth, physical control; (*of rooms*:) occupation, actual occupation; naked possession (*land*); **im** ~ **haben** to occupy, to have custody (*of s.th. or s.o.*); **in amtlichem** ~ in custodia legis, in official custody; **in** ~ **nehmen** to take into custody, to arrest; **nicht** ~ **habend** non-occupying; **politischer** ~ political detention; **polizeilicher** ~ police custody; **vorläufiger** ~ preliminary custody, provisional custody.

Gewahrsams|bruch wilful breach of

Gewährung

duty by official custodian; destruction of public records; **~inhaber** person having custody, occupier, occupant; *geduldeter* ~~: *occupant upon sufferance*; **~klausel** bailee clause; **~macht** detaining power; **~staat** detaining state.

Gewährung *f* granting, allowing; ~ **e-s Kredits** the granting of a credit, making credit facilities available; ~ **von Ansprüchen** acceptance of claims; ~ **von Unterschlupf** harbo(u)ring (*a fugitive from justice*).

Gewährvertrag *m* (contract of) indemnity.

Gewährzeichen *n* hallmark, sign of quality.

Gewalt *f* force, violence, *court*: power, *jur*: vis; **~akt** act of force, act of violence; **~aktion** violent action; **~androhung** threat of force, assault; **~anmaßung** usurpation (of state control); ~ **anwenden** to use violence, to resort to force; **~anwendung** use of force, employment of force, actual violence, assault; **~enteilung** separation of powers, sharing of power; **~enteilungslehre** trichotomy of governmental powers; **~entrennung** separation of powers; **~haber** holder of power, governing power; **~herrschaft** despotism, rule of force; **~herrscher** despot, dictator; **~kriminalität** crimes of violence; **g~los** non-violent; peaceably and quietly; **~losigkeit** non-violence; **~lösung** drastic solution, forcible solution; **~maßnahmen** violent measures; **~opferentschädigung** public compensation of victims of violent crime; **g~sam** by violent means, violently; **~streich** coup; **~tat** act of violence; **~tätigkeiten** acts of violence, outrage, vandalism; **~tätigkeit gegen Abgeordnete** restraining members of Parliament; **~verbot** prohibition of the use of (military) force; **~verbrechen** violence, heinous crime, forcible crime; **~verbrecher** violent criminal; **~verhältnis** relationship of subordination; **~ver-**

Gewerbe

zicht non-aggression (*treaty*); **absolute** ~ absolute power; **ausführende** ~ executive power; **ausübende** ~ executive power, administrative power; **durch ~ oder Drohung** by violence or threats of injury; **elterliche** ~ *obs: cf elterliche Sorge,* parental power, paternal power; **gesetzgebende** ~ legislative power; **höchste** ~ supreme authority, supremacy; **höhere** ~ force majeure; **körperliche** ~ physical force; **nackte** ~ brute force, violence; **oberste** ~ supreme authority; **öffentliche** ~ public authority, public power, act of state; **physische** ~ physical violence, force; **rechtsprechende** ~ judicial power, judiciary; **richterliche** ~ judicial power; **tatsächliche** ~ actual force, physical control; **unmittelbare** ~ direct control, physical force; **unter Anwendung von** ~ by force, using violence; **unwiderstehliche** ~ irresistible force; **väterliche** ~ paternal power; **verfassungsgebende** ~ constitutional authority; **verfassungsmäßige** ~ constitutional power; **vollziehende** ~ executive power.

Gewässer *n pl* waters; **~aufsicht** public waters control; **~reinhaltung** maintenance of water quality; **~schutz** water pollution control, prevention of water pollution; **~schutzbeauftragter** water pollution control officer; **~verschmutzung** water pollution; **inländische** ~ inland waters; **neutrale** ~ neutral waters; **öffentliche** ~ public waters; **schiffbare** ~ navigable waters; **stehende** ~ dormant waters; **unterirdische** ~ subterranean waters, underground waters.

Gewerbe business, trade and industry, trade or occupation, small-scale industry, industrial or commercial enterprise; gainful economic activity; **~abfall** industrial waste (*or* refuse); **~amt** trade supervision department; **~anmeldung** registration of a business or

367

Gewerbeanzeige

trade; ~**anzeige** application for registration of a business or trade; ~**arzt** medical inspector of factories; ~**aufsicht** industrial control, trade inspection, Inspector of Factories; ~**aufsichtsamt** trade supervisory office; ~**aufsichtsbehörde** trade supervisory authority; ~**aufsichtsdienst** trade inspection; ~**ausübung** the carrying on of a trade or profession, doing business; ~**bank** tradesmen's bank, industrial bank; ~**befugnis** right to carry on a trade or business, licence to trade; ~ **belästigender Art** noxious trade; ~**berechtigung** right to carry on a trade or business, licence to trade; ~**beschränkung** restriction on commercial activities; ~**betrieb** business enterprise, business establishment, industrial or commercial enterprise, commercial undertaking; *belästigender* ~~: *noxious enterprise*; *stehender* ~~: *stationary enterprise*; ~**erlaubnis** trade licence, licence for the operation of a business; ~**ertrag** income from trade or industry; ~**ertragssteuer** municipal trade earnings tax; ~**förderung** promotion of trade and industry; ~**freiheit** economic freedom (*liberty to establish and carry on any trade or industry*); ~**gebiet** industrial park, trading area, zone for economic activities; ~**geheimnis** trade secret; ~**gehilfe** industrial employee, craftsman, workman; ~**gruppe** category of trade or industry; ~**kapital** trading capital; stock in trade, *calculated for assessing Gewerbesteuer qv*; ~**kapitalsteuer** municipal trade capital tax, *trade tax computed on the basis of the capital of an enterprise*; ~**konzession** business licence; ~**lehrer** vocational (school) teacher; ~**lohnsummensteuer** *municipal trade tax based on the total volume of wages paid,* payroll tax; ~**müll** industrial waste; ~ **oder Beruf** trade or calling; ~**ordnung** industrial code, trade law, trade regulations; ~**raum** industrial or

Gewerbesteuer

commercial premises; ~**recht** trade-and-industry law; **g~rechtlich** pertaining to trade-and-industry law; ~**schein** (itinerant) trading licence; ~~ *für den Einzelhandel*: *retail licence*; ~**schule** trade school, technical school; ~**sperre** non-admission to a trade, freeze on admission to a trade; ~**steuer** → *Gewerbesteuer*; ~**tätigkeit** industrial and commercial activities; ~**treibende(r)** businessman, person carrying on a trade or industry; *kleine* ~*e, pl,* tradespeople; *selbständige* ~*e*: (*self-employed*) *independent contractors, independent businessmen*; ~**überwachung** supervision of trade and industry; ~**unfallversicherung** industrial accident insurance; ~**untersagung** prohibition of further trade activity; ~**verbotsverfahren** banning action; ~**verlust** trading loss; ~**wesen** (matters of) trade and industry; ~**zentralregister** central (federal) register of trade and industrial offences; ~**zulassung** trading licence, permission to operate a trade or industry, trade permit; ~**zweig** branch of industry or trade, (any) form of gainful activity, line (of business); **ambulantes** ~ itinerant trade; **anmeldungspflichtiges** ~ business or trade subject to compulsory registration; **dienstleistendes** ~ service-rendering occupation, a service trade; **ein** ~ **ausüben** to carry on a trade; **ein** ~ **betreiben** to carry on a trade or industry, to pursue a trade; **graphisches** ~ printing trade; **handwerksähnliches** ~ quasi-craft, small-scale trade; **keramisches** ~ ceramics industry; **konzessioniertes** ~ licensed trade; **selbständiges** ~ independent trade or business; **verarbeitendes** ~ manufacturing industry (*or* trade).

Gewerbesteuer *f* (municipal) trade tax, commercial earnings tax; ~**ausgleich** equalization of revenue from trade tax; ~**befreiung** exemption from trade tax; ~**be-**

gewerblich / **gewillkürt**

scheid trade tax revenue order; **~-Durchführungsverordnung** trade tax implementing ordinance; **~erklärung** trade tax return; **~gesetz** trade tax law; **~meßbescheid** trade tax assessment; **~pflicht** trade tax liability; *unbeschränkte ~~*: *unlimited trade tax liability (for residents)*; **~richtlinien** guiding principles for trade tax, trade tax guidelines.

gewerblich *adj* commercial, industrial, trade (*attrib*).

gewerbsmäßig *adj* professional; *adv* professionally, on a commercial basis; **~ betreiben** to make a business of sth.

Gewerbsmäßigkeit *f* commercial nature, occupational nature (*of some activity*).

Gewerbsunzucht *f* prostitution, lewd practices.

Gewerke *m* member of a mining company (*or* mining partnership).

Gewerkenbuch *n* register of members of a mining company (*or* mining partnership).

Gewerkenversammlung *f* general meeting of members of a mining company (*or* mining partnership).

Gewerkschaft *f* (1) mining company, mining partnership.

Gewerkschaft *f* (2) trade union, labo(u)r union; *pl also*: organized labour; **berufsgebundene ~** craft union; **gesamtstaatliche ~** national union; **internationale ~** international union.

Gewerkschaftler *m* unionist, trade union member.

gewerkschaftlich *adj* union (*attrib*).

Gewerkschafts|bank trade union bank, labour bank; **~beauftragter** shop steward; **~beiträge** union membership fees (*or* dues); **~beitritt** union affiliation; **~bewegung** unionism, trade union movement; **~bindung** commitment to a union, closed-shop character; *ohne ~~*: *non-union*; **~bund** Trades Union Congress, Federation of Labor; **~forderung** demand by the union(s); **~führer** trade union leader, labour leader; **~funktionär** union official; **~kartell** (powerful) combination between unions; **~mitglied** trade unionist; union member; **~ordnung** union regulations; **~organisation** labo(u)r organization, structure of a union; **~politik** trade union policy; **~recht** labo(u)r union law; **~sekretär** trade union secretary; **~umlagen** union assessments; **~veranstaltung** union meeting; **~verband** federation of unions; **~vertreter** union representative, trade union delegate; **~wesen** (trade) unionism; **~zugehörigkeit** labo(u)r union affiliation, union membership; **~zwang** closed-shop system.

Gewicht *n* weight; **~ nach Verpackung** boxed weight; **ausgeladenes ~** off-loaded weight; **eingeladenes ~** on-loaded weight; **genaues ~** true weight; **nach ~** by weight; **zollpflichtiges ~** dutiable weight; **zu hohes ~** overload, excess weight.

Gewichts|abgang loss of weight; **~abnahme** loss of weight, decrease in weight; **~abweichung** tolerance; **~akkord** piece work rate according to weight; **~angabe** declaration of weight; **~bescheinigung** weight certificate; **~gesetz** law on weights and measures; **~grenze** weight limit; **~kontrolleur** check weighter; **~manko** deficiency in weight, shortweight, loss in weight; **~note** weight note; **~schwund** loss of weight, shrinkage; **~tonne** freight ton, deadweight ton (*ship*), short ton (*2000 lbs*); **~überschreitung** exceeding the allowed weight, excess weight; **~verlust** loss in weight; **~verzollung** (charging) duty based on weight; **~wert** value per unit of weight; **~zoll** specific duty (based on weight); **~~bar**: *chargeable by weight*; **~~satz**: *tariff-rate based on weight*.

gewichten *v/t* to weight.

Gewichtung *f* weighting.

gewillkürt *adj* voluntary.

Gewinn *m* profit, gain, return, earnings, revenue, yield; ~**abführung** transfer of profit, profit transfer, surrender of profits; ~**abführungsvertrag** profit transfer agreement; ~**abrechnungsgemeinschaft** (profit-) pool; ~**abschluß** profit balance; ~**abschöpfung** siphoning-off of profits, skimming-off of extra profits; ~**e abwerfen** to yield gains, to yield a profit; ~**ansammlung** accumulation of profits; ~**anspruch** claim to distribution of earnings, dividend right; ~**anteil** profit share, *ins*: profit commission; *aufgeschobener* ~~: *deferred bonus*; **g**~**anteilberechtigt** *adj* entitled to a share in the profit(s); ~**anteilschein** dividend coupon, dividend-right coupon, scrip dividend, dividend warrant; ~**anteil-Staffel** graded scale of profit commission; ~**aufschlag** (profit) mark-up; ~**aufstockung** increase in capital resources out of profits; ~**ausfall** loss of profit; ~**ausfallversicherung** loss of profit insurance; ~**ausfall- und fortlaufende Geschäftskostenversicherung** loss of profit and overhead insurance; ~**ausgleichssystem** profit pass-over *(the protected traders receive part of the sales profit)*; ~**ausschließungsvereinbarung** non-profit agreement, profit-exclusion agreement; ~**ausschüttung** distribution of profits, paying out of profits; ~**aussichten** profit prospects; ~**ausweis** disclosure of earnings; ~**berechnung** calculation of the profit, assessment of profit; **g**~**berechtigt** *adj* entitled to a share of profits; ~**berechtigung** entitlement to a profit, participating rights; **g**~**beteiligt** *adj* participating, profit-sharing; ~**beteiligung** → *Gewinnbeteiligung*; ~**e beziehen** to derive profits; **g**~**bezogen** *adj* profit-related; ~**bezugsrecht** right to participate in the profits, right to draw a share of profits; ~**bilanz** balance sheet showing profits, earnings statement; **g**~**bringend** *adj* profitable, lucrative; ~**e aus der Veräußerung von Vermögen** capital gains; ~**einbehalt** undistributed profits, ploughing back profits; ~**entgang** loss of profits; ~**entnahme** withdrawal of profits; ~~*n* *für den Verbrauch*: *profits used for consumption*; ~**e entnehmen** to draw on profits; ~**ergebnis** result (profits), winning results *(racing etc)*; ~**ermittlung** determination of profits, ascertainment of profits; ~**erwartung** expected profits; *spekulative* ~~: *conjectural profits, paper profits*; ~ **erzielen** to make a profit; ~**e ~**: *to draw profits from*; ~**erzielung** making of profits, realization of profits, attainment of profits; ~~*sabsicht*: *profit motive intention to make profits*; ~**feststellung** ascertainment of profits, assessment of profit, determination of net profit; ~~*sverfahren*: *method of ascertaining profits*; ~**gemeinschaft** (profit) pool, group that shares the pooled profits; ~**herausgabe** surrender of profits; ~ **im Verhältnis zu investiertem Kapital** return on investment; ~**jahr** year of profit; ~**konjunktur** boom, prosperity, trend of business profitability; ~**konto** earned surplus account, capital surplus account; ~**lage** profit-and-loss position, earnings base; ~**liste** list of winners, list of winning numbers; ~**marge** profit margin, rate of return; ~**masse** total profits; ~**mitnahme** profit taking, realization of profits; *große* ~~: *scoop*; ~ **mitnehmen** to take profits; ~**obligation** participating debenture, participating bond, income bond, dividend bond; ~~**- oder Einkommensermittlung** calculation of taxable profits or income; ~**plan** *ins* bonus system; ~~**-Pooling** pooling of profits, profit pooling; ~**provision** commission on the profits; ~**quote** profit margin, profit ratio; ~**realisierung** realization of profits, profit-taking; ~**rech-**

nung profit account, surplus account; **~rücklage** retained income, reserves formed out of profits; **~saldo** profit balance; **~satz** profit mark-up; **~schuldverschreibung** participating debenture, participating bond, income bond, dividend bond; *indexierte ~~*: *indexed income bonds*; **~schwelle** break-even point; **~spanne** profit margin, return on sales, trade margin; **~spiel** gambling game; **~spitze** peak of profits, maximum profit; **~steigerung** increase in profits, rise in profits; **~steuern** taxes on profits; *~~ auf nicht ausgeschüttete Gewinne*: *undistributed profits tax*; **~streben** pursuit of profit, profit motive; *kaufmännisches ~~*: *mercantile pursuit of profit*; **~sucht** greed for profit, avarice; **g~süchtig** greedy, acquisitive, profit-seeking; **~teilung** sharing of profits, pooling of profits, division of profits; **~thesaurierung** retention of earnings, profit retention, ploughing (*US*: plowing) back profits; **~~ und Verlustbeteiligung** sharing in profits and losses; **~ und Verlust zu gleichen Teilen teilen** to share profits and losses equally, to share and share alike; **~~ und Verlustkonto** profit and loss account; **~~ und Verlustrechnung** profit and loss account, profit and loss statement, income statement; **~~ und Verlustübernahmevertrag** profit and loss assumption agreement; **~überschuß** profit balance; **~verheimlichung** concealment of profits; **~verlagerung** earnings shift, shift in earnings; **~verschleierung** concealment of profits; **~verteilung** profit distribution; **~verwendung** appropriation of profits; *~~srücklage*: *profit utilization reserve*; **~verwirklichung** realization of profits; **~vorschau** earnings estimate, estimate of earnings; **~ vor Steuern** pre-tax profit; **~vortrag** (profit) brought forward (retained); **~ziehung** drawing of winning numbers, drawing for a premium; **~zone** profitable phase, profits wedge (*in cost accounting*); *die ~~ erreichen*: *to break even, to be in the black*; **~(e) zurechnen** to allocate profits, to attribute profits to ...; **~zurechnung** allocation of profits; **abrechnungspflichtiger ~** profit subject to accounting; **aleatorischer ~** a problematical profit; **am ~ beteiligt sein** to have a share in profits, to participate in profits; **am ~ teilnehmen** to participate in profits; **angemessener ~** fair (*or* reasonable) profit; **ausgeschütteter ~** distributed profit; **ausgewiesener ~** disclosed profit; **ausschüttungsfähiger ~** distributable profit, profits available for distribution; **bruchteilige ~e** *exch* fractional gains; **buchmäßiger ~** accounting profit; **den ~verteilen** to allocate the profits; **einbehaltene ~e** retained profits, undistributed profits; **entfallender ~** attributable profits; **entgangener ~** lost profits, loss of profits, loss of earnings (*lat*: *lucrum cessans*); **erwarteter ~** anticipated profit; **eventueller ~** contingent profit; **für den entgangenen ~ entschädigt werden** to be compensated for lost profit; **geheimgehaltener ~** secret profits; **gewerblicher ~** industrial and commercial profits; **imaginärer ~** imaginary profit, paper profit; **kalkulatorischer ~** imputed profit; **landwirtschaftliche ~e** agricultural profits; **mit ~ abschließen** to close the accounts with a profit; **mit ~absicht** with gainful intent, with the intention of making a profit; **mit ~ verkaufen** to sell at a premium, to sell at a profit; **müheloser ~** easy profit; **nicht ausgeschütteter ~** undistributed profit, undivided profits; **nicht entnommener ~** undrawn profit, undistributed profits, profits ploughed back (into the business); **nicht realisierte ~e** unrealized profits; **nicht zugewiesener ~** unappropriated profit; **nicht**

zweckgebundener ~ available surplus, unappropriated profits; **periodenfremde ~e und Verluste** profits and losses not relating to the period under review; **realisierte ~e** realized profits, realized income; **rechnerischer ~** calculated profit, paper profit; **stehengebliebener ~**profit left in the business; profits ploughed back into a business; **steuerpflichtiger ~** taxable profits; **tatsächlicher ~** actual profit; **thesaurierter ~** accumulated income, retained earnings, profits ploughed back into the business; **unerlaubte ~e** illicit profits; **unerwartete ~e** windfall profits; **unlauterer ~** sordid gains; **unverteilter ~** undistributed profit; **unversteuerter ~** pretax profit; **verdeckter ~** disguised profit; **verteilungsfähiger ~** distributable profit; **vorgetragener ~** profits brought forward, accumulated surplus; **vorweggenommener ~** anticipated profit; **wucherischer ~** usurious profits; **zu erwartender ~** expected profit; **zugeflossene ~e** accrued profits.

Gewinnbeteiligung *f* profit-sharing, participation in profits, participation in earnings; **~ der Arbeitnehmer** employee profit-sharing; **mit ~** with profits *(policy)*; **mit ~ ausgestattet** conferring a right to participate in profits; **ohne ~** without profits, non-participating *(policy)*.

Gewinnbeteiligungs|fonds profit-sharing fund; **~kartell** gross-money pool; **~pacht** profit related rent; **~plan** profit-sharing plan *(or* scheme); **~rechte** participating rights; **~vertrag** participating contract.

gewinnen *v/t* to win, to profit, to gain, to earn, to acquire.

Gewissen *n* conscience; **nach bestem ~** to the best of one's belief.

Gewissens|bisse remorse, compunction, pangs of remorse; **~entscheidung** decision taken for reasons of conscience; **~erforschung** examination of one's conscience; **~frage** issue of conscience; **~freiheit** freedom of conscience; **~gründe** grounds of conscience; *aus ~~n: for conscience sake, Verweigerung aus ~~n: refusal as a conscientious objector;* **~konflikt** inner conflict; **~not** moral dilemma; **~notstand** (state of) moral dilemma; **~pflicht** moral duty; **~sache** matter of conscience; **~zwang** moral constraint.

gewogen *adj* weighed; weighted *(statistics)*.

Gewohnheit *f* habit, custom, usage.

Gewohnheits|dieb habitual thief; **g~mäßig** *adj* habitual; **~mäßigkeit** habitualness, habitual character; **~recht** consuetudinary law, legal custom, customary law; **~rechtssatz** customary rule of law; **~täter** habitual offender, persistent offender; **~trinker** habitual drunkard, alcoholic; **~verbrecher** habitual criminal, outlaw.

gewunden *adj* devious *(testimony)*.

gewünscht *adj* desired, intended; *wie ~: as (and when) required.*

gezahlt *adj* paid (up).

gezeichnet *adj* signed, subscribed.

Gezeiten *pl* tide, ebb and flow; **~wasser** tidal water(s); **~wechsel** turn of the tide, tidal change; **~zone** littoral zone.

gezielt *adj* ad hoc, purposeful, purposive; aimed *(shot)*.

gezwungen *adj* forced, constrained.

Gießkannenprinzip *n* (= *Gießkannenpolitik*) sprinkling, "watering-can" method *(of public grants)*; "a little for everyone" principle, indiscriminate policy of providing subsidies; regionally indiscriminate allocation of resources; *nach dem ~~ verteilen: to distribute something in "watering-can fashion" (or: in ad hoc fashion).*

Gift *n* poison; **~ beibringen** to administer poison; **~beibringung** administering poison; **~~** *mit Mordvorsatz*: administering poison with intent to murder; **~buch** book on poisons *(pharmacy)*; **~kammer**

security room for storing poisons; ~**mischer** poisoner; ~**mord** murder by poisoning; ~**müll** toxic waste; ~**schein** certificate authorizing the purchase of poison; ~**untersuchung** poison test; g~**verdächtig** suspected of being poisonous.

Gilde *f* guild, corporation; ~**nhaus** guildhall; ~**nmitglied** guildsman; ~**nversammlung** *hist* guildhall sittings.

Gipfelkonferenz *f* summit conference; ~~-*Diplomatie*: summitry.

Gipfelwert *m* peak.

giral *adj, adv* by way of bank transfer.

Giralgeld *n* bank deposit money, book money deposit currency, (*US*) check book money.

Girant *m* endorser (= *indorser*), backer.

Giratar *m* endorsee (= *indorsee*).

Giratkonossementennehmer *m* endorsee of a bill of lading.

girierbar *adj* endorsable, negotiable.

girieren *v/t* to endorse, to negotiate; blanko ~: to endorse generally, to endorse in blanc.

Girierung *f* transfer by endorsement, negotiation.

Giro *n* endorsement (= *indorsement*); giro; credit transfer, bank transfer; ~**anweisung** credit transfer order; ~**auftrag** credit transfer order, instruction to make a bank transfer; ~**ausgleichsstelle** bank transfer clearing office; ~**bank** clearing bank; „~" **bestätigt**" "endorsement confirmed"; ~ **e-r Bank** bank endorsement, credit transfer from bank to bank; ~-**Einlage** deposit on a current account, deposit by credit transfer, giro deposit; „~ **fehlt**" "endorsement required"; ~**gelder** funds available for credit transfer (*or* for bank giro); ~**gläubiger** creditor by endorsement; ~**guthaben** credit balance on current account, giro balance; ~**kasse** clearing bank, clearing house of public savings banks; ~**konto** current account (*in a bank*), clearing account, giro account; ~**kunden** customers attached to a bank clearing system, customers' giro balance; ~**netz** giro system; ~-**Obligo** contingent liability of the endorser (*of bill exchange or note*); ~ **ohne Gewähr** endorsement without recourse; ~ **ohne Haftung** endorsement without recourse; ~ **ohne Obligo** endorsement without recourse; „~ **ohne Verbindlichkeit**" qualified endorsement; ~**provision** credit transfer commission; ~**ring** (interbank) credit transfer system; ~**sammeldepot** collective safe-deposit of negotiable securities; ~**sammelkasse** collective safe-deposit agency; ~**sammelverwahrung** collective safe-deposit of negotiable securities; ~**schuldner** debtor by endorsement; ~**stelle** giro centre, credit transfer clearing house; ~**überweisung** credit transfer, bank transfer; ~**verkehr** credit transfers under the giro system; ~**vertrag** bank giro contract; ~**zahlung** payment by credit transfer (= *bank transfer*); ~**zettel** giro transfer slip; ~**zentrale** giro centre, central saving banks' clearing house; **beschränktes** ~ qualified endorsement; **gewöhnliches** ~ regular endorsement; **ordnungsgemäßes** ~ proper endorsement.

Glas *n* glass, glassware.

Glas|- **und Schmuckwarenindustrie** glassware, ornament and trinket industry; ~**versicherung** plate glass insurance; **feuersicheres** ~ fire-proof glass; **kugelsicheres** ~ bullet-proof glass; **splittersicheres** ~ security glass, shatter-proof glass; „**Vorsicht** ~" "Glass! Handle with care".

Glaser *m* glazier, glass-worker; ~**arbeiten** glazing; ~**meister** master glazier.

Glaserei *f* glazier's shop, glazing business.

Glatteis *n* black ice, icy conditions on the roads; ~**gefahr** danger of ice; danger, ice!

glattstellen *v/t* to even up, to balance, to realize, to settle, to liquidate a position, to close a position, to clear; to take in (stock) without charging contango; to continue (bargain) at even; to close *(future transactions)* by equivalent spot transactions.

Glattstellung *f* closing of a speculative position; realization; ~**sauftrag** realization order; ~**sgeschäft** evening-up transaction; ~**sverkauf** realization sale, sell-off; *e–n ~~ vornehmen*: *to sell off*; **zur** ~ in full satisfaction.

Glaube *m* faith, belief, persuasion; **böser** ~ bad faith, malice, mala fide; **guter** ~ bona fide, good faith; *im guten ~n handeln*: *to act in good faith*; **jemandem ~n schenken** to give s. o. credit, to believe s. o.; **öffentlicher** ~ public faith, full faith and credit, public reliance.

Glaubens|artikel articles of religion; ~**bekenntnis** creed, religious beliefs, confession of faith; ~**freiheit** freedom of faith, freedom of religion; ~**gemeinschaft** religious body, common religion, denomination; ~**richtung** persuasion, religious belief, shade of religious opinion; ~**wechsel** change of religion, change of faith.

glaubhaft *adj* credible, believable, reliable; ~ **machen** to substantiate by prima facie evidence, to make credible.

Glaubhaftigkeit *f* credibility, believability, acceptability.

Glaubhaftmachung *f* substantiation by prima facie evidence, substantial evidence, authentication.

Gläubiger *m* creditor (= *cr, pl : cr–s*), obligee, ~**abfindung** settlement with one's *cr–s*; ~**anfechtung** *cr–'s* avoidance of debtor's transactions *(transferring property to a third party)*, avoidance of a preference; ~**anfechtungsgesetz** Creditors' Avoidance of Transfers Act *(German law of 1898, still in force)*; ~**anspruch** creditor's claim; *e–n ~~ vereiteln*: *to defeat a creditor*; ~**aufgebot** public notice to all *cr–s (of a debtor or an estate)*; ~**aufruf** public notice to *cr–s*, ~**ausschuß** committee of *cr–s*, committee of inspection; ~**befriedigung** satisfaction of *cr-s*; ~**begünstigung** preference of a *cr*, preferential transfer, fraudulent preference; ~**behinderung** hindering or defrauding *cr–s*; ~**beirat** committee of *cr–s*, board of inspection; ~**benachteiligung** defeating of a *cr*; hindering and delaying a *cr*; ~**bestechung** bribery of *cr–s*; ~**bevorzugung** preference of a *cr*, voidable preference, fraudulent preference; ~ **der Wandelschuldverschreibungen** holders of the convertible bonds; ~**gefährdung** jeopardizing a *cr's* interests; ~**gemeinschaft** body of *cr–s*; ~**kündigungsrecht** *cr's* right to call for immediate repayment; ~**land** *cr* state; ~**position** *cr* position; ~**rang** ranking of *cr–s*; ~**recht** right of a *cr*, title as a *cr*, *cr's* claim; ~**register** register of creditors (*or* mortgagees); ~**schädigung** prejudicial treatment of *cr–s*; ~**schutz** protection of (*outside*) *cr–s*; (*of companies and partnerships*); ~**sicherung** providing security for *cr–s*; ~**staat** *cr* state, *cr* country; ~**streit** conflict among *cr–s*; ~**verluste** *cr* losses; ~**versammlung** meeting of *cr–s*, general assembly of *cr–s*; ~**vertreter** representative of the *cr–s*; ~**verzeichnis** schedule of *cr–s*, list of *cr–s*; ~**verzug** *cr's* delay in accepting performance, creditor's delay, mora accipiendi; ~**wechsel** subrogation (of *cr– s*); **absonderungsberechtigter** ~ secured *cr*; **bereits vorhandene** ~ antecedent *cr–s*; **betreibender** ~ prosecuting *cr*; **bevorrechtigter** ~ preferred *cr*, *cr* by priority, preferential *cr*, privileged *cr*; **die** ~ **befriedigen** to satisfy (the) *cr–s*; **diverse** ~ sundry *cr–s*; **doppelt gesicherter** ~ doubly secured *cr*; **e–n** ~ **begünstigen** to prefer a *cr*; **mit ~n e–n Vergleich schließen** to compound a settlement with one's creditors; **nicht befriedigter** ~ unsatisfied *cr*; **nichtbevorrechtigter** ~ non-privileged *cr*, ordinary *cr*; **säumiger** ~ indulgent *cr*, *cr* delaying the enforcement of his claim; **seine** ~ **hinhalten** to put off one's *cr–s*; to delay one's *cr–s*; **sichergestellter** ~ secured *cr*; **sonstige** ~ other *cr–s*; **zweitrangiger** ~ secondary *cr*.

Gläubigerin *f* female creditor, creditrix; creditor company (*or* firm).

glaubwürdig *adj* credible, trustworthy, authentic.

Glaubwürdigkeit *f* credibility, trustworthiness, veracity; ~ **des Angeklagten** truth and veracity of accused; ~ **des Zeugen** credibility of witness, veracity of witness; **~sgrad** degree of belief, degree of credibility; **~lücke** credibility gap; **~sgutachten** expert opinion on credibility; **die ~ e–s Zeugen erschüttern** to impeach a witness, to shake a witness's credibility.

gleichartig *adj* analogous, similar, homogeneous, kindred, of the same kind (quality, description), uniform.

Gleichartigkeit *f* similarity, equality in kind, homogeneity.

gleichbedeutend *adj* equivalent, synonymous.

Gleichbehandlung *f* equal treatment, equality of treatment, non-discrimination; **~sgrundsatz** principle of equal treatment; ~ **von Arbeitnehmern** equal employment opportunity, equality in employment relations; **steuerliche** ~ equal tax treatment.

gleichberechtigt *adj* equally entitled, having equal rights.

Gleichberechtigung *f* equal rights, equal status, equality (of rights); ~ **der Ehegatten** equal rights for spouses, equality of rights in marriage; ~ **der Geschlechter** sex equality, equal rights for both sexes; **~sgesetz** Act according equal rights to women; *pl* ~~e: sex equality legislation; **~sgesetz für Lohnzahlung** Equal Pay Act.

gleichbleibend *adj* constant, unchanging, steady, staunch.

gleichförmig *adj* uniform, of equal configuration, invariable.

gleichgerichtet *adj* parallel, similarly aligned, aiming in the same direction.

gleichgestellt *adj* on the same footing, of equal rank, analogous.

Gleichgestellter *m* (*der Gleichgestellte*) person of equal rank.

Gleichgewicht *n* equilibrium, balance; **~spreis** equilibrium price; **~sspiel** process of equilibration; **~szins** equibilibrium interest rate; **marktwirtschaftliches** ~ free-market equilibrium; **ökologisches** ~ ecological equilibrium, ecological balance; **politisches** ~ balance of power; **wirtschaftliches** ~ economic equilibrium.

gleichgewichtig *adj* even, balanced.

Gleichheit *f* equality, parity; ~ **vor dem Gesetz** equality before the law, equality in law; **~sgrundsatz** principle of equality before the law, principle of equality, rule of uniformity; **~ssatz** principle of equality.

gleichlautend *adj* identically worded, of the same tenor, idem sonans.

gleichmachen *v/t* to make equal, to level, to equalize.

Gleichmacherei *f* egalitarianism.

gleichmäßig *adj* uniform, equal, even, pari passu (*creditors*).

Gleichmäßigkeit *f* uniformity, regularity; **~sklausel** uniformity clause.

gleichordnen *v/t* to co-ordinate.

Gleichordnungskonzern *m* horizontal combination (of companies).

gleichrangig *adj* pari passu, of equal status; ~ **mit** = *ranking pari passu with*.

gleichschalten *v/t* to bring into line with, to force into conformity, to co-ordinate, to align.

Gleichschaltung *f* making (political

Gleichschrift / **Gnade**

opponents) toe the line, enforced political conformity (*of organizations under Nazi regime*), co-ordination.

Gleichschrift *f* duplicate, true copy.

gleichsetzen *v/t* to treat as equivalent to, to equate; *etw ist gleichzusetzen: sth. is tantamount to.*

gleichstellen *v/t* to grant equality of status, to place on the same footing as, to put on a par with, to treat as equal, to put in the same category.

Gleichstellung *f* placing on an equal footing, the according of equal status; ~ **der Frauenarbeit** equality for women labour, equal pay for women.

gleichwertig *adj* equivalent, of equal value.

Gleichwertigkeit *f* equivalence, equal value, equal standard; ~**sgrundsatz** principle of equivalence.

gleichzeitig *adj* simultaneous, concurrent.

Gleichzeitigkeit *f* simultaneousness, concurrence, contemporaneity.

gleichziehen *v/i* to draw level with, to catch up with.

Gleitklausel *f* sliding-scale clause.

Gleitschutzvorrichtung *f* anti-skid device(s).

Gleitzeit *f* flexitime.

Gleitzoll *m* sliding-scale tariff.

Glied *n* limb, member, bodily member, link; ~ **e-r Beweiskette** link in a chain of evidence; ~**ertaxe** rate of dismemberment benefit (*accident ins*); ~**erverlust** loss of limbs, dismemberment; ~**staat** individual state (of a federation), constituent state, federal unit.

gliedern *v/t* to arrange, to subdivide, to classify, to organize.

Gliederung *f* subdivision, arrangement, breakdown, classification; ~**der Jahresbilanz** composition of the annual balance sheet; ~ **nach Sachgebieten** functional classification; ~**smerkmale** constituent elements, criteria of classification; ~**sschemata** forms of tables for diagrammatic analysis; **berufliche** ~ breakdown of occupations, occupational classification; **bundesstaatliche** ~ federal subdivisions, federal structure; **die regionale** ~ the regional pattern.

global *adj* global, world-wide, overall, across the board; ~ **betrachtet** regarded as a whole; ~ **bewilligt** voted as a lump sum.

Global|abrechnung comprehensive calculation, aggregate calculation; ~**aktie** multiple share certificate; ~**angebot** comprehensive offer; ~**aussage** broad statement, overall proposition; ~**betrag** round sum, overall amount, en bloc amount; ~**bewilligung** bloc vote, bloc appropriation; ~**darlehen** global loan, blanket loan, loan en bloc, lump-sum loan; ~**darstellung** overall picture, general presentation; ~**einsparung** overall cut, all-round cut; ~**finanzierung** bloc financing; ~**geschäft** package deal; ~**information** comprehensive information, all-inclusive information; ~**kontingent** global quota, overall quota; ~**kredit** blanket credit, bloc credit, lump-sum credit (*or* loan); ~**kürzung** all-round cut, across-the-board cut; ~**police** blanket policy; **g**~**statistisch** according to the overall statistics; ~**steuer** single tax, comprehensive tax; ~**steuerung** overall (economic) steering; ~**summe** overall total; ~**urteil** all-embracing conclusion; ~**versicherung** blanket insurance, all risk insurance; ~**vertrag** overall agreement, lump-sum contract; ~**zession** general assignment (*of all rights and claims*), blanket assignment.

Glossar *n* glossary.

Glücksspiel *n* game of chance, gaming, gambling, lottery; ~**gerät** gambling device; **verbotenes** ~ unlawful gambling.

GmbH *f* (German) private limited company; **GmbH & Co KG** (*German*) *limited partnership, the general partner being a GmbH.*

Gnade *f* mercy, pardon, clemency; ~

vor Recht ergehen lassen to temper justice with mercy.

Gnaden|akt act of clemency; **~ausschuß** clemency board, parole board; **~behörde** clemency board; **~empfehlung** recommendation of mercy (*or* of leniency); **~erlaß** act of grace; **~erweis** (act of) pardon; **~~ mit Auflagen**: conditional pardon; **~frist** period of grace, grace period, days of grace, extra time allowed; *ohne ~~*: *unreprievable*; **~gesuch** plea of pardon, plea for clemency, clemency petition; **~instanz** board of pardon(s), clemency board, authority having the prerogative of mercy; **~recht** prerogative of mercy, power of pardoning; **~sachen** clemency petition matters; **~schuß** coup de grâce, mercy shot; **~splitting** „mercy" splitting tax allowance *(after death of spouse)*; **~stelle** board of pardon, clemency board; **~tod** mercy killing; **~weg** official channels for clemency petitions.

Gold *n* gold (= *g*); **~abfluß** efflux of *g*, *g* outflow; **~agio** *g* premium, premium price of *g*; **~ankaufspreis** buying price of *g*; **~arbitrage** arbitrage in *g*; **~ausfuhrpunkt** *g* export point, exports specie point; **~ausfuhrverbot** embargo on *g* exports; **~barren** *g* bar; **~barrenwährung** *g* bullion standard; **~basis** *g* basis; **~bestand** *g* holdings; **~bewegungen** *g* flow, *g* movements; **~blockländer** *g* bloc countries; **~deckung** *g* backing, *g* coverage; **~devisenwährung** *g*-exchange standard; **~dollar** *g* (standard) dollar; **~einfuhrpunkt** import *g* point; **~einschußpflicht** liability to make contributions in *g*, obligation to make *g* inpayments; **~garantie** *g* backing, guarantee in terms of *g*; **~gehalt** *g* content; **g~gerändert** gilt-edged; **~hortung** hoarding of *g*;; ~ **in Barren** ingot *g*; **~kernwährung** *g* bullion standard; **~klausel** *g* clause; **~kurs** *g* rate, *g* price; **~mine** *g* mine; **~minenaktien** gold-mining shares, *g* shares; **~münze** *g* coin; **~münzenklausel** *g* coin clause; **~münzparität** *g* coin standard, *g* coin parity; **~option** option to buy *g*; **~parität** *g* parity; **~~sklausel**: *g parity clause*; **~prägung** minting of *g*; **~preis** *g* price; **~punkt** *g* point, specie point, bullion point; *oberer ~~*: *g export point*; *unterer ~~*: *g import point*; **~reserve** *g* reserve; **~schatz** hoard of *g*; **~schulden** *g* debts, debts in *g* bullion; **~sovereign** *g* sovereign; **~standard** *g* standard; **~umlaufwährung** *g* specie standard; **~vorrat** stock of *g*, *g* supply; **~währung** *g* standard currency; **~währungsland** *g* standard country; **~währungsobligation** *g* bond; **~wert** *g* value, value of *g*; **~wertgarantie** (outright) gold-value guarantee; **~wertklausel** *g* clause; **~zertifikat** *g* certificate; **~zufluß** in flow of *g*, *g* influx; **gemünztes Gold** *g* in the form of coins; **rohes** ~ unrefined *g*.

Goodwill *m* goodwill, intangible value, *cf Firmenwert*.

Gösch *f* jack, ship's flag.

Gott *m* God, Lord; ~ **der Allmächtige** God (the) Almighty, Almighty God; ~ **der Allmächtige und Allwissende** God the Almighty and Omniscient *(oath)*; **so wahr mir** ~ **helfe** so help me God; *~~ dir ~~*: *so help you God*.

Gottes|dienstordnung order of service, ritual, liturgy; **~dienststörung** disturbance of public (*or* religious) worship; **~gnadentum** divine right of kings; *von* ~ *Gnaden*: *by the grace of God*; **~lästerung** blasphemy, blasphemous libel, profanity.

Gouverneursrat Governing Council.

Grabschändung *f* desecration of a grave.

Grabstätte *f* burial-place, tomb.

Grabungsschutzgebiet *n* protected site for archeological excavations.

Grad *m* degree, grade; ~ **der Beweisführung** standard of proof; ~

Graduiertenförderung   **Grenzkapazität**

der Neuheit degree of novelty; ~ **der Verwandtschaft** (degree of) relationship; ~ **des Verschuldens** level of fault.

Graduiertenförderung *f* promotion of graduates (*in the scientific and artistic fields*).

Graf *m* count, (*GB*) earl; **~enstand** count's rank, status of a count; **~enwürde** countdom, earldom.

Grafschaft *f* county, (*GB*) shire; **~samt** county office.

Gratifikation *f* gratuity, bonus, staff bonus, ex gratia payment.

gratis *adj, adv* gratuitous, gratis, without payment, free of charge, free, uncharged for.

Gratis|aktie capital bonus, bonus stock, bonus share, scrip bonus; ~~n: *stock dividend (etc.)*; ~~n *verteilen*: *to make distributions in stock*; *ausschließlich* ~~n : *ex stock dividend*; **~anteil** bonus unit; **~lieferung** supply free of charge; **~obligation** bonus bond; **~probe** free trial; **~zuteilung** bonus allotment.

Graubuch *n* grey book.

grausam *adj* cruel, brutal.

Grausamkeit *f* cruelty; **seelische ~** mental cruelty.

Grauzone *f* grey area, grey legal area.

gravierend *adj* aggravating, serious.

greifbar *adj* ready-to-hand; tangible.

Gremium *n* body, group, panel; **autonomes, sich selbst ergänzendes ~** non-elective self-perpetuating body; **beratendes ~** advisory body; **ein beschlußfähiges ~ bilden** to constitute a quorum.

Grenz|abfertigung customs clearance (at a border); **~abkommen** frontier agreement; **~abmarkung** demarcation of a boundary (*or* frontier); **~abschnitt** section of the border district; **~abstand** clear space from the boundary-line; ~~sanspruch (*land owner's*) *right, that structures are kept at a distance from his boundary line*; **~abstützung** support of adjoining land (*at a slope*); **~anbieter** marginal seller;

~änderung change in the borders; **~anlage** frontier installation(s); **~arbeiter** frontier worker; **~arbeitnehmer** frontier zone worker; **~aufsicht** frontier surveillance; **~ausgangszollstelle** frontier customs office of exit; **~ausgleichszahlungen** monetary compensatory amounts (*EEC*); **~ausweis** frontier pass; **~bahnhof** border (railway) station, frontier station; **~baum** boundary tree; **~beamte** frontier officials; **~begehung** perambulation, processioning; **~behörde** frontier authority; **~bereich** frontier, frontier area, border district; *fig* marginal sector; **~bereinigung** frontier adjustment (rectification); **~berichtigung** rectification of a boundary; **~betrieb** enterprise at the border; marginal enterprise; **~bevölkerung** frontier population, inhabitants of border regions; **~bewachung** border supervision; **~bewohner** inhabitants of border regions; **~bezirk** frontier district; **~bezugskosten** marginal cost of acquisition, marginal factor, **~bürger** border district inhabitant, *hist* inborow and outborow; **~eigentum** border property; **~erlaubnis** special frontier pass; **~ertrag** marginal income, marginal yield, marginal profit; ~~ *des Kapitals*: *marginal yield on capital*; ~~*sboden*: *marginal land*; **~fahndung** frontier search and investigation; **~fall** marginal case; **~feststellungsklage** petition to establish the border line, *hist*: writ de perambulatione facienda; **~formalitäten** border formalities; **~frage** boundary question, the problem of the national border; **~fluß** boundary river; **~forderung** frontier claim, territorial claim; **~führung** border demarcation; **~gänger** frontier commuter, border crosser, frontier worker; **~gebiet** frontier area, frontier zone, border area; **~gewässer** boundary water(s); **~kapazität** marginal production capacity;

378

Grenzkonflikt / **Grenzziehung**

~**konflikt** border dispute; ~**kontrolle** border control, *pl also:* border checks; ~**kosten** marginal costs, differential costs; ~**kostenkalkulation** marginal costing; ~**kostenlehre** differential costing, marginal costing; ~**kostenrechnung** marginal costing; ~**kreditnehmer** marginal borrower; ~**krieg** border war; ~**kurs** marginal rate; ~**land** frontier (area), border land, area adjoining frontier; ~**landbetrieb** border-area enterprise, firm located close to the frontier; ~**landfonds** Border Area Fund *(for subsidies)*; ~**leistungsfähigkeit** marginal efficiency; ~**linie** boundary line, division; ~**marke** boundary mark; ~**markierung** demarcation; ~**mauer** division wall, boundary wall; ~**nachbarn** adjoining owners; ~**nachfrager** marginal purchaser; ~**nutzen** marginal utility; *abnehmender* ~~: *diminishing marginal utility*; ~**nutzung** marginal use, marginal utilization; ~**nutzungstheorie** marginal theory of value; ~**passierschein** frontier laissez-passer; ~**plankostenrechnung** standard marginal costing; ~**planungsrechnung** marginal analysis; ~**polizei** border police; ~**posten** border patrolman, border outpost; ~**produkt** marginal product; ~**produktivität** marginal productivity; ~**produzent** marginal producer; least efficient producer; ~**punkt** limit point; ~**rain** grass strip marking a boundary, boundary verge; ~**rate** marginal rate; ~**recht** law of boundaries; ~**regelung** boundary determination; ~**regionen** frontier regions; ~**scheidungsgericht** neighbourhood court meeting *(held on the boundary)*; ~**scheidungsklage** petition to fix a boundary; ~**schmuggel** smuggling (across a boundary); ~**schutz** border protection corps, border police service, border security patrol; ~**schutzbeamter** border police-officer; ~**schutzkommando** Federal Border Guard Command; ~**sicherung** border protection; ~**sperre** frontier barrier, ban on border crossing, closure of the border; ~**stein** boundary stone; ~**steinentfernung** unlawful removal of boundary stones; ~**steinversetzung** unlawful shifting of boundary stones; ~**stelle** border post; ~**streifen** balk *(unploughed land between fields)*; ~**streitigkeit** frontier dispute; ~**stückkosten** marginal unit cost; ~**übergangsschein für Kraftfahrzeuge** triptyque; ~**überbau** building over the boundary line; ~**übergang** frontier crossing-point; ~**übergangsstelle** crossing-point, point of entry; **g~übergreifend** transfrontier; **g~überschreitend** *adj* cross-border, cross-frontier, transfrontier; ~**überschreitung** frontier crossing, border crossing; ~**übertritt** crossing of borders, frontier passage; ~**übertrittskontrolle** border check; ~**übertrittsschein** border-crossing pass *(motor vehicles)*; ~**überwachung** frontier control (*or* supervision); ~**umgang** perambulation, boundary procession; ~**verbraucher** marginal consumer; ~**vereinbarung** border agreement; ~**verhältnis** marginal relationship; ~**verkäufer** marginal seller; ~**verkehr** border traffic; *kleiner* ~~: *local frontier crossing (in border districts)*, frontier zone traffic; ~**verlauf** border (line), (where the border runs); ~**verletzung** violation of the border, frontier violation; ~**vermarkung** demarcation of boundary-line; ~**vermessung** surveying the boundaries; ~**verrückung** shifting boundary lines; ~**vertrag** frontier treaty; ~**verwirrung** wilfully causing boundary problems; ~**wache** frontier guard; ~**wert** marginal value, critical value, prescribed value; ~**zeichen** boundary mark, landmark; ~**ziehung** determination of the boundary, marking out; ~**zwi-**

schenfall border incident; ~**zollamt** border customs-house; ~**zollstelle** frontier customs office.

Grenze *f* frontier, border, borderline, boundary (*real estate*), abuttals, limit, margin; ~ **der Rentabilität** break-even point; ~ **zwischen Recht und Unrecht** dividing line between right and wrong; **an der** ~ **liegender Fall** borderline case; **äußere** ~ out-boundary, frontier, border; **die** ~ **überschreiten** to cross the border; **ethnische** ~ ethnic boundary; **geliefert** ~ delivered to frontier; **grüne** ~ frontier traversing open country; **natürliche** ~ natural boundary; **obere** ~ upper limit.

Grenzer *m* border patrolman, customs officer at the border.

Greueltat *f* atrocity, outrage.

Grob|analyse rough analysis, proximate analysis; ~**blech** heavy plate; ~**einstellung** rough tuning-in, rough adjustment; **g**~**gerechnet** *adj* roughly (calculated), as a rough estimate; ~**heiten** crude remarks.

Groll *m* grudge, anger, resentment, sense of grievance.

Groß|abnehmer bulk buyer, quantity buyer; ~**abschluß** large contract, large deal; ~**aktionär** major shareholder; ~**anlagenbau** large-scale plant engineering and construction; ~**anlagengeschäft** large-scale construction business; ~**auftrag** major order; ~**bank** major bank, big bank, big banking house, national bank, internationally operative commercial bank; ~**banksystem** large-bank system; ~**bauer** big farmer, owner of a large farm; ~**baustelle** large-scale building site; ~**behälterversand** transport (*or* transit) of large containers; ~**betrieb** large concern, large enterprise; ~**betriebsvorteil** advantage of large-scale operation; ~**bürgertum** upper middle-class, wealthy bourgeoisie; ~**detailleur** large retailer; ~**einkauf** bulk purchase, wholesale purchase; ~**einkäufer** wholesale buyer; ~**eltern** grandparents; ~**elternteil** grandparent; ~**enkel** *m*: great-grandson, *pl*: great-grandchildren; ~**enkelin** great-granddaughter; ~**europa** Greater Europe, integrated Europe; ~**fahndung** manhunt, dragnet; ~**filialist** chain-store owner; ~**format** large size; ~**grundbesitz** large-scale land-ownership, large estate holdings, extensive landed property; land-owning class(es), landed aristocracy; ~**grundbesitzer** big land-owner, big landed proprietor, owner of large estates; ~**handel** → *Großhandel;* ~**händler** wholesaler, wholesale trader, wholesale dealer, wholesale distributor, merchant wholesaler, industrial distributor; ~**herzog** grand duke; ~**herzogin** grand duchess; ~**herzogtum** grand duchy, Grand Duchy; ~**hofmeister** Lord High Steward (*GB*); ~**industrie** big industry, large-scale industry, big business; **g**~**jährig** of age, of full age, of legal age; ~~ **werden**: to become of (full) age, to reach majority; ~**jährigkeit** majority, legal age; ~**kanzlei** legal clinic; ~**kapitalist** tycoon, capitalist; ~**konsortium** large combine, group, syndicate; ~**konzern** conglomerate, merger corporation; ~**kraftwerk** super-power station (*over 50 MW*); ~**kredit** big loan, big credit; ~**kreuz** grand cross (*decoration*); ~**kunde** big customer; ~**lebenbranche** ordinary life assurance, Ordinary Business (O. B.); ~**lebensversicherung** ordinary life insurance, Ordinary Business (O. B.); ~**lieferant** large supplier, major supplier; ~**macht** great power; ~**markt** supermarket, superstore, wholesale market; ~**packung** family size package, giant package; ~**plastik** monumental sculpture; ~**projekt** large-scale project; ~**raumbüro** open-plan office; ~**raumflugzeug** jumbo jet, wide-body aircraft; ~**raumpolitik** „sphere of influ-

Größe

ence" politics; ~**razzia** sweap; ~**reihenfertigung** high-volume production; ~**schaden** heavy loss, large loss, major damage; ~**schiffahrtsweg** major inland waterway; ~**siegel** great seal; ~**stadtentwicklung** large-city development, metropolitan development; ~**stadtverwaltung** administration of a large city, metropolitan administration; ~**- und Einzelhändler** wholesale and retail distributor; ~**verbraucher** large-scale consumer, bulk consumer; ~~~**nachlaß**: *discount for large-scale consumers*; ~**verdiener** high earner; ~**verfahren** mass trial; ~**vorhaben** large project, giant project; ~**wirtschaftsraum** large economic region.

Größe *f econ*: size, quantity; **gangbare** ~ fair size; **genormte** ~ standardized size; **marktgängige** ~ commercial size; **nicht-gangbare** ~ odd size; **vorschriftsmäßige** ~ prescribed size.

Große Beschwerdekammer *f pat* Enlarged Board of Appeal.

Größen|angabe statement of size; ~**gliederung** classification by size; ~**klasse** size-category; ~**ordnung** order of magnitude; ~**schichtung** classification according to size; ~**struktur** structure according to size, make-up according to categories of size; ~**verhältnis** scale, ratio, proportion; ~**vorteile** economics of scale; ~**wahn**, megalomania, delusions of grandeur.

Großhandel *m* wholesale business, wholesale trade.

Großhandels|firma wholesale firm, wholesaler; ~**index** index of wholesale prices; ~**lager** wholesale stock; ~**preis** wholesale price, trade price, invoice price; ~**rabatt** trade allowance, wholesale discount; ~**spanne** wholesale margin; ~**vertreter** wholesale representative.

Grossist *m* wholesaler.
Grube *f min*: mine, pit.

Grundhandelsgeschäft

Gruben|arbeiter miner; ~**entleerung** emptying of sewage (*percolation*) basin; ~**industrie** mining industry; ~**vorstand** mining board; ~ **und Flöze** pits and veins.

Grün|fläche park area, grass-covered open space; ~~~**nplanung**: *open space planning*; ~**gürtel** green belt; ~**land** grassland, meadows and pastures; ~**landwirtschaft** grassland husbandry; ~**streifen** grass verge, centre strip (*on parkway*); ~**zone** green belt, open-space zone.

Grund *m* (1) (*pl*: *Gründe* = ~*e*) reason, ground, cause, basis, foundation, motive, occasion; ~**ausbildung** basic instruction, basic training; ~**ausstattung** basic facilities; ~**bedarf** basic requirements; ~**bedeutung** primary meaning; ~**bedingung** basic condition; ~**bedürfnisse** needs; ~**begriff** fundamental concept, elementary term; ~**bestand** basic stock, basic inventory; ~**betrag** basic amount, basic figure; ~ **und Steigerungsbetrag**: *basic amount and increment*; *gezahlte* ~**beträge**: *basic payments*; ~**bogen** daily reconciliation sheet; ~**buchung** original entry; ~**e anführen** to state (*or* adduce) reasons; ~**e angeben** to show reasons, to give reasons; ~**einstellung** fundamental attitude; ~**e vorbringen** to advance reasons, to advance arguments, to set forth grounds; *plausible* ~**e** ~: *to advance convincing arguments;* ~**freiheit** basic liberty; ~**freiheitsrechte** constitutional liberties; ~**gebühr** basic fee, basic rate, flat rate, (subscription) rental; ~~ *nach Anschlußwerten*: *installed load tariff;* ~**gedanke** basic idea, key note, rationale ; ~**gehalt** basic salary; ~**gerechtigkeit** natural justice; ~**geschäft** underlying transaction; ~**gesetz** Basic (Constitutional) Law (*D*), constitution, fundamental law, organic law; *im* ~~ *verankert*: *enshrined in the Basic Law;* ~**handelsgeschäft** general commercial transaction (*cf buying and selling etc*); ~**interventionspreis** basic intervention price; ~**kapital** nominal authorized capital, share capital; registered capital; *esp US*: capital stock, general stock; ~**kosten** basic costs; ~**lage** basis, substratum; ~~ *der Gegenseitigkeit*: *basis of reciprocity*; ~~ *der Preisberechnungen*: *basis of costing*; *auf paritätischer* ~~: *on the basis of equality*; *auf rechtlicher* ~~: *on a legal basis, on legal authority*; ~**lagenforschung** basic research; ~**linie** underlying tendency, basic trend; ~**lohn** basic wage, basic rate of pay; ~**lohnsatz** basic pay rate, (*US: base pay rate*); **g**~**los** without cause, for no reason; unfounded; ~**miete** basic rent, initial standard rent; ~**nahrungsmittel** basic foodstuffs; ~**norm** basic norm; ~**ordnung** constitutional system; *demokratische* ~~: *democratic constitutional system*; ~**patent** master patent, basic patent; ~**pflichten** basic (constitutional) duties; ~**postulat** fundamental requirement; ~**prämie** basic rate, basic premium; ~**preis** floor price, standard price, basic price; ~**prinzipien** fundamental principles; ~**rate** basic rate; ~**rechte** constitutional civil rights, basic rights; ~**rechtsgarantien** constitutional guarantees of civil rights; ~**rechtskatalog** list of civil rights enshrined in the Basic Law (D); ~**rente** basic (social security) pension; ~**richtlinie** basic directive; ~**satz** → Grundsatz; ~**schule** *GB*: primary school, *US*: elementary school, grade school; ~**schulerziehung** primary education, elementary (= grade) school education; ~**stock** basis, basic stock; ~~*vermögen*: *basic property*; ~**stoff** → Grundstoff; ~**stufe** junior stage; ~**tarif** basic rate, basic tariff; ~**tatbestand** general statutory definition of a crime; ~**- und Hauptschulunterricht** elementary education; ~**urteil** judgment on the basis of the cause of action (*reserving the amount to a later decision*); ~**verfassung** basic state, basic condition; ~**vergütung** basic remuneration, basic compensation, basic salary; ~**versorgung** („*soziales Netz*") floor of protection; ~**vertrag** main contract; Basic Treaty; ~**wasser** underground waters; ~**wasserabsenkung** decline in the ground-water level; ~**wehrdienst** regular military service; ~**wehrdienstpflichtiger** service draftee man; ~**zug** (*pl Grundzüge*) trend, fundamental feature; *pl* trends, outline (*publication*); ~~ *der Konjunktur*: *basic cyclical trend*; **allgemeine staatspolitische** ~**e** grounds of overall national policy; **anscheinend plausible** ~**e** ostensible reasons; **auf** ~ **eigener Aussagen überführt** self-convicted; **auf** ~ **e-s Irrtums** due to an error; **auf** ~ **von** by virtue of, by reason of, pursuant to; **aus** ~**en** ... for reasons; *aus rechtlichen* ~*en*: *on legal grounds*; **ausschlaggebender** ~ overriding reason, decisive reason; **der konkrete** ~ the actual reason; **erhebliche** ~**e** substantial grounds, just cause; **genau angegebener** ~ specific cause; **gesetzlicher** ~ lawful cause; **gewichtiger** ~ good reason; **gleich aus welchem** ~ for whatever reason; **hinreichender** ~ probable cause; **legitimer** ~ legitimate reason; **mit** ~**en versehen** stating the reasons (*for the court's decision*); **ohne ausreichenden** ~ without sufficient cause; **ohne berechtigten** ~ without good (*or* just) cause; **ohne rechtfertigenden** ~ without justification, without just cause; **ohne rechtlichen** ~ without lawful cause, without legal reason(s); **ohne triftigen** ~ without reasonable excuse, without reasonable cause; **ohne vertretbaren** ~ without reasonable cause; **stichhaltiger** ~ sound reason, good and sufficient cause; tenable argument; *nicht* ~~: *unsound reason*; **triftiger** ~

Grund | **gründen**

good reason, sound reason, sufficient cause, good (and sufficient) cause; *pl*: valid grounds; **überzeugender** ~ convincing reason; **unhaltbarer** ~ untenable ground; **verfahrensrechtlicher** ~ procedural ground; **vertretbarer** ~ justifiable reason; **wichtiger** ~ important reason, grave and weighty reason, special reason.

Grund *m* (2) land, soil, real estate, property; ~**abtretung** surrender of land; ~**akten** title-deeds, land register files; ~**besitz** real property, property holding; real estate, land holding, ~**besitzer** land owner; possessor of real estate; property holder; ~**besitzwertverzeichnis** valuation list; ~**buch** → *Grundbuch*; ~**dienstbarkeit** easement, real servitude; ~~ *der öffentlichen Hand*: *public easement*; *auf ein Unterlassen gerichtete* ~~: *negative easement*; *beschränkt persönliche* ~~: *restricted easement (entitlement to a person)*; *privatrechtliche* ~~: *private easement*; *wechselseitige* ~~: *cross easement*; ~**eigentum** freehold property, real estate ownership, property in land, fee simple (absolute); ~~ *der öffentlichen Hand*: *public domain*; *rechtsmängelfreies* ~~: *good record title*; *unbelastetes* ~~: *unencumbered real estate*; ~~*sübertragung transfer of fee simple, conveyance of land*; ~**eigentümer** land owner, owner of real estate; ~~ *als Eigenbesitzer*: *owner–occupier*; ~**erwerb** acquisition of land; ~~*s- und Nebenkosten: real-estate purchase and incidental costs*; ~**erwerbssteuer** (real estate) transfer tax; ~**fläche** area (of ground), surface of the ground (*or land*), floor space; ~**freibetrag** basic exemption; ~**herr** lord of the manor, owner of an estate, landed proprietor; ~**herrschaft** manorial estate, manor, seigniory; ~**kredit** real-estate credit; ~**kreditanstalt** mortgage bank; ~**last** land charge, rent charge; ~**pacht** lease, land lease; ~**pächter** tenant, landholder; ~**pfand** → *Grundpfand*; ~**rente** ground rent; ~**schuld** → *Grundschuld*; ~**steuer** → *Grundsteuer*; ~**stück** → *Grundstück*; ~ **und Boden** grounds, land, soil, landed property; ~**verkehrssteuer** real-estate transactions tax; ~**vermögen** landed property, real property, property in land, real estate; ~**wert** value of the soil, value of the land; ~**wertssteigerung** real-estate appreciation; **auf fremdem** ~ in alieno solo, on foreign soil; **erschlossener** ~ improved land; **unerschlossener** ~ raw land; **verpachteter** ~ leased land.

Grundbuch *n* Land Register (= *LR*), land title register, real-estate register; ~**abschrift** land certificate, copy of the entry at the *LR*; ~**amt** Land Registry, district land registry; real-estate recording office; ~**auszug** land register extract, copy of the *LR*; ~~ *über Belastungen: charge certificate*; ~**bereinigung** general rectification of the *LR*; ~**berichtigung** rectification of the *LR* (*individual case*); ~~*sklage: action for rectification of the LR*; ~**bescheinigung** *LR* certificate; ~**bezirk** Land Register district; ~**blatt** *LR* folio; ~**einsicht** inspection of the *LR*; ~**eintragung** entry in the *LR*, recording in the *LR*; ~**löschung** cancellation of an entry in the *LR*, deletion of an entry in the *L R*; ~**ordnung** Land Registry Act; ~**recht** land registry law, law of real-estate recording; ~**richter** land registry judge; ~**sachen** cases involving the *LR*; ~**sperre** *temporary prohibition of recording in the LR*; ~**umschreibung** transfer entry in the *LR*; ~**verfahren** land registry proceedings; ~**verfügung** *LR* Regulations; ~**vermutung** presumption of correct *LR* entry; ~**zwang** compulsory (land) registration; recording of real-estate.

gründen *v/t* to found, to form, to promote, to establish, to institute, to incorporate, to launch.

Gründer founder, promoter (of a company), incorporator; ~**aktien** founders' shares, founders' stock, promotional stock; ~**anteil** founders' participation, founder's share certification; ~**anteilschein** founder's share; ~**bericht** promotion report, statutory report, formation report; ~**genossenschaft** association of founders; ~**gesellschaft** association of founders; ~**haftung** company promoter's liability; ~**konjunktur** company-floating boom; ~**konsortium** promoting syndicate; ~**lohn** founders' fee (*for services during the formation of a company*); ~**obligation** founder's bond; ~**vereinigung** association of founders; ~**vergütung** promotion money; ~**zeit** period of promoterism; *German business-floating boom in the 1870s and 1880s.*

Grundpfand *n* real-estate mortgage, charge on real property; ~**besteller** mortgagor of real estate; ~**brief** official mortgage certificate; ~**darlehen** mortgage loan; ~**forderung** mortgage claim, personal debt under a mortgage; ~**gläubiger** mortgagee; ~**recht** lien on (real) property, mortgage; *erstrangiges* ~~: *first mortgage*; *nachstelliges* ~~: *junior mortgage*; *rangnächstes* ~~: *subsequent mortgage*; *mit e-m* ~~ *belasten*: *to encumber with a mortgage*; *ein* ~~ *löschen*: *to dismortgage*; **g**~**rechtlich gesichert** secured by a mortgage; ~**schuld** mortgage debt; ~**schuldner** mortgagor; ~**sicherheit** mortgage security.

Grundsatz (*pl Grundsätze* = ~*e*) principle, maxim, tenet, rule, policy; ~**bestimmung** regulation of principle; ~ **der festen Verbindung** "genuine link" principle (*between ship and state of registration*); ~ **der Fristenkongruenz** hedging principle; ~ **der Gegenseitigkeit** principle of reciprocity; ~ **der identischen Norm** double criminality rule (*extradition law*); ~ **der Mehrheitsentscheidung** majority rule; ~ **der Notwendigkeit der Erschöpfung des innerstaatlichen Rechtswegs** local remedies rule; ~ **der Öffentlichkeit** principle of publicity of proceedings (*or* public hearings); ~ **der Steuergerechtigkeit** the principle of fiscal justice; ~ **des fairen Verfahrens** principle of fair trial; ~**entscheidung** decision of principle, decision on a matter of principle; leading case; ~**e ordnungsmäßiger** (= *ordnungsgemäßer*) **Buchführung** generally accepted accounting principles, sound accounting practice, ~**erklärung** statement of policy, declaration of principles; ~**frage** question of principle, fundamental issue; ~**gesetzgebung** framework legislation; ~**kommission** policy commission; ~**programm** platform, policy statement, basic program(me); ~**urteil** leading decision, judgment creating a legal precedent; ~**vereinbarung** memorandum of understanding, open contract, policy agreement; **aktienrechtliche** ~**e** principles of company law; **allgemein anerkannte** ~**e** generally accepted principles; **aus** ~ on principle, as a matter of principle; **beherrschender** ~ overriding principle; **behördliche** ~**e** principles applied in the public service; **billigkeitsrechtliche** ~**e** maxims of equity; **eiserne** ~**e** cast-iron principles; **moralische** ~**e** ethical principles, moral code; **nach allgemeinen** ~**en** pursuant to general principles; **nach gleichen** ~**en wie** on the same footing, along the lines of (the same principles); **nach kaufmännischen** ~**en** according to business principles; **oberster** ~ leading principle; **standesrechtliche** ~**e** canons of professional ethics.

grundsätzlich *adj* fundamental, basic, *adv*: as a matter of principle, in principle, in essence; categorically.

Grundschuld *f* land charge, *abstract*

Grundsteuer / **Grundstück**

land charge for a money payment, mortgage; ~**brief** land charge certificate; ~**forderung** claim secured by land charge; ~**gläubiger** party entitled to a land charge, holder of a land charge, mortgagee; ~**löschung** resurrender (*or* cancellation) of land charge.

Grundsteuer *f* land tax, real property tax, real-estate tax, landed property tax, tax on land and buildings; ~**ablösung** redemption of land-tax; ~**ausfallvergütung** compensation for loss of land tax; ~**ausgleich** equalization of land tax revenue; ~**befreiung** exemption from land tax; ~**beamter** *revenue official in charge of land tax matters*; ~-**Durchführungsverordnung** land tax law implementing ordinance; ~**erlaß** land tax waiver; ~**freiheit** exemption from land tax; ~**gesetz** land tax law (*empowering local authorities to charge land tax and regulating the taxation*); ~**kataster** land tax cadastral register; ~**pflicht** land tax liability; ~**reinertrag** net revenue from land tax; ~**rolle** land tax register (of real estate); ~**vergünstigung** land tax relief.

Grundstoff *m* raw material, primary product; ~**industrie** primary industry, raw (materials) industry; ~**preis** raw-material price; ~**sektor** basic industry sector; ~**wirtschaft** basic (materials) industry; **inländische** ~**e** domestic raw materials.

Grundstück *n* piece of real estate, plot of real land (and structures); real property unit, a property, *pl*: (real) property; premises; ~ **des Berechtigten** dominant tenement (*easement*), real estate belonging to the entitled party; **abgeschlossenes** ~ enclosure, enclosed premises; **abgeräumtes** ~ cleared site; **angrenzendes** ~ abutting land, adjacent property, adjoining land; **bebaute** ~**e** developed real estate, land and buildings; **befriedetes** ~ enclosed premises, *pl*: enclosed lands; **belastetes** ~ encumbered real estate, encumbered property; **beschlagnahmtes** ~ requisitioned property; **buchungsfreie** ~**e** unregistered land, land not subject to land registration; **dienendes** ~ servient tenement (*servitude*), servient estate; **dinglich mit dem** ~ **verbunden** running with the land; joined in rem; **eigengenutzte** ~**e** self-used real estate, owner-occupied land; **eingefriedetes** ~ enclosed premises, fenced-in land; **ein** ~ **belasten** to encumber an estate; **ein** ~ **beleihen** to lend on mortgage; **ein** ~ **räumen und herausgeben** to quit and yield up (*or* surrender) premises; **einheitliches** ~ real estate forming one unit, uniform piece of land; **erschlossenes** ~ improved property, developed land; **gemeindeeigenes** ~ municipal property, parish property; **gemeindefreie** ~**e** area outside of local authority jurisdiction; **gemischtgenutzte** ~**e** real estate of mixed use, real property used for various purposes (*residential and trade or industry*); **gepachtetes** ~ leased land, tenement, leasehold estate; **gewerbliches** ~ industrial premises; **herrenlose** ~**e** ownerless real estate, estate in abeyance, derelict land; **herrschendes** ~ dominant tenement, dominant estate (*servitude*); **hypothekarisch belastetes** ~ mortgaged property; **landwirtschaftliche** ~**e** agricultural land; **mit dem** ~**gekoppelt** running with the land, linked with land ownership; **nicht umfriedetes** ~ unenclosed ground; **nicht verkehrssicheres** ~ dangerous premises; **rückwärtige** ~**e** back lands; **umfriedetes** ~ close, enclosed premises, fenced-in land; **unbebautes** ~ unbuilt land, lot, plot of unbuilt ground, idle land, vacant land; *unbebaute und bebaute* ~*e*: *land and buildings*; **unbelastetes** ~ unencumbered real estate; **unerschlossenes** ~ unimproved property; **ungenützte**, ~ vacant

Grundstücksabstützung   **Grundstücksverkehr**

land; **verlassenes** ~ disclaimed property, abandoned land, vacant possession; **verpachtetes** ~ leased land, rented land; **voll erschlossenes** ~ fully serviced site; **zuwegloses** ~ landlocked plot.

Grundstücks|abstützung lateral support; ~**auflassung** = *Auflassung (1)* qv; ~**auflassungsurkunde** → *Auflassung (1)*; ~**ausfahrt** property exit; ~**belastung** encumbrance (of land), charge on real property; ~**benutzung** use of land; ~**beschreibung** description of property; ~**besitz** possession of real estate, occupation of land or buildings, real property holdings; ~**besitzer** real-estate owner, possessor of real estate; ~**bestandteile** integral parts of the premises; *wesentliche* ~~: *immovable fixtures*; ~**beteiligung** shares in real-estate holdings, real-estate participation; ~**bewertung** valuation of real estate, site value appraisal; ~**eigentum** land ownership, property holding, fee simple (absolute in possession), freehold estate, title to land; ~**eigentümer** real-estate owner, owner in fee simple; ~**eigentumsurkunden** documents of title to land, title deeds; ~**einkünfte** land revenue, income from real estate; ~**enteignung** expropriation of land; ~**entschädigung** compensation for land-expropriation; ~**erschließungsgesellschaft** property developers; ~**erschließungsplan** land-development project; ~**erwerb** property purchase, acquisition of real estate; ~**fläche** surface area of a property (*or* plot of land); ~**gemeinschaft** joint holding of real estate; ~**geschäfte** real-estate transactions; ~**gesellschaft** real-estate company; g~**gleich** equivalent to real property; ~**grenze** property boundary, abuttal; ~**gruppen** classes of property; real-estate categories; ~**herausgabeklage** droitural action; ~**inanspruchnahme** utilization of real

estate, (forced) use of land (*by the state or military forces*); ~**kauf** purchase of real estate; ~**käufer** purchaser of land; ~**kaufvertrag** contract for sale of land; ~**klage** action founded on real-estate rights; ~**last** charge on land, encumbrance; ~*en*: *rates, taxes and outgoings; kommunale* ~~*en*: *local land charges; öffentliche* ~~*en*: *public burdens, public land charges;* ~**makler** real-estate broker, realtor (*US*), estate agent (*GB*); ~**markt** real-estate market, property market; ~**mitbesitzer** *pl* joint possessors of real-estate, joint tenants; (*loosely*:) joint real-estate owners; ~**miteigentümer** co-owners of real estate, tenants in common; ~**nießbrauch** usufruct of land, life estate; ~**nutzung** land use; ~**pacht** land lease, leasehold; ~**parzelle** parcel of land, plot, lot; ~**preis** real-estate price, cost of land; ~**preisüberwachung** real-estate price control; ~**räumungsklage** action for recovery of land, action for possession (of real estate); ~**recht** law of real property; title to real-estate, interest in land; ~**schätzer** land valuer, real-estate appraiser; ~**spekulant** speculator in property, real estate operator; ~**spekulation** real-estate venture; ~**steuer** = *Grundsteuer qv*; ~**teilfläche** plot, parcel of land; ~**teilung** partition of real estate; ~**teilvermächtnis** bequest partly consisting of land; ~**überlassung** surrender of real estate; ~**übertragung** conveyance, transfer of land; ~**umsätze** property sales turnover; ~**unterlagen** title deeds, real-estate records; ~**urkunden** title deeds, real-estate records; ~**veräußerer** transferor of real estate; ~**veräußerung** real-estate transfer, surrender of real property, sale of real estate; ~**veräußerungsrecht** right to convey; ~**veräußerungsurkunde** instrument of conveyance; ~**verkehr** real-estate transactions; ~**verkehrs-**

386

Gründung | **Gültigkeitsbedingung**

genehmigung official permission to transfer real property; ~**verkehrsgesetz** regulating real estate transactions; ~**verkehrsrecht** real-estate transactions law; ~**vermögen** real property, realty, immovable property; ~**verpfändung** mortgaging of land; ~**versicherung** real-property insurance; ~**versteigerung** sale of land by auction; ~**verwalter** estate manager; ~**verwaltung** estate management, real-property management; ~**verzeichnis** list of real-estate holdings; ~**wert** value of the real estate, land value, site value; *steuerlicher* ~~: *assessable site value*; ~**wertermittlung** real-estate value assessment; ~**zinsen** revenue from land; ~**zubehör** accessory to realty fixtures and fittings of the premises.

Gründung *f* establishment, foundation, formation, organization, flotation, incorporation.

Gründungs|akt act of foundation (*etc* →*Gründung*); ~**aktien** initial shares, original shares; ~**aufwand** formation expenses; ~**ausschuß** promotion committee; ~**bericht** report on the foundation, statutory report (of incorporation).; ~**bescheinigung** certificate of incorporation; ~**bilanz** commencement, balance sheet; ~**einlage** original investment; ~**fonds** foundation fund; ~**gemeinkosten** promotion (*or* foundation) overhead(s); ~**geschäft** company promotion business; ~**gesellschaft** pre-incorporation business association; ~**gesetz** basic ordinance, foundation statute, organic Act; ~**jahr** year of establishment; ~**kapital** original capital, capital on formation; ~**konsortium** promoting syndicate, underlying syndicate; ~**kosten** formation (*or* promotion) expenses; ~**mitglied** original member, subscriber member; ~**protokoll** minutes of the foundation meeting; ~**prüfer** company formation auditor; ~**prüfung** company formation audit; ~**schwindel** fictitious foundation of a company; ~**urkunde** formation deed, certificate of incorporation, memorandum of association (*company Ltd*), partnership certificate, foundation charter; ~**versammlung** promotional meeting, constituent assembly; ~**vertrag** foundation agreement.

Gruppe *f* group, panel, scale; *mil* squad; ~ **Ökologie** Ecological Panel, ecological committee.

Gruppen|abschluß group accounts, group financial statements; ~**abschreibung** composite-life method of depreciation, group depreciation; ~**akkord** group piece work; ~**arbeitsverhältnis** group employment; ~**bewertung** group valuation; ~**bildung** formation of groups; ~**denken** thinking in terms of particular groups; ~**egoismus** sectional self-interest; ~**einteilung** dividing-up into groups; ~**freistellung** group exemption; ~**index** index for a group, sub-index; ~**interessen** group interests; ~**lebensversicherung** group insurance; ~**leiter** head of group; ~**mietvertrag** non-exclusive occupation agreement; ~**versicherung** group insurance, collective insurance; ~**verteiler** group distributor; ~**wahl** employee-representation election by groups (*or* classes); ~**n-Wohnungsüberlassungsvertrag** non-exclusive occupation agreement; **fachliche** ~ specialized sections.

gültig *adj* valid, in force, authentic; ~ **nur bei Vertragsabschluß** subject to contract.

Gültigkeit *f* validity, legal force, authenticity, effectiveness; **die** ~ **verlängern** to extend the validity.

Gültigkeits|bedingung pre-conditions of (legal) validity; ~**bereich** extent of validity, scope of application; ~**dauer** validity term, period of validity, duration, term of validity, life (*of an agreement*); ~~-*e-r Offerte*: *duration of offer*; ~**erforder-**

nis(se) prerequisites of validity; ~**erklärung** validation, legalization, certification of validity; ~**verlängerung** extension of validity; ~**vermutung** presumption of validity; ~**voraussetzung** prerequisites of validity.

Gummiknüppel *m* (rubber) truncheon.

Gunst *f* favour (*US: favor*), good will; **zu ~en Dritter** for the benefit of third persons (*or* others); **zu ~ von** for the benefit of, in favour of.

Günstigkeitsprinzip *n* (*permissible*), deviation for employee's benefit from collective bargaining agreement.

Gurt *m* seat belt; ~**anlegepflicht** compulsory use of seat belts, belting (obligation); ~**muffel** *person who can't be bothered to wear a seat belt*; ~**zwang** compulsory use of seat belts.

Gut *n* (*pl* → *Güter*) landed property; property; sth of value, asset, goods (*pl*) (*economics*); **eingebrachtes ~** dotal property (*marriage*), wife's premarital property, property brought in (by spouse upon marriage); **heimgefallenes ~** escheat; **herrenloses ~** ownerless property; **herrenlos gewordenes ~** unclaimed property, disclaimed property, derelict property, abandoned property, discarded property.

Gutachten *n* expert opinion, appraisal report (*of valuer*), expertise; **~ e-s Sachverständigen** expert opinion, expertise; **ablehnendes ~** adverse opinion; **ärztliches ~** medical opinion, medical award; **demoskopisches ~** public opinion poll; **ein ~ abgeben** to render an opinion, to give an opinion; **ein ~ einholen** to take an opinion, to ask for an expertise; **ein ~ erstatten** to furnish an expert opinion, to give an expert opinion; **erbbiologisches ~** expert opinion on hereditary factors (*in paternity suits*); **fachärztliches ~** medical specialist's opinion, expert medical opinion; **gerichtsmedizinisches ~** opinion of a specialist in forensic medicine; **medizinisches ~** medical opinion; **psychiatrisches ~** psychiatric opinion; **technisches ~** technical opinion.

Gutachter *m* expert, valuer, assessor, ~**ausschuß** committee of experts; ~**kommission** panel of experts; ~**tätigkeit** an expert's advisory services, an expert's advice; ~**verfahren** (expert) advisory procedure.

gutachtlich *adj* expert, by an expert opinion; **sich ~ äußern**: *to give an expert opinion on sth.*

gutbringen *v/t* to credit.

Gutdünken *m* discretion; **nach ~ des Gerichts** at the discretion of the court; **nach eigenem ~ handeln** to act at one's own discretion, to be the sole judge of sth.

Güte *f* (1) quality, grade, class; ~**anforderungen** quality requirements, quality standards; ~**aufpreis** (additional) price for quality; ~**bestimmung** quality designation; ~**klassen** quality categories, quality grades; ~**klassenbezeichnung** grade label; ~**klasseneinteilung** making quality categories, grading; ~**marke** certification mark; ~**prüfung** quality test; ~**überwachung** quality control; ~**vorstellung** concept of quality; ~**zeichen** mark of quality, quality label, certification mark, sign of quality, brand; **handelsübliche ~ und Beschaffenheit** good merchantable quality and condition; **von erster ~** first class, first rate.

Güte *f* (2) amicableness, kindness, good nature; ~**antrag** request for conciliatory proceedings; petition for an amicable settlement; ~**stelle** conciliation office; ~**und Schiedsordnung** rules of conciliation and arbitration; ~**termin** conciliatory first hearing at labour court; ~**verfahren** conciliatory proceedings; ~**verhandlung** conciliatory hearing, hearing for purposes of reaching a settlement; ~**versuch** attempt to reach an amicable settlement.

Güter *pl* goods, commodities, assets, valuable matters; *cf Gut*; ~**abfertigung** dispatching of goods; goods office, freight office; ~**abwägung** balancing consideration of legally protected values; ~**annahme** goods (receiving) office, freight (receiving) office; ~**ausgabe** goods (delivery) office, freight (delivery) office; ~**austausch** exchange of commodities; ~**bahnhof** goods station, freight depot, freight yard; ~**beförderung** transport of goods, shipment, freight service; ~**besichtiger** commodity surveyor; ~**bündel** batch of commodities; ~ **der gewerblichen Wirtschaft** industrial goods; ~ **des gehobenen Bedarfs** luxuries and semi-luxuries; ~ **des täglichen Bedarfs** necessaries; ~ **des Massenkonsums** mass-consumption goods; ~**erzeugung** production (of goods); ~**expedition** dispatch, forwarding agency; ~**fernverkehr** long-distance transport, *(US)* long haul trucking; *gewerblicher* ~~: *commercial long-distance transport*; ~**fernverkehrsgesetz** long-distance transport Act; ~**freigabe** freight release; ~ **für Messen und Ausstellungen** exhibits at trade fairs; ~**gemeinschaft** community of property; *eheliche* ~~: *marital community of property*; *fortgesetzte* ~~: *continued marital community of property (after the death of a spouse)*; ~**kraftverkehr** road haulage, truckage, transport of goods by road; ~~**sunternehmer**: *road haulage operator*; ~**kreislauf** circulation of goods; ~**menge** volume of freight; *beförderte* ~~: *volume of freight handled*; ~**nahverkehr** short-distance goods traffic, short haul transportation; ~**pflegeschaft** property curatorship *(curator bonis)*; ~**recht** → *Güterrecht*; ~**schuppen** goods shed; ~**spediteur** freight forwarder; ~**stand** → *Güterstand*; ~**tarif** goods rates, freight tariff, commodity rates; ~**transport** carriage of goods, freight transportation; ~**transportversicherung** insurance of goods in transit, freight insurance; ~**trennung** separation of property, (marital regime of) separation of goods; *vertragliche* ~~: *conventional separation of goods (by notarial deed)*; ~**umschlag** goods turnover, transhipment; ~ **und Dienstleistungen** goods and services; ~**- und Kapitalverkehr** goods and capital movement; ~**-und Pflichtenabwägung** appreciation of values and obligations *(by a judge)*; ~~ **und Warenverkehr** goods and capital movement; ~**verkehr** transportation of goods, freight traffic, goods traffic; *öffentlicher* ~~: *public transport*; *werkseigener* ~~: *goods carried in works' own vehicles*; ~**versicherung** cargo insurance, freight insurance; ~**verteilung** distribution of goods; ~**volumen** total goods available (*or* carried); ~**waggon** waggon, box waggon, freight car; ~**zug** goods train, freight train; **bewegliche** ~ movable goods, personal property; **feuergefährliche** ~ inflammable goods; **frachtintensive** ~ goods with large freight element; **gefährliche** ~ dangerous goods, dangerous cargo; **langlebige** ~ durables, durable goods; **lebensnotwendige** ~ essentials; *nicht* ~~: *non-essentials;* **seetriftige** ~ flotsam, goods from a shipwreck at sea; **sperrige** ~ bulky goods; **strandtriftige** ~ goods from stranded ship; **unwirtschaftliche** ~ uneconomic goods, onerous goods; **weniger lebenswichtige** ~ less essentials; **wertbeständige** ~ goods of lasting value; **zollfreie** ~ free goods.

Güterrecht *n* law of matrimonial property (regimes); ~**sregister** marriage property register, register of marriage settlements; ~**sstatut** the proper law applicable to matrimonial property *(int. private law)*; ~**svereinbarung** matrimonial property agreement (deed), marriage settlement; **~sverhältnis** matrimonial property relation; **~vertrag** matrimonial property agreement, marriage settlement; **eheliches ~** law of matrimonial property, matrimonial regime; **gesetzliches ~** statutory regime in ordinary; **immaterielle ~e** intangible property rights; **vertragliches ~** contractual regime, conventional marital regime, marital property settlement.

Güterstand *m* system of marital property, matrimonial (property) regime; **~ der Verwaltung und Nutznießung** *(former)* statutory regime of administration and usufruct *(by husband of wife's property)*; **ehelicher ~** matrimonial (property) regime; **gesetzlicher ~** statutory regime of matrimonial property, statutory regime in ordinary; **vertraglicher ~** marriage settlement, matrimonial regime elected by agreement.

Gutgewicht *n* allowance on weight.

Gutglaubens|erwerb *m* bona fide acquisition, acquisition by innocent buyer without notice, *or* by bona fide purchaser; **~schutz** bona fide rights protection, protection of good faith.

gutgläubig *adj, adv* bona fide, in good faith, without notice, innocent, credulous; **~ handeln**: *to act in good faith*; **~ und redlich handeln**: *to act innocently and honestly*.

Gutgläubigkeit *f* credulity, good faith; **jmds ~ ausnützen** to take advantage of s.o.

Guthaben *n* credit balance, balance in s.o.'s favour, funds; **~bewegungen** changes in credit balances; **~ freigeben** to unfreeze funds; **~inhaber** holder of a credit balance; **~klausel** sufficient funds proviso; **~saldo** credit balance; **ausstehende ~** *pl* outstanding accounts; **ein ~ ausweisen** to show a (credit) balance; **ein ~ pfänden** to garnish an account; **eingefrorene ~** *pl* frozen assets; **erworbenes ~** credit balance on acquired account; **kein ~** no assets, no funds *(on bank account)*; **nicht zurückgefordertes ~** unclaimed balance; **täglich fälliges ~** sight deposit; **ursprüngliches ~** credit balance on original account; **verfügbare oder flüssige ~** cash or liquid assets; **verzinsliches ~** interest-bearing account having a credit balance.

gutheißen *v/t* to sanction, to approve, to authorize.

gut-nachbarlich *adj* good-neighbo(u)rly.

gütlich *adj* amicable, friendly, conciliatory, out-of-court.

Gutschein *m* credit note, (gift) voucher, coupon, gift token.

gutschreiben *v/t* to credit, to place to the credit of, to enter *(a sum)* to one's credit.

Gutschrift *f* credit entry; credit note, refund credit slip *(retail trade)*; **~(s)anzeige** credit advice, credit note; **~(s)aufgabe** advice of credit, credit advice; **vorläufige ~** short entry.

Guts|haus manor (house); **~herr** lord of the manor, landlord, landed proprietor; **~herrenrechte** manorial rights; **~pächter** tenant farmer; **~parzelle** parcel of land of an estate; **~übernahme** take-over of landed estate(s); **~verwalter** land steward, estate manager, land owner's manager (steward).

Gymnasium *n* academic secondary school, grammar school; *US approx: high school including junior college.*

H

Haag *m* (*Den* ~, *der* ~, *im* ~) The Hague.
Haager | ~ **Minderjährigenschutzabkommen** Hague Convention concerning the protection of minors; ~ **Konventionen** Hague Conventions; ~ **Landkriegsordnung** Hague Land Warfare Convention, Hague Regulations; ~ **Musterabkommen** Hague Agreement concerning the International Deposit of Industrial Designs and Models; ~ **Regeln** Hague Rules; ~ **Übereinkommen über den Zivilprozeß** Hague Convention on Civil Procedure (*1924, bills of lading*).
Haarnadelkurve *f* hairpin bend, hairpin curve.
Haarrisse *m/pl* hairline cracks.
Haarspalterei *f* hair-splitting, sophism.
Habe *f* belongings, possessions, effects, goods, property; **alle meine** ~ all I am worth, every thing I am possessed of; **bewegliche** ~ movables, personal estate, articles of personal property; **keine pfändbare** ~ nulla bona; **meine restliche** ~ what remains, the residue of my belongings; **meine übrige** ~ = *meine restliche* ~ *q v*; **persönliche** ~ personal effects, personal belongings; **unbewegliche** ~ immovables, real estate.
Haben *n* credit balance, credit side, credit; ~**buchung** credit entry; ~**posten** credit item; ~**saldo** credit balance; ~**zins(en)** credit interest, interest on deposits; ~**zinssatz** creditor interest rate, credit rate, deposit rate.
Habgier *f* greed, cupidity, covetousness, avarice.
Habilitation *f* (formal) promotion to professorial status, promotion to a university chair.

Habseligkeiten *f/pl* belongings, personal belongings, effects.
Hab und Gut *n* belongings, goods, property; **fremdes** ~ property belonging to another person.
Hader *m* quarrel, deep resentment, enmity, feud, strife.
Hafen *m* (*pl* **Häfen**) harbour (*US: harbor*), port; ~**abgaben und** ~**gebühren** port dues and charges; ~**amt** port authority, harbour authority; ~**angelegenheiten** piers and harbours; ~**anlagen** port installations, dock installations; ~**anlauferlaubnis** liberty of a port (*other than the port of destination*); ~**arbeiter** dock worker, docker; ~**becken** dock; ~**behörde** port authority; ~**dienstleistung** port service; ~**einrichtungen** port facilities; ~**gebiet** port area; ~**gebühren** port charges, port duties, port dues, pierage, dockage, groundage; ~**gelder** = ~*gebühren q v*; ~**gericht** port court; ~**gesundheitsamt** port health authority; ~**gesundheitsbescheinigung** bill of health; ~**instandhaltungsabgaben** pierage; ~ **kai** quay; *amtlicher* ~: *official quay;* ~**kapitän** port captain, harbour master; ~**kommandant** harbour master; ~**konnossement** port bill of landing; ~**lotse** harbour pilot; ~**meister** harbour master; ~**ordnung** port regulations; ~**passierschein** pass for the harbour area, harbour pass; ~**polizei** harbour police; ~**schlepper** tug, tug boat; ~**sperre** embargo, prohibition to use a port; ~**stadt** sea port; ~**- und Landeordnungen** port regulations; ~**usance** local port customs, port usage; ~**verwaltung** port administration; ~**zoll** port duties, port dues; ~**zollbeamter** boarding clerk, port customs-officer; **an-**

Haft

zulaufende ~ *pl* ports of call; **e-n ~ anlaufen,** to call at a port, to put into port; **im ~bereich** in port.

Haft *f* confinement, custody, detention; **~anordnung** remand order, order for arrest; **~anstalt** prison; **~aufhebung** release from custody; **~aufschub** stay of imprisonment; **~befehl**→*Haftbefehl*; **~beschwerde** complaint against an order for arrest; **~dauer** term of imprisonment, duration of detention; **~entlassung** discharge of prisoner, discharge from custody, release from custody; ~~ *gegen Sicherheitsleistung: release on bail;* ~~*sbeschluß: order for release from detention;* **~entschädigung** – compensation payment for deprivation of liberty; **~fortdauer** remand in custody, further detention; *die* ~~ *anordnen: to remand the accused in custody, to recommit;* **~grund** reason for arrest; **~kaution** bail, bail bond; **~lokal** detention room, guardhouse; **~ ohne Sprecherlaubnis** incommunicado-confinement of prisoner; **~prüfung** review of a remand in custody, review under writ of habeas corpus; **~prüfungsgericht** remand court; **~prüfungstermin** remand hearing; **~prüfungsverfahren** review of remand cases, remand proceedings, habeas corpus proceedings; *im* ~~ *vorgeführt werden: to appear on remand;* **~raum** prison cell; **~recht** law of arrest; **~richter** committing magistrate; **~sache** case where accused is under arrest; **~schäden** injuries caused by detention; **~strafe** (*now: Freiheitsstrafe qv*) imprisonment, short jail sentence; *e-e* ~~ *verhängen: to impose a term of imprisonment;* **~untauglichkeit** disability for imprisonment, unfitness to undergo detention; **~verschonung** refraining from enforcement of arrest, allowing accused to stay out of prison; ~~ *gegen Kaution zulassen: to grant bail, to remand on bail;* **~vollzug** execution of a prison sentence; **~zeit** term of imprisonment, duration of detention; **~zelle** remand cell, prison cell, **aus der ~ entlassen** to release from prison, to set free; **die ~ anordnen** to make an order for the arrest (of s.o.), to remand s.o. in custody; **die ~ antreten** to begin (serving) one's sentence; **in ~** under arrest, in custody; **in ~ halten** to keep in custody, to detain; **jmdn aus der ~ befreien** to liberate s.o. from custody, free s.o., set s.o. free.

haftbar *adj* liable, legally liable, responsible for, chargeable; **~ für Substanzschäden** impeachable for waste; **beschränkt ~ sein** to have limited liability; **gesamtschuldnerisch ~** jointly and severally liable; **gesamtverbindlich ~** jointly and severally liable; **jmdn ~ machen** to render a person liable; **persönlich ~** personally liable (*with one's own property*); **primär ~** primarily liable, liable in the first degree; **samtverbindlich ~** jointly and severally liable, liable in solidum; **solidarisch ~** jointly and severally liable, liable in solidum; **strafrechtlich ~** criminally liable; **subsidär ~** liable in the second degree; **unmittelbar ~** primarily responsible, directly liable.

Haftbarkeit *f* liability, responsibility.

Haftbefehl *m* warrant of arrest; **~ gegen Flüchtige** escape warrant; **e-n ~ aufrechterhalten** to remand the accused in custody; **e-n ~ ausfertigen** to execute a warrant of arrest; **e-n ~ erlassen** to issue (*or: to sign*) a warrant of arrest.

haften *v/i* to incur a liability, to be liable (for), to answer (for); **persönlich ~ für** to be personally liable for, to be individually answerable for; **solidarisch ~** to be jointly and severally liable; **strafrechtlich ~** to incur criminal liability; **unbeschränkt ~** to be liable without limitation.

haftend *adj* liable, answerable, accountable; **unbeschränkt persönlich ~** (wholly and) personally liable.

Haftender *m (der Haftende)* obligor, person liable, party liable; **persönlich** ~ **e-r Handelsgesellschaft** personally liable partner; **primär** ~ person primarily liable; **selbstschuldnerisch** ~ primary debtor, directly suable person.

Haftfreistellung indemnity, *cf Haftungsfreistellung.*

Häftling *m* person under arrest, prisoner, prison inmate, detainee; ~**shilfe** prisoners' assistance; ~**shilfegesetz** assistance of persecuted German prisoners; ~**süberwachung** surveillance of prison inmates.

Haftpflicht *f* third party indemnity, legal liability, public liability; ~ **des Arbeitgebers** employer's liability; ~**gesetz** public liability Act; ~**prozeß** liability case, indemnity case; ~**recht** liability law; ~**risiko** third party risk; ~**sacharbeiter** employee in charge of accident cases; ~**verband** liability insurers association; ~**verbindlichkeiten** public liability obligations, obligations from third party risks; ~**versicherer** liability insurer, third party (risk) insurer; ~**versicherung** liability insurance, third party (liability) insurance, insurance against third party risks, third party indemnity insurance; *allgemeine* ~~: *public liability insurance*; *berufliche* ~~: *professional indemnity insurance*; *persönliche* ~~*personal liability insurance*; → *Kfz*~~; ~**versicherung mit Kaskoversicherung** automobile personal liability and property damage insurance; ~**versicherung mit Vollkaskoversicherung** (fully) comprehensive insurance; ~**versicherungsgesetz für Unternehmer** Employers' Compulsory Insurance Act; **allgemeine** ~ general liability; **beschränkte** ~ limited liability; **gesetzliche** ~ third party indemnity, legal liability, public liability; **unbeschränkte** ~ unlimited liability; **vertragliche** ~ contractual liability.

haftpflichtig *adj* liable, subject to public liability.

Haftpflichtiger *m (der Haftpflichtige)* the liable party.

Haftsumme *f* sum by which liability is limited, guaranteed amount, liability maximum of limited partner.

Haftung *f* liability; ~ **auf Schadensersatz** liability for damages; ~ **aus unerlaubter Handlung** liability in tort, tortious liability, liability for unlawful acts; ~ **aus Vertrag** liability in contract, contractual liability; ~ **bei Einsturz von Gebäuden** liability for damage caused by collapse of buildings; ~ **bei Personen- und Sachschaden** liability for personal injury and damage to property; ~ **des Tierhalters** liability of the keeper of an animal; ~ **des Wiederverkäufers** liability of the reseller; ~ **für den Erfüllungsgehilfen** vicarious liability (for a person used in the performance of one's contractual obligation); ~ **für Dritte** vicarious liability; ~ **für die Durchführung** responsibility for enforcement; ~ **für Mängel der Lieferung** liability for defects in the goods delivered; ~ **für Schaden** liability for loss; ~ **für Tierschäden** liability for damage done by animals; ~ **für Verkehrssicherheit** occupiers' liability (for safety of buildings), liability for safety of premises; ~ **für Verrichtungsgehilfen** respondeat superior, vicarious liability in tort; ~ **für Verschulden e-s Dritten** legal responsibility for the fault of another; ~ **ohne Verschulden** strict liability; ~ **von Privatpersonen** responsibility of individuals; **aus der** ~ **ausscheiden** to cease to have liability; to be released from liability; **außervertragliche** ~ non-contractual liability; **beschränkte** ~ limited liability, limitation of liability; *mit* ~*r* ~: *limited, with limited liability*; **deliktische** ~ tortious liability; **die** ~ **ablehnen** to deny (the) reponsibility, to repudiate the liability, to disclaim

Haftungsansprüche Dritter

(all) warranties; **die ~ übernehmen** to undertake (the) liability, to assume (the) responsibility; **die ~ verteilen** to apportion liabilities; **dingliche ~** liability in rem; **durch die ~ gedeckt** covered by the guarantee, falling under the liability; **e-e ~ übernehmen** to undertake liability; **e-e weitergehende ~** a more far-reaching liability; **gesamtschuldnerische ~** joint and several liability; **gesetzliche ~** statutory liability, legal liability; **keine ~ für** not accountable, not liable; **keine ~ haben** not to incur any liability, not to be liable; **ohne ~** not liable, without any liability; **persönliche ~** personal liability, private liability, individual liability; **seine ~ ausschließen** to exclude one's liability, **seine ~ beschränken** to limit one's liability; **solidarische ~** joint and several liability; **stellvertretende ~** vicarious liability; **strafrechtliche ~** criminal liability; **strenge ~** strict liability; **subsidiäre ~** secondary liability; **unbeschränkte ~** unlimited liability; **vertragliche ~** contractual liability; **von der ~ befreien** to discharge from liability; **zivilrechtliche ~** civil liability, liability under civil law.

Haftungs|ansprüche Dritter third party liability claims; ~**anteil** share in the liability, proportion of the liability; ~~**klausel** *exclusion of liability clause, disclaimer clause; non-warranty clause;* ~**ausschluß** exclusion of liability, exemption from liability; ~**befreiung** exemption from liability; ~**bescheid** commitment advice (*to directors etc*) for tax arrears; ~**beschränkung** limitation of liability; ~**dauer** indemnity period; ~**durchgriff** exceptional direct liability of director or shareholder; ~**erklärung** warranty declaration, declaration concerning liability; ~**fonds** company's liability guarantee fund; ~**freistellung** indemnity, release from liability;

~~**svertrag**: *contract of indemnity;* ~**gemeinschaft** group bearing joint liability; ~**grenze** limit of liability (*or* indemnity); ~**grund** cause of liability, liability-basis; ~**kapital** stock capital, share capital, capital stock as security; ~**klage** action based on liability; ~**kredit** direct-commitment credit; ~**minderung** reduction of liability; ~**obligo** liability, special liability reserve; ~**privileg** privileged position as to liability; ~**prozeß** liability suit; ~**quote** commitment quota, liability quota; ~**recht** the law concerning liability; ~**regelungen** liability regime; ~**risiko** the risk of liability; ~**schuldner** liable party; ~**streitigkeit** litigation concerning liability; ~**summe** liability coverage; ~**träger** party liable; ~**übernahme** assumption of liability, indemnity; ~**übernahmevertrag** indemnity agreement, assumption of liability agreement; ~**umfang** extent of liability, accountability; ~**verbindlichkeiten** liabilities, commitments; ~**verteilung** distribution of liability; ~**verzicht** waiver of liability; ~~**sklausel**: *liability waiver clause;* ~**vorschriften** liability regulations; ~**zugeständnis** admission of liability.

Hagel|schaden *m* damage caused by hail; ~**versicherung** hail insurance, hail storm insurance, insurance against damage by hail.

halb|amtlich *adj* semi-official, quasi official, officious; ~**blütig** half-blood; **H~bruder** half brother, uterine brother; ~~ *mütterlicherseits: half brother from the mother's side;* ~~ *väterlicherseits: half brother from the father's side;* ~**bürtig** of the half blood; **H~deckung** half-cover (*by compulsory social insurance contributions of the insured time, minimum 60 months*); **H~erzeugnis** semi-finished product, *pl. etw.*: work-in-progress; **H~fabrikat** primary product, *pl* semi-manufacture, work in progress; **H~fertigfabri-**

Halde — **Handlanger**

kate semi-finished articles; H~fertigwaren semi-finished goods, semi-manufactured goods; H~invalide partly disabled person; H~jahresabschluß midyear settlement; H~jahrescoupon half-yearly coupon; H~jahresdividende mid-year dividend, six-monthly dividend; ~jahresgeld six-month money, loans for six months; ~part half share, fifty-fifty; H~pension demi-pension, half-pension (*at hotel*: bed, breakfast and lunch or dinner); ~strafaussetzung conditional discharge after serving half the sentence; H~schwester half sister; H~tagsarbeiter part-timer; half-time worker; H~tagsbeschäftigung half-day job, half-time employment part-time job; H~teilungsgrundsatz *tax* rule of splitting *total income of husband and wife*; H~waise half-orphan, *orphan who lost one parent only;* H~waren semi-finished goods; H~zeitbeschäftigung part-time job, half-day job; H~zeug semi-finished goods, semi-finished products.

Halde *f* dump, pithead stock, stockpile; ~nbestände stocks on the dumps; ~nbevorratung stockpiling; ~ngelände dumping ground; **auf** ~**nehmen** to dump, to stockpile.

Hälfte *f* half, either of two equal parts; ~anteil half share.

Halskrause *f* necklace *(terrorism)*

Halt! Vorfahrt beachten Stop: Give way.

haltbar *adj* durable, lasting, hardwearing, non-perishable, tenable (*argument*); **beschränkt** ~ semi-durable; **sachlich nicht** ~ not tenable.

Haltbarkeit *f* durability, imperishable nature *(of food stuffs)*; solidity, stability, resistance to wear, service life, tenability (*argument*); ~sprüfung endurance test.

Halte|gurt safety belt; ~**linie** stop line *(at road junction);* ~**schild** stop sign; ~**signal** stop signal; ~**stelle** stop, station; ~**verbot** "no stopping", stopping restriction.

halten *v/t* to hold, to keep, to maintain, to remain stable, to consider, to deem; **auf dem laufenden** ~ to keep posted; **schadlos** ~ to indemnify; *sich* ~~: *to take recourse against s. o.; to recover one's losses from s. o.;* **sich links** ~ to keep to the left; **sich rechts** ~ to keep to the right.

Halter *m* holder, registered user *(of motor vehicle); the person who is regularly in charge of a vehicle;* operator; keeper *(animal);* ~**haftung** liability of the registered user of a vehicle (cf Halter).

Haltlinie *f* stop line *(traffic).*

Hammelsprung *m parl* (vote by) division; *im* ~ *abstimmen: to divide (v. i.).*

Hammer *m* hammer; gavel; **unter den** ~ **bringen** to auction off.

Hamsterkauf *m* hoarding purchase.

Hand *f (pl. Hände =* ~*e*) hand; ~**akte** reference file, *desk folder with essential documents from the file;* ~**anlegen** to lend a hand; ~**arbeit** manual work; ~**arbeiter** manual worker; ~**betrieb** manual operation; ~**bibliothek** reference library; ~**blatt** flysheet; ~**buch** manual, reference book; ~**fesseln** manacles; ~**feuerwaffen** small arms; h~**gefertigt** hand made; ~**geld** earnest, earnest money, token payment, hand money, bounty *(on enlistment);* ~~ *geben: to give s.th. in earnest;* ~**gepäck** personal luggage, hand luggage *(or* baggage); ~**gepäckaufbewahrung** *GB:* left luggage office, railway luggage office; *US:* cloak room, baggage room; ~**gepäckkontrolle** baggage control, h~**geschrieben** handwritten; h~**greiflich** violent; ~**greiflichkeit** violence; ~**habe** occasion (for taking action), grounds; h~**haben** to handle, to manipulate; ~**habung** manipulation, handling; ~ **in** ~ **gehen** to be accompanied by, to act in coordination; ~**kasse** petty cash; ~**langer** help(er), accomplice,

395

stooge; ~**langerdienste** henchman's work, dirty work; ~**schellen** handcuffs, shackles; ~**schenkung** executed gift, donation by manual delivery, manual gift; ~**schlag** handshake; *durch* ~~: *by shaking hands*; ~**schreiben** handwritten letter; ~**schrift** handwriting, hand, chirography; *unleserliche* ~~: *illegible handwriting*; ~~*probe*: *handwriting specimen*; ~~*envergleich*: *comparison of handwriting specimens (for identity)*; h~**schriftlich** handwritten; ~**siegel** signet; ~**skizze** rough drawing; ~**steuerung** manual control; ~**streich** sudden attack, coup de main, surprise raid; ~- **und Spanndienste** *hist* statute labour; ~**verkauf** executed sale, open sale, over-the-counter sale; ~**vermittlung** manual exchange; ~**waffe** small weapon; ~**werk** → *Handwerk*; ~**wörterbuch** handy reference dictionary, (concise) dictionary; ~**zeichen** gesture by the hand, show of hands *(voting)*, manual sign *(signature)*, scroll; ~**zettel** hand bill; **aus erster** ~ first hand; **aus zweiter** ~ second hand; **die letzte** ~ **an etwas anlegen** to give the finishing touch (to), to finalize; **die öffentliche** ~ the public sector, the state, public funds, public authorities; *von der* ~*n* ~*unterstützt werden*: *to be supported from public funds*; **freie** ~ **lassen** to leave the decision to someone's discretion; **in andere** ~**e übergehen** to change hands, to pass into other hands; **in zweite** ~ into fresh hands; **kurzerh**~ out of hand; **mit der** ~ by hand, manually; **mit leeren** ~**en kommen** to come empty-handed; **mit leichter** ~ without forcing the issue; **mit starker** ~ **regieren** to rule with a firm hand; **öffentliche** ~ → *die öffentliche Hand*; **tote** ~ dead hand, mortmain; **unter der** ~ privately, by private arrangement *(purchase)*; **von langer** ~ **vorbereitet** planned well in advance; **zu** ~**en von** attention: ..., for the attention of ... *(F.A.O.)*; **zur gesamten** ~ (to be held) jointly, as joint property, as joint owners; **zur linken Hand** morganatic *(marriage)*; **zu treuen** ~**en** to the care of ..., on trust.

Handel *m* trade, commerce, dealing; ~ **mit Bezugsrechten** rights dealings; ~ **mit Gift** trade in poison; ~ **mit nicht notierten Wertpapieren** over-the-counter trading; ~ **treiben** to trade, to engage in business; ~ **und Gewerbe** trade and industry; ~ **und Handwerk** trade and handicraft; ~ **und Verkehr** trade and commerce; ~ **unter Kurs** dealings at rates below the official price; **ausgeglichener** ~ balanced trade; **außerbörslicher** ~ unofficial trading in stocks and shares; **e**-**n** ~ **abschließen** to strike a bargain; **erlaubter** ~ lawful trade; **freier** ~ free trade; *im* ~*n* ~ *beziehbar*: *available in the shops*; **intervalutarischer** ~ cross-exchange dealings, dealings across the exchanges; **mittelständischer** ~ middle-class trade, small-scale trading; **rechtswidriger** ~ illegal trade; **sichtbarer** ~ visible trade; **unerlaubter** ~ illicit trading; **unsichtbarer** ~ invisible trade; **zum amtlichen** ~ **zugelassen** admitted to official trading, officially marketable; **zwischenstaatlicher** ~ international trade.

handelbar *adj* marketable; **börsenmäßig** ~ admitted to the stock exchange.

Handeln *n* action, acting; ~ **auf Befehl** acting under orders; ~ **auf eigene Gefahr** acting at one's own risk, assumed risk; **befehlsgemäßes militärisches** ~ acting under superior orders; **fahrlässiges** ~ active negligence, acting negligently; **freiwilliges** ~ voluntary action; **gemeinsames** ~ common action; **gewinnsüchtiges** ~ acting out of greed; **gutgläubiges** ~ innocent action, acting in good faith; **planvolles** ~ planned action; **rechtswidriges** ~ unlawful action,

handeln

malfeasance; **schuldloses** ~ innocent action.

handeln *v/i(1)* to act; **gutgläubig und redlich** ~ to act innocently and honestly; **im eigenen Namen** ~ in one's own name, to act on one's own behalf; **in fremdem Namen** ~ to act as agent, to act on behalf of another; **recht** ~ to do right; **unter Zwang** ~ to act under duress; **vorsätzlich** ~ to act wilfully (and knowingly).

handeln *v/i(2)* to trade, to do business, to bargain; **herunter** ~ to trade down; **mit sich ~ lassen** to be willing to come to terms.

Handelndenhaftung *f* liability of person's acting *before completion of incorporation*.

Handels|abkommen trade agreement; **~adreßbuch** trade directory; **~agent** commercial agent; **~akzept** trade acceptance; **~amtsblatt** Commercial Gazette; **~artikel** *pl* goods, commercial articles; *gesetzlich geschützte* ~~: *patented articles*; **~attaché** commercial attaché; **~aufschlag** mark-up; **~auskunft** commercial agency report; **~bank** commercial bank, trade-financing bank, private credit bank; **~bedingungen** trade conditions; **~bericht** trade report; **~beschränkung** trade restriction; **~betrieb** commercial enterprise, commercial firm; **~bezeichnung** trade name, brand, commercial name; **~beziehungen** trade relations, trade connections; **~bilanz** (1) trade balance, balance of trade; *aktive* ~~: *active trade balance (favourable trade balance)*; *passive* ~~: *adverse (= passive) trade balance*; *ungünstige* ~~: *unfavourable trade balance*; **~bilanz** (2) commercial balance sheet (*as distinguished from tax balance sheet*); ~~*gewinn: commercial profit;* **~blatt** trade journal, financial paper; **~blockade** trade blockade; commercial blockade; **~brauch** commercial usage; **~brief** business letter; **~bücher** books of account; **~bürgschaft**

Handelskonkurrent

commercial surety; **~defizit** trade deficit; **~delegation** trade delegation; **~einheit** trading unit; **h~einig werden** to strike a bargain, to come to terms; **~embargo** trade embargo; **~erlaubnis** trading permit; **~erleichterungen** trade concessions; **h~fähig** *adj* tradable (= tradeable), marketable, negotiable, merchantable; **~firma** commercial undertaking, commercial firm, mercantile establishment, business house; firm-name, style; *gelöschte* ~~: *extinct firm*; **~flagge** merchant flag; **~flotte** merchant fleet; **~forderung** commercial claim; **~frau** business woman, feme-sole trader, woman who runs her own business; **~freiheit** freedom of trade, freedom of commerce; **~gebiet** trading area; **~gebrauch** trade use, commercial use; **~gehilfe** clerk, commercial employee; **~genossenschaft** trading co-operative; **~gepflogenheit** = ~*brauch q.v.*; **~gericht** commercial court; **~gerichtsbarkeit** commercial jurisdiction; **~geschäft** commercial transaction; *pl* commercial dealings; trading firm, commercial enterprise, trading business; **~gesellschaft** trading association, company, commercial partnership (or company); *offene* ~~ → *Offene Handelsgesellschaft*; **~gesetzbuch** commercial code; **~gewerbe** commercial enterprise; **~gewicht** commercial weight; **~gewinn** trading profit; **~gewohnheiten** = ~*brauch q.v.*; **~gläubiger** trade creditor; **~gut** merchandise **~güter** goods, commodities; **~hafen** (trading) port; **~haus** trading firm; **~hemmnis** trade barrier, obstacle to trade; **~kammer** chamber of commerce, *US*: board of trade; *Internationale* ~~: *International Chamber of Commerce*; **~kauf** mercantile sale; **~klasse** grade; *gesetzliche* ~~*n: legal grades of consumer goods*; **~klauseln** trade terms, abbreviated trading clauses; **~konkurrent**

397

Handelskorrespondenz

competitor (in business); ~**korrespondenz** commercial correspondence; ~**kredit** commercial credit; ~**kreditbrief** commercial letter of credit; ~**krieg** trade war, tariff war; ~**macht** commercial power; ~**makler** mercantile broker; broker (*commodities and/or securities*); ~**marine** merchant marine; ~**marke** brand, brand name; *eingetragene* ~~: *registered trade mark*; h~**mäßig** relating to trade; ~**maßnahmen** trade measures; *präferenzielle* ~~: *preferential trade measures*; ~**messe** trade fair; ~**minister** US: Secretary of Commerce; ~**ministerium** Ministry of Commerce, *GB*: Ministry of Trade and Industry *US*: Department of Commerce; ~**mission** trade mission, trade delegation; ~**monopol** trade monopoly, commercial monopoly; ~**muster** trade sample; ~**nachrichten** commercial news; ~**name** trade name, business name; *eingetragener* ~~: *registered name*; ~**niederlassung** commercial establishment, trading post; ~**organisation** trade organization; ~**papier** commercial document; ~**parität** commercial parity; ~**partner** trade partner, trading partner; ~**platz** commercial town, trading centre; ~**politik** trade policy, commercial policy; *freiheitliche* ~~: *liberal trade policy*; h~**politisch** from the point of view of trade policy, relating to trade; ~**präferenzen** trade preferences; ~**praktiken** trade practices; ~**prämie** trade bonus; ~**preis** retail price, market price; ~**rabatt** trade discount; ~**rechnung** commercial invoice; *ordnungsgemäße* ~~: *commercial invoice in proper form*; ~**recht** commercial law, mercantile law; h~**rechtlich** pursuant to commercial law; ~**register** commercial register; ~~ *für Körperschaften*: *register of companies*; ~~~**anmeldung**: *application for registration in the commercial register*; ~~~**auszug**: *excerpt (trans-*

Handelsusance

cript or photocopy) from the commercial register; ~~~**eintragung**: *entry in the commercial register* ~~~**verfügung** *Commercial Register Regulations*; ~**reisender** commercial traveller; travelling salesman, travelling representative; ~**richter** associate (*lay*) commercial judge, judge in a commercial court; ~**risiko** trade risk; ~**risikoversicherung** commercial insurance; ~**sachen** commercial causes (*court*); commercial shipping; commercial affairs, mercantile affairs; ~**schiff** merchant-vessel, merchant-ship; ~**schiffahrt** merchant shipping, maritime commerce; ~~~**svorschriften**: *maritime regulations*; ~**schranke** trade barrier; ~**schuld** commercial debt; ~**schule** commercial school, business school; *höhere* ~~: *senior commercial school*; ~**schutzgesetz** trade protection law; ~**sitte** = ~*brauch q.v.*; ~**spanne** margin, operating margin, trade margin, wholesale margin; ~**sperre** embargo; *e–e* ~~ *aufheben*: *to lift an embargo*; ~**stand** commerce, commercial class, trading class, merchants; ~**statistik** trade statistics, trade returns; ~**strom** flow of trade; ~**stufe** marketing stage; ~**tonnage** freight tonnage; ~**überschuß** trade surplus; h~**üblich** customary in trade, in accordance with ordinary trade usage, according to normal business practice; ~**übung** commercial practice; ~**umsatz** business turnover, sales; h~**- und branchenüblich** customary in trade and in this branch; ~**- und Dienstleistungsbilanz** balance of payments for goods and services; ~**- und Gewerbefreiheit** freedom of trade and industry, free economy; ~**- und Zahlungsbilanz** balance of commerce and of payments, balance of trade and of payments; ~**unternehmen** commercial enterprise, commercial concern, commercial undertaking, trading enterprise, trading concern; ~**usance** trade usage; ~**verbin-**

handeltreibend / **Handlung**

dung trade relations; ~**verbot** embargo; ~**verkehr** commerce, trade, commercial intercourse; *ausgewogener* ~~: *balanced trade*; *innergemeinschaftlicher* ~~: *intra-Community trade*; *normaler* ~~: *ordinary course of trade*; ~**verlagerungen** switch in trade, trade diversion (*EEC*); ~**vertrag** treaty of commerce, commercial treaty, trade agreement, trading agreement; ~**vertreter** commercial representative, commercial agent, trade representative; ~~ *mit Delkredere*: *delcredere agent*; ~~ *gesetz*: *Law for Commercial Representatives*; ~~~*recht*: *law of commercial agency*; ~~~*vertrag*: *agency contract*; ~**vertretung** sales agency, mercantile agency, commercial agency business; ~**vollmacht** commercial power; ~**volumen** trading volume; ~**vorschriften** trade regulations; ~**ware** merchandise, commercial goods; ~**wechsel** trade acceptance, trade bill, trade paper, commercial bill of exchange; *erstklassiger* ~~: *prime trade bill*; ~**wege** trade channels; ~**welt** the world of commerce, the business community; ~**wert** commercial value, market value, trade value, trading value, commercial quality; ~**zentrum** trade centre; ~**zweig** business line.

handeltreibend *adj* trading, engaged in trade, commercial.

Händler *m* trader dealer, tradesman, *exch* jobber; ~ **mit eigenem Lager** stockist; ~**geschäfte** dealings, dealer transactions; ~**marke** own brand, private brand; ~**provision** dealer allowance; ~**rabatt** dealer's discount, dealer's rebate; ~**spanne** dealer margin; **ambulanter** ~ itinerant trader, street trader, hawker; **autorisierter** ~ authorized dealer, franchised dealer; **fliegender** ~ street trader, pedlar (*US*: peddler).

Händlerin *f* tradeswoman.

Handlung *f* (*1*) (physical) act, action; ~ **e-s Dritten** act of a third party; ~**en gegen ausländische Staaten** actions taken against foreign states; ~**en und Unterlassungen** acts and forbearances, acts and omissions; ~ **oder Duldung** things suffered or done; **angefochtene** ~ contested act, avoided act; **außergerichtliche** ~ extra-judicial act; **betrügerische** ~ fraudulent act; **böswillige** ~ malicious act; **eigene strafbare** ~ substantive independent offence (*committed by an accomplice*); **e-e den Kausalzusammenhang unterbrechende** ~ intervening act; **einseitige** ~ unilateral act, one party's act; **fahrlässige** ~ negligent act, act of negligence; **feindliche** ~ (act of) hostility, hostile act; **fortgesetzte** ~ successive act, continued act; *in* ~*r* ~: *continually acting*; **gesetzliche** ~ act in law, lawful act; **hoheitsrechtliche** ~ act of state, sovereign act; **irgendeine** ~ any act or thing done; **konkludente** ~ implied act, action implying intention; **kriegerische** ~ act of war; ~~*en*: *acts of war, warlike operations*; **(e-e jmdm) obliegende** ~ an act incumbent upon s. o., a person called on to act; **offenkundige** ~ overt act; **rechtsgestaltende** ~ operative act, *act which directly affects legal relations*; **rechtswidrige** ~ unlawful act, wrongful act; **richterliche** ~ judicial act; **schädigende** ~ injurious act, harmful act, an act which causes damage; **schuldhafte** ~ culpable act, wrongful act; **staatsfeindliche** ~ act hostile to the state; **strafbare** ~ criminal act, punishable act, **unerlaubte** ~ tort, tortious act, actionable tort, delict, civil offence; (*non-technically*:) forbidden act, illicit act, wrongful act, offence; **unfreundliche** ~ unfriendly act; **unsittliche** ~ immoral act; **unzüchtige** ~ indecency; indecent act; ~~*en*: *lewdness, indecent liberties*; **verfassungsfeindliche** ~ seditious act, act directed against the constitutional order, subversive act; **vorbereitende** ~ preparatory act; **vorsätzliche** ~ wilful act, intentional act, volun-

Handlung

tary act; **widerrechtliche** ~ illegal act; **willenlose** ~ involuntary act; **zumutbare** ~ reasonable act.

Handlung f (2) shop, store.

Handlungs|**agent** *obs for Handelsvertreter qv*, mercantile agent; **h~befugt** entitled to act; **~bevollmächtigter** commercial employee (acting for the firm), authorized agent, managing agent; **~ermessen** discretion to act; **h~fähig** capable (of acting), entitled to act; **~fähigkeit** capacity to act, power to act; **~freiheit** liberty of action, freedom of action; **~haftung** liability for acts done, liability for a public disturbance; **~gehilfe** commercial assistant, shop assistant; **~lehre** doctrine of criminal responsibility; *finale ~~: doctrine of criminal liability for intended wrongs only*; **~lehrling** commercial apprentice; **~pflicht** duty to act; **~reisender** travelling salesman, commercial traveller, travelling agent; **h~unfähig** incapable of acting, unfit to act, incompetent to act; **~unfähigkeit** incapacity, incompetence to act; **~unkosten** operating expenses; **~vollmacht** commercial power, mercantile power or agency (*limited to usual transactions*); **~weise** line of action, mode of procedure, conduct; *böswillige ~~: malicious actions; rücksichtslose ~~: reckless conduct; unbillige ~~: inequitable line of actions, unconscionable transactions.*

handschriftlich *adj* hand-written, in one's own handwriting; **~geändert** manuscript-amended.

Handschuhehe f marriage by proxy.

Handwerk n handicraft, craft, the trade of an artisan, trade; **das politische** ~ state-craft; **dienstleistendes** ~ service-rendering craft, service trade.

Handwerker m craftsman, artisan, *US:* tradesman; **~innung** trade guild, craft guild; **~kredit** credit facilities for craftsmen; **~lebens-**

Härte

versicherung life assurance for craftsmen; **~versicherungsgesetz** Craftsmen's Insurance Act (*1960*).

Handwerks|**arbeit** craftwork, handicraft work; **~ausbildung** vocational training for handicrafts (*or* for a trade); **~betrieb** handicraft business, handicraft shop; **~brauch** craft usage; **~genossenschaft** craftsmen's cooperative; **~geselle** *hist* journeyman; skilled craftsman; **~innung** craft guild; **~lehre** (craft) apprenticeship; **~lehrling** apprentice (to a craftsman); **~kammer** Chamber of Handicrafts; **~karte** craftsmen's card; **h~mäßig** workmanlike, conforming to the rules of a craft; **~meister** master craftsman; **~ordnung** Handicrafts Code (*of 1953, as amended in 1965*); **~rolle** Register of Craftsmen; **~unternehmen** handicrafts enterprise, craftsman's firm; **~zeug** tools of the trade, hand tools, implements of a trade; **~zweig** branch of the handicrafts.

Hang m inclination, disposition, propensity; **~täter** habitual offender; **krimineller** ~ general malice, criminal disposition, criminal nature.

Hängeplakat n hanger-card.

Hängeschild n hanging sign.

Harmonisierung f harmonization; *schrittweise ~~: stage-by-stage harmonization*.

Härte f hardship, severity; **~ausgleich** hardship allowance; **~beihilfe** hardship allowance; ~ **des Urteils** severity of a sentence; **~fall** case of hardship, hardship case; *schwerer ~~: serious hardship; ungewöhnlicher ~~: exceptional hardship*; **~fonds** hardship fund; **~klausel** hardship clause, clause devised to relieve hardship; **~n mildern** to relieve hardship; **~milderungsklage** application for relief from hardship, legal action to obtain relief from hardship; **~novelle** amendment dealing with cases of hardship; **~regelung** set-

400

tlement of hardship cases, regulation for hardship cases; **unbillige** ~ inequitable hardship; **ungebührliche** ~ undue hardship; **unnötige** ~ unnecessary hardship; **unzumutbare** ~ unreasonable hardship, exceptional hardship.

Hartgeld *n* coin, coined money, *US*: hard money.

Hartwährungsländer *n/pl* hard-currency countries, strong-currency countries.

Haschisch *n* hashish, cannabis.

Haufen *m* heap, pile, great quantity, crowd; **bewaffneter** ~ armed mob, armed crowd.

Haupt|abschluß annual statement of accounts; ~**abschlußübersicht** condensed version of financial statements; ~**ader** *min* original vein; ~**aktionär** principal shareholder; h~**amtlich** full-time; ~**anklagepunkt** main charge, count (of a charge); ~**anliegen** main objective; ~**anmeldung** basic (*or* main) application; ~**anspannung** major strain; ~**anspruch** main claim; ~**antrag** main request, main petition; ~**art** principal category; ~**begründung** primary grounds for an action; ~**belastung** peak (*power, traffic*); ~**beruf** regular occuption, main profession; ~**beschäftigung** chief occupation; ~**bestandteil** chief ingredient, essential part; ~**betrag** principal amount; principal (sum) ~**betrieb** main plant, principal place of business; ~**bilanz** general balance sheet; ~**buch** general ledger, *pl*: ~**bücher**: *ledger records*; ~~*auszug*: *ledger abstract*; ~~*konten*: *control accounts*; ~**buchhaltung** general bookkeeping department; ~**einnahmequelle** main source of income; ~**entschädigung** basic compensation; ~~*sberechtigter*: *person entitled to basic compensation*; ~**erbe** principal heir (*or* beneficiary); ~**erfindung** main invention; ~**ernährer** main breadwinner; ~**fach** main subject; ~**feldwebel** sergeant major, *US*: sergeant 1st class; ~**feststellung** principal finding of loss (*due to war etc*); ~~*szeitpunkt*: *time of reference for the principal finding of loss*; principal assessment (of values); ~**filiale** main branch; ~**forderung** principal claim, chief claim, main demand; ~**fundstelle** key authority; ~**fürsorgestelle** head office for public assistance; ~**geschäftsbereich** core business; ~**geschäftsführer** managing director; ~**geschäftssitz** principal office, headquarters, principal place of business; ~**geschäftsstelle** principal office; ~**gläubiger** chief creditor, major creditor; ~**industriezweige** staple industries; ~**inhalt** subject-matter, gist; ~~ *der Klage*: *gist of the action*; ~**intervenient** intervening party; *third party claiming the subject matter from two litigants*; ~**intervention** interpleader summons (*third-party intervention against two litigants claiming the object of the lawsuit*); ~**kasse** cashier's department, maintill, main ticket box (*theatre*); ~**kassierer** chief cashier, head teller (*bank*) treasurer; ~**kläger** chief plaintiff; ~**konto** principal account, *pl* (~ ~*en*): general ledger accounts; ~**kostenstelle** cost centre, cost department; ~**lieferant** main supplier, main contractor, prime contractor, original contractor; ~**mangel** principal defect, main fault; ~**merkmal** chief criterion, key feature; ~**miete** chief tenancy; ~**nachfrage** principal demand; ~**niederlassung** main branch, principal place of business, principal establishment, ~**organe** principal organs (of an association); ~**patent** original patent, parent patent; ~**pflicht** main duty, principal obligation; ~**plan** main plan, master budget; ~~ *und Nachtrag*: *main and supplementary budgets*; ~**police** original policy; ~**positionen** principal items; ~**post** general post office; ~**produkt** main product, chief product, staple commodity;

Hauptprozeß

~**prozeß** the main trial; ~**prozeßbevollmächtigter,** lead attorney, senior counsel; ~**prüfer** *pat* examiner in chief, chief examiner, primary examiner; ~**prüfungsamt** Main Audit Office; ~**quartier** headquarters; ~**recht** primary right; ~**rücklage** principal reserve fund; ~**sache** → *Hauptsache*; ~**sachgebiete** principal fields; ~**schöffe** foreman of the jury, chief lay judge; ~**schuld** principal debt, chief blame; ~**schuldiger** (*der* ~*schuldige*) person chiefly to blame, chief offender; ~**schuldner** principal debtor, primary obligee; *Ausfall des* ~~*s*: *principal's default*; ~**schule** upper division of elementary school; secondary modern school (*formerly*: *Volksschuloberstufe*); ~**sicherheit** primary security; ~**sitz** head office, headquarters; ~**sparte** main line (*of commercial activity*) ~**spediteur** principal forwarding agent, direct forwarding agent; ~**stadt** capital; ~**steuermonat** month of major tax receipts; ~**steuertermin** main tax maturity, big tax date; ~**strecke** trunk line; ~**subunternehmer** higher tier subcontractor; ~**summe** principal sum; ~**täter** principal offender; ~**termin** trial date, trial; main hearing; ~**träger** main support, mainstay; ~**umschlagplatz** staple place, principal market; ~**und Hilfsvorbringen** primary and secondary allegations, disjunctive allegations; ~**- und Staatsaktion** a matter of high policy; ~**unternehmer** prime contractor, general contractor, original contractor; ~**unterstützungsempfänger** person in receipt of unemployment benefit; ~**urlaubssaison** peak holiday period; ~**veranlagung** basic assessment, general assessment; ~~*szeitpunkt*: *date of basic assessment*; ~~*szeitraum*: *basic assessment period*; ~**verantwortung** principal responsibility; ~**verbindlichkeit** principal obligation; ~**verbraucher** principal consum-

Hauptsache

er; ~**verdiener** principal (wage) earner, breadwinner; ~**veredelungserzeugnisse** main compensating products; ~**verfahren** main proceedings; ~**verhandlung** trial process, trial, trial of indictment; *ergebnislose* ~~: *abortive trial*; *Gang der* ~~: *trial procedure*; *zur* ~~*laden*: *to summon for trial*; ~**verkehrsstraße** traffic artery, trunk road, classified road, main road, dual carriageway; main thoroughfare (*city*); ~**verkehrszeit** peak hours; ~**vermieter** head lessor, main lessor; ~**versammlung** general meeting (of shareholders), stockholders' meeting; *ordentliche* ~~: *ordinary general meeting, regular stockholders' meeting*; *außerordentliche* ~~: *special meeting, extraordinary general meeting*; ~~*auf Antrag der Aktionäre*: *requisitioned meeting, general meeting called by the shareholders*; ~**versicherer** direct writing company, primary insurer; ~**versicherung** direct insurance, master policy (*group insurance*); ~**vertrag** main contract, original contract; ~**verwaltung** chief administration (office), central administration; ~**vollmacht** original power of attorney, primary powers; ~**vorstand** executive board, presiding office, governing board; ~**wache** police office; ~**werk** major work, chief work; ~**wohnsitz** principal residence; ~**zahlungstermin** principal date for payment; ~**zeuge** key witness, principal witness; ~~*der Anklage*: *crown witness*; ~**zollamt** principal customshouse; ~**zug** basic trend; ~**zweck** primary purpose; ~**zweigstelle** parent branch.

Hauptsache *f* principal claim, chief point, main issue, cause of action; ~**betrag** principal money, face amount; ~**erledigung** disposal of the cause of action (*by events occurring during the litigation*); ~**forderung** principal claim, unpaid principal; ~ **nebst Zinsen** principal and interest; ~**schuld** principal obligation; ~**verfahren** principal proceedings; **die ~ für erledigt erklären** to declare that the cause of action has been disposed of; **in der ~ entscheiden** to give judgment on the main issue (*as distinguished from costs, enforceability*); **zur ~ verhandeln** to plead on the main issue.

Haus *n* (*pl* **Häuser** = ~**er**) house, building; ~**angestellte(r)** domestic servant, household employee; *dipl:* *private* ~: *private servants*; ~**arbeit** household work, home work (*for school*); ~**arbeitstag** day off for housewives; ~**arrest** home confinement, detention at one's own house; ~**arzt** family physician, family doctor; ~**bank** principal banker, house bank, the firm's bank, a person's bankers; *unsere* ~~: *our bankers*; ~**bau** housebuilding, home construction; ~**besetzer** squatter(s); ~**besetzung** adverse occupation of residential premises, squatting; ~**besitz** *jur* possession of a house; *econ* house-property, residential property; ~**besitzer** proprietor of a house, landlord, home-owner; ~**besitzervereinigung** association of landlords; ~**bestand** housing stock; ~**besuch** home visit, home call; ~**diebstahl** domestic theft; ~**durchsuchung** searching of a house, search of a building; ~~*sbefehl: search warrant;* ~**eigentum** home ownership; ~**eigentümer** house owner, landlord, property owner; ~~*haftpflichtversicherung: property owners' liability insurance;* ~**friedensbruch** criminal trespass, unlawful entry; ~**gebrauch** domestic use; ~**gehilfen** domestic servants; ~**geld** out-patient's allowance; prisoners' personal money account; ~**gemeinschaft** the (community of) occupants of a house, family-household; ~**genosse** fellow-lodger, fellow-tenant, occupant of a house; ~**gerät** household utensil, household gadget, domestic appliance; ~**gewalt** control of a building, right of possession of premises; ~**gewerbe** business from home, cottage industry; ~**gewerbetreibender** worker from home; ~**halt** → *Haushalt (1)* and *Haushalt (2) respectively;* ~**haltung** → *Haushaltung;* ~**jurist** in-house lawyer; ~**makler** real estate broker, real estate agent; ~**marke** private brand, own brand, house brand; ~**meister** caretaker, janitor; ~**mitteilung** in-house memo, memorandum; ~**müll** domestic refuse, domestic rubbish; ~**objekte** house property (*offered by broker*); ~**ordnung** house rules; ~**personal** domestic servants; *dienstliches* ~~ *dipl: service staff;* ~**plakette** house plate; ~**post** interoffice mail; ~**rat** → *Hausrat;* ~**recht** domiciliary rights, right as master of the house, power of the keys; *das* ~~ *verletzten: to commit trespass, to violate the householder's sphere of authority;* ~**schild** house plate; ~**schlüssel** front-door key, latch key; *unerlaubtes Anfertigen von* ~~*n: unauthorized key-making;* ~**stand** household, domestic status; ~**strafe** internal penalty (*imposed by a company etc*); ~**suchung** house search; search of premises; ~**suchungsbefehl** search warrant; ~**suchungsprotokoll** police record of a search; ~**tür** front door, street door, outer door; ~**türgeschäfte** front door business, door-to-door sales; transactions by canvassers; ~**türwiderrufsgesetz** Act on the Right to Cancel front door transactions; ~ **und Hof** house and farm; ~**vater** head of the household; ~**verbot** order to stay away (*from a place of entertainment*), off-limits order; ~**vermietung** letting of houses; ~**vermögen** property in the form of houses; ~**verwalter** property manager, caretaker; ~**verwaltung** property management; ~~*sdienst: property managment service* ~~*sfirma: management company;* ~**wesen** household cerns); ~**wirt** house-owner, landlord, les-

Haushalt

sor; ~**wirtschaft** home economics, domestic science, household practice, household; **h~wirtschaftlich** household, domestic; ~**wirtschaftslehre** home economics, domestic science; ~**zeitschrift** house journal, house organ, staff magazine; ~**zinssteuer** tax on house rents; ~**zustellung** home delivery; **alleinstehendes** ~ detached house; **aus königlichem** ~ of royal descent; **bewohntes** ~ occupied house; **frei** ~ free delivery, free domicile, free house; **frei** ~ **verzollt** free at domicile after clearance through customs; **Hohes** ~! honourable members of the House; **regierendes** ~ the reigning house; **von**-~-**zu**-~ from warehouse to warehouse; ~~~~**klausel**: *warehouse to warehouse clause*.

Haushalt *m* (1) household; ~**sgeräte** household equipment, non-consumable household goods, yellow goods *(US)*; ~**szulage** household allowance; **gemeinsamer** ~ common household; **privater** ~ private household.

Haushalt *m* (2) budget; **ausgeglichener** ~ balanced budget; **außerordentlicher** ~ special budget; **das** ~**s-Ist** the budget as it is, the actual budget; **kommunaler** ~ local authorities' budget; **öffentliche** ~**e** (budgets of) public authorities; **ordentlicher** ~ ordinary budget; **unausgeglichener** ~ unbalanced budget, adverse budget; **zum ordentlichen** ~ **gehörig** part of the ordinary budget, above-the-line.

Haushalts(1)|**abnehmer** household-consumer(s); ~**abwässer** domestic effluents; ~**angehörige** members of the household, family group; ~**artikel** household articles; ~**besteuerung** taxes imposed per household; ~**einkommen** income of individual households; ~**einrichtung** household furniture; ~**führung** housekeeping; *doppelte* ~~: *double housekeeping*; ~**gegenstände** household goods, house-

Haushaltsansatz

hold effects; ~**geld** housekeeping money, household allowance; ~**geräte** household utensils, domestic appliances; ~**hilfe** domestic help, domestic servant, maid; ~**kosten** family expenses; ~**liste** list of household effects; ~**packung** family-size package; ~**rechnung** housekeeping account, household budget, family budget; ~**trennung** separation of households, maintaining separate households; ~**versicherung** householder's comprehensive insurance; ~**vorstand** head of the household, householder; ~**waren** household articles, hardware; ~**zulage** housekeeping allowance; ~**zwecke** housekeeping purposes. housekeeping.

Haushalts(2)|**ansatz** budget estimate; ~**ausgaben** budgetary expenditure; ~**ausgleich** the balancing of the budget; ~**ausschuß** budget committee, *US* appropriations committee; ~**befugnisse** budgetary powers; ~**behörde** budgetary authority; ~**beratung** budget debate; ~**bericht** financial report; ~**beschluß** vote on accounts; ~**bewilligung** budgetary vote, appropriation; ~**debatte** budget debate; ~**defizit** fiscal deficit, budgetary deficit; ~**einnahmen** budget revenue; ~**erklärung** financial statement; ~**freibetrag** household allowance; **h~fremd** extra-budgetary; ~**gebarung** handling of budgetary expenditure; ~**gesetz** Budget Act; ~**grundsätze** basic budgetary rules; ~**hilfe** domestic help; ~**jahr** fiscal year, financial year, budgetary year; ~**kürzung** cut in the budget; ~**lage** budgetary position; **h~mäßig** budgetary; ~**mittel** public funds, budget monies; ~~ *bewilligen*: *to vote supplies*; ~**ordnung** budget regulations; ~**plan** budget; *den* ~~*vorlegen*: *to open the budget*; *Entwurf des* ~~*s*: *draft butget, budget estimates*; *ordentlicher* ~~: *ordinary budget*; *Titel des* ~~*s*: *item of the* *budget*; ~**politik** budgetary policies; ~**prüfung** public audit; ~**rechnung** management account; ~**recht** budget law; **h**~**rechtlich** pursuant to budgetary law; ~**rede** budget speech; ~**rest** unexpended balance of budget funds; ~**satzung** local government (annual) budget bill; ~-**Soll** the budget as intended, the planned budget; **h**~**technisch** relating to budgetary procedure; ~*e Fehler: budgetary errors;* ~**titel** budgetary item, budgetary vote; ~**verfahren** budgetary procedure(s); ~**überschreitung** exceeding budgetary allocations; ~**überschuß** budget surplus, unappropriated budget; ~**volumen** size of the budget, total budget; ~**voranschlag** budget estimate; ~**vorlage** finance bill; ~**vorschriften** budgetary provisions; ~**wesen** budgetary matters.

Haushaltung *f* housekeeping, household; *pl:* ~*en: households, residential customers;* ~**en der Arbeitnehmer** households of employed persons; ~**sbuch** housekeeping book; ~**sbudget** household budget; ~**skosten** household expenses.

Hausieren *n* itinerant peddling, door-to-door selling, hawking.

hausieren *v/i* to peddle, to hawk.

Hausierer *m* pedlar (*US:* peddler).

Hausierschein *n GB:* pedlar's licence (*US:* peddler's license).

Hausierverbot *n* no peddling!

Häusler *m* cottager; ~**recht** ancient agricultural tenancy right ≈ *copyhold*.

Hausrat *m* household effects; ~**ersatzbeschaffung** replacement of household effects; ~ **und sonstige persönliche Habe** household and personal effects; ~ **und Wohnbedarf** household effects and furnishings.

Hausrats|beschaffung procurement of household effects; ~**entschädigung** compensation for household effects (*lost or destroyed during the war*); ~**hilfe** grant for obtaining household effects; ~**sachen** proceedings concerning the matrimonial home and household effects; ~**teilung** dividing-up the matrimonial household effects; ~**teilungsverfahren** proceedings to divide up matrimonial household effects; ~**verlust** loss of household effects (*due to war or expulsion*); ~**versicherung** household effects insurance, householder's comprehensive insurance, (house) contents insurance; ~**verteilung** distribution of household effects (*as between spouses or divorced persons*).

Hausse *f* boom, bull market, upward tendency, rise; ~**bewegung** upward tendency, bull movement; ~**börse** bull market; ~**einfluß** bullish influence; ~**engagement** bull account, the long account; ~**geschäft** bull transaction; ~**partei** operators for a rise; ~**position** long position, bull position; ~**spekulant** operator for a rise, bull, speculator for a rise; ~**spekulation** speculation for a rise, bull operation; ~**stimmung** bullish mood, boom mentality; ~**tendenz** bullish tendency; **auf** ~ **disponieren** to buy for a rise; **auf** ~ **spekulieren** operate for a rise; **plötzliche** ~ sudden rise, fireworks.

Haussier *m* operator for a rise, bull.

Havarie *f* average, loss by sea, sea damage, damage by sea, ship damage, statement of average; ~**agent** average agent; ~**attest** certificate of average; ~**aufmachung** settlement of average, assessment of sea damage; ~**berechnung** average assessment; ~**bericht** damage report; ~**dispacheur** average adjuster; ~**erklärung** average statement, ship's protest, captain's protest; ~**Experte** average surveyor, loss surveyor; **h**~**frei** *adj* free from average; ~**gelder** average charges; ~-**grosse-Aufopferung** general average; ~-**grosse-Beitrag** general-average contribution; ~**grosse-Einschuß** general average deposi-

Haverei | **Heim**

tion; ~**-grosse-Klausel** general average clause; ~**-grosse-Regelung am fremden Bestimmungshafen** foreign general average *(FGA)*; ~**grosse-Schaden** general average loss; ~**-grosse-Verpflichtungsschein** general-average bond; ~**gutachten** (sea) damage survey; ~**klausel** average clause; ~**-Kommissar** average agent, claims agent, average adjuster, surveyor; ~**regelung** average adjustment; ~**regulierer** average adjuster, claims settling agent for maritime losses; ~**schaden** average, sea damage; ~**schein** average certificate, average bond; ~**verschreibung** average bond; ~**verteilung** average distribution; ~**vertrag** average agreement; ~**zertifikat** survey report; **allgemeine** ~ general average; **besondere** ~ particular average; **einfache** ~ ordinary average; **frei von besonderer** ~ free from particular average; **frei von** ~ free from average; **gemeinschaftliche** ~ general average; **große** ~ general average, gross average; **große** ~**versicherung** general average bond; **kleine** ~ particular average, petty average; **mit besonderer** ~ with particular average *(W.P.A.)*, with average *(W.A.)*; **nicht gegen große und besondere** ~ **versichert** free of all average.

Haverei *f statutory term for Havarie qv.*

Hazardeur *m* gambler, adventurer.

Hebe|berechtigung entitlement to charge (rates); ~**gebühr** a lawyer's (*or* notary's) collection fee; ~**rolle** assessment roll, taxpayers' list; ~**satz** tax factor *(fixed by the municipality)*, municipal multiples, collection multiplier; ~**stelle** collection office *(of a public authority)*.

Heeres|bedarf army requirements; ~**bestände** army stores; ~**gefolge** camp followers, camp retainers; ~**lieferant** army contractor, army supplier; ~**verpflegungsamt** quartermaster general's department; ~**waffenamt** army ordnance department; ~**zeugamt** army ordnance department.

Heft|apparat stapler; ~**klammer** staple, clip, paper clip; ~ **mit Kontrollabschnitten** counterfoil book.

Hege *f* care and protection of game *(in the forest etc)*; ~**zeit** close season.

Hehler *m* receiver (of stolen goods), handler, "fence", intaker.

Hehlerei *f* receiving stolen goods, dishonest handling; ~**begehen** to receive stolen goods; ~ **im Rückfall** receiving of stolen property recidivism; third or subsequent offence of receiving; **gewerbsmäßige** ~ receiving (of stolen goods) for gain.

Heil|anstalt sanatorium, hospital; ~**bad** spa, health resort; ~**behandlung** therapeutic treatment; ~**berufe** medical professions; ~**hilfsberufe** auxiliary medical vocations; ~**fürsorge** medical care; ~**gehilfe** male nurse; ~**gewerbe** therapeutic vocations; ~**kostenversicherung** medical insurance; ~**mittel** medicine; ~**praktiker** licenced non-medical practitioner, *(not being a medical doctor)*; practitioner of alternative medicine, physiotherapist; ~**quelle** mineral spring; ~**- und Pflegeanstalt** mental institution, mental hospital; ~**verbot** prohibition from practising medicine, *or* of the exercise of a medical profession; ~**verfahren** medical treatment, method of therapy; ~**wesen** medical care.

Heilung *f* cure; *(also legally speaking)*.

Heim *n* home, hostel; ~**arbeit** homework, outwork, cottage industry; ~**arbeiter** outworker, homeworker; ~**aufsicht** supervision of homes and hostels; ~**beirat** advisory committee of a home for the aged; ~**erziehung** institutional upbringing in a home, education in an approved school; ~**fahrt** → *Heimfahrt*; ~**fall** → *Heimfall*; ~**förderung** public aid for youth centres; ~**industrie** home industry; ~**kehrer** → *Heimkehrer*;

Heimat / **Heizöl**

~stätte → *Heimstätte*; ~**textilien** household textile furnishings; ~**unterbringung** providing residential care, committing s. o. to an institution; ~**vertrag** contract concerning residence and care in old people's home *or* nursing clinic.

Heimat *f* homeland, native land, native country; ~**berechtigung** right of abode, right to live in one's native land; ~**boden** native soil; ~**börse** home stock exchange; ~**film** sentimental film with a regional background; ~**gemeinde** native town, native village; ~**hafen** home port, port of registry, registered port, port of documentation; ~**land** native country, one's own country; ~**loser** homeless person; ~**ort** native place, home town, native town, native village; ~**recht** right to live in one's native country; lex patriae (*intern. private law*); ~**staat** state of origin, home state; ~**urlaub** home leave; ~**vertriebener** displaced person, refugee, expellee, (*esp. a person expelled from ethnic-German territories*).

Heimfahrt *f* journey home, passage home, homeward journey.

Heimfall *m* reversion, escheat, devolution; ~**anspruch** right of reversion, reversionary claim; ~ **bei Erbpachtgrundstücken** lease reversion; ~**recht** (right of) reversion, right of reverter, estate in reversion, right of escheat (*crown, lord*); ~**sberechtigter** reversioner, remainderman; ~**sklage** writ of escheat *of the lord of the manor*; ~**sklausel** reversion clause, defeasance clause; ~**srecht** = *Heimfallrecht qv*; ~**srente** reversionary annuity.

heimfallen *v/t* to revert, to escheat.

Heimkehrer *m* homecoming prisoner of war, repatriate, repatriated prisoner of war; ~**bescheinigung** certificate of detention as prisoner of war; ~**gesetz** Act to regulate matters of returned prisoners of war; ~**hilfe** assistance to former prisoners of war, P. O. W. assistance.

heimlich *adj* clandestine, surreptitious, secret.

Heimlichkeit *f* furtiveness, stealth, surreptitiousness, secrecy.

Heimschaffung *f* repatriation, bringing s. o. (*or sth*) home; ~**sbescheinigung** repatriation certificate.

Heimstätte *f* homestead; ~**n-Genossenschaft** homestead cooperative; ~**nwesen** homestead matters.

Heimtücke *f* perfidy, treachery.

heimtückisch *adj* treacherous, insidious, perfidious.

Heirat *f* marriage.

heiraten *v/t* to marry, *v/i* to get married, to marry; **nicht standesgemäß** ~ to marry below one's station.

Heirats|abfindung marriage settlement; ~**alter** marriageable age, marrying age; ~**antrag** proposal (of marriage), offer of marriage; ~**anzeige** wedding announcement, notice of marriage; advertisement for a marriage partner; ~**beihilfe** marriage grant; ~**buch** register of marriages; ~**eintrag** entry in the register of marriages; ~**erlaubnis** marriage licence, permission to marry; **h~fähig** nubile, marriageable; ~**frequenz** frequency rate of marriages; ~**gut** dowry; ~**register** register of marriages; ~**schein** marriage certificate; ~**schwindler** person making a fraudulent offer of marriage; ~**urkunde** marriage certificate; ~**vermittler** marriage broker; ~**vermittlung** procurement of marriage, matchmaking, arrangement of marriage, marriage brokage, marriage bureau, marriage agency; ~**vertrag** marriage agreement, articles of marriage; ~**zuschuß** marriage allowance, marriage grant.

heißen *v/i* to be called, to be named, one's name is ...; *das heißt: that is to say*, i. e. (*id est*), to wit.

Heizkostenbeihilfe *f* heating expenses subsidy.

Heizöl *n* heating oil, fuel oil, oil-fuel;

~steuer heating oil tax, tax on fuel oil.

Heizung f heating; **die ~ bedienen** to be in charge of heating.

Heizungs|abrechnung (annual) account for heating expenses; **~anlage** heating installation, heater; **~keller** boiler room (*of central heating*); **~kosten** heating cost; **~technik** heating engineering.

Hektar m hectare (*equal to 10000 square meters*); **~höchstsatz** maximum rate per hectare; **~satz** rate per hectare.

Helfer m helper, assistant; **~ in Steuersachen** tax consultant.

Helfershelfer m accomplice, accessory, aider and abettor.

Heller m penny, cent, farthing; **auf ~ und Pfennig bezahlen** to pay scot and lot, to pay (off) all one's debts.

Helsinki Schlußakte f Helsinki Final Act.

Hemmnis n (*pl Hemmnisse = ~se*) obstacle; impediment, hindrance; **~se für den internationalen Handel** obstacles to international trade, restraints on international trade.

Hemmschwelle f (threshold of self-restraint.

Hemmung f inhibition, obstruction, restraint, curb; **~ der Ersitzungsfrist** interruption (suspension) of the period of prescriptive acquisition (*not counted for the prescriptive title*); **~ der Verjährung** suspension of the Statute of Limitations; **psychologische ~en** psychological inhibitions.

Henker m executioner, hangman.

herabsetzbar *adj* reducible.

herabsetzen v/t to reduce, to lower; to disparage, to revile.

Herabsetzung f reduction, lowering; disparagement; **~ der Geheimhaltungsstufe** downgrading of security classification; **~ der Strafe** reduction in sentence; **~ der Vermächtnisse** abatement of legacy; **~ des Grundkapitals** reduction of capital, capital-cut.

Herabstufung f downgrading.

Herabwürdigung f disparagement.

Herabzonung f zoning-down.

Heraldik f heraldry.

Heranbildung f occupational training (*in the plant*); **~ von Nachwuchskräften** training of junior staff, training of the rising generation.

herantragen v/t to supply, to submit, to approach s. o. with sth.

Heranwachsende *pl* young adults, juvenile adults, young adult offenders.

heranziehen v/t to call upon, to enlist the services (of).

Heranziehung f calling-upon, making use of, enlistment of s. o.'s services; **~ allgemeiner Grundsätze** reference to general principles; **~ zur Steuer** subjecting (s. o.) to taxation, liability to taxes.

Herausfahren n moving out (*street traffic*).

herausfinden v/t to find out, to detect, to discover.

herausfordern v/t to challenge, to provoke.

Herausforderung f provocation, challenge; **~ zum Zweikampf** challenge to fight a duel.

Herausgabe f surrender, delivery up; the giving up of possession, restoration; (*e-r beweglichen Sache*) specific restitution; disgorgement; **~anspruch** claim for possession, right to recovery of sth, claim for the surrender of sth, claim for restitution of property; **~klage** action to recover the possession of sth; **~ ~** *wegen widerrechtlicher Besitzentziehung*: (*action of*) replevin; **~pflicht** obligation to restore possession to s. o.; **~schuldner** party liable to surrender property; **~vollstreckung** execution to seize and return an object; **~verweigerung** refusal to surrender, detainer; **die ~ verlangen** to claim possession, to ask for the restoration of sth.

Herausgeber m publisher, editor of a colletive work.

herausreden v/reflex to talk one's way out of sth, to prevaricate.

herausschinden v/t to extract, to wrangle sth.
herausstellen v/t to emphasize v/reflex: to appear, to come to light; *sich als richtig ~: to come true, finally to appear to be correct.*
herausverlangen v/t to claim recovery of possession, to reclaim.
herauswirtschaften v/t to manage to earn sth, to achieve a surplus.
herbeiführen v/t to bring about, to cause.
Herbeiführung f causation, initiation, inducement; ~ **des Selbstmords** procuring suicide; ~ **e-r Straftat** initiation of a crime (*by an agent provocateur*); **beschleunigte** ~ precipitation; **fahrlässige** ~ negligent causation of sth.
Herberge f hostel, inn.
Herbst|belebung autumn upswing; **~ferien** autumn holiday; **~ultimo** last day of the third quarter.
Hereinnahme f taking in, taking on deposit, purchase; ~ **von Wechseln** discounting of bills.
hereinnehmen v/t to take in, to take into stock.
Hereinnehmer m taker, acceptor.
hergestellt pp, adj made, produced, manufactured; **einwandfrei** ~ of good construction, of proper workmanship.
Herkommen n ancestry, origin.
herkömmlich adj customary, traditional, conventional; **~erweise** (adv) according to custom, traditionally.
Herkunft f origin, provenance, derivation; **gesellschaftliche** ~ social background; **von unbekannter** ~ of obscure origin, of unknown origin.
Herkunfts|angaben indication of origin; **~bescheinigung** certificate of origin; **~bezeichnung** indication of origin, mark of origin; **~land** country of origin; **~nachweis** proof of origin; **~ort** place of origin, place of provenance; **~täuschung** misrepresentation of origin; **~zeichen** mark of origin.
Hermeneutik f hermeneutics (*the science of the art of construction and interpretation*).
herrenlos adj abandoned, ownerless, unclaimed (*goods*), derelict.
Herrensitz m mansion house, manor.
Herr Richter! Your Honour.
Herrichten n site preparation (*construction work*).
Herrschaft f domination, reign, regency; ~ **der Mehrheit** majority rule; ~ **des Pöbels** ochlocracy, mob rule; ~ **des Rechts** rule of law; ~ **über die Meere** command of the sea; **territoriale** ~ territorial power; **vermögensrechtliche** ~ property control.
Herrschafts|ausübung (exercise of) domination, jurisdiction (of the State); **~gebiet** sovereign territory; **~gewalt** dominium, power of control, power to rule; **~recht** domain, right of domination, ownership right; *lebenslängliches ~~ an e-m Grundstück*: life estate.
herrschen v/i to rule, to reign, to control.
herrschend v/t dominant, prevailing, controlling, prevalent.
Herrscher m ruler, potentate, monarch.
Herrscherhaus n (reigning) dynasty, royal family; **regierendes** ~ ruling house, reigning dynasty.
herrühren von v/i to emanate from.
herstammen v/i to stem from, to come from, to be derived from.
herstellen v/t to make, to manufacture, to produce.
Hersteller m maker, producer, manufacturer; **~finanzierung** financing of production; **~garantie** manufacturer's guarantee; **~marke** manufacturer's brand; **~typenbescheinigung** production certificate (*aeroplane*); **~werbung** producer advertising; ~ **und Baujahr** make and year; **~zeichen** (manufacturer's) trade mark; **~zusatzsteuer** surtax on manufacturers.
Herstellung f production, manufacturing, manufacture, making.
Herstellungs|aufwand production

herumlungern

expenses; ~**bereitschaft** production readiness; ~**jahr** year of manufacture; ~**gemeinkosten** production overheads; ~**klage** action for specific performance; ~**kosten** manufacturing costs, production costs; ~~**berechnung**: *calculation of production costs*; ~**land** producer country; ~**lizenz** manufacturing licence; ~**monopol** production monopoly; ~**ort** place of production; ~**patent** process (of production) patent; ~**preis** manufacturing price, production price; ~**prozeß** production process; ~**recht** manufacturing right(s), right of production; ~**unternehmen** production enterprise, manufacturer; ~**verbot** ban on production; ~**verfahren** manufacturing process, production method; *geschütztes* ~~: *proprietary industrial process*; ~**vertrag** production agreement; ~**wert** cost value, value of production.

herumlungern *v/i* to loiter.

Herumstehen *n* standing around, loitering.

herumtreiben *v/reflex* to loiter.

Herumtreiber *m* loafer, tramp.

herunterkommen *v/i* to get run down, to fall into disrepair.

heruntersetzen *v/t* to reduce, to scale down.

Heruntersetzung *f* reduction.

Hetze *f* agitation, baiting; ~ **gegen die Juden** Jew-baiting.

Hetzer *m* agitator, rabble-rouser; **staatsgefährdender** ~ seditionmonger.

Hetzrede *f* inflammatory speech.

Heuer *f* pay for sailors, wages; ~**buch** (seaman's) pay-book; ~**büro** seamen's employment agency; ~**note** advance note; ~**schein** (seaman's) certificate of engagement; ~**stelle** seamen's employment agency, shipping office; ~**vertrag** shipping articles, ship's articles.

Hexenprozeß *m* witch-trial; ~**verfolgung** witch-hunt(ing).

Hieb- und Stoßwaffe cut-and-thrust weapon.

hierauf *adv* hereupon.

Hilfsaktion

hierdurch *adv* hereby, herewith, by these presents; ~ **wird bekannt gemacht** this is to notify, notice is hereby given; ~ **wird bestätigt** this is to certify.

hiermit *adv* hereby, herewith.

Hilfe *f* help, aid, assistance; ~**leistung** salvage, assistance, rescue work; ~~**spflicht**: *duty to render aid*; *ärztliche* ~~**en**: *medical services*; *unterlassene* ~~: *failure to render aid, failure to come to the rescue*; ~**ruf** call for help; ~**stellung** provision of aid; **ärztliche erste** ~ medical first aid; **ausländische** ~ **in Anspruch nehmen** to call on outside assistance; **bedingte** ~ conditional aid; **ersatzweise** ~ makeshift form of assistance; **finanzielle** ~ financial (aid and) assistance; **gegenseitige** ~ mutual aid; **jmdm** ~ **leisten** to grant s. o. aid and assistance; **technische** ~ technical assistance; **um** ~ **ersuchen** to pray for aid, to ask for assistance.

Hilfs|aktion relief action; ~**anspruch** ancillary claim, alternative claim; ~**antrag** plea in the alternative, auxiliary request, auxiliary motion; motion for alternative relief, precautionary motion; ~**arbeiter** unskilled worker; ~**arzt** assistant medical practitioner (*acting in an emergency*); ~**aufrechnung** precautionary set-off; ~**beamter** auxiliary official; ~~ *der Staatsanwaltschaft*: *auxiliary official of the Public Prosecutor* (*i.e. the police*); **h~bedürftig** in need of assistance, helpless; ~**bedürftigkeit** need of assistance, helplessness; ~**begründung** precautionary argument in support of the claim; **h~bereit** ready to help, willing to help; helpful; ~**bereitschaft** readiness to help, helpfulness; ~**betrieb** ancillary plant; ~**beweismittel** auxiliary evidence; ~**bremse** secondary brake, emergency brake; ~**dienst** auxiliary service, emergency service, voluntary help scheme; ~**einwendung** substitute plea; ~**gemeinschaft** relief commission, re-

410

Himmelfahrtkommando   **hinhalten**

lief group; ~**geschworener** deputy juror, talesman; ~**industrie** auxiliary industry; ~**kasse** relief fund; *gewerbliche* ~~~*n*: *commercial relief schemes*; ~**konstruktion** auxiliary arrangement, precautionary argument; ~**konto** subsidiary account; ~**kräfte** unskilled workers, helpers; ~**lieferung** aid delivery; ~**lohn** remuneration for assistance, salvage pay, indirect labour; ~**maßnahmen** emergency measures, remedial measures; ~**mitglieder** deputy members; ~**mittel** remedy, *pl* remedies, resources; ~**organ** subsidiary organ, auxiliary organization; ~**organisation** relief organization; ~**person** helper; ~**personal** supporting staff, help, assistants, auxiliary personnel; ~**polizei** auxiliary police; ~**polizist** auxiliary policeman, special constable; ~**produkt** auxiliary product; ~**programm** relief programme; *militärisches* ~~~: *military assistance programme*; ~**quellen** resources; ~**redakteur** sub-editor; ~**referent** assistant head of section; ~**richter** assistant judge, specially commissioned judge; ~**schöffe** reserve juror, deputy lay judge; ~**schule** special school for retarded children; ~**spruchkörper** relief panel of judges; ~**stelle** aid centre; ~**stoff** accessory material; ~**tatsache** accessory fact; ~**vorbringen** precautionary alternative allegations (*or* averment), alternative submission; **h~weise** by an alternative method, alternatively, in the alternative, by way of precaution; ~**werk** welfare organization, relief organization; ~**widerklage** precautionary cross-petition; ~**williger** civilian volunteer (*with military forces*).

Himmelfahrtkommando *n* suicide mission, extremely risky mission.

hinaufsetzen *v/t* to raise, to mark up.

hinauslaufen *auf v/t* to amount *to*.

hinausschieben *v/t* to defer, to postpone, to delay.

Hinausschiebung *f* deferment, postponement; ~ **der Zahlungsfälligkeiten** postponement of payments, postponement of maturity dates.

hinauswerfen *v/t* to dismiss, to give s. o. the sack, to throw s. o. out.

Hinauswurf *m* sack, instant dismissal.

hinausziehen *v/t* to protract, to draw out.

hinauszögern *v/t* to retard, to delay.

Hinblick *m only in*: *im* ~ *auf*: *in view of, in the light of, whereas, with regard to, against the background of.*

hindern *v/t* to hinder, to impede, to hamper.

Hindernis *n* impediment, obstacle; **gesetzliches** ~ legal impediment, legal obstacle; **steuerliche ~se** fiscal obstacles; **unheilbares** ~ irreparable impediment, absolute impediment; **unvermeidbares** ~ unavoidable impediment.

Hinderung *f* impediment, hindrance, obstacle; ~**sgrund** obstacle, reason for non-attendance; *gesetzlicher* ~~: *statutory bar*.

hineininterpretieren *v/t* to read sth into (*a text*).

hineinlesen *v/t* to read sth into (*a text*), to imply.

Hinfahrt *f* journey there, outward journey; **nur für die** ~ one-way.

hinfällig *adj* frail, infirm, void; now useless, superseded, no longer applicable, invalid.

Hinfälligkeit *f* frailty, infirmity, weakness; invalidity.

Hinfracht *f* outward freight, outward cargo.

Hingabe *f* devotion; abandon, surrender, giving up, delivery; ~ **an Erfüllungs Statt** delivery in full discharge (*of the obligation*), transfer of sth in lieu of performance; ~ **an Zahlungs Statt** delivery (to be accepted) as payment, transfer of sth in lieu of payment; **durch** ~ **des Pfandes** by way of a pledge; **gegen** ~ **von** on delivery of.

hingeben *v/reflex* to surrender, to yield; to give oneself to (*a lover*).

hinhalten *v/t* to delay, to defer, to put off, to hold in suspense.

Hinhaltetaktik *f* delaying tactics, stalling tactics.
hinlänglich *adv* sufficiently, adequately.
hinnehmen *v/t* to put up with, to suffer, to acquiesce (in).
hinneigen *v/i* to be inclined to.
hinreichend *adj* satisfactory, adequate.
Hinreise *f* journey there, outward journey, voyage out; **auf der** ~ **begriffen** outward bound.
hinrichten *v/t* to execute, to put to death.
Hinrichtung *f* execution; ~ **auf dem elektrischen Stuhl** electrocution; ~ **durch den Strang** hanging, execution by hanging; ~ **ohne Verfahren** execution without trial.
Hinrichtungs|befehl death warrant; ~**kommando** execution squad, firing squad; ~**stätte** place of execution; ~**termin** execution date.
Hinsicht *f* regard, respect; **in jeder** ~ to all intents and purposes, in all respects; **in rechtlicher und tatsächlicher** ~ in fact and in law; **in tatsächlicher** ~ in point of fact.
hinsichtlich *prep* with respect to, concerning, with reference to.
Hintansetzung *f* disregard, putting sth last.
Hinterbliebenen|bezüge surviving dependants' benefits; ~~ *für Witwen*: *widows' benefits*; ~**entschädigung** compensation for surviving dependants; ~**fürsorge** welfare service for surviving dependants; ~**rente** survivors' pension, pension for surviving dependants; ~~ *anspruch*: *survivors' pension rights*, ~~-*empfänger*: *recipient of survivor's pension*; ~**versicherung** survivorship insurance; ~**versorgung** provision for dependants; survivor's pension.
Hinterbliebener *m* (*der Hinterbliebene*) surviving dependant, survivor.
Hintergebäude *n* rear building, outhouse.
Hinterhalt *m* ambush, trap; **im** ~ **liegen** to lie in wait.

Hinterland *n* hinterland, back lands, back country.
hinterlassen *v/t* to leave, to bequeath.
Hinterlassenschaft *f* estate, inheritance, the property left by the deceased.
hinterlegen *v/t* to deposit to make a deposit, to pay into court, to lodge (*sth with s.o. as security*); **gerichtlich** ~ to pay into court, to deposit in court; **treuhänderisch vorläufig** ~ to place in escrow (*subject to certain conditions*).
Hinterleger *m* depositor, bailor.
Hinterlegung *f* depositing (lodging of a), deposit, lodgment, bailment; ~ **der Ratifikationsurkunden** deposit of the instruments of ratification; ~ **von Geldern bei Gericht** payment into court; ~ **von Pflichtexemplaren** filing of required copies (*of a publication*); **gerichtliche** ~ deposit in court, payment into court; **vorläufige** ~ **e-r Urkunde** (delivery in) escrow, provisional deposit of a document.
Hinterlegungs|befugnis authority to deposit; ~**benachrichtigung** notice of payment in (*or* of) deposit; ~**bescheinigung** deposit receipt; receipt of deposit; ~**bestätigung** acknowledgment of deposit; ~**gebühr** deposit fee; ~**gelder** monies deposited (*in the custody of a court*), monies paid into court, trust money; ~**gericht** depositary court; ~**geschäfte** deposit transactions; ~**kasse** deposit agency, lodgment office; ~**kosten** charges for court deposit; ~**masse** deposited assets; ~**nummer** deposit number, number of deposit; ~**ordnung** Court Deposit Regulations (*of 1937*); ~**ort** place of deposit, place of lodgment; ~**recht** law as to depositing in court; ~**schein** depositing certificate; ~**stelle** depositary institution, depositary authority, office for court deposits, lodgment office; *amtliche* ~~: *official depositary*; *gerichtliche* ~~: *office for court deposits*, *zuständige* ~~: *appropriate*

Hinterlieger

depository; **~summe** sum on deposit, sum paid into court; **~urkunde** certificate of deposit; **~vereinbarung** deposit agreement; **~verfügung** lodgment order, order accepting a deposit in court; **~vertrag** contract of deposit; **~zeit** time of deposit.

Hinterlieger *m* owner of rear property.

Hinterlist *f* deceit, treachery.

hinterlistig *adj* deceitful, insidious, treacherous.

Hintermann *m* backer, subsequent endorser, person behind the scenes.

Hintersasse *m* villein.

Hintertürchen *n* loophole (in the law), escape clause, backdoor.

hinterziehen *v/t* to evade (*tax, duty etc*), to defraud.

Hinterziehung *f* (tax) evasion, defraudation, embezzlement.

Hin- und Rückfahrkarte *f* return ticket, round-trip ticket.

Hin- und Rückflug *m* flight there and back, outbund and inbound flight.

Hin- und Rückreise *f* outward and homeward journey, round trip.

Hin- und Rückweg *m* way there and back; *auf ~~~ passieren*: to pass and repass.

hin und zurück *adv* there and back, return.

hinwegsehen *v/i* to overlook, to ignore it (*just this time*).

hinwegsetzen *v/reflex* (*sich ~ über etw*) to disregard.

hinwegtäuschen *v/t* to mislead (s. o. regarding sth).

Hinweis *m* hint, reference, indication, allusion, announcement, lead; **~pflicht** duty to warn, duty to draw attention to sts; **~schild** sign; **~zeichen** directional sign, informative sign; **geschäft~mäßiger ~** business notice.

hinweisen *v/t* (*auf*) to indicate, to draw attention to, to bring to s. o.'s knowledge, to point out (emphatically), to refer to.

hinzögern *v/t* to delay (*proceedings*).

Hochachtung

Hinzuerwerb *m* complementary acquisition.

hinzufügen *v/t* to add, to append.

Hinzufügung *f* addition.

hinzukommen *v/i* to be added, to ensue.

hinzurechnen *v/t* to add, to include.

Hinzurechnung *f* addition, inclusion; **~sbetrag** amount added, addition, additional amount.

Hinzuschlagen *n* addition; *das ~ von Zinsen zum Kapital*: *capitalization of interest*.

hinzuschlagen *v/t* to add, to append.

hinzusetzen *v/t* to add, to subjoin, to append.

Hinzutreten *n* additional occurance; **~ weiterer Umstände** if other circumstances occur (intervene).

hinzuverklagen *v/t* to add defendants.

Hinzuwahl *f* co-option, election of an additional member.

hinzuwählen *v/t* to elect (as) an additional member, to co-opt.

hinzuziehen *v/t* to call in; to consult.

Hinzuziehung *f* calling-in, consultation, enlisting the services (of).

Hirtenbrief *m* pastoral letter.

Histogramm *n* histogram (*statistics*) bar chart, bar graph.

Hoch|**achtung** esteem; **h~achtungsvoll** Yours truly, Yours faithfully; **~adel** peerage, higher nobility; **~bau** surface engineering, structural engineering; **~bauingenieur** structural engineer; **~bauunternehmen** building firm, construction firm, contractors; **h~beanspruchbar** *adj* able to withstand high stress; **~betrieb** intense activity; **~finanz** high finance, world of high finance, leading financial circles; **~format** upright; **~kapitalismus** heyday of capitalism, mature capitalism; **~kommissar** High Commissioner; **~konjunktur** boom, boom conditions, prosperity; **~rechnung** computer forecast, extrapolation; expansion; *pauschale ~~*:

413

global expansion; ~**saison** peak season; ~**schul-** →*Hochschul-*; ~**schule** → *Hochschule*; ~**see** → *Hochsee*; ~**spannungsmast** high tension electricity pylon; ~**stapelei** fraud, imposture, (high-class) swindling, confidence trick; ~**stapler** fraud, impostor, swindler, con(fidence)-man; ~**touristik** mountaineering; ~**- und Tiefbau** structural and civil engineering; h~**verräterisch** seditious, treasonable; ~**verrat** sedition, high treason, treason by internal upheaval; ~**verratsprozeß** state trial; h~**verschuldet** debt-ridden, highly indebted; ~**wassergeschädigter** sufferer from flood damage; ~**wasserschutz** flood prevention; ~**wasserversicherung** flood insurance; h~**wertig** *adj* high-grade, high-quality; ~**zinsphase** period of high interest rates; ~**zinspolitik** high-interest policy; ~**zöllner** protectionist, advocate of high customs duties; ~**zollpolitik** protectionist policy.

Hochschul|ausbildung university *or:* college training, tertiary education; ~**dozent** university teacher, professor; ~**gesetz** University and College Act; ~**lehrer** university professor, university teacher; ~**politik** (government) policy on university education; ~**rahmengesetz** basic university (status) Act; ~**recht** law of academic institutions, university legislation; ~**reife** university entrance (*or* matriculation) level of education; *GB*: General Certificate of Education (GCE), Advanced (A) Level, ("A" level); *fachgebundene* ~: *subject-specific matriculation;* ~**studium** university or college education, studies at a university or college, academic studies; ~**verband** association of university professor ~**verfassung** university constitution and organisation; ~**zulassungsrecht** Act governing admission to university.

Hochschule *f* institution of higher learning; university, college; ~ **für Lehrerbildung** teachers' training college; **pädagogische** ~ teachers' training college; **technische** ~ college of advanced technology; technical university.

Hochsee *f* the high seas, open sea; ~**fischerei** deep-sea fishing; ~**fischereiboot** trawler; ~**schiff** seagoing ship, deep-sea vessel; ~**schiffahrt** ocean-carrying trade, high-seas navigation; ~**schlepper** ocean-going tug; h~**tüchtig** *adj* sea-going, ocean-going; ~**verkehr** ocean transportation.

Höchst|alter maximum age; ~**altersgrenze** maximum age limit; ~**angebot** highest offer, last offer; ~**beitrag** maximum contribution, maximum premium; ~**belastung** permissible load; *zulässige* ~~: *safety load;* ~**belastungssatz** peak rate *(psychological)* breaking point (of a tax); ~**betrag** maximum amount, limit, ceiling amount; ~*beträge für Schadensersatz*: *limitation of damages;* ~**betragsbürgschaft** limited guarantee, suretyship up to a maximum amount; ~**betragshypothek** maximum-sum mortgage, closed mortgage, running-account mortgage; ~**betragsschiffshypothek** maximum-sum bottomry bond; ~**bietender** highest bidder; ~**dauer** maximum duration; ~**ertragsalternative** transfer earnings; ~**fall** maximum; ~**flußreaktor** very high flux reactor; ~**gebot** best offer, highest bid, maximum bid, closing bid; ~**gebühr** maximum fee; ~**geschwindigkeit** maximum speed, speed limit; ~**gewicht** maximum weight, weight limit; ~**grenze** upper limit; ~**haftungssumme** maximum liability (*ins*); ~**kontingent** maximum quota; ~**kurs** peak price; ~**ladegewicht** maximum (weight of) load; ~**laufzeit** maximum (remaining) life; ~**leistung** maximum output, supreme achievement, highest efficiency; ~**lohn-**

Hof

grenze wage ceiling; ~**maß** maximum dimension; ~**mengenregelung** system of quantitative limitation; ~**miete** maximum rent, rent limit; h~**persönlich** *adj* strictly personal, strictly private, „eyes only"; ~**prämie** maximum premium; ~**preis** maximum price, highest price, ceiling price, peak price; *gesetzlicher* ~~: *ceiling price*; ~**quote** maximum quota; h~**richterlich** *adj* (decision) by the supreme court; ~**ruhegehalt** maximum pension; ~**satz** upper limit; ~**schadensmöglichkeit** maximum possible loss; ~**schuld** maximum indebtedness, highest amount of debt outstanding; ~**stand** peak level, record level, an all-time high; ~**strafe** maximum penalty, maximum sentence; ~**tarif** maximum rate (*or* tariff); ~**verbrauchertarif** maximum demand tariff; ~**versicherungssumme** maximum sum insured; ~**wert** maximum figure, maximum value; ~**zahl** maximum figure; ~**zinssätze** maximum interest rates.

Hof *m* (1) (*pl Höfe* ~*e*) farm; ~**erbfolge** farm succession; ~**folgezeugnis** farm succession certificate; ~**eordnung** law on inheritance of agricultural estates; ~**erecht** law of entailed succession of agricultural estates; ~**erolle** list of entailed estates (*cf* ~*eordnung*); ~**raum** messuage; ~**übergabe** surrender of farm to successor, farm transfer; ~**veräußerung** conveyance of a farm, alienation of a farm; ~**wirtschaft** farming; **auslaufender** ~ farm in liquidation; **frei** ~ free (to) farmyard.

Hof *m* (2) court; ~**amt** court office; ~**kanzlei** Chancellery; ~**lieferant** purveyor to the Royal Household; ~**marschall** *GB*: Lord Chamberlain; ~**zeremoniell** court etiquette.

Hoffnungskauf *m* speculative purchase.

Höflichkeit *f* courtesy; ~**sbesuch** formal call, courtesy visit; ~**sform** etiquette, decorum, proprieties; ~**sformel** complimentary close; **internationale** ~**en** international courtesies.

Höhe *f* amount, extent; ~ **der Gefängnisstrafe** period of imprisonment, term of imprisonment; ~ **der Kosten** incidence of costs, amount of the costs; ~ **der Verschuldung** amount of indebtedness; ~ **des Kredits** credit line; ~ **des Schadens** the amount of the damage; ~ **des Schadensersatzes** quantum (of damages); ~ **des Streitwerts** amount in dispute, amount of the assessed value of the litigation; ~ **des Zinsfußes** rate of interest, interest rate.

Hohe Behörde *f* High Authority.

Hoheit *f* sovereignty, supreme power, supreme authority.

hoheitlich *adj* sovereign, national.

Hoheits|akt act of state, sovereign act; *staatlicher* ~~: *act of state*; ~**befugnis** sovereign power; ~**bereich** domestic jurisdiction, national territory; ~**betrieb** public utility company (*operated by a public authority*); enterprise vested with public authority; ~**flagge** national flag; ~**gebiet** national territory, sovereign territory, territory under sovereign jurisdiction; ~**gewalt** sovereign power, territorial sovereignty; ~~ *über die Fischerei*: *jurisdiction over fisheries*; ~**gewässer** territorial waters, jurisdictional waters, national waters; *ausländisches* ~~: *foreign waters*; ~**grenze** state border, territorial frontier; ~**handlung** sovereign act, act of state; ~**recht** sovereign right, dominion, rights and attributes of sovereignty; *königliches* ~~: *royal prerogative*; ~**tätigkeit** state activity; ~**träger** organ of sovereign power, (public) authority; ~**verletzung** violation of sovereign rights; ~**verwaltung** public administration, public authority; ~**zeichen** national emblem, sovereign emblem.

Hohe Kommission *f* High Commission.

Höher|bewertung mark-up, upward revaluation; valuation at a higher level, appreciation of assets, writing up; ~**gruppierung** reclassification in a higher category, upgrading; ~**versicherung** increased insurance, insurance at a higher insurance rate.

Hoher Kommissar *m* High Commissioner.

Hohlpreiskalkulation *f* hollow costing (*material is made available to subcontractors free of charge*).

Hökerhandel *m* huckstering, street trade, hawking, peddling.

Holdinggesellschaft *f* holding company.

Holdingmarke *f* trade mark of a holding company.

holographisch *adj* holograph, holographic.

Holschuld *f liability to be discharged at the domicile of the debtor, debt to be collected at debtor's address.*

Holz *n* wood; timber, *US*: lumber; ~**arbeiter** woodworker; ~**auktion** timber auction; ~**bearbeitungswerkstatt** woodworking shop; ~**bearbeitungsindustrie** woodworking industry; ~**einschlag** timber-cutting, amount of timber to be felled; ~**entnahmegerechtigkeit** common of estovers; ~**ertrag** yield of timber; ~**erzeugung** wood production, timber production; ~**faserplatte** wood-fibre board; ~**frevel** illegal cutting of timber; ~**handel** timber trade; ~**händler** timber merchant; ~**industrie** timber industry; ~**lager** wood yard; ~**marktkunde** marketing of wood; ~**nutzung** utilization of wood, exploitation of wood and timber resources; ~**transport** timber transport; ~**verarbeitung** wood processing; ~**verarbeitungsindustrie** woodworking industry; ~**veredelung** wood processing; ~**wolle** (long thin) wood shavings, *US*: excelsior.

Honorant *m* acceptor for honour, acceptor supra protest.

Honorar *n* fee, professional fee, professional charge; ~**abrede** understanding concerning professional charges, agreement on fees; ~**aufteilung** fee splitting; ~**festsetzung** court assessment of fees; ~**forderung** professional charge, fee payable; ~**konsul** honorary consul; ~**konsulat** honorary consulate; ~**professor** honorary (extraordinary) professor; ~**rechnung** bill for (professional) services, bill of costs, fee note; ~**vereinbarung** agreement on fees (*for a lawyer*); ~**verteilungsmaßstab** ratio for splitting fees; ~**vertrag** agreement on remuneration, fee contract; ~**vorschuß** retainer, fees paid in advance, payment on account.

Honorat *m* person honoured, *on whose behalf a bill of exchange is accepted or paid.*

honorieren *v/t* to honour; **nicht** ~ to dishonour.

Hopfen|anbau hop growing, cultivation of hops; ~**anbaugebiet** hop-growing district; ~**händler** hop merchant; ~**kommissionär** hop factor; ~**pflücker** hop-picker.

Hörensagen *n* hearsay; **vom** ~: *by hearsay.*

Hörertest *m* audience research.

Hörigkeit *f* bondage, serfdom, servitude.

Hörverlust *m* loss of hearing.

Hörvermögen *n* (power of) hearing, faculty of hearing.

horten *v/t* to hoard, to stockpile.

Hortung *f* hoarding, accumulation, stockpiling; ~**skäufe** hoarding purchases; ~**spolitik** hoarding policy.

Hotel|anmeldung registration at a hotel; ~**aufnahmevertrag** hotel accommodation agreement; ~**besitzer** hotel proprietor; ~**fachschule** catering and hotel-management school; ~ **garni** bed and breakfast hotel, guest house; ~**gewerbe** hotel industry, hotel trade; ~**nachweis** hotel information service, list of hotels; ~**ord-**

nung hotel regulations; **~pension** residential hotel, private hotel; guest house; **~quartier** hotel accommodation; **~spesen** hotel expenses; **~- und Gaststättengewerbe** catering trade.

Hubraum *m* cubic capacity, piston displacement, cylinder capacity of the engine; **~steuer** automobile tax based on cylinder capacity.

Huckepack|system *n* piggy-back export scheme, pick-a-back system; **~verkehr** combined road and rail transport, piggy-back traffic, roll-on (roll-off) service; **~werbung** piggybacks.

Huldigung *f* homage; **~seid** oath of allegiance.

Humanexperiment *n* experiment on (or with) human beings.

Hunde|abgabe dog tax; **~besitzer** dog-owner; **~biß** dog-bite; **~führer** dog-handler; **~halter** keeper of a dog, person in charge of a dog; **~haltererlaubnis** dog licence; **~marke** dog tag; **~steuer** dog tax; **~streife** dog patrol.

Hunger|blockade hunger blockade; **~lohn** starvation-wages, pittance; „peanuts"; *für e–n ~ arbeiten*: *to work for peanuts*; **~revolte** food riot; **~streik** hunger strike; **~tod** starvation, death from starvation.

Hupverbot *n* prohibition from sounding one's horn, no hooting!

Hürde *f* obstacle, barrier; **handelspolitische ~n** trade barriers.

Hure *f* whore, prostitute, strumpet, harlot.

Hurenviertel *n* brothel quarter, red-light district.

Hurerei *f* whoring, prostitution, fornication.

Hüter *m* keeper, guardian; **~ des Gesetzes** guardian of the law, arm of the law, policeman.

Hütte *f* smelting works, foundry, metallurgical plant.

Hütten|arbeiter foundryman, steelworker, worker in a smelting works; **~betrieb** = *Hütte qv*; **~industrie** iron and steel industry; **~technik** metallurgical engineering; **~werk** metallurgical plant, smelting works, iron and steel works, steelworks.

Hygienegesetz *n* Sanitary Act.

Hypothek *f* (*Hypotheken→ Hypotheken-*) mortgage, mortgage charge; mortgage loan; hypothec (*referring to continental law*); **aus e-r ~ vollstrecken** to foreclose a mortgage; **e-e ~ ablösen** to dismortgage, to redeem a mortgage, to take over a mortgage; **e-e ~ aufnehmen** to take up (*or* out) a mortgage, to mortgage; **e-e ~ bestellen** to create a mortgage, to grant a mortgage; *jmdm e-e ~ bestellen*: *to grant a mortgage to s.o.*; *e-e nachrangige ~ bestellen*: *to submortgage*; **e-e ~ löschen** to cancel a mortgage (*in the land register*), to discharge a mortgage; **e-e ~ tilgen** to redeem a mortgage; **erststellige ~** first mortgage; **im Range vorgehende ~** prior mortgage; **mit e-r ~ belasten** to encumber with a mortgage, to mortgage; **mit ~en belastbar** mortgageable; **nachrangige ~** junior mortgage; mortgage lower in priority; **nachstellige ~** = *nachrangige qv*; **zweite ~** second mortgage; **zweitstellige ~** second mortgage.

Hypothekar|anlagen mortgage loan investments; **~darlehen** mortgage loan; **~satz** mortgage interest rate; **~verschuldung** mortgage borrowing.

hypothekarisch *adj* as a mortgage, by way of mortgage.

Hypotheken|anleihe mortgage loan; **~anstalt** mortgage bank; **~auszahlung** payment of mortgage loan monies (*to mortgagor*); **~bank** mortgage bank; **~bankgesetz** Mortgage Banks Act; **~belastung** encumbrance by mortgage; **~bestellung** execution of a mortgage, granting of a mortgage; **~bestellungsurkunde** mortgage deed; **~bewilligung** grant of a mortgage; **~brief** mortgage certificate (*issued by the Land Register*); **~damnum** mortgage discount;

Hypothekendarlehen

~**darlehen** mortgage loan, loan on mortgage; *ein ~~ aufnehmen*: *to lend on mortgage*; *erstklassige ~~*: *first-mortgage loans*; ~**forderung** mortgage debt; **h~frei** *adj* unmortgaged; ~**geld** mortgage loan money; ~**gewinnabgabe** levy on mortgage (revaluation of currency) profits; *~nbefreiung*: *exemption from levy on mortgage profits*; ~**gläubiger** mortgagee, mortgage creditor; ~**klage** foreclosure action (*action to acquiesce in the enforcement of the mortgage*); ~**kredit** mortgage loan; ~**laufzeit** mortgage term, duration of a real estate mortgage; ~**makler** mortgage broker; ~**markt** mortgage (loan) market; ~**pfandbrief** mortgage bond, mortgage debenture; ~**register** register of mortgages (*kept by mortgage banks*); ~**schätzer** mortgage appraiser; ~**schuld** debt secured by mortgage, mortgage debt; ~**schulden** mortgages payable; ~**schuldner** mortgagor; ~**schuldverschreibung** mortgage bond; ~**stelle** rank of a mortgage; ~**stock** portfolio of mortgages, mortgage loan portfolio; ~**tilgung** mortgage redemption, satisfaction of mortgage; ~**übernahme** taking over of a mortgage, acceptance of a mortgage; ~**urkunde** mortgagedeed, indenture of mortgage; ~**valuta** mortgage loan money (*paid to the borrower*), mortgage loan proceeds; ~**verkehr** mortgage transactions by banks, mortgage business; ~**verschuldung** mortgage indebtedness; ~**versicherung** mortgage insurance; ~**versicherungsanstalt** mortgage insurance company; ~**verteilung** apportioning of mortgages (*on various properties*), mortgage apportionment; ~**zins** mortgage interest; ~**zusage** mortgage-loan commitment.

Hypothekenzusage

I

Idealkonkurrenz *f* (nominal) coincidence of offences *more than one offence* (= *Tateinheit qv*).
Idealverein *m* non-profit (incorporated) association, members club.
Ideenverbindung *f* association of ideas, linking of ideas.
Identifikation *f* identification ~**snummer** VAT registration number (EC commen market).
identifizierbar *adj* identifiable.
identifizieren *v/t* to identify.
Identifizierung *f* identification; ~ **durch Handballenabdruck** (identification by) palmprint evidence.
Identität *f* identity; **seine ~ nachweisen** to establish one's identity; **seine ~ verheimlichen** to conceal one's identity.
Identitäts|ausweis identity card, pass; ~**beweismittel** identifying evidence; ~**feststellung** identification; ~**irrtum** mistaken identity, error de persona; ~**karte** identification card; ~**nachweis** proof of identity; certificate of identity; ~**prüfung** examination of identity; ~**täuschung** imposture, impersonation; ~**verwechslung** mistaken identity, mistake in identity.
ignorieren *v/t* to ignore, to disregard, to flout.
Ignorieren *n* deliberate disregard.
Ignorierung *f* deliberate disregard.
illegal *adj* illegal, unlawful.
Illegalität *f* illegality, unlawfulness, illegal status.
illegitim *adj* illegitimate, improper.
Illegitimität illegitimacy, illegitimate birth.
illiquid *adj* short of liquid assets, non-liquid, insolvent.
Illiquidität *f* illiquidity, non-liquidity, shortage of liquid assets, insolvency.
Illiquidisierung *f* making illiquid, increasing illiquidity.

illoyal *adj* disloyal, treacherous.
Illoyalität *f* disloyalty, perfidy.
Imitationsware(n) *f* counterfeit goods.
Immaterialgüter *n/pl* intangibles, intangible assets, incorporeal things.
Immaterialgüterrecht *n* industrial property law; the law of incorporeal things; incorporeal right, incorporeal assets, *pl* incorporeal chattels.
Immaterialschaden *m* non-physical damage, incorporeal damage.
immateriell *adj* intangible, incorporeal.
Immatrikulation *f* matriculation, enrolment (at a university) ~**sbescheinigung** matriculation certificate.
immatrikulieren *v/reflex* to matriculate, to enrol at a university.
immerdauernd *adj* permanent.
Immission *f* immission, intrusion of noxious substances or noise *(from adjacent property)* ~**srichtwerte** limits for noxious substances emanating from real estate; ~**sschutz** protection against noxious intrusions ~~**beauftragter**: *warden to control noxious intrusions;* ~~**recht**: *law on environmental protection against noxious intrusions.*
Immobiliar|anlage property investment; ~**arrest** attachment of real property *(by execution lien)*; ~**erbe** heir to real property, inheritor of real estate; ~**investmentfonds** real estate (investment) trust; ~**klage** action concerning real estate; ~**kredit** loan (credit) secured by real property, real estate credit, credit on landed property; ~**schaden** damage to real estate; ~**sicherheit** real security; ~**vermögen** real assets, real property, real estate, immovables; ~**versicherung** real-estate in-

Immobilien / **Import**

surance; ~**zwangsvollstreckung** execution upon real estate (*execution sale, execution lien, or receivership*).

Immobilien *f/pl* immovables, real estate, immovable property, landed property; ~**anlagegesellschaft** real-estate (investment) trust; ~**branche** real estate industry; ~**büro** real-estate agency; ~**firma** estate agency; ~**fonds** real-property investment fund; ~**fonds-Zertifikat** property bond; ~**geschäfte** property transactions; ~**gesellschaft** real-estate company; ~**handel** real-estate trade; ~**händler** real-estate agent, real-estate dealer; ~**konsortium** real estate syndicate; ~**makler** real-estate agent; real-estate broker, realtor (*US*); ~**markt** real-estate market, property market; ~**recht** realproperty law; ~**trust** real property trust; ~**verkauf** sale of property; ~**-Zertifikat** real property investment fund, certificate.

Immunität *f* immunity; ~**en und Vorrechte** immunities and privileges; ~**sgesetz** immunity statute; ~**sklausel** immunity clause, escape clause; ~ **von Diplomaten** diplomatic immunity; **die** ~ **aufheben** to waive immunity; **diplomatische** ~ diplomatic immunity; **gerichtliche** ~ jurisdictional immunity, immunity from prosecution; **mit** ~ **ausgestattet** vested with immunity, enjoying immunity; **parlamentarische** ~ parliamentary immunity; **staatshoheitliche** ~ sovereign immunity; **zivilrechtliche** ~ immunity from suit.

Immutabilität *f* immutability (*of public acts by private agreement*).

Imperialismus *m* imperialism.

Imperium *n* empire.

Impf|**aktion** vaccination campaign; ~**bezirk** vaccination district; ~**buch** vaccination register; ~**gesetz** vaccination law; ~**pflicht** obligatory vaccination; ~**schaden** vaccine damage; ~**schein** vaccination certificate; ~**zeugnis** vaccination certificate; ~**zwang** compulsory vaccination.

implizieren *v/i* to imply

Imponderabilien *f/pl* imponderabilia, imponderables, intangible factors.

Import *m* importation, import; ~**abgabe** import duty; ~**agent** import agent; ~**akkreditiv** import letter of credit; ~**anreiz** import incentive; ~**antrag** application for import permit; ~**artikel** imports; ~**aufnahmefähigkeit** import capacity; ~**ausgleichsbetrag** import price adjustment levy; ~**ausgleichsgesetz** law on import price adjustment; ~**bedarf** import requirements; ~**beschränkung** import restriction; ~**bewilligungsantrag** application for import permit; ~**drosselung** throttling down of imports, import restrictions; ~**erklärung** bill of entry; ~**finanzierung** import financing; ~**firma** import house, importing firm; ~**handelsfirma** → *Importfirma qv*; **i**~**intensiv** involving a high proportion of imports; ~**konnossement** inward bill of lading; ~**kontingent** import quota; ~**kontingentierung** imposition of import quotas, import quota system; ~**kredit** import credit; ~**kreditbrief** import letter of credit; ~**lizenz** import licence, import permit; ~**quote** import quota; ~**restriktion** import restrictions; ~**schleuse** import sluice, import channels; ~**schonfrist** temporary import ban, import suspension (*to protect domestic producers temporarily*); ~**sog** pull of imports; ~**überschuß** import surplus, *surplus of imports over exports;* ~**verbot** import prohibition, ban on imports; ~**verlagerung** import shift; ~**vertreter** import agent; ~**ware** imported goods, imports; ~**wirtschaft** import trade, importers; ~**zoll** import duty; **kreditierte** ~**e** imports on credit; **symbolische** ~**e** token imports; **unsichtbare** ~**e** invisible imports.

Importeur *m* importer; **freie ~ e** outside importers.

importieren *v/t* to import.

Impressum *n* imprint, masthead.

in absentia *adv* in absentia.

Inaktivierung *f* placing on a retired status, inactivation; sterilization (of funds), neutralization.

Inangriffnahme *f* tackling sth, taking a matter in hand.

Inanspruchnahme *f* utilization, availment, recourse, use (of resources); **~ der Gerichte** resort to the courts; **~ des Kapitalmarktes** tapping the capital market; **~ der Priorität** claiming priority; **~ der Quote** drawings on the quota; **~ der Zentralbank** recourse to the Central Bank; **~ e–r Garantie** implementation of a guarantee; **~ e–r Kreditlinie** availment of a credit line; **~ e–s Kredits** recourse to a credit; **~ öffentlicher Mittel** employment of public funds; **~ von Dienst- und Sachleistungen** requisitioning of goods and services; **~ von Kredit für die Firma** drawing on credit for the firm; **~ von Vergünstigungen** taking advantage of concessions.

Inaugenscheinnahme *f* inspection, taking a (judicial) view, examination.

Inbegriff *m* embodiment, essence, quintessence, aggregate.

inbegriffen *adj*; **alles ~** terms inclusive, inclusive terms; **mit ~** implied, implicit.

Inbesitznahme *f* taking possession, entry *(of real estate)*.

Inbetrachtziehung *f* taking into consideration.

Inbetriebnahme *f* commencement of operations, opening.

Inbrandsetzen *n* setting fire to, arson.

Indemnität *f* *(parl)* exemption from criminal responsibility; **~ des Parlamentsberichts** immunity of parliamentary reports; **~sbeschluß** act of indemnity; **~sgesetz** Indemnity Act.

Index *m* index; **~anleihe** index-linked loan; **~bindung** indexation, indexing; **~ der Aktienkurse** index of stocks and shares; **~ der Außenwerte** trade-weighted index; **~ der Einzelhandelspreise** retail price index; **~ der Großhandelspreise** whole-sale price index; **~ der Industrietätigkeit** industrial index; **i~gebunden** index-linked; **~ kirchlich verbotener Schriften** Expurgation Index; **~klausel** index clause, escalator clause; **~lohn** index-linked wage; **~preis** index-linked price; **~reihe** column of index figures; *die maßgeblichen ~~n: the relevant indices*; **~rente** index-linked pension; **~währung** index-linked currency; **~ziffer** index number; **gewogener ~** weighted index; **ungewogener ~** unweighted index, non-weighted index; **wirtschaftlicher ~** economic index.

Indienststellung *f* commissioning (*warship*), putting into service.

Indikation indication; legal justification for an abortion; **medizinische ~** abortion on medical grounds; **soziale ~** permissible abortion for social reasons.

Indiskretion *f* indiscretion, indiscreet remark, *pol*: leakage; **gezielte ~** deliberate leakage.

Individual|abrede individual agreement, non-standard agreement; **~anspruch** personal claim, private claim; **~eigentum** ownership by individual, individual property; **~einkommen** individual income; **~entscheidung** individual decision, separate decision; **~haftung** individual liability, liability of private individual; **~rechtsgut** individual legal asset; **~versicherung** individual insurance, private insurance; **~vertrag** contract between individuals; individually stipulated contract, non-standard contract; **~sphäre** private life, personal affairs; **~vorlage** private member's bill; *streitig gewordene ~~n: opposed business*.

Indiz *n* indication, indicium, matter

Indizienbeweis

of circumstantial evidence, pointer; ~**tatsachen** facts of circumstantial evidence.
Indizienbeweis *m* circumstantial evidence, proof by circumstantial evidence.
Indizierung *f* placing on the list of prohibited books.
indossabel *adj* endorsable; **nicht** ~ unendorsable, not negotiable.
Indossament *n* endorsement; ~ **nach Protest** endorsement supra protest, endorsenent under protest; ~ **ohne Gewähr** endorsement without recourse; ~ **ohne Haftung** endorsement without recourse; ~ **ohne Obligo** endorsement without recourse, qualified endorsement, "without recourse"; ~ **ohne Obligo** restrictive endorsement; ~**schuldner** debtor by endorsement; ~**shaftung** endorser's liability; ~**sverbindlichkeiten** liabilities from endorsement; ~**svollmacht** power to endorse; **beschränktes** ~ qualified endorsement; **durch** ~ **übertragbar** transferable by endorsement; **gefälschtes** ~ forged endorsement; **irreguläres** ~ irregular endorsement; **ordnungsgemäßes** ~ proper endorsement.
Indossant *m* endorser; **nachfolgender** ~ subsequent endorser; **vorgehender** ~ previous endorser.
Indossatar *m* endorsee, holder by endorsement.
indossierbar *adj* endorsable.
indossieren *v/t* to endorse.
Indossierer *m* endorser.
Indossierung *f* endorsement.
in dubio pro reo giving the accused the benefit of the doubt.
Industrie *f* industry, branch of industry; ~**abwässer** trade effluent; ~**aktien** industrial shares, industrial equities, industrial stock; ~**anlage** industrial plant; ~**anleihe** industrial loan; ~**arbeiter** (industrial) worker, factory worker, shop floor worker; ~**arbeiterlöhne** industrial wages; ~**ausstoß** industrial output; ~**bank** industrial bank;

Industriestandort

~**beratung** management consultancy, management guidance; ~**beratungsdienst** industrial advisory service; ~**berichterstattung** industrial reports; ~**beschäftigte** industrial work-force, persons employed in industry; ~**erzeugnis** article of manufacture, *pl* manufactured goods; ~**finanzierung** financing of industry; ~**firma** industrial firm, industrial enterprise; ~**förderung** promotion of industry; ~**förderungsgesellschaft** industrial development company; ~**gebiet** industrial region, industrial district, industrial estate; ~**gelände** industrial site; ~**gesellschaft** industrial company; (*sociology*:) industrial society; ~**gewerkschaft** industrial union, vertical union; "~ ~ *Bergbau*": *Union of Miners*; "~~ *Metall*": *Metal Workers Union;* **i**~**eigen** *adj* industry-owned; ~**kartelle** industrial cartels; ~**kaufmann** industrial trader, commercial employee in industry; ~**kontenrahmen** uniform accounting system for (German) industry; ~**kredit** industrial credit, loans to industry; ~**kreditbank** industrial credit bank; ~**land** industrial country; ~~~*er mit harter Währung*: *strong-currency industrial countries;* ~**lieferant** supplies of industrial firms, industrial contractor; ~**magnat** tycoon; ~**meister** certificated foreman; ~**messe** trade fair; ~**müll** industrial refuse; ~**normen** standards in industry; *Deutsche Industrienormen* (*DIN*): *German Industrial Standards;* ~**obligation** industrial bond, corporate bond; ~**papier** industrial security; ~**park** industrial estate, trading estate, industrial park; ~**produktion** industrial output, industrial production; ~**siedlung** industrial estate, trading estate; company housing project; ~**spionage** industrial espionage; ~**staat** industrial state, industrial country; ~**standard** level of industrial activity, industrial standard; ~**standort** location

industriell / **Informationsamt**

of an industry; ~**tarif** industrial tariff (*electricity*); ~**tätigkeit** industrial activity; ~ **und Handel** trade and industry; ~**- und Handelskammer** Chamber of Industry and Commerce; ~**- und Handelstag** Association of Chambers of Commerce; ~**unternehmen** industrial undertaking, industrial enterprise; ~**verband** industrial association, trade organization, association of manufacturers; ~~~**prinzip**: *industrial union principle, principle of representation by comprehensive industrial organizations;* ~**verlagerung** relocation of industry; ~**vermögen** industrial properties, industrial assets; ~**waren** manufactured goods; ~**werbung** industrial advertising; ~**werte** industrial securities, industrials; ~**wirtschaft** industry, the industrial sector; ~**zeitalter** industrial age, industrial era; ~**zusammenschluß** industrial combine; ~**zweig** branch of manufacture; **bearbeitende** ~ manufacturing industry, processing industry; **einheimische** ~ home industry; **eisenschaffende** ~ iron and steel industry; **elektrotechnische** ~ electrical equipment industry, electrical engineering industry; **ernährungswichtige** ~ essential food industry; **exportintensive** ~ industry producing mainly for export; **heimische** ~ domestic industries; **holzbe- und verarbeitende** ~ wood-working and wood-processing industries; **metallverarbeitende** ~ metal industries; **mittlere** ~ medium-scale industry; **notleidende** ~ industry in distress; **stahlverarbeitende** ~ steel industry; **verarbeitende** ~ finishing industry, processing industry, manufacturing industry; **weiterverarbeitende** ~ processing industry, finishing industry.

industriell *adj* industrial.

Industrieller *m* industrialist, manufacturer.

Ineligibilität *f* ineligibility

in flagranti *adv* red-handed, in the very act.

Inflation *f* inflation; **dosierte** ~ gradual inflation; **durch Lohnsteigerung bedingte** ~ wage-push inflation; **galoppierende** ~ galopping inflation, runaway inflation; **hausgemachte** ~ home-made inflation, domestic inflation; **preisgestoppte** ~ price-controlled inflation; **schleichende** ~ creeping inflation, gradual inflation; **trabende** ~ trotting inflation; **verdeckte** ~ disguised inflation; **zurückgestaute** ~ suppressed inflation.

Inflations|ausgleich allowance for inflation; ~**ausgleichssicherung** inflation proofing; ~**bekämpfung** struggle against inflation, anti-inflationary policy; **i~dämpfend** *adj* inflation-curbing; ~**druck** inflationary pressure; ~**erscheinung** inflationary symptom, sign of inflation; ~**frei** *adj* non-inflationary; ~**gefälle** inflation-rate differential; ~**gewinn** profit from inflation; ~**krise** inflationary crisis; ~**politik** inflationary policy; ~**rate** inflation rate, percentage of inflationary increase, *zweistellige* ~~: *double-digit inflation rate*; ~**rechnung** allowance for inflation in cost accounting; ~**schub** inflationary push; ~**sicherung** hedge against inflation; ~**spirale** inflationary spiral.

inflatorisch *adj* inflationary.

Informant *m* informant; informer; ~**enhaftung** liability of press informants; ~**enschutz** protection of disclosure of press informants.

Information *f* information, piece of information, knowledge; **allgemein zugängliche** ~**en** information in the public domain; **kursbeeinflussende** ~ price-sensitive information; **mit Vorrechten verbundene** ~**en** privileged information.

Informations|amt information office; ~**austauschvereinbarung** information agreement (*among bidders*); ~**bedürfnis** need for infor-

Infrastruktur — **Inhaber**

mation (*in the public interest*); ~**beschaffung** obtaining information; ~**besprechung** briefing conference; ~**büro** information office; ~**dienst** information service; ~**eingriff** interference with information (*by public authorities*); ~**freiheit** freedom of information; ~**honorar** fee for information; ~**interesse** the general public's interest in having freely available information; ~**leistung** information service; provision of information; ~**lücke** communication gap, Cack of information; ~**ministerium** Central Office of Information; ~**netze** information networks; ~**pflicht** duty to provide information, statutory requirement to furnish information; ~**quelle** source of information; *geheime* ~~: *confidential source of information;* ~**recht** right to (obtain) information; right to be informed; ~**schriften** information literature; ~**stelle** information bureau, information office; ~**system** information system; ~**verarbeitung** data processing; *sonstige einschlägige* ~**en** other relevant information; **ungesperrte** ~ unclassified information.

Infrastruktur *f* infrastructure; ~**vorhaben** infrastructure projects.

Ingangsetzung *f* start-up.

Ingebrauchnahme *f* starting to use sth, initial operation.

Ingenieur *m* engineer; ~**bau** construction engineering, civil engineering; ~**büro** (firm of) consulting engineers, (engineering) consultancy office; ~**wissenschaften** engineering; ~**gesetz** law concerning engineers; **beratender** ~ consulting engineer; **leitender** ~ chief engineer.

Ingerenzpflicht *f* obligation to impose (and enforce) compliance with the (constitutional) law.

Inhaber *m* bearer, holder, possessor, occupier, proprietor; ~**aktie** bearer share (certificate); ~**anteilschein** investment certificate made out to bearer; ~ **e-r Planstelle** holder of an established post, occupant of a regular position, regularly employed official; ~ **e-r Vollmacht** holder of a power of attorney; ~ **e-s Eigenwechsels** note holder; ~**e-s Passes** bearer of a passport; ~**e-s Warenzeichens** owner of a trade mark; ~ **e-s Wechsels** holder of a bill of exchange; *gutgläubiger* ~~~: → *gutgläubiger* ~; ~ **e-s Zwischenscheins** scrip holder, owner of interim certificate; ~**grundschuld** bearer land charge, land charge (*by way of mortgage*) evidenced by bearer-certificate; ~**hypothek** mortgage evidenced by bearer-certificate; ~**indossement** endorsement (over) to bearer; ~**klausel** bearer clause; ~**konnossement** negotiable bill of lading made out to bearer; ~**kreditbrief** open letter of credit; ~**lagerschein** negotiable warehouse receipt made out to bearer; ~**obligation** bearer bond, bond made out to bearer, interchangeable bond; ~**papier** negotiable instrument made out to bearer, bearer paper, bearer instrument, bearer bond; ~**police** bearer-policy; ~**scheck** bearer cheque; ~**schuldverschreibung** bearer bond, debenture bond; ~**solawechsel** promissory note made out to bearer; ~**versicherungspolice** insurance policy made out to bearer; ~**wechsel** bearer bill, bill payable to bearer, promissory note made out to bearer; ~**zeichen** bearer token; ~**zertifikat** certificate made out to bearer; **an den** ~ **zahlen** to pay to bearer; **auf den** ~ **ausstellen** to make out to bearer; **auf den** ~ **lauten** to be payable to bearer; **bösgläubiger** ~ mala fide holder; **eingetragener** ~ registered holder; **faktischer** ~ actual holder; **gegenwärtiger** ~ present holder, current owner; **gutgläubiger** ~ holder in good faith, bona fide holder, innocent holder for value; **jeweiliger** ~ holder for the time being; **legitimierter** ~ lawful holder, holder in due course; **nach-**

inhaftieren / **Inkompetenz**

folgender ~ subsequent holder; **rechtmäßiger** ~ lawful holder; **zahlbar an den** ~ payable to bearer.
inhaftieren *v/t* to arrest, to take into custody, to imprison, to incarcerate, to put in jail.
Inhaftierung *f* arrest, confinement, imprisonment; ~**squote** rate of incarceration; **vorbeugende** ~ preventive arrest.
Inhaftnahme *f* = Inhaftierung qv.
Inhalt *m* contents, subject matter; ~ **der Patentansprüche** terms of the claims; ~ **e-r Vereinbarung** subject matter of an agreement; **i**~**lich** in substance, in its contents; ~**sangabe** statement of contents; ~**sbeschreibung** description of contents; ~**irrtum** mistake as to the substance (*of a declaration*); ~**skontrolle** *von allgemeinen Geschäftsbedingungen* fair and reasonable test, terms control; **i**~**slos** devoid of substance; **des** ~, **daß ...** to the effect that; **nach dem** ~ **des Urteils** in accordance with the terms of the judgment; **sachlicher** ~ factual content; **seinem ganzen** ~ **nach** in all its particulars, in all its details; **wesentlicher** ~ essence, tenor, substance; **zum** ~ **haben** to purport.
Initial|werbung pioneering advertising; ~**zündung** initial ignition, priming the pump.
initiativ *adj* on one's own initiative, enterprising, initiatory.
Initiativ|antrag *m* private member's bill, notice of motion, proposed measure; ~**recht** to initiate legislation, right of (legislative) initiative, right to initiate proceedings (*or* measures).
Initiative *f* initiative; **aus eigener** ~ on one's own initiative (*or* motion); **die** ~ **beflügeln** to stimulate action, to encourage initiative; **privatwirtschaftliche** ~ private-business initiative; **unternehmerische** ~ entrepreneurial initiative.
Initiator *m* promoter, initiator.
injustitiabel *adj* nonjusticiable.

Inkasso *n* collection (*of bills*); cash against documents (*foreign trade*); ~**abtretung** assignment for (the purpose of) collection; ~**agent** collecting agent; ~**akzept** acceptance for collection; ~**auftrag** order for collection; ~**bank** collecting bank; ~**beamter** collecting official; ~**beauftragter** authorized collecting agent; ~**bevollmächtigter** authorized collecting agent; ~**büro** debt collection agency; ~**dienst** collection service; ~**erträge** proceeds of collection; ~**gebühr** collection charge; ~**geschäft** collecting business; ~**giro** "only for collection" endorsement, endorsement for collection; ~**indossament** "only for collection" endorsement, endorsement for collection; ~**kommission** collection in one's own name on behalf of another; ~**konten** accounts for the collection of payments; ~**mandat** order for collection, encashment order; ~**provision** collecting commission; ~**spesen** collecting charges; ~**tratte** bill drawn for collection; ~**unternehmen** debt-collecting agency; ~**vollmacht** power to collect, authority to collect; ~ **von Schecks** cheque collection; ~**wechsel** bill drawn for collection; ~**zession** assignment for (the purpose of) collection; ~ **zum Pariwert** par collection; **zum** ~ **von Kundenzahlungen berechtigt sein** to be entitled to collect payments from customers; **zum** ~ **vorzeigen** to present for collection.
Inkaufnahme *f* tacit acceptance, acquiescence.
Inklusivpreis *m* inclusive terms.
Inkognito-Adoption *f* anonymous adoption (*adoption without disclosing the identity of the adoptive parents to the mother of the child*).
Inkompatibilität *f* incompatibility (of office).
inkompetent *adj* incompetent, inefficient, not competent.
Inkompetenz *f* incompetence, inefficiency.

Inkonsequenz *f* inconsistency, inconsequence.

Inkorporation *f* incorporation (*of associations*); admission to a student's fraternity.

Inkraftbleiben *n* (the) remaining in force.

Inkraftsetzung *f* putting into operation, carrying into effect, enactment; **erneute** ~ revalidation; **vorläufige** ~ provisional introduction.

Inkrafttreten *n* entry into force; ~ **e-s Gesetzes** coming into force of a law, entry into force of an Act; ~ **e-s Vertrages** effective date of an agreement; **bei** ~ on entry into force; **bei** ~ **des Gesetzes** when the law (*or* Act) comes into effect (*or* becomes operative); **mit** ~ upon coming into force.

inkriminieren *v/t* to charge, to incriminate; *inkriminierend: incriminating; inkriminiert: incriminated, being the subject of a charge or suspicion.*

Inland *n* home country, interior of a state; **im** ~ within the country, domestically, at home.

Inländer *m* national (*of the state of residence*), national resident, native inhabitant of the home country; ~**behandlung** national treatment; ~**diskriminierung** discrimination against one's own nationals; ~**konvertibilität** convertibility for national residents.

inländisch *adj* internal, domestic, national, home-made.

Inlands|absatz domestic sales, sales in the home market, home sales; ~**anleihe** internal loan; ~**anmeldung** registration in home country; ~**aufenthalt** stay in one's home country; ~**auflage** national print run, domestic edition; ~**auftrag** inland order, order for the home market, *pl also*: domestic ordering, orders from domestic customers; **i**~**bedingt** due to internal causes, for domestic reasons; ~**belieferung** supplies to domestic customers; ~**besitz** internal holding, property held by residents; ~**bestellung** home-market order, order from a domestic customer; ~**beteiligung** capital investment in a domestic enterprise; ~**bezug** domestic connecting factor; ~**bruttosozialprodukt** gross domestic product; ~**einkommen** domestic income; ~**emission** internal issue, domestic issue; ~**erzeuger** home producer; ~**erzeugnis** domestic product, *agric* domestic produce; ~**erzeugung** production within the country, domestic production; ~**flugpreis** domestic air fare; ~**forderungen** domestic trade debtors; ~**gebühr** inland charge, domestic charge, domestic rate; ~**gesellschaft** domestic corporation, company domiciled inside the country; ~**hafen** domestic port; ~**investitionen** domestic investments; ~**kapital** domestic capital, capital available within the country; ~**kapitalmittel** sources of capital available within the country, domestic capital resources; ~**konjunktur** internal economic trends, internal business situation; ~**markt** home market, domestic market; ~**nachfrage** domestic demand; ~**porto** inland postage; ~**postanweisung** domestic postal money order, inland postal money order; ~**postverkehr** domestic postal service, internal mail service; ~**preis** domestic price, home-market price, internal price; ~**produkt** domestic product, *agr* domestic produce; ~**produktion** domestic production, home manufacture, internal production; ~**strecke** route inside the country; ~**tarif** inland rate, internal rate; ~**unternehmen** domestic enterprise; ~**verbindlichkeiten** internal liabilities, domestic liabilities, liabilities owed to creditors within the country; ~**verbrauch** home consumption, domestic consumption; ~**verbraucher** domestic consumer; ~**verfügbarkeit** available domestic supply; ~**verkehr** inland traffic; ~**vermögen** domestic property,

inliegend | **Inserat**

property situate within the country; ~**verschuldung** internal indebtedness (*of a country*), local debts; ~**vertreter** domestic agent; ~**währung** internal currency, local currency; ~**wechsel** domestic bill of exchange, inland bill (of exchange), domestic exchange; ~**wert** home value, value within the country, domestic valuation; **i~wirksam** *adj* producing effects inside the country, domestically effective; ~**wirkung** domestic effect; ~**zahlung** payment within the country.

inliegend *adj* enclosed, as an enclosure.

in natura *adj* in kind, in specie.

Innehaben *n* tenure, occupancy; **tatsächliches** ~ actual occupation.

innehaben *v/t* to hold, to occupy, to possess.

Innen|ausbau interior finishing; ~**ausstatter** interior designer; ~**ausstattung** interior finishing, interior decoration, ~**bereich** internal sphere, inner part of a community; *im* ~~: *intramural; internal;* ~**divergenz** city conflicting decisions of the same court; ~**finanzierung** internal financing; ~**finanzierungsmittel** internal financing resources; ~**gesellschaft** subpartnership, undisclosed association; ~**gesellschafter** internal partner; ~**haftung** internal liability (*of public servant to his superior authority*); ~**ladung** inboard cargo; ~**minister** Minister of the Interior, Interior Minister, *GB* Home Secretary, *US* Secretary of the Interior; ~**ministerium** Ministry of the Interior, *GB* Home Office, *US* Department of the Interior; ~**politik** domestic policy, (internal) politics; ~**revision** internal audit; ~**revisor** internal auditor; ~**stadt** city, innercity, town centre; ~~-*gebiet:* inner urban area; ~**umsatz** internal turnover, intercompany sales; ~**umsatzerlöse** proceeds from internal turnover (*of a group*); ~**verhältnis** internal relationship, relation inter se (*of partners etc.*), internal arrangements; *im* ~~: *inter partes*.

inner|betrieblich *adj* internal, within the firm (company, plant), in-house; ~**deutsch** inner-German, intra-German, ~**ehelich** interspousal; ~**europäisch** intra-European; ~**gemeinschaftlich** intra-Community; ~**halb** *prep* within; ~ *von 30 Tagen:* within 30 days; ~**organisatorisch** operational; ~**staatlich** national, municipal, intra-state; ~**städtisch** intra-city, municipal; within a town; ~~-*e Lagen:* in-town sites; ~**wirtschaftlich** as regards the country's internal economy, domestic.

innewohnend *adj* inherent, intrinsic.

Innovationsfähigkeit *f* innovativeness.

Innung *f* guild, craft guild.

Innungs|ausschuß craft-guild committee; ~**krankenkasse** craft-guild health insurance; ~**schiedsgericht** craft-guild arbitration court; ~**verband** association of craft guilds.

inoffiziell *adj* unofficial, non-official; off-the-record.

Inpfandnahme *f* accepting a pledge.

Inpflichtnahme *f* imposition of an obligation (*by the state*), recruitment.

Inquisition *f* inquisition, official inquiry; ~**smaxime** principle of ex-officio judicial investigation, inquisitorial system; ~**sprozeß** inquisitorial proceedings, court proceedings based on ex-officio investigation, inquisitorial trial; ~**sverfahren** inquisitorial proceedings.

Inrechnungstellung *f* invoicing; ~ **von Anwaltsgebühren** fee charging.

Insasse *m* inmate, occupant, dweller; passenger; ~**nunfallversicherung** passenger accident insurance.

insbesondere *adv* especially, in particular, particularly, in particular but not limited to.

Inserat *n* advertisement, announcement, notice inserted in a news-

Inserent

paper; ~**preisliste** rate card, advertisement price list; **amtliches** ~ official advertisement.
Inserent *m* advertizer.
inserieren *v/i* to put an advertisement (in a paper), to advertize.
Insertionskosten *pl* advertizing charges.
Insich|geschäft *n* self-dealing, self-contracting, acting as principal and agent; ~**prozeß** inter se proceedings (*between public bodies*).
Insider *m* insider, ~**delikte** insider offences; ~**handel** insider trading; ~**regeln** insider trading directives.
Insignien *pl* insignia.
insolvent *adj* insolvent.
Insolvenz *f* insolvency; ~**en** business failures; ~**niveau** level of insolvency; ~**recht** insolvency law; ~**risiko** risk of insolvency; ~**schutz** protection of employees in case of insolvency; ~**sicherung** insolvency insurance, *compulsory participation in insolvency fund for old-age pension schemes*.
Inspekteur *m* inspecting officer, inspector.
Inspektion *f* inspection, check, service check; ~**sbefugnis** visitorial power, power of inspection.
Inspektor *m* inspector, superintendent, overseer; ~**en der Gesundheitsämter** sanitary inspectors.
inspizieren *v/t* to inspect, to examine, to check.
Installateur *m* fitter, plumber.
Installation *f* installation, plumbing and house-fitting; ~**sarbeiten** plumbing, sanitary installation work; ~**sartikel** sanitary fixtures and fittings.
„**Instandbesetzung**" *f squatting in dilapidated tenement under pretext of doing repair work (a pun)*.
Instandhaltbarkeit *f* maintainability.
instandhalten *v/t* to maintain, to keep in good repair.
Instandhaltung *f* maintenance, maintenance and repair, upkeep, preservation; ~**sarbeiten** maintenance works, repairs; *notwendige*

Institut

~~: *necessary repairs;* ~**sintervall** maintenance interval; ~**skosten** maintenance costs; ~**srücklage** reserve for future repairs (*condominium*); ~**srückstellung** provision for repairs; ~**szeitfolge** period of maintenance; **laufende** ~ continual maintenance; **vorbeugende** ~ preventive maintenance.
instandsetzen *v/t* to repair.
Instandsetzung *f* repairs, reconditioning, renovation, redecorating; ~**anspruch** right to have sth. repaired; ~**sarbeiten** repairs; ~**sdarlehen** loan for repair and maintenance work; ~**dauer** repair time; ~**skosten** expenses for repair and maintenance work; ~**spflicht** obligation to repair.
Instanz *f* instance; level of authority; ~**en überspringen** to leapfrog, to bypass official channels; ~**enweg** stages of appeal, official channels; *den* ~~ *nicht einhalten: to ignore channels*; ~**enzug** sequence of courts, successive stages of appeal; *administrativer* ~~: *administrative channels*; ~**vollmacht** *authority of counsel limited to one court instance*; **alle** ~ **durchlaufen** to pass through all instances; **an die erste** ~ **zurückverweisen** to remand (*or* refer) the case back to the court of first instance; **beaufsichtigende** ~ supervising authority; **bundesstaatliche** ~**en** federal authorities; **erste** ~ court of first instance, trial court; **fiskalpolitische** ~**en** authorities concerned with fiscal policy; **höchste** ~ court of last resort, final court of appeal; **höhere** ~ higher court, appellate court; *e–e höhere* ~ *anrufen: to appeal to a higher court*; **letzte** ~ court of last resort, final court of appeal; *in* ~*r* ~: *in the last instance*; **obere** ~ higher instance; **untere** ~ lower instance, the lower court, the court below; **zuständige** ~ the proper authority *or* instance.
Institut *n* institute; ~ **für Chemisch-Technische Unter-**

428

Institution / **Interessenabwägung**

suchungen Federal Institute for Chemical and Technical Investigations; ~ **für Nuklearmedizin** Institute for Nuclear Medicine; ~ **für Sozialmedizin und Epidemiologie** Institute for Social Medicine and Epidemiology; ~ **für Strahlenhygiene** Institute for Radiation Health; ~ **für Veterinärmedizin** Institute for Veterinary Medicine; ~ **für Wasser-, Boden- und Lufthygiene** Institute for Water, Soil, and Air Hygiene.

Institution *f* institution; **~en der Kapitalvermittlung** transmitters of capital; **~slehre** theory of business structures; **~sverband** association of institutions; **e–e rechtlich einheitliche** ~ an institution forming a legal entity; **fiskalische und parafiskalische ~en** governmental and quasi-governmental institutions; **öffentliche ~en** public institutions, public services; **staatliche ~en** governmental institutions; state *or* national institutions.

institutionell *adj* institutional, *relating to an established system or arrangement*.

instruieren *v/t* to instruct, to brief.

Instruktionsfehler *f* mistake in the instructions (*by manufacturer as to proper use of product*).

Instrument *n* instrument, device, appliance; ~ **der Konjunkturpolitik** the means of giving effect to cyclical policy; *or* instruments; **kreditpolitisches** ~ instrument of credit policy.

Instrumentarium *n* instrumentality set of instruments; **konjunkturpolitisches** ~ economic policy tools; **kreditpolitisches** ~ means of enforcing credit policy, measures of credit policy.

Integration *f* integration; **~sfunktion** integrating function; **vertikale** ~ vertical integration; **wirtschaftliche** ~ economic integration, absorption.

integrieren *v/t* to integrate.

Integrität *f* integrity; **körperliche** ~ physical integrity; **territoriale** ~ territorial inviolability.

integrieren *v/t* to integrate, to absorb, to complete.

Intendant *m* general manager, director; (general), *(of a theatre, radio and television corporation)*.

Intensivhaltung *f* intensive rearing *(in cages etc)*.

Intensivstation *f* intensive care unit.

Interbank|aktiva *n/pl* inter-bank assets; **~rate** inter-bank rate (*Euromarket*); **~verflechtung** interlocking arrangements between banks.

Interbankenmarkt *m* interbank market.

Interesse *n* interest, concern, stake, regard; ~ **am Ausgang des Rechtsstreits** interest in the result of a case; ~ **der Allgemeinheit** general interest of the public; **allgemeines** ~ common interest; **berechtigtes** ~ legitimate interest, justified interest; **eigenes** ~ own interest, private interest; **fehlendes** ~ lack of interest; **finanzielles** ~ pecuniary (*or* financial) interest; **gemeinsames** ~ common interest; **im** ~ **der Kürze** for the sake of brevity; **im** ~ **des Mandanten** in the client's interest; **öffentliches** ~ public interest; *im ~n ~:* (*expedient*) *in the public interest, for the public benefit; im ~n* ~ *liegend: conducive to the public good; gegen das ~e* ~ *verstoßend: contrary to the public interest;* **ohne** ~ **für die Öffentlichkeit** of no public concern; **rechtliches** ~ legal interest, lawful interests; **versicherbares** ~ insurable interest; **versicherungsfähiges** ~ insurable interest; **versichertes** ~ interest insured; **wirtschaftliches** ~ economic interest.

Interessen|abwägung weighing of interests; **~ausgleich** balance of interests, settlement of conflicting interests; **~gebiet** sphere of influence; **~gemeinschaft** community of interests, joint venture; **~gruppen** interest groups, pressure groups, vested interests; **~juris-**

prudenz 'jurisprudence (*or:* theory) of interests' (*taking the interests of the parties into account*); ~**käufe** support buying, buying by special interests; ~**kollision** conflict of interests, clash of interests; ~**konflikt** conflict of interests; ~**lage** nature of the interests involved; ~**politik** policy based on one's own interests; ~**quoten-Soll** required quotas (of participation); ~**sphäre** sphere of interest; ~**verband** association representing common interests; interest group, pressure group; ~**vereinigung** association of interested parties, community of interests; ~**verknüpfung** joining of interests, linking of interests; ~**vertreter** agent for special interests, lobbyist; ~**vertretung** representation of interests, body representing interests, special pleading; **i**~**nwahrend** safeguarding of interests; ~ **wahren** to safeguard interests; ~**wahrnehmung** representation (of s.o.'s interests); ~**wahrung** safeguarding of interests; ~**widerstreit** conflict of interests; ~**zusammenführung** pooling of interests; **entsprechend den ~ des Unternehmers handeln** act in the principal's best interests; **gesellschaftseigene ~** the company's (*or* partnership's) own interests; **jmds ~ beeinträchtigen** to impair s.o.'s interests; **jmds ~ wahrnehmen** to attend to a person's interests; ~**wahrnehmung** protection *or* safeguarding of interests; **kollidierende ~** conflicting interests; **lebenswichtige ~** vital interests; **widerstreitende ~** conflicting interests.

Interessent *m* (the) interested party, party concerned, potential customer (*or* purchaser); *pl* ~**en**: parties interested, interested parties; ~**enpapier** security manipulated by interested parties, manipulated shares, vested-interest paper.

Interims|aktie provisional share certificate; ~**ausschuß** interim committee; ~**bilanz** interim balance sheet; ~**dividende** interim dividend; ~**kabinett** interim cabinet; ~**konto** suspense account, interim deposit account; ~**quittung** provisional receipt; ~**regierung** provisional government, interim government; ~**schein** interim certificate, (provisional) scrip; *auf den Namen lautender* ~~: *registered scrip*; ~**vertrag** interim agreement, provisional management contract.

interkonfessionell *adj* inter-denominational.

interlokal *adj* interregional.

international *adj* international, world-wide.

Internationale *f* the Internationale (*socialist hymn*); international marxist movement.

Internationale | **Arbeitsorganisation** International Labour Organization; ~ **Atomenergie-Organisation** International Atomic Energy Agency; ~ **Bank für Wiederaufbau und Entwicklung** International Bank for Reconstruction and Development (*World Bank*); ~ **Energie-Agentur** International Energy Agency; ~ **Entwicklungsorganisation** International Development Association; ~ **Fernmeldesatellitenorganisation** International Telecommunications Satellite Organization; ~ **Fernmelde-Union** International Telecommunication Union; ~ **Finanz-Corporation** International Finance Corporation; ~ **Handelskammer** International Chamber of Commerce; ~ **Hydrographische Konferenz** International Hydrographic Conference; ~ **Hydrographische Organisation** International Hydrographic Organization; ~ **Kaffee-Organisation** International Coffee Organization; ~ **Kakao-Organisation** International Cocoa Organization; ~ **Kautschukstudiengruppe** International Rubber Study Group; ~ **Kommission für Be- und Entwässerung** International Commission on Irrigation

Internationale Kommission   **Internationaler Weizenrat**

and Drainage; ~ **Kommission für das Zivilstandswesen** International Commission on Civil Status; ~ **Kommission für die Nordwestatlantische Fischerei** International Commission for the Northwest Atlantic Fisheries; ~ **Kommission für landwirtschaftliche Industrien** International Commission for Agricultural Industries; ~ **Kommission zum Schutze des Rheins gegen Verunreinigung** International Commission for the Protection of the Rhine against Pollution; ~ **Kriminalpolizeiliche Organisation** International Criminal Police Organization; ~ **Organisation für das gesetzliche Messwesen** International Organization of Legal Metrology; ~ **Organisation für Normung** International Organization for Standardization; ~ **Pappelkommission** International Poplar Commission; ~ **Recherchenbehörde** *pat* International Searching Authority; ~ **Regeln** International Regulations; ~ **Studiengruppe für Blei und Zink** International Lead and Zinc Study Group; ~ **Studienzentrale für die Erhaltung und Restaurierung von Kulturgut** International Centre for the Study of the Preservation and Restoration of Cultural Property; ~ **Union für die Erhaltung der Natur und der natürlichen Hilfsquellen** International Union for Conservation of Nature and Natural Resources; ~ **Zivilluftfahrt-Organisation** International Civil Aviation Organization.

Internationaler | **Ausschuß für den Internationalen Suchdienst** International Commission for the International Tracing Service; ~ **Ausschuß zur Frequenzregistrierung** International Frequency Registration Board; ~ **Baumwoll-Beratungsausschuß** International Cotton Advisory Committee; ~ **Beratender Ausschuß für den Funkdienst** International Radio Consultative Committee; ~ **Beratender Ausschuß für den Telegraphen- und Fernsprechdienst** International Telegraph and Telephone Consultative Committee; ~ **Eiswachdienst im Nordatlantik** International Ice Patrol Service in the North Atlantic, North Atlantic Ice Patrol; ~ **Entschädigungsfonds für Ölverschmutzungsschäden** International Oil Pollution Compensation Fund; ~ **Fonds für Agrarentwicklung** International Fund for Agricultural Development; ~ **Gerichtshof** International Court of Justice; ~ **Jugendaustausch- und Besucherdienst der Bundesrepublik Deutschland eV** International Youth Exchange and Visitors' Service of the Federal Republic of Germany; ~ **Kaffeefonds** International Coffee Fund; ~ **Kaffeerat** International Coffee Council; ~ **Kakaorat** International Cocoa Council; ~ **Militärgerichtshof** International Military Tribunal; ~ **Museumsrat** International Council of Museums; ~ **Normenausschuß** *m* International Standardization Organization; ~ **Rat** International Council; ~ **Rat für Meeresforschung** International Council for the Exploration of the Sea; ~ **Rat Wissenschaftlicher Vereinigungen** International Council of Scientific Unions; ~ **Sozialdienst** International Social Service; ~ **Suchdienst** International Tracing Service; ~ **Verband für die Veröffentlichung der Zolltarife** International Union for the Publication of Customs Tariffs; ~ **Verband für die Zusammenarbeit auf dem Gebiet des Patentwesens** International Patent Cooperation Union; ~ **Verband zum Schutz des gewerblichen Eigentums** International Union for the Protection of Industrial Property; ~ **Währungsfonds** International Monetary Fund; ~ **Weizenrat** In-

Internationales / **Interventionsakzept**

ternational Wheat Council; ~ **Zinnrat** International Tin Council; ~ **Zuckerrat** International Sugar Council.

Internationales | Abkommen über den Schutz der ausübenden Künstler, der Hersteller von Tonträgern und der Sendeunternehmen *(1961)* Rome Convention for the Protection of Performers, Producers of Phonograms and Broadcasting Organizations; ~ **Amt für Rebe und Wein** International Vine and Wine Office; ~ **Arbeitsamt** International Labour Office *ILO*; ~ **Ausstellungsbüro** International Exhibitions Bureau; ~ **Baumwoll-Institut** International Institute for Cotton; ~ **Büro für geistiges Eigentum** International Bureau of Intellectual Property; ~ **Büro für Maß und Gewicht** International Bureau of Weights and Measures; ~ **Energieprogramm** International Energy Program; ~ **Erziehungsbüro** International Bureau of Education; ~ **Hydrographisches Büro** International Hydrographic Bureau; ~ **Institut für Führungsaufgaben in der Technik** International Institute for the Management of Technology; ~ **Institut für die Vereinheitlichung des Privatrechts** International Institute for the Unification of Private Law; ~ **Kälteinstitut** International Institute of Refrigeration; ~ **Komitee vom Roten Kreuz** International Committee of the Red Cross; ~ **Rotes Kreuz** International Red Cross; ~ **Statistisches Institut** International Statistical Institute; ~ **Suchtstoff-Kontrollamt** International Narcotics Control Board; ~ **Tierseuchenamt** International Office of Epizootics; ~ **Weinamt** International Wine Office; ~ **Zentrum zur Beilegung von Investitionsstreitigkeiten** International Centre for Settlement of Investment Disputes.

internationalisieren *v/t* to internationalize, to grant international status.

Internatsschule *f* boarding school, public school *(GB)*; **private** ~: *privately owned boarding school*, public school *(GB)*.

internieren *v/t* to intern.

Internierter *n* *(der Internierte)* detainee, internee, prisoner.

Internierung *f* internment, detention; ~**sbefehl** internment order; ~**shaft** detention in an internment camp, internment; ~**slager** internment camp.

Internist *m* specialist in internal medicine, internist.

interparlamentarisch *adj* interparliamentary.

Interpellant *m* interpellator.

Interpellation *f* interpellation; ~**srecht** right of interpellation.

interpellieren *v/i* to interpellate.

interpolieren *v/i* to interpolate.

Interpretation *f* interpretation, construction; ~**svorschrift** canon of construction, rule of interpretation.

interpretieren *v/t* to interpret, to construe.

Interregnum *n* interregnum.

intervalutarisch *adj* inter-currency, cross-exchange, across the exchange.

intervenieren *v/t* to intervene, to intercede, to interfere, to interpost.

Intervenient *m* intervener, intervening party.

Intervention *f* intervention, intercession, interference, interposition, *com* acceptance for honour, acceptance supra protest; *pl (exch) also*: pegging operations; **bewaffnete** ~ armed intervention.

Interventionismus *m* system of state interference in economic affairs.

Interventions|akzept acceptance for honour, acceptance supra protest, acceptance upon protest; ~**berechtigter** party entitled to intervene; ~**bestand** holding acquired by intervention (on the market); ~**grenze** intervention limit; ~**käufe** support purchases; ~**klage** action of replevin, action

Interzession

of intervention, action of third party opposition; ~**konsortium** intervening syndicate; ~**krieg** war of intervention; ~**kurs** intervention rate; ~**politik** policy of intervention, (or of interference); ~**punkt** intervention point (*by central bank*), intervention level, support point; peg; ~**recht** right of intervention; ~**verbot** prohibition of intervention (*int law*).

Interzession *f* intercession, pledge for the debt of another.

Intestat *n* intestacy.

Intestats|erbe heir under the rules of intestacy, heir by intestate succession; ~**erbfolge** intestate succession; ~**erblasser** intestate; ~**nachlaß** intestate estate, *estate of a deceased who died without leaving a will*.

Intimsphäre *f* sphere of (utmost) privacy; **Verletzung der** ~ infringement of privacy.

Intrigant *m* intrigant, intriguer, schemer.

Intrige *f* intrigue, underhand plotting, machination.

intrigieren *v/t* to intrigue, to carry on an underhand plot or scheme.

Invalide *m* invalid, (physically) disabled person; ~**nmarke** social insurance stamp *obs*; ~**nrente** disability pension; ~**nversicherung** national disability insurance for workers, workmen's compensation insurance.

Invalidität *f* disablement, physical disability, invalidity, invalidism; **dauernde** ~ permanent disablement; **vollständige** ~ complete disablement, 100% invalidity.

Invaliditäts|grad degree of disability; ~**rente** disablement pension, invalidity pension; ~**versicherung** disability insurance; ~**wahrscheinlichkeit** disability rate; ~**zusatzversicherung** additional invalidity insurance.

Inventar *n* inventory, stock; list of the deceased's assets and liabilities; ~**aufnahme** stock-taking; ~**aufstellung** making (or drawing up) an inventory; ~**bewertung** inven-

Inventur

tory valuation; ~**buch** stock book, stock ledger; ~**erbe** *heir who has inventorized the estate*; ~**errichtung** filing an inventory (*law of succession*); ~**frist** inventory period (*law of succession*); ~**kurs** inventory rate; ~**liste** inventory list; ~**gegenstand** inventory item; ~**kredit** credit for the purchase of working equipment; ~**posten** inventory item; ~**prüfung** inventory audit, inventory control; ~**recht** legal provisions concerning inventories; ~**untreue** fraudulent inventorizing of an estate (*by an heir*); ~**veränderung** change in business inventory; *bereinigte* ~~*en*: *net change in business inventories*; ~**verfehlungen** unlawful manipulations concerning inventories; ~**verlust** inventory loss; ~**verzeichnis** inventory, inventory list, inventory sheet; ~**wert** inventory value; ~**wertberichtigung** inventory revaluation; ~**wertschwankung** inventory fluctuation; **ein** ~ **aufnehmen** to take stock, to take an inventory of; **landwirtschaftliches** ~ farm stock; **lebendes** ~ livestock; **lebendes und totes** ~ livestock, implements and machinery, live-stock and dead-stock; **totes** ~ dead-stock; **unverkäufliches** ~ dead-stock.

inventarisieren *v/t* to inventory, to make (or draw up) an inventory.

Inventur *f* taking inventory, physical inventory, stock-taking; ~**ausverkauf** stock-taking sale, clearance sale, pre-inventory sale; ~**bestandsaufnahme** physical count of inventory; ~**bewertung** inventory valuation; ~**differenz** inventory discrepancy; inventory balance; ~ **durch körperliche Bestandsaufnahme** physical inventory; ~**erstellung** stock-taking; ~**prüfung** inventory verification, inventory audit; ~**system** stock control; ~**verkauf** clearance sale, stock-taking sale; pre-inventory sale; ~**wert pro Einheit** inventory value per unit.

433

Inverkehrbringen *n* putting into circulation, spreading, uttering, marketing; ~ **von Falschgeld** uttering counterfeit money.

Inverzugsetzung *f* giving notice of default, demanding overdue payment, request for overdue performance, declaration of default.

investieren *v/i, v/t* to invest.

Investierung *f* investment, investing; ~**svorhaben** investment project; **inländische** ~**en im Ausland** German investments abroad.

Investigationsrecht *n* right of investigation.

Investition *f* investment, capital investment, investing (*of capital, money etc*); ~**en der öffentlichen Hand** public investments, public capital expenditure; **betriebliche** ~**en** capital projects; **maschinelle und bauliche** ~**en** capital expenditure on machinery and on building; **risikoarme** ~**en** investments entailing little risk, safe investments.

Investitions|abschreibungen investment (= *inv*) depreciation allowance; ~**anleihe** *inv* loan; ~**anreiz** *inv* incentive; ~**antrag** *inv* proposal; ~**aufsicht** *inv* supervision (*of electricity companies by the state*); ~**aufwand** *inv* expenditure; ~**aufwendung** *inv* expenditure; ~**bank** *inv* bank; ~**bedarf** need for *inv; aufgestauter* ~~: *accumulated need for inv;* ~**beihilfe** *inv* grant; ~**bereich** field of capital *inv*; ~**beurteilung** capital project evaluation; ~**chancen** *inv* prospects; ~**darlehen** permanent loan; ~**dispositionen** capital *inv* (dispositions); ~**fähigkeit** *inv* capacity; ~**finanzierung** *inv* financing, financing of capital projects; ~**fonds** *inv* fund; ~**förderung** *inv* backing, *inv* funding; ~**freigabe** release of funds for *inv* purposes; ~**freudigkeit** readiness to incur capital expenditure; ~**geschäft** *inv* transaction; ~**güter** capital goods, *inv* goods, *inv* property; ~**güter-Fertigwaren** finished capital goods; ~**güterindustrie** capital-goods industry; ~**güterkonjunktur** trend in capital goods; ~**güter-Rohstoffe** raw materials for capital goods; ~**haushalt** extraordinary or capital budget; ~**hilfe** *inv* aid; ~**hilfe-Abgabe** *inv* assistance levy; ~**hilfegesetz** Inv Assistance Act; ~**impuls** incentive to invest; ~**kapital** invested capital, capital for *inv*; ~**klima** climate for investing; ~**konjunktur** boom in capital *inv* business, trends in the *inv* field; ~**kontrolle** *inv* control, capital spending control, *inv* steering; ~**kosten** cost of *inv*, capital cost; ~**kredit** *inv* credit, capital *inv* loan, loan to finance capital projects; ~**leistungen** *inv* effected, *inv* performance; ~**lenkung** direction of capital *inv; staatliche* ~~: *government direction of capital inv;* ~**meldepflicht** duty to report on intended investments; ~**mittel** investable resources, *inv* funds; ~**müdigkeit** reluctance to invest; ~**nachfrage** demand for *inv;* ~**nachholbedarf** lag in *inv*, pent-up demand for *inv;* ~**neigung** propensity (*or* tendency) to invest; ~**neuling** novice investor; ~**niveau** level of *inv;* ~**periode** *inv* period; ~**plan** *inv* plan, capital development budget; ~**politik** *inv* policy; ~**prämie** (capital) *inv* premium; ~**projekt** *inv* project, capital expenditure plan; ~**quote** rate of *inv*, *inv* ratio; ~**rate** rate of gross *inv* to GNP (*at market prices*); ~**rechnung** capital expenditure account, *inv* calculation, capital budgeting; ~**risiko** risk of investing, *inv* risk; ~**rücknahme** disinvestment; ~**schema** pattern of *inv*; ~**schutz** (international) protection of *inv*; ~**-Schwerpunkt** priority in capital *inv*; ~**spritze** *inv* boost; ~**steuer** capital *inv* tax; ~**tätigkeit** *inv*, *inv* activity; ~**träger** investor; ~**umlage** betterment levy; ~**vorgang** (capital) *inv* operation; ~**vorhaben** capital project, *inv* project; ~**vorranggesetz** Investment Priority Act (*regarding restitu-*

Investitur

tion of expropriated property in the former East Germany); ~**williger** party wishing to engage in *inv*, prospective investor; ~**zulage** *inv* (tax) allowance; ~**zuschuß** capital *inv* grant, capital grant.

Investitur *f* investiture.

Investivlohn *m* investable wage (*employees' incentive scheme*).

Investment *n* investment (*in an investment trust*); ~**anteil** investment fund share (*or* unit certificate); ~**bank** investment company; ~**fonds** → *Investmentfonds*; ~**geschäft** investment fund business; ~**gesellschaft** → *Investmentgesellschaft*; ~**papier** unit certificate (of an investment company); ~**sparen** saving through investment companies, investment fund saving; ~**trust** investment trust, mutual fund; ~**vermittler** investment broker; ~**zertifikat** investment fund certificate.

Investmentfonds *m* investment fund, mutual fund *(US)*, unit trust *(GB)*, fixed fund, unit investment trust; ~ **mit auswechselbarem Portefeuille** flexible fund, managed fund; ~ **mit auswechselbarem Wertpapierbestand** flexible fund, managed fund; ~ **mit begrenzt auswechselbarem Portefeuille** semi-fixed fund; ~ **mit begrenzter Emissionshöhe** closed-end fund; ~ **mit unbeschränkter Anteilsemission** open-end fund.

Investmentgesellschaft *f* investment company; ~ **mit breitgestreutem Portefeuille** general management trust, unit trust with assorted portfolio; ~ **mit gesetzlicher Risikoverteilung** diversified company; ~ **mit konstantem Anlagekapital** closed-end investment trust; ~ **ohne gesetzliche Anlagestreuung** non-diversified company.

Investor *m* investor.

Inzahlungnahme *f* trade-in, taking sth in part exchange.

Inzest *m* incest.

Inzident|feststellungsklage *f* = *Zwischenfeststellungsklage qv*.

ipso jure *adv* by operation of law, ipso jure, by act of law.

irreführen *v/t* to mislead, to deceive.

irreführend *adj* misleading, deceiving.

Irreführung *f* misleading (*customers, the public*), intentional misrepresentation, fraudulent representation; deception.

irrelevant *adj* irrelevant, immaterial.

Irrelevanz *f* irrelevance, inapplicability.

Irrenanstalt *f* lunatic asylum, mental institution, mental hospital.

irreversibel *adj* irreversible, final non-appealable on points of law.

irrig *f* erroneous, mistaken, incorrect.

Irrläufer *m* mis-sent item.

Irrsinn *m* insanity, lunacy.

Irrtum *m* mistake, error; ~ **im Beweggrund** mistake as to motivation; ~ **im Motiv** mistake as to motivation; ~ **über den Vertragsgegenstand** mistake as to the subject matter of the contract; ~ **über die Eheschließung** error regarding the contract of marriage; ~ **über die Natur des Geschäfts** error in negotio, mistake as to the nature of the transaction; ~ **über die Person** error in persona, mistake in identity; ~ **über die Strafbarkeit** mistake as to the punishability of an act; ~ **über e-e Tatsache** mistake of fact, factual error; ~ **über e-e unwesentliche Eigenschaft** irrelevant mistake; ~ **über e-e wesentliche Eigenschaft** mistake as to an important quality (*or* property), mistake on the subject matter; ~ **vorbehalten** save error and omission, barring errors; *Irrtümer und Auslassungen vorbehalten*: errors and omissions excepted (e.a.o.e.); **auf e-m ~ beruhen** to be due to a mistake; **beachtlicher ~** material mistake; substantial error; **e-n ~ klarstellen** to clear up a mistake, to clarify the situation; **e-n ~ richtigstellen** to rectify an error; **ent-**

irrtümlich

schuldbarer ~ excusable mistake, venial offence; **erwiesener** ~ clearly proven mistake; **offenbarer** ~ obvious error, clear mistake; **rechtlicher** ~ mistake in law; **rechtserheblicher** ~ legally relevant mistake, bona fide mistake; **sachlicher** ~ mistake of fact, factual error; **sich auf** ~ **berufen** to assert that one was mistaken, to plead mistake, to allege the existence of an error; **tatsächlicher** ~ mistake of fact, factual error; **unbeachtlicher** ~ immaterial mistake, unimportant error; **wesentlicher** ~ material mistake, error on an important point, grave error.

irrtümlich *adj* mistaken, erroneous, inadvertent.

Irrtums|anfechtung avoidance on account of mistake; **~erregung** deception; **~vorbehalt** clause excepting errors; **~wahrscheinlichkeit** error probability, likelihood of a mistake (occurring).

Isolationismus *m* isolationism.
Isolationsfolter *f* "isolation torture"; *inhumane treatment by lengthy solitary confinement.*
Isolierhaft *f* solitary confinement.
Isolierzelle *f* solitary confinement cell *(for prisoners held incommunicado).*
Ist|ausgabe actual expenditure; **~bestand** actual stock, stock in hand, actual amount, present figure; **~betrag** actual amount; **~bilanz** actual balance sheet; **~einnahmen** actual receipts, actual takings; **~kosten** actual costs (and expenses); **~leistung** actual output, actual performance; **~prämie** actual premium; **~reserve** actual reserve, de facto reserve; **~stärke** actual strength; **~stunden** actual man-hours; **~versteuerung** actual payment of *(turnover)* taxes; **~wert** true value, actual value, actual cash value; **~zeit** time taken, actual time; **~zustand** „as is" condition.

J

Ja *n* yes, affirmative (answer); ~-**Stimme** affirmative vote, aye, pro; vote for; ~**wort** approval, consent, acceptance of a marriage proposal; **ein schlichtes ~ oder Nein** a simple yes or no; **mit ~ antworten** to answer yes, to answer in the affirmative, to affirm.

Jagd|ausübung hunting; ~**ausübungsberechtigter** holder of a hunting licence; ~**behörden** hunting authorities; ~**beirat** hunting advisory commission; ~**berechtigter** person authorized to hunt, holder of a hunting licence; ~**berechtigung** hunting authorization, shooting rights; ~**beschränkungen** hunting restrictions; ~**bezirk** hunting district; ~**erlaubnis** game licence, hunting licence; ~**erlaubnisschein** hunting licence (certificate); ~**gebiet** hunting ground; ~**genossenschaft** *official association of proprietors of hunting rights;* ~**gesetz** game law, hunting law; ~**inhaber** proprietor of hunting rights; ~**ordnung** hunting regulations; ~**pacht** lease of a hunting ground; ~**pächter** game tenant, shooting tenant; ~**pachtvertrag** hunting lease; ~**recht** game law, hunting right; ~**regal** prerogative of hunting, proprietary hunting rights; ~**revier** hunting district, hunting ground; ~**schaden** damage caused by hunters; ~**schutz** game and hunting protection (regulations); ~**schein** hunting licence, game licence, shooting licence; ~**schutz** game and hunting protection (regulatious); ~**steuer** tax on hunting; ~**vergehen** game trespass; ~**vorstand** *president of a Jagdgenossenschaft qv;* ~**waffenschein** hunting weapons licence; ~**wesen** hunting; ~**wilderei** poaching; ~**zeit** hunting season, shooting season.

Jahr *n* year; ~**buch** yearbook; *statistisches* ~~: *statistical abstract*; ~**gang** year, age-group (by year); ~**markt** *m* fair, fun fair; **anrechnungsfähiges ~** year of coverage; **auf drei ~e gewählt** elected for a term of three years; **aufeinanderfolgende ~e** successive years; **auf zehn ~e vermietet** let for ten years; **bürgerliches ~** civil year; **das laufende ~** the current year; **das vergangene ~** the previous year; **das vorvergangene ~** the penultimate year; two years previous; **nach ~ und Tag** after a year and a day; **pro ~** per year, per annum.

Jahres|abonnement annual subscription; ~**abgrenzung** year-end deferrals; ~**abrechnung** yearly account, annual statement of accounts; ~**abschluß** annual accounts, annual financial statements, annual balance sheet and profit and loss account; ~**abschlußbuchung** entry made at annual closing of accounts; ~**abschlußprüfung** annual audit; ~**abschlußzahlungen** end-of-year payments; ~**abschreibung** annual depreciation (charge); ~**arbeitslohn** annual wage; ~**arbeitsverdienst** annual earnings; ~**ausgleich** annual wage-tax adjustment; ~**beitrag** annual contribution, annual subscription; ~**bericht** annual report, annual statement; ~**bericht nebst Bilanz und Gewinn- und Verlustrechnung** annual statement of income and surplus; ~**betrag** annual amount; ~**bilanz** annual balance sheet, balance sheet for the fiscal year; ~**dividende** annual di-

437

Jahresdurchschnitt / **judikatorisch**

vidend; ~**durchschnitt** yearly average, annual average; ~**durchschnittsverdienst** annual average earnings; ~**einkommen** annual income, total net income; ~**endbeanspruchung** credits taken at the end of the year; ~**ergebnis** net annual profit, annual (financial) results; ~~**wert**: *annual value*; ~**erhebung** annual assessment, annual review; ~**ertrag** annual proceeds, annual income, yearly output; ~**fehlbetrag** loss for the year, annual deficit; ~**förderung** annual output; ~**freibetrag** annual allowance; ~**frist** period of one year; *binnen* ~~: *within a year; nach* ~~: *after one year*; ~**gebühr** annual fee, renewal fee, annuity; ~**gehalt** annual salary; ~**gewinn** year's earnings, annual profit; ~**hauptversammlung** annual general meeting; ~**haushalt** annual budget; ~**hinzurechnungsbetrag** annual surcharge, annual addition; ~**höchstspitze** annual peak; ~**honorar** annual fee; ~**lizenzgebühr** annual licence fee, annual royalty; ~**lohn** annual wage, year's wages; *garantierter* ~~: *guaranteed annual wage*; ~**lohnrunde** annual round of wage bargaining; ~**lohnsteuer** annual wage tax; ~**lohnsteuerausgleich** annual wage tax adjustment; ~**miete** annual rent (*tenancy*); ~**pacht** annual rent (*under a lease*), annual lease payment; *auf* ~~ *vergeben: to farm out*; ~**periode** yearly period; ~**police** annual policy; ~**prämie** annual bonus *paid to employees, ins* annual premium; ~**produktion** annual output; ~**punkt** annual point; ~**rate** annual instalment, yearly rate; ~**rechnung** computation on a yearly basis, yearly account; ~**rente** annuity, pension per year; ~**reingewinn** annual net profit; ~**rente** annual income from capital; ~**rhythmus** yearly (economic) cycle; ~**rohmiete** gross annual rent(al); ~**schluß** end of the year; ~**schlußbuchung** year-end entry; ~**schlußdividende** year-end dividend; ~**soll** required performance for the year, annual target; ~**steuer** annual tax; ~**steuerschuld** tax debt for the year; ~**tag** anniversary date; ~**tagung** annual conference; ~**überschuß** annual surplus, net income for the year; *vergleichbarer* ~~: *net income on a comparative basis*; ~**übersicht** annual review; ~**ultimo** end of the year; ~**umsatz** annual turnover, annual volume; ~**urlaub** annual leave; ~**vergütung** annual pay; ~**versammlung** annual (general) meeting, ordinary meeting; ~**versicherung** annual policy; ~**vertrag** contract for one year; ~**wert** annual value; ~**zahl** year-date, year; ~**zahlung** yearly payment; ~**zeit** season; *stille Jahreszeit: quiet season*; ~**zeitraum** period of one year, twelve-month period; ~**zins** annual interest; *effektiver* ~~: *annual percentage rate (APR)*.

Jedermann-Aktien-Plan *m* Personal Equity Plan.

Jedermann-Einfuhren *pl* "everyman imports", small-scale imports permitted without licence.

je nachdem *conj* as the case may be, depending.

jeweilig *adj* current, respective *s.o.* or *sth*, for the time being.

jeweils *adv* at the time, each time, in each case, in the individual case, from time to time.

Jeweiligkeitsklausel *f* clause to adapt general agreements to the current state.

jobben *v/i* exchange gambling, to do odd jobs.

Jobber *m* jobber.

Job-Vermittlung *f* temping agency.

Journal *n* journal (*bookkeeping*), book of original entries; ~**beleg** journal voucher.

Jubiläums|gabe anniversary bonus; ~**geld** anniversary bonus; ~**schrift** anniversary publication; ~**verkauf** anniversary sale; ~**zuwendung** anniversary bonus.

judikatorisch *adj* judicial, legal.

Judikative f judiciary.
Judikatur f practice of the courts, case law, judicature.
judizieren v/i to adjudicate, to administer justice, to dispense justice, to rule.
Jugend f youth, young people, the young generation, juveniles; ~**amt** youth welfare office; ~**amtsgesetz** Youth Welfare Office Act; ~**arbeitslosigkeit** unemployment among school leavers; ~**arbeitsschutz** protection of minors in employment; ~**arbeitsschutzgesetz** Employment of Young Persons Act; ~**arrest** detention of juvenile delinquents; ~**fürsorge** child welfare, youth welfare; ~**fürsorgeverein** youth welfare association; j~**gefährdend** adj morally harmful for adolescents; ~**gefängnis** prison for juvenile delinquents, reformatory; ~**gericht** juvenile court; ~**gerichtsbarkeit** jurisdiction over juveniles; ~**gerichtsgesetz** Juvenile Court Act; ~**gerichtshilfe** juvenile court assistance (*by youth office, assisting the judge on youth psychology and field work*); ~**gerichtsverfahren** juvenile court proceedings, procedure in juvenile courts; ~**gerichtsverhandlung** trial in a juvenile court; ~**hilfe** youth welfare; ~**jagdschein** hunting licence for minors; ~**kammer** juvenile division of a criminal court; ~**kriminalität** juvenile delinquency; ~**organisation** youth service; ~**pflege** youth welfare; ~**pfleger** youth welfare worker; ~**psychiatrie** psychiatry for young persons; ~**psychologe** guidance counsel; ~**psychologie** youth psychology; ~**richter** juvenile-court judge; ~**sache** juvenile-court case; ~**sachverständiger** expert on juvenile cases; ~**schöffe** juror in a juvenile case; ~**schöffengericht** juvenile court with lay assessors; ~**schutz** protection of children and young persons (*health, immoral influences*); ~**schutzgesetz** Protection of Young Persons Act (*D. of 1957*); ~**staatsanwalt** public prosecutor in juvenile court; ~**strafanstalt** prison for juvenile offenders; ~**strafe** young offender sentence, prison sentence for juveniles; ~**strafkammer** trial court in juvenile cases; ~**strafrecht** criminal law relating to young offenders; ~**strafsachen** juvenile-court cases; ~**straftat** juvenile offence; ~**strafverfahren** proceedings in juvenile court; ~**strafvollzug** execution of juvenile-court sentences; ~**verband** youth association; ~**verfahren** court procedure in juvenile cases; ~**verfehlung** juvenile offence; ~**vertreter** representative of young employees (*in works council*); ~**vertretung** representation of young employees (*in work's council*); ~**wohlfahrt** youth welfare; ~**wohnheim** hostel (for apprentices and young workers).
jugendlich adj youthful, young.
Jugendlicher m young person, (*from 14 to 18 incl*) juvenile, adolescent.
Juli-Ultimo m (the settlement at) the end of July.
Juliusturm m Julius Tower, national hoard, national coffer, *reserves in the national treasury*.
Jungfernrede f maiden speech.
Jungschein m *certificate committing issuer of new shares to deliver them directly to a securities bank.*
Juniorpartner m junior partner.
Junktim n mutual condition, package deal; tandem law; tandem relationship, a linked deal.
Junktimklausel package deal clause, joint performance clause, reciprocal clause.
Jura pl (the study and teaching of) law; ~**student** law student; ~ **studieren** to study law, to read law.
juridisch adj juridical.
Jurimetrie f jurimetrics.
Jurisdiktion f jurisdiction, judical power.
Jurisprudenz f jurisprudence.
Jurist m legally trained person, law-

Juristenausbildung / **Juwelenversicherung**

yer, jurist (*jurisprudence*); ~ **im Angestelltenverhältnis** staff lawyer, employed lawyer, in-house lawyer (or legal adviser).

Juristen|ausbildung legal training; ~**beruf** (the) legal profession; ~**jargon** legalese; ~**kommission** commission of legal experts; ~**latein** law Latin, lawyer's Latin; ~**laufbahn** legal career; ~**recht** juridical law, law for lawyers; ~**sprache** legal language, legalese, legal terminology; ~**stand** (the) legal profession; ~**tag** law congress; ~**vereinigung** law association.

juristisch *adj* juridical, legal, de jure juristic, *adv* legally; ~ *einwandfrei*: *legally watertight*; ~ *ausgedrückt*: *in legal parlance*; ~ *unmöglich*: *legally impossible*; ~**e Person** → *person*.

Jury *f* jury, panel of experts.

justitiabel *adj* capable of being adjudicated, justiciable.

Justitiabilität *f* capacity of being adjudicated.

Justitiar *m* legal staff lawyer, in-house lawyer, permanent legal adviser, permanent attorney, legal officer; ~**abteilung** legal department.

Justitium *n* suspension of the administration of justice in courts.

Justiz *f* justice, the judiciary, the administration of justice, judicature; ~**angestellter** court employee; ~**apparat** judicial machinery; ~**Assistent** law department assistant; ~**ausbildung** training for judicial service; ~**beamter** judicial officer, law officer; ~**behörde** judicial authority; ~**beitreibungsordnung** court-fee collection ordinance; ~**dienst** judicial service; ~**freiheit** freedom from the jurisdiction of the courts; ~**gesetze** administration of justice laws; ~**gewährungsanspruch** right to have justice administered; ~**gewalt** judicial power, judicial authority; power of the court; ~**hilfswachtmeister** assistant court sergeant; ~**hoheit** supreme judicial power; ~**inspektor** court inspector (*medium-rank court official*), administrative court employee; ~**irrtum** error of justice, judicial error, miscarriage of justice; ~**kritik** criticism of the courts; ~**minister** minister of justice, *GB*: ≈ Lord Chancellor, *US*: Attorney General; ~**ministerium** ministry of justice, *US*: Department of Justice; ~**mord** judicial murder; ~**oberinspektor** senior court official; ~**pflege** administration of justice; ~**pressestelle** press office of the judicial authorities; ~**rat** *obs* judicial counsellor; ~**reform** judicial reform; ~**schüler** court trainee; ~**sekretär** court assistant; ~**skandal** travesty of justice; ~**verbrechen** judicial crime; ~**versehen** inadvertent mistake on the part of the court; ~**verwaltung** administration of justice; ~**verwaltungsabgaben** administrative expenses of the judicial authorities; ~**verwaltungsakt** administrative judicial act; ~**verwaltungsentscheidung** administrative judicial decision; ~**verwaltungskosten** administrative judicial expenditures; ~**verwaltungssachen** matters in the field of judicial administration; ~**verwaltungsverfahren** procedure in the field of judicial administration; ~**verweigerung** denial of justice; ~**vollzugsanstalt** (*JVA*) prison; ~**wachtmeister** court sergeant, tipstaff; ~**wesen** administration of justice; **der** ~ **überstellen** to commit for trial; **käufliche** ~ venal justice, corrupt justice, justice open to bribery, corruption of the courts.

Juwelenversicherung *f* jewellery insurance, insuring of jewels.

K

Kabel|adresse cable address; **~antwort** cable reply; **~auftrag** cable order; **~auszahlungen** cable transfers; **~brief** cabled letter; **~buch** Ocean Cable Register; **~fernsehen** cable television; **~fernsehgesellschaften** multiple system operators *(MSO);* **~kurs** cable rate; **~netz** cable network; **~pilotprojekt** cable TV pilot scheme; **~überweisung** cable transfer.

Kabinetts|ausschuß cabinet committee; **~beschluß** cabinet decision; **~chef** chef de cabinet, cabinet secretary; **~entwurf** cabinet bill *(for legislation);* **~frage** question involving a motion of confidence; **~justiz** judicial decisions by the monarch, arbitrary government; **~krise** cabinet crisis; **~minister** cabinet minister; **~mitglied** cabinet member; **~order** cabinet decree, order in council; **~prinzip** principle of government by committee; **~rang** cabinet rank; **~referat** Cabinet Liaison Division; **~siegel** privy seal; **~sitz** seat in the cabinet; **~sitzung** cabinet meeting; **~umbildung** reshuffle in the cabinet; *e–e ~~ vornehmen: to change (or reshuffle or revamp) the cabinet;* **~verfügung** cabinet decree, order in council; **~vorlage** proposal to the cabinet.

Kabotage *f* cabotage.

Kader *m* cadre, key personnel, skeleton staff.

Kadi *m sl* judge; **zum ~gehen** to go to court, to take legal action.

kaduzieren *v/t* to declare forfeited.

Kaduzierung *f* forfeiture of shares, cancellation, declaring void; **~ von Aktien** cancellation of shares, forfeiture of share certificates.

kahlpfänden *v/t* to take away all leviable goods by execution.

Kahlschlag *m* clear felling, clear cutting; **~sanierung** radical urban redevelopment scheme.

Kai *m* quay, wharf, dock, pier; **~ablieferungsschein** wharf's receipt; **~empfangsbestätigung** dock receipt, quay receipt; **~empfangsschein** dock receipt, quay receipt; **~gebühren** dock dues, dockage, wharfage charges, berthage; **~geld** = **~gebühren** *qv;* **ab ~** ex quay; **ab ~ (unverzollt)** ex quay (duties on buyer's account); **ab ~ verzollt** ex quay (duty paid); **frei auf den ~** free on quay; **öffentlicher ~** public wharf.

Kaiser *m* emperor.

Kaiserreich *n* empire, the second German Empire (1871–1918).

Kalamitätsnutzungen *f/pl* forestry revenue due to natural catastrophes.

Kalender|jahr calendar year, civil year; **~jahrrechnung** accounts per calendar year; **~monat** calendar month; **~quartal** quarter of the calendar year; *am Ersten jedes ~~s: at conventional quarters, on the first day of each calendar quarter;* **~tag** calendar day, natural day, civil day; *laufende ~e: running days;* **k~täglich** per calendar day.

Kalfaktor *m a person doing low work, esp. in a prison (trusty), school or hospital.*

Kaliber *n* gauge, calibre, size.

Kalkül *n* scheming, plotting, purposeful calculation.

Kalkulation *f* calculation, estimate, cost accounting, costing, cost estimate; **marktwirtschaftliche ~** computation of market prospects; **pauschale ~** blanket costing, flat-rate costing.

Kalkulations|abteilung costing department, cost department; **~aufschlag** mark-up; **~aufschlagssatz** mark-up percentage; **~basis** basis

441

Kalkulator

for calculation; ~**büro** estimating office; ~**daten** costing data, calculation data; ~**fehler** error in one's calculations, miscalculation; ~**irrtum** calculation mistake, miscalculation; k~**mäßig** from the point of view of calculating costs; ~**norm** costing standard; ~**schema** accounts code structure, model costing account; ~**stichtag** costing reference date; ~**stundensatz** calculated hourly rate; ~**tabelle** spread sheet; ~**überholung** costing update (result); ~**unterlagen** costing data, cost-accounting records.

Kalkulator *m* cost accountant.

kalkulatorisch *adj* imputed, calculated, for costing purposes.

kalkulieren *v/i, v/t* to calculate, to compute, to estimate, to reckon.

Kälte|anlage refrigeration plant; ~**erzeugung** refrigeration; ~**industrie** refrigeration industry; ~**ingenieur** refrigeration engineer; ~**schutzmittel** anti-freeze.

Kaltlagerung *f* cold storage.

kaltmachen *v/t* to bump off, to liquidate, to kill off.

Kameradendiebstahl *m* theft from a fellow-soldier, theft from a workmate.

Kammer *f* (court) chamber, court division, court panel; ~ **für Außenhandel** Chamber for Foreign Trade; ~ **für Baulandsachen** chamber for building-land matters (*a court division for expropriation of land for public purposes etc*); ~ **für Handelssachen** commercial court; ~ **für Wertpapierbereinigung** Securities Validation Tribunal; ~**gericht** (=) Berlin Court of Appeal; ~**gesetze** legislation concerning professional bodies; ~**gutachten** expert opinion by a professional chamber (*or* society); ~**sitzung** full session; ~**versammlung** general meeting of the Bar Association; ~**vorlage** adjournment into court; ~**vorsitzender** presiding judge; ~**wahl** bar association elections; **Erste** ~ *parl*: lower chamber; **Zweite** ~ *parl*: upper chamber.

Kanzelmißbrauch

Kämmerer *m* treasurer (*of a local government unit*).

Kampf|abstimmung vote on a controversial issue, crucial vote, division, hard fought vote; ~**gruppe** task force; ~**handlung** military action, fighting, *pl also*: action, hostilities; ~**kündigung** labour conflict dismissal; ~**moral** morale; ~**offerte** highly competitive offer, cut-rate price; ~**parität** fighting parity; ~**preis** cut-rate price, dumping price, cut-throat competition price; ~**richter** umpire, referee; ~**tarif** aggressive rate scale, tarif de combat; ~**zoll** penal rate, retaliatory duty.

Kanal|abgaben canal tolls; ~**arbeiter** sewerman; *pl pol caucus members of the German Social Democratic Party (SPD)*; ~**dampfer** cross-channel steamer; ~**durchfahrschein** passing ticket, canal dues; ~**gebühren** effluent fees, drainage charge, canal dues; ~**schleuse** canal lock; ~**tunnelanteile** Eurotunnel shares.

Kanalisation *f* sewers, sewerage, draining, (main) drainage, *river*: canalization.

Kandidat *m* candidate, applicant; ~**enaufstellung** nomination; *erstmalige* ~~: *fresh nomination*; ~**enliste** list of candidates, ticket (*US*); **e-n** ~**en aufstellen** to nominate, to present a candidate, to put up a candidate, to submit a candidate.

Kandidatur *f* candidacy, candidature.

kandidieren *v/i* to be a candidate, to stand for (*election, parliament*), to run for office.

Kannkaufmann *m* optionally registrable trader (*agricultural or forestry operators with optional registration as merchant in the Commercial Register*).

Kannvorschrift *f* discretionary clause, optional rule, permissive provision.

Kanonenschußregel *f* cannon-shot rule (*int. law*).

kanonisch *adj* canonical.

Kanonist *m* canonist, canon lawyer.

Kanzelmißbrauch *m* misuse of the

Kanzlei   **Kapitalbesitzer**

pulpit (*by delivering political sermons*).
Kanzlei *f* law office, chambers, firm (of lawyers), professional premises (*of lawyer, tax consultant*); record office, *hist* chancellery; ~**abteilung** secretarial department; ~**arbeit** administrative work; ~**beamter** clerk (*in public service*); ~**besprechung** office conference; ~**bogen** foolscap; ~**mitarbeiter** paralegal; ~**ort** place of office, official domicile; ~**personal** office staff (*in a law office*); ~**schrift** engrossing hand; ~**sprache** officialese; ~**stil** legal style, „officialese"; ~**vorsteher** senior clerk (*law office*).
Kanzler *m* chancellor; registry clerk; ~**amt** chancellery; ~**kandidatur** bid for chancellorship.
Kapazität *f* capacity; **freie** ~ unused capacity; **ungenützte** ~ idle capacity.
Kapazitäts|auslastung capacity utilisation, use of capacities; ~**ausnützung** utilization of capacity, employment of capacity; ~~~**sgrad**: *operating rate, the level utilizing capacities*; ~**effekt** effect on capacity; ~**grenze** limit of capacity; **k**~**mäßig** as regards capacity; ~**nutzungsgrad** load factor; ~**überhang** surplus of unused capacity.
Kapital *n* capital, capital stock; principal, principal moneys; ~**abfindung** lump-sum settlement, lump-sum compensation, monetary compensation; ~**abfluß** outflow of capital; ~**abgabe** capital levy; *besondere* ~~: *ad hoc capital levy*; ~**ablösung** redemption of capital, substitution of capital; ~**abschöpfung** skimming-off of surplus capital, absorption of surplus capital; ~**abtragung** redemption of capital, repayment of principal; ~**abwanderung** exodus of capital, capital drain; ~**abzug** withdrawal of capital; ~**anlage** → *Kapitalanlage*; ~**anleger** investor; ~~~*schutz*: *investment protection*; ~~~ *letzter Hand*:

ultimate investor(s); ~**ansammlung** accumulation of capital, accumulation of funds; ~**ansammlungsvertrag** capital accumulation agreement; ~**anteil** capital share, equity share; ~**anteilschein** share certificate, stock certificate, share; **k**~**arm** *adj* short of capital, lacking in capital; ~ **aufbringen** to raise capital; ~**aufbringer** provider of capital, investor; ~**aufbringung** raising of capital; ~**aufnahme** taking up of capital, long-term borrowing; ~**aufstockung** increase of capital stock; ~**aufwand** capital expenditure, capital provided for investment; ~**aufwendungen** capital expenditure; ~ **aus etwas schlagen** to capitalize on sth, to make capital out of sth, to exploit; ~**ausfallrisiko** loan loss risk; ~**ausfuhr** export of capital; ~**ausschüttung** distribution of capital, stock dividend (*US*); ~**ausstattung** capital equipment, capital resources, capitalization; ~**ausweitung** capital expansion; ~**auszahlung aus einer Lebensversicherung** capital received from payment of a life insurance; ~**basis** basic capital requirements, foundation of capital structure; ~**bedarf** capital requirements, demand for investment capital; *aktueller* ~~: *current need for capital*; ~**belastung** lien(s) on the capital; ~**bereitstellung** making capital funds available, provision of loan capital, holding capital funds for a customer's disposal; ~~~*skonto: temporary account for available capital;* ~~~*skosten*: *loan commitment charges*; ~~~*sprovision*: *commitment commission*; ~**berichtigung** capital adjustment; ~**berichtigungs-Aktien** shares issued for the adjustment of capital; ~ **beschaffen** to procure capital, to raise capital; ~**beschaffung** raising of capital, procurement of capital; ~**beschaffungskosten** capital procurement costs; ~**besitz** capital holding; ~**besitzer** stockholder, capital

Kapitalbestand

proprietor; ~**bestand** total capital (resources); ~**beteiligung** participation in nominal capital, equity participation, equity investment; ~**beteiligungsgesellschaft** equity investment company, capital investment company; ~**betrag** principal amount, capital sum; ~~ e-r *Beteiligung*: *principal amount of a participation*; ~**betragsberechnung** computation of capital sum; ~**bewegung** capital movement, flow of capital; ~**bilanz** balance of capital transactions, net capital movement, capital account; *Belastung der* ~~: *charge on capital account*; ~**bildung** formation of capital, accumulation of capital; *freie* ~~: *formation of private savings capital*; *freiwillige* ~~: *voluntary capital formation*; *stille* ~~: *formation of undisclosed capital*; ~**bindung** tying up of capital, tied up capital; ~**bonus** capital bonus, stock dividend; ~**decke** capital cover, capital resources; ~**deckungsstock** capital cover fund; ~**deckungsverfahren** funding; ~**dienst** debt service; ~**dienstverpflichtung** obligation to provide service on capital; ~**eigner** *pl* owners of the capital stock, share (stock) holders, proprietors; ~ **einbringen** to bring in capital, to invest, to contribute capital; ~**einbringung** contribution of capital, capital input; ~**einbuße** capital loss; ~**einfuhr** importation of capital, inflow of foreign capital; ~**einkünfte** investment income, unearned income; ~**einlage** capital contribution, (proprietor's) capital holding, invested capital; ~**einsatz pro Beschäftigten** capital labour rate; ~**einschuß** subsequent contribution to capital, paid-up capital; ~**einzahlung** payment as capital investment, capital input; ~**embargo** ban on capital exports, capital embargo; ~**empfehlungsliste** list of recommended capital projects; ~**entnahme** withdrawal of capital; ~**entwertungskonto** capital depreciation account; ~**erhal-**

Kapitalherabsetzung

tung capital maintenance; *nominelle* ~~: *financial capital maintenance*; *substantielle* ~~: *physical capital maintenance*; ~**erhöhung** increase in stock (*or*) share capital; ~~ *durch Neueinlagen*: *increase in share capital by subscriptions*; *bedingte* ~~: *conditional increase in capital*; ~~ *durch Umwandlung von Rücklagen, Gewinnen oder Rückstellungen*: *increase in share capital by capitalization of reserves, profits and other funds*; ~**erhöhungskosten** capital-increase expenses; ~**ertrag** (*pl*: ~*erträge*) income from capital, capital yield, investment income, revenue from capital; *pl also*: investment income, proceeds from capital; *inländische* ~~*e*: *domestic capital gain*; *steuerabzugspflichtige* ~~*e*: *capital yields subject to withholding tax*; ~**erträgnis** = ~*ertrag qv*; ~**ertragsbilanz** balance of investment income, net investment income; ~**ertragsteuer** → *Kapitalertragsteuer*; ~**export** transfer of capital abroad, export of capital; ~**fehlleitung** misdirection of capital, misdirected investment; ~**festlegung** tying-up of capital; ~**flucht** capital flight, exodus of capital; ~~*währung*; ~**forderung** capital claim, capital due; ~**freisetzung** liberation (*or* freeing) of capital, making capital freely available; ~**geber** lender of capital, investor, financier; ~**gesellschaft** corporation, corporate enterprise, joint stock company (incorporated) company; *staatseigene* ~~: *wholly government-owned corporation*; ~**gewinn** capital gain, profit derived from capital; ~**gewinnabgabe** capital gains levy, capital gains tax; ~**güter** capital goods, capital assets; ~**güterindustrie** capital goods industry; ~ **herabsetzen** to reduce the capital; ~**herabsetzung** reduction of capital, capital reduction; *ordentliche* ~~: *ordinary capital reduction (reduction of nominal value of shares and repayment to shareholders)*; *vereinfachte* ~~: *simplified capital reduction (no repayment to shareholders)*;

Kapitalhilfe

~**hilfe** aid by increase in capital; **k~intensiv** *adj* heavily capitalised, capital-intensive; ~**intensivierung** enlarging the amount of capital, increasing the capital ratio; ~**investierung** capital investment; ~**investition** capital investment; ~**isation** → *Kapitalisation*; ~**isierung** → *Kapitalisierung*; ~**knappheit** shortage of capital; ~**koeffizient** capital output ratio, capital coefficient; ~**konto** (a partner's) capital account, proprietary account; ~**konzentration** concentration of capital (ownership); ~**kraft** sound capital position, strength of capital resources; **k~kräftig** *adj* well funded, in good financial standing, financially powerful; ~**kreditbeschaffung** obtaining credit for capital resources; ~ **kündigen** to recall capital, to call in the capital; ~**lebensversicherung** capital-sum life assurance, endowment (insurance) policy; ~**leistung** payment of capital, capital transaction; ~**lenkung** direction of capital, investment control; ~**lücke** capital gap; ~**macht** power of capital, capital-holding power; ~**mangel** lack of capital; ~**markt** → *Kapitalmarkt*; ~**mehrheit** majority of shares, majority stockholding; ~**mittel** capital resources; ~**nachfrage** demand for capital; ~**nachfragender** party seeking capital; ~**not** lack of capital; ~**nutzung** utilization of capital; ~**nutzungsentschädigung** service charge for the use of money; ~**nutzungsertrag** capital yield, return on invested capital; ~**rendite** return on capital employed, ratio of capital yield; ~**rentabilität** earning power of capital employed; ~**rente** annuity, pension from capital yield; ~**rentner** a person living from capital yield, person with private means; ~**reserven** reserve funds, capital reserves; ~**rückfluß** reflux of capital, pay-off; ~~*berechnung*: *payback method*; ~~*dauer*: *payback period*, *pay-off period*; ~**rückwan-**

Kapitalverkehr

derung reflux of capital, return of capital from abroad, repatriation of capital; ~**rückzahlung** payback of capital, repayment of principal; ~**sammelbecken** capital reservoir; ~**sammelstelle** institutional investor, capital depository; ~~ *für Spargelder*: *savings depository*; *amtliche* ~~: *official depository*; ~**schnitt** capital write down; ~**schöpfung** creation of capital; ~**schuld** capital debt, principal, capital amount of the debt; ~**schwund** dwindling of assets; ~**spritze** cash injection; ~**stau** piling-up of investment capital, capital pile-up; ~**steuer** tax on capital, capital levy, capital tax; ~**steuerung** directing the flow of capital, investment control; ~**struktur** financial structure, structure of capital resources; ~**substanz** real capital, genuine capital assets, net worth; ~**tilgung** redemption of capital; ~**titel** capital market security; ~**transfer** transfer of capital, capital transfer; ~**übertragung** capital transfer; ~**umdisposition** rearrangement of (capital) investments, reinvestment; ~**umlauf** circulation of capital; ~**umlenkung** re-direction of capital; ~**umsatz** capital turnover, employment of capital; ~**umschichtung** redistribution of investments, regrouping of capital, recapitalization; ~**umschlag** capital turnover; ~**umstellung** capital reorganization; ~**umstrukturierung** recapitalization, (recap); ~ **und Schuldteile** capital and current liabilities; ~**verbindlichkeit** capital liability, principal obligation; ~**verbrechen** capital crime, felony; ~**verflechtung** interlocking capital arrangements, interlocking of capital interests, intercorporate stockholding; *intensive* ~~: *highly interlocking capital arrangements*; ~**verkehr** capital transactions, capital movements; *grenzüberschreitender* ~~: *trans-frontier capital movements*; ~~*sbesteuerung*:

445

Kapitalverknappung

capital transfer taxes; ~~*kontrolle: control of the movement of capital;* ~~*steuern:* → *Kapitalverkehrsteuer;* ~**verknappung** shortage of investment capital; ~**verlust** capital loss, capital impairment; ~**verlustkonto** capital loss account; ~**vermittlung** provision of capital (*by agents or banks*), acting as intermediary in the provision of capital; ~**vermögen** capital assets; ~**versicherung** insurance for a lump sum, endowment insurance, capital-sum (life) assurance; ~~ *auf den Todes- und Erlebensfall: whole life and endowment insurance;* ~**verteilung** distribution of capital (*on liquidation*); ~**vertreter** shareholders' representative(s); ~**verwässerung** watering of stock, equity dilution, dilution of capital; ~**verwendung** capital appropriation, employment of capital, placement of funds; ~**verzinsung** interest on capital accounts; ~**verzinsungssatz** rate of return on capital; ~**wert** capital value, capitalized value, cash value (*policy*); ~~ *e-r Rente: present value;* ~~*berechnung: calculation of capital value;* ~**wertzuwachs** capital appreciation; ~**zahlung** payment out of capital; ~**zeichnung** subscription for capital issue, stock (*or* share) subscription; ~**zins** interest on capital, rate of interest; ~**zinspolitik** interest policy (*in the capital market*), policy concerning interest on capital; ~**zufluß** influx of capital; ~**zufuhr** capital accrual (*or* input) ~**zuführung** contribution, of additional capital; ~**zusammenlegung** capital consolidation; ~**zusammensetzung** capital structure; ~**zuschuß** capital subsidy, capital contributions, grant; ~**zustrom** influx of capital; ~**zuwachs** capital gain; ~~ *aus Werterhöhungen: appreciation surplus;* ~**zuwachssteuer** capital-gains tax, capital tax; **abrufbares** ~ callable capital; **amortisiertes** ~ sinking fund capital; **angelegtes** ~ invested capital; **arbeitendes** ~ working capital; **auf-**

Kapitalanlage

gerufenes ~ called-up capital; **ausgewiesenes** ~ stated capital; **bedingtes** ~ potential capital; **begebenes** ~ issued capital, (*US:*) outstanding capital; **blockiertes** ~ blocked capital, frozen capital; **brachliegendes** ~ idle capital; **eigengebildetes** ~ self-made capital; **einbezahltes** ~ paid-up capital; **eingebrachtes** ~ capital brought in; **eingefrorenes** ~ frozen capital, blocked capital; **eingezahltes** ~ paid-up capital, paid-in capital; **eingesetztes** ~ capital employed; **flüssiges** ~ available funds, liquid funds; **genehmigtes** ~ authorized capital, authorized stock, authorized issue; **gezeichnetes** ~ subscribed capital; **langfristiges** ~ long-term capital; **nicht begebenes** ~ unissued capital (*GB*), *auch:* potential capital (*US*); **privates** ~ privately-owned capital; **risikotragend angelegtes** ~ capital employed at risk; **stimmberechtigtes** ~ voting stock; **totes** ~ unproductive capital, idle capital, dead assets; **umlaufendes** ~ floating capital, circulating capital; **ungenutztes** ~ unemployed capital; **verantwortliches** ~risk-bearing capital; **verwässertes** ~ watered stock, diluted capital; **volleingezahltes** ~ fully paid-up capital.

Kapitalanlage *f* investment, capital investment, financial investment, employment of funds, employment of capital; ~~**Bankgeschäfte** investment banking; ~**nbetrug** investment fraud; ~**gesellschaft** investment trust, investment company; ~~ *mit eigenverantwortlicher Anlageverwaltung: management trust;* ~**güter mit beschränkter Lebensdauer** limited-life assets; ~ **in Investmentzertifikaten** unitized investment; ~**vertrag** investment contract; ~**verwaltungs-Gesellschaft** closed-end investment company; **kurzfristige** ~ short-term investment; **langfristige** ~ long-term investment, permanent

446

Kapitalertragssteuer   **Karriere**

investment; **mündelsichere** ~ gilt-edged investment, authorized investment, widow-and-orphan stock; **nicht ablösbare** ~ non-commutable investments, irredeemable capital investments; **notleidende** ~ defaulted investments; **private** ~ private investment, private placement; **sichere** ~ safe investment.

Kapitalertragssteuer *f* capital-yield tax, tax on unearned income, tax on income derived from capital; ~**abzug** tax deduction from capital income; ~**anmeldung** capital-yield tax declaration; ~**bescheinigung** capital-yield tax acknowledgment; ~ **im Steuerabzugsverfahren** withholding tax on dividends and interest, withholding tax on capital income.

Kapitalisation *f* capital resources, capitalization (= *capitalisation*): *total capital funds invested in a corporation*.

kapitalisieren *v/t* to capitalize.

Kapitalisierung *f* capitalization (= *capitalisation*); ~ **der Erträge** capitalization of yields, converting proceeds into capital; ~ **der Rente** capitalization of pension annuities (*into a lump sum*); ~ **der Zinsen** capitalization of interest.

Kapitalisierungs anleihe capital loan, blocked loan; ~**basis** yield basis, basis for capitalization; ~**faktor** capitalization factor; ~**satz** capitalization factor; ~**vertrag** capitalization agreement.

Kapitalist *m* capitalist.

kapitalistisch *adj* capitalist(ic).

Kapitalmarkt *m* capital market, long-term credit market; ~**dirigismus** regimentation of the capital market; ~**dispositionen** employment of funds in the capital market; ~**empfehlungsliste** list of issues recommended for the capital market; ~**förderungsgesetz** Capital Market Promotion Act; ~**intervention** intervention in the capital market; ~**klima** capital market conditions; **k**~**mäßig** *adj* relating to the capital market; ~**pflege** nursing of the capital market; **k**~**politisch** *adj* relating to capital market policy; ~**publikum** the investing public; ~**verhältnisse** conditions in the capital market; ~**marktzins** rate of interest in the capital market, the price of money; *freier* ~~: *open rate, open market rate*; **den** ~ **anzapfen** to tap the capital market; **florierender** ~ a flourishing capital market; **gehemmter** ~ restricted capital market; **sich des** ~**es bedienen** to have recourse to the capital market.

Kapitalverkehrssteuer *f* capital transfer tax, tax on capital transactions; ~**amt** Capital Transfer Tax Office; ~**gesetz** Capital Transfer Tax Act; ~**prüfung** tax audit for Capital Transfer Tax.

Kapitulation *f* capitulation, surrender; ~**sbedingungen** surrender terms; ~**surkunde** instrument of surrender; **bedingungslose** ~ unconditional surrender.

Kapo *m* foreman, trusty, prisoner in charge of a work-detail (*esp. in a concentration camp*).

Kappung *f* upper limit, ceiling; ~**grenze** upper limit, global rent increase limit (*over 3 years*).

Karenz *f* qualifying period, waiting time, time of competitive restriction; ~**entschädigung** compensation for the duration (*or* period) of non-competition; ~**frist** restraint of competition period, *ins* waiting period, qualifying period; ~**klausel** restraint of competition clause; ~**tage** days of a qualifying period; ~**zeit** *ins* waiting period, period of non-availability; period of restraint; **bezahlte** ~ compensated restraint of competition (*of former employee etc*).

Kargoversicherung *f* cargo insurance, freight insurance.

karitativ *adj* charitable, eleemosynary.

Karriere *f* career; ~**diplomat** career diplomat, professional diplomat(ist); ~**macher** careerist, "climber".

447

Karosseriebau *m* bodywork engineering, coach building; ~**firma** car body firm.

Kartei *f* card index, card catalog (= *catalogue*); ~**karte** index card; ~**kasten** filing case, card index box.

Kartell *n* (1) cartel, combine, loose combination, monopoly agreement, combination in restraint of trade; ~**abkommen** cartel agreement; ~**abrede** cartel understanding; ~**amt** Cartel Office; ~**amtsverfahren** cartel proceedings, proceedings at the Cartel Office; ~**anmeldung** registration of a cartel agreement; ~**anteile** cartel interests; ~**aufsicht** supervision of cartels; ~**ausschuß** anti-trust committee; ~**beamte** cartel authority officers; ~**behörde** cartel authority, antitrust division, Monopolies Commission; ~**beirat** cartel advisory committee; ~**beteiligung** cartel participation; ~**gericht** restrictive practices court, cartel court; ~**gesetz** cartel law, anti-trust law, *cf Gesetz gegen Wettbewerbsbeschränkungen*; ~**gesetzgebung** antitrust laws, anti-cartel legislation; ~**klage** antitrust action; ~**kündigung** cartel relinquishment; ~**mitglied** member of a cartel; ~**politik** antitrust policy, cartel-policy; ~**quote** pool quota; ~**recht** cartel law; ~**register** register of cartels; ~**sache** cartel case; ~**senat** cartel division (*of German appellate court or supreme court*); ~**verbot** (general) prohibition of cartels; ~**vereinbarung** cartel agreement, price-fixing agreement; ~**verfahren** anti-trust proceedings, ~**verordnung** Cartel Ordinance, cartel decree; ~**verträge** cartel agreements; ~**-Verwaltungssache** administrative cartel matter.

Kartell *n* (2) *hist* cartel, written challenge (*duel*); ~**träger** challenge-bearer.

Kartellierung *f* formation of cartels.

Karten|glücksspiel (card-)game of chance; ~**kundschaft** credit-card customers; ~**skizze** sketch-map; ~**steuer** tax on playing cards; ~**vorverkauf** advance booking (*theatre, opera, concerts, etc*); ~**wirtschaft** the rationing system.

kaschieren *v/t* to conceal, to cover up, to hide, to mask.

Kaserne *f* (military) barracks (*sg or pl*); ~**narrest** confinement to barracks.

kasernieren *v/t* to quarter (troops) in barracks; to compel (prostitutes) to live in licensed brothels.

Kasko *n* short for ~*versicherung qv*; ~**police** automobile damage policy, hull policy; ~ **und Maschinen** hull and machinery; ~**versicherer** insurer against damage to automobile, hull underwriter; ~**versicherung** collision damage insurance, own vehicle insurance, comprehensive insurance; *mar* hull insurance.

Kassa|buch cash book; *kleines* ~~: *petty book*; ~**devisen** spot exchange; ~**frist** deadline for cash payment; ~**fuß** cash value *of currencies with fluctuating exchange rates*; ~**geschäft** cash transaction, spot deal, cash sale; ~**handel** spot dealings; ~**kauf** cash purchase; ~**konto** cash account; ~**kurs** current published quotation, cash quotation, spot (exchange) quotation, spot rate, spot price, cash price; ~**lieferung** spot delivery, cash on delivery; ~**makler** private broker *dealing only on behalf of clients*; ~**markt** cash market, spot market; ~**Notierung** spot quotation; ~**papiere** securities for cash dealings; ~**ware** spots; ~**werte** securities quoted on the spot market.

Kassation *f* reversal, quashing (*of lower court's decision*); cashiering (*a military officer*); ~**sgericht** court of cassation, court of appeal, court of last resort.

Kasse *f* cash, cash box, strong box; cash register, till, check out; cashier's desk (*or* counter), pay desk; pay office, cashier's office bursar's office (*university, college*);

~ **gegen Dokumente** cash against documents; ~ **machen** to do the till, to balance the cash; **die ~ abnehmen** to balance the cash; **die ~ stürzen** to count the cash; **gegen ~** for cash; **gemeinsame ~** common fund, joint purse, common purse; **gemeinschaftliche ~** = *gemeinsame ~ qv*; **netto ~** net cash; **öffentliche ~** public treasury, national health insurance; **per ~** spot, on spot terms, for cash; **rechtsfähige ~** incorporated financial agency; **rein netto ~** net cash without discount.

Kassen|abschluß balancing of accounts, cash results; ~**abstimmung** reconciliation of cash; ~**anweisung** voucher for payment, pay voucher, petty cash voucher, cash order (*directive concerning payment of public funds*); treasury bill, treasury certificate; ~**arzt** panel doctor, social health insurance doctor; National Health (Insurance) doctor; ~**ärztliche Vereinigung** Association of Panel Doctors; ~**arztrecht** legislation applicable to doctors registered with social health insurance bodies; ~**arztwahl** choice among panel doctors; ~**ausgang** cash disbursement, petty cash voucher; ~**beamter** cashier, teller; ~**beleg** (journal) voucher, cash voucher; ~**bericht** cash report, treasurer's financial report; ~**bestand** cash in hand, cash holding, cash balance; ~**bilanz** cash account, cash balance; ~**budget** cash budget; ~**buch** cash journal, cash book; ~**buchhalter** cash accountant; ~**darlehen** cash loan; ~**defizit** cash deficit; ~**differenzkonto** over and short account; ~**disposition(en)** cash arrangements, handling of cash holding(s); ~**eingänge** cash receipts, takings; ~**eingangsbeleg** cash receipt; ~**einnahmen** cash receipts, takings; ~**fehlbetrag** cash deficit, cash short fall, *pl (also)*: cash shorts; ~**führer** treasurer; ~**führung** handling the cash; being in charge of the cash; ~**fülle** glut of cash; ~**gebarung** cash management, handling of cash payments and receipts, cash transactions; ~**geschäft** cash deal, cash transaction, spot deal; ~**guthaben** cash in hand, cash balance; ~**haltung** cash management; ~**konto** cash account, cashier's account; ~**kredit** cash advance, cash lendings, central bank advance (*by Federal Bank to governmental agencies*), Government's loan facility with Central Bank; short-term loan; ~**kreditzusage** cash advance facility, assurance of overdraft facility; ~**kurs** spot rate; ~**lage** cash position, position of liquid assets; ~**leistung** health insurance benefits; ~**liquidität** liquidity; ~**manko** cash deficit, shortfall of cash, adverse cash balance; ~~*versicherung: errors and omissions insurance;* ~**mittel** (cash) funds; ~**obligation** bank-issued medium-term note, fixed-rate note; ~**patient** panel patient, health service patient; ~**pfändung** levying upon cash funds; *e-e ~~ vornehmen: to seize the till;* ~**praxis** medical practice admitting (national) health service patients; ~**prüfer** (cash) auditor, internal auditor; ~**prüfung** cash audit, cash check; ~**quittung** receipt, cashier's receipt; *US:* sales check; ~**rabatt** cash discount; ~**raub** bank robbery; ~**revision** cash audit, cash stock-taking, audit of the cash account; ~**revisor** cash auditor; ~**saldo** cash balance; ~**satzung** regulations of health insurance organization, fund rules; ~**scheck** bank cheque, cashier's cheque; open cheque, cashable cheque, (open) uncrossed cheque; ~**schein** treasury certificate, deposit certificate; = *Kassenobligation qv*; health service cheque; ~**schlager** jack-pot winner, blockbuster (*US*); ~**skonto** cash discount; ~**sollbestand** required cash balance; ~**status** cash position; ~**stelle** cashier's office, paymaster; ~**stunden** banking

Kassette

hours, business hours; ~**sturz** counting the cash, checking the day's takings; ~~ *machen*: *to make up the cash, to check the cash in hand*; ~**system** checkout facility (*at a supermarket*); ~**haltungsplan** estimate of cash requirements; ~**überschuß** cash surplus, excess cash; ~**übertritt** change of health insurance; ~**umsatz** cash turnover, cash transactions; ~**verband** association of health insurance boards; ~**verein** clearing house, security-clearing institution; ~**verkehr** over-the-counter business, cash movements; ~**verlust** cash loss, missing cash, cash deficit; ~**verlustentschädigung** compensation for missing cash; ~**verwalter** treasurer, cashier; ~**verwaltung** treasury, public finance department; ~**vorschuß** cash advance; ~**wart** treasurer; ~**wesen** cash accounting; ~**zettel** receipt, sales check; ~**zugehörigkeit** membership of a public health-insurance organization; ~**zuständigkeit** competence of a social health insurance organization; ~**zwang** compulsory social health insurance.

Kassette *f* cassette, audio-cassette, video cassette.

Kassiber *m* smuggled prison message.

kassieren *v/t, v/i* to cash, to collect, to take (money).

Kassierer *m* cashier, (receiving) teller; checkout clerk (*self-service store*).

Kästchen *n* compartment on a printed form, blank, box.

Kastenwagen *m* box van, delivery van.

Kastration *f* castration.

Kasuistik *f* casuistry, case law.

Katalog *m* catalogue; ~**-Geschäft** mail-order business; ~**preis** list price; **nach** ~ as per catalogue; **nach Sachgebieten geordneter** ~ classified catalogue; **systematischer** ~ subject catalogue.

Kataster *m* cadastral land survey, field book; ~**amt** cadastral office, land survey office; ~**auszug** ex-

Kauf

cerpt from a cadastral map; ~**beamter** surveyor and valuer, official at the cadastral office; ~**bewertung** cadastral valuation; ~**buch** cadastral register, lot book, land survey register; ~**ertrag** cadastral income; ~**gesetz** land survey Act; ~**plan** cadastral survey map; ~**planeinheit** cadastral unit, (*US:*) plot *or* plat; ~**steuer** cadastral tax; ~**verzeichnis** docket, public index map; ~**wert** cadastral value, land value.

Katastrophen|fall catastrophe, unforeseen calamity; ~**gebiet** disaster area; ~**risiko** catastrophe hazard; ~**schutz** disaster control service; ~**versicherung** insurance against catastrophes.

Kauf *m* (*pl*: *Käufe* = ~*e*) purchase; sale (*law of sale*); ~**abrechnung** *exch* bought note; ~**abschluß** bargain, conclusion of contract of sale; ~~ *durch Handschlag*: *sale by clasp of hand*; *fester* ~~: *outright sale*; ~**akte** purchase-deed; ~**angebot** offer to buy, bid; ~**anreiz** buying incentive; ~**antrag** offer to buy; ~**anwärter** prospective purchaser; ~**anwartschaftsvertrag** provisional sales contract, contract for the purchase of an expectancy; ~ **auf Abruf** purchase with deferred delivery subject to call; ~ **auf Baisse** purchase for the fall; ~ **auf Besicht** sale (for inspection and) on approval; ~ **auf Probe** sale on approval, sale or return, memorandum sale, sale on trial; ~**auftrag** buying order, purchase order; *limitierter* ~ – *oder Verkaufsauftrag*: *stop-loss order*; ~ **auf Umtausch** sale or exchange; ~ **auf Zeit** purchase for a temporary period; ~ **auf Ziel** purchase on credit, credit sale; ~**ausweis** certificate of purchase; ~**belebung** increase in sales; ~ **bricht nicht Miete** sale subject to existing tenancies; ~**brief** deed of purchase; bill of sale (*ships*); ~**eigenheim** freehold property (*for sale, or*: *privately purchased*); ~ **e–s Anwartschaftsrechtes** purchase of an expectancy; ~**empfehlung** recommendation to purchase; *exch* buy recommendation; ~ **gegen bar** cash purchase; ~**gegenstand**, subject-matter of the sale, object sold; object of purchase, sales article; ~**geld** purchase money; ~**geldforderung** claim for the purchase price; ~ **geldhypothek** purchase money mortgage; ~**gelegenheit** opportunity to buy; ~**gesuch** request to buy, offer to buy; ~**gewohnheit** buying habit; ~**gut** purchased goods, goods bought; ~**haus** department store; ~**interesse** interest in purchasing; inclination to buy; ~**interessent** prospective buyer, would-be purchaser; intending purchaser, potential purchaser; ~**lohn** cost of outside labour; ~**kraft** → *Kaufkraft*; ~**kredit** loan to finance purchases; ~**kurs** buying rate; ~**leute** merchants, tradesmen; ~**lizenz** buying licence; ~**lust** inclination to buy, spending spree; ~**mann** → *Kaufmann*; ~**miete** hire-purchase; ~ **mit Rückgaberecht** sale and return, memorandum sale; ~**mittel** purchasing funds; ~ **nach Beschreibung** sale by description; ~ **nach Katalog** catalogue sale; ~ **nach Probe** sale by sample; ~ **nach Warenbeschreibung** purchase by description; ~**neigung** inclination to buy; ~**option** buyer's option, option to purchase, call option; ~**orgie** spending spree; ~**potential** purchasing power; ~**preis** → *Kaufpreis*; ~**rausch** purchasing mania, spending spree; ~**recht** right of purchase; law on sales; ~**reflektant** intending purchaser, potential buyer; ~**sache** bought object, object of sale; ~**schein** certificate of sale; ~**steuer** purchase tax; ~**stimmung** buying mood; ~**summe** purchase money, total price; ~**unlust** sales resistance, disinclination to buy; ~ **unter Ausschluß von (sämtlichen) Gewährleistungsansprüchen** sale with all faults; ~ **unter Eigentumsvorbehalt** conditional sale agreement, sale subject to reservation of title (*or* of ownership); ~**urkunde** purchase deed; ~**verhalten** purchasing pattern; ~**verhandlung** sales negotiation; ~~*en führen*: *to negotiate a sale*; ~**verpflichteter** person who has agreed to buy goods; ~**verpflichtung** obligation to purchase; purchase commitment; ~**vertrag** → *Kaufvertrag*; ~ **von beweglichen Sachen** purchase of goods; ~ **von sofort lieferbaren Produkten** (*bzw. Devisen*) *exch* spot purchase; ~**vorrecht** purchase privilege; ~**vorvertrag** agreement for purchase, preliminary contract of sale; **k~weise** *adv* by way of purchase; ~**welle** sales boom, buying surge; ~**wert** purchase money, value of the purchased item; ~ „**wie besehen**" sale on inspection; ~ **wie Ware steht und liegt** sale with all faults; ~**zentrum** shopping centre, supermarket; ~ **zur Probe** trial sale, sale of a sample; ~ **zur späteren Auslieferung** forward purchase; ~**zwang** obligation to buy; „*Kein* ~~": *no obligation, "inspection invited"*; **e-n** ~ **abschließen** to conclude a contract of sale; **fester** ~ firm sale, definite sale; *e-n festen* ~ *abschließen*: *to buy outright, to conclude a firm sale*; **durch** ~ **erwerben** to acquire by purchase; **freier** ~ voluntary purchase, voluntary sale, sale by private treaty; **lebhafte ~e** *exch* active buyers.

kaufbereit *adj* inclined to buy, ready to buy, in a spending mood.

kaufen *v/t*, *v/i* to buy, to purchase; **auf Besicht** ~ to buy subject to inspection; **auf Probe** ~ → *Probe;* **auf Ziel** ~ → *Ziel*; **billig** ~ to buy cheap(ly), to buy at a low price; **fest** ~ to make a firm purchase; **für feste Rechnung** ~ → *Rechnung*; **gegen bar** ~ to purchase for cash; **von der Stange** ~ to buy ready-made, to buy off the shelf; **zu** ~ **gesucht** required; **zur Probe** ~ → *Probe*.

Käufer *m* buyer, purchaser, vendee (*real property*); ~**abruf** *exch* buyer's call; ~ **e-r Rückprämie** *exch* taker for a put; ~ **e-r Stellage** *exch* taker for a put and call; ~ **e-r Vorprämie** giver for a call; ~ **e-s Wechsels** purchaser of a note, purchaser of an unendorsed bill; ~**gruppe** category of buyers; ~**land** purchasing country; ~**mangel** lack of buying orders; ~**markt** buyer's market; ~**pflicht** purchaser's obligation; ~**recht** purchaser's right; ~**schicht** class of buyers; ~**streik** buyers' strike; ~**verhalten** purchasing behaviour, purchase pattern; ~**widerstände** consumer resistance; **der ~ trägt die Gefahr** goods are at buyer's risk, the risk shall be borne by the purchaser; **der spätere ~** subsequent purchaser; **gutgläubiger ~** bona fide purchaser, good faith purchaser, innocent purchaser without notice; **möglicher ~** potential buyer; **nach ~s Wahl** at buyer's option; **nachfolgender ~** subsequent purchaser; **schnell entschlossener ~** ready buyer, quickly decided purchaser; **umsichtiger ~** discriminating buyer, prudent customer; **ungenannter ~** undisclosed buyer; **unschlüssiger ~** undecided purchaser (shopper).

Käuferin *f* (woman) shopper, female buyer.

Kauffahrteischiff *n* merchant ship, trading vessel.

Kauffahrteischiffahrt *f* commercial navigation.

Kauffrau *f* business woman.

Kaufkraft *f* buying power, purchasing power, spending power; ~ **abschöpfen** to absorb buying power, to take money out of circulation; ~**abschöpfung** absorbing surplus purchasing power; ~**ausgleich** compensation for loss of purchasing power; ~**entzug** drain on purchasing power; ~**erhöhung** increase in purchasing power; ~**kennzahlen** purchasing power indices; ~**minderung** reduction in purchasing power; ~**parität** purchasing power parity; ~**schöpfung** creating purchasing power; ~**schwund** loss of purchasing power; ~**überhang** excess purchasing power; **überschüssige ~ abschöpfen** to skim off (*or* tax away) surplus purchasing power.

käuflich *adj* available for sale; venal, corrupt, bribable; ~ **erwerben** to acquire by purchase.

Käuflichkeit *f* venality, corruptibility, bribability.

Kaufmann *m* merchant, trader, dealer, businessman; ~**kraft Eintragung** (status of a) merchant by virtue of entry in the Commercial Register; ~ **werden** to go into business, to become a businessman; **ordentlicher ~** responsible businessman; respectable member of the business community; **selbständiger ~** independent dealer, established businessman, proprietor of a business.

kaufmännisch *adj* commercial, mercantile; ~ **verantwortet** justified on grounds of sound business practice.

Kaufmanns|eigenschaft merchant status, business qualification; ~**beruf** the commercial profession, business occupation; ~**gehilfenbrief** commercial training certificate; ~**gemeinschaft** association of businessmen; ~**stand** the business community, the commercial profession.

Kaufpreis *m* purchase price, purchase money; ~**bereithaltung** tender of the price; ~ **bezahlt** price paid; ~**forderung** purchase-money claim; ~**genehmigung** approval of the purchase price; ~**gläubiger** unpaid seller; ~**hypothek** purchase-money mortgage; ~**minderung** diminution of price, reduction in purchase price; ~**rückzahlung** refund of purchase price; ~**schuld** debt in respect of purchase price obligation; **den ~ mindern** to reduce the purchase price (*because of faulty goods*); **der ~ wird**

wie folgt belegt the purchase price shall be paid as follows.

Kaufvertrag *m* contract of purchase, contract of sale; document of a contract of sale; ~ **mit Auflassung** contract of sale of land including conveyance; ~ **ohne Eigentumsvorbehalt** absolute sales contract; ~ **ohne Mißbrauchsabsicht** bona fide sale; ~ **unter Eigentumsvorbehalt** conditional sales contract; **vom** ~ **zurücktreten** to cancel *or* to rescind the contract of sale.

kausal *adj* causal.

Kausal|haftung liability for the consequences; ~**kette** (chain of) causation, chain of cause and effect; ~**zusammenhang** causal connection, causal relation, causal link, causation.

Kausalität *f* causality, causation; ~**sgesetz** law of cause and effect.

Kaution *f* (security) deposit, financial bond; bail bond, bail; ~ **des Mieters** tenant's security deposit; ~ **stellen** to furnish security; to provide bail; ~ **übernehmen** to go bail; ~ **zur Haftverschonung anbieten** to tender bail; **gegen** ~ **auf freiem Fuß sein** to be out on bail; **ohne** ~ **von der Untersuchungshaft verschont werden** to be released on one's own recognizance; **ungenügende** ~ insufficient bail.

kautionsfähig *adj* eligible to be released on bail; eligible to stand bail.

Kautions|gestellung providing bail, providing security; ~**hypothek** mortgage for a contingent liability; ~**kredit** credit as security for a contingent liability; ~**leistung** providing security *or* bail; ~**regreß** recourse of guarantee; ~**stellung** providing bail, providing security; *nicht zur ~~ zugelassen*: non-bailable; *sich nach ~~auf freiem Fuß befinden*: to be out on bail; ~**summe** amount of security, bond-money, bail; ~**versicherung** guarantee insurance, surety and fidelity insurance; ~**versicherungsgesellschaft** surety company; ~**verpflichtung** bail commitment; ~**wechsel** collateral bill of exchange, collateral note.

Kellerwechsel *m* accommodation bill, kite, spurious note, bogus bill, windmill.

Kennbuchstabe *m* distinguishing letter, identification letter, registration letter.

Kennenmüssen negligent ignorance of sth; imputed (*or* deemed) knowledge.

Kennkarte *f* identity card, identification card *now: Personalausweis qv*.

kenntlich *adj* identifiable; ~ *machen*: *to mark, to identify*.

Kenntlichmachung *f* identification, marking, disclosure of ingredients.

Kenntnis *f* knowledge, notice, information; ~ **auf Grund e-r Mitteilung** express notice; ~ **des Gerichts** judicial knowledge, judicial notice, judicial cognizance; ~ **erlangen** to become aware of, to obtain knowledge of sth; ~ **geben** to give notice of, to notify, to inform, to bring to s.o.'s attention; ~ **haben von** to have notice of, to be aware of; **aus eigener** ~ from firsthand knowledge; **erworbene** ~ acquired knowledge; **etwas zur** ~ **bringen** to bring to (a person's) knowledge (*or* attention), to notify; **gesetzlich vermutete** ~ constructive notice; **in voller** ~ **der Tatumstände** with full knowledge of the factual circumstances; **jmden von etw in** ~ **setzen** to inform s.o. of sth; **nicht patentfähige** ~**se** non-patentable information; **ohne meine** ~ without my knowledge; **patentfähige** ~ patentable information; **sich** ~ **von etw verschaffen** to obtain information on sth; **sichere** ~ positive knowledge, actual notice; **tatsächliche** ~ actual notice; **tatsächlich vermutete** ~ presumptive notice; **unterstellte** ~ constructive notice, imputed (*or* implied) knowledge; **vermutliche** ~ presumptive notice, presumed knowledge; **vertrauliche** ~**se** confidential information; **von etwas** ~ **nehmen** to

Kenntnisnahme

take notice of sth; **zur ~ nehmen** to take note of sth, to note sth; **zur ~ und weiteren Veranlassung** for information and further action; **zurechenbare ~** constructive notice, imputed knowledge.

Kenntnisnahme *f* taking notice of sth; **~möglichkeit** opportunity to take notice *(of terms and conditions)*; **mit der Bitte um ~** please take note, kindly note; **zur ~** for (your) information, for the attention of ...; **zur gefälligen ~** for your kind attention, for information.

Kennung identifying symbols.

Kennwort *n* password; special and distinctive word.

Kennzahl *f* code number, index number, key, box number, reference number; **wirtschaftliche ~en** economic statistical data.

Kennzeichen *n* distinguishing feature; (automobile) registration number; licence plate, registration plate; identification mark, emblem; **~mißbrauch** abuse of registration plates; **~schutz** protection of official identification marks *(against forgery etc)*; **amtliche ~** registration number, licence plate; **besondere ~** special peculiarities; **~~ e-r Erfindung:** marked features of an invention; **polizeiliches ~** licence plate.

kennzeichnen *v/t* to mark, to designate, to label, to characterize.

kennzeichnend *adj* distinctive, characteristic, typical.

Kennzeichnung *f* identification.

Kennzeichnungs|bestimmungen labelling provisions; **~funktion** distinguishing function; **~kraft** distinguishing force; **~leuchtfeuer** landmark beacon; **~vorschriften** labelling requirements.

Kennziffer *f* = *Kennzahl qv.*

Keramik *f* ceramics, pottery.

Kerbholz *n* tally(-stick), criminal record; **etw auf dem ~ haben** to have a criminal record.

Kerker *m* dungeon, *Austr* imprisonment in a penitentiary; **~ bei Wasser und Brot** imprisonment on bread and water (diet); **lebenslänglich ~** imprisonment for life, a life sentence.

Kern|anlagen nuclear installations; **~arbeitszeit** core time *(all employees present at work)*; **~brennstoff** nuclear fuel; **~gebiet** central municipal area, city; **~energie** nuclear energy; **~~agentur**: Nuclear Energy Agency; **~~system**: nuclear power system; **~explosion** nuclear explosion; **~fächer** common core subjects; **~frage** fundamental issue, key question; **~funktion** basic function, key function; **~gesellschaft** parent company *(of a group)*, central company; **~krafteinrichtungen** nuclear facilities; **~materialien** nuclear materials; **~posten** essential item; **~punkt** crucial point, point at issue; **~unrecht** basic unlawfulness; **~unterricht** core lessons; **~waffenmitbesitz** sharing of nuclear weapons; **~waffensperrvertrag** (nuclear) non-Proliferation Treaty.

Kette *f* chain, association; **~narbeitsvertrag** chain employment relationship *(successive short-term agreements)*; **~nbrief** chain letter; **~ngeschäft** chain store; **~nhandel** chain trade; **~nunfall** pile-up; **an die ~ legen** to arrest *(a ship)*.

Keule *f* club, cudgel; **elektrische ~** stun gun.

Kfz = *Kraftfahrzeug qv*; **~führer** driver.

KG = *Kommanditgesellschaft qv.*

Killerviren *m/pl* killer viruses *(electronic data)*.

Kilometer|geld allowance per kilometre, mileage allowance; **~pauschale** flat mileage rate; **~stand** number of kilometres covered *or* clocked *(by a vehicle)*, mileage.

Kind *n* (pl *Kinder* = *~er*) child, infant; **angenommenes ~** adopted child; **durch nachfolgende Eheschließung legitimiertes ~** child legitimated by subsequent marriage *(per matrimonium subsequens)*; **eheliches ~** legitimate child; **für ehe-**

Kinderarbeit / **Kirchenabgabe**

lich erklärtes ~ legitimized child; **gemeinschaftliches** ~ mutual child; **heimatlose, verwahrloste** ~**er** waifs and strays; **körperbehinderte** ~**er** disabled children; **leibliches** ~ natural child; **nachgeborenes** ~ afterborn child; **neugeborenes** ~ newly-born child, new-born child; **nichteheliches** ~ illegitimate child, child born out of wedlock; **uneheliches** ~ illegitimate child, child born out of wedlock; **ungeborenes** ~ unborn child; **unterhaltsberechtigtes** ~ child entitled to maintenance, dependant child; **vaterloses** ~ fatherless child, orphan; **voreheliche** ~**er der Ehegatten** antenati.

Kinder|arbeit child labour; ~**aussagen** testimony by children, children's depositions; ~**aussetzung** desertion of children; ~**ausweis** children's identification paper; ~**beihilfe** child allowance; ~**betreuer** child-minder; ~**betreuung** looking after children, care of children, child-minding; ~**ermäßigung** reduction for children (*transport etc*); tax relief for children; ~**erziehung** bringing-up (of children); ~~**szeit:** *time spent on the up-bringing of children;* ~**freibetrag** child allowance (= *deductions from the sum of taxable earnings*); ~**garten** nursery school, kindergarten; ~**geld** child benefit *monthly grant from the state for each child;* ~**geldgesetz** Child Benefit Act (*D: of 1975 as amended*); ~**handel** traffic in children; ~**hilfswerk der Vereinten Nationen** United Nations Children's Fund; ~**krankheiten** teething troubles, initial problems (*of a firm*); ~**krippe** day nursery for infants; **k**~**los** childless, without issue; ~**pflegerin** children's nurse; ~**psychiater** child psychiatrist; ~**psychologe** children's psychologist, child psychologist; ~**renten** periodical payments for children; ~**spielplatz** playground; ~**sterblichkeit** infant mortality; ~**unterhaltszahlungen** children's maintenance payments; ~**zulage** additional allowance for children, (contractual) children's allowance; ~**zuschlag** children's (bonus) allowance; ~**zuschuß** child (supplementary) benefit.

Kindes|alter childhood, infancy; ~**annahme** adoption; ~**aussetzung** abandoning a child; ~**bewegungen** quickening (*before birth*); ~**entführung** child abduction; ~**entziehung** wrongful removal of child; ~**kinder** grandchildren; ~**mißbrauch** child abuse; ~**mißhandlung** child abuse; ~**mord** infanticide, murder of a child; ~**mutter** (= *Kindsmutter*) mother of an illegitimate child; ~**namen** (the) child's name; ~**raub** child stealing, child kidnapping; *erpresserischer* ~~: *kidnapping children (for the purpose of ransom);* ~**recht** child law; ~**unterhalt** child support; maintenance for child(ren); ~**tötung** killing of one,'s illegitimate baby; ~**umgang** access (to children); ~**unterschiebung** substitution of child; ~**vater** (= *Kindsvater*) father of an illegitimate child; *der vermutliche* ~~: *the putative father;* ~**verderber** child molester; ~**verhältnis** parent and child relationship, parental relationship; ~**vermögen** children's property, a child's estate; ~**vernachlässigung** child neglect; ~**wille** the child's will; ~**wohl** the wellbeing of a child, child's welfare.

Kindschaftssachen *f/pl* parent and child cases, child custody cases.

Kirch|geld *n* church contribution (*apart from church taxes*).

Kirchen|abgabe church tax and contributions; ~**amt** ecclesiastical office; ~**ämterkauf** *hist* simony; ~**aufsicht** State supervision of churches; ~**austritt** withdrawal from church membership; ~**baulast** *obligation to finance the maintenance and repair of churches;* ~**behörden** ecclesiastical (*or* church)

Kiste | **Klage auf Wandelung**

authorities; ~**beamte** administrative church officials; ~**buch** church register; parish register; ~**buchauszug** extract from the parish register; ~**diebstahl** theft from a church; ~**einkommensteuer** church income tax; ~**freiheit** constitutional church liberty; ~**gebühren** church fees; ~**gemeinde** parish, congregation; ~**gericht** ecclesiastical court; ~**gesetz** church statute; ~**gut** church property; ~**hoheit** sovereign church rights; ~**mitgliedschaft** church membership; ~**ordnung** internal church constitution; ~**recht** canon law, ecclesiastical law, law spiritual; *äußeres* ~~: *external ecclesiastical law*; ~**schändung** sacrilege, profanation of a church, defilement of a church; ~**sprengel** (Protestant) church district; ~**staat** Pontifical State, Vatican, Papal State; ~**steuer** church tax; ~**strafen** canonical church penalities; ~**verfassung** church constitution; ~**umlagen** assessments for church contributions; ~**vermögen** ecclesiastical property; ~**vertrag** church agreement (*usually between the Protestant Church and the German State*); ~**vorstand** parochial church council; ~**zucht** disciplinary measurer of (protestant) churches.

Kiste *f* case, box; chest (*measure for tea*).

Kladde *f* waste-book (*in bookkeeping*); note-book; scribbling pad.

klagbar *adj* actionable, recoverable (by law), suable; **nicht** ~ unenforceable, non-actionable.

Klagbarkeit *f* suability, actionability, admissibility for legal action.

Klage *m* action, civil action, lawsuit, statement of claim; principal cause; ~**abweisung** dismissal of action, judgment against the plaintiff; ~**abweisungsantrag** motion to dismiss the action (*or* case); ~**änderung** amendment of action, amendment of pleadings; ~ *durch neuen Sachvortrag*: *new cause of action*; ~**androhung** threat of legal proceedings; ~**ankündigung** notice of action; ~**anspruch** claim (of the action); ~**anstrengung** bringing of an action, instituting an action; ~**antrag** demand for relief, prayer for relief, the relief prayed for, motion for judgment, *dem* ~~ *stattgeben*: *to find for the plaintiff; unbezifferter* ~~: *unliquidated claim (for relief);* ~**antwort** defendant's plea, answer to complaint, defence (to statement of claim); ~ **auf Anerkennung der Vaterschaft** paternity suit; ~ **auf Anfechtung der Ehelichkeit** petition for a declaration of illegitimacy; ~ **auf Aufhebung der Ehe** petition for annulment of marriage, annulment of marriage proceedings; ~ **auf Aufhebung des Vertrages** petition for rescission of contract, action for cancellation of contract; ~ **auf Besitzeinräumung** action for possession; ~ **auf Eigentumsverschaffung** action to gain title, action to transfer ownership; ~ **auf Einräumung des Besitzes** action for possession, action of detinue, action of ejectment; ~ **auf Herausgabe** action for restitution, action for possession; ~ **auf Leistung der Einzahlung auf Aktien** action for calls (on shares); ~ **auf Löschung** *action to enforce expunging an entry from official register;* ~ **auf Mietzahlung** rent action; ~ **auf Naturalerfüllung** action for specific performance; ~ **auf Nutzungsentschädigung** action for compensation for use and occupation; ~ **auf Rechnungslegung** action for an account render; ~ **auf Rückgabe** action for restitution; ~ **auf Schadenersatz** action for damages; *die* ~ *geht auf Schadensersatz*: *the action is for damages*; ~ **auf Unterlassung** prohibitory action; ~ **auf Unterlassung der Störung** action to restrain a nuisance; ~ **auf Vertragserfüllung** action for specific performance; ~ **auf Wandelung** rehibitory action, action for cancellation of a contract of sale;

Klage auf Wiedereinräumung

~ **auf Wiedereinräumung des Besitzes** action of replevin, action for possession, action of conversion; ~ **auf Wiederherstellung der ehelichen Gemeinschaft** petition for restitution of conjugal rights, suit for restitution of conjugal community; ~ **auf Widerruf der Schenkung** action seeking to revoke a gift; ~ **auf Zahlung von Pachtrückständen** action for arrears of rent; ~ **auf Zahlung** action for a money claim, suit for a debt; ~ **aus Eigentum** action based on ownership, petitory action; ~ **aus Geschäftsführung ohne Auftrag** action on the grounds of negotiorum gestio; ~**ausschlußfrist** preclusive deadline for filing an action; ~ **aus Schuldurkunden** debenture action; ~ **aus unerlaubter Handlung** action in tort, action ex delicto; ~ **aus ungerechtfertigter Bereicherung** actio sine causa, action to make restitution for unjust enrichment; ~ **aus Vertrag** action based on contract, action ex contractu; ~**beantwortung** answer, statement of defence, defendant's plea; ~**befugnis** right of action, standing to sue; ~**begehren** prayer for relief, relief sought, plaintiff's claim; ~**begründung** statement of claim, plaintiff's statement of grounds for claim; ~**berechtigung** entitlement to the claim; ~**betrag** amount of claim; ~ **des Drittbegünstigten** action by a third-party beneficiary; ~ **einreichen** to bring an action, to file an action (*or* writ), to file a suit; ~**einreichung** filing of an action, (*or* suit *or* writ); ~**ergänzung** supplemental complaint, amendment to statement of claim; ~ **erheben** to file a suit, to bring an action; ~**erhebung** commencement of an action, issue of the writ of summons, originating process, filing of an action (*or* suit); ~**erweiterung** extension of the plaintiff's claim; ~**erwiderung** answer, statement

Klage vor einem Schiedsgericht

of defence, defence; *e–e* ~~*einreichen*: to respond; *unschlüssige* ~~: *irrelevant defence*; ~~ *und Widerklage*: answer and cross-petition; ~**erzwingung** legal pressure to obtain criminal prosecution; ~~*sverfahren*: proceedings to force the public prosecution to prefer criminal charges; ~**frist** deadline *or* time-limit for filing suit, time frame for taking action (*or* commencement of proceedings); ~ **führen** to complain; ~ **gegen Nachahmer** action against imitators; ~**gegenstand** subject matter of an action; ~**grund** cause of action; *selbständig e–n* ~~ *bildend*: *actionable per se*; ~ **im ordentlichen Verfahren** plenary action, action in ordinary proceedings; ~ **in Prozeßstandschaft** representative action; ~**möglichkeit** legal remedy; ~**nhäufung** joinder of actions; *subjektive* ~~: *joinder of parties*; *objektive* ~~: *joinder of causes of action, joinder of claims*; *unzulässige* ~~: *improper cumulation of actions*; ~**nverbindung** joinder (of causes of action); ~**partei** plaintiff, party plaintiff; ~**patent** patent sued upon; ~**recht** right of action; ~**rubrum** title of a cause, title of an action; ~**rücknahme** withdrawal of an action, voluntary discontinuance of an action; ~~ *mit Anspruchsverzicht: retraxit*; ~**sache** action, matter, litigation; ~**nschema** types of action; ~**schrift** statement of claim, originating petition; ~**schriftsatz** statement of claim, petition; ~**sperre** bar to the action; ~**summe** amount sued for; ~**veranlassung** occasion prompting the action, cause of legal proceedings; ~**verbindung** → ~*nverbindung*; ~**verfahren** action, proceedings, procedure in an action; ~**verwirkung** laches in bringing suit; ~**verzicht** waiver of an action, notice of discontinuance; *vereinbarter* ~~: *pactum de non petendo*; ~ **vor e–m Schiedsgericht** application for an award by arbitration;

Klagevoraussetzung

~**voraussetzung** prerequisites for taking legal action; ~**weg** litigation, recourse to law; *auf dem* ~~: *by taking legal proceedings*; *den* ~~ *beschreiten: to resort to litigation*; ~ **wegen Besitzstörung** action for trespass; ~ **wegen falscher Herkunftsangabe** passing-off action, action for false statement of origin; ~ **wegen Vertragsverletzung** action for breach of contract; ~**zurücknahme** = ~*rücknahme qv*; ~**zustellung** service of the writ; **anhängige** ~ pending case, pending action, petition at issue; **bösgläubige** ~ vexatious action; **deliktische** ~ tort action; **die** ~ **ist begründet** the action is (well) founded; **die** ~ **ist zulässig** the action is admissible; **dingliche** ~ action in rem, real action; **durch** ~ **zu erlangen** recoverable by action; e-e ~ **abweisen** to dismiss an action, to dismiss a petition, to dismiss a case; *e-e* ~ *kostenpflichtig abweisen*: *to dismiss an action with costs*; e-e ~ **anerkennen** to admit a claim; e-e ~ **ausdehnen auf jmdn** to join a person as defendant; e-e ~ **begründen** to state one's claim, to found an action; e-e ~ **fallen lassen** to discontinue the action; e-e ~ **ist unzulässig** an action is inadmissible; e-e ~ **ist zulässig** an action; is (procedurally) admissible; e-e ~ **substantiieren** to substantiate an action; e-e ~ **unterlassen** to refrain from taking action; e-e ~ **zurücknehmen** to withdraw an action, to drop an action; **erfolglose** ~ unsuccessful action, abortive proceedings; **frivole** ~ frivolous claim, vexatious proceeding; **jmdm mit e-r** ~ **drohen** to threaten s. o. with legal action; **mit seiner** ~ **abgewiesen werden** to lose a case, to have one's case dismissed; **negatorische** ~ action for an injunction; **öffentliche** ~ charge, indictment, action by the state, public action; **persönliche** ~ personal action; **petitorische** ~ petitory action, action to enforce

458

Kläger

one's claim; **possessivische** ~ possessory action; **possessorische** ~ possessory action; **privatrechtliche** ~ private action, civil action; **schikanöse** ~ vexatious action; **schuldrechtliche** ~ personal action, action in personam; **sich auf die** ~ **einlassen** to enter an appearance, to defend a case; **sich e–r** ~ **enthalten** to refrain from taking legal action; **streitige** ~ contested action; **unabhängige** ~ independent action; **unzulässige** ~ (procedurally) inadmissible action, an action that does not lie; **verbundene** ~**n** concomitant actions; **vergebliche** ~ abortive action; **vermögensrechtliche** ~ action based on a property claim; **verspätete** ~ action barred by lapse of time; **zusätzliche** ~ supplementary claim, extra claim.

klagen *v/i* to bring an action, to sue, to commence proceedings, to go to court, to take legal action; ~ **und verklagt werden** to sue and be sued (*in the firm's name*); **auf Schadensersatz** ~ → *Schadensersatz*; **auf Zahlung** ~ → *Zahlung*; **erfolgreich** ~ to sue successfully.

Kläger *m* plaintiff, petitioner, claimant; ~ **bei Anwaltszwang** plaintiff compulsorily represented by a lawyer; ~, **dem Prozeßkostenhilfe bewilligt ist** legally-aided plaintiff; ~ **für eine Rechtsgemeinschaft** representative plaintiff; ~ **in Prozeßstandschaft** nominal plaintiff; **aktivlegitimierter** ~ proper plaintiff; **als** ~ **auftreten** to appear as the plaintiff; **anwaltschaftlich vertretener** ~ plaintiff suing through (*or* represented by) a lawyer; **den** ~ **mit seiner Klage abweisen** to dismiss the plaintiff's claim, to nonsuit the plaintiff; **für den** ~ **erscheinen** to appear for the plaintiff; **minderjähriger** ~ infant plaintiff; **nicht anwaltschaftlich vertretener** ~ plaintiff acting (*or* appearing) in person; **nicht prozeßfähiger** ~ plaintiff under a dis-

Klägerin / **Kleinabnehmertarif**

ability; **prozeßfreudiger** ~ suit-happy plaintiff, litigious person; **zugunsten des** ~**s entscheiden** to find for the plaintiff.

Klägerin *f* female plaintiff.

Klaglosstellung *f* depriving s. o. of a cause of action (*by payment etc*).

Klammerdefinition *f* definition in brackets.

Kläranlage *f* disposal works, waste-treatment plant, (sewage) purification plant.

klären *v/t* to clarify, to clear up, to make clear.

Klarschriftleser *m* optical character reader.

Klarsichtpackung *f* transparent pack, blister pack, bubble pack.

klarstellen *v/t* to clarify, to elucidate.

Klarstellung *f* clarification, elucidation.

Klärung *f* clarification, clearing up; ~ **der schwebenden Fragen** the clarification of outstanding questions.

Klasse *f* class, order; **die herrschenden** ~**en** the ruling classes.

Klassen|bearbeiter official in charge of a class (*of applications*); ~**justiz** class justice: *administration of justice influenced by class interests*; ~**kampf** class war(fare); ~**verzeichnis** classification list.

Klassierung *f* grading.

Klassifikation *f* classification; ~**sangabe** classification; **Internationale** ~ International Patent Classification (IPC).

klassifizierbar *adj* classifiable, assortable; **nicht** ~ nondescript, unclassifiable.

klassifizieren *v/t* to classify, to categorize, to schedule.

Klassifizierung *f* classification, gradation, assortment, sorting.

klauen *v/t* to pinch, to pilfer, to steal.

Klauerei *f* petty thievery.

Klausel *f* clause, proviso, provision, stipulation; ~: „**beiderseitiges Verschulden**" "both to blame" collision clause; ~ **für Zusatzleistung bei Unfalltod** accidental death benefit clause; ~**verbote** prohibited clauses (in general terms and condition); **bedingte** ~ conditional clause; **salvatorische** ~ saving clause, escape clause; **unbedingte** ~ unconditional clause; **vorgedruckte** ~ printed clause; **zwingende** ~ mandatory provision, mandatory clause.

Kleckerkonten *n/pl* mini-volume customer accounts.

Kleidergeld *m* clothing allowance.

Klein|abnehmertarif flat-rate tariff; ~**aktie** baby share, *pl* penny shares; ~**aktionär** small shareholder; ~**anzeige** classified ad(vertisement); ~**arbeit** detailed work, spade-work; *handelspolitische* ~~: *detailed trade negotiations*; ~**bank** small bank; *dubiose* ~~: *shoe-string bank*; ~**bauernhof** small-holding; ~**betrag** small sum; ~**betrieb** small enterprise; *funktionsschwacher* ~~: *inefficient small firm*; *landwirtschaftlicher* ~~: *small-holding*; ~**darlehensgeschäft** granting of small personal loans, money-lending business; ~**diebstahl** petty theft (**or** larceny), pilferage; ~**einfuhr** small import, import of goods of small value; ~**eisenbranche** hardware trade; ~**forderungen** small debts; ~**gartenwesen** allotment holding; ~**gedrucktes** (*das Kleingedruckte*) (the) small print, fine print; ~**geld** (small) change, loose cash; ~**gewerbe** small(-scale) craft; business; ~**gewerbetreibende(r)** small-scale trader; ~**handel** retail trade; ~**handelsspanne** retail-trade margin (*or* mark-up); ~**händler** shopkeeper; ~**kaufleute** small-scale traders; ~**konto** small account; ~**kredit** small loan, small-scale lending, loan for personal use; ~**kreditbank** small-scale lending bank; ~**kreditgeschäft** small-scale lending; ~**kreditwesen** money lending; ~**landwirt** small holder; ~**laster** pick-up truck; ~**lebensversicherung** industrial life-insurance, industrial life policy; ~**lieferwagen** van, pickup; ~**makler** odd

Kleinstbetrag

lot dealer; **~obligationen** baby bonds; **~pacht** tenancy of small holdings; **~pächter** small holder; **~preisgeschäft** low-price (*or* cut-price) store; **~reparaturen** small repair work, small-scale repairs; **~schaden** small loss; small-scale damage; **~siedlerstelle** small holding; **~siedlung** small housing estate; **~siedlungsträger** organization financing small holdings (*or* small housing estates); **~sparer** small saver; **~staaterei** particularism; **~stück** fractional amount; **~verbraucher** small consumer; **~verkauf** small-lot selling, retail selling; **~wagen** subcompact car; **~vieh** small stock; **~wohnung** small flat; **~wohnungsbau** construction of small housing estates.

Kleinst|betrag very small amount, minimum amount; **~betrieb** small business, small-holding; *landwirtschaftlicher* **~~**: *farm of minimum size*; **~format** miniature size, very small size; **~hypothek** very small-scale mortgage; **~siedlung** minimum-sized holding; **~wohnung** small flat, flatlet, mini-apartment.

Klemmbrett *n* clip board (*court interpreters*).

Kleptomane *m* kleptomaniac.

Kleptomanie *f* kleptomania.

Klerus *m* (the) clergy, ecclesiastical authorities, the Church.

Klient *m* client; **e-n ~en betreuen** to serve a client; **ohne ~en** briefless, without clients.

Klientel *f* clientele.

Klientin *f* (woman) client.

Klima-Bergverordnung *f regulations for underground air conditions in mines*.

Klinkenputzen *n* canvassing, door-to-door selling.

Klischeeherstellung *f* photoengraving.

Knapphaltung *f* keeping money tight.

Knappheit *f* shortage, tightness; **~skurs** policy of tightness (*of tight money etc*).

Knappschaft *f* social miners' and

460

Kohlenabgabe

mine-employees' insurance; (society of) miners; **~skasse** miners' provident fund, miners' insurance; **~srente** miners' social insurance pension; **~sverband** miners' social insurance association; **~sversicherung** miners' (health and pension) insurance.

Knastbruder *m* jailbird, habitual law breaker.

Knebel *m* gag.

knebeln *v/t* to gag.

Knebelungsvertrag *m* (= *Knebelvertrag*) oppresive contract, adhesion contract.

Know-how *m* know-how; **~-Abtretung** assignment of know-how; **~geber** grantor of know-how; **~nehmer** grantee of know-how.

Koalition *f* coalition.

Koalitions|freiheit freedom of association, right of coalition; **~~** *für Gewerkschaften*: *trade union freedom*; **~kabinett** coalition cabinet; **~partei** coalition party; **~recht** right of association; **~regierung** coalition government; **~wahlliste** mixed ticket; **~zwang** compliance with coalition agreement.

Kodeschlüssel *m* key to a code, code-book.

Kodetelegramm *n* code telegram.

Kodex *m* codex, code.

Kodifikation *f* codification.

kodifizieren *v/t* to codify.

Kodifizierung *f* codification; **~sgesetz** codifying statute.

Kodizill *n* codicil (*to a will*).

Koexistenz *f* co-existence; **friedliche ~** peaceful co-existence.

Kohlegewinnung *f* coal extraction.

Kohlen|abgabe coal levy (*to support coal mining industry*); **~bergarbeiterstreik** coal strike; **~bergbauleitung** coal mining administration; **~einsatz** utilization of coal, amount of coal used, coal input; **~förderung** coal output; **~halden** pithead stocks of coal, coal stockpiles; **~knappheit** coal shortage; **~pfennig** "coal penny", *nominal excise tax on energy supply to subsidize coal industry*; **~verflüssi-**

Kollaborateur   „**Komitee für das Erbe der Welt**"

gung *f* hydrogenation of coal; ~**versand** coal transport; ~**vorkommen** coal deposit; ~**zeche** coal mine, colliery.

Kollaborateur *m pol* collaborator.

kollationieren *v/t* to collate, to compare (*proofs, translation*), to check.

Kollationierung *f* collating, checking, word-by-word comparison.

Kollege *m* colleague, fellow worker; *mein verehrter* ~: *my learned friend, my dear colleague*; ~**nrabatt** employees' discount, fellow-publisher's discount, trade discount (*within a profession*).

Kollegial|behörde board, *authority organized on the collegial principle*; ~**gericht** panel of judges; ~**herrschaft** polygarchy; ~**prinzip** board-majority principle; principle of collective responsibility, collegial principle; ~**system** board system, collegial system (*of top management*).

Kollektion *f com* fashion collection, range of goods, assortment.

Kollektiv|anzeige composite advertisement; ~**arbeitsvertrag** collective labour (*US: labor*) agreement; ~**beleidigung** defamation of a group of persons, collective defamation (*or* libel); ~**delikt** collective crime; ~**eigentum** collective ownership, joint ownership; ~**einbürgerung** collective naturalization; ~**geldstrafe** combined fine; ~**gesellschaft** collective society, general partnership; ~**güter** public goods, collective goods; ~**haftung** collective liability; ~**handlungsvollmacht** joint power of attorney; ~**klage** multi-plaintiff action; collective action; ~**klausel** joint clause; ~**marke** collective mark (*trade mark*); ~**note** collective note; ~**prokura** joint commercial power of representation; ~**sanktion** collective sanction; ~**schuld** *pol* collective guilt; ~**sparen** group saving; ~**strafe** collective punishment; ~**Unfallversicherung** group accident insurance; ~**verantwortung** collective responsiblity; ~**versicherung** blanket insurance, group insurance; ~**vertrag** collective bargaining agreement; ~**vertragsverhandlungen** collective bargaining; ~**vollmacht** joint power of attorney; ~**wirtschaft** collective economy, socialized economy; ~**zeichen** collective trade mark; ~**zeichnung** joint signature; ~**zeichnungsbefugnis** joint authority to sign.

Kollektivierung *f* collectivization.

kollidieren *v/i* to collide, to crash.

Kollision *f* collision, conflict.

Kollisions|gefahr risk of collision; ~**haftpflicht** mandatory accident insurance, legal accident liability; ~**norm** conflict-of-laws rule; ~**patent** interfering patent; ~**prozeß** accident case; ~**recht** conflict of laws; ~**versicherung** *mar* collision insurance.

Kollo *n* parcel.

Kollusion *f* collusion; ~**sgefahr** danger of collusion; ~**sprozeß** agreed case; collusive proceedings.

Kolonial|amt Colonial office; ~**anleihe** colonial bond; ~**beamter** colonial officer; ~**besitz** colonial possessions; ~**gebiet** colonial territory; ~**gesellschaft** colonial company, chartered company *hist*: *promotion company for the colonies*; ~**herrschaft** colonial rule; ~**ministerium** colonial office; ~**politik** colonial policy; ~**vertrag** treaty concerning colonies; ~**verwaltung** colonial administration; ~**waren** groceries; ~**werte** colonials, colonial stocks.

Kolonialismus *m* colonialism.

Kolonnenspringer *m* queue jumper.

Kombattanten *m/pl* combatants.

Kombinat *n* combine, integrated plant.

Kombination *f* combination.

Kombinations|element element of a combination; ~**erfindungspatent** combination patent; ~**schloß** combination lock; ~**wirkung** combined effect.

„**Komitee für das Erbe der Welt**" *n* "the World Heritage Committee".

Kommandant *m* (*Luftfahrzeug*) pilot-in-command.
Kommandantur *f* headquarters, military command, H. Q.
Kommandeur *m* commanding officer; ~ **der Militärpolizei** provost-marshal.
Kommandit|aktiengesellschaft *f* partnership limited by shares; ~**aktionär** *limited-liability shareholder in partnership limited by shares*; ~**anteil** limited partner's interest (*or* share); ~**beteiligung** participation (*or* interest) in a limited partnership, limited-partner's holding; ~**einlage** limited-partnership capital contribution, limited partner's holding; ~**gesellschaft** limited partnership; ~**gesellschaft auf Aktien** partnership limited by shares; ~**kapital** capital contributed by the limited partners, limited-liability partnership capital.
Kommanditist *m* limited partner; ~**enanteil** *m* limited partner's interest (*in the firm's capital*).
Kommastelle *f* decimal place, decimal figure.
Kommissar *m* inspector, commissary.
Kommission *f* (1) commission; ~ **der Europäischen Gemeinschaften** Commission of the European Communities; ~ **für die Fischerei im Nordostatlantik** North-East Atlantic Fisheries Commission; **die** ~ **damit befassen** bring the matter before the Commission; **e-e** ~ **einsetzen** to appoint a commission; **gemischte** ~ mixed commission, joint commission; **paritätische** ~ joint commission of equally strong delegations.
Kommission *f* (2) commission, consignment, factorage; **in** ~ **geben** to consign, to place on consignment; **in** ~ **liefern** to supply sth on sale or return; **in** ~ **nehmen** to take sth on a commission basis.
Kommissionär *m* commission merchant; factor; commission agent; **selbsteintretender** ~ self-contracting commission merchant (*or* agent).

Kommissions|agent commission agent; ~**aufsicht** the state's (*German Land's*) supervisory power over local government agencies; ~**basis** on consignment, on sale or return; ~**buch** order book; ~**einkauf** purchase on commission, purchase on consignment; ~**geschäft** commission business, business on account of another person; ~**gut** goods consigned, articles on consignment; ~**handel** factorage, agency business; ~**konto** consignment account; ~**lager** consignment stock; ~**pfandrecht** factor's lien; ~**provision** factorage, remuneration for consignment sale; ~**rechnung** consignment invoice; ~**satz** (amount of the) factor's commission; ~**verkauf** sale on commission; ~~ *mit Selbsteintrittsrecht*: *sale with self-contracting right*; ~**verlag** commissioned publishers; publishing on commission; ~**vertrag** factor's agreement, consignment agreement; ~**ware** consignment goods, goods on commission; ~**wechsel** bill drawn for account of a third party; **k**~**weise** *adj* on an agency basis, on commission.
Kommittent *m* consignor, principal.
kommunal *adj* municipal, communal.
Kommunal|abgaben rates, municipal charges, local taxes and fees; ~**abgabennachforderung** supplementary rate demand; ~**anleihe** municipal loan; ~**bank** municipal bank; ~**beamter** municipal officer, local government official; ~**behörde** local authority, municipal authority, local government agency; ~**betrieb** municipal undertaking, public utility enterprise; ~**darlehen** municipal loan; ~**deckung** security for debts of local authorities, cover through a public authority's guarantee; ~**geschäft** local government transaction; ~**körperschaft** municipal corporation); ~**kredit** loan (*or* credit facilities) granted to a local authori-

Kommune   **Kondominium**

ty; ~**kreditanstalt** municipal bank; ~**kreditinstitut** communal loan bank; ~**leistungen** local services; ~**obligation** municipal bond, municipal debenture; ~**recht** local government law, local law; ~**schuldverschreibung** municipal bond; ~**steuer** local tax, municipal tax; ~**verband** association of local government bodies; ~**verfassung** constituion of local authorities; ~**verfassungsstreit** litigation between local government bodies, (*concerning the lawfulness of their functions*); ~**verschuldung** indebtedness of local authorities, municipal debts; ~**verwaltung** local government; ~**wahlen** local government elections, municipal elections; ~**wirtschaft** economic activities of local government agencies.

Kommune *f* municipality, local government body; commune.

Kommuniqué *n* communiqué, official bulletin.

Kommunmauer *f* party-wall, common wall, shared wall.

Kompensation *f* compensation, off-setting, set-off, barter; satisfaction (*for a defamatory act or word*); ~**seinrede** plea of retorsion; ~**sgeschäft** barter transaction, offsetting transaction, compensation trading; ~**skredit** compensating credit.

kompensieren *v/t*, *v/i* to compensate, to offset, to counterbalance; to make amends for, to make up for.

kompetent *adj* competent, responsible, relevant, appropriate.

Kompetenz *f* competence, responsibility, jurisdiction; ~**abgrenzung** jurisdictional limits; ~**artikel** objects clause (*in memorandum of association*); ~**bereich** sphere of jurisdiction; ~-**Kompetenz** (= *Kompetenzkompetenz*) competence for jurisdictional conflicts; ~**konflikt** jurisdictional conflict; *bejahender* ~~: *two courts claiming jurisdiction*; *negativer* ~~: *two courts denying jurisdiction, negative conflict of jurisdiction*; ~**konfliktsgericht(shof)** court having power to decide on jurisdictional problems between courts; ~**streitigkeit** jurisdictional conflict; ~**überschreitung** exceeding one's competence (*or* jurisdiction), acting ultra vires; ~**zuweisung** allocation of jurisdiction; **ausschließliche** ~ (*pol*) plenary power.

Komplementär *m* general partner, personally liable partner, full partner, unlimited partner; ~**anteil** general partner's interest (*in the partnership capital*).

Komplementärgüter *n/f* complementary goods, joint demand goods;

Komplice *m* (= *Komplize*) accomplice, particeps criminis.

Komplott *n* plot, conspiracy; **ein** ~ **schmieden** to plot, to conspire; **ein** ~ **vereiteln** to foil a plot.

Komponente *f* component, component part, element, factor; **evolutorische** ~ evolutive component; **undulatorische** ~ recurring element (*of a development*), recurrently fluctuating element (*e.g. seasonal movement*).

Komprimierung *f* condensation; ~ **der Gewinnspanne** narrowing the profit margin.

Kompromiß *m* compromise; ~**freudigkeit** willingness to compromise; **k~los** *adj* uncompromising; ~**vorschlag** compromise proposal, suggestion to meet s. o. half way.

kompromittieren *v/t* to injure one's reputation, to compromise.

Kompromittierung *f* disclosure of dishonorable facts, defamation.

Komputer →*Computer*.

Kondemnation *f* condemnation (*of ship*).

Konditionen *f/pl* terms (and conditions), scale of rates and charges; ~**gefüge** structure of rates and terms; ~**kartell** condition–fixing cartel (*agreed uniform application of standard terms*); ~**vereinbarung** agreement on sales conditions.

Konditionsgeschäft *n* sale and return.

Kondominium *n* condominium, joint sovereignty, country gov-

erned jointly by two or more states.
Konfektions|abteilung ready-made department; ~**artikel** ready-made clothes; ~**größe** standard size; ~**industrie** clothing industry; ~**ware** ready-to-wear clothes, ready-made clothes, off-the-peg clothes.
Konferenz *f* conference, meeting; ~**teilnehmer** delegate conference; e–e ~ **beenden** to close a meeting; e–e ~ **einberufen** to convene (*or* call) a meeting; e–e ~ **halten** to hold a meeting.
konferieren *v/i* to hold a meeting.
Konfession *f* religious belief; ~**sschule** denominational school.
Konfiskation *f* seizure, confiscation; ~**sgut** confiscated goods, prize.
konfiszieren *v/t* to confiscate, to seize.
Konfiszierung *f* seizure, confiscation.
Konflikt *m* conflict; ~**mittler** mediator, intermediary, conciliator; ~**slösung** resolution of conflict; **bewaffneter** ~ armed conflict, hostility; **offener** ~ open conflict.
Konfrontation *f* confrontation, clash.
konfrontieren *v/i* to confront, to face.
Konfusion *f* confusion, confusion of debts (*upon death*).
Konglomerat *n* conglomeration, conglomerate; mixed bag.
Kongreß *m* congress, the Congress.
König *m* king, monarch.
Königin queen; **regierende** ~ queen regnant, reigning queen.
Königs|friede pax regis, the king's (queen's) peace; ~**mord** regicide; ~**mörder** regicide; ~**standarte** royal standard; ~**treuer** royalist; ~**würde** regality, royal dignity.
Konjunktur *f* economic situation, economic trends, market conditions, level of business activity; ~**ablauf** economic cycle, trends of the economy; ~**abschwächung** slackening of economic activity, economic recession; ~**abschwung** cyclical downturn, contraction, decline in economic activity; ~**analyse** analysis of economic trends; ~**änderung** change in economic trends; k~**anfällig** *adj* sensitive to cyclical influences; ~**anstieg** increase in economic activity, upward economic trend; ~**aufschwung** improving business situation, economic upswing, economic recovery; cyclical upswing; ~**ausgleichsrücklage** compulsory anticyclical reserve; ~**aussichten** economic prospects; ~**belebung** economic recovery; ~**beobachtung** observation of economic trends; ~**beruhigung** easing of economic strains; ~**besserung** increase in business, improvement of the economic situation; k~**bestimmend** *adj* determining the economic trends; ~**bewegung** economic trend; ~**bild** the general economic situation; ~**bremse** economic brake(s); ~**dämpfung** curbing the boom; ~**debatte** economic-policy debate; ~**diagnose** economic trend analysis; ~**dynamik** business cycle dynamics; ~**einbruch** setback in economic activity, recession; ~**empfindlichkeit** sensitivity to economic fluctuations; ~**entwicklung** trend in business, economic trend, conjunctural development; ~**erholung** rebound; ~**erwartungen** expected future business trends; ~**faktor** cyclical factor; ~**flaute** dull spell, economic slackness, business stagnation; ~**förderung** cyclical stimulation; ~**forscher** specialist in cyclical research, business cycle analyst; ~**forschung** business trend research; ~**gestaltung** shaping of economic policy; ~**gewinne** boom profits; ~**impuls** stimulus to economic activity; ~**institut** economic research institute; ~**jahr** boom year; ~**klima** economic climate, economic temperature; ~**kurve** cyclical trend; ~**lage**

Konjunkturmodell

economic situation, trend of the economy; **~modell** cyclical model; **~mulde** trough in the economic trend; **~nervosität** nervousness about the economic outlook; **k~neutral** *adj* cyclically balanced; **~optimismus** optimism about business prospects; **~phase** phase of the business cycle; **~politik** business cycle policy, economic policy, conjunctural policy; *aktive* ~~: *positive counter-cyclical policy;* *monetäre* ~~: *counter-cyclical monetary policy;* **~politiker** economic policy-maker; **k~politisch** *adj* relating to economic (*or* cyclical) policy; **~prognose** economic forecasting; **~programm** economic policy program(me), anticyclical program(me); **k~reagibel** *adj* responsive to cyclical trends, fluctuationreactive; **~regulativ** economic regulator; **~rat** economic policy council (*German federal government*); **~reserve** contingency reserves for business policy; **~risiko** business (cycle) risk; **~rückgang** economic recession, decline in business, setback; **~rückschlag** business slump, setback, economic dip; **~schatten** sluggish economic activity; **~schwankungen** cyclical fluctuations; **~sensibilität** sensitivity to cyclical factors; **~spritze** pump priming; **~statistik** statistics on business trends; **~steuerung** economic management, cycle riding; **~stimulus** business incentives, stimulation of economic activity; **~stockung** economic slowdown; **~stütze** support for economic activity; **k~symptomatisch** symptomatic of the economic trend; **~tal** trough of the trade cycle, downward cycle; **~theoretiker** economist specializing in cyclical trends; **~theorie** theory of economic trends; **~therapie** counter-cyclical treatment, counter-cyclical compensatory policy; **~tief** low point of the business cycle; **~vorhersage** economic fore-

Konkurrenz

casting; **~überhitzung** overheating of the economic atmosphere, overheating of the boom; **~umbruch** radical break in the economic trend; **~verfall** economic downturn; **~verlangsamung** economic slowdown; **~verlauf** cyclical trend, run of business; **~welle** trade cycle undulation; **~wende** general upswing of the economy; **~ziffer** economic index, index showing cyclical trends; **~zügelung** curbing the boom; **~zuschlag** boom surtax; **~zyklus** trade cycle, business cycle, economic cycle; **die ~ intensivieren** to stimulate economic activity; **expansive ~** boom; **nachlassende ~** declining economy; **rückläufige ~** declining economic activity, recession, slump; **schwächer werdende ~** declining economic activity.

konkludent *adj* implied, tacit; *~es Handeln*: *action implying intention*.

Konkordat *n* concordat; *agreement between the Vatican and a government.*

konkret *adj* concrete, tangible, real.

konkretisieren *v/t* to make definite, to put into concrete form; to appropriate (*fungible goods*).

konkretisiert *adj, pp* appropriated, particular; made definite, spelled out, specified.

Konkretisierung *f* appropriation, putting into specific terms, encapsulation; **~ der Gattungsschuld** appropriation of unascertained goods.

Konkubinat *n* concubinage, illicit cohabitation, man-mistress relationship.

Konkurrent *m* competitor; **~en ausschalten** to outbid one's competitors, to defeat one's competitors; **~enklage** legal action by a competitor; action against unfair award to competitor; **als ~ auftreten** to compete, to set up competition.

Konkurrenz *f* competition, concurrence, jurisdictional conflict, rivalry; **~angebot** competitive bid, offer

465

konkurrieren / **Konkursvermerk**

from a competing firm; ~**ausschluß** exclusion of competition; ~**beschränkungen** restraint on competition; ~**betrieb** competing business; ~**druck** pressure of competition; ~**erzeugnis** competing product, rival product; k~**fähig** *adj* able to meet competition, competitive; ~**fähigkeit** competitiveness, competitive position, ability to compete; ~**firma** competing firm, competitive firm, rival firm; ~**geschäft** competing business, competing store; ~**kampf** competition, competitive struggle, trade rivalry; ~**klausel** agreement not to compete, restraint of competition clause; ~**preis** competitive price; ~**unternehmen** competing enterprise, rival business; ~**verbot** restraint of competition, prohibition of competition; ~ **von Verpflichtungen** conflict of obligations; **latente** ~ latent (potential) competition; **ruinöse** ~ destructive competition, cut-throat competition; **zur** ~ **abwandern** to switch to a rival firm, to move to a competitor.

konkurrieren *v/i* to compete.

Konkurs *m* bankruptcy (*natural persons*), compulsory winding-up (*companies*); ~**anfechtung** rescission by the trustee in bankruptcy; ~ **anmelden** to file a petition in bankruptcy, to commence winding-up proceedings; ~**anmeldung** filing (*or* presentation) of a bankruptcy petition; ~~ *durch den Schuldner*: *voluntary petition (in bankruptcy)*; ~**antrag** bankruptcy petition; ~**antragspflicht** obligation to file a bankruptcy petition; ~**ausfallgeld** substitute pay in the event of insolvency (*of the employer*); ~**beschlag** attachment of bankrupt's asset; bankruptcy freeze; ~**dividende** dividend in bankruptcy, quota of distribution in bankruptcy; ~**erklärung** declaring oneself bankrupt, declaration of bankruptcy; ~ **eröffnen** to adjudicate s.o. (a) bankrupt; ~**eröffnung**

adjudication (of bankruptcy), *GB*: order of adjudication; ~~ *beantragen*: *to file a bankruptcy petition*; ~**eröffnungsantrag** filing (*or* presentation) of a petition in bankruptcy; ~~ *des Gemeinschuldners*: *debtor's petition*; ~**eröffnungsbeschluß** order of adjudication *GB*, adjudication of bankruptcy *US*; ~**fähigkeit** capacity to be subject to bankruptcy; ~**forderung** provable debt, provable claim, claim, debt provable in bankruptcy, claim in bankruptcy; *bevorrechtigte* ~~: *preferred claim*; *gewöhnliche* ~~: *ordinary debt in bankruptcy*; ~~ *anmelden*: *to lodge proof in bankruptcy*; ~**gericht** bankruptcy court; ~**gläubiger** creditor in bankruptcy; *betreibender* ~~: *petitioning creditor*; ~**grund** cause of bankruptcy, sufficient ground for bankruptcy proceedings; ~**handlung** act of bankruptcy; ~ **machen** to go bankrupt, to become bankrupt; ~**masse** bankrupt's estate; ~**ordnung** Bankruptcy Act; ~**quote** dividend in bankruptcy, percentage of recovery, dividend on a bankrupt's estate; ~**recht** law relating to bankruptcy; k~**reif** *adj* (hopelessly) insolvent; ~**richter** judge at a bankruptcy court, referee in bankruptcy; ~**schuldner** debtor in bankruptcy, bankrupt, adjudicated bankrupt; ~**schuldnerverzeichnis** list of adjudicated bankrupts; ~**sperre** temporary blocking of bankruptcy proceeding by composition application; ~**status** an insolvent debtor's statement of affairs; ~**straftat** bankruptcy offence; ~**tabelle** schedule of creditors (of a bankrupt), bankruptcy schedule; ~**verfahren** bankruptcy proceedings, ~~ *mangels Masse einstellen*: *to dismiss the petition in bankruptcy for insufficiency of assets*; ~**vergehen** bankruptcy offence; ~**vergleich** composition in bankruptcy; ~**verlust** loss due to bankruptcy; ~**vermerk** entry of pending bankruptcy in land register;

~**verschleppung** (criminal) delay (of company director) in filing bankruptcy petition; ~**verwalter** trustee (*or* receiver *or* administrator) (in bankruptcy); *vorläufiger* ~~: *receiver in bankruptcy*; ~**verwaltung** administration of a bankrupt's estate by bankruptcy trustee; ~**verwertung** disposal of assets from the bankrupt's estate; ~**voraussetzung** prerequisites for a bankruptcy adjudication; ~**vorrecht** preference, privilege (in bankruptcy proceedings).

Konmorienten|vermutung *f* presumption of simultaneous death (*in fatal accident*); ~**klausel** simultaneous death clause.

Können *n* skill, aptitude, talent; **fachmännisches** ~ usual ability of an expert, usual ability of the person skilled in the art.

Konnexität *f* coherence.

Konnivenz *f* connivance, suborning an inferior to commit a criminal offence.

Konnossement bill of lading, B/L; ocean bill of lading, order bill of lading; ~ **gegen Kasse** cash against bill of lading; ~ **ohne Vorbehalt** clean bill of lading; **durchgehendes** ~ through bill of lading; **echtes** ~ clean bill of lading; **ein** ~ **gegen Revers reinzeichnen** to sign a clean bill of lading against counter-indemnity; **laut** ~ as per bill of lading; **reines** ~ clean bill of lading; **unreines** ~ foul *or* claused *or* dirty bill of lading.

Konossements|bestimmungen stipulations on a bill of lading; ~**garantie** letter of indemnity; ~**indossament** endorsement of a bill of lading; ~**ladung** the cargo shipped under a bill of lading; ~**teilschein** split bill of lading (*split B/L*); ~**vermerk** remark endorsed on a bill of lading.

Konsens *m* consensus; agreement, meeting of the minds.

konsenspflichtig *adj* subject to mutual agreement.

Konsensualvertrag *m* consensual contract, *contract completed by the mere agreement of the parties.*

Konservativer *m* Conservative, Tory.

Konserven|fabrik packing house (*meat*), tinning factory; cannery; ~**fabrikation** *GB*: tinning, *US*: canning; ~**industrie** tin industry, can industry.

Konsignator *m* consignee, recipient of goods.

Konsignation *f* consignment.

Konsignations|ausfuhr export of consignment goods; ~**beschaffung** consignment purchasing; ~-**Depot von Reiseschecks** travellers' cheques held in stock; ~**geschäft** sale on consignment; ~**konto** consignment account, commission account; ~**lager** stock of consignment goods, consignment stock; ~**sendung** consignment shipment; ~**verkauf** consignment sale; ~**vertrag** contract of consignment; agreement on consignment stock; **k**~**weise** *adv* by way of consignment; ~**ware** consignment goods, consigned goods.

Konsolidation *f* consolidation, confusion of title; funding.

konsolidieren *v/t* to consolidate, to fund.

Konsolidierung *f* consolidation, funding; ~ **schwebender Schulden** funding of floating debts; ~**sanleihe** funding loan; ~**skredit** consolidation credit, funding credit; ~**kreis** extent of consolidation; ~**splazierung** syndication.

Konsols *pl* consols, (= *Consolidated Stock* = *Consolidated Annuities of the British National Debt*).

Konsorte *m* associate, syndicate member.

konsortial *adj* consortial, syndicate.

Konsortial|anleihe syndicated loan; ~**anteil** underwriting share, share in a syndicate; ~**aufwendungen** underwriting expenses; ~**banken** syndicate member banks; ~**beteiligung** underwriting share, share in a syndicate, syndicate participation, partnership in a syndi-

konsortialiter / **Konsum**

cate; ~**führer** lead manager, lead bank; syndicate leader, co-manager; ~**geschäft** business on joint account, underwriting transaction, syndicate operation; ~**konto** syndicate account; ~**kredit** syndicate credit, syndicated loan; ~**-Kreditlinien** syndicate credit lines; ~**marge** issuing banks' commission; ~**mitglied** syndicate member; ~**provision** underwriter's commission; ~**vertrag** consortium agreement.

konsortialiter *adv* in the form of a syndicate, by way of a syndicate, on behalf of a syndicate.

Konsortium *n* syndicate, pool; **ausgebendes** ~ distributing syndicate.

Konspiration *f* plot, conspiracy.

konspirativ *adj* conspirational.

konspirieren *v/t* to conspire, to plot.

konstatieren *v/t* to state, to find, to put on record, to delare.

konstituieren *v/i, v/reflex* to be constituted.

konstituierend *adj* constitutive (effect).

konstituiert *pp, adj* constituted; **ordnungsgemäß** ~ duly constituted by law.

Konstitution *f* condition, constitution, → *Verfassung*.

konstruieren *v/t* to design, to construct, to plan.

Konstruktion *f* design, construction, structure, set-up, scheme, device, arrangement; ~ **der Gegenwertmittel** the set-up in connection with counterpart funds.

Konstruktions|büro drawing office, engineering department; ~**fehler** design fault, fault in the construction, structural defect; ~**ingenieur** design engineer; ~**merkmal** constructional feature, design feature; ~**prinzipien** design philosophy, principles underlying the design; ~**technik** design engineering; ~**typ** type of design; ~**- und Betriebsabteilungen** design and production departments; ~**überprüfung** design review; ~**vereinfachung** simplification of design;

~**zeichnung** production drawing, detailed drawing, workshop drawing.

Konsul *m* consul; **übergeordneter** ~ superintending consular officer.

Konsular|abkommen consular treaty; ~**abteilung** consular section (*in an embassy*); ~**agent** consular agent; ~**beamter** consular officer; ~**bezirk** consular district; ~**gebühren** consular fees, consular charges; ~**gericht** consular court, consular tribunal, ~**korps** consular corps; ~**matrikel** consular register; ~**recht** consular law; right to maintain consular representation; ~**schutz** consular protection; ~**sichtvermerk** consular visa; ~**status** consular status; ~**vertrag** consular convention, consular treaty; ~**vertreter** consular representative; ~**vertretung** consular representation.

konsularisch *adj* consular.

Konsulat *n* consulate.

Konsulats|angehöriger consulate employee, member of the consular staff; ~**beamter** consular officer; ~**befugnisse** jurisdiction of the consulate; ~**dienst** consular service; ~**faktura** consular invoice; ~**gebühren** consular fees, consular charges; ~**sekretär** clerical assistant (in the consular service); ~**sichtvermerk** consular visa; ~**vertrag** consular convention, consular treaty; ~**verweser** acting consul.

Konsultation *f* consultation.

Konsultations|einrichtungen consultative machinery; ~**gesellschaft** consultancy company; ~**pflicht** obligatory consultation; duty to consult (*or* advise); ~**recht** right to be consulted; ~**verfahren** consultation procedure.

Konsultativpakt *m* consultative pact.

konsultieren *v/i* to consult, to seek s. o.'s advice, to enquire.

Konsum *m* consumption; co-op (=*coop*), consumer co-operative society; ~**artikel** consumer goods;

gewerbliche ~~: *consumer goods produced by industry*; ~**befriedigung** satisfaction of consumers' wishes; *totale* ~~: *total utility*; ~**finanzierung** consumer credit, hire-purchase finance; ~**freudigkeit** propensity to consume; ~**genossenschaft** consumer co-operative society, co-op (= *coop*) retail society; ~**gesellschaft** consumer society; ~**gewohnheiten** consumer habits; ~**güter** consumer goods; *dauerhafte* ~~: *durable consumer goods*; *kurzlebige* ~~: *shortlived consumer goods*; *langlebige* ~~: *durable consumer goods*; ~**güterkonjunktur** state of business in consumer goods; ~**gütermesse** trade fair for consumer goods; ~**konjunktur** boom in consumer goods; ~**kraft** power to consume, consumption capacity; ~**kredit** consumer credit; ~**kreditgenossenschaft** consumer credit co-operative; ~**quote** consumption ratio; ~**schatten** fields not touched by consumer goods boom, neglected fields; ~**sphäre** consumer goods class; ~**stoß** jump in consumption; ~**subvention** consumer goods subsidy; ~**verein** consumer co-operative (society), co-op (= *coop*); ~**vermögen** consumption capital; ~**verzicht** voluntary reduction in consumption; ~**ware** consumer goods.

Konsumenten|einkommen consumer income; ~**geld** consumers' money; ~**handel** consumer co-operative trade; ~**kredit** consumer credit; ~**preis** retail price; ~**schutz** consumer safety.

konsumieren *v/t* to consume, to absorb.

konsumtiv *adj* relating to consumption.

Kontaktmann *m* (*Presse*) source, informant; (*bei Werbeagenturen*) account executive.

Kontaktsperre *f* confinement incommunicado, solitary confinement.

Kontaktstelle point of contact, contact agency.

Kontaktstudium *n* further professional studies for the purpose of keeping up to date, continuing education.

Konten *n/pl* → *Konto*; ~**abbuchung** automatic debit; ~**abgleichung** balancing of accounts; ~**abschluß** closing of accounts; ~ **abstimmen** to reconcile accounts; ~**abstimmung** reconciliation of accounts, adjustment of accounts, accounting equation; ~**aufgliederung** account classification; ~**aufteilung** accounts specification; ~ **ausgleichen** to square accounts; ~ **bereinigen** to adjust accounts; ~**blatt** account sheet; ~ **des Auslandsgeschäftes** foreign business accounts; ~**fälschung** falsification of accounts; ~**führer** person in charge of the account; ~**führung** account-keeping; ~**glattstellung** adjustment of accounts, squaring of accounts; ~**gruppe** account group; ~**inhaber** holder of a banking account, depositor; ~ **in laufender Rechnung** balances on current accounts; ~**klasse** class of account; ~**manipulation** account manipulation, juggling or fiddling of accounts; ~**pfändung** garnishment of accounts (in a bank); ~**plan** chart of accounts; ~**rahmen** accounting plan, standard form of accounts; ~**regulierung** squaring of accounts, settlement of outstanding accounts; ~**saldo** balance; ~**schiebung** fiddling accounts, account manipulation; ~**sparen** deposit account saving; ~**sperre** freezing of accounts; *e-e* ~~ *aufheben: to unfreeze an account*; ~**stand** balance of an account; ~**übertrag** carry-over from an account; ~**umschreibung** movements between accounts, transfer from one account to another; ~**unstimmigkeiten** discrepancies between accounts; ~**wahrheit** truthfulness (and accuracy) of (*taxpayer's*) accounts; ~**zusammenlegung** pooling of accounts, merger of accounts; **bewegte** ~ active accounts; *fiskali-*

Konterbande

sche ~ public authorities' accounts; **interne** ~ intercompany accounts; **steuerbegünstigte** ~ accounts eligible for tax privileges; **transferfähige** ~ transferable accounts.
Konterbande *f* contraband goods.
konterkarieren *v/t* to counteract.
kontieren *v/t* to allocate (to an account).
Kontierung *f* allocation (to an account).
Kontiguitätszone *f* contiguous zone, adjacent zone.
Kontingent *n* quota, allotment; ~**bescheid** decision on the granting of a quota, allocation award; ~**beschränkungen** quota limitations; ~**flüchtling** accepted quota refugees *(for humanitarian reasons)*; ~**e globalisieren** to lump the quotas together, to combine the quotas; **k~mäßig** *adj* in the form of quotas, according to quota.
kontingentieren *v/t* to make subject to quota, to limit, to fix a quota, to ration.
kontingentiert *adj* subject to quota; **nicht** ~ non-quota.
Kontingentierung *f* quota restrictions, fixing of quotas, rationing.
Kontinuität *f* continuity, consistency; ~**serklärung** declaration of continuity; ~**prinzip** principle of continuity.
Konto *n* (*pl* **Konten** *qv*) account; ~**abschluß** closing an account; ~**abstimmung** = *Kontenabstimmung qv*; ~**abtretung** assignment of an account; ~**aufstellung** statement of account; ~**auszug** statement (of account); bank statement; ~**belastung** debit; ~**berichtigung** correction of an account; ~**bestand** balance held on account; ~**bezeichnung** title of an account; ~**eröffnung** opening an account; **k~führend** *adj* account-keeping; ~**führer** keeper of an account, person in charge of an account, account manager; ~**führung** account management; ~**führungsgebühr** account maintenance charge; service charge; ~**führungsprovision**

470

Konto

charge for handling a customer's account; ~ **für Sonderverwendungen** special disbursement account; ~**für Unvorhergesehenes** contingent account; ~**gegenbuch** pass-book, deposit book; ~**guthaben** credit balance; ~ **in brit. Währung** sterling account; ~**inhaber** account holder; ~**korrent** → *Kontokorrent*; ~**nummer** account number, code number; ~ **mit laufenden Umsätzen** active account; ~ **ohne Bewegung** inactive account; ~ **pro Diverse** sundries account; ~**spesen** account charges, bank charges; ~**stand** account balance; ~**überschrift** account title; ~**übertrag** internal transfer; ~**übertragungszeitraum** posting period; ~**überziehung** overdrawing of an account; ~**umsatz** account turnover; ~**unterlagen** account files; ~**verbindung** accounting relationship; ~ **„Verschiedenes"** sundries account; ~**vollmacht** written power of disposal over a bank account; ~ **zur vorläufigen Verbuchung unklarer Posten** overs and shorts; **à** ~(= *akonto*) on account, as a down-payment, as a part-payment; **abgeschlossenes** ~ closed account; **auf ein** ~ **einzahlen** to pay into an account; **ausgeglichenes** ~ balanced account; **belastetes** ~ debited account; **e-m** ~ **gutschreiben** to credit an account (with sth); **ein** ~ **abschließen** to make up an account, to rule off an account, to strike a balance; **ein** ~ **anlegen** to open an account; **ein** ~ **ausgleichen** to balance an account, to adjust an account; **ein** ~ **belasten** to charge an account, to debit an account; **ein** ~ **eröffnen** to set up an account, to open an account; **ein** ~ **glattstellen** to square an account, to discharge an account; **ein** ~ **mit einem Betrag erkennen** to credit an account with an amount; **ein** ~ **sperren** to stop an account, to freeze an account; **ein** ~ **überziehen** to overdraw an account;

Kontokorrent   **Kontrollabschnitt**

ein ~ unterhalten to keep an account, to have an account; **fingiertes ~** fictitious account; **gemeinsames ~** joint account; **gesperrtes ~** frozen account; **kreditorisches ~** account showing a credit balance; **laufendes ~** current account; **offenes ~** open account, current account, drawing account; **rückständiges ~** delinquent account; **ruhendes ~** inactive account; **totes ~** dead account, nominal account, inactive account, impersonal account; **über ein ~ verfügen** to operate an account; **überzogenes ~** overdrawn account; **umsatzloses ~** dormant account, inactive account, dead account; **von e-m ~ abheben** to (with)draw from an account; **zusammenfassendes ~** summary account.

Kontokorrent *n* current account; **~auszug** statement of account; **~bestätigung** account stated; **~buch** accounts receivable ledger, accounts payable ledger; **~debitor** debtor on overdraft; **~einlagen** current deposits; **~ gewähren** to advance on current account; **~gläubiger** trade creditor; **~geschäft** overdraft business; **~konto** current account; *überzogenes ~~ overdraft (o/d) on current account*; **~kredit** current account credit, advance on current account, overdraft, overdraft (o/d) facility, open account credit terms; *~~ gewähren: to grant open account credit terms*; **~limit** overdraft limit; **~saldo** balance on current account; **~verbindlichkeiten** liability on current account; **~verkehr** current account business, *or* transactions; **~vertrag** current account agreement, mercantile account-stated agreement; **~vorbehalt** current account reservation; *reservation of ownership until all current liabilities have been discharged*; **~zinsen** interest on current account.

kontra *prep* versus.

Kontrabular-Ersitzung *f* acquisitive prescription as against the land register entry; acquisition of title in the land register by adverse possession.

kontradiktorisch *adj* contentious, adversarial, contradictory.

Kontrahent *m* contracting party.

kontrahieren *v/i* to contract, to agree; **mit sich selbst ~** to contract with oneself, to act as principal and agent.

Kontrahierungs|freiheit *f* freedom to contract, liberty to enter into a contract; **~zwang** obligation to contract, legal compulsion to enter into a contract (*public service companies*).

Kontraktabschlüsse *m/pl* contracts placed.

kontraktbestimmt *adj* determined by contract, contractual.

kontraktbrüchig *adj* in breach of contract.

Kontraktfrist *f* contractual period.

kontraktgebunden *adj* contractually committed, bound by (the) contract.

kontraktiv *adj* restrictive, tight.

Kontroll|abschnitt counterfoil, stub; **~abteilung** inspection department; **~amt** control office; **~ausschuß** committee of control, supervisory committee; audit board; **~befugnisse** supervisory powers; **~behörde** supervisory authority; **~gebiet** control area; **~karte** time card (working time); **~kommission** control commission; **~konto** control account; **~liste** check list; **~mann** patrolman; **~maßnahmen** arrangements for inspection; **~mechanismen** controls; **~mitteilung** information for a cross check; **~muster** counter sample; **~nummer** reference number, code number; **~organ** controlling body; **~prüfung** check, test; **~punkt** checkpoint; **~rat** Control Council; **~ratgesetz** Control Council Act; **~recht** right of verification; **~stelle** check-point; **~übernahme** takeover; **~uhr** time clock; **~zeichen** check mark; **~zwecke** verification purposes.

471

Kontrolle *f* checking, checkup, surveillance, supervision, inspection, screening, control; **gerichtliche** ~ judicial restraint; **parlamentarische** ~ parliamentary control.

Kontrolleur *m* ticket-inspector, supervisor, compliance officer; guard.

Kontroverse *f* controversy; **e-e** ~ **austragen** to fight a controversial issue; **e-e** ~ **beilegen** to settle a controversy, to resolve a controversy.

Kontumaz *f* contumacy, default.

Kontumazial|urteil judgment rendered in the absence of the defendant; ~**verfahren** proceedings in the absence of the defendant.

Konturkarte *f* contour map.

Konvention *f* convention, treaty; ~ **von Rom** Rome Convention (1928).

Konventional|scheidung divorce by consent; ~**strafe** *f* penalty, penalty stipulated, conventional penalty, penalty under contract, penalty for non-fulfilment, (*imprecise*:) (agreed) liquidated damages; ~**strafklausel** penalty clause; ~**zinsen** *m pl* stipulated interest.

konventionell *adj* conventional.

Konversion *f* conversion.

Konversions|angebot conversion offer; ~**anleihe** convertible loan; ~**ausgabe** conversion issue; ~**kasse** conversion office, clearing house; ~~ *für deutsche Auslandsschulden*: *Conversion Office for German External Debts*; ~**klausel** convertibility clause; ~**prämie** conversion premium; ~**recht** right of conversion; ~**schuldverschreibungen** conversion bonds; **echte** ~ effective conversion; **zwangsweise** ~ compulsory conversion.

konvertibel *adj* convertible.

Konvertibilität *f* convertibility.

konvertierbar *adj* convertible; **beschränkt** ~ of limited convertibility; **frei** ~ freely convertible; **nicht** ~ inconvertible.

Konvertierbarkeit *f* convertibility; **beschränkte** ~ limited convertibility.

konvertieren *v/t* to convert.

Konvertierung *f* conversion; ~**sangebot** conversion offer; ~**srisiko** exchange transfer risk.

Konvolut *n* bundle of papers, scroll, roll.

konzedieren *v/t* to concede.

Konzentration *f* concentration, integration; **horizontale** ~ horizontal integration; **industrielle** ~ concentration of industries; **vertikale** ~ vertical integration.

Konzept *n* concept, first draft; ~**papier** draft paper, scrap paper.

Konzern *m* group (of affiliated companies) trust (*US*); ~**abschluß** consolidated financial statements, group accounts; ~**aktien** shares of a group of companies; ~**ausgleich** intercompany squaring; ~**banken** banks owned by a group; ~**bedarf** group requirements; ~**betriebsrat** group works council; ~**beziehungen** (intra-)group relations; ~**bilanz** consolidated balance sheet, combined financial statement, group balance sheet; ~**buchführung** group accounting; ~**buchgewinn** intercompany profit, consolidated profit; **k~eigen** captive; ~**entflechtung** decartelization; ~**firmen** affiliates, offshoots, subsidiary firms; ~**forderungen** intercompany receivables; ~**fremder** outsider to a group; ~**geschäfte** inter-company operations; ~**gesellschaft** affiliated company, group company; ~**gewinn** consolidated (unappropriated net) income, consolidated profit, **k~intern** *adj* intra-group, within the group; ~**jurist** corporation lawyer; ~**konto** group account; ~**lagebericht** group management report; ~**leitung** central management of a group; ~**rechnungslegung** consolidated (group) accounting; ~**recht** law concerning industrial groups; ~**spitze** principal company in a

472

Konzertierung / **Kopf**

group; ~**statut** the law governing a group of companies; ~**syndikus** in-house lawyer for a group of companies; ~**überschuß** consolidated surplus; ~**umsatz** group turnover; ~**unternehmen** group member-company; ~**verbindlichkeiten** intercompany liabilities; ~**verflechtung** (interlocking) group integration; ~**verlust** consolidated loss; ~**verrechnungsweise** intercompany pricing, intragroup settlements; ~**vorbehalt** multiple reservation; extended group reservation of ownership *(for all outstanding accounts of the group)*; ~**werte** shares in subsidiary companies; ~**zusammenhänge** interlocking holdings.

Konzertierung *f* harmonization; ~**sverfahren** conciliation procedure, harmonization procedure.

Konzertzeichner *m* stag, concert party.

Konzertzeichnung *f* stagging.

Konzession *f* licence to trade, charter, concession, franchise, commercial privilege; ~ **zum Verkauf alkoholischer Getränke über die Straße** off licence; **e–e** ~ **beantragen** to apply for a licence *(etc → Konzession)*; **e–e** ~ **entziehen** to withdraw *(or* revoke*)* a licence, to disfranchise; **e–e** ~ **erteilen** to grant a licence (concession *etc)*; **ohne** ~ non-licensed *(alcoholic beverages)*; **öffentlich-rechtliche** ~ licence, charter, franchise, business concession under public law; **vorläufige** ~ interim licence.

konzessionieren *v/t* to license, to grant a licence, to franchise, *US (also)*: to grant a concession.

konzessioniert *adj* licensed.

Konzessionierung *f* licensing, granting a franchise *or (US)* a concession.

Konzessions|abgabe licence tax, royalty, municipal compensation; *zusätzliche* ~~: additional *(or)* overriding royalty*; ~**entziehung** revocation of a licence, withdrawing of a licence; ~**entzug** revocation of a licence, withdrawing of a licence; ~**erteiler** licensor, franchiser; ~**erteilung** licensing, granting of a charter, issue of licences; ~**gebühr** concession fee, licence fee, royalty; ~**inhaber** concessionaire, concessionary, franchisee, licensed person, person duly licensed, holder of a licence; ~**pflicht** obligation to grant a licence; ~**steuer** franchise tax; ~**system** franchise system; ~**urkunde** charter, organization certificate, licence document; ~**vergabe** grant of a charter *(or* franchise*)*, issue of a licence; ~**vertrag** charter agreement, franchise agreement.

Kooperation *f* cooperation; ~**sfibel** *official guidelines governing (permissible) intercompany cooperation*.

Kooptationsrecht *n* right of cooption.

kooptieren *v/t* to co-opt.

Kooption *f* co-option.

Koordinationsausschuß *m* coordinating committee, steering committee.

Koordinierung *f* coordination; ~**smaßnahmen** coordinating measures, trade-off; ~**sstudie** trade-off study.

Kopf *m* head, title, heading; ~**arbeiter** brain worker; ~**bahnhof** terminal (station); ~**betrag** per capital quota; ~**bogen** letterheaded paper, *normierter* ~~: *standardized front page (pat)*; ~**filiale** main branch; ~**geld** poll-money, allowance per person *(upon change of currency)*, head money *(to catch convict)*; ~**höhe** headroom; ~**jäger** head hunter; executive search consultant; ~**mehrheit** majority of members present; ~**pauschale** lump-sum allowance per head; ~~**-Produktivität** per capita productivity; ~**quote** quota per capita, amount per person; ~**rechnen** mental arithmetic; ~**stärke** strength; ~**steuer** personal tax, poll tax, community charge; ~**teil** individual quota; *nach* ~~**en**: *per capita*; ~**wasserzeichen** watermark in the

473

Kopflosigkeit

form of a head; ~**zahl** number per capita; ~**zahlung** head count; ~**zeitung** leading newspaper of a syndicated group; **pro** ~ (= *nach Köpfen*) per capita, per head of population.

Kopflosigkeit *f* rashness.

Kopie *f* copy, duplicate, carbon (copy), transcript, print *(film)*, imitation; **beglaubigte** ~ certified copy; **wortgetreue** ~ precise copy, word-for-word copy.

kopieren *v/t* to copy, to duplicate.

Kopiergerät *n* copying machine.

Kopierschutz *m* protection against unauthorized copying; ~**technik** technology for protection against copying.

Kopplungs|geschäft *n* tie-in arrangement, linked transaction, package deal; ~**klausel** tie-in clause; ~**produkt** tied product; ~**verbot** prohibition of tying arrangement; ~**werbung** advertising for tied products; ~**verkauf** tie-in sale, combination sale.

Korbwährung *f* basket currency.

körperbehindert *adj* physically handicapped, disabled.

Körperbehindertenpauschale *f* lump-sum tax benefit for disabled persons.

Körperbehinderter *m* disabled person, handicapped person.

Körperbehinderung *f* physical defect.

Körperbeschädigter *m* disabled person, physically handicapped person.

Körperbeschädigung *f* physical injury; **unfallbedingte** ~ injury by accident.

Körperschäden *m* personal injury bodily harm, physical injury.

Körperschaft *f* (de jure) corporation, incorporated body, body corporate, incorporated group; ~ **des öffentlichen Rechts** public-law corporation, statutory corporation, statutory body; ~ **im Rechtssinne** de jure corporation; ~**saufsicht** state supervision of (public-law) corporations; **beratende** ~ consulting body; **bundesunmittelbare** ~ federal corporation; **gemeinnützige** ~ non-profit corporation; **gesetzgebende** ~ legislative body, legislature; **kommunale** ~**en** municipal corporate bodies; **mildtätige** ~ charitable corporation, charitable society; **öffentliche** ~ public authority; **öffentlich-rechtliche** ~ public-law corporation, statutory corporation, statutory body; **privatrechtliche** ~ private-law corporation; **parlamentarische** ~**en** legislative bodies; **rechtsfähige politische** ~ independent body politic; **sich in e-r** ~ **zusammenschließen** to become incorporated; **steuerbegünstigte** ~ corporation enjoying tax benefits; **steuerpflichtige inländische** ~ taxable domestic corporation.

Körperschaftssteuer *f* corporation (or corporate) income tax; ~-**Durchführungsverordnung** corporation tax implementing ordinance; ~**erklärung** corporation (income) tax return; ~**gesetz** Corporation Income Tax Act; ~**pflicht** corporation (income) tax liability; **beschränkte** ~~: *limited corporation tax liability (inland income only)*; k~**pflichtig** *adj* subject to corporation tax; *beschränkt* ~~: *territorially liable to corporation tax*; *with limited liability to pay corporation tax*.

Körperverletzung *f* physical injury, personal injury, bodily harm; ~ **erleiden** to sustain injury; ~ **im Amt** bodily injury caused by an officer of the law; ~ **mit Einwilligung** inflicting bodily injury with consent (*volenti non fit injuria*); ~ **mittels e-r Waffe** bodily injury inflicted using a weapon; ~ **mittels e-s gefährlichen Werkzeugs** bodily injury caused using a dangerous instrument; ~ **mit Todesfolge** fatal injury; **fahrlässige** ~ negligent bodily injury; **gefährliche** ~ dangerous bodily injury, grievous bodily harm; **gewaltsame** ~ assault and battery, bodily

Korporationsrecht   **Kosten des Prüfens**

injury by violence; **schwere** ~ (causing) grievous bodily harm; **unfallbedingte** ~ accidental injury; **vorsätzliche** ~ wilfully causing bodily harm, intentional bodily harm.

Korporationsrecht *n* the right to form bodies corporate.

Korrespondentreeder *m* shipowner's permanent representative.

Korrespondenz *f* correspondence; ~**abteilung** correspondence department; ~**anwalt** communicating lawyer (*solicitor who communicates with the trial lawyer and the client*) ~**bank** correspondent bank; ~**gebühr** correspondence fee; ~**scheck** correspondence cheque; ~**versicherung** foreign insurance, agent, insurance brought about by correspondence (with foreign insurer); **geschäftliche** ~ commercial correspondence, business letters.

korrumpieren *v/t* to corrupt, to debauch, to lead astray.

Korruption *f* corruption, corrupt practices.

Kost *f* food, board; *exch*: pension, carrying over; ~**gänger** paying guest for meals; ~**geber** person who provides daily meals (*in return for payment*); *exch*: giver-on, lender (of stock), payer of contango; ~**geschäft** continuation, carrying over (business); contango business, take-in transaction; ~**nehmer** *exch*: taker, borrower (of stock); receiver of contango; ~ **und Logis** room and board, board and lodging; ~**wechsel** bill in pension, bill on deposit.

Kostbarkeiten *f/pl* valuables, precious things.

Kosten *pl* cost, costs, expenses, outlay, charges; ~**abwälzung auf die Preise** cost increases to be passed on in prices; ~**analyse** account analysis; ~**anordnung** costs order; ~**ansatz** statement of court costs; cost breakdown; ~**anschlag** estimate, quotation; *e-n* ~~ *machen*: *to give an estimate*; *zu geringer* ~~: *underestimate*; ~**anteil** portion of the cost(s), share of the costs; ~**artenrechnung** cost type accounting; ~ **auferlegen** to impose costs; ~**auferlegung** assessment of costs, costs order; ~ **aufgliedern** to itemize costs, to give a breakdown of costs; ~**aufgliederung** cost break-down; ~**aufhebung** (*approx*) no costs, *splitting of court costs with each side paying their own costs*; ~**auflage** condition as to costs; ~**aufriß** cost survey; ~ **aufschlüsseln** to break down expenses; ~**aufstellung** statement of costs; ~**aufwand** expense incurred; *unmittelbarer* ~~: *direct expense*; ~**ausgleichung** assessment of costs (*by taxing master*); ~**ausgleichsbetrag** cost-assessment amount; ~**ausgleichszuschlag** cost equalization surcharge; ~**beamter** taxing master; **k~bedingt** *adj* determined by the costs, cost-induced; ~**befreiung** cost exemption; ~**beitreibung** recovery of costs; ~**berechnung** calculation of cost; costing; cost accounting, statement of costs; ~**bereinigung** clearing up of accounts; ~**beschluß** costs order; ~**bestandteile** cost components; ~ **bestreiten** to defray costs; ~**beteiligung** assuming a share of the costs; ~**dämmung** cost containment; ~**dämpfung** curbing cost expansion, cost containment; ~**deckung** cost recovery, covering of costs; ~ **decken** to cover the costs; ~**deckungsprinzip** cost covering principle, self-cost system; ~**degression** cost degression, regressive cost trend, degression in scales for costs and fees; ~**denken** thinking in terms of costs, cost consciousness; ~ **der allgemeinen Geschäftsführung** management costs; ~ **der Kapitalbeschaffung** capital procurement costs; ~ **der Lagerhaltung** storage cost; ~ **der Rechtsverfolgung** costs of litigation; ~ **der Luftfrachtbeförderung** cost of air freight; ~ **der notariellen Wechselvorlage** expense of noting; ~ **des Prüfens**

Kosten des Rechtsstreits   **Kostenspirale**

costs of checking; ~ **des Rechtsstreits** = ~ *des Verfahrens gv;* ~ **des Verfahrens** costs and expenses of the suit (*or* action), expensae litis; ~**einsparung** cost saving; economy, saving; ~**druck** cost push; pressure of costs; ~**einheit** cost unit; ~**eintreibung** (compulsory) collection of costs; ~**entscheidung** costs order; ~~ *ergeht nicht*: *no order as to costs*; ~**entwicklung** cost trend; ~**erlaß** waiver of costs; ~**-Erlös-Relation** relationship between costs and selling prices; ~**ermittlung** costing, cost calculation; ~**ersatz** reimbursement of costs and expenses; ~**ersatzanspruch** claim for reimbursement of costs and expenses; ~**ersparnis** saving of expenses, cost saving, economizing on costs; ~**erstattung** reimbursement of costs and expenses, refund of costs; *gegenseitige* ~~: *reciprocal costs*; ~**erstattungsanspruch** entitlement to costs; k~**erstattungsfähig** taxable; ~**faktor** cost factor; ~ **festsetzen** to tax the costs, to allow costs; ~**festsetzung** determination of costs, fixing of costs, awarding of costs; taxation of costs (*court*); ~**folge** consequence as to costs; ~**frage** question of costs; k~**frei** *adj* free of charge(s); ~**freiheit** exemption from costs; ~ **für die Leichterung und Handhabung** lightering and handling charges; ~ **für die Leichterung und die Verbringung an Land** lighterage and wharfage charges; ~ **für die Löschung** unloading costs; ~**gefälle** differential in costs; ~ **gegeneinander aufheben** to split the costs (*each side bearing half the court costs and its own lawyer's fees and expenses*); ~**gesetz** Court Costs Act; k~**günstig** cost-effective, cheap, good value for money; ~**haftung** liability for costs; ~**haftungserklärung** undertaking to pay costs; ~**höchstbeträge** maximum charges; ~**kategorien** cost categories, types of cost; ~**konto** account of charges; ~**kontrolle** rein on costs, expenses control; ~**kurve** cost line, cost curve; ~**Leistungs-Verhältnis** cost-to-performance ratio; k~**los** *adj* free of charge; without charge; ~**marken** stamps for payment of court fees; ~**miete** minimum rent, sufficient rent for covering costs; *manipulierte* ~~: *manipulated rent allegedly covering costs only*; ~**minderung** reduction in costs; ~**moral** morality in claiming expenses, conscientiousness with regard to costs; ~**nachzahlung** subsequent payment of costs; k~**näher** *adj* adjusted more closely to costs; ~**niederschlagung** waiving court costs; ~**-Nutzen-Analyse** cost-benefit analysis; ~**-Nutzen-Verhältnis** cost-benefit ratio; ~**ordnung** Regulations on Ex-parte Costs; ~**pflicht** obligation to pay the costs; ~~ *des Unterlegenen*: *costs follow the event*; k~**pflichtig** with costs, liable to pay the costs; ~~ *abweisen*: *to dismiss with costs*; ~**preis** cost price, original cost; ~**-Preisschere** cost-and-price scissors; ~**rechnung** (1) bill of costs, bill for services, bill of charges, statement of charges; ~**rechnung** (2) cost accounting, costing; ~~ *für Einzelfertigung*: *job cost system*; ~~**ssystem**: *job cost system*; ~~**ssystem mit vorausgeschätzten Kosten**: *estimate cost system*; ~**recht** law concerning court costs; ~**rechtsprechung** court decisions on cost problems; ~**regelung** regulation concerning costs; ~**risiko** costs risk; ~**sachen** cases involving taxation of costs; ~**sammelblatt** job cost sheet; ~**satz** cost unit rate; ~**schätzungen** estimates of costs; ~**schuldner** party liable for costs; ~**schwelle** transfer cost (*change of location*); ~**senkung** lowering costs; ~**sicherheitsleistung** costs bond; ~**spaltung** splitting of costs; k~**sparend** *adj* cost-saving, economic; ~ **spielen keine Rolle** costs are irrelevant (*or* are of no consequence); ~**spirale** spiral(l)ing

Kostensprung — **kotieren**

of costs; ~**sprung** jump in costs; ~**stand** level of costs; ~**steigerung** cost increase; ~**stelle** cost centre; ~**titel** cost taxation order (*enforceable*); ~**teilung** dividing the cost burden, sharing costs; ~**träger** funding agency (*for social or public services*); cost-inducing item (*accounting*; cost unit (*cheque*); ~**tragung** apportionment of costs, bearing the costs; ~**übernahme** defraying costs and expenses; ~**überschlag** estimate (of costs); ~**überschreitung** exceeding the agreed price, exceeding the cost limit; ~**überwachung** expense control; ~**überwälzung** passing costs, passing cost increases (*on to buyers, tenants*); ~**umlegung** apportionment of costs, assessment of expenses; ~ **und Auslagen** charges, costs and expenses; ~**unterdeckung** cost deficit; ~**urteil** costs order; ~**verfahren** proceedings as to costs; ~**vergleich** court settlement on the costs of a case; ~**vergleichsmiete** economic rent, rent equivalent to similar tenancies; ~**verzeichnis** cost schedule; ~**voranschlag** preliminary estimate (of costs), estimated charges; ~**vorschuß** retainer (*lawyer*), payment on account, advance of lawyer's fees, advance on costs; ~**vorschußpflicht** obligation to make advance payments as to costs; ~**wert** cost value; ~**wesen** matters concerning costs; ~**wirksam** cost-effective; ~**wirksamkeitsanalyse** effectiveness analysis, cost-efficacy analysis; ~**wirkungen** impact of costs; ~**zahlung** payment of costs; ~ **zu (abgeschriebenen) Buchwerten** amortized cost; ~ **zu gleichen Teilen tragen** costs shall be borne in equal parts; ~ **zur Folge haben** to involve expense; ~ **zurückerstatten** to refund (the) expenses; ~**zuschlag** excess charge; **abzüglich** ~ less charges; **aktivierte** ~ capitalized costs; **anomale** ~ untypical costs; **angefallene** ~ expenses incurred, accrued costs; **anteilige** ~ prorated costs; **anteilig zu verrechnende** ~ costs to be prorated; **auf** ~ **und Gefahr** at the risk and cost; **auf** ~ **von** on account of, at the expense of; **auferlegte** ~ costs imposed (by the court); **auflaufende** ~ accruing costs; **auf meine** ~ at my expense; **außergerichtliche** ~ out-of-court expenses; **die** ~ **ersetzen** to refund the costs; **die** ~ **tragen** to bear the costs; **direkte** ~ direct cost, specific cost; **direkt zurechenbare** ~ directly apportionable costs; **einmalige** ~ non-recurring costs; **eintreibbare** ~ collectible charges, recoverable costs; **entstandene** ~ expense incurred; **entstehende** ~ accruing costs; **erstattungsfähige** ~ party and party costs; **fällige** ~ payable costs and expenses; **feste** ~ fixed costs, overhead, overhead expenses, overhead charges, volume cost; **festsetzbare** ~ taxable costs; **fixe** ~ nonvariable expenses *viz feste* ~; **gewöhnliche** ~ ordinary expense; **historische** ~ historic(al) costs; **jmdn zu den Kosten verurteilen** to award the costs against s. o.; **kalkulatorische** ~ imputed costs, expenses assumed for costing purposes; **konstante** ~ standing charges; **kumulierende** ~ accruing costs; **laufende** ~ current expenses, recurring costs; **leistungsabhängige** ~ variable costs; **nicht anderweitig erstattete** ~ expense not otherwise received; **ohne** ~ no costs (*on bill of exchange*); without expenses, incur no expenses; **sämtliche** ~ full costs; **sich** ~ **aufbürden** to incur costs and expenses voluntarily; **Sowieso-**~ costs arising in any case; **über die** ~ **entscheiden** to order costs; **überfällige** ~ overdue costs; **variable** ~ variable costs; **vorprozessuale** ~ costs incurred before action; **zu den** ~ **verurteilt sein** to be ordered to pay the costs.

Kote *f* bench mark, height notation.
kotieren *v/t* (1) *exch* to admit (*shares,*

kotieren *etc*) to official quotation, to fix (*price*), to quote (*price*).

kotieren *v/t* (2) to measure altitudes (*or* spot heights); to indicate ultimate (*or* spot height) numbers, to place bench marks.

Kotierung *f* (1) admission (*of shares, etc*) to official quotation.

Kotierung *f* (2) indication of spot heights (*or* bench marks).

Koupon *m* = *Kupon qv*.

Kraft *f* (*pl Kräfte* = ~e) strength, power, force; ~**ebedarf der Wirtschaft** labour requirements of industry; ~**emangel** labour shortage; ~**epotential** potential labour force; **außer** ~ **sein** to be out of force, (to have been) repealed; **außer** ~ **setzen** to repeal, to invalidate, to abrogate, to set aside, to cancel, to overrule, to rescind; **außer** ~ **treten** to become inoperative, to become ineffective, to expire, to lapse; **familieneigene** ~**e** family labour; **freie** ~**e** available labour; **gleichgewichtsstörende** ~**e** disequilibrating forces; **in** ~ **in** force; **in** ~ **bleiben** to remain in force, to remain valid, to remain effective; **in** ~ **sein** to be in force, to be in operation, to be effective; **in** ~ **setzen** to put into force, to put into operation; **in** ~ **treten** to enter into force, to take effect, to come into operation; **in** ~ **treten lassen** to make effective, to make operative; **marktbestimmende** ~**e** forces governing market trends; **normative** ~ **des Faktischen** power of de facto conditions to establish rules of law; **rückwirkende** ~ retroactive effect, retrospective effect, retrospective force; *mit* ~*r* ~: *with retroactive effect, retroactively*; **sich nach besten** ~**en bemühen** to use one's best endeavours *or* offorts.

kraft *prep* by operation of, by virtue of, in virtue of, on the strength of, by right of.

Kraftdroschke *f* taxi.

Kraftfahr|industrie automobile industry; ~**sachverständiger** motor vehicle expert; ~**unfall** automobile accident, motor vehicle accident, road traffic accident; ~**versicherung** motor insurance, automobile insurance.

Kraftfahrer *m* motorist, driver; ~**eignung** suitability as a driver of motor vehicles.

Kraftfahrt-Bundesamt *n* Federal Office for Motor Traffic.

Kraftfahrzeug *n* motor vehicle; ~**anmeldung** motor vehicle registration; ~**brief** motor vehicle registration book, certificate of title to a motor vehicle, manufacturer's statement of origin *US*; ~**eigentümer** owner of a motor vehicle; ~**entwendung** (unauthorized use (*or* temporary theft) of a motor vehicle; ~**fahndung** tracing of stolen vehicles; ~**führer** operator of a motor vehicle; ~**gesetz** Motor Vehicle Act; ~**haftpflicht** motor vehicle third party liability; ~**haftpflichtversicherung** motor vehicle liability insurance, third party insurance; ~**haftung** motor vehicle third-party liability; ~**halter** registered user of a motor vehicle, *person in charge of a motor vehicle*; keeper of a motor vehicle; ~**industrie** automobile industry; ~**kennzeichen** licence (*US* license) plate, number plate; ~**klasse** class of motor vehicle (*for tax purposes*); ~**kosten** cost of motor vehicle maintenance; ~**papiere** motor vehicle documents; ~**schein** motor vehicle registration certificate; ~**steuer** motor vehicle tax; ~~*vergehen*: *motor vehicle tax offence*; ~**überwachung** control of motor vehicle safety; ~**unfall** motor vehicle accident; ~**verkehr** motor vehicle traffic, vehicular traffic; ~**vermietung** renting of motor cars; ~**versicherung** automobile insurance, motor car insurance, motor insurance; ~~ *mit Prämien für unfallfreies Fahren*: *merit pricing system*; ~**zulassung** licensing of motor vehicles, motor vehicle licensing; ~**zulassungsstelle**

kraftlos   **Krankenhaus**

motor vehicle licensing office; **ein ~ abmelden** to cancel the registration of a motor vehicle registration; **ein ~ führen** to drive, to operate a motor vehicle; *verkehrsgefährdendes Führen e-s ~s: dangerous driving.*

kraftlos *adj* invalid, inoperative, void, inefficacious; **für ~ erklären** to declare void.

Kraftloserklärung *f* invalidation, declaration of invalidity, forfeiture, cancellation; **~ von Wertpapieren** invalidation of securities.

Kraftloswerden *n* ceasing to be effective, invalidation.

Kraftrad *n* motor cycle.

Kraftstoff *m* fuel, propellant; **~behälter** fuel tank; **~diebstahl** theft of fuel; **~industrie** fuel industry; **~lager** fuel depot; **~verbrauch** fuel consumption; **~zufuhr** fuel supply.

Kraftverkehr road transport, road traffic; **~sabgaben** motor vehicle duties; **~sordnung** road traffic ordinance.

Kraftwagen *m* motor vehicle; **~beförderung** motor transport; **~benutzung** use of a motor vehicle; **~kolonne** convoy, column of motor vehicles; **~kosten** automobile expenses; **~verkehr** road haulage; *gewerblicher ~~: road-haulage contractors.*

Krakeeler *m* brawler, rowdy.

Kranführer *m* crane operator.

krank *adj* ill, sick; **jmdn ~ schreiben** to certify s. o. unfit to work due to illness; **sich ~ melden** to report sick; **~feiern** to go sick for trivial reasons, to malinger (*on the pretence of sickness*), to feign illness.

Kranken|anstalt public hospital; *gemeinnützige ~~en: non-profitmaking hospital organizations;* **~ausfallquote** illness frequency rate; **~beförderung** transport of patients; **~behandlung** medical treatment; **~beihilfe** sickness relief; **~blätter** medical record; **~fahrstuhl** chair wheel; **~fürsorge** medical care; **~geld** sickness benefit; **~geldzuschuß** additional allowance to sickness benefit; **~geldanspruch** entitlement to sickness benefit; **~geschichte** medical record; **~haus** → *Krankenhaus;* **~hilfe** medical care; **~karte** sickness card; **~kasse** health insurance (fund *or* scheme *or* company); *kaufmännische ~~: health insurance for commercial employees;* **~kassenarzt** panel doctor; **~kassenbeiträge** contributions to health insurance; **~pflege** medical care; **~pflegeanstalt** (*GB*) nursing home; **~pflegegesetz** Nursing of Patients Act; **~pfleger** nurse, male nurse; **~pflichtversicherung** statutory sickness insurance; **~schein** sick-certificate (*entitling to medical treatment*), health service cheque; **~schwester** nurse; *staatlich geprüfte ~~: state registered nurse;* **~stuhl** wheel chair; **~tagegeld** daily allowance during sickness; **~tagegeldversicherung** daily benefits insurance; **~transportdienst** ambulance service; **~überwachung** surveillance of persons who have reported sick; **~unterstützung** assistance during illness; **~urlaub** sick leave; *bezahlter ~~: paid sick leave;* **~versicherung** health insurance, sickness insurance; *soziale ~~: social health insurance;* **~versicherung der Rentner** health insurance for social security pensioners; **~versicherungsbezüge** health insurance benefits; **~versicherungsgesellschaft** health insurance company; **~versicherungsträger** organization in charge of health insurance; **~versorgungsleistungen** health care benefits; **~versorgungsträger** health care provider; **~zusatzversicherung** supplementary sickness insurance.

Krankenhaus *n* hospital; **~aufnahme** admission to a hospital; **~aufnahmevertrag** hospitalization agreement; **~behandlung** hospital treatment; *stationäre ~~: hospitalization, in-patient treatment;* **~kostenversicherung** hospital

Krankfeiern / **Kreditbeschaffung**

costs insurance; ~**ordnung** hospital regulations; ~**pflege** hospital care; ~**pflegekosten** hospital ward costs, nursing costs; ~**pflegesatz** hospital per diem charge; ~**tagegeld-Versicherung** hospital per diem allowance insurance; ~**versorgung** hospital provision; ~**vertrag** hospitalization contract; **gemeinnütziges** ~ non-profit hospital.

Krankfeiern *n* feigning illness, malingering.

Krankheit *f* disease, illness, sickness; **angeborene** ~ congenital disease; **ansteckende** ~ contagious disease; **ekelerregende** ~ repulsive disease; **meldepflichtige** ~ notifiable disease; **quarantänepflichtige** ~ disease subject to quarantine regulations; **schwere** ~ serious illness; **simulierte** ~ feigned disease; **übertragbare** ~ contagious disease.

Krankheits|ausgleichszahlung (*des Arbeitgebers*) sick pay; ~**fall** case (of illness); ~**kosten** medical costs; ~**unterhalt** financial support for divorced spouse in case of illness; ~**urlaub** sick leave; ~**verhütung** prevention of illness; ~**vorsorge** health care; ~**zeit** period of illness.

Kranzgeld *n* compensation upon breach of promise, for lost chastity, indemnity for defloration.

Krawall *n* trouble, tumultuous demonstration, uproar; ~**schäden** riot damage, vandalism (damage).

Kredit *m* (*pl Kredite*) credit, credit balance, credit standing, credit line, facility, loan, loan advance; ~**absicherung** providing collateral security for credit; ~**aktion** lending scheme, lending arrangements; k~**aktiv** *adj* active in granting credit; ~**anschwärzung** defamation to ruin a person's credit standing; ~**anspannung** strain on credit; ~**anstalt** bank, credit institution, loan corporation; ~~ *des öffentlichen Rechts*: public loan corporation; *landschaftliche* ~~*en*: *regional banks*; ~**anteil** credit portion;

~**antrag** loan application, application for credit facilities; ~**apparat** credit system; *öffentlich-rechtlicher* ~~: *official credit institutions*; ~**aufblähung** credit inflation, over-expansion of credit; ~**aufnahme** borrowing, raising of credit, making use of credit facilities; ~ **aufnehmen** to borrow, to take out a loan, to obtain credit; ~**aufsicht** official supervision of credit institutions; ~**auftrag** agreement to provide a credit-extending arrangement; ~**ausdehnung** credit expansion; ~**ausfall** loan loss; ~**ausfallrückstellung** loan-loss provision; ~**auskunft** credit information, banker's reference, status enquiries and reports, credit report, trade reference; *gegenseitige* ~~: *credit interchange*; ~**auskunftei** credit bureau, credit reference agency, commercial agency; ~**auskunftsbeurteilung** credit rating, credit scoring; ~**auslese** credit selection, selectivity in the granting of credit; ~**ausreichung** loan accomodation; ~**ausschuß** credit committee, loans committee; ~**ausweitung** expansion of credit; ~**automatismus** automatic granting of credit; ~**bank** commercial bank, credit bank; *private* ~~*en*: *ordinary commercial banks*; ~**beanspruchung** borrowing, strain on credit, making use of credits; ~**bearbeiter** loans officer; ~**bearbeitung** processing of applications for credits, loan processing; ~~*sprovision: credit processing charge*; ~**bedarf** borrowing needs, credit requirements, borrowing demand; ~~*splan: credit requirements plan*; *öffentlicher* ~~: *public sector credit requirement(s)*; ~**bedingungen** terms of credit; *günstige* ~~: *favourable terms*; ~**bedürfnis** credit requirements; ~**bereich** area of lending; k~**bereit** *adj* disposed to grant credits; ~**bereitschaft** readiness to grant credits; *passive* ~~: *readiness to borrow*; ~**bereitstellung** allocation of credit funds; ~**beschaffung** pro-

480

Kreditbeschränkungen   **Kreditmarktverschuldung**

curement of credit facilities; ~~*sprovision: credit procurement fee*; ~**beschränkungen** credit restrictions; ~**besicherung** security for a loan; ~**bestätigung** facility letter; ~**betrag** amount of credit, principal (sum); ~**betrug** obtaining credit by false pretences; ~**bewegungen** shifts in credit volume; ~**bewilligung** granting of credit; ~**beziehung** mutual debtor-creditor relationship; ~**bremse** restraint on credit; ~**brief** credit advice, circular credit *(for bank customers to draw money at other banks while away on business trips etc)*; ~**bürgschaft** loan guarantee, credit guarantee; ~**deflation** credit squeeze, deflation due to a lack of credit; ~**dirigismus** credit regimentation; ~**drosselung** credit squeeze; ~**einengung** credit restrictions; ~**einräumung** granting of credit (facilities); ~**einschränkung** restriction of credit; ~**engagement** credit commitment; ~**entwicklung** movement in borrowings, trend in lending; ~**erleichterung** easing of credit terms; ~**eröffnung** opening of a credit; ~~*svertrag: credit agreement;* ~**expansion** credit expansion; ~**fähigkeit** credit standing, solidity, borrowing power, financial reliability, creditworthiness; ~**fall** case in which a loan is granted; ~**fazilität** credit facility; ~**finanzierung** borrowing, financing by way of credit; ~**förderung** trade facilities, promotion of credit expansion; ~**form** type of credit; ~ **geben** to give credit; ~**geber** extender of credit, lender, creditor, financial backer; *letztbereiter* ~~: *marginal lender*; ~**gebühren** loan charges, credit charges; ~**gefährdung** impairment of credit standing; ~**geld** fiduciary money; ~**genossenschaft** credit co-operative, mutual loan society; *gewerbliche* ~~: *commercial credit co-operative*; *ländliche* ~~: *rural credit co-operative*; ~**geschäft** transaction on credit, credit operation; ~ **gewähren** to grant credit; ~**gewährung** extension of credit, lending, granting credit; *objektgebundene* ~~: *earmarked credit*; ~**gewerbe** banking, the banking sector, credit institutions, financial services industry; ~**grenze** credit limit, credit line, credit ceiling, credit margin; ~**hai** loan shark; ~**hergabe** lending, granting credit; ~**hilfen** aid by credit, credit facilities; ~**inanspruchnahme** credit use, recourse to credit; ~**inflation** credit inflation; ~**informationsdienst auf Gegenseitigkeit** watch and warning service, credit interchange; ~**institut** bank, banking institution, financial institution, credit institution; *erstverwahrendes* ~~: *credit institution acting as initial depository*; *landwirtschaftliches* ~~: *farm mortgage company*; *staatliches* ~~: *government banking institution*; ~**kapazität** lending capacity; ~**karte** credit card, charge card; ~**kartenbesitzer** credit card holder; ~**kauf** purchase on credit, credit sale; ~**knappheit** credit stringency; ~**kommission** credit commission; ~**komponente** credit factor; ~**konditionen** credit terms; ~**kontingentierung** credit rationing, allocation of credit by quotas; ~**konto** credit account, loan account, personal account, drawing account; ~**kosten** charges for credits, credit cost; ~**kunde** borrowing customer, credit customer; ~**kündigung** withdrawal of credit, withdrawal notice, termination of credit; ~**laufzeit** period of credit, term of loan; ~**lenkung** credit control, distribution of credit; ~**limit** credit limit; ~**linie** credit line, line of credit, credit limit; *offene* ~~: *unspent credit balance*; ~**lockerung** easing of credit; ~**makler** credit broker, financial agent; ~**marge** credit margin, credit limit; ~**markt** credit market; ~**marktmittel** market resources; ~**marktverschuldung** market in-

kreditmäßig / **Kreditverpflichtung**

debtedness; k~mäßig *adj, adv* by way of credit; ~mittel borrowed monies, loan funds; *etatisierte ~~: amounts to be borrowed, as shown in the estimates*; ~möglichkeit credit facilities, credit resources; ~nachfrage demand for credit, credit requirements; ~nachsuchender applicant for credit; ~nahme borrowing, making use of credit facilities; ~nebengewerbe ancillary credit business; ~nehmer borrower, debtor; *letzter ~~: final borrower*; k~neutral *adj* not affecting credit (*or* credit standing); ~not credit shortage; ~note credit note; ~obergrenze credit ceiling, credit limit; ~or → *Kreditor*; ~papier credit instrument; ~plafond credit ceiling, credit limit, credit line, loan ceiling; ~politik credit policy; *restriktive ~~: restrictive credit policy*; *staatliche ~~: government's credit policy*; k~politisch *adj* relating to credit policy; ~posten credit item; ~potential lending capacity, capacity to grant credit, power of credit creation; ~preise lending rates; ~prolongation extension of credit; ~programm lending programme; ~protokoll credit memorandum; ~provision arrangement fee, credit commission; ~prüfung investigation of creditworthiness; ~quellen credit (re)sources; ~rahmen credit limit, credit line; ~restriktion credit restriction; ~richtlinie credit standards, credit rules; ~richtsätze regulations on credit; ~risiko credit risk, exposure; ~rückflüsse loan repayments, amortization received on lendings; ~rückführung reduction in the volume of credit; ~sachbearbeiter bank employee in charge of credits, loan officer; ~saldo credit balance, outstanding balance of loan; ~schädigung discredit, defamation of business reputation; ~schöpfung creation of credit; ~schutz credit protection; ~schutzverein trade protection society; ~schwindel obtaining credit by false pretences; ~selektion selection as between borrowers, credit selection; ~sicherheit security for a loan; ~sicherung security, collateral security; *auswechselbare ~~: floating security*; ~sonderkonto special loan account; ~spanne credit ceiling; ~sperre credit freeze; ~spielraum available margin of credit; ~spitzenbetrag maximum amount of credit; ~spritze credit injection, shot of credit; ~status credit standing; ~stop ban on new lending, credit restraints; ~summe credit limit, sum borrowed; ~täuschung obtaining credit by false pretences; k~technisch *adj* (technically) relating to credit; ~tilgung repayment of credit, loan repayment; ~überschreiten to exceed one's credit limit; ~ überziehen to overstep one's credit, to overdraw one's account; ~überziehung credit overdrawing; ~umfang extent of credit; ~umschuldung rescheduling of a loan, converting the type of a loan; ~unterlage credit basis, credit information; ~unternehmen credit institution; k~unwürdig *adj* unworthy of credit; ~valuta loan monies, account owed under a credit (scheme); ~verein (industrial) loan society; ~vereinbarung credit agreement, credit arrangement; ~verflechtung interlocking credit relationships; ~verfügbarkeit availability of loans; ~vergabe granting credit facility; ~verkauf credit sale, sale on credit, deferred payment sale; ~verkehr credit transactions, credit business; ~verknappung credit tightness; ~ verlängern to renew a credit, to extend a credit; ~verlängerung credit extension; ~vermittler money broker, credit broker; ~vermittlung arranging credit facilities, credit brokerage; ~vermittlungsgebühr commission for arranging credit facilities; ~verpflichtung lending obligation, obligation to grant credit; **~versicherung** credit insurance, bad debts insurance, fidelity and guarantee insurance; **~versorgung** credit supply; **~verteuerung** increase in credit costs; **~vertrag** credit contract, credit agreement, credit arrangement; **~verwaltung** credit management; **~verwendung** application of loan funds; use of credit; **~volumen** volume of credit, total credit outstanding; **~wechsel** bill of exchange accepted on a credit basis; **~wesen** credit system, lending business; **~wesengesetz** Act regulating banking and credit business (D 1976); **~wirtschaft** credit economy; **~wucher** usury; **k~würdig** adj credit-worthy; **~würdigkeit** credit worthiness, credit status; credit position, credit standing; **~~sbeurteilung**: credit scoring; **~zinsen** credit rates, lending rates; ~~ der Banken: the banks' lending rates; **~zügel** credit restrictions; **~zusage** commitment to grant credit, promise of credit; terminierte ~~: credit promise for future date; **auf ~** on credit, on credit basis; **auf ~ kaufen** to buy on credit; **auf ~ verkaufen** to sell on credit; **ausgelegte ~e** loans which have been granted; **befristeter ~** credit with fixed repayment, credit limited in time; **durchgeleiteter ~** loan passed on to a borrower; **durchlaufende ~e** loans in transit; **e-n ~ aufnehmen** to borrow, to take up a loan, to obtain credit facilities; **e-n ~ ausschöpfen** to make full use of a credit; **e-n ~ eröffnen** to open credit facilities; **eingefrorene ~e** frozen credits; **gedeckter ~** secured credit, secured loan; **kurzfristiger ~** short-term credit; **landesverbürgter ~** a Land-guaranteed credit, term loan; **längerfristiger ~** relatively long-term credit, term loan; **langfristiger ~** long-term credit; **mittelfristiger ~** medium-term credit: (loans from three to ten years); **mittelständischer ~** loans to small-scale trade and industry; **öffentlicher ~** credit by (or to) public authorities; **rechtsverbindlich zugesagter ~** credit promised with legally binding effect; **revolvierender ~** revolving credit; **rückführungspflichtiger ~** credit subject to reduction; **transitorischer ~** temporary credit, transmitted loan; **ungedeckter ~** unsecured credit, open credit; **unverbriefter ~** uncertificated credit, informal credit; **unverzinslicher ~** interest-free credit; **unwiderruflicher ~** irrevocable credit; **verbilligter ~** subsidized credit; **widerruflicher ~** revocable credit; **zweckbestimmter ~** restricted-use credit.

kreditär adj credit, pertaining to credit.

kreditieren v/t to credit.

Kreditierung f crediting, credit advice.

Kreditor m pl → Kreditoren creditor, tender.

Kreditoren m/pl creditors, deposits, accounts payable, bills payable (bills of exchange); **~buch** creditors' ledger, purchase ledger; **~buchhalter** voucher clerk; **~buchhaltung** accounts payable department; **~ in laufender Rechnung** account current creditors; **~journal** purchase register; **~konto** creditor account.

kreditorisch adj creditor, non-borrowing, credit-side.

Kreis m district, county; **~aufgaben** functions assigned to a district (or county); **~ausschuß** district committee, county council standing committee; **~beamte** district (or county) officials; **~bediensteter** employee of a county council; **~brandinspektor** district fire inspector; **~brandmeister** district fire chief; **~bürger** district inhabitant, local inhabitant; **~direktor** deputy clerk of the county council; **~gebiet** territory of a district, county area; **~gericht** county court, district court; **~handwer-**

kerschaft district crafts guild; ~**haushalt** budget of a district (*or* county); ~**hoheit** autonomous status of a district (*or* county); ~**lasten** district public expenditures; ~**ordnung** county constitution; ~**organe** administrative organs of a district authority (*or* county); ~**präsident** chairman of the county (*or* district) council, county district commissioner; ~**rat** county councillor (*Bavaria*); district committee (*Baden-Württemberg*); ~**satzung** district (*or* county) by-laws; ~**schulbehörde** district (*or* county) school board; ~**sparkasse** district (*or* county) savings bank; ~**stadt** county seat; ~**straße** secondary (*or* link) road; ~**tag** county council, district council; ~**tagswahl** local government election, election of district (*or* county) councillors; ~**umlage** district (*or* county) assessment; ~**verband** joint district administrative organisation; ~**verordnung** district ordinance, county ordinance; ~**verwaltung** county council (administration); ~**verwaltungsbehörde** county board, administrative authority of a district (*or* county); ~**wehrersatzamt** district draft board; ~**wohnungspfleger** district (*or* county) housing officer.

Kreisdiagramm *n* pie chart (*statistics*).

Kreislaufschema *n* circular flow scheme.

Kreisverkehr *m* roundabout.

Kreuz|fahrer cruise ship passenger; ~**fahrt** cruise ~~-**en-Schiff:** cruise ship; ~**parität** cross rate, cross exchange; ~**tabulierung** cross-tabulation; ~**verhör** cross-examination; *ins* ~~ *nehmen:* to cross-examine.

Kreuzung *f* crossing, cross roads, intersection; ~ **ohne Kreisverkehr** intersection without a roundabout; **niveaugleiche** ~ level crossing; **rechtwinklige** ~ T-junction.

Kreuzungs|bahnhof junction; ~**bereich** intersection; **k**~**frei** *adj* free of crossings, intersection-free; ~**mittelpunkt** point of intersection.

Krieg *m* war; ~**führung** waging war, war operations; ~ **ohne Kriegserklärung** undeclared war; **allgemeiner** ~ general war, public war; **begrenzter** ~ limited war; **im** ~ **befindlich** engaged in war, at war; **kalter** ~ cold war.

Kriegs|-Abweichungsklausel war deviation clause; ~**ächtung** outlawing war, ban on war; ~**anfälligkeit** proneness to wars; ~**anleihe** war bond, war loan; ~**beschädigter** war-invalid; ~**beute** war-booty, prize; ~**bräuche** customs of war; ~**dienst** war service; ~**dienstverweigerer** conscientious objector; ~**dienstverweigerung** conscientious objection; ~**dienstzeit** time served in war; ~**einsatz** active military service, military operations; ~**einwirkung** effects of war; ~**entschädigung** war indemnity, benefit for war-invalids; ~**ereignisse** events of war; ~**erklärung** declaration of war; ~**folgelasten** public burdens resulting from war, war-induced damages; ~**folgen** consequences of war; ~**folgengesetz** War Consequences Act; ~**folgelasten** consequential war burdens; ~**folgerenten** war pensions; ~**folgeschäden** war-induced damage; ~**fristengesetz** Act on Time Limits in War; ~**führung** warfare; *psychologische* ~~: *psychological warfare*; ~**gebiet** war region, operational zone; ~**gebrauch** war customs; ~**gefahr** danger of war; *ins*: ~~-*en*: perils of war; ~**gefangenenentschädigung** compensation for prisoners of war; ~**gefangener** prisoner of war; ~**gefangenschaft** (war) captivity, status of a prisoner of war, time of detention as prisoner of war; ~**gericht** military tribunal, court martial; ~**gesetz** wartime law, emergency law; ~**gesetzgebung** war legislation; ~**gewinnler** war profiteer; ~**gewinn-**

Kriegsgewohnheitsrecht / **Krisenanfälligkeit**

steuer war profits tax; ~**gewohnheitsrecht** the customs and usages of war; ~**gräber** war graves; ~**gräberfürsorge** War Graves' Commission; ~**handlungen** hostilities; ~**heimkehrer** home-coming prisoner of war, repatriated prisoner of war; ~**hetzer** warmonger; ~**hinterbliebene** surviving dependants (of war victims); ~**invaliden** war pensioners, wardisabled persons; ~**klausel** war risk clause; ~**konterbande** contraband of war; ~**lasten** burdens of war; ~**list** stratagem (of war); ~**marine** navy; ~**maßnahme** war measure; ~**material** war material; *überschüssiges* ~~: *surplus war property*; ~**müdigkeit** war weariness; ~**notrecht** war-time emergency law; ~**opfer** war victim; ~**opferfürsorge** care for war victims; ~**opferversorgung** pensions scheme for war victims; ~**opferversorgungsgesetz** Act on War Victims' Pensions; ~**partei** the hawks, those in favour of war; ~**potential** war potential; ~**recht** law of war, the laws and customs of war; martial law (*internal*); ~**reserve** *ins* reserve for war risk; ~**risiko** risk of war, war risk, *ins* war hazard; ~~ *ist Sache des Käufers*: *war risk for buyer's account*; *pl* ~**risiken**: *perils of war*; ~**risikoklausel** war clause, war risk clause; ~**risikoversicherung** war risk insurance; ~**rücklage** *ins* war reserve; ~**sachgeschädigter** *person who has suffered property damage through war*; ~**sachschaden** war damage to property; ~**schaden** war damage; ~**schadenrente** war indemnification pension; ~**schauplatz** theatre of war; ~**schuld** war guilt; ~**schulden** war debts; ~**sterbefall** death of insured person due to war; ~**steuern** war taxes; ~**straftat** war crime; ~**straftäter** war criminal; ~**teilnehmer** war veteran; ~**teuerung** war-time price increase; ~**treiber** warmonger; ~**verbot** prohibition of agressive war; ~**verbrechen** war crime; *herkömmliche* ~ *conventional war crimes*; ~**verbrecher** war criminal; ~**verfassung** emergency constitution in war; ~**verletzung** war injury, war service injury; *zivile* ~~: *civilian war injury*; ~**verluste** war casualties; ~**verordnungen** defence regulations; ~**verrat** war treason, treachery in war; ~**verschollenheit** presumption of death due to war; ~**versehrtenrente** veterans' disablement pension; ~**versehrter** disabled soldier, disabled veteran; ~**versicherung** insurance against war risk; ~**versicherungsgemeinschaft** war risks pool; k~**verwendungsfähig** *adj* fit for active service; ~**vorbereitung** preparations for war; ~**waffen** weapons of war, military weapons; ~**waffenbuch** register of military weapons; ~**waffenherstellung** production of war weapons; ~**waffenliste** war-weapons list; ~**waise** war orphan; ~**wirtschaft** war-time economy, war economy; ~**ziel** war aims; ~**zulage** combat allowance, war bonus; ~**zustand** state of war, belligerency; *sich im* ~~ *befinden*: *to be at war* (*with*).

Kriminal|abteilung („*Kripo*") criminal investigation department; ~**beamter** police detective; ~**inspektor** police inspector, detective inspector; ~**politik** criminological policy; ~**polizei** criminal police, *GB* Scotland Yard, criminal investigation department; ~**prävention** crime prevention; ~**statistik** criminal statistics; ~**strafe** penalty for a criminal offence, punishment.

Kriminalisierung *f* criminalization.

Kriminalist *m* investigation specialist, detective.

Kriminalistik *f* criminology.

Kriminalität *f* criminality, delinquency, incidence of crime; **organisierte** ~ organized crime, racketeering.

Krisen|anfälligkeit proneness to crises; ~**fall** emergency; k~**fest** *adj* crisis-proof, slump-proof; **~festigkeit** ability to withstand crises; **~frachtzuschlag** emergency freight surcharge; **k~geschüttelt** *adj* crisis-ridden; **~gesetzgebung** emergency legislation; **~herd** trouble spot, (political) storm-centre; **~jahr** year of crisis, depression year; **~kartell** cartel to meet a structural crisis (*of a business*); **~paket** emergency package of measures; **~sitzung** emergency session; **~stab** emergency headquarters, crisis staff, crisis management group; **k~unempfindlich** *adj* immune to crises; **~unterstützung** depression-aid.

Kron|anwalt Attorney General, Solicitor General; **~beamter** servant of the Crown; **~recht** royal prerogative; **~zeuge** witness for the crown, key witness; witness who „turned state", gives State's evidence (*tending to incriminate accomplices for a promise of immunity or lesser sentence, introduced D 1990 in anti-terrorism legislation*).

Krönung *f* coronation; **~seid** coronation oath; **~sinsignien** regalia.

Kugelschreiber *m* ball-point pen, ball pen.

Kuhhandel *m pol* horse trading.

Kühl|anlage cold storage plant, refrigerating plant; **~gut** chilled cargo, refrigerated items; **~güterversicherung** cold storage insurance; **~ladung** refrigerated cargo; **~schiff** refrigerator ship; **~truhe** deep-freezer chest; **~wagen** refrigerated truck, refrigerated car.

kulant *adj* obliging, accommodating.

Kulanz *f* willingness to do favours, accommodation, generosity; **~deckung e-s unerwünschten Risikos** covering an undesired risk as a favour; **~leistung** accommodation, favour in business dealings, courtesy, act of generosity; **~regelung** arrangement on accommodating terms, liberal settlement; **~zahlung** ex gratia payment.

Kulisse *f exch* outside operators, operators dealing for their own account, professional traders, unofficial market.

Kultivierung *f* cultivation, tillage; **~smethode** mode of tillage.

Kultur|abkommen cultural convention; **~austausch** cultural exchanges; **~bau** land improvement; **~denkmal** cultural monument; **~gut** cultural property, cultural heritage; *nationales* **~~**: *national treasures*; **~hoheit** educational autonomy; **~land** arable land; **~landmarke** man-made landmark; **~landschaft** cultivated landscape, man-made landscape; **~leistung** cultural service, educational achievement; **~politik** cultural diplomacy; **~schaffende** persons (*or* people) engaged in cultural activities; **~staat** civilized nation; **~volk** civilized nation.

Kultus|gemeinde *f* religious community, congregation; **~minister** minister of (*or*) for education (and cultural affairs); **~ministerium** ministry of education (and cultural affairs); **~ministerkonferenz** standing conference of (the German) ministers of education (and cultural affairs).

Kumpel *m* miner, fellow-worker.

Kumulation *f* cumulation, accumulation.

Kumulations|prinzip cumulative system of penalties; **~wahlrecht** cumulative voting.

kumulativ *adj* cumulative, accumulative.

Kumulativaktie *f* cumulative preference share.

kumulieren *v/i* to accumulate, to be added to.

Kumulierung *f* cumulation, combined effect.

kündbar *adj* determinable, terminable, subject to notice of termination, redeemable (*bonds etc*), subject to redemption; **jederzeit ~** terminable at any time, terminable at will, at call, subject to call (*deposit*).

Kündbarkeit *f* terminability, redeemability.

Kunde *m* (*pl Kunden* = **~n**; → *Kun-*

den) customer, client; **fester** ~ regular customer; **gelegentlicher** ~ chance customer, occassional customer; **möglicher** ~ potential customer; **wichtiger** ~ key customer; **zahlungsfähiger** ~ solvent client, wealthy customer; **zuverlässiger** ~ loyal customer, reliable customer.

Kunden|abwerbung enticing customers away, poaching customers; ~**arbeit** custom work, customized work; custom; ~**außenstände** customers' accounts receivable; ~**bedienung** serving of customers; ~**beeinflussung** suggestive selling, influencing customers' choice; k~**belastend** burdening the customer; ~**berater** adviser to customers, adviser on customer's problems; ~**beratungsdienst** customer advisory service; ~**besuch** calling on customers; ~**betreuung** customer service, customer cultivation; ~**bonus** discount for customers; ~**buch** customer/client ledger; ~**buchführung** customer accounting; ~**dienst** customer service, after-sales service; *technischer* ~~: *field engineering service, after-installation service*; ~**dienstabteilung** (customer) service department; ~**dienstzentrale** service center; ~**einlagen** customers' ordinary deposits; ~**fang** canvassing, enticing customers, pressure salesmanship; ~**fänger** drummer, tout, puller-in; ~**finanzierung** financing for customers; ~**finanzierungsbank** discount company; ~**finanzierungsgesellschaft** money lending company, finance house; ~**forderung** account receivable; *abgetretene* ~~*n: assigned accounts receivable*; *verpfändete* ~~*en: pledged accounts receivable*; ~**geschäft** business done for customers; ~**kartei** customer file; ~**karteikarte** customers' card; ~**konto** depositor's account, personal account, charge account; ~**kredit** consumer credit, consumer financing, retail credit; ~**kreditbank** hire-purchase finance house, instalment credit company; ~**kreditfinanzierungsgesellschaft** personal finance company, hire-purchase finance house; ~**kreditkonto** drawing account; ~**kreditvertrag** debtor-creditor agreement; ~**kreis** range of customers, clientele; *fester* ~~: *regular customers*; ~~~*schutz: protection of agent's regular clientele*; ~**liste** list of customers; ~**parkplatz** customer car park; ~**rabatt** discount for customers; ~**saldenkontrolle** audit of customer's outstanding accounts; ~**scheck** customer's cheque; ~**schutz** protection of patronage, non-interference with another's customer-relations; ~**stamm** regular customers, regular clientele; ~**stammentschädigung** compensation for loss of clientele; ~**test** consumer survey; ~**umsätze** turnover on customers' accounts; ~**verlust** loss of custom; ~**wechsel** customer's bill, trade bill, private bill, commercial bill, *pl* bills receivable; ~**werber** canvasser, travelling salesman; ~**werbung** touting, soliciting customers, canvassing; ~**zahlung** payment from customer: ~~ *auf Anderkonto: escrow deposit*, payment of customer to a trust account; ~**zeitschrift** magazine for customers; ~**zuführung** bringing (*or* introducing) customers, gaining custom.

Kundgebung *f* demonstration.

kundig *adj* skilful, expert.

kündigen *v/t* to give notice of termination, to terminate, to determine, to give notice to quit (*tenancy*); to call up for redemption; **ordentlich** ~ to give notice of termination; **fristlos** ~ to terminate without notice, to dismiss summarily, to sack.

Kündigender *m* (*der Kündigende*) the person giving notice to terminate.

Kündigung *f* termination, notice to terminate, notice to quit (*tenancy*), notice of dismissal (*employer*), denunciation (*treaty*); calling-in, giving notice of withdrawal; ~ **aus**

wichtigem Grund termination for an important (*or* special) reason, termination without notice, for grave cause; ~ **durch den Vermieter** notice to quit; ~ **durch den Verpächter** notice to quit; ~ **e–r Anleihe** calling in a loan, redemption of a loan; ~ **e–s Bankguthabens** notice of withdrawal (*of a bank-account balance*); ~ **e–s Darlehens** redemption of a loan; ~ **e–s Vertrages** notice to terminate a contract; ~ **nach Belieben** termination for convenience; ~ **von Einlagen** notice of withdrawal of funds (*or* capital contributions); ~ **von Staatsverträgen** denunciation of treaties; ~ **von Wertpapieren** notice of redemption; ~ **zum Jahresende** notice expiring at the end of the year; **auf jederzeitige** ~ terminable at will, at call; **auf tägliche** ~ at call, on call (money); **außerordentliche** ~ extraordinary (*or* special) termination; **betriebsbedingte** ~ business structure related dismissal, dismissal due to operational requirements; **einvernehmliche** ~ mutually agreed termination; **fristlose** ~ termination without notice, instant dismissal, summary dismissal; **monatliche** ~ a month's notice; **nahegelegte** ~ involuntary resignation; **ohne** ~ **rückzahlbar** (re)payable at call; **ordentliche** ~ notice to terminate, termination subject to (*legal or contractual*) period of notice; **ordnungsgemäße** ~ (*Arbeitgeber*) dismissal by notice, due notice; **sozial ungerechtfertigte** ~ socially unjustified (*or* unfair) dismissal; **vierteljährliche** ~ **zum Quartalsende** quarter notice, 3 months' notice to the end of a calendar quarter; **14tägige** ~ a fortnight's notice; 14 days' notice; **vereinbarte** ~ mutually agreed; **vorzeitige** ~ early (*or* premature) termination; **willkürliche** ~ arbitrary dismissal.

Kündigungs|abfindung severance pay, payment in lieu of notice, termination benefit; ~**begründung** statement of reasons for dismissal; ~**entschädigung** severance pay, compensation for loss of employment; ~**frist** → *Kündigungsfrist*; ~**geld** notice deposit; ~**grund** reason for termination; ~**klausel** (contractual) clause on unilateral termination, break clause; ~**möglichkeit** provision for termination; ~**recht** right of notice, right of termination, right to call for repayment, right of cancellation; ~**schreiben** letter containing notice of termination, letter of dismissal, dismissal notice; ~**schutz** protection against unfair dismissal *or* socially unjustified termination of tenancy; ~**schutzklage** action against unfair dismissal; ~**schutzvorschriften** dismissal protection regulations; ~**-Spareinlagen** savings deposits at notice; ~**sperrfrist** period in which redemption is barred, non-calling period; ~**termin** last date for giving notice, (required) period of notice; ~**verbot** restriction on giving notice, ban on giving notice.

Kündigungsfrist *f* notice period; withdrawal notice; ~ **von 1 Monat** a month's notice; **angemessene** ~ reasonable notice; **gesetzliche** ~ statutory period of notice, lawful period of notice; **mit einjähriger** ~ **abhebbar** withdrawable at one year's notice; **tarifliche** ~ period of notice fixed by a collective agreement; **wöchentliche** ~ seven days' notice.

Kundmachung *f* announcement, notice; **öffentliche** ~ public announcement.

Kundschaft *f* customers, clientele, patronage; ~**seinlagen** customers' deposits.

Kundschafter *m* scout, spy.

Kunst|faser synthetic fibre, man-made fibre; ~**fehler** unskilful treatment; *ärztlicher* ~~: *medical malpractice, unskilful treatment, maltreatment (on the part of a doctor)*; ~**fertigkeit** skilfulness, skill, dexterity, art; ~**förderung** promotion of arts; ~**freiheit** freedom of art; ~**gegenstand** work of art, objet d'art; ~**geheimnis** trade secret; ~**gewerbe** arts and crafts, applied art; ~**gewerbetreibender** artist-craftsman, industrial artist, commercial artist; ~**glied** artificial limb, prosthesis; ~**griff** trick, dodge; ~**handwerk** arts and crafts; ~**hochschule** academy of arts; ~**maler** painter; ~**markt** art market; ~**schutz** legal protection of works of art, copyright for works of art, artistic copyright; ~**schutzfähigkeit** qualification for artistic copyright; ~**stoff** plastics, synthetic material; ~**stoffindustrie** plastics industry; ~**urheberrecht** copyright for works of art, artistic copyright; ~**werk** work of art, artistic work; *literarisches* ~~: *literary work; plastisches* ~~: *plastic work*; ~**wert** artistic value; ~**wort** invented word, technical term; *juristisches* ~~: *nomen juris, legal term*.

Künstler *m* artist; **ausübende** ~ performing artists; **darstellender** ~ performer; ~**name** pen-name, nom de plume, stage name, assumed name, pseudonym (of author).

Kupon *m* coupon, dividend warrant; ~**s abtrennen** to detach coupons; ~**bogen** coupon sheet; ~**einlösung** coupon service; ~**kasse** coupon-paying department; ~**schneiden** detaching of coupons; ~**steuer** coupon tax, withholding tax; ~**steuergesetz** Coupons Tax Act; ~**termin** coupon date, dividend coupon date; ~**zahlstelle** paying agents for coupons; **ausstehender** ~ outstanding coupon; **fällig werdender** ~ maturing coupon; **ohne** ~ ex coupon.

Kuppelei *f* procuring, pandering; ~ **treiben** to procure for another the gratification of lust, to pander.

Kuppler *m* procurer, pander(er).

Kupplerin *f* procuress, panderess.

Kur|**abgabe** = ~*taxe qv*; ~**anlagen** health resort facilities; ~**anstalt** sanatorium; ~**aufenthalt** stay at a health resort; ~**beitrag** = ~ *taxe qv*; ~**kostenversicherung** insurance for convalescence costs in a spa; ~**mittel** applications for a cure at a spa; ~**ort** health resort, spa; ~**taxe** health resort tax.

kurant *adj* current, saleable, marketable.

Kuratel *n* tutelage, guardianship.

Kurator *m* trustee, curator, administrator, guardian.

Kuratorium *n* board of trustees, board of governors; ~ **Deutsche Altershilfe** German Foundation for the Care of the Aged; ~ **für das Bankgewerbe** Board for Banking.

Kurier *m* courier, diplomatic courier; ~**abteilung** foreign messengers service; ~**dienst** courier service, messenger service; ~**gepäck** diplomatic pouch, diplomatic bag; **diplomatischer** ~ diplomatic courier.

Kurpfuscher *m* quack (doctor).

Kurrentschrift *f* long hand, ordinary writing, cursive script.

Kurs *m* (1) course, policy; ~**abweichung** deviation (from the course); ~**wagen** through coach, through carriage; ~**wechsel** change in policy; **der agrarpolitische** ~ farming policy; **politischer** ~ policy, orientation of policy.

Kurs *m* (2) rate, quotation, market price, market rate, exchange rate; ~**abbröckelung** slight drop in market prices; ~**abschlag** markdown; ~**abschwächung** weak market; ~**angleichung** adjustment of rates; ~**anstieg auf breiter Front** price rises across the board; ~**aufschwung** upturn in quotations; ~**ausschläge** erratic price swings; ~**befestigung** stiffening of prices; ~ **bei telegrafischer Auszahlung** cable rate; ~**begrenzung** price limit; ~**bericht** stock exchange report; ~**besserung** improvement in prices, exchange advance; ~**beständigkeit** steadiness in prices; ~**bewegungen** price

Kursbildung

movements; ~**bildung** formation of rates, fixing of prices, price range determination; ~**bindung** pegging of exchange rates; ~**blatt** stock market report, over the counter report, list of quotations; *amtliches* ~~: *official price list*; ~**buch** railway time-table, railway guide; ~**bukkel** bulge; ~**depesche** exchange telegram; ~**depression** depressed rates (prices); *vorübergehende* ~~: sag; ~**deroute** collapse of prices, general fall in prices; ~**differenz** difference in rates, differences in exchange, spread; ~**e der Rentenwerte** quotations for fixed-interest securities; ~**druck** downward pressure on prices; ~**e drücken** to pull down prices; ~**einbruch** slump, (sudden) price fall; ~**einbuße** price decline, price loss, drop in prices; ~**entwicklung** trend in quotations, price movement; ~**erholung** recovery of the market, rally in prices, recovery in prices; ~**e stützen** to peg (exchange) quotations; ~**festigung** recovery in prices; ~**festsetzung** rate fixing, price determination; ~**feststellung** determination of exchange rate; ~ **für Termingeschäfte** forward price; ~**gefüge** price structure, structure of market rates; ~ **gestrichen** trading stopped; ~**s-Gewinn** stock price gain, rise in market rates, market profit, exchange profits; profit on exchange; *e-n* ~~ *verzeichnen*: *to score an advance*; ~**gewinn-Verhältnis** price-earnings ratio; ~**grenze** limit of the exchange rate; ~**index** price index, stock-exchange index; ~**intervention** exchange intervention; ~**korrektur** corrective price adjustment; ~**limit** limited price, price limit; k~**mäßig** *adj*, *adv* in terms of quotation, relating to prices; ~**makler** official (exchange) broker; ~**manipulation** market rigging; stock jobbing; ~**niveau** price level; ~**notierung** market quotation, price quotation; *e-e* ~~ *aussetzen*: *to stop a quotation*;

Kurszettel

~**notiz** market quotation; ~**parität** exchange parity; ~**pflege** price nursing, regulation of the market (*by interventions*), supporting purchases; k~ **reagibel** price-sensitive; ~**regulierung** regulation of the market, action to regulate market quotations; ~**risiko** foreign exchange risk, price risk; ~**rückgang** decline in prices, market decline, fall in stocks; ~**schwankungen** fluctuations of market rates; ~**sicherung** rate support, forward covering of rates, exchange rate guarantee, hedging; ~**sicherungsgeschäft** rate-fixing business, hedging (transaction); ~**sicherungsklausel** exchange rate fluctuation clause; ~**spanne** difference in quotations; ~**spekulant** market operator, premium hunter; ~**sprung** spurt, bull movement *pl also*: gyrations; ~**stabilität** (exchange) market stability; ~**stand** level of quotations, price level; ~**steigerung** price advance, rise, ~**struktur** exchange rate structure; ~**sturz** share fallout, slump (in prices); ~**stützung** price support, price pegging, exchange pegging; ~**tabelle** table of exchanges, quotation board; ~**tag** date determining the rate; ~**tendenz** tendency of prices, trend in prices; ~**treiber** rigger, market maker; ~**treiberei** bull campaign, forcing up prices, share pushing; ~**übersteigerung** excessive rise in prices; ~**verbesserung** improvement in the market rates, improvement of a quotation; ~**verfall** collapse of prices, sudden decline of the market; ~**verlust** loss on the stock-exchange, loss in prices, loss on securities; ~**verlustversicherung** insurance against loss by exchange fluctuations; ~**verwässerung** watering of stock-exchange rates; ~**wert** current price, quoted value, list price, market value; ~**zettel** list of quotations, stock exchange list, share list, stock list, price list; *amtlicher* ~~: *quoted list*; ~**zusammen-**

Kurtoisie | **Küstenstaat**

bruch collapse of the market, price collapse; ~**zuschlag** contango rate, continuation rate, carrying-over rate; **amtlicher** ~ official quotation, official rate of exchange; **anziehender** ~ rising market rate; **außerbörslicher** ~ unofficial quotation, curb price; **außer** ~ **setzen** to demonetize, to recall, to withdraw from circulation; **äußerste** ~**e** the finest rates; **den** ~ **stützen** to support an exchange rate; **die** ~**e reagieren empfindlich** prices are quick to react; **echter** ~ true rate; **e–n** ~ **notieren** to mark a price; **fallender** ~ dropping price, falling price; **fester** ~ firm price; **garantierter** ~ guaranteed exchange rate; **gedrückter** ~ depressed market rate; **gehaltener** ~ maintained rate; **gesetzlicher** ~ legal rate, legally fixed exchange rate; **gestützter** ~ supported exchange rate; **getätigter** ~ effected rate of exchange; **grauer** ~ grey rate; **haussierende** ~**e** soaring prices; **im** ~ **stehen** to quote; **letzter** ~ closing price; **limitierter** ~ limited price; **nachbörsliche** ~**e** street prices, prices after hours; **niedrigster** ~ lowest rate, bottom price; **notierter** ~ quoted price, price quoted; **schwankender** ~ flexible rate; **sinkende** ~**e** sagging prices; **steigende** ~**e** rising prices, rising market; **ungünstiger** ~ unfavourable exchange rate; **variabler** ~ variable exchange rate; **wieder in** ~ **setzen** to remonetize.

Kurtoisie *f* courtesy; **völkerrechtliche** ~ international comity.

Kurve *f* curve (*math, statistics*) bend, corner (*road*); **gefährliche** ~ dangerous bend; **scharfe** ~ sharp bend; **unübersichtliche** ~**n** deceptive bends, blind bends; **eine** ~ **schneiden** to cut a bend (*or corner*).

Kurz|anschrift abbreviated address; ~**anzeige** small ad; ~**arbeit** short time; short-time work, short hours; **k**~**arbeiten** to be on short-time; ~**arbeiter** short-time worker, short-timer; ~**arbeitergeld** compensation (*paid by job office*) for workers put on short time; ~**arbeiterunterstützung** support for short-time workers; ~**arbeitsvereinbarung** short-time (work) agreement; ~**arrest** short-term detention (for juvenile offenders); ~**erkrankung** short-time illnes; ~**fassung** abridged version, summary; ~~ *e–s Patents*: title of a patent; **k**~**fristig** *adj, adv* short-term, at short notice; ~**fristigkeit** short-term (nature); ~**kredit** short-term credit; ~**läufer** short-dated bond *pl also*: shorts; **k**~**lebig** transitory; ~**prüfung** short-time test, accelerated test; ~**referat** short report, brief outline; ~**schrift** shorthand; ~**schriftaufzeichnungen des Protokollführers** shorthand writer's notes, official shorthand notes; ~**streckenfracht** short haul; ~**titel** short title (*of an Act*); ~**urlaub** brief holiday, short break; short leave; ~**waren** haberdashery (*GB*), notions (*US*) ~**warenhandlung** haberdashery (*GB*); ~**zeitarrest** detention for short periods; ~**zeitbeobachtung** short-time observation (*testing*).

Kürzung *f* cut, curtailment, reduction, abridgment; ~ **des Ruhegehalts** pension reduction; ~ **von Vermächtniszuwendungen** abatement of legacies; **eigenschöpferische** ~ fair abridgment.

Küsten|fischerei coastal fishery, inshore fishing; ~**gewässer** coastal waters; ~**grenzen** maritime frontiers; ~**handel** intercoastal trade; ~**hoheitsgewässer** coastal (territorial) waters, marine belt; ~**land** littoral state, coastal state; ~**leuchtfeuer** coast beacon; ~**meer** territorial sea; ~**nähe** proximity to the coast, offshore; ~**patrouille** shore patrol; ~**polizei** coast guard; ~**radar** shore-based radar; ~**schiffahrt** coastal shipping, cabotage; ~**schutz** coast protection, shore protection, coastal defence; ~**sockel** maritime shelf, continental shelf; ~**staat** lit-

Küstenstreife

toral state, coastal state; ~**streife** shore patrol; ~**streifen** sea-shore (*between side-marks*); ~- **und Nahverkehrsschiff** home trade ship, coastal trader; ~**vermessung** coast geodetic survey, coast-survey; ~**verteidigung** coastal defence; ~**wachboot** coastal patrol vessel; ~**wachstation** coast guard station.

Kux

Kustos *m* custodian, curator, caretaker.

Kux *m* registered mining share: *registered mining share of no par value in a „Gewerkschaft" (1) qv, subject to contributions by the shareholders;* ~**anteil** registered mining share; ~**schein** mining share certificate.

L

Lade|fähigkeit load capacity, cargo tonnage, carrying capacity, hold volume; **~frist** loading days, time allowed for loading; **~geschäft** loading business, loading and unloading; **~gewicht** load, shipping weight; **~gut** cargo; **~kai** cargo dock; **~kosten** lading charges; **~linie** water line, load line; **~liste** manifest, shipper's manifest, freight list; **~luke** cargo hatch; **~marke** load line, plimsoll mark, freeboard mark; **~papiere** shipping papers, shipping documents; **~platz** place of shipment, loading berth; **~rampe** loading ramp; **~raum** freight space, (ship's) hold, cargo space, hold, cargo compartment; **~rost** pallet; **~schein** inland-waterways bill of lading, shipping note; **~stelle** loading berth; **~tätigkeit** loading; **~tonnage** load displacement; **~vermögen** loading capacity; **~verzeichnis** cargo list; **~verzögerung** delay in loading; **~zeit** time for loading.

Laden *m* shop, store, retail store; **~angestellter** shop assistant; **~besitzer** shopkeeper, storekeeper; **~besitzerin** tradeswoman; **~dieb** shoplifter, shop thief; **~diebstahl** shoplifting; **~einbruch** breaking into a shop; **~einrichtung** shop fittings; **~front** shop front; **~geschäft** shop, store; **~hüter** slow mover, old stock, „shelf-warmer", cats and dogs, non-moving items; **~inhaber** shop owner, tradesman; **~kasse** till *elektronische ~: point of sale terminal*; **~kette** chain of retail stores; **~lokal** shop premises; **~mädchen** salesgirl; **~miete** store rental; **~preis** retail price; **~preisschutz** protection of the published price; **~räume** shop premises; **~schluß** shop closing (time); **~schlußgesetz** Shop Hours Act, Shop Closing Act; **~schlußzeit** closing hour; **~verkäufer** sales clerk; **~vollmacht** shop assistants' usual authority *(legal presumption)*.

laden *v/t* to summon s. o., to serve a summons on s. o.; **gerichtlich ~** to issue a summons; **jmdn ~ lassen** to take out a summons against s. o.; **ordnungsgemäß ~** duly summon to appear, to order an appearance.

Ladung *f* (1) summons (to appear), subpoena, notice of hearing; **~ als Zeuge** subpoena for a witness; **~ des Beklagten** notice to appear; **~ durch öffentliche Zustellung** public citation, summons by publication; **~ mit abgekürzter Frist** summons at short notice; **~ mit Aufforderung zur Stellungnahme** summons and order to show cause; **~sbeamter** summoner; **~sbuch** cause-book; **~sfrist** minimum period of notice before a court hearing; notice period for summons; **~skanzlei** subpoena office; **~smangel** faulty summons; **~sschreiben** letter containing a summons; **~szustellung** service of summons; **~ unter Strafandrohung** writ of subpoena, subpoena; **~ zum Termin** notice of trial, summons to appear at the hearing; **~ zur mündlichen Verhandlung** notice of trial *(after preliminary pleadings)*; **erneute ~** repeated (*or* fresh) summons, resummons; **förmliche ~** subpoena; **nochmalige ~** resummons; **trotz ~ nicht vor Gericht erscheinen** to fail to appear, to be contumacious; **unmittelbare ~** personal summons; **vereinfachte ~** simplified process.

Ladung *f* (2) cargo, freight, load; loading, shipment, stowage;

Ladungsaufkommen   **Lagerhaus**

feuergefährliche ~ inflammable cargo; **gefährliche** ~ dangerous cargo; **in Säcke gefüllte** ~ bag cargo; **nicht deklarierte** ~ undeclared cargo; **sperrige** ~ bulky cargo; **volle** ~ full and complete cargo (*ship*); **zahlende** ~ revenue freight, paying cargo.

Ladungs|aufkommen tonnage loaded; ~**aufseher** supercargo; ~**empfänger** consignee; ~**gewicht** load, shipping weight; ~**gläubiger** consignee; ~**hafen** port of loading, port of departure; ~**interessent** party interested in cargo; ~**kontrolleur** tallyman; ~**manifest** shipper's manifest; ~**papiere** documents relating to cargo; ~**pfandrecht** cargo lien; ~**police** cargo policy; ~**schäden beim Löschen** damage to cargo in discharging; ~**schäden durch Seewurf und Aufopferung** damage to cargo by jettison and sacrifice; ~**steg** pier; ~**träger** carrier; ~**verzeichnis** freight list, carrier's manifest, shipper's manifest; ~**wert** value of cargo.

Lage *f* position, situation; site, situs; ~**bericht** briefing, situation report; ~**besprechung** discussion of the situation, headquarters conference; ~**plan** site plan, ground plan, plan showing position; **außenpolitische** ~ the foreign situation; **finanzielle** ~ financial positon; **gespannte** ~ tense atmosphere; **innerstädtische** ~ in-town site; **kritische** ~ critical situation, crisis; **in günstiger** ~ well situated; **je nach** ~ **des Falles** as the case may be; **liquiditätspolitische** ~ liquidity situation; **mißliche** ~ uncomfortable situation, dilemma, scrape; **nach** ~ **der Akten entscheiden** to decide on the strength of the records (*non-appearance of parties*); **örtliche** ~ location; **peinliche** ~ embarrassing situation; **rechtliche** ~ status, legal position; **steuerliche** ~ tax status, tax position; **tatsächliche** ~ **der Dinge** actual state of affairs.

Lager *n* (1) store, stock, store-room, warehouse; ~**abbau** stock reduction; ~**auffüllung** replenishment of stocks; ~**aufstockung** replenishment of stocks, stockpiling; ~**bedingungen** storing conditions; ~**behälter** storage container; ~**bestand** inventories, stocks, stock of merchandise, stock-in-hand, stock in trade; ~**bestandsaufnahme** stocktaking; ~**bestandsbewertung** inventory valuation; ~**bestandsfortschreibung** updating of inventory; ~**bestandsführung** inventory control; ~**bestandskarte** stock record card; ~**bestandsverzeichnis** inventory (list); ~**bestandswert** inventory value; ~**bildung** storing, stockpiling, accumulation of stocks; ~**buch** stock book, warehouse book, store book, store ledger; ~**buchhaltung** stock records department, stores accounting; ~**butter** cold-storage butter; ~**dauer** duration of storage; ~**dispositionen** storage dispositions; ~**empfangsschein** warehouse receipt; warehousekeeper's certificate, warehousekeeper's receipt; **l~fähig** *adj* fit for storage, storable; ~**fähigkeit** storage capacity, suitability for storage; ~**finanzierungsdarlehen** inventory loan; ~ **für den aktiven Veredelungsverkehr** inward-processing warehouse; ~**gebühren** storage charges; ~ **gegen Zoll- bzw. Steuersicherung** bonded warehouse; ~**geld** storage charges, storage, warehouse charges; ~**geschäft** warehousing, storage business; ~**gut** stored goods, warehouse goods, goods in storage; ~**halle** warehouse, storage building; ~**halter** warehousekeeper, *US:* warehouseman; ~**halterkonnossement** custody bill of lading; ~**halterpfandrecht** warehousekeeper's lien, *US:* warehouseman's lien; ~**haltung** warehousing, stockkeeping; ~**haus** warehouse, storehouse, storage depot, depository; *öffentliches ~ ~*: public warehouse; **~hausgebühr** storage charges; **~hausgenossenschaft** cooperative warehouse association; **~hausgesellschaft** warehousing company; **~hof** storage yard; **~index** index of stocks in hand; **~investition** inventory investment; **~kartei** stock index, stock file; **~konto** warehouse account, store account; **~kosten** storage expenses, inventory carrying cost; **~liste** stock sheet; **~nummer** storage number, stock number; **~pfandschein** warehouse warrant (*issued as security for a loan*); **~platz** storage room, storage yard; **~politik** stock-carrying policy, inventory policy; **~raum** storage space, store-room, stockroom; **~rauminhaber** occupier of store-room; **~räumung** (stock) clearance; **~risiko** risk inherent in carrying stock, storage risk; **~rechnung** warehouse account; **~restbestand** left over, residue of stock; **~schein** warrant for goods, warehousekeeper's warrant, *US:* warehouse receipt; **~schuppen** storage shed; **~stätte** (*mining*) deposit; *abbauwürdige ~ ~*: productive bed; **~überwachung** storage control, monitoring of inventory; **~umsatz** inventory turnover; **~umschlag** stock turnover, inventory turnover; **~veralterung** obsolescence of stock; **~versicherung** storage insurance; **~vertrag** warehousing contract, storage contract; **~verwalter** warehouse keeper, warehouse manager; **~vorrat** stock, supply; **~vorrichtungen** storage facilities; **~wertänderung** variation in inventory prices; **~wirtschaft** stock control; **~zeit** period of storage, storing time; **~zugang** addition to stocks; **~zunahme** growth of inventory; **l~zyklisch** relating to the stock cycle; **~zyklus** stock cycle, inventory cycle; **ab** ~ ex warehouse; **am** ~ in stock; **auf** ~ in stock, in store; **auf ~halten** to keep in stock, to stock; **ein ~ liquidieren** to sell out; **nicht am ~** not in stock, out of stock; **überhöhte ~** inflated stocks; **zu viel auf ~ haben** to overstock.

Lager *n* (2) camp, prison camp, detention camp; **~insasse** camp inmate.

Lagerei *f* warehousing, storage service; **~gewerbe** warehousing.

Lagerist *m* stockkeeper, storeroom clerk, storekeeper.

Lagerung *f* storing, storage, warehousing; (*von Schadstoffen*) tipping.

Laie *m* layman; **~nbeisitzer** lay assessor; **~nrichter** non-professional judge, lay judge; **~nstand** laity.

Land *n* (1) land, soil, landed property, rural district, region; the countryside; **~abfindung** compensation for land, compensation in the form of land; **~abgabe** surrender of farm land; **~abgaberente** annuity to farmer who surrendered his holdings; **~adel** landed gentry; **~arbeiter** agricultural labourer, farm worker; **~arbeitertarif** wage scale for farm workers; **~aristokratie** landed gentry, landocracy; **~aufteilung** dividing-up of land; **~ausnutzung** (intensity of) land use; **~beschädigung** shore damage; **~beschaffung** land procurement; **~beschaffungsgesetz** Land Procurement Act; **~beschaffungsverfahren** land procurement proceedings; **~besitz** landholding, tenant's possession of land; *imprecisely*: property, landed property, real estate; *gemeinsamer ~ ~*: multiple tenure; *teilbarer ~ ~*: severable lands; **~besitzer** occupier of land, land owner; **~bevölkerung** rural population; **~bezirk** rural district; **~eier** free-range eggs (*opp. = battery eggs*); **~eskultur** land improvement; **~eskulturkredit** land improvement loan; **~fahrzeug** land vehicle; **~flucht** rural exodus, drift from the land, absconding of peasants; **~fracht** freight charge for land, land-borne freight; **~frachtvertrag** contract of carriage

Landfriedensbruch   **Landtag**

by land; ~**friedensbruch** rioting, civil disorder; ~ **für Verkehrszwecke** land for public transport requirements; ~**gang** shore leave; ~**gangausweis** shore leave pass; ~**gangsgelder** seamen's shore allowance; ~**gemeinde** rural community, parish; ~**gewinnung** reclamation of land; ~**gut** agricultural estate, country estate; ~**jugend** rural youth; ~**krankenkasse** rural health insurance board; ~**krankenkassenpflichtiger** person subject to compulsory rural health insurance; ~**kreis** *approx*: administrative county, county, administrative district, rural district; ~**kreisbehörde** county authority; ~**kreisordnung** county constitution; ~**kreiswahl** county council election; ~**krieg** land warfare, war on land; ~**lieferungsverband** agricultural supply association; ~**maschinen** agricultural machinery; ~**messer** land surveyor; ~**- oder Schiffsentladeseite** ashore or overside; ~**pacht** tenure of land, farm tenancy; ~**pachtgesetz** Farm Tenancies Act; ~**pachtvertrag** farm lease, agricultural lease; ~**parzelle** parcel of land, plot (of land), lot; ~**polizei** state police, rural police; ~**polizeidirektion** state police headquarters; ~**rat** (=) county president, chief executive of a county, county council chairman; ~**ratsamt** county office district authority; district administrator's office; ~**recht** *hist* common law (*in Germany*); ~**reform** land reform; ~**schaden** damage to the soil, damage to the shore; ~**schenkung** land grant; ~**sitz** country seat; ~**straße** common highway, "B" road, country road; ~ ~ *I. Ordnung:* "*B*"*road;* ~ ~ *II. Ordnung: country road;* ~**streicher** vagrant; ~**streicherei** vagrancy; ~**streitkräfte** land forces, army; ~**transport** carriage by land, land carriage; ~**transportversicherung** insurance of goods in transit by land; ~**- und Forstwirte** farmers and foresters; ~**- und Forstwirtschaft** agriculture and forestry; ~**verkehr** land transport; ~**vermesser** surveyor; ~**vermessung** ordnance survey, land survey; ~**volk** rural population; ~**weg** overland route, by land; ~**wirt** → *Landwirt;* ~**wirtschaft** → *Landwirtschaft;* ~**zunahme** accretion; ~**zustellung** rural postal delivery, ~**zuteilung** assignment of land; ~**zuwachs** accretion; ~**zuweisung** land grant, assignment of land; **an ~ bringen** to put ashore; **bebautes ~** built-up area; **brachliegendes ~** fallow, under-used land; **gerodetes ~** cleared forest-land; **melioriertes ~** improved land; **nächstgelegenes ~** nearest land; **selbst bewirtschaftetes ~** home farm; **unentwickeltes ~** undeveloped land; **verpachtetes ~** leased land.

Land *n* (2) (*pl Länder =* ~*er*) country, state, member-state, Land; ~ **des Gesellschaftssitzes** country of the registered office; ~ **des steuerlichen Wohnsitzes** country of fiscal domicile; ~**eranleihen** bonds of German states (*Länder*); ~**erbank** State bank; ~**erbeamte** state officials, Länder officials; ~**erfinanzverwaltungen** Länder taxation authorities; ~**ergrenzen** national borders, Länder borders; ~**ergruppe** group of (associated) countries; ~**erhaushalte** Länder budgets; ~**erkonkordate** *concordats (treaties) between German states and the Vatican;* ~**ermittel** Länder cash resources; ~**erparlamente** Land parliaments; ~**er-Staatsangehörigkeit** state-citizenship (*citizenship in a German state or Land*); ~**frieden** public peace; ~**friedensbruch** breach of the public peace, public violence, public disorder *aktive Teilnahme an ~ ~: riotous act;* ~**gericht** regional court, (higher) district court; ~**gerichtspräsident** (=) *president of a Landgericht qv;* ~**tag** → *Landtag;* ~**er und Bund** the German

Landegebühr **Landessitte**

Länder and the Federal Government; ~**zwang** public coercion, threats to public peace; **assoziiertes** ~ associated country; **außereuropäische** ~**er** non-European countries; **außer** ~**es aufhalten** to stay abroad; **des** ~**es verweisen** to relegate, to deport; **devisenschwaches** ~ country short of foreign exchange; **finanzschwächere** ~**er** the financially weaker Länder (*or* countries); **industrieschwaches** ~ industrially undeveloped country; **kriegführendes** ~ nation at war, belligerent country; **reservestarke** ~**er** countries with strong reserve positions; **steuerstarke** ~**er** countries (Länder) with large tax revenues; **währungsschwaches** ~ soft-currency country; **währungsstarkes** ~ strong-currency country.

Landegebühr *f* landing tax, landing fee.

Länderei *f* estate, landed property, plantation, country property.

Landes|abgaben state taxes, internal taxes; ~**amt** state office, Land agency; ~**amt für Denkmalspflege** Land (state) Authority for the Preservation of Ancient Monuments (*Bavaria*); ~**amt für Verfassungsschutz** Land (state) security office; ~**arbeitsamt** regional labour office; ~**arbeitsgericht** (Land) employment appeals tribunal; ~**arbeitsstock** regional unemployment insurance fund; ~**aufnahme** topographical survey; ~**ausgleichsamt** Land equalization of burdens office; ~**bank** Land bank, regional bank; ~**baudarlehen** Land building loan, provincial building loan; ~**beamtenrecht** Land civil service law; ~**behörde** Land authority; *oberste* ~ ~: *supreme Land authority;* ~**berufsgericht** supreme Land professional tribunal; ~**bodenkreditanstalt** (*Bavarian*) Land mortgage bank; ~**brandversicherungsanstalt** Land fire insurance board; ~**ebene** Land level; ~**entschädigungsamt** Land compensation office (*for Nazi persecutees*); ~**entwicklungsplan** Land development plan; ~**farben** national colours, Land colours; ~**feuerwehrunterstützungskasse** Land fire-brigade relief fund; ~**finanzämter** Land tax offices; ~**gesetz** (Land) state law; ~**gesetzgebung** state legislation, Land laws; ~**grenze** national border, Land border; ~**herr** sovereign, ruler; ~**hoheit** national sovereignty, state autonomy; ~**interesse** national interest, (Land) state interest; ~**justizverwaltung** Land administration of justice; ~**kasse** Land treasury, Land cash office; ~**kinderklausel** preference to native children clause; ~**kreditanstalt** (=) *semi-public bank in a German state*; ~**kreditausschuß** Land credit committee; ~**kreditgarantiegemeinschaft des Handwerks** Land credit guarantee association for handicrafts; ~**kriminalamt** (Land) state criminal investigation department; ~**kulturerbe** National Heritage; ~**kunde** study of the geography and civilization of a country (*politology*); ~**liste** list of party candidates for (German) Land elections; ~**medienanstalt** state media authority; ~**minister** (Land) state minister; ~**mittel** (Land) state resources; ~**organisationsgesetz** Land administrative organization Act; ~**personalausschuß** (Land) state civil service selection board; ~**planung** regional planning in a German state; ~**planungsgesetz** Land Planning Act; ~**planungsstelle** Land planning agency; ~**prüfungsamt** Land examination authority; ~**recht** Land law, state law; ~**regierung** Land government, state government; ~**rentenbank** Land mortgage bank; ~**rentenbrief** Land annuity bond; ~**schiedsamt** Land arbitration office; ~**sitte** national custom;

497

Landessprache

~**sprache** national language; ~**sozialgericht** (=) regional social insurance appeals tribunal; ~**steuern** (Land) state taxes; ~**strafgesetze** (Land) state penal laws; ~**straßenbaubehörde** Land road construction authority; ~**vater** sovereign, popular elder statesman; ~**verband** Land association; ~**verfassung** Land constitution; ~**verfassungsgericht** (Land) state constitutional court; ~**verfassungsgerichtsbarkeit** jurisdiction of Land constitutional courts; ~**verfassungsrecht** Land constitutional law; ~**verordnung** state ordinance, Land ordinance; ~**verrat** treason; *publizistischer* ~ ~: *treasonable publication*; ~**verräter** traitor; ~**versicherungsamt** (Land) state (supervisory) insurance authority; ~- ~**versicherungsanstalt** Land social insurance board (for workers); ~**verteidigung** national defence; ~**vertretung** representation of a Land, Land mission; ~**verwaltung** Land administration; ~**verwaltungsgericht** Land administrative tribunal; ~**verweisung** expulsion (*of an alien*), exclusion order ~**wahlausschuß** (Land) state elections committee; ~**wahlgesetz** (Land) state elections law; ~**wahlleiter** chief election officer for state elections, state-elections returning officer; ~**wahlordnung** (Land) state elections rules; ~**wahlrecht** (Land) state elections law; ~**währung** national currency; ~**wappen** national coat of arms, Land coat of arms; ~**wohl** the public good, common weal, public interest, general public benefit; ~**wohnungsordnung** (Land) state housing regulations; ~**zentralbank** Land central bank; ~**zinsfuß** current official interest rate for the country (or Land); ~**zugehörigkeit** nationality, Land jurisdiction.

Landschaft *f* landscape, countryside, rural district; ~**gestalter** landscape engineer, landscape gardener; ~**sökologie** natural ecology;

~**sverband** agricultural association.

Landschaftsschutz *m* landscape protection; ~**gebiete** landscape areas; ~**verordnung** landscape protection ordinance.

Landsmannschaft *f* regional association, regional refugee association.

Landstreicherei *f* vagrancy.

Landtag *m* Land Parliament, State Parliament, Landtag; ~**sabgeordneter** member of a Landtag *qv*; ~**spräsident** speaker of a Landtag *qv*, Landtag President; ~**swahl** elections for a Landtag *qv*, Landtag elections.

Landung *f* landing; ~**skosten** landing charges, landing fee.

Landwirt *m* farmer, peasant farmer, agriculturist; **marktorientierte** ~**e** commercially motivated farmers.

Landwirtschaft *f* agriculture, farming, farming sector.

landwirtschaftlich *adj* agricultural.

Landwirtschafts|amt board of agriculture; ~**ausschuß** agricultural executive committee; ~**bank** agricultural bank, land bank; ~**behörden** agricultural authorities; ~**berater** agricultural consultant; ~**brief** agricultural mortgage bond; ~**betrieb** farm, agricultural undertaking; ~**darlehen** agricultural loan; ~**erzeugnisse** agricultural products; ~**förderungsgesetz** promotion of agriculture Act; ~**genossenschaft** farmers' cooperative association; ~**gericht** agricultural tribunal; ~**gesetz** agricultural law; ~**jahr** agricultural year; ~**kammer** Chamber of Agriculture; ~**minister** minister of agriculture, Secretary of Agriculture; ~**ministerium** ministry of agriculture, *US:* department of agriculture; ~**politik** agricultural policy; ~**rat** official agricultural expert; ~**recht** agricultural law; ~**sachen** farm-law cases; ~**treibender** farmer, agriculturist; ~**verband** farmers' association; ~**swissenschaftler** agronomist.

langatmig *adj* long-winded.

längerfristig *adj* relatively long term.
Langfinger *m* pickpocket.
langfristig *adj* long-term.
langjährig *adj* of long standing, of long duration, longstanding.
Langläufer *m/pl* long maturities, long-term bonds.
langlebig *adj* long-lived, lasting, durable, long-term.
Langlebigkeit *f* longlife, durability; ~ **von Schadstoffen** persistence of pollutants.
Langsamstreik *m* „go-slow" (strike).
Längsmarkierungen *f/pl* longitudinal markings.
Längsschnitt *m* longitudinal section.
Langschrift *f* longhand, ordinary writing.
längsseits *prep* alongside.
Längsseite *f* long side (*building*), broad side (*ship*); **ab ~ Schiff** from alongside ship; **frei ~ Seeschiff** free alongside ship, F. A. S.
langwierig *adj* lengthy, protracted, dilatory, wearisome, unending.
Langzeitprognose *f* long-range forecast.
Lärm *m* noise; ~**bekämpfung** noise abatement; ~**einwirkung** noise impact, noise level; ~**isolierungsbeihilfe** noise insulation grant; ~**schutz** → *Lärmschutz*; **ruhestörender ~** disturbing noise.
Lärmschutz *m* protection against (from) noise; ~**bereich** noise abatement zone; ~**wand** noise protection wall; ~**wall** noise barrier, noise protection embankment.
Last *f* load, burden, charge, onus; ~**anhänger** goods trailer, freight trailer; ~**fahrzeug** goods vehicle; ~**kraftwagen** *GB*: lorry *US*: truck; ~**schrift** debit advice, debit entry; ~**schriftanzeige** debit note; debit memo, charge slip; ~**schriftbeleg** debit voucher; ~**schriftposten** debit item; ~**schriftverfahren** *n* debit charge procedure, direct debiting; ~**- und andere Nutzfahrzeuge** trucks, tractors and trailers; ~**- und Gutschriften** debit and credit entries; ~**wagen** = *Lastkraftwagen qv*; ~**wagenfahrer** teamster (*US*), truck driver, lorry driver; **prozessuale ~** procedural burden; **zur ~ legen** to charge, to impute, to accuse of.

Lasten *f/pl* charges, burden, encumbrances; ~**aufzug** hoist, goods lift, freight lift; ~**ausgleich** → *Lastenausgleich;* ~**beihilfe** hardship relief allowance; ~**berechnung** statement of public charges (*tenancy*); ~**erhöhung** increase in public charges; **l~frei** *adj* unencumbered, free from encumbrances, without charge of any kind; ~**freiheit** freedom from encumbrances; ~**heft** (tender) specifications; ~**teilung** burden sharing; ~**tragung** payment of the charges, the bearing of the charges; ~**übergang** transfer of encumbrances, passing of liability for public charges (*conveyance*); ~**zuschuß** hardship allowance; **dauernde ~** permanent charges; **jährliche ~** annual charges; **öffentliche ~** public charges, rates and taxes; **soziale ~** social (insurance etc) charges; **vertragliche ~** onerous covenants; **zu ~ des Empfängers** on receiver's account; **zusätzliche ~** additional burden(s).

Lastenausgleich *m* burden-sharing, equalization of (war) burdens.
Lastenausgleichs|abgabe equalization of war burdens levy; ~**amt** Equalization of War Burdens Office; ~**bank** Equalization of War Burdens Bank; ~**berechtigter** equalization of war burdens beneficiary; ~**fond** Equalization of War Burdens Fund; ~**gesetz** Equalization of War Burdens Act; ~**verfahren** equalization of war burdens proceedings; ~**-Vermögensabgabe** property levy for equalization of war burdens; ~**versicherung** equalization of war burdens insurance; ~**zahlungen** equalization of war burdens payments.
Laster *n* vice.

lästig *adj* annoying, onerous, burdensome.
Lastigkeit *f* trim, relative heaviness, tendency to preponderate.
Lästigkeit *f* annoyance, nuisance.
latent *adj* latent, potential.
Laternengarage *f* parking under a streetlight.
Laubenkolonie *f* allotment garden, allotment colony.
Lauf *m* course, operation; ~**bahn** → *Laufbahn,* ~ **der Gerechtigkeit** course of justice; ~ **e-r Frist** running of a term, running of a period; ~**kundschaft** passing trade, casual customers, occasional customers, irregular customers; ~**zeit** → *Laufzeit;* ~**zettel** control slip, inter-office slip, routing slip, tracer; transit record sheet (*rail transport*); **der ~ der Verjährungsfrist** the running of time for the purposes of the Statute of Limitations.
Laufbahn *f* career, civil service career; ~**aussichten** career outlook, occupational prospects; ~**bewerber** civil service applicant; ~**gruppe** service class; civil service group; ~**recht** civil service career regulations, ~**strafe** disciplinary penalty affecting promotion; ~**verordnung** civil service promotion ordinance, ~**vorschriften** career and promotion rules; ~**wechsel** change of career, switch in jobs.
Laufzeit *f* term, currency, life, duration, period to run, time to run to maturity date; ~ **des Mietvertrages** term of the tenancy; ~ **e-r Anleihe** period of a loan; ~ **e-r Hypothek** mortgage term; ~ **e-r Police** term of a policy, ~ **e-r Versicherung** currency of policy, term of the policy; ~ **e-s Akkreditivs** term of a letter of credit; ~ **e-s Films** running time of a film; ~ **e-s Patents** term of a patent; ~ **e-s Vertrages** term of an agreement, duration of a contract; ~ **e-s Wechsels** term of a bill, tenor of a bill; **mit sechsmonatiger** ~ with a term of six months; ~**umstrukturierung** change of term; **vertragliche ~** contract period; **zehnjährige ~** term of ten years.
Lausch|angriff illicit wiretapping operation, surreptitious electronic surveillance; ~**operation** wiretapping (operation), electronic surveillance.
Lauscher *m* eavesdropper.
laut *prep* per, as per, pursuant to, according to.
lauten *v/i* to read, to be worded; ~**d auf** denominated in, made out to; **wie folgt ~** to be worded as follows, to run (*or* read) as follows.
Lauterkeitsregeln *f/pl* rules of fair trading.
Läuterung *f* purging; ~**seid** purgatory oath; ~**surteil** *hist* judgment based on purgatory oath; ~**sverfahren** purgatory oath proceedings, *proceeding to force a litigant to swear to the truth of his statements; hist*.
Leasing *n* leasing; ~**geber** lessor; ~**gegenstand** leasing item, leased equipment; subject matter of leasing contract; ~**makler** leasing broker; ~**nehmer** lessee; ~**raten** rental payments; ~**vertrag** leasing contract; **Anlagen~** equipment leasing; **Fahrzeug~** vehicle leasing; **Finanzierungs~** finance lease; **Operating~** operational leasing; operating lease.
Leben *n* life, existence, living; **eheliches ~** conjugal life; **im öffentlichen wie im privaten ~** in public as in private affairs; **sein ~ versichern** to take out a life policy, to insure one's life; **verbundene ~ ins** joint lives; **versichertes ~** insured life.
leben *v/i* to live, to be alive; *solange ich lebe:* during my life; **getrennt ~** to live apart, to be separated; **nicht getrennt ~** to live together.
lebend *adj* living, alive.
Lebender *m* (*der Lebende*) living person, *pl: the living; unter Lebenden: inter vivos.*
Lebendgeburt *f* live birth, live-born child.

Lebendgewicht *n* live weight.
Lebens|abend old age, autumn of life, evening of one's life; **~ansprüche** material demands, basic requirements; **~alter** age; **~arbeit** one's life's work; **~arbeitszeit** working life; **~aufgabe** mission in life, life's work; **~aufwand** style of living, living expenses; *unvertretbar aufwendiger ~ ~: unjustifiable extravagance in living*; **~bedarf** necessities of life; **~bedingungen** conditions of life, living conditions; **~bedürfnisse** necessities of life, basic needs; *die allgemeinen ~ ~: the ordinary necessities of life*; **~berechtigung** right to exist, raison d'etre; **~beruf** occupation for life, lifelong career; **~bescheinigung** certificate of existence, life certificate, *certificate stating that a person is alive*; **~chance** chance of survival; **~dauer** life (span), physical life, length of life; (equipment); useful life; *auf ~ ~: for life; mutmaßliche ~ ~: probable life; wahrscheinliche ~ ~: probable life; auf die ~ ~ e–s Dritten: pur autre vie*; **~erwartung** life expectancy, expectation of life; mean time before failure *(MTBF)*; *abgekürzte ~ ~: reduced life expectancy*; l**~fähig** *adj* capable of living, viable, capable of surviving; *wirtschaftlich ~: economically viable*; **~fähigkeit** viability, capability of survival; **~frist** term of life, span of life; **~führung** conduct, line of conduct, style of living; **~führungskosten** living expenses; **~führungsschuld** criminal conduct; **~gefahr** danger to life; mortal danger; **~gefährdend** *adj* dangerous to life, perilous, involving danger to life and limb; critical; **~gefährdung** endangering life, mortal danger; **~gefährte** common law spouse, lifetime *or* live-in companion; **~gefährtin** common-law wife; **~gemeinschaft** cohabitation, cohabitee, partnership for life; live-in couple; *eheänliche ~~: concubinage, common law marriage; eheliche ~~ conjugal life, conjugal community; ehelose ~~: extra-marital cohabitation*; **~genuß** enjoyment of life; **~gewohnheiten** way of living, habits; **~grundlage** basis of existence; **~haltung** → *Lebenshaltung;* **~jahr** year of one's life, *das 18. ~ ~ nicht vollendet haben: to be under eighteen years of age;* **~kampf** struggle for live; l**~länglich** lifelong, for life; limited by life of a person; **~lauf** course of life; personal record, personal background, curriculum vitae; bio sheet; resumé, history *(machine)*; **~laufakte** service records; **~leistung** life achievement; **~mittel** → *Lebensmittel;* **~nachstellung** preparation for murder; **~nachweis** proof of life, certificate that a person is alive; **~ordnung** way of life, rules of life; **~qualität** quality of life, quality of living conditions; **~raum** living space; *(biol)* biotope; habitat; **~recht** right to exist; **~rente** life pension; **~rettung** rescue, life-saving; **~risiko** risk to life, life contingency; **~standard** standard of living, living standard; **~stellung** station in life, position in life, social status, lifelong position; **~stufe** age-level; **~umstände** environment, situation in life; **~unterhalt** livelihood, living, maintenance, subsistence, keep, support; **~vermutung** presumption of life; **~wandel** (moral) conduct, kind of life; *e–n ehrlosen ~ ~ führen: to lead a disreputable life; unbescholtener ~ ~: orderly life;* **~zeit** natural life, lifetime; *auf ~ ~: for life; auf ~ ~ e–s Dritten: pur autre vie;* **~zeitprinzip** principle of civil servant's life-long relation to the state; **~zeugnis** certificate of life.
Lebenshaltung *f* standard of living, style of living; lifestyle; **~s-Gleitklausel:** index-linked clause; **~sindex** cost of living index; **~skosten** cost of living, living expenditures, subsistence expense; **~spreisindex** consumer price index, cost-of-living index; **~sniveau** style of life.

Lebensmittel *n/pl* food, articles of food, victuals, groceries, provisions; ~**abteilung** food department; ~-**Bestrahlungsverordnung** ordinance regulating the exposure of foodstuffs to electronic rays: ~**betrieb** food store, food industry enterprise; ~**bevorratung** stockpiling of foodstuffs; ~**bewirtschaftung** food control, food rationing; ~**branche** food trade, food business, grocery trade; ~**einzelhandel** grocer, retail trade; ~**fälschung** food adulteration; ~**geschäft** food store, grocery; ~**gesetz** Foodstuffs Act; ~**großhandel** whole sale food trade; ~**handel** grocery business, food trade; ~**händler** grocer; ~**industrie** food processing industry, food manufacturing industry; ~**karte** food ration card; ~**lieferant** supplier of groceries; ~**marke** brand of food; ~**recht** law relating to food production and distribution; ~**spende** food donation; ~**überwachung** food supervision, control of the purity and hygiene of food; ~**- und Bedarfsgegenständegesetz** Act on Foodstuffs and Goods in Daily Use; ~**verfälschung** adulteration of foodstuffs; ~**verkauf** sale of foodstuffs; ~**vergiftung** food poisoning; ~**verkehr** distribution and handling of food; ~**versorgung** food supply; ~**vorrat** food supply; **dauerhafte** ~ non-perishable foodstuffs; **nicht zum Verzehr geeignete** ~ not suitable for consumption.

Lebensretter *m* rescuer (*of a person*), life saver.

Lebensversicherung *f* life assurance, *US*: life insurance; ~ **auf den Erlebensfall** endowment insurance; ~ **auf den Todesfall** whole life assurance, ordinary life insurance; ~ **auf Gegenseitigkeit** mutual life insurance; ~ **für Staatsangestellte** govermental life insurance; ~ **gegen Einmalprämie** single-premium insurance; ~ **mit abgekürzter Prämienzahlung** limited-pay life insurance; ~ **mit gestaffelten Prämienzahlungen** graded premium policy; ~ **mit Gewinnbeteiligung** life insurance with profits, participating life policy; ~ **ohne ärztliche Untersuchung** non-medical policy; ~ **ohne Gewinnbeteiligung** non-participating life insurance; ~ **ohne Rückkaufswert** term policy; **befristete** ~ fixed-term assurance; **beitragslos gestellte** ~ extended policy; **gegenseitige** ~ mutual life insurance; **gemischte** ~ combined endowment and whole life insurance; **große** ~ ordinary life assurance; **normale** ~ ordinary life policy.

Lebensversicherungs|agent underwriter, life insurance representative; ~**ansprüche** rights under a life assurance, life insurance claims; ~**gesellschaft** life assurance company, life insurance company; ~**gesellschaft auf Gegenseitigkeit** mutual life insurance company; ~**police** life assurance policy *GB*; life insurance policy; *US*; ~ ~ **auf den Todesfall**: *whole-life policy*; ~**prämie** life insurance premium; ~**summe** life insurance sum; ~**treuhandfond** life trust; ~**unternehmen** life insurance company; ~**verein auf Gegenseitigkeit** mutual life insurance company; ~**vertrag** life insurance contract.

Leckage *f* leakage; ~-**Klausel** leakage clause; ~ **und Bruch** leakage and breakage; **frei von** ~ free from leakage.

ledig *adj* single, unmarried.

Ledige *f* unmarried female, spinster, femme sole, a single woman.

Lediger *m* (*der Ledige*) bachelor, unmarried man, a single man.

Leer|abgabe short selling, bear sale; ~**aktie** unpaid share; ~**fahrt** empty run, unloaded drive; ~**formel** empty phrase; ~**fracht** dead freight; ~**gang** neutral, neutral position (*gears*); ~**gewicht** dead

legal

weight, empty weight, unladen weight; ~ ~ des Fahrzeugs: unladen weight of the vehicle; ~**gut** empties; ~ ~ zurück: empties returned; ~ ~ wird nicht zurückgenommen: empties are not taken back; ~**gutrücksendung** return of empties; ~**kauf** uncovered sale; ~**lauf** neutral, neutral position (gears); running idle, unproductiveness, idleness, idle time; ~**packung** dummy, empty package; ~**rabatt** discount for empty ship; ~**stehen** unoccupancy; l~**stehend** adj vacant, unoccupied, unpossessed; ~**tabelle** dummy table; ~**tonnage** deadweight tonnage; ~**übertragung** pro forma transfer, „empty" assignment; trade-mark assignment, separate from the enterprise (void); ~**verkauf** selling stocks short, short sale, bear sale; ~**verkaufsposition** short position; ~**zimmer** vacant room, unfurnished room.

legal adj legal, lawful.

Legaldefinition f legal definition, statutory definition.

Legalisation legalization, consular authentication; ~**sklausel** attestation clause, authentication clause.

legalisieren v/t to make lawful, to legalize, to authenticate.

Legalisierung f legalization, authorization.

Legalität f legality, lawfulness; **außerhalb der** ~ outside the law, unlawful, non-lawful.

Legalitätsprinzip principle of mandatory prosecution (principle that every person suspected of an offence must be prosecuted).

Legalservitut n easement, servitude required by law.

Legalzession f assignment by operation of law.

Legat n legacy, bequest; devise (real estate); ~**aussetzung** granting of a legacy; ~**sentziehung** ademption; **ein** ~ **aussetzen** to grant a legacy.

Legatar m legatee, devisee, beneficiary.

Legierungsgesetz n Alloy Act.

legislativ adj legislative.

Lehrabschlußprüfung

Legislativbefugnisse f/pl legislative powers.

Legislative f legislative power, legislative, legislature.

Legislaturperiode f parliamentary term, legislative period, life of a Parliament.

legitim adj legitimate.

Legitimation f evidence of authority, identification of an officer of the law, lawful entitlement, declaration of legitimacy; ~ **durch nachfolgende Eheschließung** legitimation by subsequent marriage, legitimatio per subsequens matrimonium.

Legitimations|aktionär proxy-shareholder (voting in his own name); ~**funktion** identity-establishing function, title-evidencing function; ~**karte** identification card, special sales licence; ~**papier** non-negotiable document of entitlement (e.g. savings-bank book), title-evidencing instrument; ~**srecht** law of legitimation; ~**schein** licence (for canvassing), distribution licence; ~**übertragung** transfer of right to vote, delegation of authority; ~**wirkung** legitimating effect, effect of establishing s. o. as bona fide holder in due course; ~**zeichen** token of identity, warrant token.

legitimieren v/t to authorize, to legitimate, to make lawful; v/reflex to prove one's identity, to show one's papers.

legitimiert adj authorized, entitled; **aktiv** ~ entitled to the claim, entitled to sue; **nicht aktiv** ~ not entitled to the claim, not entitled to sue; **passiv** ~ capable of being sued (as the right party defendant).

Legitimierung f legitimation, proof of identity.

Legitimität f legitimacy, legal standing; ~**sprinzip** principle of legitimacy; das monarchische ~ ~: the principle of monarchic legitimacy.

Lehen n fief, feud, feudal tenure.

Lehr|abschlußprüfung final apprenticeship examination; ~**amt** office of teacher, teaching appointment;

teaching profession; *geistliches ~ ~: ministry, magisterium*; **~amtsanwärter** candidate for a teaching appointment, junior teacher; **~amtskandidat** = *~amtsanwärter qv;* **~amtsprüfung** teaching diploma examination; **~prüfungszeugnis** teaching diploma; **~anstalt** educational establishment, school; *höhere ~~: secondary school;* **~auftrag** (junior) lectureship; teaching assignment; **~beauftragter** (junior) lecturer; **~befähigung** teaching qualification, authority to teach; **~berechtigung** authorization to teach; **~betrieb** apprentice workshop, apprentice-training firm, training establishment; **~brief** articles of apprenticeship; **~buch** text-book; **~fach** teaching profession, education (*casa subject*); **~freiheit** freedom of teaching, freedom to teach according to one's conscience; **~gang** course; **~geld** apprenticeship premium; *fig: ~ ~ zahlen: = to pay dearly for one's wisdom;* **~herr** master, employer; **~körper** teaching staff; **~kraft** teacher *pl*: teaching staff; **~krankenhaus** teaching hospital; **~ling** → *Lehrling;* **~mädchen** girl-apprentice; **~meinung** doctrine, teaching, authority; **~mittel** educational equipment and materials, *esp school books;* ~~ *freiheit: free supply of school books;* teaching aids; **~personal** teaching staff; **~plan** syllabus, curriculum; **~satz** theorem, maxim, principle; **~stand** teaching profession; **~stelle** apprenticeship (place); **~stuhl** chair, professorship; **~stuhlinhaber~** holder of a chair, holder of a professorship; **~tätigkeit** teaching; **~- und Lernjahre** years of apprenticeship and learning the trade; **~veranstaltung** class, lecture; **~verhältnis** apprenticeship; **~verpflichtung** teaching obligation, obligation to lecture; **~vertrag** apprenticeship; contract articles of apprenticeship; **~werkstatt** training workshop, apprenticeship

workshop; inplant training centre; **~zeit** apprenticeship; **~zweck** aim of teaching, teaching goal.

Lehre *f* academic teaching; doctrine; apprenticeship; **~ von der Teilnichtigkeit** doctrine of severance; **~ zum technischen Handeln** *pat* technical teaching: *dem Fachmann vermittelte ~~~: technical teaching imparted to a person skilled in the art;* **herrschende ~** the prevailing (academic) opinion (*or* doctrine); **in der ~** articled, undergoing apprenticeship training.

Lehrer *m* teacher; **~bildung** teachers' training; **~bildungsanstalt** teachers' training college; college of education; **~seminar** *obs for Lehrerbildungsanstalt qv;* **~stand** teaching profession; **~stelle** teaching appointment, teaching job; **~verband** teachers' association; **~überschuß** teacher glut, surplus of teachers; **~zimmer** staff room.

Lehrling *m* apprentice; **gewerblicher ~** industrial apprentice; **kaufmännischer ~** commercial apprentice, junior clerk.

Lehrlings|ausbildung apprenticeship training; **~ausschuß** apprenticeship training committee; **~haltung** employment of apprentices; **~heim** hostel for apprentices; **~rolle** register of apprentices (*at the Chamber of Commerce*); **~vergütung** payment of apprentices; **~verhältnis** apprenticeship.

Leib|eigener serf, bondsman; **~eigenschaft** serfdom, bondage; **~gedinge** (agricultural) life endowment (*to retired farmer*); **~rente** life annuity (*periodical payments during the remaining life of the entitled party*); **~rentenempfänger** life annuitant; **~rentenversicherung** annuity life insurance; **~rentenvertrag** contract of annuity for life; **~ und Leben** life and limb; **~wächter** bodyguard; **~zucht** = *Leibgedinge qv.*

Leibes|erben heirs of the body; **~erziehung** physical education, physical training; **~frucht** foetus, em-

Leiche | **leisten**

bryo, unborn child; ~**strafe** corporal punishment; ~**visitation** bodily search.
Leiche *f* corpse, dead body, the remains.
Leichen|ausgrabung exhumation, disinterment; ~**beschauer** coroner; *ärztlicher* ~ ~: *pathologist performing a post-mortem examination, medical examiner;* ~**bestatter** undertaker; ~**diebstahl** body-snatching; ~**fledderei** plundering the dead, stealing from a dead body; ~**halle** mortuary; ~**öffnung** post-mortem examination, autopsy; ~**paß** corpse transport permit; ~**raub** body-snatching; ~**räuber** body-snatcher; ~**schänder** desecrator of dead bodies, necrophile; ~**schändung** abuse of the dead, desecration of a dead body, necrophilia (= *necrophilism*); ~**schau** autopsy, post-mortem examination; post-mortem certificate; ~**starre** rigor mortis, post-mortem rigidity; ~**teil** part of a dead body; ~**überführung** transportation of the body; ~**verbrennung** cremation.
Leicht|bau lightweight construction; ~**behälter** lightweight container; ~**beton** lightweight concrete; ~**betonware** lightweight concrete products; ~**faß** lightweight barrel; ~**güterzug** light goods train; ~**industrie** light industry; ~**last** lightweight, light load; ~**matrose** ordinary seaman, ordinary sailor; ~**metallindustrie** light metalls industrie; ~**metallware** light-metal goods.
Leichter *m* lighter, barge; ~**gebühr** lighterage; ~**geld** lighterage; ~**schiffer** lighterman; ~**transportgewerbe** lighterage.
Leichtern *n* lighterage.
Leichterung *f* lightering.
leichtfertig *adj* extremely careless, reckless, frivolous.
Leichtfertigkeit extreme carelessness, hazardous negligence, inadvertent negligence, recklessness, frivolity, *bewußte* ~ ~: *wilful negligence.*

leichtgläubig *adj* credulous, gullible.
Leichtgläubigkeit credulity, credulousness, gullibility.
leichtverderblich *adj* perishable.
Leichtverderblichkeit *f* perishability.
Leid *n* anguish, suffering; **seelisches** ~ mental suffering.
Leidenschaft *f* passion; **aus** ~ **handeln** to act in the heat of passion.
Leih|arbeit loan employment, ~**arbeiter** loaned-out workers, loaned servant; ~**arbeitnehmer** loaned employee, ~**arbeitskraft** loaned employee, loaned servant; ~**arbeitsverhältnis** loan out employment, body shop agreement; ~**basis** trial and return basis; ~**behälter** loan-container; ~**bibliothek** lending library; ~**emballagen** loan-containers; ~**frist** lending period; ~**gabe** painting (*etc*) on loan; ~**gebühr** lending fee; ~**geld** loan money; ~**haus** pawnshop; ~**kapital** loan capital, outside capital; ~**lieferungen** loaned supplies; ~**mutter** →*Leihmutter*, ~**mutterschaft** →*Leihmutterschaft;* ~**Pacht-System** *hist* lend-lease-system (*2nd world war*); ~**schein** pawn ticket (*pawnshop*), lending ticket, borrowing slip (*library*); ~**vertrag** gratuitous hire contract; ~**wagen** hire-car, rented car; ~**wagengeschäft** car rental business; ~**wagenmarkt** car rental market; ~**waren** equipment lent to customers; **l**~**weise** *adv* on loan, by way of lending; ~**zeit** lending period; ~**zins** loan interest rate.
Leihe *f* gratuitons hire (gratuitous) lending of sth.
leihen *v/t* to lend sth (to be returned to loan out (money).
Leihmutter *f* surrogate mother.
Leihmutterschaft *f* surrogacy, womb leasing; ~**sgesetz** Surrogacy Arrangements Act *GB 1985;* ~**sverhältnis** surrogacy; ~**vermittlung** surrogacy brokerarge (*or* agency).
leisten *v/t* to render, to perform, to

505

effect, to accomplish, to achieve, to produce.
Leistender *m* (*der Leistende*) the person providing a service.
Leistung *f* performance, the obligation (to be) performed; effort, achievement, accomplishment; output; benefit, merit; ~ **als Maßstab** performance regarded as a yardstick; ~ **an Erfüllungs Statt** performance in full discharge of the obligation; ~ **aus der Sozialversicherung** social insurance benefits; ~ **des Entgelts** provision of the consideration, payment for the services; **~en, die gegen Entgelt erbracht werden** services provided for remuneration; **~en im Kapitalsektor** payments in connection with capital; ~ **je Arbeitskraft** output per worker; **~en von Fall zu Fall** benefits varying from one case to another, ad hoc payments; ~ **e-r Dauerschuld** continuing performance; ~ **in Person** personal performance; ~ **von Sacheinlagen** paying-up of shares in kind, capital contributions in kind; ~ **Zug um Zug** performance conditional upon counter-performance; **bankbetriebliche** ~**en** banking services; **bauwirtschaftliche** ~ amount of building done; **beitragspflichtige** ~**en** contributory benefits; **doppelte** ~ **bei Unfalltod** double accident benefit, double indemnity; **eigenschöpferische** ~ **e-s Schriftwerkes** literary merit; **entsprechende** ~**en** corresponding benefits; **fakultative** ~ alternative performance; **freiwillige soziale** ~**en** fringe benefits (*paid by employer*), perquisites, „perks"; **geldwerte** ~ performance having monetary value; **gewerbliche** ~**en** commercial and industrial services; **gute** ~**en** proficiency (*education*), a good standard; **produktive** ~**en** grants for productive purposes, productive achievements; **soziale** ~**en** social benefits, payments for social purposes; **steuerbare** ~**en** taxable benefits; **steuerpflichtige** ~**en** taxable benefits; **tatsächliche** ~ actual performance; **teilbare** ~ severable performance; **übliche** ~**en** ordinary services; **unentgeltliche** ~ gratuitous performance, *pl* gratuitous services, unrequited deliveries and remittances; **unmögliche** ~ impossibility of performance; **unteilbare** ~ indivisible (*or* unseverable) performance; **vereinbarte** ~ contracted work and deliveries, agreed performance, agreed services; **vermögenswirksame** ~**en** capital-building fringe benefits; asset-forming contributions *or* allowances; **vertraglich geschuldete** ~ (performance under a) contractual obligation; **werkvertragliche** ~ contract work, work and labour; **wiederkehrende** ~**en** recurring benefits, recurring payments; **Zug um Zug** ~ performance subject to counter-performance; mutual performance.
Leistungs|abfall falling off in performance, decline in performance, drop in power output; **l~abhängig** performance-related; dependent on efficiency; ~**abstimmung** balancing of comparative workload; ~**analyse** value analysis; ~**anforderung** demand for performance; requisition note; ~**anforderungen** standards (*or* requirements) of performance; ~**angebot** tender, offer of performance; ~**annahme** acceptance (of goods and services); ~**anreiz** incentive; ~**anspruch** right to recovery, right to benefit, entitlement to benefits; ~**aufforderung** request to perform; ~**austausch** exchange of goods and services; ~**auszeichnung** achievement award; ~**bedarf** required output; ~**befreiung** exemption from performance; ~**begriff** notion of performance; ~**berechnung** calculation of services, statement of account for services; power rating (*electricity supply*); **l~berechtigt** entitled to benefits; ~**berechtigter** person enti-

Leistungsberechtigung   **Leistungsträger**

tled (*to services, benefits*); ~**berechtigung** entitlement to benefits; *erworbene* ~ ~: *accrued benefits*; ~**bescheid** administrative demand for payment; requisition order; ~**beschreibung** performance (*or* work) specifications; ~**bewertung** performance appraisal, efficiency rating, assessment of performance; ~**bezieher** recipient of benefits; ~**bilanz** (balance on) current account; net position on goods and services (*in the balance of payments*) ~ ~ *defizit: current account payments deficit*; ~**dauer** indemnity period; ~**diagramm** performance chart, indicator diagram; ~**druck** pressure to perform; ~**effekt** useful output, effective output; ~**einheit** unit of performance, work unit; production unit; power unit; ~**einkommen** income from services, factor income; ~**einsatz** application of effort, work input; ~**einstufung** performance rating, merit rating; ~**empfänger** recipient of benefits; beneficiary; ~**entgelt** compensation; ~**erbringer** supplier, contractor; ~**ermittlung** output evaluation; ~**erschleichung** fraudulent obtaining of benefits (*or* a performance); ~**erstellung** performance; l~**fähig** *adj* efficient, capable; ~**fähigkeit** → *Leistungsfähigkeit*; ~**fall** case of entitlement to benefit, benefit case; ~**feststellung** declaration of entitlement to benefits; ~**freiheit** exemption from performance; ~**frist** performance period, time for performance; ~**garantie** performance guarantee; ~**gebot** command to render services; ~**gefahr** performance risk; ~**gefälle** variation in (regional) performance; ~**gegenstand** object of performance; l~**gerecht** just, conforming to performance, performance-related; ~**gesellschaft** achievement-oriented society; ~**gewicht** power-to-weight ratio; ~**grad** performance efficiency, performance index; ~**grenze** limit of performance, output maximum; ~**herstellung** production of goods and services; ~**klage** action to enforce a right (or claim), action for (affirmatory) relief; ~**konkurrenz** competition to produce results; ~**kontrolle** efficiency check, efficiency verification, monitoring individual's performance; ~**kraft** economic capacity; ~**lohn** payment by results, incentive pay, incentive wage; ~**motivation** achievement motivation; ~**nachweis** evidence that a requirement has been duly complied with, track record, proof of payment; ~**niveau** standard of performance; l~**orientiert** achievement-oriented; ~**ort** place of performance; ~**pflicht** obligation to perform, obligation to render services, obligation to pay; ~**pflichtiger** person liable to make payments or render services, contributor; ~**prämie** incentive bonus, production bonus, efficiency premium; ~**prämiensystem** efficiency bonus plan; ~**prinzip** efficiency principle, merit system, promotion according to merit, output principle; ~**prüfung** efficiency test, proficiency test; ~**querschnitt** cross-section of productive performance; ~**rente** real-value pension; ~**reserve** reserve capacity; ~**schau** trade exhibition; ~**schild** rating plate; ~**schuldner** obligor, person obliged to render performance; ~**schutzrecht** *law against exploitation of accomplishments of another*; law of industrial property and copyright protection; ~**soll** production target; ~**stand** level of performance; ~**standard** standard of performance; ~**steigerung** increase in performance, increase in output, increase in efficiency; ~**störung** default in performance (*breach of contract, default, impossibility etc*); events of default; ~**streben** effort to achieve sth; ~**teil** part of the supplies and services to be rendered; ~**träger** body or agency ad-

507

Leistungsüberschuß   **Leiter**

ministering services or benefits, administering body, responsible organisation for providing benefits; ~**überschuß** surplus on goods and services; ~**- und Kapitalbilanz** balance of transactions in goods, services, donations and capital; ~**- und Kapitalverkehr** transactions in goods, services, donations and capital; ~**- und Soziallohn** fully earned wage and socially subsidized wage; ~**urteil** judgment granting affirmative relief (*as distinguished from a declaratory judgment*); ~**verbot an Drittschuldner** third party order, garnishee order; ~**verbrauch** *electr* power consumption; ~**vermögen** economic capacity; ~**versprechen** promise to perform sth; ~**verwaltung** administration of community services; ~**verweigerung** refusal to perform; ~**verweigerungsrecht** right to withhold performance, recoupment; ~**verzeichnis** performance specifications, specification schedule, description of (*studio*) services, bill of quantities; ~**verzögerung** delay in performance; ~**verzug** statutory delay in performance (*after demand or a fixed calendar date*); ~**volumen** volume of production and services, volume of output; ~**voraussetzungen** eligibility for benefits, requirements for entitlement to benefits; ~**vorgabe** standard of performance; ~**vorsprung** superior efficiency; ~**wettbewerb** competition, competition based on relative efficiency, competitive production; competition in performance; ~**wille** will to work and to produce, will-power to be efficient; ~**zeit** time of performance, time limit for performance; ~**zulage** efficiency bonus; ~**zusage** promise of performance.

Leistungsfähigkeit *f* efficiency, productive efficiency; achievement potential, capacity, ability to pay; ~**sprinzip** efficiency principle; ability-to-pay principle; **betriebliche** ~ operating efficiency; **finanzielle** ~ financial capacity; **mangelnde** ~ inefficiency; ~**treuepflicht** requirement to comply with agreed standards (of performance); **wirtschaftliche** ~ economic efficiency, business capacity, entrepreneurial skill.

Leit|bild ideal, guiding principle; ~**devise** key currency; ~**emission** signpost issue, lead-giving security issue; ~**entscheidung** precedent; ~**faden** manual, guide; ~**fall** leading case, lead case; seminal case; ~**gedanke** fundamental idea; ~**kurs** central rate; ~**linie** guideline; guiding line (*traffic*); *unterbrochene* ~ ~: *broken guiding line*; ~**pfosten** guide post, *vs* delineator; ~**planken** crash barriers; ~**prinzip** leading principle; ~**satz** head note, syllabus, guiding principle; ~**stelle** head office; ~**vermerk** route instructions; *mit* ~ ~ *versehen: routed* (*postal service*); ~**währung** lead currency, reserve currency; ~**zins(satz)** key lending rate(s) key interest rate, prime rate.

Leiter *m* head, head of department, chief, director; ~ **der Abteilung** ... Head of the ... Division; ~ **der Abteilung Absatzförderung** marketing manager; ~ **der Anzeigenabteilung** advertisement sales executive; ~ **der Einkaufsabteilung** head of purchasing department; ~ **der Datenverarbeitung** data processing manager; ~ **der Entwicklungsabteilung** development manager; ~ **der Exportabteilung** export manager; ~ **der Finanzabteilung** treasurer, finance director; ~ **der konsularischen Vertretung** head of consular post; ~ **der Pressestelle** press officer, press attaché; ~ **der Rechtsabteilung** head of legal department; general counsel; ~ **der Verkaufsabteilung** sales manager, sales and marketing director, sales director, sales executive; ~ **der Versammlung** chairman of the meeting; ~ **der Versandabteilung** shipping clerk; ~ **der Vertriebs-**

abteilung marketing manager; ~ **des Beschaffungsamtes** procurement officer; ~ **des Finanzwesens** head of the accounting department, chief accountant; ~ **des Hafenamtes** surveyor of the port; ~ **des Lohnbüros** payroll manager; ~ **des Ministerbüros** Principal Private Secretary; ~ **des Patentamts** Commissioner of the Patent Office; ~ **des Rechnungswesens** accounting supervisor; **kaufmännischer** ~ business manager; **stellvertretender** ~ deputy chief; **technischer** ~ technical director; **verantwortlicher** ~ responsible manager.

Leitung f direction, management; **~sbefugnis** managerial power; **~sfunktion** executive function; **~skosten** managerial costs; **~s- oder Überwachungsorgane** managerial or supervisory posts; ~ **von Behörden** administrative management; **unter der** ~ **von** under the direction of, headed by.

Leitungsnetz n distribution network, grid.

Leitungswasserversicherung f water pipe insurance.

Lenk|einschlag m turn, angle of wheel steered; **~flugkörper** guided missile; **~rad** steering wheel; **~säule** steering column; **~vorrichtung** steering mechanism; **~zeit** permitted total driving time.

lenken v/t to guide, to direct, to control, to rule; to drive, to steer.

Lenker m driver, steersman.

Lenkung f guidance, direction, control; steering; **autoritäre** ~ control by the authorities, authoritative steering.

Lenkungs|ausschuß steering committee; **~maßnahme** measure of control; **~vorschriften** (market) control regulations.

leoninisch adj leonine.

Lernbeeinträchtigte m/f/pl slow learners.

Lernmittel n/pl educational aids, school requisites: *equipment and materials used by pupils*; **~freiheit** free provision of school books (*and other materials used in school*).

Lesart f reading, interpretation (*of a legal text etc*); **falsche** ~ misreading, misconstruction; **nach dieser** ~ on this reading of the facts, pursuant to this version; **verschiedene ~en** different interpretations.

Lesbarkeit f legibility.

Leseunkundiger m (*der Leseunkundige*) person unable to read, illiterate.

Lesezirkelwerbung f advertising in circulating magazines.

Lesung f reading; ~ **e-s Gesetzesentwurfs** reading of a bill; **erste** ~ first reading; **in dritter** ~ **verabschiedet** passed after the third reading.

Letzt|angebot last offer; **~begünstigter** ultimate beneficiary; **l~berechtigt** adj last entitled; **~bietender** last and highest bidder; **l~genannt** adj last named, last mentioned; **l~instanzlich** = *letztinstanziell qv*; **l~instanziell** adj of (the) last instance; **~lebender** survivor; **l~rangig** last ranking; **~verbrauch** ultimate consumption; **~verbraucher** ultimate consumer; **~verteiler** ultimate distributor, retailer; **~verwender** ultimate user; **l~willig** adj testamentary.

letztlich adv finally, in the last analysis, eventually, in the long run.

Leuchtfeuergeld n light dues.

Leuchtwerbung f illuminated advertizing, neon advertising.

Leugnen n denial, disavowal.

leugnen v/t to deny, to refuse to acknowledge, to repudiate.

Leumund m reputation, repute; **allgemeiner** ~ general reputation; **einwandfreier** ~ good repute, good moral character; **guter** ~ good reputation, good character; **schlechter** ~ ill repute, bad reputation.

Leumunds|beweis evidence of character, character evidence; *ab-*

Liberaler

träglicher ~ ~: negative evidence of character; **~szeuge** character witness, referee for one's character; **~szeugnis** reference, certificate of good character.

Liberaler *m (der Liberale)* liberal, Liberal, member of a liberal party.

liberalisieren *v/t* to liberalize, to decontrol, to deregulate.

Liberalisierung *f* liberalization, deregulation; **~sstand** degree of liberalization.

Liberalismus *m* liberalism.

Liberalität *f* liberality.

Liberalitätszahlung *f* ex gratia payment.

liberiert *adj* fully paid up, negotiable.

Librierung *f* payment under subscription.

Licht|recht easement of light, bye-laws concerning the right to light; **~reklame** illuminated advertising, neon light advertising; **~signal** light signal, flash signal, traffic light; **~spiel** photoplay, film, picture; **~stärke** intensity of light emitted *(headlight)*.

Lidlohn *m* arrears of wages *(during bankruptcy)*.

Liebes|brief love letter; **~erklärung** declaration of love, confession of love; **~gabe** gift, charitable gift; ~ **~sendung:** *gift package;* **~heirat** love match, marriage for love; **~paarbelauscher** voyeur, person spying on lovers; **~paragraph** punishable failure to help accident victim *(German Penal Code)*; **~verhältnis** love affair.

Liebhaberei *f* hobby, occupation just for fun *(tax law)*.

Liebhaberpreis *m* fancy price, connoisseur's price, collector's price.

Liebhaberwert *m* collector's value, sentimental value, pretium affectionis.

Liefer|angebot tender of delivery; **~anweisung** delivery order; **~auftrag** purchase order; **l~bar** *adj* deliverable, available, ready for delivery; *kurzfristig ~: available for prompt delivery; nicht mehr ~: no longer on sale;* **~barkeit** deliverability, availability; **~barkeitsbescheinigung** certificate of deliverability; **~bedingungen** sales conditions, terms and conditions of sale, sales terms, trade terms; terms of delivery; **~begünstigung** priority with regard to delivery; **l~bereit** *adj* ready for delivery; **~bereitschaft** readiness to deliver, readiness for delivery; **~bezirk** service area, market; **~buch** delivery book; **~dienst** supply service; **~einheit** delivery unit; **~fähigkeit** ability to deliver, output capacity; **~firma** supplies (firm), seller; **~frist** time for delivery, delivery period; **~fristüberschreitung** failure to keep the delivery date; **~garantie** performance guarantee, guarantee of supply; delivery guarantee; **~gegenstand** article of sale, delivery item; **~geschäft** delivery transaction, transaction for supply of goods; **~gewicht** net weight, delivery weight; **~hafen** delivery port; **~kaution** delivery bond; **~klausel** delivery term; **~konsortium** suppliers' syndicate; **~kosten** delivery cost, delivery charges; **~kredit** supplier's credit, credit allowed by supplier; **~land** supplier country; **~liste** delivery schedule; **~menge** quantity to be delivered, quantity delivered; **~normen** delivery regulations, delivery standards, *standards of size, weight and packing for delivery;* **~ort** place of delivery; point of delivery; **~plan** delivery schedule; **~posten** lot, delivery item, supply item; **~preis** agreed price, contract price, price of delivery; **~rückstand** delay in delivery, backlog in delivery; **~schein** delivery note, advice note, supply note; **~sperre** restriction on the supply of goods, refusal to deal, embargo; **~spesen** delivery cost; **~termin** date of delivery, delivery deadline; **~- und Leistungsforderungen** trade debtors; **~- und Leistungsgeschäfte** deliveries and services rendered; **~- und Leistungsverbindlichkeiten**

Lieferant

trade creditors; ~**verlangen** demand for delivery; ~**vertrag** supply agreement, contract for supply of goods; contract for future delivery, contract to sell; *ein nicht befristeter ~ ~: open-ended contract*; ~**verweigerung** withholding delivery, refusal to deliver; ~**verzögerung** late delivery, delayed delivery; ~**verzug** undue delay in delivery, default in delivery; ~**vorschriften** delivery instructions; ~**werk** supplying factory, supplying plant; *ab ~ ~: ex works*; ~**zeit** time of delivery, lead time *(from ordering to delivery date)*; *die ~ ~ einhalten: to deliver within the specified time*; ~**zusage** delivery promise.

Lieferant *m* supplier, purveyor, seller, contractor.

Lieferanten|eingang goods entrance, tradesmen's entrance; ~**kartei** card index of suppliers; ~**konto** suppliers' account; ~**kredit** trade credit, suppliers' credit; ~**kreditkonto** drawing account, suppliers' trade credit account; ~**liste** vendor' list, list of suppliers; ~**rechnung** invoice, suppliers' invoice; *offene ~ ~en: outstanding accounts of tradesmen (or: suppliers)*; ~**schuld** debt due to a supplier; ~**skonto** trade discount, discount allowed by the supplier; ~**ziehung** bill drawn in connection with supply of goods.

Lieferer *m* supplier.

liefern *v/t* to deliver, to supply, to provide, to yield; **neu** ~ to redeliver, to deliver again.

Lieferung *f* delivery, supply, provision; ~ **anbieten** to tender delivery; ~**en des Auslandes** goods delivered by foreign countries; ~ **erfolgt auf Abruf** goods are deliverable on call; ~ **erfolgt gegen Akkreditiv** delivery will follow on receipt of a letter of credit; ~ **frei Haus** delivery free domicile; ~ **gegen Barzahlung** cash on delivery; ~ **im Streckengeschäft** drop shipment (delivery); ~ **und Aufstellung** supply and erection (*or* installation); ~**en und Leistungen** deliveries and services; **aufgeschobene** ~ deferred delivery; **auf zukünftige** ~ **verkaufen** to sell for future delivery; **bei** ~ upon delivery; **freie** ~ delivery free of charge; **für zukünftige** ~ **verkaufen** to sell for future delivery; **gegen sofortige** ~ **kaufen** to buy outright; **innerbetriebliche** ~ internal delivery; **kurzfristige** ~ short delivery, delivery at short notice; **mangelhafte** ~ defective delivery, defective goods supplied; **nicht termingerechte** ~ non-delivery in due contract time; **ordnungswidrige** ~ misdelivery, faulty delivery; **rückständige** ~ overdue delivery; **sofortige** ~ prompt delivery; **steuerfreie** ~**en** tax-exempt supplies; **termingerechte** ~ delivery by the due date; **unvollständige** ~ short delivery, incomplete delivery; **verrechnete** ~**en** deliveries charged to an account (or compensated); **verspätete** ~ late delivery; **vorzeitige** ~ premature delivery; **zahlbar bei** ~ payable on delivery, C. O. D.

Lieferungs|anforderung request for delivery, requisition, request to supply; ~**angebot** = *Lieferangebot qv*; ~**annahme** taking delivery, acceptance of delivery; ~**auftrag** purchase order; ~**bedingungen** = *Lieferbedingungen qv*, terms of delivery; *allgemeine ~ ~: general terms of delivery*; ~**garantie** = *Liefergarantie qv*, guarantee in respect of deliveries; ~**genehmigung** delivery permit; ~**geschäft** transaction concerning future delivery, time bargain, delivery; ~**kauf** purchase for future delivery; ~**kosten** delivery expenses; ~**ort** place of delivery; ~**umfang** items covered by the contract; ~**verpflichtung** obligation to deliver, obligation to supply goods; ~**vertrag** = *Liefervertrag qv*; ~**verzug** = *Lieferverzug qv*; ~**zustand** condition as supplied.

Liege|gebühren = *Liegegeld qv* ~**geld** demurrage; ~**platz** berth;

511

Liegenschaft   **Liquidationsanteilschein**

~**tage** lay days, lying days, running days; ~**wagen** couchette; ~**zeit** lay days, running days, idle time, idle period.
Liegenschaft *f* real estate, real property, *pl* ~*en*: landed property, realty, immovables, immovable property, real property holdings, real assets.
Liegenschafts|anteil (undivided) share of land; ~**dienst** real estate service; ~**fonds** real estate investment fund; ~**konto** property account; ~**nutzung** use of real estate; ~**recht** real property law, law of real property; interest in landed property, title to real estate; ~**übertragung** conveyance; ~**- und Inventarverzeichnis** property record.
Liga *f* league; ~ **der Rotkreuzgesellschaften** League of Red Cross Societies.
Limit *n* limit, price limit, margin; ~**auftrag** limited order; ~**preis** limited price; ~**setzung** stop order; **das** ~ **erhöhen** to raise the limit; **ein** ~ **festsetzen** to fix a limit; **ein** ~ **einhalten** to keep (*or* remain) within a limit; **ein** ~ **vorschreiben** to give a limit.
limitieren *v/t* to limit, to restrict.
Linie *f* line, course, policy; ~**nagent** shipping line agent; ~**nfahrt** liner traffic; ~**nflug** scheduled flight; ~**nfrachtraten** liner rates; ~**n-Konnossementsbedingungen** shipping-line bill-of-lading terms; ~**nschiffahrt** regular navigation, shipping line service; ~~*skonnossement*: liner bill of lading; ~**ntreue** fidelity to the party line; ~**nverkehr** regular scheduled service, regular navigation, scheduled airline service; *öffentlicher* ~ ~ *public transport service vehicles; vereinbarter* ~ ~: *agreed services*; **in absteigender** ~ in the descending line; **in aufsteigender** ~ in the ascending line; **in gerader** ~ in the direct line; **kreditpolitische** ~ credit policy; **mittlere** ~ average trend; **offene** ~ unutilized (credit) line; **punktierte** ~ dotted line; **re-**

striktive ~ restrictive policy; **ununterbrochene** ~ continuous line.
Links|abbiegen (*n*) left turn; ~**abbieger** vehicle turning left; ~**abbiegersignal** left-turn signal; ~**abweichler** *pol* deviationist to the left; ~**anwalt** *pej* pettifogger; ~**fahrgebot** *GB:* law of the road, driving on the left; ~**intellektueller** *pol* left-wing intellectual; ~**kartell** *pol* left-wing conspiracy; ~**kurs** *pol* policy tending toward the left; ~**politiker** leftist; ~**radikaler** leftist radical; ~**regierung** left-wing government; ~**stimmen** left-wing votes; ~**unterzeichneter** signatory on the left; ~**verkehr** left-hand traffic.
liquid *adj* (= *liquide*) liquid, having liquid assets, solvent.
Liquidation *f* liquidation, winding-up, realization; bill for services rendered; **freiwillige** ~ voluntary winding-up; **in** ~ **gehen** to be wound up; **stille** ~ voluntary liquidation, amicable liquidation.
Liquidations|anteilschein liquidation certificate; ~**santrag** petition for liquidation; ~**ausverkauf** clearance sale; ~**beschluß** winding-up resolution, resolution to wind up, *court:* winding-up order; ~**bilanz** liquidation balance sheet; ~**eröffnungsbilanz** opening balance sheet of a firm in liquidation; ~**erlös** liquidation proceeds; ~**gesellschaft** company in liquidation; ~**gewinn** winding-up profit; ~**guthaben** clearing balance; ~**kasse** clearing house; ~**konto** realization and liquidation account, settlement account; ~**kurs** making-up price, settling rate; ~**masse** total assets of a company in liquidation; ~**plan** scheme of liquidation; ~**quote** liquidating dividend, liquidating distribution; ~**rente** liquidation annuity; ~**tag** settlement day, day of settlement; ~**verfahren** liquidation proceedings; ~**vergleich** winding-up composition arrangement, *with full surrender of assets to creditors* (*discharging*

debtor); **~verkauf** sale of a bankrupt's assets; **~vorrecht** preference (on liquidation); **~wert** liquidation (*or* realization) value, winding up value.

Liquidator *m* liquidator, receiver, liquidating partner; **gerichtlich bestellter** ~ official liquidator.

liquidieren *v/t* to liquidate, to wind up, to realize, to convert into cash.

Liquidisierung *f* increase in liquidity.

Liquidisierungs|periode period of increasing liquidity; **~prozeß** process of increasing liquidity; **~tendenz** tendency towards increasing liquidity; **~welle** phase of growing liquidity.

Liquidität *f* liquidity, liquid resources, financial solvency; ~ **des Unternehmenssektors** corporate sector liquidity; ~ **ersten Grades** first grade liquidity.

Liquiditäts|abschöpfung absorption of liquidity; **~anspannung** strains on liquidity; **~ausgleich** liquidity equalization; **~ausstattung** liquidity allocation, allocation of funds; **~ausweis** liquidity statement; **~ausweitung** newly created liquidity; **~beengung** reduction in liquidity; **~belastung** pressure on liquidity, strain on liquidity; **~beschaffung** cash procurement; **~bindung** immobilization of liquid funds, absorbing liquidity; **~budget** cash budget; **~decke** extent of liquidity; **~engpaß** cash squeeze; **~erfordernisse** liquidity requirements; **~erhaltung** maintenance of liquidity; **~gefälle** different levels of liquidity; **~grad** degree of liquidity; **~guthaben** balance of liquid resources; **~hemmung** drag on liquidity; **~hilfe** help with liquidity problems; **~klemme** liquidity squeeze, cash-flow squeeze; **~koeffizient** liquidity ratio; **~kredit** loan to maintain liquidity; **~lage** liquidity position; **~mangel** cash shortage; lack of cash, cash deficiency; **~papier** liquidity paper; **~politik** liquidity policy, liquidity rules; **l~politisch** from the point of view of liquidity policy; **~probleme** cash flow problems; **~prognose** cash forecast; **~reserve** liquid reserve; **~risiko** risk to liquidity; **~sicherung** measures safeguarding liquidity; **~spielraum** margin of available liquidity; **~spritze** cash injection; **~status** state of liquidity, cash statement; **~steuerung** cash management; **~theorie** liquidity preference theory; **~überhang** excess liquidity; **~umschichtung** transfer of liquidity, liquidity switch; **~verhältnis** quick asset ratio; **~verkauf** sale for the purpose of raising liquid funds; **~verzicht** sacrifice of liquidity; **~vorliebe** liquidity preference; **~vorschrift** liquidity rule; **~vorsorge** liquidity provision; **l~wirksam** *adj* affecting liquidity; **~zustrom** liquidity afflux.

Liste *f* list, panel, schedule, roll; ~ **der Abgangsdaten** list of sailings; ~ **der börsenfähigen Effekten** official list; ~ **der Kandidaten** list of candidates; „~ **des gefährdeten Erbes der Welt**" "List of World Heritage in Danger"; **in e-e** ~ **aufnehmen** to include in a list, to list, to add to a list; **schwarze** ~ black list; *auf der ~n* ~ *stehen: to be blacklisted; in e-e* ~ ~ *aufnehmen: to blacklist*; **von der** ~ **streichen** to strike off the list, to expunge from a list, to strike off the roll, to delete from the list.

Listen|aufstellung making up a list; **~führer** leading candidate; **~grundpreis** basic list price; **~preis** list price, scheduled price; *diskriminierender* ~~: *rate discrimination; festgesetzter* ~~: *posted price*; **~wahl** list voting, election by party-tickets; **~wahlschein** party column ballot.

Literatur *f* literature, the works consulted; **~angaben** bibliographical data; **~nachweisverzeichnis** bibliography, list of references; **einschlägige** ~ pertinent litera-

Lizenz

ture; **juristische** ~ legal literature; **unzüchtige** ~ obscene literature; **verwendete** ~ books consulted.

Lizenz *f* licence, permit; ~**abgabe** royalty, licence fee; ~**abkommen** licence agreement; ~~ *auf Gegenseitigkeit: cross licence agreement*; ~**abrechnung** royalty statement; ~ **auf ein Patent** licence under a patent; ~**ausgabe** licensed edition, edition published under licence; ~**austausch** cross-licensing; ~**bau** licensed construction, licensed design, manufactured under licence; **l~bereit** *adj* ready to grant a licence; ~**bewilligung** granting of a licence, licensing; ~**dauer** term of a licence; ~**einnahmen** royalties (received); ~**einräumung** granting of a licence, licensing; ~**entziehung** revocation of a licence; ~**entzug** revocation of a licence; ~**erteilung** granting of a licence; ~**fertigung** licensed construction, manufactured under licence; **l~frei** *adj* requiring no licence, royalty-free; ~**geber** licensor, grantor of a licence; ~**gebiet** territory (subject to a licence); ~**gebühr** licence fee, royalty; ~ ~**en für Urheberrechte**: *copyright royalties; laufende* ~ ~ *(auf den Umsatz): continuing royalty on sales;* ~**gegenstand** subject matter under a licence, licensed object; ~**gewährung** licensing; *gegenseitige* ~ ~: *cross-licensing;* ~**inhaber** licensee, licence holder; *alleiniger* ~ ~: *sole licensee;* ~**nehmer** licensee, licence holder; **l~pflichtig** *adj* subject to licence; ~**presse** licensed press (*occupied Germany after 1945*); ~**stopp** stoppage of licence issuing; ~**vereinbarung** licence agreement; ~**vergabe** grant of licence; ~**vergabegesellschaft** franchise company; ~**verlängerung** renewal of a licence; ~**vertrag** licence agreement, licensing agreement; ~**verwertung** exploitation of a licence; ~**vorschriften** licence requirements; ~**zahlung** royalty payment; **ausschließliche** ~ exclusive licence; **e–e** ~ **erteilen** to grant a licence; **einfache** ~ non-exclusive licence; **gebührenfreie** ~ royalty-free licence; **gegenseitige** ~**en** cross licences; **unbeschränkte** ~ unrestricted licence; **unentgeltliche** ~ royalty-free licence; **vertragliche** ~ contractual licence.

lizensieren *v/t* to license, to permit.

Lizensierung *f* licensing, granting of a licence.

LKW *m* (= *Lastkraftwagen*) lorry, *US*: truck; ~**-Stückgutladung** less-than-truck load; **frei** ~ free on truck, F. O. T.

Lobbyismus *m* lobbyism.

Lobbyist *m* lobbyist, government relations manager.

lochen *v/t* to punch, to perforate.

Locher *m* punch, perforator.

Lochkarte *f* punched card.

Lochkarten|buchführung punched-card bookkeeping; ~**index** punched-card index; ~**schlüssel** punched-card code; ~**umrechner** punched-card computer; ~**verfahren** punched-card method.

Lock|artikel loss-leader; article displayed to attract customers; ~**effekt** exaggerated enticement effect; ~**mittel** bait, decoy; ~**spitzel** agent provocateur, stool pigeon; ~**vogel** decoy, bait; ~**vogelangebot** advertizing offer with a loss-leader, bait; ~**vogelwerbung** advertizing by enticement, bait and switch tactics advertizing.

loco *adv* at hand, in stock, spot, for delivery; ~ **sigilli** loco sigilli, instead of a seal (L. S.).

Loco-Geschäft spot transaction; ~**Preis** spot price.

Logbuch *n* ship's log (book), decklog.

Lohn *m* (*pl Löhne* ~**e**) wage, pay, remuneration; ~**abhebung** drawing of wages; ~**abkommen** wage agreement, pay agreement; ~**abrechnung** wage accounting, earnings statement, pay slip; ~**abrechnungszeitraum** wage accounting period; ~**abschlüsse** wage settlements; ~**abtretung** wage assignment; ~**abzug** wage deduction, payroll deduction (*tax and social in-*

Lohnangleichung   **lohnpolitisch**

surance contributions withheld from wage and/or salary); ~**angleichung** wage adjustment; ~**anreiz** wage incentive; ~**ansatz** wage rate; ~**anspruch** wage claim; ~**anstieg** wage increase; *genereller ~ ~: across-the-board wage increase*; ~**anteilsanweisung** allotment note; ~**arbeit** (manual) labour; farmed-out work; ~**arbeiter** hired man, wage-earner; ~**aufbesserung** wage increase; ~**auftrag** commission order, farmed-out contract, farming-out agreement; *~aufträge vergeben: to farm out work to sub-contractors*; ~**auftrieb** upward tendency in wages, wage upturn; ~**auseinandersetzung** wage dispute; ~**ausfall** loss of wage, loss of pay, dead time; ~**ausfallentschädigung** compensation for lost earnings; ~**ausgleich** compensatory wage adjustment; *bei vollem ~ ~: (reduced working hours) without proportionate wage reduction, at full pay*; ~**ausgleichskasse** wage equalization fund; ~**auszahlung** payment of wages; ~**auszahlungsbeleg** payroll voucher; l~**bedingt** *adj* due to wage movements, due to the burden of wages; ~**beleg** pay slip; ~**berechnung** calculation of wages; ~**bestätigung** wage statement; l~**bezogen** wage-related; ~**bildung** development of wages, remuneration structure; ~**bücher** wage account books; ~**buchhalter** payroll clerk, wage accountant, wage payment clerk; ~**buchhaltung** payroll accounting; ~**buchhaltungsrevision** payroll audit; ~**büro** pay office; ~**druck** wage pressure; ~**e für Ausfallstunden und Ausbildung** wages for hours not worked and for training; ~**druckinflation** wage-push inflation; ~**einbehaltung** withholding of wages; ~**empfänger** wage earner; ~**entwicklung** development of wages; ~**erhebung** wage statistics; ~**erhöhung** wage increase, raise, pay rise; *allgemeine ~~: across-the-board wage increase;*

massive ~ ~en: large-scale wage increases; rückwirkende ~ ~: retroactive wage increase; ~**erhöhungswelle** spate of wage increases; ~**e und Gehälter** wages and salaries; ~**fertigungsvertrag** farmed-out production contract; ~**forderung** wage claim; ~**fortzahlung** continuation of wage payments; *~ ~ bei Krankheit: sick pay*; ~**fortzahlungsgesetz** continuation of wage payments (during sickness) Act; ~**gefälle** pay differential, wage differential; ~**gefüge** wage structure; ~**gelder** wage payments; *einbehaltene ~ ~: withheld wages, holdback pay*; ~**gesetz** wage law; *(econ) ehernes ~ ~: subsistence theory*; ~**gleichheit** principle of equal pay to men and women; ~**gruppe** wage bracket, wage group; ~**gruppenverfahren** grading scheme; ~**höhe** wage level; ~**höchstgrenze** wage ceiling; ~**indexierung** wage indexation; ~**intensität** payload ratio, proportion of wages to costs; ~**kampf** wage dispute; ~**klage** legal action for wages; ~**klasse** wage group; ~**konto** wage account, wage-earner's account; ~**kontrolle** wage control; ~**kosten** cost of labour, labour costs, payload, gross wages costs; ~**kosteninflation** wage-push inflation; ~**kostenzuschuß** wage subsidy; ~**kürzung** wage cut, reduction in wages; ~**leitlinien** wage guidelines; ~**liste** payroll, payroll book, pay sheet, payment book; ~**mäßigung** wage restraint; ~**nachweis** evidence of wages paid; ~**nachzahlung** retroactive payment of wages; back-pay; ~**nebenkosten** ancillary wage costs; ~**niveau** wage level; ~**niveauunterschied** wage differential; ~**pfändung** garnishment of wages; ~**pfändungsbeschluß** order for attachment of earnings, wage garnishment order; ~**pfändungstabelle** permissible wage garnishment scale; ~**politik** wage policy; l~**politisch** *adj* relating to

515

Lohn-Preis-Spirale

wage policy; ~-**Preis-Spirale** wage-price spiral, wage spiral; ~**register** register of wages; ~**runde** general wage-increase, a new across-the-board wage increase; ~**satz** wage rate, rate of pay; *normaler* ~ ~: *standard wage rate; überhöhter* ~ ~: *penalty rate (overtime)*; ~**scheck** wage cheque, *US*: pay check; ~**schiebung** fraudulent preference by wage manipulations; ~**schiebungsvertrag** employment agreement involving fraudulent wage stipulations *(to hinder creditors)*; ~**schlichtung** wage arbitration; ~**schlüssel** wage criterion; ~**schneider** jobbing tailor; ~**skala** wage-scale; *gleitende* ~ ~: *sliding wage-scale*; ~**steuer** → *Lohnsteuer*; ~**stop** wage freeze; ~**streifen** pay slip; ~**stückkosten** unit labour costs; ~**stufe** wage group, wage level, wage bracket; ~**stunden** hours of paid work, wage hours; *vergütete arbeitsfreie* ~ ~: *time paid for but not worked*; ~**stundennachweis** time check; ~**summe** aggregate wages, total wages, total wage bill; ~**summensteuer** municipal trade tax on payroll, payroll tax; ~**tabelle** pay scale, wage schedule, table of wages; ~**tarif** scale of wages, rate of pay, wages schedule; ~**tüte** wage packet, pay envelope; ~- **und Arbeitsbedingungen** conditions of employment and wage rates; ~ **und Gehaltsabrechnung** pay statement; ~- **und Gehaltsfortzahlung** continuation of wage and salary payments *(during first six weeks' illness, initial sickness period)*; ~- **und Gehaltsliste** payroll payment sheet; ~- **und Preisrunde** all-round rise in wages and prices; ~ **und Gehaltsschulden** wages and salaries owing; ~- **und Preisüberwachung** wage and price controls; ~**untergrenze** wage floor, minimum wage level; ~**unterschiede** wage differentials; ~**ungerechtigkeit** wage discrimination; ~**veredelung** contract

Lohnsteuer

processing work, commission processing; *aktive* ~ ~: *processing of goods for foreign account; passive* ~~: *processing of goods abroad for domestic account*; ~**veredelungsgeschäft** commission processing; ~**veredelungsverkehr** commission processing (transactions); ~**vereinbarung** wage agreement; ~**verhandlungen** wage negotiations, wage bargaining; ~**verwirkung** forfeiture of wages; ~**volumen** wage-total; ~**welle** round of wage increases; ~**zahlung** pay, payment of wages; *ungekürzte* ~ ~: *full pay*; ~**zahlungszeitraum** wage-payment period; ~**zeit** time paid, time for which wages are paid; ~**zettel** wage slip; ~**zulage** premium pay, bonus; ~**zurückhaltung** wage restraint; ~**zuschlag** extra pay, premium (pay), bonus; **durchschnittlicher** ~ average wage; **fertigungsbezogener** ~ production-related wages; **fester** ~ fixed wage(s); **garantierter** ~ guaranteed wage; **gleitender** ~ wage(s) based on a sliding scale; **ortsüblicher** ~ standard wage; **rückständiger** ~ back pay.

Lohnsteuer *f* employment tax, wage tax, PAYE-tax, income tax on wages and salaries; ~**abführung** deducted wage-tax remittance; ~**abrechnungen** payroll records, wage-tax accounts; ~**abzug** payroll deduction, tax withheld *(from wages and salaries)*; ~**abzugspflichtiger** withholding agent, party liable to withhold wage tax; ~**anmeldung** report of wage-tax deductions, wage-tax return; ~**außenprüfung** external wage-tax audit; ~**bemessung** assessment of wage taxes; ~**bescheinigung** certificate of wage-tax deductions; ~**durchführungsverordnung** wage-tax implementing ordinance *(or order)*; ~**ermäßigung** wage tax reduction; ~**freibetrag** personal allowance, wage-earners' tax allowance; ~**freiheit** exemption from wage tax; ~**jahresausgleich**

annual adjustment of wage tax; *gemeinsamer ~ ~*: *joint annual adjustment of wage tax*; ~**jahrestabelle** annual wage-tax table; ~**karte** wage tax card, *card showing pay and tax deducted*; ~**nachforderung** additional wage tax claim (*from tax office*); ~**pflicht** wage tax liability, obligation to withhold wage tax; *unbeschränkte ~ ~*: *unlimited wage tax liability (for residents)*; ~**pflichtiger** person subject to wage tax; ~**richtlinien** wage tax rules; ~**rückvergütung** wage tax refund; ~**satz** withholding rate; ~**system** wage tax system, withholding system, pay as you earn system (P. A. Y. E.); ~**tabelle** wage-tax table, withholding tax table; ~**überweisungsblatt** wage-tax remittance form; **einbehaltene** ~ retained wage tax; **nachzuentrichtende** ~ wage tax to be paid subsequently.

Löhnung *f* payment of wages; pay, soldier's pay; ~**stag** pay day.

Lokal|augenschein inspection of the scene (*of the crime or the accident*), official inspecting of the premises; ~**bank** local bank; ~**behörde** local authority; ~**blatt** local paper; ~**konnossement** local bill of lading; ~**patriot** parochialist, local patriot, particularist; ~**patriotismus** parochialism; ~**redakteur** (*US*) city editor; ~**termin** viewing scene of the crime, court's inspection, on-the-spot investigation; ~**werte** local securities, local equities.

Lokalisierung *f* residence requirement, locally concentrated activity.

Loko|geschäft spot transaction, local transaction, spot bargain; ~**kauf** spot purchase; ~**kurs** spot price; ~**markt** spot market; ~**preis** price loco, spot price; ~**waren** spots.

Lombard *m* collateral, collateral loan, collateral advance; ~**anleihe** collateral loan; ~**bank** loan bank; ~**bestand** collateral holdings; ~**darlehen** loan on (*or* against) collateral, collateral loan; ~**debitoren** collateral-loan debtors, carryover loans; ~**depot** collateral security deposit; ~**entnahmen** drawings on advances against securities; **l~fähig** *adj* eligible as collateral; ~**forderungen** collateral loans, advances against security; ~**geschäfte** advances on securities, (collaterally secured) loan transactions; ~**inanspruchnahme** amount of advances taken against securities (*and outstanding accounts*); ~**kredit** lombard loan *GB*, collateral loan *US*; ~**pfand** security for an advance; ~**satz** rate for loans on collateral, lombard rate (*of the central bank, i. e. The German Federal Bank*), Lombard rate, the Lombard; ~**schein** hypothecation certificate; ~**verkehr** collateral lending (or loan) business; ~**verzeichnis** Lombard Register (*list of securities admitted as collateral by the German Federal Bank*); ~**vorschüsse** loans on securities; ~**wechsel** bill serving as security for an advance, collateral security note; ~**zinssatz** lombard lending rate.

lombardieren *v/t v/i* to lend money on collateral, to accept as collateral.

Lombardierung *f* accepting collateral; borrowing (from the central bank) against securities.

Londoner Schuldenabkommen *m* London Agreement on German External Debts.

Lordkanzler *m* Lord Chancellor.

Lordsiegelbewahrer *m* Lord Privy Seal.

Loroguthaben *n* credit balance on loro account.

Lorokonto *n* loro account (*the current account of another bank*).

Los *n* lot, section (*public work*); ~**anleihe** loan eligible for lottery premium, lottery loan; **durch das** ~ by drawing lots, by casting lots; **durch das** ~ **entscheiden** to decide by lot; ~**vergabe** awarding by lots; ~**vertrieb** lottery sale.

Lösch|anlage (*1*) fire-extinguishing equipment; ~**arbeiten** fire fighting; ~**ordnung** fire service regula-

Löschbescheinigung / **Lotsenamt**

tions; ~**kommando** fire-brigade detachment.
Lösch|bescheinigung (2) landing certificate; ~**ende** end of discharge; ~**erlaubnis** discharging permit; ~**hafen** port of delivery, port of entry; ~**kosten** unloading charges; ~**platz** unloading berth, place of discharge; ~**risiko** unloading risk; ~**tage** lay days.
Löschen n (1) deletion, cancellation, obliteration.
Löschen n (2) discharge, unloading; ~ **der Ladung** breaking bulk.
löschen v/t (1) to delete, to expunge, to extinguish, to cancel, to deregister, to remove from a register, to vacate (the register); *von Amts wegen gelöscht: deleted ex officio*.
löschen v/t (2) to unload, to discharge.
Löschung f (1) deletion, cancellation, deregistration; ~ **e-r Dienstbarkeit** release (*or* discharge) of an easement; extinction of an easement in the land register; ~ **e-r Eintragung** cancellation of an entry, deletion of an entry, deregistration; ~ **e-r Hypothek** cancellation of a mortgage in the land register; ~ **e-s Kontos** closing of an account; ~ **e-s Warenzeichens** cancellation of a trademark; ~ **von Amts wegen** ex officio cancellation of an entry; **freiwillige** ~ cancellation of an entry by consent; **gerichtliche** ~ cancellation of an entry by court order, ex officio deregistration.
Löschung f (2) unloading, landing (goods); ~ **e-r Ladung** discharge of cargo, unloading; ~**serlaubnis** landing order; ~**shafen** port of discharge; ~**skosten** discharging fee, wharfage charges; ~**sort** unloading point; **franco** ~ landed terms.
Löschungs|ankündigung advance notice of cancellation (*of an item in a public register*); ~**anspruch** *right to have an entry expunged from a register,* cancellation right; ~**antrag** request for cancellation, request for deregistration, application to have a register entry (*such as a mortgage*) cancelled (*i. e. expunged from the register by underlining in red ink*), application for revocation (*patent*); ~**anzeige** notice of cancellation in a public register; ~**bescheinigung** certificate of cancellation of an entry *in a public register;* ~**bewilligung** consent to the cancellation of an entry *in a public register;* ~ ~ *für e–e Hypothek: release of mortgage, memorandum of satisfaction;* l~**fähig** sufficient to have (Land Register) entry cancelled; sufficient to discharge a mortgage; ~**klage** petition to cancel an entry in a public register; ~**pflicht** obligation to have a registered item cancelled (*usually a mortgage entered in the Land Register*); ~**verfahren** cancellation procedure, procedure for removal from a public register; ~**vermerk** cancellation note (*of an entry in a register*); memorandum of satisfaction; ~**vormerkung** cautionary entry to ensure future cancellation (*of prior charge when repaid*).
Loseblatt|ablage loose-leaf filing system; ~**ausgabe** loose-leaf edition; ~**buchführung** loose-leaf system of book-keeping; ~**buchhaltung** = ~*buchführung qv*; ~**katalog** loose-leaf catalogue; ~**konto** loose-leaf account; ~**sammelmappe** loose-leaf binder; ~**sammlung** loose-leaf; ~**system** loose-leaf system.
Lösegeld n ransom, ransom money; ~**vertrag** ransom bill.
loskaufen v/t to buy the release *of a prisoner,* to ransom, v/reflex to buy oneself out (*of army*).
Loskurs m price fixed by lot.
lossagen v/reflex to dissociate from, to secede from, to break with.
Lösung f solution; ~**sweg** method of solution.
Losvertrieb m lottery sale.
Lotsen|amt pilotage authority; *Zuständigkeitsbereich e–s* ~ ~ *es: pilotage jurisdiction;* ~**boot** pilot boat; ~**brüderschaft** licensed pilots' association; ~**dampfer** pilot vessel; ~**dienst** pilot service, pilotage;

Lotterie

pilot service for motorists, driver-guide service; ~**flagge** pilot jack, pilot flag; ~**freiheit** free pilotage; ~**gebühr** pilotage, pilot's fee; ~**geld** pilotage; ~ ~ *für Auslotsen: pilotage outwards;* ~ ~ *für Einlotsen: pilotage inwards;* ~**gewerbe** pilot's profession; ~**lohn** load manage; ~**patent** pilots's licence; ~**signale** pilot signals; ~**vergütung** pilotage; ~**vorschrift** pilotage law; ~**zulassungsurkunde** pilotage certificate; ~**zwang** compulsory pilotage.

Lotterie *f* lottery; ~**anleihe** loan eligible for lottery premium; ~**einnehmer** lottery agent; ~**gewinn** lottery winnings, (lottery) prize, winning ticket; ~**los** lottery ticket; ~**spiel** lottery, playing lottery; ~**steuer** lottery tax; ~**stichprobe** lottery sample (*statistics*); ~**unternehmer** promoter of lotteries, lottery agent; ~**vertrag** lottery contract; **öffentliche** ~ public lotteries; **steuerpflichtige** ~**n** taxable lotteries.

Löwenanteil *m* lion's share.

Lücke *f* gap, omission, blank, vacancy, loophole; ~**nbüßer** stopgap; ~**nhaftigkeit** incompleteness, fragmentary character; ~**nlosigkeit** completeness, uninterrupted nature; **e-e** ~ **im Gesetz** a loophole in the law, legal gap.

Luft|aufsicht air-traffic control; ~**beförderung** air carriage, transportation by air; ~**brücke** air lift; ~**ersatzverkehr** transport of air cargo by land, trucking; ~**fahrer** pilot, aviator; ~**fahrerschein** pilot's licence; ~**fahrt** → *Luftfahrt;* ~**fahrzeug** → *Luftfahrzeug;* ~**fracht** → *Luftfracht;* ~**herrschaft** air supremacy, control of the air; ~**hoheit** air sovereignty; ~**hoheitsgebiet** territorial air space; ~**inspektion** aerial inspection; ~**kabotage** aerial cabotage; ~**korridor** air corridor; ~**navigation** air navigation; ~**piraterie** air piracy, hijacking; ~**post** = *Luftpost;* ~**privatrecht** private law of aviation; ~**raum** air space; ~**raumüberwachung** air traffic control; ~**raumverletzung** violation of one's air space; ~**recht** law, concerning the air space; ~**reinhaltung** preservation of clean air; ~**reinigungsanlagen** air purification plants; ~**reiseverkehr** air travel; ~**schacht** air shaft, air course, ventilation shaft; ~**schutz** → *Luftschutz;* ~**sperrgebiete** prohibited aerial space; ~**stützpunkt** air base; ~**tauglichkeit** airworthiness; ~~~*szeugnis: air worthiness certificate;* ~**taxe** air taxi; ~**transport** air transport; ~**transportbrief** = ~*frachtbrief qv;* ~**transportunternehmer** air carrier; ~**transporttarif** air cargo rates; ~**tüchtigkeit** airworthiness; ~**tüchtigkeitszeugnis** certificate of airworthiness; ~**unfallversicherung** air accident insurance; ~**verbindungen** air links; ~**verkehr** → *Luftverkehr;* ~**verpestung** air pollution; ~**verschmutzung** air pollution; ~**verschollenheit** unexplained absence after air accident *(for more than 3 months);* ~**versicherung** air-risk insurance; ~**verteidigung** air defence; ~ **verunreinigung** air pollution; ~**weg** flight route; *auf dem* ~~: *by air;* ~**zuführung** air supply, ventilation; ~**zwischenfall** air incident.

Luftfahrt *f* aviation; aeronautics; ~**abkommen** aviation convention; ~**behörden** aviation authorities; ~**-Bundesamt** Federal Office of Civil Aeronautics, Federal Aviation Authority; ~**einrichtungen** aviation facilities; ~**elektronik** avionics; ~**gesellschaft** airline, air company; ~**gesetzgebung** aviation legislation; ~**hindernisse** aviation impediments; ~**kommission** Air Navigation Commission; ~**recht** aviation law; ~**srisiko** aviation risk; ~**unternehmen** aviation enterprise, airline; ~**versicherung** aviation insurance, flight insurance; ~**werte** *exch* aircrafts.

Luftfahrzeug *n* aircraft; ~**halter** aircraft licence holder, person in charge of an aircraft; ~**rolle** register of aircraft; ~**srechtegesetz** Law on Rights in Respect of Aircraft (D 1959).

Luftfracht *f* air freight, air cargo, air carriage; ~**branche** air freight industry; ~**brief** airbill, air consignment note, air waybill; ~**führer** air carrier; ~**recht** air carriage law; ~**spedition** air freight forwarding; ~**tarif** air cargo rate; ~**verkehr** air transportation, air traffic.

Luftpost *f* air mail; ~**brief** air mail letter; ~**dienst** air mail service; ~**einlieferungsschein** air mail receipt; ~**empfangsbescheinigung** air consignment note; ~**leichtbrief** air letter; ~**paket** air parcel; ~**zuschlag** air surcharge.

Luftschutz *m* air-raid protection; ~**anlagen** air-raid protection installations, air-raid shelters; ~**bauten** air-raid protection structures; ~**dienst** air-raid protection service; ~**hilfsdienst** air-raid protection service; ~**stollen** underground air-raid shelter; ~**warndienst** air-raid warning service.

Luftverkehr *m* air traffic, air transport.

Luftverkehrs|abkommen aviation treaty; ~**betrieb** airline, carrier; ~**gesellschaft** airline (company), air carrier, carrier; ~**gesetz** civil aviation law; ~**ordnung** rules of the air; ~**verwaltung** civil aviation board; ~**weg** flight route, airway; ~**-Zulassungs-Ordnung** Ordinance regulating admission to civil aviation.

Lüge *f* lie; ~**ndetektor** lie detector; ~**ngebäude** fabric of lies, tissue of lies; ~**ngewebe** web of lies; ~**nmärchen** a tall story, cock-and-bull story; **e-e faustdicke** ~ a monstrous lie, a whopping lie; **e-e glatte** ~ a downright lie; **jmdn der** ~ **bezichtigen** to call s. o. a liar; **sich in** ~**n verstricken** to get entangled in lies.

lügen *v/i* to lie, to tell a lie (*or* lies); ~**, daß sich die Balken biegen** to tell a monstrous lie, to lie like the devil; **unverschämt** ~ to tell a blatant lie.

Lügner *m* liar; **gemeiner** ~ dirty liar, rotten liar.

lukrativ *adj* lucrative, profitable.

Lumpensammler *m* rag and bone dealer.

Lustbarkeiten *f/pl* public entertainments.

lustlos *adj exch* dull, stagnant, quiet, flat.

Lustlosigkeit *f exch* dullness, stagnancy.

Lustmord *m* sex murder, sexually motivated murder.

Lustmörder *m* rapist-killer, sex murderer.

Luxus|artikel fancy article, luxury article; ~**ausführung** de luxe model, de luxe finish; ~**gegenstand** luxury article; ~**steuer** luxury tax.

lynchen *v/t* to lynch.

Lynchjustiz lynch-law, mob-law, gibbet law.

M

Machart *f* style, design, make.
Machbarkeitsstudie *f* feasibility study.
Machenschaften *f/pl* machinations, intrigues, practices; **betrügerische** ~ deceptive practices, fraudulent practices; **dunkle** ~ sinister intrigues; **korrupte** ~ corrupt practices; **verbrecherische** ~ criminal practices.
Macher *m pol*: wire-puller, prime mover, boss, man of action.
Macht *f* (*pl Mächte* ~*e*) power; ~**anmaßung** usurpation of power; ~**anspruch** claim to power; ~**apparat** machinery of power; ~**ausübung** exercise of power; *willkürliche* ~ ~: *arbitrary power*; ~**befugnis** authority; *aus eigener* ~ ~: *on one's own authority*; ~**bereich** sphere of power, sphere of influence, jurisdiction; ~**beschränkung** limitation of powers; ~**beteiligung** power sharing; ~**demonstration** show of force; ~ **der Verwaltung** administrative power; ~**entfaltung** display of power; ~**ergreifung** seizure of power; ~**gleichgewicht** balance of power; ~**gruppe** powerful group, pressure group; ~**haber** ruler, person in power; ~**kampf** struggle for power; ~**konzentration** power concentration; ~**politik** power politics; ~**mißbrauch** abuse of power; ~**probe** test of power, trial of strength; ~**spruch** fiat, peremptory order; ~**stellung** powerful position, position of strength; ~**übernahme** seizure of power, assumption of power; ~**überschreitung** exceeding one's authority, acting ultra vires; ~**vakuum** power vacuum; ~**vollkommenheit** authority; *aus eigener* ~ ~: *on one's own authority;* ~**wort** word(s) of authority; ~**zentrum** centre of power; ~**zusammenballung** concentration of power; *wirtschaftliche* ~ ~: *concentration of economic power*; **alliierte** ~**e** Allied powers; **an der** ~ **sein** to be in power; **ausländische** ~ foreign power; **die** ~ **ausüben** to exercise power; **die** ~ **ergreifen** to seize power; **die** ~ **übernehmen** to take over power; **kriegführende** ~ belligerent power; **neutrale** ~ neutral power, neutral state; **unbeschränkte** ~ absolute power; **vertragsschließende** ~**e** signatory powers; **weltliche** ~ temporal power; **wirtschaftliche** ~ economic power.
Machwerk *n* a poor piece of work, botch, a miserable job.
Mädchen|handel white slave traffic, white slave trade, white slavery; ~**händler** white slave trader; ~**jahre** girlhood; ~**name** maiden name.
Madrider Markenabkommen *n* Madrid Trade Mark Convention *The Arrangement of Madrid Concerning the International Registration of Trade Marks* (*1891*).
Magazin *n* magazine; store room, stack room, "morgue"; ~**arbeiter** warehouseman; ~**verwalter** storekeeper, warehouse keeper.
Magistrat *m* municipal authority, municipal council; ~**sbeschluß** municipal decree; ~**smitglied** municipal councillor.
Magna Charta *f* Magna Charta Libertatum, the Great Charter (*1215*).
Magnetschwebebahn *f* magnetic hover train.
Mahn|bescheid default summons, summary notice to pay; ~**bescheidsantrag** application for a default summons; ~**brief** reminder (letter), letter requesting payment,

mahnen — **Mandat**

dunning letter, demand note; ~**frist** deadline for payment; ~**gebühr** dunning charge; ~**kosten** expenses of reminding a debtor, collection expenses; ~**schreiben** = *Mahnbrief qv*; ~**verfahren** summary proceedings for recovery of debt or liquidated demand, default action; ~**wesen** dunning, dunning activity; ~**zettel** reminder slip, short request for payment, prompt note.

mahnen *v/t* to dun, to remind of, to warn, to request payment.

Mahnung *f* reminder, warning, (legal) demand, dunning notice; ~ **zur Zahlung** demand for payment, notice to pay; **erste** ~ first reminder; **letzte** ~ final demand letter before action.

Majestät *f* majesty; ~**sbedrohung** threat to the Sovereign; ~**sbeleidigung** lèse-majesty, laesa majestas; ~**sverbrechen** high treason.

Majorat *n* primogeniture, majorat, estate (in) tail devolving to the eldest son; ~ **im Mannesstamm** estate tail male; ~**serbe** heir in right of primogeniture; ~**sgut** entailed estate, estate devolving by right of primogeniture; ~**sherr** tenant in tail.

majorisieren *v/t* to overrule by a majority, to outvote.

Majorisierung *f* defeating by majority vote; *majorisiert: outvoted;* ~**sprinzip** majoritarianism.

Majorität *f* majority, majority of votes cast, *cf Mehrheit;* ~**skäufe** stock purchases for the purpose of acquiring a majority stake.

Makel *m* taint, flaw.

makellos *adj* flawless, impeccable, faultless, free from fault.

Makellosigkeit *f* impeccability, faultlessness.

Makler *m* broker, (estate) agent; ~**buch** broker's journal; ~**büro** broking firm's office, estate agent's office; ~**courtage** broker's commission; ~**firma** broker's firm, firm of stock brokers, jobbing house, estate agents; ~**gebühr** brokerage, broker's charges; agent's fee; ~**geschäft** brokerage, broking, brokerage operation; ~ **in kleineren Effektenposten** odd lot broker; ~**kammer** brokers' professional organization; ~**lohn** broker's (*or* agent's) commission, broker's (*or* agent's) fee, brokerage; ~**ordnung** professional rules and regulations for brokers; ~**provision** broker's (*or* agent's) commission; ~**schranke** broker's bar (*at stock exchange*); ~**stand** *exch* pitch; ~**usancen** brokerage practices; ~**vertrag** contract with a broker, brokerage agreement, brokerage contract; *exch:* contract note; **amtlich zugelassener** ~ licensed broker; **freier** ~ outside broker, independent broker (*or* agent); street broker; **nicht an der Börse zugelassener** ~ unlicensed broker; **staatlich vereidigter** ~ officially sworn broker; **vereidigter** ~ sworn broker.

Makulatur *f* printer's waste, painter's overs.

Makulierung *f* pulping (*of unsaluble books*).

Malstaffel *f* quantity discount for advertisement (*for repeats*).

Management *n* management, team of managers; ~-**Vertrag** management agreement; ~-**Trust** flexible trust.

Manager *m* manager; ~**krankheit** hypertension; (managerial) stress; ~**system** managerial system.

Mandant *m* client (*of a lawyer, a tax consultant etc*); ~**enschutzklausel** *f* client confidentiality clause (*lawyer's staff clause*); **zahlungsunwilliger** ~ client reluctant to pay (his lawyer's fee).

Mandat *n* retainer, engaging the services of a lawyer, professional agreement with a lawyer; mandate; seat (*in parliament*); **auf sein** ~ **verzichten** to give up one's seat; **ein** ~ **ausüben** to act on behalf of a client; **ein** ~ **erringen** to secure a seat; **ein** ~ **übernehmen** to assume a mandate; **sein** ~ **niederle-**

Mandatar / **mangels**

gen to vacate one's seat, to discontinue one's services as a lawyer, to terminate one's retainer; **sein ~ zur Verfügung stellen** to resign from one's attorneyship; **von e–m ~ entbinden** to disengage a lawyer, to cease instructing a lawyer.

Mandatar *m* mandatary, mandatory (*one to whom a mandate has been given, who undertakes without compensation to perform certain duties*); **~macht** mandatory power; **~staaten** Mandatory States.

Mandats|ausübung exercise of a mandate, action as a lawyer *or* attorney-atlaw; **~entzug** termination of a mandate, disengagement of a lawyer, withdrawal of mandate; **~gebiet** mandated territory; **~niederlegung** withdrawal of lawyer from client-relationship; **~verhältnis** client-lawyer relationship; **~verlust** loss of a client (*of a lawyer*), loss of a mandate; **~verteilung** distribution of mandates.

Mandierung *f* employment of counsel, brief; retainer of a lawyer; **~sgebühr** retaining fee.

Mangel *m* (*pl: Mängel qv*) defect, physical defect, fault flaw, vice, imperfection; lack, want, deficiency, need, shortage, shortcoming; **~ an Arbeitskräften** shortage of labour; **~ an Bestimmtheit** lack of certainty; **~ an Beweisen** lack of proof; *aus ~ ~ ~*: *for lack of proof, for want of evidence;* **~ an Beweiskraft** lack of probative force; **~ an Enthaltsamkeit** incontinence; **~ an Geld** lack of money, shortage of money; **~ an Masse** lack of assets (of an estate); **~ an Schlüssigkeit** inconclusiveness; **~ an Sorgfalt** lack of care, want of diligence; **~anspruch** claim arising from a defect; **~beruf** shortage occupation (*scarcity of skilled personnel*); **~ der Vollmacht** lack of authority, insufficiency of the power of attorney; **~folgeschaden** consequential harm caused by a defect, consequential damages; **m~frei** *adj* free from defect(s), faultless; **~freiheit** faultlessness, flawlessness; **m~haft** *adj* faulty, defective, imperfect, inadequate, flawed, *vorwerfbar ~ negligently defective;* **~haftigkeit** defectiveness, faultiness, inadequacy, imperfection; **~ im Recht** defect of title, lack of legal basis; **~klausel** warranty clause; *versteckte ~ ~*: *latent defect clause;* **~lage** shortage; **~ware** goods in short supply, scarce articles; **e–m ~ abhelfen** to remedy a defect; **e–n ~ beheben** to remedy a defect; **e–n ~ geltend machen** to raise a claim for breach of warranty; **erkennbarer ~** apparent defect, patent defect; **geheimer ~** hidden defect, hidden fault, latent defect; **e–n ~ heilen** to cure (*or* remedy, *or* rectify) a defect; **geringfügiger ~** minor defect; **grober ~** serious defect; **heimlicher ~ =** *geheimer Mangel qv;* **innerer ~** intrinsic defect, inherent flaw, inherent vice; **nicht äußerlich erkennbarer ~** latent defect, defect not apparent; **offener ~** patent defect; **unheilbarer ~** irremediable defect; **verborgener ~ =** *geheimer Mangel qv;* **versteckter ~ =** *geheimer Mangel qv.*

Mängel (*sing: Mangel qv*) *m/pl;* **~ansprüche** warranty claims; **~anzeige** notification (*or* notice) of defects; **~ beheben** to remedy defects, to make good defects; **~beseitigung** correction, remedying faults; **~einrede** defence based on warranty for defects; plea that goods are defective; **~gewähr(leistung)** warranty for defects *or*: faults; **~haftung** liability for defects, warranty for defects; **~rüge** notification (*or* notice) of defects, deficiency claim, complaint (about defects); **~rügefrist** notification period for defects; **mit allen ~n** with all faults; **ohne offenkundige ~** without any apparent faults; **zur Wandlung berechtigende ~** redhibitory defects.

mangels *prep* for lack of, for want of,

in the absence of, in default of, without.

Manifest *n* manifest, shipping bill, ship's manifest, *pol:* manifesto, *hist:* das Kommunistische ~: the Communist Manifesto.

Manifestation *f* manifestation.

manipulieren *v/t* to manipulate, to rig *(the market)*.

Manipulation *f* manipulation, sharp practices; ~**sbestand** general fund, working fund; ~**sgebühr** handling charge; ~**sreserve** reserve for manœuvre; ~ **der Zollverschlüsse** tampering with customs seals.

Manko *n* shortage, deficiency; ~**geld** cashier's allowance for shortages; ~**haftung** liability for a cash shortage.

Mannesstamm *m* male line.

Mannstollheit *f* nymphomania.

Mantel *m* bare shell, skeleton; ~**abtretung** blanket assignment (of receivables); ~**gesetz** covering law, framework law, omnibus law; ~**gründung** formation of an off-the-shelf company; ~**kauf** purchase of the "bare shell" (inactive company); ~**gesellschaft** shell corporation, corporate shell; ~**note** covering note; ~**police** global policy; ~**tarif** industry-wide collective bargaining agreement, framework collective agreement; ~**tarifvertrag** industry-wide collective bargaining agreement, framework collective agreement; ~**vertrag** master agreement, framework agreement, skeleton agreement; ~**zession** blanket assignment (of receivables).

Marathondebatte *f* talkathon, filibuster, non-stop debate.

Margarine|steuer *f* margarine tax; ~**ausgleichsabgabe** *f* margarine price equalization levy.

Marge *f* margin, mark-up, difference, spread.

Marginalien *f/pl* marginal notes, marginalia.

Marine|akademie naval college; ~**angelegenheiten** naval affairs; ~**attaché** naval attaché; ~**haushalt** navy estimates; ~**minister** Minister of Naval Affairs *GB:* Under-Secretary of State (Royal Navy), *US:* Secretary of the Navy; ~**ministerium** Ministry of Naval Affairs, *US:* Department of the Navy; *GB:* the Admiralty, MOD (Navy); ~**nachrichtendienst** naval intelligence; ~**offizier** naval officer; ~**recht** naval law; ~**stützpunkt** naval base; ~**wehrrecht** naval law.

Marionetten|regierung puppet government; ~**staat** puppet state.

Mark *f (pl Marken)* march, marches, borderland.

Marke *f* mark, landmark, trade mark, distinctive name, trade name, brand, brand name; ticket, voucher, check, stamp, chit; **abgestempelte** ~ used stamp; **bevorzugte** ~ favorite brand; **erstklassige** ~ first-class brand; **geschützte** ~ registered trade mark.

Marken|abkommen trade mark convention; ~**akzeptanz** brand acceptance; ~**anmeldung** filing a trade-mark registration; ~**artikel** branded merchandise, branded goods, proprietary articles; ~**benzin** branded petrol, premium grade petrol; ~**erzeugnis** branded article, firstclass product(s); ~**etikett** brand label; ~**firma** established firm, firm with well-known trade name; ~**inhaber** trade-mark proprietor, proprietor of a trade mark, proprietor of a brand; ~**nahrungsmittel** patent foods; ~**name** brand name; ~**recht** law of trademarks; title to a trade mark; ~**schokolade** brand chocolate; ~**schutz** trademark protection; ~**schutzrecht** law of trade marks; ~**waren** branded articles, proprietary goods; ~**zeichen** = *Warenzeichen qv.*

Marketenderware *f* goods sold to military personnel; *US:* Post Exchange (PX) goods.

Marketing *n* marketing.

Markscheide *f* boundary, march.

Markscheiden *n* underground surveying.

Markscheider *m* mine surveyor.

Markt *m* (*pl Märkte ~e*) market; **~abgrenzung** (mutual) market delimitation; **~abrede** marketing arrangement; **~abschottung** market isolation; **~absprache** (underhand) marketing agreement, informal understanding about sales; **~analyse** market analysis; **~anteil** market share, sales quota, slice of the market; **~aufteilung** allocation; **~ausdehnung** expansion of the market, **~ausgleich** evening out the market; establishment of market equilibrium; **~ausweitung** expansion of the market; **~bank** bank serving a market; **~beeinflussung** influencing of the market; **~befestigung** market consolidation; **m~beherrschend** market-dominating; **~beherrschung** market control, domination of the market; **~belebung** buoyancy; **~beobachtung** observation of the market; **~bericht** market report; **~beschickung** supplying the market, market supplies; **m~bestimmend** *adj* determining the market, market-determinant (*factor, influence*); **~beteiligte** parties trading in the market, market participants; **~bilanz** net market position; **~chancen** sales possibilities, marketing opportunities; **~durchdringung** market penetration; **~einfluß** influence on the market; **~einkauf** shopping on the market; **~elastizität** market flexibility; **~enge** market narrowness; **~entwicklung** market development; **~erschließung** opening of new markets, tapping new markets; **m~fähig** *adj* marketable, saleable, sound; *nicht ~ ~: unmarketable, unsound;* **~fähigkeit** marketability; **~forschung** market research, field survey, consumer investigation; **~freiheit** free market principle; **m~fühlig** *adj* sensitive to market trends; **~führer** market leader; **~ für unnotierte Werte** market for unquoted securities; **m~gängig** *adj* marketable, merchantable; **~gebiet** territorial market, marketing area; **~gefälle** flow of the market, direction of market trend; **~gefüge** structure of the market, pattern of marketing; **~geld** stallage; **~geltung** acceptance in the market, market standing; **m~gemäß** *adj* in conformity with the market; **~gemeinde** rural township, market town; **m~gerecht** *adj* in conformity with the market, based on the demands of the market, fair (*price*); **~geschehen** market activities; **~händler** marketman; **~jahr** market year; **~klima** climate of the market; **m~konform** *adj* in conformity with the market, in line with the market; *nicht ~ ~ sein: to be counter to market practice;* **~konstellation** market situation; **m~konträr** *adj* incompatible with the market, contrary to market developments; **~konzentration** concentration of the market; **~kurs** market price; **~lage** market situation, state of the market; *gesamtwirtschaftliche ~ ~: the position of the market as a whole; einmalig günstige ~ ~: uniquely favorable market situation;* **~leistung** effectiveness of the market, market output; *landwirtschaftliche ~ ~: marketed farming output;* **~lücke** niche (in the market), untapped market; *e-e ~ ~ schließen: to fill a gap in the market;* **m~mäßig** *adj* relating to the market, marketable; **~mechanismus** marketing machinery; **~miete** (open) market rent, **~monopol** monopoly of the market; **~nachfrage** demand in the market; **m~nahe** *adj* close to the market, in close accord with market facts; **~nähe** market proximity, closeness to the market; **~ordnung** market organization, market régime, market regulation; *landwirtschaftliche ~ ~: régime of the agricultural market;* **~ordnungsgesetz** market-regulating law; **~ordnungsstelle** market-regulating agency; **~ordnungsware** goods subject to market regula-

Marktorientierung — **offener Markt**

tions, *andienungspflichtige* ~ ~: (*controlled*) *goods which must be offered to official buyers;* ~**orientierung** market orientation; ~**partner** market member; ~**pflege** cultivating the market, market support; ~**politik** market policy; *offene* ~ ~: *open market policy;* **m**~**politisch** *adj* from the point of view of market policy; ~**polizei** market police; ~**preis** market price; *freier* ~ ~: *free market price, competitive price;* ~**produktion** production for the market; **m**~**reagibel** *adj* sensitive to the market; ~**recht** market right, law concerning markets; **m**~**regelnd** *adj* regulating the market; ~**regelung** market regulation; **m**~**reif** *adj* ready for the market, fully developed; ~**sättigung** saturation of the market; ~**schreier** booster, puffer, barker; ~**schwankung** market fluctuation; ~**schwemme** glut on the market; ~**situation** market (situation): *gleichgewichtige* ~ ~: *balanced market;* ~**spannungen** strains in the markets; ~**standort** market place; ~**stellung** market position; *beherrschende* (= *überragende*) ~~: *dominating market position;* ~**studie** study of the market, market study; ~**stützung** market support; ~**tag** market day; **m**~**-technisch** technical; ~~*e Erholung: technical rally;* ~**tendenz** market tendency; ~**transparenz** market transparency; ~**übersicht** market view; ~**- und Messeabgabe** "pitching-pence"; ~**untersuchung** market investigation, market research, area sampling; *stichprobenartige* ~ ~: *haphazard sampling;* ~**verband** marketing association; ~**verbot** market prohibition; ~**verengung** market shortage; ~**verfassung** state of the market; ~**verflechtung** integration of the markets; ~**verhältnis** market ratio; *pl* ~ ~*se: market conditions;* ~**verkehr** market transactions; ~**verschiebung** shift of the market; ~**versorgung** supply of the market, market supplies; ~**versteifung** stiffening of the market, narrowing of the market; ~**verzerrung** market distortion; ~**volumen** size of the market; ~**wert** market value, marketable value, commercial value, exchange value, trade value; ~**widerstand** market resistance; ~**wirtschaft** (free) market economy, uncontrolled economy, free enterprise economy; *freie* ~ ~: *free market economy; soziale* ~ ~: *social market economy;* ~**zerrüttungen** market distortions; ~**zettel** market quotations, market note; ~**zins** current interest rate; **agrarischer** ~ agricultural market; **amtlicher** ~ official market; **auf den** ~ **bringen** to launch on the market, to market; **auf den** ~ **werfen** to unload (sth on the market); **aufnahmebereiter** ~ receptive market; **ausländische** ~**e** foreign markets; ~ ~ *gewinnen:* to conquer foreign markets, to penetrate foreign markets; **beschränkter** ~ restricted market; **den** ~ **abtasten** to sound out the market, to explore the market; **den** ~ **beherrschen** to control the market, to dominate the market; **den** ~ **erkunden** to study the market; **den** ~ **überschwemmen** to flood the market; **Der Gemeinsame** ~ The Common Market; **einheimischer** ~ home market, domestic market; **einheitlicher** ~ uniform market; **e-n neuen** ~ **erschließen** to open up a new market; to develop a new market; **enger** ~ limited market; **fester** ~ steady market; **freier** ~ open market; **gedrückter** ~ depressed market; **geschlossener** ~ closed market; **gewerblicher** ~ market for industrial goods; **grauer** ~ grey market; **heimischer** ~ domestic market; **homogener** ~ homogenous market, uniform market; **lebhafter** ~ brisk market, active market; **leerer** ~ no stock available, empty market; **lockerer** ~ easy market; **lustloser** ~ inactive market, dull market, flat market; **offener** ~ open market, public

marodieren

market; **öffentlicher** ~ public market; **reagible** ~**e** sensitive markets; **ruhiger** ~ calm market; **schwacher** ~ weak market; **schwarzer** ~ black market; **theoretisch vollkommener** ~ (theoretically) perfect market; **übersättigter** ~ glutted market, flooded market; **unbearbeiteter** ~ virgin market, unexplored market.

marodieren *v/t* to maraud, to pillage.

martern *v/t* to torture.

Marterung *f* torture.

Martinshorn *n* police (car) siren.

Masche *f* racket, trick, gimmick.

Maschinen|anlage machinery, plant; ~**arbeit** machine work; ~**ausfall** failure of machinery; ~**ausfallzeit** machine idle-time; ~**bau** →*Maschinenbau;* ~**bediener** (machine) operator; ~**bruchversicherung** insurance against breakdown of machinery; ~**buchführung** mechanized bookkeeping; ~**einsatzplan** work ahead schedule; ~**fabrik** engineering works, machine factory; ~**fach** mechanical engineering; ~**führer** operator; ~**gruppe** production unit, set of machines; ~**haftpflichtversicherung** machinery insurance; ~**leistung** machine capacity; ~**park** (stock of) machinery, mechanical equipment; ~**pistole** submachine-gun, tommy-gun; ~**saal** machine-shop, engineeroom; **hauswirtschaftliche** ~ mechanical appliances for use in the home, domestic appliances.

Maschinenbau *m* mechanical engineering, machine construction; ~**industrie** engineering industry; ~**ingenieur** mechanical engineer; ~**werte** mechanical engineering shares.

Maske *f* mask, disguise; ~**nverleih** (*m*) costume hire, costume rental (*shop*).

Maß|anfertigung making to measure; ~**akkord** piece rate by measure (or quantity); ~**angaben** measurements data; ~**arbeit** making to

Masse

measure, made-to-measure suit; ~**einheit** unit of measurement; ~**fracht** freighting on measurement; ~**gabe** instruction, directive; *mit der* ~: *on the understanding, subject to the proviso; nach* ~: *pursuant to, according to, in compliance with, in accordance with;* **m**~**gebend** *adj* authoritative, authentic, relevant, applicable; **m**~**geblich** *adj* definitive, authoritative; ~ *sein: to be authoritative, to override; in gleicher Weise* ~: *equally authentic;* ~**geblichkeit** authority, controlling importance; ~~**sprinzip**: *principle of the dependency of the tax balance sheet on the commercial balance sheet;* **m**~**geschneidert** made-to-measure; ~**halteappell** austerity appeal, appeal for self-restraint (*in spending*); ~**haltigkeit** accuracy of size; ~**nahme** → *Maßnahme;* ~**regel** → *Maßregel;* **m**~**-regeln** → *maßregeln;* ~**stab** standard, test measure, scale (*of map*); *feinere Maßstäbe: more detailed criteria;* ~**stabstreue** accuracy in scale; ~**system** system of measures, system of units; ~**toleranz** tolerance; ~**e und Gewichte** *n/pl* weights and measures; ~**- und Gewichtsgesetz** Act on weights and measures.

Masse *f* mass, crowd, volume, bulk; (bankrupt's) estate, assets; ~**anspruch** preferential claim (*to be satisfied directly out of the estate*); ~**darlehen** loan for insolvent estate (*for current transactions*); ~**forderung** post-adjudication claim against a bankrupt's estate; ~**gläubiger** post-adjudication preferred creditor, *creditor of claims directly to be discharged by trustee;* ~**kosten** costs of bankruptcy *including cost of living allowance to bankrupt and family;* ~**schulden** direct debts of the bankruptcy estate (*to be satisfied by the trustee*); ~**verwalter** trustee in bankruptcy, administrator of a bankrupt's estate; ~**verzeichnis** list of assets (of the estate); **mangels** ~ (for) insufficiency of assets.

Massen|abfertigung mass processing (of people), handling of mass applicant; ~**änderungskündigung** multiple notice of termination to effect a variation of employment terms; ~**angebot** large-scale supply; ~**ankauf** bulk buying; ~**arbeitslosigkeit** mass unemployment; ~**armut** pauperism; ~**artikel** bulk articles, mass-produced articles; ~**aufgebot** levy en masse, large crowd of supporters; ~**aufmarsch** mass parade; ~**aussperrung** general lockout; ~**bedarfsartikel** articles in mass demand; ~**bedarfsgüter** commodities in mass demand; ~**beförderung** mass transportation; ~**berechnung** calculation of quantities; bill of quantity; ~**bewegung** mass movement; ~-**einbürgerung** mass naturalization; ~**einkommen** incomes of the general population; ~**entlassungen** mass dismissals, compulsory mass redundancies; ~**ermittlung** quantity surveying, calculation of quantities; ~**fabrikation** mass production; ~**flucht** flight en masse, mass exodus, mass escape; ~**geschäft** retail banking; ~**gesellschaft** mass society; ~-**grab** mass grave, common grave; ~**güter** bulk goods; *agrarische* ~~: *agricultural bulk goods; frachtintensive* ~~: *bulk goods on which the freight is heavy; mit unverpackten* ~~*n beladen: laden in bulk*; ~**gütertransport** bulk goods transport; ~**gutschiff** bulk freighter; ~**herstellung** mass production; ~**hinrichtung** mass execution; ~**informationsmittel** means of mass communication; ~**karambolage** mass collision, pile-up, multi-car crash; ~**kaufkraft** purchasing power of the general population, mass purchasing power; ~**kommunikationsmittel,** mass communication media; ~**konsum** general consumption, mass-consumption; ~**kundgebung** mass demonstration; ~**kündigung** mass dismissals; ~**lieferung** bulk consignment; ~**medien** mass media, means of mass communication; ~**nahrungsmittel** bulk foodstuffs; ~**organisation** mass organization; ~**panik** mass panic, crowd panic; ~**partei** party with mass support, large party; ~**produktion** mass production, production in bulk; ~**psychologie** mass psychology; ~**publikum** mass audience; ~**quartier** mass accommodation; ~**streik** general strike; ~**suggestion** mass suggestion; ~**terror** mass terror; ~**tourismus** mass tourism; ~**veranstaltung** mass rally; ~**verbrechen** mass crime; ~**verfolgung** mass persecution; ~**verhaftungen** mass arrests; ~**verkauf von Effekten** unloading, large-scale selling of equities; ~**verkehr** very heavy traffic; ~**verkehrsmittel** mass transit, means of public transport, mass transportation facilities; -~**vernichtungswaffen** weapons of mass destruction; ~**versammlung** mass rally; ~**verteilung** liquidating distribution; ~**vertrieb** mass selling; ~**verzeichnis** schedule of quantities (*in a tender or building contract*); ~**wahn** mass delusion; ~**ware** mass-produced goods.

Mäßigungspflicht *f* (public servant's) duty to be politically moderate.

Maßnahme *f* action, measure, step; ~**n der Betriebsleitung** managerial decisions; ~ **des Gerichts** act of court; ~**gesetz** statute for a specific provision; ~**n ergreifen** to take measures, to take action, to adopt measures; ~**n gleicher Wirkung** measures having equivalent effect; ~**nkomplex** set of measures; ~**n unterlassen** to refrain from action, to abstain from measures; **bevölkerungspolitische** ~**n** population policies, demographic policies; **dirigistische** ~**n** authoritarian measures, dirigistic measures; **diskriminierende** ~**n** discriminatory measures; **einschneidende** ~**n** sweeping

Maßregel / **Material**

measures, radical action; **einstweilige** ~n temporary measures; **etwa erforderlich werdende** ~n any necessary measures; **feindliche** ~n enemy measures, hostile acts; **geeignete** ~n appropriate steps, appropriate action; **geldpolitische** ~n measures of monetary policy; **gerichtliche** ~n **ergreifen** to take court action; **gesetzgeberische** ~n legislative measures; **gezielte** ~ selective measure; **handelspolitische** ~n trade policy steps; **hoheitliche** ~n acts of sovereignty; **investitionspolitische** ~n measures in the field of investment policy; **kriegsähnliche** ~n measures short of war, quasi-war measures; **marktwidrige** ~ action in disregard of market conditions, measure contrary to free market principles; **polizeiliche** ~ police action; **sofort vollziehbare** ~n immediately enforceable measures; **soziale** ~n welfare measures, social measures; **staatliche** ~n governmental action; **steuerliche** ~n fiscal measures; acts of taxation; **steuerpolitische** ~n measures of fiscal policy; **strengere** ~n more drastic measures; **unaufschiebbare** ~n urgent measures, unpostponable steps; **vertrauensbildende** ~n confidence-building measures; **vorbereitende** ~n preliminaries; **vorbeugende** ~n precautionary measures, preventive measures; **vorsorgliche** ~ safeguarding measure; **wettbewerbshemmende oder -verzerrende** ~n measures restricting or distorting competition.

Maßregel *f* rule, regulation, penalty, disciplinary action; ~**n der Sicherung und Besserung** measures for the prevention of crime and the reformation of offenders; **einstweilige** ~n provisional measures, interlocutory orders, interim measures.

maßregeln *v/t* to discipline, to reprimand, to punish.

Maßregelung *f* disciplinary reprimand, formal rebuke; ~**sverbot** stipulation forbidding company penalties after strikes; ban on victimization.

Material *n* material, *coll*: materials, stock; ~**abgang** material withdrawals; ~**anforderung** material requisition; ~**aufstellung** bill of materials; ~**aufwand** material used; ~**ausgabe** issue of materials; ~**bedarf** material requirements; ~**bedarfsplanung** materials budget; ~**beistellung** supply of materials; ~**bereitstellungsplan** supply-of-materials plan; ~**bestand** stock of material; ~**empfangsbescheinigung** materials receiving report; ~**ersparnis** saving of material; ~**fehler** defective material, defect in material; ~**gemeinkosten** indirect material costs; ~**gemeinkostenzuschlag** material cost burden rate; ~**konto** material stores account; ~**lager** stores, contractor's store, supplies in factory; ~**lieferant** materials supplier; ~**liste** bill of materials; ~**mangel** shortage of materials, shortage of securities on offer; ~**nachweisverfahren** materials accountability system; ~**preisabweichung** materials price variance; ~**prüfung** testing of materials, material control; ~**prüfungsamt** materials testing office; ~**schwierigkeit** difficulty in procuring materials; ~**schwund** wastage; ~ **und Arbeitslöhne** material and labour; ~**verarbeitung** working of material, processing of material, workmanship concerning materials; ~**verbrauch** material usage, consumption of materials; ~**verlust** wastage, loss of materials; ~**wert** value of raw material; ~**wiederverwendung** recycling of materials; ~ **zu Beweiszwecken** evidential material; **flottantes** ~ shares on offer; **fluktuierendes** ~ floating supply of securities on offer; **herauskommendes** ~ new issues; **minderwertiges** ~ materials of poor quality; **nicht frist-**

gerecht geliefertes ~ late delivery of material; **rollendes** ~ rolling stock; **urkundliches** ~ documentary evidence.

Materialismus *n* materialism; **dialektischer** ~ dialectical materialism; **historischer** ~ historical materialism.

Materie *f* subject-matter, material.

materiell *adj* substantive, in concrete terms; ~ **bedeutsam** of practical significance; **~-rechtlich** substantive, relating to substantive law.

Mätressentestament *n* last will in favour of one's mistress.

Matrosenheuer *f* seamen's wages.

Mauer *f* wall, brick wall; ~**werk** masonry, brick work; ~**schwamm** dry rot; **feuerfeste** ~ fire proof partition wall; **gemeinschaftliche** ~ party wall.

Maul- und Klauenseuche *f* foot and mouth disease.

Maulwurf *m* mole (*secret agent*).

Maut *f* toll; ~**brücke** toll bridge; **m~pflichtig** *adj* subject to toll charges; ~**recht** tollage; ~**straße** toll-road.

Maximal|belastung peak load; ~**forderung** maximum claim; ~**grenze** maximum, upper limit; ~**hypothek** = *Höchstbetragshypothek qv*; ~**schaden** maximum damage, upper limit of damage.

Maxime *f* dictum.

maximieren *v/i* to fix a maximum, to fix a retention limit, to maximize.

Mechanismus *m* mechanism, apparatus, machinery; ~**des Verfahrens** procedural machinery.

Medaillenverordnung *f* decree concerning honours and medals.

Medien *n/pl* (the) media; ~**angehörige** media staff members; ~**ordnung** media regulations; ~**recht** media law; ~**verbund** media grid.

Medikamenten|herstellung production of medicine; ~**mißbrauch** abuse of medical drugs.

Medio|abrechnung mid-month settlement; ~**ausweis** mid-monthly statement; ~**geld** short-term credit for mid-month settlement; ~**geschäft** business for mid-month settlement; ~**liquidation** mid-monthly settlement; ~**wechsel** fortnightly bill.

Medizin *f* medicine, medical science; **gerichtliche** ~ forensic medicine, medical jurisprudence.

Meer *n* ocean, the high seas, the open sea; ~**enge** straits, channel; ~**engenabkommen** the Convention of Montreux (1936), the Straits Convention; ~**engendurchfahrt** straits passage; ~**engenvertrag** The Straits Convention (1841); ~**engenkommission** straits commission.

Meeres|arm arm of the sea, inlet; ~**bergbau** deep-sea mining; ~**bodensperrvertrag** treaty on denuclearization of the ocean floor; ~**forschung** marine research, exploration of the sea; ~**freiheit** freedom of the seas; ~**grenze** sea frontier; ~**grund** seabed; ~**höhe** (height above) sea level; ~**umwelt** marine environment; ~**verschmutzung** marine pollution by dumping; ~~ *vom Land aus; marine pollution from land-based sources*.

Megafon *n* megaphone, speaking trumpet.

Mehr|anbau additional cultivation; ~**anfall** increase (*in work etc*); ~**ankäufe** excess of purchases over sales; ~**anspruch** additional claim; ~**arbeit** extra work, additional work; ~**arbeitslöhne** extra pay, overtime pay; ~**arbeitsverbot** prohibition of overtime; ~**arbeitsvergütungen** overtime pay; ~~ *für Anwesenheitsstunden: overtime pay for hours worked*; ~**arbeitszeit** overtime; ~**arbeitszuschlag** bonus paid for extra work; ~**aufwand** additional expenditure, additional outlay, extra trouble; ~**aufwendungen** extra expenses, additional expenditure; ~**ausgabe** increase in expenditure, extra expense; ~**bedarf** additional demand, additional requirements;

Mehrbelastung / **Mehrheit**

~**belastung** extra burden, additional charge; *nachträgliche* ~~: *supplementary charge; e-e ~~ ausgleichen: to offset an additional charge*; ~**beschäftigung** higher level of employment; ~**bestand** additional stock, additional supply; ~**betrag** additional amount, excess amount; ~**bietender** outbidder; **m~deutig** *adj* ambiguous; ~**deutigkeit** ambiguity, equivocation; *grundlegende* ~~: *ambiguity upon the factum; offenkundige* ~~: *patent ambiguity; offensichtliche* ~~: *patent ambiguity; versteckte* ~~: *latent ambiguity*; ~**ehe** plural marriage, polygamous marriage; ~**einnahme** surplus of receipts; ~**entnahme** excess withdrawal; ~**erlös** excess proceeds; ~**erlösabführung** transfer of excess proceeds; ~**ertrag** surplus, over-proceeds, extra proceeds, surplus profits; ~**export** increase in exports, additional exports; ~**facharbitrage** compound arbitrage; ~**belegung** multiple occupancy; ~ **fachbeschäftigter** person engaged in several occupations; ~**fachbesteuerung** recurrent taxation, multiple taxation; ~**fachbezieher** recipient of several types of benefit (*social ins*); ~**fachkonten** multiple accounts; ~**fachtäter** recidivist, multiple offender; ~**fachüberlassung** granting possession to several people; time share arrangement; ~**fachversicherung** multiple insurance, double indemnity; ~**fahrtenausweis** multiple ticket; ~**familienhaus** multi-family building; ~**farbendruck** polychrome print(ing); ~**felderwirtschaft** multi-field system; ~**förderung** extra output; ~**frontenkrieg** war on several fronts; ~**gebot** overbid, higher bid; referential bid; difference between the reserve price and the highest bid; ~**gewicht** excess weight, overweight, surplus weight; ~**gewinn** excess profits; ~**heit** → *Mehrheit*, majority; ~**jahresforschungsprogramm** multi-year research programme; ~~**jahresprogramm** multi-annual programme; **m~jährig** *adj* lasting several years, long-standing; ~**kosten** additional expenses, additional charges; ~**leistungen** increased performance, increased efficiency, additional benefit (*ins*); ~**lieferung** increased delivery, additional delivery; **m~ oder weniger** more or less, (or) thereabouts; ~**parteiensystem** multiple party system; ~**phasensteuer** multi-stage tax; *kumulative* ~~: *cumulative multistage tax system*; **m~prozentig** of (*or* by) more than one per cent, by several percentage points; ~**schichtenbetrieb** working in several shifts, multiple shift operation; ~**schichtkosten** multiple shift costs; **m~seitig** *adj* multilateral; **m~sprachig** *adj* multilingual; ~**staatenangehörigkeit** multi nationality, intercitizenship; ~**staater** person of more than one nationality; ~**stimmenaktie** = *Mehrstimmrechtsaktie qv*; ~**stimmenwahlrecht** plural vote, plural voting right, multiple voting right, weighted voting right; ~**stimmrechtsaktie** multiple-vote share, share with weighted voting right; supervoting share(s); ~**stückpakkung** multipack; **m~stufig** *adj* multistage; multi-phase; ~**verbrauch** additional consumption, excess consumption, ~**verkehr** sexual intercourse with several men *during period of conception (paternity case)*; ~~*szeuge: witness of a woman's sexual relation with a man (or men other than the putative father)*; ~**völkerstaat** multinational state; ~**wert** added value, additional value, increment value; appreciated surplus; ~~ *e-s Grundstücks durch Zusammenlegung: plottage increment*; ~**wertsteuer** → *Mehrwertsteuer*; ~**zahl** majority; ~**zwecktransporte** multimodal transport facilities; ~**zweckverband** multi-purpose joint authority.

Mehrheit *f* majority; ~ **der Erben**

531

plurality of heirs; ~ **nach Köpfen** majority of members; ~ **von Ja-stimmen** affirmative vote, the ayes have it; ~ **von Tätern** co-principals; several persons participating in one crime; ~ **von Unternehmern** group of business owners; **absolute** ~ absolute majority; **arbeitsfähige** ~ working majority; **die erforderliche** ~ the requisite majority; **die ~ haben** to be in, *or* have, the majority; **die ~ ist dafür** the ayes have it; **einfache** ~ majority vote, simple majority; **erforderliche** ~ necessary majority; **knappe** ~ bare majority, narrow majority; **kommt e-e ~ nicht zustande** failing a majority; **mit e~r** ~ **von** by a majority of; **mit ~ beschlossen** carried by a majority of votes; **qualifizierte** ~ special majority, qualified majority; **relative** ~ relative majority, US: plurality; *majority in relation to other (unelected) candidates*; **sichere** ~ comfortable majority; **über e-e ~ verfügen** to command a majority; **überwältigende** ~ overwhelming majority; **überwiegende** ~ vast majority; **verfassungsändernde** ~ majority sufficient to modify the constitution; **zahlenmäßige** ~ numerical majority.

Mehrheits|aktionär majority *or* controlling shareholder; **~ansicht** majority opinion; **~beschluß** majority vote, decision of the majority, resolution adopted by a majority of votes; *gewöhnlicher* ~~: *ordinary resolution*; **~besitz** majority holding; **~beteiligung** majority stake, majority participation, majority interest, majority holding; **~entscheid** majority decision; **~gesellschaft** majority shareholder; partner holding the majority of capital; **~grundsatz** majority principle, principle of majority rule; **~herrschaft** majority rule; **~parteien** majority parties; **~votum** majority opinion; **~wahl** majority vote (system);

~wahlrechtssystem majority vote system, „first-past-the-post" system.

Mehrwertsteuer *f* (*MWSt*) value added tax (VAT); **~befreiung** zero-rating; **~-Gesamtbelastung** total amount of VAT; **~-Vorbelastung** prior VAT charges; **die ~ in e-r Rechnung ausweisen** to indicate VAT in an invoice.

meiden *v/t* to avoid, to keep away from, to shun.

Meidung *f* avoidance; **bei ~ e-r Strafe von** ... under penalty of ...

Meineid *m* perjury, false oath; **~verfahren** prosecution for perjury; **e-n ~ leisten** to commit perjury; **e-n ~ schwören** to swear falsely; **zum ~ verleiten** to suborn to commit perjury.

meineidig *adj* perjured; ~ **werden** to perjure oneself.

Meineidiger *m* (*der Meineidige*) perjurer, person who has committed perjury.

Meinung *f* opinion; **abweichende** ~ dissenting opinion; **die ablehnende ~ aufgeben** to recede from an opinion (*legislative chamber*); **e-e ~ abgeben** to render an opinion; **einhellige** ~ general concurrence of opinion; **herrschende** ~ dominant opinion; **irrige** ~ mistaken idea; **öffentliche** ~ public opinion; **übereinstimmende** ~ consensus of opinion; **vorbehaltslose** ~ unhedged opinion; **vorgefaßte** ~ preconceived notion (opinion), fixed opinion; preconception.

Meinungs|änderung change of opinion, change of mind; *radikale* ~~: *volte face*. **~äußerung** statement of opinion, expression of opinion; *freie* ~~ *unterdrücken*: *to gag, to supress freedom of opinion*; **~äußerungsfreiheit** freedom of opinion; freedom to express one's opinion; **~austausch** exchange of views; **~befragung** opinion poll; **~bildung** forming of one's opinion, forming of public opinion;

Meistbegünstigung

~**forschung** public opinion research; ~~*sgutachten: expertise of public opinion research*; ~**freiheit** freedom of opinion, freedom of expression; ~**kauf** *exch* speculative buying; ~**monopol** monopolistic concentration of the media; **m~neutral** neutral as to opinion, independent, impartial, objective; ~**streit** conflict of opinion; ~**umfrage** opinion poll; ~~*spezialist* psephologist; ~**verkauf** *exch* speculative selling; ~**verschiedenheit** difference of opinion, disagreement, dissent; *sämtliche* ~~*en: all matters in difference; unbedeutende* ~~*en: minor differences;* ~**vielfalt** diversity of opinion, a wide range of opinions.

Meistbegünstigung *f* most favoured nation treatment; ~**sklausel** most favoured nation clause; ~**sprinzip** most favoured nation principle; ~**ssatz** most favoured nation rate; ~**svolltarif** most favoured nation tariff; ~**szollsatz** most favoured nation tariff.

meistbietend *adj* highest bidding, *(after the noun:)* bidding highest.

Meistbietender *m (der Meistbietende)* the highest bidder, best bidder, outbidder; *dem* ~*n zuschlagen: to knock down to the highest bidder*.

Meister *m* master, master craftsman, ~**arbeit** master work; ~**brief** master craftsman's certificate; ~**prüfung** master craftsman's qualifying examination; ~**recht** master craftsman's rights; ~**stück** masterpiece; ~**titel** title of master craftsman *(title of master baker, master tailor etc)*; ~**würde** mastership, rank of master (craftsman).

Meistgebot *n* highest bid.

Melde|amt registration office; ~**behörde** registration office, district recruitment centre; ~**bestätigung** confirmation of registration with the police; ~**bestimmungen** notification regulations, registration regulations; ~**bogen** registration form; ~**daten** registration data; ~**formular** registration form; ~**frist** time for registering; ~**geheimnis** confidentiality of registration office data; ~**gesetz** Registration Act; ~**kartei** registration card index, register; ~**pflicht** compulsory registration, duty to report; ~~ *für Ausländer: aliens' registration formalities*; **m~pflichtig** *adj* notifiable, reportable, declarable *(customs)*, obliged to register, subject to reporting (to); ~**pflichtiger** *(der Meldepflichtige)* person liable to report, registrant; ~**recht** law of residence registration; ~**register** register of residents; ~**schein** registration form, certificate of registration; ~**stelle** registration office; ~**termin** reporting date; ~**- und Ausweiswesen** (matters of) registration and identification papers; ~**vorschriften** registration rules, regulations concerning registration with authorities; ~**wesen** registration matters, registration of residents; *polizeiliches* ~~*: the system of registration (of residents) with the police*; ~**zeit** time for registration; check-in time; ~**zettel** registration form.

melden *v/t* to report, to register, to give notice to register, *v/reflex* to report, to register, to enrol *(US: -ll)*; **sich freiwillig** ~ to volunteer.

Meldung *f* report; information; news; ~**seingang** receipt of a report, receipt of a return; **dienstliche** ~ official report; **eingehende** ~**en** incoming messages; **polizeiliche** ~ police report; **rechtzeitige** ~ report in time.

Melioration *f* land improvement, soil improvement; ~**sarbeiten** land improvement works; ~**sdarlehen** loan for agricultural land improvement; ~**sfonds** public fund for agricultural land improvement; ~**skredit** agricultural land improvement credit.

meliorieren *v/t* to improve the quality of arable land.

Memorandum *n* memorandum.

Menge *f* quantity, quantum, amount; **etwa gleiche** ~**n** roughly equal

Mengenabsatz / **Metageschäft**

amounts; **gewinnbringende ~n** paying quantities.
Mengen|absatz quantity sale; quantity sold; **~abschreibung** depreciation based on the quantitative output, unit-of-production method of depreciation; **~abweichung** quantity variance; volume discrepancy; **~angabe** indication of quantities; **~beschränkung** quantitative restriction(s); **~bonus** volume discount; **~effekt** quantity effect; **~einheit** unit of quantity; **~einkauf** bulk buying; **~geschäft** volume banking business, standardized banking services; retail banking; **~index** quantity index; **~kauf** quantity buying; **~~vertrag**: *quantity purchase agreement*; **~kennzeichnung** quantity marking (*on packages*); **~konjunktur** quantity boom, expansion boom, growing output, increased demand boom; **~kontrolle** quantity control; *buchmäßige ~~*: *unit control*; **~kostenrechnung** marginal costing; **~leistung** quantitative output; **m~mäßig** *adj* quantitative, in terms of quantity; **~nachlaß** quantitative rebate; **~preis** bulk price; **~prüfung** verification of quantity; **~rabatt** quantity volume discount, volume merchandise allowance; **~rechnung** volume accounting; **~staffelung** quantity scale; **~stufen-Kaufvertrag** progressive volume purchase agreement; **~tarif** bulk supply tariff; **~vorgabe** production standard; **~vorschrift** quantitative regulations.
Menschen|ansammlung crowd of people, gathering; **~führung** leadership, management; **~gedenken** living memory; *seit ~~*: *within living memory*; **~handel** slave traffic, trade in human beings; **~leben** human life; **~menge** crowd; **~raub** kidnapping; *~~ gegen Lösegeld*: *kidnapping for ransom*; **~räuber** kidnapper; **~recht** human right, manmade law; **~rechtsbeschwerde** appeal to the Human Rights Commission; **~rechtskonvention** Human Rights Convention; **~schinder** torturer, slave driver; **~verstand** human intelligence; *gesunder ~~*: *common sense*; **~würde** human dignity.
Menschlichkeitsverbrechen *n* crime against humanity.
Mentalreservation *f* mental reservation.
Merkantilismus *n* mercantilism.
Merkblatt *n* leaflet, explanatory notes, instruction card.
merklich *adj* appreciable; *kaum ~*: *small, trifling, trivial*.
Merkmal *n* indication, criterion, characteristic feature, **~sanalyse** *pat* feature table style; **besondere ~e** distinguishing features; **kennzeichnende ~e** characterizing features (*pat*); **spezifische ~e** special characteristics, specific features; **technische ~e** technical features.
Merkposten *m* reminder item, nominal figure, depreciated item at a nominal valuation, pro-memoria item.
Mesalliance *f* mésalliance.
Meß|apparat measuring device; **~fehler** error in measurement; **~fühler** sensor; **~genauigkeit** accuracy of measuring; **~gerät** measuring tool; **~instrumente** measuring instruments; **~station** monitoring station; *nukleare ~~*: *fall-out-station*; **~tischblatt** ordnance map; **~zahl** index number; **~ziffer** = **~zahl** *qv*; **~~** *der Preise*: *price index*.
Messe *f* trade fair, trade show, trade exhibition; **~amt** trade fair administration, trade fair office; **~gelände** exhibition site; **~halle** exhibition hall; **~leitung** trade fair management; **~stand** exhibition stand, stand at a trade fair; **~vertrag** exhibition contract (*trade fair*).
Messe- und Marktsachen *f/pl* trade fair and market matters.
Meta|geschäft joint business venture, transaction on joint account, fifty-fifty business; **~konto** joint account of a *Metageschäft qv*; **~kredit** credit on joint account.

Metall|arbeit metalwork, work in metal; ~**arbeiter** metal-worker; ~**bau** metal construction; ~**bearbeitung** metal-working; ~**berufe** occupations in the metal industry; ~**geld** metal currency; coins, specie; ~**industrie** metal industry, non-ferrous metals industry; ~**kunde** metallurgy; ~**münze** metal coin; ~**notierungen** metal quotations, metal prices; ~**probe** assay; ~**verarbeitung** metal processing, metal working; ~**währung** metallic standard, metallic currency; ~**waren** hardware, metal goods.

Meterware f piece goods, material sold by the metre (US: meter).

Metist m party engaging in a *Metageschäft qv*.

Meuchelmord m treacherous murder, foul assassination.

Meuchelmörder m treacherous murderer, foul assassin.

Meuterei f mutiny; ~ **von Gefangenen** prison mutiny.

Meuterer m mutineer, participant in prison mutiny.

meutern v/i to mutiny, to mutineer.

Miet|ablösung key money, compensation to outgoing tenant; ~**abtretung** assignment of rent; ~**anlagen** rental equipment; ~**anlagengeschäft** leasing activities; ~**anpassung** rent adjustment, rent review; ~**aufhebung** tenancy termination (by court); ~**aufhebungsklage** petition to have a tenancy terminated; ~**aufwand** expense involved in renting; ~**ausfall** loss of rent; ~**ausfallversicherung** insurance against loss of rent; ~**ausfallwagnis** risk of loss of rent; ~**auto** hired car; ~**beendigung** termination of tenancy; ~**beihilfe** rent subsidy; ~**besitz** possession as a tenant, tenancy, leasehold; ~**bindungsanordnung** rent-fixing order; ~**bücherei** subscription library; ~**dauer** term of tenancy (*or* lease); ~**droschke** taxi(-cab); ~**einigungsamt** rent-mediation tribunal; ~**einigungssachen** rent-mediation cases; ~**einnahmen** rent receipts; ~**erhöhung** increase in rent, rent increase; ~~*svereinbarung rent-increase agreement*; ~**ertrag** rental income, rental return; ~**ertragswert** rental value; ~**fläche** rented floor space; **m**~**frei** *adj* rent-free; ~**garantie** rent guarantee; ~**gebäude** multiple dwelling, tenement, block of flats; ~**gebühr** rental fee; ~**gegenstand** leased object, rented property, demised premises; ~**geld** rent; ~**geldentschädigung** compensation for loss of rent income; ~**grundstück** property let for rent, demised premises; ~**(s)haus** apartment building, block of flats, tenement (house); ~**herabsetzung** rent reduction; ~**höhe** amount of rent; ~**inkasso** rent collection; ~**kauf** hire-purchase; ~**kaution** security for rent, rent deposit; ~**kosten** rent, hiring charge, rental fee; ~**kündigung** notice of termination of tenancy, notice to quit (by landlord); ~**nachlaß** remission of rent; ~**nebenkosten** ancillary costs (of tenancy); ~**objekt** = *Mietgegenstand qv*; ~**preis** rent, hire; ~**preisbindung** rent control; ~**preiserhöhung** = ~*erhöhung qv*; ~**preisfreigabe** decontrolling of rents; ~**preiskontrolle** rent control; ~**preispolitik** rent policy; ~**preisrecht** law on controlled rents; ~**preisüberhöhung** overcharging of rent; ~**räume** rented premises, demised premises, lodgings; ~**recht** law of tenancy; *soziales* ~~: *law on socially just tenancies*; ~**rückgang** rent reduction; ~**rückstände** arrears of rent; ~**sache** = ~*gegenstand qv*; ~**sätze** rental rates; ~**schuld** debts to pay rent, rent-debit, arrears of rent; ~**spiegel** representative list of rents; ~**skaserne** (large) tenement house; ~**streitigkeiten** tenancy disputes; ~**(en)- und Berechnungsverordnung** rent and rent-calculation regulations;

~- und Lastenbeihilfen grants for rents and public charges; **~- und Pachtrecht** landlord and tenant law; **~vereinbarung** tenancy agreement; lease (agreement); **~verfügung** tenancy order; **~verhältnis** tenancy, landlord and tenant relationship; *monatliches ~~: month-to- month-tenancy; (gerichtl.) verlängertes ~~: continuation tenancy;* **~verhandlungen** negotiations about a tenancy agreement; **~verlängerung** extension of tenancy (*or* lease), renewal of tenancy term; **~verlängerungsrecht** option to renew a tenancy; **~vertrag** tenancy agreement, lease; hiring agreement; **~vorauszahlung** prepayment of rent, rent payment in advance; **~wagen** hired car; **~wagenkosten** costs of a hired car (*after accident*); **~wagenverleih** hire-car service; **m~weise** *adj* by way of tenancy (*or* hire); **~wert** rental value; *steuerlicher ~~: assessed rental;* **~wohngrundstück** property for rented accommodation (*or* residential letting); **~wohnhaus** apartment building, tenement; **~wohnung** apartment, flat, dwelling; *pl* housing for rent; **~wohnverhältnisse** rented accommodation; **~wucher** usurious rent, charging exorbitant rent; **~zahlung** payment of rent; **~zeit** term of (the) tenancy; (*or* lease) *noch nicht abgelaufene ~~* unexpired term; **~zins** rent, rental, hire (*movables*); **~zinsforderung** claim for rent; **~zinsstop** rent freeze; **~zuschlag** extra charges on the rent; **~zuschuß** rent subsidy.

Miete *f* tenancy, hire; rent; **~ für e-e Etagenwohnung** rent for an apartment; **~ mit automatischer Erhöhungsklausel** progressive rent clause; **angemessene ~** fair rent; **ausbedungene ~** rent reserved; **die ~ kündigen** to give notice to terminate the tenancy (*or* lease); to give notice to quit; **fällige ~** rent due; **freie ~n** private sector rents; **gesetzlich zulässige ~** standard rent, legal rent; **Kostendeckende ~** cost-covering rent; **rückständige ~** rent arrears; **vereinbarte ~** agreed rent; **zur ~** on hire, to be let; **zur ~ wohnen** to live in rented accommodation.

mieten *v/t* to rent (*room, apartment*), to lease (*house*), to hire (*car, movables*), to charter (*ship, aircraft*).

Mieter *m* tenant, lessee, lodger, hirer (*movables*); charterer (*ship, aeroplane*); **~darlehen** loan by tenant to landlord; **~haftpflichtversicherung** tenant's liability insurance; **~kaution** tenant's deposit; **~leistungen** improvements and contributions by the tenant; *noch nicht abgewohnte ~~: unexhausted improvements;* **~rechte** tenant's rights; **~schutz** legal protection of tenants (*against notice to quit*), security of tenure; **~schutzgesetz** Protection of Tenants Act (*D, no longer in force*); **~vereinigung** tenant's association; **~vormerkliste** housing list; **~zuschuß** tenant's contribution (to building costs); **bereits vorhandener ~** sitting tenant; **dem ~ kündigen** to give notice of termination to the tenant; **gewerblicher ~** business tenant; **neuer ~** incoming tenant.

Mietling *m* hireling, mercenary.

Mikrofilmlesegerät *n* microfilm (*or* microfiche) reader.

Milch|ertrag milk yield; **~gesetz** Milk Act (*relating to milk production and distribution*); **~leistung** milking capacity; **~mädchenrechnung** overoptimistic estimate, simpleminded reasoning, exorbitant charge; **~panscher** adulterator of milk; **~produkte** dairy products; **~sammelstelle** milk collection centre; dairy; **~- und Fettgesetz** Milk and Fats Act, *German market régime for dairy products and fats;* **~verarbeitung** milk processing; **verbrauch** milk consumption; **~verordnung** ordinance concerning milk production; **~verpackung** packaging of milk, milk container, milk package; **~vieh** dairy

mildern

cattle; ~**viehherde** dairy herd; ~**wirtschaft** dairy industry, dairy farming.

mildern v/t to mitigate.

mildernd adj mitigating, extenuating, alleviating.

Milderung f extenuation, mitigation, alleviation; ~**sgrund** mitigation cause, ground for clemency; **auf ~ der Strafe plädieren** to plead in mitigation.

mildtätig adj charitable, kindhearted.

Mildtätigkeit f charity.

Militär n the military, armed forces, army; ~**akademie** military academy; ~**attaché** military attaché; ~**ausschuß** military committee; ~**behörde** military authority, military office; ~**bündnis** military alliance; ~**dienst** military service; ~ *ableisten: to serve (in the armed forces), to do one's military service;* ~**diktatur** military dictatorship; ~**führerschein** military driving licence; ~**gebiet** military zone; ~**gefängnis** military prison, US: stockade; ~**gericht** military tribunal, military commission, military court; ~**gerichtsbarkeit** military jurisdiction; ~**gerichtshof** military tribunal; ~**gewalt** military power, power of command; ~**gouverneur** military governor; ~**haushalt** military budget; ~**hilfe** military aid; ~**junta** military junta; ~**konvention** military convention; ~**luftfahrt** military aviation; ~**mission** military mission; ~**paß** service record book; ~**person** member of the armed forces; ~~**en**: *military personnel; für ~~en gesperrt: off limits;* ~**pflicht** compulsory military service, conscription; ~**polizei** military police; ~**regierung** military government; ~**richter** military judge; judge of a military tribunal; ~**staat** military state, stratocracy; ~**staatsanwalt** judge advocate; ~~ *in der Hauptverhandlung: trial judge advocate;* ~**strafgesetzbuch** military penal code; ~**strafrecht** military penal

Minderaufkommen

law; **m~tauglich** adj fit for active service, able-bodied; ~**tauglichkeit** fitness for military service, fitness for active service; ~**testament** military testament, soldier's will, sailor's will; ~**vergehen** offence against military law; ~**verwaltung** military administration, military government; ~**wesen** military matters; ~**zeit** time in the forces, military service.

Miliz f militia, special reserve.

Milliarde f milliard, a thousand million, US: billion; ~**nkredit** loan of one milliard (billion) or more.

Millionen|anleihe loan of several millions, enormous loan; ~**erbschaft** inheritance worth millions; ~**konkurs** bankruptcy involving millions in debts; ~**kredit** credit of one or several millions.

Minder|aufkommen revenue loss; ~**ausgabe** reduction of expenditure; **m~belastet** adj less incriminated; **m~bemittelt** adj low-income, poor; *fig* stupid; ~**betrag** deficit, shortage, shortfall; ~**bewertung** reduction in valuation; ~**einnahmen** shortfall in receipts, deficiency in receipts; ~**erlös** deficiency in proceeds; ~**ertrag** deficiency in proceeds; ~**gewicht** reduced weight, underweight, weight below a limit; ~**heit** → *Minderheit;* **m~jährig** adj minor, infant under age; ~**jähriger** *(der Minderjährige)* minor, young person, infant; *unterhaltsbedürftiger ~~: minor in need of maintenance; vernachlässigter ~~: neglected minor;* ~**jährigkeit** minority, infancy; ~**kaufmann** small trader, non-registrable merchant; ~**kosten** reduced cost; ~**leistung** deficient output, loss of efficiency; ~**lieferung** short shipment, short supply, part delivery; ~**nutzung** under-utilization; ~**umsatz** falling off in sales, reduced turnover; ~**ung** → *Minderung;* ~**wert** decrease in value, depreciation; *merkantiler ~~: loss in value upon resale (damaged automobile); technischer ~~: technical*

537

Minderheit

depreciation; ~**wertig** *adj* of small value, cheap, inferior; ~**wertigkeit** inferiority; ~**zahl** minority; *in der* ~~ *sein: to be in the minority;* ~**zahlung** reduction of payment, underpayment.

Minderheit *f* (*pl. Minderheiten* ~*en*) minority; ~**enfrage** minorities problem; ~**enrechte** rights of (*national, ethnic, religious etc*) minorities; ~**enschutz** protection of minorities; ~**enstatut** statute of minorities; ~**svotum** minority opinion, dissenting opinion; **in der** ~ **sein** to be outnumbered, to be in the minority; **nationale** ~ ethnic minority; **religiöse** ~ religious minority; **sprachliche** ~ linguistic minority; **völkische** ~ ethnic minority.

Minderheits|aktionär minority shareholder; ~**ansicht** minority opinion; ~**bericht** minority report; ~**beteiligung** minority participation, minority interest, minority holding; ~**gesellschafter** minority shareholder; ~**paket** minority holding; ~**partei** minority party; ~**recht** minority rights; ~**regierung** minority government, minority rule; ~**schutz** protection of minority rights.

mindern *v/t* to diminish, to reduce, to decrease; to demand a reduction.

Minderung *f* diminution, reduction, shrinkage; diminution of the (purchase) price *due to defect*; ~ **der Erwerbsfähigkeit** impairment of earning capacity.

Minderungs|anspruch warranty-claim for a reduction in the purchase (*or* contract) price; ~**klage** action for reduction in purchase price (*due to defects in the article sold*); ~**recht** right to a reduction in price due to a defect in the article sold.

Mindest|abnahme minimum purchasable amount; ~**abstand** minimum distance, minimum clearance; ~**akkordsatz** minimum job rate, minimum piece rate; ~**alter** minimum age, age limit; ~**anforderungen** minimum requirements;

Mindestrendite

~**angebot** lowest bid, lowest admissible offer; ~**arbeitsbedingungen** minimum working conditions; ~**auflage** guaranteed minimum circulation; ~**ausstattung** minimum equipment; ~**bargebot** minimum cash bid; ~**bedarf** minimum requirements; ~**bedingung** minimum condition; ~**beitrag** minimum contribution; ~**bestand** minimum stock, minimum inventory level; ~**besteuerung** minimum taxation; ~**betrag der Haushaltszulage** the minimum head-of-household allowance; ~**courtagesatz** minimum broker's commission; ~**deckung** minimum cover; ~**dividende** guaranteed dividend; ~**einkommen** minimum income; ~**einlage** minimum deposit; ~**einschluß** minimum margin requirements; ~**ertrag** lowest yield; ~**forderung** minimum claim; ~**freibetrag** minimum exemption, minimum standard deduction; ~**gebot** lowest bid, reserved price (*auction*); *ohne* ~~: *without reserve;* ~**gebühr** minimum fee; ~**gehalt** 1) minimum salary; ~**gehalt** 2) minimum content; ~**geschwindigkeit** minimum speed; ~**grenze** (lowest) limit; ~**größe** minimum size; ~**guthaben** minimum balance; ~**inventar** basic stock; ~**kapazität** marginal capacity, minimum performance; ~**kapital** minimum capital; ~**kleinverkaufspreis** minimum retail price; ~**lizenz** minimum royalty; ~**lohn** minimum wage, wage floor; ~**maß** minimum; ~**monatsentgelt** monthly minimum remuneration; ~**nennbetrag** minimum nominal sum; ~**preis** minimum price, lowest price, reserve price (*auction*); ~**prozentsatz** minimum percentage; ~**prüfstoff** *pat* minimum documentation; ~**prüfungsnoten** lowest-possible pass marks; ~**rand** minimum margin (*on documents*); ~**rendite** required rate of return, cut-off rate;

538

Mindestreserve

minimum yield; **~reserve** → *Mindestreserve;* **~saldogebühren** minimum balance charges; **~satz** minimum rate; **~sparsumme** minimum savings figure; **~strafe** minimum sentence; **~steuer** minimum tax; **~steuersatz** minimum tax rate; **~streitwert** lowest value of a matter in dispute; **~stundenlohn** minimum hourly wage (rate); **~umsatz** minimum turnover; **~unterstützungssatz** minimum allowance; **~urlaubsgesetz** Act (or statute) on minimum paid holiday; **~verdienst** minimum pay; **~vermögen** minimum (prescribed) assets; **~versicherungszeit** minimum period of insurance cover; **~voraussetzung** minimum prerequisite; **~wert** minimum value; **~wiederverkaufspreis** minimum resale price; **~zahl** minimum figure; *beschlußfähige* **~~**: *quorum;* **~zeichnung** minimum subscription.

Mindestreserve *f pl* **~n** safety fund, statutory reserve, minimum reserve(s), required reserve(s), minimum cash reserve; **~anforderung** minimum reserve requirements; **~dispositionen** arrangements to maintain minimum reserves; **~einlagen** minimum reserve deposits; **~erhöhung** increase in the minimum reserve requirement; **~npolitik** minimum reserve policy, policy as to bank's minimum reserve ratio; **~satz** required minimum reserve ratio; **~(n)system** safety fund system, minimum reserve system; **bei der Zentralbank hinterlegte und gesperrte ~n** special deposits.

Mineral|gewinnungsrechte rights to exploit mineral resources; **~lagerstätte** mineral deposit; **~öl** (mineral) oil, petroleum; **~ölbesteuerung** petroleum taxation; **~ölsteuer** mineral oil tax; **~ölsteuergesetz** mineral oil tax law; **~vorkommen** mineral deposits.

Minister *m* minister, Secretary of State, *US*: Secretary; **~anklage** impeachment of a minister; **~ausschuß** ministerial committee; **~ebene** ministerial level; **~konferenz** ministerial conference, conference of (Länder) ministers; **~ ohne Geschäftsbereich** minister without portfolio; **~präsident** premier, prime minister, *D*: minister-president *(of one of the Länder);* **~resident** resident minister; **~sessel** ministerial post, portfolio; **~verantwortung** ministerial responsibility; **bevollmächtigter ~** minister plenipotentiary.

Ministerial|beamter departmental official; **~beauftragter** ministerial commissioner *(for schools);* **~direktor** Director (General); **~dirigent** Assistant Director; **~erlaß** departmental order, ministerial order; **~rat** Ministerial Counsellor; **~runderlaß** interdepartmental order, departmental circular; **~zulage** extra pay for departmental officers.

Ministerium *n* ministry, government department, executive department; **von ~ zu Ministerium** interdepartmental, interministerial.

Minna *f (short for Grüne Minna)* Black Maria *(prison van).*

Minus|bestand stock deficit, **~betrag** deficiency, shortage, deficit; **~korrektur** downward adjustment; **~punkt** minus point; disadvantage; **~saldo** negative balance, deficit balance.

Misch|anbau growing of mixed crops; **~bestand** mixed growth *(forest);* **~betriebe** mixed enterprise; **~ehe** mixed marriage; **~fläche** mixed residential and business zone *US (or* area, *GB);* **~geldsystem** mixed money system; **~heirat** intermarriage; **~konzern** conglomerate, mixed enterprise; **~kredit** mixed credit; **~lagerung** common storage of goods belonging to different customers; **~preis** composite price, mixed price, blended price;

Mischling — **Mißtrauen**

~**tatbestände** mixed sets of facts; mixed statutory elements (*of an offence, a statutory provision*), hybrid provision; ~**verfahren** mixed proceedings, hybrid proceedings; ~**verwaltung** administration by interlocking authorities, mixed (Federal and Land) administration; ~**wald** mixed forest, forest of different species of trees; ~**zinssatz** composite interest rate.

Mischling *m* a person of mixed race; half-caste, half-breed; ~**skind** half-breed child, half-caste child.

mißachten *v/t* to disregard, to despise, to hold in contempt.

Mißachtung *f* disrespect, disregard, contempt; ~ **des Gerichts** contempt of court; *der ~~~ schuldig sein: standing in contempt.*

Mißbildung *f* deformity, malformation.

mißbilligen *v/t* to disapprove of.

Mißbilligung disapprobation, disapproval; ~**santrag** motion of censure; ~**svotum** vote of censure.

Mißbrauch *m* abuse, improper use; ~ **der Amtsgewalt** misuse of official authority, abuse of office; ~ **der Befehlsbefugnis** abuse of military authority; ~ **der Befugnis, über fremdes Vermögen zu verfügen** abuse of power over third party assets, breach of trust; ~ **des Arbeitsverhältnisses** abuse of status of employment; ~ **des Berufs** misuse of profession, professional malpractice; ~ **des Dienstverhältnisses zur Unzucht** abusing one's office or position to commit indecency; ~ **des Ermessens** abuse of discretionary power; ~ **des richterlichen Ermessens** abuse of judicial discretion; ~ **e-s Patents** abuse of a patent; ~ **e-s Rechts** misuse of a right; ~ **geschützter Daten** misuse of protected data; ~ **im Amt** abuse of office; ~ **öffentlicher Gelder** misapplication of public funds; ~**saufsicht** supervision to preclude abuses; control of abusive practices; ~**kontrolle** control of abusive practices; ~**sprinzip** principle of abuse; ~**verfahren** abuse proceedings (*cartel law*); ~ **von Ausweispapieren** improper use of identity papers; ~ **von Marktmacht** abuse of market power; ~ **wirtschaftlicher Macht** abuse of economic power; **sexueller** ~ **von Kindern** sexual abuse of children.

mißbrauchen *v/t* to abuse, to misuse.

mißbräuchlich *adj* abusive, (making) wrongful use.

mißdeuten *v/t* to misinterpret, to misconstrue, to place a wrong construction on.

Mißdeutung *f* misinterpretation, misconstruction.

Mißerfolg *m* failure, fiasco.

Mißernte *f* crop failure.

Missetat *f* misdeed, wrongful act.

Missetäter *m* culprit, delinquent, wrongdoer.

Mißfallen *n* disapproval, disfavour.

Mißgeburt *f* monster, monstrosity.

Mißgeschick *n* misfortune.

Mißgriff *m* blunder, bad mistake.

mißhandeln *v/t* to abuse, to ill-treat.

Mißhandlung *f* maltreatment, ill-treatment, abuse; ~ **von Abhängigen** maltreatment of dependent children and defenceless persons; ~ **von Kindern** cruelty to children; ~ **schwere** ~ extreme cruelty.

Mißhelligkeit *f* unpleasantness, disagreement, discord, dissension.

Mission *f* mission; **diplomatische** ~ diplomatic mission; **geheime** ~ secret mission.

Missions|angehöriger member of a (*diplomatic or consular*) mission, *pl*: ~**angehörige**: mission staff; ~**chef** head of mission; *e-n ~~ beglaubigen: to accredit a head of mission.*

Mißkredit *m* discredit, disrepute; *in* ~ *bringen: to discredit, to bring into disrepute.*

Mißstand *m* nuisance, grievance, deplorable state of affairs; ~**suntersuchungen** investigation of a grievance; *e-n* ~ *beseitigen* to remedy a grievance.

Mißtrauen *n* distrust, want of confi-

mißtrauen

dence; ~**santrag** motion of no confidence, motion of censure; ~**sgrundsatz** principle of mistrusting other road users (*in complying with traffic regulations*) ~**svotum** vote of no confidence; *konstruktives* ~~ *"constructive" vote of no confidence (coupled with the vote for a new Federal Chancellor).*

mißtrauen *v/i* to distrust, to mistrust, to be suspicious of.

Mißverhältnis *n* disproportion; ~ **zwischen Eigenkapital und Fremdkapital** disproportion between one's capital resources and indebtedness; **im auffälligen** ~ conspicuously out of proportion.

mißverständlich *adj* ambiguous, liable to be misunderstood.

Mißverständlichkeit *f* ambiguity, likelihood of being misunderstood.

Mißverständnis *n* misunderstanding; **ein** ~ **ausräumen** to remove a misunderstanding.

mißverstehen *v/t, v/reflex* to misunderstand, to misapprehend.

Mißwirtschaft *f* mismanagement, maladministration.

Mitangeklagter *m* (*der Mitangeklagte*), co-accused, co-defendant, joint defendant.

Mitanmelder *m pl*: joint applicants (*for a patent*).

Mitarbeit *f* collaboration, help, assistance, participation; ~ **der Ehegatten** marital collaboration; **kostenlose** ~ unpaid work; **zur** ~ **heranziehen** to engage s.o.'s services, to call on s.o.'s advice, to ask s.o. to help.

Mitarbeiter *m* staff member, staffer, fellow worker, colleague, (fellow) employee; contributor (*press*); *pl also*: staff; ~-**Aktienbeteiligungsplan** employee share scheme, stock option plan for staff members; ~**förderung** personnel development; ~ **im Außendienst** field worker, sales representative, *pl*: field staff; ~ **im Innendienst** *pl*: in-house staff; ~**schaft** staff, personnel; ~**stab** staff; ~ **und Mitarbeiterinnen** men and women

mitbestimmen

employees, colleagues; ~**vertretung** staff representation; **ausländische** ~ foreign employees, non-German personnel; **erfahrener** ~ experienced colleague; **freiberuflicher** ~ free-lance contributor; **hauptamtlicher** ~ full-time member of the staff; **juristischer** ~ legal assistant; **kaufmännischer** ~ commercial employee, clerk; **leitende** ~ *pl* executive personnel, managerial staff; **nebenamtlicher** ~ part-time member of the staff; **übertariflicher** ~ employee paid above collective bargaining rates; **unbezahlte** ~ voluntary staff.

Mitausschließlichkeitsrecht *n* co-exclusive right.

Mitautor *m* co-author.

Mitbegründer *m* co-founder, co-originator.

Mitbeklagter *m* (*der Mitbeklagte*) co-defendant (*civil proceedings*).

Mitbelastung *f* incrimination jointly with another; joint encumbrance (*on several plots of real estate*).

mitbenutzen *v/t* to share in the use of, to use jointly.

Mitbenutzer *m/pl* joint users, concurrent users.

Mitbenutzung *f* joint use, concurrent use; ~**srecht** right of joint use, concurrent user.

Mitberechtigter *m* (*der Mitberechtigte*) jointly entitled person, co-beneficiary.

Mitberechtigung *f* joint entitlement; ~ *am Geschäftsanteil: joint holding of a share.*

Mitbeschuldigter *m* (*der Mitbeschuldigte*) co-accused, co-defendant.

Mitbesitz *m* joint possession, joint tenancy (*land, houses*).

mitbesitzen *v/i, v/t* to hold jointly, to posses jointly, to own jointly.

Mitbesitzer *m* joint holder(s), joint proprietor(s).

mitbestimmen *v/i* to exercise co-determination rights, to have an influence on decisions, to have a voice in the management, *mitbestimmt: co-determined by employees.*

541

Mitbestimmung *f* co-determination, participatory decision making, employee participation in management; ~**sgesetz** Co-determination (in Industry) Act; ~**srecht** right of co-determination in industry, right to have a say in management; **betriebliche** ~ employee participation in company operations, industrial democracy; **paritätische** ~ parity co-determination, management-labour parity; **überbetriebliche** ~ external co-management *or* co-determination.

mitbeteiligt *adj* associated with, privy to (crime), taking part in, s. o., to get a lift.

Mitbeteiligter *m* (*der Mitbeteiligte*) participant, associate, accomplice.

Mitbeteiligung *f* participation, worker participation, joint interest, copartnership.

Mitbewerber *m* competitor, contestant.

Mitbewohner *m* coinhabitant, fellow lodger.

Mitbieten *n* (participation in) bidding, competitive bidding.

Mitbietungsrecht *n* right to bid; ~~ *des Verkäufers: right to reserved bid.*

Mitbürge *m* co-surety, co-guarantor, joint guarantor; co-sponsor.

Mitbürger *m* fellow citizen(s), fellow townsman.

Mitbürgschaft *n* co-suretyship, collective guarantee.

Miteigentum *n* co-ownership, joint ownership, common ownership, common property, joint property, condominium; ~ **an Grundstücken** co-ownership in land; ~ **nach Bruchteilen**, tenancy in common, co-ownership by fractional shares; ~**santeil** co-ownership share; *Tausendstel-* ~~: *per mille interest*; ~ **zur gesamten Hand** joint ownership; **quotenmäßiges** ~ proportionate share in ownership.

Miteigentümer *n* co-owner, co-proprietor, joint owner, part-owner, fellow-owner, *pl also:* common owners; ~**gemeinschaft** association of co-owners; ~ **nach Bruchteilen** *pl* fractional co-owner(s), tenants in common, part owners; ~ **sein** to hold concurrently, to hold as co-owners; ~ **zur gesamten Hand** joint co-owners.

Miterbe *m* co-heir, joint heir, fellow heir; ~ **sein** to inherit jointly; ~**nanteil** joint share in an inheritance; ~**ngemeinschaft** = *Erbengemeinschaft qv*.

Miterbin *f* co-heiress.

Miterfinder *m* joint inventor, fellow inventor, co-inventor.

Miterfinderschaft *f* joint inventorship.

mitfahren *v/i* to travel along with s. o., to get a lift.

Mitfahrer *m* fellow-traveller, (car)-passenger; ~**zentrale** car passenger agency.

mitfinanzieren *v/t* to help to finance, to join in the financing of, to finance part of.

mitführen *v/t* to carry (*documents*); to join in the management, to act as joint trader (*business*).

Mitführen *n* carrying, taking along.

Mitgarant *m* joint guarantor, co-guarantor.

Mitgefangener *m* co-prisoner.

Mitgeschäftsführer *m* co-manager, co-director (*GmbH*).

Mitgesellschafter *m* co-partner, fellow partner, co-investor, co-shareholder.

Mitgift *f* trousseau, dowry, marriage portion; ~**jäger** fortune hunter, dowry hunter; ~**versicherung** dowry insurance.

Mitgläubiger *m* co-creditor; joint creditor.

Mitglied *n* member, card holder; ~ **auf Lebenszeit** life member; ~ **des Oberhauses** peer; ~ **des Parteivorstandes** party official, member of the party executive; ~**er müssen geschlossen ihr Amt niederlegen** members shall resign as a body; ~ **kraft Amtes** ex officio member; ~**sabzeichen** membership badge; ~**sbeitrag** membership fee; ~**schaft** → *Mitglied-*

schaft; **~schein** membership certificate; **~sland** member country; **~snummer** membership number; **~spapiere** securities representing membership (*i. e. shares*); **~(s)staat** member state, member nation; **aktives ~** active member; **als ~ aufnehmen** to admit as a member; **als ~ ausscheiden** to cease to be a member, to withdraw one's membership; **angeschlossenes ~** affiliate member; **assoziiertes ~** associate member; **ausscheidendes ~** withdrawing member; *pl also*: members withdrawing; **beigeordnetes ~** associate member; **beratendes ~** consultant member; **ehrenamtliches ~** honorary member; **ein ~ ausschließen** to expel a member; **eingetragenes ~** enrolled member, registered member; **förderndes ~** subscribing member; **geschäftsführendes ~** managing member (*of the board etc*); **hinzugewähltes ~** elected member, cooptee; **korrespondierendes ~** consultant member; **neues ~** new member, entrant; **nominelles ~** nominal member, pro forma member; **ordentliches ~** regular member, full member; **planmäßiges ~** regular member; **proforma ~** pro forma member, nominal member; **stellvertretendes ~** deputy member; **ursprüngliches ~** initial member; **zahlendes ~** supporter, paying member; **zuwiderhandelndes ~** non-complying member.

Mitglieder|abwerbung raiding; **~beiträge** membership fees, dues, subscription(s); **~klasse** class of members, occupational class (*insurance*); **~kreis** the members; *aus dem ~~: from among the members;* **~recht** membership rights; **~vermögen** property of the members, members' assets; **~versammlung** members' meeting, meeting of members, body of members; *außerordentliche ~~: extraordinary meeting;* **~vertreterversammlung** *ins* member's representatives meeting; **~verzeichnis** list of members; **~werbung** canvassing for members, touting for new members, raiding.

Mitgliedschaft *f* membership; **~ bei der Börse** exchange seat; **beitragsfreie ~** free membership, contribution-free membership; **die ~ erwerben** to become a member, to acquire membership; **die ~ kündigen** to give notice of termination of membership, to opt out; **korporative ~** corporate membership.

Mitgliedschafts|antrag application for membership; **~ausweis** membership card; **~recht** right of membership, membership rights; **~verhältnis** membership relation; **~voraussetzungen** qualification for membership; **~zwang** compulsory membership.

Mitgründer *m* joint founder, cofounder.

Mithaft *f* joint arrest; joint attachment (*levy of execution*).

mithaften *v/i* to be jointly liable.

Mithäftling *m* fellow prisoner.

Mithaftung *f* joint liability.

Mitherausgeber *m* joint editor, co-editor, joint publisher.

Mitherrschaft *f* joint rule, co-rule.

Mithöreinrichtung *f* monitoring device, a "bug".

Mitinhaber *m* co-owner, co-proprietor; **~ e-r Lizenz** joint licensee; **~ e-s Patents** joint patentee.

Mitinteressent *m* interested party.

Mitkandidat *m* running mate, fellow candidate.

Mitkläger *m* co-plaintiff, joint plaintiff.

Mitkontrahent *m* co-contractor, co-contracting party.

Mitläufer *m* fellow traveller, hanger-on, sympathizer; **~effekt** band wagon effect.

Mitmieter *m* joint tenant, co-tenant.

Mitnahme *f* taking away, removal, profit taking, cashing in.

mitnehmen *v/t* to take away; to cash in (on profits).

Mitpächter *m* joint tenant, co-tenant).

543

Mitreeder *m* co-owner of a ship.
Mitschneiden *n* (unauthorized) tape recording, bugging.
mitschneiden *v/t* to record on a tape recorder (stealthily), to record (surreptitiously), to bug.
Mitschuld *f* joint guilt; contributory negligence.
mitschuldig *adj* jointly guilty; **beiderseits** ~ in pari delicto.
Mitschuldiger *m* (*der Mitschuldige*) jointly guilty party, accomplice.
Mitschuldner *m* joint debtor, co-debtor.
Mitsichführen *n* carrying, taking along.
Mitspracherecht *n* a say, voice (in the management), right of representation, right of co-determination.
mitstimmen *v/i* to take part in the voting, to exercise one's vote, to join in the vote.
Mittäter *m* joint offender, joint perpetrator, co-principal (= *co-principal*), particeps criminis, principal in the first degree, accomplice; **selbständiger Mittäter** (*zivilrechtl*) concurrent tortfeasor.
Mittäterschaft *n* joint commission of crime, complicity, perpetration as co-principal(s).
mitteilen *v/t* to inform, to notify, to advise, to communicate, to impart, to transmit.
Mitteilender *m* (*der Mitteilende*) the person giving notice (*etc cf mitteilen*).
mitteilsam *adj* communicative, talkative, voluble.
Mitteilung *f* information, notice, notification, communication, advice; ~ **der Unzustellbarkeit** notice of non-service; **~sblatt** official bulletin, newsletter; **~spatent** communicated patent; **~spflicht** duty to report, duty to inform, *pl also* notification duties; ~ **über nicht erfolgte Zahlung** advice of non-payment; **amtliche** ~ official communication, official notice; **dem Aussageverweigerungsrecht unterliegende** ~ privileged communication; **erforderliche** ~ due notice; **gegenteilige** ~ notification to the contrary; **innerbetriebliche** ~ inter-office (*or* internal) communication; **jmdm von etwas ~ machen** to inform s. o. of sth; **mündliche** ~ verbal communication, oral information; **öffentliche** ~ public notice, advertisement; **sachdienliche ~en** pertinent information; **schriftliche** ~ notice in writing, written communication; **telegrafische** ~ telegraphic communication; **ohne vorherige** ~ without prior notice; **urkundliche ~en** documentary communications; **vertrauliche** ~ confidential communication.
Mittel *n* (1) means; **berauschende** ~ intoxicants, drugs, **ein ~ zum Zweck** a means to an end; **empfängnisverhütende** ~ contraceptives; **unzulässige** ~ unallowed means, non-permissible methods;
Mittel *pl* (2) resources, funds, means, finances, appropriations; **~ansammlung** accumulation of funds; **~aufbringung** raising of money; **~aufnahme** borrowing, raising of funds; **~aufkommen** accrual of resources, yield of revenue, composition of resources; **~beschaffung** borrowing, raising funds; **~einsatz** employment of funds; **~entzug** withdrawal of funds; **m~los** *adj* destitute, impecunious; **~losigkeit** lack of means, destitution, impecuniousness; **~losigkeitszeugnis** poverty certificate, lack-of-means certificate; **~überhänge** surplus resources; **~überlassung** lending, assignment of assets; **~verwendung** employment of resources; **~zuweisung** allocation of funds, appropriation of funds; grant-in-aid; **aufgenommene** ~ borrowed funds; **bereitgestellte** ~ funds made available; **beträchtliche** ~ ample means; **bewilligte** ~ appropriated funds; **durchlaufende** ~ transmitted monies; **eigene** ~

(one's) own resources, capital and reserves; **eingeplante** ~ earmarked capital; **einwandfreie** ~ permissible methods; **entsprechend terminierte** ~ resources available for corresponding periods; **erforderliche** ~ required funds, necessary appropriations; **erststellige** ~ monies lent on first mortgage; **finanzielle** ~ financial resources; **flüssige** ~ liquid resources, liquid funds, available funds, liquid assets; **frei verfügbare** ~ spare cash; **fremde** ~ borrowed funds, funds from outside sources; **gemeingefährliche** ~ means endangering the public; **greifbare** ~ quick assets, ready means; **haftende** ~ liable funds; **kapitalmarktreife** ~ funds ready for employment on the capital market; **längerfristige** ~ medium-term loans; **liquide** ~ = *flüssige* ~ *qv*; **öffentliche** ~ public funds; **private** ~ private means, private capital; **staatliche** ~ state resources, government(al) resources; **überschüssige** ~ surplus funds; **verfügbare** ~ available means (*or* funds); **zugesagte** ~ promised funds; **zweckentfremdete** ~ diverted funds, misused funds; **zweckgebundene** ~ earmarked funds.

Mittel|abstandslinie equidistance line (*maritime law*); ~**behörden** regional authorities; ~**betrieb** medium-sized enterprise; **m~fristig** *adj* medium-term; ~**gang** aisle (*cinema*); ~**gebühr** standard medium fee; ~**größe** medium size; ~**kurs** mean rate (*between buying and selling rate*), middle market quotation (*securities*), central rate, middle price; ~**linie** centre line. ~**punkt der Lebensinteressen** centre of vital interests; ~**punktschule** central rural school, centralized regional school; ~**schule** (=) intermediate school, *US:* junior high school; ~**smann** middleman, intermediary, go-between; ~**sorte** medium quality, middling; ~**sperson** middleman, intermediary, go-between; ~**stand** → *Mittelstand;* ~**streifen** central reservation, highway, median (*strip*); ~**wert** mean (value), average value; *arithmetischer* ~~: *arithmetic mean*; *gewogener* ~~: *weighted average*.

mittelbar *adj* indirect, consequential, remote.

Mittelbarkeit *f* indirectness.

Mittelstand *m* middle classes, bourgeoisie; *gewerblicher* ~~: *small and medium-sized business, small-scale industry*; **gehobener** ~ the upper middle-classes.

mittelständisch *adj* middle-class, small to medium-sized (*enterprises*).

Mittelstands|ausschuß small businessmen's committee; ~**hilfe** assistance for small-scale traders; ~**politik** policy towards the middle classes, policy on small-scale industry; **m~politisch** *adj* relating to middle-class interests; ~**programm** middle-class programme.

Mittlertätigkeit *f* role of intermediary, broker's activities.

Mitunternehmer *m* joint contractor, co-partner, co-owner of a business enterprise; ~**anteil** interest in a jointly-owned business, co-partnership interest; ~**schaft** *f* joint ownership of a business enterprise, co-partnership.

mitunterschreiben *v/t* to sign together with another party, to sign jointly, to co-sign.

Mitunterschrift *f* joint signature, co-signature, counter-signature.

Mitunterzeichner *m* co-signatory, one of several signatories.

Mitunterzeichnung *f* = *Mitunterschrift qv*.

Miturheber *m* co-author, joint copyright-holder.

Miturheberrecht *n* joint copyright.

Miturheberschaft *f* joint authorship, co-authorship.

Mitursache *f* concurrent cause, contributing factor, additional cause.

mitverantwortlich *adj* jointly responsible, co-responsible.

Mitverantwortung *f* joint responsibility, co-responsibility.

Mitverbundener m (*der Mitverbundene*) party jointly committed.

Mitverfasser m joint author, co-author.

Mitverklagen n joinder of party defendant, adding as a defendant.

mitverklagen v/t to sue jointly, to add as a defendant.

Mitverpflichteter m (*der Mitverpflichtete*) jointly obligated party, jointly committed party.

Mitverschluß m dual control, dual control lock.

Mitverschulden n contributory negligence, US: comparative negligence: **beiderseitiges** ~ mutual contributory negligence.

mitversichern v/t to insure (*s.o. or sth*) together with (*s.o. or sth*), to insure jointly.

Mitversicherer m co-insurer.

Mitversicherung co-insurance.

Mitverteidiger co-defence counsel, additional defence counsel.

Mitverursachung contributory causation, additional cause.

Mitverwaltung participation in the management, sharing in the administration, joint administration.

Mitvormund m co-guardian, joint guardian.

mitwirken v/i to help to do sth, to contribute, to co-operate, to take part in.

mitwirkend adj concurrent, contributory.

Mitwirkender m (*der Mitwirkende*) participant, helper.

Mitwirkung f participation, help, co-operation; ~**spflicht** duty to cooperate; ~**srecht** right to participate in the administration, right to participate in the performance; ~**sverbot** ban on participation in management; **echte** ~ playing a genuine part; **gutachtliche** ~ advisory assistance by an expert.

Mitwissen n privity, knowledge (*of a secret or crime*).

Mitwisser m privy, person who has knowledge of another's crime; confidant, accessory.

Mitwisserschaft f privity or knowledge, knowledge of another's crime.

Mitzeichner m co-subscriber, joint underwriter, co-signatory.

Mitzeichnung f joint subscription, joint underwriting, co-signature, counter-signature.

Mitzessionar m co-assignee.

Möbel n piece of furniture, *pl* furnishings; ~**bau** furniture making; ~**fernverkehr** long-distance removal, long-haul movers; ~**geschäft** furniture store; ~**spedition** removal contractors, moving company; ~**transport** furniture transport, removal.

Mobiliar n furniture, furnishings.

Mobiliar|erbe heir to personal estate; ~**hypothek** chattel mortgage; ~**klage** action for movables, action for replevin; ~**kredit** loan on movable property; ~**pfandrecht** pledge, chattel mortgage; ~**pfändung** levy of execution, distress on movable goods, seizure of chattels; ~**schuld** obligation to supply movables; ~**sicherheit** chattel mortgage, collateral security over movable goods; ~**steuer** tax on movable property; ~**vermögen** movables, personal property, furniture; ~**versicherung** furniture insurance, contents insurance; insurance on household goods; ~**zwangsvollstreckung** levy of execution (on movable goods).

Mobilien f/pl movables, goods and chattels, personal property.

Mobilisierungszusage f promise of rediscount (*by Central Bank*).

Mobilität f mobility; **berufliche** ~ occupational mobility.

Modalitäten f/pl terms of procedure, arrangements, terms of agreement, details.

Mode|artikel fashion goods; ~**geschäft** fashion house, fashion store, fashion shop; ~**schmuck** costume jewellery, dress jewellery, fashion jewellery; ~**schule** school of fashion design; ~**spionage** fashion spying; ~**waren** novelties, fancy goods, fashion articles.

Modell *n* model, pattern, prototype; ~**bau** making of models; ~**bauer** model-maker, pattern maker; ~**macher** model-maker, pattern maker; ~**schutz** legal protection for models and patterns, protection as registered designs; ~**studien** pilot studies; ~**zeichnung** model drawing.

Modelleur *m* pattern maker.

Modernisierung *f* modernization, streamlining; ~**sbeihilfe** improvement grant; ~**darlehen** home improvement loan.

Mogelpackung *f* cheating pack, deceptive packaging.

Möglichkeit *f* possibility, practicability, feasibility, opportunity; ~ **der Nichtteilnahme** (chance of) opting out; ~ **der vorzeitigen Ablösung** option for compounding by making a lump-sum advance payment; **entfernte** ~ remote possibility, off-chance; **objektive** ~**en** practical possibilities; **unbegrenzte** ~**en** unlimited opportunities.

Mole *f* pier, mole, jetty.

Molkereigenossenschaft *f* co-operative dairy.

Molkereiprodukte *n/pl* dairy products.

Molotow-Cocktail *m* molotov cocktail, petrol bomb.

Moment *n* (*pl Momente* = ~*e*) factor, element; **anregende** ~**e** encouraging factors, stimulating features; **ausschlaggebendes** ~ determining cause; **beunruhigendes** ~ cause for disquiet; **konjunkturelle** ~ cyclical factors; **retardierendes** ~ retarding factor, delaying factor.

Monarch *m* monarch, sovereign.

Monarchie *f* monarchy; **absolute** ~ absolute monarchy; **konstitutionelle** ~ constitutional monarchy; **parlamentarische** ~ constitutional monarchy with parliamentary government.

Monarchismus *m* monarchism.

Monarchist *m* monarchist, royalist.

Monat *m* month, calendar month; **im letzten** ~ last month; ultimo; **laufender** ~ current month; **pro** ~ per month, monthly; **vom ersten des** ~**s an** on or after the first of the month.

Monats|abschluß monthly settlement; ~**abschnitt** period of a month; ~**ausweis** monthly return, monthly report; ~**bericht** monthly report, monthly bulletin; ~**bilanz** monthly balance, monthly return; ~**durchschnitt** monthly average; ~**endstand** end-of-month figure; ~**frist** period of a month, monthly period, a month's time; *binnen* ~~: *within the period of a month*; ~**gehalt** monthly salary; ~**geld** loan for one month, loan repayable within one month, monthly allowance; ~**karte** monthly ticket; ~**kompensation** monthly settlement; ~**lohn** monthly wages; ~**lohnsteuertabelle** monthly wage tax table; ~**mittel** monthly mean; ~**rate** monthly payment, monthly instalment (= installment); ~**rhythmus** monthly cycle, month-to-month trend; ~**ultimo** on the last of the month, end-of-month settlement; ~**umsatz** monthly turnover; ~**verdienst** monthly earnings; ~**wechsel** monthly allowance (for students from parents); ~**wert** monthly value, *pl* monthly data; *rechnerischer* ~~: *computed monthly value*.

monetär *adj* monetary.

Monetarismus *m* monetarism.

monetisieren *v/t* to turn into money.

Monierbauweise *f* reinforced-concrete method of building.

monieren *v/t* to remind (*s. o. of sth*), to give a reminder, to complain.

Monitum *n* query, reminder, warning, complaint.

monogam *adj* monogamous.

Monogamie *f* monogamy.

monokausal *adj* having only one cause, involving a single cause.

Monokultur *f* single-crop farming.

Monometallismus *m* monometallism (*currency*).

Monopol *n* monopoly; ~**abgabe**

Montage / **Mortalität**

monopoly levy; ~**betrieb** monopoly enterprise; ~**erzeugnis** proprietary article; ~**gesellschaft** monopoly company; ~**gesetzgebung** monopoly legislation; ~**gewinn** monopoly profits; ~**gut** proprietary article; ~**inhaber** holder of a monopoly, monopolist; ~**jäger** *US:* trust buster; ~**kapital** monopoly capital; ~**kapitalismus** monopoly capitalism; ~**kommission** Monopolies Commission (*German statutory advisory body of independent experts*); ~**mißbrauch** improper use of monopoly, abuse of monopoly; ~**preis** monopoly price; ~**recht** monopoly right, law of monopoly; ~**sache** monopoly case; ~**stellung** monopoly position; ~**vereinbarung** monopoly agreement; ~**vergehen** offence against anti-trust laws, monopoly offence; ~**ware** monopoly goods; ~**zuwiderhandlung** monopoly offence, infringement against anti-trust laws; **staatliches** ~ government monopoly; **totales** ~ perfect monopoly.

Montage *f* assembly (work), subassembly, installation; ~**abteilung** assembly department; ~**betrieb** assembly shop, assembly plant; ~**fabrik** subassembly factory, assembly plant; ~**firma** assembly firm; ~**gebühren** installation charges; ~**gehälter** installation salaries; ~**löhne** installation wages; ~**gruppe** unit assembly; ~**kosten** installation costs; ~**tätigkeit** assembly work; ~**werkstatt** assembly shop.

Montan|aktien mining shares, shares in the iron and coal industries; ~**anleihe** European Coal and Steel Community loan; ~**bereich** the coal and steel sector; coal and steel industries; ~**entflechtung** decartelization of the German coal and steel industries; ~**gemeinschaft** Coal and Steel Community; ~**gesellschaften** coal and steel companies; ~**industrie** coal and steel industries; ~**länder** countries of the European Coal and Steel Community; ~**mitbestimmungsgesetz** (*D 1951*) Coal and Steel Co-Determination Act; ~**papiere** securities of the coal and steel industries; ~**umlage** European Coal and Steel Community levy; ~**union** Coal and Steel Pool; ~**unionsumlage** = *Montanumlage qv;* ~**werte** coal mining and steel shares.

Monteur *m* fitter, mechanic.

Moorschutzrecht *n* law for the protection of moors.

Moral *f* morals, moral code; **allgemeine** ~ public morals.

Moratorium *n* moratorium.

Mord *m* murder, capital murder, first-degree murder; ~**anklage** murder charge; ~**anschlag** murderous plot; ~ **auf Bestellung** contract murder, murder for hire; ~**brand** setting fire with intention to kill; ~**dezernat** homicide commission, police department handling murder cases; ~**drohung** threat of murder; ~**gier** lust to kill; ~**kommando** killer squad; ~**kommission** homicide squad; ~**komplott** conspiracy to commit murder; ~**lust** murderous lust, bloodlust; ~**prozeß** murder trial; ~**verdacht** suspicion of murder; ~**versuch** attempt to murder, homicidal attempt; ~**vorsatz** malice aforethought; **des ~es an jmdm angeklagt sein** to be indicted for the murder of s. o.; **gedungener** ~ assassination; **gewöhnlicher** ~ non-capital murder; **politischer** ~ political murder, assassination; **versuchter** ~ attempted murder; **wegen ~es verurteilen** to convict of murder.

Mörder *m* murderer, murderer in the first degree; ~**bande** gang of murderers; ~**grube** den of cutthroats; **gedungener** ~ hired murderer, hired assassin.

Morgen *m ancient agricultural square measure of different sizes; approx one acre.*

Mortalität *f* mortality; ~**s|tafel** decrement table.

Motiv *n* motive, inducement; ~**irrtum** error in motivation, error in the inducement.

motivieren *v/i* to motivate.

Motivierung *f* motivation, statement of reasons.

Motor|enbau engine manufacturing; ~**en und Fahrzeugwerte** motor and vehicle-building shares; ~**fahrrad** moped; ~**fahrzeug** motor vehicle; ~**kraftstoff** motor fuel; ~**leistung** engine capacity, engine make (*for tax purposes*).

Motorisierung *f* motorization, spread of car ownership.

Mühewaltung *f* trouble taken; *für Ihre* ~ *dankend:* thanking you for the trouble you have taken (*or: for your trouble*).

Mühlen|besitzer owner of a (corn) mill; ~**industrie** flour-milling industry; ~**recht** prerogative to operate a mill; ~**regal** = ~*recht qv*.

Müll|abfuhr refuse collection, rubbish collection, collection of waste, *US:* garbage collection; ~**abfuhrmann** refuse collector, rubbish man, dustbin man, dust man; ~**abladeplatz** refuse pit, rubbish tip, *US:* dumping ground; ~**ablagerung** dumping refuse; ~**beseitigung** disposal of refuse, garbage disposal *unbefugte* ~~: *unlicensed disposal of waste*; ~**deponie** official dumping ground; garbage dump (*US*) refuse tip, rubbish tip (*GB*); ~**quote** garbage quota; ~**verbrennung** waste incineration, refuse incineration; ~**verbrennungsanlage** waste incinerator, refuse incinerator; ~**schlucker** waste chute; ~**tonne** refuse bin, dustbin, *US:* garbage can; ~**wagen** rubbish lorry, refuse collection lorry, *US:* garbage truck.

Multikausalität *f* multiple causation.

Multis *pl* multinationals.

Mündel *n* ward, protected person; ~**geld** trust money (for a ward), ward's money; **m**~**sicher** *adj* eligible for trusts (*for wards*), gilt-edged; ~~ *angelegtes Geld:* authorized investments; ~**sicherheit** trustee investment status (*of securities*), eligibility for trust investment; ~**vermögen** ward's property; ~**wertpapiere** securities invested for a ward, investments on trust.

mündig *adj* of age; **jmdn für** ~ **erklären** to declare s. o. to have reached majority; ~ **werden** to come of age, to reach majority.

Mündigkeit *f* full age, majority, responsible age; ~**salter** majority; ~**serklärung** declaring a person to be of age.

mündlich *adj* verbal, oral, viva voce, nuncupative (*will*), *adv also:* by word of mouth.

Mündlichkeit *f* orality, oral proceedings, oral presentation; ~**grundsatz** principle of orality; ~**sprinzip** = ~*sgrundsatz qv*.

Mundraub *m obs* petty larceny of food, theft of small quantities of food (*for immediate consumption*).

Mundwerbung *f* word-of-mouth sales promotion, canvassing.

Munition *f* ammunition; ~**sfabrik** munitions factory; ~**slager** ammunition dump; ~**sverwaltung** control of ammunition.

Muntbruch *m obs* breach of parental authority by removing a child.

Münz|amt mint; ~**automat** slot machine; ~**delikt** coinage offence; ~**direktor** warden of the mint; ~**einheit** coin denomination; ~**einnahmen** seigniorage; ~**einwurf** slot; insertion of a coin; ~**fälschung** coin counterfeiting; ~**fernsehen** pay television, pay-as you-see (television), pay-per-view TV, Payola; ~**fernsprecher** public telephone, coin-operated telephone, *US:* pay phone; ~**fund** treasure trove of coins; ~**fuß** standard of coinage: *ratio of the standard weight (of gold, silver) to the number of coins to be struck;* ~**geld** coins, metal money; ~**gerechtigkeit** prerogative of coinage; ~**gesetz** coinage law; monetary law; ~**gold** monetary gold; ~**gutschrift** amount

Münze   **Mustervordruck**

credited to government on account of coinage; ~**hoheit** coining prerogative (*of sovereign, state*), monetary sovereignty, right of coinage; ~**metalldepot** coinage metal depository; ~**metallprüfanstalt** assay office; ~**monopol** monopoly of the right of coinage; ~**parität** parity of coins; ~**prägung** minting; ~**regal** coining prerogative (of sovereign), coinage prerogative; ~**rohling** planchet; ~**silber** standard silver; ~**sorten** types of coins, foreign coins; ~**sortiermaschine** coin assorter; ~**tankstelle** coin-operated petrol station (*or:* filling station) (*US: gasoline station*); ~**telefon** pay phone, coin-operated telephone; ~**umlauf** coin circulation; ~**- und Barrengold** gold coin and bullion; ~**verbrechen** coinage crime; ~**verfälschung** debasement of currency; ~**vergehen** coinage offence; ~**verringerung** impairing coins; ~**verschlechterung** debasement of currency, debasement of coinage; ~**waschsalon** coin laundry; coin-operated launderette; ~**wäscherei** coin-operated launderette; ~**wechsel** change of coins; ~**wechselschwindel** ringing the changes; ~**wechsler** change machine; ~**wert** assay value; ~**wertprüfung** assay; ~**wesen** coinage, minting; ~**zähler** coinmeter.

Münze *f* (*pl Münzen* = ~n) coin; mint; ~ *mit gesetzlich vorgesehenem Feingehalt*: *standard coin*; **gesetzliche** ~ lawful coins, sterling; **in barer** ~ **zahlen** to pay in specie, to pay all; **in** ~**n** in specie, in the form of coins; **untergewichtige** ~ subweight coin; **vollwichtige** ~ standard money.

Musikverlagsvertrag *m* music publisher's agreement; ~**werk** musical composition.

Muß|bestimmung mandatory regulation, compulsory provision, obligatory regulation, peremptory provision; ~**heirat** shotgun marriage; ~**kaufmann** mandatory merchant: *businessman having the status of a merchant by virtue of his activities;* ~**leistungen** obligatory benefits; ~**vorschrift** = ~*bestimmung qv.*

Muster *n* sample, model, pattern, specimen, precedent; ~**anforderungskarte** sample request card; ~**anmeldung** filing of a design for registration; ~**arbeitsvertrag** model employment contract; ~**ausstellung** trade exhibition; ~**betrieb** model plant, model enterprise; *landwirtschaftlicher* ~~: *model farm, pilot farm;* ~**brief** specimen letter; ~**buch** sample book; ~**dekoration** model display; ~**dienstordnung** model service regulations; ~**exemplar** specimen, specimen copy, precedent; ~**fall** model case, precedent; ~**formular** specimen form; **m**~**getreu** *adj* true to specimen; ~**gut** model farm; ~**haus** show house; ~**karte** sample card; ~**klauseln** model clauses; ~**koffer** salesman's sample case; ~**kollektion** collection of samples, collection of patterns, assortment of patterns; ~**lager** display of samples; ~**los** plot lot (*stat*); ~**messe** trade fair; sample exhibition; ~**mietvertrag** standard tenancy, agreement; ~ **ohne Wert** sample post, sample not for sale; sample, no commercial value, "not for sale" sample without value; ~**prozeß** representative proceeding, model suit, test action, test case; ~**rabatt** discount on samples, sample rebate; ~**register** register of designs, (ornamental) designs register; ~**rolle** register of designs; official crew list, muster roll; ~**satzung** model articles of association; ~**schutz** protection of registered designs; ~~ *begehren: to apply for a design patent;* ~**sendung** sample parcel, sample consignment; ~**stück** sample (item), specimen; ~ **unter versiegeltem Verschluß** sealed sample; ~**vertrag** model contract, standard contract; ~**vordruck** specimen form; ~**vor-**

schriften standard procedure, standard regulations; ~**wohnung** show flat *(for inspection)*; ~ **ziehen** to sample; ~**zieher** sampler; ~**ziehung** sampling, taking samples *(for quality control)*; ~**zulassung** acceptance of designs, design certificate; **gewerbliches** ~ commercial sample; **nach** ~ **kaufen** to buy by sample; **nach** ~ **verkaufen** to sell by sample.

Musterung *f* preinduction physical examination, mustering, recruitment, registration for the draft; ~**sausschuß** recruiting board, *US*: draft board; ~**sbescheid** decision by the recruiting board (*US*: draft board); ~**sverfahren** recruitment procedure.

muten *v/i* to apply for a mining concession.

mutmaßen *v/i* to presume, to surmise, to assume, to imagine.

mutmaßlich *adj* presumed, presumable, presumptive, putative, alleged; *adv*: presumably, presumedly, assumedly.

Mutmaßung *f* conjecture, speculation.

Mutter *f* mother; ~**gesellschaft** parent company, parent enterprise; ~**institut** parent institution; ~**land** mother country; ~**leib** venter, maternal body, womb; *vom* ~~*e an: from one's birth*; ~**mal** birthmark; ~**mord** matricide; ~**pflicht** maternal duty; ~**recht** matriarchy; ~**schaft** → *Mutterschaft*; ~**schutz** → *Mutterschutz*; ~**sprache** native tongue; ~**teil** maternal portion *(inheritance)*; parent and subsidiary (companies); ~**- und Tochter** parent and subsidiary (companies); **ledige** ~ unmarried mother; **leibliche** ~ (own) mother; **werdende** ~ expectant mother.

Mutterpause *f* reproducible copy; ~*n der Ausführungszeichnungen: reproducible copies of working drawings*.

Mutterschafts|ansprüche maternity rights; ~**geld** maternity grant; ~**hilfe** natal care; maternity grant; ~**urlaub** maternity leave; ~**versicherung** maternity insurance.

Mutterschutz *m* protection of the working mother; ~**frist** maternity protection period; ~**gesetz** Maternity Protection Act; ~**lohn** substitute wage payments during maternity.

Mutung *f* application for a mining concession, mining location prospect; ~ **abstecken** to peg out a claim, to stake out a mining claim; ~**sanspruch** mining claim, reward claim; ~**srecht** mining licence, prospecting rights.

Mutwillen *m* wantonness, mischievousness.

mutwillig *adj* wanton, mischievous.

Mutwilligkeit *f* = *Mutwillen qv*.

N

Nachabstimmung *f* subsequent vote, re-vote.

nachaddieren *v/t* to check the addition of, to add up again.

nachahmen *v/t* to imitate, to copy.

Nachahmer *m* imitator.

Nachahmung *f* imitation, plagiarism; ~ **in jeder Form ist verboten** reproduction in any form is forbidden; ~ **von Warenzeichen** imitation of trade marks; **freie** ~ free imitation; **sklavische** ~ colourable imitation (*US: colorable*), design piracy, a close copy, servile imitation; **täuschende** ~ fraudulent imitation; **unbefugte:** ~ **e-s Geschmacksmusters** piracy of design; **vor ~en wird gewarnt** beware of imitations!

Nachanmeldung *f* supplementary registration, further declaration, (*pat*) subsequent application.

Nacharbeit *f* touching-up, follow-up work; refinishing operation.

nacharbeitbar *adj pat* reproducible.

nacharbeiten *v/t* to re-treat (*rejected goods*), to reproduce (*an invention*).

Nachbar|eigentümer adjacent owner; **~gefahr** contiguity risk, danger to adjacent property; **~grundstück** adjacent land, adjacent property; **~interessen** neighbour's interests; **~klage** action against (interference by) a neighbour; **~kreis** adjoining county, neighbouring district; **~recht** neighbour law (*law concerning neighbours and interests of adjoining owners*); **~schaftsladen** convenience store; neighbourhood shop, corner shop; **~schutz** adjoining owners' legal protection; **~staat** neighbouring state, adjacent country.

Nachbau *m* imitation; copy, duplication, reproduction, reverse engineering; construction under licence, *construction taking an existing object as a model*; **lizenzweiser** ~ construction under licence; **sklavischer** ~ servile imitation, *cf sklavische Nachahmung;* **unerlaubter** ~ unlicensed reproduction, unlawful imitation.

nachbauen *v/t* to imitate, to copy, to duplicate, to reproduce.

nachbearbeiten *v/t* to re-work (*US:* rework), to process further, to re-machine, to re-treat, to finish, to dress, to reprocess.

Nacharbeitung *f* further processing, finishing, re-treatment, *cf nachbearbeiten.*

nachbehandeln *v/t* to give further treatment, to apply secondary treatment, *med* to give after-treatment.

Nachbehandlung *f* subsequent treatment, follow-up treatment, *med* after-care.

nachbekommen *v/t* to receive later, to get replacements.

nachbelasten *v/t* to debit subsequently, to charge subsequently.

Nachbelastung *f* additional charge, subsequent debit.

Nachbenutzung *f* subsequent use.

nachbessern *v/t* to remedy a defect (*by contractor*), to mend, to correct, to touch up, to improve subsequently, to re-treat, to amend defects.

Nachbesserung *f* subsequent improvement, remedying a defect, correction, amendment; **~sanspruch** the right to be given an opportunity to remedy a fault; **~sfrist** period for remedying defects, cure period; **~spflicht** contractor's obligation to remedy defects (*before acceptance*); **~srecht** *contractor's right to be given the opportunity to remedy defects*; **~sverlangen** request for cure, (subsequent) request to remedy a defect.

552

nachbestellen *v/t* to reorder, to order an additional quantity.

Nachbestellung *f* repeat order, further order, reorder, additional order.

Nachbesteuerung *f* supplementary taxation.

Nachbewilligung *f* supplementary grant, supplementary vote, additional allowance, supplementary allowance.

nachbezahlen *v/t* to pay later, to pay arrears, to pay extra.

Nachbezugsrecht *n* right to a cumulative dividend.

nachbilden *v/t* to reproduce, to copy, to make a replica (*of sth*).

Nachbildung *f* reproduction, copy, imitation, replica; ~**srecht** right of adaptation; **offensichtliche** ~ obvious imitation; **widerrechtliche** ~ unlawful imitation.

Nachbörse *f* after-hours market, street market, kerb market, *US*: curb market.

nachbörslich *adj* after-market, after official hours; street ..., curb ...

nachbringen *v/t* to file afterwards, to submit after the hearing.

nachbuchen *v/t* to enter an additional item, to enter subsequently (*after the accounts have been closed*), to make an additional booking, to book an additional passage.

Nachbuchung *f* additional entry, additional booking.

Nachbürge *m* collateral surety, surety for a surety, secondary surety.

Nachbürgschaft *f* sub-suretyship, secondary guarantee.

nachdatieren *v/t* to post-date; to back-date; *but also*: to ante-date.

Nachdeckungspflicht *f* obligation to provide additional cover.

Nachdeklaration *f* post-entry (*customs*), subsequent delaration.

Nachdruck *m* reproduction, reprint; ~**recht** copyright, licence to reprint, permission to reproduce under copyright; ~~ **für Zeitschriften:** magazine rights; ~**erlaubnis** permission to reproduce (*or* reprint) an article (etc); ~ **verboten** copyright, not to be reprinted; **heimlicher** ~ surreptitious edition; **unberechtigter** ~ unauthorized reprint; **unerlaubter** ~ pirated edition, piracy copy, fraudulent impression, counterfeit edition; **unveränderter** ~ reprint.

nachdrucken *v/t* to reprint, to reproduce; **unbefugt** ~ to pirate.

Nachdrucker *m* reprinter, pirate.

nachehelich *adj* post-nuptial.

Nacheid *m* oath after statement, oath administered after testimony.

Nacheile *f* pursuit.

Nachemission *f* follow-up issue.

nachentrichten *v/t* to pay retrospective contributions (*social insurance etc*), to pay retrospectively.

Nachentrichtung *f* subsequent remittance, retrospective payment (*of contributions*).

Nacherbe *m* reversionary (*or* subsequent) heir; ~**fall** subsequent inheritance; ~**folge** reversionary (*or* subsequent) succession; ~**recht** expectant interest of a reversionary (*or* subsequent) heir; ~**schaft** estate of a reversionary (*or* subsequent) heir; ~**envermerk** caution (*in land register*) to protect reversionary (*or* subsequent) heirs.

Nacherhebung *f* subsequent assessment, subsequent levy.

Nacherwerber *m* subsequent acquirer, subsequent taker.

Nachfassen *n* follow-up, reminder; ~ **bei Nichtbeantwortung** follow-up of those who have not replied.

nachfassen *v/i* to follow up, to approach again, to remind.

Nachfeststellung *f* subsequent statement, subsequent assessment.

Nachfinanzierung *f* supplementary financial assistance.

Nachfolge *f* succession; ~**bank** successor bank; ~**firma** successor firm, successor in business; ~**gesellschaft** successor company; ~ **im Amt** succession in office; ~**klausel** successorship clause (*partnership agreement clause vesting a partner's share in his successors upon*

Nachfolger

death); ~**konferenz** follow-up conference; ~**ordnung** system of succession (*in office*); ~**organisation** successor organization; ~**recht** right of succession; ~**schuldner** successor debtor; ~**staat** successor state; ~**treuhänder** successor trustee; ~**verhältnis** successor relationship; ~**zusatz** addition to indicate successorship (*to a firm name*); **rechtmäßige** ~ legitimate succession, legitimacy.

Nachfolger *m* successor (in title).

Nachfolgerin *f* a woman as successor, successor company.

nachfordern *v/t* to demand in addition, to make a further claim, to demand additional compensation.

Nachforderung *f* further demand, subsequent claim, supplementary claim, extra-charge, margin call; ~**sbescheid** advice concerning additional charge (*tax, dues etc*); ~**sklage** action for further payment.

nachforschen *v/i* to investigate, to trace, to inquire into.

Nachforschung *f* investigation, inquiry, tracing; ~ **an Ort und Stelle** local investigation, investigation on the spot, field investigation; ~**en anstellen** to investigate, to make inquiries, to conduct investigations; ~**en blieben ergebnislos** investigations were fruitless; ~ **nach e-r Urkunde** search for a document; ~**spflicht** the duty to investigate, obligation to make inquiries; **genaue** ~**en** close investigations; **polizeiliche** ~**en** police investigations; **sich den** ~**en entziehen** to evade investigations.

Nachfrage *f* demand, inquiry, request, requirements; ~**analyse** demand analysis, study of demand; ~**änderung** change in demand; ~**ballung** accumulated demand, piling up of demand; ~**belebung** growth in demand; ~**bremse** check (exercised) on demand, curbing demand; ~**dynamik** dynamic force of demand, pull of demand; ~**effekt** effect on demand, impact upon demand; ~**elastizität** flexibility of demand; ~**entwicklung** trend in demand; ~**funktion** demand function; ~**kurve** graph showing demand; ~**lücke** unsatisfied demand; ~**macht** power of demand; ~**menge** quantity demanded; ~**monopol** demand monopoly; ~ **nach Verkehrsmöglichkeiten** demand for traffic facilities; ~**rückgang** decline in demand; ~**schöpfung** demand creation; ~**seite** the demand side, the buyer's side; ~**sog** demand pull; ~**stau** accumulated demand, backlog of unmet demand; ~**steuerung** demand management; ~**stoß** sudden increase in demand; ~**überhang** excess demand; ~**vorrat** reservoir of demand; ~**welle** flood of demand; **anhaltende** ~ persistent demand; **die** ~ **befriedigen** to meet demand, to cover demand (*for sth*); **die** ~ **übersteigt das Angebot** demand exceeds supply; **gleichbleibende** ~ steady demand; **hektische** ~ keen demand; **innere** ~ domestic demand, demand within the country; **kaufwillige** ~ genuine demand, demand backed by the desire to buy; **lebhafte** ~ brisk demand; **laufende** ~ current demand; **lustlose** ~ sluggish demand; **saisonbedingte** ~ seasonal demand; **schwache** ~ slack demand; **stürmische** ~ keen demand; **wachsende** ~ increase in demand, growing demand.

Nachfrager *m* inquirer, interested party, potential customer, prospective buyer.

Nachfrist *f* additional period of time *for completion or remedying defects;* extension of the original term, grace period, additional respite, final deadline; ~ **gewähren** to grant grace, to extend the original term; ~**gewährung** extension of delay; ~ **setzen** to fix a final deadline, to grant a respite.

Nachgangshypothek *f* junior mortgage.

Nachgeben *n* yielding, making concessions; **gegenseitiges** ~ accomodation on each side, mutual yielding.

nachgeben *v/i* to yield, to give in; **stillschweigend** ~ to acquiesce.

nachgeboren *adj* after-born, puisne; posthumous (*child born after his father's death*).

Nachgeborener *m* (*der Nachgeborene*) post natus, person born after an event.

Nachgebühr *f* additional charge, surcharge on unfranked or insufficiently franked mail, postage due, excess postage.

nachgemacht *adj* imitated, counterfeit, copied.

nachgeordnet *adj* subordinate, lower.

Nachgeschäft *n* follow-up transaction, follow-up deal.

nachgewiesen *adj* proven, established as true.

nachgiebig *adj* indulgent, yielding, ready to give in.

Nachgiebigkeit *f* indulgence, yielding nature.

Nachgiro = *Nachindossament qv*.

Nachgründung *f* post-formation acquisition of capital goods (*to be included in the capital stock*).

Nachhaftung *f* continuing (*or* follow-up) liability of withdrawing partner.

Nachhaltigkeit *f* persistence, perseverence; persistent effort to do business.

Nachhol|arbeit work to make up for arrears; **~bedarf** pent-up demand, backlog demand, accumulated demand; **~frist** additional time granted to make up for arrears; **~impuls** belated impulse; **~konjunktur** boom based on the satisfaction of backlog demand; **~verbot** *prohibition to make up for lost working time by speeding up production*.

Nachholung *f* making up for lost working time, catching-up with; ~ **der Erfindernennung** subsequent identification of the inventor.

Nachindossament *n* post-maturity endorsement, endorsement of overdue (*or dishonoured*) bill of exchange, post-endorsement.

Nachindossant *m* subsequent endorser.

Nachkalkulation *f* ex-post costing, re-estimate on the basis of historical cost, actual cost accounting.

Nachkomme *m* descendant, *pl* ~**n:** descendants, issue, offspring; **~n hinterlassen** to die leaving issue; **ältester männlicher** ~ eldest male issue; **ältester männlicher** ~ **gerader Linie** eldest male lineal descendant; **die betreffenden** ~**n** such issue, the descendants in question; **eheliche** ~**n** legitimate issue; **erbberechtigte** ~**n** descendants entitled to inherit; **männliche** ~**n im Mannesstamm** male issue; **ohne** ~**n** without issue, issueless; **sonstige** ~**n** other issue of my body.

Nachkommenschaft *f* offspring, issue, progeny; **~sschäden** damage suffered by offspring.

Nachkömmling *m* after-born child, post natus, child born after an event, descendant.

Nachkonjunktur *f* delayed boom.

nachkonstitutionell *adj* post-constitutional (*i. e. enacted after the German Basic Law*).

Nachkontrolle *f* further check, subsequent checking, re-checking.

Nachkriegswirtschaft *f* post-war economy, post-war industry.

Nachlaß *m* (1) (deceased person's) estate, decedent's estate, inheritance; **~angelegenheit** probate matters; **~anspruch** claim arising out of an estate; **~aufteilung nach Stämmen** distribution *of the estate* per stirpes; **~auseinandersetzung** partition of a succession, distribution and partition (*of an estate*); **~besitz** (the deceased's) estate, possession of the estate; **~bewertung** valuation of the estate; **~eigenschuld** *debt of the estate for which heir is personally liable;* **~forderung** claim by the estate, debt due to the estate; ~**gegenstand** item forming part of the estate; ~**gericht** probate court, *US also:* surrogate's court; ~**gerichtsregister** testamentary office; ~**gläubiger** creditor of the estate; ~**grundstück** inherited real estate; ~**haftung** liability of the estate assets; ~**inventar** schedule of estate assets; ~**konkurs** bankruptcy administration of an insolvent estate; bankruptcy of the estate; ~ **nach Abzug von Vermächtnissen** remainder of the estate; ~**pfleger** provisional administrator of the estate; ~**pflegschaft** provisional administration of estate; ~**prozeßpfleger** administrator pendente lite; ~**recht** probate law; ~**register** probate registry; ~**richter** probate judge; ~**sache** matter of the estate, ~**schuld** debt of the estate, deceased's debt; ~**schuldner** debtor of the estate; ~**verbindlichkeiten** liabilities of the estate; ~**verfahren** administration suit, probate action, probate proceedings; ~**vergleich** *composition proceedings to avoid compulsory liquidation of an estate;* ~**vermögen** assets of a deceased person, estate; ~**verteilung** distribution of the estate; ~**veruntreuung** subtraction of legacies; ~**verwalter** administrator, receiver *on behalf of the creditors of the estate;* ~**verwalterin** administratrix; ~**verwaltung** administration of the estate on behalf of creditors; ~**verzeichnis** estate inventory; ~**wert** value of the inheritance; ~**wesen** probate matters; ~**wohnsitz** domicile of succession; **aus meinem** ~ from my estate; **beweglicher** ~ personal estate; **den** ~ **teilen** to partition the estate; **der** ~ **fällt an die gesetzlichen Erben** the estate devolves by intestacy; **der** ~ **geht auf den ältesten Sohn über** the estate devolves upon the eldest son; **e-n** ~ **abwickeln** to wind up the estate; **e-n** ~ **auseinandersetzen** to settle an estate, to wind up an estate; **e-n** ~ **verwalten** to administer an estate; **erbenloser** ~ estate without any heirs, vacant succession; **herrenloser** ~ vacant succession; **liquider** ~ solvent estate; **mein gesamter** ~ everything I die possessed of, my entire estate; **restlicher** ~ residue; **treuhänderisch verwalteter** ~ trust estate; **unbeweglicher** ~ real property of an estate; **unverteilter** ~ undivided estate.

Nachlaß *m* (2) discount, price reduction, allowance, abatement (*of taxes after assessment*); ~ **für Vorauszahlung** anticipation (rate).

nachlässig *adj* careless, negligent.

Nachlässigkeit *f* carelessness, neglect, negligence; ~ **bei der Geltendmachung von Rechten**, laches; **grobe** ~ gross negligence.

Nachleistung *f* subsequent performance, additional services.

Nachlese *f* gleaning (*field*), second selection.

nachliefern *v/t* to furnish additional (objects), to deliver subsequently.

Nachlieferung *f* additional supply, subsequent delivery, replacement, update.

nachlösen *v/t* to buy a ticket en route (*or: on arrival*), to pay an additional fare, to pay on the train.

Nachlöseschalter *m* excess fare window, *office for the payment of fares on arrival.*

nachmachen *v/t* to copy, to imitate.

Nachmann *m* subsequent endorser.

Nachmieter *m* new tenant, subsequent tenant.

Nachmietrecht *n* option to renew tenancy.

Nachmonat *m* subsequent month, following month.

nachmustern *v/t* to re-examine s. o. for fitness for military service.

Nachnahme *f* cash on delivery (C. O. D.), collect on delivery, payment on delivery; ~**begleitschein** C. O. D. form; ~**betrag** amount to be collected on delivery; ~**brief** C. O. D. letter; ~**dienst** C. O. D. service; ~**paket** collect on delivery package, C.O.D. package; **~sendung** C.O.D. consignment *US:* registered C.O.D. mail; **~spesen** C.O.D. charges; **gegen ~** cash on delivery (C.O.D.), collect on delivery, payment on delivery; **gegen ~ der Kosten** expense charged forward; **mit e–r ~ belasten** to send C.O.D.

Nachname *m* surname, last name, family name.

Nachpächter *m* new tenant, subsequent tenant.

Nachpachtrecht *n* option to renew lease.

Nachpatent *n* later-dated patent.

nachpfänden *v/i* to levy again (*at the same debtor's place*).

Nachpfändung *f* renewed levy of execution, second distress.

Nachporto *n* additional (*or* extra) postage.

nachprägen *v/t* to coin again, to issue newly-minted coins, to copy coins.

Nachprägung *f* repeated coining, counterfeit coining.

nachprüfen *v/t* to check, to examine, to review, to re-examine, to audit, to scrutinize; **auf Richtigkeit ~** to verify; **gerichtlich ~** to review judicially; **nochmals ~** to re-examine.

Nachprüfung *f* examination, re-examination, review, audit, scrutiny; **~ auf dem Verwaltungswege** administrative review; **~ der Einfuhrgeschäfte** subsequent control of imports; **~srecht** right to review; right of verification; **~sverfahren** procedure on review; **öffentliche ~** public inquiry; **richterliche ~** judicial review.

Nachrang *m* subsequent (*or* lower) ranking (*of securities or creditors or liabilities*).

nachrangig *adj* inferior, subordinated, secondary, of lower rank, of lower priority, of lesser importance.

Nachrangigkeit *f* lower priority, lesser importance, lower ranking.

Nachrecherche *f pat* further search, additional search.

nachrechnen *v/t* to check the calculation, to re-calculate.

Nachrechnung *f* re-calculation; supplementary invoice.

Nachrede *f* talk about s.o., aspersion, calumny; **üble ~** defamatory remark, slander, calumny.

nachreichen *v/t* to file (*send, hand in*) later (*or* subsequently), to file at a later date.

Nachreichung *f* subsequent presentation.

Nachrevision *f* post-audit.

Nachricht *f* message, information, news, news item, notice; **~ erhalten** to receive notice; **~ erteilen** to give notice, to notify; **e–e ~ hinterlassen** to leave a message; **wir bitten um ~** please let us know, please inform us; **verschlüsselte ~en** messages in code or cipher.

Nachrichten|abteilung news department, news division; **~beschaffung** collection of information; **~büro** news agency, press agency; **~dienst** information service; **geheimer ~~**: *intelligence service*; **verfassungsverräterischer ~~**: *treasonable information service*; **~mittler** conveyor of (illegal) messages (*or* communications); **~netz** communications network; **~offizier** intelligence officer; **~schutz** legal protection of confidential information, data secrecy; **~sperre** news ban, prohibition of informing the media, news bar; **~sprecher** news reader, news announcer; **~übermittlung** transmission of news and information; **~verbindungen** communications; **~wesen** communication system, communications; **~zensur** censorship of the news.

nachrichtlich *adv* for information, blind copy to.

Nachrücken *n* moving up, filling a vacated post; **~ e–r Hypothek** advancement of ranking due to repayment of prior mortgage.

nachrücken *v/i* to move up (*into vacated seat, position etc*).
Nachrüstung *f* (nuclear) arms modernization.
Nachsaison *f* post season.
Nachschaden *m* consequential damage, subsequent damage.
Nachschau *f* inspection), follow-up examination, closer look.
Nachschieben *f* later submission, subsequent presentation; ~ **von Gründen** subsequent submission of argument, adducing reasons subsequently.
nachschieben *v/t* to submit subsequently, to adduce subsequently.
nachschießen *v/t* to make a further contribution, *exch* to remargin.
Nachschlagewerk *n* reference book.
Nachschlüssel *m* duplicate key, false key, picklock, skeleton key; ~**diebstahl** theft by using false keys.
nachschnüffeln *v/i* to snoop around (*after s.o.*), to spy on.
Nachschrift *f* postscript.
Nachschub *m* supply, reinforcement; ~**bedarf** supply requirements; ~**klausel** clause to secure seller's reserved property by additional measures (*preservation, replenishment of stocks, proceeds*); ~**lager** supply depot, supply dump.
Nachschulung *f* follow-up training, retraining.
Nachschuß *m* additional contribution (*beyond original amount*), additional payment, additional assessment, further cover, further margin; ~**aufforderung** call on contributories; ~**forderung** marginal call (*for additional cash*); ~**haftung** reserve liability, liability to effect further contributions; ~**klausel** safety clause (*mutual insurance*); ~**pflicht** liability to assessment, liability to make further contributions, reserve liability; ~~ *e-s Vorschußnehmers:* borrower's obligation to provide further cover; *mit beschränkter* ~~: limited guarantee; ~**verbindlichkeiten** assessments payable; ~**zahlung** payment of further contribution, re-margining.

nachschußpflichtig *adj* assessable, liable to further contributions; **nicht** ~ non-assessable.
Nachsende|antrag application for redirection, application to have one's mail forwarded; ~**adresse** forwarding address, accomodation address *GB*, temporary mailing address.
nachsenden *v/t* to forward, to send on; **bitte** ~! please forward; **nicht** ~! not to be forwarded, to await arrival.
Nachsendung *f* redirection, forwarding of mail; ~**gebühr** redirection fee, forwarding fee.
Nachsicherung *f* subsequent increase in collateral, additional collateral.
Nachsicht *f* indulgence, forbearance, lenience, toleration; ~**gewährung** granting further time, granting indulgence.
nachsichtig *adj* indulgent, forbearing, lenient, tolerant.
Nachsorge *f* aftercare; ~**auflage** aftercare condition.
Nachspann *m* end title.
Nachsichtwechsel *m* after-sight bill.
Nachspiel *n* unpleasant consequences; **gerichtliches** ~ legal consequences.
nachsprechen *v/i* to repeat, to say (the following words) after s.o.; *sprechen Sie mir nach!: repeat the following (words) after me!*
nächst|berechtigt next in order of entitlement, next entitled; ~**bereit** next-prepared; ~**berufen** next-entitled, next in line; **N**~**berufener** *m* (*der Nächstberufene*) next-entitled party, next in line; ~**folgend** next; **N**~**gebot** nearest bid given, closest bid given; ~ **höher** next highest; ~**liegend** (located) nearest; most obvious; ~**offen** next open, next free, next unoccupied.
nachstehend *adj* following, *adv* hereinafter, thereafter; ~**bezeichnet** (**als**) hereinafter called (*or* referred to as); ~ **genannt** hereinafter called.
nachstellig *adj* junior, not having priority.

Nachstellungen *f/pl* unwelcome advances, persecution.

Nachsteuer *f* supplementary tax, subsequently levied tax, tax payable after reassessment.

nachsuchen *v/i* to request, to petition.

Nachsuchung *f* request, petition.

Nacht|arbeit night-work; ~**arbeiter** night-worker; ~**arbeitsverbot** prohibition of night-work (*e.g. for children etc*); ~**arbeitszuschlag** night-work premium; ~**asyl** night-shelter, lodging house; ~**backverbot** prohibition of baking at night; ~**börse** evening trade; ~**briefkasten** night safe, night-time mail box (*at court building*); ~**diebstahl** theft at night-time (*aggravation*); ~**dienst** night duty; ~**fahrt** overnight journey, overnight drive; ~**fluchtgrund** (assumed) danger of escape during the night; ~**gebühr** night rate; ~**post** night mail; ~**ruhe** silence at night-time, night's rest; ~**schalter** night counter, night booking office; ~**schicht** night-shift, "grave-yard shift"; ~**streckenbefeuerung** route beacons for night-time-flying service; ~**stromtarif** night-time tariff for electricity, restricted hours traffic; ~**tarif** night tariff, night charge; ~**tresor** night safe; ~**wächter** night watchman; ~**zeit** night-time; ~**zuschlag** night hour premium.

Nachtat *f* subsequent lesser offence; **straflose** ~ not punishable subsequent lesser offence.

Nachteil *m* disadvantage, disbenefit, detriment, drawback; ~**ausgleich** compensation for detrimental effects (of dismissal); ~**sverbot** prohibition of adverse discrimination; exclusion of prejudice; **e–n** ~ **in Kauf nehmen** to put up with a disadvantage, to accept a disadvantage; **erheblicher** ~ material detriment; **zum** ~ **e–s Dritten** to the disadvantage of a third party.

nachteilig *adj* detrimental, disadvantageous.

Nächtigung *f* overnight stay.

Nachtrag *m* supplement, addendum, postscript.

nachtragen *v/t* to add, to supplement.

nachträglich *adj* subsequent, additional, belated, ex post facto.

Nachtrags|anklage supplementary charge; ~**bestimmung** annex, additional clause (*last will*), codicillary clause; ~**bewilligung** supplementary expenditure, appropriation; ~**buchung** subsequent entry; ~**gesetz** amendment, amending Act; ~**haushalt** supplementary budget, interim budget; ~**klage** supplemental (statement of) claim; ~**kredit** supplementary credit; ~**liquidation** subsequent bill for professional charges; ~**police** additional policy, subsequent policy, supplementary policy; addendum to a policy; ~**testament** codicil; ~**urkunde** supplemental deed; ~**verfügung** amending instructions; ~**verteilung** subsequent distribution, later distribution.

Nachtrunk *m* subsequent drink *to conceal level of blood alcohol*.

Nachunternehmer *m* subcontractor.

Nachuntersuchung *f* subsequent examination, re-examination.

Nachurlaub *m* extended leave.

Nachveranlagung *f* subsequent assessment.

Nachverfahren *n* subsequent proceedings (after conditional judgment).

Nachvermächtnis *n* reversionary legacy.

Nachvermächtnisnehmer *m* reversionary legatee.

nachveröffentlicht *adj pat* post-published.

Nachverrechnung *f* after-clearing.

Nachversicherung *f* subsequent insurance, payment of retrospective contributions (to social insurance); ~**sfall** requirement for admission of insurance contributions; ~**szeiten** periods to which retrospective (social insurance) contributions apply; subsequent insurance period.

Nachversteuerung *f* payment in settlement of tax arrears, additional assessment, subsequent taxation.

nachverzollen *v/t* to pay extra duties for undeclared merchandise, to pay subsequent duty on an article.

Nachverzollung *f* subsequent payment of customs duty.

Nachwahl *f* by-election.

Nachweis *m* proof, evidence; ~ **der Aushändigung** proof of delivery; ~ **der Echtheit** proof of authenticity; ~ **der Empfangsberechtigung** proof of authority to accept (*remittance, mail etc*); ~ **der Identität** proof of identity; ~ **der Staatsangehörigkeit** proof of nationality; ~ **der Zahlungsunfähigkeit** proof of inability to pay; ~ **führen** to furnish proof, to produce evidence; ~**klausel** evidence clause; ~**makler** *broker who need only disclose an opportunity for a transaction (to earn his commission)*; ~**pflicht** obligation to present evidence, accountability, obligation to account for expenditure; ~**provision** broker's commission earned for disclosing an opportunity for a transaction (*realized subsequently*); ~**verteilung** subsequent distribution of (newly discovered) assets; **bei** ~ **von** on proof of, upon proof; **bis zum** ~ **des Gegenteils** unless there is proof to the contrary, subject to evidence to the contrary; **buchmäßiger** ~ as evidenced by the books; **den** ~ **erbringen** to bear evidence, to produce evidence (of sth) to evidence; **lückenlose** ~**e** complete evidence, airtight case; **mangels** ~**es** failing proof, if proof is lacking.

nachweisbar *adj* demonstrable, provable, capable of demonstration, ascertainable.

nachweisen *v/t* to prove, to demonstrate, to establish.

nachweislich *adj* provable; *adv* provably.

Nachweisung *f* documents, documentary proof.

Nachwiegen *n* check weighing, reweighing.

nachwiegen *v/t* to reweigh, to check the weight.

Nachwirkung *f* after-effect.

Nachwucher *m* profiting from usurious acts of another.

Nachwuchsförderung *f* promotion of young talent, promotion of the up and coming generation.

Nachwuchskräfte *f/pl* young persons (in a firm), junior members of the staff, management trainees.

nachzahlen *v/t* to pay in arrears, to pay retrospectively, to pay a surcharge.

Nachzahlung *f* subsequent payment, back pay, additional contribution; payment of arrears; ~**saufforderung** call for further contributions; ~**spflicht** obligation to make up for a deficiency, obligation to reimburse legal aid.

Nachzählung *f* recount, second counting.

Nachzeichnung *f* subsequent subscription.

Nachzensur *f* post-publication censorship.

Nachzug ~ **ausländischer Familienangehöriger** subsequent immigration of family dependants; family reunion; ~**salter für Kinder** (upper) age limit for children to join their parents.

Nachzugsaktie *f* deferred share, *pl*: deferred stock.

Nadelgeld *n* pin-money.

Nagelprobe *f* acid test, crucial test.

Nah|auslosung compensation for travel-time to and from (relatively near) employee's home; ~**bereich** close range, immediate sphere of influence; ~**erholungsgebiet** recreational area near a population centre, local recreational facilities; ~**fischerei** local fishing; ~**schnellverkehr** rapid transit, local fast traffic; ~**- und Fernverkehrstransport** long and short haul; ~**verkehr** short haul, short-distance transport, local (suburban) traffic; ~**ziel** immediate objective; ~**zone** local traffic zone.

nahestehen *v/i* to be closely connect-

Nahezu-Bargeld *n* quasi-cash.
Nährstand *m* agriculture, the agricultural occupations.
Nährstoffeinheit *f* nutrition unit.
Nahrungsmittel *n* food, foodstuff; **~ fälschen** to adulterate food; **~fälschung** food adulteration; **~grundstoff** basic foodstuff; **~handwerk** food-processing trade; **~hilfe** food aid; **~hilfe-Ausschuß** food aid committee; **~hilfe-Übereinkommen** food aid convention; **~industrie** food industry; **~rohstoff** basic foodstuff, raw material used in the production of foodstuffs; **~ und Genußmittel** *n/pl* food, beverages and tobacco; **biologisches ~** organic food; **hochwertige ~** high-grade foodstuffs; **tierisches ~** foodstuff of animal origin; animal food.
Nahrungsverweigerung *f* refusal to take food.
Nahtstelle *f* point of union, point of contact, linkage point, interface.
Name *m* name, own name, family name; **~ der Redaktion bekannt** name withheld; **~ des Ausstellers** name of maker; **~ und Anschrift sind der Redaktion bekannt** name and address supplied; **angenommener ~** assumed name, alias, pseudonym; **auf den ~n jmds eintragen** to register in s. o.'s name; **auf den ~n lauten** to be made out in the name of s. o.; **dem ~n nach** nominal, by name, according to name; **der richtige ~** the true name; **falscher ~** false name, pseudonym, alias; **gesetzlich geschützter ~** proprietary name, legally protected name; **im eigenen ~n** in one's own name; **im eigenen ~n für fremde Rechnung** in one's own name but for the account of another, on commission; **im eigenen ~n klagen** to sue in one's own name; **im fremden ~n** in the name of another, as agent(s) only; **im ~n der Firma zeichnen** to sign for the firm; **im ~n des Gesetzes** in the name of the law; **im ~n jmds auftreten** to go under the name of s. o.; **im ~ und für Rechnung des Unternehmers** in the name and on behalf of the principal; **im ~ von** in the name of, on behalf of; **in fremdem ~n für fremde Rechnung** in the name and for the account of another, as agent; **jmdn mit ~ nennen** to call s. o. by name, to name; **nur dem ~n nach** purely nominally, in (*or* by) name only; **ohne ~n** anonymous; **seinen ~n angeben** to state one's name; **rechtlich geschützter ~** legally protected name, a registered name, a copyrighted name; **unter dem ~n von** under the name of; **vollständiger ~** full name, legal name.
namenlos *adj* anonymous, nameless (*brand*).
namens *prep* in the name of, on account of, on behalf of non-name.
Namens|adoption adoption to give the child a name; **~aktie** personal share, registered share; *vinkulierte* **~~:** *not freely transferable registered share*; **~anbringung** legal requirement to display proprietor's name (*near shop entrance*); **~änderung** change of name; **~angabe** indication of name; **~aufruf** call-over; roll call; **~ehe** nominal marriage (*to obtain name of husband*); **~erteilung** naming; **~firma** personal firm-name (*firm-name consisting of the name or names of natural persons*); **~führung** (constant) use of a name; **~gebung** naming, christening; name-giving ceremony, nomenclature; **n~gleich** *adj* having the same name; **~gleichheit** identity of name; **~indossament** special endorsement; **~irrtum** misnomer, mistake in names; **~konnossement** non-negotiable bill of lading; **~lagerschein** warehouse warrant made out to a named person; **~liste** list of names, nominal roll, rota; **~mißbrauch** misuse of name, using a false name as an impostor;

namentlich

~**nennung** mentioning of a name, statement of names; ~**obligation** registered bond, debenture made out to a named person; ~**papier** document made out to a named individual, registered security; ~**pfandbrief** registered mortgage bond; ~**recht** right to the use of a name; ~**schild** name plate; ~**schuldverschreibung** registered bond, registered debenture; *auswechselbare* ~~*en: interchangeable bonds*; ~**schutz** legal protection of names; ~**tag** name-day, Saint's day; ~**unterschrift** signature; ~**verwechslung** confusion of names; ~**verzeichnis** list of names, index of names, nominal list; ~**wechsel** change of name; ~**zeichnung** signature; ~**zertifikat** registered certificate; ~**zug** form of signature.

namentlich *adj* (mentioned) by name.

namhaft *adj* renowned, well-known, substantial.

Namhaftmachung *f* naming, identification, designation.

nämlich *conj* id est (i.e.), that is to say, viz., to wit, namely.

Nämlichkeit *f* identity; ~**sbescheinigung** certificate of identity; ~**snachweis** proof of the unaltered character (of temporarily imported goods); ~**sprüfung** verification of identity; ~**szeichen** identification mark; ~**szeugnis** certificate of identity, certificate of unaltered character of goods.

Nansenpaß *m* Nansen passport (for stateless persons).

Narkosewaffe *f* stun gun.

Narkotikum *n pl*: *Narkotika* (= ~*a*), narcotic, drug, anaesthetic; **gesundheitsgefährdende** ~**a** dangerous drugs; **süchtigkeitsbildende** ~**a** habit-forming narcotic drugs.

Nasciturus *m* child en ventre sa mère, unborn child.

Nassauer *m* sponger, parasite.

National|bewußtsein national consciousness, sense of national identity; ~**budget** national budget; ~**einkommen** national income, national revenue; ~**farben** national colours; ~**feiertag** national holiday; ~**flagge** national flag, ensign; ~**hymne** national anthem; ~**ökonom** economist, political economist; ~**ökonomie** economics, national economy, political economy; ~**produkt** national product; ~**rat** National Council; member of the National Council (*Sw*, *A*); ~**sozialismus** national socialism; ~**staat** nation state; ~**versammlung** National Assembly.

Nationalität *f* nationality; ~**enfrage** problem of national minorities; ~**enprinzip** nationality principle, rule that a person is subject to the law of his nationality; ~**enstaat** multi-national state; ~**szeichen** international registration plate, national mark.

Nato *f* NATO; ~-**Doppelbeschluß** Nato twin-track decision; ~-**Truppenstatut** NATO Status of Forces Agreement.

Natur|boden natural soil, uncultivated soil; ~**denkmal** natural monument; ~**ereignis** natural event, natural phenomenon, act of nature; ~**erscheinung** natural phenomenon; ~**erzeugnis** natural product, *pl* (*also*): natural produce; *gewerbliche* ~~*se: industrial crops*; ~**gabe** gift of nature, talent; ~**gesetz** natural law, law of nature; ~**haushalt** eco system; ~**katastrophe** natural disaster; ~**kautschuk** natural rubber; ~**kostladen** biological food store; ~**kraft** power of nature; ~**ökologie** natural ecology; ~**produkt** natural product; ~**raum** physical region; ~**recht** law of nature, natural law; "**n~rein**" *adj* pure, unadulterated; ~**schätze** natural resources; ~**schutz** → *Naturschutz*; ~**stoff** natural product; ~**stofferfindung** inventory of a natural product (*by induced mutation etc*).

Natural|abgabe levy in kind; ~**ausgleich** compensation in kind; ~**di**-

naturalisieren / **Nebenerwerbstätigkeit**

vidende dividend payable in kind; **~einkommen** income in kind; **~entlohnung** remuneration in kind; **~erfüllung** specific performance, performance in kind; **~ersatz** replacement in kind, recovery in kind; **~ertrag** yield (of the sort); **~form** original form; **~leistung** payment in kind; **~lohn** wages in kind, remuneration in kind; **~obligation** imperfect obligation, unenforceable obligation, debt of honour; **~pacht** *US*: share-cropping, lease where rent is paid in kind, rent in kind; **~~pächter** share tenant; sharecropper; **~rabatt** discount by supply of extra articles free of charge; **~reichnisse** natural resources; **~restitution** restoration, compensation for damage in kind, restitution in kind; **~steuer** tax paid in kind; **~tausch** barter; **~vergütung** remuneration in kind; *e-e ~~ leisten*: to pay in kind; **~wirtschaft** closed household economy, economy based on self-production and barter, moneyless economy; **~zins** rent payable in kind.

naturalisieren *v/t* to naturalize.
Naturalisierung *f* naturalization.
Naturschutz *m* nature preservation, nature protection; **~behörde** nature preservation authority; **~gebiet** nature preservation area, nature reserve, national park; **~gesetz** nature preservation law, conservation law(s).

navigationsunfähig *adj* unmanoeuvrable, out of control, unnavigable.
ne bis in idem prohibition against double jeopardy.
Nebel|scheinwerfer *m* fog light(s), fog lamp, fog headlight; **~schlußleuchte** rear foglight; **~warnung** fog signal.
Neben|abrede additional agreement, subsidiary agreement, collateral agreement(s); *mündliche ~~*: *verbal collateral agreements;* (informal) understanding, side agreement, subagreement; **~absicht** secondary motive; **~amt** additional function, secondary office, part-time job; **~anschluß** extension; **~anspruch** secondary claim, subsidiary claim; **~antrag** secondary petition for additional relief; **~artikel** side-line article; **~ausgaben** incidental expenses; **~bahn** branch railway, branch line; **~bedeutung** connotation, secondary meaning; **~befugnisse** incidental powers; **~begriff** auxiliary concept; **~bemerkung** side remark, incidental remark, passing remark; **~berechtigter** secondarily entitled party; **~beruf** secondary occupation, side line; **n~beruflich** *adj* as a secondary occupation; **~beschäftigung** secondary activities, spare-time work, side-line, part-time job; *unerlaubte ~~*: *moonlighting*; **~bestandteile** auxiliary constituents; **~bestimmungen** incidental provisions; **~beteiligte** secondary parties; **~betrieb** subsidiary establishment, subsidiary enterprise, branch; **~beweis** accessory proof; **~bezüge** fringe benefits, perquisites, "perks"; **~börse** curb exchange, provincial stock exchange; **~buch** auxiliary book; **~buchkonto** secondary account; **~bürge** co-surety, collateral surety, additional bail; **~bürgschaft** co-surety, collateral guarantee; **~effekt** side result; **~einander fahren** driving (*or* riding) side by side (*two or three abreast*); **~einkommen** secondary income, extra income, additional income; **~einkünfte** casual earnings, perquisites, additional income; **~einnahmen** additional income, extra income; **~erfindung** collateral invention; **~erwerb** secondary occupation, sparetime job; **n~erwerblich** incidental(ly) to one's main business or profession; **~erwerbsbetrieb** smallholding, additional business; **~erwerbslandwirt** part-time farmer; **~erwerbslandwirtschaft** smallholding; **~erwerbsstelle** subsidiary earning position; **~erwerbstätigkeit** subsidiary gainful activity;

~**erzeugnis** byproduct; spin-off (*also fig*), co-product, ~**folge** incidental consequence; ~**forderung** incidental claim; ~**frage** secondary question, side issue; ~**frau** secondary wife, concubine; ~**gebäude** adjacent building, outbuilding, outhouse, annexe; ~**gebrauch(szweck)** accessory use; ~**gebühren** supplementary charges, extra charges; ~**geschäft** side line, sundry business; ~**gewässer** dependent seas; ~**gewerbe** ancillary trade; ~**intervenient** intervening party; ~**intervention** intervention (*by third party to support one of the litigants*); ~**interventionsverfahren** (intervention by) third party proceedings; ~**kasse** petty cash fund; ~**klage** accessory prosecution (*by injured party*); ~**kläger** additional private prosecutor; ~**konto** subsidiary account; ~**kosten** additional expenses, outgoings, incidental expenses; utilities (*tenancy contract*); ~**kostenpauschale** lump sum to cover incidental expenses; ~**kriegsschauplatz** secondary theatre of war; ~**leistung** performance of an additional service, *pl also*: fringe benefits, additional services; ~**leistungsgesellschaft** company with additional service obligations of shareholders; ~**linie** side line; connecting line; ~**markt** side-line market, parallel market; ~**papiere** coupons; ~**partei** subsidiary party, joint litigant; ~**patent** collateral patent; ~**pflicht** secondary obligation, accessory obligation; ~**platz** place of insignificant importance, outlying place, out-of-town point; ~**produkt** = ~*erzeugnis qv;* ~**postamt** sub post-office; ~**recht** accessory right, subsidiary right, secondary right, peripheral right; ~**register** secondary register; ~**sache** collateral matter, subordinate matter, matter of secondary importance, secondary cause, minor point; **n**~**sächlich** *adj* incidental, unimportant, minor; ~**sächlichkeit** minor point, triviality; ~**schaden** collateral damage; ~**sicherheit** secondary security, collateral security; ~**stelle** suboffice, branch-office; ~**steuer** minor tax; ~**strafe** supplementary penalty; ~**strafrecht** law on supplementary penalties; ~**straße** side street, minor road, secondary road; ~**strekke** byroute, connecting line, branch railway; ~**tat** incidental offence; *konsumierte* ~~: *lesser offence;* ~**täter** independent perpetrator (*of an offence*); ~**tätigkeit** = *Nebenbeschäftigung qv;* ~**umstand** incidental circumstance; ~**urkunde** supporting document, ancillary document; annex, schedule; ~**verdienst** additional earnings, incidental earnings, casual earnings, extra profit; ~**vereinbarung** collateral agreement; ~**verfahren** collateral proceedings, ancillary proceedings, interlocutory proceedings; ~**verpflichtung** additional obligation; ~**versicherung** additional insurance; ~**vertrag** subsidiary contract, accessory contract; ~**vormund** co-guardian, second guardian; ~**vorschlag** incidental proposal, additional proposal; ~**werte** sundry securities; ~**wirkung** collateral effect, incidental consequence, incidental result; ~**zentrum** district centre; ~**zweck** secondary object.

Negativ|attest negative clearance certificate, negative confirmation; cerificate of non-applicability of a restraint; ~**beweis** negative evidence; ~**erklärung** negative declaration; ~**klausel** negative pledge clause: *undertaking by a bank to refrain from issuing additional secured debentures;* ~**zins** negative interest.

negatorisch *adj* negating, denying, prohibiting.

negieren *v/t* to negate.

negoziabel *adj* negotiable, marketable.

negoziierbar *adj* negotiable; *nicht* ~: *non-negotiable*.

Negoziierbarkeit *f* negotiability.

Negoziierung *f* negotiation.

Negoziierungsanzeige

Negoziierungs|anzeige advice of negotiation; **~ermächtigung** authority to negotiate; **~auftrag** order to negotiate; **~kredit** drawing authorization, letter of authority, negotiation credit.
Nehmer *m* taker, buyer, investor.
Neigung *f* inclination, tendency, propensity; **kriminelle ~** criminal leanings; **schädliche** proclivity (*to sth harmful*), destructive leanings, damaging tendency.
Neinstimme *f* negative vote, *pl* the noes.
Nekrophilie *f* necrophilism.
Nennbetrag *m* nominal amount, face value.
Nennkapital *n* nominal capital.
Nennonkel *m* a nominal uncle.
Nenntante *f* nominal aunt.
Nennung *f* naming, mention, designation *esp pl*: credits (*film*).
Nennwert *m* nominal amount, nominal value, par value, face value, par, nominal par; **~aktie** par-value share, nominal-value share; **n~los** *adj* no par (value), non-par value; **~parität** nominal parity; **~~ von** *Banknoten*: parity of notes.
Nepotismus *m* nepotism.
Nepp *m* daylight-robbery.
neppen *v/t* to fleece s. o., to dupe, to swindle.
Nerven|anspannung suspense, strain; **~arzt** neurologist; **~klinik** mental hospital, neuropathic hospital, psychiatric and neurological clinic; **~krieg** war of nerves; **~schock** mental shock, nervous shock.
netto *adj* net, after all deductions, without deductions; **rein ~** net without any discount.
Netto|-Anlageinvestition net investment in fixed assets; **~auslandsinvestition** net foreign investment; **~auslandsposition** net external monetary position; **~-Ausschüttung** net payment, net relevant distribution; **~beanspruchung** net borrowing; **~bestände** net holdings; **~betrag** net amount, net sum, clear amount,

Nettowährungsreserven

clear money; **~betriebsgewinn** net operating income; net operating profit; **~betriebsverlust** net operating loss; **~bezüge** net salary; **~bilanz** balance of balances; **~dienstbezüge** net remuneration; **~dividende** net dividend; **~einkünfte** net earnings; **~einnahmen** net receipts, net income; **~entschädigung** net indemnity, net compensation; **~erdöleinfuhren** net oil imports; **~erlös** net proceeds; **~ersparnis** net savings; **~ertrag** net yield, *pl* (*also*): net earnings; **~ertragswertberechnung** net earnings rule; **~finanzierungsdefizite** net financial deficit; **~gewicht** net weight; **~gewinn** net profit; **~grenzprodukt** marginal net product; **~guthaben** net holdings; **~inventarwert** net asset value; **~kredit** (*ohne Gebühren und Kosten*) proceeds of credit; **~kurs** net price; **~lohn** net wage(s), take-home pay, effective wage payment(s); **~miete** net rent; **~pacht** net rental for a lease; **~prämie** net premium, net level annual premium; **~preis** net price, trade price (*list price less trade discount*); zum **~~**: straight; **~produktion** net production; **~produzentenanteil** producer's net share; **~raumgehalt** net tonnage; **~registertonne** net registered ton; **~rendite** net yield, after-tax yield; **~rente** net annual return; **~reserve** net reserves; **~schaden** net loss; **~sozialprodukt** net social product, net national product; **~sparzins** net rate of interest on savings; **~steuerbelastung** net burden of taxes; **~umsatz** net turnover, net sales, net returns; **~umsatzerlöse** net sales; **~umsatzrendite** net earnings as a percentage of sales; **~verdienst** take-home pay; **~verlust** net loss, clear loss; **~vermögen** net assets; **~verzinsung** net interest (return); net return; *interest after deduction of withholding tax;* **~-Volkseinkommen** net national income; **~währungsreserven** net official

565

Netz — **Neuzulassung**

monetary assets; ~**warenumsatz** net sales; ~**wert** net value; ~**-Wertzuwachs** net added value; ~**zins** pure interest, net interest; ~**zinsklausel** net interest clause, pure interest clause.

Netz *n* network, system; ~**karte** area season ticket, network card; **das soziale ~** social (-security) network, system of welfare-state facilities, floor of protection.

Neu|abschluß fresh business, new order booked; ~**anschaffung** new acquisition; ~**auflage** new edition, reissue, republication; ~**aufnahme** admission of new members; ~**aufschluß** fresh exploitation (*of a mine*); ~**ausgabe** new edition, reissue; ~**ausrüstung** retooling, re-equipment; ~**auszeichnung** remarking (goods for sale); ~**bau** newly built house; new works; ~**baumietenverordnung** *ordinance regulating publicly subsidized tenancies on controlled rents in newly-built houses (D: 1975)*; ~**bauten** newly-built houses, new buildings; ~**begebung** new issue; ~**berechnung** updating, recalculation; ~**besetzung** new appointment, filling of a vacancy; *regelmäßige* ~~: *normal replacement*; ~**bestellung** repeat order, fresh order; ~**bewertung** revaluation, reassessment, reappraisal; ~~*srücklage: revaluation reserve*; ~~*srückstellung: special revaluation reserve*; ~**bewilligung** fresh appropriation; ~**bildung** reorganization, reshaping, reshuffle; ~**druck** republication, reprint, reimpression; ~**einstellung** fresh engagement, engagement of new personnel; ~**einteilung** reclassification; reapportionment; ~**eintragung** new registration; fresh entry in a register; ~**eintritte** new entrants; ~**emission** new issue of shares (*or* bonds); ~**erwerb** new acquisition; ~**erwerbungen** accessions, future additions; n~**fassen** *v/t* to redraft, to reword; ~**fassung** revised text, update; ~**festsetzung** revised text; ~**festsetzung** fixing of a new price, redetermination, realignment; ~~ *von Preisen: repricing*; ~**feststellung** restatement, fresh ascertainment; ~**formulierung** rewording, restatement; ~**fundierung** refunding; n~ **für alt** new for old; ~**geschäft** new business, fresh transaction; ~**gestaltung** reshaping, recasting; ~**gliederung** reorganization; new structure, rearrangement; ~**gründung** new foundation, newly established business; ~~ *durch Bareinlagen: new formation by cash subscriptions*; ~**investition** new investment, fresh capital expenditure; ~**kalkulation** recosting; ~**landwirt** pioneer farmer, newly set-up farmer; ~**lieferung** fresh supplies, redelivery; ~**ordnung** reform, rearrangement, reconstruction; ~~ *des Geldwesens: currency reform*; ~**orientierung** reorientation, new departure, realignment; ~**placierung** placing securities in fresh hands, putting securities back on the market; ~**regelung** revised arrangements, rearrangement, reorganization, reform; ~~*sgesetz: amending law*; ~**siedlung** new farm, newly established settlement, new housing project; ~**veranlagung** reassessment, post-assessment n~**vermieten** *v/t* to re-let; ~**vermietung** re-letting, letting new premises, granting a new tenancy; n~**veröffentlichen** to republish; n~**verpachten** *v/t* to re-lease; ~**verpachtung** granting a new lease, leasing for a new term; ~**verplanung** expenditure freshly voted; ~**verputzen** *n* replastering; ~**verschuldung** newly incurred indebtedness; ~**verteilung** redistribution; ~**wahl** new elections; ~~*en veranlassen: to go to the country*; ~**wert** original value, value when new; ~**wertschaden** damage equivalent to the value of a newly bought article; ~**wertversicherung** replacement value insurance; ~**zugang** fresh business, new accrual, new admission, accession; ~**zulassung** new registration;

newly licensed car; ~**zusammenschluß** reamalgamation; ~**zuteilung** reallocation.

Neuerung *f* innovation.

Neuheit *f* novelty, novel matter; ~ **der Erfindung** novelty of invention; **die** ~ **verneinen** to negate the novelty; **mangelnde** ~ want of (*or* lack of) novelty; **mangels** ~ due to lack of novelty.

Neuheits|aufkommen total of new inventions; ~**beweis** proof of novelty; ~**mangel** lack of novelty, want of novelty; ~**merkmal** novel feature; ~**prüfung** examination for novelty; ~**recherche** search as to novelty; ~**rest** retaining feature of recognized novelty, inventive difference; **n**~**schädlich** detrimental to novelty, novelty-destroying; ~**schädlichkeit** infringement of novelty, bar to novelty; ~**wert** novelty value, innovative value.

Neuling *m* newcomer, novice; ~**investor** novice investor.

neutral *adj* neutral, disinterested, impartial.

Neutralität *f* neutrality, neutral status; **bewaffnete** ~ armed neutrality; **ständige** ~ permanent neutrality; **wohlwollende** ~ friendly neutrality, benevolent neutrality.

Neutralitäts|abkommen neutrality agreement; ~**bruch** breach of neutrality; violation of neutrality; ~**erklärung** declaration of neutrality; ~**gesetze** neutrality laws; ~**politik** policy of neutrality; ~**status** neutral status; ~**verletzung** violation of neutrality; ~**zeichen** emblem of neutrality.

Nicht|abgabe failure to submit, non-submission, non-delivery; ~**-Abkommensland** non-agreement country, non-clearing country; ~**abnahme** failure to take delivery; non-acceptance, refusal to accept; ~~*entschädigung*: *compensation for failure to take delivery*; ~**achtung** non-observance, disregard; ~~ *des Gerichts*: *contempt of court;* **n**~**amtlich** *adj* non-official, unofficial; ~**anerkennung** non-recognition, non-acknowledgment; ~**angriffspakt** non-aggression pact; ~**annahme** non-acceptance; ~**anrainerstaat** non-littoral state; ~**antritt** failure to appear to serve a sentence; ~**anwendbarkeit** non-applicability; ~**anwendung** non-application; ~**anwesenheit** absence; ~**anzeige** failure to inform, failure to report sth. to the police; ~~ *von Verbrechen*: *non-disclosure of crimes, misprision of felony*; ~**ausführung** non-execution; ~**aushändigung** non-delivery, refusal to hand sth. over; ~**ausschöpfung** non-exhaustion; ~**ausschüttung von Dividenden** passing of the dividend, forgoing payment of dividend; ~**außenberuf** indoor calling; ~**ausübung** non-use, failure to exercise; ~~ e-s *Patents*: non-working (*or* non-exploitation) of a patent; ~**banken** non-banks, non-bank customers, parties other than banks; ~**bankenkundschaft** non-bank customers; ~**beachten** non-observance, failure to comply with (*a regulation*), non-adherence to; ~**beachtung** non-observance, disregard (for); ~~ *der verkehrsüblichen Sorgfalt*: *want of ordinary care*; ~~ *von Verkehrsanweisungen*: *ignoring directions*; ~~ *von Verkehrszeichen*: *ignoring traffic signs*; ~**beantwortung** failure to answer, non-response; ~**befolgung** non-compliance; *bei* ~~: *failing to comply with*; ~**beitreibbarkeit** uncollectibility, irrecoverability, impossibility of collecting; ~**beiwohnung** non-access; ~**benutzung** non-use, non-user; ~**berechtigter** non-entitled person, unauthorized person; ~**berücksichtigung** disregard; ~**bestehen** non-existence; ~**besteuerung** non-taxation; ~**bestreiten** non-denial, no contention; ~**deutscher** non-German, a non-German citizen, an alien; ~**diskriminierung** non-discrimination; ~~ *im Außenhandel: fair trade*; ~~*sklausel: non-discrimination clause;* ~**durchsetzbarkeit** unenforce-

Nichtehe   **Nichtverantwortlicher**

ability; ~**ehe** non-existent marriage; ~**ehelicher** illegitimate person; ~**ehelichkeit** illegitimacy; **n**~**eidlich** *adj* unsworn, not under oath; ~**eigentümer** non-owner; ~**eingreifen** non-intervention; ~**einhaltung** non-compliance; ~~ *von Förmlichkeiten hinnehmen*: *to waive formalities*; ~**einigung** nonagreement; *bei* ~~ *in default of agreement*; ~**einklagbarkeit** unenforceability; ~**einlassung** non-appearance; ~**einlösung** non-payment, dishonour(ing), failure to redeem; ~**einmischung** non-intervention; ~**einmischungspolitik** policy of non-interference, hands-off policy; ~**einräumung** non-delivery, failure to grant (*possession, a right etc*); ~**eintragung** non-registration; ~**eintreffen** failure to arrive; *bei* ~~ *keine Kaufverpflichtung: no arrival no sale*; ~**eintreibung** failure to collect; ~**eintritt** non-occurrence; ~~ *e-r Bedingung: non-occurrence of a contingency*; ~**erfolgen** non-occurrence; ~~ *des Geschlechtsverkehrs: non-intercourse*; ~**erfüllung** non-performance, non-fulfil(l)ment, failure to perform; ~~ *von Verpflichtungen: failure to fulfil obligations*; ~~ *der Zahlungsverpflichtung non-payment*; *bei* ~~ (*also*:) *on default*; ~**erhebung** refraining from levying; ~**erneuerung** non-renewal; ~**erscheinen** non-appearance, non-attendance, default of appearance, failure to appear; ~**erschöpfung des innerstaatlichen Rechtswegs** non-exhaustion of domestic remedies; ~**erweislichkeit** unprovability; ~**fachmann** layman, outsider, non-expert; ~**gebrauch** non-use, non-user, disuse; ~**gemeinschaftsländer** countries other than those of the Community; ~**genehmigung** non-approval; ~**gewährung** refusal to grant sth.; **n**~**gewerblich** *adj* non-commercial, non-trading; ~**gewerkschaftler** non-union worker; ~**haftung** non-liability,

exemption from liability; ~**honorierung** dishono(u)ring; ~**kaufmann** non-merchant, non-trader; ~**kenntnis** ignorance, lack of knowledge, absence of notice; *schuldhafte* ~~: *negligent ignorance*; ~~ *tatsächlicher Umstände*: *ignorance of fact*; ~**klagbar** *adj* non-suable; ~**kombattant** non-combatant; **n**~**kommerziell** *adj* non-commercial; ~**konvertierbarkeit** inconvertibility; ~**kriegführung** non-belligerency; ~**leistung** non-performance, failure to perform, default; *bei* ~~ (*also*:) *on default*; *versehentliche* ~~: *inadvertent default*; ~**lieferung** non-delivery; ~**mitglied** non-member; ~**nennung** remaining nameless; ~~ *des Erfinders beantragt* ~~: *the inventor requests to remain nameless*; **n**~**obligatorisch** non-compulsory; ~**offenbarung** non-disclosure; **n**~**offenbarungspflichtig** immune from disclosure; ~**öffentlichkeit** non-admission of the public; privacy; ~**organisierte** non-unionists; ~**rechtsfähig** *adj* unincorporated; ~**rückwirkung** non-retroactivity; ~**schlüssigkeit** inconclusivess, „no case to answer"; ~**schuld** non-existing debt; ~**schuldigerklärung** plea of not guilty, general issue; ~**schuldvermutung** presumption of innocence; ~**seßhafte** persons without fixed abode; ~**steuerpflichtiger** non-taxable person; ~**störer** *m* non-disturber, *person not committing a disturbance or violation of public order;* ~**straftat** non-punishable act; ~**teilnehmerland** non-participating country; ~- **übereinstimmung** non-conformity, variance; **n**~**übertragbar** *adj* non-transferable, non-assignable; non-negotiable; ~**unternehmen** parties other than enterprises; ~**unterzeichner** non-signer, non-signatory; ~**unterzeichnerregierung** non-signatory government; ~**veranlagungsverfügung** non-assessment order; ~**verantwortlicher** non-responsible party; ~**veräußerung** non-alienation; ~**verbreitung** non-proliferation, non-dissemination; ~**vereidigung** non-administration of the oath; ~**verfolgung** non-prosecution; ~**verfügbarkeit** non-availability; ~**verhandeln** failure to argue the case in court, refusal to negotiate; ~**verlängerung** discontinuing, non-renewal; ~**vermarktung** withholding s.th. from the market; ~**vermögensrechtlich** *adj* not concerning property rights, non-pecuniary; ~**verpfändungsklausel** negative pledging clause; ~**versicherung** non-insurance; ~**vertragsstaaten** non-contracting states; ~**verwendung** non-use, disuse; ~**vollstreckbarkeit** non-enforceability; ~**vollziehung** non-execution; n~ **vorbestraft** having no criminal record; ~**vorbestrafter** person without a criminal record; ~**vorhandensein** non-existence; *bei* ~~ *e–s Gegenbeweises: in the absence of proof to the contrary*; ~**vorlage** non-presentation, non-submission; ~**vorlegung** non-presentation, non-submission; ~**wählbarkeit** incapacity of being elected, ineligibility; ~**wähler** non-voter; ~**weiterbetreiben e-s Prozesses** abandonment of action; ~**weitergabevertrag** nonproliferation treaty; ~**wissen** ignorance, lack of knowledge; *mit* ~~ *bestreiten: to raise the plea of lack of knowledge*; *schuldhaftes* ~~: *voluntary ignorance, culpable ignorance*; *schuldloses* ~~: *bona fide without notice*; n~**wissend** *adj* ignorant, having no knowledge of sth.; ~**wohngebäude** non-residential building; ~**zahlung** non-payment, failure to pay, default of payment; *bei* ~~: *in default of payment*; ~**zugehörigkeit** non-membership, disaffiliation; ~**zugestehen** non-admission; ~**zulassung** non-admission (*to the bar, of an appeal etc*); ~~ *zur amtlichen Notierung: non-quotation*; ~**zulassungsbeschwerde** complaint against denial of leave to appeal; ~**zustimmung** non-consent; ~**zutreffendes streichen** delete what is inapplicable.

nichtig *adj*, void, null and void, absolutely void; ~ **gegenüber Dritten** void as against any third person; ~ **machen** to avoid, to nullify, to render void; **für** ~ **erklären** to nullify; **insgesamt** ~ void pro toto; **teilweise** ~ void pro tanto; **von Anfang an** ~ void from the beginning, void ab initio.

Nichtigerklärung *f* declaration of nullity, annulment.

Nichtigkeit *f* nullity, absolute nullity; **heilbare** ~ curable nullity; **relative** ~ relative nullity, contestability; **teilweise** ~ partial nullity.

Nichtigkeits|beschwerde nullity appeal; ~**einrede** plea of nullity; ~**entscheidung** decision on a plea of nullity; ~**erklärung** annulment, nullification, declaration of annulment; ~**grund** ground of nullity, reason for nullity; ~**gründe** *pat* grounds for revocation; ~**klage** proceedings for annulment (*new trial*), nullity suit, invalidity suit, action for cancellation; ~**prozeß** proceedings for annulment, nullity suit; ~**senat** patent appeal court: *court division for nullity (of patents) suits*; ~**urteil** decree of nullity, declaration of nullity; ~**verfahren** nullity proceedings, invalidation suit; ~**urteil** decree of nullity, nullity ruling.

Niederkunft *f* accouchement, confinement, delivery, childbirth.

niederlassen *v/reflex* to establish a business, to settle down.

Niederlassung *f* place of business, business establishment; branch; ~**en an den Offshore-Finanzplätzen** offshore branches (*banking*); ~ **im Ausland** foreign branch; **gewerbliche** ~ business establishment.

Niederlassungs|abkommen convention on establishment, treaty on settlement and residence; ~**bereich** *region within which a company may do business and keep branches*; ~**be-**

niederlegen

schränkung restriction on freedom of establishment; **~bewilligung** permission to settle, permission to establish a business; **~freiheit** right of establishment, freedom of settlement; **~netz** branch network; **~ort** place of business; **~recht** law of establishment, right of establishment, right of settlement, *right to choose one's place of business and residence*; **~vertrag** treaty governing settlement and residence, treaty on establishment.

niederlegen *v/t* to lay down, to resign (from an office), to set forth; to deposit; **schriftlich ~** to set down in writing, to reduce to writing.

Niederlegung *f* resignation (*from office*); deposit (*of a document at post office, court or police station as substituted service*); **~ des Mandats** to give up a mandate, to cease acting as s. o.'s lawyer.

niederschlagen *v/t* to suppress, to quell (*riot*), to quash (*prosecution*), to cancel (*public fees, costs*).

Niederschlagung *f* suppression; quashing, waiver.

niederschreiben *v/t* to write down, to put down, to set down, to record, to register; *etwas vollständig ~~*: *to write sth out (in full)*.

Niederschrift *f* record, minutes, written statement, memorandum; **gerichtliche ~** court record; **notarische ~** notarial record, notarial protocol; **vereinbarte ~** agreed minutes.

Niederschutzgebiet *n* low-protection area.

Niederstwertprinzip *n* cost-or-market rule; *rule of cost or market, whichever is lower*; minimum value principle; lower-of-cost-or-market rule *zum ~ at the lower of cost or market*.

Niederträchtigkeit *f* maliciousness, viciousness, malice.

Niedriglohnland *n* low-wage country.

Niedrigsteuergebiet *n* area of low taxation, tax haven.

Nominalbeteiligung

Niedrigzinspolitik *f* policy of low interest rates.

Niemandsland *n* terra nullius, no-man's land.

Nießbrauch *m* usufruct, usufructuary enjoyment, beneficial interest; **~ an Grundstück** usufruct of landed property; **~ an Inbegriff von Sachen** usufruct of an aggregate of things; **~ auf Lebenszeit** usufruct for life, usufructuary life estate; **~bestellung** grant of usufruct, declaration of uses; **~ für den überlebenden Ehegatten** usufruct for life to the surviving spouse, life interest to surving spouse; **den ~ ausüben** to exercise the right of usufruct; **e-n ~ bestellen** to grant a (right of) usufruct; **lebenslänglicher ~** usufruct for life, life interest; **mit e-m ~ belasten** to burden (property) with a right of usufruct.

Nießbraucher *m* usufructuary, beneficiary under a right of usufruct.

Nießbrauchs|berechtigter = *Nießbraucher qv*; **~recht** right of usufruct; *gesetzliches ~~*: *legal usufruct*; *gestaffeltes ~~*: *shifting usufruct (or: use)*; **~vermächtnis** usufructuary legacy, life interest.

Nihilist *m* nihilist.

Niveau *n* level, standard, status; **hohes sittliches ~** high standard of ethics, high moral standard.

nivellieren *v/t* to level, to make even; **nach unten ~** to level down.

Nivellierungskauf *m* equalizing purchase.

noch nicht in Kraft still-not-in-force.

Nochgeschäft *n* repeat option business, option to double, call-of-more, put of more: *option to buy or sell multiples (of previously bought or sold securities)*; **~ in Käufers Wahl** buyer's option to double.

nolens-volens *adv* willingly or unwillingly.

Nomenklatur *f* nomenclature.

nominal *adj* nominal, in terms of money.

Nominal|beteiligung nominal par-

nominell

ticipation; ~**betrag** nominal amount, nominal value, amount at par value, face value; ~**einkommen** nominal income; ~**kapital** nominal capital, registered capital; ~**kurs** quoted price; ~**satz** nominal rate; ~**verzinsung** nominal interest; ~**wert** par value, nominal par, nominal value, face value; ~**zinsen** nominal interest return; ~**zinsfuß** nominal rate of interest; ~**zinssatz** nominal rate (of interest).

nominell *adj* nominal, by name, titular.

nominieren *v/t* to nominate.

Nominierter *m* nominee, appointee.

Nominierung *f* nomination.

Non-valeur *f* worthless security.

Nörgelei *f* nagging, carping, faultfinding, niggling criticism.

nörgelsüchtig *adj* nagging, querulous, carping, niggling.

Norm *f (pl Normen = ~en)* norm, standard, standard of performance, standard of quality; rule, legal provision, statutory rule; ~**blatt** standard sheet; ~**enausschuß** standards committee, standards institution; ~**enkartell** standardization cartel; ~**enkollision** conflict of laws; ~**enkontrolle** judicial review of the constitutionality of laws, test of constitutionality; ~**enkontrollverfahren** judicial proceedings on the constitutionality of laws; ~**enprüfung** verification of standards, maintenance; ~**en und Typen** standards and types; ~- ~~*kartell: standardization cartel, cartel for uniform industrial standards*; ~**enverband** standards association; ~**envorschrift** standard specification; ~**klarheit** clarity of legal rules; explicit standards; ~**kontingent** standard quota; ~**maße** standard measures; ~**-Rediskontkontingent** standard rediscount quota; ~**satz** standard rate; ~**schrift** standard style of lettering; **n**~**unterschreitend** substandard; ~**vordruck** standard printed form; ~**wert** standard; *in* ~~*en ausdrücken: to standardize*; **n**~**widrig** *adj*

Normalisation

non-standard; ~**zeile** standard length (of a line); **anerkannte** ~**en** established standards; **arbeitsrechtliche** ~**en** labour standards; **formaljuristische** ~ technical rule of law, formal legal rule; **sachenrechtliche** ~ rule under the law of property; **sachlichrechtliche** ~ rule of substance; **schuldrechtliche** ~ rule under the law of obligations (*or* contract); **zwingende** ~ mandatory rule, obligatory provision.

normal *adj* normal, regular, ordinary; **geistig** ~ of sound mind, sane, compos mentis.

Normalabschreibung normal (calculated) depreciation, flat rate depreciation; ~**arbeitszeit** regular time, regular working hours; ~**ausführung** standard make, standard design, regular model; ~**benzin** regular petrol, regular fuel; ~**breite** normal width; ~**brief** standard letter; ~**ertrag** normal yield; ~**erzeugung** normal output; ~**fall** normal case, standard occurrence; ~**format** standard size, standard format; ~**gewicht** standard weight; **n**~**groß** *adj* standard-sized; ~**größe** standard size; ~**konditionen** usual terms and conditions; ~**kontenplan** standard scheme of accounts; ~**kosten** normal cost; ~~ *pro Einheit: standard unit cost*; ~**kraftstoff** regular-grade motor fuel, normal petrol; ~**leistung** normal output; ~**lohn** regular pay, standard remuneration; ~**maß** standard measure; ~**police** standard policy; ~**post** surface mail; ~**preis** normal price, standard price; ~**satz** regular rate, standard rate; ~**spur** standard gauge; ~**stundentarif** standard time rates, standard hourly rate of pay; ~**verbrauch** normal consumption; ~**verbraucher** average consumer; ~**verteilung** normal distribution; ~**verzinsung** regular rate of interest, nominal yield; ~**wert** normal value, standard value; ~**zeit** standard time.

Normalisation *f* standardization.

Normalisierung *f* normalization, return to normal conditions; ~**zeichen** signs of a return to normality, evidence of normal conditions.

Normativ|bedingungen standard conditions; ~**bestimmungen** standard regulations, standard provisions.

normen *v/t* to standardize.

normieren *v/t* to standardize, to normalize, to lay down as a rule.

Normung *f* standardization.

Nostrifikation naturalization; recognition of foreign diploma.

Nostro|geschäft business done for our own account; ~**guthaben** credit balance on a nostro account, credit balance with other banks, nostro balance; ~**transaktion** operation for own account; ~**verbindlichkeit** nostro liability, due to banks; ~**verpflichtungen** due to banks.

Not *f* need, want, poverty, distress, emergency; ~**abgabe** emergency levy; ~**adressat** drawee in case of need, referee in case of need: *als* ~~ *intervenieren: to intervene in case of need*; ~**adresse** referee in case of need; ~**akzept** acceptance in case of need; ~**anzeige** notice of dishonour; ~**aufnahme** emergency *(for refugees)*, entry permit; emergency admission *(hospital)*; ~~*gesetz law on entry and residence permits for German refugees*; ~~*lager: temporary reception camp*; ~~*verfahren: emergency reception procedure*; ~**ausgang** emergency exit, fire exit; ~**ausstieg** escape hatch, emergency exit, emergency door; ~**bedarf** necessaries, essential requirements; ~**bedarfseinrede** plea of destitution, plea of necessity; ~**behelf** makeshift, stopgap; ~**bekanntmachung** emergency announcement; ~**bestellung** emergency appointment; ~**betrieb** emergency operation; ~**betrug** petty fraud due to need; ~**bremse** emergency brake; ~**diebstahl** petty theft due to need, pilferage; ~**dienst** emergency service, emergency duty; ~**dienstpflichtiger** person recruited for emergency service; ~**einsatzkommando** emergency squad; ~**entwendung** pilfering due to need; petty larceny out of need; ~**erbrecht** compulsory right of inheritance; ~**fall** emergency, exigence; ~**fallbehandlung** emergency treatment; ~**frist** strict (statutory) time limit *(which cannot be extended)*; ~**fristzeugnis** certificate of absence of appeal: *court certificate that appeal has not been filed within statutory period;* ~**geld** emergency currency, emergency money, scrip (money); ~**gemeinschaft** *association formed in times of need*; ~**geschäftsführer** emergency director *(appointed by the court to fill vacancy)*; ~**gesetzgebung** emergency legislation; ~**hafen** port of refuge, port of distress, port of anchorage; ~~*klausel: port of refuge clause;* ~**helfer** helper in need: *person warding off an attack from another, rescuer;* ~**hilfe** help in an emergency; defence of another from imminent attack; ~**hilfedienst** rescue service; ~**klausel** escape clause; ~**lage** (state of) emergency, state of need, exigence, distressed circumstances; ~**landung** emergency landing, forced landing; **n~leidend** needy; defaulting, dishonoured, delinquent, ailing; ~**leistungsgesetz** emergency relief law; ~**leitungsrecht** *emergency right to lay conduits (piper, lines) across another's land;* ~**lösung** temporary solution, emergency solution; ~**lüftungssystem** means of emergency ventilation; ~**lüge** white lie; ~**maßnahme** emergency measure, stopgap; ~**operation** emergency operation; ~**opfer** emergency levy; ~**parlament** emergency parliament; ~**programm** emergency plan, austerity program(me); ~**recht** emergency law, emergency legislation; ~**ruf** emergency call, distress call; helpline; ~**rufsäule** emergency telephone box; ~**schlachtung** emergency slaugh-

Notalgeld

ter (*of injured animal etc*); ~**schrei** cry of distress; ~**signal** distress signal; ~**stand** → *Notstand*; ~**stromanlage** emergency power unit; ~**testament** nuncupative (= oral) will (*in testator's last sickness or in an emergency*); ~**tötung** emergency slaughter; ~**trauung** emergency marriage celebration; ~**treppe** emergency staircase; ~**und Dringlichkeitsfall** case of need and urgency; ~ **und Gefahr** trouble and danger; ~**unterkunft** temporary accommodation, makeshift accommodation; ~**veräußerung** compulsory disposal; ~**verglasung** emergency glass fitting; ~**verkauf** emergency sale, compulsory sale; ~**verordnung** emergency decree; ~**verpfändung der Schiffsladung** repondentia; ~**verwalter** emergency administrator; ~**vorrat** emergency supply; ~**vorstand** temporary (court-appointed) board; ~**weg** way of necessity, emergency route; ~~**recht**: *right of access, easement of access;* ~**wehr** self-defence, privilege of self-defence; *berechtigte* ~~: (*justified*) *self-defence*; ~**wehrexzeß** excessive self-defence; ~**wehrlage** situation justifying self-defence; *extreme* ~~: *retreat to the wall*; ~**wehrrecht** right of self-defence, privilege of self-defence; ~**wohnung** emergency accommodation, makeshift dwelling; ~**zeit** period of emergency; ~**zucht** → *Notzucht*; ~**zurückbehaltungsrecht** extended right of retention (*apprehension of insolvency*), right of stoppage in transitu; ~**zustand** state of emergency, state of distress.

Notalgeld *n* bank notes.

Notar *m* notary, notary public; ~**anderkonto** notarial trust account; account kept by a notary in his own name for a third party; ~**assessor** junior notary; ~**kammer** chamber of notaries, professional association of notaries; ~**siegel** notary's seal; ~**tag** annual congress of notaries; ~**vertreter** deputy notary; **amtierender** ~ officiating notary; **beurkundender** ~ recording notary; **der mitwirkende** ~ the notary acting in this matter, officiating notary.

Notariat *n* notary's office.

Notariats|akt notarial instrument, notarial act; ~**angelegenheiten** notarial matters; ~**angestellter** notarial employee; ~**beamter** notarial officer; ~**gebühr** notary's fee, *pl* (*also*): notarial charges; ~**kosten** notarial charges; ~**ordnung** regulations for notaries; ~**protokoll** notarial instrument, notarial record of the proceedings; ~**recht** law for notaries, law relating to notarial functions; ~**siegel** notary's seal; ~**urkunde** notarial instrument, notarially recorded document, notarial deed; ~**verfassung** organization of the profession of notaries; ~**verweser** administrator for a (defunct) notary; ~**zwang** mandatory notarial proceedings.

notariell *adj* notarial; ~ **beglaubigt** → *beglaubigt;* ~ **beurkundet** → *beurkundet.*

notarisch *adj* notarial.

Note *f* note, bank note; mark (*school*); **diplomatische** ~ diplomatic note.

Noten|aufruf calling in of notes; ~**ausgabe** issue of bank notes; ~**ausgaberecht** issuing power; ~**austausch** exchange of notes; ~**bank** note-issuing bank; bank of issue, central bank; ~**bankgeld** central bank money; ~**bankinstrumentarium** power of the central bank; ~**bankprivileg** note-issuing privilege, right of issue; ~**bankwesen** central banking; ~**deckung** cover of note circulation; ~**durchschnitt** average marks; ~**emission** issue of bank notes, note issue; ~ **monopol** note-issuing privilege; ~**regal** prerogative of issuing bank notes; ~**reserve** reserve to cover bank notes; ~**rückfluß** reflux of bank notes; ~**umlauf** circulation of bank notes, notes in circulation; ~**wechsel** exchange of notes.

notieren *v/t* to note, to make a note, to write down; to quote, to list; *v/i*: to stand at; *notiert werden*: *to be quoted at the exchange*; **amtlich** ~ to list officially.

notiert *adj* listed, quoted; **nicht** ~ not listed, unlisted, unquoted, unregistered.

Notierung *f* quotation; ~ **in Bruchteilen** split quotation; **amtliche** ~ official quotation; **erste** ~ opening quotation; **genannte** ~ nominal quotation; **zur** ~ **zugelassen** admitted to the stock exchange.

Notifikation *f* notification, notice; notice of dishonour; ~**spflicht** notification requirement, duty to give notice; ~**surkunde** certification instrument.

notifizieren *v/t* to notify.

Notifizierung *f* notification, noting; ~**sdatum** date of noting.

nötigen *v/t* to coerce, to compel, to put under duress.

Nötigung *f* undue pressure, duress, coercion; unlawful compulsion; ~ **durch Drohung** duress under a threat; ~ **im Amt** unlawful compulsion by a public official; ~**sstand** state of duress; *im* ~~ *handeln*: *to act under duress*; ~ **von Beamten** coercion of officials; ~ **von Gesetzgebungsorganen** use of force and threats against legislative bodies; ~ **von Parlamentsmitgliedern** intimidation of MPs; ~ **zur Unzucht** indecent assault; **auf Grund e–r** ~ under duress; **unter** ~ **handeln** to act under duress.

Notiz *f* note, quotation; **amtliche** ~ official listing; ~ **ohne Umsätze** nominal quotation.

Notizblock *n* scratch pad *US*, scribbling book, notebook *GB*.

notleidend *adj* needy, poor, distressed, in sufferance.

notleiden lassen *v/t* to hold in suspense (*bill of exchange*).

notorisch *adj* notorious.

Notstand *m* emergency, state of emergency, (urgent), necessity; excuse of necessity, irresistible compulsion; **e–n** ~ **erklären** to proclaim a state of emergency; **öffentlicher** ~ public emergency; **nationaler** ~ national emergency; **strafrechtlicher** ~ plea of necessity in criminal law; **übergesetzlicher** ~ extra-statutory necessity.

Notstands|arbeiten unemployment relief projects; ~**beihilfe** emergency assistance grant; ~**bestimmungen** emergency provisions; ~**einsatz** emergency action, emergency operation; ~**exzeß** acts not excused by the (existing state of) emergency; ~**gebiet** distressed area, emergency area, development area; ~**gesetze** emergency laws; ~**gesetzgebung** emergency legislation; ~**land** distressed country, distressed area; ~**maßnahmen** emergency measures; ~**sondersitzung** special emergency session; ~**- und Sanierungsprogramm** distress and rehabilitation programme; ~**vorhaben** unemployment relief project; ~**vorlage** emergency bill.

notwendig *adj* necessary, requisite; ~**enfalls** *adv* in case of necessity, in case of need; ~ **machen** to necessitate; ~ **sein** to be required; ~ **und geeignet** necessary and proper; ~ **und zweckmäßig** necessary and expedient.

Notwendigkeit *f* necessity, need; **absolute** ~ absolute necessity, stringent necessity; **dringende** ~ urgent necessity, absolute need.

Notzucht *f* rape; ~ **mit Todesfolge** rape resulting in death; ~**täter** rapist, ravisher; ~**versuch** attempt to rape.

notzüchtigen *v/t* to rape, to commit rape.

Novation *f* novation, renewal, substitution of debt; ~**svertrag** substituted contract.

Novelle *f* re-enactment, supplementary law, amending statute.

Novellierung *f* re-enactment of a law (*with amemdments*); ~**svorschlag** proposed amendment, proposal for re-enactment.

Null nought, zero; **~kopie** first print (*film*); **~kuponanleihe** Zero Bonds; **~saldo** zero balance; **~satz** nil rate band; **~serie** pilot lot; **~stellung** zeroing; **~tarif** fare-free transport; **~tarifzölle** zero tariffs; **~wachstum** zero growth; **n~ und nichtig** null and void.

nulla poena sine lege no crime without a law: *no crime unless there is a statute for it.*

Nullifizierung *f* nullification.

numerieren *v/t* to number; **laufend ~** to number consecutively.

numeriert *adj* numbered; **fortlaufend ~** consecutively numbered.

numerisch *adj* numerical.

Numerus clausus *m* (numerically) restricted admission (*to university or profession*), numerus clausus.

Nummer *f* number, serial number, sub-item; **~ndepot** numbered custody account; **~nfolge** sequence of numbers; **~nkonto** numbered account; **~nschild** number plate, licence plate; **laufende ~** running number, serial number, consecutive number; **nicht mehr benützte ~n** inactive numbers, no longer used numbers.

Nuntiatur *f* nunciature.

Nuntius *m* nuncio.

Nur-Hausfrau f (exclusively a) housewife.

Nutz|anwendung practical application; **n~bar** *adj* useful; **~~ machen**: *to utilize;* **~barkeit** usefulness, utility; **~barmachung** utilization, exploitation, industrial application, reclamation (*soil*), cultivation; **n~bringend** *adj* useful, benefical; **~dauer** useful (*or* service) life; **~effekt** practical effect, useful effect; **~fahrt** loaded run, business trip; **~fahrzeug** commercial vehicle; **~fläche** usable floor-space, used area; **~holz** timber; **~~rechte**: *timber rights;* **~kosten** fixed costs apportioned to productive capacity; **~last** payload, useful load, loading capacity, permitted load; **höchstzulässige ~~**: *maximum permissible payload;* **~lastfahrzeug** load-carrying vehicle; **~leistung** effective performance, output; **n~los** *adj* useless, unavailing; **~losigkeit** non-utility, disutility, uselessness; **~nießer** usufructuary, beneficiary, user; *lebenslänglicher ~~*: *life beneficiary;* **~nießung** use, usufruct; **~nießungsrecht** right of usufruct; **~pfand** = *Nutzungspfand qv;* **~schwelle** break-even point; **~tier** (economically) useful animal; **~- und Zuchtvieh** animals for stock and breeding purposes; **~verwaltung** (matrimonial regime of husband's) administrative and usufructuary rights (*formerly enjoyed by husband over wife's property*); **~wert** utility (value), useful value.

Nutzen *m* utility, usefulness, benefit, advantage, profit; **~ bringen** to benefit; **~ e-r Erfindung** utility of an invention; **~-Kosten-Analyse** profit cost analysis; **~maximum** maximum utility, total utility; **~schwelle** break-even point; **abnehmender ~** diminishing utility; **e-n ~ abwerfen** to be of use, to yield a benefit; **gemeinsamer ~** mutual advantage; **öffentlicher ~** public use; **wirtschaftlicher ~** economic value.

nützlich *adj* useful, expedient.

Nützlichkeit *f* utility, usefulness; **~serwägungen** utilitarian considerations.

Nutzung *f* use, utilization, emoluments (*fruits plus advantages*); *pl:* (*Nutzungen = ~en*) *also:* possession and enjoyment, profits; **~ des Eigenbesitzers** beneficial use; **~ und Besitz** use and occupation; **~ von Abwärme** waste heat utilization; **alleinige ~** entire use, exclusive use; **bauliche ~** use for building purposes; **die ~en haben** to use and enjoy sth.; **die ~en ziehen** to draw the profits (and enjoy the benefits); **eigene ~** own use and benefit; **gemeinsame ~** joint use and benefit; **gemischtwirtschaftliche ~** mixed residential and non-residential use; **immerwährende ~**

Nutzungsänderung / **Nutzungsrecht**

permanent use and profits; **landwirtschaftliche ~** agricultural use; **lebenslängliche ~en** use and profits for life; **ungestörte ~** quiet enjoyment; **wirtschaftliche ~** economic use.

Nutzungs|änderung change of user; change of utilization; **~art** type of use, application (*of invention*); **~aufgabe** discontinuance of use, desuetude; **~ausfall** loss of use; **~ausübung** user; **~befugnis** right of beneficial use; **~dauer** operating life, useful life, duration of use; *betriebsgewöhnliche ~~*: ordinary useful life; *durchschnittliche ~~*: average life; *gewöhnliche ~~*: expected life; *wirtschaftliche ~~*: economic life; *technische ~~*: physical life; **~entgang** loss of use, loss of enjoyment; **~entnahme** withdrawal for own use (*or: use only*); **~entschädigung** compensation for use; occupation rent; **~ertrag** revenue for the use of sth.; **~gebot** requirement to use land (*according to official development plan*); **~gebühr** charge for the use and benefit, rental; **~gemeinschaft** association for joint utilization; **~genossenschaft** agricultural co-operative; **~grad** degree of productivity, yield; **~güter** durable consumer goods; **~maß** extent of use; **~maximum** utility optimum; **~möglichkeit** possible use; **~pfand** antichresis, Welsh mortgage; **~recht** → *Nutzungsrecht*; **~satz** rate of exploitation, percentage of utilization; **~schaden** damage through deprivation of use, loss of use, loss of user; **~überlassungsvertrag** agreement on the surrender of the use and benefit of sth.; **~untersagung** restraint of use, ban on use of sth; **~vergütung** working interest, compensation for the exploitation rights; **~verhältnis** owner and user relationship; *gesetzliches ~~*: statutory tenancy; **~verlust** loss of usufruct, loss of use, loss of fruits and benefits; **~vermächtnis** legacy of usufruct; **~vertrag** permission for use contract, use and occupation contract; **~wert** utility value, useful value, value in use, enjoyment value.

Nutzungsrecht *n* right of use and enjoyment (*of property*); beneficial interest; **auflösend bedingtes lebenslängliches ~** determinable life interest; **ausschließliches ~** exclusive right of exploitation; **unbeschränktes ~** beneficial use, unlimited use of.

O

Oasenländer *n/pl* tax-havens.
obdachlos *adj* homeless, shelterless.
Obdachlosen|asyl hostel for the homeless, night shelter; "dosshouse"; **~behörde** department for homeless persons; **~einweisung** admission to a hostel for the homeless; **~heim** hostel for the homeless, house of refuge, common lodging house, night shelter.
Obdachloser *m* (*der Obdachlose*) homeless person.
Obdachlosigkeit *f* homelessness.
Obduktion *f* autopsy, post-mortem examination; **e-e ~ vornehmen** to conduct an autopsy, to perform a post-mortem examination.
obduzieren *v/t* = *e-e Obduktion vornehmen qv*.
oben *adv* above, hereinbefore, ante, supra (*in citations*).
obenerwähnt *adj* above-mentioned, above-named, aforesaid.
obengenannt *adj* above-mentioned, above-named.
Ober|amtmann chief inspector, senior clerical officer; **~amtsrichter** chief magistrate judge; **~anspruch** overriding claim; **~aufsicht** superintendence, supervision; **~ausschuß** senior committee; **~befehl** supreme command; **~begriff** generic term, nomen collectivum; *pat* characterizing portion, preamble (*of a claim*); **~buchhalter** chief accountant; **~bundesanwalt** Chief Public Attorney; **~bürgermeister** lord mayor; **~eigentum** title paramount, eminent domain; **~eigentümer** superior owner; **~finanzbezirk** regional revenue district; **~finanzdirektion** superior finance directorate; **~finanzkasse** Chief Tax Collector's Office; **~finanzpräsident** president of an Oberfinanzdirektion *qv*; **~flächenschaden** surface damage; **~flächenwasser** surface waters; **~gericht** higher court; **~gerichtsvollzieher** senior bailiff, high bailiff; **~gesellschaft** principal company, primary company; **~grenze** upper limit, ceiling, cap; **~gutachten** decisive expert opinion; **~haus** upper house, upper chamber, House of Lords, Senate; **~hausmitglieder** members of the House of Lords; *lebenslängliche* **~~**: life peers; **~herrschaft** supremacy, dominion; **~hofmeister** Lord Chamberlain of the Household; **~hoheit** supremacy; **~~** *des* (*brit.*) *Parlaments*: sovereignty of Parliament; **~justizkasse** Court Funds Office; **~kleidung** outer wear, outer garments; **~kommando** high command, supreme command; **~landesgericht** Regional Appeal Court, Higher Regional Court; **~lehen** tenure in capite; **~lehnsherr** overlord; **~leitung** overhead wires; **~lieger** supra-riparian; **~postdirektion** Superior Postal Directorate; **~prüfungsamt** High Board of Examination; **~realschule** secondary technical school; **~rechnungshof** public audit department; **~regierungsrat** senior executive officer; **~schiedsrichter** umpire; **~schule** secondary school; **~staatsanwalt** Senior Public Prosecutor, Director of Public Prosecutions, attorney general; **~steuerinspektor** senior tax inspector; **~studiendirektor** headmaster of a secondary school, principal of a high school (*as a civil service rank*); **~stufe** senior forms, upper classes, senior high school; **~versicherungsamt** regional social insurance board; **~verwaltungsgericht** higher administrative court, administrative appeals

577

tribunal; ~**ziel** main (*or* prime) objective.

Obhut *f* care, charge, care and protection, custody; ~**spflicht** duty to exercise proper care; ~**sverhältnis** custodial relationship; **etwas in ~ nehmen** to take charge of sth.

Objekt *n* object, thing, item of property; *comm*: transaction, property (*real estate*); ~**besteuerung** taxation of specific property; **o~bezogen** object related, in rem, real; ~**kredit** loan against specific security; ~**steuer** impersonal tax, tax levied on specific property; **beleihungsfähiges ~** property suitable as security (for loans), mortgageable property; **betriebsfremdes ~** asset not related to the business.

objektiv *adj* objective, practical, disinterested; unbiased.

objektivieren *v/t* to approach (more) objectively, to rationalize.

Objektivität *f* objectivity, impartiality.

obliegen *v/i* to be incumbent upon.

obliegend *adj* incumbent (upon s. o.).

Obliegenheit *f* obligation, incidental obligation, incumbency, responsibility; ~**sverletzung** non-observance of an incidental obligation (*to be fulfilled by the insured party*) ~**sverstoß** =*sverletzung qv*.

Obligation *f* obligation; debenture, bond; ~**enbuch** bonds register; ~**en der öffentlichen Hand** public stocks; ~**en einlösen** to redeem bonds; ~**enfonds** bond investment trust; ~**srecht** law of obligations; ~**srendite** redemption yield; ~**enverschuldung** bonded indebtedness, debts in the form of bonds; ~ **mit Tilgungsplan** sinking fund bond; ~ **mit zusätzlicher Gewinnbeteiligung** participating bond; ~**sanleihe** loan on debentures; ~**sausgabe** bond issue, issue of debentures; ~**sgläubiger** bond holder, bond creditor, debenture creditor; ~**srecht** = *Obligationenrecht qv*; **kündbare ~en** redeemable bonds; **kurzfristige ~en** short-term bonds; **mündelsichere ~en** gilt-edged stock; **nicht einklagbare ~** unenforceable obligation; **sich selbst amortisierende ~en** self-liquidating paper; **steuerfreie ~en** tax-exempt bonds; **ungetilgte ~en** outstanding securities; **unkündbare ~en** irredeemable debentures.

Obligationär *m* debenture holder, bond-holder, debenture creditor.

Obligationenrecht *n* law of obligations, law of contract.

obligatorisch *adj* obligatory, mandatory; **es ist nicht ~** it may be dispensed with, it is optional.

Obligo *n* engagement, liability, commitment; **ohne ~** without obligation (*on our part*), without commitment, without recourse, sans recours (*bill of exchange*); **unter dem ~ früherer Zusagen** committed by earlier promises.

Obmann *m* chairman, umpire, foreman (*jury*).

Obrigkeit *f* public authority, magistracy, government; ~**sdenken** excessive deference (to public officials), servility; ~**sstaat** authoritarian state.

obrigkeitlich *adj* governmental, magisterial, authoritarian, *adv*: by high authority.

observieren *v/t* to place under surveillance, to stake out, to observe, to shadow.

obsiegen *v/i* to succed, to win a case.

Obsoleszenz *f* obsolescence.

obsolet *adj* obsolete.

Obst|bau *m* fruit growing; ~**baugenossenschaft** fruit grower's cooperative; ~**handel** *m* fruit trade; ~**konserve** preserved fruit, tinned fruit; ~**verwertungsbetrieb** fruit-processing plant.

Obstruktion *f* obstruction; ~ **betreiben** to obstruct, to practise obstructionism; ~**spolitik** obstructionism; ~~~ *betreiben*: to stonewall, to practise obstructionism; ~**spolitiker** obstructionist; ~**sverzögerung** vexatious delay.

Ochlokratie f ochlocracy, mob rule.
Oder-Konto n joint account with full power of disposal of each party.
Ödfläche f wasteland, barren land.
Ödland n wasteland, uncultivated land, barren land; **~kultivierung** reclamation of wasteland.
offen adj open, unsettled, unexempted, overt, outstanding, unobstructed (view); undecided.
offenbar adj evident, apparent, plain, manifest.
Offenbaren n disclosing, disclosure, ~ **fremder Geheimnisse** disclosing the secrets of another.
offenbaren v/t to divulge, to disclose, to make full disclosure of; **deutlich und vollständig** ~ to disclose in a manner sufficiently clear and complete.
Offenbarung f disclosure; ~ **des Standes der Technik** prior art disclosure; **eidliche** ~ disclosure on (or under) oath; **erstmalige** ~first disclosure; **nichtschriftliche** ~ non-written disclosure; **unbefugte** ~ **fremder Geheimnisse** disclosing the secrets of another without authority; **unschädliche** ~**en** non-prejudicial disclosures.
Offenbarungs|eid obs oath of disclosure; **~pflicht** duty to disclose, positive duty of candour; **~gehalt** pat disclosure (content); **~versicherung** statutory declaration of disclosure, affidavit of means (statement in lieu of an oath).
Offene Handelsgesellschaft f (OHG): general (mercantile) partnership.
offenkundig adj obvious, manifest, clear.
Offenkundigkeit f notoriety, notoriousness, obviousness; **die** ~ **feststellen** to take judicial notice of sth.
offenlassen v/t to leave open, to leave in abeyance, to leave undecided.
offenlegen v/t to disclose, to reveal.
Offenlegung f disclosure, discovery; ~ **der Erfindung** disclosure of the invention; ~ **des Schuldnervermögens** discovery of debtor's assets; **~spflicht** duty of disclosure, duty to acertain solvency of borrower; **~sschrift** (pat) application papers laid open to public inspection, first publication; published application, printed publication of the unexamined application; **vollständige** ~ full (or complete) disclosure.
Offenmarkt|geschäfte open-market operations; **~papier** open-market paper: securities bought or sold in open-market transactions; **~politik** open-market policy; **~-Titel** open-market paper.
offensichtlich adj obvious, self-evident, clear.
offenstehen v/i to stand open, to be open, to be due, to remain outstanding.
offenstehend adj outstanding, owing.
öffentlich adj public, adv: in public; in open court; **~e Hand** → Hand; **nicht** ~ private, in camera, in chambers.
Öffentlichkeit f the public, the general public; availability for public inspection, publicity; public character; ~ **bei der Gerichtsverhandlung** publicity of trial; ~ **des Verfahrens** publicity of proceedings; **an die** ~ **kommen** to become generally known; **die** ~ **ausschließen** to close the court, to sit in camera; **die** ~ **wiederherstellen** to readmit the public to the court room, to restore publicity; **etwas an die** ~ **bringen** to give sth. publicity; **in der breiten** ~ among the general public; **in die** ~ **dringen** to become known.
Öffentlichkeits|arbeit public relations work; **~beziehungen** public relations; **~grundsatz** principle of public trial; **~prinzip** principle of public trial; **~schaden** loss of publicity.
öffentlich-rechtlich adj (under) public law.
Offerent m offeror.
offerieren v/t to offer, to tender.

579

offeriert *adj* offered, tendered, *exch:* "sellers".
Offerte *f* offer, tender; ~**nskizze** sketch accompanying an offer; **freibleibende** ~ offer without obligation; **zur Abgabe e-r** ~ **auffordern** to invite an offer.
Offizial|delikt public offence, offence requiring public prosecution; ~**klage** public prosecution; ~**maxime** principle of ex officio proceedings; accusatory principle; ~**verteidiger** court-assigned defence counsel, public defender.
Offizier *m* officer, military officer, commissioned officer; **höherer** ~ senior officer.
Offiziers|bewerber officer candidate; ~**dienstgrad** officer's rank; ~**-laufbahn** officer's career; ~**patent** officer's commission; ~**rang** officer's rank.
offiziös *adj* semi-official.
Öffnungszeiten *f/pl* opening hours.
Offshore|-Aufträge offshore purchase order (*German spelling also: Off-shore-Auftrag*); ~**-Banken** offshore banks; ~**-Bohrung** offshore drilling, offshore borehole; ~**-Finanzplätze** offshore centres; ~**-Kauf** offshore purchase; ~**-Steuerabkommen** Offshore Tax Agreement (*US Forces in Germany*); ~**-Steuergesetz** Offshore Tax Law.
Ohne-Rechnung-Geschäft *n* non-invoiced transaction (*for tax evasion purposes*), non-recorded deal.
ohne weiteres *adv* ipso jure.
Ohrenzeuge *m* ear-witness, auricular witness.
Ohrfeige *f* slap (in the face), box on the ear.
Okkupation *f* occupation; ~**sgebiet** occupied territory; ~**smacht** occupying power; ~**sschaden** damage caused by the occupying forces; **derivative** ~ derivative occupation; **originäre** ~ original occupation.
okkupieren *v/t* to occupy.
Öko|logie *f* ecology, ~**system der Gewässer** aquatic ecosystem.
Ökonometrie *f* econometrics.

Öl|aktien oil shares; ~**bedarf** demand for oil; ~**beheizung** oil heating; ~**bohrinsel** oil rig; ~**boykott** oil boycott, oil sanction; ~**einfuhr** oil imports; ~**erschließung** unlocking oil; ~**feld** oil field; ~**förderung** oil production; ~**gesellschaft** oil company; ~**gewinnung** oil extraction, oil production; ~**hafen** tanker terminal; ~**industrie** oil industry; ~**katastrophe** oil-spill disaster; ~**leitung** oil pipeline, oil pipe; ~**lieferung** oil shipment, *pl also*: oil supplies; ~**prospektion** oil prospecting, oil exploration; ~**quelle** oil well; ~**raffinerie** oil refinery; ~**sperre** oil embargo; ~**spur** oil trace, patch of oil; ~**suche** prospecting for oil; ~**terminmarkt** oil futures market; ~**verschmutzung** oil pollution, oil fouling; ~ ~ *des Meeres: pollution of the sea by hydrocarbon discharge*; ~**verschmutzungsabkommen** International Convention for the Prevention of Pollution of the Sea by Oil.
Oligarchie *f* oligarchy.
Oligopol *m* oligopoly; **unvollständiges** ~ parallel pricing.
Oligopolist *m* oligopolist.
Ombudsmann *m* ombudsman.
Omniumversicherung all-risk insurance, combined insurance.
Onkelehe *f* cohabitation of elderly couple (*disguised as uncle and aunt relationship for the children and designed to preserve pension benefits to the woman*).
Operations|kostenversicherung surgical fees insurance; ~**kostenzuschuß** subsidy towards operation costs; ~**narbe** post-operative scar: ~**verweigerung** refusal to submit to an operation.
Opfer|entschädigungsgesetz Crime Victims Compensation Statute; ~**schutz** protection of crime victims; ~**stockdieb** pilferer of offertory boxes.
Opium|mohn *m* opium poppy; ~**stellen** opium agencies.

Opponent *m* opposer, objector.
opponieren *v/i* to be opposed to.
Opportunitätsprinzip *n* principle of discretionary prosecution (*public prosecutor may refrain from prosecuting lesser offences etc*).
Opposition *f* opposition, party in opposition, parliamentary opposition.
Oppositions|bewegung opposition movement; ~**führer** leader of the opposition; ~**liste** stopping list (*lost or stolen securities*); ~**partei** opposition party; ~**politiker** politician of the opposition party.
Optant *m* party exercising an option, party making a choice.
optieren *v/i* to opt, to elect, to make a choice, to select.
Optimierung *f* optimization.
Option *f* option, right of choice, right of first refusal; ~ **beim ersten Verkaufsfall** first option, right of first refusal; **bedingte** ~ qualified option; **e-e** ~ **einräumen** to grant an option; **handelbare** ~ traded option; **ungesicherte** ~ naked option.
Options|anleihe option loan, *bond with an option to be converted into shares;* ~**ausübung** exercise of option; ~**berechtigter** optionee, grantee of an option; ~**börse** options exchange; ~**dauer** option period; ~**empfänger** optionee; ~**erklärung** grant of an option; ~**frist** option period; ~**geber** grantor of an option; ~**geschäft** option dealing; ~~ **mit Termindevisen**: *option forward*; ~**gewährer** grantor of an option; ~**handel** trading in options; ~**klausel** option clause, first refusal clause; ~**nehmer** taker of an option; ~**recht** option right, right of option, right to opt; ~**schein** subscription warrant, warrant issue, stock purchase warrant; ~ **verkäufer** writer (of an option); ~**vertrag** option agreement; ~**zeit** option period.
ordentlich *adj* ordinary, regular, orderly, business-like *adv* properly.

Orden- und Ehrenzeichen *pl* medals and decorations.
Order *f* order: *indication of transferee on negotiable instrument;* order (to buy or sell securities); ~**klausel** order clause, pay to order clause; *negative* ~~: *'not to order' clause;* ~**konnossement** order bill of lading; ~**lagerschein** negotiable warehouse receipt, warehousekeepers' warrant; ~**papier** order paper, instrument to order, instrument negotiable by endorsement; *geborenes* ~~: *original order paper; gekorenes* ~~: *order paper by act of party; kaufmännische* ~~*e*: *documents of title to goods;* ~**police** policy made out to order; ~**scheck** order cheque, cheque to order; ~**schuldverschreibung** order bond, negotiable bond, registered bond made out to order; **an die** ~ **des Ausstellers zahlen** pay to order; **an eigene** ~ to one's own order; **an** ~ to order, to the order of; **an** ~ **lauten** to be made out to order; **an** ~ **lautend** made out to order, payable to order; **bis auf Widerruf gültige** ~ open order; **limitierte** ~ stop order, limited order; **unlimitierte** ~ unlimited order; **zahlbar an** ~ payable to order.
Ordinarius *m* (full) professor (*at a university*), professor-in-ordinary.
Ordner *m* (1) steward, prefect, marshal.
Ordner *m* (2) file, standing file.
Ordnung *f* order, arrangement, system; **der** ~ **halber** for order's sake; **der guten** ~ **halber** for the sake of good order; **die marktwirtschaftliche** ~ the free-market system; **die** ~ **aufrechterhalten** to maintain order; **e-e sinnvolle** ~ a sensible arrangement; **intervalutare** ~ intercurrency system; **öffentliche** ~ public order; **soziale** ~ social order; **verfassungsmäßige** ~ constitutional order; **zur** ~ **rufen** to name (a member), to call to order.
Ordnungs|behörden regulatory authorities, police authorities;

ordre public / **Organ**

~**dienst** steward's work, service for public order; ~**geld** administrative fine, disciplinary fine; o~**gemäß** *adj* orderly, proper; *adv*: duly, in due form, properly; ~**gemäßheit** propriety, regularity; *die* ~~ *der Vollstreckungsmaßnahmen*: *enforcement is being carried out in a regular manner*; ~**gewalt** police authorities; ~**haft** (*or* arrest); confinement for contempt of court (*or* disobedience); ~**hüter** guardian of public order, policeman; o~**mäßig** = *ordnungsgemäß qv*; ~**mäßigkeit** regularity, compliance with regulations; ~**maßnahme** measure to maintain (public) order; ~**merkmal** aid to classification; ~**polizei** regular police, uniformed police; ~**prinzip** regulating principle; ~**recht** regulatory law, administrative rules, law of administrative penalties; ~**ruf** call to order, naming a member; ~**strafe** administrative penalty, penalty for infringement of regulations, penalty for contempt of court; ~**strafverfahren** administrative penalty proceedings; ~**system** system of organization; system of classification; ~**vorschriften** administrative rules; o~**widrig** *adj* disorderly, irregular, contrary to regulations; ~**widrigkeit** regulatory offence: *offence against police and administrative regulations*; summary offence; *pl also*: breach of regulations; ~**widrigkeitsgesetz** Regulatory Offences Act: *Law against infringements of police and administrative regulations*.

ordre public *n* (=) public policy.

Organ *n* organ institution, agency, body; ~**aufbau** organic structure, organization; ~**e der Gemeinschaft** the competent bodies of the Community; ~**e der öffentlichen Meinungsbildung** media, instruments which shape public opinion; ~ **der Rechtspflege** judicial body, organ of the administration of justice; ~**e der politischen Zusammenarbeit** political co-operation machinery; ~**firma** firm integrated in a group; closely affiliated firm; ~**gemeinschaft** group of integrated companies; ~**gesellschaft** company integrated in a group; ~**haftung** responsibility for executive organs; ~**klage** action of one public body against another; intra-company legal action; ~**kredite** *credits given by a bank to its own executives or closely connected companies or firms*; ~**leihe** *lending of an administrative organ to another public authority;* ~**schaft** integrated inter-company relation (*with tax unity*), relationship between interlocking companies; ~**schaftsabrechnung** accounting settlement between integrated companies; ~**schaftsverhältnis** integrated inter-company relationship, relationship between interlocking companies; ~**schaftsverrechnung** integrated inter-company settlement of accounts, settlement between interlocking companies; ~**schaftsvertrag** agreement between interlocking companies, contract concerning the integration of a subsidiary; ~**spende** anatomical gift (*by will*), organ donation; ~**spender** organ donor; ~**streit** litigation between two public bodies; ~**streitverfahren** court proceedings between administrative bodies; ~**verhältnis** interlocking relationship, integrated relationship with a subsidiary; ~**vertrag** integration agreement with a subsidiary, intergroup agreement; ~**wille** intent of an executive organ, intention to integrate a subsidiary; **amtliches** ~ official organ (*for public notices*); **ausführendes** ~ executive organ; **beratendes** ~ consulting body, consultative body; **ein paritätisch zusammengesetztes parlamentarisches** ~ a parliamentary body with equal representation; **gesetzgebende** ~**e** legislative organs, the legislature; **nachgeordnete** ~**e** subsidiary organs; **offizielles** ~ official organ; **paritätische** ~**e** joint

Organigramm   **Ort**

bodies with equal membership; **staatliches** ~ state organ, state agency; **ständiges** ~ permanent institution; **untätiges** ~ inactive body; **vollziehendes** ~ executive organ.

Organigramm *n* organizational chart.

Organisation *f* organization; ~ **der Vereinten Nationen für Erziehung, Wissenschaft und Kultur** United Nations Educational, Scientific and Cultural Organization (*UNESCO*); ~**Erdölexportierender Länder** Organization of the Petroleum Exporting Countries *OPEC;* ~ **für Wirtschaftliche Zusammenarbeit und Entwicklung** Organization for Economic Cooperation and Development (*OECD*); **beigeordnete** ~ associate agency; **gemeinnützige** ~ non-profit organization; **internationale** ~**en** international organizations; **maßgebliche europäische** ~**en** representative European bodies; **nichtstaatliche** ~**en** non-governmental organizations; **verbotene** ~ prescribed organization; **zwischenstaatliche** ~**en** intergovernmental bodies.

Organisations|abteilung administration and coordination department, organization and methods department; ~**akt** act of establishment, act of foundation; ~**ausschuß** organization committee, steering committee; ~**fehler** faulty organization; ~**form** organizational form; ~**gemeinschaft** management association; ~**gewalt** organizational power, power to create governmental bodies; ~**klausel** closed-shop clause (*in a collective agreement*), clause concerning union-membership; ~**kosten** foundation expenses, pre-incorporation expenses, costs of promotion; ~**mittel** organizational aid; ~**plan** organization chart, organization diagram; ~**probleme** management problems; ~**recht** right to form associations, law concerning

organizations; ~**schaubild** organization chart, organization tree; ~**talent** organizing ability; ~**verbrechen** crime committed by an organization (*irrespective of membership*); ~**umstellung** change of business system.

organisatorisch *adj* organizational.

organisieren *v/t, v/i* to organize, to form an organization, to establish; **gewerkschaftlich** ~ to organize, to unionize.

organisiert *adj* organized; unionized; **nicht** ~ not organized, non-union.

Organismus *m* organism, system; **der marktwirtschaftliche** ~ the free-enterprise market system.

Orientierungs|programm program(me) of orientation; ~**preis** (merely) informative price, introductory price; ~**rahmen** guidelines, long-term program(me); ~**stufe** orientation stage (*to test aptitude for secondary school education*).

Original *m* original; ~**abfüllung** estate-bottled, brewery-bottled; ~**ausfertigung** original document; *zweite* ~~: *duplicate original;* ~ **e-s Schriftsatzes** the original of a brief; ~**faktura** original invoice; ~**fracht** original freight; ~**gerätehersteller** original equipment manufacturer (OEM); ~**handschrift** autograph; ~**klischee** master plate, original block; ~**police** original policy; ~**tara** tare determined by the sender; ~**testament** original will; ~**text** original text; ~**unterschrift** original signature; ~**urkunde** original document; ~**verpackung** original package, original wrapping; ~**wechsel** original bill of exchange; ~**zahl** original figure; **im** ~ in the original; **nach dem** ~ **bearbeitet** adapted from the original, based on the original.

originär *adj* original, inborn, initial.

Ort *m* place, position, location, situs; ~ **der Ausfertigung** place of execution; ~ **der Leistung** place of performance; ~ **der Leitung** place of management; ~ **der Niederlas-**

Ortsangabe ... **Ortschaft**

sung place of establishment; ~ **der tatsächlichen Geschäftsleitung** place of effective management; ~ **des Vertragsabschlusses** place of (conclusion of) contract; ~**e mit Asylrecht** privileged places; ~**schaft** → *Ortschaft*; **am angeführten** ~ (*a.a.O.*) loco citato (*loc. cit.*), op. cit., ibidem (*ibid*); **am** ~ in place, in the same locality; **an** ~ **und Stelle** on the spot, in situ; **der** ~ **des steuerbaren Umsatzes** the place of taxable transactions; **öffentlicher** ~ public place; **ungefährdeter** ~ place of safety.

Orts|angabe indication of place, address; **o**~**ansässig** *adj* resident; ~**ansässiger** (*der Ortsansässige*) resident; ~**anwesenheit** on the spot presence; ~**ausschuß** local committee; ~**behörden** local authorities; ~**besichtigung** local inspection, visit to the scene, inspection on the spot; ~**bezeichnung** geographical name; ~**bezirk** local district; ~**brief** local letter; ~**clearing** interbank clearing; ~**durchfahrt** main road for through traffic; ~**form** *the proper legal form at the place where the transaction is entered into or the instrument is made;* ~**gebiete** built-up areas; ~**gebrauch** local custom, local usage, local trade rules; ~**gericht** local court; ~**gespräch** local call; ~**kennzahl** *US:* ZIP code, *GB* postal code; ~**klasseneinteilung** locality classification; ~**krankenkasse** (=) local branch of national health insurance; ~**lohn** local wage; ~**name** name of place; ~**netzkennzahl** prefix (number); S.T.D. code (standard telephone dialling code); ~**planungsbehörde** local planning authority; ~**planungsgebiet** local development area; ~**polizei** local police; ~**polizeibehörde** local police authority; ~**recht** local law; lex loci actus (*the law of the place where the transaction has been entered into);* ~**satzung** local statutes, local by(e)-laws; ~**schild** place-name sign; ~**straße** street; ~**tafel** place-name sign, place identification sign; ~**tarif** local rates; ~**termin** hearing on site, court inspection of the scene, physical inspection by the court; **o**~**üblich** *adj* customary in the locality, in conformity with local custom; ~**üblichkeit** local practice; ~**umbenennung** change of place name; ~**umgehung** (town *or* village) bypass; ~**verkehr** local traffic; ~**verkehrsbereich** local service area, local rate zone; ~**vertreter** resident agent; ~**verwaltung** local administration; ~**verweis** order of removal; ~**wechsel** change of locality; ~**zeit** local time; ~**zulage** local bonus, residential allowance; ~**zuschlag** local bonus, local cost-of-living allowance, weighting allowance.

Ortschaft *f* place, town, village, locality; **geschlossene** ~ built-up area, urban area.

P

Pacht *f* lease (*granting use and profits*), leasehold; rent; ~**abkommen** lease agreement; ~ **auf Lebenszeit** lease for life; ~**ausfallversicherung** leasehold insurance; ~**bedingungen** terms of a (the) lease; ~**besitz** leasehold; *landwirtschaftlicher* ~~: *agricultural holding*; ~**besitzer** tenant; *unmittelbarer* ~~: *sitting tenant, tenant in occupation under a lease;* ~**betrieb** (farming of) leasehold property; ~**dauer** term of lease, duration of leasehold; ~**einnahmen** rent receipts from a lease; ~**ertrag** rental return from leaseholds, rental revenue; ~**ertragswert** rental value of leasehold property; ~**gebiet** leasehold area, leased territory; ~**gegenstand** leased property, the leased item, the demised premises; ~**grundstück** leasehold property, leasehold estate, leased property, the demised premises; ~**jahr** year of lease; ~**kredit** credit for leaseholders; ~**kreditgeber** lender to leaseholders; ~**kreditgesetz** Leasehold Credit Act; ~**kreditinstitut** leasehold credit institution; ~**kreditsachen** leasehold credit cases; ~**land** leased land, land on lease; ~**minderung** reduction of rent, abatement of rent; ~**preis** amount of leasehold rent; ~**recht** leasehold law; leasehold right, tenant's rights; ~**rückstände** arrears of rent (for leasehold property); ~**schutz** agricultural tenant's protection; security of tenure; ~**schutzordnung** *ordinance concerning agricultural tenant's protection procedure;* ~**urkunde** lease, instrument of lease, covenant of lease; ~**verhältnis** tenancy, tenure, relationship of landlord and tenant, lease tenure; *lebenslängliches* ~~: *tenancy for life;* ~**verlängerung** extension of (leasehold) tenancy, renewal of lease; ~**vertrag** lease, lease contract, leasehold tenancy agreement; *landwirtschaftlicher* ~~: *farm lease*; *langfristiger* ~~: *long lease*; ~**wert** rental (letting) value, letting value of leasehold property; ~**wesen** leasehold matters; ~**zeit** term of lease, period of lease; *restliche* ~~: *unexpired term (of lease)*; ~**zins** rent, leasehold rent, farm rent; *nomineller* ~~: *nominal rent, peppercorn rent*; ~**zubehör** tenant's fixtures; **in ~ geben** to let by lease; **in ~ nehmen** to take on lease; **landwirtschaftliche ~** farming lease.

pachten *v/t* to take on lease; to hire, to rent.

Pächter *m* leaseholder, lessee; *landwirtschaftlicher* ~: *agricultural tenant, tenant farmer*; *neuer* ~: *incoming tenant*; *weichender* ~: *outgoing tenant*; ~-**Inventarpfandrecht** lien on tenant farmer's working assets; ~**kaution** bond to perform lease; ~**pfandrecht** lessee's statutory lien; ~**schutz** legal protection for tenant farmers (upon termination of tenancy); **lebenslänglicher ~** life tenant.

Pack *m* pack; **ein ~ Wolle** a pack of wool (*240 pounds = 108.86 kg*).

Pack|leinwand packcloth, packing sheet; ~**maschine** packer; ~**papier** wrapping paper; ~**stück** package; ~**tuch** packcloth, packing sheet; ~**zettel** packing slip.

Päckchen *n* small parcel, (small) packet.

Packung *f* packing, wrapper; package, pack, packaging; ~**sbeilage** package insert; ~**sgestaltung** packaging (design).

pacta sunt servanda *lat* (=) agreements must be observed.

pactum *m* (*lat*) pact, agreement, contract; ~ **de non cedendo** (=)

agreement forbidding an assignment; ~ **de non petendo** (=) an agreement not to sue.

Päderastie *f* pederasty.

Paket *n* parcel; package (*deal*); ~**adresse** address on a parcel, address for parcels, (gummed) parcel (post) label; ~**annahme** parcels receiving office; ~**handel** (*exch*) dealing in large lots, large-lot dealing; ~**inhaltsliste** packing list; ~**karte** parcel mailing form, parcel dispatch note; ~**liste** list of parcels; ~**police** package policy; ~**porto** parcel postage: ~**post** parcel post, *US*: fourth-class mail; ~**postversicherung** parcel post insurance; ~**schalter** parcels counter; ~**sendung** parcel; ~**umschlagstelle** parcel rerouting centre; ~ **von Verhandlungsangeboten** *pol* package offer; ~**zuschlag** additional price for a block of shares; ~**zustellung** parcel delivery.

Pakt *m* pact, covenant; ~ **zur gegenseitigen Hilfeleistung** mutual assistance pact; **e-n** ~ **schließen** to conclude a pact.

Palette *f* pallet; ~**nladung** pallet load.

palettieren *v/t* to load (*or* store) on pallets.

Pamphlet *n* polemical pamphlet, lampoon, satirical article.

Panaschieren *n* preferential voting for different candidates, split voting.

panaschieren *v/i* to split one's vote, to cast one's vote for candidates of different parties.

Pandekten *pl* the Digests, the Pandects.

Panik *f* panic, scare; ~**kauf** panic buying, scare buying; ~**mache** scare-mongering; ~**macher** alarmist, scare-monger.

Panne *f* mechanical breakdown, engine trouble, failure; ~**ndienst** breakdown service; ~**hilfe** breakdown service; ~**nkoffer** breakdown kit; ~**nwarnschild** warning triangle.

panschen *v/t* to adulterate.

Panzer *m* armour; tank; ~**faust** bazooka; ~**glas** bullet-proof laminated glass; ~**grenadier** infantryman in an armoured division; ~**grenadierdivision** armoured infantry division; ~**knacker** tank buster; safe-cracker; ~**schrank** safe; ~**schrankklausel** iron-safe clause.

Papier *n* paper, document, instrument; *pl* ~*e*, *also*: securities; identity papers; ~**effekten** paper securities; ~**fabrik** paper mill; ~**geld** paper money, paper currency, notes, *US* folding money; ~**geldumlauf** circulation of notes; ~**geldwährung** paper money standard, fiduciary standard; *unterwertige* ~~: scrip; ~**handel** paper trade; ~**industrie** paper industry; ~**klammer** paper clip; ~**kram** paper work; ~**krieg** red tape, bureaucracy; ~**patent** paper patent; ~**tiger** *pol* paper tiger; ~**währung** paper currency, paper standard, fiduciary standard; ~**waren** paper goods, stationery; ~**wert** book value, purely nominal value (*of a treaty etc*); ~**werte** paper securities; ~**zoll** paper duty; **bankfähiges** ~ bank paper, paper eligible for discount at a bank; **begebbares** ~ negotiable instrument; **börsengängige** ~**e** stock exchange securities, marketable securities (on stock exchange); **diskontfähiges** ~ paper eligible for discount; **festverzinsliche** ~**e** fixed-interest-bearing securities; **hoch rentierende** ~**e** securities yielding a high return, high-yielding securities; **indossable** ~**e** securities transferable by endorsement; **marktfähige** ~**e** marketable securities; **mündelsichere** ~**e** trustee stock, trustee securities.

Paradewert *m* window-dressing figure (*or* value).

parafiskalisch *adj* quasi-governmental.

Paragraph *m* section (*of a statute*), clause (*of a contract*), paragraph; ~**engestrüpp** tangled mass of regulations; ~**enreiter** pettifogger, legalist, stickler; ~**enreiterei** redtapism, pettifogging; ~**enüberschrift** section heading *(statute)*, clause heading *(contract)*; ~**enzeichen** section mark, §; **gemäß** ~ **242 BGB** pursuant to section 242 of the German Civil Code; **unter e-n** ~**en fallen** to fall within a section.

Parallel|buchung parallel posting; ~**buchungsbeleg** posting reference; ~**fall** parallel case; ~**gesetzgebung** parallel legislation; ~**verhalten** parallelism of action, parallel conduct; **bewußtes** ~~: conscious parallelism; ~**verkehr** competing traffic (*e.g. road and rail*); ~**vorlage** companion bill; ~**währung** parallel currency; ~**wertung** comparative valuation.

Paraphe *f* initials.

paraphieren *v/t* to initial (*a treaty*).

Paraphierung *f* initialling of treaty.

Parentel *f* parentela, *the sum of persons who trace descent from one ancestor*, family root; ~**enerbfolge** succession per stirpes, parentelic succession; ~**system** (= ~*ensystem*) system of succession per stirpes, system of parentelic succession.

pari *adv* par; ~ **notieren** to quote at par; **über** ~ above par, at a premium; **unter** ~ at a discount, below par.

Pari|ausgabe issue at par; ~**einlösungssystem** par redemption system; ~**emission** issue at par, par issue; ~**grenze** parity (limit); ~**kurs** par price, parity; *zum* ~~: at par; ~**plätze** *places where cheques are collected by banks free of charge*; ~**rückzahlung** redemption at par; ~**wert** parity, par value.

Pariser | **Seerechtsdeklaration** The Declaration of Paris on Maritime Warfare *(1856)*; ~ **Verband** (*Verband zum Schutz des gewerblichen Eigentums*) Paris Union; ~**Verbandsübereinkunft** Union Convention, Paris Convention; ~ **Verbandsübereinkunft über gewerblichen Rechtsschutz** = *Pariser Verbandsübereinkunft zum Schutz des gewerblichen Eigentums qv*; ~ **Verbandsübereinkunft zum Schutz des gewerblichen Eigentums** Paris Convention for the Protection of Industrial Property; ~ **Verträge** The Paris Treaties (*1954, ending military government in West Germany etc*); ~ **Währungsklub** Paris Club, Group of Ten.

Parität *f* parity; ~**engitter** parity grid; **anpassungsfähige** ~**en** adjustable par values; **Londoner** ~ London equivalent (*foreign exchange quotations*); **rechnerische** ~ calculated parity (*value*).

paritätisch *adj* equally represented, on an equal footing, at par.

Paritäts|klausel parity clause, national treatment clause; ~**kurs** parity price; ~**preis** parity price; ~**punkt** parity point; ~**tabelle** parity table.

Park|abholdienst parking valet service; ~**beschränkung** parking restriction, limited parking; ~**bucht** parking bay; ~**gebühr** parking fee; ~**haus** multi-storey carpark; *US*: parking garage; ~**kralle** wheel clamp; ~**leitlinien** parking lines; ~**lücke** gap between parked cars; ~**möglichkeiten** parking, parking facilities; ~**platz** car park, parking lot; ~**scheibe** parking disk (*or* disc); ~**schein** car-park ticket; ~**streifen** lay-by; ~**sünder** parking offender; ~**uhr** parking meter; ~**uhrbereich** parking meter zone; ~**verbot** no parking; ~**verbotsschild** "no parking" sign; ~**vorschriften** parking regulations; ~**zeit** parking period.

Parkanlagen *f/pl* (public) park, ornamental grounds.

Parken *n* parking, street parking; ~ **in doppelter Reihe** double parking; **enges** ~ shoehorn parking; tight parking.

Parkett *n exch* floor.

Parlament *n* parliament; **das** ~ **einberufen** to summon a Parliament, to convene a Parliament, to con-

Parlamentär | **Partei**

voke Parliament; **das ~ ist vertagt** Parliament is prorogued; **das ~ tagt** P. is sitting; **für das ~ kandidieren** to put up for Parliament, to stand for Parliament, to run for Parliament.

Parlamentär *m* parlementaire, bearer of the flag of truce; **~flagge** flag of truce, white flag.

Parlamentarier *m* member of parliament, parliamentarian.

parlamentarisch *adj* parliamentary.

Parlamentarismus *m* parliamentarism, parliamentarianism.

Parlaments|abgeordneter member of parliament, M. P.; **~anklage** impeachment; **~auflösung** dissolution of Parliament; **~ausschuß** parliamentary committee; **~bannmeile** parliamentary precincts; **~berichte** parliamentary reports; **~beschluß** resolution adopted by Parliament (*or* by the House of Commons); **~debatte** parliamentary debate; **~direktor** clerk of the House (*GB*); **~eröffnung** opening of parliament; *feierliche ~~:* State opening of Parliament; **~ferien** parliamentary recess; **~fraktion** parliamentary party; **~frieden** inviolacy of Parliament; *Verletzung des ~~s:* parliamentary trespass; **~hoheit** parliamentary sovereignty; **~immunität** parliamentary immunity, parliamentary privilege; **~korruption** corrupt practices in Parliament; **~mehrheit** parliamentary majority; **~mitglied** member of parliament; **~nötigung** obstruction of members, obstruction of parliamentary proceedings; **~opposition** parliamentary opposition; **~präsident** Speaker; **~privilegien** parliamentary privilege(s); **~protokoll** minutes of parliamentary proceedings, *GB*: "Hansard" Reports; *US*: Congressional Record; **~reform** parliamentary reform; **~sitz** seat (in parliament); **~sitzung** Parliament sitting; **~verurteilung** bill of attainder; **~vorlage** parliamentary bill; **~wachtmeister** serjeant; **~wahl** parliamentary election; **~wahlkreis** parliamentary borough, parliamentary constituency.

Parole *f* password; slogan, catchphrase.

Partei *f* party, *pl Parteien* (*=en*); *die ~n:* the parties concerned, the parties hereto, litigant parties, the parties to a dispute; the parties to a contract;; **~abrede** stipulation, understanding between the parties; **~abzeichen** party badge; party insignia; **~apparat** party machinery; **~ausschuß** caucus, committee of a political party; **~autonomie** power of the parties to determine the applicable provisions, party autonomy; **~basis** grassroots level (*of a political party*); **~behauptung** allegation (of a party); **~betrieb** (principle of) party prosecution; **~buch** party membership card; **~buchwirtschaft** nepotism, party political favouritism, party politics; **~disziplin** party discipline; **~~ wahren:** to toe the line; **~-Eid** suppletory oath (*oath sworn by one of the parties*), a party's oath; **e-s Rechtsstreits** litigant, litigator, party to a dispute; **~einvernahme** interrogation or examination of a party (by the judge); **~ ergreifen** to take the part of, to take party against; **p~fähig** *adj* capable of being a party in a lawsuit; **~fähigkeit** capacity to be a party in a law-suit, capacity to sue and be sued; **~flügel** wing of a party; **~führer** leader of a party, party leader; **~führung** party leadership; **~funktionär** party official; **~gänger** partisan, (devoted) party supporter; **~genosse** member of a party, party member; **~handlung** act of party; **~jargon** party-jargon; **~kongreß** party conference, party congress; **~kurs** party line; **~linie** party line; **p~los** *adj* unattached; **~mann** party man; **~mitglied** party member; *eingetragenes ~~: enrolled member of a party;* **~-eneid** = *Partei-Eid qv;* **~enprivileg** party

588

parteiisch / **Partie**

privilege, privileges of political parties; ~**organ** party organ; ~**organisation** party organization; ~**politik** party-politics; **p~politisch** party-political; ~**programm** party-programme, platform; ~**proporz** (in) proportions of party strength; ~**prozeß** *civil procedure based on the system of party prosecution*; *case where parties need no counsel in court*; ~**system** political party system; ~**verbot** prohibition of a party, ban on a party; ~**envereinbarung** contractual stipulation, agreement by the parties; ~**vernehmung** interrogation of a party (*by the judge*); ~**verrat** prevarication; double-crossing of a client by a lawyer; ~~ *begehen*: *to prevaricate*; ~**versammlung** party rally; ~**versammlungsbeschluß** party resolution; ~**volk** the rank and file of a party; ~**vorbringen** statements by the parties, party-allegations; ~**vorstand** executive committee of the party; ~**vortrag** pleadings by a party, party-allegations; ~**wechsel** change of party (*in law-suit*), substitution of parties; defection (*political*); ~**wille** (*presumed*) intention of the parties (*of a contract*); ~**zentrale** party headquarters; ~**zugehörigkeit** party membership; **abgewiesene** ~ unsuccessful plaintiff; **antragstellende** ~ applicant, mover; **beklagte** ~ defendant (party), party defendant; **berechtigte** ~ entitled party; **beschwerte** ~ the party aggrieved; **beteiligte** ~ party involved, interested party; **betreibende** ~ prosecuting party, plaintiff; **bürgerliche** ~**en** middle class parties, middle-of-the-road parties; **den ~en Gelegenheit zur Stellungnahme geben** to hear the parties, to give the parties the opportunity to state their case; **die aktiv legitimierte** ~ the real party, the entitled party; **die betreffenden** ~**en** the respective parties, the parties concerned; **die eigentliche** ~ the proper party, dominus litis; **die erschienene** ~ the appearing party; **die erstgenannte** ~ party of the first part, the former party; **die Hohen Vertragsschließenden** ~**en** The High Contracting Parties; **die kostenpflichtige** ~ the party liable for the costs; **die** ~**en belehren** to caution the parties, **die** ~**en sind bestrebt** the parties are desirous; **die richtige** ~ the proper party; **ersuchende** ~ requesting party; **ersuchte** ~ requested party; **geladene** ~ the summoned party; **in Verzug befindliche** ~ party in default; **klägerische** ~ complaining party, plaintiff; **obsiegende** ~ successful party, successful litigant, prevailing party; **replizierende** ~ repliant; **politische** ~ political party; **säumige** ~ defaulting party, party in default, defaulter; **streitig gegen e–e** ~ in adversum; **unterlegene** ~ unsuccessful party, losing party, defeated party; **unterliegende** ~ = *unterlegene* ~ *qv*; **verfassungswidrige** ~**en** unconstitutional parties; **verpflichtete** ~ party liable, obligated party; **vertraglich verpflichtete** ~ party liable under a contract, contractually obligated party; **vertragsbrüchige** ~ party in breach, defaulting party; **vertragsschließende** ~ contracting party; **vertragstreue** ~ non-defaulting party, party who abides by the terms of an agreement.

parteiisch *adj* partial, biased.
parteilich *adj* partial, partisan, onesided.
Parteilichkeit *f* partiality, bias.
parteilos *adj* independent (*politician*), non-party.
Partenreederei *f* shipowning partnership.
Partialschaden *m* partial loss, particular average.
Partie *f* (1) parcel, lot; ~**handel** *exch* spot business; ~**kauf** sale by lot; ~**provision** lot money; ~**ware** job goods, goods bought in one lot, substandard goods; ~ **wird landseitig gelöscht** this lot to be discharged on (to) the quay; **in ~n verkaufen** to sell in lots.

Partie *f* (2) gang (of workers); ~**führer** foreman (of a gang of workers).

Partikulier *m* master of a riverboat, (independent) barge-owner; ~**schiffahrt** privately-owned inland shipping.

Partizipationsschein *m* participating receipt.

Partner *m* partner, co-partner, party, fellow-member; ~**land** member country, partner country; *bilaterale* ~**länder**: *countries with bilateral agreements*; ~**stadt** linked town, twinned city; ~**tausch** exchange of partners, "partner swapping"; **geschäftsführender** ~ managing partner, acting partner; **pro forma** ~ partner in name.

Partnerschaft *f* partnership.

Parzelle *f* parcel of land, fractional tract of land, lot, plot.

parzellieren *v/t* to subdivide, to parcel (out), to divide into lots.

Parzellierung *f* parcellation.

Paß *m* passport; ~**abfertigung** passport inspection; ~~**sstelle**: *passport inspection point*; ~**behörden** passport office, passport authorities; ~**beschränkung** passport restriction, restricted use of passport; ~**eintrag** endorsement on passport; ~**ersatz** substitute passport document, replacement passport, document as passport; ~**fälschung** passport forgery; ~**freiheit** passports not required, *exemption from the requirement to show one's passport*; ~**gebührenverordnung** ordinance on passport-fees; ~**inhaber** holder of a passport, passport holder; ~**kontrolle** passport inspection, passport check; ~**nummer** passport number; ~**pflicht** obligation to carry a passport; ~**recht** passports law; ~**register** register of issued passports; ~**stelle** passport office; ~**vergehen** offence against the passport regulations, contravention of the passport regulations; ~**verordnung** passport ordinance; ~**versagung** refusal to issue a passport to s.o.; ~**wesen** passport matters; ~**zwang** legal requirement to carry one's passport; **e-n** ~ **beantragen** to apply for a passport; **einheitlicher** ~ uniform passport; **gültiger** ~ valid passport.

Passagier|beförderung passenger transport; ~**einschiffung** embarkation; ~**gut** passenger luggage; ~**liste** list of passengers; ~**meile** passenger mile; ~**räume** passenger accommodation; ~**schiffahrt** passenger shipping; **zahlender** ~ fare-paying passenger.

Passant *m* passerby.

Passierschein *m* pass, permit, laissez-passer; ~**stelle** pass office, checkpoint.

passiv *adj* passive, on the liabilities side, showing a deficit; ~ **legitimiert** → *legitimiert*.

Passiv|-Bereich deficit area; ~**bilanz** unfavourable (or adverse) balance (*of trade*); ~~**-Diskrepanz** minus-difference; ~**gelder** borrowings; *kurzfristige* ~~: *short-term liabilities*; ~**geschäft** transaction creating a liability; deposit business (*banks*), deposit banking; borrowing transaction; ~**handel** passive trade, import trade; ~**konto** account payable, liability account; ~**kredit** borrowing; ~**legitimation** answerability as the proper party; ~**masse** liabilities; ~**-Periode** deficit period, period with adverse balances; ~**posten** liability item, deficit item, debit item: ~~ *der Rechnungsabgrenzung*: *deferred credits to income, prepaid unearned income*; ~**prozeß** defendant's lawsuit, litigation as a defendant; ~**saldo** debit balance; ~**seite** liabilities side; ~**zinsen** interest payable, credit interest (*paid by bank*); ~**wechsel** bill payable.

Passiva *pl* liabilities; **antizipative** ~, accrued expenses, accrued payables; **transitorische** ~ prepaid income, deferred revenue, earned revenue, deferred assets.

passivieren *v/t* to enter on the liabilities side (of the balance sheet),

Passivierung to carry as a liability (*or* a debit), to include on the liabilities (*or* debit) side.

Passivierung *f* inclusion on the liabilities (*or* debit) side, increase in indebtedness, carrying as a liability; ~ **der Kapitalbilanz** deterioration of the capital-transaction balance; ~ **im Warenaußenhandel** (appearance of) a deficit on trade, incurring a foreign trade deficit; **~spflicht** obligation to disclose liabilities on the balance sheet; **~stendenz** tendency to (incur a) deficit.

Patenschaft *f* sponsorship.

Patent *n* patent, letters patent; **~abgabe** royalty; **~amt** Patent Office, *US*: Commissioner of Patents; **p~amtlich** *adj* approved by the Patent Office; **~amtsentscheidung** ruling of the Patent Office; „**~ angemeldet**" "patent applied for"; **~anmelder** applicant for a patent, patent applicant, intended patentee, claimant; **~anmeldung** patent application, application for letters patent, filing of a patent application; ~~ *läuft: patent pending*; *nationale* ~~: *application for a national patent*; *schwebende* ~~: *patent pending*; **~anteil** part interest in a patent; **~anspruch** patent claim, *Zweckgebundener* ~~: *patent claim bound (or directed) to a specific purpose*; **~antrag** patent application; **~anwalt** → *Patentanwalt*; **~aufgabe** abandonment of patent; **~ausschuß** Patents Board; **~austausch** cross-licensing of patents, exchange of patents; **~austauschvertrag** patent exchange agreement, cross-licensing agreement; **~ausübung** use of a patent, patent exploitation; *unterlassene* ~~: *non-use of a patent, non-user of a p.*; **~begehren** wish to obtain a patent, patent claim; **p~begründend** substantiating a patent claim; **~berichte** patent reports; **~berichterstatter** patent investigator; **~berichtigung** patent amendment; **~berühmung** patent adver-

tizing, arrogation of patent; **~beschränkung** voluntary restriction on extent of patent claim; **~beschreibung** patent specification, patent description; *vorläufige* ~~: *provisional specification*; **~besitzer** patent owner; **~blatt** Patent Office Journal; **~büro** patent law firm, patent agents; **~dauer** life of a patent, duration of a patent; **~einspruch** interference, opposition (to a patent); **~einspruchsverfahren** opposition proceedings, interference proceedings; ~~ *wegen offenkundiger Vorbenutzung: public use proceedings*; **~entziehung** revocation of a patent; **~erschleichung** surreptitious obtainment of a patent; **~erteilung** issue of a patent, grant of a patent; ~~*sanspruch: claim to the grant of a patent*; ~~*sverfahren: patent granting procedure*; **~fach** patent branch; **p~fähig** *adj* patentable; **~fähigkeit** patentability; **~gebühr** patent fee, royalty; **~gegenstand** object matter of a patent, patented article; **~gemeinschaft** patent pool; **~gericht** patent court; **~gerichtsverfahren** patent court proceedings; **~gesetz** patent law, Patent Act; **~gesetzgebung** patent legislation; **~gutachten** expert report on a patent; **~hindernis** bar to patentability; **~inhaber** patent owner, patent holder, patentee; *alleiniger* ~~: *sole patentee;* **~inhalt** contents of patent; **~kartell** patent cartel; **~klage** patent action, patent proceedings; **~klasse** patent class, patent category; **~klassifikation** patent classification; **~kosten** patent charges; **~laufzeit** term of a patent; **~lizenz** patent licence, licence under a patent; ~~ *ohne technische Nebenleistungen: bare patent licence, clean patent licence;* **~lizenzabgabe** royalty (on patents); **~lizenzvertrag** patent licence agreement; **~löschung** revocation of a patent, cancellation of a patent; ~~*sklage: petition for patent cancellation*; **~makler** patent-right dealer;

~**mißbrauch** misuse of a patent; ~**monopol** patent monopoly; ~**nichtigkeitsklage** plea of nullity, nullity suit, *GB* action for revocation of a patent, writ of scire facias to repeal letters of patent; ~**nichtigkeitsverfahren** proceedings for revocation (of a patent), nullity proceedings; ~**prozeß** patent litigation; ~**prüfer** patent examiner; ~**recht** patent law, patent right; *nationales* ~~: *national law concerning patents*; ~**rechtler** expert on patent law; **p**~**rechtlich geschützt** patented; ~**rezept** nostrum; ~**richter** patent court judge; ~**rolle** register of patents, Patent Register, Patent Roll; ~**sachen** patent cases; ~**schrift** printed patent specification, *pl also*: patent documents; *endgültige* ~~: *complete patent specification*; *europäische* ~~: *specification of the European patent*; *vorläufige* ~~: *provisional patent spezification*; ~**schriftenauszug** abridgment of patents; ~**schutz** patent protection; *bestehender* ~~: *active patent*; ~**streit** patent contest; ~**streitkammer** patent court; ~**streitsache** patent case, patent suit, patent litigation; ~**sucher** intended patentee; ~**übertragung** assignment of patent; ~**unteranspruch** subclaim of a patent; ~**urkunde** letters patent, patent certificate; ~**verbesserung** improvement; ~**verfahren** patent procedure; ~**verkauf** sale of a patent; ~**verlängerung** extension of (a) patent; ~**verletzer** infringer of a patent; *vermeintlicher* ~~: *assumed infringer*; ~**verletzung** infringement of patent, patent infringement; *mittelbar* ~~: *contributory infringement of a patent*; ~**verletzungsklage** infringement suit, infringement proceedings; ~**verletzungsstreit** patent infringement proceedings; ~**verruf** slander of patent; ~**versagung** refusal of patent; ~**vertrag** patent agreement; ~**verweigerung** patent barred, refusal to issue a patent; ~**verwer**-**tung** patent exploitation, exploitation of a patent; ~**verzicht** abandonment of patent; ~ **von Weltbedeutung** universal patent; ~**vorwegnahme** anticipation, anticipatory reference; ~**wesen** patent system; ~**widerruf** revocation of a patent; ~**zeichnung** patent drawing; ~**zusammenarbeitsvertrag** Patent Cooperation Treaty PCI, *1970 (international protection of inventions)*; ~**zusammenfassung** patent consolidation, patent summary; ~**abgelaufenes** ~ expired patent; **älteres** ~ earlier patent, prior patent; **auf ein** ~ **verzichten** to abandon a patent; **bahnbrechendes** ~ pioneer patent; **das ältere** ~ the earlier patent; **das jüngere abhängige** ~ the subsequent dependent patent; **einheitliches** ~ unitary patent; **ein** ~ **anmelden** to apply for a patent; **ein** ~ **aufrechterhalten** to maintain a patent; **ein** ~ **erhalten** to take out (*or* obtain) a patent; **ein** ~ **erteilen** to issue a patent; **ein** ~ **für nichtig erklären lassen** to nullify a patent; **ein** ~ **nutzen** to exploit a patent; **ein** ~ **verlängern** to extend a patent; **ein** ~ **verletzen** to infringe a patent; **ein** ~ **versagen** to refuse a patent; **ein** ~ **verwerten** to exploit a patent; **entgegengehaltenes** ~ reference patent, cited patent; **erloschenes** ~ expired patent; **gemeinsames** ~ joint patent; **grundlegendes** ~ basic patent; **gültiges** ~ patent in force, active patent, valid patent; **jmdm ein** ~ **erteilen** to grant a patent to s. o.; **jüngeres** ~ subsequent patent; **laufendes** ~ pending patent; **mangelhaftes** ~ defective patent; **nationales** ~ national patent; **nebeneinander bestehende** ~**e** co-existing patents; **nutzloses** ~ paper patent; **parallel laufendes** ~ collateral patent; **rechtsgültiges** ~ valid patent; **regionales** ~ regional patent; **selbständiges** ~ independent patent; **streitgegenständliches** ~ litigious patent; **strittiges**

Patentanwalt

~ disputed (litigious) patent; **verbrauchtes** ~ patent which has become common knowledge, lapsed patent; **verfallenes** ~ lapsed patent.

Patentanwalt *m* patent agent, patent attorney, patent lawyer; **~sbüro** patent law firm, patent agent's office; **~sgesetz** Patent Agents Act; **~skammer** Chartered Institute of Patent Agents; **~skanzlei** patent agent's office.

patentierbar *adj* patentable.

Patentierbarkeit *f* patentability.

patentieren *v/t* to patent; ~ *lassen:* to take out a patent, to patent sth.

Patentierung *f* the granting of a patent, issue of a patent; **~sverfahren** patent procedure.

Paternalismus *m* paternalism.

Patient in ambulanter Behandlung out-patient; ~ **in stationärer Behandlung** in-patient.

Patron *m* patron, sponsor, protector.

Patronat *n* patronage, sponsorship; **~serklärung** letter of awareness, „comfort letter"; **~sfirma** sponsor (*radio, television*); **~sherr** patron, lord of the manor, squire.

Patronin *f* patroness.

Pattsituation *f pol* stalemate, deadlock, cul de sac.

Pausch|besteuerung lump-sum taxation, taxation based on average figures, lump-sum deduction; **~-betrag** lump sum, global amount, flat fee; ~~ *für Sonderausgaben: standard allowance for special expenditures (insurance premiums etc)*; **~beträge für Werbungskosten:** *lump sums for professional expenses*; **~festsetzung** global assessment; **~satz** overall rate, lump-sum charge; **~steuer** blanket-rate tax, lump-sum tax; **~vergütung** overall compensation, flat-rate compensation; **~zahlung** lump-sum payment.

pauschal *adj* global, overall, lump-sum, compounded, all-included, all-in.

Pauschal|abfindung lump-sum settlement, lump-sum compensation; **~abgeltung** compounded settle-

Pauschalabfindung

ment; **~abrechnung** lump-sum settlement, flat-rate accounting; **~-abschreibung** overall depreciation; **~abzug** flat-rate deduction, fixed deduction, all-in deduction; **~beitrag** flat-rate fee, lump-sum contribution; **~besteuerung** lump-sum taxation, taxation based on average figures; **~betrag** lump sum, global sum, blanket amount; *durch Zahlung e-s ~~es abgelten: to discharge by a lump-sum payment*; **~bezugsvertrag zur Bedarfsdeckung** requirement contract; **~deckung** blanket cover; **~delkredere** global delcredere, overall provision for contingent losses; **~entgelt** lump-sum remuneration; **~entlohnung** lump-sum remuneration; **~entschädigung** lump-sum compensation; **~fracht** lump-sum freight, flat-rate freight; **~freibetrag** standard deduction (*tax*), flat-rate exemption; **~gebühr** flat fee; **~genehmigung** blankert licence; **~honorar** flat(-rate) fee, lump-sum payment for professional services; **~leistung** flat-rate benefit; **~lizenz** bloc licence; **~lohn** flat-rate wage;~ **police** blanket policy; **~prämie** all-inclusive premium, flat(-rate) bonus; **~preis** all-inclusive price; **~regelung** flat-rate scheme; **~regulierung** lump-sum settlement (*by insurance*); **~reise** all-expense tour, package tour; ~~*veranstalter: package tour operator;* ~~*dienste: tourist package services;* ~~*tourist: package tourist;* **~-rückstellungen** overall provisions; **~satz** lump-sum rate, blanket rate, overall rate; **~steuer** flat-rate tax; **~summe** lump sum; **~tarif** flat-rate tariff; **~vergütung** fixed allowance; **~vermächtnis** indefinite legacy; **~versicherung** blanket policy insurance, global insurance; **~versicherungspolice** block policy; **~vertrag** lump-sum contract, all-inclusive contract, blanket agreement; **~wert** global value, overall value; **~wert-**

593

berichtigung overall adjustment, general allowance for doubtful accounts; ~**zahlung** lump-sum payment, ~**zuwendung** lump-sum gift; ~**zuweisung** lump-sum appropriation.

Pauschale *f* lump sum, flat charge, standard allowance.

pauschalieren *v/t* to express as a round sum, to liquidate in a lump sum.

Pauschalierung *f* consolidation into a lump sum, lump-sum payment, lump-sum distribution; flat rate charge.

Peer *m* peer; ~ **auf Lebenszeit** life peer; ~**swürde** peerage.

Pegel *m* level indicator, gauge; ~**stand** water mark, water level.

Peitschenschlag *(Schleudertrauma) m* whiplash.

pekuniär *adj* pecuniary.

Pendelverkehr *m* shuttle service.

Pendler *m* commuter; ~**einzugsbereich** *m* commuter zone; (*or* area) ~**verkehr** commuting, commuter traffic.

Pension *1 (1)* guest house, lodging house, pension (*on the Continent*); board and lodgings; ~**sgast** boarder, lodger.

Pension *f (2)* retirement pension, civil pension; **lebenslängliche** ~ life pension.

Pensionär *m* pensioner.

pensionieren *v/t* to pension off; *sich* ~ *lassen: to retire (on a pension); wegen Erreichens der Altersgrenze* ~: *to superannuate.*

Pensionierung *f* retirement; ~**salter** retiring age, retirement age; **vorgezogene** ~ early retirement; **vorzeitige** ~ early retirement.

Pensions|**alter** pensionable age, retirement age, retiring age; ~**anordnungen** pension regulations; ~**anspruch** entitlement to a pension; ~**anwartschaft** accrued pension rights; right in future pension benefits; *unverfallbare* ~~: *vested pension right;* **p**~**berechtigt** pensionable, entitled to a pension, entitled to superannuation, eligible for a pension; ~**berechtigung** pension right, entitlement to a pension, eligibility for a pension; ~**bestimmungen** pension provisions; ~**bezüge** pension (payments), retirement benefits; ~**dienstalter** pensionable age; ~**empfänger** pensioner; ~**ergänzungsversicherung** supplementary retirement pension insurance; **p**~**fähig** pensionable; ~**festsetzungsbehörde** retirement pension board; ~**fonds** pension fund, staff pension fund, retirement fund, pension(s) trust; ~**geber** pledgor under a repurchase agreement; ~**geschäft** pension transaction: *sale of securities subject to repurchase*; repurchase agreement, securities-repurchase pact; securities tender buy back; repos; ~**kasse** staff pension fund, *also* → ~*fonds;* betriebliche ~~: *staff pension fund, employer's pension f., company's pension f.;* gemeinsame ~~: *pension pool;* ~**nehmer** pledgee under a repurchase agreement; ~**plan** pension plan, pension scheme; *beitragsfreier* ~~: *non-contributory pension plan; beitragspflichtiger* ~~: *contributory pension scheme;* ~**ordnung** pension regulations; ~**rückstellung** pension reserve, provision for pensions: *pl also: pension provisions*; ~**satz** pension rate; ~~**-Sicherungs-Verein** (= *German obligatory pensions guarantee corporation;* ~**system** = ~*plan qv;* ~**verpflichtung** pension obligation(s); ~**versicherung** old-age pension insurance; ~**versprechen** promise to grant a pension; ~**wechsel** bill of exchange deposited with a bank as security for a loan; ~**zusage** pension commitment.

per *prep* through, by, per; ~ *Adresse*: care of *(c/o);* ~ *Saldo* → *Saldo;* ~ *sofort: immediately*.

peremptorisch *adj* peremptory, strict, commanding.

perfektionieren *v/t* to perfect, to make perfect (*or* more nearly perfect).

Perfektionismus *m* perfectionism.

Periode *f* period (of time).
Perioden|abgrenzung allocation to applicable accounting period; delimitation of accounting periods; **~bilanz** periodic statement; **~erfolg** balance by accounting period; **p~fremd** not belonging to the accounting period; **~gewinn** profit in a stated period; **~kosten** cost for an accounting period; **~leistung** quantitative result during an accounting period; **~rechnung** accounting by definite period.
periodisch *adj* periodical, at stated periods, regular.
Periodizität *f* periodicity.
peripher *adj* peripheral, on the fringe, on the outskirts.
perpetuatio fori (principle of) continued jurisdiction.
„Persilschein" *m pol* whitewashing certificate.
Person *f* person; ~ **mit Auslandswohnsitz** non-resident; **abgängige** ~ missing person; **an der ~ haftend** attached to the person, personal; **an die ~ gebunden sein** to subsist in the person (*a right*); **ansässige** ~ resident; **anweisungsbefugte** ~**en** authorizing officers; **arbeitsscheue** ~ idle person; **aufzeichnungspflichtige** ~ person obliged to keep books; **bedachte** ~ person remembered in a will, beneficiary, legatee; **bevollmächtigte** ~ authorized person, authorized agent; **bundesgebietsfremde** ~**en** persons other than residents of the Federal Republic; **fiktive** ~ fictitious person; **für seine** ~ in his personal capacity; **geeignete** ~ fit person; **geisteskranke** ~ person of unsound mind; **im Vertragstaat ansässige** ~ resident of a Contracting State; **in der Ausbildung stehende** ~ trainee; **in eigener** ~ in person, in propria persona; **in** ~ in person, personally; ~ ~ *erscheinen: to appear in person;* **in Haft befindliche** ~ person under arrest; **jugendliche** ~**en** young persons, youths, adolescents; **juristische** ~ legal entity, juristic person, juridical person, corporate body; ~ ~ *des öffentlichen Rechts: juristic person under public law, public-law corporation, legal entity under public law;* ~ ~ *des Privatrechts: juristic person governed by private law;* **maßgebende** ~ the person who matters, the crucial person; **natürliche** ~ natural person, physical person, individual; *die* ~**n** ~**en** *e–s Landes: the individual inhabitants of a country;* **nicht geschäftsfähige** (*erwachsene*) ~ incapacitated person; **nicht verwandte** ~ not-related person; **physische** ~ natural person; **rauschgiftsüchtige** ~**en** drug addicts; **repatriierte** ~ repatriate; **rückerstattungspflichtige** ~ restitutor; **übel beleumundete** ~ person of ill fame; **unbescholtene** ~ person of unblemished character; **unerwünschte** ~ undesired person; an undesirable alien; **unzuverlässige** ~ unreliable person; **verdrängte** ~ displaced person; **verschleppte** ~ displaced person; kidnapped person; **versicherte** ~ insured (person); **von** ~ **bekannt** of known identity.
persona | grata persona grata (*diplomat*); ~ **ingrata** = *persona non grata qv;* ~ **non grata** persona non grata, unwelcome (*or* unacceptable) person (*diplomat*).
Personal *n* personnel, staff, employees; **~abbau** staff reduction; job cutting; **~abteilung** staff department, personnel department, personnel management, staff administration, human resources department; **~adelsstand** life peerage; **~akte** personal file, personal dossier, *pl also: personnel records;* employee records; ~~~**neinsicht**: right to inspect one's personal file; **~angaben** personal data; **~angelegenheiten** personnel matters; **~anmeldung** reporting personnel; **~anwerber** recruiter; **~aufwand** = ~*aufwendungen qv;* **~aufwendungen** personnel expense, salaries and wages, employment expense, labour ex-

595

Personalien

pense; staff expenditure; ~**ausgaben** = ~*aufwendungen qv*; ~**ausweis** identity card, *pl also*: identity papers; certificate of identification; ~ *für Ausländer: alien's identity card, behelfsmäßiger-~: provisional identity card;* ~**bedarf** personnel requirements; ~**bereich** personnel administration; ~**beschaffung** recruitment; ~**beschreibung** personal particulars, description; ~**bestand** staff, total of persons employed; *(dipl)* ~~ *der Mission: size of the mission;* ~**beurteilung** personnel merit rating; ~**bogen** personal record sheet; ~**buch** staff book; ~**buchhaltung** personnel accounting; ~**büro** personnel office; ~**chef** personnel director, personnel manager, staff manager; ~**einsparung** personnel cut, staff savings; ~**fragebogen** preliminary application form, questionnaire; ~**freisetzung** personnel lay off; ~**führung** personnel management; ~**fürsorgefonds** staff provident fund; ~**gemeinkosten** employment overhead costs; ~**geschäft** independent firm, firm in a personal name; ~**gesellschaft** partnership *(general or limited partnership)*, firm; *nicht gewerbliche ~~: non-trading partnership*; ~**gutachterausschuß** service appointment advisory committee: *consultation committee for highranking military appointments;* ~**haft** personal arrest, detention; ~**handelsgesellschaft** (business) partnership; ~**hoheit** personal sovereignty, ultimate jurisdiction for appointments, power to appoint and dismiss staff; ~ **im Außendienst** field staff; ~**kartei** personnel card file; ~**knappheit** staff shortage, manpower shortage; ~**konzession** licence granted to a named individual; ~**kosten** personnel expense, labour costs; *anteilige ~~: pro rata labour costs;* ~**kredit** personal loan, personal credit (agreement); loan on personal security, fiduciary loan; ~~*abteilung: personal loan department;*

Personenbeförderung

~**mangel** = ~*knappheit qv*; ~**nebenkosten** incidental personnel cost *(social insurance etc)*; ~**ordnung** staff regulations; ~**papiere** identification documents; ~**planung** personnel planning, manpower planning; ~**politik** employment policy; ~**prinzip** principle of staff policy; ~**rat** staff council *(of a public authority)*; ~**sachbearbeiter** personnel officer, staff manager; ~**sicherheiten** personal securities; ~**stand** number of persons employed; ~**statut** the law applicable to the person, personal statute *(int. private law)*; staff regulations; ~**steuer** personal tax; ~**umbesetzung** switch in personnel, a reshuffle; ~**union** personal union, identity of membership; ~**versammlung** staff meeting; ~**vertretung** staff representation *(in public authorities)*, personnel committee; ~~*sgesetz: Staff Representation (in public service) Act;* ~~*ssachen: staff representation proceedings;* ~**verwaltung** personnel administration, staff management; ~**wesen** personnel management; **bautechnisches** ~ building-engineering personnel; **das erforderliche** ~ the staff required; **leitendes** ~ managerial staff, senior staff; **subalternes** ~ subordinate personnel.

Personalien *f/pl* personal data; **jmds** ~ **feststellen** to establish a person's identity.

Personen|beförderung carriage of passengers, passenger transportation; ~**beförderungsentgelt** (passenger) fare; ~**beförderungsgesetz** Passenger Transport Act (*on streets and roads*); ~**beförderungsvertrag** passenger (conveyance) contract; ~**beschreibung** description of wanted persons; ~**feststellung** identification; ~**firma** personal firm-name; ~**gemeinschaft** association; ~**gesamtheit** aggregate of persons; ~**gesellschaft** = *Personalgesellschaft qv*; **p~gleich** identical (in person), one and the same person, ~**gleichheit** identity; ~**hehlerei** shielding of a criminal, concealing a person after the crime, protection of a criminal; ~-**Kautionsversicherung** fidelity bond insurance; ~**kilometer** passenger-kilometres; ~**konto** personal account; ~**kraftfahrzeug** motor vehicle for persons; ~**kraftwagen** motor car, (passenger) car; ~**kreis** category of people; circle (of people); *begünstigter* ~~: *category of beneficiaries;* ~**kult** personality cult; ~**nahverkehr** short-distance passenger transport; ~**name** (personal) name; ~**recht** law concerning persons (*or* individuals); ~**rufanlage** staff calling system; ~**schaden** physical injury, personal injury; ~**sorge** legal custody of the child, care and custody (of a child); ~**sorgeberechtigter** person having the care and custody of a child, custodial parent; ~**sorgerecht** the right of care and custody of a child; ~**stand** →*Personenstand;* ~**steuer** personal tax; tax imposed on individuals; ~**tarif** passenger rates, passenger fares; ~-**transport** passenger transport (or carriage); ~**überprüfung** review of personal records; ~- **und Güterverkehr** passenger und goods traffic; ~- **und Sachbeschädigung** personal injury or damage to property; ~**verband** association (of individuals); ~**vereinigung** association (of individuals); *nichtrechtsfähige* ~~*ty:* unincorporated society; ~**verkehr** passenger traffic, passenger transport; *freier* ~~: *freedom of movement for persons; öffentlicher* ~~: *public (passenger) transport;* ~**versicherung** personal insurance (*life, sickness and accident insurance*); ~**verzeichnis** register of persons; ~**verwechslung** mistaken identity.

Personenstand *m* (a person's) legal, status, personal status.

Personenstands|**änderung** change of personal status (*e.g. by marriage, divorce, adoption etc*), ~**angelegenheit** a matter concerning one's personal status (*registrar of births, deaths, and marriages*); ~**bücher** registers of births, deaths, and marriages; ~**fälschung** fraudulent alteration of a person's legal status ~**gesetz** Law on Personal Status *registration of births, marriages, and deaths;* ~**klage** action concerning personal status; ~**recht** law of personal status, ~**register** personal register, register of births, marriages and deaths; ~**urkunden** personal registration certificates; ~**wesen** matters of personal status.

Personifikation *f* impersonation.

personifizieren *v/t* to impersonate, to personify, to imitate.

persönlich *adj* personal, private; *adv* personally, in person, in personam, in propria persona.

Persönlichkeit *f* personality.

Persönlichkeits|**entfaltung** development of personality; *freie* ~~; *free development of one's personality, pursuit of happiness;* ~**mangel** personality defect; ~**recht** right of personality, personal rights, *right to protection of one's individual sphere of life (privacy, name etc);* ~**schutz** legal protection of personality; ~**spaltung** split personality; ~**untersuchung** inquiry into s. o's personality; ~**verletzung** violation of personal rights, violation of one's individual sphere of life; ~**wahl** election of an individual candidate, direct election of candidates, „first past the post" election, election of one candidate per constituency; ~**wandlung** change of personality.

Petent *m* petitioner, suppliant.

Petition *f* petition; ~**sausschuß** committee on public petitions; ~**srecht** right of petition.

Petitum *n* demand, request, petition, prayer (*the remedy asked for*).

Petschaft *n* signet, seal.

Pfalzgrafschaft county palatine, palatinate.

Pfand *n* pawn, pledge, security, collateral, the pledged item, ~**ab-**

pfändbar / **Pfandbrief**

stand return unsatisfied, certificate of nulla bona; ~**abstandsbescheinigung** = *Pfandabstand qv*; ~**abstandserklärung** = *Pfandabstand qv*; ~**auslösungsrecht** right to redeem a pledge, equity of redemption (*mortgage*); ~**besitzer** pawnee, pledgee, holder of a pledge; ~**besteller** pledgor, pawnor; ~**bestellung** pledging, pawning; ~**bestellungsurkunde** certificate of pledge; ~**brief** → *Pfandbrief;* ~ **bruch** → *Verstrickungsbrüchiger;* ~**buch** register of charges; ~**einlösung** redemption of a pledge, taking out of pawn; ~**depot** pledged securities deposit; ~**entstrickung** release of pawn, release from a lien; ~**erstreckung** extension of a lien; ~~**sklausel**: *after-acquired clause;* ~**forderung** debt secured by pledge, mortgage claim; ~**freigabe** release from pledge, restoration of goods taken in distraint, release from lien, release from mortgage restrictions; ~**geber** pledgor, pawnor; ~**gegenstand** pledged object, pledged item, mortgaged property; ~**geld** money advanced under a pledge; ~**gläubiger** pledgee, pawnee, lienor, lienholder; ~**gut** pledged property; ~**haft** attachment; ~**halter** pawnee, pledgee; ~**haus** pawnshop; ~**hinterlegung** delivery as a pawn, deposit of pledged item; ~**indossament** pledge endorsement; ~**inhaber** holder of a pledge, pawnee, bailee; ~**kehr** unlawful recovery of pledged goods; ~**leihanstalt** pawnshop, loan office; ~**leihe** pawnbroking; ~**leiher** pawnbroker; ~**leihhaus** pawnshop; ~**lokal** storage place for distrained goods; ~**mißbrauch** fraudulent use of a pawn; ~**nehmer** pledgee, holder of pledged property, pawnee; ~**objekt** pledged article, pledged property; ~**recht** → *Pfandrecht;* ~**sache** pledged property; ~**schein** pawn-ticket, pawn-receipt; ~**schuldner** pledgor, pawnor; ~**siegel** bailiff's stamp; ~**stück** pledged article, pawn; ~**unterschlagung** conversion of a pledge to own use; ~**urkunde** certificate of pledge, letter of lien, letter of hypothecation; ~**veräußerung** disposal of pledged property; ~**verfall** forfeiture of pledged property, foreclosure; ~~**skündigung**: *notice of foreclosure;* ~~**serklärung**: *foreclosure order;* ~~**sverfahren**: *foreclosure proceedings;* ~**verkauf** distress sale, foreclosure sale, sale of pledged property; ~**vermittler** pawnbroker; ~**verschleppung** unlawful removal of pledged property; ~**versteigerung** auction of distrained (*or* pledged) goods; ~**verstrickung** attachment under a lien; ~**vertrag** contract of pledge, contract of lien; ~**verwahrung** custody of pledged goods; ~**verwertung** realization of a pledge, realization of goods taken in execution, realization of distrained goods; *e-e* ~~ *vornehmen*: to enforce a lien; *freihändiges* ~~*recht*: power to sell; ~**verwirkung** forfeiture of pledged property; **p**~**weise** *adv* by way of pledge; **als** ~ **besitzen** to have a lien over sth to hold in pledge; **als ~ nehmen** to take in pledge, to take in pawn; **ein ~ auslösen** to redeem a pawn; **ein ~ einlösen** to redeem a pawn, to take out of pledge; **verfallenes ~** forfeited pledge; **zum ~e geben** = *verpfänden qv*.

pfändbar *adj* leviable, distrainable, subject to execution, non-exempt (from execution), attachable.

Pfändbarkeit *f* attachability, liability to distress (*or* execution).

Pfandbrief *m* mortgage bond, mortgage-bank bond; ~**agio** mortgage bond discount; ~**anleihe** mortgage bond issue; ~**anstalt** mortgage bank; ~**ausstattung** mortgage bond terms; ~**darlehen** loans secured by mortgage collateral; ~**gläubiger** mortgage-bond holder; ~**hypothek** mortgage serving as collateral for mortgage bonds; ~**inhaber** mortgage-bond holder;

pfänden

~**umlauf** mortgage bonds outstanding.

pfänden *v/t* to levy (execution upon), to distrain (upon goods), to attach (a debt), to seize goods under distress; **bei jmdn** ~ **lassen** to levy execution against s. o.

Pfandrecht *n* lien, lien in rem, right of lien; ~ **an beweglichen Sachen** chattel mortgage; ~ **an e-r Sache** lien over an item; ~ **des Frachtführers** carrier's lien; ~ **des Gastwirts** innkeeper's lien; ~ **des Vermieters** landlord's lien; **älteres** ~ senior lien; **besitzloses** ~ non-possessory lien; **gesetzliches** ~ lien by operation of law, statutory lien; **gesetzlich vermutetes** ~ implied lien; **gewillkürtes** ~ conventional lien; **gleichrangige** ~**e** concurrent liens; **kaufmännisches** ~ mercantile lien; **nachrangiges** ~ junior lien; **rechtsgeschäftliches** ~ conventional lien, pledge; **sich aus e-m** ~ **befriedigen** to obtain satisfaction from a lien.

Pfändung *f* levy of execution, distress, levy of distress, distraint; ~ **der Früchte auf dem Halm** seizure of unharvested crops by way of execution; ~ **und Überweisung von Forderungen** garnishment, attachment and (judicial) transfer of garnished claims; **die** ~ **aufheben** to lift the seizure; **fruchtlose** ~ nulla bona, unproductive levy of execution.

Pfändungs|anordnung writ of fieri facias (*fi. fa.*); order of attachment, distraint order, judgment execution; ~**anzeige** notice of execution; ~**auftrag** writ of execution, warrant of execution; ~**bericht** *report of bailiff concerning his levy of execution*, fieri feci, return of writs; ~**beschränkungen** restrictions on execution, exemptions from execution; ~**freigrenze** limit of exemption from execution (*necessities of life etc*); ~**gebühr** bailiff's fee for execution; ~**gläubiger** attaching creditor, judgment creditor (*during execution upon a debtor's property*);

Pflege

~**grenze** maximum limit for executions; ~**pfandrecht** execution lien, lien by attachment; ~**protokoll** bailiff's return (*or* record) (*of the levying of an execution*), fieri feci; ~**schuldner** debtor under a levy of execution, distrainee; ~**schutz** exemption from distraint, exemption (*of debtor's property or income*) from execution; ~- **und Überweisungsbeschluß** garnishment order; order of attachment and transfer of garnished claim; ~**verfügung** garnishee order (*from tax office*); ~**versuch erfolglos** no goods, nulla bona.

Pflanzen|gesundheitszeugnis phytosanitary certificate; ~**patent** plant patent; ~**schutz** → *Pflanzenschutz;* ~**sorten und Tierarten** plant and animal varieties; ~**züchtung** plant breeding.

Pflanzenschutz *m* plant protection, protection of natural flora; ~**bestimmungen** plant-health provisions; ~**mittel** pesticide, pest control agent; ~-**Organisation für Europa und den Mittelmeerraum** European and Mediterranean Plant Protection Organization; ~-**recht** plant protection law *p*~~~*lich:* phytopathological; ~-**warte** plant protection station.

Pflege *f* care, nursing, maintenance, cultivation; ~ *des Exports:* promotion *of exports;* ~**anstalt** nursing home; ~**bedürftiger** person needing care and attention; ~**befohlener** protected person, charge, ward; ~**eltern** foster parents; ~**entschädigung** care allowance; ~**erlaubnis** permission to take over the care and custody of a person; ~**fall** case requiring nursing; ~**fallversicherung** insurance to cover long term (at home *or*) nursing home care; ~**geld** nursing fee, allowance for nursing attendance; ~**heim** nursing home; ~**kind** foster child; ~**kinderwesen** matters concerning foster children; ~**kindschaftsverhältnis** foster relationship, fostering; ~**kosten** nursing charges,

599

expenses of nursing; p~**leicht** *adj* easy to clean, easy to look after; ~**mutter** foster mother; ~**satz** hospitalization cost rate (*per day and patient*), daily cost of maintenance in home for the aged: ~**vater** foster father; ~**vertrag** care contract; ~**zulage** additional nursing allowance.

Pfleger *m* curator, temporary guardian, ward custodian; *hospital etc*: male nurse.

pfleglich *adj* careful, circumspect.

Pflegling *m* ward, person subject to wardship.

Pflegschaft *f* curatorship, tutelage, trusteeship, wardship; ~**sbestellung** wardship order; ~**smasse** estate under curatorship; ~**ssachen** curatorship (*or* wardship) cases; **befreite** ~ exempted wardship.

Pflicht *f* duty, obligation; ~**aktie** qualifying share; ~**altersversorgung** compulsory old-age pension scheme; ~**angaben** required disclosures; ~**auffassung** sense of duty; ~**aufgaben** absolute obligations, unavoidable duties, legally required functions; ~**beitrag** compulsory contribution; ~**bekanntmachung** obligatory announcement; obligatory stock exchange notice; ~**besuch** compulsory attendance; p~**bewußt** *adj* dutiful, having a sense of duty; ~**blatt** official journal for notices; proper journal for obligatory announcements (*of a company etc*); ~**einlage** compulsory contribution (*to capital of a firm or company*); ~**enabwägung** the weighing of conflicting duties; ~**en des Treuhänders** fiduciary duties; ~**enheft** duties record book, software specifications; ~**en im eigenen Wirkungskreis** original duties (*local authorities*); ~**enkollision** conflict of duties, clash of responsibilities; ~**en und Rechte** rights and obligations; ~**erfüllung** discharge of obligation, fulfilment of one's duty, performance of one's duty; ~**exemplar** statutory copy, presentation copy, ~**exemplarrecht** copyright privilege (*cf Library of Congress*); ~**fach** compulsory subject; ~**feuerwehr** compulsory fire service; p~**gemäß** *adj* dutiful, *adv* in accordance with one's duty, dutifully; ~**grenze** limit of one's duty, compulsory contribution limit; ~**lager** compulsory stock; ~**leistung** standard insurance benefit; p~**mäßig** *adj* obligatory, compulsory; ~**mitglied** compulsory member; ~**mitgliedschaft** compulsory membership; ~**notstandsreserven** emergency reserve commitment (*oil*); ~**prüfung** compulsory examination (*of insurance companies*); ~**quote** compulsory quota; ~**reserven** required reserves, statutory reserves, minimum reserves; p~**schuldig** *adj* dutiful; ~**sozialbeiträge** compulsory social welfare contributions; ~**stunden** prescribed (number of) lessons; ~**teil** → *Pflichtteil*; ~**treue** loyality, faithful observance of one's duties; ~**übung** compulsory course (*at university*); ~**-untersuchung** obligatory medical examination (*insurance*); ~**verbände** associations with compulsory membership; p~**vergessen** *adj* neglectful of one's duty; ~**vergessenheit** dereliction of duty, neglect of one's duty; ~**verletzung** neglect of one's duty, breach of duty, failure to comply with one's duties, misfeasance; *fortgesetzte* ~~: *continued breach of duty*; *grobe* ~~: *gross breach of duty, gross neglect of duty*; ~**versäumnis** neglect of duty, dereliction of duty, shortcoming, default; ~**versicherung** compulsory insurance (scheme), obligatory insurance, statutory insurance; *soziale* ~~*en*: *obligatory social insurance institutions*; ~**verstoß** violation of duty; ~**verteidiger** official defence counsel, court-appointed counsel, assigned counsel; *e-n* ~~ *beiordnen: to assign counsel for the defence*; *e-n* ~~ *bestimmen: to designate a counsel for the defence*;

~**verteidigung** court-assigned defence; ~**vorlesung** compulsory lecture, non-optional lecture; **p~widrig** *adj* contrary to one's duty, in breach of one's duty, undutiful, disloyal; ~**widrigkeit** violation of duty, breach of duty; ~ **zum Handeln** positive duty; ~ **zur Abrechnung** obligation to render account; ~ **zur Hilfeleistung** duty to assist *(emergency)*; ~ **zur Vorlage von Urkunden** obligation to present documents; **ausdrückliche** ~ express obligation; **bedingte** ~ conditional obligation; **die sich aus seinem Amt ergebenden ~en** obligations arising from one's office; **eheliche** ~ conjugal duty, marital duty; **gesetzliche** ~ legal obligation, statutory duty; **nicht zwingend vorgeschriebene** ~ non-prescribed duty, non compulsory duty; **primäre** ~ primary obligation; **privatrechtliche** ~ private law duty; **seine** ~ **ausüben** to do one's duty, to discharge one's duty; **seine** ~ **erfüllen** to fulfil one's duty, to do one's duty; **seine** ~ **verletzen** to fail in one's duty, to neglect one's duty; **seine ~en vernachlässigen** to be remiss in one's duties; **sittliche** ~ moral obligation, natural obligation; **stillschweigende** ~ implied obligation; **vertragliche** ~ contractual obligation, obligation under a contract; **vorrangige** ~ overriding duty; **zwingende** ~ absolute obligation, compulsion.

pflichtig *adj* due, to be bound, to be under an obligation (to), to be committed (to).

Pflichtiger *m (der Pflichtige)* obligated person, obligor, debtor, person under a duty.

Pflichtigkeit *f* obligation, commitment.

Pflichtteil *m* compulsory portion, *(money compensation in lieu of inheritance for disinherited descendants, parents or spouse)*.

Pflichtteils|anspruch entitlement to a compulsory portion; ~**berechtigter** person entitled to a compulsory portion; ~**ergänzung** augmentation of the compulsory portion; ~**ergänzungsanspruch** right to augmentation of compulsory portion *(in view of testator's donations)*; ~**entziehung** deprivation of the right to compulsory portion; ~**last** burden of (having to pay) compulsory portion; ~**recht** right to a compulsory portion.

Pflücker *m* picker.

Pflug|genossenschaft ploughing pool, agricultural cooperative; ~**recht** right of ploughman to encroach upon adjoining land *(US: plow)*.

Pfründe *f* sinecure, *eccl*: benefice, prebend; ~**nbesetzungsrecht** right of patronage; ~**nrecht** right to a benefice; ~**nstiftung** endowment; ~**nverleihungsrecht** patronage.

Pfund *n* (metric) pound; pound sterling.

Phantasiewort *n* fancy word *(trade marks)*, imaginary word, made-up word.

Phantombild *n* identikit picture.

Photogrammetrie *f* photogrammetry, photographic surveying.

Pier *m* pier, jetty; ~**geld** pierage.

Pirat *m* pirate.

Piratensender *m* pirate radio station.

Piraterie *f* piracy.

Placet *n* = *Plazet qv*.

plädieren *v/i* to plead, to address the court, to sum up.

Plädieren *n* pleading, summing-up.

Plädoyer *n* oral pleading, argument of counsel, address by counsel, pleading; ~ **des Staatsanwalts** prosecution counsel's speech; **mit dem** ~ **beginnen** to open the pleadings; **Reihenfolge der ~s** order of speeches; **sein** ~ **als Verteidiger halten** to address the court for the defence.

Plafond *m* ceiling, limit, line; ~-**Liberalisierung** limited liberalisation.

plafondieren *v/t* to impose a limit.

Plagiat *n* plagiarism, literary piracy;

Plagiator

ein ~ **begehen** to commit plagiarism, to lift, to copy.
Plagiator *m* plagiarist, plagiarizer.
plagiieren *v/i* to plagiarize.
Plakat *n* poster, placard, broad sheet; ~**ankleben verboten!** post no bills!; ~**anschlag** bill-posting, placard; ~**-säule** advertisement pillar; ~**träger** sandwich man; ~**wand** hoarding, billboard; ~**werbung** poster advertizing.
Plakette *f* badge, medal.
Plan *m* plan; schedule; scheme; map; ~**änderung** modification of a plan; ~**ansatz** planned appropriation, budget estimate; ~**defizit** estimated deficit, budget deficit; ~**durchführung** implementation of plan; ~**erfüllung** fulfilment of production targets; ~**feststellung** project approval (public works), *official determination and approval of a plan for public works projects (highways, canals airports etc)*. ~**feststellungsverfahren** public works planning procedure, project-determination procedure; ~**kostenrechnung** budget accounting, standard costing; **p~mäßig** *adj* according to plan, as planned, as scheduled; ~**pause** blueprint; ~**quadrat** grid square, ~**rechnung** estimate; ~**satz** set of planning documents; ~**soll** plan target; ~**spiel** management business game, planning game, ~**-stelle** established post; ~**wirtschaft** planned economy, controlled economy; ~**wirtschaftler** advocate of planned economy; ~**zeichen** plan notation; ~**ziel** planned output, production objective, target, *pl also*: objectives of the plan; **rechtsverbindlicher** ~ legally binding plan; **totgeborener** ~ dead-on-arrival plan, useless/hopeless plan from the start, a non-starter.
Planung *f* planning; ~ **der gegenständlichen Umwelt** physical planning; **langfristige** ~ long-term planning; **regionale** ~ regional planning; **staatliche** ~ state planning; **städtebauliche** ~ town

Plazet

planning; **volkswirtschaftliche** ~ economic planning.
Planungs|abteilung planning department; ~**amt** planning department; ~**ansatz** planning approach; ~**ausschuß** planning committee; ~**behörde** planning authority; ~**bereich** planning sector; ~**ermessen** discretionary planning power; ~**fehler** design defect; ~**gebiet** planning area; ~**gebot** (mandatory) requirement to submit a (development) plan; ~**hoheit** planning competence; ~**instanz** planning authority; ~**kosten** costs of planning; ~**recht** planning law; ~**soll** target; ~**-stelle** planning agency; ~**träger** planning agency; ~**verband** association for planning purposes, planning group; ~**vorschriften** planning regulations.
Platz|akzept local acceptance; ~**anweiser** usher; ~**bedarf** space requirement; ~**bedingungen** local terms, *naut* berth terms; ~**gebrauch** local trade usage; *pl* ~*gebräuche*: local trade rules; ~**geschäft** spot contract, local transaction; ~**handel** local trade, spot business; ~**karte** reserved seat ticket; ~**kauf** local purchase, spot purchase; ~**kurs** spot-market price, spot rate; ~**makler** spot broker: ~**reservierung** booking, reservation of seats; ~**scheck** local cheque, locally drawn cheque; *cheque payable at the place where drawn;* ~**übertragung** local transfer; ~**usance** local usage, local practice; *pl also*: local trade rules; ~**veränderung** change of location; removal (*of insured objects*); ~**verkauf** sale on the spot; ~**vertreter** local agent, town traveller; ~**wechsel** local bill, town bill *US: bill of exchange payable at place of issue.*
plausibel *adj* plausible, arguable.
Plausibilität *f* plausibility, arguability; ~**skontrolle** *f (von gespeicherten Daten)* validity check;
Plazet *n* assent, approval; placet (*vote of assent in church or university assembly*).

plazierbar *ajd* placeable; *nicht* ~: **unplaceable**.

plazieren *v/t* to place, to position, to seat.

Plazierung *f* placing, placement; ~**sfähigkeit** ability to place securities; ~**geschäft** security-placing business; ~**skonsortium** selling group, selling syndicate; distributing syndicate; ~**kurs** placing price.

Plebiszit *n* plebiscite.

pleite *adj* broke, bankrupt.

Pleite *f* smash, bust, failure, bankruptcy, „flop"; ~**firma** bust firm; ~**geier** threat of bankruptcy; ~**welle** wave of bankruptcies, spate of bankruptcies.

Plenar|ausschuß plenary committee; ~**entscheidung** plenary decision, per totam curiam, decision by the full court; ~**saal** plenary hall, main assembly hall, full session hall, floor of the House; ~**sitzung** full session, trial at bar, plenary court, plenary session; ~~ *des Gerichts*: sitting in banc, session in pleno; ~**versammlung** plenary assembly, plenary meeting.

Plenum *n* plenary sitting (*or* session), full session, full court, plenum; ~**sdiskussion** floor discussion.

Plombe *f* lead seal, metal seal.

plombieren *v/t* to seal (*container, wagon etc*).

Plombierung *f* (official) sealing.

Plünderer *m* looter, pillager, marauder.

plündern *v/t*, *v/i* to plunder, to loot, to maraud, to pillage, to rifle.

Plünderung *f* pilferage, looting, pillage, plundering, spoliation, rapine; **kriegsrechtliche** ~ spoliation.

Pluralismus *m pol* pluralism.

plus *adv* plus; ~ *minus Null*: nil either way.

Plus *n* plus, surplus, advantage, increase, rise, upward movement. ~**korrektur** upward adjustment.

Plutokratie *f* plutocracy.

Pockenschutzimpfung *f* smallpox vaccination.

Podium *n* platform; ~**sdiskussion** panel discussion.

Polemik *f* sharp dispute, polemics, bitter controversy.

polemisch *adj* polemic, argumentative.

polemisieren *v/i* to engage in polemics.

Police *f* (insurance) policy; ~**nausfertigung** original policy, issue of policy; ~**ndarlehen** loan against policy (*or* policies); ~**nformular** blank policy; ~**ninhaber** policy holder, policy owner; ~**nregister** policy book; ~ **ohne Nachschußpflicht** non-assessable policy; ~ **ohne Wertangabe** unvalued policy, open policy; ~ **ohne Zurückweisungsrecht** indisputable policy; ~ **über e-e Überlebensversicherung** joint life policy; **abgelaufene** ~ expired policy; **befristete** ~ term insurance (policy), **beitragsfreie** ~ free policy; **laufende** ~ open policy, floating policy; **nicht eingelöste** ~ policy not taken up; uncashed policy; **nicht gewinnberechtigte** ~ without profits policy, non-participating policy; **offene** ~ open policy, floating policy; **prämienfreie** ~ free policy, paid-up policy; **prolongierte** ~ extended policy; **rückdatierte** ~ backdated policy; **taxierte** ~ valued policy; **unwiderruflich gewordene** ~ incontestable policy.

Poliklinik *f* policlinic, outpatients' department (at a local hospital).

Politechnikum *n* technical college, technical high school.

Politesse *f* traffic warden.

Politik *f* politics; policy; ~ **auf weite Sicht** long-range policy; ~ **der Einkommensbegrenzung** (the) pay restraint policy; ~ **der guten Nachbarschaft** good-neighbour policy; ~ **der Mitte** policy of the middle road; ~ **der offenen Tür** open-door policy; ~ **der Versöhnung** policy of conciliation; ~ **des Abwartens** policy of wait and see; ~ **des billigen Geldes** policy

Politikaster

of cheap money; ~ **des knappen Geldes** policy of tight money; ~ **des teuren Geldes** tight money policy; **auswärtige** ~ foreign policy; **e–e** ~ **aktivieren** to revive a policy; **gemeinsame** ~ common policy; **internationale** ~ international politics.

Politikaster *m* armchair politician, coffeehouse politician.

Politiker *m* politician; ~ **im Ruhestand** elder statesman; **käuflicher** ~ venal politician, corrupt politician.

Politikum *n* political issue, matter of politics, political affair.

politisch *adj* political.

Polizei *f* police, police force, police service, police station; **~aktion** police operation, police raid; **~anordnung** police order; **~aufgaben** police functions; **~aufgabengesetz** Police Functions Act; **~aufgebot** police detachment, contingent of police; **~aufsicht** police surveillance; **~ausrüstung** police equipment; **~auto** patrol car; **~beamter** police officer, constable; **~beamtin** woman police officer; **~behörde** police authority; **~bericht** police report; **~bezirk** precinct; **~dienst** police service; **~dienstkräfte** police force, members of the police; **~dienststelle** police office, police station; **~einsatz** police operation, police raid; **~eskorte** police escort; **~exzeß** outrageous behaviour by the police; **~fahrzeug** police vehicle; **~falle** plant, police trap, sting; **~funk** police radio (network); **~funktionen** police functions; *Ausübung von ~~*: policing; **~gefängnis** police prison, police cell, slammer; **~gewahrsam** police custody, police detention; **~gewalt** police power; **~haft** police custody **~hund** police dog; **~knüppel** (policeman's) truncheon, *US*: night stick, club, "billy"; **~kommissar** police superintendent; **~kordon** police cordon; **~kräfte** police officers, police force; **~melder** police alarm,

Polygamie

police box; **~organisationsgesetz** Police Organization Act; **~posten** police picket, police guard; **~präsident** police chief, head of the police department; **~präsidium** police headquarters; **~rat** senior police official; **~recht** police law; **~revier** police district, police precinct; police station; **~richter** police justice, magistrate; **~schule** police training school; **~schüler** police cadet; **~schutz** police protection; **~spitzel** police informer, spotter, plant, police spy, stool pidgeon; **~staat** police state; **~stock** club; **~streife** police patrol; **~stunde** closing hours *(for public houses, bars etc)*, statutory closing time; **~truppe** constabulary; **~verfügung** police order; **~verordnung** police ordinance; **~verwahrung** police detention; **~verwaltung** police administration; **~verwaltungsgesetz** Police Administration Act; **~verwendung** employment of the police, police operations; **~-V-Mann** super grass; **~vollzugsbeamter** police officer, law enforcement officer; **~wache** police station; **~wachtmeister** police sergeant; **~wesen** police system, police matters; **~widrigkeit** infringement of police regulations; **~zwang** compulsion by the police; **politische** ~ political police; **sich der** ~ **stellen** to surrender to the police, to give oneself up to the police; **von der** ~ **festgenommen werden** to be arrested by the police, to be pulled in by the police; **von der** ~ **verhört werden** to be questioned by the police; **von der** ~ **vernommen werden** to be questioned by the police.

polizeilich *adj* police ..., of the police, by the police.

Polizist *n* policeman, police officer, patrolman, cop (*US sl*); ~ **in Zivil** plain-clothes policeman.

Polizistin *f* policewoman.

Polyandrie *f* polyandry.

Polygamie *f* polygamy, plural marriage.

Polygraph *m* polygraph, lie detector.
Polypol *n* polypoly.
Polyzentrismus *m* policy of regionalism, polycentrism.
pönalisieren *v/t* to penalize, penalizing.
Pool *m* pool; **~bildung** pooling; **~vertrag** pooling agreement.
Popularklage *f* taxpayer's suit, relator action; **~verfahren** procedure in a taxpayer's suit, taxpayer's proceedings.
Pornographie *f* pornography.
pornographisch *adj* pornographic, obscene.
Portefeuille *n* portfolio; **~-Effekten** portfolio securities; **~-Eintritt** taking up the portfolio; **~-Prämienreserve** portfolio premium reserve; **~-Rückzug** withdrawal of portfolio; **~-Überweisung** transfer of portfolio securities; **~versicherung** portfolio insurance; **~wechsel** portfolio bill; **~umschichtung** portfolio switching.
Porto *n* postage; **~ablösung** settling of postal charges by block payment; **~buch** postage book; **~erhöhung** raising of postal rates; **p~frei** *adj* postage-free, exempt from postage; **~freiheit** exemption from postage, free post; **~gebühren** postage rates, postal; **~hinterziehung** defrauding postage, non-payment of due postage; **~kasse** petty cash, petty-cash box, imprest fund; **p~pflichtig** *adj* liable to postage; **~spesen** postage expenses; **~ und Verpackung** postage and packing: **~vergütung** refunding of postage; **~zuschlag** extra postage.
Position *f* position, item, heading; **~en des Zolltarifs** headings in the customs tariff; **~sauflösung** liquidation of commitments; **~slösung** closing of position(s); **gesonderte ~** separate item.
Positivismus *m* positivism, strict adherence to enacted law.
possessorisch *adj* possessory.

Post *f* Post Office, postal service, post, mail; **~abholer** post collector; caller for mail; **~abholung** post collection, collection of mail; **~abkommen** postal agreement; *Internationales ~~*: *Postal Convention;* **~ablage** letter rack, mail tray, post basket; **~antwortschein** (international) reply coupon; **~agentur** postal agency, sub-post-office; **~amt** post office; **~amtsvorsteher** postmaster; **~anschrift** postal address, mailing address; **~anstalt** post office; **~anweisung** postal remittance, money order, post-office order, postal order; *internationale ~~ International Payment GB;* internationale Eil-~~: *International Rapid Payment;* telegraphische ~~: *telegraph money order;* **~ausgabe** mail delivery at the counter; **~ausgang** outgoing mail; **~barscheck** postal cheque; **~beamter** postal employee, post-office clerk; post-office official, postal officer; **~bediensteter** postal employee; **~beförderung** postal transport; *normale ~~: ordinary course of post*; **~begleitpapiere** post-office despatch notes; **~behörde** postal authorities; **~bezirk** postal district; **~bote** postman, *US:* mailman; **~diebstahl** mail theft; **~dienst** postal service, mail service; **~eingang** incoming mail; **~einlieferungsbuch** postal receipt book; **~einlieferungsschein** postal receipt, post-office receipt, certificate of posting; **~-fach** post-office box (*P.O. box*), private box (*at post office*); **~fehler** mistake by the postal service; **~forderungen** post-office demands; **~-freistempler** franking machine; **~gebühren** postage, *pl*: postal rates, postal charges, mailing charges; **~gebührenfreiheit** exemption from postal charges; **~geheimnis** secrecy of mail, postal confidentiality; **~giro** postal giro transfer; **~girodienst** National Giro (Bank); **~gut** mail matter, objects in postal custody;

605

~**haftpflicht** third-party liability of postal service; ~**halter** postmaster; ~ **heimlich öffnen** to tamper with mail; ~**hilfsstelle** sub-post-office, postal agency; ~**hoheit** postal prerogative; ~**karte** postcard; ~~*ngröße: postcard size;* ~**kasten** postbox, mail box; p~**lagernd** *adj* poste restante, left till called for; ~**lauf** course of mail; *time during which a letter is normally in transit;* ~**laufkredit** mail credit *(credit allowed by one bank to another pending the arrival of the relevant documents mailed to the bank);* ~**laufzeit** message delivery time; ~**leitzahl** postal code, post code, *US* zip code; ~**leitzone** *US* zip area; ~**minister** Postmaster General; ~**ministerium** post-office department; ~**monopol** post monopoly; ~**ordnung** postal regulations; ~**paket** parcel *(sent through the post)*, postal parcel; ~**privileg** postal privilege; ~**protestauftrag** *order to the Post Office to protest a bill of exchange;* ~**raub** mail robbery; ~**recht** postal law, legal provisions concerning the postal services; ~**regal** postal privilege, postal monopoly; ~**reglement** postal regulations; ~**route** (post(al) route; ~**sache** postal matter, postal item, mail; ~**sack** mail bag; ~**schalter** (post-office) counter; ~**scheck** → *Postscheck;* ~**schein** post-office receipt; ~**schließfach** post-office box, private box; ~**schnellgut** express parcel; ~**sendung** mail item, mail matter, postal consignment; *unzustellbare* ~~: *letter which cannot be delivered; dead letters;* ~**sortierer** mail sorter; ~**sparbuch** postal savings book, post-office bank book; ~**spareinlagen** postal savings deposits; ~**sparer** post-office saver; ~**sparguthaben** postal savings deposit; ~**sparkasse** post-office savings bank, postal savings bank, National Savings bank *GB*; ~**sparkassenamt** postal savings bank office; ~**sparkassendienst** postal savings bank service;

~**sparkassensystem** postal savings system; ~**sparkassenvermögen** postal savings bank funds; ~**sperre** suspension of mail; *suspension of permission to receive or send any mail (prison);* ~**stempel** postmark, postal mark, post-office hand stamp; ~**tarif** postage rates; ~**überwachungsdienst** postal censorship; ~**überweisung** postal giro transfer, post remittance; ~**- und Fernmeldewesen** post and telecommunications; ~**- und Portovergehen** postal offence; ~**verbindung** postal connection, postal link; ~**verein** Postal Union; ~**verkehr** postal service; ~**vermerk** official endorsement by post office; ~**vermögen** property of the post office; ~**versand** despatch of mail, sending (*or* delivery) by mail, transmission by post; *vom* ~~ *ausgeschlossen: non-mailable; zum* ~~ *zugelassen: mailable;* ~**versandauftrag** mail order; ~**versandkatalog** mail-order catalogue; ~**versendung** sending by post (*cf* ~*versand*); ~**verwaltung** postal administration; ~**vollmacht** postal power of attorney, written authorization to receive mail; ~**vorschriften** postal regulations; ~**wagen** mail van, postal van, mail coach; ~**weg** postal route, post road; *auf dem* ~~: *by post;* p~**wendend** *adv* by return of post, by return (of) mail, immediate reply; ~**wertsendung** insured packet; ~**wertversicherung** registered mail insurance; ~**wertzeichen** (postage) stamp, postal stamp; ~**wurfsendung** unadressed mailing, bulk mail, sample packet, direct-mail advertising; mail distribution, post-office mailing; ~**zahlungsverkehr** postal money-transfer system, postal giro system; ~**zeitungsdienst** postal newspaper (delivery) service; ~**zensur** postal censorship, censorship of the mail; ~**zentrale** mailing department; ~**zustellbezirk** postal zone, postal district; ~**zustellung** postal delivery, service through the post office; *schnelle* ~~: *prompt postal delivery*; ~**zustellungsadresse** postal address, post-office address; ~**zustellungsverordnung** *ordinance concerning service (of writs etc) by the post office*; ~**zwang** postal monopoly, postal privilege; **ausgehende** ~ outgoing mail; **eingehende** ~ incoming mail; **gewöhnliche** ~ unrecorded mail; **mit der** ~ **aufgeben** to post; **zur Postbeförderung nicht zugelassen** unmailable (matter).

postalisch *adj* postal.

Posten *m (1)* post, position, job, office; ~ **im Justizdienst** judical post; ~**jäger** a "climber", careerist, career ambitious person.

Posten *m(2)* item, entry, posting, caption; lot; ~**gebühr** commission on entries; ~**kalkulation** item-costing; ~-**Statistik** statistics of items of business handled; **durchlaufende** ~ mutually offsetting items, items which are debited and credited in equal amounts; **e-n** ~ **auf einem Konto verbuchen** to pass an entry to an account; **e-n** ~ **gutschreiben** to credit an item, **transitorische** ~ deferred items; **vorläufige** ~ suspense items, provisional items.

Postliminium *n int* postliminium, postliminy; *(post-war) restoration of captured property to rightful owner.*

postnumerando *adj, adv* (payable) in arrears.

Postscheck *m* giro cheque, ~**amt** postal giro office, *GB*: = National Giro centre; ~**dienst** National Giro; ~**guthaben** postal giro account balance; ~**konto** postal giro account, post transfer account, postal cheque account; ~**verkehr** giro system, postal giro transfer; ~**teilnehmer** postal giro account holder, holder of a postal cheque account; ~**vermögen** postal giro funds.

Postulat *n* demand, postulate, requirement, precondition.

postulationsfähig *adj* right in court, entitled to appear and address the court, having the right of audience.

Postulationsfähigkeit *f* (right of) audience, locus standi, capacity to conduct a case in court; **mangelnde** ~ non-ability (to appear and conduct a case in court).

postulieren *v/t* to demand, to stipulate, to require.

Potential *n* potential, capacity; **wirtschaftliches** ~ economic potential.

potenzieren *v/t* to raise to a higher power, to intensify; to reinforce, to strengthen.

Potestativbedingung *f* potestative condition.

Präambel *f* preamble.

Präbende *f eccl* prebend.

Präfektur *f* prefecture.

Präferenz *f* preference, preferential treatment; ~**berechtigung** entitlement to preference; ~**satz** preferential rate; ~**höchstspanne** maximum margin of preference.

Präge|anstalt *f* mint; ~**gebühr** mintage; ~**siegel** impressed seal; ~**stempel** raised seal, impressed stamp; coining die; ~**stock** punch *(minting).*

pragmatische Sanktion *f* Pragmatic Sanction *(1713, hereditary unity of Austria).*

Präjudiz *n* prejudice; **ohne** ~ without prejudice.

Präjudizienrecht *n* case law, law based on precedents.

präjudizieren *v/t* to prejudice, to establish a legal precedent (for), to prejudge a case.

präkludieren *v/t* to preclude, to bar, to foreclose.

Präklusion *f* preclusion, bar, foreclosure; ~**swirkung** preclusive effect.

Präklusivfrist *f* absolute deadline *(barring all further presentation to the court),* final deadline, time allowed for insured party to claim or take legal action.

Praktikant *m* trainee, student employee.

Praktiken *f/pl* practices; **mißbräuchliche** ~ abusive practices.

Praktiker *m* practical (business) man, practitioner.
Praktikum *n* practical training, work experience, on-the-job training.
praktizieren *v/t, v/i* to practise; **freiberuflich** ~ to free-lance, to work as a freelance, to practise independently, to be self-employed.
Prälegat *n* preferential legacy.
Prämie *f* premium, bonus, *exch*: option, money prize; ~ **für Produktionsstillegung** non-production bonus; ~ **für Verbesserungsvorschläge** bonus for improvement suggestions; **ausstehende** ~ outstanding premium; **gleitende** ~ sliding-scale premium; **kostendeckende** ~ net premium; **nicht verdiente** ~ unearned bonus, unearned premium; **ohne** ~ ex bonus; **rückständige** ~ overdue premium, premium in arrears; **verbrauchte** ~ earned premium; **verdiente** ~ earned premium; **umsatzabhängige** ~ sales related bonus.
Prämien|abrechnung accounting for the premiums; ~**abschlag** reduction in premium, premium rebate; ~**akkordlohn** piece rate plus bonus; ~**angleichungsklausel** variable premium rates clause; ~**anleihe** lottery loan, premium bond; ~**aufgabe** abandonment of the option money; ~**aufkommen** premium income (*insurance*); ~**außenstände** outstanding premiums; ~-**Bausparen** building-society saving with benefit of premiums; ~**befreiung** waiver of premium; ~**begünstigung** bonus-advantage, benefit of a premium; ~**berechtigter** person entitled to a savings-bonus; ~**brief** option contract; ~**depot** (interest-bearing) deposit for insurance payments; ~**einnahmen** premium income; ~**erhöhung** increase in premiums; ~**erklärungstag** *exch* option day, declaration day; ~**festsetzung** rate making; **p~frei** *adj* free from payment of further premiums; paid-up; ~**geschäft** premium transaction (*right to withdraw against premium*); stock exchange options, option dealing; ~**gutschrift** premium credit entry; ~**händler** *exch* option dealer; ~-**Istbetrag** actual amount of premium; ~**käufer** option buyer; ~**kurs** option rate, option price; ~**lohn** premium (incentive) wage, bonus payment; ~**lohnsystem** premium (incentive) system, reward system, bonus system of wages; ~**los** lottery bond; ~**makler** privilege broker (*US*); ~**nachzahlung** subsequent payment of premium; ~**papier** premium bond; ~**plan für betriebliche Verbesserungsvorschläge** suggestion system; ~**rabatt** premium rebate; ~**rate** premium instalment; ~**rechnung** premium note, renewal notice; ~**reserve** policy reserve, unearned premium reserve; ~**reservefonds** reserve value fund; ~**rückerstattung** (no-claim) premium refund; ~**rückgewähr** premium refund, return of premium; ~**rückgewährungspolice** return premium policy; ~**rückstand** premium arrears; ~**rückvergütung** return of premium; ~~ *bei schadenfreiem Verlauf;* "no-claim" bonus; ~**satz** *exch* option rate; rate of premium; *zeitlich begrenzter* ~~: term rate; ~-**Schatzanweisung** premium treasury bond; ~**schein** premium bond; ~**schuldverschreibung** premium bond; ~**sparen** bonus-aided saving, saving under (*the Federal Government's*) bonus scheme, saving with benefit of premiums; ~-**Sparvertrag** bonus savings contract; ~**steuer** premium tax; ~**stücklohn** piece incentive rate; ~**stundung** deferment of payment of premiums; ~**überschuß** net premium income; ~-**übertrag** premium reserve carried forward from previous year; ~-**verkäufer** *exch* taker of an option; ~**versicherung** proprietary insurance; ~**volumen** total of pre-

Pranger   **Preis**

miums collected; ~**vorauszahlung** advance payment of the premium; ~**werte** option stock, premium securities; ~**ziehung** premium drawing; ~**zahler** giver of the rate; ~**zahlung** payment of premiums (*or: of a premium*); ~**zeitlohn** time rate plus bonus; ~**zuschlag** extra premium, hazard bonus.

Pranger *m* pillory.

pränumerando *adv* payable in advance, beforehand, before a given date.

Prärogativ *n* prerogative; ~**rechte der Krone** royal perogatives, jura regia.

Präsentant *m* presenting party, presenter.

Präsentation *f* presentation; ~**srecht** right of proposal (*to an office*).

Präsentierer *m* presenter (of a bill of exchange etc), party presenting.

Präsentierung *f* presentation.

Präsenz *f* presence, attendance, number present; ~**geld** attendance fee; ~**liste** list of persons present.

Präses *m eccl* chairman.

Präsident *m* president, chairman; ~ **des Patentamts** *GB*: Comptroller General of Patents, Designs and Trade Marks; *US*: Commissioner of Patents; ~**enanklage** *US*: impeachment proceedings against the President; **amtierender** ~ acting president; **der gewählte** ~ president elect; **geschäftsführender** ~ managing president; **stellvertretender** ~ vice-president.

Präsidentschaft *m* presidency; ~**skandidat** presidential candidate; ~**swahl** presidential election.

Präsidial|ausschuß general (presidential) committee; ~**demokratie** presidential democracy; ~**erlaß** presidential decree; ~**rat** presidential council; ~**regierung** presidential government; ~**system** presidential system.

präsidieren *v/i* to preside (over), to chair, to head.

Präsidium *n* presiding committee, presiding board, executive body, presidium, chairmanship, the chair.

Präsumption *f* presumption, presupposition.

Prätendent *m* pretender, claimant; ~**enstreit** interpleader issue.

Prävarikation *f* prevarication.

Prävention *f* prevention, the act of preventing.

Präventiv|krieg preventive war; ~**maßnahme** preventive measure; ~**zensur** pre-censorship.

Praxis *f* practice, practical experience; **p~bezogen** practical, realistic; **p~fern** *adj* remote from actual practice, purely theoretical; **p~fremd** *adj* out of step with actual practice; ~**vertreter** locum (doctor); **e-e** ~ **eröffnen** to hang out one's shingle, to set up in practice; **hauptberufliche** ~ full-time private practice; **seine** ~ **aufgeben** to retire from practice; **ständige** ~ established practice.

Präzedenz *f* precedence; ~**entscheidungen** legal precedents, legal authorities; ~**fall** precedent, judicial precedent, (leading case, leading decision; *(or relevant or applicable)* **einschlägiger** ~~: *pertinent precedent*; **ohne** ~~: *without precedent, unprecedented*; **politischer** ~~: *political precedent*.

präzisieren *v/t* to state more precisely, to specify, to clarify, to set out in clear terms, to define, to spell out.

Präzisierung *f* rendering more precise, stating in greater detail.

Präzision *f* precision; ~**sarbeit** precision work; ~**sinstrument** precision instrument; ~**schleuder** lethal catapult; ~**swerkzeug** precision tool; ~**swaffe** precision weapon.

Preis *m* (1) price (= *p, pl: prices* = *p–s*); ~**abbau** *p* cut; ~**abrede** understanding as to *p–s*; ~ **ab Schacht** pit-head *p*; ~**abschlag** markdown; ~**abschöpfung** *p* adjustment levy; ~**abschöpfungsmaßnahme** *p* adjustment levy; ~ **ab Erzeuger** fac-

609

tory *p;* ~**absicherungsgeschäfte** hedging agreement; ~ **ab Speicher** ex-warehouse *p;* ~**absprache** *p*–fixing; ~ **ab Werk** factory *p;* ~**angabe** indication of *p;* ~**anfrage** *p* inquiry; ~**angebot** quoted *p,* quote; *absolut niedrigstes* ~~: *rock-bottom price; verbindliches* ~~: *firm quotation;* ~**angleichung** *p* adjustment; ~**anhebung** upward adjustment of *p–s;* ~**ankündigung** *p* announcement; ~**anpassung** adjustment of *p–s;* ~**anreiz** *p* appeal, *p* incentive; ~**anstieg** *p* increase; ~**aufgliederung** breakdown of the *p;* ~**aufschlag** addition to *p,* extra *p,* additional charge, *p* supplement; ~**auftrieb** up-ward trend of *p–s,* buoyancy in *p–s;* ~**ausgleich** *p* compensation, *p* equalization; ~~*smaßnahmen: price compensation;* ~~*sprinzip: principle of compensatory prices;* ~**auszeichnung** *p*-marking, labelling *(of prices), p* tag, *p* mark, *p* label; ~~*spflicht: obligation to indicate the price of goods;* ~**basis** *p* basis; *auf e–e gleiche* ~~ *bezogen: in terms of a like price basis;* ~ **bei Anlieferung** landed *p;* ~ **bei Ratenzahlung** *GB:* hire purchase *p, US:* deferred payment *p, p* by instalments; ~ **bei sofortiger Lieferung** spot *p;* ~ **bei Übernahme am Lagerort** loco *p;* ~**behörde** *p*-control authority; *p*~**bereinigt** price-level adjusted; ~**beruhigung** tendency towards *p* stability, *p* steadying, levelling out of *p-s;* **p**~**bestimmend** *adj p*-determining; ~**bewegung** movement in *p–s;* **p**~**bezogen** *adj* related to *p–s,* linked to *p–s, p*-linked; ~**bildung** *p* formation, *p* determination; *gebundene* ~~: *price fixing; marktwirtschaftliche* ~~: *market price formation; nichtdirigistische* ~~: *uncontrolled price formation;* ~**bildungsstelle** *p* administration office; ~**bindung** control of *p–s, p* fixing; ~~ *der zweiten Hand: resale price maintenance;* ~~*svertrag: price fixing agreement; vertikale* ~~: *resale price maintenance, vertical price fixing;*

horizontale ~~: *collective resale price maintenance;* ~**brecher** *p*-cutter, person who undercuts competitors, *p*-cutting article; ~**differenz** difference in *p–s, p* variance; ~**differenzierung** *p* discrimination; ~**differenzkonto** *p* variance account; ~**disziplin** self-imposed *p* restraint; ~**druck** (downward) pressure on *p–s;* upward pressure on *p–s;* price yoke; ~**drückerei** *p* cutting; ~**dumping** *p* dumping; ~**durchschnitt** average *p; mittlerer* ~~: *average of mean prices;* ~ **der Verkehrsleistungen** transport charges; ~**e drücken** to run down *p–s;* ~**einbruch** abrupt *p* reduction, collapse in *p–s;* ~ **einschließlich Bedienung** *p* inclusive of service; ~ **einschließlich Gemeinkosten** overhead *p (einschließlich Generalunkosten und Nebenkosten);* ~ **einschließlich Lieferkosten** including delivery *p* ~ **einschließlich Porto und Verpackung** *p* inclusive of postage and packing; ~**elastizität** *p* elasticity, elasticity of *p–s;* ~**empfehlung** *p* recommendation; ~**entwicklung** trend in *p–s,* movement in *p–s; inlandsbedingte* ~~: *movement in prices due to domestic causes;* ~**entzerrung** straightening out of *p* distortions, *p* rectification; ~**erhöhung** increase in *p–s, p* boost, mark-up, rise in *p–s;* ~**ermäßigung** reduction in *p–s;* ~**ermittlung** *p* ascertainment, *p* determination, *p* calculation; ~**erwartung** expected *p,* expectation regarding *p, pl:* views as to *p* prospects; ~**etikett** *p* label, *p* tag; ~**explosion** *p* explosion, *p* jump; ~**fächer** *p* range; ~**festsetzung** *p* fixing, fixing of *p–s;* ~**findung** *p* determination, *p* calculation; ~**flexibilität** flexibility of *p–s;* ~ **frei Bestimmungshafen** landed *p;* ~ **freibleibend** *p* subject to change without notice, *p* without engagement; ~**freigabe** unfreezing of *p–s,* decontrol of *p–s;* ~ **frei Bestimmungsort** free domicile price; ~ **frei Haus** *des Käufers bzw Impor-*

Preis

teurs rendu p, *p* free to the door; ~ **frei Grenze** free-at-frontier price; ~**führer** *p* leader; ~**führerschaft** *p* leadership; ~**führung** *p* leadership; ~ **für Einfuhrgüter** (*einschließlich Transport, Abladung und Zoll*) landed price; ~ **für unverzollte Ware im Zollager** in-bond *p*; ~**garantie** *p* guarantee; ~**gefälle** difference in *p*, *p* gap; *Ausebnung des ~~s: levelling out of the price differential;* ~**gefüge** *p* structure; ~**gegenüberstellung** comparative *p* table, *p* comparison; ~**gestaltung** *p* formation, pricing; ~**gestellung** *p* setting; **p~gestoppt** *adj* price-controlled, *p*-frozen; ~**gleichgewicht** equilibrium in *p–s*; ~**gleitklausel** escalation clause, *p* variance clause, sliding-*p* clause; ~**grenze** *p* limit; *obere ~~: maximum price, price ceiling; untere ~~: minimum price, price floor;* ~**gruppe** *p* group, *p* category; **p~günstig** *adj* reasonably-priced, cheap, good value; ~**herabsetzung** *p* cutting; *starke ~~: roll back;* ~**e hochtreiben** to push up *p–s*, to boost *p–s*; ~**index** *p* index; *~~währung: isometric standard;* ~**informationsabsprache** *p*-reporting agreement; ~**informationssystem** open *p* system; ~**kalkulation** *p* calculation; *~~ einschließlich Gemeinkosten und Risikofaktor: full cost pricing; ~~ssystem: pricing system;* ~**kampf** *p* war; ~**kartell** restrictive agreement on *p–s*; *p* ring, *p* cartel, *p*-fixing agreement; ~**klasse** *p* category; ~**klausel** *p* clause; ~**konjunktur** *p* boom, period of rising *p–s*; ~**kontrolle** *p* control, regulation of *p–s*; *Aufhebung der ~~: lifting of price control;* ~**konvention** *p* agreement; ~-**Kosten Schere** *p*/cost gap; ~**krieg** *p*-cutting war; ~**kritik** *p*-consciousness, a critical attitude towards *p–s;* ~**lage** *p* range; ~**lawine** avalanche of *p* increases; ~**lenkung** *p* administration, control of *p–s;* ~**limit** *p* limit; *ein ~~ festsetzen: to fix a price limit;* ~**liste** *p* list, list of

p–s, *p* catalogue, current *p–s* tariff; ~-**Lohn-Gefüge** *p*-wage structure; ~**mechanismus** *p* mechanism; ~**meßzahl** *p* index; ~**minderung** reduction in the purchase *p*; ~**minderungsklage** action for a *p* reduction; ~**nachlaß** rebate, discount, *p* reduction; **p~neutral** *adj* neutral as regards the effect on *p–s*; ~**niveau** *p* level; ~**niveaustabilität** overall *p* level stability; ~**notierung** quotation; ~**obergrenze** *p* ceiling; ~ **per Einheit** unit *p*; ~ **per Stück** unit pricing; ~**politik** *p* policy, policy on *p–s*; *dirigistische ~~: planned policy of price controls, governmental price policy;* **p~politisch** *adj* as regards *p* policy; ~**polster** *p* cushion; ~**prüfung** verification of *p–s*; ~**rat** Price Council; **p~reagibel** *adj* sensitive to *p* (changes); ~**recht** law concerning controlled *p–s*; ~**regelung** *p* regulation; ~**regulierung** *p* control; *kartellähnliche ~~: cartel-type regulation;* ~**reihe** series of *p–s*, *p* indices; ~**relationen** *p* ratios; *~~ im Außenhandel: terms of trade;* ~**risiko** risk of changed *p–s*; ~**rückgang** fall in *p–s*, depreciation; ~**ruhe** *p* stability; ~**runde** all-round rise in *p–s*; ~**schaukelei** manipulated *p* fluctuation, bait-and-switch campaign; ~**schere** *p* gap, *p* scissors, disparity between *p* indices (*of different commodities*), fluctuating ratio between *p–s*; ~**schild** *p* tag, *p* label, *p* ticket; ~**schleuderei** *p* slashing, undercutting of *p–s*; ~**schub** general *p* increase; ~**schwankungen** fluctuations in *p*, variations in *p–s*; ~**senkung** *p* reduction, *p* decrease; ~**skala** *p* range; ~**spanne** *p* margin; ~**spiegel** *p*-level; ~**spirale** upward spiral movement in *p–s*; ~**e stabil halten** to stabilize *p–s*; ~**stabilität** *p* stability, stability of *p–s*; ~**staffel** *p* range; ~**steigerung** *p* increase, *p* advance *p* rise; *~~srate: rate of price increase; ~~srücklage: contingent reserve for price increases; ~~stendenz: upward*

Preis **Preis**

price tendency; nachfragebedingte ~~: *demand-induced upward price tendency;* ~**stellung** quoting a *p*, pricing, (terms of) quotation; ~**stopp** *p* freeze; ~**sturz** slump in *p–s*; ~**struktur** *p* structure; ~**stützung** *p* support, subsidy; ~~*saktion: price support measures;* ~~*smaßnahmen: price support measures, valorization scheme*; ~**theorie** *p* theory; **p**~**treibend** *adj p*-enhancing, tending to push up *p–s*; ~**treiber** (price-)booster, *p*-raising manipulator, inflator; ~**treiberei** forcing up of *p–s*, deliberate overcharging; ~**überhöhung** overcharging, making excessive *p–s*; ~**überwachung** *p* supervision, *p* control; ~**umschwung** reversal in *p–s*; ~**unterbietung** underselling, undercutting, dumping; ~**unterschied** *p* differential; ~**vereinbarung** *p*-fixing agreement; ~**verfall** *p* collapse; ~**vergehen** offence against *p* regulations; ~**vergleich** comparison between *p–s*, *p* comparison; ~**vergünstigung** quoting an especially favourable *p*, *p* allowance, *p* concession; ~**verhalten** *p* behaviour; ~**verlust** loss in *p*; ~**e verstehen sich ohne Abzug** terms net cash, *p–s* net; ~**verstoß** infringement of *p* regulations; ~**verzeichnis** *p* list; ~**verzerrung** *p* distortion; ~**verzollt** duty-inclusive price; ~ **vor Abzug der Belastungen** gross *p*; ~**vorbehalt** *p* reserve, *p* reservation; ~**vorstellung** *p* expectation; ~**vorschriften** *p* regulations; ~**welle** wave of *p* increases; ~**wucher** outrageous overcharging, profiteering; ~**zettel** *p* label, *p* tag, *p* ticket; ~**zugeständnis** *p* concession; ~**zuschlag** extra charge; **ab-Werk-** *p* at factory, *p* ex works; **aktueller** ~ latest price; **allgemeiner** ~ general *p*; **amtlicher** ~ official *p*; **angebotener** ~ offering *p*; **angegebener** ~ quoted *p*; **angemessener** ~ fair *p*, reasonable *p*, equitable *p*; **angestrebter** ~ target *p*; **annehmbarer** ~ acceptable *p*; **ausbedungener** ~

p agreed upon, stipulated *p*; **auskömmlicher** ~ good enough *p*, remunerative *p*; **äußerster** ~ lowest *p*; **bewirtschaftete** ~ administered *p–s*; **Börsen- oder Markt~** market *p*, exchange or market *p*; **den ~ bestimmen** to fix the *p*; **der ~ spielt keine Rolle** *p* is no object; **echter** ~ real *p*; **effektiver** ~ real *p*; **e–n ~ aushandeln** to negotiate a *p*; **e–n ~ berechnen** to calculate a *p*; to charge a *p*; **e–n ~ bestimmen** to make a *p*; **e–n ~ festsetzen** to set a *p*, to determine a *p*; **e–n hohen ~ erzielen** to fetch a high *p*; **e–n höheren ~ erzielen** to fetch a higher *p*; **e–n ~ verlangen** to demand a *p*; **eingependelter stabiler** ~ long-run normal *p*; **einkaufswirksame** ~**e** *p–s* as per purchasing date; **empfohlener** ~ recommended *p*, suggested *p*; **ermäßigter** ~ reduced price; **erster** ~ opening *p*; initial *p*, original *p*; **erzielter** ~ *p* obtained; **fallender** ~ dropping *p*, falling *p*; **fakturierter** ~ invoiced *p*; **fester** ~ fixed *p*, no reductions; **gebotener** ~ offer *p*; **gebundener** ~ maintained *p*, controlled *p*, fixed *p*; **geforderter** ~ asked *p*, charge; **gegenwärtiger** ~ prevailing *p*, present *p*; **geltender** ~ current *p*, present *p*; **gestaffelter** ~ adjustable *p*; **gestützter** ~ supported *p*, pegged *p*; **herrschender** ~ prevailing *p*; **in jeweiligen ~en** at current *p–s*; **inlandsbestimmter** ~ domestic *p*; **in Rechnung gestellter** ~ the *p* invoiced; **jahreszeitlich gestaffelte** ~**e** *p–s* graduated according to the seasons; **konkurrenzfähiger** ~ competitive *p*; **letzter** ~ lowest limit, final offer; **marktgerechter** ~ fair market *p*; **marktnahe** ~**e** *p–s* in conformity with market levels; **nach dem ~ fragen** to ask the *p (of s.th)*; **nachgebende** ~**e** easing *p–s*; **nachgeordnete** ~**e** dependent *p* structure; **niedrigster** ~ lowest *p*, bottom *p*; **ruinöser** ~ cut-throat *p*; **scharf kalkulierter** ~ close *p*, finely computed *p*; **stabiler** ~

612

stable *p*, stationary *p*; **theoretischer** ~ nominal *p*; **überhöhter** ~ excessive *p*, exorbitant *p*; **üblicher** ~ usual *p*, prevailing *p*, going *p*; **unangemessener** ~ unreasonable *p*; **unerschwinglicher** ~ prohibitive *p*; **unter** ~ priced below cost; **verbindlicher** ~ operative *p*; **vereinbarter** ~ *p* agreed upon; **vom** ~ **nachlassen** to take off the *p*, to reduce the *p*; **vorgelagerte** ~**e** *p*–*s* at the earlier stages; **vorgeschriebener** ~ statutory sales *p*, controlled *p*; **vorherrschender** ~ ruling *p*, prevailing *p*; **wucherischer** ~ usurious *p*; **zu niedriger** ~ inadequate *p*, unreasonably low *p*.

Preis *m* (2) prize, award; ~**ausschreiben** competition, prize contest; ~**frage** question put in a competition; the vital question; ~**richter** adjudicator (*in a competition*); ~**träger** prizewinner; ~**verleihung** awarding of a prize (*or* prizes), prize-giving.

Preisgabe *f* disclosure, giving away, abandonment, surrender, relinquishment; ~**recht** right to abandon; ~ **von Staatsgeheimnissen** disclosure of official secrets.

preisgeben *v/t* to reveal, to disclose, to give away, to surrender, to abandon, to relinquish, to give up.

preislich *adj* as regards the price, in terms of price.

Prekareihandel *m* precarious commerce, secret trade between belligerents under neutral flag.

Premierminister *m* prime minister.

Presse *f* the press, the newspapers; ~**abteilung** press department; ~**amt** press department, press office; ~**attaché** press attaché; ~**auskunft** information for the press; ~**ausweis** press card, press pass; ~**bericht** press report, report in the press; ~**betrieb** newspaper enterprise; ~**delikt** offence by press publication; ~**dienst** news service, press service, press agency; ~**erklärung** press release, statement to the press; ~**ente** canard; ~**erzeugnisse** products of the newspaper industry; ~**fehde** paper warfare; ~**freigabe** press release; ~**freiheit** freedom of the press, liberty of the press; ~**geheimnis** privilege of journalists, right of an editor not to disclose the source of his information; ~**geplauder** journalist gossip; ~**gesetz** Press Act; ~**information** press release; ~**inhaltsdelikt** substantive press offence; press publication constituting a criminal offence; ~**kampagne** press campaign ~**mappe** press kit; ~**postgut** *US*: second-class mail; ~**rat** press council; ~**recht** press law; ~**referent** press officer, press and public relations officer; ~**sekretär** press secretary; ~**sprecher** spokesman, press officer; ~**stelle** press office, public information office; ~**stimmen** press comments; ~**tribüne** *parl* press gallery; press platform; ~**- und Informationsamt der Bundesregierung** German Federal Press and Information Office; ~**unternehmen** newspaper enterprise; ~**verband** press association; ~**vergehen** offence by press publication; **verlautbarung** press release; ~**wesen** the press, the newspaper world; ~**zensur** press censorship; **überregionale** ~ national press.

Pression *f* (undue) pressure, undue influence, coercive measure.

Primadiskonten *pl* prime banker's acceptances, prime acceptances.

prima facie *adv*, *adj* (=) prima facie, at first sight.

Primage *f* = *Primgeld qv*.

Primanota *f* journal, daybook.

Primapapiere *n/pl* prime paper, prime acceptances.

Primarate *f* prime rate.

Primär|energie primary energy; ~**geschäft** new issue business; ~**händler** market maker; ~**liquidität** *f* primary liquidity; cash ratio (*banks*); ~**markt** primary market; ~**reserve** *f* primary reserve.

Primat *m or n* primacy.

Primawechsel *m* first (of) exchange, original bill of exchange, first bill of exchange.

Primgeld *n* primage, *a payment made for care in loading and unloading ship*.

Primogenitur *f* primogeniture.

Prinzip *n* principle; ~ **der Bilanzkontinuität** principle of accounting consistency; ~ **der freien Beweiswürdigung** the principle of free appreciation of evidence; ~ **des Haushaltsausgleichs** principle of the balanced budget.

Prinzipal *m* principal, head of a business, employer, boss.

Prinzregent *m* prince regent.

Priorität *f* priority, precedence; ~ **beanspruchen** *pat* to claim priority for an application; **innere** ~ *(pat)* internal priority.

Prioritäts|aktie preference share, preferred share; ~**ankündigung** notice for priority; ~**anleihe** preference bond, preferential loan; ~**anspruch** priority claim, prior claim; ~**beanspruchung** prior claim; ~**belege** priority documents; ~**datum** priority date; ~**dividende** preferred dividend; ~**erklärung** declaration of priority; ~**erklärungsfrist** time for filing priority; ~**gläubiger** preferred creditor, privileged creditor; ~**grundsatz** principle of priority; ~**obligationen** preference bonds; ~**recht** right of priority, preference; ~**streit** dispute about priority; ~**tag** priority date; ~**zession** prior assignment.

Prise *f* prize, naval prize, prize of war.

Prisen|anteil prize money, share in the prize; ~**geld** prize bounty, prize money; ~**gericht** prize court; ~**güter** prize goods; ~**kommando** prize crew; ~**offizier** boarding officer; ~**ordnung** regulations governing prizes; ~**recht** prize law; ~**rückeroberung** rescue of a prize; ~**sache** prize case, prize cause(s); ~**verteilung** prize giving.

Pritsche *f* plank-bed; floor, platform *(lorry, truck)*; ramp; ~**nwagen** pick-up truck.

privat *adj* private, personal.

Privat|abhebungen personal drawings; ~**angelegenheit** personal matter, private concern; *pl*: personal affairs; ~**anleihe** personal loan; ~**anschrift** home address, private address; ~**anschluß** private siding *(railway)*, private extension *(tel)*; ~**audienz** private audience; ~**bank** private bank, commercial bank; ~**bankgeschäft** private banking business; ~**bankier** private banker, individual banker; ~**beamter** privately employed official; ~**besitz** private property; *im* ~~: *privately owned*; ~**betrieb** private undertaking; ~**darlehen** personal loan; ~**detektiv** private detective, private investigator; ~**diskont** *m* discount-rate for first-class bills; ~**diskonten** prime acceptances, first-class bills of exchange; **p**~**diskontfähig** *adj* qualifying as prime acceptance, eligible for the prime acceptance market; ~**diskontgesellschaft** private discount company; ~**diskontmarkt** prime acceptance market; ~**dozent** (=) private lecturer; ~**eigentum** private property, private ownership, private belongings; ~**eigentümer** private owner; ~**einfahrt** private driveway; ~**einkommen** individual income, private income; ~**einkünfte** types of individual income, total individual income; ~**einlage** private deposit; ~**entnahme** (private) drawing *or* withdrawal; ~**ersparnisse** personal savings; ~**fahrt** private use of a car; ~**firma** private firm, private business, family business; ~**fluß** private river, private stream; ~**gebrauch** private use, personal use; ~**geheimnis** private secret, confidential information; ~**geschäft** private transaction; ~**gewässer** private waters; ~**grundstück** private property, private estate; ~**gutachten** privately obtained expert opinion; ~**gutachter** expert

privatisieren

employed by one of the parties; ~**haftpflichtversicherung** personal liability insurance; ~**haus** private dwelling house; ~**haushalt** private household; ~**industrie** private industry, private-enterprise industry; ~**initiative** private initiative; ~**interesse** personal interest; ~**kapital** private capital, private industry, private equity capital; ~**kapitalismus** private capitalism; ~**klage** private prosecution (*for certain minor offences against individuals*); ~**kläger** private prosecutor; ~**klägerin** private prosecutrix; ~**klagesachen** private prosecution cases; ~**klinik** private hospital, nursing home; ~**konto** private account; personal account; ~**kontenbuch** personal ledger; ~**krankenanstalt** private hospital; ~**kredit** personal loan, instalment credit; ~**krieg** private war; ~**kunde** private customer; ~**kundschaft** private clientele, private customers; ~**lehrer** private tutor; ~**mann** private person, private gentleman; ~**papiere** private papers; ~**person** individual, private person; *als* ~~: *in one's private capacity*; ~**pfändung** levy of execution by private creditor; ~**pier** private wharf; ~**plazierung** private placement; ~**praxis** private practice; ~**publikum** individual members of the public; private investors; ~**recht** → *Privatrecht*; ~-**Rechtsschutz-Versicherung** insurance against legal costs incurred by individuals; ~**sanatorium** privately-owned sanatorium, nursing home; ~**schatulle** privy purse; p~**schriftlich** *adj* holographic, under hand, handwritten; ~**schulden** personal debts (*of a partner*); ~**schule** → *Privatschule*; ~**sekretärin** private secretary; ~**sektor** private sector of the economy; ~**sender** private enterprise radio; ~**sparen** personal savings; ~**sphäre** private life, privacy; ~**station** private ward; ~**straße** private road; ~**testament** private will, holograph(ic) will; ~**unternehmen** private undertaking; ~**urkunde** private document: *document made by a private party*; ~**verbrauch** personal consumption; ~**vermögen** personal assets, private fortune; ~**versicherer** private underwriter, private insurer; ~**versicherung** private insurance, commercial insurance; ~**vorlage** private bill, personal bill; ~**weg** private footpath, private way, private road; ~**wirtschaft** private enterprise, private sector (of the economy); ~**wohnung** private residence, residential flat; ~**zwecke** private use; social, domestic and recreational purposes.

privatisieren *v/t* to convert to private ownership, to (re)privatize *privatisiert werden: going private.*

Privatisierung *f* privatisation, conversion to private ownership, denationalization.

Privatrecht *n* private law; ~**snorm** rule of private law; ~**sverhältnis** relationship under private law; ~**sweg** recourse to civil courts; **interlokales** ~ statutory interlocal conflict rules; **internationales** ~ private international law, conflict of laws; **interzonales** ~ interzonal conflict of laws rules.

privatrechtlich *adj* pursuant to private law, private-law ...

Privatschul|e *f* private school, *GB*: independent school, public school; *US*: endowed school; ~**leistungsgesetz** Provision for Private Schools Act; ~**träger** private-school maintenance body; **gemeinnützige** ~**e** non-profit making private school.

Privileg *n* privilege, special right.

privilegieren to privilege, to grant a privilege.

Privilegierter *m* privileged person.

Privilegierung *f* privileges, granting privileges.

Proband *m* probationer.

Probe *f* test, trial; sample, specimen; ~**angebot** trial offer; ~**arbeit** specimen of one's work, test piece;

~**abstimmung** test ballot, straw vote; ~**abzug** proof, proof-sheet; ~**anlage** pilot plant; ~**anstellung** probationary employment; ~**antrag** trial proposal, trial application; ~**arbeitsvertrag** probationary employment contract; ~**arbeitsverhältnis** employment on trial; ~**auftrag** trial order; ~**belastung** test load; ~**bestellung** trial order, sample order; ~**bilanz** trial balance; *bereinigte ~~: closing trial balance;* ~**bohrung** test drilling; ~**dienst** probationary service; ~**druck** proof, trial impression; ~**ehe** trial marriage; ~**entnahme** sampling; ~**n entnehmen** to sample, to take samples; ~**exemplar** specimen copy, sample copy, complimentary copy; ~**fahrt** test drive; test run, trial run; ~**fall** test case; ~**heft** specimen copy; ~**gut** sample, test material, specimen; ~**kauf** trial purchase, sale on approval; sale by sample; ~**käufer** trial buyer; ~**lauf** trial run; ~**lehrzeit** probationary apprenticeship; ~**lieferung** trial shipment; ~**modell** pattern design; ~**muster** check sample, reference pattern; ~**nnahme** sampling; ~**nummer** specimen copy; ~**nverteilung** sampling; ~**pakkung** trial package; ~**schacht** prospecting shaft; ~**schuß** practice shot; ~**sendung** trial lot; ~**stück** sample, specimen, pattern, test piece; ~**untersuchung** testing of a specimen, pilot study; ~**vertrag** tentative agreement; ~**zeit** trial period, test period, probationary period; **auf** ~ on approval, on probation, on trial; ~~ *kaufen: to buy on trial;* ~**entnommene** ~ pricked sample; **nach** ~ per sample, by sample; **zur** ~ as a sample.

Problem *n* problem; ~**darstellung** presentation of the problem, definition of the problem; ~**lösung** solution of a (*or* the) problem; **juristisches** ~ legal problem; **linguistische** ~**e** semantic problems, linguistic problems; **offenes** ~ open problem; **übergeordnetes** ~ overriding problem; **vielschichtiges** ~ a complex problem, a knotty problem.

Produkt *n* product, produce *(agricultural)*; ~ **des gehobenen Bedarfs** high-quality product; ~**einheit** unit of output; *letzte ~~: marginal unit;* ~**haftpflichtversicherung** product-liability insurance; ~**haftung** product liability; ~**innovation** product innovation; ~**koppelung** product link; ~**name** product name; ~**palette** range of products; ~**piraterie** product piracy; ~**überprüfung** product review; ~**verbesserungsmitteilung** product improvement bulletin; ~**warnung** warning against potentially dangerous products; **das gesamtwirtschaftliche** ~ the national product; **landwirtschaftliche** ~**e** agricultural products; **nachgeordnete** ~**e** products at later stages of manufacture; **tierisches** ~ animal product.

Produkten|börse commodity market; ~**großhandel** wholesale produce market; ~**handel** produce trade; ~**makler** produce broker, merchandise broker.

Produktion *f* production, output, outturn; ~ **an der Kostengrenze** marginal production; **die gesamtwirtschaftliche** ~ total national production; **gewerbliche** ~ industrial and handicraft production; **kapitalintensive** ~ heavily capitalized production; **nachhinkende** ~ output that is lagging behind, lagging production; **nachziehende** ~ production following the trend; **volkswirtschaftliche** ~ national product.

Produktions|anlagen production facilities, production plant, production equipment; ~**apparat** productive apparatus, production facilities; ~**aufnahme** going into production; ~**ausdehnung** expansion in output; ~**ausfall** loss of production; ~**belebung** stimulation of production; ~**bereich**

branch of production; ~**betrieb** manufacturing firm, production plant; ~**bezogen** *adj* production-oriented, ~**breite** product diversification; ~**dispositionen** production decisions; ~**drosselung** curtailment of production, curbing production; ~**einheit** unit of production, production unit; ~**einrichtungen** productive equipment; ~**einstellung** production stop; ~**elastizität** resilience of output, flexibility of output; ~**engpaß** producton bottleneck; ~**entfaltung** expansion of production; ~**entwicklung** development of production, production (trend); ~**erfahrung** manufacturing know-how; ~**ergebnis** productive output; ~**erhebung** census of production; ~**faktoren** factors of production, production factors; p~**fördernd** *adj* calculated to expand production; ~**funktion** production function; ~**glättung** production smoothing; ~**gemeinkosten** production overhead; ~**genossenschaft** production cooperative; ~**gesellschaft** manufacturing company; ~**grundlagen** bases of production; ~**güter** (intermediate) producer goods, pre-production goods; ~**güterindustrie** pre-producergoods industry; ~**höhe** production level; ~**index** production index; ~**kapazität** productive capacity; ~**kartell** production cartel; ~**koeffizient** production coefficient; ~**kosten** production cost; ~**kostenkontrolle** manufacturing cost control; ~**kostentheorie** theory of production costs; ~**kredit** credit to finance production; ~**kürzung** production cutback; ~**leistung** output; *die inländische* ~~: *the gross domestic product; volkswirtschaftliche* ~~: *the country's output;* ~**leiter** production manager; ~**leitung** plant management; p~**mäßig** *adj* in terms of production; ~**mittel** means of production, producer goods, production goods, productive equipment;

~**optimum** optimum production; ~**potential** productive capacity; ~**prozeß** phases of production; p~**reif** *adj* ready for production; ~**reserven** reserves of productive capacity; ~**risikoversicherung** production risks insurance; ~**rückgang** production decline, production setback; ~**spitze** output record; ~**stadium** manufacturing stage; ~**stand** level of output; ~**standard** standard of production; ~**steigerung** production increase; ~**steuern** taxes linked to production; ~**stopp** shutdown in production, output ceiling; ~**stufen** stages of production; ~**technik** production engineering; p~**technisch** *adj* relating to production technique; ~**termin** production date; ~**überschuß** production surplus; ~**umstellung** switch in production, production change-over; ~**verfahren** production method(s); ~**verlangsamung** production slowdown; ~**vertrag** production contract, manufacturing agreement; ~**vorschriften** manufacturing directions; ~**wert** value of production; ~**zahlen** output figures; ~**zentrum** centre of production; ~**ziel** output target, production target; ~**zweig** line of producton; ~~*aufgabe: line dropping;* ~**zyklus** production cycle.

produktiv *adj* productive, fruitful.

Produktiv|**genossenschaft** production cooperative, cooperative for production and sale; ~**kapital** productive capital; ~**kraft** productive factor, productive strength; ~**kredit** credit granted for productive purposes, production-financing loan; ~**vermögen** productive assets.

Produktivität *f* productivity, productive efficiency, productiveness; ~**sgewinn** productivity gain; **volkswirtschaftliche** ~ overall productivity.

Produktivitäts|**abnahme** diminishing productivity; ~**bindung** linking of s.th. to productivity; ~**ent-**

Produzent   **Prolongation**

wicklung trend in productivity; ~**faktor** productivity factor; ~**gefälle** productivity differential; ~**grenze** limit to productivity, marginal productivity; ~**mittel** productivity programme funds ~**rat** productivity council; ~**rente** productivity-linked pension; ~**sonderprojekt** special productivity project; ~**steigerung** improvement in productivity; ~**zuwachs** productivity increase, rise in productivity.

Produzent *m* producer, manufacturer; ~**enbereich** manufacturers' sphere; ~**engeld** producers' money (*or* funds); ~**engewinn** producers' surplus; ~**enhaftung** product liability.

produzieren *v/t* to produce, to manufacture, to make.

Professor *m* professor; **außerordentlicher** ~ professor not holding a chair; **ordentlicher** ~ university professor.

Profi *m* professional.

Profil *n* profile; tread.

profilieren *v/t* to present in clear outline, to make more pronounced, *v/reflex* to distinguish oneself, to make a name for oneself.

Profilierung *f* clear outlining, presentation in clear outline, self-presentation, gaining prominence.

Profilneurose *f* (excessive) preoccupation with one's personal image.

Profilrinnen *f/pl* (*der Lauffläche*) tread grooves.

Profit *m* profit; ~**gier** greed for profit; ~**macher** profiteer; ~**macherei** profiteering; ~**rate** rate of profit; ~**streben** profit-seeking, profiteering.

profitieren *v/i* to profit, to make a profit, to benefit.

pro forma (=) for the sake of form, as a matter of form, merely as a formality, simulated.

Proforma|anteil qualifying share, dummy share; ~**faktura** pro forma invoice (*also: pro-forma, proforma*); ~**-Indossament** pro forma endorsement, straw name; ~**rech-nung** pro forma invoice, pro forma account, simulated account; ~**verfahren** pro forma trial, sham trial; ~**verkauf** pro forma sale; ~**wechsel** pro forma bill, accommodation bill.

Programmhandel *m* (*elektronischer Aktienindex-Terminhandel*) program trading.

programmieren *v/t* to programme.

Programmierverbund *m* programme link, programming pool.

Progression *f* progression, progressive scale; **steile** ~ steep progression.

Progressions|satz rate of progression; ~**stufe** stage of progression; *hohe* ~~: high progressive scale; ~**vorbehalt** reservation to apply progressive tax rate.

Progressiv|lohn *m* progressive wage rate; ~**steuer** graduated tax, progressive tax.

Prohibitionismus *m* prohibitionism.

Prohibitivzoll *m* prohibitive tariff.

Projekt *n* project, scheme, planning scheme; ~**finanzierung** project funding; *p* ~**gebunden** project-tied, project-linked; ~**gruppe** project team; ~**leiter** project manager; ~**leitung** project management; ~**reife** final stage of planning, pre-production stage maturity; ~**studie** feasibility study; ~**träger** project sponsor; ~**vorschlag** project proposal, draft scheme; **grenzübergreifende** ~**e** trans-frontier projects, international projects.

Proklamation *f* proclamation; **gemeinsame** ~ joint declaration; **königliche** ~ royal proclamation.

proklamieren *v/t* to proclaim.

Prokura *f* (=) general commercial power of representation, per pro; collection endorsement; ~**unterschrift** signature per pro; ~**zeichnung** (*Wechsel*) signature per pro(curation).

Prokurist *m* (=) person vested with, general commercial power (of representation).

Prolongation *f* prolongation, renewal, extension of maturity (*or* running period). ~**srecht** right of renewal; *mit* ~~: *renewed if required*; ~**ssatz** renewal rate; ~**stag** continuation day; contango day.

prolongieren to prolong, to renew, to extend, to continue, to carry over.

Promille *n* per mille; blood alcohol, content per 1000th; ~**grenze** blood alcohol limit, prescribed blood alcohol level.

Prominententribüne *f* distinguished guests' gallery.

Promotion *f* awarding a doctorate, conferring a doctorate upon s. o., graduation.

promovieren *v/i* to obtain a doctorate, to take one's doctor's degree.

Promovierung *f* obtaining a doctorate.

Promptgeschäft *n* spot transaction, cash transaction.

promulgieren *v/i* to promulgate, to proclaim.

Propaganda *f* propaganda, publicity; ~**schrift** propagandistic publication, propaganda pamphlet; **staatsgefährdende** ~ seditious propaganda; **subversive** ~ subversive propaganda.

Propagandist *m* propagandist, propaganda agent.

propagieren *v/t* to propagate, to advocate, to make publicity for.

Propatriapapier *n* (*formerly*) foolscap.

Propergeschäft *n* trade for one's own account.

Properhändler m trader, person trading in his own name, trader on own account.

Proponent *m* proposer, supporter.

proportional *adj* proportionate, proportional, rateable (= *ratable, US*).

Proportionalwahlrechtssytem *n* proportional representation.

Proporz *m* proportional holding of offices (*by coalition party, by denomination etc*), proportional representation.

pro rata *adj, adv* pro rata, proportional(ly), rateable (rateably); ~ **temporis** (=) in proportion to the time, proportionate to the relative period.

Proratelung *f* prorating; ~ **von Zahlungen** prorating of payments.

Prorogation *f* prorogation of jurisdiction, prorogated jurisdiction, mutual agreement as to jurisdiction, ouster of jurisdiction; ~**svertrag** jurisdiction agreement (*to try the case before an otherwise incompetent court*), prorogated jurisdiction agreement.

Proskription *f hist* proscription.

Prospekt *m* prospectus, brochure, offering brochure, pamphlet; ~**ersatzerklärung** statement in lieu of prospectus; ~ **für die Zulassung zum Börsenhandel** prospectus (for admission to the stock exchange); ~**haftung** legal liability for the statements in the prospectus; ~**material** pamphlets, descriptive or illustrative literature; ~**zwang** requirement to publish an issuing propectus.

prospektieren *v/i* to prospect (*for oil etc*), to explore.

Prospektierung *f* prospecting; ~**svertrag** prospecting contract.

Prospektor *m* prospector.

Prosperität *f* prosperity, affluence.

Prostituierte *f* prostitute, common prostitute; ~, *die auf den Strich geht: street walker; hooker (US)*.

Prostitution *f* prostitution; ~ **als Straßenstrich**: *street walking, curb prawling*.

protegieren *v/t* to patronize, to sponsor, take s. o. under one's wings.

Protektion *f* patronage.

Protektionismus *m* protectionism; **nationalstaatlicher** ~ nationalistic protectionism.

Protektor *m* patron, sponsor.

Protektorat *n* protectorate, protectorship; ~**sgebiet** protected territory, protectorate; **völkerrechtliches** ~ protectorate under international law.

Protest *m* protest, act of protest, Pro-

619

testation; **~anzeige** notification of protest, advice of dishonor; **~aufnahme** protesting; *nachträgliche ~~: extending a protest*; *subsequent (or later) protestation*; ~ **erheben** to protest, to lodge a protest, (*generally:*) to raise a protest, to protest; **~erhebung** protestation, protesting, entering (of) a protest, noting and protesting; **~frist** statutory period for noting and protesting a bill; **~gebühr** protest fee; **~gläubiger** protester; **~kosten** protest charges, protest fee, expenses of noting and protest, expenses of protest; ~ **mangels Annahme** protest for non-acceptance; ~ **mangels Lieferung** protest for non-delivery; ~ **mangels Sicherheitsleistung** protest for better security; ~ **mangels Zahlung** protest for non-payment; **~note** note of protest; **~notifizierung** noting (a bill), notice of protest; **~-Solawechsel** protested note; **~urkunde** protest certificate, certificate of protestation, (note of) protest; **~vermerk** notation on a bill of exchange; **~verzicht** waiver of protest; **~wechsel** protested bill; **~zahlung** payment under protest; **formell ~ erheben** to formally protest; to enter a protest (*bill of exchange*); **nach ~** supra protest; **ohne ~** without protest; **rechtzeitig erhobener ~** protest in due course; **unter ~** supra protest; **zu ~ gehen** to go to protest; **zu ~ gehen lassen** to dishono(u)r, to let a bill be protested; **zu spät erhobener ~** past due protest.

Protestat *m* addressee of a protest, person against whom a bill of exchange has been protested.

protestierbar *adj* protestable.

protestieren *v/i* to protest, to enter a protest, to note (*a bill*); **~ lassen** to get protested.

Protokoll *n* minutes (*of a meeting*), report of proceedings, record (*of the proceedings*), protocol (*intern. law, dipl. service*), procès-verbal; **~abschriften** copies of the proceedings; **~abteilung** protocol section, protocol department; **~aufnahme** taking down of the minutes, reporting the proceedings; **~berichtigung** rectification of the minutes, rectification of the record; **~buch** minute book, records of the proceedings; **~chef** chief of protocol; **~führer** court reporter, court stenographer, recording clerk; person who keeps the minutes, keeper of the minutes; **~ über die Beweisaufnahme** record of the evidence; **das ~ aufnehmen** to keep the minutes; **das ~ führen** to keep the minutes; **das ~ liegt zur Unterzeichnung auf** the protocol is open for signature; **das ~ verlesen** to read out the minutes; **das ~ wurde verlesen, genehmigt und unterschrieben** the recorded statement was read (to the parties), approved and signed (by them); **etw zu ~ erklären** to depose, *to make a statement which is reduced to writing by a duly-qualified official;* **etw zu ~ geben** to have s.th. recorded; **etw zu ~ nehmen** to record, to put s.th. down on record; **im ~ festhalten** to note s.th. in the record; **im ~ vermerken** to record in the minutes; **polizeiliches ~** statement before the police, police report, police records.

protokollieren *v/t, v/i* to take down the minutes, to enter in the minute book, to take down a statement, to record (*the testimony*); **~ lassen** to leave on record, to have s.th. entered in the record.

Protokollierung *f* keeping minutes, recording, entry in the minutes; drawing up a protocol, recording; **gerichtliche ~** recording in court, court reporting.

Prototyp *m* prototype.

Provision *f* commission, agent's commission, factorage, brokerage; **~ des Auktionators** auctioneer's fees; **geheime ~** kickback; **geteilte ~** split commission; **vertragliche ~** contract percentage,

Provisionsagent   **Prozeß**

contractually agreed commission; **vorbehaltlose** ~ straight commission.

Provisions|agent agent (on a commission basis), commercial agent, commission agent; ~**anspruch** entitlement to commission, accrued commission; ~**basis** commission basis; ~**beteiligungsvereinbarung** commission-sharing agreement; ~**einnahmen** commissions earned; ~**forderungen** commissions receivable; p~**frei** *adj* free of commission; ~**geschäft** business on a commission basis ~**guthaben** accrued commission, credit balance on commission account; ~**nota** commission note; p~**pflichtig** *adj* liable to commission, subject to commission; ~**reisender** commercial traveller, travelling salesman; ~**rückgewähr** refunding the commission; ~**satz** rate of commission; ~**überschuß** net commissions received; ~**vertreter** commission agent, travelling salesman; ~**zahlung** payment of commission.

provisorisch *adj* provisional, pro tem, for the time being.

Provisorium *n* provisional arrangement, makeshift arrangement.

Provokateur *m* agent provocateur.

Provokation *f* provocation.

provozieren *v/t* provoke.

Prozent *n* per cent; ~**bruchteil** fraction in per cent; ~**kurs** price expressed as a percentage of the nominal value; ~**notierung** percentage quotation; ~**satz** percentage rate.

Prozeß *m* (*pl: Prozesse:* ~*e*) lawsuit, legal proceedings, action, suit, trial, litigation, litigation proceedings; procedure; ~**ablauf** the course of the proceedings; ~**abweisung** dismissal of an action; ~**agent** law agent; ~**akte** case record; ~**anwalt** trial lawyer; ~**aufrechnung** set-off during court proceedings; ~**beendigung** conclusion of trial; ~**beginn** commencement of the proceedings, the beginning of the action; ~**behauptung** allegation, statement (to the court), assertion, contention; ~**beistand** next friend; ~**beitritt** intervention; ~**beschleunigung** speeding up the trial; ~~~*sgesetz: Speedy Trials Act*; ~**betrug** deceitful plea, deceiving the court, malicious use of process; ~**bevollmächtigter** counsel, attorney of record, attorney for the action; *der* ~~~*e des Klägers: counsel for the plaintiff*; ~**dauer** duration of a lawsuit; ~**durch Eideshelfer** *hist* trial by compurgation; ~ **durch Zweikampf** *hist* trial by wager of battle; ~**eid** oath in litem; ~**erlös** proceeds of an action; ~**ergebnis** result of the proceedings; recovery; p~**fähig** legally capable of conducting proceedings (*in one's own name*); ~**fähigkeit** capacity to sue and be sued (*in one's own name*); ~**flut** surge of litigation, ~**fortsetzungsbeschluß** order to carry on proceedings; p~**freudig** litigious; ~**führender** litigant; ~**führung** → *Prozeßführung;* ~**gebühr** general fee for court proceedings (*of a German lawyer*) *gerichtliche* ~~~: *plaint fee;* ~**gegenstand** subject (matter) of an action; ~**gegner** opposing party, the other side, adverse party; ~**gericht** trial court, court before which an action is tried; ~**handlung** step in the proceedings, pleading(s); p~**hindernd** *adj* impeding an action, barring an action; ~**hindernis** impediment to an action, bar of trial; ~**kosten** → *Prozeßkosten;* ~**kunst** the art of conducting a lawsuit, art of pleading; ~**lage** stage of proceedings; ~**lawine** spate of lawsuits, avalanche of cases; ~**leitung** direction of the proceedings; ~**mandat** trial brief; ~**maxime** principles of procedure; ~**mißbrauch** malicious use of process; ~**ökonomie** procedural economy, economy in litigation; ~**ordnung** code of procedure, rules of court, Practice Act, Judges' Rules *GB*, rules of practice; ~**partei** party, litigant, party to an

621

action, party to a suit, litigating party, party to litigation, party to the proceedings, *pl: (also)* contending parties; *obsiegende ~~: the successful party; unterlegene ~~: the unsuccessful party;* ~**pfleger** guardian ad litem, administrator at litem, official solicitor, next friend *(for a minor)*; ~**phase** stage of trial; ~**praxis** court practice; ~**recht** law of procedure, procedural law, adjective law; *internationales ~~: international law of procedure*; ~**regel** procedural rule; ~**risiko** the risk of losing a case; ~**sache** cause, case; ~**schriftsätze** pleadings; ~**standschaft** standing to sue doctrine, litigation in one's own name but on another's behalf, representative action; ~**standschaftsklage** derivative action (*or* suit), representative action, action in one's own name but on another's behalf; ~**stoff** the subject matter of the litigation; ~**strafe** penalty for non-observance of procedural requirements; ~**sucht** litigiousness; ~**taktik** lawyer's tactics during the legal proceedings; p~**technisch** *adj* procedural, relating to procedural techniques; ~**trennung** severance of actions; p~**unfähig** *adj* incapable of acting in legal proceedings; ~**unfähigkeit** incapacity to act in legal proceedings; *Einwendung der ~~: plea of incapacity (plea that a party is not of age or not mentally fit to act in court)*; ~**unterbrechung** discontinuance; ~**urteil** judgment on procedural grounds; *klageabweisendes ~~; dismissal without prejudice*; ~**verbindung** joinder of actions; ~**vergleich** court settlement, compromise in court; ~**verhalten** trial conduct, behaviour in court; ~**verlauf** course of the proceedings; ~**verschleppung** protracting of a lawsuit, delaying the proceedings, dilatory methods; ~**vertreter** counsel *(for the plaintiff, for the defendant)*; ~**vertretung** legal representation in court; ~**verzeichnis** case-book, register of court cases; ~**verzicht** waiver of action; ~**vollmacht** authority to represent a party in an action, power of attorney for legal proceedings, warrant to sue and defend; ~**voraussetzungen** procedural requirements; ~**vorbereitung** preparation of the case, preparation for trial, instructions for brief; ~**vorschrift** procedural rule; ~ **wegen e-r Berühmung** jactitation suit; ~**zinsen** interest on claim during litigation; **anhängiger** ~ pending lawsuit (*etc cf Prozeß*); **den** ~ **wiederaufnehmen** to continue the case, to resume the case; **e-m** ~ **beitreten** to join an action; **e-n** ~ **anhängig machen** to institute an action; **e-n** ~ **auslösen** to trigger litigation; **e-n** ~ **betreiben** to carry on a lawsuit, to conduct a lawsuit, to prosecute an action; **e-n** ~ **einleiten** to institute an action, to start legal proceedings, to take out a writ; **e-n** ~ **einstellen** to stop a lawsuit; **e-n** ~ **führen** to conduct a case, to maintain an action; **e-n** ~ **neu aufrollen** to retry a case; **e-n** ~ **persönlich führen** to act in person; **e-n** ~ **unterbrechen** to discontinue an action; **e-n** ~ **verlieren** to lose one's case; **e-n** ~ **verschleppen** to protract an action; **für die Dauer des** ~**es** pending the lawsuit, pending action; **im** ~ **unterliegen** to be unsuccessful, to be defeated in a lawsuit; **in e-n** ~ **verwickelt sein** to be involved in litigation (*or* in an action); **laufende** ~**e** pending cases; **mit e-m** ~ **bedrohen** to threaten to take legal action; **schikanöser** ~ vexatious suit; **s-n** ~ **gewinnen** to win one's case; **sich in e-n** ~ **einlassen** to enter an appearance; **solange der** ~ **schwebt** pending the lawsuit; **streitiger** ~ defended suit.

Prozeßführung *f* conduct of a case, trial conduct; ~**sbefugnis** locus standing, standi to sue; ~**klausel** *clause restricting the right to take legal action, allowing one only to sue the leading insurer of a group*; ~**srecht**

Prozessieren authority to conduct litigation, right to sue, standing to sue; **mutwillige und schikanöse** ~ malicious and vexatious proceedings; **streitige** ~ litigious proceedings.

Prozessieren *n* litigation; **böswilliges** ~ malicious prosecution; **erneutes** ~ renewed litigation.

prozessieren *v/i* to litigate, to sue.

Prozeßkosten *pl* costs of an action, cost of litigation, costs of a lawsuit, legal costs, law costs, law charges; ~**hilfe** (civil) legal aid; ~**hilfebescheinigung** legal aid certificate; ~**hilfeempfänger** assisted person, ~**hilfegesetz** Legal Aid and Advice Act; ~**sicherheit** security for costs (of action); ~~ *für die Rechtsmittelinstanz: security for costs of appeal;* ~~*sleistung: furnishing security for costs of action;* ~**vorschuß** advance payment of costs; suit money (*to wife in a divorce suit etc*).

prozessual *adj* procedural.

Prüf|amt testing authority; ~**anlagen** test systems; ~**anstalt** testing institute; ~**attest** certificate of inspection; ~**beamter** testing officer; ~**befund** test result; ~**bericht** test report; ~**gerät** testing instrument, testing apparatus; ~**kosten** costs of testing; ~**lasten** test loads; ~**liste** check list; ~**nachweis** checking record; ~**normen** standards for testing; ~**plakette** inspection sticker, safety inspection sticker; ~**stelle** testing agency, examining agency, regulatory agency; (*or* board); ~**verfahren** testing method, test procedure; ~**vermerk** accountant's certificate; ~**vorrichtung** testing device; ~**zeichen** test mark, certification mark.

prüfbar *adj* testable, verifiable.

prüfen *v/t* to test, to inspect, to examine, to review, to investigate, to look into s.th., to study; to audit; **genau** ~ to examine in detail, to investigate thoroughly, to scrutinize, to test strictly; **von Amts wegen** ~ to consider ex officio, to consider without application; **wohlwollend** ~ to consider favourably.

Prüfer *m* tester, searcher, examiner, reviewer, inspector, auditor; ~**bericht** auditor's report, test inspector's report; ~**bilanz** tax auditor's balance sheet; **betriebseigener** ~ private accountant; **externer** ~ independent auditor; **sachverständiger** ~ expert examiner; **technisch qualifizierter** examiner; **technisch vorgebildeter** ~ *pat* technical examiner, **unabhängiger** ~ independent (*or* external) auditor.

Prüfung *f* examination, inspection, check, test, review, consideration, investigation; auditing, audit; ~ **an Ort und Stelle** spot check; ~ **der Betriebstätigkeit** operational audit; ~ **der Echtheit** verification of authenticity; ~ **der Liquidität** acid test, test of liquidity; ~ **der Neuheit** *pat* examination for (of) novelty; ~ **der Ware** examination of goods; ~ **des Erfindungsanspruchs** examination of invention; **bei nochmaliger** ~ on re-examination; **e-e** ~ **ablegen** to undergo an examination; **internationale vorläufige** ~ *pat* international preliminary examination; **nach** ~ **festgestellt** examined and found (to be ...); **nochmalige** ~ reconsideration, verification; **sachgemäße** ~ **ohne Zeitdruck** proper unhurried consideration; **stichprobenweise** ~ test audit, vouching, sample testing, testing at random; **übliche** ~ ordinary inspection, customary inspection; **vorläufige** ~ *par* preliminary examination; **zeitraffende** ~ accelerated test.

Prüfungs|abteilung *par* examining division (section, department); ~**akten** examination records; ~**amt** examining authority; ~**angelegenheiten** examination matters; ~**anstalt** testing laboratory; ~**antrag** request for exami-

Prügelstrafe | **Putativdelikt**

nation; ~**arbeit** examination paper; ~**aufsicht** invigilator; ~**ausschuß** examination board, screening panel, board of review, selection board; ~**beamter** tester, inspector; ~**bedingungen** examination requirements; test conditions; ~**behörde** examining authority; ~**bericht** examination report, test report, audit report, auditor's report; ~**bescheid** *pat* examiner's action, official action; ~**bescheinigung** test certificate, auditor's certificate; ~**entscheidung** decision upon the examination; ~**ergebnis** examination results, test results; ~**fahrt** test drive, trial run; ~**folge** sequence of tests; ~**gebühr** examination fee, charge for the test(s); ~**gesellschaft** firm of auditors, auditing company; ~**kommission** examining commission; ~**liste** list of examination candidates; ~**maßnahmen** test measures; ~**maßstab** test standard; ~**ordnung** rules relating to examinations, regulations for the conduct of an examination; ~**note** (examination) mark; ~**pflicht** obligation to examine, requirement to conduct an examination; ~**recht** right to examine; ~**richtlinien** auditing standards; *par* examination guidelines; ~**stelle** examining board, examining section, examining bureau; ~**termin** date of the examination, public examination of the debtor; ~**verband** auditing association, audit group; ~**verfahren** examination procedure, auditing procedure; ~**vermerk** auditor's certificate, certificate of audit; *uneingeschränkter* ~~: *clean audit certificate;* ~**versuch** test; ~**voraussetzungen** qualifying requirements for an examination; ~**vorschriften** rules of examination; ~**wesen** examination matters, auditing; ~**zeitraum** period under review, audit period; ~**zeugnis** examination certificate.

Prügelstrafe *f* corporal punishment, flogging, whipping.

624

Pseudonym *n* pseudonym, assumed name, fictitious name.

Psychologie *f* psychology; **gerichtliche** ~ forensic psychology.

Publikationsbefugnis right to publish (*e.g. an apology*).

Publikum *n* public, audience, readership, visitors; ~**sanlage** popular investment, investment favoured by the general public; ~**sgesellschaft,** publicly held corporation, open corporation; **das private** ~ private investors; **dem** ~ **zugänglich** open to the public.

Publizität *f* publicity; public disclosure; ~**sprinzip** principle of public disclosure; ~**svorschriften** disclosure rules.

Pufferstaat *m* buffer state.

Punkt *m* point, dot, spot, full stop; item; ~ **der Tagesordnung** item on the agenda; ~**diagramm** scatter diagram; ~**e e-s Vertrages** clauses of a contract; ~**system** points system; **aufklärungsbedürftiger** ~ a point to be investigated; **der wesentliche** ~ main point, crucial point, crunch point; **dunkler** ~ dubious point, obscure matter; **heikle** ~**e** delicate issues; **kritischer** ~ point of critical importance, the deciding juncture; **springender** ~ **der Klageschrift** the decisive point of the statement of claim; **streitiger** ~ point at issue, matter in dispute; **strittiger** ~ point at issue; **toter** ~ deadlock, stalemate; **unerledigte** ~**e** unfinished business; **wunder** ~ **der Beweisführung** weak point in the evidence, the Achilles heel.

Punktation *f* agreement on the basic terms of a contract, heads of agreement.

Putativ|delikt putative crime, imaginary offence; ~**ehe** putative marriage; ~**notstand** imaginary necessity: *situation erroneously regarded as an emergency;* ~**notwehr** imaginary self-defence: *self-defence in the mistaken belief that one is being attacked;* ~**vater** putative father.

Putsch *m* coup d'état, revolt, putsch.
putschen *v/i* to revolt, to carry out a coup d'état, to carry out a putsch.

Putschist *m* insurgent, rebel, participant in a coup d'état.
Pyromane *m* pyromaniac.
Pyromanie *f* pyromania, incendiarism.

Q

Quadruplik f surrebutter.
quälen v/t to torture, to torment.
Quälerei f torture, cruel maltreatment.
Qualifikation f qualification, level of ability, eligibility (description); classification (*international private law*); ~ **zum Richteramt** qualification to hold judicial office; ~**sfreiheit** cy-pres doctrine: *construction of a will according to testator's presumed intention*.
qualifizieren v/t to specify, to qualify, to describe, to designate; to apply the appropriate law (*international private law*), to aggravate (*crime*).
qualifiziert adj qualified, specified; aggravated; skilled.
Qualität f quality, grade, class; **einwandfreie** ~ acceptable quality; **einwandfreie** ~ acceptable quality; **erste** ~ first-class quality, first-choice quality, first-rate quality; **geringere** ~ inferior quality; **handelsübliche** ~ commercial standard, merchantable quality; **mittlere** ~ medium quality; **vereinbarte** ~ agreed quality; **zugesicherte** ~ promised quality, assured quality.
qualitativ adj qualitative, as regards quality, in quality.
Qualitäts|abweichung off standard, variation in quality, deviation in quality; ~**anforderungen** quality requirements; ~**arbeit** high-quality workmanship, work of superior craftsmanship; ~**auflagen** quality assurance requirements; **q~bewußt** adj quality-conscious; ~**erzeugnis** quality product, high-quality product; ~**fehler** quality defect, defective quality; ~**förderung** measures to improve quality; ~**grenzlage** quality level; ~**konkurrenz** competing in terms of quality; ~**kontrolle** quality control, acceptance sampling; ~**lücke** quality gap; ~**mangel** quality defect; ~**muster** representative sample; ~**norm** quality standard; ~**prüfung** quality test; ~ ~ *vorbehalten: quality subject to approval;* ~**sicherung** quality; ~**übereinstimmung** compliance with quality standards; ~**unterschreitung** off standard, below standard; ~**vorschrift** quality specification; ~**ware** high-quality goods, high-class products; ~**zeugnis** quality certificate; ~**zirkel** quality circle; ~**zuschlag** quality supplement, extra-charge for quality grade, surcharge for quality.
Quantität f quantity, amount; ~**smangel** deficiency (in quantity), shortage.
Quarantäne f quarantine; ~**bestimmungen** quarantine regulations; ~**flagge** quarantine flag, yellow flag; ~**hafen** quarantine harbour; **q~pflichtig** subject to quarantine; ~**risiko** quarantine risk; ~**sperre** sanitary cordon, cordon sanitaire; ~**station** quarantine station; ~**verletzung** violation of quarantine regulations, breaking quarantine; **unter** ~ **stellen** to quarantine, to put into quarantine; **Verhängung der** ~ imposing quarantine regulations.
Quartal n quarter (of a year), calendar quarter.
Quartals|abschluß end of the quarter; quarterly settlement of account, quarterly statement of accounts; quarterly profit and loss account; ~**bericht** quarterly report; ~**dividende** quarterly dividend; ~**schluß** end of quarter, end of a calender quarter; ~**tag** quarter day; ~**termin** quarter day, end of quarter; **q~weise** adj, adv quarterly;

Quartier | **Quotenabdeckung**

~**zahler** quarterly payer; ~**zahlung** quarterly payment.

Quartier *n* quarters, billet; accommodation; ~**amt** billeting office; ~**macher** billeting officer; ~**meister** quartermaster; ~**schein** billet, billeting paper, accommodation bill; ~**sleute** landlords of a billet; ~**zettel** billet.

Quasi|delikt quasi-tort; ~-**Geld** near-money, quasi money; ~**kontrakt** quasi contract; ~**monopol** near monopoly, quasi-monopoly; ~**rente** quasi-rent, quasi-income from capital; ~**splitting** splitting of spouses future pension rights (*by family court*); ~**verbindlichkeit** quasi-obligation; ~-**Versicherer** quasi-insurer; **q**~**vertraglich** quasi-contractual.

Quelle *f* origin, source; **aus amtlichen** ~**n** from official sources; **aus guter** ~ on good authority; from a reliable source; **zuverlässige** ~ reliable authority, reliable source.

Quellen|abzug deduction at source; *mit dem* ~~ *ist die Einkommensteuer abgegolten: the levy is in full discharge of personal income tax;* ~**abzug auf Dividenden und Zinsen** deduction at source on dividends and interest; ~**angabe** indication of source, sources used, source documentation; citing of sources; ~**belegung** source documentation; ~**besteuerung** taxation at source, tax deduction at source; ~**forschung** study of source material; ~**material** source material; ~**nachweis** indication of sources used; acknowledgments; ~**schutzgebiet** protection of spring-water area (*from surface pollution*); ~**staat** source country; ~**steuer** withholding tax; pay-as-you-earn tax, PAYE-tax; ~**steuerabzug** deduction at source; ~**steuerbefreiung** exemption from deduction at source.

Querschnitt *m* cross section; ~**sanalyse** cross-sectional analysis; **repräsentativer** ~ representative cross section.

Querschnittslähmung *f* paraplegia, paralysis of the lower limbs.

Querulant *m* quarreller, querulous person, troublemaker; ~**enwahn** querulous paranoia.

querulatorisch *adj* querulous, quarrelsome, vexatious.

Querverkehr *m* crossing traffic.

Querzahlungen *fpl* cross payments.

quittieren *v/t* to receipt, to give a receipt for, to acknowledge receipt of.

quittiert *adj* receipted, receipt given; **nicht** ~ unreceipted.

Quittung *f* (written) receipt; ~ **des Gerichtsvollziehers** seizure note; ~ **über den gesamten Betrag** receipt in full; ~ **über die Restzahlung** receipt for the balance; **e-e** ~ **ausstellen** to write out a receipt; **e-e** ~ **erteilen** to issue a receipt; **gegen** ~ against receipt; **gültige** ~ good receipt; **löschungsfähige** ~ mortgage discharge (receipt); statutory receipt *entitling one to cancel mortgage entry in Land Register;* **vorläufige** ~ provisional receipt.

Quittungs|aussteller person giving receipt, receptor; ~**buch** receipt book; ~**erteilung** issuing of a receipt; ~**formular** receipt form; ~**stempel** receipt stamp.

Quorum *n* quorum; *kommt das* ~ *nicht zustande: in the absence of a quorum; in the event that there is no quorum.*

quota litis lawyer's agreed share of the recovery (*as fee*).

quotal *adj* proportionate, on a quota basis, rateable.

Quote *f* quota, proportional share; ~ **der Ersparnisse** ratio of saving; **e-e** ~ **einhalten** to keep within the agreed quota; **in gleichen** ~**n** pari passu.

Quotelung *f* proportional assessment, proportional distribution (*of costs*).

Quoten|abdeckung quota cover; ~**aktie** share without par value; ~**einwanderer** quota immigrant (*USA*); ~-**Exzedentenvertrag** quota surplus reinsurance agreement; ~**frau** „quota" female (*to comply with quota regulations*);

627

~-rückversicherung quota reinsurance; **~stichprobe** quota sample; **~träger** quota-holder; **~überschreitung** exceeding the quota; **~urteil** distributive finding in the judgment; **~vereinbarung** quota (of women) arrangement; **~vermächtnis** legacy of a share of the estate; **~verteilung** distribution by quotas; **~vertrag** quota-share insurance; **~vorrecht** preferential quota of damages (*to which social insurance bodies and other assignees by operation of law are entitled*).

Rabatt *m* discount, rebate, reduction; ~ **bei Barzahlung** cash discount; ~ **bei Inzahlungnahme** trade-in allowance, discount for part exchange; ~ **bei Mengenabnahme** quantity discount, discount for bulk buying; ~ **für Stammkunden** discount for regular customers, patronage discount, ~ **für Wiederverkäufer** trade discount.

Rabatt|gesetz Act on Discounts; **r~fähig** subject to discount, discountable, eligible for a discount; **~flugpreise** discount fares; **~gewährung** granting of a discount; discount allowance; **~gruppe** discount bracket; **~kartell** discount cartel, agreed uniform rebates (*cartel to enforce uniform discounts*); **~laden** discount store; **~marke** trading stamp; **~sparverein** patronage savings association: *association of retail merchants with a common discount policy*; **~staffel** scale of discounts; **~stufe** discount level; **~vereinbarung** discount agreement; **~verstoß** infringement of discount regulations; **e-n ~ gewähren** to grant a discount; **mit ~** at a discount; **ohne ~** straight, without discount.

Rabulist *m* hair-splitter, equivocator, pettifogger (*lawyer*).

Rabulistik *f* hairsplitting, pettifogging, equivocation.

Rache *f* revenge, vengeance; **~akt** act of revenge, act of vengeance; **~gedanke** thought of revenge.

Rachgier *f* lust for revenge.

Radar|falle *f* radar trap, speed trap; **~warngerät** (electronic) radar warning device.

Radau *m* racket, rumpus, tumult, uproar, row.

Rädelsführer *m* ringleader, leader of a gang; **~schaft** leadership of a gang, leadership of a conspiracy.

Radierstelle *f* erasure.

Radierung *f* erasure (*on a document*).

Radikalenerlaß *m* ordinance restricting employment of radicals in public service.

Radikalismus *m* radicalism, extremism.

Radweg *m* (compulsory) cycle track.

Raffinerie *f* refinery.

raffinieren *v/i* to refine.

Rahmen *m* scope, framework, setting; **~abkommen** skeleton agreement; ~ **der Beschäftigung** scope of employment; ~ **e-s Gesetzes** scope of an Act; **~gebühr** sliding-scale fee *with a lower and upper limit;* **~gesetz** framework law, global law; **~gesetzgebung** framework legislation; **~kompetenz** competence (*of federal parliament*) to issue framework legislation; **~kredit** blanket credit, credit line, global credit; **~organisation** skeleton organization; **~planung** overall planning; **~police** master policy; **~programm** outline programme; **~recht** fundamental-principle right, general right; **~richtlinie** outline policy; **~tarif** skeleton tariff; **~tarifvertrag** skeleton wage agreement; **~vertrag** basic agreement, general agreement, skeleton contract, framework agreement, master agreement; **~vorschriften** general regulations, policy rules; **im ~** within the scope, within the ambit, within the limits, within the framework; **~~ der Amts- oder Berufstätigkeit:** (*acting*) *within the scope of office or employment;* **~~ der Vollmacht:** *within the scope of authority;* **~~***ihrer Befugnisse: within the limits of their authorities;* **~~***dieses Gesetzes: for the purpose(s) of this Act;* **~~ des üblichen Geschäftsverkehrs:** *in the ordinary course of business;* **~~** *seines Zweckes: within the framework of its terms of reference.*

Raiffeisen|banken rural banking co-operatives; ~**verband** Association of Farmers' Credit Co-operatives.

Ramsch *m* jumble, rummage; ~**verkauf** jumble-sale, *US:* rummage sale; ~**ware** joblot goods, odds and ends.

Randale *f* rampage.

randalieren *v/i* to make a row, to rampage.

Randalierer *m* rowdy, roisterer, brawler.

Rand|bemerkung marginal note, side note; *am Rande bemerkt: as per margin;* ~**figur** accessory, accomplice, second-stringer; ~**gebiete** peripheral areas; ~~ *eingemeinden: to absorb neighbouring districts (in a city)*; ~**gemeinde** peripheral village (*or* town); ~**staat** peripheral state; ~**vermerk** marginal note, annotation; ~**zeche** marginal mine; ~**zuwendungen** fringe benefits, perks.

Rang *m* ranking, rank, status, order, station; tier (*administration*); **r~älter** *adj* senior, higher in priority; **r~ältest** *adj* highest in seniority; ~**ältester** most senior in rank, highest in priority; ~**änderung** change in priority (*mortgages in the land register*); **r~besser** of prior rank, higher in priority; ~**einräumung** granting of a better priority (*mortgages in the land register*); ~ **e–r Forderung** priority of a debt, rank of a debt; ~ **e–r Hypothek** rank of a mortgage, priority status of a mortgage (*in land register*); ~**folge** seniority order of priority (*entries in public register*), order of precedence; **r~gleich** *adj* of equal rank; **r~jünger** junior, subsequent; ~**liste** list of precedency; **r~niedrigst** *adj* of lowest rank, of lowest priority; ~**ordnung** seniority, ranking, order of priorities, order of precedence, pecking order; ~~ *der Forderung: ranking of claims;* ~~ *von Pfandrechten: priority of liens;* ~**rücktritt** withdrawal to lower rank, giving-up a position of priority; retreat in rank, subordination; ~**stelle** specific rank, place in order of priority; ~**stellenvermerk** priority note (*in land register*); ~**verhältnis** rank, priority; ~**verlust** loss of priority, forfeiture of seniority, reduction to a lower rank; ~**vorbehalt** (entry of) reservation of priority (*in case of cancellation of an entry in land register*); ~**vermerk** priority notice (entry); ~**vorteil** advance; **ersten ~es** primary, first-ranking; first rate, top class; **gesellschaftlicher ~** social standing; **hoher ~** high rank, eminence; **im ~ aufrücken** to move up in priority (*or* rank); **im ~ gleichstehen** to rank pari passu; **im ~ nachstehen** to rank behind; **im ~ vorgehen** to have priority (over); **im ~ vorstehen** to rank before, to rank in priority.

Rasse *f* race; racial group; breed.

Rassen|diskriminierung racial discrimination, racialism, racism; ~**fanatiker** fanatical racialist, racist; ~**gegensätze** racial antagonism; ~**gleichheit** racial equality; ~**haß** racial hatred; ~**gesetz** racial law; ~**gesetzgebung** racial legislation; ~**hetze** stirring-up racial hatred; ~**krawall** race riot; ~**lehre** racial theory, racial doctrine; ~**politik** racial policy; ~**schande** race defilement (*sexual intercourse between persons of different races, esp Nazi Germany, between "Aryans" and Jews*); ~**schranken** racial barriers; ~**trennung** racial segregation; ~**unruhen** racial disturbances; ~**verfolgung** racial persecution; ~**vorurteil** racial prejudice.

Rasterfahndung *f* search for wanted persons by (screening) scanning devices.

Rasur *f* erasure (*document*), deletion.

Rat *m (1)* advice, counsel; ~**erteilung** (giving of) advice; ~**geber** counsellor, adviser; ~**suchender** s. o. seeking advice; **juristischer ~** legal advice; **kostenloser ~** gratuitous (*or* free) advice; **unabhängiger fachmännischer ~** independent expert advice.

Rat *m(2)* council; ~ **der Westeuro-**

päischen Union Council of Western European Union, WEU Council; ~ **für die Zusammenarbeit auf dem Gebiete des Zollwesens** Customs Co-operation Council; ~ **für gegenseitige Wirtschaftshilfe** *(RGW)* Council for Mutual Economic Assistance.

Ratazins *m* broken-period interest.

Rate *f* instalment, part-payment; rate *(proportion)*; ~ **der aufgeklärten Fälle** rate of cases solved, detection rate; **in ~n** by instalments; **~~ zahlen**: to pay by instalments; **in festgesetzten ~n** by fixed instalments; **überfällige ~** past due instalment.

Raten|kauf instalment purchase, purchase on the instalment system, instalment sale; hire purchase; **~kredit** instalment sales credit, credit repayable by instalments; **~rückstand** arrears of instalments; **~spareinlagen** saving-by-instalments deposits; **~sparvertrag** saving-by-instalments contract; **~vereinbarung** agreement for payment in instalments; **~zahlung** payment by instalments; **~zahlungsbeschluß** order to pay by instalments; **~zahlungsgeschäft** instalment trading, hire purchase; **~zahlungskredit** = *~kredit qv*.

Rathaus *n* town hall, city hall; **~partei** local political party; **~verbot** prohibition to enter the town hall *(for certain individuals)*.

Ratifikation *f* ratification; **~surkunde** ratification instrument, instrument of ratification; **~sverfahren** ratification proceedings; **der ~ bedürfen** to be subject to ratification.

ratifizieren *v/t* to ratify, to validate.

Ratifizierung *f* ratification, validation, validating statute; **nachfolgende ~** subsequent ratification.

Ratio *f* logical reason, sense, underlying purpose, rationale.

Ration *f* ration.

rationalisieren *v/i* to rationalize, to render more efficient.

Rationalisierung *f* rationalization, rational development, efficiency drive, cut-back; **innerbetriebliche ~** internal company rationalization.

Rationalisierungs|effekt effect of rationalization; **~fachmann** efficiency expert; **~förderung** state grant for rationalization schemes *(in coal mining)*; **~güter** goods used for rationalization; **~investition** capital investment for rationalization purposes; **~kartell** cartel for rationalization purposes, rationalization cartel; **~konjunktur** rationalization boom; **~kuratorium** rationalization board; **~maßnahmen** rationalization measures, productivity measures; cut-back measures; **~schutz** protection of employees in case of rationalization redundancy; **~test** test for rationalization purposes; *innerbetrieblicher ~~*: intra-firm comparison; **~versuche** rationalization tests.

rationell *adj* efficient, economical.

rationieren to ration.

Rationierung *f* rationing.

Rats|herr town councillor, municipal councillor; **~mitglied** councillor, assemblyman; **~schreiber** town clerk; **~versammlung** assembly of the town council; **~vorsitzender** chairman of municipal council.

Ratsgebühr *f* fee for legal advice, legal consultancy fee.

Raub *m* robbery; **~ auf öffentlichen Wegen** robbery committed on a public road; **~bau** predatory exploitation, over-exploitation; **~~** *am Boden treiben*: to exhaust the soil; **~~** *an Fischbeständen*: devastation of fishery resources; **~druck** pirate(d) edition; **~ mit Marterung** robbery with torture; **~mord** murder and robbery, *murder committed in the course (or furtherance) of a robbery*; **~mörder** robber committing murder, murderous robber; **~platte** pirated record, pirate recording, bootleg record; **~überfall** armed robbery, stick-up; **~überfallversicherung** insurance against rob-

rauben   **Räumungsanordnung**

bery; **bewaffneter** ~ armed robbery; **schwerer** ~ robbery with aggravation.
rauben to commit robbery, to rob, to maraud.
Räuber *m* robber; **~bande** gang of robbers, predatory band.
räuberisch *adj* predatory, rapacious.
Rauch|bekämpfungsvorschriften smoke control regulations; **~belästigung** smoke nuisance; **~gehalt** percentage of smoke in the air; **~verbot** ban on smoking, prohibition of smoking; no smoking!; **~vergiftung** smoke poisoning; **~waren** *(1)* tobacco products; **~waren** *(2)* furs, peltry.
Rauferei *f* brawl, affray, fight, scuffle.
Raufhandel *m* joint assault, affray *(resulting in death or grievous bodily harm)*.
Raum *m* (pl *Räume* = ~*e*) space, room, area, region; **~aufteilung** floor plan; **~ersparnis** space saving; **~fahrt** space travel, astronautics; **~fahrtindustrie** space industry; **~forschung** space research; **~kosten** expenditure on office space; **~nachfolger** successor to the premises; **~nebenkosten** incidental expenses for accommodation; **~not** shortage of housing, shortage of business premises; **~ordnung** → *Raumordnung*; **~pflege** domestic service; **~planung** regional planning, land-use planning; **~recht** space law; **~sicherungsvertrag** storage security contract; **~tarif** tariff based on the required space *(for transportation of goods)*; **~tiefe** depth of a room; **~transport** orbital transportation; **~verteilung** allocation of rooms; **gemeinschaftliche ~e** jointly used rooms, communal room; **gewerbliche ~e** business premises; **lichter ~** clearance; **umbauter ~** building volume, cubic content; enclosed area; **umfriedeter ~** enclosed area, enclosure; **umschlossener ~** room, enclosed space.

räumen *v/t* to evacuate, to vacate, to clear, to dispossess, *v/i* to yield up, to quit, to surrender *(premises)*.
Raumordnung *f* regional planning; **~sbehörde** regional planning authority; **~sgesetz** Regional Planning Act; **~sklausel** proviso for regional planning; **~spläne** regional planning charts; **~spolitik** urban and regional policy, **~sprogramm** regional planning programme, general development order, planning class; **~sverfahren** regional planning procedure.
Räumpflicht *f duty to clear street (or footpaths) from snow and ice.*
Räumung *f* removal, evacuation, eviction, dispossession *(tenants)*, clearance *(stocks)*; **gewaltsame ~** forcible eviction; **zur ~ zwingen** to evict, to dispossess.
Räumungs|anordnung eviction order; **~anspruch** right to have premises vacated, right to dispossess (or evict) a tenant; **~aufschub** stay of eviction; **~auftrag** writ of possession, instruction to enforce an eviction; **~ausverkauf** major disposal auction; **~befehl** eviction order, order for possession; **~frist** deadline for vacating the premises; **~gläubiger** ejector, evicting landlord; **~klage** action for possession (of premises), possession proceedings, eviction proceedings, dispossession proceedings; **~kosten** costs incurred by evacuation of premises, costs of eviction; **~prozeß** possession proceedings; **~schuldner** person required to vacate premises, person to be evicted, evicted person; **~schutz** (equitable) protection against eviction, **~titel** eviction order; **~urteil** judgment for possession (of premises), eviction order; **~verfahren** eviction proceedings; **~vergleich** court settlement requiring tenant to vacate premises; **~verkauf** clearance sale; **~verzug** delay in vacating premises *(after termination of tenancy)*; **~vollstreckung** eviction, enforcement of orders for possession.

Rauschgift *n* narcotic drug, narcotic, drug, dope, dangerous drug(s); ~**delikte** drug offences; ~**-Durchsuchungsbefehl** warrant to search for drugs; ~**handel** drug dealing, drug traffic, dope peddling, narcotics traffic; ~**händler** trafficker in drugs, narcotics dealer, pusher, drug pedlar, drug merchant; ~**nehmen** to take drugs, to be on drugs; ~**schmuggel** dope smuggling, narcotics smuggle; ~**suchhund** dope-attuned dog; ~**sucht** drug addiction; ~**süchtiger** drug addict, dope fiend, narcotic; ~ **verabreichen** to administer narcotic drugs, to dope; ~**vergehen** narcotics offence, drugs offence.

Rauschmittel *n* intoxicant, intoxicating drug; ~**abgabe** passing intoxicating drugs; **ein die Widerstandskraft lähmendes** ~ overpowering drug.

Rauschtat *f* offence of intoxication.

rausschmeißen *v/t* to throw out, to sack, to fire.

Rausschmeißer *m* bouncer.

Rausschmiß *m* sacking, sack, firing.

Rayonchef *m* floor walker.

Razzia *f* police raid, round-up.

Reagibilität *f* proneness to react, sensitiveness (*market etc*), responsiveness.

Reaktion *f* reaction, response; reactionary movement, reactionary forces; ~**sgeschwindigkeit** speed of response; ~**szeit** reaction time, thinking distance; **marktmäßige** ~ free-market reaction; **unwiderstehliche** ~ uncontrollable impulse.

Reaktionär *m* reactionary.

Reaktivierung *f* reactivation, rehabilitation; recall to the service, recommissioning; ~ **der Diskontpolitik** restoring bank-rate policy to active use.

Reaktor *m* atomic reactor; ~**sicherheitskommission** reactor safety commission; ~**unfall** atomic reactor accident.

real *adj* real, in terms of real value, in real terms, actual, true.

Real|akt physical act; ~**angebot** tender; ~**berechtigung** *f* object-related licence; ~**einkommen** real income, real earnings; ~**erlös** actual yield, real return; ~**gemeinde** village community with common real property; ~**gewerbsberechtigung** trade franchise attached to the land; ~**injurie** insult by physical act (*slap, spitting in the face*); ~**kapital** real capital, effective capital, nonmonetary capital, physical capital, tangible fixed assets; ~**kauf** executed sale, sale, executed purchase; ~**kaufkraft** effective purchasing power; ~**konkurrenz** = *Tatmehrheit qv;* ~**kredit** credit secured by a charge on (real or personal) property; real-estate loan; ~**kreditinstitut** real-estate credit institution, mortgage bank; ~**last** land charge *conveying right to recurrent payments or services*; ~**lohn** real wages, wages in real terms, actual wages; ~**politik** realistic political approach, realistic policies, policy based on realities; ~**politiker** realist in political affairs, realistic politician; ~**rechte** real-estate rights, real-estate encumbrances, object-related rights; ~**schule** intermediate modern secondary school, US: junior high school; ~**splitting** de facto splitting (*of tax for maintenance payments to ex-wife*); ~**statut** lex rei sitae; real statute; ~**steuer** impersonal tax, real tax, *esp.* land tax and trade tax; ~**teilung** physical partition (of estate); ~**union** real union, merger of offices; ~**vermögen** real assets, realty; real wealth; ~**vertrag** executed contract; *völkerrechtlicher* ~~: *paction;* ~**wert** actual value, intrinsic value, real value; ~**zins** real interest rate, running yield, yield with allowance for redemption.

Realien *f/pl* real properties, real estate.

realisierbar *adj* realizable, convertible into money, recoverable; **nicht** ~ not realizable, unrecoverable, non-convertible; **sofort** ~ easily marketable.

realisieren *v/t* to put into practice, to materialize, to implement; to convert into money, to realize; to liquidate, to cash in on projects.

Realisierung *f* realization, liquidation, selling, implementation; ~ **e-r Forderung** successful collection.

Realisation *f* realization, conversion into money, selling; **~skonto** realization and liquidation account; **~sverkauf** liquidating sale; **~swelle** wave of selling, bout of selling; **~swert** value on realization.

Reassekuranz *f* reinsurance.

Reassortierung *f* replenishing the assortment, rearranging the assortment.

Rebell *m* rebel, insurgent.

Rebellion *f* revolt, rebellion.

Rechen|fehler arithmetical error, error in calculation; **~stift** slate pencil, critical appraisal of expenses; **~werk** arithmetic, arithmetical system, accounting, accountancy, set of accounts; **~zentrum** computer centre.

Rechenschaft *f* account, rendering of account; ~ **ablegen** to render account, to account for; **~fordern** to call to account, to demand an explanation; ~ **verlangen** to call to account, to demand an explanation; **zur ~ ziehen** to call to account.

Rechenschafts|bericht account, statement of account, report and statement of account; **~legung** rendering of account; **~legungspflicht** liability to account, accountability; **~pflicht** accountability, liability to account (for); **r~pflichtig** *adj* liable to account (for).

Recherche *f* search; investigation (*by journalist, detective etc*); ~ **auf Neuheit** search as to novelty; ~ **internationaler Art** worldwide search; **~nabteilung** search division; **~namt** *pat* search authority; **~nbericht** search report; **~nexemplar** search copy; **~ngebühr** search fee; **ausgedehnte ~** extensive search; **ergänzende** **Europäische ~** *pat* supplementary European search; **internationale ~** international search.

Recherscheur *m* investigator, researcher.

rechnerisch *adj* calculated, computable, notional.

Rechnung *f* bill, sales bill, invoice, statement of account, note; ~ **in doppelter Ausfertigung** invoice in duplicate; ~ **legen** to render (an) account; ~ **und Gefahr** account and risk; *auf Ihre ~~~: for your account and risk*; ~ **und Gegenrechnung** debit and credit; **alte ~** the last accounting period, now closed; **auf ~ von** on account of; **auf die ~ setzen** to score; **auf e-r ~ stehen** to appear in an account; **auf fremde ~** for account of a third party, as agent only; **auf feste ~** at a fixed price; **auf neue ~ vortragen** to carry forward to a new account; **ausstehende ~en** outstanding invoices, unpaid bills; **die ~ begleichen** to foot the bill, to pay the bill, to settle an account; **die ~en vorlegen** to produce the accounts (*or* the invoices); **e-e ~ als unrichtig zurückweisen** to return an invoice (*or* a bill) for incorrectness; **e-e ~ aufstellen** to draw up an account; **e-e ~ ausstellen** to issue an account, to make out an invoice, to invoice, to make out a bill; **e-e ~ in Ordnung befinden** to agree with an invoice; to pass an account; **e-e ~ prüfen** to verify an account, to check a bill; **e-e ~ quittieren** to receipt a bill; **e-e ~ spezifizieren** to itemize an account; **e-e ~ vorlegen** to present a bill, to submit an account; **fingierte ~** pro forma invoice; **für eigene ~** for one's own account; **für feste ~ kaufen** to buy firm; **für fremde ~** for another's account; **für gemeinsame ~** for joint account, on joint account; **für ~ e-s anderen** = *für fremde ~ qv*; **für ~ von** for the account of, on account of; **getrennte ~** separate account, Dutch treat (*in restaurant etc*); **in**

Rechnungsabgrenzung

engl. Pfund zahlbare ~en invoices payable in sterling; **in ~ stellen** to invoice, to charge; *jmdm ~~~: to put down to a person's account, to pass to a person's account;* **~~ gestellt**; *billed, invoiced;* **längst fällige ~** past due account, long outstanding account; **laufende ~** current account, running account, open account; **laut ~** as per account; **laut ausgestellter ~** as per account rendered; **laut erhaltener ~** as per account received; **laut vorgelegter ~** per account rendered; **nächste ~** next account; **neue ~** a new accounting period; **nicht in ~ gestellt** not charged, not invoiced; **offene ~** outstanding account, unsettled account, trader's running account; **offenstehende ~** outstanding account; unsettled account; **pro-forma ~** pro-forma invoice; **provisionsfreie ~** without deduction for commissions; **prüffähige ~** verifiable invoice; **quittierte ~** receipted bill; **rückdatierte ~** back-dated (or predated) invoice; **spezifizierte ~** specified *or* itemized account; **überfällige ~** overdue (*or* delinquent) account; **überhöhte ~** excessive bill, stiff bill; **überschlägige ~** rough calculation; **unbewegliche ~** open account, unpaid invoice, back bill; **vordatierte ~** post-dated invoice; **vorläufige ~** provisional invoice.

Rechnungs|abgrenzung → *Rechnungsabgrenzung;* **~ablegung** rendering of account, accounting; **~abschluß** closing of accounts, closing the books, statement of account, accounts agreed upon; **~abteilung** billing (*or* accounts) department; **~austausch** substitution of invoices; **~auszug** extract of account; **~beamter** accounting official; **~beleg** voucher; **~betrag** amount invoiced, invoice amount, amount of invoice; **~bogen** tally sheet; **~datum** date of invoice; **~defizit** accounting deficit; **~durchschlag** copy (of) invoice;

~einheit unit of account; **~einzugsverfahren** direct debiting; **~empfang** receipt of invoice; **~ergebnis** result of calculation; **~erteilung** rendering an account, invoicing; **r~fähig** billable; **~fehler** accounting mistake, calulation mistake; **~formular** printed account form, billhead; **~führer** accounting officer, person in charge of the account(s); **~führung** accounting, keeping of accounts; **~gebühren** accounting charges; **~gewicht** billed weight; **~gutschrift** credit to the account, credit note; **~halbjahr** half of the financial year; **~hof** audit office, Auditor General, Court of Auditors, *US:* General Accounting Office; **~jahr** financial year, accounting year, fiscal year; **~legung** → *Rechnungslegung;* **r~mäßig** *adj* in accordance with the account; **~nachlaß** discount on the account; **~nachweis** accounting evidence; **~nummer** invoice number; **~periode** accounting period; **~position** invoice item, item on the account, accounting position; **~posten** item of account, item of a bill, invoice item; accounting unit; **~~ aufaddieren:** *to sum up the items;* **~~ nachprüfen:** *to check the items of the invoice;* **~preis** invoiced price, invoice price; **~prüfer** auditor; *amtlicher ~~: government accountant; externer ~~: outside auditor;* **~prüfung** → *Rechnungsprüfung;* **~rückstand** account in arrears; **~sachverständiger** accounting expert; **~saldo** balance (of an invoice); **~stelle** accounts department, accounting office; **~stellung** billing; submission of account, bill rendered, presenting an invoice; *überhöhte ~~: overbilling;* **~summe** invoice amount sum payable; **~tag** audit day; **~überschuß** accounting surplus; **~vierteljahr** quarter of the financial year; **~vorgang** accounting operation; previous accounts; **~vorlage** submission of account, presentation of the in-

Rechnungsabgrenzung

voice; ~**vordruck** invoice form, billhead; ~**wert** invoice value, value as per invoice; ~**wesen** → *Rechnungswesen*; ~**zinsfuß** interest-rate for accounting purposes; ~**zettel** slip.

Rechnungsabgrenzung *f* apportionment between accounting periods, separation of items applicable to a future accounting period, deferral, deferred charges to operations; ~**posten** *pl.* transitory items, deferred items, suspense items, items applicable to a future accounting period; *aktive* ~~: *prepaid expenses passive* ~: *deferred liability items*; **aktive** ~ prepaid expenses; **passive** ~ deferred credits to income.

Rechnungslegung *f* rendering an account, accounting; ~ **im Prozeß** rendering an account during litigation; ~**sbeschluß** order to render an account; ~**sklage** action for an account, account render; ~**spflicht** liability to render an account; ~**spublizität** public disclosure of accounts; ~**s- und Aufklärungsbeschluß** accounts and inquiries; ~ **und Rechnungsprüfung** presenting and auditing accounts; **abschließende** ~ full account, final accounting; **detaillierte** ~ detailed account; **periodengerechte** ~ accounting on an accrual basis *related to accounting periods*; **zukünftige** ~ prospective account, future accounting.

Rechnungsprüfung *f* audit, auditing of accounts, post audit examination of accounts; ~**samt** auditing office; ~**sausschuß** auditing committee, public accounts committee; ~**sbehörden** auditing authorities; ~**swesen** audit system; e-e ~ **vornehmen** to audit (accounts); **vorläufige** provisional audit; **stichprobenweise** ~ random (test) audit.

Rechnungswesen *n* accounting, accounting system, accountancy; **betriebliches** ~ cost accounting, internal accounting; **industrielles** ~ industrial accounting; **kaufmännisches** ~ business accounting; **kommunales** ~ municipal accounting; **öffentliches** ~ public accounting, public accounts.

Recht

Recht *n* law; right; ~ **am eingerichteten und ausgeübten Gewerbebetrieb** right to one's business establishment; ~ **am Gemeinschaftseigentum** common interest (in condominium property); ~ **an e-m Grundstück** an interest in land, (or real property), real estate right; ~ **an unbeweglichen Sachen** title to landed property, real estate right; ~ **auf Ämterbesetzung** patronage; ~ **auf anwaltschaftliche Beratung** right to consult with counsel; ~ **auf Arbeit** right to work; ~ **auf Aufrechnung** right to set-off; ~ **auf Ausbeutung** right to work; (*or* exploit) *a mine etc* ~ **auf Benennung von Beobachtern** right to designate observers; ~ **auf Benutzung** right to use, (right of) user; ~ **auf Besitz** possessive right, right of possession; ~ **auf das Patent** title to the patent; ~ **auf Entnahme von Mineralien** right to extract minerals; ~ **auf Ernte der eigenen Saat** right to emblements; ~ **auf Gegendarstellung** right of reply; right to a counter-statement; ~ **auf Gehör** right to be heard, right of audience (*in court*); ~ **auf Hinzuziehung e-s Verteidigers** right to consult (and be defended by) a lawyer of one's choice; counsel; ~ **auf Leben** right to live; ~**auf Leistungsverweigerung** right of refusal to perform; ~ **auf persönliche Sicherheit** right to personal safety; ~ **auf rechtliches Gehör** right to be heard; ~ **auf Schadenherabsetzung** right to reduction of damage; ~ **auf Seßhaftigkeit** status of irremovability; ~ **auf ungehinderten Zutritt** right of free entry (*or* access); ~ **auf ungestörte Nutzung** right to quiet enjoyment; ~ **auf Urkundenvorlage** power to call for documents, right of discovery; ~ **auf**

Vorlage von Urkunden = ~ *auf Urkundenvorlage qv*; ~ **auf vorzugsweise Befriedigung** right to preferential satisfaction (*of lienholder in bankruptcy*); ~ **behalten** to be right after all, to maintain one's right; ~ **der belegenen Sache** lex situs; ~ **der Berufung auf Anwaltsgeheimnis** professional privilege, solicitor's privilege; ~ **der Beweisführung** law of evidence; ~ **der Einsichtnahme** right to inspection of documents; ~ **der Erfindereigenschaft** right of inventorship; ~ **der ersten Wahl** (right of) first choice; ~ **der ersten Ablehnung** right of first refusal; ~ **der Flaggenkontrolle** right of visit; ~ **der freien Zufahrt** right of ingress, egress, and regress, right of access; ~ **der Freizügigkeit** freedom of movement; ~ **der Gegenäußerung** right to reply (*or* answer), right of counter-statement; ~ **der Schuldverhältnisse** law of obligations; ~ **der Stellvertretung** law of agency; ~ **der unerlaubten Handlung** law of torts; ~ **des Ausschlusses der Öffentlichkeit** right of privacy; ~ **des Bestellers zur Ersatzvornahme** option of owner to complete works (*building*), right of customer to effect (a) substitute performance; ~**e des Ehemannes** marital rights (*of husband*); ~ **des Erfüllungsortes** law of the place of performance; ~ **des Erstgeborenen** rule of primogeniture; ~ **des freien Zugangs zum Meer** right of free access to the sea; ~ **des freihändigen Verkaufs** power of sale (*of mortgaged property or attached goods*), right to sell by private contract; ~ **des geistigen Eigentums** intellectual property; ~ **des Gerichtsstandes** lex fori; ~ **des Nacherben** expectant interest as a reversionary heir, right(s) of the subsequent heir; ~ **des Überlebenden** right of survivor; ~ **des Urhebers** author's right(s), right(s) of copyright owner; ~ **des Vertragsortes** lex loci contractus, lex loci actus; ~ **des Vorerben** right(s) of the provisional heir; ~ **des Wirkungsstaates** law of the state where the agent acts; ~ **des Wohnsitzes** law of domicile; ~**e an fremder Sache** jura in re aliena; ~**e Dritter** third party rights; ~**e einklagen** to enforce one's rights by legal action, to sue for one's rights; ~**e geltend machen** to assert rights, to vindicate one's rights; ~**e mit Gewinnbeteiligung** rights conferring a share of the profits, profit-sharing rights; ~**e übergehen lassen auf** to subrogate; ~**e und Pflichten** rights and obligations; ~~~ *aus e–m Vertrag*: rights and obligations arising under a contract; ~**e und Verbindlichkeiten** rights and obligations; ~**e wahren** to preserve (the) rights; **r~los** *adj* rightless, without rights, without legal remedy; ~**losigkeit** lawlessness ~**schaffen** to create law; ~ **sich anwaltschaftlich vertreten zu lassen** right to counsel (of one's choice); right to be represented by a lawyer; ~ **sprechen** to adjudicate, to administer the law, to dispense justice; ~**sprechung** → *Rechtsprechung;* **r~ und billig** just and equitable, right and proper; ~ **zum Auftreten vor Gericht** (*vgl. Postulationsfähigkeit*) right of audience in court; ~ **zum ausschließlichen Vertrieb** exclusive distribution, right; sole right of sale; ~ **zum Getrenntleben** right to separation; ~ **zur freien Würdigung** right of free appraisal; ~ **zur Gewährung von Unterlizenzen** right to grant sublicences; ~ **zur Vertretung vor Gericht** right of audience in court; **abdingbares** ~ disposable right; **abgeleitete** ~**e** derivative rights; **absolutes** ~ absolute right, absolute interest (*in sth*); **abstraktes** ~ abstract right, bare right; **abtretbares** ~ assignable right; **akzessorisches** ~ accessory right, incidental right, secondary right; **alle** ~**e vorbehalten** all rights reserved; **alleiniges** ~ sole right; **allgemein anerkanntes** ~ common right, general law, generally accepted right, generally recognized legal rule; **allgemein geltendes** ~ general law; **allgemeines** ~ general right; **allodiales** ~ allodial right; **älteres** ~ prior right; **altes** ~ ancient law; **angeborenes** ~ inherent right; **anerkanntes** ~ established law, vested right; **anwachsendes** ~ accruing right; **anwendbares** ~ applicable law, governing law; **auf ausländisches** ~ **abstellen** to refer to foreign law as authoritative; **auf ein** ~ **verzichten** to disclaim a right, to renounce a (one's) right, to relinquish a right, to waive a right; **auf seinem** ~ **beharren** to stand on one's right; **auf seinem** ~ **bestehen** to insist on one's rights; **aus eigenem** ~ in one's own right, sui juris; ~~~ *besitzen: to hold in one's own right*; **aus fremdem** ~ (in) autre droit; **ausländisches** ~ foreign law; **ausschließlich aller** ~**e** ex all (rights), excluding all rights; **ausschließliches** ~ absolute right, exclusive right; **bedingtes** ~ conditional right, contingent interest; **beschränkt dingliches** ~ equitable interest in property, property interest limited to its holder; **beschränktes** ~ limited right, limited interest, qualified right; **besseres** ~ better right, outstanding title; **bürgerliches** ~ civil law; **das** ~ **anwenden** to apply the law; **das** ~ **beugen** to deviate from justice, to pervert the course of justice; **das** ~ **der belegenen Sache** lex loci rei sitae, lex situs: *the law of the place where the thing is situate*; **das** ~ **der freien Zufahrt** ingress, egress and regress; **das** ~ **durchsetzen** to enforce the law; **das** ~ **ist erloschen** the right has lapsed; **das** ~ **verdrehen** to twist the law; **dem** ~ **Wirksamkeit verleihen** to make the law effective, to enforce; **die sich aus ... ergebenden** ~**e** the rights ensuing from the law; **dingliches** ~ right in rem, real right; **dispositives** ~ optional rules, flexible law, jus dispositivum; **durch Geburt erworbenes** ~ right acquired by birth; **eheliches** ~ marital right, conjugal right (*mostly pl*); **ein** ~ **abtreten** to assign a right; **ein** ~ **aufgeben** to abandon a right, to waive a right, to relinquish a right, to renounce a right, to disclaim a right; *seine* ~*e* ~: *(also) to yield one's rights*; **ein** ~ **einräumen** to grant (s. o.) a right (*or* privilege); **ein** ~ **entziehen** to deprive (s. o.) of a right; **ein** ~ **fällt an** a right arises, a right accrues; **ein** ~ **geht auf jmdn über** a right is vested in a person, a right is transferred to s. o.; **ein** ~ **geht unter** a right extinguishes; **ein** ~ **geltend machen** to assert a right, to assert a title; **ein** ~ **haben** to have a right, to hold a right, to be entitled; **ein** ~ **herleiten von** to derive a right from; **ein** ~ **stützen auf** to establish a right on a basis of; **ein** ~ **verleihen** to grant a privilege, to vest a right (*in s. o.*); **ein** ~ **verletzen** to infringe a right; *jmds* ~~ *to infringe s. o. 's right*; **ein** ~ **wird erworben** a right is acquired, a right accrues to s. o.; **e-s** ~**es verlustig gehen** to become disentitled, to lose one's right, to forfeit a right; **einklagbare** ~**e** legally enforceable rights; **einschlägiges** ~ pertinent law, relevant provisions; **elterliche** ~**e** parental rights; **ersessenes** ~ prescriptive right, right derived from long possession, right acquired by adverse possession; **es mit dem** ~ **nicht genau nehmen** to stretch the law; **formelles** ~ legal right, strict right; procedural law, adjective law; **fremdes** ~ foreign law, right of another; **für** ~ **erkennen** to hold, to adjudicate; **gegenwärtiges** ~ present right; **geltendes** ~ prevailing law, law in force for the time being, law of the land; **gemeines** ~ common law; **gemeinsames** ~ joint right, undivided right; **gerichtlich durchsetzbares** ~ judicial right, enforceable right; **geschriebenes** ~ written law, statutory law; **gesetztes** ~ statutory law, statute law; **gleiche ~e genießen** to enjoy equal rights; **grundlegendes** ~ fundamental right; **grundstücksgleiches** ~ full legal title to land; **gutgläubig erworbenes** ~ bona fide acquired right; **höchstpersönliches** ~ strictly personal right, strictly private right; **ich lasse mir mein ~ nicht nehmen** I insist on my rights; **immaterielles** ~ intangible right; **in die ~e eintreten** to be subrogated to (s. o.'s) rights; **in fremdem** ~ en autredroit; **in jmds ~e eingreifen** to infringe s. o.'s rights, to interfere with s. o.'s rights; **in jmds ~e eintreten** to be subrogated to, to enter into the rights of, to succeed to the rights of s. o.; **inländisches** ~ national law, domestic law, municipal law, internal law; **innerstaatliches** ~ national law, domestic law, municipal law, internal law; **in seine ~e wiedereinsetzen** to reinstate (to s.o.'s rights); **internationales** ~ international law; **interzonales** ~ interzonal law (*Germany*); **jmdm ein ~ aberkennen** to deprive s. o. of a right; **jmdm ein ~ absprechen** to deny s. o. a right; **jmdn in seine ~e wiedereinsetzen** to reinstate s. o. in his rights; **kodifiziertes** ~ codified law; **künftiges** ~ future right; **künstlerische ~e** artistic rights; **lebenslängliches** ~ life interest, title for life; **lokales** ~ local law; **materielles** ~ substantive law; substantial (*or material*) right; **mit allen ~en** with all rights; **mit e–m Grundstück verbundene ~e** rights that run with the land; **nach deutschem** ~ under the German law, by German law; **nach geltendem** ~ under the law in force; **nachgiebiges** ~ flexible law, jus dispositivum; **nach künftigem** ~ de lege ferenda; **nationales** ~ national law, domestic law, internal law; **natürliches** ~ natural right; **nicht übertragbares** ~ non-transferable right;: **objektives** ~ (objective) law; impartial law; **obligatorisches** ~ relative right, right in personam, right arising out of an obligation; **offenbares** ~ clear right, manifest right; **öffentliches** ~ public law; **originäres** ~ original right, inherent right; **persönliches** ~ private right, personal right; **politisches** ~ political right; **positives** ~ positive law; **possessorisches** ~ possessory right; **privates** ~ private right; **rangbesseres** ~ superior title; **ranghöchstes** ~ paramount title **rangschlechteres** ~ junior right; **relatives** ~ relative right; **reversibles** ~ reversible right; **römisches** ~ Roman Law; **sachliches** ~ substantive law; **salisches** ~ Salic Law; **sämtliche ~e** all rights, all the estate, all the interest; **schottisches** ~ Scots law; **sich auf ein ~ berufen** to assert a right; **sich ~ verschaffen** to obtain justice; **sich ~e vorbehalten** to reserve rights; **staatliches** ~ law of the country, public law; **staatsbürgerliche ~e** political right, rights of citizenship, civic rights, citizen's rights; **selbständiges** ~ independent right; **stärkeres** ~ superior title, better right; **streitiges** ~ disputed right; **strenges** ~ strict law, cogent law, jus strictum; **subjektives** ~ (*an individual's*) right, entitlement; **subjektiv-dingliches** ~ right ad rem, right in rem; **subsidiär geltendes** ~ subsidiary law; **übertragbares** ~ transferable right, assignable right; **unabdingbares** ~ peremptory law, inalienable right; **unangreifbares** ~ established right, indefeasible right; **uneingeschränktes** ~ absolute law, absolute right; **ungeschriebenes** ~ unwritten law; **ungeteiltes** ~ undivided right; **unkörperliches** ~ intangible right; **unveräußerliches** ~ inalienable (= *unalienable*) right; **unverjährbares** ~ right that cannot become statute-barred, permanent right, imprescriptible right;

unvollkommenes ~ imperfect right; **veräußerliches** ~ alienable right; **verbrieftes** ~ vested title, chartered title; **verliehenes** ~ granted title; **verwandtes** ~ related right; closely similar law; **vollkommenes** ~ perfect right; **von e–m** ~ **Gebrauch machen** to avail oneself of a right; **von** ~**s wegen** according to law, by law, de jure, by right, in the name of the law, according to law; **vorbeugendes** ~ preventive (*or* preventative) law; **vorkonstitutionelles** ~ pre-constitutional law; **widerruflich gewährtes** ~ revocable right; **wohlbegründetes** ~ vested right, well established right; **wohlerworbenes** ~ vested right, vested interest, *pl also*: well (*or* duly) acquired rights; **zukünftiges** ~ expectant interest, future right; **zu** ~ **bestehen** to be valid in law, to be good in law; **zwingendes** ~ cogent law, binding law; **zwischenstaatliches** ~ international law; interstate law (*US*).

Rechter *m* (*der Rechte*) rightist, member of the right wing (of the party).

rechtfertigen *v/t* to justify, to vindicate; **erneut** ~ to revindicate, to reaffirm.

Rechtfertigung *f* justification, vindication; ~ **des eigenen Verhaltens** self-justification; ~**sgrund** legal justification; ~**smöglichkeit** justifiability.

rechtlich *adj* legal, in law, de jure; ~ **oder tatsächlich** in law or in fact; ~ **und tatsächlich** in fact and in law; ~ **unmöglich** legally impossible; ~ **verpflichtet** bound by law, legally bound.

rechtmäßig *adj* lawful; rightful, as of right, legal.

Rechtmäßigkeit *f* lawfulness, legality.

Rechts|abteilung legal department; ~**abtretung** assignment (of rights), ~**akt** legally relevant act (or conduct); ~**amt** municipal legal office; ~**analogie** (application of) analogous law; ~**änderung** change in the law, alteration of rights; ~**änderungsklage** action for modification of rights; ~**angelegenheit** legal matter, matter of law, matter for legal consideration; ~**angleichung** unification of law, assimilation of laws, harmonization of legal provisions; ~**anschauung** legal view; ~**anspruch** legal claim, right; ~**antragsstelle** special applications office, issuing office, (*at the local court*); ~**anwalt** → *Rechtsanwalt*; ~-**anwendung** application of law; ~**argument** legal argument, point of law; ~**auffassung** legal opinion, legal viewpoint; ~**aufsicht** supervisory control, legal supervision, supervision on points of law; ~**aufsichtsbehörde** supervisory authority (*on points of law*); ~**ausführungen** legal argument, legal submissions; *mündliche* ~~: *oral argument, oral pleadings* (*on points of law*); *schriftliche* ~~: *brief on points of law, legal brief*; ~**auskunft** legal information; ~**auslegung** legal interpretation; ~**äußerung** legal comment; ~**ausschuß** committee on legal affairs, law committee, judiciary committee; ~**ausübung** exercise of a right; *unzulässige* ~~: *estoppel, equitable estoppel, improper exercise of a right*; ~**ausübungsfrist** time limit for asserting one's rights, deadline for legal remedies; ~**basis** legal foundation; ~**begehren** petition, request for a legal remedy; ~**begriff** legal concept, legal term, nomen juris; **r**~**begründend** establishing a right; ~**behelf** → *Rechtsbehelf*; ~**beistand** legal practitioner (for minor matters); legal assistance; ~**belehrung** instructing s. o. on his legal rights, caution; ~**berater** legal adviser; ~ **beratung** legal advice; ~**beratungsmißbrauchsgesetz** law against unlicensed legal practice; ~**beratungsstelle** legal aid office; ~**bereinigung** repealing obsolete statutes; ~~**sgesetz**: *Act to* *abolish obsolete legislation;* ~**beschwerde** appeal on points of law (*from an order by a court or tribunal*); ~**beschwerdeverfahren** procedure for appeals on points of law (*cf Rechtsbeschwerde*); ~**besitz** civil possession, naked possession, theoretical possession; ~**besitzer** holder of a right; ~**besorgung** legal services, conduct of legal matters; ~**bestand** (legal) validity, legal existence; ~**betreuung** legal assistance, looking after s. o.'s rights; ~**beugung** perverting the course of justice; ~**beziehung** legal relationship, legal relations; *die internen* ~~*en der Parteien: the rights of the parties inter se*; ~**bibliothek** law library; ~**bindungswille** intentin to create legal relations; ~**blindheit** recklessly ignoring the law; ~**brauch** legal custom; ~**brecher** law-breaker, criminal, trespasser; ~**bruch** violation of the law, breach of the law, infringement; ~**büro** law office; ~**charakter** legal character, legal nature; ~**denken** legal thinking; ~**dezernat** municipal legal department; ~**einheit** legal uniformity, legal unity; ~**eintritt** subrogation of rights; ~**einwand** plea, objection, demurrer; ~**empfinden** sense of justice; *gesundes* ~~: *natural sense of justice, natural equity*; ~**entscheid** legal decision; **r**~**erheblich** *adj* legally relevant, relevant in law; ~**erheblichkeit** relevancy in law; ~**erlebnis** experience of a legal affair; ~**erwerb** acquisition of a right (*or* rights), acquisition of title, vesting; ~~ *durch Verarbeitung: right by specification;* **r**~**fähig** having legal capacity, possessing legal personality; ~**fähigkeit** (legal) capacity, capacity to acquire and hold rights and duties; ~~ *verleihen: to grant juristic personality, to incorporate; völkerrechtliche* ~~: *international personality*; ~**fall** legal case, law case; *e–n* ~~ *behandeln: to handle a case;* ~**fehler** legal mistake, error in law; *revisibler*

~~: *reversible error;* **r**~**fehlerhaft** *adj* legally mistaken, incorrect on a point of law, erroneous in (point of) law, flawed; ~**figur** legal entity, legally defined concept, legal concept; ~**fiktion** legal fiction; ~**findung** legal finding; ~**folge** legal consequence, ~**folgenbelehrung** cautioning (*or* warning) as to the legal consequences (*of an act or omission*); ~**form** legal form; ~**formularbuch** book of legal forms, book of legal precedents; ~**fortbildung** further legal education; ~**frage** legal question, point of law, legal issue; *streitige* ~~: *issue of law, controversial legal point*; ~**frieden** law and order, public peace; undisturbed administration of the law; ~**gang** practice of the court, court proceedings; ~**garantie** legal guarantee, warranty of title; ~**gebiet** field of law, legal sphere; ~**gedanke** legal concept, policy of the law; ~**gefährdung** imperilment of the law, danger to justice; ~**gefühl** sense of justice, sense of what is right and wrong; **r**~**gelehrt** *adj* versed in law, skilled in the law; ~**gelehrter** legal scholar; ~**geltungswille** intention of legal effect; ~**gemeinschaft** legal community, unity of interest, joint holding; **r**~**genügend** *adj* legally sufficient, adequate under existing law; ~**genuß** enjoyment of a right; ~**geschäft** → *Rechtsgeschäft*; ~**geschichte** legal history, history of law; ~**gespräch** legal discussion; **r**~**gestaltend** *adj* legally operative; ~**gestaltung** shaping the law; influencing the legal status by court decisions; ~**gestaltungsklage** action to change the legal status; ~**gewohnheit** legal custom, judicial custom; ~**gleichheit** equality before the law, equality of rights; ~**grund** cause in law, legal basis, legal ground; ~**grundlage** legal basis, legal foundation; ~**grundsatz** principle of law, legal principle, legal maxim, *pl also* canons (of law); **r**~**gültig** *adj* legally valid; *für*

641

Rechtsabteilung

~~ *erklären: to validate;* ~**gültigkeit** legal validity; ~**gut** object of legal protection (*such as life, property, honour*); ~**güterabwägung:** *weighing the legal merits;* ~**gutachten** (legal) opinion, counsel's opinion, legal expertise; ~**handlung** (objective) act *as manifestation of a person's will;* r~**hängig** sub judice, pending (before a court), under judicial determination; ~**hängigkeit** lis pendens, pendency (of a claim); *anderweitige* ~~: *another action pending; für den Fall der* ~~: *pending suit; nach* ~~ *post litem motam; vor* ~~: *before pendency of the claim; während* ~~: *in an action, pending action, while proceedings are pending, hanging the process, pending final decision;* ~**hilfe** → *Rechtshilfe;* ~**informatik** information processing in law; ~**inhaber** holder of a right, entitled person; ~**institut** legal institution (*such as marriage, administration etc*); ~**irrtum** (innocent) mistake of the law; error of law, judicial error, misconception of the law; *außerstrafrechtlicher* ~~: *mistake of law other than criminal law; unverschuldeter* ~~: *innocent mistake of the law;* ~**kenntnisse** knowledge of law; ~**kollision** conflict of laws; ~**kontinuität** continuity of (the) law; ~**kontrolle** legal review; legal supervision; ~**kraft** → *Rechtskraft;* ~**kräftig** *adj* final and conclusive, absolute (*decree*); indefeasible, unappealable, non-appealable; *formell* ~~: *unappealable, non-reversible, non-appealable; materiell* ~~: *res judicata; noch nicht* ~~: *pending appeal, not yet final;* ~**kreis** legal system; r~**kundig** *adj* versed in law; ~**kundiger** person with a knowledge of the law, person versed in the law; ~**lage** legal position, legal situation, juridical position; ~**leben** legal affairs, legal system, law; ~**lehrbuch** legal textbook, compendium of law; ~**lehre** jurisprudence; ~**lehrer** lecturer in law, professor of law; ~**lücke** gap in the law, shortcoming in the law, defi-

ciency in the law; ~**mangel** legal imperfection in title; *arglistiger* ~~; *fraud in title;* ~**mängelgewähr** warranty of title, warranty of quiet enjoyment; ~**mängelhaftung** liability for sound title, warranty of title; ~**maxime** legal maxim; ~**mißbrauch** abuse of law, abusive exercise of a right; abuse of title, conduct subject to estoppel; ~**mittel** → *Rechtsmittel;* ~**nachfolge** succession, succession in title, legal succession, devolution; ~~ *durch Erbgang: devolution by inheritance;* ~~ *bei Tod: devolution upon death;* ~**nachfolgeklausel** subrogation clause; ~**nachfolger** successor, legal successor, successor in title, successor in interest; *pl also*: heirs and assigns; ~**nachteil** legal detriment, legal disadvantage, prejudice; ~**natur** legal nature, legal status; ~**norm** legal norm, rule of law, legal rule, statutory provision; ~**objekt** legal object; object of a right; ~**ordnung** legal system, legal regime; lex; ~~ *der Vornahme der Handlung: lex loci actus;* ~**persönlichkeit** legal personality, legal person, legal entity, juridical personality; corporate personality; ~~ *haben: to be a subject of law, to be a legal entity; öffentliche* ~~: *legal personality under public law;* ~**pflege** administration of justice, administration of the law; ~**pflegeakte** judicial acts; ~**pflegedelikte** offences against the administration of justice; ~**pflegeministerium** general ministry of justice; ~**pfleger** judicial officer, adjudicatory officer, clerk of court; ~~ *im Konkursgericht: referee in bankrupty;* ~**pflegergesetz** *Act (D, 1959) concerning the office of Rechtspfleger qv (delegating minor judicial functions to them);* ~**pflicht** legal duty, duty in law, legal obligation; ~~*merkmale: cirteria of legal obligation;* ~~ *zum Handeln: legal duty to act;* ~**philosoph** legal philosopher; ~**philosophie** philosophy of law, legal philosophy; ~**politik** legal policy, policy of law; **r~politisch** *adj* pertaining to legal policy; **~position** legal position, legal situation; **~positivismus** legal positivism, positivist theory of law; **~praxis** legal practice, practice of the courts; **~quellen** sources of the law; **~reform** law reform; **~sache** law case, cause, litigation, legal matter, legal suit; *anhängige ~~: pending case; bürgerliche ~~: civil case; nichtstreitige ~~n: non-contentious legal matters;* **~satz** legal rule, legal provision, legal norm; **~schein** appearance of a right or legal position; **~scheinshaftung** estoppel by representation, *liability for creating the appearance of a right or entitlement;* **~scheinvollmacht** agency by estoppel; **~schöpfung** creation of laws, law-making, judge-made law, legal innovation; **~schutz** protection of the law; → *Rechtsschutz;* **~setzung** legislation; *abgeleitete ~~: secondary legislation;* **~setzungsbefugnis** legislative authority; **~sicherheit** legal security, public safety, law and order, certainty of the law, consistency of the law; **~sinn** legal meaning, juristic sense; **~sprache** legal parlance, legal language; **~sprichwort** legal proverb, legal maxim; **~staat** constitutional state, state governed by the rule of law, state where law and order prevails; *sozialer ~~: social constitutional state;* **r~~staatlich** *adj* determined by the rule of law, constitutional; **~staatlichkeit** a condition where the rule of law is maintained, **~staatsgefährdung** endangering the constitutional state; **~staatsprinzip** principle of due course of law; **~stand** legal status; **~standpunkt** legal point of view; **~status** legal status; **~statut** legal statute; **~stellung** legal position, (legal) status; **~stillstand** paralysis of the legal system; **~streit** litigation, legal proceedings, lawsuit; *anhängige ~~: pending action, pending litigation, lis pendens; bürgerlicher ~~: civil action, civil case;* **~streitigkeit** legal dispute, litigation; *~~en vor den ordentlichen Gerichten: ordinary civil causes; anhängige ~~en: pending litigation; bürgerlicher ~~: civil case;* **~student** student of law; **~studium** study of law; **~subjekt** the person acting in legal matters, legal personality, holder of rights; **~system** legal system; **~terminologie** legal terminology; **~title** (legal) title; **~träger** instrumentality, holder of a right, legal entity: *person or body in whom a right is vested;* **~übergang** devolution of title, vesting (of title), transmission of rights; *gesetzlicher ~~: subrogation, transfer of title by operation of law;* **~überlieferung** legal tradition; **~übertragung** assignment *(of a right or of rights),* transfer of title; **~- und Geschäftsfähigkeit** legal capacity; **~- und Verwaltungsausschuß** legal and administrative committee; **~- und Verwaltungsvorschriften** legal regulations and administrative rules; **r~unerheblich** *adj* legally irrelevant; **r~unfähig** *adj* legally incapable, legally disqualified; **~unfähigkeit** legal incapacity; **r~ungültig** *adj* legally invalid, void; **~ungültigkeit** (legal) invalidity; **~unkenntnis** ignorance of (the) law; **~unsicherheit** legal uncertainty, uncertainty as to what the law is; **~unterworfener** person subject to the law; **r~unwirksam** *adj* invalid, legally ineffective; *~~ machen: to render invalid, to vitiate, to rescind, to annul;* **r~verbindlich** *adj* legally binding, binding (in law); *nicht ~~ of no legal force, non-binding;* **~verbindlichkeit** legal force, binding effect; **~verdreher** person who twists the law, prevaricator, pettifogger; **~verdrehung** pettifoggery, prevarication, twisting the law; **~vereinheitlichung** unification of law, harmonization of laws; **~verfolgung** prosecution, prosecution of an action; *böswillige ~~: malicious prosecution;* **r~vergleichend** *adj* comparing laws, legally comparative; ~**vergleichung** comparative law, comparing laws, comparative jurisprudence; ~**verhältnis** legal relationship, *vertragsähnliches* ~~: *quasi contractual relationship*; ~**verkehr** legal relations; ~**verletzung** breach of the law violation of law; infringement of rights (*or* of a right); *e–e* ~~ *verfolgen: to sue for an infringement;* ~**verlust** loss of a right, forfeiture of right, lapse of a right, lapse of title; ~**vermutung** presumption of law; ~**verordnung** minister's order, statutory instrument, legal regulation, decree, ordinance, statutory order, *pl also*: statutory rules and orders; ~**verteidigung** defence (*in civil cases*); ~**verwahrung** reservation of a right, legal protest; ~**verweigerung** refusal of justice, denial of justice; ~**verwirkung** forfeiture of a right; ~**verzicht** disclaimer of a right, waiver; ~**vorbehalt** legal reservation, reservation of rights, legal proviso; ~**vorgang** legal process, legal case, case history; ~**vorgänger** legal predecessor; predecessor in title; ~**vorschrift** legal provision, legislative provision, *pl also* legislation, legal requirements; *innerdeutsche* ~~: *provision of domestic German law; innerstaatliche* ~~*en: domestic and local laws, national legislation*; ~**vorstellung** legal concept; ~**vorteil** legal benefit, benefit of a law; ~**vortrag** legal argument; ~**wahlklausel** choice-of-law clause; ~**weg** → *Rechtsweg*; ~**wesen** legal system, administration of justice; **r~widrig** *adj* unlawful, contrary to law, illegal; ~~ *handeln: to act illegally;* ~**widrigkeit** unlawfulness, illegality, illegal act; ~**wirklichkeit** legal reality; **r~wirksam** *adj* legally effective, operative, with effect (as of/from); ~~ *machen: to perfect; sofort* ~~: *immediately effective*; ~**wirksamkeit** legal validity; operative date; ~**wissenschaft** jurisprudence; *vergleichende* ~~: *comparative jurisprudence*; ~**wissenschaftler** academic lawyer, legal scholar; **r~wissenschaftlich** *adj* juristic, jurisprudential, in legal theory; ~**wirkung** legal effect, (legal) operation; ~**wohltat** legal benefit, benefit of the law; *die* ~~ *des „in dubio pro reo": the benefit of the doubt; die* ~~ *der Inventarerrichtung: the benefit of the inventory*; ~**zug** instance, (recourse to) legal process; ~**zustand** legal state, legal condition, legal status, legal position, legal situation; ~**zuständigkeit** jurisdiction, competence.

Rechtsanwalt *m* lawyer, advocate, *GB*: solicitor, barrister, *US*: attorney at law, counsel, legal counsel, counsellor at law; ~ **eigener Wahl** solicitor of one's choice, counsel of one's own choice; ~**schaft** (the) bar, the legal profession, the legal fraternity; ~**sgebühr** lawyer's fee, *pl also*: legal fees; ~**sgebührenordnung** Attorneys' Fee Ordinance; ~**skammer** chamber of lawyers, Bar Association, German law society; ~**skanzlei** law office(s), firm of lawyers, law firm; ~**ssozietät** firm of lawyers, law firm, law partnership; ~**svergütung** lawyer's remuneration (*or* fee); ~**versorgung** (*compulsory*) pension scheme for lawyers; ~**vertrag** contract for the services of a lawyer, retainer; **der** ~ **des Beklagten** counsel for the defendant, defendant's lawyer/solicitor/barrister; **der** ~ **des Klägers** counsel (lawyer) for the plaintiff; **e–n** ~ **beiordnen** to assign a counsel (lawyer) *to a legally aided party;* **e–n** ~ **mandieren** to retain a lawyer, to engage the services of a lawyer, to instruct a lawyer.

Rechtsbehelf *m* legal redress, legal remedy, judicial remedy; ~ **in Verwaltungsangelegenheiten** administrative remedy; ~**sbelehrung** advising s. o. of legal remedies; **auf e–n** ~ **verzichten** to waive a remedy; **ausreichender** ~

adequate legal remedy; **außergerichtlicher** ~ extrajudicial remedy; **außerordentlicher** ~ extraordinary remedy; **innerstaatlicher** ~ domestic remedy; **kein** ~ no recourse, no legal remedy; **wahlweise zulässiger** ~ alternative remedy, permissible remedy.

Rechtschaffenheit *f* integrity, honesty, probity.

Rechtsfahrgebot *n* rule to drive on the right.

Rechtsgeschäft *n* legal transaction, legal (*or* juristic) act, private act; ~**e vornehmen** to engage in transactions; ~ **unter Lebenden** transaction inter vivos; ~ **von Todes wegen** transaction mortis causa; **abstraktes** ~ abstract juristic act: *transaction isolated from underlying contractual obligations;* **anfechtbares** ~ voidable act, voidable transaction; **annahmebedürftiges** ~ legal act requiring acceptance (*in order to become valid*); **bedingtes** ~ act subject to a condition, conditional legal transaction; **befristetes** ~ legal transaction limited in time; act subject to time-limit; **ein** ~ **abschließen** to conclude a transaction; **einseitiges** ~ unilateral juristic act; **einseitig verpflichtendes** ~ unilaterally obligating legal transaction; **entgeltliches** ~ transaction for value; **fiduziarisches** ~ fiduciary transaction; **höchstpersönliches** ~ strictly personal transaction; **kausales** ~ underlying transaction; **nichtiges** ~ void legal act, void transaction; **sittenwidriges** ~ immoral transaction, transaction contra bonos mores; **unzulässiges** ~ inadmissible transaction, unlawful act or transaction; **zweiseitiges** ~ bilateral act, bilateral transaction, two-party transaction; **zustimmungsbedürftiges** ~ legal transaction subject to approval.

rechtsgeschäftlich by act of the party (*or* parties); (*acc. to context:*) contractual, voluntary.

Rechtshilfe *f* mutual judicial assistance, legal assistance, inter-court assistance, mutual administrative assistance; relief, legal redress; ~**ersuchen** letters rogatory; ~~ **zur Zeugenvernehmung**: *letters rogatory, rogatory commission;* ~**gewährung** granting of mutual judicial assistance; ~ **in Strafsachen** mutual assistance in criminal matters; ~**richter** commissioned judge; ~**verkehr** relations of mutual judicial assistance; ~**vertrag** mutual judicial assistance treaty; ~**verfahren** mutual judicial assistance procedure, letters rogatory; ~**weg** recourse to mutual judicial assistance, judicial process carried out through a foreign court.

Rechtskraft *f* res judicata, legal force, finality of a decision, non-appealability: ~ **erlangen** to become final and absolute, to become non-appealable, to become res judicata; ~ **haben** to be final and absolute, to be non-appealable; ~ **verleihen** to make absolute, to give legal effect to; ~**wirkung** res judicata effect; ~**zeugnis** certificate of indefeasibility: *certificate that a judgment has become non-appealable;* **formelle** ~ non-appealability; **materielle** ~ res judicata; *mit* ~*r* ~: *with prejudice, with final force and effect.*

Rechtsmittel *n* right of appeal, appeal, resort to a higher court or authority; ~**antrag** petition of appeal, appellant's motion; ~**begründung** (pleadings of) grounds of appeal; ~**begründungsfrist** time-limit for filing (pleadings of) grounds of appeal; ~**behörde** board of review; ~**belehrung** instructions about a person's right to appeal; ~**berechtigter** person entitled to appeal; ~**beschränkung** restriction of an appeal; ~ **des innerstaatlichen Rechts** judicial remedy under national law; ~**einlegung** lodging an appeal; *bei* ~~: *upon appeal;* ~**entscheidung** decision upon appeal, decision of the appellate court;

~erklärung statement of appeal; **r~fähig** *adj* appealable; *nicht ~~: without appeal, non-appealable, unappealable*; **~fähigkeit** reviewability; **~frist** time for appeal, period for appeal; **~gebühr** fee of the appellate instance; **~gericht** appellate court; **~instanz** appellate instance, appeal authority, board of review; **~kläger** appellant; **~kosten** costs of appeal; **~schrift** appellant's pleadings supporting his appeal, petition for review; **~verfahren** appeal procedure, appellate proceedings; *innerstaatliche ~~: domestic remedies*; **~verzicht** waiver of right to appeal; **~weg** appeal procedure, resort to a higher court (*or* review authority); *der ~~ ist erschöpft: remedies have been exhausted*; **~zulassung** leave to appeal; **auf ~ verzichten** to waive the right to appeal; **außerordentliches ~** extraordinary resort to an upper court; **das ~ der Revision** right of appeal on a point of law; **dem ~ stattgeben** to allow the appeal; **des ~s verlustig erklärt werden** to be informed that the right to appeal has lapsed; **des ~s verlustig gehen** to lose one's right to appeal; **ein ~ einlegen** to appeal, to lodge an appeal, to appeal against (*or* from) a decision to a higher court, to appeal from an administrative body (*to a superior authority*); **ein ~ ist nicht gegeben** no appeal shall lie; **e-m ~ unterliegen** to be subject to appeal; **über ~ entscheiden** to decide as appellate instance, to decide on appeal.

Rechtsprechung *f* adjudication, dispensation of justice, court decisions, precedents, established case law, leading cases; **~befugnis** judicial power, authority to render decisions; **~slehre** case law jurisprudence; **~sorgan** judicial organ, court; **~ssammlungen** law reports; **~sübersicht** legal update; **~ und Rechtslehre** legal authorities; **anerkannte ~** ruling cases, established case law; **aufgegebene ~** overruled precedents; **feststehende ~** established practice, settled practice, case law; **herrschende ~** prevailing case law, ruling case(s); **höchstrichterliche ~** supreme court practice, precedents of the highest courts of the land; **nach der ~** as specified by the courts; **ständige ~** invariable practice, unchanged line of case law, continuous holding.

Rechtsradikaler *m* right-wing extremist.

Rechtsschutz *m* judicial relief, legal protection, protection of the law, legal redress, insurance for legal costs, **~anspruch** right to judicial relief, remedial right, right to legal and equitable relief, right to legal redress; **~bedürfnis** requirement to seek judicial relief; **~begehren** petition for relief by the court, the relief sought; **~interesse** legitimate interest in the proceedings; **~versicherer** insurer for legal costs and expenses; **~versicherung** legal expenses insurance, insurance for legal costs, **gewerblicher ~** industrial property law, legal protection of industrial property rights, industrial property protection.

Rechtsüberholen *n* overtaking on the right.

Rechtsunterzeichner *m* person whose signature appears to the right, name on the right.

Rechtsweg *m* legal process, recourse to the law, access to the courts (of law), resort to the courts, (*or to* litigation); **~entscheidung** decision as to the course of justice; **~garantie** guarantee of access to the courts; **den ~ ausschließen** to exclude (*or* oust) the jurisdiction of the courts; **den ~ beschreiten** to take legal measures, to go to law, to resort to litigation, to institute legal proceedings; **ordentlicher ~** resort to the general courts of law; **unter Ausschluß des ~s** any recourse to courts of law being excluded.

rechtzeitig *adj* timely, *adv* in due

Rechtzeitigkeit

time, (just) in time, on time, in good time.
Rechtzeitigkeit *f* timeliness.
Redaktion *f* editing; editorial department, editorial staff; production department (*television*), production team.
Redaktions|ausschuß drafting committee, editorial committee; **~geheimnis** right of editor not to disclose his source of information, editor's privilege, editor's right to refuse testimony; **~gemeinschaft** editorial pool, joint editing; **~schluß** editorial deadline; **~schwanz** editorial comment added to a published counter-statement; **~stab** editorial staff, editors; **~statut** editorial regulations.
Rede|freiheit liberty of speech, freedom of speech, liberty of discussion; **~zeit** speaking time.
Rediskont *m* rediscount; **r~fähig** eligible for rediscount; **~fazilität,** discount window; **~kontingent** rediscount quota; *freies ~~:* unused *rediscount quota*; **~kredit** rediscount credit, rediscounting; **~linie** rediscount line; **~papier** rediscountable paper; **~plafond** rediscount quota, rediscount line; **~satz** rediscount rate; **~titel** rediscounted bill; **~zusage** undertaking to rediscount, rediscounting promise.
rediskontierbar *adj* rediscountable.
rediskontieren *v/t* to rediscount (= *re-discount*).
redlich *adj* honest, right-thinking *adv also:* in good faith.
Redlichkeit *f* honesty, fairness, good faith, probity.
Reede *f* roadstead, roads; **~hafen** open roadstead port.
Reeder *m* shipowner; **~haftpflicht** shipowner's legal liability; **~haftung** liability of shipowner(s).
Reederei *f* joint *ownership and operation of a ship* shipping trade, shipping business; shipping company, shipowning firm, shipping office, ship's office; **~betrieb** shipping

Refinanzierungsbank

business; **~flagge** house flag; **~leiter** manager of a shipping company; **~verband** chamber of shipping; **~vertrag** contract with the shipowner; **~vertreter** shipping agent (*abroad*).
Reexport *m* re-export (= *reexport*); **~verbote** prohibition of re-exporting.
Refaktie *f* allowance for loss, tret, payment for breakage, shrinkage.
REFA-Studie *f* time and motion study, works study.
Referat *n* report, paper; section, subject department, field of work; **~sleiter** head of a section, head of a (subject) department, head of division; **ein ~ halten** to deliver a paper.
Referendar *m* trainee lawyer, trainee in the judicial service.
Referendum *n* referendum.
Referent *m* subject specialist, head of section, reporter, rapporteur, reader of a paper; desk officer, specialist adviser; reporting judge; **~enentwurf** ministerial draft bill; **persönlicher ~** personal secretary, private secretary (*of a minister etc*).
Referenz *f* reference; **~jahr** basis year, year of reference; **~kurs** rate referred to; **~niveau** posted level; **~periode** period of reference.
refinanzieren *v/t* to refinance, to cover financing, to finance by recourse to other financial sources; to refund.
Refinanzierung *f* refinancing; cover financing; refunding; **~bei der Zentralbank** recourse to the Central Bank.
Refinanzierungs|bank refinancing bank; **~bedarf** refinancing requirements; **~hypothek** wraparound mortgage; **~kontingent** Central Bank assistance quota; **~kosten** costs of cover financing; **~kredit** covering credit, refinancing credit; **~limit** rediscount quota *at the Central Bank*; **~linie** rediscount line; **~quelle** source of funds to finance lenders; *letzte*

647

Reflation   **Regentschaft**

~~: *bank of last resort*; ~**zinssatz** rate of interest paid for (*bank's*) borrowed resources; ~**zusage** promise to provide refinancing (*or* covering) facilities.

Reflation *f* reflation.

Reflektant *m* interested party, prospective customer, prospective buyer, potential purchaser.

Reflexbewegungen *f/pl* reflex movement, *pl also*: automatism.

Reform *m* reform; ~**bewegung** reform movement; ~**en des Gesetzgebers** legislative reforms; ~**gesetz** reform law; ~**vorhaben** intended reform; ~**vorlage** reform bill; **durchgreifende** ~ radical reform; **überfällige** ~ overdue reform.

reformatio in peius worsening of sentence on appeal.

refundieren *v/t* to refund.

Refundierung *f* refunding.

Regal *m* prerogative right of use (*or* exploitation).

Regel *f* rule, guiding rule, canon, observance; ~**ausführung** standard design; ~**bedarf** regular maintenance required; ~**fall** normal case; ~**gebühr** standard fee; ~**lehrverpflichtung** minimum lecturing requirement; ~**lohn** normal wage or salary (*as basis of disability pension*); ~**leistung** normal (health insurance) benefits, normal allowance, ~**n der gesetzlichen Erbfolge** canons of intestate succession; ~**n der ordnungsgemäßen Bewirtschaftung** rules of goods husbandry; ~**n des Seerechts** sealaws; ~**satz** standard rate, regular maintenance-payment rate; ~**satzverordnung** ordinance on regular maintenance payment amounts (*for illegitimate children*); ~**strafandrohung** normal penalty provided by law; ~**studienzeit** standard length of university studies; ~**stundenmaß** regular number of lessons required of a teacher; ~**vorschriften** regulations; ~**wert** ordinary value, ordinary amount; **r~widrig** *adj* irregular; ~**widrigkeit** irregularity, violation of the rules; offence against the rules, contravention of the regulations; **anerkannte** ~**n der Technik** accepted engineering standards; **die** ~ **ist ausnahmslos** there is no exception to the rule; **diese** ~ **findet keine Anwendung** this rule does not apply; **e-e feste** ~ a firmly established rule; **e-e** ~ **aufstellen** to establish a rule; **in der** ~ as a rule; **sich an e-e** ~ **halten** to adhere to a rule; **strenge** ~ hard and fast rule.

Regelung *f* regulation, settlement, adjustment, ruling; ~ **der Grenzfrage** settlement of the border question; ~ **der Sprachenfrage** the rules governing the languages; ~ **des Verkehrs** traffic control; ~**sangebot** offer of settlement; ~**slücke** a gap *in the provisions of the agreement*; ~**sstreitigkeit** litigation about a (new) regulation; ~ **von Rechsstreitigkeiten** settlement of disputes; ~ **von Verbindlichkeiten** settlement of obligations; **abweichende gesetzliche** ~**en** (any) statutory regulations to the contrary; **abweichend von der früheren** ~ deviating from the former regulation; **befriedigende** ~ acceptable settlement; **bei der derzeitigen** ~ in the current system; **devisenpolitische** ~**en** arrangements on foreign exchange policy; **friedensvertragliche** ~ peace settlement; **gesetzliche** ~ statutory regulation, regulation by law, legal provisions; **gütliche** ~ amicable settlement; **vergleichsweise** ~ compromise, agreed settlement, negotiated settlement; **vertragliche** ~ settlement by (mutual) agreement, contractual determination, contractual rule.

regeln *v/t* to regulate, to settle, to put in order, to order, to regularize, to control, to arrange.

regelnd *adj* regulatory, regulative.

Regen *m* rain; **saurer** ~ acid rain.

Regent *m* ruler, sovereign, regent.

Regentschaft *f* regency, regentship; ~**srat** regency council.

648

Regenversicherung f rain insurance; ~**spolice** pluvius policy, rain insurance policy.

Regie f *econ* management, administration; job work; state control; ~**arbeit** scheduled work, *work for which time and materials are charged,* (building in) daywork; ~**betrieb** ancillary municipal enterprise, public undertaking, publicly owned and operated enterprise (*without independent legal status*); öffentlicher ~~: *publicly owned enterprise;* ~**investitionen** capital investment in publicly owned enterprises; ~**kosten** overhead costs, overhead expenses, administrative costs; working expenses; ~**verwaltung** excise office; ~**zettel** time sheet.

regieren *v/t* to govern.

Regierende *pl* (*die Regierenden*) the ins, the party in power, the governing party.

Regierung f government, central government; the government of the country; reign, rule; **an die ~ kommen** to come into office; **aufständische ~** insurgent government; **auslaufende ~** outgoing government; **de-facto ~** government de facto; **de jure ~** de jure government; **derzeitige ~** government of the day, current government; **die neue ~** the incoming government; **die ~ bilden** to form the government; **die ~ stürzen** to overthrow the government; **die vertragsschließenden ~en** the contracting governments; **ersuchende ~** the requesting (= *requisitioning*) government; **ersuchte ~** the requested government; **parlamentarische ~** parliamentary government; **feindliche ~** hostile government; **provisorische ~** provisional government; **rechtmäßige ~** de jure government, legitimate government; **unterzeichnende ~en** signatory governments; **verfassungsmäßige ~** constitutional government.

Regierungs|abkommen executive agreement, intergovernmental agreement; ~**akt** governmental (*as distinguished from adminstrative*) act; ~**antritt** entry upon office; ~**apparat** government machinery; ~**aufsicht** governmental supervision, governmental control; ~**auftrag** government contract; ~**bank** front bench, treasury bench, ministerial bench; ~**beamter** government official; ~**beauftragter** state agent; ~**beihilfe** government grant, state grant; ~**bezirk** provincial administrative district; ~**bildung** formation of a government; ~**chef** head of a government; ~**delegation** government(al) delegation; ~**ebene** government level; ~**entwurf** ministerial bill; ~**erklärung** government statement of policy; policy statement of the federal chancellor (*or other head of government*) before parliament; **r~fähig** *adj* capable of governing, capable of forming a government; **r~feindlich** *adj* antigovernment; ~**form** form of government, government; *demokratische* ~~: *democratic government; parlamentarische* ~~: *parliamentary government;* ~**gebäude** government building; ~**gewalt** government power; ~**gutachten** expert opinion from the government side; ~**handlung** act of government; ~**haushalt** government budget; ~**käufe** government purchases; ~**koalition** government coalition; ~**konferenz** (inter)governmental conference; *zwischenstaatliche* ~~: *intergovernmental conference;* ~**kreise** governmental circles; ~**krise** governmental crisis; ~**kunst** statesmanship; ~**lager** government camp; ~**maßnahmen** governmental measures; ~**mehrheit** governmental majority, majority sufficient to form the government; ~**mitglied** member of the government; government minister; ~**organ** government agency, government body; official newspaper (*representing the government's policy*); ~**partei** party in power, governing

Regime

party; ~**partner** partner in a coalition government; ~**politik** governmental policy, policy of the government; ~**präsident** president of the regional administration; ~**programm** government programme; ~**sitz** seat of government; ~**sprecher** government spokesman; ~**stelle** government office; ~**sturz** fall of the government; ~**system** governmental system; system of government, form of government; r~**treu** *adj* loyal to the government, loyalist; ~**übereinkommen** intergovernmental agreement; ~**übernahme** coming into power, coming into office; ~**umbildung** government reshuffle; ~**vereinbarung** intergovernmental arrangement; ~**verlautbarung** government announcement; ~**vertreter** government representative; ~**vertretung** government mission, government representatives; ~**vizepräsident** vicepresident of regional state administration; ~**vorlage** government bill, *pl also*: government business; ~**wechsel** change of government; ~**zeit** term (*or* period) of government, regency, regnal years, regime.

Regime *n* regime; **autoritäres** ~ authoritarian regime; **totalitäres** totalitarian regime.

Regional|**bank** regional bank, provincial bank; ~**börse** provincial exchange; ~**clearing** provincial clearing; ~**organisation** regional multistate organization; ~**politik** regional policy; ~**planung** town and country planning; regional development policy; ~**presse** regional press; ~**sender** local channel station; ~**verband** regional association; ~**wirtschaft** regional economic situation.

Regionalisierung *f* regionalization.

Regisseur *m* director.

Register *n* register, registry; ~**abschrift** copy of a register entry; *beglaubigte* ~~: *certified copy from the register*; ~**auszug** abstract

Regreß

from a register; ~**beamter** registry official; ~**behörden** registry authorities; ~**brief** *naut* certificate of registry, registration certificate; ~**buch** docket; register folio; ~ **der Grundstücksbelastungen** register of charges, ~ **der Rentenschulden** register of annuities; ~**einsicht** inspection of the register; ~**eintragung** entry in the register, registration; ~**führer** registrar, employee in charge of a register; ~**gebühr** registration fee, registration charge; ~**gericht** registry court; ~**hafen** port of registry; ~**nummer** registry number; ~**pfandrecht** registered lien; *lien which comes into existence by public registration*; ~**richter** judge in charge of the Court Registry, Section; ~**sache** case in a registry court; ~**tonne** register ton; ~**vorschriften** registry rules; **im** ~ **löschen** to strike off the register, to cancel in the register, to deregister; **öffentliches** ~ public register, public book; **zum** ~ **anmelden** to apply for registration, to file for registration, to register.

Registrator *m* filing clerk, recorder.

Registratur *f* filing department, archives; ~**beamter** file clerk, filing officer.

registrieren *v/t* to register, to record.

registrierfähig *adj* recordable.

Registrierkasse *f* cash register; ~**ndiebstahl** till tapping.

Registrierung *f* registration, recording; ~**szwang** compulsory registration; **internationale** ~ **von Übereinkünften** registration of conventions.

Reglement *n* regulations, rules.

reglementieren *v/t* to regulate, to put under control, to regiment.

Regreß *m* recourse, remedy over; ~**anspruch** right of recourse; ~**anspruchsversicherung** recourse indemnity insurance; ~**forderung** claim of recourse; ~**klage** action for recourse; ~ **nehmen** to have recourse, to assert a remedy over; ~**nehmer** person seeking recourse; ~**pflicht** liability to recourse; **r~pflichtig** *adj* liable to recourse; ~**pflichtiger** party liable to recourse, indemnitor; ~**prozeß** third party proceedings; ~**recht** right of recourse; ~**risiko** third party risk; ~**schuldner** party liable to recourse, indemnitor; ~**verzichtsvereinbarung** knock-for-knock agreement (*insurance*); **im ~weg** by recourse; **ohne ~** without recourse, no recourse.

regulär *adj* regular, normal, usual, standard.

Regulativ *n* means of regulation, regulating effect.

regulativ *adj* regulatory, regulative.

regulieren *v/t* to regulate, to adjust, to settle, to discharge; to regularize.

Regulierung *f* regulation, adjustment, settlement, discharge; **~ e–s Schadens** settlement of a claim, claim settlement; **~ e–s überzogenen Kontos** remittance of cover, **~ e–s Versicherungsfalles** claim settlement; **bei der ~** in process of adjustment; **pauschale ~** global settlement, flat-rate settlement.

Regulierungs|abkommen settlement agreement; ~**beamter** settling official, claim adjuster; ~**beauftragter** claim adjuster; ~**kosten** costs of the claim settlement; ~**verhandlung** negotiation for the disposal of a damage claim (with an insurance company).

Rehabilitand *m* person on a rehabilitation scheme.

rehabilitieren *v/t* to rehabilitate.

Rehabilitierung *f* rehabilitation, personal discharge; ~**chance** opportunity to wipe the slate clean; ~ **von Aktien** restoring shares to their former standing; **berufliche ~** vocational rehabilitation.

rei vindicatio *f* (=) *action for recovery of property*.

Reibung *f* friction; ~**sverlust** loss as a result of friction; **wirtschaftlicher ~skoeffizient** economic friction.

Reich *n* realm, empire, (German) Reich.

Reichs|abgabenordnung German Tax Code; ~**gericht** *hist* Supreme Court of the German Reich; ~**konkordat** *hist* the Reich Concordat (*1933 with the Holy See*); ~**leistungsgesetz** Reich Requisition Law (1939); ~**präsident** President of Germany, Reich President; ~**recht** (*pre–1945*) national law of Germany; ~**tag** *hist* German Diet, Reichstag; ~**verfassung** Constitution of the German Reich (1871–1945); ~**versicherungsordnung** (*RVO*) German National Insurance Code.

Reifen *m* tyre (= *tire US*); ~**panne** flat tyre, puncture; ~**profil** tread; **abgefahrene ~** worn-down tyres.

Reifeprüfung *f* school leaving examination (*qualifying for university admission*), „A" levels (*G.B.*); baccalaureate; ~**szeugnis** school leaving certificate (*at German secondary schools*), German secondary school diploma.

Reiheneckhaus *n* end-of-terrace house.

Reiheneigenheim *n* (individually owned) terraced house.

Reihenfolge *f* sequence, consecutive order; **~ der Eintragungen** order of registration, sequence of registrations; **~ der Indossamente** order of endorsements.

Reihenhausgruppe *f* terrace.

Reihenregreß *n recourse against other parties of a bill in consecutive order*.

Reihenrückgriff *m* recourse in order of endorsers.

Reimport *m* reimportation.

Rein|dividende dividends net; ~**einkommen** net income; **~~ nach Steuern**: *net income after taxes*; ~**erlös** net proceeds; ~**ertrag** net yield, net proceeds, net revenues, net balance, net profits; **~~ der Gesamtrechnung**: *overall net surplus*: **jährlicher ~~**: *net annual proceeds*; ~**gewicht** net weight; ~**gewinn** net profits, net gain, surplus profit, surplus earnings, operating surplus; **unverteilter ~~**: *unappropriated surplus, undistributed net income*;

~**nachlaß** residuary estate, net estate; ~**schrift** fair copy, engrossment; ~**überschuß** net surplus; ~**verdienst** net earnings; ~**verlust** net loss; ~**vermächtnis** residuary gift; ~**vermögen** net assets, net worth; **r**~**waschen** v/t to clear, to whitewash; **r**~**zeichen** v/t to sign clear (*bill of lading*).
Reinheitsgebot *n* "purity commandment" (*German beer*).
Reinigungseid *m* purgative oath.
reinvestieren v/t, v/i to reinvest, v/t to plough (*US: plow*) back earnings.
Reinvestierung *f* reinvestment, plough-back (*US: plow-back*).
Reinvestition *f* reinvestment.
Reise|agent travel agent; ~**agentur** travel agency; ~-**Akkreditiv** traveller's letter of credit; ~**andenken** travel souvenirs; ~**ausweis** traveller's identification card, passport; *pl also*: travel documents; ~**bedarf** articles of personal use of a traveller (*or tourist*); ~**beilage** travel supplement; ~**beschränkungen** travelling restrictions; ~**büro** travel agency; ~**bus** coach; ~**charter** voyage charter; ~**devisen** travel allowances in foreign currencies; ~**diplomatie** shuttle diplomacy, diplomacy by travel; ~**entschädigung** travel allowance; ~**erleichterungen** travelling facilities; **r**~**fähig** *adj* capable to travel, ready for sea; ~**gelder** travel funds; ~**gepäck** baggage, *US*: luggage, passenger's luggage, ordinary luggage; ~**gepäckdiebstahl** larceny of baggage (luggage), theft of luggage; ~**gepäckversicherung** baggage insurance, luggage insurance; ~**gesetz** Tourist Travel Act; ~**gewerbe** itinerant trade, itinerant occupation, trade with no fixed place of business; ~**gewerbebetrieb** itinerant business; ~**gewerbekarte** licence for an itinerant trade (*or occupation*), hawker's licence; ~**kosten** travel and subsistence expenses, travel expenses, out-of-town travel expenses; ~**kostenersatz** reimbursement of travel expenses; ~**kostenpauschale** travel allowance; ~**kostenvergütung** reimbursement of travel expenses; ~**kostenvorschuß** travel advance; ~**krankenversicherung** traveller's health insurance; ~**kreditbrief** worldwide letter of credit, traveller's letter of credit; ~**leiter** tour manager, local representative of tour operators; ~**mitbringsel** travel souvenirs and gifts; ~**muster** commercial traveller's sample; ~**paß** passport; ~**passagier** passenger; ~**police** voyage (*or* travel) policy; ~**prospekt** travel brochure, travel leaflet; ~**route** travel route, itinerary; ~**scheck** traveller's cheque (*US: check*); ~**schmuggel** smuggling by tourists; ~**sperre** travel ban; ~**spesen** travel expenses; ~**spesenabrechnung** statement of travel expenses; ~**spesenpauschale** travel allowance; ~**unfallversicherung** traveller's accident insurance; ~**unternehmen** firm of tour operators; ~**unternehmer** tour operator; ~**veranstalter** tour organizer; ~**veranstaltungsvertrag** package tour cotract; ~**vergünstigungen** concessionary travel facilities; ~**verkehr** travelling, passenger travel, tourist travel; ~**verkehrsbilanz** balance of travel transactions; ~**vermittler** travel agent; ~**vermittlung** arranging tourist bookings; ~**versicherung** travel insurance, voyage insurance, tourist policy; ~**versicherungspolice** travel insurance policy, tourist policy; ~**vertrag** tourist travel agreement, travel (tour) contract; contract of tourism; ~**vertragsgesetz** (*D 1979*) Travel Tour Contracts Act; ~**vertreter** travelling agent, travelling salesman; ~**weg** route, itinerary; ~**wetterversicherung** tourist weather insurance, insurance against bad weather on holiday; ~**zahlungsmittel** tourist's means of payment; ~**zeit** travel season, season of holiday travel,

tourist season; travelling time; ~**ziel** destination; ~**zuschuß** travelling allowance.

Reisender m (*der Reisende*) traveller, travelling agent, sales agent.

Reißwolf m shredder; ~**vernichtung** shredding.

Reitwechsel m fictitious bill, kite.

Reitweg m bridle-path, bridle-way.

Reizstoffsprühgerät n aerosol tear-gas projector, spray gun for irritant agents.

Reklamation f complaint, claim; ~**en entgegennehmen** to receive representations, to receive complaints; **berechtigte** ~ legitimate complaint, justifiable complaint.

Reklame f advertising, publicity, sales promotion; ~**anpreisungen** puffs, puffery; ~**artikel** advertizing article; ~**fachmann** publicity expert; ~**feldzug** advertizing campaign; ~**gegenstände** advertizing material; ~**preis** cut-rate price; ~**schild** advertizing sign; ~**schlepp** air-poster towing; ~**schrift** publicity pamphlet, advertizing letters, *pl also*: promotional literature; ~**- und Verkaufsberater** publicity and sales consultant; ~**wand** advertisement hoarding; ~**zettel** advertising leaflet, throwaway.

Rekommerzialisierung recommercialization.

Rekonstruktion f reconstruction, reorganization; ~ **e-s Verbrechens** reconstruction of a crime, re-enactment of a crime.

rekrutieren v/t to recruit.

Rekrutierung f recruitment, enlistment, enlisting.

Rekta|indossament restrictive endorsement (*prohibiting further negotiation*); ~**klausel** not-to-order clause, non-negotiable clause, non-negotiability notice; restrictive clause; ~**konnossement** straight bill of lading, non-negotiable b. o. l.; ~**lagerschein** non-negotiable warehouse receipt; ~**papier** instrument "not to order", unendorsable title, non-negotiable instrument, instrument in favour of a specified beneficiary only; ~**scheck** non-negotiable cheque, cheque payable only to named payee; ~**schuldverschreibung** registered debenture; ~**wechsel** non-negotiable bill of exchange.

Rektorenkonferenz f standing conference of German university presidents (*GB: vice-chancellors*).

Rekurs m recourse.

Relegation f expulsion (of a student).

relegieren v/t to expel (a student).

relevant adj relevant, pertinent, material, significant, appropriate.

Relevanz f relevancy, relevance, significance.

Religions|ausübung practice of religion; **freie** ~~: *freedom of worship*; ~**diener** minister of religion; ~**freiheit** religious liberty, religious freedom; ~**gemeinschaft** religious group, church; ~**gesellschaft** religious society; ~**mündigkeit** age of child's personal determination in religions and church matters; ~**recht** law of religious organizations; ~**unterricht** religious education, religious instruction; ~**wechsel** change of religion; religious conversion; ~**vergehen** offence against religious institutions; ~**zugehörigkeit** religious affiliation.

Reliquidisierung f restoration of liquidity.

Rembours m payment of overseas goods, documentary acceptance (*in foreign trade*), payment by means of a documentary acceptance credit, banker's acceptance; ~**akzeptkonto** documentary acceptance account; ~**auftrag** order to open a documentary acceptance credit; ~**benachrichtigung** documentary acceptance-credit advice; ~**ermächtigung** authority to open a documentary acceptance credit; ~**geschäft** documentary payment business, transaction based on documentary acceptance credit, financing by documentary acceptance credit (*overseas trade*); bill-of-lading financing; ~**kredit** documentary acceptance credit; ~**regreß** recourse by an endorser against prior endorsers (*bill of exchange*); ~**rückgriff** = ~-*regreß qv;* ~**schuld** debt under a documentary acceptance credit; ~**schuldner** debtor under a documentary acceptance credit; ~**stelle** agent for documentary acceptance credits; ~**tratte** documentary acceptance, documentary bill; ~**verbindlichkeit** indebtedness on documentary acceptance credit; ~**verschuldung** indebtedness on documentary acceptance credit.

Remedur *f* remedy, correction, redress.

Remisier *m* half-commission man.

Remittenden *pl* return copies, returns.

Remittent *m* payee of a bill of exchange; **fiktiver** fictitious payee; **gemeinsame** ~**en** joint payees; **unbenannter** ~ unnamed payee.

remittieren *v/t* to return (goods); to remit.

remonetisieren *v/t* to convert into money, to bring back into circulation (*coin*).

Remonetisierung *f* reconversion (of capital assets) into money, bringing back into circulation (*coin*).

Remonstration *f* remonstrance, formal protest, representation; ~**spflicht** public officer's duty to remonstrate (*with his superior against an unlawful measure*).

Remontage *f* re-erection of dismantled plant, re-assembly.

Rendant *m* accountant, treasurer.

Rendite *f* yield, return (*investment*), lucrativeness, income basis; ~**abstand** yield gap; *negativer* ~~: reverse yield gap; ~ **auf eingesetztes Kapital** return on capital employed; ~**basis** profit basis, profitability; ~**gefälle** difference between yields, yield differential; ~**haus** tenement building, commercial property; ~**lage** position as to yield; ~ **nach Steuern** post-tax yield; ~**objekt** lucrative investment; ~**satz** rate of investment return; ~ **vor Steuern** pre-tax yield.

Renegat *m* renegade, turncoat.

Rennwett|steuer betting tax, racing tax; ~- **und Lotteriegesetz** Racing-Bets and Lotteries Act; ~- **und Lotteriesteuer** betting and lottery tax.

Rennwette *f* sweepstake, racing bet, bet on a race.

Renommee *n* reputation.

renovieren *v/t* to renovate, to overhaul, to redecorate (*rooms*), to refurbish, to restore to good condition.

Renovierung *f* renovation, refurbishment, redecoration; ~**skosten** renovation expenses, redecorating expenses; ~**spflicht** (tenant's) obligations to redecorate.

rentabel *adj* profitable, paying, lucrative, worthwhile.

Rentabilität *f* profitability, earning power, earning capacity, lucrativeness.

Rentabilitäts|analyse return analysis, yield analysis, analysis of profits; ~**berechnung** profitability calculation, estimate of prospective profits, cost accounting; ~**gesichtspunkte** considerations of profit, profit aspects; ~**grenze** break-even point, limit of profitability, marginal profit; ~**interesse** need to ensure a yield; ~**rechnung** profitability accounting, calculation of the net returns, ~**schwelle** lower limit of profitability, break-even point; ~**standpunkt** point of view of profitability.

Rente *f* pension, social insurance pension, contributory pension; periodical payment; annuity (from capital etc); *pl* bonds, fixed-interest securities (*exch*) *economics*: economic rent; **abgeleitete** ~ pension derived from another person; ~ **ohne Beitragspflicht** non-contributory pension; ~**haus** income property, tenement; **ablösbare** ~ redeemable annuity; **aufgeschobene** ~ deferred annuity, deferred pension; **dynamische** ~ (wage-) index-linked pension; **e-e** ~ **ablösen** to redeem

Rentenabfindung

an annuity; **e–e ~ kapitalisieren** to capitalize an annuity; **ewige ~** perpetual annuity; **kündbare ~** terminable annuity, redeemable annuity; **lebenslängliche ~** life annuity, life pension; **nachschüssige ~** ordinary annuity; **nicht ablösbare ~** irredeemable annuity; **sofort fällige ~** immediately payable annuity; **temporäre ~** temporary annuity; **unablösbare ~** irredeemable annuity; **unkündbare ~** non-terminable annuity, irredeemable annuity; **zeitlich begrenzte ~** annuity for a fixed term.

Renten|abfindung *lump-sum settlement in discharge of an annuity or pension claim*; ~**ablösung** redemption of an annuity; ~**alter** pensionable age, retirement age; ~**anleihe** annuity bond, consols; *unkündbare* ~~: *perpetual bond*; *irredeemable loan*; *pl also, funded debt*; ~**änderung** change of a pension; ~**anpassung** adjustment of pension (*to gross employment income*); ~**anpassungsgesetz** Pension Adjustment Act; ~**anspruch** pension claim; *unübertragbarer* ~~: *unassignable pension rights*; ~**anspruchsberechtigter** person entitled to a pension, annuitant; ~**anstalt** annuity credit institution; ~**antrag** application for a pension; ~**anwartschaft** accrued future pension rights, ~**aufbesserung** improvement in pensions, pension increase; ~**ausgleichsforderung** annuity equalization claim; ~**ausschuß** social insurance pensions committee; ~**automatismus** automatic character of (social insurance) pensions; ~**bank** *hist* central bank (*after World War I*); public mortgage bank, land annuity bank; ~**barwert** annuity discounted to reflect its cash value, present value of annuity; ~**beginn** initial date of pension payments; ~**behörde** pensions authority; ~**bemessungsgrundlage** basis for computing pensions; ~**berater** consultant on pensions; ~**beratung** consultation on pension rights; ~**berechnung** computation of pensions; ~**berechtigter** person entitled to a pension, grantee of an annuity; ~**bescheid** ruling on a pension application; ~**besteuerung** taxing of pensions and annuities; ~**beträge** amount of the annuity (*or* of the pension); ~**bezieher** recipient of a pension, pensioner; ~**bezug** regular receipt of a pension; ~*sberechtigung: entitlement to receive full pension benefits,* ~**bezugszeiten** periods of pension payments; ~**brief** annuity certificate, rent charge certificate, land annuity bond; ~**empfänger** recipient of a pension, pensioner, annuitant; ~**entziehung** forfeiture of a pension; ~**erhöhung** pension increase; ~**erwartung** probable future pension, expected pension; ~**fall** event when pension becomes due, pension case, *pl*: number of pensions awarded.; ~**fonds** fixed-interest security investment fund, bond fund (*US*); ~**gewährung** granting of a pension; ~**gut** estate charged with an annuity, farm for which purchaser paid by terminable annuity; ~**Kapitalversicherung** endowment insurance with life annuity option; ~**kurs** bond price; ~**lasten** annuity charge; ~**leistungen** pension benefits, annuity payments; ~**markt** bond market, gilt-edged market; ~**mehrbetrag** pension increase; ~**nachzahlung** supplementary pension payment, payment of pension arrears; ~**neurose** compensation neurosis, pension neurosis; ~**papier** fixed-interest security, bond; ~**pfändung** garnishment of pension; ~**police** annuity policy; ~**reallast** realty charge, land charge imposing recurrent obligations (*money, services, food etc*); ~**reform** reform of social security pensions, pension reform; ~**rückforderung** repayment claim for pensions (*received without justification*); ~**schein** annuity certificate; ~**schenkung** gift of annuity rights

rentieren | **Repräsentant**

(*or* pension rights); ~**schuld** annuity charge (on land), annuity land charge; ~**schuldbrief** annuity-charge certificate; ~**schuldforderung** indebtedness in respect of an annuity charge; ~**schuldgläubiger** holder of an annuity charge; ~**schuldverschreibung** annuity bond; ~**splitting** splitting future accrued pension rights (*upon divorce*); ~ **umstellen** to recalculate pensions; ~**umstellung** conversion of social security pensions (*currency reform*); ~**- und Unterstützungszahlungen** pension and social assistance benefits, public transfer payments; ~**urteil** judgment for periodical payments; ~**verschreibung** annuity bond; ~**versicherung** pension insurance fund, social pension insurance; ~~ *der Angestellten: Salaried Employees' Pension Insurance*; ~~ *der Arbeiter: Wage Earners' Pension Insurance*; *gesetzliche* ~~: *national pension insurance scheme*; *knappschaftliche* ~~: *miners' pension insurance*; *soziale* ~~: *social (national) pension insurance*; ~**versicherungsträger** pension insurance institution; ~**vertrag** contract of annuity; ~**vorschußzahlung** advance payment of retirement pension; ~**wert** fixed-interest security, bond; ~**zahlung** pension payment, pension benefit, annuity payment; ~**zusammensetzung** elements of a pension; ~**zuschußkasse** supplementary pension fund.

rentieren *v reflex* to yield a surplus, to be profitable, to be worthwhile, to "pay off"; **sich gerade noch** ~ to break even.

Rentner *m* pensioner, social-insurance pensioner, holder of pension rights; ~**krankenversicherung** social health insurance for pensioners.

Renvoi *m* renvoi; *return-reference to another country's law, referring back to the law of the forum* (*Conflict of Laws*).

Reparatur *f* (*pl Reparaturen* = ~**en**) repair, repairing, repair work; ~**auftrag** repair order; **r~bedürftig** *adj* in need of repair, in want of repair; ~**bedürftigkeit** disrepair; ~**kosten** cost of repairs, repair(ing) charges; ~**leistung** performance of repair services; ~**schein** repair ticket; ~**vertrag** contract for repairs; ~**werkstatt** repair shop, repair workshop; **in** ~ under repair; **bauliche** ~**en** structural repairs; **unentbehrliche** ~**en** necessary repairs; **laufende** ~**en** running repairs, regular repairs.

reparierbar *adj* repairable; **nicht mehr** ~ beyond repair.

reparieren *v/t* to repair.

repartieren *v/t* to apportion, to allot, to scale down an allotment.

Repartierung *f* apportionment, allotment, scaling down; **scharfe** ~ heavy scaling down.

Repartition *f* = *Repartierung qv*; ~**ssteuer** apportioned tax.

repatriieren *v/t* to repatriate.

Repatriierung *f* repatriation; ~ **von Auslandsbonds** repatriation of external bonds.

Repetitor *m* coach, tutor: *qualified person who coaches (law) students*.

Replik *f* (plaintiff's) replication (*to defendent's answer*).

replizieren *v/i* to reply, to make one's reply.

Report *m exch* contango, contango rate, continuation rate, carryover transaction; ~**geber** person carried over, buyer who pays to delay settlement; ~**geld** contango; ~**geschäft** jobbing in contangos, contango transaction, carry-over business; ~**kredit** loan for a contango transaction; ~**kurs** rate of contango; ~**nehmer** person carrying over; ~**prämie** contango; ~**satz** contango rate, rate of contango; ~**tag** contango day, making-up day, continuation day; **in** ~ **geben** to give in continuation; **in** ~ **nehmen** to take in contango.

Repräsentant *m* representative, resident agent; ~**enhaus** House of Representatives (*US*).

Repräsentanz f representative agency, representation.
Repräsentation f representation, status symbol.
Repräsentations|aufwendungen representational expenses, expenses for social representation, entertainment expenses; ~**gelder** allowance for social duties; ~**haftung** vicarious liability; ~**kosten** representational expenses, expenses of social representation, entertainment expenses; ~**pflichten** social functions, social responsibilities; ~**prinzip** principle of representation.
repräsentativ adj representative, typical, presentable, representational.
Repräsentativ|auswahl sampling; ~~ *nach Wahrscheinlichkeitsregeln: probability sample*: ~**erhebung** statistical sample, collection of sample statistics, sample investigation; ~**system** (system of) representative government; ~**umfrage** representative poll.
Repressalie f (act of) retaliation, reprisal.
Repressivaufsicht f remedial supervision (*by state over local an thorities*).
reprivatisieren v/t to denationalize (again), to reprivatize.
Reprivatisierung f reprivatization, restoration to private ownership, denationalization.
Reproduktion f reproduction; ~**srecht** right of reproduction.
reproduzieren v/t to reproduce, to duplicate.
Reptilienfonds m secret government funds, US: slush fund, secret service money; *funds at the disposal of the Chancellor for which no public accounting is required.*
requirieren v/t to requisition.
Requisition f requisitioning.
Requisitions|bescheid notice of requisitioning; ~**entschädigung** compensation for requisitioning; ~**recht** law of requisition, right of requisitioning; ~**schaden** damage caused by requisitions; ~**vergütung** compensation for requisition.

Reservat n reservation, reserved right; ~**srecht** prerogative right (*or* power); **alliierte** ~**e** matters reserved to the Allied Powers, (the Allies') reserved rights.
Reserve f reserve, reserve supply, reserve fund, reserve capital, reserve stock; ~**bank** reserve bank; ~**fonds** reserve fund, safety fund; ~**forderung** reserve claim; ~ **für besondere Fälle** contingency fund; ~ **für schwebende Versicherungsfälle** reserve for pending claims; ~**kapital** capital reserve(s); ~**klassen** reserve classes; ~**konto** reserve account; ~**meldung** reserve statement; ~**nabbau** reduction of the reserves; ~**n auffüllen** to replenish the reserves; ~**nausweis** reserve statement; ~**nbestimmungen** reserve requirements; ~**nbildung** accumulation of reserves; ~**n-Einsatz** reserves actually maintained; ~**nerhöhung** increase in reserves; ~**offizier** reserve officier, ~**satz-Staffel** reserve ratio scale; ~**-Soll** required reserve, reserve requirements; ~**stellung** allocation to reserve fund, reserve position; ~**überweisung** allocation to reserve fund; ~**vorschriften** reserve requirements; ~**währung** reserve currency; ~**währungsguthaben** reserve currency balance; **ausgewiesene** ~ disclosed reserve, visible reserve; **außerordentliche** ~ surplus reserve; **die angesammelte** ~ the reserve accrued; **freie** ~ excess reserve, available reserve; **gesetzliche** ~ legal reserve fund; **offene** ~**n** visible reserves; **remonetisierbare** ~**n** reserves capable of reconversion into money; **satzungsmäßige** ~ reserve required by the articles of association; **stille** ~**n** hidden reserves, latent reserves, hidden assets, undisclosed reserves.
reservieren v/t to reserve, to set aside, to make a reservation.
Resident m resident, permanent representative, minister resident.

Residenzpflicht residence requirement, obligation to reside within the precincts of the court (*of a lawyer*).
resignieren *v/i* to resign from office.
Resignation *f* resignation (from office).
Resolution *f* resolution; ~**sentwurf** draft resolution.
Resolutivbedingung *f* resolutory condition (*causing contract to lapse*), dissolving condition.
resozialisieren *v/t* to rehabilitate.
Resozialisierung social adjustment, rehabilitation and settlement, aftercare, resettlement of offenders.
Respekttage *m/pl* days of grace, days of respite (*for the payment of a bill of exchange*).
Ressentiment *n* sense of grievance, resentment, feeling of resentment, hard feeling.
Ressort *n* department, sphere of authority, purview, desk, division; ~**abkommen** interministerial agreement; ~**bedenken** departmental objections; ~**besprechung** departmental conference; ~**chef** head of department; ~**denken** thinking in terms of departmental interests; ~**egoismus** selfishness among governmental departments, excessive "compartmentalization"; ~**leiter** head of department, group executive; ~**minister** departmental minister; ~**politik** departmental policy; ~**prinzip** principle of departmental responsibility; ~**verteilung** distribution of responsibilities; ~**verhandlung** interdepartmental negotiation.
ressortieren *v/i* to be responsible for, to come within the scope of.
Ressourcen *f/pl* resources, economic assets.
Rest *m* rest, remnant, remainder, residue, residuum; ~**abgeltung** residuary discharge; ~**arbeitslosigkeit** residual unemployment; ~**ausfuhrzahlung** remaining export payment; ~**bestand** remaining stock, remainder, *pl also*: oddments; ~**betrag** balance, balance of an account, residual amount, remainder of an account; *noch nicht ausbezahlter* ~~: undisbursed balance; *geschuldeter* ~~: *balance due*; ~**buchwert** net book value, residual cost; ~**dividende** remaining dividend, liquidation dividend; ~**einzahlungsverpflichtung** remaining calls, contingent liability in respect of unpaid portion, uncalled capital; ~**erwerbsfähigkeit** residual earning capacity; ~**forderung** residual claim, claim for the remaining balance, outstanding amount, unpaid balance; ~**gebührenanspruch** claim for the remainder of the fees; ~**gewinn** balance of profit; ~**größe** residual amount, residue; ~**gut** remnants of an estate; ~**guthaben** remaining credit balance; ~**kapital** residual capital; ~**kaufgeld** → *Restkaufgeld*; ~**kaufhypothek** purchase money mortgage, vendor's lien; ~**laufzeit** remaining term, unexpired remainder; residual term; ~**lebensdauer** remaining useful life; ~**lieferung** back order; ~**masse** residual (*or* remaining) assets and liabilities; ~**nachlaß** residuary estate, residual estate; *zum* ~~: *rechnen*: *to carry to residue*; ~**nutzungsdauer** remaining useful life, remaining service life; ~**parkzeit** remaining parking time; ~**partie** odd lot; ~**posten** residual item, remainders; job lot; ~**profiltiefe** residual depth of tread; ~**prozeß** residue of action (*after part-judgment*); ~**quote** residual quota, final payment, final dividend; ~**risiko** inherent residual risk (*of technical defect*); ~**saldo** remaining balance; ~**schuld** residual debt, balance owing *pl also*: surviving debts; ~**versicherung**: *residual mortgage debt (life) insurance*; ~**strafe** unserved portion of the penalty, remainder of the sentence; ~**summe** balance, remainder, balance account; ~**urlaub** residual leave; remainder of holiday, holiday left over; ~**vermächtnis** residuary gift; ~**vermögen** residual assets; *mein*

Restanten

~~: *the entire balance of my estate;* ~**wert** residual value, salvage value, value after depreciation; *kalkulatorischer* ~~: *calculated residual value;* ~**wirtschaft** rump economy; ~**zahlung** final payment, payment of the balance; **nicht aufteilbarer** ~ residue.

Restanten *m/pl* leavings, odd lots, dead stock, drawn bonds which have not been collected; delinquent debtors.

Restehändler *m* seller of remnants, *exch* piece broker.

Resteverkauf *m* sale of remnants.

restitutio in integrum (=) restoration to the previous condition; *(with respect to lapse of statutory period, on the grounds of force majeure etc).*

Restitution *f* restitution, restoration of property; **äußere** ~ external restitution.

Restitutionsanspruch claim for the restitution (of property), ~**grund** fatal error; harmful error (giving entitlement to a new trial); ~**klage** proceedings for restitution (*new trial*); ~**recht** law of restitution, petition for a new trial; ~**schaden** restitution damage: *losses due to restoration of property under the Restitutions Acts.*

Restkaufgeld *n* balance of purchase price, residual purchase money; ~**darlehen** residual purchase-money loan; ~**hypothek** purchase-money mortgage, mortgage to secure balance of purchase price; ~**obligation** purchase-money bond; ~**rente** purchase annuity; ~**schuldschein** purchase-money note.

Restriktion *f* restriction; ~**smaßnahmen** restrictive measures; **quantitative** ~ quota, restrictive quota.

Retentionsrecht *n* right of retention, possessory lien.

Retorsion *f* retorsion (= *retortion*), retaliation, reprisal, tit-for-tat; ~**szoll** retaliatory tariff, duty of retortion.

Revier

Retortenbaby *n* test tube baby.
Retourenbuch *n* returns-book.
Retourewaren *f/pl* goods returned.
Retrozedent *m* retrocedent, reassignor.
retrozedieren *v/t* to retrocede, to assign back.
Retrozession *f* retrocession, reassignment; ~**svertrag** retrocession agreement.
Retrozessionar *m* retrocessionary; *the original assignor to whom a right is reassigned.*

Rettungs|**aktion** rescue operation, bailout; ~**bohrung** rescue shaft, escape shaft; ~**dienst** life saving service, rescue service; ~**fonds** bailout fund; ~**geld** salvage-money; ~**mannschaft** rescue party, search party; ~**weg** (way to an) emergency exit, fire exit; ~**wesen** rescue services, life-saving.

Reue *f* remorse, repentance, contrition; **tätige** ~ active regret, active repentance (*coupled with a timely attempt to avert the consequences of the act*); ~~ *bei Falschaussage: timely correction of false statements.*

Reugeld *n* forfeit-money.

revalidieren *v/i* to become operative again, to become valid again.

Revalierung *f* cover, recourse; ~**sanspruch** right of indemnity; *claim of a drawee against maker of a bill of exchange; claim of surety who has discharged the obligation against the debtor;* ~**sgeschäft** covering transaction; ~**sklage** action for indemnity (*of drawee against maker of a bill of exchange or of surety against original debtor*).

revalorisieren *v/t* to revalorize (currency etc).

Revalorisierung revalorization.

Revaluation *f* revaluation.

Revers *m* written undertaking, release, acknowledgement.

revidieren *v/t* to revise, to review.

Revier *n* police district, *US*: police precinct; mining district, forestry district; ~**inhaber** district forestry officer; ~**verwaltung** district forestry office.

659

Revindikation revindication, action for the return of property.

revindizieren *v/t* to revindicate.

revisibel *adj* appealable (on points of law).

Revisibilität *f* appealabilty (on points of law), suitability for writ of certiorari (*US*).

Revision *f* (1) appeal on points of law, proceedings in error, writ (*now GB*: order) of certiorari, writ of error, assignment of errors; ~ **einlegen** to lodge an appeal on points of law; **die ~ zulassen** to grant leave to appeal on points of law; **die ~ ist zulässig** leave to appeal on questions of law is granted, an appeal on points of law shall lie.

Revision *f* (2) auditing, accounting control; ~**sabteilung** auditing department; ~**sgesellschaft** auditing company; ~**sklausel** revision clause; ~**sverband** association of auditors; ~**sverfahren** auditing procedure, auditing methods; **außerbetriebliche ~** external audit; **betriebsinterne ~** internal audit; **innerbetriebliche ~** internal audit.

Revisionismus *m* revisionism.

Revisions|antrag motion for judgment in an appeal (on points of law); ~**anwalt** lawyer specialized in appeals on points of law, counsel admitted to the German Supreme Court; ~**begründung** grounds for appeal (on points of law); ~**begründungsfrist** time for filing grounds for appeal (on points of law); ~**begründungsschrift** brief containing the grounds of appeal on points of law; ~**beklagter** respondent in an appeal on points of law; ~**beschluß** order granting leave to appeal (on points of law), order of certiorari, writ of certiorari; ~**beschwerde** appeal on points of law against a court order; ~**entscheidung** appellate decision on points of law; ~**fähigkeit** appealability on points of law; ~**fehler** reversible error; ~**frist** statutory period for lodging an appeal on points of law; ~**gericht** final appeal court; court of last resort, ~**grund** reversible error, *reason on which appeal on points of law is based*; *absoluter ~~: fundamental error, automatic error*; ~**instanz** court of last resort, *instance where appeals on points of law are heard*; ~**kläger** appellant in; an appeal on points of law; ~**konferenz** revision conference; ~**recht** rules concerning appeals on points of law; ~**richter** appellate judge in error proceedings; ~**schrift** notice of appeal on points of law; ~**summe** minimum value of claim required for appeal on points of law; ~**zulassung** order granting leave to appeal on points of law; ~~*antrag: petition for leave to appeal.*

Revisor *m* auditor, revisor, chartered accountant.

Revolte *f* revolt.

revoltieren *v/i* to revolt.

Revolution *f* revolution; ~**sgericht** revolutionary tribunal; ~**sregierung** revolutionary government; ~**srat** revolutionary executive committee.

Revolving-Akkreditiv *n* revolving letter of credit.

Revolving-Kredit *m* revolving credit, revolving fund.

Rezensent *m* (book)reviewer.

Rezept|gebühr (nominal) prescription charge; ~**pflicht** obligation to present a prescription (*when buying medicine*); **r~pflichtig** *adj* obtainable only on prescription.

Rezeption *f the gradual taking-over of a foreign system of law esp. of the Roman law;* reception desk.

Rezession *f* recession, slump.

Reziprozitätsgeschäft reciprocal transaction, reciprocal deal.

Reziprozitätsrückversicherung reciprocal reinsurance.

R-Gespräch *n* reverse charge call.

Rheinschiffahrt *f* navigation on the Rhine; ~**sgericht** Navigation on the Rhine Tribunal; ~**ssachen** cases involving navigation on the Rhine.

Richt|geschwindigkeit recommended speed, posted advisory speed, maximum advisory speed; ~**kosten** standard cost; ~**kurs** reference rate; ~**linie** → *Richtlinie*; ~**maß** nominal dimension, standard; ~**menge** target figure, prescribed quantity; ~**preis** leading price, recommended retail price, suggested price, target price, provisional price; *empfohlener* ~~: *recommended retail price*; ~**punkt** aiming point, point of alignment; ~**satz** → *Richtsatz*; ~**schnur** guide-line, guide, guiding principle, canon; ~**strahl** directional beam; ~**wert** standard value, guiding figure, approximate-value production standard, reference point; ~**zahl** guiding figure, governing figure, index figure.

richten *v/i* to judge, to sit in judgment, to adjudicate, to adjudge, to sentence judicially.

Richter *m* judge *pl* the judiciary; ~**ablehnung** objection (*or* challenge) to a judge; ~**amt** judgeship, office of (a) judge, justiceship, judicial function; ~**amtsbezeichnungen** official designations of judges; ~**anklage** impeachment of a judge; ~ **auf Lebenszeit** judge for life; ~ **auf Probe** judge on probation; ~**bank** judge's seat, judgement seat, bench; ~**bestechung** bribery of a judge, corruption of judges; ~ **der 1. Instanz** judge of the first instance, trial judge; ~ **der Rechtsmittelinstanz** appellate judge, judge ad quem; ~**dienst** judicial service; ~**dienstgericht** *disciplinary tribunal for judges*; ~**eid** judge's oath; ~**gesetz** Law on the Judiciary; ~ **in e-m Bürotermin** judge in chambers; ~**kollegium** the judiciary, a body of judges, the Bench; ~ **kraft Auftrags** commissioned judge; ~**rat** council of judges; ~**recht** judge-made law; case law; ~**schaft** the Bench, judiciary; ~**spruch** judgment, judicial finding, judge's decision, court ruling; ~**stand** judiciary, the Bench; ~**tag** (German) annual congress of judges; ~**vertretung** judges' representative body; ~**vorlage** case stated, *submitted by judges on their own motion*; ~**vorbehalt** requirement of judicial authority (*for searches, arrests*); ~**wechsel** change of judge (*during proceedings*); ~**wahlausschuß** electoral committee for judges; ~**würde** justiceship, dignity of a judge; ~**zimmer** chambers, the judge's office; **aufsichtsführender** ~ supervising judge; **ausscheidender** ~ retiring judge; **beauftragter** ~ commissioned judge, official referee; **beisitzender** ~ associate judge; **berichterstattender** ~ reporting judge (*preparing the judgment*); **dem** ~ **vorgeführt werden** to be brought before the judge; **e-n** ~ **ablehnen** to challenge a judge, to object to a judge; **erkennender** ~ trial judge; **ersuchter** ~ requested judge; **geistlicher** ~ ecclesiastical judge; **gerechter** ~ even-handed judge; **gesetzlicher** ~ legally competent judge; **im Bürowege entscheidender** ~ judge in chambers; **jmdn als** ~ **einsetzen** to appoint s.o. as a judge; **jmdn zum** ~ **ernennen** to appoint a person as a judge; **kommissarischer** ~ commissioned judge; **nebenamtlicher** ~ part-time judge; **ordentlicher** ~ regular judge; **parteiischer** ~ biassed judge, partial judge; **unvoreingenommener** ~ impartial judge; **vor den** ~ **bringen** to bring to justice, to take to court; **vorsitzender** ~ presiding judge; **zuständiger** ~ competent judge.

richterlich *adj* judicial, of a judge, adjudicative.

Richtfest *n* celebration of completion of the main structure, topping-out ceremony.

richtig *adj* correct; **sachlich** ~ correct in substance.

Richtigbefund certification of correctness; ~**anzeige** reconciliation statement.

richtigstellen *v/t* to rectify, to amend, to correct.
Richtigstellung *f* rectification; ~sbuchung (period-end) adjusting entry.
Richtigkeit *f* correctness, accuracy; **die ~ an Eides Statt versichern**, to assure the correctness in lieu of on oath; **die ~ der Abschrift wird beglaubigt** certified true copy, copy certified correct; **die ~ der Aussage bezweifeln** to doubt the truth of the testimony; **die ~ seiner Angaben beweisen** to prove one's statements to be true; **für die ~ der Abschrift** certified as a true copy.
Richtlinie *f* directive, guidance, guiding principle; ~nentwurf draft directive; ~n erlassen to issue directives; ~nkompetenz authority to decide on government policy, power to issue guidelines; ~n mißachten to defy the rulings; **allgemeine ~n** general policy; **e~e ~ erlassen** to issue a directive; **einheitliche ~n** uniform rules; **einheitliche ~n und Gebräuche** uniform customs and practice; **geeignete ~n** appropriate directives; **internationale ~n** international standards; **standesrechtliche ~n** code of professional conduct.
Richtpreis *m* recommended retail price; standard (agricultural) price.
Richtsatz *m* guiding rate, standard rate *pl also* comparative data; ~miete controlled standard rent; ~norm standard.
Richtung *f* direction; ~ **der Investitionen** aim of investments.
Richtungs|änderung change of direction; ~änderungsanzeige indication of change of direction; ~anzeige directional sign; ~anzeiger direction indicator; ~kampf struggle over policy.
Richtzeichen *n* directional sign.
Ries *n* ream (*paper*).
Riesenkredit *m* jumbo loan.
Rikambio *m* re-exchange; ~wechsel re-exchange bill, redraft.

Rimesse *f* re-exchange bill *by way of recourse on prior endorser*, remittance.
Rinderauftrieb *m* number of cattle coming onto the market.
Ring|bahn circular railway, circular tramline; ~straße ring road;, circular road; ~tausch exchange between several parties (*apartments*); ~verkehr multilateral dealings.
Rinnverlust *m* leakage, allowance for leakage.
Risiko *n* (*pl Risiken* = ~*n*) risk, peril, adventure, jeopardy; ~abschätzung estimation of the risk; ~abwälzung shifting of risk; ~änderung change of the risk; ~aufklärung risk disclosure, advice on potential risk of an operation; ~ausgleich(ung) compensation of risks, risk sharing; ~auslese selection of risks; ~ausschluß exclusion of risks; ~~ **bei Gebäudeeinsturz**: fallen building clause; ~ausschlußklausel excepted perils clause; ~beginn commencement of risk; ~begrenzung limitation of risks; ~begrenzungsklausel limitation of risks clause; ~beherrschung risk management; **r~bereit** *adj* prepared to take a risk; ~beseitigung elimination of risks; ~deckung covering a risk, insuring against a risk; ~erhöhung added peril; ~garantie indemnity; ~geschäft speculative enterprise; ~gruppe special risk category (*or* group); ~haftung liability for risk; ~häufung accumulation of risks; ~-Investition investment at risk, investment in venture capital; ~kapital risk capital, venture capital; ~lebensversicherung term policy; ~marge risk margin; ~mischung spreading of risks, diversification of risk; ~patient patient at risk, patient in (a) critical condition; ~prämie risk premium; ~-Rückstellungen contingency reserves; ~schwelle point where risk begins; ~steigerung increase of hazard; ~streuung spreading of risks, diversification (of risk); ~summe amount at risk; ~träger

risk-bearer; **~tragung** bearing the risk, risk carrying; **~übergang** passing of the risk; **~übernahme** assumption of risk, taking risk, coverage; *volle* ~~: *full coverage*; **~übertragung** transfer of risk; **~umtauschversicherung** convertible term insurance; **~verbindung** linkage of risk; **~vergütung** compensation for the risk; **~versicherung** insurance, risk insurance; **~verteilung** allocation of risk, risk spread, diversification of risk, distribution of risk; **~vertrag** hazardous contract; **~zuschlag** risk markup, additional risk premium; **akutes** ~ immediate risk; **auf** ~ **des Käufers** at buyer's risk, let the buyer beware; **ausgeschlossenes** ~ risk excluded, hazard not covered; **außerökonomische** ~**n** non-economic risks; **berufliches** ~ occupational risk; **das** ~ **übernehmen** to assume the risk; **ein** ~ **auf sich nehmen** to run a risk; **ein** ~ **decken** to cover a risk; **ein** ~ **eingehen** to bear a risk; **ein** ~ **laufen** to run a risk; **ein** ~ **tragen** to incur a risk; **ein** ~ **versichern** to underwrite a risk, to insure against a risk; **erhebliches** ~ substantial risk; **erhöhtes** ~ aggravated risk; **gedecktes** ~ risk covered; **gewöhnliches** ~ normal risk; **handelsübliches** ~ customary risk; **kalkuliertes** ~ calculated risk; **kaufmännisches** ~ commercial risk; **mittleres** ~ median risk, average risk; **nicht versicherbares** ~ uninsurable risk; **nicht versichertes** ~ uninsured risk, uncovered risk; **nicht versicherungsfähiges** ~ uninsurable risk; **objektives** ~ actual risk; **ungedecktes** ~ uninsured risk; **unternehmerisches** ~ business risk; **unversicherbares** ~ uninsurable risk; **versicherbares** ~ insurable risk, fair risk; **versichertes** ~ insured risk; **wirtschaftliches** ~ commercial risk.

ristornieren *v/t* to reverse an erroneous entry, to cancel by making a contra-entry.

Ristorno *n* reverse of an erroneous entry, cancellation by making a contra-entry.

Ritter|dienste knight service; **~gut** manor, nobleman's estate; **~gutsbesitzer** lord of the manor; **~kreuz** Knight's Cross; **~schaft** knights, knighthood; **~stand** knighthood, rank of a knight.

Ritual|gesetze ritual law; **~mord** ritual murder.

Robe *f* gown, robe.

Roboter *m* robot; **~einsatz** robotization, use of robots.

Rodung *f* clearing woodland, cleared woodland, clearing; **~sprämie** bonus for uprooting.

Roh|bau → *Rohbau*; **~betrag** gross amount; **~bilanz** rough balance, trial balance; **~entwurf** rough sketch, rough draft; **~energie** basic energy; **~ertrag** gross surplus, gross proceeds; **~gewicht** gross weight; **~gewinn** gross profits, balance of profits and gains; ~~*quotient*: *gross profit ratio*; **~material** raw material, bulk material, raw materials; **~produkt** prime product, raw product, rude produce; **~stoff** → *Rohstoff*; **~überschuß** gross surplus; **~vermögen** gross assets; **~verlust** gross loss.

Rohbau *m* bare structure, shell of a building; **~abnahme** acceptance of the structural work of a builder; **~gewerbe** building trade excluding finishing work; ~ **ohne Ausbau** bare construction without finishing work; **im** ~ **fertiggestellt** structurally complete.

Röhrchen *n* test tube; „*ins Röhrchen blasen*": *to take a breath test, to take a breathalyzer test, "to blow into the bag"*.

Rohrfernleitung *f* pipeline.

Rohrpost *f* pneumatic post, pneumatic dispatch.

Rohstoff *n* raw material(s), primary product(s); *Roh-, Hilfs- und Betriebsstoffe*: *raw materials and supplies*; **~abkommen** commodity agreement; **~-Ausgleichslager** buffer stocks of primary products;

Rollfeld

~**gewinnungsbetrieb** extractive enterprise; ~**handel** trade in raw materials, commodity trade; ~**hortung** stockpiling of raw materials; ~**kreditermächtigung** raw material credit authorization; ~**notierungen** commodity prices; ~**quellen** natural resources; ~**stadium** raw material stage; ~**verein** co-operative society for combined purchases of raw materials; ~**versorgung** supply of raw materials; ~**vorkommen** raw materials deposits; **agrarisch erzeugte** ~**e** agricultural produce, industrial crops; **gewerbliche** ~**e** industrial raw materials; **inländische** ~**e** home-produced raw materials; **internationale** ~**abkommen** world agreements on primary commodities; **nachwachsende** ~**e** industrial crops.

Roll|feld airfield, airstrip, taxistrip, taxiway, operational area of airport; ~**fuhrdienst** *collection and delivery service to and from railway freight depot*; ~**fuhrunternehmen** rail express agency, door-to-door service; ~**fuhrunternehmer** haulage contractor; ~**geld** charge for goods transport *to and from railway freight depot*; ~**gut** local freight, cases and casks, carted goods; ~**kommando** flying squad; flying pickets; ~**splitt** loose gravel.

Rolle *f* roll, scroll, register.

Rotwelsch *n* thieves' cant, thieves' latin, patter.

Routine|arbeit routine work; ~**untersuchung** routine check-up; *(med., jur.)* mundane test.

Rowdytum *n* vandalism, hooliganism.

Royalist *m* royalist, monarchist.

Royalismus *m* royalism, monarchism.

Rubrik *f* rubric, section of a newspaper, column, heading; **in** ~**en einteilen** to rubricate.

rubrizieren *v/t* to rubricate.

Rubrum *n* recitals, title reference, heading (of a case), recital of parties, premises *(of a deed)*.

Rückabtretung

Ruchlosigkeit *f* heinousness, profanity, enormity (of a crime).

Rück|abtretung *(to)*; retrocession, reassignment, return-assignment, assignment back; ~**abtretungsempfänger** retrocessionary *(person to whom a claim is assigned back)*; ~**abwicklung** reversed transaction, finalizing a reversed transaction; ~**antwort** reply; ~**antwortkarte** reply-paid postcard, business reply card; ~**antwortschein** reply coupon; ~**auflassung** reconveyance *(to the original transferor)*, redemise; ~**äußerung** reply; ~**berufung** recall; ~**beziehung** retrospectivity, retrospective effect; ~**blick** retrospective view, review, look back; ~**buchung** contra-entry, reverse entry, cancellation by contra-entry, reversing entry; ~**bürge** counter-surety, surety for a surety, counter-guarantor, collateral surety; ~**bürgschaft** counter-suretyship, counter-guarantee, back-to-back guarantee; **r**~**datieren** *v/t* to backdate, to antedate; ~**datierung** backdating, antedating; **r**~**decken** *v/t* to cover, to reinsure; ~**deckung** covering, reinsurance, provision of cover; ~**enteignung** retro expropriation, expropriation for restitution purposes; ~**entflechtung** reversal of decartelization; ~**ersatz** reimbursement; **r**~**erstatten** to refund, to reimburse; ~**erstattung** → *Rückerstattung*; ~**fahrscheinwerfer** reversing light, *US*: backup light; ~**fahrt** return trip *(or* journey); ~**fall** → *Rückfall*; **r**~**fällig** *adj* recidivous, relapsing; ~~ *werden: to relapse*; ~**fälligkeitsquote** reoffending rate; ~**fälliger** *(m, der Rückfällige)* backslider, recidivist; ~**fälligkeit** recidivism; ~**flug** return flight, inward flight; ~**fluß** reflux, return flow; ~**forderung** claim for recovery; ~~**sklausel**: *recovery clause*; ~~**srecht**: *right to restitution*; ~**fracht** freight home, homeward freight, return freight, return car-

Rückabtretung   **Rückabtretung**

go; ~**frage** query, request for further particulars; ~**führung** → *Rückführung*; ~**gabe** return, redelivery; ~**gabenanordnung** return order; ~**gaberecht** return privilege; **r**~**gabepflichtig** *adj* returnable; **r**~**gängig** *adj* reversible; ~~ *machen: to cancel, to reverse*; *nicht* ~~ *zu machen: irreversible*; ~**gängigmachung** cancellation, reversal; ~**garantie** back-to-back guarantee, counter-guarantee; ~**gewähr** return, restitution; ~**gewähranspruch** claim for restitution; ~**gewährung** return, restitution; **r**~**gliedern** *v/t* to reintegrate, to reincorporate; ~**gliederung** reincorporation; ~**griff** → *Rückgriff*; ~**halt** backing, support, encouragement; ~**haltebecken** retaining reservoir; ~**holung** clawback (*tax*); ~**indossament** endorsement to a prior endorser; ~**kauf** → *Rückkauf*; ~**kehr** return; ~**kehrhilfe** repatriation grant; ~**kehrpflicht** obligation to return; ~**ladung** homeward freight, return cargo; ~**lage** → *Rücklage*; ~**lieferung** redelivery, return delivery, return shipping; mandatory return of a temporaily extradicted prisoner; ~**nahme** → *Rücknahme*; **r**~**nehmbar** *adj* withdrawable, returnable, redeemable; *nicht rücknehmbar: non-redeemable*; ~**pacht** leaseback; ~**porto** return postage; ~**prämie** put, put premium, premium for the put, money paid for the put option, seller's option to double; ~~ *kaufen: to give for the put*; ~~ *mit Nachliefern: put of more*; ~**prämiengeschäft** put option, option deal for the put; ~**rechnung** debit for returned item, re-exchange, return account, *receipt given to endorser for return of the bill*, back calculation (*blood alcohol*); ~**ruf**, return call, recall; manufacturer's recall of faulty products; ~**rufaktion** recall operation (*because of faulty parts*); ~**rufschreiben** letter of recall; ~**rufsrecht** (right of) stoppage in transitu, right of recall; ~**rufungsrecht** jus evocandi (*to require return of a national from abroad*); ~**schaffung** expenses of returning asylum seekers to their home country; ~**scheck** returned (dishonoured) cheque; ~**schein** recorded delivery form, return receipt, receipt of delivery, acknowledgment of service, proof of re-exportation; ~**schlag** setback, relapse; ~**schluß** inference, conclusion; ~**seite** back, rear, reverse, off board; *siehe* ~~: *see back, see over, see overleaf, for further details see back; p. t. o. = please turn over*; ~**sendung** return shipment, reconsignment, return cargo; ~~ *von Leergut: return of empties*; ~**sicht** → *Rücksicht*; **r**~**sichtslos** *adj* ruthless, reckless, wanton, inconsiderate; ~**sichtslosigkeit** recklessness, wantonness, ruthlessness, inconsiderateness; ~**spiegel** driving mirror, rearview mirror; ~**sprache** consultation, conference; ~~ *nehmen mit: to consult with, to check with, to confer with, refer back to*; ~**stand** → *Rückstand*; **r**~**ständig** *adj* overdue, unpaid, behind with one's payments; ~**standsanzeige** notice of arrears; ~**standsverzeichnis** list of arrears, list of outstanding debts; ~**stau** backlog; congestion of waiting vehicles; hold-up; **r**~**stellen** *v/t* to set aside, to reserve, to make allowance, to make provision (*for contingencies etc*); ~**stellung** → *Rückstellung*; ~**strom** reflux, flooding back; ~**stufung** down grading; ~**trag** carrying back, backdating (*in accounting*); ~**transport** back haul (*same route*); ~**tritt** → *Rücktritt*; ~**übereignung** reconveyance to the former owner, transfer of ownership back (*to*); ~**übernehmer** receiver of returned goods; **r**~**übersetzen** *v/t* to translate back (*into the original language*); ~**übersetzung** translation back (*into the original language*); **r**~**übertragen** to transfer back (*to*), to reconvey, to redemise, to reassign;

Rückerstattung

~**übertragung** transfer back (*to*); reconveyance, assignment; ~**umstellung** reversal of conversion; ~**verflechtung** recartelization; ~**verfolgbarkeit** traceability; ~**vergütung** reimbursement, refund, refunding, repayment, re-allowance, rebate, drawback (*customs*); r~**versetzen** to transfer back, to move back to the former position, to change to former status; ~**versetzung** transfer back, moving to former position, changing to former status; ~**versicherer** reinsurer; r~**versichern** to reinsure; ~**versicherung** → *Rückversicherung*; ~**verweisung** referring back, renvoi (*international private law*), recommitment (*committee*), remand, cross-reference; ~**wanderer** repatriate, person returning to his own country, returning emigrant; ~**wanderung** migration back (*to*), return migration; ~**waren** goods returned, returned goods; ~**warenbuch** purchase returns journal; ~**wärts**|... → *Rückwärts*|...; ~**wechsel** re-exchange bill (*drawn by holder of dishonoured bill on a prior endorser*); unpaid bill of exchange (*returned to customer of the bank*), protested bill (*or note*); ~**wechselkosten** bill-back charges; ~**weisung** final rejection (*quality testing*); r~**wirken** v/i to have retroactive (*or* retrospective) effect; r~**wirkend** *adj* retrospective, retroactive, nunc pro tunc, now for then; ~**wirkung** retroactive (*or* retrospective) force, retroactive effect, retroactivity; reaction, repercussion; r~**zahlbar** *adj* repayable; ~**zahlung** → *Rückzahlung*; ~**zoll** drawback, customs drawback (*upon re-exporting*); ~**zollgüter** debentured goods; ~**zollschein** customs debenture; ~**zug** withdrawal, retirement.

Rückerstattung *f* restitution; refund, reimbursement; ~ **in natura** specific restitution of property; ~ **von Vermögen** restitution of property (*or* assets).

Rückgriff

Rückerstattungs|**anspruch** claim for restitution; ~**berechtigter** restitutee, person entitled to restitution; ~**beschluß** restitution order; ~**gericht** Restitution Tribunal; ~**pflichtiger** restitutor; ~**recht** law of restitution, restitutory right; ~**schäden** losses due to restitution orders; ~**stück** restituted bond; ~**system** refund system; ~**verfahren** restitution proceedings; ~**vergleich** restitution compromise.

Rückfall *m* repeat offence, second and subsequent offence; recidivism; ~**diebstahl** larceny recidivism, stealing as a repeated offence; ~**hehlerei** receiving (*or* handling) of stolen goods as repeated offender; ~**kriminalität** recidivism; ~**schärfung** increase in penalty in cases of recidivism; ~**strafe** penalty for recidivism; ~**tat** repeated offence; ~**täter** repeat offender, second and subsequent offender, recidivist; ~**verjährung** limitation of time for aggravation due to recidivism (*5 years after previous offence*); ~**voraussetzungen** statutory requirements for recidivism.

Rückführung *f* repatriation, restoration, reduction of debt, feedback; ~ **von Kapital** repatriation of capital, return of capital.

Rückführungs|**aktion** reduction of debt scheme; ~**betrag** (amount of) reduction; ~**kontingent** quota of redemption, reduction quota; ~**kosten in die Heimat** passage home; ~**soll** desired quota of reduction (*of indebtedness*).

Rückgriff *m* recourse; ~ **auf den Indossanten** recourse to the endorser; ~ **auf die Reserven** drawing on reserves; ~ **mangels Annahme** recourse for non-acceptance; ~**mangels Zahlung** recourse in default of payment; ~ **nehmen** to have recourse to; ~**sanspruch** claim under a right of recourse; ~**sforderung** claim under a right of recourse; ~**shaftung** liability upon recourse; **mit**

Rückkauf

~~: *with recourse*; ~**smöglichkeit** recourse basis; ~**srecht** right of recourse, right of relief; ~**sschuldner** secondary party, party liable upon recourse.

Rückkauf *m* buy back, repurchase; redemption, ~**swert** policy value.

Rückkaufs|ankündigung notice of intention to redeem; ~**berechtigung** surrender privilege (life assurance); ~**fristen** periods for repurchase; ~**gesellschaft** repurchase company; ~**kurs** redemption price; ~**preis** redemption price; ~**recht** right to repurchase, right of redemption; ~**vertrag** repurchase agreement; ~**wert** surrender value (*of an insurance policy*), equity under the policy, redemption value (*securities*), paid-up value.

Rücklage *f* reserve, reserve fund; *pl auch*: surplus reserves, appropriated retained earnings; ~**guthaben** reserve balance; ~**nbildung** creation of reserves; ~**nkonto** reserve account; ~**nsatz** reserve ratio; ~**soll** required level of reserves; ~**vermögen** reserve assets, reserve fund property; ~**nzuweisung** allocation to reserves; **allgemeine** ~ general reserve, general purpose contingency reserve, unappropriated surplus; **außerordentliche** ~ extraordinary reserve; **freie** ~ free reserves, available reserve; **gesetzliche** ~ statutory reserve fund; *pl also*: *statutory reserves*; **offene** ~**n** disclosed reserves, published reserve funds, reserves shown on the balance sheet; **satzungsmäßige** ~ reserves required by the Articles (of Association); **stille** ~**n** secret reserves, hidden reserves; **versicherungstechnisch** ~**n** actuarial reserves; **zweckgebundene** ~ earmarked fixed-purpose reserve surplus.

Rücknahme *f* taking back, withdrawal, retraction, repurchase; ~ **der Anklage** withdrawal of the charge; ~ **der Berufung** withdrawal of appeal, abandonment of appeal; ~ **der Widerklage** discontinuance of counterclaim; ~ **des Rechtsmittels** abandonment of appeal; ~ **des Strafantrages** withdrawal of charges, withdrawal of petition for prosecution; ~ **e-r Klage** withdrawal of an action (*or* petition), abandonment of action; ~ **e-s Angebots** revocation of an offer; ~**garantie** repurchase guarantee; ~**kurs** redemption price, bid price; ~**preis** repurchase price, buy back price, redemption price; bid price (*investment*); ~**recht** right to the return of sth, right of redemption; ~**verpflichtung** obligation to repurchase (*or* buy back); ~**verzicht** renunciation of right to have deposit returned.

Rücksicht *f* respect, regard, consideration; **aus** ~ **gegen** in deference to; with respect to; **mit** ~ **auf** considering that, with regard to; **ohne** ~ **auf** irrespective of, regardless of, without consideration for; ~~~ *die Kosten*: *regardless of costs*; ~~~ *Dritte*: *independent of any other person*; ~~~ *etwa anderslautende vorstehende Bestimmungen*: *notwithstanding anything in the foregoing provisions*; to the contrary *ohne* ~ *darauf, ob versicherbares Interesse besteht*: interest or no interest.

rücksichtlich *prep* in view of.

Rücksichtnahme *f* (showing) consideration, (for), (due) respect (for).

Rückstand *m* backwardness; arrears; backlog; **im** ~ **sein** to be in arrears, to be behind, shortfall; leeway *Rückstände also*: residue, subsisting substances.

Rückstau *m* tailback.

Rückstellung *f* special (*or specific*) reserve, provision, special contingency reserve, set-aside, reserve fund, contingent fund, offsetting reserve; *pl also*: provisions for accrued liabilities; liability reserves, appropriated surplus, ~ **für Abschreibungen** provision for depreciation, allowance for depreciation, depreciation reserve;

Rücktritt

~en für Altersruhegeldverpflichtungen pension reserve; ~ für Betriebskostenmehrungen operating reserve; ~ für Devisenschwankungen allowance for exchange fluctuations; ~ für die Auffüllung des Lagerbestandes provision for stock replenishment; ~ für Dividendennachzahlungen reserve for deferred dividends; ~ für Dubiosen provision for doubtful accounts, doubtful debts provision, reserve for bad debts; ~ für Ersatzbeschaffung reserve for replacements; ~ für Kursverluste reserve for loss on exchange rates; ~ für Mietausfall allowance for loss of rent; ~ für Nichtvorhergesehenes reserve for contingencies, contingent reserve; ~ für Pensionsanwartschaften pension reserve; ~ für Prozeßkosten reserve for litigation costs; ~ für Ruhegehaltsverpflichtungen pension reserve; ~ für Schuldentilgung debt reduction reserve; ~en für Steuern amounts set aside for tax liabilities; ~ *für Steuern von Einkommen: provision for income tax*; ~ für strittige Forderungen claim reserve; ~ für Überalterung provision for obsolescence; ~ für Umstellungskosten reserve for conversion costs; ~ für uneinbringliche Forderungen bad-debt reserve; ~ für unvorhergesehene Ausgaben provision for contingencies; ~ für Verluste loss reserve; ~ für Wertberichtigungen revaluation reserve; ~ für Wertminderung der Vorräte reserve for inventory price decline; ~ für Wiederbeschaffung reserve for replacements; ~ für zweifelhafte Forderungen doubtful debts reserve; ~skonto reserve account, contingent account, appropriation account; ~~ *für unvorhergesehene Verpflichtungen; reserve account for unforeseen liabilities*; ~ wegen Erschöpfung von Bodenschätzen depletion reserve; e-e ~ bilden set up a reserve.

Rücktritt *m* resignation, retirement from office; withdrawal; abandonment of priority; ~ vom Versuch withdrawal from attempted crime, abandoning an attempt; ~ vom Vertrag repudiation of contract, revocation of contract, cancellation of an agreement, rescission of contract; den ~ anbieten to tender one's resignation.

Rücktritts|drohung threat of resignation; ~erklärung notice of repudiation of contract, notice of cancellation; announcement of resignation, letter of resignation; ~frist escape period, period allowed for cancellation; ~gesuch offer of resignation; ~klausel escape clause, cancellation clause; ~recht right of cancellation, right to withdraw from a contract, right to cancel an undertaking, right to repudiate a contract; ~verzichtklausel indisputability clause (*ins*); ~vorbehalt reservation of the right to cancel, escape clause.

Rückversicherung *f* reinsurance, reinsurance company; in ~ gegebene Versicherung policy covered by reinsurance; obligatorische ~ compulsory reinsurance; unkündbare ~ flat reinsurance, non-terminable reinsurance.

Rückversicherungs|anstalt reinsurance company; ~anteil reinsurance share; ~bestand reinsured business, reinsured portfolio; ~gesellschaft reinsurance company; ~konsortium reinsurance syndicate; ~makler reinsurance broker; ~option facultative reinsurance, reinsurance option; ~police reinsurance policy; ~prämie reinsurance premium; ~träger reinsurer, reinsurance company; ~vertrag contract of reinsurance, reinsurance agreement, Reinsurance Treaty (*Germany with Russia 1887*).

Rückwärtsversicherung insurance providing retroactive coverage.

Rückzahlung *f* repayment, refund; ~ e-r Anleihe repayment of a loan; ~ e-r Hypothek redemption of a mortgage; ~ **von Kapital** return of capital; **fristgemäße** ~ repayment on (*or* by) due date; **vorzeitige** ~ early repayment.

Rückzahlungs|agio premium payable on redemption, redemption charge; ~**anspruch** repayment claim; ~**frist** time for repayment, deadline for repayment; ~**gewinn** premium on redemption; ~**klausel** repayment clause, redemption clause; ~**kurs** redemption price; ~**pflicht** repayment obligation; ~**prämie** redemption premium; ~**provision** redemption commission; ~**tag** repayment date, day of redemption; ~**wert** redemption value.

Ruf *m* reputation; ~**ausbeutung** exploitation of the reputation of another; ~**mord** character assassination; ~**schaden** damage to reputation; ~**schädigung** damage to reputation, injurious falsehood; ~~ *e-s Konkurrenten: defamation of a competitor's reputation*; **guter** ~ good reputation; **makelloser** ~ spotless reputation, unblemished character; **schlechter** ~ bad reputation, disrepute.

Rufbereitschaft *f* being on call.

Rufname *m* Christian name, first name, given name.

Rüge *f* rebuke, reprehension, reprimand; objection, exception, plea; ~ **der mangelnden Substantiierung** application for further and better particulars; ~ **der Unzuständigkeit** jurisdictional plea; ~ **e-s Vorgesetzten** reprimand by a superior; ~**frist** time (limit) for claims; ~**obliegenheit** = ~*pflicht qv*; ~**pflicht** requirement to give notice of defects; ~**recht** right to make a claim (for defects etc), right to raise an objection.

rügen *v/t* to object, to reprimand, to rebuke, to criticise, to notify a defect, to censure, to denounce.

Ruhe *f* quietude, quiet, rest, (public) peace; ~**gehalt** → *Ruhegehalt*; ~**geld** → *Ruhegeld*; „~ **im Gerichtssaal"** oyez, order in the court room; ~**pause** break, rest period; ~**stand** → *Ruhestand*; ~**störer** disturber of the peace, rioter, disorderly person; ~**störung** breach of the peace, disorder, disturbance of (the) peace; *nächtliche* ~~: *disturbance of the peace at night*; ~**tag** day of rest, day off, closing day; ~**zeit** time of rest, rest period, off-season; public peace and order; **die öffentliche** ~ **stören** to break the peace; **öffentliche** ~ **und Ordnung** public peace and order; *die* ~~ *bewahren: to keep the peace*; **öffentliche** ~ **und Sicherheit** public peace (and quiet), the Queen's peace; **sich zur** ~ **setzen** to retire.

Ruhegehalt *n* pension, retirement pension, retired pay; ~ **wegen Dienstunfähigkeit** invalidity pension; ~**sanspruch** pension rights; ~~*e aberkennen: to deprive s. o. of his right to a pension*; ~**sberechtigung** entitlement to a pension; ~**sempfänger** pensioner; ~**sverlust** forfeiture of pension, loss of pension.

Ruhegeld *n* pension (money), retirement benefit; ~**anpassung** pension adjustment (to price level); ~**anwartschaft** future pension rights; ~**bezüge** retirement income; ~**empfänger** recipient of a pension, pensioner; ~**ordnung** pension scheme; *betriebliche* ~~: *company pension scheme*; ~**verpflichtung** pension liability; ~**versprechen** pension promise.

Ruhen *n* suspension, stay; ~ **der Verjährung** suspension (of the running) of time of limitation; ~ **des Anspruchs** suspension (*or* stay) of (the) claim; ~ **des Verfahrens** suspension of (the) proceedings; ~**svorschriften** legal provisions concerning the suspension of proceedings.

ruhen *v/i* to rest, to be inactive, to be dormant, to be suspended *v/t* to stay.

Ruhestand *m* retirement; ~**salter** retirement age; ~**sbeamter** retired

Rumpfgeschäftsjahr   **Rutschspur**

---

official, retired civil servant; ~**sversorgung** retirement pension; **einstweiliger** ~ provisional retirement; **in den** ~ **treten** to retire (on a pension); **in den** ~ **versetzen** to pension off, to be retired; **vorgezogener** ~ early retirement; **vorzeitiger** ~ early retirement.

Rumpf|geschäftsjahr short financial year, abbreviated financial year; ~**jahr** partial year, incomplete year; ~**parlament** rump parliament; ~**rechnungsjahr** part financial year, abbreviated financial year.

Rund|brief circular, circular letter; ~**erlaß** circular order; ~**erneuerung** retread, tyre reconditioning; ~**frage** enquiry by circular; ~**funk** → *Rundfunk*; ~**reisebillet** round trip ticket; ~**schreiben** circular letter; (office) memo (randum); ~**verfügung** circular order; ~**umverteidigung** all-round defence.

Rundfunk|anstalt radio station, broadcasting corporation; *öffentlich-rechtliche* ~~: *public broadcasting corporation*; ~**empfangsanlage** radio receiving installation; ~**recht** broadcasting legislation, law of broadcasting; ~**staatsvertrag** German (interstate) Broadcasting Convention; ~**werbung** radio and television advertizing.

Rüstungs|auftrag defence contract; ~**beschränkung** limitation of armaments; ~**betrieb** defence plant; ~**güter** armament supplies; *Verkauf von* ~~*n*: *defence sales*, sale of arms; ~**haushalt** defence budget; ~**hilfsaufträge** off-shore orders; ~**industrie** defence industry; ~**kontrolle** armament control; ~**produktion** arms production; ~**werte** defence stocks; ~**wirtschaft** defence economy.

Rutschen *n* skidding slipping, sliding.

rutschen *v/i* to skid, to slip, to slide.

Rutschspur *f* skid mark.

S

Sabotage *f* sabotage; **~abwehr** counter-sabotage; **~akt** act of sabotage; **~verdacht** suspicion of sabotage.

Sach|abweisung dismissal of action on the merits; **~anlage** real investment, material asset; *pl also*: (tangible) fixed assets, physical assets; buildings, plant and machinery; **~anlagevermögen** tangible fixed assets, physical assets; **~antrag** motion for judgment, substantive motion; *e-n ~~ stellen: to ask for relief*; **~aufklärung** clarification of the facts and circumstances; *weitere ~~: amplification*; **~aufklärungspflicht** duty (of the court) to clarify the case; **~aufruf** the calling of the case, calendar call; **~aufwendungen** expenditure on materials, expenditure in kind; **~ausgaben** expenditure on materials, expenditure in kind; **~ausschüttung** distribution in kind; **~bearbeiter** official (*or* employee) in charge (*of a matter*), subject specialist, person handling sth; partner concerned in the transaction (*law firm*); desk officer, executive clerk, executive officer; **~befugnis** entitlement to a cause of action; authority to claim; **~behandlung** handling, processing; **~bereich** field of jurisdiction, sphere, scope, purview; **~bericht** case report; **~beschädigung** damage to property; *vorsätzliche ~~: criminal damage (to property)*; **~bezüge** non-cash remuneration, remuneration in kind, benefits in kind; **~darstellung** statement of the facts; **s~dienlich** *adj* expedient, pertinent, suitable, relevant; **~dienlichkeit** expediency, pertinency, suitability, relevancy; **~dividende** property dividend, dividend payable in property, dividend in kind; **~eigentum** of property ownership; **~einlage** non-cash capital contribution, contribution in kind, contribution in kind; **~entscheidung** decision on the merits, substantive decision; **~entziehung** removal of property, deprivation of property; **~fahndung** tracing of stolen property; **~firma** firm (*or* company) name derived from the object of the enterprise, objective firm name; **~form** material form; **~frage** issue, question of merit; **~früchte** natural fruits; **~gebiet** subject, subject group, subject area, field of work, field of reference; **s~gemäß** *adj* appropriate (to the case), proper, suitable; **~gesamtheit** aggregate (of things), impersonal entity; **~geschädigter** person who has suffered property damage; **~gründung** formation of a company on the basis of non-cash contributions; **~gruppe** group of subjects, subject-category; **~güter** material goods, goods (*excluding services*); **~haftung** liability for risks arising from property; **~hehlerei** receiving stolen property; **~herrschaft** physical control; *uneingeschränkte ~~: quiet enjoyment of possession*; **~inbegriff** aggregate of things, entirety of things; **~investition** investment in physical assets, real investment; **~kapital** tangible fixed assets, capital stock, real capital; capital in kind; **~katalog** subject catalogue; **~kenntnis** expert knowledge, proficiency, knowledge of the facts; **~konto** impersonal account, nominal account; **~kredit** credit based on collateral security; **~kunde** special knowledge, technical competence, expert knowledge, professional expertise, expert skill, proficiency, *~~ nachweis: proof of basic business skills*;

angemessene ~~: *fair knowledge or skill*; *praktische* ~~: *practical knowledge*; *technische* ~~: *technical skill*; s~**kundig** *adj* proficient, skilled, expert, technically competent; ~**lage** factual position, state of affairs, position of the case, facts and circumstances; *nach* ~~ *entscheiden*: *to decide according to the present position of the case, to decide as matters stand*; ~**legitimation** legitimacy as the proper party; ~**leistung** non-cash benefit; performance in kind, benefit(s) in kind; ~**leistungsvertrag** contract for the supply of goods and services; ~**leitung** direction of the proceedings; ~**lohn** wages in kind, compensation in kind; ~**mangel** defect of quality, fault; ~**mängelhaftung** liability for defects, implied warranty for proper quality; ~**mittel** physical resources, non-monetary resources; ~**nähe** factual relationship; ~**nießbrauch** usufruct (of things belonging to another), perfect usufruct; ~**normen** provisions of substantive law; ~**normrückverweisung** renvoi; ~**patent** patent protecting a physical contrivance; ~**pfand** pledge of a chattel, chattel mortgage; ~**prüfung** examination of the case (on the merits), *pat*: substantive examination; ~**register** subject index; ~**rüge** assignment of error concerning substantive law; ~**schaden** property damage, damage to property, actual loss; ~**schäden-Haftpflichtversicherung** property-damage liability insurance; ~**schadensrisiko** property risk; ~**schadensversicherung** property (damage) insurance, material damage insurance; ~**schuld** obligation in kind; ~**steuern** impersonal taxes; taxes on objects; ~**substanz** physical substance; ~**übernahmen** related acquisitions in kind; ~- **und Rechtsvortrag** submissions of law and facts; ~- **und Streitstand** position of the stage of the proceedings; ~**urteil** judgment on the merits of the case; ~**verhalt** → *Sachverhalt*; ~**verhältnis** factual relationship; ~**vermögen** → *Sachvermögen*; ~**versicherung** property insurance, *pl also*: insurance companies other than life insurance companies; s~**verständig** *adj* expert, authoritative, competent; ~**verständigen**|... → *Sachverständigen*|...; ~**verständiger** → *Sachverständiger*; ~**verzeichnis** subject index; ~**vortrag** statement of facts, factual submissions, allegations; ~**wert** → *Sachwert*; ~**widrigkeit** impropriety, irrelevancy, unfitness for the particular purpose, incorrectness; ~**walter** agent, private attorney, administrator, trustee (*in composition proceedings*); ~**walterschaft** mandate, administration, trusteeship, procuracy; ~**wucher** usurious enrichment, predatory dealing; *gewerbmäßiger* ~~: *professional predatory dealing*; ~**zusammenhang** (factual) connection; ~**zuwendung** allowance in kind; ~**zwänge** factual restraints, compelling factual reasons.

Sache *f* (1) thing, physical object, res, *pl also*: things in possession; ~**nmehrheit** plurality of things; ~**nrecht** law of property, law of things, real law; **belegene** ~ property situate(d) at; **beschlagnahmte** ~ attached property (item); **bestimmte** ~ specific thing; **bewegliche** ~ movable, chattel, *pl also*: personal property, tangibles; **derelinquierte** ~ abandoned chattel; **die** ~ **ist untergegangen** the goods have perished; **eingebrachte** ~**n** contributed items; tenants' personal property; **fremde** ~ third-party property, property (item) belonging to another, outside assets; **gepfändete** ~**n** attached goods; **gestohlene** ~ stolen goods; **herrenlose** ~ ownerless property, derelict property; res nullius; **leicht verderbliche** ~**n** perishable goods; **nicht vertretbare** ~**n** non-fungible things, specific property items; **öffentliche ~** public property; **sich e–e ~ rechtswidrig zueignen** to convert sth unlawfully to one's own benefit; **unbewegliche ~n** immovables, real property; **unpfändbare ~n** property exempt from execution, non-attachable items; **unveräußerliche ~** non-transferable property, inalienable property; **verbrauchbare ~n** consumables, consumable things; **verkehrsfähige ~** marketable thing; **verlorene ~n** lost things; **vertretbare ~n** fungibles.

Sache *f* (2) matter, case, cause; **anhängige ~** pending case; **der ~ nach** on the real facts, in reality; **die ~ absetzen** to discontinue the proceedings; **die ~ an ein höheres Gericht abgeben** to refer the case to a higher (*or* superior) court; **die ~ aufrufen** to call the next case; **die fragliche ~** the case in question; **die ~ ging fehl** the action failed; **die oben erwähnte ~** the above-mentioned matter; **e–e ~ zurückverweisen** to remand a case(*US*); to remit a case (to), to refer a case back to; **e–r ~ nachgehen** to look into a matter to follow up s.th; **einseitig zu verhandelnde ~** undefended case; **entscheidungsreife ~** a case that is ripe for decision; **gemeinsame ~** common cause; **in der ~** on the merits of a case; in the matter; **in eigener ~** in one's own cause (*or* case), on one's own behalf; **~ ~ aussagen:** *to give evidence as the defendant* (*or: as a party*); *to testify on one's own behalf*; **in e–r ~ verhandeln** to sit on a case, to hear a case; **in ~n re**, in the matter of, in the case of ...; **laufende ~n** current cases; **neben der ~ liegend** irrelevant, not pertinent; **nicht in der ~ selbst** not on the merits; **nicht streitige ~** non-litigious case; **nicht zur ~ gehörig** off the point, irrelevant; **rechtskräftig entschiedene ~** res judicata; **schwebende ~** pending case; **streitbefangene ~** pending case; **unerledigte ~** outstanding matter; **verwiesene ~n** remitted actions; **vorliegende ~** matter in hand, case in hand (*or* in question); *in vorliegender ~: in the instant case*; **zur Entscheidung anstehende ~** case at issue; **zur ~ gehörig** pertinent, to the point; **zur ~ kommen** to come to the point, to get down to business; **zur ~ selbst ausführen** to plead on the merits; **zur ~ sprechen** to speak to the point; **zur ~ vernehmen** to examine (*a witness, a party*) with regard to the matter itself.

sachlich *adj* factual, objective, material; on the merits; **~ richtig** (certified as) factually *or* substantially correct; **~zuständig** competent as regards the subject matter.

Sachlichkeit *f* objectivity, essentiality, impartiality, matter-of-fact attitude.

Sachverhalt *m* state of facts, the factual situation; facts of the case, the facts and circumstances, statement of facts; **~sdarstellung** explanation of the case, statement of the facts of the case; **der wirkliche ~** the real facts; **im Urteil festgestellter ~** findings of fact; **technischer ~** technical facts and circumstances; **vereinbarter ~** agreed statement of facts; **vorstehender ~** the foregoing facts; **zuständigkeitsbegründender ~** jurisdictional facts.

Sachvermögen *n* material assets, physical *or* tangible property; **~ der Volkswirtschaft** national wealth in material assets; **~swert** tangible value; **ausländisches ~** foreign material wealth; **bewegliches ~** movable material assets, movables; **inländisches ~** domestic physical property.

Sachverständigen|aussage expert testimony; **~ausschuß** expert committee, committee of experts; **~beirat** advisory council of experts; **~bericht** expert opinion; **~beweis** expert evidence, evidence produced by an expert, evidence by expert opinion; ~**eid** the oath sworn by an expert (*concerning the impartiality of his opinion*); ~**entschädigung** compensation for the services of an expert; ~**gebühr** expert's fee; ~**gremium** committee of experts; ~**gruppen** groups of experts; ~**gutachten** expert opinion, report submitted by an expert, **e-n ~~~ einholen**: *to ask for an expert opinion, to call the evidence of an expert*; ~**kammer** panel of experts; ~**leistung** performance rendered by an expert, an expert's contribution; ~**prozeß** trial by expert; trial where expert testimony is crucial; ~**rat** council of experts, panel of experts; ~**-Untersuchungen** methodical investigations by an expert (*or* experts); ~**verfahren** insurance determination based on arbitral award of an expert; ~**vergütung** remuneration for the expert, a specialist's fees; ~**wissen** expertise.

Sachverständiger *m* expert, specialist; **amtlicher** ~ official referee, officially appointed expert; **beeidigter** ~ sworn expert, sworn appraiser; **durch e-n ~n begutachten lassen** to ask for an (expert) opinion; **e-n ~n beiziehen** to call an expert; **e-n ~n bestellen** to appoint an expert; **e-n ~n zu Rate ziehen** to consult an expert; **gerichtlich bestellter** ~ court (appointed) expert; **kaufmännischer** ~ commercial appraiser, economic expert; **öffentlich bestellter** ~ publicly appointed expert.

Sachwert *m* physical *or* material asset, real value, intrinsic value, value-retaining capital investment; *dem ~e nach*: *in terms of real value*; *Flucht in ~e*: *flight into real assets;* ~**anleihe** loan on collateral security, mortgage-bond issue; ~**denken** thinking in terms of material assets; ~**dividende** property dividend; **s~gesichert** *adj* secured by property, secured by collateral; ~**klausel** property-value index clause; **s~mäßig** *adj* in terms of real value, in real terms; ~**psychose** material-value psychosis, frantic efforts to protect savings by investment in tangible property.

Sackgasse *f* impasse, blind alley, dead end, cul de sac.

Safe (*n or m*) safe, safe-deposit box, strong-box; ~**miete** hire of a safe, private safe renting.

Saison *f* season, time of year; **s~abhängig** *adj* seasonal, subject to seasonal influences (*or* fluctuation); ~**abschlag** seasonal reduction; ~**arbeiter** seasonal worker, seasonal labourer; ~**arbeitslosigkeit** seasonal unemployment; ~**arbeitsverhältnis** seasonal employment (relationship); ~**artikel** seasonal article, seasonal item; ~**ausschlag** seasonal deviation; ~**ausverkauf** seasonal sale, seasonal clearance sale; ~**bedarf** seasonal demand; **s~bedingt** *adj* seasonal, due to the season/time of year; **s~bereinigt** *adj* seasonally adjusted, adjusted to take account of seasonal fluctuation; ~**bereinigung** seisonal adjustment; **s~berichtigt** *adj* seasonally adjusted; ~**beschäftigung** seasonal employment; ~**betrieb** seasonal business; ~**eröffnung** start/beginning of the season; ~**geschäft** seasonal business; ~**kredit** seasonal credit; ~**schlußverkauf** end-of-season sale, clearance sale; ~**schwankung** seasonal fluctuation; ~**tendenz** seasonal tendency; ~**tief** seasonal low (point); ~**verkauf** seasonal sale; ~**verlauf** seasonal movement; ~**wanderung** seasonal flow of labour; **außerhalb der** ~ out of season, in the off-season; **tote** ~ dull season, off-season.

Salden|abstimmung balance reconciliation; ~**bilanz** trial balance.

saldieren *v/t* to balance, to settle, to strike the balance.

Saldierung *f* balancing of accounts.

Saldo *m* (*pl*: *Salden* = ~*n*), account balance; ~**abdeckung** payment of the (a) balance; ~**aner-**

kenntnis acceptance of the statement of account, account stated; ~**auszug** statement of account; ~ **der Kapitalbilanzen** balance of capital transactions; ~ **der laufenden Übertragungen** net current transfers; ~ **der nicht erfaßbaren Posten und der statistischen Ermittlungsfehler** errors and omissions; ~**guthaben** credit balance, balance in favour of, balance in the black; ...; ~ **laut Gewinn- und Verlustrechnung** balance as per profit and loss account; ~**nbilanz** trial balance, rough balance; ~**nspalte** residual column; ~**quittung** receipt for the balance; ~**schuld** balance due; ~**übertrag** = ~*vortrag qv*; ~**vorbehalt** overall reservation of title, *title retention until all outstanding accounts have been paid;* ~**vortrag** balance brought (*or* carried) forward, carry-forward; ~**zahlung** payment of (the) balance, payment per account; ~ **zu Ihren Gunsten** balance in your favour; ~ **zu Ihren Lasten** your debit balance; **den** ~ **vortragen** to carry forward the balance; **e-n** ~ **anerkennen** to accept the statement of account; **e-n** ~ **aufweisen** to show a balance; **e-n** ~ **ausgleichen** to settle a balance; **e-n Saldo ziehen** to strike a balance; **beglichener** ~ account settled; **fälliger** ~ account payable; **kassenmäßiger** ~ cash balance; **per** ~ as per balance, on balance; **täglicher** ~ daily balance; **verfügbarer** ~ balance at your disposal; **vorgetragener** ~ balance carried forward.

Sammelaktion fund-raising campaign; ~**anerkennung** collective recognition; ~**anleihe** joint loan; ~**aufgebot** collective publication of banns; collective notice of forfeiture; ~**auftrag** collective order; ~**becken** reservoir; ~**begriff** collective term, nomen collectivum; ~**bestand** total orders on hand; ~**bestellung** collective order, omnibus order, centralized buying; ~**bezeichnung** collective title; ~**buchung** collective entry; ~**depot** collective -custody; collective deposit; ~**depotkonto** collective deposit (of securities) account; ~**einbürgerung** group naturalization; ~**einkauf** collective buying, group buying, multiple purchase; ~**erbschein** joint certificate of inheritance; ~**fahrschein** group ticket, party ticket; ~**girokonto** combined deposit account; ~**gut** miscellaneous goods consolidated; ~**heizung** central heating system; ~**inkasso** centralized collection; ~**kasse** general pay office, main cash desk; ~**kauf** centralized buying; ~**klausel** omnibus clause, dragnet clause; ~**konnossement** collective (*or:* omnibus, grouped, consolidated) bill of lading; ~**konto** collective account; ~**ladung** collective (*or* grouped) shipment, mixed consignment, joint cargo, groupage; ~**ladungsspedition** pool car service; ~**lager** collecting point depot; ~**lagerung** combined storage; ~**lebensversicherung** group life insurance; ~**lohnkonto** group wage account; ~**name** collective name; ~**nummer** main number, multiline telephone number; ~**packung** variety pack; ~**paket** collective uniform package *or* parcel of a collective consignment; ~**paß** collective passport; ~**police** group policy, package policy, general policy; ~~ *für Wagenpark:* fleet policy; ~**position** collective item; ~**posten** aggregate item, collective item; ~**preis** blanket price; ~**revers** collective written undertaking; ~**schuldverschreibung** general bond, comprehensive bond; ~**sendung** groupage consignment, combined shipment; ~**stelle** collecting agency; collecting point; ~**tarif** group rate, class rate; ~**termin** date for court hearing of several cases; ~**transport** collective transport; ~**überweisung** combined bank transfer; ~**urkunde** global certifi-

Sammlung

cate, collective instrument, collective document of title; ~**verfügung** combined administrative act; ~**vermögen** combined (*or* collective) assets; ~**verpflichtung** collective obligation; ~**versicherung** group insurance, collective insurance; ~**versicherungsvertrag** master group contract (*of insurance*); ~**verwahrung** collective centralised custody (*or safe keeping*) of securities; ~**verwaltung** collective securities management; ~**visum** group visa; ~**werk** compilation; ~**wert** global value; ~**wertberichtigung** global loss provisions; ~**zahlungsauftrag** combined payment orders.

Sammlung *f* *(1)* compilation, collection; *(2)* (charity) collection.

samtverbindlich *adj* jointly and severally liable.

sanieren *v/t* to restore to financial soundness, to reconstruct, to reorganize, to rehabilitate, to revitalize.

Sanierung *f* capital reconstruction, financial rehabilitation, reorganization (*companies*); urban renewal; ~ **der Währung** currency reform, restoration of the currency to financial soundness.

Sanierungs anordnung rehabilitation order; ~**bilanz** reconstruction account, reorganization statement; ~**darlehen** reorganization loan; s~**fähig** capable of being reorganized; ~**fonds** reorganization fund; ~**gebiet** redevelopment area, slum clearance district; ~**gewinn** reorganization profit; ~**konsortium** reconstruction syndicate; ~**maßnahmen** urban renewal measures, reorganizing measures; ~**plan** reorganisation plan, scheme of reconstruction, financial rescue plan; ~**prospekt** reorganization prospectus; ~**umgründung** reconstruction and reorganization of a company; ~**vergleich** reorganization settlement.

Sanktion *f* sanction, penal sanction; ~**sbefugnis** power to impose sanctions.

676

Satzungsänderung

sanktionieren *v/t* to sanction, to ratify, to confirm.

Satelliten betreiber satellite operator; ~**funkanlagen** satellite communications; ~**netz** satellite network.

Satisfaktion *f* satisfaction, amends.

Sattel anhänger *m* semi-trailer; ~**kraftfahrzeuge** articulated vehicles; ~**zug** articulated lorry, *US*: trailer truck.

Sättigung *f* saturation, satiation; ~**spunkt** *m* saturation point.

Satz *m* (pl *Sätze* = ~*e*) rate, proportion; set; **einheitlicher** ~ uniform rate; **ermäßigter** ~ reduced rate; **fester** ~ fixed rate; **geltender** ~ applicable rate, current rate; **unterschiedliche** ~**e** differing rates, varying rates; **vollständiger** ~ full set (*of bills of lading etc*); **zum** ~ **von** at the rate of, to the amount of.

Satzung *f* charter, constitution, memorandum and articles, articles of association, articles of incorporation, *US*: charter, charter and by-laws, standing rules (*of an association*); ~ **der Vereinten Nationen** United Nations Charter; **autonome** ~ autonomous legislation, local statutes; **bewehrte** ~**en** local regulations containing penalty provisions.

Satzungs änderung alteration (*or* change) of articles of association, amendment of the charter; ~**autonomie** autonomous regional legislation, freedom to form articles of association at pleasure; ~**berichtigung** rectification of the articles of association (*charter, by-laws*); ~**bestimmung** provision of the articles (*charter etc*); ~~ *über die Kapitalstruktur: capital clause*; s~**gemäß** in conformity with the memorandum and articles (*charter etc*); ~**gewalt** right of local authorities to enact bye-laws; ~**mangel** defect in the articles of association (etc); ~**recht** statutory law, local bye-laws; ~**verletzung** violation of the memorandum and articles, infringement of the charter s~**widrig**

Säuberung / **Schaden**

contrary to the articles of association, in breach of the rules.
Säuberung f purge; ~**saktion** purge; mopping-up action (*military*); ~**swelle** massive purge.
Säuferraserei f delirium tremens, mania a potu.
Säulengraphik f column diagram, bar chart.
säumig *adj* defaulting, dilatory, remiss; ~ **sein** to default (on one's payments), to be in default of.
Säumigkeit f dilatoriness.
Säumnis f default, delay, dilatoriness; ~ **des Beklagten** default by defendant; ~**folgen** consequences of default; ~**urteil** default judgment; ~**verfahren** default proceedings; ~**zuschlag** penalty for delay, default surcharge.
Schablone f pattern design, stencil.
Schachtelbeteiligung inter corporate capital holdings, participation in an affiliated company (*of 25% minimum*); capital interlocking; ~**dividende** dividend received from an interrelated company; ~**gesellschaft** affiliated company, interrelated company; ~**privileg** group relief, affiliation privilege, affiliation privilege; ~**vergünstigung** = ~*privileg qv*.
Schaden *m* damage, loss, injury, harm; ~**abwendungskosten** cost of averting the damage; ~**abwicklung** claims adjustment; ~**anfall** occurrence of loss; ~**anzeige** notice of loss; ~**attest** certificate of damage; ~**begutachtung** appraisal of damage; ~ **durch inneren Verderb** damage by intrinsic defects; ~**einschuß** cash payment of share of loss; ~**ersatz** → *Schadensersatz*; ~**exzedent** excess of loss, losses exceeding a specified limit; ~**exzedentdeckung** loss excess cover; ~**exzedentenversicherung** excess of loss reinsurance; ~ **jeder Art** loss or damage of whatever kind; ~ **ohne Verschulden** damage caused without fault; ~**satz** loss ratio; **s**~**stiftend** *adj* damaging, ~**stifter** tortfeasor,

damaging party; ~**teilungsabkommen** repartition agreement; ~ **zufügen** to inflict damage, to inflict injury; **adäquater** ~ proximate damage; **als Totalverlust geltender** ~ constructive total loss; **ästhetischer** ~ aesthetic damage (*by disfigurement etc*); **außergewöhnlicher** ~ exceptional loss; **den** ~ **abdecken** to settle the damage claim, to cover the loss; **den** ~ **abschätzen** to assess (*or* estimate) the damage; **den** ~ **berechnen** to compute the damage; **den** ~ **festsetzen** to assess the damage; **den** ~ **tragen** to bear the loss; *den* ~ *trägt: the loss falls on* ...; **den** ~ **wiedergutmachen** to undo the damage, to make good the damage; **der gesamte** ~ the total loss; **ein** ~ **ist entstanden** a loss has occurred; **e-n** ~ **abfinden** to settle a claim, to adjust a claim; **e-n** ~ **abwenden** to avert damage; **e-n** ~ **anmelden** to give notice of a claim; **e-n** ~ **erleiden** to suffer a loss; **e-n** ~ **haben** to sustain a loss; **e-n** ~ **regulieren** to adjust (a) damage; **e-n** ~ **verursachen** to occasion a loss, to cause damage; **e-n** ~ **wiedergutmachen** to remedy (a) damage, to afford compensation for (a) damage; **eingetretener** ~ loss incurred, actual damage or loss; **einklagbarer** ~ actionable loss; **empfindlicher** ~ serious loss; **entstandener** ~ resulting damage, damage incurred; **erlittener** ~ damage or loss suffered, sustained loss; **erstattungsfähiger** ~ reimbursable damage or loss, recoverable damage or loss, damage eligible for compensation; **festgestellter** ~ ascertained damage, established loss; **formaler** ~ petty damage, pro forma damage; **für e-n** ~ **aufkommen** to make good a loss, to reimburse a loss, to pay for damages; **für e-n** ~ **eintreten** to answer for a loss; **geringfügiger** ~ negligible damage; **immaterieller** ~ non-physical damage, non-material damage; intangible damage; **materieller** ~ physical damage, actual damage or loss, tangible loss; **mittelbarer** ~ indirect damage, consequential damage; **nicht versicherter** ~ uninsured loss; **nicht voraussehbarer** ~ unforeseeable damage; **nicht wieder gutzumachender** ~ irrepairable damage; **nomineller** ~ nominal damage; **physischer** ~ actual loss, physical loss; **regulierter** ~ settled claim; **seelischer** ~ mental damage, mental anguish; **tatsächlicher** ~ actual damage; **unersetzbarer** ~ irrecoverable loss; **unmittelbarer** ~ direct loss or damage, actual damage; **vermeidbarer** ~ avoidable damage; **wirtschaftlicher** ~ economic loss; **zufälliger** ~ accidental loss (or damage).

Schadens|abfindung indemnification, claim adjustment; ~**abteilung** claims department, disputed claims office; ~**abwälzung** redistribution of loss; ~**abwicklung** loss adjustment, settlement of claims; ~**anfall** incidence of loss; ~**anspruch** = *Schadensersatzanspruch qv*; ~**anzeige** notice of loss; ~**aufstellung** statement of damage, list of losses; ~**ausgleich** settlement of a damage claim, compensation for damage; *voller und angemessener* ~~: *full and fair compensation for loss*; ~**begriff** concept of damage; s~**begründend** causing damage, damaging; ~**behebungspflicht** duty to rectify the loss, requirement to make good a loss; ~**bekämpfung** minimizing losses, moves to prevent damage; ~**betrag** amount of loss (or damage); ~**bevorschussung** advance compensation; ~**büro** claims department, adjustment bureau; ~**eintritt** incidence of loss, occurrence of the damaging event; ~**ereignis** loss occurrence, damaging event; ~**erledigung** claims adjustment; ~**erwartung** anticipated damage, expectation of loss; ~**-Exzedenten-Rückversicherung** excess loss reinsurance; ~**-Exzedenten-Vertrag** loss excess treaty; ~**fall** damaging event, claim; ~**feststellung** ascertainment of damage; ~**feuer** unfriendly fire; ~**folgen** damaging consequences, implication of the damage; ~**forderung** damage claim; ~**freiheitsrabatt** no-claims bonus; ~**freiheitsrabattsystem** no-claims bonus system; ~**haftung** liability for damages; ~**häufigkeit** frequency of damaging events; ~**höhe** extent of damage, amount of loss; ~**kommission** claims commission; ~**liquidation** liquidation of damage; ~**maximum** maximum damage; loss limit; ~**meldung** damage report, notice of damage; *unverzügliche* ~~: *immediate notice*; ~**meldungsformular** claim form; ~**merkmal** element of damage; ~**minderung** minimizing loss, reduction of damage, mitigation; ~**minderungspflicht** duty to minimize damages, mitigation of loss, doctrine of avoidable consequences; ~**nachweis** proof of loss; ~**ort** location of loss; ~**papiere** records of the damage; ~**protokoll** certificate of damage; ~**prüfung** damage survey; ~**quote** loss ratio; ~**referent** claims agent; ~**regulierer** claims agent, claims adjuster, average adjuster; ~**regulierung** claim settlement, loss settlement, loss adjustment, adjustment of damages, adjustment of average (*ship*); ~**rente** periodical payments as damages; ~**reserve** loss reserve, liability on outstanding claims, reserve for outstanding claims; ~**rücklage** = ~*reserve qv*; ~**sachbearbeiter** claims handler; ~**sachverständiger** insurance adjuster; ~**schätzung** appraisal of damage, loss assessment; ~**summe** amount of loss; ~**taxierung** loss assessment; ~**teilung** loss sharing, mutual participation in losses; ~**teilungsverband** inter-insurance exchanges; ~**umfang** extent of loss; ~**umschichtung** redistribution of loss (*or* damage); ~**ursache** cause of loss; ~**verhütung** prevention of loss (*or* damage); ~**versicherung** indemnity insurance, insurance against damages, compensation insurance; ~**verteilung** loss repartition; ~**sverteilungsklausel** contribution clause; ~**verursachung** the causing of the damage; ~**wahrscheinlichkeit** probability of loss, likelihood of damage; ~**zufügung** infliction of damage, imposing damage.

Schadensersatz *m* compensation for damage, damages, compensatory damages, indemnification; ~**anspruch** damage claim, claim for damages, compensation claim, ~**anspruch aus unerlaubter Handlung** tortious claim for damages; ~**ansprüche geltend machen** to claim damages; ~**anspruch wegen positiver Vertragsverletzung** claim for defaulting in performance of contract, damage claim for breach of contract; ~**aufwand** compensation costs; ~ **ausschließen** to exclude any damage claim; ~ **beantragen** to claim (for) damages; ~**berechtigter** party entitled to damages, indemnitee; ~ **erhalten** to recover damages; ~**erlangung** recovery of damages; ~**forderung** damage claim, claim for damages; ~ **für Spätfolgen** remote damages; ~ **in Geld** pecuniary damages; ~**klage** action for damages; ~**klage wegen Nichterfüllung** action of assumpsit, action for damage due to non-performance; ~**klage wegen Verkehrsunfalls** legal action for damages arising out of a road accident; traffic accident case; RTA case; ~**leistung** indemnification, recovery of damages; ~**pflicht** liability for damages, liability to make good a loss; **s~pflichtig** *adj* liable for damages, liable to pay damages, liable to indemnify; ~**pflichtiger** party liable for damages; ~**summe** amount of damages; ~ **wegen Nichterfüllung** damages for non-performance; ~ **wegen unerlaubter Handlung** damages in tort; ~ **zuerkennen** to award damages; ~ **zusprechen** to award damages; **adäquater** ~**anspruch** compensatory damages; **auf** ~ **erkennen** to award damages; **auf** ~ **klagen** to sue for damages; **doppelter** ~ double damages; **e-n** ~**anspruch haben** to be entitled to damages; **gesetzlich begründeter** ~**anspruch** lawful damages; **großzügig bemessener** ~ generous damages, generous compensation; **jmdn auf** ~ **in Anspruch nehmen** to claim damages from s. o.; **jmdn auf** ~ **verklagen** to sue s. o. for damages; **pauschalierter** ~ liquidated damages, lump-sum damages, lump-sum award; **unbezifferter** ~ indeterminate damages, unliquidated damages; **vereinbarter** ~ agreed damages; **zu** ~ **verurteilen** to award damages by court judgment; **zugesprochener** ~ damages awarded, damages granted.

schadhaft *adj* defective, faulty, damaged.

Schädiger *m* wrongdoer, damaging party, tortfeasor.

Schädigung *f* injury, impairment; ~**sabsicht** intent (*or* intention) to cause damage, actual malice; **fahrlässige** ~ actionable negligence; **nicht wiedergutzumachende** ~ irreparable injury.

schädlich *adj* detrimental, injurious, harmful, damaging, noxious, pernicious.

Schädling *m* pest, destructive insect, parasite; ~**sbekämpfung** pest control.

schadlos *adj* free from loss; ~ **halten** to hold harmless; to indemnify; *sich* ~~: *to recover one's loss.*

Schadlosbürgschaft *f* guarantee, indemnity.

Schadloshaltung *f* indemnification, indemnity; ~**serklärung** declaration of indemnity; ~**sgarantie** indemnity bond; ~**sklausel** indemni-

Schadlosstellung

ty clause, hold-harmless clause; ~**sverpflichtung** indemnity bond, obligation to hold s. o. harmless (against *or* from).
Schadlosstellung *f* indemnification.
Schadstoff *m* pollutant, harmful substance.
Schaffen *n* work, creative activities, **das graphische** ~ creative commercial art.
schaffen *v/t* to create, to produce, to make, to effect; **beiseite** ~ to put away, to remove, to take away, to secrete, to get rid of.
Schaffott *n* scaffold.
Schaffung *f* creation, production; ~ **von Arbeitsplätzen** job creation, creation of jobs.
Schall|dämpfung sound-insulation; ~**schutz** protection from noise, sound absorbing devices; ~**zeichen** (*Kfz*) audible warning devices.
Schalter *m* counter; ~**automat** teller terminal; ~**beamter** counter-clerk; *auszahlender* ~~: *paying cashier*; ~**dienst** counter service; ~**geschäft** counter transaction; ~**schluß** closing of the counters; ~**stunden** banking hours; ~**verkehr** over-the-counter trading.
Schaltjahr *n* leap year.
Schamgefühl *n* sense of shame.
Scham- und Geschlechtsteile (the) privy parts.
Schande *f* disgrace, ignominy, opprobrium.
schänden *v/t* to ravish, to rape; to desecrate, to profane.
Schändung *f* ravishment, rape; desecration.
Schank|erlaubnis licence to sell alcoholic beverages; ~**gefäß** mug, glass; ~**konzession** = *Schankerlaubnis qv*; ~**wirtschaft** licenced premises.
scharf machen to prime (*bomb*).
Scharfrichter *m* executioner.
Schatten|kabinett shadow cabinet, shadow government, would-be cabinet; ~**kapital** shadow capital (*in reserves*); ~**quote** shadow quota; ~**seite** dark side, seamy side

Schatzwechsel

shady side; ~**wirtschaft** shadow economy, underground economy, twilight economy, submerged economy.
Schatz *m* treasure, treasure trove; ~**fund** treasure trove; ~**regal** state entitlement to a treasure trove.
Schätz|akkord fixing of piece-work rates by appraisers; ~**beamter** appraiser, assessor; ~**betrag** estimated amount; ~**tarif** estimated rates.
Schatzamt *n* Treasury, Exchequer, *US*: Treasury Department.
Schatzanweisung *f* treasury bond (*or* note); **auslosbare** ~ drawable treasury bond; **unverzinsliche** ~ non-interest-bearing treasury bond; **verzinsliche** ~ interest-bearing treasury bond.
schätzbar *adj* appraisable, estimable, computable.
Schätzbarkeit *f* appraisability, computability, assessability.
schätzen *v/t* to estimate, to appraise.
Schätzer *m* appraiser, valuer; **beeidigter** ~ sworn appraiser.
Schatzmeister *m* treasurer.
Schätzpreis *m* estimated price.
Schätzstelle *f* appraisal office (*for value of used cars*).
Schätzung *f* appraisal, estimate, valuation; ~ **von Grundstücken** valuation of property; real estate appraisal; **amtliche** ~ official appraisal; **durch** ~ **feststellen** to ascertain by valuation; **eigene** ~ one's own estimate (*estimate made by a bank itself*); **fundierte** ~ an informed estimate; **gerichtliche** ~ judicial valuation; **grobe** ~ gestimate; rough estimate; **gutachterliche** ~ expert appraisal; **vorsichtige** ~ safe estimate, conservative estimate.
Schätzungs|befugnis authority to appraise; ~**kosten** cost of estimate (*or* valuation); ~**protokoll** appraisal record; ~**wert** estimated value.
Schatzwechsel *m* Treasury bill; ~**kredit** borrowing on treasury bills.

Schätzwert *m* estimated value, appraised value.
Schaubild *n* diagram, graph.
Schauerleute *pl* stevedores, dock workers.
Schauermann *m* stevedore.
Schaufenster|arrangement window dressing; (*or* decoration); ~**auslage** window display; ~**einbruch** smash-and-grab raid; ~**reklame** shop-window (*US shop window or window display*) advertising; ~**werbung** shop-window advertising; ~**wettbewerb** window-display competition.
Schaukasten *m* display case.
Schaukelpolitik *f* seesaw policy, back-and-forth measures.
Schaumünze *f* medal.
Schaumwein *m* sparkling wine; ~**bezeichnung** designation of sparkling wines.
Schauplatz *m* scene, scene of the event.
Schauprozeß *m* show-trial.
Schausteller *m* exhibitor, showman (*at fairs*), public entertainer.
Schaustellung *f* exhibition, display.
Schauvorstellung *f* public entertainment, show.
Scheck *m* cheque, *also US*: check; ~**abrechnungsverkehr** clearance of cheques, cheque clearing; ~**aussteller** drawer of a cheque, maker of a cheque; ~**ausstellungsmaschine** cheque-writing machine; ~**bereicherungsanspruch** *compensation claim for uncollectable cheque against drawer*; ~**bestätigung** certification of cheque(s); ~**betrug** cheque fraud, issuing bad cheques; ~**bezogener** drawee of a cheque; ~**bürgschaft** cheque guarantee; ~**deckungsanzeige** advice of fate; ~**duplikat** duplicate cheque; ~**einlösung** payment of a cheque, cashing of a cheque; ~**einreichung** presentaiton of a cheque; ~~*sfrist presentation period for a cheque*; ~**einreichungsformular** cheque paying-in slip; ~**einzahlung** payment in of a cheque; ~**einzug** cheque collection; ~**empfänger** recipient of a cheque; ~**erklärung** designation as a cheque; ~**fähigkeit** capacity to draw cheques; *aktive* ~~: *capacity to draw cheques*; *passive* ~~: *capacity to be the drawee of cheques*; ~**fälschung** forging (of) cheques, alteration of checks; ~**formular** cheque form; ~**geld** cheque money; ~**gesetz** Cheques Act; ~**haftung** liability for a cheque; ~**heft** cheque book; ~**inhaber** bearer of a cheque; ~**inkasso** cheque collection; ~**karte** cheque (guarantee) card; ~**kartenbetrug** cheque card fraud; ~**kartenmißbrauch** misuse of cheque cards; ~**klage** summary action based on a cheque; ~**konto** cheque account, checking account; ~**leiste** cheque counterfoil, cheque stub; ~**mahnbescheid** default summons based on a cheque; ~ **mit Rechnungsabschnitt** voucher cheque; ~**nehmer** recipient of a cheque; ~**protest** protesting a cheque; ~**prozeß** cheque proceedings (*summary action based on an unpaid cheque*); ~**recht** law on negotiable instruments, law concerning cheques; ~**reiterei** cheque kiting; ~**sperrung** stop payment, stopping (of) a cheque, revocation of payment on a cheque; ~**summe** amount of the cheque; ~**umlauf** cheques in circulation; ~**verkehr** cheque transactions; ~**verrechnung** (cheque) clearing; ~**verrechnungsstelle** clearing house; ~**zahlung** payment by cheque; ~**ziehung** drawing of a cheque; ~**zinsen** interest on cheques; **allgemein gekreuzter** ~ crossed cheque; **besonders gekreuzter** ~ specially crossed cheque, cheque with a special crossing; **bestätigter** ~ certified check, confirmed cheque; **e-n** ~ **ausstellen** to write out a cheque; **e-n** ~ **einziehen** to collect a cheque; **e-n** ~ **sperren** to stop a cheque; **eingelöster** ~ paid cheque; **gefälschter** ~ forged cheque; **gekreuzter** ~ crossed cheque; **gesperrter** ~ stopped

cheque; **girierfähiger** ~ negotiable cheque; **nicht eingelöster** ~ dishonoured cheque, unpaid cheque; **retournierter** ~ returned cheque; **rückdatierter** ~ back dated (*or* antedated) cheque; **überfälliger** ~ stale cheque, overdue cheque; **ungedeckter** ~ uncovered cheque, bad cheque; dud cheque; **verspätet vorgelegter** ~ out-of-date cheque; **vordatierter** ~ post-dated cheque; **vorsätzlich ausgestellter ungedeckter** ~ flash cheque.

Scheidemünze *f* small coin, divisional coin, subsidiary coin.

scheiden *v/t* to divorce; **sich ~ lassen** to get a divorce, to get divorced.

Scheidung *f* divorce, dissolution of marriage; ~ **aus beiderseitigem Verschulden** divorce with both parties being at fault; ~ **im einseitigen Verfahren** ex parte divorce; ~ **nach dem Zerrüttungsprinzip** divorce without reference to fault; ~ **ohne Verschulden** no-fault divorce; ~ **wegen Verschuldens** divorce on grounds of guilt; **auf ~ erkennen** to grant a divorce; **auf ~ klagen** to petition for divorce; **der ~ widersprechen** to oppose the divorce; **die ~ begehren** to seek a divorce; **die ~ aussprechen** to grant a divorce decree, to pronounce a divorce decree; **einverständliche ~** mutually agreed divorce, divorce by mutual consent; **streitige ~** defended divorce; **unstreitige ~** uncontested divorce.

Scheidungs|antrag petition for divorce; ~**begehren** petition for divorce; *dem ~~ stattgeben: to grant a divorce*; ~**beklagter** (= *Antragsgegner*) respondent in divorce proceedings; ~**folgen** legal consequences of divorce; ~**folgesachen** ancillary consequential matters of a divorce (*custody, maintenance, pensions etc*); ~**grund** ground for divorce; ~**klage** petition for divorce; *~~ erheben: to file a divorce suit*; ~**kläger** (= *Antragsteller*) petitioner (for divorce); ~**prozeß** divorce proceedings; ~**rate** divorce rate; ~**recht** law of divorce; ~**richter** divorce judge; ~**statut** applicable national divorce law; ~**urteil** divorce decree; *ein ~~ erlassen: to grant a divorce*; *rechtskräftiges ~~:* (*non-appealable*) decree absolute of divorce; ~**vereinbarung** divorce settlement; ~**verfahren** divorce suit, divorce proceedings; *ein ~~ einleiten: to start divorce proceedings*; ~**widerklage** cross-petition for divorce.

Schein|adoption fictitious adoption; ~**angebot** fictitious offer (*to attract customers*); ~**argument** sophism, specious argument; ~**asylant** bogus refugee, bogus asylum seeker; ~**auktion** mock auction; ~**beantwortung** sham answer; ~**bieter** mock bidder; ~**bilanz** fictitious balance sheet; ~**blüte** fictitious boom; ~**dividende** fictitious dividend; ~**ehe** fictitious marriage, mock marriage, sham marriage; ~**einrede** sham defence; ~**erbe** presumptive heir; ~**faktura** pro forma invoice; ~**firma** bogus firm; ~**flüchtling** bogus refugee; ~**forderung** fictitious claim; ~**gebot** feigned bid, straw bid, sham bid, rigged bid; *das Abgeben von ~~en: by-bidding*; ~**geschäft** fictitious bargain, sham transaction, dummy transaction; ~**gesellschaft** dummy corporation; ~**gesellschafter** nominal partner; ostensible partner, ~**gewinn** apparent (book) profit, illusory profit; inflationary profit; ~**grund** specious reason, pretence, ostensible reason; ~**handlung** fictitious act, sham act; ~**kauf** fictitious purchase, simulated sale, mock purchase; ~**kaufmann** ostensible merchant; ~**konjunktur** pseudo prosperity, quasi prosperity; ~**kurs** fictitious price; ~**mietvertrag** sham tenancy; ~**pistole** imitation firearm, dummy pistol; ~**prozeß** fictitious action, mock trial, sham trial; ~**quittung** pro forma receipt; ~**tätigkeit** dummy activity; ~**testament** sham last will and testament; ~**tod** apparent death, suspended animation; ~**urteil** fictitious judgment; ~**vertrag** sham contract, feigned contract, fictitious contract; ~**vollmacht** ostensible agency, apparent authority; ~**waffe** sham weapon.

Scheinwerfer *m* headlight(s) (*automobile*); searchlight (*police, military*).

Scheitelpunkt *m* peak, crest; ~ **e–r Kuppe** crest of a hill.

Scheitern *n* failure, miscarriage; ~ **der Ehe** irretrievable breakdown of marriage.

scheitern *v/i* to fail, to miscarry, to be frustrated (by).

Schemabrief *m* standard letter, form letter.

schenken *v/t* to make a gift, to make a present, *to make sb a present of sth;* to donate.

Schenker *m* donor, donator (*charity*).

Schenkerin *f* donatrix.

Schenkung *f* gift, donation, present; ~ **auf den Todesfall** gift in contemplation of death, donatio mortis causa; ~ **unter e-r Auflage** gift sub modo, gift subject to a condition (*to be fulfilled by the donee, or subject to a proviso*); ~ **unter Lebenden** gift between the living, gift inter vivos; ~ **von Todes wegen** gift in contemplation of death, gift causa mortis; **bedingte** ~ gift sub modo, conditional donation; **bedingungslose** ~ unconditional (*or* outright) gift; **belastende** ~ onerous donation; **echte** ~ personal gift, genuine gift; **e-e** ~ **machen** to donate, to make a gift of sth; **e-e** ~ **widerrufen** to revoke a donation; **indirekte** ~ indirect donation; **letztwillige** ~ testamentary gift; **mildtätige** ~ charitable gift; **mittelbare** ~ indirect donation; **reine** ~ genuine donation; **remuneratorische** ~ remunerative gift, gift in recognition of past services; **sofort vollzogene** ~ outright gift; **testamentarische** ~ testamentary gift; **verschleierte** ~ concealed donation; **vorbehaltslose** ~ outright gift; **widerrufene** ~ revoked donation.

Schenkungs|anfechtung avoidance of a gift, contesting a donation; ~**annahme** acceptance of a gift; ~**empfänger** donee; ~**land** bounty lands; ~**steuer** gift tax, tax on donations; ~~ **und Erbschaftssteuer** inheritance tax (*IHT*) *GB formerly*: capital transfer tax (CTT); ~**urkunde** deed of donation; deed of gift; ~**versprechen** promise to make a gift, executory donation; ~**vertrag** contract of donation; ~**vollzug** execution of donation, (actual) presentation of a gift; **s~weise** *adv* by way of (a) gift as (a) donation; ~**widerruf** revocation of a gift, revocation of a donation.

Scherzgeschäft *n* transaction entered into as a joke, "a joke".

Schicht *f* shift, work shift, tour of duty; ~**arbeit** shift work(ing); ~**ausfall** shifts not worked; ~**betrieb** shift operation; ~**leistung** output per shift; ~~ *je Mann:* output per man-shift; ~~ *unter Tage:* output per underground man-shift; ~**lohn** pay for shift work, pay per shift; ~**prämie** shift premium, extra-pay for shift work; ~**unterricht** instruction in shifts, school attendance in shifts; ~**wechsel** change-over (of shifts); ~**zeit** shift hours, number of hours worked in a shift; ~**zulage** shift premium, extra pay for shift work, shift allowance; ~**zuschlag** = ~*zulage qv*.

schicken *v/t* to send, to consign, to forward, to dispatch.

Schicklichkeit *f* propriety, decorum, tact, decency.

Schickschuld *f obligation involving the dispatch of what is owed, debt which may be discharged by remittance.*

Schieber *m* racketeer.

Schiebung *f* racket, graft, raket(eering); ~**sanfechtung** avoidance of transaction to defraud creditors; ~**sgeld** racket money; ~**sgeschäft** racket (business), profiteering, put-up job.

schiedlich *adv* by arbitration; **~-friedlich** by amicable arrangement.
Schieds|abkommen arbitration agreement; **~abrede** arbitration clause; **~amt** arbitration board; **~antrag** request for arbitration; **~ausschuß** arbitral committee, arbitration committee; **~gericht** → *Schiedsgericht*; **s~gerichtlich** *adj, adv* by arbitration; **~gerichtsbarkeit** → *Schiedsgerichts* ...; **~gutachten** arbitrator's expert opinion, factual arbitral award; **~gutachter** adjudicator, (expert) arbitrator, quasi arbitrator; **~instanz** arbitration body, arbitral authority; **~klausel** arbitration clause, obligation to arbitrate, future disputes clause; *gemischte ~~*: *joint clause*; **~kommission** arbitration commission; **~mann** ombudsman, official referee; **~obmann** umpire, third arbitrator; **~ordnung** arbitration rules; **~parteien** parties to arbitration, parties to a submission; **~regeln** arbitration rules; **~richter** arbitrator; **~richterkollegium** board of arbitrators; **s~richterlich** *adj* arbitral; **~richterliste** panel of arbitrators; **~richtertätigkeit** arbitrator's actions; **~sachen** arbitration matters; **~spruch** arbitration award; *e-n ~~ fällen*: *to render an award, to make an award*; *~~ als Teilurteil*: *partial award*; **~stelle** arbitration board; **~- und Schlichtungsvertrag** treaty of arbitration and conciliation; **~- und Vermittlungsausschuß** arbitration and mediation committee; **~verfahren** arbitration proceedings; **~vergleich** settlement in arbitration proceedings; **~vereinbarung** arbitration agreement; **~vertrag** arbitration agreement, agreement to go to arbitration, arbitration clause.
Schiedsgericht *n* arbitration tribunal, court of arbitration, arbitral tribunal; *ein ~ anrufen* to refer to arbitration; *durch ~ regeln* to settle by arbitration; **gemischtes ~** mixed arbitration board; **paritätisches ~** arbitration tribunal on a parity basis; **ständiges ~** permanent court of arbitration.
Schiedsgerichts|barkeit arbitration, arbitral jurisdiction; *berufsständische ~~*: *professional arbitration*; *freiwillige ~~*: *voluntary arbitration*; *internationale ~~*: *international arbitration, international arbitral jurisdiction*; **~hof** court of arbitration; *Ständiger Internationaler Schiedsgerichtshof*: *Permanent Court of Arbitration*; **~instanz** court of arbitration, arbitral tribunal; **~klausel** arbitration clause; **~kosten** cost of arbitration, arbitration fee; **~ordnung** arbitration code, rules of arbitration; **~ort** place of arbitration; **~vereinbarung** arbitration agreement; **~verfahren** arbitration proceedings; **~vertrag** arbitration agreement, arbitration treaty; **~vorlage** appeal to arbitration, submission to arbitration; **~wesen** arbitration; **~zwang** compulsory arbitration.
Schießen *n* shooting, firing, combat practice firing.
schießen *v/i* to shoot, to fire; **scharf ~** to shoot in earnest.
Schiff *f* ship, vessel, boat; **~arrestierungsbeamter** detaining officer; **~bau** ship building; **~~hilfe** shipyard aid; **~befrachtungsvertrag** contract of affreightment; **~bruch** shipwreck; **~park** shipping fleet, tonnage; **auslaufendes ~** outward-bound vessel; *das ~ ausklarieren* to clear the ship; *ein ~ löschen* to unload a ship; *ein ~ mit Beschlag belegen* to embargo a ship, to arrest a ship; **fahrplanmäßiges ~** scheduled ship; **frei ans ~** free alongside ship; **frei ~** free on board, free on steamer; **havariertes ~** ship under average; **seetüchtiges ~** sound ship, seaworthy vessel; **seuchenfreies ~** healthy ship; **vorfahrtsberechtigtes ~** privileged vessel.
Schiffbarkeit *f* navigability; **~sgrenze** navigation head.

Schiffahrt *f* navigation, shipping, shipping business, shipping trade; ~ **und Luftfahrt** sea and air transport.

Schiffahrts|abgaben navigation dues; ~**abkommen** navigation agreement, treaty of navigation; ~**agent** shipping agent; ~**angelegenheiten** maritime matters; ~**betrieb** shipping company, shipping enterprise; ~**gebühren** shipping dues; ~**gericht** naval court, navigation court; ~**gesellschaft** shipping company, navigation company; ~**gesetz** Navigation Act; ~**kanal** ship-channel; ~**konferenz** shipping conference, navigation conference; ~**linie** shipping line; ~**recht** navigation law; ~**regeln** rules of navigation, rules of the road at sea; ~**rinne** talweg (= *thalweg*); ~**risiko** dangers of navigation, sea risk, shipping hazards; ~**route** navigation route, shipping lane; ~**sachen** navigation cases, admiralty cases; ~**sperre** embargo on ships; ~**straße** navigation route, ocean lane; ~**- und Flußordnung** shipping and river regulations; ~**unternehmen** shipping enterprise; ~**vertrag** maritime contract; ~**weg** sea-lane, water-way; ~**werte** shipping shares.

Schiffer *m* ship's master, master; ~**patent für große Fahrt** master's patent; ~**patent für kleine Fahrt** mate's patent.

Schiffs|abgaben navigation dues; ~**abladeplatz** unloading place; ~**abwässer** sewage from ships; ~**agent** ship's agent; ~**agentur** shipping agency; ~**anteil** ship's part; ~**arrest** restraint of ship, seizure of a ship, civil embargo; ~**artikel** shipping articles; ~**attest** inland waters navigation certificate, certificate that vessel is in sound condition; ~**ausrüstung** ship's equipment, ship-chandlery; ~**bank** ship loan bank, ship mortgage bank; ~**bauwerk** ship under construction; ~**bauregister** ship construction register; ~**bausubvention** ship construction subsidy; ~**bedarf** ship's supplies; ~**bedarfshandlung** ship-chandlery; ~**befrachter** freighter; charterer, consignor; ~**befrachtung** affreightment; ~**besatzung** ship's crew; ~**besichtiger** ship surveyor, ship and cargo surveyor; ~**bodmerei** bottomry; ~**bodmereigläubiger** bottomry-bond holder; ~**brief** ship's passport, ship letter; ~**dunstschaden** sweat damage; ~**durchsuchung** search of a ship; ~**eichung** gauging of a ship; ~**eigner** shipowner; ~**eintragung** registration of vessels; ~**flagge** ship's flag; ~**fracht** (ship's) freight, cargo; ~**frachtbrief** bill of lading; ~**führer** shipmaster, (ship's) captain; ~**führung** running of a ship; ~**gefährdung** endangering of ships, jeopardizing of a ship; ~**gläubiger** ship's creditor; ~**gläubigerrecht** maritime lien; ~**händler** shipbroker; ~**hypothek** ship mortgage, mortgage of a vessel; ~**hypothekenbank** ship mortgage bank; ~**hypothekenforderung** ship mortgage claim; ~**hypothekengläubiger** ship mortgagee; ~**inspektion** marine survey, inspection of a ship; ~**inspektor** ship's inspector; ~**inventar** ship's inventory; ~**journal** ship's log (book); ~**kapitän** captain, master of a ship; ~**kaskoversicherer** hull underwriter; ~**kaskoversicherung** hull policy, hull insurance; ~**klasse** class of ship; ~**klasseattest** classification certificate; ~**klassifikation** ship's classification; ~**kollision** collision between ships; ~**konnossement** (ship's) bill of lading; ~**ladung** shipload, cargo; ~**landeplatz** quay; ~**leute** sailors; ~**lieferant** ship chandler; ~**liegeplatz** loading berth; ~**liste** shipping list; ~**löschplatz** discharging berth, landing place, unloading place; ~**makler** shipping agent, ship's agent, shipbroker; ~**maklergeschäft** ship

Schikane — **Schlechterfüllung**

brokerage; ~**manifest** ship's manifest; ~**mannschaft** (ship's) crew; ~**maschinenbau** marine engineering; ~**meßbrief** tonnage certificate; ~**meßschein** tonnage certificate; ~**mietvertrag** charter of a vessel, charter-party; ~**musterrolle** ship's articles; ~**notsignal** ship's distress signal; ~**papiere** ship's papers; ~**part** ship's part, share in a ship, interest in a vessel; ~**paß** ship's passport (*for neutral vessel*), sea letter; ~**passage** sea voyage; (ship) passenger fare; ~**personal** ship's officers and crew, ship's personnel, crew; ~**pfandbrief** ship mortgage bond, bottomry bond; ~**pfandbriefbank** ship mortgage bank; ~**pfandrecht** maritime lien (*ship and cargo*); ~**police** marine policy, policy of marine insurance; ~**raum** tonnage, hold; ~**reeder** shipowner; ~**register** register of ships, marine register; ~**registerbehörde** marine registry office; ~**registerbrief** ship's register, ship's certificate; ~**registerordnung** marine registry regulations; ~**registersache** marine registry proceedings; ~**reise** sea journey, voyage; ~**risikodarlehen** *loan to shipowner to be repaid only upon successful termination of the voyage*; ~**rumpf** hull, body of a ship; ~**sachverständiger** nautical assessor; ~**seite** shipside; ~**sicherheit** maritime safety; ~**sicherheitsausschuß** maritime safety committee; ~**tagebuch** log-book, ship's journal, sea journal; ~**unfall** collision at sea; ~**verkehr** shipping, navigation; ~**verlust** loss of a ship at sea; ~**vermieter** charterer; ~**vermietung an Dritte** outside charter; ~**verschollenheit** presumptive loss of a ship; ~**versicherung** hull insurance; ~**versicherungspolice** ship (insurance) policy; ~**verzeichnis** shipping list; ~**vorräte** ship's stores, marine stores; ~**wechsel** bottomry bond; ~**werft** shipbuilding yard, shipyard, dockyard; ~**zahlmeister** purser; ~**zertifikat** certificate of registry; ~**zettel** shipping order, shipping note; ~**zeugnis** ship's certificate, survey of a vessel; ~**zimmermann** ship's carpenter; ~**zubehör** ship's equipment, appurtenances; ~**zubehörhändler** ship chandler; ~**zusammenstoß** collision at sea.

Schikane *f* chicanery, vexation, harrassment; ~**verbot** prohibition of chicanery.

schikanieren *v/t* to use chicanery, to vex, to annoy, to harass.

schikanös *adj* vexatious, purposely annoying, spiteful, contumalious.

Schild *n* (1) sign, signboard, nameplate.

Schild *m* (2) shield.

schildern *v/t* to give an account, to describe, to narrate, to report.

Schilderung *f* description, recital, account, report, statement.

schimpflich *adj* disgraceful, dishonourable; insulting, abusive.

Schimpfworte *n/pl* words of vituperation, abusive language.

Schirmherr *m* sponsor, patron.

Schirmherrschaft *f* patronage, sponsorship.

Schlaf abteil sleeping compartment; ~**gelegenheit** sleeping accommodation; ~**stadt** dormitory-suburb, commuter town; bedroom community (*US*); ~**stelle** overnight accommodation, a night's lodging.

Schlag *m* blow, punch, stroke, slap, *pl also*: beating; ~**baum** toll bar; ~**loch** pot-hole; ~**ring** knuckleduster; ~**stock** truncheon, riot stick, baton.

schlagen *v/t*, *v/i* to beat, to strike, to knock, to hit.

Schläger *m* thug, ruffian; warden who habitually beats up prisoners.

Schlägerei *f* row, affray, brawl, free-for-all.

Schlagwort *n* catch-word, slogan.

Schlampe *f* slut, slattern, slovenly woman.

Schlamperei *f* sloppy work, negligence, slovenliness; mess.

Schlechterfüllung *f* faulty performance, legally insufficient performance, failure to fulfil obligation properly; ~**leistung** poor workmanship, insufficient performance.

Schlechterstellung *f* discrimination, inferior position.

Schlechtwetter|geld bad-weather pay, bad-weather allowance; ~**versicherung** *f* insurance against bad weather.

Schleich|bezug undercover sale of fixed-priced articles; ~**handel** clandestine trade; ~**händler** clandestine trader, black marketeer; ~**reklame** surreptitious advertizing, camouflaged advertizing; ~**werbung** camouflaged advertizing, indirect product placement.

Schlepp|dienst towing service, tug and tow; ~**fischerei** trawling; ~**kahn** barge; ~**lohn** towage; ~**netzfahndung** drag-net technique; ~**netzfischerei** trawling; ~**netzmethode** drag-net technique; ~**schiff** lighter, tow-boat; ~**schiffahrt** towage; ~**schiffahrtsunternehmer** towage contractor.

Schlepper *m* (1) tractor; tugboat.

Schlepper *m* (2) tout (*night club*).

Schleuder|angebot cut-rate offer; bargain; ~**ausfuhr** dumping; ~**gefahr!** slippery road! ~**preis** cut-rate price, underprice, give-away price, under-cost price; ~**verkauf** sale at give-away prices, dumping; ~**ware** catch-penny articles, cut-rate goods, shoddy goods.

Schleudern *n* skid, skidding, spin, sideslip (*automobile*).

schleudern *v/i* (*traffic*) to skid, to spin, to swerve.

Schleuse *f* lock, gate (*canal*); sluice, sluice-gate (*dam*); ~**ngeld** lockage, lock dues.

Schliche *pl* tricks, dodges.

schlicht *adj* simple, plain.

schlichten *v/t* to conciliate, to settle amicably, mediate, to settle by mediation.

Schlichter *m* mediator, conciliator, friendly arbitrator, amicable compositeur.

Schlichtung *f* mediation, conciliation.

Schlichtungs|abkommen mediation agreement; ~**amt** conciliation board; ~**ausschuß** mediation committee, grievance committee; ~**befugnis** power to negotiate for a settlement; ~**gespräch** mediation talks; ~**stelle** mediation agency; ~**vereinbarung** mediation agreement, conciliated agreement; ~**verfahren** conciliation proceedings proposed by a mediator; ~**verhandlungen** settlement negotiations; ~**vorschlag** offer of mediation; ~**wesen** mediation in industrial conflicts.

Schließfach *n* post office box (= *P.O. box*); safe-deposit box (*bank*); luggage locker; ~**miete** hire of a safe-deposit box, safe-deposit facilities; safe-deposit box rent.

Schließung *f* closing, shutdown (*plant*).

Schlosser *m* locksmith; mechanic; ~**gehilfe** journeyman locksmith, mechanic; ~**handwerk** locksmith's trade; ~**innung** locksmith's guild; ~**meister** master locksmith.

Schlosserei *f* locksmith's shop.

Schlupfwinkel *m* hideout, hiding place; haunt; secret nook.

Schluß *m* the end, conclusion, termination, close; ~**abnahme** final acceptance; ~**abrechnung** final settlement, final account; ~**abstimmung** final vote; ~**akte** final act; ~**antrag** final submissions, final motion, motion for judgment; ~**bearbeitung** finish; ~**bericht** final report; ~**besprechung** concluding conference; ~**bestand** closing stock; ~**bestimmung** final provision, final clause; concluding provision; ~**bilanz** final balance sheet, concluding balance, closing balance sheet; ~**buchung** closing entry; ~ **der Debatte beantragen** to move the closure; ~**dividende** final dividend; ~**empfehlungen** Final Recommendations (*Helsinki*); ~**erbe** final heir, reversionary heir;

Schlüsseleinbehalt

~**formel** formal ending; ~**inventar** closing inventory; ~**klausel** final clause, concluding clause, testimonium clause (*deed*); ~**kurs** closing rate, closing price, final quotation; *festgestellter* ~~: *reported closing price*; ~**leuchte** tail-light, rear light; ~**licht** tail-lamp, tail-light, rear light; ~**memorandum** final act; ~**note** broker's note, sale note, purchase contract, selling contract; ~**notierung** closing price, closing quotation; ~**plädoyer** summing up, (argument in) summation, closing arguments, closing speech, final submissions; ~~ *des Staatsanwalts: (Crown or State) prosecutor's summing-up*; ~**protokoll** final protocol; ~**quittung** receipt for the balance; ~**quote** liquidation dividend; ~**rechnung** final account; ~**schein** = ~*note qv*; ~**sitzung** closing session, final sitting; ~**tag** closing day; ~**termin** final date, deadline, closing time, final meeting of creditors (*in bankrupty*); ~- **und Übergangsbestimmungen** concluding and transitional provisions; ~**urteil** final judgment (*after a part-judgment*); ~**verhandlung** final hearing; ~**vereinbarung** closing agreement; ~**verkauf** end-of-season sale, clearance sale, seasonal sale; ~**vermögensübersicht** final survey of assets; ~**verteilung** final distribution; ~**vortrag** final address, closing address (*or* speech), summing-up; ~**wort** last word, final words (*of defendant at trial*); ~**zahlung** final payment.

Schlüsseleinbehalt retention of key ~**gewalt** *obs* wife's (statutory) authorization to purchase necessaries (*in her husband's name*); ~**industrie** key industry, basic industry; ~**information** key information, crucial information; ~**kind** latchkey child; ~**kraft** key man, *pl also*: key personnel; ~**position** key job, strategic position; ~**stellung** key position; ~**telegramm** cipher telegram; telegram in code; ~**werte** economic indicators; ~**zahl** code figure, quota figure; ~**zuweisungen** quota allocations of funds, rate support grant.

schlüsselfertig *adj* ready for immediate occupancy, turnkey.

Schlußfolgerung *f* conclusion; **zwingende** ~ compelling conclusion; inescapable conclusion.

schlüssig *adj* conclusive, convincing, issuable, logical; **nicht** ~ inconclusive, irrelevant to the issue.

Schlüssigkeit logical coherence (of an argument), a good case, a proper cause of action; ~**prüfung** testing the merits of the case, testing whether a complaint states a proper cause of action; **die** ~ **e-s Anspruchs prüfen** to examine the merits of a claim.

schmähen *v/t* to revile, to abuse, to calumniate, to vilify.

Schmähkritik *f* libellous cirticism, insulting criticism, calumny.

Schmähschrift *f* libellous publication, libellous pamphlet, lampoon.

Schmähung *f* revilement, abuse, invective, calumny, vilification.

schmälern *v/t* to reduce, to curtail, to encroach upon, to diminish.

Schmälerung *f* reduction, curtailment, encroachment.

Schmalfilmrechte *n/pl* substandard film rights.

Schmerz *m* (*pl Schmerzen* = ~*en*) pain, *pl also*: pain and suffering; ~**ensgeld** compensation for pain and suffering, solatium, solace, smart money; **körperliche** ~**en** physical pain and suffering; **voraussichtliche** ~**en** prospective pain, foreseeable pain.

schmieren *v/t*, *v/i* to pay graft money, to bribe, to pay a bribe, to „oil s. o.'s palm".

Schmiergeld *n* grease money, pay off, graft, bribe (-money), slush money, palm oil, sweetener, kickback (*coll.*).

Schmuck|gegenstände (items of) jewellery, bijouterie; ~**sachen** jewellery, (cheap) trinkets; ~**versicherung** jewellery insurance;

Schmuggel

~waren jewellery, ornaments and trinkets.

Schmuggel *m* smuggling, illegal trade; ~bande gang of smugglers; ~gut smuggled goods; ~schiff smuggler; ~unwesen widespread smuggling; **bandenmäßiger ~** smuggling by gangs, organized smuggling; **gewerbsmäßiger ~** organized smuggling, smuggling as a business.

schmuggeln *v/i, v/t* to smuggle.

Schmuggler *m* smuggler.

Schmutz|geld extra pay for dirty work, dirt money; ~kampagne mudslinging campaign; ~konkurrenz (extremely) unfair competition; ~**literatur** filth, obscene literature; ~stoffe pollutants; ~- **und Schundgesetz** law against filthy and obscene publications; ~zulage extra pay for dirty work.

Schnee|ballsystem snow-ball system, chain-letter system, pyramid selling, pyramid sales scheme; ~glätte packed snow; ~matsch slush; ~**räumpflicht** legal obligation to remove snow (*from one's sidewalk, from public streets etc*); ~räumung snow removal; ~verwehung snow drift; ~zaun snow fence.

Schnell|bericht urgent report, summary report; ~dienst express service; expediting service; ~**frachtgüterzug** freightliner, liner train; ~gericht police court; ~**imbiß mit Straßenverkauf** take-away food shop; ~richter (police) magistrate; ~straße express highway, speedway; ~strecke high-speed line; ~**testverfahren** sample-check procedure; ~verfahren summary proceedings, summary trial; ~verkehr fast moving traffic, high speed traffic; ~**verkehrsstraße** express highway, speedway.

Schnitt|ansicht sectional view; ~holz sawn timber; ~muster dress pattern; ~waren drapery, dry goods; ~warenhändler draper, dry goods dealer.

Schreibauslagen

Schnupftabaksteuer *f* snuff tax.

Schock *m* shock; ~schaden impairment of health due to shock; **seelischer ~**, *mental shock, psychological shock, mental breakdown*.

Schöffe *m* lay assessor (*in a criminal court*), lay magistrate; ~**namt** the position of lay assessor in court; ~**nauslosung** selection of lay assessors by lot; ~**ngericht** (=) magistrates' court, *criminal court with a professional judge and two lay assessors;* ~**nliste** court panel for lay judges.

Schonfrist *f* period of grace.

Schönheits|fehler minor blemish, flaw in the finish; ~**reparaturen** interior redecoration; ~~ *vornehmen: to decorate* (*apartment, rented house*); *notwendige ~~: essential interior redecoration*.

Schonzeit *f* close season; period of convalescence.

Schonvermögen *n* residual essential household goods and funds (*exempt from contribution*).

Schöpfer *m* creator, originator, inventor; **~ e-r Erfindung** originator of an invention.

Schöpfung *f* creation; **eigentümliche ~** individually distinct creation.

Schotterstraße *f* metalled road.

Schraffierung *f* (oblique) hatching.

Schrägstreifen *m/pl* oblique parallel lines.

Schranke *f* gate, bar (*in court, parliament etc*); **trennende ~n** divisive issues, dividing barriers.

Schrankfach *n* letter box *for lawyers in court buildings*; bank safe; ~miete renting of safes, rent for a safe.

Schrebergarten *m* allotment (garden).

Schrecken *m* horror, terror, fright; ~**sherrschaft** reign of terror, terror regime.

Schreckschußwaffe *f* warning shot pistol, blank (cartridge) pistol.

Schrecksekunde *f* reaction time, thinking distance (*when braking*).

Schreib|auslagen clerical expenses, copying charge; ~fehler clerical

689

Schreiben

error, misspelling, typing mistake, "typo", slip of the pen; **~gebühren** charges for copying; **~gehilfe** an aid to help a disabled person write; **~kraft** typist, shorthand and copy typist, *pl*: clerical staff; **~mappe** writing case, portfolio; **~maschinenmanuskript** typescript; **~saal** typing room, typing pool; **~schrift** long hand; **~unfähigkeit** inability to write; **~unkundiger** illiterate person; **~versehen** = ~*fehler qv*; **~waren** stationery; **~warenhändler** stationer; **~weise** spelling; *fehlerhafte* ~~: *wrong spelling, misspelling.*

Schreiben *n* writing, letter, note, memorandum; **amtliches** ~ official letter; **beanstandetes** ~ letter complained of; **beleidigendes** ~ insulting (or libellous) letter; **fingiertes** ~ fictitious letter, sham letter.

Schreiber *m* writer, author, novelist.

Schrift *f* (*pl Schriften* = ~*en*) writing; pamphlet, publication; **~bild** typeface; **~enreihe** series of publications; **~form** writing, written form, in writing and signed; *gesetzliche* ~~: *Statute of Frauds, statutory written form*; *gewillkürte* ~~: *mutually agreed written form (for amendments, additions etc)*; *in* ~~: *in writing (and signed)*; *vorgeschriebene* ~~; *prescibed or required written form (suretystip etc)*; **~formklausel** stipulation requiring written form (*for any changes or amendments*); **~führer** secretary, keeper of the minutes; **~gutachten** opinion by a handwriting expert, graphological expertise; **~inhalt** substance of a publication; **~leiter** editor; **~leitertätigkeit** editorial work; **~leitung** editorial office, editorial staff; **~proben** handwriting specimens; **~sachverständiger** handwriting expert, forensic handwriting examiner; **~satz** → *Schriftsatz*; **~schild** name-board (*over a shop*), shingle (*US*); **~steller** professional writer, *juristischer* ~~: *legal writer*; **~stellername** pen-name, nom de plume; **~stück** writing, memorandum, written document, paper; *amtliche* ~*stücke*: *official papers, official documents*; *eigenhändiges* ~~: *holograph*; *unterschriebenes* ~~: *signed document*; *vertrauliches* ~~: *confidential document*; **~vergleichung** comparison of handwriting; **~verkehr** correspondence; *den* ~~ *abbrechen: to discontinue the correspondence*; **~wechsel** correspondence; **~werk** literary work, literary composition; *originäres* ~~: *original literary work*; **~zeichen** character, letter, graphic symbol; **~zeichengesetz** Typographical Copyright Act; **beschimpfende ~en** libellous publications; **ehrenrührige ~** libellous publication, libel, disparaging publication; **fette ~** bold face, bold type; **hochverräterische ~en** treasonable publications; **leserliche ~** legible handwriting; **obszöne ~en** obscene publications; **schamlose ~en** obscene literature; **staatsgefährdende ~en** seditious literature, seditious publications; **unzüchtige ~en** obscene books or papers, obscene writings, obscene publications; **verfassungsfeindliche ~en** seditious publications.

schriftlich *adj* written, in writing, "black on white".

Schriftlichkeit *f* written form; requirement that sth shall be in writing.

Schriftsatz *m* (*pl Schriftsätze* ~*e*) brief, written pleading; **~wechsel** exchange of pleadings; **e-n ~ einreichen** to file a brief, to submit a written statement; **bestimmender ~** (important) procedural brief (or pleading); substantive pleading, **ergänzender ~** supplemental pleading; **nachgereichter ~** subsequently filed brief (or written pleading); **vorbereitende ~e** pleadings.

Schrifttum *n* literature, legal writers, pertinent works of (legal) experts.

Schritt *m* step, measure; ~ **für Schritt** step by step, gradually; by

Schrott

degrees; **~geschwindigkeit** walking pace, dead slow, speed of a pedestrian; ~ **halten** to keep pace; to keep in step; to keep up with; **die erforderlichen ~e** necessary remedial action, the required measures; **diplomatischer ~** diplomatic step, diplomatic move, démarche; *pl also*: (diplomatic) representations; **einleitende ~e** introductory steps, initial steps, preliminary measures; **erster ~** the first step, the initiative; **geeignete ~e** appropriate steps; **gerichtliche ~e** legal action; **maßgeblicher ~** the decisive step.

Schrott *m* scrap; **~handel** scrap business; **~händler** scrap dealer, junk dealer; **~verkäufe** scrap sales; **~wert** scrap value, junk value, salvage value.

Schrumpfung *f* contraction, shrinkage.

Schubschiffahrt *f* pusher barge navigation.

Schul(*cfSchule*)|**abgänger** school leaver; **~abgangsalter** school-leaving age; **~abgangszeugnis** school certificate, school leaving certificate; **~absolventen** school leavers; **~amt** board of education; **~aufsicht** school inspectorate, school inspection department; **~aufsichtsbehörde** board of education; **~aufsichtsgesetz** School Inspection Act; **~ausbildung** school education, school training, schooling; **~behörde** education authority; **~beirat** school board; **~beispiel** test case, perfect example; **~besuch** school attendance; **~bildung** school education, school training; **~~ an öffentlichen Schulen**: *public education*; *höhere ~~*: *secondary education*; **~einzugsgebiet** school catchment area; **~entlassungsalter** school-leaving age; **~ferien** school holidays, school vacation; **~finanzierungsgesetz** school financing Act; **~fremdenprüfung** examination of external students (or pupils); **~geld** tuition (fee), school fee;

Schuld

~geldfreiheit free school education, exemption from school fees; **~helfer** temporary assistant teacher; **~hoheit** supreme authority in school matters; **~impfung** vaccination of school children; **~inspektion** inspection of schools; **~jahr** school year, year at school; **~laufbahn** schooling, school life; **~leistungen** school performance; **~note** mark, grade; **~ordnung** school regulations; **~organisationsgesetz** schools Act, schools organization law; **~pflicht** compulsory education, compulsory attendance at school; **~~alter**: *compulsory school age*; **s-pflichtig** *adj* of school age; **~pflichtiger** child of school age, child required to attend school; **~praktikant** trainee teacher; **~recht** law of school education; **~schluß** close of school, end of school; **~schwänzer** truant; **~schwänzerei** truancy; **~sprengel** school district; **~strafe** school punishment, disciplinary school penalty; **~streik** strike by pupils (*or* their parents); **~träger** school administrative body; **~system** educational system, school system; *allgemeinbildendes ~~*: *general school system*; **~verhältnis** relationship between school and pupils (students); **~versäumnis** non-attendance at school, truancy; **~verwaltung** school administration; **~wesen** schooling, school system, school matters; *öffentliches ~~*: *public education, public schooling*; **~zeugnis** school certificate; **~zwang** compulsory school attendance.

Schuld *f* (*pl*: *Schulden* → *Schulden*) debt, indebtedness, obligation, liability; guilt, fault, blame; **~ablösung** refunding of a debt; **~anerkenntnis** acknowledgment of indebtedness, certificate of indebtedness, IOU (*I owe you*); *negatives ~~*: *acknowledgment of non-indebtedness, full discharge*; **~aufnahme** borrowing, taking up of a loan; **~ausschließungsgrund** lawful

691

Schuld

excuse, reason precluding punishability (*lack of criminal responsibility, error, necessity, et al*); ~**ausschluß** exemption from liability for negligence; ~**ausspruch** verdict of guilty; ~**auswechslung** substitution of debt novation; ~**begleichungsurkunde** acknowledgment of satisfaction; ~**beitreibung** collection of debts; ~**beitritt** additional assumption of debt; ~**bekenntnis** admission of guilt; ~**bescheinigung** certificate of indebtedness; ~**beweis** proof of guilt, inculpatory evidence; *der ~~ ist nicht gelungen: the guilt has not been established beyond reasonable doubt*; ~**bewußtsein** guilty knowledge, guilty mind, mens rea, consciousness of guilt, guilt-stricken sense; ~**brief** borrower's bond or note, certificate of indebtedness; ~**buch** debt register; ~**bucheintragung** entry in the debt register; ~**buchforderung** debt register claim, registered debt, government-inscribed debt; ~**buchgiroverkehr** transfers on the Federal Debt Register; ~**entlastung** discharge from an obligation; ~**erlaß** remission of debt; ~**fähigkeit** criminal capacity; ~**forderung** claim for payment of a debt; ~**frage** question of guilt; ~**gefängnis** debtor's prison; ~**geständnis** admission of guilt; ~ **haben** to be at fault, *the fault lies with s.o.*; ~**haft** imprisonment pending the payment of a debt; ~**höhe** amount of indebtedness; ~**interlokut** separate finding of guilt (*before sentence*); ~**klage** action on a debt, writ of assumpsit; ~**konto** debit account; ~**lehre** doctrine of guilt; s~**los** *adj* innocent, not guilty, guiltless; ~**losigkeit** innocence; ~ **mit Konventionalstrafklausel** penal obligation; ~**mitübernahme** cumulative assumption of debt; ~**nachlaß** part release from debt, allowance of a reduction of the debt; ~**posten** debititem; ~**prinzip** (*Scheidung*) fault principle, matrimonial offence

doctrine; ~**recht** law of obligations; s~**rechtlich** under the law of obligations, obligatory; ~**saldo** debit balance; ~**schein** → *Schuldschein*; s~ **sein** to be at fault; ~**spruch** verdict of guilty, finding of guilt, conviction; *e-n ~~ bestätigen: to uphold a conviction*; ~**statut** the law governing contractual obligations (*intern. private law*); ~**strafrecht** *criminal law based on the doctrine of mens rea*; system of criminal law based on the requirement of personal guilt; ~**summe** total amount of debt; ~**teil** part of debt item of indebtedness; ~**tilgung** discharge of a debt, redemption, satisfaction of debts; *~~splan: redemption plan*; ~**titel** instrument of indebtedness, proof of indebtedness, judicial title of indebtedness; ~**turm** *hist* debtor's prison; ~**übernahme** assumption of indebtedness, *befreiende ~~: assumption of a debt with full discharge of original debtor; kumulative ~~: cumulative assumption of a debt*; ~**übertragung** assignment of a debt, transfer of indebtedness; ~**umschaffung** novation; ~**umwandlung** conversion of a debt; ~**- und Forderungsposten** liability and asset items; ~**unfähigkeit** criminal incapacity, incapacity of being guilty of an offence; ~**urkunde** instrument of indebtedness, evidence of indebtedness, certificate of indebtedness, debt certificate; ~~ *mit Verpfändungsklausel: debenture, mortgage bond*; ~**urteil** judgment for the recovery of a debt; ~**verhältnis** obligation, relationship under the law of obligations; ~**vermutung** presumption of guilt; ~**verpflichtung** obligation; ~**verpflichtungsschein** promissory note, certificate of indebtedness; ~**verschreibung** → *Schuldverschreibung*; ~**versprechen** promise to fulfil an obligation, promise to pay, recognition of liability; ~**vertrag** contract for a debt, contract for personal liability; ~**vorwurf** imputa-

Schulden

tion of wrong, blame; ~**zahlung** payment of debt; ~**zinsen** interest on debts; ~**zuweisung** allocation of blame, apportioning of blame; **antizipatorische** ~ accrued liability; **aufgeschobene** ~ deferred liability; **aufteilbare** ~ severable obligation, apportionable debt; **ausstehende** ~ outstanding debt, outstanding balance; **bereits bestehende** ~ (already) existing debt; **bewehrte** ~ penal obligation; subject to a penalty (*in case of non-performance*); **buchmäßige** ~ book debt; **die** ~ **abstreiten** to deny blame; **die** ~ **auf e–n anderen abwälzen** to put the blame onto s. o. else; to find a scape goat; **die** ~ **auf jmdn schieben** to shift the blame onto s. o. else; **die** ~ **des Angeklagten ist hinreichend bewiesen** the guilt of the accused has been established beyond reasonable doubt; **die** ~ **zugeben** to admit guilt, to confess; **dingliche** ~ real obligation, ad rem obligation; **dinglich gesicherte** ~ debt secured by a mortgage or pledge; debt secured by collateral; **e–e** ~ **anerkennen** to acknowledge a debt; **e–e** ~ **anwachsen lassen** to allow a debt to grow; **e–e** ~ **begleichen** to settle a debt; **e–e** ~ **bezahlen** to pay a debt; *seine* ~*en bezahlen*: *to meet one's debts, to discharge one's liabilities*; **e–e** ~ **eingehen** to contract a debt, to incur a liability; **e–e** ~ **eintreiben** to collect a debt, to recover a debt; **e–e** ~ **erfüllen** to satisfy a debt, to perform an obligation; **e–e** ~ **erlassen** to release (s. o.) from a debt (*or* claim), to waive a debt (*or* claim); remit a debt, to remit a claim; **e–e** ~ **übernehmen** to assume a debt; **e–e** ~ **zurückbezahlen** to pay off a debt, to pay back a debt; **fällige** ~ due debt, matured debt; **frühere** ~ antecedent debt, previous debt; **fundierte** ~ funded debt, bonded debt; **getilgte** ~ (discharged) debt, redeemed debt; **höchst persönliche** ~ strictly personal obligation; **jmdm die** ~ **geben** to blame s. o., to put the blame on s. o.; **jmdn e–r** ~ **entheben** to release s. o. from a liability; **konsolidierte** ~ consolidated debt; **laufende** ~ current debt, pending debt; **nicht bezahlte** ~ undischarged debt; **nicht fundierte** ~ unfunded debt; **persönliche** ~ private debt; **samtverbindliche** ~ joint and several obligation; (*or* debt); **schwebende** ~ floating charge (*or* debt); **teilbare** ~ divisible obligation; **überwiegende** ~ severable debt (*or* liability), predominance of guilt; **uneinbringliche** ~ non-recoverable debt; **unteilbare** ~ inseverable debt (*or* liability), indivisible obligation; **unverbriefte** ~ non-bonded debt; **unverzinsliche** ~ non-interest-bearing debt, passive debt; **verbriefte** ~ bonded debt, debt evidenced by documents; **verwirkte** ~ stale debt; **verzinsliche** ~ interest-bearing debt, active debt.

Schulden *f/pl* debts, liabilities; ~**abkommen** agreement on debts, arrangement with creditors; ~**ablösung** redemption of debts; ~**aufnahme** borrowing; *staatliche* ~~: *government borrowing*; ~**aufschlüsselung** debt break down; ~**bereinigung** settlement of debts; ~ **der öffentlichen Hand** public debts, debts by public authorities; ~**dienst** debt service; **s~frei** *adj* free of debts, without debt; ~ **gehen auf jmdn über** debts devolve on a person; ~**haftung** liability for debts; ~**handhabung** debt management; ~**last** burden of debts, total debts; ~ **machen** to incur debts, to contract debts; ~**masse** total of indebtedness; ~**regelung** debt settlement, debt-adjusting; ~**regulierung** settlement of debts; ~**rückzahlung** repayment of debts, debt repayment; ~**stillhalteabkommen** moratorium, debt standstill; ~**strukturpolitik** debt management; ~ **tilgen** to repay one's debts; ~ **tilgung** repayment of debts, redemption of debts, (*also pl*) debt redemption; ~**tilgungsfonds** sinking fund; ~**übernahme** assumption of liabilities; ~ **übernehmen** to take over liabilities, to assume debts; ~**verwaltung** debt management; ~**verzeichnis** register of debts; **für** ~ **haften** to be liable for debts; **in** ~ **geraten** to run into debt; **unbezahlte** ~ unpaid debts; **voreheliche** ~ antenuptial debts.

schulden *v/t* to owe, to be in debt.

schuldhaft *adj* culpable, negligent, faulty.

schuldig *adj* guilty; owing, payable; ~ **sein** to be guilty, to owe, to be indebted; ~ **sprechen** to find guilty; **allein**~ solely guilty; **nicht** ~ not guilty; *sich für* ~~~ *erklären:* to plead "*not guilty*"; **sich für** ~ **erklären** to plead guilty; **sich** ~ **bekennen** to plead guilty; **überwiegend** ~ predominantly guilty.

Schuldiger *m* (*der Schuldige*) the party at fault, the guilty party.

Schuldigerklärung *f* plea of guilty.

Schuldner *m* debtor, obligor, party liable; ~**begünstigung** unlawful preference for a debtor, showing favour to one particular debtor; ~**gewinn** profit accruing to debtors; ~**land** debtor country; ~**liste** credit default register; ~**nötigung** (unlawful) harassment of debtors; ~**schaft** indebtedness, being in debt; ~**schutz** protection of debtor, mitigation of hardship for innocent debtors; ~**vermögen** debtor's property; ~**vernehmung** discovery in aid of execution, questioning of a debtor; ~**verzeichnis** list of insolvent debtors; ~**verzug** debtor's delay, culpable delay by obligor, default, mora debitoris; **persönlicher** ~ contractual debtor, personal debtor; **säumiger** ~ debtor who is in arrears, defaulting debtor; **zahlungsunfähiger** ~ insolvent debtor, defaulting debtor, debtor unable to pay; **zahlungsunwilliger** ~ "won't pay" debtor, unwilling debtor.

Schuldnerin *f* debitrix, a female debtor.

Schuldschein *m* memorandum of debt, borrower's note; promissory note; I. O. U. (= *I owe you*), note of debt; ~**darlehen** non-bonded loan, loan against borrower's note, loan by private treaty, promissory note bond; ~**forderung** claim covered by a promissory note; ~ **für e-n Vorschuß** advance note; ~**inhaber** note holder; ~ **mit Bürgschaft** note with surety; ~ **mit Unterwerfungsklausel** judgment note; ~ **mit Zinseszinsklausel** note providing for compound interest; **dinglich gesicherter** ~ collateral note; **e-n** ~ **bezahlen** to pay a debt under a promissory note; **gesiegelter** ~ bond, debenture deed; **kurzfristige** ~**e** short-term notes; **mittelfristige** ~**e** medium-term notes; **überfälliger** ~ overdue I. O. U., overdue promissory note; **ungesicherter** ~ plain bond, non-secured promissory note.

Schuldverschreibung *f* debenture bond, bond, debenture, debt certificate; ~ **auf den Inhaber** bearer bond, debenture to bearer; ~**en ausgeben** to float a bond-issue; ~ **mit Gewinnbeteiligung** participating bond; ~**sgläubiger** bond-holder, creditor in respect of a bond; ~ ~**svorkauf** bond sold in advance of issue; **auf engl. Pfund laufende** ~ sterling bond; **ausgeloste** ~**en** drawn bonds; **e-e** ~ **ausstellen** to issue a bond; **ertragssteuerfreie** ~**en** bonds exempt from the capital yield tax, tax-free bonds; **festverzinsliche** ~**en** fixed-interest bearing bonds; **gestückelte** ~ fractional debenture; **hypothekarisch gesicherte** ~ mortgage debenture, mortgage bond; **kommunale** ~**en** municipal bonds; **kündbare** ~ redeemable bond; **marktfähige** ~**en** marketable bonds; **mündelsichere** ~ eligible bond, gilt-edged bond; **öffentliche** ~ stock, bond issued by a public authority; **ungesicherte** ~

simple bond, non-secured bond; **unkündbare** ~ irredeemable bond; **unverzinsliche** ~**en** interest-free bonds, passive bonds; **verkehrsfähige** ~ marketable bond; **zinstragende** ~ active bond, interest-bearing debt certificate.

Schule *f* school, educational establishment, college; ~ **in freier Trägerschaft** independent school; **allgemeinbildende** ~ school offering general education; **berufsbildende** ~ vocational school (*or* college); **höhere** ~ secondary school, grammar school; **öffentliche** ~ (publicly) maintained school, State school; **private** ~ independent school, private school *GB*: public school; **weiterführende** ~ secondary school.

Schüler|lotse *m* school traffic warden; lollipop-man; ~**mitverantwortung** pupils' co-participation.

Schulung *f* training, further education (on courses); **politische** ~ political education.

Schund *m* smut, shoddy goods, trash, rubbish.

Schüren *n* (= *Schürung f*) formenting, fomentation.

schüren *v/t* to foment, to arouse.

Schürf|erlaubnis prospecting permit; ~**ermächtigung** prospecting authorization; ~**feld** prospecting location; ~**konzession** prospecting licence; ~**recht** prospecting rights, right to work minerals, right of search, mining rights; ~**rechtsdienstbarkeit** mineral servitude; ~**rechtsvergütung** prospecting fee; ~**stelle** prospecting site; ~**steuer** prospecting tax; ~**vertrag** prospecting agreement.

Schürfen *n* prospecting.

schürfen *v/i* to prospect.

Schürfer *m* prospector.

Schurke *m* scoundrel, rogue, villain.

Schußwaffe *f* firearm; ~**ngebrauch** making use of firearms.

Schußwechsel *m* shoot-out, exchange of fire (*or* shots).

Schutt *m* rubble, debris, detritus; ~**abladeplatz** *m* dump.

Schütt-aus-Hol-zurück-Verfahren pay out/take back procedure (*corporation accounts*).

Schutz *m* protection; ~**aktien** defensive share-issue, shares issue to prevent third-party control; ~**anordnungen** safety regulations; ~**art** type of protection; ~ **auf Ausstellungen** protection at exhibitions (*of patent rights*); ~**aufsicht** protective custody; ~**befohlener** ward, person under the custody of another, protégé, charge, ~**begehren** request for protection, patent claims; ~**behauptung** self-serving statement, exculpatory statement; ~**bereich** area of protection, extent of protection, restricted (military) area; ~~**sverfahren**: *establishment of a restricted area*; *räumlicher* ~~: *territorial scope of protection*; *sachlicher* ~~: *extent of protection*; ~**bestimmung** protective clause; ~**brief** letter of safe conduct; motorist's letter of protection; ~**bündnis** defensive alliance; ~**dauer** time of protection, duration of protection (*patent*), life of a patent; ~**dauerverlängerung** extension of protection; ~ **der lebenden Schätze** conservation of living resources; ~ **der Privatsphäre** protection (*or* right) of privacy; ~ **des Persönlichkeitsrechts** right of privacy; ~ **e-s Patents** scope of a patent; **s**~**fähig** *adj* capable of being protected, patentable, copyrightable; ~**fähigkeit** protectability, patentability, copyrightability; ~**frist** copyright period; ~**gebiet** protectorate, dependent territory; ~**gegenstand** subject matter for which protection is sought; ~ **geistigen Eigentums** protection of intellectual property; ~**geld** protection money; ~**gelderpressung** protection racket; ~**gesetz** protective law, protective legislative provision (*the violation of which entitles to damages*); ~ **gewähren** to afford protection, to furnish protection, to safeguard; ~**frist** time of protection, period of protection, term (=

695

schützen | **Schwangerschaft**

duration) of patent (*or copyright etc*); ~**gebiet** protectorate, dependent territory; ~**gebühr** nominal price (*pamphlet etc*): protection money (*gangsters*); ~**geleit** safe conduct; ~**gesetz** protective law, remedial statute; ~**haft** protective custody, preventive detention; ~**helm** protective headgear (*or* helmet), ~**herr** protector, patron; ~**herrschaft** protectorate, patronage; ~**hoheit** suzerainty; ~**impfung** general vaccination, immunization; ~**insel** traffic island; ~**klausel** protective clause, hedge clause, safeguard(ing) clause, saving clause; ~**kleidung** protective clothing; s~**los** *adj* unprotected, defenceless, undefendable; ~**macht** protective power, protecting state; ~**marke** trade mark (= *trademark*); ~**maßnahmen** protective measures; *handelspolitische* ~~: *measures to protect trade*; ~**polizei** police force, constabulary; ~**recht** →*Schutzrecht;* ~**schild** riot shield (*police*); ~**schrift** caveat; anticipatory brief against an expected ex parte injunction (*filed in court*); ~**stätte** sanctuary; ~**umfang** scope of protection; ~**- und Trutzbündnis** defensive alliance; ~**verband** trade-protection society; ~**vereinigung für Wertpapierbesitz** Association for the Protection of Security Holders; ~**vermerk** interim caveat; ~**verpackung** protective packing; ~**verwaltung** protective administration; ~ **von Werken der Literatur und Kunst** protection for literary and artistic works; ~**vorrichtung** protective device, safety device; ~**wald** protective forest (*erosion, climate, avalanches etc*); ~**wirkung** protective character; ~**würdig** meriting protection; ~**zoll** protective tariff, protective duty; ~**zöllner** protectionist; ~**zollpolitik** protectionism; ~**zollsystem** protectionism; **diplomatischer** ~ diplomatic protection; **finanzieller** ~ financial protection; **gegenseitiger** ~ mutual protection; **vertraglicher** ~ contractual protection; **vorläufiger** ~ provisional protection, temporary protection.

schützen *v/t* to protect, to safeguard, to shield: **patentrechtlich** ~ to patent; **urheberrechtlich** ~ to copyright.

Schutzrecht *n* right of protection, protective right, protected privilege; proprietary right, industrial property right, patent, copyright, ~**sinhaber** proprietor of industrial right, party entitled to industrial property right(s), owner of a patent (*or copyright etc*); ~**skosten** royalties; ~**slizenz** licence concerning industrial property rights; ~**surkunde** certificate of industrial property right; ~**sverletzung** infringement of industrial property rights; ~**sverwarnung** warning against infringement of industrial property right; ~**sverwertungsgesellschaft** company for the exploitation of industrial property rights; **gewerbliche** ~**e** industrial property rights; industrial rights, industrial property; **vorläufiges** ~ right of provisional protection.

schwächen *v/t* to weaken, to impair, to diminish, to debilitate.

Schwachsinn *m* feeble-mindedness, mental deficiency, dementia, subnormality.

Schwachsinniger *m* feeble-minded person, mentally deficient person, mentally handicapped person.

Schwägerschaft *f* in-laws relationship by affinity; ~**sgrad** degree of affinity; ~ **in der Seitenlinie** collateral affinity.

Schwamm *m* rot, dry rot (*in buildings*).

schwanger *adj* pregnant.

Schwangere *f* pregnant woman, expectant mother; ~**nberatungsstelle** ante-natal clinic, pregnancy advisory service; ~**nfürsorge** antenatal care.

Schwangerschaft *f* pregnancy; ~**sabbruch** termination of preg-

Schwängerung

nancy, (induced) abortion; ~s**bei-hilfe** aid to expectant mothers; ~**sunterbrechung** = ~*sabbruch qv.*; e–e ~ **voll austragen** to carry a pregnancy to full term; **außereheliche** ~ pregnancy per alium, pregnancy out of wedlock.

Schwängerung *f* causing pregnancy, causing conception, impregnation.

Schwankungs|bereich range; ~**breite** amplitude of fluctuation, band of fluctuation; spread; ~**sklausel** fluctuating clause; currency adjustment clause; ~**kurs** fluctuating price; ~**rückstellung** special reserve for exchange-rate fluctuations; ~**spitze** margin of fluctuation.

Schwarz|arbeit clandestine work, illicit work, moonlighting; unrecorded employment; ~**arbeiter** clandestine worker, moonlighter; ~**brennerei** illicit distillery; ~**fahrer** fare dodger; ~**fahrt** travel(l)ing without payment; unauthorized use of a motor vehicle; ~**flug** unauthorized flight; ~**handel** illicit trade, black-market trade, underground economy; ~**händler** black-market dealer, blackmarketeer, black market operator; ~**hörer** radio pirate; student attending courses without paying tuition; ~**kauf** illicit purchase, black-market sale; ~**schlachtung** unlawful slaughtering; ~**sender** secret transmitter, unlicensed transmitter; private broadcaster; ~**verbriefung** (*unlawful*) *conveyance at lower price than actually agreed*; ~**zahlung** under-the-table payment, under the counter payment.

schwebend *adj* suspended, unliquidated, unfunded.

Schwebezeit *f* period of suspense, transitional period, interim period.

Schweige|geld hush-money; ~**marsch** silent protest march; ~**pflicht** pledge of secrecy, professional discretion; *ärztliche* ~~: *medical confidentiality*; ~**recht** a right to silence.

Schweigen *n* silence, keeping silent; ~ **bedeutet Zustimmung** silence denotes consent (*to commercial letter of confirmation*); **zum** ~ **bringen** to silence.

Schweizerische Eidgenossenschaft *f* Swiss Confederation.

Schwelle *f* threshold; ~**nland** threshold country; newly industrialized country; developing country; ~**preis** threshold price.

Schwemme *f* glut, oversupply.

Schwer|arbeit hard work, heavy work (*or* labour), hard manual labour; ~**arbeiter** heavy labourer; ~**behinderter** invalid, severely handicapped person, serverely disabled (person); ~**beschädigter** permanently disabled person (*due to war or public service*); ~**gewicht** main weight, preponderance; heavyweight; ~**gut** heavy load, heavy cargo; ~**gutladefähigkeit** deadweight cargo (capacity); ~**industrie** heavy industry; ~**kriegsbeschädigter** war invalid; ~**kriminalität** serious crime; ~**pflegebedürftigkeit** nursing need in disability cases; ~**punkt** emphasis, point of gravity; ~~ *des Vertragsverhältnisses* (*IPR* center of gravity doctrine); ~~*programm: sectors of priority, areas of emphasis*, ~~ *staatsanwaltschaft*; *centralized* (*or specialized*) *prosecution*; ~~*streik: selective strike, pin-point strike*; ~**verbrecher** felon, major criminal; ~**verletztenzulage** extra pay for seriously injured employees; ~**verletzter** seriously injured person; ~**wassereaktor** heavy-water reactor.

Schwere *f* gravity, seriousness (*of the offence*).

Schwester|bank associated bank, sister banking institution; ~**firma** affiliate, associated firm, related company; ~**gesellschaft** sister company, brother-sister corporation; ~**institut** affiliated organization; ~**schiff** sister ship; ~**unternehmen** affiliated undertaking, associated enterprise.

Schwimmbagger *m* dredge.
Schwimmdock *n* floating dock.
schwimmend *adj* afloat; **auf Hamburg** ~ afloat, bound for Hamburg.
Schwindel *m* swindle; ~**firma** bogus firm, bogus company; ~**geschäft** fraudulent transaction; ~**maklerfirma** bucket shop; ~**manöver** fraudulent trick, fraudulent stratagem; ~**preis** fraudulent price.
Schwindler *m* swindler, rogue, confidence man, crook.
schwören *v/i* to swear, to take the oath, ~, **die reine Wahrheit zu sagen, nichts zu verschweigen und nichts hinzuzufügen** to swear to tell the truth, the whole truth and nothing but the truth; **bei Gott dem Allmächtigen** ~ to swear by Almighty God; **falsch** ~ to commit perjury; to swear falsely; **jmdn** ~ **lassen** to administer the oath upon s. o.
Schwund *m* diminution, shrinkage, leakage; ~**satz** rate of shrinkage, rate of wastage, rate of waste; ~**vergütung** leakage (money); **bei der Herstellung eintretender** ~ production losses; **natürlicher** ~ natural loss, normal loss, natural waste.
Schwur *m* oath, vow; ~**finger** fingers raised in taking the oath; ~**gericht** criminal chamber of the regional court (*for grave offences*), crown court; ~**gerichtssitzung** *session of the Schwurgericht q.v.*; ~**hand** raised hand; **vorsätzlich falscher** ~ wilfully swearing falsehood; perjury.
See|amt Maritime Investigation, Board *(for shipping accidents)*; ~**arbeitsrecht** maritime employment law; ~**beförderungsvertrag** marine contract, ocean transport contract; ~-**Berufsgenossenschaft** Seamen's Accident Prevention and Insurance Authority; ~**blockade** maritime blockade, naval blockade; ~**brief** ship's passport; ~**brauch** maritime usage, maritime custom; ~**darlehen** bottomry loan; ~**durchgang** sea passage; ~**fahrt** navigation; ~**fahrtsbuch** seaman's passport, discharge book; ~**fischerei** sea fishing, ocean fishing; ~**flagge** maritime flag; ~**fracht** sea freight, maritime freight; *pl*: ~~**en**: marine *freight rates*, marine *freights*; ~**frachtbrief** ocean bill of lading, bill of lading; ~**frachtgeschäft** carriage of goods by sea, affreightment; ~**frachtrecht** law of carriage of goods by sea; ~**fracht- und Gewinnausfallversicherung** freight and profits policy; ~**frachtvertrag** shipment contract, contract of carriage of goods by sea; ~**freihafen** maritime free port; ~**gebrauch** maritime usage, maritime custom; ~**gefahr** marine risk, risks of the sea, hazards of the sea; ~**gefecht** naval action; ~**gericht** admiralty court; ~**gerichtsbarkeit** maritime jurisdiction; ~**gesundheitserklärung** maritime declaration of health; ~**grenze** maritime boundary *or* frontier; ~**grundstück** riparian property, lakeside property; ~**hafen** sea port, maritime port, harbour; ~**hafenplätze** seaport towns, seaports; ~**handel** maritime trade, seaborne trade, maritime commerce, shipping trade; ~**handelskredit** maritime commerce credit; ~**handelsrecht** shipping law; ~**herrschaft** naval supremacy; ~**hoheitsgebiet** maritime domain; ~**kanal** ship canal; ~**kaskoversicherung** maritime hull insurance; ~**kasse** seamen's pension insurance board *(compulsory insurance for seamen)*; ~**konossement** ocean bill of lading; ~-**Krankenkasse** maritime health insurance (fund); ~**krieg** naval war; ~**kriegsrecht** law of naval warfare; ~**küste** seashore, coast, coast line; ~**leute** seamen, sailors; ~~ *anheuern:* to engage seamen; ~**lotse** ship's pilot; ~**macht** naval power, maritime power; ~**mann** seaman,

sailor, mariner; **~mannsamt** shipping commissioner, seamen's administrative board; **~mannsbrauch** maritime usage, seamen's custom; *sailor's tradition;* **~mannsheim** home for sailors, sailors' hostel; **~mannsordnung** regulations for masters and seamen, maritime regulations; **~mannstestament** sailor's (*or* mariner's) will; **~meile** sea mile, nautical mile *(1.853 km);* **~not** distress at sea; ~~*dienst: obligation to come to the rescue of ships in distress; rescue operations;* ~~*ruf: distress signal S. O. S.; aus* ~~ *retten: to rescue;* **~paß** ship's passport; **~passagevertrag** sea passage contract; **~pfandrecht** maritime lien; **~prisenrecht** naval prize law; **~protest** ship's protest, protest by the shipmaster, captain's report; **~räuber** pirate; **~räuberei** piracy (on the high seas); **~recht** laws of the sea, maritime law, marine law, shipping law, admiralty law; *hanseatisches* ~~: *Hanseatic Laws of the Sea; internationales* ~~: *maritime international law;* **~rechtsabkommen** convention of the law of the sea; **~rechtssache** admiralty case, maritime matter; **~reise** sea passage, voyage; **~risiko** = ~*gefahr qv;* **~schaden** sea damage, average; ~~*berechnung: computation of sea damage;* **~schiedsgericht** marine arbitral tribunal; **~schiff** ocean-going vessel (*or* ship); **~schiffahrt** sea navigation, maritime shipping; **~schiffahrtsbetrieb** merchant marine company, shipping company; **~schiffer** ship's captain, commanding officer of a ship; **~straße** maritime route, ocean course; **~straßenordnung** rules of the road (at sea); **~testament** nuncupative will in distress at sea; **~transport** marine transport, seaborne transport; **~transportgefahr** maritime perils, hazards of the sea; **~transportgeschäft** shipping trade, marine transport, maritime shipping; **~transportversicherer** marine underwriter, underwriter of oversea shipments; **~transportversicherung** marine insurance; **~transportversicherungsvertrag** marine insurance contract; **s~tüchtig** *adj* seaworthy; *nicht* ~~: *unseaworthy;* **~tüchtigkeit** seaworthiness; **~tüchtigkeitsbescheinigung** general safety certificate; **~uferanlage** sea bank, bank of a lake; **~- und Landfrachten** freight and carriage; **~- und Landtransport** sea and land carriage; **~unfall** maritime casualty, sea accident, accident at sea; **~unfallversicherung** accidents-at-sea insurance; **s~untauglich** *adj* unseaworthy; **~untauglichkeit** unseaworthiness; ~~*serklärung: condemnation;* **s~untüchtigkeit** *adj* unseaworthy; **~untüchtigkeit** unseaworthiness; **~verkehr** ocean traffic, sea transit; **~vermessung** hydrographic survey; **~vermögen** property at sea (*of shipowner*); **~verpackung** seaworthy packing, seaport packing; **~verschollenheit** *long unexplained disappearance of seamen or ship's passengers,* presumption of death due to perils of the sea; **~versicherer** marine insurer, marine underwriter; **~versicherung** (ocean) marine insurance; **~versicherungspolice** marine policy; **~versicherungsrecht** marine insurance law; **~versicherungstransportpolice** marine transport insurance policy; **~versicherungsvertrag** marine insurance contract, contract of sea insurance; **~wasserstraße** ocean route, ocean lane; **~wechsel** bill, respondentia bond; **~weg** ocean route, sea route, ocean course; *auf dem* ~~ *befördert: seaborne;* **~wurf** jettison, jettisoning, jettisoned goods; **~zeichen** sea mark, nautical mark; **~zoll** customs levied at the coast; **~zollhafen** port of entry (*for customs clearance*).

Seh|bereich visual range, vision; ~**leistung** visual performance; ~**prüfung** sight test, optometry; ~**störung** impaired vision; ~**vermögen** sight, vision, visual range.
Seilschaft *f pol* the old boys' network.
Seiten|abstand lateral distance; *ausreichender* ~~: *sufficiently wide berth*: ~**einsteiger** irregular entrant; ~**kanal** side canal; ~**linie** collateral line; ~**rand** margin, side; ~**sprung** extramarital escapade; ~**streifen** (hard) shoulder; *begehbare* ~~ *suitable verges for pedestrians*; ~**verwandter** collateral relative; ~**wind** cross wind; **der Verkehrsrichtung entgegengesetzte Seite** the side opposite to that of the direction of traffic, the side facing the traffic; **vorgeschriebene Seite für das Vorbeifahren** overtake (or pass) on this side.
Sekretariat *n* secretariat, secretary's office; ~**sinspektor** secretarial assistant.
Sektion *f* section, group; dissection, autopsy, post-mortem (examination); ~**seinwilligung** consent to a post-mortem examination.
Sektor *m* sector, section; **der kommunale** ~ the local authorities; **der öffentliche** ~ the public, the public sector; **im gewerblichen und industriellen** ~ in trade and industry; **wirtschaftlicher** ~ branch of economic activity.
Sektsteuer *f* champagne tax, tax on sparkling white wine.
Sekundant *m* second (*duelling*).
sekundär *adj* secondary.
Sekundär|bereich secondary field, secondary industries, capital goods industries; ~**emission** secondary offering; ~**forschung** desk research; ~**liquidität** secondary liquidity; ~**markt** secondary market; ~**reserven** secondary reserves; ~**wirkung** secondary effect, "spin-off".
Sekundarabschluß *m* intermediate (school) leaving certificate.

selbständig *adj* self-employed, independent, self-supporting; original.
Selbständiger *m* (*der Selbständige*) self-employed person, independent person.
Selbst|abholer self-collector; ~**abholung** self-collection; ~**ablehnung** self-disqualification by a judge; recusation; ~**abtreibung** abortion brought about by the pregnant woman herself; ~**anfertigung** self-made product; ~**anklage** self-accusation; ~**anmelder** applicant in his own name; ~**anzeige** self-accusation reported to the police, self-accusation of tax evasion; ~**aufbringungsbetrag** *additional contribution by aided person for himself*; s~**auferlegt** self-imposed; ~**auflösung** voluntary winding up; ~**aufopferung** self-sacrifice; ~**auskunft** disclosure of one's personal and financial data; ~**bedarf** personal requirements; ~**bedienung** self-service; ~**bedienungsgroßhandel** self-service wholesale trade; ~**bedienungsladen** self-service store; ~**befreiung** liberation without outside help, prison breaking; ~**begünstigung** obtaining (improper) benefits for oneself; ~**behalt** excess, own risk (*automobile insurance*), co-insurance, retention, self-retention; ~**behaltsklausel** own-risk clause, franchise clause, excess clause; ~**beherrschung** self-restraint, power of self-control; s~**beigebracht** *adj* self-inflicted; ~**bekenntnis** voluntary confession; ~**belastung** self-incrimination; ~**belieferung** obtaining supplies oneself; ~**belieferungsvorbehalt** reservation as to oneself obtaining delivery; ~**beschränkung** self-restraint, voluntary restraint; ~**beschuldigung** self-accusation; ~**bestimmung** self-determination; ~**bestimmungsrecht** right of self-determination; ~**beteiligung** *assuming part of the risk oneself, cf* ~*behalt*; ~**bewirtschaftung** self-management (*farm*); ~**bezich-**

Selbstabholer

tigung self-incrimination; ~**bindung** self-engagement, self-commitment; ~**einschätzung** self-assessment; ~**eintritt** *agent contracting in his own name and for his own benefit*; adopting a transaction for oneself, dealing for one's own account; ~**eintrittsrecht** (agent's) right to take over a transaction for oneself; ~**entzündung** spontaneous combustion; ~**erhaltung** self-preservation; ~**erwerber** *person acquiring s.th. for himself*; s~**erworben** *adj* self-acquired; ~**fahrer** owner-driver; self-propelled craft; self-propelling chair; s~**finanzieren** to finance out of one's own resources; ~**finanzierung** self-financing, financing out of retained earnings; ~**gefährdung** self-endangering; *unnötige* ~~: *unnecessary exposure (to danger)*; ~**gefährdung durch Verwahrlosung** self-neglect; ~**gefährlichkeit** intrinsic danger (to oneself); ~**genügsamkeit** selfsufficiency, modesty; s~**gerecht** *adj* self-righteous; ~**gerechtigkeit** self-righteousness; s~**haftend** *adj* at one's own risk, liable for oneself; ~**herrschaft** independent rule; ~**herrscher** autocratic ruler; ~**hilfe** self-redress, self-help; attack in defence of property; ~**hilfeverkauf** sale without resort to legal process, emergency sale, selling out, resale on buyer's default to take delivery; ~**hilferecht** right of self-redress; ~**justiz** acting as one's own judge; applying the law of the jungle; ~**kontrahent** party contracting as principal and agent, self-contracting party; ~**kontrahieren** (*n*) self-dealing, acting as principal and agent; s~**kontrahieren** *v/i* to act as principal and agent; ~**kontrolle** self-control, self-regulation, ~**korrektur** automatic adjustment, automatic correction; ~**kosten** own costs, self-cost, prime cost, original cost, cost price; ~~ *des Verkäufers: selling cost, seller's own costs*; ~**kostenerstattungspreis** cost reimbursement price; ~**kostenpreis** cost price, prime cost; ~**mord** suicide; ~**mordabsicht** intent to commit suicide; suicidal intent; ~**mörder** suicide; felo-de-se; ~**mordkandidat** potential suicide, suicidal person; ~**mordklausel** suicide clause, suicide sane or insane; ~**mordversuch** suicide attempt; ~**potenzierung** automatic increase, snowball growth; ~**rechtfertigung** self-justification; ~**regierung** self-government; ~**regulierung** self-regulation; ~**schuldner** principal (*or* primary) debtor; ~**schuldnerisch** directly liable, owing as a principal (*or* primary) debtor; ~**schußanlage** shrapnel-firing anti-escape device, automatically triggered shotguns; ~**schüsse** self-firing explosions; trap guns; ~**steigerungskräfte** self-regulating forces; ~**ständigkeit** independence; ~**steigerung** automatic growth; ~**täuschung** self-deception; ~**tilgung** self-amortization, self-liquidity; ~**tötung** suicide; ~**unterricht** self-instruction; ~**veranlagung** self-assessment (for taxation); s~**veranlagungspflichtig** *adj* self-assessable; ~**verbrauch** private consumption; ~**vereitelung** self-induced frustration; ~**verlag** publication by the author; *im* ~~ *erschienen*: *published by the author*; ~**verschuldet** through one's own fault, caused by one's personal negligence; ~**versenkung** scuttling; ~**versicherer** self-insurer, private insurer, co-insurer; ~**versicherung** self-insurance, private insurance, coinsurance; *vereinbarte* ~~: *coinsurance clause*; s~**versorgend** *adj* self-supporting; ~**versorger** own producer, self-supporter; ~**versorgung** self-sufficiency ~~ *mit Öl: self-sufficiency in oil supplies;* autarky; ~**verständlichkeit** self-evident truth, self-evidence; matter of course, truism, foregone conclusion; ~**verstümmelung** self-mutilation, maiming oneself, voluntary

Seltenheitswert — **Seuchenbekämpfung**

mutilation, self-inflicted wounds; ~**verteidigung** self-defence; ~**verwaltung** self-administration, self-government, autonomy; ~**verwaltungskörperschaft** self-governing body, autonomous corporation; ~**verwaltungsorgane** self-governing bodies; ~**verwaltungsrecht** right of (local) self-government; ~**zahler** self-pay patient; ~**zweck** end in itself, object in itself.

Seltenheitswert *m* scarcity (*or* rarity) value.

Senat *m* senate, appellate court division; **akademischer** ~ university convocation (*or* senate); **die vereinigten** ~**e** the plenum (*supreme court*).

Senator *m* senator; minister (*head of executive department in Berlin, and/or Hanseatic Cities*).

Senats|direktor permanent secretary (*municipal government of Berlin*); ~**enquete** senate inquiry; ~**mandat** senatorial seat; ~**mitglied** member of the senate, senator; ~**präsident** (*formerly:*) presiding judge (*of a division of the court of appeal*); ~**sitz** senatorial seat; ~**sitzung** session of the senate, (superior) court session; ~**verwaltung** governmental administration (*of Berlin*); ~**vorsitzender** presiding judge of a division of a court of appeal; ~**wahlen** senatorial elections.

Sende|erlaubnis *f* transmission licence; ~**genehmigung** = *Sendeerlaubnis qv;* ~**leitung** transmissions management; ~**recht** broadcasting rights; ~**zeit** (daily) airtime.

Sendung *f (1)* shipment, consignment; ~ **als Frachtgut** consignment by goods train; ~ **e–s Geldbetrages** remittance; ~ **gegen Barzahlung** cash on delivery; **unzustellbare** ~ undeliverable mail.

Sendung *f (2)* broadcast, transmission, programme: **e–e** ~ **des Werbefunks** a commercial broadcast.

Seniorenheim *n* senior citizens' accommodation.

Seniorpartner *m* senior partner.

Senkungsschaden *m* subsidence damage, damage caused by settlement of the ground.

Sensationspresse *f* yellow press, stunt press, cheap tabloids.

Separatfriede *m* separate peace.

Separatismus *m* separatism.

Separatist *m* separatist, secessionist.

Separatkonto *n* special account.

Sequester *m* sequestrator, official receiver; ~ *für die Dauer des Rechtsstreits: receiver pendente lite;* ~**pfandrecht** official receiver's lien; ~**vermögen** sequestrated property; ~**verwaltung** receivership by a sequestrator.

Sequestration *f* sequestration, official (temporary) receivership; *gerichtliche* ~: *receiving order.*

Sequestratur *f* sequestration.

sequestrierbar *adj* sequestrable.

sequestrieren *v/t* to sequestrate.

Serien|anleihe serial loan, serial bonds issue; ~**artikel** mass-produced article; ~**bauprogramm** multiple production series programme; ~**fertigung** (continuous) series-type production; ~**güter** series-produced goods, mass produced goods; ~**herstellung** = *Serienfertigung qv;* s~**mäßig** in series, serial standard, regular; ~**muster** representative sample; ~**nummer** serial number; ~**obligation** serial bond; ~**preisgeschäft** penny store; ~**rabatt** frequency discount; ~**reife** production stage.

Servitut *n* servitude, easement; ~**enablösung** commutation of easements; **öffentlich-rechtliches** ~ public easement; **völkerrechtliches** ~ international servitude.

Servolenkung *f* power-assisted steering.

seßhaft *adj* settled, sedentary.

Seßhaftmachung *f* settlement, settling down; ~**sgesetz** law on the settlement of migrants.

Seuchen|bekämpfung epidemics control; ~**gefahr** danger of an epidemic; ~**gesetz** epidemics con-

Sexualdelikt   **Sicherheitsabkommen**

trol act; ~**polizei** epidemics control inspectorate, sanitary authorities; ~**verhütung** prevention of epidemics.
Sexual|delikt sexual offence; ~**strafrecht** penal (*or* criminal) law on sexual offences; ~**verbrechen** sex crime; ~**verbrecher** sexual criminal.
Sezession *f* secession; ~**skrieg** war of secession.
Sezessionist *m* secessionist.
Sezierung *f* dissection.
Sichausschweigen *n* keeping silent, stonewalling.
Sicheinfügen *n* compliance, attitude of team-membership.
Sicherheit *f (1)* safety, security; ~ **am Arbeitsplatz** safe working conditions, industrial safety; ~**des Arbeitsplatzes** job security; ~ **hat Vorrang** safety first; **die öffentliche ~ und Ordnung wiederherstellen** to restore law and order; **nationale ~** national security; **öffentliche ~** public safety (*or* security); **persönliche ~** personal security; **soziale ~** social security.
Sicherheit *f (2)* security, collateral security; ~ **durch Hinterlegung** security by payment into court; ~**en an Grundstücken** real securities; ~**en anschaffen** to supply collateral; ~**en bestellen** to supply collateral, to provide security for money; ~ **für e-e Forderung** security for a debt; ~**gewähren** to secure; ~ **leisten** to provide security, to post a bond; ~**sdepot** guarantee fund, premium reserve; **ausreichende ~** sufficient security; **dingliche ~** lien secured by property, security in rem, collateral security, underlying security; **gegen ~** against security, by way of security; ~ *hypothekarische ~: on mortgage security;* ~ ~ *freilassen: to release on bail;* **hochwertige ~** high-grade security; **hypothekarische ~** security by mortgage.
Sicherheits|abkommen defensive alliance, security agreement; ~**ab-**

stand safe distance, (maintenance of) adequate distance between cars; ~**arrest** preventive custody; ~**beamter** security officer; safety inspector; ~~ *im Flugzeug: sky marshall;* ~**beauftragter** security commissioner; ~**bereich** security zones; ~**bescheid** security clearance; **s~bildend** security-building (*pol*); ~**denken** safety first attitude; ~**dienst** intelligence service, security service; security agency (*factory*); ~**einbehalt** retention of security; ~**einrichtungen** safety installations; **s~empfindlich** sensitive; ~**faktor** safety factor; ~**filmgesetz** safety film law (*for motion pictures*); ~**flächen** safety area; ~**fonds** collateral fund; ~**garantie** security guarantee; ~**gurt** safety belt; ~**hinterlegung** guarantee deposit; ~**klausel** escape clause; ~**konto** margin account; ~**kontrolle** security control, safety check; ~**leistung** → *Sicherheitsleistung;* ~**manko** security lapse; ~**marge** safety margin, collateral security margin; ~**maßnahmen** security measures, safety precautions, precautionary measures; ~**maßregeln** security measures, precautionary measures; ~**normen** safety rules, safety standards; ~**pakt** security pact, defence pact; ~**partnerschaft** security partnership; ~**programm** defence programme; ~**rat** Security Council; ~**recht** security interest; ~**reserven** contingency reserves, security reserves; ~**risiko** security risk; ~**rücklage** contingency reserve, security reserve; ~**spanne** safety margin; ~**system** security system; *gesamteuropäisches* ~~: *all-European security system; kollektives* ~~: *collective security system;* ~**technologie** safety technology; ~**verwahrung** preventive custody (*for dangerous habitual criminals*); ~**vorkehrungen** safety precautions, security precautions; ~**vorrichtungen** safety appliances; ~**vorschriften** safety regulations;

bautechnische ~~*en*: structural safety requirements; ~**wechsel** collateral bill; ~-**Zulassungsschild** safety approval notice; ~**zuschlag** security surcharge.

Sicherheitsleistung *f* lodging of security, provision of security; bail, judicial bond, ~ **bei Gericht** judicial bond; ~ **des Submittenten** performance bond, performance guarantee; ~ **durch Testamentsvollstrecker** administration bond; ~ **für Prozeßkosten** security for costs; ~ **im Zivilprozeß** civil bail, security in a civil case; **gegen** ~ on (*or* against) security.

sichern *v/t* to secure, to provide security (for); **dinglich** ~ to secure by collateral, to secure (by a right) in rem; **hypothekarisch** ~ to secure by mortgage (*or* charge).

sicherstellen *v/t* to ensure, to make sure; to guarantee, to warrant, to impound, to put in safe custody.

Sicherstellung *f* security, provision of emergency services and supplies, safeguarding, providing collateral.

Sicherung *f* provision of security, protection, safeguarding; ~ **der Familie** family protection, safeguarding the maintenance of the family; ~ **der Ruhegeldverpflichtungen** covering the pension liabilities; ~ **des Arbeitsplatzes** job security; ~ **des Beweises** securing (the maintenance of) evidence; ~ **des Friedens** safeguarding peace; ~ **gegen Verlust** cover against loss; ~ **und Besserung** public security and correction; **bankmäßige** ~ normal banking security, bank safeguards.

Sicherungs|abrede agreement on the provision of collateral; ~**abtretung** assignment by way of security (*of a claim or debt*); ~**beschlagnahme** attachment by way of security; ~**eigentum** security by transfer of ownership, conditional ownership, title transferred as security; ~**eigentümer** owner of property transferred as collateral security; ~**fonds** safety fund;

~**geber** party furnishing security, mortgagor of a chattel or interest; ~**gegenstand** collateral, item serving as security; ~**gelder** funds pledged as security; ~**geschäft** secured transaction; ~**grundschuld** land charge serving as collateral; ~**gut** property serving as security, mortgaged property; ~**haft** precautionary detention; ~**hypothek** collateral mortgage, lien by way of mortgage; ~**klausel** escape clause, safeguarding clause; ~**maßnahmen** measures of public security; ~**mittel** means of providing security, the security provided; ~**nehmer** *party to whom security has been furnished,* secured party; ~**patent** confirmation patent; ~**pflicht** safety obligation; ~**recht** security right, right to protection from risks; ~**scheck** memorandum cheque; ~**schein** security note; ~**stempel** authentication stamp; ~**treuhand** trust for purpose of security; ~**übereignung** transfer of ownership by way of security, conditional bill of sale; ~**übereignungsurkunde** bill of sale, trust deed; ~-**und Überwachungsmaßnahmen** safeguards and controls; ~**verfahren** confinement proceedings (*of mentally disabled offender*), safeguarding proceedings; ~**verkauf** hedge selling, sale to obtain cover; ~**verwahrter** prisoner under preventive (*or* precautionary) detention; ~**verwahrung** preventive/detention (*of habitual offenders*), extended sentence of imprisonment; ~**vollstreckung** provisional attachment; ~**vorkehrungen** protective measures, safeguards; ~**zession** fiduciary assignment.

Sicht *f* sight, vision; ~**einlage** demand deposit; *pl* ~*en also: current accounts*; ~**fahrgebot** legal requirement to adjust speed to visibility conditions; ~**feld** (driver's) field of vision; ~**gelder** demand deposits; ~**guthaben** credit balance payable on demand; sight balance; ~**papier**

Sickerwasser

demand note; ~**tage** days of grace; ~**tratte** sight draft, draft at sight, demand draft; ~**verbindlichkeiten** liabilities payable at sight or on demand; ~**vermerk** visa; ~**wechsel** bill payable on demand; sight bill, sight draft; ~**weite** visibility, range of vision; **auf** ~ on demand, on sight, at sight; **auf kurze** ~ at short sight, in the short term; **auf lange** ~ in the long run, (in the) long term; **behinderte** ~ obscured vision; **bei** ~ at sight, on presentation, on demand.

Sickerwasser n percolating water.

sieben v/t screen (*candidates*).

Siebung f screening; ~ **der Aufträge** screening the orders.

Siechtum n lingering illness, invalidism, languishing (state).

siedeln v/i to settle, to form housing estates; **wild** ~ to squat.

Siedler m settler, colonizer, homecrofter, homesteader (*US*); ~**stelle** settler's holding, homestead; **unberechtiger** ~ squatter.

Siedlung f housing development, housing estate, settlement, resettlement, small holding, housing project.

Siedlungs|bank housing development bank; ~**behörde** resettlement administration; ~**gebiete** housing development area; ~**gemeinschaft** housing development association, group of settlers; ~**genossenschaft** cooperative land society, homestead cooperative; ~**gesellschaft** homestead corporation, land settlement society; ~**gesetz** Housing Development Act, Homestead Act; ~**kredit** land settlement credit; ~**land** housing development land, settlement area; ~**maßnahmen** measures to promote settlement schemes; ~**programm** settlement scheme; ~**recht** the law of agricultural settlements; ~**unternehmen** housing and land settlement enterprise; ~**vorkaufsrecht** right of pre-emption for homestead land; ~**wesen** land settlement.

Simulierung

Siegel n seal, signet; ~**abdruck** imprint of a seal; ~**abnahme** removal of a seal; ~**bruch** breaking official seals; ~ **der Verschwiegenheit** seal of secrecy; ~**fälschung** forging seals; ~**führung** use of seal; ~**marke** paper seal, wafer; ~**verfälschung** forging seals; **ein** ~ **anbringen** to affix a seal; **ein** ~ **beidrücken** to affix a seal; **ein** ~ **brechen** to unseal, to break a seal; **ein** ~ **erbrechen** to break a seal; **mit e-m** ~ **versehen** to seal; **unverletztes** ~ unbroken seal.

siegeln v/t to seal, to affix a seal.

Siegelung f sealing, affixing of a seal, impressment of a seal.

siehe vide; ~ **oben** supra, see above; ~ **unten** infra, see below.

Signal n signal, sign indication, pointer; ~**code** signal book; ~**wirkung** signalling effect, sth serving as a signal; **ein** ~ **beachten** to obey a signal, to pay heed to a signal; **ein** ~ **überfahren** to overshoot a signal, to skip the lights.

Signatar m signatory (power); ~**mächte** signatory powers; ~**staat** signatory state.

signieren v/t to initial.

Signierung f initial(l)ing, autographing.

Silber n silver; ~**bergwerk** silver mine; ~**gehalt** silver content; ~**geld** silver currency, silver coins; ~**geldwährung** silver currency, silver standard; ~**geschirr** silver plate; ~**münze** silver coin; ~**punkt** silver point; ~**sachen** silver, silver goods; ~**währung** silver standard; ~**waren** silver goods, silverware; **gediegenes** ~ solid silver; **gemünztes** ~ coined silver; **ungemünztes** ~ silver bullion; **verarbeitetes** ~ wrought silver.

Simonie f simony.

Simulant m simulator of illness, malingerer, sham.

simulieren v/i to simulate, to feign disease, to malinger, to sham.

Simulierung f simulation, pretending to be ill, malingering, feigning illness.

Simultangründung one-step incorporation, *standard method of incorporation with the founders taking over all shares*; ~**haftung** simultaneous liability, direct and primary liability; ~**schule** non-denominational school; ~**verhältnis** simultaneous relationship; ~**zulassung** simultaneous admission (of a lawyer) at a lower and higher court.

„**singen**" to squeal (*at police interrogation*).

Sinn *m* sense, meaning; ~ **des Gesetzes** ratio legis, meaning of the law; ~**gehalt** essential meaning; gist (invention), substance, **den** ~ **haben** to mean, to purport, to signify, to denote; **im juristischen** ~ in the legal sense; **im rechtlichen** ~**e** in the legal sense, for legal purposes; **im** ~**e der Gesetzgebung** in accordance with the purpose of the legislation; **im** ~**e des Gesetzes** within the meaning of the Act; **im** ~**e des Vorschlags** on the lines of the proposal; **im** ~**e dieses Vertrages** for the purposes of this agreement; **im engeren** ~ in a narrower sense; **übertragener** ~ figurative meaning, metaphorical sense; **wörtlicher** ~ literal meaning.

Sinnestäuschung *f* illusion, hallucination, mental delusion.

sinngemäß *adj* (*adv*) according(ly), analogous(ly), mutatis mutandis.

sinnlos *adj* senseless, meaningless, needless, pointless.

sinnvoll *adj* meaningful, significant; **wenig** ~ unsuitable, of little significance.

sinnwidrig *adj* illogical.

Sippe *f* clan, kin, kinship, relations.

sistieren *v/t* to stay, to suspend.

Sistierung *f* stay of execution (*civil*), stay of proceedings, nolle prosequi.

Sitte *f* custom, mores, morality, observance; **gute** ~**n** public morals, good manners, morality, public policy; *gegen die* ~**n** ~*n:* contra bonos mores, contrary to morality, against public morals, unconscionable.

Sitten|gesetz moral law, rules (or code) of ethics; ~**lehre** moral philosophy, ethics; ~**polizei** vice squad; ~**strafrecht** criminal law of immorality; ~**strolch** sex molester; ~**verderbnis** corruption of public morals.

sittenwidrig *adj* contra bonos mores, against morals, immoral, unethical, unconscionable, offending against good morals.

Sittenwidrigkeit *f* immorality, unconscionability, violation of moral principles, violation of boni mores.

Sittlichkeit *f* morality, good morals, public decency, public morals; ~**sdelikt** offence against morality, sexual offence; ~**sverbrechen** sex crime; ~**sverbrecher** sex criminal; ~**svergehen** sexual offence.

Sitz *m(1)* chair, seat, membership; ~ **in e-m Verwaltungsrat** seat on a board; „~**redakteur**" imprisoned editor; ~**verteilung** allotment of seats; **freiwerdende** ~**e** vacancies; **ständiger** ~ permanent seat.

Sitz *m(2)* principal place of business, registered seat, registered office, corporate domicile; ~ **der Geschäftsleitung** place of management; ~ **der Niederlassung** commercial domicile; ~ **des Unternehmens** business seat, registered office; ~**staat** country of corporate domicile, country in which (a company) has its registered office; ~**verlegung** change of corporate domicile; *von Gesellschaften ins Ausland:* emigration of companies; **juristischer** ~ legal domicile, registered office; **satzungsmäßiger** ~ registered office.

Sitz|blockade sit-down blockade; ~**ordnung** seating plan, prescribed seats; ~**streik** sit-down strike; *mehrtägiger* ~~: stay-in-strike.

Sitzung *f* session, sitting, meeting, hearing, conference; ~ **unter Ausschluß der Öffentlichkeit** hearing in camera, closed session; **außerordentliche** ~ emergency session, extraordinary meeting; **die** ~ **eröffnen** to open (the) court; **die** ~ **ist eröffnet** the court is in session;

Sitzungsgeld / **Solawechsel**

die ~ **leiten** to preside (over), to chair; die ~ **unterbrechen** to adjourn the hearing, to take a recess; e–e ~ **abhalten** to sit, to hold a session; e–e ~ **anberaumen** to fix a date for a hearing; to schedule a meeting, to fix a meeting; **feierliche** ~ formal meeting; **gemeinsame** ~ joint session; **in der** ~ at the hearing, in the presence of the court; **nichtöffentliche** ~ closed session; in ~r ~: *in camera*; **öffentliche** ~ public hearing, hearing in open court; **ordentliche** ~ regular session; **vertagte** ~ adjourned meeting, further hearing.

Sitzungs|geld attendance fee; ~**gewalt** authority to maintain order in the court room (*or* at a meeting); ~**liste** the court's agenda, paper of causes, trial list; ~**ort** place of meeting; ~**niederschrift** minutes of proceedings, record of trial, trial record; ~**pause** recess; ~**periode** session, sittings, term; ~~ e–s Gerichts: term of court, law term; außerhalb der ~~: out of term; ~~ des Parlaments; session of parliament; Beendigung der ~~: prorogation of parliament; ordentliche ~~: ordinary session; ~**polizei** (judge's) power of maintaining order in the courtroom; ~**programm** order paper, agenda; ~**protokoll** minutes of proceedings, record of trial, trial record; ~**saal** court room, conference hall; ~**schluß** adjournment, close of the meeting; endgültiger ~~: adjournment sine die; ~**tage** days of session; ~**tagegelder** sessional per diem allowance; ~**tantieme** sessional allowance; ~**unterlagen** documents and papers for the session; ~**vertreter** deputy for the hearing; ~**zeit** stated term; ~**zeiten** sittings; ~**zimmer** council room, board room; ~**zwang** compulsory attendance at a meeting, compulsory meeting.

Skandalpresse *f* gutter press, yellow journalism, tabloids.

Skibruchversicherung *f* ski-breakage insurance.

Sklavenarbeit *f* slave labour.

Sklaverei *f* slavery, bondage, serfdom.

Skontierung *f* deduction of cash discounts; ~**stag** settlement day; ~~ für Termingeschäfte: name day.

Skonto (*m or n*) cash discount, prompt-payment discount ~**abzug** deduction of cash discount; ~**frist** discount period; ~ **gewähren** to allow a cash discount; ~**schinderei** taking unjustified cash discounts; ~**verzicht** foregoing the cash discount; **echtes** ~ genuine discount.

Skontration *f* settlement clearing.

Skontro *n* auxiliary ledger (*stocktaking*).

Skripturhaftung *f* liability for the correctness of (commercial) documents.

Sockel|betrag flat rate, basic amount, ~**finanzierung** provision of basic finance.

Sodomie *f* sodomy, buggery, crime against nature, bestiality.

Sofort|abschreibung immediate write-off (*equipment of small value*); ~**abzug** immediate deduction (*tax*), deduction at source; ~**auftrag** rush job; ~**bedarf** immediate requirements; ~**darlehen** immediate loan; ~**hilfe** immediate aid; ~**kontrolle** verification on the spot; ~**kredit** emergency credit; ~**maßnahmen** instant measures, prompt steps; ~**programm** immediate program(me), emergency aid program(me); ~**verfahren** summary proceedings; ~**vollzug** immediate enforcement.

Solange-Beschluß *m* resolution pending review (*of constitutionality*).

Solawechsel *m* negotiable promissory note (*often: promissory note, or: note*), negotiable note, promissory note made out to order; ~ **mit Prolongationsvereinbarung** note with agreement to execute renewal; **diskontierter** ~ discounted note; **girierter** ~ endorsed promissory note; **überfälliger** ~ past due note.

Sold *m* soldier's pay; ~**buch** (military) pay book.
Soldaten|beruf military profession; ~**gesetz** (*D 1975*) the Army Law; ~**laufbahn** military career; ~**laufbahnverordnung** Military Career Ordinance (*D 1977*); ~**recht** military law as regards soldiers; ~**testament** soldier's (nuncupative) will; ~**versorgung** *social and financial care, assistance and pension rights for members of the Armed Forces.*
Söldner *m* mercenary.
Solidaritätsbeitrag solidarity contribution (*as additional tax after reunification of Germany*).
Solidar|bürgschaft joint and several guarantee; ~**haftung** joint and several liability; ~**schuldner** joint and several debtor; ~**verbindlichkeit** joint and several liability; ~**verpflichtung** joint and several obligation.
solidarisch *adj* solidary, joint and several; *sich* ~ *erklären mit: to identify oneself with.*
Solidaritätsmechanismen *m/pl* (*int.*) common instruments.
Soll *n* debit, debit side; target, output target; ~**aufkommen** estimated yield, expected yield; ~**bestand** target inventory, calculated assets, calculated number, nominal balance; presumed assets; ~**bilanz** balance sheet as it ought to be, nominal balance; ~**buch** debit book; ~**einnahmen** supposed receipts, estimated receipts, receipts due; ~**erfüllung** achievement of goals, attainment of targets; ~**fertigungszeit** planned manufacturing time; ~**gewicht** standard weight; ~**-Ist-Vergleich** target-performance comparision; ~**kaufmann** businessman (*or* enterprise) required to be recorded in the Commercial Register; ~**kosten** target costs, standard costs; ~**kostenrechnung** budget accounting, standard costing; ~**leistung** nominal output, standard of performance, planned target; ~**menge** prescribed quantity, production target; ~**posten** debit item; ~**prämie** premium due; ~**seite** debit side; ~**-Saldo** debit balance; ~**seite** debit side; ~**spalte** debit column; ~**stärke** required strength, theoretical strength, effective authorized strength, establishment; ~**system** *system of debiting agents with total premiums collectible*; ~ **und Haben** debit and credit, balance of the account; ~**vorgabe** target; ~~~*n im Verkauf: sales quotas*; ~**vorschrift** directory provision, directory statute; ~**wert** target amount; nominal amount; desired value, required figure, theoretical value; ~**zahlen** target figures; ~**zeit** required time; ~**ziffern** required figures, target figures; ~**zinsen** lending debit interest, interest on the debit balance; ~**zinssatz** lending rate, debit rate; **im** ~ **stehen** to be on the debit side.
solvent *adj* solvent, able to pay.
Solvenz *f* solvency, ability to pay.
Sommer|bevorratung accumulation of stocks during the summer; ~**fahrplan** summer time-table; ~**halbjahr** summer term, second and third quarters of the calendar year; ~**pause** summer recess, summer break, summer slack season, summer slump; ~**schlußverkauf** summer sale; ~**weg** unpaved side road, road with unpaved shoulders, fineweather road.
Sonder|abgabe special levy, special assessment, special contribution; ~**abmachung** separate agreement, side agreement; ~**abkommen** special agreement; ~**abnehmervertrag** special consumers' agreement; ~**abrechnung** special settlement (*newly introduced securities*); ~**abschreibungen** special depreciation allowances, additional capital allowance; ~**aktion** special scheme, special campaign; ~**anfertigung** special design, item manufactured to order; ~**angebot** special offer, special bargain, bargain sale, preference offer; premium offer; ~~~*e zur Absatzförderung: pro-*

Sonderabgabe

motional offers, stimulative sales; ~**anknüpfung** special connecting factor *(to national law)*; ~**anlagen** special-purpose equipment; ~**anstalten** special institutions; ~**arbeit** special work; ~**aufsicht** special supervision; ~**aufgaben** special assignments, special tasks; ~**auftrag** special order; ~**aufwendungen** extra costs, extra expense; ~**ausgabe** specially allowed tax deduction, special expenses ~~**n-pauschale**: *standard deduction for special expenses (such as insurance premiums)*; *als* ~~ *abzugsfähig: deductible as a special expense; pauschalierte* ~~: *overall allowance for special expenses*; ~**ausschüttung** extra distribution; ~**ausstattung** optional equipment, extras; ~**ausverkauf** bargain sale, special sale; ~**ausweis** special pass, authorized credentials; ~**bearbeitung** special treatment; ~**beauftragter** special representative; ~**bedarf** special needs *(in addition to regular maintenance)*; ~**bedingungen** special terms (or conditions); ~**befreiungsvorschriften** special exemption rules; ~**behandlung** special treatment, privileged treatment; ~**behörde** special administrative board; ~**beilage** special supplement; ~**belastung** special charge, specific lien; ~**bestellung** special order; ~**besteuerung** special assessment; ~**bestimmung** special regulation, exceptional provision; ~**betriebsmittel** special operating resources provided by third parties; ~**betriebsvermögen** separate business assets *(made available by a partner to firm)*; ~**bilanz** special purpose balance sheet; ~**botschafter** envoy extraordinary, ambassador extraordinary, special envoy; ~**bevollmächtigter** special envoy, plenipotentiary; ~**delikte** special statutory offences; ~**depot** separate deposit; *im* ~~ *verwahrtes Gold: earmarked gold*; ~**dividende** extra dividend; ~**druck** special impression, special edition; ~**eigentum** separate ownership, single real property unit *(in a multiple-unit building)*, individual ownership of an apartment; ~**eigentümer** separate owner of individual unit of a condominium *(multiple unit building)*; ~**einkommenszahlung** special income payment; ~**einnahmen** specific revenues; ~**einzelkosten** special direct costs; ~**erbfolge** special succession to property (upon death); ~**erhebung** special investigation; special collection; ~**erlaubnis** special permit; ~**ermächtigung** special authorization; ~**ermäßigung** special price reduction; ~**fall** special case, exception to the rule; ~**fonds** special fund; ~**freibetrag** special (tax) exemption; ~**frieden** separate peace; ~**gebiet** preserve, special; ~**gebühr** extra fee; ~**gefahren** particular dangers (or risks), extraneous perils; ~**gehaltszahlung** extra salary payment; ~**genehmigung** special permit, special clearance, special licence; ~**gericht** special tribunal; ~**gerichtsbarkeit** jurisdiction of special tribunals, emergency jurisdiction; ~**gerichtsurteil** judgment by a special tribunal; ~**gesetz** special statute, private Act; ~**gesetzgebung** special legislation; ~**gewinn** extra profit; ~**gewinnsteuer** excess profits levy, excess profits tax, windfall (profits) tax; ~**gut** separate property *(of one of the spouses)*; ~**gutachten** special expert opinion; ~**haushalt** special budget, special-purpose budget; ~**heiratserlaubnis** special marriage licence; ~**honorar** extra fee; ~**institut** specialized institute; ~**kasse** special fund; ~**klasse** extra class; ~**konkurs** compulsory winding-up of segregated business units; ~**konditionen** special terms; *keine* ~~: *no special terms; at arm's length*; ~**konjunktur** special boom; *nationale* ~~: *domestic boom*; ~**kontingent** special quota; ~**konto** separate account, special account; ~**kosten** special costs;

Sonderabgabe

~**kredit** special-purpose loan; special credit (operation); ~**leistung** special service, additional service; extra performance; ~**linie** special line; ~**liquidation** special settlement; ~**maßnahmen** special measures; ~**minister** minister without portfolio, specially designated minister; ~**müll** special refuse; bulky waste material; ~**nachfolge** singular succession, succession as to particular assets; ~**nachfolger** subrogee, singular successor, successor in interest, successor to specific rights and obligations; ~**nachlaß** special rebate, special discount; ~**niederschrift** special record; ~**nutzung** separate use *especially by condominium part owner of a portion of community property*; ~~**sgebühr** *charge for the separate use (of)*; ~**opfer** special sacrifice; ~**organisation** specialized agency (UNO); ~**posten** separate item; ~**prämie** premium bonus; ~**preis** exceptional price, special offer; ~**prüfer** special auditor; ~**prüfung** specially arranged examination; ~**rabatt** special discount; ~**recht** special right, privilege; special law; *diskriminierendes* ~~: *special discriminatory law*; ~**rechtsklausel** subrogation clause, liberties clause, special privileges clause; ~**rechtsnachfolge** subrogation, assignment, succession to specific rights and obligations; *gewillkürte* ~~: *conventional subrogation*; ~**rechtsnachfolger** subrogee, singular successor, successor in interest, successor to specific rights and obligations; ~**regel** special rule; ~**regelung** special regulation, special provision, special arrangements; ~~ *für Ausländer: special treatment of foreign nationals*; ~**revision** special audit; ~**risiko** special hazard; ~**rücklage** special contingency reserve, extraordinary reserve, provident reserve, special reserve (fund); ~**rückstellung** special reserve; ~**schicht** extra shift; ~**schuldverschreibung** special bond; ~**schule** special school (*for handicapped or retarded children*); ~**schutz** special protection; ~**sitzung** special session, special meeting; ~**status** special status; ~**statut** special law; ~**stelle** special agency, special office; special department; ~**stellung** special position, privileged position;~ **steuer** special tax; ~**strafkammer** special criminal division (*of a regional court*); ~**tarif** preferential rate, exceptional rate, special tariff; ~~ *für günstige Versicherungsrisiken: preferred risks*; ~**termin** special session, special date; ~**umlage** special assessment; ~**urlaub** special leave, compassionate leave; ~**verbrauchssteuern im grenzüberschreitenden Reiseverkehr** excise duties levied during the international transit of travellers; ~**vereinbarung** special agreement; ~**verfahren** special proceedings; ~**vergünstigung** special favo(u)r; special privilege; ~**vergütung** bonus, special remuneration, extra pay, premium pay; ~**verkauf** (special) sale, rummage sale; ~**vermächtnis** specific legacy; ~**vermögen** special fund, separate property, separate assets; ~~ *von öffentlichen Versorgungsbetrieben: utility fund; zweckgebundenes* ~~: *working capital fund*; ~**verordnung** separate ordinance; ~**vertrag** special contract; ~**vertragskunden** special customers; ~**verwahrung** separate safekeeping, special deposit; ~**vollmacht** special power of attorney; ~**vorschrift** special regulation, special requirement(s); ~**vorteil** special advantage; ~**vorzugsaktie** cumulative preference share; ~**votum** separate opinion; ~**wechselsteuer** exchange surcharge; ~**wertberichtigung** special loss provision; ~**wunsch** special wish, special request; ~**zahlung** special payment, extra payment; ~**ziehungsrecht** special drawing right;

~ziehungsrechts-Abteilung Special Drawing Rights Department; ~zinsen special interest; ~zoll surcharge on customs duties; ~zulage special bonus, merit increase; ~zustellung special service, special delivery; ~zuwendung special grant.

sondieren *v/t* to probe, to sound out, to explore.

Sondierung *f* probing, (*pl also:*) soundings, exploratory talks.

Sonnenenergie *f* solar energy.

Sonntags\|arbeit Sunday work; ~**arbeitsverbot** prohibition of work on Sundays; ~**fahrverbot** *prohibition to drive on Sundays and public holidays (for heavy vehicles)*; ~**gewerbe** *trade allowed on Sundays and public holidays;* ~**ruhe** Sunday closing, dominical rest; ~**zuschlag** Sunday supplement, extra charge for work on Sundays.

Sorge *f* care, solicitude, concern; ~**berechtigter** person having the care and custody (of s. o.); ~ **für die Person** care and custody of a person; ~**pflicht** obligation to care for (a child); ~**recht** custody, custody right; ~ **tragen für** to take care of sth.; to ensure sth.; ~**rechtsabänderung** change in the terms of parental care and custody; ~**rechtsentscheidung** court ruling on parental care and custody; ~**rechtsregelung** regulation concerning the child's care and custody; ~**rechtsverfahren** custody proceedings; **elterliche** ~ parental care and custody.

sorgen *v/i* to take care of, to provide for, to make due preparation for.

Sorgfalt *f* care, prudence, circumspection; ~ **e-s ordentlichen Kaufmanns** due diligence of a prudent businessman; a business-like manner; ~**smaßstab** standard of care; ~**spflicht** duty of care; ~**spflicht gegenüber dem Nächsten** neighbour principle; ~**spflichtverletzung** breach of the duty of care; ~ **üben** to exercise proper care; ~ **wie in eigenen Angelegenheiten** care as applied in one's own affairs; *diligentia quam in suis;* **angemessene** ~ reasonable care; **ausreichende** ~ adequate (*or* sufficient) care; **äußerste** ~ extraordinary care, utmost care; **besondere** ~ special care; **die im Verkehr erforderliche** ~ reasonable care, ordinary prudence, proper care and attention, due diligence, ~~~~~ *beachten: to exercise proper care;* **erforderliche** ~ due care; **fachmännische** ~ **anwenden** to take workmanlike care; **größtmögliche** ~ utmost care; **hinreichende** ~ proper care; **jede zumutbare** ~ all reasonable care; **mangelnde** ~ want (*or* lack) of care; **notwendige** ~ proper care, the required care and diligence; **übliche** ~ ordinary duty of care; **unterlassene** ~ failure to exercise due care and attention; **verkehrsübliche** ~ ordinary care, proper care, due care and attention.

sorgfältig *adj* careful, diligent.

Sorte *f* sort, kind, type variety, grade, *pl also:* foreign notes and coins, foreign cash.

Sorten\|abteilung foreign currency department; ~**geschäft** dealings in foreign notes and coins; ~**handel** dealings in foreign notes and coins; ~**händler** exchange jobber; ~**kasse** foreign currency cash department; ~**kurs** rate of exchange for notes and coins; ~**liste** list of (protected) seed varieties; ~**problem** problem of supplying goods of the required grades; ~**schutz** (plant) varieties patent; ~**schutzrechte** plant varieties protective rights; ~**schutzkontrolle** plant variety patent register; ~**wahl** grading; ~**zahl** number of varieties; ~**zettel** statement of specie, bill of specie.

sortieren *v/t* to assort, to sort.

Sortiermaschine *f* sorter, sorting machine.

Sortierung *f* assortment.

Sortiment *n* line of goods, range of goods, assortment, product mix, variety; **breites ~ der Güter** wide range of goods; **hereingenommene ~e** lines of goods taken into stock; **knappe ~e** little stock in hand.

Sortimenter *m* retail bookseller.

Sortiments|abhängigkeit dependence on the supply of a special brand of goods; **~abteilung** new book department; **~buchhändler** retail bookseller; **~-Buchhandlung** retail bookshop; **~erweiterung** diversification, broadening one's variety of goods; **~handel** single-line trade, wholesale trade, retail trade (*books*).

Souterrain *n* basement; **~räume** underground rooms; **~wohnung** basement flat, basement dwelling.

Souverän *m* sovereign.

souverän *adj* sovereign.

Souveränität *f* sovereignty; **~sakt** act of a sovereign state; **~sbeschränkung** restriction of sovereign rights; **~srecht** sovereign right; **~sverletzung** violation of sovereign rights; **äußere ~** (external) sovereignty; **nationale ~** national sovereignty; **parlamentarische ~** parliamentary sovereignty; **volle ~** full sovereignty.

Sozial|abgaben social security contributions, *US*: social security tax; **~amt** social services office, (social) welfare office; **~anspruch** social welfare claims; claims of partners inter se (*arising from their relationship*); **~arbeit** welfare work, social work; **~arbeiter** social worker; **~aufwand** social expenditure, social benefits; **~ausgaben** social expenditure; **~bedürftigkeit** indigence, poverty; **~beirat** social insurance advisory board (*at ministerial level*), **~beiträge** social insurance contributions, **~belastung** burden of social charges; **~bericht** annual social insurance report (*to the German parliament*); **~betreuer** social worker, welfare officer; **~bilanz** corporate socio-economic accounting, social balance sheet; **~bindung** restrictions on individual property rights for the benefit of society; ties with one's social environment; **~bonus** social bonus, discount for low-income subscribers; **~demokrat** social democrat; **~demokratie** social democracy; **~einrichtung** welfare institution; *pl also*: social services; **~etat** budget for social services; **~fonds** welfare funds, charitable fund; social fund; **~fürsorge** social welfare, public welfare; **~gefüge** social structure; **~geheimnis** confidential nature of social insurance data; **~gericht** social security tribunal, DHSS-court (*GB*); **~gerichtsbarkeit** jurisdiction for social security litigation; **~gerichtsgesetz** (*D 1975*): *law concerning social security tribunals and their procedure*; **~gerichtsverfahren** procedure in social security tribunals; **~gesetzbuch** Social Security Code (*comprehensive codification of all social insurance and welfare legislation*); **~gesetzgebung** social welfare legislation; **~haushalt** budget for social and welfare expenditure, social (services) budget; **~hilfe** → *Sozialhilfe*; **~klausel** social hardship clause *in favour of the tenant*; **~kommunalobligation** municipal bond to finance social services, communal bond to finance housing; **~kontrakt** social contract, social compact; **~kosten** social welfare costs, employee benefit costs, social expenditure; *allgemeine ~~*: *general employee benefits and facilities*; **~kredit** credit extended to socially weak persons; **~last** social charges, the burden of social expenditure; **~leistungen** social security benefits; *freiwillige ~~*: *voluntary welfare payments, fringe benefits*; *gesetzliche ~~*: *social insurance contributions required by law*; **~medizin** social medicine, medical care for social purposes; **s~medizinisch** medico-social; **~minister** Minister for Social Services; **~ordnung** social system, social order; **~papiere** bonds for social services, housing

Sozialhilfe | **Sozialversicherungsabgabe**

bonds; ~**partner** employers and employed, both sides of industry, management and labour (*or* work force); ~**pflichtigkeit des Eigentums** (constitutional) principle that ownership involves (social) obligations; ~**philosophie** social philosophy; ~**plan** social redundancy plan; ~**politik** social policy; s~**politisch** *adj* socio-political; ~**produkt** national product, social product; ~**prognose** rehabilitation prospects (*of an offender*); ~**programm** welfare program(me); ~**psychologie** social psychology; ~**rabatt** discount on social grounds, discount for low-income subscribers; ~**rat** social council; ~**recht** social welfare law, social legislation, law concerning social problems; ~**rechtsweg** access to social security tribunal and appellate courts; ~**reform** social reform; ~**rente** social insurance pension, social security pension; ~**rentenreform** social insurance pensions reform; ~**rentner** social insurance pensioner; ~**richter** social security tribunal judge; ~**staat** welfare state, state based on social justice, social state; ~**staatsprinzip** principle of social justice and the welfare state; ~**station** welfare centre; ~**system** social security (system); ~**verbindlichkeiten** social services liabilities; ~**verpflichtungen** partners' obligations inter se (*arising from their relationship*); ~**versicherung** → *Sozialversicherung*; ~**vertrag** social contract, social compact; ~**verwaltung** social security authorities; ~**verwaltungsrecht** administrative social security law; ~**wahlen** social insurance assembly elections (*of delegates*); ~**wesen** social services; ~**widrigkeit** unsocial conduct; harsh and unconscionable action, socially unjustified action; ~**wissenschaften** social sciences; ~**wohnung** council home, socially subsidized flat, public-assistance dwelling; ~**zulage** welfare allowance, fringe benefit; ~**zuschlag** allowances based on the domestic status of employees; ~**zuschuß** social grant, supplementary benefit.

Sozialhilfe *f* public welfare, public assistance, social assistance; supplementary benefits, social welfare benefits; ~~ *beziehen: to be in receipt of Supplementary Benefits (GB), to be on social security;* ~**ausschuß** public welfare committee; **s~ berechtigt** eligible for social assistance, eligible for supplementary benefit *GB*, entitled to social assistance, eligible for welfare; ~**bezieher** recipient of social assistance, welfare recipient, person on social security; ~**gesetz** Federal Public Welfare Act (*D 1987*); ~**recht** public welfare law; ~**richtsatz** standard rate for public welfare benefits; ~**träger** *authorities financially responsible for public welfare.*

sozialisieren *v/t* to socialize, to nationalize.

Sozialisierung *f* socialization, nationalization.

Sozialversicherung *f* (contributory) social insurance scheme; national insurance.

Sozialversicherungs|abgabe social security contribution, social security tax (*US*); ~**abzüge** social security payroll deductions; ~**anpassungsgesetz** social insurance adaptation Act; ~**ansprüche** the rights to social security benefits; ~**beitrag** social security contribution, *US also:* (federal) social security tax; ~**bezüge** social insurance benefits; ~**gesetz** *GB*: social security (*or* National Insurance) Act, social security legislation; ~**grenze** income limit for compulsory social insurance; ~**leistungen** social insurance services and benefits, social security benefits; ~~ *bei Arbeitsunfall: industrial injuries benefits;* ~**ministerium** department of social security; ~**pflicht** compulsory social insurance; s~**pflichtig** subject to social insurance (contributions); ~**rente** social insurance

713

pension; ~**versicherungsträger** social insurance institution, **freiwillige** ~ voluntary membership in a social insurance scheme.
Sozietät *f* professional partnership, society, association.
Sozius *m* partner, associate; ~**fahrer(in)** pillion passenger.
Spaltenaddition *f* footing.
Spaltgesellschaft *f* split company (*due to expropriation of part of the company*), breakup company.
Spaltungstheorie *f* splitting-up doctrine (*expropriation in part*).
Spanne *f* margin, spread, difference.
Spannung *f* *pol* tension, friction; ~**sfall** case of emergency short of war; ~**sklausel** (pro rata) adjustment clause (*of equivalent services in escalator clauses*).
Spar|anlage savings holding, savings investment; ~**anreiz** savings incentive; ~**aufkommen** total savings; ~**bon** savings certificate; ~**bonds** savings bonds; ~**brief** savings bank certificate; ~**buch** pass-book, savings bank book; ~**eckzins** basic savings rate; ~**einlage** savings deposit, savings account ~~*nzugänge: accruals of savings deposits*; ~**förderung** tax incentives for (private) saving; ~**freudigkeit** propensity to save; ~**geld** savings, savings deposits; ~**geschäft** savings business; ~**giroverkehr** transfer of funds via the savings banks, savings banks' giro system; ~**guthaben** savings account, savings-bank deposits, credit balance of a savings account; ~**institut** savings institution; ~**kapital** savings capital; ~**kasse** → *Sparkasse*; ~**konto** (pass-book) savings account; ~*en der privaten Haushalte: savings accounts of private account-holders*; ~**leistung** saving, total saving, achieved savings; ~**marke** savings stamp; trading stamp; ~**maßnahmen** economizing measures; ~**menge** volume of savings, quantity of savings; ~**mittel** savings, saved resources, accrued savings; ~**neigung** propensity to save; ~**politik** savings policy; economy-mindedness; **s**~**politisch** *adj* relating to savings policy; ~**prämie** savings premium; ~**prämien-Vertrag** premium-savings contract; ~**programm** cost-cutting drive, economy programme; ~**quote** saving rate, saving ratio; ~~ *der privaten Haushalte: personal saving ratio*; ~**rücklage** savings reserve; ~**schwein** piggy bank; ~**tätigkeit** saving, saving activity; ~**verein** savings club, provident society, thrift society; ~**verkehr** saving; savings-banks transactions; ~**vertrag** saving agreement, savings-plan (agreement); ~~ *mit festgelegten Sparraten: instalment savings plan; prämienbegünstiger* ~~: *premium-aided savings agreement*; ~**vorgang** saving process; ~**werbung** savings propaganda; ~**wesen** saving, savings system; ~**wille** will to save; ~**ziele** objects of saving, saving targets; ~**zinsen** interest on savings deposits; ~**zugang** accrual of savings; ~**zwang** compulsory saving.
Sparen *n* saving, thrift; ~ **im Lohnabzugsverfahren** save as you earn; **prämienbegünstigtes** ~ premium-aided saving.
sparen *v/t, v/i* to save; to economize.
Sparer *m* saver; ~**freibetrag** tax allowance for savers; ~**schutz** legal protection of savings accounts.
Sparkasse *f* savings bank; **kommunale** ~ municipal savings bank; **öffentliche** ~ public savings bank.
Sparkassen|buch savings-bank book, pass-book; ~**geschäft** savings business; ~**gesetz** savings-bank Act; ~**guthaben** savings-bank deposit(s); ~**kredit** savings-bank credit; ~~**ordnung** savings-bank regulations; ~**- und Giroverband** (=) *savings banks and their clearing association*.
Sparsamkeit *f* economy, thrift.
Sparte *f* line of business; column.
Spätaussiedler *m* post-war repatriated person from Eastern Europe.

Spätfolgen f/pl remote consequences (of an injury).

Spätheimkehrer m late-returning prisoner of war (P. O. W.).

Spediteur m forwarder, forwarding agent, forwarding merchant, removal man (or firm); ~**bedingungen** forwarders' conditions; *Allgemeine Deutsche* ~~: *General German Forwarders' Conditions*; ~ **Empfangsquittung** forwarder's receipt; ~-**Empfangsschein** forwarder's receipt; ~**übernahmebescheinigung** forwarder's receipt, forwarding agent's certificate of receipt.

Spedition f forwarding, business of forwarding, forwarding trade, removal.

Speditions|agent forwarding firm's agent, shipper's representative removal agency; ~**auftrag** forwarding order, shipping order; ~**büro** forwarding office, shipping office, shipping agency; ~**firma** forwarding agency, forwarding firm, transport agency; ~**geschäft** forwarding agency, (the) forwarding trade; ~**gesellschaft** forwarding company, transport company; ~**gewerbe** forwarding trade; ~**kosten** forwarding charges; ~**provision** forwarding commission; ~**rechnung** note of charges for forwarding; ~**versicherung** forwarder's risk insurance; ~**versicherungsschein** forwarder's risk insurance policy, forwarding insurance policy; ~**vertrag** forwarding contract, contract with a forwarding agent.

Speiserolle f captain's record of food for the crew.

Speisewirtschaft f restaurant.

Spekulant m speculator, speculative dealer, stock exchange gambler, operator, bear, bull; **kurzfristiger** ~ free rider.

Spekulation f speculation, venture, punt, stock jobbing; **berufsmäßige** ~ professional speculation, professional stock-exchange operations; **e–e** ~ **riskieren** to take a (speculative) risk; **gewagte** ~ hazardous (or daring) speculation.

Spekulations|aktien speculative shares, floating stock; ~**druck** speculative pressure; ~**geschäft** speculative venture, speculative transaction; ~**gewinn** speculative profit; *plötzlicher* ~~: *killing*; ~**kapital** venture capital, risk-bearing capital; ~**kauf** speculative buy (or purchase) *pl also*: speculative buying; ~**papiere** speculative securities, speculative stock; ~**risiko** speculative risk; ~**steuer** gambling tax, tax on speculative gains; ~**verlust** gambling loss, loss caused by speculation; ~**versicherung** speculative underwriting; ~**wert** speculative value, speculative share; ~**zwecke** speculative purposes.

spekulativ *adj* speculative.

spekulieren *v/i* to speculate, to gamble, to play the market.

Spende f charity (or public benefit) contribution, donation, gift *(for charitable or non-profit making purposes)*; ~**nabzug** deduction of donations from taxable income *(for charity etc)*; ~**naffäre** political donations scandal; ~**naufruf** appeal for donations, charity appeal; ~**n bescheinigung** *tax relevant* receipt of a public benefit donation; donation receipt; ~**nempfänger** recipient of a donation, donee; ~**höchstbetrag** maximum tax allowance for donations.

Sperr|auftrag stop order, stop payment; ~**bezirk** prohibited area *for prostitution,* restricted area; ~**depot** frozen deposit account; blocked safe-deposit, blocked security deposit; ~**erklärung** instruction to stop payment *(on a cheque etc)*; ~**fläche** restricted area; ~**frist** blocked period, waiting period *(insurance),* qualifying period, period of ineligibility, period of exclusion from benefits; period of non-negotiability; ~**gebiet** prohibited area, restricted area; prohibited zone; ~**gut** bulky goods; ~**guthaben** frozen account; ~**jahr** twelve-month ban, restrictive year, wait-

sperren

ing period of one year; ~**konto** frozen (*or* stopped *or* blocked) account; ~**klausel** restrictive clause, minimum percentage clause *for admission of a party to a parliamentary body*; ~**mark** blocked marks; ~**minorität** voting veto, vetoing stock, blocking minority; ~**müll** bulky refuse, bulky waste; ~**patent** blocking-off patent; ~**stücke** blocked units; ~**stunde** closing hour, curfew; ~**vermerk** note of blocking, non-negotiability notice; inhibition (*on a register*); ~**wirkung** blocking effect, freezing effect; ~**zeit** period when unemployment benefits are stopped; period of ineligibility; ~**zoll** prohibitive duty.

sperren *v/t* to block, to suspend, to exclude from benefits, to countermand, to stop payment on a cheque.

Sperrigkeitszuschlag *m* additional charge for handling bulky goods.

Sperrung *f* blockage, stoppage, freezing; ~ **e–s Schecks** stoppage of payment, stopping a cheque.

Spesen *pl* expenses, out-of-pocket expenses, charges; per diem (allowance); ~**abrechnung** expense report, list of expenses; ~ **aufschlüsseln** to specify (*or* to itemize) expenses, to break down expenses; ~**aufstellung** statement of expenses, specification of disbursements; s~**frei** *adj* free of expenses; ~**konto** expense account; ~**pauschale** expense allowance; ~**rechnung** note of expenses; ~**ritter** expense-account fiddler; ~**satz** daily expense allowance; ~**unwesen** expenses racket, malpractice in connection with expense accounts; ~ **vergüten** to reimburse expenses incurred; ~**vorschuß** advance payment for expenses; ~**zettel** expense voucher; **abzüglich der** ~ charges deducted, less charges.

Spezial|**anfertigung** special manufacture, custom made; ~**arbeiter** qualified worker; ~**artikel** special article, shopping goods, specialty goods, specialty; ~**ausbildung**

Spiegelglasversicherung

special training; ~**bank** specialized commercial bank; ~**bestimmung** special provision; ~**einkaufsermächtigung** special purchasing authorization; ~**erzeugnis** specialty product, specialty; ~-**Fachgeschäft** one-line business; ~-**Fahndungsliste** most wanted list; ~**fahrzeug** special-purpose vehicle; ~**gebiete** speciality, special field, special line; ~**geschäft** one-line business, single-line store; ~**gesetz** special law, private statute; ~**gütermesse** specialized trade fair; ~**handel** special trade; ~**kenntnisse** special knowledge; ~~ *der Herstellung: manufacturing know-how*; ~**markt** fair, special market; ~**prävention** deterrent effect on a particular offender; ~**risiko** special risk; ~**rückversicherung** facultative reinsurance, special risk reinsurance; ~**sachen** specific goods; ~**strafgesetz** special penal (*or* criminal) statute; ~**vollmacht** special power of attorney; ~**wert** specialty (*share, stock exchange*), special stock; ~**wissen** special knowledge, technical knowledge.

spezialisieren *v/t reflex* to specialize.

Spezialisierung *f* specialization; ~**skartell** cartel calling for specialization of enterprises.

Spezialität *f* speciality; ~**sprinzip** *principle that rights in rem are specifically attached to a thing*.

Spezies|**kauf** sale of specific (*or* ascertained) goods; ~**schuld** determinate obligation, specific obligation; *als* ~~: *in specie*; ~**vermächtnis** specific legacy, specific gift.

Spezifikation *f* specification; ~**skauf** sale subject to buyer's specifications.

spezifizieren *v/t* to specify, to particularize, to give full particulars.

Spezifizierung *f* specification(s), full particulars, itemization, detailed statement; ~ **von Patenteinsprüchen** notice of objections.

Spiegelglasversicherung *f* plate-glass-insurance.

Spiel *n* game, gambling, play; ~**automat** gambling machine, slot machine, one-armed bandit; ~**bank** casino, kursaal, gambling house; ~**bank-Abgabe** (combined) kursaal levy; ~**banksteuer** tax on gambling establishments; ~**film** feature film, feature (motion picture); ~**hölle** gambling den; ~**kasino** (gaming) casino; ~**lokal** common gaming house; ~**raum** latitude; margin; *kassenmäßiger* ~~: *cash margin*; ~**regeln** rules of the game; ~**salon** gaming house, kursaal; ~**schuld** gambling debt, gaming debt, play debt; ~**straße** street for playing, street used as a playground; ~ **und Wette** wagering and gambling; ~- **und Wettverträge** gaming and wagering contracts; ~**unternehmer** common gambler; ~**vertrag** gaming contract; ~**warenmesse** toy industry fair; **abgekartetes** ~ put-up job.

Spielzeugwaffe imitation firearm.

Spillage *f* spillage, waste.

Spillgeld *n* spillage, charge for spillage.

Spion *m* spy, agent.

Spionage *f* espionage, spying; ~**abwehr** counter-espionage, counter-intelligence; ~ **treiben** to spy, to engage in espionage activities; ~-**ring** spy ring.

Spitzel *m* informer, common informer, stool pigeon, undercover agent, spy, gumshoe (*US, sl.*), snooper, ferret, "snitcher".

Spitzen|anlage first-class investment; ~**ausgleich** settlement of balance; evening-out of the peaks; ~**beanspruchung** peak-load (conditions); ~**bedarf** peak demand, marginal requirements; ~**belastung** peak load, maximum rate ~~*szeit: peak period*; ~**betrag** maximum amount; ~**einkommen** top income; ~**ergebnis** top achievement, record level; ~**fabrikat** top-quality product, first-class product; ~**finanzierung** provision of residual finance; ~**führungskraft** top executive; ~**gehalt** top-level salary, top salary; ~**gespräch** top level talks; ~**gremium** leading group, top management team, controlling organ; ~**gruppe** leading group; ~**gruppenwerbung** top group advertising aimed at; ~**institut** leading institution; ~**kandidat** leading candidate; ~**klasse** top quality, best quality; ~**kraft** top-level employee; ~**kräfte** high-calibre staff; ~**leistung** peak performance, maximum output, top work; ~**lohn** peak wage, top wage(s); ~**manager** top manager; *datensachverständiger* ~~: *top manager with EDP background*; ~**marke** brand leader; ~**nachfrage** residual demand; ~**organisation** top-level organization, leading collective bargaining group; ~**papier** leading stock; ~**politiker** leading politician, prominent politician; ~**qualität** top quality, best quality; **regulierung** adjustment of fractional amounts; evening-out of peaks; ~**verkauf** peak sales; ~**satz** maximum rate, top tax rate; ~**preis** peak price, top price; ~**verband** central organization, central association; *kommunaler* ~~: *local authority association*; ~**versorgung** standby supply (electricity); ~**werte** leaders, leading shares, blue chips; ~**zeit** peak period, peak hours.

Spitzfindigkeit *f* quibble, sophism, sophistry; **juristische** ~ pettifogging.

Split *m* split, splitting.

Splitter|aktionär ultra-small shareholder, person with a modest shareholding; ~**bombe** fragmentation bomb; ~**siedlung** scattered housing; ~**gruppe** splinter group, small faction; ~**partei** splinter party; ~**siedlungen** scattered housing.

Splitting *n* splitting; ~**verfahren** income tax splitting (*between husband and wife*); ~**Vergünstigung** splitting privilege.

Spotkurs *m* spot price.

Spottpreis ridiculously low price.
Sprachregelung *f* official position, official version, official wording.
Sprachreise *f* language learning trip.
Sprachwerk *n* literary work.
Sprech|anlage intercom; ~**erlaubnis** visitor's permit (*prison*); ~**filmrechte** talking motion picture rights; ~**stunde** hours open for consultation, hours of attendance; ~**tage** out-of-town consultation days; ~**verbot** no speaking; ~**zeit** speaking time; ~**zimmer** consulting room.
Sprecher *m* spokesman; ~**ausschuß** representative committee of executive employees; ~ **der Bundesregierung** spokesman of the German Federal Government.
Sprengel *m* district; parish; ~**arzt** district physician, local doctor.
Sprengkammer demolition chamber ~**kommando** bomb disposal squad; ~**ladung** explosive charge; ~**meister** blaster; ~**mittel** explosives, demolition material; ~**stoff** → *Sprengstoff*; ~**wirkung** explosive effect.
Sprengstoff *m* explosive; ~**anschlag** bomb attack, bomb outrage; ~**brief** letter bomb; ~**delikte** offences involving the use of explosives; ~**erlaubnisschein** permit to use explosives; ~**gesetz** Explosive Substances Act; ~**paket** parcel bomb; ~**recht** law on explosives; ~**register** register of licensed users of explosives; ~**verbrechen** felonies committed with explosives; ~**verkehrsordnung** explosives transmittal ordinance; ~**verwendungsordnung** explosives (use) ordinance.
Sprengung *f* blasting; *pol*: break-up, dispersal; ~ **e-r Gesetzgebungsversammlung** breaking-up of a legislative assembly.
Sproß *m* issue, scion, offspring.
Spruch *m* award, verdict, judgment; ~**ausschuß** grievance committee, mediation committee; ~**behörde** conciliation board; ~**kammer** denazification court; ~**körper** panel of judges; ~**reife** ripeness for court decision; ~**richter** trial judge; ~**termin** date for pronouncing a decision; ~**verfahren** administrative decision procedure.
Sprungregress *m* recourse against one of the previous endorsers (*other than the last-preceding one*).
Sprungrevision *f* leap-frog appeal, leap frogging, leap frog procedure.
Spur *f* (1) trace; track; ~**ensicherung** preserving traces; **s**~**los** *adj* traceless, without leaving a trace; ~**en verfolgen** to pursue leads (*or* clues); **die ~en verwischen** to remove the traces; **ohne ~en zu hinterlassen** to leave without a trace.
Spur *f* (2) lane; ~ **für Linksabbieger** filter lane (*for those turning left*); ~ **halten** keeping to one's lane (in traffic); ~**wechsel** change of lane; **in der ~ bleiben!** keep in your lane!
Spürbarkeit *f* noticeable influence (*of restrictive practices*).
Spürhund *m* detector dog, sniffer dog.
Staat *m* state; ~ **e-s Staatenbundes** confederated state; ~**en mit Rechtsverkehr** states where one drives on the right; **abhängiger ~** dependent state; **absolut regierter ~** absolutely governed state, autocratic state; **anspruchstellender ~** claimant State; **antragstellender ~** applicant country; **assoziierter ~** associated state; **assoziierungsfähiger ~** associable state; **ausländischer ~** foreign state; **befreundeter ~** friendly state, friendly nation; **blockfreier ~** non-aligned state; **der ersuchende ~** the requesting state, the state making the application, applicant state; **der ersuchte ~** the requested state; **dem ~ anheimfallen** to revert to the state; **fremder ~** foreign state; **halbsouveräner ~** semi-sovereign state; **kriegführender ~** belligerent state:; **neutraler ~** neutral state; **neutralisierter ~** neutralized state; **nicht-regionale ~en** non-

regional countries; **Sanktionen verletzende ~en** sanction breakers; **selbständiger ~** independent state; **souveräner ~** sovereign state, independent sovereign state; **vertragschließender ~** contracting state.

Staaten|bildung formation of states; **~bund** federation, permanent confederacy of supreme governments; **~dienstbarkeit** international servitude; **~gemeinschaft** community of states; comity of nations; **~gleichheit** equal sovereignty (of states); **~haftung** liability of states; **~~** *aus Verschulden: inculpation of states*; **~immunität** sovereign immunity (of states); **~klage** (European Court) action against a member state; **~konferenz** conference of states; **~loser** stateless person; **~losigkeit** statelessness; **~nachfolge** succession of states; **~~** *ohne Übernahme der Verbindlichkeiten des Vorgängers: negative succession*; **~sukzession** succession of states; **~verantwortlichkeit** state responsibility; **~verbindung** federation (*or* combination) of states.

staatlich *adj* state, governmental, national.

Staats|abgaben tribute; fiscal dues, public revenue charges; **~abkommen** government agreement(s); **~akt** act of state, governmental act; *feierlicher* **~~**: *state ceremony*; **~angehöriger** → *Staatsangehöriger;* **~angehörigkeit** → *Staatsangehörigkeit;* **~angestellter** government employee, civil servant; **~anleihe** government bonds, government loan, national bond issue, public bonds, bank annuities, **~~***papiere: public funds;* **~anwalt** prosecutor, public prosecutor, *US also*: district attorney; **~~** *beim Militärgericht: judge advocate;* **~anwaltschaft** prosecution, department of public prosecution, Director of Public Prosecutions, Crown Proscution Service (*GB*); **~anzeiger** official bulletin, official gazette; **~apparat** state machinery; **~archiv** public record office, public records, state archives; **~aufgaben** state functions; **~aufsicht** governmental supervison; **~aufsichtsbehörde** state supervisory authority; **~auftrag** public contract, government contract; *geheimhaltungsbedürftiger* **~~**: *restricted government contract*; **~ausgaben** national expenditure, government expenditure, public expenditures, government spending; **~bank** government bank, national bank, state-owned central bank; **~bankenkonten** central bank accounts; **~bankrott** national bankruptcy, national insolvency; **~beamter** government official, civil servant, public official; **~beauftragter** government agent, state commissioner; **~bediensteter** civil servant; **~begräbnis** state funeral; **~behörde** governmental authority; **~besitz** public property, public domain, possessions of the state; **~besuch** state visit; **~betrieb** state enterprise, national enterprise; publicly owned enterprise; **~bürger** citizen; national; **~** *mit Wohnsitz im Ausland: non-resident citizen*; **~bürgerrechte** civil (*or* civic) rights, citizens' rights; **~bürgschaft** government guarantee; **~bürgerurkunde** certificate of citizenship; **~chef** executive head, head of state; **~darlehen** public loan, government(al) loan; **~dienst** public service, civil service; **~dienstbarkeit** state servitude; **~domäne** state farm; public domain; **~druckerei** government printer, government printing office; **s~eigen** *adj* state owned, government owned; **~eigentum** state ownership, government ownership, public ownership, national ownership; state property, state owned property, national property, public property, government property; *im* **~~** *befindlich: state owned;* **~einkünfte** state revenue, public revenue, government revenue, government income; **~ein-**

Staatsabgaben

nahmen state revenue, government income, cf *~einkünfte*; **~einrichtungen** state institutions; **~empfang** public reception; **~erbrecht** escheat: *right of the state to inherit in the absence of heirs or beneficiaries*; **~fehlbetrag** national budget deficit; **~feiertag** national (bank) holiday; **~feind** public enemy; **~finanzen** state finances, public finances, national finances; **~finanzwirtschaft** governmental finance; **~flagge** national flag; **~form** form of government; *repräsentative ~~: representative government; republikanische ~~: republican government*; **~forst** national forests; **~führung** government; **~garantie** government guarantee; **~gebäude** public building; **~gebiet** national territory, state territory; **~gefährdend** *adj* subversive; **~gefährdung** endangering of the state, threat to the security of the state, sedition; **~gefängnis** state prison; **~geheimnis** official secret, state secret; *ein ~~ ausspähen: to obtain an official secret by espionage*; **~geld** public funds; fiduciary money standard; **~gerichtshof** state tribunal, constitutional court; **~geschäfte** official business, state affairs; **~gewalt** state authority, state power; **~grenze** national border, state border; **~grund** public lands; **~gründung** formation of (a, the) state; **~haftung** government liability, state responsibility *~~sklage: state action*; **~handel** state monopoly trading, governmental trade; **~handelsland** Socialist state; state-trading country, country with a controlled Socialist economy; *pl also: centrally planned economies*; **~handelsschiff** State-merchant ship; **~haushalt** national budget, government(al) budget; public accounts; **~hoheit** sovereignty, sovereign power; **~hoheitsakt** act of state, sovereign act, act of sovereignty; **~hoheitsgebiet** national territory, territory of a sovereign state; **~interesse** national interest, public interest; **s~intern** intra-government; **~intervention** state intervention; **~kanzlei** state chancellery; **~kapitalismus** state capitalism; **~kasse** public treasury; *der ~~ die Kosten auferlegen: to direct that payment of the costs should be made out of public funds; to award the costs against the state*; **~kassenschein** treasury certificate, treasury bill; **~kirche** national church, state church, the Established Church (*GB*); **~kirchenrecht** public law concerning religious bodies, law concerning church-and-state relations; **~kommissar** state commissioner, government commissioner; **~konkurs** national bankruptcy; **~kontinuität** continuity of states; **~kontrolle** state control, government control; **~konzession** state licence; **~kosten** public expense; *auf ~~: at public expense*; **~kredit** government credit (*or* loan); **~kunst** statesmanship; **~land** public lands; **~lasten** public burdens; **~lehre** political science; **~leistung** performance by the state; **~leitung** government; **~lenkung** state management, government control; **~lotterie** state-lottery; **~macht** state power, governmental power; **~mann** statesman; **s~männisch** *adj* statesmanlike; **~maschinerie** state machinery; **~minister** minister of state; (departmental) minister (*in the German Länder*); permanent secretary of state; **~ministerium** state ministry; **~monopol** state monopoly, fiscal monopoly; **~notstand** national emergency; **~notwehr** national self-defence, act of self-defence by a state; **~oberhaupt** head of state; **~oberkasse** exchequer department; **~obligationen** government stocks, public bonds; **~ordnung** system of government, governmental system; **~organ** government organ; state institution; **~papiere** government securities, government bonds, public securities; *konsolidierte* ~~: *consols*; ~**politik** national policy, state policy, government policy; s~**politisch** *adj* concerning government policy, from a national policy point of view; ~**präsident** President (*of a nation or state*); ~**prüfung** state examination; *juristische* ~~: *state examination in law*; ~**quote** public-sector share; ~**raison** public policy, reasons of state, national interest; ~**rat** state councillor; council of state; ~**ratsvorsitzender** chairman of the council of state; ~**rechnung** public accounts, budget accounts; ~**rechnungswesen** public accounts; ~**recht** law of the state (*and its organs*), constitutional law; ~**regierung** state government of a state; ~**religion** state religion; ~**rente** government pension; ~**säckel** (*m*) public purse, common purse; ~**schatz** public treasury; ~**schiff** state-owned vessel; public vessel, public ship; ~**schuld** national debt, public debt; ~**schuldbuch** register of public debts, national debt ledger; ~**schuldenaufnahme** state borrowing, government borrowing; ~**schuldendienst** servicing of the national debts; ~**schuldenrisiko** sovereign-debt risk; ~**schuldenverwaltung** administration of the public debts; ~**schutz** (state) security; ~**schutzbehörden** state security authorities; ~**schutzdelikte** security-related offences; ~**schutzsachen** security-related matters (*or* cases); ~**schutzsenat** division at Oberlandesgericht for security matters; ~**sekretär** state secretary, under-secretary of state, assistant secretary; ~**sector** the public sector; ~**sicherheit** national security; ~**sicherheitsdienst** state security police; ~**siegel** state seal; *das große* ~~: the *Great Seal*; ~**stellung** government appointment, civil service position; ~**straße** state highway; ~**streich** coup d'état; ~**sukzession** succession of states;

~**symbol** national emblem, emblem of sovereignty; ~**system** governmental system; ~**titel** public loan issue(s), government securities; ~**trauer** national mourning; ~**treue** allegiance to a state; ~**unternehmen** state-owned enterprise; ~**urkunde** public document, *pl also*: public records, state papers; ~**verbrauch** consumption by public agencies, level of current government expenditure on goods and services; ~**verbrechen** state crime, political crime; crime of treason; ~**verdrossenheit** general disaffection with the government; ~**verfassung** constitution (of a, the, state); ~**verleumdung** defamation of the state; ~**vermögen** public property, state assets, national domain; ~**verrat** treason; ~**verschuldung** indebtedness of a (the) state; (international) convention, ~**vertrag** treaty, international treaty, international convention, interstate agreement; ~~ *mit unmittelbarer innerstaatlicher Wirkung: self-executing treaty*; ~**verwaltung** public administration; ~**volk** body politic; the people constituting a nation, the leading national element; ~**vorbehalt** reservation for the state; ~**wappen** national coat of arms, emblem of sovereignty; ~**wirtschaft** state economy, public sector of the economy; national economy; ~**wirtschaftsprinzip** statism; ~**wirtschaftssystem** statism, system of state-controlled economy; ~**wissenschaft** political science, science of government; ~**wohl** public benefit, benefit of the state; ~**ziel** fundamental aim of state policy; ~~-**bestimmung**: *basic policy clause of the constitution*; ~**zugehörigkeit** nationality; ~**zugehörigkeitszeichen** nationality mark; ~**zuschuß** government(al) grant, grant-in-aid, exchequer grant; ~~ *an Gemeinden: rate support grant*.

Staatsangehöriger *m* (*der Staatsangehörige*) national, citizen, sub-

Staatsangehörigkeit

ject; ~**kraft Einbürgerung** naturalized citizen; ~ **kraft Geburt** natural-born subject; birthright citizen; **ausländischer** ~ foreign national (or subject); **deutscher** ~ German national, German citizen.
Staatsangehörigkeit f nationality, citizenship; **ausländische** ~ foreign nationality; ~ **der USA** United States citizenship; ~**durch Geburt** citizenship by birth; ~**kraft Abstammung** citizenship by descent; **deutsche** ~ German nationality; **die** ~ **aberkennen** to expatriate, to be deprived of one's citizenship; **die** ~ **aufgeben** to renounce one's citizenship, to give up one's nationality; **doppelte** ~ dual nationality, dual citizenship; **für eine** ~ **optieren** to opt for a nationality; **gültige** ~ effective nationality.
Staatsangehörigkeits|ausweis certificate of nationality; official identity card showing nationality; ~**behörde** public authority in charge of nationality matters; ~**gesetz** (German) Nationality Act; ~**option** choice of nationality; ~**recht** law of nationality and citizenship; ~**urkunde** certificate of nationality; ~**verzicht** renunciation of citizenship, waiver of national status.
Stadt f (pl **Städte** = ~e) town, city, municipality; ~**anleihe** municipal loan; ~**autobahn** urban motorway; ~**bahn** city railway, interurban railway; ~**baurat** municipal building officer; ~**bevölkerung** urban population; ~**bezirk** urban district, parish, ward; ~**bild** townscape; ~**büro** town office; ~**direktor** city manager (US), town clerk; ~**entwicklung** town development; ~**erneuerung** urban renewal; urban re-development; ~**etag** congress of municipalities, cities' assembly; ~**gebiet** urban area; ~**gemeinde** municipality, township; ~**gericht** municipal court, petty sessional court; ~**grundstück** town property; ~**haus** guildhall, town house;

722

Staffelanleihe

~**jugendamt** municipal youth welfare office; ~**kämmerer** town treasurer; ~**kernsanierung** rehabilitation of inner city housing; ~**kreis** country borough; ~ **mit Marktrecht** market town; ~**parlament** municipal assembly, town (or city) council; ~**planung** town planning, city planning; ~**polizei** municipal police; ~**polizeichef** head of the municipal police, town sergeant; ~**präsident** chairman of the town council; ~**privileg** municipal privilege; ~**randgebiete** city outskirts; ~**randlage** edge-of-town location; ~**randsiedlung** suburban settlement; ~**rat** town council, council, town councillor; ; ~**sanierung** urban redevelopment; slum clearance; ~**schulrat** chief education officer (of a town); ~**sparkasse** municipal savings bank; ~**staat** city state (Hamburg, Bremen); ~**umland** urban hinterland; ~**väter** (the) city fathers; ~**verordnetenversammlung** town council; ~**verordneter** town councillor; ~**verordnung** (municipal) by-law; ~**verwaltung** town management, municipal administration; ~**werke** public utilities; ~**zweigstelle** city sub-branch; **kreisangehörige** ~ non-county borough; **kreisfreie** ~ autonomous municipality, county borough.
Städtebauförderungsgesetz n Act for the Promotion of Urban Construction.
Staffel|anleihe graduated-interest loan; ~**auszug** equated abstract of accounts; ~**bauordnung** zoning ordinance; ~**form** echelon formation; staggered form; ~**gebühren** differential rates; ~**gewinnanteil** graded profit commission; ~**miete** step-up lease, graduated rent; ~**preis** graduated price, sliding scale price; ~**rechnung** equated account, single-column account; ~**skonto** progressive discount rates; ~**tarif** graduated tariff, differential tariff, graduated tariff; ~**zinsen** day-to-day interest calcu-

staffeln   **Standardabweichung**

lation; daily interest (rate); ~**zinsrechnung** daily balance interest calculation.
staffeln *v/t* to graduate, to scale.
Staffelung *f* gradation, differentiation, spacing out; ~ **der Laufzeiten** spacing out the periods of validity; **jahreszeitliche** ~ seasonal gradation.
Stahl|aktien steel shares, steel stock; ~**fach** safe-deposit box; ~**fachabteilung** safe-deposit vault; ~**gewinnung** steel manufacture, steel production; ~**industrie** steel industry; ~**kammer** safe-deposit box, strong room, safe room, steel vault, vault, safe vault; ~**kartell** steel cartel; ~**konsortium** steel consortium; ~**lieferungen** steel supplies; ~**produktion** steel production; ~**verbraucher** user of steel; ~**werte** steel shares, steel stock(s).
Stamm *m* stock, permanent staff; parentela (*law of succession*); *nach Stämmen*: per stirpes, according to the rule of representation (intestacy); ~**aktie** ordinary share, equity share, common share, *pl US*: common stock, ordinary stock, general stock, equities; ~**aktiendividende** dividend on common shares (stock); ~**aktionär** ordinary shareholder, ordinary stockholder; ~**anteil** = *Stammaktie qv*; ~**anmeldung** basic application; ~**arbeiter** regular worker, permanent labour; ~**baum** family tree table of descent, pedigree, lineage, gradus parentelae; ~**belegschaft** permanent staff, body of permanent workers; ~**buch** family register, family album; ~**dividende** ordinary dividend; ~**einlage** original capital share *in a private limited company*; original capital contribution; ~**entschädigung** basic compensation; ~**esrecht** tribal lands law; ~**firma** original firm, parent firm; ~**gast** regular customer; ~~ *sein: to patronize*; ~**gesellschaft** parent company; ~**gruppe** skeleton staff; ~**gut** family estate; ~**halter** son and heir; ~**haus** chief house, parent firm, parent store; ~**kapital** nominal capital of a German private limited company (*GmbH*); registered capital, original capital; ~**kunde** regular customer; ~~ *sein: to patronize*; ~**kundschaft** regular customers, clientele; ~**lieferant** regular supplier; ~**order** regular customers' order; ~**patent** original patent, parent patent; pioneer patent; ~**personal** permanent staff, skeleton staff; ~**rolle** military enrol(l)ment register; ~**vermögen** basic assets; ~ **von Facharbeitern** permanent staff of skilled workers; ~**wert** original value; **männlicher** ~ male stock.
Stand *m* (*gen. Standes* → *Standes*)- status, position, station, level, social standing position in life; ~ **am Jahresende** position at end of year; ~ **der Aktiven und Passiven** statement of assets and liabilities; ~ **der Dinge** (present) state of affairs; ~ **der Konjunktur** state of the economy; ~ **der neuesten Erkenntnisse** current knowledge; ~ **der Technik** prior art (*patent application*), state of technology, background art; state of the art; ~ **des Verfahrens** stage of proceedings; ~**gebühren** market dues; ~**geld** pitch fee, demurrage; ~**gericht** summary court martial, drumhead trial; ~**licht** parking lights; ~**ort** → *Standort*; ~**platz** stand, parking space; taxi rank; ~**recht** martial law; ~~ *verhängen: to proclaim martial law*; **s**~**rechtlich** *adj* under martial law, ~ *erschießen: to court-martial and shoot*; ~**sicherheit** stability; **auf dem neuesten** ~ up to date; **geistlicher** ~ Holy Orders; **jetziger** ~ present position, status quo; **im vorigen** ~ in statu quo ante; in the prior position; **in den vorigen** ~ **setzen** to restore to the prior condition.
Standard|abweichung standard deviation; ~**aktien** standard shares, leading stocks, blue chips; ~**bestimmung** standard provision,

usual term; ~**brief** form letter, standardized letter, standard letter; ~**dienstvertragsbedingungen** standard terms and conditions of employment; ~**formular** standard form; ~**klausel** standard clause; ~**kosten** standard cost; *optimale* ~~: *ideal standard*; ~**vertrag** standard-form contract; ~**waren** standard goods; staple articles; ~**werbetarife** standard media rates; ~**werte** standard securities, standard stocks.

standardisieren *v/t* to standardize.

Standardisierung *f* standardization.

Standarte *f* standard, banner; guidon.

Standbesitzer *m* stallholder.

Standby-Vereinbarung *f* standby agreement.

Stander *m* pennant.

Standes|bezeichnung description of social position, social rank; ~**ehre** professional honour; ~**fall** personal status case, personal registry matter; ~**gepflogenheiten** professional etiquette (*or* code of conduct); ~**gericht** professional tribunal; ~**gerichtsbarkeit** jurisdiction of professional tribunals; ~**pflicht** professional duty, obligation to observe professional etiquette (*or* code of conduct); ~**recht** canons of professional etiquette; ~**regeln** professional code of conduct, etiquette of the profession, canons of professional etiquette; ~**richtlinien** code of (professional) conduct; Code of Professional Responsibilities (*GB*); ~**vereinigung** professional society; ~**vertretung** professional representation; s~**widrig** *adj* unprofessional, unethical; ~**widrigkeit** professional misconduct, breach of professional conduct.

Standesamt *m* registrar's office, registrar of births, deaths and marriages, registry office; office of matters of personal status.

Standesamts|bezirk registry district; ~**register** register of births, deaths and marriages; ~**sachen** *matters dealt with by the registrar of births, deaths, and marriages*; ~**verwaltung** *administration of the registry office for births, deaths and marriages*; ~**wesen** vital statistics.

Standesbeamter *m* Registrar General, superintendent registrar, registrar of births, deaths and marriages, registrar of vital statistics; ~ **für Eheschließungen** (marriage) registrar.

Ständige Kommission zur Sicherung der Luftfahrt Permanent Commission for the Safety of Air Navigation.

Standort *m* location, site; ~**ortbedingungen** conditions applying to the locality, local conditions; ~**bestimmung** determination of the location, site determination; ~**faktoren** location factors; s~**gebunden** *adj* location-specific; ~**gunst** locational advantage, ~**politik** regional economic policy, location policy; ~**präferenz** locational preference; ~**verlegung** change of location; ~**vorteil** locational advantage; ~**wahl** choice of location, siting.

Stapelungsgewicht stacking weight.

Stapelvollmacht *f* blank power of attorney (*for future clients*).

Stapelware *f* staple commodities, basics.

Starterlaubnis take-off clearance; ~**gleichheit** equality of starting conditions; ~**hilfe** start-up help; initial aid, launching assistance, pump-priming finance; ~**kapital** initial capital, start-up capital, seed money; ~**staat** launching State; ~**verbot** take-off ban.

Statistik *f* statistics; ~**geheimnis** secrecy of statistical data.

Statistisches Bundesamt *n* Federal Statistical Office.

stattgeben *v/i* to allow, to permit, to grant.

statthaft *adj* admissible, permissible.

statuieren *v/t* to establish, to lay down, to constitute.

Status *m* status, standing, social standing; statement of condition, statement of assets and liabilities, financial statement; ~ **der Bank** the bank's standing (*or* status); ~ **der Beamten** established civil servant status; ~**beirat** staff regulations committee; ~**deutsche** "status Germans" (*ethnic Germans admitted to former Reich territory*); ~ **e-s Gemeinschuldners** *bankrupt's* statement of affairs; ~**klage** (*declaratory*) action to determine the personal status (*e.g. legitimacy*); ~**prüfung** statement analysis; ~**sachen** cases relating to personal status, legal status cases; ~**symbol** sign (*or* symbol) of social status; ~**urteil** judgment on status; ~**zahlen** figures of a financial statement; **bilanzmäßiger** ~ state of the books; **ehelicher** ~ status of legitimacy, married status; **finanzieller** ~ financial status, statement of present financial condition; **gesetzlicher** ~ legal status, legal standing.

Statut *n (pl Statuten)* constitution, articles of association, charter, set of regulations; governing law; *also pl*: by-laws, rules and regulations; ~ **der Beamten** staff regulations for officials; ~**enkollision** conflict of laws; ~**enwechsel** change of jurisdiction.

statutarisch *adj* according to regulations, laid down in regulations.

Stau *m* congestion, traffic queue tailback, traffic jam.

Stauattest *n* (certificate of) stowage.

Staubniederschlag *m* deposition of air-borne solid matter.

stauen *v/t* to trim, to stow away; **seemäßig** ~ to trim the hold.

Stauer *m* stevedore; ~**attest** certificate of stowage; ~**lohn** stowage; ~**schein** stevedore's certificate.

stechen *v/i, v/t* to stab, to thrust.

Stechen *n* clocking (*factory*).

Stechkarte *f* clocking-in card.

Stechuhr *f* time clock, check clock.

Steckbrief *m* warrant of apprehension, "wanted" circular, (*or* poster), description notice.

steckbrieflich gesucht wanted by the police (under a warrant of arrest).

stehlen *v/t* to steal, to purloin, to commit larceny, to "pinch".

Stehlgutliste *f* list of stolen goods.

Stehlsucht *f* kleptomania.

steigern *v/t* to increase, to enhance, to augment.

Steigerungsbetrag *m* rate of increase, increment.

Steigung *f* ascent, upward slope gradient, rise; ~ **oder Gefälle von 16%** upward or downward gradient of 16 per cent; **starke** ~ steep ascent.

Steinbruch *m* quarry.

Steinigung *f* stoning.

Steinkohle *f* hard coal; ~**bergwerk** hard-coal colliery; ~**förderung** hard-coal output.

Steinschlag *m* falling rocks.

Stellage *f* put and call, straddle; ~**geber** seller of a put and call, seller of a spread; ~**geschäft** put and call (option), spread, double option, straddle; ~**kurs** put and call price; ~**nehmer** buyer of a spread.

Stelle *f* job, post, place, locality, position, site, agency; **an anderer** ~ in alio loco; **an** ~ **dessen** in lieu of, instead of; **an die** ~ **setzen** to replace; **an die** ~ **treten** to replace, to supersede, to be superseded by; to step into the shoes of; **an erster** ~ in the first place, primo loco; **an** ~ **von** in stead of, in lieu of; **buchführende** ~ accounting department; **fachliche** ~**n** technical agencies; **freie** ~ (job) vacancy; **freiwerdende** ~ expected vacancy; **intergouvernementale** ~**n** intergovernmental agencies; **kompetente** ~ competent office; **kursstützende** ~ price-supporting agency; **nachgeordnete** ~**n** subsidiary bodies; **offene** ~ (job) vacancy; vacant job; **öffentlich-rechtliche** ~**n** public authorities; **politische** ~**n** political authorities; **quasi-öffentliche** ~**n** quasi-public institutions; **sachkundige** ~**n** competent bodies; **von amtlichen** ~**n** from official quarters.

Stellen|abbau reduction of staff, job cutting; **~angebot** offer of employment, job offer, (job) vacancy; *pl*: situations vacant; **~anzeige** employment ad (job); **~ausschreibung** announcement of a vacancy; **~ausschreibungspflicht** obligation to give notice of vacancies, posting; **~beschreibung** job description; **~besetzung** placement, posting; **~besetzungsplan** staffing schedule; **~bewerber** job seeker, job candidate, job applicant; **~gesuche** situations wanted, positions wanted, employment wanted; **~markt** employment market; labour market; **~nachweis** employment bureau; **~~dienst**: *job-referral service*; **~plan** staff establishment, staffing schedule; **~suche** looking for a job, job-hunting; **~vergebungsrecht** patronage; **~vermittlung** job placement; employment agency, placement agency; **~vermittlungsmonopol** exclusive right to arrange job-placements, **~wert** priority, significance; **~zulagen** allowance for service.

Stellfläche *f* shelf-space, storage space.

Stellgeschäft *n* put and call, spread, straddle.

Stellkurs *m* put and call price.

Stellplatz *m* parking position, parking space, parking lot; **überdachter ~** covered parking.

Stellung *f* position, standing, status; **~durch Protektion erhalten** to get a job by one's good connections; **~ im Beruf** occupational status; **~nahme** → *Stellungnahme*; **~ nehmen** to express a view, to give an opinion, to comment; **amtliche ~** official status; **beherrschende ~** dominant position; **gesellschaftliche ~** social status; **grundbuchrechtliche ~** position in the land register (*rank, priority*); **güterrechtliche ~** status of marital property (régime); **in e-e ~ wiedereinsetzen** to reinstate in an office; **leitende ~** executive position, managerial capacity; **marktbeherrschende ~** dominant market power; **organrechtliche ~** position as executive (of a corporation), **pensionsberechtigte ~** pensionable employment; **rechtliche ~** legal position; **soziale ~** social standing, social status, **statusrechtliche ~** legal status; **untergeordnete ~** subordinate position, lower standing.

Stellungnahme *f* opinion, view(s), observations; reaction, comment **~~** *abgeben: to state one's position; to give one's opinion*; **~n bzw. Empfehlungen** opinions or recommendations; **ablehnende ~** dissenting opinion, rejection, declining comments; **abweichende ~** dissenting opinion; **e-e ~ einreichen** to file one's observations; **Gelegenheit zur ~** opportunity to give an explanation, opportunity to express one's views; **gemeinsame ~** joint opinion; **gutachtliche ~** expert opinion, advisory opinion; *e-e ~ ~ einholen: to ask for an opinion*; **mit Gründen versehene ~** reasoned opinion; **parteiliche ~** biased view, partisan opinion; **positive ~** favourable opinion; **schriftliche oder mündliche ~n** written or oral observations; **schriftliche ~** comments in writing, written observations; **zu Ihrer ~** for your comments.

stellvertretend *adj* vicarious, acting, deputizing, deputy.

Stellvertreter *m* representative, agent, proxy, deputy, locum (tenens); **~ des Bundeskanzlers** Deputy Federal Chancellor; **~krieg** agents' war; **jmdn zu seinem ~ einsetzen** to appoint s. o. as one's deputy; **privatrechtlicher ~** private agent; **selbstkontrahierender ~** self-contracting agent; procurator in rem suam.

Stellvertretung *f* (relationship of) principal and agent, agency, representation, attorneyship, proxy; **die ~ ausüben** to stand proxy for; **gewillkürte ~** agency by private

Stempel

act; **mittelbare** ~ indirect agency; **verdeckte** ~ undisclosed agency, undisclosed principal; **wirkliche** ~ actual agency.

Stempel *m* stamp, imprint, (rubber) seal; ~**abgabe** stamp duty; ~**bogen** stamp paper; ~**freiheit** exemption from stamp duty; ~**geld** stamp duty; unemployment pay; ~**kissen** ink (*or* stamps) pad; ~**marke** fee stamp, inland revenue stamp; ~~ *für Wechsel und Inhaberpapiere*: bills of exchange stamp; ~**papier** stamp paper; ~**steuer** stamp duty, stamp tax; s~ ~*frei*: *exempt from stamp duty*; s~ ~*pflichtig*: *liable to stamp duty*; ~**steuergesetze** stamp acts; ~**steuermarke** stamp, inland revenue stamp, fee stamp; ~**uhr** time clock, checkclock.

stempeln *v/t* to stamp, to postmark; to clock in (*factory*); ~ **gehen** *v/i* to be on the dole.

Sterbe|alter age of death; ~**bett** death bed; ~**beihilfen** death benefit; ~**buch** register of deaths; ~**fall** death, decease, exitus; ~**fallversicherung** life assurance, insurance payable at death; ~**geld** death benefit, death grant; ~**geldbeitrag** funeral-cost insurance contribution; ~**geldversicherung** funeral-cost insurance; ~**hilfe** euthanasia; ~**kasse** burial fund; ~**monat** month of death; ~**rate** death rate; ~**register** register of (the) deaths, death records; ~**sakramente** last rites, last sacraments; ~**tafel** mortality table, mortuary table, graduated life table; ~**urkunde** certificate of death, death certificate; ~**versicherung** burial fund death grant, burial (expenses) insurance; ~**wahrscheinlichkeit** probable time of death, probability of death, probable death rate; ~**ziffer** death rate, rate of mortality.

Sterblichkeit *f* mortality, death rate.

Sterilisierung *f* sterilization, asexualization (*male*).

Steuer *f* tax, internal revenue tax; ~**abfindung** tax settlement; ~**abgrenzung** deferred taxation; ~**abkommen** tax treaty, tax convention, tax agreement; ~**ablieferung** tax remittance, transfer of tax proceeds, revenue transfer; ~**abschreibung** tax write-off; ~**abwälzung** tax burden transfer clause (*in loan agreements etc*); ~**abzug** deduction for taxes, deduction of tax, tax deduction at source, withholding rate; income-tax relief; ~**abzugsbescheinigung** withholding tax certificate; s~**abzugsfähig** tax deductible; ~**abzugsbescheid** withholding tax notice; ~**abzugssystem** pay as you earn (P.A.Y.E.), system of tax deductions at source; withholding tax system; ~**abzugsverfahren** tax deduction at source; ~**amnestie** amnesty for tax offenders; ~**änderungsgesetz** Taxation Amendment Act; ~**anfall** tax incidence, tax yield; ~**anmeldung** tax statement; ~**anpassungsgesetz** Tax Adaption Act; ~**anrechnung** tax credit (*esp. for foreign taxes*); ~**anreize** tax incentives; ~**anspruch** tax claim, right to taxation; ~**anteile** tax portion; ~**anwaltschaft** tax lawyers; ~**arrest** attachment for tax debts; ~ **auf das bewegliche Vermögen** personal property tax; ~**aufkommen** revenue from taxation, tax revenue, tax yield, internal revenue; s~~*sneutral*: *revenue neutral;* ~**aufschlag** surtax; ~**aufschub** suspension of payment of (the) tax; ~**aufsicht** tax supervision; ~**aufsichtsverfahren** tax supervision proceedings; ~**aufstellung** tax statement; ~**ausfall** shortfall in tax revenue, revenue loss, revenue shortfall; ~**ausgleich** equalizing tax revenue, revenue sharing; ~**ausländer** non-resident (for tax purposes); person(s) not resident (*in Germany*) for tax purposes; ~**ausnutzung** exploitation of tax resources; ~**ausschuß** taxation committee, inland revenue committee; ~**aussetzung** deferral of payment

Steuer   **Steuer**

of tax; ~**ausweis** tax statement; ~**banderole** stamped revenue band; ~**basis** tax base, basis for taxation; ~**beamter** tax man, inspector of taxes, revenue officer; **s~befreit** *adj* exempt from tax; ~**befreiung** tax exemption, freedom from tax; *wechselseitige ~ ~: reciprocal exemption from tax;* **s~begünstigt** *adj* entitled to tax relief, enjoying tax relief; ~**begünstigung** tax relief; tax concession; ~**behörde** internal revenue service, taxing authority, tax authority; ~**beitreiber** tax collector; ~**beitreibung** compulsory collection of taxes; ~**belastung** tax burden; ~**bemessungsgrundlage** basis of assessment; ~**berater** tax adviser, tax consultant; ~**berechnung** computation of tax; ~**berechtigter** party entitled to the tax revenue; ~**berechtigung** entitlement to the tax revenue; ~**bescheid** tax-assessment notice, tax demand; ~**betrag** amount of tax; ~**betrug** tax fraud, tax evasion; ~**bevollmächtigter** tax representative, tax consultant; ~**bewertung** tax valuation; ~**bewilligungsrecht** tax allocation right; ~**bezirk** tax district, assessment district; ~**bilanz** tax balance sheet, balance sheet for taxation purposes, fiscal balance sheet; ~**buchführung** tax accounting; ~**bürge** guarantor for tax debts; ~**bürger** tax-payer; ~**delikt** *n* tax offence; ~**destinatar** prospective tax payer; ~**differenzierung** differential treatment in taxation; ~**druck** pressure of taxation, burden of taxation; ~**einheitswert** standard rating value; ~**einnahmen** public revenue, revenue receipts, tax receipts; *gemeindeeigene ~ ~: tax proceeds due to the local authority;* ~**einsparung** tax saving; ~**einspruch** tax appeal; ~**eintreiber** tax collector; ~**einziehung** tax collection; ~**entlastung** tax relief; ~**entrichtung** payment of tax; ~**erhebung** tax levy, tax collection; ~~**srecht**:

right to levy taxes; ~**erhöhung** tax increase, increase in taxation; *lineare ~ ~: linear increase in taxes;* ~**erklärung** tax return, tax declaration; *getrennte ~ ~: separate return; unrichtige ~ ~: false return;* ~~**sfrist**: *period for filing tax return;* ~~**spflicht**: *obligation to file tax return;* ~~**stermin**: *tax-filing date, due date for tax return;* ~**erlaß** tax abatement; ~**erleichterung** tax relief; ~**ermäßigung** tax reduction, tax relief; *degressive ~ ~: graduated tax relief;* ~**ermittler** tax investigator; ~**ermittlung** tax investigation; ~**ersparnis** tax saving; ~**erstattung** tax rebate; refund(ing) of tax; ~**ertrag** tax yield, tax revenue; ~**erträgnisse** tax yield, tax revenue; **s~fähig** taxable; ~**fahnder** tax inspector, (official) tax investigator; ~**fahndung** (bureau of) investigation of tax offences; ~**fahndungsbeamter** tax investigator; ~**fahndungsdienst** tax investigation service; ~**fall** tax taxation case; ~**festsetzung** tax assessment; ~**fiskus** taxation authorities; ~**flucht** tax-motivated flight *(from a country)*, tax evasion by absconding; ~**forderung** tax debt, fiscal claim; ~**formular** tax form; ~**fragen** questions of taxation; **s~frei** *adj* free of tax, tax-free, tax-exempt, exempt from taxation; ~**freibetrag** personal allowance, tax allowance, tax-exempt amount; *~ ~ für e-e Haushälterin: housekeeper's allowance; persönlicher ~ ~: personal allowance (or exemption);* ~**freigrenze** exemption limit; ~**freiheit** non-taxability, tax-exemption, immunity from taxation; fiscal immunity; *persönliche ~ ~: fiscal immunity;* ~**gefährdung** inchoate tax evasion; ~**gefälle** tax differential; tax differences; ~**gegenstand** subject of taxation, taxable product; ~**geheimnis** tax secrecy; ~**gerechtigkeit** fairness in the application of tax laws, equitable taxation; ~**gerichtsverfahren** revenue tribunal proceedings;

Steuer

~**gesetz** tax law, tax statute, fiscal law, Finance Act; *pl also*: revenue statutes, tax legislation; ~**gesetzgebung** tax legislation; ~**gesetzvorlage** Finance Bill, revenue bill; ~**grundlage** basis of taxation; s ~ **günstig** tax efficient; ~**guthaben** tax credit; ~**gutschein** tax credit certificate; ~**gutschrift** tax credit; ~**haftung** tax liability; ~**harmonisierung** tax harmonization; ~**hebebezirk** taxing district; ~**hehler** tax-fraud abettor; ~**hehlerei** purchasing (*or* handling) tax-evaded goods; ~**helfer** tax consultant; ~**herabsetzung** tax abatement; ~**hinterzieher** tax evader, tax dodger; ~**hinterziehung** defraudation of the revenue; fiscal fraud, tax fiddling, fraudulent tax evasion; ~**hoheit** taxing power, power to levy taxes; sovereign-right of taxation; ~**inländer** resident (tax payer); ~**inspektor** tax inspector; ~**jahr** tax year, taxable year; ~**jurist** tax lawyer; ~**karte** tax card, wage-tax card; ~**klasse** tax class, tax bracket; ~**klausel** recission clause to avoid unforseen tax effect; ~**kraft** taxable capacity; revenue-raising power; ~**kurs** price for tax purposes; ~~**werte**: *price for taxation figures*; tax-law training course; ~**kürzung** tax cut; ~**lager** bonded warehouse for untaxed goods; ~**last** tax burden, fiscal charges; *auf die ~ ~ anrechnen*: *to set-off against tax due;* ~**lehre** theory of taxation; s~**lich** *adj* fiscal, relating to taxation; ~ ~~**rechnerisch**: *as calculated for tax purposes*; ~**liste** tax list, list of taxpayers; ~**lücke** tax loophole; ~**mahnschreiben** tax reminder (letter); ~**marke** revenue stamp; ~**maßstab** standard of taxation; ~**meldepflicht** legal obligation to file tax returns; ~**merkmal** tax coding; ~**meßbescheid** assessment notice; notice of ratable value; ~**meßbetrag** basic assessment figure; ~**meßzahl** tax index number, tax reference; ~**mindereinnahmen** revenue shortfall, decrease in tax receipts; ~ **mit proportionalem Tarif** taxation at a constant rate; ~**mittel** fiscal resources, tax proceeds, tax revenue, public funds; ~**monopol** fiscal tax monopoly; ~**moral** taxpayer's honesty; ~**nachforderung** subsequent tax demand; ~**nachlaß** tax rebate, tax abatement, tax relief; ~**nachzahlungen** additional tax payments; ~**n auf Dienstleistungen** taxes on services; ~**n eintreiben** to collect (*or* exact) taxes; ~**n erheben** to levy taxes; ~**neutralität** impartial taxation, equitable fiscal policy; ~**n hinterziehen** fraudulently to evade payment of taxes; ~**normen** (legal) tax provisions, fiscal norms; ~**novelle** tax amendment law; ~**n vom Wertzuwachs** taxes on capital gains (*or* appreciation); capital gains tax; ~**n weiterbelasten** to re-debit taxes, to charge a tax liability to s. o. else; ~**oase** tax haven, tax shelter, tax oasis; ~**objekt** taxable property, thing taxed; taxable item; ~**ordnung** tax system; ~**ordnungswidrigkeit** breach of tax regulations; s~**orientiert** *adj* influenced by tax considerations; ~**pächter** farmer general (*hist.*); ~**pauschalierung** lump-sum taxation; ~**periode** taxable period; ~**pfändung** distress for taxes; ~**pflicht** tax liability, liability to pay taxes; *beschränkte ~~*: *restricted (domestic) tax liability; sachliche ~~*: *objective tax-liability; unbeschränkte ~~*: *residents' full tax liability, unrestricted tax liability;* s~**pflichtig** *adj* taxable, liable to tax(ation), subject to taxation; *beschränkt ~~*: *subject to restricted taxation (domestic assets); unbeschränkt ~~*: *subject to unrestricted taxation;* ~**pflichtiger** tax-payer, taxable person; *beschränkt ~~*: *non-resident taxpayer; buchführender ~~*: *tax payer who keeps books; inländischer ~~*: *resident taxpayer; säumiger ~~*: *taxpayer in arrears; unbeschränkt ~~*: *resident taxpayer;*

Steuer   **Steuer**

~**plakette** tax disc; ~**politik** fiscal policy, taxation policy; s~**politisch** relating to tax (policy); ~**privilegien** tax privileges; ~**progression** progressive increase in taxation; ~~**sstufe**: *rate band; tax bracket; heimliche* ~~: *fiscal drag (through inflation), bracket creep; überspannte* ~~: *excessively steep progressive scale of taxation;* ~**prozeß** tax lawsuit, tax litigation; ~**prüfer** tax inspector; ~**prüfung** tax inspector's investigation; ~**-PS-Leistung** engine rating; ~**quellen** sources of taxation; *ergiebige* ~~: *productive sources of revenue;* ~**quote** taxation ratio *(of tax revenue to national product);* ~**recht** law of taxation, revenue law, fiscal law, tax law; ~**rechtsstreit** tax proceedings, tax litigation, lawsuit in a tax tribunal; ~**reform** tax reform; ~**regelung** tax regulations; ~~ *für Alkohol: tax system for alcohol;* ~**reserve** provision for taxation, tax reserve; ~**rhythmus** (regular) timing of tax payments; ~**richtlinien** administrative tax regulations; ~**rückerstattung** tax refund; ~**rückstände** tax arrears, back taxes, delinquent taxes, tax delinquency; ~**rückstellung** provision for tax(ation), tax reserve; ~**rückvergütung** tax refund, tax rebate; ~**sachen** taxation (matters); ~**sachverständiger** tax expert; ~**satz** rate of taxation, tax rate, *normaler* ~~: *standard rate of taxation;* ~**säumnis** tax delinquency, dilatoriness in effecting tax payments; ~**säumniszuschlag** tax penalty; ~**schätzung** estimated tax (assessment), tax revenue estimate; ~**schraube** increasing tax burden, tax screw; ~**schuld** tax debt, tax due; *rückständige* ~ ~: *arrears of taxes;* ~**schuldner** tax debtor, taxpayer, person liable for taxes; ~**schuldnerschaft** tax liability; s~**schwach** *adj* fiscally weak, (*month*) of low tax receipts; ~**senkung** tax reduction, tax cut; ~**sicherung** security for taxes;

~**skonto** tax discount; ~~-**Soll** amount of tax liability; ~**staffelung** tax graduation; s~**stark** *adj* having a large tax revenue, fiscally strong; ~**strafe** penalty for tax offence; ~**strafrecht** criminal law in relation to tax offences; ~**strafsachen** revenue offences, tax-offence cases; ~**straftat** revenue offence, tax offence; ~**strafverfahren** criminal prosecution for tax offences; ~**stufe** tax bracket, tax grade; ~**stundung** tax deferral; ~**subjekt** taxpayer, taxable person (*or* entity *or* subject); ~**system** tax system, fiscal system; ~**tabelle** tax table; ~**tarif** tax scale, tax rate; s~**technisch** *adj* relating to taxation methods; ~**termin** tax payment date; ~**träger** tax-levying authority; ~**transparenz** transparency of taxes, intelligibility of the taxation system; ~**überschuß** tax surplus; ~**überwälzung** tax shifting, passing the tax-burden to others; ~**umgehung** tax avoidance; ~**unbedenklichkeitsbescheinigung** tax clearance certificate; s~**unschädlich** *adj* tax-neutral, not attracting tax, without effect on tax; ~**unschädlichkeit** tax neutrality; ~**veranlagung** tax assessment; ~**veranlagungszeitraum** assessment period; ~**verband** combined revenue collection; ~**verbindlichkeiten** taxation liabilities; ~**verfahren** tax proceedings, proceedings for a tax offence; ~**vergehen** criminal tax offence; ~**vergünstigung** tax concession, tax privilege, tax allowance, preferential tax treatment; fiscal advantage; ~ ~ *für Kapitalanlagen: investment allowance; gestaffelte* ~ ~**en**: *graded tax concessions;* ~**vergütung** tax rebate; ~**verkoppelung** linking of taxes; ~**verkürzung** unlawful reduction of tax assessment; ~**verwaltung** revenue authorities, tax administration; ~**verwaltungsakt** administrative fiscal act; ~**vollstreckungsrecht** tax enforcement law; ~**vorausschät-**

730

Steuermannsquittung | **Stichprobe**

zung tax estimate; **~vorauszahlung** advance tax collection, prepayment of taxes (*before annual assessment*); **~vorlage** tax bill, finance bill, revenue bill; **~vorschriften** tax regulations, tax provisions; **~vorteile** tax advantages, tax benefits, tax privileges; **~wert** value for tax purposes; **~wesen** taxation, fiscal matters, tax system; **~widerstand** resistance to taxation; **s~wirksam** *adj* tax efficient; **~wohnsitz** residence for tax purposes, tax home; **~zahler** taxpayer, ratepayer; *säumiger ~ ~: dilatory taxpayer;* **~zahlung** payment of taxes; *anonyme ~ ~en: conscience money; pauschalierte ~ ~en: lump-sum tax payments*; **~zeichen** revenue stamp; **~zeichenfälschung** forging of revenue stamps; **~zerlegung** break-down of taxes; **~zuschlag** additional tax, surcharge; **~zuwiderhandlung** violation of the tax laws, tax offence; **~zwangsverkauf** tax sale; forced sale because of tax; **anrechenbare ausländische ~n** deductible foreign taxes; **ausländische ~** foreign tax; **ausweispflichtige ~n** taxes subject to obligatory publication; **bundeseigene ~** federal tax; **degressive ~** degressive tax; **der ~ unterworfen** taxable; subject to taxation; **die auf ... lastenden ~n** the tax burden on ...; **die ~n hinterziehen** to defraud the revenue, to fraudulently evade payment of taxes; **direkte ~n** direct tax; **einbehaltene ~** tax withheld, tax deducted at source; **e-e ~ abwälzen** to pass on a tax, to shift a tax (on to); **e-e ~ erheben** to tax, to impose a tax (on); **e-e ~ erhöhen** to raise a tax, to increase a tax (rate); **e-e konjunkturreagible ~** a tax which is sensitive to economic trends; **e-e ~ zurückerstattet erhalten** to recover tax, to get a tax refund, **e-r ~ unterliegen** to be liable for tax, to be subject to tax; **einzelstaatliche ~** state tax (*US*); **fällige ~n** due taxes; **gestaffelte ~** prorated tax, taxes on a sliding scale; **gewinnabhängige ~n** profit-related (or profit-dependent) taxes; **hinterzogene ~n** defrauded tax; **indirekte ~** indirect tax, excise duties; **jährlich zu entrichtende ~** (*auf Aktien und Schuldverschreibungen*) compulsory annual duty (*payable on shares and bonds*); **kommunale ~n** local taxes; **ländereigene ~n** a Federal Land's own taxes, state taxes; **latente ~n** deferred taxes, offsetting tax, *temporary tax differential between tax balance sheet and commercial balance sheet;* **mit e-r ~ belegen** to impose a tax (on sth.); **persönliche ~** direct taxes, personal taxes; **progressive ~** graduated tax, progressive tax; **staatliche ~n** public taxes; **veranlagte ~n** assessed taxes, scheduled taxes; taxes levied by assessments; **verschleierte ~** concealed tax; **zur ~ veranlagen** to assess s. o. for tax.

Steuermannsquittung *f* mate's receipt.

Stich|datum relevant date, qualifying date **~entscheid** tie-breaking decision, casting vote; final decision *in respect of competing applicants or conflicting awards;* **s~haltig** *adj* sound, valid, conclusive, relevant; **~haltigkeit** soundness, validity, conclusiveness, relevancy; **~monat** relevant month, sample month; **~probe** → *Stichprobe;* **~tag** relevant date, reckonable date, settlement day, record date; computation date, key date, fixed date, qualifying date, target date; **~~smiete**: rent on the relevant date; **~waffe** stabbing weapon, thrust weapon; **~wahl** second ballot, decisive ballot (*between two candidates*); run-off vote; **~wunde** stab wound.

Stichprobe *f* spot check, sampling, sample taken offhand, random sample, random test, random examination, probability sample; **~ aus e-m Querschnitt** sample from a cross-section; **~ von Haushalten**

sample of households; **ausgewogene** ~ proportionate sampling; **gewichtete** ~ weighted sample, balanced sample; **kontrollierte** ~ controlled sampling; **repräsentative** ~ representative sample; **zu klein gewählte** ~ ~**n** undersampled.

Stichproben|auswahl sampling (procedure), sampling method; ~~ *nach Gruppen stratified sample; mehrfache* ~~~: *multiple sampling;* ~**basis** sample census; ~**entnahme** random sampling, bulk sampling; ~**entnehmen** to take samples at random; ~**erhebung** random sample survey, random sampling; ~**fehler** sampling error; ~**mittelwert** sample mean; ~**plan** sample design; ~**raum** sample space; ~**verfahren** spot-check system.

Stief|bruder step-brother; ~**eltern** step-parents, ~**elternteil** step-parent; ~**kind** step-child; ~**kindschaftsverhältnis** step relationship; ~**mutter** step-mother; ~**sohn** step-son; ~**tochter** step-daughter; ~**vater** step-father.

stiften *v/t* to endow, to found, to institute, to donate, to establish.

Stifter *m* founder, institutor, originator, donor; ~**verband** endowment association, founder's association; ~**wille** founder's intention.

Stiftung *f* (*incorporated*) foundation, endowed institute; endowment, public trust; ~ **des bürgerlichen Rechts** incorporated foundation; ~ **des öffentlichen Rechts** foundation under public law; ~ **für e–e Bildungsanstalt** educational trust; **gemeinnützige** ~ community trust; **kirchliche** ~ ecclesiastical charitable trust; **mildtätige** ~ charitable endowment, charitable foundation; **nichtöffentliche** ~ private endowment; **öffentliche** ~ public foundation; **örtliche** ~ local foundation; **wohltätige** ~ charitable endowment, charitable foundation.

Stiftungs|aufsicht supervision of a foundation; ~**aufsichtsbehörde** supervisory authority for foundations and endowments; ~**beamter** foundation officer; ~**beirat** advisory board of the foundation; ~**gelder** endowment funds; ~**geschäft** endowment (transaction); ~ ~ *unter Lebenden: endowment inter vivos*; ~**gesetz** endowments and foundations act; ~**organe** statutory organs of a foundation; ~**rat** board of trustees; ~**recht** law on foundations and endowments; ~**satzung** charter of a (the) foundation; ~**urkunde** foundation instrument; ~**vermögen** endowment property, endowment fund; ~**versammlung** general meeting of the foundation; ~**vertrag** endowment contract, foundation agreement.

Still|geld nursing benefit; ~**fähigkeit** ability to nurse; ~**zeit** lactation (period), nursing period.

Stillhalte|abkommen standstill agreement, moratorium, cooling-off agreement; ~**anordnungen** moratorium instructions; ~**kommission** standstill commission; ~**konsortium** standstill syndicate; ~**kredit** standstill credit; ~**schulden** frozen debts; ~**vereinbarung** moratorium, letter of licence.

stillhalten *v/i* to grant a moratorium, to postpone enforcement of claims.

Stillhalter *m* writer of an option, taker of an option.

Stillhaltung *f* prolongation of credits, refraining from enforcement.

Stillegung *f* shutdown, closing down; ~**svergütung** bonus for closing down; ~**sversicherung** insurance against business closure; ~ **von Nebenbahnen** closing down branch lines.

stilliegen *v/i* to lie idle, to remain dormant.

Stillstand *m* stoppage, deadlock, standstill, stagnation.

stillstehend *adj* idle, unused, inactive, stagnant, dormant.

Stillschweigen *n* silence, secrecy.

stillschweigend *adj* tacit, implied; ~ *enthalten sein: to be implied*.

Stimm|abgabe → *Stimmabgabe;* **s-~berechtigt** *adj* entitled to vote; carrying voting rights, voting; *nicht ~ ~: not entitled to vote, nonvoting (shares);* **~berechtigung** right to vote; **~bevollmächtigter** proxyholder; **~bevollmächtigung** proxy; **~bezirk** electoral district; **~bindungsvertrag** voting trust agreement; **~enthaltung** non-voting, abstention; **~karte** poll card; voting card; **~kreis** constituency, electoral district; **~ordnung** voting rules; **~recht** → *Stimmrecht;* **~schein** certificate of proxy, voting form; **~verbot** prohibition of voting; **~zählung** counting of votes; **~zettel** ballot paper, voting paper; *ungültiger ~ ~: void (invalid) voting paper.*

Stimmabgabe *f* voting, vote-casting, poll, polling; **~ durch Handheben** voting by show of hands; **~ durch Sicherheben** (*bzw Sitzenbleiben*), vote by rising (*or remaining seated, respectively*); **~ durch Vertreter** vote by proxy; **geschlossene ~** block vote; **geteilte ~** split vote; **irrtümliche ~** erroneous vote; **schriftliche ~** vote by correspondence, written polling, postal vote.

Stimme *f* vote; **~n auf mehrere Kandidaten verteilen** to split votes; **abgegebene ~n** votes cast, votes polled; **ausschlaggebende ~** casting vote; **beratende ~** consultative voice; *mit ~ r ~: in a consultant capacity;* **die ~ des Vorsitzenden ist entscheidend** (= *maßgebend*) the chairman shall have a casting vote; **einfache ~** basic vote; **gültige ~** valid vote; **sich der ~ enthalten** to abstain from voting; **ungültige ~** void vote; **unsichere ~n** floating vote, undecided voters.

Stimmen|auszählung counting of votes; **~einheit** unanimity, unanimous vote; **~fang** vote-catching; **~fänger** vote-catcher; **~fängerei** vote-catching method; **~gleichheit** equality of votes, tie; **~häufung** cumulation of votes; **~kauf** buying of votes; **~mehrheit** majority of votes, majority vote; *einfache ~ ~: simple majority; mit ~ ~ entscheiden: to decide by a majority of votes; relative ~ ~: plurality;* **~vereinigung** pooling of votes; **~wanderung** poll permutations; **~werber** canvasser; **~werbung** touting, canvassing.

stimmen *v/i* to vote; **geschlossen für etw ~** to vote solidly for.

Stimmlosigkeit *f* aphonia.

Stimmrecht *n* voting right, right to vote, vote, franchise, voting power, suffrage; **abgeleitetes ~** derivative vote; **allgemeines ~** universal suffrage; **das ~ verleihen** to enfranchise; **doppeltes ~** double vote; **Verlust des ~s** disqualification from voting, loss of voting rights.

Stimmrechts|aktie share; **~ausschluß** disqualification from voting; **~ausübung** voting, exercising the right to vote; **~ ~ durch Vertreter:** *voting by proxy;* **~bindung** voting commitment; **s~los** *adj* nonvoting, voteless; **~mißbrauch** abuse of voting rights; **~treuhänder** voting trustee; **~vollmacht** proxy (paper).

Stimmungswechsel *m* change of mood.

Stockdarlehen *n* permanent loan.

Stockdegen *m* sword stick.

Stoffpatent *n* patent for a material substance.

Stollenmundloch *n* pit head.

Stockwerkseigentum flat ownership, ownership of an entire floor.

Stopppreis *m* ceiling price, frozen price.

Stoppschild *n* stop sign.

Störanfälligkeit *f* susceptibility (*or* tendency) to breakdown.

stören *v/t* to disturb, to annoy, to interfere with, to pester.

störend *adj* disturbing, annoying, offensive.

Störer *m* disturber, intruder, troublemaker.

Störfaktor *m* disturbant, disturbing factor.

Störfall *m* radioactive leak (*in nuclear reactor*); **~verordnung** *f* Regulation on Disruptions of Operations (*nuclear reactors*).

stornieren *v/t* to cancel, to annul, to countermand, to revoke.

Stornierung *f* cancellation, countermanding; counter-order; ~ **e–s Auftrags** cancellation of an order, withdrawal of an order.

Storno *n* cancellation, contra entry, offsetting entry, reversing entry; **~buchung** reversing entry.

Störsender *m* jamming station.

Störung *f* disturbance, annoyance, disorder, trespass, nuisance; ~ **der Geistestätigkeit** unbalanced mind, mental deficiency; *krankhafte ~ ~ ~: mental derangement, mental disturbance;* ~ **der Nachtruhe** disturbance of repose, disturbance at night-time; ~ **der öffentlichen Sicherheit und Ordnung** disturbance of the peace; ~ **der Religionsausübung** disturbance of public worship; ~ **der Sonntagsruhe** disturbance of Sunday peace; sabbath violation; ~ **der Totenruhe** interference with bodily remains, defilement of graves; ~ **der Zahlungsbilanz** maladjustment in the balance of payments; ~ **des Arbeitsfriedens** disturbance of peaceful industrial relations; ~ **des öffentlichen Friedens** disturbing the public peace; violation of the public peace; ~ **des Verkehrs** traffic disruption; **~en im Gleichgewicht** disequilibria (*balances of payments etc*); ~ **im Postdienst** irregularities in the mail service; ~ **öffentlicher Betriebe** disturbing public services; **~sbeseitigung** abatement of a nuisance; **~sstelle** telephone repair service station, operator; ~ **von Amtshandlungen** disturbance of official functions; ~ **von Wahlen** interference with elections; **erratische ~en** erratic disruptions; **rechtserhebliche** ~ actionable nuisance; **schwerwiegende** ~ serious disturbance; **vorüber**gehende **~en** temporary difficulties.

Stoß|angebot concentrated offering, massive offering; **~auftrag** urgent order, rush order; **~bedarf** urgent heavy demand; **~kraft** impact, thrust; **~trupp** combat patrol; **~waffe** weapon for stabbing; **~wirkung** shock effect; **~zeit** peak hours, rush hours, peak period.

Straf|akte (criminal)case file, case record; **~aktion** punitive action; **~änderung** change of penalty, commutation of sentence; **~androhung** punitive sanction, criminal sanction; *gesetzliche ~ ~: legislative sanction; unter ~ ~: under penalty of . . .; jmdn unter ~ ~ laden: to subpoena s. o.;* **~anrechnung** allowance for the served part of another sentence; **~anstalt** penal institution, prison; **~antrag** demand for prosecution; demand (by the prosecutor) for a penalty; **~antragsfrist** statutory period to file a demand for prosecution; **~antragsrecht** entitlement to demand prosecution; **~antritt** commencement of prison sentence; **~anwendung** application of penal sanction; **~anzeige** (criminal) information, complaint of an offence, denunciation; *e–e ~ ~ erstatten:* to lay an information, to report an offence to the police; **~arrest** short-term military imprisonment; **~arten** types of penalty (*or* sentence); **~aufhebungsgründe** reasons for withdrawing punishment; **~aufschub** suspension of commencement of a sentence, postponement of execution, respite in punishment; **~ausschließungsgründe** legal reasons for exemption from punishment; **~aussetzung** suspension of sentence; ~ ~ *zur Bewährung: (suspension of sentence on) probation;* ~ ~ *gewähren: to suspend a sentence; einstweilige ~ ~: temporary suspension;* **~aussetzungsbeschluß zur Bewährung** probation order; **~ausstand** unserved portion of a sen

Strafakte

tence; s~**bar** → *strafbar*; ~**barkeit** → *Strafbarkeit*; ~**befehl** fixed penalty order, order for summary punishment; ~**befehlsverfahren** summary punishment, order proceedings; ~**befugnis** power to punish, power to sentence; ~**bemessung** assessment of punishment (to be imposed); ~**bescheid** an administrative order inflicting a penalty; ~**beschluß** order to inflict punishment; ~**bestimmung** penal (*or* criminal) provision; *pl also: penal laws*; ~**dauer** duration of punishment, length of a prison term; ~**entlassener** discharged prisoner; *auf Bewährung bedingt* ~ ~: *probationer*; ~**entlassung** discharge (from prison); *bedingte* ~ ~: *conditional discharge*; ~**erhöhungsmerkmal** aggravating circumstance; ~**erkenntnis** sentence (imposed by the court); ~**erlaß** remission of penalty, remittal of a penalty, pardon; *bedingter* ~ ~: *conditional discharge, binding over on probation*; *teilweiser* ~ ~: *remission of part of a sentence*; ~**ermäßigung** abatement of penalty, reduction in sentence; ~**erschwerungsgrund** aggravating circumstance; ~**expedition** punitive expedition; s~**fällig** *adj* liable to punishment, delinquent; *erneut* ~ *werden: to reoffend*; ~**fälligkeit** liability to punishment; ~**festsetzung** fixing of the sentence, assessment of punishment; ~**frage** the question of sentencing; s~**frei** exempt from punishment, free from punishment, scot-free; ~**freiheit** impunity, immunity from criminal prosecution, amnesty; ~**freiheitsgesetz** impunity law, amnesty law; ~**gebühr** penalty; ~**gefangener** criminal prisoner (under a sentence), prison inmate; *entlassener* ~ ~: *discharged prisoner, ex-convict*; ~**geld** fine; penalty; ~**gericht** criminal court, criminal division; *pl* courts of criminal jurisdiction; ~**gerichtsbarkeit** criminal jurisdiction, penal jurisdiction; ~**gesetz** criminal law, penal law,

Strafakte

criminal statute, penal statute; ~**gesetzbuch** penal code, criminal code; ~**gesetzgebung** penal legislation; ~**gewalt** punitive power, power to sentence; ~**haft** penal confinement, imprisonment, punitive detention (*juveniles*); *aus der* ~ ~ *entlassen: discharged from prison*; ~**haftentschädigung** compensation for unjustified imprisonment; ~**herabsetzung** reduction of sentence; ~**kammer** criminal court, criminal division; ~**justiz** criminal justice (system), penal justice, penal jurisdiction; ~**klage** penal action, criminal charge indictment; ~**klageverbrauch** ne bis in idem (*double jeopardy*), (plea of) *autrefois acquit and autrefois convict*; ~**klausel** penalty clause; ~**kolonie** convict settlement; ~**lager** penal camp, prison camp; s~**los** unpunished, exempt from punishment; ~ *bleiben: to go unpunished*; ~**losigkeit** impunity, immunity, exemption from punishment; ~**makel** blemish, taint of a previous conviction; ~**mandat** ticket, summons issued to (traffic) offender; ~**maß** degree of penalty, sentence, measure of sentence, measure of punishment; *das* ~ ~ *festsetzen: to (fix the) sentence*; *zu niedriges* ~ ~: *inadequate sentence*; ~**maßberufung** appeal against sentence; ~**maßverkündung** sentencing, ~**maßnahmen** punitive measures; ~**mildernd** *adj* mitigating, extenuating; ~**milderung** *f* mitigation (of sentence), extenuation; ~ ~**sgründe**: *grounds for mitigation*; s~**mündig** *adj* of criminally responsible age; ~**mündigkeit** age of reason, the beginning of criminal responsibility, age of criminal capacity; ~**nachlaß** reduction of sentence; ~**norm** penal provision; ~**porto** penalty postage; ~**prozeß** criminal procedure, criminal proceedings; *e–n* ~ ~ *führen: to try a case*; ~**prozeßordnung** code of criminal procedure, (rules of) criminal procedure; ~**prozeßrecht**

Strafakte

law of criminal procedure; ~**rahmen** range of punishment; ~**recht** → *Strafrecht*; **s**~**rechtlich** *adj* penal, according to criminal law; ~ ~ *verantwortlich*: *criminally responsible, doli capax*; ~**register** register of convictions; ~ ~ *ohne Vermerk*: *no entry in the register of convictions*; ~**registerauszug** extract from the register of convictions; ~**registerbehörde** *authority in charge of keeping the register of convictions*; ~**registerverordnung** register of convictions ordinance; ~**rest** remainder of a sentence, unserved portion of a sentence; ~**richter** criminal court judge; ~**sache** criminal case; criminal matter; ~**sanktion** punitive (*or* criminal) sanction; **s**~**schärfend** *adj* aggravating; ~**schärfung** aggravation (of sentence), increasing the severity of the sentence; ~**schärfungsgründe** aggravating circumstances; ~**senat** high criminal court, criminal division of the court of appeal, criminal division of the German Bundesgerichtshof; ~**tat** → *Straftat*; ~**tatbestand** facts constituting an offence, corpus delicti, statutory definition of a crime, elements of a crime; *konsumierter* ~ ~: *included (lesser) offence*; ~**täter** delinquent, offender; *geisteskranker* ~ ~: *criminal lunatic*; *defective delinquent*; *jugendlicher* ~ ~: *juvenile delinquent*; *politischer* ~ ~: *political offender*; ~**tilgung** deletion from the criminal record; extinction of previous convictions; ~**umwandlung** commutation of sentence; **s**~**unmündig** *adj* doli incapax, below the age of criminal responsibility; ~**unmündigkeit** age below criminal responsibility, criminal incapacity due to young age; ~**unterbrechung** interruption in serving a sentence; ~**urteil** conviction and sentence, penal judgment, judgment of a criminal court, judgment of conviction; *ein* ~ ~ *aufheben*: *to quash a conviction*; *ein* ~ ~ *bestätigen*: *to uphold a conviction*; *ein* ~ ~ *fällen*:

to pass a sentence; ~**verbüßung** serving a sentence, serving one's term in prison; *sich der* ~ ~ *entziehen*: *to evade punishment*; ~**verbüßungszeit** length of sentence (to be) served, served (part of the) sentence; ~**verdächtiger** criminal suspect; ~**vereitelung** compounding crime; obstruction of criminal prosecution, prevention of punishment; ~**verfahren** → *Strafverfahren*, ~**verfolgung** → *Strafverfolgung*; ~**verfügung** penal order, disciplinary penalty; ~**verhandlung** (criminal) trial, hearing before a criminal court; ~**verjährung** limitation of criminal prosecution, bar to prosecution due to lapse of time; ~**verkürzung** reduction (of service) of a sentence; ~**verlangen** request for punishment (*by a foreign government*); ~**vermerk** criminal record; **s**~**verschärfend** aggravating; ~**verschärfung** aggravation of sentence; ~**verschärfungsgrund** aggravating circumstances; ~**versetzung** transfer for disciplinary reasons; ~**verteidiger** defence counsel, criminal practitioner, criminal lawyer; ~**verteidigung** (criminal) defence; ~**vollstreckung** → *Strafvollstreckung*; ~**vollzug** → *Strafvollzug*; ~**vorbehalt** reserved punishment; ~**vorschrift** penal (*or* criminal) provisions, penal regulation; **s**~**würdig** punishable, deserving punishment; ~**würdigkeit** qualification for punishment, eligibility for punishment; ~**zeit** term, penal term, prison term, time of sentence, time to be served, „stretch"; ~**zelle** prison cell; ~**zettel** penalty notice; traffic ticket; ~**zins** penalty, penal interest; ~**zoll** penalty duty, penal duty; ~**zumessung** sentencing, determination of penalty (*or* punishment); ~**zumessungsgründe** considerations as to the award of punishment, reasons for the length of the sentence awarded; ~**zuständigkeit** jurisdiction in

strafbar / **Straftat**

criminal cases; **~zweck** object of punishment, purpose of punishment, aim of sentence.

strafbar *adj* punishable, liable to prosecution; *sich ~ machen: to incur a penalty, to be liable to prosecution.*

Strafbarkeit *f* criminality, punishability, criminal nature.

Strafe *f* punishment, penalty, sentence; **~nhäufung** cumulative sentences; **~n werden gleichzeitig verbüßt** sentences run concurrently; **~ ohne Freiheitsentzug** noncustodial sentence; **~ unbestimmter Höhe** indeterminate sentence; **angemessene ~** reasonable sentence, adequate punishment, appropriate punishment; **auferlegte ~** sentence imposed; **auf ~ erkennen** to award a sentence; **bei ~ von** under penalty of, upon pain of; **die ~ antreten** to appear at prison to serve a sentence; **die vom Gesetz angedrohte ~** the punishment laid down by law; **e-e ~ erlassen** to remit (*or* waive) a penalty (*or* punishment); **e-e ~ herabsetzen** to reduce a sentence; **e-e ~ umwandeln** to commute a sentence (*or* penalty); **e-e ~ verbüßen** to serve a sentence; **e-e ~ verhängen** to pass sentence (on), to inflict a penalty (on), to impose a penalty (on); **e-e ~ voll verbüßen** to complete one's sentence; **e-e ~ verwirken** to incur a punishment (*or* penalty); **e-e ~ vollstrecken** to execute a sentence; **e-e ~ zuerkennen** to award a punishment; **e-e ~ zumessen** to mete out punishment; **e-e ~ zur Bewährung aussetzen** to place on probation, to suspend a sentence on probation; **e-e zusätzliche ~ verhängen** to superimpose a punishment; **empfindliche ~** severe punishment; **entehrende ~** dishonorable punishment; **erkannte ~** sentence awarded (*or* imposed); **exemplarische ~** exemplary punishment; **gerechte ~** condign penalty, appropriate punishment; just and lawful sentence; **geringfügige ~** slight penalty, modest penalty; **gesetzliche ~** lawful punishment, statutory punishment; **keine ~ ohne Gesetz** nulla poena sine lege; **körperliche ~** corporal punishment; **lebenslängliche ~** life sentence; **milde ~** lenient punishment; **mit e-r ~ belegen** to penalize, to subject to a penalty; **mit ~ bedroht sein** to carry a penalty; **nicht zur Bewährung ausgesetzte ~** immediate sentence; **schwere ~** heavy sentence; **seine ~ absitzen** serve one's sentence, to do one's time; **sich e-r ~ entziehen** to evade punishment; **übermäßig harte ~** harsh sentence, excessive sentence (*or* penalty); **verjährte ~** penalty barred by lapse of time; **verschärfte ~** increased penalty, stricter punishment; **verwirkte ~** incurred penalty, sentence awarded; **vollzogene ~** enforced sentence, executed sentence, **von ~ absehen** to remit an offence; **zu e-r ~ verurteilen** to sentence, to impose a penalty; **zwingend vorgeschriebene ~** mandatory sentence.

strafen *v/t* to punish, to penalize.

strafend *adj* punitive, corrective.

Sträfling *m* prisoner, prison inmate, convict.

Strafrecht *n* criminal law, penal law; **~ssystem** penal system; **formelles ~** law of criminal procedure; **internationales ~** international criminal law; **materielles ~** substantive criminal law.

Strafrechts|änderungsgesetz Criminal Law Amendment Act; **~irrtum** mistake of law in a criminal case, error as to the criminal nature of an act; **~notstand** emergency in criminal law, plea of necessity; **~pflege** administration of penal justice; **~praxis** practice of the criminal courts; **~reform** penal reform; **~schutz** protection afforded by the penal laws; **~system** penal system; **~theorie** theory of criminal jurisprudence.

Straftat *f* criminal act, punishable

737

Strafverfahren | **Strafvollzugsabteilung**

act, criminal offence, crime; ~**bestandsmerkmale** elements of the offence, characteristics constituting the criminal act; ~**en gegen die öffentliche Ordnung** offences against public order; ~**en gegen die Person** offences against the person; ~**en und Ordnungswidrigkeit auf öffentlichen Straßen** street offences; ~ **im ersten Rückfall** second offence; **atomare** ~ nuclear crime; **auf politischen Beweggründen beruhende** ~ offence inspired by political motives; **auslieferungsfähige** ~**n** extraditable crimes; **bundesrechtliche** ~ federal offence, federal crime; **die schwerere** ~ the higher offence; **die zur Last gelegte** ~ the alleged offence; **erhebliche** ~ notable crime, serious offence; **erstmalige** ~ first offence; **fahrlässige** ~ negligent offence; **fortgesetzte** ~ continued offence; **gesetzliche** ~**bestände** statutory offences; **im Rausch begangene** ~ offence committed while under the influence of intoxicating liquors; „**keine** ~ **ohne Gesetz**" nulla poena sine lege; nullum crimen rule; **konsumierte** ~ necessarily included offence; **militärische** ~**en** military offences; **mit Geldstrafe bedrohte** ~ offence punishable by a fine; **nachfolgende** ~ subsequent offence; **neue** ~ fresh offence; **politische** ~ political offence; **unerledigte** ~**en** outstanding offences; **unvollendete** ~ inchoate offence; **vollendete** ~ offence committed, accomplished crime.

Strafverfahren *n* criminal procedure; criminal proceeding(s), criminal action, criminal suit, penal proceeding(s), penal suit; ~**srecht** law of criminal procedure; ~**sreform** reform of criminal procedure; **abgekürztes** ~ summary trial; **anhängiges** ~ pending prosecution, pending criminal case; **beschleunigtes** ~ summary trial, accelerated criminal proceedings; **ein** ~ **betreiben** to pursue criminal proceedings; **ein** ~ **einleiten** to institute criminal proceedings; **ein** ~ **einstellen** to drop a prosecution, to withdraw a charge, to remit an offence, to cease criminal proceedings.

Strafverfolgung *f* prosecution, public prosecution, prosecution of criminal offences; **die** ~ **einstellen** to stop the prosecution, to discontinue the prosecution; **die** ~ **niederschlagen** to quash the proceedings, to stop the proceedings; **die** ~ **unterdrücken** to quash prosecution; **öffentliche** ~ official prosecution; **sich der** ~ **entziehen** to evade justice.

Strafverfolgungs|ankündigung notice of intended prosecution; ~**beamter** prosecution officer; ~**behörde** prosecution, criminal prosecution authority; *GB* Director of Public Prosecutions; Crown Prosecution Service; *US* (*also*) district attorney; ~**verjährung** limitation of criminal prosecution.

Strafvollstreckung *f* penal execution, execution of a sentence; ~**sbehörde** public authority for penal execution; ~**sleiter** director of penal execution; ~**svereitelung** thwarting (or obstructing) the execution of sentences; ~**sverjährung** bar of execution of punishment due to lapse of time; **die** ~ **aussetzen** to suspend the execution of a sentence.

Strafvollzug *m* execution of a custodial sentence, imprisonment, prison regime; **offener** ~ open prison, non-confinement facility.

Strafvollzugs|abteilung department of correction; ~**anstalt** penal institution, prison, correctional institution; ~**beamter** prison officer, prison guard, prison inspector; ~**bedienstete** prison staff; ~**behörde** penal administration, prison authority; ~**gesetz** Prison Act, Treatment of Offenders Act; ~**grundsätze** prison policy; ~**ordnung** prison regulations;

Strahlenbelastung

~**recht** law of prison administration; ~**system** prison system, correctional system (US), penological system; ~**wissenschaft** penology.

Strahlen|belastung level of radioactivity; ~**gefahr** radiation hazard; ~**geschädigter** radiation victim; ~**pass** radiation record (*or* passport) ~**schädigung** injury from radiation; ~**schutz** radiation protection, radiation safety devices, radiation shielding; ~**schutzbeauftragter** radiation protection commissioner; ~**schutzverordnung** radiation protection ordinance.

Strahlungs|verbrechen radiation crime; ~**gefahr** radiation hazard, exposure hazard; ~**risiko** radiation hazard, exposure hasard; ~**schädigung** radiation injury.

Strand|gut salvage goods, stranded goods; ~**recht** right of salvage; ~**vogt** wreck commissioner, wreck master, receiver of wreck.

Strandungsordnung *f* law of wreckage.

Strang *m* rope, cord.

Strangulation *f* strangulation.

strangulieren *v/t* to strangle, to choke.

Straße *f* street; road, highway; ~ **mit Gegenverkehr** two-way street; ~ **mit Schnellverkehr** main road, road with fast traffic; **befahrbare** ~ road fit for traffic; **e-e** ~ **dem Verkehr freigeben** to open a street; **e-e** ~ **unterhalten** to keep a street/road in good repair; **enge kurvenreiche** ~ winding road; **mautpflichtige** ~ toll road, turnpike road; **öffentliche** ~ public street, public road, common way; public thoroughfare; **steile** ~ steep road, precipitous road; **zweispurige** ~ two-lane road.

Straßen|anlieger frontager, owner of wayside property, abutting property owner; ~**anliegerbeitrag** frontage assessment; ~**arbeiten** street works, road works, road repair; ~**auflauf** street brawl;

Straßenanlieger

~**aufsicht** traffic surveillance, street control; ~**aufsichtsbehörde** overseer of highways, roads commission; ~**bankett** road embankment; ~**bau** → *Straßenbau;* ~**behörden** highway authorities, road authorities; ~**belag** road surface; ~**benutzung** use of streets and public roads; ~**benutzungsgebühr** road toll; ~**bezeichnungsschilder** road identification signs; ~**block** block of houses; ~**darbietungen** street performances; ~**decke** paving, highway surface; ~**dichte** density of the road network; ~**dienst** road patrols; ~**fahrzeug** road vehicle; ~**fläche** road surface; ~**gesetze** Highway Acts; ~**güterverkehr** road haulage, haul goods traffic; ~**einmündung** street (*or* road) junction; ~**handel** street trading, street vending; ~**händler** street trader, huckster; ~ ~ *mit Obst und Gemüse; costermonger;* ~**kostenbeitrag** assessment for street maintenance; ~**kriminalität** street crime; ~**kreuzung** road crossing; ~**kundgebung** street demonstration; ~**lage** road holding; ~**mädchen** street walker; ~**markierung** road marking; ~**meister** surveyor of highways; ~**netz** network of roads, road system; ~**prostitution** soliciting; ~**raub** highway robbery, assault; ~**räuber** highway robber, brigand; ~**räuberei** brigandage, highway-robbery; ~**recht** law of public streets and roads; ~**reklame** street advertizing; ~**sammlung** street collection; ~**sperre** road block, (street) barricade; ~**umleitung** detour, diversion; ~**- und Wasserbauamt** Roads and Waterways Office; ~**-und Wegenetz** road system; ~**unkostenbeitrag** paving rate, assessment for road maintenance; ~**unterhaltsabgabe** highway rate, road maintenance contribution (*by adjoining owners*); ~**unterhaltsverpflichteter** person (*or* authority) liable to keep (the road in repair);

739

~**unterhaltungszuschüsse** road maintenance grants; ~**verkauf** hawking, street vending; ~**verkäufer** hawker; ~**verkaufsstand** pitch; ~**verkehr** → *Straßenverkehr*; ~**zoll** road toll, turnpike charges.

Straßenbau *m* road works, road construction; ~**amt** road board, highway board, highway department, road construction office; ~**beamter** road construction supervisor; ~**finanzierungsgesetz** Financing of Roadbuilding Act; ~**investitionen** capital expenditure on roadbuilding; ~**last** road construction and maintanance liability; ~**verwaltung** administration of road construction.

Straßenverkehr road traffic, road transport.

Straßenverkehrs|behörde road traffic authority; ~**delikt** traffic offence, highway offence; ~**gefährdung** endangering road traffic; ~**haftung** road user's liability; ~**gesetz** road traffic law; ~**ordnung** Road Traffic Regulations; ~**recht** traffic law; ~**regeln** rules of the road; ~**sicherheit** road safety; ~**teilnehmer** road user; ~**zeichen** road sign(s), traffic sign; ~-**Zulassungs-Ordnung** Road Traffic Licensing Regulations.

Strategie *f* strategy; ~ **der kleinen Schritte** policy (*or* strategy) of gradualism; ~**kommission** political strategy commission.

Streben *n* pursuit, endeavour, push; ~ **nach Glück** pursuit of happiness, quest for happiness.

Strecke *f* route, track, line; *min* roadway, gallery, drift; ~**ngeschäft** chain-of-delivery business (*successive traders of same goods*); ~**nstillegung** railway closure; **auf freier** ~ somewhere on the line; **e-e** ~ **abgehen** to pace off a track; **e-e** ~ **zu Fuß zurücklegen** to walk.

strecken *v/t* to prolong, to extend the maturity.

Streckung *f* protraction, stretching, spreading, extension; **zeitliche** ~ spreading over a period.

streichen *v/t* to delete, to eliminate, to cancel, to expunge; to strike off.

Streichung *f* deletion, elimination, cancellation, obliteration, erasure.

Streifband *n* wrapper, postal wrapper, cover; ~**depot** jacket custody, individual (safe custody) deposit of securities, segregational (*or* individual) safe custody account.

Streife *f* patrol; ~**ndienstwagen** patrol car, squad car.

Streifschuß *m* graze, grazing shot.

Streik *f* strike; ~**ankündigung** strike notice; ~**arbeit** strike-breaking work, emergency work during a strike; ~**aufruf** call to strike; ~**ausschuß** strike committee; ~**befehl** strike order; ~**beteiligung** strike turnout; ~**bewegung** organized strikes; ~**brecher** strike breaker, *pej* scab, blackleg; ~**drohung** strike threat; ~**geld** strike pay; ~**kasse** strike fund, war chest; ~**leitung** strike committee; **s**~**lustig** *adj* eager to strike; ~**posten** picket, picketeer; ~ ~ *aufstellen*: *to picket*; ~ ~ *stehen*: *to picket*; ~ ~ *von Betriebsfremden*: *stranger picketing*; *gewaltlosen* ~ ~ *stehen*: *peaceful picketing*; *mobile* ~ ~: *flying pickets*; ~**recht** (the) right to strike, freedom to strike; ~**risiko** risk of strikes; ~**risikoversicherung** strike (risk) insurance; ~**tage** days of strike, lost work days due to strikes; ~**unterstützungsfonds** strike (support) fund; ~**verbot** prohibition of strikes, ban on strikes (*or* a strike); ~**verbotsklausel** no-strike clause; ~**versicherung** strike insurance; ~**wache** picket; ~ **wegen Abgrenzungskämpfen** jurisdictional strike; ~**welle** wave of strikes, spate of strikes; **e-n** ~ **abbrechen** to call off a strike; **e-n** ~ **ausrufen** to call a strike, to declare a strike; **genehmigter** ~ authorized strike, official strike; **in den** ~ **treten** to walk out, to come out on strike; **Schwerpunkt**~ selective strike; **unangekündigter** ~ unannounced strike; **widerrechtlicher** ~ illegal

streiken

strike; **wilder** ~ wildcat strike, illegal strike, walkout.

streiken *v/i* to strike, to lay down tools, to walk out.

Streikender *m* striker.

Streit *m* dispute, controversy; **s~befangen** *adj* in litigation, in dispute, pending; *noch* ~ ~: *unadjudged*; ~**befangenheit** pendency of the matter; ~**beilegng** settlement of a dispute; ~**betrag** amount involved in the case; ~**entscheidung** decision of the case; ~**erledigung** peaceful disposal of a conflict; ~**fall** litigation, case, dispute; ~**frage** issue, question at issue; question in dispute, point of controversy; *rechtliche* ~ ~: *issue (at law)*; *tatsächliche* ~ ~: *issue of fact*; ~**gegenstand** object at issue, subject of litigation, subject of the dispute; subject matter of the proceedings, matter in controversy, matter in dispute; **s~gegenständlich** belonging to the case; present, said; ~**gehilfe** party intervening on the side of a litigant; ~**genosse** joint litigant, joint plaintiff, *pl also*: coparties; *notwendige* ~ ~*n*: *necessary parties, indispensable parties*; ~**genossenschaft** joinder of parties; *notwendige* ~ ~: *compulsory joinder*; ~**helfer** party intervening on the side of a litigant; ~**hilfe** intervention on the side of a litigant; ~**objekt** = *Streitgegenstand qv*; ~**patent** contested (opposed, challenged) patent, patent in suit; ~**partei** party to the dispute, litigant, contending party; ~**punkt** point at issue, matter in dispute, issue; ~**sache** action, ~**stoff** matter in controversy, area of dispute; ~**verfahren** litigation contentious proceedings, procedure in defended cases; ~**verhältnis** plaintiff-defendant relationship, relationship between litigants; ~**verkündender** person giving notice to intervene; ~**verkündeter** *(der Streitverkündete)* person notified (of a possibility) of intervention, additional party; ~**verkündung** third party

Strich

notice *US*: third party complaint; third party practice, ~**wert** value (of the matter) in dispute (*or* being litigated jurisdictional value; amount involved in the particular case; ~**wertfestsetzung** assessment of value in dispute (*etc cf Streitwert*); **außer** ~ beyond dispute; **äußerst kleinlicher** ~ niggardly dispute; **den** ~ **verkünden** to give third party notice, to interplead; **e-n** ~ **beilegen** to settle a dispute, to compromise; **juristischer** ~ legal dispute, legal issue.

streiten *v/i* to litigate, to dispute, to argue, to contend, to fight.

streitig *adj* litigious, in dispute, controversial, at issue; debatable, argumentative; **nicht** ~ noncontentious, uncontroversial.

Streitigkeit *f* dispute, quarrel; ~**en durch ein Schiedsgericht entscheiden lassen** to settle a dispute by arbitration; **arbeitsrechtliche** ~ labour dispute; **e-e** ~ **beilegen** to settle a dispute, to sink a controversy; **nicht justitiable** ~ non-justiciable dispute; **nichtvermögensrechtliche** ~ non-pecuniary dispute; **öffentlich-rechtliche** ~ public-law dispute; **vermögensrechtliche** ~**en** pecuniary cases; **völkerrechtliche** ~ international legal dispute.

Strenge *f* severity, severeness, stringency; ~ **des Gesetzes** severity of the law, rigour of the law, harshness of the law, stringency of the law.

Streubesitz *m* diversified holdings; widespread shareholdings.

Streubreite *f* extent of diversification, cover *(public relations)*, spread.

Streugrenze *v/t* limit of variation.

Streu|pflicht obligation to strew sand (*or other suitable materials*) on (*or* to grit) icy surfaces; ~**recht** right to have icy *or snow covered* pavements strewn *with sand or salt* (*or gritted*).

Streuung *f* diversification, spread; ~**sbreite** range of dispersion.

Strich *m* street prostitution, soliciting; **auf den ~ gehen** to walk the streets.

Strichcode *m* bar-code.

Strichliste *f* tally list, check-list; **~nzählung** tally.

strittig *adj* = *streitig qv*.

Strittigkeit *f* disputability, contestable nature.

Strohmann *m* man of straw, figurehead, nominee; dummy, stooge; **~-Aktienbeteiligung** nominee shareholdings; **~aktionär** dummy stockholder, nominee shareholder; **~ als Kläger** nominal plaintiff; **~gesellschaft** dummy company, nominee company; **~-Gesellschafter** nominal partner.

Strom *m* (1) current, electricity, electric power; **~abnehmer** consumer of electricity; **~abschaltung** power cut; **~anschluß** power supply terminal; **~anschlußkosten** power installation costs; cost of being connected with electricity supply; **~ausfall** power failure; **~bilanz** net position on electricity; **~darbietung** supply of electric current; **~entwendung** dishonest abstraction of electricity; **~klemme** shortage of electric current; **~lieferung** power supply, electricity supply; **~lieferungsunterbrechung** interruption of electricity (*or* power) supply; **~lieferungsvertrag** contract for the supply of electricity; **~rechnung** electricity bill; **~sperre** power cut, power shutdown; **~tarif** electricity tariff; **~verbrauch** electricity consumption, power consumption; **~versorgung** power supply, electricity supply; **~versorgungsbezirk** public power district; **~zähler** electricity meter; **~zahlungsboykott** boycott of paying electricity bills.

Strom *m* (2) river; **~anliegerstaat** riparian state; **~polizei** river police; **internationaler ~** international river; **schiffbarer ~** navigable river.

Struktur|krise structural crisis; **~anpassung** structural adjustment; **~politik** policy for the improvement of regional structure; **~verbesserung** improvement of regional structure; **~vertrieb** multilevel selling (*US*), pyramid system (*GB*); **~wandel** structural change, fundamental change.

Stubenarrest *m* confinement to one's room, confinement to quarters.

Stück *n* piece, individual item, unit article; **~aktie** individual share certificate; **~arbeit** piecework; **~konto** shares account; **~emangel** shortage of offerings, uncovered position; **~everzeichnis** schedule of deposited securities; **~gebühren** charges for handling individual items; **~geld** notes and coins; **~gut** → *Stückgut*; **~kalkulation** product cost; **~kosten** unit cost; **~liste** itemized list; **~lizenz** per unit royalty; **~lizenzgebühr** per unit royalty; **~lohn** piece wages, wage on piece-work basis, job wage; **~lohnverfahren** differential piece rate system; **~nummer** serial number, bond number, certificate number; **~notierung** (stock exchange) quotation per unit; **~preis** price per item, unit price, piece price; **~preiskategorie** per unit price category; **~prüfung** detailed inspection (*item by item*); **~schuld** determinate obligation, obligation to supply individual objects; **~steuer** specific tax; **~vermächtnis** bequest of an individual object; **s~weise** by the piece, by parcels; **~zahl** number of items, number of units; **~zeit** time required per unit of production; **~zins** broken interest, interest for broken period, accrued interest, interest on shares, interest on bonds; *mit ~en*: *cum interest*; *ohne ~en*: *ex interest*; **~zoll** specific duty; **aus freien ~en** of one's (own) free will, willingly, unsolicited; **effective ~e** actual securities, actual bonds (*as documents*); **einwandfreies ~** good delivery (*securities*); **fehlerhafte ~e** rejects, imperfect items; **per ~** by the piece.

stückeln *v/t* to subdivide, to fragment, to denominate.

Stückelung *f* subdivision, indication of denomination, division into shares, fragmentation, denomination(al) unit.

Stückgut *n* small consignments, part-load, general cargo, less-than-carload lot (l.c.l.); **~befrachtung** consignment of general cargo; **~fracht** less-(than)-carload freight, general cargo; **~lieferung** general cargo delivery, drop shipment (delivery); **~tarif** general goods tariff; **~versand** shipment as less-than-carload lot; **~zustellung** less-than-carload delivery.

Studentenwerk *n* student welfare organization, student(s') union, student relief organization.

Studien|beihilfe educational grant; student grant, scholarship; **~fach** field of study, subject (of study), **~förderung** financial assistance for students; **~gang** course of studies; **~gebühr** tuition fee; **~kolleg** preparatory university courses; **~kommission** study commission, research group; **~kosten** cost of (college or) university studies; **~reform** academic studies reform, reform of university studies.

Stufen|gründung incorporation by stages, gradual incorporation; **~klage** action by stages; **~plan** graduated plan, phased plan; **~regreß** recourse by stages; **~tarif** graded tariff; **s~weise** *adv*, gradatim, gradually, by stages, step by step.

Stumm- und Tonfilmrechte silent and sound dialogue rights.

Stunde *f* hour, lesson; **aktuelle ~** special session on a topical issue (*debate on request*), question time; **jede ~ oder angefangene ~** each hour or fraction thereof.

stunden *v/t* to grant indulgence to a debtor, to give time, to allow time, to grant a respite, to defer.

Stunden|durchschnitt average per hour; **~honorar** hourly rate; **~hotel** house of ill fame, (disguised) brothel; **~leistung** output per hour; **~liste** time sheet; **~lohn** →*Stundenlohn*; **~-Produktivität** productivity per man-hour; **~satz** hourly rate; **~tarif** hourly rate; **~verdienst** hourly earnings; **~zettel** time sheet.

Stundenlohn *m* hourly wage, hourly rate; **~arbeiten** time work; **~satz** hourly rate; **~verrechnungssätze** regular time work charges; **~zuschlag** extra charge for time work, tariflicher ~ ~: standard hourly wage.

Stundung *f* allowing additional time for performance (*or* payment), **~ gewähren** to grant a delay *etc*, *cf Stundung*; **~ von Geldstrafen** time to pay fines; **befristete ~** extension of the term of payment.

Stundungs|erleichterung facility granted for postponing payment, respite; **~frist** period of extension; **~gesuch** request for an extension of time, request for a respite; **~kredit** credit granted by permitting deferred payment; **~nehmer** party to whom deferment is allowed; **~vergleich** compromise involving additional time for payment; **~vertrag** extension agreement, letter of respite; **~zinsen** interest charged during agreed delay.

Sturmschädenversicherung storm and tempest insurance.

Sturz *m* abrupt fall, drop, collapse; overthrow; **~helm** crash helmet.

stürzen *v/i* to fall, to have a fall, to drop, to slump; *v/t* to overthrow; to depose, to force to resign, to bring down; „nicht ~!" this side up!

Sturzgüter *n/pl* goods that *must not be handled roughly or turned upside down*, fragile goods.

Stütz|anleihe bailment loan; **~kurs** supported price, pegged rate; **~mauer** supporting wall; **~preis** supported price, cushioning price, pegged price; **~punkt** base, support-price level; **~unterricht** remedial tuition.

Stützungsaktion supporting action,

life boat operation; ~ ~ *der Banken: banking support*; ~**käufe** supporting purchases, support purchases, backing; ~**kredit** emergency credit, standby credit; ~**maßnahme** support operation; ~**operation** support operation; ~**preis** support price, supported price, pegged price; ~**vereinbarung** support arrangements; ~**vorrichtung** supporting appliance.

Subemissionvertrag *m* sub-underwriting agreement.

Subemittent *m* sub-underwriter.

subeventuell *adj* as a subordinate alternative, as a second alternative.

Subjekt *n* subject, individual; legal entity, issue.

subjektiv *adj* subjective.

Submission *f* tender, contractor's offer, contractor's submission.

Submissions|absprache bid rigging; ~**angebot** tender, tender offer, contractor's offer, bid; ~**bedingungen** terms of tender, conditions of tender; ~**bewerber** tenderer, bidder; ~**garantie** tender guarantee; ~**offerte** tender, contractor's offer; ~**preis** contract price; ~**termin** tender closing date; ~**verfahren** tender procedure, competitive bidding procedure, public tender; ~**vergebung** allocation by tenders, allocation of contract, award of contract; ~**vertrag** tender agreement; ~**weg** method of tender; *auf dem* ~ ~*e: by tender*.

Submittent *m* tenderer, bidder; *der billigste* ~: *the lowest bidder*.

submittieren *v/i* to submit tenders, to tender.

Subrogation *f* subrogation.

subsidiär *adj* subsidiary, subordinate; (*loosely:*) alternative.

Subsidiarität *f* subsidiary nature, subsidiary character.

Subsidiärklausel *f* subsidiary clause.

Subsidie *f* subsidy.

Subskribent *m* subscriber.

Subskription *f* subscription.

Subskriptions|angebot proposal for subscription; ~**anzeige** prospectus for a new publication; ~**frist** time limit for subscriptions; ~**preis** subscription list price; ~**recht** privilege of subscription.

substantiieren *v/t* to particularize, to specify, to state full particulars, to give full details, to put flesh on the bones.

Substantiierung *f* statement of particulars, substantiation; ~**sauflage** order for further and better particulars; **genügende** ~ particularity; **mangelnde** ~ failure to state full particulars.

Substanz *f* substance, instrinsic value, assets, resources; ~**erhaltung** maintenance of assets, preservation of substance; ~**minderung** depletion of assets; decrease of capital value; ~**steuer** tax on the substance of property; ~**verlust** depletion of assets, asset erosion, waste; ~**verringerung** depletion of assets; ~**verschlechterung** depletion of assets, waste; ~**verzehr** depletion of assets, consumption in use; ~**wert** tangible value, intrinsic value, material value, net value of tangible assets, real value; ~~**klausel** *material value clause;* ~ ~*zuwachs: growth of real value.*

substituieren *v/i* to deputize.

Substituierung *f* substitution.

Substitut *f* substitute, replacement.

Substitution *f* substitution; ~**sgüter** substitutes.

subsumieren *v/t* to subsume.

Subsumtion *f* subsumption; ~**sirrtum** error of subsumption.

Subunternehmer *m* subcontractor; ~**vertrag** subcontract; **an e–n** ~ **vergeben** to subcontract.

Subunternehmung *f* subcontractor's business undertaking.

Subvention *f* subsidy, grant; ~**betrug** fraudulently obtaining subsidies; ~**sjäger** subsidy seeker; ~**richtlinien** directives on granting subsidies; ~**vergabe** granting of subsidies; **offene** ~ overt subsidy.

subventionieren *v/t* to subsidize.

subventionsfähig *adj* subsidizable.

subversiv *adj* subversive.

Suchanzeige wanted ad; **~arbeitslosigkeit** frontal unemployment, search unemployment; **~kartei** tracing file; **~liste** list of missing persons; list of wanted persons; **~meldung** announcement about missing persons; **~trupp** search party; **~vermerk** search notice, wanted notice.

Suche *f* search, hunt (for).

suchen *v/t* to seek, to search.

Sucht *f* mania, addiction, craving.

Süchtiger *m* (drug) addict.

Suchtstoff *m* drug, narcotic drug; **~sendungen** consignments of drugs.

Suggestivfrage *f* leading question.

Sühne *f* atonement, expiation; conciliation; **~bescheinigung** certificate of a conciliation attempt; **~richter** judge at a conciliation hearing; **~termin** conciliation hearing; **~verfahren** conciliation proceedings; **~verhandlung** conciliation hearing; **~versuch** attempt at reconciliation (*spouses*).

sühnen *v/t* to atone (for), to expiate, to satisfy, to make up for.

Sukzession *f* succession; **~sstaat** succession state, succeeding state.

Sukzessivgründung foundation of a joint-stock company by stages, *cf Stufengründung*; **~lieferung** successive delivery, delivery by instalments, multiple delivery; **~lieferungsvertrag** multiple delivery contract.

summarisch *adj* summary.

Summe *f* sum, sum total, total, total amount, amount, aggregate amount; **~ der Aktiva** total assets; **e-e bestimmte ~** a given sum; **runde ~** round sum, even sum; **überwiesene ~** remittance; **veranschlagte ~** estimated amount.

Summenaktie share issued for a fixed amount, *share having a par value expressed in money*; **~bilanz** turnover balance; **~depot** collective (mixed) deposit, irregular deposit; **~rabatt** quantity premium; **~tabelle** cumulative table; **~vermächtnis** pecuniary legacy, bequest of a sum of money; **~versicherung** endowment insurance, insurance in terms of fixed sums.

Superdividende super-dividend, surplus dividend, bonus; **~kargo** supercargo; **~kraftstoff** premium-grade motor fuel; **~markt** supermarket, multiple store; **~provision** overriding commission; **~treibstoff** premium grade petrol, super (grade) petrol.

supranational *adj* supranational.

Surrogat *n* substitute, alternative.

Surrogation *f* surrogation, substitution, replacement; **~ kraft Gesetzes** substitution by operation of law; **~srecht** right of substitution; **dingliche ~** substitution in rem.

suspendieren *v/t* to suspend, to stay.

Suspendierung *f* suspension, stay, reprieve, respite.

Suspensivbedingung *f* suspensive condition, suspensory condition, condition precedent.

Suspensiveffekt *m* suspensory effect.

Süßwasserfischerei *f* freshwater-fishing; **~nutzung** use of fresh water.

Suzerän *m* suzerain.

Suzeränität *f* suzerainity.

Swapabkommen swap agreement; **~-Abschluß** swap transaction; **~-Fazilität** swap facility; **~geschäft** swap transaction; **~satz** swap rate.

Swing *m* swing (*under an offset agreement*); **~-Grenze** swing, limit of the swing; **~überschreitung** exceeding the swing.

Switchgeschäft *n* switch, switched transaction.

Sympathiestreik *m* sympathy strike.

Syndikalismus *m* (anarcho-)syndicalism.

Syndikat *n* syndicate, consortium; **~preis** underwriting price; **~sbeteiligung** participation in a consortium; **~sführung** lead management; **~vertrag** underwriting agreement, consortium agreement, syndicate agreement.

Syndikus staff lawyer in-house

Syndizierung   **System**

lawyer, legal officer, (*of a company*), standing counsel; ~**anwalt** staff lawyer, in-house lawyer; in-house counsel, senior staff lawyer, litigation counsel.

Syndizierung *f* syndication.

Synode *f* synod, church council.

System *n* system; ~ **der eigenen Mittel** own-resources system; ~ **der Steuervorauszahlungen** system of advance tax payments; ~ **des gespaltenen Satzes** system of the double rate; ~**vergleich** comparitive advertizing as to procedures or systems (*of products, appliances, goods*).

T

Tabelle *f* table, scale; index; register; list of claims proved in bankruptcy; **amtliche** ~ official scale; **versicherungsstatistische** ~ actuarial table.

Tabularbesitz *m* possession *coupled with entry in land register.*

Tabularersitzung *f* acquisition of title by being *(wrongly)* entered in the land title register for more than 30 years.

Tadelsantrag *m* motion of censure.

Tadelsvotum *n* vote of censure.

Tafelgeschäft *n* over-the-counter transaction *(at a bank).*

Tag *m* day, date; ~ **der Besitzübertragung** date of transfer of possession; ~ **der ersten Zulassung** date of first registration; ~ **der Wertstellung** value date; ~ **des Eigentumsübergangs** vesting day; ~ **des Inkrafttretens** enactment date, effective date, date of coming into force; ~- **und Nachtstromtarif** night-and-day tariff; ~ **wechsel** day bill, *bill payable on a specified date;* **gerichtsfreier** ~ non-judicial day, dies non juridicus; **laufende** ~**e** consecutive days; **pro** ~ per diem; **volle** ~**e** clear days; **wetterabhängige** ~**e** weather working days *(wwd).*

Tage|bau surface working, open-cast mining, open-pit mining, stripmining; ~**buch** journal, book of original entries; ~**buchblatt** record sheet; ~**geld** attendance fee, daily allowance; daily subsistence allowance, per diem; ~**löhner** worker, day labourer; **über** ~ above ground, surface.

tagen *v/i* to sit, to hold a meeting, to be in session *(court),* to meet.

Tages|abrechnung daily cash settlement; ~**auftrag** order valid today; ~**ausweis** daily return *(banking);* ~**auszug** daily statement; ~**befehl** order of the day; ~**belastung** daily load; ~**bericht** daily report; ~**bestände** daily balances; ~**einlagen** call deposits; ~**einnahme** daily receipt, daily return; ~**erholung** day-trip recreation; ~**förderung** daily output *(mining);* ~**geld** day-to-day money, money for one day, call money, money at call; ~~*satz: rate for day-to-day money, call rate;* ~**geldversicherung** daily benefits insurance (when hospitalized); ~**geschäft** business of one day, cash receipts for one day; ~**heimschule** all-day school; ~**kalkulation** current cost calculation; ~**kauf** day order; ~**kurs** current rate, present price, quotation of the day, current quotation, market value; ~**leistung** daily output; ~**lichtzeit** natural day, daylight hours; ~**lohn** daily wage, a day's wages; ~**lohnsteuertabelle** wage-tax scale for daily wages; ~**mutter** child minder; ~**notierung** daily quotation; ~**ordnung** → *Tagesordnung;* ~**pendler** daily commuter; ~**planung** daily planning; ~**politik** current politics, politics of the day, current affairs; ~**preis** current price, present price, ruling price, actual price; ~**produktion** daily output; ~**rate** average daily amount; ~**satz** daily rate, per diem allowance; daily fine, penalty per day; *daily rate for a fine;* ~**schicht** day-shift; ~**stätte** day-care centre; ~**stempel** date stamp; ~**spunkt** item on the agenda; ~**umsatz** turnover per day, daily sales, daily returns; ~**wechsel** = *Tagwechsel qv;* ~**wert** current value, prevailing rate; ~**zinsen** interest on daily balances, daily interest.

Tagesordnung *f* agenda, business to be transacted, order paper *(parl),* order of the day; *unerledigte* ~~*e: unfinished business;* **auf der** ~ **stehen**

Tagung

to be at issue, to be on the agenda; **auf die ~ setzen** to put on the agenda, to place on the agenda; **die ~ festsetzen** to fix the agenda; **in die ~ eintreten** to proceed to the agenda, to get down to business; **von der ~ absetzen** to remove from the agenda, to delete from the agenda; **zum nächsten ~spunkt übergehen** to proceed to next business; **zur ~ übergehen** to proceed to the order of the day.

Tagung *f* meeting, convention.

Takt|betrieb fixed cycle operation; **~fahrplan** regular(-interval) time table; **~fertigung** (fixed) cycle operation (*in assembly line production*); **~straße** assembly line.

Talar *m* robe, gown.

Talentsucher *m* head hunter.

Talon *m* renewal coupon.

Talsohle trough, lowest point of a recession (*or* depression).

Tank|bodenbestand storage tank bottom(s); **~-Scheck** filling-station cheque; **~stelle** petrol station, *US*: gas station; **~stellenbetrug** fraudulent non-payment of petrol/gasoline.

Tante-Emma-Laden *m* the (old) neighbourhood store, corner shop, mum and pop store (*US*).

Tantieme *f* profit-orientated extra pay; director's bonus; management bonus, author's royalty.

Tanz|lustbarkeiten dancing (amusements); **~verbot** *n* no dancing, dancing prohibited, dancing not allowed.

Tara *n* tare; **~gewicht** tare weight; **~ vergüten** to tare; **~vergütung** allowance for tare; *zusätzliche ~~: super tare;* **handelsübliche ~** customary tare; **reine ~** actual tare.

Tarif *m* scale, rate scale, scale of charges, wage scale, tariff (*customs*), tax scale; table of fares; schedule of charges; **~abkommen** collective agreement, industrial agreement; **~abschluß** conclusion of a collective pay agreement; **~änderung** change in rates; **~angehörige** employees covered by collective

Tarif

agreements; **~angestellter** employee remunerated according to collective agreements; **~ansätze** collective wage rates, collectively agreed wage rates; **~ausschuß** collective bargaining agencies committee; **~autonomie** collective bargaining autonomy; **t~ besteuert** fully taxed at standard rate; **~bestimmung** collective bargaining term; **~einstufung** classification rating; **~erhöhung** increase of standard wage, increase of tariff; **~fähigkeit** collective bargaining capacity; **~festsetzung** tariff making, collective wage formation; **~freigabe** decontrol of rates; **~freiheit** freedom of collective bargaining; **~ für Mustersendungen** sample rate; **~ für Schichtarbeit** shift rates; **~gehalt** collectively agreed salary; **~gestaltung** collective wage formation; **~genehmigung** permission to charge (energy) rates; **~gruppe** tax bracket, wage group; **~herabsetzung** rate cutting, reduction in agreed rate; **~hoheit** right to conclude collective agreements (*unions and employers*); **~kampf** wage dispute; **~klasse** tariff category, wage class; **~klausel** tariff provision, collective wage agreement clause; **~kommission** rate commission, tariff commission; **~krieg** dispute over tariffs; wage dispute, fares war (*aviation*); **~lohn** standard wage, standard wage rate, collectively agreed wage; **~lohnvereinbarung** collective wage agreement; **~mauern** tariff walls; **~normen** provisions of collective wage agreements, collective agreement norms; **~nummer** tariff item; **~ordnung** fee scale, collective wage system; **~paket** collective bargaining package; **~partner** the parties to a collective wage agreement (*unions and management*), collective bargaining; **~politik** policy for wages and salaries; **~positionen** tariff headings; **~preis** scale rate, standard price;

~**progression** progressive increase in tax scales; ~**recht** collective bargaining law; right under a collective agreement; ~**reduktion** reduction of rate or scale; ~**register** Official Collective Agreements Register; ~**rente** collectively agreed retirement pension; ~**rubrik** rating column; ~**runde** round of collective bargaining; ~**satz** standard rate, tariff rate, collective wage rate, class rate; ~**schema** tariff scheme; ~**schiedsgericht** collective bargaining arbitration tribunal; ~**senkung** lowering of scale of rates, rate reduction, tariff reduction; ~**spanne** range of rates; ~**staffelung** scale graduation; ~**statistik** tariff statistics, statistics relative to collective wage agreements; ~**streitigkeiten** collective wage disputes; ~**stufen** grades of tariff, grades of taxable earnings; zones (*public transport*); ~**stundenlohn** standard hourly rate; ~**system** tariff system of fares, collective wage system; ~**überwachung** supervision of tariffs, supervision of the scale of charges; ~**unterbietung** price-cutting (*by public utilities or carriers*); ~**unterschied** wage differential, rate differential; ~**verband** rate-making pool; ~**verbund** joint rates; ~**vereinbarung** collective bargaining agreement, rating agreement; ~**vereinheitlichung** standardization of tariffs; ~**vereinigung** collective bargaining association; ~**verhandlungen** collective bargaining; ~**verhandlungspartner** bargaining agent, opposite number of (collective bargaining) negotiations; ~**verordnung** tariff ordinance; ~**verstoß** contravention of collectively agreed provisions; ~**vertrag** collective agreement, collective bargaining contract, collective wage agreement; **t~vertraglich** *adj* collectively agreed, under a collective wage agreement; ~**vertragsgesetz** (*D 1949*) Collective Bargaining Contracts Act; ~**vertragspartei** party to a collective wage agreement, bargaining unit, collective bargaining party; ~**vertragssache** collective bargaining case; ~**vorschrift** tariff rule; ~**wert** tariff value; ~**wesen** collective bargaining system; ~**zeit** duration of a collective bargaining agreement; ~**zoll** tariff duty; ~**zwang** compulsory collective bargaining; **gleitender** ~ sliding scale, sliding tariff; **gültiger** ~ tariff in force; **tageszeitlich gestaffelter** ~ time-of-day tariff.

Tarifierung *f* tariff classification, fixing of insurance rates, classification; ~ **erschwerter Risiken** determination of insurance rates for increased risks.

tariflich *adj*, according to collective agreement, on the agreed scale, pursuant to the tariff.

Tarnorganisation *f* cover organization, camouflage organization.

Taschen|buch pocket book (edition), paper back; ~~*rechte: publishing rights for a pocket book edition*; ~**dieb** pickpocket, pursesnatcher, purloiner; ~**diebstahl** pocket picking; ~**geld** pocket money; ~~*paragraph: pocket money rule for minors*; ~**pfändung** *f* levying upon the debtor's purse; ~**rechner** handheld (*or* pocket) calculator.

Tastentelefon *n* push-button telephone.

Tastversuch *m* tentative experiment.

Tat *f* act, deed, offence; ~**bericht** statement of facts; ~**bestand** → *Tatbestand*; ~**beteiligter** particeps criminis, participant in a crime, accomplice; ~**einheit** unity of crime, commission (*of several offences, nominal coincidence of offences*), by one and the same act; *in* ~~ *mit: in coincidence with*; ~**frage** question of fact, point of fact, issue of fact; ~**gehilfe** accessory, aider and abettor, secondary party; ~~ *vor der Tat: accessory before the fact*; ~**handlung** act(s) constituting the offence; ~**irrtum** mistake of fact, factual mistake; ~**mehrheit** plurality of

Tatbestand — **Täter**

acts; joinder of offences; *in ~~ committed as separate offences but joined in one indictment;* ~**motiv** motive of the crime, inducement; ~**ort** scene (of the crime), place of the commission of an offence; ~**ortbesichtigung** viewing scene of the crime, (local) inspection of the scene of the crime; ~**richter** trial judge; ~**sache** → *Tatsache;* ~**seite** aspect of an offence; *innere ~~: mental element;* ~**umstand** circumstance; *subjektiver ~~: mental element;* ~**umstände** facts and circumstances, res gestae, set of circumstances; *auf Grund besonderer ~~: due to particular circumstances;* ~**verdacht** → *Tatverdacht;* ~**verdächtiger** suspected person, suspect, suspected offender; *flüchtiger ~~: fugitive offender;* ~**waffe** weapon used for the crime; ~**zeit** time of the offence, material time; **an Tötung grenzende** ~ act falling short of homicide; **auf frischer** ~ flagrante delicto, in the very act, red-handed; ~ ~~ *ertappen: to catch in the very act, to take red-handed;* ~ ~ ~ *ertappt (also:) found committing;* **die zur Last gelegte** ~ the alleged offence; **eine und dieselbe** ~ single act, one and the same act; **einmalige** ~ unrepeated act, "one-off" act; **innerhalb der Gerichtsbarkeit begangene** ~ act done within the jurisdiction; **nach dem Recht dieses Gebietes strafbare** ~ an offence which is cognizable under the law of this territory; **nach der** ~ after the fact; **offenkundige** ~ overt act; **vollendete** ~ accomplished offence, completed offence; **vor der** ~ before the fact; **zur Last gelegte** ~ alleged offence.

Tatbestand *m* the facts, facts of the case, statement of facts, general findings, findings of fact *(in a judgment)*, summary of the facts, res gestae; statutory definition of an offence, elements of an offence, body of the offence; ~ **e-r strafbaren Handlung** statutory definition of an offence; the acts constituting the offence; ~ **e-s Delikts** statutory definition of an offence; **den** ~ **erfüllen** to amount to an offence, to constitute an offence; **den** ~ **e-s Versuchs vollenden** to amount to an attempt; **gesetzlicher** ~ statutory definition of an offence; **objektiver** ~ material substance of a crime, physical elements of (the commission of) an offence, corpus delicti; **subjektiver** ~ mental element(s) (of an offence); *den* ~*n* ~ *nachweisen: to prove scienter.*

Tatbestands|angabe particulars of the charge, summary of the facts and circumstances; ~**aufnahme** fact finding, taking down the facts of the case; ~**fehler** error in fact; ~**feststellungen** findings of fact; ~**irrtum** factual mistake, mistake as to the type of offence; ~**merkmal** ingredient of an offence, element of an offence, constituent fact, *pl also:* operative facts; *äußere ~~e: actus reus; subjectives ~~: mental element.*

Täter *m* perpetrator, offender, actor, delinquent, *(torts:)* tortfeasor, *(crimes)* criminal; malefactor; ~**mehrheit** several offenders *(committing the same offence);* ~**persönlichkeit** the personal characteristics of the offender; ~**schaft** commission of the offence, perpetration; *in mittelbarer ~~ handeln: to act through an agent, to commit a crime indirectly;* ~~**svoraussetzung**: *legal requirements of the perpetration of a crime;* ~**typ** type of perpetrator (*or* offender); ~**wille** offender's intention to commit a crime; **den** ~ **beherbergen** to accommodate the felon, to provide accommodation for a criminal; **flüchtiger** ~ fugitive offender; **geistesgestörter** ~ defective delinquent; **jugendlicher** ~ juvenile offender, youthful offender, juvenile delinquent; **mittelbarer** ~ indirect perpetrator, *a person committing an offence through the medium of an innocent agent;* **nicht vorbestrafter** ~ first offender;

rückfälliger ~ recidivist, second and subsequent offender; **tatnaher ~** physically involved culprit, actual perpetrator; **unmittelbarer ~** actual offender.

tätig *adj* active, in active practice, acting; **~ sein** to act, to work; **anwaltschaftlich ~** active in the law, practising as a lawyer; **geschäftlich ~** engaged in business; **von sich aus ~ werden** acting on one's own initiative.

tätigen *v/t* to transact, to effect.

Tätiger *m (der Tätige)*; **freiberuflich ~** practitioner, professional man, self-employed (person), free-lance(r).

Tätigkeit *f* activity, activities, occupation, operation, service, work; **~en im Rahmen der öffentlichen Gewalt** activities as public authorities; **auf Gewinn gerichtete ~** gainful activity, activity directed at profit, trade or business carried on for purposes of profit; **anwaltschaftliche ~** practice of law, attorneyship; **beratende ~** advisory service; **berufliche ~** occupation; **e-e ~ ehrenamtlich ausüben** to serve on an honorary basis; **ehrenamtliche ~** honorary activity; **entgeltliche ~** remunerated activity; **erfinderische ~** inventive work; **freiberufliche ~** free-lance work, self-employment, *pl also*: (activities of) the liberal professions; **gefahrgeneigte ~** (extra-)hazardous employment; **geschäftliche ~** economic activity, business activity; **e-e ~ ~ ausüben**: *to work in business, to transact business*; **gewerbliche ~** commercial activity, industrial activity; trade and commerce, trade or business, gainful activity, pursuit of a trade; **e-e ~ ~ ausüben**: *to carry on a trade or business;* **handwerkliche ~en** activities of craftsmen; **hauptberufliche ~** full-time job; **kaufmännische ~** mercantile pursuits, business activity; **mehrjährige ~** activities over several years; **regelmäßig ausgeübte berufliche ~en** regular occupation; **richterliche ~** judicial action; **schöpferische ~** creative work; **schriftstellerische ~** work as an author, literary work; **selbständige ~** activities as self-employed person, self-employment; **staatsfeindliche politische ~** subversive political activity; **treuhänderische ~** fiduciary service, activities carried out in a trust capacity; **umstürzlerische ~** subversive activities; **unselbständige ~** paid employment.

Tätigkeits|bereich sphere of activity, field of operation, area of operation, range of action; **~bericht** action report, progress report; **~beschreibung** job description; **~delikt** offence by commission; **~feld** = *~bereich qv*; **~gebühr** fee for professional services; **~merkmal** occupational characteristic; **~profil** job profile.

Tätigwerden *n* action, taking action.

Tätlichkeiten physical violence, assault and battery; **~ gegen Familienangehörige** domestic violence; **beleidigende ~** indignity (= *indignities*) to the person, insults with violence.

Tatsache *f* fact; **~nbehauptung** allegation of fact, factual claim; **~nfrage** question of fact; **~ngeständnis** admission; **~ninstanz** trial court, nisi prius court; **~nirrtum** error of fact, factual error; **~n leugnen** to traverse, to deny the facts; **~nmaterial** factual data; **~nschilderung** narrative (of facts); **~nstoff** facts of the case, matter in pais; **~nverdrehung** prevarication, travesty of facts; **~nvermutung** presumption of fact; **~nvortrag** allegations, narratio; **~n vortragen** to state facts; **als ~ hinstellen** to aver, to present as a fact; **ausgemachte ~** definitely a fact; **äußere ~** physical fact; **belastende ~** incriminatory fact; **bereits bewiesene ~** proven fact; **beweiserhebliche ~** evidentiary fact; **die entscheidende ~** the decisive fact, the principal fact, **e-e ~**

beschwören to swear to a fact; **einschlägige** ~n relevant facts; **entlastende** ~ exculpatory fact; **feststehende** ~ established fact; **gerichtsnotorische** ~n facts of which the court has judicial knowledge; **nackte** ~n hard facts; **neue** ~n **berücksichtigen** to take fresh facts into consideration; **neue** ~n **und Beweismittel** fresh facts and evidence; **neue** ~n **vorbringen** to adduce new (fresh) facts; **nicht entscheidungserhebliche** ~n immaterial facts; **offenkundige** ~ obvious fact; **physische** ~ physical fact; **rechtsändernde** ~ dispositive fact; **rechtsbegründende** ~ constitutive fact, fact establishing a right; **vollendete** ~ accomplished fact; **von der** ~ **ausgehen** starting from the premise that; **wesentliche** ~ material fact; **zugestandene** ~ admitted fact, admission.

tatsächlich *adj* actual, factual, *adv also*: in fact, in reality.

Tatverdacht *m* suspicion of a criminal offence; **ausreichender** ~ reasonable suspicion, justifiable cause; **dringender** ~ strong suspicion; **hinreichender** ~ probable cause, reasonable suspicion of an offence; **kein ausreichender** ~ not found; **mangels** ~ **freisprechen** to pass an honorary acquittal, to dismiss honorably.

Taube *f pol* dove, a "wet".

taubstumm *adj* deaf and dumb.

Taubstummer *m* (*der Taubstumme*) deaf and dumb person, deaf mute.

Taufname *m* Christian name.

Taufschein *m* certificate of baptism.

tauglich *adj* fit, capable, qualified, serviceable; ~ **zum Dienst mit der Waffe** fit for military service.

Tauglichkeit *f* suitability, fitness, capacity, qualification, usefulness; ~**sgrad** degree of fitness; ~**szeugnis** certificate of fitness, qualifying certificate; ~ **zum gewöhnlichen Gebrauch** merchantable quality; ~ **zum vertragsgemäßen Gebrauch** fitness for the agreed use; **körperliche** ~ physical fitness.

Tausch barter, exchange, swap; ~**gemeinschaft** system of free exchange; ~**geschäft** barter transaction, exchange deal, switch; ~**grundstück** exchange land; ~**handel** interchange, barter trade; ~**verkauf** swapping sale, swap; ~**verkehr** bartering; ~**vertrag** barter agreement; ~**verwahrung** mutual custody; ~**wert** value in exchange; ~**wirtschaft** barter economy.

täuschen *v/t* to deceive, to delude.

Täuschung *f* deceit, deception, fraudulent misrepresentation; ~ **bei der Eheschließung** procuring marriage by deceit; ~**sabsicht** fraudulent intent, intent to deceive; ~**shandlung** deceptive act; ~**smanöver** artifice, feint; ~**sversuch** attempt to deceive, attempt to defraud; ~ **über e-n Nebenumstand** collateral deceit; ~ **über e-n wesentlichen Umstand** material deceit; ~ **zur Umgehung der Wehrpflicht** fraudulent draft evasion (*USA*), fraudulent attempt to avoid conscription (*GB*); **absichtliche** ~ deceit, wilful deception; **arglistige** ~ deceit, fraudulent misrepresentation, malicious deceit; **landesverräterische** ~ forgery endangering the state, treacherous forgery; **vorsätzliche** ~ wilful deception; **zum Zwecke der** ~ with intent to deceive; **zur** ~ **bestimmt** calculated to deceive; **zwecks** ~ deceptive.

Tautologie *f* tautology.

Tauwetter *n pol* thaw, detente.

Tauziehen *n pol* tug-of-war.

Taxator *m* appraiser, valuer.

Taxe *f* rate, charge; valuation, appraisal; tariff; assessment.

Taxi|besitzer taxi operator; ~**konzession** taxi licence, licence to operate a taxi (service); ~**stand** taxi rank, cabstand, taxi stand.

taxieren *v/t* to appraise, to estimate, to value, to rate, to assess; *nicht taxiert: unvalued*.

Taxkurs *m* estimated quotation, valuation of price, estimation price.

Taxwert *m* appraised value, estimated value, rough value.
Techniker *m* engineer, technician.
Technische Anleitung/Luft (*TA-Luft, 1974*) Technical Directive on Air Pollution Control; ~ **zum Schutz gegen Lärm** (*1968*) Technical Directive on Noise Abatement.
Technische Nothilfe *f* (=) *organization for the maintenance of supplies in an emergency*.
Technischer Überwachungsverein *m* = *TÜV qv* Technical Inspection Agency.
Technisierung *f* technicalization, mechanization.
Technologie|kriminalität techno banditry; **~raub** techno banditry; **~-Räuber** technobandit; **~transfer** technology transfer; **~-Überlassungsvertrag** technology transfer agreement.
Teigwaren *f/pl* farinaceous products.
Teil *m* part, portion, share; party; **~abladung** partial shipment; **~abrechnung** partial account; **~abschnitt** subsection, part of a transaction; **~abtretung** partial assignment; **~aktie** fraction of a share, stock scrip; **~akzept** partial acceptance; **~anmeldung** divisional (patent) application; **~annahme** partial acceptance; **~-Arbeitskräfte** part-time workers, part-time employees; **~arbeitsloser** partially unemployed; **~ausbau** partial extension; **~ausgabe** subedition; slice, tranche (of bonds); **~baugenehmigung** partial building permit; **~begnadigung** partial pardon; **~bereich** particular sector, subdivision; **~berufung** appeal in part; **~beschäftigung** part-time employment; **~bescheid** interim decision; **~besitz** part possession; **~betrag** partial amount, instalment; **~betrieb** separate division of a business; **~bilanz** section of the balance sheet, balance sheet for part of the enterprise; **~eigentum** part-ownership; **~eigentümer** part-owner; **~eigentumsgrundbuch** land title register for commercial condominium units; **~entschädigung** part-compensation, reduced earnings allowance; **~entscheidung** decision on part of an action; **~erbschein** fractional certificate of inheritance (*for an individual co-heir*); **~ergebnis** part-result, interim operating result; **~erhebung** sample inquiry; **~finanzierungskredit** instalment sales credit; **~fläche** fractional tract of land; **~fortführungsanmeldung** continuation-in-part application (*part, US*); CIP-application; **~frage** facet (of an issue), part (of a question); **~gebiet** branch, subsection, localized area; **~geständnis** partial confession; **~gesellschaft** independent division of a company; **~grundstück** part of a plot of land; **~gutschein** fractional bonus certificate, fractional debt certificate; **t~haben** → *teilhaben;* **~haber** → *Teilhaber;* **~haberschaft** → *Teilhaberschaft;* **~haftung** partial liability, partial commitment; **~haftungskredit** credit covering a partial commitment; **~havarie** particular average (P. A.); **~haverei** = *Teilhaverie qv;* **~index** subindex; **~indossament** partial endorsement; **~institut** part institution; **~invalidität** partial disability, partial incapacity; **~inventur** departmental stocktaking, sectional inventory; **~klage** action for a part of the claim, part-action; **~leistung** part performance; **~lieferung** part shipment, partial delivery; **~lieferungsvertrag** multiple delivery contract; **~lohn** part of a wage; **~markt** sectional market, market forming part of a larger market; **~masse** part of a bankrupt's estate; **~montage** subassembly; **~münzen** divisional coin, subsidiary coin; **~nahme** → *Teilnahme;* **t~nehmen** → *teilnehmen;* **~nehmer** → *Teilnehmer;* **~nichtigkeit** partial nullity; **~nichtigkeitsklausel**, severability clause; **~obligation** fractional bond, par-

ticipation certificate; ~**pacht** lease for a share of the property, share tenancy; ~**pächter** part-tenant, particular tenant, sharecropper; ~**quittung** receipt in part; ~**recht** partial right; ~**rechtsnachfolge** partial succession; ~**regelung** piecemeal arrangement; ~**rente** proportional part of the pension; ~**rückzahlung** repayment in part; ~**schaden** partial loss, part damage; *frei von* ~~: *free from particular average;* ~**schlußrechnung** final invoice in part; ~**schuld** part of the debt; ~**schuldschein** promissory note for a part of the debt, partial bond; ~**schuldverschreibung** partial debenture; ~**scrips** fractional scrip; ~**sektor** subdivision, sub-branch, compartment; ~**sendung** consignment in part, partial shipment; ~**steuerbescheid** partial tax assessment; ~**storno** partial cancellation, partial reserve; ~**strecke** fare stage; ~**streik** sectional strike, local strike; ~**summe** partial sum, subtotal; ~**unternehmen** part of the business, part-enterprise; ~**unwirksamkeit** partial invalidity; ~**urteil** part-judgment; ~**veräußerung** transfer of a part; ~**vereinbarung** partial agreement; ~**verkauf** partial sale; ~**verlust** partial loss; t~**versichert** *adj* partially insured; ~**versicherung** partial insurance; ~**versteuerung** taxation in part; ~**verurteilung** verdict on a part of the charge; ~**vollstreckung** execution in part; ~**waffenstillstand** truce, partial armistice; ~**werk** part of a work; *urheberrechtsfähiges* ~~: *copyrightable part*; ~**wert** value of a part, fractional value; going concern value of individual assets; ~**wertabschreibung** write-off (*or allowable tax deprecation*) on individual assets (*at going concern value*); ~**zahlung** → *Teilzahlung*; ~**zeit** part-time work, reduced working hours; ~~**beschäftigter**: *part-time worker*; ~~**beschäftigung**: *part-time employment*; ~**ziffer** sub-index; **allgemeiner** ~ general part; **der nichtschuldige** ~ the party not at fault, the innocent party; **der proportionale** ~ the proportional area (*of the scale*); **der schuldige** ~ the party at fault, the guilty party; **frei verfügbarer** ~ freely disposable part; **kennzeichnender** ~ characterizing portion; **nicht rückversicherter** ~ **des Risikos** retained risk; **patentfähiger** ~ patentable part, subordinate integer; **pfändbarer** ~ leviable part, items subject to execution; **rechtsgestaltender** ~ operative part; **streitender** ~ litigating party, party to the dispute; **verfügender** ~ operative part; **vertragschließender** ~ contracting party; **wesentlicher** ~ substantive part; **zu gleichen** ~**en** in equal parts, in equal shares, in equal portions, share-and-share-alike; ~ ~ ~**en beteiligt sein**: to participate equally.

teilbar *adj* separable, severable, divisible.

Teilbarkeit *f* separability, divisibility, severability.

teilen *v/t* to divide, to part, to partition, to separate, to sever.

teilhaben *v/i* to participate, to have a share in, to share in.

Teilhaber *m* partner, copartner, participant, participator, joint proprietor; ~ **auf gemeinsame Rechnung** partner in joint account; ~**versicherung** business partnership insurance; **aktiver** ~ active partner; **e-n** ~ **abfinden** to buy out a partner; **jüngerer** ~ junior partner; **stiller** ~ silent partner, sleeping partner, secret partner; **tätiger** ~ active partner.

Teilhaberschaft *f* participation, partnership, association, joint proprietorship.

Teilnahme *f* participation, complicity; ~**berechtigung** right to participate; ~**lehre** principal and accessory, participation (in crime), complicity theory.

Teilnahmslosigkeit *f* stolidity, apathy, indifference, passiveness.

teilnehmen *v/i* to take part, to participate; **gemeinsam** ~ to share jointly, to have together.

Teilnehmer *m* participant, participator, accomplice, accessory, party to an offence; joint holder; ~**gemeinschaft** community of joint holders; ~**staaten** participating countries; ~**versammlung** meeting of joint holders; **ausscheidender** ~ outgoing participant.

Teilung *f* division, partition, separation; ~**der Anmeldung** division of the application (*pat*).

Teilungs|anordnung (testator's) instructions to apportion the estate; words of severance; ~**auflassung** deed of partition; ~**begehren** notice of desire to sever; ~**erklärung** declaration of division (or severance); ~**genehmigung** permission for a partition (of land); ~**klage** action for partition, action for apportionment; ~**masse** estate to be divided up, estate to be apportioned; ~**niederschrift** memorandum of partition; ~**plan** scheme of partition, scheme of distribution; ~**sache** partition-matter; ~**urkunde** deed of partition; ~**vertrag** partition agreement; severance agreement; ~**verfahren** procedure of partitioning, partition action, apportionment procedure; ~**versteigerung** compulsory partition by public auction.

Teilzahlung *f* part payment, instalment (*US: installment*).

Teilzahlungs|bank instalment (*US: installment*) credit institution; ~**darlehen** loan to finance instalment-purchase(s); ~**finanzierung** instalment (sale) financing; ~**finanzierungsgesellschaft** consumer finance company; ~**kredit** instalment (sale financing) credit; ~**kreditbank** instalment finance company, instalment credit institution; ~**system** instalment system, tally system; ~**wechsel** instalment sale financing bill.

Telefon|beantworter telephone answering machine; ~**buch** telephone directory, phone book; ~**dienstmonopol** telephone monopoly; ~**einrichtung(en)** telephone equipment; ~**gebühren** telephone charges; ~**geheimnis** secrecy of telephone communications; ~**grundgebühr** basic rate for telephone subscribers; ~**handel** trade transacted by telephone; interoffice trade, over-the-counter trade; ~ **mit Lautsprecherverstärkung** speaker telephone; ~**zelle** telephone booth, callbox telephone box, kiosk; ~**rechnung** telephone bill; ~**tarif** telephone rate, scale of telephone charges; ~**verkehr** telephone dealings; ~**netz** telephone network; ~**werbung** canvassing by telephone; ~**zentrale** switchboard (*hotel etc*), exchange.

Telefonist *m* telephone operator.

Telegrafen|amt telegraph office; ~**dienst** telegraph system; ~**gebühren** telegraph service charges; ~**geheimnis** secrecy of telegraph communications; ~**netz** telegraph system, telegraph network.

Telekolleg *n* TV-College (*vocational studies*).

Telegramm *n* telegram, wire, cable; ~**adresse** telegram address, telegraphic address, cable address, abbreviated address; ~**annahme** telegram reception; ~**anschrift** = ~*adresse qv*; ~**beschlagnahme** confiscation of telegram message(s); ~**formular** telegram form; ~ **mit bezahlter Rückantwort** reply paid telegram, prepaid telegram; wire collect; ~ **mit Empfangsbenachrichtigung** telegram with notice of delivery; **gewöhnliches** ~ deferred telegram; **kollationiertes** ~ readback telegram; **offenes** ~ telegram in plain language; **unchiffriertes** ~ telegram in plain language; **verschlüsseltes** ~ code telegram, cipher telegram; **vom Amt zugesprochenes** ~ telegram by telephone.

tel quel *adj* (*wie die Sache steht und liegt*) = *tel quel*.

Telquel-Kurs *m* tel quel rate.

Tendenz *f* tendency, trend; special purpose; **~angabe** indication of tendency; **~betriebe** *enterprises in the field of politics, the press, education, the Churches etc, not fully subject to the Betriebsverfassungsgesetz qv;* **~schutz** partial exemption from co-determination by employees; **~umschwung** trend reversal; **~unternehmen** *qv* **~betriebe;* **deutliche ~** distinct tendency; **konjunkturelle ~** cyclical trend, trend of business development; **steigende ~** uptrend; **wirtschaftliche ~** economic trend.

tendenziell *adj* showing a tendency, tending to (*grow, improve*).

Tenor *m* tenor, operative part, substance; **~ des Urteils** operative part of the judgment, the "held".

Termin *m* (*1*) date, appointed time, fixed time, trial date, date for the hearing; court hearing; date for a meeting, appointment; **~ beim Einzelrichter** date of reference; **t~gerecht** *adj, adv* in due time, according to schedule; **~gründe** reasons of time commitments, (reasons of) deadlines; **~kalender** desk calendar, diary, appointment book; (*court:*) cause list, trial list, docket, trial docket; **~plan** date plan, time schedule; **~sache** transaction subject to a deadline, urgent matter; **~sanberaumung** setting down for trial, fixing a date for the hearing (*generally*); appointment; *frühzeitige ~~:* advancement of trial; **~saufhebung** cancelling the date of a hearing; **~sbestimmung** = *~sanberaumung qv;* **~schwierigkeiten** difficulties as to timing, problems of keeping time limits; scheduling problems; **~sladung** fixed-date summons; **~sliste** (trial) docket, trial list, cause list; **~stag** date of the hearing, trial date, law day; **~ steht an für** (*Datum*) the hearing has been fixed for (*date*); **~stunde** hour of cause; **~überwachung** deadline control, tracing of maturities; **~verlängerung** extension of time; **~verlegung** adjournment of trial, postponement of date of hearing; **~versäumnis** failure to appear; *versehentliches ~versäumnis:* inadvertent *default;* **~vertreter** locum; **~wahrung** attendance at court hearings; **~ zur Hauptverhandlung** date of trial; **außerordentlicher ~** adjournment day, date for a special hearing; **auswärtiger ~** out-of-town appointment; **der nächste ~** next appointment; **e-n ~ anberaumen** to fix a date for the hearing, to set down the action for trial, to docket a case; **e-n ~ ansetzen** = *e-n ~ anberaumen qv;* **e-n ~ festsetzen** = *e-n ~ anberaumen qv;* **e-n ~ setzen** to fix a day, to fix a deadline; **e-n ~ verlegen** to adjourn (the date of the hearing); **e-n ~ wahrnehmen** to attend a court hearing; **festgesetzter ~** place and time designated; **früher erster ~** preliminary hearing (*civil case*); **letzter ~** closing date, peremptory day, dies ad quem; **neuer ~** adjournment day, new date for a hearing; **planmäßiger ~** target date; **vorgezogener ~** expedited hearing; **zu e-m bestimmten ~** at a set date, on a pre-arranged date.

Termin *m* (*2*) date of a forward transaction; **~abschlag** forward discount; **~abschluß** forward contract; **~angebot** offer for a forward contract; **~auftrag** forward order, order for the account; *~~ auf Monatsfrist:* month order; **~börse** futures exchange; **~devisen** foreign exchange for forward delivery; **~effekten** forward stocks; **~einlage** time deposit, fixed term deposit (*or* investment); **~einwand** defence of non enforceability of futures trading, plea of marginal gambling in futures; **~gelder** time deposits; fixed term deposits; **~geldkonto** time deposit account; **~geldsatz** time deposit rate; **~geschäft** forward exchange transaction, futures contract, settlement bargain, time settlement deal;

terminieren

pl also: trading in futures, forward operations, futures, futures market; ~**handel** forward business dealings; futures trading, dealing in futures *cf* ~*geschäft;* ~**händler** pit trader *(commodities)*, option writer; ~**kauf** forward contract, forward buying, forward purchase, purchase for future delivery; *e–n* ~~ *tätigen:* to buy forward; ~**käufer** forward buyer; ~**kommissionär** futures commission man; ~**konto** account for forward transactions; ~**kontrakt** contract of futures; ~**kurs** forward rate, settlement price, price for the account; ~**lieferung** forward delivery, future delivery; ~**markt** forward market, futures market, terminal market, options market; ~**notierung** forward quotation; ~**pfunde** forward sterling; ~**preis** future price; ~**satz** future rate; ~**spekulation** speculation in futures; ~**sicherung** forward cover, hedging operations in a forward market, hedging in the futures market; ~**verkauf** forward sale, selling forward, sale for future delivery, future sale; ~**verkäufer** forward seller; ~**verpflichtung** future obligation, obligation under a forward transaction; ~**wechsel** time draft, term bill; **auf** ~ **kaufen** to purchase for future delivery, to purchase forward, to buy for the account; **auf** ~ **verkaufen** to sell for the settlement.

terminieren *v/i* to specify a date, to assign a day for trial, to set down.

Terminierung *f* timing, setting a final date; listing of cases; **rechtzeitige** ~ early timing, proper timing.

terminlich *adj* as to timing, timely, with regard to final dates.

Terminologie *f* terminology, nomenclature; **juristische** ~ legal terminology, legal terms.

Terminus technicus *m* technical term, word of art, special phrase.

Terraingesellschaft *f* real estate company, site-holding company.

Territorial|gewässer territorial waters; ~**hoheit** territorial sovereignty; ~**recht** regional law; ~**staat** territorial state, state comprising fixed territory; ~**statut** locus regit actum.

Territorialität *f* territoriality; ~**sprinzip** principle of territoriality *(confining effect of expropriation)*.

Terror *m* terror; ~**aktion** terrorist campaign; ~**angriff** terror raid, terrorist attack.

Terrorismusbekämpfung *f* suppression of terrorism, counter terrorism, anti-terrorist action.

Terrorist *m* terrorist; ~**engesetze** laws against terrorist activities.

Tertiawechsel *m* third of exchange, triplicate bill of exchange.

Test|befragung opinion poll, straw vote; ~**betrieb** enterprise to be tested, test factory; ~**muster** test specimen; ~**projekt** pilot project; ~**-, Prototyp- und Demonstrationsanlagen** test, prototype and demonstration facilities; ~**-Stopp** test ban *(nuclear tests)*; ~**unterlagen** test materials; ~**zeichen** test mark.

Testament *n* testament, will, last will (and testament); **t~los** *adj* intestate; **außerordentliches** ~ extraordinary testament, nuncupative will; **Berliner** ~ (=) mutual will of spouses *appointing each other as heir and the child(ren) as subsequent heir(s)*; **durch** ~ **vermachen** to bequeath; **ein** ~ **anfechten** to contest a will; **ein** ~ **aufsetzen** to draw up a will; **ein** ~ **eröffnen** to open a will; **ein** ~ **errichten** to testate, to write a will, to execute a will; **ein** ~ **machen** to make a will; **ein** ~ **umstoßen** to vitiate a will; **ein** ~ **unterdrücken** to suppress a will; **ein** ~ **unterschlagen** to suppress a will; **ein** ~ **vollziehen** to implement a last will; **ein** ~ **widerrufen** to revoke a will; **eigenhändiges** ~ holographic will; **eigenschriftliches** ~ holographic will; **Eröffnung e–s** ~**s** proving of a will; **gegenseitiges** ~ reciprocal will, mutual will, double will;

testamentarisch   **Textilfabrik**

geheimes ~ secret testament; **gemeinsames** ~ joint will, conjoint will, common will; **gemeinschaftliches** ~ = *gemeinsames Testament. qv;* **gültiges** ~ valid will; **holografisches** ~ holographic will; **in e-m ~ bedacht werden** to take a benefit under a will, to benefit by a will; **jmdn im ~ bedenken** to include a person in a will, to remember s. o. in one's will; **mein (hiermit errichtetes)** ~ this my will; **mündliches** ~ verbal testament, nuncupative will; **notariell beurkundetes** ~ notarial will; **öffentliches** ~ notarial will, will made in the presence of, and recorded by, a notary; **ohne Hinterlassung e-s ~s sterben** to die intestate; **späteres** ~ later will; **verschlossenes** ~ sealed will; **wechselbezügliches** ~ reciprocal will, joint and mutual will.

testamentarisch *adj* testamentary.

Testaments|änderung alteration of will; ~**anfechtung** contesting of a will, avoidance of will, contest of probate; ~**anfechtungsprozeß** proceedings to contest a will; ~**bestätigung** probate; ~**bestimmung** testamentary clause; ~**erbe** testamentary heir; ~**eröffnung** opening of will, proving of a will; ~**errichtung** the making of a will; ~**fälschung** forgery of a will; ~**hinterlegung** deposit of wills; ~**nachtrag** codicil; ~**nachweis** proof of will; ~**recht** the law concerning testaments, probate law; ~**urkunde** testamentary instrument; ~**vollstrecker** → *Testamentsvollstrecker;* ~**widerruf** revocation of a will; ~**zeuge** witness to a will, attesting witness.

Testamentsvollstrecker *m* executor; ~**zeugnis** letters testamentary; **befreiter** ~ executor without statutory restrictions; **gegenständlich beschränkter** ~ special executor; **letztwillig eingesetzter** ~ (instituted) executor.

Testamentsvollstreckerin *f* executrix, female executor.

Testamentsvollstreckung executorship.

Testat *m* attestation, official certificate.

Testator *m* testator.

testen *v/t* to test, to examine.

testieren *v/i* to testate, to make a will, to dispose by will; to attest.

Testierender *m* (*der Testierende*) testator, testate, person making a will; *in Hörweite des ~n: in the presence of the testator.*

testierfähig *adj* having testamentary capacity, capable of disposing capacity, being of sound and disposing mind and memory.

Testier|fähigkeit testamentary capacity, capacity to make a will; ~**freiheit** testamentary freedom; ~**unfähigkeit** testamentary incapacity; ~**wille** testamentary intention.

Teuerung *f* general increase in prices; ~**szulage** cost-of-living bonus, cost-of-living grant, cost-of-living allowance.

Teufelskreis *m* vicious circle.

Text *m* text, wording, tenor; ~ **des Wechsels** tenor of the bill, body of the note; ~**entwurf** draft text; ~**lücke** blank space; ~**teil** textual part; ~**verarbeitung** word processing, text processing; ~**vergleich** text comparison, collation; **der englische ~ entscheidet** the English text prevails; **der englische und deutsche Text ist gleich maßgebend** the English and German texts are equally authentic (authoritative); **der maßgebende** ~ the controlling text, the prevailing text; **hinzuzusetzender** ~ addendum; **kommentierter** ~ annotated text; **maschinengeschriebener** ~ typescript; **maßgeblicher** ~ authentic text, prevailing text; **nichtamtlicher Verhandlungs~** informal negotiating text; **verbindlicher** ~ authentic text; **verschlüsselter** ~ coded text.

Textil|fabrik textile factory; ~**geschäft** textile business; ~**hausrat**

Textilien

textile house-furnishings; ~**industrie** textile industry; ~**kennzeichnungsgesetz** Textile Labelling Act; ~**messe** textile goods fair; ~**sektor** textile trade, textile industry; ~**verarbeitung** textile processing; ~**veredelung** textile finishing; ~**ware** textile goods, soft goods; ~**wirtschaft** textile industry and trade.

Textilien *pl* textiles, textile goods, drapery.

Textierung *f* drafting, wording, copywriting.

thesaurieren *v/t, v/i* to retain income, to accumulate profits; to plough back (*profits into reserves*), to reinvest.

Thesaurierung *f* accumulation of profits, capitalisation of profits, ploughing-back of profits; ~**sfond** growth fund, non-expendable trust fund, accumulative trust; ~**splan** voluntary, accumulation plan; ~**streuhand** accumulation trust.

Thron *m* throne; ~**anwärter** pretender to the throne; ~**besteigung** accession to the throne, elevation to the throne; ~**besteigungsrat** Accession Council; ~**folge** succession to the throne, devolution of crown; ~**folgegesetz** Act of Settlement (1701); ~**folger** successor to the throne; ~**prätendent** pretender to the throne; ~**rede** speech from the throne; ~**verzicht** disclaimer to the throne, abdication of the throne; **den** ~ **besteigen** to ascend to the throne.

Tickerdienst *m* ticker service.

Tief|**bau** civil engineering (work); ~**bauingenieur** civil engineer; ~**bauunternehmen** civil engineering enterprise; ~**bohrunternehmen** well-sinking enterprise; ~**gang** draught; ~**garage** underground carpark; ~**kühlanlage** deep-freeze storage centre; ~**ladeanhänger** flat-bed trailer; ~**see** → *Tiefsee* . . .; ~**wasserzeichen** low water mark.

Tiefsee|**bergbau** deep-sea mining;

Tilgung

~**boden** deep-sea floor, deep ocean floor, abyssal floor; ~**fischerei** deep-sea fishery.

Tiefstkurs *m* lowest price, lowest rate, minimum price.

Tiefstwert *m* lowest point, a low.

Tier *n* animal, beast; ~**besamung** insemination; ~**halter** minder (of an animal), keeper of an animal; ~**halterhaftung** liability for animals; ~**heim** asylum for animals; ~**hüter** (employed) keeper of an animal, animal attendant; ~**körper** carcase, carcass, dead animal; *krankheitsverdächtiger* ~~: *suspected carcase*; ~**mißhandlung** cruelty to animals, animal abuse; ~**quälerei** cruelty to animals; ~**schaden** damage caused by animals; ~**schadenhaftung** liability for animals; ~**schutz** protection of animals; ~**schutzgesetz** Prevention of Cruelty to Animals Act, Animal Protection Act; ~**seuchenbekämpfung** prevention of epidemics among animals; ~**seuchengesetz** Epizootic Diseases Act; ~**versicherung** livestock insurance; ~**versuche** experiments on animals, animal testing; ~**zuchtrecht** the law of animal breeding; **streunendes** ~ stray; **zum Vergnügen gehaltene** ~**e** pet animals.

tilgbar *adj* repayable, amortizable; redeemable, subject to redemption; **nicht** ~ irredeemable; **vorzeitig** ~ redeemable in advance.

tilgen *v/t* to repay, to pay off a debt, to redeem, to amortize, to retire; to extinguish, to cancel; **anteilmäßig** ~ to pay off pro rata.

Tilgung *f* repayment, sinking, paying off, redemption, settlement; amortization; clearance (*of a record*); ~ **e-r Anleihe** redemption of a loan; ~ **e-r Hypothek** redemption of a mortgage; ~ **im Strafregister** erasure, extinction of entry for previous convictions; ~**klausel** repayment clausel; ~ **von Verbindlichkeiten** payment of debts; **planmäßige** ~ contractual redemption,

Tilgungsabkommen   **Tod**

regular repayment; **planmäßige und außerplanmäßige ~en** regular and additional redemption payments; **vorzeitige ~** prepayment, advance repayment.

Tilgungsabkommen redemption agreement; **~anleihe** redeemable loan, redemption loan, amortization loan, sinking fund loan, sinking fund bond; **~art** type of amortization; **~aufforderung** call for redemption; **~aussetzung** redemption break; **~bedingungen** terms of amortization; **~bescheinigung** certificate of redemption; **~beträge** redemption monies, amortization payments; **~darlehen** redeemable loan, amortizable loan, loan redeemable by scheduled repayments; **~datum** redemption date (*bonds*); **~dauer** payback period; **~eingänge** repayment of loans, incoming redemption; **~erlös** redemption yield; **~fälligkeit** maturity of redemption payments, date of redemption; **~fonds** redemption fund, sinking fund; **t~frei** *adj* free from redemption; **~gesetz** Redemption Act; **~grundschuld** land charge to secure an amortization loan; **~hypothek** instalment mortage; **~kredit** amortizable loan; **~kurs** redemption rate, redemption price; **~lasten** required amortization payments; **~lebensversicherung** mortgage (redemption) life insurance; **~leistung** amortization, amortization payment; **~modalitäten** repayment terms; **~plan** redemption plan, redemption schedule, redemption table, sinking fund table; redemption arrangements; **~quote** quota of debt reduction, redemption quota; **~rate** amortization instalment, redemption instalment; **~recht** right to redeem; **~rücklage** reserve for sinking fund, redemption reserve, amortization reserve; **~schema** sinking-fund table, redemption plan; **~schuld** debt subject to amortization; **~schuldverschreibung** sinking fund debenture; **~soll** redemption target (*or* requirement); repayment requirements; **~streckung** repayment extension, rescheduling of debts, deferral of payment; **~termin** repayment date; **~vereinbarung** redemption agreement; **~zahlung** repayment of debt, payment of redemption instalment; **~zeit** redemption time, pay-back period.

Tippgeber *m* tipper (*insider dealing*).

Tischvorlage *f* ad hoc proposal, room document.

Titel *m* title, heading, caption; enforceable judgment *or* instrument *short for* Vollstreckungstitel *qv, pl also* securities; **~anmeldung** (*Urh*) registration of title (*of a new publication*); **~führung** use of a title; *unbefugte ~~: unlawful assumption of a title*; **~schutz** copyright protection of titles; **~seite** title page; **akademischer ~** university degree; **ehrenhalber verliehener ~** honorary title; **vollständiger ~** full title; **vollstreckbarer ~** = *Vollstreckungstitel qv.*

tituliert *adj* legally enforceable *by execution.*

Tochtergesellschaft *f* subsidiary (company), underlying company; **100%ige ~** wholly-owned subsidiary; **mehrheitliche ~** majority-owned subsidiary.

Tod *m* death, decease, exitus; **~ durch den Strang** death by hanging; **~ durch Fahrlässigkeit** negligent homicide; **t~krank** terminally ill; **angesichts des ~es** in contemplation of death, in the face of death; **dem ~e nah** in extremis; **den ~ finden** to meet one's death, to die; **gewaltsamer ~** violent death; **im Augenblick des ~es** in articulo mortis; **mit dem ~e bestraft werden** to be sentenced to death; **nach dem ~e** post mortem; **natürlicher ~** natural death, death from natural causes; **unnatürlicher ~** unnatural death, violent death; **von ~es wegen** by will,

Todesangst

mortis causa; **zum ~e verurteilen** to sentence to death, to condemn to death.

Todes|angst fear of death; *in ~ängsten: in fear of one's life;* **~anzeige** obituary notice, notice of death; **~bestimmung** determination of death; **~beweis** proof of death; **~blässe** deathly pallor; **~datum** date of death; **~dosis** lethal dose; **~erklärung** (official) declaration of death; **~fall** death, event of death, fatality; *im ~~: upon death, in the event of death, in case of death;* **~falle** death trap; **~fallkapital** (capital) sum payable on death; **~fallprämie** mortuary dividend; **~fallrente** annuity at death; **~fallversicherung** whole life insurance, assurance payable at death; **~folge** fatal outcome, fatal result; **~gefahr** deadly peril; **~kampf** death struggle, agony; **~kandidat** prisoner awaiting execution, doomed man; **~krankheit** last sickness; illness leading to death; **~kugel** fatal bullet; **~marsch** death march; **~nachweis** proof of death; **~nähe** nearness of death, impending death; **~not** agony; **~opfer** person killed, casualty; **~risiko** risk to one's life; **~schuß** deadly shot, a shot meant to kill; *gezielter ~~: the use of deadly force (authorizing the police to shoot to kill);* **~stoß** death blow; **~strafe** capital punishment, death penalty, supreme penalty; *bei ~~: on penalty of death; mit ~~ bedroht: punishable by death;* **~tag** day (*or* anniversary) of death, day of a person's death; **~ursache** cause of death; **~urteil** death sentence; **~vermutung** presumption of death, presumptive death; **~verursachung** causing death; *zufällige ~~: accidental death;* **~verursachung durch Rauschgift** manslaughter by an unlawful and dangerous drug; **~zeit** time of death; **~zelle** death cell.

tödlich *adj* fatal, mortal, lethal.

Toleranz *f* tolerance, toleration, allowed variation; **~bewilligung** al-

Totalisator

lowed variation; **~gesetz** Toleration Act (*GB 1689*); **~grenze** tolerable limit, limit of tolerance, plus and minus limits; **~ zwischen Waagen** scale tolerance; **zulässige ~** total tolerance.

Tombola *f* raffle, tombola.

Tonatelier *n* sound studio.

Tonbandaufnahme *f* tape recording, audio recording.

Tonkunst *f* music, musical art.

Tonnage *f* tonnage; **aufgelegte ~** idle shipping, laid up vessels.

Tonnen|fracht ton freight, freight charged by the ton; **~geld** tonnage dues; **~gehalt** displacement ton; **~kilometer** ton kilometre(s) (*US: kilometer(s)*); **~meile** ton mile.

Tontine *f* tontine fund; **~gesellschaft** tontine assurance company; **~versicherung** (*mit befristeter Gruppenlebensversicherung, Anwachsungsrecht für die während der Versicherungsdauer überlebenden Versicherungsnehmer*) tontine policy; **~nvertrag** contract of tontine.

Tonträger *m* sound recording tape; **~rechte** sound record rigths.

Torschlußpanik *f* last-minute panic, rush before the doors close.

Tortur *f* torture; **jmdn der ~ unterwerfen** to subject s. o. to torture, to torture.

tot *adj* dead; **~geboren** *adj* stillborn (child); abortive (thing); **T~geburt** still birth, stillborn child; **T~schlag** → *Totschlag;* **für ~ erklären** to declare dead; **physisch ~** actually dead, clinically dead.

Total|ausverkauf clearance sale, closing-down sale; **~geschädigter** person who has lost his entire property; **~invalidität** total invalidity; **~schaden** total loss, actual total loss, write-off (*accident*); *haftet nur bei ~schäden: warranted free of all average;* **~verlust** total loss, total wreck; *als ~~ geltender Schaden → Schaden; konstruktiver ~~: constructive total los; physischer ~~: actual total loss, physical loss.*

Totalisator *m* totalizator, totalizer, tote.

761

totalität *adj* totalitarian.
Toten|beschauer coroner; **~bestattung** burial; **~bett** death-bed; **~fürsorge** obituary care, entitlement to arrange funeral rites; **~geruch** cadaverous smell; **~haus** mortuary; **~kopf** death's head, skull and cross bones (*danger sign*); **~liste** list of casualties, obituary, necrology; **~schein** death certificate, certification of death; **~starre** rigor mortis.
töten *v/t* to kill, to put to death; **aus Geschlechtslust ~** to kill in order to gratify one's sexual urge; **aus Habgier ~** to kill out of greed; **heimtückisch ~** to kill treacherously.
Toto *m* football pools; **~gewinne** winnings on the football pools, totalizator winnings; **~schein** football pool coupon.
Totschlag *m* manslaughter, wilful homicide (*less than murder*); **~ im Affekt** manslaughter committed in the heat of passion; **~sversuch** homicidal attempt; **versuchter ~** homicidal attempt, attempted manslaughter.
Totschläger *m* committer of manslaughter; killer; manslayer; blackjack, cosh, sap.
Tötung *f* killing, homicide; **~ auf Verlangen** killing another person at his own request; **~ aus Notwehr** killing in self-defence, homicide se defendo; **~ beim Zweikampf** killing someone in a duel; **~ der Leibesfrucht** (criminal) abortion, feticide, foeticide; **~ e-s Menschen** homicide; **entschuldbare ~** excusable homicide; **fahrlässige ~** homicide caused by negligence, negligent homicide, killing by negligence; **grobfahrlässige ~** killing by gross negligence; **nichtrechtswidrige ~** lawful homicide; **schuldlose zufällige ~** excusable accidental homicide; **unbeabsichtigte ~** unintentional homicide, involuntary homicide, involuntary manslaughter; **ungewollte ~** involuntary homicide; **unverschuldete ~** killing by misadventure; **vorsätzliche ~** wilful homicide; **zufällige ~** involuntary manslaughter, casual homicide, killing by misadventure.
Tötungs|absicht intent to kill; **~delikte** homicide offences; **~handlung** the act of killing; **~verbrechen** felonious homicide; **~versuch** homicidal attempt; **~vorsatz** intent to kill.
Touristen|ausgabe tourist expenditure; **~gepäckversicherung** tourists' baggage insurance; **~gutschein** tourist voucher; **~konjunktur** tourist boom; **~verkehr** tourism, tourist travel; **~visum** tourist visa; **~wesen** tourism.
Touristik *f* tourism, tourist industry; **~unternehmer** tour operator.
Trabantenstadt *f* satellite town.
traditio brevi manu *f* (=) transfer of title by constructive delivery (*to the person who already holds possession*).
Tradition *f* tradition; delivery; handing over; **~spapier** negotiable document of title, transferable title-conferring instrument.
Träger *m* (*1*) bearer, holder, subject, agency, legally and economically responsible body, organization responsible for the provision of services; **~ der Arbeitsvermittlung** organization responsible for the placing of unemployed persons; **~ der gesetzlichen Rentenversicherungen** organization(s) responsible for social pension insurance; **~ der Investitionshilfe** agency responsible for investment assistance; **~ der Kapitalbildung** creators of capital; **~ der Konjunkturentwicklung** promoter of economic activity; **~ der ländlichen Siedlung** rural settlement agencies; **~ der öffentlichen Gewalt** agencies in whom state power is vested; **~ der Sozialversicherung** social insurance agency; **~ der Straßenbaulast** body responsible for road maintenance; **~ der Straßenunterhaltslast** party liable to repair of streets and roads;

Träger   **Transport**

~ **des Geld- und Kreditverkehrs** money and capital transfer agencies; ~ **des Markenrechts** trade mark holder; ~ **des sozialen Wohnungsbaus** agencies in charge of publicly assisted housing programmes; ~**gesellschaft** sponsoring company, supporting company; ~ **öffentlicher Unterstützungen** organization(s) responsible for providing public assistance; ~**organisationen** sponsoring agencies; ~ **von Rechten und Pflichten** subject of rights and duties; **ausländischer** ~ foreign holder (*of exchange balances*); **örtlicher** ~ local supporting organization; **überörtliche** ~ regional supporting organizations.

Träger *m* (2) porter; stretcher bearer; deliverer of newspapers; ~**gebühren** porterage, ~**lohn** porterage, porter's wages.

Trägerschaft *f* financial basis, functional basis, sponsorship.

Tragfähigkeit *f* load capacity; ~ *e–s Schiffes in Gewichtstonnen*: dead weight carrying capacity.

Traktandenliste *f* agenda.

Tramp|fahrt tramping trade; ~**geschäft** tramping; tramp shipping; ~**reeder** tramp-ship owner; ~**schiffahrt** tramp navigation, occasional navigation; ~**schiffahrtsroute** trading voyage; ~**verkehr** tramping trade.

Tranche *f* tranche (*normal block of shares*); ~ **e–r Anleihe** tranche of a bond issue; ~ **eines Kontingents** quota share.

Transaktion *f* transaction, operation.

Transfer *f* transfer; ~**agent** transfer agent; ~**aufschub** delay in transfer; ~**begünstigter** recipient of transfer, beneficiary of a transfer; ~**bewilligung** transfer licence; **t~fähig** *adj* transferable; ~**garantie** guarantee of foreign exchange transfer; ~**kosten** transfer cost; ~**leistung** effective transfer; ~~ *im Kapitalsektor*: transfer on capital account; ~**lockerung** relaxation of restrictions on the transfer (*of capital etc*); ~**moratorium** transfer moratorium; ~**risiko** transfer risk, risk of currency transfer; ~**zahlungen** transfer payments, remittances in foreign currency.

transferierbar *adj* transferable.

transferieren *v/t* to transfer, to transfer abroad, to remit.

Transferierung *f* transferring, transfer (*into foreign currency*).

Transit|abfertigung transit clearance; ~**abgaben** transit charges; ~**ausfuhr** transit exports (*channelled through third countries*); third-country export; ~**blatt** transit voucher, transit counterfoil; ~**delikte** transfrontier offences; ~**durchfahrt** transit passage; ~**einfuhr** transit import(s) (*channelled through third countries*); ~**einkäufe** transit purchases; ~**erklärung** transit declaration; ~**fracht** transit (*or* through) freight; ~**güter** goods in transit; ~**hafen** transit port; ~**handel** transit trade, third-country trade, entrepôt trade; ~**händler** transit trader; ~**konnossement** transit bill of lading; ~**ladung** transit cargo; ~**lager** transit store, entrepôt; ~**preis** cross-rate; ~**verkauf** sale through third country, sale in a third country; ~**verkehr** transit trade, international transit, transit traffic; ~**versand** transit dispatch; ~**ware** goods in transit; ~**weg** transit route; *im ~~e*: *in the course of merchanting trade*; ~**zeugnis** certificate of transit; ~**zoll** duty on goods in transit.

Transiteur *m* transit trader.

transitorisch *adj* transitory, transitional, deferred.

Transport *m* transportation, transport, shipment, haulage, conveyance; ~**anlage** conveying machinery; ~**(e) auf dem Seeweg** carriage by sea; ~ **auf dem Wasserweg** transport by water, waterage; ~**bedingungen** terms of freight, terms and conditions of transportation; ~**bilanz** net position on transport; ~**fahrzeuge** hauling equipment; ~**firma** = ~*unter-*

763

nehmen qv; ~**gefahr** transport hazard, transport risk, risk of conveyance; ~~*en im Straßenverkehr*: *perils of the road*; ~**gefährdung** endangering public transport; ~**gefäß** transport vessel; ~**geschäft** transport business, shipping trade; ~**gewerbe** haulage sector, carrying trade, shipping trade; ~**gut** cargo, shipment; ~~ *bei Verladung in einwandfreiem Zustand*: *shipped in good order and condition*; ~**haftung** carrier's liability; ~**kapazität** transport capacity; ~**kosten** transport charges, carrying charges, cost of carriage; *US*: ~~ *per Güterwagen*: *wagonage*; ~**makler** freight broker (*or* agent); ~**mittel** means of transport; ~**möglichkeit** transport facilities; ~**papiere** shipping papers; ~**raum** cargo space; ~**risiko** = ~*gefahr qv*; ~**sachverständiger** transportation expert; ~**schaden** transport damage, damage in transit; ~**steuer** transport tax; ~**tarif** transportation rate; ~**unfähigkeit** unfitness for transportation; ~**verlust** transportation loss; ~**versicherung** transport insurance; ~**versicherungspolice** transport insurance policy; ~**vertrag** contract of carriage; ~**vorschriften** forwarding instructions, shipping instructions; ~**unternehmen** carrier, operating company, haulage company; ~**weg** transport route, voyage, distance over which goods are transported; ~**wesen** transportation (system), public service transport; **auf dem** ~ in transit, in transitu; **beim** ~ **beschädigt** damaged in transit, damaged en route.

Trassant *m* drawer.

Trassat *m* drawee.

Trassierungs|kredit draft credit, documentary acceptance credit; ~**provision** drawing commission.

Tratte *f* draft, a drawn bill without acceptance; ~**nankaufsermächtigung** authority to purchase bills of exchange; ~**navis** advice of a draft; ~ **ohne Dokumente** clean draft; **dokumentäre** ~ documentary draft; **nicht dokumentäre** ~ clean draft, non-documentary draft.

Trauschein *m* marriage certificate, certificate of marriage.

Trauung *f* marriage ceremony, solemnization of marriage; **kirchliche** ~ church wedding ceremony; **standesamtliche** ~ civil marriage, marriage at a registry office.

Trauzeuge *m* witness to a marriage, best man.

Treffgenauigkeit *f* accuracy (*statistics*).

Treibgut *n* flotsam.

Treibhauseffekt *f* greenhouse effect.

Treibnetzfischerei *f* drift netting.

Treibstoff *m* fuel, petrol, gasoline; ~**einnahme** fuelling (*ship*); ~**lager** fuel dump; ~**monopol** fuel monopoly; ~**steuern** fuel taxes; ~**verbrauch** fuel consumption; ~**versorgung** fuel supply.

Trend *m* trend, tendency; ~**verlagerung** basic change in a trend, switch in trends; ~**wende** trend reversal.

trennbar *adj* separable, detachable.

Trennbarkeit *f* separability.

trennen *v/t*o separate, to sever, to disconnect, to disunite, to disassociate, to divide.

Trennmauer *f* partition-wall.

Trennung *f* separation, severance (*etc cf trennen*); ~ **der Gewalten** separation of powers; ~ **mehrerer Rechtsstreitigkeiten** severance of actions, separation of actions; ~ **vom Bande der Ehe** (= *Scheidung*) divorce a vinculo matrimonii; ~ **von Tisch und Bett** divorce a mensa et thoro, legal separation, separation from bed and board; **einverständliche** ~ separation by consent; **gerichtliche** ~ judicial separation.

Trennungs|entschädigung separation allowance, severance allowance; absence money, compensation for double housekeeping; ~**frist** minimum period of separation (*before divorce petition can be filed*) ~**geld** = ~*entschädigung qv*;

Tresor   **Treu und Glauben**

~**grund** reason for the separation; ~**sunterhalt** maintenance (*or* alimony) during the separation of spouses; ~**vereinbarung** separation agreement; ~**zulage** = ~*entschädigung qv*.

Tresor *m* safe-deposit box, safe; ~**anlagen** vaults; ~**raum** vault; ~**steuer** safe deposit tax; ~**verwahrung** safe deposit.

Treubruch *m* breach of faith, breach of trust, disloyalty, perfidy, infidelity.

Treue *f* loyalty, fidelity, allegiance, faithfulness; ~**eid** oath of allegiance; ~**erklärung** trust declaration; ~**pflicht** duty to be loyal, allegiance; *Verletzung der ~~: breach of faith, disloyalty*; ~**prämie** loyalty bonus, *bonus for long years of service, bonus to long-standing customers*; ~**rabatt** discount for long-standing customers, patronage discount; ~**vergütung** = ~*prämie qv*; ~**verhältnis** fiduciary relation, relation of good faith; **eheliche** ~ conjugal (*or* marital) fidelity.

Treugeber *m* cestui que trust, trustor, settlor, donor, the maker of a trust, beneficiary under a trust, grantor of a trust, creditor in trust.

Treugut *n* trust property, trust estate, goods in trust.

Treuhand *f* trust; ~**anstalt** institutional trustee, Trusteeship Administration, Trustee Administrative Authority (*privatization agency*); ~**bank** trust bank; ~**begünstigung** beneficial interest; ~**beteiligung** trusteeship participation; ~**bindung** trust obligation; ~**eigentum** trust property; ~**eigentümer** owner as trustee; ~**gebiet** trusteeship territory; ~**gebühren** trust fees, fees paid to a trustee; ~**gelder** trust fund, trust moneys; ~**geschäft** fiduciary transaction; ~**gesellschaft** trust company; auditing company; ~**konto** trust account, escrow deposit; ~**kredit** loan on a trust basis; ~ **mit Tätigkeitspflicht** active trust; ~**pflichten** fiduciary obligations, trustees' duties; ~**rat** Trusteeship Council; ~**schaft** trusteeship; ~**schaftsabkommen** trusteeship agreement; ~**sonderkonto** special trust account; ~**urkunde** trust deed, deed of trust, trust instrument; ~**verhältnis** trust relationship, fiduciary relation; *gesetzlich vermutetes ~~: implied trust; vereinbartes ~~: express trust*; ~**vermögen** trust property, property held in trust, trust assets; ~**vertrag** trust agreement, trust deed, fiduciary contract; ~**verwahrer** fiduciary custodian, stakeholder; ~**verwaltung** trusteeship; *gerichtlich angeordnete ~~: court trust*; ~~ *zur Verhinderung von Verschwendung: spendthrift trust*; ~**zertifikat** trust certificate; **auf letztwilligem Wunsch beruhende** ~ precatory trust; **auftragsgebundene** ~ special trust; **gemeinnützige** ~ public trust; **letztwillige** ~**bestellung** testamentary trust; **rangbessere** ~ overriding trust, priority trust.

Treuhänder *m* trustee, person in trust; ~**ausschuß** committee of trustees; ~**eigenschaft** fiduciary capacity; capacity as trustee; ~**rat** trust council; **als** ~ in fiduciary capacity, in trust for, in the capacity as trustee; **als** ~ **verwalten** to hold on trust; **e-n** ~ **bestellen** to appoint a trustee; **e-n** ~ **einsetzen** to appoint a trustee; **ehrenamtlicher** ~ honorary trustee; **gewillkürter** ~ private trustee; **uneigennütziger** ~ volunteer (trustee).

treuhänderisch *adj* fiduciary, in trust, upon trust, on trust; ~ **verwalten** to administer in a fiduciary capacity.

Treupflicht *f* duty of loyalty (*to a company or partnership or employer*).

Treu und Glauben good faith; **auf** ~ in good faith; **gegen** ~ **verstoßen** to act in breach of good faith; **nach** ~ according to the requirements of good faith; **Verstoß gegen** ~ contrary to the rule of good faith; **wider** ~ contrary to good faith.

Tribunal *n* tribunal.
Tribüne *f* platform.
Tribut *m* tribute, offering.
Trichinenschau examination for trichinosis.
Trichotomie *f* trichotomy.
Trick *m* trick, dodge, artifice, gimmick; ~**diebstahl** larceny committed by means of a trick, confidence trick.
Triebtäter *m* pathological sex offender.
triftig *adj* valid, sound, conclusive.
Triftigkeit *f* validity, soundness, cogency, plausibility.
Trimm *m* trim (*ship*).
Trinken *n* drinking; *gewohnheitsmäßiges* ~: habitual consumption of alcohol, regular heavy drinking.
Trinker *m* heavy drinker, drunkard; ~**fürsorgestelle** institution for the care of alcoholics; ~**heilanstalt** asylum for inebriates, institution for the treatment of chronic alcoholics, drunks' asylum; ~**psychose** mania a potu.
Trinkgeld *n* tip, gratuity.
Trinkwassergewinnung *f* abstraction of drinking water.
Triplik *f* surrejoinder, triplicatio.
Triplikat *n* triplicate.
triplizieren *v/i* surrejoin.
Triptyk *n* (= *Triptik*) triptyque, passport for motor vehicles.
Trittbrettfahrer *m* free rider (*also fig*), opportunist.
Trittschall *m* impact sound of footsteps.
Trivialforderung *f* small claim (*or* petty).
Trocken|dock dry dock; ~**fäule** dry rot; ~**gewicht** dry weight; ~**legen** drainage; ~**siegel** embossed seal; ~**stempel** embossed seal.
Trödelhandel *m* second-hand goods trade.
Tropen|ausführung tropical finish; ~**ausweis** certificate of fitness for use in the tropics; ~**ausrüstung** tropical equipment; t~**fest** *adj* suitable for the tropics, tropics-resistant, tropicalized; ~**risiko** risk of tropical conditions; ~**verwendungsfähigkeit** fitness for service in tropical climate; ~**zulage** extra pay for service in the tropics.
Trostpreis *m* consolation prize.
Troygewicht *n* troy weight (*precious stones, medicines*).
Truckverbot *n* prohibition of violating the Truck Acts (*i.e. ban from paying wages in the form of goods or services instead of money*).
Trugschluß *n* false syllogism, fallacy, sophism, false conclusion.
Trümmerbeseitigung *f* rubble clearance, clearing débris.
Trunkenbold *m* drunkard, alcoholic.
Trunkenheit *f* drunkenness, intoxication, inebriation; *Zustand der* ~: *state of intoxication;* ~ **am Steuer** drunkenness while in charge of a motor vehicle; ~ **im Verkehr** drunkenness in traffic; ~**sdelikt** drink-driving offence; ~**sfahrt** drunken driving *GB*; drunk driving *US*; driving while intoxicated (*DWI*), *US*; ~**stäter** drink-driving offender; **selbstverschuldete** ~ voluntary drunkenness.
Trunksucht *f* dipsomania, chronic alcoholism, habitual drunkenness, habitual intemperance.
Trunksüchtiger *m* dipsomaniac, alcoholic, habitual drunkard.
Truppen|abbau reduction of armed forces; ~**dienstgericht** court martial; ~**gattung** branch of the armed forces; ~**übungsplatz** army training ground; ~**versorgung** troops supply; ~**verschiebung** troop redeployment; ~**vertrag** Forces Convention.
Trust *m* trust combine, pool.
Tuberkulose|bekämpfung tuberculosis control; ~**hilfe** aid to tuberculosis patients; ~**versorgungswerk** welfare organization for tuberculosis patients.
Tüchtigkeit *f* efficiency, proficiency, skill.
Tumult *m* turmoil, rampage, pandemonium, riot, uproar, civil commotion; ~**risiko** risk of riot; ~**schäden** riot damage; ~**schädengesetz** *GB*: Riot Damages Act;

~schadenversicherung riot insurance; **~schutzkleidung** riot gear.

Tun *n* action, commission, activities.

tunlich *adj* expedient, convenient, suitable; **für ~ halten** to think fit, to consider suitable.

Tür *f* door; **feuerhemmende ~** fire door, fire security door.

Turnus *m* rotation, rota, turn; **t~mäßig** *adj* rotational, *adv* by rotation, in turns; **im zweijährigen ~** biennially, every two years.

TÜV *m* = *Technischer Überwachungsverein qv*; **~bescheinigung** certificate of road-worthiness, MOT certificate *(GB)* **~plakette** MOT disc.

Typen|bereinigung simplification of design; **~beschränkung** limitation of varieties; **~betriebserlaubnis** operating permit for the type of machine (or vehicle); **~muster** representative sample; **~prüfung** qualification inspection, type acceptance test; **~reihe** production series.

U, Ü

Übel *n* evil, grievance, misfortune; **ein empfindliches** ~ great discomfort.

Übeltat *f* misdeed, wrong.

Übeltäter *m* wrong-doer, malefactor; **unverbesserlicher** ~ incorrigible rogue.

Überabschreibung *f* over-depreciation.

Überalterung *f* obsolescence, superannuation; ~ **der Wirtschaftsgüter** product obsolescence; **technische** ~ functional obsolescence.

Überangebot *n* over-supply, excess supply, glut.

überantworten *v/t* to deliver up, to hand over, to surrender (*to the police*).

Überantwortung *f* surrender (*to the police*), handing over.

überarbeiten *v/t* to rework, to revise, to touch up, to polish (up).

Überarbeitung *f* reworking, revision; overwork (*strain*).

Überbau *m* superstructure, projecting part; building over the boundary line; ~**rente** periodic compensation for having built over the boundary line.

Überbeanspruchung *f* overstraining, excessive demand.

überbelegen *v/t* to overbook, to accommodate more than the permitted number of occupiers, to overcrowd.

Überbelegung *f* overcrowding, filling beyond capacity, living in overcrowded conditions.

Überbeschäftigung *f* over-employment; overwork, excessive work.

Überbestand *n* excess stock.

Überbesteuerung *f* excessive taxation, over-taxation.

überbetrieblich *adj* inter-company, covering more than a single enterprise, supra-plant.

Überbevölkerung *f* over-population.

überbewerten *v/t* to overvalue; to overstate (*one's position*).

Überbewertung *f* overvaluation, overstating.

überbezahlen *v/t* to overpay.

überbezirklich *adj* supra-regional.

überbieten *v/t* to overbid, to outbid.

überbord *adj* overboard, overside; **Ü~-Auslieferungsklausel** *f* overside delivery clause; **Ü~lieferung** *f* ashore or overside.

Überbringer *m* deliverer, bearer; *durch* ~: *per bearer*; ~**klausel** bearer clause; ~**scheck** bearer cheque.

überbrücken *v/t* to bridge, to overbridge, to tide over.

Überbrückung *f* interim aid, temporary assistance, tiding over, stop-gap.

Überbrückungs|abkommen interim aid agreement; ~**beihilfe** interim aid, tideover allowance, temporary grant; ~**darlehen** bridging loan; ~**hilfe** temporary relief; ~**kredit** stop-gap loan, bridging credit (*or loan*); interim credit.

Überbuchung *f* overbooking.

Überbürdung *f* charging another party (with sth), passing on (a liability); **unter** ~ **der Kosten auf die Staatskasse** awarding the costs against the state; ~**splan** tide-me-over plan.

überdauern *v/t* to outlast, to outwear.

Überdeckung *f* excess cover, surplus cover.

Überdenkungsfrist *f* cooling-off period (*industrial disputes*).

Überdividende *f* superdividend, surplus dividend, bonus dividend.

überdurchschnittlich *adj* better-than-average, above-average.

übereignen *v/t* to transfer ownership, to pass title.

Übereignung *f* transfer of ownership, passing of title, making over; ~**surkunde** document of transfer of title, absolute bill of sale; **absolute** ~ outright transfer of title *or* of ownership.

Übereinkommen *n* agreement, treaty, convention; ~ **über das Mindestalter in gewerblichen Betrieben** Minimum Age in Industry Convention; **ein** ~ **kündigen** to terminate *or* denounce a treaty; **internationales** ~ international convention; **neugefaßtes** ~ new revising Convention.

übereinkommen *v/i* to agree, to reach an agreement.

Übereinkunft *f* convention, pact, agreement; **internationale** ~ international agreement.

übereinstimmen *v/i* to agree, to concur, to accord, to be in accordance with, to conform to, to be in conformity with, to answer to; **nicht** ~ to disagree, to dissent, not to be in conformity with.

übereinstimmend *adj* conformable, in harmony (with), consistent (with), in conformity (with); **im wesentlichen** ~ in substantial agreement (with).

Übereinstimmung *f* accord, agreement, accordance; **in** ~ **mit** in accordance with, in keeping with; **mangelnde** ~ disagreement, lack of conformity.

Überemission *f* over-issue.

Überentschädigung *f* over-compensation.

Übererlös *m* surplus proceeds.

Übererzeugung *f* overproduction.

Überfahrt *f* sea passage; ~**sgelder** passage moneys; **glückliche** ~ safe passage, a safe journey.

Überfall *m* raid; ~**kommando** riot squad, emergency squad, flying squad; **bewaffneter** ~ hold-up, armed raid; **hinterlistiger** ~ perfidious assault, treacherous assault;. **nächtlicher** ~ assault at nighttime.

überfallen *v/t* to assault, to raid.

überfällig *adj* overdue, past due, out of time; ~ **sein** to be overdue; to lie over (*bill of exchange*).

Überfinanzierung *f* overfinancing.

Überfischen *n* over-fishing.

Überfliegen *n* flight over a territory, overflight.

Überfliegungsrecht *n* = *Überflugsrecht* right to fly over a territory; right of overflight.

überflügeln *v/t* to exceed, to outstrip, to outperform.

Überflug *m* overflight; ~**srecht** right of overflight.

Überfluß *m* overabundance, surplus, overplus; ~**gesellschaft** abundance economy, society of overabundance, society of excessive affluence, a highly affluent society.

überfordern *v/t* to overcharge, to overtax.

Überforderung *f* excessive demand, excessive charge, overcharging, overtaxing, overstraining.

Überfracht *f* overfreight, excess freight.

Überfremdung *f* excessive foreign influence, (excessive) foreign penetration, substantial foreign control.

überführen *v/t* (1) to transfer, to ferry, to transport (*from one place to another*).

überführen *v/t* (2) to prove s.o.'s guilt.

Überführung *f* (1) transfer, conveyance, transport (*from one place to another*); ~ **in ein Gefängnis** transfer to prison, committing a.p. to jail; ~ **in Gemeineigentum** nationalization; ~**sersuchen** request for the transfer (*of a prisoner etc*); ~**sfahrt** transfer (trip); ~**kosten** funeral transport charges.

Überführung *f* (2) proof of s.o.'s guilt; ~**sstück** exhibit (*proving guilt*).

Überführungsrecht *n* wayleave (*over the land of another*).

Übergabe delivery, hand delivery, delivery of possession, surrender; ~ **als Sicherheit** delivery by way of security, delivery as a pledge; ~**bedingungen** terms of surrender; ~**bescheinigung** receipt of delivery, bill of transfer; **~bilanz** premerger balance sheet; **~ durch Abtretung des Herausgabeanspruchs** constructive delivery by assigning the right to possession; **~probefahrt** handing-over test run; **~protokoll** record of delivery of possession; **~surrogat** constructive delivery, substitute for delivery; **~verweigerung** refusal to surrender sth; **bedingungslose ~** unconditional surrender, unconditional delivery; **bis zur ~** pending delivery; **mittelbare ~** constructive delivery; **physische ~** actual delivery; **tatsächliche ~** actual delivery, manual delivery; **zahlbar bei ~** payable on delivery.

Übergang *m* (1) transmission, devolution, transition, reversion; **~ der Gefahr** passing of risk; **~ des Eigentums** passing of title, devolution of title, transmission of ownership, vesting of title; **~ e-s Vermögens** devolution of the estate; **~skonto** suspense account; **~sregelung** transitional rules (*or* provisions); **~szeit** transitional period; **~ von Todes wegen** transmission on death, transfer by death; **~ zur Tagesordnung** passing to the order of the day, beginning with the business of the meeting, dealing with points of the agenda.

Übergang *m* (2) crossing; **~ für Fußgänger** pedestrian crossing; **~spunkt** crossing, check-point.

Übergangs|arbeitslosigkeit transitional unemployment, temporary unemployment; **~beschäftigung** temporary employment, interim employment; **~bestimmungen** transitional provisions; **~budget** transitional budget; **~geld** severance pay, bridging benefits; **~gesetz** interim law; **~haushalt** interim budget; **~hilfe** temporary assistance, bridging loan; **~kabinett** caretaker cabinet; **~posten** suspense item, transitory item; **~regelung** transitional arrangement; **~regierung** provisional government, caretaker government, interregnum; **~- und Schlußbestimmungen** transitional and concluding provisions; **~vorschriften** temporary provisions, transitional regulations; **~zahlung** transitional payment; **~zeit** transitional period, period of transition; **~zustand** transitional stage, transitional state.

übergeben *v/t* to deliver, to hand over, to give up, to surrender.

Übergebot *n* higher bid, outbidding.

übergehen *v/i* to devolve, to pass, to vest (in), to subrogate; to skip, to disregard, to omit, to pass over; **ineinander ~** to blend, to merge; **zu etwas ~** to proceed to, to pass on to.

Übergehung *f* passing over, omission, neglect.

übergeordnet *adj* overriding, superior, paramount.

übergesetzlich *adj* supra-statutory, above codified law.

Übergewicht *n* excess weight, overweight; overbalance, predominance.

Übergewinn *n* excess profit, superprofit; **~steuer** excess profits tax.

übergreifen *v/i* to encroach (upon), to overlap.

Übergriff *m* encroachment, interference, incursion, inroad, impingement, infringement.

Übergröße *f* oversize, outsize.

Überhaft *f* superimposed custody, additional confinement pending investigation.

Überhandnehmen *n* excessive spreading, prevalence.

Überhang *m* (1) excess, backlog; **~ an Aufträgen** backlog of orders; **~ an Investitionen** excess of capital investments; **~mandat** extraordinary additional seat in parliament.

Überhang *m* (2) overhang (*overhanging branches and roots extending into neighbour's land*).

Überhitzung *f* overheating (*of the economy*).

Überhöhung *f* excess, excessive rise; **~ des Zinsniveaus** excessively high interest rates.

Überholen *n* passing, overtaking; ~ **verboten** no overtaking; **falsches** ~ improper overtaking; **zum ~ ansetzen** to begin to overtake.
überholen *v/t* (*1*) to overtake (*a car*).
überholen *v/t* (*2*) to overhaul (*an engine*).
Überholung *f* overhaul; **~sarbeit** overhauling.
Überholverbot *n* prohibition of overtaking; no passing!
Überindustrialisierung *f* overindustrialization.
Überinvestition *f* over-investment.
Überkapazität *f* excess capacity, overcapacity.
Überkapitalisation *f* overcapitalization.
überkapitalisieren *v/t* to overcapitalize.
Überkapitalisierung *f* overcapitalization.
Überkonjunktur *f* super-boom, overheated boom.
Überkreuzverflechtung *f* interlocking (directorships).
überladen *v/t* to overload; to transship, *adj* overladen.
Überladung *f* overloading; transshipment.
Überlandstrom *m* long-distance electricity supply.
Überlappung *f* overlap.
überlassen *v/t* to hand over, to deliver, to leave, to yield, to cede to, to abandon, to surrender, to entrust, to submit; **leihweise ~** to lend.
Überlassung *f* handing-over, cession, delivery, surrender, relinquishment, abandonment; **~sanspruch** right to have (infringing) copies surrendered; **~surkunde** transfer deed; **~svertrag** agreement on transfer of possession; **schenkungsweise ~** donation; **unentgeltliche ~** gratuitous surrender of sth, disposal without consideration; **~ von Verkaufsrechten** franchising; **~ von Wirtschaftsgütern** transfer of assets.
überlasten *v/t* to overload.
Überlastung *f* excessive weight, overload, overburdened condition; **~sgeld** charge for excessive weight.
überlaufen *v/i* to desert (to the enemy), to defect.
Überläufer *m* deserter, *pol* turncoat, defector, renegade.
Überlebens|fall (in) case of survival; **~rente** joint and survivor annuity, two-life annuity, annuity on the last survivor; **~vermutung** presumption of survival, presumption of survivorship; **~versicherung** survivorship insurance; *wechselseitige ~~*: *joint life insurance*; **~wahrscheinlichkeit** probability of surviving.
Überlegung *f* deliberation, consideration, premeditation; **bei nochmaliger ~** on second thoughts; **nach reiflicher ~** after careful consideration; **steuerliche ~en** tax considerations.
Überleitung *f* transition; **~sanzeige** notice of transfer, notice of statutory assignment (of maintenance rights); **~sgesetz** Transference Act, Transitional Act; **~sregelung** transitional regulation (*or* provisions); **~svertrag** transference convention; **~svorschrift** transitional regulation.
Überliegegeld *n* demurrage.
Überliegetage *m/pl* extra lay-days.
Überliegezeit *f* demurrage (days), extra lay-days.
Überliquidität *f* excess liquidity.
Übermaßverbot *n* prohibition of excessiveness (*on the part of courts or public authorities*); rule of reasonableness.
Übermittlung *f* transmission, communication; **~sfehler** mistake in communicating (*a message etc*); **~sgebühr** transmittal fee; **~irrtum** error of transmission; **fernschriftliche ~** telex transmission; **telegrafische ~** wire communication; **unrichtige ~** incorrect transmittal.
Übermüdung *f* fatigue, overfatigue.
Übernachfrage *f* excessive demand; **~inflation** demand-pull inflation.

Übernachtungen *f/pl* overnight reservations, overnight stays.

Übernachtungs|geld overnight accommodation allowance, reimbursement of hotel expenses; **~kosten** hotel allowances, hotel expense, accommodation costs.

Übernahme *f* assumption, take-over, absorption; **~angebot** take-over bid; tender offer, *unfreundliches ~~:* hostile offer; **~beschluß** take-over resolution; **~ der Regierungsgewalt** assumption of government; **~ e–r Emission** underwriting commitment; **~ e–r Gesellschaft** take-over of a company; **~ e–s Amts** succession to an office; **~faszilität** underwriting facility; **~garantie** underwriting commitment guarantee; **~gebühr** assumption fee *(mortgage);* **~gesetz** Adoptive Act, Adopting Act; **~hai** takeover shark; **~klausel** assumption clause; **~konossement** received (for shipment) bill of lading (B/L); **~konsortium** underwriting syndicate, security-taking syndicate; **~kurs** underwriting price, take-over price; **~objekt** takeover target; **~pirat** predator, corporate raider; **~preis** take-over price, acceptance price; **~probe** acceptance test; **~provision** underwriting commission; **~recht** right to take over; **~risiko** risk of non-acceptance (by the purchaser), buyer's rejection risk; **~spekulant** suitor; **~schuldner** cost-debtor *due to assumption of liability for legal expenses*; **~syndikat** underwriting syndicate; **~vertrag** take-over agreement.

übernational *adj* supranational.

übernehmen *v/t* to take over, to assume, to adopt, to accept.

Übernehmer *m* transferee, surrenderee, assignee.

Übernennwertausgabe *f* issue above par.

Überordnungsverhältnis *n* relationship of superiority.

überörtlich *adj* regional, non-local.

Überpariemission *f* issue above par.

überparteilich *adj* non-party, non-partisan, above party lines.

Überparteilichkeit *f* impartiality.

Überpfändung *f* excessive distraint.

Überpreis *m* excessive price.

Überproduktion *f* overproduction.

überproportional *adj* disproportionately large, unbalanced.

Überprovision *f* overriding commission.

überprüfen *v/t* to review, to check, to reconsider, to screen *(security)*, to vet, to audit, to revise, to re-examine.

Überprüfer *m* inspector, revisor *(translation),* checker.

Überprüfung *f* review, check, audit; reconsideration; screening; **~ e–s Urteils durch die Rechtsmittelinstanz** review on appeal; **~sausschuß** review board; **~sbefugnis** revisory power; **~sbehörde** board of review, revising authority; **~srecht** right of review; **~suntersuchung** additional medical examination; **vereinbarte nachträgliche ~ von Rechnungen** renegotiation *(government contracts).*

Überqueren *n* crossing, traversing, transit across; **unachtsames ~ e–r Kreuzung** jay walking.

überragen *v/i* to surpass, to overreach.

Überraschungs|entscheidung surprise decision; **~gewinne** windfall profits; **~streik** guerilla strike, wildcat strike.

überreden *v/t* to persuade.

Überredung *f* persuasion; **~skunst** art of persuasion; **friedliche ~** peaceful persuasion; **~ zum Selbstmord** procuring suicide.

überregional *adj* supra-regional.

überreichen *v/t* to hand over, to present, to submit; **eigenhändig ~** to hand over personally.

Überreichung *f* presentation.

Überrest *m* remainder, residue.

übersaisonmäßig *adj* more than seasonal, all-year . . .

Übersättigung *f* oversaturation, glut.

Überschallschaden *m* damage caused by sonic booms.
überschätzen *v/t* to overvalue.
Überschicht *f* extra shift.
Überschlagsrechnung *f* rough estimate, approximate calculation.
überschreiben *v/t* to transfer in a register, to transfer by deed, to convey.
Überschreibung *f* transfer in a register, conveyance.
Überschreiten der Geschwindigkeitsgrenze exceeding the speed limit, speeding; ~ **der Grenze** crossing the border.
Überschreitung *f* excess, transgression; ~ **der Amtsbefugnisse** overstepping of one's official powers; ~ **der Notwehr** exceeding the bounds of justifiable self-defence; going beyond self-defence; ~ **der Satzungsbefugnisse** acting ultra vires; ~ **der Vollmacht** exceeding one's powers.
Überschuldung *f* overindebtedness, excess of liabilities over assets.
Überschuß *m* (*pl Überschüsse* ~*e*) surplus, overplus, surplus value, excess; credit balance, balance in hand, net balance; ~**besteuerung** surplus taxes; ~**beteiligung** sharing the surplus, participation in net proceeds; ~**bildung** formation of surpluses; *fiskalische* ~~: *formation of surpluses out of revenue*; ~ **der Leistungsbilanz** surplus on goods and services; ~ **der Zahlungsbilanz** external surplus; ~**einkünfte** (taxable) net income; ~**gebiet** surplus area, area producing a surplus; *landwirtschaftliches* ~~: *agricultural surplus area*; ~**gelder** surplus funds; ~**güter** surplus goods; ~**-Politik** policy of budgeting for a surplus, policy aiming for a surplus; ~**rechnung** net income method; ~**reserve** surplus fund, excess reserve, surplus reserve; ~**wasser** surplus water; ~**wirtschaft** economy of abundance; **mit e-m** ~ **abschließen** to close with a surplus (profit); **rechnerischer** ~ surplus as shown by the accounts.

Überschwerung *f* overburdening (of estate), over-encumbrance.
Übersee|hafen transatlantic harbo(u)r; ~**handel** overseas trade, maritime commerce, sea-borne trade; ~**kabel** transmarine cable; ~**länder** overseas countries; ~**märkte** overseas markets; ~**reise** ocean voyage; ~**transport** overseas shipment, ocean shipment; ~**verpackung** packing for export.
Übersendbarkeit *f* transmissibility.
übersenden *v/t* to send, to transmit, to remit, to forward.
Übersender *m* sender, consignor, remitter, forwarder.
Übersendung *f* transmittal, consignment, remittance; ~**sbericht** prosecution's report upon criminal appeal.
Übersetzer *m* translator; **beeidigter** ~ sworn translator; **freiberuflicher** ~ free-lance translator; **öffentlich bestellter** ~ officially certified translator; **vereidigter** ~ sworn translator.
Übersetzung *f* translation; ~**sdoppel** copies of translation(s); ~**fehler** mistranslation; **sinngetreue** ~ faithful translation; ~**srecht** right of translation; **beglaubigte** ~ certified translation; **maßgebliche** ~ authentic translation; **wörtliche** ~ literal translation.
Übersicherung *f* excessive collateral (for a debt).
Übersicht *f* survey, overall survey, outline; ~**splan** layout plan, general location plan, general survey chart; ~**szeichnung** outline drawing; ~ **über das Vermögen und die Schulden** financial statement of assets and liabilities; **politische** ~ political survey; **statistische** ~ statistical digest; **vergleichende** ~ comparative table, synopsis.
Übersiedler *m|pl* East Germans resettling in West (*or* united) Germany.
Übersiedlungs|beihilfe removal allowance; ~**gut** removal goods; ~**kosten** relocation expenses.

Überspekulation *f* overspeculation, overtrading, undue speculation.

überstaatlich *adj* supra-national; international; supra-governmental.

überstellen *v/t* to remand, to transfer (*prisoners*).

Überstellung *f* transmission (*of prisoner*), remand, rendition.

Übersteuer *f* super-tax, surtax.

überstimmen *v/t* to outvote, to vote down, to override (*a vote or veto*).

Überstunden *f/pl* overtime, excess hours; ~**genehmigung** overtime authorization; ~**tarif** overtime rate; ~**verbot** ban on overtime; ~**vergütung** overtime pay; ~**zuschlag** overtime premium.

übertariflich *adj* above the general wage scale, supra-tariff.

überteuern *v/t* to charge excessive prices, to overcharge, to render too expensive.

Überteuerung *f* overcharge, excessive prices.

Übertrag *m* subtotal carried forward; transfer entry; brought forward; ~ **auf neue Rechnung** brought forward to new account.

übertragbar *adj* transferable, transmissible, assignable; **nicht** ~ non-transferable, non-assignable.

Übertragbarkeit *f* transferability, assignability.

übertragen *v/t* to transfer, to transmit, to convey, to assign, to alienate, to confer, to pass, to transcribe, to post, to negotiate; **käuflich** ~ to transfer by way of sale.

Übertragung *f* transfer, transmission, conveyance, assignment, making-over, transport, alienation, transcription, negotiation; ~ **aus dem Stenogramm** transcript; ~ **der Zuständigkeit** transfer of jurisdiction; ~ **des Urheberrechts** assignment of copyright; ~ **durch letztwillige Verfügung** disposition by will; ~ **e-r Forderung** assignment of a claim; ~ **e-s im Streit befangenen Gegenstandes** transfer of action; ~ **e-s Patents** assignment of a patent; ~ **von Grundstücksrechten** conveyance, common assurance; ~ **von Hoheitsrechten** transfer (*or* surrender) of sovereign rights; ~ **von Zuständigkeiten** conferring of powers; **gesetzliche** ~ conveyance by operation of law; **rechtsgeschäftliche** ~ transfer by a transaction, assignment; **unentgeltliche** ~ gratuitous transfer; **wertpapiermäßige** ~ negotiation.

Übertragungs|**akt** act of transfer; ~**datum** vesting date; ~**erfindung** invention by adaptation; ~**erklärung** act of assignment; ~**formular** transfer form; ~**gebühr** transfer fee; ~**patent** patent of adaptation; ~**urkunde** instrument of transfer, deed of transfer, deed of assignment; vesting deed, deed of grant, bill of sale; ~**verfügung** vesting order; ~**vermerk** transfer entry.

übertreten *v/t* to infringe, to transgress, to violate, to breach.

Übertretung *f* infringement, breach, transgression.

Überversicherung *f* excess insurance, overinsurance.

Übervölkerung *f* overpopulation.

übervorteilen *v/t* to overreach, to take unfair advantage of.

Übervorteilung *f* overreaching, taking unfair advantage.

Überwachung *f* supervision, surveillance, monitoring; superintendence; ~ **der Warenausgänge** inspection of outgoing goods.

Überwachungs|**abteilung** safety engineering department; ~**beamter** supervisor, superintendent; **ü**~**bedürftig** requiring supervision; subject to supervision; ~**befugnis** supervisory power; ~**pflicht** duty of supervision; ~**stelle** control board; ~**vorschriften** technical control regulations.

überwältigen *v/t* to overcome, to overpower, to overwhelm.

überwälzen *v/t* to pass on, to shift (*the tax*), to roll over.

Überwälzung *f* shifting of a tax burden, roll-over relief.

überweisen *v/t* to remit, to transfer, to remand, to assign.

Überweisung *f* remittance, bank-transfer, cashless transfer payments; ~ **auf ein Konto** transfer to an account, remittance to an account; ~ **der gepfändeten Forderung** judicial transfer of garnisheed claim to creditor; ~ **e-r Sache an ein Schiedsgericht** reference to arbitrators; ~ **per Scheck** transfer by cheque, payment by cheque; **telegrafische** ~ telegraphic transfer, remittance by cable, cable transfer; **um** ~ **wird gebeten** please remit.

Überweisungs|abteilung giro money-transfer department; ~**auftrag** order for remittance, transfer order; ~**begleitzettel** remittance slip; ~**beschluß** transfer order, garnish; ~**betrag** amount of the remittance; ~**empfänger** remittee; ~**kredit** transfer credit; ~**möglichkeit** transfer facility; ~**träger** transfer slip; ~**- und Einzugsverkehr** bank payments and collections; ~**verkehr** inter-bank money transfer.

Überwiegen *n* preponderance.

überwiegen *v/i* to outbalance, to outweigh, to prevail.

überwiegend *adj* preponderant, predominant.

Überzahlung *f* excess payment.

überzeichnen *v/t* to over-subscribe, to subscribe in excess.

Überzeichnung *f* over-subscription, excess-application.

überzeugen *v/t* to convince, to persuade, to satisfy (*the court*).

überzeugend *adj* convincing, conclusive; **nicht** ~ unconvincing, inconclusive.

Überzeugung *f* conviction; ~**sfähigkeit** demonstrative force, conclusiveness; ~**skraft** persuasive force, power to convince; ~**stäter** offender convinced by conviction; perpetrator convinced of the rightfulness of his cause; **feste** ~ firm belief; **freie** ~ independent conviction; **vertretbare** ~ reasonable belief; **zur** ~ **des Gerichts** to the satisfaction of the court.

überziehen *v/t* to overdraw.

Überziehung *f* overdrawing, overdraft; ~ **e-s Bankkontos** overdraft (o/d); ~**sklausel** overdraft clause; ~**skredit** overdraft facility, advance on current account; ~**sprovision** overdraft (o/d) commission; ~**zinsen** interest on overdraft.

üblich *adj* usual, customary, ordinary, conventional.

üblicherweise *adv* customarily.

übrig *adj* residuary, residual.

übrigbleibend *adj* residual.

Übung *f* practice, usage.

Ufer|anlieger riparian (owner); ~**anliegerechte** riparian rights; ~**bewohner** riparian resident (*or* inhabitant); ~**geld** pierage; ~**grundstück** riparian tenement; ~**linie** shoreline; ~**staat** littoral state, riparian state.

ultimativ *adv* by way of an ultimatum, categorically.

Ultimatum *n* ultimatum.

Ultimo *m* end of month, the last weekday of the month, month-end closing; ~**abschluß** end-of-month settlement, monthly settlement; ~**abrechnung** end-of-month settlement; ~**abwicklung** end-of-month settlement; ~**anforderung** funds needed for end-of-month settlement; ~**ausgleich** end-of-month adjustment; ~**bedarf** end-of-month requirements; ~**fälligkeit** end-of-month maturity; ~**geld** end-of-month settlement loan; ~**geschäft** transaction for end-of-month settlement; ~**glattstellung** end-of-month position squaring; ~**kurs** end-of-month stock-exchange rate; ~**liquidation** end-of-month settlement; ~**regulierung** end-of-month settlement; **per** ~ for the monthly settlement.

umadressieren *v/t* to redirect, to re-consign, to re-address.

Umadressierung *f* redirection, reconsignment, re-addressing.

umarbeiten *v/t* to rework.

Umbau *m* rebuilding, reconstruction, recasting.

umbenennen v/t to rename, to redesignate.
Umbenennung f change of name, redesignation.
umbilden v/t to recast, to reshuffle, to reorganize.
Umbildung f reform, transformation, reshuffle (of cabinet).
umbringen v/t to kill, to put to death.
Umbruch m radical change.
umbuchen v/t to change a reservation; to change a bookkeeping entry; to transfer to a different account.
Umbuchung f change in reservation; transfer of an entry, book transfer.
umdatieren v/t to change the date.
umdeuten v/t to give a different interpretation, to reinterpret.
Umdeutung f change of meaning by a different interpretation (of); reinterpretation; equitable conversion (*of void transaction into valid one*).
umdirigieren v/t to reconsign, to redirect.
umdisponieren v/t to redispose, to alter the disposition, to make new arrangements.
Umdisposition f redisposition, rearrangement, rescheduling.
Umfang m extent, range, volume, coverage; ~ **der Haftung** extent of liability; ~ **der Vollmacht** scope of power, extent of a power-of-attorney; ~ **des Schadens** extent of the damage; ~ **des Verschuldens** extent of the fault; ~ **e-r Versicherung** coverage of a policy; ~ **e-s Patents** scope of a patent; **in vollem** ~ in its entirety, in full.
umfassen v/t to comprise, to include to cover.
Umfassungsmauer f enclosing wall.
Umfeldverschmutzung f pollution of the environment.
umfinanzieren v/t to refinance, to roll over.
Umfinanzierung f refinancing, conversion of debts, refunding, debt rescheduling rollover.
umfirmieren v/t to change the firm's (*or* company's) name.

Umfirmierung f change of a firm's (*or* company's) name.
umflaggen v/i to reflag.
Umflaggen n reflagging.
umformulieren v/t to rephrase, to redraft, to restate, to reword.
Umformulierung f rephrasing, redrafting, restatement.
Umfrage f general inquiry, opinion poll; ~**ergebnis** survey data; ~**teilnehmer** poll respondent; **statistische** ~ statistical inquiry.
umfriedet adj enclosed, fenced in.
Umfriedung f enclosure, fence.
Umgang m access to (see) a child; ~**sberechtigter** person entitled to have access to a child; ~**srecht** right of access (to children); visitation rights; ~**sregelung** regulation (*or* arrangment) of access to a child; ~**sverbot** prohibition to contact a child.
Umgebungsschutz m environmental protection (*of cultural monument*).
umgehen v/t to circumvent.
umgehend adj immediate, adv forthwith.
Umgehung f circumvention, elusion, evasion; ~**sgeschäft** transaction for the purpose of evading a law; ~**sverbot** ban of circumvention, prohibition of evasion.
Umgehungsstraße f bypass.
umgemeinden v/t to transfer a (*part of a*) *local community to a neighbouring one*, to reallocate a local community or part thereof.
Umgemeindung f redistribution of local authorities, reallocation of local communities (*or parts thereof*).
Umgesiedelte pl resettled persons.
Umgestaltung f change, restructuring.
umgliedern v/t to rearrange, to reallocate, to change the organizational structure.
Umgliederung f rearrangement, reallocation, change of organizational structure.
umgrenzen v/t to border, to enclose.
Umgrenzung f enclosure, boundary.
umgründen v/t to convert to a different legal form, to reorganize.

Umgründung *f* conversion to another (corporate) form, reorganization.

Umgruppierung *f* regrouping.

Umhüllung *f* wrapping, packaging.

Umkehr *f* reversal; ~ **der Beweislast** reversal of the burden of proof; **~schluß** argumentum e contrario.

Umlade|gebühren reloading charges; **~konossement** trans-shipment bill of lading; **~platz** transfer point, rehandling yard; **~schuppen** trans-shipment shed; **~station** transfer station.

umladen *v/t* to reload, to trans-ship.

Umlage *f* (special) assessment, levy, (cost-covering) contribution; **~beschluß** resolution imposing an assessment; **~kasse** assessment (insurance) company; **u~pflichtig** *adj* assessable, subject to contribution; *nicht ~~: non-assessable*; **~satz** rate of contribution; **~schlüssel** assessment formula; **~schuldner** assessee; **~verfahren** (adjustable) contribution procedure, assessment system; **rückständige ~n** delinquent special assessments; **zweckgebundene ~** special assessment, earmarked assessment.

Umlauf *m* circulation; "please circulate"; **u~fähig** *adj* fit for circulation, marketable, negotiable; **~fähigkeit** negotiability, negotiable character; **~fonds** revolving fund; **~kapital** floating capital, active capital; circulating capital; **~mittel** circulating media; **~sgeld** current money; **~(s)geschwindigkeit** velocity of circulation, rate of turnover, income velocity; **~verfahren** circularizing; **~vermögen** current assets, revolving assets, working capital, operating assets, floating assets, current receivables; **~zeit** period for turnaround, turn-around time; **im ~** in circulation, afloat; **im ~ befindlich** outstanding, in circulation; **in ~ bringen** to put into circulation, to circulate, to market.

umlegen *v/t* (*1*) to apportion, to assess; to regroup, to reclassify.

umlegen *v/t* (*2*) to kill instantly, to shoot to death; *sl* to bump off.

Umlegung *f* reapportionment, regrouping, passing on, transfer; real estate amalgamation and reapportioning; ~ **der Mehrkosten** apportionment of additional costs; **~sausschuß** assessment committee.

umleiten *v/t* to divert, to redirect.

Umleitung *f* detour, diverted, traffic, reconsignment, siphoning (off).

Ummeldung *f* registration of one's new address, re-registration (of address).

umplazieren *v/t* to place afresh, to reallocate, to re-place.

Umplazierung *f* reallocation.

umprogrammieren *v/t* to rearrange the programme, to re-programme.

Umprogrammierung *f* rearrangement of the programme.

Umrandung *f* frame; **fette ~** thick frame, heavy frame.

umrechnen *v/t* to convert, to recalculate, to re-reckon.

Umrechnung *f* conversion, recalculation, translation.

Umrechnungs|kurs rate of exchange, parity (of exchange), conversion rate; *nomineller ~~: nominal exchange*; **~satz** conversion ratio, rate of conversion; **~tabelle** conversion table; **~verhältnis** ratio of conversion, exchange ratio.

Umsatz *n* (*pl Umsätze; ~e*) turnover, volume of trade, sales, trading; **~ausfall** loss of sales; **~ausgleichssteuer** turnover equalization tax; **~belebung** increase in turnover, business pick-up; **~besteuerung** taxation of turnover; **~beteiligung** commission on turnover, participation in sales; **~bonus** deferred rebate (based on turnover); **~e im Dienstleistungsbereich** turnover in services; **~e im Großhandel** wholesale trading; **~erlös(e)** sales, proceeds from turnover; **~gebühr** turnover charge; **~geschwindigkeit** trading pace; **~häufigkeit**

Umsatzsteuer

rate of turnover; **~kapazität** sales capacity; **u~los** *adj* without sales; **~lizenz** licence based on turnover; **~pacht** percentage lease; **~prämie** sales premium; **~provision** turnover commission; **~quote** turnover ratio; **~rückgang** drop in sales, slump in sales; **~schwund** falling off in turnover; **~statistik** sales statistics; **~steigerung** increase in turnover, sales increase; **~steuer** → *Umsatzsteuer*; **~volumen** sales volume; **~verlagerung** shifting of sales, switch(ing) in turnover; **fingierter ~** fictitious sales; **gute ~e** brisk sales; **interner ~** intercompany sales; **konzerninterner ~** intercompany sales; **„ohne ~"** no sales; **schwache ~e** light trading; **steuerbarer ~** taxable turnover; **steuerfreie ~e** exempted supplies; **steuerpflichtiger ~** taxable turnover; **tauschähnlicher ~** quasi-barter transaction; **unsichtbare ~e** invisible transactions; **volkswirtschaftliche ~e** the country's total turnover.

Umsatzsteuer *f* turnover tax, value-added tax; (*loosely:*) sales tax, purchase tax; **~ abwälzen** to pass on value-added tax *to the customer (as part of the price)*; **~ auf Güter des gehobenen Bedarfs** purchase tax; **~befreiung** exemption from turnover tax; **~bescheid** turnover-tax notice; **~-Durchführungsbestimmung** Turnover Tax Regulation; **~erklärung** turnover-tax return; **~erstattung** rebate of turnover tax; **~freiheit** exemption from turnover tax; **~gesetz** Turnover Tax Act; Value Added Tax Act; **~ im Einzelhandel** retail sales tax; **~; nicht inbegriffen** turnover net of tax; **~pflicht** turnover tax liability; **~rückvergütung** turnover-tax refund; **~vergütung** turnover-tax refund; **~-Verordnung** Turnover Tax Regulation; **~voranmeldung** turnover-tax advance return.

umschichten *v/t* to regroup, to shift.
Umschichtung *f* reapportionment, shifting, regroupment, restructuring.

Umschlag *m* transshipment, turn-round handling (of goods); **~bahnhof** marshalling yard, trans-shipment terminal; **~hafen** port of trans-shipment; **~platz** distribution centre, trans-shipment point; **~sfirma** trans-shipping firm; **~sgeschwindigkeit** turnover rate, speed of turnover; **~shäufigkeit** turnover (ratio), turnover frequency; **~sort** place of trans-shipment; **~sspesen** handling charges; **~verkehr** trans-shipment business.

umschreiben *v/t* to transcribe, to change a register entry, to amend.
Umschreibung *f* transcription, change of registration; **~sgebühr** transfer duty, re-registration charge.

umschulden *v/t* to refinance, to refund, to roll over, to reschedule a debt, to transfer debt to another debtor (or lender).
Umschuldung debt refunding, debt rescheduling, debt restructuring, debt renegotiation, debt conversion; **~saktion** debt restructuring operation; **~sanleihe** rescheduling funding loan, funding bonds; **~skredit** refunding credit; **längerfristige ~** conversion into medium-term debt.

Umschüler *m* vocational retrainee.
Umschulung *f* occupational retraining, vocational adjustment; **~sprogramm** vocational retraining scheme.

Umschwung *m* reversal, swing back, backlash, landslide.
umseitig *adj, adv* overleaf.
Umsetzung *f* transfer of duties, transfer to a different position.
Umsicht *f* discretion, circumspection, prudence, care.
umsichtig *adj* prudent, circumspect.
Umsiedler *m* resettler, resettled person; *ethnic German transferred from German-occupied territory by German authories during 2nd World War and resettled elsewhere.*

Umsiedlung *f* resettlement.
Umsiedlungs|aktion resettlement scheme; **~beihilfe** resettlement allowance; **~gebiet** resettlement territory.
Umstand *m* (*pl Umstände*: ~*e*) circumstance, factor; **außergewöhnliche ~e** exceptional circumstances; **belastende ~e** aggravating circumstances, aggravation; **besondere ~e** particular circumstances; **den ~en nach annehmen** to have reasonable grounds to assume; **den jeweiligen ~en nach** as the circumstances may require; **erschwerende ~c** aggravating circumstances; **je nach den ~en** according to circumstances, as the case may be; **mildernde ~e** extenuating circumstances, mitigating circumstances; **~ ~ zubilligen**: to allow extenuating circumstances; **nähere ~e** particulars, details; **schadenersatzerhöhende ~e** aggravation of damages; **sich aus den ~en ergeben** to arise from the facts and circumstances; **strafmildernde ~e vortragen** to plead in mitigation; **strafverschärfende ~e** aggravation, aggravated circumstances; **unter den obwaltenden ~en** under the prevailing circumstances; **unter sonst gleichbleibenden ~en** other things being equal; **unvorhergesehene ~e** unforeseen circumstances; **versicherungswichtiger ~** material representation.
Umsteige|karte transfer ticket; **~verbindung** connection.
umstellen *v/t* to convert, to change over, to recalculate, to translate.
Umstellung *f* change, conversion, currency conversion, reorganization.
Umstellungs|bestand post-conversion total; **~betrag** amount resulting from conversion; **~bilanz** (post)-conversion balance sheet; **~gewinn** profit resulting from (currency) conversion; **~gesetz** Currency Conversion Act (*Reichsmark to D-Mark 1948*);

~grundschuld (currency) conversion land charge; **~kosten** conversion costs; **~kredit** loan to finance currency conversion burdens; **~maßnahme** measure for readjustment; **~rechnung** conversion account; **~sachen** currency conversion litigation; **~satz** conversion rate; **~schwierigkeiten** transitional problems; **~tag** date of currency conversion.
umstrukturieren *v/t* to reorganize, to restructure, to revamp, to reshape.
Umstrukturierung *f* restructuring, reconstruction, reorganization.
umstufen *v/t* to regrade, to change the classification, to upgrade.
Umstufung *f* regrading.
umstürzlerisch *adj* subversive.
Umtausch *m* exchange; conversion; **~ nicht gestattet** no goods exchanged; **~vorbehalt** subject to change, exchange proviso; **~ zum Nennwert** conversion at nominal value; **kein ~** all sales final.
Umtausch|aktion conversion operation, conversion scheme; **~obligationen** refunding bonds, redemption bonds; **~recht** option of exchange, right to exchange; conversion right; **~stück** security given in exchange; **~transaktion** conversion operation; **~verhältnis** exchange rate.
umtauschbar *adj* convertible, exchangeable.
Umtriebe *m/pl* subversive activities; machinations, intrigues; **staatsfeindliche ~** subversive activities.
umverteilen *v/t* to redistribute (*property*).
Umverteilung *f* redistribution, income redistribution; **~sbesteuerung** redistributive taxation.
umwandeln *v/t* to commute, to convert, to transform.
Umwandlung *f* transformation, conversion, commutation, change of corporate form; merger, absorption; **formwechselnde ~** conversion of form; **steuerbegünstigte ~** tax-privileged reorganization;

779

Umwandlungsantrag

übertragende ~ reorganization of a company involving a take-over.
Umwandlungs|antrag application for permission to change (the corporate form); **~gebühr** *pat* conversion fee; **~klausel** convertibility clause; **~recht** conversion right; **~steuergesetz** (*D 1976*) Mergers and Reorganization Tax Act; **~stichtag** effective date of conversion.
Umweg *m* detour, indirect way.
Umwelt|bundesamt Federal Environmental Agency; **~-Altlasten** pollution caused by previous owner (*or* administration); **~einflüsse** environmental influences; **~fragen** environmental affairs; **u~freundlich** non-polluting, environmentally friendly (*or* benign); **~haftpflicht** statutory liability for environmental damage; **~haftung** environmental liability; **~kriminalität** offences involving environmental damage; **~politik** environmental policy; **~schäden** environmental damage; **~schutz** environmental protection; environmental control; **~strafrecht** environmental penal law; **~verschmutzung** environmental pollution; *grenzüberschreitende* ~~: cross-frontier (*or: transboudary*) pollution; **~verträglichkeitsprüfung** environmental impact assessment, examination of environmental acceptability.
umwerten *v/t* to revalue, to convert; **im Verhältnis 1:2** ~ to convert in the ratio 1:2.
Umzäunung *f* fence, enclosure.
Umzugs|beihilfe removal allowance, relocation allowance, relocation benefits, relocation package; **~gut** removal goods, household effects in transit; **~kosten** removal costs, relocation expenses; **~kostenbeihilfe** = ~*beihilfe qv*; **~kostenentschädigung** compensation for transfer (to new location).
unabdingbar *adj* unalterable, indispensable, not subject to change, absolute, categorical, mandatory.

Unanfechtbarkeit

Unabdingbarkeit *f* unchangeability, absoluteness.
unabhängig *adj* independent, self-supporting, separate.
Unabhängiger *m* (*der Unabhängige*) independent person, self-employed; **finanziell** ~ person of independent means.
Unabhängigkeit *f* independence; **~ der Gerichte** independence of the courts; **~serklärung** Declaration of Independence (*US: 1776*); **richterliche** ~ judicial independence; **wirtschaftliche** ~ economic independence, self-sufficiency.
unabkömmlich *adj* indispensable, in a reserved occupation, exempt from military service due to profession or occupation.
Unabkömmlichkeit *f* indispensability; **~sstellung** exemption from military service due to profession or occupation; **~sverfahren** *proceedings for exemption from military duty due to indispensability*; **berufliche** ~ occupational deferment, reserved occupation.
unablösbar *adj* irredeemable.
unabsetzbar *adj* irremovable; non-deductible (tax).
unabsichtlich *adj* unintentional, accidental.
unabtretbar *adj* not transferable, non-assignable.
Unabtretbarkeit *f* non-assignability, non-transferability; **~svereinbarung** covenant against assignment.
unabweisbar *adj* irrefusable, absolutely necessary; unobjectionable, irrefutable.
unabwendbar *adj* inevitable.
Unabwendbarkeit *f* inevitability.
unachtsam *adj* careless, inadvertent; inattentive, heedless.
Unachtsamkeit *f* carelessness, inattention, inadvertence, heedlessness.
unanfechtbar *adj* non-appealable; non-contestable (*insurance*).
Unanfechtbarkeit *f* res judicata, non-appealability; incontestability (*insurance*); **~sklausel** incontestable clause, non-contestable clause.

unangebracht inappropriate, unsuitable, inapposite.

unangefochten *adj* unchallenged.

unangemessen *adj* unsuitable, inappropriate, unreasonable, unfair.

Unangemessenheit *f* unsuitability, inappropriateness, unreasonableness.

unangreifbar *adj* unchallengeable, indefeasible, incontestable.

unannehmbar *adj* unacceptable.

unanständig *adj* indecent, obscene.

Unanständigkeit *f* indecency, obscenity.

unantastbar *adj* irreproachable, untouchable, inviolable.

unanwendbar *adj* inapplicable.

Unanwendbarkeit *f* inapplicability.

unaufgefordert *adj* unsolicited, unrequested, unsummoned.

unaufhebbar *adj* indefeasible, non-repealable.

Unaufklärbarkeit *f* impossibility to clear up a matter.

unauflöslich *adj* indissolvable, insoluble.

unaufmerksam *adj* inattentive, inadvertent.

Unaufmerksamkeit *f* inattentiveness, inadvertence.

unaufschiebbar *adj* unpostponable; unreprievable (*execution of death sentence*), non-reprievable.

Unaufschiebbarkeit *f* inpostponability, impossibility of postponement.

unausführbar *adj* impracticable.

Unausführbarkeit *f* impracticability.

unausgefüllt *adj* unfilled, blank.

unausgeglichen *adj* unsettled (*bill, account*).

unausgenutzt *adj* idle, not sufficiently used, unused.

unausgeschüttet *adj* undistributed.

unausgewogen *adj* unbalanced.

Unausgewogenheit *f* imbalance, disequilibrium.

unauslöschlich *adj* indelible.

unbar *adj* cashless.

unbeabsichtigt *adj* inadvertent, unintentional.

unbeanstandet *adj* unopposed, not objected to, unchallenged; ~ **lassen** to pass, not to object to.

unbebaut *adj* unbuilt (on), undeveloped, vacant.

unbedacht *adj* thoughtless, indiscreet, improvident.

Unbedachtsamkeit *f* inadvertency, indiscretion, improvidence.

unbedenklich *adj* unobjectionable.

Unbedenklichkeitsbescheinigung *f* clearance certificate, certificate of non-objection, negative clearance certificate.

unbedingt *adj* unconditional, unreserved, absolute, imperative.

unbeeidigt *adj* unsworn.

unbefangen *adj* unbiassed, unprejudiced, objective.

unbefristet *adj* unlimited, for an unlimited period, for an indefinite period of time.

unbefugt *adj* unauthorized, without authority.

Unbefugter *m* (*der Unbefugte*) unauthorized person.

unbegeben *adj* unissued.

unbeglaubigt *adj* unauthenticated, unattested.

unbeglichen *adj* unsatisfied, undischarged, unpaid, unsettled.

unbegründet *adj* unfounded.

Unbegründetheit *f* unfoundedness, lack of merit, implausibility.

unbehelligt *adj* unmolested, scotfree.

unbehoben *adj* unclaimed; unremedied.

Unbekannter (*der Unbekannte*) unknown person.

unbelastet *adj* unencumbered, uncharged; **politisch** ~ politically clear.

unbenannt *adj* innominate, undesignated.

unbenommen *adj* unrestrained, free; *es ist Ihnen* ~: *you are at liberty* ...

unbenutzt *adj* unused, unoccupied, dormant.

unbeobachtet *adj* unobserved, unwitnessed, not noticed.

unberechenbar *adj* incalculable.

Unberechenbarkeit *f* incalculability.

unberechtigt *adj*, unjustified, unentitled, unauthorized, unwarranted.

unbereinigt *adj* unadjusted, unsettled.
unberücksichtigt *adj* unconsidered, disregarded, neglected.
unberührt *adj* (1) unaffected; ~ *von diesem Gesetz bleiben die Vorschriften* ...: nothing in this Act shall affect the provisions of ...
unberührt *adj* (2) chaste, virgin.
Unberührtheit *f* virginity.
unbeschadet *prep* notwithstanding, irrespective of, without affecting, without prejudice to, not in derogation of, saving.
unbeschädigt *adj* undamaged, intact.
unbeschäftigt *adj* unemployed, out of work, idle, jobless.
unbescholten *adj* unblemished, chaste, blameless.
Unbescholtenheit *f* chastity; integrity, good name.
unbeschränkt *adj* unrestricted, unlimited, unqualified.
unbesehen *adj* without previous examination, without inspection.
unbesetzt *adj* vacant, not occupied.
unbesichert *adj* unsecured.
unbesoldet *adj* unsalaried, unpaid.
unbestätigt *adj* unconfirmed.
unbestechlich *adj* incorruptible, unbribable, honest, upright.
Unbestechlichkeit incorruptibility.
unbestellbar *adj* non-deliverable.
Unbestellbarkeit *f* non-deliverability; **~smeldung** advice of non-delivery.
unbesteuert *adj* untaxed.
unbestimmbar *adj* indeterminable, indefinable.
Unbestimmbarkeit *f* uncertainty, indefiniteness, incalculability, indeterminable nature.
unbestimmt *adj* indefinite, indeterminate, unascertained, unliquidated.
Unbestimmtheit *f* indefiniteness, vagueness, uncertainty.
unbestraft *adj* unpunished, not previously convicted, without any previous convictions.
unbestreitbar *adj* undeniable, incontestable, indisputable, beyond dispute.
unbestritten *adj* undisputed, uncontested, uncontended.
unbeteiligt *adj* unconcerned, indifferent; not involved.
unbeweglich *adj* immovable.
unbewiesen *adj* unproved, not proven.
unbewohnbar *adj* uninhabitable.
unbewohnt *adj* unoccupied, uninhabited.
Unbewohntsein *n* vacancy, unoccupancy.
unbewußt *adj* unaware, unwitting, involuntary, unjust, unreasonable.
unbezahlt *adj* unpaid.
unbeziffert *adj* non-enumerated, unliquidated.
unbillig *adj* inequitable.
Unbilligkeit *f* inequity; **grobe ~** gross inequity.
unbotmäßig *adj* recalcitrant.
Unbotmäßigkeit *f* insubordination, recalcitrance.
unbrauchbar *adj* useless, unsuitable.
Unbrauchbarkeit *f* uselessness, inapplicability, unsuitability.
Unbrauchbarmachung *f* rendering unservicable, wreckage; denaturation.
Undank *m* ingratitude; **grober ~** gross ingratitude, ungratefulness.
undatiert *adj* undated, not dated.
undelegierbar *adj* non-delegable.
Und-Konto *n* joint account.
undurchführbar *adj* impracticable, not feasible.
Undurchführbarkeit *f* impracticability, non-feasibility.
undurchsetzbar *adj* unenforceable.
unecht *adj* not genuine, false, spurious.
Unechtheit *f* ungenuineness, falseness, spuriousness.
unehelich *adj* illegitimate; **~ geboren** born out of wedlock.
Unehelichkeit *f* illegitimacy.
unehrlich *adj* dishonest.
Unehrlichkeit *f* dishonesty.
uneidlich *adj* unsworn.
uneigennützig *adj* disinterested, altruistic, selfless.
Uneigennützigkeit *f* disinterestedness, altruism.

uneigentlich *adj* not in the proper sense, figurative.
uneinbringlich *adj* uncollectible, irrecoverable.
Uneinbringlichkeit *f* impossibility of collection.
uneingelöst *adj* uncollected, unredeemed, dishonoured.
uneingeschränkt *adj* unrestricted, unqualified.
uneinheitlich *adj* non-uniform, irregular.
Uneinheitlichkeit *f* lack of uniformity.
uneinig *adj* disunited, at variance.
Uneinigkeit *f* disunity, disagreement, discord.
uneinklagbar *adj* unenforceable, not actionable.
uneinlösbar *adj* irredeemable.
uneinträglich *adj* unremunerative, unprofitable.
uneintreibbar *adj* uncollectible, irrecoverable.
unentgeltlich *adj* gratuitous, free, without payment, free of charge.
Unentgeltlichkeit *f* gratuitousness.
unentschieden *adj* undecided, pending, in limbo.
unentschuldbar *adj* inexcusable.
unentschuldigt *adj* unexcused, without reasonable excuse, without valid excuse.
unerfüllbar *adj* unrealizable, impossible.
unerfüllt *adj* unfulfilled, unperformed.
unerheblich *adj* immaterial, irrelevant; **rechtlich ~ für die Entscheidung** irrelevant to the issue.
Unerheblichkeit *f* irrelevancy.
unerhoben *adj* unclaimed, unlevied.
unerläßlich *adj* indispensable.
unerlaubt *adj* not permitted, illicit, illegal, unauthorized.
unerledigt *adj* undisposed of, unfinished, outstanding, undischarged (*debt*), unsettled, unfinished, pending.
Unerledigtes *n* unfinished business.
unerreichbar *adj* unattainable, unachievable, inaccessible, unavailable (*witness*), beyond reach of a summons.

unerschlossen *adj* undeveloped.
Unersetzbarkeit *f* irreplaceableness, irretrievability, uniqueness.
unersetzlich *adj* irreplaceable, irretrievable.
unersitzbar *adj* imprescriptible.
Unersitzbarkeit *f* imprescriptibility.
unerträglich *adj* intolerable, unbearable, insufferable.
unerwachsen *adj* minor.
Unerreichbarkeit *f* inaccessibility, unattainability; *witness:* unavailability.
unerwiesen *adj* unproved, unproven, not established by evidence.
Unerwiesenheit *f* unproveness, lack of proof.
unfachmännisch *adj* unskilled, unprofessional.
unfähig *adj* incapable, unable, unfit, not qualified, ineligible; **~ zur Bekleidung e-s Richteramtes** not qualified to hold judicial office.
Unfähigkeit *f* incapacity, incapability, inability, unfitness, ineligibility; **~ der Amtsausübung** inability to act in an officialcapacity; **~ zur Bekleidung e-s öffentlichen Amtes** disqualification from holding public office.
Unfall *m* accident (= *acc*), misadventure; **~abteilung** emergency ward (for *acc–s*); **~ am Arbeitsplatz** *acc* at work; **u~anfällig** *adj acc*-prone; **~anzeige** reporting an *acc*, notification of an *acc*; **~ausgleich** compensation for an *acc*; **~ außerhalb der Arbeitszeit** off-the-job *acc*; **~bericht** *acc* record; **~beteiligter** person involved in an *acc*; **~ durch Übermüdung** fatigue *acc*; **~(s)entschädigung** compensation for *acc–s*, *acc* indemnity, *acc* benefit; **~ereignis** occurrence of the *acc*; **~fahrer** driver involved in an *acc*; **~flucht** leaving the scene of an *acc*, absconding after an *acc*, hit-and-run driving; **u~frei** *adj acc*-free; **~fürsorge** *acc* welfare work; **u~gefährdet** *adj acc*-prone; **~haftpflicht** legal liability for *acc–s*; **~häufigkeit** *acc* frequency; **~hinterbliebenenversorgung** care for

unfertig

surviving dependants of *acc* victims; ~**last** burdens of an *acc*; ~**meldung** notice of *acc*; ~ **mit Todesfolge** fatal *acc*, *acc* resulting in death; ~**neigung** *acc* proneness; ~**neurose** *acc* psychosis; ~**opfer** *acc* victim; ~**ort** place (*or* scene) of *acc*; *acc* scene; ~**reaktion** traumatic reaction; ~**rente** *acc* injury benefit, *acc* annuity, periodical payments (as compensation) for an *acc*; ~**risiko** *acc* hazard, *acc* risk; ~**ruhegehalt** retirement pension due to an *acc*; ~**schaden** *acc* damage; ~**schilderung** statement about the *acc*; ~**schutz** protection against *acc*–*s*; ~**sstätte** place of *acc*; ~**station** first aid post; ~**statistik** *acc* statistics; ~**stelle** site (*or* scene) of an *acc*, *acc* scene; ~**(s)tod** accidental death, death by *acc*; ~**- und Berufskrankheitsversicherung** *acc* and occupational disease insurance schemes; ~**untersuchung** *acc* investigation; ~**ursache** cause of (the) *acc*; ~**ursachenforschung** *acc* analysis (research); ~**verhütung** *acc* prevention, prevention of *acc*–*s*; ~**- ~svorschriften**: regulations for prevention of *acc*–*s*; ~**verletzter** person injured by an *acc*; ~**(s)verletzung** injury by *acc*; ~**vermeidung** *acc* avoidance; ~**versicherung** personal *acc* insurance, casualty insurance, public *acc* insurance; ~**versicherungspflicht** compulsory *acc* insurance; ~**versicherungsträger** organization in charge of *acc* insurance; ~**verzeichnis** list of *acc*–*s*; ~**(s)zeit** time of *acc*; ~**zeuge** witness to an *acc*; ~**ziffer** *acc* frequency rate; **auf Ermüdung zurückzuführender** ~ *acc* due to fatigue; **außerbetrieblicher** ~ non-occupational *acc*; private *acc*, off-the-job *acc*; **dienstlicher** ~ *acc* while on official duty; **e–n** ~ **abwenden** to avert an *acc*; **entschädigungspflichtiger** ~ *acc* entitling to compensation; **fingierter** ~ simulated *acc*; **inszenierter** ~a staged *acc*; **selbstverschuldeter** ~ ~ *acc* due to one's own fault; **tödlicher** ~ fatal *acc*;

784

Ungerechtigkeit

unabwendbarer ~ unavoidable *acc*.
unfertig *ad*, unfinished, incomplete.
unfrankiert *adj* unstamped.
unfrei *adj* unfree, not free, covenanted; not prepaid (letter).
unfreiwillig *adj* involuntary.
Unfrieden *m* discord, trouble.
Unfug *m* mischief, nuisance; **grober** ~ public mischief, vandalism, common nuisance, public nuisance.
unfundiert *adj* unsubstantiated, unconsolidated, floating.
ungeachtet notwithstanding, regardless of, irrespective of, despite, in spite of.
ungeahndet *adj* unpunished.
ungeboren *adj* unborn, en ventre sa mère.
Ungeborener (*m, der Ungeborene*) unborn person.
Ungebühr *f* impropriety, misconduct; ~ **vor Gericht** misbehaviour in court, contempt of court.
ungebührlich *adj* improper, unseemly, disorderly.
ungebunden *adj* uncommitted, not earmarked free, not tied.
ungedeckt *adj* unsecured, uncovered.
ungeeignet *adj* unsuitable, unsuited, unfit, inappropriate.
Ungeeignetheit *f* unsuitability, unfitness, improvidence, inappropriateness.
ungeheuerlich *adj* monstrous, atrocious.
ungehörig *adj* improper.
Ungehörigkeit *f* impropriety.
Ungehorsam *m* disobedience, failure to obey, insubordination; ~**sfolgen** consequences of insubordination; **ziviler** ~ civil disobedience.
ungehorsam *adj* disobedient, nonobservant.
ungelernt *adj* unskilled.
ungelöscht *adj* undischarged, not deregistered, not removed from the register, not deleted.
ungerecht *adj* unjust.
ungerechtfertigt *adj* unjustified.
Ungerechtigkeit *f* injustice; **grobe** ~ gross injustice.

ungeregelt *adj* unregulated, uncontrolled, unofficial.

ungeschehen *adj* undone; ~ **machen**: *to undo, to make sth undone.*

ungeschmälert *adj* uncurtailed, unimpaired.

ungeschoren *adj* unpunished, scot-free.

ungesetzlich *adj* illegal, unlawful.

Ungesetzlichkeit *f* illegality, unlawfulness.

ungesetzmäßig *adj* contrary to law, unlawful, illegal.

ungesiegelt *adj* unsealed.

ungestört *adj* undisturbed, *adv (also:)* peaceably and quietly.

ungestraft *adj* unpunished, with impunity.

ungesühnt *adj* unatoned, unpunished, unexpiated.

ungesund *adj* unhealthy, unwholesome.

ungeteilt *adj* undivided.

ungiriert *adj* without endorsement.

unglaubwürdig *adj* untrustworthy, incredible, unbelievable.

Unglaubwürdigkeit *f* incredibility, untrustworthiness.

Ungleichgewicht *n* disequilibrium, imbalance; **regionale ~e** regional imbalances; **wirtschaftliches ~** economic imbalance.

Ungleichheit *f* inequality; ~ **der Bildungschancen** inequality of educational opportunities.

Unglücksfall *n* misfortune, misadventure, accident.

Ungnade *f* disgrace, disfavour.

ungültig *adj* invalid, ineffective; ~ **machen** to invalidate, to vitiate, to obliterate, to set aside; ~ **wegen Unklarheit** void due to uncertainty; **für ~ erklären** to cancel, to invalidate, to rescind.

Ungültigkeit *f* invalidity; **~serklärung** invalidation, cancellation, annulment, avoidance; ~ **wegen Formmangels** voidness due to lack of prescribed form.

unhaltbar *adj* untenable, indefensible.

unheilbar *adj* incurable.

Uniformträger person in uniform; **~verbot** ban on (political) uniforms.

Unikat *n* sole original, unique (thing).

uninteressiert *adj* unconcerned, uninterested.

Unionsland member country of a union; **~parteien** union parties; *esp D: the Christian Democratic parties*; **~priorität** union priority.

Universalbank all-purpose bank, full-services bank, all-round bank; **~beschluß** unanimous resolution of all condominium owners; **~erbe** universal heir, universal legatee; sole heir; **~erbschaft** universal inheritance, universal legacy; **~sukzession** universal succession, universal representation; **~vermächtnis** universal legacy; **~verpfändung** blanket mortgage, general mortgage; **~versammlung** full general meeting; **~versicherung** comprehensive insurance, all-risks policy; **~vollmacht** universal agency, universal power of attorney.

Universitätsabschluß university degree; **~bildung** university education; **~laufbahn** university career; **~satzung** university statutes; **~verwaltung** university administration.

unkaufmännisch *adj* unbusinesslike.

unkenntlich *adj* unidentifiable, disfigured; ~ **machen** to deface, to obliterate.

Unkenntlichmachen *n* = *Unkenntlichmachung qv.*

Unkenntlichmachung *f* obliteration, spoliation.

Unkenntnis *f* ignorance; ~ **des Gesetzes** ignorance of the law; *sich auf ~ ~ ~ berufen: to plead ignorance of the law*; ~ **des Gesetzes schützt vor Strafe nicht** ignorance of the law is no defence; ~ **tatsächlicher Art** ignorance of fact; ~ **von Tatumständen** ignorance of the existence of factual circumstances; **fahrlässige ~** negligent ignorance; **schuldhafte ~** voluntary ignorance, culpable ignorance.

unkeusch *adj* unchaste.
Unkeuschheit *f* unchastity, lack of chastity.
unklagbar *adj* non-actionable.
Unklagbarkeit *f* non-actionability; ~ **von Eheversprechen** unenforeability of promise to marry.
unklar *adj* unclear, obscure, blurred, ambiguous.
Unklarheit *f* lack of clarity, ambiguity, uncertainty.; **~enregel** rule concerning uncertainty (*in pleading, documents*).
unkompensiert *adj* not compensated, unadjusted, unoffset (*balance sheet*).
unkonvertierbar *adj* unconvertible.
unkonzessioniert *adj* unlicensed, non-licensed.
unkörperlich *adj* incorporeal, immaterial; spiritual.
Unkosten *pl* expense(s), outlay; **~anfall** incurrence of expense; ~ **bestreiten** to defray (the) expenses, to bear the expense; **~beteiligung** sharing expenses; **~beitrag** contribution to the expenses; **~belege** expense vouchers; ~ **haben** to incur expenses; **~konto** expense account; ~ **niedrig halten** to control expenses, to keep down the expense; **~satz** expense ratio; **~spezifizierung** breakdown of expenses; ~ **umlegen** to apportion expenses, to divide expenses, to assess expenses; **~vergütung** reimbursement of expenses; **~verteilung** allocation of expenses; **abzugsfähige** ~ deductible expenses; **allgemeine** ~ overhead expenses, overheads; **bleibende** ~ basic expenditure, overhead expenses; **feste** ~ fixed costs, overhead expenses; **laufende** ~ current expenses; **sich** ~ **machen** to go to expense.
unkündbar *adj* non-cancellable, non-callable, non-redeemable, irredeemable, not subject to termination.
unkundig *adj* unacquainted, without knowledge, ignorant.
unlauter *adj* dishonest, unfair.
unleserlich *adj* illegible.

unleugbar *adj* undeniable.
unlöschbar *adv* indelibly.
unmerklich *adj* imperceptible, gradual.
unmißverständlich *adj* unmistakable, blunt.
unmittelbar *adj* direct, immediate; ~ **bevorstehend** imminent.
Unmittelbarkeit *f* immediacy, directness, bluntness.
unmöglich *adj* impossible; **physisch** ~ physically impossible; **rechtlich** ~ legally impossible.
Unmöglichkeit *f* impossibility (= *imp*); ~ **der Erfüllung** *imp* of performance; ~ **der Leistung** *imp* of performance; ~ **der Vertragserfüllung** *imp* of performance of a contract; **absolute** ~ absolute *imp*; **faktische** ~ physical *imp*; **nachträgliche** ~ subsequent *imp*, subsequent frustration; **nachträgliche** ~ **der Erfüllung** subsequent *imp* of performance; **objektive** ~ absolute, physical *imp*; **offenbare** ~ manifest *imp*; **praktische** ~ practical *imp*; **rechtliche** ~ legal *imp*; **subjektive** ~ relative *imp*; **relative** ~ relative *imp*; **tatsächliche** ~ *imp* in fact; **teilweise** ~ partial *imp*; **ursprüngliche** ~ initial *imp*.
unmoralisch *adj* immoral.
unmündig *adj* under age, not of age, minor.
Unmündiger *m* (*der Unmündige*) minor.
Unmündigkeit *f* minority.
Unnachgiebigkeit *f* intransigence, firmness.
unnotiert *adj* unlisted.
unparteiisch *adj* impartial, neutral, unprejudiced, even-handed.
Unparteiischer *m* (*der Unparteiische*) referee.
Unparteilichkeit *f* impartiality, neutrality.
unpatentiert *adj* unpatented.
unpfändbar non-leviable, judgment-proof, exempt from seizure.
Unpfändbarkeit *f* exemption from execution, exemption from seizure; **~sbestimmungen** exemption laws.

unplanmäßig *adj* not planned, unscheduled.
unpräjudiziell *adj* without prejudice.
unproduktiv *adj* unproductive, idle.
unquittiert *adj* unreceipted.
unrationell *adj* inefficient, wasteful.
Unrecht *n* wrong, injustice; **u~mäßig** *adj* wrongful; **~mäßigkeit** wrongfulness; **~sbewußtsein** guilty knowledge, consciousness of the wrongful character of one's doings, mens rea; *fehlendes ~~*: inability to perceive legal wrong; **~svereinbarung** wrongful agreement; **ein ~ beseitigen** to remedy a wrong; **jmdm geschieht ~** s. o. suffers an injustice; **schreiendes ~** travesty of justice; **völkerrechtliches ~** offences against international law; **vorsätzlich begangenes ~** positive wrong, wilfully committed wrong; **zu ~** wrongfully, unjustly.
unredlich *adj* dishonest, in bad faith, underhand.
Unredlichkeit *f* dishonesty.
unregelmäßig *adj* irregular.
Unregelmäßigkeiten *f/pl* irregularities.
unqualifiziert *adj* unqualified, unsound.
unrentabel *adj* unprofitable, uneconomical, submarginal, not remunerative.
unrentierlich *adj* not remunerative, not yielding a return.
unrichtig *adj* mistaken, erroneous.
Unrichtigkeit *f* mistake, incorrectness; **~ der Bücher** incorrect accounting; **~ der Steuererklärung** incorrectness of the tax return; **offenbare ~en** obvious mistakes.
Unruhe *f* disturbance(s), disorder(s), unrest, *pl* (*also*): public disturbances, public disorder, riot; **~ schüren** to foment disturbance; **~stifter** disturber, trouble-maker, demagogue, trouble-monger; **innere ~n** civil turmoil.
unsachgemäß *adj* improper, unskillful.
unsachlich *adj* unobjective, irrelevant, unrealistic, unbusinesslike.

unschädlich *adj* harmless, without any detrimental effects; **~er Stoff** innocent material.
Unschädlichkeitszeugnis *n* clearance certificate, certificate of harmlessness.
unschätzbar *adj* inestimable, incalculable, immense.
Unschätzbarkeit *f* inestimableness, incalculability.
unschicklich *adj* improper, in bad form; indecent, unseemly, indecorous, unbefitting.
Unschicklichkeit *f* impropriety.
unschlüssig *adj* inconclusive, non liquet, non sequitur; impertinent.
Unschlüssigkeit *f* inconclusiveness, failure to state a proper cause of action, irresolution.
Unschuld *f* innocence; **~beteuerung** protestation of innocence; **~svermutung** presumption of innocence; **erwiesene ~** proved innocence; **seine ~ beteuern** to protest one's innocence.
unschuldig *adj* innocent; **sich für ~ erklären** to plead not guilty.
Unselbständiger *m* employed person, (working) employee.
Unsicherheitsmoment *n* element of uncertainty, uncertainty factor.
Unsinn *m* nonsense, *parl*: rubbish.
unsittlich *adj* immoral, indecent.
Unsittlichkeit *f* immorality, indecency.
unsolide *adj* dissipated, loose (living); untrustworthy, unreliable.
unsozial *adj* asocial, anti-social.
unständig *adj* not permanent, temporary.
unstatthaft *adj* inadmissible, improper.
Unstatthaftigkeit *f* impropriety, inadmissibility, improper nature.
Unstimmigkeit *f* dissent, discrepancy; inconsistency, friction.
unstofflich *adj* insubstantial.
unstreitig *adj* undisputed, beyond dispute, indisputable, without dispute, undenied, undefended; **~ stellen** to stipulate (*during trial*).
unsubstantiiert *adj* unparticularised, unsubstantiated, unspecified.

untätig *adj* inactive, dormant, idle.
Untätigkeit *f* inactivity, inaction, idleness; ~ **e-r Behörde** administrative inaction; ~**sbeschwerde** complaint about inaction; ~**sklage** court action on the grounds of administrative inaction.
untauglich *adj* unfit, unsuitable, incapable; ~ **machen** to incapacitate.
Untauglichkeit *f* unfitness, unsuitability, incapacity.
untaxiert *adj* unassessed.
unteilbar *adj* indivisible, unseparable, inseverable.
Unteilbarkeit *f* indivisibility, unseparability.
Unter|absatz subparagraph; ~**abschnitt** subsection, subclause, subparagraph, subdivision; ~**abteilung** sub-division; ~**abteilungsleiter** head of sub-division; ~**agent** subagent; ~**aktionär** indirect shareholder; ~**anspruch** subclaim, subordinate claim; ~**auftrag** subcontracting order; ~**auslastung** subutilization, idle capacity; ~**beamter** subordinate official; ~**bau** substructure, basement; **u~bauen** *v/t* to support, to underpin; ~**baugruppe** subassembly; ~**begriff** subterm; ~**belegung** insufficient occupation; ~**beschäftigung** underemployment, working below capacity, slack; ~**bestand** shortage of stock; ~**beteiligung** sub-participation, subshare, sub-partnership; **u~bevollmächtigen** *v/t* to delegate one's authority, to appoint a subagent; ~**bevollmächtigter** subagent, agent by delegation; ~**bevollmächtigung** delegation of powers; **u~bewerten** to underrate, to undervalue; ~**bewertung** underrating, undervaluation; ~**bezahlung** underpayment; **u~bieten** *v/t* to underbid, to undersell, to undercut, to dump; ~**bietung** *f* price cutting, underselling, undercutting; ~**bilanz** deficit balance, adverse balance; **u~binden** → *unterbinden*; ~**bindung** → *Unterbindung*; **u~brechen** → *unterbrechen*; ~**brechung** → *Unterbrechung*; **u~breiten** → *unterbreiten*; **u~bringen** → *unterbringen*; ~**bringung** → *Unterbringung*; **u~chartern** *v/t* to subcharter; ~**deckung** cover shortage, deficient cover; ~**drücken** → *unterdrücken*; ~**drückung** → *Unterdrückung*; **u~entwickelt** *adj* underdeveloped, developing; ~**ernährung** nutritional deficiency; **u~fertigen** → *unterfertigen*; ~**fertigung** → *Unterfertigung*; ~**finanzierung** inadequate financial basis, lack of equity capital; ~**frachtführer** subcarrier; ~**frachtvertrag** contract of recharter, contract with a subcarrier, sub-contract of affreightment; **u~frankieren** *v/t* to underpay the postage, understamp (*a letter*); **u~frankiert** *adj* postage underpaid, understamped; ~**führung** underpass; ~**gang** → *Untergang*; ~**gebener** subordinate; **u~geordnet** *adj* subordinate; ~**gewicht** short weight, underweight; **u~gliedern** to subdivide, to break down; ~**gliederung** subdivision, breaking down; ~**grundbewegung** underground movement; ~**gruppe** subgroup; subassembly; ~**halt** → *Unterhalt*; ~**haltung** → *Unterhaltung*; ~**händler** → *Unterhändler*; ~**handlung** → *Unterhandlung*; ~**haus** → *Unterhaus*; ~**kalkulation** cut costing, unreasonably low costing; **u~kapitalisiert** *adj* undercapitalized; ~**kapitalisierung** undercapitalization; ~**kasse** subordinate accounting agency; ~**konsorte** subsidiary member of a syndicate, sub-underwriter; ~**konto** sub-account; ~**kostenpreis** lower-than-cost price; ~**lage** → *Unterlage*; ~**lassen** → *Unterlassen*; **u~lassen** → *unterlassen*; ~**lassung** → *Unterlassung*; ~**lehensgewährung** subfeudation; ~**lieferant** subcontractor (for the supply of goods); **u~liegen** → *unterliegen*; ~**lizenz** sub-licence (= *sublicence, US: sublicense*); ~**lizenzgeber** sublicensor (= *sublicensor*); ~**lizenznehmer** sub-licensee (= *sublicen-*

unterbinden / **Unterbringung**

see); ~**miete** subtenancy, undertenancy; ~**mieter** subtenant, undertenant, lodger; ~**mietverhältnis** subtenancy; ~**mietvertrag** subtenancy contract; ~**mietzuschlag** extra charge for permission to sublet; **u~nehmen** → *unternehmen*; ~**nehmen** → *Unternehmen (1), (2)*; ~**nehmer** → *Unternehmer*; ~**nehmung** → *Unternehmung*; ~**offizier** non-commissioned officer; **u~optimal** *adj* less than optimal; **u~ordnen** *v/t, v/reflex* to subordinate (sth; oneself); ~**ordnung** subordination, subjection; ~**pacht** sublease, underlease, sub-term; ~**pächter** sublessee, subtenant, undertenant; **u~ pari** below par; ~**pariemission** below-par issue, inferior issue, issue at a discount; ~**position** sub-item; ~**posten** sub-item; ~**prozeßbevollmächtigter** substitute (counsel), deputy lawyer; ~**richtung** → *Unterrichtung*; **u~sagen** → *untersagen*; ~**sagung** → *Untersagung*; **u~schätzen** to underrate, to underestimate; **u~scheiden** → *unterscheiden*; ~**scheidung** → *Unterscheidung*; **u~schieben** → *unterschieben*; ~**schiebung** → *Unterschiebung*; ~**schied** → *Unterschied*; **u~schlagen** → *unterschlagen*; ~**schlagung** → *Unterschlagung*; ~**schlupf** → *Unterschlupf*; **u~schreiben** → *unterschreiben*; ~**schrift** → *Unterschrift*; **u~stellen** → *unterstellen*; ~**stellung** → *Unterstellung*; **u~stützen** → *unterstützen*; ~**stützung** → *Unterstützung*; **u~suchen** → *untersuchen*; ~**suchung** → *Untersuchung*; ~**tan** *m* subject; **u~tariflich** *adj* below-standard wage rate; ~**teilen** to subdivide; ~**teilung** subdivision; ~**titel** subhead(ing); ~**treuhand** sub-trust; ~**typ** subcategory; **u~verfrachten** to subcharter, to reload, to re-ship; ~**vergabe** contracting out, farming out; ~**vermächtnis** sublegacy; **u~vermieten** to sublet; ~**vermieter** sublessor; ~**vermietung** subletting; ~**verpächter** sublessor; ~**verpachtung** sublease, underlease; **u~verpfänden** to submortgage, to repledge; ~**verpfändung** sub-charge, sub-mortgage, subpledge; ~**versicherer** sub-underwriter; **u~versichern** to underinsure; ~**versicherung** underinsurance; ~**versorgung** deficiency in supply; ~**vertrag** subcontract, subsidiary contract; ~**vertreter** subagent; ~**vertretung** subagency; ~**vollmacht** → *Untervollmacht*; **u~werfen** to subject (to), to submit; ~**werfung** → *Unterwerfung*; **u~zeichnen** → *unterzeichnen*; ~**zeichner** → *Unterzeichner*; ~**zeichnung** → *Unterzeichnung*.

unterbinden *v/t* to stop sth, to prevent sth, to forestall, to obviate.

Unterbindung *f* injunction (from ...) prevention; ~**sgewahrsam** preventive police custody, preventive detention.

unterbrechen *v/t* to discontinue, to disconnect, to interrupt.

Unterbrechung *f* discontinuance, discontinuation, interruption; ~ **der diplomatischen Beziehungen** suspension of diplomatic relations; ~ **der Sitzung** suspension of sitting, adjournment of the meeting; ~ **der Verjährung** interruption of the running of time for purposes of limitation; interruption of the Statute of Limitations; ~ **des Kausalzusammenhangs** novus actus interveniens, break in the chain of causation; ~ **des Strafvollzugs** suspension of execution; ~ **des Verfahrens** suspension of proceedings, interruption of the sitting; ~ **e-s Prozesses** abatement of proceedings; **mit** ~**en** intermittently.

unterbreiten *v/t* to submit, to propound, to refer to.

unterbringen *v/t* to accommodate, to place, to commit.

Unterbringung *f* accommodation, placement, commitment; ~ **e-r Anleihe** placement of a loan issue; ~ **in e-m Arbeitshaus** confine-

unterdrücken / **Unterhaltsanspruch**

ment to a work house; ~ **in e–r Heil- und Pflegeanstalt** confinement to an institution for cure and care; **~sbeschluß** place of safety order; **~sverfahren** commitment proceedings; ~ **von Aufträgen** placement of orders; **angemessene** ~ appropriate accommodation; **ausreichende anderweitige** ~ suitable alternative accommodation; **auswärtige** ~ accommodation out of town; **einstweilige** ~ provisional commitment; **sofortige** ~ immediate commitment; **vorläufige** ~ temporary commitment, provisional custody.

unterdrücken v/t to suppress, to oppress, to repress; to crush.

Unterdrückung f suppression, repression, oppression; ~ **der Meinungsfreiheit** suppression of opinion; ~ **des Personenstandes** concealment of personal status; ~ **von Beweismaterial** suppression of evidence; ~ **von Tatsachen** concealment of facts; ~ **von Urkunden** suppression of documents.

unterfertigen v/t to execute, to sign, to append signatures.

Unterfertiger m (*der Unterfertigte*) (the) undersigned, signatory.

Unterfertigung f execution, signing (and sealing).

Untergang m loss, destruction; ~ **der vertragsgegenständlichen Sache** destruction of subject matter of the contract; **zufälliger** ~ loss by accident, accidental loss.

Untergebener m subordinate.

untergeordnet adj subordinate, junior.

Unterhalt m maintenance, alimony, sustenance, subsistence, support; ~ **gewähren** to provide maintenance; **angemessener** ~ reasonable maintenance, appropriate support; **Dauer** ~ → *Dauer*; **freier** ~ free board and lodging; **für jmds** ~ **sorgen** to provide for somebody; **gesetzlicher** ~ statutory maintenance; **lebenslänglicher** ~ lifelong maintenance; **nachehelicher** ~ maintenance after termination of marriage; **notdürftiger** ~ bare necessities of life; **standesgemäßer** ~ maintenance suitable to one's station in life (*or* social position), comfortable maintenance; **u~n~ leisten**: *to provide suitably*; **vorläufiger** ~ maintenance pending suit; alimony pendente lite (*during divorce proceedings*).

unterhalten v/t to support, to provide maintenance, to maintain.

Unterhalts|anspruch right of maintenance, maintenance claim; **~ausfalleistungen** payments (benefits) in lieu of maintenance; **~bedarf** required maintenance, maintenance requirements; **u~bedürftig** adj requiring (*or* in need of) maintenance; **~bedürftigkeit** necessitous circumstances; **~beihilfe** maintenance allowance, maintenance grant; **~beitrag** allowance; **~bemessung** assessment of amount of maintenance; **u~berechtigt** adj entitled to maintenance; **~berechtigter** person entitled to maintenance, dependant; **~empfänger** recipient of maintenance; **~ersatzanspruch** claim in lieu of maintenance; **~fonds** alimentary trust; **~forderung** claim for maintenance, maintenance claim; **~geld** maintenance amount (allowance); **~gläubiger** person entitled to receive maintenance; **~hilfe** maintenance assistance, subsistence payment; **~klage** action for support, petition for maintenance; **~kläger** plaintiff in a maintenance case; **~kosten** cost of maintenance, living expenses; **~pfleger** custodian for alimony; **~pflegschaft** official guardianship for (recovery of) maintenance payments; **~pflicht** maintenance obligation, liability to maintain, liability to (provide) support, obligation to maintain; **gegenseitige ~~**: *mutual maintenance obligations*; *gesetzliche* **~~**: *legal duty to support* **~~** *ohne Rücksicht auf Verschulden*: *maintenance regardless of fault*; **u~pflichtig** adj liable to maintain; **~pflichtiger** person li-

Unterhaltung

able to provide maintenance; ~**pflichtverletzung** violation of maintenance obligation, non-support; ~**quelle** source of livelihood; ~**quote** percentage of income subject to maintenance; ~**rente** maintenance assistance pension, periodical payments for maintenance; ~**rückstände** maintenance arrears; ~**sache** maintenance case, affiliation case (*of illegitimate child*); ~**sicherung** providing security for maintenance obligations, substitute maintenance to dependants of draftees; ~**urteil** maintenance order, affiliation order (*illegitimate child*); ~**vereinbarung** maintenance agreement; ~**verfahren** maintenance proceedings; ~**verletzung** neglect to maintain, failure to provide maintenance, breach of maintenance obligation; non-support; ~**vertrag** maintenance agreement; contract in respect of alimony; ~**verzicht** waiver of maintenance right; ~**vollstreckung** enforcement of maintenance; ~**zahlungen** maintenance payments; ~**vorschuß** advance maintenance payments; ~**zuschuß** subsistence allowance, living allowance; **einstweilige Anordnung auf** ~**zahlung** (*an Ehegatten*) maintenance order pending suit.

Unterhaltung *f* upkeep, maintenance; ~**skosten** maintenance expenses, cost of upkeep; ~**slast** (street) maintenance charges; ~**spflicht** maintenance obligation (*streets, public buildings, schools etc*), covenant to repair.

Unterhändler negotiator (*for a truce etc*).

Unterhandlung *f* negotiation, parley.

Unterhaus *n* (the) House of Commons (*GB*), lower chamber (of parliament), (the) lower house; ~**abgeordneter** member of parliament, M.P.; ~**debatte** debate in the House of Commons; ~**sitzung** session of the House; ~**wahlen** general elections; **das** ~ **vertagt**

Unterlassungsanspruch

sich parliament rises; **für das** ~ **kandidieren** to stand for parliament, to run for election.

Unterlage *f* supporting document, underlying security, (*pl also:*) records, papers, documentation; **beweiskräftige** ~ substantiating document; **buchmäßige** ~ accounting records; **die** ~**n liefern** to supply the documents; **durch einschlägige** ~**n belegen** to support by the relevant documentary evidence; to produce vouchers; **nachgereichte** ~**n** later documents; **technische** ~**n** technical data; **vorschriftsmäßige** ~**n** regular documents.

Unterlassen *n* failure to do sth., omission, nonfeasance; ~ **e-r Mitteilung** failure to notify; **schuldhaftes** ~ culpable neglect, non-feasance, passive negligence.

unterlassen *v/t* to desist, to leave sth undone, to omit to do sth, to refrain (from doing), to forbear, to fail to do.

Unterlassung *f* forbearance, omission, default, neglect, non-performance, failure to do sth, failure to comply with a requirement, non-act; ~ **der Anzeige (e-r strafbaren Handlung)** misprision, failure to report a criminal offence; ~ **der Hilfeleistung** failure to help *or* to rescue; **auf** ~ **gerichtete einstweilige Verfügung** restraining order; **auf** ~ **klagen** to petition for a restraining order; **pflichtgemäße** ~ due restraint; **schuldhafte** ~ wrongful failure to act, nonfeasance; **vorsätzliche** ~ wilful default, wilful neglect.

Unterlassungs|anspruch right to (a) forbearance, right to require s. o. to refrain from acting; ~**befehl** a cease and desist order; ~**delikt** crime by omission; ~**erklärung** declaration of discontinuance; *strafbewehrte* ~~: *declaration of discontinuance with a penalty clause*; ~**gebot** prohibitory order, mandatory requirement to cease and desist from doing sth; ~**klage** pro-

Unterliegen

hibitory action, suit for discontinuance, bill quia timet; **~pflicht** duty to refrain from doing sth, duty of forbearance, negative duty; obligation to desist; *vertragliche* **~~**: *negative covenant*; **~urteil** prohibitory decree, restraint order; **~verfügung** cease and desist order, stop notice; negative injunction.

Unterliegen *n* defeat, non-success.

unterliegen *v/i* to be defeated; to be subject to, to be governed by.

unterliegend *adj* losing, defeated; subjacent.

Unternehmen *n* (1) business undertaking, enterprise, business establishment; **~ der gewerblichen Wirtschaft** commercial enterprise; **~ privaten Rechts** private-law enterprise; **abhängiges ~** dependent enterprise; **ausländisches ~** foreign enterprise; **beherrschendes ~** controlling enterprise; **beherrschtes ~** controlled enterprise, subsidiary; **belegschaftseigenes ~** common ownership enterprise; **buchführendes ~** accounting entity; **bundesunmittelbares ~** directly operated federal government enterprise; **ein ~ abwickeln** to wind up a business enterprise; **federführendes ~** pilot contractor, leading undertaking; **gemeinnütziges ~** non-profit-making enterprise; **gemischtes ~** mixed enterprise; **gemischt-wirtschaftliches ~** part privately and part publicly owned enterprise, mixed enterprise; **geschäftliches ~** business venture, commercial enterprise, business undertaking; **gewerbliches ~** commercial enterprise, commercial undertaking; **gewinnbringendes ~** paying concern, remunerative enterprise; **herrschendes ~** dominant enterprise; **im öffentlichen Interesse liegendes ~** business undertaking involving a public interest; **in Betrieb befindliches ~** going concern; **inländisches ~** domestic enterprise; **in Mehrheitsbesitz stehende ~** enterprises held by a majority; **kaufmännisches ~** trade establishment, commercial enterprise; **kleine und mittlere ~** small and middling firms; **laufendes ~** operating concern, going concern; **lebendes ~** going concern; **mit Mehrheit beteiligte ~** enterprises holding a majority interest; **marktbeherrschendes ~** market-dominating enterprise; **mittelständische ~** medium-sized business; **öffentliches ~** publicly owned enterprise, public sector enterprise; **privatwirtschaftliches ~** privately owned enterprise, private sector enterprise; **rentables ~** remunerative undertaking; **staatliches ~** state-owned enterprise; **verbundene ~** related enterprises, connected enterprises; affiliated enterprises; **verstaatlichtes ~** nationalized enterprise; **wechselseitig beteiligte ~** mutually participating enterprises.

Unternehmen *n* (2) activity, operation(s); **~sdelikt** the offence of undertaking to commit a wrongful act; **~shaftung** operational liability (*of railways, funiculars*); **~ gegen den Bestand der Bundesrepublik** treasonable activity against the Federal Republic; **~ gegen die verfassungsmäßige Ordnung** activities against the constitutional order.

Unternehmens|berater management consultant; **~beratung** management consulting; **~~** *durch Wirtschaftsprüfer*: *management accountancy*; **~beauftragter** in-house safety commissioner (*of a company*); **~bereich** division; **~besteuerung** taxation of business enterprises; **~bilanzen** corporate balance sheets; **~ebene** company level; **~einheit** unity of an enterprise (*for tax purposes*); **~ertrag** earnings of an enterprise; **~form** (legal) form of enterprise; **~forschung** operations research (*US*), company research (*GB*); **~führung** management (of an enterprise); **~gegen-**

stand object(s) of a business; ~**gewinn** business profit, equity earnings, corporate profits; ~**kapital** equity capital, equity plus borrowed capital; ~**leitung** management; ~**nachfolge** succession to an enterprise (*or* business); ~**spitze** top management; ~**vereinigung** association of undertakings, (commercial or industrial) federation; ~**verfassung** internal legal structure of an enterprise, constitution of a company; ~**verflechtungen** inter-company relationships, business interlinking; ~**vertrag** company-transfer agreement; ~**zusammenschluß** business merger; consolidation of enterprises; (*auf Marktbeherrschung gerichteter*) ~~: *trust;* horizontaler ~~: *lateral combination.*

Unternehmer *m* entrepreneur, employer, industrialist, business owner, manufacturer; independent contractor; ~**disposition** entrepreneurial action; ~**einkommen** entrepreneurial income, business-ownership income; ~**freiheit** free enterprise; ~**fürsorgeaufgaben** social entrepreneurial responsibility; ~**geist** entrepreneurial spirit; ~**gewinn** profit from operations, entrepreneur's profit, business profit; ~**haftpflichtversicherung** employer's liability insurance; ~**haftung** contractor's liability, producer's liability; ~**kredit** contractor loan; ~**leistung** entrepreneurial service; ~**lohn** earnings of management, entrepreneur's remuneration; ~**pfandrecht** artisan's lien, mechanic's lien; ~**risiko** entrepreneurial risk; ~**testament** last will the owner of a business (*to settle the continuation after his death*); ~**tum** entrepreneurship; *freies* ~~: *free enterprise;* ~ **und Arbeitnehmer** employers and employed; ~**verband** employers' association, trade association; ~**versicherung** employers' liability insurance; ~**verzeichnis** list of employers; ~**wagnis** entrepreneurial risk; ~**wechsel** change of ownership at a business enterprise; ~**wirtschaft** system of private enterprise; **ausländischer** ~ foreign contractor; **inländischer** ~ domestic business owner, domestic entrepreneur; **selbständiger** ~ self-employer, independent contractor, private trader.

Unternehmerin *f* woman executive, business woman.

unternehmerisch *adj* entrepreneurial, commercial.

Unternehmung *f* business, enterprise, undertaking.

Unterordnung *f* subordination; ~**skonzern** vertical integration.

Unterricht *m* school instruction, teaching; ~**vertrag** contract to provide educational instruction.

Unterrichtung *f* briefing, information; **gegenseitige** ~ exchange of information.

untersagen *v/t* to forbid, to interdict, to inhibit, to restrain (from).

Untersagung *f* prohibition, inhibition, interdiction; ~**sbescheid** prohibition notice; ~**srecht** right to forbid; ~**sverfügung** prohibition order; **befristete** ~ **der Berufsausübung** suspense from exercise of profession or trade.

unterschätzen *v/t* to underrate, to underestimate, to fail to appreciate.

unterscheidbar *adj* distinct, distinctive.

unterscheiden *v/t* to distinguish, to discriminate, to differentiate (between).

Unterscheidung *f* distinction, discrimination; **u**~**sfähig** distinctive; ~**sfähigkeit** distinctiveness (*trade mark*); ~**skraft** distinctiveness; ~**smarke** distinctive trade mark; ~**smerkmal** distinctive device, distinctive criterion, *pl also:* distinguishing characteristics; distinctive characteristic; ~**snummer** identification number; ~**svermögen** discernment; ~**szeichen** distinctive sign; distinguishing mark(s); ~~ **des Zulassungsstaates:** *distinguishing sign of the State of registration.*

Unterschieben *n* fraudulent sub-

Unterschiebung

stituting; ~ **e–s Kindes** foisting a child upon another.

Unterschiebung *f* fraudulent substitution, personation, false attribution.

Unterschied *m* difference, distinction, disparity; ~**e der Rechtsvorschriften** disparities in ... legal provisions; ~**e steuerlicher Art** disparities in tax systems; ~**sbetrag** differential amount; ~**slosigkeit** indiscrimination; **kaum merklicher** ~ no appreciable difference; **sachlicher** ~ difference of fact; **strukturelle** ~**e** structural disparities.

unterschiedlich *adj* discriminative, discriminatory.

Unterschiedlichkeit *f* differential, different character, variability.

unterschlagen *v/t* to misappropriate, to embezzle, to peculate.

Unterschlagung *f* fraudulent appropriation, misappropriation, embezzlement; peculation; ~ **im Amt** embezzlement in office.

Unterschlupf *m* place of shelter, hideout, hiding-place.

unterschreiben *v/t* to sign, to undersign, to subscribe; **eigenhändig** ~ to sign personally, to sign in one s own hand.

unterschrieben *adj* signed, executed; **rechtsverbindlich** ~ properly subscribed, duly executed.

Unterschrift *f* signature; ~**enfolge** alternat; ~**en unter diesen Vertrag setzen** to sign this Treaty; „~ **fehlt"** "signature missing"; ~ **in Vertretung** signature by proxy; ~ **in Vollmacht** signature by procuration; ~ **leisten** to affix one's signature, to sign on the dotted line „~ **ungenau"** "signature differs"; **eigenhändige** ~ personal signature, autograph(ic) signature, manuscript signature; **gefälschte** ~ forged signature; **gemeinschaftliche** ~ joint signature; **ohne** ~ unsigned; **seine** ~ **nicht anerkennen** to disown one's signature; „**unvollständige** ~" "signature incorrect", incomplete signature;

Unterstützungsangebot

zur ~ **bereit liegend** open for signature; **zur** ~ **vorlegen** to submit for signature.

Unterschrifts|befugnis power to sign; ~**beglaubigung** attestation of signature, verification of execution; ~**berechtigung** authority to sign (for ...); ~**fälschung** forgery of signature; ~**probe** specimen signature; **u**~**reif** *adj* open for signature, ready for signature; ~**seite** signature page; ~**stempel** signature stamp; ~**vollmacht** power to sign, entitlement to sign; ~**verzeichnis** list of authorized signatures; ~**vollmacht** authority to sign documents; ~**vorlage** specimen signature; submission for signature; ~**zeuge** subscribing witness, attesting witness.

Unterschutzstellung *f* placing under the protection (*of a public authority*); making s. b. a ward of court.

unterstellen *v/t* to impute, to insinuate, to presume, to imply; **als wahr** ~ to beg the question, to proceed on the footing that it is true; to take sth for granted.

Unterstellung *f* imputation, insinuation, innuendo, reflection, presumption, implication, supposition, assumption.

unterstützen *v/t* to support, to assist, to aid and assist, to stand by.

Unterstützung *f* support, assistance, backing, aid; benefit; ~ **bei wirtschaftlicher Notlage** assistance in case(s) of financial need; ~ **des Beweises** corroboration of evidence; **finanzielle** ~ financial aid; **gegenseitige** ~ reciprocal assistance; **großangelegte internationale** ~ international assistance on a large scale; **öffentliche** ~ public aid and support; **staatliche** ~ government aid, state aid.

Unterstützungs|angebot offer of assistance; ~**aufwendung** benefit payment; **u**~**berechtigt** entitled to public support; ~**berechtigter** person entitled to public support; ~**einrichtung** welfare fund, welfare institution; ~**empfänger**,

794

welfare beneficiary; ~**fall** case of public welfare, needy person in receipt of public support; ~**fonds** relief fund, protective trust; ~**kasse** benefit society, provident fund, relief fund, benevolent club; ~**leistung** public assistance payments, (welfare) benefits; ~**pflicht** duty to support; ~**satz** rate of (the supplementary) benefit; ~**verein** benevolent society, aid society; ~**zahlung** relief payment, benefit payment, remittance for maintenance purposes.

untersuchen v/t to investigate, to examine, to test, to scrutinize.

Untersuchung f inquiry, examination, test, probe, investigation, inquest, scrutiny; ~ **der Werbewirksamkeit** impact study, study of advertizing impact; ~ **zum Abstammungsbeweis** paternity test; **amtliche** ~ official inquiry; **ärztliche** ~ medical examination; **demoskopische** ~ field research *for public opinion poll*; **eingehende** ~ close examination, detailed investigation; **förmliche** ~ formal inquiry; **gerichtliche** ~ judicial inquiry, judicial investigation; **inoffizielle** ~ informal investigation, unofficial inquiry; **körperliche** ~ physical examination; **ordnungsgemäße** ~ due inquiry; proper examination; **psychiatrische** ~ psychiatric examination.

Untersuchungs|anstalt testing institution; ~**ausschuß** investigating committee, committee of inquiry, fact-finding committee; ~**bericht** test report; investigation report; ~**ergebnis** result of investigation, test result; ~**führer** examiner, inspector; ~**gefangener** remand prisoner, person remanded in custody, person held in pre-trial confinement, person held in custody pending further investigations, person detained for trial; ~**gefängnis** remand prison; ~**grundsatz** inquisitorial system; ~**haft** → *Untersuchungshaft*; ~**häftling** = ~*gefangener qv*; ~**handlungen** investigation, test actions; ~**kommission** commission of enquiry; ~**maxime** (principle of) inquisitorial procedure; ~**pflicht** duty to examine *ex officio*; ~**richter** (*before 1974, abrogated*) committing magistrate, examining magistrate; investigating magistrate.

Untersuchungshaft f remand, pre-trial custody, pretrial detention during investigation, pre-trial custody; **aus der ~ vorgeführt werden** to appear on remand; **die ~ anrechnen** to make allowance for the pre-trial confinement; **in ~ nehmen** to arrest pending further investigations; **in ~ sein** to be on remand, to be held in pre-trial confinement.

Unterversicherung f under-insurance.

Untervollmacht f sub-authorisation, substitute power of attorney, power of substitution.

Unterweisung f briefing, (adequate specific) instruction.

Unterweltkriminalität f racketeering, underground crime.

Unterwerfung f submission; ~**serklärung** submission to immediate execution, judgment note; ~**sklausel** submission to execution clause (*in a German notarial deed*); ~**sverfahren** repressive procedure, voluntary submission to (tax) penalty proceedings.

unterzeichnen v/t to sign, to undersign, to subscribe, to append signatures, to sign on the dotted line.

Unterzeichner m signatory, subscriber, (the) undersigned; ~**regierung** signatory government; ~**staat** signatory state.

unterzeichnet adj signed, subscribed; **eigenhändig ~** signed in (one's) own hand; **von mir ~** witness my hand, given under my hand, signed by me personally.

Unterzeichnung f signature, execution (deed); ~ **des Grundstückskaufvertrages** real estate closing, the signing of a contract of sale of

land; ~**sprotokoll** protocol of signature.
untilgbar *adj* irredeemable.
Untilgbarkeit *f* irredeemability.
untreu *adj* disloyal, unfaithful.
Untreue *f* disloyalty, dishonest dealings (by agent or trustee), defalcation, criminal breach of trust, unfaithfulness, infidelity.
unüberlegt *adj* unpremeditated, imprudent, thoughtless.
Unüberlegtheit *f* imprudence, indiscretion, thoughtlessness.
unübertragbar *adj* non-transferable.
Unübertragbarkeit *f* non-transferability.
unüberwindlich *adj* insuperable.
unumgänglich *adj* unavoidable, indispensable.
Unumgänglichkeit *f* absolute necessity.
unumschränkt *adj* unlimited, unrestricted.
unumstößlich *adj* unalterable.
ununterbrochen *adj* uninterrupted.
unverändert *adj* unaltered, unchanged.
unverantwortlich *adj* irresponsible.
Unverantwortlichkeit *f* irresponsibility, lack of due responsibility.
unverausgabt *adj* unexpended.
unveräußerlich *adj* unalienable, inalienable.
Unveräußerlichkeit *f* inalienability.
unverbesserlich *adj* incorrigible.
unverbindlich *adj* not binding, non-committed, (*also adv:*) without obligation, without engagement.
unverborgen *adj* unhidden, patent.
unverbrieft *adj* non-bonded, not in the form of a deed, unrecorded.
unverbürgt *adj* unauthenticated.
unverdächtig *adj* unsuspicious, beyond suspicion.
unverdient *adj* unearned, undeserved, unmerited.
unvereinbar *adj* incompatible, irreconcilable, repugnant.
Unvereinbarkeit *f* incompatibility, repugnancy.
unvererblich *adj* not heritable.
unverfallbar *adj* non-forfeitable, non-lapsable.

Unverfallbarkeit *f* non-forfeitability.
unverfolgbar *adj* exempt from prosecution, unenforceable.
Unverfolgbarkeit *f* exemption from prosecution, unenforceability.
unvergällt *adj* undenatured.
unverhältnismäßig *adj* disproportionate, unbalanced.
Unverhältnismäßigkeit *f* disproportion, disparity, unreasonableness.
unverheiratet *adj* unmarried.
Unverheiratete *f* unmarried woman, spinster.
Unverheirateter *m* (*der Unverheiratete*) bachelor, unmarried man.
unverjährbar *adj* not subject to the statute of limitations.
Unverjährbarkeit *f* incapacity to become statute-barred.
unverjährt *adj* not statute-barred.
unverkäuflich *adj* unsaleable, not for sale.
Unverkäuflichkeit *f* unsaleability.
unverkauft *adj* unsold, unbought.
unverkennbar *adj* unmistakable.
unverkürzt *adj* unabbreviated.
unverlangt *adj* unsolicited (*offer, manuscript*).
unverletzlich *adj* inviolable.
Unverletzlichkeit *f* inviolability; ~ **diplomatischer Kurierbeutel** inviolability of the diplomatic pouch.
unvermeidlich *adj* inevitable, unavoidable.
unvermietbar *adj* untenantable, unsuitable for letting.
unvermietet *adj* tenantless.
Unvermögen *n* inability to comply with sth, incapacity.
unvermögend *adj* destitute, impecunious, without means.
Unvermögensfall *m* case of inability *or* incapacity.
unvermutet *adj* unexpected, unforeseen, sudden.
unveröffentlicht *adj* unpublished, unreported.
unverpachtet *adj* tenantless.
unverpackt *adj* unpacked, loose, in bulk, without packing.
unverpfändet *adj* unpledged, unmortgaged.

unverplant *adj* unallocated, not included in planning or budgeting.
unverschämt *adj* impudent, impertinent, insolent.
Unverschämtheit *f* impudence, impertinence, insolence.
unverschlossen *adj* unlocked (*room*); unsealed (*letter*).
unverschuldet *adj* blameless; undeserved, arising through no fault of (*ours, mine*), without fault, faultless.
unversehrt *adj* unharmed, undamaged, safe and sound, intact.
Unversehrtheit *f* intactness, freedom from injury (*or* damage), integrity, sound condition.
unversetzbar *adj* not transferable (*to other post or location except with civil servant's consent*).
Unversetzbarkeit exemption from transfer (*to other place or occupation*), irremovability.
unversichert *adj* uninsured.
unversiegelt *adj* unsealed.
unversöhnlich *adj* irreconcilable, unappeasable.
Unversöhnlichkeit *f* irreconcilability, implacability.
unversteuert *adj* untaxed.
unverteilt *adj* undistributed.
unverträglich *adj* incompatible.
Unverträglichkeit *f* incompatibility.
Unverwirkbarkeit *f* non-forfeitability, exclusion of estoppel.
unverzichtbar *adj* not subject to renunciation, unabandonable.
unverzinslich *adj* non-interest-bearing, interest-free.
unverzollt *adj* uncleared, duty unpaid.
unverzüglich prompt, forthwith, without delay.
Unverzüglichkeit *f* promptness.
unvollziehbar *adj* unenforceable.
Unvollziehbarkeit *f* unenforceability.
unvollzogen *adj* executory, unconsummated, uncompleted.
unvordenklich *adj* immemorial.
unvoreingenommen *adj* free from bias, unbiassed, impartial, unprejudiced.

Unvoreingenommenheit *f* impartiality, freedom from bias.
unvorhergesehen *adj* unforeseen.
Unvorhergesehenes *n* unforeseen events, *bal* contingent expenses.
unvorhersehbar *adj* unforeseeable, unimaginable.
Unvorhersehbarkeit *f* unforeseeability.
unvorsichtig *adj* imprudent, inadvertent, careless.
Unvorsichtigkeit *f* imprudence, carelessness.
unwählbar *adj* ineligible.
Unwählbarkeit *f* ineligibility.
unwahr *adj* untrue, untruthful, false.
Unwahrheit *f* untruth, untruthfulness, falsehood.
unwandelbar *adj* unchangeable.
Unwandelbarkeit *f* unchangeability.
unweigerlich *adj* inevitable, unavoidable; automatic.
Unwesen *n* evil practices, sinister activities.
unwesentlich *adj* immaterial, nonessential, irrelevant, insubstantial, unimportant.
Unwetterschaden *m* damage due to tempests, damage caused by a thunderstorm.
unwiderlegbar *adj* irrefutable, irrebuttable, conclusive, definitive.
Unwiderlegbarkeit *f* irrefutability.
unwiderrufen *adj* unrescinded, unrevoked, unchallenged.
unwiderruflich *adj* irrevocable, unrecallable, irreversible.
Unwiderruflichkeit *f* irrevocability.
unwidersprochen *adj* uncontradicted, unopposed.
unwiederbringlich *adj* irretrievable.
unwirksam *adj* ineffective, inoperative, invalid, inefficacious, nugatory; **schwebend** ~ provisionally invalid.
Unwirksamkeit *f* ineffectiveness, invalidity; ~ **e–s Vermächtnisses** invalidity of legacy; ~**serklärung** repudiation, rescission, annulment; ~ **von Verträgen durch lange Nichtanwendung** desuetude of treaties; **relative** ~ ineffectiveness as between the parties.

unwirtschaftlich *adj* uneconomic(al), unproductive, inefficient.
Unwirtschaftlichkeit *f* unproductiveness, inefficiency, non-profitability.
unwissend *adj* ignorant, uninformed.
Unwissenheit *f* ignorance; **~ schützt vor Strafe nicht** ignorance (of the law) is no defence; **sich auf ~ berufen** to plead ignorance.
Unze *(28,35 gr.)* ounce.
Unzeit *f* the wrong time; **~gebühr** extra fee for acting during unusual hours; **zur ~** at the wrong time, inopportunely, prematurely.
unzensiert *adj* uncensored.
unziemlich *adj* improper, unbecoming, unseemly.
Unzucht *f* indecency, illicit sexual practices; lewd acts, lewdness, debauchery, fornication; **~ mit Abhängigen** indecency with dependants; **~ mit Minderjährigen** indecency with minors; **~ mit Tieren** bestiality; **~ treiben** to carry on illicit sexual practices; **~ unter Drohung** indecency by threats; **~ zwischen Männern** indecency between males, sodomy between men; **gewerbsmäßige ~** prostitution; **schwere ~** gross indecency, serious lewd acts; **widernatürliche ~** unnatural offence.
unzüchtig *adj* indecent, obscene, lewd, lascivious.
Unzüchtigkeit *f* indecency, obscenity, lewdness, lasciviousness.
unzugänglich *adj* inaccessible.
unzulänglich *adj* inadequate, insufficient.
Unzulänglichkeit *f* inadequacy, insufficiency, *pl. also*: shortcomings.
unzulässig *adj* inadmissible, undue, out of order, not allowed, barred, bad, illicit, impermissible.
Unzulässigkeit *f* inadmissibility, impermissibility, inappropriateness; bar, hindrance; **~ der Klage** (procedural) bar to the action; *the action does not lie*; **~~ feststellen**: *striking the action out*; **~ der Strafverfolgung** bar to trial; **~ der Strafvollstreckung** bar to execution of a sentence; **~ der Zwangsvollstreckung** bar to civil execution.
unzumutbar *adj* unreasonable, unacceptable, outrageous.
Unzumutbarkeit *f* unreasonableness, unacceptability.
unzurechnungsfähig *adj* doli incapax, incapable of criminal intention, not criminally responsible, non compos (mentis); **jmdn für ~ erklären** to declare a person to be of unsound mind (non compos mentis).
Unzurechnungsfähige *m* (*der Unzurechnungsfähige*) person not criminally responsible for his actions; **~ wegen Geisteskrankheit** person of unsound mind, person non compos mentis.
Unzurechnungsfähigkeit *f* mental incapacity, incapability of distinguishing between right and wrong; **~ wegen Geistesschwäche oder Geistesgestörtheit** mental incapacity; **altersbedingte ~** senile incapacity.
unzureichend *adj* inadequate, insufficient.
unzuständig *adj* incompetent, not-responsible; **sich für ~ erklären** to decline jurisdiction.
Unzuständigkeit lack of jurisdiction, non-competence; **funktionelle ~** lack of jurisdiction over the type of case; **örtliche ~** lack of local jurisdiction, improper venue; **sachliche ~** lack of jurisdiction over the subject-matter *depending on amount involved*.
unzustellbar *adj* undeliverable, impossible to be served.
Unzustellbarkeit *f* undeliverability, impossibility of service; **~smeldung** return of nihil.
unzuträglich *adj* unsuitable, unwholesome, unhealthy.
Unzuträglichkeit *f* unsuitability, unwholesomeness, disharmony.
unzuverlässig *adj* unreliable, untrustworthy, unsound.

Unzuverlässigkeit *f* unreliability, unsoundness, untrustworthiness.
unzweckmäßig *adj* inexpedient, inappropriate.
Unzweckmäßigkeit *f* inexpedience, inappropriateness.
unzweideutig *adj* unambiguous, unequivocal, explicit, quite clear.
unzweifelhaft *adj* indubitable, undoubtful, beyond doubt.
Urabstimmung *f* strike ballot, strike vote.
Uraufführung *f* first performance, first theatrical release, premiere.
Uraufzeichnungen *f/pl* records of original entry.
Urbarmachung *f* (original) cultivation, reclamation.
Urbeleg *m* original document, source document.
Urerzeuger *m* primary producer.
Urerzeugung *f* primary production.
Urgewicht *n* original weight.
Urgroßeltern great-grandparents; *Urgroßmutter: great-grandmother; Urgroßvater: great-grandfather.*
Urheber *m* author, originator, creator; ~**benennung** the naming of the author; ~**bezeichnung** indication of authorship, droit moral; ~**ehre** author rights of honour; ~**nennung** authorship credit; author's droit moral; ~**persönlichkeitsrecht** inherent rights of the author rights of paternity; ~**rolle** register of copyright(s); ~**schaft** authorship, origination; ~ **von Werken der Tonkunst** composer of musical works; **mutmaßlicher** ~ presumptive originator, presumed author.
Urheberrecht *n* copyright (law), proprietary right, author's right, literary property; ~ **an Bühnenwerken** dramatic copyright; ~ **an Werken der bildenden Kunst** artistic copyright; ~ **an Werken der Schauspielkunst** copyright in dramatic works, ~ **an Werken der Tonkunst** copyright in musical works; **bestehendes** ~ subsisting (*or* existing) copyright; **erloschenes** ~ lapsed copyright; **gesetzliches** ~ statutory copyright; **literarisches** ~ literary copyright; **originäres** ~ original copyright.
Urheberrechts|eintragung registration of copyright; ~**gesetz** Copyright Act (*D, 1965*); ~**inhaber** holder of copyright, copyright owner, copyright proprietor; ~**klage** copyright action; ~**lizenzgebühren** copyright royalties; ~**schiedsstelle** performing rights tribunal; ~**schutz** copyright protection; *vorläufiger* ~~: *ad interim copyright;* ~**schutzfrist** term (*or* period) of copyright protection; ~**streitsache** copyright case, copyright litigation; ~**übertragung** assignment of copyright; ~**verlängerung** renewal of copyright; ~**verletzung** infringement of copyright, breach of copyright; ~~*sfall: copyright infringement case;* ~**vermerk** copyright notice; ~**vermutung** presumption of copyright; ~**vertrag** copyright agreement; ~**verwertungsgesellschaft** copyright collecting society; ~**verzicht** waiver of copyright.
Urkartei *f* original card index.
Urkund *obs only in:* **zu** ~ **dessen** in witness whereof, in verification whereof.
Urkunde *f* document (legal), instrument, certificate; **abhandengekommene** ~ lost document; **amtliche** ~ official document; **begebbare** ~ negotiable instrument; **beglaubigte** ~ authenticated document; **beweiserhebliche** ~ evidentiary document, relevant document; **echte** ~ authentic document; **e-e** ~ **aufsetzen** to draw up an instrument; **e-e** ~ **begeben** to deliver a deed, to negotiate a document; **e-e** ~ **beibringen** to produce a document, to present a document; **e-e** ~ **einsehen** to inspect a document; **e-e** ~ **entwerfen** to draft a document; **e-e** ~ **errichten** to execute an instrument; **e-e** ~ **legalisieren** to legalize a document: *to authenticate a document by certification of signature of attesting*

official by superior officer or diplomatic agency; **e–e ~ unterdrücken** to suppress a document; **e–e ~ unterfertigen** to execute an instrument (*or* document), to execute a deed; **e–e ~ unterzeichnen** to sign a document; **e–e ~ verfälschen** to forge an instrument; **e–e vorlegen** to produce a document, to tender a document; *e–e ~ zu Beweiszwecken ~: to submit a document in evidence*; **e–e ~ zerstören** to destroy a document; **e–e ~ zu den Akten reichen** to file a document; **eigenhändig geschriebene ~** holograph; **eigenschriftliche ~** holograph, holographic instrument; **eingetragene ~** registered deed, recorded instrument; **gefälschte ~** forged document, false instrument; **notarielle ~** notarial act, notarial instrument; **öffentlich beglaubigte ~** officially authenticated document; **öffentliche ~** official document, public document, public record; *document issued by a public authority*; **privatschriftliche ~** private document; **rechtsförmliche ~** legal document; **standesamtliche ~** document issued by a registrar's office; **unechte ~** fabricated document; **unvollständige ~** inchoate instrument, incomplete instrument; **verfälschte ~** forged instrument; **vollstreckbare ~** (directly) enforceable instrument; **vorprozessuale ~** pretrial document.

Urkunden|aufbewahrung safekeeping of documents; **~aushändigung** delivery of documents; **~beschädigung** spoliation, partial destruction of a document; **~beweis** documentary evidence, proof by documents, written evidence; **~einsicht** inspection of documents; **~entwurf** draft (of a) document; **~fälscher** forger; **~fälschung** forgery of an instrument (*or* document), altering a document with intent to defraud; **~~ begehen**: *to falsify a document*; **~mahnbescheid** default summons based on documents; **~prozeß** trial by the record, proceedings restricted to documentary evidence; **~rolle** (notary's) document register; **~sammlung** *(a notary's)* collection (*or* file) of documents; **~sprache** the official language of (notarial) documents; **~steuer** documents tax, stamp duty; **~unterdrückung** suppression of documents, interception of documents; **~unterschlagung** abstraction of documents; **~verfasser** draftsman; **~vernichtung** spoliation, destruction of a document; **~vorlage** production of documents, discovery of documents; *Aufforderung zur ~~*: *notice to produce*; **~vorlegung** production of documents.

urkundlich *adj* documentary, by formal deed; **~** *adv* **dessen** in witness thereof.

Urkunds|beamter clerk of the court, authenticating (*or* recording) official; **~~** *der Geschäftsstelle*: *clerk of the court's office, clerk of the court*; **~person** authenticator; **~papiere** documentation; **~sachen** cases restricted to documentary evidence; **~zeuge** attesting witness.

Urlaub *m* leave, leave of absence, holiday, vacation, *mil*: furlough; **~ von der Haftanstalt** ticket-of-leave system; **ausbezahlter ~** salary in lieu of leave; **bezahlter ~** paid vacation, holiday with pay, paid holiday, vacation with pay, leave with pay; **tariflicher ~** standard holiday with pay, paid holiday pursuant to a collective wage agreement; **unbezahlter ~** unpaid holiday; **vertaner ~** spoilt holiday.

Urlauber *m* holiday maker.

Urlaubs|abgeltung pay in lieu of vacation; **~anspruch** entitlement of leave, leave claim, vacation privilege; **~berechtigung** eligibility for vacation; **~bescheinigung** (employer's) vacation certificate; **~entgelt** vacation pay, regular salary or wage paid during vacations; **~erteilung** granting of (time for) a

Urliste | **Urteil**

vacation; ~**-Fehlschicht** workers' absence on holiday (during a shift); ~**geld** additional vacation pay; holiday bonus; ~**gesetz** (*German*) *law concerning leave of absence and vacations for employed persons;* ~**gesuch** application for leave; ~**häufung** bunching of holiday periods; ~**jahr** holiday year, year for which vacation is reckoned; sabbatical year (*universities*); ~**konjunktur** holiday boom; ~**plan** vacation schedule; ~**schaden** damage suffered by spoilt holiday; ~**schein** ticket-of-leave; ~**sperre** stoppage of leave; ~**übertragung** carry forward of vacation (*or* holiday) rights; ~**vergütung** holiday remuneration; ~**vertretung** vacation substitute, vacation replacement.

Urliste *f* original list.

Urmaß *n* standard measure, master gauge.

Urmaterial prime matter, primary data.

Urne *f* urn, *pol* ballot box; ~**ngang** polls, general elections.

Urprodukte *n/pl* primary products.

Urproduktion *f* primary production.

Ursache *f* cause; ~ **und Wirkung** cause and effect; **adäquate** ~ adequate cause; **dazwischentretende** ~ intervening cause; **die entscheidende** ~ the determining cause; **e-e nicht feststellbare** ~ an undetermined cause; **entfernte** ~ remote cause; **letzte** ~ ultimate cause; **nicht vorausgesehene** ~ unforeseen cause; **nicht vorausgesehene** ~ unforeseeable cause; **unmittelbare** ~ immediate cause, proximate cause, direct cause; **unmittelbare und alleinige** ~ direct and sole cause.

ursächlich *adj* causal, causative.

Urschrift *f* original, original text; ~ **der Vereinbarung** original agreement; **geschehen in drei** ~**en** done in three original texts; **geschehen in zwei** ~**en** done in duplicate; **in einer** ~ in a single original; **in einer** ~ **abgefaßt** drawn up in a single original.

urschriftlich *adj* original.

ursprünglich *adj* original, initial.

Ursprünglichkeit *f* originality.

Ursprungs|angabe statement of origin; ~**anstalt** originating institution, bank of issue; ~**bestimmung** determination of origin; ~**bezeichnung** designation of origin, mark of origin, marking country of origin, origin mark; ~**eigenschaft** status of origin; ~**erklärung** declaration of origin; ~**fälschung** counterfeiting; ~**land** country of origin, state of origin; ~**nachweis** documentary evidence of origin; ~**ort** point of origin; ~**patent** original patent, pioneer patent; ~**regeln** rules of origin; ~**täuschung** holding out; ~**waren** originating products; ~**wert** original value, unadjusted data; ~**wohnsitz** domicile of origin; ~**zeichen** mark of origin; ~**zeugnis** certificate of origin; ~**zuerkennung** qualification for origin.

Urteil *n* judgment, decree, verdict and sentence, adjudication; ~ **auf Schadenersatz** judgment for damages; ~ **auf Zahlung** money judgment; ~ **des Schiedsgerichts** (arbitral) award; ~ **durch ranggleiche Richter** judgment of his peers; ~ **im streitigen Verfahren** defended judgment; ~ **im unstreitigen Verfahren** consent judgment; ~ **mit dinglicher Wirkung** judgment in rem; ~ **mit Wirkung für und gegen alle** judgment with absolute effect; judgment in rem; **abänderndes** ~ altering judgment, *judgment involving a change of the lower court's decision;* **abgewogenes** ~ balanced judgment; **absprechendes** ~ judgment of dismissal; **aus e-m** ~ **vollstrecken** to enforce a judgment; **ausgeglichenes** ~ balanced judgment; **ausländisches** ~ foreign judgment; **bedingtes** ~ conditional judgment; **bestätigendes** ~ confirmatory decision (of the ap-

801

Urteilsaufhebung

pellate court); **durch ~ zuerkennen** to award by judgment; **ein ~ abändern** to alter a judgment; **ein ~ abgeben** to give an opinion; **ein ~ anfechten** to appeal from a judgment; **ein ~ aufheben** to set aside a judgment, to reverse a judgment; **ein ~ aussprechen** to render a judgment, to pronounce a judgment; **ein ~ bestätigen** to confirm a judgment (*or* sentence); **ein ~ erkennt etwas zu** a judgment awards sth (*to the plaintiff*); **ein ~ erlangen** to obtain a judgment; **ein ~ erlassen** to render (a) judgment, to enter (a) judgment, to deliver a judgment; **ein ~ erwirken** to obtain a judgment; **ein ~ fällen** to render judgment, to adjudicate; **ein ~ kassieren** to quash a judgment; **ein obsiegendes ~ erreichen** to obtain a judgment in one's favour; **ein ~ verkünden** to pronounce (a) judgment; **ein ~ vollstrecken** to enforce a judgment; **e-m ~ vorgreifen** to prejudice the determination by a court; **erstinstanzliches ~** judgment by the court of first instance, judgment by the trial court; **freisprechendes ~** (judgment of) acquittal; **gegen ein ~ Berufung einlegen** to appeal from a judgment; **irriges ~** erroneous judgment; **klageabweisendes ~** judgment of dismissal, judgment of non-suit, order to dismiss; **mildes ~** lenient sentence; **nachträglich verkündetes ~** reserved judgment; **nicht vollstreckbares ~** unenforceable judgment; **noch nicht rechtskräftiges ~** judgment subject to appeal; **obsiegendes ~** judgment in one's favour; **~~ des Klägers**: *judgment for the plaintiff*; **rechtsfehlerhaftes ~** erroneous judgment; **rechtsgestaltendes ~** judgment changing legal status; **rechtsgültiges ~** valid judgment, valid sentence; **rechtskräftiges ~** judgment admitting of no appeal, non-appealable judgment; final and absolute judgment (*or* decree); **reformatorisches ~** reformatory judgment; **schuldrechtliches ~** judgment in personam; **sich mit e–m ~ abfinden** to acquiesce in a judgment, to accept a verdict; **sich mit e–m ~ bescheiden** to acquiesce in a judgment; **über ein ~ beraten** to deliberate on a judgment; **unüberlegtes ~** rash judgment; **vollstreckbares ~** enforceable judgment; **vorläufig vollstreckbares ~** provisionally enforceable judgment (*pending appeal*); **zu mildes ~** over-lenient sentence.

Urteils|aufhebung setting-aside of, *or* reversal of a judgment, quashing of a judgment; **~ausfertigung** court-sealed copy of a judgment, engrossed copy of the judgment; **~begründung** reasons for the judgment, ratio decidendi, findings of law (of a judgment); **~beratung** deliberation of judgment; **~ergänzung** supplementation of the judgment; **~fähigkeit** strength of judgment; **~fällung** rendition of judgment, delivery of judgment; **~findung** adjudicative process; deliberations leading to a court decision; **~forderung** judgment claim, enforceable claim of a court judgment; **~formel** operative part of a judgment; **~gebühr** court fee for the judgment; **~gründe** reasons for judgment, grounds for a judgment, ratio decidendi; **~kopf** title of a judgment; **~kraft** discernment; **~register** judgment-book; **u~reif** *adj* ready for judgment; **~resümee** syllabus held, headnote; **~schelte** public criticism of a judgment; **~schuld** judgment debt; **~schuldner** judgment debtor; **~spruch** judgment, verdict, sentence; **~summe** sum adjudged (to be paid), sum recovered; **~staat** state where the judgment was rendered; **~tenor** operative part of a judgment; **~verfahren** proceedings leading to a judgment; **~verkündung** pronouncement of judgment, delivery of a judgment; rendition of judgment, passing of

Urwahl

judgment; **~vermögen** discernment, judgment; **~vollstreckung** execution of a judgment, enforcement of a judgment; **~zustellung** service of the judgment.

Urwahl *f* direct vote, primary election.

Usance *f* usage, habitual practice; völkerrechtliche **~n** international usage.

Usowechsel *m* bill at usance, usance draft.

Usurpation *f* usurpation.

Usurpator *m* usurper.

usurpieren *v/t* to usurp.

V

Vakanz *f* vacancy.
validieren *v/t* to validate (*securities*).
Validierung *f* validation.
Valoren *f/pl* valuables, securities; **~versicherung** insurance of valuables.
valorisieren *v/t* to valorize.
Valuta *f* value, foreign exchange, rate of exchange; foreign notes; value date, availability date; amount of mortgage loan; mortgage money, loan proceeds; **~abschluß** currency transaction; **~anleihe** loan in foreign currency, currency bonds; **~ausgleichsfonds** exchange equalization account; **~-Exporttratte** export draft in foreign currency; **~forderung** currency claim; **~gewinn** profit in foreign exchange; **~guthaben** holdings in foreign currency, foreign currency credit balance, balances with foreign bankers; **~klausel** value given clause, "value received" clause; foreign currency stipulation; **~konto** foreign currency account; **~kredit** foreign currency loan; **~kupon** foreign currency coupon; **v~mäßig** *adj* from the standpoint of foreign exchange policy; **~notierung** quotation of exchange; **~risiko** exchange risk; **~schuld** foreign currency debt; **v~schwach** *adj* soft-currency (*country*); **v~stark** *adj* hard-currency (*country*); **~tag** value date, effective date of credit entry; **~verhältnis** underlying debt relationship; **~verlust** currency loss; **~wechsel** foreign exchange bill, currency bill; **ankaufsfähige ausländische ~** purchasable foreign currency; **franko ~** free of payment, without any return consideration; **goldwertige ~** gold currency.

valutarisch *adj* relating to foreign exchange (currency).
Valuten|arbitrage arbitration of exchange; **~geschäft** dealing in foreign notes and coin; **~kurs** rate of exchange.
valutieren *v/i* to value, to state the value date, to amount to (*indebtedness under a mortgage*); to extend a loan.
Valutierung *f* value, stating the value, value date; **~stag** value date, settlement date.
Vandalismus *m* vandalism.
variabel *adj* variable, floating.
Variante *f* variant, different reading, different version.
Vasall *m* vassal; **~enstaat** vassal state, dependent state.
Vater *m* father, procreator; **~land** native country, mother country, fatherland; **~mord** patricide, parricide; **leiblicher ~** biological father, natural father.
Vaterschaft *f* paternity, fatherhood; **~sanerkennung** acknowledgment of paternity, recognition of paternity; **~sanfechtungsklage** suit for contesting paternity; **~sfeststellung** determination of paternity, affiliation; **~sfeststellungsurteil** declaration of parentage; **~sirrtum** erroneous assumption of paternity; **~sklage** legal action to establish paternity, affiliation proceedings, paternity suit; **~snachweis** proof of paternity; **~sprozess** paternity suit; **~svermutung** presumption of paternity; **die ~ behaupten** to affiliate, to claim paternity; **die ~ bestreiten** to deny paternity; **die ~ feststellen** to establish paternity; **eheliche ~** paternity in marriage; **nichteheliche ~** illegitimate paternity.
väterlich *adj* parental; **v~erseits** on the father's side, agnate.

verabreden *v/t*, to agree, to concert *v/reflex*, to make an appointment, to conspire.

verabredet *adj* mutually understood; **vorher** ~ preconcerted.

Verabredung *f* appointment, engagement, concerted action, conspiracy; ~ **einer Straftat** criminal conspiracy, conspiracy (to commit a crime); ~ **zum Mord** conspiracy to commit murder; ~ **zum Selbstmord** suicide pact.

verabreichen *v/t* to administer (*poison*).

verabsäumen *v/i* to neglect, to omit, to fail to meet, to (be in) default.

Verabsäumung *f* default, failure, neglect.

verabschieden *v/t* to discharge, to retire, to pension off, to place on the retired list (*officer etc*); to pass, to enact, to adopt (*legislation*).

Verabschiedung *f* discharge (*officer*); passing (*bill*), passage, enactment (*legislation*), adoption (*resolution*); ~ **e-s Gesetzes** passage of a bill, enactment.

verächtlich machen *v/t* to bring into contempt, to disparage.

Verächtlichmachung *f* disparagement, defamation; ~ **des Gerichts** contempt of court; ~ **von Personen** defamation (of persons), damaging a person's reputation.

veralten *v/i* to become obsolete, to become antiquated.

Veralterungsabschreibung *f* depreciation for obsolescence.

veraltet *adj* obsolete, out of date, defunct, stale, antiquated.

verändern *v/t* to change, to vary, to alter, to amend.

Veränderung *f* change (in *or* of), modification, alteration, variation (in); ~ **der Bedingungen** change of conditions; ~ **der Rechtsgrundlage** change of the legal basis; ~ **des Gesellschaftszwecks** change in the objects of a company; ~ **des Personenstandes** change of personal status; ~ **des rechtlichen Gesichtspunktes** change of the legal assessment; ~**smeldung** notice of a change, report on alterations; ~**snachweis** official record of changes; ~**ssperre** temporary prohibition to change sth (*structure of a building*), development freeze, preservation order; **geldwirtschaftliche** ~ change in monetary conditions; **gewaltsame** ~ violent change; **institutionelle** ~**en** institutional changes; **jahreszeitlich bedingte** ~ seasonal variation.

verankern *v/t* to anchor, to root in; **gesetzlich** ~ to embody in a law; **statutarisch** ~ to embody in the articles of association.

veranlagen *v/t* to assess (*income tax*); **zusammen** ~ to assess jointly (*married couple*).

Veranlagter *m* (*der Veranlagte*) income-tax payer, assessed person.

Veranlagung *f* (1) disposition, inclination; **bösartige** ~ general malice; **krankhafte** ~ pathological predisposition; **kriminelle** ~ criminal disposition.

Veranlagung *f* (2) (tax) assessment; ~ **zur Gemeindesteuer** assessment for local rates (*GB*); **gemeinsame** ~ joint (income tax) assessment; **getrennte** ~ separate income tax assessment of spouses.

Veranlagungs|bescheid tax assessment notice; ~**bezirk** area of assessment; **v**~**fähig** *adj* leviable; ~**grundlage** basis of assessment; ~**jahr** year of assessment; ~**objekt** property subject to assessment, item of assessment; ~**periode** period of assessment; ~**richtlinien** assessment directives; **v**~**technisch** *adj* related to the method (*or* timing) of assessment; ~**wert** assessment value; ~**zeitpunkt** date of assessment; ~**zeitraum** assessment period, fiscal period, taxable period.

veranlassen *v/t* to cause and procure, to induce, to actuate, to occasion, to prompt; *veranlaßt durch:* occasioned by, actuated by.

Veranlassung *f* initiation, instance, cause, inducement, direction, insti-

veranschlagen

gation; **auf seine** ~ on his initiative; **auf** ~ **des Gerichts** upon the court's own motion; **auf** ~ **von** by direction of, at the instance of, at the instigation of; **aus gegebener** ~ in view of the circumstances, as the occasion requires; **zur weiteren** ~ for further action, for appropriate action.

veranschlagen *v/t* to estimate, to appraise, to assess; **zu hoch** ~ to overrate.

Veranschlagung *f* estimate, rating, assessment; ~**szeitraum** chargeable accounting period.

Veranstalter *m* organizer, promoter; broadcaster.

verantworten *v/t, v/reflex* to answer (*a charge*), to account (for), to stand for; **sich** ~ **müssen** to be answerable (for).

verantwortlich *adj* answerable, responsible, accountable, liable; ~ **machen** to hold s.o. responsible; ~ **sein für** to answer for, to be liable for; **strafrechtlich** ~ criminally responsible (*or* liable), doli capax.

Verantwortlicher *m* (*der Verantwortliche*) person responsible (for), person having superintendence entrusted to him; **unmittelbar** ~ direct superior; person in charge.

Verantwortlichkeit *f* responsibility, accountability; **strafrechtliche** ~ criminal responsibility.

Verantwortung *f* responsibility; ~ **ablehnen** to decline (all) responsibility; ~ **tragen** to bear responsibility; **behördliche** ~ administrative responsibility; **die** ~ **für etwas übernehmen** to assume responsibility for sth; **die** ~ **tragen** to be responsible for; **jmdn aus der** ~ **entlassen** to discharge s.o. from responsibility; **jmdn zur** ~ **ziehen** to hold (*or* to make) s.o. responsible; **strafrechtliche** ~ criminal responsibility; **zivilrechtliche** ~ civil liability, civil responsibility.

Verantwortungsbereich *m* sphere of responsibility, field of jurisdiction; **v~bewußt** *adj* responsible, con-

Veräußerung

scious of one's responsibilities; ~**bewußtsein** acceptance of one's responsibilities; ~**freude** readiness to take responsibility; ~**gefühl** sense of responsibility; **v~los** *adj* irresponsible; **v~voll** *adj* responsible.

verarbeiten *v/t* to use material for work, to process, to make (material) into s.th., to use up.

Verarbeiter *m* processor, person (*or* firm) using material for production.

Verarbeitung *f* specification (acquisition of title by) conversion of material into a new article; working-up, processing; workmanship.

Verarbeitungsanweisung job order; ~**bestand** work-in-progress; ~**betrieb** manufacturing plant, processing enterprise, processing plant; ~**industrie** processing industries; ~**kosten** processing expenses; ~**stufe** stage of manufacture, stage of processing, processing stage; ~**verbot** processing prohibition.

verauktionieren *v/t* to auction, to put up for auction.

Verausgaben *n* = *Verausgabung qv.*

verausgaben *v/t* to expend, to spend, to show as expenditure.

Verausgabung *f* expenditure, disbursement; ~ **von Mitteln** disbursement of funds.

verauslagen *v/t* to pay expenses in advance (for s.o. else).

Verauslagung *f* temporary payment for another (*to be reimbursed*), out-of-pocket expense(s); ~ **von Beträgen und Sachaufwendungen** expenditure in money and in kind.

Veräußerer *m* transferor, assignor, grantor, vendor, seller, person disposing of property.

veräußerlich *adj* disposable, alienable, transferable, sellable, assignable.

veräußern *v/t* to transfer, to dispose, to alienate, to assign, to sell.

Veräußerung *f* alienation, disposal, transfer, assignment, sale; **freihän-**

dige ~ disposal by private agreement (*or* treaty); **schenkungsweise** ~ transfer by way of gift; **unentgeltliche** ~ gratuitous transfer, assignment without consideration.

Veräußerungsǀanzeige notice of alienation; ~**befugnis** power of alienation, dispositive power, power of disposition, power of sale; power to assign; ~**beschränkung** restriction (on the right of disposal); ~**erlös** proceeds from sale; ~**geschäfte** dealings involving alienation; ~**gewinn** capital gain on disposal, profit on sale; ~~ *von Investitionsgütern*: *capital profit*; ~**gewinnsteuer** capital gains tax; ~**mitteilung** notice of transfer to others; ~**recht** right of disposal, right of alienation; ~**sperre** temporary restraint on alienation, period of prohibition of sale, stop order; ~**verbot** total (*or* direct) prohibition of transfer, restraint on alienation; *gesetzliches* ~~: *statutory restraint on alienation*; *vertragliches* ~~: *pactum de non alienando*; ~**verlust** loss upon disposal, loss upon sale; ~**vorbehalt** reservation of the right of disposal; ~**wert** realization value, sale value, liquidation value; salvage value.

Verbalangebot *n* verbal offer.

Verbalbeleidigung *f* gross insult (*using obscene language*).

Verbalkontrakt *m* oral (*or* verbal) agreement.

Verbalnote *f* note verbale.

Verballhornung *f* distortion of a name *making it sound absurd*.

Verband *m* (*pl Verbände* = ~**e**) association federation, confederation, union, convention; ~ **zum Schutz der Rechte der Urheber an ihren Werken der Literatur und Kunst** Union for the Protection of the Rights of Authors in their Literary and Artistic Works; ~ **zum Schutz des gewerblichen Eigentums** (*Pariser Verband*) Union for the Protection of Industrial Property (*Paris Union*); **angeschlossene** ~**e** affiliated organizations; **karitative** ~**e** charitable institutions.

Verbandsǀklage legal action instituted by an association *in the interest of its members or the general public*, group action; ~**land** union-country, convention-country; association member-country; ~**marke** collective mark, certification mark, trade mark of a group; ~**priorität** convention priority; ~**satzung** articles of association (of a federation); ~**staat** union-state, federation state; ~**tarif** joint scale of charges; ~**übereinkunft zum Schutz des gewerblichen Eigentums** Convention for the Protection of Industrial Property; ~**wesen** (system of) associations; ~**zeichen** collective trade mark; *trade mark for use by members of a trade association*; ~**zeitschrift** trade paper.

verbannen *v/t* to banish.

Verbannter *m* (*der Verbannte*) exile, exiled person.

Verbannung *f* banishment, exile, deportment.

verbeamten *v/t* to grant the status of an established civil servant.

verbergen *v/t* to conceal, to hide.

verbessern *v/t* to rectify, to amend, to improve, to better.

Verbesserung *f* correction, rectification, amendment, improvement, betterment; amelioration; ~**en nach dem Stand der Technik** technological improvement; **ausgesprochene** ~ real improvement; **bauliche** ~**en** structural improvements; **organisatorische** ~ improvement in organization; **patentfähige** ~ patentable improvement; **technische** ~ technical improvement.

Verbesserungsǀerfindung invention of improvement, invention involving a real improvement; ~**frist** time-limit for correction; ~**mittel** means of improvement, improver; ~**patent** patent of improvement,

improvement patent; **~vorschläge** suggestions for improvement.

verbieten *v/t* to prohibit, to forbid, to proscribe, to enjoin (from), to disallow, to ban, to outlaw.

verbietend *adj* inhibitory, prohibitive, prohibitory.

Verbietungsrecht *n* right to prohibit sth.

verbilligen *v/t* to cheapen, to lower the price.

Verbilligung *f* price reduction, cheapening, making cheaper; **~sbeitrag** price-reduction subsidy; **~sschein** price-reduction certificate; **~szuschuß** price-reduction subsidy.

Verbinden *n* combination, (the act of) connecting; **das ~ von Erfindungselementen ohne neue Funktion** juxtaposition.

verbinden *v/t* to combine, to join, to associate, to unite, to connect.

verbindlich *adj* binding, compulsory; **~ machen** to confirm as binding, to obligate; **gleichermaßen ~** equally authentic (*text*); **nicht ~** of no binding force, non-obligatory.

Verbindlichkeit *f* obligation, liability, commitment; validity, binding character; *pl also*: outstanding liabilities, accounts payable; **~en an Beteiligungsgesellschaften** liabilities towards associated companies; **~en aus Gewährleistungsverträgen** liabilities arising from indemnities; **~en aus Lieferungen und Leistungen** creditors (trade), trade creditors; **~en aus Warenlieferungen** suppliers (*balance sheet*); **~en aus juristischer Personen** corporate obligations; **~ ohne Konventionalstrafklausel** single obligation, obligation without penalty clause; **~serklärung** declaration of commitment; **bedingte ~en** contingent liabilities; **befristete ~en** time liabilities; **e-e ~ eingehen** to assume an obligation, to enter into an engagement; **e-e ~ erfüllen** to discharge (*or* fulfil) an obligation; **e-e ~ erledigen** to discharge an obligation; **entstandene, noch nicht fällige ~en** accruals payable; **fällige ~en** matured liability; **frei von ~en** not liable, free from liabilities; **gleichrangige ~en** liabilities of equal priority; **konsolidierte ~en** funded debts, consolidated debts; **kurzfristige ~** short-term obligations; *pl also*: *current liabilities*; **langfristige fundierte ~en** fixed liabilities, funded debt; **langfristige ~** long-term obligation; *pl also*: *long-term liabilities, long-term debts*; **laufende ~en** current liabilities; **offene ~en** outstanding debts; **rechtsgültige ~** valid obligation; **reservepflichtige ~en** reserve-carrying liabilities, liabilities subject to the reserve requirements; **seinen ~en nachkommen** to meet one's obligations; **täglich fällige ~en** liabilities payable on demand; **unbedingte ~** actual (*or* direct) liability, unconditional obligation; **vertragsmäßige ~** contractual obligation; **voreheliche ~en** antenuptial debts, pre-marriage debts.

Verbindung *f* combination, accession, connexion (connection), tie, link, association; **~ durch Verarbeitung** adjunction; **~ von Prozessen** consolidation of proceedings, joinder of actions; **geheime ~en** secret societies; **miteinander in ~ treten** to intercommunicate, to form a link.

Verbindungs|amt liaison office; **~aufgaben** liaison duties; **~ausschuß** liaison committee; **~mann** contact man; **~offizier** liaison officer; **~stelle** liaison office; **~wege** communications.

Verbleib *m* stay, whereabouts, destination; **~squote** retention rate; **~ von Ausrüstungen und Vorräten** disposition of equipment and supplies; **„zum ~"** to be retained.

verbodmen *v/t* to hypothecate (*ship, cargo*).

verborgen *adj* hidden, concealed, latent; **nicht ~** unconcealed, overt, manifest.

Verböserung *f* deterioration (*of appellant's position*).

Verbot *n* prohibition, interdiction, proscription, ban; ~ **der Doppelbestrafung** double jeopardy clause; ~ **der Vorausverfügung** restraint on anticipation; ~ **der Warenursprungsfälschung** prohibition of passing off (*unfair trade doctrine*); ~ **rückwirkender Strafgesetze** ex post facto clause, prohibition on retroactive criminal legislation; ~ **unterschiedlicher Behandlung** ban on discriminatory treatment; **absolutes** ~ outright ban; **ein** ~ **aufheben** to lift a ban; **gerichtliches** ~ prohibitory order, negative injunction; **gesetzliches** ~ statutory prohibition; **polizeiliches** ~ police ban.

verboten *adj* forbidden, prohibited, illegal, illicit; **gesetzlich** ~ forbidden by law.

Verbots|bestimmung prohibition, prohibitory provision; **~gesetz** prohibiting law, negative statute, prohibitory enactment, legal provision containing a prohibition, statutory ban; **~gesetzgebung** proscriptive legislation; **~irrtum** error as to the prohibited nature of an act; **~liste** prohibited list, list of prohibitions; **~recht** right to prohibit; **~tafel** prohibitory sign; **~verfügung** banning order; **~zeichen** prohibitory sign.

Verbrauch *m* consumption, use; ~ **des gehobenen Bedarfs** consumption of luxury and semi-luxury goods; ~ **von Dienstleistungen** amount spent on services; **privater** ~ expenses of private consumption; **pro-Kopf-**~ per capita consumption; **staatlicher** ~ government consumption; **zum** ~ **im Inland** for home use.

verbrauchbar *adj* consumable.

verbrauchen *v/t* to consume.

Verbraucher *m* consumer; **~abgabe** excise duty; **~ausgaben** consumer spending; *private* ~ ~: *personal consumption*; **~befragung** consumer inquiry; **~benachteiligung** unfair consumer practices; **~betrieb** firm using the goods; **~einheit** spending unit; **~erwartung** customers' expectations; **~genossenschaft** consumers' co-operative; **~gewohnheit** spending habit; **~gruppe** consumer group, category of consumers; **~höchstpreis** retail ceiling price; **~industrie** consumer goods industry; **~kaufkraft** spending capacity; **~kredit** consumer credit; **~kreditgesetz** Consumer Credit Act; **~land** consumer country; **~markt** market-situation determined by consumers; **~nachfrage** consumer demand; **~preisindex** consumer price index; **~preisniveau** retail price level; **~schicht** category of consumers; **~schutz** consumer protection; **~schutzaktion** consumer campaign; **~schutzgesetz** Consumer Protection Act; **~schutztendenz** consumerism; **~täuschung** deception of consumers; **~test** consumer survey; **~verbände** consumers' associations; **~verträge** consumer contracts; **gewerbliche** ~ consumers in trade and industry; **marginaler** ~ marginal consumer.

Verbrauchs|abgabe excise (duty); **~artikel** article(s) of consumption; **~aufwendung** expenditure on consumption; **~ausgabe** expenditure on consumption, consumer expenditure; **v~bedingt** *adj* due to consumption; **~bereich** consumers; **~bild** pattern of consumption; **~einkommen** income available for consumption; **~freudigkeit** propensity to consume; **~gestaltung** consumption pattern; **~gewohnheiten** consumer habits, consumption pattern; **~güter** consumer goods; *gewerbliche* ~~: *industrially produced consumer goods*; *technische* ~~: (*the more*) *durable consumer goods*; **~güterindustrie** consumer-goods industry; **~güterkonjunktur** consumer-goods business trends; **~gütersektor** industries producing consumer goods;

Verbrechen / **Verbreitung**

~**konjunktur** trends of consumption, level of consumption; ~**land** consumer country; ~**nachfrage** consumer demand; v~**nah** *adj* closely related to consumer habits; **v~orientiert** *adj* orientated towards consumption, producing for consumption; ~**preise** retail prices; ~**quote** consumption ratio; ~**recht** right to consume (*or* use up) sth; ~**reserven** consumption-potential; ~**sättigung** saturation of consumer demand; ~**schema** pattern of consumption; ~**sektor** consumer goods sector; ~**steuer** excise tax, excise duty, tax on consumption; ~**steueraufschub** delaying excise control; **v~steuerfrei** *adj* unexcised, exempt from excise tax; ~**struktur** pattern of consumption; ~**symptom** indicator of consumption; ~**umschichtung** shift in consumption; ~**verlagerung** shift in consumption; ~**wirtschaft** consumer-goods sector, consumption-orientated economy.

Verbrechen *n* major (*or* serious) crime, indictable offence, felony; ~ **am untauglichen Objekt** abortive crime; ~ **auf offener Straße** street crime; ~ **gegen den Frieden** crime against peace; ~ **gegen die Menschlichkeit** crime against humanity; ~ **und Vergehen gegen die öffentliche Ordnung** felonies and misdemeanours against the public order; ~ **und Vergehen gegen die Person** felonies and misdemeanours committed against a person; ~ **und Vergehen gegen die Sicherheit des Staates und wider die öffentliche Ordnung** felonies and misdemeanours (committed) against the State and public order; ~ **und Vergehen gegen die Sittlichkeit** felonies and misdemeanours against morality and decency; ~ **und Vergehen im Amt** felonies and misdemeanours in office; **das ~ rechtfertigt die höchste Strafe** the crime justifies the (imposition of the) maximum penalty; **e-s ~s schuldig sprechen** to find s. o. guilty of a crime; **e–m ~ Vorschub leisten** to aid and abet; **ein ~ verüben** to perpetrate a crime; **gemeingefährliche ~** crimes entailing a danger to the community (at large); **jmdn e-s ~s überführen** to convict a person of a crime, to find s.o. guilty of a crime; **jmdn zu e–m ~ verleiten** to entice s.o. into committing a crime; **politisches ~** political crime; **selbständiges ~** independent crime, substantive felony; **versuchtes ~** attempted crime; **vollendetes ~** accomplished crime.

Verbrechens|bekämpfung crime-combatting, suppression of crime, crime busting; the fight against crime; ~**häufung** accumulation of crime; ~**schadensversicherung** crime insurance; ~**statistik** crime statistics; ~**verhütung** crime prevention; ~**vorsatz** felonious (*or* criminal) intent(ion).

Verbrecher *m* felon, (major) criminal, culprit; ~**album** rogues' gallery, mug book; ~**bande** gang (of criminals); **e-n ~ verbergen** to harbour (*or* to conceal) a criminal; **gemeingefährlicher ~** public enemy; **rückfälliger ~** recidivist, second and subsequent offender of a major crime; **unverbesserlicher ~** incorrigible criminal.

verbrecherisch *adj* criminal, felonious.

Verbrechertum *n* criminals, criminality; **berufsmäßiges ~** professional crime.

verbreiten *v/t* to disseminate, to disperse, to propagate, to spread.

Verbreiter *m* disseminator, promulgator; ~ **von Skandalgeschichten** scandal monger.

Verbreitung *f* dissemination, proliferation, dispersal, prevalence; ~**sort** place of distribution (*or* dissemination); ~**srechte** rights of distribution; ~**sverbot** prohibition of dissemination (*of seditious propaganda*); ~ **von falschem Geld** putting counterfeit money into circulation; ~ **von Kenntnissen** advancement of knowledge; ~ **unzüchtiger Schriften** dissemination of obscene writings; **freie ~ von Ideen** free flow of ideas.

Verbrennung *f* incineration, burning; ~ **ersten Grades** first degree burn; ~**sanlage** incinerator.

verbriefen *v/t* to record before a notary; to issue as a funded obligation, to certify; to acknowledge in writing, to document.

Verbriefung *f* embodiment in a notarial document, recording (of a deed) before a notary, formal conclusion of a contract (*conveyance*); ~**skosten** (*bei Auflassung*) conveyancing costs; ~ **von Buchkrediten** conversion of credits into security form.

verbringen *v/t* to commit (*to an institution*), to transfer.

Verbringung *f* committal; transfer, transportation; ~ **an Bord** loading on board; ~ **an Land** wharfing, unloading of a ship's cargo; ~**sgewahrsam** police custody; ~**sverbot** ban on dissemination of prohibited (propaganda) materials.

verbuchen *v/t* to post, to make an entry, to enter in the books, to register.

Verbuchung *f* entry; posting (entering) in the books, the making of an entry, inclusion in the books; ~**stitel** heading under which an item is booked (entered).

Verbund *m* combination, interlocking system, inter-operation, pool; ~**gefüge** coherent structure; ~**geschäft** linked deal; ~**netz** linked supply system, electricity grid; ~**produkt** joint product; ~**sache** joint proceedings (*in matrimonial and incidental matters*); ~**strompreis** centrally authorized price of electricity; ~**starif** joint rates; ~**unternehmen** network enterprises; ~**werbung** association advertising, combined advertising; ~**wirtschaft** coordinated industrial system, interlinked business enterprises, vertical integration.

verbunden *adj* connected, linked, united; affiliated; **fest** ~ adherent, firmly connected (with).

Verbundenheit *f* solidarity; ~~ *Europas mit den überseeischen Ländern*: solidarity which binds Europe with countries overseas.

verbündet *adj* allied.

Verbündeter *m* (*der Verbündete*) ally, allied state, allied power, confederate.

verbürgen *v/t*, to guarantee, to warrant, to stand surety for; *v/reflex*: to stand surety (for), to accept a guarantee (for).

Verbuschung *f* excessive growth of shrubs (*nature preservation*).

verbüßen *v/t* to serve one's sentence, to complete one's sentence.

Verbüßung *f* completion of one's sentence; **gleichzeitige ~ von Freiheitsstrafen** (serving of) concurrent terms, concurrent sentences.

Vercharterung *f* chartering (of a vessel).

Verdacht *m* suspicion; ~**säußerung** expression of suspicion; ~**skündigung** *termination of employment based on a strong suspicion of an offence*; ~**smoment** suspicious factor, suspicious circumstance; **begründeter ~** suspicion based on a good reason, justifiable suspicion; **dringender ~** strong suspicion; **e-n ~ zerstreuen** to dispel (a) suspicion; **grundloser ~** gratuitous suspicion; **hinreichender ~** (upon) reasonable suspicion; **in ~ geraten** to incur suspicion; **in ~ stehen** to be suspected; **über jeden ~ erhaben** beyond suspicion; **unbegründeter ~** unfounded suspicion; **unter ~ stehen** to be suspected.

verdächtig *adj* suspect, suspected, suspicious.

verdächtigen *v/t* to cast suspicion upon s.o., to suspect s.o. of sth.

Verdächtiger *m* (*der Verdächtige*), suspect, person suspected of (having committed) a crime.

Verdächtigung *f* casting suspicion (upon s.o); suspecting s.o. (of); ~

wider besseres Wissen intentional casting of unfounded suspicion upon another person (*with knowledge of the true facts*); **politische** ~ casting political suspicion upon another person.

Verdatung *f* computerization.

verdeckt *adj* covered, concealed, undisclosed.

Verdeckung *f* concealment, covering-up; **~sabsicht** intention to conceal.

Verderb *m* spoilage, deterioration, waste; **gewöhnlicher** ~ normal deterioration; **innerer** ~ inherent (*or* spontaneous, *or* natural) deterioration.

verderben *v/t, v/i* to spoil, to vitiate.

verderblich *adj* perishable; **nicht** ~ non-perishable.

Verderblichkeit *f* perishability; **leichte** ~ inherent (*or* intrinsic) deterioration.

verderbt *adj* debauched, perverse.

Verdeutlichung *f* elucidation, explication, clarification.

verdienen *v/t* to earn, to gain, to deserve.

Verdienst *m* (*1*) earnings income, gain; **v~abhängig** earnings-related; **~ausfall** loss of earnings; **~aussichten** earnings prospects; **~einbuße** loss of income; **~grenze** limit of earnings; **~möglichkeit** potential earnings, earning capacity; **~obergrenze** upper earnings limit; **~sicherungsklausel** standard wage maintenance clause (*in case of piece work*); **~spanne** margin, sales margin, profit margin, margin of profit; **tatsächlicher** ~ actual earnings; **tariflicher** ~ standard earnings under collective wage agreements.

Verdienst *n* (*2*) merit, desert(s).

verdingen *v/reflex* to go into service (with), to bind oneself as servant.

Verdingung *f* hire, hiring out; contract for services; **~sordnung** standard official contracting terms; ~~ *für Bauleistungen (VOB)*: *standard building contract terms; contractual scale of building performance.*

Verdrängungstonne *f* displacement ton.

Verdrängungswettbewerb *m* displacement competition.

verdrehen *v/t* to pervert, to distort (*the truth, meaning*), to twist.

Verdrehung *f* distortion, perversion.

verdunkeln *v/t* to obscure, to prevaricate, camouflage.

Verdunkelung *f* obscuration, suppression of evidence; (danger of) collusion; ~ **e-r Straftat** suppressing evidence of a crime; **~sgefahr** risk of suppression of evidence, danger of collusion.

veredeln *v/t* to refine, to finish, to process.

Veredelung finishing, refining, refinement, processing, job processing; **aktive** ~ inward processing; **passive** ~outward processing.

Veredelungs|betrieb processing enterprise, finishing plant; **~erzeugnis** finished product, processed product, compensated product; **~industrie** processing industry, finishing industry, refining industry; **~land** processing country; **~lohn** payment for processing; **~steuer** processing tax; **~verfahren** finishing process; **~verkehr** processing trade, across-the-border processing; **~werk** finishing plant; **~wert** value added by processing; **~wirtschaft** processing trade, finishing industry; *tierische* ~~: *stock-raising and dairy farming*.

verehelichen *v/reflex* to marry, to get married.

Verehelichung *f* (celebration of) marriage, solemnization of marriage.

vereidigen *v/t* to administer an oath, to swear in.

vereidigt *adj* sworn; **vorschriftsmäßig** ~ duly sworn.

Vereidigung *f* administration of the oath, swearing in, oath-taking ceremony; **auf** ~ **verzichten** to dispense with an oath.

Verein (membership) association,

society, club; **eingetragener** ~ (*e. V.*) registered society, incorporated society, incorporated association; membership corporation **gemeinnütziger** ~ non-profit-making association, charitable organization; **nicht eingetragener** ~ non-incorporated body, unincorporated society; unregistered society; **nicht rechtsfähiger** ~ unincorporated association; **rechtsfähiger** ~ incorporated society (*or* association).

vereinbar *adj* compatible, reconcilable, consistent.

vereinbaren *v/t* to agree, to come to an agreement, to stipulate; **förmlich** ~ to stipulate in a formal agreement; **schriftlich** ~ to stipulate in writing.

Vereinbarkeit *f* compatibility, reconcilability.

vereinbart *adj* agreed (upon), stipulated, negotiated, pactional; **erklärt wie** ~ agreed and declared; **es gilt als** ~ it is deemed to be agreed that; **soweit nichts anderes** ~ failing an agreement to the contrary, unless otherwise agreed, save as otherwise provided; **vertraglich** ~ stipulated by contract, contractually agreed; **wie** ~ as stipulated.

Vereinbarung *f* agreement (= *agr*), contract, stipulation; *int also*: convention; memorandum of understanding; ~ **auf Gegenseitigkeit** reciprocal *agr*; ~ **auf Treu und Glauben** bona fide *agr*, gentlemen's *agr*; ~ **des Erfüllungsort(e)s** appointment of a place of performance (or fulfilment); ~ **e-r Konventionalstrafe** stipulation of a contract penalty; ~ **e-r Vertragsstrafe** stipulation of a contract penalty; ~ **e-s Schiedsgerichts** submission to arbitration; ~ **ohne Gegenleistung** naked contract; **~sdarlehen** loan by *agt*, conventional loan; **v~sgemäß** as agreed, in accordance with our agreement, pursuant to (our) contract; ~ **über das Getrenntleben** separation *agr*, articles (*or* deed) of separation; ~ **über Preisbindung** price fixing *agr*, ~ **von pauschaliertem Schadensersatz** liquidated damages clause; ~ **zur Vermeidung der Doppelbesteuerung** double taxation arrangements, convention for the avoidance of double taxation; ~ **zur Zusammenarbeit** co-operative arrangement; **ausdrückliche** ~ express *agr*, explicit *agr*; **außergerichtliche** ~ out-of-court settlement; **bestehende ~en** existing *agr–s*; **e-e** ~ **aufheben** to abrogate (*or* to cancel, *or* to annul) a stipulation (*or* an *agr*); **e-e** ~ **treffen** to reach (*or* to conclude) an *agr*; **entgegenstehende ~en** any *agr* to the contrary; **formlose** ~ understanding, informal *agr*; **gegenseitige** ~ mutual *agr*; **gemäß** ~ as per *agr*, pursuant to the *agr*; **je nach** ~ as may be agreed; **mangels abweichender** ~ unless otherwise agreed; in the absence of any *agr* to the contrary; **mangels besonderer** ~ in the absence of some express stipulation; **mangels gegenteiliger** ~ in the absence of any provision to the contrary; **maßgebende ~en** agreements which are material (for this purpose); **mündliche** ~ oral (*or* verbal) *agr*, **nachträgliche ~en** subsequent *agr–s*; **privatschriftliche** ~ *agr* under hand, handwritten *agr*; **schuldrechtliche** ~ *agr* under the law of obligations (contractual *agr*); **sich an e-e** ~ **halten** to keep to an *agr*, to stand by one's *agr*; **stillschweigende** ~ tacit understanding, implied *agr* **unbeschadet anderweitiger** ~ unless otherwise agreed; **ursprüngliche** ~ original *agr*; **verbotene ~en** prohibited *agr–s*; **vertragliche** ~ contractual *agr*; **völkerrechtliche** ~ convention, treaty, international *agr*; **vorbehaltlich ausdrücklicher** ~ subject to express stipulation; **vorbehaltlich gegenteiliger** ~ subject to stipulation to the contrary; **vorherige** ~ previous *agr*; **vorläufige** ~ interim *agr*; provisional *agr;* **wettbewerbsbeschränkende ~en** *agr–s* in restraint of competition.

vereinheitlichen *v/t* to standardize, to unify, to secure uniformity, to harmonize.

Vereinheitlichung *f* standardization, unification, achievement of uniformity, harmonization.

vereinigen *v/t* to unite, to combine, *v/reflex* to associate, to combine.

vereinigt *adj* united.

Vereinigte Große Senate German Federal (Supreme) Court in plenary session; ~ **Internationale Büros zum Schutz des geistigen Eigentums** United International Bureaux for the Protection of Intellectual Property; ~ **Internationale Büros zum Schutz des gewerblichen, literarischen und künstlerischen Eigentums** United International Bureaux for the Protection of Industrial, Literary and Artistic Property.

Vereinigung *f* association, federation, organization; amalgamation, union, merger, confusion; ~ **der Arbeitgeber** employers' association; ~ **mehrerer Hypotheken** consolidation of mortgages; **~sfreiheit** freedom to form associations; **~srecht** right to form associations; **~szeitplan** timetable for unity; ~ **von Aktien** consolidation of shares; ~ **von Forderung und Schuld** confusion of debts; ~ **von Grundstücken** real estate consolidation (by merging several plots); ~ **von Rechten in e-r Person** merger of rights; ~ **von Wertpapierinhabern** association of security holders; **gemeinnützige** ~ non-profit association; **kriminelle ~en** criminal societies (*or* associations); **rechtsfähige** ~ incorporated association; **terroristische** ~ terroristic combination; **verbotene** ~ prohibited association, unlawful society, unlawful organization; **verfassungsfeindliche** ~ seditious group, anti-constitutional organization; **widerrechtliche** ~ unlawful association; **wohltätige** ~ benevolent society.

vereinnahmen *v/t* to receive, to collect.

Vereinnahmung *f* receipt, collection.

Vereins|auflösung disincorporation, dissolution of a club; **~beitrag** club dues, membership fee; **~freiheit** freedom of association; **~gesetz** Act regulating clubs and associations; **~kasse** club treasurer's office, society funds; **~mitglied** member of an association, club member; **~mitgliedschaft** membership (of an association or club); **~recht** law of associations; law governing societies; *öffentliches* **~~:** *law of public organizations;* **~register** (court) register of associations, register of societies; **~sachen** society matters; **~satzung** regulations of a society (*or* association); **~sperre** club embargo; embargo on further club membership; **~sstrafe** penalty of a club; **~sverbot** prohibition of an association; **~vermögen** society assets, club property; **~vorsitzender** president of an association, club chairman; **~vorstand** association's president; executive committee of an association; **~wesen** clubs and societies.

Vereiteln n = *Vereitelung qv;* ~ **der Zwangsvollstreckung** frustration (*or* prevention) of civil execution.

vereiteln *v/t* to defeat, to thwart, to prevent, to frustrate.

Vereitelung *f* frustration, prevention; ~ **der Befriedigung von Gläubigern** frustrating the satisfaction of creditors, hindering and delaying creditors; ~ **des Beweises** = *Beweisvereitelung qv.*

Verelendungstheorie *f* pauperization theory.

vererbbar *adj* hereditary.

vererben *v/t* to bequeath, to leave, to pass on by inheritance.

vererblich *adj* inheritable, hereditable.

Vererblichkeit *f* inheritability.

Vererbung *f* inheritance, heredity, transmission by succession.

Verfahren *n* (1) procedure (*law of procedure*); proceedings (*individual case*), suit; ~ **bei Rechtshilfeersuchen** procedure for letters rogatory; ~ **der Beweisaufnahme** procedure for taking evidence; ~ **in Ehesachen** procedure in matrimonial cases, matrimonial causes; ~ **in familienrechtlichen Angelegenheiten** domestic proceedings; ~ **in Nichtigkeitssachen** nullity proceedings; ~ **mit Geschworenen** jury trial; ~ **nach Einweisung** post-commitment hearing (*institution*); ~ **über dingliche Rechte** = *dingliches* ~ *qv*; ~ **vor dem Patentamt** patent office procedure; ~ **wegen Aufenthaltsverbots** administrative proceedings to expel; **abgekürztes** ~ summary proceedings; **angemessenes** ~ appropriate procedure; **anhängiges** ~ pending case (*or* proceedings); **beschleunigtes** ~ summary procedure, accelerated proceedings, speedy proceedings; **das** ~ **aussetzen** to stay (the) proceedings (*or* action), to suspend proceedings; **das** ~ **beschleunigen** to expedite the proceedings; **das** ~ **einstellen** to quash proceedings, to withdraw the charge; to dismiss a case; ~~ *wegen Geringfügigkeit einstellen:* to *discontinue proceedings in view of the insignificance of the matter*; **das** ~ **niederschlagen** to quash the proceedings; **das** ~ **unterbrechen** to discontinue the proceedings; **das** ~ **wiederaufnehmen** to reopen a case, to try a case de novo; **dingliches** ~ proceedings in rem, suit in rem; **ein** ~ **anstrengen** to take proceedings; **ein** ~ **betreiben** to prosecute a case, to proceed with an action; **ein** ~ **einleiten** to institute proceedings; **ein** ~ **ruhen lassen** to let proceedings rest; **ein** ~ **wird anhängig** a case becomes pending in court, proceedings arise; **fehlerhaftes** ~ flawed proceedings; irregular proceedings; **geeignete** ~ appropriate machinery; **gerechtes** ~ fair trial; **gerichtliches** ~ proceedings in court, judicial action; judicial procedure, court procedure; **in das** ~ **eintreten** to intervene in the proceedings; **in e-m schwebenden** ~ pendente lite; **inquisitorisches** ~ inquisitorial procedure; **kontradiktorisches** ~ adversary procedure; **kurzes** ~ summary proceedings, short trial; **langwieriges** ~ lengthy procedure; **mündliches** ~ oral proceedings, verbal process; **nichtstrafrechtliches** ~ non-penal proceedings; **nichtstreitiges** ~ non-contentious proceedings; **objektives** ~ in rem proceedings (*condemnation and confiscation of items*); **ordentliches** ~ ordinary proceedings, main trial; standard procedure; general court procedure; **ordnungsgemäßes** ~ due process of law; **parlamentarisches** ~ parliamentary practice, parliamentary procedure; **rechtshängiges** ~ active proceedings, pending proceeding's; **rechtliches** ~ legal procedure; **rechtsstaatliches** ~ due process of law; **schiedsrichterliches** ~ arbitration (procedure), arbitration (proceedings); **schriftliches** ~ written proceedings; **schwebendes** ~ pending proceedings (*or* case); **strafrechtliches** ~ criminal procedure; **streitiges** ~ litigious procedure, litigation, litigious proceedings; **summarisches** ~ summary proceedings, summary action; **ungerechtes** ~ unfair trial; **unübliches** ~ irregular proceedings, *or* procedure; **vollkommen neues** ~ fresh proceedings, action de novo, a completely fresh trial; **während des** ~**s** in the course of the proceedings; ~~ *schwebenden* ~: *pendente lite*; **wiederaufgenommenes** ~ revived action.

Verfahren *n* (2) method, process, operation, treatment, technique; ~ **bei der Zahlung** method of payment; ~ **für gedankliche Tätigkeiten** (*PatG*) method for performing mental acts; **~snummer** processing number; **~spatent** process patent; **ein ~ einschlagen** to go through a process; **gesetzlich geschütztes ~** proprietary process; **mechanisches ~** mechanical process; **patentfähiges ~** patentable process; **patentiertes ~** patented process; **traditionelles ~** established procedure; **üblicher ~** customary procedure.

verfahren v/i to proceed; **ordnungsgemäß ~** to proceed in a regular manner.

Verfahrens|änderung change in procedure; **~antrag** procedural motion, interlocutory application, adjective motion; motion on a point of order; **~art** type of procedure; **~ausschuß** committee on procedure; **~beschluß** procedural order; **~bestimmung** procedural provision, pl also: rules of procedure; **~beteiligte** parties to the proceedings; **~einstellung** dismissal, withdrawal of the charge; *einstweilige ~~*: *suspension of proceedings*; **~erfindung** invention of a process; **~fehler** procedural error, pl also: formal irregularities in the proceedings; **~fortsetzung** resuming the hearing, resumption of the trial; **~frage** point of order, procedural question, question of procedure; **~freiheit** free choice of procedure; **~frist** procedural time-limit; **~gang** course of procedure; **~grundrechte** fundamental procedural rights; **~hindernis** procedural bar, hindrance to proceedings; **~kosten** cost(s) of the proceedings; *die ~~ verteilen*: *to apportion the costs*; **~mangel** procedural mistake, error of procedure; *e-m ~~ abhelfen*: *to rectify (or: correct) a procedural mistake*; **v~mäßig** adj procedural, adjective, adv as regards procedure; **~merkmal** element of procedure; **~norm** rule (of procedure), procedural norm; **~ordnung** rules of procedure; rules of practice, code of procedure; **~patent** method patent, process patent; **~raffinesse** procedural niceties; **~recht** law of procedure, procedural law, adjective law; **v~rechtlich** adj procedural; **~regel** rule, procedural rule, rule of procedure, pl. also: rules of procedure; **~rüge** procedural objection; **~schritt** stage in the proceedings; **~sicherungen** procedural safeguards; **~sprache** language of the proceedings; **v~technisch** adj technical; **~trick** procedural device; **~verordnung** ordinance on procedure; **~verschleppung** delaying the progress of the proceedings; **~verstoß** irregularity; *formaler ~~*: *legal irregularity*; *wesentlicher ~~*: *material irregularity*; *auf die Folgen des ~~es verzichten*: *to waive the irregularity*; **~voraussetzungen** procedural preconditions; **~vorschriften** rules of procedure, procedure requirement; *gerichtliche ~~*: *rules of court*.

Verfall m (1) forfeiture; maturity (*bill of exchange*), due date; lapse (*policy*); **~datum** sell-by-date; **~e-s Patents** forfeiture of a patent; **~ e-s Pfandes** forfeiture of a pledge; **~frist** preclusive deadline (or period); **~klausel** cancellation clause; accelerating clause (*in the sense of Fälligkeitsklausel q.v.*); **~pfand** forfeiture pledge; **~serklärung von Aktien** cancellation of shares; **~stag** day of maturity, expiration date (*policy*); **~stermin** maturity, expiry date; **~svertrag** forfeiture agreement; **~szeit** time of expiration; **mit ~sandrohung** on pain of forfeiture; **nach ~** when overdue (*bill of exchange*).

Verfall m (2) decay, dilapidation.

verfallen v/i forfeit, to become forfeited; to expire, to lapse; to expire, to cease to be valid.

verfallen adj overdue, forfeited, lapsed, expired.

verfälschen to falsify, to forge, to adulterate (*food, wine*).

Verfälschung f falsification, forging, adulteration.

verfassen *v/t* to draft, draw up, to prepare.

Verfasser *m* author, writer; **~anteil** (author's) royalty; **~eigenschaft** authorship.

Verfassung *f (1)* condition, state.

Verfassung *f (2)* constitution; **bundesstaatliche ~** federal constitution; **demokratische ~** democratic constitution; **geschriebene ~** written constitution; **ungeschriebene ~** unwritten constitution.

Verfassungs|änderung amendment to the constitution, constitutional amendment; **~auftrag** constitutional directive *(to the state organs)*; **~beschwerde** constitutional complaint, petition to constitutional court *based on allegation of infringement of constitutional right*; **~bruch** violation of the constitution; **~feind** enemy of the democratic constitutional order; extremist; **v~feindlich** *adj* inimical to the constitution, seditious, anti-constitutional; **~garantie** constitutional guarantee; **v~gebend** *adj* constituent, creating constitutional law; **v~gemäß** *adj* constitutional, compatible with the constitution; **~gericht** constitutional court; **~gerichtsbarkeit** jurisdiction of the constitutional court; **~gerichtshof** Supreme Constitutional Court; **~geschichte** constitutional history; **~grundsätze** constitutional principles; **~klage** action to have a bill declared unconstitutional, action in a constitutional court; **~konflikt** constitutional conflict; **~kontrolle** check as to constitutionality, control of constitutionality; **v~mäßig** *adj* constitutional; **~mäßigkeit** constitutionality; **~organ** entity created under the constitution, constitutional organ; **~recht** constitutional law; **~srechtler** constitutional lawyer; **~reform** constitutional reform; **~richter** constitutional court judge; **~schutz** protection of the constitutional order; (Office for the) Protection of the Constitution; (German) intelligence service against subversive activities; **~staat** constitutional state (system); **~streit** constitutional conflict; **~streitigkeiten** litigation in constitutional matters; **~treue** loyalty to the constitution; **~urkunde** constitutional charter, instrument of the constitution; **~verrat** treason against the constitution; **v~widrig** *adj* unconstitutional, anti-constitutional; **~widrigkeit** unconstitutionality, contravention of the constitution, unconstitutional act; **~wirklichkeit** constitutional reality; **~zusatz** constitutional amendment.

Verfechter *m* supporter, partisan.

Verfehlung *f* (minor) offence, misdemeanour, lapse.

verfemen *v/t* to outlaw, to ostracize, to send to Coventry.

Verfilmungsrecht(e) *n/pl* film rights, screen(ing) rights.

Verflechtung *f* integration, interlocking, inter-connections, interdependence; **vertikale ~** vertical combination, vertical integration; **~ der Volkswirtschaften** interpenetration of national economies; **~ wirtschaftlicher Interessen** interpenetration of industrial interests.

verfolgbar *adj* actionable, subject to prosecution, suable.

verfolgen *v/t* to pursue, to prosecute, to persecute; **gerichtlich ~** to prosecute; **politisch ~** to persecute for political reasons; **steckbrieflich ~** to search, to conduct a police search; **~ verfolgt werden**: *to be wanted by the police*; **strafrechtlich ~** to charge with an offence, to prosecute.

Verfolger *m* pursuer, persecutor.

Verfolgter *m (der Verfolgte)* persecutee; **politisch ~** political persecutee; **politisch, rassisch oder aus religiösen Gründen ~** person persecuted for political, racial or religious reasons.

Verfolgung *f* pursuit, prosecution; persecution; **~srecht** right of stop-

verfrachten

page in transitu, right of pursuing title; ~~ *über die Staatsgrenze: right of hot pursuit (across the border)*; **~sverjährung** limitation of prosecutions; **~szwang** compulsory prosecution of criminal offences; **~ Unschuldiger** prosecution (*or* persecution) of innocent persons; **~ von Zuwiderhandlungen** prosecution for contraventions; **disziplinarische ~** disciplinary prosecution; **gerichtliche ~** (judicial) prosecution; **politische ~** persecution for political reasons.

verfrachten *v/t* to transport goods (by sea).

Verfrachter *m* shipper.

Verfrachtung *f* carriage of goods by sea; **~svertrag** contract of maritime transport of goods, contract of affreightment.

verfügbar *adj* available, disposable; **~e** *Arbeiter manpower resources, labour resources;* **~e** *Mittel available cash, liquid funds.*

Verfügbarkeit *f* availability, disposability.

verfügen *v/i* to direct, to order, to decree; to deal with, to dispose (of sth), to have sth at one's disposal; **letztwillig ~** to dispose by will; **testamentarisch ~** to dispose by will.

Verfügung *f* (1) direction, order, decision, instruction; **~en von hoher Hand** acts decreed by public authorities; **amtliche ~** official direction; **~sanspruch** entitlement to an interim order (*or* injunction); **auf Grund gerichtlicher ~** by order of the court; **einstweilige ~** interim injunction; provisional injunction, interlocutory injunction; ~~ *auf Unterlassung: prohibitory injunction*; **gerichtliche ~** court order, order of the court; ~~, *sich zu äußern: order to show cause*; **gesetzliche ~** decree, ordinance, statutory instrument; **laut ~** as directed, as ordered; **polizeiliche ~** police order; **prozeßleitende ~** order for directions; **richterliche ~** judicial or-

Verfügungsbefugnis

der, order of the court; *pl also*: rulings of the court.

Verfügung *f* (2) disposal, disposition, transfer (*of possession, a thing, ownership, rights*); transaction (*in rem*); **~ angesichts des Todes** transfer in contemplation of death; **~ e-s Nichtberechtigten** disposition by a non-entitled party; **~ unter Lebenden** disposition (*or* transaction) inter vivos; **~ von Todes wegen** disposition mortis causa: *testament and/or deed of succession (Erbvertrag)*; **begünstigende ~** beneficial disposition; disposition with a preference; fraudulent conveyance; **freie ~** free disposition; **korrespektive ~en** reciprocal dispositions; **letztwillige ~** last will, testament; **letztwillige ~ gegen Lebensverlängerung** living will; **rechtsgeschäftliche ~** contractual disposition, voluntary disposition; **schriftliche ~** order in writing; **testamentarische ~** testamentary disposition; **unentgeltliche ~** gratuitous disposition; **wechselbezügliche ~en** reciprocal dispositions; **wechselseitige ~en** reciprocal dispositions; **widerrechtliche ~en** illegal transactions; **zur ~ stellen** to place at s.o.'s disposal, to make available; **zwingend vorgeschriebene ~** obligatory disposition.

Verfügungs|befugnis power of disposal; power of disposition; **~berechtigter** party entitled to dispose of sth, authorized agent; **~berechtigung** authority to dispose (*of sth.*); **~bereitschaft** readiness of being at s.o.'s disposal, readiness to serve in the Armed Force at any time; **~sbeschränkung** restraint on disposal, limitation of the right to dispose of sth; **~einkommen** disposable income; **~gewalt** power of disposition, control, power of disposal; possession, order of disposition (*bankrupt*); *unbeschränkte* ~~: *full and absolute control*; **~geschäft** disposition; *the act of transferring, encumbering or discharging*; ~**grund** urgency of applying for an interim injunction; ~**macht** disposing power, disposing capacity; ~**recht** right of disposal, power of disposition; *das alleinige* ~~: *the sole right of disposition*; *das* ~~ *haben: to have power of disposal of*; ~**sperre** prohibition on disposal, restraining order; ~**unfähigkeit** legal disability to dispose; ~**verbot** restraint on disposition, restraining order; *vorläufiges* ~~: *stop order*.

verführen *v/t* to mislead, to seduce, to entice, to lead astray.

Verführung *f* enticement, seduction; ~ **e–s** (*e–r*) **Minderjährigen** seduction of a minor.

Vergabe *f* placing, contracting, award (*of contract*), allocation (*of funds*), grant; ~ **im Submissionsweg** allocation by tenders; ~**verordnung** (*uniform*) regulations on limited university admission; ~ **von Stipendien** award of scholarships (*or grants*); **beschränkte** ~ limited tender; **freie** ~ open invitation to tender.

vergällen *v/t* to denature.

Vergällung *f* denaturing; ~**smittel** denaturing agent.

Vergangenheit *f* the past, previous record; **schlechte** ~ bad record.

vergeben *v/t* to award (*a contract*).

Vergehen *n* criminal offence, misdemeano(u)r (*subject to imprisonment or a fine*); ~ **gegen die Landesverteidigung** offence against national defence; ~ **im Amte** criminal offence in public office; **politisches** ~ political offence; **schweres** ~ indictable offence; ~~ *gegen fremde Patentrechte: grave infringement of another's patent rights*; **sittenwidriges** ~ offence against morality; **vorsätzliches** ~ wilful offence; **verabscheuungswürdiges** ~ heinous crime.

vergehen *v/reflex* to commit a grave offence, to violate, to commit an indecent assault, to commit an outrage.

vergelten *v/t* to retort, to retaliate.

Vergeltung *f* retaliation, reprisal, retribution; ~**sgesetz** retaliatory law; ~**smaßnahmen** reprisals, retaliatory measures; ~**sprinzip** principle of retaliation; ~**srecht** law of reprisal, right of retaliation, right of retorsion; ~**szoll** retaliatory tariff; ~ **üben** to retaliate, to take reprisals.

vergewaltigen *v/t* to rape, to ravish.

Vergewaltigung *f* rape, ravishment; ~ **durch den eigenen Ehemann** marital rape; **mehrfache** ~ gang-rape.

vergewissern *v/reflex* to make certain, to make sure.

vergiften *v/t* to poison, to administer poison.

Vergiftung *f* poisoning; **gemeingefährliche** ~ environmental poisoning, spreading poisonous substances dangerous to the public.

Vergleich *m* (1) comparison; ~**sbilanz** comparative balance sheet; ~**sgrundstück** comparable property; ~**smiete** equivalent comparative rent (*of similar premises*); ~**smuster** reference sample; ~**subject** comparable property (*or* flat); ~**sstichproben** matched samples; ~**swert** comparison-figure, comparative value; ~**szeitraum** comparable period, period taken as basis of comparison; **schiefer** ~ false analogy.

Vergleich *m* (2) settlement, compromise, composition, arrangement; ~ **anmelden** = ~*santrag stellen*; → *Vergleichsantrag*; ~ **mit den Gläubigern** composition with creditors; arrangement with one's creditors; ~ **zur Abwendung des Konkurses** composition with creditors to avert bankruptcy; **außergerichtlicher** ~ private settlement, out-of-court settlement, pre-trial settlement, (amicable) arrangement; **e–n** ~ **annehmen** to accept a compromise, to agreee to a settlement; **e–n** ~ **eingehen** to reach a settlement; **e–n** ~ **perfekt machen** to finalize a settlement, to make a compromise arrangement watertight; **e-n ~ schließen** to compromise, to reach a settlement; **gerichtlicher ~** court settlement; **gütlicher ~** amicable arrangement *or* settlement.

vergleichen *v/reflex* to reach a compromise.

Vergleichs|angebot settlement offer; **~antrag** petition to institute composition proceedings; **~~ stellen**: *to file for insolvency protection (composition proceedings), to file for protection (from creditors) under Chapter 11 of the Bankruptcy Code (US)*; **~basis** basis for a compromise; **~bedingungen** terms of composition; **~beispiel** comparative example; **v~bereit** *adj* prepared to negotiate a settlement; **~bereitschaft** readiness to come to a compromise; **~garant** guarantor of a composition offer; **~gebühr** (counsel's) fee for negotiating a settlement; **~gericht** court for composition proceedings; **~gläubiger** creditor in composition proceedings; **~maßstab** standard unit for comparison, bench mark (*US*); **~ordnung** Composition Code (*of procedure for arrangements between debtor and creditors*); **~person** comparator; **~miete** amount of rent for comparison; **~plan** scheme of arrangement; **~quote** composition dividend, dividend on a composition settlement; **~status** statement of affairs in composition proceedings; **~schuldner** debtor under a composition arrangement; **~termin** (meeting of creditors) hearing in composition proceedings; **~- und Schiedsordnung** rules of conciliation and arbitration; **~~** *der Internationalen Handelskammer*: *Conciliation and Arbitration Rules of the International Chamber of Commerce*; **~verfahren** composition proceedings (*to avert bankruptcy*), *int*: conciliation proceedings; *gerichtliches* **~~**: *judicial composition, US: "Chapt 11" receivership*; **~versuch** comparative test; **~verwalter** receiver (*composition proceedings*); **~vorschlag** settlement offer, suggestion of a compromise; proposal in composition proceedings; **v~weise** *adj, adv* by way of compromise (*or* settlement); **~wohnung** comparable accomodation; **~zahl** comparative figure.

Vergnügungs|industrie entertainment industry, leisure industry; **~park** amusement park; **~reise** pleasure trip, pleasure cruise; **~stätte** place of public entertainment (= *öffentliche* **~~**); **~steuer** entertainment tax, entertainment duty, amusement tax.

vergriffen *adj* sold out, out of print, out of stock.

Vergleichbarkeit *f* comparability, reproducibility (*quality testing*).

Vergünstigung *f* special allowance, special benefit, privilege, concession; **betriebliche ~en** fringe benefits, perks; **entsprechende ~en** like benefits; **steuerliche ~en** tax concessions; **tarifliche ~en** special rates, reduced fare.

vergüten *v/t* to remunerate, to reimburse, to refund, to compensate, to reward.

Vergütung *f* emolument, remuneration, pay, payment, reimbursement, compensation, royalty, refund, refunded amount; **~ der Überstunden** remuneration for overtime; overtime pay; **~ für Ausfallzeiten** compensation for interruption of career; **~en für die Ausbeutung von Bodenschätzen** natural resource royalties; **~ für schnelles Entladen** dispatch money; **angemessene ~** fair reward, fair compensation, reasonable *or* adequate remuneration; **~~ für Teilleistung**: *quantum meruit*; **gegen ~ von** in consideration of, on payment of; **kassenärztliche ~** panel doctor's fees; **ohne ~** without (giving) compensation (therefor), without consideration; **sonstige ~en** any other consideration; **veränderliche ~** variable remuneration; **wiederkehrende ~en** periodic payments.

Vergütungs|anspruch claim for re-

verhaften

muneration, compensation demand; *urheberrechtliche* ~~e: copyright royalties; **~auftrag** payment order; **~bescheid** notice of reimbursement; **~festsetzung** fixing of lawyer's fee by the court; **~liste** schedule of remuneration; **~paket** remuneration package; **~satz** rate of remuneration; *~sätze für Leihfahrzeuge*: rental rates, rental charges.

verhaften *v/t* to apprehend, to arrest, to place under arrest, to take into custody; **erneut** ~ to rearrest.

Verhaftung *f* apprehension, arrest, taking into custody; **~ auf frischer Tat** immediate arrest, arrest during the commission of the act, caught red-handed; **~ ohne Haftbefehl** arrest without a warrant; **~ wegen Fluchtverdachts** arrest due to suspicion of escape; **~ wegen Verdunklungsgefahr** arrest due to likelihood of (collusion or) suppression of evidence.

Verhalten *f* demeanour, conduct, attitude, behaviour; **~ auf dem Markt** behaviour on the market; **~smuster** behaviour(al) patterns; **~spielraum** scope of conduct; **~sstudie** behaviour study; **~sweise** conduct, practice; **abgestimmtes** ~ collusive conduct, concerted action, concerted practices; a coordinated approach; **angemessenes** ~ befitting conduct, appropriate behavio(u)r; **aufgabenorientiertes** ~ task-oriented behaviour; **berufsständisches** ~ professionalism; **berufswidriges** ~ unprofessional conduct, professional misconduct; **betrügerisches** ~ fraudulent behaviour; **bewußtes gleichgerichtetes** ~ conscious parallelism of action; **bundesfreundliches** ~ (a Land's) friendly attitude to the Federal Government; **ehewidriges** ~ matrimonial misconduct; **ehrkränkendes** ~ insulting behaviour; **fahrlässiges** ~ negligence; **fehlerhaftes** ~ misconduct; **gehorsamsverweigerndes** ~ insubordinate conduct; **gesetzwid-**

Verhaltensforschung

riges ~ illegal conduct; **gewinnsüchtiges** ~ profiteering; **gleichförmiges** ~ unvarying behaviour; **konkludentes** ~ implied conduct, conduct leading to the conclusion (of); **marktgerechtes** ~ action in conformity with market trends; **ordnungsgemäßes** ~ orderly behaviour; **ordnungswidriges** ~ disorderly conduct; **rechtswidriges** ~ illegal conduct, guilty conduct; **redliches** ~ fair dealing; **schlüssiges** ~ conduct from which the intention may be implied; **schuldbewußtes** ~ guilty conduct; **schuldhaftes** ~ fault, culpable conduct; **schuldminderndes provozierendes** ~ (partial) defence of provocation; **sittenwidriges** ~ immoral conduct; **sozialadäquates** ~ conduct in conformity with social needs; **standesgemäßes** ~ (proper) professional conduct; **standeswidriges** ~ unprofessional conduct, violation of professional standards; malpractice, breach of professional etiquette; **unbotmäßiges** ~ disorderliness, insubordinate behaviour; **unehrenhaftes** ~ infamous conduct; **unerhörtes** ~ outrageous conduct; **ungebührliches** ~ improper (*or indecent*) behaviour (*in court*); **ungehöriges** ~ improper conduct; **unredliches** ~ dishonest conduct; **unsittliches** ~ immoral conduct, indecency; **untadeliges** ~ irreproachable conduct, conduct beyond reproach; **vertragswidriges** ~ acting in breach of contract; **wettbewerbsbeschränkendes** ~ anti-competitive practices; **wohlanständiges** ~ good order and decorum.

verhalten *v/reflex* to conduct oneself, to behave; **sich fair** ~ to be fair, to observe the rules of fairness; **sich opportunistisch** ~ to temporize, to act in an opportunistic manner; **sich ordnungswidrig** ~ to act improperly; **sich vorschriftswidrig** ~ to commit irregularities.

Verhaltens|forschung (economic)

Verhältnis   **Verhandlung**

behaviour research; **~kodex** code of practice, (UN) directives on social business practice; international code of conduct; **~ maßregeln** rules of conduct, instructions for negotiations; **~normen** standards of behaviour; *völkerrechtliche ~~*: *international standards*; **~regeln** code of practice; **~weise** conduct, usual practice.

Verhältnis *n* (*pl Verhältnisse*) relation, relationship, proportion, ratio; **~berechnung** calculating by proportion, calculation of pro rata shares; **v~mäßig** *adj* proportional, reasonable; **~mäßigkeit** commensurability, reasonableness; *~~ e-r Entscheidung: reasonableness of a decision*; **~ von Obligationen und Vorzugsaktien zu Stammaktien** leverage; **~wahl** proportional representation, proportional vote; **~wahlrecht** law of proportional representation; **~wahlsystem** proportional representation; **~werte** ratios, relatives; **~zahl** ratio, proportional factor; *statistische ~~*: *statistic ratio (balance sheet analysis)*; **ärmliche ~se** indigent (*or* impecunious) circumstances; **beidseitig verpflichtendes ~** reciprocal obligation; **beschränkte ~se** strained circumstances; **eheähnliches ~** de facto marriage, a quasi-marriage; **ehebrecherisches ~** adulterous relationship; **gute ~se** easy circumstances; **im gleichen ~** in equal proportions; **im richtigen ~** proportionate, in the right proportion; **im ~ zu** as between, in proportion to; *~~~ Dritten: vis-à-vis third parties*; **obligatorisches ~** relationship under the law of obligations (*contract, quasi-contract, tort*); **persönliche ~se** personal circumstances; **über seine ~se leben** to overspend; **unter den derzeitigen steuerlichen ~sen** with taxes as they now stand; **unter den gegebenen ~sen** under the prevailing circumstances; **vermögensrechtliche ~se** financial relations, pecuniary relationship; **vertragsähnliches ~** quasi-contractual relationship.

Verhandeln *n* negotiating, bargaining; **rein geschäftsmäßiges ~** dealing at arm's length, a purely business negotiation, businesslike talks.

verhandeln *v/i* to negotiate, to participate in a court hearing, to plead before the court, to hear (*a case*); (*notary:*) to record, to execute; **mündlich ~** to conduct a court hearing, to plead in court.

Verhandlung *f* negotiation; judicial hearing, court hearing, legal conference; *mil* parley; **~ des Falles** hearing of the case; **~en beginnen** to open negotiations, to start talks; **~ vor der Kammer** proceedings before the full court; **abgesonderte ~en** separate negotiations; **abgetrennte ~** separate trial (*against co-accused*); **außergerichtliche ~en** out-of-court negotiations; **die ~ aussetzen** to suspend the hearing, to stay the hearing; **die ~ eröffnen** to open the hearing; **die ~ leiten** to conduct the proceedings; **die ~ schließen** to close the court, to close the hearing; **die ~ vertagen** to adjourn the hearing; **diese ~en werden aufgenommen** such negotiations shall be undertaken; **direkte ~en** direct negotiations; **erneute ~** proceedings de novo, rehearing, reopened hearing; **gerichtliche ~** court hearing; **in ~en eintreten** to enter into negotiations, to engage in negotiations; **kontradiktorische ~** adversarial procedure; **langwierige ~en** protracted negotiations; **mündliche ~** hearing, court hearing, trial (*in civil proceedings*); **nichtöffentliche ~** trial in camera; **nichtstreitige ~** (proceedings in an) uncontested case, undefended case, non-contentious (ex parte) hearing; **nochmalige ~** re-hearing; **öffentliche ~** (hearing in) open court, in curia, public trial; **persönliche ~ unter vier Augen** one-to-one negotiations; **schwebende ~en** negotiations in progress; **streitige** ~ adversarial hearing; defended trial; **vorvertragliche** ~**en** antecedent negotiations; **zur** ~ **anstehen** to come up for trial.

Verhandlungs|angebot overture, offer to negotiate, offer to enter into negotiations; ~**akten** court (*or* trail) record; ~**ausschuß** negotiating committee; ~**basis** basis of the negotiations; asking price; **v**~**bereit** *adj* open to negotiation; ~**bereitschaft** readiness to negotiate, willingness to negotiate; ~**bericht** report of the negotiations; ~**dolmetschen** interpreting of dialogues; ~**eröffnung** overture, start of the negotiations; **v**~**fähig** *adj* fit (*or* capable) to proceed; ~**fähigkeit** capacity to proceed (*or* act) in court; ~**frieden** negotiated peace; ~**führer** negotiator, bargaining agent; ~**führung** conduct of the negotiations, conduct of the proceedings; *gerechte* ~~: *granting a fair hearing*; ~**gebühr** (lawyer's) fee for pleading in court, sitting fee, hearing fee; ~**gegenstand** subject matter of the negotiation; ~**grundlage** basis for the negotiations; ~**grundsatz** principle of party presentation (*i.e. not ex officio*); ~**leitung** chairmanship, conduct of the proceedings; ~**liste** list of cases; cause list; ~**maxime** principle of party presentation; ~**niederschrift** record of the proceedings, joint minutes; ~**ort** place of the negotiations; ~**paket** package deal; ~**partner** negotiating party; ~**plan** format; ~**position** negotiating position; ~**protokoll** written record of proceedings, trial record, minutes of the hearing (*or* of the proceedings); ~**punkte** agenda, points of negotiation, points to negotiate; **v**~**reif** *adj* ready for negotiation; ~**runde** set of negotiations; contracting parties' session; ~**spielraum** margin for negotiations; ~**sprache** official language, working language, language for negotiations; ~**stärke** negotiating strength; ~**termin** date of hearing, hearing, day of appearance; *e-n* ~~ *anberaumen: to fix a date for the hearing, to assign a day for trial*; ~**tisch** negotiating table; ~**unfähigkeit** unfitness to plead, inability to follow the proceedings; ~**vertreter** substitute lawyer for a hearing, locum; ~**vollmacht** authority to negotiate, negotiating power.

Verhängen *n* imposition, infliction; ~ **des Standrechts** proclamation of martial law.

verhängen *v/t* to impose, to inflict.

Verhängung e-r Strafe imposition of a sentence (*or* penalty).

Verharmlosung *f* making sth (e.g. violence) appear to be harmless.

verheimlichen *v/t* to conceal, to dissimulate, to suppress, to hide.

Verheimlichung *f* concealment, suppression; ~ **e-s Kindes** concealing a (newly-born) child; ~ **gestohlener Sachen** concealing stolen property.

verheiratet *adj* married.

Verheiratung *f* marriage.

verhindern *v/t* to prevent, to hinder.

Verherrlichung *f* glorification.

Verhinderung *f* hindrance, prevention, inability to attend; ~**sgrund** reason for inability to attend.

Verhöhnung des Rechts making a mockery of the law.

Verhör *n* interrogation, questioning; **beim** ~ **auspacken** to "squeal", to crack under interrogation; **verschärftes** ~ third degree practices.

verhören *v/t* to interrogate, to question.

verhüten *v/t* to prevent.

Verhütung *f* prevention; contraception; ~**smittel** contraceptive.

Verhüttung *f* smelting.

verifizieren *v/t* to verify, to authenticate, to check, to certify.

Verifizierung *f* verification, collation.

verjährbar *adj* prescriptible, subject to the Statute of Limitations.

Verjährbarkeit *f* limitation of actions, prescription under the Statute of Limitations, unenforceability due to lapse of time; limitation of prosecution.

verjähren *v/t* to become statute-barred.

verjährt *adj* statute-barred, barred by the Statute of Limitations.

Verjährung *f* limitation of actions; ~ **der Strafverfolgung** bar to prosecution by lapse of time, limitation of prosecution; ~ **der Strafvollstreckung** bar to execution due to lapse of time; ~ **einwenden** to plead (*or* to invoke) the Statute of Limitations, **~sfrist** (statutory) period of limitation; **~shemmung** suspension of the running of time (for purposes) of limitation; **~unterbrechung** interruption of the running of the period of limitation (*period begins anew*); **~svorschriften** statutory limitation rules, provisions of the Limitation Act; *GB*, statutes of limitation *US*; **~szeit** period of limitation, term of prescription; ~ **von Geldforderungen** limitation of actions for a debt; **anspruchsvernichtende** ~ extinction prescription, exclusion due to limitation; **der** ~ **unterliegen** to be subject to the Statute of Limitations, to become statute-barred; **die** ~ **beginnt** the period of limitation begins to run; **die** ~ **hemmen** to suspend the limitation; **die** ~ **unterbrechen** to interrupt the running of the period of limitation (*the statutory period of limitation begins anew*).

verkalkulieren *v/reflex* to miscalculate.

Verkauf *m* sale, vending; ~ **auf Baisse** bear sale, short sale; ~ **auf Grund e-r Ausschreibung** sale by tender; ~ **auf Kreditbasis** credit sale; ~ **auf Rechnung** sale on account; invoiced sale; ~ **auf Ziel** fixed-date, credit sale; ~ **beweglicher Sachen** sale of goods; ~ **durch Mittelsleute** sale via middlemen; ~ **für zukünftige Lieferung** sale for future delivery; ~ **gegen bar** cash sale; ~ **in Bausch und Bogen** outright sale; ~ **mit Rückkaufsrecht** sale with the option to repurchase; ~ **mit sofortigem Eigentumsübergang** outright sale, sale with immediate transfer of ownership; ~ **mit Vorbehalt des Wiederkaufs** sale with option to repurchase; ~ **mit Zugaben** sale with free gifts; ~ **ohne Zwischenhändler** direct sale; ~ **schamloser Schriften an Jugendliche** sale of obscene publications to young people; ~ **unter der Hand** private sale, underhand sale; ~ **unter Eigentumsvorbehalt** conditional sale (with reservation of ownership); ~ **unter Selbstkosten** sale below cost price; ~ **von Restauflagen** remainder sale; ~ **wie die Ware steht und liegt** "as is" sale; ~ **zur sofortigen Lieferung** sale for prompt (*or* immediate) delivery; ~ **zu Verlustpreisen** selling at a loss; **~e zwecks Gewinnrealisierung** profit-taking sales; **außergerichtlicher** ~ sale out of court; **bedingter** ~ conditional sale; **einmaliger** ~ one-off sale; **freier** ~ private sale, sale on the open market; **freihändiger** ~ private sale, sale by private contract (*i.e. not auction*), sale by private treaty; **gerichtlicher** ~ judicial sale; **leichter** ~ quick sale, easy sale; **rascher** ~ quick sale; **vorrangiger** ~ priority sale (*trading of securities*); **zum** ~ for sale; **zum** ~ **anbieten** to offer for sale, to offer to sell; **zum** ~ **aufgeben** to give a selling order; **zum** ~ **aufliegen** to be available for sale; **zum** ~ **hergerichtet** made up for sale; **zum** ~ **übernehmen** to accept for selling.

verkaufen *v/t* to sell, to vend; ~ **oder beliefern** to sell or supply; **anderweitig** ~ to sell to another person, to sell elsewhere; **auf Kredit** ~ to sell on credit; **auf Ziel** ~ to sell on (a limited period of) credit; **bestens** ~ to sell at the best price (obtainable); **freihändig** ~ to sell privately, to sell by private contract; **ganz** ~ to sell outright; **gegen bar** ~ to sell for cash; **geräumt** ~ to sell with vacant possession; **in Bausch und Bogen** ~ to sell outright; **leer** ~ to go short, to sell short; **loko** ~ to sell for spot delivery; **mehr** ~ **als lieferbar** to oversell; **meistbietend** ~ to sell to the highest bidder; **schwarz** ~ to sell under the counter, to sell on the black market; **sich gut** ~ **lassen** to sell readily, to find a ready market; **sich schwer** ~ to sell hard, to be a slow mover; **teuer** ~ to sell at a good price; **unter dem Wert** ~ to sell below value; **zu** ~ for sale.

Verkäufer *m* seller, vendor, salesman, salesperson, shop assistant; ~ **im Außendienst** outside salesman; ~**markt** sellers' market; ~**pfandrecht** unpaid seller's lien; **gewerbsmäßiger** ~ (professional) salesman.

Verkäuferin *f* saleslady, sales girl, sales clerk *US*.

verkäuflich *adj* saleable (= *salable*) merchantable; for sale; **schwer** ~ hard to sell.

Verkäuflichkeit *f* saleability, marketability.

Verkaufs|abrechnung sales account, account sales, sold note; ~**abschluß** conclusion of a sale, actual sale; *pl also*: selling transactions; ~**agentur** sales agency; ~**aktion** sales campaign, drive; ~**analyse** sales analysis; ~**angebot** sales offer, offer for sale, offer to sell; ~**anlagen** sales facilities; ~**anzeige** announcement of sale; ~**argument** selling point, sales argument; ~**auftrag** sales order, order to sell, selling order; *exch: limitierter* ~~: *stop-order selling*; ~**auslagen** sales display; ~**automat** vending machine; ~**bedingungen** conditions (*or* terms) of sale, sales conditions, selling conditions; *allgemeine* ~~: *general conditions of sale*; ~**bemühungen** sales efforts; ~**berater** sales consultant; ~**berechtigung** right to sell; ~**broschüre** sales manual; ~**buch** sold ledger;

~**büro** sales office, selling agency; ~**einheit** sales unit; ~**einrichtung** selling unit, sales outlet; ~**erlös** proceeds of sale, sale proceeds; ~**fall** purchase contingency; **v**~**fertig** *adj* ready for sale, saleable; ~**förderung** sales promotion; ~**förderungskampagne** sales drive; ~**gebiet** trading area; ~**gegenstände** articles for sale, articles (*or* goods) sold; ~**gemeinschaft** joint sales agency; ~**genossenschaft** marketing co-operative; ~**geschäfte** sales transactions; ~~ *vermitteln: to negotiate contracts of sale*; ~**gespräch** sales talk; ~**gewinn** profit on a sale; ~**gruppe** selling syndicate; ~**journal** sold ledger, sales register; ~**kampagne** sales drive, sales campaign; ~**kapazität** selling capacity; ~**kartell** marketing cartel; ~**kommission** commission for sale, commission charged on sale, bailment for sale; ~**kommissionär** consignment merchant (*or* commission merchant) entrusted with a sale, factor, selling agent; ~**kontingent** sales quota; ~**kunst** (the art of) salesmanship; ~**kurs** selling rate; ~**leistung** sales performance; ~**leiter** sales manager; ~**lizenz** licence to sell; ~**methode** sales method; *aggressive* ~~*n: high-pressure salesmanship*; ~**monopol** sales monopoly; ~**niederlassung** sales agency, sales branch; chain store's shop; ~**note** sold note; ~**object** sold property, property for sale, subject matter of the contract of sale; ~**option** seller's option, selling option; *exch:* put (option); ~**organisation** sales organization; ~**personal** sales staff, sales personnel; ~**prämie** push money, sales premium; ~**preis** sales price, selling price; ~~ *vorstellung*: asking price; ~**prospekt** sales prospectus; ~**provision** sales commission, commission on sales; ~~ *des Maklers: selling brokerage*; ~**punkt** point of sale; ~**recht** selling rights, right to sell, right of disposal; ~**schub** wave of selling, a surge in sales; ~**strategie** sales strategy, marketing; ~**schlager** quick-selling article, runner; ~**sollsumme** sales target; ~**spanne** sales margin; ~**stelle** sales agency, sales point; ~**tag** date of sale, selling day; ~**technik** sales technique, salesmanship; ~**termin** date (*or* time limit) set for sale; ~**umsatzplan** sales budget; ~**unkosten** marketing costs; ~**urkunde** sales document, bill of sale (*ships*); ~**veranstaltung** trade fair; ~**verbot** ban on sales, embargo; ~**vereinbarung** agreement to sell, sales agreement; ~**versprechen** promise to sell; ~**vollmacht** power to sell, authority to sell; ~**werbung** sales promotion, sales publicity; ~**wert** marketable value, selling value, sales value; *gewöhnlicher* ~~: *saleable value, actual cash value, market-selling value*; ~**zwang** obligation to sell, sale under compulsion, compulsory selling.

Verkehr *m* transport, traffic; intercourse, transactions; ~ **mit Arzneimitteln** transactions involving medicine, sale of medicine; ~ **mit Gefangenen** contacts with prisoners; ~ **mit Grundstücken** real estate transactions; ~ **zwischen dritten Ländern** cross traffic, cross trade; **außerehelicher** ~ extramarital intercourse; **außer** ~ withdrawn from circulation; **außer** ~ **setzen** to withdraw from circulation, to take off the road; **betrügerisch in** ~ **bringen** to market with fraudulent intent; **den** ~ **umleiten** to divert traffic, to reroute traffic; **diplomatischer** ~ diplomatic intercourse; **ehebrecherischer** ~ adulterous intercourse; **ehelicher** ~ conjugal (*or* marital) intercourse; **einspuriger** ~ single lane (*or* file) traffic; **fahrplanmäßiger** ~ regular service; **freier** ~ free circulation; **gewerblicher** ~ commercial transport; **grenzüberschreitender** ~ border-crossing traffic; **inländischer** ~ domestic transport; **in** ~ **bringen** to put into circulation; **mündlicher** ~ verbal intercourse; **öffentlicher** ~ public traffic, public transport; **persönlicher** ~ **mit den Kindern** personal access to the children; **ruhender** ~ stationary traffic, *parked, or standing vehicles in public streets*; **überörtlicher** ~ regional traffic, supra-local traffic; **vierspuriger** ~ four-lane traffic.

verkehren *v/i* to deal with, to have relations with, to associate with, to have intercourse with.

Verkehrs|abkommen traffic convention; ~**ampel** traffic signal, traffic light; ~**amt** tourist office; ~**anlagen** transport installations, transportation facilities; ~**anschauung** general attitude, generally accepted standards; ~**anstalt** public transport authority; ~**anwalt** correspondence lawyer (*between trial lawyer and client*); ~**aufkommen** volume of traffic; ~**auffassung** = ~sanschauung; ~**ausgaben** traffic expenditure, fares; ~**bedarf** current demand for transport, traffic requirements; ~**bedürfnis** normal requirements of traffic; ~**behinderung** obstruction of traffic; ~**behörden** transport authorities; ~**beruhigung** strict reduction in traffic; ~**beschränkungen** traffic restrictions; ~**betrieb** transport undertaking, transport service; ~**chaos** traffic breakdown, traffic chaos; ~**delikt** traffic offence; *strafpunktepflichtiges* ~~: *endorsable* (*indorsable*) *traffic offence*; ~**dichte** traffic density, density of traffic; ~**disziplin** discipline of road users, road behaviour; ~**einheit** unit for commercial transactions; ~**einrichtungen** transport facilities; ~**erziehung** education of road users; **v**~**fähig** *adj* marketable, negotiable; *nicht* ~~: *non-marketable, non-negotiable*; ~**fähigkeit** marketability, negotiability, negotiable character; ~**fahrzeug** passenger transport vehicle; *öffentliche* ~~*e*: *public service vehic-*

les; ~**fläche** traffic area; ~**fund** finding of lost articles in public places; ~**gefährdung** dangerous driving; ~**geltung** general acceptance in trade; ~**gesetzgebung** traffic legislation; ~**gewerbe** transport industry; v~**günstig** *adj* in a favourable position as regards transport facilities; ~**haftpflicht** legal liability in transport and traffic; ~**haftung** liability in traffic cases; ~**hindernis** traffic obstacle; ~**hypothek** ordinary mortgage; ~**insel** traffic island, refuge; ~**investition** capital expenditure on communications; ~**kontrolle** road check; ~**knotenpunkt** traffic junction; ~**lage** location in respect of transport facilities; ~**lärm** traffic noise, ~~~*schutz protection against traffic noise*; ~**leistung** volume of traffic, transport services; ~**lichtzeichen** traffic light signals; ~**minister** Minister of Transport; ~**ministerium** Ministry of Transport; ~**mittel** means of transport; *öffentliche* ~~: *public transport(ation)*; ~**nachfrage** traffic demand; ~**netz** transportation network; ~**opfer** victim(s) of traffic accidents; ~**ordnung** traffic regulations, rules of traffic, regulatory system for transport; ~**ordnungswidrigkeit** traffic violation; ~**papier** negotiable paper; ~**planung** traffic planning; ~**politik** transport policy; ~**polizei** traffic police, traffic control squad; ~**recht** (1) road traffic law; ~**recht** (2) visiting rights, right of access; ~**regelung** traffic regulations; ~**richtung** direction of traffic; ~**rücksichtnahme** courtesy of the road, drivers' courtesy, consideration in traffic; ~**sachverständiger** traffic expert; ~**schild** traffic sign; ~**schutzmann** patrol-man, traffic policeman; v~**sicher** *adj* roadworthy; *nicht* ~~: *unsafe for traffic, unroadworthy, technically unsafe for general use*, public safety, transport safety; ~**sicherheit** safety for general use;

public safety; transport safety; safety for roadworthiness, relability for transport; *mangelnde* ~~~: *lack of safety, unroadworthiness*; ~**sicherungspflicht** duty to maintain safety, duty of care toward third parties; ~**sitte** common usage; ~**spitze** peak traffic, rush hour; ~**stau** traffic jam, traffic congestion; ~**steuern** taxes on transfer of property, transfer duties; taxes on transactions; ~**stockung** traffic holdup, traffic jam; ~**störung** disruption, stoppage of traffic; ~**strafsachen** penal traffic cases; ~**strom** flow of traffic; ~**sünder** persistent traffic offender; ~**sünderkartei** official register of traffic offenders; ~**tarife** transport charges; ~**teilnehmer** road user; ~**träger** transport undertaking, transport authority, carrier; ~**tüchtig** *adj* roadworthy; ~**tüchtigkeit** roadworthiness; ~**übertretung** traffic violation; ~**übung** general usage; ~**- und Versorgungstarife** rates charged for transport and public utility services; ~**unfall** traffic accident, road accident, street accident; ~**unfallprozeß** (road) traffic accident case; ~~ *mit Verletzung von Fußgängern*: *accident case involving injuries to pedestrians*; *running-down case*; ~**unternehmer** carrier; *nicht ansässige* ~~: *non-resident carriers*; ~**unterricht** traffic instruction, *compulsory attendance at police traffic tuition*; ~**verband** transport pool; ~**verbindungen** transport links; ~**verbot** traffic prohibition, ban on traffic; ~**verbund** metropolitan transit; ~**verein** tourist agency, association for the promotion of local tourism; ~**verlagerung** displacement of traffic; shift of trade; ~**verletzung** traffic violation; ~**vorschriften** traffic regulations; ~**wacht** road patrol; ~**weg** traffic route, service road; ~**wert** trade value, current value, open market value, fair market value, current market price; ~**wertschätzung**

verkennen

appraisal of trade value, estimate of current value; ~**wesen** traffic, transport and communications; **v~widrig** *adj* contrary to traffic regulations; ~**widrigkeit** traffic violation; ~**wirtschaft** transport industry; free market economy, commerce; ~**zählung** traffic census; ~**zeichen** traffic sign, sign post, road sign; *pl also:* signs and signals; ~**zentralregister** central register of traffic violations (*at Flensburg*); ~**zulassung** road licence.

verkennen *v/t* to fail to appreciate, to misjudge; **nicht** ~ to be fully aware of, to appreciate fully.

Verkennung *f* misjudgment, misapprehension; ~ **der Tatsachen** misjudgment, misapprehension of the facts; **offensichtliche** ~ obvious misapprehension.

verketzern *v/t pol* to malign, to brand as a heretic.

verklagbar *adj* suable, liable to action, actionable.

verklagen *v/t* to take legal proceedings against, to sue s.o., to bring an action (against s.o.), to take out a summons (against s.o.).

Verklappung *f* ocean dumping.

verklaren to make protest.

Verklarung *f* ship's protest, sea protest; protest by the shipmaster (*to preserve evidence*); ~**sprotokoll** deed of sea protest (*or* of ship's protest).

verklausulieren *v/t* to safeguard by clauses, to express in complicated terms.

verklausuliert *adj* stipulated in detail, hedged in by clauses.

Verknappung tightness, shortage; **künstliche** ~ self-induced shortage.

verkörpern *v/t* to embody, to impersonate.

Verkörperung *f* embodiment, personification; impersonation.

Verköstigung *f* board, food.

Verkrüppelung crippling, maiming.

verkünden *v/t* to read out, to pronounce (*judgment*), to hand down, to promulgate (*a law*), to proclaim.

Verkündung announcement, publication, promulgation, proclamation, pronouncement; ~ **des Strafurteils** pronouncement of sentence; ~ **e-s Gesetzes** promulgation of a law; ~ **e-s Urteils** pronouncing judgment; ~**stermin** date for the pronouncement of a decision.

verkuppeln *v/t* to procure.

Verkupplung *f* procuration.

Verkürzung *f* abridgment, shortening; ~ **e-r Frist**: *abridgment of time, reduction in a stipulated period of time*; ~ **der Arbeitszeit bei vollem Lohnausgleich** reducing working hours without corresponding decrease in pay.

Verlade|anlage loading plant; ~**bahnhof** loading station, forwarding station; ~**dokument** shipping document; *reines* ~~: *clean shipping document*; ~**einheit** loading unit; ~**flughafen** airport of dispatch; ~**hafen** port of loading, port of embarkation, port of shipment; ~**kosten** loading expenses, shipping charges, forwarding charges; ~**order** shipping order; ~**ort** place of shipment (*or* loading); ~**papiere** shipping documents; ~**rampe** loading platform; ~**risiko** loading risk; ~**schein** consignment note, dispatch note, shipping note; ~**schluß** closing for cargo; ~**station** place of shipment.

verladen *v/t* to load, to ship.

Verlader *m* freighter, shipper, forwarder.

Verladung *f* loading, stowage, shipping, shipment, dispatch; ~**sfrist** period of shipment; ~**skonnossement** bill of lading; ~**skosten** forwarding charges; ~**sort** place of shipment; ~**spapiere** shipping documents; ~**splatz** place of shipment; ~**szeugnis** shipping certificate; **fehlerhafte** ~ improper stowage.

Verlag *m* publishing firm, publishing house, publishers; ~**geber** au-

verlagern

thor *in relation to a publisher*; ~**nehmer** publisher *in relation to an author*.

verlagern *v*|*reflex* to dislocate, to relocate, to switch.

Verlagerung *f* dislocation, relocation; ~ **der Beweislast** shifting of the burden of proof.

Verlags|**abteilung** publishing department; ~**agent** literary agent; ~**anstalt** publishing company; ~**buchhandel** publishing business; ~**buchhändler** publisher; ~**erzeugnisse** published printed products; ~**geschäfte** publishing business; ~**gesetz** Publishing Act; ~**gewerbe** publishing trade; ~**lizenz** publisher's licence; ~**lektor** publisher's reader; ~**recht** right to publish, publishing rights; publishing law; ~**verhältnis** author-publisher relationship; ~**vertrag** author-publisher agreement, publishing contract; ~**zeichen** publisher's mark, imprint.

verlangen *v*/*t* to demand, to claim, to assert, to require.

verlängerbar *adj* renewable, extendable.

verlängern *v*/*t* to prolong, to extend, to renew; **stillschweigend** ~ to extend automatically, to extend by implication.

Verlängerung *f* prolongation, extension, renewal, protraction; ~ **der Abgabefrist** extension of time for the filing of a return; ~ **der Fristen** extended deadlines, deferment of (the) final dates; ~ **der Gültigkeitsdauer** extension of validity; ~ **der Laufzeit e-s Darlehens** renewal of a loan; ~ **der Lieferfristen** lengthening of delivery periods; ~ **der Polizeistunde** extension of permitted licensing hours; ~ **der Rechtsmittelfrist** extension of time for appeal; ~ **der Wechselprotestmöglichkeit** extension of protest; ~ **der Mietverhältnisses** renewal of a tenancy (*or* lease); ~ **e-r Bescheinigung** extension of certificate; ~ **e-s Patents** renewal of a patent; ~ **e-s Wechsels** prolongation of a bill of exchange; **stillschweigende** ~ tacit renewal (*tenancy*).

Verlängerungs|**eintrag** renewal endorsement (*passport*); ~**gebühr** renewal fee; ~**klausel** continuation clause, extension clause, renewal clause; *automatische* ~~: *provision for automatic renewal*; ~**option** option of renewal; ~**police** extension policy; ~**recht** right to renew; ~**stück** allonge (*bill of exchange*); ~**zeitraum** period of extension; ~**zettel** allonge (*bill of exchange*).

Verlassen *n* leaving, departure, desertion; ~ **Schwangerer** abandoning a pregnant woman; **böswilliges** ~ desertion, malicious abandonment; **grundloses** ~ desertion, voluntary abandonment.

verlassen *v*/*t* to desert, to abandon.

Verlassenschafts|**gericht** (*Austria*) probate court; ~**kurator** custodian of a deceased's estate, administrator.

Verläßlichkeitskaution *f* fidelity guarantee.

Verlaufsstatistik *f* flow statistics.

verlautbaren *v*/*i* to announce officially, to declare.

Verlautbarung *f* (official) announcement; ~**srecht** (government's) right to have broadcasting time for public announcements; **amtliche** ~ official announcement.

Verlegenheitslösung *f* makeshift solution, emergency arrangements.

Verleger *m* publisher; ~**verband** publishers' association.

Verlegung *f* transfer, postponement; ~ **der Hauptverhandlung** postponement of trial; ~ **des Sitzes** relocation of the registered office; ~ **e-s Termins** postponement of the date of a hearing; ~ **des Wohnsitzes** transfer of residence.

Verleih *m* distribution; ~**gesell-**

verleihen   **Verletzung**

schaft distribution company; **~kopie** release print.
verleihen *v/t* (*1*) to lend, to hire out.
verleihen *v/t* (*2*) to confer, to bestow.
Verleiher *m* lender, money-broker, pawnbroker; distributor (*films*).
Verleihung *f* conferment, bestowal, grant; **~surkunde** charter, award of honours, diploma; *königliche ~~*: *royal charter*.
verleiten *v/t* to suborn, to inveigle.
Verleitung *f* subornation (*to crime, esp perjury*), seduction, inducement; ~ **zum Meineid** subornation of perjury, persuading s. o. to commit perjury; ~ **zum militärischen Ungehorsam** subornation to insubordination; ~ **zum Vertragsbruch** procuring breach of contract, interference with (subsisting) contract; ~ **zur Auswanderung** inducing s. o. to emigrate; ~ **zur Falschaussage** subornation of false testimony, fabricating false evidence; ~ **zu strafbaren Handlungen** solicitation to commit crimes, procuring an offence, subornation.
verlesen *v/t* to read out (aloud).
Verlesung *f* reading (out), reading aloud; **~sprotokoll** *record of a document that has been read out to the parties*; **auf die ~ wird verzichtet** taken as read.
verletzen *v/t* to violate, to infringe, to injure, to impair.
Verletzer *m* infringer, the injuring party.
Verletzte|r *m* (*der Verletzte*) the injured party, the wronged party; **~ngeld** allowance to an injured person, injury grant; **~nrente** injured person's pension, periodic payments to an injured party; **der in seinen Rechten ~** the person aggrieved, the aggrieved party.
Verletzung *f* injury, infringement, breach, violation, infraction; ~ **der Amtspflicht** → *Amtspflichtverletzung*; ~ **der Amtsverschwiegenheit** breach of official secrecy; ~ **der Anzeigepflicht** failure to disclose, non-disclosure; non-observance of statutory duty to provide information; ~ **der Aufsichtspflicht** failure to supervise (*children*); ~ **der ehelichen Pflichten** breach of matrimonial duties; ~ **der Formvorschriften** non-compliance with the procedure, non-compliance with formal requirements; ~ **der Geschlechtsehre** violation of sexual honour; ~ **der gesetzlichen Sorgfaltspflicht** lack of proper care, negligence; ~ **der Gewährleistungspflicht** breach of warranty; ~ **der Instandhaltungspflicht** permissive waste; ~ **der Neutralität** violation of neutrality; ~ **der Obhutspflichten** non-observance of duty to keep sth in good order; ~ **der öffentlichen Ruhe und Ordnung** offence against law and order; ~ **der Schweigepflicht** breach of professional discretion (*or* secrecy); ~ **der Sonn- und Feiertagsruhe** breaking the sabbath; ~ **der Sorgfaltspflicht** lack of proper care, negligence; ~ **der Standespflicht** breach of professional ethics; ~ **der Unterhaltspflicht** failure to fulfil one's statutory maintenance obligation; non-support; ~ **der Vertragspflicht** breach of contract; ~ **der Vertraulichkeit** breach of confidentiality; ~ **des Anstandes** indecency, outrage upon decency; ~ **des Berufsgeheimnisses** breach of professional duty of confidentiality; ~ **des Briefgeheimnisses** breach of confidentiality in letters; ~ **des Friedens** violation of the peace; ~ **des Luftraums** interference with airspace, violation of the sovereignty of the air; ~ **des Personenstandes** violation of personal status, infringement of civil status; ~ **des Post- und Fernmeldegeheimnisses** violation of the secrecy of the postal and telecommunications; ~ **des Schamgefühls** grossly offending s. o.'s sense of shame; ~ **des Steuergeheimnisses** breach of

tax confidentiality; ~ **des Urheberrechts** copyright infringement; ~ **des Wahlgeheimnisses** violation of a secret ballot; ~ **e-r Gewährleistungspflicht** breach of warranty; ~ **e-s gewerblichen Schutzrechtes** infringement of an industrial property right; ~ **e-s Patents** patent infringement; ~ **von Grundrechten** violation of constitutional rights; ~ **von Warenzeichenrechten** trade-mark infringement; ~ **wesentlicher Formvorschriften** non-observance of essential formalities; **äußerlich sichtbare** ~ visible injury; **lebensgefährliche** ~**en** critical injuries, life-endangering injuries; **offenkundige** ~ public infringement, visible injury; **tödliche** ~ fatal injury; **unfallsbedingte** ~ injury caused by the accident, sudden or violent injury.

Verletzungs|absicht intention to cause harm, malicious intent; ~**art** type of injury; ~**delikte** offence of causing an injury; ~**folgen** effects of the injury; ~**handlung** injurious act, infringing act; ~**klage** action for infringement, infringement suit (*industrial property rights*); ~**prozess** infringement suit; ~**streit** infringement litigation.

verleugnen *v/t* to disown, to deny.

verleumden *v/t* to calumniate, to slander, to vilify, to malign.

Verleumder *m* calumniator, slanderer; traducer.

verleumderisch *adj* defamatory, libellous, slanderous.

Verleumdung *f* defamation, defamatory statement, calumny, vilification; ~ **der Bundeswehr** vilification of the Federal Armed Forces; ~ **des Bundespräsidenten** vilification of the President of the Federal Republic; ~**skampagne** smear(ing) campaign, campaign of slander, vicious campaign of libel or slander; ~**sklage** action for defamation; ~**sprozess** defamation suit, libel suit; ~**staktik** smear device, slandering tactics; ~ **von Staatseinrichtungen** defamation of state institutions; **geschäftliche** ~ business slander.

Verlierer *m* loser, unsuccessful party.

verloben *v/reflex* to become engaged, to get engaged.

Verlöbnis *n* engagement, betrothal (*poet.*), mutual promise to marry; ~**bruch** breach of promise (of marriage); **ein** ~ **aufheben** to break off an engagement.

verlobt *adj* engaged (to be married).

Verlobte *f* fiancée, intended wife.

Verlobter *m* (*der Verlobte*) fiancé, betrothed.

Verlobung *f* engagement (to marry); ~**sgeschenke** engagement presents.

verlocken *v* to inveigle, to entrap.

verlosen *v/t* to draw lots, to dispose by lots.

Verlosung *f* drawing lots; drawing for redemption; ~**liste** list of drawings (*of bonds*); ~**svertrag** raffle contract.

Verlust *m* loss; ~**abschluß** loss shown in annual accounts, balance deficit; ~**abzug** deduction of loss(es); ~ **an Lebensqualität** loss of amenity; ~**anteil** share in the loss; ~**anzeige** report of loss of missing item, announcement of a loss; ~ **auf dem Transport** loss in transit; ~**ausgleich** loss-compensation, making-up for a loss, loss offsetting; ~**begrenzungsauftrag** stop-loss order; ~**bestätigung** certificate of loss; ~**bilanz** balance-sheet showing a loss; ~**deckung** loss covering; ~ **der bürgerlichen Ehrenrechte** forfeiture of civic rights, deprivation of civic rights; ~ **der Kundschaft** loss of custom; ~ **der öffentlichen Ämter** loss of public offices; ~ **der Sprechfähigkeit** aphasia, loss of the power of speech; ~ **der Staatsangehörigkeit** loss of nationality; ~ **der Voraussetzung für ein Amt** disqualification from public office; ~ **der Zeugnisfähigkeit** disqualification from being a witness; ~ **der Zeugungsfähigkeit** loss of capaci-

831

verlustig | **vermeintlich**

ty of procreation; ~ **des Arbeitsplatzes** loss of job, job loss; ~ **des Pensionsanspruches** disqualification from pension-rights; ~ **des Sehvermögens** loss of sight; ~ **des Wahlrechts** disqualification from voting; ~ **e–s Rechts** loss of a right; ~**eintragung** red ink entry; ~**geschäft** a losing business, a transaction involving a loss; ~**jahr** a year marked by a loss; ~**liste** death roll, casualty list; ~**maßstab** loss measure; ~**nachweis** proof of loss; ~**preis** price at a loss, losing price; *zu e–m* ~~: *at a loss*; ~**quellenrechnung** calculation of losses caused by operational deficiencies; ~**rechnung** compilation of loss(es); ~**risiko** risk of loss; ~**rückstellung** loss reserve; ~**rücktrag** loss carryback; ~**saldo** loss balance, debit balance; ~**spitze** marginal loss, loss residue; ~**stück** lost security; ~**übernahme** loss takeover; assumption of loss(es), transferred losses; ~**verteilung** loss apportionment; ~ **von Absatzgebieten** loss of markets; ~**vortrag** (tax) loss carryforward, carry over; ~~ *oder -rücktrag: carrying losses forward to subsequent years or back to previous years*; ~**zeit** time of losses, waiting time (*stoppage of production*); ~**zuweisung** allocation of loss; ~**zuweisungsgesellschaft** tax loss company, project write-off company; **buchmäßiger** ~ book-loss, loss on paper; **e–n** ~ **abdecken** to make good a loss, to cover a loss; **e–n** ~ **erleiden** to suffer a loss, to sustain a loss; **e–n** ~ **in Kauf nehmen** to take a loss, to accept a loss; **ersetzbarer** ~ recoverable loss; **mit** ~ at a loss, at a sacrifice; **mit** ~ **abschließen** to close at a loss, to show a loss; **schwerer** ~ severe loss; **sich für e–n** ~ **schadlos halten** to retrieve a loss; **steuerlich abzugsfähiger** ~ deductible loss; **steuerlicher** ~ tax loss; **uneinbringlicher** ~ irretrievable loss; **unersetzlicher** ~ irreparable loss; irrecoverable loss.

verlustig *adj* deprived (of), having incurred a loss; lapsed; ~ *erklären: to declare devoid of, to declare to have lost (or: forfeited sth).*

Verlustigerklärung *f* declaration of forfeiture, official statement of loss (*of right to appeal*).

vermachen *v/t* to bequeath, to devise.

Vermächtnis *n* legacy, bequest; ~**anfall** devolution of a legacy; ~**anspruch** claim to a legacy; ~**berechtigter** legatee, devisee; ~ **e–s Geldbetrages** pecuniary legacy; ~**geber** legator; ~ **mit Auflagen** modal legacy, bequest accompanied by directions; ~**nehmer** legatee, recipient of a legacy; ~~ *e–s Einzelvermächtnisses: specific legatee;* ~**unwürdigkeit** disqualification from receiving a legacy for moral reasons; **ausgefallenes** ~ lapsed legacy (*predeceased beneficiary*); **bedingtes** ~ conditional legacy; **bestimmtes** ~ specific legacy; **betagtes** ~ deferred legacy; **ein** ~ **annehmen** to accept a legacy, to take under a bequest; **ein** ~ **ausschlagen** to refuse to accept a legacy; **ein** ~ **aussetzen** to grant (*or provide*) a legacy, to make a bequest; **gemeinschaftliches** ~ joint legacy; **generelles** ~ indefinite legacy; **unbedingtes** ~ unqualified legacy.

vermählen *v/reflex* to marry, to get married, to wed.

Vermählung *f* wedding, marriage.

vermarken *v/t* to mark the border.

vermarkten *v/t* to market, to distribute.

Vermarktung *f* marketing; ~**stricks** marketing ploys.

Vermarkung *f* marking out.

Vermassung *f* treating as one mass, lumping together.

vermeidbar *adj* avoidable.

vermeiden *v/t* to avoid, to prevent.

Vermeidung *f* avoidance; ~ **der Doppelbesteuerung** avoidance of double taxation; ~ **von Härten** prevention of hardship.

vermeintlich *adj* putative, reputed, supposed, imagined.

Vermengung f blending together; comminglement, mixing together.

Vermerk m note, notation, remark; entry.

vermerken v/t to note, to make a note of sth.

vermessen v/t to survey (*boundaries of lands*).

Vermesser m surveyor.

Vermessung f (land) surveying, survey.

Vermessungs|amt surveyor's office, land surveying office, cadastral office; ~**beamter** surveying official; ~**marke** survey mark; tonnage mark; ~**plan** survey; ~**pflock** bench mark; ~**protokoll** verification of survey; ~**punkt** fixed point; ~**schein** certificate of survey; ~**wesen** surveying; ~**zeichen** survey mark, bench mark.

vermietbar *adj* tenantable.

Vermietbarkeit f suitability for letting.

vermieten v/t to let, to let on lease, to hire out (*chattels*), to rent (*out*) (*US*).

Vermieter m landlord, lessor; letter, hirer out; ~**haftpflichtversicherung** landlord's liability insurance; ~**kündigung** notice to quit; ~**pfandrecht** landlord's lien; ~**vereinigung** association of landlords.

Vermieterin f landlady.

Vermietung f letting; hiring (out); ~ **und Verpachtung** letting and leasing; ~ **von Betriebsanlagen** plant leasing.

Vermischung f mixing, blending, commingle; intermingling, commixtion; confusion, merger; ~ **von beweglichen Sachen** commixtion, intermixture of goods (*of various owners*).

Vermißtenanzeige missing person advertisement, information to the police that a person is missing; ~**suchdienst** service for tracing missing persons.

Vermißter m missing person.

vermittelbar *adj* placeable, employable, capable of placing; **schwer**~ hard-to-place.

vermitteln v/t to introduce, to place, to bring together, to arrange, to find work for; v/i to act as intermediary, to mediate, to go between.

vermittelnd *adj* conciliatory, intermediary, mediatory.

Vermittler m mediator, intermediary, interceder; go-between, middleman, conciliator; agent, broker; placement officer; ~**provision** agent's commission; **nur als** ~ as agent only.

Vermittlung f mediation, intercession; conciliation; agency, services of a broker; placing, placement; *int* good offices; ~ **von Adoptionen** placement (of children) for adoption; **die** ~ **anbieten** to offer one's good offices (*international law*); **durch** ~ **von** through the instrumentality of, via, by the introduction of, through; **gewerbsmäßige** ~ commercial agency.

Vermittlungs|agent (soliciting) agent, *authorized to arrange (but not to conclude a business transaction)*; ~**angebot** offer of mediation; ~**auftrag** mediation mission; ~**ausschuß** mediation committee, conference committee; ~**behörde** placement agency, authority in charge of placement of adoptees; ~**dienste** *int* good offices; ~**gebühr** introduction charge; ~**gehilfe** assistant in negotiations; ~**geschäft** agency business; ~**makler** real estate agent, broker (*employed contingent on success in negotiating a transaction*); ~**monopol** *exclusive legal anthority (of German labour office) to act as employment agency*; job placement monopoly; ~**provision** commission (for negotiating a transaction); ~**stelle** liaison office, mediation agency; ~**vertreter** (soliciting) agent, representative for the purpose of arranging business; ~**vorschlag** proposal for a settlement, compromise proposal, offer of mediation.

Vermögen n wealth, property, ef-

Vermögen

fects, fortune, assets; ~ **besitzen** to own property, to be wealthy; ~ **der Gesellschaft** partnership assets, corporate assets; ~ **der öffentlichen Hand** public property; ~ **in Sachform** assets in kind; ~ **juristischer Personen** corporate assets; ~ **natürlicher Personen** assets of natural persons; ~ **übertragen** to assign property, to transfer assets; ~ **verwalten** to administer property; **aufzeichnungspflichtiges** ~ property to be recorded in the books, registerable assets; **ausländisches** ~ foreign property, assets abroad; **bares** ~ liquid assets, assets in cash form; **beschlagnahmtes** ~ blocked property, confiscated assets; **bewegliches** ~ movable property, personal property, goods and chattels; **das gesamte** ~ total assets, real and personal effects; *mein ~s ~: everything I am possessed of (last will)*; **das öffentliche** ~ public wealth; **das restliche** ~ remainder of any monies, the rest of my assets; **das ~ einschließlich der Verbindlichkeiten** net assets after allowance for liabilities; **eheliches** ~ marital property; **eigenes** ~ one's own property, one's own assets; **eerbtes** ~ inherited property; **ertragloses** ~ onerous property, profitless property; **feindliches** ~ enemy property; **flüssiges** ~ liquid assets; **forstwirtschaftliches** ~ forest property; **gemeinschaftliches** ~ common property; **gewerbliches** ~ trading and industrial property; **inländisches** ~ domestic property, resident's property and assets situate inside the country; **land- und forstwirtschaftliches** ~ farm and forestry holdings; **mit seinem ganzen ~ haften** to be liable with one's entire assets; **öffentliches** ~ public wealth, property owned by public authorities; **persönliches** ~ individual property, private property; **pfändbares** ~ non-exempt property, distrainable assets; **sonstiges** ~ further assets, miscellaneous assets; **steuerpflichtiges** ~ taxable property; **über sein** ~ **verfügen** to dispose of one's property; **umlaufendes** ~ current assets, ready capital; **unbewegliches** ~ immovables, real estate, immovable property, real assets, capital represented by immovable property; **väterliches** ~ paternal property; **vererbliches** ~ inheritable property, property passing on death; **verfügbares** ~ disposable capital (*or* assets); **vermögensteuerpflichtiges** ~ assets subject to property (*or* wealth) tax; **verpfändbares** ~ mortgageable property.

Vermögens|abgabe property levy (*under Equalization of War Burdens legislation*); **~absonderung** segregation of property; **~anfall** accession of property; **~angabe** property declaration, summary of means, notification of assets; **~anlage** investment; **~anreicherung** accumulation of wealth; increase of net worth, growth in one's assets; **~anwachsung** accession of property; **~arten** types of property; **~aufgabe** surrender of one's entire property; **~aufstellung** statement of assets and liabilities, statement of affairs; **~auseinandersetzung** property settlement, liquidation and division of property, partition of net assets; apportionment of assets and liabilities; **~ausweis** statement of assets, financial statement; **~besitz** (holding of) property, assets; **~bestand** existing assets; **~bestandteil** property item, part of the assets; **~besteuerung** taxation of wealth; **~beschlagnahme** property confiscation; **~bewegung** capital transactions, transfer of assets; **~bewertung** valuation of property, valuation of net assets; **~bilanz** asset and liability statement, asset and liability position; **~bildung** creation of wealth, formation of wealth, capital building; *volkswirtschaftliche ~~: aggregate wealth formation*; **~bildungsgesetz**

Vermögen

Formation of Wealth Law (*tax-free contributions to employee*); **~bindung** commitment of assets, tying-up of wealth; *satzungsmäßige ~~: allocation of funds as required by the articles of association*; **~delikt** offence involving property, crime against property; **~einlage** capital investment; **~einkommen** income from capital; **~einnahmen** receipts from capital assets; **~entziehung** forfeiture of property, confiscation of property; **~erklärung** statement of one's assets and liabilities; **~erträgnis** investment income, income from property; **~erwerb** acquisition of wealth, take-over of total assets; **~gegenstand** (*pl ~gegenstände = ~e*) item of property; property item; asset; *bewegliche ~~e: goods and chattels*; *immaterielle ~~e: incorporeal property, intangible assets*; *kirchliche ~~e: ecclesiastical things*; *unpfändbare ~~e: exempt property*; **~gerichtsstand** asset-based jurisdiction; **~güter** assets, goods; *reale ~~: tangible assets*; **~haftung** liability with all of one's property; **~hinterziehung** fraudulent alienation; **~interesse** pecuniary interest; **~komplex** body of assets; **~konto** property account; **~lage** financial situation; **~liste** assets log; **v~los** *adj* impecunious; **~losigkeit** absence of property, lack of funds, insolvency; **~masse** total assets, estate, funds, accumulation of wealth; **v~mäßig** *adj* relating to wealth, pecuniary; **~mehrung** augmentation of property, increase in one's assets, increase in net worth; **~nachfolger** successor in property rights; **~nachteil** pecuniary loss, pecuniary disadvantage; **~nachweis** financial position statement; **~neubewertung** reassessment of property values; **~objekt** asset, property item; **~offenbarung** (debtor's) disclosure of property (*all assets and liabilities*); **~offenbarungsverfahren** *proceedings for the disclosure of a debtor's assets*; **~recht** economic right(s); proprietary interest, property right; pecuniary right; **~rechnung** calculation of net worth; **~reserve** capital reserve; **~rücklage** capital reserve; **~schaden** property loss, pecuniary loss, damage to one's property; **~schadensversicherung** consequential loss insurance, insurance against pecuniary damage; **~sorge** statutory duty of care for a minor's property; looking after a minor's property; **~stand** net position on assets and liabilities, financial state, pecuniary status; **~status** financial status, asset and liability statement, pecuniary status; **~steuer** → *Vermögenssteuer*; **~stock** main property fund; **~strafen** fines levied on property; **~struktur** asset structure; **~teile** elements of capital; **~träger** property holder; **~transaktion** property transaction; capital transaction; **~übergang** transfer of all assets and liabilities; **~übernahme** take-over of the aggregate of property, take-over of capital; **~übersicht** summary of assets and liabilities, financial statement; *durch eidliche Erklärung bekräftigte ~~: statement of affairs verified by affidavit*; **~übertragung** transfer of one's property (as a whole), assignment of assets; *gläubigerbegünstigende ~~: preferential assignment of assets*; *treuhänderische ~~: trust settlement*; **~umschichtung** regrouping of assets; **~umverteilung** redistribution of wealth; **~- und Ertragslage** financial position and operating results; **~veränderung** change in net assets; **~veräußerung** alienation of one's assets (as a whole); **~verbindlichkeit** capital liability; **~verfall** dwindling of assets, financial collapse; pecuniary deterioration; **~verfügung** disposition of property, pecuniary disposition; **~verfügungsbeschränkung** restraint on dealings with property; **~vergleich** property comparison, comparison of assets; **~verhältnisse**

835

Vermögenssteuer | **Vernehmung**

financial (*or* pecuniary) circumstances; ~**verkehr** transfer of property, property transactions; ~**verkehrssteuer** (property) transfer tax, property transactions tax; ~**verlust** loss of one's wealth, pecuniary loss; ~**vermehrung** increase in wealth; ~**verschiebung** (fraudulent) transfer of assets; ~**verschlechterung** deterioration in one's financial position; ~**verschleierung** concealment of assets; ~**verwahrer** custodian, depositary of property; ~**verwalter** administrator, guardian of property, receiver; manager of an estate; ~**verwaltung** administration of property, investment management; receivership; ~**verwaltungsgesellschaft** asset-administering company, property-managing company; ~**verzeichnis** inventory of property, schedule of property (*especially that of a judgment debtor*), statement of all property; ~**vorteil** pecuniary benefit (*or* advantage), capital gain; *e-n* ~~ *erlangen: to gain a pecuniary advantage*; *rechtswidriger* ~~: *unlawful enrichment, unlawful gain*; ~**wert** asset, net asset value; *pl also*: resources, property holdings, property assets; ~*e der Bank*: bank assets; *immaterielle* ~~*e*: *intangible assets*; *monetäre* ~~*e*: *monetary assets*; *verfügbare* ~~*e*: *ready assets*; **v**~**swirksam** *adj* asset-forming, capital-forming; ~**zuführung** addition to assets, accession of property; ~**zusammenrechnung** computed total of assets; ~**zuwachs** wealth increment, capital gains, increase in wealth, asset growth.

Vermögenssteuer *f* wealth tax, (general) property tax, capital tax; ~**änderungsgesetz** law to amend wealth tax law; ~**gesetz** wealth tax law; ~**richtlinien** wealth tax directives; ~**veranlagung** assessment of the wealth tax; ~**vorauszahlungen** advance payments of wealth tax, wealth tax prepayments.

Vermummung *f* masking, hiding one's face; ~**sverbot** ban on masks and disguises at demonstrations.

vermuten *v/t* to presume, to assume.

vermutlich *adj* presumable, putative.

Vermutung *f* presumption, assumption; ~ **des Überlebens** presumption of survival; **e-e** ~ **entstehen lassen** to raise a presumption; **e-e** ~ **widerlegen** to rebut (*or* to disprove, to refute) a presumption; **gesetzliche** ~ presumption of law, statutory presumption; **tatsächliche** ~ factual presumption; **unwiderlegbare** ~ irrebuttable (*or* non-rebuttable) presumption, irrefutable assumption; **widerlegbare** ~ rebuttable presumption, refutable assumption; **zwingende** ~ compelling presumption.

vernachlässigen *v/t* to neglect.

Vernachlässigung *f* neglect; ~ **der Aufsichtspflicht** neglect of one's supervisory duties; ~ **der Unterhaltspflicht** failure to provide maintenance, non-support; ~ **von Schutzbefohlenen** neglect of persons placed in one's care and custody.

vernehmen *v/t* to examine, to interrogate; to question (*by the police*); **jmdn eidlich** ~ to examine someone on oath.

Vernehmung *f* examination, interrogation, questioning; ~ **der Beteiligten** examination of the parties; ~ **des Angeklagten zur Sache** examination of the defendant concerning the substance of the charge; ~ **e-s Sachverständigen** interrogation of an expert; ~ **e-s Zeugen** examination of a witness; ~ **mit Suggestivfragen** interrogation involving the use of leading questions; ~**sbeamter** interrogator; ~**sbeschluß** order for the interrogation (*of a suspect*); **v**~**sfähig** *adj* fit to be examined; in a physical condition to undergo an interrogation; ~**sprotokoll** record of interrogation; ~**srichter** examining magistrate; ~ **zur Beschuldigung** arraignment, hearing

verneinen / **verpfändbar**

the defendant about the charge; ~ **zur Person** examination (of witness, defendant) about his personal status; **eidliche** ~ examination on oath; **öffentliche** ~ public examination; **polizeiliche** ~ police interrogation; **richterliche** ~ judicial examination; **uneidliche** ~ examination (*of a witness*) not under oath.

verneinen *v/t* to answer in the negative, to deny, to negate, to negative.

verneinend *adj* negative.

Verneinung *f* negative answer, negation.

Vernichtbarkeit *f* voidability (*deed*).

vernichten *v/t* to destroy, to annihilate, to eliminate.

Vernichtung *f* destruction, annihilation; ~**sprotokoll** written record of destruction (*of documents, substances, etc*); ~**swettbewerb** cutthroat competition; ~ **von Akten** destruction of records.

Vernunft *f* reason, reasonableness, rationality; ~**sehe** marriage of convenience; ~**sregeln** rules of reason.

vernünftig *adj* reasonable.

veröffentlichen *v/t* to publish, to promulgate (*a law*).

Veröffentlichung *f* publication, promulgation (*of a law*); ~ **des Aufgebots** publication of the banns; ~**sblatt** official gazette; ~**datum** publication date, date of publication; ~**sgebühr** *pat* publication fee; ~**srecht** right of publication, *pl also* publishing rights; ~**svorschriften** disclosure provisions; **amtliche** ~ official publication, public notice; **internationale** ~ *pat* international publication; **mit der** ~ **rechtswirksam werden** to become effective upon publication; **nicht zur** ~ **bestimmt** off the record; **nicht zur** ~ **geeignet** unfit for publication, unfit to print, unprintable; **pornografische** ~ obscene book or paper, pornographical publication; **regelmäßig erscheinende** ~**en** periodical publications; **unzüchtige** ~ indecent publication.

verordnen *v/t* to ordain, to decree.

Verordnung *f* ordinance, statutory instrument; executive order, ministerial order; *pl also*: subordinate legislation, official regulations; ~**en erlassen** to issue regulations; to issue ministerial orders; ~ **mit Gesetzeskraft** statutory instruments; ~**sblatt** official gazette, gazette of ordinances; ~**srecht** decree law, subordinate legislation; **städtische** ~ municipal ordinance.

verpachten *v/t* to lease, to let on lease.

Verpächter *m* lessor; ~**pfandrecht** lessor's lien.

Verpachtung *f* lease, leasing, letting on lease; ~ **e-s Patents** lease of a patent; ~ **von Fischerei- und Jagdrechten** leasing of fishing and hunting rights.

Verpacken *n* packing, wrapping.

verpacken *v/t* to pack (up), to wrap up.

Verpacker *m* packer, packing agent.

verpackt *adj* packed; **handelsüblich** ~ packed as usual in the trade, packed to normal commercial standards; **seemäßig** ~ packed for transportation by sea.

Verpackung *f* packing, packaging; ~ **für Ozeantransport** ocean packing; ~ **in Kisten** crating; ~**sanweisung** packing instructions; ~**sgewicht** tare weight; ~**sgestaltung** packaging; ~**skosten** packing charges; ~**sleinwand** bale-cloth; ~**stechnik** package engineering; ~**szettel** packing slip; **mangelhafte** ~ defective packing; **ohne** ~ packing extra, without packing; **seemäßige** ~ seaworthy packing; **wiederverwendungsfähige** ~ re-usable packaging (*or* packing).

verpanschen *v/t* to adulterate (*wine, milk*), to "doctor".

Verpanschung *f* adulteration of beverages.

verpfändbar *adj* pawnable, suitable

verpfänden

as pledge, assignable by way of pledge.

verpfänden *v/t* to pawn, to pledge (*as collateral security*); to hock, to mortgage; **sich etw ~ lassen** to take in pawn; **weiter~** to repledge.

Verpfänder *m* pawnor, pledgor, mortgagor.

verpfändet *adj* pledged, pawned, in pawn, mortgaged; **nicht ~**: *unmortgaged, free from pledge or pawn*.

Verpfändung *f* pawning, pledging, mortgaging, hypothecation; **~ der Beteiligung** assignment of the share by way of mortgage; **~ der Ernte auf dem Halm** crop mortgage; **~ e-s Patents** assignment of a patent by way of mortgage; **~ e-s Schiffs** bottomry, pledging a ship as security; **~serklärung** (declaration of) pledge; **~sgrenze** mortgaging limit; **~sklausel** pledging clause; *negative ~~*: *negative pledging clause (promise not to encumber assets)*; **~surkunde** letter of hypothecation; **~svertrag** contract of pledge; *obligatorischer ~~*: *equitable mortgage*; **~ von Außenständen** pledge of accounts; **~ von beweglichen Sachen** pledge of chattels; **etw aus der ~ auslösen** to take sth out of pledge, to redeem; **formlose ~** equitable charge (*title deeds*).

verpfeifen *v/t* (*sl*) to "squeak", to inform (against s. o.).

verpflegen *v/t* to provide food, to cater for.

Verpflegung *f* provisions, food supply, board, victualling; **~sentschädigung** per diem allowance.

verpflichten *v/t* to obligate, to engage, to commit, to put under an obligation; *v/reflex* to undertake, to obligate oneself, to commit oneself, to agree (to); **sich vertraglich ~** to bind oneself by contract, to enter into a contract.

verpflichtend *adj* obligatory; **einseitig ~** unilaterally obligating, onerous, one-sided.

verpflichtet *adj* indebted, liable, obligated, committed; **gesetzlich ~** legally bound, bound by law, legal-

Verpflichtung

ly obligated; **urkundlich ~** liable under an indenture; **vertraglich ~** bound by contract, contractually obligated; contractually committed.

Verpflichteter *m* (*der Verpflichtete*) obligor, obligated party, party liable; **als zahlungsfähig bekannter ~** party known to be solvent.

Verpflichtung *f* obligation (= *obl*), undertaking, commitment, engagement, liability, duty; **~en erfüllen** to meet one's *obl–s*; to discharge one's duties; **~en nicht erfüllen** to fail in one's *obl–s*, to be derelict in one's duties; **~sermächtigung** commitment authority, commitment appropriation; **~sgeschäft** undertaking, transaction constituting an obligation; executory transaction; **~ zu e-r Unterlassung** *obl* to refrain from doing sth; **~ zur Duldung** *obl* to tolerate sth; **~ zur Vorlage e-r Urkunde** duty to produce a document; **~ zur Vornahme e-r Handlung** *obl* to perform an act; **abstrakte ~** independent covenant, absolute (*or* abstract) *obl*; **akzessorische ~** accessory *obl*, dependent (*or* secondary) *obl*; **ausdrückliche ~** express *obl*, explicit commitment; **aus e-r ~ entlassen** to release from an *obl*; **außenpolitische ~en** foreign commitments; **befristete ~** *obl* subject to a time-limit; **bedingte ~** conditional *obl*; **bewehrte ~** penal *obl*, *obl* subject to a penalty clause; **dingliche ~** real *obl*, in rem *obl*; **e-e ~ abgelten** to discharge (*or* settle) an *obl*; **e-e ~ auferlegen** to impose an *obl*; **e-e ~ auf sich nehmen** to incur an *obl* (*or* a liability); **e-e ~ eingehen** to undertake (*or* to enter into) an *obl*; **~en ~**: *to incur obligations, to incur liabilities*; **e-e ~ übernehmen** to undertake (*or* to assume) an *obl*; **einfache ~** simple *obl*; **eingegangene ~en** liabilities incurred; **einseitige ~** unilateral *obl*; **entstandene ~** accrued liability;

838

feierliche ~ solemn undertaking; **finanzielle** ~ pecuniary *obl, pl also*: pecuniary liabilities; **gegenseitige** ~ mutual (*or* reciprocal) *obl*; **geldliche** ~**en** pecuniary liabilities, financial *obl–s*; **gemeinsame** ~ joint *obl*; **gemeinschaftliche** ~ joint *obl*; **gesamtverbindliche** ~ joint and several *obl*; **gesellschaftliche** ~ social engagement; **gesetzliche** ~ legal *obl*, statutory *obl*; **handelsvertragliche** ~**en** *obl–s* under trade agreements; **internationale** ~ international commitment; **in** ~**en eintreten** to assume liabilities as debtor; **jmdn von seiner** ~ **befreien** to discharge s. o. from his *obl–s*, to release s. o. from his liabilities; **laufende** ~ current engagement; **mit e-m Recht verbundene** ~**en** liabilities attaching to a right; **moralische** ~ moral *obl*, ethical duty; **nicht einklagbare** ~ imperfect *obl*; non-actionable *obl*; **öffentlich-rechtliche** ~ *obl* under public law; **persönliche** ~ personal obligation; **primäre** ~ primary *obl*; **rechtlich durchsetzbare** ~ perfect *obl*, enforceable *obl*; **rechtliche** ~ legal *obl*; **samtverbindliche** ~ joint and several *obl*; **satzungsgemäße** ~ *obl* under the memorandum and articles (of association); **schwer zu erfüllende** ~ onerous *obl*; **seine** ~**en erfüllen** to meet one's *obl–s*; **sekundäre** ~ secondary *obl*; **sich auf** ~**en berufen** to invoke *obl–s*; **solidarische** ~ joint and several *obl*; **stillschweigende** ~ implied *obl* (*or* engagement), tacit *obl*; **terminierte** ~ commitment maturing at a future date, *obl* as from a specified date; **unbedingte** ~ unconditional (*or* pure) *obl*; **unbewehrte** ~ single *obl*, naked bond; **unmittelbare** ~ direct *obl*, primary liability, direct commitment, personal liability; **vertragliche** ~ contractual *obl* (*or* engagement); **völkerrechtliche** ~ international *obl*, requirement under international law; **von e-r** ~ **befreien** to release from an *obl*; **von e-r** ~ **entbinden** to release from an *obl*; **voreheliche** ~**en** ante-nuptial debts, pre-marital *obl–s*; **zwingende** ~ absolutely binding *obl*, compulsory *obl*.

Verpflichtungs|eid promissory oath; ~**erklärung** formal obligation; ~**geschäft** executory agreement; ~**klage** action for the issue of an administrative act; ~**kredit** guarantee credit (*bank assuming liability*); ~**schein** promissory document, liability bond; certificate of obligation; *kaufmännischer* ~~: *mercantile promise*; ~**schreiben** written undertaking; ~**übernahme** assumption of an obligation; ~**urteil** judgment commanding the defendant to do some positive act.

verplomben *v/t* to seal.

Verprobung *f* trial balance.

Verramschen *n* selling at cut-rate prices, dumping (products).

Verrat *m* treason, betrayal, treachery; ~ **militärischer Geheimnisse** betrayal of military secrets, military treason; ~ **von Staatsgeheimnissen** betrayal of state secrets.

verraten *v/t* to betray, to divulge.

Verräter *m* traitor, betrayer (of).

verräterisch *adj* treacherous, treasonable, perfidious.

verrechnen *v/t* to settle, to set off, to account for, to charge, to invoice, *v/reflex* to miscalculate.

Verrechnung *f* settlement, placing to the account, clearing, compensation, (mutual) set-off; **nur zur** ~ (*on cheque*) account payee only, for deposit only; **schwebende** ~ item in course of settlement.

Verrechnungs|abkommen offset agreement, clearing agreement; ~**ausland** foreign country covered by a clearing agreement, clearing countries abroad; ~**bilanz** clearing balance, offset account balance; ~**defizit** clearing deficit; ~**devise** offset (account) currency; ~**dollar** clearing dollar; ~**einheit** unit of account, clearing unit; ~**einrede** offset plea, defence that the account

verrichten / **Versand**

has already been settled; ~**geschäfte** offsetting transactions; ~**guthaben** clearing balance, offset account balance; ~**kasse** clearing house, clearing office; ~**konto** clearing account, offset account; ~**kredit** offset credit; ~**kurs** settlement rate; ~**land** clearing agreement country, clearing country, offset-account country; ~**position** offsetting item; ~**posten** offsetting item; *wechselseitige* ~~: *mutually offsetting items*; ~**preis** price; *innerbetrieblicher* ~~: *internal transfer price*; ~**raum** clearing area; ~**saldo** clearing balance, offset balance; ~**satz** invoice price rate, cost rate; ~**scheck** collection-only cheque, account-payee-only cheque, ~ crossed cheque; ~**schuld** clearing debt, debt under a clearing agreement, debit balance; ~**spitze** clearing balance, balance on clearing account; ~**stelle** clearing office; ~**steuer** withholding tax; ~**tag** settlement day, day of settlement; ~**verfahren** clearing system; ~**verkehr** clearing (system), clearing transactions; ~**vertrag** (agreement for) mutual settlement of accounts; ~**vorgang** clearing, settlement; ~**währung** clearing (agreement) currency; ~**wege** clearing channels; ~**wert** trade-in value.

verrichten *v/t* to perform, to carry out, to effect, to execute.

Verrichtung *f* the doing of sth, discharge of a function, transaction; ~**sgehilfe** vicarious agent *with respect to tortious liability*.

Verruf *m* disrepute; ~**erklärung** boycott declaration.

Versagen *n* failure; ~ **der Bremse** failure of the brake.

Versagung *f* denial, refusal; ~ **der Einreiseerlaubnis** refusal of entry permit; ~ **der Hilfe gegenüber e-r Schwangeren** withholding help from a pregnant woman.

versammeln *v/reflex* to assemble, to meet.

Versammlung *f* meeting, gathering, assembly; ~ **der Europäischen Gemeinschaften** European Assembly; ~ **unter freiem Himmel** open-air meeting; **außerordentliche** ~ extraordinary meeting; **beratende** ~ consultative (*or* deliberative) assembly; **die** ~ **leiten** to preside over the meeting; **e-e formgerecht einberufene** ~ a duly convened meeting; **e-e** ~ **einberufen** to convene a meeting; **e-e** ~ **vertagen** to adjourn a meeting; **gemeinsame** ~ common assembly; **gesetzgebende** ~ legislative assembly; **konstituierende** ~ constituent assembly; **öffentliche** ~ public meeting, public gathering; **ordentliche** ~ ordinary meeting; **politische** ~ political assembly; **unerlaubte** ~ unlawful assembly; **verbotene** ~ unlawful assembly; **verfassungsgebende** ~ constitutional assembly; **widerrechtliche** ~ unlawful assembly; **zulässige** ~ lawful meeting.

Versammlungs|erlaubnis permission (*or* licence) to hold a meeting; ~**erlaubniserteilung** licensing of a meeting; ~**freiheit** freedom of meeting, right of assembly; ~**gesetz** law regulating public meetings; ~**leiter** person in charge of (*or organizer of*) a public meeting; ~**recht** right of assembly; law of meetings; ~**stätte** assembly room; ~**störung** disturbance of (public) meetings; ~**termin** date of the assembly; ~**verbot** prohibition of assembly, ban on public meetings.

Versand *m* consignment, dispatch, shipping, shipment, transport, mailing; ~**abteilung** shipping *or* forwarding department; ~ **an bestimmte Empfänger** straight shipment (*not to order*); ~**anschrift** address for shipments, parcels address; ~**anweisungen** shipping instructions, instructions for despatch; ~**anzeige** dispatch note, notice of consignment, shipping advice; ~**art** mode of dispatch; ~**auftrag** shipping order, dispatch order; ~**ausfuhrerklärung** export shipping declaration; ~**avis** advice of dispatch, shipping note; ~**bahnhof** forwarding station; ~**bedingungen** shipping terms; v~**bereit** *adj* ready for shipment; ~**bereitstellungskredit** packing credit; ~**bestellung** mail order (buying), postal shopping; ~**buch** shipping book; v~**fähig** *adj* transportable; ~**flughafen** shipping airport; ~**form** manner of delivery; ~**gebühr** forwarding charge; ~**geschäft** mail-order business; ~**hafen** shipping port; ~**handel** mail-order business; ~**haus** mail-order firm, catalogue company ~~**niederlassung** catalogue shop; ~**kauf** sale to destination according to buyer's instructions; mail-order sale; ~~**lieferant**: *mail-order supplier*; ~**kosten** shipping expense, delivery expenses, forwarding expenditure; ~**land** = *Versendungsland qv*; ~**liste** packing list; ~**mitteilung** forwarding note, advice of dispatch, shipping advice; ~**ort** = *Versendungsort qv*; ~**papiere** shipping documents; ~**raum** shipping room; ~**rechnung** shipping invoice; ~**schein** dispatch (*or* shipping) note; ~**spesen** forwarding charges, shipping expense(s); ~**termin** shipping date (*or* time); ~**vorschriften** forwarding instructions; ~**weg** routing; ~**ziel** destination (of shipment), goal.

versäumen *v/t* to miss, to fail to appear, to fail to attend.

Versäumnis *n* default, default of appearance, non-attendance, neglect, omission, failure to perform; ~**entscheidung** judgment by default; ~**kosten** fees accruing due to default of appearance; ~**urteil** judgment by default; ~~ *wegen Nichtanzeige der Verteidigungsbereitschaft*: *judgment in default of notice of intention to defend; ein ~~ beantragen: to move for a judgment by default; ein ~~ gegen sich ergehen lassen: to suffer default*; ~**verfahren** default proceedings; ~**zwischenurteil** interlocutory judgment by default; **unverschuldetes** ~excusable default.

Versäumung *f* failure to observe (*a time-limit, date etc*).

Verschachtelung *f* interlocking, pyramiding.

verschaffen *v/t* to procure, to obtain, to secure, to acquire.

Verschaffen *n* procurement; ~ **von Staatsgeheimnissen** obtaining state secrets.

Verschaffung *f* procurement; ~ **der Gelegenheit zur Unzucht** procuring opportunities for illicit sexual relations; ~**svermächtnis** demonstrative legacy.

verschärfen *v/t* to sharpen, to aggravate, to tighten.

Verschärfung *f* aggravation, intensification, stiffening; ~ **des Wettbewerbs** intensification (*or* accentuation) of competition.

verscheiden *v/i* to die, to pass away, to decease.

Verschiebebahnhof *n* shunting station.

Verschiebung *f* displacement, postponement; ~ **der Ladung** shift of stowage; ~ **der Nachfrage** shift in demand.

Verschiedenes *n* general (*or* other) business (*agenda*), miscellaneous.

Verschiedenheit *f* disparity.

verschiffen *v/t* to ship.

Verschiffer *m* shipper.

verschifft *adj* loaded, afloat.

Verschiffung *f* shipping, shipment.

Verschiffungs|anzeige shipping advice; ~**auftrag** shipping order; ~**dokumente** shipping documents shipping papers; ~**gewicht** shipment weight; ~**hafen** port of shipment; *benannter* ~~: *named port of shipment*; ~**muster** shipment sample; ~**tag** shipping date; ~**wert** shipping value.

Verschlechterung *f* deterioration, impairment, a change for the worse, worsening; ~**sverbot** *n* prohibition to worsen appellant's position (*by the court*).

verschleiern *v/t* to conceal, to disguise, to mask, to hide.

Verschleierung *f* concealment, disguise.

Verschleiß *m* wear and tear; ~**ausfall** loss through wear and tear, wear-out failure, breakdown through use; ~**erscheinung** signs of wear and tear.

verschleppen *v/t* (1) to delay unduly, to protract.

verschleppen *v/t* (2) to kidnap, to carry off, to abduct against one's will.

Verschleppter *m* (*der Verschleppte*) *pol*: displaced person, *crim*: kidnapped person.

Verschleppung *f* (1) protraction, dilatory tactics, procrastination; ~ **des Verfahrens** delaying the proceedings; ~**absicht** intention to delay the proceedings; ~**staktik** dilatory tactics.

Verschleppung (2) kidnapping, displacement, abduction.

verschleudern *v/t* to waste, to dissipate, to squander; to sell at dumping (*or* ruinous) prices.

Verschleuderung *f* dissipation, squandering, selling at dumping (*or* ruinous) prices; ~ **von Familienhabe** squandering of family property.

Verschlimmerungsantrag *m* application for an increase in war injury benefits due to a worsening of the disablement.

verschlüsseln *v/t* to code, to encipher.

Verschlußsache *f* restricted matter, classified information; ~**nanweisung** federal regulation concerning classified (secret) matters; ~**nverordnung** security regulations.

Verschlußverletzung *f* breaking of seals.

verschmelzen *v/i* to merge, to amalgamate, to fuse.

Verschmelzung *f* merger, amalgamation, fusion; ~ **durch Aufnahme** amalgamation; ~ **durch Neubildung** consolidation; ~ **durch Neugründung** reorganization-merger.

Verschmutzung *f* pollution; ~**sschaden** damage by pollution.

verschollen *adj* missing, presumed dead, untraceable.

Verschollener *m* untraceable person, a person who has disappeared completely, absentee of unknown whereabouts.

Verschollenheit *f* protracted disappearance; ~ **e-s Schiffes** presumptive loss of a ship; ~**serklärung** report of a person's long-lasting disappearance; ~**sgesetz** Law on Missing Persons; ~**ssachen** *court proceedings concerning missing persons and presumption of death.*

Verschonung *f* relief, saving; ~ *von der Untersuchungshaft durch Sicherheitsleistung: granting bail.*

Verschrottung *f* junking, scrapping.

Verschubung *f* transfer of prisoners.

Verschulden *n* fault, blame; ~ **bei Vertragsschluß** culpa in contrahendo; ~**shaftung** liability for fault (*liability for wilful or negligent wrongdoing*); ~**sprinzip** fault principle (*divorce*); ~ **beiderseitiges** ~ mutual fault; "both to blame"; ~~ *der Parteien: both parties (spouses) equally at fault;* **fahrlässiges** ~ negligence; **fremdes** ~ fault of another party; **geringfügiges** ~ slight fault; **grobes** ~ gross negligence; **ihn trifft das** ~ the fault lies with him; **jmds** ~ fault attributable to s. o.; **jmds** ~ **überwiegt** someone's fault outweighs (that of the other party); **konkurrierendes** ~ concurrent negligence; **mitwirkendes** ~ contributory negligence; **nautisches** ~ negligence by persons in charge of a ship, nautical negligence; **ohne jedes** ~ without anybody's fault, without anyone being at fault; **sittliches** ~ moral fault, blame; **strafrechtliches** ~ criminal guilt, blame under criminal law.

verschulden *v/reflex* to get into debt.

verschuldet *adj* in debt, indebted; caused by one's own fault; **hoch** ~ heavily indebted, debt-ridden.

Verschuldung *f* indebtedness, level of debt, amount of indebtedness; ~**sgrad** debt ratio; ~**sgrenze** ceiling for (public) debts; **die ~ abwickeln** to liquidate the indebtedness; **echte ~** net indebtedness; **langfristige ~** long-term indebtedness; **näher bezeichnete ~** specified indebtedness; **zugelassene ~** legal debt margin (*for local authorities*).

Verschuldungs|grenze borrowing limit; **~hebel** leverage; **~möglichkeit** borrowing capacity, borrowing facilities; **~neigung** tendency to incur debts, propensity to assume liabilities; **~rate** rate of increase of indebtedness; **~spielraum** debt margin; **~vorgang** debt-incurring process, the incurring of debts; **~vorwurf** blame.

verschwägert *adj* related (*or* connected) by marriage.

Verschwägerter *m* (*der Verschwägerte*) in-law, person related by marriage.

Verschweigen *n* keeping silent about sth, withholding information; **~ der Wahrheit** withholding of the truth; **~ von Ehehindernissen** concealing of legal impediments to marriage; **~ von Tatsachen** suppression of facts; **arglistiges ~** malicious non-disclosure.

verschweigen *v/t* to conceal, to withhold (*the truth, information etc*), to suppress (*material facts*), to keep silent (*about sth.*); **sich ~** to commit laches, to lose rights by keeping silent.

Verschweigung *f* laches, estoppel by laches; **~seinrede** plea of estoppel by laches as against a creditor (*of the estate a deceased person*).

verschwenden *v/t* to dissipate, to squander, to waste.

Verschwender *m* spendthrift.

Verschwendung *f* waste, squander, dissipation, prodigality, profligacy; **~ssucht** prodigality, squandermania, profligacy.

verschwiegen *adj* discreet.

Verschwiegenheit *f* discretion, secrecy; **~spflicht** obligation of secrecy; **ärztliche ~spflicht** a doctor's duty of confidentiality.

verschwören *v/reflex* to conspire, to plot.

Verschwörer *m* conspirator, plotter.

Verschwörung *f* conspiracy, plot; **~ gegen die Sicherheit des Staates** conspiracy against state security.

Versehen *n* inadvertence, (accidental) error; **aus ~** inadvertently.

versehentlich *adj* inadvertent; *adv* inadvertently, by mistake.

versehrt *adj* physically disabled.

Versehrte|r *m* (*der Versehrte*) physically disabled person; **~nunterstützung bei Gliederverlust** dismemberment benefit.

Versehrtheit *f* disablement.

Verselbständigung *f* achievement of autonomy, independence.

versenden *v/t* to send off, to dispatch, to forward, to send to another destination; to ship to another place; *versandt, aber noch nicht in Rechnung gestellt:* shipped not billed.

Versender *m* sender, consignor.

Versendung *f* dispatch, shipment, transportation (*to buyer's address*), transmission; **~ entzündlicher Waren** sending inflammables; **~ mit der Post** mailing, dispatch by post; **~ von Gütern** transmission of goods.

Versendungs|anzeige forwarding advice, notice of shipment; **~art** mode of forwarding dispatch; **~geschäft** forwarding business; **~kauf** sale to destination according to buyer's instructions; **~kosten** = *Versandkosten qv*; **~land** country of consignment, country of dispatch; **~ort** place of consignment, shipping point.

Versenkung | von Atommüll dumping of radioactive waste.

Versetzen *n* pawning, pledging.

versetzen *v/t* (1) to relocate, to transfer to another post; **zeitweilig ~** to second (*civil servants, officers*).

versetzen *v/t* (2) to pawn, to pledge.

Versetzung *f* transfer to another post; transposition; moving up to a higher school class; **~ in den Anklagestand** arraignment; **~ in**

versicherbar

den einstweiligen Ruhestand placing on non-active status; ~ in den Ruhestand pensioning; ~ in den Wartestand placing on non-active status pending new assignment; ~sgesuch application for a transfer (to another post); e-e ~ beantragen to apply for a transfer; strafweise ~ transfer to another post as a disciplinary measure.

versicherbar *adj* insurable.

Versicherer *m* assurer, insurer, underwriter.

versichern *v/t* (1) to insure, to assure, to underwrite; höher ~ to rate up, to insure at higher rate.

versichern *v/t* (2) to assure, to affirm; to asseverate; eidlich ~ to affirm under oath.

versichert *adj* insured; anderweitig ~ insured elsewhere.

Versichertenältester *m* social insurance deputy.

Versichertendividenden *f/pl* dividends to policy-holders.

Versicherter *m* (*der Versicherte*) person insured, (the) insured, the insured party; freiwillig ~ voluntary contributor (*social insurance*).

Versicherung *f* (1) (= *ins*) insurance, assurance, underwriting; ~ auf den Todesfall whole life policy, straight life assurance; ~ auf den Todes- und Erlebensfall endowment assurance; ~ auf festen Termin term assurance; ~ auf fremdes Leben assurance on the life of another person; ~ auf Gegenseitigkeit mutual *ins*; ~en im Luftverkehr air *ins*; ~ für bestimmte Zeitdauer term assurance; ~ für fremde Rechnung *ins* for another person's account; ~ für Rechnung, für wen es angeht *ins* for the account of whom it may concern; ~ für stationäre Krankenhausbehandlung hospitalization *ins*; ~ gegen Betriebsunterbrechung business interruption *ins*; ~ gegen Kriegsgefahr war risk *ins*; ~ gegen Raubüberfall personal hold-up *ins*; ~ gegen Wasserschaden aus Feuerlösch-

Versicherungsablauf

anlagen sprinkler leakage *ins*, ~ mit begrenzter Prämienzahlung limited payment policy; ~ mit beschränktem Risiko limited policy; ~ mit Gewinnbeteiligung *ins* with profits; ~ mit Gewinnbeteiligungsgarantie guaranteed dividend policy; ~ mit Selbstbehalt contributory *ins*; ~ ohne Gewinnbeteiligung *ins* without profits; aufgeschobene ~ deferred assurance; bedingte ~ contingent *ins*; direkte ~ direct *ins* business; e-e ~ abschließen to effect *ins*, to take out an *ins* policy; e-e ~ läuft ab an *ins* contract expires, a policy lapses; freiwillige ~ voluntary membership of a social *ins* scheme, non-mandatory *ins*; gewinnbeteiligte ~ a with-profits *ins*; mehrfache ~ multiple *ins*; öffentliche ~en public-law *ins* bodies, social *ins* institutions; prämienfreie ~ insurance without further premium obligations; privatrechtliche ~ private non-mandatory *ins*; voll eingezahlte ~ paid-up *ins*.

Versicherung *f* (2) positive assertion, assurance, protestation; ~ an Eides Statt statutory declaration (*or* affirmation) in lieu of an oath; ~ auf den Diensteid invoking the oath of office; ~ der Richtigkeit von tatsächlichen Angaben affirmative warranty; ehrenwörtliche ~ attestation on hono(u)r, word of honour; eidesstattliche ~ statutory declaration (or affirmation) in lieu of an oath, *imprecisely*: affidavit: *e-e* ~~ *abgeben*: to execute an affirmation *etc*, to swear an affidavit; eidliche ~ adjuration; affidavit, assurance under oath, sworn declaration; feierliche ~ asseveration, solemn assurance, affirmation.

Versicherungs|ablauf expiration of policy; ~agent *ins* agent; ~akquisiteur *ins* canvasser; ~aktie *ins* company share; ~amt Insurance Office; ~anspruch *ins* claim; ~anstalt *ins* company, (public) *ins* corporation; ~anteilschein fractional

Versicherung

ins certificate; **~antrag** *ins* proposal; **~aufsichtsamt** Supervisory Insurance Board; **~aufsichtsbehörde** *ins* supervisory authority; **~aufsichtsgesetz** *ins* supervision law; **~bedingungen** *ins* conditions, terms of a policy; *allgemeine ~~*: *general conditions of insurance*; **~beginn** commencement of *ins* cover; **~beirat** advisory council for *ins* supervision; **~beitrag** *ins* premium; **~berechtigter** beneficiary of *ins*; **~berechtigung** entitlement under a policy; **~bestand** total amount of assurances effected, *ins* portfolio; **~bestätigung** confirmation of *ins* cover, insurance certificate; **~betrug** *ins* fraud; **~courtage** *ins* brokerage commission; **~darlehen** policy loan; **~dauer** term of *ins*; *noch nicht abgelaufene ~~*: *unexpired term of ins*; **~deckung** *ins* cover(age); *~~ ab*: *cover commences*; **~einrichtungen** *ins* facilities; **~entgelt** amount of the *ins* premium *(including certain duties and expenses)*; **~entschädigung** compensation paid by an *ins* company; **~ergänzungsverordnung** supplementary *ins* regulations; **v~fähig** *adj* insurable; eligible for insurance; **~fähigkeit** insurability; **~fall** (occurrence of) event insured against; **~forderung** *ins* claim; **v~frei** exempt from insurance, exempt from the obligation to insure; **~freiheit** exemption from (social) *ins*; **~garant** policy underwriter; **~gegenstand** subject-matter insured, insured item; **~genossenschaft** co-operative *ins* society; **~geschäft** *ins* business, underwriting; **~gesellschaft** *ins* company; **~gesellschaften auf Aktien** stock *ins* companies; **~gesellschaften auf Gegenseitigkeit** friendly societies, mutual *ins* companies; **~gewerbe** *ins* business, the *ins* branch; **~inspektor** *ins* claims adjuster; **~interesse** insurable interest; *volles ~~ zugestanden*: *full interest admitted*; **~jahre** *ins* years; **~kalkulation** actuarial calculation; **~kammer** *ins* board, public *ins* corporation; **~karte** *ins* card; **~kennzeichen** *ins* identification mark; **~klasse** class of *ins*; **~kosten** *ins* expenses; **~kredit** loan from an *ins* company; **~lastregelungen** provisions relating to the apportionment of insurance burdens; **~leistung** *ins* benefits, idemnification payments; **~makler** *ins* broker, a person's agent to find suitable *ins* cover; **~marke** social *ins* stamp; **~mathematik** actuarial theory; **~mathematiker** actuary; *amtlicher ~~*: *officially appointed actuary*; **v~mathematisch** *adj* actuarial; **~medizin** medico-actuarial science; **~nachweis** proof (or evidence) of *ins* policy; **~nehmer** person taking out *ins*; the insured; *ins* policyholder; **~ordnung** regulations for (social) *ins*; **~nummer** *ins* number; **~periode** period of *ins*; **~pflicht** compulsory coverage; obligation (or duty) to insure; insurance liability income limit *(social insurance)*; *allgemeine ~~*: *general obligatory ins*; **r~pflichtig** compulsorily insured; subject to compulsory *ins*; **~pflichtiger** person subject to compulsory *ins*; **~police** *ins* policy, policy of *ins*; *laufende ~~*: *floating policy*, *verfallene ~~*: *lapsed policy*; **~prämie** (*ins*) premium; **~prämiensatz** *ins* rate; **~recht** *ins* law; **~risiko** insured risk; *laufende ~~en*: *pending risks*; **~rückkauf** redemption of policy; **~rückkaufwert** surrender value; **~schaden** damage covered by *ins*; **~schein** *ins* policy; *vorläufiger ~~*: *insurance note*; **~schutz** *ins* cover; *~~ vorläufig aufgehoben*: *out of benefit*; *sofortiger ~~*: *immediate benefit*; **~sparen** saving through *ins*, saving coupled with life assurance policy; **~steuer** *ins* tax; **~steuerpflicht** *ins* tax liability; **~summe** sum insured, amount insured; insured value, insurance money; amount covered, limit of indemnity; *doppelte ~~ bei Unfalltod*: *double indemnity in the*

845

versiegeln | **Versorgungsamt**

event of accidental death; ~**taxe** *ins* value; ~**technik** actuarial practice; **v~technisch** *adj* actuarial; ~**träger** insurer, underwriter, *ins* institution; *öffentlichrechtlicher ~~: public insurance institution*; ~**unterlagen** *ins* papers, *ins* records; ~**unternehmen** *ins* business-enterprise, *ins* company; ~**verband** association of insurers; ~**verein** *ins* association; ~~ *auf Gegenseitigkeit: mutual insurance association; friendly insurance company*; ~**verhältnis** *ins* relationship; ~**verlängerung** extension of policy; *automatische ~~: extended-term insurance*; ~**verlust** underwriting deficit, loss of policy cover; ~**verordnung** *ins* regulations; ~**vertrag** (*pl ~e*) contract of *ins*, *ins* agreement; underwriting contract; ~~*e abschließen: to effect insurances*; ~**vertragsgesetz** Insurance Act (*D, of 1908 as amended*); ~**vertreter** *ins* agent; *ins* representative; ~**vorvertrag** agreement for *ins*; ~**werber** *ins* canvasser; ~**wert** insured value, *ins* value; ~**wesen** *ins* matters, *ins* system; ~**wirtschaft** *ins* business, *ins* branch; ~**zeit** period of *ins,* period insured, term of *ins*; *beitragsfreie ~~: free insurance period; zurückgelegte ~~en: periods of coverage completed*; ~**zugehörigkeit** membership of an *ins* scheme; ~**zwang** liability to insure, compulsory *ins*; ~**zweig** *ins* branch.

versiegeln *v/t* to seal; *gerichtlich* ~ to affix seals (to), to put under seal.

versiegelt *adj* sealed, under seal.

Versiegelung *f* official sealing; ~**sprotokoll** record of official sealing (*of premises*); **amtliche** ~ official sealing; **gerichtliche** ~ official sealing by court order.

versilbern *v/t* to convert into cash, to reduce to money, to sell, to turn to account.

Versitzgrube *f* percolation basin, sewage basin, cess pool.

Versitzung *f* extinctive prescription; ~**sfrist** time of extinctive prescription.

versöhnen *v/t* to reconcile, to conciliate, to placate, to appease.

Versöhnung *f* reconciliation.

versorgen *v/t* to provide, to supply (with), to maintain, to take care of.

Versorger *m* provider, breadwinner.

Versorgung *f* (public) support (*esp: retirement pensions of civil servants, war victims etc.*), provision, supply, care; **grenzüberschreitende ärztliche** ~ trans-frontier medical care; **kassenärztliche** ~ medical care provided by panel doctors; **lebenslängliche** ~ support for life, life pension; **soziale** ~ social security support.

Versorgungs|amt public support and pensions administration; ~**anlagen** public-utility installations, utility systems; ~**anspruch** entitlement to a pension; ~**anstalt** pension fund institution; ~**anwartschaft** pension expectancy, future pension rights; ~**ausgleich** statutory equalization of (old-age) pensions *upon dissolution of marriage; isolierter ~~: separate court ruling on pensions equalization (divorce)*; ~**bedarf** *der Gemeinschaft an . . .* requirements *of the Community* as regards the supply *of . . .*; **v~berechtigt** *adj* entitled to maintenance, entitled to a pension; ~**berechtigter** person entitled to public support; ~**bereich** service area; ~**betrieb** public utility (enterprise); *öffentlicher ~~: public utility (enterprise)*; ~**bezug** pension, maintenance benefits; ~**dienstalter** (length of) pensionable service; ~**dienste** public utility services; ~**ehe** *marriage designed to obtain spouse's retirement benefits;* ~**einrichtung** pension scheme, pension organization; ~**empfänger** pensioner, beneficiary under a pension scheme; recipient of benefit; ~**engpaß** supply bottleneck; ~**fall** event giving rise to retirement benefits; ~**freibetrag** personal tax exemption for retirement benefits; ~**gebiet** supplies area; ~**gesetz** Act on public support and pensions; ~**industrie** public utility

verspätet / **Versteigerungsantrag**

industry; ~**kasse** pension fund; ~**klemme** supply difficulties, shortage(s); ~**krankengeld** disabled person's entitlement to sickness pay; ~**krise** critical supply position; ~**lage** supply situation; ~**leistung** public support benefit; ~**lücke** gap in supplies; **v**~**mäßig** *adj* as regards supplies; ~**monopol** utility monopoly; ~**ordnung** Public Support and Pensions Regulations; ~**rente** life annuity to provide for old age or infirmity; ~**sachen** public pension cases; ~**satz** pension rate, maintenance rate; ~**schiff** supply ship; ~**schuld** (public) support obligation; ~**schwierigkeiten** difficulty in providing supplies; ~**staat** welfare state; *der totale* ~~: *the 100% welfare state*; ~**standard** standard of supplies available; ~**tarife** rates charged for supply of municipal services (*electricity, gas, water*); ~**träger** pension-paying institution, pension fund; ~**- und Absatzbedingungen** conditions under which goods are procured and marketed; ~**unternehmen** public utility (undertaking); ~**verpflichtung** pension obligation; ~**verwaltung** public pensions authority; ~**werk** pension scheme, company pension scheme; *innerbetriebliches* ~~: *internal pensions scheme*; ~**werke** utilities; ~**werte** *exch* public utilities, shares in public utilities; ~**wesen** public utilities; ~**wirtschaft** public utilities; ~**zusage** employer's pension commitment; ~**zuschuß** additional allowance for maintenance.

verspätet *adj* late, belated; out of time.

Verspätungs|schaden damage caused by delay; ~**zinsen** interest on arrears; ~**zuschlag** extra charge for delay.

Versprechen *n* promise, undertaking, pledge, voluntary undertaking; ~**sempfänger** promisee; ~**sgeber** promisor; **bindendes** ~ binding promise; **ernst gemeintes** ~ serious promise; **unbedingtes** ~ unconditional promise.

versprechen *v/t* to promise.

Versprechender *m* (*der Versprechende*) promisor, the promising party.

Versprechungen *n/pl* promissory representations, promises.

verstaatlichen *v/t* to nationalize.

Verstaatlichung *f* nationalization, transfer to state ownship.

Verstädterung *f* urbanization.

verständigen *v/reflex* to reach an understanding, to come to an agreement; to make o.s. understood.

Verständigung *f* understanding, arrangement; **zur** ~ **kommen** to come to terms, to reach an understanding, to make an arrangement.

Verständigungs|bereitschaft readiness to come to an understanding; ~**politik** policy of mutual understanding, policy of rapprochement; ~**verfahren** procedure of mutual consultation.

verstauen *v/t* to stow (away).

Verstauung *f* stowage.

Versteigerer *m* auctioneer; ~**gewerbe** (the) auctioneering trade.

versteigern *v/t* to auctioneer, to auction off, to sell by public auction, to sell by public sale, to put up for auction; *versteigert werden: to come under the hammer etc*; **meistbietend** ~ to auction off to the highest bidder; **öffentlich** ~ to put on public sale, to sell by public auction.

versteigert *adj* sold by auction.

Versteigerung *f* auction, sale by auction, public sale; **freiwillige** ~ private auction; **gerichtliche** ~ sale by the court, judicial sale; **öffentliche** ~ public auction, public sale.

Versteigerungs|antrag application for public auction; ~**bedingungen** terms of public auction; ~**beschreibung** particulars of public auction; ~**erlös** proceeds of an auction; ~**gericht** the court in charge of a public sale; ~**gewerbe** the auctioneering trade, the auctioneering branch; ~**limit** limit for bidding; *unteres* ~~: *reserve price, upset price*;

847

~**ort** place of auction; ~**protokoll** record of the auction; ~**termin** auction day, date of the auction; ~**verfahren** auctioneering procedure; ~**vermerk** entry of public auction (*in a public register*); ~**zeit** time of auction.

Verstetigung *f* institutionalization, stabilization, consolidation.

versteuerbar *adj* taxable, rateable.

versteuern *v/t* to pay tax (on sth), to pay duty (on sth); to impose a tax.

versteuert *adj* tax-paid, taxed.

Versteuerung imposition of a tax, payment of tax; ~**swert** taxable value.

verstorben *adj* deceased, late, defunct, dead, departed, ob (= *obit*).

Verstorbener *m* (*der Verstorbene, f: die Verstorbene*) the deceased, decedent.

Verstoß *m* infringement, contravention, offence, violation, breach; ~ **gegen das Gesetz** breach of the law; ~ **gegen die Denkgesetze** defiance of the rules of logic; ~ **gegen die guten Sitten** infringement of bonos mores, offence against public morals, breach of public policy; ~ **gegen die öffentliche Ordnung** violation of public order, violation of public peace; ~**e** (*Verstöße*) **gegen diese Grundsätze** contravention of these principles; ~ **gegen die Verkehrsvorschriften** traffic offence; ~ **gegen e-n Vertrag** breach of contract; ~ **gegen Parkvorschriften** parking offence.

verstoßen *v/i* (*1*) to contravene, to infringe, to violate, to infract; **gegen § 32** ~ to contravene section 32.

verstoßen *v/t* (*2*) to cast out, to breach, to be in breach of, to expel, to repudiate.

Verstoßung *f* casting off, expulsion, disownment, repudiation.

verstricken *v/t* to entangle, to inculpate, to ensnare.

Verstrickung *f* entanglement, inculpation, involvement; attachment by execution; imposition of an execution lien; ~**sbruch** interference with attachment; *unlawful destruction or conversion of property under distress or judicial execution.*

Verstromung *f* gaining of electricity from coal.

verstümmeln *v/t* to mutilate, to maim; to garble (report).

Verstümmelung *f* mutilation.

Versuch *m* attempt; test, trial; ~ **der Begehung e-r Straftat** attempt to commit a crime; ~ **e-r strafbaren Handlung** attempt to commit a crime; ~ **und Irrtum** trial and error; **e-n** ~ **darstellen** to amount to an attempt; **fruchtloser** ~ futile attempt; **strafbarer** ~ criminal attempt; **untauglicher** ~ attempt impossible of fulfilment; **von e-m** ~ **zurücktreten** to abandon an attempt.

versuchen *v/t* to attempt.

Versuchs|anlage pilot plant; ~**anstalt** research institute, experimental station; ~**ballon** trial balloon; ~**bedingungen** test conditions; ~**betrieb** trial operation, pilot plant; ~**bohrung** test drilling; ~**ergebnis** test results; ~**fahrt** trial run; ~**gelände** test site; ~**handlung** acts amounting to an attempt, attempt; ~**modell** test model; ~**projekt** pilot scheme; ~**serie** test series; ~**stadium** experimental stage, trial period; **im** ~~: undergoing trials; ~**zwecke** experimental purposes.

vertagen *v/t* to adjourn, to prorogue, to put off, to postpone; **auf unbestimmte Zeit** ~ to adjourn sine die, to adjourn indefinitely; **erneut** ~ to readjourn; **sich** ~ to stand adjourned, to be adjourned; **terminlos** ~ to adjourn sine die.

Vertagung *f* adjournment, deferment, prorogation, postponement; ~ **auf die nächste Legislaturperiode** prorogation; ~ **auf unbestimmte Zeit** adjournment sine die; ~ **beantragen** to apply for deferment of the hearing; ~ **des Gerichts** rising of court; ~ **der Verhandlung** adjournment of trial; ~ **der Parlamentssitzung**

adjournment of the House; **~santrag** motion of adjournment; **~ wegen Beschlußunfähigkeit** adjournment due to lack of quorum; count-out; **um ~ bitten** to ask for a deferment of the hearing.

Vertauschung *f* **von Waren** substitution of goods (*customs*).

verteidigen *v/t* to defend, *v/reflex* to defend oneself, to act as one's own defence counsel; **geschickt ~** to set up a good (*or* clever) defence.

Verteidiger *m* (defence) counsel, defence attorney; **bestellter ~** retained defence counsel, privately appointed defence counsel; **e-n ~ bestellen** to appoint a counsel for the defence, to choose one's defence counsel; **erster ~** leading counsel; **gerichtlich bestellter ~** official defence counsel; **gewillkürter ~** privately appointed defence counsel; **~ausschuß** committee of defence counsels.

Verteidigung *f* (*1*) defence (in court), justification; **~ gegen rechtswidrigen Angriff** defence to avert an unlawful attack; **~sgrund** plea of defence; **~smittel** means of defence; **~splädoyer** defence speech; **~sschrift** statement of defence; **~ vor Gericht** defence in court; **die ~ niederlegen** to discontinue the defence, to withdraw from the defence; **die ~ übernehmen** to take over the defence; **notwendige ~** compulsory representation by defence counsel (*ordered by the court*); **zur ~ von** in the defence of; **zur ~ vorbringen** to set up as a defence, to advance as defence; **zu seiner ~** in one's own defence.

Verteidigung *f* (*2*) military defence.

Verteidigungs|abkommen defence pact; **~anlagen** national defences; **~ausgaben** defence expenditure; **~beitrag** defence contribution; **~bereitschaft** preparedness; **~bündnis** defensive alliance; **~etat** defence appropriations, defence budget; **~fall** state of national emergency where war is imminent (*requiring defence measures*), the case of war; **~folgekosten** defence-induced costs; **~güter** defence material, defence items; **~haushalt** military budget; **~minister** (the) Secretary of State for Defence (*GB*), (the) Secretary of Defense (*US*); **~ministerium** Ministry of Defence (*GB*), Department of Defense (*US*); **~notstand** national emergency for the defence of the country; **~rat** National Defence Council.

verteilbar *adj* available for distribution, capable of distribution.

verteilen *v/t* to distribute, to apportion, to allocate; **anteilig ~** to distribute on a pro rata basis.

Verteiler *m* distributor, distribution list; **~gewerbe** distributing trade; **~kette** distribution chain; **~liste** mailing list; **~netz** distribution network; **~schlüssel** distribution key (*formula*).

Verteilung *f* distribution, marketing, allocation, disaggregation, apportionment, spread; **~ der Zuständigkeit** allocation of responsibility; **~ des Nachlasses** distribution of the estate; **anteilige ~** pro-rata distribution; **ausgewogene ~** balanced distribution; **quotenmäßige ~** pro-rata distribution.

Verteilungs|beschluß order of distribution; **~bilanz** calculation of supplies and requirements; **~dividende** dividend for the creditors; **v~fähig** distributable; **~kampf** struggle for income; struggle for a bigger share of national income; **~kartell** marketing cartel; **~konto** distribution account; **~kosten** costs of distribution; **~masse** fund available for distribution; **~maßstab** scale of distribution; *pl also* sharing criteria; **~modus** method of distribution (*or* apportionment); **~netz** distribution network, distribution system; **~plan** scheme of distribution; **~prozeß** process of distribution; **~quote** distribution quota, distribution rate; **~schlüssel** distribution key, apportion-

verteuern

ment formula; ~**stelle** distributing agency; retail shop; ~**streitigkeiten** disputes about distribution; ~**verfahren** proceedings for partition and distribution.

verteuern v/t to raise prices.

Verteuerung f price increases, price rises, increase in the cost (of).

verteufeln v/t pol: to malign, to expose to a smear campaign, to smear.

Verteufelung f vilification, disparagement (*of opponent*).

Vertikalkonzern m vertical combine.

Vertrag m contract (= c; pl Verträge = c–s), agreement, treaty; ~ **auf Lebenszeit** life c; ~ **in gesiegelter Form** c under seal; ~ **mit dem Generalunternehmer** prime c; ~ **mit Höchstpreisklausel** cost-plus c; ~ **mit rückwirkender Kraft** c with retroactive effect; ~ **mit Wahlschuld** alternative c; ~ **ohne Nebenabreden** entire c, c without any side agreements; ~ **über die Abgabe e-s Konsortialangebots** joint tender agreement; ~ **über e-e schlüsselfertige Wohnung** "turn-key" c; ~ **vom ...** agreement (made and) dated the ...; ~ **zugunsten Dritter** agreement in favour of a third party; ~ **zu Lasten Dritter** c imposing a burden on a third party; **aleatorischer** ~ aleatory c; **anfechtbarer** ~ impeachable c; avoidable agreement; **atypische** ~**e** innominate c–s, untypical c–s; **ausdrücklicher** ~ express c; **aus e–m** ~ under a c, contractual; **aus e–m** ~ **entlassen** to release from a c; **aus e–m** ~ **klagen** to sue on a c; **aus** ~ ex contractu; **ausgewogener** ~ fair and reasonable c; **auswärtige** ~**e** external treaties, treaties with foreign countries; **bedingter** ~ conditional c; **befristete** ~**e** c–s of limited duration; **beurkundeter** ~ agreement recorded before a notary, notarized c; deed; **bürgerlich-rechtlicher** ~ civil c; **der** ~ **ist dem Recht von ...** un-

Vertrag

terworfen the c is governed by the law of ...; **der vorliegende** ~ the present agreement; **die Römischen** ~**e** the Treaty of Rome; **dinglicher** ~ real c, agreement in rem; **ein** ~ **enthält** a c involves ...; **ein** ~ **läuft ab** a c expires; **e–m** ~ **beitreten** to accede to a convention; **e–n** ~ **abschließen** to enter into an agreement, to enter into a c, to conclude a c; **e–n** ~ **als ungültig behandeln** to repudiate a c; **e–n** ~ **anfechten** to avoid a c; **e–n** ~ **aufheben** to cancel a c by mutual agreement; **e–n** ~ **aufsetzen** to draw up a c; **e–n** ~ **brechen** to break a c, to violate a c; **e–n** ~ **erfüllen** to fulfil a c, to perform a c (*or* an agreement); **e–n** ~ **formulieren** to draw up a c, to work out the text of an agreement; **e–n** ~ **kündigen** to terminate a c; **e–n** ~ **schließen** to conclude a c, to make a c; **e–n** ~ **unterzeichnen** to sign a c, to execute a c; **e–n** ~ **verlängern** to extend a c, to renew a c, to prolong a c; **e–n** ~ **verletzen** to breach a c (*or* treaty), to commit a breach of c; **einheitlicher** ~ entire c, uniform agreement; **einseitig verpflichtender** ~ unilateral c; **einseitig unterzeichneter** ~ unilaterally signed agreement, inchoate agreement; **entgeltlicher** ~ onerous c; **erfüllter** ~ executed c, performed c; **fehlerhafter** ~ defective agreement; **fingierter** ~ fictitious c; **formbedürftiger** ~ formal c, c subject to formal requirements; **förmlicher** ~ formal c; **formfreier** ~ informal c, simple c; **gegenseitiger** ~ reciprocal agreement; **gemischter** ~ mixed c, (*agreement containing various elements of contract-types; e.g. sale, service and letting in hospitalization*); **in den** ~ **aufnehmen** to embody in the agreement; **interner** ~ internal-relationship c, agreement inter se; **konkludent geschlossener** ~ implied (in fact) c; **laufender** ~ running c, current c; **laut** ~ under the c, according to the c, as per agree-

vertraglich — **Vertragsablauf**

ment; **lediglich schriftlicher ~** agreement under hand only; **leonischer ~** leonine c; **mehrseitiger ~** multilateral agreement, multilateral treaty; **mündlicher ~** verbal agreement, oral agreement; **nicht erfüllter ~** unperformed c, executory c; **nicht förmlicher ~** informal c; **nicht klagbarer ~** unenforceable agreement; **noch zu erfüllender ~** executory agreement; **notarieller ~** agreement in the form of a notarial deed, c recorded before a notary; notarial deed; **normativer ~** lawmaking treaty, rule-establishing c, standard-setting c; **obligatorischer ~** contractual agreement; **öffentlich-rechtlicher ~** c governed by public law; **schriftlicher ~** c in writing, written agreement; **schwebend unwirksamer ~** provisionally invalid agreement; **seerechtlicher ~** marine c; **selbständiger ~** independent c; **sich durch ~ verpflichten** to commit oneself by c; **sittenwidriger ~** immoral c, agreement contra bonos mores; **stillschweigender ~** implied c; **synallagmatischer ~** synallagmatic c, reciprocal agreement; **teilbarer ~** divisible c; **typische ~e** nominate c–s, typical c–s; **unbefristeter ~** c for an indefinite period of time; **unentgeltlicher ~** gratuitous c; **unteilbarer ~** entire c, c which is not severable; **unter e–n ~ fallen** to fall within the scope of an agreement; **unvollkommen zweiseitiger ~** imperfectly reciprocal agreement; **völkerrechtlicher ~** treaty; **vollkommen zweiseitiger ~** wholly bilateral c; **von einem ~ zurücktreten** to rescind a c, to resile from a c, to cancel an agreement, to withdraw from an agreement; **vorausgehender ~** pre-contract; **vorehelicher ~** antenuptial agreement; **widerrechtlicher ~** illegal c; **zweiseitiger ~** bilateral c; **zweiseitig verpflichtender ~** reciprocal c, mutual c, commutative

contract; **zwischenstaatliche ~e** (international) treaties.

vertraglich adj contractual, by contract, by treaty, by agreement, ex contractu, as agreed; **~ festgelegt** stipulated by contract, (as) contracted, contractually agreed.

Vertrags|ablauf expiration (or expiry) of an agreement or contract, (contract = c); **~abrede** (informal) contractual stipulation; **~abschluß** conclusion of c; v~**ähnlich** quasi-contractual; **~änderung** alteration of a c, variation; **~anfechtung** rescission, avoidance of c, vitiation of c; **~angebot** offer (to enter into an agreement), contractual offer; ein ~~ machen: to offer, to make an offer; **~annahme** acceptance of the contractual offer; **~annullierung** rescission of c, quashing of a c, cancellation of an agreement; **~anpassung** adaptation (or adjustment) of contract (to changed conditions); **~anspruch** contractual claim, contract right; **~anteil** treaty quota; **~antrag** offer, proposal; **~arzt** c surgeon; **~aufhebung** mutually agreed termination (or cancellation) of a c; **~auflösung** termination of c, dissolution of c; ~~ durch Gerichtsurteil: equitable rescission; **~auslegung** construction of the terms of the c, interpretation of a c; **~bedingung** contractual term, stipulation of c, pl: terms of c; (in den) üblichen ~~en: usual clauses; stillschweigend vereinbarte ~~: implied term; **~beendigung** termination of c; **~beginn** commencement of the contractual relationship; **~beitritt** accession (to a treaty); **~bereitschaft** readiness to contract (v/i); **~bestand** total policies outstanding; **~bestandteil** part of a c; wesentlicher ~~: essential part of a contract, (essential) condition of a contract; **~bestimmung** stipulation of c, term, clause, provision (of a c); auflösende ~~: rescissory clause (of a contract); gegenteilige ~~: contrary stipulation; sich an ~~en halten: to stand by the terms of a contract; **~be-**

Vertrags~

ziehungen contractual relations; **~bruch** breach of *c*, breach of a treaty, breach of (an) agreement; *vorweggenommener ~~: anticipatory breach (of contract)*; **~dauer** duration of *c*, term of *c*; *bestimmte ~~: fixed term*; **~entwurf** draft agreement, draft *c*; **~erbe** heir conventional; **~erfordernisse** essentials of a *c*; **~erfüllung** performance of *c*, fulfilment of the terms of a *c*; *mangelnde ~~: failure of performance*; *weitgehende ~~: substantial performance*; **~firma** contracting firm; **~formeln** (usual) contractual clauses; *handelsübliche ~~: trade terms*; **~fortsetzung** renewal (of *c*); **~freiheit** contractual liberty, liberty to contract (*v/i*), freedom of *c*; **~gebiet** territory covered by a treaty; contract territory (*agent, licence*); **~gegenstand** subject (matter) of the *c*; **~gegner** the other party to an agreement, (the other) contract(ing) party; **v~gemäß** in conformity with the contract; **~gemäßheit** conformity (*of the goods*) with the *c*; **v~gerecht** conforming to the *c*; **~grundlage** basis of agreement; **~haftung** contractual liability; **~händler** authorized dealer, appointed dealer, distributor; **~hilfe** judicial assistance for the adjustment of contracts (*to grant relief to debtors*); **~hypothek** contractual mortgage; **~inhalt** subject of the *c*; *wesentlicher ~~: material points of a contract, essence of the agreement*; **~interesse** interest in the performance of a *c*; *positives ~~: positive interest; fulfilment interest, value of the performance*; *negatives ~~: the position as if the contract had not been entered into*; **~jahr** year of the *c*; *c* year; **~kirchenrecht** treaty-based law between the state and religious bodies; **~klage** action (based) on *c*, actio(n) ex contractu, contractual suit; contractual claim; **~klausel** contractual clause, *c* clause, stipulation; **~konsens** agreement (between parties to a *c*); **~konzern** business combine on a contractual basis; **~mächte** treaty powers, contracting states; **v~mäßig** *adj*, *adv* contractual, according to *c*, as stipulated; **~miete** contractually agreed rent; **~niederschrift** written text of the agreement; **~partei** contracting party, party to a contract, party to an agreement (*or* contract); *pl also*: the parties hereto; *die abtretende ~~: the assigning party*; *die Hohen ~~n: the High Contracting Parties*; *die unmittelbaren ~~n: parties and privies*; *empfangende ~~: recipient party*; **~partner** party to a *c*; **~pfandrecht** lien by agreement, conventional lien, **~pflicht** contractual obligation; **~prämie** stipulated premium; **~praxis** practice in the law of *c*; **~preis** *c* price; **~recht** law of *c*; right under a *c*, contractual right; *pl: international law also*: treaty rights; *internationales*: *~~ conventional international law*; **v~rechtlich** *adj* contractual, pertaining to the law of *c*; **~regelung** contractual arrangement; **~rücktritt** rescission of *c*, repudiation of *c*; **~schluß** conclusion of *c*; **~schuld** *c* debt; **~schuldner** debtor under the agreement; **~sparen** contractual saving; **~sprache** language used in the *c*, *c* language, official language of the *c*; **~staat** contracting state; *benannter ~~: designated contracting state*; **~statut** the proper law of the contract, governing law; **~strafe** (conventional) penalty, contractual penalty; **~~versicherung**: *contract penalty insurance*; **~teil** party to a *c*, contracting party; **~termin** contractual deadline; **v~treu** *adj* abiding by a *c*; **~treue** observance of *c–s*, contractual fidelity, loyalty to treaty; **~typ** type of *c*; **~übernahme** the taking-over of a *c* (as a whole); **~unterzeichnung** execution of a *c*, signing of a *c* (*or* treaty); **~urkunde** contractual document, contractual instrument, indenture; **~verbindung** combination of contracts; interrelation of contracts; **~verhältnis** contractual relationship; *faktisches ~~: de facto contractual rela-*

tionship; *gesetzlich fingiertes* ~~: *contract implied by law*; *stillschweigendes* ~~: *implied contract*; *unmittelbares* ~~: *privity of contract*; ~**verlängerung** extension (*or* prolongation) of a *c*; ~**verletzung** breach of *c*, violation of *c*; *positive* ~~: *special breach of contract, breach of contract (other than delay or impossibility), faulty contractual performance*; ~~ *durch Erfüllungsverweigerung*: *repudiatory breach of contract*; ~**verpflichtung** contractual obligation; ~**versprechen** contractual promise; assumpsit; *Erneuerung des* ~~*s*: *new promise*; ~**vorschlag** *c* proposal; ~**werk** complete contract, set of agreements, contractual system; **v~tragswidrig** *adj* in violation of the contract, contrary to the *c*; not in accordance with the *c*; not conforming to the *c*; *c*-breaching; ~**widrigkeit** breach of *c*; ~**wille** intention of the contracting parties; ~**zeit** term of the *c*, contractual period, duration of the agreement; ~**zusatz** additional clause, marginal note; supplement; ~**zweck** purpose (*or* object) of a *c*.

Vertrauen *n* reliance, trust; **in vollem** ~ in full confidence; **jmds** ~ **mißbrauchen** to misuse s.o.'s confidence; **sein** ~ **entziehen** to withdraw one's confidence (from); **sich das** ~ **erschleichen** to obtain s.o.'s trust by false pretences.

Vertrauens|amt position of trust; ~**antrag** motion for a vote of confidence; ~**anwalt** counsel of choice; ~**arzt** medical examiner (*nominated by an insurance company*), medical referee; ~**bereich** sphere of confidence; **v~bildend** confidence-building; ~**bildung** confidence-building; ~**bruch** breach of faith, breach of confidence, indiscretion; ~**frage** question of confidence; *die* ~~ *stellen*: *to ask for a vote of confidence*; ~**grundsatz** principle of mutual reliance on reasonably safe driving of other road users; ~**häftling** trusty; ~**interesse** interst due to reliance on trustworthiness; ~**mann** confidential agent; deputy of a group; ~~ *der Polizei*: *confidential police agent, police informer*; ~**person** reliable person, person enjoying s.o.'s confidence; ~**schaden** detriment due to futile reliance on a promise, damage caused by breach of trust; ~**schadenversicherung** commercial fidelity insurance; ~**schutz** legal protection of (*protecting person relying on the principle of* good faith), protection for bona fide acts, protection of (public) confidence; ~**stelle** position of trust; ~**stellung** confidential post, position of trust, fiduciary position; ~**verhältnis** confidential relation(ship), fiduciary relation; ~**votum** vote of confidence; ~**werbung** institutional advertizing; **v~würdig** *adj* trustworthy, reliable; ~**würdigkeit** trustworthiness, reliability.

vertraulich *adj* confidential, private and confidential; **streng** ~ strictly confidential, in strict confidence, sub rosa.

Vertraulichkeit *f* confidentiality; **Recht über Schutz der** ~ law of confidence; **unzulässige** ~**n** improper familiarities.

vertreiben *v/t* (*1*) to drive away, to expel, to displace, to dispossess, to oust, to repulse.

vertreiben *v/t* (*2*) to market, to distribute, to trade in …

Vertreibung *f* expulsion, displacement, dispossession, ouster; ~**s-schaden** damage due to expulsion.

vertretbar *adj* (*1*) justifiable, tenable, arguable, defensible, reasonable; **nicht** ~ indefensible; **rechtlich** ~ legally justifiable; **sozial** ~ justifiable from a social point of view.

vertretbar *adj* (*2*) fungible, exchangeable; **nicht** ~ specific, non-fungible.

Vertretbarkeit *f* justifiability, warrantableness; fungibility, fungible nature.

vertreten *v/t* to represent, to act (for), to deputize (for); to justify, to warrant, to answer (for); **e–e Firma** ~ to be agent to a firm; **gerichtlich** ~ to represent in court, to represent judicially, to appear for; **jmden** ~ to stand in for s. o., to deputize for s. o.; **nicht zu** ~ **haben** not to be responsible for; **vor Gericht** ~ = *gerichtlich* ~ *qv supra*.

vertreten *adj* represented; **anwaltschaftlich** ~ represented by counsel (*or* by an attorney); **gerichtlich und außergerichtlich** ~ represented in and out of court; **nicht anwaltschaftlich** ~ lawyerless, acting in person (not represented by a lawyer).

vertretend *adj* representative.

Vertretener *m* (*der Vertretene*) the represented party, the principal (*of an agent*), principal.

Vertreter *m* agent, (*business*) representative, ~**bericht** agent's report; ~**besuch** sales call; "~~*e zwecklos*": "*no agents*"; ~**bezirk** agent's territory; ~ **der Anklage** counsel for the prosecution, prosecuting counsel; ~ **des Staatsanwalts** deputy prosecutor; ~ **e–r Bank** bank's representative; ~**fixum** salesman's fixed remuneration; ~**konto** representative's account; ~**kosten** representatives expenses; ~ **ohne Vertretungsmacht** agent without authority; ~**organisation** association of; representatives *or* salesmen; ~**provision** (agent's) commission, agency fee; ~**stab** sales force; ~**versammlung** meeting of representatives; ~**vertrag** agency agreement; ~ **von Amts wegen** ex officio representative; **alleiniger** ~ sole representative; **bevollmächtigter** ~ authorized representative; **diplomatischer** ~ diplomatic representative, diplomatic agent; **einstweiliger** ~ provisional representative; **gesetzlicher** ~ statutory agent, legal representative; **jmdn zu seinem** ~ **bestellen** to constitute s. o. one's agent, to appoint s. o. one's proxy; **örtlicher** ~ local agent; **rechtmäßiger** ~ lawful representative; **ständiger** ~ regular agent, standby, permanent representative; **vollmachtloser** ~ agent without authority; **zugelassener** ~ professional representative, licenced agent.

Vertretung *f* representation; agency; proxy; substitution; ~ **der Anteilseigner** representation of ownership (*or* of capital); ~ **des Kindes** legal authority to represent the child (*parents, guardian*); ~ **ohne Vertretungsmacht** unauthorized agency; **amtliche** ~ official representation; **berufene** ~ authorized representative body; **berufsständische** ~ professional representation; **die** ~ **ablehnen** to decline to act (as lawyer); **die** ~ **niederlegen** to resign the representation, to cease acting for; **diplomatische** ~ diplomatic representation; **diplomatische und konsularische** ~**en** diplomatic and consular posts (*or* missions); **gerichtliche und außergerichtliche** ~ legal and general representation; **gesetzliche** ~ legal representation, statutory agency; **in** ~ through, by, by attorney, by proxy, per pro, per procuration; ~~ *kontrahieren: to contract as s.o.'s agent*; **offene** ~ disclosed agency; **rechtliche** ~ legal representation; **ständige anwaltschaftliche** ~ permanent legal representation.

Vertretungs|befugnis power of representation, authority to act for (*or* to represent); ~**behörde** representing authority; ~**berechtigter** authorized representative; ~**büro** office of an agency; ~**eigenschaft** representative capacity; ~**macht** representative authority, power of agency; ~~ *kraft Rechtsscheins: authority by estoppel, ostensible authority, agency by estoppel*; *gegenseitige* ~~: *reciprocal power of representation*; *gesetzliche* ~~: *agency by operation of law*; *gewillkürte* ~~: *agency by act of party, power of attorney*; *mangelnde* ~~: *lack of authority*; *unbe-*

schränkte ~~: *unlimited authority*; ~**organ** representative body; ~**verhältnis** agency (relationship); *stillschweigendes* ~~: *implied agency*; ~**vollmacht** power of attorney; ~**wille** intention to act on behalf of another; ~**zwang** compulsory representation (*by a lawyer*).

Vertrieb *m* distribution, sales; ~ **über ausgewählten Händlerkreis** selective distribution, selective selling; ~ **über das Telefon** telesales, telemarketing; **gewerbsmäßiger** ~ commercial distribution.

Vertriebener *m* (*der Vertriebene*), expellee, expelled person, displaced person.

Vertriebs|anzeige notification of sales; ~**ausgaben** selling expense; ~**berater** marketing consultant; ~**bindung** distribution ties, tied distribution; ~**büro** selling agency; ~**firma** marketing firm, distributor; ~**gebiet** sales territory, trading area; ~**gemeinkosten** selling overheads; ~**gesellschaft** marketing company, sales company, distribution company; ~**kosten** marketing costs, distribution costs, selling expenses; ~**leiter** sales manager; ~**leitung** sales management; ~**lizenz** distribution licence; ~**methoden** selling methods; ~**organisation** marketing organization, sales management; ~**recht** right of sale, *pl also*: distribution rights; *alleiniges* ~~: *sole distribution right*; ~**verbot** sales prohibition, ban on sales; ~**vereinbarung** marketing agreement, selling arrangement; ~**wesen** distribution, selling (arrangements).

verüben *v/t* to commit, to perpetrate, to carry out.

Verübung *f* perpetration, commission.

verunglimpfen *v/t* to disparage, to defame, to revile, to smear.

Verunglimpfung *f* disparagement, defamation, detraction, *pol* smear; ~ **der Gesetzgebungsorgane** disparagement of the legislature; ~ **der Staatsorgane** disparagement of state institutions, slandering state institutions; ~ **des Andenkens Verstorbener** reviling the memory of the dead; ~ **des Bundespräsidenten** vilification of the President of the Federal Republic; ~ **von Hoheitszeichen** casting disparagement upon national emblems; ~ **von Toten** reviling the memory of the dead.

Verunreinigung *f* pollution; ~ **e-s Gewässer** water pollution.

verunstalten *v/t* to disfigure; to deform, to mutilate.

Verunstaltung *f* disfiguration, disfigurement, spoilage.

veruntreuen *v/t* to misappropriate, to embezzle.

Veruntreuer *m* peculator, defalcator, embezzler.

Veruntreuung *f* misappropriation, defalcation, peculation, fraudulent conversion, malversation; ~ **im Amte** misappropriation in a public office.

verursachen *v/t* to cause, to bring about, to give rise to.

Verursachung *f* causation; ~**sprinzip** causation principle.

verurteilen *v/t* to sentence, to convict; to adjudge, to condemn; *verurteilt werden*: *to stand convicted, to be sentenced*; **im voraus** ~ to precondemn; **lebenslänglich** ~ to sentence to life imprisonment; **zivilrechtlich** ~ to adjudge.

Verurteilter *m* (*der Verurteilte*) person convicted; ~, **dessen Strafe zur Bewährung ausgesetzt ist** probationer; **lebenslänglich** ~ "lifer", person serving a life sentence, prisoner for life.

Verurteilung *f* conviction, judgment of conviction; a judgment (against s. o.), adjudication; ~ **im Ausland** foreign conviction; ~ **in Abwesenheit** conviction in absentia; ~ **mangels Einwendungen** nihil dicit; ~ **wegen Rückfalls** second or subsequent conviction; ~ **zu den Kosten** order to bear the costs of the proceedings; ~ **zum Tode** death sentence; ~ **zu Schadener-**

vervielfältigen — **Verwaltung**

satz judgment for damages, a judgment to recover damages; ~ **zur Zahlung des Rechnungssaldos** award of balance due on account; **kostenpflichtige** ~ judgment with costs; **zivilrechtliche** ~ delivery of a civil judgment against a person.

vervielfältigen *v/t* to duplicate, to mimeograph, to reproduce.

Vervielfältigung *f* reproduction, multiplication, duplication; **~s-recht** right to reproduce, right of reproduction.

verwahren *v/t* to keep in safe custody, to hold (*or* to have) in custody.

verwahren *v/reflex* to protest against.

Verwahrer *m* bailee, depositary, custodier, custodian; **~pfandrecht** bailee's lien; **~regierung** depositary government.

Verwahrlosung *f* neglect, dilapidation, complete disrepair; **sittliche** ~ moral neglect.

Verwahrregierung *f* depositary government.

Verwahrung *f* (1) custody; safe custody, deposit, safekeeping; compulsory detention; **~slager** temporary store (*customs*); ~ **von Diebeswerkzeug** safe-keeping of tools designed for the commission of larceny, looking after a burglar's tools; **amtliche** ~ official custody; **gerichtliche** ~ judicial custody, court custody; *in* ~*r* ~: *in custodia legis*; **gewerbliche** ~ commercial bailment; **in** ~ **geben** to deposit, to place in custody, to bail; *in treuhänderische* ~~: *to give in trust, to give in escrow (deed)*; **in** ~ **nehmen** to take into custody; **öffentlich-rechtliche** ~ public law deposit; **regelmäßige** ~ regular deposit; **unentgeltliche** ~ naked bailment, regular deposit, gratuitous deposit, naked deposit; **unregelmäßige** ~ irregular deposit; **vorläufige** ~ provisional committal to an institution; summary reception order.

Verwahrung *f* (2) protest, protestation (against).

Verwahrungs|beschluß reception order, restriction order; civil commitment (*or* confinement) order; urgency order (*committal of insane person*); **~bruch** breach of official custody; **~buch** custody ledger; **~geschäft** safekeeping transaction, custody transaction; **~gesetz** Act regulating committal to an institution; **~konto** custody account; **~ort** place of deposit, repository; **~vertrag** contract of deposit, contract of bailment.

verwalten *v/t* to administer, to manage; **getrennt** ~ to manage separately; **schlecht** ~ to mismanage; **treuhänderisch** ~ to administer in a fiduciary capacity; *verwaltet werden: to be under trust*.

verwaltend *adj* administrative.

Verwalter *m* administrator, manager, steward, receiver, custodian; **~amt** administratorship; **~genehmigung** approval of an administrator; ~ **von Wohnungseigentum** (condominium) management agent; **gerichtlicher** ~ judicial receiver; **treuhänderischer** ~ trustee, fiduciary administrator; **von Amts wegen eingesetzter** ~ ex officio administrator.

Verwaltung *f* administration, management; ~ **der gesperrten Vermögen** blocked properties administration; ~ **der Wirtschaft** economic administration, business management; ~ **durch e-n Treuhänder** stewardship (*or* management) of a trustee; ~ **durch Grundpfandgläubiger** receivership on behalf of mortgagors; ~ **e-s Nachlasses** administration of an inheritance; ~ **für gegenseitige Sicherheit** mutual security agency; ~ **von Kapitalanlagen** investment management; **allgemeine** ~ public administration; **bundeseigene** ~ federal administration; **die** ~ **betreffend** administrative; **gerichtliche** ~ judicial ad-

Verwaltungsabkommen   **Verwaltungs~**

ministration; **öffentliche** ~ public administration, public service; **örtliche** ~ local government; **treuhänderische** ~ trust administration; *unter ~r ~ halten: to hold on trust;* **vorläufige** ~ receivership.

Verwaltungs|abkommen executive agreement, administrative agreement, inter-agency agreement; inter-departmental agreement; **~akt** administrative act (*or* decision), administrative determination; order of a civil authority; *fehlerhafter ~~: impeachable admistrative act*, administrative error; **~aktien** management shares, dead stock, treasury stock, stock held in treasury, shares standing at board's disposal; **~angehörige** public servants; **~angelegenheit** administrative business; **~anordnung** administrative directive, administrative order; **~apparat** administrative machinery; **~aufbau** organization of the administration; **~aufwand** administrative expense; **~ausschuß** managing committee, administrative committee; **~ausgaben** administrative expenditure; **~autonomie** self-administration, devolution, home rule (*pol*); **~beamter** administrative official; **~behörde** public authority, administrative agency, administrative body, executive agency; **~sbehördlich** administrative; **~beirat** advisory board; **beschwerde** appeal against an administrative decision, complaint about a public office; **~bezirk** administrative district; **~dienst** civil service; *höherer ~~ administrative class of the civil service*; **~direktor** executive director; **~einheit** administrative unit, political subdivision; **~entscheidung** administrative decision, administrative determination, **~ermessen** administrative discretion; **~fachmann** administration expert; **~formalitäten** administrative formalities; **~funktion** administrative function, regulatory function; **~gebiet** administrative territory, political subdivision; **~gebühr** service charges, management fee; **~gemeinkosten** administrative overhead, overhead; **~gericht** administrative court, administrative tribunal; **~gerichtsbarkeit** system of administrative tribunals; jurisdiction of an administrative court; **~gerichtshof** Higher Administrative Court, administrative court of justice; **~gerichtsordnung** regulations governing administrative courts; **~gerichtsverfahren** administrative court procedure; **~geschäfte** administrative transactions; **~gesellschaft** managing company, management company; **~grundsätze** principles of administrative practice; **~handlung** administrative action; **~haushalt** administrative budget; **~hilfe** mutual administrative assistance; **~hilfsdienste** administrative support services; **~klage** administrative court action; **~kompetenz** jurisdiction for administration; **~kosten** management expenses, administrative overheads, administrative expenses; **~kräfte** administrative personnel, office staff; **~lehre** science of management and administration; **~organ** administrative organ, administrator; **~personal** administrative personnel; staff; **~praktiken** administrative practices; **~prinzip** principle of organization (*or* administration); **~privatrecht** rules for private-law transactions of public bodies, **~rat** board of management, board of directors; **~ratsmitglied** director, member of the board of administration; **~ratsvorsitzender** chairman of the board; **~recht** administrative law; **~rechtspflege** practice of administrative law; **~rechtsrat** administrative law counsellor; **~rechtsweg** recourse to administrative tribunals; *den ~~ ausschöpfen: to exhaust administrative remedies;* **~reform** reform of public administration; **~richter** adjudicator, judge at an administrative tribunal; ~**richtlinie** administrative directive; ~**sachen** administration business; ~**sitz** seat of administration, head office; ~**stelle** administrative authority; ~**strafverfahren** (rules of) administrative penalty procedure; ~**streitigkeiten** civil administrative litigation; v~**technisch** *adj* relating to administration (techniques), administrative; ~**träger** administrative organ, executive body, administrative body, administrator; ~**treuhand** administrative trust; ~**übung** administrative custom; ~**union** combined administration; ~**unkosten** administrative expense; overheads; ~**unrecht** infractions of administrative rules, administrative offence; ~**vereinbarung** = ~*abkommen qv*; ~**verfahren** administrative process, administrative procedure, administrative proceedings, administrative practice; ~**verfügung** administrative ruling; ~**verordnung** administrative regulation, regulation of an executive department, statutory order; ~**vertrag** contract for management services, investment management contract; ~**vollmacht** management authorization; ~**vollstreckungsgesetz** Administration Enforcement Act; ~**vollstreckungsverfahren** administrative enforcement procedure; ~**vollzug** administrative enforcement, execution of administrative tasks; ~**vorschrift** regulatory provision, administrative rule; *pl also: administrative regulations*; ~**weg** administrative channels; ~**zustellung** administrative service (of notices); ~**zwang** administrative compulsion; ~~*s verfahren: regulations concerning the application of administrative compulsion*; ~**zweig** branch of the administration.

verwandt *adj* related by blood, akin; **in der Seitenlinie** ~ related in the collateral line; **in gerader Linie** ~ related in the direct line.

Verwandte *pl* (*die Verwandten*) relatives, relations, kindred, kin; ~ **in absteigender Linie** lineal descendents, issue; ~ **aufsteigender Linie** lineal ascendents; **halbbürtige** ~ relatives of the half blood; **nächste** ~ next of kin; first and nearest kindred; **nahe** ~ near relatives; **vollbürtige** ~ relatives of the whole blood; **weitläufiger** ~**r** remote kinsman.

Verwandtschaft *f* kin, kindred relation by blood, propinquity, consanguinity, kinship, relatives; ~ **im weiteren Sinne** affinitas affinitatis; ~ **in gerader Linie** relations by lineal descent; ~**sgrad** degree of kin, degree of consanguinity, (degree of) relationship; *verbotene* ~~*e: prohibited degrees (of consanguinity)*; ~**snähe** proximity of blood, ~**sverhältnis** kinship.

verwarnen *v/t* to warn, to admonish, to reprimand.

Verwarnung *f* warning, warning notice, admonition, reprimand, caution *subject to the imposition of a charge;* ~**sgebühr** charge for a warning notice, police ticket; ~**sgeld** warning charge (*for a traffic offence*); police ticket; **gebührenpflichtige** ~ warning notice, a charge subject to payment of ticket; **rechtzeitige** ~ fair warning; **strenge** ~ severe reprimand.

verwässern *v/t* to dilute, to water down; to gloss over.

Verwechslungsgefahr *f* possibility (*or risk*) of confusion.

verweigern *v/t* to deny, to refuse, to decline; *grundlos verweigert: unreasonably refused, unjustifiably refused*.

Verweigerung *f* refusal, denial; ~ **der Annahme** refusal to accept; ~ **der ehelichen Lebensgemeinschaft** denial of marital community; ~ **der Eidesleistung** refusal to take an oath; ~ **der Genehmigung** refusal to confirm, disaffirmance; ~ **der Patenterteilung** patent barred; ~ **der Zahlung** refusal to pay; ~ **der Zeugenaussage** refusal of testimony; ~ **des**

Verweildauer   **Verwertung**

ehelichen **Verkehrs** denial of (marital) intercourse; ~ **des Gehorsams** refusal to obey, insubordination; ~ **des Zeugnisses** refusal to give evidence; **im** ~**sfall** in case of refusal.

Verweildauer *f* length of stay (in hospital), period of hospitalization.

Verweis *m* reprimand, censure; **e–n** ~ **erteilen** to reprimand; **e–n scharfen** ~ **erteilen** to rebuke; **strenger** ~ severe reprimand.

verweisen *v/t* to refer to, to remit, to remand; to relegate (*compulsory departure*).

Verweisung *f* remittal, referral, transfer of a case, remand, removal, removal of cause; banishment, expulsion; ~ **an den Einzelrichter** adjournment into chambers; ~ **an den Rechtspfleger** transfer of a case to the master; ~ **an die Kammer für Handelssachen** transfer to the Commercial List; ~ **des Rechtsstreits** transfer of proceedings (*or* ... of action); transfer of a case, remand, removal of cause; ~ **e–s Beklagten aus dem Prozeß** striking out a defendant (*by interlocutory judgment*); ~**santrag** motion to remit to another court, application to refer a case to another court; ~**sbeschluß** order for transfer of action, order of reference, remitter; ~**sverfügung** = ~**sbeschluß** *qv*.

verwendbar *adj* usable, utilizable, suitable, serviceable, appropriate.

Verwendbarkeit *f* usefulness, utility, suitability, serviceability; **praktische** ~ practical utility.

verwenden *v/t* to make use of, to employ, to put to use.

Verwender *m* user, imposer of standard terms and conditions; **gewerblicher** ~ industrial user.

Verwendung *f* use, utilization, employment, appropriation; *pl* ~**en** outlay for repair, maintenance and improvement (*of rented premises*); ~ **auf das Anlagevermögen** capital outlay; ~ **der Steuereinnahmen** (re)employment of tax revenue; ~ **des Reingewinns** allocation of the net profit; **freie** ~ unrestricted use; **gewerbliche** ~ industrial use; **mißbräuchliche** ~ improper use; **notwendige** ~**en** necessary outlay; **rationelle** ~ efficient use; **unsachgemäße** ~ misuse; **zu alleiniger** ~ for one's sole use; **zur besonderen** ~ for special duty (*officer*); **zweckgebundene** ~ restricted use.

Verwendungs|anspruch claim to the reimbursement of outlay (*on rented premises*); ~**auflage** instructions as to use, condition for the appropriation of funds; ~**beschränkung** restriction as to use; ~**dauer** service life; ~**erfindung** new use invention; **v**~**gebunden** *adj* tied to a particular use; ~**grundsätze** principles of utilization; ~**möglichkeit** possible use; *hauptsächliche* ~~**en**: *principal use, uses of the invention*; ~**nachweis** proof of employment of funds; ~**schein** (*EG*) document for temporary importation; ~**zweck** use, purpose, end use.

verwerfen *v/t* to turn down, to dismiss, to disallow; to reject.

verwerflich *adj* reprehensible, damnable, nefarious, immoral.

Verwerflichkeit *f* turpitude, damnability, reprehensibility.

Verwerfung *f* rejection, dismissal disallowance; ~ **der Buchführung** rejection of the accounts; ~**skompetenz** power to reject a remedy.

verwertbar *adj* utilizable, useful; **gewerblich** ~ new and useful.

Verwertbarkeit *f* usability, utility; **gewerbliche** ~ (commercial) utility; **marktmäßige** ~ marketability, saleability.

verwerten *v/t* to use, to utilize, to exploit, to turn to account, to realize.

verwertet *adj* used, realized; **nicht** ~ unrealized.

Verwertung *f* utilization, realization, exploitation; ~ **e–s Patents** exploitation of a patent; ~ **gepfändeter Gegenstände** realization of objects seized; **~srechte** exploitation rights; ~ **von Erfindungen** exploitation of inventions; **bestmögliche** ~ optimal use; **industrielle** ~ industrial exploitation; **zur** ~ **im Auftragsgeschäft** for realization on a commission basis.

Verwertungs|anlage utilizing plant; **~genossenschaft** marketing co-operative; **~gesellschaft** exploitation company, performing rights society; **~möglichkeiten** ways of employing (sth); **~moratorium** extension of time to dispose (of collateral or mortgage of property); **~protokoll** record of utilization; **~recht** right of exploitation, power of sale; **~sperre** ban on sale, ban on utilization; **~sverbot** ban on utilization, prohibition of disposal; **~zwang** compulsory exploitation (*of collateral*), prohibition to use as evidence (*or* disposal).

Verwesung *f* putrefaction, decomposition; **~sgeruch** odour (*or* smell) of putrefaction.

Verwicklung *f* entanglement, complication, involvement; **außenpolitische ~en** foreign entanglements, involvement abroad.

verwickeln *v/t* to entangle in, to involve, to implicate.

verwickelt *adj* complicated, complex, intricate.

verwiegen *v/t* to weigh (out).

Verwiegung *f* weighing.

verwirken *v/i* to forfeit, to become estopped (from), to incur a penalty.

verwirkt *adj* imposed (*penalty*), deserved (*punishment*); stale, forfeited (*rights*); ~ **sein** to be forfeited, to be estopped.

Verwirkung *f* forfeiture, equitable estoppel, laches, doctrine of waiver; ~ **durch Duldung** acquiescence; ~ **der elterlichen Gewalt** forfeiture of parental power; ~ **e-s Rechts** forfeiture of a right; **~sklausel** estoppel clause, forfeiture clause, defeasance clause.

Verwirrung *f* confusion, imbroglio, obfuscation; **geistige** ~ (mental) aberration.

verwitwet *adj* widowed.
Verwitwete *f* widow, widowed woman.
Verwitweter *m* (*der Verwitwete*) widower.
verworfen *adj* depraved, corrupt.
Verworfenheit *f* turpitude, baseness.
Verwundung *f* wound, war injury.
Verzehr *m* consumption of food, eating; **~zwang** obligation to order a meal; **für menschlichen ~ ungeeignet** unfit for human consumption.
verzeichnen *v/t* to record, to schedule, to list, to register.
Verzeichnis *n* schedule, register, itemized list; ~ **der Anlagewerte** schedule of investments; ~ **der Aktionäre** register of members; ~ **der verschifften Waren** shipping note; ~ **des Inventars** inventory; **tabellarisches** ~ schedule.
verzeihen *v/t* to condone.
Verzeih|ung *f* condonation.
Verzerrung *f* distortion; ~ **der Wettbewerbsstellung** distortion of the competitive position.
Verzicht renouncement, renunciation, waiver, disclaimer; ~ **auf die Einrede der Vorausklage** waiver of the benefit of discussion; *waiver of surety's plea of prior enforcement of guaranteed claim against the principal debtor*; ~ **auf die Erbschaft** disclaimer of inheritance; ~ **auf die Staatsangehörigkeit** renunciation of nationality; ~ **auf e-n Anspruch leisten** to waive a claim; ~ **auf Pfändungsschutz** waiver of exemption; **~erklärung** waiver, notice of disclaimer, dispensing notice; **~~sformular**: renunciation form; **~klausel** disclaimer clause (*of a contract*), waiver clause; **~leistender** renouncing party; **~leistung** renunciation, waiver, disclaimer; ~~ **unter Eid**: abjuration; **~schreiben** letter of renunciation; **~surkunde** waiver, (deed of) renunciation; **ohne ~ auf den Klageanspruch** with survival of cause of action.

verzichten v/i to renounce, to waive; *es kann darauf verzichtet werden: it may be dispensed with (or waived)*.

verziehen v/i to move away; *falls verzogen: in case of change of address; unbekannt verzogen: moved to an unknown address, no trace*.

verzinsen v/t to pay interest (on); v/reflex to bear interest, to yield interest.

verzinslich adj (adv) at interest, interest-bearing, interest-yielding.

Verzinsung f (payment of) interest, interest rate, rate of interest; interest return; **feste** ~ fixed interest; interest at a fixed rate; **marktgemäße** ~ interest in line with market conditions.

verzogen pp → *verziehen*.

verzögerlich adj dilatory.

verzögern v/t to delay, to retard, to protract.

Verzögerung f delay, protraction, retardation, time lag; ~**sabsicht** intention to delay proceedings; ~**sgebühr** court fee for causing delay in proceedings; ~**spolitik** dilatory policy; ~**sstreifen** deceleration lane; ~**staktik** stalling tactics, delaying tactics; **unerhörte** ~ inordinate delay; **vorsätzliche** ~ deliberate delay; **zu erwartende** ~ expected delay.

verzollen v/t to pay duty (on), to clear through customs.

verzollt adj duty-paid, customs-cleared, customs-paid.

Verzollung f customs clearance, ~**sgebühren** customs clearance charges; ~**sgrundlagen** elements of customs charges; ~**skosten** clearance charges; ~**spapiere** clearance papers; ~**sstelle** customs station, duty collection point; ~**svorschriften** rules for customs clearance; ~**swert** customs value.

Verzug m default, *(unexcused or statutory)* delay; **in ~ geraten** to be overdue, to be in delay (or default).

Verzugs|entschädigung compensation for damage resulting from delay (or default); ~**fall** case of delay (or default), event of default; ~**folge** consequences of delay (or default); ~**gebühren** delinquency charges; ~**kosten** delinquency charges; ~**schaden** damage caused by default, damage caused by delay; ~**strafe** penalty for delay, default fine; ~**tage** days of delay; ~**zinsen** interest for late payment, interest on deliquent accounts, interest on arrears, default interest.

Veto n veto; ~**recht** right of veto, veto power; *ein ~~ ausüben: to execute a veto*; **v~berechtigt** veto-bearing; **absolutes** ~ absolute veto; **aufschiebendes** ~ suspensive veto; **ein ~ einlegen** to veto, to interpose one's veto; **ein ~ überstimmen** to override a veto, to outvote a veto; **punktuelles** ~ item veto; **trotz des ~s beschließen** to override a veto.

Vetter m cousin; ~ **ersten Grades** first cousin; ~**nwirtschaft** nepotism, favouritism; ~ **zweiten Grades** cousin twice removed; **leiblicher** ~ first cousin, cousin german.

Videoaufzeichnung f video taping.

Videokopierdiebstahl m video piracy.

Vieh n (pl) livestock; ~**bestand** number (or quantity) of livestock; ~**gewährschaftsrecht** livestock warranty law; ~**handel** trade in livestock; ~**hof** stockyard; ~**kauf** sale of livestock; ~**pacht** lease of livestock; ~**pächter** leaseholder of livestock; ~**seuche** infectious disease among farm animals, cattle-plague, rinderpest; ~**triebweg** driftway; ~**- und Fleischgesetz** Livestock and Meat Act (D: 1977); ~**versicherung** livestock insurance; ~**zucht** animal husbandry, livestock breeding; ~**zuchtbetrieb** stock farm.

Vielseitigkeit f versatility, diversification, variety.

Vielvölkerstaat n multinational state, state with multiple nationalities.

Viererausschuß m committee of four, quadripartite committee.

Viermächte|abkommen quadripartite agreement, four-power agreement; ~**ausschuß** quadripartite committee, four-power committee; ~**erklärung** Four-Power Declaration (*5. June 1945*); ~**konferenz** four-power conference; ~**status** quadripartite status; ~**vertrag** four-power agreement.

Vierteljahr *n* quarter, calender quarter.

Vierteljahres|abonnement quarterly subscription; ~**bericht** quarterly report (*or* statement); ~**beträge** quarterly contributions; ~**dividende** quarterly dividend; ~**zahlung** quarterage.

Viktimologie *f* branch of criminology dealing with victims of crime.

Vindicatio *f* vindicatio (*the claiming of a thing as one's own*).

Vindikations|klage suit for the recovery of property, action of detinue; ~**legat** claimable legacy (*legacy creating a right against the heir for the surrender of the bequeathed object*); ~**zession** assignment of the right to claim the surrender of sth (*a form of ownership transfer*).

vindizieren *v/t* to claim ownership of, to demand the surrender of sth.

Vinkulation *f* restriction of transferability, limitation of transfer.

vinkulieren *v/t* to restrict the transferability (of), to tie, to block.

Vinkulierung *f* restriction of transferability; limitation of transfer (*of shares*); ~ **von Aktien** restriction on the transfer of shares.

visieren to verify, to visa (*a passport*).

Visitenkarte *f* visiting card, professional card.

Visitation *f* official inspection; ~**srecht** right of approach (*to ships*).

Visum *n* visa; *zur wiederholten Einreise berechtigendes* ~; multiple entry visa; ~**sabteilung** visa office; ~**sausstellung** issue of a visa, granting a visa; ~**sgebühr** visa fee; ~**sverlängerung** extension of visa; ~**zwang** obligation to hold a visa.

Vize|kanzler vice-chancellor; ~**konsul** vice-consul; ~**präsident** vice-president.

V-Mann *m* confidential agent, undercover agent.

VOB → *Verdingungsordnung*.

Vogel|-Strauß-Politik ostrich policy; **den** ~ **zeigen** to tap one's forehead (*as a sign of contempt*).

vogelfrei *adj hist* outlawed; **für** ~ **erklären** to proscribe, to outlaw.

Vogelfreier *m* (*der Vogelfreie*) outlaw.

Volatilität *f* volatility, volatile conditions *exch*.

Volk *n* (the) people, nation.

Völker|bund League of Nations; ~**bundssatzung** covenant of the League of Nations; ~**gemeinschaft** community of nations; ~**gewohnheitsrecht** customary international law; ~**haß** national hatred, ethnic hatred; ~**krieg** world war, battle of the nations; ~**mord** genocide; ~**recht** → *Völkerrecht*; ~**rechtler** expert on (public) international law; ~**strafrecht** international criminal law, (national) law dealing with international crimes; ~**vertragsrecht** (the) law of international agreements.

Völkerrecht *n* (public) international law, law of nations; jus gentium; ~ **im Kriege** the law(s) of war, the customs and usages of war; ~**skommission** International Law Commission; ~**snorm** rule of international law; ~**spraxis** practice of international law; ~**ssubjekt** international person; subject of international law; ~**sverletzung** violation of international law.

völkerrechtlich *adj* under (in, of, pertaining to) international law.

Volks|abstimmung plebiscite, referendum; ~**aktie** people's share, *low-denomination share for small savers (issued to privatize large public enterprises)*; ~**aufgebot** levée en masse; ~**aufklärung** public enlightenment, propaganda; ~**aufstand** uprising of the people, popular uprising; ~**bank** coop bank, banking co-operative; ~**befragung** referendum, poll, canvassing; ~**begehren** (popular) initiative: *petition by a certain percentage of the electorate to initiate legislation*; ~**betrug** deceiving the people; ~**charakter** national character; ~**demokratie** people's democracy; ~**deutscher** person of German ethnic origin, ethnic German; ~**eigentum** socialist state's property, people's property; ~**einkommen** national income; ~**entscheid** plebiscite, referendum; ~**erhebung** uprising of the people; national uprising; ~**feind** public enemy; ~**front** popular front, people's front; ~**gemeinschaft** national community; ~**genosse** fellow countryman (*Nazi jargon*); ~**gesundheit** public health; ~**gruppe** ethnic group; ~**herrschaft** democracy; ~**hochschule** adult education courses, university extension courses; ~**justiz** people's justice; mob law, lynch law; ~**kammer** chamber of deputies *of the former German Democratic Republic*; ~**kapitalismus** popular capitalism; ~**meinung** popular opinion; ~**partei** popular party; „*Deutsche* ~~": *German Liberal party (1918-1933)*; ~**pflegeberufe** public welfare callings; ~**polizei** people's police *of the former German Democratic Republic*; ~**republik** people's republic; ~**schädling** public enemy; ~**schulbildung** elementary education; ~**schule** primary school, grade school (*US*), public elementary school; ~**schulpflicht** compulsory education in (public) elementary schools; ~**souveränität** sovereignty of the people, national sovereignty; ~**trauertag** memorial day, day of national mourning; ~**verhetzung** stirring up hatred against national, ethnic, racial or religious groups; ~**vermögen** national wealth; ~**verrat** (national) treason, betrayal of the nation; ~**versammlung** popular assembly, public meeting; ~**versicherung** industrial life assurance; ~**vertreter** representative of the people, parliamentarian; ~**vertretung** parliamentary representation, parliament; ~**wille** popular will; ~**wirt** economist, graduate in economics; ~**wirtschaft** national economy, political economy, economies; ~**wirtschaftler** (political) economist; **v**~**wirtschaftlich** *adj* economic; ~**wirtschaftslehre** political economy, economics; ~**wirtschaftspolitik** national economic policy; ~**wohl** national welfare; ~**wohlfahrt** national well-being; ~**zählung** census, population census ~~*gesetz*: *National Census Act;* ~**zugehöriger** national; *deutscher* ~~: (*ethnic*) *German*; ~**zugehörigkeit** ethnic origin.

Voll|arbeitskräfte fully qualified workers, full-time workers; ~**auslastung** full capacity operation; ~**ausschüttung** full distribution; of profits; ~~*sgebot*: legal requirement to distribute all net profits; **v**~**berechtigt** *adj* fully entitled, having a good title; **v**~**beschäftigt** *adj* employed on a full-time basis; ~**beschäftigung** full employment; ~**bewertung** taking at full value, complete assessment; **v**~**bürtig** *adj* of the whole blood; ~**eigentum** absolute ownership, plenum dominum, estate in fee simple; ~**eigentümer** absolute owner, unrestricted owner, legal owner, outright owner, owner of the fee simple; ~**einzahlung** payment in full; ~**erbe** unrestricted heir; ~**erwerbslandwirt** full-time farmer; ~**ersatz** full replacement; ~**giro** = ~*indossament qv*; **v**~**gültig** *adj* fully valid; ~**hafter** general partner, person subject to unlimited liability; ~**indossament** full endorsement, endorsement in full, special endorsement, direct endorsement; ~~ *mit Rektaklausel*: *restrictive endorsement*; ~**invalidität** total incapacity, permanent and total disability; **v**~**jährig** *adj* of full age; ~ *werden*: *to attain full age, to attain one's majority*; *für* ~ *erklären*: *to*

vollenden   **Vollmacht**

emancipate; ~**jährigenadoption** adoption of an adult person; ~**jähriger** person of full age; ~**jährigkeit** full age, majority; ~*serklärung: declaration of majority, emancipation*; *bei Erreichung der* ~~: *on attaining one's majority, on coming of age*; ~**jährigwerden** coming of age; attaining one's majority; ~**jurist** fully qualified lawyer, *person with the legal qualifications of a jugde or lawyer*; ~**kaskoversicherung** fully comprehensive insurance; ~**kaufleute** *pl of* ~*kaufmann q.v.* ~**kaufmann** fully qualified merchant (*under German Commercial Code*); ~**kostenrechnung** absorption costing, actual cost system; ~**macht** → *Vollmacht*; ~**mitgliedschaft** full membership; ~**rausch** complete drunkenness ~**recht** full legal rights; ~**rente** full retirement pension; ~**sitzung** plenary session, plenary meeting; ~**trunkenheit** total intoxication; ~**versammlung** plenary assembly, plenary meeting; ~**waise** orphan (*who has lost both parents*); **v**~**wertig** *adj* up to standard, fully effective; *nicht* ~~: *substandard*; ~**wertversicherung** insurance at full value.

vollenden *v/t* to accomplish, to consummate, to complete.

vollendet *adj* accomplished (*crime*), perfect; **nicht** ~ incomplete, inchoate, unfinished.

Vollendung *f* accomplishment, completion, perfection, consummation; ~ **e-r Tat** accomplishment of an offence; consummation of felony; ~ **e-s Verbrechens** accomplishment of the crime, commission of offence, completion of an offence; ~ **e-s Versuchs** completion of an attempt; **die** ~ **der Tat abwenden** to avert the accomplishment (*of an offence*); **mit** ~ **des 30. Lebensjahres** upon attaining the age of 30.

Vollmacht power of agency, power, authority, authorization, power of attorney, proxy, certificate of authority; ~ **des Anwalts** a lawyer's power of attorney; ~ **erteilen** to confer (or to grant) a power of attorney to s.o., to authorize s.o.; ~**geber** grantor of a power (of attorney), principal; ~**indossament** restrictive endorsement, procuration endorsement; ~**nehmer** holder of a power of attorney, mandatary, proxy; ~**prüfungsausschuß** credentials committee; ~ **vorlegen** to produce power of attorney, to submit evidence of one's authority; ~ **zum Vergleichsabschluß** power to compromise; ~ **zur Aufnahme von Krediten** borrowing authority; **auf Grund der mir erteilten** ~ in pursuance of the powers conferred upon me; **ausdrückliche** ~ express authority; **außerordentliche** ~**en** extraordinary powers; **beschränkte** ~ limited authority; **die** ~ **niederlegen** to divest oneself of one's power of attorney; **die** ~ **überschreiten** to exceed one's authority; **die** ~ **vorlegen** to produce one's authority; **e-e** ~ **widerrufen** to withdraw powers of attorney; **erkennbar erteilte** ~ manifest authority; **faktische** ~ actual authority; **ihre als gut und gehörig befundenen** ~**en** their full powers, found to be in good and due form; **in jmds** ~ **handeln** to act as s.o.'s agent, to act on behalf of s.o.; **in** ~ on behalf of, acting under a power of attorney; **in** ~ **kontrahieren** to contract as a person's agent; **in** ~ **unterschreiben** to sign by proxy, to sign as plenipotentiary, to sign as agent; **jmdn mit e-r** ~ **ausstatten** to confer powers upon s.o.; **mangelnde** ~ absence of authority, lack of authority; **notarielle** ~ notarial power; **ordnungsgemäße** ~ proper authorization; **reine** ~ bare authority; **schriftliche** ~ written authority; **stillschweigende** ~ implied authority, tacit procuration; **unbegrenzte** ~ unlimited power; **unbeschränkte** ~ full power of attorney, carte blanche; **unwider-**

rufliche ~ irrevocable proxy, irrevocable power of attorney.

Vollmachts|beschränkung limitation of authority; ~**entzug** withdrawal of power of attorney, revocation of authority; ~**formular** power of attorney form, authorization form; ~**indossament** procuration endorsement; ~**inhaber** holder of a power of attorney, attorney-in-fact; ~**mißbrauch** abuse of one's power of attorney; ~**spediteur** authorized recipient of transport goods; ~**statut** lex auctoritatis: *the law of that country in which the agent actually makes use of the power (private international law)*; ~**überschreitung** excess of authority, ultra vires action; ~**übertragung** delegation of powers (*or* of authority); ~**unterschrift** procuration signature; ~**urkunde** power of attorney, letter of attorney, written power of agency, written authority, proxy (power); ~**verhältnis** relationship between principal and agent; ~**widerruf** withdrawal of power of attorney.

Vollständigkeits|erklärung statement of completeness (and accuracy) in an audit; ~**klausel** *f* (*"keine Nebenabreden"*) entire contract clause.

vollstreckbar *adj* enforceable (by execution); **für** ~ **erklären** to declare enforceable by execution, to grant a writ of execution; **nicht** ~ non-enforceable; **sofort** ~ self-executing, immediately enforceable; **vorläufig** ~ provisionally enforceable (*pending an appeal*).

Vollstreckbarerklärung *f* leave to issue execution, writ of execution.

Vollstreckbarkeit *f* enforceability by execution; ~**sverfahren** execution proceedings, proceedings to obtain leave of execution (*of a foreign judgment etc*); ~ **von ausländischen Urteilen auf Gegenseitigkeit** reciprocal enforcement of judgments; **mangelnde** ~ lack of enforceability; **vorläufige** ~ provisional enforceability.

vollstrecken *v/t* to enforce, to execute, to carry out.

Vollstreckung *f* enforcement, execution; ~ **aus e-m Grundpfandrecht** foreclosure (action); ~ **aus e-m Schiedsurteil** execution on an award; ~ **aus e-m Urteil** execution under a judgment, enforcement of a judgment; ~ **aus Forderungen und Rechten** execution of a debt or enforcement of rights; ~ **ausländischer Schiedssprüche** enforcement of foreign arbitral awards; ~ **des Todesurteils** execution of the death sentence; ~ **durch Herausgabe an den Gerichtsvollzieher** execution by sequestration; ~ **durch Räumung** execution by writ of possession, eviction by bailiff; ~ **durch Wegnahme** execution by writ of delivery; ~ **durch Versteigerung** sale under execution; ~ **e-s Testaments** execution of a will; ~ **gegen Sicherheitsleistung** execution on bond; ~ **in bewegliche Sachen** levy of execution, execution under a writ of fieri facias; ~ **in Gegenstände Dritter** foreign attachment; ~ **richterlicher Entscheidung** enforcement of judgment delivered by a court; **auf Grund e-r** ~ under an execution; **die** ~ **aussetzen** to suspend (the measures of) execution; **die** ~ **betreiben** to issue execution, to carry out the execution; **die** ~ **vorläufig einstellen** to suspend execution; **durch** ~ **erfassen** to extend the execution; **fruchtlose** ~ abortive execution; **unzulässige** ~ illegal execution, illegal enforcement.

Vollstreckungs|abkommen treaty concerning enforcement of foreign judgments; ~**abwehr** defence against excution; ~**abwehrklage** action to oppose execution; ~**anordnung** writ of execution; ~**anspruch** right to obtain execution;

vollziehbar   **Vollzugsanstalt**

~**aufschub** stay of execution, respite, reprieve (*death sentence*); ~~ gewähren: *to grant a stay (of execution)*; ~~~**sgesuch**: *petition for reprieve*; ~**auftrag** writ of execution, instructions to bailiff (*US: sheriff*) to levy execution; fieri facias (*fi. fa.*); *den* ~~ *erteilen*: (*also*) *to issue the execution*; ~**auslagen** incidental expenses of execution; ~**aussetzung** suspension of execution, stay of execution; ~**beamter** bailiff, sheriff; ~**beendigung** completion of execution; ~**befehl** order for execution, summary payment warrant (*now: Vollstreckungsbescheid qv*); ~**behinderung** obstructing the due process of the law; ~**behörde** law enforcement authorities; ~**bescheid** enforceable default summons; ~**beschluß** writ of execution; ~**beschränkungen** restrictions on execution; ~**beschwerde** appeal against an order in execution proceedings; ~**einstellung** suspension of execution; *gerichtliche* ~~ *judicial suspension of execution*; ~**erinnerung** complaint against a measure of execution; ~**erschleichung** malicious use of process; ~**fähigkeit** subjectibility to execution; ~**forderung** judgment claim; ~**fristen** time limits for compliance with a judgment; ~**gebühr** fee for execution; ~**gegenklage** = ~*abwehrklage qv*; ~**gläubiger** judgment creditor, execution of civil claims; ~**gericht** court competent for execution of civil judgments; ~**grundlage** enforceable instruments (*as basis of execution*); ~**handlung** process of execution; ~**instanz** court instance for civil execution; ~**klausel** court certificate of enforceability, writ of execution; *Erteilung der* ~~: *issuing execution*; ~**kosten** costs of the execution; ~**leiter** official in charge of enforcement; ~**maßnahmen** enforcement measures; ~**organ** official organ for enforcement by execution; ~**pfandrecht** execution lien, judicial lien; ~**recht** law of enforcement of civil judgment; ~**schuld** judgment debt, execution debt; ~**schuldner** judgment debtor; ~**schutz** debtor's relief from judicial execution; ~**schutzantrag** application for relief against execution; ~**titel** (judicially) enforceable instrument (*judgment or other instrument entitling s. o. to obtain execution*), title for execution, execution deed; ~**vereitelung** obstructing execution; frustrating execution; ~**verfahren** enforcement process; ~**verjährung** limitation of sentence, statute-barring of execution; ~**vermerk** notice of attachment by execution.

vollziehbar *adj* enforceable, executable.

Vollziehbarkeit *f* enforceability, executability.

vollziehen *v/t* to execute, to enforce, to put in force; to consummate (*marriage*).

Vollziehung *f* execution, enforcement, consummation; ~ **der Ehe** consummation of marriage; ~ **des Haftbefehls** prison committal; ~ **e-r Schenkung** perfection of a gift; ~**sbescheid** enforcement notice; ~**sfrist** time limit on enforcement; ~**sbeamter** bailiff, collection officer; ~**sordnung** implementing ordinance; **in** ~ **dieses Gesetzes handeln** acting in the execution of this Act.

vollzogen *adj* executed, carried out; **nicht** ~ unexecuted, non-executed, unenforced, not carried out.

Vollzug *m* enforcement, execution, consummation; **außer** ~ **setzen** to stay *or* suspend the execution.

Vollzugs|anstalt penal institution; ~**aufschub** deferral of enforcement; stay of execution; ~**beamter** enforcement officer, prison officer; ~**behörde** enforcement agency; prison authority; ~**bedienstete** prison staff; ~**bericht** report, return (of enforcement officer); ~**dienst** enforcement officers' service; ~**gebühr** fee for completion of a notarial act; **~gewalt** executive power; **~hilfe** interpolice assistance; **~klausel** executive clause; **~kosten** enforcement costs; **~meldung** report of execution, report that order has been carried out; **~ordnung** enforcement regulations; **~organ** executive organ, enforcement agency; *polizeiliche ~~~e: police departments*; **~polizei** (the) police; **~untauglichkeit** unfitness for prison custody.

Volontär *m* (unpaid) trainee.

Vomhundertsatz *m* percentage rate.

von jetzt ab henceforth.

Vorab|ausschüttung advance dividend; **~entscheidung** *f* interlocutory decision, preliminary ruling; *~~~ über den Grund: interlocutory judgment on the substance of the claim*; **~kosten** off-the-top costs in advance; **~schiedsspruch** interim arbitral award.

Voralarm *m* early warning.

Voranfrage *f* preliminary request for information (*or* guidance); outline application for planning permission; **~zulassung** preliminary admission, advanced licence, granting of permission in advance.

Vorangehendes *n* (*das Vorangehende*) the foregoing, the premises.

Vorankündigung *f* advance notice; **~smaterial** pre-publication material; **~szeichen** advance sign.

Voranmelder *m* prior applicant (*pat*).

Voranmeldung *f* previous application (*pat*), preliminary return; booking a person-to-person call.

Voranschlag *m* estimate, preliminary estimate, pre-estimate; *überschlägiger ~*: rough estimate.

Voranzeige *f* advance notice, preliminary announcement.

Vorarbeiter *m* foreman.

Voraus *m* preferential right (*of surviving spouse to household goods and wedding presents*).

Voraus|abtretung assignment of future claim, anticipatory assignment; **~abstimmung** internal private vote; **~abzug** prior deduction, deduction at source; **~belastung mit Spesen** front-end loading; **~berechnung** pre-calculation, projection; **~bestellung** advance order; **v~bezahlen** *v/t* to prepay, to pay in advance; **v~bezahlt** *adj* prepaid; **~bilanz** proforma balance sheet; **v~datieren** *v/t* to post-date, to date forward; **v~disponieren** to make arrangements in advance, to buy ahead; **~dispositionen** advance arrangements; **~empfang** advance receipt; **~entnahme** prior withdrawal, preferential benefit; **~entrichtung** prepayment; **~entwicklung** advance development; **~erfüllung** pre-fulfilment; **~erhebung** collection in advance; **~festsetzung** advance fixing; **v~gesetzt** *adj*, *prep*, presupposed, provided (that), subject to; *es wird ferner ~*: provided further that; **~haftung** primary liability; **~kasse** cash before delivery; **~klage** → *Einrede der ~klage*; **~leistung** advance performance, advance fulfilment, prepayment; **~planung des Bedarfs** advance scheduling of requirements; **~prämie** advance premium; **~rechnung** pro forma invoice, account rendered beforehand; **~schätzung** forecast; **~schau** forecast, preview; **v~sehbar** *adj* foreseeable; **~sehbarkeit** foreseeability; **v~setzen** *v/t* to presuppose; **~setzung** → *Voraussetzung*; **~sicht** foresight, providence; **~verfügung** anticipatory disposal, advance disposal; *~~~ über Vermögenserträge*: anticipation of property proceeds; **~vermächtnis** preference (*or* preferential) legacy; **~zahlung** prepayment, payment in advance, advance payment.

Voraussetzung *f* precondition, presupposition, prerequisite; **~en für ein Amt** eligibility for office; **buchmäßige ~en** accounting requirements; **die ~en erfüllen** to comply with the requirements, to fulfil the qualifications, to meet (certain) conditions; **e-e ~ für die**

Gültigkeit a condition of validity; **erforderliche steuerliche ~en** necessary fiscal conditions; **gesetzliche ~en** legal (*or* statutory) requirements; **persönliche ~en** personal qualifications; **sofern die ~en gegeben sind** in so far as the requirements are fulfilled; **unabdingbare ~** essential prerequisite, mandatory requirement; **unbedingte ~** absolute precondition, *or* prerequisite; **unter der stillschweigenden ~** on the tacit understanding that, on the implicit understanding; **verfassungsmäßige ~en** constitutional requirements; **verfahrensrechtliche ~en** (completion of) the procedures required; **von der ~ ausgehen** to proceed on the assumption; **zur ~ haben** to presuppose.

Voravis *n* preliminary advice.

Vorbedacht *m* premeditation, premeditated design, aforethought.

Vorbedingung *f* precondition, prerequisite, condition precedent.

Vorbefassung *f* referral for a preliminary ruling; prior involvement (*of judge in an investigation*).

Vorbehalt *m* reservation, proviso; **~ der Haftung** subject to limitation of liability (*of the heir*); **~ der Nachprüfung** subject to review (*tax assessment*); **~ der Rechte** reservation of one's rights; **~e zum Ausdruck bringen** to express reservations; **~ für den Kriegsfall** war clause; **geheimer ~** mental reservation; **grundlegender ~** fundamental reservation; **mit dem ~** with the reservation that, reserving, subject to the proviso that, always provided that, save that; **ohne ~** without reserve, absolute, unconditional; **~~ kontrahieren**: to contract absolutely; **stiller ~** mental reservation; **üblicher ~** usual reservation (or caution); **unter ~** with reservation, with the proviso, provided that, under protest, subject to; **~ dem üblichen ~**: with the usual proviso; **~ dem ~ des Eingangs**: subject to collection of the proceeds; **~ diesem ~**: subject to this; **~~ unterzeichnen**: to sign under reserve.

vorbehalten *v/t* to reserve (*the right*).

vorbehaltlich *adv* subject to, provided that, with the proviso, with reservation.

Vorbehalts|erklärung reservation, proviso; **~gut** paraphernal property, privileged property, separate property of a spouse; **~~ der Ehefrau**: (*formerly*) *paraphernal property, paraphernalia*; *extra-dotal property*; **~~ für Frau und Kinder**: *wife's equity*; **~kauf** conditional sale; **~käufer** conditional purchaser; **~kauf-Schuldschein** conditional sale note; **~klausel** reservation clause, reservation, proviso clause, saving clause; **~rechte** reserved rights; **~urteil** provisional judgment, conditional judgment, judgment subject to a change (*in subsequent proceedings by the same court*); **~verkäufer** conditional vendor, person who sells subject to reservation.

vorbehaltlos *adj* unconditional, unreserved; *adv also*: without reservation, unreservedly.

Vorbelastung *f* prior charge, previous charge; **~sverbot** illegality of pre-incorporation burdens; **standortbedingte ~en** handicaps due to location.

Vorbemerkung *f* preliminary statement, initial remarks, preamble.

vorbenannt *adj* aforesaid, mentioned above.

Vorbenutzer *m* prior user.

Vorbenutzung *f* prior use, prior user; *offenkundige ~*: notorious use, prior notorious use, prior public use; **~srecht** right resulting from prior use of the invention.

Vorbereitungs|arbeiten preparatory work; **~dienst** preparatory service; **~handlungen** acts preparatory to the commission of an offence; **~jahr** preparatory year; **~treffen** preparatory meeting; **~zeit** preparation time, make-ready time (*engineering*), lead time.

Vorbescheid *m* preliminary ruling, ruling in an interim action (*patents*), first official notification, preliminary communication, previous official notification, outline (building) permission.

vorbeschrieben *adj* disclosed in a prior art reference *pat.*

Vorbesitzer *m* prior holder, previous owner.

Vorbesprechung *f* preliminary discussion, preparatory conference.

Vorbestellung *f* reservation, advance booking, advance order; ~**spreis** subscription-list price.

vorbestraft *adj* previously convicted, having a criminal record; ~ **sein** to have a criminal record, to have previous convictions; **einschlägig** ~ previously convicted for the same type of offence; **mehrfach** ~ **sein** to have several previous convictions; **nicht** ~ without criminal record, without previous conviction.

Vorbestrafter *m* (*der Vorbestrafte*) previously convicted person, person with a criminal record; **mehrfach** ~ person with a (considerable) criminal record, recidivist.

Vorbeugehaft *f* preventive detention.

vorbeugen *v/i* to prevent, to preclude, to forestall, to pre-empt.

vorbeugend *adj* preventive, precautionary, pre-emptive.

Vorbeugung *f* prevention; ~**shaft** preventive detention; ~**smaßnahmen** precautionary measures.

Vorbilanz *f* trial balance, preliminary balance sheet.

Vorbildung *f* education, educational background; **juristische** ~ legal education, legal background, legal training.

Vorbörse *f* pre-market dealings, market before hours, kerb (*US: curb*) market.

Vorbringen *n* statement, arguments, submission, pleading; allegation; ~ **von neuen Beweisen** production of fresh evidence; **beleidigendes** ~ scandalous matter; **das** ~ **der Parteien** the arguments submitted by the two sides, the submissions of the (two) parties; **frivoles** ~ **des Beklagten** frivolous defence; **nachträgliches** ~ subsequent averments (*or* arguments); **neues** ~ novel pleadings, fresh arguments; **nicht entscheidungserhebliches** ~ irrelevant allegation; **sachlich-rechtliches** ~ submissions on substantive law, submissions on the merits of the case, issuable plea; **schriftsätzliches** ~ pleadings; **tatsächliches** ~ allegation(s) (of fact); **überflüssiges** ~ surplusage, superfluous arguments; **unerhebliches** ~ immaterial averment, irrelevant pleading; **verspätetes** ~ late submissions.

vorbringen *v/t* to submit, to allege, to state, to set forth, to propound, to adduce, to propose, to offer (to the court); **einredeweise** ~ to plead by way of defence (*by answer or affirmatively*).

vordatieren *v/t* to post-date (*later than the actual date*), to date in advance, to predate, to antedate.

Vorder|haus front building; ~**mann** man in front; superior; previous holder (*bill of exchange*); ~**richter** previous court, lower court, judge of the lower court, trial judge, original judge; ~**seite** front, front page, obverse; ~**sitz** front seat.

Vordienstzeit *f* period of time prior to service.

Vordiplom *n* intermediate diploma.

Vordividende *f* interim dividend, initial dividend.

vordringlich *adj* (extremely) urgent, of urgent priority, priority (item).

Vordruck *m* (printed) form; ~**satz** set of printed forms; **e-n** ~ **ausfüllen** to complete a form.

vorehelich *adj* antenuptial, premarital.

Voreid *m* promissory oath; *oath taken by the witness before his statement*.

Voreigentümer *m* previous owner, predecessor in title.

869

Voreindeckung f advance covering, precautionary buying.

voreingenommen adj partial, biassed, prejudiced.

Voreingenommenheit f bias, partiality, prejudice.

Voreintragung f preceding entry.

Voreltern pl ancestors.

Vorempfang m advance receipt, property received before distribution, advancement.

vorenthalten v/t to withhold.

Vorenthaltung f withholding, retention, denial.

Vorentscheidung preliminary decision, precedent judgment.

Vorentwurf m preliminary draft, rough draft.

Vorerbe m provisional heir; **befreiter** ~ exempt provisional heir (*exempt from fiduciary restrictions except for gifts*); **beschränkter** ~ fiduciary provisional heir.

Vorerbschaft f provisional succession; **befreite** ~ exempt provisional succession, *cf befreiter Vorerbe*.

Vorerfinder m prior inventor.

Vorerhebung f preliminary investigation, exploratory survey.

Vorerkrankungen f/pl pre-insurance illnesses.

Vorermittlungen f/pl previous investigations, preliminary investigations.

vorerwähnt adj aforesaid.

Vorerwerb m previous acquisition.

Vorerzeugnis n product for further processing, primary product.

Vorfahre m progenitor, ancestor.

Vorfahrt f right of way; ~ **beachten!** give way; major road ahead; ~**srecht** right of way, priority, right of priority on the road; ~**sstraße** priority road, through road; **abknickende** ~ right-of-way street turn; **die** ~ **gewähren** to give way; **Ende der** ~ end of priority.

Vorfaktur f pro forma invoice.

Vorfall m occurrence, event.

Vorfälligkeitsentschädigung f prepayment indemnity.

vorfertigen v/t to prefabricate.

Vorfertigung f prefabrication.

vorfinanzieren v/t to prefinance, to provide interim financing.

Vorfinanzierung f prefinancing, preliminary financing, interim financing, anticipatory credit; ~**saktion** anticipatory financing scheme, anticipatory credit arrangement; ~**skredit** pre-finance credit, preliminary credit, anticipatory credit, pre-shipment credit, credit to finance initial costs; ~**szusage** promise to grant preliminary credit, assurance of interim credit.

Vorfracht f precarriage, original freight; ~**konnossement** preliminary freight bill of lading.

Vorfrage f preliminary question.

Vorfrieden provisional peace; ~**svertrag** preliminary peace treaty.

vorführen v/t (1) to exhibit, to present, to submit.

vorführen v/t (2) to bring before the judge.

Vorführung f (1) exhibition, performance; **gewerbliche** ~ performance for profit.

Vorführung f (2) compulsory attendance enforced by officials or police, leading s. o. into the court room; ~**sbefehl** warrant to take a person to the court room, order to bring s. o. before a judge, warrant to produce prisoner for trial; ~~ *im Haftprüfungsverfahren*: writ of habeas corpus; **polizeiliche** ~ **von Verdächtigen** identification parade; **zwangsweise** ~ compulsory attendance.

Vorführwagen m demonstration car; test-drive car.

Vorgabe f handicap, advance time, performance target, given standard; ~**zeit** lead time, time allowed (*piece work*).

Vorgang m course of events, operation, proceeding, case record; dossier, job-file; ~**sschreiben** last letter, previous letter; **aktenmäßiger** ~ proceedings in the record, case record file.

Vorgänger *m* predecessor; ~ **im Amt** predecessor (in office); **~schuldner** preceding debtor.

vorgeben *v/t* to pretend, to purport.

vorgeblich *adj* ostensible, purported.

Vorgehen *n* line of action, official steps; **abgestimmtes** ~ concerted approach; **eigenmächtiges** ~ unauthorized action, arbitrary action; **einverständliches** ~ agreed action; **gemeinschaftliches** ~ concerted action.

vorgehen *v/i (1)* to take action, to proceed; **energisch** ~ to take a strong line; **gerichtlich** ~ to take proceedings, to take judicial action; **summarisch** ~ to take summary proceedings.

vorgehen *v/i (2)* to rank before, to take precedence, to have priority (over); **im Rang** ~ to rank before, to override, to take precedence.

vorgelesen *prep, adj* read (to s.o.), read out, read aloud; ~, **genehmigt und unterschrieben** read out, agreed to and signed.

vorgenannt *adj* said, aforesaid.

Vorgeschichte *f* genesis, previous history, record; **zweifelhafte** ~ bad record, dubious record.

Vorgeschlagener *m (der Vorgeschlagene)* nominee.

vorgeschoben *adj* pretended, sham, advanced as a man of straw.

vorgeschrieben *adj* required, officially prescribed, stipulated; **gesetzlich** ~ required by law, provided by law.

vorgesehen *adj* envisaged, provided for, designated; **nicht anderweitig** ~ not otherwise provided for; **nicht** ~ unprovided for, not envisaged.

Vorgesetztenverhältnis *n* relationship of superior to subordinate.

Vorgesetzter *m* superior, senior officer, senior in rank, principal.

Vorgesprächsrunde *f* preliminary meeting.

vorgreifen *v/i* to anticipate.

vorgreiflich *adj* prejudicial, of prior importance, anticipatory.

Vorgreiflichkeit *f* prejudicial effect.

Vorgriff *m* anticipation; **~skontingent** *n* advance quota; **v~sweise** *adv* in anticipation, as an advance instalment.

Vorgründungs|bericht statement in lieu of prospectus; **~gesellschaft** pre-incorporation association; **~gewinn** pre-incorporation profit; **~vertrag** pre-incorporation contract, promotion agreement.

Vorhaben *n* project, undertaking; **schwebende** ~ pending projects; **sich selbst amortisierende** ~ self-liquidating projects.

Vorhaftung *f* prior liability, prior commitment.

Vorhalt *m* query, argumentative question, putting s.th. to the witness; **~ekosten** precautionary (damage-preventing) costs, expenses of keeping sth available; **e-n machen** to put it to (the witness).

vorhalten *v/t* to put it to (the witness); to rebuke, to censure, to remonstrate.

Vorhaltung *f* remonstrance, censure, rebuke, *pl also*: representations; **~en machen** to remonstrate (with), to make representations (to), to expostulate, to object.

Vorhand first option *(to purchase)*.

Vorhängeschloß *n* padlock.

Vorherrschaft *f* predominance.

vorherrschen *v/i* to predominate, to prevail.

vorherrschend *adj* predominant, prevalent, prevailing.

Vorhersagedienst *m* forecasting service.

Vorindossant *m* previous endorser.

Vorindustrie *f* industrial supplier.

Vorinstanz *f* court below, lower court.

Vorjahr *n* previous year, last year; **~esabschnitt** preceding annual period; **~niveau** level of the previous year; **~esvergleich** comparison with the year before.

Vorkalkulationskarte *f* product-cost card.

Vorkasse *f* cash in advance; **gegen** ~ against cash in advance.

Vorkauf *m* pre-emption, right of

pre-emption; ~**sberechtigter** pre-emptor, pre-emption claimant, person entitled to a right of pre-emption; ~**sklausel** pre-emption clause, first refusal clause; ~**srecht** → *Vorkaufsrecht*; ~**svertrag** pre-emption contract, convenant to convey.

Vorkaufsrecht right of pre-emption, pre-emptive right, preferential right to purchase, right of first refusal; **auf Grund e-s ~ erwerben** to pre-empt; **dingliches ~** real right of pre-emption; **ein ~ erwerben** to buy a right of pre-emption; **e-m ~ unterliegend** pre-emptible.

Vorkehrung *f* arrangement, precaution, precautionary measure; ~**en treffen** to take precautions, to make arrangements.

Vorkenntnis *f* previous knowledge, precognition, *pl also*: educational background, basic knowledge; ~**klausel** (disclouse of) previous knowledge clause (*broker's contract*).

Vorkommen *n* incidence; deposit(s).

Vorkommnis *n* occurrence; *keine besonderen* ~**se**: *no unusual occurrences.*

Vorkonnossement *n* initial bill of lading.

Vorkonto *n* preliminary account.

Vorkosten *pl* preliminary costs, preceding costs.

Vorkriegs|anleihe pre-war loan; ~**miete** pre-war rent; ~**preisniveau** pre-war price level; ~**stand** pre-war level; ~**verbindlichkeiten** pre-war debts.

vorladen *v/t* to summon, to issue a summons, to subpoena.

Vorladung *f* summons, writ of summons to appear, cital, subpoena; *behördliche* ~: *administrative request to appear*; ~**sbefehl** (writ of) summons, writ; **e-e ~ erwirken** to take out a summons; **polizeiliche ~** police summons.

Vorlage *f* (*1*) presentation, production, submission; **~ ans Schiedsgericht** reference (to the court of arbitration); ~**bericht** statement of case; ~**beschluß** order to refer the matter (*or* case) to another authority (*or* court); **~ e-s Schecks** presentation of cheque; ~**frist** time limit for submission; ~**ort** place of presentment; ~**pflicht** duty of presentation; liability to produce (*or* to present) a document (*or* instrument); **v~pflichtig** *adj* under a duty to produce (*or* to present) sth.; to discover; ~**termin** date for submission (*of sth.*); **~ zur Ehrenannahme** presentment to acceptor for honour; **bei ~** at sight, on presentation, when presented; **~~** *zahlbar: payable at sight*; **erneute ~** resubmission . . .

Vorlage *f* (*2*) bill (*legislation*); ~**nentwurf** draft bill; **e-e ~ durchbringen** to pilot a bill (*through parliament*); **e-e ~ einbringen** to introduce a bill; **unstreitige ~** unopposed bill.

Vorlage *f* (*3*) advance, outlay; ~**provision** commission charged on cash outlays; **in ~ treten** to advance funds; **kurzfristige ~** short-term advance.

Vorlagenmißbrauch *m* abuse of designs and patterns.

Vorläufer *m* precursor.

vorläufig *adj* provisional, interim, temporary, ad hoc.

Vorleben *n* antecedents, record, past life.

vorlegen *v/t* to submit, to produce (*document*), to adduce (*evidence*), to propound (*a question*).

Vorlegung *f* presentation, production; ~**sbescheinigung** certificate of presentation, noting (*bill or cheque*); ~**spapier** *commercial instrument which must be presented in order to be honoured;* **~ von Urkunden und sonstigen Beweismitteln** production of evidence, documentary or otherwise; **~ zur Annahme** presentation for acceptance; **~ zur Zahlung** presentation for payment.

Vorleistung *f* advance performance, preferential treatment; ~**sklausel** contract clause requiring prior performance.

vorlesen v/t to read out, to read aloud, to read to s. o.

Vorlesungspflicht f notary's obligation to read document aloud to the parties.

Vorletzter (e, s) penultimate.

Vorlieferant m supplier (of the seller).

vorliegen v/i to be present, to be before the court, to be at hand.

vorliegend adj present, instant, at issue, given, existing.

Vorlizenz f preliminary licence.

Vormachtstellung f hegemony, supremacy, domination.

Vormann m previous endorser, preceding endorser, previous holder.

Vormaterial n preliminary material, primary material.

vormerken v/t to note, to register, to mark down.

Vormerkliste f list of reservations, waiting list.

Vormerkprovision f reservation commission, booking commission.

Vormerkung f priority caution, priority notice (*land register*), note, registration; ~ **zum Protest** note for protest; **e-e ~ eintragen lassen** to put in a caveat, to have a caution entered.

Vormonat m previous month.

Vormund m guardian, legal guardian, tutor; ~ **e-s Geisteskranken** guardian of a lunatic, receiver; ~ **e-s Minderjährigen** guardian of an infant; **befreiter ~** exempted guardian; **gesetzlicher ~** statutory guardian, legally appointed guardian; **unbeschränkter ~** general guardian; **vorläufiger ~** provisional guardian; **weiblicher ~** tutrix.

Vormundschaft f guardianship, tutorship, tutelage, wardship; **v~lich** adj tutorial; ~ **über Minderjährige** guardianship for (of) minors; **befreite ~** exempted guardianship; **e-n ~ bestellen** to appoint a guardian; **gesetzliche ~** legal guardianship; **unter ~ stehen** to be under the care of a guardian; **unter ~ stellen** to place under the care of a guardian, to receive into guardianship; **vorläufige ~** provisional guardianship (*mental case*), temporary guardianship.

Vormundschafts|abteilung guardianship department; **~behörde** guardianship authority; **~gericht** guardianship court, guardians' court, orphan's court; **~ ~ für Geisteskranke**: *Court of Protection*; **~rat** board of guardians; **~richter** judge of a court of guardianship; **~sachen** wardship cases, guardianship cases.

Vornahme f undertaking, execution, perpetration; ~ **des Steuerabzugs** making a tax-deduction; **~klage** action for specific performance; ~ **unzüchtiger Handlungen** defilement, perpetration of indecencies; ~ **von Buchungen** posting entries, making entries (*in a ledger*).

Vorname m Christian name, forename, first name, name (*as distinguished from surname*).

vornehmen v/t to undertake, to do, to effect; **feierlich ~** to solemnize (*marriage*).

vornummeriert adj pre-numbered.

Vorpatent n prior patent.

Vorpfändung f provisional garnishment; prior attachment.

Vorprämie f *exch* buyer's option, premium for the call; ~ **kaufen** *exch* to give for the call; **~ngeschäft** trading in calls, option deal for the call, call option; *kombiniertes Vor- und Rückprämiengeschäft*: *straddle*; **~nkurs** call price.

Vorprodukt n product for further processing.

Vorprotest m (*e-s Wechsels*) noting a bill.

Vorprüfer m preliminary examiner.

Vorprüfung f preliminary search; preliminary audit; feasibility study; pre-audit, pre-liminary audit; **~sverfahren** pre-liminary search (proceeding).

Vorrang m priority, preference, precedence, seniority; ~ **haben** to take priority (over); to antecede; **mit ~ behandeln** to accord priority treat-

873

vorrangig / **Vorschrift**

ment to; **mit ~ vor** ranking in priority over, with priority over.

vorrangig *adj* of better rank, paramount, having higher priority, in preference (to), higher-ranking.

Vorrangstellung *f pol* hegemony; pre-eminence, predominance, priority.

Vorrat *m* (*pl: Vorräte = ~e*) stock, store, stockpile; **~sschutz** storage protection (*for agricultural products*); **gehortete ~e** hoarded stocks, stockpile; **staatliche ~e** public stores; **auf ~ emittieren** to issue "for stock"; **solange ~ reicht** first come first served (basis).

vorrätig *adj* in stock, available.

Vorrats|abbau inventory decumulation, reduction in stocks; **~aktien** disposable shares, company's own shares; **~ansammlung** accumulation of stocks, stockbuilding; **~einkünfte** hedge buying; **~haltung** storing, stockpiling; **~investition** inventory, investment for future need; **~kauf** stockpiling purchase, stockbuilding purchase; **~kontingente** reserved quotas, quotas to be held in reserve; **~kredit** stockpiling credit, inventory-financing loan; **~lager** stores, stockpile; **~politik** stockpiling policy; **~pfändung** collective garnishment of future claims; **~raum** storeroom; **~stelle** storage agency; **~~nwechsel**: *storage agency bill*; **staatliche ~~**: *state storage agency*; **~teilung** advance partition (*for condominium units*); **~überhang** stock carried over, surplus stock; **~vermögen** stock-in-trade, inventories (*book-keeping*); **~wirtschaft** stockpiling; **~zeichen** reserve trade mark.

Vorrecht *n* privilege, prerogative.

Vorredner *m* last speaker.

Vorrichtung *f* device, apparatus; **~spatent** device patent.

Vorruhestandsregelung *f* early retirement scheme.

Vorrüstung *f* nuclear arms build-up.

Vorsaison *f* pre-season, early season, last season, previous season.

Vorsatz *m* (wrongful) intent, intention; **aus den Tatumständen gefolgerter ~** implied intent; **bedingter ~** contingent intent; **den ~ haben** to intend; **in dem ~** ... as the essential objective ... (*preamble*); **konkreter ~** specific intent; **rechtswidriger ~** unlawful intent; **strafrechtlicher ~** criminal intent.

vorsätzlich *adv* with intent; wilfully and knowingly.

Vorschaden *f* pre-existing damage (*or* injury).

Vorschaltdarlehen *n* provisional loan.

Vorschau *f* forecast; **~ergebnisrechnung** projected income statement.

vorschieben *v/t* to plead as an excuse; to use s. o. as a front.

vorschießen *v/t* to advance.

Vorschlag *m* proposal, suggestion; **~sentwurf** draft proposal; **~sliste** nomination list; **~srecht** right of presentation (*or* nomination); **~swesen** (employee) suggestion system; **e-m ~ beipflichten** to concur with a proposal; **e-n ~ annehmen** to adopt a proposal; **e-n ~ positiv beurteilen** to consider a proposal favourably; **e-n ~ unterbreiten** to submit a proposal, to put forward a suggestion; **e-n ~ verwerfen** to reject a proposal; **in den ~ übernehmen** to incorporate in the proposal; **konkreter ~** definitive proposal, specific suggestion, firm proposal.

vorschlagen *v/t* to propose, to propound; to nominate, suggest.

Vorschlagender *m* (*der Vorschlagende*) proposer, presenter, propounder, nominator.

vorschreiben *v/t* to prescribe, to direct, to stipulate, to order.

Vorschrift *f* provision, instruction, prescription, precept, regulation, rule, directive; **~en durch Rechtsverordnung** rules by statutory instruments, statutory orders; **~en e-s Vertrages** provisions of a contract; **~en erlassen** to impose (*or* lay down) regulations (*or* rules);

vorschriftsgemäß / Vorserie

~en mildern to relax requirements; ~en über die Bildung von Rücklagen reserve requirements; allgemeine ~en general rules; absolut bindende ~ hard and fast rule; aktienrechtliche ~en provisions of company law; arbeitsrechtliche ~en labour legislation rules; baurechtliche ~en building regulations; den ~en entsprechen to conform to statutory regulations, to comply with the rules, to be in accordance with the provisions; die ~en berücksichtigen to observe the rules, to adhere to the rules; dispositive ~en non-mandatory provisions, permissive provisions, optional rules, optional provisions; e-e ~ durchführen to comply with a legal requirement; e-e ~ umgehen to evade a rule; e-e ~ verletzen to disobey a rule, to break a law, to infringe a rule; e-e ~ zu weit auslegen to stretch a rule; e-r ~ nachkommen to comply with a legal requirement; ergänzende ~en supplementary regulations, additional provisions; geltende ~en regulations in force; gemeinsame ~en provisions common (to), joint provisions; gesetzliche ~ statutory provision, statutory rule, statutory requirement; *pl also*: statutory regulations; *e-e ~~ verletzen: to infringe a law; nach ~r ~: as the law directs;* gesundheitsrechtliche ~en health provisions; innerstaatliche ~en domestic regulations; landesrechtliche ~en Land legislation, the rules of Land laws; laut ~ in accordance with regulations; materiellrechtliche ~ provision of substantive law; ortspolizeiliche ~en local police regulations; patentamtliche ~en patent rules; polizeiliche ~en police regulations; prozeßrechtliche ~ = *prozessuale qv;* prozessuale ~ procedural rule, *pl also*: rules of procedure; rules of practice; seerechtliche ~en admiralty regulations; staatliche ~en government regulations; steuerrechtliche ~ fiscal provision; unbeschadet der ~en in nothing (in this Act) shall affect *(the law relating to ...);* verfassungsrechtliche ~en constitutional requirements; widersprechende ~en conflicting rules; zu Grunde liegende ~en the regulations underlying (the agreement); zwingende ~ peremptory (*or* mandatory) rule (*or* regulation).

vorschrifts|gemäß as prescribed, duly, in accordance with the regulations, according to regulations, according to directions; ~mäßig regular, normal, prescribed; *nicht ~~: nonconforming, not meeting the requirements;* ~widrig improper, irregular, non-observant, *attr* against the rules; V~widrigkeit irregularity; V~zeichen regulatory sign.

Vorschub *m* abetment, furtherance (*of crime*), aiding and abetting; ~leistung aiding and abetting.

Vorschule *f* preparatory school, junior school, infant school.

Vorschuß *m (pl Vorschüsse: ~e)* advance, advance payment, payment in advance, payment on account, advance disbursement, wage (*or* salary) advance, retainer (*or* retaining) fee, down payment for professional services; ~ auf Seefracht advance on freight; ~berechnung computation of advances; ~konto advance account; ~ kurzfristiger Kredite advance; ~ leisten to pay (*court fees etc*) in advance; ~leistung payment of sth in advance; ~pflicht obligation to make advance payments (*cf on commissions earned*); v~weise *adj, adv* by way of advance; ~zahlung advance payment; als ~ by way of advance; fester ~ advance of fixed amount, advance for a fixed period; unverzinsliche ~e interest-free advances, advances without interest.

vorschützen *v/t* to pretend, to plead as a pretext, to use as an excuse.

vorsehen *v/t* to provide, to plan, to envisage, to earmark; *in Artikel 1 vorgesehen: provided by article 1.*

Vorserie *f* pilot production.

Vorsicht *f* caution, prudence, precaution, discretion; ~**smaßnahme** precautionary measure; *polizeiliche* ~~ *n: police precaution;* ~**smaßregel** precautionary measure; ~**sprinzip** principle of conservatism; **die übliche** ~ the usual caution.

vorsichtig *adj* cautious, circumspect, careful.

Vorsitz *m* chair, chairmanship, presidency; **den** ~ **führen** to take the chair, to preside; **den** ~ **haben** to preside (*over*), to act as chairman; **den** ~ **übergeben** to pass the chair; **den** ~ **übernehmen** to take the chair; **der** ~ **wird von ... nacheinander wahrgenommen** the office of President shall be held by ... in turn; **unter dem** ~ **von** presided over by, (*Mr A*) in the chair, (*Mr A*) taking the chair, chaired by (*Mr A*).

Vorsitzender *m* chairman, president; presiding judge; ~ **des Gerichts** presiding judge, president of the court; **stellvertretender** ~ deputy chairman; **stimmberechtigter** ~ chairman with voting power.

Vorsitzer *m* chairman (*of the board*).

Vorsorge *f* provision, precaution, providence, advance arrangements; ~**aufwendungen** expenses of a provident nature; ~**maßnahmen** precautionary measures; ~**pauschale** contingency sum, provisional lump-sum; ~**unterhalt** maintenance to provide for retirement; ~**untersuchung** preventive medical checkup, prophylactic medical examination; ~**verein** mutual benefit society.

vorsorglich *adj* precautionary, provident, by way of precaution; **höchst** ~ ex abundante cautela, out of extreme caution.

Vorspalte *f* previous column, preceding column.

Vorspann *m* credit titles (*film*); ~**angebot** enticement offer of minor article (tied with main article); ~**benennung** screen credits.

vorspiegeln *v/t* to pretend, to delude; to feign, to simulate.

Vorspiegelung *f* pretending, pretence, fraudulent representation; ~ **falscher Tatsachen** fraudulent misrepresentation, fraudulent representation, false pretences, wilful misrepresenation, fraudulent statement.

Vorspruch *m* preamble.

Vorstand *m* directorate, management board, executive board (of management); ~ **e-r Kapitalgesellschaft** executive board of a corporation, board of management; **geschäftsführender** ~ managing board, chief executive manager.

Vorstands|**aktien** management shares; ~**bericht** the report (and accounts) of the directors; ~**funktion** top-executive function; ~**genehmigung** board approval; ~**kollege** fellow board-member; ~**mitglied** → *Vorstandsmitglied*; ~**sitz** directorship; ~**sitzung** directors' meeting, board-meeting, meeting of the board (of directors); ~**sprecher** spokesman for the board of directors, company spokesman; ~**vorsitzender** chairman of the board of directors, president (of a corporation); executive board president, chief executive; *stellvertretender* ~~: *deputy chairman of the board; executive vice-president;* ~**zimmer** board room.

Vorstandsmitglied *n* director, member of the board, board-member, executive officer; **ausscheidendes** ~ retiring director; **betriebsunabhängiges** ~ independent director; **geschäftsführendes** ~ managing director, managing member of the executive committee; **lebenslängliches** ~ life director; **ordentliches** ~ full member of the board (*of management etc*).

vorstehen *v/i* to preside (over), to be the head of, to supervise.

vorstehend *adj* aforementioned, aforesaid, hereinbefore mentioned; **wie** ~ **erwähnt** as aforesaid.

Vorstehendes *n* (*das Vorstehende*) the premises, the foregoing.

Vorsteher *m* head, supervisor, governor, principal.

vorstellig *adj* remonstrative, expostulatory; ~ **werden** to make representations, to remonstrate, to intervene (*for s. o.*), to call (upon).

Vorstellung *f* representation, remonstration(s); **~sgespräch** interview; introductory interview; **~skosten** (job) interview costs; **diplomatische ~en** diplomatic representations, intercession.

Vorstellungskraft *f* imaginative faculty, imagination, power of imagination.

Vorsteuer *f* input tax, prior turnover tax, previously paid value-added tax.

Vorstrafe *f* previous conviction, prior conviction; **~nliste** record of convictions, criminal record; **~nregister** list of previous convictions; **einschlägige ~n** similar (previous) offences.

Vorstudie *f* pilot study, feasibility study.

Vortagsnotierung *f* quotation of the previous day.

Vortat *f* prior offence.

Vortäuschen *n* simulation, feigning, pretence; ~ **e-r Straftat** simulating the commission of a punishable act, feigning commission of a crime.

vortäuschen *v/t* to simulate, to feign.

Vorteil *m* advantage, benefit; **~sannahme** acceptance of benefit by public official; **~sausgleichung** offsetting losses by advantages due to the damaging event; **geldwerte ~e** benefits in money's worth; **~sgewährung** granting of an undue advantage; **~sversprechen** promise of an undue advantage, promise of preferential treatment; **zu beiderseitigem ~** to their mutual benefit, of mutual benefit.

vorteilhaft *adj* advantageous, beneficial, remunerative.

Vortermin *m* previous maturity.

Vortest *m* pilot study.

Vortrag *m* (1) pleadings, submission(s), argument, report; **~srecht** author's right of public oral presentation of a work; **frivoler ~** frivolous pleading; **mündlicher ~** oral delivery, oral argument; **schriftsätzlicher ~** pleadings; *ausreichend substantiierter ~~*: sufficient particularity of pleadings; **sorgfältig abgewogener ~** carefully considered submissions; **unseriöser ~** spurious submissions.

Vortrag *m* (2) carrying forward, carry-forward; ~ **auf neue Rechnung** account carried forward, balance carried forward to new account, amount carried forward.

vortragen *v/t* (1) to submit, to plead, to speak, to state; **hilfsweise ~** to plead in the alternative; **materiellrechtlich ~** to adduce reasons of substantive law, to plead to the merits; **schlüssig ~** to make out a prima facie case; **schriftsätzlich nochmals ~** to replead.

vortragen *v/t* (2) to bring forward.

Vortragsrecht *n* right of oral presentation in public, right of public citation.

Vortragsreise *f* lecture tour.

Vortransport *m* precarriage (*auch pl*).

Vortritt *m* precedence; **~srecht** preaudience; right of precedence; **den ~ haben** to precede, take precedence over s. o.

Vorumsatz *m* previous turnover.

Voruntersuchung *f* preliminary examination, preliminary proceeding, pre-trial procedure, proceeding before trial.

Vorurteil *n* bias, bias(s)ed opinion, preconceived opinion, prejudice.

vorurteilslos *adj* unbias(s)ed, impartial, unprejudiced.

Vorverfahren *n* pre-trial process, preliminary proceedings, prior proceeding.

vorverfügen *v/i* to dispose in advance, to arrange beforehand.

Vorverhandlung *f* preliminary proceedings, preliminary trial; *pl also*: preliminary talks, antecedent *or* preliminary negotiations.

Vorverkauf *m* advance sale, sale effected in advance; pre-emption; ~**svertrag** pre-emption contract.

vorverlegen *v/t* to accelerate, to fix a prior date.

vorveröffentlicht *adj* previously published, pre-published.

Vorveröffentlichung *f* previous publication.

vorverschlüsseln *v/t* to pre-code.

Vorversicherung *f* previous insurance; ~**szeit** required pre-insurance period.

Vorversterben *n* prior death.

vorversterben *v/i* to predecease.

Vorversterbender *m* (*der Vorversterbende*) the first to die.

Vorverstorbene(r) *m* (*der Vorverstorbene*) (the) predeceased.

Vorversuch *m* pilot experiment, preliminary test.

Vorvertrag *m* preliminary agreement, preliminary contract, memorandum of agreement, memorandum of understanding; binder (*insurance*).

Vorverurteilung *f* advance conviction (*by media*).

Vorwahl *f* preliminary election; pre-election; *pl also*: primary elections, primaries.

Vorwahlnummer *f* code number, dialling code, area code.

Vorwand *m* pretext; **als ~ dienen** to serve as a pretext; **unter falschem ~** on false pretences.

Vorwarnung *f* early warning.

Vorwärtsverteidigungstrategie *f* forward strategy.

Vorweg|befriedigungsrecht preferential claim, preference right; ~**belastung** prior charge; ~**bewilligung** appropriation to provide funds in advance; ~**entnahme** drawing(s), premature drawing before distribution of profits; ~**nahme** anticipation; **v~nehmen** *v/t* to anticipate; ~**pfändung** anticipated levy of execution; ~**vollzug** advance implementation.

Vorwegweiser *m* advance direction sign.

vorwerfen *v/t* to reproach a person with, to charge a person with, to blame s. o.

vorwiegend *adj* preponderant, prevailing, paramount.

Vorwurf *m* (*pl*: *Vorwürfe* ~*e*) reproach, rebuke, charge; ~**e erheben** to reproach, to remonstrate; ~**e ausräumen** to rebut the charges, to repudiate the charges.

vorzeigen *v/t* to produce, to present, to show, to submit.

Vorzeigepflicht *f* obligation to produce sth for inspection.

Vorzeiger *m* presenter.

vorzeitig *adj* premature, advance.

Vorzensur *f* pre-censorship.

Vorzug *m* preference, priority.

Vorzugs|aktie → *Vorzugsaktie*; ~**aktionär** preference shareholder *GB*; ~**angebot** preference offer; ~**bedingungen** preference terms; ~**behandlung** preferential treatment; ~**dividende** preferred dividend, preferential (*or* preference) dividend; ~**diskontsatz** preferential discount rate; ~**gläubiger** preferential creditor; ~**klage** action for preferential satisfaction; ~**klausel** preferential clause; ~**kurs** preferential price (*or* rate); ~**pfandrecht** prior lien; ~**preis** private price, special price; ~**rabatt** preferential discount; ~**recht** preferential right, prior right, preemptive right; ~**stimmrecht** preferential vote; ~**tarif** preferential rate (*or* tariff); ~**zins** concessionary interest rate, preferential interest; ~**zoll** preferential duty (*or* tariff), differential duty.

Vorzugsaktie *f* preference share; *pl*: preferred stock *US*; ~**n mit Dividendengarantie** preference shares with guaranteed dividends; ~**n mit Gewinnbeteiligung** participating preference shares; ~**n mit Umtauschberechtigung** convertible preferred stock; ~**n ohne Nachbezugsrecht** non-cumulative preferred stock; **gewöhnliche** ~**n** ordinary preferred shares; **kumulative** ~**n**

cumulative preference shares, cumulative preferred stock; **nichtkumulative ~n** non-cumulative preference shares; **partizipierende ~n** participating preference shares, participating preferred stock.

Vostrokonto *n* vostro account, their account.

Votum *n* vote, opinion; assent.

W

Waage f scales; ~ **der Gerechtigkeit** the scales of justice.

Wach|dienst m watch; ~**hund** guard dog; ~**- und Schließgesellschaft** protection service, firm of watchmen and private guards; ~**verfehlung** neglect of duty while on guard; ~**vorschriften** guard regulations.

Wache f guard, escort; police station.

Wachstum n growth; ~ **der Volkswirtschaft** economic growth; **angestrebtes** ~ growth target; **ausgewogenes** ~ balanced growth; **gleichgewichtiges** ~ even growth; **verlangsamtes wirtschaftliches** ~ slower economic growth; **volkswirtschaftliches** ~ the overall economic growth; **überdurchschnittliches** ~ above-average growth (rate).

Wachstums|aktien growth shares (stocks); ~**flaute** stagnation; ~**fonds** growth fund, cumulative fund; w~**sfreundlich** growth-promoting; ~**impulse** stimulus to growth; ~**industrie** growth industry; ~**perspektiven** growth perspectives; ~**rate** rate of growth; ~**steigerung** upturn in growth; ~**trend** growth performance; ~**werte** growth shares; ~**ziele** growth targets.

Waffe f arm, weapon; ~**n bei sich führen** to be armed; **gefährliche** ~ offensive weapon, dangerous weapon; **konventionelle** ~ conventional weapon; **tödliche** ~ deadly weapon, lethal weapon.

Waffen|amt Ordnance Department; ~**ausfuhrverbot** arms embargo; ~**besitz** possession of (fire-)arms; ~**gebrauch** use of arms; ~**gesetz** Weapons Act (*D*: 1976); ~**gewalt** force of arms; ~**gleichheit** equal fighting chances; equal fire power; ~**handel** traffic in arms; ~**händler** (fire) arms dealer; ~**lager** store of arms, arsenal; ~**lieferung** arms delivery; ~**offizier** ordnance officer; ~**recht** the law concerning weapons; ~**ruhe** truce, cease-fire; ~**schein** firearms certificate (*or*: fire arm certificate), gun licence, shot gun certificate; ~**schmuggel** arms smuggling, gun running; ~**stillstand** armistice, truce, cease-fire; suspension of hostilities; ~~**sabkommen**: *armistice agreement*; ~~**sverhandlungen**: *armistice negotiations*; ~**versteck** cache.

Wagen|besitzer car owner; ~**halter** = *Kraftfahrzeughalter qv*; ~**haltung** upkeep of car; ~**kolonne** line of cars; ~**papiere** motor vehicle documents; ~**park** rolling stock, vehicle fleet; ~**standgeld** (rail) truck demurrage charge; ~**vermietung** rent-a-car, car hire.

Waggon m carriage, car, freight car, truck; ~**ladung** wagon load, truck load, carload; ~**teilladung** less than carload (*l.c.l.*); **ab** ~ **am Verladekai beim Schiff** ex cars from alongside steamer; **frei** ~ f.o.r. = free on rail, free on truck.

Wagnis n risk, venture, hazard; ~**kapital** venture capital; ~**zuschlag** extra premium for unusual risks; **gemeinsames** ~ joint venture; **sich auf kein** ~ **einlassen** to take no risks, to play safe.

Wägeordnung f weighing regulations.

Wahl f (1) choice, election, selection, option; ~**anwalt** counsel of one's own choice; ~**befugnis** right of choice, authority to elect (*or* choose); ~ **des richtigen Zeitpunkts** timing, choice of the right moment; ~**fach** elective subject, choice of subject, chosen subject, optional subject; ~**feststellung** alternative findings; **w~frei** *adj* optional; **~freiheit** free choice; **~gerichtsbarkeit** diversity of jurisdiction (*parties of different nationalities*); **~gerichtsstand** elective venue, forum of choice; **~heimat** adopted home country; **~konsul** honorary consul, unsalaried consul; **~recht** right to elect, option right; **~schuld** alternative obligation; **~vermächtnis** alternative legacy; **~verteidiger** counsel of one's own choice; **~verteidigung** defence by counsel; **w~weise** *adj* optional, as an alternative, alternatively; **~wohnsitz** domicile of choice; **die ~ haben** to have the option (*or* choice); **freie ~ des Arbeitsplatzes** free choice of employment; **im ~fall** where there is an option, where a choice is available; **jmdm die ~ lassen** to leave the choice to someone; **nach freier ~** at one's discretion; **nach ~** at the option (of); **nach ~ des Käufers** at buyer's option; **nach ~ des Verkäufers** at seller's option; **zweite ~** seconds (*product*).

Wahl *f* (2) election(s), vote, poll, polling, ballot; **~ablehnung** challenging a vote, contesting an election; **~alter** voting age; **~anfechtung** challenging an election, election contest; **~anfechtungsklage** election petition (*GB*); **~ankündigung** announcement of a (forthcoming) election; **~ansprache** election speech, address to electors; **~ausschließung** disqualification from voting; **~ausschreibung** election writ; **~ausschuß** election committee, election board, returning board; **~ausweis** election (*or* voting) card; **~auswertung** evaluation of election returns; **~beamter** elected public officer, incumbent of an elective office; **~beauftragter** election commissioner; **~beeinflussung** influencing of election (results); **~behinderung** obstruction of polling; **~beisitzer** polling clerk; **~bekanntmachung** election announcement; **w~berechtigt** *adj* entitled to vote; *passiv ~~:* eligible for election, qualified to be elected; **~berechtigter** (registered) qualified elector, (qualified) voter, s. o. with a right to vote; **~berechtigung** electoral capacity; **~bericht** return of vote, report on elections; **~beteiligung** election turnout, poll; *geringe ~~:* small poll; *große ~~:* heavy poll; **~betrug** election fraud, electoral corrupt practices; **~bewerber** election candidate; **~bezirk** polling district, electoral district, legislative district, electoral ward; *manipulierte ~~sabgrenzung:* gerrymander; **~brief** election paper for postal vote; **~dauer** polling time, duration of the election; **~delikte** voting offences; **~ durch Akklamation** vote by acclamation; **~ durch Handaufheben** vote by show of hands; **~ durch Wahlmänner** election by electors; **~ durch Zuruf** vote by acclamation; **~einspruch** objection to an election (result), challenging a vote; **~enthaltung** abstention from voting; **~erfolg** success at the polls; **~ergebnis** election returns, outcome of an election; **w~fähig** *adj* of voting age, eligible (for election); **~fähigkeit** capacity to vote, eligibility (for office); **~fälschung** election fraud; **~gang** ballot; *erster ~~:* first voting, first ballot; *zweiter ~~:* second ballot; **~gebiet** electoral district; **~geheimnis** secrecy of elections; **~gesetz** electoral law, Ballot Act; Representation of the People Act (*GB*); **~handlung** voting; **~helfer** assistant election officer; **~kabine** polling booth; **~kampagne** election campaign; **~kampf** election campaign; **~kampfbeauftragter** election agent; **~kampfkosten** expenses of an election campaign; **~kandidatur** election candidacy; **~kartei** electorals register; **~korruption** illegal election practices; **~kosten** election expense; **~kreis** election district, representative district, (parliamentary)

Wahl **Wahl**

constituency; ~**kreisausschuß** election district committee; ~**kreisabgrenzung** districting; ~**kreiseinteilung** election district division, apportionment; ~**kreisleiter** district election officer; ~**kuvert** envelope for ballot paper; ~**leiter** election officer, returning officer; ~**leitung** election headquarters; ~**liste** list of electors; list of candidates; ticket (*US*); ~**lokal** polling station, polling place; ~**lokomotive** vote catcher, a great vote-getter; ~**mandat** electoral mandate; ~**manifest** election manifesto; ~**manipulierung** manipulation of elections; ~**mann** electoral delegate, delegate to an electoral committee, elector (*US*); ~**männerausschuß** committee of electors *to choose the federal constitutional court judges;* ~**männerkollegium** electoral college (*US*); ~**manöver** electioneering manoeuvre; ~ **mit Namensaufruf** vote by roll call; ~**modus** mode of election; ~**monarchie** elective monarchy; ~**niederlage** electoral defeat, defeat at the polls; ~**nötigung** electoral coercion; ~**ordnung** election regulations; ~**organe** electoral agencies; ~**periode** electoral period; ~**pflicht** compulsory voting, duty to take part in an election; **w~pflichtig** *adj* of voting age; ~**programm** election platform, election manifesto; ~**propaganda** election propaganda; ~**prüfer** election auditor, scrutineer, election supervisor; ~**prüfung** election scrutiny; ~**prüfungsausschuß** committee for election supervision; ~**prüfungsbehörde** electoral revising authority; ~**prüfungsgesetz** Review of Elections Act (*D:* 1951); ~**quotient** electoral ratio; ~**raum** polling station, polling place; ~**recht** ~ *Wahlrecht;* ~**rede** election speech; ~**redner** electioneer, stumper (*US*); ~**reform** election reform; ~**schein** ballot, ballot paper, voting certificate, mail ballot; ~~*e* *zur Briefwahl:* absentee ballot, postal ballot papers; *ungültiger* ~~: *void ballot paper, "scratch ticket";* ~**schwindel** election fraud; ~**sieg** victory at the polls, electoral victory; ~**sprengel** constituency; ~**statistik** election statistics; ~**stimmberechtigung** right to vote; ~**stimme** vote; *sich um* ~~*n bewerben:* to solicit voters, to canvass voters; ~**stimmenwerber** canvasser; ~**system** election system, electoral system, elective system; ~**tag** election date; ~**taktiker** electioneer; ~**täuschung** electoral fraud, deception of voters, *false statement as to the candidates;* ~**umschlag** envelope for ballot paper; ~**unfähigkeit** incapacity to vote; ~**unterlagen** election papers; ~**untersuchungskommission** Electoral Commission; ~**urne** ballot box, urn, voting box; ~**verfahren** electoral procedure, electoral process; ~**verhinderung** interference with elections; ~**versammlung** election rally; ~**versprechen** pre-election promise, election pledge; ~**vorbereitungsurlaub** electioneering leave; ~**vorgang** electoral procedure; ~**vorschläge** nominations (for the election); ~**vorschlagsliste** nomination paper; ~**vorstand** election committee; ~**vorsteher** election officer; ~**werbung** election propaganda; ~**zählung** vote count; ~**zeit** election time, voting hours; period for which a person is elected, term of office; ~**zelle** polling booth; ~**zettel** ballot paper, ballot; **allgemeine** ~ general elections, universal suffrage; **direkte** ~ direct voting; **e-e** ~ **ausschreiben** to call an election, to go to the country; **geheime** ~ secret ballot; **gesamtdeutsche** ~**en** all-German elections; **jmdn zur** ~ **vorschlagen** to nominate s. o. for election; **knappe** ~ close election, close result; **offene** ~ open ballot; **sich e-r** ~ **stellen** to stand (*for parliament*), to be a can-

882

wählbar / **Wahrscheinlichkeit**

didate, to contend a nomination; **zur ~ schreiten** to proceed to the vote, to begin the poll.

wählbar *adj* eligible (for election), electable; **nicht ~** inelectable, non-eligible.

Wählbarkeit *f* eligibility.

wählen *v/i* to vote; to go to the polls; *v/t* to elect, to choose.

Wähler *m* elector, voter; **~bestechung** bribing voters, corrupt electoral practices; **~gruppen** categories of voters; **~initiative** voters' initiative; **~liste** register of voters, list of voters, electoral register; **~nötigung** undue pressure on electors; **~schaft** voters, electorate; **~schwund** electoral rot, dwindling numbers of voters; **~stamm** steady voters; **~täuschung** deception of voters (*during polling*); **~verzeichnis** electoral register; **eingetragene ~** registered voters; **nicht im Wahlkreis wohnender ~** non-resident voter; **unbestimmte ~** floaters; **wehrdienstangehöriger ~** military service voter, armed forces voter.

Wählerin *f* (female) voter.

Wahlrecht *n* voting right, right to vote, vote; electoral franchise; suffrage; electoral law; **~sgrundsätze** principles governing the law of elections; **~sverleihung** enfranchisement; **~sverlust** *deprivation of the right to vote and of the eligibility for public office*; **aktives ~** right to vote, (electoral) franchise; **aktives und passives ~** right to vote and to stand for election; **allgemeines, gleiches, geheimes und direktes ~** universal, equal, secret and direct suffrage; **allgemeines, gleiches ~** right of universal suffrage, "one person, one vote"; **allgemeines ~** electoral franchise, universal suffrage; **beschränktes ~** restricted right to vote; **das ~ entziehen** to disfranchise, to withdraw the right to vote; **das ~ verleihen** to enfranchise; **direktes ~** right to vote directly (*for a candidate or party*); **passives ~** right to stand for election, eligibility; *Fehlen des ~n ~s: incapacity for election, non-eligibility*.

Wahn|delikt acts committed under the erroneous assumption of punishability; **~vorstellung** *f* insane delusion.

Wahrhaftigkeit *f* veracity (*of witness*), truthfulness.

Wahrheit *f* truth, verity; **die reine ~** the plain truth, nothing but the truth, *the whole truth and nothing but the truth*; **die ~ beweisen** to prove the truth, to give evidence for the truth of the facts alleged; **die ~ ermitteln** to ascertain the truth; **die ~ sagen** to tell the truth; **die ~ unterdrücken** to suppress the truth; **die ~ verdrehen** to prevaricate; **reine ~** plain truth; **zur ~ ermahnen** to admonish s. o. to tell the truth.

Wahrheits|beweis proving the truth, evidence of the truth; **~ermittlung** finding out the truth, ascertaining the facts; **~findung** finding-out the truth; **~pflicht** duty to tell the truth; obligation to be truthful (*in pleadings*); **w~widrig** *adj* untruthful, mendacious.

wahrnehmbar *adj* discernible, appreciable, noticeable, audible.

wahrnehmen *v/t* to assert, to safeguard (*interests*); to discern, to notice, to observe.

Wahrnehmung *f* safeguarding; observation, perception; **~ berechtigter Interessen** exercising legitimate interests, justification by fair comment; privileged occasion, justification and privilege; **in ~ ~ ~**: *privileged, on a privileged occasion; sich auf ~ ~ ~ berufen:* to plead justification and privilege; **~ der Interessen** safeguarding the interests (of); **~sgesetz** Law on Authors' Societies; **~ von Aufgaben** discharging one's responsibilities, exercise of one's functions.

Wahrscheinlichkeit *f* probability; **~sauswahl** probability sampling; **~sbeweis** proof of likelihood, balance of probabilities; **~srechnung**

probability calculus; **mit an Sicherheit grenzender** ~ with the utmost probability, based on a strong presumption of proof, with virtual certainty.

Wahr|spruch *m* verdict (of the jury); ~**unterstellung** taking sth for granted, assumption of truthfulness.

Wahrung *f* observance, adherence, safeguarding; ~ **von Geschäftsgeheimnissen** keeping of trade secrets; **die** ~ **der Interessen** safeguarding of interests.

Währung *f* currency; **ausländische** ~ foreign currency; **frei konvertierbare** ~ freely convertible currency; **frei verwendbare** ~ freely usable currency; **fremde** ~ foreign currency, foreign exchange; **gebundene** ~ currency subject to control; **gesetzliche** ~ lawful currency; **gesteuerte** ~ managed currency; **harte** ~ hard currency; **heimische** ~ domestic currency; **in deutscher** ~ in German currency; **knappe** ~**en** scarce currencies; **manipulierte** ~ managed currency; **schwache** ~ soft currency; **stabile** ~ stable currency; **stabilisierte** ~ stabilized currency; **staatlich kontrollierte** ~ state-controlled currency; **unterbewertete** ~ undervalued currency; **weiche** ~ soft currency.

Währungs|abkommen monetary agreement; ~**abteilung** foreign exchange department; ~**abstieg** currency deterioration; ~**abwertung** exchange depreciation, devaluation; ~~ *aus Wettbewerbsgründen*: *competitive devaluation*; ~**änderungsklausel** alteration of currency clause; ~**angleichung** adjustment of exchange rates, currency adjustment; ~**anleihe** loan in foreign currency; ~**aufwertung** revaluation; ~**ausgleich** currency conversion compensation; ~-**Ausgleichsbetrag** monetary compensatory amount; ~**ausgleichsfonds** exchange equalization account (*GB*), exchange stabilization fund (*US*); ~**ausgleichskonto** exchange equalization account; ~**ausschuß** monetary committee; ~**bandbreiten** currency bands; ~**bank** bank of issue, currency-issuing bank, central bank; ~**barkredit** (foreign) currency advance; ~**bereich** currency area; ~**bestimmungen** currency regulations; ~**block** monetary bloc; ~**deckung** backing support for a currency; ~**einheit** monetary unit, currency unit, monetary standard; ~**einrichtungen** monetary institutions; ~**entwertung** currency depreciation, (currency) devaluation; ~**fonds** (international) monetary fund; ~**gebiet** monetary area, currency area; ~**geld** standard money, legal tender money; ~**gesetz** currency law; ~**gesundung** monetary rehabilitation, currency reform; ~**gewinn** profit on foreign exchange fluctuations; ~**guthaben** balance in currency; ~**hoheit** monetary sovereignty; ~**hüter** guardian of the currency (*central bank*); ~**inflation** monetary inflation; ~**klausel** currency clause; ~**kommission** foreign exchange clause, currency commission; ~-**Kongruenz** identity of currency; ~**konto** (foreign) currency account; ~**kredit** (foreign) loan or credit; ~**krise** monetary crisis, currency crisis; ~**kurs** exchange rate; ~**kursstabilität** exchange stability; ~**lage** monetary situation, monetary scene; ~**manipulation** currency manipulation; **w**~**mäßig** *adj* monetary, as regards currency, relating to currency; ~**mechanismus** monetary mechanism; ~**option** currency option, choice of currency; ~**parität** par rate of exchange; monetary parity, exchange rate parity, currency parity; ~**politik** monetary policy; **w**~**politisch** *adj* as regards monetary policy; monetary; ~~ *neutral*: *neutral in monetary effect*; ~**rechnungseinheit** currency unit; ~**reform** currency reform, monetary reform;

~**reserve** monetary reserve, currency reserve (*gold and foreign exchange holding*); ~**risiko** currency risk, exchange rate risk; ~**sanierung** currency rehabilitation; ~**schuldner** foreign-currency debtor; ~**schwankungen** currency fluctuations; ~**sicherung** safeguarding one's currency, protection of one's foreign exchange position; ~**sicherungsgeschäft** currency hedging arrangements; ~**sicherungsklausel** exchange guarantee clause, currency safeguarding clause; ~**souveränität** monetary sovereignty; ~**stabilität** currency stability; ~**standard** monetary standard; ~~ *nach Kaufkrafttabellen: tabular standard*; ~**stichtag** appointed day for the (West German) Currency Reform; ~**sturz** fall in the exchange rate; ~**system** monetary system; ~**umbenennung** redenomination of currency; ~**umstellung** currency conversion; ~**union** monetary union, currency union; ~**unruhen** currency unrest; ~**verfall** currency erosion, currency decline; ~**verfassung** monetary conditions, monetary set-up; ~**verlust** (foreign) exchange loss; ~**wechsel** currency bill; ~**wesen** currency matter, monetary system; ~~-**Wirtschafts- und Sozialunion** Economic, Monetary and Social Union; ~**zerfall** currency decline.

Waisen|anstalt orphanage, ~**beihilfe** (non-recurrent) orphanage allowance; ~**geld** orphans' pension; ~**haus** orphanage; ~**kasse** orphans' fund; ~**kind** orphan; ~**rente** orphans' pension.

Wald|bau silviculture, forestry; ~**beschädigung** damage to the forest; ~**besitz** forest holding, forest ownership; ~**besitzer** forest owner; holder of forest possession; ~**bestand** forest stand; *abgewirtschafteter* ~~: *deteriorated forest*; ~**bewirtschaftung** forest management forestry; ~**brandschutz** protection from forest fires; ~**erwerb** acquisition of a forest, profits from silviculture; ~**erzeugnisse** products of the forest; ~**früchte** products (or fruits) of the forests; ~**gebiet** forest land; ~**gemeinschaft** joint group of forest owners; ~**pfennig** forest levy; ~**schutz** forest preservation, forest protection provisions; ~**sterben** dying forests syndrome; ~**umwandlung** conversion of forest(s) to a different use; ~**weg** forest path; ~**weiderechte** rights of forest pasture.

Wand|flächenreklame outdoor advertizing; ~**plakat** wall poster; ~**schild** wall sign; ~**zeitung** wall newspaper; **tragende** ~ load-bearing wall, supporting wall.

Wandel|anleihe f = *Wandelschuldverschreibung qv*; ~**obligation** = *Wandelschuldverschreibung qv*; ~**parität** conversion parity (*convertible issue, convertible bonds*); ~**prämie** conversion premium (*conversion parity/share price*); ~**recht** right of conversion, conversion privilege, warrant, conversion right; ~**schuldverschreibung** f convertible debenture; *pl* convertible bonds, convertible loan stock, convertibles.

wandeln v/t to repudiate the contract.

Wandelung f repudiation of contract *for breach of warranty*, redhibition, cancellation of contract (*sale, work performance*); ~**sklage** action to dissolve contract (*of sale etc*), redhibitory action.

Wander|arbeit migrant labour; ~**arbeitnehmer** migrant worker; ~**ausstellung** travelling exhibition; ~**bewegung** migration, wave of migrants; ~**freiheit** freedom of movement; ~**gewerbe** itinerant trade; ~**gewerbeschein** hawker's licence; ~**gewerbetreibender** itinerant vendor, itinerant trader, pedlar (*US*: peddler); ~**versicherung** transferable insurance periods;

Wanderung f migration; ~**sgewinn**

Wanzen f/pl bugs (*also as electronic devices*).

Wappen n coat of arms, insignia; **das königliche** ~ royal arms; **übernommenes** ~ adoptive arms.

Ware f merchandise, product, goods; ~n abnehmen to take delivery of goods; ~n absetzen to place goods; ~n auf Lager goods in stock, warehouse goods; ~n beleihen to raise money on the security of goods, to lend money on goods; ~n des nichtalltäglichen Bedarfs special goods, shopping goods; ~n des täglichen Bedarfs convenience good, every day items (*or* goods); ~n etikettieren to label goods, to docket goods; ~n liefern to supply goods, to deliver goods; ~n des gewerblichen Sektors commercial and industrial goods; ~ mit Gemeinschaftscharakter Community goods; ~ ohne Gemeinschaftscharakter non-Community-goods; ~ ohne Ursprungseigenschaft non-originating product; ~ unbestimmbaren Ursprungs product of undertermined origin; ~n unter Zollverschluß bonded goods; ~n zweiter Qualität seconds; abgabepflichtige ~n chargeable goods; anmeldepflichtige ~n goods to declare; bearbeitete ~ processed goods; bewirtschaftete ~ rationed commodity; devisenbringende ~n goods capable of earning foreign exchange; die uns bemusterte ~ the goods of which we have received samples; die ~ dem Frachtführer aushändigen to place the goods in the custody of the carrier; die ~ prüfen to inspect the goods; durchgeführte ~(n) goods in transit; eingelagerte ~n goods in warehouse, stored goods; einheimische ~n inland commodities, domestic goods; entzündliche ~n inflammables; gängige ~n goods in general supply, marketable goods; gepfändete ~ distrained goods; gesetzlich zulässige ~ lawful merchandise; gewichtszollbare ~n goods chargeable by weight; havarierte ~ averaged (sea-damaged) goods; heimische ~n domestic goods, inland goods; home-produced goods; hochwertige ~n high-grade goods; in ~ bezahlen to pay in kind; in ~n in kind; in Zahlung gegebene ~n trade-in, in part-exchange; karten-bezahlte ~ goods paid with credit cards; kontingentierte ~n quota goods; leicht abzusetzende ~ goods with a ready sale, easily marketable goods; mangelhafte ~n defective goods; minderwertige ~n inferior goods, shoddy goods; nicht abgeholte ~ unclaimed merchandise, uncollected goods; nicht verderbliche ~ non-perishable commodity; ortskennzeichnende ~n goods indicating place of origin; preisgebundene ~n price-maintained goods; preisgestützte ~n price-supported goods, goods enjoying price-support; reguläre ~ staple stock, regular line of goods; schwimmende ~n goods afloat; sofort lieferbare ~n disposable goods; unbestellte ~ unsolicited goods; unveredelte ~n goods in unaltered state, goods in their natural condition, unrefined goods, unprocessed goods; unverkäufliche ~n dud stock, unsaleable items; unverzollte ~n duty-unpaid goods, goods in bond, undeclared goods; verbrauchsnahe ~n goods close to the ultimate consumer; verderbliche ~n perishable goods, articles of a perishable nature; veredelte ~n processed goods, improved goods; weiße ~ white goods (*household equipment*); zollfreie ~n duty-free goods; zollpflichtige ~n dutiable goods, goods to be declared.

Waren|abgabe sale, supply of goods; ~~ *nur bei komplettem Sortiments-*

Waren~ **Waren~**

kauf: full line forcing; ~**absendung** dispatch of goods; ~**anmeldung** declaration of goods; ~**art** article, type of goods; ~**artenvergleich** competitive comparison of types of goods; ~**ausfall** finished articles, goods produced; ~**ausfuhr** exportation of goods; ~**ausgang** outgoing goods, consignment of goods; ~**ausgangsbuch** ledger of outgoing goods; ~**ausgangskontrolle** inspection of outgoing merchandise; ~**ausstattung** presentation of goods, get-up of goods; ~**austausch** exchange of goods; ~**automat** (automatic) vending machine; ~**beförderung** carriage of goods, transport of goods; ~**begleitschein** document accompanying goods, waybill; ~**beschreibung** trade description; ~**bestand** stock (in hand), stock in trade; *balance sheet*: goods, wares and merchandise; *veränderlicher* ~~: *shifting stock of merchandise*; ~**bezeichnung** description of goods, distinctive name, trade name; ~**börse** commodity exchange; ~~ *mit Terminhandel: futures market*; ~**diebstahl** shoplifting; ~**dividende** commodity dividend; ~**durchfuhr** transit of goods; ~**einfuhr** importation of goods; ~**eingänge** goods received, incoming goods; ~**eingangsbescheinigung** delivery receipt, certificate of arrival of goods, delivery verification; ~**eingangsbuch** ledger of incoming merchandise, purchase journal, suppliers' ledger; ~**eingangskonto** purchase account; ~**einheit** goods unit; ~**einsatz** cost of goods sold; ~**einzelhandel** retail trade; ~**empfänger** receiver of goods, consignee of goods; ~**etikett** trade label; ~**fonds** commodity fund; ~**forderungen** trade accounts receivable, trade debtors; ~**forschung** merchandising research; ~**führer** carrier; ~**gattung** class of goods, category of merchandise; ~**genossenschaft** consumers' co-operative; ~**geschäfte** commodities trading; ~**gewinn** trading profit; ~**gleichartigkeit** equal nature of goods; ~**gruppe** products category; ~**handel** merchandise trade, commodity trading; ~*sdefizit: merchandise trade deficit*; ~**haus** department store; ~**hausaktien** department store shares; ~**hausdieb** shop thief, shoplifter; ~**hausdiebstahl** shoplifting; ~**haussteuer** department store tax; ~**herstellerhaftung** product liability; ~**hersteller-Kennzeichnung** branding of manufacturer; ~**kauf** sale of goods; ~**kaufvertrag** agreement for the sale of goods; ~**klasse** class of goods, grade designation marking; ~**klasseneinteilung** classification of goods; ~**kontingent** goods quota; ~**konto** merchandise account, goods account; ~**korb** *stat* basket of goods: *average choice of consumer goods per family unit*; ~~*formel: basket formula*; ~**kredit** trade credit, commercial credit; lending on goods; produce lending; ~~ *aufnehmen: to establish credit with a company*; ~**kreditgenossenschaft** consumers' credit co-operative, industrial co-operative; ~**kreditkonzern** consumer credit group; ~**kreditschuldschein** trade customer's note; ~**kreditsolawechsel** trade customer's note; ~**kunde** merchandise technology, product analysis; ~**lager** stock-in-hand, stock-in-trade, stock of goods, goods in hand, stock of merchandise; ~**lagerbuch** warehousebook, stock-book; ~**lieferant** supplier of goods, holder of order for goods; ~**lieferungen** goods deliveries; ~**lieferungen und Leistungen** goods delivered and services (rendered) by trade creditors; ~**lombard** advance on goods, loan based on the security of goods; ~**lombardkredit** secured revolving credit, commodity collateral loan; ~**makler** produce broker, merchandise broker; ~**manifest** goods manifest; ~**markt** com-

887

modity market, produce market; ~**merkmale** descriptive standard; ~**muster** commercial sample; ~**normung** standardization of retail goods; ~**- oder Traditionspapiere** goods or documents of title to goods; ~**papiere** documents relating to goods; instruments of title in respect of goods; ~**partie** parcel of goods, lot; ~**posten** item, lot (of goods); ~**probe** sample, pattern; *zurückbehaltene* ~~*n: reference patterns*; ~**probenverteilung** novelty advertizing, free gift advertizing; ~**prüfung** quality inspection, examination of goods; ~**rechnung** (commercial) invoice; ~**rohertrag** gross trading profit; ~**rückvergütung** rebate for purchased goods (*paid as premium to cooperative members*); ~**schuld** commercial debt, debt for goods; ~**schulden** trade accounts payable; ~**seetransport** carriage of goods by sea; ~**sendung** consignment of goods; ~**sortiment** line of goods, assortment of goods; ~**struktur** pattern of goods, range of goods; ~**terminbörse** commodity futures exchange; ~**termingeschäft** commodity futures trading; ~**terminhandel** commodity futures trading; ~**terminmarkt** commodity futures market; ~**terminoption** commodity futures option; ~**test** goods quality test; ~**umsatz** merchandise turnover, sales turnover; ~**umsatzsteuer** sales tax; ~**umschlag** movement of goods, turnover of goods; ~**- und Dienstleistungsbilanz** balance of payments for goods and services; ~**- und Dienstleistungsverkehr** transfer of goods and services; ~**- und Zahlungsabkommen** trade and payments agreement; ~**unterscheidung** product differentiation; ~**verbindlichkeiten** *bal* accounts payable (*US*); ~**verkauf** sale of goods; ~**verkaufskonto** sales account; ~**verkehr** trade, movement of goods; *freier* ~~: *free movement of goods; begünstigter* ~~: *preferential trade; innergemeinschaftlicher* ~~: *intra-community trade;* ~**vermittler** middleman; ~**verpfändung** hypothecation of goods, mortgaging of goods; ~**versendung** consignment of goods; ~**versicherung** insurance of goods, insurance of merchandise; ~**vertrieb** marketing, distribution of goods; ~**verzeichnis** list of goods, commodity index; *Internationales* ~~ *für den Außenhandel: Standard International Trade Classification*; ~**vorräte** stocks, stocked goods; ~**wechsel** bill on goods, commercial (*or* mercantile) paper, trade acceptance; *bankgirierter* ~~: *commercial bill endorsed by a bank*; ~**werbung** product advertising; ~**wert** value of the goods, commodity value; ~**zeichen** → *Warenzeichen*; ~**zoll** customs duty; ~**zustellung** delivery of goods; ~**zurückhaltung** holding goods off the market, withholding (available) goods, retention of goods; ~**zusammenstellung** set (of goods).

Warenzeichen *n* trade mark (*GB*); *US*: *trademark*; ~**abteilung** (*des Patentamts*) Trade Marks Registry (*GB*); ~**benutzer** user of a trade mark; *eingetragener* ~~: *registered user*; ~**benutzungsrecht** right to use a trade mark; ~**eintragung** registration of trade marks; ~**gebühren** trade mark registration fees; ~**gesetz** (*WZG, D: 1968*) Trade Marks Act (*GB*), Trademark Act (*US*); ~**inhaber** proprietor of a trade mark, owner of the mark; ~**lizenz** trade-mark licence; ~**recht** law of trade marks, trade mark law, right in a trade mark; ~**rolle** trade mark register; ~**schutz** trade mark protection, legal protection of trade marks; ~**streitsachen** trade mark disputes; ~**verletzung** infringement of a trade mark; ~**vorschriften** Trademark Rules of Practice (*US*); **eingetragenes** ~ registered trade mark, certification trade mark; **ein**

~ **anmelden** to apply for registration of a trade mark; **ein ~ eintragen** to register a trade mark; **geschütztes ~** protected trade mark; **irreführendes ~** deceptive mark; **nicht deutlich unterscheidbare ~** non-distinctive marks; **notorisches ~** commonly known trade mark; **spezifisch unterscheidbares ~** distinctive mark; **unterscheidungskräftiges ~** distinguishing trade mark; **verbundene ~** associated trade marks, linked trade marks.

Wärme|dämmung heat insulation, thermal insulation; **~- und Schallschutzunterlagen** thermal and sound-proofing insulation documents.

Warn|anlage warning device; **~arbeitskampf** warning strike (or lockout); **~bake** warning sign at level crossing; **~blinkanlage** warning flasher, flashing amber light signal, hazard warning lights; **~blinker** anti-collision lights; **~blinklicht** hazard (or warning) lights; **~dienst** warning service; **~dreieck** warning triangle; **~einrichtung** means for giving warning; **~schild** warning notice; **~signal** warning signal; on-signal (*air raid alarm*); **~streik** warning strike, token strike, demonstration strike; **~vorrichtung** warning system (or device); **~zeichen** warning sign; *akustisches ~~*: *audible warning device*; *optisches ~~*: *luminous warning* (*device*).

warnen *v/t* to warn, to caution.

Warnung *f* warning, notice; **ernste ~** solemn warning.

Warte|frist waiting time, period of delay, period of courtesy wait (*for lawyer to attend*); **~geld** demurrage; inactive status pay; **~liste** waiting list; **~pflicht** duty to wait for the police (at scene of accident); **~schlange** queue; **~stand** inactive status, provisional retirement; **~standsbeamter** official in provisional retirement; **~zeit** waiting period, qualifying period; *navig*: lay-days, days of demurrage; standby-time.

Wartung *f* service, servicing, maintenance, upkeep; **~sfreundlichkeit** maintainability; **~skosten** maintenance charges, maintenance activity costs; **~sschlamperei** maintenance laxity; **~svertrag** service agreement, service contract; **rechtzeitige ~** pre-accident maintenance; **unvorhergesehene ~sprobleme** emergency service problems.

Waschsalon *m* launderette.

Waschzettel *m* blurb, laudatory slip.

Wasser|anschlüsse water mains; **~bau** hydraulic engineering; **~bauamt** waterway engineering office; **~benutzungsrecht** water privilege; **~buch** water-rights register; **~entnahmeanspruch** water right claim; **~entnahmegebiet** water catchment area; **~fahrzeug** watercraft, vessel, ship; **~fracht** waterage, charge for carriage by water; water-borne transport; **~frachtführer** water carrier; **~gefahr** water hazard; **~geld** water rate; **~gesetz** Water Act; **~gewinnungsgebiet** water gathering grounds; **~haushalt** water supply (and consumption), water resources; **~haushaltsgesetz** Water Resources Act (*D: 16. 10. 1976*); **~kraft** hydro-electric power; **~kraftwerk** hydropower plant; **~lauf** watercourse; **~ordal** *hist* water ordeal; **~polizei** water guard, river police; **~recht** law concerning water; water-right; **~schaden** damage by water; **~schadensversicherung** water damage insurance; **~schutzgebiet** water conservation area; **~schutzpolizei** water guard, river police; **~sicherstellung** safe-guarding water resources; **~stand** water level; *~~smarke*: *water mark*; *oberer normaler ~~*: *high water mark*; **~straßen** (inland) waterways; *~~-Maschinenamt*: *Waterway Machinery and Equipment Office*; **~straßennetz** navigable network; **~- und**

Schiffahrtsamt Local Office for Waterways and Shipping; ~- **und Schiffahrtsdirektion** (Regional) Directorate for Waterways and Shipping; ~**verband** water board; ~**verschmutzung** water pollution; ~**versorgung** water supply; ~**versorgungsanlage** water works; ~**weg** waterway, water route; ~**wehr** flood control unit; ~**werfer** water canon, water gun; ~**werk** (municipal) water company; ~**wirtschaft** water management; water supply and regulation, economics of water supply and distribution; ~**wirtschaftsamt** water resources board; ~**wirtschaftsverwaltung** department of water supply; ~**zeichen** water-mark; ~**zolldienst** customs waterguard service.

Wechsel *m (1)* change, reversal; exchange; ~**automat** currency converter; ~**beziehung** reciprocity, interrelation; ~ **des Flaggenstaates** transfer to another flag; ~ **des Wohnorts** change of residence; ~**fälle** vicissitudes, contingencies, ups and downs (of life); ~**geld** (small) change; ~**geldfalle** money-changing trap *fraudulent trick of asking to change a bank note and keeping it while pocketing the small change*; ~**geschäft** exchange business; ~**kurs** → *Wechselkurs*; ~**lagen** alternating phases; ups and downs; **turnusmäßiger** ~ rotation; ~**makler** exchange broker; ~**pari** parity of exchange; ~**parität** parity of exchange; ~**platz** place of exchange; ~**schicht** rotating shift; **w~seitig** *adj* reciprocal; ~**seitigkeit** reciprocity; ~**spiel** interplay, reciprocal action; ~**stelle** exchange agency; ~**stube** bureau de change, foreign exchange counter; ~**wähler** floating voter, *pl also* the floating vote; **w~weise** *adj* alternating; ~**wirkung** reciprocal action, interaction; ~**wirtschaft** rotation of crops, alternate husbandry.

Wechsel *m (2)* bill (of exchange), draft, (promissory) note; ~**abschrift** transcript (*or* copy) of a bill; ~**akzept** acceptance (of a bill); ~**akzeptant** acceptor (of a bill); ~**annahme** acceptance (of a bill); ~**arten** types of bills of exchange and promissory notes; ~ **auf kurze Sicht** short bill, short dated bill; ~**ausfertigung** drafting of a bill; original of a bill; *zweite* ~~: *redraft*; ~**aussteller** drawer (*or* issner) of a bill, maker of a bill (*or* note); ~**bestand** bill holdings; ~**betrag** sum payable (*in a bill or note*); ~**bezogener** drawee (of bill); ~**blankett** blank bills, skeleton bill; ~**brauch** usance in negotiable instruments; ~**buch** discount ledger; ~**bürge** collateral acceptor, guarantor on a bill (*or* note), bill surety; ~**bürgschaft** bill guarantee, commitment to meet a bill; ~~ *leisten: to guarantee a bill of exchange;* ~**courtage** bill brokerage; ~**debitoren** bills receivable; ~**delkredere** delcredere for a bill; ~**depot** deposit of bills; ~**diskont** discounts of drafts, prepaid discount; ~**diskontierung** discounting of acceptances; ~**diskontkredit** credit by way of discount of bills; ~**diskontsatz** bill rate, rate of discount, bill discounting rate; ~**drittausfertigung** third of exchange; ~**duplikat** duplicate bill, second of exchange; ~**einreicher** presenter of a bill; ~**einzugspesen** bill collection charges; ~**erklärung** data on a bill of exchange; ~**erneuerung** renewal of a bill; ~**erstausfertigung** first of exchange; **w~fähig** legally capable of being a party to a bill of exchange; ~**fähigkeit** legal capacity of being a party to a bill of exchange; ~**fälligkeit** maturity of a bill; ~**forderung** bill-based claim, claim arising out of a bill of exchange or promissory note; *pl also*: bills receivable, notes receivable; *e-e* ~~ *einziehen: to collect a bill;* ~**frist** usance, duration of a bill; ~**garant** guarantor of a bill of exchange; ~**geber** drawer (*or* issuer) of a bill, maker of a bill; ~**gesetz** Bills of

Exchange Act (*D: 21. 6. 1933*); ~**girant** endorser of a bill of exchange; ~**gläubiger** creditor in respect of a bill of exchange (*or* note); ~**haftung** liability of the parties to a bill of exchange; ~ **in ausländischer Währung** foreign exchange acceptance; ~ **in einer Ausfertigung** sole bill; ~**inhaber** holder of a bill (*or* note); *gutgläubiger (rechtmäßiger)* ~~: *holder for value without notice; rechtmäßiger* ~~: *holder in due course;* ~**inkasso** collection of bills of exchange; ~ **in mehrfacher Ausfertigung** bills in a set; ~**klage** legal action based on a (*dishonoured*) bill of exchange; ~**klausel** the word bill of exchange (*Wechsel*) or equivalent on the face of a bill; ~**kopie** copy (*or* duplicate) of a bill; ~**kopierbuch** discount ledger; ~**kredit** credit on bills, draft credit, acceptance credit; discount credit; ~**lombard** collateral loan based on a bill of exchange; lending on (security of) bills; ~**mahnbescheid** default summons based on a bill of exchange or promissory note; ~**makler** bill broker, discount broker; **w**~**mäßig** *adj* arising out of a bill, complying with the formal requirements of bills of exchange; ~ **mit fester Laufzeit** bill with a fixed maturity; ~ **mit Finanzierungszusage** bill with a promise of discount; ~**nehmer** payee of a bill of exchange; ~**obligo** contingent liability on bills of exchange; ~**pension** loan against pledged bill of exchange subject to a repurchase clause; ~**portefeuille** bill holding, bill portfolio; ~**prolongation** renewal of a bill of exchange, prolongation of a bill *by postponing expiry date;* ~**protest** protest (of a bill), noting of a bill; ~~ *beurkunden: to note a bill;* ~**protestanzeige** notice of dishonour; ~**protesturkunde** certificate of protest, (record of) protest *recorded by a notary public or bailiff (Gerichtsvollzieher);* ~**provision** *statutory charge payable to the party protesting the bill;* ~**prozeß** summary bill-enforcement procedure, summary enforcement of bills of exchange; proceeding based on a bill of exchange or promissory note; bill of exchange case; ~**recht** law on bills of exchange and promissory notes; ~**rediskontierung** rediscounting bills of exchange (*by central bank*); ~**regreß** recourse (against a prior endorser of a bill); ~**reiter** bill jobber; ~**reiterei** drawing and redrawing, kite-flying; ~~ *treiben: to trade in bills, to draw and redraw bills;* ~**rembours** (documentary) acceptance credit; ~**respekttage** days of respite; ~**rückgriff** = *Wechselregress qv*; ~**sachen** court cases in bill of exchange proceedings; ~**schuld** debt on a bill of exchange or promissory note; ~**schuldner** party liable on a bill (*or* note); ~**spekulant** bill jobber; ~**spesen** discount expenses, cost of bills of exchange and/or notes; ~**stempelsteuer** stamp duty on bills of exchange; ~**steuer** stamp duty on bills of exchange; ~**steuermarke** bill stamp; ~**strenge** strict rules for bills of exchange; ~**summe** sum payable under a bill of exchange (*or* note); ~**trassierung** drawing of a bill; ~**verbindlichkeiten** bills payable; commitments arising from bills of exchange and/or notes; ~**verbundener** party to a bill of exchange; ~**verfall** maturity of a bill of exchange or note; ~**verfallbuch** bills payable book, acceptance maturity tickler (*US*); ~**verjährung** limitation of rights in respect of bills of exchange; ~**vermutung** presumption in favour of bona fide holder of a bill of exchange; ~**verpflichteter** party liable on a bill of exchange (*or* note); ~**verpflichtungen** obligations arising out of bills of exchange and/or notes; ~**vollstreckungsbefehl** enforceable default summons based on a bill of exchange or note; *now:*

~*vollstreckungsbescheid qv*; ~**vollstreckungsbescheid** *present term for:* ~*vollstreckungsbefehl qv*; ~**vorlage** presenting a bill of exchange; ~**zahlungsbefehl** = ~*mahnbescheid qv*; ~**ziehung** drawing of a bill of exchange; ~**zinsen** (statutory) interest on matured bills of exchange and/or notes; **angenommener** ~ accepted bill, bill of acceptance; **avalierter** ~ backed bill, guaranteed promissory note; **bankfähiger** ~ bankable bill, bank paper; **bezahlter** ~ discharged bill; **bundesbankfähige** ~ bills eligible for re-discount (by the German Federal Bank); **diskontfähiger** ~ eligible bill of exchange; **diskontierter** ~ discounted bill; **domizilierter** ~ domiciled bill; **eigener** ~ (negotiable) promissory note; **eigentrassierter** ~ bill drawn by the maker on himself, self-drawn bill; **e-n** ~ **an den Vormann zurückgeben** to redraw a bill; **e-n** ~ **auf den Vormann ziehen** to redraw; **e-n** ~ **ausstellen** to issue a bill; ~~~ *auch: to draw a bill of exchange on*; **e-n** ~ **begeben** to negotiate a bill; **e-n** ~ **domizilieren** to domicile a bill; **e-n** ~ **einlösen** to pay a bill; **e-n** ~ **honorieren** to honour a bill of exchange; **e-n** ~ **nehmen auf** to draw a bill of exchange on; **e-n** ~ **nicht einlösen** to dishonour a bill; **e-n** ~ **nicht honorieren** to dishonour a bill; **e-n** ~ **platzen lassen** to dishonour a bill; **e-n** ~ **protestieren** to protest a bill; ~~~ *lassen: to have a bill protested*; **e-n** ~ **vorlegen** to present a bill; **e-n** ~ **vor Verfall einlösen** to anticipate a bill; **e-n** ~ **zahlbar stellen** to domicile a bill; **e-n** ~ **zum Akzept vorlegen** to present a bill for acceptance; **e-n** ~ **zur Annahme vorlegen** to present a bill for acceptance; **e-n** ~ **zur Diskontierung einreichen** to present a bill for discount; **einwandfreier** ~ approved bill; **erstklassiger** ~ prime bill; **fälliger** ~ due and payable bill of exchange; acceptance due; **fälliger, nicht eingelöster** ~ bill dishonoured by non-payment; **fällig gewesener** ~ overdue bill; **gezogene oder eigene** ~ bills or notes; **gezogener** ~ bill of exchange, draft; **girierter** ~ endorsed bill of exchange, endorsed note; **gültiger** ~ subsisting bill; **Handels**~ ordinary bill; **kurzfristiger** ~ short bill; **langfristiger** ~ long-dated bill; **nicht akzeptierter** ~ bill dishonoured by non-acceptance; **nicht bankfähiger** ~ unbankable paper; **nicht bezahlter** ~ bill dishonoured by non-payment; **nicht diskontierfähiger** ~ ineligible paper, non-discountable bill; **nicht dokumentärer** (*Inkasso-*)~ clean draft; **nicht eingelöster** ~ unpaid bill, dishonoured bill; **nicht honorierter** ~ dishonoured bill; **noch nicht fälliger** ~ unexpired bill; **notleidender** ~ dishonoured bill, bill in distress, bill in suspense; **offener** ~ acceptance receivable; blank bill; **prima** ~ fine bill; **protestierter** ~ bill noted for protest; **quittierter** ~ receipted bill of exchange; **rediskontfähiger** ~ eligible bill; **rediskontierter** ~ rediscounted bill (*by central bank*); **schlichter** ~ clean draft; **trassierteigener** ~ self-accepted bill of exchange; (*drawn by the maker on himself cf eigentrassiert*) **trockener** ~ promissory note; **überfälliger** ~ past due bill, overdue bill; **umlaufender** ~ bill in circulation; **unvollständig ausgefüllter** ~ incomplete bill, inchoate bill; **verfallener** ~ matured bill; **verpfändeter** ~ pawned bill of exchange; **weitergegebener** ~ endorsed bill; **zentralbankfähiger** ~ eligible bill of exchange; **zweiter** ~ redraft.

Wechselkurs *m* exchange rate; ~**ausschläge** currency fluctuations, currency ups and downs; ~**bandbreite** spread between the intervention points of exchange rates; ~ **der Devisen** foreign exchange rates; ~**garantie** exchange rate guarantee; ~**korrektur** exchange-rate adjustment; ~**regelungen** exchange arrangements; ~**schwankungen** exchange-rate fluctuations; ~**steuerung** exchange-rate management; ~**system** system of exchange rates; ~**umrechnung** conversion of exchange rates; ~**verlust** exchange loss; **amtlicher** ~ official exchange rate; **der handelsgewogene** ~ the trade-weighted exchange rate; **effektive** ~**e seit dem Washingtoner Realignment** effective post-Smithsonian exchange rates; **festgesetzter** ~ fixed rate of exchange; **freier** ~ freely fluctuating exchange rate; **frei veränderlicher** ~ floating exchange rate; **gestaffelte** ~**e** differentiated rates of exchange; **Londoner** ~ London rates; **mehrfache** ~**e** multiple exchange rates; **paritätisch liegende** ~**e** unified cross-rate structure (of exchange rates); **zum jetzigen** ~ **umrechnen** to convert at the present rate.

Weg *m* way, passage; *fig* channel; means; manner; ~**abweichungsklausel** deviation clause; ~**ebau** construction of country roads and lanes; ~**ebaulast** public charge to build and maintain country roads and lanes; ~**egeld** travelling expenses, fares; ~**egesetze** laws concerning country roads and lanes; ~**ekosten** infrastructure costs (*transportation*); ~**erecht** private way; right of way, right of passage ~~ *für Reiter*: bridle path; ~~**sfahrzeuge**: *vehicles absolutely entitled to the right of way* (*police, military, fire brigade, emergency*); ~**eunfall** (*social-insurance covered*) accident en route; ~**ezeit** walking time, travelling time; ~**ezoll** toll; ~**weiser** direction sign, signpost, road sign; ~~**tafel**: *guide board*; **auf diplomatischem** ~**e** through diplomatic channels; **auf gerichtlichem** ~**e** by judicial means; **beschränkt öffentlicher** ~ semipublic country road; **öffentlicher** ~ public thoroughfare.

Wegfall *m* cessation, abolition, lapse; ~ **der Geschäftsgrundlage** frustration of contract; ~ **des Arbeitsplatzes** loss of job; job loss, redundancy; ~ **e–s Erben** lapse of an heir (*predeceased heir*); ~ **e–s Vermächtnisses** lapse of gift (*or legacy*).

wegfallen *v/i* to cease (to exist); to be cancelled, to be deleted; to become void, to lapse, to expire.

Wegfertigung *f* disposal.

Weglassen *n* omission; **versehentliches** ~ accidental omission.

weglegen *v/t* to file (away).

Wegnahme *f* taking away sth from s. b., (actual) taking (*in criminal law*); removal; ~ **als Selbsthilfe** recaption, retaking by reprisal; ~**recht** the right to take sth away, right to repossess; tenant's right to remove fixtures (*installed by him*); **widerrechtliche** ~ unlawful taking.

wegnehmen *v/t* to take (away), to dispossess (s. o. of sth.), to remove sth.

wegschaffen *v/t* to get rid of, to make away with, to carry away.

wegschleichen *v/reflex* to sneak away, to steal away, to abscond.

wegsteuern *v/t* to skim off by taxation, to tax away.

Wegweiser *m* direction sign, road sign.

Wegwerf|behälter *m* one-trip container, no-return packet; ~**gesellschaft** throw-away society; ~**rechte** junking rights.

wegwerfen *v/t* to discard.

Wegzug *m* removal (to another location).

Wehr|auftrag defence mission; ~**beauftragter** Parliamentary Commissioner for the Armed Forces; ~**beschwerdeordnung** Military Grievance Code; ~**dienst** → *Wehrdienst*; ~**disziplinaranwalt** provost-marshal; ~**disziplinarordnung** military disciplinary code; ~**disziplinarrecht** military disciplinary law; ~**dorf** fortified village; ~**ersatzwesen** recruiting and

Wehrdienst

replacement (of military personnel); **~etat** military budget; **~gesetz** Military Service Act; **~gerechtigkeit** equity in conscription; **~kraftzersetzung** incitement to disaffection (in the armed forces), demoralization of the armed forces; **~kreis** military district; **~macht** *the Armed Forces of the German Reich*; **~mittel** military resources, military funds; **~mittelbeschädigung** damage to military installations and equipment; **~mittelsabotage** sabotage of military equipment or resources; **~paß** service book; **~pflicht** compulsory military service; **~pflichtentziehung** draft dodging (*US*), evading military service; **~pflichterfassung nach Musterung** selective service; **~pflichtiger** person liable to perform military service; **~recht** military law; **~sold** military pay, soldier's pay; **~stammrolle** service roster; **~steuer** defence tax; **~strafgericht** court martial; **~strafgesetz** military penal code; **~strafrecht** military penal law; **~technik** defence technology; **~überwachung** surveillance of drafting; **~übungen** military manoeuvres; **w~untauglich** *adj* unfit for military service; **w~unwürdig** *adj* ineligible for military service.

Wehrdienst *m* military service, national service; **~ausnahmen** exemptions from military service; **~beschädigter** person injured while on military duty; **~beschädigung** disability incurred during military duty; **~erfassung** enlistment service; **~gericht** court martial; **~senat** military board of review; **~unfähigkeit** disablement for military service; **w~untauglich** *adj* unfit for military service; **~verhältnis** service status; **~verweigerer** conscientious objector; **~verweigerung** refusal to serve in the armed forces as a combatant; **~zeit** period of military service.

Weide|dienstbarkeit easement of pasture, pasture rights; **~frevel** damage to meadow-land; **~land** meadow-land, pasture; **~pacht** pastoral lease; **~recht** right of pasturage, grazing rights, pasture rights, **~wirtschaft** pastoral economy.

Weigerung *f* refusal, denial; **~sgrund** reason for refusal; **~srecht** right of refusal; **glatte ~** outright refusal; **im Falle der ~** in case of refusal; **willkürliche ~** arbitrary refusal.

Weihnachts|freibetrag tax-free allowance for Christmas; **~geld** Christmas bonus; **~gratifikation** Christmas bonus; **~spendenaufrufe** Christmas appeals.

Wein|anbau viticulture, viniculture, wine-growing; **~ausschank** sale of wine on licensed premises; **~bau** viniculture, viticulture, wine-growing; **~baukataster** vineyards survey register; **~fälschung** adulteration of wine; **~geist** spirit(s) of wine; **~gesetz** (the Federal German) Wine Act; **~handel** wine trade; **~händler** wine merchant; **~kommissionär** wine commission merchant; **~pantschen** wine doctoring, adulteration of wine; **~wirtschaftsgesetz** Viniculture and Wine Trade (Supervision) Act.

Weißbuch *n* white paper.

Weisung *f* instruction, directive, order; **~en als Bewährungsauflage** directions of probation; **~en einholen** to ask for instructions; **~en erteilen** to give instructions; **an keine ~en gebunden** not to be bound by any (mandatory) instructions; **auf ~ von** by order of, as directed by; **e-e ~ geben** to order and direct; **von ~en abweichen** to deviate from instructions; **vorbehaltlich anderer ~en** pending instructions.

Weisungs|befugnis power of control, authority (to give directions), occupational control; **w~gebunden** *adj* bound by instructions, non-discretionary; **~gebundenheit** duty to comply with instructions, occupational control; **w~ge-**

mäß *adj*, *adv* in accordance with instructions; ~**kompetenz** managerial authority, occupational control; ~**recht** authority, right to give instructions; **w**~**unterworfen** *adj* subject to control; ~**verhältnis** subordination, relationship of control.

Weiter|arbeit continued production, continued employment; ~**beförderer** on-carrier; **w**~**begeben** *v/t* to negotiate (further), to renegotiate; ~**begebung** further endorsement, renegotiation; ~**beglaubigung** follow-up certification; ~**behandlungsgebühr** *pat* fee for further processing; ~**benutzung** continued use; ~**benutzungsrecht** right of continued use; ~**berechnung** passing on a charge, on-debiting; ~**beschäftigung** continued employment, retention of staff for future employment; ~~*sanspruch*: *right to continuation of employment during dismissal proceedings*; **w**~**bestehen** *v/i* to remain in existence; ~**bildung** further education, adult education, advanced training, in-service training; ~~ *von Führungskräften*: *executive training, managerial courses*; ~**entwicklung** follow-up development, further development; ~**führung** continuation; ~**gabe** transmission, passing on, dissemination; ~~ *von Handelswechseln*: *rediscounting of commercial bills*; ~~ *von Informationen*: *transmission of information*; *nicht zur* ~~ *bestimmt*: *to be retained*; ~**geben** passing on, relaying; ~~ *von Falschgeld*: *passing of counterfeit money*; ~**gehen** moving on; *zum* ~~ *auffordern*: *to order s.o. to move on*; ~**geltung** continuation, continued validity; ~**kommen** advancement; **w**~**leiten** *v/t* to pass on, to transmit onward; ~**leitung** transmission, passing on, redispatch; ~**lieferant** subsequent supplier, subsequent seller; ~**lieferung** supply to subpurchaser, delivery to a third party; **w**~**plazieren** *v/t* to distribute (*issue of securities*); ~**sendung** reconsignment; ~**transport** onward transport; **w**~**verarbeiten** *v/t* to (re)process; ~**verarbeiter** processor, processing firm; ~**verarbeitung** (re)processing; **w**~**veräußern** *v/t* to resell, to transfer to a third party; ~**veräußerung** further disposal, resale; ~**veredelung** supplementary processing; ~**verfolgen** to prosecute further (*pat application*); ~**vergabe** farming out, subcontracting; **w**~**vergeben** sublet (*a contract*); ~**verkauf** resale; **w**~**verkaufen** *v/t* to resell (*to a third party*); ~**verladung** loading for further shipment, onward shipment; ~**verleihen** to on-lend sth; **w**~**vermieten** *v/t* to re-let; ~**vermietung** re-letting; ~**verpachten** *v/t* to re-lease; ~**verpachtung** re-leasing, re-letting; ~**verrechnung** further (*or* subsequent) charge, passing-on of a charge (*or* expense item); ~**versand** onward shipment; **w**~**versenden** to reship; ~**versicherter** person who continues his (social) insurance payments voluntarily; ~**versicherung** continued insurance; *freiwillige* ~~: *continued voluntary insurance*; ~**versteuerung** passing-on of a tax; ~**verweisung** referring the case to the law of a third country; ~**verwendung** continued use; ~**wälzung** passing on to others (*of a burden*); ~**zahlung** continued payment *without loss of remuneration*.

weitschweifig *adj* long-winded, prolix, verbose, diffuse.

Weitschweifigkeit *f* prolixity, diffuseness, verbosity.

Welle|nberg cyclical peak; ~**ntal** cyclical trough; *grüne* ~ synchronized traffic lights, linked (traffic) lights.

Weltanschauung *f* philosophy of life, ideology; ~**sfreiheit** freedom to choose (and adhere to) philosophical beliefs; ~**sgemeinschaften** philosophical groups.

Welt|bank *f* World Bank; (= *Internationale Bank für Wiederaufbau und*

Entwicklung: International Bank for Reconstruction and Development); ~**bedarf** world requirements; ~**fangertrag** world fish catch; ~**firma** firm of world-wide reputation; ~**frieden** world peace; ~**geltung** world standing, world-wide recognition, world-wide repute; ~**gerichtshof** world court ~**geschäft** global business, world trade; ~**gesundheitsorganisation** World Health Organization (WHO); ~**handel** world trade, international trade; ~**handelspreis** price of world trade, international price; ~**handelswaren** world-market goods, goods in world-wide demand; ~**hilfsverband** International Relief Union; ~**konjunktur** world-wide economic trends; ~**markt** world market, international market; ~**marktnotierung** international quotation; ~**marktpreise** world market prices; ~**organisation für geistiges Eigentum** World Intellectual Property Organisation (*WIPO*); ~**organisation für Meteorologie** World Meteorological Organisation; ~**patent** universal patent; ~**postverein** Universal Postal Union; ~**produktion** global production; ~**raum** → *Weltraum*; ~**recht** world law, world-wide law, universal law; ~**rechtspflegeprinzip** principle of international prosecution of (world-wide) crimes; ~**rechtsprinzip** principle of world-wide application of law; ~**regierung** world government; ~**reich** (world-wide) empire; ~**sicherheitsrat** Security Council; ~**urheberrechtsabkommen** Universal Copyright Convention; ~**verkehr** international traffic; ~**währungsfonds** International Monetary Fund (IMF); ~**warenmärkte** world commodity markets; ~**wirtschaft** world economy; ~**wirtschaftsgipfel** world economic summit; ~**wirtschaftskrise** world economic crisis, world-wide depression.

Weltraum *m* aerospace, space; ~**gegenstand** space object; ~**industrie** aerospace industry; ~**politik** space policy; ~**recht** (outer) space law; ~**tätigkeiten** activities in the space field; ~**vertrag** space treaty.

wen es angeht to whom it may concern.

Wende *f* turning point, turning, turn-round, economic turnaround; a change for the better, a general upswing, basic recovery; ~**fläche** turnaround; ~**hals** turncoat; ~**punkt** turning point, landmark; ~**verbot** prohibition of U-turns.

wenden *v/i* to make a U-turn.

Werbe|**abteilung** publicity department, promotion department; ~**agent** publicity agent; ~**akquisiteur** advertising canvasser, space salesman; ~**aktion** publicity campaign; ~**antwort** return, (business) reply mail; ~**antwortkarte** business reply card; ~**artikel** advertising novelty; ~**atelier** commercial studio; ~**beirat** publicity advisory board; ~**berater** advertizing consultant, publicity man; ~**budget** advertising budget; ~**drucksache** advertising matter; ~**einblendung** spot announcement; ~**einnahmen** advertizing revenue; ~**erfolgskontrolle** advertizing effectiveness study, advertizing control; ~**erfolgsprognose** forecast of advertizing effectiveness; ~**etat** advertizing budget; ~**fachmann** advertising expert, publicity expert; ~**fahrt** (free *or* cheap) trip for sales promotion; ~**feldzug** publicity campaign; ~**fernsehen** *TV* advertising spots ~**firma** publicity firm, advertizing agency; ~**funk** radio advertising, commercial broadcasting; ~**gemeinschaft** advertizing pool; ~**geschenk** sales promotion (*or* good will) gift, gift for advertizing; ~**gespräch** sales talk; ~**grafik** commercial art; ~**kampagne** publicity campaign; ~**kosten** publicity expenses; ~**leiter** advertising man-

werben | **Werk**

ager; ~**mittel** publicity medium, publicity aid; ~**muster** advertising sample; ~**nummer** complimentary copy, publicity copy; ~**plakat** advertizing poster; show bill; ~**preis** introductory price, "kneeldown price"; ~**preisausschreiben** advertizing contest; ~**prospekte** promotional literature, advertizing prospectuses; ~**rabatt** advertizing allowance; ~**spezialist** publicity expert; ~**rat** Advertizing Standards Board; ; ~**spot** advertizing spot, commercial; ~**tätigkeit** activity in publicity; advertizing; ~**texter** ad writer, copy-writer; ~**träger** advertizing vehicle, advertizing medium; ~**treibender** advertiser; ~**verbot** restraint on publicity, ban on publicity; ~**verkauf** promotional selling; ~**woche** promotional week; ~**zwecke** publicity purposes.

werben *v/i* to advertize, to engage in promotional activities; *v/t* to recruit, to enlist *(members)*.

Werbung *f* publicity, sales promotion, advertizing; ~ **am Verkaufsort** point-of-sale advertizing; ~ **betreiben** to solicit orders, to engage in promotional activities; ~ **durch Musterverteilung** free trial sampling; ~ **durch Postversand** direct-mail advertizing; ~ **durch Postwurfsendung** direct-mail advertizing; **geballte** ~ mass advertizing; **herabsetzende** ~ disparaging (*or* knocking) advertizing; **mißbräuchliche** ~ improper solicitation; **reißerische** ~ loud publicity; **repräsentative** ~ prestige advertizing; **sensationelle** ~ stunt advertizing, gimmick, sensational advertizing; **unerlaubte** ~ illicit advertizing; **unterschwellige** ~ subliminal advertizing; **vergleichende** ~ comparative advertisements, discriminatory advertizing.

Werbungs|aktion advertizing campaign, publicity campaign, canvassing campaign; ~**kampagne** canvassing campaign; ~**kosten** publicity costs; income-related expenses *(for tax purposes)*, professional outlay; ~**kostenpauschale** overall allowance for income-related expenses; ~**mittel** advertizing media, publicity vehicles, publicity aids; ~**mittler** publicity agent; ~**rundschreiben** advertizing circular; ~**verbot** restraint on publicity.

Werdegang *m* personal background, career, curriculum vitae; **beruflicher** ~ career pattern, job history.

Werft *f* dockyard, shipyard; ~**arbeiter** docker.

Werk *n (1)* work, performance; ~**auftrag** work by order; ~ **der Bildhauerkunst** sculpture; ~ **der Schauspielkunst** dramatic work; ~ **der Theaterkunst** dramatic work; **w~gerecht** *adj* good and workmanlike; ~**leistung** work performance, industrial service; ~**lieferung** contractor's labour and materials; ~**lieferungsvertrag** contract for work done and materials supplied; ~**löhne** labour; ~**stoff** (working) material; *hochbeanspruchbarer* ~~: *high stress material*; ~**stoffprüfamt** (Industrial) Material Testing Office; ~**stoffverarbeitung** materials processing (industrial) use of materials; ~**studenten** working students; ~**unternehmer** contractor, manufacturer; ~**unterricht** handicrafts lessons; ~**vertrag** contract for services *(by independent contractor)*; contract to achieve sth; contract to produce a result; ~**vertragsunternehmer** (independent) contractor; **choreographisches** ~ choreographic work; **gemeinfreie** ~**e** works in public domain; **mildtätige** ~**e** works of charity; **nachgelassene** ~**e** posthumous works; ~**schriftstellerische** ~**e** literary works.

Werk *n (2)* plant, works, factory; ~**abnahmeprotokoll** final inspection record; ~**ausschuß** works committee; ~**bahn** factory railway; ~**dienstwohnung** tied accommodation (*of employed person*); ~**fernverkehr** company-owned long distance transport, interworks long-distance traffic; ~**feuerwehr** company-fire brigade; ~**halle** workshop; ~**leitung** factory management; ~**meister** (shop) foreman; ~**sanlage** factory installation(s); ~**sarzt** factory surgeon, company doctor; ~**sbesetzung** factory sit-down, occupation of a factory (*or* plant); ~**schutz** works protection force, works police; ~**sgüterprüfdienst** company goods inspection service; ~**shafen** private factory harbour; ~**skonsumanstalten** company-owned consumer shops; ~**sleiter** works manager; ~**spionage** industrial espionage; ~**statt** → *Werkstatt*; ~**svertreter** manufacturer's agent; ~**verkehr** company operated transport; ~**wohnung** service occupancy, company-owned dwelling; **ab** ~ ex works, ex factory, free at point of dispatch.

Werkstatt *f* workshop; ~**arbeit** shop work; ~**fertigung** job shop production, custom manufacturing; ~**für Behinderte** sheltered workshop; ~**montage** shop assembly; ~**zeichnung** workshop drawing; **beschützende** ~ sheltered workshop.

Werktag *m* workday, working day.

Werkzeug *n* tool(s); ~**maschinenindustrie** machine tools industry; ~**- und Maschinenausstattung** tooling; ~**versicherung** tool insurance; **schuldloses** ~ innocent agent.

Wert *m* value, worth; valuable object, asset, *pl. also*: *securities* (*traded on the stock exchange*); value date; ~ **als pari** issue at par; ~**angabe** statement of value, declaration of value; ~**ansatz** carrying value, valuation (of asset), value shown; ~ **auf Faktura** value as per invoice; ~**aufholungsgebot** requirement to reinstate orginal values (*in later balance sheet*); ~**aufstockung** appreciation in value; ~**ausgleich** compensation of equal value; compensation for the loss of value; ~**begriff** concept of value; ~**berechnung** calculation of the value; ~**berichtigung** allowance for depreciation, writedown, accrued depreciation, accumulated depreciation, value adjustment, valuation allowance; allowance for doubtful accounts, bad debt allowance; ~~ *auf Darlehen: loan loss provisions*; ~~ *auf Forderungen: reserve for bad debts*; ~~ *auf Vorratsvermögen: inventory reserve*; *steuerliche* ~~: *value adjustment for taxation purposes*; ~**berichtigungskonto** adjustment of property account, offset account; **w**~**beständig** *adj* of stable value; ~**beständigkeit** stability of value; ~~*sklausel*: *stable value clause*; ~**bestimmung** valuation, determination of value; ~**brief** insured letter; ~ **des Anlagevermögens** net tangible asset value; ~ **des Streitgegenstandes** value of the matter in dispute; ~ **e-r Zeugenaussage** weight of testimony, value of evidence; ~**einheit(en)** unit(s) of value; ~ **erhalten** value received (*bank account*); ~**erhaltung** maintenance of value; ~**erhöhung** increase in value, appreciation; ~~ *des Anlagevermögens*: *capital appreciation*; ~~ *von Wohnhäusern*: *improvement of houses*; ~**ermittlung** ascertainment of the value, valueing; ~**ersatz** substitution by an object of equal value, substituted item of value, compensation for the value of sth; ~**ermittlung** valuation, determination of the value; ~**festsetzung** fixing of the value; ~**fortschreibung** revaluation for further accounting; **w**~**frei** value-free, neutral, abstract; ~**gegenstand** object of value, valuable, thing of value; ~**grenze** limit for the value; maximum value; ~**gutachten** expert opinion on the (true) value of sth; ~**haltigkeit** intrinsic value; ~**herabsetzung** reduction in value; **~ in Geld** monetary value; **~klausel** valuation clause; **w~los** *adj* worthless, valueless; **~marke** token coin; **w~mäßig** *adv* in terms of value, ad valorem; **~maßstab** standard of value, measure of value; **~messer** standard of value; **~minderung** impairment in value, depreciation (*or* decline) in value; **~muster** sample of value; **~münze** token coin; **~paket** insured parcel (with value declared); **~papier** → *Wertpapier*; **~paradox** paradox of value; **~rechte** (uncertificated) loan stock rights; **~sachen** valuables; **w~schaffend** *adj* asset-creating, productive; **~schätzung** esteem, appraisal, appreciation; **~schöpfung** creation of wealth, net product, value added; **~schriften** securities; **~sendung** consignment with value declared; valuable consignment; **~sicherung** value guarantee, stable-value arrangement; protection from inflationary loss; indexing arrangement; **~~sklausel**: *stable value clause*; **~skala** table of values; **~steigerung** enhancement in value, appreciation in value, increase in value, improvement; **~stellung** availability date, value date; **~~stag**: *value date*; **~stempel** revenue stamp; **~steuer** ad valorem tax; **~taxe** estimate of value; **~urteil** opinion, judgment, critical comment, value judgment; *gutgläubiges ~~ fair comment*; **~verbesserung** improvement of value, increased value; **~verhältnisse** value relationships; **~verlust** loss in value; decrease in value; **~verminderung** decrease in value; **~verschlechterung** deterioration (in value); **~vorschriften** valuation regulations; **~zeichen** postal stamp, token of value; **~zeichenautomat** stamp machine; **~zeichenfälschung** forgery of postal stamps; **~zoll** ad valorem duty (*or* tariff); **~zuschlag** increment-of-value charge, valuation charge; **~zuwachs** increase in value; increment value, unearned increment; **~zuwachssteuer** increment value tax, increment tax; **abgeschriebener ~** written-down value; **angemessener ~** fair value, fair and reasonable value; **bleibender ~** lasting value; **bereinigte ~e** adapted figures; **börsennotierte ~e** officially quoted securities; **den ~ vermindern** to deteriorate, to reduce in value; **die ~e aus den Sicherungen entlassen** to release the assets from the charges; **echter ~** true value, real value; **effektiver ~** effective value, real value; **errechneter ~** computed value; **festverzinsliche ~e** fixed-interest-bearing securities, bonds; **fiktiver ~** fictitious value; **finanzieller ~** monetary value; **fremde ~e** foreign securities; **führende ~e** leading shares, leaders; **gehaltene ~e** firm stock; **gemeiner ~** ordinary value, fair market value; **gewöhnlicher ~** ordinary value; **gesetzlich festgelegter ~** statutory value; **immaterieller ~** intangible value; **im ~ steigen** to improve in value; **im ~e von** in the amount of; **innerer ~** worth, inherent value, intrinsic value; **kalkulatorischer ~** imputed value; **künstlerischer ~** artistic merit; **maßgebender ~** decisive value; **materieller ~** tangible value; **objektiver ~** real value; **unnotierte ~e** unlisted securities; **unter ~ deklarieren** to enter short; **ursprünglicher ~** original value; **variable gehandelte ~e** variable-price securities; **versicherbarer ~** insurable value; **versicherter ~** insured value; **wirtschaftlicher ~** economic value; **zufälliger ~** adventitious value, fortuitous value; **zurückgerechneter ~** commuted value.

Wertpapier *n* security (*usually pl*), document (*or certificate*) of value, instrument *evidencing an asset or property interest; often used in the narrower sense of* negotiable instrument; instrument of value (*representing a* *right or asset*); **~absatz** sales of securities, marketing of securities; **~analyse** securities research; **~anlage** investment in securities; **~art** category of securities; **~beratung** investment counselling; **~bereinigung** validation of securities, revalorization of securities; **~besitz** securities holdings; **~besitzer** securities holder; **~bestand** security holdings, portfeuille; **~börse** stock exchange, securities exchange; *amtliche* ~~: *recognized stock exchange*; **~darlehen** loan on collateral securities; **~depot** deposit of securities (for safe custody); ~~*konto: safe custody account of negotiable instruments; offenes* ~~: *ordinary deposit of securities; verschlossenes* ~~: *sealed deposit of securities*; **~e des Anlagevermögens** investment securities; **~e beleihen** to borrow on securities; **~e des Handelsrechts** mercantile paper(s), commercial paper; **~e einziehen** to declare securities forfeited; **~emission** issue of securities, floating of an issue; **~e mit festem Ertrag** fixed-yield securities; **~e mit kurzer Laufzeit** short-term securities; **~e mit schwankendem Ertrag** variable-yield securities; **~ersterwerb** original acquisition of securities; **~finanzierung** financing through securities; **~fonds** security fund; **~gesetz** Securities Act, negotiable instruments and securities law; **~handel** jobbing, securities trade; **~händler** dealer in securities, jobber, trader; **~kredit** credit on the collateral of securities; **~kurszettel** list of security prices; **~makler** stock broker; **~markt** securities market; **~-Mitteilungen** securities bulletin; **~pensionsgeschäft** credit transaction under repurchase agreement of securities; **~placement** placing of securities; **~-Portefeuille** security holdings, (securities) portfolio; *gestreutes* ~~: *diversified portfolio*; **~recht** law relating to negotiable instruments and other securities; **~sammelbank** securities clearing and deposit bank; **~schwindel** securities fraud; **~sparen** investment saving, saving through securities; **~steuer** stamp duty on securities, securities tax (on first acquisitions); **~termingeschäft** forward transactions in securities; **~umsatzsteuer** securities transfer tax; **~unterbringung** placing of securities; **~verkäufe an Private** private placement of securities; **~vermögen** property in the form of securities; *ausgewogenes* ~~: *balanced portfolio of assets*; **~verwahrungsversicherung** securities insurance; **~verwaltung** portfolio management; **~zins** interest on bonds, rate of interest obtainable on securities; **ausgeloste ~e** bonds drawn for redemption; **ausländische ~e** foreign securities; **auslosbares ~** lottery bond; **begebbares ~** negotiable instrument; **beleihungsfähige ~e** assessable securities; **beliehene ~e** pledged securities; **börsenfähige ~e** listed securities, marketable securities; ~~*e zu Ankaufskursen: securities at cost*; **börsengängige ~e** stock exchange securities; **erstklassige ~e** first-class stock, gilt-edged securities; **festverzinsliche ~e** fixed-interest-bearing securities, bonds; **gut eingeführte ~e** seasoned securities; **handelsfähige ~e** negotiable securities; **international gehandelte ~e** interbourse securities; **kaufmännisches ~** commercial instrument; **lombardierte ~e** pledged securities, collateral securities; **marktfähige ~e** marketable securities; **mündelsichere ~e** trustee securities, gilt-edged securities, authorized securities, "widow-and-orphan stock"; **nachschußpflichtige ~e** assessable securities; **nicht börsenfähige ~e** unquoted investments; **nicht einlösbares ~** non-redeemable security; **nicht handelbare ~e** non-marketable securities; **nicht notierte ~e** unlisted securities;

nicht umlauffähige ~e non-marketable securities; **notierte** ~e quoted (*or* listed) securities; **notleidendes** ~ investment in default; **selten gehandelte** ~e inactive securities; **stimmberechtigte** ~e voting securities; **stimmrechtlose** ~e non-voting securities; **tarifbesteuerte** ~e securities subject to tax on the normal scale; **umlauffähige** ~e negotiable securities, negotiable instruments; **unkotierte** ~e unlisted securities; **verkehrsfähiges** ~ negotiable instrument; **verlosbare** ~e redeemable securities; **verpfändete** ~e pledged securities; **verzinsliche** ~e interest-bearing securities; **zum Börsenhandel zugelassene** ~e listed securities.

Wertung *f* appraisal, evaluation, valuation, estimate.

Wesens|gleichheit *pat* identity; ~**merkmal** *n* criterion, essentiality.

wesentlich *adj* of the essence, material, substantial, fundamental, vital.

Westeuropäische Union *f* Western European Union.

Westminster-Statut *n* Statute of Westminster (*1931*).

Wett|annahme betting office; ~**annahmestelle** betting office, bookmaker's (= bookies) office; ~**buch** betting book; ~**gemeinschaft** pari mutuel; ~**lokal** poolroom; ~**marke** token; ~**salon** betting house; ~**schein** betting slip; ~**steuer** betting tax; ~**schuld** betting debt; ~**vertrag** gaming contract; ~**zahlung** paying out.

Wettbewerb *m* competition; **freier** ~ free competition; **in** ~ **treten** to compete, to enter into competition; **lauterer** ~ fair competition; **redlicher** ~ fair competition; **ruinöser** ~ destructive competition; **scharfer** ~ keen competition; **schmarotzerischer** ~ parasitic competition; **publizistischer** ~ competition between publishers; **unlauterer** ~ unfair competition, unfair trading; **unverfälschter** ~ pure competition; **wesentlicher** ~ substantial competition, real competition.

Wettbewerbs|abkommen (non-)competition agreement; ~**abrede** informal (*or* secret) competition arrangement, understanding concerning competition; ~**anreize** competitive incentives; ~**bedingungen** terms (*or* conditions) of competition; ~**beschränkung** restraint of competition, restraint of trade, market restraint; *pl also*: restrictive practices; stifling of competition; ~**charakter** competitive nature; ~**druck** stress of competition; **w~fähig** *adj* able to meet competition; competitive; ~**fähigkeit** competitive strength, competitive ability, competitiveness; ~**freiheit** freedom of competition; **unvollkommene** ~~: *imperfect competition*; ~**gleichheit** competitive equality; ~**handlung** act of competition; ~**hüter** guardians of free competition; ~**klausel** non-competition clause; competition clause; restraint clause; ~**lage** competitive position; ~**nachteil** competitive disadvantage; **w~neutral** of no influence on the competitive position; ~**ordnung** system for regulating competition, competition code; ~**preis** competitive price; ~**prinzip** principle of free competition; ~**rabatt** competition rebate; ~**recht** law on competition; legislation on competition; ~**regeln** competition rules; code of fair competition; ~**schutz** protection of fair competition; ~**spielraum** competitive range; ~**stellung** position to compete; ~**system** competitive system; ~**tarife** tariffs fixed to meet competition; ~**verbot** covenant not to compete, restraint of competition; ~**verbotsklausel** restraint of competition clause; ~**verfälschung** distortion of competition; ~**verhältnisse** competitive relations; ~**verhinderung** unreasonable restraint of trade; ~**verzerrung** distortion of competition;

~**vorteil** competitive advantage; **w~widrig** *adj* contrary to fair competition; ~**wirtschaft** competitive economy, free-market economy.

Wette *f* bet, wager, punt.

Wetten *n* betting, wagering; **verbotenes** ~ (illegal) betting.

wetten *v/i* to bet, to wager.

Wetter *n* weather; ~**amt** weather bureau; ~**meldung** weather forecast; ~**vorhersage** weather forecasting; **außerordentlich schlechtes** ~ exceptionally inclement weather; **falls es das** ~ **zuläßt** weather permitting.

wettmachen *v/t* to compensate.

Wettrüsten *n* arms race.

Widerbeklagter *m* cross-defendant.

Widerklage *f* cross-action, cross-complaint; ~**forderung** counterclaim; **e-e** ~ **erheben** to bring a cross-action.

Widerkläger *m* cross-petitioner, cross-claimant.

widerlegbar *adj* disprovable, rebuttable, refutable; **nicht** ~ irrefutable, irrebuttable.

Widerlegbarkeit *f* refutability, rebuttability.

widerlegen *v/t* to refute, to rebut, to disprove, to repudiate.

Widerlegung *f* refutation, rebuttal, disproof; ~**sbeweis** evidence in rebuttal, disproof.

widernatürlich *adj* unnatural, perverse.

widerrechtlich *adj* unlawful.

Widerrechtlichkeit *f* unlawfulness.

Widerruf *m* retraction, revocation, countermand; ~ **der Strafaussetzung** revocation of probation; ~ **der Vertretungsmacht** revocation of agency; ~ **der Zulassung** revocation of licence to practise; ~ **der Zustimmung** revocation of the consent; ~ **des Angebots** withdrawal of the offer; ~ **des Geständnisses** retraction of the confession; ~ **des Testaments** revocation of will; ~ **e-r Schenkung** revocation of a gift; ~ **e-r Vollmacht** revocation of an authority, cancellation of power of attorney; ~ **e-s Vermächtnisses** ademption of a legacy; ~ **e-s Verzichts** withdrawal *or* retractation of a renunciation; ~ **falscher Aussagen** retraction of false statements; ~**sgründe** grounds of revocation; ~**klage** action for a retraction (*or* revocation); ~**sklausel** contestable clause (ins); ~**srecht** power of revocation; ~**svorbehalt** proviso of cancellation; **bis auf** ~ until cancelled, subject to withdrawal.

widerrufen *v/t* to withdraw, to revoke, to retract, to countermand; **öffentlich** ~ to recant.

widerruflich *adj* revocable, precarious, at s. o.'s pleasure.

Widerruflichkeit *f* revocability.

Widersacher *m* opponent, adversary, foe.

widersetzen *v/reflex* to oppose, to resist.

widersetzlich *adj* contumacious.

Widersetzlichkeit *f* insubordination, refractoriness.

widersinnig *adj* absurd.

Widerspenstigkeit *f* recalcitrance, refractory nature, refractoriness.

widersprechen *v/i* to oppose, to contradict, to object.

widersprechend *adj* contradictory.

Widerspruch *m* objection, protest, opposition, counter-notice, caveat; discrepancy, contradiction, variance; ~ **einlegen** to lodge a protest, to file an objection; ~ **erheben** to object, to oppose; to raise objections; ~**stelle** board of appeals; ~ **zweier Gesetze** antinomy; **auf** ~ **stoßen** to meet with opposition; **im** ~ **stehend** repugnant, conflicting; **innerer** ~ inconsistency, self-contradiction; **offener** ~ open (*or* flagrant) contradiction, contradiction in terms.

widersprüchlich *adj* contradictory, equivocal, inconsistent, illogical.

Widersprüchlichkeit *f* contradictoriness, equivocality; ~ **der Behauptungen** repugnancy of allegations.

Widerspruchs|bescheid ruling on an

Widerstand

objection (*or* interference); ~**freiheit** consistency; ~**frist** time-limit for filing an objection; ~**klage** = *Drittwiderspruchsklage qv*; **w**~**los** *adj* unequivocal; ~**recht** right to object; ~**verfahren** *administrative proceedings reviewing an individual administrative decision upon a protest by the party aggrieved*; *pat*: proceedings of interference; **w**~**voll** *adj* contradictory; *in sich* ~~: *self-contradictory*.

Widerstand *m* resistance; ~ **gegen Beamte** resisting public officers; ~ **gegen die Staatsgewalt** obstructing an officer, resistance to state authority; ~ **gegen Notzuchtversuch** resisting rape; ~ **gegen Vollstreckungsbeamte** obstructing enforcement officers; ~ **leisten** to put up resistance; **bewaffneter** ~ armed resistance; **den** ~ **brechen** to overcome resistance by force; **passiver** ~ passive resistance.

Widerstands|bewegung resistance movement; **w**~**fähig** *adj* capable of resisting, offering resistance; ~**fähigkeit** tenacity, durability; ~**kämpfer** resistance fighter; ~**kraft** strength to resist; ~**leistung bei Verhaftung** resisting arrest, forcible resistance to arrest; ~**nest** pocket of resistance; ~**punkt** resistance point; ~**recht** right to resist (*unconstitutional activities*).

widerstreitend *adj* conflicting.

Widerwillen *m* loathing, repugnance, distaste, unwillingness.

widerwillig *adj* reluctant, unwilling.

widmen *v/t* to dedicate, to devote.

Widmung *f* dedication; ~ **als öffentliche Straße** declaration as a public road, dedication of way.

widrigenfalls *adv* failing which, in default whereof.

wie|besehen as inspected; ~**besichtigt** as inspected; ~ **dem auch sei** be that as it may; ~ **gehabt** as usual; ~ **gesagt** as mentioned before; ~ **sich's gehört** as is proper and fitting.

Wieder|abdruck (additional) reprint; **w**~**abtreten** *v/t* to reassign; ~**anlage** reinvestment; **w**~**anlegen** *v/t* to reinvest; ~**anlagerabatt** reinvestment discount; ~**annäherung** rapprochement; ~**annahme** reacceptance; **w**~**annehmen** *v/t* to reaccept, to resume possession; ~**aufarbeitung** reprocessing, ~**aufarbeitungsanlage** reprocessing plant *for fuel from (light water) reactors,* nuclear reprocessing plant; ~**aufbau** reconstruction, rebuilding; ~**auffüllung** replenishment; ~**aufgreifen** resumption (of the matter); renewed treatment, taking up sth again, renewed recourse to; ~**aufhebung** repeal; ~**aufleben** revival; ~~ *e-r Versicherung: reinstatement (of policy)*; ~**auflebensklausel** revival-clause *of claims against fraudulent bankrupt (which had been settled)*; ~**aufnahme** → *Wiederaufnahme*; **w**~**aufnehmen** *v/t* to resume; ~**aufrüstung** rearmament; ~**aufschwung** economic recovery, upswing, rebound; ~**ausfuhr** re-exportation; ~**ausfuhrhandel** re-export trade; ~**austritt** (repeated) withdrawal; ~**belebung** revival; ~**berufung** reappointment (*board member etc*); ~**beschaffung** replacement (*cf. Wiederbeschaffungs ...*); **w**~**bringlich** *adj* retrievable; **w**~**einberufen** *v/t* to reconvene; ~**einberufung** reconvening (*a meeting*); recalling to the colours; **w**~**einbürgern** *v/t* to repatriate; ~**einbürgerung** renaturalization; ~**einfuhr** reimportation; ~**eingliederung** rehabilitation, resettlement, re-integration; berufliche ~~ *vocational rehabilitation*; ~**eingliederungsfonds** resettlement fund; ~**einlagerung** rewarehousing; ~**einlieferung** recommittal; **w**~**einräumen** *v/t* to resume (possession), to re-allow; ~**einräumung** resumption (of possession), re-entry; ~**einrichter** *in East Germany, a new farmer on formerly expropriated ground* ~**einrichtung** refurnishing; ~~**sbeihilfe**: *grant for setting up a new household*; **w**~**einsetzen** *v/t* to reinstate, to reinstall;

~**einsetzung** → *Wiedereinsetzung*; **w~einstellen** to re-employ, to re-engage; ~**einstellung** re-employment, re-engagement; ~**eintritt** re-opening, re-entry; ~~ *in den Besitz*: re-entry; ~~ *in die mündliche Verhandlung*: *re-opening the hearing*; ~**einweisung** recommitment; ~**erhebung** renewed assessment (*tax*); **w~erlangbar** *adj* recoverable; **w~erlangen** *v/t* to recover, to reacquire, to retrieve; ~**erlangung** recovery, recapture, reacquisition; ~**ernennung** reappointment; **w~eröffnen** *v/t* to reopen; ~**eröffnung** reopening; **w~erstatten** *v/t* to refund, to reimburse; ~**erteilung** reissue, new grant; ~~ *der Fahrerlaubnis*: *reissue of driving licence*; ~**erwerb** reacquisition; ~**gabe** account, rendition; *mechanische* ~~: *mechanical reproduction, playback*; *wörtliche* ~~: *literal repetition, verbatim account*; **w~gefangennehmen** *v/t* to recapture; ~**gewährung** renewed grant; ~**gewinnung** retrieval, recovery, salvage; ~**gutmachung** → *Wiedergutmachung*; **w~herstellen** *v/t* to restore; ~**herstellung** restoration, repair; ~~ *der ehelichen Lebensgemeinschaft*: *restitution of conjugal life*; ~~ *des früheren Zustands*: *restoration to the former condition*; ~~ *verfallener Patente*: *restoration of lapsed patents*; ~**herstellungsanspruch** right (*or* claim) of restitution, restoration right; ~**erkennungstest** recognition test (*advertizing*); ~**holbar** *adj* repeatable, reproducible, capable of being reproduced; ~**holung** repetition, reiteration; *im* ~~*sfall*: *in the event of a repeated offence*; ~**holungsgefahr** danger of recurrence, danger of recidivism; ~**skurs** refresher course; ~**holungstäter** repeat offender, repeater, recidivist; ~**inbesitznahme** repossession, re-entry (*land*), regress; ~**ingangsetzung** re-starting; ~**inkraftsetzung** re-enactment; ~**inkrafttreten** revival, renewed coming into force;

~**inkurssetzung** reconditioning, putting into circulation again; **w~instandsetzen** *v/t* to repair; ~**instandsetzung** repair; ~**kauf** repurchase; **w~kaufen** *v/t* to repurchase; ~**käufer** repurchaser; ~**kaufsrecht** right to repurchase; **w~kehrend** *adj* recurring, periodic, periodical; *periodisch* ~: *periodical*; ~**kehrschuldverhältnis** regulary renewed obligation; ~**nutzbarmachung** salvage, recycling; ~**umstellung** reconversion; ~**vereinigung** reunification; ~**vergeltungsrecht** right of reprisal; ~**verhaftung** rearrest; ~**verheiratung** remarriage; *bis zu ihrer* ~~: *until she shall marry again*; ~**verkauf** resale; *nicht zum* ~~ *bestimmt*: *not intended for resale*; **w~verkaufen** *v/t* to resell; ~**verkäufer** reseller, dealer; dealer's buyer; *an* ~~ *verkaufen*: *to sell to the trade*; ~**verkäuferpreis** trade price; ~**verkäuferrabatt** trade discount; ~**verkaufspreis** resale price; ~**verkaufsrecht** right of resale; ~**verleihung der Staatsangehörigkeit** repatriation; ~**vermietung** reletting; ~**veröffentlichung** republication; ~**versöhnung** reconciliation; ~**vertagung** readjournment; ~**verwendung** reuse; ~**verwertung** recycling, salvage; ~**vorlage** resubmission; *zur* ~~: *to be resubmitted*; ~**vorlagemappe** follow-up file; ~**vorlagenliste** tickler; ~**vorlegungsfrist** period for resubmission; ~**wahl** re-election; *sich zur* ~~ *stellen*: *to stand for re-election*; **w~wählbar** *adj* eligible for re-election; **w~wählen** *v/t* to re-elect; *nicht wiedergewählt*: *unreturned*; **w~zulassen** *v/t* to readmit; ~**zulassung** readmission.

Wiederaufnahme *f* resumption, re-opening; ~**antrag** motion for a new trial; ~ **der Arbeit** resumption of work; ~ **der diplomatischen Beziehungen** resumption of diplomatic relations; ~ **der Geschäftstätigkeit** resumption of business; ~ **der mündlichen Verhandlung** reopening of the hearing, continuation of the trial; ~ **der Verhandlungen** resumption of negotiations; ~ **der Zahlungen** resumption of payments; ~ **des Verfahrens** reopening of appeal, revival of action, new trial, trial de novo; *die ~~ anordnen: to order a new trial*; ~ **e-s Prozesses** revivor, reopening of the proceedings (*which had been suspended*); ~**verfahren** (proceedings of a) new trial; *ein ~~ beantragen: to file a motion for a new trial*.

wiederaufnehmen *v/t* to resume, to reopen.

Wiederbeschaffungs|anspruch claim for replacement; ~**kosten** replacement cost, repurchase cost; ~**preis** repurchase price, replacement price; ~**prinzip** current cost accounting; ~**rücklage** replacement reserve, replacement fund; ~**wert** replacement value, replacement cost, reproduction value; ~~ *abzüglich Abschreibungen: fair value*.

Wiedereinsetzung *f* reinstatement, reinstalment, restoration, restitution; re-establishment; ~ **e-s Patents** re-establishment of a patent; ~ **in den Besitz** repossession, re-entry; ~ **in den vorigen Stand** restoration, reinstatement, restitution to the previous condition (*lapse of a deadline*); *lat*: restitutio in integrum; ~~ *gewähren: to reinstate a case*; ~ **in ein Amt** reinstatement in an office; ~ **in seine Rechte** restoration of one's rights; ~**sgebühr** *pat* fee for re-establishment for rights.

Wiedergutmachung *f* reparation, indemnification, compensation, redress, indemnity.

Wiedergutmachungs|abkommen agreement on compensation (*for racial, political or religious persecutees of the Naziregime*); ~**sanspruch** compensation claim (*submitted by persecutees*); ~**sberechtigter** person entitled to compensation for persecution; ~**sgelder** indemnification monies; ~**skammer** Court Division for Compensation of Racial Persecutees; ~**skommission** Commission for Compensation of Persecutees; ~**srecht** law of compensation of Nazi persecutees; ~**szahlungen** compensation payments to persecutees.

Wiege|gebühr weighing fee; ~**geld** weighing charge, weighage; ~**ordnung** weighing regulations; ~**schein** weight note, attestation of weight; ~**stempel** weighing stamp.

Wild *n* wild animals, game; ~**dieb** poacher; ~**dieberei** poaching; ~**gatter** game fence, paddock, game preserve; ~**handel** game dealing; ~**hüter** gamekeeper; ~**schaden** damage caused by game; ~**schadenssachen** case of damage by game; **jagdbares** ~ fair game.

Wilderei *f* poaching; ~**gerät** poaching equipment; **nächtliche** ~ night poaching.

Wildern *n* poaching.

wildern *v/i* to poach.

Wille *m* will, volition, intent; intention; ~ **der Parteien** intention of the parties; ~ **des Gesetzgebers** legislative intent, intention of the legislature; **böser** ~ ill will; **der wirkliche** ~ the real (*or* true) intention; **freier** ~ free will; **letzter** ~ last will; **mit** ~**n** voluntarily, with intent, willingly.

Willens|akt voluntary act, act of volition, spontaneous act; ~**anspannung** effort of willpower; ~**äußerung** manifestation of a person's will; ~**beeinflussung** influencing a person's will; **unzulässige** ~ undue influence; ~**bereich** range of volition; ~**bestimmung** determination of one's intent; *freie* ~~: *free determination of one's will*; ~**betätigung** volitional act; ~**bildung** creating an intention; ~**einigung** meeting of (the) minds, concurrence of will; agreement, consensus (ad idem); ~**entscheidung** voluntary decision; ~**erklärung** → *Willenserklärung*; ~**freiheit** free-

Willenserklärung

dom of volition, freedom of will; **~handlung** voluntary act, act of volition; **~kraft** will power; **~mangel** imperfect (*or* erroneous) expression of intention (*due to mistake, fraud, threat*); lack of willpower; **~richtung** intention; **~theorie** doctrine of real intention; **~übereinstimmung** concurrence of will, agreement, accord, consensus (ad idem); *fehlende ~~: non-agreement, dissent.*

Willenserklärung *f* expression of will, *legally relevant* manifestation of intent, (private) act, act and deed; **~ in öffentlich beglaubigter Form** authenticated act; **amtsempfangsbedürftige ~** act requiring communication to an authority (*or* registry); **ausdrückliche ~** express act of party; **mehrseitige ~en** consensual acts; **einseitige ~** unilateral act (of party); **empfangsbedürftige ~** act requiring communication; **hoheitliche ~** act of state; **mangelnde ~** deficient act; **nicht ernstlich gemeinte ~** jocular expression of intention, jocular act; **rechtsgeschäftliche ~** private act *with intention to create legal relations*, utterance or expression resulting in legal coseequences; **stillschweigende ~** implied act; implied expression of intention; **zweiseitige ~** bilateral act, bilateral transaction.

Willkür *f* arbitrariness; **~akt** arbitrary act; **~herrschaft** arbitrary rule; **~justiz** arbitrary justice, Star-Chamber-justice; **~maßnahmen** arbitrary measures; **~verbot** prohibition of arbitrary decision-making.

willkürlich *adj* arbitrary, wanton.

Windenergie *f* energy gained from the wind.

Windhundverfahren *n* first-come, first-serve method (*of granting subsidies*).

Windprotest *m unsuccessful attempt to have a bill protested due to payee's unknown whereabouts.*

Wirkung

Winkeladvokat *m* pettifogging lawyer, shyster.

Winker direction indicator, blinker.

Winter|bauförderung promotion of building in winter time; **~fahrplan** winter time-table; **~geld** winter compensation money (*to construction workers*); **~pause** lay-off in winter, winter break.

Winzer *m* wine-grower; **~genossenschaft** wine-growers' cooperative.

Winzigkonten *n/pl* petty accounts.

wirken *v/i* to operate; *wirkt für und gegen:* is operative for and against.

wirksam *adj* effective, effectual, operative, valid; **~ gegen** effective as against, effective vis-a-vis; **~ werden** to take effect, to become effective; **ohne weiteres ~** automatically operative.

Wirksamkeit *f* validity, effectiveness, operative effect; **~serklärung** ratification, acknowledgment of validity.

Wirksamwerden *n* the coming into force, entry into force.

Wirkung *f* effect; **~ e-s Vertrages** operation of a contract; **~ gegenüber Dritten** effect as against third parties; **~ kraft Gesetzes** effect by virtue of law, statutory effect; **~ kraft Vertrages** contractual force; **auflösende ~** resolutory effect, dissolving effect; **aufschiebende ~** suspensory *or,* suspensive effect; **befreiende ~** discharging effect; *mit ~r ~: with the effect of a (full) discharge;* **beschränkte ~** limited operation; **bindende ~** binding effect; **deklarative ~** declaratory effect; **dingliche ~** in rem, running with the land; **fortzeugende ~** continuously generative effect; **gesetzliche ~** statutory effect; **illiquidisierende ~** effect in reducing liquidity; **konstituierende ~** constitutive effect; **mit steuerlicher ~** with effect for tax purposes; **mit ~ für und gegen alle** binding on all persons, absolutely effective; **mit ~ vom** with effect from, effective as of; **rechtliche ~** legal effect; **schuldbefreiende ~** debt-discharging effect, acting as a full discharge; **sofortige ~** immediate effect; mit ~*r* ~: *effective immediately, with immediate effect*; **unmittelbare ~** direct effect; *durch ~~ des Gesetzes:* by direct statutory effect; by act and operation of law.

Wirkungs|bereich sphere (*or:* ambit) of operation; **~haftung** direct liability for the effects (*of inadequate function*); **~kreis** purview, province, sphere of activity, sphere of functions; *allseitiger ~~: universal sphere of functions*; *eigener ~~: original competence*; *häuslicher ~~: domestic sphere*; *übertragener ~: delegated sphere of functions*; **w~los** *adj* ineffectual, ineffective, without effect; **~losigkeit** ineffectiveness, inefficacy; **~radius** effective range; **~statut** lex causae, governing law: *the legal system governing the transaction.*

Wirren *pl* disorders, disturbances, trouble, civil commotion, upheaval.

Wirtschaft *f* economy, economic system, trade and industry, business sector; **die gütererzeugende ~** economy consisting of all producers of goods; **einheimische ~** the domestic economy; **exportorientierte ~** the exporting industries; **freie ~** free enterprise (economy), free market economy; **gelenkte ~** state-influenced economy,; **gemischte ~** mixed economy; **gewerbliche ~** trade and industry, trade economy; **heimische ~** domestic economy, indigenous industry; **mittelständische ~** middle-class enterprises; **öffentliche ~** public (sector of the) economy; **staatlich gelenkte ~** governmentally guided economy, semi-controlled economy.

wirtschaften *v/t* to manage, to engage in economic activity.

Wirtschaftler *m* economist.

wirtschaftlich *adj* economic, economically efficient, commercial.

Wirtschaftlichkeit *f* commercial efficiency, profitability, financial management; **~sberechnung** profitability calculation, economic appraisal; **~sprüfung** examination of profitability; **~s- und Umweltschutzuntersuchungen** economic and environmental studies.

Wirtschafts|abkommen treaty of commerce, economic accord, trade and payments agreement; **~ablauf** the economic process; **~ankurbelung** pump priming; **~anpassung** economic adjustment; **~anstieg** growth in economic activity, economic up-turn; **~aufbau** economic reconstruction; **~ausgleich** economic adjustment; **~ausschuß** economic affairs committee, business committee; employees' committee for management (*co-determination*); **~behörde** economic agency; **~beihilfen** grants to trade and industry; **~belange** economic interests, business interests; **~belebung** economic recovery; **~berater** economic advisor; **~bereich** economic field, sector of the economy; *eng verflochtener ~~: a sector integrated into the economy as a whole*; **~besprechungen** trade talks; **~betrieb** business enterprise; *~~ der öffentlichen Hand:* public (*or* government) enterprise; **~beziehungen** economic ties, trade relations; **~bilanz** trade balance; **~block** economic bloc; **~blüte** prosperity; **~boss** tycoon; **~einheit** economic entity, economic unity; **~entwicklung** economic development; **~ergebnis** internal operating results; **~fachzeitschrift** trade magazine, business publication; **~faktor** economic factor; **~fluß** flow of trade; **~förderung** promotion of trade; **~form** economic system (*or* structure); **~forschung** economic research; **~führer** economic lead-

Wirtschaftsabkommen

er; ~**führung** management; *einwandfreie* ~~ *e–s landwirtschaftlichen Betriebes*: good husbandry; ~**gebiet** economic area; ~**geld** household allowance, housekeeping allowance, housekeeping money; ~**genossenschaft** co-operative society, industrial co-operative; ~**geographie** economic geography; ~**geräte** household appliances; ~**geschehen** economic process, economic events, economic activities; ~**geschichte** economic history; ~**gesetz** law in the economic field, economic law; ~**gesetzgebung** economic legislation; ~**gruppe** business group, trade group; ~**gut** → *Wirtschaftsgut*; ~**hilfe** economic aid; ~**indikatoren** economic indicators; ~**interessen** economic interests; ~**jahr** fiscal year, accounting year, financial year; ~**jurist** business lawyer, commercial lawyer; industrial lawyer; ~**kabinett** economic cabinet; ~**kampf** economic struggle (*or* battle); ~**kommission** economic commission; ~**kraft** economic power, economic strength; *eigenständige* ~~: *intrinsic economic strength*; ~**kreise** business circles; business community; ~**kreislauf** economic circulation; ~**krieg** economic warfare (*or* battle), ~**kriminalität** white-collar crime; ~**krise** economic crisis; recession; ~**lage** economic situation, economic conditions; ~**leben** economic life, business life, economic activities; ~**leistung** economic effort, economic achievement; ~**lenkung** regulation of business, steering of economic development; ~**liberalismus** economic liberalism; ~**macht** economic power; ~**minister** economics minister, Minister of Economics (*or* of Economic Affairs); ~**ministerium** ministry of economic affairs; ~**ordnung** economic system; ~**ordnungsrecht** economic regulatory law; ~**plan** economic plan, economic management plan; ~**planung** economic planning; ~**politik** economic policy; *antizyklische* ~~: *anti-cyclical economic policy*; *marktpolitische* ~~: *market policy, policy of the free market economy*; *wachstumsfreundliche* ~~: *growth-promoting economic policy*; ~**politiker** person professionally engaged in economic policy, economic policy-maker; ~**praktiken** economic practices; ~**praxis** economic practice; ~**potential** economic potential; ~**produkt** economic product; ~**programm** economic programme; ~**prozess** economic process; trial in a business case, *pl* commercial litigation; ~**prüfer** chartered accountant; accountant, certified accountant (*GB*), certified public accountant (*US*), (professional) auditor; *unabhängiger neutraler* ~~: *independent auditor*; ~**prüfung** audit; ~**prüfungsgesellschaft** auditing company; firm of auditors, firm of chartered accountants; ~**rat** economic council; ~**raum** economic area, market; *gemeinsamer* ~~: *common market*; ~**recht** business law, commercial law; ~**redakteur** financial editor; ~**sabotage** economic sabotage; ~**sanktionen** economic sanctions; ~**schule** business school; junior business high school; ~**sicherstellungsgesetz** Economic Emergency Act (*D: 3 Oct. 1968*); ~**spion** business spy, industrial spy; ~**spionage** industrial and commercial espionage; ~ **statistik** economic statistics; ~**stockung** economic stagnation; ~**strafgesetz** Economic Offences Act (*D: 3 June 1975*); ~**strafkammer** court division for business offences; ~**strafrecht** penal law concerning business offences; ~**strafsachen** cases involving business offences; ~**tätigkeit** economic activity; ~**streitigkeiten** business disputes; ~**struktur** economic structure; ~**system** economy, economic system; *einheitliches* ~~: *integrated economy*; ~**theorie** economic theory;

Wirtschaftsgut / **Wohl**

~**treibende** businessmen, business circles; ~**trend** economic trend; ~**treuhänder** business trustee; ~**überschuß** economic surplus; ~**- und Haushaltsführung** economic activity and budgets; ~**- und Sozialrat** Economic and Social Council; ~**- und Währungsunion** Economic and Monetary Union; ~**unternehmen** business enterprise; ~ *und Private: the business and private sectors*; ~**verband** trade association; ~**verbrechen** grave economic offence, white-collar crime; ~**vereinigung** trade association; ~**verfassung** economic system, economic order; ~**vergehen** economic offence; ~**verkehr** trade, economic transactions, commerce; ~**verwaltung** economic administration; ~**verwaltungsrecht** adminstrative law concerning trade and industry; ~**volumen** total economic activity; ~**wachstum** economic growth; ~~*sraten: rates of expansion in the economies*; ~**weg** farm road; ~**werbung** business publicity, trade advertizing; ~**wert** economic value; ~**wissenschaft** economics, political economy; ~**wunder** economic miracle; ~**zahlen** economic figures (*or* data); ~**zweig** sector of the economy.

Wirtschaftsgut *n* (*pl* ~*güter,* ~*er*) asset, economic asset, business asset; **geringwertige** ~**er** low-value assets; **kurzlebige** ~**er** non-durable goods; **langlebige** ~**er** durable goods, durables; **nicht buchungsfähige** ~**er** non-ledger assets.

Wissen *n* knowledge; ~ **bestreiten** to deny (*or* disclaim) all knowledge; ~**sgebiet** field of knowledge; **meines** ~**s nicht** not to my knowledge; **mit seinem** ~ **und Willen** with his knowledge and consent; **mit** ~ **und Wollen** volitional, wilfully and knowingly; **nach (meinem)** ~ **und Gewissen** according to my knowledge and belief, to the best of my knowledge and belief; **ohne** ~ **und Willen** without one's knowledge and consent; **praktisches** ~ industrial know-how; **wider besseres** ~ against one's better knowledge; **technisches** ~ technical knowledge, industrial know-how.

wissen *v/t* to know, to be aware of, to realize; to remember; **etw nicht** ~ not to know sth, to be unaware of sth.

Wissenschaft *f* science, the scientific world; ~**sminister** minister of science; ~**srat** (advisory) scientific council; „~**ssteuer**" knowledge tax (*VAT on books etc.*).

wissentlich *adv* knowingly.

Witwen|abfindung widow's compensation; ~**altersgeld** widow's (*social insurance*) retirement pension; ~**beihilfe** (*non-recurrent*) aid to widow (*whose husband was killed by occupational accident*); ~**geld** widow's benefits, widow's pension, widow's allowance; ~**leibgedinge** dower; ~**pflichtteil** widow's compulsory portion; ~**privileg** widow's privilege to continue husband's business; ~**rente** widow's (*social insurance*) pension; ~**- und Waisengeld** compassionate allowance; life insurance benefits to widows and orphans; ~**versicherung** widows' insurance.

Witwerrente *f* widower's (social insurance) pension.

Wochen|abschluß weekly closing of the accounts; ~**arbeitstunden** weekly working hours; ~**arbeitszeit** working week; weekly hours of work; ~**ausweis** weekly return (*bank*); ~**bericht** weekly report, weekly return; ~**beiträge** weekly dues; ~**geld** maternity allowance; ~**hilfe** maternity benefit; ~**karte** weekly (season) ticket; ~**lohn** weekly wage; ~**lohnsteuertabelle** wage-tax table for weekly wages; ~**markt** weekly market; ~**pflegerin** visiting nurse (after childbirth); ~**-Stichtag** weekly return date; ~**tag** weekday; ~**übersicht** weekly review; ~**umsatz** weekly sales; ~**verdienst** weekly earnings.

Wohl *n* welfare, weal; **das öffent-**

909

Wohlbefinden

liche ~ the public good, public welfare.

Wohl|befinden well-being, physical comfort; **w~behalten** *adv* safe and sound; **w~erworben** *adj* duly acquired, established, vested; **~fahrt** → *Wohlfahrt*; **w~geordnet** *adj* ordered; **w~habend** *adj* well off, affluent, wealthy; **~habenheit** wealthy circumstances, prosperity; **~stand** → *Wohlstand*; **~tat** benefit; **~täter** benefactor, donor; **w~tätig** *adj* philanthropic; **~tätigkeit** → *Wohltätigkeit*; **w~überlegt** *adj* well-considered; **w~unterrichtet** *adj* well-informed; **w~verdient** *adj* merited, well-earned; ~ **verhalten** good behaviour; **w~wollend** *adj* benevolent, well-meaning.

Wohlfahrt *f* welfare, public welfare, social welfare; **soziale** ~ social welfare.

Wohlfahrts|einrichtungen social sevices, public welfare institutions, charities; **~pflege** public welfare, charitable activities; *freie* ~~: *private charity*; *voluntary charitable work*; **~staat** welfare state; **~tätigkeit** charitable activity, charity; **~verband** provident society, welfare association.

Wohlstand *m* affluance, wealth, prosperity; **~sgefälle** wealth gap, differential in affluance; **~sgesellschaft** affluent society.

Wohltätigkeit *f* charity.

Wohltätigkeits|anstalt charitable institution; **~aufführung** charity performance; **~fond** charitable fund; **~organisation** charitable institution; *öffentliche* ~~: *public benevolent institution*; **~stiftung** charitable trust; **~verein** charitable society, friendly society; **~verkauf** charity bazaar; **~vorstellung** charity performance; **~zweck** charitable purpose.

Wohlwollenserklärung *f* letter of comfort.

Wohn|anlage apartment building, group of apartment buildings; **~baudarlehen** home construction

Wohnanlage

loan; **~bauprojekt** housebuilding project; **~bausparer** member of a building society; **~bau-Sparvertrag** building savings agreement; **~bedarf** accommodation requirements, furnishings, home requisites; **~berechtigung** residence right, entitlement to accommodation; **~berechtigung** certificate of eligibility for publicly supported (council) accommodation; **~bevölkerung** resident population; **~bezirk** residential district; **~element** item of interior decoration (*or* fitting); **~fläche** floor space, floor area; **~gebäude** residential building; **~gebiet** residential area; **~geld** (public) housing benefit, rent allowance; condominium contributions (*for joint expenses*); w~~*fähig*: *allowable in computing the housing benefit*; **~gemeinde** residential community; **~gemeinschaft** shared house, flat sharing, group of flat mates, common household; ~~*smitglieder*: *flat mates*; **~grundstück** residential plot, residential property; **~haus** residential building, dwelling house, domestic building; **~heim** hostel, lodging house, ~~ *für Nichtseßhafte*: *resettlement unit*; **~lage** residential location; **~möglichkeiten** housing accommodation; **~ort** place of residence, legal residence, place of abode; *derzeitiger* ~~: *current residence*; **~ortwechsel** change of address, change of residence; **~partei** co-occupant of a house, co-tenant; **~raum** → *Wohnraum*; **~recht** right of habitation, right of residence; *dingliches* ~~: *a right of habitation running with the land*; **~schlafzimmer** bed-sit(ter), bed-sitting-room; **~siedlung** residential development, residential cluster, housing estate, *städtische* ~~: *urban housing estate, urbanization*; **~sitz** → *Wohnsitz*; **~ung** → *Wohnung*; **~viertel** residential quarter; **~wagen** caravan; ~~*abstellplatz*: *caravan site*; **~zwecke** residential purposes; domestic purposes; *für ~~ geeignet:* (reasonably) *fit for human habitation; für ~~ ungeeignet: unfit for human habitation; für ~~ unzumutbar: not reasonably fit for human habitation.*

Wohnen *n* living, dwelling, inhabitation, accommodation; **mietfreies** ~ rent-free accommodation.

wohnen *v/i* to dwell, to live, to reside, to be domiciled, to lodge.

wohnhaft *adj* resident, ordinarily resident; *nicht hier ~:* non-resident.

Wohnraum *m* residential space, housing accommodation, domestic premises; **~bewirtschaftung** housing control; **~kündigungsschutz** legal protection of tenant's rights of occupation; **~miete** residentual tenancy; residential rent; **~sanierungsgebiet** slum clearance area, housing action area; district scheduled for rehabilitation; **~versorgung** supply of accommodation; **~zuteilung** allotment of dwellings; **geeigneter** ~ suitable accommodation; **möblierter** ~ furnished accommodation; **preisgebundener** ~ rent-controlled housing; **unmöblierter** ~ unfurnished accommodation; **vermieteter** ~ rented accommodation, lodgings.

Wohnsitz *m* domicile, legal residence, permanent abode, settled abode; ~ **der gewerblichen Niederlassung** commercial domicile; **~erfordernis** residence requirement, residential qualification; **~finanzamt** tax office at one's place of residence; **~gemeinde** the local authority of one's place of residence; ~ **im Rechtssinn** legal domicile; ~ **oder gewöhnlichen Aufenthalt haben in** to be resident in, to reside in; **~staat** state of habitual residence, state of domicile; **~statut** lex domicilii; **~verlegung** transfer of domicile, change of habitual residence; **abgeleiteter** ~ domicile of dependency, derivative domicile; **dienstlicher** ~ official residence; **ehelicher** ~ conjugal domicile, matrimonial residence, the place of the matrimonial home; **e–n ~ begründen** to establish a domicile, to elect a domicile, to establish one's place of habitual residence; **fester** ~ habitual residence, fixed abode, settled abode; **fiktiver** ~ constructive domicile; **gemeinsamer ehelicher** ~ matrimonial domicile; **gesetzlicher** ~ domicile by operation of law; **gewillkürter** ~ elected domicile, domicile of choice; **gewöhnlicher** ~ habitual residence; **mehrfacher** ~ more than one habitual residence; **mit** ~ **in** domiciled, residing at; **ohne festen** ~ without a fixed place of abode, of no fixed abode, of no settled address; **seinen** ~ **in haben** to be habitually resident in, to reside at (*or* in), to be domiciled at; ~~ *im Ausland haben: to be domiciled abroad*; **ständiger** ~ permanent place of, of abode (*or* residence); **steuerlicher** ~ tax home, fiscal domicile, domicile for tax purposes; **ursprünglicher** ~ domicile of origin, natural domicile, domicile by birth; **zweiter** ~ second place of residence.

Wohnung *f* lodging, dwelling, residence, (living) accommodation, place of abode, apartment, flat, residential unit (*esp. pl*); ~ **im Hause des Dienstherren** service occupation, tied cottage; **abgeschlossene** ~ self-contained flat; **bezugsfertige** ~ dwelling ready for occupation; **eheliche** ~ marital home, matrimonial home; **freie** ~ non-controlled accommodation; **frei finanzierte** ~ privately financed dwelling; **leerstehende** ~ idle tenement, vacant dwelling; **mietergeschützte** ~ (statutorily) protected tenancy; **öffentlich geförderte ~en** subsidized accommodation; **schlüsselfertige** ~ dwelling ready for occupation, house ready for immediate occupancy; **steuerbegünstigte ~en** tax-aided accommodation; **unterbelegte ~en** under-occupied dwellings; **werkseigene** ~ company-owned dwelling.

Wohnungs|amt accommodation office, housing department, public housing agency; **~angabe** address, stating one's address; **~anschrift** private address, (residential) address; **~aufsicht** public surveillance of the housing situation; **~sbau** → *Wohnungsbau*; **~bedarf** housing requirements; **~behörden** housing authorities; **~beihilfe** housing grant, rent allowance, rent rebate; **~beschaffungskredit** housing credit; **~besetzung** squatting in houses, unlawful entry and occupation of dwellings; **~bindungsgesetz** Controlled Tenancies Act (*social housing, D: 31. 1. 1974*); **~defizit** housing shortage; **~durchsuchung** search of habitation; **~eigentum** ownership of an apartment, property in a freehold flat, strata estate, strata title; stratum; condominium (*US*); (*separate ownership of individual apartment in multiple-unit building*); **~eigentumsgesetz** Condominium Act; (*D: 15. 3. 1951*); **~eigentümer** owner of a condominium flat (*or* freehold flat); **~eigentümergemeinschaft** commonhold association, condominium association; **~eigentümerversammlung** statutory meeting of condominium owners; **~einbruchsversicherung** home (*or* house) burglary insurance; **~einheit** accommodation unit; **~einrichtung** household furniture and fittings, furniture and fixtures; **~erbbaurecht** heritable lease of a dwelling (*entered in the land title register*); **~erhebung** housing census; **~genossenschaft** cooperative housing society; **~gesellschaft** housing society, real estate company, house-building society; **~grundbuch** condominium register (*as part of the land register*); **~grundstück** residential real estate (*or* property); **~inhaber** occupant of a flat; **~losigkeit** homelessness;

~makler estate agent, real estate broker; **~markt** housing market; *freier ~~: private rental sector*; **~miete** (residential) rent; **~mieter** (residential) tenant, tenant of a flat; **~müll** domestic rubbish, house refuse; **~nachweis** accommodation registry; housing register, lists of available accommodation; **~not** (extreme) housing shortage; **~nutzer** occupant (of a dwelling); **~nutzung** use of housing accommodation; **~räumung** eviction, vacating of a flat (*or* appartment); **~recht** landlord and tenant law; **~suchender** house hunter, person looking for accommodation; **~tausch** exchange of apartments; **~tür** front door; *~geschäfte: transactions at one's door step;* **~- und Siedlungsunternehmen** housing development company, estate company; **~unternehmen** housing company; *gemeinnütziges ~~: non-profit housing enterprise*; **~vermittlung** estate agent, housing agency; **~wechsel** change of residence; **~wert** value for dwelling purposes; **~wesen** housing; **~wirtschaft** housing industry; **~zuschuß** rental allowance; **~zwangswirtschaft** housing control, rent control.

Wohnungsbau *m* dwelling house construction, residential construction, house-building; **~behörden** public housing authorities; **~beihilfe** basic residual subsidy for housing construction; **~darlehen** house-building loan; **~ der öffentlichen Hand** public housing; **~finanzierung** home financing; **~förderung** government aid for residential building; **~genehmigung** housebuilding permit, residential planning permission; **~genossenschaft** housebuilding cooperative; **~gesellschaft** house-building company, house-building association; **~gesetze** housing laws; **~hypothek** mortgage loan for housing; **~konjunktur** housing boom;

Wollbörse

~**kredit** housing credit; ~**kreditanstalten** housing loan institutions; ~**ministerium** Ministry of Housing; ~**politik** housing policy; ~**prämie** housing (*or* house-building) premium ~-**Prämiengesetz** House-Building Premiums Law; (*D: 28. 8. 1974*); ~**programm** residential building programme, house-building programme; ~ **unternehmen** housing company; **freifinanzierter** ~ privately financed housing; **gemeinnütziger** ~ non-profit house-building; **gewerblicher** ~ commercial residential building; **sozialer** ~ low-rent housing, council housing, local authority flats; state-assisted housing schemes, subsidized house-building; **steuerbegünstigter** ~ tax-privileged housing construction.

Wollbörse *f* wool-hall.

Wort *n* word; ~**auslegung** literal construction; ~-**Bild-Zeichen** word-picture mark, combination trade mark of word and symbol (logo); ~**bruch** breaking one's word; ~**entziehung** order to relinquish the floor (*US*); ~**erfindung** invented word; ~**erteilung** recognition (*by the Speaker*); catching the speaker's eye; ~**führer** spokesman; ~ **für Wort** verbatim; **w**~**getreu** *adj* verbatim, word for word, exact, true; ~**klauberei** quibble, verbalism; ~~ **treiben:** *to quibble*; ~**laut** → *Wortlaut*; ~**meldung** request for leave to speak; ~**protokoll** textual protocol, verbatim minutes, verbatim report; ~**verdreher** prevaricator; ~**verdrehung** prevarication, equivocation; ~-**Warenzeichen** = *Wortzeichen qv*; **w**~**wörtlich** *adj* literal; ~**zeichen** word trademark, distinctive word, slogan trade-mark; **ärgerniserregende** ~**e** offensive language; **auf das** ~ **verzichten** to waive one's right to speak; **beleidigende** ~**e** defamatory words, injurious words; **das gegebene** ~ the pledged word; **das letzte** ~ the last word; **das letzte** ~ **haben** to have the last word; to make the final plea; **das** ~ **entziehen** to stop s. o. speaking, to order s. o. to relinquish the floor; **das** ~ **ergreifen** to begin to speak, *US parl*: to take the floor; **das** ~ **erteilen** to allow s. o. to speak, to recognize (*chairman, speaker*), to admit to the floor (*US*); **das** ~ **führen** to lead the discussion; **das** ~ **haben** to be allowed to speak, to have the floor; **durch** ~ **und Tat** by word and deed; **eindeutiges** ~ overt word; **einschränkende** ~**e** words of limitation (*last will*); **erdachtes** ~ invented word; **gegenstandslose** ~**e** vestigial words (*in a statute*); **in** ~**e fassen** to put into words, to formulate, to phrase; **in** ~**en** in words, in letters (*figures on cheques etc*); **jmdm das** ~ **abschneiden** to cut s. o. short; **jmdm das** ~ **überlassen** to yield to, to give way to; **rechtsgestaltende** ~**e** operative words; **sein** ~ **nicht einlösen** to fail to keep one's word; **sich zu** ~ **melden** to ask for leave to speak, to claim the floor (*US*); **unzüchtige** ~**e** obscene words; **vertragsbegründende** ~**e** words of contract.

Wortlaut *m* wording, tenor, text; ~ **von Verträgen** language of treaties; **amtlicher** ~ official text; **authentischer** ~ authentic text; **der englische** ~ **ist maßgebend** the English text prevails; **gegenwärtiger** ~ current text; **genauer** ~ exact text, precise terms, literal text; **gleich welchen** ~**s** however worded; **im vollen** ~ **zitieren** to quote verbatim; **jeder** ~ **ist gleichermaßen verbindlich** both texts are equally authentic; **nach dem** ~ **des Formulars** in accordance with the form; **nach dem** ~ **eines Gesetzes** pursuant to the provisions, according to the wording of an Act; **sich genau an den** ~ **halten** to stick to the text; **ursprünglicher** ~ original wording, original tenor; **verbindlicher** ~

wörtlich

authentic text; **wobei jeder ~ gleichermaßen verbindlich ist** all texts being equally authentic.

wörtlich *adj* verbatim, verbal, literal; *adv* word for word.

Wucher *m* usury, usurious dealings, loan sharking; **~darlehen** usurious loan; **~geschäft** usurious transaction, extortionate credit transaction; **~gewinn** extortionate profit; **~kreditgeschäft** extortionate credit transaction; **~preis** ransom price, exorbitant price; **~vertrag** usurious contract; **~zinsen** usurious interest.

Wucherer *m* usurer.

wucherisch *adj* usurious.

Wuchsaktie *f* growth stock.

Wunde *f* wound; **an seinen ~n sterben** to die from one's injuries; **jmdm e-e ~ beibringen** to inflict a wound on s. o.; **tödliche ~** fatal injury (*or* wound).

Wunsch *m* wish, request; **auf allgemeinen ~** by general request; **auf eigenen ~ ausscheiden** to leave (the service) at one's own request, to retire of one's own accord; **auf ~** upon request; **auf ~ gegen besondere Rechnung** optional (*or* at request) at extra cost; **von dem ~e beseelt** .... desiring ...; **von dem ~e geleitet** moved by the desire; **von dem ~e getrieben** ... actuated (*or* driven) by the desire ...; **w~gemäß** *adv* as (and when) requested.

Würde *f* dignity, distinction; **~ des Gerichts** dignity of the court; **~ des Menschen** dignity of man, human dignity, **e-e ~ verleihen** to bestow an honour (on s. o.); **richterliche ~** the dignity of judgeship.

würdigen *v/t* to appreciate, to assess, to consider, to weigh; to acknowledge, to pay tribute to.

Würdigung *f* appreciation, assessment, valuation, consideration; **~ der Erfindungshöhe** appreciation of the inventive merit; **kritische ~** critical appraisal; **verständige ~** true assessment, reasoned appreciation, sound appraisal.

Wurfkörper *m* projectile, missile.

Wurfsendung *f* direct mail (advertising), house-to-house delivery (of advertising matter).

Würgegriff *m* stranglehold.

würgen *v/t* to choke, to strangle.

Z

Zahl *f* figure, number; **aufschlußreiche ~en** sensitive figures; **rote ~en aufweisen** to be in the red.

Zahl|grenze (payment) zone limit, fare stage limit; **~karte** postal money order; **~kind** *a child for whom a parent receives child benefit*, qualifying child; **~meister** bursar, purser (*ship*); **~stelle** paying agent, disbursing agency, paying office, pay counter, cashier's office; appointed paying agent, domicile (*bill of exchange*); **~stellenwechsel** branch (*or* domiciled) bill; **~tag** pay-day, settling day; *pl also* term days; **~vaterschaft** maintenance obligation for illegitimate child *regardless of actual descent*.

Zähl|bogen tally sheet, census paper; **~kind** *a child to be counted (regardless of entitlement to child benefit)*; **~tag** day of the count.

zahlbar *adj* payable, due; **~ an den Inhaber** payable to bearer; **~ an dessen Order** payable to order; **~ bei Aufforderung** payable on demand; **~ bei Fälligkeit** payable on maturity, cash at maturity; **~ bei Lieferung** payable on delivery; **~ bei Sicht** payable on presentation; **~ bei Vorlage** payable on presentation; **~ machen (in)** to domicile (at) (*bill of exch.*); **~ nach Sicht** payable after sight; **~ ohne Kündigung** payable on demand; **~ zuzüglich Einzugsspesen** payable with collection charges; **in bar ~** payable in cash; **nachträglich ~** payable in arrears; **pränumerando ~** payable in advance; **sofort ~** payable immediately (*or* forthwith), spot cash; **im voraus ~** payable in advance.

Zahlbarkeit *f* payability.

Zahlbarstellung *f* domiciliation (*bill of exchange*).

zahlen *v/t*, *v/i* to pay, to make payment; **~ Sie an mich** pay self (*cheque*); **bar ~** to pay cash; **im voraus ~** to pay in advance; **in Raten ~** to pay by instalments; **schwarz ~** to pay under the table.

Zahlen|aufstellung numerical statement; **~folge** numerical order, numerical sequence; **~lotto** numbers game, lottery; **z~mäßig** *adj* numerical; **~stempel** numbers stamp; **~verdrehung** transposition; **~werk** set of figures, computation; **~wert** numerical value.

Zahler *m* payer; **pünktlicher ~** prompt payer; **säumiger ~** slow payer, defaulter; **schlechter ~** slow payer, defaulter.

Zähler *m* meter (*electricity, gas, water*); teller, counter (*person*); **~stand** meter reading.

Zahlung *f* payment (= *p*, *pl*: *p–s*); **~ anmahnen** to press for *p*, to dun for *p*; **~ auf dem Postwege** remittance by post; **~ bei Fälligkeit** *p* when due; **~ bei Kaufabschluß** *p* on completion of purchase; **~ bei Lieferung** *p* on delivery; **~ bei Vorlage des Wechsels** *p* on demand, *p* on presentation of the bill; **~ binnen 7 Tagen nach Rechnungsdatum** *p* within 7 days of invoice date (= *prompt cash*); **~ durch Dauerüberweisung** *p* by automatic bill paying order; **~ durch Einzugsermächtigung** *p* by direct debit; **~en einstellen** to stop *p–s*; **~en entgegennehmen** to receive *p–s*, to accept *p–s*; **~en im Bankverkehr** interbank *p–s*; **~en im Kapitalsektor** *p–s* on capital account; **~en im Kapitalverkehr** financial *p–s*; **~ gegen Dokumente** cash against documents; documents against *p*; **~ in Gold** specie *p*; **~ leisten** to make *p*, to effect (a) *p*; **~ nach Leistungsabschnitten** progress payments; ~ **ohne Bestimmung der Anrechnung** indefinite *p*; ~ **unter Protest** *p* supra protest; ~ **unter Vorbehalt** *p* under reserve; ~ **vor Fälligkeit** *p* before maturity; ~ **Zug-um-Zug** *p* on contemporaneous performance; back-to-back *p, p* pari passu, ~**en zum Parikurs** parity *p–s*; **anteilige** ~ pro rata *p*; **an** ~**s statt** in lieu of *p*; in place of *p*; ~~~ *hingeben: to give in payment*; **auf** ~ **klagen** to sue for *p*, to sue for the recovery of money; **aufgeschobene** ~ deferred *p*; **bargeldlose** ~ cashless *p*; **die** ~**en aussetzen** to suspend *p–s*; **die** ~**en einstellen** to stop *p–s*, to suspend *p–s*; **die** ~ **stunden** to allow a deferral in *p*; **e-e** ~ **entgegennehmen** to accept *p*; **e-e** ~ **leisten** to make a *p*; **eingegangene** ~ *p* received; **einmalige** ~ a one off *p*, non-recurring *p*; **erste** ~ initial *p*; **fällige** ~ due *p*; **freiwillige** ~ voluntary *p*; **gegen** ~ **von** on *p* of; **gestundete** ~ deferred *p*; **glatte** ~ clean *p*; **in** ~ **nehmen** to take in *p*, to receive in *p*; **irrtümliche** ~ *p* by mistake; **jmdn zur** ~ **drängen** to push s. o. for *p*, to press for *p*; **laufende** ~**en** current *p–s*; **liquiditätsneutrale** ~**en** *p–s* which are neutral in their effect on liquidity; **mangels** ~ for want of *p*, in default of *p*, failing *p*, for non-*p*; ~~ *protestiert: protested for non-payment*; **massierte** ~**en** a block of *p–s*; **multilaterale** ~**en** multilateral *p–s*; **nachträgliche** ~ *p* in arrears, subsequent *p*; **ordnungsgemäße** ~ proper *p*; **prompte** ~ prompt *p*; **regelmäßige** ~**en** periodical *p–s*, regular *p–s*; **regelmäßig wiederkehrende** ~**en** periodical *p–s*, periodically recurring *p–s*; **rückständige** ~ overdue *p*, outstanding *p*; **sofortige** ~ immediate *p*; **sofortige** ~ **bei Lieferung** spot cash; **symbolische** ~ token *p*; **teilweise** ~ partial *p*; **terminbedingte** ~**en** *p–s* owed on fixed dates; **verspätete** ~ late *p*; **vergleichsweise** ~ **e-r Abfindung** settlement in a lump sum; **vorbehaltslose** ~ direct *p*, unconditional *p*; **wiederkehrende** ~**en** periodical *p–s*; **zeitlich gestaffelte** ~ *p* by instalments; **zur** ~ **auffordern** to demand *p*, to call for *p*; **zur** ~ **herangezogen werden** to be called upon to pay; **zur** ~ **mahnen** to dun for *p*, to demand *p* immediately; **zusammengezogene** ~**en** block *p–s*.

Zahlungs|abkommen payments (= *p–s*) agreement; ~**abschnitt** stub, counterfoil; ~**abwicklung** handling of payments; ~**adresse** address for payment (= *p*), domicile of a bill; ~**anerbieten** tender of *p*; ~**angebot** tender of *p*; ~**anordnung** order for *p*; ~**anspruch** pecuniary claim, liquidated demand; ~**antrag** application for *p*; ~**anweisung** order for *p* (of money), postal payment order, order to pay, instruction to pay; *keine* ~~: *no instruction to pay*; ~**anzeige** advice of payment received; ~**aufforderung** request (*or* demand) for *p*, notice to pay; ~**aufschub** deferral of *p*, moratorium, debt deferral; ~**gewähren**: *to grant a respite*; ~**auftrag** instructions to pay, order for *p, p, order*; *internationaler* ~~: *international money order*; ~**ausgänge** outgoing *p–s*, cash disbursements; ~**bedingungen** terms of *p*; ~~~, *die Barzahlung vorschreiben: cash terms*; ~**befehl** *now*: *Mahnbescheid qv*; ~**beleg** voucher (for *p*); ~**berechtigter** payee, party entitled to *p*; ~**bereitschaft** willingness to pay; ~**bestätigung** confirmation of *p*; ~**bilanz** → *Zahlungsbilanz*; ~**eingänge** *p–s* received, incomings; ~**einstellung** cessation of *p–s*, default in *p*, suspension of *p–s*, stoppage in *p–s*; ~**empfänger** recipient of *p*, payee; **z~empfangsberechtigt** *adj* entitled to receive *p*; ~**erleichterungen** easy terms, *p* facilities, relief from payment obligation; ~**ermächtigung** authority to make *p–s,* payment appropriation;

z~fähig *adj* solvent; ~fähigkeit solvency, capacity to pay; ~freigrenze free quota *(foreign exchange)*; ~frist *p* deadline, time for *p*, term of *p*; *letzte* ~~ *final respite; übliche* ~~*en: conventional terms*; ~gewohnheiten customary terms of *p*; z~halber *adv* in *p* *(pending full discharge of the debt)*; ~klage action for the recovery of money; ~klausel *p* clause; z~kräftig *adj* financially sound; ~kredit time allowed for *p*, credit term; ~mittel means of *p*, instrument(s) of *p*; ~~*umlauf: notes and coin in circulation; money supply; ausländische* ~~: *foreign currencies; gesetzliches* ~~: *legal tender, lawful currency*; ~modalitäten terms of *p*; ~moral payment behavior; ~moratorium moratorium; ~nachweis proof of *p*; evidence of *p*; ~ort place of *p*, domicile *(bill of exchange)*; ~pflicht obligation to pay, monetary obligation; z~pflichtig *adj* liable to pay, committed to pay; ~pflichtiger debtor, payer, party liable to pay; ~rangfolge order for payment *(bankruptcy)*; ~rückstand outstanding *p*, delay in *p*; *pl also:* arrears; ~schuldner debtor; ~schwierigkeiten financial difficulties; ~sperre blocking, stoppage for *p*, stop *p*; ~stockung temporary delay of *p–s*; ~system *p–s* system; ~tag day of *p*, payday, settlement day; *account day (stock exchange: 4th day after the order); maßgebender* ~~: *relevant date of p (date to be considered as the date on which p is made)*; ~termin time (fixed) for *p*; time of *p*; *mittlerer* ~~: *average due date*; ~überschuß surplus; ~überweisung money order, bank transfer; z~unfähig unable to pay, insolvent; in failing circumstances; ~unfähiger insolvent, „can't pay"; ~unfähigkeit insolvency, inability to pay due debts; *amtsbekannte* ~~: *notorious insolvency*; ~unwilligkeit unwillingness to pay; ~urteil money judgment; ~verbindlichkeit financial obligation; ~verbot freezing of *p–s*; prohibition to make *p–s*; ~~ *an Drittschuldner: garnishment, garnishee order*; ~vereinbarung *p–s* agreement; ~verhalten *p* behaviour; ~verkehr money transfers, *p–s, p* transactions; *allgemeiner* ~~: *general p–s (system); bargeldloser* ~~: *cashless money transfer, non-cash transactions, cashless p–s; freier* ~~: *free foreign exchange; gebundener* ~~ *payments through clearing channels*; ~verpflichtung financial obligation; *die* ~~*en einhalten: to meet the p–s; seinen* ~~*en nachkommen: to meet one's p–s; to keep up one's p–s*; ~versäumnis failure to pay; ~versprechen promise to pay, undertaking to pay; ~verweigerung refusal to pay, repudiation of a debt; dishonour by non-payment; ~verzögerung delay in *p*; ~verzug default in *p*, (undue) delay in *p*; ~ vor Fälligkeit payment before maturity; ~weise mode of *p*; ~wille willingness to pay; ~zeit time for *p*; ~ziel time allowed for *p*, period for payment; *offenes* ~~: *open terms*; ~zusage undertaking to pay.

Zahlungsbilanz *f* balance of payments; ~defizit external deficit; ~gleichgewicht balance of payments equilibrium; ~krise crisis in the balance of payments; ~politik balance of payments policy; ~schwankung fluctuation in the balance of payments; ~spielraum scope for fluctuations in the balance of payments; ~überschuß external surplus, balance of payments surplus; **ausgeglichene** ~ exchange equilibrium; **globale** ~ overall balance of payments; **kranke** ~ unsound balance of payments; **unausgeglichene** ~ imbalance in payments, disequilibrium in the balance of payments.

zänkisch *adj* querulous.

Zauderpolitik *f* Fabian policy, attentisme, a policy of "wait-and-see".

Zebrastreifen *m* zebra crossing, safety zone, pedestrian crossing.

Zech|anschlußraub pilfering a (drunken) guest (*at a bar or restaurant*), robbing a drunk; **~prellerei** absconding without paying for one's meal.

Zeche *f* (1) (coal) mining company; **~nstillegung** pit closure.

Zeche *f* (2) restaurant bill; **seine eigene ~ zahlen** to pay one's own bill; *jeder zahlt seine eigene ~: let's have a Dutch treat (vs)*.

Zedent *m* assignor, transferor of a right (*or* claim), ceding company.

zedieren *v/t* to assign (*a right, claim*), to transfer, to cede.

Zehnerclub The Group of Ten.

Zehnt *m* tithes; **~ablösung** commutation of tithes; **~berechtigter** occupier of tithes.

Zehr|geld food allowance; **~kosten** food expenses (*messenger etc.*).

Zeichen *n* sign, token; trade mark; **~fähigkeit** qualification as a trade mark; **~geld** representative money, money tokens; token money; **~inhaber** = *Warenzeicheninhaber qv*; **~mißbrauch** misuse of a trade mark; **~rolle** Trade Mark Register; **~schutz** trade-mark protection; **~übereinstimmung** trademark identity; **~ und Weisungen** instructions (*traffic*); **mit ~ und Nummern versehen** marked and numbered; **notorisches ~** → *Warenzeichen*; **unterscheidungsfähiges ~** distinctive mark.

zeichnen *v/t* to draw; to sign; to subscribe; **per procura ~** to sign by procuration.

Zeichner *m* (1) draftsman, graphic artist.

Zeichner *m* (2) subscriber, original subscriber.

Zeichnung *f* (1) drawing, diagram; **~sblatt** sheet of drawings; **graphische ~** graph; **technische ~** technical drawing; **verspätet eingereichte ~en** late-filed drawings.

Zeichnung *f* (2) subscription; signature, signing; **~ von Aktien** subscription to shares; **~ von Kapitalanteilen** capital stock subscription; **freie ~** public subscription; **öffentliche ~** public issue; **zur ~ auflegen** to invite subscriptions, to offer for subscription.

Zeichnungs|angebot subscription offer; **~aufforderung** invitation to make subscriptions; **~bedingungen** terms of subscription; **~befugnis** authority to sign; **z~berechtigt** *adj* authorized to sign; **~berechtigung** authority to sign for (*the firm, the public agency etc*); **~bescheinigung** application receipt; **~betrag** amount subscribed; **~bevollmächtigter** duly authorized signatory; **~einladung** invitation to prospective subscribers; **~frist** subscription period; **~grenze** underwriting limit; **~kurs** issue price, rate for subscriptions; **~liste** subscription list, list of subscribers; **~preis** issue price; **~prospekt** underwriting prospectus; **~recht** authority to sign (*for the firm etc*); **~schein** subscription form, subscription order blank, subscription certificate.

Zeit *f* time; **~ablauf** lapse of time, passage of time, expiration of a period; *durch ~~ beendet: determined by lapse of time*; **~abschnitt** period; *erster ~~: initial period; in regelmäßigen ~~en: at stated times, periodically*; **~angabe** exact time, date; **~anteilig** by time quota; **~arbeit** temporary employment, time-work, **~~leisten**: *to temp*; **~~sfirma**: *temporary employment agency*; **~akkord** time piecework system; **~arbeiter** temporary worker; **~aufwand** time involved, time (spent on something); **~berechnung** calculation of time, computation of a period; **~beschränkung** time limit; **~bestimmung** stipulation as to time, dating; **~charter** time charter, catch time charter; **~dauer** time, time spent, duration; **~ der Zustellung** time of service; **~folge** sequence of dates, timetable; **~fracht** time freight; **~frachtvertrag** time charter;

Zeitungsabonnement   **Zentralagentur**

~gebühr time charge; z~gemäß *adj* timely; up to date; z~gerecht *adj* timely, in due time; ~geschäft time bargain, forward deal, futures transaction; ~geschichte contemporary history; ~gesetz temporary law; ~karte season ticket; ~kostenkalkulation time costing; z~lebens *adj* for life; ~lohn time rate, time wages; ~~sätze: *time rates*; ~not time constraints, lack of time; *in* ~~ *sein: to be pressed for time*; ~pacht fixed-term lease; ~personalvermittlung temporary job placement agency, temping office; ~plan time-table; ~punkt point (*or* moment) in time, moment, date; ~~ *der Inbetriebnahme: in service date; der maßgebliche* ~~: *the material time; der entscheidungserhebliche* ~~: *the material time; zum gegenwärtigen* ~~: *now; zum jeweiligen* ~~: *for the time being, at the respective time*; ~raum period of time; *festgesetzter* ~~: *fixed period*; ~rechnung chronology, calendar time, era; ~rente terminable annuity, annuity (*or* disability pension) for a certain period; ~soldat serviceman on a fixed term; ~stempel automatic time stamp; ~strafe (punishment by) a term of imprisonment; ~studie work study; ~stufen time-scales; ~- und Bewegungsstudie time and motion study; ~verlust loss of time; ~~~*entschädigung: compensation for loss of time*; ~versäumnis loss of time, delay; ~versicherungspolice time policy; ~vertrag fixed term contract; ~wechsel time draft; ~wert present (usable) value, current value; ~wertentschädigung compensation at current value; ~ zu gewinnen suchen to temporize; auf unbegrenzte ~ for an unlimited period, in perpetuity; auf unbestimmte ~ for an indefinite period, sine die; ~~~ *vertagen: to adjourn sine die*; auf ~ temporary; die ~ zwischen den Jahren limbo period; e~e angemessene ~ vorher a reasonable time beforehand; einrechnungsfähige ~ time during which conception could occur; festgesetzte ~ time allowed, fixed period; gerichtsfreie ~en court vacations; nicht ausgenutzte ~ dead time, unused time; tote ~ dead time; unvordenkliche ~ time immemorial; verstreichende ~ time elapsing; zu bestimmter ~ at a given time, at a fixed time; zu gegebener ~ in due course; zur festgesetzten ~ at the fixed time; zur gehörigen ~ in due time; zur rechten ~ in due time; zur ~ for the time being, at present, currently, at the moment.

Zeitungs|abonnement subscription to a newspaper: ~ausschnittdienst, clipping service; ~beilage insert, supplement; ~bunde newspaper (*for posted service*), wrappings (*or* packages); ~krieg newspaper war; ~post second-class mail; ~reklame newspaper advertisement; ~verleger newspaper publisher; ~werbung newspaper advertizing.

Zellenhaft *f* confinement to a prison cell.

zensieren *v/t* to censure, to expurgate.

Zensor *m* censor, expurgator.

Zensur *f* censorship; ~behörde censor's office; ~verbot (*constitutional*) prohibition of censorship (*of the press*); ~vorschriften censor's regulations; von der ~ freigegeben passed by censor.

Zentral|agentur central agency; ~amt central office; ~~ *für den internationalen Eisenbahnverkehr:* Central Office for International Railway Transport; ~bank → *Zentralbank*; ~behörde central office; national agency; ~~ *für den gewerblichen Rechtsschutz:* Central Industrial Property Office; ~büro executive office; ~einkauf centralized purchasing; ~kartei central card index; ~kasse central credit institution; ~kommission central commission; ~~ *für die Rheinschiffahrt:* Central Com-

Zentralbank   **Zeuge**

mission for the Navigation on the Rhine; ~**organ** official party organ; ~**regierung** central government; ~**register** central penal register; ~**staat** unitary state; ~**stelle** central office; ~~ *für Arbeitsvermittlung Central Office for Inter-regional Job Placements*; ~~ *für die Vergabe von Studienplätzen: Central Office for the Allocation of Places in High Education*; ~**verband** national union, central association.

Zentralbank *f* Central Bank; ~**diskont** (Central Bank) discount rate; ~~-**Diskontierung** discounting by Central Bank; ~**fähig** acceptable to monetary authority, eligible for discounting by the Central Bank; ~**kredit** Central Bank credit; ~**rat** Central Bank Council; ~**rediskontierung** rediscounting by central banks.

zerlegen *v/t* to dismantle, to disassemble, to break down (into components); *teilweise zerlegt: semi-knocked-down* (*SKD*); *vollständig zerlegt: completely-knocked-down* (*CKD*).

Zerlegung *f* dismantlement, disassembly, apportioning of trade tax standard (*among several local authorities*); reallocation.

Zermürbungs|**politik** policy of attrition; ~**krieg** war of attrition.

Zero-Bonds *m/pl* zero coupon bonds.

zerreden *v/t* to talk s.th. to death .

Zerreißprobe *f* tensile test; gruelling test.

Zerrüttung *f* disintegration, breakdown (of marriage), disruption; ~ **der Ehe** → *Ehezerrüttung*; ~**sprinzip** principle of entitlement to divorce in case of irretrievable breakdown of the marriage.

Zersetzung *f* subversion, disintegration, decay; **verfassungsverräterische** ~ treasonable subversion against the constitution; **verräterische** ~ **der Bundeswehr** treasonable subversion of the Federal Armed Forces.

Zersiedlung *f* over-fragmentation,

ribbon development, urban sprawl, overflow of the towns into the countryside, unplanned settlement in the open country.

Zerstörung *f* destruction, devastation, demolition; ~ **fremder Sachen** destroying things belonging to another person; ~ **gepfändeter Sachen** destroying things which have been attached; ~**swut** vandalism, impulse to destroy; ~ **von Bauwerken** destruction of building structures.

zerstückeln *v/t* to dismember, to disintegrate, to fragment.

Zerstückelung *f* fragmentation.

Zertifikat *n* certificate; ~**inhaber** unit-holder, certificate holder.

Zession *f* assignment (of debts), transfer (*of a right, claim*); ~**skredit** assignment credit; ~**surkunde** instrument of assignment; ~**sverbot** convenant against assignment; **offene** ~ disclosed assignment; **stille** ~ undisclosed assignment.

Zessionar *m* assignee (*pl: assigns*), transferee, cessionary; ~**schuldner** assigned debtor, debtor of the assignment; **nur als** ~ without recourse (*bill of exchange*).

Zeter und Mordio *hist* hue and cry.

Zeugamt *n* arsenal, ordnance depot.

Zeuge *m* witness (= *w*; *pl*: *witnesses* = *w-s*); ~ **bei der Unterschriftsleistung** attesting *w*; ~ **der Anklage** *w* for the prosecution; ~ **vom Hörensagen** hearsay witness; ~ **mit Aussageverweigerungsrecht** privileged *w*; **abgelehnter** ~ *w* rejected by a party; **als** ~ **aussagen** to testify; **als** ~ **beeidigt** sworn in as a *w*; **als Polizeispitzel aussagender** ~ supergrass testifying police informer; **als** ~ **wahrnehmen** to witness; **auf e-n** ~**n einwirken** to influence a *w*; **ausbleibender** ~ *w* who fails to appear; **aussagepflichtiger** ~ compellable *w*; **beeidigter** ~ sworn *w*; **die** ~**n anhören** to hear the evidence; **eigener** ~ friendly *w*; **e-m** ~**n gegenübergestellt werden** to be

920

Zeugenablehnung **Zeugnis**

confronted with a *w*; **e-m ~n Glauben schenken** to believe a *w*; **e-n ~n auf die Probe stellen** to try to impeach a *w*; **e-n ~n aufrufen** to call a *w* (into the witness box); **e-n ~n beeiden** to swear in a *w*, to swear a *w* (in); **e-n ~n beeinflussen** to influence a *w*, to dissuade a *w*, to tamper with a *w*; **e-n ~n benennen** to offer a *w* (*giving his name and address to the court*), to nominate a *w*; **e-n ~n erneut vernehmen lassen** to recall a *w*; **e-n ~n hören** to hear (the evidence of) a *w*; **e-n ~n ins Kreuzverhör nehmen** to cross-examine a *w*; **e-n ~n kommissarisch vernehmen** to examine a witness on commission (*letters rogatory*); **e-n ~n laden** to summon a *w*; **e-n ~ stellen** to produce a *w*; **e-n ~n unbeeidigt lassen** to leave a *w* unsworn; **e-n ~n verhören** to interrogate a *w*; **e-n ~n vernehmen** to examine a *w*, to question a *w*; **e-n ~n zur Wahrheit ermahnen** to admonish a *w* to speak the truth; **feindlicher ~** hostile (*or* adverse) *w*; **freimütiger ~** plain-spoken *w*, a frank *w*; **geeigneter ~** competent *w*; suitable *w*; **geladener ~** a *w* who has been summoned; **gewöhnlicher ~** non-expert *w*; **glaubwürdiger ~** reliable *w*, credible *w*; **meineidiger ~** forsworn *w*; **neutraler ~** neutral *w*; disinterested *w*; **sachverständiger ~** expert *w*, skilled *w*; scientific *w*; **spontan erscheinender ~** voluntary *w*, volunteer *w*; **übereifriger ~** swift *w*, zealous *w*; **unbeeidigter ~** unsworn *w*; **unbeteiligter ~** disinterested *w*; **unentschuldigt ausgebliebener ~** an absent *w* without excuse, contumacious *w*; **verläßlicher ~** reliable *w*, unimpeachable *w*; **von der Verteidigung benannter ~** *w* for the defence; **widersetzlicher ~** unwilling *w*, contumacious *w*; **widerspenstiger ~** unwilling *w*; **zulässiger ~** competent *w*.

Zeugen|ablehnung objection to a *w*; **~aufruf** calling the *w-s*; **~aussage** (oral) testimony, statement by a *w*; *pl also*: oral testimony; *eidliche ~~*: testimony under oath; *gegenbeweisliche ~~*: rebuttal testimony; *schriftliche ~~*: deposition; *uneidliche ~~*: unsworn statement of a *w*; *widersprechende ~~n*: conflicting testimonies; **~beeidigung** swearing in of a *w*, administering the oath to a *w*; **~beeinflussung** tampering with *w-s*; bringing influence to bear on *w-s*; **~befragung** examination of a *w*; **~benennung** giving name and address of an offered *w*; **~bestechung** bribing of *w-s*; **~beweis** testimonial evidence, evidence of *w-s*, proof by *w-s*; **~eid** witness' oath; oath sworn by a *w*; **~einvernahme** examination of *w-s*; **~entschädigung** compensation to *w-s* (*for expenses, time*); conduct money; **~formel** attestation clause (*acknowledgement*); **~gebühren** compensation for *w-s*; **~indemnität** privilege of witness; **~ladung** *w* warrant, summoning of a *w*, summons of a *w*; subpoena of *w*, subpoena ad testificandum; **~manipulation** interference with *w-s*; manipulation of *w-s*; **~nötigung** intimidation of *w-s*; **~protokoll** transcript of the oral evidence; **~stand** *w* box, (*w*) stand; **~testament** ordinary will (before attesting *w-s*); *mündliches ~~*: oral will; **~vereidigung** swearing in of *w*; **~vermerk** attestation; **~vernehmung** examination of *w-s*, viva voce examination of *w-s*; *~~ durch beauftragten Richter*: taking evidence on commission; **~vorschuß** advance payment into court of compensation for *w-s* (*or* of conduct money for w-s).

Zeugnis *n* certificate, testimony, testimonial, credentials; school report; **~fähigkeit** competency of a witness; **~pflicht** duty to testify; **z~unfähig** *adj* incapable of being a witness, unable to testify; **~unfähigkeit** incapacity to testify; **~verweigerung** refusal to give evidence; **~verweigerungsrecht** the right to refuse to give evidence, privilege of witnesses (*to decline to answer questions*); *auf sein* ~~ *verzichten: to waive one's privilege*; **~zwang** enforcement of duty to testify; **ärztliches** ~ medical certificate.

Zeugung *f* procreation, generation; **~sakt** progenitive act; **~sfähigkeit** procreative capacity; **~sunfähigkeit** impotence.

Zickzack|fahren zigzagging; **~kurs** zigzag course; *politischer* ~~: *zigzag policy, seesaw policy*.

Ziehschein *m* certificate of seaman's wages.

Ziehung *f* drawing; redemption of bonds by lot; **~sermächtigung** drawing authorization; **~sliste** drawing list (*of lottery*); **~srecht** drawing right(s).

Ziel *n* time for payment, credit; operational target; **~bestimmung** target provision, objective; **~gesellschaft** target company (*takeover bid*); **~gruppe** target population; **~kauf** purchase on deferred payment terms; **~konflikt** conflicting goals; conflict of objective; **~land** country of destination; **~ort** place of destination; **~tratte** term draft; *auf* ~ *kaufen* to buy on terms, to buy on credit; **offene ~e** open-account terms.

Ziffer *f* number; sub-item, sub-clause (*in contracts*), subparagraph, subsection (*in enactments, schedules*).

Zimmerherr *m* lodger.

Zimmermiete *f* letting of furnished rooms; rent for a furnished room.

Zins *m* (*pl Zinsen* = **~en**) interest (= *int*); **~abbau** general reduction of *int* rates; **~abgrenzung** limitation of *int* by phases; *antizipative* ~~: *deferred interest*; **~abschlagssteuer** interest tax deducted at source (at a flat-rate); **~abzug** *int* deduction; **~anpassung** adjustment of *int* rates; **~anspruch** *int* claim; **~arbitragegeschäfte** interest-rate arbitrage dealings; **~aufstellung** *int* statement; **~auftrieb** upsurge in *int* rates; **~aufwand** *int* expense; **~aufwendungen** *int* payments; **~ausstattung** rate of *int* of a loan; **~bedingungen** terms of *int*; **~befestigung** hardening of *int* rates; **~beihilfe** aid to alleviate *int* burden; **~beleg** *int* voucher; **~berechnung** calculation of *int*; **~berechnungsklausel** *int* calculation formula (*or* stipulation); **~berichtigung** adjustment of *int* rates; **~bestandteil** *int* component; **~bindung** linking the *int* rate (to) fixed *int* period; **~bogen** talon *int* sheet; **~bogensteuer** talon tax; **~bonus** *int* premium; **~degression** *int* rate decline; **~differenz** spread; **~divisor** *int* divisor; **~en berechnen** to charge *int*; *~en dürfen nicht berechnet werden*: *no interest shall be chargeable*; **~en bringen** to bear *int*; **~endienst** *int* service; **~en tragen** to bear *int*; **z~entragend** *adj* *int*-bearing; **~en von der Hauptsache** *int* on principal; **~ersparnis** saving of *int*; *volkswirtschaftliche* ~~: *overall saving of int*; **~erträge** income from *int*; *transitorische* ~~: *unearned int*; **~eszinsen** compound *int*, *int* on the *int*; **~forderung** claim for *int*, *int* receivable; **z~frei** *adj* free of *int*; **~en für Fremdkapital** loan *int*; **~fuß** rate of *int*, *int* rate; *gesetzlicher* ~~: *legal* (*interest*) *rate*; *üblicher* ~~: *standard int*; *übermäßiger* ~~: *excessive int rate*; *vereinbarter* ~~: *agreed int rate*; **~garantie** guaranteed *int*; **~gefälle** *int* differential; **~gefüge** structure of *int* rates; **~gleitklausel** sliding rate of *int* clause, *int* escalator clause; **~gutschrift** credit entry for accrued *int*; **~hypothek** *int*-bearing mortgage; **~klausel** provision concerning *int*; **~kupon** *int* coupon, *int* warrant; **~last** *int* burden; **z~los** *adj* without *int*, non-interest-bearing; **~marge** *int* margin, spread; **~rechnung** interest statement, computation of *int*; **~relationen** relative levels of *int*; **~rückstände** arrears on *int*; **~satz** rate of *int*, *int* rate; ~~ *für Auslei-*

hungen: lending rates; ~*sätze für Wohnbaudarlehen: home loan rates;* ~*sätze für kurzfristige Einlagen: short-term interest rates;* derzeitiger ~~: *current (or: going) rate of interest;* reagible ~*sätze: sensitive rates of interest;* ~**schaden** loss of interest receipts *due to default or breach;* ~**schein** *int* coupon; *int* warrant, *int* ticket; ~**schwankungen** fluctuations in *int* rates; ~**senkung** reduction of the *int* rate; ~~ *im Passivgeschäft: reduction of interest rates paid for borrowings;* ~**spanne** interest margin; *margin between the rates of interest earned and those paid;* ~**spiegel** interest-rate level; ~**stufe** *int* band; ~**tabelle** table of *int, int* table; ~**termin** *int* payment date; **z~tragend** *adj int* bearing; ~**umwandlung** conversion of *int (into capital);* **z~verbilligt** benefitting from subsidized *int;* **z~variabel** at a changeable *int* rate; ~**verbindlichkeiten** *int* obligations, *int* payable; ~**vereinbarung** agreement concerning *int;* **z~vergünstigt** at reduced *int* rates, at subsidized *int* rates; ~**vergütung** *int* credited, allowance for *int;* ~**vermerk** statement concerning *int;* ~**verzicht** waiver of *int;* ~**waldungen** forest under tenure; ~**wucher** usury; ~**zahl** *multiplication of capital by number of days divided by 100,* interest product; ~**zahlung** *int* payment; **anfallende** ~**en** accruing *int;* **aufgelaufene** ~**en** accrued *int;* **auflaufende noch nicht fällige** ~**en** accruing *int;* **die** ~**en kapitalisieren** to include accrued *int* in the capital sum; **ex** ~**en** without *int;* **fällige** ~**en** *int* payable; **feste** ~**en** fixed *int;* **fundierte** ~**en** consolidated *int;* **gegen** ~**en ausleihen** to lend on *int;* **gesetzliche** ~**en** statutory *int;* **gesetzlich zulässiger** ~ legal *int;* **gestaffelte** ~**en** graduated *int;* **gestundete** ~**en** *int* with additional time allowed for payment; **gewöhnliche** ~**en** simple *int,* ordinary *int (not compound int);* **kal-** **kulatorische** ~ *int* computed in advance, imputed *int;* **laufende** ~**en** current *int;* **marktgerechte** ~**en** *int* rates in line with the capital market; **marktkonforme** ~**en** = *marktgerechte* ~ *qv;* **mit** ~**en zurückzahlen** to return with *int;* **ohne demnächst fällige** ~**en** ex *int;* **ohne** ~**en** ex *int;* **plus** ~**en** with *int;* **reine** ~**en** true *int;* **rückständige** ~**en** outstanding *int;* **steuerfreie** ~**en** tax-free *int;* **transitorische** ~ deferred *int,* transferred *int;* **vereinbarte** ~**en** contract *int,* agreed *int;* **vertragliche** ~**en** contractually agreed *int;* **zeitanteilige** ~ pro rata *int;* broken-period *int;* **zugerechnete** ~**en** imputed *int.*

Zirkular|kreditbrief circular letter of credit; ~**note** circular letter.

Zirkaauftrag *m* near order, approximate limit order.

Zitierweise *f* method of citation.

Zitterpartie *f (elections)* cliff-hanger.

Zivil|behörden civil authorities; ~**bevölkerung** civilian population; ~**blinde** *persons who are blind due to non-military causes,* blind civilians; ~**dienst** non-military service by conscientious objectors; ~**dienstverpflichteter** conscientious objector undergoing civilian service; ~**ehe** civil marriage, registry-office marriage; ~**fahnder** plain-clothes detective; ~**gericht** civil court; ~**gerichtsbarkeit** civil jurisdiction; ~**gesetzgebung** civil legislation; ~**haft** custody for non-criminal reasons; ~**internierter** civilian detainee; ~**kammer** civil division, civil chamber, civil court of a Landgericht; ~**klage** civil action, civil suit, civil case; ~**kleidung** civilian clothes, plain clothes; ~**komputation** statutory rules as to computation of periods; ~**liste** civil list; ~**mäkler** real estate broker *(or* agent*);* ~**prozeß** civil proceedings, civil case, law suit, civil trial; civil procedure; ~**prozeßordnung** code of civil procedure; ~**prozeßrecht** law *(or* rules*)* of civil procedure; ~**recht**

Zögern / **Zoll**

civil law, private law; ~**rechtler** common lawyer; **z**~**rechtlich** *adj* relating to (*or* according to) civil law (*or* common law and equity); ~**rechtsweg** access to the civil courts; ~**richter** judge for civil cases; ~**sache** civil case; ~**schutz** civil defence; ~**schutzkorps** civil defence corps; ~**senat** civil division of a superior court; ~**streitigkeiten** civil litigation; ~**trauung** civil marriage; ~**urteil** judgment (in a civil case); ~**verfahren** civil procedure; ~**verwaltung** civil administration, civil rule.

Zögern *n* hesitation, procrastination, delay; **ohne schuldhaftes** ~ without undue delay, promptly; **schuldhaftes** ~ unreasonable delay.

zögern *v/i* to hesitate, to procrastinate, to delay.

Zölibat *m or n* celibacy; ~**sklausel** clause prohibiting marriage of employees (*void*).

Zoll *m* (*p*: *Zölle* = ~*e*) (customs) duty, external duty, tariff; customs administration; ~**abbau** tariff dismantling; ~**abfertigung** → *Zollabfertigung*; ~**abfertigungsstelle** customs office, examination station; ~**abgaben** customs duties; **z**~**abgabenpflichtig** *adj* subject to customs duty; ~**abkommen** customs convention; ~**agent** customs agent; ~**amt** customs office; ~**amtsvorsteher** head of customs office; ~**anmeldung** customs declaration, goods declaration; ~**anschluß** customs exemption, customs enclave; ~**anschlußgebiet** customs-free zone; ~**aufkommen** customs revenue; ~**aufschlag** extra duty; ~**aufsicht** customs supervision; ~**ausfuhrerklärung** declaration outwards, outward manifest, export specification; ~**ausgangserklärung** entry outwards, shipper's manifest; ~**auskunft** preclearance inquiry; ~**ausland** foreign customs territories; territory beyond customs borders; ~**auslieferungsschein** customs warrant;

~**ausschluß** customs enclave; ~**aussetzung** suspension of customs duties; ~**bahnhof** railway station with customs facilities, customs station; ~**beamter** customs officer, customs inspector; ~**befreiung** exemption from customs duties; ~**betriebsprüfung** inspection of a firms records by customs officer; ~**befund** particulars of examination by customs officer; ~**begleitpapier** customs documents accompanying the product(s); ~**behandlung** customs treatment, customs clearance; *benachteiligende* ~~: *tariff discrimination*; ~**behörde** (the) customs, customs authorities, board of customs and excise; ~**belastung** incidence of customs duties; ~**beschau** customs examination, physical control; ~**bescheid** notice of assessment; ~**bestimmungen** tariff regulations; ~**bewertungsbeamter** general appraiser; ~**binnenland** inland customs area; ~**deklarant** party who makes a customs declaration; ~**deklaration** customs declaration, declaration of goods, ~**delikt** customs offence, contravention of customs regulations; ~**einfuhrerklärung** inward manifest, customs declaration for import; ~**eingangsschein** customs entry certificate; ~**einnahmen** customs revenue; ~**einnehmer** customs collector; ~**einschlußgebiet** bonded area; ~**erhebung** collection of duties; ~**erhöhung** tariff increase; ~**erklärung** customs declaration; ~**erleichterungen** customs facilities; ~**ermäßigung** tariff reduction; ~**fahnder** customs investigator; ~**fahndung** customs investigation, preventive service; ~**fahndungsdienst** customs investigation service; ~**fahndungsstelle** customs investigation office; ~**festsetzung** assessment of duty; ~**formalitäten** customs formalities; **z**~**frei** *adj* free of customs duties, duty-

Zoll

free; ~**freigebiet** (customs)free zone; ~**freiheit** exemption from customs duty; ~**freiladen** duty-free shop; ~**freischreibung** agreed customs-exemption; ~**gebiet** customs territory; ~**gebühren** customs duties; ~**gemeinschaft** customs union; ~**gesetz** tariff law, customs act; ~**gesetzgebung** tariff legislation; ~**gewahrsam** attachment by the customs authorities; temporary possession by the customs authorities; ~**gewicht** dutiable weight; ~**grenzbezirk** customs surveillance zone; ~**grenzdienst** customs frontier service; ~**grenze** customs frontier, customs border; ~**gut** dutiable goods; ~~ *abfertigen: to clear goods*; ~**hilfsperson** person duly authorized to assist customs; ~**hinterziehung** customs fraud; concealment of dutiable goods; ~**hoheit** customs jurisdiction; ~**inland** domestic customs territory; ~**kennzeichen** customs plate (*temporary registration*); ~**kontingent** tariff quota; ~**kontrolle** customs control, customs inspection; ~**lager** (*Zollager*) customs warehouse; bonded warehouse; ~**lagerung** (*Zollagerung*) customs warehousing; ~**meldepflichtiger** person liable to declare dutiable goods, declarant; ~**nomenklatur** (customs) nomenclature; ~**nummer** customs clearance number; ~**ordnung** customs regulations; ~**ordnungswidrigkeit** contravention of customs regulations (*incurring administrative fines*); ~**papier** customs document; ~**passierschein** customs pass, carnet de passage; landing order; triptych; ~**plafonds** customs ceiling; z~**pflichtig** *adj* dutiable, liable to customs duties; non-exempt; ~**plombe** customs seal; ~**politik** tariff policy; ~**präferenz** customs tariff preference; ~**protektionismus** (tariff) protectionism; ~**quittung** customhouse receipt (*or* customs house), *also*: GB docket; ~**recht** customs legislation; customs law; ~**rechnungsgut** goods subject to customs invoice; ~**revision** customs inspection; ~**rückvergütung** drawback; customs refund (*or* reimbursement); ~**satz** tariff rate, rate of duty; *autonome* ~*sätze: autonomous* (*or: unilateral*) *tariff rates*; *pauschale* ~~: *flat-rate duty*; *vertraglicher* ~~: *treaty tariff*; ~**scheinheft** pass-book; ~**schloß** customs lock; ~**schnur** customs seal string; ~**schuld** amount due to customs, customs debt; ~**schuldner** party liable to duty; ~**schranken** customs barriers; ~**schuppen** customs shed; ~**schutz** protection by tariffs, tariff protection; ~**senkung** tariff reduction, tariff cut; z~**sicher** tamper-proof (*for customs purposes*); ~**speicher** bonded-goods warehouse; ~**stelle** customs station, customs office; ~**strafe** customs penalty; ~**streitverfahren** tariff proceedings; ~**system** customs regime, tariff system; ~**tara** customs tare; ~**tarif** (customs) tariff, book of rates; ~~**anpassung**: *tariff adjustment*; ~~**kennziffer**: *tariff code*; ~~ *schema: nomenclature*; *gemeinsamer* ~~: *common customs tariff*; ~**transit** customs transit; ~**übereinkommen** customs convention; ~**übertretung** customs violation; ~**überwachung** customs control; ~- **und Steuervergehen** fiscal offence; ~**union** customs union; ~**unterschied** tariff differential; ~**verband** tariff union; ~**veredelung** processing in bond; ~**verein** customs (*or* tariff) union; ~**verfahren** customs procedure; ~**vergehen** customs offence, infringement of the customs regulations; ~**verhandlungen** tariff negotiations; ~**verkehr** customs procedure; ~**verordnung** customhouse regulation; ~**versandgut** goods in customs transit; ~**verschluß** (customs) seal; *unter* ~~: *customs-locked*; ~**verschlußschein** warehouse bond; ~**vertrag** tariff

925

treaty, customs treaty; ~**verwahrung** safe custody in bond; ~**verwaltung** customs administration; ~**vordruck** customs form; ~**vorschriften** customs regulations; ~**wert** customs (assessment) value, dutiable value, value declared; ~**wertermittlung** valuation for duty purposes; ~**zugeständnisse** tariff concessions; ~**zuschlag** additional duty; ~**zuwiderhandlung** customs offence; **ad valorem** ~ ad valorem duty; **diskriminierende** ~**e** discriminating duties; **gleitende** ~**e** sliding tariff rates; **mit hohen** ~**en belastet** bearing a heavy duty; **mit** ~ **belegen** to levy duty on; **nach Gewicht erhobener** ~ poundage; **pauschaler** ~ flat-safe duty.

Zollabfertigung f customs clearance, customs control, customs formalities, customs operations; ~**sförmlichkeiten** customs clearance procedure; ~**sformular** official customs clearance form; ~**gebühren** customs clearance charges; ~**shafen** port of entry; ~**sstelle** examination station.

Zubehör n accessory, removable fixture, appurtenant, chattel appurtenant to a principal thing, incident; ~**pfandrecht** appurtenance lien; ~**teile** accessories.

zubilligen v/t to accord, to allow, to grant, to concede.

Zubringer m feeder, feeder road; conveyor.

Zubuße f additional contribution, fresh supply of funds, allowance.

Zucht f breeding, stock breeding; ~**bestimmungen** breeding regulations; ~**mittel** disciplinary means.

Zuchthaus n obs penitentiary; ~**strafe** (now: Freiheitsstrafe) penal servitude; **lebenslänglich** ~ (now: Freiheitsstrafe) imprisonment for life.

Zuchthäusler m (colloq) jailbird, ex-convict.

züchtigen v/t to chastise, to punish physically (by slapping, caning etc pupils, children).

Züchtigung f chastising, corporeal punishment (of pupils, children); **gesetzlich zulässige** ~ lawful correction ~**srecht** right of chastisement, discipline.

Zuchtlosigkeit f disorderliness; debauchery, lack of discipline.

Zuchtmittel n means of correction (of juvenile offenders).

Zucker|abschöpfung levy on sugar; ~**börse** sugar exchange; ~**gesetz** Sugar Commerce Act (D., 1951); ~**industrie** sugar industry; ~**steuer** sugar tax.

Zudringlichkeit f importunity, impertinence.

Zudularsystem n (= Besteuerung nach Einkommensarten) schedular system (= separate taxes for categories of income).

zueignen v/reflex to appropriate (for one's use), to acquire.

Zueignung f appropriation (for one's own use and benefit); ~**sabsicht** intention of appropriating sth, intention of acquiring.

zuerkennen v/t to award (by a judge); to grant (benefits).

Zuerkennung f attribution, award, grant; ~ **von Unterhalt** award of maintenance.

Zufahrt f approach, access, vehicular access, drive, driveway. ~**srecht** right of access by vehicles; ~**sstraße** access road, approach road; ~**sweg** approach, drive, driveway; ~~**e zum Hafen**: harbour approaches; **ohne** ~ land-locked.

Zufall m accident, accidental happening, chance, contingency; **unabwendbarer** ~ inevitable accident.

zufallen v/i to devolve upon, to vest in, to accrue to.

zufällig adj accidental, incidental, casual; ~ **oder irrtümlich** by accident or mistake.

Zufalls|auswahl random sampling, lottery sampling; ~**bekanntschaft** chance acquaintance, pickup; ~**einnahmen** windfall receipts;

zufließen / **Zukunftsaussichten**

~**erfindung** chance discovery; ~**haftung** liability for accidental event; ~**schaden** casualty loss; ~**stichprobe** random sample; ~**zahl** random number.

zufließen *v/i* to accrue, to derive (from), to flow (to).

Zuflucht *f* refuge, shelter; ~**sort** place of refuge, place of shelter; ~**sstätte** place of refuge.

zufriedenstellen *v/t* to satisfy.

Zufriedenstellung *f* satisfaction, gratification, contentment.

zuführen *v/t* to supply.

Zuführung *f* supply, feeding, allocation, transfer, appropriation; ~ **in die Rücklagen** allocation to reserves.

Zugabe *f* free gift, bonus; makeweight (*added in weighing*); premium; *pl also*: premium selling; ~**angebot** premium offer; ~**gutschein** free gift coupon; ~**verbot** prohibition of free gift with sales; ~**verordnung** Regulation governing free gifts (*with sales*); ~**wesen** selling with free gift.

Zugang *m* (1) receipt, arrival (*of mail, message*).

Zugang *m* (2) access;~**srecht** right of access; ~ **zu den Gerichten** access to the courts of law; **freier ~ zum Meer** free access to the sea; **sich betrügerisch ~ verschaffen** to obtain entry by fraud; **sicherer ~** safe means of access.

Zugang *m* (3) (*pl Zugänge = ~e*), addition, *pl also*: accruals (*to stock*), subsequent additions; ~**sjahr** year of acquisition; year of accrual; ~**sschranken** entry barrier, entry restrictions; ~**s- und Abgangsrate** replacement rate; ~ **zum Lagerbestand** incoming stocks; **zukünftige** ~**e** future additions.

zugeben *v/t* to admit, to concede.

zugegebenermaßen *adv* admittedly.

zugehörig *adj* pertinent, appendant, appurtenant.

Zugehörigkeit *f* close relationship; affinity, membership, affiliation; ~ **zu e-r Partei** party affiliation; **politische ~** political affiliation.

zugelassen *adj* admitted (*to the Bar*), legally qualified, eligible; permitted; **nicht ~** unadmitted, non-eligible; not permitted, inadmissible.

Zügellosigkeit *f* licentiousness, incontinence, dissoluteness.

zügig *adj* expeditious, prompt, rapid.

zugeschrieben *adj* ascribed, attributed; added (*on a register*).

zugestanden *adj* admitted, acknowledged; **nicht ~** not admitted, unacknowledged.

Zugeständnis *n* admission, acknowledgment, concession; **beiläufiges ~** incidental admission.

zugestehen *v/t* to admit, to concede.

zugestellt *adj* served (upon), delivered; **nicht ~** not served, undelivered; **ordnungsgemäß ~** duly served.

Zugewinn *m* accrued gain, (net) property increment (*of a spouse during marriage*), net post-marital acquisitions; ~**sausgleich** equalization of accrued gains (*splitting spouses' property increments on divorce or death*); **vorzeitiger ~~:** anticipatory equalization of accrued gains; ~**ausgleichsanspruch** accrued gains equalization claim: *claim to half of the balance of the Zugewinn qv.*

zügig *adj* expeditous, prompt.

Zugriff *m* grip; quick action; seizure; ~**sbereitschaft** alertness, readiness to effect a seizure or an arrest; ~**sbesteuerung** direct taxation; ~**smöglichkeiten** access to the general resources; opportunities for successful execution.

Zug-um-Zug reciprocal and simultaneous, concurrent, conditional upon the counter-performance; *cf Erfüllung, Leistung*.

Zugbetrieb *m* train operation; **schaffnerloser ~** driver-only train operation.

Zuhälter *m* pimp, procurer, souteneur.

Zuhälterei *f* procuration of women, pandering, procuring.

Zukauf *m* additional purchase.

Zukunfts|aussichten future prospects; ~**planung** forward plan-

927

Zulage

ning; ~**projekt** project for the future; ~**sicherung** to make provision for future needs.

Zulage f extra pay, increase in salary, allowance, bonus, premium; ~ **für behinderte Kinder** handicapped child allowance; ~ **für unterhaltsberechtigte Kinder** dependant child allowance; **ruhegehaltsfähige** ~ pensionable allowance.

zulassen v/t to admit, to allow, to tolerate; to grant leave (*to appeal etc*), to concede.

zulässig *adj* admissible, proper: available (*remedy*), receivable (*in evidence*); **für** ~ **erklären** to admit, to grant leave; **gesetzlich** ~ permitted by law, legal, legally admissible.

Zulässigkeit f admissibility, permissibility; sufficiency, propriety; ~ **der Antragstellung** sufficiency of motion; ~ **der Eintragung** registrability; ~ **des Beweisangebots** admissibility of evidence; ~ **des Rechtsweges** access to the courts; ~ **von Beweismitteln** admissibility of evidence.

Zulassung f admission, admission to practice, admission to the roll (*or* bar), licence, certification, permission, permit, leave; qualifying procedure; ~ **der Revision** leave to appeal on points of law; ~ **der Vollstreckung zur Nachtzeit** noctanter, permission to levy execution at night; ~ **des Rechtsanwalts** admission to the bar; ~ **e-r Klage** court's acceptance of an action (as procedurally correct); ~ **von Kraftfahrzeugen** licensing of motor vehicles; ~ **von Wertpapieren an der Börse** listing of securities; ~ **zum Börsenhandel** admission to the Stock Exchange; ~ **zum Geschäftsbetrieb** licence to operate, permission to trade; ~ **zur Anwaltschaft** admission to the bar (*or* roll), bar admission; ~ **zur Personenbeförderung** licence to carry passengers; **bauaufsichtliche** ~ permit by building

Zulieferbetrieb

authorities; **die** ~ **entziehen** to strike off the roll (*or* register), to debar; **einstweilige** ~ temporary admission; **vorläufige** ~ provisional admission; **zeitweilige** ~ temporary admission.

Zulassungs|antrag application for admission; ~**ausschuß** entrance qualifications committee; ~**bedingungen** requirements for admission; ~**behörde** licensing authority; ~**bescheid** official listing notice (*exch*); ~**beschränkung** restriction on admission; ~**bezeichnung** approval reference; ~**bezirk** licensing district; ~**diplom** qualifying diploma; ~**entzug** strikeoff, decertification (*engineering design*); **z~fähig** qualified to be admitted (*or* listed *or* licensed), eligible; *nicht* ~~: *non-eligible*; ~**frist** deadline for admission (*or* qualification); ~**gebühren** licensing fees; ~**hindernis** a bar to obtaining leave, an obstacle to admission; ~**nummer** permit number; ~**ordnung** licensing regulations; ~**pflicht** obligatory admission, obligation to submit to admission control; ~**prüfung** type acceptance test; certification test, licensing test; ~**revision** appeal on points of law by leave of the court; ~**schein** registration certificate; ~**schild** licence plate; ~**sperre** general restriction of admission (*to an institution or profession*); ~**staat** state of registration (*motor vehicle*); ~**stelle** licensing bureau, admission board; admissions office (*stocks, vehicles*); ~**urkunde** document of admission, license certificate; licence, practising certificate (*solicitor*); ~**verfahren** admission procedures, qualification procedure, system of approval; ~**verweigerung** refusal to admit, non-admission; ~**voraussetzungen** admission requirements, entrance requirements.

Zuliefer|betrieb (ancillary) supplier firm, feeder plant, manufacturing subsidiary; ~**ungsindustrie** sup-

plying industry; **~vertrag** (sub) supplies contract.
Zulieferer *m* supplier, subsupplier.
„zum ersten, zum zweiten und zum letzten!" "going, going, gone" (*auction*).
zumessen *v/t* to award, to mete out (*punishment*); to apportion, to allot (*time*); to measure out.
Zumessung *f* inflicting, awarding (*sentence*).
zumutbar *adj* reasonable, appropriate, acceptable.
Zumutbarkeit *f* reasonableness, appropriateness, acceptability; **~sprüfung** reasonableness test.
Zumutung *f* imposition, unreasonable request (*or* untenable situation).
Zuname *m* surname, family name.
Zunft *f* guild; **~geheimnis** trade secret; **~gewerbe** incorporated trade(s); **~ordnung** guild regulations; **~recht** law on guilds; **~rolle** guild roll; **~zwang** compulsory guild membership; **~wesen** system of guilds.
zunutze *adv* profitably, advantageously; **sich ~ machen** to turn to account, to utilize, to take advantage of, to benefit from.
zuordnen *v/t* to allocate, to allot.
Zuordnung *f* allocation, allotment; **periodengerechte ~** allocation to the proper accounting period.
zurechenbar *adj* attributable (to), imputable.
Zurechenbarkeit *f* accountability, responsibility; **~szusammenhang** connection of accountability.
zurechnen *v/t* to attribute, to allocate, to ascribe to, to charge with; *zugerechnet werden: to be attributable to.*
Zurechnung *f* imputation, attribution, accountability, allocation; **~szusammenhang** connection of responsibility, accountable connection.
zurechnungsfähig *adj* criminally responsible, doli capax.
Zurechnungsfähigkeit *f* responsible capacity, tortious and/or criminal responsibility; **beschränkte ~** limited criminal responsibility; **verminderte ~** diminished criminal responsibility; **z~unfähig** *adj* not criminally responsible; **~unfähigkeit** *f* incapacity for criminal responsibility.
Zurechnungsunfähigkeit *f* = *Schuldunfähigkeit qv.*
zurechtweisen *v/t* to reprimand, to rebuke.
Zurechtweisung *f* reprimand, rebuke.
Zurruhesetzung *f* retirement.
Zurschaustellen *n* exposure, exhibition, display; **sittenwidriges ~** indecent exhibition.
zurück|abtreten to reassign, to retrocede; **~behalten** to retain, to withhold; **Z~behaltung** retention, withholding; **Z~behaltungsrecht** → *Zurückbehaltungsrecht*; **~bezahlt** repaid; *nicht ~~: not repaid, unredeemed*; **~bezogen** retrospective; **~bleibend** residuary; **~datieren** to backdate; **~erstatten** to reimburse, to restore, to restitute; **~erstattung** reimbursement; **~erstattungsanspruch** restitution claim, claim to restitutionary recovery; **~erwerben** to reacquire; **~fallend** revertible; **~fordern** to reclaim, to revindicate; **~führen (auf)** to ascribe (to); **~geben** to return, to redeliver; **~gewähren** to restore; **~gewinnen** to regain, to recoup, to win back; **~greifen** to take recourse to, to fall back upon; **~kaufen** to buy back, to repurchase; **Z~legung** completion; **~~ von Versicherungszeiten**: *completion of (social) insurance periods*; **Z~nahme** withdrawal, retraction, revocation, recantation; **~nehmen** to take back, to withdraw, to revoke, to retract; **~rufen** to recall, to redeem; **~schiebung** return-removal *of illegal entrant*; **~senden** to return, to send back, to remand (*a case*), to reconsign; **~stellen** to defer, to postpone, to pigeonhole, to shelve, to stand over; to exempt from service tem-

porarily; ~~ *bis auf weiteres: to defer until further notice; vorsorglich* ~~: *to defer by way of precaution;* **Z~stellung** deferment, postponement; **~stufen** to downgrade; **Z~stufung** downgrading; **~trassieren** to redraw; **~treten** to resign (*from office*); to withdraw; to rescind, to repudiate (*a contract*), to cancel (*an agreement, an order*); **~übertragen** to retransfer, to reconvey, to convey back; **~verlangen** to reclaim; **~verweisen** to remand (*to a lower court*), to recommit, to refer back, *esp*: to refer back to the law of the forum (*renvoi*); **Z~verweisung** remand, remanding a case, recommitment, recommittal (*to a committee*); renvoi (*to law of the forum*); **~weisen** to repudiate, to refute, to refuse, to disallow (*a claim*), to dismiss (*appeal, petition*); *als unbegründet* ~: *to dismiss on the merits; als unzulässig* ~; *to dismiss on procedural grounds, to throw out; to strike out;* **Z~weisung** repudiation, refusal, refutation, rejection, disallowance, dismissal (*action, appeal*); **Z~werfen** roll-back; **~wirken** to have retroactive (*or* retrospective) effect; **~zahlbar** repayable, refundable; **~zahlen** to repay, to refund; **Z~zahlung** repayment; **~ziehen** to retract, to withdraw, to retire, to take back.

Zurückbehaltungsrecht *n* right of retention, retaining lien; **~ des Anwalts an den Urkunden des Mandanten** attorney's retaining lien, solicitor's lien, lien over documents; **~ des Handwerkers** mechanic's lien, craftsman's lien; **~ des Verkäufers** seller's lien, vendor's lien; **kaufmännisches ~** mercantile lien, commercial lien (*in personam*).

Zurückhaltung *f* self-restraint.

Zuruf *m* acclamation; **durch ~** (*also:*) *viva voce;* **offener ~** open outcry *exch.*

Zurverfügungstellung *f* putting sth. at s. o.'s disposal, making sth available to s. o.

Zusage *f* acceptance, promise, commitment, undertaking, engagement; **~n bei Vertragsabschluß** promissory representations; **z~fähig** eligible, suitable for approval, grantable; **bindende ~** binding promise; **klare ~** definite promise; **konkrete ~** firm assurance, assurance in black and white.

zusagen *v/t* to promise, to commit oneself to do sth.

Zusammenarbeit *f* co-operation, collaboration; **~svertrag** Cooperation Treaty; **grenzübergreifende ~** transfrontier co-operation; **jede zweckdienliche ~** all appropriate forms of co-operation; **paritätische ~** co-operation on the basis of equality.

Zusammenbruch *m* collapse, breakdown; **geschäftlicher ~** commercial failure.

Zusammenfassung *f* abstract, summary, synopsis, précis, résumé; **~ des Sachverhalts** summary of the facts.

Zusammenhang *m* (*pl Zusammenhänge* = **~e**) coherence, connection, continuity; **soweit sich aus dem ~ nichts anderes ergibt** unless the context otherwise requires; **untrennbarer ~** inseparable link; **ursächlicher ~** causal connection, causality; **verbundwirtschaftliche ~e** economic links; **wenn der ~ es zuläßt** whenever the context so admits or requires.

zusammenhängend *adj* coherent, relevant, germane, continuous.

zusammenhanglos *adj* incoherent.

Zusammenhangslosigkeit *f* incoherence.

Zusammenkunft *f* (*pl Zusammenkünfte* = **~e**) meeting; **geheime ~** secret meeting; **regelmäßige ~e** periodical meetings; **zwanglose ~** informal gathering.

Zusammenleben *n* living together; **eheähnliches ~** cohabitation (*as husband and wife*).

Zusammenlegung *f* amalgamation, merger, combination.

Zusammenprall *m* collision, crash; clash.

Zusammenrechnung *f* addition, aggregation; ~ **der Einkünfte** total income treated as one (*married couples*).

zusammenrotten *v/reflex* to gang up, to riot, to form a riotous assembly, to band together.

Zusammenrottung *f* riotous assembly, riot, mob.

zusammenschließen *v/reflex* to join, to associate, to combine.

Zusammenschluß *m* association. combine, combination; merger, consolidation; ~**vorhaben** merger project; **horizontaler** ~ horizontal combine; **lockerer** ~ loose combination; **loser** ~**e** loose combination; **vertikaler** ~ vertical combine.

Zusammensetzung *f* composition, make-up; ~ **der Repräsentativauswahl** sample make-up; ~ **der Unterausschüsse** composition of the subcommittees; ~ **des Gerichts** composition of the panel of judges.

Zusammenstoß *m* (*pl Zusammenstöße = ~e*) collision, crash, smash-up; ~ **auf See** collision at sea.

Zusammentreffen *n* concurrence; ~ **mehrerer Freiheitsstrafen** merger of offences; ~ **mehrerer Geldstrafen** several fines (*awarded in the same case*); ~ **mehrerer strafbarer Handlungen** coincidence of offences; ~ **von Umständen** coincidence of circumstances.

Zusammenveranlagung *f* joint assessment (*of married couples to income tax*).

Zusammenwachsen *n* interpenetration, growing together.

Zusammenwirken *n* joint action; **bewußtes und gewolltes** ~ acting jointly and wilfully, acting in conspiracy; **planvolles** ~ action by design, acting in collusion.

Zusammenwohnen *n* living together, cohabitation.

zusammenwohnen *v/t* to live together, to cohabit.

Zusatz *m* addition, added matter, addendum; subjoinder, annex, adjunct, rider (*bill*); ~**abkommen** supplementary agreement; ~**anmeldung** additional application; ~**antrag** supplementary motion; ~**arbeiten** extra work; ~**artikel** supplementary article; ~**ausbildung** additional training; *erforderliche* ~~: *additional training requirements*; ~**ausrüstung** add-on (*or* additional, *or* extra) equipment; ~**bedarf** additional need, additional requirement; ~**bedingung** additional condition (*or* provision); ~**berechnung** added computation; ~**bestimmung** additional clause; additional provision; ~**betrag** additional amount; ~**blatt** continuation sheet; ~**dividende** additional dividend, superdividend; ~**entschädigung** additional compensation; ~**erfinderschein** inventor's certificate of addition; ~**finanzierung** front-end financing, provision of extra funds; ~**frage** follow-up question, supplementary question; ~**gebühr** additional fee, surcharge; ~**gebrauchszertifikat** utility certificate of addition; ~**gesetz** supplemental Act; ~**geräte** add-on (or additional or extra) equipment; ~**haftpflichtversicherung** umbrella policy; ~**kasse** additional (sickness) insurance; ~**klausel** additional clause, rider; ~**kapazität** additional (production) capacity; ~**leistungen** extra work and material, additional services; ~**name** epithet, nickname; ~**patent** patent of addition, additional patent; ~**police** additional policy; ~**prämie** extra premium; ~**protokoll** supplementary protocol; ~**rente** supplementary pension; ~**steuer** surtax; ~**stoff** additive; ~**stoff-Zulassungsverordnung** Ordinance on Permitted Additives; ~**strafe** extra punishment; ~**teile** add-on components; ~**vereinbarung** additional (*or* supplemental) agreement; ~**vergütung** extra pay, additional

931

remuneration; **~vermächtnis** accumulative legacy; **~vermerk** superimposed clause; **~versicherung** supplementary insurance; *Hüttenknappschaftliche* **~~**: *Steelworkers' Supplementary Pension Insurance*; **~versorgung** supplementary retirement provision; **~vertrag** supplementary contract; **~ zu e-m Testament** codicil; **~ zu e-r Police** addendum to a policy.

zusätzlich *adj* additional, supplementary, ancillary, extra.

zuschieben *v/t* to lay (*the blame*) upon.

zuschießen *v/t* to contribute towards; to supply additionally, to add to.

Zuschlag *m* (1) excess charge, surcharge; **~sgebühr** *pat* additional fee; surcharge; **~skalkulation** distributive cost accounting; **~sprämie** additional premium, extra bonus; **mit ~ belegen** to surcharge; **tariflicher ~** collectively agreed extra-payment.

Zuschlag *m* (2) the fall of the hammer, adjudication; acceptance of bid; the award of the contract (*tenders*); **~ an den Submittenden** acceptance of tender; **~serteilung** adjudication (*public sale*); **~sfrist** deadline for adjudication; **~sgebot** adjudication price; **~(s)preis** hammer price; **~sprotokoll** record of adjudication; **den ~ erteilen** to award a contract, to knock down, to strike off; **den ~ erhalten** to obtain sth as the highest bidder; to be awarded (*a contract*).

zuschlagen *v/t* to award (*contract, auction*); to knock down (to).

zuschreibbar *adj* attributable, imputable, ascribable.

zuschreiben *v/t* to ascribe, to attribute (to); to impute, to add to the Land Register unit.

Zuschreibung *f* property addition, inventory addition, *adding plot of real estate to a larger unit in the land register*; appreciation (*value*).

Zuschuß *m* (*pl Zuschüsse:* **~e**) grant-in-aid, grant, contribution, subsidy, allowance; **~bedarf** subsidy requirements; **~betrieb** subsidized enterprise, deficit operation; **~e des Bundes** federal subsidies, federal grants-in-aid; **~ pro Kopf** capitation grant; **nicht rückzahlbare ~e** non-repayable grants; **staatlicher ~** government grant; **verlorener ~** non-repayable grant; irrecoverable contribution (*by tenant, public authority etc*).

zusenden *v/t* to forward (to s. o.), to send to s. o.'s home.

Zusendung *f* sending to s. o.'s address, forwarding.

zusetzen *v/i* to lose money (on sth.).

zusichern *v/t* to assure, to reassure; to represent and warrant; to warrant, to promise, to guarantee.

Zusicherung *f* assurance, reassurance, representation, warranty, promise, guarantee; **~ der Rechtsmangelfreiheit** warranty of title; **~ des ungestörten Besitzes** warranty of quiet enjoyment; **~ e-r Eigenschaft** warranty of a quality; **schriftliche ~** written warranty, written promise.

zusprechen *v/t* to award, to adjudicate, to adjudicate, to grant.

Zustand *m* condition, state; **äußerlich in einwandfreiem ~** in apparent good order and condition; **baulicher ~** state of repair; **beschädigter ~** damaged condition; **betriebsbereiter ~** operating condition, working order; **betriebsfähiger ~** operating condition, working order; **bewohnbarer ~** habitable state of repair, condition fit for human habitation; **derzeitiger ~** present state, present condition, current state; **einsatzbereiter ~** operating condition; **einstweiliger ~** temporary state (of affairs); **einwandfreier äußerer ~** apparent external good order and condition; **einwandfreier ~** perfect condition; flawless state, *in* **~n ~ versetzen**: *to put in repair, to rectify*; **fahrbereiter ~** efficient state to resume service (*vessel*),

Zustandekommen

roadworthy condition (*vehicle*); **gesetzloser** ~ anarchy; **im gegenwärtigen** ~ in the actual (*or* present) state; **in betrunkenem** ~ in a state of intoxication; **in e-m guten pfleglichen** ~ in well-kept condition; **in e-m zum Tode führenden** ~ in a terminal condition; **in gebrauchsfähigem** ~ in a serviceable condition; **in gutem** ~ in good repair, in good order and condition, sound (condition); **in ordentlichem** ~ in good order and condition, in fair repair; **in ordnungsgemäßem** ~ **halten** to keep in (a fit state of) repair; **in reisefähigem** ~ in a fit state to travel; **in seetüchtigem** ~ in navigable condition, seaworthy; **in wohnlichem** ~ in tenantable repair; **jeweiliger** ~ current state; **kriegsähnlicher** ~ quasi-war conditions, a state just short-of-war; war-like circumstances; **lieferfähiger** ~ deliverable state; **mangelfreier** ~ perfect condition, faultless condition; impeccable; **neuwertiger** ~ (condition) as new; **polizeimäßiger** ~ a condition in compliance with police regulations; **schlechter** ~ disrepair, bad condition; **übergabefähiger** ~ deliverable state; **vermietungsfähiger** ~ tenantable repair; **vorheriger** ~ status quo ante, former state.

Zustandekommen *n* materialization; ~ **von Beschlüssen** adoption of acts (resolutions).

zuständig *adj* competent, responsible, relevant; ~ **sein** to be competent, to have jurisdiction; **ausschließlich** ~ **sein** to have exclusive jurisdiction; **örtlich** ~ **sein** to have jurisdiction at a place, to be locally competent, to have venue; **sachlich** ~ **sein** to have jurisdiction over the subject matter.

Zuständigkeit *f* jurisdiction (= *j*), competence, sphere of *j*; administrative responsibility, scope of authority, province; ~ **als Rechtsmittelinstanz** appellate *j*; ~ **auf Grund einer Vereinbarung** *j* on the basis of an agreement; ~ **der örtlichen Gerichte** *j* of the local courts; ~ **der Zivil-Gerichte** *j* of the civil courts; ~ **in Ehesachen** matrimonial *j*; ~ **in erster Instanz** first-instance (*or* initial) *j*; ~ **in Nachlaßsachen** probate *j*; ~ **in Strafsachen** criminal *j*; **allgemeine** ~ general *j*; **ausschließliche** ~ exclusive *j*; **die** ~ **bestreiten** plead incompetence; **die** ~ **e-s Gerichts vereinbaren** to agree to submit to the *j* of a court; **erstgerichtliche** ~ first-instance (*or* initial) *j*; **funktionelle** ~ limited *j* over the type of case; **implizierte** ~**en** implied powers; **in der** ~ **konkurrieren mit** have concurrent *j* with; **inländische** ~ national *j*; domestic *j* **innerhalb meiner** ~ within my province; **internationale** ~ international *j*; **mangelnde** ~ want of *j*; lack of *j*; **örtliche** ~ venue, local *j*; territorial *j*; **die** ~~ **begründen**: *to lay the venue, to justify choice of venue;* **sachliche** ~ *j* over the subject (-matter), *j* relating to the value of the claim; *j* ratione materiae; **seine** ~ **verneinen** to disclaim one's competence; **subsidiäre** ~ subsidiary *j*; alternative *j*; **unbeschränkte** ~ plenary *j*; **unmittelbare** ~ direct *j*; **unter die** ~ **fallen** to be within the competence of; **vorbehaltene konkurrierende** ~ reserved federal legislative competence concurrent with the Länder, pendent *j*.

Zuständigkeits|begrenzung limitation of *j*; ~**bereich** sphere of responsibility, purview, ambit, province; ~~ *e-s Ausschusses*: *terms of reference*; ~**beschränkung** limitation of authority; ~**erfordernisse** requirements as to *j*; ~**erklärung** assumption of *j*; ~**erweiterung** extension of *j*; ~**frage** jurisdictional question; ~**grenze** ambit, limit of *j*; ~**klausel** jurisdiction(al) clause; ~**lücke** jurisdictional gap; ~**streit** conflict about *j*, jurisdictional dispute; ~**überschreitung**

exceeding one's competence, acting ultra vires; ~**vereinbarung** agreement as to *j*; *j* clause; ~**verteilung** allocation of responsibility; ~**voraussetzung** requirement(s) as to *j*.

zustehen *v/i* to be entitled to.

Zustell|amt delivery post office; ~**bezirk** postal district; ~**anschrift** mailing address, postal address; address for service; ~**dienst** delivery service; ~**gebühr** delivery charge, cartage; ~**postamt** delivery post office.

zustellen *v/t* to deliver *(postal and general)*; to serve upon *(judicial, administrative)*.

Zusteller *m* postman; process server, writ server, the person who served.

Zustellung *f* service, service of process; postal, delivery, distribution; ~ **an die Person des Empfängers selbst** personal service; ~ **der Klageschrift** service of process; ~ **durch Aufgabe zur Post** constructive service by mailing, *posted by process-server to non-resident's address (exceptional)*; ~ **durch Einwurf in den Briefkasten des Empfängers** service by insertion through the letter box; ~ **durch Postaufgabe** = ~ *durch Aufgabe zur Post qv*; ~ **durch Postniederlegung** (constructive) service by depositing the document at local post office; ~**en oder Mitteilungen gelten als erfolgt, wenn** ... notifications or communications shall be deemed to have been made when ...; ~ **im Ausland** service abroad; ~ **von Amts wegen** official service, service ex officio; ~ **von Anwalt zu Anwalt** service between solicitors; **binnen 30 Tagen nach** ~ within 30 days of service; **die** ~ **an den Beklagten vornehmen** to serve *sth upon* the defendant; **die** ~ **bewirken** to effect service; **diplomatische** ~ service through diplomatic channels; **eigenhändige** ~ personal service; **erneute** ~ re-service; **fehlende** ~ default of service; **gerichtliche** ~**en vornehmen** to effect service by the court, to serve process; **nicht ordnungsmäßige** ~ irregularity in service; **öffentliche** ~ service by publication, substituted service, public notification; ~~ *durch Zeitungsinserat*: substituted service by advertisement; **ordnungsgemäße** ~ due service, regular service; **persönliche** ~ personal service; *durch* ~~ *geladen*: summoned personally; **vereinfachte** ~ simplified service by mail.

Zustellungs|adresse address for service; ~**arten** types of service; ~**beamter** writ-server, process-server; ~**behinderung** obstructing service; ~**bestätigung** return of service, acknowledgment of service, acceptance of service; ~**bevollmächtigter** process agent, person authorized to accept service, registered agent for service of process; ~~ **bzw. Ladungsmängel** defective notice; ~**empfänger** recipient *(of postal or judicial service)*; ~ **ersuchen** request for service; ~**gebühr** delivery charge; ~**mangel** irregularity in service, defective service, default of service; *unheilbarer* ~~: irreparable irregularity in the service *(of)*; ~**nachweis** (due) proof of service, evidence of service, acknowledgment of service, ~**organ** competent agency for effecting service, process-server; ~**ort** place of service; ~**tag** return day; ~**urkunde** certificate of service, return of service; notice of delivery; ~**vereitelung** impeding the service of process; ~**verfahren** regulations for the service of documents; ~**vertreter** person authorized to accept service; ~**zeit** time of service.

zustimmen *v/i* to assent, to agree to.

Zustimmender *m, der Zustimmende, die Zustimmende(n)* the consenting party *(parties)*.

Zustimmung *f* assent, consent; ~**serklärung** notice of assent *(or* consent); ~**sgesetz** Act of the *Bundestag* requiring the consent of the

Bundesrat; **ausdrückliche ~** explicit consent; **behördliche ~** official consent; **die ~ einstweilen verweigern** to withhold consent provisionally; **eigenhändige, schriftliche ~** one's own consent in writing; **einhellige ~** unanimous consent; **elterliche ~** parental consent; **konkludente ~** constructive consent; **mit ~ von** with (the advice and) consent of; **mündliche ~** verbal consent; **nachträgliche ~** subsequent consent, sanction; **schriftliche ~** written consent; **stillschweigende ~** implied consent, tacit consent; **volle ~** unreserved consent, full consent; **vorbehaltlose ~** consent without reserve; **vorherige ~** previous consent; *~ schriftliche ~: prior written consent.*

Zutat *f* ingredient, additive; **~enverzeichnis** list of ingredients (*of food*).

zuteilen *v/t* to allocate, to allot, to apportion, to assign.

Zuteilung *f* allotment, allocation, apportionment; **~santrag** application for allotment; **~sanzeige** letter of allotment; **~speriode** basic period (*Special Drawing Rights*); ration period; **~squote** ratio of allotment; **z~sreif** available for drawdowns; **~sschein** allotment letter; **repartierte ~** scaled-down allotment, partial allotment.

Zutritt *m* access, admittance, entry, approach; **~ gestattet** entry permitted; in limits (*military*); **~ nur mit Sonderausweis** admittance by authorized credentials (*or* special permit) only; **~srecht** right of access; **~ streng verboten** strictly no entry; **~ verboten** no entry, keep out!; (*mil:*) off limits (*US*), out of bounds (*GB*).

zuverlässig *adj* reliable, trustworthy, faithful, loyal.

Zuverlässigkeit *f* reliability, trustworthiness, faithfulness; **~grad** dependability, reliability; **~snachweis** proof of personal reliability; **~sprobe** endurance test.

zuvorkommen *v/i* to anticipate, to forestall, to preclude, to pre-empt.

Zuwachs *m* accrual, accretion, increase; **~rate** rate of increment; **~recht** right to the accretion.

Zuwahl *f* co-opting, co-optation, additional election.

Zuwanderung *f* influx by migration; **~sdruck** pressure caused by new immigrants.

zuweisen *v/t* to assign, to allocate, to allot, to apportion.

Zuweisung *f* assignment, allocation, allotment, apportionment; **~en an Rücklagen** funds earmarked for the reserves; **~en zum Tilgungsfonds** sinking-fund contributions; **gerichtliche ~** judicial allocation (*of accommodation or land*).

zuwenden *v/t* to bestow, to bequeath, to grant, to make an allowance, to allow.

Zuwendung *f* bestowal, bequest, gift, grant, allowance; **~en aus öffentlichen Mitteln** grants from public funds; **~streuhand** beneficial trust, trust for purposes of donation; **~ von Todes wegen** bequest, testamentary gift, disposition mortis causa; **einmalige ~** non-recurring allowance; **freigiebige ~** charitable gift; **laufende ~en** periodical allowance; **letztwillige ~** bequest, testamentary gift; **unabtretbare ~** non-transferable provision; **unentgeltliche ~** gift, gratuitous grant.

zuwiderhandeln *v/i* to contravene, to disobey (*the law*), to offend, to infringe, to infract.

Zuwiderhandlung *f* contravention, non-compliance, infraction, infringement; **vermutete ~** suspected infringement.

zuzahlen *v/i* to make an additional payment.

Zuzahlung *f* additional contribution.

zuziehen *v/t* to call in, to consult in addition, to enlist the services of.

Zuziehung *f* calling in, additional consultation.

Zuzug *m* migration (*to a city*), tak-

ing-up one's residence; ~**sbeschränkung** restriction of entry (for aliens to join their family); ~**sgenehmigung** permit to take up one's residence (in).
zuzüglich *prep* plus, *adj* additional.
Zwang *m* compulsion, coercion; ~ **zu Deckungskäufen** bear squeeze (*at a loss*); **gerichtlicher** ~ judicial compulsion; **moralischer** ~ moral compulsion; **ökonomischer** ~ economic necessity; **physischer** ~ physical force; **psychischer** ~ mental compulsion, mental duress; **unmittelbarer** ~ direct compulsion, force; **widerrechtlicher physischer** ~ inadmissible physical duress.
Zwangs|abgabe compulsory levy (*or* contribution); ~**ablieferung** compulsory delivery; ~**abmeldung** compulsory deregistration (*of an entry in a register*); ~**abtretung** compulsory assignment, forced cession (*of territory*); ~**angebot** compulsory offer; ~**anheuerung** impressment; ~**anleihe** compulsory loan, forced loan; ~**arbeit** forced labour, compulsory labour; hard labour (*as a punishment*); ~**aufenthalt** forced stay, detention; ~**auflage** requisition; ~**ausgleich** compulsory settlement; ~**behandlung** compulsory medical (examination and/or) treatment; ~**beitrag** compulsory contribution; ~**beitreibung** forcible collection; ~**beurlaubung** (compulsory) suspension from office, compulsory unpaid leave; ~**bewirtschaftung** public control, controlled management; ~**eintragung** compulsory registration; ~**enteignung** (compulsory) expropriation; ~~**srecht**: right of eminent domain; **z**~**ernährt** force fed; ~**ernährung** force feeding; ~**erwerbsbehörde** acquiring authority; ~**geld** coercive payment (*to enforce public duty*); ~**haft** coercive detention; ~**handlung** coercive action; ~**hypothek** execution lien (*upon the debtor's land*), mortgage registered to enforce judgment debt; ~**innung** (craftsmen's) guild with compulsory membership; ~**jacke** straight-jacket; ~**kapitalbildung** compulsory capital formation; ~**kartell** compulsory cartel; ~**kurs** compulsory rate; ~**lage** position of constraint, necessity; ~**liquidation** compulsory winding-up, involuntary liquidation; ~**liquidator** liquidator in winding-up by court; ~**lizenz** licence of right, compulsory licence; ~**lotse** compulsory pilot; ~**maßnahme** coercion, measures of compulsion; ~**maßregeln** measures of compulsion; ~**mitgliedschaft** compulsory membership; ~**mittel** means of coercion, coercive methods; ~**pensionierung** mandatory retirement; ~~**räumung** eviction; ~~**sauftrag**: *dispossession warrant*; *die* ~~ *gegen e-n Mieter durchführen*: to eject (= evict) a tenant; ~**rechte** coercive rights; ~**regulierung** forced settlement; ~**rekrutierung** impressment; ~**rotation** forced rotation; ~**rückkauf** compulsory redemption (*of bonds*); ~**schlichtung** compulsory settlement of disputes, compulsory mediation; ~**sparen** compulsory saving; ~**strafe** coercive penalty; ~**teilung** compulsory partition; ~**umsiedlung** compulsory resettlement; ~**veranlagung** compulsory tax assessment; ~**verfahren** coercive proceedings, compulsory measures; ~**vergleich** compulsory settlement, bankruptcy composition; ~**verhör** compulsory interrogation; ~~**verkauf** sale, judicial sale; ~**verschickung** deportation; ~**verschleppung** forced deportation, kidnapping; ~**versicherung** compulsory insurance; **z**~**versteigern** to sell by public auction *to enforce executiv*; ~**versteigerung** → *Zwangsversteigerung*; ~**verwalter** official receiver; ~**verwaltung** judicially enforced receivership; ~**verwertung** coercive utilization, compulsory disposal; compulsory

Zwangsversteigerung

working (*patent*); ~**vollstreckung** → *Zwangsvollstreckung*; ~**vorführung** compulsory attendance before a judge; ~**vorlage** referral; ~**wirtschaft** controlled economy; ~**wohnsitz** compulsory domicile, allocated domicile.

Zwangsversteigerung *f* execution sale by public auction, compulsory auction, foreclosure sale; ~**serlös** proceeds of foreclosure sale; ~**sgesetz** (*ZVG 20. 5. 1898*), Compulsory Auction of Immovable Property Act; ~**sverfahren** compulsory auction of immovable property procedure (*or* proceedings); ~**svermerk** foreclosure notice (*in land register*); ~ **von Grundstücken** compulsory auction of landed property, foreclosure sale.

Zwangsvollstreckung *f* execution (*of judgment, decree or other enforceable instrument*), enforcement, final process; ~ **aus Urteil** enforcement of judgment, execution of judgment; ~ **aus Zahlungstiteln** enforcement of judgment debts; ~ **durch Wegnahme** execution by writ of delivery; ~ **in das bewegliche Vermögen** general execution; ~ **in das unbewegliche Vermögen** execution imposed on debtor's immovable property; ~**sklausel** writ of execution; ~**sverfahren** execution proceedings, measures of execution; ~**sverkauf** distress sale, forced sale; **der** ~ **unterliegend** liable to execution; **die** ~ **betreiben** to levy execution, to issue execution (against), to have execution issued, to commence execution; **die** ~ **einstellen** to terminate the process of execution; **die** ~ **vorläufig einstellen** to stay the execution; **erfolglose** ~ unsatisfied execution; **nicht der** ~ **unterworfen** judgment-proof, exempt from execution.

Zweck *m* (*pl: Zwecke* = ~*e*) purpose, aim, object, end; ~**bestimmung** appropriation, application, ear-

Zweck

marking (*for a specific purpose*), specification of aim (objects); ~**bindung** earmarking for specific purpose, tying funds to an object; **z**~**dienlich** expedient; ~ **e-r Gesellschaft** object(s) of a company; ~ **e-r Zahlung** purpose (*or* object) of a payment; ~**entfremdung** misuse, conversion for an improper use, *unlawfully using private accommodation for commercial or other nonresidential purposes*; ~**erklärung** declaration of purpose (*of a bank loan*); ~**erreichung** accomplishment of purpose; ~**heirat** marriage of convenience; **z**~**mäßig** *adj* expedient, suitable; ~**mäßigkeit** expedience; ~*serwägungen: considerations of expendiency* (*or: suitability*); *aus* ~*sgründen: as a matter of convenience*; ~**propaganda** propaganda with a specific target; ~**verband** special-purpose association, special association, ad hoc group, specialized administrative union; *gemeindlicher* ~~: *special administrative union of local authorities* (*or: district*); ~**vereitelung** frustration; intentional prevention from reaching an aim; ~**vermächtnis** legacy for a designated purpose; ~**vermögen** special-purpose fund, ad hoc fund; ~**zuwendung** allowance subject to special conditions (as to its use); **begünstigter** ~ (tax-)-favoured purpose; **dem** ~ **entsprechen** to answer the purpose, to be suitable (or fit) for the purpose; **diplomatische** ~**e** diplomatic purposes; **erlaubter** ~ lawful purpose; **förderungswürdige** ~**e** purposes eligible for a grant; **gemeinnützige** ~**e** non-profit-making (*or* charitable) purposes (in the public interest); **geschäftlicher** ~ business purpose; **gesetzlich zulässiger** ~ lawful purpose; **gewerblicher** ~ commercial purpose; **mildtätige** ~**e** charitable purposes; **nützliche** ~**e** utilitarian purposes; **öffentliche** ~**e** public purposes; **seelsorgerische** ~**e** pious uses; **staatspolitische** ~**e** aims of public policy; **steuerbegünstigte** ~e tax-aided purposes; **widerrechtlicher** ~ illegal purpose; **wohltätige** ~e charitable purposes; **zu diesem** ~ to this end, for this purpose.

Zwei|drittelmehrheit two-thirds majority; ~**familienhaus** two-family house, (*US*:) duplex; ~**kammersystem** bicameral system; ~**kampf** duel; trial by battle (*ordeal*); ~~ *mit tödlichen Waffen*: *duel with deadly weapons*; ~**metallsystem** bi-metallism; ~**parteiensystem** two-party system; ~**schichten-Betrieb** double-shift working; **z**~**seitig** *adj* bilateral; ~**staatentheorie** "two-state theory" (*of two independent German states*); **z**~**stellig** *adj* double-digit, two figure (number); double figure.

zweideutig *adj* equivocal, ambiguous, dubious.

Zweideutigkeit *f* duplicity, ambiguity, equivocality, dubiety.

Zweifel *m* doubt; ~ **ausräumen** to remove doubts, to eliminate misgivings; ~ **beseitigen** to eliminate doubts; ~**sfall** doubtful case; *im* ~~ *soll der englische Text zugrunde gelegt werden: the English text shall prevail in case of doubt*; **außer allem** ~ beyond all doubt; **begründeter** ~ reasonable doubt, rational doubt; **berechtigter** ~ legitimate doubt; **im** ~ in case of doubt, in dubio; ~~ *zugunsten des Angeklagten entscheiden: to give the accused the benefit of the doubt*; **nicht unerheblicher** ~ reasonable doubt, justifiable doubt.

Zweig|anstalt branch (establishment); ~**betrieb** operating branch of an enterprise; ~**gesellschaft** branch of a company, affiliate; ~**niederlassung** branch establishment, branch; ~**organisation** affiliate; ~**stelle** agency, branch office, suboffice; ~~**nnetz**: *branch network*.

zweigleisig *adj* bifurcated, double track.

Zweit|ausbildung second vocational (*or* educational) training; ~**ausfertigung** duplicate; ~**begünstigter** secondary beneficiary; ~**erwerb** second hand purchase; ~**schrift** copy; ~**schuldner** additional debtor; ~**stimme** a second vote; ~**verdiener** secondary earner; ~**wohnung** second home, second residence.

Zwerg|betrieb dwarf enterprise; ~**schule** one-room school.

zwingen *v/t* to compel, to force, to coerce.

zwingend *adj* obligatory, peremptory, imperative, compulsory.

Zwischen|ablesung intermediate reading; ~**abnahme** acceptance of part-performance, in-process inspection; ~**abrechnung** intermediate account; ~**abschluß** interim closing balance; ~**aufenthalt** transitory stay, stop-over; ~**ausschuß** interim committee; ~**ausweis** interim return; **z**~**behördlich** *adj* intergovernmental departments, between authorities; interagency; ~**benutzung** intermediate exploitation (*or* use), intervening user; ~**bericht** interim report, progress report; ~**bescheid** interim notice; ~**besitzer** temporary possessor, interim owner; **z**~**betrieblich** *adj* intercompany, between firms; ~**bilanz** interim financial statement, interim balance sheet; ~**dividende** interim dividend; ~**entscheidung** interlocutory decision, intermediate order; ~**ergebnis** intermediate result; ~**erledigung** provisional handling ~**fall** incident; ~**feststellungsklage** petition for an interlocutory declaration; ~**feststellungsurteil** interlocutory declaratory judgment, order declaring rights; ~**finanzierung** interim financing, bridging loan (*or* finance); ~**frage** interruption; interpellation; *e–e* ~~ *stellen: to interpellate*; **z**~**geschaltet** intermediary; ~**geschoß** mezzanine; ~**handel** intermediate trade; intermediate (wholesale) trade; ~**händler** middleman, agent, intermediary; ~**käufer** intermediate buyer; ~**konten** suspense accounts, deferred accounts; ~**kredit** interim loan, intermediate credit, bridging loan; ~**lager** interim storage (*of nuclear waste*); ~**lagergebühr** houseage; ~**lagerung** intermediate storage; ~**landung** stop-over; *ohne* ~~: *non-stop*; ~**nutzung** intervening use; ~**personen** intermediaries; ~**produkterfindung** invention of intermediate product(s); ~**prüfung** interim check; interim examination; ~**quittung** interim receipt; ~**ruf** interjection, interruption (*of a speaker*); *durch* ~~*e provozieren*: *to heckle*; ~**rufer** heckler; ~**satz** intermediate rate; **z~schalten** to interpose; ~**schein** provisional receipt, scrip; ~**spediteur** intermediate forwarding agent; **z~staatlich** → *zwischenstaatlich*; ~**streit** interlocutory proceedings; ~**summe** subtotal; ~**träger** informer, confidential agent; ~**unternehmer** intermediate entrepreneur; ~**urteil** interlocutory judgment (*or* decree); ~**verdienst** middleman's profit; ~**verfahren** interlocutory proceedings; ~**verfügung** interim order; ~**verkauf** intermediate sale; ~~ *vorbehalten*: *subject to prior sale*; ~**verkäufer** intermediate seller; ~**vermietung** interim letting, interim tenancy; ~**verpächter** intermediary lessor; ~**vertrag** provisional agreement; ~**vertreter** intermediate agent; ~**verwahrer** escrow agent; stakeholder; ~**wahlen** off-year elections, by-elections; ~**zeugnis** provisional testimonial; ~**zins** interim interest.

zwischenstaatlich *adj* intergovernmental, international, cross-national, *US also*: interstate; **Z~e Beratende Seeschiffahrts-Organisation** Intergovernmental Maritime Consultative Organization; **Z~r Ausschuß für Urheberrechte** Intergovernmental Copyright Committee; **Z~s Komitee für Europäische Auswanderung** Intergovernmental Committee for European Migration.